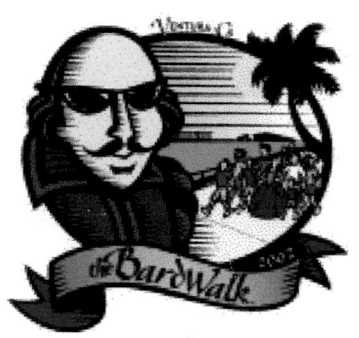

This book donated by
Barnes & Noble Booksellers
for
BardWalk 2002
presented by
Rubicon Theatre Company
Education Outreach Programs
April 20, 2002

Shakespeare

The Complete Works

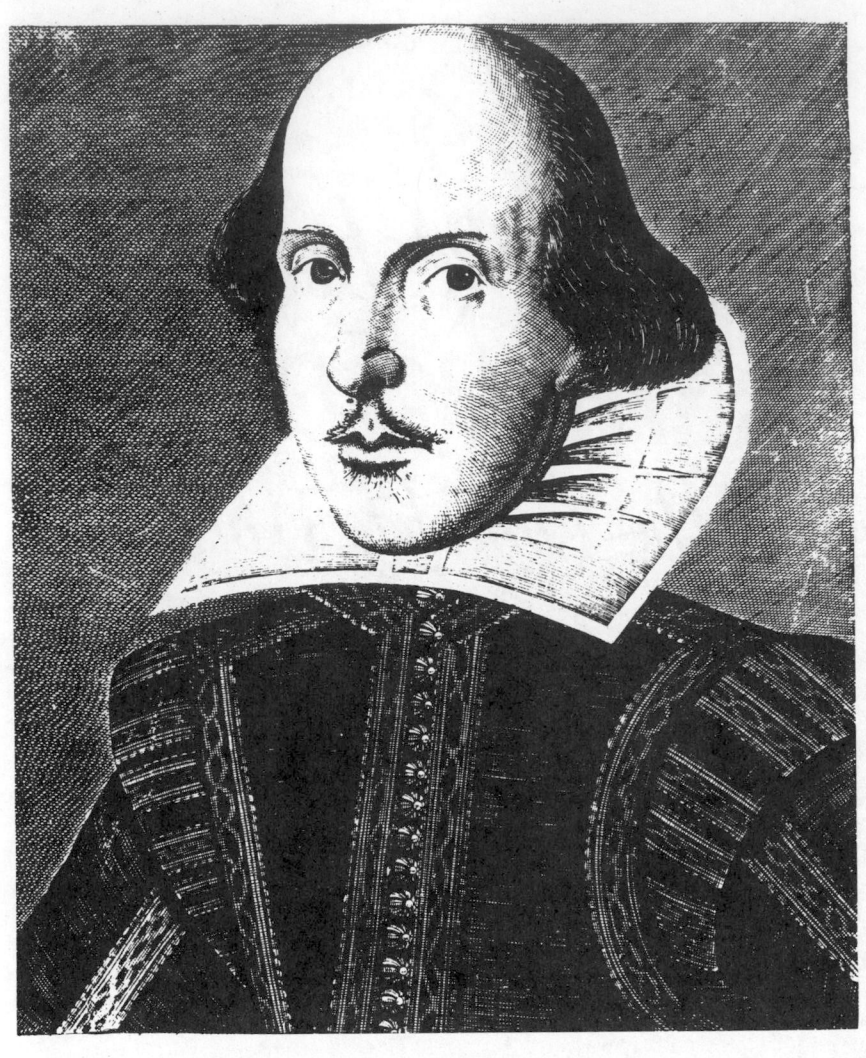

TO THE READER.

THIS FIGURE, THAT THOU HERE SEEST PUT,
  IT WAS FOR GENTLE SHAKESPEARE CUT;
WHEREIN THE GRAVER HAD A STRIFE
  WITH NATURE, TO OUT-DO THE LIFE:
O, COULD HE BUT HAVE DRAWN HIS WIT
  AS WELL IN BRASS, AS HE HATH HIT
HIS FACE; THE PRINT WOULD THEN SURPASS
  ALL, THAT WAS EVER WRIT IN BRASS.
BUT, SINCE HE CANNOT, READER, LOOK,
  NOT ON HIS PICTURE, BUT HIS BOOK.
                              BEN: JONSON.

William Shakespeare

The Complete Works

The Edition of
The Shakespeare Head Press
Oxford

MetroBooks

This edition published by MetroBooks,
an imprint of Friedman/Fairfax Publishers.

1994 MetroBooks

ISBN 1-58663-556-5

Printed and bound in the United States of America

02 03 04 05 06 07 MC 23 22 21 20 19 18 17

HAW

For bulk purchases and special sales, please contact:
Friedman/Fairfax Publishers
Attention: Sales Department
230 Fifth Avenue, Suite 700-701
New York, NY 10001
212/685-6610 Fax 212/685-3916

Visit our website:
www.metrobooks.com

THE CONTENTS

In this volume the Plays are arranged in the chronological order of their composition. Naturally, no claim to finality is made in a subject so beset with difficulties, but the sequence may be taken as fairly representing the general results of recent research. The time-honoured division into Comedies, Histories and Tragedies, dating from the First Folio and since universally followed, has been abandoned, in the belief that there were room and need for an edition that should enable readers to approach the body of the plays, not as a static monument of achievement, but as a vital and growing organism revealing the evolution of the poet's personality and genius.

NOTE

The text used for this edition is that prepared by the late Arthur Henry Bullen for the Stratford Town Edition, to print which he founded the Shakespeare Head Press in 1904.

v

To the Most Noble and Incomparable Pair of
Brethren,

WILLIAM

EARL OF PEMBROKE, &C., LORD CHAMBERLAIN
TO THE KING'S MOST EXCELLENT MAJESTY,

AND PHILIP

EARL OF MONTGOMERY, &C., GENTLEMAN OF
HIS MAJESTY'S BED-CHAMBER; BOTH KNIGHTS
OF THE MOST NOBLE ORDER OF THE GARTER,
AND OUR SINGULAR GOOD LORDS.

Right Honourable,

WHILST *we study to be thankful in our particular for the many favours we have received from your L.L., we are fallen upon the ill fortune, to mingle two the most diverse things that can be, fear and rashness; rashness in the enterprise, and fear of the success. For when we value the places your H.H. sustain, we cannot but know their dignity greater than to descend to the reading of these trifles; and while we name them trifles, we have deprived ourselves of the defence of our dedication. But since your L.L. have been pleased to think these trifles something heretofore, and have prosecuted both them and their author living with so much favour, we hope that (they outliving him, and he not having the fate, common with some, to be executor to his own writings) you will use the like indulgence toward them you have done unto their parent. There is a great difference whether any book choose his patrons, or find them: this hath done both. For so much were your L.L. likings of the several parts when they were acted, as before they were publish'd, the volume ask'd to be yours. We have but collected them, and done an office to the dead, to procure his orphans guardians; without ambition either of self-profit or fame; only to keep the memory of so worthy a friend and fellow alive as was our* SHAKESPEARE, *by humble offer of his plays to your most noble patronage. Wherein, as we have justly observed no man to come near your L.L. but with a kind of religious address, it hath been the height of our care, who are the presenters, to make the present worthy of your H.H. by the perfection. But there we must also crave our abilities to be consider'd, my Lords. We cannot go beyond our own powers. Country hands reach forth milk, cream, fruits, or what they have; and many nations, we have heard, that had not gums and incense, obtain'd their requests with a leaven'd cake. It was no fault to approach their gods by what means they could: and the most, though meanest, of things are made more precious when they are dedicated to temples. In that name, therefore, we most humbly consecrate to your H.H. these remains of your servant* SHAKESPEARE, *that what delight is in them may be ever your L.L., the reputation his, and the faults ours, if any be committed by a pair so careful to show their gratitude both to the living and the dead as is*

Your Lordships' most bounden,

JOHN HEMINGE,
HENRY CONDELL.

TO THE GREAT VARIETY OF READERS

FROM the most able to him that can but spell: there you are number'd. We had rather you were weigh'd: especially when the fate of all books depends upon your capacities; and not of your heads alone, but of your purses. Well, it is now public; and you will stand for your privileges, we know,—to read and censure. Do so, but buy it first. That doth best commend a book, the stationer says. Then how odd soever your brains be or your wisdoms, make your license the same, and spare not. Judge your six-pen'orth, your shillings-worth, your five-shillings-worth at a time, or higher, so you rise to the just rates, and welcome. But, whatever you do, buy. Censure will not drive a trade, or make the jack go. And though you be a magistrate of wit, and sit on the stage at *Black-friars* or the *Cock-pit*, to arraign plays daily, know, these plays have had their trial already, and stood out all appeals, and do now come forth quitted rather by a decree of court than any purchased letters of commendation.

It had been a thing, we confess, worthy to have been wish'd, that the author himself had lived to have set forth and overseen his own writings. But, since it hath been ordain'd otherwise, and he by death departed from that right, we pray you do not envy his friends the office of their care and pain, to have collected and publish'd them; and so to have publish'd them as where before you were abused with divers stolen and surreptitious copies, maim'd and deform'd by the frauds and stealths of injurious impostors, that exposed them, even those are now offer'd to your view cured and perfect of their limbs, and all the rest absolute in their numbers as he conceived them; who, as he was a happy imitator of Nature, was a most gentle expresser of it: his mind and hand went together; and what he thought, he utter'd with that easiness, that we have scarce received from him a blot in his papers. But it is not our province, who only gather his works and give them you, to praise him. It is yours that read him: and there we hope, to your divers capacities, you will find enough both to draw and hold you; for his wit can no more lie hid than it could be lost. Read him, therefore; and again and again: and if then you do not like him, surely you are in some manifest danger not to understand him. And so we leave you to other of his friends, whom if you need, can be your guides: if you need them not, you can lead yourselves and others. And such readers we wish him.

JOHN HEMINGE,
HENRY CONDELL.

To the memory of the deceased author
MASTER W. SHAKESPEARE

SHAKESPEARE, *at length thy pious fellows give*
The world thy works; thy works, by which outlive
Thy tomb thy name must: when that stone is rent,
And time dissolves thy Stratford *monument,*
Here we alive shall view thee still; this book,
When brass and marble fade, shall make thee look
Fresh to all ages; when posterity
Shall loathe what's new, think all is prodigy
That is not Shakespeare's, *every line, each verse,*
Here shall revive, redeem thee from thy hearse.
Nor fire, nor cank'ring age,—as Naso *said*
Of his,—thy wit-fraught book shall once invade:
Nor shall I e'er believe or think thee dead,
Though miss'd, until our bankrout stage be sped—
Impossible—with some new strain t'out-do
Passions of Juliet *and her* Romeo;
Or till I hear a scene more nobly take,
Than when thy half-sword-parleying Romans
  spake:
Till these, till any of thy volume's rest,
Shall with more fire, more feeling be exprest,
Be sure, our Shakespeare, *thou canst never die,*
But, crown'd with laurel, live eternally.

L. DIGGES.

To the memory of
MASTER W. SHAKESPEARE

WE *wonder'd*, Shakespeare, *that thou went'st*
  so soon
From the world's stage to the grave's tiring-room:
We thought thee dead; but this thy printed worth
Tells thy spectators that thou went'st but forth
To enter with applause. An actor's art
Can die, and live to act a second part:
That's but an exit *of mortality,*
This a re-entrance *to a plaudite.*

I. M.

THE NAMES OF THE PRINCIPAL
ACTORS IN ALL THESE PLAYS

William Shakespeare.
Richard Burbadge.
John Heminge.
Augustine Phillips.
William Kempt.
Thomas Poope.
George Bryan.
Henry Condell.
William Slye.
Richard Cowly.
John Lowine.
Samuel Crosse.
Alexander Cooke.
Samuel Gilburne.
Robert Armin.
William Ostler.
Nathan Field.
John Underwood.
Nicholas Tooley.
William Ecclestone.
Joseph Taylor.
Robert Benfield.
Robert Goughe.
Richard Robinson.
John Shancke.
John Rice.

To the memory of my beloved, the author,

MASTER WILLIAM SHAKESPEARE

AND WHAT HE HATH LEFT US

TO draw no envy, Shakespeare, on thy name,
Am I thus ample to thy book and fame;
While I confess thy writings to be such
As neither man nor Muse can praise too much:
'Tis true, and all men's suffrage: but these ways
Were not the paths I meant unto thy praise;
For seeliest ignorance on these may light,
Which, when it sounds at best, but echoes right;
Or blind affection, which doth ne'er advance
The truth, but gropes, and urgeth all by chance;
Or crafty malice might pretend this praise,
And think to ruin where it seem'd to raise:
These are as some infamous bawd or whore
Should praise a matron:—what could hurt her
    more?
But thou art proof against them; and, indeed,
Above the ill fortune of them or the need.
I, therefore, will begin. Soul of the age,
The applause, delight, the wonder of our stage,
My Shakespeare, rise! I will not lodge thee by
Chaucer or Spenser, or bid Beaumont lie
A little further, to make thee a room:
Thou art a monument without a tomb,
And art alive still, while thy book doth live,
And we have wits to read, and praise to give.
That I not mix thee so, my brain excuses,—
I mean, with great but disproportion'd Muses;
For if I thought my judgement were of years,
I should commit thee surely with thy peers,
And tell how far thou didst our Lyly outshine,
Or sporting Kyd, or Marlowe's mighty line:
And though thou hadst small Latin and less
    Greek,
From thence to honour thee I would not seek
For names; but call forth thundering Aeschylus,
Euripides, and Sophocles to us,
Pacuvius, Accius, him of Cordova, dead,
To life again, to hear thy buskin tread
And shake a stage; or when thy socks were on,
Leave thee alone for the comparison
Of all that insolent Greece or haughty Rome
Sent forth, or since did from their ashes come.
Triumph, my Britain! thou hast one to show,
To whom all scenes of Europe homage owe.
He was not of an age, but for all time;
And all the Muses still were in their prime,
When, like Apollo, he came forth to warm
Our ears, or like a Mercury to charm.
Nature herself was proud of his designs,
And joy'd to wear the dressing of his lines;
Which were so richly spun, and woven so fit,
As since she will vouchsafe no other wit:
The merry Greek, tart Aristophanes,
Neat Terence, witty Plautus, now not please;
But antiquated and deserted l.e,
As they were not of Nature's family.
Yet must I not give Nature all; thy art,
My gentle Shakespeare, must enjoy a part:
For though the poet's matter nature be,
His art doth give the fashion; and that he

Who casts to write a living line, must sweat,—
Such as thine are,—and strike the second heat
Upon the Muses' anvil; turn the same,
And himself with it, that he thinks to frame;
Or, for the laurel, he may gain a scorn,—
For a good poet's made, as well as born:
And such wert thou. Look how the father's face
Lives in his issue; even so the race
Of Shakespeare's mind and manners brightly
    shines
In his well-turned and true-filed lines;
In each of which he seems to shake a lance,
As brandish'd at the eyes of ignorance.
Sweet Swan of Avon, what a sight it were
To see thee in our waters yet appear,
And make those flights upon the banks of
    Thames,
That so did take Eliza and our James!
But stay, I see thee in the hemisphere
Advanced, and made a constellation there:
Shine forth, thou star of poets, and with rage
Or influence chide or cheer the drooping stage;
Which, since thy flight from hence, hath mourn'd
    like night,
And despairs day, but for thy volume's light.

BEN: JONSON

UPON THE LINES AND LIFE OF THE FAMOUS SCENIC POET

MASTER WILLIAM SHAKESPEARE

THOSE *hands which you so clapp'd, go now
    and wring,*
You Britons *brave; for done are* Shakespeare's *days,*
His days are done that made the dainty plays,
Which made the Globe of heaven and earth to ring
Dried is that vein, dried is the Thespian *spring,*
Turn'd all to tears, and Phœbus *clouds his rays:*
That corpse, that coffin, now bestick those bays,
Which crown'd him poet *first, then* poets' *king.*
If tragedies *might any* prologue *have,*
All those he made would scarce make one to this;
Where Fame, *now that he gone is to the grave—*
Death's *public tiring-house—the* Nuntius *is:*
For, though his line of life went soon about,
The life yet of his lines shall never out.

HUGH HOLLAND

THE FIRST PART OF
KING HENRY THE SIXTH

DRAMATIS PERSONAE

KING HENRY THE SIXTH.

DUKE OF GLOSTER, *uncle to the King, and Protector.*

DUKE OF BEDFORD, *uncle to the King, and Regent of France.*

THOMAS BEAUFORT, *Duke of Exeter, great-uncle to the King.*

HENRY BEAUFORT, *great-uncle to the King, Bishop of Winchester, and afterwards Cardinal.*

JOHN BEAUFORT, *Earl of Somerset, afterwards Duke.*

RICHARD PLANTAGENET, *son of Richard late Earl of Cambridge, afterwards Duke of York.*

EARL OF WARWICK.

EARL OF SALISBURY.

EARL OF SUFFOLK.

LORD TALBOT, *afterwards Earl of Shrewsbury.*

JOHN TALBOT, *his son.*

EDMUND MORTIMER, *Earl of March.*

SIR JOHN FASTOLFE.

SIR WILLIAM LUCY.

SIR WILLIAM GLANSDALE.

SIR THOMAS GARGRAVE.

MAYOR OF LONDON.

WOODVILLE, *Lieutenant of the Tower.*

VERNON, *of the White-Rose or York faction.*

BASSET, *of the Red-Rose or Lancaster faction.*

A LAWYER.—MORTIMER'S KEEPERS.

CHARLES, *Dauphin, and afterwards King, of France.*

REIGNIER, *Duke of Anjou, and titular King of Naples.*

DUKE OF BURGUNDY.

DUKE OF ALENÇON.

BASTARD OF ORLEANS.

GOVERNOR OF PARIS.

MASTER-GUNNER OF ORLEANS, *and his* SON

GENERAL *of the French forces in Bourdeaux.*

A FRENCH SERGEANT.   A PORTER.

AN OLD SHEPHERD, *father to Joan la Pucelle.*

MARGARET, *daughter to Reignier, afterwards married to King Henry.*

COUNTESS OF AUVERGNE.

JOAN LA PUCELLE, *commonly called Joan of Arc.*

LORDS, WARDERS OF THE TOWER, HERALDS.

OFFICERS, SOLDIERS, MESSENGERS *and* ATTENDANTS.

FIENDS *appearing to La Pucelle.*

SCENE—*Partly in England, and partly in France.*

ACT I. SCENE I.

Westminster Abbey.

Dead march.   Enter the Funeral of KING HENRY THE FIFTH, *attended on by the* DUKE OF BEDFORD, *Regent of France; the* DUKE OF GLOSTER, *Protector; the* DUKE OF EXETER, *the* EARL OF WARWICK, *the* BISHOP OF WINCHESTER, HERALDS, *&c.*

DUKE OF BEDFORD.

HUNG be the heavens with black, yield day to night!
Comets, importing change of times and states,
Brandish your crystal tresses in the sky,
And with them scourge the bad revolting stars
That have consented unto Henry's death!
Henry the Fifth, too famous to live long!
England ne'er lost a king of so much worth.

DUKE OF GLOSTER.

England ne'er had a king until his time.
Virtue he had, deserving to command:
His brandisht sword did blind men with his beams;
His arms spread wider than a dragon's wings;
His sparkling eyes, replete with wrathful fire,
More dazzled and drove back his enemies
Than mid-day sun fierce bent against their faces.
What should I say? his deeds exceed all speech:
He ne'er lift up his hand, but conquered.

DUKE OF EXETER.

We mourn in black: why mourn we not in blood?
Henry is dead, and never shall revive:
Upon a wooden coffin we attend;
And death's dishonourable victory
We with our stately presence glorify,
Like captives bound to a triumphant car.
What! shall we curse the planets of mishap
That plotted thus our glory's overthrow?
Or shall we think the subtle-witted French
Conjurers and sorcerers, that, afraid of him,
By magic verses have contrived his end?

BISHOP OF WINCHESTER.

He was a king blest of the King of kings.
Unto the French the dreadful judgement-day
So dreadful will not be as was his sight.
The battles of the Lord of hosts he fought:
The church's prayers made him so prosperous.

DUKE OF GLOSTER.

The church! where is it? Had not churchmen pray'd,
His thread of life had not so soon decay'd:
None do you like but an effeminate prince,
Whom, like a schoolboy, you may overawe.

BISHOP OF WINCHESTER.

Gloster, whate'er we like, thou art Protector,
And lookest to command the prince and realm.
Thy wife is proud; she holdeth thee in awe,
More than God or religious churchmen may.

DUKE OF GLOSTER.

Name not religion, for thou lovest the flesh;
And ne'er throughout the year to church thou go'st,
Except it be to pray against thy foes.

I

DUKE OF BEDFORD.

Cease, cease these jars, and rest your minds in
   peace!
Let's to the altar:—heralds, wait on us:—
Instead of gold, we'll offer up our arms;
Since arms avail not, now that Henry's dead.—
Posterity, await for wretched years,
When at their mothers' moist eyes babes shall
   suck;
Our isle be made a marish of salt tears,
And none but women left to wail the dead.—
Henry the Fifth! thy ghost I invocate;
Prosper this realm, keep it from civil broils!
Combat with adverse planets in the heavens!
A far more glorious star thy soul will make
Than Julius Cæsar or bright—

Enter a MESSENGER.

MESSENGER.

My honourable lords, health to you all!
Sad tidings bring I to you out of France,
Of loss, of slaughter, and discomfiture:
Guienne, Champagne, Rheims, Rouen, Orleans,
Paris, Guysors, Poictiers, are all quite lost.

DUKE OF BEDFORD.

What say'st thou, man! before dead Henry's corse
Speak softly, or the loss of those great towns
Will make him burst his lead, and rise from death.

DUKE OF GLOSTER.

Is Paris lost? is Rouen yielded up?
If Henry were recall'd to life again,
These news would cause him once more yield the
   ghost.

DUKE OF EXETER.

How were they lost? what treachery was used?

MESSENGER.

No treachery; but want of men and money.
Amongst the soldiers this is muttered,
That here you maintain several factions;
And, whilst a field should be dispatcht and fought,
You are disputing of your generals:
One would have lingering wars, with little cost;
Another would fly swift, but wanteth wings;
A third thinks, without expense at all,
By guileful fair words peace may be obtain'd.
Awake, awake, English nobility!
Let not sloth dim your honours new-begot:
Cropt are the flower-de-luces in your arms;
Of England's coat one half is cut away.

DUKE OF EXETER.

Were our tears wanting to this funeral,
These tidings would call forth their flowing tides.

DUKE OF BEDFORD.

Me they concern; Regent I am of France.—
Give me my steeled coat! I'll fight for France.
Away with these disgraceful wailing robes!
Wounds will I lend the French, instead of eyes,
To weep their intermissive miseries.

Enter a SECOND MESSENGER.

SECOND MESSENGER.

Lords, view these letters, full of bad mischance.
France is revolted from the English quite,
Except some petty towns of no import:
The Dauphin Charles is crowned king in Rheims;
The Bastard of Orleans with him is join'd;
Reignier, duke of Anjou, doth take his part;
The Duke of Alençon flieth to his side.

DUKE OF EXETER.

The Dauphin crowned king! all fly to him!
O, whither shall we fly from this reproach?

DUKE OF GLOSTER.

We will not fly, but to our enemies' throats:—
Bedford, if thou be slack, I'll fight it out.

DUKE OF BEDFORD.

Gloster, why doubt'st thou of my forwardness?
An army have I muster'd in my thoughts,
Wherewith already France is overrun.

Enter a THIRD MESSENGER.

THIRD MESSENGER.

My gracious lords, to add to your laments,
Wherewith you now bedew King Henry's
   hearse,
I must inform you of a dismal fight
Betwixt the stout Lord Talbot and the French.

BISHOP OF WINCHESTER.

What! wherein Talbot overcame? is't so?

THIRD MESSENGER.

O, no; wherein Lord Talbot was o'erthrown:
The circumstance I'll tell you more at large.
The tenth of August last, this dreadful lord,
Retiring from the siege of Orleans,
Having full scarce six thousand in his troop,
By three-and-twenty thousand of the French
Was round encompassed and set upon.
No leisure had he to enrank his men;
He wanted pikes to set before his archers;
Instead whereof, sharp stakes, pluckt out of
   hedges,
They pitched in the ground confusedly,
To keep the horsemen off from breaking in.
More than three hours the fight continued;
Where valiant Talbot, above human thought,
Enacted wonders with his sword and lance:
Hundreds he sent to hell, and none durst stand
   him;
Here, there, and every where, enraged he flew:
The French exclaim'd, the devil was in arms;
All the whole army stood agazed on him:
His soldiers, spying his undaunted spirit,
'A Talbot! a Talbot!' cried out amain,
And rusht into the bowels of the battle.
Here had the conquest fully been seal'd up,
If Sir John Fastolfe had not play'd the coward:
He, being in the vaward,—placed behind,
With purpose to relieve and follow them,—
Cowardly fled, not having struck one stroke.
Hence grew the general wrack and massacre;
Enclosed were they with their enemies:
A base Walloon, to win the Dauphin's grace,
Thrust Talbot with a spear into the back;
Whom all France, with their chief assembled
   strength,
Durst not presume to look once in the face.

DUKE OF BEDFORD.

Is Talbot slain? then I will slay myself,
For living idly here in pomp and ease,
Whilst such a worthy leader, wanting aid,
Unto his dastard foemen is betray'd.

THIRD MESSENGER.

O, no, he lives; but is took prisoner,
And Lord Scales with him, and Lord Hunger-
   ford:
Most of the rest slaughter'd or took likewise.

DUKE OF BEDFORD.

His ransom there is none but I shall pay:
I'll hale the Dauphin headlong from his throne,—
His crown shall be the ransom of my friend;
Four of their lords I'll change for one of ours.—
Farewell, my masters; to my task will I;
Bonfires in France forthwith I am to make,
To keep our great Saint George's feast withal:
Ten thousand soldiers with me I will take,
Whose bloody deeds shall make all Europe quake.

THIRD MESSENGER.

So you had need; for Orleans is besieged;
The English army is grown weak and faint:
The Earl of Salisbury craveth supply,
And hardly keeps his men from mutiny,
Since they, so few, watch such a multitude.

DUKE OF EXETER.

Remember, lords, your oaths to Henry sworn,
Either to quell the Dauphin utterly,
Or bring him in obedience to your yoke.

DUKE OF BEDFORD.

I do remember it; and here take my leave,
To go about my preparation.   [*Exit.*

DUKE OF GLOSTER.

I'll to the Tower, with all the haste I can,
To view th' artillery and munition;
And then I will proclaim young Henry king.
    [*Exit.*

DUKE OF EXETER.

To Eltham will I, where the young king is,
Being ordain'd his special governor;
And for his safety there I'll best devise.   [*Exit.*

BISHOP OF WINCHESTER.

Each hath his place and function to attend:
I am left out; for me nothing remains.
But long I will not be Jack-out-of-office:
The king from Eltham I intend to steal,
And sit at chiefest stern of public weal.   [*Exit.*

SCENE II.

France. Before Orleans.

Sound a flourish. Enter CHARLES, ALENÇON,
and REIGNIER, *marching with drum and* SOL-
DIERS.

CHARLES.

MARS his true moving, even as in the heavens,
So in the earth, to this day is not known:
Late did he shine upon the English side;
Now we are victors, upon us he smiles.
What towns of any moment but we have?
At pleasure here we lie, near Orleans;
Otherwhiles the famisht English, like pale ghosts,
Faintly besiege us one hour in a month.

DUKE OF ALENÇON.

They want their porridge and their fat bull-
    beeves:
Either they must be dieted like mules,
And have their provender tied to their mouths,
Or piteous they will look, like drowned mice.

REIGNIER.

Let's raise the siege: why lie we idly here?
Talbot is taken, whom we wont to fear:
Remaineth none but mad-brain'd Salisbury;
And he may well in fretting spend his gall,—
Nor men nor money hath he to make war.

CHARLES.

Sound, sound alarum! we will rush on them.
Now for the honour of the forlorn French!—
Him I forgive my death that killeth me
When he sees me go back one foot or fly. [*Exeunt.*
*Here alarum; they are beaten back by the English
    with great loss. Enter* CHARLES, ALENÇON,
REIGNIER, *and others.*

CHARLES.

Who ever saw the like? what men have I!—
Dogs! cowards! dastards!—I would ne'er have
    fled,
But that they left me midst my enemies.

REIGNIER.

Salisbury is a desperate homicide;
He fighteth as one weary of his life.
The other lords, like lions wanting food,
Do rush upon us as their hungry prey.

DUKE OF ALENÇON.

Froissart, a countryman of ours, records,
England all Olivers and Rowlands bred
During the time Edward the Third did reign.
More truly now may this be verified;
For none but Samsons and Goliases
It sendeth forth to skirmish. One to ten!
Lean raw-boned rascals! who would e'er suppose
They had such courage and audacity?

CHARLES.

Let's leave this town; for they are hare-brain'd
    slaves,
And hunger will enforce them be more eager:
Of old I know them; rather with their teeth
The walls they'll tear down than forsake the siege.

REIGNIER.

I think, by some odd gimmers or device,
Their arms are set like clocks, still to strike on;
Else ne'er could they hold out so as they do.
By my consent, we'll even let them alone.

DUKE OF ALENÇON.

Be it so.
    Enter the BASTARD OF ORLEANS.

BASTARD OF ORLEANS.

Where's the Prince Dauphin? I have news for
    him.

CHARLES.

Bastard of Orleans, thrice welcome to us.

BASTARD OF ORLEANS.

Methinks your looks are sad, your cheer appall'd:
Hath the late overthrow wrought this offence?
Be not dismay'd, for succour is at hand:
A holy maid hither with me I bring,
Which, by a vision sent to her from heaven,
Ordained is to raise this tedious siege,
And drive the English forth the bounds of France.
The spirit of deep prophecy she hath,
Exceeding the nine sibyls of old Rome:
What's past and what's to come she can descry.
Speak, shall I call her in? Believe my words,
For they are certain and unfallible.

CHARLES.

Go, call her in. [*Exit* BASTARD.] But first, to try
    her skill,
Reignier, stand thou as Dauphin in my place:
Question her proudly; let thy looks be stern:
By this means shall I sound what skill she hath.
    [*Retires.*

Enter the BASTARD OF ORLEANS, *with* JOAN
LA PUCELLE.
REIGNIER.
Fair maid, is't thou wilt do these wondrous feats?
JOAN LA PUCELLE.
Reignier, is't thou that thinkest to beguile me?
Where is the Dauphin?—Come, come from be-
hind;
I know thee well, though never seen before.
Be not amazed, there's nothing hid from me:
In private will I talk with thee apart.—
Stand back, you lords, and give us leave awhile.
REIGNIER.
She takes upon her bravely at first dash.
JOAN LA PUCELLE.
Dauphin, I am by birth a shepherd's daughter,
My wit untrain'd in any kind of art.
Heaven and our Lady gracious hath it pleased
To shine on my contemptible estate:
Lo, whilst I waited on my tender lambs,
And to sun's parching heat display'd my cheeks,
God's mother deigned to appear to me,
And, in a vision full of majesty,
Will'd me to leave my base vocation,
And free my country from calamity.
Her aid she promised, and assured success:
In complete glory she reveal'd herself;
And, whereas I was black and swart before,
With those clear rays which she infused on me
That beauty am I blest with which you see.
Ask me what question thou canst possible,
And I will answer unpremeditated:
My courage try by combat, if thou darest,
And thou shalt find that I exceed my sex.
Resolve on this,—thou shalt be fortunate,
If thou receive me for thy warlike mate.
CHARLES.
Thou hast astonisht me with thy high terms:
Only this proof I'll of thy valour make,—
In single combat thou shalt buckle with me;
And if thou vanquishest, thy words are true;
Otherwise I renounce all confidence.
JOAN LA PUCELLE.
I am prepared: here is my keen-edged sword,
Deckt with five flower-de-luces on each side;
The which at Touraine, in Saint Katharine's
churchyard,
Out of a deal of old iron I chose forth.
CHARLES.
Then come, o' God's name; I fear no woman.
JOAN LA PUCELLE.
And, while I live, I'll ne'er fly from a man.
[*Here they fight and* JOAN LA PUCELLE
overcomes.
CHARLES.
Stay, stay thy hands! thou art an Amazon,
And fightest with the sword of Deborah.
JOAN LA PUCELLE.
Christ's mother helps me, else I were too weak.
CHARLES.
Whoe'er helps thee, 'tis thou that must help me:
Impatiently I burn with thy desire;
My heart and hands thou hast at once subdued.
Excellent Pucelle, if thy name be so,
Let me thy servant, and not sovereign, be:
'Tis the French Dauphin sueth to thee thus.

JOAN LA PUCELLE.
I must not yield to any rites of love,
For my profession's sacred from above:
When I have chased all thy foes from hence,
Then will I think upon a recompense.
CHARLES.
Meantime look gracious on thy prostrate thrall.
REIGNIER.
My lord, methinks, is very long in talk.
DUKE OF ALENÇON.
Doubtless he shrives this woman to her smock;
Else ne'er could he so long protract his speech.
REIGNIER.
Shall we disturb him, since he keeps no mean?
DUKE OF ALENÇON.
He may mean more than we poor men do know:
These women are shrewd tempters with their
tongues.
REIGNIER.
My lord, where are you? what devise you on?
Shall we give over Orleans, or no?
JOAN LA PUCELLE.
Why, no, I say, distrustful recreants!
Fight till the last gasp; I will be your guard.
CHARLES.
What she says, I'll confirm: we'll fight it out.
JOAN LA PUCELLE.
Assign'd am I to be the English scourge.
This night the siege assuredly I'll raise:
Expect Saint Martin's summer, halcyon days,
Since I have entered into these wars.
Glory is like a circle in the water,
Which never ceaseth to enlarge itself,
Till, by broad spreading, it disperse to naught.
With Henry's death the English circle ends;
Dispersed are the glories it included.
Now am I like that proud-insulting ship
Which Cæsar and his fortune bare at once.
CHARLES.
Was Mahomet inspired with a dove?
Thou with an eagle art inspired, then.
Helen, the mother of great Constantine,
Nor yet Saint Philip's daughters, were like thee.
Bright star of Venus, faln down on the earth,
How may I ever worship thee enough?
DUKE OF ALENÇON.
Leave off delays, and let us raise the siege.
REIGNIER.
Woman, do what thou canst to save our honours;
Drive them from Orleans, and be immortalized.
CHARLES.
Presently we'll try:—come, let's away about it:—
No prophet will I trust, if she prove false. [*Exeunt.*

SCENE III.
London.　Before the Tower.

Enter the DUKE OF GLOSTER, *with his* SERVING-
MEN *in blue coats.*

DUKE OF GLOSTER.
I AM come to survey the Tower this day:
　Since Henry's death, I fear, there is convey-
ance.—
Where be these warders, that they wait not here?
Open the gates; 'tis Gloucester that calls.
[*Servants knock.*

FIRST WARDER [*within*].
Who's there that knocks so imperiously?
FIRST SERVING-MAN.
It is the noble Duke of Gloucester.
SECOND WARDER [*within*].
Whoe'er he be, you may not be let in.
FIRST SERVING-MAN.
Villains, answer you so the lord Protector?
FIRST WARDER [*within*].
The Lord protect him! so we answer him:
We do no otherwise than we are will'd.
DUKE OF GLOSTER.
Who willed you? or whose will stands but mine?
There's none Protector of the realm but I.—
Break up the gates, I'll be your warrantize:
Shall I be flouted thus by dunghill grooms?
[GLOSTER'S *men rush at the Tower-gates,
and* WOODVILLE, *the Lieutenant, speaks
within.*
WOODVILLE.
What noise is this? what traitors have we here?
DUKE OF GLOSTER.
Lieutenant, is it you whose voice I hear?
Open the gates; here's Gloster that would enter.
WOODVILLE.
Have patience, noble duke; I may not open;
The Cardinal of Winchester forbids:
From him I have express commandement
That thou nor none of thine shall be let in.
DUKE OF GLOSTER.
Faint-hearted Woodville, prizest him 'fore me,—
Arrogant Winchester, that haughty prelate,
Whom Henry, our late sovereign, ne'er could
brook?
Thou art no friend to God or to the king:
Open the gates, or I'll shut thee out shortly.
SERVING-MEN.
Open the gates unto the lord Protector:
Or we'll burst them open, if that you come not
quickly.
Enter to the PROTECTOR *at the Tower-gates* WIN-
CHESTER, *and his* MEN *in tawny coats.*
BISHOP OF WINCHESTER.
How now, ambitious Humphrey! what means this?
DUKE OF GLOSTER.
Peel'd priest, dost thou command me to be shut
out?
BISHOP OF WINCHESTER.
I do, thou most usurping proditor,
And not Protector, of the king or realm.
DUKE OF GLOSTER.
Stand back, thou manifest conspirator,
Thou that contrivedst to murder our dead lord;
Thou that givest whores indulgences to sin:
I'll canvass thee in thy broad cardinal's hat.
If thou proceed in this thy insolence.
BISHOP OF WINCHESTER.
Nay, stand thou back; I will not budge a foot:
This be Damascus, be thou cursed Cain,
To slay thy brother Abel, if thou wilt.
DUKE OF GLOSTER.
I will not slay thee, but I'll drive thee back:
Thy scarlet robes as a child's bearing-cloth
I'll use to carry thee out of this place.
BISHOP OF WINCHESTER.
Do what thou darest; I beard thee to thy face.

DUKE OF GLOSTER.
What! am I dared, and bearded to my face?—
Draw, men, for all this privileged place;
Blue-coats to tawny-coats.—Priest, beware your
beard;
I mean to tug it, and to cuff you soundly:
Under my feet I'll stamp thy cardinal's hat;
In spite of Pope or dignities of church,
Here by the cheeks I'll drag thee up and down.
BISHOP OF WINCHESTER.
Gloster, thou wilt answer this before the Pope.
DUKE OF GLOSTER.
Winchester goose! I cry, a rope! a rope!—
Now beat them hence; why do you let them
stay?—
Thee I'll chase hence, thou wolf in sheep's
array.—
Out, tawny-coats!—out, scarlet hypocrite!
Here GLOSTER'S *men beat out the* CARDINAL'S
men, and enter in the hurly-burly the MAYOR OF
LONDON *and his* OFFICERS.
MAYOR OF LONDON.
Fie, lords! that you, being supreme magistrates,
Thus contumeliously should break the peace!
DUKE OF GLOSTER.
Peace, mayor! thou know'st little of my wrongs:
Here's Beaufort, that regards nor God nor king,
Hath here distrain'd the Tower to his use.
BISHOP OF WINCHESTER.
Here's Gloucester, a foe to citizens;
One that still motions war, and never peace,
O'ercharging your free purses with large fines;
That seeks to overthrow religion,
Because he is Protector of the realm;
And would have armour here out of the Tower,
To crown himself king, and suppress the prince.
DUKE OF GLOSTER.
I will not answer thee with words, but blows.
[*Here they skirmish again.*
MAYOR OF LONDON.
Naught rests for me, in this tumultuous strife,
But to make open proclamation:—
Come, officer; as loud as e'er thou canst.
OFFICER [*cries*].
All manner of men assembled here in arms this
day against God's peace and the king's, we
charge and command you, in his highness' name,
to repair to your several dwelling-places; and not
to wear, handle, or use any sword, weapon, or
dagger, henceforward, upon pain of death.
DUKE OF GLOSTER.
Cardinal, I'll be no breaker of the law:
But we shall meet, and break our minds at large.
BISHOP OF WINCHESTER.
Gloster, we'll meet; to thy dear cost, be sure:
Thy heart-blood I will have for this day's work.
MAYOR OF LONDON.
I'll call for clubs, if you will not away:—
This cardinal's more haughty than the devil.
DUKE OF GLOSTER.
Mayor, farewell: thou dost but what thou mayst.
BISHOP OF WINCHESTER.
Abominable Gloster! guard thy head;
For I intend to have it ere long.
[*Exeunt, severally,* GLOSTER *and* WIN-
CHESTER *with their* SERVING-MEN.

MAYOR OF LONDON.
See the coast clear'd, and then we will depart.—
Good God, these nobles should such stomachs
     bear!
I myself fight not once in forty year.   [*Exeunt.*

SCENE IV.

France. Before Orleans.

Enter, on the walls, the MASTER-GUNNER OF
ORLEANS, *and his* BOY.

MASTER-GUNNER OF ORLEANS.
Sirrah, thou know'st how Orleans is besieged,
And how the English have the suburbs won.
BOY.
Father, I know; and oft have shot at them,
Howe'er unfortunate I miss'd my aim.
MASTER-GUNNER OF ORLEANS.
But now thou shalt not. Be thou ruled by me:
Chief master-gunner am I of this town;
Something I must do to procure me grace.
The prince's espials have informed me
How the English, in the suburbs close intrencht,
Wont, through a secret grate of iron bars
In yonder tower, to overpeer the city;
And thence discover how with most advantage
They may vex us with shot or with assault.
To intercept this inconvenience,
A piece of ordnance 'gainst it I have placed;
And even these three days have I watcht, if I
Could see them.
Now do thou watch, for I can stay no longer.
If thou spy'st any, run and bring me word;
And thou shalt find me at the governor's.   [*Exit.*
BOY.
Father, I warrant you; take you no care;
I'll never trouble you, if I may spy them.   [*Exit.*

Enter SALISBURY *and* TALBOT *on the turrets, with*
SIR WILLIAM GLANSDALE, SIR THOMAS GAR-
GRAVE, *and others.*

EARL OF SALISBURY.
Talbot, my life, my joy, again return'd!
How wert thou handled being prisoner,
Or by what means got'st thou to be released,
Discourse, I prithee, on this turret's top.
LORD TALBOT.
The Duke of Bedford had a prisoner
Called the brave Lord Ponton de Santrailles;
For him was I exchanged and ransomed.
But with a baser man-of-arms by far,
Once, in contempt, they would have barter'd me:
Which I, disdaining, scorn'd; and craved death
Rather than I would be so vile-esteem'd.
In fine, redeem'd I was as I desired.
But, O, the treacherous Fastolfe wounds my heart!
Whom with my bare fists I would execute,
If I now had him brought into my power.
EARL OF SALISBURY.
Yet tell'st thou not how thou wert entertain'd.
LORD TALBOT.
With scoffs, and scorns, and contumelious taunts.
In open market-place produced they me,
To be a public spectacle to all:
Here, said they, is the terror of the French,
The scarecrow that affrights our children so.
Then broke I from the officers that led me,

And with my nails digg'd stones out of the
To hurl at the beholders of my shame: [ground,
My grisly countenance made others fly;
None durst come near for fear of sudden death.
In iron walls they deem'd me not secure;   [spread,
So great fear of my name 'mongst them was
That they supposed I could rend bars of steel,
And spurn in pieces posts of adamant:
Wherefore a guard of chosen shot I had,
That walkt about me every minute-while;
And if I did but stir out of my bed,
Ready they were to shoot me to the heart.

Enter the BOY *with a linstock.*

EARL OF SALISBURY.
I grieve to hear what torments you endured;
But we will be revenged sufficiently.
Now it is supper-time in Orleans:
Here, through this grate, I count each one,
And view the Frenchmen how they fortify:
Let us look in; the sight will much delight thee.—
Sir Thomas Gargrave and Sir William Glansdale,
Let me have your express opinions
Where is best place to make our battery next.
SIR THOMAS GARGRAVE.
I think, at the north gate; for there stand lords.
SIR WILLIAM GLANSDALE.
And I, here, at the bulwark of the bridge.
LORD TALBOT.
For aught I see, this city must be famisht,
Or with light skirmishes enfeebled.

[*Here they shoot.* SALISBURY *and* SIR
THOMAS GARGRAVE *fall down.*

EARL OF SALISBURY.
O Lord, have mercy on us, wretched sinners!
SIR THOMAS GARGRAVE.
O Lord, have mercy on me, woful man!
LORD TALBOT.
What chance is this that suddenly hath crost us?
Speak, Salisbury; at least, if thou canst speak:
How farest thou, mirror of all martial men?
One of thy eyes and thy cheek's side struck off!—
Accursed tower! accursed fatal hand
That hath contrived this woful tragedy!
In thirteen battles Salisbury o'ercame;
Henry the Fifth he first train'd to the wars;
Whilst any trump did sound, or drum struck up,
His sword did ne'er leave striking in the field.—
Yet livest thou, Salisbury? though thy speech
     doth fail,
One eye thou hast, to look to heaven for grace:
The sun with one eye vieweth all the world.—
Heaven, be thou gracious to none alive,
If Salisbury wants mercy at thy hands!—
Bear hence his body; I will help to bury it.—
Sir Thomas Gargrave, hast thou any life?
Speak unto Talbot; nay, look up to him.—
Salisbury, cheer thy spirit with this comfort;
Thou shalt not die whiles—
He beckons with his hand, and smiles on me,
As who should say, 'When I am dead and gone,
Remember to avenge me on the French.'—
Plantagenet, I will; and, like thee, Nero,
Play on the lute, beholding the towns burn:
Wretched shall France be only in my name.

[*Here an alarum, and it thunders and
     lightens.*

What stir is this? what tumult's in the heavens?
Whence cometh this alarum and this noise?

Enter a MESSENGER.

MESSENGER.

My lord, my lord, the French have gather'd head:
The Dauphin, with one Joan la Pucelle join'd,—
A holy prophetess new risen up,—
Is come with a great power to raise the siege.

[*Here* SALISBURY *lifteth himself up and
groans.*

LORD TALBOT.

Hear, hear how dying Salisbury doth groan!
It irks his heart he cannot be revenged.—
Frenchmen, I'll be a Salisbury to you:—
Pucelle or puzzel, dolphin or dogfish,
Your hearts I'll stamp out with my horse's heels,
And make a quagmire of your mingled brains.—
Convey me Salisbury into his tent:
And then try what these dastard Frenchmen dare.

[*Alarum. Exeunt.*

SCENE V.

The same.

Here an alarum again: and TALBOT *pursueth the*
DAUPHIN, *and driveth him: then enter* JOAN LA
PUCELLE, *driving Englishmen before her, and
exit after them: then enter* TALBOT.

LORD TALBOT.

WHERE is my strength, my valour, and my
force?
Our English troops retire, I cannot stay them;
A woman clad in armour chaseth them.
Here, here she comes.

Enter LA PUCELLE.
I'll have a bout with thee;
Devil or devil's dam, I'll conjure thee:
Blood will I draw on thee,—thou art a witch,—
And straightway give thy soul to him thou serv-
est.

JOAN LA PUCELLE.

Come, come, 'tis only I that must disgrace thee.

[*They fight.*

LORD TALBOT.

Heavens, can you suffer hell so to prevail?
My breast I'll burst with straining of my courage,
And from my shoulders crack my arms asunder,
But I will chastise this high-minded strumpet.

[*They fight again.*

JOAN LA PUCELLE.

Talbot, farewell; thy hour is not yet come:
I must go victual Orleans forthwith.

[*A short alarum: then enter the town, with*
SOLDIERS.

O'ertake me, if thou canst; I scorn thy strength.
Go, go cheer up thy hunger-starved men;
Help Salisbury to make his testament:
This day is ours, as many more shall be.   [*Exit.*

LORD TALBOT.

My thoughts are whirled like a potter's wheel;
I know not where I am, nor what I do;
A witch by fear, not force, like Hannibal,
Drives back our troops, and conquers as she lists:
So bees with smoke, and doves with noisome
stench,
Are from their hives and houses driven away.

They call'd us, for our fierceness, English dogs;
Now, like to whelps, we crying run away.

[*A short alarum.*

Hark, countrymen! either renew the fight,
Or tear the lions out of England's coat;
Renounce your soil, give sheep in lions' stead:
Sheep run not half so timorous from the wolf,
Or horse or oxen from the leopard,
As you fly from your oft-subdued slaves.

[*Alarum. Here another skirmish.*

It will not be:—retire into your trenches:
You all consented unto Salisbury's death,
For none would strike a stroke in his revenge.—
Pucelle is enter'd into Orleans,
In spite of us or aught that we could do.
O, would I were to die with Salisbury!
The shame hereof will make me hide my head.

[*Exit* TALBOT. *Alarum, retreat.*

SCENE VI.

The same.

Flourish. Enter, on the walls, LA PUCELLE,
CHARLES, REIGNIER, ALENÇON, *and* SOL-
DIERS.

JOAN LA PUCELLE.

ADVANCE our waving colours on the walls;
Rescued is Orleans from the English:—
Thus Joan la Pucelle hath perform'd her word.

CHARLES.

Divinest creature, Astræa's daughter,
How shall I honour thee for this success?
Thy promises are like Adonis' gardens,
That one day bloom'd, and fruitful were the
next.—
France, triumph in thy glorious prophetess!—
Recover'd is the town of Orleans:
More blessed hap did ne'er befall our state.

REIGNIER.

Why ring not out the bells aloud throughout the
town?
Dauphin, command the citizens make bonfires,
And feast and banquet in the open streets,
To celebrate the joy that God hath given us.

DUKE OF ALENÇON.

All France will be replete with mirth and joy,
When they shall hear how we have play'd the
men.

CHARLES.

'Tis Joan, not we, by whom the day is won;
For which I will divide my crown with her;
And all the priests and friars in my realm
Shall in procession sing her endless praise.
A statelier pyramis to her I'll rear
Than Rhodope's of Memphis ever was:
In memory of her when she is dead,
Her ashes, in an urn more precious
Than the rich-jewell'd coffer of Darius,
Transported shall be at high festivals
Before the kings and queens of France.
No longer on Saint Denis will we cry,
But Joan la Pucelle shall be France's saint.
Come in, and let us banquet royally,
After this golden day of victory.

[*Flourish. Exeunt.*

ACT II. SCENE I.

France.   Before Orleans.

Enter a SERGEANT *of a band, with two* SEN-
TINELS.

SERGEANT.

SIRS, take your places, and be vigilant:
If any noise or soldier you perceive
Near to the walls, by some apparent sign
Let us have knowledge at the court-of-guard.

FIRST SENTINEL.

Sergeant, you shall. [*Exit* SERGEANT.] Thus are
poor servitors—
When others sleep upon their quiet beds—
Constrain'd to watch in darkness, rain, and cold.

Enter TALBOT, BEDFORD, BURGUNDY, *and*
FORCES, *with scaling-ladders, their drums beating a dead march.*

LORD TALBOT.

Lord regent, and redoubted Burgundy,—
By whose approach the regions of Artois,
Walloon, and Picardy are friends to us,—
This happy night the Frenchmen are secure,
Having all day caroused and banqueted:
Embrace we, then, this opportunity,
As fitting best to quittance their deceit,
Contrived by art and baleful sorcery.

DUKE OF BEDFORD.

Coward of France!—how much he wrongs his
fame,
Despairing of his own arm's fortitude,
To join with witches and the help of hell!

DUKE OF BURGUNDY.

Traitors have never other company.—
But what's that Pucelle, whom they term so
pure?

LORD TALBOT.

A maid, they say.

DUKE OF BEDFORD.

A maid! and be so martial!

DUKE OF BURGUNDY.

Pray God she prove not masculine ere long;
If underneath the standard of the French
She carry armour, as she hath begun.

LORD TALBOT.

Well, let them practise and converse with spirits:
God is our fortress, in whose conquering name
Let us resolve to scale their flinty bulwarks.

DUKE OF BEDFORD.

Ascend, brave Talbot; we will follow thee.

LORD TALBOT.

Not all together: better far, I guess,
That we do make our entrance several ways;
That, if it chance the one of us do fail,
The other yet may rise against their force.

DUKE OF BEDFORD.

Agreed: I'll to yond corner.

DUKE OF BURGUNDY.

And I to this.

LORD TALBOT.

And here will Talbot mount, or make his
grave.—
Now, Salisbury, for thee, and for the right
Of English Henry, shall this night appear
How much in duty I am bound to both.

[*Cry,* St. George! A Talbot !

SENTINEL.

Arm! arm! the enemy doth make assault!

*The French leap o'er the walls in their shirts. Enter,
several ways, the* BASTARD OF ORLEANS,
ALENÇON, *and* REIGNIER, *half ready and half
unready.*

DUKE OF ALENÇON.

How now, my lords! what, all unready so?

BASTARD.

Unready! ay, and glad we scaped so well.

REIGNIER.

'Twas time, I trow, to wake and leave our beds,
Hearing alarums at our chamber-doors.

DUKE OF ALENÇON.

Of all exploits since first I follow'd arms,
Ne'er heard I of a warlike enterprise
More venturous or desperate than this.

BASTARD.

I think this Talbot be a fiend of hell.

REIGNIER.

If not of hell, the heavens, sure, favour him.

DUKE OF ALENÇON.

Here cometh Charles: I marvel how he sped.

BASTARD.

Tut, holy Joan was his defensive guard.

Enter CHARLES *and* LA PUCELLE.

CHARLES.

Is this thy cunning, thou deceitful dame?
Didst thou at first, to flatter us withal,
Make us partakers of a little gain,
That now our loss might be ten times so much?

JOAN LA PUCELLE.

Wherefore is Charles impatient with his friend?
At all times will you have my power alike?
Sleeping or waking, must I still prevail,
Or will you blame and lay the fault on me?
Improvident soldiers! had your watch been good,
This sudden mischief never could have faln.

CHARLES.

Duke of Alençon, this was your default,
That, being captain of the watch to-night,
Did look no better to that weighty charge.

DUKE OF ALENÇON.

Had all your quarters been as safely kept
As that whereof I had the government,
We had not been thus shamefully surprised.

BASTARD.

Mine was secure.

REIGNIER.

And so was mine, my lord.

CHARLES.

And, for myself, most part of all this night,
Within her quarter and mine own precinct
I was employ'd in passing to and fro,
About relieving of the sentinels:
Then how or which way should they first break
in?

JOAN LA PUCELLE.

Question, my lords, no further of the case,
How or which way: 'tis sure they found some
place
But weakly guarded, where the breach was
made.
And now there rests no other shift but this,—
To gather our soldiers, scatter'd and dispersed,
And lay new platforms to endamage them.

Alarums. Enter an English SOLDIER, *crying,* A
   Talbot! a Talbot! *They fly, leaving their clothes
   behind.*

SOLDIER.

I'll be so bold to take what they have left.
The cry of Talbot serves me for a sword;
For I have loaden me with many spoils,
Using no other weapon but his name.   [*Exit.*

SCENE II.

Orleans. Within the town.

Enter TALBOT, BEDFORD, BURGUNDY, *a* CAP-
   TAIN, *and others.*

DUKE OF BEDFORD.

THE day begins to break, and night is fled,
   Whose pitchy mantle over-veil'd the earth.
Here sound retreat, and cease our hot pursuit.
                              [*Retreat sounded.*

LORD TALBOT.

Bring forth the body of old Salisbury,
And here advance it in the market-place,
The middle centre of this cursed town.
Now have I paid my vow unto his soul;
For every drop of blood was drawn from him,
There hath at least five Frenchmen died to-night.
And that hereafter ages may behold
What ruin happen'd in revenge of him,
Within their chiefest temple I'll erect
A tomb, wherein his corpse shall be interr'd:
Upon the which, that every one may read,
Shall be engraved the sack of Orleans,
The treacherous manner of his mournful death,
And what a terror he had been to France.
But, lords, in all our bloody massacre,
I muse we met not with the Dauphin's Grace,
His new-come champion, virtuous Joan of Arc,
Nor any of his false confederates.

DUKE OF BEDFORD.

'Tis thought, Lord Talbot, when the fight began,
Roused on the sudden from their drowsy beds,
They did, amongst the troops of armed men,
Leap o'er the walls for refuge in the field.

DUKE OF BURGUNDY.

Myself—as far as I could well discern
For smoke and dusky vapours of the night—
Am sure I scared the Dauphin and his trull,
When arm in arm they both came swiftly running,
Like to a pair of loving turtle-doves,
That could not live asunder day or night.
After that things are set in order here,
We'll follow them with all the power we have.

Enter a MESSENGER.

MESSENGER.

All hail, my lords! Which of this princely train
Call ye the warlike Talbot, for his acts
So much applauded through the realm of France?

LORD TALBOT.

Here is the Talbot: who would speak with him?

MESSENGER.

The virtuous lady, Countess of Auvergne,
With modesty admiring thy renown,
By me entreats, great lord, thou wouldst vouchsafe
To visit her poor castle where she lies,
That she may boast she hath beheld the man
Whose glory fills the world with loud report.

DUKE OF BURGUNDY.

Is it even so? Nay, then, I see our wars
Will turn unto a peaceful comic sport,
When ladies crave to be encounter'd with.—
You may not, my lord, despise her gentle suit.

LORD TALBOT.

Ne'er trust me, then; for when a world of men
Could not prevail with all their oratory,
Yet hath a woman's kindness over-ruled:—
And therefore tell her I return great thanks,
And in submission will attend on her.—
Will not your honours bear me company?

DUKE OF BEDFORD.

No, truly; it is more than manners will:
And I have heard it said, unbidden guests
Are often welcomest when they are gone.

LORD TALBOT.

Well then, alone, since there's no remedy,
I mean to prove this lady's courtesy.—
Come hither, captain. [*Whispers.*] You perceive
   my mind?

CAPTAIN.

I do, my lord, and mean accordingly.   [*Exeunt.*

SCENE III.

Auvergne. Court of the Castle.

Enter the COUNTESS *and her* PORTER.

COUNTESS OF AUVERGNE.

PORTER, remember what I gave in charge;
   And when you've done so, bring the keys to me.

PORTER.

Madam, I will.   [*Exit.*

COUNTESS OF AUVERGNE.

The plot is laid: if all things fall out right,
I shall as famous be by this exploit
As Scythian Tomyris by Cyrus' death.
Great is the rumour of this dreadful knight,
And his achievements of no less account:
Fain would mine eyes be witness with mine
   ears,
To give their censure of these rare reports.

Enter MESSENGER *and* TALBOT.

MESSENGER.

Madam,
According as your ladyship desired,
By message craved, so is Lord Talbot come.

COUNTESS OF AUVERGNE.

And he is welcome. What! is this the man?

MESSENGER.

Madam, it is.

COUNTESS OF AUVERGNE.

             Is this the scourge of France?
Is this the Talbot, so much fear'd abroad,
That with his name the mothers still their babes?
I see report is fabulous and false:
I thought I should have seen some Hercules,
A second Hector, for his grim aspect
And large proportion of his strong-knit limbs.
Alas, this is a child, a silly dwarf!
It cannot be this weak and writhled shrimp
Should strike such terror to his enemies.

LORD TALBOT.

Madam, I have been bold to trouble you;
But since your ladyship is not at leisure,
I'll sort some other time to visit you.   [*Going.*

9

COUNTESS OF AUVERGNE.
What means he now?—Go ask him whither he
goes.
MESSENGER.
Stay, my Lord Talbot; for my lady craves
To know the cause of your abrupt departure.
LORD TALBOT.
Marry, for that she's in a wrong belief,
I go to certify her Talbot's here.
Enter PORTER *with keys.*
COUNTESS OF AUVERGNE.
If thou be he, then art thou prisoner.
LORD TALBOT.
Prisoner! to whom?
COUNTESS OF AUVERGNE.
To me, blood-thirsty lord;
And for that cause I train'd thee to my house.
Long time thy shadow hath been thrall to me,
For in my gallery thy picture hangs:
But now the substance shall endure the like;
And I will chain these legs and arms of thine,
That hast by tyranny, these many years,
Wasted our country, slain our citizens,
And sent our sons and husbands captivate.
LORD TALBOT.
Ha, ha, ha!
COUNTESS OF AUVERGNE.
Laughest thou, wretch? thy mirth shall turn to
moan.
LORD TALBOT.
I laugh to see your ladyship so fond
To think that you have aught but Talbot's
shadow
Whereon to practise your severity.
COUNTESS OF AUVERGNE.
Why, art not thou the man?
LORD TALBOT.
I am, indeed.
COUNTESS OF AUVERGNE.
Then have I substance too.
LORD TALBOT.
No, no, I am but shadow of myself;
You are deceived, my substance is not here;
For what you see is but the smallest part
And least proportion of humanity:
I tell you, madam, were the whole frame here,
It is of such a spacious lofty pitch,
Your roof were not sufficient to contain 't.
COUNTESS OF AUVERGNE.
This is a riddling merchant for the nonce;
He will be here, and yet he is not here:
How can these contrarieties agree?
LORD TALBOT.
That will I show you presently.
[*Winds his horn. Drums strike up: a peal
of ordnance. Enter* SOLDIERS.
How say you, madam? are you now persuaded
That Talbot is but shadow of himself?
These are his substance, sinews, arms, and
strength,
With which he yoketh your rebellious necks,
Razeth your cities, and subverts your towns,
And in a moment makes them desolate.
COUNTESS OF AUVERGNE.
Victorious Talbot! pardon my abuse:
I find thou art no less than fame hath bruited,
And more than may be gather'd by thy shape.
Let my presumption not provoke thy wrath;
For I am sorry that with reverence
I did not entertain thee as thou art.
LORD TALBOT.
Be not dismay'd, fair lady; nor misconster
The mind of Talbot, as you did mistake
The outward composition of his body.
What you have done hath not offended me:
Nor other satisfaction do I crave,
But only, with your patience, that we may
Taste of your wine, and see what cates you have;
For soldiers' stomachs always serve them well.
COUNTESS OF AUVERGNE.
With all my heart; and think me honoured
To feast so great a warrior in my house.　[*Exeunt.*

SCENE IV.
London. The Temple-garden.

Enter the EARLS OF SOMERSET, SUFFOLK, *and*
WARWICK; RICHARD PLANTAGENET, VER-
NON, *and a* LAWYER.

RICHARD PLANTAGENET.
GREAT lords and gentlemen, what means this
silence?
Dare no man answer in a case of truth?
EARL OF SUFFOLK.
Within the Temple-hall we were too loud;
The garden here is more convenient.
RICHARD PLANTAGENET.
Then say at once if I maintain'd the truth;
Or else was wrangling Somerset in th' error?
EARL OF SUFFOLK.
Faith, I have been a truant in the law,
And never yet could frame my will to it;
And therefore frame the law unto my will.
EARL OF SOMERSET.
Judge you, my Lord of Warwick, then, between
us.
EARL OF WARWICK.
Between two hawks, which flies the higher pitch;
Between two dogs, which hath the deeper mouth;
Between two blades, which bears the better
temper;
Between two horses, which doth bear him best;
Between two girls, which hath the merriest eye;—
I have, perhaps, some shallow spirit of judge-
ment:
But in these nice sharp quillets of the law,
Good faith, I am no wiser than a daw.
RICHARD PLANTAGENET.
Tut, tut, here is a mannerly forbearance:
The truth appears so naked on my side,
That any purblind eye may find it out.
EARL OF SOMERSET.
And on my side it is so well apparell'd,
So clear, so shining, and so evident,
That it will glimmer through a blind man's eye.
RICHARD PLANTAGENET.
Since you are tongue-tied and so loth to speak,
In dumb significants proclaim your thoughts:
Let him that is a true-born gentleman,
And stands upon the honour of his birth,
If he suppose that I have pleaded truth,
From off this brier pluck a white rose with me.

EARL OF SOMERSET.
Let him that is no coward nor no flatterer,
But dare maintain the party of the truth,
Pluck a red rose from off this thorn with me.
        EARL OF WARWICK.
I love no colours; and, without all colour
Of base-insinuating flattery,
I pluck this white rose with Plantagenet.
        EARL OF SUFFOLK.
I pluck this red rose with young Somerset;
And say withal, I think he held the right.
        VERNON.
Stay, lords and gentlemen, and pluck no more,
Till you conclude that he, upon whose side
The fewest roses are cropt from the tree,
Shall yield the other in the right opinion.
        EARL OF SOMERSET.
Good Master Vernon, it is well objected:
If I have fewest, I subscribe in silence.
        RICHARD PLANTAGENET.
And I.
        VERNON.
Then, for the truth and plainness of the case,
I pluck this pale and maiden blossom here,
Giving my verdict on the white rose side.
        EARL OF SOMERSET.
Prick not your finger as you pluck it off,
Lest, bleeding, you do paint the white rose
  red,
And fall on my side so, against your will.
        VERNON.
If I, my lord, for my opinion bleed,
Opinion shall be surgeon to my hurt,
And keep me on the side where still I am.
        EARL OF SOMERSET.
Well, well, come on: who else?
        A LAWYER [to SOMERSET].
Unless my study and my books be false,
The argument you held was wrong in you;
In sign whereof I pluck a white rose too.
        RICHARD PLANTAGENET.
Now, Somerset, where is your argument?
        EARL OF SOMERSET.
Here in my scabbard; meditating that
Shall dye your white rose in a bloody red.
        RICHARD PLANTAGENET.
Meantime your cheeks do counterfeit our
  roses;
For pale they look with fear, as witnessing
The truth on our side.
        EARL OF SOMERSET.
                        No, Plantagenet,
'Tis not for fear; but anger that thy cheeks
Blush for pure shame to counterfeit our roses,
And yet thy tongue will not confess thy error.
        RICHARD PLANTAGENET.
Hath not thy rose a canker, Somerset?
        EARL OF SOMERSET.
Hath not thy rose a thorn, Plantagenet?
        RICHARD PLANTAGENET.
Ay, sharp and piercing, to maintain his truth;
Whiles thy consuming canker eats his falsehood.
        EARL OF SOMERSET.
Well, I'll find friends to wear my bleeding roses,
That shall maintain what I have said is true,
Where false Plantagenet dare not be seen.

        RICHARD PLANTAGENET.
Now, by this maiden blossom in my hand,
I scorn thee and thy faction, peevish boy.
        EARL OF SUFFOLK.
Turn not thy scorns this way, Plantagenet.
        RICHARD PLANTAGENET.
Proud Pole, I will; and scorn both him and thee.
        EARL OF SUFFOLK.
I'll turn my part thereof into thy throat.
        EARL OF SOMERSET.
Away, away, good William de la Pole!
We grace the yeoman by conversing with him.
        EARL OF WARWICK.
Now, by God's will, thou wrong'st him, Somer-
  set;
His grandfather was Lionel Duke of Clarence,
Third son to the third Edward King of England:
Spring crestless yeomen from so deep a root?
        RICHARD PLANTAGENET.
He bears him on the place's privilege,
Or durst not, for his craven heart, say thus.
        EARL OF SOMERSET.
By Him that made me, I'll maintain my words
On any plot of ground in Christendom.
Was not thy father, Richard Earl of Cambridge,
For treason executed in our late king's days?
And, by his treason, stand'st not thou attainted,
Corrupted, and exempt from ancient gentry?
His trespass yet lives guilty in thy blood;
And, till thou be restored, thou art a yeoman.
        RICHARD PLANTAGENET.
My father was attached, not attainted,
Condemn'd to die for treason, but no traitor;
And that I'll prove on better men than Somerset,
Were growing time once ripen'd to my will.
For your partaker Pole, and you yourself,
I'll note you in my book of memory,
To scourge you for this apprehension:
Look to it well, and say you are well warn'd.
        EARL OF SOMERSET.
Ah, thou shalt find us ready for thee still;
And know us, by these colours, for thy foes,—
For these my friends, in spite of thee, shall wear.
        RICHARD PLANTAGENET.
And, by my soul, this pale and angry rose,
As cognizance of my blood-drinking hate,
Will I for ever, and my faction, wear,
Until it wither with me to my grave,
Or flourish to the height of my degree.
        EARL OF SUFFOLK.
Go forward, and be choked with thy ambition!
And so, farewell, until I meet thee next.   [Exit.
        EARL OF SOMERSET.
Have with thee, Pole.—Farewell, ambitious
  Richard.   [Exit.
        RICHARD PLANTAGENET.
How I am braved, and must perforce endure it!
        EARL OF WARWICK.
This blot, that they object against your house,
Shall be wiped out in the next parliament,
Call'd for the truce of Winchester and Gloster:
And if thou be not then created York,
I will not live to be accounted Warwick.
Meantime, in signal of my love to thee,
Against proud Somerset and William Pole,
Will I upon thy party wear this rose:

And here I prophesy,—this brawl to-day,
Grown to this faction, in the Temple-garden,
Shall send, between the red rose and the white,
A thousand souls to death and deadly night.

RICHARD PLANTAGENET.
Good Master Vernon, I am bound to you,
That you on my behalf would pluck a flower.

VERNON.
In your behalf still will I wear the same.

A LAWYER.
And so will I.

RICHARD PLANTAGENET.
Thanks, gentle sir.
Come, let us four to dinner: I dare say
This quarrel will drink blood another day.
                                        [Exeunt.

SCENE V.

The Tower of London.

Enter MORTIMER, *brought in a chair, and*
GAOLERS.

EDMUND MORTIMER.
KIND keepers of my weak decaying age,
Let dying Mortimer here rest himself.—
Even like a man new-haled from the rack,
So fare my limbs with long imprisonment;
And these grey locks, the pursuivants of death,
Nestor-like aged, in an age of care,
Argue the end of Edmund Mortimer:
These eyes—like lamps whose wasting oil is
        spent—
Wax dim, as drawing to their exigent:
Weak shoulders, overborne with burdening grief;
And pithless arms, like to a wither'd vine
That droops his sapless branches to the ground:
Yet are these feet—whose strengthless stay is
        numb,
Unable to support this lump of clay—
Swift-winged with desire to get a grave,
As witting I no other comfort have.—
But tell me, keeper, will my nephew come?

FIRST GAOLER.
Richard Plantagenet, my lord, will come:
We sent unto the Temple, unto his chamber;
And answer was return'd that he will come.

EDMUND MORTIMER.
Enough: my soul shall then be satisfied.—
Poor gentleman! his wrong doth equal mine.
Since Henry Monmouth first began to reign,
Before whose glory I was great in arms,
This loathsome sequestration have I had;
And even since then hath Richard been obscured,
Deprived of honour and inheritance.
But now, the arbitrator of despairs,
Just death, kind umpire of men's miseries,
With sweet enlargement doth dismiss me hence:
I would his troubles likewise were expired,
That so he might recover what was lost.

Enter RICHARD PLANTAGENET.

FIRST GAOLER.
My lord, your loving nephew now is come.

EDMUND MORTIMER.
Richard Plantagenet, my friend, is he come?

RICHARD PLANTAGENET.
Ay, noble uncle, thus ignobly used,
Your nephew, late-despised Richard, comes.

EDMUND MORTIMER.
Direct mine arms I may embrace his neck,
And in his bosom spend my latter gasp:
O, tell me when my lips do touch his cheeks,
That I may kindly give one fainting kiss.—
And now declare, sweet stem from York's great
        stock,
Why didst thou say, of late thou wert despised?

RICHARD PLANTAGENET.
First, lean thine aged back against mine arm;
And, in that ease, I'll tell thee my disease.
This day, in argument upon a case,
Some words there grew 'twixt Somerset and
        me;
Among which terms he used his lavish tongue,
And did upbraid me with my father's death:
Which obloquy set bars before my tongue,
Else with the like I had requited him.
Therefore, good uncle, for my father's sake,
In honour of a true Plantagenet,
And for alliance sake, declare the cause
My father, Earl of Cambridge, lost his head.

EDMUND MORTIMER.
That cause, fair nephew, that imprison'd me,
And hath detain'd me all my flowering youth
Within a loathsome dungeon, there to pine,
Was cursed instrument of his decease.

RICHARD PLANTAGENET.
Discover more at large what cause that was;
For I am ignorant, and cannot guess.

EDMUND MORTIMER.
I will, if that my fading breath permit,
And death approach not ere my tale be done.
Henry the Fourth, grandfather to this king,
Deposed his nephew Richard,—Edward's son,
The first-begotten and the lawful heir
Of Edward king, the third of that descent:
During whose reign, the Percies of the north,
Finding his usurpation most unjust,
Endeavour'd my advancement to the throne:
The reason moved these warlike lords to this
Was, for that—young King Richard thus re-
        moved,
Leaving no heir begotten of his body—
I was the next by birth and parentage;
For by my mother I derived am
From Lionel Duke of Clarence, the third son
To King Edward the Third; whereas he
From John of Gaunt doth bring his pedigree,
Being but fourth of that heroic line.
But mark: as, in this haughty-great attempt,
They laboured to plant the rightful heir,
I lost my liberty, and they their lives.
Long after this, when Henry the Fifth,
Succeeding his father Bolingbroke, did reign,
Thy father, Earl of Cambridge, then derived
From famous Edmund Langley, duke of York,
Marrying my sister, that thy mother was,
Again, in pity of my hard distress,
Levied an army, weening to redeem
And have install'd me in the diadem:
But, as the rest, so fell that noble earl,
And was beheaded.   Thus the Mortimers,
In whom the title rested, were supprest.

RICHARD PLANTAGENET.
Of which, my lord, your honour is the last.

EDMUND MORTIMER.
True; and thou seest that I no issue have,
And that my fainting words do warrant death:
Thou art my heir; the rest I wish thee gather:
And yet be wary in thy studious care.

RICHARD PLANTAGENET.
Thy grave admonishments prevail with me:
But yet, methinks, my father's execution
Was nothing less than bloody tyranny.

EDMUND MORTIMER.
With silence, nephew, be thou politic:
Strong-fixed is the house of Lancaster,
And, like a mountain, not to be removed.
But now thy uncle is removing hence;
As princes do their courts, when they are cloy'd
With long continuance in a settled place.

RICHARD PLANTAGENET.
O, uncle, would some part of my young years
Might but redeem the passage of your age!

EDMUND MORTIMER.
Thou dost, then, wrong me,—as that slaughterer
    doth
Which giveth many wounds when one will kill.
Mourn not, except thou sorrow for my good;
Only, give order for my funeral:
And so, farewell; and fair be all thy hopes,
And prosperous be thy life in peace and war!
                                        [Dies.

RICHARD PLANTAGENET.
And peace, no war, befall thy parting soul!
In prison hast thou spent a pilgrimage,
And like a hermit overpast thy days.—
Well, I will lock his counsel in my breast;
And what I do imagine, let that rest.—
Keepers, convey him hence; and I myself
Will see his burial better than his life.
    [Exeunt GAOLERS, bearing out the body of
    MORTIMER.
Here dies the dusky torch of Mortimer,
Choked with ambition of the meaner sort:—
And for those wrongs, those bitter injuries,
Which Somerset hath offer'd to my house,
I doubt not but with honour to redress;
And therefore haste I to the parliament,
Either to be restored to my blood,
Or make my ill th' advantage of my good. [Exit.

ACT III. SCENE I.

London. The Parliament House.

Flourish. Enter KING HENRY, EXETER, GLOS-
TER, WARWICK, SOMERSET, *and* SUFFOLK;
the BISHOP OF WINCHESTER, RICHARD
PLANTAGENET, *and others.* GLOSTER *offers
to put up a bill;* WINCHESTER *snatches it,
tears it.*

BISHOP OF WINCHESTER.
COMEST thou with deep-premeditated lines,
    With written pamphlets studiously devised,
Humphrey of Gloster? If thou canst accuse,
Or aught intend'st to lay unto my charge,
Do it without invention, suddenly;
As I with sudden and extemporal speech
Purpose to answer what thou canst object.

DUKE OF GLOSTER.
Presumptuous priest! this place commands my
    patience,
Or thou shouldst find thou hast dishonour'd me.
Think not, although in writing I preferr'd
The manner of thy vile outrageous crimes,
That therefore I have forged, or am not able
Verbatim to rehearse the method of my pen:
No, prelate; such is thy audacious wickedness,
Thy lewd, pestiferous, and dissentious pranks,
As very infants prattle of thy pride.
Thou art a most pernicious usurer;
Froward by nature, enemy to peace;
Lascivious, wanton, more than well beseems
A man of thy profession and degree;
And for thy treachery, what's more manifest,—
In that thou laid'st a trap to take my life,
As well at London-bridge as at the Tower?
Beside, I fear me, if thy thoughts were sifted,
The king, thy sovereign, is not quite exempt
From envious malice of thy swelling heart.

BISHOP OF WINCHESTER.
Gloster, I do defy thee.—Lords, vouchsafe
To give me hearing what I shall reply.
If I were covetous, ambitious, or perverse,
As he will have me, how am I so poor?
Or how haps it I seek not to advance
Or raise myself, but keep my wonted calling?
And for dissension, who preferreth peace
More than I do,—except I be provoked?
No, my good lords, it is not that offends;
It is not that that hath incensed the duke:
It is, because no one should sway but he;
No one but he should be about the king;
And that engenders thunder in his breast,
And makes him roar these accusations forth.
But he shall know I am as good—

DUKE OF GLOSTER.
                                As good!
Thou bastard of my grandfather!—

BISHOP OF WINCHESTER.
Ay, lordly sir; for what are you, I pray,
But one imperious in another's throne?

DUKE OF GLOSTER.
Am I not lord Protector, saucy priest?

BISHOP OF WINCHESTER.
And am not I a prelate of the church?

DUKE OF GLOSTER.
Yes, as an outlaw in a castle keeps,
And useth it to patronage his theft.

BISHOP OF WINCHESTER.
Unreverent Gloster!

DUKE OF GLOSTER.
                        Thou art reverent
Touching thy spiritual function, not thy life.

BISHOP OF WINCHESTER.
This Rome shall remedy.

EARL OF WARWICK.
                        Roam thither, then.

EARL OF SOMERSET.
My lord, it were your duty to forbear.

EARL OF WARWICK.
Ay, see the bishop be not overborne.

EARL OF SOMER
Methinks my lord should be religious,
And know the office that belongs to such.

EARL OF WARWICK.
Methinks his lordship should be humbler;
It fitteth not a prelate so to plead.
EARL OF SOMERSET.
Yes, when his holy state is toucht so near.
EARL OF WARWICK.
State holy or unhallow'd, what of that?
Is not his Grace Protector to the king?
RICHARD PLANTAGENET [aside].
Plantagenet, I see, must hold his tongue,
Lest it be said, 'Speak, sirrah, when you should;
Must your bold verdict enter talk with lords?'
Else would I have a fling at Winchester.
KING HENRY.
Uncles of Gloster and of Winchester,
The special watchmen of our English weal,
I would prevail, if prayers might prevail,
To join your hearts in love and amity.
O, what a scandal is it to our crown,
That two such noble peers as ye should jar!
Believe me, lords, my tender years can tell
Civil dissension is a viperous worm
That gnaws the bowels of the commonwealth.
      [A noise within, 'Down with the tawny-coats!'
What tumult's this?
EARL OF WARWICK.
                    An uproar, I dare warrant,
Begun through malice of the bishop's men.
      [A noise again within, 'Stones! stones!'
                    Enter MAYOR.
MAYOR.
O, my good lords,—and virtuous Henry,—
Pity the city of London, pity us!
The bishop and the Duke of Gloster's men,
Forbidden late to carry any weapon,
Have fill'd their pockets full of pebble-stones,
And, banding themselves in contrary parts,
Do pelt so fast at one another's pate,
That many have their giddy brains knockt out:
Our windows are broke down in every street,
And we, for fear, compell'd to shut our shops.
      Enter SERVING-MEN, in skirmish, with bloody
                    pates.
KING HENRY.
We charge you, on allegiance to ourself,
To hold your slaughtering hands and keep the
      peace.—
Pray, uncle Gloster, mitigate this strife.
FIRST SERVING-MAN.
Nay, if we be forbidden stones, we'll fall to it
with our teeth.
SECOND SERVING-MAN.
Do what ye dare, we are as resolute.
                    [Skirmish again.
DUKE OF GLOSTER.
You of my household, leave this peevish broil,
And set this unaccustom'd fight aside.
THIRD SERVING-MAN.
My lord, we know your Grace to be a man
Just and upright; and, for your royal birth,
Inferior to none but to his majesty:
And, ere that we will suffer such a prince,
So kind a father of the commonweal,
To be disgraced by an inkhorn mate,
We, and our wives, and children, all will fight,
And have our bodies slaughter'd by thy foes.

FIRST SERVING-MAN.
Ay, and the very parings of our nails
Shall pitch a field when we are dead. [Begin again.
DUKE OF GLOSTER.
                    Stay, stay, I say!
An if you love me, as you say you do,
Let me persuade you to forbear awhile.
KING HENRY.
O, how this discord doth afflict my soul!—
Can you, my Lord of Winchester, behold
My sighs and tears, and will not once relent?
Who should be pitiful, if you be not?
Or who should study to prefer a peace,
If holy churchmen take delight in broils?
EARL OF WARWICK.
Yield, my lord Protector; yield, Winchester;
Except you mean, with obstinate repulse,
To slay your sovereign, and destroy the realm.
You see what mischief, and what murder too,
Hath been enacted through your enmity;
Then be at peace, except ye thirst for blood.
BISHOP OF WINCHESTER.
He shall submit, or I will never yield.
DUKE OF GLOSTER.
Compassion on the king commands me stoop;
Or I would see his heart out, ere the priest
Should ever get that privilege of me.
EARL OF WARWICK.
Behold, my Lord of Winchester, the duke
Hath banisht moody discontented fury,
As by his smoothed brows it doth appear:
Why look you still so stern and tragical?
DUKE OF GLOSTER.
Here, Winchester, I offer thee my hand.
KING HENRY.
Fie, uncle Beaufort! I have heard you preach
That malice was a great and grievous sin;
And will not you maintain the thing you teach,
But prove a chief offender in the same?
EARL OF WARWICK.
Sweet king!—the bishop hath a kindly gird.—
For shame, my Lord of Winchester, relent!
What, shall a child instruct you what to do?
BISHOP OF WINCHESTER.
Well, Duke of Gloster, I will yield to thee;
Love for thy love, and hand for hand I give.
DUKE OF GLOSTER [aside].
Ay, but, I fear me, with a hollow heart.
See here, my friends and loving countrymen;
This token serveth for a flag of truce
Betwixt ourselves and all our followers:
So help me God, as I dissemble not!
BISHOP OF WINCHESTER [aside].
So help me God, as I intend it not!
KING HENRY.
O loving uncle, kind Duke of Gloucester,
How joyful am I made by this contract!—
Away, my masters! trouble us no more;
But join in friendship, as your lords have done.
FIRST SERVING-MAN.
Content: I'll to the surgeon's.
SECOND SERVING-MAN.
                    And so will I.
THIRD SERVING-MAN.
And I will see what physic the tavern affords.
                    [Exeunt SERVING-MEN, MAYOR, &c

EARL OF WARWICK.
Accept this scroll, most gracious sovereign,
Which in the right of Richard Plantagenet
We do exhibit to your majesty.

DUKE OF GLOSTER.
Well urged, my Lord of Warwick:—for, sweet
prince,
An if your Grace mark every circumstance,
You have great reason to do Richard right;
Especially for those occasions
At Eltham-place I told your majesty.

KING HENRY.
And those occasions, uncle, were of force:
Therefore, my loving lords, our pleasure is,
That Richard be restored to his blood.

EARL OF WARWICK.
Let Richard be restored to his blood;
So shall his father's wrongs be recompensed.

BISHOP OF WINCHESTER.
As will the rest, so willeth Winchester.

KING HENRY.
If Richard will be true, not that alone,
But all the whole inheritance I give
That doth belong unto the house of York,
From whence you spring by lineal descent.

RICHARD PLANTAGENET.
Thy humble servant vows obedience
And humble service till the point of death.

KING HENRY.
Stoop, then, and set your knee against my foot;
And, in reguerdon of that duty done,
I girt thee with the valiant sword of York:
Rise, Richard, like a true Plantagenet,
And rise created princely Duke of York.

RICHARD PLANTAGENET.
And so thrive Richard as thy foes may fall!
And as my duty springs, so perish they
That grudge one thought against your majesty!

ALL.
Welcome, high prince, the mighty Duke of York!

EARL OF SOMERSET [aside].
Perish, base prince, ignoble Duke of York!

DUKE OF GLOSTER.
Now will it best avail your majesty
To cross the seas, and to be crown'd in France:
The presence of a king engenders love
Amongst his subjects and his loyal friends,
As it disanimates his enemies.

KING HENRY.
When Gloster says the word, King Henry goes;
For friendly counsel cuts off many foes.

DUKE OF GLOSTER.
Your ships already are in readiness.
[Sennet. Flourish. Exeunt all except EXETER.

DUKE OF EXETER.
Ay, we may march in England or in France,
Not seeing what is likely to ensue.
This late dissension grown betwixt the peers
Burns under feigned ashes of forged love,
And will at last break out into a flame:
As fester'd members rot but by degree,
Till bones and flesh and sinews fall away,
So will this base and envious discord breed.
And now I fear that fatal prophecy
Which in the time of Henry named the Fifth
Was in the mouth of every sucking babe,—
That Henry born at Monmouth should win all,
And Henry born at Windsor should lose all:
Which is so plain, that Exeter doth wish
His days may finish ere that hapless time.   [Exit.

SCENE II.

France. Before Rouen.

Enter LA PUCELLE *disguised, with four* SOL-
DIERS, *with sacks upon their backs.*

JOAN LA PUCELLE.
THESE are the city-gates, the gates of Rouen,
   Through which our policy must make a
   breach:
Take heed, be wary how you place your words;
Talk like the vulgar sort of market-men
That come to gather money for their corn.
If we have entrance,—as I hope we shall,—
And that we find the slothful watch but weak,
I'll by a sign give notice to our friends,
That Charles the Dauphin may encounter them.

FIRST SOLDIER.
Our sacks shall be a mean to sack the city,
And we be lords and rulers over Rouen;
Therefore we'll knock.   [Knocks.

WATCHMAN [within].
Qui va là?

JOAN LA PUCELLE.
Paysans, pauvres gens de France,—
Poor market-folks, that come to sell their corn.

WATCHMAN [opening the gates].
Enter, go in; the market-bell is rung.

JOAN LA PUCELLE.
Now, Rouen, I'll shake thy bulwarks to the
ground.   [LA PUCELLE, &c., enter the town.
Enter CHARLES, *the* BASTARD OF ORLEANS,
ALENÇON, REIGNIER, *and* FORCES.

CHARLES.
Saint Denis bless this happy stratagem!
And once again we'll sleep secure in Rouen.

BASTARD OF ORLEANS.
Here enter'd Pucelle and her practisants;
Now she is there, how will she specify
Where is the best and safest passage in?

REIGNIER.
By thrusting out a torch from yonder tower; [is,—
Which, once discern'd, shows that her meaning
No way to that, for weakness, which she enter'd.
Enter LA PUCELLE *on the top, thrusting out a
torch burning.*

JOAN LA PUCELLE.
Behold, this is the happy wedding-torch
That joineth Rouen unto her countrymen,
But burning fatal to the Talbotites.   [Exit.

BASTARD OF ORLEANS.
See, noble Charles, the beacon of our friend;
The burning torch in yonder turret stands.

CHARLES.
Now shine it like a comet of revenge,
A prophet to the fall of all our foes!

REIGNIER.
Defer no time, delays have dangerous ends;
Enter, and cry 'The Dauphin!' presently,
And then do execution on the watch.
   [Alarum. They enter.
An alarum. Enter TALBOT *in an excursion.*

LORD TALBOT.
France, thou shalt rue this treason with thy tears,
If Talbot but survive thy treachery.—
Pucelle, that witch, that damned sorceress,
Hath wrought this hellish mischief unawares,
That hardly we escaped the pride of France.
　　　　　　　　　　　　　　　[Exit.
An alarum: excursions. BEDFORD *brought in sick
in a chair. Enter* TALBOT *and* BURGUNDY
without: within LA PUCELLE, CHARLES, *the*
BASTARD OF ORLEANS, ALENÇON, *and* REI-
GNIER, *on the walls.*
JOAN LA PUCELLE.
Good morrow, gallants! want ye corn for bread?
I think the Duke of Burgundy will fast,
Before he'll buy again at such a rate:
'Twas full of darnel;—do you like the taste?
DUKE OF BURGUNDY.
Scoff on, vile fiend and shameless courtezan!
I trust ere long to choke thee with thine own,
And make thee curse the harvest of that corn.
CHARLES.
Your Grace may starve, perhaps, before that
　　time.
DUKE OF BEDFORD.
O, let no words, but deeds, revenge this treason!
JOAN LA PUCELLE.
What will you do, good greybeard? break a lance,
And run a tilt at death within a chair?
LORD TALBOT.
Foul fiend of France, and hag of all despite,
Encompast with thy lustful paramours!
Becomes it thee to taunt his valiant age,
And twit with cowardice a man half dead?
Damsel, I'll have a bout with you again,
Or else let Talbot perish with his shame.
JOAN LA PUCELLE.
Are ye so hot, sir?—yet, Pucelle, hold thy peace;
If Talbot do but thunder, rain will follow.
　　　　[TALBOT *and the rest whisper together in
　　　　counsel.*　　　　　　　[speaker?
God speed the parliament! who shall be the
LORD TALBOT.
Dare ye come forth and meet us in the field?
JOAN LA PUCELLE.
Belike your lordship takes us, then, for fools,
To try if that our own be ours or no.
LORD TALBOT.
I speak not to that railing Hecate,
But unto thee, Alençon, and the rest;
Will ye, like soldiers, come and fight it out?
DUKE OF ALENÇON.
Signior, no.
LORD TALBOT.
Signior, hang!—base muleters of France!
Like peasant foot-boys do they keep the walls,
And dare not take up arms like gentlemen.
JOAN LA PUCELLE.
Away, captains! let's get us from the walls;
For Talbot means no goodness by his looks.—
God b' wi' you, my lord! we came but to tell you
That we are here.
　　　[Exeunt LA PUCELLE, &c., from the walls.
LORD TALBOT.
And there will we be too, ere it be long,
Or else reproach be Talbot's greatest fame!—

Vow, Burgundy, by honour of thy house—
Prickt on by public wrongs sustain'd in France—
Either to get the town again or die;
And I,—as sure as English Henry lives,
And as his father here was conqueror,—
As sure as in this late-betrayed town
Great Cœur-de-lion's heart was buried,—
So sure I swear to get the town or die.
DUKE OF BURGUNDY.
My vows are equal partners with thy vows.
LORD TALBOT.
But, ere we go, regard this dying prince,
The valiant Duke of Bedford.—Come, my lord,
We will bestow you in some better place,
Fitter for sickness and for crazy age.
DUKE OF BEDFORD.
Lord Talbot, do not so dishonour me:
Here will I sit before the walls of Rouen,
And will be partner of your weal or woe.
DUKE OF BURGUNDY.
Courageous Bedford, let us now persuade you.
DUKE OF BEDFORD.
Not to be gone from hence; for once I read,
That stout Pendragon, in his litter, sick,
Came to the field, and vanquished his foes:
Methinks I should revive the soldiers' hearts,
Because I ever found them as myself.
LORD TALBOT.
Undaunted spirit in a dying breast!—
Then be it so:—heavens keep old Bedford safe!—
And now no more ado, brave Burgundy,
But gather we our forces out of hand,
And set upon our boasting enemy.
　　　[Exeunt all but BEDFORD and ATTEN-
　　　DANTS.
　　An alarum: excursions. Enter SIR JOHN FAS-
　　　TOLFE *and a* CAPTAIN.
CAPTAIN.
Whither away, Sir John Fastolfe, in such haste?
SIR JOHN FASTOLFE.
Whither away! to save myself by flight:
We are like to have the overthrow again.
CAPTAIN.
What! will you fly, and leave Lord Talbot?
SIR JOHN FASTOLFE.
　　　　　　　　　　　　　　　　　Ay,
All the Talbots in the world, to save my life.
　　　　　　　　　　　　　　　　　[Exit
CAPTAIN.
Cowardly knight! ill fortune follow thee!　　[Exit
　　Retreat: excursions. LA PUCELLE, ALENÇON,
　　　and CHARLES *fly.*
DUKE OF BEDFORD.
Now, quiet soul, depart when heaven please,
For I have seen our enemies' overthrow.
What is the trust or strength of foolish man?
They that of late were daring with their scoffs,
Are glad and fain by flight to save themselves.
　　　[BEDFORD *dies and is carried in by two in
　　　his chair.*
　　An alarum. Enter TALBOT, BURGUNDY, *and
　　　the rest.*
LORD TALBOT.
Lost and recover'd in a day again!
This is a double honour, Burgundy:
Yet heavens have glory for this victory!

16

DUKE OF BURGUNDY.

Warlike and martial Talbot, Burgundy
Enshrines thee in his heart, and there erects
Thy noble deeds, as valour's monuments.

LORD TALBOT.

Thanks, gentle duke. But where is Pucelle now?
I think her old familiar is asleep:
Now where's the Bastard's braves, and Charles
   his gleeks?
What, all amort? Rouen hangs her head for grief,
That such a valiant company are fled.
Now will we take some order in the town,
Placing therein some expert officers;
And then depart to Paris to the king,
For there young Henry with his nobles lie.

DUKE OF BURGUNDY.

What wills Lord Talbot pleaseth Burgundy.

LORD TALBOT.

But yet, before we go, let's not forget
The noble Duke of Bedford late deceased,
But see his exequies fulfill'd in Rouen:
A braver soldier never couched lance,
A gentler heart did never sway in court:
But kings and mightiest potentates must die,
For that's the end of human misery.   [Exeunt.

SCENE III.

The plains near Rouen.

Enter CHARLES, *the* BASTARD OF ORLEANS,
ALENÇON, LA PUCELLE, *and* FORCES.

JOAN LA PUCELLE.

DISMAY not, princes, at this accident,
   Nor grieve that Rouen is so recovered:
Care is no cure, but rather corrosive,
For things that are not to be remedied.
Let frantic Talbot triumph for a while,
And like a peacock sweep along his tail;
We'll pull his plumes, and take away his train,
If Dauphin and the rest will be but ruled.

CHARLES.

We have been guided by thee hitherto,
And of thy cunning had no diffidence:
One sudden foil shall never breed distrust.

BASTARD OF ORLEANS.

Search out thy wit for secret policies,
And we will make thee famous through the
   world.

DUKE OF ALENÇON.

We'll set thy statue in some holy place,
And have thee reverenced like a blessed saint:
Employ thee, then, sweet virgin, for our good.

JOAN LA PUCELLE.

Then thus it must be; this doth Joan devise:
By fair persuasions, mixt with sugar'd words,
We will entice the Duke of Burgundy
To leave the Talbot and to follow us.

CHARLES.

Ay, marry, sweeting, if we could do that,
France were no place for Henry's warriors;
Nor should that nation boast it so with us,
But be extirped from our provinces.

DUKE OF ALENÇON.

For ever should they be expulsed from France,
And not have title of an earldom here.

JOAN LA PUCELLE.

Your honours shall perceive how I will work
To bring this matter to the wished end.
   [*Drum sounds afar off.*
Hark! by the sound of drum you may perceive
Their powers are marching unto Paris-ward.
*Here sound an English march.   Enter, and pass over
   at a distance,* TALBOT *and his* FORCES.
There goes the Talbot, with his colours spread,
And all the troops of English after him.
French march.   Enter the DUKE OF BURGUNDY
   and his FORCES.
Now in the rearward comes the duke and his:
Fortune in favour makes him lag behind.
Summon a parley; we will talk with him.
   [*Trumpets sound a parley.*

CHARLES.

A parley with the Duke of Burgundy!

DUKE OF BURGUNDY.

Who craves a parley with the Burgundy?

JOAN LA PUCELLE.

The princely Charles of France, thy countryman.

DUKE OF BURGUNDY.

What say'st thou, Charles? for I am marching
   hence.

CHARLES.

Speak, Pucelle, and enchant him with thy words.

JOAN LA PUCELLE.

Brave Burgundy, undoubted hope of France!
Stay, let thy humble handmaid speak to thee.

DUKE OF BURGUNDY.

Speak on; but be not over-tedious.

JOAN LA PUCELLE.

Look on thy country, look on fertile France,
And see the cities and the towns defaced
By wasting ruin of the cruel foe!
As looks the mother on her lowly babe
When death doth close his tender dying eyes,
See, see the pining malady of France;
Behold the wounds, the most unnatural wounds,
Which thou thyself hast given her woful breast!
O, turn thy edged sword another way;
Strike those that hurt, and hurt not those that
   help!
One drop of blood drawn from thy country's
   bosom
Should grieve thee more than streams of foreign
   gore:
Return thee, therefore, with a flood of tears,
And wash away thy country's stained spots.

DUKE OF BURGUNDY [*aside*].

Either she hath bewitcht me with her words,
Or nature makes me suddenly relent.

JOAN LA PUCELLE.

Besides, all French and France exclaim on
   thee,
Doubting thy birth and lawful progeny,
Who join'st thou with, but with a lordly nation,
That will not trust thee but for profit's sake?
When Talbot hath set footing once in France,
And fashion'd thee that instrument of ill,
Who then but English Henry will be lord,
And thou be thrust out like a fugitive?
Call we to mind,—and mark but this for proof,—
Was not the Duke of Orleans thy foe?
And was he not in England prisoner?

But when they heard he was thine enemy,
They set him free, without his ransom paid,
In spite of Burgundy and all his friends.
See, then, thou fight'st against thy countrymen,
And join'st with them will be thy slaughter-men.
Come, come, return; return, thou wandering
    lord;
Charles and the rest will take thee in their arms.
            DUKE OF BURGUNDY [aside].
I'm vanquished; these haughty words of hers
Have batter'd me like roaring cannon-shot,
And made me almost yield upon my knees.—
Forgive me, country, and sweet countrymen!
And, lords, accept this hearty kind embrace:
My forces and my power of men are yours:—
So, farewell, Talbot; I'll no longer trust thee.
            JOAN LA PUCELLE [aside].
Done like a Frenchman: turn, and turn again!
            CHARLES.
Welcome, brave duke! thy friendship makes us
    fresh.
            BASTARD OF ORLEANS.
And doth beget new courage in our breasts.
            DUKE OF ALENÇON.
Pucelle hath bravely play'd her part in this,
And doth deserve a coronet of gold.
            CHARLES.
Now let us on, my lords, and join our powers;
And seek how we may prejudice the foe. [Exeunt.

                SCENE IV.

            Paris.   The palace.

Enter the KING, GLOSTER, WINCHESTER,
    YORK, SUFFOLK, SOMERSET, WARWICK,
    EXETER, VERNON, BASSET, etc. To them, with
    his SOLDIERS, TALBOT.

            LORD TALBOT.
MY gracious prince,—and honourable peers,—
    Hearing of your arrival in this realm,
I have awhile given truce unto my wars,
To do my duty to my sovereign:
In sign whereof, this arm—that hath reclaim'd
To your obedience fifty fortresses,
Twelve cities, and seven walled towns of strength,
Beside five hundred prisoners of esteem—
Lets fall his sword before your highness' feet,
                            [Kneeling.
And with submissive loyalty of heart
Ascribes the glory of his conquest got
First to my God, and next unto your Grace.
            KING HENRY.
Is this the Lord Talbot, uncle Gloster,
That hath so long been resident in France?
            DUKE OF GLOSTER.
Yes, if it please your majesty, my liege.
            KING HENRY.
Welcome, brave captain and victorious lord!
When I was young,—as yet I am not old,—
I do remember how my father said
A stouter champion never handled sword.
Long since we were resolved of your truth,
Your faithful service, and your toil in war;
Yet never have you tasted our reward,

Or been reguerdon'd with so much as thanks,
Because till now we never saw your face:
Therefore, stand up; and, for these good deserts,
We here create you Earl of Shrewsbury;
And in our coronation take your place.
        [Sennet. Flourish. Exeunt all except VER-
            NON and BASSET.
            VERNON.
Now, sir, to you, that were so hot at sea,
Disgracing of these colours that I wear
In honour of my noble Lord of York,—
Darest thou maintain the former words thou
    spakest?
            BASSET.
Yes, sir; as well as you dare patronage
The envious barking of your saucy tongue
Against my lord the Duke of Somerset.
            VERNON.
Sirrah, thy lord I honour as he is.
            BASSET.
Why, what is he? as good a man as York.
            VERNON.
Hark ye; not so: in witness, take ye that.
                            [Strikes him.
            BASSET.
Villain, thou know'st the law of arms is such,
That whoso draws a sword, 'tis present death,
Or else this blow should broach thy dearest
    blood.
But I'll unto his majesty, and crave
I may have liberty to venge this wrong;
When thou shalt see I'll meet thee to thy cost.
            VERNON.
Well, miscreant, I'll be there as soon as you;
And, after, meet you sooner than you would.
                            [Exeunt.

            ACT IV.   SCENE I.

        Paris.   A room of state in the palace.

Enter the KING, GLOSTER, EXETER, YORK,
    SUFFOLK, SOMERSET, WINCHESTER, WAR-
    WICK, TALBOT, the GOVERNOR OF PARIS
    and others.

            DUKE OF GLOSTER.
LORD bishop, set the crown upon his head.
            BISHOP OF WINCHESTER.
God save King Henry, of that name the sixth!
            DUKE OF GLOSTER.
Now, governor of Paris, take your oath,—
                        [GOVERNOR kneels
That you elect no other king but him;
Esteem none friends but such as are his friends,
And none your foes but such as shall pretend
Malicious practices against his state:
This shall ye do, so help you righteous God!
        [Exeunt GOVERNOR and his TRAIN.
    Enter SIR JOHN FASTOLFE.
            SIR JOHN FASTOLFE.
My gracious sovereign, as I rode from Calais,
To haste unto your coronation,
A letter was deliver'd to my hands,
Writ to your Grace from th' Duke of Burgundy.
            LORD TALBOT.
Shame to the Duke of Burgundy and thee!

I vow'd, base knight, when I did meet thee next,
To tear the garter from thy craven's leg,—
                        [Plucks it off.
Which I have done,—because unworthily
Thou wast installed in that high degree.—
Pardon me, princely Henry, and the rest:
This dastard, at the battle of Patay,
When but in all I was six thousand strong,
And that the French were almost ten to one,—
Before we met, or that a stroke was given,
Like to a trusty squire, did run away:
In which assault we lost twelve hundred men;
Myself, and divers gentlemen beside,
Were there surprised and taken prisoners.
Then judge, great lords, if I have done amiss;
Or whether that such cowards ought to wear
This ornament of knighthood, yea or no.
      DUKE OF GLOSTER.
To say the truth, this fact was infamous,
And ill beseeming any common man,
Much more a knight, a captain, and a leader.
      LORD TALBOT.
When first this order was ordain'd, my lords,
Knights of the Garter were of noble birth,
Valiant and virtuous, full of haughty courage,
Such as were grown to credit by the wars;
Not fearing death, nor shrinking for distress,
But always resolute in most extremes.
He, then, that is not furnisht in this sort
Doth but usurp the sacred name of knight,
Profaning this most honourable order,
And should—if I were worthy to be judge—
Be quite degraded, like a hedge-born swain
That doth presume to boast of gentle blood.
      KING HENRY.
tain to thy countrymen, thou hear'st thy doom!
Be packing, therefore, thou that wast a knight:
Henceforth we banish thee, on pain of death.
                [Exit FASTOLFE.
And now, my lord Protector, view the letter
Sent from our uncle Duke of Burgundy.
      DUKE OF GLOSTER.
What means his Grace, that he hath changed his
    style?
No more but, plain and bluntly, 'To the king'?
Hath he forgot he is his sovereign?
Or doth this churlish superscription
Pretend some alteration in good will?
What's here?—*[Reads]* 'I have, upon especial
    cause,—
Moved with compassion of my country's wrack,
Together with the pitiful complaints
Of such as your oppression feeds upon,—
Forsaken your pernicious faction,
And join'd with Charles, the rightful King of
    France.'
O monstrous treachery! can this be so,—
That in alliance, amity, andoaths,
There should be found such false dissembling
    guile?
      KING HENRY.
What! doth my uncle Burgundy revolt?
      DUKE OF GLOSTER.
He doth, my lord; and is become your foe.
      KING HENRY.
Is that the worst this letter doth contain?

      DUKE OF GLOSTER.
It is the worst, and all, my lord, he writes.
      KING HENRY.
Why, then, Lord Talbot there shall talk with him,
And give him chastisement for this abuse.—
How say you, my lord? are you not content?
      LORD TALBOT.
Content, my liege! yes, but that I am prevented,
I should have begg'd I might have been employ'd.
      KING HENRY.
Then gather strength, and march unto him
    straight:
Let him perceive how ill we brook his treason,
And what offence it is to flout his friends.
      LORD TALBOT.
I go, my lord; in heart desiring still
You may behold confusion of your foes.   *[Exit.*
    Enter VERNON AND BASSET.
      VERNON.
Grant me the combat, gracious sovereign!
      BASSET.
And me, my lord, grant me the combat too!
      DUKE OF YORK.
This is my servant: hear him, noble prince!
      EARL OF SOMERSET.
And this is mine: sweet Henry, favour him!
      KING HENRY.
Be patient, lords; and give them leave to speak.—
Say, gentlemen, what makes you thus exclaim?
And wherefore crave you combat? or with whom?
      VERNON.
With him, my lord; for he hath done me wrong.
      BASSET.
And I with him; for he hath done me wrong.
      KING HENRY.
What is that wrong whereof you both complain?
First let me know, and then I'll answer you.
      BASSET.
Crossing the sea from England into France,
This fellow here, with envious carping tongue,
Upbraided me about the rose I wear;
Saying, the sanguine colour of the leaves
Did represent my master's blushing cheeks,
When stubbornly he did repugn the truth
About a certain question in the law
Argued betwixt the Duke of York and him;
With other vile and ignominious terms;
In confutation of which rude reproach,
And in defence of my lord's worthiness,
I crave the benefit of law of arms.
      VERNON.
And that is my petition, noble lord:
For though he seem with forged quaint conceit
To set a gloss upon his bold intent,
Yet know, my lord, I was provoked by him;
And he first took exceptions at this badge,
Pronouncing that the paleness of this flower
Bewray'd the faintness of my master's heart.
      DUKE OF YORK.
Will not this malice, Somerset, be left?
      EARL OF SOMERSET.
Your private grudge, my Lord of York, will out,
Though ne'er so cunningly you smother it.
      KING HENRY.
Good Lord, what madness rules in brain-sick
    men,

When for so slight and frivolous a cause
Such factious emulations shall arise!—
Good cousins both, of York and Somerset,
Quiet yourselves, I pray, and be at peace.

DUKE OF YORK.

Let this dissension first be tried by fight,
And then your highness shall command a peace.

EARL OF SOMERSET.

The quarrel toucheth none but us alone;
Betwixt ourselves let us decide it, then.

DUKE OF YORK.

There is my pledge; accept it, Somerset.

VERNON.

Nay, let it rest where it began at first.

BASSET.

Confirm it so, mine honourable lord.

DUKE OF GLOSTER.

Confirm it so! Confounded be your strife!
And perish ye, with your audacious prate!
Presumptuous vassals, are you not ashamed
With this immodest clamorous outrage
To trouble and disturb the king and us?—
And you, my lords,—methinks you do not well
To bear with their perverse objections;
Much less to take occasion from their mouths
To raise a mutiny betwixt yourselves:
Let me persuade you take a better course.

DUKE OF EXETER.

It grieves his highness:—good my lords, be
  friends.

KING HENRY.

Come hither, you that would be combatants:
Henceforth I charge you, as you love our favour,
Quite to forget this quarrel and the cause.—
And you, my lords, remember where we are;
In France, amongst a fickle wavering nation:
If they perceive dissension in our looks,
And that within ourselves we disagree,
How will their grudging stomachs be provoked
To wilful disobedience, and rebel!
Beside, what infamy will there arise,
When foreign princes shall be certified
That for a toy, a thing of no regard,
King Henry's peers and chief nobility
Destroy'd themselves, and lost the realm of
  France!
O, think upon the conquest of my father;
My tender years; and let us not forgo
That for a trifle that was bought with blood!
Let me be umpire in this doubtful strife.
I see no reason, if I wear this rose,
                    [Putting on a red rose.
That any one should therefore be suspicious
I more incline to Somerset than York:
Both are my kinsmen, and I love them both:
As well they may upbraid me with my crown,
Because, forsooth, the King of Scots is crown'd.
But your discretions better can persuade
Than I am able to instruct or teach:
And therefore, as we hither came in peace,
So let us still continue peace and love.—
Cousin of York, we institute your Grace
To be our regent in these parts of France:—
And, good my Lord of Somerset, unite
Your troops of horsemen with his bands of foot:—
And, like true subjects, sons of your progenitors,

Go cheerfully together, and digest
Your angry choler on your enemies.
Ourself, my lord Protector, and the rest,
After some respite, will return to Calais;
From thence to England; where I hope ere long
To be presented, by your victories,
With Charles, Alençon, and that traitorous rout.
  [Flourish. Exeunt KING, GLOSTER, SOM-
      ERSET, WINCHESTER, SUFFOLK, and
      BASSET.

EARL OF WARWICK.

My Lord of York, I promise you, the king
Prettily, methought, did play the orator.

DUKE OF YORK.

And so he did; but yet I like it not,
In that he wears the badge of Somerset.

EARL OF WARWICK.

Tush, that was but his fancy, blame him not;
I dare presume, sweet prince, he thought no
  harm.

DUKE OF YORK.

An if I wist he did,—but let it rest;
Other affairs must now be managed.
      [Exeunt YORK, WARWICK, and VERNON.

DUKE OF EXETER.

Well didst thou, Richard, to suppress thy voice;
For, had the passions of thy heart burst out,
I fear we should have seen decipher'd there
More rancorous spite, more furious raging broils,
Than yet can be imagined or supposed.
But howsoe'er, no simple man that sees
This jarring discord of nobility,
This shouldering of each other in the court,
This factious bandying of their favourites,
But that he doth presage some ill event.
'Tis much when sceptres are in children's hands;
But more when envy breeds unkind division;
There comes the ruin, there begins confusion.
                                        [Exit.

SCENE II.

Before Bourdeaux.

Enter TALBOT, *with trump and drum.*

LORD TALBOT.

GO to the gates of Bourdeaux, trumpeter;
  Summon their general unto the wall.
Trumpet sounds. Enter GENERAL *and others aloft*
English John Talbot, captains, calls you forth,
Servant in arms to Harry King of England;
And thus he would,—Open your city-gates;
Be humble to us: call my sovereign yours,
And do him homage as obedient subjects;
And I'll withdraw me and my bloody power:
But, if you frown upon this proffer'd peace,
You tempt the fury of my three attendants,
Lean famine, quartering steel, and climbing fire;
Who, in a moment, even with the earth
Shall lay your stately and air-braving towers,
If you forsake the offer of our love.

GENERAL.

Thou ominous and fearful owl of death,
Our nation's terror, and their bloody scourge!
The period of thy tyranny approacheth.
On us thou canst not enter but by death;
For, I protest, we are well fortified,
And strong enough to issue out and fight:

If thou retire, the Dauphin, well appointed,
Stands with the snares of war to tangle thee:
On either hand thee there are squadrons pitcht,
To wall thee from the liberty of flight;
And no way canst thou turn thee for redress,
But death doth front thee with apparent spoil,
And pale destruction meets thee in the face.
Ten thousand French have ta'en the sacrament
To rive their dangerous artillery
Upon no Christian soul but English Talbot.
Lo, there thou stand'st, a breathing valiant man,
Of an invincible unconquer'd spirit!
This is the latest glory of thy praise
That I, thy enemy, due thee withal;
For ere the glass, that now begins to **run**,
Finish the process of his sandy hour,
These eyes, that see thee now well-coloured,
Shall see thee wither'd, bloody, pale, and dead.
                              [*Drum afar off.*
Hark! hark! the Dauphin's drum, a warning bell,
Sings heavy music to thy timorous soul;
And mine shall ring thy dire departure out.
                    [*Exeunt* GENERAL, *etc.*
                    LORD TALBOT.
He fables not; I hear the enemy:—
Out, some light horsemen, and peruse their
    wings.—
O, negligent and heedless discipline!
How are we parkt and bounded in a pale,—
A little herd of England's timorous deer,
Mazed with a yelping kennel of French curs!
If we be English deer, be, then, in blood;
Not rascal-like, to fall down with a pinch,
But rather, moody-mad and desperate stags,
Turn on the bloody hounds with heads of steel,
And make the cowards stand aloof at bay:
Sell every man his life as dear as mine,
And they shall find dear deer of us, my friends.—
God and Saint George, Talbot and England's
    right,
Prosper our colours in this dangerous fight!
                              [*Exeunt.*

SCENE III.
Plains in Gascony.

Enter a MESSENGER *that meets* YORK. *Enter*
YORK *with trumpet and many* SOLDIERS.
                    DUKE OF YORK.
ARE not the speedy scouts return'd again,
That dogg'd the mighty army of the Dau-
                    MESSENGER.   [phin?
They are return'd, my lord; and give it out
That he is marcht to Bourdeaux with his power,
To fight with Talbot: as he marcht along,
By your espials were discovered
Two mightier troops than that the Dauphin
    led;
Which join'd with him, and made their march for
    Bourdeaux.
                    DUKE OF YORK.
A plague upon that villain Somerset,
That thus delays my promised supply
Of horsemen, that were levied for this siege!
Renowned Talbot doth expect my aid;
And I am louted by a traitor villain,
And cannot help the noble chevalier:

God comfort him in this necessity!
If he miscarry, farewell wars in France.
                    Enter SIR WILLIAM LUCY.
                    SIR WILLIAM LUCY.
Thou princely leader of our English strength,
Never so needful on the earth of France,
Spur to the rescue of the noble Talbot,
Who now is girdled with a waist of iron,
And hemm'd about with grim destruction:
To Bourdeaux, warlike duke! to Bourdeaux, York!
Else, farewell Talbot, France, and England's
    honour.
                    DUKE OF YORK.
O God, that Somerset—who in proud heart
Doth stop my cornets—were in Talbot's place!
So should we save a valiant gentleman
By forfeiting a traitor and a coward.
Mad ire and wrathful fury make me weep,
That thus we die, while remiss traitors sleep.
                    SIR WILLIAM LUCY.
O, send some succour to the distrest lord!
                    DUKE OF YORK.
He dies, we lose; I break my warlike word;
We mourn, France smiles; we lose, they daily
    get;
All long of this vile traitor Somerset.
                    SIR WILLIAM LUCY.
Then God take mercy on brave Talbot's soul;
And on his son young John, who two hours since
I met in travel toward his warlike father!
This seven years did not Talbot see his son;
And now they meet where both their lives are
    done.
                    DUKE OF YORK.
Alas, what joy shall noble Talbot have
To bid his young son welcome to his grave?
Away! vexation almost stops my breath,
That sunder'd friends greet in the hour of
    death.—
Lucy, farewell: no more my fortune can,
But curse the cause I cannot aid the man.
Maine, Blois, Poictiers, and Tours, are won away,
Long all of Somerset and his delay.
                    [*Exit with* FORCES.
                    SIR WILLIAM LUCY.
Thus, while the vulture of sedition
Feeds in the bosom of such great commanders,
Sleeping neglection doth betray to loss
The conquest of our scarce-cold conqueror,
That ever-living man of memory,
Henry the Fifth:—whiles they each other cross,
Lives, honours, land, and all, hurry to loss. [*Exit.*

SCENE IV.
Other plains in Gascony.

Enter SOMERSET, *with his* ARMY; *an* OFFICER *of*
TALBOT'S *with him.*
                    EARL OF SOMERSET.
IT is too late: I cannot send them now:
This expedition was by York and Talbot
Too rashly plotted; all our general force
Might with a sally of the very town
Be buckled with: the over-daring Talbot
Hath sullied all his gloss of former honour
By this unheedful, desperate, wild adventure:

York set him on to fight and die in shame,
That, Talbot dead, great York might bear the
    name.
OFFICER.
Here is Sir William Lucy, who with me
Set from our o'er-matcht forces forth for aid.
Enter SIR WILLIAM LUCY.
EARL OF SOMERSET.
How now, Sir William! whither were you sent?
SIR WILLIAM LUCY.
Whither, my lord? from bought and sold Lord
    Talbot;
Who, ring'd about with bold adversity,
Cries out for noble York and Somerset,
To beat assailing death from his weak legions:
And whiles the honourable captain there
Drops bloody sweat from his war-wearied limbs,
And, in advantage lingering, looks for rescue,
You, his false hopes, the trust of England's
    honour,
Keep off aloof with worthless emulation.
Let not your private discord keep away
The levied succours that should lend him aid,
While he, renowned noble gentleman,
Yields up his life unto a world of odds:
Orleans the Bastard, Charles, Burgundy,
Alençon, Reignier, compass him about,
And Talbot perisheth by your default.
EARL OF SOMERSET.
York set him on, York should have sent him aid.
SIR WILLIAM LUCY.
And York as fast upon your Grace exclaims;
Swearing that you withhold his levied host,
Collected for this expedition.
EARL OF SOMERSET.
York lies; he might have sent and had the horse;
I owe him little duty, and less love;
And take foul scorn to fawn on him by sending.
SIR WILLIAM LUCY.
The fraud of England, not the force of France,
Hath now entrapt the noble-minded Talbot:
Never to England shall he bear his life;
But dies, betray'd to fortune by your strife.
EARL OF SOMERSET.
Come, go; I will dispatch the horsemen straight;
Within six hours they will be at his aid.
SIR WILLIAM LUCY.
Too late comes rescue; he is ta'en or slain:
For fly he could not, if he would have fled;
And fly would Talbot never, though he might.
EARL OF SOMERSET.
If he be dead, brave Talbot, then, adieu!
SIR WILLIAM LUCY.
His fame lives in the world, his shame in you.
                              [*Exeunt.*

SCENE V.

The English camp near Bourdeaux.

Enter TALBOT *and* JOHN *his son.*

LORD TALBOT.

O YOUNG John Talbot! I did send for thee
    To tutor thee in stratagems of war,
That Talbot's name might be in thee revived
When sapless age and weak unable limbs
Should bring thy father to his drooping chair.
But,—O malignant and ill-boding stars!—

Now thou art come unto a feast of death,
A terrible and unavoided danger:
Therefore, dear boy, mount on my swiftest horse;
And I'll direct thee how thou shalt escape
By sudden flight: come, dally not, be gone.
JOHN TALBOT.
Is my name Talbot? and am I your son?
And shall I fly? O, if you love my mother,
Dishonour not her honourable name,
To make a bastard and a slave of me!
The world will say, he is not Talbot's blood,
That basely fled when noble Talbot stood.
LORD TALBOT.
Fly, to revenge my death, if I be slain.
JOHN TALBOT.
He that flies so will ne'er return again.
LORD TALBOT.
If we both stay, we both are sure to die.
JOHN TALBOT.
Then let me stay; and, father, do you fly:
Your loss is great, so your regard should be;
My worth unknown, no loss is known in me.
Upon my death the French can little boast;
In yours they will, in you all hopes are lost.
Flight cannot stain the honour you have won;
But mine it will, that no exploit have done:
You fled for vantage, every one will swear;
But, if I bow, they'll say it was for fear.
There is no hope that ever I will stay,
If, the first hour, I shrink and run away.
Here, on my knee, I beg mortality,
Rather than life preserved with infamy.
LORD TALBOT.
Shall all thy mother's hopes lie in one tomb?
JOHN TALBOT.
Ay, rather than I'll shame my mother's womb.
LORD TALBOT.
Upon my blessing, I command thee go.
JOHN TALBOT.
To fight I will, but not to fly the foe.
LORD TALBOT.
Part of thy father may be saved in thee.
JOHN TALBOT.
No part of him but will be shamed in me.
LORD TALBOT.
Thou never hadst renown, nor canst not lose it.
JOHN TALBOT.
Yes, your renowned name: shall flight abuse it?
LORD TALBOT.
Thy father's charge shall clear thee from that
    stain.
JOHN TALBOT.
You cannot witness for me, being slain.
If death be so apparent, then both fly.
LORD TALBOT.
And leave my followers here, to fight and die?
My age was never tainted with such shame.
JOHN TALBOT.
And shall my youth be guilty of such blame?
No more can I be sever'd from your side
Than can yourself yourself in twain divide:
Stay, go, do what you will, the like do I;
For live I will not, if my father die.
LORD TALBOT.
Then here I take my leave of thee, fair son,
Born to eclipse thy life this afternoon.

Come, side by side together live and die;
And soul with soul from France to heaven fly.
                                          [*Exeunt.*

SCENE VI.

A field of battle.

Alarum: excursions, wherein TALBOT'S SON *is
hemm'd about, and* TALBOT *rescues him.*

LORD TALBOT.

SAINT George and victory! fight, soldiers, fight:
    The regent hath with Talbot broke his word,
And left us to the rage of France his sword.
Where is John Talbot?—Pause, and take thy
    breath;
I gave thee life, and rescued thee from death.

JOHN TALBOT.

O, twice my father, twice am I thy son!
The life thou gavest me first was lost and done,
Till with thy warlike sword, despite of fate,
To my determined time thou gavest new date.

LORD TALBOT.

When from the Dauphin's crest thy sword struck
    fire,
It warm'd thy father's heart with proud desire
Of bold-faced victory. Then leaden age,
Quicken'd with youthful spleen and warlike rage,
Beat down Alençon, Orleans, Burgundy,
And from the pride of Gallia rescued thee.
The ireful bastard Orleans—that drew blood
From thee, my boy, and had the maidenhood
Of thy first fight—I soon encountered,
And, interchanging blows, I quickly shed
Some of his bastard blood; and, in disgrace,
Bespoke him thus,—'Contaminated, base,
And misbegotten blood I spill of thine,
Mean and right poor, for that pure blood of mine
Which thou didst force from Talbot, my brave
    boy:'—
Here, purposing the Bastard to destroy,
Came in strong rescue. Speak, thy father's
    care,—
Art thou not weary, John? how dost thou fare?
Wilt thou yet leave the battle, boy, and fly,
Now thou art seal'd the son of chivalry?
Fly, to revenge my death when I am dead:
The help of one stands me in little stead.
O, too much folly is it, well I wot,
To hazard all our lives in one small boat!
If I to-day die not with Frenchmen's rage,
To-morrow I shall die with mickle age:
By me they nothing gain, an if I stay,—
'Tis but the shortening of my life one day:
In thee thy mother dies, our household's name,
My death's revenge, thy youth, and England's
    fame:
All these, and more, we hazard by thy stay;
All these are saved, if thou wilt fly away.

JOHN TALBOT.

The sword of Orleans hath not made me smart;
These words of yours draw life-blood from my
    heart:
On that advantage, bought with such a shame,—
To save a paltry life, and slay bright fame,—
Before young Talbot from old Talbot fly,
The coward horse that bears me fall and die!
And like me to the peasant boys of France,

To be shame's scorn and subject of mischance!
Surely, by all the glory you have won,
An if I fly, I am not Talbot's son:
Then talk no more of flight, it is no boot;
If son to Talbot, die at Talbot's foot.

LORD TALBOT.

Then follow thou thy desperate sire of Crete,
Thou Icarus; thy life to me is sweet:
If thou wilt fight, fight by thy father's side;
And, commendable proved, let's die in pride.
                                          [*Exeunt.*

SCENE VII.

Another part of the field.

Alarum: excursions. Enter old TALBOT *led by a*
SERVANT.

LORD TALBOT.

WHERE is my other life?—mine own is
    gone;—
O, where's young Talbot? where is valiant
    John?—
Triumphant death, smear'd with captivity,
Young Talbot's valour makes me smile at thee:—
When he perceived me shrink and on my knee,
His bloody sword he brandisht over me,
And, like a hungry lion, did commence
Rough deeds of rage and stern impatience;
But when my angry guardant stood alone,
Tendering my ruin, and assail'd of none,
Dizzy-eyed fury and great rage of heart
Suddenly made him from my side to start
Into the clustering battle of the French;
And in that sea of blood my boy did drench
His over-mounting spirit; and there died
My Icarus, my blossom, in his pride.

SERVANT.

O my dear lord, lo, where your son is borne!
    Enter SOLDIERS, *with* JOHN TALBOT *borne.*

LORD TALBOT.

Thou antic death, which laugh'st us here to
    scorn,
Anon, from thy insulting tyranny,
Coupled in bonds of perpetuity,
Two Talbots, winged through the lither sky,
In thy despite, shall scape mortality.—
O thou whose wounds become hard-favour'd
    death,
Speak to thy father, ere thou yield thy breath!
Brave death by speaking, whether he will or no;
Imagine him a Frenchman and thy foe.—
Poor boy! he smiles, methinks, as who should say,
Had death been French, then death had died
    to-day.—
Come, come, and lay him in his father's arms:
My spirit can no longer bear these harms.
Soldiers, adieu! I have what I would have,
Now my old arms are young John Talbot's grave.
                                          [*Dies.*

Enter CHARLES, ALENÇON, BURGUNDY, BAS-
TARD, LA PUCELLE, *and* FORCES.

CHARLES.

Had York and Somerset brought rescue in,
We should have found a bloody day of this.

BASTARD OF ORLEANS.

How the young whelp of Talbot's, raging-wood,
Did flesh his puny sword in Frenchmen's blood!

JOAN LA PUCELLE.
Once I encounter'd him, and thus I said,
'Thou maiden youth, be vanquisht by a maid':
But, with a proud majestical high scorn,
He answer'd thus, 'Young Talbot was not born
To be the pillage of a giglot wench':
So, rushing in the bowels of the French,
He left me proudly, as unworthy fight.

DUKE OF BURGUNDY.
Doubtless he would have made a noble knight:
See, where he lies inhearsed in the arms
Of the most bloody nurser of his harms!

BASTARD OF ORLEANS.
Hew them to pieces, hack their bones asunder,
Whose life was England's glory, Gallia's wonder.

CHARLES.
O, no, forbear! for that which we have fled
During the life, let us not wrong it dead.

Enter SIR WILLIAM LUCY, *attended; a French*
HERALD *preceding.*

SIR WILLIAM LUCY.
Herald, conduct me to the Dauphin's tent,
To know who hath obtain'd the glory of the day.

CHARLES.
On what submissive message art thou sent?

SIR WILLIAM LUCY.
Submission, Dauphin! 'tis a mere French word;
We English warriors wot not what it means.
I come to know what prisoners thou hast ta'en,
And to survey the bodies of the dead.

CHARLES.
For prisoners ask'st thou? hell our prison is.
But tell me whom thou seek'st.

SIR WILLIAM LUCY.
Where is the great Alcides of the field,
Valiant Lord Talbot, Earl of Shrewsbury,—
Created, for his rare success in arms,
Great Earl of Washford, Waterford, and Valence;
Lord Talbot of Goodrig and Urchinfield,
Lord Strange of Blackmere, Lord Verdun of
   Alton,
Lord Cromwell of Wingfield, Lord Furnival of
   Sheffield,
The thrice-victorious Lord of Falconbridge;
Knight of the noble order of Saint George,
Worthy Saint Michael, and the Golden Fleece;
Great Marshal to Henry the Sixth
Of all his wars within the realm of France?

JOAN LA PUCELLE.
Here is a silly-stately style indeed!
The Turk, that two-and-fifty kingdoms hath,
Writes not so tedious a style as this.—
Him that thou magnifiest with all these titles,
Stinking and fly-blown, lies here at our feet.

SIR WILLIAM LUCY.
Is Talbot slain,—the Frenchmen's only scourge,
Your kingdom's terror and black Nemesis?
O, were mine eyeballs into bullets turn'd,
That I, in rage, might shoot them at your faces!
O, that I could but call these dead to life!
It were enough to fright the realm of France:
Were but his picture left amongst you here,
It would amaze the proudest of you all.
Give me their bodies, that I may bear them
   hence,
And give them burial as beseems their worth.

JOAN LA PUCELLE.
I think this upstart is old Talbot's ghost,
He speaks with such a proud-commanding spirit.
For God's sake, let him have 'em; to keep them
   here,
They would but stink, and putrefy the air.

CHARLES.
Go, take their bodies hence.

SIR WILLIAM LUCY.
I'll bear them hence: but from their ashes shall be
   rear'd
A phœnix that shall make all France afeard.

CHARLES.
So we be rid of them, do with 'em what thou
   wilt.—
And now to Paris, in this conquering vein:
All will be ours, now bloody Talbot's slain.
   [*Exeunt.*

ACT V. SCENE I.

London. The palace.

Enter KING, GLOSTER, *and* EXETER.

KING HENRY.
HAVE you perused the letters from the Pope,
   The emperor, and the Earl of Armagnac?

DUKE OF GLOSTER.
I have, my lord: and their intent is this,—
They humbly sue unto your excellence
To have a godly peace concluded of
Between the realms of England and of France.

KING HENRY.
How doth your Grace affect their motion?

DUKE OF GLOSTER.
Well, my good lord; and as the only means
To stop effusion of our Christian blood,
And stablish quietness on every side.

KING HENRY.
Ay, marry, uncle; for I always thought
It was both impious and unnatural
That such immanity and bloody strife
Should reign among professors of one faith.

DUKE OF GLOSTER.
Beside, my lord, the sooner to effect
And surer bind this knot of amity,
The Earl of Armagnac—near kin to Charles,
A man of great authority in France—
Proffers his only daughter to your Grace
In marriage, with a large and sumptuous dowry.

KING HENRY.
Marriage, uncle! alas, my years are young!
And fitter is my study and my books
Than wanton dalliance with a paramour.
Yet, call th' ambassadors; and, as you please,
So let them have their answers, every one:
I shall be well content with any choice
Tends to God's glory and my country's weal.

Enter a LEGATE *and two* AMBASSADORS, *with*
WINCHESTER *in a Cardinal's habit.*

DUKE OF EXETER [*aside*].
What! is my Lord of Winchester install'd,
And call'd unto a cardinal's degree?
Then I perceive that will be verified
Henry the Fifth did sometime prophesy,—
'If once he come to be a cardinal,
He'll make his cap co-equal with the crown.'

KING HENRY.

My lords ambassadors, your several suits
Have been consider'd and debated on.
Your purpose is both good and reasonable;
And therefore are we certainly resolved
To draw conditions of a friendly peace;
Which by my Lord of Winchester we mean
Shall be transported presently to France.

DUKE OF GLOSTER.

And for the proffer of my lord your master,
I have inform'd his highness so at large,
As, liking of the lady's virtuous gifts,
Her beauty, and the value of her dower,
He doth intend she shall be England's queen.

KING HENRY [to the AMBASSADORS].

In argument and proof of which contract,
Bear her this jewel, pledge of my affection.—
And so, my lord Protector, see them guarded,
And safely brought to Dover; where, inshipt,
Commit them to the fortune of the sea.

[Exeunt KING, GLOSTER, EXETER, and
AMBASSADORS.

CARDINAL.

Stay, my lord legate: you shall first receive
The sum of money which I promised
Should be deliver'd to his holiness
For clothing me in these grave ornaments.

LEGATE.

I will attend upon your lordship's leisure.

CARDINAL [aside].

Now Winchester will not submit, I trow,
Or be inferior to the proudest peer.
Humphrey of Gloster, thou shalt well perceive
That neither in birth or for authority
The bishop will be overborne by thee:
I'll either make thee stoop and bend thy knee,
Or sack this country with a mutiny.   [Exeunt.

SCENE II.

France. Plains in Anjou.

Enter CHARLES, BURGUNDY, ALENÇON, BAS-
TARD, LA PUCELLE, and FORCES.

CHARLES.

THESE news, my lords, may cheer our droop-
ing spirits:
'Tis said the stout Parisians do revolt,
And turn again unto the warlike French.

DUKE OF ALENÇON.

Then march to Paris, royal Charles of France,
And keep not back your powers in dalliance.

JOAN LA PUCELLE.

Peace be amongst them, if they turn to us;
Else, ruin combat with their palaces!

Enter a MESSENGER.

MESSENGER.

Success unto our valiant general,
And happiness to his accomplices!

CHARLES.

What tidings send our scouts? I prithee, speak.

MESSENGER.

The English army, that divided was
Into two parties, is now conjoin'd in one,
And means to give you battle presently.

CHARLES.

Somewhat too sudden, sirs, the warning is;
But we will presently provide for them.

DUKE OF BURGUNDY.

I trust the ghost of Talbot is not there:
Now he is gone, my lord, you need not fear.

JOAN LA PUCELLE.

Of all base passions, fear is most accurst:—
Command the conquest, Charles, it shall be
thine;
Let Henry fret, and all the world repine.

CHARLES.

Then on, my lords; and France be fortunate!

[Exeunt.

SCENE III.

Before Angiers.

Alarum: excursions. Enter LA PUCELLE.

JOAN LA PUCELLE.

THE regent conquers, and the Frenchmen fly.—
Now help, ye charming spells and periapts;
And ye choice spirits that admonish me,
And give me signs of future accidents,—
You speedy helpers, that are substitutes
Under the lordly monarch of the north,
Appear, and aid me in this enterprise!   [Thunder.

Enter FIENDS.

This speedy and quick appearance argues proof
Of your accustom'd diligence to me.
Now, ye familiar spirits, that are cull'd
Out of the powerful legions under earth,
Help me this once, that France may get the field.

[They walk, and speak not.

O, hold me not with silence over-long!
Where I was wont to feed you with my blood,
I'll lop a member off, and give it you,
In earnest of a further benefit,
So you do condescend to help me now.

[They hang their heads.

No hope to have redress?—My body shall
Pay recompense, if you will grant my suit.

[They shake their heads.

Cannot my body nor blood-sacrifice
Entreat you to your wonted furtherance?
Then take my soul,—my body, soul, and all,
Before that England give the French the foil.

[They depart.

See, they forsake me! Now the time is come,
That France must vail her lofty-plumed crest,
And let her head fall into England's lap.
My ancient incantations are too weak.
And hell too strong for me to buckle with:
Now, France, thy glory droopeth to the dust.

[Exit.

Excursions. LA PUCELLE and YORK fight hand to
hand: LA PUCELLE is taken. The French fly.

DUKE OF YORK.

Damsel of France, I think I have you fast:
Unchain your spirits now with spelling charms,
And try if they can gain your liberty.—
A goodly prize, fit for the devil's grace!
See, how the ugly witch doth bend her brows,
As if, with Circe, she would change my shape!

JOAN LA PUCELLE.

Changed to a worser shape thou canst not be.

DUKE OF YORK.
O, Charles the Dauphin is a proper man;
No shape but his can please your dainty eye.
JOAN LA PUCELLE.
A plaguing mischief light on Charles and thee!
And may ye both be suddenly surprised
By bloody hands, in sleeping on your beds!
DUKE OF YORK.
Fell banning hag, enchantress, hold thy tongue!
JOAN LA PUCELLE.
I prithee, give me leave to curse awhile.
DUKE OF YORK.
Curse, miscreant, when thou comest to the
  stake.
                                        [Exeunt.
Alarum. Enter SUFFOLK, with MARGARET in his
                hand.
EARL OF SUFFOLK.
Be what thou wilt, thou art my prisoner.
                                  [Gazes on her.
O fairest beauty, do not fear nor fly!
For I will touch thee but with reverent hands,
And lay them gently on thy tender side.
I kiss these fingers for eternal peace.
                            [Kissing her hand.
Who art thou? say, that I may honour thee.
MARGARET.
Margaret my name, and daughter to a king,
The King of Naples,—whosoe'er thou art.
EARL OF SUFFOLK.
An earl I am, and Suffolk am I call'd.
Be not offended, nature's miracle,
Thou art allotted to be ta'en by me:
So doth the swan her downy cygnets save,
Keeping them prisoner underneath her wings.
Yet, if this servile usage once offend,
Go, and be free again as Suffolk's friend.
                                [She is going.
O, stay!—[aside] I have no power to let her
  pass;
My hand would free her, but my heart says
  no.
As plays the sun upon the glassy streams,
Twinkling another counterfeited beam,
So seems this gorgeous beauty to mine eyes.
Fain would I woo her, yet I dare not speak:
I'll call for pen and ink, and write my mind:—
Fie, de la Pole! disable not thyself;
Hast not a tongue? is she not here thy prisoner?
Wilt thou be daunted at a woman's sight?
Ay, beauty's princely majesty is such,
Confounds the tongue, and makes the senses
  rough.
MARGARET.
Say, Earl of Suffolk,—if thy name be so,—
What ransom must I pay before I pass?
For I perceive I am thy prisoner.
EARL OF SUFFOLK [aside].
How canst thou tell she will deny thy suit
Before thou make a trial of her love?
MARGARET.
Why speak'st thou not? what ransom must I
  pay?
EARL OF SUFFOLK [aside].
She's beautiful, and therefore to be woo'd;
She is a woman, therefore to be won.

MARGARET.
Wilt thou accept of ransom—yea or no?
EARL OF SUFFOLK [aside].
Fond man, remember that thou hast a wife;
Then how can Margaret be thy paramour?
MARGARET.
I were best to leave him, for he will not hear.
EARL OF SUFFOLK [aside].
There all is marr'd; there lies a cooling-card.
MARGARET.
He talks at random; sure, the man is mad.
EARL OF SUFFOLK [aside].
And yet a dispensation may be had.
MARGARET.
And yet I would that you would answer me.
EARL OF SUFFOLK [aside].
I'll win this Lady Margaret. For whom?
Why, for my king: tush, that's a wooden
  thing!
MARGARET.
He talks of wood: it is some carpenter.
EARL OF SUFFOLK [aside].
Yet so my fancy may be satisfied,
And peace established between these realms.
But there remains a scruple in that too;
For though her father be the King of Naples,
Duke of Anjou and Maine, yet is he poor,
And our nobility will scorn the match.
MARGARET.
Hear ye, captain,—are you not at leisure?
EARL OF SUFFOLK.
It shall be so, disdain they ne'er so much:
Henry is youthful, and will quickly yield.—
Madam, I have a secret to reveal.
MARGARET [aside].
What though I be enthrall'd? he seems a
  knight,
And will not any way dishonour me.
EARL OF SUFFOLK.
Lady, vouchsafe to listen what I say.
MARGARET [aside].
Perhaps I shall be rescued by the French;
And then I need not crave his courtesy.
EARL OF SUFFOLK.
Sweet madam, give me hearing in a cause—
MARGARET [aside].
Tush, women have been captive ere now.
EARL OF SUFFOLK.
I prithee, lady, wherefore talk you so?
MARGARET.
I cry you mercy, 'tis but *quid* for *quo*.
EARL OF SUFFOLK.
Say, gentle princess, would you not suppose
Your bondage happy, to be made a queen?
MARGARET.
To be a queen in bondage is more vile
Than is a slave in base servility;
For princes should be free.
EARL OF SUFFOLK.
                                And so shall you,
If happy England's royal king be free.
MARGARET.
Why, what concerns his freedom unto me?
EARL OF SUFFOLK.
I'll undertake to make thee Henry's queen;
To put a golden sceptre in thy hand,

26

And set a precious crown upon thy head,
If thou wilt condescend to be my—
      MARGARET.
                      What?
      EARL OF SUFFOLK.
His love.
      MARGARET.
I am unworthy to be Henry's wife.
      EARL OF SUFFOLK.
No, gentle madam; I unworthy am
To woo so fair a dame to be his wife,
And have no portion in the choice myself.
How say you, madam,—are ye so content?
      MARGARET.
An if my father please, I am content.
      EARL OF SUFFOLK.
Then call our captains and our colours forth!—
              [Troops come forward.
And, madam, at your father's castle-walls
We'll crave a parley, to confer with him.
  A parley sounded. Enter REIGNIER on the walls.
See, Reignier, see, thy daughter prisoner!
      REIGNIER.
To whom?
      EARL OF SUFFOLK.
  To me.
      REIGNIER.
          Suffolk, what remedy?
I am a soldier, and unapt to weep
Or to exclaim on fortune's fickleness.
      EARL OF SUFFOLK.
Yes, there is remedy enough, my lord:
Consent—and, for thy honour, give consent—
Thy daughter shall be wedded to my king;
Whom I with pain have woo'd and won thereto;
And this her easy-held imprisonment
Hath gain'd thy daughter princely liberty.
      REIGNIER.
Speaks Suffolk as he thinks?
      EARL OF SUFFOLK.
              Fair Margaret knows
That Suffolk doth not flatter, face, or feign.
      REIGNIER.
Upon thy princely warrant, I descend
To give thee answer of thy just demand.
      EARL OF SUFFOLK.
And here I will expect thy coming.
          [Exit REIGNIER from the walls.
  Trumpets sound.   Enter REIGNIER, below.
      REIGNIER.
Welcome, brave earl, into our territories:
Command in Anjou what your honour pleases.
      EARL OF SUFFOLK.
Thanks, Reignier, happy for so sweet a child,
Fit to be made companion with a king:
What answer makes your Grace unto my suit?
      REIGNIER.
Since thou dost deign to woo her little worth
To be the princely bride of such a lord;
Upon condition I may quietly
Enjoy mine own, the counties Maine and An-
  jou,
Free from oppression or the stroke of war,
My daughter shall be Henry's, if he please.
      EARL OF SUFFOLK.
That is her ransom,—I deliver her;

And those two counties I will undertake
Your Grace shall well and quietly enjoy.
      REIGNIER.
And I again, in Henry's royal name,
As deputy unto that gracious king,
Give thee her hand, for sign of plighted faith.
      EARL OF SUFFOLK.
Reignier of France, I give thee kingly thanks,
Because this is in traffic of a king:—
[aside] And yet, methinks, I could be well content
To be mine own attorney in this case.—
I'll over, then, to England with this news,
And make this marriage to be solemnized.
So, farewell, Reignier: set this diamond safe
In golden palaces, as it becomes.
      REIGNIER.
I do embrace thee, as I would embrace
The Christian prince King Henry, were he here.
      MARGARET.
Farewell, my lord: good wishes, praise, and
  prayers
Shall Suffolk ever have of Margaret.   [Going.

      EARL OF SUFFOLK.
Farewell, sweet madam: but, hark you, Marga-
  ret,—
No princely commendations to my king?
      MARGARET.
Such commendations as becomes a maid,
A virgin, and his servant, say to him.
      EARL OF SUFFOLK.
Words sweetly placed and modestly directed.
But, madam, I must trouble you again,—
No loving token to his majesty?
      MARGARET.
Yes, my good lord,—a pure unspotted heart,
Never yet taint with love, I send the king.
      EARL OF SUFFOLK.
And this withal.   [Kisses her.
      MARGARET.
That for thyself:—I will not so presume
To send such peevish tokens to a king.
         [Exeunt REIGNIER and MARGARET.
      EARL OF SUFFOLK.
O, wert thou for myself!—But, Suffolk, stay;
Thou mayst not wander in that labyrinth;
There Minotaurs and ugly treasons lurk.
Solicit Henry with her wondrous praise:
Bethink thee on her virtues that surmount,
And natural graces that extinguish art;
Repeat their semblance often on the seas,
That, when thou comest to kneel at Henry's feet,
Thou mayst bereave him of his wits with wonder.
                [Exit.

      SCENE IV.
  Camp of the DUKE OF YORK in Anjou.

  Enter YORK, WARWICK, and others.

      DUKE OF YORK.
BRING forth that sorceress condemn'd to burn.
    Enter LA PUCELLE, guarded,
      and a SHEPHERD.
      SHEPHERD.
Ah, Joan, this kills thy father's heart outright!
Have I sought every country far and near,
And, now it is my chance to find thee out,

Must I behold thy timeless-cruel death?
Ah, Joan, sweet daughter Joan, I'll die with thee!
JOAN LA PUCELLE.
Decrepit miser! base ignoble wretch!
I am descended of a gentler blood:
Thou art no father nor no friend of mine.
SHEPHERD.
Out, out!—My lords, an please you, 'tis not so;
I did beget her, all the parish knows:
Her mother liveth yet, can testify
She was the first fruit of my bachelorship.
EARL OF WARWICK.
Graceless! wilt thou deny thy parentage?
DUKE OF YORK.
This argues what her kind of life hath been,—
Wicked and vile; and so her death concludes.
SHEPHERD.
Fie, Joan, that thou wilt be so obstacle!
God knows thou art a collop of my flesh;
And for thy sake have I shed many a tear:
Deny me not, I prithee, gentle Joan.
JOAN LA PUCELLE.
Peasant, avaunt!—You have suborn'd this man,
Of purpose to obscure my noble birth.
SHEPHERD.
'Tis true, I gave a noble to the priest
The morn that I was wedded to her mother.—
Kneel down and take my blessing, good my girl.
Wilt thou not stoop? Now cursed be the time
Of thy nativity! I would the milk
Thy mother gave thee when thou suck'dst her
    breast,
Had been a little ratsbane for thy sake!
Or else, when thou didst keep my lambs a-field,
I wish some ravenous wolf had eaten thee!
Dost thou deny thy father, cursed drab?
O, burn her, burn her! hanging is too good. [Exit.
DUKE OF YORK.
Take her away; for she hath lived too long,
To fill the world with vicious qualities.
JOAN LA PUCELLE.
First, let me tell you whom you have condemn'd:
Not one begotten of a shepherd swain,
But issued from the progeny of kings;
Virtuous and holy; chosen from above,
By inspiration of celestial grace,
To work exceeding miracles on earth.
I never had to do with wicked spirits:
But you,—that are polluted with your lusts,
Stain'd with the guiltless blood of innocents,
Corrupt and tainted with a thousand vices,—
Because you want the grace that others have,
You judge it straight a thing impossible
To compass wonders but by help of devils.
No, misconceived! Joan of Arc hath been
A virgin from her tender infancy,
Chaste and immaculate in very thought;
Whose maiden blood, thus rigorously effused,
Will cry for vengeance at the gates of heaven.
DUKE OF YORK.
Ay, ay:—away with her to execution!
EARL OF WARWICK.
And hark ye, sirs; because she is a maid,
Spare for no fagots, let there be enow:
Place barrels of pitch upon the fatal stake,
That so her torture may be shortened.

JOAN LA PUCELLE.
Will nothing turn your unrelenting hearts?—
Then, Joan, discover thine infirmity,
That warranteth by law to be thy privilege.—
I am with child, ye bloody homicides:
Murder not, then, the fruit within my womb,
Although ye hale me to a violent death.
DUKE OF YORK.
Now heaven forfend! the holy maid with child!
EARL OF WARWICK.
The greatest miracle that e'er ye wrought:
Is all your strict preciseness come to this?
DUKE OF YORK.
She and the Dauphin have been juggling:
I did imagine what would be her refuge.
EARL OF WARWICK.
Well, go to; we'll have no bastards live;
Especially since Charles must father it.
JOAN LA PUCELLE.
You are deceived; my child is none of his;
It was Alençon that enjoy'd my love.
DUKE OF YORK.
Alençon! that notorious Machiavel!
It dies, an if it had a thousand lives.
JOAN LA PUCELLE.
O, give me leave, I have deluded you:
'Twas neither Charles, nor yet the duke I named,
But Reignier, king of Naples, that prevail'd.
EARL OF WARWICK.
A married man! that's most intolerable.
DUKE OF YORK.
Why, here's a girl! I think she knows not well,
There were so many, whom she may accuse.
EARL OF WARWICK.
It's sign she hath been liberal and free.
DUKE OF YORK.
And yet, forsooth, she is a virgin pure.—
Strumpet, thy words condemn thy brat and thee:
Use no entreaty, for it is in vain.
JOAN LA PUCELLE.
Then lead me hence—with whom I leave my
    curse;
May never glorious sun reflex his beams
Upon the country where you make abode;
But darkness and the gloomy shade of death
Environ you, till mischief and despair
Drive you to break your necks or hang yourselves
                     [Exit, guarded
DUKE OF YORK.
Break thou in pieces, and consume to ashes,
Thou foul accursed minister of hell!
    Enter CARDINAL BEAUFORT, attended.
CARDINAL BEAUFORT.
Lord regent, I do greet your excellence
With letters of commission from the king.
For know, my lords, the states of Christendom,
Moved with remorse of these outrageous broils,
Have earnestly implored a general peace
Betwixt our nation and the aspiring French;
And here at hand the Dauphin and his train
Approacheth, to confer about some matter.
DUKE OF YORK.
Is all our travail turn'd to this effect?
After the slaughter of so many peers,
So many captains, gentlemen, and soldiers,
That in this quarrel have been overthrown,

And sold their bodies for their country's benefit,
Shall we at last conclude effeminate peace?
Have we not lost most part of all the towns,
By treason, falsehood, and by treachery,
Our great progenitors had conquered?—
O, Warwick, Warwick! I foresee with grief
The utter loss of all the realm of France.
                EARL OF WARWICK.
Be patient, York: if we conclude a peace,
It shall be with such strict and severe covenants
As little shall the Frenchmen gain thereby.
        Enter CHARLES, ALENÇON, BASTARD, REI-
            GNIER, *and others.*
                    CHARLES.
Since, lords of England, it is thus agreed
That peaceful truce shall be proclaim'd in
    France,
We come to be informed by yourselves
What the conditions of that league must be.
                DUKE OF YORK.
Speak, Winchester; for boiling choler chokes
The hollow passage of my prison'd voice,
By sight of these our baleful enemies.
            CARDINAL BEAUFORT.
Charles, and the rest, it is enacted thus:
That, in regard King Henry gives consent,
Of mere compassion and of lenity,
To ease your country of distressful war,
And suffer you to breathe in fruitful peace,—
You shall become true liegemen to his crown:
And, Charles, upon condition thou wilt swear
To pay him tribute, and submit thyself,
Thou shalt be placed as viceroy under him,
And still enjoy thy regal dignity.
            DUKE OF ALENÇON.
Must he be, then, a shadow of himself?
Adorn his temples with a coronet,
And yet, in substance and authority,
Retain but privilege of a private man?
This proffer is absurd and reasonless.
                    CHARLES.
'Tis known already that I am possest
With more than half the Gallian territories,
And therein reverenced for their lawful king:
Shall I, for lucre of the rest unvanquisht,
Detract so much from that prerogative,
As to be call'd but viceroy of the whole?
No, lord ambassador; I'll rather keep
That which I have than, coveting for more,
Be cast from possibility of all.
                DUKE OF YORK.
Insulting Charles! hast thou by secret means
Used intercession to obtain a league,
And, now the matter grows to compromise,
Stand'st thou aloof upon comparison?
Either accept the title thou usurp'st,
Of benefit proceeding from our king,
And not of any challenge of desert,
Or we will plague thee with incessant wars.
        REIGNIER [*aside to* CHARLES].
My lord, you do not well in obstinacy
To cavil in the course of this contract:
If once it be neglected, ten to one
We shall not find like opportunity.
        DUKE OF ALENÇON [*aside to* CHARLES].
To say the truth, it is your policy

To save your subjects from such massacre
And ruthless slaughters as are daily seen
By our proceeding in hostility;
And therefore take this compact of a truce,
Although you break it when your pleasure serves.
            EARL OF WARWICK.
How say'st thou, Charles? shall our condition
    stand?
                    CHARLES.
It shall;
Only reserved, you claim no interest
In any of our towns of garrison.
                DUKE OF YORK.
Then swear allegiance to his majesty;
As thou art knight, never to disobey
Nor be rebellious to the crown of England,—
Thou, nor thy nobles, to the crown of England.
So, now dismiss your army when ye please;
Hang up your ensigns, let your drums be still,
For here we entertain a solemn peace.   [*Exeunt.*

SCENE V.

London.   The royal palace.

Enter SUFFOLK *in conference with the* KING;
    GLOSTER *and* EXETER.

                KING HENRY.

YOUR wondrous rare description, noble earl,
    Of beauteous Margaret hath astonisht me:
Her virtues, graced with external gifts,
Do breed love's settled passions in my heart:
And like as rigour of tempestuous gusts
Provokes the mightiest hulk against the tide,
So am I driven, by breath of her renown,
Either to suffer shipwrack, or arrive
Where I may have fruition of her love.
            EARL OF SUFFOLK.
Tush, my good lord,—this superficial tale
Is but a preface of her worthy praise;
The chief perfections of that lovely dame—
Had I sufficient skill to utter them—
Would make a volume of enticing lines,
Able to ravish any dull conceit:
And, which is more, she is not so divine,
So full-replete with choice of all delights,
But, with as humble lowliness of mind,
She is content to be at your command;
Command, I mean, of virtuous chaste intents,
To love and honour Henry as her lord.
                KING HENRY.
And otherwise will Henry ne'er presume.
Therefore, my lord Protector, give consent
That Margaret may be England's royal queen.
                DUKE OF GLOSTER.
So should I give consent to flatter sin.
You know, my lord, your highness is betroth'd
Unto another lady of esteem:
How shall we, then, dispense with that contract,
And not deface your honour with reproach?
            EARL OF SUFFOLK.
As doth a ruler with unlawful oaths;
Or one that, at a triumph having vow'd
To try his strength, forsaketh yet the lists
By reason of his adversary's odds:
A poor earl's daughter is unequal odds,
And therefore may be broke without offence.

DUKE OF GLOSTER.
Why, what, I pray, is Margaret more than that?
Her father is no better than an earl,
Although in glorious titles he excel.
EARL OF SUFFOLK.
Yes, my lord, her father is a king,
The King of Naples and Jerusalem;
And of such great authority in France,
As his alliance will confirm our peace,
And keep the Frenchmen in allegiance.
DUKE OF GLOSTER.
And so the Earl of Armagnac may do,
Because he is near kinsman unto Charles.
DUKE OF EXETER.
Beside, his wealth doth warrant a liberal dower,
Where Reignier sooner will receive than give.
EARL OF SUFFOLK.
A dower, my lords! disgrace not so your king,
That he should be so abject, base, and poor,
To choose for wealth and not for perfect love.
Henry is able to enrich his queen,
And not to seek a queen to make him rich:
So worthless peasants bargain for their wives,
As market-men for oxen, sheep, or horse.
Marriage is a matter of more worth
Than to be dealt in by attorneyship;
Not whom we will, but whom his Grace affects,
Must be companion of his nuptial bed:
And therefore, lords, since he affects her most,
It most of all these reasons bindeth us,
In our opinions she should be preferr'd.
For what is wedlock forced but a hell,
An age of discord and continual strife?
Whereas the contrary bringeth bliss,
And is a pattern of celestial peace.
Whom should we match with Henry, being a king,
But Margaret, that is daughter of a king?
Her peerless feature, joined with her birth,
Approves her fit for none but for a king:
Her valiant courage and undaunted spirit—
More than in women commonly is seen—
The answer our hope in issue of a king;

For Henry, son unto a conqueror,
Is likely to beget more conquerors,
If with a lady of so high resolve
As is fair Margaret he be linkt in love.
Then yield, my lords; and here conclude with me
That Margaret shall be queen, and none but she.
KING HENRY.
Whether it be through force of your report,
My noble Lord of Suffolk, or for that
My tender youth was never yet attaint
With any passion of inflaming love,
I cannot tell; but this I am assured,
I feel such sharp dissension in my breast,
Such fierce alarums both of hope and fear,
As I am sick with working of my thoughts.
Take, therefore, shipping; post, my lord, to
    France;
Agree to any covenants; and procure
That Lady Margaret do vouchsafe to come
To cross the seas to England, and be crown'd
King Henry's faithful and anointed queen:
For your expenses and sufficient charge,
Among the people gather up a tenth.
Be gone, I say; for, till you do return,
I rest perplexed with a thousand cares.—
And you, good uncle, banish all offence:
If you do censure me by what you were,
Not what you are, I know it will excuse
This sudden execution of my will.
And so, conduct me where, from company,
I may revolve and ruminate my grief.   [Exit.
DUKE OF GLOSTER.
Ay, grief, I fear me, both at first and last.
    [Exeunt GLOSTER and EXETER.
EARL OF SUFFOLK.
Thus Suffolk hath prevail'd; and thus he goes,
As did the youthful Paris once to Greece,
With hope to find the like event in love,
But prosper better than the Trojan did.
Margaret shall now be queen, and rule the king;
But I will rule both her, the king, and realm.
    [Exit.

THE SECOND PART OF
KING HENRY THE SIXTH

DRAMATIS PERSONAE

KING HENRY THE SIXTH.
HUMPHREY, *Duke of Gloster, his uncle.*
CARDINAL BEAUFORT, *Bishop of Winch ster,
  great-uncle to the King.*
RICHARD PLANTAGENET, *Duke of York.*
EDWARD *and* RICHARD, *his sons.*
DUKE OF SOMERSET.
DUKE OF SUFFOLK.
DUKE OF BUCKINGHAM.
LORD CLIFFORD.
YOUNG CLIFFORD, *his son.*
EARL OF SALISBURY.
EARL OF WARWICK.
LORD SCALES.
LORD SAY.
SIR HUMPHREY STAFFORD, *and* WILLIAM
  STAFFORD, *his brother.*
SIR JOHN STANLEY.
VAUX.
MATTHEW GOUGH.
A SEA-CAPTAIN, MASTER, *and* MASTER'S-
  MATE, *and* WALTER WHITMORE.
TWO GENTLEMEN, *prisoners with Suffolk.*
ALEXANDER IDEN, *a Kentish gentleman.*

JOHN HUME *and* JOHN SOUTHWELL, *two
  priests.*
ROGER BOLINGBROKE, *a conjurer.*
THOMAS HORNER, *an armorer.* PETER, *his man.*
CLERK OF CHATHAM.
MAYOR OF SAINT ALBAN'S.
SAUNDER SIMPCOX, *an impostor.*
JACK CADE, *a rebel.*
GEORGE BEVIS, JOHN HOLLAND, DICK *the
  butcher,* SMITH *the weaver,* MICHAEL, *&c.,
  his followers.*
TWO MURDERERS.

MARGARET, *Queen to King Henry.*
ELEANOR, *Duchess of Gloster.*
MARGERY JOURDAIN, *a witch.*
WIFE *to Simpcox.*

LORDS, LADIES, *and* ATTENDANTS, PETI-
  TIONERS, ALDERMEN, *a* HERALD, *a* BEADLE,
  SHERIFF, *and* OFFICERS, CITIZENS, PRENTI-
  CES, FALCONERS, GUARDS, SOLDIERS, MES-
  SENGERS, *&c.*
A SPIRIT.

SCENE—*In various parts of England.*

ACT I. SCENE I.

London. A room of state in the palace.

Flourish of trumpets: then hautboys. Enter the
KING, DUKE OF GLOSTER, SALISBURY,
WARWICK, *and* CARDINAL BEAUFORT, *on
the one side; the* QUEEN, SUFFOLK, YORK,
SOMERSET, *and* BUCKINGHAM, *on the other.*

DUKE OF SUFFOLK.

AS by your high imperial majesty
    I had in charge at my depart for France,
As procurator to your excellence,
To marry Princess Margaret for your Grace;
So, in the famous ancient city Tours,
In presence of the Kings of France and Sicil,
The Dukes of Orleans, Calaber, Bretagne, and
  Alençon,
Seven earls, twelve barons, and twenty reverend
  bishops,
I have perform'd my task, and was espoused:
And humbly now, upon my bended knee,
In sight of England and her lordly peers,
Deliver up my title in the queen
To your most gracious hands, that are the sub-
  stance
Of that great shadow I did represent;
The happiest gift that ever marquess gave,
The fairest queen that ever king received.

KING HENRY.

Suffolk, arise.—Welcome, Queen Margaret:
I can express no kinder sign of love
Than this kind kiss.—O Lord, that lends me life,
Lend me a heart replete with thankfulness!

For Thou hast given me, in this beauteous face,
A world of earthly blessings to my soul,
If sympathy of love unite our thoughts.

QUEEN MARGARET.

Great King of England, and my gracious lord,—
The mutual conference that my mind hath had,
By day, by night, waking and in my dreams,
In courtly company or at my beads,
With you, mine alder-liefest sovereign,
Makes me the bolder to salute my king
With ruder terms, such as my wit affords
And over-joy of heart doth minister.

KING HENRY.

Her sight did ravish; but her grace in speech,
Her words yclad with wisdom's majesty,
Make me from wondering fall to weeping joys;
Such is the fulness of my heart's content.—
Lords, with one cheerful voice welcome my love.

ALL [*kneeling*].
Long live Queen Margaret, England's happiness!
                                          [*Flourish.*

QUEEN MARGARET.

We thank you all.

DUKE OF SUFFOLK.

My lord Protector, so it please your Grace,
Here are the articles of contracted peace
Between our sovereign and the French king
  Charles.
For eighteen months concluded by consent.

DUKE OF GLOSTER [*reads*].

Imprimis, It is agreed between the French king
Charles, and William de la Pole, marquess of
Suffolk, ambassador for Henry King of England,

31

—that the said Henry shall espouse the Lady Margaret, daughter unto Reignier King of Naples, Sicilia, and Jerusalem; and crown her Queen of England ere the thirtieth of May next ensuing. *Item*, that the duchy of Anjou and the county of Maine shall be released and deliver'd to the king her father—   [*Lets the paper fall.*
KING HENRY.
Uncle, how now!
        DUKE OF GLOSTER.
                        Pardon me, gracious lord;
Some sudden qualm hath struck me at the heart,
And dimm'd mine eyes, that I can read no further.
        KING HENRY.
Uncle of Winchester, I pray, read on.
        CARDINAL BEAUFORT [*reads*].
Item, It is further agreed between them, that the duchies of Anjou and Maine shall be released and deliver'd over to the king her father; and she sent over of the King of England's own proper cost and charges, without having any dowry.
        KING HENRY.
They please us well.—Lord marquess, kneel down:
We here create thee the first Duke of Suffolk,
And girt thee with the sword.—Cousin of York,
We here discharge your Grace from being regent
I' th' parts of France, till term of eighteen months
Be full expired.—Thanks, uncle Winchester,
Gloster, York, Buckingham, Somerset,
Salisbury, and Warwick;
We thank you all for this great favour done,
In entertainment to my princely queen.
Come, let us in; and with all speed provide
To see her coronation be perform'd.
        [*Exeunt* KING, QUEEN, *and* SUFFOLK.
        DUKE OF GLOSTER.
Brave peers of England, pillars of the state,
To you Duke Humphrey must unload his grief,—
Your grief, the common grief of all the land.
What! did my brother Henry spend his youth,
His valour, coin, and people in the wars?
Did he so often lodge in open field
In winter's cold and summer's parching heat,
To conquer France, his true inheritance?
And did my brother Bedford toil his wits,
To keep by policy what Henry got?
Have you yourselves, Somerset, Buckingham,
Brave York, Salisbury, and victorious Warwick,
Received deep scars in France and Normandy?
Or hath mine uncle Beaufort and myself,
With all the learned council of the realm,
Studied so long, sat in the council-house
Early and late, debating to and fro
How France and Frenchmen might be kept in awe?
And was his highness in his infancy
Crowned in Paris in despite of foes?
And shall these labours and these honours die?
Shall Henry's conquest, Bedford's vigilance,
Your deeds of war, and all our counsel die?
O peers of England, shameful is this league!
Fatal this marriage! cancelling your fame,
Blotting your name from books of memory,
Razing the characters of your renown.

Defacing monuments of conquer'd France,
Undoing all, as all had never been!
        CARDINAL BEAUFORT.
Nephew, what means this passionate discourse,
This peroration with such circumstance?
For France, 'tis ours; and we will keep it still.
        DUKE OF GLOSTER.
Ay, uncle, we will keep it, if we can;
But now it is impossible we should:
Suffolk, the new-made duke that rules the roast,
Hath given the duchies of Anjou and Maine
Unto the poor King Reignier, whose large style
Agrees not with the leanness of his purse.
        EARL OF SALISBURY.
Now, by the death of Him that died for all,
These counties were the keys of Normandy:—
But wherefore weeps Warwick, my valiant son?
        EARL OF WARWICK.
For grief that they are past recovery:
For, were there hope to conquer them again,
My sword should shed hot blood, mine eyes no tears.
Anjou and Maine! myself did win them both;
Those provinces these arms of mine did conquer:
And are the cities, that I got with wounds,
Deliver'd up again with peaceful words?
Mort Dieu!
        DUKE OF YORK.
For Suffolk's duke, may he be suffocate,
That dims the honour of this warlike isle!
France should have torn and rent my very heart,
Before I would have yielded to this league.
I never read but England's kings have had
Large sums of gold and dowries with their wives;
And our King Henry gives away his own,
To match with her that brings no vantages.
        DUKE OF GLOSTER.
A proper jest, and never heard before,
That Suffolk should demand a whole fifteenth
For costs and charges in transporting her!
She should have stay'd in France, and starved in France,
Before—
        CARDINAL BEAUFORT.
My Lord of Gloster, now ye grow too hot:
It was the pleasure of my lord the king.
        DUKE OF GLOSTER.
My Lord of Winchester, I know your mind;
'Tis not my speeches that you do mislike,
But 'tis my presence that doth trouble ye.
Rancour will out: proud prelate, in thy face
I see thy fury: if I longer stay,
We shall begin our ancient bickerings.—
Lordings, farewell; and say, when I am gone,
I prophesied—France will be lost ere long. [*Exit.*
        CARDINAL BEAUFORT.
So, there goes our Protector in a rage.
'Tis known to you he is mine enemy;
Nay, more, an enemy unto you all;
And no great friend, I fear me, to the king.
Consider, lords, he is the next of blood,
And heir-apparent to the English crown:
Had Henry got an empire by his marriage,
And all the wealthy kingdoms of the west,
There's reason he should be displeased at it.
Look to it, lords; let not his smoothing words

Bewitch your hearts; be wise and circumspect.
What though the common people favour him,
Calling him 'Humphrey, the good Duke of
  Gloster;'
Clapping their hands, and crying with loud
  voice,
'Jesu maintain your royal excellence!'
With 'God preserve the good Duke Humphrey!'
I fear me, lords, for all this flattering gloss,
He will be found a dangerous Protector.

DUKE OF BUCKINGHAM.
Why should he, then, protect our sovereign,
He being of age to govern of himself?—
Cousin of Somerset, join you with me,
And all together, with the Duke of Suffolk,
We'll quickly hoise Duke Humphrey from his
  seat.

CARDINAL BEAUFORT.
This weighty business will not brook delay;
I'll to the Duke of Suffolk presently. [Exit.

DUKE OF SOMERSET.
Cousin of Buckingham, though Humphrey's
  pride
And greatness of his place be grief to us,
Yet let us watch the haughty cardinal:
His insolence is more intolerable
Than all the princes in the land beside:
If Gloster be displaced, he'll be Protector.

DUKE OF BUCKINGHAM.
Or thou or I, Somerset, will be Protector,
Despite Duke Humphrey or the cardinal.
  [Exeunt BUCKINGHAM and SOMERSET.

EARL OF SALISBURY.
Pride went before, ambition follows him.
While these do labour for their own preferment,
Behoves it us to labour for the realm.
I never saw but Humphrey duke of Gloster
Did bear him like a noble gentleman.
Oft have I seen the haughty cardinal—
More like a soldier than a man o' th' church,
As stout and proud as he were lord of all—
Swear like a ruffian, and demean himself
Unlike the ruler of a commonweal.—
Warwick, my son, the comfort of my age,
Thy deeds, thy plainness, and thy housekeep-
  ing,
Have won the greatest favour of the commons,
Excepting none but good Duke Humphrey:—
And, brother York, thy acts in Ireland,
In bringing them to civil discipline;
Thy late exploits done in the heart of France,
When thou wert regent for our sovereign,
Have made thee fear'd and honour'd of the
  people:—
Join we together, for the public good,
In what we can, to bridle and suppress
The pride of Suffolk and the cardinal,
With Somerset's and Buckingham's ambition;
And, as we may, cherish Duke Humphrey's
  deeds,
While they do tend the profit of the land.

EARL OF WARWICK.
So God help Warwick, as he loves the land,
And common profit of his country!

DUKE OF YORK [aside].
And so says York, for he hath greatest cause.

EARL OF SALISBURY.
Then let's make haste away, and look unto the
  main.

EARL OF WARWICK.
Unto the main! O father, Maine is lost,—
That Maine which by main force Warwick did
  win,
And would have kept so long as breath did last!
Main chance, father, you meant; but I meant
  Maine,—
Which I will win from France, or else be slain.
  [Exeunt WARWICK and SALISBURY.

DUKE OF YORK.
Anjou and Maine are given to the French;
Paris is lost; the state of Normandy
Stands on a tickle point, now they are gone:
Suffolk concluded on the articles;
The peers agreed; and Henry was well pleased
To change two dukedoms for a duke's fair
  daughter.
I cannot blame them all: what is't to them?
'Tis thine they give away, and not their own.
Pirates may make cheap pennyworths of their
  pillage,
And purchase friends, and give to courtezans,
Still revelling, like lords, till all be gone;
While as the silly owner of the goods
Weeps over them, and wrings his hapless hands,
And shakes his head, and trembling stands aloof,
While all is shared, and all is borne away,
Ready to starve, and dare not touch his own:
So York must sit, and fret, and bite his tongue,
While his own lands are bargain'd for and sold
Methinks the realms of England, France, and
  Ireland
Bear that proportion to my flesh and blood
As did the fatal brand Althæa burn'd
Unto the prince's heart of Calydon.
Anjou and Maine, both given unto the French!
Cold news for me; for I had hope of France,
Even as I have of fertile England's soil.
A day will come when York shall claim his own;
And therefore I will take the Nevils' parts,
And make a show of love to proud Duke Hum-
  phrey,
And, when I spy advantage, claim the crown,
For that's the golden mark I seek to hit:
Nor shall proud Lancaster usurp my right,
Nor hold the sceptre in his childish fist,
Nor wear the diadem upon his head,
Whose church-like humours fits not for a crown.
Then, York, be still awhile, till time do serve:
Watch thou and wake, when others be asleep,
To pry into the secrets of the state;
Till Henry, surfeiting in joys of love,
With his new bride and England's dear-bought
  queen,
And Humphrey with the peers be faln at jars:
Then will I raise aloft the milk-white rose,
With whose sweet smell the air shall be perfumed;
And in my standard bear the arms of York,
To grapple with the house of Lancaster;
And, force perforce, I'll make him yield the
  crown,
Whose bookish rule hath pull'd fair England
  down. [Exit.

SCENE II.

The same.   *The* DUKE OF GLOSTER'S *house.*

Enter DUKE HUMPHREY *and his Wife* ELEANOR.

DUCHESS OF GLOSTER.

WHY droops my lord, like over-ripen'd corn
    Hanging the head at Ceres' plenteous load?
Why doth the great Duke Humphrey knit his
    brows,
As frowning at the favours of the world?
Why are thine eyes fixt to the sullen earth,
Gazing on that which seems to dim thy sight?
What seest thou there? King Henry's diadem,
Enchased with all the honours of the world?
If so, gaze on, and grovel on thy face,
Until thy head be circled with the same.
Put forth thy hand, reach at the glorious gold:—
What, is't too short? I'll lengthen it with mine;
And, having both together heaved it up,
We'll both together lift our heads to heaven,
And never more abase our sight so low
As to vouchsafe one glance unto the ground.

DUKE OF GLOSTER.

O Nell, sweet Nell, if thou dost love thy lord,
Banish the canker of ambitious thoughts!
And may that thought, when I imagine ill
Against my king and nephew, virtuous Henry,
Be my last breathing in this mortal world!
My troublous dream this night doth make me sad.

DUCHESS OF GLOSTER.

What dream'd my lord? tell me, and I'll requite
    it
With sweet rehearsal of my morning's dream.

DUKE OF GLOSTER.

Methought this staff, mine office-badge in court,
Was broke in twain; by whom I have forgot,
But, as I think, 'twas by the cardinal;
And on the pieces of the broken wand
Were placed the heads of Edmund duke of
    Somerset,
And William de la Pole, first duke of Suffolk.
This was my dream: what it doth bode, God
    knows.

DUCHESS OF GLOSTER.

Tut, this was nothing but an argument
That he that breaks a stick of Gloster's grove
Shall lose his head for his presumption.
But list to me, my Humphrey, my sweet duke:
Methought I sat in seat of majesty
In the cathedral church of Westminster,
And in that chair where kings and queens are
    crown'd;
Where Henry and Dame Margaret kneel'd to
    me,
And on my head did set the diadem.

DUKE OF GLOSTER.

Nay, Eleanor, then must I chide outright:
Presumptuous dame, ill-nurtured Eleanor!
Art thou not second woman in the realm,
And the Protector's wife, beloved of him?
Hast thou not worldly pleasure at command,
Above the reach or compass of thy thought?
And wilt thou still be hammering treachery,
To tumble down thy husband and thyself
From top of honour to disgrace's feet?
Away from me, and let me hear no more!

DUCHESS OF GLOSTER.

What, what, my lord! are you so choleric
With Eleanor, for telling but her dream?
Next time I'll keep my dreams unto myself,
And not be checkt.

DUKE OF GLOSTER.

Nay, be not angry, I am pleased again.

Enter a MESSENGER.

MESSENGER.

My lord Protector, 'tis his highness' pleasure
You do prepare to ride unto Saint Alban's,
Whereas the king and queen do mean to hawk.

DUKE OF GLOSTER.

I go.—Come, Nell,—thou wilt ride with us, I'm
    sure.

DUCHESS OF GLOSTER.

Yes, my good lord, I'll follow presently.

    [*Exeunt* GLOSTER *and* MESSENGER.

Follow I must; I cannot go before,
While Gloster bears this base and humble mind.
Were I a man, a duke, and next of blood,
I would remove these tedious stumbling-blocks,
And smooth my way upon their headless necks;
And, being a woman, I will not be slack
To play my part in Fortune's pageant.—
Where are you there, Sir John? nay, fear not, man,
We are alone; here's none but thee and I.

Enter HUME.

JOHN HUME.

Jesus preserve your royal majesty!

DUCHESS OF GLOSTER.

What say'st thou? majesty! I am but grace.

JOHN HUME.

But, by the grace of God, and Hume's advice,
Your Grace's title shall be multiplied.

DUCHESS OF GLOSTER.

What say'st thou, man? hast thou as yet con-
    ferr'd
With Margery Jourdain, the cunning witch,
With Roger Bolingbroke, the conjurer?
And will they undertake to do me good?

JOHN HUME.

This they have promised,—to show your high-
    ness
A spirit raised from depth of under-ground,
That shall make answer to such questions
As by your Grace shall be propounded him.

DUCHESS OF GLOSTER.

It is enough; I'll think upon the questions:
When from Saint Alban's we do make return,
We'll see these things effected to the full.
Here, Hume, take this reward; make merry, man,
With thy confederates in this weighty cause.

    [*Exit.*

JOHN HUME.

Hume must make merry with the duchess' gold;
Marry, and shall. But, how now, Sir John Hume!
Seal up your lips, and give no words but mum:
The business asketh silent secrecy.
Dame Eleanor gives gold to bring the witch:
Gold cannot come amiss, were she a devil.
Yet have I gold flies from another coast:—
I dare not say, from the rich cardinal,
And from the great and new-made Duke of
    Suffolk;
Yet I do find it so: for, to be plain,

They, knowing Dame Eleanor's aspiring humour,
Have hired me to undermine the duchess,
And buzz these conjurations in her brain.
They say,—A crafty knave does need no broker;
Yet am I Suffolk and the cardinal's broker.
Hume, if you take not heed, you shall go near
To call them both a pair of crafty knaves.
Well, so it stands; and thus, I fear, at last
Hume's knavery will be the duchess' wrack,
And her attainture will be Humphrey's fall:
Sort how it will, I shall have gold for all.   [*Exit.*

SCENE III.

The same.   The palace.

Enter PETER, *and other* PETITIONERS.

FIRST PETITIONER.

MY masters, let's stand close: my lord Protector will come this way by and by, and
then we may deliver our supplications in the quill.

SECOND PETITIONER.
Marry, the Lord protect him, for he's a good
man! Jesu bless him!

PETER.
Here 'a comes, methinks, and the queen with him.
I'll be the first, sure.

Enter SUFFOLK *and* QUEEN.

SECOND PETITIONER.
Come back, fool; this is the Duke of Suffolk, and
not my lord Protector.

DUKE OF SUFFOLK.
How now, fellow! wouldst any thing with me?

FIRST PETITIONER.
I pray, my lord, pardon me; I took ye for my lord
Protector.

QUEEN MARGARET.
For my lord Protector! Are your supplications to
his lordship? Let me see them:—what is thine?

FIRST PETITIONER.
Mine is, an't please your Grace, against John
Goodman, my lord cardinal's man, for keeping
my house, and lands, and wife and all, from me.

DUKE OF SUFFOLK.
Thy wife too! that's some wrong, indeed.—
What's yours?—What's here! [*reads*] 'Against
the Duke of Suffolk, for enclosing the commons
of Melford.'—How now, sir knave!

SECOND PETITIONER.
Alas, sir, I am but a poor petitioner of our whole
township.

PETER [*presenting his petition*].
Against my master, Thomas Horner, for saying
that the Duke of York was rightful heir to the
crown.

QUEEN MARGARET.
What say'st thou? did the Duke of York say he
was rightful heir to the crown?

PETER.
That my master was? no, forsooth: my master
said that he was; and that the king was an usurper.

DUKE OF SUFFOLK.
Who is there? [*Enter* SERVANT.]—Take this
fellow in, and send for his master with a pursuivant presently.—We'll hear more of your
matter before the king.

[*Exit* SERVANT *with* PETER.

QUEEN MARGARET.
And as for you, that love to be protected
Under the wings of our Protector's Grace,
Begin your suits anew, and sue to him.

[*Tears the supplications.*

Away, base cullions!—Suffolk, let them go.

ALL.
Come, let's be gone.   [*Exeunt* PETITIONERS.

QUEEN MARGARET.
My Lord of Suffolk, say, is this the guise,
Is this the fashion in the court of England?
Is this the government of Britain's isle,
And this the royalty of Albion's king?
What, shall King Henry be a pupil still,
Under the surly Gloster's governance?
Am I a queen in title and in style,
And must be made a subject to a duke?
I tell thee, Pole, when in the city Tours
Thou rann'st a tilt in honour of my love,
And stolest away the ladies' hearts of France,
I thought King Henry had resembled thee
In courage, courtship, and proportion:
But all his mind is bent to holiness,
To number *Ave-Maries* on his beads:
His champions are the prophets and apostles;
His weapons, holy saws of sacred writ;
His study is his tilt-yard, and his loves
Are brazen images of canonized saints.
I would the college of the cardinals
Would choose him Pope, and carry him to Rome,
And set the triple crown upon his head:—
That were a state fit for his holiness.

DUKE OF SUFFOLK.
Madam, be patient: as I was cause
Your highness came to England, so will I
In England work your Grace's full content.

QUEEN MARGARET.
Beside the haught Protector, have we Beaufort
The imperious churchman, Somerset, Buckingham,
And grumbling York; and not the least of these
But can do more in England than the king.

DUKE OF SUFFOLK.
And he of these that can do most of all
Cannot do more in England than the Nevils:
Salisbury and Warwick are no simple peers.

QUEEN MARGARET.
Not all these lords do vex me half so much
As that proud dame, the lord Protector's wife.
She sweeps it through the court with troops of
ladies,
More like an empress than Duke Humphrey's
wife:
Strangers in court do take her for the queen:
She bears a duke's revenues on her back,
And in her heart she scorns our poverty:
Shall I not live to be avenged on her?
Contemptuous base-born callet as she is,
She vaunted 'mongst her minions t' other day,
The very train of her worst wearing gown
Was better worth than all my father's lands,
Till Suffolk gave two dukedoms for his daughter.

DUKE OF SUFFOLK.
Madam, myself have limed a bush for her,
And placed a quire of such enticing birds,
That she will light to listen to the lays,

And never mount to trouble you again.
So, let her rest: and, madam, list to me;
For I am bold to counsel you in this.
Although we fancy not the cardinal,
Yet must we join with him and with the lords,
Till we have brought Duke Humphrey in dis-
grace.
As for the Duke of York,—this late complaint
Will make but little for his benefit.
So, one by one, we'll weed them all at last,
And you yourself shall steer the happy helm.
Sound a sennet. Enter the KING, DUKE HUM-
PHREY, CARDINAL BEAUFORT, BUCKING-
HAM, YORK, SOMERSET, SALISBURY, WAR-
WICK, *and the* DUCHESS OF GLOSTER.
KING HENRY.
For my part, noble lords, I care not which;
Or Somerset or York, all's one to me.
DUKE OF YORK.
If York have ill demean'd himself in France,
Then let him be denay'd the regentship.
DUKE OF SOMERSET.
If Somerset be unworthy of the place,
Let York be regent; I will yield to him.
EARL OF WARWICK.
Whether your Grace be worthy, yea or no,
Dispute not that: York is the worthier.
CARDINAL BEAUFORT.
Ambitious Warwick, let thy betters speak.
EARL OF WARWICK.
The cardina''s not my better in the field.
DUKE OF BUCKINGHAM.
All in this presence are thy betters, Warwick.
EARL OF WARWICK.
Warwick may live to be the best of all.
EARL OF SALISBURY.
Peace, son!—and show some reason, Bucking-
ham,
Why Somerset should be preferr'd in this.
QUEEN MARGARET.
Because the king, forsooth, will have it so.
DUKE OF GLOSTER.
Madam, the king is old enough himself
To give his censure: these are no women's
matters.
QUEEN MARGARET.
If he be old enough, what needs your Grace
To be Protector of his excellence?
DUKE OF GLOSTER.
Madam, I am Protector of the realm;
And, at his pleasure, will resign my place.
DUKE OF SUFFOLK.
Resign it, then, and leave thine insolence.
Since thou wert king,—as who is king but thou?—
The commonwealth hath daily run to wrack;
The Dauphin hath prevail'd beyond the seas;
And all the peers and nobles of the realm
Have been as bondmen to thy sovereignty.
CARDINAL BEAUFORT.
The commons hast thou rackt; the clergy's bags
Are lank and lean with thy extortions.
DUKE OF SOMERSET.
Thy sumptuous buildings, and thy wife's attire,
Have cost a mass of public treasury.
DUKE OF BUCKINGHAM.
Thy cruelty in execution

Upon offenders hath exceeded law,
And left thee to the mercy of the law.
QUEEN MARGARET.
Thy sale of offices and towns in France—
If they were known, as the suspect is great—
Would make thee quickly hop without thy head.
[*Exit* GLOSTER. *The* QUEEN *drops her fan.*
Give me my fan: what, minion! can ye not?
[*She gives the* DUCHESS *a box on the ear.*
I cry you mercy, madam; was it you?
DUCHESS OF GLOSTER.
Was't I! yea, I it was, proud Frenchwoman:
Could I come near your beauty with my nails,
I'ld set my ten commandments in your face.
KING HENRY.
Sweet aunt, be quiet; 'twas against her will.
DUCHESS OF GLOSTER.
Against her will! good king, look to 't in time;
She'll hamper thee, and dandle thee like a baby:
Though in this place most master wear no
breeches,
She shall not strike Dame Eleanor unrevenged.
[*Exit.*
DUKE OF BUCKINGHAM.
Lord cardinal, I will follow Eleanor,
And listen after Humphrey, how he proceeds:
She's tickled now; her fury needs no spurs,
She'll gallop fast enough to her destruction.
[*Exit.*
Enter GLOSTER.
DUKE OF GLOSTER.
Now, lords, my choler being over-blown
With walking once about the quadrangle,
I come to talk of commonwealth affairs.
As for your spiteful false objections,
Prove them, and I lie open to the law:
But God in mercy so deal with my soul,
As I in duty love my king and country!
But, to the matter that we have in hand:—
I say, my sovereign, York is meetest man
To be your regent in the realm of France.
DUKE OF SUFFOLK.
Before we make election, give me leave
To show some reason, of no little force,
That York is most unmeet of any man.
DUKE OF YORK.
I'll tell thee, Suffolk, why I am unmeet:
First, for I cannot flatter thee in pride;
Next, if I be appointed for the place,
My Lord of Somerset will keep me here,
Without discharge, money, or furniture,
Till France be won into the Dauphin's hands:
Last time, I danced attendance on his will
Till Paris was besieged, famisht, and lost.
EARL OF WARWICK.
That can I witness; and a fouler fact
Did never traitor in the land commit.
DUKE OF SUFFOLK.
Peace, headstrong Warwick!
EARL OF WARWICK.
Image of pride, why should I hold my peace?
Enter HORNER, *the Armourer, and his man* PETER,
guarded.
DUKE OF SUFFOLK.
Because here is a man accused of treason:
Pray God the Duke of York excuse himself!

DUKE OF YORK.
Doth any one accuse York for a traitor?
KING HENRY.
What mean'st thou, Suffolk? tell me, what are
these?
DUKE OF SUFFOLK.
Please it your majesty, this is the man
That doth accuse his master of high treason:
His words were these,—that Richard duke of
York
Was rightful heir unto the English crown,
And that your majesty was an usurper.
KING HENRY.
Say, man, were these thy words?
THOMAS HORNER.
An 't shall please your majesty, I never said nor
thought any such matter: God is my witness, I
am falsely accused by the villain.
PETER [holding up his hands].
By these ten bones, my lords, he did speak them
to me in the garret one night, as we were scouring
my Lord of York's armour.
DUKE OF YORK.
Base dunghill villain and mechanical,
I'll have thy head for this thy traitor's speech.—
I do beseech your royal majesty,
Let him have all the rigour of the law.
THOMAS HORNER.
Alas, my lord, hang me, if ever I spake the words.
My accuser is my prentice; and when I did cor-
rect him for his fault the other day, he did vow
upon his knees he would be even with me: I have
good witness of this; therefore, I beseech your
majesty, do not cast away an honest man for a
villain's accusation.
KING HENRY.
Uncle, what shall we say to this in law?
DUKE OF GLOSTER.
This is my doom, my lord, if I may judge:
Let Somerset be regent o'er the French,
Because in York this breeds suspicion;
And let these have a day appointed them
For single combat in convenient place,
For he hath witness of his servant's malice:
This is the law, and this Duke Humphrey's
doom.
KING HENRY.
Then be it so.—My Lord of Somerset,
We make your Grace regent over the French.
DUKE OF SOMERSET.
I humbly thank your royal majesty.
THOMAS HORNER.
And I accept the combat willingly.
PETER.
Alas, my lord, I cannot fight; for God's sake, pity
my case! The spite of man prevaileth against me.
O Lord, have mercy upon me! I shall never be
able to fight a blow: O Lord, my heart!
DUKE OF GLOSTER.
Sirrah, or you must fight, or else be hang'd.
KING HENRY.
Away with them to prison; and the day
Of combat shall be the last of the next
month.—
Come, Somerset, we'll see thee sent away.
[*Exeunt.*

SCENE IV.

The same. GLOSTER's *garden.*

Enter MARGERY JOURDAIN, HUME, SOUTH-
WELL, *and* BOLINGBROKE.

JOHN HUME.
COME, my masters; the duchess, I tell you,
expects performance of your promises.
ROGER BOLINGBROKE.
Master Hume, we are therefore provided: will her
ladyship behold and hear our exorcisms?
JOHN HUME.
Ay, what else? fear you not her courage.
ROGER BOLINGBROKE.
I have heard her reported to be a woman of an
invincible spirit: but it shall be convenient,
Master Hume, that you be by her aloft, while we
be busy below; and so, I pray you, go in God's
name, and leave us. [*Exit* HUME.] Mother Jour-
dain, be you prostrate, and grovel on the earth;—
John Southwell, read you;—and let us to our
work.
Enter DUCHESS *aloft;* HUME *following.*
DUCHESS OF GLOSTER.
Well said, my masters; and welcome all. To this
gear,—the sooner the better.
ROGER BOLINGBROKE.
Patience, good lady; wizards know their times:
Deep night, dark night, the silent of the night,
The time of night when Troy was set on fire;
The time when screech-owls cry, and ban-dogs
howl,
And spirits walk, and ghosts break up their
graves,—
That time best fits the work we have in hand.
Madam, sit you, and fear not: whom we raise,
We will make fast within a hallow'd verge.
[*Here do the ceremonies belonging,* and make
the circle; BOLINGBROKE *or* SOUTH-
WELL *reads,* Conjuro te, &c. *It thun-
ders and lightens terribly; then the* SPIRIT
riseth.
SPIRIT.
Adsum.
MARGERY JOURDAIN.
Asmath,
By the eternal God, whose name and power
Thou tremblest at, answer that I shall ask;
For, till thou speak, thou shalt not pass from
hence.
SPIRIT.
Ask what thou wilt:—that I had said and done!
ROGER BOLINGBROKE [reading out of a
paper].
'First of the king: what shall of him become?'
SPIRIT.
The duke yet lives that Henry shall depose;
But him outlive, and die a violent death.
[*As the* SPIRIT *speaks,* SOUTHWELL
writes the answer.
ROGER BOLINGBROKE.
'What fates await the Duke of Suffolk?'
SPIRIT.
By water shall he die, and take his end.
ROGER BOLINGBROKE.
'What shall befall the Duke of Somerset?'

SPIRIT.
Let him shun castles;
Safer shall he be upon the sandy plains
Than where castles mounted stand.—
Have done, for more I hardly can endure.

ROGER BOLINGBROKE.
Descend to darkness and the burning lake!
False fiend, avoid!

[Thunder and lightning. Exit SPIRIT.
Enter the DUKE OF YORK *and the* DUKE OF
BUCKINGHAM, *with their* GUARD, *and break in.*

DUKE OF YORK.
Lay hands upon these traitors and their trash.—
Beldam, I think we watcht you at an inch.—
What, madam, are you there? the king and
commonweal
Are deeply indebted for this piece of pains:
My lord Protector will, I doubt it not,
See you well guerdon'd for these good deserts.

DUCHESS OF GLOSTER.
Not half so bad as thine to England's king.
Injurious duke, that threatest where's no cause.

DUKE OF BUCKINGHAM.
True, madam, none at all:—what call you this?—
[Showing her the papers.
Away with them! let them be clapt up close,
And kept asunder.—You, madam, shall with us.—
Stafford, take her to thee.—
We'll see your trinkets here all forthcoming.—
Away!

[Exeunt, above, DUCHESS *and* HUME,
guarded.   Exeunt, below, SOUTHWEL,
BOLINGBROKE, *&c., guarded.*

DUKE OF YORK.
Lord Buckingham, methinks you watcht her
well:
A pretty plot, well chosen to build upon!
Now, pray, my lord, let's see the devil's writ.
What have we here?   *[Reads.*
'The duke yet lives that Henry shall depose;
But him outlive, and die a violent death.'
Why, this is just
Aio te, Æacida, Romanos vincere posse.
Well, to the rest:
'Tell me what fate awaits the Duke of Suffolk?
By water shall he die, and take his end.—
What shall betide the Duke of Somerset?
Let him shun castles;
Safer shall he be upon the sandy plains
Than where castles mounted stand.'
Come, come, my lords;
These oracles are hardly attain'd,
And hardly understood.
The king is now in progress towards Saint
Alban's,
With him the husband of this lovely lady:
Thither goes these news, as fast as horse can
carry them,—
A sorry breakfast for my lord Protector.

DUKE OF BUCKINGHAM.
Your Grace shall give me leave, my Lord of
York,
To be the post, in hope of his reward.

DUKE OF YORK.
At your pleasure, my good lord.—Who's within
there, ho!

Enter a SERVANT.
Invite my Lords of Salisbury and Warwick
To sup with me to-morrow night.—Away!
[Exeunt.

ACT II. SCENE I.
Saint Alban's.

Enter the KING, QUEEN, GLOSTER, CARDINAL,
and SUFFOLK, *with* FALCONERS *hallooing.*

QUEEN MARGARET.
BELIEVE me, lords, for flying at the brook,
I saw not better sport these seven years' day:
Yet, by your leave, the wind was very high;
And, ten to one, old Joan had not gone out.

KING HENRY.
But what a point, my lord, your falcon made,
And what a pitch she flew above the rest!—
To see how God in all His creatures works!
Yea, man and birds are fain of climbing high.

DUKE OF SUFFOLK.
No marvel, an it like your majesty,
My lord Protector's hawks do tower so well;
They know their master loves to be aloft,
And bears his thoughts above his falcon's pitch.

DUKE OF GLOSTER.
My lord, 'tis but a base ignoble mind
That mounts no higher than a bird can soar.

CARDINAL BEAUFORT.
I thought as much: he would be above the
clouds.

DUKE OF GLOSTER.
Ay, my lord cardinal,—how think you by that?
Were it not good your Grace could fly to heaven?

KING HENRY.
The treasury of everlasting joy!

CARDINAL BEAUFORT.
Thy heaven is on earth; thine eyes and thoughts
Beat on a crown, the treasure of thy heart;
Pernicious Protector, dangerous peer,
That smooth'st it so with king and commonweal!

DUKE OF GLOSTER.
What, cardinal, is your priesthood grown per-
emptory?
Tantæne animis cælestibus iræ?
Churchmen so hot? good uncle, hide such malice;
With such holiness can you not do it?

DUKE OF SUFFOLK.
No malice, sir; no more than well becomes
So good a quarrel and so bad a peer.

DUKE OF GLOSTER.
As who, my lord?

DUKE OF SUFFOLK.
            Why, as you, my lord,
An 't like your lordly lord-Protectorship.

DUKE OF GLOSTER.
Why, Suffolk, England knows thine insolence.

QUEEN MARGARET.
And thy ambition, Gloster.

KING HENRY.
            I prithee, peace,
Good queen, and whet not on these furious peers
For blessed are the peacemakers on earth.

CARDINAL BEAUFORT.
Let me be blessed for the peace I make,
Against this proud Protector, with my sword!

DUKE OF GLOSTER [*aside to* CARDINAL].
Faith, holy uncle, would 'twere come to that!
CARDINAL BEAUFORT [*aside to* GLOSTER].
Marry, when thou darest.
DUKE OF GLOSTER [*aside to* CARDINAL].
Make up no factious numbers for the matter;
In thine own person answer thy abuse.
CARDINAL BEAUFORT [*aside to* GLOSTER].
Ay, where thou darest not peep: an if thou
  darest,
This evening on the east side of the grove.
KING HENRY.
How now, my lords!
CARDINAL BEAUFORT.
              Believe me, cousin Gloster,
Had not your man put up the fowl so suddenly,
We had had more sport.—[*aside to* GLOSTER]
        Come with thy two-hand sword.
DUKE OF GLOSTER.
True, uncle.
CARDINAL BEAUFORT [*aside to* GLOSTER].
Are ye advised?—the east side of the grove?
DUKE OF GLOSTER [*aside to* CARDINAL].
Cardinal, I am with you.
KING HENRY.
Why, how now, uncle Gloster!
DUKE OF GLOSTER.
Talking of hawking; nothing else, my lord.—
[*aside to* CARDINAL] Now, by God's mother,
  priest, I'll shave your crown for this,
Or all my fence shall fail.
CARDINAL BEAUFORT [*aside to* GLOSTER].
             Medice, teipsum;
Protector, see to 't well, protect yourself.
KING HENRY.
The winds grow high; so do your stomachs,
  lords.
How irksome is this music to my heart!
When such strings jar, what hope of harmony ?
I pray, my lords, let me compound this strife.
Enter a TOWNSMAN *of St. Alban's, crying,*
        A miracle!
DUKE OF GLOSTER.
What means this noise?
Fellow, what dost thou proclaim?
TOWNSMAN.
A miracle! a miracle!
DUKE OF SUFFOLK.
Come to the king, and tell him what miracle.
TOWNSMAN.
Forsooth, a blind man at Saint Alban's shrine,
Within this half-hour, hath received his
  sight;
A man that ne'er saw in his life before.
KING HENRY.
Now, God be praised, that to believing souls
Gives light in darkness, comfort in despair!
Enter the MAYOR *of St. Alban's and his brethren,*
  bearing SIMPCOX, *between two in a chair, his*
  WIFE *and a multitude following.*
CARDINAL BEAUFORT.
Here comes the townsmen on procession,
To present your highness with the man.
KING HENRY.
Great is his comfort in this earthly vale,
Although by his sight his sin be multiplied.

DUKE OF GLOSTER.
Stand by, my masters:—bring him near the
  king;
His highness' pleasure is to talk with him.
KING HENRY.
Good fellow, tell us here the circumstance,
That we for thee may glorify the Lord.
What, hast thou been long blind, and now re-
  stored?
SAUNDER SIMPCOX.
Born blind, an't please your Grace.
WIFE.
              Ay, indeed was he.
DUKE OF SUFFOLK.
What woman is this?
WIFE.
        His wife, an't like your worship.
DUKE OF GLOSTER.
Hadst thou been his mother, thou couldst have
  better told.
KING HENRY.
Where wert thou born?
SAUNDER SIMPCOX.
At Berwick in the north, an't like your Grace.
KING HENRY.
Poor soul, God's goodness hath been great to
  thee:
Let never day nor night unhallow'd pass,
But still remember what the Lord hath done.
QUEEN MARGARET.
Tell me, good fellow, camest thou here by
  chance,
Or of devotion, to this holy shrine?
SAUNDER SIMPCOX.
God knows, of pure devotion; being call'd
A hundred times and oftener, in my sleep,
By good Saint Alban; who said, 'Simpcox,
  come,—
Come, offer at my shrine, and I will help
  thee.'
WIFE.
Most true, forsooth; and many time and oft
Myself have heard a voice to call him so.
CARDINAL BEAUFORT.
What, art thou lame?
SAUNDER SIMPCOX.
          Ay, God Almighty help me!
DUKE OF SUFFOLK.
How camest thou so?
SAUNDER SIMPCOX.
          A fall off of a tree.
WIFE.
A plum-tree, master.
DUKE OF GLOSTER.
        How long hast thou been blind?
SAUNDER SIMPCOX.
O, born so, master.
DUKE OF GLOSTER.
        What, and wouldst climb a tree?
SAUNDER SIMPCOX.
But that in all my life, when I was a youth.
WIFE.
Too true; and bought his climbing very dear.
DUKE OF GLOSTER.
Mass, thou lovedst plums well, that wouldst
  venture so.

SAUNDER SIMPCOX.
Alas, good master, my wife desired some damsons,
And made me climb, with danger of my life.
DUKE OF GLOSTER.
A subtle knave! but yet it shall not serve.—
Let me see thine eyes: wink now; now open
them:—
In my opinion yet thou see'st not well.
SAUNDER SIMPCOX.
Yes, master, clear as day, I thank God and Saint
Alban.
DUKE OF GLOSTER.
Say'st thou me so? What colour is this cloak of?
SAUNDER SIMPCOX.
Red, master; red as blood.
DUKE OF GLOSTER.
Why, that's well said. What colour is my gown
of?
SAUNDER SIMPCOX.
Black, forsooth; coal-black as jet.
KING HENRY.
Why, then, thou know'st what colour jet is of?
DUKE OF SUFFOLK.
And yet, I think, jet did he never see.
DUKE OF GLOSTER.
But cloaks and gowns, before this day, a many.
WIFE.
Never, before this day, in all his life
DUKE OF GLOSTER.
Tell me, sirrah, what's my name?
SAUNDER SIMPCOX.
Alas, master, I know not.
DUKE OF GLOSTER.
What's his name?
SAUNDER SIMPCOX
I know not.
DUKE OF GLOSTER.
Nor his?
SAUNDER SIMPCOX.
No, indeed, master.
DUKE OF GLOSTER.
What's thine own name?
SAUNDER SIMPCOX.
Saunder Simpcox, an if it please you, master.
DUKE OF GLOSTER.
Then, Saunder, sit there, the lyingest knave in
Christendom. If thou hadst been born blind,
thou mightst as well have known all our names as
thus to name the several colours we do wear.
Sight may distinguish of colours; but suddenly to
nominate them all, it is impossible.—My lords,
Saint Alban here hath done a miracle; and would
ye not think his cunning to be great that could
restore this cripple to his legs again?
SAUNDER SIMPCOX.
O master, that you could!
DUKE OF GLOSTER.
My masters of Saint Alban's, have you not
beadles in your town, and things call'd whips?
MAYOR OF ST. ALBAN'S.
Yes, my lord, if it please your Grace.
DUKE OF GLOSTER.
Then send for one presently.
MAYOR OF ST. ALBAN'S.
Sirrah, go fetch the beadle hither straight.
[Exit an ATTENDANT.

DUKE OF GLOSTER.
Now fetch me a stool hither by and by. [A stool
brought out.] Now, sirrah, if you mean to save
yourself from whipping, leap me over this stool
and run away.
SAUNDER SIMPCOX.
Alas, master, I am not able to stand alone:
You go about to torture me in vain.
Enter a BEADLE with whips.
DUKE OF GLOSTER.
Well, sir, we must have you find your legs.—
Sirrah beadle, whip him till he leap over that
same stool.
BEADLE.
I will, my lord.—Come on, sirrah; off with your
doublet quickly.
SAUNDER SIMPCOX.
Alas, master, what shall I do? I am not able to
stand.
[After the BEADLE hath hit him once, he
leaps over the stool and runs away; and
they follow and cry, A miracle!
KING HENRY.
O God, seest Thou this, and bearest so long?
QUEEN MARGARET.
It made me laugh to see the villain run.
DUKE OF GLOSTER.
Follow the knave; and take this drab away.
WIFE.
Alas, sir, we did it for pure need.
DUKE OF GLOSTER.
Let them be whipt through every market-town
till they come to Berwick, from whence they came.
[Exeunt MAYOR, BEADLE, WIFE, &c.
CARDINAL BEAUFORT.
Duke Humphrey has done a miracle to-day.
DUKE OF SUFFOLK.
True; made the lame to leap and fly away.
DUKE OF GLOSTER.
But you have done more miracles than I;
You made in a day, my lord, whole towns to fly.
Enter BUCKINGHAM.
KING HENRY.
What tidings with our cousin Buckingham?
DUKE OF BUCKINGHAM.
Such as my heart doth tremble to unfold.
A sort of naughty persons, lewdly bent,—
Under the countenance and confederacy
Of Lady Eleanor, the Protector's wife,
The ringleader and head of all this rout,—
Have practised dangerously against your state,
Dealing with witches and with conjurers:
Whom we have apprehended in the fact;
Raising up wicked spirits from under ground,
Demanding of King Henry's life and death,
And other of your highness' privy-council,
As more at large your Grace shall understand.
CARDINAL BEAUFORT.
And so, my lord Protector, by this means
Your lady is forthcoming yet at London.
[aside to GLOSTER] This news, I think, hath
turn'd your weapon's edge;
'Tis like, my lord, you will not keep your hour.
DUKE OF GLOSTER.
Ambitious churchman, leave to afflict my heart:
Sorrow and grief have vanquisht all my powers;

And, vanquisht as I am, I yield to thee,
Or to the meanest groom.
KING HENRY.
O God, what mischiefs work the wicked ones,
Heaping confusion on their own heads thereby!
Gloster, see here the tainture of thy nest;
And look thyself be faultless, thou wert best.
QUEEN MARGARET.
DUKE OF GLOSTER.
Madam, for myself, to heaven I do appeal,
How I have loved my king and commonweal:
And, for my wife, I know not how it stands:
Sorry I am to hear what I have heard:
Noble she is; but if she have forgot
Honour and virtue, and conversed with such
As, like to pitch, defile nobility,
I banish her my bed and company,
And give her, as a prey, to law and shame,
That hath dishonour'd Gloster's honest name.
KING HENRY.
Well, for this night we will repose us here:
To-morrow toward London back again,
To look into this business thoroughly,
And call these foul offenders to their answers;
And poise the cause in justice' equal scales,
Whose beam stands sure, whose rightful cause
    prevails.   [*Flourish. Exeunt.*]

SCENE II.

London. The DUKE OF YORK'S *garden.*

Enter YORK, SALISBURY, *and* WARWICK.

DUKE OF YORK.   [wick'
NOW, my good Lords of Salisbury and War-
    Our simple supper ended, give me leave,
In this close walk, to satisfy myself,
In craving your opinion of my title,
Which is infallible, to England's crown.
EARL OF SALISBURY.
My lord, I long to hear it at full.
EARL OF WARWICK.
Sweet York, begin: and if thy claim be good,
The Nevils are thy subjects to command.
DUKE OF YORK.
Then thus:—
Edward the Third, my lords, had seven sons:
The first, Edward the Black Prince, Prince of
    Wales;
The second, William of Hatfield; and the third,
Lionel duke of Clarence; next to whom
Was John of Gaunt, the duke of Lancaster;
The fifth was Edmund Langley, duke of York;
The sixth was Thomas of Woodstock, duke of
    Gloster;
William of Windsor was the seventh and last.
Edward the Black Prince died before his father;
And left behind him Richard, his only son, [king;
Who, after Edward the Third's death, reign'd as
Till Henry Bolingbroke, duke of Lancaster,
The eldest son and heir of John of Gaunt,
Crown'd by the name of Henry the Fourth,
Seized on the realm, deposed the rightful king,
Sent his poor queen to France, from whence she
    came,
And him to Pomfret,—where, as all you know,
Harmless Richard was murder'd traitorously.

EARL OF WARWICK.
Father, the duke hath told the truth;
Thus got the house of Lancaster the crown.
DUKE OF YORK.
Which now they hold by force, and not by right;
For Richard, the first son's heir, being dead,
The issue of the next son should have reign'd.
EARL OF SALISBURY.
But William of Hatfield died without an heir.
DUKE OF YORK.
The third son, Duke of Clarence,—from whose
    line   [daughter,
I claim the crown,—had issue, Philippe, a
Who married Edmund Mortimer, earl of March:
Edmund had issue, Roger earl of March;
Roger had issue, Edmund, Anne, and Eleanor.
EARL OF SALISBURY.
This Edmund, in the reign of Bolingbroke,
As I have read, laid claim unto the crown;
And, but for Owen Glendower, had been king,
Who kept him in captivity till he died.
But, to the rest.
DUKE OF YORK.
            His eldest sister, Anne,
My mother, being heir unto the crown,
Married Richard earl of Cambridge; who was son
To Edmund Langley, Edward the Third's fifth
    son.
By her I claim the kingdom: she was heir
To Roger earl of March; who was the son
Of Edmund Mortimer; who married Philippe,
Sole daughter unto Lionel duke of Clarence:
So, if the issue of the elder son
Succeed before the younger, I am king.
EARL OF WARWICK.
What plain proceeding is more plain than this?
Henry doth claim the crown from John of Gaunt,
The fourth son; York doth claim it from the third.
Till Lionel's issue fails, his should not reign:
It fails not yet, but flourishes in thee,
And in thy sons, fair slips of such a stock.—
Then, father Salisbury, kneel we together;
And, in this private plot, be we the first
That shall salute our rightful sovereign
With honour of his birthright to the crown.
BOTH.
Long live our sovereign Richard, England's king!
DUKE OF YORK.
We thank you, lords. But I am not your king
Till I be crown'd, and that my sword be stain'd
With heart-blood of the house of Lancaster;
And that's not suddenly to be perform'd,
But with advice and silent secrecy.
Do you as I do in these dangerous days:
Wink at the Duke of Suffolk's insolence,
At Beaufort's pride, at Somerset's ambition,
At Buckingham, and all the crew of them,
Till they have snared the shepherd of the flock,
That virtuous prince, the good Duke Humphrey:
'Tis that they seek; and they, in seeking that,
Shall find their deaths, if York can prophesy.
EARL OF SALISBURY.
My lord, break we off; we know your mind at full.
EARL OF WARWICK.
My heart assures me that the Earl of Warwick
Shall one day make the Duke of York a king.

DUKE OF YORK.

And, Nevil, this I do assure myself,—
Richard shall live to make the Earl of Warwick
The greatest man in England but the king.

[*Exeunt.*

SCENE III.

A hall of justice.

Sound trumpets. Enter the KING, *the* QUEEN,
GLOSTER, YORK, SUFFOLK, *and* SALISBURY;
the DUCHESS OF GLOSTER, MARGERY JOUR-
DAIN, SOUTHWELL, HUME, *and* BOLING-
BROKE, *under guard.*

KING HENRY.

STAND forth, Dame Eleanor Cobham, Glos-
ter's wife:
In sight of God and us, your guilt is great:
Receive the sentence of the law, for sins
Such as by God's book are adjudg'd to death.—
[*to* JOURDAIN, *&c.*] You four, from hence to
prison back again;
From thence unto the place of execution:
The witch in Smithfield shall be burnt to ashes,
And you three shall be strangled on the gallows.—
You, madam, for you are more nobly born,
Despoiled of your honour in your life,
Shall, after three days' open penance done,
Live in your country here, in banishment,
With Sir John Stanley, in the Isle of Man.

DUCHESS OF GLOSTER.

Welcome is banishment; welcome were my death.

DUKE OF GLOSTER.

Eleanor, the law, thou seest, hath judged thee:
I cannot justify whom the law condemns.—
[*Exeunt the* DUCHESS *and the other
prisoners, guarded.*
Mine eyes are full of tears, my heart of grief.
Ah, Humphrey, this dishonour in thine age
Will bring thy head with sorrow to the ground!—
I beseech your majesty, give me leave to go;
Sorrow would solace, and mine age would ease.

KING HENRY.

Stay, Humphrey duke of Gloster: ere thou go,
Give up thy staff: Henry will to himself
Protector be; and God shall be my hope,
My stay, my guide, and lantern to my feet:
And go in peace, Humphrey,—no less beloved
Than when thou wert Protector to thy king.

QUEEN MARGARET.

I see no reason why a king of years
Should be to be protected like a child.—
God and King Henry govern England's helm!—
Give up your staff, sir, and the king his realm.

DUKE OF GLOSTER.

My staff! here, noble Henry, is my staff:
As willingly do I the same resign
As e'er thy father Henry made it mine;
And even as willingly at thy feet I leave it
As others would ambitiously receive it.
Farewell, good king: when I am dead and gone,
May honourable peace attend thy throne! [*Exit.*

QUEEN MARGARET.

Why, now is Henry king, and Margaret queen;
And Humphrey duke of Gloster scarce himself,
That bears so shrewd a maim; two pulls at once,—
His lady banisht, and a limb lopt off:

This staff of honour raught, there let it stand
Where it best fits to be,—in Henry's hand.

DUKE OF SUFFOLK.

Thus droops this lofty pine, and hangs his
sprays;
Thus Eleanor's pride dies in her youngest days.

DUKE OF YORK.

Lords, let him go.—Please it your majesty,
This is the day appointed for the combat;
And ready are the appellant and defendant,
The armourer and his man, to enter the lists,
So please your highness to behold the fight.

QUEEN MARGARET.

Ay, good my lord; for purposely therefore
Left I the court, to see this quarrel tried.

KING HENRY.

O' God's name, see the lists and all things fit;
Here let them end it; and God defend the right!

DUKE OF YORK.

I never saw a fellow worse bested,
Or more afraid to fight, than is the appellant,
The servant of this armourer, my lords.

Enter, at one door, HORNER, *the Armourer, and
his* NEIGHBOURS, *drinking to him so much that
he is drunk: and he enters with a drum before
him and his staff with a sandbag fasten'd to it;
and at the other door* PETER, *his man, with a
drum and sandbag, and* PRENTICES *drinking
to him.*

FIRST NEIGHBOUR.

Here, neighbour Horner, I drink to you in a cup
of sack: and fear not, neighbour, you shall do well
enough.

SECOND NEIGHBOUR.

And here, neighbour, here's a cup of charneco.

THIRD NEIGHBOUR.

And here's a pot of good double-beer, neighbour:
drink, and fear not your man.

THOMAS HORNER.

Let it come, i' faith, and I'll pledge you all; and
a fig for Peter!

FIRST PRENTICE.

Here, Peter, I drink to thee: and be not afraid.

SECOND PRENTICE.

Be merry, Peter, and fear not thy master: fight
for credit of the prentices.

PETER.

I thank you all: drink, and pray for me, I pray
you; for I think I have taken my last draught in
this world.—Here, Robin, an if I die, I give thee
my apron:—and, Will, thou shalt have my hammer:—and here, Tom, take all the money that I
have.—O Lord bless me, I pray God! for I am
never able to deal with my master, he hath learnt
so much fence already.

EARL OF SALISBURY.

Come, leave your drinking, and fall to blows.—
Sirrah, what's thy name?

PETER.

Peter, forsooth.

EARL OF SALISBURY.

Peter! what more?

PETER.

Thump.

EARL OF SALISBURY.

Thump! then see thou thump thy master well.

THOMAS HORNER.

Masters, I am come hither, as it were, upon my
man's instigation, to prove him a knave, and myself an honest man: and touching the Duke of
York, I will take my death, I never meant him
any ill, nor the king, nor the queen: and therefore,
Peter, have at thee with a downright blow!

DUKE OF YORK.

Dispatch:—this knave's tongue begins to double.
—Sound, trumpets, alarum to the combatants!

[Alarum. They fight, and PETER *strikes
him down.*

THOMAS HORNER.

Hold, Peter, hold! I confess, I confess treason.

[Dies.

DUKE OF YORK.

Take away his weapon.—Fellow, thank God, and
the good wine in thy master's way.

PETER.

O God, have I overcome mine enemy in this presence? O Peter, thou hast prevail'd in right!

KING HENRY.

Go, take hence that traitor from our sight;
For by his death we do perceive his guilt:
And God in justice hath reveal'd to us
The truth and innocence of this poor fellow,
Which he had thought to have murder'd wrong-
fully.—
Come, fellow, follow us for thy reward.

[Sound a flourish.   Exeunt.

SCENE IV.

A street.

Enter GLOSTER *and his* MEN, *in mourning
cloaks.*

DUKE OF GLOSTER.   [cloud;

THUS sometimes hath the brightest day a
    And after summer evermore succeeds
Barren winter, with his wrathful nipping cold:
So cares and joys abound, as seasons fleet.—
Sirs, what's o'clock?

SERVING-MAN.

'Tis almost ten, my lord.

DUKE OF GLOSTER.

Ten is the hour that was appointed me
To watch the coming of my punisht duchess:
Uneath may she endure the flinty streets,
To tread them with her tender-feeling feet.
Sweet Nell, ill can thy noble mind abrook
The abject people gazing on thy face
With envious looks, still laughing at thy shame,
That erst did follow thy proud chariot-wheels
When thou didst ride in triumph through the
streets.
But, soft! I think she comes; and I'll prepare
My tear-stain'd eyes to see her miseries.

Enter the DUCHESS *of* GLOSTER *barefoot, in a
white sheet, with verses pinn'd on her back, and
a taper burning in her hand; with* SIR JOHN
STANLEY, *the* SHERIFF, *and* OFFICERS.

SERVING-MAN.

So please your Grace, we'll take her from the
sheriff.

DUKE OF GLOSTER.

No, stir not, for your lives; let her pass by.

DUCHESS OF GLOSTER.

Come you, my lord, to see my open shame?
Now thou dost penance too. Look how they
gaze!
See how the giddy multitude do point,
And nod their heads, and throw their eyes on
thee!
Ah, Gloster, hide thee from their hateful looks,
And, in thy closet pent up, rue my shame,
And ban thine enemies, both mine and thine!

DUKE OF GLOSTER.

Be patient, gentle Nell; forget this grief.

DUCHESS OF GLOSTER.

Ah, Gloster, teach me to forget myself!
For, whilst I think I am thy married wife,
And thou a prince, Protector of this land,
Methinks I should not thus be led along,
Mail'd up in shame, with papers on my back,
And follow'd with a rabble, that rejoice
To see my tears and hear my deep-fet groans.
The ruthless flint doth cut my tender feet;
And when I start, the envious people laugh,
And bid me be advised how I tread.
Ah, Humphrey, can I bear this shameful yoke?
Trow'st thou that e'er I'll look upon the world,
Or count them happy that enjoy the sun?
No; dark shall be my light, and night my day;
To think upon my pomp shall be my hell.
Sometime I'll say, I am Duke Humphrey's wife;
And he a prince, and ruler of the land:
Yet so he ruled, and such a prince he was,
As he stood by, whilst I, his forlorn duchess,
Was made a wonder and a pointing-stock
To every idle rascal follower.
But be thou mild, and blush not at my shame;
Nor stir at nothing, till the axe of death
Hang over thee, as, sure, it shortly will;
For Suffolk,—he that can do all in all
With her that hateth thee and hates us all,—
And York, and impious Beaufort, that false priest,
Have all limed bushes to betray thy wings,
And, fly thou how thou canst, they'll tangle thee:
But fear not thou, until thy foot be snared,
Nor never seek prevention of thy foes.

DUKE OF GLOSTER.

Ah, Nell, forbear! thou aimest all awry;
I must offend before I be attainted:
And had I twenty times so many foes,
And each of them had twenty times their power,
All these could not procure me any scathe,
So long as I am loyal, true, and crimeless.
Wouldst have me rescue thee from this reproach?
Why, yet thy scandal were not wiped away,
But I in danger for the breach of law.
Thy greatest help is quiet, gentle Nell:
I pray thee, sort thy heart to patience;
These few days' wonder will be quickly worn.

Enter a HERALD.

HERALD.

I summon your Grace to his majesty's parliament,
Holden at Bury the first of this next month.

DUKE OF GLOSTER.

And my consent ne'er askt herein before!
This is close dealing.—Well, I will be there.

[Exit HERALD.

My Nell, I take my leave:—ind, master sheriff,
Let not her penance exceed the king's commission.

SHERIFF.
An't please your Grace, here my commission
stays;
And Sir John Stanley is appointed now
To take her with him to the Isle of Man.

DUKE OF GLOSTER.
Must you, Sir John, protect my lady here?

SIR JOHN STANLEY.
So am I given in charge, may't please your Grace.

DUKE OF GLOSTER.
Entreat her not the worse, in that I pray
You use her well: the world may laugh again;
And I may live to do you kindness, if
You do it her: and so, Sir John, farewell.

DUCHESS OF GLOSTER.
What, gone, my lord, and bid me not farewell!

DUKE OF GLOSTER.
Witness my tears, I cannot stay to speak.

[Exeunt GLOSTER and his MEN.

DUCHESS OF GLOSTER.
Art thou gone too? all comfort go with thee!
For none abides with me: my joy is death,—
Death, at whose name I oft have been afeard,
Because I wisht this world's eternity.
Stanley, I prithee, go, and take me hence;
I care not whither, for I beg no favour,
Only convey me where thou art commanded.

SIR JOHN STANLEY.
Why, madam, that is to the Isle of Man;
There to be used according to your state.

DUCHESS OF GLOSTER.
That's bad enough, for I am but reproach,—
And shall I, then, be used reproachfully?

SIR JOHN STANLEY.
Like to a duchess, and Duke Humphrey's lady;
According to that state you shall be used.

DUCHESS OF GLOSTER.
Sheriff, farewell, and better than I fare,—
Although thou hast been conduct of my shame.

SHERIFF.
It is my office; and, madam, pardon me.

DUCHESS OF GLOSTER.
Ay, ay, farewell; thy office is discharged.—
Come, Stanley, shall we go?

SIR JOHN STANLEY.
Madam, your penance done, throw off this sheet,
And go we to attire you for our journey.

DUCHESS OF GLOSTER.
My shame will not be shifted with my sheet:
No, it will hang upon my richest robes,
And show itself, attire me how I can.
Go, lead the way; I long to see my prison.

[Exeunt.

ACT III. SCENE I.

The Abbey at Bury St. Edmund's.

Sound a sennet. Enter KING, QUEEN, CARDINAL
BEAUFORT, SUFFOLK, YORK, BUCKINGHAM,
SALISBURY, *and* WARWICK *to the Parliament.*

KING HENRY.
I MUSE my Lord of Gloster is not come:
'Tis not his wont to be the hindmost man,
Whate'er occasion keeps him from us now.

QUEEN MARGARET.
Can you not see? or will ye not observe
The strangeness of his alter'd countenance?
With what a majesty he bears himself;
How insolent of late he is become,
How proud, how peremptory, and unlike him-
self?
We know the time since he was mild and affable;
And, if we did but glance a far-off look,
Immediately he was upon his knee,
That all the court admired him for submission:
But meet him now, and, be it in the morn,
When every one will give the time of day,
He knits his brow, and shows an angry eye,
And passeth by with stiff unbowed knee,
Disdaining duty that to us belongs.
Small curs are not regarded when they grin;
But great men tremble when the lion roars,—
And Humphrey is no little man in England.
First note, that he is near you in descent;
And, should you fall, he is the next will mount.
Me seemeth, then, it is no policy,—
Respecting what a rancorous mind he bears,
And his advantage following your decease,—
That he should come about your royal person,
Or be admitted to your highness' council.
By flattery hath he won the commons' hearts;
And when he please to make commotion,
'Tis to be fear'd they all will follow him.
Now 'tis the spring, and weeds are shallow-
rooted;
Suffer them now, and they'll o'ergrow the garden,
And choke the herbs for want of husbandry.
The reverent care I bear unto my lord
Made me collect these dangers in the duke.
If it be fond, call it a woman's fear;
Which fear if better reasons can supplant,
I will subscribe, and say I wrong'd the duke.
My Lord of Suffolk, Buckingham, and York,
Reprove my allegation, if you can;
Or else conclude my words effectual.

DUKE OF SUFFOLK.
Well hath your highness seen into this duke;
And, had I first been put to speak my mind,
I think I should have told your Grace's tale.
The duchess, by his subornation,
Upon my life, began her devilish practices:
Or, if he were not privy to those faults,
Yet, by reputing of his high descent,—
As, next the king, he was successive heir,
And such high vaunts of his nobility.—
Did instigate the bedlam brain-sick duchess
By wicked means to frame our sovereign's fall.
Smooth runs the water where the brook is deep;
And in his simple show he harbours treason.
The fox barks not when he would steal the lamb.
No, no, my sovereign: Gloster is a man
Unsounded yet, and full of deep deceit.

CARDINAL BEAUFORT.
Did he not, contrary to form of law,
Devise strange deaths for small offences done?

DUKE OF YORK.
And did he not, in his Protectorship,
Levy great sums of money through the realm
For soldiers' pay in France, and never sent it?
By means whereof the towns each day revolted.

DUKE OF BUCKINGHAM.
Tut, these are petty faults to faults unknown,
Which time will bring to light in smooth Duke
  Humphrey.
KING HENRY.
My lords, at once:—the care you have of us,
To mow down thorns that would annoy our foot,
Is worthy praise: but—shall I speak my con-
  science?—
Our kinsman Gloster is as innocent
From meaning treason to our royal person
As is the sucking lamb or harmless dove:
The duke is virtuous, mild, and too well given
To dream on evil, or to work my downfall.
QUEEN MARGARET.
Ah, what's more dangerous than this fond
  affiance!
Seems he a dove? his feathers are but borrow'd,
For he's disposed as the hateful raven:
Is he a lamb! his skin is surely lent him,
For he's inclined as is the ravenous wolf.
Who cannot steal a shape that means deceit?
Take heed, my lord: the welfare of us all
Hangs on the cutting short that fraudful man.
Enter SOMERSET.
DUKE OF SOMERSET.
All health unto my gracious sovereign!
KING HENRY.
Welcome, Lord Somerset. What news from
  France?
DUKE OF SOMERSET.
That all your interest in those territories
Is utterly bereft you: all is lost.
KING HENRY.
Cold news, Lord Somerset: but God's will be
  done!
DUKE OF YORK [*aside*].
Cold news for me; for I had hope of France
As firmly as I hope for fertile England.
Thus are my blossoms blasted in the bud,
And caterpillars eat my leaves away:
But I will remedy this gear ere long,
Or sell my title for a glorious grave.
Enter GLOSTER.
DUKE OF GLOSTER.
All happiness unto my lord the king!
Pardon, my liege, that I have stay'd so long.
DUKE OF SUFFOLK.
Nay, Gloster, know that thou art come too soon,
Unless thou wert more loyal than thou art:
I do arrest thee of high treason here.
DUKE OF GLOSTER.
Well, Suffolk, well, thou shalt not see me blush
Nor change my countenance for this arrest:
A heart unspotted is not easily daunted.
The purest spring is not so free from mud
As I am clear from treason to my sovereign:
Who can accuse me? wherein am I guilty?
DUKE OF YORK.
'Tis thought, my lord, that you took bribes of
  France,
And, being Protector, stay'd the soldiers' pay;
By means whereof his highness hath lost France.
DUKE OF GLOSTER.
Is it but thought so? what are they that think it?
I never robb'd the soldiers of their pay,

Nor ever had one penny bribe from France.
So help me God, as I have watcht the night,—
Ay, night by night,—in studying good for
  England!
That doit that e'er I wrested from the king,
Or any groat I hoarded to my use,
Be brought against me at my trial-day!
No; many a pound of mine own proper store,
Because I would not tax the needy commons,
Have I dispursed to the garrisons,
And never askt for restitution.
CARDINAL BEAUFORT.
It serves you well, my lord, to say so much.
DUKE OF GLOSTER.
I say no more than truth, so help me God!
DUKE OF YORK.
In your Protectorship you did devise
Strange tortures for offenders, never heard of,
That England was defamed by tyranny.
DUKE OF GLOSTER.
Why, 'tis well known that, whiles I was Pro-
  tector,
Pity was all the fault that was in me;
For I should melt at an offender's tears,
And lowly words were ransom for their fault.
Unless it were a bloody murderer,
Or foul felonious thief that fleeced poor pas-
  sengers,
I never gave them condign punishment:
Murder, indeed, that bloody sin, I tortured
Above the felon or what trespass else.
DUKE OF SUFFOLK.
My lord, these faults are easy, quickly answer'd:
But mightier crimes are laid unto your charge,
Whereof you cannot easily purge yourself.
I do arrest you in his highness' name;
And here commit you to my lord cardinal
To keep, until your further time of trial.
KING HENRY.
My Lord of Gloster, 'tis my special hope
That you will clear yourself from all suspect:
My conscience tells me you are innocent.
DUKE OF GLOSTER.
Ah, gracious lord, these days are dangerous!
Virtue is choked with foul ambition,
And charity chased hence by rancour's hand;
Foul subornation is predominant,
And equity exiled your highness' land.
I know their complot is to have my life;
And, if my death might make this island happy,
And prove the period of their tyranny,
I would expend it with all willingness:
But mine is made the prologue to their play;
For thousands more, that yet suspect no peril,
Will not conclude their plotted tragedy.
Beaufort's red sparkling eyes blab his heart's
  malice,
And Suffolk's cloudy brow his stormy hate;
Sharp Buckingham unburdens with his tongue
The envious load that lies upon his heart;
And dogged York, that reaches at the moon,
Whose overweening arm I have pluckt back,
By false accuse doth level at my life:—
And you, my sovereign lady, with the rest,
Causeless have laid disgraces on my head,
And with your best endeavour have stirr'd up

My liefest liege to be mine enemy:—
Ay, all of you have laid your heads together—
Myself had notice of your conventicles—
And all to make away my guiltless life.
I shall not want false witness to condemn me,
Nor store of treasons to augment my guilt;
The ancient proverb will be well effected,—
A staff is quickly found to beat a dog.

CARDINAL BEAUFORT.
My liege, his railing is intolerable:
If those that care to keep your royal person
From treason's secret knife and traitors' rage
Be thus upbraided, chid, and rated at,
And the offender granted scope of speech,
'Twill make them cool in zeal unto your Grace.

DUKE OF SUFFOLK.
Hath he not twit our sovereign lady here
With ignominious words, though clerkly couch'd,
As if she had suborned some to swear
False allegations to o'erthrow his state?

QUEEN MARGARET.
But I can give the loser leave to chide.

DUKE OF GLOSTER.
Far truer spoke than meant: I lose, indeed;—
Beshrew the winners, for they play'd me false!
And well such losers may have leave to speak.

DUKE OF BUCKINGHAM.
He'll wrest the sense, and hold us here all day:—
Lord cardinal, he is your prisoner.

CARDINAL BEAUFORT.
Sirs, take away the duke, and guard him sure.

DUKE OF GLOSTER.
Ah, thus King Henry throws away his crutch,
Before his legs be firm to bear his body!
Thus is the shepherd beaten from thy side,
And wolves are gnarling who shall gnaw thee first.
Ah, that my fear were false! ah, that it were!
For, good King Henry, thy decay I fear.
                [Exit GLOSTER, guarded.

KING HENRY.
My lords, what to your wisdoms seemeth best
Do or undo, as if ourself were here.

QUEEN MARGARET.
What, will your highness leave the parliament?

KING HENRY.
Ay, Margaret; my heart is drown'd with grief,
Whose flood begins to flow within mine eyes;
My body round engirt with misery,—
For what's more miserable than discontent?—
Ah, uncle Humphrey, in thy face I see
The map of honour, truth, and loyalty!
And yet, good Humphrey, is the hour to come
That e'er I proved thee false, or fear'd thy faith.
What louring star now envies thy estate,
That these great lords, and Margaret our queen,
Do seek subversion of thy harmless life?
Thou never didst them wrong, nor no man
    wrong:
And as the butcher takes away the calf,
And binds the wretch, and beats it when it strays,
Bearing it to the bloody slaughter-house;
Even so, remorseless, have they borne him hence:
And as the dam runs lowing up and down,
Looking the way her harmless young one went,
And can do naught but wail her darling's loss;
Even so myself bewails good Gloster's case

With sad unhelpful tears; and with dimm'd eyes
Look after him, and cannot do him good,—
So mighty are his vowed enemies.
His fortunes I will weep; and, 'twixt each groan,
Say, 'Who's a traitor, Gloster he is none.'   [Exit.

QUEEN MARGARET.
Fair lords, cold snow melts with the sun's hot
    beams.
Henry my lord is cold in great affairs,
Too full of foolish pity: and Gloster's show
Beguiles him, as the mournful crocodile
With sorrow snares relenting passengers;
Or as the snake, roll'd in a flowering bank,
With shining checker'd slough, doth sting a
    child,
That for the beauty thinks it excellent.
Believe me, lords, were none more wise than I,—
And yet herein I judge mine own wit good,—
This Gloster should be quickly rid the world,
To rid us from the fear we have of him.

CARDINAL BEAUFORT.
That he should die is worthy policy;
But yet we want a colour for his death:
'Tis meet he be condemn'd by course of law.

DUKE OF SUFFOLK.
But, in my mind, that were no policy:
The king will labour still to save his life;
The commons haply rise to save his life;
And yet we have but trivial argument,
More than mistrust, that shows him worthy
    death.

DUKE OF YORK.
So that, by this, you would not have him die.

DUKE OF SUFFOLK.
Ah, York, no man alive so fain as I!

DUKE OF YORK [aside].
'Tis York that hath more reason for his death.—
But, my lord cardinal, and you, my Lord of
    Suffolk,—
Say as you think, and speak it from your souls,—
Were't not all one, an empty eagle were set
To guard the chicken from a hungry kite,
As place Duke Humphrey for the king's Pro-
    tector?

QUEEN MARGARET.
So the poor chicken should be sure of death.

DUKE OF SUFFOLK.
Madam, 'tis true; and were't not madness, then,
To make the fox surveyor of the fold?
Who being accused a crafty murderer,
His guilt should be but idly posted over,
Because his purpose is not executed.
No; let him die, in that he is a fox,
By nature proved an enemy to the flock,
Before his chaps be stain'd with crimson blood,
As Humphrey, proved by reasons, to my liege,
And do not stand on quillets how to slay him:
Be it by gins, by snares, by subtlety,
Sleeping or waking, 'tis no matter how,
So he be dead; for that is good deceit
Which mates him first that first intends deceit.

QUEEN MARGARET.
Thrice-noble Suffolk, 'tis resolutely spoke.

DUKE OF SUFFOLK.
Not resolute, except so much were done;
For things are often spoke, and seldom meant:

But, that my heart accordeth with my tongue,—
Seeing the deed is meritorious,
And to preserve my sovereign from his foe,—
Say but the word, and I will be his priest.

CARDINAL BEAUFORT.

But I would have him dead, my Lord of Suffolk,
Ere you can take due orders for a priest:
Say you consent, and censure well the deed,
And I'll provide his executioner,—
I tender so the safety of my liege.

DUKE OF SUFFOLK.

Here is my hand, the deed is worthy doing.

QUEEN MARGARET.

And so say I.

DUKE OF YORK.

And I: and now we three have spoke it,
It skills not greatly who impugns our doom.

Enter a POST.

POST.

Great lords, from Ireland am I come amain,
To signify that rebels there are up,
And put the Englishmen unto the sword:
Send succours, lords, and stop the rage betime,
Before the wound do grow uncurable;
For, being green, there is great hope of help.

CARDINAL BEAUFORT.

A breach that craves a quick expedient stop!
What counsel give you in this weighty cause?

DUKE OF YORK.

That Somerset be sent as regent thither:
'Tis meet that lucky ruler be employ'd;
Witness the fortune he hath had in France.

DUKE OF SOMERSET.

If York, with all his far-fet policy,
Had been the regent there instead of me,
He never would have stay'd in France so long.

DUKE OF YORK.

No, not to lose it all, as thou hast done:
I rather would have lost my life betimes
Than bring a burden of dishonour home
By staying there so long till all were lost.
Show me one scar character'd on thy skin:
Men's flesh preserved so whole do seldom win.

QUEEN MARGARET.

Nay, then, this spark will prove a raging fire,
If wind and fuel be brought to feed it with:—
No more, good York;—sweet Somerset, be
   still:—
Thy fortune, York, hadst thou been regent there,
Might happily have proved far worse than his.

DUKE OF YORK.

What, worse than naught? nay, then, a shame
   take all!

DUKE OF SOMERSET.

And, in the number, thee that wishest shame!

CARDINAL BEAUFORT.

My Lord of York, try what your fortune is.
Th' uncivil kerns of Ireland are in arms,
And temper clay with blood of Englishmen:
To Ireland will you lead a band of men,
Collected choicely, from each county some,
And try your hap against the Irishmen?

DUKE OF YORK.

I will, my lord, so please his majesty.

DUKE OF SUFFOLK.

Why, our authority is his consent;

And what we do establish he confirms:
Then, noble York, take thou this task in hand.

DUKE OF YORK.

I am content: provide me soldiers, lords,
Whiles I take order for mine own affairs.

DUKE OF SUFFOLK.

A charge, Lord York, that I will see perform'd.
But now return we to the false Duke Humphrey.

CARDINAL BEAUFORT.

No more of him; for I will deal with him,
That henceforth he shall trouble us no more.
And so break off; the day is almost spent:
Lord Suffolk, you and I must talk of that event.

DUKE OF YORK.

My Lord of Suffolk, within fourteen days
At Bristol I expect my soldiers;
For there I'll ship them all for Ireland.

DUKE OF SUFFOLK.

I'll see it truly done, my Lord of York.

[*Exeunt all except* YORK.

DUKE OF YORK.

Now, York, or never, steel thy fearful thoughts,
And change misdoubt to resolution:
Be that thou hopest to be; or what thou art
Resign to death,—it is not worth th' enjoying:
Let pale-faced fear keep with the mean-born
   man,
And find no harbour in a royal heart.
Faster than spring-time showers comes thought
   on thought;
And not a thought but thinks on dignity.
My brain, more busy than the labouring spider,
Weaves tedious snares to trap mine enemies.
Well, nobles, well, 'tis politicly done,
To send me packing with an host of men:
I fear me you but warm the starved snake,
Who, cherisht in your breasts, will sting your
   hearts.
'Twas men I lackt, and you will give them me:
I take it kindly; yet be well assured
You put sharp weapons in a madman's hands.
Whiles I in Ireland nourish a mighty band,
I will stir up in England some black storm,
Shall blow ten thousand souls to heaven or hell;
And this fell tempest shall not cease to rage
Until the golden circuit on my head,
Like to the glorious sun's transparent beams,
Do calm the fury of this mad-bred flaw.
And for a minister of my intent
I have seduced a headstrong Kentishman,
John Cade of Ashford,
To make commotion, as full well he can,
Under the title of John Mortimer.
In Ireland have I seen this stubborn Cade
Oppose himself against a troop of kerns,
And fought so long, till that his thighs with darts
Were almost like a sharp-quill'd porpentine;
And, in the end being rescued, I have seen
Him caper upright like a wild Morisco,
Shaking the bloody darts as he his bells.
Full often, like a shag-hair'd crafty kern,
Hath he conversed with the enemy,
And, undiscover'd, come to me again,
And given me notice of their villainies.
This devil here shall be my substitute;
For that John Mortimer, which now is dead,

In face, in gait, in speech, he doth resemble:
By this I shall perceive the commons' mind,
How they affect the house and claim of York.
Say he be taken, rackt, and tortured,
I know no pain they can inflict upon him
Will make him say I moved him to those arms.
Say that he thrive,—as 'tis great like he will,—
Why, then from Ireland come I with my strength,
And reap the harvest which that rascal sow'd;
For, Humphrey being dead, as he shall be,
And Henry put apart, the next for me.   [*Exit.*

SCENE II.

Bury St. Edmund's.   A room of state.

*Enter two or three running over the stage, from the
murder of* DUKE HUMPHREY.

FIRST MURDERER.

RUN to my Lord of Suffolk; let him know
We have dispatcht the duke, as he command-
SECOND MURDERER.   [ed.
O, that it were to do!—What have we done?
Didst ever hear a man so penitent?
FIRST MURDERER.
Here comes my lord.
Enter SUFFOLK.
DUKE OF SUFFOLK.
Now, sirs, have you dispatcht this thing?
FIRST MURDERER.
Ay, my good lord, he's dead.
DUKE OF SUFFOLK.
Why, that's well said. Go, get you to my house;
I will reward you for this venturous deed.
The king and all the peers are here at hand:—
Have you laid fair the bed? is all things well,
According as I gave directions?
FIRST MURDERER.
'Tis, my good lord.
DUKE OF SUFFOLK.
Away! be gone.   [*Exeunt* MURDERERS.
Sound trumpets.   Enter the KING, *the* QUEEN,
CARDINAL BEAUFORT, SOMERSET, LORDS,
and others.
KING HENRY.
Go, call our uncle to our presence straight;
Say we intend to try his Grace to-day,
If he be guilty, as 'tis published.
DUKE OF SUFFOLK.
I'll call him presently, my noble lord.   [*Exit.*
KING HENRY.
Lords, take your places; and, I pray you all,
Proceed no straiter 'gainst our uncle Gloster
Than from true evidence of good esteem
He be approved in practice culpable.
QUEEN MARGARET.
God forbid any malice should prevail,
That faultless may condemn a nobleman!
Pray God he may acquit him of suspicion!
KING HENRY.
I thank thee, Meg; these words content me much.
Enter SUFFOLK.
How now! why look'st thou pale? why tremblest
thou?
Where is our uncle? what's the matter, Suffolk?
DUKE OF SUFFOLK.
Dead in his bed, my lord; Gloster is dead.

QUEEN MARGARET.
Marry, God forfend!
CARDINAL BEAUFORT.
God's secret judgement:—I did dream to-night
The duke was dumb, and could not speak a word.
[*The* KING *swoons.*
QUEEN MARGARET.
How fares my lord?—Help, lords! the king is
dead.
DUKE OF SOMERSET.
Rear up his body; wring him by the nose.
QUEEN MARGARET.
Run, go, help, help!—O Henry, ope thine eyes!
DUKE OF SUFFOLK.
He doth revive again:—madam, be patient.
KING HENRY.
O heavenly God!
QUEEN MARGARET.
How fares my gracious lord?
DUKE OF SUFFOLK.
Comfort, my sovereign! gracious Henry, com-
fort!
KING HENRY.
What, doth my Lord of Suffolk comfort me?
Came he right now to sing a raven's note,
Whose dismal tune bereft my vital powers;
And thinks he that the chirping of a wren,
By crying comfort from a hollow breast,
Can chase away the first-conceived sound?
Hide not thy poison with such sugar'd words:
Lay not thy hands on me; forbear, I say;
Their touch affrights me as a serpent's sting.
Thou baleful messenger, out of my sight!
Upon thy eyeballs murderous tyranny
Sits in grim majesty, to fright the world.
Look not upon me, for thine eyes are wound-
ing:—
Yet do not go away:—come, basilisk,
And kill the innocent gazer with thy sight;
For in the shade of death I shall find joy,—
In life but double death, now Gloster's dead.
QUEEN MARGARET.
Why do you rate my Lord of Suffolk thus?
Although the duke was enemy to him,
Yet he, most Christian-like, laments his death:
And for myself,—foe as he was to me,—
Might liquid tears, or heart-offending groans,
Or blood-consuming sighs recall his life,
I would be blind with weeping, sick with groans,
Look pale as primrose with blood-drinking sighs,
And all to have the noble duke alive.
What know I how the world may deem of me?
For it is known we were but hollow friends:
It may be judged I made the duke away;
So shall my name with slander's tongue be
wounded,
And princes' courts be fill'd with my reproach.
This get I by his death: ay me, unhappy!
To be a queen, and crown'd with infamy!
KING HENRY.
Ah, woe is me for Gloster, wretched man!
QUEEN MARGARET.
Be woe for me, more wretched than he is.
What, dost thou turn away, and hide thy face?
I am no loathsome leper?—look on me.
What, art thou, like the adder, waxen deaf?

Be poisonous too, and kill thy forlorn queen.
Is all thy comfort shut in Gloster's tomb?
Why, then, Dame Margaret was ne'er thy joy:
Erect his statua, and worship it,
And make my image but an alehouse sign.
Was I for this nigh wrackt upon the sea,
And twice by awkward winds from England's
   bank
Drove back again unto my native clime?
What boded this but well-forewarning winds
Did seem to say,—'Seek not a scorpion's nest,
Nor set no footing on this unkind shore'?
What did I then but cursed the gentle gusts,
And he that loosed them forth their brazen caves;
And bid them blow towards England's blessed
   shore,
Or turn our stern upon a dreadful rock?
Yet Æolus would not be a murderer,
But left that hateful office unto thee:
The pretty-vaulting sea refused to drown me;
Knowing that thou wouldst have me drown'd on
   shore,
With tears as salt as sea, through thy unkindness:
The splitting rocks cower'd in the sinking sands,
And would not dash me with their ragged sides;
Because thy flinty heart, more hard than they,
Might in thy palace perish Margaret.
As far as I could ken the chalky cliffs,
When from thy shore the tempest beat us back,
I stood upon the hatches in the storm;
And when the dusky sky began to rob
My earnest-gaping sight of thy land's view,
I took a costly jewel from my neck,—
A heart it was, bound in with diamonds,—   [it;
And threw it towards thy land:—the sea received
And so I wisht thy body might my heart:
And even with this I lost fair England's view,
And bid mine eyes be packing with my heart,
And call'd them blind and dusky spectacles,
For losing ken of Albion's wished coast,
How often have I tempted Suffolk's tongue—
The agent of thy foul inconstancy—
To sit and witch me, as Ascanius did
When he to madding Dido would unfold
His father's acts commenced in burning Troy!
Am I not witcht like her? or thou not false like
   him?
Ay me, I can no more! die, Margaret!
For Henry weeps that thou dost live so long.
   Noise within. Enter WARWICK, SALISBURY,
   and many COMMONS.
          EARL OF WARWICK.
It is reported, mighty sovereign,
That good Duke Humphrey traitorously is mur-
   der'd
By Suffolk and the Cardinal Beaufort's means.
The commons, like an angry hive of bees
That want their leader, scatter up and down,
And care not who they sting in his revenge.
Myself have calm'd their spleenful mutiny,
Until they hear the order of his death.
          KING HENRY.
That he is dead, good Warwick, 'tis too true;
But how he died God knows, not Henry:
Enter his chamber, view his breathless corpse,
And comment then upon his sudden death.

          EARL OF WARWICK.
That shall I do, my liege.— Stay, Salisbury,
With the rude multitude till I return.   [*Exit.*
          KING HENRY.
O Thou that judgest all things, stay my
   thoughts,—
My thoughts, that labour to persuade my soul
Some violent hands were laid on Humphrey's life!
If my suspect be false, forgive me, God;
For judgement only doth belong to Thee.
Fain would I go to chafe his paly lips
With twenty thousand kisses, and to rain
Upon his face an ocean of salt tears,
To tell my love unto his dumb deaf trunk,
And with my fingers feel his hand unfeeling:
But all in vain are these mean obsequies;
And to survey his dead and earthy image
What were it but to make my sorrow greater?
   [WARWICK *draws the curtains and shows*
     DUKE HUMPHREY *in his bed.*
          EARL OF WARWICK.
Come hither, gracious sovereign, view this body.
          KING HENRY.
That is to see how deep my grave is made;
For with his soul fled all my worldly solace,
And seeing him, I see my life in death.
          EARL OF WARWICK.
As surely as my soul intends to live   [Him
With that dread King that took our state upon
To free us from His Father's wrathful curse,
I do believe that violent hands were laid
Upon the life of this thrice-famed duke.
          DUKE OF SUFFOLK.
A dreadful oath, sworn with a solemn tongue!
What instance gives Lord Warwick for his vow?
          EARL OF WARWICK.
See how the blood is settled in his face!
Oft have I seen a timely-parted ghost,
Of ashy semblance, meagre, pale, and bloodless,
Being all descended to the labouring heart;
Who, in the conflict that it holds with death,
Attracts the same for aidance 'gainst the enemy;
Which with the heart there cools, and ne'er re-
   turneth
To blush and beautify the cheek again.
But see, his face is black and full of blood;
His eyeballs further out than when he lived,
Staring full ghastly like a strangled man;
His hair uprear'd, his nostrils stretcht with
   struggling;
His hands abroad display'd, as one that graspt
And tugg'd for life, and was by strength subdued:
Look, on the sheets his hair, you see, is sticking;
His well-proportion'd beard made rough and
   rugged,
Like to the summer's corn by tempest lodged
It cannot be but he was murder'd here;
The least of all these signs were probable.
          DUKE OF SUFFOLK.
Why, Warwick, who should do the duke to
   death?
Myself and Beaufort had him in protection;
And we, I hope, sir, are no murderers.
          EARL OF WARWICK.
But both of you were vow'd Duke Humphreys'
   foes;

And you, forsooth, had the good duke to keep:
'Tis like you would not feast him like a friend;
And 'tis well seen he found an enemy.

QUEEN MARGARET.
Then you, belike, suspect these noblemen
As guilty of Duke Humphrey's timeless death.

EARL OF WARWICK.
Who finds the heifer dead and bleeding fresh,
And sees fast by a butcher with an axe,
But will suspect 'twas he that made the slaughter?
Who finds the partridge in the puttock's nest,
But may imagine how the bird was dead,
Although the kite soar with unbloodied beak?
Even so suspicious is this tragedy.

QUEEN MARGARET.
Are you the butcher, Suffolk?—where's your
knife?
Is Beaufort term'd a kite?—where are his talons?

DUKE OF SUFFOLK.
I wear no knife to slaughter sleeping men;
But here's a vengeful sword, rusted with ease,
That shall be scoured in his rancorous heart
That slanders me with murder's crimson
badge:—
Say, if thou darest, proud Lord of Warwickshire,
That I am faulty in Duke Humphrey's death.

[Exeunt CARDINAL, SOMERSET, and others.

EARL OF WARWICK.
What dares not Warwick, if false Suffolk dare
him?

QUEEN MARGARET.
He dares not calm his contumelious spirit,
Nor cease to be an arrogant controller,
Though Suffolk dare him twenty thousand times.

EARL OF WARWICK.
Madam, be still,—with reverence may I say;
For every word you speak in his behalf
Is slander to your royal dignity.

DUKE OF SUFFOLK.
Blunt-witted lord, ignoble in demeanour!
If ever lady wrong'd her lord so much,
Thy mother took into her blameful bed
Some stern untutor'd churl, and noble stock
Was graft with crab-tree slip; whose fruit thou
art,
And never of the Nevils' noble race.

EARL OF WARWICK.
But that the guilt of murder bucklers thee,
And I should rob the deathsman of his fee,
Quitting thee thereby of ten thousand shames,
And that my sovereign's presence makes me mild,
I would, false murderous coward, on thy knee
Make thee beg pardon for thy passed speech,
And say it was thy mother that thou meant'st,—
That thou thyself wast born in bastardy;
And, after all this fearful homage done,
Give thee thy hire, and send thy soul to hell,
Pernicious blood-sucker of sleeping men!

DUKE OF SUFFOLK.
Thou shalt be waking while I shed thy blood,
If from this presence thou darest go with me.

EARL OF WARWICK.
Away even now, or I will drag thee hence:
Unworthy though thou art, I'll cope with thee,
And do some service to Duke Humphrey's ghost.

[Exeunt SUFFOLK and WARWICK.

KING HENRY.
What stronger breastplate than a heart untainted!
Thrice is he arm'd that hath his quarrel just;
And he but naked, though lockt up in steel,
Whose conscience with injustice is corrupted.

[A noise within.

QUEEN MARGARET.
What noise is this?

Enter SUFFOLK and WARWICK, with their
weapons drawn.

KING HENRY.
Why, how now, lords! your wrathful weapons
drawn
Here in our presence! dare you be so bold?—
Why, what tumultuous clamour have we here?

DUKE OF SUFFOLK.
The traitorous Warwick, with the men of Bury,
Set all upon me, mighty sovereign.

EARL OF SALISBURY [to the COMMONS at
the door].
Sirs, stand apart; the king shall know your
mind.—
Dread lord, the commons send you word by me,
Unless false Suffolk straight be done to death
Or banished fair England's territories,
They will by violence tear him from your palace,
And torture him with grievous lingering death.
They say, by him the good Duke Humphrey
died;
They say, in him they fear your highness' death;
And mere instinct of love and loyalty—
Free from a stubborn opposite intent,
As being thought to contradict your liking—
Makes them thus forward in his banishment.
They say, in care of your most royal person,
That if your highness should intend to sleep,
And charge that no man should disturb your
rest,
In pain of your dislike, or pain of death;
Yet, notwithstanding such a strait edict,
Were there a serpent seen, with forked tongue,
That slily glided towards your majesty,
It were but necessary you were waked;
Lest, being suffer'd in that harmful slumber,
The mortal worm might make the sleep eternal:
And therefore do they cry, though you forbid,
That they will guard you, whe'r you will or no,
From such fell serpents as false Suffolk is;
With whose envenomed and fatal sting,
Your loving uncle, twenty times his worth,
They say, is shamefully bereft of life.

COMMONS [within].
An answer from the king, my Lord of Salisbury!

DUKE OF SUFFOLK.
'Tis like the commons, rude unpolisht hinds,
Could send such message to their sovereign:
But you, my lord, were glad to be employ'd,
To show how quaint an orator you are:
But all the honour Salisbury hath won
Is, that he was the lord ambassador
Sent from a sort of tinkers to the king.

COMMONS [within].
An answer from the king, or we will all break in!

KING HENRY.
Go, Salisbury, and tell them all from me,
I thank them for their tender loving care;

And had I not been cited so by them,
Yet did I purpose as they do entreat;
For, sure, my thoughts do hourly prophesy
Mischance unto my state by Suffolk's means:
And therefore,—by His majesty I swear,
Whose far unworthy deputy I am,—
He shall not breathe infection in this air
But three days longer, on the pain of death.
                    [Exit SALISBURY.
                    QUEEN MARGARET.
O Henry, let me plead for gentle Suffolk!
                    KING HENRY.
Ungentle queen, to call him gentle Suffolk!
No more, I say: if thou dost plead for him,
Thou wilt but add increase unto my wrath.
Had I but said, I would have kept my word;
But when I swear, it is irrevocable.—
If after three days' space thou here be'st found
On any ground that I am ruler of,
The world shall not be ransom for thy life.—
Come, Warwick, come, good Warwick, go with
    me;
I have great matters to impart to thee.
        [Exeunt all except QUEEN and SUFFOLK.
                    QUEEN MARGARET.
Mischance and sorrow go along with you!
Heart's discontent and sour affliction
Be playfellows to keep you company!
There's two of you; the devil make a third!
And threefold vengeance tend upon your steps!
                    EARL OF SUFFOLK.
Cease, gentle queen, these execrations,
And let thy Suffolk take his heavy leave.
                    QUEEN MARGARET.
Fie, coward woman, and soft-hearted wretch!
Hast thou not spirit to curse thine enemies?
                    DUKE OF SUFFOLK.
A plague upon them! wherefore should I curse
    them?
Would curses kill, as doth the mandrake's groan,
I would invent as bitter-searching terms,
As curst, as harsh, and horrible to hear,
Deliver'd strongly through my fixed teeth,
With full as many signs of deadly hate,
As lean-faced Envy in her loathsome cave:
My tongue should stumble in mine earnest
    words;
Mine eyes should sparkle like the beaten flint;
Mine hair be fixt on end, as one distract;
Ay, every joint should seem to curse and ban:
And even now my burden'd heart would break,
Should I not curse them. Poison be their drink!
Gall, worse than gall, the dainties that they
    taste!
Their sweetest shade a grove of cypress-trees!
Their chiefest prospect murdering basilisks!
Their softest touch as smart as lizards' stings!
Their music frightful as the serpent's hiss,
And boding screech-owls make the consort full!
All the foul terrors in dark-seated hell—
                    QUEEN MARGARET
Enough, sweet Suffolk; thou torment'st thyself;
And these dread curses—like the sun 'gainst
    glass,
Or like an overcharged gun—recoil,
And turn the force of them upon thyself.

                    EARL OF SUFFOLK.
You bade me ban, and will you bid me leave?
Now, by the ground that I am banisht from,
Well could I curse away a winter's night,
Though standing naked on a mountain-top,
Where biting cold would never let grass grow,
And think it but a minute spent in sport.
                    QUEEN MARGARET.
O, let me entreat thee, cease! Give me thy hand,
That I may dew it with my mournful tears;
Nor let the rain of heaven wet this place,
To wash away my woful monuments.
O, could this kiss be printed in thy hand,
                    [Kisses his hand.
That thou mightst think upon these by the seal,
Through whom a thousand sighs are breath'd for
    thee!
So, get thee gone, that I may know my grief;
'Tis but surmised whiles thou art standing by,
As one that surfeits thinking on a want.
I will repeal thee, or, be well assured,
Adventure to be banished myself:
And banished I am, if but from thee.
Go; speak not to me; even now be gone.—
O, go not yet!—Even thus two friends condemn'd
Embrace, and kiss, and take ten thousand leaves,
Lother a hundred times to part than die.
Yet now farewell; and farewell life with thee!
                    DUKE OF SUFFOLK.
Thus is poor Suffolk ten times banished,—
Once by the king, and three times thrice by thee.
'Tis not the land I care for, wert thou thence;
A wilderness is populous enough,
So Suffolk had thy heavenly company:
For where thou art, there is the world itself,
With every several pleasure in the world;
And where thou art not, desolation.
I can no more:—live thou to joy thy life;
Myself no joy in naught but that thou livest.
                    Enter VAUX.
                    QUEEN MARGARET.
Whither goes Vaux so fast? what news, I prithee?
                    VAUX.
To signify unto his majesty
That Cardinal Beaufort is at point of death;
For suddenly a grievous sickness took him,
That makes him gasp, and stare, and catch the
    air,
Blaspheming God, and cursing men on earth.
Sometime he talks as if Duke Humphrey's
    ghost
Were by his side; sometimes he calls the king,
And whispers to his pillow, as to him,
The secrets of his overcharged soul:
And I am sent to tell his majesty
That even now he cries aloud for him.
                    QUEEN MARGARET.
Go tell this heavy message to the king.
                    [Exit VAUX.
Ay me! what is this world! what news are these!
But wherefore grieve I at an hour's poor loss,
Omitting Suffolk's exile, my soul's treasure?
Why only, Suffolk, mourn I not for thee,
And with the southern clouds contend in tears,—
Theirs for the earth's increase, mine for my
    sorrows?

Now get thee hence: the king, thou know'st, is
  coming;—
If thou be found by me, thou art but dead.

DUKE OF SUFFOLK.

If I depart from thee, I cannot live;
And in thy sight to die, what were it else
But like a pleasant slumber in thy lap?
Here could I breathe my soul into the air,
As mild and gentle as the cradle-babe
Dying with mother's dug between its lips:
Where, from thy sight, I should be raging mad,
And cry out for thee to close up mine eyes,
To have thee with thy lips to stop my mouth;
So shouldst thou either turn my flying soul,
Or I should breathe it so into thy body,
And then it lived in sweet Elysium.
To die by thee were but to die in jest;
From thee to die were torture more than death:
O, let me stay, befall what may befall!

QUEEN MARGARET.

Away! though parting be a fretful corrosive,
It is applied to a deathful wound.
To France, sweet Suffolk: let me hear from thee;
For wheresoe'er thou art in this world's globe,
I'll have an Iris that shall find thee out.

DUKE OF SUFFOLK.

I go.

QUEEN MARGARET.

      And take my heart with thee.

DUKE OF SUFFOLK.

A jewel, lockt into the woful'st cask
That ever did contain a thing of worth.
Even as a splitted bark, so sunder we:
This way fall I to death.

QUEEN MARGARET.

      This way for me.

              [*Exeunt severally.*

SCENE III.

The CARDINAL'S *bedchamber.*

Enter the KING, SALISBURY, *and* WARWICK *to
the* CARDINAL *in bed.*

KING HENRY.

HOW fares my lord? speak, Beaufort, to thy
   sovereign.

CARDINAL BEAUFORT.

If thou be'st Death, I'll give thee England's
  treasure,
Enough to purchase such another island,
So thou wilt let me live, and feel no pain.

KING HENRY.

Ah, what a sign it is of evil life,
Where death's approach is seen so terrible!

EARL OF WARWICK.

Beaufort, it is thy sovereign speaks to thee.

CARDINAL BEAUFORT.

Bring me unto my trial when you will.
Died he not in his bed? where should he die?
Can I make men live, whe'r they will or no?
O, torture me no more! I will confess.—
Alive again? then show me where he is:
I'll give a thousand pound to look upon him.—
He hath no eyes, the dust hath blinded them.—
Comb down his hair; look, look! it stands upright,
Like lime-twigs set to catch my winged soul!—

Give me some drink; and bid the apothecary
Bring the strong poison that I bought of him.

KING HENRY.

O Thou eternal Mover of the heavens,
Look with a gentle eye upon this wretch!
O, beat away the busy-meddling fiend
That lays strong siege unto this wretch's soul,
And from his bosom purge this black despair!

EARL OF WARWICK.

See how the pangs of death do make him grin!

EARL OF SALISBURY.

Disturb him not, let him pass peaceably.

KING HENRY.

Peace to his soul, if God's good pleasure be!—
Lord cardinal, if thou think'st on heaven's bliss,
Hold up thy hand, make signal of thy hope.—
He dies, and makes no sign:—O God, forgive
  him!

EARL OF WARWICK.

So bad a death argues a monstrous life.

KING HENRY.

Forbear to judge, for we are sinners all.—
Close up his eyes, and draw the curtain close;
And let us all to meditation.   [*Exeunt*

ACT IV. SCENE I.

The coast of Kent.

*Alarum. Fight at sea. Ordnance goes off. Ent
a* CAPTAIN, *a* MASTER, *a* MASTER'S-MAT
WALTER WHITMORE, *and others; with the*
SUFFOLK *and others, prisoners.*

CAPTAIN.

THE gaudy, blabbing, and remorseful day
  Is crept into the bosom of the sea;
And now loud-howling wolves arouse the jades
That drag the tragic melancholy night;
Who, with their drowsy, slow, and flagging wing
Clip dead men's graves, and from their misty jav
Breathe foul contagious darkness in the air.
Therefore bring forth the soldiers of our prize;
For, whilst our pinnace anchors in the Downs,
Here shall they make their ransom on the sand,
Or with their blood stain this discolour'd shore.
Master, this prisoner freely give I thee;—
And thou that art his mate, make boot of this;—
The other [*pointing to* SUFFOLK], Walter Whit-
  more, is thy share.

FIRST GENTLEMAN.

What is my ransom, master? let me know.

MASTER.

A thousand crowns, or else lay down your head.

MASTER'S-MATE.

And so much shall you give, or off goes yours.

CAPTAIN.

What, think you much to pay two thousand
  crowns,
And bear the name and port of gentlemen?—
Cut both the villains' throats;—for die you
  shall:—
The lives of those which we have lost in fight
Be counterpoised with such a petty sum!

FIRST GENTLEMAN.

I'll give it, sir; and therefore spare my life.

SECOND GENTLEMAN.

And so will I, and write home for it straight.

WALTER WHITMORE.
I lost mine eye in laying the prize aboard,
[to SUFFOLK] And therefore, to revenge it, shalt
    thou die;
And so should these, if I might have my will.
CAPTAIN.
Be not so rash; take ransom, let him live.
DUKE OF SUFFOLK.
Look on my George,—I am a gentleman:
Rate me at what thou wilt, thou shalt be paid.
WALTER WHITMORE.
And so am I; my name is Walter Whitmore.
How now! why start'st thou? what, doth death
    affright?
DUKE OF SUFFOLK.
Thy name affrights me, in whose sound is death.
A cunning man did calculate my birth,
And told me that by *water* I should die:
Yet let this not make thee be bloody-minded;
Thy name is *Gualtier*, being rightly sounded.
WALTER WHITMORE.
Gualtier or *Walter*, which it is, I care not:
Never yet did base dishonour blur our name,
But with our sword we wiped away the blot;
Therefore, when merchant-like I sell revenge,
Broke be my sword, my arms torn and defaced,
And I proclaim'd a coward through the world!
                    [*Lays hold on* SUFFOLK.
DUKE OF SUFFOLK.
Stay, Whitmore; for thy prisoner is a prince,
The Duke of Suffolk, William de la Pole.
WALTER WHITMORE.
The Duke of Suffolk muffled up in rags!
DUKE OF SUFFOLK.
Ay, but these rags are no part of the duke:
Jove sometime went disguised, and why not I?
CAPTAIN.
But Jove was never slain, as thou shalt be.
DUKE OF SUFFOLK.
Obscure and lowly swain, King Henry's blood,
The honourable blood of Lancaster,
Must not be shed by such a jaded groom.
Hast thou not kist thy hand, and held my stirrup?
Bare-headed plodded by my foot-cloth mule,
And thought thee happy when I shook my head?
How often hast thou waited at my cup,
Fed from my trencher, kneel'd down at the
    board,
When I have feasted with Queen Margaret?
Remember it, and let it make thee crest-faln,
Ay, and allay this thy abortive pride:
How in our voiding-lobby hast thou stood,
And duly waited for my coming forth?
This hand of mine hath writ in thy behalf,
And therefore shall it charm thy riotous tongue.
WALTER WHITMORE.
Speak, captain, shall I stab the forlorn swain?
CAPTAIN.
First let my words stab him, as he hath me.
DUKE OF SUFFOLK.
Base slave, thy words are blunt, and so art thou.
CAPTAIN.
Convey him hence, and on our long-boat's side
Strike off his head.
DUKE OF SUFFOLK.
        Thou darest not, for thy own.

CAPTAIN.
Yes, Pole.
DUKE OF SUFFOLK.
Pole!
CAPTAIN.
Pole! Sir Pole! lord!
Ay, kennel, puddle, sink; whose filth and dirt
Troubles the silver spring where England drinks
Now will I dam up this thy yawning mouth
For swallowing the treasure of the realm:
Thy lips, that kist the queen, shall sweep the
    ground;
And thou, that smiledst at good Duke Hum-
    phrey's death,
Against the senseless winds shalt grin in vain,
Who, in contempt, shall hiss at thee again:
And wedded be thou to the hags of hell,
For daring to affy a mighty lord
Unto the daughter of a worthless king,
Having neither subject, wealth, nor diadem.
By devilish policy art thou grown great,
And, like ambitious Sylla, overgorged
With gobbets of thy mother's bleeding heart.
By thee Anjou and Maine were sold to France;
The false revolting Normans thorough thee
Disdain to call us lord; and Picardy
Hath slain their governors, surprised our forts,
And sent the ragged soldiers wounded home.
The princely Warwick, and the Nevils all,—
Whose dreadful swords were never drawn in
    vain,—
As hating thee, are rising up in arms: [crown
And now the house of York—thrust from the
By shameful murder of a guiltless king
And lofty proud-encroaching tyranny—
Burns with revenging fire; whose hopeful colours
Advance our half-faced sun, striving to shine,
Under the which is writ *Invitis nubibus.*
The commons here in Kent are up in arms:
And, to conclude, reproach and beggary
Is crept into the palace of our king,
And all by thee.—Away! convey him hence.
DUKE OF SUFFOLK.
O, that I were a god, to shoot forth thunder
Upon these paltry, servile, abject drudges!
Small things make base men proud: this villain
    here,
Being captain of a pinnace, threatens more
Than Bargulus, the strong Illyrian pirate.
Drones suck not eagles' blood, but rob bee-hives:
It is impossible that I should die
By such a lowly vassal as thyself.
Thy words move rage and not remorse in me:
I go of message from the queen to France;
I charge thee waft me safely cross the Channel.
CAPTAIN.
Walter,—
WALTER WHITMORE.
Come, Suffolk, I must waft thee to thy death.
DUKE OF SUFFOLK.
Gelidus timor occupat artus:—it is thee I fear.
WALTER WHITMORE.
Thou shalt have cause to fear before I leave thee.
What, are ye daunted now? now will ye stoop?
FIRST GENTLEMAN.
My gracious lord, entreat him, speak him fair.

DUKE OF SUFFOLK.
Suffolk's imperial tongue is stern and rough,
Used to command, untaught to plead for
   favour.
Far be it we should honour such as these
With humble suit: no, rather let my head
Stoop to the block than these knees bow to
   any,
Save to the God of heaven and to my king;
And sooner dance upon a bloody pole
Than stand uncover'd to the vulgar groom.
True nobility is exempt from fear:—
More can I bear than you dare execute.

CAPTAIN.
Hale him away, and let him talk no more.

DUKE OF SUFFOLK.
Come, soldiers, show what cruelty ye can,
That this my death may never be forgot!—
Great men oft die by vile besonians:
A Roman sworder and banditto slave
Murder'd sweet Tully; Brutus' bastard hand
Stabb'd Julius Cæsar; savage islanders
Pompey the Great; and Suffolk dies by pirates.

[Exeunt WHITMORE and others with SUF-
   FOLK.

CAPTAIN.
And as for these whose ransom we have set,
It is our pleasure one of them depart:—
Therefore come you with us, and let him go.

[Exeunt all except the FIRST GENTLEMAN.
Enter WHITMORE with SUFFOLK'S body.

WALTER WHITMORE.
There let his head and lifeless body lie,
Until the queen his mistress bury it.   [Exit.

FIRST GENTLEMAN.
O barbarous and bloody spectacle!
His body will I bear unto the king:
If he revenge it not, yet will his friends;
So will the queen, that living held him dear.

[Exit with the body.

SCENE II.

Blackheath.

Enter GEORGE BEVIS and JOHN HOLLAND.

GEORGE BEVIS.
COME, and get thee a sword, though made
of a lath: they have been up these two days.

JOHN HOLLAND.
They have the more need to sleep now, then.

GEORGE BEVIS.
I tell thee, Jack Cade the clothier means to dress
the commonwealth, and turn it, and set a new nap
upon it.

JOHN HOLLAND.
So he had need, for 'tis threadbare. Well, I say it
was never merry world in England since gentlemen came up.

GEORGE BEVIS.
O miserable age! virtue is not regarded in handi-
crafts-men.

JOHN HOLLAND.
The nobility think scorn to go in leather aprons.

GEORGE BEVIS.
Nay, more, the king's council are no good workmen.

JOHN HOLLAND.
True; and yet it is said,—labour in thy vocation;
which is as much to say as,—let the magistrates
be labouring men; and therefore should we be
magistrates.

GEORGE BEVIS.
Thou hast hit it; for there's no better sign of a
brave mind than a hard hand.

JOHN HOLLAND.
I see them! I see them! There's Best's son, the
tanner of Wingham,—

GEORGE BEVIS.
He shall have the skins of our enemies, to make
dog's-leather of.

JOHN HOLLAND.
And Dick the butcher,—

GEORGE BEVIS.
Then is sin struck down like an ox, and iniquity's
throat cut like a calf.

JOHN HOLLAND.
And Smith the weaver,—

GEORGE BEVIS.
Argo, their thread of life is spun.

JOHN HOLLAND.
Come, come, let's fall in with them.
Drum. Enter CADE, DICK Butcher, SMITH the
   Weaver, and a SAWYER, with infinite numbers.

JACK CADE.
We John Cade, so term'd of our supposed
father,—

DICK [aside].
Or rather, of stealing a cade of herrings.

JACK CADE.
For our enemies shall fall before us,—inspired
with the spirit of putting down kings and princes,
—Command silence.

DICK.
Silence!

JACK CADE.
My father was a Mortimer,—

DICK [aside].
He was an honest man, and a good bricklayer.

JACK CADE.
My mother a Plantagenet,—

DICK [aside].
I knew her well; she was a midwife.

JACK CADE.
My wife descended of the Lacies,—

DICK [aside].
She was, indeed, a pedler's daughter, and sold
many laces.

SMITH [aside].
But now of late, not able to travel with her furr'd
pack, she washes bucks here at home.

JACK CADE.
Therefore am I of an honourable house.

DICK [aside].
Ay, by my faith, the field is honourable; and there
was he born, under a hedge,—for his father had
never a house but the cage.

JACK CADE.
Valiant I am.

SMITH [aside].
'A must needs; for beggary is valiant.

JACK CADE.
I am able to endure much.

DICK [*aside*].

No question of that; for I have **seen** him whipt three market-days together.

JACK CADE.

I fear neither sword nor fire.

SMITH [*aside*].

He need not fear the sword; for his coat is of proof.

DICK [*aside*].

But methinks he should stand in fear of fire, being burnt i' th' hand for stealing of sheep.

JACK CADE.

Be brave, then; for your captain is brave, and vows reformation. There shall be in England seven half-penny loaves sold for a penny: the three-hoop'd pot shall have ten hoops; and I will make it felony to drink small beer: all the realm shall be in common; and in Cheapside shall my palfrey go to grass: and when I am king,—as king I will be,—

ALL.

God save your majesty!

JACK CADE.

I thank you, good people:—there shall be no money; all shall eat and drink on my score; and I will apparel them all in one livery, that they may agree like brothers, and worship me their lord.

DICK.

The first thing we do, let's kill all the lawyers.

JACK CADE.

Nay, that I mean to do. Is not this a lamentable thing, that of the skin of an innocent lamb should be made parchment? that parchment, being scribbled o'er, should undo a man? Some say the bee stings: but I say, 'tis the bee's wax; for I did but seal once to a thing, and I was never mine own man since.—How now! who's there?

Enter some, bringing in the CLERK OF CHATHAM.

SMITH.

The clerk of Chatham: he can write and read and cast accompt.

JACK CADE.

O monstrous!

SMITH.

We took him setting of boys' copies.

JACK CADE.

Here's a villain!

SMITH.

Has a book in his pocket with red letters in't.

JACK CADE.

Nay, then, he is a conjurer.

DICK.

Nay, he can make obligations, and write court-hand.

JACK CADE.

I am sorry for't: the man is a proper man, of mine honour; unless I find him guilty, he shall not die.—Come hither, sirrah, I must examine thee: what thy name?

CLERK OF CHATHAM.

Emmanuel.

DICK.

They use to write it on the top of letters:—'twill go hard with you.

JACK CADE.

Let me alone.—Dost thou use to write thy name?

or hast thou a mark to thyself, like an honest plain-dealing man?

CLERK OF CHATHAM.

Sir, I thank God, I have been so well brought up that I can write my name.

ALL.

He hath confest: away with him! he's a villain and a traitor.

JACK CADE.

Away with him, I say! hang him with his pen and inkhorn about his neck.

[*Exit one with the* CLERK.

Enter MICHAEL.

MICHAEL.

Where's our general?

JACK CADE.

Here I am, thou particular fellow.

MICHAEL.

Fly, fly, fly! Sir Humphrey Stafford and his brother are hard by, with the king's forces.

JACK CADE.

Stand, villain, stand, or I'll fell thee down. He shall be encounter'd with a man as good as himself: he is but a knight, is 'a?

MICHAEL.

No.

JACK CADE.

To equal him, I will make myself a knight presently. [*Kneels.*] Rise up Sir John Mortimer. [*Rises.*] Now have at him!

Enter SIR HUMPHREY STAFFORD *and his* BROTHER, *with drum and* SOLDIERS.

SIR HUMPHREY STAFFORD.

Rebellious hinds, the filth and scum of Kent, Markt for the gallows, lay your weapons down; Home to your cottages, forsake this groom:— The king is merciful, if you revolt.

BROTHER.

But angry, wrathful, and inclined to blood, If you go forward; therefore yield, or die.

JACK CADE.

As for these silken-coated slaves, I pass not: It is to you, good people, that I speak, Over whom, in time to come, I hope to reign; For I am rightful heir unto the crown.

SIR HUMPHREY STAFFORD.

Villain, thy father was a plasterer; And thou thyself a shearman,—art thou not?

JACK CADE.

And Adam was a gardener.

BROTHER.

And what of that?

JACK CADE.

Marry, thus:—Edmund Mortimer, Earl of March, Married the Duke of Clarence' daughter,—did he not?

SIR HUMPHREY STAFFORD.

Ay, sir.

JACK CADE.

By her he had two children at one birth.

BROTHER.

That's false.

JACK CADE.

Ay, there's the question; but I say 'tis true: The elder of them, being put to nurse,

Was by a beggar-woman stoln away;
And, ignorant of his birth and parentage,
Became a bricklayer when he came to age:
His son am I; deny it, if you can.

DICK.
Nay, 'tis too true; therefore he shall be king.

SMITH.
Sir, he made a chimney in my father's house, and
the bricks are alive at this day to testify it; therefore deny it not.

SIR HUMPHREY STAFFORD.
And will you credit this base drudge's words,
That speaks he knows not what?

ALL.
Ay, marry, will we; therefore get ye gone.

BROTHER.
Jack Cade, the Duke of York hath taught you this.

JACK CADE [aside].
He lies, for I invented it myself.
Go to, sirrah, tell the king from me, that, for his
father's sake, Henry the Fifth, in whose time boys
went to span-counter for French crowns, I am
content he shall reign; but I'll be Protector over
him.

DICK.
And furthermore, we'll have the Lord Say's head
for selling the dukedom of Maine.

JACK CADE.
And good reason; for thereby is England main'd,
and fain to go with a staff, but that my puissance
holds it up. Fellow kings, I tell you that that Lord
Say hath gelded the commonwealth, and made it
an eunuch: and more than that, he can speak
French; and therefore he is a traitor.

SIR HUMPHREY STAFFORD.
O gross and miserable ignorance!

JACK CADE.
Nay, answer, if you can:—the Frenchmen are our
enemies; go to, then, I ask but this,—can he that
speaks with the tongue of an enemy be a good
counsellor, or no?

ALL.
No, no; and therefore we'll have his head.

BROTHER.
Well, seeing gentle words will not prevail,
Assail them with the army of the king.

SIR HUMPHREY STAFFORD.
Herald, away; and throughout every town
Proclaim them traitors that are up with Cade;
That those which fly before the battle ends
May, even in their wives' and children's sight,
Be hang'd up for example at their doors:—
And you that be the king's friends, follow me.
[Exeunt the two STAFFORDS and SOLDIERS.

JACK CADE.
And you that love the commons, follow me.
Now show yourselves men; 'tis for liberty.
We will not leave one lord, one gentleman:
Spare none but such as go in clouted shoon;
For they are thrifty honest men, and such
As would—but that they dare not—take our parts.

DICK.
They are all in order, and march toward us.

JACK CADE.
But then are we in order when we are most out of
order. Come, march forward!   [Exeunt.

SCENE III.
Another part of Blackheath.

*Alarums to the fight, wherein both the STAFFORDS
are slain. Enter CADE and the rest.*

JACK CADE.
WHERE'S Dick, the butcher of Ashford?

DICK.
Here, sir.

JACK CADE.
They fell before thee like sheep and oxen, and
thou behavedst thyself as if thou hadst been in
thine own slaughter-house: therefore thus will I
reward thee,—the Lent shall be as long again as
it is; and thou shalt have a licence to kill for a
hundred lacking one a week.

DICK.
I desire no more.

JACK CADE.
And, to speak truth, thou deservest no less. This
monument of the victory will I bear [*putting on
SIR HUMPHREY's brigandine*]; and the bodies
shall be dragg'd at my horse heels till I do come
to London, where we will have the mayor's sword
borne before us.

DICK.
If we mean to thrive and do good, break open the
gaols, and let out the prisoners.

JACK CADE.
Fear not that, I warrant thee.—Come, let's
march towards London.   [*Exeunt.*

SCENE IV.
London.   The palace.

*Enter the KING with a supplication, and the
QUEEN with SUFFOLK's head; the DUKE OF
BUCKINGHAM and the LORD SAY.*

QUEEN MARGARET.
OFT have I heard that grief softens the mind,
And makes it fearful and degenerate;
Think therefore on revenge, and cease to weep.
But who can cease to weep, and look on this?
Here may his head lie on my throbbing breast:
But where's the body that I should embrace?

DUKE OF BUCKINGHAM.
What answer makes your Grace to the rebels'
supplication?

KING HENRY.
I'll send some holy bishop to entreat;
For God forbid so many simple souls
Should perish by the sword! And I myself,
Rather than bloody war shall cut them short,
Will parley with Jack Cade their general:—
But stay, I'll read it over once again.

QUEEN MARGARET.
Ah, barbarous villains! hath this lovely face
Ruled, like a wandering planet, over me,
And could it not enforce them to relent,
That were unworthy to behold the same?

KING HENRY.
Lord Say, Jack Cade hath sworn to have thy head.

LORD SAY.
Ay, but I hope your highness shall have his.

KING HENRY.
How now, madam!

Still lamenting, and mourning for Suffolk's death?
I fear me, love, if that I had been dead,
Thou wouldest not have mourn'd so much for me.
            QUEEN MARGARET.
No, my love, I should not mourn, but die for
   thee.

Enter a MESSENGER.
            KING HENRY.
How now! what news? why comest thou in such
   haste?

            MESSENGER.
The rebels are in Southwark; fly, my lord!
Jack Cade proclaims himself Lord Mortimer,
Descended from the Duke of Clarence' house;
And calls your Grace usurper openly,
And vows to crown himself in Westminster.
His army is a ragged multitude
Of hinds and peasants, rude and merciless:
Sir Humphrey Stafford and his brother's death
Hath given them heart and courage to proceed:
All scholars, lawyers, courtiers, gentlemen,
They call false caterpillars, and intend their death.
            KING HENRY.
O graceless men! they know not what they do.
            DUKE OF BUCKINGHAM.
My gracious lord, retire to Killingworth,
Until a power be raised to put them down.
            QUEEN MARGARET.
Ah, were the Duke of Suffolk now alive,
These Kentish rebels would be soon appeased!
            KING HENRY.
Lord Say, the traitor hateth thee;
Therefore away with us to Killingworth.
            LORD SAY.
So might your Grace's person be in danger;
The sight of me is odious in their eyes:
And therefore in this city will I stay,
And live alone as secret as I may.

Enter a second MESSENGER.
            SECOND MESSENGER.
Jack Cade hath gotten London-bridge;
The citizens fly and forsake their houses:
The rascal people, thirsting after prey,
Join with the traitor; and they jointly swear
To spoil the city and your royal court.
            DUKE OF BUCKINGHAM.
Then linger not, my lord; away, take horse.
            KING HENRY.
Come, Margaret; God, our hope, will succour us.
            QUEEN MARGARET.
My hope is gone, now Suffolk is deceased.
         KING HENRY [*to* LORD SAY].
Farewell, my lord: trust not the Kentish rebels.
            DUKE OF BUCKINGHAM.
Trust nobody, for fear you be betray'd.
            LORD SAY.
The trust I have is in mine innocence,
And therefore am I bold and resolute.   [*Exeunt.*

SCENE V.

The same. The Tower.

Enter LORD SCALES *upon the Tower, walking.
Then enter two or three* CITIZENS *below.*
            LORD SCALES.
How now! is Jack Cade slain?

            FIRST CITIZEN.
No, my lord, nor likely to be slain; for they have
won the bridge, killing all those that withstand
them: the lord mayor craves aid of your honour
from the Tower, to defend the city from the
rebels.
            LORD SCALES.
Such aid as I can spare, you shall command;
But I am troubled here with them myself,—
The rebels have assay'd to win the Tower.
But get you to Smithfield, and gather head,
And thither I will send you Matthew Gough:
Fight for your king, your country, and your lives;
And so, farewell, for I must hence again. [*Exeunt.*

SCENE VI.

The same. Cannon-street.

Enter JACK CADE *and the rest, and strikes his staff
on London-stone.*
            JACK CADE.
NOW is Mortimer lord of this city. And here,
sitting upon London-stone, I charge and
command, that, of the city's cost, the pissing-
conduit run nothing but claret wine this first
year of our reign. And now henceforward it shall
be treason for any that calls me other than Lord
Mortimer.

Enter a SOLDIER, *running.*
            SOLDIER.
Jack Cade! Jack Cade!
            JACK CADE.
Knock him down there.   [*They kill him.*
            SMITH.
If this fellow be wise, he'll never call ye Jack
Cade more: I think he hath a very fair warning.
            DICK.
My lord, there's an army gather'd together in
Smithfield.
            JACK CADE.
Come, then, let's go fight with them: but first,
go and set London-bridge on fire; and, if you can,
burn down the Tower too. Come, let's away.
                       [*Exeunt.*

SCENE VII.

The same. Smithfield.

Alarums. MATTHEW GOUGH *is slain, and all the
rest. Then enter* JACK CADE, *with his company.*
            JACK CADE.
SO, sirs:—now go some and pull down the
Savoy; others to the inns of court; down
with them all.
            DICK.
I have a suit unto your lordship.
            JACK CADE.
Be it a lordship, thou shalt have it for that word.
            DICK.
Only, that the laws of England may come out of
your mouth.
         JOHN HOLLAND [*aside*].
Mass, 'twill be sore law, then; for he was thrust
in the mouth with a spear, and 'tis not whole yet.
          SMITH [*aside*].
Nay, John, it will be stinking law; for his breath
stinks with eating toasted cheese.

JACK CADE.

I have thought upon it, it shall be so. Away, burn all the records of the realm: my mouth shall be the parliament of England.

JOHN HOLLAND [*aside*].

Then we are like to have biting statutes, unless his teeth be pull'd out.

JACK CADE.

And henceforward all things shall be in common.

Enter a MESSENGER.

MESSENGER.

My lord, a prize, a prize! here's the Lord Say, which sold the towns in France; he that made us pay one-and-twenty fifteens, and one shilling to the pound, the last subsidy.

Enter GEORGE BEVIS, *with the* LORD SAY.

JACK CADE.

Well, he shall be beheaded for it ten times.—Ah, thou say, thou serge, nay, thou buckram lord! now art thou within point-blank of our jurisdiction regal. What canst thou answer to my majesty for giving up of Normandy unto Monsieur Basimecu, the dauphin of France? Be it known unto thee by these presence, even the presence of Lord Mortimer, that I am the besom that must sweep the court clean of such filth as thou art. Thou hast most traitorously corrupted the youth of the realm in erecting a grammar-school: and whereas, before, our forefathers had no other books but the score and the tally, thou hast caused printing to be used; and, contrary to the king, his crown, and dignity, thou hast built a paper-mill. It will be proved to thy face that thou hast men about thee that usually talk of a noun and a verb, and such abhominable words as no Christian ear can endure to hear. Thou hast appointed justices of peace, to call poor men before them about matters they were not able to answer. Moreover, thou hast put them in prison; and because they could not read, thou hast hang'd them; when, indeed, only for that cause they have been most worthy to live. Thou dost ride in a foot-cloth, dost thou not?

LORD SAY.

What of that?

JACK CADE.

Marry, thou ought'st not to let thy horse wear a cloak, when honester men than thou go in their hose and doublets.

DICK.

And work in their shirt too; as myself, for example, that am a butcher.

LORD SAY.

You men of Kent,—

DICK.

What say you of Kent?

LORD SAY.

Nothing but this,—'tis *bona terra, mala gens.*

JACK CADE.

Away with him, away with him! he speaks Latin.

LORD SAY.

Hear me but speak, and bear me where you will. Kent, in the Commentaries Cæsar writ, Is term'd the civill'st place of all this isle: Sweet is the country, beauteous, full of riches; The people liberal, valiant, active, wealthy;

Which makes me hope you are not void of pity. I sold not Maine, I lost not Normandy; Yet, to recover them, would lose my life. Justice with favour have I always done; Prayers and tears have moved me, gifts could never. When have I aught exacted at your hands, But to maintain the king, the realm, and you? Large gifts have I bestow'd on learned clerks, Because my book preferr'd me to the king: And, seeing ignorance is the curse of God, Knowledge the wing wherewith we fly to heaven, Unless you be possest with devilish spirits, You cannot but forbear to murder me: This tongue hath parley'd unto foreign kings For your behoof,—

JACK CADE.

Tut, when struck'st thou one blow in the field?

LORD SAY.

Great men have reaching hands: oft have I struck Those that I never saw, and struck them dead.

GEORGE BEVIS.

O monstrous coward! what, to come behind folks?

LORD SAY.

These cheeks are pale for watching for your good.

JACK CADE.

Give him a box o' th' ear, and that will make 'em red again.

LORD SAY.

Long sitting to determine poor men's causes Hath made me full of sickness and diseases.

JACK CADE.

Ye shall have a hempen caudle, then, and the help of hatchet.

DICK.

Why dost thou quiver, man?

LORD SAY.

It is the palsy, and not fear, provokes me.

JACK CADE.

Nay, he nods at us, as who should say, I'll be even with you: I'll see if his head will stand steadier on a pole, or no. Take him away, and behead him.

LORD SAY.

Tell me wherein have I offended most? Have I affected wealth or honour? speak. Are my chests fill'd up with extorted gold? Is my apparel sumptuous to behold? Whom have I injured, that ye seek my death? These hands are free from guiltless blood-shed-
ding. This breast from harbouring foul deceitful
thoughts. O, let me live!

JACK CADE [*aside*].

I feel remorse in myself with his words; but I'l bridle it: he shall die, an it be but for pleading so well for his life.—Away with him! he ha a familiar under his tongue; he speaks not o God's name. Go, take him away, I say, and strik off his head presently; and then break into hi son-in-law's house, Sir James Cromer, and strik off his head, and bring them both upon two pole hither.

ALL.

It shall be done.

LORD SAY.

Ah, countrymen! if when you make your prayers,
God should be so obdurate as yourselves,
How would it fare with your departed souls?
And therefore yet relent, and save my life.

JACK CADE.

Away with him! and do as I command ye.

[Exeunt some with LORD SAY.

The proudest peer in the realm shall not wear a
head on his shoulders, unless he pay me tribute;
there shall not a maid be married, but she shall
pay to me her maidenhead ere they have it: men
shall hold of me in capite; and we charge and
command that their wives be as free as heart can
wish or tongue can tell.

DICK.

My lord, when shall we go to Cheapside, and
take up commodities upon our bills?

JACK CADE.

Marry, presently.

ALL.

O, brave!

Enter one with the heads.

JACK CADE.

But is not this braver?—Let them kiss one another, for they loved well when they were alive.
Now part them again, lest they consult about
the giving-up of some more towns in France.
Soldiers, defer the spoil of the city until night:
for with these borne before us, instead of maces,
will we ride through the streets; and at every
corner have them kiss.—Away!   [Exeunt.

SCENE VIII.

Southwark.

Alarum and retreat. Enter again CADE and all his
rabblement.

JACK CADE.

UP Fish-street! down Saint Magnus'-corner!
kill and knock down! throw them into
Thames!—[Sound a parley.] What noise is this I
hear? Dare any be so bold to sound retreat or
parley, when I command them kill?

Enter BUCKINGHAM and OLD CLIFFORD.

DUKE OF BUCKINGHAM.

Ay, here they be that dare and will disturb thee:
Know, Cade, we come ambassadors from the king
Unto the commons whom thou hast misled;
And here pronounce free pardon to them all
That will forsake thee and go home in peace.

OLD CLIFFORD.

What say ye, countrymen? will ye relent,
And yield to mercy whilst 'tis offer'd you;
Or let a rebel lead you to your deaths?
Who loves the king, and will embrace his pardon,
Fling up his cap, and say, 'God save his majesty!'
Who hateth him, and honours not his father,
Henry the Fifth, that made all France to quake,
Shake he his weapon at us, and pass by.

ALL.

God save the king! God save the king!

JACK CADE.

What, Buckingham and Clifford, are ye so
brave?—And you, base peasants, do ye believe
him? will you needs be hang'd with your pardons

about your necks? Hath my sword therefore broke
through London gates, that you should leave me
at the White Hart in Southwark? I thought ye
would never have given out these arms till you
had recover'd your ancient freedom: but you are
all recreants and dastards, and delight to live in
slavery to the nobility. Let them break your backs
with burdens, take your houses over your heads,
ravish your wives and daughters before your
faces: for me, I will make shift for one; and so,
God's curse light upon you all!

ALL.

We'll follow Cade! we'll follow Cade!

OLD CLIFFORD.

Is Cade the son of Henry the Fifth,
That thus you do exclaim you'll go with him?
Will he conduct you through the heart of France,
And make the meanest of you earls and dukes?
Alas, he hath no home, no place to fly to;
Nor knows he how to live but by the spoil,
Unless by robbing of your friends and us.
Were't not a shame, that whilst you live at jar,
The fearful French, whom you late vanquished,
Should make a start o'er seas, and vanquish you?
Methinks already in this civil broil
I see them lording it in London streets,
Crying 'Viliago!' unto all they meet.
Better ten thousand base-born Cades miscarry
Than you should stoop unto a Frenchman's
   mercy.
To France, to France, and get what you have lost;
Spare England, for it is your native coast:
Henry hath money, you are strong and manly;
God on our side, doubt not of victory.

ALL.

A Clifford! a Clifford! we'll follow the king and
Clifford.

JACK CADE[aside].

Was ever feather so lightly blown to and fro
as this multitude? the name of Henry the Fifth
hales them to an hundred mischiefs, and makes
them leave me desolate. I see them lay their heads
together to surprise me: my sword make way for
me, for here is no staying.—In despite of the
devils and hell, have through the very middest of
you! and heavens and honour be witness, that no
want of resolution in me, but only my followers'
base and ignominious treasons, makes me betake
me to my heels.   [Exit.

DUKE OF BUCKINGHAM.

What, is he fled? Go some, and follow him;
And he that brings his head unto the king
Shall have a thousand crowns for his reward.—

[Exeunt some of them.

Follow me, soldiers: we'll devise a mean
To reconcile you all unto the king.   [Exeunt.

SCENE IX.

Killingworth Castle.

Sound trumpets. Enter KING, QUEEN, and
SOMERSET, on the terrace.

KING HENRY.

WAS ever king that joy'd an earthly throne,
And could command no more content than
No sooner was I crept out of my cradle   [I?

But I was made a king, at nine months old:
Was never subject long'd to be a king
As I do long and wish to be a subject.
Enter BUCKINGHAM *and* OLD CLIFFORD.
DUKE OF BUCKINGHAM.
Health and glad tidings to your majesty!
KING HENRY.
Why, Buckingham, is the traitor Cade surprised?
Or is he but retired to make him strong?
Enter, below, multitudes, with halters about their
necks.
OLD CLIFFORD.
He is fled, my lord, and all his powers do yield;
And humbly thus, with halters on their necks,
Expect your highness' doom, of life or death.
KING HENRY.
Then, heaven, set ope thy everlasting gates,
To entertain my vows of thanks and praise!—
Soldiers, this day have you redeem'd your lives,
And show'd how well you love your prince and
    country:
Continue still in this so good a mind,
And Henry, though he be infortunate,
Assure yourselves, will never be unkind:
And so, with thanks and pardon to you all,
I do dismiss you to your several countries.
ALL.
God save the king! God save the king!
Enter a MESSENGER.
MESSENGER.
Please it your Grace to be advertised
The Duke of York is newly come from Ireland;
And with a puissant and a mighty power
Of gallowglasses and stout kerns
Is marching hitherward in proud array;
And still proclaimeth, as he comes along,
His arms are only to remove from thee
The Duke of Somerset, whom he terms a traitor.
KING HENRY.
Thus stands my state, 'twixt Cade and York
    distrest;
Like to a ship that, having scaped a tempest,
Is straightway calm'd, and boarded with a
    pirate:
But now is Cade driven back, his men dispersed;
And now is York in arms to second him.—
I pray thee, Buckingham, go and meet him;
And ask him what's the reason of these arms.
Tell him I'll send Duke Edmund to the
    Tower;—
And, Somerset, we will commit thee thither,
Until his army be dismist from him.
DUKE OF SOMERSET.
My lord,
I'll yield myself to prison willingly,
Or unto death, to do my country good.
KING HENRY.
In any case, be not too rough in terms;
For he is fierce, and cannot brook hard language.
DUKE OF BUCKINGHAM.
I will, my lord; and doubt not so to deal
As all things shall redound unto your good.
KING HENRY.
Come, wife, let's in, and learn to govern better;
For yet may England curse my wretched reign.
[*Flourish.   Exeunt.*

SCENE X.
Kent. IDEN'S *garden.*

Enter CADE.
JACK CADE.
FIE on ambition! fie on myself, that have a
sword, and yet am ready to famish! These five
days have I hid me in these woods; and durst not
peep out, for all the country is laid for me; but now
am I so hungry, that if I might have a lease of my
life for a thousand years, I could stay no longer.
Wherefore, on a brick-wall have I climb'd into
this garden, to see if I can eat grass, or pick a
sallet another while, which is not amiss to cool a
man's stomach this hot weather. And I think this
word 'sallet' was born to do me good: for many a
time, but for a sallet, my brain-pan had been
cleft with a brown bill; and many a time, when I
have been dry, and bravely marching, it hath
served me instead of a quart-pot to drink in; and
now the word 'sallet' must serve me to feed on.
Enter IDEN, *and his* MEN *behind.*
ALEXANDER IDEN.
Lord, who would live turmoiled in the court,
And may enjoy such quiet walks as these?
This small inheritance my father left me
Contenteth me, and worth a monarchy.
I seek not to wax great by others' waning;
Or gather wealth, I care not with what envy:
Sufficeth that I have maintains my state,
And sends the poor well pleased from my gate.
JACK CADE [*aside*].
Here's the lord of the soil come to seize me for
a stray, for entering his fee-simple without leave
—Ah, villain, thou wilt betray me, and get a
thousand crowns of the king by carrying my
head to him! but I'll make thee eat iron like an
ostrich, and swallow my sword like a great pin
ere thou and I part.
ALEXANDER IDEN.
Why, rude companion, whatsoe'er thou be,
I know thee not; why, then, should I betray thee?
Is't not enough to break into my garden,
And, like a thief, to come to rob my grounds,
Climbing my walls in spite of me the owner,
But thou wilt brave me with these saucy terms?
JACK CADE.
Brave thee! ay, by the best blood that ever was
broacht, and beard thee too. Look on me well
I have eat no meat these five days; yet, come thou
and thy five men, and if I do not leave you all as
dead as a door-nail, I pray God I may never eat
grass more.
ALEXANDER IDEN.
Nay, it shall ne'er be said, while England stands,
That Alexander Iden, an esquire of Kent,
Took odds to combat a poor famisht man.
Oppose thy steadfast-gazing eyes to mine,
See if thou canst outface me with thy looks:
Set limb to limb, and thou art far the lesser;
Thy hand is but a finger to my fist;
Thy leg a stick compared with this truncheon;
My foot shall fight with all the strength thou
    hast;
And if mine arm be heaved in the air,
Thy grave is digg'd already in the earth.

As for words,—whose greatness answers words,
Let this my sword report what speech forbears.
        JACK CADE.
By my valour, the most complete champion that
ever I heard!—Steel, if thou turn the edge, or cut
not out the burly-boned clown in chines of beef
ere thou sleep in thy sheath, I beseech God, on
my knees, thou mayst be turn'd to hobnails.
[Here they fight. CADE falls.] O, I am slain!
famine and no other hath slain me: let ten
thousand devils come against me, and give me
but the ten meals I have lost, and I'ld defy them
all. Wither, garden; and be henceforth a burying-
place to all that do dwell in this house, because
the unconquer'd soul of Cade is fled.
        ALEXANDER IDEN.
Is't Cade that I have slain, that monstrous traitor?
Sword, I will hallow thee for this thy deed,
And hang thee o'er my tomb when I am dead:
Ne'er shall this blood be wiped from thy point;
But thou shalt wear it as a herald's coat,
To emblaze the honour that thy master got.
        JACK CADE.
Iden, farewell; and be proud of thy victory.
Tell Kent from me, she hath lost her best man;
and exhort all the world to be cowards,—for I,
that never fear'd any, am vanquisht by famine,
not by valour.   [Dies.
        ALEXANDER IDEN.
How much thou wrong'st me, heaven be my
        judge.   [thee!
Die, damned wretch, the curse of her that bare
And as I thrust thy body in with my sword,
So wish I, I might thrust thy soul to hell.
Hence will I drag thee headlong by the heels
Into a dunghill, which shall be thy grave,
And there cut off thy most ungracious head;
Which I will bear in triumph to the king,
Leaving thy trunk for crows to feed upon.
        [Exeunt IDEN, dragging out the body, and
        SERVANTS.

ACT V. SCENE I.

Fields between Dartford and Blackheath.

*Enter YORK and his army of Irish, with drum
and colours.*

        DUKE OF YORK.
FROM Ireland thus comes York to claim his
        right,
and pluck the crown from feeble Henry's head:
Ring, bells, aloud; burn, bonfires, clear and bright;
To entertain great England's lawful king.
Ah, *sancta majestas!* who would not buy thee dear?
Let them obey that know not how to rule;
This hand was made to handle naught but gold.
I cannot give due action to my words,
Except a sword or sceptre balance it:
A sceptre shall it have,—have I a soul,—
On which I'll toss the flower-de-luce of France.
        Enter BUCKINGHAM [aside].
Whom have we here? Buckingham, to disturb
        me?
The king hath sent him, sure: I must dissemble.
        DUKE OF BUCKINGHAM.
York, if thou meanest well, I greet thee well.

        DUKE OF YORK.
Humphrey of Buckingham, I accept thy greeting.
Art thou a messenger, or come of pleasure?
        DUKE OF BUCKINGHAM.
A messenger from Henry, our dread liege,
To know the reason of these arms in peace;
Or why thou, being a subject as I am,
Against thy oath and true allegiance sworn,
Should raise so great a power without his leave,
Or dare to bring thy force so near the court.
        DUKE OF YORK [aside].
Scarce can I speak, my choler is so great:
O, I could hew up rocks, and fight with flint,
I am so angry at these abject terms;
And now, like Ajax Telamonius,
On sheep or oxen could I spend my fury!
I am far better born than is the king,
More like a king, more kingly in my thoughts:
But I must make fair weather yet awhile,
Till Henry be more weak, and I more strong.—
Buckingham, I prithee, pardon me,
That I have given no answer all this while;
My mind was troubled with deep melancholy.
The cause why I have brought this army hither
Is, to remove proud Somerset from the king,
Seditious to his Grace and to the state.
        DUKE OF BUCKINGHAM.
That is too much presumption on thy part:
But if thy arms be to no other end,
The king hath yielded unto thy demand;
The Duke of Somerset is in the Tower.
        DUKE OF YORK.
Upon thine honour, is he prisoner?
        DUKE OF BUCKINGHAM.
Upon mine honour, he is prisoner.
        DUKE OF YORK.
Then, Buckingham, I do dismiss my powers.—
Soldiers, I thank you all; disperse yourselves;
Meet me to-morrow in Saint George's field,
You shall have pay and every thing you wish.—
And let my sovereign, virtuous Henry,
Command my eldest son, nay, all my sons,
As pledges of my fealty and love;
I'll send them all as willing as I live:
Lands, goods, horse, armour, any thing I have,
Is his to use, so Somerset may die.
        DUKE OF BUCKINGHAM.
York, I commend this kind submission:
We twain will go into his highness' tent.
        Enter KING HENRY and ATTENDANTS.
        KING HENRY.
Buckingham, doth York intend no harm to us,
That thus he marcheth with thee arm in arm?
        DUKE OF YORK.
In all submission and humility
York doth present himself unto your highness.
        KING HENRY.
Then what intends these forces thou dost bring?
        DUKE OF YORK.
To heave the traitor Somerset from hence;
And fight against that monstrous rebel Cade,
Who since I heard to be discomfited.
        Enter IDEN, with CADE'S head.
        ALEXANDER IDEN.
If one so rude and of so mean condition
May pass into the presence of a king,

Lo, I present your Grace a traitor's head,
The head of Cade, whom I in combat slew.
> KING HENRY.

The head of Cade!—Great God, how just art
    Thou!—
O, let me view his visage, being dead,
That living wrought me such exceeding trouble.—
Tell me, my friend, art thou the man that slew
    him?
> ALEXANDER IDEN.

I was, an't like your majesty.
> KING HENRY.

How art thou call'd? and what is thy degree?
> ALEXANDER IDEN.

Alexander Iden, that's my name;
A poor esquire of Kent, that loves his king.
> DUKE OF BUCKINGHAM.

So please it you, my lord, 'twere not amiss
He were created knight for his good service.
> KING HENRY.

Iden, kneel down. [He kneels.] Rise up a knight.
We give thee for reward a thousand marks;
And will that thou henceforth attend on us.
> ALEXANDER IDEN.

May Iden live to merit such a bounty,
And never live but true unto his liege!
> KING HENRY.

See, Buckingham! Somerset comes with the
    queen:
Go, bid her hide him quickly from the duke.
> Enter QUEEN MARGARET and SOMERSET.
> QUEEN MARGARET.

For thousand Yorks he shall not hide his head,
But boldly stand, and front him to his face.
> DUKE OF YORK.

How now! is Somerset at liberty?   [thoughts,
Then, York, unloose thy long-imprison'd
And let thy tongue be equal with thy heart.
Shall I endure the sight of Somerset?—
False king! why hast thou broken faith with me,
Knowing how hardly I can brook abuse?
King did I call thee? no, thou art not king;
Not fit to govern and rule multitudes,
Which darest not, no, nor canst not rule a traitor.
That head of thine doth not become a crown;
Thy hand is made to grasp a palmer's staff,
And not to grace an awful princely sceptre.
That gold must round engirt these brows of
    mine;
Whose smile and frown, like to Achilles' spear,
Is able with the change to kill and cure.
Here is a hand to hold a sceptre up,
And with the same to act controlling laws.
Give place: by heaven, thou shalt rule no more
O'er him whom heaven created for thy ruler.
> DUKE OF SOMERSET.

O monstrous traitor!—I arrest thee, York,
Of capital treason 'gainst the king and crown:
Obey, audacious traitor; kneel for grace.
> DUKE OF YORK.

Wouldst have me kneel? first let me ask of these,
If they can brook I bow a knee to man.—
Sirrah, call in my sons to be my bail:
> [Exit an ATTENDANT.

I know, ere they will have me go to ward, [ment.
They'll pawn their swords for my enfranchise-

> QUEEN MARGARET.

Call hither Clifford; bid him come amain,
To say if that the bastard boys of York
Shall be the surety for their traitor father.
> [Exit BUCKINGHAM.
> DUKE OF YORK.

O blood-bespotted Neapolitan,
Outcast of Naples, England's bloody scourge!
The sons of York, thy betters in their birth,
Shall be their father's bail; and bane to those
That for my surety will refuse the boys!
See where they come: I'll warrant they'll make it
    good.
> Enter EDWARD and RICHARD.
> QUEEN MARGARET.

And here comes Clifford to deny their bail.
> Enter OLD CLIFFORD and his SON.
> OLD CLIFFORD.

Health and all happiness to my lord the king!
> [Kneels.
> DUKE OF YORK.

I thank thee, Clifford: say, what news with thee?
Nay, do not fright us with an angry look:
We are thy sovereign, Clifford, kneel again;
For thy mistaking so, we pardon thee.
> OLD CLIFFORD.

This is my king, York, I do not mistake;
But thou mistakest me much to think I do:—
To Bedlam with him! is the man grown mad?
> KING HENRY.

Ay, Clifford; a bedlam and ambitious humour
Makes him oppose himself against his king.
> OLD CLIFFORD.

He is a traitor; let him to the Tower,
And chop away that factious pate of his.
> QUEEN MARGARET.

He is arrested, but will not obey;
His sons, he says, shall give their words for him.
> DUKE OF YORK.

Will you not, sons?
> EDWARD.

Ay, noble father, if our words will serve.
> RICHARD.

And if words will not, then our weapons shall.
> OLD CLIFFORD.

Why, what a brood of traitors have we here!
> DUKE OF YORK.

Look in a glass, and call thy image so:
I am thy king, and thou a false-heart traitor.—
Call hither to the stake my two brave bears,
That with the very shaking of their chains
They may astonish these fell-lurking curs:
Bid Salisbury and Warwick come to me.
> Enter the EARLS OF WARWICK and SALISBURY
> OLD CLIFFORD.

Are these thy bears? we'll bait thy bears to death,
And manacle the bear-ward in their chains,
If thou darest bring them to the baiting-place.
> RICHARD.

Oft have I seen a hot o'erweening cur
Run back and bite, because he was withheld;
Who, being suffer'd with the bear's fell paw,
Hath clapt his tail between his legs and cried:
And such a piece of service will you do,
If you oppose yourselves to match Lord War-
    wick.

OLD CLIFFORD.
Hence, heap of wrath, foul indigested lump,
As crooked in thy manners as thy shape!
DUKE OF YORK.
Nay, we shall heat you thoroughly anon.
OLD CLIFFORD.
Take heed, lest by your heat you burn yourselves.
KING HENRY.
Why, Warwick, hath thy knee forgot to bow?—
Old Salisbury,—shame to thy silver hair,
Thou mad misleader of thy brain-sick son!—
What, wilt thou on thy death-bed play the ruffian,
And seek for sorrow with thy spectacles?—
O, where is faith? O, where is loyalty?
If it be banisht from the frosty head,
Where shall it find a harbour in the earth?—
Wilt thou go dig a grave to find out war,
And shame thine honourable age with blood?
Why art thou old, and want'st experience?
Or wherefore dost abuse it, if thou hast it?
For shame! in duty bend thy knee to me,
That bows unto the grave with mickle age.
EARL OF SALISBURY.
My lord, I have consider'd with myself
The title of this most renowned duke;
And in my conscience do repute his Grace
The rightful heir to England's royal seat.
KING HENRY.
Hast thou not sworn allegiance unto me?
EARL OF SALISBURY.
I have.
KING HENRY.
Canst thou dispense with heaven for such an
oath?
EARL OF SALISBURY.
It is great sin to swear unto a sin;
But greater sin to keep a sinful oath.
Who can be bound by any solemn vow
To do a murderous deed, to rob a man,
To force a spotless virgin's chastity,
To reave the orphan of his patrimony,
To wring the widow from her custom'd right;
And have no other reason for this wrong,
But that he was bound by a solemn oath?
QUEEN MARGARET.
A subtle traitor needs no sophister.
KING HENRY.
Call Buckingham, and bid him arm himself.
DUKE OF YORK.
Call Buckingham, and all the friends thou hast,
I am resolved for death or dignity.
OLD CLIFFORD.
The first I warrant thee, if dreams prove true.
EARL OF WARWICK.
You were best to go to bed and dream again,
To keep thee from the tempest of the field.
OLD CLIFFORD.
I am resolved to bear a greater storm
Than any thou canst conjure up to-day;
And that I'll write upon thy burgonet,
Might I but know thee by thy household badge.
EARL OF WARWICK.
Now, by my father's badge, old Nevil's crest,
The rampant bear chain'd to the ragged staff,
This day I'll wear aloft my burgonet,—
As on a mountain-top the cedar shows,

That keeps his leaves in spite of any storm,—
Even to affright thee with the view thereof.
OLD CLIFFORD.
And from thy burgonet I'll rend thy bear,
And tread it under foot with all contempt,
Despite the bear-ward that protects the bear.
YOUNG CLIFFORD.
And so to arms, victorious father,
To quell the rebels and their complices.
RICHARD.
Fie! charity, for shame! speak not in spite,
For you shall sup with Jesu Christ to-night.
YOUNG CLIFFORD.
Foul stigmatic, that's more than thou canst tell.
RICHARD.
If not in heaven, you'll surely sup in hell.
[Exeunt severally.

SCENE II.
Saint Alban's.

Alarums to the battle. Enter WARWICK.

EARL OF WARWICK.
CLIFFORD of Cumberland, 'tis Warwick calls!
An if thou dost not hide thee from the bear,
Now,—when the angry trumpet sounds alarum,
And dead men's cries do fill the empty air,—
Clifford, I say, come forth and fight with me!
Proud northern lord, Clifford of Cumberland,
Warwick is hoarse with calling thee to arms.
Enter YORK.
How now, my noble lord! what, all a-foot?
DUKE OF YORK.
The deadly-handed Clifford slew my steed;
But match to match I have encounter'd him,
And made a prey for carrion kites and crows
Even of the bonny beast he loved so well.
Enter OLD CLIFFORD.
EARL OF WARWICK.
Of one or both of us the time is come.
DUKE OF YORK.
Hold, Warwick, seek thee out some other chase,
For I myself must hunt this deer to death.
EARL OF WARWICK.
Then, nobly, York; 'tis for a crown thou fight'st.—
As I intend, Clifford, to thrive to-day,
It grieves my soul to leave thee unassail'd.   [Exit.
OLD CLIFFORD.
What seest thou in me, York? why dost thou
pause?
DUKE OF YORK.
With thy brave bearing should I be in love,
But that thou art so fast mine enemy.
OLD CLIFFORD.
Nor should thy prowess want praise and esteem,
But that 'tis shown ignobly and in treason.
DUKE OF YORK.
So let it help me now against thy sword,
As I in justice and true right express it!
OLD CLIFFORD.
My soul and body on the action both!
DUKE OF YORK.
A dreadful lay!—address thee instantly.
[They fight.   OLD CLIFFORD *falls*
OLD CLIFFORD.
La fin couronne les œuvres.   [Dies

DUKE OF YORK.
Thus war hath given thee peace, for thou art still.
Peace with his soul, heaven, if it be thy will! [*Exit.*
Enter YOUNG CLIFFORD.
YOUNG CLIFFORD.
Shame and confusion! all is on the rout;
Fear frames disorder, and disorder wounds
Where it should guard. O war, thou son of hell,
Whom angry heavens do make their minister,
Throw in the frozen bosoms of our part
Hot coals of vengeance!—Let no soldier fly:
He that is truly dedicate to war
Hath no self-love; nor he that loves himself
Hath not essentially, but by circumstance,
The name of valour.—O, let the vile world end,
[*Seeing his father's body.*
And the premised flames of the last day
Knit earth and heaven together!
Now let the general trumpet blow his blast,
Particularities and petty sounds
To cease!—Wast thou ordain'd, dear father,
To lose thy youth in peace, and to achieve
The silvery livery of advised age,
And, in thy reverence and thy chair-days, thus
To die in ruffian battle?—Even at this sight
My heart is turn'd to stone: and while 'tis mine,
It shall be stony. York not our old men spares;
No more will I their babes: tears virginal
Shall be to me even as the dew to fire;
And beauty, that the tyrant oft reclaims,
Shall to my flaming wrath be oil and flax.
Henceforth I will not have to do with pity:
Meet I an infant of the house of York,
Into as many gobbets will I cut it,
As wild Medea young Absyrtus did:
In cruelty will I seek out my fame.—
Come, thou new ruin of old Clifford's house.
[*Taking up the body.*
As did Æneas old Anchises bear,
So bear I thee upon my manly shoulders;
But then Æneas bare a living load,
Nothing so heavy as these woes of mine.   [*Exit.*
Enter RICHARD and SOMERSET to fight.
SOMERSET is kill'd.
RICHARD.
So, lie thou there;—
For underneath an alehouse' paltry sign,
The castle in Saint Alban's, Somerset
Hath made the wizard famous in his death.—
Sword, hold thy temper; heart, be wrathful still:
Priests pray for enemies, but princes kill.   [*Exit.*
Fight. Excursions. Enter KING, QUEEN, and
others.
QUEEN MARGARET.
Away, my lord! you are slow; for shame, away!
KING HENRY.
Can we outrun the heavens? good Margaret, stay.
QUEEN MARGARET.
What are you made of? you'll nor fight nor fly:
Now is it manhood, wisdom, and defence,
To give the enemy way; and to secure us
By what we can, which can no more but fly.
[*Alarum afar off.*

If you be ta'en, we then should see the bottom
Of all our fortunes: but if we haply scape,—
As well we may, if not through your neglect,—
We shall to London get: where you are loved;
And where this breach, now in our fortunes made,
May readily be stopt.
Enter YOUNG CLIFFORD.
YOUNG CLIFFORD.
But that my heart's on future mischief set,
I would speak blasphemy ere bid you fly:
But fly you must; uncurable discomfit
Reigns in the hearts of all our present part.
Away, for your relief! and we will live
To see their day, and them our fortune give:
Away, my lord, away!   [*Exeunt.*

SCENE III.

Fields near Saint Alban's.

Alarum. Retreat. Enter YORK, RICHARD, WAR-
WICK, *and* SOLDIERS, *with drum and colours.*

DUKE OF YORK.
OLD Salisbury, who can report of him,—
That winter lion, who in rage forgets
Aged contusions and all brush of time,
And, like a gallant in the brow of youth,
Repairs him with occasion? This happy day
Is not itself, nor have we won one foot,
If Salisbury be lost.
RICHARD.
My noble father,
Three times to-day I holp him to his horse,
Three times bestrid him, thrice I led him off,
Persuaded him from any further act:
But still, where danger was, still there I met
him;
And like rich hangings in a homely house,
So was his will in his old feeble body.
But, noble as he is, look where he comes.
Enter SALISBURY.
EARL OF SALISBURY.
Now, by my sword, well hast thou fought to-day;
By th' mass, so did we all.—I thank you, Richard:
God knows how long it is I have to live;
And it hath pleased him that three times to-day
You have defended me from imminent death.—
Well, lords, we have not got that which we have:
'Tis not enough our foes are this time fled,
Being opposites of such repairing nature.
DUKE OF YORK.
I know our safety is to follow them;
For, as I hear, the king is fled to London,
To call a present court of parliament.
Let us pursue him, ere the writs go forth:—
What says Lord Warwick? shall we after them?
EARL OF WARWICK.
After them! nay, before them, if we can.
Now, by my faith, lords, 'twas a glorious day:
Saint Alban's battle, won by famous York,
Shall be eternized in all age to come.—
Sound drums and trumpets;—and to London
all:
And more such days as these to us befall! [*Exeunt.*

THE THIRD PART OF
KING HENRY THE SIXTH

DRAMATIS PERSONAE

KING HENRY THE SIXTH.
EDWARD, *Prince of Wales, his son.*
LOUIS XI., *King of France.*
DUKE OF SOMERSET.
DUKE OF EXETER.
EARL OF OXFORD.
EARL OF NORTHUMBERLAND.
EARL OF WESTMORELAND.
LORD CLIFFORD.
RICHARD PLANTAGENET, *Duke of York.*
EDWARD, *Earl of March, afterwards King Edward IV.,*
EDMUND, *Earl of Rutland,*
GEORGE, *afterwards Duke of Clarence,*
RICHARD, *afterwards Duke of Gloster,* } *his sons.*
DUKE OF NORFOLK.
MARQUESS OF MONTAGUE.
EARL OF WARWICK.
EARL OF PEMBROKE.
LORD HASTINGS.
LORD STAFFORD.

SIR JOHN MORTIMER, } *uncles to the Duke of*
SIR HUGH MORTIMER, } *York.*
HENRY, *Earl of Richmond, a youth.*
LORD RIVERS, *brother to Lady Grey.*
SIR WILLIAM STANLEY.
SIR JOHN MONTGOMERY.
SIR JOHN SOMERVILLE.
TUTOR TO RUTLAND. MAYOR OF YORK.
LIEUTENANT OF THE TOWER. A NOBLEMAN.
TWO KEEPERS. A HUNTSMAN.
A SON THAT HAS KILL'D HIS FATHER.
A FATHER THAT HAS KILL'D HIS SON.

QUEEN MARGARET.
LADY GREY, *afterwards Queen to Edward IV.*
BONA, *sister to the French Queen.*

SOLDIERS, ATTENDANTS, MESSENGERS,
WATCHMEN, &c.

SCENE—*During part of the third Act in France;
during the rest of the Play in England.*

ACT I. SCENE I.

London.   The Parliament-house.

Alarum.   Enter the DUKE OF YORK, EDWARD, RICHARD, NORFOLK, MONTAGUE, WARWICK, *and* SOLDIERS.

EARL OF WARWICK.

I WONDER how the king escaped our hands.
DUKE OF YORK.
While we pursued the horsemen of the north,
He slily stole away, and left his men:
Whereat the great Lord of Northumberland,
Whose warlike ears could never brook retreat,
Cheer'd up the drooping army; and himself,
Lord Clifford, and Lord Stafford, all a-breast,
Charged our main battle's front, and, breaking in,
Were by the swords of common soldiers slain.
EDWARD.
Lord Stafford's father, Duke of Buckingham,
Is either slain or wounded dangerous;
I cleft his beaver with a downright blow:
That this is true, father, behold his blood.
                    [*Showing his bloody sword.*
MARQUESS OF MONTAGUE [*to* YORK,
                    showing his].
And, brother, here's the Earl of Wiltshire's blood,
Whom I encounter'd as the battles join'd.
RICHARD.
Speak thou for me, and tell them what I did.
    [*Throwing down the* DUKE OF SOMER-
    SET'S *head.*
DUKE OF YORK.
Richard hath best deserved of all my sons.—
But, is your Grace dead, my Lord of Somerset?
DUKE OF NORFOLK.
Such hap have all the line of John of Gaunt!
RICHARD.
Thus do I hope to shake King Henry's head.

EARL OF WARWICK.
And so do I.—Victorious Prince of York,
Before I see thee seated in that throne
Which now the house of Lancaster usurps,
I vow by heaven these eyes shall never close.
This is the palace of the fearful king,
And this the regal seat: possess it, York;
For this is thine, and not King Henry's heirs'.
DUKE OF YORK.
Assist me, then, sweet Warwick, and I will;
For hither we have broken in by force.
DUKE OF NORFOLK.
We'll all assist you; he that flies shall die.
DUKE OF YORK.
Thanks, gentle Norfolk:—stay by me, my
    lords;—
And, soldiers, stay, and lodge by me this night.
EARL OF WARWICK.
And when the king comes, offer him no violence,
Unless he seek to thrust you out perforce.
                    [*They go up.*
DUKE OF YORK.
The queen, this day, here holds her parliament,
But little thinks we shall be of her council:
By words or blows here let us win our right.
RICHARD.
Arm'd as we are, let's stay within this house.
EARL OF WARWICK.
The bloody parliament shall this be call'd,
Unless Plantagenet, duke of York, be king,
And bashful Henry deposed, whose cowardice
Hath made us by-words to our enemies.
DUKE OF YORK.
Then leave me not, my lords; be resolute;
I mean to take possession of my right.
EARL OF WARWICK.
Neither the king, nor he that loves him best,
The proudest he that holds up Lancaster,
Dares stir a wing, if Warwick shake his bells.

65

I'll plant Plantagenet, root him up who dares:—
Resolve thee, Richard; claim the English crown.
Flourish. *Enter* KING HENRY, CLIFFORD,
    NORTHUMBERLAND,   WESTMORELAND,
    EXETER, *and the rest.*

KING HENRY.

My lords, look where the sturdy rebel sits,
Even in the chair of state! belike he means—
Backt by the power of Warwick, that false peer—
To aspire unto the crown, and reign as king.—
Earl of Northumberland, he slew thy father,
And thine, Lord Clifford; and you both have
    vow'd revenge
On him, his sons, his favourites, and his friends.

EARL OF NORTHUMBERLAND.

If I be not, heavens be revenged on me!

LORD CLIFFORD.

The hope thereof makes Clifford mourn in steel.

EARL OF WESTMORELAND.

What, shall we suffer this? let's pluck him down:
My heart for anger burns: I cannot brook it.

KING HENRY.

Be patient, gentle Earl of Westmoreland.

LORD CLIFFORD.

Patience is for poltroons, such as he:
He durst not sit there, had your father lived.
My gracious lord, here in the parliament
Let us assail the family of York.

EARL OF NORTHUMBERLAND.

Well hast thou spoken, cousin: be it so.

KING HENRY.

Ah, know you not the city favours them,
And they have troops of soldiers at their beck?

DUKE OF EXETER.

But when the duke is slain, they'll quickly fly.

KING HENRY.

Far be the thought of this from Henry's heart,
To make a shambles of the parliament-house!
Cousin of Exeter, frowns, words, and threats
Shall be the war that Henry means to use.
Thou factious Duke of York, descend my
    throne,
And kneel for grace and mercy at my feet;
I am thy sovereign.

DUKE OF YORK.

        Thou'rt deceived; I'm thine.

DUKE OF EXETER.

For shame, come down: he made thee Duke of
    York.

DUKE OF YORK.

'Twas my inheritance, as the earldom was.

DUKE OF EXETER.

Thy father was a traitor to the crown.

EARL OF WARWICK.

Exeter, thou art a traitor to the crown
In following this usurping Henry.

LORD CLIFFORD.

Whom should he follow but his natural king?

EARL OF WARWICK.

True, Clifford; and that's Richard duke of York.

KING HENRY.

And shall I stand, and thou sit in my throne?

DUKE OF YORK.

It must and shall be so: content thyself.

EARL OF WARWICK.

Be Duke of Lancaster; let him be king.

EARL OF WESTMORELAND.

He is both king and Duke of Lancaster;   [tain.
And that the Lord of Westmoreland shall main-

EARL OF WARWICK.

And Warwick shall disprove it. You forget
That we are those which chased you from the
    field,
And slew your fathers, and with colours spread
Marcht through the city to the palace-gates.

EARL OF NORTHUMBERLAND.

No, Warwick, I remember it to my grief;
And, by his soul, thou and thy house shall rue it.

EARL OF WESTMORELAND.

Plantagenet, of thee, and these thy sons,   [lives
Thy kinsmen, and thy friends, I'll have more
Than drops of blood were in my father's veins.

LORD CLIFFORD.

Urge it no more; lest that, instead of words,
I send thee, Warwick, such a messenger
As shall revenge his death before I stir.

EARL OF WARWICK.

Poor Clifford! how I scorn his worthless threats!

DUKE OF YORK.

Will you we show our title to the crown?
If not, our swords shall plead it in the field.

KING HENRY.

What title hast thou, traitor, to the crown?
Thy father was, as thou art, Duke of York;
Thy grandfather, Roger Mortimer, Earl of
    March:
I am the son of Henry the Fifth,
Who made the Dauphin and the French to stoop,
And seized upon their towns and provinces.

EARL OF WARWICK.

Talk not of France, sith thou hast lost it all.

KING HENRY.

The lord Protector lost it, and not I:
When I was crown'd I was but nine months old.

RICHARD.

You are old enough now, and yet, methinks, you
    lose.—
Father, tear the crown from the usurper's head.

EDWARD.

Sweet father, do so; set it on your head.

MARQUESS OF MONTAGUE [*to* YORK].

Good brother, as thou lovest and honourest
    arms,
Let's fight it out, and not stand cavilling thus.

RICHARD.

Sound drums and trumpets, and the king will fly.

DUKE OF YORK.

Sons, peace!

KING HENRY.

Peace thou! and give King Henry leave to speak.

EARL OF WARWICK.

Plantagenet shall speak first: hear him, lords;
And be you silent and attentive too,
For he that interrupts him shall not live.

KING HENRY.

Think'st thou that I will leave my kingly throne,
Wherein my grandsire and my father sat?
No; first shall war unpeople this my realm;
Ay, and their colours—often borne in France,
And now in England to our heart's great sorrow—
Shall be my winding sheet.—Why faint you, lords?
My title's good, and better far than his.

EARL OF WARWICK.
Prove it, Henry, and thou shalt be king.
KING HENRY.
Henry the Fourth by conquest got the crown.
DUKE OF YORK.
'Twas by rebellion against his king.
KING HENRY [aside].
I know not what to say; my title's weak.—
Tell me, may not a king adopt an heir?
DUKE OF YORK.
What then?
KING HENRY.
An if he may, then am I lawful king;
For Richard, in the view of many lords,
Resign'd the crown to Henry the Fourth,
Whose heir my father was, and I am his.
DUKE OF YORK.
He rose against him, being his sovereign,
And made him to resign his crown perforce.
EARL OF WARWICK.
Suppose, my lords, he did it unconstrain'd,
Think you 'twere prejudicial to his crown?
DUKE OF EXETER.
No; for he could not so resign his crown
But that the next heir should succeed and reign.
KING HENRY.
Art thou against us, Duke of Exeter?
DUKE OF EXETER.
His is the right, and therefore pardon me.
DUKE OF YORK.
Why whisper you, my lords, and answer not?
DUKE OF EXETER.
My conscience tells me he is lawful king.
KING HENRY [aside].
All will revolt from me, and turn to him.
EARL OF NORTHUMBERLAND.
Plantagenet, for all the claim thou lay'st,
Think not that Henry shall be so deposed.
EARL OF WARWICK.
Deposed he shall be, in despite of all.
EARL OF NORTHUMBERLAND.
Thou art deceived: 'tis not thy southern power,
Of Essex, Norfolk, Suffolk, nor of Kent—
Which makes thee thus presumptuous and
    proud—
Can set the duke up, in despite of me.
LORD CLIFFORD.
King Henry, be thy title right or wrong,
Lord Clifford vows to fight in thy defence:
May that ground gape, and swallow me alive,
Where I shall kneel to him that slew my father!
KING HENRY.
O Clifford, how thy words revive my heart!
DUKE OF YORK.
Henry of Lancaster, resign thy crown.—
What mutter you, or what conspire you, lords?
EARL OF WARWICK.
Do right unto this princely Duke of York;
Or I will fill the house with armed men,
And over the chair of state, where now he sits,
Write up his title with usurping blood.
[He stamps with his foot, and the SOLDIERS
    show themselves.
KING HENRY.
My Lord of Warwick, hear me but one word:—
Let me for this my life-time reign as king.

DUKE OF YORK.
Confirm the crown to me and to mine heirs,
And thou shalt reign in quiet while thou
    livest.
KING HENRY.
I am content: Richard Plantagenet,
Enjoy the kingdom after my decease.
LORD CLIFFORD.
What wrong is this unto the prince your son!
EARL OF WARWICK.
What good is this to England and himself!
EARL OF WESTMORELAND.
Base, fearful, and despairing Henry!
LORD CLIFFORD.
How hast thou injured both thyself and us!
EARL OF WESTMORELAND.
I cannot stay to hear these articles.
EARL OF NORTHUMBERLAND.
Nor I.
LORD CLIFFORD.
Come, cousin, let us tell the queen these news.
EARL OF WESTMORELAND.
Farewell, faint-hearted and degenerate king,
In whose cold blood no spark of honour bides.
EARL OF NORTHUMBERLAND.
Be thou a prey unto the house of York,
And die in bands, for this unmanly deed!
LORD CLIFFORD.
In dreadful war mayst thou be overcome,
Or live in peace, abandon'd and despised!
[Exeunt NORTHUMBERLAND, CLIFFORD,
    and WESTMORELAND.
EARL OF WARWICK.
Turn this way, Henry, and regard them not.
DUKE OF EXETER.
They seek revenge, and therefore will not yield.
KING HENRY.
Ah, Exeter!
EARL OF WARWICK.
    Why should you sigh, my lord?
KING HENRY.
Not for myself, Lord Warwick, but my son,
Whom I unnaturally shall disinherit.
But, be it as it may:—I here entail
The crown to thee, and to thine heirs for ever;
Conditionally, that here thou take an oath
To cease this civil war, and, whilst I live,
To honour me as thy king and sovereign,
And neither by treason nor hostility
To seek to put me down, and reign thyself.
DUKE OF YORK.
This oath I willingly take, and will perform.
EARL OF WARWICK.
Long live King Henry!—Plantagenet, embrace
    him.
KING HENRY.
And long live thou, and these thy forward sons!
DUKE OF YORK.
Now York and Lancaster are reconciled.
DUKE OF EXETER.
Accurst be he that seeks to make them foes!
[Sennet. Here they come down.
DUKE OF YORK.
Farewell, my gracious lord; I'll to my castle.
EARL OF WARWICK.
And I'll keep London with my soldiers.

DUKE OF NORFOLK.
And I to Norfolk with my followers.
MARQUESS OF MONTAGUE.
And I unto the sea, from whence I came.
[*Exeunt* YORK *and his* SONS, WARWICK,
NORFOLK, MONTAGUE, SOLDIERS,
and ATTENDANTS.
KING HENRY.
And I, with grief and sorrow, to the court.
DUKE OF EXETER.
Here comes the queen, whose looks bewray her
anger:
I'll steal away.   [*Going.*
KING HENRY.
Exeter, so will I.   [*Going.*
Enter QUEEN MARGARET *and the* PRINCE OF
WALES.
QUEEN MARGARET.
Nay, go not from me; I will follow thee.
KING HENRY.
Be patient, gentle queen, and I will stay.
QUEEN MARGARET.
Who can be patient in such extremes?
Ah, wretched man! would I had died a maid,
And never seen thee, never borne thee son,
Seeing thou hast proved so unnatural a father!
Hath he deserved to lose his birthright thus?
Hadst thou but loved him half so well as I,
Or felt that pain which I did for him once,
Or nourisht him as I did with my blood,
Thou wouldst have left thy dearest heart-blood
there,
Rather than have made that savage duke thine
heir,
And disinherited thine only son.
PRINCE OF WALES.
Father, you cannot disinherit me:
If you be king, why should not I succeed?
KING HENRY.
Pardon me, Margaret;—pardon me, sweet son:—
The Earl of Warwick and the duke enforced me
QUEEN MARGARET.
Enforced thee! art thou king, and wilt be forced?
I shame to hear thee speak. Ah, timorous wretch!
Thou hast undone thyself, thy son, and me;
And given unto the house of York such head,
As thou shalt reign but by their sufferance.
To entail him and his heirs unto the crown,
What is it, but to make thy sepulchre,
And creep into it far before thy time?
Warwick is chancellor, and the lord of Calais;
Stern Falconbridge commands the narrow seas;
The duke is made Protector of the realm;
And yet shalt thou be safe? such safety finds
The trembling lamb environed with wolves.
Had I been there, which am a silly woman,
The soldiers should have toss'd me on their pikes
Before I would have granted to that act.
But thou preferr'st thy life before thine honour:
And seeing thou dost, I here divorce myself
Both from thy table, Henry, and thy bed,
Until that act of Parliament be repeal'd,
Whereby my son is disinherited.
The northern lords that have forsworn thy colours
Will follow mine, if once they see them spread;
And spread they shall be,—to thy foul disgrace,

And utter ruin of the house of York.
Thus do I leave thee.—Come, son, let's away;
Our army is ready; come, we'll after them.
KING HENRY.
Stay, gentle Margaret, and hear me speak.
QUEEN MARGARET.
Thou hast spoke too much already; get thee gone.
KING HENRY.
Gentle son Edward, thou wilt stay with me?
QUEEN MARGARET.
Ay, to be murder'd by his enemies.
PRINCE OF WALES.
When I return with victory from the field,
I'll see your Grace: till then I'll follow her.
QUEEN MARGARET.
Come, son, away; we may not linger thus.
[*Exeunt* QUEEN MARGARET *and the*
PRINCE.
KING HENRY.
Poor queen! how love to me and to her son
Hath made her break out into terms of rage!
Revenged may she be on that hateful duke,
Whose haughty spirit, winged with desire,
Will cost my crown, and like an empty eagle
Tire on the flesh of me and of my son!
The loss of those three lords torments my heart:
I'll write unto them, and entreat them fair:—
Come, cousin, you shall be the messenger.
DUKE OF EXETER.
And I, I hope, shall reconcile them all.
[*Exeunt.*

SCENE II.

Sandal Castle, near Wakefield.

Enter RICHARD, EDWARD, *and* MONTAGUE.

RICHARD.
BROTHER, though I be youngest, give me
leave.
EDWARD.
No, I can better play the orator.
MARQUESS OF MONTAGUE.
But I have reasons strong and forcible.
Enter the DUKE OF YORK.
DUKE OF YORK.
Why, how now, sons and brother! at a strife?
What is your quarrel? how began it first?
EDWARD.
No quarrel, but a slight contention.
DUKE OF YORK.
About what?
RICHARD.
About that which concerns your Grace and us,—
The crown of England, father, which is yours.
DUKE OF YORK.
Mine, boy? not till King Henry be dead.
RICHARD.
Your right depends not on his life or death.
EDWARD.
Now you are heir, therefore enjoy it now:
By giving the house of Lancaster leave to breathe,
It will outrun you, father, in the end.
DUKE OF YORK.
I took an oath that he should quietly reign.
EDWARD.
But, for a kingdom, any oath may be broken:
I would break a thousand oaths to reign one year.

RICHARD.
No; God forbid your Grace should be forsworn.
DUKE OF YORK.
I shall be, if I claim by open war.
RICHARD.
I'll prove the contrary, if you'll hear me speak.
DUKE OF YORK.
Thou canst not, son; it is impossible.
RICHARD.
An oath is of no moment, being not took
Before a true and lawful magistrate,
That hath authority over him that swears:
Henry had none, but did usurp the place;
Then, seeing 'twas he that made you to depose,
Your oath, my lord, is vain and frivolous.
Therefore, to arms! And, father, do but think
How sweet a thing it is to wear a crown;
Within whose circuit is Elysium,
And all that poets feign of bliss and joy.
Why do we linger thus? I cannot rest
Until the white rose that I wear be dyed
Even in the lukewarm blood of Henry's heart.
DUKE OF YORK.
Richard, enough; I will be king, or die.—
Brother, thou shalt to London presently,
And whet-on Warwick to this enterprise.—
Thou, Richard, shalt to the Duke of Norfolk,
And tell him privily of our intent.—
You, Edward, shall unto my Lord Cobham,
With whom the Kentishmen will willingly rise:
In them I trust; for they are soldiers,
Witty, courteous, liberal, full of spirit.—
While these are thus employ'd, what resteth more,
But that I seek occasion how to rise,
And yet the king not privy to my drift,
Nor any of the house of Lancaster?
Enter a MESSENGER.
But, stay: what news?—Why comest thou in such
post?
MESSENGER.
The queen with all the northern earls and lords
Intend here to besiege you in your castle:
She is hard by with twenty thousand men;
And therefore fortify your hold, my lord.
DUKE OF YORK.
Ay, with my sword. What! think'st thou that we
fear them?—
Edward and Richard, you shall stay with me;—
My brother Montague shall post to London:
Let noble Warwick, Cobham, and the rest,
Whom we have left protectors of the king,
With powerful policy strengthen themselves,
And trust not simple Henry nor his oaths.
MARQUESS OF MONTAGUE.
Brother, I go; I'll win them, fear it not:
And thus most humbly I do take my leave.
[Exit.
Enter SIR JOHN and SIR HUGH MORTIMER.
DUKE OF YORK.
Sir John and Sir Hugh Mortimer, mine uncles!
You are come to Sandal in a happy hour;
The army of the queen mean to besiege us.
SIR JOHN MORTIMER.
She shall not need, we'll meet her in the field.
DUKE OF YORK.
What, with five thousand men?

RICHARD.
Ay, with five hundred, father, for a need:
A woman's general; what should we fear?
[A march afar off.
EDWARD.
I hear their drums: let's set our men in order,
And issue forth, and bid them battle straight.
DUKE OF YORK.
Five men to twenty!—though the odds be great,
I doubt not, uncle, of our victory.
Many a battle have I won in France,
Whenas the enemy hath been ten to one:
Why should I not now have the like success?
[Alarum. Exeunt.

SCENE III.

Field of battle near Sandal Castle.

Alarums. Enter RUTLAND *and his* TUTOR.

EARL OF RUTLAND.
AH, whither shall I fly to scape their hands?
Ah, tutor, look where bloody Clifford comes!
Enter CLIFFORD *and* SOLDIERS.
LORD CLIFFORD.
Chaplain, away! thy priesthood saves thy life.
As for the brat of this accursed duke,
Whose father slew my father,—he shall die.
TUTOR.
And I, my lord, will bear him company.
LORD CLIFFORD.
Soldiers, away with him!
TUTOR.
Ah, Clifford, murder not this innocent child,
Lest thou be hated both of God and man!
[Exit, forced off by SOLDIERS.
LORD CLIFFORD.
How now! is he dead already? or is it fear
That makes him close his eyes?—I'll open them.
EARL OF RUTLAND.
So looks the pent-up lion o'er the wretch
That trembles under his devouring paws;
And so he walks, insulting o'er his prey,
And so he comes, to rend his limbs asunder.—
Ah, gentle Clifford, kill me with thy sword,
And not with such a cruel threatening look!
Sweet Clifford, hear me speak before I die!—
I am too mean a subject for thy wrath:
Be thou revenged on men, and let me live.
LORD CLIFFORD.
In vain thou speak'st, poor boy; my father's blood
Hath stopt the passage where thy words should
enter.
EARL OF RUTLAND.
Then let my father's blood open it again:
He is a man, and Clifford, cope with him.
LORD CLIFFORD.
Had I thy brethren here, their lives and thine
Were not revenge sufficient for me;
No, if I digg'd up their forefathers' graves,
And hung their rotten coffins up in chains,
It could not slake mine ire nor ease my heart.
The sight of any of the house of York
Is as a fury to torment my soul;
And till I root out their accursed line,
And leave not one alive, I live in hell.
Therefore—   [Lifting his hand.

EARL OF RUTLAND.
O, let me pray before I take my death!—
To thee I pray; sweet Clifford, pity me!

LORD CLIFFORD.
Such pity as my rapier's point affords.

EARL OF RUTLAND.
I never did thee harm: why wilt thou slay me?

LORD CLIFFORD.
Thy father hath.

EARL OF RUTLAND.
But 'twas ere I was born.
Thou hast one son,—for his sake pity me;
Lest in revenge thereof,—sith God is just,—
He be as miserably slain as I.
Ah, let me live in prison all my days;
And when I give occasion of offence,
Then let me die, for now thou hast no cause!

LORD CLIFFORD.
No cause!
Thy father slew my father; therefore, die.
                    [*Stabs him.*

EARL OF RUTLAND.
Di faciant, laudis summa sit ista tuæ!   [*Dies.*

LORD CLIFFORD.
Plantagenet! I come, Plantagenet!
And this thy son's blood cleaving to my blade
Shall rust upon my weapon, till thy blood,
Congeal'd with this, do make me wipe off both.
                    [*Exit.*

SCENE IV.

Another part of the field.

Alarums.   Enter RICHARD, DUKE OF YORK.

DUKE OF YORK.
THE army of the queen hath got the field:
My uncles both are slain in rescuing me;
And all my followers to the eager foe
Turn back, and fly, like ships before the wind,
Or lambs pursued by hunger-starved wolves.
My sons,—God knows what hath bechanced
   them:
But this I know, they have demean'd themselves
Like men born to renown by life or death.
Three times did Richard make a lane to me,
And thrice cried, 'Courage, father! fight it
   out!'
And full as oft came Edward to my side,
With purple falchion, painted to the hilt
In blood of those that had encounter'd him:
And when the hardiest warriors did retire,
Richard cried, 'Charge! and give no foot of
   ground!'
And cried, 'A crown, or else a glorious tomb!
A sceptre, or an earthly sepulchre!'
With this, we charged again: but, out, alas!
We bodged again: as I have seen a swan
With bootless labour swim against the tide,
And spend her strength with over-matching
   waves.   [*A short alarum within.*
Ah, hark! the fatal followers do pursue;
And I am faint, and cannot fly their fury:
And were I strong, I would not shun their fury:
The sands are number'd that make up my life;
Here must I stay, and here my life must end.

Enter the QUEEN, CLIFFORD, NORTHUMBER-
         LAND, *and* SOLDIERS.

Come, bloody Clifford,—rough Northumber-
   land,—
I dare your quenchless fury to more rage:
I am your butt, and I abide your shot.

EARL OF NORTHUMBERLAND.
Yield to our mercy, proud Plantagenet.

LORD CLIFFORD.
Ay, to such mercy as his ruthless arm,
With downright payment, show'd unto my father.
Now Phaethon hath tumbled from his car,
And made an evening at the noontide prick.

DUKE OF YORK.
My ashes, as the phœnix, may bring forth
A bird that will revenge upon you all;
And in that hope I throw mine eyes to heaven,
Scorning whate'er you can afflict me with.
Why come you not? what! multitudes, and fear?

LORD CLIFFORD.
So cowards fight when they can fly no further;
So doves do peck the falcon's piercing talons;
So desperate thieves, all hopeless of their lives,
Breathe out invectives 'gainst the officers.

DUKE OF YORK.
O Clifford, but bethink thee once again,
And in thy thought o'er-run my former time;
And, if thou canst for blushing, view this face,
And bite thy tongue, that slanders him with
   cowardice
Whose frown hath made thee faint and fly ere this!

LORD CLIFFORD.
I will not bandy with thee word for word,
But buckle with thee blows, twice two for one.
                    [*Draws.*

QUEEN MARGARET.
Hold, valiant Clifford! for a thousand causes
I would prolong awhile the traitor's life.—
Wrath makes him deaf:—speak thou, Northum-
   berland.

EARL OF NORTHUMBERLAND.
Hold, Clifford! do not honour him so much
To prick thy finger, though to wound his heart:
What valour were it, when a cur doth grin,
For one to thrust his hand between his teeth,
When he might spurn him with his foot away?
It is war's prize to take all vantages;
And ten to one is no impeach of valour.
         [*They lay hands on* YORK, *who struggles.*

LORD CLIFFORD.
Ay, ay, so strives the woodcock with the gin.

EARL OF NORTHUMBERLAND.
So doth the cony struggle in the net.

DUKE OF YORK.
So triumph thieves upon their conquer'd booty;
So true men yield, with robbers so o'ermatcht.

EARL OF NORTHUMBERLAND.
What would your Grace have done unto him
   now?

QUEEN MARGARET.
Brave warriors, Clifford and Northumberland,
Come, make him stand upon this molehill here,
That raught at mountains with outstretched arms,
Yet parted but the shadow with his hand.—
What! was it you that would be England's king?
Was't you that revell'd in our parliament,

And made a preachment of your high descent?
Where are your mess of sons to back you now?
The wanton Edward, and the lusty George?
And where's that valiant crook-back prodigy,
Dicky your boy, that with his grumbling voice
Was wont to cheer his dad in mutinies?
Or, with the rest, where is your darling Rutland?
Look, York: I stain'd this napkin with the blood
That valiant Clifford, with his rapier's point,
Made issue from the bosom of the boy;
And if thine eyes can water for his death,
I give thee this to dry thy cheeks withal.
Alas, poor York! but that I hate thee deadly,
I should lament thy miserable state.
I prithee, grieve, to make me merry, York;
Stamp, rave, and fret, that I may sing and dance.
What! hath thy fiery heart so parcht thine
    entrails
That not a tear can fall for Rutland's death?
Why art thou patient, man? thou shouldst be
    mad;
And I, to make thee mad, do mock thee thus.
Thou wouldst be fee'd, I see, to make me sport:
York cannot speak, unless he wear a crown.—
A crown for York!—and, lords, bow low to
    him:—
Hold you his hands, whilst I do set it on.—
           [*Putting a paper crown on his head.*
Ay, marry, sir, now looks he like a king!
Ay, this is he that took King Henry's chair;
And this is he was his adopted heir.—
But how is it that great Plantagenet
Is crown'd so soon, and broke his solemn oath?
As I bethink me, you should not be king
Till our King Henry had shook hands with death.
And will you pale your head in Henry's glory,
And rob his temples of the diadem,
Now in his life, against your holy oath?
O, 'tis a fault too-too unpardonable!—
Off with the crown, and, with the crown, his head;
And, whilst we breathe, take time to do him dead.
           LORD CLIFFORD.
That is my office, for my father's sake.
           QUEEN MARGARET.
Nay, stay; let's hear the orisons he makes.
           DUKE OF YORK.
She-wolf of France, but worse than wolves of
    France,
Whose tongue more poisons than the adder's
    tooth!
How ill-beseeming is it in thy sex
To triumph, like an Amazonian trull,
Upon their woes whom fortune captivates!
But that thy face is, vizard-like, unchanging,
Made impudent with use of evil deeds,
I would assay, proud queen, to make thee blush:
To tell thee whence thou camest, of whom
    derived,
Were shame enough to shame thee, wert thou
    not shameless.
Thy father bears the type of King of Naples,
Of both the Sicils and Jerusalem;
Yet not so wealthy as an English yeoman.
Hath that poor monarch taught thee to insult?
It needs not, nor it boots thee not, proud queen;
Unless the adage must be verified,—

That beggars mounted run their horse to death.
'Tis beauty that doth oft make women proud;
But, God he knows, thy share thereof is small:
'Tis virtue that doth make them most admired;
The contrary doth make thee wonder'd at:
'Tis government that makes them seem divine;
The want thereof makes thee abominable:
Thou art as opposite to every good
As the Antipodes are unto us,
Or as the south to the septentrion.
O tiger's heart wrapt in a woman's hide!
How couldst thou drain the life-blood of the
    child,
To bid the father wipe his eyes withal,
And yet be seen to bear a woman's face?
Women are soft, mild, pitiful, and flexible;
Thou stern, obdurate, flinty, rough, remorseless.
Bidd'st thou me rage? why, now thou hast thy
    wish;
Wouldst have me weep? why, now thou hast thy
    will:
For raging wind blows up incessant showers,
And when the rage allays, the rain begins.
These tears are my sweet Rutland's obsequies;
And every drop cries vengeance for his death,
'Gainst thee, fell Clifford, and thee, false French-
    woman.
           EARL OF NORTHUMBERLAND.
Beshrew me, but his passion moves me so
That hardly can I check my eyes from tears.
           DUKE OF YORK.
That face of his the hungry cannibals
Would not have toucht, would not have stain'd
    with blood:
But you are more inhuman, more inexorable,—
O, ten times more,—than tigers of Hyrcania.
See, ruthless queen, a hapless father's tears:
This cloth thou dipp'dst in blood of my sweet
    boy,
And I with tears do wash the blood away.
Keep thou the napkin, and go boast of this:
And, if thou tell'st the heavy story right,
Upon my soul, the hearers will shed tears;
Yea, even my foes will shed fast-falling tears,
And say, 'Alas, it was a piteous deed!'—
There, take the crown, and, with the crown, my
    curse;
           [*Giving back the paper crown.*
And in thy need such comfort come to thee
As now I reap at thy too cruel hand!—
Hard-hearted Clifford, take me from the world:
My soul to heaven, my blood upon your heads!
           EARL OF NORTHUMBERLAND.
Had he been slaughter-man to all my kin,
I should not for my life but weep with him,
To see how inly sorrow gripes his soul.
           QUEEN MARGARET.
What, weeping-ripe, my Lord Northumberland?
Think but upon the wrong he did us all,
And that will quickly dry thy melting tears.
           LORD CLIFFORD.
Here's for my oath, here's for my father's death.
           [*Stabbing him.*
           QUEEN MARGARET.
And here's to right our gentle-hearted king.
           [*Stabbing him.*

DUKE OF YORK.

Open Thy gate of mercy, gracious God!
My soul flies through these wounds to seek out
    Thee.   [*Dies.*

QUEEN MARGARET.

Off with his head, and set it on York gates;
So York may overlook the town of York.

                        [*Flourish. Exeunt.*

ACT II. SCENE I.

A plain near Mortimer's Cross in Herefordshire.

*A march.   Enter EDWARD, RICHARD, and their
POWER.*

EDWARD.

I WONDER how our princely father scaped,
    Or whether he be scaped away or no
From Clifford's and Northumberland's pursuit:
Had he been ta'en, we should have heard the
    news;
Had he been slain, we should have heard the
    news;
Or had he scaped, methinks we should have heard
The happy tidings of his good escape.—
How fares my brother? why is he so sad?

RICHARD.

I cannot joy, until I be resolved
Where our right valiant father is become.
I saw him in the battle range about;
And watcht him how he singled Clifford forth.
Methought he bore him in the thickest troop
As doth a lion in a herd of neat;
Or as a bear, encompast round with dogs,—
Who having pincht a few, and made them cry,
The rest stand all aloof, and bark at him.
So fared our father with his enemies;
So fled his enemies my warlike father:
Methinks, 'tis prize enough to be his son.—
See how the morning opes her golden gates,
And takes her farewell of the glorious sun!
How well resembles it the prime of youth,
Trimm'd like a younker prancing to his love!

EDWARD.

Dazzle mine eyes, or do I see three suns?

RICHARD.

Three glorious suns, each one a perfect sun;
Not separated with the racking clouds,
But sever'd in a pale clear-shining sky.
See, see! they join, embrace, and seem to kiss,
As if they vow'd some league inviolable:
Now are they but one lamp, one light, one sun.
In this the heaven figures some event.

EDWARD.

'Tis wondrous strange, the like yet never heard of.
I think it cites us, brother, to the field,—
That we, the sons of brave Plantagenet,
Each one already blazing by our meeds,
Should, notwithstanding, join our lights together,
And over-shine the earth, as this the world.
Whate'er it bodes, henceforward will I bear
Upon my target three fair-shining suns.

RICHARD.

Nay, bear three daughters:—by your leave I
    speak it,
You love the breeder better than the male.

Enter one blowing.

But what art thou, whose heavy looks foretell
Some dreadful story hanging on thy tongue?

MESSENGER.

Ah, one that was a woful looker-on
Whenas the noble Duke of York was slain,
Your princely father and my loving lord!

EDWARD.

O, speak no more! for I have heard too much.

RICHARD.

Say how he died, for I will hear it all.

MESSENGER.

Environed he was with many foes;
And stood against them as the hope of Troy
Against the Greeks that would have enter'd Troy.
But Hercules himself must yield to odds;
And many strokes, though with a little axe,
Hew down and fell the hardest-timber'd oak.
By many hands your father was subdued;
But only slaughtered by the ireful arm
Of unrelenting Clifford and the queen,
Who crown'd the gracious duke in high despite;
Laugh'd in his face; and when with grief he wept,
The ruthless queen gave him to dry his cheeks
A napkin steeped in the harmless blood
Of sweet young Rutland, by rough Clifford slain:
And after many scorns, many foul taunts,
They took his head, and on the gates of York
They set the same; and there it doth remain,
The saddest spectacle that e'er I view'd.

EDWARD.

Sweet Duke of York, our prop to lean upon,
Now thou art gone, we have no staff, no stay!—
O Clifford, boisterous Clifford, thou hast slain
The flower of Europe for his chivalry;
And treacherously hast thou vanquisht him,
For hand to hand he would have vanquisht
    thee!—
Now my soul's palace is become a prison:
Ah, would she break from hence, that this my
    body
Might in the ground be closed up in rest!
For never henceforth shall I joy again,
Never, O never, shall I see more joy!

RICHARD.

I cannot weep; for all my body's moisture
Scarce serves to quench my furnace-burning
    heart: [burden;
Nor can my tongue unload my heart's great
For selfsame wind that I should speak withal
Is kindling coals that fires all my breast,
And burns me up with flames that tears would
    quench.
To weep is to make less the depth of grief:
Tears, then, for babes; blows and revenge for
    me!—
Richard, I bear thy name; I'll venge thy death,
Or die renowned by attempting it.

EDWARD.

His name that valiant duke hath left with thee;
His dukedom and his chair with me is left.

RICHARD.

Nay, if thou be that princely eagle's bird,
Show thy descent by gazing 'gainst the sun:
For chair and dukedom, throne and kingdom say;
Either that is thine, or else thou wert not his.

March. *Enter* WARWICK, MONTAGUE, *and their*
ARMY.
EARL OF WARWICK.
How now, fair lords! What fare? what news
  abroad?
RICHARD.
Great Lord of Warwick, if we should recount
Our baleful news, and at each word's deliverance
Stab poniards in our flesh till all were told,
The words would add more anguish than the
  wounds.
O valiant lord, the Duke of York is slain!
EDWARD.
O Warwick, Warwick! that Plantagenet,
Which held thee dearly as his soul's redemption,
Is by the stern Lord Clifford done to death.
EARL OF WARWICK.
Ten days ago I drown'd these news in tears;
And now, to add more measure to your woes,
I come to tell you things sith then befaln.
After the bloody fray at Wakefield fought,
Where your brave father breathed his latest gasp,
Tidings, as swiftly as the posts could run,
Were brought me of your loss and his depart.
I, then in London, keeper of the king,
Muster'd my soldiers, gather'd flocks of friends,
And very well appointed, as I thought,   [queen,
Marcht toward Saint Alban's to intercept the
Bearing the king in my behalf along;
For by my scouts I was advertised
That she was coming with a full intent
To dash our late decree in parliament
Touching King Henry's oath and your succession.
Short tale to make,—we at Saint Alban's met,
Our battles join'd, and both sides fiercely fought:
But whether 'twas the coldness of the king,
Who lookt full gently on his warlike queen,
That robb'd my soldiers of their heated spleen;
Or whether 'twas report of her success;
Or more than common fear of Clifford's rigour,
Who thunders to his captives blood and death,
I cannot judge: but, to conclude with truth,
Their weapons like to lightning came and went;
Our soldiers—like the night-owl's lazy flight,
Or like an idle thrasher with a flail—
Fell gently down, as if they struck their friends.
I cheer'd them up with justice of our cause,
With promise of high pay and great rewards:
But all in vain; they had no heart to fight,
And we, in them, no hope to win the day;
So that we fled; the king unto the queen;
Lord George your brother, Norfolk, and myself,
In haste, post-haste, are come to join with you;
For in the marches here we heard you were
Making another head to fight again.
EDWARD.
Where is the Duke of Norfolk, gentle Warwick?
And when came George from Burgundy to
  England?
EARL OF WARWICK.
Some six miles off the duke is with his power;
And for your brother, he was lately sent
From your kind aunt, Duchess of Burgundy,
With aid of soldiers to this needful war.
RICHARD.
'Twas odds, belike, when valiant Warwick fled:

Oft have I heard his praises in pursuit,
But ne'er till now his scandal of retire.
EARL OF WARWICK.
Nor now my scandal, Richard, dost thou hear;
For thou shalt know this strong right hand of
  mine
Can pluck the diadem from faint Henry's head,
And wring the awful sceptre from his fist,
Were he as famous and as bold in war
As he is famed for mildness, peace, and prayer.
RICHARD.
I know it well, Lord Warwick; blame me not:
'Tis love I bear thy glories makes me speak.
But in this troublous time what's to be done?
Shall we go throw away our coats of steel,
And wrap our bodies in black mourning-gowns,
Numbering our Ave-Maries with our beads?
Or shall we on the helmets of our foes
Tell our devotion with revengeful arms?
If for the last, say 'Ay,' and to it, lords.
EARL OF WARWICK.
Why, therefore Warwick came to seek you out;
And therefore comes my brother Montague.
Attend me, lords. The proud insulting queen,
With Clifford and the haught Northumberland,
And of their feather many moe proud birds,
Have wrought the easy-melting king like wax.
He swore consent to your succession,
His oath enrolled in the parliament;
And now to London all the crew are gone,
To frustrate both his oath, and what beside
May make against the house of Lancaster.
Their power, I think, is thirty thousand strong:
Now, if the help of Norfolk and myself,
With all the friends that thou, brave Earl of
  March,
Amongst the loving Welshmen canst procure,
Will but amount to five-and-twenty thousand,
Why, *Via!* to London will we march amain;
And once again bestride our foaming steeds,
And once again cry, 'Charge! upon our foes!'
But never once again turn back and fly.
RICHARD.
Ay, now methinks I hear great Warwick speak:
Ne'er may he live to see a sunshine day,
That cries, 'Retire,' if Warwick bid him stay.
EDWARD.
Lord Warwick, on thy shoulder will I lean;
And when thou faint'st,—as God forbid the
  hour!—
Must Edward fall, which peril heaven forfend!
EARL OF WARWICK.
No longer Earl of March, but Duke of York:
The next degree is England's royal throne;
For King of England shalt thou be proclaim'd
In every borough as we pass along;
And he that throws not up his cap for joy,
Shall for the fault make forfeit of his head.
King Edward,—valiant Richard,—Montague,—
Stay we no longer, dreaming of renown,
But sound the trumpets, and about our task.
RICHARD.
Then, Clifford, were thy heart as hard as
  steel,—
As thou hast shown it flinty by thy deeds,—
I come to pierce it, or to give thee mine.

EDWARD.

Then strike up drums:—God and Saint George
for us!

Enter a MESSENGER.

EARL OF WARWICK.

How now! what news?

MESSENGER.

The Duke of Norfolk sends you word by me
The queen is coming with a puissant host,
And craves your company for speedy counsel.

EARL OF WARWICK.

Why, then it sorts, brave warriors: let's away.

[*Exeunt.*

SCENE II.

Before York.

Flourish. Enter the KING, QUEEN, *the* PRINCE
OF WALES, CLIFFORD, *and* NORTHUMBER-
LAND, *with drum and trumpets.*

QUEEN MARGARET.

WELCOME, my lord, to this brave town of
York.
Yonder's the head of that arch-enemy
That sought to be encompast with your crown:
Doth not the object cheer your heart, my lord?

KING HENRY.

Ay, as the rocks cheer them that fear their
wrack:—
To see this sight, it irks my very soul.—
Withhold revenge, dear God! 'tis not my fault,
Nor wittingly have I infringed my vow.

LORD CLIFFORD.

My gracious liege, this too much lenity
And harmful pity must be laid aside.
To whom do lions cast their gentle looks?
Not to the beast that would usurp their den.
Whose hand is that the forest bear doth lick?
Not his that spoils her young before her face.
Who scapes the lurking serpent's mortal sting?
Not he that sets his foot upon her back.
The smallest worm will turn being trodden on,
And doves will peck in safeguard of their brood.
Ambitious York did level at thy crown,
Thou smiling while he knit his angry brows:
He, but a duke, would have his son a king,
And raise his issue, like a loving sire;
Thou, being a king, blest with a goodly son,
Didst yield consent to disinherit him,
Which argued thee a most unloving father.
Unreasonable creatures feed their young;
And though man's face be fearful to their eyes,
Yet, in protection of their tender ones,
Who hath not seen them, even with those wings
Which sometime they have used in fearful flight,
Make war with him that climb'd unto their nest,
Offering their own lives in their young's defence?
For shame, my liege, make them your precedent!
Were it not pity that this goodly boy
Should lose his birthright by his father's fault,
And long hereafter say unto his child,
'What my great-grandfather and grandsire got
My careless father fondly gave away'?
Ah, what a shame were this! Look on the boy;
And let his manly face, which promiseth
Successful fortune, steel thy melting heart
To hold thine own, and leave thine own with him.

KING HENRY.

Full well hath Clifford play'd the orator,
Inferring arguments of mighty force.
But, Clifford, tell me, didst thou never hear
That things ill-got had ever bad success?
And happy always was it for that son
Whose father for his hoarding went to hell?
I'll leave my son my virtuous deeds behind;
And would my father had left me no more!
For all the rest is held at such a rate
As brings a thousand-fold more care to keep
Than in possession any jot of pleasure.—
Ah, cousin York! would thy best friends did know
How it doth grieve me that thy head is here!

QUEEN MARGARET.

My lord, cheer up your spirits: our foes are nigh,
And this soft courage makes your followers faint.
You promised knighthood to our forward son:
Unsheathe your sword, and dub him presently.—
Edward, kneel down.

KING HENRY.

Edward Plantagenet, arise a knight;
And learn this lesson,—draw thy sword in right.

PRINCE OF WALES.

My gracious father, by your kingly leave,
I'll draw it as apparent to the crown,
And in that quarrel use it to the death.

LORD CLIFFORD.

Why, that is spoken like a toward prince.

Enter a MESSENGER.

MESSENGER.

Royal commanders, be in readiness:
For with a band of thirty thousand men
Comes Warwick, backing of the Duke of York;
And in the towns, as they do march along,
Proclaims him king, and many fly to him:
Darraign your battle, for they are at hand.

LORD CLIFFORD.

I would your highness would depart the field:
The queen hath best success when you are absent.

QUEEN MARGARET.

Ay, good my lord, and leave us to our fortune.

KING HENRY.

Why, that's my fortune too; therefore I'll stay.

EARL OF NORTHUMBERLAND.

Be it with resolution, then, to fight.

PRINCE OF WALES.

My royal father, cheer these noble lords,
And hearten those that fight in your defence:
Unsheathe your sword, good father; cry, 'Saint
George!'

March. Enter EDWARD, GEORGE, RICHARD,
WARWICK, NORFOLK, MONTAGUE, *and*
SOLDIERS.

EDWARD.

Now, perjured Henry! wilt thou kneel for grace,
And set thy diadem upon my head;
Or bide the mortal fortune of the field?

QUEEN MARGARET.

Go, rate thy minions, proud insulting boy!
Becomes it thee to be thus bold in terms
Before thy sovereign and thy lawful king?

EDWARD.

I am his king, and he should bow his knee;
I was adopted heir by his consent:
Since when, his oath is broke; for, as I hear,

You, that are king, though he do wear the crown,
Have caused him, by new act of Parliament,
To blot out me, and put his own son in.

LORD CLIFFORD.

And reason too:
Who should succeed the father but the son?

RICHARD.

Are you there, butcher?—O, I cannot speak!

LORD CLIFFORD.

Ay, crook-back, here I stand to answer thee,
Or any he the proudest of thy sort.

RICHARD.

'Twas you that kill'd young Rutland, was it not?

LORD CLIFFORD.

Ay, and old York, and yet not satisfied.

RICHARD.

For God's sake, lords, give signal to the fight.

EARL OF WARWICK.

What say'st thou, Henry, wilt thou yield the
crown?

QUEEN MARGARET.

Why, how now, long-tongued Warwick! dare you
speak?
When you and I met at Saint Alban's last,
Your legs did better service than your hands.

EARL OF WARWICK.

Then 'twas my turn to fly, and now 'tis thine.

LORD CLIFFORD.

You said so much before, and yet you fled.

EARL OF WARWICK.

'Twas not your valour, Clifford, drove me thence.

EARL OF NORTHUMBERLAND.

No, nor your manhood that durst make you stay.

RICHARD.

Northumberland, I hold thee reverently.—
Break off the parle: for scarce I can refrain
The execution of my big-swoln heart
Upon that Clifford there, that cruel child-killer.

LORD CLIFFORD.

I slew thy father,—call'st thou him a child?

RICHARD.

Ay, like a dastard and a treacherous coward,
As thou didst kill our tender brother Rutland;
But ere sun set I'll make thee curse the deed.

KING HENRY.

Have done with words, my lords, and hear me
speak.

QUEEN MARGARET.

Defy them, then, or else hold close thy lips.

KING HENRY.

I prithee, give no limits to my tongue:
I am a king, and privileged to speak.

LORD CLIFFORD.

My liege, the wound that bred this meeting here
Cannot be cured by words; therefore be still.

RICHARD.

Then, executioner, unsheathe thy sword:
By Him that made us all, I am resolved
That Clifford's manhood lies upon his tongue.

EDWARD.

Say, Henry, shall I have my right, or no?
A thousand men have broke their fasts to-day
That ne'er shall dine unless thou yield the crown.

EARL OF WARWICK.

If thou deny, their blood upon thy head;
For York in justice puts his armour on.

PRINCE OF WALES.

If that be right which Warwick says is right,
There is no wrong, but every thing is right.

RICHARD.

Whoever got thee, there thy mother stands;
For, well I wot, thou hast thy mother's tongue.

QUEEN MARGARET.

But thou art neither like thy sire nor dam;
But like a foul mis-shapen stigmatic,
Markt by the Destinies to be avoided,
As venom toads, or lizards' dreadful stings.

RICHARD.

Iron of Naples hid with English gilt,
Whose father bears the title of a king,—
As if a channel should be call'd the sea,—
Shamest thou not, knowing whence thou art ex‑
traught,
To let thy tongue detect thy base-born heart?

EDWARD.

A wisp of straw were worth a thousand crowns,
To make this shameless callet know herself.—
Helen of Greece was fairer far than thou,
Although thy husband may be Menelaus;
And ne'er was Agamemnon's brother wrong'd
By that false woman as this king by thee.
His father revell'd in the heart of France,
And tamed the king, and made the dauphin stoop;
And had he matcht according to his state,
He might have kept that glory to this day;
But when he took a beggar to his bed,
And graced thy poor sire with his bridal-day,
Even then that sunshine brew'd a shower for him,
That washt his father's fortunes forth of France,
And heapt sedition on his crown at home.
For what hath broacht this tumult but thy pride?
Hadst thou been meek, our title still had slept;
And we, in pity of the gentle king,
Had slipt our claim unto another age.

GEORGE.

But when we saw our sunshine made thy spring,
And that thy summer bred us no increase,
We set the axe to thy usurping root;   [selves,
And though the edge hath something hit our‑
Yet, know thou, since we have begun to strike,
We'll never leave till we have hewn thee down,
Or bathed thy growing with our heated bloods.

EDWARD.

And, in this resolution, I defy thee;
Not willing any longer conference,
Since thou deniest the gentle king to speak.—
Sound trumpets!—let our bloody colours wave!—
And either victory, or else a grave.

QUEEN MARGARET.

Stay, Edward.

EDWARD.

No, wrangling woman, we'll no longer stay;
These words will cost ten thousand lives this day.

[*Exeunt.*

SCENE III.

*A field of battle between Towton and Saxton, in
Yorkshire.*

Alarum.   Excursions.   Enter WARWICK.

EARL OF WARWICK.

FORSPENT with toil, as runners with a race,
I lay me down a little while to breathe;

For strokes received, and many blows repaid,
Have robb'd my strong-knit sinews of their
     strength,
And, spite of spite, needs must I rest awhile.
     Enter EDWARD, *running.*
          EDWARD.
Smile, gentle heaven! or strike, ungentle death!
For this world frowns, and Edward's sun is
     clouded.
          EARL OF WARWICK.
How now, my lord! what hap? what hope of good?
     Enter GEORGE.
          GEORGE.
Our hap is loss, our hope but sad despair;
Our ranks are broke, and ruin follows us:
What counsel give you? whither shall we fly?
          EDWARD.
Bootless is flight,—they follow us with wings;
And weak are we, and cannot shun pursuit.
     Enter RICHARD.
          RICHARD.
Ah, Warwick, why hast thou withdrawn thyself?
Thy brother's blood the thirsty earth hath drunk,
Broacht with the steely point of Clifford's lance;
And, in the very pangs of death, he cried,
Like to a dismal clangor heard from far,
'Warwick, revenge! brother, revenge my death!'
So, underneath the belly of their steeds,
That stain'd their fetlocks in his smoking blood,
The noble gentleman gave up the ghost.
          EARL OF WARWICK.
Then let the earth be drunken with our blood:
I'll kill my horse, because I will not fly.
Why stand we like soft-hearted women here,
Wailing our losses, whiles the foe doth rage;
And look upon, as if the tragedy
Were play'd in jest by counterfeiting actors?
Here on my knee I vow to God above,
I'll never pause again, never stand still,
Till either death hath closed these eyes of mine,
Or fortune given me measure of revenge.
          EDWARD.
O Warwick, I do bend my knee with thine;
And in this vow do chain my soul to thine!—
And, ere my knee rise from the earth's cold face,
I throw my hands, mine eyes, my heart to Thee,
Thou setter-up and plucker-down of kings,—
Beseeching Thee, if with Thy will it stands
That to my foes this body must be prey,
Yet that Thy brazen gates of heaven may ope,
And give sweet passage to my sinful soul!—
Now, lords, take leave until we meet again,
Where'er it be, in heaven or in earth.
          RICHARD.
Brother, give me thy hand;—and, gentle Warwick,
Let me embrace thee in my weary arms:
I, that did never weep, now melt with woe
That winter should cut off our spring-time so.
          EARL OF WARWICK.
Away, away! Once more, sweet lords, farewell.
          GEORGE.
Yet let us all together to our troops,
And give them leave to fly that will not stay;
And call them pillars that will stand to us;
And, if we thrive, promise them such rewards
As victors wear at the Olympian games:

This may plant courage in their quailing breasts;
For yet is hope of life and victory.—
Forslow no longer, make we hence amain.
                              [*Exeunt.*

          SCENE IV.
     Another part of the field.
Excursions. Enter RICHARD *and* CLIFFORD.
          RICHARD.
NOW, Clifford, I have singled thee alone:
     Suppose this arm is for the Duke of York,
And this for Rutland; both bound to revenge,
Wert thou environ'd with a brazen wall.
          LORD CLIFFORD.
Now, Richard, I am with thee here alone:
This is the hand that stabb'd thy father York;
And this the hand that slew thy brother Rutland;
And here's the heart that triumphs in their death,
And cheers these hands that slew thy sire and
     brother,
To execute the like upon thyself;
And so, have at thee!
     [*They fight.* WARWICK *comes;* CLIFFORD
     flies.
          RICHARD.
Nay, Warwick. single out some other chase;
For I myself will hunt this wolf to death.
                              [*Exeunt.*

          SCENE V.
     Another part of the field.
     Alarum. Enter KING HENRY *alone.*
          KING HENRY.
THIS battle fares like to the morning's war,
     When dying clouds contend with growing
     light,
What time the shepherd, blowing of his nails,
Can neither call it perfect day nor night.
Now sways it this way, like a mighty sea
Forced by the tide to combat with the wind;
Now sways it that way, like the selfsame sea
Forced to retire by fury of the wind:
Sometime the flood prevails, and then the wind;
Now one the better, then another best;
Both tugging to be victors, breast to breast,
Yet neither conqueror nor conquered:
So is the equal poise of this fell war.
Here on this molehill will I sit me down.
To whom God will, there be the victory!
For Margaret my queen, and Clifford too,
Have chid me from the battle; swearing both
They prosper best of all when I am thence.
Would I were dead! if God's good will were so;
For what is in this world but grief and woe?
O God! methinks it were a happy life,
To be no better than a homely swain;
To sit upon a hill, as I do now,
To carve out dials quaintly, point by point,
Thereby to see the minutes how they run,—
How many makes the hour full complete;
How many hours brings about the day;
How many days will finish up the year;
How many years a mortal man may live.
When this is known, then to divide the times:—
So many hours must I tend my flock;
So many hours must I take my rest;

So many hours must I contemplate;
So many hours must I sport myself;
So many days my ewes have been with young;
So many weeks ere the poor fools will ean;
So many months ere I shall shear the fleece:
So minutes, hours, days, months, and years,
Past over to the end they were created,
Would bring white hairs unto a quiet grave.
Ah, what a life were this! how sweet! how lovely!
Gives not the hawthorn-bush a sweeter shade
To shepherds looking on their silly sheep,
Than doth a rich-embroider'd canopy
To kings that fear their subjects' treachery?
O, yes, it doth; a thousand-fold it doth.
And to conclude,—the shepherd's homely curds,
His cold thin drink out of his leather bottle,
His wonted sleep under a fresh tree's shade,
All which secure and sweetly he enjoys,
Is far beyond a prince's delicates,
His viands sparkling in a golden cup,
His body couched in a curious bed,
When care, mistrust, and treason waits on him.

Alarum. Enter a SON *that hath kill'd his father,*
bringing in the dead body.

SON.

Ill blows the wind that profits nobody.
This man, whom hand to hand I slew in fight,
May be possessed with some store of crowns;
And I, that haply take them from him now,
May yet ere night yield both my life and them
To some man else, as this dead man doth me.—
Who's this?—O God! it is my father's face,
Whom in this conflict I un'wares have kill'd.
O heavy times, begetting such events!
From London by the king was I prest forth;
My father, being the Earl of Warwick's man,
Came on the part of York, prest by his master;
And I, who at his hands received my life,
Have by my hands of life bereaved him.—
Pardon me, God, I knew not what I did!—
And pardon, father, for I knew not thee!—
My tears shall wipe away these bloody marks;
And no more words till they have flow'd their
   fill.

KING HENRY.

O piteous spectacle! O bloody times!
Whiles lions war and battle for their dens,
Poor harmless lambs abide their enmity.—
Weep, wretched man, I'll aid thee tear for tear;
And let our hearts and eyes, like civil war,
Be blind with tears, and break o'ercharged with
   grief.

Enter FATHER, *bearing of his son.*

FATHER.

Thou that so stoutly hast resisted me,
Give me thy gold, if thou hast any gold;
For I have bought it with an hundred blows.—
But let me see: is this our foeman's face?
Ah, no, no, no, it is mine only son!
Ah, boy, if any life be left in thee,
Throw up thine eye! see, see what showers arise,
Blown with the windy tempest of my heart,
Upon thy wounds, that kills mine eye and
   heart!—
O, pity, God, this miserable age!—
What stratagems, how fell, how butcherly,

Erroneous, mutinous, and unnatural,
This deadly quarrel daily doth beget!
O boy, thy father gave thee life too soon,
And hath bereft thee of thy life too late!

KING HENRY.

Woe above woe! grief more than common grief!
O, that my death would stay these ruthful
   deeds!—
O, pity, pity, gentle heaven, pity!—
The red rose and the white are on his face,
The fatal colours of our striving houses:
The one his purple blood right well resembles;
The other his pale cheeks, methinks, presenteth..
Wither one rose, and let the other flourish;
If you contend, a thousand lives must wither.

SON.

How will my mother for a father's death
Take on with me, and ne'er be satisfied!

FATHER.

How will my wife for slaughter of my son
Shed seas of tears, and ne'er be satisfied!

KING HENRY.

How will the country for these woful chances
Misthink the king, and not be satisfied!

SON.

Was ever son so rued a father's death?

FATHER.

Was ever father so bemoan'd his son?

KING HENRY.

Was ever king so grieved for subjects' woe?
Much is your sorrow; mine ten times so much.

SON.

I'll bear thee hence, where I may weep my fill.
                    [*Exit with the body.*

FATHER.

These arms of mine shall be thy winding-sheet;
My heart, sweet boy, shall be thy sepulchre,—
For from my heart thine image ne'er shall go;
My sighing breast shall be thy funeral bell;
And so obsequious will thy father be,
E'en for the loss of thee, having no more,
As Priam was for all his valiant sons.
I'll bear thee hence; and let them fight that will,
For I have murder'd where I should not kill.
                    [*Exit with the body.*

KING HENRY.

Sad-hearted men, much overgone with care,
Here sits a king more woful than you are.
   Alarums. Excursions. Enter the QUEEN, *the*
      PRINCE, *and* EXETER.

PRINCE OF WALES.

Fly, father, fly! for all your friends are fled,
And Warwick rages like a chafed bull:
Away! for death doth hold us in pursuit.

QUEEN MARGARET.

Mount you, my lord; towards Berwick post
   amain:
Edward and Richard, like a brace of greyhounds
Having the fearful flying hare in sight,
With fiery eyes sparkling for very wrath,
And bloody steel graspt in their ireful hands,
Are at our backs; and therefore hence amain.

DUKE OF EXETER.

Away! for vengeance comes along with them:
Nay, stay not to expostulate,—make speed;
Or else come after: I'll away before.

KING HENRY.

Nay, take me with thee, good sweet Exeter:
Not that I fear to stay, but love to go
Whither the queen intends. Forward; away!

[*Exeunt.*

SCENE VI.

Another part of the field.

A loud alarum.   Enter CLIFFORD, *wounded.*

LORD CLIFFORD.

HERE burns my candle out,—ay, here it dies,
Which, whiles it lasted, gave King Henry
O Lancaster, I fear thy overthrow   [light.
More than my body's parting with my soul!
My love and fear glued many friends to thee;
And, now I fall, that tough commixture melts.
Impairing Henry, strengthening misproud York,
The common people swarm like summer flies;
And whither fly the gnats but to the sun?
And who shines now but Henry's enemies?
O Phœbus, hadst thou never given consent
That Phaethon should check thy fiery steeds,
Thy burning car never had scorcht the earth!
And, Henry, hadst thou sway'd as kings should do,
Or as thy father and his father did,
Giving no ground unto the house of York,
I and ten thousand in this luckless realm
Had left no mourning widows for our death;
And thou this day hadst kept thy chair in peace.
For what doth cherish weeds but gentle air?
And what makes robbers bold but too much lenity?—
Bootless are plaints, and cureless are my wounds;
No way to fly, nor strength to hold out flight:
The foe is merciless, and will not pity;
For at their hands I have deserved no pity.
The air hath got into my deadly wounds,
And much effuse of blood doth make me faint.—
Come, York and Richard, Warwick and the rest;
I stabb'd your fathers' bosoms,—split my breast.

[*Faints.*

Alarum and retreat.   Enter EDWARD, GEORGE,
RICHARD, MONTAGUE, WARWICK, *and* SOL-
DIERS.

EDWARD.

Now breathe we, lords: good fortune bids us pause,
And smooth the frowns of war with peaceful looks.—
Some troops pursue the bloody-minded queen,
That led calm Henry, though he were a king,
As doth a sail, fill'd with a fretting gust,
Command an argosy to stem the waves.
But think you, lords, that Clifford fled with them?

EARL OF WARWICK.

No, 'tis impossible he should escape;
For, though before his face I speak the words,
Your brother Richard markt him for the grave:
And wheresoe'er he is, he's surely dead.

[CLIFFORD *groans, and dies.*

EDWARD.

Whose soul is that which takes her heavy leave?

RICHARD.

A deadly groan, like life and death's departing.

EDWARD.

See who it is: and, now the battle's ended,
If friend or foe, let him be gently used.

RICHARD.

Revoke that doom of mercy, for 'tis Clifford;
Who not contented that he lopt the branch
In hewing Rutland when his leaves put forth,
But set his murdering knife unto the root
From whence that tender spray did sweetly spring,—
I mean our princely father, Duke of York.

EARL OF WARWICK.

From off the gates of York fetch down the head,
Your father's head, which Clifford placed there;
Instead whereof let this supply the room:
Measure for measure must be answered.

EDWARD.

Bring forth that fatal screech-owl to our house,
That nothing sung but death to us and ours:
Now death shall stop his dismal-threatening sound,
And his ill-boding tongue no more shall speak.

[SOLDIERS *bring the body forward.*

EARL OF WARWICK.

I think his understanding is bereft.—
Speak, Clifford, dost thou know who speaks to thee?—
Dark cloudy death o'ershades his beams of life,
And he nor sees nor hears us what we say.

RICHARD.

O, would he did! and so, perhaps, he doth:
'Tis but his policy to counterfeit,
Because he would avoid such bitter taunts
Which in the time of death he gave our father.

GEORGE.

If so thou think'st, vex him with eager words.

RICHARD.

Clifford, ask mercy, and obtain no grace.

EDWARD.

Clifford, repent in bootless penitence.

EARL OF WARWICK.

Clifford, devise excuses for thy faults.

GEORGE.

While we devise fell tortures for thy faults.

RICHARD.

Thou didst love York, and I am son to York.

EDWARD.

Thou pitied'st Rutland; I will pity thee.

GEORGE.

Where's Captain Margaret, to fence you now?

EARL OF WARWICK.

They mock thee, Clifford: swear as thou wast wont.

RICHARD.

What, not an oath? nay, then the world goes hard
When Clifford cannot spare his friends an oath.—
I know by that he's dead; and, by my soul,
If this right hand would buy two hours' life,
That I in all despite might rail at him,
This hand should chop it off; and with the issuing blood
Stifle the villain whose unstanched thirst
York and young Rutland could not satisfy.

EARL OF WARWICK.

Ay, but he's dead: off with the traitor's head,
And rear it in the place your father's stands.—

And now to London with triumphant march,
There to be crowned England's royal king.
From whence shall Warwick cut the sea to France,
And ask the Lady Bona for thy queen:
So shalt thou sinew both these lands together;
And, having France thy friend, thou shalt not
　　dread
The scatter'd foe that hopes to rise again;
For though they cannot greatly sting to hurt,
Yet look to have them buzz to offend thine ears.
First will I see the coronation;
And then to Brittany I'll cross the sea,
To effect this marriage, so it please my lord.

EDWARD.

Even as thou wilt, sweet Warwick, let it be;
For in thy shoulder do I build my seat,
And never will I undertake the thing
Wherein thy counsel and consent is wanting.—
Richard, I will create thee Duke of Gloster;—
And George, of Clarence:—Warwick, as ourself,
Shall do and undo as him pleaseth best.

RICHARD.

Let me be Duke of Clarence, George of Gloster;
For Gloster's dukedom is too ominous.

EARL OF WARWICK.

Tut, that's a foolish observation:
Richard, be Duke of Gloster. Now to London,
To see these honours in possession. [Exeunt.

ACT III. SCENE I.

A chase in the north of England.

Enter two KEEPERS, *with cross-bows in their
hands.*

FIRST KEEPER.

UNDER this thick-grown brake we'll shroud
　　ourselves;
For through this laund anon the deer will come;
And in this covert will we make our stand,
Culling the principal of all the deer.

SECOND KEEPER.

I'll stay above the hill, so both may shoot.

FIRST KEEPER.

That cannot be; the noise of thy cross-bow
Will scare the herd, and so my shoot is lost.
Here stand we both, and aim we at the best:
And, for the time shall not seem tedious,
I'll tell thee what befell me on a day
In this self-place where now we mean to stand.

SECOND KEEPER.

Here comes a man; let's stay till he be past.

Enter the KING, *with a prayer-book.*

KING HENRY.

From Scotland am I stoln, even of pure love,
To greet mine own land with my wishful sight.
No, Harry, Harry, 'tis no land of thine;
Thy place is fill'd, thy sceptre wrung from thee,
Thy balm washt off wherewith thou wast
　　anointed:
No bending knee will call thee Cæsar now,
No humble suitors press to speak for right,
No, not a man comes for redress of thee;
For how can I help them, and not myself?

FIRST KEEPER.

Ay, here's a deer whose skin's a keeper's fee:
This is the *quondam* king; let's seize upon him.

KING HENRY.

Let me embrace thee, sour adversity;
For wise men say it is the wisest course.

SECOND KEEPER.

Why linger we? let us lay hands upon him.

FIRST KEEPER.

Forbear awhile; we'll hear a little more.

KING HENRY.

My queen and son are gone to Ftance for aid;
And, as I hear, the great-commanding Warwick
Is thither gone, to crave the French king's sister
To wife for Edward: if this news be true,
Poor queen and son, your labour is but lost;
For Warwick is a subtle orator,
And Louis a prince soon won with moving
　　words.
By this account, then, Margaret may win him;
For she's a woman to be pitied much:
Her sighs will make a battery in his breast;
Her tears will pierce into a marble heart;
The tiger will be mild whiles she doth mourn;
And Nero will be tainted with remorse,
To hear and see her plaints, her brinish tears.
Ay, but she's come to beg; Warwick, to give:
She, on his left side, craving aid for Henry;
He, on his right, asking a wife for Edward.
She weeps, and says her Henry is deposèd;
He smiles, and says his Edward is install'd;
That she, poor wretch, for grief can speak no
　　more;
Whiles Warwick tells his title, smooths the wrong,
Inferreth arguments of mighty strength,
And in conclusion wins the king from her,
With promise of his sister, and what else,
To strengthen and support King Edward's place.
O Margaret, thus 'twill be; and thou, poor soul,
Art then forsaken, as thou went'st forlorn!

SECOND KEEPER.

Say, what art thou that talk'st of kings and
　　queens?

KING HENRY.

More than I seem, and less than I was born to:
A man at least, for less I should not be;
And men may talk of kings, and why not I?

SECOND KEEPER.

Ay, but thou talk'st as if thou wert a king.

KING HENRY.

Why, so I am—in mind; and that's enough.

SECOND KEEPER.

But, if thou be a king, where is thy crown?

KING HENRY.

My crown is in my heart, not on my head;
Not deckt with diamonds and Indian stones,
Nor to be seen: my crown is call'd content—
A crown it is that seldom kings enjoy.

SECOND KEEPER.

Well, if you be a king crown'd with content,
Your crown content and you must be contented
To go along with us; for, as we think,
You are the king King Edward hath deposed;
And we his subjects, sworn in all allegiance,
Will apprehend you as his enemy.

KING HENRY.

But did you never swear, and break an oath?

SECOND KEEPER.

No, never such an oath; nor will not now.

KING HENRY.
Where did you dwell when I was king of England?
SECOND KEEPER.
Here in this country, where we now remain.
KING HENRY.
I was anointed king at nine months old;
My father and my grandfather were kings;
And you were sworn true subjects unto me:
And tell me, then, have you not broke your oaths?
FIRST KEEPER.
No;
For we were subjects but while you were king.
KING HENRY.
Why, am I dead? do I not breathe a man?
Ah, simple men, you know not what you
    swear!
Look, as I blow this feather from my face,
And as the air blows it to me again,
Obeying with my wind when I do blow,
And yielding to another when it blows,
Commanded always by the greater gust;
Such is the lightness of you common men.
But do not break your oaths; for of that sin
My mild entreaty shall not make you guilty.
Go where you will, the king shall be commanded;
And be you kings; command, and I'll obey.
FIRST KEEPER.
We are true subjects to the king, King Edward.
KING HENRY.
So would you be again to Henry,
If he were seated as King Edward is.
FIRST KEEPER.
We charge you, in God's name, and the king's,
To go with us unto the officers.
KING HENRY.
In God's name, lead; your king's name be obey'd;
And what God will, that let your king perform;
And what he will, I humbly yield unto.   [Exeunt.

SCENE II.

London.   A room in the palace.

Enter KING EDWARD, GLOSTER, CLARENCE,
and LADY GREY.

KING EDWARD.

BROTHER of Gloster, at Saint Alban's field
This lady's husband, Sir Richard Grey, was
    slain,
His lands then seized on by the conqueror:
Her suit is now to repossess those lands;
Which we in justice cannot well deny,
Because in quarrel of the house of York
The worthy gentleman did lose his life.
DUKE OF GLOSTER.
Your highness shall do well to grant her suit;
It were dishonour to deny it her.
KING EDWARD.
It were no less; but yet I'll make a pause.
DUKE OF GLOSTER [*aside to* CLARENCE].
Yea, is it so?
I see the lady hath a thing to grant,
Before the king will grant her humble suit.
DUKE OF CLARENCE [*aside to* GLOSTER].
He knows the game: how true he keeps the
    wind!

DUKE OF GLOSTER [*aside to* CLARENCE].
Silence!
KING EDWARD.
Widow, we will consider of your suit;
And come some other time to know our mind.
LADY GREY.
Right gracious lord, I cannot brook delay:
May't please your highness to resolve me
    now;
And what your pleasure is shall satisfy me.
DUKE OF GLOSTER [*aside*].
Ay, widow? then I'll warrant you all your
    lands,
An if what pleases him shall pleasure you.
Fight closer, or, good faith, you'll catch a blow.
DUKE OF CLARENCE [*aside to* GLOSTER].
I fear her not, unless she chance to fall.
DUKE OF GLOSTER [*aside to* CLARENCE].
God forbid that! for he'll take vantages.
KING EDWARD.
How many children hast thou, widow? tell me.
DUKE OF CLARENCE [*aside to* GLOSTER].
I think he means to beg a child of her.
DUKE OF GLOSTER [*aside to* CLARENCE].
Nay, whip me, then; he'll rather give her two.
LADY GREY.
Three, my most gracious lord.
DUKE OF GLOSTER [*aside*].
You shall have four, if you'll be ruled by him.
KING EDWARD.
'Twere pity they should lose their father's lands.
LADY GREY.
Be pitiful, dread lord, and grant it, then.
KING EDWARD.
Lords, give us leave: I'll try this widow's wit.
DUKE OF GLOSTER [*aside*].
Ay, good leave have you; for you will have
    leave,
Till youth take leave, and leave you to the
    crutch.   [*Retires with* CLARENCE
KING EDWARD.
Now tell me, madam, do you love your chil-
    dren?
LADY GREY.
Ay, full as dearly as I love myself.
KING EDWARD.
And would you not do much to do them good?
LADY GREY.
To do them good, I would sustain some harm.
KING EDWARD.
Then get your husband's lands, to do them
    good.
LADY GREY.
Therefore I came unto your majesty.
KING EDWARD.
I'll tell you how these lands are to be got.
LADY GREY.
So shall you bind me to your highness' service.
KING EDWARD.
What service wilt thou do me, if I give them?
LADY GREY.
What you command, that rests in me to do.
KING EDWARD.
But you will take exceptions to my boon.
LADY GREY.
No, gracious lord, except I cannot do it.

KING EDWARD.
Ay, but thou canst do what I mean to ask.
LADY GREY.
Why, then I will do what your Grace commands.
DUKE OF GLOSTER [*aside to* CLARENCE].
He plies her hard; and much rain wears the marble.
DUKE OF CLARENCE [*aside to* GLOSTER].
As red as fire! nay, then her wax must melt.
LADY GREY.
Why stops my lord? shall I not hear my task?
KING EDWARD.
An easy task; 'tis but to love a king.
LADY GREY.
That's soon perform'd, because I am a subject.
KING EDWARD.
Why, then, thy husband's lands I freely give thee.
LADY GREY.
I take my leave with many thousand thanks.
DUKE OF GLOSTER [*aside to* CLARENCE].
The match is made; she seals it with a curt'sy.
KING EDWARD.
But stay thee,—'tis the fruits of love I mean.
LADY GREY.
The fruits of love I mean, my loving liege.
KING EDWARD.
Ay, but, I fear me, in another sense.
What love, think'st thou, I sue so much to get?
LADY GREY.
My love till death, my humble thanks, my prayers;
That love which virtue begs, and virtue grants.
KING EDWARD.
No, by my troth, I did not mean such love.
LADY GREY.
Why, then you mean not as I thought you did.
KING EDWARD.
But now you partly may perceive my mind.
LADY GREY.
My mind will never grant what I perceive
Your highness aims at, if I aim aright.
KING EDWARD.
To tell thee plain, I aim to lie with thee.
LADY GREY.
To tell you plain, I had rather lie in prison.
KING EDWARD.
Why, then thou shalt not have thy husband's lands.
LADY GREY.
Why, then mine honesty shall be my dower;
For by that loss I will not purchase them.
KING EDWARD.
Therein thou wrong'st thy children mightily.
LADY GREY.
Herein your highness wrongs both them and me.
But, mighty lord, this merry inclination
Accords not with the sadness of my suit:
Please you dismiss me, either with 'ay' or 'no.'
KING EDWARD.
Ay, if thou wilt say 'ay' to my request;
No, if thou dost say 'no' to my demand.
LADY GREY.
Then, no, my lord. My suit is at an end.

DUKE OF GLOSTER [*aside to* CLARENCE].
The widow likes him not, she knits her brows.
DUKE OF CLARENCE [*aside to* GLOSTER].
He is the bluntest wooer in Christendom.
KING EDWARD [*aside*].
Her looks do argue her replete with modesty;
Her words do show her wit incomparable:
All her perfections challenge sovereignty:
One way or other, she is for a king;
And she shall be my love, or else my queen.—
Say that King Edward take thee for his queen?
LADY GREY.
'Tis better said than done, my gracious lord:
I am a subject fit to jest withal,
But far unfit to be a sovereign.
KING EDWARD.
Sweet widow, by my state I swear to thee
I speak no more than what my soul intends;
And that is, to enjoy thee for my love.
LADY GREY.
And that is more than I will yield unto:
I know I am too mean to be your queen,
And yet too good to be your concubine.
KING EDWARD.
You cavil, widow: I did mean, my queen.
LADY GREY.
'Twill grieve your Grace my sons should call you father.
KING EDWARD.
No more than when my daughters call thee mother.
Thou art a widow, and thou hast some children;
And, by God's mother, I, being but a bachelor,
Have other some: why, 'tis a happy thing
To be the father unto many sons.
Answer no more, for thou shalt be my queen.
DUKE OF GLOSTER [*aside to* CLARENCE].
The ghostly father now hath done his shrift.
DUKE OF CLARENCE [*aside to* GLOSTER].
When he was made a shriver, 'twas for shift.
KING EDWARD.
Brothers, you muse what chat we two have had.
DUKE OF GLOSTER.
The widow likes it not, for she looks sad.
KING EDWARD.
You'ld think it strange if I should marry her.
DUKE OF CLARENCE.
To whom, my lord?
KING EDWARD.
       Why, Clarence, to myself.
DUKE OF GLOSTER.
That would be ten days' wonder at the least.
DUKE OF CLARENCE.
That's a day longer than a wonder lasts.
DUKE OF GLOSTER.
By so much is the wonder in extremes.
KING EDWARD.
Well, jest on, brothers: I can tell you both
Her suit is granted for her husband's lands.

81

Enter a NOBLEMAN.
NOBLEMAN.
My gracious lord, Henry your foe is taken,
And brought as prisoner to your palace-gate.
KING EDWARD.
See that he be convey'd unto the Tower:—
And go we, brothers, to the man that took him,
To question of his apprehension.—
Widow, go you along:—lords, use her honourably.
[Exeunt all except GLOSTER.
DUKE OF GLOSTER.
Ay, Edward will use women honourably.—
Would he were wasted, marrow, bones, and all,
That from his loins no hopeful branch may spring,
To cross me from the golden time I look for!
And yet, between my soul's desire and me—
The lustful Edward's title buried—
Is Clarence, Henry, and his son young Edward,
And all the unlookt-for issue of their bodies,
To take their rooms, ere I can place myself:
A cold premeditation for my purpose!
Why, then, I do but dream on sovereignty
Like one that stands upon a promontory,
And spies a far-off shore where he would tread,
Wishing his foot were equal with his eye;
And chides the sea that sunders him from thence,
Saying, he'll lade it dry to have his way:
So do I wish the crown, being so far off;
And so I chide the means that keeps me from it;
And so I say, I'll cut the causes off,
Flattering me with impossibilities.—
My eye 's too quick, my heart o'erweens too much,
Unless my hand and strength could equal them.
Well, say there is no kingdom, then, for Richard;
What other pleasure can the world afford?
I'll make my heaven in a lady's lap,
And deck my body in gay ornaments,
And witch sweet ladies with my words and looks.
O miserable thought! and more unlikely
Than to accomplish twenty golden crowns!
Why, love forswore me in my mother's womb:
And, for I should not deal in her soft laws,
She did corrupt frail nature with some bribe,
To shrink mine arm up like a wither'd shrub;
To make an envious mountain on my back,
Where sits deformity to mock my body;
To shape my legs of an unequal size;
To disproportion me in every part,
Like to a chaos, or an unlickt bear-whelp
That carries no impression like the dam.
And am I, then, a man to be beloved?
O monstrous fault, to harbour such a thought!
Then, since this earth affords no joy to me,
But to command, to check, to o'erbear such
As are of better person than myself,
I'll make my heaven to dream upon the crown,
And, whiles I live, t' account this world but hell,
Until my mis-shaped trunk that bears this head,
Be round impaled with a glorious crown.
And yet I know not how to get the crown,
For many lives stand between me and home:
And I—like one lost in a thorny wood,
That rents the thorns, and is rent with the thorns,
Seeking a way, and straying from the way;
Not knowing how to find the open air,
But toiling desperately to find it out—

Torment myself to catch the English crown:
And from that torment I will free myself,
Or hew my way out with a bloody axe.
Why, I can smile, and murder whiles I smile;
And cry 'Content' to that which grieves my heart;
And wet my cheeks with artificial tears,
And frame my face to all occasions:
I'll drown more sailors than the mermaid shall;
I'll slay more gazers than the basilisk;
I'll play the orator as well as Nestor;
Deceive more slily than Ulysses could;
And, like a Sinon, take another Troy:
I can add colours to the chameleon;
Change shapes with Proteus for advantages;
And set the murderous Machiavel to school.
Can I do this, and cannot get a crown?
Tut, were it further off, I'll pluck it down. *[Exit.*

SCENE III.

France. The KING'S *palace.*

Flourish. Enter LOUIS *the French king, his sister*
BONA, *his Admiral call'd* BOURBON; PRINCE
EDWARD, QUEEN MARGARET, *and the* EARL
OF OXFORD. LOUIS *sits and riseth up again.*
KING LOUIS.
FAIR Queen of England, worthy Margaret,
Sit down with us: it ill befits thy state
And birth, that thou shouldst stand while Louis
  doth sit.
QUEEN MARGARET.
No, mighty King of France: now Margaret
Must strike her sail, and learn awhile to serve,
Where kings command. I was, I must confess,
Great Albion's queen in former golden days:
But now mischance hath trod my title down,
And with dishonour laid me on the ground;
Where I must take like seat unto my fortune,
And to my humble seat conform myself.
KING LOUIS.
Why, say, fair queen, whence springs this deep
  despair?
QUEEN MARGARET.
From such a cause as fills mine eyes with tears,
And stops my tongue, while heart is drown'd in
  cares.
KING LOUIS.
Whate'er it be, be thou still like thyself,
And sit thee by our side: yield not thy neck
                  [Seats her by him.
To fortune's yoke, but let thy dauntless mind
Still ride in triumph over all mischance.
Be plain, Queen Margaret, and tell thy grief;
It shall be eased, if France can yield relief.
QUEEN MARGARET.
Those gracious words revive my drooping
  thoughts,
And give my tongue-tied sorrows leave to speak.
Now, therefore, be it known to noble Louis,
That Henry, sole possessor of my love,
Is, of a king, become a banisht man,
And forced to live in Scotland a forlorn;
While proud ambitious Edward duke of York
Usurps the regal title and the seat
Of England's true-anointed lawful king.

This is the cause that I, poor Margaret,—
With this my son, Prince Edward, Henry's
    heir,—
Am come to crave thy just and lawful aid;
And if thou fail us, all our hope is done:
Scotland hath will to help, but cannot help;
Our people and our peers are both misled,
Our treasure seized, our soldiers put to flight,
And, as thou seest, ourselves in heavy plight.

        KING LOUIS.
Renowned queen, with patience calm the storm,
While we bethink a means to break it off.

        QUEEN MARGARET.
The more we stay, the stronger grows our foe.

        KING LOUIS.
The more I stay, the more I'll succour thee.

        QUEEN MARGARET.
O, but impatience waiteth on true sorrow:—
And see where comes the breeder of my sorrow!

      Enter WARWICK, *attended.*

        KING LOUIS.
What's he approacheth boldly to our presence?

        QUEEN MARGARET.
Our Earl of Warwick, Edward's greatest friend.

        KING LOUIS.
Welcome, brave Warwick! What brings thee to
    France?   [*He descends. She ariseth.*

        QUEEN MARGARET [*aside*].
Ay, now begins a second storm to rise;
For this is he that moves both wind and tide.

        EARL OF WARWICK.
From worthy Edward, king of Albion,
My lord and sovereign, and thy vowed friend,
I come, in kindness and unfeigned love,—
First, to do greetings to thy royal person;
And then to crave a league of amity;
And lastly, to confirm that amity
With nuptial knot, if thou vouchsafe to grant
That virtuous Lady Bona, thy fair sister,
To England's king in lawful marriage.

        QUEEN MARGARET [*aside*].
If that go forward, Henry's hope is done.

        EARL OF WARWICK [*to* BONA].
And, gracious madam, in our king's behalf,
I am commanded, with your leave and favour,
Humbly to kiss your hand, and with my tongue
To tell the passion of my sovereign's heart;
Where fame, late entering at his heedful ears,
Hath placed thy beauty's image and thy virtue.

        QUEEN MARGARET.
King Louis,—and Lady Bona,—hear me speak,
Before you answer Warwick. His demand
Springs not from Edward's well-meant honest
    love,
But from deceit bred by necessity;
For how can tyrants safely govern home,
Unless abroad they purchase great alliance?
To prove him tyrant this reason may suffice,—
That Henry liveth still; but were he dead,
Yet here Prince Edward stands, King Henry's son.
Look therefore, Louis, that by this league and
    marriage
Thou draw not on thy danger and dishonour;
For though usurpers sway the rule awhile,
Yet heavens are just, and time suppresseth
    wrongs.

        EARL OF WARWICK.
Injurious Margaret!

        PRINCE EDWARD.
           And why not queen?

        EARL OF WARWICK.
Because thy father Henry did usurp;
And thou no more art prince than she is queen.

        EARL OF OXFORD.
Then Warwick disannuls great John of Gaunt,
Which did subdue the greatest part of Spain;
And, after John of Gaunt, Henry the Fourth,
Whose wisdom was a mirror to the wisest;
And, after that wise prince, Henry the Fifth,
Who by his prowess conquered all France:
From these our Henry lineally descends.

        EARL OF WARWICK.
Oxford, how haps it, in this smooth discourse,
You told not how Henry the Sixth hath lost
All that which Henry the Fifth had gotten? [that.
Methinks these peers of France should smile at
But for the rest,—you tell a pedigree
Of threescore and two years; a silly time
To make prescription for a kingdom's worth.

        EARL OF OXFORD.
Why, Warwick, canst thou speak against thy liege,
Whom thou obeyed'st thirty and six years,
And not bewray thy treason with a blush?

        EARL OF WARWICK.
Can Oxford, that did ever fence the right,
Now buckler falsehood with a pedigree?
For shame! leave Henry, and call Edward king.

        EARL OF OXFORD.
Call him my king by whose injurious doom
My elder brother, the Lord Aubrey Vere,
Was done to death? and more than so, my father,
Even in the downfall of his mellow'd years,
When nature brought him to the door of death?
No, Warwick, no; while life upholds this arm,
This arm upholds the house of Lancaster.

        EARL OF WARWICK.
And I the house of York.

        KING LOUIS.
Queen Margaret, Prince Edward, and Oxford,
Vouchsafe, at our request, to stand aside,
While I use further conference with Warwick.
              [*They stand aloof.*

        QUEEN MARGARET.
Heavens grant that Warwick's words bewitch
    him not!

        KING LOUIS.
Now, Warwick, tell me, even upon thy conscience,
Is Edward your true king? for I were loth
To link with him that were not lawful chosen.

        EARL OF WARWICK.
Thereon I pawn my credit and mine honour.

        KING LOUIS.
But is he gracious in the people's eye?

        EARL OF WARWICK.
The more that Henry was unfortunate.

        KING LOUIS.
Then further,—all dissembling set aside,
Tell me for truth the measure of his love
Unto our sister Bona.

        EARL OF WARWICK.
           Such it seems
As may beseem a monarch like himself.

Myself have often heard him say and swear
That this his love was an eternal plant,
Whereof the root was fixt in virtue's ground,
The leaves and fruit maintain'd with beauty's sun;
Exempt from envy, but not from disdain,
Unless the Lady Bona quit his pain.

KING LOUIS.
Now, sister, let us hear your firm resolve.

BONA.
Your grant, or your denial, shall be mine:—
[to WARWICK] Yet I confess that often ere this day,
When I have heard your king's desert recounted,
Mine ear hath tempted judgement to desire.

KING LOUIS.
Then, Warwick, thus,—Our sister shall be Edward's;
And now forthwith shall articles be drawn
Touching the jointure that your king must make,
Which with her dowry shall be counterpoised.—
Draw near, Queen Margaret, and be a witness
That Bona shall be wife to the English king.

PRINCE EDWARD.
To Edward, but not to the English king.

QUEEN MARGARET.
Deceitful Warwick! it was thy device
By this alliance to make void my suit:
Before thy coming, Louis was Henry's friend.

KING LOUIS.
And still is friend to him and Margaret:
But if your title to the crown be weak,—
As may appear by Edward's good success,—
Then 'tis but reason that I be released
From giving aid which late I promised.
Yet shall you have all kindness at my hand
That your estate requires, and mine can yield.

EARL OF WARWICK.
Henry now lives in Scotland at his ease,
Where having nothing, nothing can he lose.
And as for you yourself, our *quondam* queen,
You have a father able to maintain you;
And better 'twere you troubled him than France.

QUEEN MARGARET.
Peace, impudent and shameless Warwick! peace,
Proud setter-up and puller-down of kings!
I will not hence till, with my talk and tears,
Both full of truth, I make King Louis behold
Thy sly conveyance and thy lord's false love;
For both of you are birds of selfsame feather.
                    [POST *blowing a horn within.*

KING LOUIS.
Warwick, this is some post to us or thee.
          Enter the POST.

POST [*to* WARWICK].
My lord ambassador, these letters are for you,
Sent from your brother, Marquess Montague:—
[*to* LOUIS] These from our king unto your majesty:—
[*to* MARGARET] And, madam, these for you; from
   whom I know not.   [*They all read their letters.*

EARL OF OXFORD.
I like it well that our fair queen and mistress
Smiles at her news, while Warwick frowns at his.

PRINCE EDWARD.
Nay, mark how Louis stamps, as he were nettled:
I hope all's for the best.

KING LOUIS.
Warwick, what are thy news?—and yours, fair queen?

QUEEN MARGARET.
Mine such as fill my heart with unhoped joys.

EARL OF WARWICK.
Mine full of sorrow and heart's discontent.

KING LOUIS.
What! has your king married the Lady Grey?
And now, to soothe your forgery and his,
Sends me a paper to persuade me patience?
Is this th'alliance that he seeks with France?
Dare he presume to scorn us in this manner?

QUEEN MARGARET.
I told your majesty as much before: [honesty.
This proveth Edward's love and Warwick's

EARL OF WARWICK.
King Louis, I here protest, in sight of heaven,
And by the hope I have of heavenly bliss,
That I am clear from this misdeed of Edward's,—
No more my king, for he dishonours me,
But most himself, if he could see his shame.
Did I forget that by the house of York
My father came untimely to his death?
Did I let pass th' abuse done to my niece?
Did I impale him with the regal crown?
Did I put Henry from his native right?
And am I guerdon'd at the last with shame?
Shame on himself! for my desert is honour:
And, to repair my honour lost for him,
I here renounce him, and return to Henry.—
My noble queen, let former grudges pass,
And henceforth I am thy true servitor:
I will revenge his wrong to Lady Bona,
And replant Henry in his former state.

QUEEN MARGARET.
Warwick, these words have turn'd my hate to love;
And I forgive and quite forget old faults,
And joy that thou becomest King Henry's friend.

EARL OF WARWICK.
So much his friend, ay, his unfeigned friend,
That, if King Louis vouchsafe to furnish us
With some few bands of chosen soldiers,
I'll undertake to land them on our coast,
And force the tyrant from his seat by war.
'Tis not his new-made bride shall succour him:
And as for Clarence,—as my letters tell me,
He's very likely now to fall from him,
For matching more for wanton lust than honour,
Or than for strength and safety of our country.

BONA.
Dear brother, how shall Bona be revenged
But by thy help to this distressed queen?

QUEEN MARGARET.
Renowned prince, how shall poor Henry live,
Unless thou rescue him from foul despair?

BONA.
My quarrel and this English queen's are one.

EARL OF WARWICK.
And mine, fair Lady Bona, joins with yours.

KING LOUIS.
And mine with hers and thine and Margaret's:
Therefore, at last, I firmly am resolved
You shall have aid.

QUEEN MARGARET.
Let me give humble thanks for all at once.

KING LOUIS.
Then, England's messenger, return in post,
And tell false Edward, thy supposed king,
That Louis of France is sending over maskers
To revel it with him and his new bride:
Thou seest what's past,—go fear thy king withal.
BONA.
Tell him, in hope he'll prove a widower shortly,
I'll wear the willow-garland for his sake.
QUEEN MARGARET.
Tell him, my mourning-weeds are laid aside,
And I am ready to put armour on.
EARL OF WARWICK.
Tell him from me, that he hath done me wrong;
And therefore I'll uncrown him ere't be long.
There's thy reward: be gone.   [Exit POST.
KING LOUIS.
                        But, Warwick,
Thou and Oxford, with five thousand men,
Shall cross the seas, and bid false Edward battle;
And, as occasion serves, this noble queen
And prince shall follow with a fresh supply.
Yet, ere thou go, but answer me one doubt,—
What pledge have we of thy firm loyalty?
EARL OF WARWICK.
This shall assure my constant loyalty,—
That if our queen and this young prince agree,
I'll join mine eldest daughter and my joy
To him forthwith in holy wedlock-bands.
QUEEN MARGARET.
Yes, I agree, and thank you for your motion.—
Son Edward, she is fair and virtuous;
Therefore delay not, give thy hand to Warwick;
And, with thy hand, thy faith irrevocable,
That only Warwick's daughter shall be thine.
PRINCE OF WALES.
Yes, I accept her, for she well deserves it;
And here, to pledge my vow, I give my hand.
            [He gives his hand to WARWICK.
KING LOUIS.
Why stay we now? These soldiers shall be levied;
And thou, Lord Bourbon, our high-admiral,
Shalt waft them over with our royal fleet.—
I long till Edward fall by war's mischance,
For mocking marriage with a dame of France.
            [Exeunt all except WARWICK.
EARL OF WARWICK.
I came from Edward as ambassador,
But I return his sworn and mortal foe:
Matter of marriage was the charge he gave me,
But dreadful war shall answer his demand.
Had he none else to make a stale but me?
Then none but I shall turn his jest to sorrow.
I was the chief that raised him to the crown,
And I'll be chief to bring him down again:
Not that I pity Henry's misery,
But seek revenge on Edward's mockery.   [Exit.

ACT IV. SCENE I.
London. The palace.
Enter GLOSTER, CLARENCE, SOMERSET, and
MONTAGUE.
DUKE OF GLOSTER.
NOW tell me, brother Clarence, what think you
Of this new marriage with the Lady Grey?
Hath not our brother made a worthy choice?

DUKE OF CLARENCE.
Alas, you know 'tis far from hence to France;
How could he stay till Warwick made return?
DUKE OF SOMERSET.
My lords, forbear this talk; here comes the king.
DUKE OF GLOSTER.
And his well-chosen bride.
DUKE OF CLARENCE.
I mind to tell him plainly what I think.
Flourish. Enter KING EDWARD, LADY GREY, as
    Queen; PEMBROKE, STAFFORD, HASTINGS:
    four stand on one side and four on the other.
KING EDWARD.
Now, brother of Clarence, how like you our
    choice,
That you stand pensive, as half malcontent?
DUKE OF CLARENCE.
As well as Louis of France or the Earl of War-
    wick;
Which are so weak of courage and in judgement,
That they'll take no offence at our abuse.
KING EDWARD.
Suppose they take offence without a cause,
They are but Louis and Warwick: I am Edward,
Your king and Warwick's, and must have my will.
DUKE OF GLOSTER.
Ay, and shall have your will, because our king:
Yet hasty marriage seldom proveth well.
KING EDWARD.
Yea, brother Richard, are you offended too?
DUKE OF GLOSTER.
Not I:
No, God forbid that I should wish them sever'd
Whom God hath join'd together; ay, and 'twere
    pity
To sunder them that yoke so well together.
KING EDWARD.
Setting your scorns and your mislike aside,
Tell me some reason why the Lady Grey
Should not become my wife and England's
    queen:—
And you too, Somerset and Montague,
Speak freely what you think.
DUKE OF CLARENCE.
Then this is mine opinion,—that King Louis
Becomes your enemy, for mocking him
About the marriage of the Lady Bona.
DUKE OF GLOSTER.
And Warwick, doing what you gave in charge,
Is now dishonoured by this new marriage.
KING EDWARD.
What if both Louis and Warwick be appeased
By such invention as I can devise?
MARQUESS OF MONTAGUE.
Yet, to have join'd with France in such alliance
Would more have strengthen'd this our
    commonwealth
'Gainst foreign storms than any home-bred
    marriage.
LORD HASTINGS.
Why, knows not Montague that of itself
England is safe, if true within itself?
MARQUESS OF MONTAGUE.
Yes; but the safer when 'tis backt with France.
LORD HASTINGS.
'Tis better using France than trusting France:

Let us be backt with God, and with the seas
Which He hath given for fence impregnable,
And with their helps only defend ourselves;
In them and in ourselves our safety lies.
DUKE OF CLARENCE.
For this one speech Lord Hastings well deserves
To have the heir of the Lord Hungerford.
KING EDWARD.
Ay, what of that? it was my will and grant;
And for this once my will shall stand for law.
DUKE OF GLOSTER.
And yet methinks your Grace hath not done
well,
To give the heir and daughter of Lord Scales
Unto the brother of your loving bride;
She better would have fitted me or Clarence:
But in your bride you bury brotherhood.
DUKE OF CLARENCE.
Or else you would not have bestow'd the heir
Of the Lord Bonville on your new wife's son,
And leave your brothers to go speed elsewhere.
KING EDWARD.
Alas, poor Clarence! is it for a wife
That thou art malcontent? I will provide thee.
DUKE OF CLARENCE.
In choosing for yourself, you show'd your judge-
ment,
Which being shallow, you shall give me leave
To play the broker in mine own behalf;
And to that end I shortly mind to leave you.
KING EDWARD.
Leave me, or tarry, Edward will be king,
And not be tied unto his brother's will.
QUEEN ELIZABETH.
My lords, before it pleased his majesty
To raise my state to title of a queen,
Do me but right, and you must all confess
That I was not ignoble of descent;
And meaner than myself have had like fortune.
But as this title honours me and mine,
So your dislikes, to whom I would be pleasing,
Doth cloud my joys with danger and with sorrow.
KING EDWARD.
My love, forbear to fawn upon their frowns:
What danger or what sorrow can befall thee,
So long as Edward is thy constant friend,
And their true sovereign, whom they must obey?
Nay, whom they shall obey, and love thee too,
Unless they seek for hatred at my hands;
Which if they do, yet will I keep thee safe,
And they shall feel the vengeance of my wrath.
DUKE OF GLOSTER [aside].
I hear, yet say not much, but think the more.
Enter a POST.
KING EDWARD.
Now, messenger, what letters or what news
From France?
POST.
My sovereign liege, no letters; and few words,
But such as I, without your special pardon,
Dare not relate.
KING EDWARD.
Go to, we pardon thee: therefore, in brief,
Tell me their words as near as thou canst guess
them.
What answer makes King Louis unto our letters?

POST.
At my depart, these were his very words:
'Go tell false Edward, thy supposed king,
That Louis of France is sending over maskers
To revel it with him and his new bride.'
KING EDWARD.
Is Louis so brave? belike he thinks me Henry.
But what said Lady Bona to my marriage?
POST.
These were her words, utter'd with mild disdain:
'Tell him, in hope he'll prove a widower shortly,
I'll wear the willow-garland for his sake.'
KING EDWARD.
I blame not her, she could say little less;
She had the wrong. But what said Henry's
queen?
For I have heard that she was there in place.
POST.
'Tell him,' quoth she, 'my mourning-weeds are
done,
And I am ready to put armour on.'
KING EDWARD.
Belike she minds to play the Amazon.
But what said Warwick to these injuries?
POST.
He, more incensed against your majesty
Than all the rest, discharged me with these words:
'Tell him from me, that he hath done me wrong,
And therefore I'll uncrown him ere't be long.'
KING EDWARD.
Ha! durst the traitor breathe out so proud words?
Well, I will arm me, being thus forewarn'd:
They shall have wars, and pay for their presump-
tion.
But say, is Warwick friends with Margaret?
POST.
Ay, gracious sovereign; they are so linkt in friend-
ship,   [daughter
That young Prince Edward marries Warwick's
DUKE OF CLARENCE.
Belike the elder; Clarence will have the younger.
Now, brother king, farewell, and sit you fast,
For I will hence to Warwick's other daughter;
That, though I want a kingdom, yet in marriage
I may not prove inferior to yourself.—
You that love me and Warwick, follow me.
[Exit CLARENCE, and SOMERSET follows.
DUKE OF GLOSTER [aside].
Not I:
My thoughts aim at a further matter; I
Stay not for the love of Edward, but the crown.
KING EDWARD.
Clarence and Somerset both gone to Warwick!
Yet am I arm'd against the worst can happen;
And haste is needful in this desperate case.—
Pembroke and Stafford, you in our behalf
Go levy men, and make prepare for war;
They are already, or quickly will be landed:
Myself in person will straight follow you.
[Exeunt PEMBROKE and STAFFORD.
But, ere I go, Hastings and Montague,
Resolve my doubt. You twain, of all the rest,
Are near to Warwick by blood and by alliance:
Tell me if you love Warwick more than me?
If it be so, then both depart to him;
I rather wish you foes than hollow friends:

But if you mind to hold your true obedience,
Give me assurance with some friendly vow,
That I may never have you in suspect.
MARQUESS OF MONTAGUE.
So God help Montague as he proves true!
LORD HASTINGS.
And Hastings as he favours Edward's cause!
KING EDWARD.
Now, brother Richard, will you stand by us?
DUKE OF GLOSTER.
Ay, in despite of all that shall withstand you.
KING EDWARD.
Why, so! then am I sure of victory.
Now therefore let us hence; and lose no hour,
Till we meet Warwick with his foreign power.
                                        [Exeunt.

SCENE II.

A plain in Warwickshire.

Enter WARWICK *and* OXFORD, *with French*
SOLDIERS.

EARL OF WARWICK.
TRUST me, my lord, all hitherto goes well;
   The common people by numbers swarm to us.
But see where Somerset and Clarence comes!
    Enter CLARENCE *and* SOMERSET.
Speak suddenly, my lords,—are we all friends?
DUKE OF CLARENCE.
Fear not that, my lord.
EARL OF WARWICK.
Then, gentle Clarence, welcome unto Warwick;—
And welcome, Somerset:—I hold it cowardice
To rest mistrustful where a noble heart
Hath pawn'd an open hand in sign of love;
Else might I think that Clarence, Edward's
    brother,
Were but a feigned friend to our proceedings:
But welcome, sweet Clarence; my daughter shall
    be thine.
And now what rests but, in night's coverture,
Thy brother being carelessly encampt,
His soldiers lurking in the towns about,
And but attended by a simple guard,
We may surprise and take him at our pleasure?
Our scouts have found the adventure very easy:
That as Ulysses and stout Diomede
With sleight and manhood stole to Rhesus' tents,
And brought from thence the Thracian fatal
    steeds,
So we, well cover'd with the night's black mantle,
At unawares may beat down Edward's guard,
And seize himself; I say not, slaughter him,
For I intend but only to surprise him.—
You that will follow me in this attempt
Applaud the name of Henry with your leader.
                        [*They all cry*, 'Henry!'
Why, then, let's on our way in silent sort:
For Warwick and his friends, God and Saint
    George!   [*Exeunt.*

SCENE III.

EDWARD'S *camp, near Warwick.*

Enter three WATCHMEN, *to guard the* KING'S *tent.*
FIRST WATCHMAN.
COME on, my masters, each man take his stand:
   The king, by this, is set him down to sleep.

SECOND WATCHMAN.
What, will he not to bed?
FIRST WATCHMAN.
Why, no; for he hath made a solemn vow
Never to lie and take his natural rest
Till Warwick or himself be quite supprest.
SECOND WATCHMAN.
To-morrow, then, belike shall be the day,
If Warwick be so near as men report.
THIRD WATCHMAN.
But say, I pray, what nobleman is that
That with the king here resteth in his tent?
FIRST WATCHMAN.
'Tis the Lord Hastings, the king's chiefest friend.
THIRD WATCHMAN.
O, is it so? But why commands the king
That his chief followers lodge in towns about
    him,
While he himself keeps here in the cold field?
SECOND WATCHMAN.
'Tis the more honour, because more dangerous.
THIRD WATCHMAN.
Ay, but give me worship and quietness;
I like it better than a dangerous honour.
If Warwick knew in what estate he stands,
'Tis to be doubted he would waken him.
FIRST WATCHMAN.
Unless our halberds did shut up his passage.
SECOND WATCHMAN.
Ay, wherefore else guard we his royal tent,
But to defend his person from night-foes?
Enter WARWICK, CLARENCE, OXFORD, SOMER-
SET, *and French* SOLDIERS, *silent all.*
EARL OF WARWICK.
This is his tent; and see where stand his guard.
Courage, my masters! honour now or never!
But follow me, and Edward shall be ours.
FIRST WATCHMAN.
Who goes there?
SECOND WATCHMAN.
Stay, or thou diest!
        [WARWICK *and the rest cry all*, 'Warwick!
        Warwick!' *and set upon the* GUARD, *who
        fly, crying*, 'Arm! arm!' WARWICK *and
        the rest following them.*
The drum playing and trumpet sounding, enter
WARWICK, SOMERSET, *and the rest, bringing
the* KING *out in his gown, sitting in a chair.*
RICHARD *and* HASTINGS *fly over the stage.*
DUKE OF SOMERSET.
What are they that fly there?
EARL OF WARWICK.
Richard and Hastings: let them go; here is the
duke.
KING EDWARD.
The duke! Why, Warwick, when we parted last
Thou call'dst me king.
EARL OF WARWICK.
                    Ay, but the case is alter'd:
When you disgraced me in my embassade,
Then I degraded you from being king,
And come now to create you Duke of York.
Alas, how should you govern any kingdom,
That know not how to use ambassadors;
Nor how to be contented with one wife;
Nor how to use your brothers brotherly;

Nor how to study for the people's welfare;
Nor how to shroud yourself from enemies?
KING EDWARD.
Yea, brother of Clarence, art thou here too?
Nay, then I see that Edward needs must down.—
Yet, Warwick, in despite of all mischance,
Of thee thyself and all thy complices,
Edward will always bear himself as king:
Though fortune's malice overthrow my state,
My mind exceeds the compass of her wheel.
EARL OF WARWICK.
Then, for his mind, be Edward England's king:
                     [*Takes off his crown.*
But Henry now shall wear the English crown,
And be true king indeed; thou but the shadow.—
My Lord of Somerset, at my request,
See that forthwith Duke Edward be convey'd
Unto my brother, Archbishop of York.   [lows,
When I have fought with Pembroke and his fel-
I'll follow you, and tell the duke what answer
Louis and the Lady Bona send to him.—
Now, for a while farewell, good Duke of York.
KING EDWARD.
What fates impose, that men must needs abide;
It boots not to resist both wind and tide.
              [*They lead him out forcibly.*
EARL OF OXFORD.
What now remains, my lords, for us to do,
But march to London with our soldiers?
EARL OF WARWICK.
Ay, that's the first thing that we have to do;
To free King Henry from imprisonment,
And see him seated in the regal throne. [*Exeunt.*

SCENE IV.
London. The palace.
Enter QUEEN ELIZABETH *and* RIVERS.
LORD RIVERS.
MADAM, what makes you in this sudden
change?
QUEEN ELIZABETH.
Why, brother Rivers, are you yet to learn
What late misfortune is befaln King Edward?
LORD RIVERS.
What, loss of some pitcht battle against Warwick?
QUEEN ELIZABETH.
No, but the loss of his own royal person.
LORD RIVERS.
Then, is my sovereign slain?
QUEEN ELIZABETH.
Ay, almost slain, for he is taken prisoner;
Either betray'd by falsehood of his guard,
Or by his foe surprised at unawares:
And, as I further have to understand,
Is new committed to the Bishop of York,
Fell Warwick's brother, and by that our foe.
LORD RIVERS.
These news, I must confess, are full of grief;
Yet, gracious madam, bear it as you may:
Warwick may lose, that now hath won the day.
QUEEN ELIZABETH.
Till then, fair hope must hinder life's decay.
And I the rather wean me from despair,
For love of Edward's offspring in my womb:
This is it that makes me bridle passion,

And bear with mildness my misfortune's cross;
Ay, ay, for this I draw-in many a tear,
And stop the rising of blood-sucking sighs,
Lest with my sighs or tears I blast or drown
King Edward's fruit, true heir to th' English
crown.
LORD RIVERS.
But, madam, where is Warwick, then, become?
QUEEN ELIZABETH.
I am inform'd that he comes towards London,
To set the crown once more on Henry's head:
Guess thou the rest; King Edward's friends must
down.
But, to prevent the tyrant's violence,—
For trust not him that hath once broken faith,—
I'll hence forthwith unto the sanctuary,
To save at least the heir of Edward's right:
There shall I rest secure from force and fraud.
Come, therefore, let us fly while we may fly:
If Warwick take us, we are sure to die. [*Exeunt.*

SCENE V.
A park near Middleham Castle in Yorkshire.
Enter GLOSTER, HASTINGS, SIR WILLIAM
STANLEY, *and others.*
DUKE OF GLOSTER.
NOW, my Lord Hastings and Sir William
Stanley,
Leave off to wonder why I drew you hither,
Into this chiefest thicket of the park.
Thus stands the case: you know our king, my
brother,
Is prisoner to the bishop here, at whose hands
He hath good usage and great liberty;
And, often but attended with weak guard,
Comes hunting this way to disport himself.
I have advertised him by secret means,
That if about this hour he make this way,
Under the colour of his usual game,
He shall here find his friends, with horse and men,
To set him free from his captivity.
Enter KING EDWARD *and a* HUNTSMAN.
HUNTSMAN.
This way, my lord; for this way lies the game.
KING EDWARD.
Nay, this way, man: see where the huntsmen
stand.—   [rest,
Now, brother of Gloster, Lord Hastings, and the
Stand you thus close, to steal the bishop's deer?
DUKE OF GLOSTER.
Brother, the time and case requireth haste:
Your horse stands ready at the park-corner.
KING EDWARD.
But whither shall we then?
LORD HASTINGS.
To Lynn, my lord; and ship from thence to
Flanders.
DUKE OF GLOSTER.
Well guest, believe me; for that was my meaning.
KING EDWARD.
Stanley, I will requite thy forwardness.
DUKE OF GLOSTER.
But wherefore stay we? 'tis no time to talk.
KING EDWARD.
Huntsman, what say'st thou? wilt thou go along

HUNTSMAN.
Better do so than tarry and be hang'd.
DUKE OF GLOSTER.
Come then, away; let's ha' no more ado.
KING EDWARD.
Bishop, farewell: shield thee from Warwick's
frown;
And pray that I may repossess the crown.
[Exeunt.

SCENE VI.

London. The Tower.

Enter KING HENRY, CLARENCE, WARWICK,
SOMERSET, *young* RICHMOND, OXFORD,
MONTAGUE, *and* LIEUTENANT OF THE
TOWER.

KING HENRY.
MASTER lieutenant, now that God and friends
Have shaken Edward from the regal seat,
And turn'd my captive state to liberty,
My fear to hope, my sorrows unto joys,—
At our enlargement what are thy due fees?
LIEUTENANT OF THE TOWER.
Subjects may challenge nothing of their sove-
reigns;
But if an humble prayer may prevail,
I then crave pardon of your majesty.
KING HENRY.
For what, lieutenant? for well-using me?
Nay, be thou sure I'll well requite thy kindness,
For that it made my imprisonment a pleasure;
Ay, such a pleasure as incaged birds
Conceive, when, after many moody thoughts,
At last, by notes of household harmony,
They quite forget their loss of liberty.—
But, Warwick, after God, thou sett'st me free,
And chiefly therefore I thank God and thee;
He was the author, thou the instrument.
Therefore, that I may conquer fortune's spite,
By living low, where fortune cannot hurt me,
And that the people of this blessed land
May not be punisht with my thwarting stars,—
Warwick, although my head still wear the crown,
I here resign my government to thee,
For thou art fortunate in all thy deeds.
EARL OF WARWICK.
Your Grace hath still been famed for virtuous;
And now may seem as wise as virtuous,
By spying and avoiding fortune's malice,
For few men rightly temper with the stars:
Yet in this one thing let me blame your Grace,
For choosing me when Clarence is in place.
DUKE OF CLARENCE.
No, Warwick, thou art worthy of the sway,
To whom the heavens, in thy nativity,
Adjudged an olive-branch and laurel-crown,
As likely to be blest in peace and war;
And therefore I yield thee my free consent.
EARL OF WARWICK.
And I choose Clarence only for Protector.
KING HENRY.
Warwick and Clarence, give me both your hands:
Now join your hands, and with your hands your
hearts,
That no dissension hinder government:
Make you both Protectors of this land;

While I myself will lead a private life,
And in devotion spend my latter days,
To sin's rebuke and my Creator's praise.
EARL OF WARWICK.
What answers Clarence to his sovereign's will?
DUKE OF CLARENCE.
That he consents, if Warwick yield consent;
For on thy fortune I repose myself.
EARL OF WARWICK.
Why, then, though loth, yet must I be content:
We'll yoke together, like a double shadow
To Henry's body, and supply his place;
I mean, in bearing weight of government,
While he enjoys the honour and his ease.
And, Clarence, now then it is more than needful
Forthwith that Edward be pronounced a traitor,
And all his lands and goods be confiscate.
DUKE OF CLARENCE.
What else? and that succession be determined.
EARL OF WARWICK.
Ay, therein Clarence shall not want his part.
KING HENRY.
But, with the first of all your chief affairs,
Let me entreat—for I command no more—
That Margaret your queen, and my son Edward,
Be sent for, to return from France with speed;
For, till I see them here, by doubtful fear
My joy of liberty is half eclipsed.
DUKE OF CLARENCE.
It shall be done, my sovereign, with all speed.
KING HENRY.
My Lord of Somerset, what youth is that,
Of whom you seem to have so tender care?
DUKE OF SOMERSET.
My liege, it is young Henry, earl of Richmond.
KING HENRY.
Come hither, England's hope.—If secret powers
[Lays his hand on his head.
Suggest but truth to my divining thoughts,
This pretty lad will prove our country's bliss.
His looks are full of peaceful majesty;
His head by nature framed to wear a crown,
His hand to wield a sceptre; and himself
Likely in time to bless a regal throne.
Make much of him, my lords, for this is he
Must help you more than you are hurt by me.
Enter a POST.
EARL OF WARWICK.
What news, my friend?
POST.
That Edward is escaped from your brother,
And fled, as he hears since, to Burgundy.
EARL OF WARWICK.
Unsavoury news! but how made he escape?
POST.
He was convey'd by Richard duke of Gloster,
And the Lord Hastings, who attended him
In secret ambush on the forest-side,
And from the bishop's huntsmen rescued him;
For hunting was his daily exercise.
EARL OF WARWICK.
My brother was too careless of his charge.—
But let us hence, my sovereign, to provide
A salve for any sore that may betide.
[Exeunt all but SOMERSET, RICHMOND,
and OXFORD.

DUKE OF SOMERSET.
My lord, I like not of this flight of Edward's;
For doubtless Burgundy will yield him help,
And we shall have more wars before 't be long.
As Henry's late presaging prophecy
Did glad my heart with hope of this young Rich-
mond,
So doth my heart misgive me, in these conflicts
What may befall him, to his harm and ours:
Therefore, Lord Oxford, to prevent the worst,
Forthwith we'll send him hence to Brittany,
Till storms be past of civil enmity.

EARL OF OXFORD.
Ay, for if Edward repossess the crown,
'Tis like that Richmond with the rest shall down.

DUKE OF SOMERSET.
It shall be so; he shall to Brittany.
Come, therefore, let's about it speedily. [Exeunt.

SCENE VII.

Before York.

Flourish. Enter KING EDWARD, GLOSTER,
HASTINGS, and SOLDIERS.

KING EDWARD.
NOW, brother Richard, Lord Hastings, and
the rest,
Yet thus far fortune maketh us amends,
And says, that once more I shall interchange
My waned state for Henry's regal crown.
Well have we past and now repast the seas,
And brought desired help from Burgundy:
What, then, remains, we being thus arrived
From Ravenspurg haven before the gates of
York,
But that we enter, as into our dukedom?

DUKE OF GLOSTER.
The gates made fast!—Brother, I like not this;
For many men that stumble at the threshold
Are well foretold that danger lurks within.

KING EDWARD.
Tush, man, abodements must not now affright us:
By fair or foul means we must enter in,
For hither will our friends repair to us.

LORD HASTINGS.
My liege, I'll knock once more to summon them.

Enter, on the walls, the MAYOR OF YORK and his
BRETHREN.

MAYOR OF YORK.
My lords, we were forewarned of your coming,
And shut the gates for safety of ourselves;
For now we owe allegiance unto Henry.

KING EDWARD.
But, master mayor, if Henry be your king,
Yet Edward at the least is Duke of York.

MAYOR OF YORK.
True, my good lord; I know you for no less.

KING EDWARD.
Why, and I challenge nothing but my dukedom,
As being well content with that alone.

DUKE OF GLOSTER [aside].
But when the fox hath once got in his nose,
He'll soon find means to make the body follow.

LORD HASTINGS.
Why, master mayor, why stand you in a doubt?
Open the gates; we are King Henry's friends.

MAYOR OF YORK.
Ay, say you so? the gates shall then be open'd.
[They descend.

DUKE OF GLOSTER.
A wise stout captain, and soon persuaded!

LORD HASTINGS.
The good old man would fain that all were well,
So 'twere not 'long of him; but being enter'd,
I doubt not, I, but we shall soon persuade
Both him and all his brothers unto reason.

Enter the MAYOR and two ALDERMEN.

KING EDWARD.
So, master mayor: these gates must not be shut
But in the night or in the time of war.
What! fear not, man, but yield me up the keys;
[Takes his keys.
For Edward will defend the town and thee,
And all those friends that deign to follow me.

March. Enter MONTGOMERY with drum and
SOLDIERS.

DUKE OF GLOSTER.
Brother, this is Sir John Montgomery,
Our trusty friend, unless I be deceived.

KING EDWARD.
Welcome, Sir John! But why come you in arms?

SIR JOHN MONTGOMERY.
To help King Edward in his time of storm,
As every loyal subject ought to do.

KING EDWARD.
Thanks, good Montgomery: but we now forget
Our title to the crown, and only claim
Our dukedom till God please to send the rest.

SIR JOHN MONTGOMERY.
Then fare you well, for I will hence again:
I came to serve a king, and not a duke.—
Drummer, strike up, and let us march away.
[The drum begins to march.

KING EDWARD.
Nay, stay, Sir John, awhile; and we'll debate
By what safe means the crown may be recover'd.

SIR JOHN MONTGOMERY.
What talk you of debating? in few words,—
If you'll not here proclaim yourself our king,
I'll leave you to your fortune, and be gone
To keep them back that come to succour you:
Why shall we fight, if you pretend no title?

DUKE OF GLOSTER.
Why, brother, wherefore stand you on nice
points?

KING EDWARD.
When we grow stronger, then we'll make our
claim:
Till then, 'tis wisdom to conceal our meaning.

LORD HASTINGS.
Away with scrupulous wit! now arms must
rule.

DUKE OF GLOSTER.
And fearless minds climb soonest unto crowns.
Brother, we will proclaim you out of hand;
The bruit thereof will bring you many friends.

KING EDWARD.
Then be it as you will: for 'tis my right,
And Henry but usurps the diadem.

SIR JOHN MONTGOMERY.
Ay, now my sovereign speaketh like himself;
And now will I be Edward's champion.

LORD HASTINGS.
Sound trumpet; Edward shall be here pro-
claim'd:—
Come, fellow-soldier, make thou proclamation.
[*Flourish.*

SOLDIER.
Edward the Fourth, by the grace of God, king of
England and France, and lord of Ireland, &c.

SIR JOHN MONTGOMERY.
And whosoe'er gainsays King Edward's right,
By this I challenge him to single fight.
[*Throws down his gauntlet.*

ALL.
Long live Edward the Fourth!

KING EDWARD.
Thanks, brave Montgomery;—and thanks unto
you all:
If fortune serve me, I'll requite this kindness.
Now, for this night, let's harbour here in York;
And when the morning sun shall raise his car
Above the border of this horizon,
We'll forward towards Warwick and his mates;
For well I wot that Henry is no soldier.—
Ah, froward Clarence! how evil it beseems thee
To flatter Henry, and forsake thy brother!
Yet, as we may, we'll meet both thee and War-
wick.—
Come on, brave soldiers: doubt not of the day;
And that once gotten, doubt not of large pay.
[*Exeunt.*

SCENE VIII.

London. The palace.

Flourish. Enter KING HENRY, WARWICK, MON-
TAGUE, CLARENCE, EXETER, *and* OXFORD.

EARL OF WARWICK.
WHAT counsel, lords? Edward from Belgia,
With hasty Germans and blunt Hollanders,
Hath past in safety through the narrow seas,
And with his troops doth march amain to London;
And many giddy people flock to him.

EARL OF OXFORD.
Let's levy men, and beat him back again.

DUKE OF CLARENCE.
A little fire is quickly trodden out;
Which, being suffer'd, rivers cannot quench.

EARL OF WARWICK.
In Warwickshire I have true-hearted friends,
Not mutinous in peace, yet bold in war;
Those will I muster up; and thou, son Clarence,
Shalt stir in Suffolk, Norfolk, and in Kent,
The knights and gentlemen to come with thee:
Thou, brother Montague, in Buckingham,
Northampton, and in Leicestershire, shalt find
Men well inclined to hear what thou command'st:
And thou, brave Oxford, wondrous well beloved,
In Oxfordshire shalt muster up thy friends.
My sovereign, with the loving citizens,—
Like to his island girt in with the ocean,
Or modest Dian circled with her nymphs,—
Shall rest in London till we come to him.
Fair lords, take leave, and stand not to reply.
Farewell, my sovereign.

KING HENRY.
Farewell, my Hector, and my Troy's true hope.

DUKE OF CLARENCE.
In sign of truth, I kiss your highness' hand.

KING HENRY.
Well-minded Clarence, be thou fortunate!

SIR JOHN MONTGOMERY.
Comfort, my lord; and so I take my leave.

EARL OF OXFORD [*kissing* HENRY'S *hand*].
And thus I seal my truth, and bid adieu.

KING HENRY.
Sweet Oxford, and my loving Montague,
And all at once, once more a happy farewell.

EARL OF WARWICK.
Farewell, sweet lords: let's meet at Coventry.
[*Exeunt all but* KING HENRY *and* EXETER.

KING HENRY.
Here at the palace will I rest awhile.
Cousin of Exeter, what thinks your lordship?
Methinks the power that Edward hath in field
Should not be able to encounter mine.

DUKE OF EXETER.
The doubt is that he will seduce the rest.

KING HENRY.
That's not my fear; my meed hath got me fame:
I have not stopt mine ears to their demands,
Nor posted off their suits with slow delays;
My pity hath been balm to heal their wounds,
My mildness hath allay'd their swelling griefs,
My mercy dried their water-flowing tears;
I have not been desirous of their wealth,
Nor much opprest them with great subsidies,
Nor forward of revenge, though they much err'd:
Then why should they love Edward more than
me?
No, Exeter, these graces challenge grace:
And, when the lion fawns upon the lamb,
The lamb will never cease to follow him.
[*Shout within,* 'A York! A York!'

DUKE OF EXETER.
Hark, hark, my lord! what shouts are these?
Enter KING EDWARD, GLOSTER, *and* SOLDIERS.

KING EDWARD.
Seize on the shame-faced Henry, bear him hence;
And once again proclaim us king of England.—
You are the fount that makes small brooks to flow:
Now stops thy spring; my sea shall suck them dry,
And swell so much the higher by their ebb.—
Hence with him to the Tower; let him not speak.
[*Exeunt some with* KING HENRY.
And, lords, towards Coventry bend we our course,
Where peremptory Warwick now remains:
The sun shines hot; and, if we use delay,
Cold-biting winter mars our hoped-for hay.

DUKE OF GLOSTER.
Away betimes, before his forces join,
And take the great-grown traitor unawares:
Brave warriors, march amain towards Coventry.
[*Exeunt.*

ACT V. SCENE I.

Coventry.

Enter WARWICK, *the* MAYOR OF COVENTRY,
two MESSENGERS, *and others upon the walls.*

EARL OF WARWICK.
WHERE is the post that came from valiant
Oxford?—
How far hence is thy lord, mine honest fellow?

FIRST MESSENGER.
By this at Dunsmore, marching hitherward.
EARL OF WARWICK.
How far off is our brother Montague?—
Where is the post that came from Montague?
SECOND MESSENGER.
By this at Daintry, with a puissant troop.
Enter SIR JOHN SOMERVILLE.
EARL OF WARWICK.
Say, Somerville, what says my loving son?
And, by thy guess, how nigh is Clarence now?
SIR JOHN SOMERVILLE.
At Southam I did leave him with his forces,
And do expect him here some two hours hence.
[*Drum heard.*
EARL OF WARWICK.
Then Clarence is at hand; I hear his drum.
SIR JOHN SOMERVILLE.
It is not his, my lord; here Southam lies:
The drum your honour hears marcheth from
Warwick.
EARL OF WARWICK.
Who should that be? belike, unlookt-for friends.
SIR JOHN SOMERVILLE.
They are at hand, and you shall quickly know.
[*Enters the city.*
March. Flourish. Enter KING EDWARD,
GLOSTER, *and* SOLDIERS.
KING EDWARD.
Go, trumpet, to the walls, and sound a parle.
DUKE OF GLOSTER.
See how the surly Warwick mans the wall!
EARL OF WARWICK.
O unbid spite! is sportful Edward come?
Where slept our scouts, or how are they seduced,
That we could hear no news of his repair?
KING EDWARD.
Now, Warwick, wilt thou ope the city-gates,
Speak gentle words, and humbly bend thy knee,
Call Edward king, and at his hands beg mercy?
And he shall pardon thee these outrages.
EARL OF WARWICK.
Nay, rather, wilt thou draw thy forces hence,
Confess who set thee up and pluckt thee down,
Call Warwick patron, and be penitent?
And thou shalt still remain the Duke of York.
DUKE OF GLOSTER.
I thought at least he would have said the king;
Or did he make the jest against his will?
EARL OF WARWICK.
Is not a dukedom, sir, a goodly gift?
DUKE OF GLOSTER.
Ay, by my faith, for a poor earl to give:
I'll do thee service for so good a gift.
EARL OF WARWICK.
'Twas I that gave the kingdom to thy brother.
KING EDWARD.
Why, then, 'tis mine, if but by Warwick's gift.
EARL OF WARWICK.
Thou art no Atlas for so great a weight:
And, weakling, Warwick takes his gift again;
And Henry is my king, Warwick his subject.
But Warwick's king is Edward's prisoner:
And, gallant Warwick, do but answer this,—
What is the body when the head is off?

DUKE OF GLOSTER.
Alas, that Warwick had no more forecast,
But, whiles he thought to steal the single ten,
The king was slily finger'd from the deck!
You left poor Henry at the bishop's palace,
And, ten to one, you'll meet him in the Tower.
KING EDWARD.
'Tis even so; yet you are Warwick still.
DUKE OF GLOSTER.
Come, Warwick, take the time; kneel down, kneel
down:
Nay, when? strike now, or else the iron cools.
EARL OF WARWICK.
I had rather chop this hand off at a blow,
And with the other fling it at thy face,
Than bear so low a sail, to strike to thee.
KING EDWARD.
Sail how thou canst, have wind and tide thy
friend,
This hand, fast wound about thy coal-black hair,
Shall, whiles thy head is warm and new cut off,
Write in the dust this sentence with thy blood,—
'Wind-changing Warwick now can change no
more.'
Enter OXFORD, *with drum and colours.*
EARL OF WARWICK.
O cheerful colours! see where Oxford comes!
EARL OF OXFORD.
Oxford, Oxford, for Lancaster!
[*He and his* FORCES *enter the city*
DUKE OF GLOSTER.
The gates are open, let us enter too.
KING EDWARD.
So other foes may set upon our backs.
Stand we in good array; for they no doubt
Will issue out again and bid us battle:
If not, the city being but of small defence,
We'll quickly rouse the traitors in the same.
EARL OF WARWICK.
O, welcome, Oxford! for we want thy help.
Enter MONTAGUE, *with drum and colours.*
MARQUESS OF MONTAGUE.
Montague, Montague, for Lancaster!
[*He and his* FORCES *enter the city*
DUKE OF GLOSTER.
Thou and thy brother both shall buy this treason
Even with the dearest blood your bodies bear.
KING EDWARD.
The harder matcht, the greater victory:
My mind presageth happy gain and conquest.
Enter SOMERSET, *with drums and colours.*
DUKE OF SOMERSET.
Somerset, Somerset, for Lancaster!
[*He and his* FORCES *enter the city*
DUKE OF GLOSTER.
Two of thy name, both Dukes of Somerset,
Have sold their lives unto the house of York;
And thou shalt be the third, if this sword hold.
Enter CLARENCE, *with drum and colours.*
EARL OF WARWICK.
And lo, where George of Clarence sweeps along,
Of force enough to bid his brother battle;
With whom an upright zeal to right prevails
More than the nature of a brother's love!—
Come, Clarence, come; thou wilt, if Warwick
call.

[*Sound a parley; and* RICHARD *and*
CLARENCE *whisper together, and then*
CLARENCE *takes his red rose out of his*
hat and throws it at WARWICK.

DUKE OF CLARENCE.

Father of Warwick, know you what this means?
Look here, I throw my infamy at thee:
I will not ruinate my father's house,
Who have his blood to lime the stones together,
And set up Lancaster. Why, trow'st thou, War-
    wick,
That Clarence is so harsh, so blunt, unnatural,
To bend the fatal instruments of war
Against his brother and his lawful king?
Perhaps thou wilt object my holy oath:
To keep that oath were more impiety
Than Jephtha's, when he sacrificed his daughter.
I am so sorry for my trespass made,
That, to deserve well at my brother's hands,
I here proclaim myself thy mortal foe;
With resolution, wheresoe'er I meet thee,—
As I will meet thee, if thou stir abroad,—
To plague thee for thy foul misleading me.
And so, proud-hearted Warwick, I defy thee,
And to my brother turn my blushing cheeks.—
Pardon me, Edward, I will make amends;
And, Richard, do not frown upon my faults,
For I will henceforth be no more unconstant.

KING EDWARD.

Now welcome more and ten times more beloved
Than if thou never hadst deserved our hate.

DUKE OF GLOSTER.

Welcome, good Clarence; this is brother-like.

EARL OF WARWICK.

O passing traitor, perjured and unjust!

KING EDWARD.

What, Warwick, wilt thou leave the town, and
    fight?
Or shall we beat the stones about thine ears?

EARL OF WARWICK.

Alas, I am not coopt here for defence!
I will away towards Barnet presently,
And bid thee battle, Edward, if thou darest.

KING EDWARD.

Yes, Warwick, Edward dares, and leads the
    way.—
Lords, to the field; Saint George and victory!

[*Exeunt* KING EDWARD *and his* COM-
PANY. *March.* WARWICK *and his*
COMPANY *follow.*

SCENE II.

A field of battle near Barnet.

Alarums and excursions. Enter KING EDWARD,
bringing forth WARWICK, *wounded.*

KING EDWARD.

O, lie thou there: die thou, and die our fear;
For Warwick was a bug that fear'd us all.—
Now, Montague, sit fast; I seek for thee,
That Warwick's bones may keep thine company.

[*Exit.*

EARL OF WARWICK.

Ah, who is nigh? come to me, friend or foe,
And tell me who is victor, York or Warwick?
Why ask I that? my mangled body shows,

My blood, my want of strength, my sick heart
    shows,
That I must yield my body to the earth,
And, by my fall, the conquest to my foe.
Thus yields the cedar to the axe's edge,
Whose arms gave shelter to the princely eagle,
Under whose shade the ramping lion slept,
Whose top-branch overpeer'd Jove's spreading
    tree,
And kept low shrubs from winter's powerful
    wind.
These eyes, that now are dimm'd with death's
    black veil,
Have been as piercing as the mid-day sun,
To search the secret treasons of the world:
The wrinkles in my brows, now fill'd with blood,
Were liken'd oft to kingly sepulchres;
For who lived king, but I could dig his grave?
And who durst smile when Warwick bent his
    brow?
Lo, now my glory smear'd in dust and blood!
My parks, my walks, my manors that I had,
Even now forsake me; and of all my lands
Is nothing left me but my body's length!
Why, what is pomp, rule, reign, but earth and dust?
And, live we how we can, yet die we must.

Enter OXFORD *and* SOMERSET.

DUKE OF SOMERSET.

Ah, Warwick, Warwick! wert thou as we are,
We might recover all our loss again: [power;
The queen from France hath brought a puissant
Even now we heard the news: ah, couldst thou fly!

EARL OF WARWICK.

Why, then, I would not fly.—Ah, Montague,
If thou be there, sweet brother, take my hand,
And with thy lips keep in my soul awhile!
Thou lovest me not; for, brother, if thou didst,
Thy tears would wash this cold congealed blood,
That glues my lips and will not let me speak.
Come quickly, Montague, or I am dead.

DUKE OF SOMERSET.

Ah, Warwick! Montague hath breath'd his last;
And to the latest gasp cried out for Warwick,
And said, 'Commend me to my valiant brother.'
And more he would have said; and more he spoke,
Which sounded like a clamour in a vault,
That mought not be distinguisht; but at last
I well might hear, deliver'd with a groan,
'O, farewell, Warwick!'

EARL OF WARWICK.

Sweet rest his soul!—Fly, lords, and save your-
    selves.
For Warwick bids you all farewell, to meet in
    heaven.   [*Dies.*

EARL OF OXFORD.

Away, away, to meet the queen's great power!

[*Here they bear away his body.*   *Exeunt.*

SCENE III.

Another part of the field.

Flourish. Enter KING EDWARD *in triumph; with*
GLOSTER, CLARENCE, *and the rest.*

KING EDWARD.

THUS far our fortune keeps an upward course,
And we are graced with wreaths of victory.

But, in the midst of this bright-shining day,
I spy a black, suspicious, threatening cloud,
That will encounter with our glorious sun
Ere he attain his easeful western bed:
I mean, my lords, those powers that the queen
Hath raised in Gallia have arrived our coast,
And, as we hear, march on to fight with us.

DUKE OF CLARENCE.

A little gale will soon disperse that cloud,
And blow it to the source from whence it came:
Thy very beams will dry those vapours up;
For every cloud engenders not a storm.

DUKE OF GLOSTER.

The queen is valued thirty thousand strong,
And Somerset, with Oxford, fled to her:
If she have time to breathe, be well assured
Her faction will be full as strong as ours.

KING EDWARD.

We are advertised by our loving friends
That they do hold their course toward Tewks-
bury:
We, having now the best at Barnet field,
Will thither straight, for willingness rids way;
And, as we march, our strength will be aug-
mented
In every county as we go along.—
Strike up the drum; cry, 'Courage!' and away.
[_Exeunt._

SCENE IV.
Plains near Tewksbury.

Flourish. March. Enter QUEEN MARGARET,
PRINCE EDWARD, SOMERSET, OXFORD, _and_
SOLDIERS.

QUEEN MARGARET.

GREAT lords, wise men ne'er sit and wail their
loss,
But cheerly seek how to redress their harms.
What though the mast be now blown overboard,
The cable broke, the holding-anchor lost,
And half our sailors swallow'd in the flood?
Yet lives our pilot still: is't meet that he
Should leave the helm, and, like a fearful lad,
With tearful eyes add water to the sea,
And give more strength to that which hath too
much;
Whiles, in his moan, the ship splits on the rock,
Which industry and courage might have saved?
Ah, what a shame! ah, what a fault were this!
Say Warwick was our anchor; what of that?
And Montague our topmast; what of him?
Our slaughter'd friends the tackles; what of these?
Why, is not Oxford here another anchor?
And Somerset another goodly mast?
The friends of France our shrouds and tacklings?
And, though unskilful, why not Ned and I
For once allow'd the skilful pilot's charge?
We will not from the helm to sit and weep;   [no,
But keep our course, though the rough wind say
From shelves and rocks that threaten us with
wrack.
As good to chide the waves as speak them fair.
And what is Edward but a ruthless sea?
What Clarence but a quicksand of deceit?
And Richard but a ragged fatal rock?
All these the enemies to our poor bark.

Say you can swim,—alas, 'tis but awhile!
Tread on the sand,—why, there you quickly sink;
Bestride the rock,—the tide will wash you off,
Or else you famish; that's a threefold death.
This speak I, lords, to let you understand,
If case some one of you would fly from us,
That there's no hoped-for mercy with the
brothers,
More than with ruthless waves, with sands, and
rocks.
Why, courage, then! what cannot be avoided
'Twere childish weakness to lament or fear.

PRINCE EDWARD.

Methinks a woman of this valiant spirit
Should, if a coward heard her speak these words,
Infuse his breast with magnanimity,
And make him naked foil a man-at-arms.
I speak not this as doubting any here;
For did I but suspect a fearful man,
He should have leave to go away betimes;
Lest in our need he might infect another,
And make him of like spirit to himself.
If any such be here,—as God forbid!—
Let him depart before we need his help.

EARL OF OXFORD.

Women and children of so high a courage,
And warriors faint! why, 'twere perpetual
shame.—
O brave young prince! thy famous grandfather
Doth live again in thee: long mayst thou live
To bear his image and renew his glories!

DUKE OF SOMERSET.

And he that will not fight for such a hope,
Go home to bed, and, like the owl by day,
If he arise, be mockt and wonder'd at.

QUEEN MARGARET.

Thanks, gentle Somerset;—sweet Oxford, thanks.

PRINCE EDWARD.

And take his thanks that yet hath nothing else.

Enter a MESSENGER.

MESSENGER.

Prepare you, lords; for Edward is at hand,
Ready to fight; therefore be resolute.

EARL OF OXFORD.

I thought no less: it is his policy
To haste thus fast, to find us unprovided.

DUKE OF SOMERSET.

But he's deceived; we are in readiness.

QUEEN MARGARET.

This cheers my heart, to see your forwardness.

EARL OF OXFORD.

Here pitch our battle; hence we will not budge.
Flourish and march.   Enter KING EDWARD,
GLOSTER, CLARENCE, _and_ FORCES.

KING EDWARD.

Brave followers, yonder stands the thorny wood,
Which, by the heavens' assistance and your
strength,
Must by the roots be hewn up yet ere night.
I need not add more fuel to your fire,
For well I wot ye blaze to burn them out:
Give signal to the fight, and to it, lords.

QUEEN MARGARET.

Lords, knights, and gentlemen, what I should say
My tears gainsay; for every word I speak,
Ye see, I drink the water of mine eyes.

Therefore, but no more but this:—Henry, your
    sovereign,
Is prisoner to the foe; his state usurpt,
His realm a slaughter-house, his subjects slain,
His statutes cancell'd, and his treasure spent;
And yonder is the wolf that makes this spoil.
You fight in justice: then, in God's name, lords,
Be valiant, and give signal to the fight.
    [*Alarum. Retreat. Excursions. Exeunt.*

SCENE V.
Another part of the field.

Flourish. Enter KING EDWARD, GLOSTER,
CLARENCE, *and* SOLDIERS; *with* QUEEN
MARGARET, OXFORD, *and* SOMERSET, *pri-
soners.*

KING EDWARD.
LO, here a period of tumultuous broils.
    Away with Oxford to Hames Castle straight:
For Somerset, off with his guilty head.
Go, bear them hence; I will not hear them speak.

EARL OF OXFORD.
For my part, I'll not trouble thee with words.

DUKE OF SOMERSET.
Nor I, but stoop with patience to my fortune.
    [*Exeunt* OXFORD *and* SOMERSET, *guarded.*

QUEEN MARGARET.
So part we sadly in this troublous world
To meet with joy in sweet Jerusalem.

KING EDWARD.
Is proclamation made, that who finds Edward
Shall have a high reward, and he his life?

DUKE OF GLOSTER.
It is: and lo, where youthful Edward comes!
Enter SOLDIERS, *with* PRINCE EDWARD.

KING EDWARD.
Bring forth the gallant, let us hear him speak.
What! can so young a thorn begin to prick?—
Edward, what satisfaction canst thou make
For bearing arms, for stirring up my subjects,
And all the trouble thou hast turn'd me to?

PRINCE EDWARD.
Speak like a subject, proud ambitious York!
Suppose that I am now my father's mouth;
Resign thy chair, and where I stand kneel thou,
Whilst I propose the selfsame words to thee,
Which, traitor, thou wouldst have me answer to.

QUEEN MARGARET.
Ah, that thy father had been so resolved!

DUKE OF GLOSTER.
That you might still have worn the petticoat,
And ne'er have stol'n the breech from Lancaster.

PRINCE EDWARD.
Let Aesop fable in a winter's night;
His currish riddles sort not with this place.

DUKE OF GLOSTER.
By heaven, brat, I'll plague ye for that word.

QUEEN MARGARET.
Ay, thou wast born to be a plague to men.

DUKE OF GLOSTER.
For God's sake, take away this captive scold.

PRINCE EDWARD.
Nay, take away this scolding crook-back rather.

KING EDWARD.
Peace, wilful boy, or I will charm your tongue.

DUKE OF CLARENCE.
Untutor'd lad, thou art too malapert.

PRINCE EDWARD.
I know my duty; you are all undutiful:
Lascivious Edward,—and thou, perjured
    George,—
And thou, mis-shapen Dick,—I tell ye all
I am your better, traitors as ye are;—
And thou usurp'st my father's right and mine.

KING EDWARD.
Take that, thou likeness of this railer here.
    [*Stabs him.*

DUKE OF GLOSTER.
Sprawl'st thou? take that, to end thy agony.
    [*Stabs him.*

DUKE OF CLARENCE.
And there's for twitting me with perjury.
    [*Stabs him.*

QUEEN MARGARET.
O, kill me too!

DUKE OF GLOSTER.
Marry, and shall.   [*Offers to kill her.*

KING EDWARD.
Hold, Richard, hold; for we have done too much.

DUKE OF GLOSTER.
Why should she live, to fill the world with words?

KING EDWARD.
What, doth she swoon? use means for her re-
    covery.

DUKE OF GLOSTER.
Clarence, excuse me to the king my brother;
I'll hence to London on a serious matter:
Ere ye come there, be sure to hear some news.

DUKE OF CLARENCE.
What? what?

DUKE OF GLOSTER.
The Tower, man, the Tower!—I'll root 'em out.
    [*Exit.*

QUEEN MARGARET.
O Ned, sweet Ned! speak to thy mother, boy!
Canst thou not speak? O traitors! murderers!
They that stabb'd Cæsar shed no blood at all,
Did not offend, nor were not worthy blame,
If this foul deed were by to equal it:
He was a man; this, in respect, a child,—
And men ne'er spend their fury on a child.
What's worse than murderer, that I may name it?
No, no, my heart will burst, an if I speak:
And I will speak, that so my heart may burst.
Butchers and villains! bloody cannibals!
How sweet a plant have you untimely cropt!
You have no children, butchers! if you had,
The thought of them would have stirr'd up
    remorse:
But if you ever chance to have a child,
Look in his youth to have him so cut off   [prince!
As, deathsmen, you have rid this sweet young

KING EDWARD.
Away with her; go, bear her hence perforce.

QUEEN MARGARET.
Nay, never bear me hence, dispatch me here;
Here sheathe thy sword, I'll pardon thee my
    death:
What, wilt thou not?—then, Clarence, do it thou.

DUKE OF CLARENCE.
By heaven, I will not do thee so much ease.

QUEEN MARGARET.
Good Clarence, do; sweet Clarence, do thou do it.
DUKE OF CLARENCE.
Didst thou not hear me swear I would not do it?
QUEEN MARGARET.
Ay, but thou usest to forswear thyself:
'Twas sin before, but now 'tis charity.
What, wilt thou not?—Where is that devil's
butcher,
Hard-favour'd Richard?—Richard, where art
thou?
Thou art not here: murder is thy alms-deed;
Petitioners for blood thou ne'er putt'st back.
KING EDWARD.
Away, I say; I charge ye, bear her hence.
QUEEN MARGARET.
So come to you and yours, as to this prince!
[Exit, led out forcibly.
KING EDWARD.
Where's Richard gone?
DUKE OF CLARENCE.
To London, all in post; and, as I guess,
To make a bloody supper in the Tower.
KING EDWARD.
He's sudden, if a thing comes in his head.
Now march we hence: discharge the common sort
With pay and thanks, and let's away to London,
And see our gentle queen how well she fares,—
By this, I hope, she hath a son for me.   [Exeunt.

SCENE VI.

London. The Tower.

Enter KING HENRY *and* GLOSTER, *with the*
LIEUTENANT, *on the walls.*

DUKE OF GLOSTER.
GOOD day, my lord. What, at your book so
hard?
KING HENRY.
Ay, my good lord:—my lord, I should say rather;
'Tis sin to flatter; 'good' was little better:
'Good Gloster' and 'good devil' were alike,
And both preposterous; therefore, not 'good
lord.'
DUKE OF GLOSTER.
Sirrah, leave us to ourselves: we must confer.
[Exit LIEUTENANT.
KING HENRY.
So flies the reckless shepherd from the wolf;
So first the harmless sheep doth yield his fleece,
And next his throat unto the butcher's knife.—
What scene of death hath Roscius now to act?
DUKE OF GLOSTER.
Suspicion always haunts the guilty mind;
The thief doth fear each bush an officer.
KING HENRY.
The bird that hath been limed in a bush,
With trembling wings misdoubteth every bush;
And I, the hapless male to one sweet bird,
Have now the fatal object in my eye
Where my poor young was limed, was caught,
and kill'd.
DUKE OF GLOSTER.
Why, what a peevish fool was that of Crete,
That taught his son the office of a fowl!
And yet, for all his wings the fool was drown'd.

KING HENRY.
I, Dædalus; my poor boy, Icarus;
Thy father, Minos, that denied our course;
The sun, that sear'd the wings of my sweet boy,
Thy brother Edward; and thyself, the sea,
Whose envious gulf did swallow up his life.
Ah, kill me with thy weapon, not with words!
My breast can better brook thy dagger's point
Than can my ears that tragic history.
But wherefore dost thou come? is't for my life?
DUKE OF GLOSTER.
Think'st thou I am an executioner?
KING HENRY.
A persecutor, I am sure, thou art:
If murdering innocents be executing,
Why, then thou art an executioner.
DUKE OF GLOSTER.
Thy son I kill'd for his presumption.
KING HENRY.
Hadst thou been kill'd when first thou didst pre-
sume,
Thou hadst not lived to kill a son of mine.
And thus I prophesy,—that many a thousand,
Which now mistrust no parcel of my fear,
And many an old man's sigh and many a widow's,
And many an orphan's water-standing eye—
Men for their sons, wives for their husbands'
fate,
And orphans for their parents' timeless death—
Shall rue the hour that ever thou wast born.
The owl shriekt at thy birth,—an evil sign;
The night-crow cried, aboding luckless time;
Dogs howl'd, and hideous tempest shook down
trees;
The raven rookt her on the chimney's top,
And chattering pies in dismal discord sung.
Thy mother felt more than a mother's pain,
And yet brought forth less than a mother's
hope,—
An indigested and deformed lump,
Not like the fruit of such a goodly tree.
Teeth hadst thou in thy head when thou wast
born,
To signify thou camest to bite the world:
And, if the rest be true which I have heard,
Thou camest—
DUKE OF GLOSTER.
I'll hear no more: die, prophet, in thy speech:
[Stabs him
For this, amongst the rest, was I ordain'd.
KING HENRY.
Ay, and for much more slaughter after this.
O, God forgive my sins, and pardon thee!   [Dies
DUKE OF GLOSTER.
What, will the aspiring blood of Lancaster
Sink in the ground? I thought it would have
mounted.
See how my sword weeps for the poor king's
death!
O, may such purple tears be alway shed
From those that wish the downfall of our house!
If any spark of life be yet remaining,
Down, down to hell; and say I sent thee thither,
[Stabs him again
I, that have neither pity, love, nor fear.
Indeed, 'tis true that Henry told me of;

For I have often heard my mother say
I came into the world with my legs forward:
Had I not reason, think ye, to make haste,
And seek their ruin that usurpt our right?
The midwife wonder'd; and the women cried,
'O, Jesus bless us, he is born with teeth!'
And so I was; which plainly signified
That I should snarl, and bite, and play the dog.
Then, since the heavens have shaped my body so,
Let hell make crookt my mind to answer it.
I have no brother, I am like no brother;
And this word 'love,' which greybeards call
      divine,
Be resident in men like one another,
And not in me: I am myself alone.—
Clarence, beware; thou keep'st me from the light:
But I will sort a pitchy day for thee;
For I will buzz abroad such prophecies,
That Edward shall be fearful of his life;
And then, to purge his fear, I'll be thy death.
King Henry and the prince his son are gone:
Clarence, thy turn is next, and then the rest;
Counting myself but bad till I be best.—
I'll throw thy body in another room,
And triumph, Henry, in thy day of doom.
                              [Exit with the body.

SCENE VII.

London.   The palace.

Flourish.   Enter KING EDWARD, QUEEN ELIZA-
BETH, GLOSTER, CLARENCE, HASTINGS, *a*
NURSE *with the young* PRINCE, *and* ATTEN-
DANTS.

KING EDWARD.

ONCE more we sit in England's royal throne,
      Re-purchased with the blood of enemies.
What valiant foemen, like to autumn's corn,
Have we mow'd down in tops of all their pride!
Three Dukes of Somerset, threefold renown'd
For hardy and undoubted champions;
Two Cliffords, as the father and the son;
And two Northumberlands,—two braver men
Ne'er spurr'd their coursers at the trumpet's
      sound;
With them, the two brave bears, Warwick and
      Montague,

That in their chains fetter'd the kingly lion,
And made the forest tremble when they roar'd.
Thus have we swept suspicion from our seat,
And made our footstool of security.—
Come hither, Bess, and let me kiss my boy.
Young Ned, for thee, thine uncles and myself
Have in our armours watcht the winter's night;
Went all afoot in summer's scalding heat,
That thou mightst repossess the crown in peace:
And of our labours thou shalt reap the gain.

DUKE OF GLOSTER [aside].

I'll blast his harvest, if your head were laid;
For yet I am not lookt on in the world.
This shoulder was ordain'd so thick to heave;
And heave it shall some weight, or break my
      back:—
Work thou the way,—and thou shalt execute.

KING EDWARD.

Clarence and Gloster, love my lovely queen;
And kiss your princely nephew, brothers both.

DUKE OF CLARENCE.

The duty that I owe unto your majesty
I seal upon the lips of this sweet babe.

QUEEN ELIZABETH.

Thanks, noble Clarence; worthy brother, thanks.

DUKE OF GLOSTER.

And, that I love the tree from whence thou
      sprang'st,
Witness the loving kiss I give the fruit.—
[aside] To say the truth, so Judas kist his Master,
And cried, 'All hail!' whenas he meant all harm.

KING EDWARD.

Now am I seated as my soul delights,
Having my country's peace and brothers' loves.

DUKE OF CLARENCE.

What will your Grace have done with Margaret?
Reignier, her father, to the king of France
Hath pawn'd the Sicils and Jerusalem,
And hither have they sent it for her ransom.

KING EDWARD.

Away with her, and waft her hence to France.
And now what rests, but that we spend the time
With stately triumphs, mirthful comic shows,
Such as befits the pleasure of the court?
Sound drums and trumpets! farewell sour annoy!
For here, I hope, begins our lasting joy.
                              [Exeunt.

KING RICHARD THE THIRD

ACT I. SCENE I.

London.   A street.

Enter RICHARD, DUKE OF GLOSTER, *solus.*

DUKE OF GLOSTER.

NOW is the winter of our discontent
Made glorious summer by this sun of York;
And all the clouds that lour'd upon our house
In the deep bosom of the ocean buried.
Now are our brows bound with victorious wreaths;
Our bruised arms hung up for monuments;
Our stern alarums changed to merry meetings,
Our dreadful marches to delightful measures.
Grim-visaged war hath smooth'd his wrinkled front;
And now—instead of mounting barbed steeds
To fright the souls of fearful adversaries—
He capers nimbly in a lady's chamber
To the lascivious pleasing of a lute.
But I, that am not shaped for sportive tricks,
Nor made to court an amorous looking-glass;
I, that am rudely stampt, and want love's majesty
To strut before a wanton ambling nymph;
I, that am curtail'd of this fair proportion,
Cheated of feature by dissembling nature,
Deform'd, unfinish't, sent before my time
Into this breathing world, scarce half made up,
And that so lamely and unfashionable
That dogs bark at me as I halt by them;—
Why, I, in this weak piping time of peace,
Have no delight to pass away the time,

Unless to spy my shadow in the sun,
And descant on mine own deformity:
And therefore, since I cannot prove a lover,
To entertain these fair well-spoken days,
I am determined to prove a villain,
And hate the idle pleasures of these days.
Plots have I laid, inductions dangerous,
By drunken prophecies, libels, and dreams,
To set my brother Clarence and the king
In deadly hate the one against the other:
And, if King Edward be as true and just
As I am subtle, false, and treacherous,
This day should Clarence closely be mew'd up,
About a prophecy, which says that G
Of Edward's heirs the murderer shall be.
Dive, thoughts, down to my soul:—here Clarence comes.

Enter CLARENCE, *guarded, and* BRAKENBURY.

Brother, good day: what means this armed guard
That waits upon your Grace?

DUKE OF CLARENCE.

His majesty,
Tendering my person's safety, hath appointed
This conduct to convey me to the Tower.

DUKE OF GLOSTER.

Upon what cause?

DUKE OF CLARENCE.

Because my name is George.

DUKE OF GLOSTER.

Alack, my lord, that fault is none of yours;
He should, for that, commit your godfathers:—
O, belike his majesty hath some intent

That you shall be new-christen'd in the Tower.
But what's the matter, Clarence? may I know?
DUKE OF CLARENCE.
Yea, Richard, when I know; for I protest
As yet I do not: but, as I can learn,
He hearkens after prophecies and dreams;
And from the cross-row plucks the letter G,
And says a wizard told him that by G
His issue disinherited should be;
And, for my name of George begins with G,
It follows in his thought that I am he.
These, as I learn, and such-like toys as these,
Have moved his highness to commit me now.
DUKE OF GLOSTER.
Why, this it is, when men are ruled by women:—
'Tis not the king that sends you to the Tower;
My Lady Grey his wife, Clarence, 'tis she
That tempers him to this extremity.
Was it not she, and that good man of worship,
Antony Woodville, her brother there,
That made him send Lord Hastings to the Tower,
From whence this present day he is deliver'd?
We are not safe, Clarence; we are not safe.
DUKE OF CLARENCE.
By heaven, I think there's no man is secure
But the queen's kindred, and night-walking
      heralds
That trudge betwixt the king and Mistress Shore.
Heard ye not what an humble suppliant
Lord Hastings was to her for his delivery?
DUKE OF GLOSTER.
Humbly complaining to her deity
Got my lord chamberlain his liberty.
I'll tell you what,—I think it is our way,
If we will keep in favour with the king,
To be her men, and wear her livery:
The jealous o'erworn widow and herself,
Since that our brother dubb'd them gentlewomen,
Are mighty gossips in this monarchy.
SIR ROBERT BRAKENBURY.
I beseech your Graces both to pardon me;
His majesty hath straitly given in charge
That no man shall have private conference,
Of what degree soever, with his brother.
DUKE OF GLOSTER.
Even so; an please your worship, Brakenbury,
You may partake of any thing we say:
We speak no treason, man;—we say the king
Is wise and virtuous; and his noble queen
Well struck in years, fair, and not jealous;—
We say that Shore's wife hath a pretty foot,
A cherry lip, a bonny eye, a passing pleasing
      tongue;   [folks:
And that the queen's kindred are made gentle-
How say you, sir? can you deny all this?
SIR ROBERT BRAKENBURY.
With this, my lord, myself have naught to do.
DUKE OF GLOSTER.
Naught to do with Mistress Shore! I tell thee,
      fellow,
He that doth naught with her, excepting one,
Were best to do it secretly, alone.
SIR ROBERT BRAKENBURY.
What one, my lord?
DUKE OF GLOSTER.
Her husband, knave:—wouldst thou betray me?

SIR ROBERT BRAKENBURY.
I beseech your Grace to pardon me; and, withal,
Forbear your conference with the noble duke.
DUKE OF CLARENCE.
We know thy charge, Brakenbury, and will obey.
DUKE OF GLOSTER.
We are the queen's abjects, and must obey.—
Brother, farewell: I will unto the king;
And whatsoe'er you will employ me in,—
Were it to call King Edward's widow sister,—
I will perform it to enfranchise you.
Meantime, this deep disgrace in brotherhood
Touches me deeper than you can imagine.
DUKE OF CLARENCE.
I know it pleaseth neither of us well.
DUKE OF GLOSTER.
Well, your imprisonment shall not be long;
I will deliver you, or else lie for you:
Meantime, have patience.
DUKE OF CLARENCE.
                    I must perforce: farewell.
      [*Exeunt* CLARENCE, BRAKENBURY, *and*
      GUARD.
DUKE OF GLOSTER.
Go, tread the path that thou shalt ne'er return,
Simple, plain Clarence!—I do love thee so,
That I will shortly send thy soul to heaven,
If heaven will take the present at our hands.—
But who comes here? the new-deliver'd
      Hastings?
Enter HASTINGS.
LORD HASTINGS.
Good time of day unto my gracious lord!
DUKE OF GLOSTER.
As much unto my good lord chamberlain!
Well are you welcome to the open air.
How hath your lordship brookt imprisonment?
LORD HASTINGS.
With patience, noble lord, as prisoners must:
But I shall live, my lord, to give them thanks
That were the cause of my imprisonment.
DUKE OF GLOSTER.
No doubt, no doubt; and so shall Clarence too;
For they that were your enemies are his,
And have prevail'd as much on him as you.
LORD HASTINGS.
More pity that the eagle should be mew'd,
While kites and buzzards prey at liberty.
DUKE OF GLOSTER.
What news abroad?
LORD HASTINGS.
No news so bad abroad as this at home,—
The king is sickly, weak, and melancholy
And his physicians fear him mightily.
DUKE OF GLOSTER.
Now, by Saint Paul, this news is bad indeed.
O, he hath kept an evil diet long,
And overmuch consumed his royal person:
'Tis very grievous to be thought upon.
What, is he in his bed?
LORD HASTINGS.
He is.
DUKE OF GLOSTER.
Go you before, and I will follow you.
                          [*Exit* HASTINGS.
He cannot live, I hope; and must not die

Till George be packt with post-horse up to
    heaven.
I'll in, to urge his hatred more to Clarence,
With lies well steel'd with weighty arguments;
And, if I fail not in my deep intent,
Clarence hath not another day to live:
Which done, God take King Edward to His
    mercy,
And leave the world for me to bustle in!
For then I'll marry Warwick's youngest
    daughter:
What though I kill'd her husband and her father?
The readiest way to make the wench amends,
Is to become her husband and her father:
The which will I; not all so much for love
As for another secret close intent,
By marrying her which I must reach unto.
But yet I run before my horse to market:
Clarence still breathes; Edward still lives and
    reigns:
When they are gone, then must I count my gains.

                                    [*Exit.*

SCENE II.

The same. Another street.

Enter the corse of HENRY THE SIXTH, *with halberds to guard it,* LADY ANNE *being the
mourner;* TRESSEL *and* BERKELEY.

LADY ANNE.

SET down, set down your honourable load,—
    If honour may be shrouded in a hearse,—
Whilst I awhile obsequiously lament
Th' untimely fall of virtuous Lancaster.
Poor key-cold figure of a holy king!
Pale ashes of the house of Lancaster!
Thou bloodless remnant of that royal blood!
Be it lawful that I invocate thy ghost,
To hear the lamentations of poor Anne,
Wife to thy Edward, to thy slaughter'd son,
Stabb'd by the selfsame hand that made these
    wounds!
Lo, in these windows that let forth thy life,
I pour the helpless balm of my poor eyes,—
O, cursed be the hand that made these holes!
Cursed the heart that had the heart to do it!
Cursed the blood that let this blood from hence!
More direful hap betide that hated wretch,
That makes us wretched by the death of thee,
Than I can wish to adders, spiders, toads,
Or any creeping venom'd thing that lives!
If ever he have child, abortive be it,
Prodigious, and untimely brought to light,
Whose ugly and unnatural aspect
May fright the hopeful mother at the view;
And that be heir to his unhappiness!
If ever he have wife, let her be made
More miserable by the death of him
Than I am made by my young lord and thee!—
Come, now towards Chertsey with your holy
    load,
Taken from Paul's to be interred there;
And still, as you are weary of the weight,
Rest you, whiles I lament King Henry's corse.

Enter GLOSTER.

DUKE OF GLOSTER.

Stay, you that bear the corse, and set it down.

LADY ANNE.

What black magician conjures up this fiend,
To stop devoted charitable deeds?

DUKE OF GLOSTER.

Villains, set down the corse; or, by Saint Paul,
I'll make a corse of him that disobeys!

FIRST GENTLEMAN.

My lord, stand back, and let the coffin pass.

DUKE OF GLOSTER.

Unmanner'd dog! stand thou, when I command:
Advance thy halberd higher than my breast,
Or, by Saint Paul, I'll strike thee to my foot,
And spurn upon thee, beggar, for thy boldness.

LADY ANNE.

What, do you tremble? are you all afraid?
Alas, I blame you not; for you are mortal,
And mortal eyes cannot endure the devil.—
Avaunt, thou dreadful minister of hell!
Thou hadst but power over his mortal body,—
His soul thou canst not have; therefore, be gone.

DUKE OF GLOSTER.

Sweet saint, for charity, be not so curst.

LADY ANNE.

Foul devil, for God's sake, hence, and trouble us
    not;
For thou hast made the happy earth thy hell,
Fill'd it with cursing cries and deep exclaims.
If thou delight to view thy heinous deeds,
Behold this pattern of thy butcheries.
O, gentlemen, see, see! dead Henry's wounds
Open their congeal'd mouths and bleed afresh!
Blush, blush, thou lump of foul deformity;
For 'tis thy presence that exhales this blood
From cold and empty veins, where no blood
    dwells;
Thy deed, inhuman and unnatural,
Provokes this deluge most unnatural.—
O God, which this blood mad'st, revenge his
    death!
O earth, which this blood drink'st, revenge his
    death!
Either heaven with lightning strike the murderer
    dead;
Or, earth, gape open wide, and eat him quick,
As thou dost swallow up this good king's blood,
Which his hell-govern'd arm hath butchered!

DUKE OF GLOSTER.

Lady, you know no rules of charity,
Which renders good for bad, blessings for curses.

LADY ANNE.

Villain, thou know'st no law of God nor man:
No beast so fierce but knows some touch of
    pity.

DUKE OF GLOSTER.

But I know none, and therefore am no beast.

LADY ANNE.

O wonderful, when devils tell the truth!

DUKE OF GLOSTER.

More wonderful, when angels are so angry.—
Vouchsafe, divine perfection of a woman,
Of these supposed evils, to give me leave,
By circumstance, but to acquit myself.

LADY ANNE.

Vouchsafe, defused infection of a man,
For these known evils, but to give me leave,
By circumstance, to curse thy cursed self.

DUKE OF GLOSTER.
Fairer than tongue can name thee, let me have
Some patient leisure to excuse myself.
               LADY ANNE.
Fouler than heart can think thee, thou canst
   make
No excuse current, but to hang thyself.
             DUKE OF GLOSTER.
By such despair, I should accuse myself.
             LADY ANNE.
And, by despairing, shouldst thou stand excused
For doing worthy vengeance on thyself,
That didst unworthy slaughter upon others.
             DUKE OF GLOSTER.
Say that I slew them not?
             LADY ANNE.
        Why, then, they are not dead:
But dead they are, and, devilish slave, by thee.
             DUKE OF GLOSTER.
I did not kill your husband.
             LADY ANNE.
        Why, then, he is alive.
             DUKE OF GLOSTER.
Nay, he is dead; and slain by Edward's hand.
             LADY ANNE.
In thy foul throat thou liest: Queen Margaret
   saw
Thy murderous falchion smoking in his blood;
The which thou once didst bend against her
   breast,
But that thy brothers beat aside the point.
             DUKE OF GLOSTER.
I was provoked by her slanderous tongue,
That laid their guilt upon my guiltless shoulders.
             LADY ANNE.
Thou wast provoked by thy bloody mind,
That never dreamt on aught but butcheries:
Didst thou not kill this king?
             DUKE OF GLOSTER.
          I grant ye.
             LADY ANNE.
Dost grant me, hedgehog? then, God grant me
   too
Thou mayst be damned for that wicked deed!
O, he was gentle, mild, and virtuous!
             DUKE OF GLOSTER.
The fitter for the King of heaven, that hath him.
             LADY ANNE.
He is in heaven, where thou shalt never come.
             DUKE OF GLOSTER.
Let him thank me, that holp to send him thither;
For he was fitter for that place than earth.
             LADY ANNE.
And thou unfit for any place but hell.
             DUKE OF GLOSTER.
Yes, one place else, if you will hear me name it.
             LADY ANNE.
Some dungeon.
             DUKE OF GLOSTER.
        Your bed-chamber.
             LADY ANNE.
Ill rest betide the chamber where thou liest!
             DUKE OF GLOSTER.
So will it, madam, till I lie with you.
             LADY ANNE.
hope so.

DUKE OF GLOSTER.
     I know so. But, gentle Lady Anne,—
To leave this keen encounter of our wits,
And fall somewhat into a slower method,—
Is not the causer of the timeless deaths
Of these Plantagenets, Henry and Edward,
As blameful as the executioner?
             LADY ANNE.
Thou wast the cause and most accurst effect.
             DUKE OF GLOSTER.
Your beauty was the cause of that effect;
Your beauty, that did haunt me in my sleep
To undertake the death of all the world,
So I might live one hour in your sweet bosom.
             LADY ANNE.
If I thought that, I tell thee, homicide,   [cheeks.
These nails should rend that beauty from my
             DUKE OF GLOSTER.
These eyes could not endure that beauty's
   wrack;
You should not blemish it, if I stood by:
As all the world is cheered by the sun,
So I by that; it is my day, my life.
             LADY ANNE.
Black night o'ershade thy day, and death thy life!
             DUKE OF GLOSTER.
Curse not thyself, fair creature; thou art both.
             LADY ANNE.
I would I were, to be revenged on thee.
             DUKE OF GLOSTER.
It is a quarrel most unnatural,
To be revenged on him that loveth thee.
             LADY ANNE.
It is a quarrel just and reasonable,
To be revenged on him that kill'd my husband.
             DUKE OF GLOSTER.
He that bereft thee, lady, of thy husband,
Did it to help thee to a better husband.
             LADY ANNE.
His better doth not breathe upon the earth.
             DUKE OF GLOSTER.
He lives that loves thee better than he could.
             LADY ANNE.
Name him.
             DUKE OF GLOSTER.
        Plantagenet.
             LADY ANNE.
          Why, that was he.
             DUKE OF GLOSTER.
The selfsame name, but one of better nature.
             LADY ANNE.
Where is he?
             DUKE OF GLOSTER.
        Here. [She spits at him.] Why dost
   thou spit at me?
             LADY ANNE.
Would it were mortal poison, for thy sake!
             DUKE OF GLOSTER.
Never came poison from so sweet a place.
             LADY ANNE.
Never hung poison on a fouler toad.
Out of my sight! thou dost infect mine eyes.
             DUKE OF GLOSTER.
Thine eyes, sweet lady, have infected mine.
             LADY ANNE.
Would they were basilisks, to strike thee dead!

DUKE OF GLOSTER.
I would they were, that I might die at once;
For now they kill me with a living death.
Those eyes of thine from mine have drawn salt
　　tears,
Shamed their aspects with store of childish drops:
These eyes, which never shed remorseful tear,
No, when my father York and Edward wept
To hear the piteous moan that Rutland made
When black-faced Clifford shook his sword at
　　him;
Nor when thy warlike father, like a child,
Told the sad story of my father's death,
And twenty times made pause to sob and weep,
That all the standers-by had wet their cheeks,
Like trees bedasht with rain; in that sad time
My manly eyes did scorn an humble tear;
And what these sorrows could not thence exhale,
Thy beauty hath, and made them blind with
　　weeping.
I never sued to friend nor enemy;
My tongue could never learn sweet smoothing
　　words;
But, now thy beauty is proposed my fee,
My proud heart sues, and prompts my tongue to
　　speak. 　　[She looks scornfully at him.
Teach not thy lips such scorn; for they were made
For kissing, lady, not for such contempt.
If thy revengeful heart cannot forgive,
Lo, here I lend thee this sharp-pointed sword;
Which if thou please to hide in this true breast,
And let the soul forth that adoreth thee,
I lay it naked to the deadly stroke,
And humbly beg the death upon my knee.
　　[He lays his breast open; she offers at it with
　　　his sword.
Nay, do not pause; for I did kill King Henry,
But 'twas thy beauty that provoked me.
Nay, now dispatch; 'twas I that stabb'd young
　　Edward,
But 'twas thy heavenly face that set me on.
　　　　　　　　　[She falls the sword.
Take up the sword again, or take up me.
LADY ANNE.
Arise, dissembler: though I wish thy death,
I will not be thy executioner.
DUKE OF GLOSTER.
Then bid me kill myself, and I will do it.
LADY ANNE.
I have already.
DUKE OF GLOSTER.
　　　　That was in thy rage:
Speak it again, and, even with the word,
This hand, which for thy love did kill thy love,
Shall for thy love kill a far truer love;
To both their deaths shalt thou be accessary.
LADY ANNE.
I would I knew thy heart.
DUKE OF GLOSTER.
'Tis figured in my tongue.
LADY ANNE.
I fear me both are false.
DUKE OF GLOSTER.
Then never man was true.
LADY ANNE.
Well, well, put up your sword.

DUKE OF GLOSTER.
Say, then, my peace is made.
LADY ANNE.
That shalt thou know hereafter.
DUKE OF GLOSTER.
But shall I live in hope?
LADY ANNE.
All men, I hope, live so.
DUKE OF GLOSTER.
Vouchsafe to wear this ring.
LADY ANNE.
To take, is not to give.
DUKE OF GLOSTER.
Look, how this ring encompasseth thy finger,
Even so thy breast encloseth my poor heart;
Wear both of them, for both of them are thine.
And if thy poor devoted servant may
But beg one favour at thy gracious hand,
Thou dost confirm his happiness for ever.
LADY ANNE.
What is it?
DUKE OF GLOSTER.
That it may please you leave these sad designs
To him that hath more cause to be a mourner,
And presently repair to Crosby-place;
Where—after I have solemnly interr'd
At Chertsey monastery this noble king,
And wet his grave with my repentant tears—
I will with all expedient duty see you:
For divers unknown reasons, I beseech you,
Grant me this boon.
LADY ANNE.
With all my heart; and much it joys me too
To see you are become so penitent.—
Tressel and Berkeley, go along with me.
DUKE OF GLOSTER.
Bid me farewell.
LADY ANNE.
　　　　　'Tis more than you deserve;
But since you teach me how to flatter you,
Imagine I have said farewell already.
　　[Exeun LADY ANNE, TRESSEL, and
　　　BERKELEY.
DUKE OF GLOSTER.
Sirs, take up the corse.
GENTLEMEN.
　　　　　Towards Chertsey, noble lord
DUKE OF GLOSTER.
No, to White-Friars; there attend my coming.
　　　　　[Exeunt all, except GLOSTER
Was ever woman in this humour woo'd?
Was ever woman in this humour won?
I'll have her;—but I will not keep her long.
What! I, that kill'd her husband and his father,
To take her in her heart's extremest hate;
With curses in her mouth, tears in her eyes,
The bleeding witness of her hatred by;
Having God, her conscience, and these bars
　　against me,
And I no friends to back my suit withal
But the plain devil and dissembling looks,
And yet to win her,—all the world to nothing!
Ha!
Hath she forgot already that brave prince,
Edward, her lord, whom I, some three months
　　since,

Stabb'd in my angry mood at Tewksbury?
A sweeter and a lovelier gentleman—
Framed in the prodigality of nature,
Young, valiant, wise, and, no doubt, right royal—
The spacious world cannot again afford:
And will she yet abase her eyes on me,
That cropt the golden prime of this sweet prince,
And made her widow to a woful bed?
On me, whose all not equals Edward's moiety?
On me, that halt and am mis-shapen thus?
My dukedom to a beggarly denier,
I do mistake my person all this while:
Upon my life, she finds, although I cannot,
Myself to be a marvellous proper man.
I'll be at charges for a looking-glass;
And entertain a score or two of tailors
To study fashions to adorn my body:
Since I am crept in favour with myself,
I will maintain it with some little cost.
But first I'll turn yon fellow in his grave;
And then return lamenting to my love.—
Shine out, fair sun, till I have bought a glass,
That I may see my shadow as I pass.　　　[*Exit.*

SCENE III.

The palace.

Enter QUEEN ELIZABETH, RIVERS, *and* GREY.

EARL RIVERS.

H AVE patience, madam: there's no doubt his
majesty
Will soon recover his accustom'd health.

LORD GREY.

In that you brook it ill, it makes him worse:
Therefore, for God's sake, entertain good
　　comfort,
And cheer his Grace with quick and merry words.

QUEEN ELIZABETH.

If he were dead, what would betide of me?

EARL RIVERS.

No other harm but loss of such a lord.

QUEEN ELIZABETH.

The loss of such a lord includes all harms.

LORD GREY.

The heavens have blest you with a goodly son,
To be your comforter when he is gone.

QUEEN ELIZABETH.

Ah, he is young; and his minority
Is put unto the trust of Richard Gloster,
A man that loves not me nor none of you.

EARL RIVERS.

Is it concluded he shall be Protector?

QUEEN ELIZABETH.

It is determined, not concluded yet:
But so it must be, if the king miscarry.

Enter BUCKINGHAM *and* DERBY.

LORD GREY.

Here come the lords of Buckingham and Derby.

DUKE OF BUCKINGHAM.

Good time of day unto your royal Grace!

EARL OF DERBY.

God make your majesty joyful as you have been!

QUEEN ELIZABETH.

The Countess Richmond, good my Lord of
　　Derby,
To your good prayer will scarcely say amen.

Yet, Derby, notwithstanding she's your wife,
And loves not me, be you, good lord, assured
I hate not you for her proud arrogance.

EARL OF DERBY.

I do beseech you, either not believe
The envious slanders of her false accusers;
Or, if she be accused on true report,
Bear with her weakness, which, I think, proceeds
From wayward sickness, and no grounded malice.

EARL RIVERS.

Saw you the king to-day, my Lord of Derby?

EARL OF DERBY.

But now the Duke of Buckingham and I
Are come from visiting his majesty.

QUEEN ELIZABETH.

What likelihood of his amendment, lords?

DUKE OF BUCKINGHAM.

Madam, good hope; his Grace speaks cheerfully.

QUEEN ELIZABETH.

God grant him health! Did you confer with him?

DUKE OF BUCKINGHAM.

Ay, madam: he desires to make atonement
Between the Duke of Gloster and your brothers,
And betwixt them and my lord chamberlain;
And sent to warn them to his royal presence.

QUEEN ELIZABETH.

Would all were well!—but that will never be:
I fear our happiness is at the height.

Enter GLOSTER, HASTINGS, *and* DORSET.

DUKE OF GLOSTER.

They do me wrong, and I will not endure it:—
Who are they that complain unto the king
That I, forsooth, am stern, and love them not?
By holy Paul, they love his Grace but lightly
That fill his ears with such dissentious rumours.
Because I cannot flatter and speak fair,
Smile in men's faces, smooth, deceive, and cog,
Duck with French nods and apish courtesy,
I must be held a rancorous enemy.
Cannot a plain man live and think no harm,
But thus his simple truth must be abused
By silken, sly, insinuating Jacks?

EARL RIVERS.

To whom in all this presence speaks your Grace?

DUKE OF GLOSTER.

To thee, that hast nor honesty nor grace.
When have I injured thee? when done thee
　　wrong?—
Or thee?—or thee?—or any of your faction?
A plague upon you all! His royal Grace—
Whom God preserve better than you would
　　wish!—
Cannot be quiet scarce a breathing-while,
But you must trouble him with lewd complaints.

QUEEN ELIZABETH.

Brother of Gloster, you mistake the matter.
The king, of his own royal disposition,
And not provoked by any suitor else;
Aiming, belike, at your interior hatred,
That in your outward action shows itself
Against my children, brothers, and myself,
Makes him to send, that thereby he may gather
The ground of your ill-will, and so remove it.

DUKE OF GLOSTER.

I cannot tell: the world is grown so bad,
That wrens may prey where eagles dare not perch:

Since every Jack became a gentleman,
There's many a gentle person made a Jack.
QUEEN ELIZABETH.
Come, come, we know your meaning, brother
Gloster;
You envy my advancement and my friends':
God grant we never may have need of you!
DUKE OF GLOSTER.
Meantime, God grants that we have need of you:
Our brother is imprison'd by your means,
Myself disgraced, and the nobility
Held in contempt; while great promotions
Are daily given to ennoble those
That scarce, some two days since, were worth
a noble.
QUEEN ELIZABETH.
By Him that raised me to this careful height
From that contented hap which I enjoy'd,
I never did incense his majesty
Against the Duke of Clarence, but have been
An earnest advocate to plead for him.
My lord, you do me shameful injury,
Falsely to draw me in these vile suspects.
DUKE OF GLOSTER.
You may deny that you were not the cause
Of my Lord Hastings' late imprisonment.
EARL RIVERS.
She may, my lord; for—
DUKE OF GLOSTER.
She may, Lord Rivers!—why, who knows not so?
She may do more, sir, than denying that:
She may help you to many fair preferments;
And then deny her aiding hand therein,
And lay those honours on your high desert.
What may she not? She may,—ay, marry, may
she,—
EARL RIVERS.
What, marry, may she?
DUKE OF GLOSTER.
What, marry, may she! marry with a king,
A bachelor, a handsome stripling too:
I wis your grandam had a worser match.
QUEEN ELIZABETH.
My Lord of Gloster, I have too long borne
Your blunt upbraidings and your bitter scoffs:
By heaven, I will acquaint his majesty
With those gross taunts I often have endured.
I had rather be a country servant-maid
Than a great queen, with this condition,—
To be so baited, scorn'd, and stormed at:
Enter QUEEN MARGARET, *behind.*
Small joy have I in being England's queen.
QUEEN MARGARET [*aside*].
And lessen'd be that small, God, I beseech
Him!
Thy honour, state, and seat is due to me.
DUKE OF GLOSTER.
What! threat you me with telling of the king?
Tell him, and spare not: look, what I have said
I will avouch in presence of the king:
I dare adventure to be sent to th' Tower.
'Tis time to speak,—my pains are quite forgot.
QUEEN MARGARET [*aside*].
Out, devil! I remember them too well:
Thou kill'dst my husband Henry in the Tower,
And Edward, my poor son, at Tewksbury.

DUKE OF GLOSTER.
Ere you were queen, ay, or your husband king,
I was a pack-horse in his great affairs;
A weeder-out of his proud adversaries,
A liberal rewarder of his friends:
To royalize his blood I spilt mine own.
QUEEN MARGARET [*aside*].
Ay, and much better blood than his or thine.
DUKE OF GLOSTER.
In all which time you and your husband Grey
Were factious for the house of Lancaster;—
And, Rivers, so were you:—was not your husband
In Margaret's battle at Saint Alban's slain?
Let me put in your minds, if you forget,
What you have been ere now, and what you are;
Withal, what I have been, and what I am.
QUEEN MARGARET [*aside*].
A murderous villain, and so still thou art.
DUKE OF GLOSTER.
Poor Clarence did forsake his father, Warwick;
Ay, and forswore himself,—which Jesu pardon!—
QUEEN MARGARET [*aside*].
Which God revenge!
DUKE OF GLOSTER.
To fight on Edward's party, for the crown;
And for his meed poor lord, he is mew'd up.
I would to God my heart were flint, like Ed-
ward's;
Or Edward's soft and pitiful, like mine:
I am too childish-foolish for this world.
QUEEN MARGARET [*aside*].
Hie thee to hell for shame, and leave this
world,
Thou cacodemon! there thy kingdom is.
EARL RIVERS.
My Lord of Gloster, in those busy days
Which here you urge to prove us enemies,
We follow'd then our lord, our lawful king:
So should we you, if you should be our king.
DUKE OF GLOSTER.
If I should be!—I had rather be a pedlar:
Far be it from my heart, the thought of it!
QUEEN ELIZABETH.
As little joy, my lord, as you suppose
You should enjoy, were you this country's
king,—
As little joy may you suppose in me,
That I enjoy, being the queen thereof.
QUEEN MARGARET [*aside*].
As little joy enjoys the queen thereof;
For I am she, and altogether joyless.
I can no longer hold me patient.— [*Advancing*
Hear me, you wrangling pirates, that fall out
In sharing that which you have pill'd from me!
Which of you trembles not that looks on me?
If not, that, I being queen, you bow like subjects,
Yet that, by you deposed, you quake like rebels?—
Ah, gentle villain, do not turn away!
DUKE OF GLOSTER.
Foul wrinkled witch, what makest thou in my
sight?
QUEEN MARGARET.
But repetition of what thou hast marr'd;
That will I make before I let thee go.
DUKE OF GLOSTER.
Wert thou not banished on pain of death?

QUEEN MARGARET.

I was;
But I do find more pain in banishment
Than death can yield me here by my abode.
A husband and a son thou owest to me,—
And thou a kingdom,—all of you allegiance:
The sorrow that I have, by right is yours;
And all the pleasures you usurp are mine.

DUKE OF GLOSTER.

The curse my noble father laid on thee,
When thou didst crown his warlike brows with
   paper,
And with thy scorns drew'st rivers from his eyes:
And then, to dry them. gavest the duke a clout
Steept in the faultless blood of pretty Rutland;—
His curses, then from bitterness of soul
Denounced against thee, are all faln upon thee;
And God, not we, hath plagued thy bloody deed.

QUEEN ELIZABETH.

So just is God, to right the innocent.

LORD HASTINGS.

O, 'twas the foulest deed to slay that babe,
And the most merciless that e'er was heard of!

EARL RIVERS.

Tyrants themselves wept when it was reported.

MARQUESS OF DORSET.

No man but prophesied revenge for it.

DUKE OF BUCKINGHAM.

Northumberland, then present, wept to see it.

QUEEN MARGARET.

What! were you snarling all before I came,
Ready to catch each other by the throat,
And turn you all your hatred now on me?
Did York's dread curse prevail so much with
   heaven,
That Henry's death, my lovely Edward's death,
Their kingdom's loss, my woful banishment,
Could all but answer for that peevish brat?
Can curses pierce the clouds and enter heaven?—
Why, then, give way, dull clouds, to my quick
   curses!—
Though not by war, by surfeit die your king,
As ours by murder, to make him a king!
Edward thy son, that now is Prince of Wales,
For Edward my son, that was Prince of Wales,
Die in his youth by like untimely violence!
Thyself a queen, for me that was a queen,
Outlive thy glory, like my wretched self!
Long mayst thou live to wail thy children's loss;
And see another, as I see thee now,
Deckt in thy rights, as thou art stall'd in mine!
Long die thy happy days before thy death;
And, after many lengthen'd hours of grief,
Die neither mother, wife, nor England's queen!—
Rivers and Dorset, you were standers by,—
And so wast thou, Lord Hastings,—when my
   son
Was stabb'd with bloody daggers: God, I pray
   Him,
That none of you may live his natural age,
But by some unlookt accident cut off!

DUKE OF GLOSTER.

Have done thy charm, thou hateful wither'd hag!

QUEEN MARGARET.

And leave out thee? stay, dog, for thou shalt hear
   me.

If heaven have any grievous plague in store
Exceeding those that I can wish upon thee,
O, let them keep it till thy sins be ripe,
And then hurl down their indignation
On thee, the troubler of the poor world's peace!
The worm of conscience still begnaw thy soul!
Thy friends suspect for traitors while thou livest,
And take deep traitors for thy dearest friends!
No sleep close up that deadly eye of thine,
Unless it be while some tormenting dream
Affrights thee with a hell of ugly devils!
Thou elvish-markt, abortive, rooting hog!
Thou that wast seal'd in thy nativity
The slave of nature and the son of hell!
Thou slander of thy mother's heavy womb!
Thou loathed issue of thy father's loins!
Thou rag of honour! thou detested—

DUKE OF GLOSTER.

   Margaret.

QUEEN MARGARET.

   Richard!

DUKE OF GLOSTER.

     Ha!

QUEEN MARGARET.

      I call thee not.

DUKE OF GLOSTER.

I cry thee mercy, then; for did I think
That thou hadst call'd me all these bitter names.

QUEEN MARGARET.

Why, so I did; but lookt for no reply.
O, let me make the period to my curse!

DUKE OF GLOSTER.

'Tis done by me, and ends in—Margaret.

QUEEN ELIZABETH.

Thus have you breathed your curse against yourself.

QUEEN MARGARET.

Poor painted queen, vain flourish of my fortune!
Why strew'st thou sugar on that bottled spider,
Whose deadly web ensnareth thee about?
Fool, fool! thou whett'st a knife to kill thyself.
The day will come that thou shalt wish for me
To help thee curse that poisonous bunch-backt
   toad.

LORD HASTINGS.

False-boding woman, end thy frantic curse,
Lest to thy harm thou move our patience.

QUEEN MARGARET.

Foul shame upon you! you have all moved mine.

EARL RIVERS.

Were you well served, you would be taught your
   duty.

QUEEN MARGARET.

To serve me well, you all should do me duty,
Teach me to be your queen, and you my subjects:
O, serve me well, and teach yourselves that duty!

MARQUESS OF DORSET.

Dispute not with her,—she is lunatic.

QUEEN MARGARET.

Peace, master marquess, you are malapert:
Your fire-new stamp of honour is scarce current:
O, that your young nobility could judge
What 'twere to lose it, and be miserable!
They that stand high have many blasts to shake
   them;
And if they fall, they dash themselves to pieces.

DUKE OF GLOSTER.
Good counsel, marry:—learn it, learn it, marquess.

MARQUESS OF DORSET.
It touches you, my lord, as much as me.

DUKE OF GLOSTER.
Ay, and much more: but I was born so high,
Our aery buildeth in the cedar's top,
And dallies with the wind, and scorns the sun.

QUEEN MARGARET.
And turns the sun to shade;—alas! alas!—
Witness my son, now in the shade of death;
Whose bright out-shining beams thy cloudy wrath
Hath in eternal darkness folded up.
Your aery buildeth in our aery's nest:—
O God, that seest it, do not suffer it;
As it was won with blood, lost be it so!

DUKE OF BUCKINGHAM.
Peace, peace, for shame, if not for charity.

QUEEN MARGARET.
Urge neither charity nor shame to me:
Uncharitably with me have you dealt,
And shamefully by you my hopes are butcher'd.
My charity is outrage, life my shame,—
And in that shame still live my sorrow's rage!

DUKE OF BUCKINGHAM.
Have done, have done.

QUEEN MARGARET.
O princely Buckingham, I'll kiss thy hand,
In sign of league and amity with thee:
Now fair befall thee and thy noble house!
Thy garments are not spotted with our blood,
Nor thou within the compass of my curse.

DUKE OF BUCKINGHAM.
Nor no one here; for curses never pass
The lips of those that breathe them in the air.

QUEEN MARGARET.
I'll not believe but they ascend the sky,
And there awake God's gentle-sleeping peace.
O Buckingham, take heed of yonder dog!
Look, when he fawns he bites; and when he bites,
His venom tooth will rankle to the death:
Have not to do with him, beware of him;
Sin, death, and hell have set their marks on him,
And all their ministers attend on him.

DUKE OF GLOSTER.
What doth she say, my Lord of Buckingham?

DUKE OF BUCKINGHAM.
Nothing that I respect, my gracious lord.

QUEEN MARGARET.
What, dost thou scorn me for my gentle counsel?
And soothe the devil that I warn thee from?
O, but remember this another day,
When he shall split thy very heart with sorrow,
And say, poor Margaret was a prophetess!—
Live each of you the subjects to his hate,
And he to yours, and all of you to God's!   [Exit.

LORD HASTINGS.
My hair doth stand on end to hear her curses.

EARL RIVERS.
And so doth mine: I muse why she's at liberty.

DUKE OF GLOSTER.
I cannot blame her: by God's holy mother,
She hath had too much wrong; and I repent
My part thereof that I have done to her.

QUEEN ELIZABETH.
I never did her any, to my knowledge.

DUKE OF GLOSTER.
Yet you have all the vantage of her wrong.
I was too hot to do somebody good
That is too cold in thinking of it now.
Marry, as for Clarence, he is well repaid;
He is frankt up to fatting for his pains;—
God pardon them that are the cause of it!

EARL RIVERS.
A virtuous and a Christian-like conclusion,
To pray for them that have done scathe to us.

DUKE OF GLOSTER [aside].
So do I ever, being well advised;
For had I cursed now, I had cursed myself.

Enter CATESBY.

SIR WILLIAM CATESBY
Madam, his majesty doth call for you,—
And for your Grace,—and you, my noble lords.

QUEEN ELIZABETH.
Catesby, I come.—Lords, will you go with me?

EARL RIVERS.
We wait upon your Grace.
[Exeunt all except GLOSTER.

DUKE OF GLOSTER.
I do the wrong, and first begin to brawl.
The secret mischiefs that I set abroach
I lay unto the grievous charge of others.   [ness,—
Clarence,—whom I, indeed, have laid in dark-
I do beweep to many simple gulls;
Namely, to Hastings, Derby, Buckingham;
And say it is the queen and her allies
That stir the king against the duke my brother.
Now, they believe it; and withal whet me
To be revenged on Rivers, Vaughan, Grey:
But then I sigh; and, with a piece of Scripture,
Tell them that God bids us do good for evil:
And thus I clothe my naked villainy
With old odd ends stoln out of holy writ;
And seem a saint, when most I play the devil.—
But, soft! here come my executioners.

Enter two MURDERERS.

How now, my hardy, stout-resolved mates!
Are you now going to dispatch this thing?

FIRST MURDERER.
We are, my lord; and come to have the warrant,
That we may be admitted where he is.

DUKE OF GLOSTER.
Well thought upon;—I have it here about me:
[Gives the warrant.
When you have done, repair to Crosby-place.
But, sirs, be sudden in the execution,
Withal obdurate, do not hear him plead;
For Clarence is well-spoken, and perhaps
May move your hearts to pity, if you mark him.

FIRST MURDERER.
Tut, tut, my lord, we will not stand to prate;
Talkers are no good doers: be assured
We go to use our hands, and not our tongues.

DUKE OF GLOSTER.
Your eyes drop millstones, when fools' eyes drop tears:
I like you, lads;—about your business straight;
Go, go, dispatch.

FIRST MURDERER.
We will, my noble lord.   [Exeunt

SCENE IV.

The Tower.

Enter CLARENCE *and* BRAKENBURY.

SIR ROBERT BRAKENBURY.

WHY looks your Grace so heavily to-day?
DUKE OF CLARENCE.
O, I have past a miserable night,
So full of fearful dreams, of ugly sights,
That, as I am a Christian faithful man,
I would not spend another such a night,
Though 'twere to buy a world of happy days,—
So full of dismal terror was the time!
SIR ROBERT BRAKENBURY.
What was your dream, my lord? I pray you, tell
me.
DUKE OF CLARENCE.
Methought that I had broken from the Tower,
And was embarkt to cross to Burgundy;
And, in my company, my brother Gloster;
Who from my cabin tempted me to walk
Upon the hatches: thence we lookt toward
England,
And cited up a thousand heavy times,
During the wars of York and Lancaster,
That had befaln us. As we paced along
Upon the giddy footing of the hatches,
Methought that Gloster stumbled; and, in falling,
Struck me, that thought to stay him, overboard
Into the tumbling billows of the main.
Lord, Lord! methought, what pain it was to
drown!
What dreadful noise of waters in mine ears!
What ugly sights of death within mine eyes!
Methought I saw a thousand fearful wracks;
Ten thousand men that fishes gnaw'd upon;
Wedges of gold, great anchors, heaps of pearl,
Inestimable stones, unvalued jewels,
All scatt'red in the bottom of the sea:
Some lay in dead men's skulls; and, in those holes
Where eyes did once inhabit, there were crept,
As 'twere in scorn of eyes, reflecting gems,
That woo'd the slimy bottom of the deep,
And mockt the dead bones that lay scatt'red by.
SIR ROBERT BRAKENBURY.
Had you such leisure in the time of death
To gaze upon the secrets of the deep?
DUKE OF CLARENCE.
Methought I had; and often did I strive
To yield the ghost: but still the envious flood
Kept in my soul, and would not let it forth
To seek the empty, vast, and wandering air;
But smother'd it within my panting bulk,
Which almost burst to belch it in the sea.
SIR ROBERT BRAKENBURY.
Awaked you not with this sore agony?
DUKE OF CLARENCE.
No, no, my dream was lengthen'd after life;
O, then began the tempest to my soul!
I past, methought, the melancholy flood,
With that grim ferryman which poets write of,
Unto the kingdom of perpetual night.
The first that there did greet my stranger soul,
Was my great father-in-law, renowned Warwick;
Who cried aloud, 'What scourge for perjury
Can this dark monarchy afford false Clarence?'

And so he vanisht: then came wandering by
A shadow like an angel, with bright hair
Dabbled in blood; and he shriekt out aloud,
'Clarence is come; false, fleeting, perjured
Clarence,
That stabb'd me in the field by Tewksbury:
Seize on him, Furies, take him to your torments!'
With that, methought, a legion of foul fiends
Environ'd me, and howled in mine ears
Such hideous cries, that, with the very noise,
I trembling waked, and, for a season after,
Could not believe but that I was in hell,—
Such terrible impression made my dream.
SIR ROBERT BRAKENBURY.
No marvel, lord, though it affrighted you:
I am afraid, methinks, to hear you tell it.
DUKE OF CLARENCE.
O Brakenbury, I have done those things,
That now give evidence against my soul,
For Edward's sake; and see how he requites me!
O God! if my deep prayers cannot appease
Thee,
But Thou wilt be avenged on my misdeeds,
Yet execute Thy wrath in me alone;
O, spare my guiltless wife and my poor chil-
dren!—
I pray thee, gentle keeper, stay by me;
My soul is heavy, and I fain would sleep.
SIR ROBERT BRAKENBURY.
I will, my lord: God give your Grace good rest!—
[CLARENCE *sleeps.*
Sorrow breaks seasons and reposing hours,
Makes the night morning, and the noontide
night.
Princes have but their titles for their glories,
An outward honour for an inward toil;
And, for unfelt imaginations,
They often feel a world of restless cares:
So that, betwixt their titles and low names,
There's nothing differs but the outward fame.
Enter the two MURDERERS.
FIRST MURDERER.
Ho! who's here?
SIR ROBERT BRAKENBURY.
What wouldst thou, fellow? and how camest thou
hither?
FIRST MURDERER.
I would speak with Clarence, and I came hither
on my legs.
SIR ROBERT BRAKENBURY.
What, so brief?
SECOND MURDERER.
'Tis better, sir, than to be tedious.—Let him see
our commission; and talk no more.
[BRAKENBURY *reads it.*
SIR ROBERT BRAKENBURY.
I am, in this, commanded to deliver
The noble Duke of Clarence to your hands:—
I will not reason what is meant hereby,
Because I will be guiltless of the meaning.
Here are the keys;—there sits the duke asleep:
I'll to the king: and signify to him
That thus I have resign'd to you my charge.
FIRST MURDERER.
You may, sir; 'tis a point of wisdom: fare you well.
[*Exit* BRAKENBURY.

SECOND MURDERER.
What, shall we stab him as he sleeps?
FIRST MURDERER.
No; he'll say 'twas done cowardly, when he wakes.
SECOND MURDERER.
When he wakes! why, fool, he shall never wake
till the judgement-day.
FIRST MURDERER.
Why, then he'll say we stabb'd him sleeping.
SECOND MURDERER.
The urging of that word 'judgement' hath bred
a kind of remorse in me.
FIRST MURDERER.
What, art thou afraid?
SECOND MURDERER
Not to kill him, having a warrant for it; but to be
damn'd for killing him, from the which no war-
rant can defend me.
FIRST MURDERER.
I thought thou hadst been resolute.
SECOND MURDERER.
So I am, to let him live.
FIRST MURDERER.
I'll back to the Duke of Gloster, and tell him so.
SECOND MURDERER.
I pray thee, stay a while: I hope my holy humour
will change; 'twas wont to hold me but while one
tells twenty.
FIRST MURDERER.
How dost thou feel thyself now?
SECOND MURDERER.
Faith, some certain dregs of conscience are yet
within me.
FIRST MURDERER.
Remember our reward, when the deed is done.
SECOND MURDERER.
Zounds, he dies: I had forgot the reward.
FIRST MURDERER.
Where is thy conscience now?
SECOND MURDERER.
In the Duke of Gloster's purse.
FIRST MURDERER.
So, when he opens his purse to give us our reward,
thy conscience flies out.
SECOND MURDERER.
Let it go; there's few or none will entertain it.
FIRST MURDERER.
How if it come to thee again?
SECOND MURDERER.
I'll not meddle with it: it is a dangerous thing: it
makes a man a coward: a man cannot steal, but it
accuseth him; he cannot swear, but it checks him;
he cannot lie with his neighbour's wife, but it de-
tects him: it is a blushing shame-faced spirit that
mutinies in a man's bosom; it fills one full of
obstacles: it made me once restore a purse of gold,
that by chance I found; it beggars any man that
keeps it: it is turn'd out of all towns and cities for
a dangerous thing; and every man that means to
live well endeavours to trust to himself and to live
without it.
FIRST MURDERER.
Zounds, it is even now at my elbow, persuading
me not to kill the duke.
SECOND MURDERER.
Take the devil in thy mind, and believe him not:

he would insinuate with thee but to make th e
sigh.
FIRST MURDERER.
Tut, I am strong-framed, he cannot prevail with
me, I warrant thee.
SECOND MURDERER.
Spoke like a tall fellow that respects his reputa-
tion.   Come, shall we to this gear?
FIRST MURDERER.
Take him over the costard with the hilts of thy
sword, and then we will chop him in the malmsey
butt in the next room.
SECOND MURDERER.
O excellent device! make a sop of him.
FIRST MURDERER.
Hark! he stirs: shall I strike?
SECOND MURDERER.
No, first let's reason with him.
DUKE OF CLARENCE [waking].
Where art thou, keeper? give me a cup of
wine.
FIRST MURDERER.
You shall have wine enough, my lord, anon.
DUKE OF CLARENCE.
In God's name, what art thou?
FIRST MURDERER.
A man, as you are.
DUKE OF CLARENCE.
But not, as I am, royal.
FIRST MURDERER.
Nor you, as we are, loyal.
DUKE OF CLARENCE.
Thy voice is thunder, but thy looks are humble.
FIRST MURDERER.
My voice is now the king's, my looks mine own.
DUKE OF CLARENCE.
How darkly and how deadly dost thou speak!
Your eyes do menace me: why look you pale?
Who sent you hither? Wherefore do you
come?
BOTH MURDERERS.
To, to, to—
DUKE OF CLARENCE.
To murder me?
BOTH MURDERERS.
Ay, ay.
DUKE OF CLARENCE.
You scarcely have the hearts to tell me so,
And therefore cannot have the hearts to do it.
Wherein, my friends, have I offended you?
FIRST MURDERER.
Offended us you have not, but the king.
DUKE OF CLARENCE.
I shall be reconciled to him again.
SECOND MURDERER.
Never, my lord; therefore prepare to die.
DUKE OF CLARENCE.
Are you call'd forth from out a world of men
To slay the innocent? What is my offence?
Where are the evidence that do accuse me?
What lawful quest have given their verdict
up
Unto the frowning judge? or who pronounced
The bitter sentence of poor Clarence' death?
Before I be convict by course of law,
To threaten me with death is most unlawful.

I charge you, as you hope to have redemption
By Christ's dear blood shed for our grievous sins,
That you depart, and lay no hands on me:
The deed you undertake is damnable.

FIRST MURDERER.

What we will do, we do upon command.

SECOND MURDERER.

And he that hath commanded is the king.

DUKE OF CLARENCE.

Erroneous vassal! the great King of kings
Hath in the tables of His law commanded
That thou shalt do no murder: will you, then,
Spurn at His edict, and fulfil a man's?
Take heed; for He holds vengeance in His hand,
To hurl upon their heads that break His law.

SECOND MURDERER.

And that same vengeance doth He hurl on thee,
For false forswearing, and for murder too:
Thou didst receive the sacrament to fight
In quarrel of the house of Lancaster.

FIRST MURDERER.

And, like a traitor to the name of God,   [blade
Didst break that vow; and with thy treacherous
Unripp'dst the bowels of thy sovereign's son.

SECOND MURDERER.

Whom thou wert sworn to cherish and defend.

FIRST MURDERER.

How canst thou urge God's dreadful law to us,
When thou hast broke it in so dear degree?

DUKE OF CLARENCE.

Alas! for whose sake did I that ill deed?
For Edward, for my brother, for his sake:
Why, sirs,
He sends ye not to murder me for this;
For in this sin he is as deep as I.
If God will be revenged for this deed,
O, know you yet, He doth it publicly:
Take not the quarrel from His powerful arm;
He needs no indirect nor lawless course
To cut off those that have offended Him.

FIRST MURDERER.

Who made thee, then, a bloody minister,
When gallant-springing brave Plantagenet,
That princely novice, was struck dead by thee?

DUKE OF CLARENCE.

My brother's love, the devil, and my rage.

FIRST MURDERER.

Thy brother's love, our duty, and thy fault,
Provoke us hither now to slaughter thee.

DUKE OF CLARENCE.

O, if you do love my brother, hate not me;
I am his brother, and I love him well.
If you be hired for meed, go back again,
And I will send you to my brother Gloster,
Who shall reward you better for my life
Than Edward will for tidings of my death.

SECOND MURDERER.

You are deceived, your brother Gloster hates you.

DUKE OF CLARENCE.

O, no, he loves me, and he holds me dear:
Go you to him from me.

BOTH MURDERERS.

         Ay, so we will.

DUKE OF CLARENCE.

Tell him, when that our princely father York
Blest his three sons with his victorious arm,

And charged us from his soul to love each other,
He little thought of this divided friendship:
Bid Gloster think of this, and he will weep.

FIRST MURDERER.

Ay, millstones; as he lesson'd us to weep.

DUKE OF CLARENCE.

O, do not slander him, for he is kind.

FIRST MURDERER.

Right.
As snow in harvest.—Thou deceivest thyself:
'Tis he that sent us hither now to slaughter thee

DUKE OF CLARENCE.

It cannot be; for when I parted with him,
He hugg'd me in his arms, and swore, with sobs,
That he would labour my delivery.

FIRST MURDERER.

Why, so he doth, now he delivers thee
From this earth's thraldom to the joys of heaven.

SECOND MURDERER.

Make peace with God, for you must die, my lord.

DUKE OF CLARENCE.

Hast thou that holy feeling in thy soul,
To counsel me to make my peace with God,
And art thou yet to thy own soul so blind,
That thou wilt war with God by murdering
   me?—
Ah, sirs, consider, he that set you on
To do this deed will hate you for the deed.

SECOND MURDERER.

What shall we do?

DUKE OF CLARENCE.

         Relent, and save your souls.
Which of you, if you were a prince's son,
Being pent from liberty, as I am now,
If two such murderers as yourselves came to you,
Would not entreat for life? As you would beg,
Were you in my distress—

FIRST MURDERER.

Relent! 'tis cowardly and womanish.

DUKE OF CLARENCE.

Not to relent is beastly, savage, devilish.
My friend, I spy some pity in thy looks;
O, if thine eye be not a flatterer,
Come thou on my side, and entreat for me:
A begging prince what beggar pities not?

SECOND MURDERER.

Look behind you, my lord.

FIRST MURDERER.

Take that, and that [stabs him]: if all this will not
   do,
I'll drown you in the malmsey-butt within.
               [Exit, with the body.

SECOND MURDERER.

A bloody deed, and desperately dispatcht!
How fain, like Pilate, would I wash my hands
Of this most grievous guilty murder done!

       Enter FIRST MURDERER.

FIRST MURDERER.

How now! what mean'st thou, that thou help'st
   me not?
By heaven, the duke shall know how slack thou
   art!

SECOND MURDERER.

I would he knew that I had saved his brother!
Take thou the fee, and tell him what I say;
For I repent me that the duke is slain.   [Exit.

FIRST MURDERER.

So do not I: go, coward as thou art.—
Well, I'll go hide the body in some hole,
Till that the duke give order for his burial:
And when I have my meed, I will away;
For this will out, and then I must not stay.   [*Exit.*

ACT II. SCENE I.

London.   The palace.

Enter the KING, *sick, the* QUEEN, DORSET,
RIVERS, HASTINGS, BUCKINGHAM, GREY,
and others.

KING EDWARD.

WHY, so: now have I done a good day's work:
You peers, continue this united league:
I every day expect an embassage
From my Redeemer to redeem me hence;
And now in peace my soul shall part to heaven,
Since I have made my friends at peace on earth.
Rivers and Hastings, take each other's hand;
Dissemble not your hatred, swear your love.

EARL RIVERS.

By heaven, my soul is purged from grudging
   hate;
And with my hand I seal my true heart's love.

LORD HASTINGS.

So thrive I, as I truly swear the like!

KING EDWARD.

Take heed you dally not before your king;
Lest He that is the supreme King of kings,
Confound your hidden falsehood, and award
Either of you to be the other's end.

LORD HASTINGS.

So prosper I, as I swear perfect love!

EARL RIVERS.

And I, as I love Hastings with my heart!

KING EDWARD.

Madam, yourself are not exempt in this,—
Nor you, son Dorset,—Buckingham, nor you;—
You have been factious one against the other.
Wife, love Lord Hastings, let him kiss your hand;
And what you do, do it unfeignedly.

QUEEN ELIZABETH.

There, Hastings; I will never more remember
Our former hatred, so thrive I and mine!

KING EDWARD.

Dorset, embrace him;—Hastings, love lord
   marquess.

MARQUESS OF DORSET.

This interchange of love, I here protest,
Upon my part shall be inviolable.

LORD HASTINGS.

And so swear I.   [*They embrace.*

KING EDWARD.

Now, princely Buckingham, seal thou this league
With thy embracements to my wife's allies,
And make me happy in your unity.

DUKE OF BUCKINGHAM [*to the* QUEEN].

Whenever Buckingham doth turn his hate
Upon your Grace, but with all duteous love
Doth cherish you and yours, God punish me
With hate in those where I expect most love!
When I have most need to employ a friend,
And most assured that he is a friend,
Deep, hollow, treacherous, and full of guile,

Be he unto me!—this do I beg of God,
When I am cold in zeal to you or yours.

                              [*They embrace.*

KING EDWARD.

A pleasing cordial, princely Buckingham,
Is this thy vow unto my sickly heart.
There wanteth now our brother Gloster here,
To make the perfect period of this peace.

DUKE OF BUCKINGHAM.

And, in good time, here comes the noble duke.

Enter GLOSTER.

DUKE OF GLOSTER.

Good morrow to my sovereign king and queen;
And, princely peers, a happy time of day!

KING EDWARD.

Happy, indeed, as we have spent the day.
Brother, we have done deeds of charity;
Made peace of enmity, fair love of hate,
Between these swelling wrong-incensed peers.

DUKE OF GLOSTER.

A blessed labour, my most sovereign liege.
Among this princely heap, if any here,
By false intelligence or wrong surmise,
Hold me a foe;
If I unwittingly, or in my rage,
Have aught committed that is hardly borne
By any in this presence, I desire
To reconcile me to his friendly peace:
'Tis death to me to be at enmity;
I hate it, and desire all good men's love.
First, madam, I entreat true peace of you,
Which I will purchase with my duteous service;
Of you, my noble cousin Buckingham,
If ever any grudge were lodged between us;
Of you, Lord Rivers, and, Lord Grey, of you,
That all without desert have frown'd on me;—
Dukes, earls, lords, gentlemen;—indeed, of all.
I do not know that Englishman alive
With whom my soul is any jot at odds
More than the infant that is born to-night:
I thank my God for my humility.

QUEEN ELIZABETH.

A holiday shall this be kept hereafter:
I would to God all strifes were well compounded.
My sovereign lord, I do beseech your highness
To take our brother Clarence to your grace.

DUKE OF GLOSTER.

Why, madam, have I offer'd love for this,
To be so flouted in this royal presence?
Who knows not that the gentle duke is dead?
                              [*They all start.*
You do him injury to scorn his corse.

EARL RIVERS.

Who knows not he is dead! who knows he is?

QUEEN ELIZABETH.

All-seeing heaven, what a world is this!

DUKE OF BUCKINGHAM.

Look I so pale, Lord Dorset, as the rest?

MARQUESS OF DORSET.

Ay, my good lord; and no one in this presence
But his red colour hath forsook his cheeks.

KING EDWARD.

Is Clarence dead? the order was reversed.

DUKE OF GLOSTER.

But he, poor soul, by your order first died,
And that a winged Mercury did bear;

Some tardy cripple bore the countermand,
That came too lag to see him buried.
God grant that some, less noble and less loyal,
Nearer in bloody thoughts, but not in blood,
Deserve not worse than wretched Clarence did,
And yet go current from suspicion!

Enter DERBY.

EARL OF DERBY.
A boon, my sovereign, for my service done!

KING EDWARD.
I prithee, peace: my soul is full of sorrow.

EARL OF DERBY.
I will not rise, unless your highness hear me.

KING EDWARD.
Then say at once what is it thou request'st.

EARL OF DERBY.
The forfeit, sovereign, of my servant's life;
Who slew to-day a riotous gentleman
Lately attendant on the Duke of Norfolk.

KING EDWARD.
Have I a tongue to doom my brother's death,
And shall that tongue give pardon to a slave?
My brother kill'd no man,—his fault was
        thought,
And yet his punishment was bitter death.
Who sued to me for him? who, in my rage,
Kneel'd at my feet, and bade me be advised?
Who spoke of brotherhood? who spoke of love?
Who told me how the poor soul did forsake
The mighty Warwick, and did fight for me?
Who told me, in the field at Tewksbury,
When Oxford had me down, he rescued me,
And said, 'Dear brother, live, and be a king'?
Who told me, when we both lay in the field
Frozen almost to death, how he did lap me
Even in his garments, and did give himself,
All thin and naked, to the numb-cold night?
All this from my remembrance brutish wrath
Sinfully pluckt, and not a man of you
Had so much grace to put it in my mind.
But when your carters or your waiting-vassals
Have done a drunken slaughter, and defaced
The precious image of our dear Redeemer,
You straight are on your knees for pardon,
        pardon;
And I, unjustly too, must grant it you:
But for my brother not a man would speak,
Nor I, ungracious, speak unto myself
For him, poor soul. The proudest of you all
Have been beholding to him in his life;
Yet none of you would once plead for his life.—
O God, I fear Thy justice will take hold
On me, and you, and mine, and yours for this!—
Come, Hastings, help me to my closet.—Ah,
Poor Clarence!
        [*Exeunt some with* KING *and* QUEEN.

DUKE OF GLOSTER.
This is the fruit of rashness!—Markt you not
How that the guilty kindred of the queen
Lookt pale when they did hear of Clarence'
        death?
O, they did urge it still unto the king!
God will revenge it.—Come, lords, will you go
To comfort Edward with our company?

DUKE OF BUCKINGHAM.
We wait upon your Grace.   [*Exeunt.*

SCENE II.
The palace.

Enter the old DUCHESS OF YORK, *with the two*
CHILDREN *of* CLARENCE.

SON.
GOOD grandam, tell us, is our father dead?

DUCHESS OF YORK.
No, boy.

DAUGHTER.
Why do you weep so oft, and beat your breast,
And cry, 'O Clarence, my unhappy son!'

SON.
Why do you look on us, and shake your head,
And call us orphans, wretches, castaways,
If that our noble father be alive?

DUCHESS OF YORK.
My pretty cousins, you mistake me both;
I do lament the sickness of the king,
As loth to lose him, not your father's death;
It were lost sorrow to wail one that's lost.

SON.
Then, grandam, you conclude that he is dead.
The king my uncle is to blame for this:
God will revenge it; Whom I will importune
With daily prayers all to that effect.

DAUGHTER.
And so will I.

DUCHESS OF YORK.
Peace, children, peace! the king doth love you
        well:
Incapable and shallow innocents,
You cannot guess who caused your father's death.

SON.
Grandam, we can; for my good uncle Gloster
Told me, the king, provoked by the queen,
Devised impeachments to imprison him:
And when my uncle told me so, he wept,
And pitied me, and kindly kist my cheek;
Bade me rely on him as on my father,
And he would love me dearly as his child.

DUCHESS OF YORK.
Ah, that deceit should steal such gentle shapes,
And with a virtuous vizor hide deep vice!
He is my son; ay, and therein my shame;
Yet from my dugs he drew not this deceit.

SON.
Think you my uncle did dissemble, grandam?

DUCHESS OF YORK.
Ay, boy.

SON.
I cannot think it.—Hark! what noise is this?

Enter the QUEEN, *with her hair about her ears;*
RIVERS *and* DORSET *after her.*

QUEEN ELIZABETH.
O, who shall hinder me to wail and weep,
To chide my fortune, and torment myself?
I'll join with black despair against my soul,
And to myself become an enemy.

DUCHESS OF YORK.
What means this scene of rude impatience?

QUEEN ELIZABETH.
To make an act of tragic violence:—
Edward, my lord, thy son, our king, is dead!
Why grow the branches when the root is gone?
Why wither not the leaves that want their sap?

If you will live, lament; if die, be brief,
That our swift-winged souls may catch the king's,
Or, like obedient subjects, follow him
To his new kingdom of ne'er-changing night.

DUCHESS OF YORK.

Ah, so much interest have I in thy sorrow
As I had title in thy noble husband!
I have bewept a worthy husband's death,
And lived by looking on his images:
But now two mirrors of his princely semblance
Are crackt in pieces by malignant death,
And I for comfort have but one false glass,
That grieves me when I see my shame in him.
Thou art a widow; yet thou art a mother,
And hast the comfort of thy children left thee:
But death hath snatcht my husband from mine
     arms,
And pluckt two crutches from my feeble hands,—
Clarence and Edward. O, what cause have I—
Thine being but a moiety of my grief—
To over-go thy plaints and drown thy cries!

SON.

Ah, aunt, you wept not for our father's death!
How can we aid you with our kindred tears?

DAUGHTER.

Our fatherless distress was left unmoan'd;
Your widow-dolour likewise be unwept!

QUEEN ELIZABETH.

Give me no help in lamentation;
I am not barren to bring forth complaints:
All springs reduce their currents to mine eyes,
That I, being govern'd by the watery moon,
May send forth plenteous tears to drown the
     world!
Ah for my husband, for my dear lord Edward!

CHILDREN.

Ah for our father, for our dear lord Clarence!

DUCHESS OF YORK.

Alas for both, both mine, Edward and Clarence!

QUEEN ELIZABETH.

What stay had I but Edward? and he's gone.

CHILDREN.

What stay had we but Clarence? and he's gone.

DUCHESS OF YORK.

What stays had I but they; and they are gone.

QUEEN ELIZABETH.

Was never widow had so dear a loss!

CHILDREN.

Were never orphans had so dear a loss!

DUCHESS OF YORK.

Was never mother had so dear a loss!
Alas, I am the mother of these griefs!
Their woes are parcell'd, mine are general.
She for an Edward weeps, and so do I;
I for a Clarence weep, so doth not she:
These babes for Clarence weep, and so do I;
I for an Edward weep, so do not they:—
Alas, you three, on me, threefold distrest,
Pour all your tears! I am your sorrow's nurse,
And I will pamper it with lamentations.

MARQUESS OF DORSET.

Comfort, dear mother: God is much displeased
That you take with unthankfulness His doing:
In common worldly things 'tis call'd ungrateful
With dull unwillingness to repay a debt
Which with a bounteous hand was kindly lent;

Much more to be thus opposite with heaven,
For it requires the royal debt it lent you.

EARL RIVERS.

Madam, bethink you, like a careful mother,
Of the young prince your son: send straight for
     him;
Let him be crown'd; in him your comfort lives:
Drown desperate sorrow in dead Edward's grave,
And plant your joys in living Edward's throne.

Enter GLOSTER, BUCKINGHAM, DERBY, HAST-
     INGS, RATCLIFF, and others.

DUKE OF GLOSTER.

Sister, have comfort: all of us have cause
To wail the dimming of our shining star;
But none can cure their harms by wailing them.—
Madam, my mother, I do cry you mercy;
I did not see your Grace:—humbly on my knee
I crave your blessing.

DUCHESS OF YORK.

God bless thee; and put meekness in thy breast,
Love, charity, obedience, and true duty!

DUKE OF GLOSTER.

Amen;—[aside] and make me die a good old man!
That is the butt-end of a mother's blessing:
I marvel that her Grace did leave it out.

DUKE OF BUCKINGHAM.

You cloudy princes and heart-sorrowing peers,
That bear this mutual heavy load of moan,
Now cheer each other in each other's love:
Though we have spent our harvest of this king,
We are to reap the harvest of his son.
The broken rancour of your high-swoln hearts,
But lately splinter'd, knit and join'd together,
Must gently be preserved, cherisht, and kept:
Me seemeth good, that, with some little train,
Forthwith from Ludlow the young prince be fet
Hither to London, to be crown'd our king.

EARL RIVERS.

Why with some little train, my Lord of Bucking-
     ham?

DUKE OF BUCKINGHAM.

Marry, my lord, lest, by a multitude,
The new-heal'd wound of malice should break
     out;
Which would be so much the more dangerous,
By how much the estate is green and yet un-
     govern'd:
Where every horse bears his commanding rein,
And may direct his course as please himself,
As well the fear of harm as harm apparent,
In my opinion, ought to be prevented.

DUKE OF GLOSTER.

I hope the king made peace with all of us;
And the compact is firm and true in me.

EARL RIVERS.

And so in me; and so, I think, in all:
Yet, since it is but green, it should be put
To no apparent likelihood of breach,
Which haply by much company might be urged:
Therefore I say with noble Buckingham,
That it is meet so few should fetch the prince.

LORD HASTINGS.

And so say I.

DUKE OF GLOSTER.

Then be it so; and go we to determine   [Ludlow.
Who they shall be that straight shall post to

Madam,—and you, my mother,—will you go
To give your censures in this business?
  QUEEN ELIZABETH *and* DUCHESS OF YORK.
With all our hearts.
    [*Exeunt all except* BUCKINGHAM *and*
      GLOSTER.
      DUKE OF BUCKINGHAM.
My lord, whoever journeys to the prince,
For God's sake, let not us two stay at home;
For, by the way. I'll sort occasion,
As index to the story we late talkt of,
To part the queen's proud kindred from the
  prince.
     DUKE OF GLOSTER.
My other self, my counsel's consistory,
My oracle, my prophet!—my dear cousin,
I, as a child, will go by thy direction.
Towards Ludlow then, for we'll not stay behind.
                 [*Exeunt.*

SCENE III.

London. A street.

Enter two CITIZENS, *meeting.*

     FIRST CITIZEN.

GOOD morrow, neighbour: whither away so
  fast?
     SECOND CITIZEN.
I promise you I scarcely know myself:
Hear you the news abroad?
     FIRST CITIZEN.
        Ay,—that the king is dead.
     SECOND CITIZEN.
Ill news, by 'r lady; seldom comes the better:
I fear, I fear 'twill prove a giddy world.
    Enter another CITIZEN.
     THIRD CITIZEN.
Neighbours, God speed!
     FIRST CITIZEN.
       Give you good morrow, sir.
     THIRD CITIZEN.
Doth the news hold of good King Edward's
  death?
     SECOND CITIZEN.
Ay, sir, it is too true; God help, the while!
     THIRD CITIZEN.
Then, masters, look to see a troublous world.
     FIRST CITIZEN.
No, no; by God's good grace his son shall reign.
     THIRD CITIZEN.
Woe to that land that's govern'd by a child!
     SECOND CITIZEN.
In him there is a hope of government,
That, in his nonage, council under him,
And, in his full and ripen'd years, himself,
No doubt, shall then, and till then, govern well.
     FIRST CITIZEN.
So stood the state when Henry the Sixth
Was crown'd in Paris but at nine months old.
     THIRD CITIZEN.
Stood the state so? No, no, good friends, God
  wot;
For then this land was famously enricht
With politic grave counsel; then the king
Had virtuous uncles to protect his Grace.
     FIRST CITIZEN.
Why, so hath this, both by his father and mother.

     THIRD CITIZEN.
Better it were they all came by his father,
Or by his father there were none at all;
For emulation now, who shall be nearest,
Will touch us all too near, if God prevent not.
O, full of danger is the Duke of Gloster!   [proud:
And the queen's sons and brothers haught and
And were they to be ruled. and not to rule,
This sickly land might solace as before.
     FIRST CITIZEN.
Come, come, we fear the worst; all will be well.
     THIRD CITIZEN.
When clouds are seen, wise men put on their
  cloaks;
When great leaves fall, then winter is at hand;
When the sun sets, who doth not look for night?
Untimely storms make men expect a dearth.
All may be well; but, if God sort it so,
'Tis more than we deserve, or I expect.
     SECOND CITIZEN.
Truly, the hearts of men are full of fear:
You cannot reason almost with a man
That looks not heavily and full of dread.
     THIRD CITIZEN.
Before the days of change, still is it so:
By a divine instinct men's minds mistrust
Ensuing danger; as, by proof, we see
The waters swell before a boisterous storm.
But leave it all to God.—Whither away?
     SECOND CITIZEN.
Marry, we were sent for to the justices.
     THIRD CITIZEN.
And so was I: I'll bear you company.   [*Exeunt.*

SCENE IV.

London. The palace.

Enter the ARCHBISHOP OF YORK, *the young*
DUKE OF YORK, *the* QUEEN, *and the* DUCHESS
OF YORK.

     ARCHBISHOP OF YORK.

LAST night, I hear, they lay at Northampton;
  At Stony-Stratford will they be to-night;
To-morrow, or next day, they will be here.
     DUCHESS OF YORK.
I long with all my heart to see the prince:
I hope he is much grown since last I saw him.
     QUEEN ELIZABETH.
But I hear, no; they say my son of York
Has almost overta'en him in his growth.
     DUKE OF YORK.
Ay, mother; but I would not have it so.
     DUCHESS OF YORK.
Why, my young cousin, it is good to grow.
     DUKE OF YORK.
Grandam, one night, as we did sit at supper,
My uncle Rivers talkt how I did grow
More than my brother: 'Ay,' quoth my uncle
  Gloster,   [apace:'
'Small herbs have grace, great weeds do grow
And since, methinks, I would not grow so fast,
Because sweet flowers are slow, and weeds make
  haste.
     DUCHESS OF YORK.
Good faith, good faith, the saying did not hold
In him that did object the same to thee:

He was the wretched'st thing when he was young,
So long a-growing and so leisurely,
That, if his rule were true, he should be gracious.
ARCHBISHOP OF YORK.
And so, no doubt, he is, my gracious madam.
DUCHESS OF YORK.
I hope he is; but yet let mothers doubt.
DUKE OF YORK.
Now, by my troth, if I had been remember'd,
I could have given my uncle's Grace a flout,
To touch his growth nearer than he toucht mine.
DUCHESS OF YORK.
How, my young York? I prithee, let me hear it.
DUKE OF YORK.
Marry, they say my uncle grew so fast
That he could gnaw a crust at two hours old:
'Twas full two years ere I could get a tooth.
Grandam, this would have been a biting jest.
DUCHESS OF YORK.
I prithee, pretty York, who told thee this?
DUKE OF YORK.
Grandam, his nurse.
DUCHESS OF YORK.
His nurse! why, she was dead ere thou wast
born.
DUKE OF YORK.
If 'twere not she, I cannot tell who told me.
QUEEN ELIZABETH.
A parlous boy:—go to, you are too shrewd.
ARCHBISHOP OF YORK.
Good madam, be not angry with the child.
QUEEN ELIZABETH.
Pitchers have ears.
ARCHBISHOP OF YORK.
Here comes a messenger.
Enter a MESSENGER.
                                What news?
MESSENGER.
Such news, my lord, as grieves me to report.
QUEEN ELIZABETH.
How doth the prince?
MESSENGER.
                    Well, madam, and in health.
DUCHESS OF YORK.
What is thy news, then?
MESSENGER.
Lord Rivers and Lord Grey are sent to Pomfret,
With them Sir Thomas Vaughan, prisoners.
DUCHESS OF YORK.
Who hath committed them?
MESSENGER.
                                The mighty dukes
Gloster and Buckingham.
QUEEN ELIZABETH.
                    For what offence?
MESSENGER.
The sum of all I can I have disclosed;
Why or for what these nobles were committed
Is all unknown to me, my gracious lady.
QUEEN ELIZABETH.
Ay me, I see the downfall of our house!
The tiger now hath seized the gentle hind;
Insulting tyranny begins to jet
Upon the innocent and aweless throne:
Welcome, destruction, blood, and massacre!
I see, as in a map, the end of all.

DUCHESS OF YORK.
Accursed and unquiet wrangling days,
How many of you have mine eyes beheld!
My husband lost his life to get the crown;
And often up and down my sons were tost,
For me to joy and weep their gain and loss:
And being seated, and domestic broils
Clean over-blown, themselves, the conquerors,
Make war upon themselves; brother to brother,
Blood to blood, self against self:—O, prepos-
terous
And frantic outrage, end thy damned spleen;
Or let me die, to look on death no more!
QUEEN ELIZABETH.
Come, come, my boy; we will to sanctuary.—
Madam, farewell.
DUCHESS OF YORK.
                Stay, I will go with you.
QUEEN ELIZABETH.
You have no cause.
ARCHBISHOP OF YORK [*to the* QUEEN].
                    My gracious lady, go;
And thither bear your treasure and your goods.
For my part, I'll resign unto your Grace
The seal I keep: and so betide to me
As well I tender you and all of yours!
Come, I'll conduct you to the sanctuary. [*Exeunt*

ACT III. SCENE I.
London. A street.

The trumpets sound. Enter the young PRINCE
GLOSTER, BUCKINGHAM, CARDINAL BOUR
CHIER, CATESBY, *and others.*
DUKE OF BUCKINGHAM.
WELCOME, sweet prince, to London, to
your chamber.
DUKE OF GLOSTER.
Welcome, dear cousin, my thoughts' sovereign:
The weary way hath made you melancholy.
PRINCE.
No, uncle; but our crosses on the way
Have made it tedious, wearisome, and heavy:
I want more uncles here to welcome me.
DUKE OF GLOSTER.
Sweet prince, the untainted virtue of your years
Hath not yet dived into the world's deceit;
Nor more can you distinguish of a man
Than of his outward show; which, God He
knows,
Seldom or never jumpeth with the heart. ·
Those uncles which you want were dangerous;
Your Grace attended to their sugar'd words,
But lookt not on the poison of their hearts:
God keep you from them, and from such false
friends!
PRINCE.
God keep me from false friends! but they were
none.
DUKE OF GLOSTER.
My lord, the mayor of London comes to greet
you.
Enter the LORD MAYOR *and his* TRAIN.
MAYOR.
God bless your Grace with health and happy
days!

PRINCE.
I thank you, good my lord;—and thank you all.
> [MAYOR *and his* TRAIN *retire.*
I thought my mother, and my brother York,
Would long ere this have met us on the way:
Fie, what a slug is Hastings, that he comes not
To tell us whether they will come or no!

DUKE OF BUCKINGHAM.
And, in good time, here comes the sweating lord.
Enter HASTINGS.

PRINCE.
Welcome, my lord: what, will our mother come?

LORD HASTINGS.
On what occasion, God He knows, not I,
The queen your mother, and your brother York,
Have taken sanctuary: the tender prince
Would fain have come with me to meet your
   Grace,
But by his mother was perforce withheld.

DUKE OF BUCKINGHAM.
Fie, what an indirect and peevish course
Is this of hers!—Lord Cardinal, will your Grace
Persuade the queen to send the Duke of York
Unto his princely brother presently?
If she deny, Lord Hastings, go with him,
And from her jealous arms pluck him perforce.

CARDINAL BOURCHIER.
My Lord of Buckingham, if my weak oratory
Can from his mother win the Duke of York,
Anon expect him here; but if she be obdurate
To mild entreaties, God in heaven forbid
We should infringe the holy privilege
Of blessed sanctuary! not for all this land
Would I be guilty of so great a sin.

DUKE OF BUCKINGHAM.
You are too senseless-obstinate, my lord,
Too ceremonious and traditional:
Weigh it but with the grossness of this age,
You break not sanctuary in seizing him.
The benefit thereof is always granted
To those whose dealings have deserved the place,
And those who have the wit to claim the place:
This prince hath neither claim'd it nor deserved
   it;
And therefore, in mine opinion, cannot have it:
Then, taking him from thence that is not there,
You break no privilege nor charter there.
Oft have I heard of sanctuary-men;
But sanctuary-children ne'er till now.

CARDINAL BOURCHIER.
My lord, you shall o'er-rule my mind for once.—
Come on, Lord Hastings, will you go with me?

LORD HASTINGS.
I go, my lord.

PRINCE.
Good lords, make all the speedy haste you may.
> [*Exeunt* CARDINAL *and* HASTINGS.
Say, uncle Gloster, if our brother come,
Where shall we sojourn till our coronation?

DUKE OF GLOSTER.
Where it seems best unto your royal self.
If I may counsel you, some day or two
Your highness shall repose you at the Tower;
Then where you please, and shall be thought
   most fit
For your best health and recreation.

PRINCE.
I do not like the Tower, of any place.—
Did Julius Cæsar build that place, my lord?

DUKE OF BUCKINGHAM.
He did, my gracious lord, begin that place;
Which, since, succeeding ages have re-edified.

PRINCE.
Is it upon record, or else reported
Successively from age to age, he built it?

DUKE OF BUCKINGHAM.
Upon record, my gracious lord.

PRINCE.
But say, my lord, it were not register'd,
Methinks the truth should live from age to
   age,
As 'twere retail'd to all posterity,
Even to the general all-ending day.

DUKE OF GLOSTER [*aside*].
So wise so young, they say, do never live long.

PRINCE.
What say you, uncle?

DUKE OF GLOSTER.
I say, without characters, fame lives long.—
[*aside*] Thus, like the formal Vice, Iniquity,
I moralize two meanings in one word.

PRINCE.
That Julius Cæsar was a famous man;
With what his valour did enrich his wit,
His wit set down to make his valour live:
Death makes no conquest of this conqueror;
For now he lives in fame, though not in life.
I'll tell you what, my cousin Buckingham,—

DUKE OF BUCKINGHAM.
What, my gracious lord?

PRINCE.
An if I live until I be a man,
I'll win our ancient right in France again,
Or die a soldier, as I lived a king.

DUKE OF GLOSTER [*aside*].
Short summers lightly have a forward spring.

DUKE OF BUCKINGHAM.
Now, in good time, here comes the Duke of
   York.
Enter young YORK, HASTINGS, *and the*
CARDINAL.

PRINCE.
Richard of York! how fares our loving brother?

DUKE OF YORK.
Well, my dread lord; so must I call you now.

PRINCE.
Ay, brother,—to our grief, as it is yours:
Too late he died that might have kept that
   title,
Which by his death hath lost much majesty.

DUKE OF GLOSTER.
How fares our cousin, noble Lord of York?

DUKE OF YORK.
I thank you, gentle uncle. O, my lord,
You said that idle weeds are fast in growth:
The prince my brother hath outgrown me far.

DUKE OF GLOSTER.
He hath, my lord.

DUKE OF YORK.
   And therefore is he idle?

DUKE OF GLOSTER.
O, my fair cousin, I must not say so.

DUKE OF YORK.
Then he is more beholding to you than I.
DUKE OF GLOSTER.
He may command me as my sovereign;
But you have power in me as in a kinsman.
DUKE OF YORK.
I pray you, uncle, give me this dagger.
DUKE OF GLOSTER.
My dagger, little cousin? with all my heart.
PRINCE.
A beggar, brother?
DUKE OF YORK.
Of my kind uncle, that I know will give;
And being but a toy, which is no grief to give.
DUKE OF GLOSTER.
A greater gift than that I'll give my cousin.
DUKE OF YORK.
A greater gift! O, that's the sword to it.
DUKE OF GLOSTER.
Ay, gentle cousin, were it light enough.
DUKE OF YORK.
O, then, I see you will part with but light gifts;
In weightier things you'll say a beggar nay.
DUKE OF GLOSTER.
It is too heavy for your Grace to wear.
DUKE OF YORK.
I weigh it lightly, were it heavier.
DUKE OF GLOSTER.
What, would you have my weapon, little lord?
DUKE OF YORK.
I would, that I might thank you as you call me.
DUKE OF GLOSTER.
How?
DUKE OF YORK.
Little.
PRINCE.
My Lord of York will still be cross in talk:—
Uncle, your Grace knows how to bear with
    him.
DUKE OF YORK.
You mean, to bear me, not to bear with me:—
Uncle, my brother mocks both you and me;
Because that I am little, like an ape,
He thinks that you should bear me on your
    shoulders.
DUKE OF BUCKINGHAM [aside to HASTINGS].
With what a sharp-provided wit he reasons!
To m tigate the scorn he gives his uncle,
He prettily and aptly taunts himself:
So cunning and so young is wonderful.
DUKE OF GLOSTER.
My lord, will 't please you pass along?
Myself and my good cousin Buckingham
Will to your mother, to entreat of her
To meet you at the Tower and welcome you.
DUKE OF YORK.
What, will you go unto the Tower, my lord?
PRINCE.
My lord Protector needs will have it so.
DUKE OF YORK.
I shall not sleep in quiet at the Tower.
DUKE OF GLOSTER.
Why, what should you fear?
DUKE OF YORK.
Marry, my uncle Clarence' angry ghost:
My grandam told me he was murder'd there.

PRINCE.
I fear no uncles dead.
DUKE OF GLOSTER.
Nor none that live, I hope.
PRINCE.
An if they live, I hope I need not fear.
But come, my lord; and with a heavy heart,
Thinking on them, go I unto the Tower.
    [A sennet. Exeunt all but GLOSTER,
        BUCKINGHAM, and CATESBY.
DUKE OF BUCKINGHAM.
Think you, my lord, this little prating York
Was not incensed by his subtle mother
To taunt and scorn you thus opprobriously?
DUKE OF GLOSTER.
No doubt, no doubt: O, 'tis a parlous boy,
Bold, quick, ingenious, forward, capable:
He is all the mother's, from the top to toe.
DUKE OF BUCKINGHAM.
Well, let them rest.—Come hither, Catesby.
    Thou
Art sworn as deeply to effect what we intend
As closely to conceal what we impart:
Thou know'st our reasons urged upon the way;—
What think'st thou? is it not an easy matter
To make William Lord Hastings of our mind,
For the instalment of this noble duke
In the seat royal of this famous isle?
SIR WILLIAM CATESBY.
He for his father's sake so loves the prince,
That he will not be won to aught against him.
DUKE OF BUCKINGHAM.
What think'st thou, then, of Stanley? will not he?
SIR WILLIAM CATESBY.
He will do all in all as Hastings doth.
DUKE OF BUCKINGHAM.
Well, then, no more but this: go, gentle Catesby,
And, as it were far off, sound thou Lord Hastings,
How he doth stand affected to our purpose;
And summon him to-morrow to the Tower,
To sit about the coronation.
If thou dost find him tractable to us,
Encourage him, and show him all our reasons:
If he be leaden, icy-cold, unwilling,
Be thou so too; and so break off your talk,
And give us notice of his inclination:
For we to-morrow hold divided councils,
Wherein thyself shalt highly be employ'd.
DUKE OF GLOSTER.
Commend me to Lord William: tell him,
    Catesby,
His ancient knot of dangerous adversaries
To-morrow are let blood at Pomfret-castle;
And bid my friend, for joy of this good news,
Give Mistress Shore one gentle kiss the more.
DUKE OF BUCKINGHAM.
Good Catesby, go, effect this business soundly.
SIR WILLIAM CATESBY.
My good lords both, with all the heed I can.
DUKE OF GLOSTER.
Shall we hear from you, Catesby, ere we sleep?
SIR WILLIAM CATESBY.
You shall, my lord.
DUKE OF GLOSTER.
At Crosby-place, there shall you find us both.
    [Exit CATESBY.

DUKE OF BUCKINGHAM.
Now, my lord, what shall we do, if we perceive
Lord Hastings will not yield to our complots?
DUKE OF GLOSTER.
Chop off his head, man;—somewhat we will
 do:—
And, look, when I am king, claim thou of me
The earldom of Hereford, and the moveables
Whereof the king my brother stood possest.
DUKE OF BUCKINGHAM.
I'll claim that promise at your Grace's hand.
DUKE OF GLOSTER.
And look to have it yielded with all kindness.
Come, let us sup betimes, that afterwards
We may digest our complots in some form.
          [Exeunt.

SCENE II.

Before LORD HASTINGS' *house.*

Enter a MESSENGER *to the door of* HASTINGS.

MESSENGER.
My lord! my lord!—   [Knocking.
 LORD HASTINGS [within].
Who knocks?
MESSENGER.
One from the Lord Stanley.
 LORD HASTINGS [within].
What is 't o'clock?
MESSENGER.
Upon the stroke of four.
 Enter HASTINGS.
LORD HASTINGS.
Cannot thy master sleep these tedious nights?
MESSENGER.
So it appears by that I have to say.
First, he commends him to your noble self.
LORD HASTINGS.
What then?
MESSENGER.
Then certifies your lordship, that this night
He dreamt the boar had razed off his helm:
Besides, he says there are two councils held;
And that may be determined at the one
Which may make you and him to rue at th' other.
Therefore he sends to know your lordship's
 pleasure,—
If presently you will take horse with him,
And with all speed post with him toward the
 north,
To shun the danger that his soul divines.
LORD HASTINGS.
Go, fellow, go, return unto thy lord;
Bid him not fear the separated councils:
His honour and myself are at the one,
And at the other is my good friend Catesby;
Where nothing can proceed that toucheth us
Whereof I shall not have intelligence.
Tell him his fears are shallow, wanting instance:
And for his dreams, I wonder he's so simple
To trust the mockery of unquiet slumbers:
To fly the boar before the boar pursues,
Were to incense the boar to follow us,
And make pursuit where he did mean no chase.
Go, bid thy master rise and come to me;
And we will both together to the Tower,
Where he shall see the boar will use us kindly.

MESSENGER.
I'll go, my lord, and tell him what you say. [Exit.
 Enter CATESBY.
SIR WILLIAM CATESBY.
Many good morrows to my noble lord!
LORD HASTINGS.
Good morrow, Catesby; you are early stirring:
What news, what news, in this our tottering
 state?
SIR WILLIAM CATESBY.
It is a reeling world, indeed, my lord;
And I believe will never stand upright
Till Richard wear the garland of the realm.
LORD HASTINGS.
How! wear the garland! dost thou mean the
 crown?
SIR WILLIAM CATESBY.
Ay, my good lord.
LORD HASTINGS.
I'll have this crown of mine cut from my shoul-
 ders
Before I'll see the crown so foul misplaced.
But canst thou guess that he doth aim at it?
SIR WILLIAM CATESBY.
Ay, on my life; and hopes to find you forward
Upon his party for the gain thereof:
And thereupon he sends you this good news,—
That this same very day your enemies,
The kindred of the queen, must die at Pomfret.
LORD HASTINGS.
Indeed, I am no mourner for that news,
Because they have been still my adversaries:
But, that I'll give my voice on Richard's side,
To bar my master's heirs in true descent,
God knows I will not do it to the death.
SIR WILLIAM CATESBY.
God keep your lordship in that gracious mind!
LORD HASTINGS.
But I shall laugh at this a twelve-month hence,—
That they who brought me in my master's hate,
I live to look upon their tragedy.
Well, Catesby, ere a fortnight make me older,
I'll send some packing that yet think not on 't.
SIR WILLIAM CATESBY.
'Tis a vile thing to die, my gracious lord,
When men are unprepared and look not for it.
LORD HASTINGS.
O monstrous, monstrous! and so falls it out
With Rivers, Vaughan, Grey: and so 'twill do
With some men else, that think themselves as safe
As thou and I; who, as thou know'st, are dear
To princely Richard and to Buckingham.
SIR WILLIAM CATESBY.
The princes both make high account of you,—
[aside] For they account his head upon the bridge.
LORD HASTINGS.
I know they do; and I have well deserved it.
 Enter STANLEY.
Come on, come on; where is your boar-spear,
 man?
Fear you the boar, and go so unprovided?
LORD STANLEY.
My lord, good morrow;—good morrow,
 Catesby:—
You may jest on, but by the holy rood,
I do not like these several councils, I.

LORD HASTINGS.
My lord,
I hold my life as dear as you do yours;
And never in my days, I do protest,
Was it more precious to me than 'tis now:
Think you, but that I know our state secure,
I would be so triumphant as I am?
LORD STANLEY.
The lords at Pomfret, when they rode from
    London,   [sure,—
Were jocund, and supposed their states were
And they, indeed, had no cause to mistrust;
But yet, you see, how soon the day o'ercast.
This sudden stab of rancour I misdoubt:
Pray God, I say, I prove a needless coward!
What, shall we toward the Tower? the day is
    spent.
LORD HASTINGS.
Come, come, have with you.—Wot you what, my
    lord?
To-day the lords you talk of are beheaded.
LORD STANLEY.
They, for their truth, might better wear their
    heads
Than some that have accused them wear their
    hats.—
But come, my lord, let us away.
    Enter a PURSUIVANT.
LORD HASTINGS.
Go on before; I'll talk with this good fellow.
    [*Exeunt* STANLEY *and* CATESBY.
How now, sirrah! how goes the world with thee?
PURSUIVANT.
The better that your lordship please to ask.
LORD HASTINGS.
I tell thee, man, 'tis better with me now   [meet:
Than when thou mett'st me last where now we
Then was I going prisoner to the Tower,
By the suggestion of the queen's allies;
But now, I tell thee—keep it to thyself—
This day those enemies are put to death,
And I in better state than e'er I was.
PURSUIVANT.
God hold it, to your honour's good content!
LORD HASTINGS.
Gramercy, fellow: there, drink that for me.
    [*Throwing him his purse.*
PURSUIVANT.
God save your lordship!   [*Exit.*
    Enter a PRIEST.
PRIEST.
Well met, my lord; I am glad to see your honour.
LORD HASTINGS.
I thank thee, good Sir John, with all my heart.
I am in your debt for your last exercise;
Come the next Sabbath, and I will content you.
    [*He whispers in his ear.*
    Enter BUCKINGHAM.
DUKE OF BUCKINGHAM.
What, talking with a priest, lord chamberlain!
Your friends at Pomfret, they do need the priest;
Your honour hath no shriving-work in hand.
LORD HASTINGS.
Good faith, and when I met this holy man,
The men you talk of came into my mind.—
What, go you toward the Tower?

DUKE OF BUCKINGHAM.
I do, my lord; but long I cannot stay there:
I shall return before your lordship thence.
LORD HASTINGS.
Nay, like enough, for I stay dinner there.
    DUKE OF BUCKINGHAM [*aside*].
And supper too, although thou know'st it
    not.—
Come, will you go?
LORD HASTINGS.
    I'll wait upon your lordship.
       [*Exeunt.*

SCENE III.
Pomfret Castle.

Enter SIR RICHARD RATCLIFF, *with halberds,*
carrying RIVERS, GREY, *and* VAUGHAN *to death.*

SIR RICHARD RATCLIFF.

COME, bring forth the prisoners.
EARL RIVERS.
Sir Richard Ratcliff, let me tell thee this,—
To-day shalt thou behold a subject die
For truth, for duty, and for loyalty.
LORD GREY.
God keep the prince from all the pack of you!
A knot you are of damned blood-suckers.
SIR THOMAS VAUGHAN.
You live that shall cry woe for this hereafter.
SIR RICHARD RATCLIFF.
Dispatch; the limit of your lives is out.
EARL RIVERS.
O Pomfret, Pomfret! O thou bloody prison,
Fatal and ominous to noble peers!
Within the guilty closure of thy walls
Richard the Second here was hackt to death;
And, for more slander to thy dismal seat,
We give thee up our guiltless blood to drink.
LORD GREY.
Now Margaret's curse is faln upon our heads,
When she exclaim'd on Hastings, you, and I,
For standing by when Richard stabb'd her son.
EARL RIVERS.
Then cursed she Richard, then cursed she Buck-
    ingham,
Then cursed she Hastings:—O, remember, God,
To hear her prayers for them, as now for us!
And for my sister and her princely sons,
Be satisfied, dear God, with our true blood,
Which, as Thou know'st, unjustly must be spilt.
SIR RICHARD RATCLIFF.
Make haste; the hour of death is expiate.
EARL RIVERS.
Come, Grey,—come, Vaughan,—let us here
    embrace:
Farewell, until we meet again in heaven. [*Exeunt.*

SCENE IV.
London. The Tower.

Enter BUCKINGHAM, DERBY, HASTINGS, *the*
BISHOP OF ELY, RATCLIFF, LOVEL, *with*
others, at a table.

LORD HASTINGS.

NOW, noble peers, the cause why we are met
Is, to determine of the coronation.
In God's name, speak,—when is the royal day?

DUKE OF BUCKINGHAM.
Are all things ready for that royal time?
EARL OF DERBY.
It is; and wants but nomination.
BISHOP OF ELY.
To-morrow, then, I judge a happy day.
DUKE OF BUCKINGHAM.
Who knows the lord Protector's mind herein?
Who is most inward with the noble duke?
BISHOP OF ELY.
Your Grace, we think, should soonest know his
mind.
DUKE OF BUCKINGHAM.
Who, I, my lord? We know each other's faces,
But for our hearts, he knows no more of mine
Than I of yours; nor I no more of his
Than you of mine.
Lord Hastings, you and he are near in love.
LORD HASTINGS.
I thank his Grace, I know he loves me well;
But, for his purpose in the coronation,
I have not sounded him, nor he deliver'd
His gracious pleasure any way therein:
But you, my noble lords, may name the time;
And in the duke's behalf I'll give my voice,
Which, I presume, he'll take in gentle part.
BISHOP OF ELY.
In happy time, here comes the duke himself.
Enter GLOSTER.
DUKE OF GLOSTER.
My noble lords and cousins all, good morrow.
I have been long a sleeper: but, I trust,
My absence doth neglect no great design,
Which by my presence might have been con-
cluded.
DUKE OF BUCKINGHAM.
Had you not come upon your cue, my lord,
William Lord Hastings had pronounced your
part,—
I mean, your voice,—for crowning of the king.
DUKE OF GLOSTER.
Than my Lord Hastings no man might be
bolder;
His lordship knows me well, and loves me
well.—
My Lord of Ely, when I was last in Holborn,
I saw good strawberries in your garden there:
I do beseech you send for some of them.
BISHOP OF ELY.
Marry, and will, my lord, with all my heart. [*Exit.*
DUKE OF GLOSTER.
Cousin of Buckingham, a word with you.
            [*Takes him aside.*
Catesby hath sounded Hastings in our business,
And finds the testy gentleman so hot,
That he will lose his head ere give consent
His master's child, as worshipfully he terms it,
Shall lose the royalty of England's throne.
DUKE OF BUCKINGHAM.
Withdraw you hence, my lord; I'll follow you.
   [*Exit* GLOSTER, *follow'd by* BUCKINGHAM.
EARL OF DERBY.
We have not yet set down this day of triumph.
To-morrow, in my judgement, is too sudden;
For I myself am not so well provided
As else I would be, were the day prolong'd.

Enter BISHOP OF ELY.
BISHOP OF ELY.
Where is my lord the Duke of Gloucester?
I have sent for these strawberries.
His Grace looks cheerfully and smooth to-day;
There's some conceit or other likes him well,
When he doth bid good-morrow with such a
spirit.
I think there's never a man in Christendom
That can less hide his love or hate than he;
For by his face straight shall you know his heart.
EARL OF DERBY.
What of his heart perceive you in his face
By any likelihood he show'd to-day?
LORD HASTINGS.
Marry, that with no man here he is offended;
For, were he, he had shown it in his looks.
EARL OF DERBY.
I pray God he be not, I say.
Enter GLOSTER *and* BUCKINGHAM.
DUKE OF GLOSTER.
I pray you all, tell me what they deserve
That do conspire my death with devilish plots
Of damned witchcraft, and that have prevail'd
Upon my body with their hellish charms?
LORD HASTINGS.
The tender love I bear your Grace, my lord,
Makes me most forward in this noble presence
To doom th' offenders: whosoe'er they be,
I say, my lord, they have deserved death.
DUKE OF GLOSTER.
Then be your eyes the witness of their evil:
Look how I am bewitcht; behold mine arm
Is, like a blasted sapling, wither'd up:
And this is Edward's wife, that monstrous witch,
Consorted with that harlot-strumpet Shore,
That by their witchcraft thus have marked me.
LORD HASTINGS.
If they have done this thing, my gracious lord,—
DUKE OF GLOSTER.
If! thou protector of this damned strumpet,
Talk'st thou to me of 'ifs'? Thou art a traitor:—
Off with his head!—now, by Saint Paul, I swear
I will not dine until I see the same.—
Lovel and Ratcliff, look that it be done:—
The rest, that love me, rise and follow me.
   [*Exeunt all, except* HASTINGS, LOVEL, *and*
RATCLIFF.
LORD HASTINGS.
Woe, woe for England! not a whit for me;
For I, too fond, might have prevented this.
Stanley did dream the boar did raze his helm;
But I disdain'd it, and did scorn to fly: [stumble,
Three times to-day my foot-cloth horse did
And started when he lookt upon the Tower,
As loth to bear me to the slaughter-house.
O, now I need the priest that spake to me:
I now repent I told the pursuivant,
As too triumphing, how mine enemies
To-day at Pomfret bloodily were butcher'd,
And I myself secure in grace and favour.
O Margaret, Margaret, now thy heavy curse
Is lighted on poor Hastings' wretched head!
SIR RICHARD RATCLIFF.
Dispatch, my lord; the duke would be at dinner:
Make a short shrift; he longs to see your head.

LORD HASTINGS.

O momentary grace of mortal men,
Which we more hunt for than the grace of God!
Who builds his hope in air of your fair looks,
Lives like a drunken sailor on a mast,
Ready, with every nod, to tumble down
Into the fatal bowels of the deep.

LORD LOVEL.

Come, come, dispatch; 'tis bootless to exclaim.

LORD HASTINGS.

O bloody Richard!—miserable England!
I prophesy the fearfull'st time to thee
That ever wretched age hath lookt upon.—
Come, lead me to the block; bear him my head:
They smile at me who shortly shall be dead.

         [*Exeunt.*

SCENE V.

The Tower-walls.

Enter GLOSTER *and* BUCKINGHAM, *in rotten
armour, marvellous ill-favour'd.*

DUKE OF GLOSTER.

COME, cousin, canst thou quake, and change
   thy colour,
Murder thy breath in middle of a word,
And then begin again, and stop again,
As if thou wert distraught and mad with terror?

DUKE OF BUCKINGHAM.

Tut, I can counterfeit the deep tragedian;
Speak and look back, and pry on every side,
Tremble and start at wagging of a straw,
Intending deep suspicion: ghastly looks
Are at my service, like enforced smiles;
And both are ready in their offices,
At any time, to grace my stratagems.
But what, is Catesby gone?

DUKE OF GLOSTER.

He is; and, see, he brings the mayor along.

DUKE OF BUCKINGHAM.

Let me alone to entertain him.

    Enter the MAYOR *and* CATESBY.
             Lord mayor,—

DUKE OF GLOSTER.

Look to the drawbridge there!

DUKE OF BUCKINGHAM.

            Hark! a drum.

DUKE OF GLOSTER.

Catesby, o'erlook the walls.

DUKE OF BUCKINGHAM.

Lord mayor, the reason we have sent,—

DUKE OF GLOSTER.

Look back, defend thee,—here are enemies.

DUKE OF BUCKINGHAM.

God and our innocency defend and guard us!

DUKE OF GLOSTER.

Be patient, they are friends,—Ratcliff and Lovel.

Enter LOVEL *and* RATCLIFF, *with* HASTINGS'
head.

LORD LOVEL.

Here is the head of that ignoble traitor,
The dangerous and unsuspected Hastings.

DUKE OF GLOSTER.

So dear I loved the man, that I must weep.
I took him for the plainest harmless creature
That breathed upon the earth a Christian;
Made him my book, wherein my soul recorded

The history of all her secret thoughts:
So smooth he daub'd his vice with show of virtue,
That, his apparent open guilt omitted,—
I mean, his conversation with Shore's wife,—
He lived from all attainder of suspect.

DUKE OF BUCKINGHAM.

Well, well, he was the covert'st shelter'd traitor
That ever lived.
Would you imagine, or almost believe,—
Were 't not that, by great preservation,
We live to tell it you,—the subtle traitor
This day had plotted, in the council-house,
To murder me and my good Lord of Gloster?

MAYOR OF LONDON.

What, had he so?

DUKE OF GLOSTER.

What, think you we are Turks or infidels?
Or that we would, against the form of law,
Proceed thus rashly in the villain's death,
But that the extreme peril of the case,
The peace of England and our persons' safety,
Enforc'd us to this execution?

MAYOR OF LONDON.

Now, fair befall you! he deserved his death;
And your good Graces both have well proceeded,
To warn false traitors from the like attempts.
I never lookt for better at his hands,
After he once fell in with Mistress Shore.

DUKE OF BUCKINGHAM.

Yet had we not determined he should die,
Until your lordship came to see his end;
Which now the loving haste of these our friends,
Somewhat against our meaning, have prevented;
Because, my lord, we would have had you heard
The traitor speak, and timorously confess
The manner and the purpose of his treason;
That you might well have signified the same
Unto the citizens, who haply may
Misconster us in him, and wail his death.

MAYOR OF LONDON.

But, my good lord, your Grace's word shall serve,
As well as I had seen, and heard him speak;
And do not doubt, right noble princes both,
But I'll acquaint our duteous citizens
With all your just proceedings in this case.

DUKE OF GLOSTER.

And to that end we wisht your lordship here,
T' avoid the censures of the carping world.

DUKE OF BUCKINGHAM.

But since you come too late of our intent,
Yet witness what you hear we did intend:
And so, my good lord mayor, we bid farewell.

        [*Exit* MAYOR.

DUKE OF GLOSTER.

Go, after, after, cousin Buckingham.
The mayor towards Guildhall hies him in all
   post:—
There, at your meetest vantage of the time,
Infer the bastardy of Edward's children:
Tell them how Edward put to death a citizen,
Only for saying he would make his son
Heir to the crown; meaning, indeed, his house,
Which, by the sign thereof, was termed so.
Moreover, urge his hateful luxury,
And bestial appetite in change of lust;   [wives
Which stretcht unto their servants, daughters,

Even where his raging eye or savage heart,
Without control, listed to make a prey.
Nay, for a need, thus far come near my person:—
Tell them, when that my mother went with child
Of that insatiate Edward, noble York
My princely father then had wars in France;
And, by just computation of the time,
Found that the issue was not his begot;
Which well appeared in his lineaments,
Being nothing like the noble duke my father:
Yet touch this sparingly, as 'twere far off;
Because, my lord, you know my mother lives.

DUKE OF BUCKINGHAM.

Doubt not, my lord, I'll play the orator
As if the golden fee for which I plead
Were for myself: and so, my lord, adieu.

DUKE OF GLOSTER.

If you thrive well, bring them to Baynard's
   Castle;
Where you shall find me well accompanied
With reverend fathers and well-learned bishops.

DUKE OF BUCKINGHAM.

I go; and towards three or four o'clock
Look for the news that the Guildhall affords.
                  [*Exit.*

DUKE OF GLOSTER.

Go, Lovel, with all speed to Doctor Shaw,—
[*to* CATESBY] Go thou to Friar Penker;—bid
   them both
Meet me within this hour at Baynard's Castle.
    [*Exeunt* LOVEL, CATESBY, *and* RATCLIFF.
Now will I in, to take some privy order,
To draw the brats of Clarence out of sight;
And to give notice that no manner person
Have any time recourse unto the princes.   [*Exit.*

SCENE VI.

The same. A street.

Enter a SCRIVENER, *with a paper in his hand.*

SCRIVENER.

HERE is th' indictment of the good Lord
  Hastings;
Which in a set hand fairly is engross'd,
That it may be to-day read o'er in Paul's.
And mark how well the sequel hangs together:
Eleven hours I have spent to write it over,
For yesternight by Catesby was it sent me;
The precedent was full as long a-doing:
And yet within these five hours Hastings lived,
Untainted, unexamined, free, at liberty.   [gross
Here's a good world the while! Why, who's so
  that cannot see this palpable device?
Yet who so bold but says he sees it not?
Bad is the world; and all will come to naught
When such ill dealing must be seen in thought.
                  [*Exit.*

SCENE VII.

Baynard's Castle.

Enter GLOSTER *and* BUCKINGHAM, *meeting.*

DUKE OF GLOSTER.

HOW now, how now! what say the citizens?

DUKE OF BUCKINGHAM.

Now, by the holy mother of our Lord,
The citizens are mum, say not a word.

DUKE OF GLOSTER.

Toucht you the bastardy of Edward's children?

DUKE OF BUCKINGHAM.

I did; with his contract with Lady Lucy,
And his contract by deputy in France;
Th' insatiate greediness of his desires,
And his enforcement of the city wives;
His tyranny for trifles, his own bastardy,—
As being got, your father then in France,
And his resemblance, being not like the duke:
Withal I did infer your lineaments,—
Being the right idea of your father,
Both in your form and nobleness of mind;
Laid open all your victories in Scotland,
Your discipline in war, wisdom in peace,
Your bounty, virtue, fair humility;
Indeed, left nothing fitting for the purpose
Untoucht, or slightly handled, in discourse:
And when my oratory drew toward end,
I bade them that did love their country's good
Cry, 'God save Richard, England's royal king!

DUKE OF GLOSTER.

And did they so?

DUKE OF BUCKINGHAM.

No, so God help me, they spake not a word,
But, like dumb statuas or breathing stones,
Stared each on other, and lookt deadly pale.
Which when I saw, I reprehended them;
And askt the mayor what meant this wilful
  silence:
His answer was,—the people were not used
To be spoke to but by the recorder.
Then he was urged to tell my tale again,—
'Thus saith the duke, thus hath the duke in-
  ferr'd;'
But nothing spake in warrant from himself.
When he had done, some followers of mine own,
At lower end of the hall, hurl'd up their caps,
And some ten voices cried, 'God save King
  Richard!'
And thus I took the vantage of those few,—
'Thanks, gentle citizens and friends,' quoth I;
'This general applause and cheerful shout
Argues your wisdom and your love to Richard:'
And even here brake off, and came away.

DUKE OF GLOSTER.

What tongueless blocks were they! would they
  not speak?

DUKE OF BUCKINGHAM.

No, by my troth, my lord.

DUKE OF GLOSTER.

Will not the mayor, then, and his brethren,
  come?

DUKE OF BUCKINGHAM.

The mayor is here at hand. Intend some fear;
Be not you spoke with but by mighty suit:
And look you get a prayer-book in your hand,
And stand between two churchmen, good my
  lord;
For on that ground I'll make a holy descant:
And be not easily won to our request;
Play the maid's part,—still answer nay, and take it.

DUKE OF GLOSTER.

I go; and if you plead as well for them
As I can say nay to thee for myself,
No doubt we'll bring it to a happy issue.

DUKE OF BUCKINGHAM.
Go, go, up to the leads; the lord mayor knocks.
                              [*Exit* GLOSTER.
Enter the MAYOR, ALDERMEN, *and* CITIZENS.
Welcome, my lord: I dance attendance here;
I think the duke will not be spoke withal.
              Enter CATESBY.
Now, Catesby, what says your lord to my
    request?
          SIR WILLIAM CATESBY.
He doth entreat your Grace, my noble lord,
To visit him to-morrow or next day:
He is within, with two right-reverend fathers,
Divinely bent to meditation:
And in no worldly suit would he be moved,
To draw him from his holy exercise.
          DUKE OF BUCKINGHAM.
Return, good Catesby, to the gracious duke;
Tell him, myself, the mayor and aldermen,
In deep designs and matters of great moment,
No less importing than our general good,
Are come to have some conference with his
    Grace.
          SIR WILLIAM CATESBY.
I'll signify so much unto him straight.   [*Exit.*
          DUKE OF BUCKINGHAM.
Ah, ha, my lord, this prince is not an Edward!
He is not lolling on a lewd day-bed,
But on his knees at meditation;
Not dallying with a brace of courtezans,
But meditating with two deep divines;
Not sleeping, to engross his idle body,
But praying, to enrich his watchful soul:
Happy were England, would this virtuous prince
Take on himself the sovereignty thereof;
But sure I fear we shall not win him to it.
          MAYOR OF LONDON.
Marry, God defend his Grace should say us nay!
          DUKE OF BUCKINGHAM.
I fear he will. Here Catesby comes again.
              Enter CATESBY.
Now, Catesby, what says his Grace?
          SIR WILLIAM CATESBY.
He wonders to what end you have assembled
Such troops of citizens to come to him,
His Grace not being warn'd thereof before:
He fears, my lord, you mean no good to him.
          DUKE OF BUCKINGHAM.
Sorry I am my noble cousin should
Suspect me, that I mean no good to him:
By heaven, we come to him in perfect love;
And so once more return and tell his Grace.
                              [*Exit* CATESBY.
When holy and devout religious men
Are at their beads, 'tis much to draw them
    thence,—
So sweet is zealous contemplation.
Enter GLOSTER *aloft, between two* BISHOPS.
          CATESBY *returns.*
          MAYOR OF LONDON.
See, where his Grace stands 'tween two clergy-
    men!
          DUKE OF BUCKINGHAM.
Two props of virtue for a Christian prince,
To stay him from the fall of vanity:
And, see, a book of prayer in his hand,—

True ornaments to know a holy man.—
Famous Plantagenet, most gracious prince,
Lend favourable ear to our request;
And pardon us the interruption
Of thy devotion and right Christian zeal.
          DUKE OF GLOSTER.
My lord, there needs no such apology:
I rather do beseech you pardon me,
Who, earnest in the service of my God,
Neglect the visitation of my friends.
But, leaving this, what is your Grace's pleasure?
          DUKE OF BUCKINGHAM.
Even that, I hope, which pleaseth God above,
And all good men of this ungovern'd isle.
          DUKE OF GLOSTER.
I do suspect I have done some offence
That seems disgracious in the city's eye;
And that you come to reprehend my ignorance.
          DUKE OF BUCKINGHAM.
You have, my lord: would it might please your
    Grace,
On our entreaties, to amend your fault!
          DUKE OF GLOSTER.
Else wherefore breathe I in a Christian land?
          DUKE OF BUCKINGHAM.
Know, then, it is your fault that you resign
The supreme seat, the throne majestical,
The scepter'd office of your ancestors,
Your state of fortune and your due of birth,
The lineal glory of your royal house,
To the corruption of a blemish'd stock:
Whilst, in the mildness of your sleepy thoughts—
Which here we waken to our country's good—
This noble isle doth want her proper limbs;
Her face defaced with scars of infamy,
Her royal stock graft with ignoble plants,
And almost shoulder'd in the swallowing gulf
Of dark forgetfulness and deep oblivion.
Which to recure, we heartily solicit
Your gracious self to take on you the charge
And kingly government of this your land;—
Not as protector, steward, substitute,
Or lowly factor for another's gain;
But as successively, from blood to blood,
Your right of birth, your empery, your own.
For this, consorted with the citizens,
Your very worshipful and loving friends,
And by their vehement instigation,
In this just suit come I to move your Grace.
          DUKE OF GLOSTER.
I cannot tell, if to depart in silence,
Or bitterly to speak in your reproof,
Best fitteth my degree or your condition:
If not to answer, you might haply think
Tongue-tied ambition, not replying, yielded
To bear the golden yoke of sovereignty,
Which fondly you would here impose on me;
If to reprove you for this suit of yours,
So season'd with your faithful love to me,
Then, on the other side, I checkt my friends.
Therefore,—to speak, and to avoid the first,
And then, in speaking, not to incur the last,—
Definitively thus I answer you.
Your love deserves my thanks; but my desert
Unmeritable shuns your high request.
First, if all obstacles were cut away,

And that my path were even to the crown,
As the ripe revenue and due of birth;
Yet so much is my poverty of spirit,
So mighty and so many my defects,
That I would rather hide me from my greatness—
Being a bark to brook no mighty sea—
Than in my greatness covet to be hid,
And in the vapour of my glory smother'd.
But, God be thankt, there is no need of me;—
And much I need to help you, were there need;—
The royal tree hath left us royal fruit,
Which, mellow'd by the stealing hours of time,
Will well become the seat of majesty,
And make, no doubt, us happy by his reign.
On him I lay what you would lay on me,
The right and fortune of his happy stars;
Which God defend that I should wring from him!
　　　　DUKE OF BUCKINGHAM.
My lord, this argues conscience in your Grace;
But the respects thereof are nice and trivial,
All circumstances well considered.
You say that Edward is your brother's son:
So say we too, but not by Edward's wife;
For first he was contract to Lady Lucy,—
Your mother lives a witness to his vow,—
And afterward by substitute betroth'd
To Bona, sister to the King of France.
These both put by, a poor petitioner,
A care-crazed mother of a many children,
A beauty-waning and distressed widow,
Even in the afternoon of her best days,
Made prize and purchase of his wanton eye,
Seduced the pitch and height of his degree
To base declension and loath'd bigamy:
By her, in his unlawful bed, he got
This Edward, whom our manners call the prince.
More bitterly could I expostulate,
Save that, for reverence to some alive,
I give a sparing limit to my tongue.
Then, good my lord, take to your royal self
This proffer'd benefit of dignity;
If not to bless us and the land withal,
Yet to draw forth your noble ancestry
From the corruption of abusing time
Into a lineal true-derived course.
　　　　MAYOR OF LONDON.
Do, good my lord; your citizens entreat you.
　　　　DUKE OF BUCKINGHAM.
Refuse not, mighty lord, this proffer'd love.
　　　　SIR WILLIAM CATESBY.
O, make them joyful, grant their lawful suit!
　　　　DUKE OF GLOSTER.
Alas, why would you heap these cares on me?
I am unfit for state and majesty:—
I do beseech you, take it not amiss;
I cannot nor I will not yield to you.
　　　　DUKE OF BUCKINGHAM.
If you refuse it,—as, in love and zeal,
Loth to depose the child, your brother's son;
As well we know your tenderness of heart,
And gentle, kind, effeminate remorse,
Which we have noted in you to your kindred,
And egally indeed to all estates,—
Yet whether you accept our suit or no,
Your brother's son shall never reign our king;
But we will plant some other in the throne,

To the disgrace and downfall of your house:
And in this resolution here we leave you.
Come, citizens: zounds, I'll entreat no more.
　　　　DUKE OF GLOSTER.
O, do not swear, my lord of Buckingham.
　　　[*Exit* BUCKINGHAM *with the* CITIZENS.
　　　　SIR WILLIAM CATESBY.
Call him again, sweet prince, accept their suit:
If you deny them, all the land will rue it.
　　　　DUKE OF GLOSTER.
Will you enforce me to a world of cares?
Well, call them again. I am not made of stones,
But penetrable to your kind entreats,
Albeit against my conscience and my soul.
　　　　Enter BUCKINGHAM *and the others.*
Cousin of Buckingham, and you sage, grave men,
Since you will buckle fortune on my back,
To bear her burden, whe'r I will or no,
I must have patience to endure the load:
But if black scandal or foul-faced reproach
Attend the sequel of your imposition,
Your mere enforcement shall acquittance me
From all the impure blots and stains thereof;
For God He knows, and you may partly see,
How far I am from the desire of this
　　　　MAYOR OF LONDON.
God bless your Grace! we see it, and will say it.
　　　　DUKE OF GLOSTER.
In saying so, you shall but say the truth.
　　　　DUKE OF BUCKINGHAM.
Then I salute you with this royal title,—
Long live King Richard, England's worthy king!
　　　　ALL.
Amen.
　　　　DUKE OF BUCKINGHAM.
To-morrow may it please you to be crown'd?
　　　　DUKE OF GLOSTER.
Even when you please, since you will have it so.
　　　　DUKE OF BUCKINGHAM.
To-morrow, then, we will attend your Grace:
And so, most joyfully, we take our leave.
　　　　DUKE OF GLOSTER [*to the* BISHOPS].
Come, let us to our holy work again.—
Farewell, good cousin; farewell, gentle friends.
　　　　　　　　　　　　[*Exeunt.*

ACT IV. SCENE I.

London.　Before the Tower.

Enter, on one side, QUEEN ELIZABETH, DUCHESS
OF YORK, *and* DORSET; *on the other,* ANNE,
DUCHESS OF GLOSTER, *leading* LADY MAR-
GARET PLANTAGENET, CLARENCE'S *young
daughter.*

　　　　DUCHESS OF YORK.
WHO meets us here? my niece Plantagenet,
　　Led in the hand of her kind aunt of Gloster?
Now, for my life, she's wandering to the Tower,
On pure heart's love, to greet the tender princes.—
Daughter, well met.
　　　　LADY ANNE.
　　　　　　God give your Graces both
A happy and a joyful time of day!
　　　　QUEEN ELIZABETH.
As much to you, good sister! Whither away?

LADY ANNE.
No further than the Tower; and, as I guess,
Upon the like devotion as yourselves,
To gratulate the gentle princes there.
QUEEN ELIZABETH.
Kind sister, thanks: we'll enter all together:—
And, in good time, here the lieutenant comes.
Enter BRAKENBURY.
Master lieutenant, pray you, by your leave,
How doth the prince, and my young son of York?
SIR ROBERT BRAKENBURY.
Right well, dear madam. By your patience,
I may not suffer you to visit them;
The king hath straitly charged the contrary.
QUEEN ELIZABETH.
The king! who's that?
SIR ROBERT BRAKENBURY.
                        I mean the lord Protector.
QUEEN ELIZABETH.
The Lord protect him from that kingly title!
Hath he set bounds between their love and me?
I am their mother; who shall bar me from them?
DUCHESS OF YORK.
I am their father's mother; I will see them.
LADY ANNE.
Their aunt I am in law, in love their mother:
Then bring me to their sights; I'll bear thy
    blame,
And take thy office from thee, on my peril.
SIR ROBERT BRAKENBURY.
No, madam, no,—I may not leave it so:
I'm bound by oath, and therefore pardon me.
                                         [*Exit.*
Enter STANLEY.
LORD STANLEY.
Let me but meet you, ladies, one hour hence,
And I'll salute your Grace of York as mother,
And reverend looker-on, of two fair queens.—
[*to the* DUCHESS OF GLOSTER] Come, madam,
    you must straight to Westminster,
There to be crowned Richard's royal queen.
QUEEN ELIZABETH.
Ah, cut my lace asunder,
That my pent heart may have some scope to beat,
Or else I swoon with this dead-killing news!
LADY ANNE.
Despiteful tidings! O unpleasing news!
MARQUESS OF DORSET.
Be of good cheer:—mother, how fares your
    Grace?
QUEEN ELIZABETH.
O Dorset, speak not to me, get thee hence!
Death and destruction dog thee at the heels;
Thy mother's name is ominous to children.
If thou wilt outstrip death, go cross the seas,
And live with Richmond, from the reach of hell:
Go, hie thee, hie thee from this slaughter-house,
Lest thou increase the number of the dead;
And make me die the thrall of Margaret's curse,—
Nor mother, wife, nor England's counted queen.
LORD STANLEY.
Full of wise care is this your counsel, madam.—
Take all the swift advantage of the hours;
You shall have letters from me to my son
In your behalf, to meet you on the way:
Be not ta'en tardy by unwise delay.

DUCHESS OF YORK.
O ill-dispersing wind of misery!—
O my accursed womb, the bed of death!
A cockatrice hast thou hatcht to the world,
Whose unavoided eye is murderous.
LORD STANLEY.
Come, madam, come; I in all haste was sent.
LADY ANNE.
And I in all unwillingness will go.—
O, would to God that the inclusive verge
Of golden metal that must round my brow
Were red-hot steel, to sear me to the brain!
Anointed let me be with deadly venom;
And die, ere men can say, 'God save the queen!'
QUEEN ELIZABETH.
Go, go, poor soul, I envy not thy glory;
To feed my humour, wish thyself no harm.
LADY ANNE.
No! why?—When he that is my husband now
Came to me, as I follow'd Henry's corse;
When scarce the blood was well washt from his
    hands
Which issued from my other angel husband,
And that dead saint which then I weeping
    follow'd;
O, when, I say, I lookt on Richard's face,
This was my wish,—'Be thou,' quoth I, 'accurst,
For making me, so young, so old a widow!
And, when thou wedd'st, let sorrow haunt thy
    bed;
And be thy wife—if any be so mad—
More miserable by the life of thee
Than thou hast made me by my dear lord's
    death!'
Lo, ere I can repeat this curse again,
Even in so short a space, my woman's heart
Grossly grew captive to his honey words,
And proved the subject of mine own soul's
    curse,—
Which ever since hath kept mine eyes from rest;
For never yet one hour in his bed
Have I enjoy'd the golden dew of sleep,
But have been waked by his timorous dreams.
Besides, he hates me for my father Warwick;
And will, no doubt, shortly be rid of me.
QUEEN ELIZABETH.
Poor heart, adieu! I pity thy complaining.
LADY ANNE.
No more than from my soul I mourn for yours.
QUEEN ELIZABETH.
Farewell, thou woful welcomer of glory!
LADY ANNE.
Adieu, poor soul, that takest thy leave of it!
DUCHESS OF YORK [*to* DORSET].
Go thou to Richmond, and good fortune guide
    thee!—
[*to* ANNE] Go thou to Richard, and good angels
    tend thee!—
[*to* QUEEN ELIZABETH] Go thou to sanctuary,
    and good thoughts possess thee!—
I to my grave, where peace and rest lie with me!
Eighty odd years of sorrow have I seen,
And each hour's joy wrackt with a week of teen.
QUEEN ELIZABETH.
Stay yet, look back with me unto the Tower.
Pity, you ancient stones, those tender babes,

Whom envy hath immured within your walls!
Rough cradle for such little pretty ones!
Rude ragged nurse, old sullen playfellow
For tender princes, use my babies well!
So foolish sorrow bids your stones farewell.
                                        [*Exeunt.*

SCENE II.

London. The Palace.

Sound a sennet. Enter RICHARD, *in pomp, crown'd;* BUCKINGHAM, CATESBY, *a* PAGE, *and others.*

KING RICHARD.

STAND all apart.—Cousin of Buckingham,—
            DUKE OF BUCKINGHAM.
My gracious sovereign?
            KING RICHARD.
Give me thy hand. [*Here he ascendeth the throne.*]
    Thus high, by thy advice
And thy assistance, is King Richard seated:—
But shall we wear these honours for a day?
Or shall they last, and we rejoice in them?
            DUKE OF BUCKINGHAM.
Still live they, and for ever let them last!
            KING RICHARD.
Ah, Buckingham, now do I play the touch,
To try if thou be current gold indeed:—
Young Edward lives;—think now what I would
    speak.
            DUKE OF BUCKINGHAM.
Say on, my loving lord.
            KING RICHARD.
Why, Buckingham, I say, I would be king.
            DUKE OF BUCKINGHAM.
Why, so you are, my thrice-renowned liege.
            KING RICHARD.
Ha! am I king? 'tis so:—but Edward lives.
            DUKE OF BUCKINGHAM.
True, noble prince.
            KING RICHARD.
            O bitter consequence,
That Edward still should live! 'True, noble
    prince!'
Cousin, thou wert not wont to be so dull:
Shall I be plain?—I wish the bastards dead;
And I would have it suddenly perform'd.
What say'st thou now? speak suddenly, be brief.
            DUKE OF BUCKINGHAM.
Your Grace may do your pleasure.
            KING RICHARD.
Tut, tut, thou art all ice, thy kindness freezes:
Say, have I thy consent that they shall die?
            DUKE OF BUCKINGHAM.
Give me some breath, some little pause, my lord,
Before I positively speak herein:
I will resolve your Grace immediately.   [*Exit.*
    SIR WILLIAM CATESBY [*aside to another*].
The king is angry; see, he gnaws his lip.
            KING RICHARD.
I will converse with iron-witted fools
And unrespective boys: none are for me
That look into me with considerate eyes:
High-reaching Buckingham grows circumspect.
Boy!—
                    PAGE.
My lord?

KING RICHARD.
Know'st thou not any whom corrupting gold
Would tempt unto a close exploit of death?
                    PAGE.
I know a discontented gentleman,
Whose humble means match not his haughty
    mind:
Gold were as good as twenty orators,
And will, no doubt, tempt him to any thing.
            KING RICHARD.
What is his name?
                    PAGE.
                His name, my lord, is Tyrrel.
            KING RICHARD.
I partly know the man: go call him hither.
                        [*Exit* PAGE.
The deep-revolving witty Buckingham
No more shall be the neighbour to my counsels:
Hath he so long held out with me untired,
And stops he now for breath?—well, be it so.
            Enter STANLEY.
How now! what news with you?
            LORD STANLEY.
My lord, I hear the Marquess Dorset's fled
To Richmond, in those parts beyond the seas
Where he abides.
            KING RICHARD.
Come hither, Catesby:—rumour it abroad
That Anne, my wife, is very grievous sick;
I will take order for her keeping close.
Inquire me out some mean-born gentleman,
Whom I will marry straight to Clarence'
    daughter;—
The boy is foolish, and I fear not him.—
Look, how thou dream'st!—I say again, give out
That Anne my queen is sick, and like to die:
About it; for it stands me much upon,
To stop all hopes whose growth may damage me.
                        [*Exit* CATESBY.
I must be married to my brother's daughter,
Or else my kingdom stands on brittle glass:—
Murder her brothers, and then marry her!
Uncertain way of gain! But I am in
So far in blood, that sin will pluck on sin:
Tear-falling pity dwells not in this eye.
            Enter PAGE, *with* TYRREL.
Is thy name Tyrrel?
            SIR JAMES TYRREL.
James Tyrrel, and your most obedient subject.
            KING RICHARD.
Art thou indeed?
            SIR JAMES TYRREL.
                Prove me, my gracious sovereign.
            KING RICHARD.
Darest thou resolve to kill a friend of mine?
            SIR JAMES TYRREL.
Ay, my lord;
But I had rather kill two enemies.
            KING RICHARD.
Why, then thou hast it: two deep enemies,
Foes to my rest and my sweet sleep's disturbers,
Are they that I would have thee deal upon:—
Tyrrel, I mean those bastards in the Tower.
            SIR JAMES TYRREL.
Let me have open means to come to them,
And soon I'll rid you from the fear of them.

KING RICHARD.
Thou sing'st sweet music. Hark, come hither,
  Tyrrel:
Go, by this token:—rise, and lend thine ear:
                                    [Whispers.
There is no more but so:—say it is done,
And I will love thee, and prefer thee for it.
                SIR JAMES TYRREL.
I will dispatch it straight.   [Exit.
        Enter BUCKINGHAM.
        DUKE OF BUCKINGHAM.
My lord, I have consider'd in my mind
The late demand that you did sound me in.
            KING RICHARD
Well, let that rest. Dorset is fled to Richmond.
        DUKE OF BUCKINGHAM.
I hear the news, my lord.
            KING RICHARD.
Stanley, he is your wife's son:—well, look to
  it.
        DUKE OF BUCKINGHAM.
My lord, I claim the gift, my due by promise,
For which your honour and your faith is
  pawn'd;
Th' earldom of Hereford, and the movables,
The which you promised I should possess.
            KING RICHARD.
Stanley, look to your wife: if she convey
Letters to Richmond, you shall answer it.
        DUKE OF BUCKINGHAM.
What says your highness to my just request?
            KING RICHARD.
I do remember me,—Henry the Sixth
Did prophesy that Richmond should be king,
When Richmond was a little peevish boy.
A king! perhaps, perhaps—
        DUKE OF BUCKINGHAM.
My lord,—
            KING RICHARD.
How chance the prophet could not at that time
Have told me, I being by, that I should kill
  him?
        DUKE OF BUCKINGHAM.
My lord, your promise for the earldom,—
            KING RICHARD.
Richmond!—When last I was at Exeter,
The mayor in courtesy show'd me the castle,
And call'd it Rougemont: at which name I
  started,
Because a bard of Ireland told me once,
I should not live long after I saw Richmond.
        DUKE OF BUCKINGHAM.
My lord,—
            KING RICHARD.
Ay, what's o'clock?
        DUKE OF BUCKINGHAM.
I am thus bold to put your Grace in mind
Of what you promised me.
            KING RICHARD.
                Well, but what's o'clock?
        DUKE OF BUCKINGHAM.
Upon the stroke of ten.
            KING RICHARD.
                Well, let it strike.
        DUKE OF BUCKINGHAM.
Why let it strike?

KING RICHARD.
Because that, like a Jack, thou keep'st the stroke
Betwixt thy begging and my meditation.
I am not in the giving vein to-day.
        DUKE OF BUCKINGHAM.
Why, then resolve me whether you will or no.
            KING RICHARD.
Tut, tut,
Thou troublest me; I am not in the vein.
            [Exeunt all except BUCKINGHAM.
        DUKE OF BUCKINGHAM.
Is it even so? rewards he my true service
With such contempt? made I him king for this?
O, let me think on Hastings, and be gone
To Brecknock, while my fearful head is on! [Exit.

            SCENE III.
            The same.
        Enter TYRREL.
        SIR JAMES TYRREL.
THE tyrannous and bloody act is done,—
    The most arch deed of piteous massacre
That ever yet this land was guilty of.
Dighton and Forrest, whom I did suborn
To do this ruthless piece of butchery,
Albeit they were flesht villains, bloody dogs,
Melting with tenderness and mild compassion,
Wept like two children in their death's sad story.
'Lo, thus,' quoth Dighton, 'lay the gentle
  babes,'—
'Thus, thus,' quoth Forrest, 'girdling one another
Within their innocent alabaster arms:
Their lips were four red roses on a stalk,
Which in their summer beauty kist each other.
A book of prayers on their pillow lay;
Which once,' quoth Forrest, 'almost changed
  my mind;
But, O, the devil'—there the villain stopt;
When Dighton thus told on,—'We smothered
The most replenished sweet work of nature,
That from the prime creation e'er she framed.'
Hence both are gone with conscience and remorse;
They could not speak; and so I left them both,
To bear this tidings to the bloody king:—
And here he comes.
        Enter KING RICHARD.
                All health, my sovereign lord!
            KING RICHARD.
Kind Tyrrel, am I happy in thy news?
            SIR JAMES TYRREL.
If to have done the thing you gave in charge
Beget your happiness, be happy then,
For it is done.
            KING RICHARD.
But didst thou see them dead?
            SIR JAMES TYRREL.
I did, my lord.
            KING RICHARD.
            And buried, gentle Tyrrel?
            SIR JAMES TYRREL.
The chaplain of the Tower hath buried them;
But where, to say the truth, I do not know.
            KING RICHARD.
Come to me, Tyrrel, soon at after supper,
When thou shalt tell the process of their death.

Meantime, but think how I may do thee good,
And be inheritor of thy desire.
Farewell till then.
>> SIR JAMES TYRREL.
>> I humbly take my leave. [*Exit.*
>> KING RICHARD.
The son of Clarence have I pent up close;
His daughter meanly have I matcht in marriage;
The sons of Edward sleep in Abraham's bosom,
And Anne my wife hath bid the world good night.
Now, for I know the Breton Richmond aims
At young Elizabeth, my brother's daughter,
And, by that knot, looks proudly on the crown,
To her go I, a jolly thriving wooer.
>> *Enter* CATESBY.
>> SIR WILLIAM CATESBY.
My lord,—
>> KING RICHARD.
Good news or bad, that thou comest in so
>> bluntly?
>> SIR WILLIAM CATESBY.
Bad news, my lord: Ely is fled to Richmond;
And Buckingham, backt with the hardy Welsh-
>> men,
Is in the field, and still his power increaseth.
>> KING RICHARD.
Ely with Richmond troubles me more near
Than Buckingham and his rash-levied strength.
Come,—I have learn'd that fearful commenting
Is leaden servitor to dull delay;
Delay leads impotent and snail-paced beggary:
Then fiery expedition be my wing,
Jove's Mercury, and herald for a king!
Go, muster men: my counsel is my shield;
We must be brief, when traitors brave the field.
>> [*Exeunt.*

SCENE IV.
Before the palace.

Enter QUEEN MARGARET.

>> QUEEN MARGARET.
SO, now prosperity begins to mellow,
And drop into the rotten mouth of death.
Here in these confines slily have I lurkt,
To watch the waning of mine enemies.
A dire induction am I witness to,
And will to France; hoping the consequence
Will prove as bitter, black, and tragical.—
Withdraw thee, wretched Margaret: who comes
>> here?   [*Retires.*
Enter QUEEN ELIZABETH *and the* DUCHESS OF
>> YORK.
>> QUEEN ELIZABETH.
Ah, my poor princes! ah, my tender babes!
My unblown flowers, new-appearing sweets!
If yet your gentle souls fly in the air,
And be not fixt in doom perpetual,
Hover about me with your airy wings,
And hear your mother's lamentation!
>> QUEEN MARGARET [*aside*].
Hover about her; say, that right for right
Hath dimm'd your infant morn to aged night.
>> DUCHESS OF YORK.
So many miseries have crazed my voice,
That my woe-wearied tongue is still and mute.—
Edward Plantagenet, why art thou dead?

>> QUEEN MARGARET [*aside*].
Plantagenet doth quit Plantagenet,
Edward for Edward pays a dying debt.
>> QUEEN ELIZABETH.
Wilt Thou, O God, fly from such gentle lambs,
And throw them in the entrails of the wolf?
When didst Thou sleep, when such a deed was
>> done?
>> QUEEN MARGARET [*aside*].
When holy Harry died, and my sweet son.
>> DUCHESS OF YORK.
Dead life, blind sight, poor mortal living ghost,
Woe's scene, world's shame, grave's due by life
>> usurpt,
Brief abstract and record of tedious days,
Rest thy unrest on England's lawful earth,
>> [*Sitting down.*
Unlawfully made drunk with innocents' blood!
>> QUEEN ELIZABETH.
Ah, that thou wouldst as soon afford a grave
As thou canst yield a melancholy seat!
Then would I hide my bones, not rest them here.
Ah, who hath any cause to mourn but I?
>> [*Sitting down by her.*
>> QUEEN MARGARET [*coming forward*].
If ancient sorrow be most reverend,
Give mine the benefit of seniory,
And let my griefs frown on the upper hand.
If sorrow can admit society,
>> [*Sitting down with them.*
Tell o'er your woes again by viewing mine:—
I had an Edward, till a Richard kill'd him;
I had a Harry, till a Richard kill'd him:
Thou hadst an Edward, till a Richard kill'd
>> him;
Thou hadst a Richard, till a Richard kill'd him.
>> DUCHESS OF YORK.
I had a Richard too, and thou didst kill him;
I had a Rutland too, thou holp'st to kill him.
>> QUEEN MARGARET.
Thou hadst a Clarence too, and Richard kill'd
>> him.
From forth the kennel of thy womb hath crept
A hell-hound that doth hunt us all to death:
That dog, that had his teeth before his eyes,
To worry lambs, and lap their gentle blood;
That foul defacer of God's handiwork,
That excellent grand tyrant of the earth,
That reigns in galled eyes of weeping souls,—
Thy womb let loose, to chase us to our graves.—
O upright, just, and true-disposing God,
How do I thank thee, that this carnal cur
Preys on the issue of his mother's body,
And makes her pew-fellow with others' moan!
>> DUCHESS OF YORK.
O Harry's wife, triumph not in my woes!
God witness with me, I have wept for thine.
>> QUEEN MARGARET.
Bear with me; I am hungry for revenge,
And now I cloy me with beholding it.
Thy Edward he is dead, that kill'd my Edward;
Thy other Edward dead, to quit my Edward;
Young York he is but boot, because both they
Match not the high perfection of my loss:
Thy Clarence he is dead that stabb'd my
>> Edward;

And the beholders of this tragic play,
Th' adulterate Hastings, Rivers, Vaughan, Grey,
Ur timely smother'd in their dusky graves.
Richard yet lives, hell's black intelligencer;
Only reserved their factor, to buy souls,
And send them thither:—but at hand, at hand,
Ensues his piteous and unpitied end:
Earth gapes, hell burns, fiends roar, saints pray,
To have him suddenly convey'd from hence.—
Cancel his bond of life, dear God, I pray,
That I may live to say, 'The dog is dead!'

QUEEN ELIZABETH.

O, thou didst prophesy the time would come
That I should wish for thee to help me curse
That bottled spider, that foul bunch-backt toad!

QUEEN MARGARET.

I call'd thee then vain flourish of my fortune;
I call'd thee then poor shadow, painted queen;
The presentation of but what I was;
The flattering index of a direful pageant;
One heaved a-high, to be hurl'd down below;
A mother only mockt with two sweet babes;
A dream of what thou wast; a breath, a bubble;
A sign of dignity, a garish flag
To be the aim of every dangerous shot;
A queen in jest, only to fill the scene.   [brothers?
Where is thy husband now? where be thy
Where be thy two sons? wherein dost thou joy?
Who sues to thee, and cries, 'God save the
     queen'?
Where be the bending peers that flattered thee?
Where be the thronging troops that followed thee?
Decline all this, and see what now thou art:
For happy wife, a most distressed widow;
For joyful mother, one that wails the name;
For one being sued-to, one that humbly sues;
For queen, a very caitiff crown'd with care;
For one that scorn'd at me, now scorn'd of me:
For one being fear'd of all, now fearing one;
For one commanding all, obey'd of none;
Thus hath the course of justice wheel'd about,
And left thee but a very prey to time;
Having no more but thought of what thou wast,
To torture thee the more, being what thou art.
Thou didst usurp my place, and dost thou not
Usurp the just proportion of my sorrow?
Now thy proud neck bears half my burden'd yoke;
From which even here I slip my wearied head,
And leave the burden of it all on thee.
Farewell, York's wife; and queen of sad mischance:
These English woes will make me smile in France.

QUEEN ELIZABETH.

O thou well-skill'd in curses, stay awhile,
And teach me how to curse mine enemies!

QUEEN MARGARET.

Forbear to sleep the night, and fast the day;
Compare dead happiness with living woe;
Think that thy babes were fairer than they were,
And he that slew them fouler than he is:
Bettering thy loss makes the bad causer worse:
Revolving this will teach thee how to curse.

QUEEN ELIZABETH.

My words are dull; O, quicken them with thine!

QUEEN MARGARET.

Thy woes will make them sharp, and pierce like
     mine.   [Exit.

DUCHESS OF YORK.

Why should calamity be full of words?

QUEEN ELIZABETH.

Windy attorneys to their client woes,
Airy succeeders of intestate joys,
Poor breathing orators of miseries!
Let them have scope: though what they do impart
Help nothing else, yet do they ease the heart.

DUCHESS OF YORK.

If so, then be not tongue-tied: go with me,
And in the breath of bitter words let's smother
My damned son, that thy two sweet sons
     smother'd.   [Drum within.
I hear his drum:—be copious in exclaims.

Enter KING RICHARD and his TRAIN, marching,
            with drums and trumpets.

KING RICHARD.

Who intercepts me in my expedition?

DUCHESS OF YORK.

O, she that might have intercepted thee,
By strangling thee in her accursed womb,   [done!
From all the slaughters, wretch, that thou hast

QUEEN ELIZABETH.

Hidest thou that forehead with a golden crown,
Where should be branded, if that right were right,
The slaughter of the prince that owed that crown,
And the dire death of my poor sons and brothers?
Tell me, thou villain-slave, where are my children?

DUCHESS OF YORK.

Thou toad, thou toad, where is thy brother
     Clarence?
And little Ned Plantagenet, his son?

QUEEN ELIZABETH.

Where is the gentle Rivers, Vaughan, Grey?

DUCHESS OF YORK.

Where is kind Hastings?

KING RICHARD.

A flourish, trumpets! strike alarum, drums!
Let not the heavens hear these tell-tale women
Rail on the Lord's anointed: strike, I say!
            [Flourish. Alarums
Either be patient, and entreat me fair,
Or with the clamorous report of war
Thus will I drown your exclamations.

DUCHESS OF YORK.

Art thou my son?

KING RICHARD.

Ay, I thank God, my father, and yourself.

DUCHESS OF YORK.

Then patiently hear my impatience.

KING RICHARD.

Madam, I have a touch of your condition,
That cannot brook the accent of reproof.

DUCHESS OF YORK.

O, let me speak!

KING RICHARD.

     Do, then; but I'll not hear.

DUCHESS OF YORK.

I will be mild and gentle in my words.

KING RICHARD.

And brief, good mother; for I am in haste.

DUCHESS OF YORK.

Art thou so hasty? I have stay'd for thee,
God knows, in torment and in agony.

KING RICHARD.

And came I not at last to comfort you?

DUCHESS OF YORK.
No, by the holy rood, thou know'st it well,
Thou camest on earth to make the earth my hell.
A grievous burden was thy birth to me;
Tetchy and wayward was thy infancy;
Thy school-days frightful, desperate, wild, and
　　furious;
Thy prime of manhood daring, bold, and ven-
　　turous;
Thy age confirm'd, proud, subtle, bloody,
　　treacherous,
More mild, but yet more harmful-kind in hatred:
What comfortable hour canst thou name,
That ever graced me in thy company?
　　　　　KING RICHARD.
Faith, none, but Humphrey Hour, that call'd
　　your Grace
To breakfast once forth of my company.
If I be so disgracious in your eye,
Let me march on, and not offend you, madam.—
Strike up the drum.
　　　　　DUCHESS OF YORK.
　　　　　　　I prithee, hear me speak.
　　　　　KING RICHARD.
You speak too bitterly.
　　　　　DUCHESS OF YORK.
　　　　　　　Hear me a word;
For I shall never speak to thee again.
　　　　　KING RICHARD.
So.
　　　　　DUCHESS OF YORK.
Either thou wilt die, by God's just ordinance,
Ere from this war thou turn a conqueror;
Or I with grief and extreme age shall perish,
And never look upon thy face again.
Therefore take with thee my most heavy curse;
Which, in the day of battle, tire thee more
Than all the complete armour that thou wear'st!
My prayers on the adverse party fight;
And there the little souls of Edward's children
Whisper the spirits of thine enemies,
And promise them success and victory.
Bloody thou art, bloody will be thy end;
Shame serves thy life, and doth thy death attend.
　　　　　　　　　　　　　　　　　[Exit.
　　　　　QUEEN ELIZABETH.
Though far more cause, yet much less spirit to
　　curse
Abides in me; I say amen to her.　　　　[Going.
　　　　　KING RICHARD.
Stay, madam; I must speak a word with you.
　　　　　QUEEN ELIZABETH.
I have no more sons of the royal blood
For thee to murder· for my daughters, Richard,—
They shall be praying nuns, not weeping queens;
And therefore level not to hit their lives.
　　　　　KING RICHARD.
You have a daughter call'd Elizabeth,
Virtuous and fair, royal and gracious.
　　　　　QUEEN ELIZABETH.
And must she die for this? O, let her live,
And I'll corrupt her manners, stain her beauty;
Slander myself as false to Edward's bed;
Throw over her the veil of infamy:
So she may live unscarr'd of bleeding slaughter,
I will confess she was not Edward's daughter.

KING RICHARD.
Wrong not her birth, she is a royal princess.
　　　　　QUEEN ELIZABETH.
To save her life, I'll say she is not so.
　　　　　KING RICHARD.
Her life is safest only in her birth.
　　　　　QUEEN ELIZABETH.
And only in that safety died her brothers.
　　　　　KING RICHARD.
Lo, at their births good stars were opposite.
　　　　　QUEEN ELIZABETH.
No, to their lives ill friends were contrary.
　　　　　KING RICHARD.
All unavoided is the doom of destiny.
　　　　　QUEEN ELIZABETH.
True, when avoided grace makes destiny:
My babes were destined to a fairer death,
If grace had blest thee with a fairer life.
　　　　　KING RICHARD.
You speak as if that I had slain my cousins.
　　　　　QUEEN ELIZABETH.
Cousins, indeed; and by their uncle cozen'd
Of comfort, kingdom, kindred, freedom, life.
Whose hand soever lanced their tender hearts,
Thy head, all indirectly, gave direction:
No doubt the murderous knife was dull and blunt
Till it was whetted on thy stone-hard heart,
To revel in the entrails of my lambs.
But that still use of grief makes wild grief tame,
My tongue should to thy ears not name my boys
Till that my nails were anchor'd in thine eyes;
And I, in such a desperate bay of death,
Like a poor bark, of sails and tackling reft,
Rush all to pieces on thy rocky bosom.
　　　　　KING RICHARD.
Madam, so thrive I in my enterprise
And dangerous success of bloody wars,
As I intend more good to you and yours
Than ever you and yours by me were harm'd!
　　　　　QUEEN ELIZABETH.
What good is cover'd with the face of heaven,
To be discover'd, that can do me good?
　　　　　KING RICHARD.
Th' advancement of your children, gentle lady.
　　　　　QUEEN ELIZABETH.
Up to some scaffold, there to lose their heads?
　　　　　KING RICHARD.
No, to the dignity and height of honour,
The high imperial type of this earth's glory.
　　　　　QUEEN ELIZABETH.
Flatter my sorrows with report of it;
Tell me what state, what dignity, what honour,
Canst thou demise to any child of mine?
　　　　　KING RICHARD.
Even all I have; ay, and myself and all,
Will I withal endow a child of thine;
So in the Lethe of thy angry soul
Thou drown the sad remembrance of those
　　wrongs
Which thou supposest I have done to thee.
　　　　　QUEEN ELIZABETH.
Be brief, lest that the process of thy kindness
Last longer telling than thy kindness' date.
　　　　　KING RICHARD.
Then know, that from my soul I love thy
　　daughter.

QUEEN ELIZABETH.
My daughter's mother thinks it with her soul.
KING RICHARD.
What do you think?
QUEEN ELIZABETH.
That thou dost love my daughter from thy soul:
So, from thy soul's love, didst thou love her brothers;
And, from my heart's love, I do thank thee for it.
KING RICHARD.
Be not so hasty to confound my meaning:
I mean, that with my soul I love thy daughter,
And do intend to make her Queen of England.
QUEEN ELIZABETH.
Well, then, who dost thou mean shall be her king?
KING RICHARD.
Even he that makes her queen: who else should be?
QUEEN ELIZABETH.
What, thou?
KING RICHARD.
I, even I: what think you of it, madam?
QUEEN ELIZABETH.
How canst thou woo her?
KING RICHARD.
                    That would I learn of you,
As one being best acquainted with her humour.
QUEEN ELIZABETH.
And wilt thou learn of me?
KING RICHARD.
          Madam, with all my heart.
QUEEN ELIZABETH.
Send to her, by the man that slew her brothers,
A pair of bleeding hearts; thereon engrave
'Edward and York;' then haply will she weep:
Therefore present to her—as sometime Margaret
Did to thy father, steept in Rutland's blood—
A handkerchief; which, say to her, did drain
The purple sap from her sweet brother's body,
And bid her dry her weeping eyes withal.
If this inducement move her not to love,
Send her a letter of thy noble deeds;
Tell her thou madest away her uncle Clarence,
Her uncle Rivers; ay, and, for her sake,
Madest quick conveyance with her good aunt Anne.
KING RICHARD.
You mock me, madam; this is not the way
To win your daughter.
QUEEN ELIZABETH.
                There is no other way;
Unless thou couldst put on some other shape,
And not be Richard that hath done all this.
KING RICHARD.
Say that I did all this for love of her?
QUEEN ELIZABETH.
Nay, then indeed she cannot choose but hear thee,
Having bought love with such a bloody spoil.
KING RICHARD.
Look, what is done cannot be now amended:
Men shall deal unadvisedly sometimes,
Which after-hours gives leisure to repent.
If I did take the kingdom from your sons,
To make amends, I'll give it to your daughter.
If I have kill'd the issue of your womb,
To quicken your increase, I will beget

Mine issue of your blood upon your daughter:
A grandam's name is little less in love
Than is the doting title of a mother;
They are as children but one step below,
Even of your mettle, of your very blood;
Of all one pain,—save for a night of groans
Endured of her, for whom you bid like sorrow.
Your children were vexation to your youth;
But mine shall be a comfort to your age.
The loss you have is but a son being king,
And by that loss your daughter is made queen.
I cannot make you what amends I would,
Therefore accept such kindness as I can.
Dorset your son, that with a fearful soul
Leads discontented steps in foreign soil,
This fair alliance quickly shall call home
To high promotions and great dignity:
The king, that calls your beauteous daughter wife,
Familiarly shall call thy Dorset brother;
Again shall you be mother to a king,
And all the ruins of distressful times
Repair'd with double riches of content.
What! we have many goodly days to see:
The liquid drops of tears that you have shed
Shall come again, transform'd to orient pearl,
Advantaging their loan with interest
Of ten-times-double gain of happiness.
Go, then, my mother, to thy daughter go;
Make bold her bashful years with your experience;
Prepare her ears to hear a wooer's tale;
Put in her tender heart th' aspiring flame
Of golden sovereignty; acquaint the princess
With the sweet silent hours of marriage joys:
And when this arm of mine hath chastised
The petty rebel, dull-brain'd Buckingham,
Bound with triumphant garlands will I come,
And lead thy daughter to a conqueror's bed;
To whom I will retail my conquest won,
And she shall be sole victress, Cæsar's Cæsar.
QUEEN ELIZABETH.
What were I best to say? her father's brother
Would be her lord? or shall I say, her uncle?
Or, he that slew her brothers and her uncles?
Under what title shall I woo for thee,
That God, the law, my honour, and her love,
Can make seem pleasing to her tender years?
KING RICHARD.
Infer fair England's peace by this alliance.
QUEEN ELIZABETH.
Which she shall purchase with still-lasting war.
KING RICHARD.
Tell her, the king, that may command, entreats.
QUEEN ELIZABETH.
That at her hands which the king's King forbids.
KING RICHARD.
Say, she shall be a high and mighty queen.
QUEEN ELIZABETH.
To wail the title, as her mother doth.
KING RICHARD.
Say, I will love her everlastingly.
QUEEN ELIZABETH.
But how long shall that title 'ever' last?
KING RICHARD
Sweetly in force unto her fair life's end.

QUEEN ELIZABETH.
But how long fairly shall her sweet life last?
KING RICHARD.
As long as heaven and nature lengthens it.
QUEEN ELIZABETH.
As long as hell and Richard likes of it.
KING RICHARD.
Say, I, her sovereign, am her subject love.
QUEEN ELIZABETH.
But she, your subject, loathes such sovereignty.
KING RICHARD.
Be eloquent in my behalf to her.
QUEEN ELIZABETH.
An honest tale speeds best being plainly told.
KING RICHARD.
Then, plainly to her tell my loving tale.
QUEEN ELIZABETH.
Plain and not honest is too harsh a style.
KING RICHARD.
Your reasons are too shallow and too quick.
QUEEN ELIZABETH.
O, no, my reasons are too deep and dead;—
Too deep and dead, poor infants, in their graves.
KING RICHARD.
Harp not on that string, madam; that is past.
QUEEN ELIZABETH.
Harp on it still shall I till heart-strings break.
KING RICHARD.
Now, by my George, my garter, and my
   crown,—
QUEEN ELIZABETH.
Profaned, dishonour'd, and the third usurpt.
KING RICHARD.
I swear—
QUEEN ELIZABETH.
      By nothing; for this is no oath:
Thy George, profaned, hath lost his holy honour;
Thy garter, blemisht, pawn'd his knightly virtue;
Thy crown, usurpt, disgraced his kingly glory.
If something thou wouldst swear to be believed,
Swear, then, by something that thou hast not
   wrong'd.
KING RICHARD.
Now, by the world,—
QUEEN ELIZABETH.
        'Tis full of thy foul wrongs.
KING RICHARD.
My father's death,—
QUEEN ELIZABETH.
      Thy life hath that dishonour'd.
KING RICHARD.
Then, by myself,—
QUEEN ELIZABETH.
      Thyself is self-misused.
KING RICHARD.
Why, then, by God,—
QUEEN ELIZABETH.
      God's wrong is most of all.
If thou hadst fear'd to break an oath by Him,
The unity the king thy brother made
Had not been broken, nor my brother slain:
If thou hadst fear'd to break an oath by Him,
Th' imperial metal, circling now thy head,
Had graced the tender temples of my child;
And both the princes had been breathing here,
Which now, two tender bedfellows for dust,

Thy broken faith hath made a prey for worms.
What canst thou swear by now?
KING RICHARD.
         The time to come.
QUEEN ELIZABETH.
That thou hast wronged in the time o'erpast;
For I myself have many tears to wash
Hereafter time, for time past wrong'd by thee.
The children live, whose parents thou hast
   slaughter'd,
Ungovern'd youth, to wail it in their age;
The parents live, whose children thou hast
   butcher'd,
Old wither'd plants, to wail it with their age.
Swear not by time to come; for that thou hast
Misused ere used, by time misused o'erpast.
KING RICHARD.
As I intend to prosper and repent,
So thrive I in my dangerous attempt
Of hostile arms! myself myself confound!
Heaven and fortune bar me happy hours!
Day, yield me not thy light; nor, night, thy
   rest!
Be opposite all planets of good luck
To my proceeding!—if, with pure heart's love,
Immaculate devotion, holy thoughts,
I tender not thy beauteous princely daughter!
In her consists my happiness and thine;
Without her, follows to myself and thee,
Herself, the land, and many a Christian soul,
Death, desolation, ruin, and decay:
It cannot be avoided but by this;
It will not be avoided but by this.
Therefore, dear mother,—I must call you so,—
Be the attorney of my love to her:
Plead what I will be, not what I have been;
Not my deserts, but what I will deserve:
Urge the necessity and state of times,
And be not peevish-fond in great designs.
QUEEN ELIZABETH.
Shall I be tempted of the devil thus?
KING RICHARD.
Ay, if the devil tempt thee to do good.
QUEEN ELIZABETH.
Shall I forget myself to be myself?
KING RICHARD.
Ay, if your self's remembrance wrong yourself.
QUEEN ELIZABETH.
But thou didst kill my children.
KING RICHARD.
But in your daughter's womb I'll bury them:
Where, in that nest of spicery, they shall breed
Selves of themselves, to your recomforture.
QUEEN ELIZABETH.
Shall I go win my daughter to thy will?
KING RICHARD.
And be a happy mother by the deed.
QUEEN ELIZABETH.
I go.—Write to me very shortly,
And you shall understand from me her mind.
KING RICHARD.
Bear her my true love's kiss; and so, farewell.
          [*Exit* QUEEN ELIZABETH.
Relenting fool, and shallow, changing woman!
   Enter RATCLIFF; CATESBY *following*.
How now! what news?

SIR RICHARD RATCLIFF.
My gracious sovereign, on the western coast
Rideth a puissant navy; to the shore
Throng many doubtful hollow-hearted friends,
Unarm'd, and unresolved to beat them back:
'Tis thought that Richmond is their admiral;
And there they hull, expecting but the aid
Of Buckingham to welcome them ashore.
KING RICHARD.
Some light-foot friend post to the Duke of
　　Norfolk:—
Ratcliff, thyself,—or Catesby; where is he?
SIR WILLIAM CATESBY.
Here, my good lord.
KING RICHARD.
Fly to the duke.—[to RATCLIFF] Post thou to
　　Salisbury:
When thou comest thither,—[to CATESBY] Dull,
　　unmindful villain,
Why stay'st thou here, and go'st not to the duke?
SIR WILLIAM CATESBY.
First, mighty liege, tell me your highness'
　　pleasure,
What from your Grace I shall deliver to him.
KING RICHARD.
O, true, good Catesby:—bid him levy straight
The greatest strength and power he can make,
And meet me suddenly at Salisbury.
SIR WILLIAM CATESBY.
I go.　　　　　　　　　　　　　　　　　　[Exit.
SIR RICHARD RATCLIFF.
What, may it please you, shall I do at Salisbury?
KING RICHARD.
Why, what wouldst thou do there before I go?
SIR RICHARD RATCLIFF.
Your highness told me I should post before.
Enter STANLEY.
KING RICHARD.
My mind is changed.—Stanley, what news with
　　you?
LORD STANLEY.　　　　　　　　　　[ing;
None good, my liege, to please you with the hear-
Nor none so bad, but well may be reported.
KING RICHARD.
Hoyday, a riddle! neither good nor bad!
What need'st thou run so many miles about,
When thou mayst tell thy tale the nearest way?
Once more, what news?
LORD STANLEY.
　　　　　　　Richmond is on the seas.
KING RICHARD.
There let him sink, and be the seas on him,
White-liver'd runagate! what doth he there?
LORD STANLEY.
I know not, mighty sovereign, but by guess.
KING RICHARD.
Well, as you guess?
LORD STANLEY.
Stirr'd up by Dorset, Buckingham, and Ely,
He makes for England, here, to claim the crown.
KING RICHARD.
Is the chair empty? is the sword unsway'd?
Is the king dead? the empire unpossest?
What heir of York is there alive but we?
And who is England's king but great York's heir?
Then, tell me, what makes he upon the seas?

LORD STANLEY.
Unless for that, my liege, I cannot guess.
KING RICHARD.
Unless for that he comes to be your liege,
You cannot guess wherefore the Welshman
　　comes.
Thou wilt revolt, and fly to him, I fear.
LORD STANLEY.
No, mighty liege, therefore mistrust me not.
KING RICHARD.
Where is thy power, then, to beat him back?
Where be thy tenants and thy followers?
Are they not now upon the western shore,
Safe-conducting the rebels from their ships?
LORD STANLEY.
No, my good lord, my friends are in the north.
KING RICHARD.
Cold friends to me: what do they in the north,
When they should serve their sovereign in the
　　west?
LORD STANLEY.
They have not been commanded, mighty king:
Pleaseth your majesty to give me leave,
I'll muster up my friends, and meet your Grace
Where and what time your majesty shall please.
KING RICHARD.
Ay, ay, thou wouldst be gone to join with
　　Richmond:
I will not trust you, sir.
LORD STANLEY.
　　　　　　　Most mighty sovereign,
You have no cause to hold my friendship doubt-
　　ful:
I never was nor never will be false.
KING RICHARD.
Go, then, and muster men. But leave behind
Your son, George Stanley: look your faith be
　　firm,
Or else his head's assurance is but frail.
LORD STANLEY.
So deal with him as I prove true to you.　　[Exit.
Enter a MESSENGER.
MESSENGER.
My gracious sovereign, now in Devonshire,
As I by friends am well advertised,
Sir Edward Courtney, and the haughty prelate
Bishop of Exeter, his elder brother,
With many moe confederates, are in arms.
Enter a second MESSENGER.
SECOND MESSENGER.
In Kent, my liege, the Guildfords are in arms;
And every hour more competitors
Flock to the rebels, and their power grows strong.
Enter a third MESSENGER.
THIRD MESSENGER.
My lord, the army of great Buckingham—
KING RICHARD.
Out on ye, owls! nothing but songs of death?
　　　　　　　　　　　　　　　[He striketh him.
There, take thou that, till thou bring better news.
THIRD MESSENGER.
The news I have to tell your majesty
Is, that by sudden floods and fall of waters,
Buckingham's army is dispersed and scatter'd;
And he himself wander'd away alone,
No man knows whither.

KING RICHARD.

I cry thee mercy:
There is my purse to cure that blow of thine.
Hath any well-advised friend proclaim'd
Reward to him that brings the traitor in?

THIRD MESSENGER.

Such proclamation hath been made, my lord.

Enter a fourth MESSENGER.

FOURTH MESSENGER.

Sir Thomas Lovel and Lord Marquess Dorset,
'Tis said, my liege, in Yorkshire are in arms.
But this good comfort bring I to your highness,—
The Breton navy is dispersed by tempest:
Richmond, in Dorsetshire, sent out a boat
Unto the shore, to ask those on the banks
If they were his assistants, yea or no;
Who answer'd him, they came from Buckingham
Upon his party: he, mistrusting them,
Hoised sail, and made his course again for Bre-
    tagne.

KING RICHARD.

March on, march on, since we are up in arms;
If not to fight with foreign enemies,
Yet to beat down these rebels here at home.

Enter CATESBY.

SIR WILLIAM CATESBY.

My liege, the Duke of Buckingham is taken,—
That is the best news: that the Earl of Richmond
Is with a mighty power landed at Milford,
Is colder tidings, yet they must be told.

KING RICHARD.

Away towards Salisbury! while we reason here,
A royal battle might be won and lost:—
Some one take order Buckingham be brought
To Salisbury; the rest march on with me.

[Flourish. Exeunt.

SCENE V.

LORD DERBY'S *house.*

Enter DERBY *and* SIR CHRISTOPHER URSWICK.

EARL OF DERBY.

SIR Christopher, tell Richmond this from me:—
That, in the sty of this most bloody boar,
My son George Stanley is frankt up in hold:
If I revolt, off goes young George's head;
The fear of that withholds my present aid.
But, tell me, where is princely Richmond now?

SIR CHRISTOPHER URSWICK.

At Pembroke, or at Ha'rford-west, in Wales.

EARL OF DERBY.

What men of name resort to him?

SIR CHRISTOPHER URSWICK.

Sir Walter Herbert, a renowned soldier;
Sir Gilbert Talbot, Sir William Stanley;
Oxford, redoubted Pembroke, Sir James Blunt,
And Rice ap Thomas, with a valiant crew;
And many moe of noble fame and worth:
And towards London they do bend their course,
If by the way they be not fought withal.

EARL OF DERBY.

Return unto thy lord; commend me to him:
Tell him the queen hath heartily consented
He shall espouse Elizabeth her daughter.
These letters will resolve him of my mind.
Farewell.

[Exeunt.

ACT V. SCENE I.

Salisbury. An open place.

Enter the SHERIFF, *and* BUCKINGHAM, *with
halberds, led to execution.*

DUKE OF BUCKINGHAM.

WILL not King Richard let me speak with
    him?

SHERIFF.

No, my good lord; therefore be patient.

DUKE OF BUCKINGHAM.

Hastings, and Edward's children, Rivers, Grey,
Holy King Henry, and thy fair son Edward,
Vaughan, and all that have miscarried
By underhand corrupted foul injustice,—
If that your moody discontented souls
Do through the clouds behold this present hour,
Even for revenge mock my destruction!—
This is All-Souls' day, fellows, is it not?—

SHERIFF.

It is, my lord.

DUKE OF BUCKINGHAM.

Why, then All-Souls' day is my body's doomsday.
This is the day that, in King Edward's time,
I wisht might fall on me, when I was found
False to his children or his wife's allies;
This is the day wherein I wisht to fall
By the false faith of him I trusted most;
This, this All-Souls' day to my fearful soul
Is the determined respite of my wrongs:
That high All-Seer that I dallied with
Hath turn'd my feigned prayer on my head,
And given in earnest what I begg'd in jest.
Thus doth He force the swords of wicked men
To turn their own points on their masters'
    bosoms:
Thus Margaret's curse falls heavy on my neck,—
'When he,' quoth she, 'shall split thy heart with
    sorrow,
Remember Margaret was a prophetess.'—
Come, sirs, convey me to the block of shame;
Wrong hath but wrong, and blame the due of
    blame.   [Exeunt.

SCENE II.

Plain near Tamworth.

Enter RICHMOND, OXFORD, BLUNT, *and others,
with drum and colours.*

EARL OF RICHMOND.

FELLOWS in arms, and my most loving
    friends,
Bruised underneath the yoke of tyranny,
Thus far into the bowels of the land
Have we marcht on without impediment;
And here receive we from our father Stanley
Lines of fair comfort and encouragement.
The wretched, bloody, and usurping boar,
That spoil'd your summer fields and fruitful
    vines,   [trough
Swills your warm blood like wash, and makes his
In your embowell'd bosoms,—this foul swine
Lies now even in the centre of this isle,
Near to the town of Leicester, as we learn:
From Tamworth thither is but one day's march.
In God's name, cheerly on, courageous friends,
To reap the harvest of perpetual peace

By this one bloody trial of sharp war.
EARL OF OXFORD.
Every man's conscience is a thousand swords,
To fight against this guilty homicide.
SIR WALTER HERBERT.
I doubt not but his friends will turn to us.
SIR JAMES BLUNT.
He hath no friends but what are friends for fear,
Which in his dearest need will shrink from him.
EARL OF RICHMOND.
All for our vantage. Then, in God's name,
march:
True hope is swift, and flies with swallow's wings;
Kings it makes gods, and meaner creatures kings.
                                   [*Exeunt.*

SCENE III.

Bosworth field.

Enter KING RICHARD *in arms, with* NORFOLK,
the EARL OF SURREY, *and others.*

KING RICHARD.
HERE pitch our tents, even here in Bosworth
field.
My Lord of Surrey, why look you so sad?
EARL OF SURREY.
My heart is ten times lighter than my looks.
KING RICHARD.
My Lord of Norfolk,—
DUKE OF NORFOLK.
                  Here, most gracious liege.
KING RICHARD.
Norfolk, we must have knocks; ha! must we not?
DUKE OF NORFOLK.
We must both give and take, my loving lord.
KING RICHARD.
Up with my tent! here will I lie to-night;
    [SOLDIERS *begin to set up the* KING'S *tent.*
But where to-morrow? Well, all's one for that.—
Who hath descried the number of the traitors?
DUKE OF NORFOLK.
Six or seven thousand is their utmost power.
KING RICHARD.
Why, our battalia trebles that account:
Besides, the king's name is a tower of strength,
Which they upon the adverse party want.—
Up with the tent!—Come, noble gentlemen,
Let us survey the vantage of the ground;—
Call for some men of sound direction:—
Let's lack no discipline, make no delay;
For, lords, to-morrow is a busy day.   [*Exeunt.*

Enter, on the other side of the field, RICHMOND,
    BRANDON, OXFORD, *and others.   Some of the*
    SOLDIERS *pitch* RICHMOND'S *tent.*
EARL OF RICHMOND.
The weary sun hath made a golden set,
And, by the bright track of his fiery car,
Gives token of a goodly day to-morrow.—
Sir William Brandon, you shall bear my
standard.—
Give me some ink and paper in my tent:
I'll draw the form and model of our battle,
Limit each leader to his several charge,
And part in just proportion our small power.—
My Lord of Oxford,—you, Sir William Bran-
don,—

And you, Sir Walter Herbert,—stay with me.—
The Earl of Pembroke keeps his regiment:—
Good Captain Blunt, bear my good-night to him,
And by the second hour in the morning
Desire the earl to see me in my tent:
Yet one thing more, good captain, do for me,—
Where is Lord Stanley quarter'd, do you know?
SIR JAMES BLUNT.
Unless I have mista'en his colours much,—
Which well I am assured I have not done,—
His regiment lies half a mile at least
South from the mighty power of the king.
EARL OF RICHMOND.
If without peril it be possible,   [him,
Sweet Blunt, make some good means to speak with
And give him from me this most needful note.
SIR JAMES BLUNT.
Upon my life, my lord, I'll undertake it;
And so, God give you quiet rest to-night!
EARL OF RICHMOND.
Good night, good Captain Blunt. [*Exit* BLUNT.]
Come, gentlemen,
Let us consult upon to-morrow's business:
In to my tent; the air is raw and cold.
                    [*They withdraw into the tent.*

Enter, to his tent, KING RICHARD, NORFOLK,
    RATCLIFF, CATESBY, *and others.*
KING RICHARD.
What is't o'clock?
SIR WILLIAM CATESBY.
                  It's supper-time, my lord;
It's nine o'clock.
KING RICHARD.
                  I will not sup to-night.—
Give me some ink and paper.—
What, is my beaver easier than it was?
And all my armour laid into my tent?
SIR WILLIAM CATESBY.
It is, my liege; and all things are in readiness.
KING RICHARD.
Good Norfolk, hie thee to thy charge;
Use careful watch, choose trusty sentinels.
DUKE OF NORFOLK.
I go, my lord.
KING RICHARD.
Stir with the lark to-morrow, gentle Norfolk.
DUKE OF NORFOLK.
I warrant you, my lord.   [*Exit.*
KING RICHARD.
Catesby,—
SIR WILLIAM CATESBY.
My lord?
KING RICHARD.
            Send out a pursuivant-at-arms
To Stanley's regiment; bid him bring his power
Before sunrising, lest his son George fall
Into the blind cave of eternal night.
                              [*Exit* CATESBY.
Fill me a bowl of wine.—Give me a watch.—
Saddle white Surrey for the field to-morrow.—
Look that my staves be sound, and not too
heavy.—
Ratcliff,—
SIR RICHARD RATCLIFF.
My lord?

KING RICHARD.
Saw'st thou the melancholy Lord Northumberland?
SIR RICHARD RATCLIFF.
Thomas the Earl of Surrey, and himself,
Much about cock-shut time, from troop to troop
Went through the army, cheering up the soldiers.
KING RICHARD.
So, I am satisfied.—Give me a bowl of wine:
I have not that alacrity of spirit,
Nor cheer of mind, that I was wont to have.
                                        [Wine brought.
Set it down.—Is ink and paper ready?
SIR RICHARD RATCLIFF.
It is, my lord.
KING RICHARD.
Bid my guard watch; leave me.—Ratcliff,
About the mid of night come to my tent
And help to arm me.—Leave me, I say.
                        [Exeunt RATCLIFF and others.

Enter DERBY to RICHMOND in his tent; LORDS
    and GENTLEMEN.
EARL OF DERBY.
Fortune and victory sit on thy helm!
EARL OF RICHMOND.
All comfort that the dark night can afford
Be to thy person, noble father-in-law!
Tell me, how fares our loving mother?
EARL OF DERBY.
I, by attorney, bless thee from thy mother,
Who prays continually for Richmond's good:
So much for that. The silent hours steal on,
And flaky darkness breaks within the east.
In brief,—for so the season bids us be,—
Prepare thy battle early in the morning,
And put thy fortune to th' arbitrement
Of bloody strokes and mortal-staring war.
I, as I may,—that which I would I cannot,—
With best advantage will deceive the time,
And aid thee in this doubtful shock of arms:
But on thy side I may not be too forward,
Lest, being seen, thy brother, tender George,
Be executed in his father's sight.
Farewell: the leisure and the fearful time
Cuts off the ceremonious vows of love
And ample interchange of sweet discourse,
Which so-long-sunder'd friends should dwell
    upon:
God give us leisure for these rites of love!
Once more, adieu: be valiant, and speed well!
EARL OF RICHMOND.
Good lords, conduct him to his regiment:
I'll strive, with troubled thoughts, to take a
    nap,
Lest leaden slumber peise me down to-morrow,
When I should mount with wings of victory:
Once more, good night, kind lords and gentlemen.
                        [Exeunt all but RICHMOND.
O Thou, whose captain I account myself,
Look on my forces with a gracious eye;
Put in their hands Thy bruising irons of
    wrath,
That they may crush down with a heavy fall
Th' usurping helmets of our adversaries!
Make us Thy ministers of chastisement,

That we may praise Thee in the victory!
To Thee I do commend my watchful soul,
Ere I let fall the windows of mine eyes:
Sleeping and waking, O, defend me still! [Sleeps.

Enter the GHOST of PRINCE EDWARD, son to
            KING HENRY THE SIXTH.
GHOST [to KING RICHARD].
Let me sit heavy on thy soul to-morrow!
Think, how thou stabb'dst me in my prime of
    youth
At Tewksbury: despair, therefore, and die!
[to RICHMOND] Be cheerful, Richmond; for the
    wronged souls
Of butcher'd princes fight in thy behalf:
King Henry's issue, Richmond, comforts thee.
        Enter the GHOST of HENRY THE SIXTH.
GHOST [to KING RICHARD].
When I was mortal, my anointed body
By thee was punched full of deadly holes:
Think on the Tower and me: despair, and die,
Harry the Sixth bids thee despair and die!
[to RICHMOND] Virtuous and holy, be thou conqueror!
Harry, that prophesied thou shouldst be king,
Doth comfort thee in thy sleep: live, and
    flourish!
            Enter the GHOST of CLARENCE.
GHOST [to KING RICHARD].
Let me sit heavy on thy soul to-morrow!
I, that was washt to death with fulsome wine,
Poor Clarence, by thy guile betray'd to death!
To-morrow in the battle think on me,
And fall thy edgeless sword: despair, and die!
[to RICHMOND] Thou offspring of the house of
    Lancaster,
The wronged heirs of York do pray for thee:
Good angels guard thy battle! live, and flourish!
    Enter the GHOSTS of RIVERS, GREY, and
                    VAUGHAN.
GHOST OF RIVERS [to KING RICHARD].
Let me sit heavy on thy soul to-morrow,
Rivers, that died at Pomfret! despair, and die!
        GHOST OF GREY [to KING RICHARD].
Think upon Grey, and let thy soul despair!
    GHOST OF VAUGHAN [to KING RICHARD].
Think upon Vaughan, and, with guilty fear,
Let fall thy lance: despair, and die!
            ALL THREE [to RICHMOND].
Awake, and think our wrongs in Richard's
    bosom
Will conquer him!—awake, and win the day!
            Enter the GHOST of HASTINGS.
GHOST [to KING RICHARD].
Bloody and guilty, guiltily awake,
And in a bloody battle end thy days!
Think on Lord Hastings: despair, and die.
[to RICHMOND] Quiet untroubled soul, awake,
    awake!
Arm, fight, and conquer, for fair England's
    sake!
Enter the GHOSTS of the two young PRINCES.
            GHOSTS [to KING RICHARD].
Dream on thy cousins smothered in the Tower:
Let us be lead within thy bosom, Richard,

And weigh thee down to ruin, shame, and death!
Thy nephews' souls bid thee despair and die!
[*to* RICHMOND] Sleep, Richmond, sleep in peace,
   and wake in joy;
Good angels guard thee from the boar's annoy!
Live, and beget a happy race of kings!
Edward's unhappy sons do bid thee flourish.
     Enter the GHOST *of* ANNE, *his wife.*
     GHOST [*to* KING RICHARD].
Richard, thy wife, that wretched Anne thy wife,
That never slept a quiet hour with thee,
Now fills thy sleep with perturbations:
To-morrow in the battle think on me,
And fall thy edgeless sword: despair, and die!
[*to* RICHMOND] Thou quiet soul, sleep thou a
   quiet sleep;
Dream of success and happy victory!
Thy adversary's wife doth pray for thee.
     Enter the GHOST *of* BUCKINGHAM.
     GHOST [*to* KING RICHARD].
The first was I that helpt thee to the crown;
The last was I that felt thy tyranny:
O, in the battle think on Buckingham,
And die in terror of thy guiltiness!
Dream on, dream on, of bloody deeds and death:
Fainting, despair; despairing, yield thy breath!
[*to* RICHMOND] I died for hope ere I could lend
   thee aid:
But cheer thy heart, and be thou not dismay'd:
God and good angels fight on Richmond's
   side;
And Richard falls in height of all his pride.
     [*The* GHOSTS *vanish.* KING RICHARD
     starts out of his dream.
     KING RICHARD.
Give me another horse,—bind up my wounds,—
Have mercy, Jesu!—Soft! I did but dream.
O coward conscience, how dost thou afflict me!
The lights burn blue. It is now dead midnight.
Cold fearful drops stand on my trembling
   flesh.
What do I fear? myself? there's none else by:
Richard loves Richard; that is, I am I.
Is there a murderer here? No;—yes, I am:
Then fly. What, from myself? Great reason why:
Lest I revenge. What, myself upon myself?
Alack, I love myself. Wherefore? for any good
That I myself have done unto myself?
O, no! alas, I rather hate myself
For hateful deeds committed by myself!
I am a villain: yet I lie, I am not.
Fool, of thyself speak well:—fool, do not flatter.
My conscience hath a thousand several tongues,
And every tongue brings in a several tale,
And every tale condemns me for a villain.
Perjury, perjury, in the high'st degree;
Murder, stern murder, in the direst degree;
All several sins, all used in each degree,
Throng to the bar, crying all 'Guilty! guilty!'
I shall despair. There is no creature loves me;
And if I die, no soul shall pity me:
Nay, wherefore should they,—since that I myself
Find in myself no pity to myself?
     Enter RATCLIFF.
     SIR RICHARD RATCLIFF.
My lord,—

     KING RICHARD.
Who's there?
     SIR RICHARD RATCLIFF.
My lord, 'tis I. The early village-cock
Hath twice done salutation to the morn;
Your friends are up, and buckle on their arm-
   our.
     KING RICHARD.
O Ratcliff, I have dream'd a fearful dream!—
What thinkest thou,—will our friends prove all
   true?
     SIR RICHARD RATCLIFF.
No doubt, my lord.
     KING RICHARD.
        O Ratcliff, I fear, I fear!—
Methought the souls of all that I had murder'd
Came to my tent; and every one did threat
To-morrow's vengeance on the head of Richard.
     SIR RICHARD RATCLIFF.
Nay, good my lord, be not afraid of shadows.
     KING RICHARD.
By the apostle Paul, shadows to-night
Have struck more terror to the soul of Richard
Than can the substance of ten thousand soldiers
Armed in proof and led by shallow Richmond.
It is not yet near day. Come, go with me;
Under our tents I'll play the eaves-dropper,
To hear if any mean to shrink from me.
     [*Exeunt* KING RICHARD *and* RATCLIFF.

Enter the LORDS *to* RICHMOND, *sitting in his tent.*
     LORDS.
Good morrow, Richmond!
     EARL OF RICHMOND [*waking*].
Cry mercy, lords and watchful gentlemen,
That you have ta'en a tardy sluggard here.
     LORDS.
How have you slept, my lord?
     EARL OF RICHMOND.
The sweetest sleep, and fairest-boding dreams
That ever enter'd in a drowsy head,
Have I since your departure had, my lords.
Methought their souls, whose bodies Richard
   murder'd,
Came to my tent, and cried on victory:
I promise you, my heart is very jocund
In the remembrance of so fair a dream.
How far into the morning is it, lords?
     LORDS.
Upon the stroke of four.
     EARL OF RICHMOND.
Why, then 'tis time to arm and give direction.
     His oration to his SOLDIERS.
More than I have said, loving countrymen,
The leisure and enforcement of the time
Forbids to dwell upon: yet remember this,—
God and our good cause fight upon our side;
The prayers of holy saints and wronged souls,
Like high-rear'd bulwarks, stand before our
   faces;
Richard except, those whom we fight against
Had rather have us win than him they follow:
For what is he they follow? truly, gentlemen,
A bloody tyrant and a homicide;
One rais'd in blood, and one in blood establisht;
One that made means to come by what he hath,

And slaughter'd those that were the means to
help him;
A base foul stone, made precious by the foil
Of England's chair, where he is falsely set;
One that hath ever been God's enemy:
Then, if you fight against God's enemy,
God will, in justice, ward you as his soldiers;
If you do sweat to put a tyrant down,
You sleep in peace, the tyrant being slain;
If you do fight against your country's foes,
Your country's fat shall pay your pains the hire;
If you do fight in safeguard of your wives,
Your wives shall welcome home the conquerors;
If you do free your children from the sword,
Your children's children quit it in your age.
Then, in the name of God and all these rights,
Advance your standards, draw your willing
swords.
For me, the ransom of my bold attempt
Shall be this cold corpse on the earth's cold face;
But if I thrive, the gain of my attempt
The least of you shall share his part thereof.
Sound drums and trumpets, boldly and cheer-
fully;
God and Saint George! Richmond and victory!
[*Exeunt.*

Enter KING RICHARD, RATCLIFF, ATTEN-
DANTS, *and* FORCES.
KING RICHARD.
What said Northumberland as touching Rich-
mond?
SIR RICHARD RATCLIFF.
That he was never trained up in arms.
KING RICHARD.
He said the truth: and what said Surrey, then?
SIR RICHARD RATCLIFF.
He smiled, and said, 'The better for our pur-
pose.'
KING RICHARD.
He was in the right; and so, indeed, it is.
[*Clock strikes.*
Tell the clock there.—Give me a calendar.—
Who saw the sun to-day?
SIR RICHARD RATCLIFF.
           Not I, my lord.
KING RICHARD.
Then he disdains to shine; for, by the book,
He should have braved the east an hour ago:
A black day will it be to somebody.—
Ratcliff,—
SIR RICHARD RATCLIFF.
My lord?
KING RICHARD.
        The sun will not be seen to-day;
The sky doth frown and lour upon our army.
I would these dewy tears were from the ground.
Not shine to-day! Why, what is that to me
More than to Richmond? for the selfsame heaven
That frowns on me looks sadly upon him.
Enter NORFOLK.
DUKE OF NORFOLK.
Arm, arm, my lord; the foe vaunts in the field.
KING RICHARD.
Come, bustle, bustle;—caparison my horse;
Call up Lord Stanley, bid him bring his power:
I will lead forth my soldiers to the plain,

And thus my battle shall be ordered:—
My foreward shall be drawn out all in length,
Consisting equally of horse and foot;
Our archers shall be placed in the midst:
John Duke of Norfolk, Thomas Earl of Surrey,
Shall have the leading of this foot and horse.
They thus directed, we will follow
In the main battle; whose puissance on either side
Shall be well winged with our chiefest horse.
This, and Saint George to boot!—What think'st
thou, Norfolk?
DUKE OF NORFOLK.
A good direction, warlike sovereign.
This found I on my tent this morning.
[*He sheweth him a paper.*
KING RICHARD [*reads*].
'Jockey of Norfolk, be not too bold,
For Dickon thy master is bought and sold.'
A thing devised by the enemy.—
Go, gentlemen, every man unto his charge:
Let not our babbling dreams affright our souls;
Conscience is but a word that cowards use,
Devised at first to keep the strong in awe:
Our strong arms be our conscience, swords our
law.
March on, join bravely, let us to't pell-mell;
If not to heaven, then hand in hand to hell.—
His oration to his ARMY.
What shall I say more than I have inferr'd?
Remember whom you are to cope withal;—
A sort of vagabonds, rascals, and runaways,
A scum of Bretons, and base lackey peasants,
Whom their o'er-cloyed country vomits forth
To desperate ventures and assured destruction.
You sleeping safe, they bring to you unrest;
You having lands, and blest with beauteous
wives,
They would distrain the one, distain the other.
And who doth lead them but a paltry fellow,
Long kept in Bretagne at our mother's cost?
A milk-sop, one that never in his life
Felt so much cold as over shoes in snow?
Let's whip these stragglers o'er the seas again;
Lash hence these overweening rags of France,
These famisht beggars, weary of their lives;
Who, but for dreaming on this fond exploit,
For want of means, poor rats, had hang'd them-
selves:
If we be conquer'd, let men conquer us,
And not these bastard Bretons; whom our fathers
Have in their own land beaten, bobb'd, and
thumpt,
And, on record, left them the heirs of shame.
Shall these enjoy our lands? lie with our wives?
Ravish our daughters? [*Drum afar off.*] Hark! I
hear their drum.
Fight, gentlemen of England! fight, bold yeomen!
Draw, archers, draw your arrows to the head!
Spur your proud horses hard, and ride in blood;
Amaze the welkin with your broken staves!
Enter a MESSENGER.
What says Lord Stanley? will he bring his power?
MESSENGER.
My lord, he doth deny to come.
KING RICHARD.
Off with his son George's head!

DUKE OF NORFOLK.
My lord, the enemy is past the marsh:
After the battle let George Stanley die.
KING RICHARD.
A thousand hearts are great within my bosom:
Advance our standards, set upon our foes;
Our ancient word of courage, fair Saint George,
Inspire us with the spleen of fiery dragons!
Upon them! Victory sits on our helms.   [*Exeunt.*

SCENE IV.

Another part of the field.

Alarum: excursions. Enter NORFOLK *and*
FORCES; *to him* CATESBY.

SIR WILLIAM CATESBY.
RESCUE, my Lord of Norfolk, rescue, rescue!
The king enacts more wonders than a man,
Daring an opposite to every danger:
His horse is slain, and all on foot he fights,
Seeking for Richmond in the throat of death.
Rescue, fair lord, or else the day is lost!
Alarums. Enter KING RICHARD.
KING RICHARD.
A horse! a horse! my kingdom for a horse!
SIR WILLIAM CATESBY.
Withdraw, my lord; I'll help you to a horse.
KING RICHARD.
Slave, I have set my life upon a cast,
And I will stand the hazard of the die:
I think there be six Richmonds in the field;
Five have I slain to-day instead of him.
A horse! a horse! my kingdom for a horse!
[*Exeunt.*

SCENE V.

Another part of the field.

Alarum. Enter RICHARD *and* RICHMOND; *they
fight.* RICHARD *is slain. Retreat and flourish.
Re-enter* RICHMOND, DERBY *bearing the
crown, with divers other* LORDS.

EARL OF RICHMOND.
GOD and your arms be praised, victorious
friends!
The day is ours, the bloody dog is dead.
EARL OF DERBY.
Courageous Richmond, well hast thou acquit thee.

Lo, here, this long-usurped royalty
From the dead temples of this bloody wretch
Have I pluckt off, to grace thy brows withal:
Wear it, enjoy it, and make much of it.
EARL OF RICHMOND.
Great God of heaven, say Amen to all!—
But, tell me, is young George Stanley living?
EARL OF DERBY.
He is, my lord, and safe in Leicester town;
Whither, if't please you, we may now withdraw
us.
EARL OF RICHMOND.
What men of name are slain on either side?
EARL OF DERBY.
John Duke of Norfolk, Walter Lord Ferrers,
Sir Robert Brakenbury, and Sir William Brand-
on.
EARL OF RICHMOND.
Inter their bodies as becomes their births:
Proclaim a pardon to the soldiers fled
That in submission will return to us:
And then, as we have ta'en the sacrament,
We will unite the white rose and the red.
Smile heaven upon this fair conjunction,
That long have frown'd upon their enmity!—
What traitor hears me, and says not Amen?
England hath long been mad and scarr'd herself;
The brother blindly shed the brother's blood,
The father rashly slaughter'd his own son,
The son, compell'd, been butcher to the sire:
All this divided York and Lancaster,
Divided in their dire division,
O, now let Richmond and Elizabeth,
The true succeeders of each royal house,
By God's fair ordinance conjoin together!
And let their heirs—God, if Thy will be so—
Enrich the time to come with smooth-faced peace,
With smiling plenty, and fair prosperous days!
Abate the edge of traitors, gracious Lord,
That would reduce these bloody days again,
And make poor England weep in streams of
blood!
Let them not live to taste this land's increase
That would with treason wound this fair land's
peace!
Now civil wounds are stopt, peace lives agen:
That she may long live here, God say Amen!
[*Exeunt.*

TITUS ANDRONICUS

DRAMATIS PERSONAE

SATURNINUS, *son to the late Emperor of Rome,*
  afterwards emperor.
BASSIANUS, *brother to Saturninus; in love with*
  Lavinia.
TITUS ANDRONICUS, *a noble Roman, general*
  against the Goths.
MARCUS ANDRONICUS, *tribune of the people, and*
  brother to Titus.
LUCIUS,
QUINTUS,
MARTIUS, } *sons to Titus Andronicus.*
MUTIUS,
YOUNG LUCIUS, *a boy, son to Lucius.*
PUBLIUS, *son to Marcus the tribune.*
SEMPRONIUS,
CAIUS, } *kinsmen to Titus.*
VALENTINE,

AEMILIUS, *a noble Roman.*
ALARBUS,
DEMETRIUS, } *sons to Tamora.*
CHIRON,
AARON, *a Moor, beloved by Tamora.*
A CAPTAIN, TRIBUNE, MESSENGER, *and*
  CLOWN.
ROMANS *and* GOTHS.

TAMORA, *Queen of the Goths.*
LAVINIA, *daughter to Titus Andronicus.*
A NURSE, *and a black* CHILD.

SENATORS, TRIBUNES, OFFICERS, SOLDIERS,
  and ATTENDANTS.

SCENE—*Rome and the country near it.*

ACT I. SCENE I.

Rome. Before the Capitol. The Tomb of the
  Andronici appearing.

Flourish. Enter the TRIBUNES *and* SENATORS
aloft. And then enter, below, SATURNINUS *and*
his FOLLOWERS *at one door; and* BASSIANUS
and his FOLLOWERS *at the other, with drums*
and colours.

SATURNINUS.

NOBLE patricians, patrons of my right,
  Defend the justice of my cause with arms;
And, countrymen, my loving followers,
Plead my successive title with your swords:
I am his first-born son, that was the last
That ware the imperial diadem of Rome;
Then let my father's honours live in me,
Nor wrong mine age with this indignity.

BASSIANUS.

Romans,—friends, followers, favourers of my
  right,—
If ever Bassianus, Cæsar's son,
Were gracious in the eyes of royal Rome,
Keep, then, this passage to the Capitol;
And suffer not dishonour to approach
Th' imperial seat, to virtue consecrate,
To justice, continence, and nobility;
But let desert in pure election shine;
And, Romans, fight for freedom in your choice.

Enter MARCUS ANDRONICUS, *aloft, with the*
  crown.

MARCUS ANDRONICUS.

Princes,—that strive by factions and by friends
Ambitiously for rule and empery,—   [stand
Know that the people of Rome, for whom we
A special party, have, by common voice,
In election for the Roman empery,
Chosen Andronicus, surnamed Pius
For many good and great deserts to Rome:
A nobler man, a braver warrior,
Lives not this day within the city walls:
He by the senate is accited home
From weary wars against the barbarous Goths;

That, with his sons, a terror to our foes,
Hath yoked a nation strong, train'd up in arms.
Ten years are spent since first he undertook
This cause of Rome, and chastised with arms
Our enemies' pride: five times he hath return'd
Bleeding to Rome, bearing his valiant sons
In coffins from the field;
And now at last, laden with honour's spoils,
Returns the good Andronicus to Rome,
Renowned Titus, flourishing in arms.
Let us entreat,—by honour of his name,
Whom worthily you would have now succeed,
And in the Capitol and senate's right,
Whom you pretend to honour and adore,—
That you withdraw you, and abate your strength;
Dismiss your followers, and, as suitors should,
Plead your deserts in peace and humbleness.

SATURNINUS.

How fair the tribune speaks to calm my thoughts!

BASSIANUS.

Marcus Andronicus, so I do affy
In thy uprightness and integrity,
And so I love and honour thee and thine,
Thy noble brother Titus and his sons,
And her to whom my thoughts are humbled all,
Gracious Lavinia, Rome's rich ornament,
That I will here dismiss my loving friends;
And to my fortunes and the people's favour
Commit my cause in balance to be weigh'd.

[Exeunt the FOLLOWERS *of* BASSIANUS.

SATURNINUS.

Friends, that have been thus forward in my right,
I thank you all, and here dismiss you all;
And to the love and favour of my country
Commit myself, my person, and the cause.

[Exeunt the FOLLOWERS *of* SATURNINUS.

Rome, be as just and gracious unto me
As I am confident and kind to thee.—
Open the gates, and let me in.

BASSIANUS.

Tribunes, and me, a poor competitor.

[Flourish. SATURNINUS *and* BASSIANUS
  go up into the Capitol.

Enter a CAPTAIN.
CAPTAIN.

Romans, make way: the good Andronicus,
Patron of virtue, Rome's best champion,
Successful in the battles that he fights,
With honour and with fortune is return'd
From where he circumscribed with his sword,
And brought to yoke, the enemies of Rome.

Sound drums and trumpets, and then enter MAR-
TIUS *and* MUTIUS, *two of* TITUS' *sons; after
them, two* MEN *bearing a coffin cover'd with
black; then two other sons,* LUCIUS *and* QUIN-
TUS; *after them,* TITUS ANDRONICUS; *and
then* TAMORA, *the Queen of Goths, and her sons*
ALARBUS, DEMETRIUS, *and* CHIRON, *with*
AARON *the Moor, and others, as many as can be.
They set down the coffin and* TITUS *speaks.*

TITUS ANDRONICUS.

Hail, Rome, victorious in thy mourning weeds!
Lo, as the bark that hath discharged her fraught
Returns with precious lading to the bay
From whence at first she weigh'd her anchorage,
Cometh Andronicus, bound with laurel-boughs,
To re-salute his country with his tears,
Tears of true joy for his return to Rome.—
Thou great defender of this Capitol,
Stand gracious to the rites that we intend!—
Romans, of five-and-twenty valiant sons,
Half of the number that King Priam had,
Behold the poor remains, alive and dead!
These that survive let Rome reward with love;
These that I bring unto their latest home,
With burial amongst their ancestors:　　[sword.
Here Goths have given me leave to sheathe my
Titus, unkind, and careless of thine own,
Why suffer'st thou thy sons, unburied yet,
To hover on the dreadful shore of Styx?—
Make way to lay them by their brethren.—
　　　　　　　　[*They open the tomb.*
There greet in silence, as the dead are wont,
And sleep in peace, slain in your country's wars!
O sacred receptacle of my joys,
Sweet cell of virtue and nobility,
How many sons of mine hast thou in store,
That thou wilt never render to me more!

YOUNG LUCIUS.

Give us the proudest prisoner of the Goths,
That we may hew his limbs, and on a pile
Ad manes fratrum sacrifice his flesh,
Before this earthy prison of their bones;
That so the shadows be not unappeased,
Nor we disturb'd with prodigies on earth.

TITUS ANDRONICUS.

I give him you,—the noblest that survives,
The eldest son of this distressed queen.

TAMORA.

Stay, Roman brethren!—Gracious conqueror,
Victorious Titus, rue the tears I shed,
A mother's tears in passion for her son:
And if thy sons were ever dear to thee,
O, think my son to be as dear to me!
Sufficeth not, that we are brought to Rome,
To beautify thy triumphs and return,
Captive to thee and to thy Roman yoke;
But must my sons be slaughter'd in the streets,
For valiant doings in their country's cause?

O, if to fight for king and commonweal
Were piety in thine, it is in these.
Andronicus, stain not thy tomb with blood:
Wilt thou draw near the nature of the gods?
Draw near them, then, in being merciful:
Sweet mercy is nobility's true badge:
Thrice-noble Titus, spare my first-born son.

TITUS ANDRONICUS.

Patient yourself, madam, and pardon me.
These are their brethren, whom you Goths beheld
Alive and dead; and for their brethren slain
Religiously they ask a sacrifice:
To this your son is markt; and die he must,
T'appease their groaning shadows that are gone.

LUCIUS.

Away with him! and make a fire straight;
And with our swords, upon a pile of wood,
Let's hew his limbs till they be clean consumed.
　　[*Exeunt the* SONS *of* ANDRONICUS *with*
　　ALARBUS.

TAMORA.

O cruel, irreligious piety!

CHIRON.

Was ever Scythia half so barbarous?

DEMETRIUS.

Oppose not Scythia to ambitious Rome.
Alarbus goes to rest; and we survive
To tremble under Titus' threatening looks.
Then, madam, stand resolved; but hope withal,
The self-same gods, that arm'd the Queen of Troy
With opportunity of sharp revenge
Upon the Thracian tyrant in her tent,
May favour Tamora, the Queen of Goths,—
When Goths were Goths, and Tamora was
　　queen,—
To quit these bloody wrongs upon her foes.

Enter the SONS *of* ANDRONICUS *again, with their
swords bloody.*

LUCIUS.

See, lord and father, how we have perform'd
Our Roman rites: Alarbus' limbs are lopt,
And entrails feed the sacrificing fire,
Whose smoke, like incense, doth perfume the sky.
Remaineth naught, but to inter our brethren,
And with loud 'larums welcome them to Rome.

TITUS ANDRONICUS.

Let it be so; and let Andronicus
Make this his latest farewell to their souls.
　　[*Then sound trumpets and lay the coffin in
　　the tomb.*
In peace and honour rest you here, my sons;
Rome's readiest champions, repose you here,
Secure from worldly chances and mishaps!
Here lurks no treason, here no envy swells,
Here grow no damned grudges; here are no
　　storms,
No noise, but silence and eternal sleep:

Enter LAVINIA.

In peace and honour rest you here, my sons!

LAVINIA.

In peace and honour live Lord Titus long;
My noble lord and father, live in fame!
Lo, at this tomb my tributary tears
I render, for my brethren's obsequies;
And at thy feet I kneel, with tears of joy,
Shed on the earth, for thy return to Rome:

O, bless me here with thy victorious hand,
Whose fortunes Rome's best citizens applaud!
TITUS ANDRONICUS.
Kind Rome, that hast thus lovingly reserved
The cordial of mine age to glad my heart!—
Lavinia, live; outlive thy father's days,
And fame's eternal date, for virtue's praise!
Enter, below, MARCUS ANDRONICUS *and* TRI-
BUNES; SATURNINUS *and* BASSIANUS, *at-*
tended.
MARCUS ANDRONICUS.
Long live Lord Titus, my beloved brother,
Gracious triumpher in the eyes of Rome!
TITUS ANDRONICUS.
Thanks, gentle tribune, noble brother Marcus.
MARCUS ANDRONICUS.
And welcome, nephews, from successful wars,
You that survive, and you that sleep in fame!
Fair lords, your fortunes are alike in all,
That in your country's service drew your swords:
But safer triumph is this funeral pomp,
That hath aspired to Solon's happiness,
And triumphs over chance in honour's bed.—
Titus Andronicus, the people of Rome,
Whose friend in justice thou hast ever been,
Send thee by me, their tribune and their trust,
This palliament of white and spotless hue;
And name thee in election for the empire,
With these our late-deceased emperor's sons:
Be *candidatus*, then, and put it on,
And help to set a head on headless Rome.
TITUS ANDRONICUS.
A better head her glorious body fits
Than his that shakes for age and feebleness:
What should I don this robe, and trouble you?
Be chosen with proclamations to-day,
To-morrow yield up rule, resign my life,
And set abroach new business for you all?
Rome, I have been thy soldier forty years,
And led my country's strength successfully,
And buried one-and-twenty valiant sons,
Knighted in field, slain manfully in arms,
In right and service of their noble country:
Give me a staff of honour for mine age,
But not a sceptre to control the world:
Upright he held it, lords, that held it last.
MARCUS ANDRONICUS.
Titus, thou shalt obtain and ask the empery.
SATURNINUS.
Proud and ambitious tribune, canst thou tell?
TITUS ANDRONICUS.
Patience, Prince Saturnine.
SATURNINUS.
Romans, do me right;—
Patricians, draw your swords, and sheathe them
Till Saturninus be Rome's emperor.—　　　　[*not*
Andronicus, would thou wert shipt to hell,
Rather than rob me of the people's hearts!
LUCIUS.
Proud Saturnine, interrupter of the good
That noble-minded Titus means to thee!
TITUS ANDRONICUS.
Content thee, prince; I will restore to thee　[*selves.*
The people's hearts, and wean them from them-
BASSIANUS.
Andronicus, I do not flatter thee,

But honour thee, and will do till I die:
My faction if thou strengthen with thy friends,
I will most thankful be; and thanks to men
Of noble minds is honourable meed.
TITUS ANDRONICUS.
People of Rome, and people's tribunes here,
I ask your voices and your suffrages:
Will you bestow them friendly on Andronicus?
TRIBUNES.
To gratify the good Andronicus,
And gratulate his safe return to Rome,
The people will accept whom he admits.
TITUS ANDRONICUS.
Tribunes, I thank you: and this suit I make,
That you create your emperor's eldest son,
Lord Saturnine; whose virtues will, I hope,
Reflect on Rome as Titan's rays on earth,
And ripen justice in this commonweal:
Then, if you will elect by my advice,
Crown him, and say, 'Long live our emperor!'
MARCUS ANDRONICUS.
With voices and applause of every sort,
Patricians and plebeians, we create
Lord Saturninus Rome's great emperor,
And say, 'Long live our Emperor Saturnine!'
　　　　　　[*A long flourish till they come down.*
SATURNINUS.
Titus Andronicus, for thy favours done
To us in our election this day
I give thee thanks in part of thy deserts,
And will with deeds requite thy gentleness:
And, for an onset, Titus, to advance
Thy name and honourable family,
Lavinia will I make my empress,
Rome's royal mistress, mistress of my heart,
And in the sacred Pantheon her espouse:
Tell me, Andronicus, doth this motion please
　　thee?
TITUS ANDRONICUS.
It doth, my worthy lord; and in this match
I hold me highly honour'd of your Grace:
And here, in sight of Rome, to Saturnine—
King and commander of our commonweal,
The wide world's emperor—do I consecrate
My sword, my chariot, and my prisoners;
Presents well worthy Rome's imperial lord:
Receive them, then, the tribute that I owe,
Mine honour's ensigns humbled at thy feet.
SATURNINUS.
Thanks, noble Titus, father of my life!
How proud I am of thee and of thy gifts
Rome shall record; and when I do forget
The least of these unspeakable deserts,
Romans, forget your fealty to me.
TITUS ANDRONICUS [*to* TAMORA].
Now, madam, are you prisoner to an emperor;
To him that, for your honour and your state,
Will use you nobly and your followers.
SATURNINUS [*aside*].
A goodly lady, trust me; of the hue
That I would choose, were I to choose anew.—
Clear up, fair queen, that cloudy countenance:
Though chance of war hath wrought this change
　　of cheer,
Thou comest not to be made a scorn in Rome:
Princely shall be thy usage every way.

Rest on my word, and let not discontent
Daunt all your hopes: madam, he comforts you
Can make you greater than the Queen of
    Goths.—
Lavinia, you are not displeased with this?
LAVINIA.
Not I, my lord; sith true nobility
Warrants these words in princely courtesy.
SATURNINUS.
Thanks, sweet Lavinia.—Romans, let us go:
Ransomless here we set our prisoners free:
Proclaim our honours, lords, with trump and
    drum.
    [*Flourish.* SATURNINUS *courts* TAMORA
    in dumb-show.
BASSIANUS.
Lord Titus, by your leave, this maid is mine.
    [*Seizing* LAVINIA.
TITUS ANDRONICUS.
How, sir! are you in earnest, then, my lord?
BASSIANUS.
Ay, noble Titus; and resolved withal
To do myself this reason and this right.
MARCUS ANDRONICUS.
Suum cuique is our Roman justice:
This prince in justice seizeth but his own.
LUCIUS.
And that he will, and shall, if Lucius live.
TITUS ANDRONICUS.
Traitors, avaunt!—Where is the emperor's
    guard?—
Treason, my lord,—Lavinia is surprised!
SATURNINUS.
Surprised! by whom?
BASSIANUS.
            By him that justly may
Bear his betrothed from all the world away.
    [*Exeunt* BASSIANUS *and* MARCUS *with*
    LAVINIA.
MUTIUS.
Brothers, help to convey her hence away,
And with my sword I'll keep this door safe.
    [*Exeunt* LUCIUS, QUINTUS, *and* MARTIUS.
TITUS ANDRONICUS.
Follow, my lord, and I'll soon bring her back.
    [*Exeunt* SATURNINUS, TAMORA, *and her*
    SONS, *and* AARON *the Moor.*
MUTIUS.
My lord, you pass not here.
TITUS ANDRONICUS.
            What, villain boy!
Barr'st me my way in Rome?
MUTIUS.
           Help, Lucius, help!
    [TITUS *kills* MUTIUS.
Enter LUCIUS.
LUCIUS.
My lord, you are unjust; and, more than so,
In wrongful quarrel you have slain your son.
TITUS ANDRONICUS.
Nor thou, nor he, are any sons of mine;
My sons would never so dishonour me:
Traitor, restore Lavinia to the emperor.
LUCIUS.
Dead, if you will; but not to be his wife,
That is another's lawful promised love.   [*Exit.*

Enter aloft the Emperor SATURNINUS *with* TA-
MORA *and her two* SONS, *and* AARON *the
Moor.*
SATURNINUS.
No, Titus, no; the emperor needs her not,
Nor her, nor thee, nor any of thy stock:
I'll trust, by leisure, him that mocks me once;
Thee never, nor thy traitorous haughty sons,
Confederates all thus to dishonour me.
Was there none else in Rome to make a stale,
But Saturnine? Full well, Andronicus,
Agree these deeds with that proud brag of thine,
That saidst, I begg'd the empire at thy hands.
TITUS ANDRONICUS.
O monstrous! what reproachful words are these?
SATURNINUS.
But go thy ways; go, give that changing piece
To him that flourisht for her with his sword:
A valiant son-in-law thou shalt enjoy;
One fit to bandy with thy lawless sons,
To ruffle in the commonwealth of Rome.
TITUS ANDRONICUS.
These words are razors to my wounded heart.
SATURNINUS.
And therefore, lovely Tamora, Queen of Goths,—
That, like the stately Phoebe 'mongst her nymphs,
Dost overshine the gallant'st dames of Rome,—
If thou be pleased with this my sudden choice,
Behold, I choose thee, Tamora, for my bride,
And will create thee empress of Rome.
Speak, Queen of Goths, dost thou applaud my
    choice?
And here I swear by all the Roman gods,—
Sith priest and holy water are so near,
And tapers burn so bright, and every thing
In readiness for Hymenæus stand,—
I will not re-salute the streets of Rome,
Or climb my palace, till from forth this place
I lead espoused my bride along with me.
TAMORA.
And here, in sight of heaven, to Rome I swear,
If Saturnine advance the Queen of Goths,
She will a handmaid be to his desires,
A loving nurse, a mother to his youth.
SATURNINUS.
Ascend, fair queen, Pantheon.—Lords, accom-
    pany
Your noble emperor and his lovely bride,
Sent by the heavens for Prince Saturnine,
Whose wisdom hath her fortune conquered:
There shall we consummate our spousal rites.
    [*Exeunt all but* TITUS.
TITUS ANDRONICUS.
I am not bid to wait upon this bride:—
Titus, when wert thou wont to walk alone,
Dishonour'd thus, and challenged of wrongs?
Enter MARCUS, LUCIUS, QUINTUS, *and*
MARTIUS.
MARCUS ANDRONICUS.
O Titus, see, O, see what thou hast done!
In a bad quarrel slain a virtuous son.
TITUS ANDRONICUS.
No, foolish tribune, no; no son of mine,—
Nor thou, nor these, confederates in the deed
That hath dishonour'd all our family;
Unworthy brother, and unworthy sons!

LUCIUS.

But let us give him burial, as becomes;
Give Mutius burial with our brethren.

TITUS ANDRONICUS.

Traitors, away! he rests not in this tomb:—
This monument five hundred years hath stood,
Which I have sumptuously re-edified:
Here none but soldiers and Rome's servitors
Repose in fame; none basely slain in brawls:—
Bury him where you can, he comes not here.

MARCUS ANDRONICUS.

My lord, this is impiety in you:
My nephew Mutius' deeds do plead for him;
He must be buried with his brethren.

QUINTUS AND MARTIUS.

And shall, or him we will accompany.

TITUS ANDRONICUS.

'And shall'! what villain was it spake that word?

QUINTUS.

He that would vouch it in any place but here.

TITUS ANDRONICUS.

What, would you bury him in my despite?

MARCUS ANDRONICUS.

No, noble Titus; but entreat of thee
To pardon Mutius, and to bury him.

TITUS ANDRONICUS.

Marcus, even thou hast struck upon my crest,
And, with these boys, mine honour thou hast
    wounded:
My foes I do repute you every one;
So, trouble me no more, but get you gone.

MARTIUS.

He is not with himself; let us withdraw.

QUINTUS.

Not I, till Mutius' bones be buried.

[MARCUS and the SONS of TITUS k el.

MARCUS ANDRONICUS.

Brother, for in that name doth nature plead,—

QUINTUS.

Father, and in that name doth nature speak,—

TITUS ANDRONICUS.

Speak thou no more, if all the rest will speed.

MARCUS ANDRONICUS.

Renowned Titus, more than half my soul,—

LUCIUS.

Dear father, soul and substance of us all,—

MARCUS ANDRONICUS.

Suffer thy brother Marcus to inter
His noble nephew here in virtue's nest,
That died in honour and Lavinia's cause.
Thou art a Roman,—be not barbarous:
The Greeks upon advice did bury Ajax,
That slew himself; and wise Laertes' son
Did graciously plead for his funerals:
Let not young Mutius, then, that was thy joy,
Be barr'd his entrance here.

TITUS ANDRONICUS.

              Rise, Marcus, rise:—
The dismall'st day is this that e'er I saw,
To be dishonour'd by my sons in Rome!—
Well, bury him, and bury me the next.

[They put MUTIUS in the tomb.

LUCIUS.

There lie thy bones, sweet Mutius, with thy
    friends,
Till we with trophies do adorn thy tomb.

ALL [kneeling].

No man shed tears for noble Mutius;
He lives in fame that died in virtue's cause.

MARCUS ANDRONICUS.

My lord,—to step out of these dreary dumps,—
How comes it that the subtle Queen of Goths
Is of a sudden thus advanced in Rome?

TITUS ANDRONICUS.

I know not, Marcus; but I know it is,—
Whether by device or no, the heavens can tell:
Is she not, then, beholding to the man
That brought her for this high good turn so far?

MARCUS ANDRONICUS.

Yes, and will nobly him remunerate.

Flourish. Enter the Emperor SATURNINUS, TA-
MORA *and her two* SONS, *with the* MOOR *at one
door; enter at the other door,* BASSIANUS *and*
LAVINIA, *with others.*

SATURNINUS.

So, Bassianus, you have play'd your prize:
God give you joy, sir, of your gallant bride!

BASSIANUS.

And you of yours, my lord! I say no more,
Nor wish no less; and so, I take my leave.

SATURNINUS.

Traitor, if Rome have law, or we have power,
Thou and thy faction shall repent this rape.

BASSIANUS.

Rape, call you it, my lord, to seize my own,
My true-betrothed love, and now my wife?
But let the laws of Rome determine all;
Meanwhile I am possest of that is mine.

SATURNINUS.

'Tis good, sir: you are very short with us;
But, if we live, we'll be as sharp with you.

BASSIANUS.

My lord, what I have done, as best I may,
Answer I must, and shall do with my life.
Only thus much I give your Grace to know,—
By all the duties that I owe to Rome,
This noble gentleman, Lord Titus here,
Is in opinion and in honour wrong'd;
That, in the rescue of Lavinia,
With his own hand did slay his youngest son,
In zeal to you, and highly moved to wrath
To be controll'd in that he frankly gave:
Receive him, then, to favour, Saturnine,
That hath exprest himself in all his deeds
A father and a friend to thee and Rome.

TITUS ANDRONICUS.

Prince Bassianus, leave to plead my deeds:
'Tis thou and those that have dishonour'd me.
Rome and the righteous heavens be my judge,
How I have loved and honour'd Saturnine!

TAMORA.

My worthy lord, if ever Tamora
Were gracious in those princely eyes of thine,
Then hear me speak indifferently for all;
And at my suit, sweet, pardon what is past.

SATURNINUS.

What, madam! be dishonour'd openly,
And basely put it up without revenge?

TAMORA.

Not so, my lord; the gods of Rome forfend
I should be author to dishonour you!
But on mine honour dare I undertake

For good Lord Titus' innocence in all;
Whose fury not dissembled speaks his griefs:
Then, at my suit, look graciously on him;
Lose not so noble a friend on vain suppose,
Nor with sour looks afflict his gentle heart.—
[aside to SATURNINUS] My lord, be ruled by
   me, be won at last;
Dissemble all your griefs and discontents:
You are but newly planted in your throne;
Lest, then, the people, and patricians too,
Upon a just survey, take Titus' part,
And so supplant you for ingratitude,—
Which Rome reputes to be a heinous sin,—
Yield at entreats; and then let me alone:
I'll find a day to massacre them all,
And raze their faction and their family,
The cruel father and his traitorous sons,
To whom I sued for my dear son's life;
And make them know what 'tis to let a queen
Kneel in the streets and beg for grace in vain.—
Come, come, sweet emperor,—come, Androni-
   cus,—
Take up this good old man, and cheer the heart
That dies in tempest of thy angry frown.

            SATURNINUS.
Rise, Titus, rise; my empress hath prevail'd.

          TITUS ANDRONICUS.
I thank your majesty, and her, my lord:
These words, these looks, infuse new life in
   me.

             TAMORA.
Titus, I am incorporate in Rome,
A Roman now adopted happily,
And must advise the emperor for his good.
This day all quarrels die, Andronicus;—
And let it be mine honour, good my lord,
That I have reconciled your friends and you.—
For you, Prince Bassianus, I have past
My word and promise to the emperor,
That you will be more mild and tractable.—
And fear not, lords,—and you, Lavinia;—
By my advice, all humbled on your knees,
You shall ask pardon of his majesty.

   [MARCUS, LAVINIA, and the SONS of
       TITUS kneel.

             LUCIUS.
We do; and vow to heaven, and to his highness,
That what we did was mildly as we might,
Tend'ring our sister's honour and our own.

        MARCUS ANDRONICUS.
That, on mine honour, here I do protest.

           SATURNINUS.
Away, and talk not; trouble us no more.

             TAMORA.
Nay, nay, sweet emperor, we must all be friends:
The tribune and his nephews kneel for grace;
I will not be denied: sweet heart, look back.

           SATURNINUS.
Marcus, for thy sake and thy brother's here,
And at my lovely Tamora's entreats,
I do remit these young men's heinous faults.

             [Stand up.
Lavinia, though you left me like a churl,
I found a friend; and sure as death I swore
I would not part a bachelor from the priest.
Come, if the emperor's court can feast two brides,

You are my guest, Lavinia, and your friends.—
This day shall be a love-day, Tamora.

        TITUS ANDRONICUS.
To-morrow, an it please your majesty
To hunt the panther and the hart with me,
With horn and hound we'll give your Grace
   bonjour.

           SATURNINUS.
Be it so, Titus, and gramercy too.

         [Flourish. Exeunt.

ACT II. SCENE I.

Rome.   Before the palace.

Enter AARON alone.

            AARON.
NOW climbeth Tamora Olympus' top,
   Safe out of fortune's shot; and sits aloft,
Secure of thunder's crack or lightning-flash;
Advanced above pale envy's threat'ning reach.
As when the golden sun salutes the morn,
And, having gilt the ocean with his beams,
Gallops the zodiac in his glistering coach,
And overlooks the highest-peering hills;
So Tamora:
Upon her wit doth earthly honour wait,
And virtue stoops and trembles at her frown.
Then, Aaron, arm thy heart, and fit thy thoughts,
To mount aloft with thy imperial mistress,
And mount her pitch, whom thou in triumph
   long
Hast prisoner held, fetter'd in amorous chains,
And faster bound to Aaron's charming eyes
Than is Prometheus tied to Caucasus.
Away with slavish weeds and servile thoughts!
I will be bright, and shine in pearl and gold,
To wait upon this new-made empress.
To wait, said I? to wanton with this queen,
This goddess, this Semiramis, this nymph,
This siren, that will charm Rome's Saturnine,
And see his shipwrack and his commonweal's.—
Holla! what storm is this?

   Enter DEMETRIUS and CHIRON, braving
          DEMETRIUS.
Chiron, thy years wants wit, thy wit wants edge,
And manners, to intrude where I am graced;
And may, for aught thou know'st, affected be.

             CHIRON.
Demetrius, thou dost over-ween in all;
And so in this, to bear me down with braves.
'Tis not the difference of a year or two
Makes me less gracious, or thee more fortunate:
I am as able and as fit as thou
To serve, and to deserve my mistress' grace;
And that my sword upon thee shall approve,
And plead my passions for Lavinia's love.

         AARON [aside].
Clubs, clubs! these lovers will not keep the
   peace.

            DEMETRIUS.
Why, boy, although our mother, unadvised,
Gave you a dancing-rapier by your side,
Are you so desperate grown to threat your
   friends?
Go to; have your lath glued within your sheath
Till you know better how to handle it.

CHIRON.

Meanwhile, sir, with the little skill I have,
Full well shalt thou perceive how much I dare.

DEMETRIUS.

Ay, boy, grow ye so brave?   [*They draw.*

AARON [*coming forward*].

          Why, how now, lords!
So near the emperor's palace dare you draw,
And maintain such a quarrel openly?
Full well I wot the ground of all this grudge:
I would not for a million of gold
The cause were known to them it most concerns;
Nor would your noble mother for much more
Be so dishonour'd in the court of Rome.
For shame, put up.

DEMETRIUS.

       Not I, till I have sheathed
My rapier in his bosom, and withal
Thrust these reproachful speeches down his
    throat
That he hath breathed in my dishonour here.

CHIRON.

For that I am prepared and full resolved,—
Foul-spoken coward, that thunder'st with thy
    tongue,
And with thy weapon nothing darest perform.

AARON.

Away, I say!—
Now, by the gods that warlike Goths adore,
This pretty brabble will undo us all.—
Why, lords, and think you not how dangerous
It is to jet upon a prince's right?
What, is Lavinia, then, become so loose,
Or Bassianus so degenerate,
That for her love such quarrels may be broacht
Without controlment, justice, or revenge?
Young lords, beware! an should the empress
    know
This discord's ground, the music would not
    please.

CHIRON.

I care not, I, knew she and all the world:
I love Lavinia more than all the world.

DEMETRIUS.

Youngling, learn thou to make some meaner
    choice;
Lavinia is thine elder brother's hope.

AARON.

Why, are ye mad? or know ye not, in Rome
How furious and impatient they be,
And cannot brook competitors in love?
I tell you, lords, you do but plot your deaths
By this device.

CHIRON.

       Aaron, a thousand deaths
Would I propose to achieve her whom I love.

AARON.

To achieve her!—how?

DEMETRIUS.

       Why makest thou it so strange?
She is a woman, therefore may be woo'd;
She is a woman, therefore may be won;
She is Lavinia, therefore must be loved.
What, man! more water glideth by the mill
Than wots the miller of; and easy it is
Of a cut loaf to steal a shive, we know:

Though Bassianus be the emperor's brother,
Better than he have worn Vulcan's badge.

AARON [*aside*].

Ay, and as good as Saturninus may.

DEMETRIUS.

Then why should he despair that knows to court
    it
With words, fair looks, and liberality?
What, hast not thou full often struck a doe,
And borne her cleanly by the keeper's nose?

AARON.

Why, then, it seems, some certain snatch or so
Would serve your turns.

CHIRON.

       Ay, so the turn were served.

DEMETRIUS.

Aaron, thou hast hit it.

AARON.

       Would you had hit it too!
Then should not we be tired with this ado.
Why, hark ye, hark ye,—and are you such fools
To square for this? would it offend you, then,
That both should speed?

CHIRON.

Faith, not me.

DEMETRIUS.

       Nor me, so I were one.

AARON.

For shame, be friends, and join for that you jar:
'Tis policy and stratagem must do
That you affect; and so must you resolve,
That what you cannot as you would achieve,
You must perforce accomplish as you may.
Take this of me,—Lucrece was not more chaste
Than this Lavinia, Bassianus' love.
A speedier course than lingering languishment
Must we pursue, and I have found the path.
My lords, a solemn hunting is in hand;
There will the lovely Roman ladies troop:
The forest-walks are wide and spacious;
And many unfrequented plots there are
Fitted by kind for rape and villainy:
Single you thither, then, this dainty doe,
And strike her home by force, if not by words:
This way, or not at all, stand you in hope.
Come, come, our empress, with her sacred wit
To villainy and vengeance consecrate,
Will we acquaint with all that we intend;
And she shall file our engines with advice,
That will not suffer you to square yourselves,
But to your wishes' height advance you both.
The emperor's court is like the house of Fame,
The palace full of tongues, of eyes, and ears:
The woods are ruthless, dreadful, deaf, and
    dull;
There speak, and strike, brave boys, and take your
    turns;
There serve your lust, shadow'd from heaven's
    eye,
And revel in Lavinia's treasury.

CHIRON.

Thy counsel, lad, smells of no cowardice.

DEMETRIUS.

Sit fas aut nefas, till I find the stream
To cool this heat, a charm to calm these fits,
Per Styga, per manes vehor.   [*Exeunt.*

SCENE II.

A forest near Rome.

Enter TITUS ANDRONICUS *and his three* SONS, *making a noise with hounds and horns; and* MARCUS.

TITUS ANDRONICUS.

THE hunt is up, the morn is bright and gray,
  The fields are fragrant, and the woods are
Uncouple here, and let us make a bay,   [green:
And wake the emperor and his lovely bride,
And rouse the prince, and ring a hunter's peal,
That all the court may echo with the noise.
Sons, let it be your charge, as it is ours,
To attend the emperor's person carefully:
I have been troubled in my sleep this night,
But dawning day new comfort hath inspired.
Here a cry of hounds, and wind horns in a peal.
  Enter SATURNINUS, TAMORA, BASSIANUS,
  LAVINIA, DEMETRIUS, CHIRON, *and their*
  ATTENDANTS.
Many good morrows to your majesty;—
Madam, to you as many and as good:—
I promised your Grace a hunter's peal.

SATURNINUS.

And you have rung it lustily, my lords;
Somewhat too early for new-married ladies.

BASSIANUS.

Lavinia, how say you?

LAVINIA.

        I say, no;
I have been broad awake two hours and more.

SATURNINUS.

Come on, then; horse and chariots let us have,
And to our sport.—[*to* TAMORA] Madam, now
  shall ye see
Our Roman hunting.

MARCUS ANDRONICUS.

        I have dogs, my lord,
Will rouse the proudest panther in the chase,
And climb the highest promontory top.

TITUS ANDRONICUS.

And I have horse will follow where the game
Makes way, and run like swallows o'er the plain.

DEMETRIUS.

Chiron, we hunt not, we, with horse nor hound,
But hope to pluck a dainty doe to ground.
                      [*Exeunt.*

SCENE III.

A lonely part of the forest.

Enter AARON *alone, with a bag of gold.*

AARON.

HE that had wit would think that I had none,
  To bury so much gold under a tree,
And never after to inherit it.
Let him that thinks of me so abjectly
Know that this gold must coin a stratagem,
Which, cunningly effected, will beget
A very excellent piece of villainy:
And so repose, sweet gold, for their unrest
                 [*Hides the gold.*
That have their alms out of the empress' chest.
  Enter TAMORA *to the* MOOR.

TAMORA.

My lovely Aaron, wherefore look'st thou sad,
When every thing doth make a gleeful boast?
The birds chant melody on every bush;
The snake lies rolled in the cheerful sun;
The green leaves quiver with the cooling wind,
And make a chequer'd shadow on the ground:
Under their sweet shade, Aaron, let us sit,
And, whilst the babbling echo mocks the hounds,
Replying shrilly to the well-tuned horns,
As if a double hunt were heard at once,
Let us sit down and mark their yelping noise;
And—after conflict such as was supposed
The wandering prince and Dido once enjoy'd,
When with a happy storm they were surprised,
And curtain'd with a counsel-keeping cave—
We may, each wreathed in the other's arms,
Our pastimes done, possess a golden slumber;
Whiles hounds and horns and sweet melodious
  birds
Be unto us as is a nurse's song
Of lullaby to bring her babe asleep.

AARON.

Madam, though Venus govern your desires,
Saturn is dominator over mine:
What signifies my deadly-standing eye,
My silence and my cloudy melancholy,
My fleece of woolly hair that now uncurls
Even as an adder when she doth unroll
To do some fatal execution?
No, madam, these are no venereal signs:
Vengeance is in my heart, death in my hand,
Blood and revenge are hammering in my head.
Hark, Tamora,—the empress of my soul, [thee,-
Which never hopes more heaven than rests in
This is the day of doom for Bassianus:
His Philomel must lose her tongue to-day;
Thy sons make pillage of her chastity,
And wash their hands in Bassianus' blood.
Seest thou this letter? take it up, I pray thee,
And give the king this fatal-plotted scroll.—
Now question me no more,—we are espied;
Here comes a parcel of our hopeful booty,
Which dreads not yet their lives' destruction.

TAMORA.

Ah, my sweet Moor, sweeter to me than life!

AARON.

No more, great empress,—Bassianus comes:
Be cross with him; and I'll go fetch thy sons
To back thy quarrels, whatsoe'er they be.   [*Ex:*
  Enter BASSIANUS *and* LAVINIA.

BASSIANUS.

Who have we here? Rome's royal empress,
Unfurnisht of her well-beseeming troop?
Or is it Dian, habited like her,
Who hath abandoned her holy groves
To see the general hunting in this forest?

TAMORA.

Saucy controller of our private steps!
Had I the power that some say Dian had,
Thy temples should be planted presently
With horns, as was Actæon's; and the hounds
Should drive upon thy new-transformed limbs,
Unmannerly intruder as thou art!

LAVINIA.

Under your patience, gentle empress,
'Tis thought you have a goodly gift in horning;
And to be doubted that your Moor and you

Are singled forth to try experiments:
Jove shield your husband from his hounds to-day!
'Tis pity they should take him for a stag.

BASSIANUS.

Believe me, queen, your swarth Cimmerian
Doth make your honour of his body's hue,
Spotted, detested, and abominable.
Why are you sequester'd from all your train,
Dismounted from your snow-white goodly steed,
And wander'd hither to an obscure plot,
Accompanied but with a barbarous Moor,
If foul desire had not conducted you?

LAVINIA.

And, being intercepted in your sport,
Great reason that my noble lord be rated
For sauciness.—I pray you, let us hence,
And let her joy her raven-colour'd love;
This valley fits the purpose passing well.

BASSIANUS.

The king my brother shall have note of this.

LAVINIA.

Ay, for thee slips have made him noted long:
Good king, to be so mightily abused!

TAMORA.

Why have I patience to endure all this?

Enter DEMETRIUS *and* CHIRON.

DEMETRIUS.

How now, dear sovereign and our gracious
mother!
Why doth your highness look so pale and wan?

TAMORA.

Have I not reason, think you, to look pale?
These two have 'ticed me hither to this place:—
A barren detested vale you see it is;
The trees, though summer, yet forlorn and lean,
O'ercome with moss and baleful mistletoe:
Here never shines the sun; here nothing breeds,
Unless the nightly owl or fatal raven:
And when they show'd me this abhorred pit,
They told me, here, at dead time of the night,
A thousand fiends, a thousand hissing snakes,
Ten thousand swelling toads, as many urchins,
Would make such fearful and confused cries,
As any mortal body hearing it
Should straight fall mad, or else die suddenly.
No sooner had they told this hellish tale,
But straight they told me they would bind me
here
Into the body of a dismal yew,
And leave me to this miserable death:
And then they call'd me foul adulteress,
Lascivious Goth, and all the bitterest terms
That ever ear did hear to such effect:
And, had you not by wondrous fortune come,
This vengeance on me had they executed.
Revenge it, as you love your mother's life,
Or be ye not henceforth call'd my children.

DEMETRIUS.

This is a witness that I am thy son.

[*Stabs* BASSIANUS.

CHIRON.

And this for me, struck home to show my
strength. [*Stabs* BASSIANUS, *who dies.*

LAVINIA.

Ay, come, Semiramis,—nay, barbarous Tamora,
For no name fits thy nature but thy own!

TAMORA.

Give me the poniard;—you shall know, my boys,
Your mother's hand shall right your mother's
wrong.

DEMETRIUS.

Stay, madam; here is more belongs to her;
First thrash the corn, then after burn the straw:
This minion stood upon her chastity,
Upon her nuptial vow, her loyalty,
And with that painted hope she braves your
mightiness:
And shall she carry this unto her grave?

CHIRON.

An if she do, I would I were an eunuch.
Drag hence her husband to some secret hole,
And make his dead trunk pillow to our lust.

TAMORA.

But when ye have the honey ye desire,
Let not this wasp outlive, us both to sting.

CHIRON.

I warrant you, madam, we will make that sure.—
Come, mistress, now perforce we will enjoy
That nice-preserved honesty of yours.

LAVINIA.

O Tamora! thou bear'st a woman's face,—

TAMORA.

I will not hear her speak; away with her!

LAVINIA.

Sweet lords, entreat her hear me but a word.

DEMETRIUS.

Listen, fair madam: let it be your glory
To see her tears; but be your heart to them
As unrelenting flint to drops of rain.

LAVINIA.

When did the tiger's young ones teach the dam?
O, do not learn her wrath,—she taught it thee;
The milk thou suck'dst from her did turn to
marble;
Even at thy teat thou hadst thy tyranny.—
Yet every mother breeds not sons alike:
[*to* CHIRON] Do thou entreat her show a woman
pity.

CHIRON.

What, wouldst thou have me prove myself a bastard?

LAVINIA.

'Tis true,—the raven doth not hatch a lark:
Yet have I heard,—O, could I find it now!—
The lion, moved with pity, did endure
To have his princely paws pared all away:
Some say that ravens foster forlorn children,
The whilst their own birds famish in their nests:
O, be to me, though thy hard heart say no,
Nothing so kind, but something pitiful!

TAMORA.

I know not what it means.—Away with her!

LAVINIA.

O, let me teach thee! for my father's sake,
That gave thee life, when well he might have
slain thee,
Be not obdurate, open thy deaf ears.

TAMORA.

Hadst thou in person ne'er offended me,
Even for his sake am I pitiless.—
Remember, boys, I pour'd forth tears in vain
To save your brother from the sacrifice;

But fierce Andronicus would not relent:
Therefore, away with her, and use her as you
    will;
The worse to her, the better loved of me.
LAVINIA.
O Tamora, be call'd a gentle queen,
And with thine own hands kill me in this place!
For 'tis not life that I have begg'd so long;
Poor I was slain when Bassianus died.
TAMORA.
What begg'st thou, then? fond woman, let me go.
LAVINIA.
'Tis present death I beg; and one thing more
That womanhood denies my tongue to tell:
O, keep me from their worse than killing lust,
And tumble me into some loathsome pit,
Where never man's eye may behold my body:
Do this, and be a charitable murderer.
TAMORA.
So should I rob my sweet sons of their fee:
No, let them satisfy their lust on thee.
DEMETRIUS.
Away! for thou hast stay'd us here too long.
LAVINIA.
No grace? no womanhood? Ah, beastly creature!
The blot and enemy to our general name!
Confusion fall—
CHIRON.
Nay, then I'll stop your mouth.—Bring thou her
    husband:
This is the hole where Aaron bid us hide him.
[DEMETRIUS throws the body of BASSIA-
NUS into the pit; then exeunt DEMETRIUS
and CHIRON, dragging off LAVINIA.
TAMORA.
Farewell, my sons: see that you make her sure:—
Ne'er let my heart know merry cheer indeed
Till all the Andronici be made away.
Now will I hence to seek my lovely Moor,
And let my spleenful sons this trull deflow'r.
[Exit.
Enter AARON, with QUINTUS and MARTIUS.
AARON.
Come on, my lords, the better foot before:
Straight will I bring you to the loathsome pit
Where I espied the panther fast asleep.
QUINTUS.
My sight is very dull, whate'er it bodes.
MARTIUS.
And mine, I promise you; were it not for shame,
Well could I leave our sport to sleep awhile.
[Falls into the pit.
QUINTUS.
What, art thou faln?—What subtle hole is this,
Whose mouth is cover'd with rude-growing
    briers,
Upon whose leaves are drops of new-shed blood
As fresh as morning dew distill'd on flowers?
A very fatal place it seems to me.—
Speak, brother, hast thou hurt thee with the
    fall?
MARTIUS.
O brother, with the dismall'st object hurt
That ever eye with sight made heart lament!
AARON [aside].
Now will I fetch the king to find them here,

That he thereby may have a likely guess
How these were they that made away his brother.
[Exit.
MARTIUS.
Why dost not comfort me, and help me out
From this unhallow'd and blood-stained hole?
QUINTUS.
I am surprised with an uncouth fear;
A chilling sweat o'er-runs my trembling joints;
My heart suspects more than mine eye can see.
MARTIUS.
To prove thou hast a true-divining heart,
Aaron and thou look down into this den,
And see a fearful sight of blood and death.
QUINTUS.
Aaron is gone; and my compassionate heart
Will not permit mine eyes once to behold
The thing whereat it trembles by surmise:
O, tell me how it is; for ne'er till now
Was I a child to fear I know not what.
MARTIUS.
Lord Bassianus lies embrewed here,
All on a heap, like to a slaughter'd lamb,
In this detested, dark, blood-drinking pit.
QUINTUS.
If it be dark, how dost thou know 'tis he?
MARTIUS.
Upon his bloody finger he doth wear
A precious ring, that lightens all the hole,
Which, like a taper in some monument,
Doth shine upon the dead man's earthy cheeks,
And shows the ragged entrails of the pit:
So pale did shine the moon on Pyramus
When he by night lay bathed in maiden blood.
O brother, help me with thy fainting hand—
If fear hath made thee faint, as me it hath—
Out of this fell-devouring receptacle,
As hateful as Cocytus' misty mouth.
QUINTUS.
Reach me thy hand, that I may help thee out;
Or, wanting strength to do thee so much good,
I may be pluckt into the swallowing womb
Of this deep pit, poor Bassianus' grave.
I have no strength to pluck thee to the brink.
MARTIUS.
Nor I no strength to climb without thy help.
QUINTUS.
Thy hand once more; I will not loose again,
Till thou art here aloft, or I below:
Thou canst not come to me,—I come to thee.
[Falls i
Enter SATURNINUS with AARON the Moor.
SATURNINUS.
Along with me: I'll see what hole is here,
And what he is that now is leap'd into it.—
Say, who art thou that lately didst descend
Into this gaping hollow of the earth?
MARTIUS.
The unhappy son of old Andronicus;
Brought hither in a most unlucky hour,
To find thy brother Bassianus dead.
SATURNINUS.
My brother dead! I know thou dost but jest:
He and his lady both are at the lodge
Upon the north side of this pleasant chase;
'Tis not an hour since I left him there.

MARTIUS.
We know not where you left them all alive;
But, out, alas! here have we found him dead.
Enter TAMORA, *with* ATTENDANTS; TITUS
ANDRONICUS, *and* LUCIUS.
TAMORA.
Where is my lord the king?
SATURNINUS.
Here, Tamora; though grieved with killing grief.
TAMORA.
Where is thy brother Bassianus?
SATURNINUS.
Now to the bottom dost thou search my wound:
Poor Bassianus here lies murdered.
TAMORA.
Then all too late I bring this fatal writ,
[*Giving a letter to* SATURNINUS.
The complot of this timeless tragedy;
And wonder greatly that man's face can fold
In pleasing smiles such murderous tyranny.
SATURNINUS [*reads*].
'An if we miss to meet him handsomely,—
Sweet huntsman, Bassianus 'tis we mean,—
Do thou so much as dig the grave for him:
Thou know'st our meaning. Look for thy reward
Among the nettles at the elder-tree
Which overshades the mouth of that same pit
Where we decreed to bury Bassianus.
Do this, and purchase us thy lasting friends.'—
O Tamora! was ever heard the like?—
This is the pit, and this the elder-tree.—
Look, sirs, if you can find the huntsman out
That should have murder'd Bassianus here.
AARON.
My gracious lord, here is the bag of gold.
[*Showing it.*
SATURNINUS [*to* TITUS]
Two of thy whelps, fell curs of bloody kind,
Have here bereft my brother of his life.—
Sirs, drag them from the pit unto the prison:
There let them bide until we have devised
Some never-heard-of torturing pain for them.
TAMORA.
What, are they in this pit? O wondrous thing!
How easily murder is discovered!
TITUS ANDRONICUS.
High emperor, upon my feeble knee
I beg this boon, with tears not lightly shed,
That this fell fault of my accursed sons,—
Accursed, if the fault be proved in them,—
SATURNINUS.
If it be proved! you see it is apparent.—
Who found this letter? Tamora, was it you?
TAMORA.
Andronicus himself did take it up.
TITUS ANDRONICUS.
I did, my lord: yet let me be their bail;
For, by my father's reverend tomb, I vow
They shall be ready at your highness' will
To answer their suspicion with their lives.
SATURNINUS.
Thou shalt not bail them: see thou follow
me.—
Some bring the murder'd body, some the mur-
derers:
Let them not speak a word,—the guilt is plain;

For, by my soul, were there worse end than death,
That end upon them should be executed.
TAMORA.
Andronicus, I will entreat the king:
Fear not thy sons; they shall do well enough.
TITUS ANDRONICUS.
Come, Lucius, come; stay not to talk with them.
[*Exeunt.*

SCENE IV.
Another part of the forest.
Enter the Empress' SONS, DEMETRIUS *and*
CHIRON, *with* LAVINIA, *her hands cut off, and
her tongue cut out, and ravisht.*
DEMETRIUS.
SO, now go tell, an if thy tongue can speak,
Who 'twas that cut thy tongue and ravisht thee.
CHIRON.
Write down thy mind, bewray thy meaning so,
An if thy stumps will let thee play the scribe.
DEMETRIUS.
See, how with signs and tokens she can scrowl.
CHIRON.
Go home, call for sweet water, wash thy hands.
DEMETRIUS.
She hath no tongue to call, nor hands to wash;
And so let's leave her to her silent walks.
CHIRON.
An 'twere my case, I should go hang myself.
DEMETRIUS.
If thou hadst hands to help thee knit the cord.
[*Exeunt* DEMETRIUS *and* CHIRON.
Wind horns. Enter MARCUS *from hunting to*
LAVINIA.
MARCUS ANDRONICUS.
Who is this? my niece, that flies away so fast!
Cousin, a word; where is your husband?—
If I do dream, would all my wealth would wake
me!
If I do wake, some planet strike me down,
That I may slumber in eternal sleep!—
Speak, gentle niece, what stern ungentle hands
Have lopt and hew'd and made thy body bare
Of her two branches, those sweet ornaments,
Whose circling shadows kings have sought to
sleep in,
And might not gain so great a happiness
As have thy love? Why dost not speak to me?—
Alas, a crimson river of warm blood,
Like to a bubbling fountain stirr'd with wind,
Doth rise and fall between thy rosed lips,
Coming and going with thy honey breath.
But, sure, some Tereus hath deflower'd thee,
And, lest thou shouldst detect him, cut thy
tongue.
Ah, now thou turn'st away thy face for shame!—
And, notwithstanding all this loss of blood,—
As from a conduit with three issuing spouts,—
Yet do thy cheeks look red as Titan's face
Blushing to be encounter'd with a cloud.
Shall I speak for thee? shall I say 'tis so?
O, that I knew thy heart! and knew the beast,
That I might rail at him, to ease my mind!
Sorrow concealed, like an oven stopt,
Doth burn the heart to cinders where it is.
Fair Philomela, she but lost her tongue,
And in a tedious sampler sew'd her mind:

But, lovely niece, that mean is cut from thee;
A craftier Tereus, cousin, hast thou met,
And he hath cut those pretty fingers off,
That could have better sew'd than Philomel.
O, had the monster seen those lily hands
Tremble, like aspen-leaves, upon a lute,
And make the silken strings delight to kiss them,
He would not, then, have toucht them for his life!
Or, had he heard the heavenly harmony
Which that sweet tongue hath made,
He would have dropt his knife, and fell asleep
As Cerberus at the Thracian poet's feet.
Come, let us go, and make thy father blind;
For such a sight will blind a father's eye:
One hour's storm will drown the fragrant meads;
What will whole months of tears thy father's eyes?
Do not draw back, for we will mourn with thee:
O, could our mourning ease thy misery! [*Exeunt.*

ACT III. SCENE I.

Rome. A street.

Enter JUDGES, SENATORS, *and* TRIBUNES, *with*
TITUS' *two* SONS, MARTIUS *and* QUINTUS,
bound, passing on the stage to the place of execu-
tion; TITUS *going before, pleading.*

TITUS ANDRONICUS.

HEAR me, grave fathers! noble tribunes, stay!
For pity of mine age, whose youth was spent
In dangerous wars, whilst you securely slept;
For all my blood in Rome's great quarrel shed;
For all the frosty nights that I have watcht;
And for these bitter tears, which now you see
Filling the aged wrinkles in my cheeks;
Be pitiful to my condemned sons,
Whose souls are not corrupted as 'tis thought.
For two-and-twenty sons I never wept,
Because they died in honour's lofty bed.
For these, these, tribunes, in the dust I write
  [*Lieth down, and the* JUDGES *pass by him,*
    and exeunt.
My heart's deep languor and my soul's sad tears:
Let my tears stanch the earth's dry appetite;
My sons' sweet blood will make it shame and
  blush.
  [*Exeunt* SENATORS, *&c., with the* PRI-
    SONERS.
O earth, I will befriend thee more with rain,
That shall distil from these two ancient urns,
Than youthful April shall with all his showers:
In summer's drought I'll drop upon thee still;
In winter with warm tears I'll melt the snow,
And keep eternal spring-time on thy face,
So thou refuse to drink my dear sons' blood.
    Enter LUCIUS, *with his weapon drawn.*
O reverend tribunes! O gentle, aged men!
Unbind my sons, reverse the doom of death;
And let me say, that never wept before,
My tears are now prevailing orators.

LUCIUS.
O noble father, you lament in vain:
The tribunes hear you not; no man is by;
And you recount your sorrows to a stone.

TITUS ANDRONICUS.
Ah, Lucius, for thy brothers let me plead.—
Grave tribunes, once more I entreat of you,—

LUCIUS.
My gracious lord, no tribune hears you speak.

TITUS ANDRONICUS.
Why, 'tis no matter, man: if they did hear,
They would not mark me; or if they did mark,
They would not pity me. Yet plead I must:
And bootless unto them. . . .
Therefore I tell my sorrows to the stones;
Who, though they cannot answer my distress,
Yet in some sort they are better than the tribunes,
For that they will not intercept my tale:
When I do weep, they humbly at my feet
Receive my tears, and seem to weep with me;
And, were they but attired in grave weeds,
Rome could afford no tribune like to these.
A stone is soft as wax, tribunes more hard than
  stones;
A stone is silent, and offendeth not,
And tribunes with their tongues doom men to
  death.—   [*Rises.*
But wherefore stand'st thou with thy weapon
  drawn?

LUCIUS.
To rescue my two brothers from their death:
For which attempt the judges have pronounced
My everlasting doom of banishment.

TITUS ANDRONICUS.
O happy man! they have befriended thee.
Why, foolish Lucius, dost thou not perceive
That Rome is but a wilderness of tigers?
Tigers must prey; and Rome affords no prey
But me and mine: how happy art thou, then,
From these devourers to be banished!—
But who comes with our brother Marcus here?
    Enter MARCUS *and* LAVINIA.

MARCUS ANDRONICUS.
Titus, prepare thy aged eyes to weep;
Or, if not so, thy noble heart to break:
I bring consuming sorrow to thine age.

TITUS ANDRONICUS.
Will it consume me? let me see it, then.

MARCUS ANDRONICUS.
This was thy daughter.

TITUS ANDRONICUS.
          Why, Marcus, so she is.

LUCIUS.
Ay me, this object kills me!

TITUS ANDRONICUS.
Faint-hearted boy, arise, and look upon her.—
Speak, Lavinia, what accursed hand
Hath made thee handless in thy father's sight?
What fool hath added water to the sea,
Or brought a faggot to bright-burning Troy?
My grief was at the height before thou camest;
And now, like Nilus, it disdaineth bounds.—
Give me a sword, I'll chop off my hands too;
For they have fought for Rome, and all in vain;
And they have nursed this woe, in feeding life;
In bootless prayer have they been held up,
And they have served me to effectless use:
Now all the service I require of them
Is, that the one will help to cut the other.—
'Tis well, Lavinia, that thou hast no hands;
For hands, to do Rome service, is but vain.

LUCIUS.
Speak, gentle sister, who hath martyr'd thee?

MARCUS ANDRONICUS.

O, that delightful engine of her thoughts,
That blabb'd them with such pleasing eloquence,
Is torn from forth that pretty hollow cage,
Where, like a sweet melodious bird, it sung
Sweet varied notes, enchanting every ear!

LUCIUS.

O, say thou for her, who hath done this deed?

MARCUS ANDRONICUS.

O, thus I found her, straying in the park,
Seeking to hide herself, as doth the deer
That hath received some unrecuring wound.

TITUS ANDRONICUS.

It was my deer; and he that wounded her
Hath hurt me more than had he kill'd me dead:
For now I stand as one upon a rock,
Environ'd with a wilderness of sea;
Who marks the waxing tide grow wave by wave,
Expecting ever when some envious surge
Will in his brinish bowels swallow him.
This way to death my wretched sons are gone;
Here stands my other son, a banisht man;
And here my brother, weeping at my woes:
But that which gives my soul the greatest spurn,
Is dear Lavinia, dearer than my soul.—
Had I but seen thy picture in this plight,
It would have madded me: what shall I do
Now I behold thy lively body so?
Thou hast no hands to wipe away thy tears;
Nor tongue to tell me who hath martyr'd thee:
Thy husband he is dead; and for his death
Thy brothers are condemn'd, and dead by this.—
Look, Marcus! ah, son Lucius, look on her!
When I did name her brothers, then fresh tears
Stood on her cheeks, as doth the honey-dew
Upon a gather'd lily almost wither'd.

MARCUS ANDRONICUS.

Perchance she weeps because they kill'd her husband;
Perchance because she knows them innocent.

TITUS ANDRONICUS.

If they did kill thy husband, then be joyful,
Because the law hath ta'en revenge on them.—
No, no, they would not do so foul a deed;
Witness the sorrow that their sister makes.—
Gentle Lavinia, let me kiss thy lips;
Or make some sign how I may do thee ease:
Shall thy good uncle, and thy brother Lucius,
And thou, and I, sit round about some fountain,
Looking all downwards, to behold our cheeks
How they are stain'd, like meadows, yet not dry,
With miry slime left on them by a flood?
And in the fountain shall we gaze so long
Till the fresh taste be taken from that clearness,
And made a brine-pit with our bitter tears?
Or shall we cut away our hands, like thine?
Or shall we bite our tongues, and in dumb-shows
Pass the remainder of our hateful days?
What shall we do? let us, that have our tongues,
Plot some device of further misery,
To make us wonder'd at in time to come.

LUCIUS.

Sweet father, cease your tears; for, at your grief,
See how my wretched sister sobs and weeps.

MARCUS ANDRONICUS.

Patience, dear niece.—Good Titus, dry thine eyes.

TITUS ANDRONICUS.

Ah, Marcus, Marcus! brother, well I wot
Thy napkin cannot drink a tear of mine,
For thou, poor man, hast drown'd it with thine
own.

LUCIUS.

Ah, my Lavinia, I will wipe thy cheeks.

TITUS ANDRONICUS.

Mark, Marcus, mark! I understand her signs:
Had she a tongue to speak, now would she say
That to her brother which I said to thee:
His napkin, with his true tears all bewet,
Can do no service on her sorrowful cheeks.
O, what a sympathy of woe is this,—
As far from help as Limbo is from bliss!

Enter AARON *the Moor alone.*

AARON.

Titus Andronicus, my lord the emperor
Sends thee this word,—that, if thou love thy
sons,
Let Marcus, Lucius, or thyself, old Titus,
Or any one of you, chop off your hand,
And send it to the king: he for the same
Will send thee hither both thy sons alive;
And that shall be the ransom for their fault.

TITUS ANDRONICUS.

O gracious emperor! O gentle Aaron!
Did ever raven sing so like a lark,
That gives sweet tidings of the sun's uprise?
With all my heart, I'll send the emperor
My hand:
Good Aaron, wilt thou help to chop it off?

LUCIUS.

Stay, father! for that noble hand of thine,
That hath thrown down so many enemies,
Shall not be sent: my hand will serve the turn:
My youth can better spare my blood than you:
And therefore mine shall save my brothers' lives.

MARCUS ANDRONICUS.

Which of your hands hath not defended Rome,
And rear'd aloft the bloody battle-axe,
Writing destruction on the enemy's castle?
O, none of both but are of high desert:
My hand hath been but idle; let it serve
To ransom my two nephews from their death;
Then have I kept it to a worthy end.

AARON.

Nay, come, agree whose hand shall go along,
For fear they die before their pardon come.

MARCUS ANDRONICUS.

My hand shall go.

LUCIUS.

By heaven, it shall not go!

TITUS ANDRONICUS.

Sirs, strive no more: such wither'd herbs as these
Are meet for plucking up, and therefore mine.

LUCIUS.

Sweet father, if I shall be thought thy son,
Let me redeem my brothers both from death.

MARCUS ANDRONICUS.

And, for our father's sake and mother's care,
Now let me show a brother's love to thee.

TITUS ANDRONICUS.

Agree between you; I will spare my hand.

LUCIUS.

Then I'll go fetch an axe.

MARCUS ANDRONICUS.
But I will use the axe.
                    [*Exeunt* LUCIUS *and* MARCUS.
TITUS ANDRONICUS.
Come hither, Aaron; I'll deceive them both:
Lend me thy hand, and I will give thee mine.
                    AARON [*aside*].
If that be call'd deceit, I will be honest,
And never, whilst I live, deceive men so:
But I'll deceive you in another sort,
And that you'll say, ere half an hour pass.
                    [*Cuts off* TITUS' *hand.*
Enter LUCIUS *and* MARCUS *again.*
TITUS ANDRONICUS.
Now stay your strife: what shall be is dispatcht.
Good Aaron, give his majesty my hand:
Tell him it was a hand that warded him
From thousand dangers; bid him bury it;
More hath it merited,—that let it have.
As for my sons, say I account of them
As jewels purchased at an easy price;
And yet dear too, because I bought mine own.
                    AARON.
I go, Andronicus: and for thy hand
Look by and by to have thy sons with thee:—
[*aside*] Their heads, I mean. O, how this villainy
Doth fat me with the very thoughts of it!
Let fools do good, and fair men call for grace,
Aaron will have his soul black like his face. [*Exit.*
TITUS ANDRONICUS.
O, here I lift this one hand up to heaven,
And bow this feeble ruin to the earth:
If any power pities wretched tears,
To that I call!—[*to* LAVINIA] What, wouldst
    thou kneel with me?   [*prayers*;
Do, then, dear heart; for heaven shall hear our
Or with our sighs we'll breathe the welkin dim,
And stain the sun with fog, as sometime clouds
When they do hug him in their melting bosoms.
                    MARCUS ANDRONICUS.
O brother, speak with possibility,
And do not break into these deep extremes.
                    TITUS ANDRONICUS.
Is not my sorrow deep, having no bottom?
Then be my passions bottomless with them.
                    MARCUS ANDRONICUS.
But yet let reason govern thy lament.
                    TITUS ANDRONICUS.
If there were reason for these miseries,
Then into limits could I bind my woes: [flow?
When heaven doth weep, doth not the earth o'er-
If the winds rage, doth not the sea wax mad,
Threat'ning the welkin with his big-swoln face?
And wilt thou have a reason for this coil?
I am the sea; hark, how her sighs do blow!
She is the weeping welkin, I the earth:
Then must my sea be moved with her sighs;
Then must my earth with her continual tears
Become a deluge, overflow'd and drown'd:
For why my bowels cannot hide her woes,
But like a drunkard must I vomit them.
Then give me leave; for losers will have leave
To ease their stomachs with their bitter tongues.
Enter a MESSENGER, *with two heads and a hand*
MESSENGER.
Worthy Andronicus, ill art thou repaid

For that good hand thou sent'st the emperor.
Here are the heads of thy two noble sons;
And here's thy hand, in scorn to thee sent back,—
Thy griefs their sport, thy resolution mockt;
That woe is me to think upon thy woes
More than remembrance of my father's death.
                    [*Exit.*
MARCUS ANDRONICUS.
Now let hot Aetna cool in Sicily,
And be my heart an ever-burning hell!
These miseries are more than may be borne.
To weep with them that weep doth ease some
    deal;
But sorrow flouted-at is double death.
                    LUCIUS.
Ah, that this sight should make so deep a wound,
And yet detested life not shrink thereat!
That ever death should let life bear his name,
Where life hath no more interest but to breathe!
                    [LAVINIA *kisses* TITUS.
MARCUS ANDRONICUS.
Alas, poor heart, that kiss is comfortless
As frozen water to a starved snake.
                    TITUS ANDRONICUS.
When will this fearful slumber have an end?
                    MARCUS ANDRONICUS.
Now, farewell, flattery: die, Andronicus;
Thou dost not slumber: see, thy two sons' heads,
Thy warlike hand, thy mangled daughter here;
Thy other banisht son, with this dear sight
Struck pale and bloodless; and thy brother, I,
Even like a stony image, cold and numb.
Ah, now no more will I control thy griefs:
Rent off thy silver hair, thy other hand
Gnawing with thy teeth; and be this dismal sight
The closing up of our most wretched eyes:
Now is a time to storm; why art thou still?
                    TITUS ANDRONICUS.
Ha, ha, ha!
                    MARCUS ANDRONICUS.
Why dost thou laugh? it fits not with this hour.
                    TITUS ANDRONICUS.
Why, I have not another tear to shed:
Besides, this sorrow is an enemy,
And would usurp upon my watery eyes,
And make them blind with tributary tears:
Then which way shall I find Revenge's cave?
For these two heads do seem to speak to me,
And threat me I shall never come to bliss
Till all these mischiefs be return'd again
Even in their throats that have committed them.
Come, let me see what task I have to do.—
You heavy people, circle me about,
That I may turn me to each one of you,
And swear unto my soul to right your wrongs.—
The vow is made.—Come, brother, take a head;
And in this hand the other will I bear.—
Lavinia, thou shalt be employ'd in these things;
Bear thou my hand, sweet wench, between thy
    teeth.—
As for thee, boy, go get thee from my sight;
Thou art an exile, and thou must not stay:
Hie to the Goths, and raise an army there:
And, if you love me, as I think you do,
Let's kiss and part, for we have much to do.
                    [*Exeunt* TITUS, MARCUS, *and* LAVINIA.

LUCIUS.

Farewell, Andronicus, my noble father,—
The woefull'st man that ever lived in Rome:
Farewell, proud Rome; till Lucius come again,
He leaves his pledges dearer than his life:
Farewell, Lavinia, my noble sister;
O, would thou wert as thou tofore hast been!
But now nor Lucius nor Lavinia lives
But in oblivion and hateful griefs.
If Lucius live, he will requite your wrongs;
And make proud Saturnine and his empress
Beg at the gates, like Tarquin and his queen.
Now will I to the Goths, and raise a power,
To be revenged on Rome and Saturnine.   [*Exit.*

SCENE II.

A room in TITUS' *house. A banquet set out.*

Enter TITUS, MARCUS, LAVINIA, *and* YOUNG
LUCIUS, *a boy.*

TITUS ANDRONICUS.

SO, so; now sit: and look you eat no more
Than will preserve just so much strength in
us
As will revenge these bitter woes of ours.
Marcus, unknit that sorrow-wreathen knot:
Thy niece and I, poor creatures, want our
hands,
And cannot passionate our tenfold grief
With folded arms. This poor right hand of mine
Is left to tyrannize upon my breast;
Who, when my heart, all mad with misery,
Beats in this hollow prison of my flesh,
Then thus I thump it down.—
[*to* LAVINIA] Thou map of woe, that thus dost
talk in signs!
When thy poor heart beats with outrageous beat-
ing,
Thou canot not strike it thus to make it still.
Wound it with sighing, girl, kill it with groans;
Or get some little knife between thy teeth,
And just against thy heart make thou a hole;
That all the tears that thy poor eyes let fall
May run into that sink, and, soaking in,
Drown the lamenting fool in sea-salt tears.

MARCUS ANDRONICUS.

Fie, brother, fie! teach her not thus to lay
Such violent hands upon her tender life.

TITUS ANDRONICUS.

How now! has sorrow made thee dote already?
Why, Marcus, no man should be mad but I.
What violent hands can she lay on her life?—
Ah, wherefore dost thou urge the name of
hands;—
To bid Aeneas tell the tale twice o'er,
How Troy was burnt, and he made miserable?
O, handle not the theme, to talk of hands,
Lest we remember still that we have none.—
Fie, fie, how franticly I square my talk,—
As if we should forget we had no hands,
If Marcus did not name the word of hands!—
Come, let's fall to; and, gentle girl, eat this:—
Here is no drink!—Hark, Marcus, what she
says;—
can interpret all her martyr'd signs;—

She says she drinks no other drink but tears,
Brew'd with her sorrow, masht upon her
cheeks:—
Speechless complainer, I will learn thy thought;
In thy dumb action will I be as perfect
As begging hermits in their holy prayers:
Thou shalt not sigh, nor hold thy stumps to
heaven,
Nor wink, nor nod, nor kneel, nor make a sign,
But I of these will wrest an alphabet,
And by still practice learn to know thy meaning.

YOUNG LUCIUS.

Good grandsire, leave these bitter deep laments:
Make my aunt merry with some pleasing tale.

MARCUS ANDRONICUS.

Alas, the tender boy, in passion moved,
Doth weep to see his grandsire's heaviness.

TITUS ANDRONICUS.

Peace, tender sapling; thou art made of tears,
And tears will quickly melt thy life away.—
[MARCUS *strikes the dish with a knife.*
What dost thou strike at, Marcus, with thy
knife?

MARCUS ANDRONICUS.

At that that I have kill'd, my lord,—a fly.

TITUS ANDRONICUS.

Out on thee, murderer! thou kill'st my heart;
Mine eyes are cloy'd with view of tyranny:
A deed of death done on the innocent
Becomes not Titus' brother: get thee gone;
I see thou art not for my company.

MARCUS ANDRONICUS.

Alas, my lord, I have but kill'd a fly.

TITUS ANDRONICUS.

But how, if that fly had a father and mother?
How would he hang his slender gilded wings,
And buzz lamenting doings in the air!
Poor harmless fly,
That, with his pretty buzzing melody,
Came here to make us merry! and thou hast kill'd
him.

MARCUS ANDRONICUS.

Pardon me, sir; it was a black ill-favour'd fly,
Like to the empress' Moor; therefore I kill'd him.

TITUS ANDRONICUS.

O, O, O,
Then pardon me for reprehending thee,
For thou hast done a charitable deed.
Give me thy knife, I will insult on him;
Flattering myself, as if it were the Moor
Come hither purposely to poison me.—
There's for thyself, and that's for Tamora.—
Ah, sirrah!
As yet, I think, we are not brought so low
But that between us we can kill a fly
That comes in likeness of a coal-black Moor.

MARCUS ANDRONICUS.

Alas, poor man! grief has so wrought on him,
He takes false shadows for true substances.

TITUS ANDRONICUS.

Come, take away.—Lavinia, go with me:
I'll to thy closet; and go read with thee
Sad stories chanced in the times of old.—
Come, boy, and go with me: thy sight is young,
And thou shalt read when mine begin to dazzle.
[*Exeunt*

ACT IV. SCENE I.

Rome.   The garden of TITUS' *house.*

Enter YOUNG LUCIUS, *and* LAVINIA *running after him, and the* BOY *flies from her, with his books under his arm.   Then enter* TITUS *and* MARCUS.

YOUNG LUCIUS.

HELP, grandsire, help! my aunt Lavinia
Follows me every where, I know not why:—
Good uncle Marcus, see how swift she comes.—
Alas, sweet aunt, I know not what you mean.

MARCUS ANDRONICUS.

Stand by me, Lucius; do not fear thine aunt.

TITUS ANDRONICUS.

She loves thee, boy, too well to do thee harm.

YOUNG LUCIUS.

Ay, when my father was in Rome she did.

MARCUS ANDRONICUS.

What means my niece Lavinia by these signs?

TITUS ANDRONICUS.

Fear her not, Lucius:—somewhat doth she
mean:—
See, Lucius, see how much she makes of thee:
Somewhither would she have thee go with her.
Ah, boy, Cornelia never with more care
Read to her sons than she hath read to thee
Sweet poetry and Tully's Orator.

MARCUS ANDRONICUS.

Canst thou not guess wherefore she plies thee
thus?

YOUNG LUCIUS.

My lord, I know not, I, nor can I guess,
Unless some fit or frenzy do possess her:
For I have heard my grandsire say full oft,
Extremity of griefs would make men mad;
And I have read that Hecuba of Troy
Ran mad through sorrow: that made me to fear;
Although, my lord, I know my noble aunt
Loves me as dear as e'er my mother did,
And would not, but in fury, fright my youth:
Which made me down to throw my books, and
fly,—
Causeless, perhaps.—But pardon me, sweet
aunt:
And, madam, if my uncle Marcus go,
I will most willingly attend your ladyship.

MARCUS ANDRONICUS.

Lucius, I will.

[LAVINIA *turns over with her stumps the
books which* LUCIUS *has let fall.*

TITUS ANDRONICUS.

How now, Lavinia! Marcus, what means this?
Some book there is that she desires to see.
Which is it, girl, of these? Open them, boy.
But thou art deeper read, and better skill'd:
Come, and take choice of all my library,
And so beguile thy sorrow, till the heavens
Reveal the damn'd contriver of this deed.—
Why lifts she up her arms in sequence thus?

MARCUS ANDRONICUS.

I think she means that there was more than
one
Confederate in the fact; ay, more there was;
Or else to heaven she heaves them for revenge.

TITUS ANDRONICUS.

Lucius, what book is that she tosseth so?

YOUNG LUCIUS.

Grandsire, 'tis Ovid's Metamorphoses;
My mother gave it me.

MARCUS ANDRONICUS.

For love of her that's gone,
Perhaps she cull'd it from among the rest.

TITUS ANDRONICUS.

Soft! so busily she turns the leaves!
Help her:
What would she find?—Lavinia, shall I read?
This is the tragic tale of Philomel,
And treats of Tereus' treason and his rape;
And rape, I fear, was root of thine annoy.

MARCUS ANDRONICUS.

See, brother, see; note how she quotes the leaves.

TITUS ANDRONICUS.

Lavinia, wert thou thus surprised, sweet girl,
Ravisht and wrong'd, as Philomela was,
Forced in the ruthless, vast, and gloomy
woods?—
See, see:—
Ay, such a place there is, where we did hunt—
O, had we never, never hunted there!—
Pattern'd by that the poet here describes,
By nature made for murders and for rapes.

MARCUS ANDRONICUS.

O, why should nature build so foul a den,
Unless the gods delight in tragedies?

TITUS ANDRONICUS.

Give signs, sweet girl,—for here are none but
friends,—
What Roman lord it was durst do the deed:
Or slunk not Saturnine, as Tarquin erst,
That left the camp to sin in Lucrece' bed?

MARCUS ANDRONICUS.

Sit down, sweet niece:—brother, sit down by
me.—
Apollo, Pallas, Jove, or Mercury,
Inspire me, that I may this treason find!—
My lord, look here!—look here, Lavinia:
This sandy plot is plain; guide, if thou canst,
This after me, when I have writ my name
Without the help of any hand at all.

[*He writes his name with his staff, and guides
it with feet and mouth.*

Curst be that heart that forced us to this shift! —
Write thou, good niece; and here display, at last,
What God will have discover'd for revenge:
Heaven guide thy pen to print thy sorrows plain,
That we may know the traitors and the truth!

[*She takes the staff in her mouth, and guides
it with her stumps, and writes.*

TITUS ANDRONICUS.

O, do ye read, my lord, what she hath writ?—
'*Stuprum, Chiron, Demetrius.*'

MARCUS ANDRONICUS.

What, what! the lustful sons of Tamora
Performers of this heinous, bloody deed?

TITUS ANDRONICUS.

Magni dominator poli,
Tam lentus audis scelera? tam lentus vides?

MARCUS ANDRONICUS.

O, calm thee, gentle lord; although I know
There is enough written upon this earth
To stir a mutiny in the mildest thoughts,
And arm the minds of infants to exclaims.

My lord, kneel down with me; Lavinia, kneel;
And kneel, sweet boy, the Roman Hector's hope;
And swear with me,—as, with the woful fere
And father of that chaste dishonour'd dame,
Lord Junius Brutus sware for Lucrece' rape,—
That we will prosecute, by good advice,
Mortal revenge upon these traitorous Goths,
And see their blood, or die with this reproach.

TITUS ANDRONICUS.

'Tis sure enough, an you knew how.
But if you hunt these bear-whelps, then beware:
The dam will wake; and, if she wind you once,
She's with the lion deeply still in league,
And lulls him whilst she playeth on her back,
And when he sleeps will she do what she list.
You are a young huntsman, Marcus; let alone;
And, come, I will go get a leaf of brass,
And with a gad of steel will write these words,
And lay it by: the angry northern wind
Will blow these sands, like Sibyl's leaves, abroad
And where's your lesson, then?—Boy, what say
  you?

YOUNG LUCIUS.

I say, my lord, that if I were a man,
Their mother's bed-chamber should not be safe
For these bad bondmen to the yoke of Rome.

MARCUS ANDRONICUS.

Ay, that's my boy! thy father hath full oft
For his ungrateful country done the like.

YOUNG LUCIUS.

And, uncle, so will I, an if I live.

TITUS ANDRONICUS.

Come, go with me into mine armoury;
Lucius, I'll fit thee; and withal, my boy
Shall carry from me to the empress' sons
Presents that I intend to send them both:
Come, come; thou'lt do thy message, wilt thou
  not?

YOUNG LUCIUS.

Ay, with my dagger in their bosoms, grandsire.

TITUS ANDRONICUS.

No, boy, not so; I'll teach thee another course.—
Lavinia, come.—Marcus, look to my house:
Lucius and I'll go brave it at the court;
Ay, marry, will we, sir; and we'll be waited on.
  [*Exeunt* TITUS, LAVINIA, *and* YOUNG
    LUCIUS.

MARCUS ANDRONICUS.

O heavens, can you hear a good man groan,
And not relent, or not compassion him?—
Marcus, attend him in his ecstasy,
That hath more scars of sorrow in his heart
Than foemen's marks upon his batter'd shield;
But yet so just that he will not revenge:—
Revenge, ye heavens, for old Andronicus!   [*Exit.*

SCENE II.

The same. A room in the palace.

Enter AARON, DEMETRIUS, *and* CHIRON, *at one
door; at another door* YOUNG LUCIUS, *and*
ANOTHER, *with a bundle of weapons, and
verses writ upon them.*

CHIRON.

DEMETRIUS, here's the son of Lucius;
He hath some message to deliver us.

AARON.

Ay, some mad message from his mad grandfather.

YOUNG LUCIUS.

My lords, with all the humbleness I may,
I greet your honours from Andronicus,—
[*aside*] And pray the Roman gods confound you
  both!

DEMETRIUS.

Gramercy, lovely Lucius: what's the news?

YOUNG LUCIUS [*aside*].

That you are both decipher'd, that's the news,
For villains markt with rape.—May it please
  you,
My grandsire, well advised, hath sent by me
The goodliest weapons of his armoury
To gratify your honourable youth,
The hope of Rome; for so he bid me say;
And so I do, and with his gifts present
Your lordships, that, whenever you have need,
You may be armed and appointed well:
And so I leave you both,—[*aside*] like bloody
  villains.
    [*Exeunt* YOUNG LUCIUS *and* ATTENDANT.

DEMETRIUS.

What's here? A scroll; and written round about?
Let's see:—
[*Reads*] *Integer vitæ, scelerisque purus,
    Non eget Mauri jaculis, nec arcu.*

CHIRON.

O, 'tis a verse in Horace; I know it well:
I read it in the grammar long ago.

AARON.

Ay, just,—a verse in Horace;—right, you have
  it.—
[*aside*] Now, what a thing it is to be an ass!
Here's no sound jest! the old man hath found
  their guilt;
And sends them weapons wrapt about with lines
That wound, beyond their feeling, to the quick.
But were our witty empress well a-foot,
She would applaud Andronicus' conceit:
But let her rest in her unrest awhile.—
And now, young lords, was't not a happy star
Led us to Rome, strangers, and more than so,
Captives, to be advanced to this height?
It did me good, before the palace-gate
To brave the tribune in his brother's hearing.

DEMETRIUS.

But me more good, to see so great a lord
Basely insinuate and send us gifts.

AARON.

Had he not reason, Lord Demetrius?
Did you not use his daughter very friendly?

DEMETRIUS.

I would we had a thousand Roman dames
At such a bay, by turn to serve our lust.

CHIRON.

A charitable wish and full of love.

AARON.

Here lacks but your mother for to say amen.

CHIRON.

And that would she for twenty thousand more.

DEMETRIUS.

Come, let us go; and pray to all the gods
For our beloved mother in her pains.

AARON.
Pray to the devils; the gods have given us over.
[*Flourish within.*
DEMETRIUS.
Why do the emperor's trumpets flourish thus?
CHIRON.
Belike for joy the emperor hath a son.
DEMETRIUS.
Soft! who comes here?
Enter a NURSE, *with a blackamoor* CHILD.
NURSE.
Good morrow, lords:
O, tell me, did you see Aaron the Moor?
AARON.
Well, more or less, or ne'er a whit at all,
Here Aaron is; and what with Aaron now?
NURSE.
O gentle Aaron, we are all undone!
Now help, or woe betide thee evermore!
AARON.
Why, what a caterwauling dost thou keep!
What dost thou wrap and fumble in thine arms?
NURSE.
O, that which I would hide from heaven's eye,
Our empress' shame, and stately Rome's dis-
grace!—
She is deliver'd, lords,—she is deliver'd.
AARON.
To whom?
NURSE.
I mean, she is brought a-bed.
AARON.
Well, God give her good rest. What hath he sent
her?
NURSE.
A devil.
AARON.
Why, then she is the devil's dam;
A joyful issue.
NURSE.
A joyless, dismal, black, and sorrowful issue:
Here is the babe, as loathsome as a toad
Amongst the fairest breeders of our clime:
The empress sends it thee, thy stamp, thy seal,
And bids thee christen it with thy dagger's point.
AARON.
'Zounds, ye whore! is black so base a hue?—
Sweet blowse, you are a beauteous blossom, sure.
DEMETRIUS.
Villain, what hast thou done?
AARON.
That which thou canst not undo.
CHIRON.
Thou hast undone our mother.
AARON.
Villain, I have done thy mother.
DEMETRIUS.
And therein, hellish dog, thou hast undone
her.
Woe to her chance, and damn'd her loathed
choice!
Accurst the offspring of so foul a fiend!
CHIRON.
It shall not live.
AARON.
It shall not die.

NURSE.
Aaron, it must; the mother wills it so.
AARON.
What, must it, nurse? then let no man but I
Do execution on my flesh and blood.
DEMETRIUS.
I'll broach the tadpole on my rapier's point:—
Nurse, give it me; my sword shall soon dispatch
it.
AARON.
Sooner this sword shall plough thy bowels up.
[*Takes the* CHILD *from the* NURSE, *and
draws.*
Stay, murderous villains! will you kill your
brother?
Now, by the burning tapers of the sky,
That shone so brightly when this boy was got,
He dies upon my scimitar's sharp point
That touches this my first-born son and heir!
I tell you, younglings, not Enceladus,
With all his threat'ning band of Typhon's brood,
Nor great Alcides, nor the god of war,
Shall seize this prey out of his father's hands.
What, what, ye sanguine, shallow-hearted boys!
Ye white-limed walls! ye alehouse painted signs!
Coal-black is better than another hue,
In that it scorns to bear another hue;
For all the water in the ocean
Can never turn the swan's black legs to white,
Although she lave them hourly in the flood.
Tell the empress from me, I am of age
To keep mine own,—excuse it how she can.
DEMETRIUS.
Wilt thou betray thy noble mistress thus?
AARON.
My mistress is my mistress; this, myself,—
The vigour and the picture of my youth:
This before all the world do I prefer;
This maugre all the world will I keep safe,
Or some of you shall smoke for it in Rome.
DEMETRIUS.
By this our mother is for ever shamed.
CHIRON.
Rome will despise her for this foul escape.
NURSE.
The emperor, in his rage, will doom her death.
CHIRON.
I blush to think upon this ignomy.
AARON.
Why, there's the privilege your beauty bears:
Fie, treacherous hue, that will betray with blush-
ing
The close enacts and counsels of the heart!
Here's a young lad framed of another leer:
Look, how the black slave smiles upon the father,
As who should say, 'Old lad, I am thine own.'
He is your brother, lords; sensibly fed
Of that self-blood that first gave life to you;
And from that womb where you imprison'd were
He is enfranchised and come to light:
Nay, he is your brother by the surer side,
Although my seal be stamped in his face.
NURSE.
Aaron, what shall I say unto the empress?
DEMETRIUS.
Advise thee, Aaron, what is to be done,

And we will all subscribe to thy advice:
Save thou the child, so we may all be safe.
AARON.
Then sit we down, and let us all consult.
My son and I will have the wind of you:
Keep there: now talk at pleasure of your safety.
[*They sit.*
DEMETRIUS.
How many women saw this child of his?
AARON.
Why, so, brave lords! when we join in league,
I am a lamb: but if you brave the Moor,
The chafed boar, the mountain lioness,
The ocean swells not so as Aaron storms.—
But say, again, how many saw the child?
NURSE.
Cornelia the midwife and myself;
And no one else but the deliver'd empress.
AARON.
The empress, the midwife, and yourself:—
Two may keep counsel when the third's away:—
Go to the empress, tell her this I said:—
[*He kills her.*
Weke, weke!—so cries a pig prepared to th' spit.
DEMETRIUS.
What mean'st thou, Aaron? wherefore didst thou
this?
AARON.
O Lord, sir, 'tis a deed of policy:
Shall she live to betray this guilt of ours,—
A long-tongued babbling gossip? no, lords, no:
And now be it known to you my full intent.
Not far one Muliteus, my countryman,
His wife but yesternight was brought to bed;
His child is like to her, fair as you are:
Go pack with him, and give the mother gold,
And tell them both the circumstance of all;
And how by this their child shall be advanced,
And be received for the emperor's heir,
And substituted in the place of mine,
To calm this tempest whirling in the court;
And let the emperor dandle him for his own.
Hark ye, lords; you see I have given her physic,
[*Pointing to the* NURSE.
And you must needs bestow her funeral;
The fields are near, and you are gallant grooms:
This done, see that you take no longer days,
But send the midwife presently to me.
The midwife and the nurse well made away,
Then let the ladies tattle what they please.
CHIRON.
Aaron, I see thou wilt not trust the air
With secrets.
DEMETRIUS.
For this care of Tamora,
Herself and hers are highly bound to thee.
[*Exeunt* DEMETRIUS *and* CHIRON, *bear-*
ing off the dead NURSE.
AARON.
Now to the Goths, as swift as swallow flies;
There to dispose this treasure in mine arms,
And secretly to greet the empress' friends.—
Come on, you thick-lipt slave, I'll bear you hence;
For it is you that puts us to our shifts:
I'll make you feed on berries and on roots,
And feed on curds and whey, and suck the goat,

And cabin in a cave; and bring you up
To be a warrior and command a camp.   [*Exit.*

SCENE III.

The same. A public place.

Enter TITUS, MARCUS, YOUNG LUCIUS, *and*
other GENTLEMEN (PUBLIUS, SEMPRONIUS,
CAIUS), *with bows; and* TITUS *bears the arrows*
with letters at the end of them.
TITUS ANDRONICUS.
COME, Marcus, come:—kinsmen, this is the
way.—
Sir boy, now let me see your archery;
Look ye draw home enough, and 'tis there
straight.—
Terras Astræa reliquit:
Be you remember'd, Marcus, she's gone, she's
fled.—
Sirs, take you to your tools. You, cousins, shall
Go sound the ocean, and cast your nets;
Happily you may catch her in the sea;
Yet there's as little justice as at land:
No; Publius and Sempronius, you must do it;
'Tis you must dig with mattock and with spade,
And pierce the inmost centre of the earth:
Then, when you come to Pluto's region,
I pray you, deliver him this petition;
Tell him, it is for justice and for aid,
And that it comes from old Andronicus,
Shaken with sorrows in ungrateful Rome.—
Ah, Rome! Well, well; I made thee miserable
What time I threw the people's suffrages
On him that thus doth tyrannize o'er me.—
Go, get you gone; and pray be careful all,
And leave you not a man-of-war unsearcht:
This wicked emperor may have shipt her hence;
And, kinsmen, then we may go pipe for justice.
MARCUS ANDRONICUS.
O Publius, is not this a heavy case,
To see thy noble uncle thus distract?
PUBLIUS.
Therefore, my lord, it highly us concerns
By day and night t' attend him carefully,
And feed his humour kindly as we may,
Till time beget some careful remedy.
MARCUS ANDRONICUS.
Kinsmen, his sorrows are past remedy.
Join with the Goths; and with revengeful war
Take wreak on Rome for this ingratitude,
And vengeance on the traitor Saturnine.
TITUS ANDRONICUS.
Publius, how now! how now, my masters! What
Have you met with her?
PUBLIUS.
No, my good lord; but Pluto sends you word,
If you will have Revenge from hell, you shall:
Marry, for Justice, she is so employ'd,
He thinks, with Jove in heaven, or somewhere
else,
So that perforce you must needs stay a time.
TITUS ANDRONICUS.
He doth me wrong to feed me with delays.
I'll dive into the burning lake below,
And pull her out of Acheron by the heels.—
Marcus, we are but shrubs, no cedars we,

No big-boned men framed of the Cyclops' size;
But metal, Marcus, steel to the very back,   [bear:
Yet wrung with wrongs more than our backs can
And, sith there's no justice in earth nor hell,
We will solicit heaven, and move the gods
To send down Justice for to wreak our wrongs.—
Come, to this gear.—You are a good archer,
  Marcus;   [*He gives them the arrows.*
Ad Jovem, that's for you:—here, *Ad Apollinem*:—
Ad Martem, that's for myself:—
Here, boy, *To Pallas*:—here, *To Mercury*:—
To Saturn, Caius, not to Saturnine;
You were as good to shoot against the wind.—
To it, boy.—Marcus, loose when I bid.—
Of my word, I have written to effect;
There's not a god left unsolicited.

      MARCUS ANDRONICUS.
Kinsmen, shoot all your shafts into the court:
We will afflict the emperor in his pride.

      TITUS ANDRONICUS.
Now, masters, draw. [*They shoot.*]—O, well said,
  Lucius!—
Good boy, in Virgo's lap; give it Pallas.

      MARCUS ANDRONICUS.
My lord, I aim a mile beyond the moon;
Your letter is with Jupiter by this.

      TITUS ANDRONICUS.
Ha, ha!
Publius, Publius, what hast thou done?
See, see, thou hast shot off one of Taurus' horns.

      MARCUS ANDRONICUS.
This was the sport, my lord: when Publius shot,
The Bull, being gall'd, gave Aries such a knock
That down fell both the Ram's horns in the
  court;   [villain?
And who should find them but the empress'
She laught, and told the Moor he should not
  choose
But give them to his master for a present.

      TITUS ANDRONICUS.
Why, there it goes: God give his lordship joy!
  Enter a CLOWN, *with a basket, and two pigeons
      in it.*
News, news from heaven! Marcus, the post is
  come.—
Sirrah, what tidings? have you any letters?
Shall I have justice? what says Jupiter?

      CLOWN.
Ho, the gibbet-maker! he says that he hath taken
them down again, for the man must not be
hang'd till the next week.

      TITUS ANDRONICUS.
But what says Jupiter, I ask thee?

      CLOWN.
Alas, sir, I know not Jupiter; I never drank with
him in all my life.

      TITUS ANDRONICUS.
Why, villain, art not thou the carrier?

      CLOWN.
Ay, of my pigeons, sir; nothing else.

      TITUS ANDRONICUS.
Why, didst thou not come from heaven?

      CLOWN.
From heaven! alas, sir, I never came there: God
forbid I should be so bold to press to heaven in
my young days. Why, I am going with my pigeons

to the tribunal plebs, to take up a matter of brawl
betwixt my uncle and one of the emperial's men.

      MARCUS ANDRONICUS.
Why, sir, that is as fit as can be to serve for your
oration; and let him deliver the pigeons to the
emperor from you.

      TITUS ANDRONICUS.
Tell me, can you deliver an oration to the emperor with a grace?

      CLOWN.
Nay, truly, sir, I could never say grace in all my
life.

      TITUS ANDRONICUS.
Sirrah, come hither: make no more ado,
But give your pigeons to the emperor:
By me thou shalt have justice at his hands.
Hold, hold; meanwhile here's money for thy
  charges.—
Give me pen and ink.—
Sirrah, can you with a grace deliver a supplication?

      CLOWN.
Ay, sir.

      TITUS ANDRONICUS.
Then here is a supplication for you. And when
you come to him, at the first approach you must
kneel; then kiss his foot; then deliver up your
pigeons; and then look for your reward. I'll be at
hand, sir; see you do it bravely.

      CLOWN.
I warrant you, sir, let me alone.

      TITUS ANDRONICUS.
Sirrah, hast thou a knife? come, let me see it.—
Here, Marcus, fold it in the oration;
For thou hast made it like an humble suppliant:—
And when thou hast given it to the emperor,
Knock at my door, and tell me what he says.

      CLOWN.
God be with you, sir; I will.   [*Exit.*

      TITUS ANDRONICUS.
Come, Marcus, let us go.—Publius, follow me.
           [*Exeunt.*

SCENE IV.

The same. Before the palace.

Enter SATURNINUS, TAMORA, DEMETRIUS,
  CHIRON, LORDS, *and others; the* EMPEROR
  brings the arrows in his hand that TITUS *shot at*
  him.

      SATURNINUS.
WHY, lords, what wrongs are these! was ever
    seen
An emperor in Rome thus overborne,
Troubled, confronted thus; and, for the extent
Of egal justice, used in such contempt?
My lords, you know, as do the mightful gods,
However these disturbers of our peace
Buzz in the people's ears, there naught hath past,
But even with law, against the wilful sons
Of old Andronicus. And what an if
His sorrows have so overwhelm'd his wits,—
Shall we be thus afflicted in his wreaks,
His fits, his frenzy, and his bitterness?
And now he writes to heaven for his redress:
See, here's *To Jove*, and this *To Mercury*;
This *To Apollo*; this *To the god of war*;—
Sweet scrolls to fly about the streets of Rome!

What's this but libelling against the senate,
And blazoning our injustice every where?
A goodly humour, is it not, my lords?
As who would say, in Rome no justice were.
But if I live, his feigned ecstasies
Shall be no shelter to these outrages:
But he and his shall know that justice lives
In Saturninus' health; whom, if she sleep,
He'll so awake, as she in fury shall
Cut off the proud'st conspirator that lives.

TAMORA.

My gracious lord, my lovely Saturnine,
Lord of my life, commander of my thoughts,
Calm thee, and bear the faults of Titus' age,
Th' effects of sorrow for his valiant sons, [heart;
Whose loss hath pierced him deep and scarr'd his
And rather comfort his distressed plight
Than prosecute the meanest or the best [become
For these contempts.—[aside] Why, thus it shall
High-witted Tamora to gloze with all:
But, Titus, I have toucht thee to the quick,
Thy life-blood out: if Aaron now be wise,
Then is all safe, the anchor's in the port.—

Enter CLOWN.

How now, good fellow! wouldst thou speak with us?

CLOWN.

Yea, forsooth, an your mister-ship be emperial.

TAMORA.

Empress I am, but yonder sits the emperor.

CLOWN.

'Tis he.—God and Saint Stephen give you god-
den: I have brought you a letter and a couple of
pigeons here.   [SATURNINUS reads the letter.

SATURNINUS.

Go, take him away, and hang him presently.

CLOWN.

How much money must I have?

TAMORA.

Come, sirrah, you must be hang'd.

CLOWN.

Hang'd! by'r lady, then I have brought up a neck
to a fair end.   [Exit, guarded.

SATURNINUS.

Despiteful and intolerable wrongs!
Shall I endure this monstrous villainy?
I know from whence this same device proceeds:
May this be borne,—as if his traitorous sons,
That died by law for murder of our brother,
Have by my means been butcher'd wrongfully?—
Go, drag the villain hither by the hair;
Nor age nor honour shall shape privilege:
For this proud mock I'll be thy slaughter-man;
Sly frantic wretch, that holp'st to make me great,
In hope thyself should govern Rome and me.

Enter AEMILIUS.

What news with thee, Aemilius?

AEMILIUS.

Arm, my lords,—Rome never had more cause!
The Goths have gather'd head; and with a power
Of high-resolved men, bent to the spoil,
They hither march amain, under conduct
Of Lucius, son to old Andronicus;
Who threats, in course of this revenge, to do
As much as ever Coriolanus did.

SATURNINUS.

Is warlike Lucius general of the Goths?

These tidings nip me; and I hang the head
As flowers with frost, or grass beat down with
  storms:
Ay, now begins our sorrows to approach:
'Tis he the common people love so much;
Myself hath often heard them say—
When I have walked like a private man—
That Lucius' banishment was wrongfully,
And they have wisht that Lucius were their
  emperor.

TAMORA.

Why should you fear? is not your city strong?

SATURNINUS.

Ay, but the citizens favour Lucius,
And will revolt from me to succour him.

TAMORA.

King, be thy thoughts imperious, like thy name.
Is the sun dimm'd, that gnats do fly in it?
The eagle suffers little birds to sing,
And is not careful what they mean thereby,
Knowing that with the shadow of his wings
He can at pleasure stint their melody:
Even so mayst thou the giddy men of Rome.
Then cheer thy spirit: for know, thou emperor,
I will enchant the old Andronicus
With words more sweet, and yet more dangerous,
Than baits to fish, or honey-stalks to sheep;
Whenas the one is wounded with the bait,
The other rotted with delicious feed.

SATURNINUS.

But he will not entreat his son for us.

TAMORA.

If Tamora entreat him, then he will:
For I can smooth, and fill his aged ear
With golden promises; that, were his heart
Almost impregnable, his old ears deaf,
Yet should both ear and heart obey my tongue.—
[to AEMILIUS] Go thou before, be our ambassador:
Say that the emperor requests a parley
Of warlike Lucius, and appoint the meeting
Even at his father's house, the old Andronicus.

SATURNINUS.

Aemilius, do this message honourably;
And if he stand on hostage for his safety,
Bid him demand what pledge will please him best.

AEMILIUS.

Your bidding shall I do effectually.   [Exit.

TAMORA.

Now will I to that old Andronicus,
And temper him, with all the art I have,
To pluck proud Lucius from the warlike Goths.
And now, sweet emperor, be blithe again,
And bury all thy fear in my devices.

SATURNINUS.

Then go successantly, and plead to him.
    [Exeunt.

ACT V. SCENE I.

Plains near Rome.

Flourish. Enter LUCIUS, with an army of GOTHS,
with drum and colours.

LUCIUS.

APPROVED warriors, and my faithful friends,
I have received letters from great Rome,
Which signify what hate they bear their emperor,
And how desirous of our sight they are.

Therefore, great lords, be, as your titles witness,
Imperious, and impatient of your wrongs;
And wherein Rome hath done you any scathe,
Let him make treble satisfaction.

FIRST GOTH.

Brave slip, sprung from the great Andronicus,
Whose name was once our terror, now our
    comfort;
Whose high exploits and honourable deeds
Ingrateful Rome requites with foul contempt,
Be bold in us: we'll follow where thou lead'st,—
Like stinging bees in hottest summer's day,
Led by their master to the flow'red fields,—
And be avenged on cursed Tamora.

GOTHS.

And as he saith, so say we all with him.

LUCIUS.

I humbly thank him, and I thank you all.—
But who comes here, led by a lusty Goth?

Enter a GOTH, *leading of* AARON *with his* CHILD
in his arms.

SECOND GOTH.

Renowned Lucius, from our troops I stray'd
To gaze upon a ruinous monastery;
And, as I earnestly did fix mine eye
Upon the wasted building, suddenly
I heard a child cry underneath a wall.
I made unto the noise; when soon I heard
The crying babe controll'd with this discourse:
'Peace, tawny slave, half me and half thy dam!
Did not thy hue bewray whose brat thou art,
Had nature lent thee but thy mother's look,
Villain, thou mightst have been an emperor:
But where the bull and cow are both milk-white,
They never do beget a coal-black calf.
Peace, villain, peace!'—even thus he rates the
    babe,
'For I must bear thee to a trusty Goth;
Who, when he knows thou art the empress' babe,
Will hold thee dearly for thy mother's sake.'
With this, my weapon drawn, I rusht upon him,
Surprised him suddenly; and brought him hither,
To use as you think needful of the man.

LUCIUS.

O worthy Goth, this is the incarnate devil
That robb'd Andronicus of his good hand;
This is the pearl that pleased your empress' eye;
And here's the base fruit of his burning lust.—
Say, wall-eyed slave, whither wouldst thou
    convey
This growing image of thy fiend-like face?
Why dost not speak? what, deaf? not a word?—
A halter, soldiers! hang him on this tree,
And by his side his fruit of bastardy.

AARON.

Touch not the boy,—he is of royal blood.

LUCIUS.

Too like the sire for ever being good.—
First hang the child, that he may see it sprawl,—
A sight to vex the father's soul withal.—
Get me a ladder.

[*A ladder brought, which* AARON *is made*
to ascend.

AARON.

Lucius, save the child,
And bear it from me to the empress.

If thou do this, I'll show thee wondrous things.
That highly may advantage thee to hear:
If thou wilt not, befall what may befall,
I'll speak no more but—vengeance rot you all!

LUCIUS.

Say on: an if it please me which thou speak'st,
Thy child shall live, and I will see it nourisht.

AARON.

An if it please thee! why, assure thee, Lucius,
'Twill vex thy soul to hear what I shall speak;
For I must talk of murders, rapes, and massacres,
Acts of black night, abominable deeds,
Complots of mischief, treason, villainies
Ruthful to hear, yet piteously perform'd:
And this shall all be buried in my death,
Unless thou swear to me my child shall live.

LUCIUS.

Tell on thy mind; I say thy child shall live.

AARON.

Swear that he shall, and then I will begin.

LUCIUS.

Who should I swear by? thou believest no god:
That granted, how canst thou believe an oath?

AARON.

What if I do not? as, indeed, I do not;
Yet, for I know thou art religious,
And hast a thing within thee called conscience,
With twenty popish tricks and ceremonies,
Which I have seen thee careful to observe,
Therefore I urge thy oath; for that I know
An idiot holds his bauble for a god,
And keeps the oath which by that god he swears,
To that I'll urge him:—therefore thou shalt vow
By that same god, what god soe'er it be,
That thou adorest and hast in reverence,—
To save my boy, to nourish and bring him up;
Or else I will discover naught to thee.

LUCIUS.

Even by my god I swear to thee I will.

AARON.

First know thou, I begot him on the empress.

LUCIUS.

O most insatiate and luxurious woman!

AARON.

Tut, Lucius, this was but a deed of charity
To that which thou shalt hear of me anon.
'Twas her two sons that murder'd Bassianus;
They cut thy sister's tongue, and ravisht her,
And cut her hands, and trimm'd her as thou
    saw'st.

LUCIUS.

O detestable villain! call'st thou that trimming?

AARON.

Why, she was washt, and cut, and trimm'd; and
   'twas
Trim sport for them that had the doing of it.

LUCIUS.

O barbarous, beastly villains, like thyself!

AARON.

Indeed, I was their tutor to instruct them:
That codding spirit had they from their mother,
As sure a card as ever won the set;
That bloody mind, I think, they learn'd of me,
As true a dog as ever fought at head.—
Well, let my deeds be witness of my worth.
I train'd thy brethren to that guileful hole,

Where the dead corpse of Bassianus lay:
I wrote the letter that thy father found,
And hid the gold within the letter mention'd,
Confederate with the queen and her two sons:
And what not done, that thou hast cause to rue,
Wherein I had no stroke of mischief in it?
I play'd the cheater for thy father's hand;
And, when I had it, drew myself apart,   [laughter:
And almost broke my heart with extreme
I pried me through the crevice of a wall
When, for his hand, he had his two sons' heads;
Beheld his tears, and laught so heartily,
That both mine eyes were rainy like to his:
And when I told the empress of this sport,
She swounded almost at my pleasing tale,
And for my tidings gave me twenty kisses.

FIRST GOTH.
What, canst thou say all this, and never blush?

AARON.
Ay, like a black dog, as the saying is.

LUCIUS.
Art thou not sorry for these heinous deeds?

AARON.
Ay, that I had not done a thousand more.
Even now I curse the day—and yet, I think,
Few come within the compass of my curse—
Wherein I did not some notorious ill:
As, kill a man, or else devise his death;
Ravish a maid, or plot the way to do it;
Accuse some innocent, and forswear myself;
Set deadly enmity between two friends;
Make poor men's cattle break their necks;
Set fire on barns and hay-stacks in the night,
And bid the owners quench them with their tears.
Oft have I digg'd up dead men from their graves,
And set them upright at their dear friends' doors,
Even when their sorrows almost was forgot;
And on their skins, as on the bark of trees,
Have with my knife carved in Roman letters,
'Let not your sorrow die, though I am dead.'
Tut, I have done a thousand dreadful things
As willingly as one would kill a fly;
And nothing grieves me heartily indeed,
But that I cannot do ten thousand more.

LUCIUS.
Bring down the devil; for he must not die
So sweet a death as hanging presently.
     [AARON is brought down from the ladder.

AARON.
If there be devils, would I were a devil,
To live and burn in everlasting fire,
So I might have your company in hell,
But to torment you with my bitter tongue!

LUCIUS.
Sirs, stop his mouth, and let him speak no more.
     Enter a GOTH.

THIRD GOTH.
My lord, there is a messenger from Rome
Desires to be admitted to your presence.

LUCIUS.
Let him come near.
     Enter AEMILIUS.
Welcome, Aemilius: what's the news from Rome?

AEMILIUS.
Lord Lucius, and you princes of the Goths,
The Roman emperor greets you all by me;

And, for he understands you are in arms,
He craves a parley at your father's house,
Willing you to demand your hostages,
And they shall be immediately deliver'd.

FIRST GOTH.
What says our general?

LUCIUS.
Aemilius, let the emperor give his pledges
Unto my father and my uncle Marcus,
And we will come.—March, away!
     [Flourish.   Exeunt

SCENE II.

Rome.   Before TITUS' house.

*Enter TAMORA and her two SONS, DEMETRIUS
and CHIRON, disguised.*

TAMORA.
THUS, in this strange and sad habiliment,
I will encounter with Andronicus,
And say I am Revenge, sent from below
To join with him and right his heinous wrongs.
Knock at his study, where, they say, he keeps,
To ruminate strange plots of dire revenge;
Tell him Revenge is come to join with him,
And work confusion on his enemies.
     [*They knock and TITUS opens his study
     door.*

TITUS ANDRONICUS.
Who doth molest my contemplation?
Is it your trick to make me ope the door,
That so my sad decrees may fly away,
And all my study be to no effect?
You are deceived: for what I mean to do
See here in bloody lines I have set down;
And what is written shall be executed.

TAMORA.
Titus, I am come to talk with thee.

TITUS ANDRONICUS.
No, not a word: how can I grace my talk,
Wanting a hand to give it action?
Thou hast the odds of me; therefore no more.

TAMORA.
If thou didst know me, thou wouldst talk with
     me.

TITUS ANDRONICUS.
I am not mad; I know thee well enough:
Witness this wretched stump, witness these
     crimson lines;
Witness these trenches made by grief and care;
Witness the tiring day and heavy night;
Witness all sorrow, that I know thee well
For our proud empress, mighty Tamora:
Is not thy coming for my other hand?

TAMORA.
Know, thou sad man, I am not Tamora;
She is thy enemy, and I thy friend:
I am Revenge; sent from th' infernal kingdom,
To ease the gnawing vulture of thy mind,
By working wreakful vengeance on thy foes.
Come down, and welcome me to this world's
     light;
Confer with me of murder and of death:
There's not a hollow cave or lurking-place,
No vast obscurity or misty vale,
Where bloody murder or detested rape

Can couch for fear, but I will find them out;
And in their ears tell them my dreadful name,—
Revenge,—which makes the foul offenders quake.
TITUS ANDRONICUS.
Art thou Revenge? and art thou sent to me,
To be a torment to mine enemies?
TAMORA.
I am; therefore come down, and welcome me.
TITUS ANDRONICUS.
Do me some service, ere I come to thee.
Lo, by thy side where Rape and Murder stand;
Now give some surance that thou art Revenge,—
Stab them, or tear them on thy chariot-wheels;
And then I'll come and be thy wagoner,
And whirl along with thee about the globe.
Provide thee two proper palfreys, black as jet,
To hale thy vengeful wagon swift away,
And find our murderers in their guilty caves:
And when thy car is loaden with their heads,
I will dismount, and by the wagon-wheel
Trot, like a servile footman, all day long,
Even from Hyperion's rising in the east
Until his very downfall in the sea:
And day by day I'll do this heavy task,
So thou destroy Rapine and Murder there.
TAMORA.
These are my ministers, and come with me.
TITUS ANDRONICUS.
Are these thy ministers? what are they call'd?
TAMORA.
Rapine and Murder; therefore called so,
'Cause they take vengeance of such kind of men.
TITUS ANDRONICUS.
Good Lord, how like the empress' sons they are!
And you, the empress! but we worldly men
Have miserable, mad, mistaking eyes.
O sweet Revenge, now do I come to thee;
And, if one arm's embracement will content thee,
I will embrace thee in it by and by.   [*Exit above.*
TAMORA.
This closing with him fits his lunacy:
Whate'er I forge to feed his brain-sick fits,
Do you uphold and maintain in your speeches,
For now he firmly takes me for Revenge;
And, being credulous in this mad thought,
I'll make him send for Lucius his son;
And, whilst I at a banquet hold him sure,
I'll find some cunning practice out of hand,
To scatter and disperse the giddy Goths,
Or, at the least, make them his enemies.—
See, here he comes, and I must ply my theme.
Enter TITUS, *below.*
TITUS ANDRONICUS.
Long have I been forlorn, and all for thee:
Welcome, dread Fury, to my woeful house:—
Rapine and Murder, you are welcome too:—
How like the empress and her sons you are!
Well are you fitted, had you but a Moor:—
Could not all hell afford you such a devil?—
For well I wot the empress never away
But in her company there is a Moor;
And, would you represent our queen aright,
It were convenient you had such a devil:
But welcome, as you are. What shall we do?
TAMORA.
What wouldst thou have us do, Andronicus?

DEMETRIUS.
Show me a murderer, I'll deal with him.
CHIRON.
Show me a villain that hath done a rape,
And I am sent to be revenged on him.
TAMORA.
Show me a thousand that have done thee wrong,
And I will be revenged on them all.
TITUS ANDRONICUS.
Look round about the wicked streets of Rome;
And when thou find'st a man that's like thyself,
Good Murder, stab him; he's a murderer.—
Go thou with him; and when it is thy hap
To find another that is like to thee,
Good Rapine, stab him; he's a ravisher.—
Go thou with them; and in the emperor's court
There is a queen, attended by a Moor;
Well mayst thou know her by thy own proportion,
For up and down she doth resemble thee:
I pray thee, do on them some violent death;
They have been violent to me and mine.
TAMORA.
Well hast thou lesson'd us; this shall we do.
But would it please thee, good Andronicus,
To send for Lucius, thy thrice-valiant son,
Who leads towards Rome a band of warlike
          Goths,
And bid him come and banquet at thy house;
When he is here, even at thy solemn feast,
I will bring in the empress and her sons,
The emperor himself, and all thy foes;
And at thy mercy shall they stoop and kneel,
And on them shalt thou ease thy angry heart.
What says Andronicus to this device?
TITUS ANDRONICUS.
Marcus, my brother! 'tis sad Titus calls.
Enter MARCUS.
Go, gentle Marcus, to thy nephew Lucius;
Thou shalt inquire him out among the Goths:
Bid him repair to me, and bring with him
Some of the chiefest princes of the Goths;
Bid him encamp his soldiers where they are:
Tell him the emperor and the empress too
Feast at my house, and he shall feast with them.
This do thou for my love; and so let him,
As he regards his aged father's life.
MARCUS ANDRONICUS.
This will I do, and soon return again.   [*Exit.*
TAMORA.
Now will I hence about thy business,
And take my ministers along with me.
TITUS ANDRONICUS.
Nay, nay, let Rape and Murder stay with me;
Or else I'll call my brother back again.
And cleave to no revenge but Lucius.
TAMORA [*aside to* DEMETRIUS *and* CHIRON].
What say you, boys? will you abide with him,
Whiles I go tell my lord the emperor
How I have govern'd our determined jest?
Yield to his humour, smooth and speak him
          fair,
And tarry with him till I turn again.
TITUS ANDRONICUS [*aside*].
I know them all, though they suppose me mad,
And will o'er-reach them in their own devices,—
A pair of cursed hell-hounds and their dam.

DEMETRIUS [*aside to* TAMORA].
Madam, depart at pleasure; leave us here.
TAMORA.
Farewell, Andronicus: Revenge now goes
To lay a complot to betray thy foes.
TITUS ANDRONICUS.
I know thou dost; and, sweet Revenge, farewell.
[*Exit* TAMORA.
CHIRON.
Tell us, old man, how shall we be employ'd?
TITUS ANDRONICUS.
Tut, I have work enough for you to do.—
Publius, come hither, Caius, and Valentine!
Enter PUBLIUS, CAIUS, *and* VALENTINE.
PUBLIUS.
What is your will?
TITUS ANDRONICUS.
Know you these two?
PUBLIUS.
The empress' sons,
I take them, Chiron and Demetrius.
TITUS ANDRONICUS.
Fie, Publius, fie! thou art too much deceived.—
The one is Murder, Rape is the other's name;
And therefore bind them, gentle Publius:—
Caius and Valentine, lay hands on them:—
Oft have you heard me wish for such an hour,
And now I find it; therefore bind them sure,
And stop their mouths, if they begin to cry. [*Exit.*
[PUBLIUS, &c., *lay hold on* CHIRON *and*
DEMETRIUS.
CHIRON.
Villains, forbear! we are the empress' sons.
PUBLIUS.
And therefore do we what we are commanded.—
Stop close their mouths, let them not speak a
word.
Is he sure bound? look that you bind them fast.
Enter TITUS, *with a knife, and* LAVINIA, *with a
basin.*
TITUS ANDRONICUS.
Come, come, Lavinia; look, thy foes are bound.—
Sirs, stop their mouths, let them not speak to
me;
But let them hear what fearful words I utter.—
O villains, Chiron and Demetrius!
Here stands the spring whom you have stain'd
with mud;
This goodly summer with your winter mixt.
You kill'd her husband; and, for that vile fault,
Two of her brothers were condemn'd to death,
My hand cut off, and made a merry jest;
Both her sweet hands, her tongue, and that more
dear
Than hands or tongue, her spotless chastity,
Inhuman traitors, you constrain'd and forced.
What would you say, if I should let you speak?
Villains, for shame you could not beg for grace.
Hark, wretches! how I mean to martyr you.
This one hand yet is left to cut your throats,
Whilst that Lavinia 'tween her stumps doth hold
The basin that receives your guilty blood.
You know your mother means to feast with me,
And calls herself Revenge, and thinks me mad:—
Hark, villains! I will grind your bones to dust,
And with your blood and it I'll make a paste;

And of the paste a coffin I will rear,
And make two pasties of your shameful heads;
And bid that strumpet, your unhallow'd dam,
Like to the earth, swallow her own increase.
This is the feast that I have bid her to,
And this the banquet she shall surfeit on;
For worse than Philomel you used my daughter,
And worse than Progne I will be revenged:
And now prepare your throats.—Lavinia, come.
[*He cuts their throats.*
Receive the blood: and when that they are dead,
Let me go grind their bones to powder small,
And with this hateful liquor temper it;
And in that paste let their vile heads be baked.
Come, come, be every one officious
To make this banquet; which I wish may prove
More stern and bloody than the Centaurs' feast.
So:—now bring them in, for I'll play the cook,
And see them ready 'gainst their mother comes.
[*Exeunt, bearing the dead bodies.*

SCENE III.

Court of TITUS' *house: tables set out.*

Enter LUCIUS, MARCUS, *and* GOTHS, *with*
AARON *prisoner.*

LUCIUS.

UNCLE Marcus, since it is my father's mind
That I repair to Rome, I am content.
FIRST GOTH.
And ours with thine, befall what fortune will.
LUCIUS.
Good uncle, take you in this barbarous Moor,
This ravenous tiger, this accursed devil;
Let him receive no sustenance, fetter him,
Till he be brought unto the empress' face,
For testimony of her foul proceedings:
And see the ambush of our friends be strong;
I fear the emperor means no good to us.
AARON.
Some devil whisper curses in my ear,
And prompt me that my tongue may utter forth
The venomous malice of my swelling heart!
LUCIUS.
Away, inhuman dog! unhallow'd slave!—
Sirs, help our uncle to convey him in.
[*Exeunt some* GOTHS *with* AARON.   *Flour-
ish within.*
The trumpets show the emperor is at hand.
Enter SATURNINUS *and* TAMORA, *with*
AEMILIUS, TRIBUNES, SENATORS, *and others.*
SATURNINUS.
What, hath the firmament more suns than one?
LUCIUS.
What boots it thee to call thyself a sun?
MARCUS ANDRONICUS.
Rome's emperor, and nephew, break the parle;
These quarrels must be quietly debated.
The feast is ready, which the careful Titus
Hath ordain'd to an honourable end,
For peace, for love, for league, and good to Rome:
Please you, therefore, draw nigh, and take your
places.
SATURNINUS.
Marcus, we will.
[*Hautboys. A table brought in.*

Enter TITUS, *like a cook, placing the meat on the
table, and* LAVINIA *with a veil over her face,*
YOUNG LUCIUS, *and others.*

TITUS ANDRONICUS.

Welcome, my gracious lord: welcome, dread
    queen;
Welcome, ye warlike Goths; welcome, Lucius;
And welcome, all: although the cheer be poor,
'Twill fill your stomachs; please you eat of it.

SATURNINUS.

Why art thou thus attired, Andronicus?

TITUS ANDRONICUS.

Because I would be sure to have all well,
To entertain your highness and your empress.

TAMORA.

We are beholding to you, good Andronicus.

TITUS ANDRONICUS.

An if your highness knew my heart, you were.—
My lord the emperor, resolve me this:
Was it well done of rash Virginius
To slay his daughter with his own right hand,
Because she was enforced, stain'd, and deflower'd?

SATURNINUS.

It was, Andronicus.

TITUS ANDRONICUS.

Your reason, mighty lord?

SATURNINUS.

Because the girl should not survive her shame,
And by her presence still renew his sorrows.

TITUS ANDRONICUS.

A reason mighty, strong, and effectual;
A pattern, precedent, and lively warrant,
For me, most wretched, to perform the like:—
Die, die, Lavinia, and thy shame with thee;
                      [He kills her.
And with thy shame thy father's sorrow die!

SATURNINUS.

What hast thou done, unnatural and unkind?

TITUS ANDRONICUS.

Kill'd her, for whom my tears have made me
    blind.
I am as woeful as Virginius was,
And have a thousand times more cause than he
To do this outrage;—and it now is done.

SATURNINUS.

What, was she ravisht? tell who did the deed.

TITUS ANDRONICUS.

Will't please you eat? will't please your highness
    feed?

TAMORA.

Why hast thou slain thine only daughter thus?

TITUS ANDRONICUS.

Not I; 'twas Chiron and Demetrius:
They ravisht her, and cut away her tongue;
And they, 'twas they, that did her all this wrong.

SATURNINUS.

Go fetch them hither to us presently.

TITUS ANDRONICUS.

Why, there they are both, baked in that pie;
Whereof their mother daintily hath fed,
Eating the flesh that she herself hath bred.
'Tis true, 'tis true; witness my knife's sharp point.
                   [He stabs the EMPRESS.

SATURNINUS.

Die, **frantic wretch, for this accursed deed!**
                        [Kills TITUS.

LUCIUS.

Can the son's eye behold his father bleed?
There's meed for meed, death for a deadly deed!
    [Kills SATURNINUS.   *A great tumult.*
    LUCIUS, MARCUS, *and others go up into*
    a gallery.

MARCUS ANDRONICUS.

You sad-faced men, people and sons of Rome,
By uproar sever'd, like a flight of fowl
Scatter'd by winds and high tempestuous gusts,
O, let me teach you how to knit again
This scatter'd corn into one mutual sheaf,
These broken limbs again into one body;
Lest Rome herself be bane unto herself,
And she whom mighty kingdoms court'sy to,
Like a forlorn and desperate castaway,
Do shameful execution on herself.
But if my frosty signs and chaps of age,
Grave witnesses of true experience,
Cannot induce you to attend my words,—
[*to* LUCIUS] Speak, Rome's dear friend: as erst
    our ancestor,
When with his solemn tongue he did discourse
To love-sick Dido's sad-attending ear
The story of that baleful-burning night
When subtle Greeks surprised King Priam's
    Troy,—
Tell us what Sinon hath bewitcht our ears,
Or who hath brought the fatal engine in
That gives our Troy, our Rome, the civil
    wound.—
My heart is not compact of flint nor steel;
Nor can I utter all our bitter grief,
But floods of tears will drown my oratory,
And break my utterance, even in the time
When it should move you to attend me most,
And force you to commiseration.
Here 's Rome's young captain, let him tell the
    tale;
While I stand by and weep to hear him speak.

LUCIUS.

Then, gracious auditory, be it known to you
That Chiron and the damn'd Demetrius
Were they that murdered our emperor's brother;
And they it were that ravished our sister:
For their fell faults our brothers were beheaded,
Our father's tears despised, and basely cozen'd
Of that true hand that fought Rome's quarrel
    out,
And sent her enemies unto the grave.
Lastly, myself unkindly banished,
The gates shut on me, and turn'd weeping out,
To beg relief among Rome's enemies;
Who drown'd their enmity in my true tears,
And oped their arms to embrace me as a friend:
I am the turn'd forth, be it known to you,
That have preserved her welfare in my blood;
And from her bosom took the enemy's point,
Sheathing the steel in my adventrous body.
Alas, you know I am no vaunter, I;
My scars can witness, dumb although they are,
That my report is just and full of truth.
But, soft! methinks I do digress too much,
Citing my worthless praise: O, pardon me;
For when no friends are by, men praise them-
    selves.

MARCUS ANDRONICUS.
Now is my turn to speak. Behold this child,—
> [*Pointing to the* CHILD *in the
> arms of an* ATTENDANT.

Of this was Tamora delivered;
The issue of an irreligious Moor,
Chief architect and plotter of these woes:
The villain is alive in Titus' house,
Damn'd as he is, to witness this is true.
Now judge what cause had Titus to revenge
These wrongs, unspeakable, past patience,
Or more than any living man could bear.
Now you have heard the truth, what say you,
   Romans?
Have we done aught amiss,—show us wherein,
And, from the place where you behold us plead-
   ing,
The poor remainder of Andronici
Will, hand in hand, all headlong hurl ourselves,
And on the ragged stones beat forth our brains,
And make a mutual closure of our house.
Speak, Romans, speak; and if you say we shall,
Lo, hand in hand, Lucius and I will fall.
AEMILIUS.
Come, come, thou reverend man of Rome,
And bring our emperor gently in thy hand,
Lucius our emperor; for well I know
The common voice do cry it shall be so.
ROMANS.
Lucius, all hail, Rome's royal emperor!
MARCUS ANDRONICUS [*to* ATTENDANTS].
Go, go into old Titus' sorrowful house,
And hither hale that misbelieving Moor,
To be adjudged some direful-slaughtering
   death,
As punishment for his most wicked life.
> [*Exeunt some* ATTENDANTS.
LUCIUS, MARCUS, &c., *descend.*
ROMANS.
Lucius, all hail, Rome's gracious governor!
LUCIUS.
Thanks, gentle Romans: may I govern so,
To heal Rome's harms, and wipe away her woe!
But, gentle people, give me aim awhile,—
For nature puts me to a heavy task:—
Stand all aloof;—but, uncle, draw you near,
To shed obsequious tears upon this trunk.—
O, take this warm kiss on thy pale cold lips,
> [*Kissing* TITUS.
These sorrowful drops upon thy blood-stain'd
   face,
The last true duties of thy noble son!
MARCUS ANDRONICUS.
Tear for tear, and loving kiss for kiss,
Thy brother Marcus tenders on thy lips:

O, were the sum of these that I should pay
Countless and infinite, yet would I pay them!
LUCIUS.
Come hither, boy: come, come, and learn of us
To melt in showers: thy grandsire loved thee
   well:
Many a time he danced thee on his knee,
Sung thee asleep, his loving breast thy pillow;
Many a story hath he told to thee,
Meet and agreeing with thine infancy;
In that respect, then, like a loving child,
Shed yet some small drops from thy tender spring,
Because kind nature doth require it so:
Friends should associate friends in grief and woe:
Bid him farewell; commit him to the grave;
Do him that kindness, and take leave of him.
YOUNG LUCIUS.
O grandsire, grandsire! even with all my heart
Would I were dead, so you did live again!—
O Lord, I cannot speak to him for weeping;
My tears will choke me, if I ope my mouth.
Enter ATTENDANTS *with* AARON.
AEMILIUS.
You sad Andronici, have done with woes:
Give sentence on this execrable wretch,
That hath been breeder of these dire events.
LUCIUS.
Set him breast-deep in earth, and famish him;
There let him stand, and rave, and cry for food:
If any one relieves or pities him,
For the offence he dies. This is our doom:
Some stay to see him fasten'd in the earth.
AARON.
O, why should wrath be mute, and fury dumb?
I am no baby, I, that with base prayers
I should repent the evils I have done:
Ten thousand worse than ever yet I did
Would I perform, if I might have my will:
If one good deed in all my life I did,
I do repent it from my very soul.
LUCIUS.
Some loving friends convey the emperor hence,
And give him burial in his father's grave:
My father and Lavinia shall forthwith
Be closed in our household monument.
As for that ravenous tiger, Tamora,
No funeral rite, nor man in mourning weeds,
No mournful bell shall ring her burial;
But throw her forth to beasts and birds of prey:
Her life was beast-like, and devoid of pity;
And, being so, shall have like want of pity.
See justice done on Aaron, that damn'd Moor,
By whom our heavy haps had their beginning:
Then, afterwards, to order well the state,
That like events may ne'er it ruinate.   [*Exeunt.*

THE COMEDY OF ERRORS

DRAMATIS PERSONAE

SOLINUS, *Duke of Ephesus.*
AEGEON, *a merchant of Syracuse.*

ANTIPHOLUS OF EPHESUS, } *twin brothers and*
ANTIPHOLUS OF SYRACUSE, } *sons to Aegeon and Aemilia.*

DROMIO OF EPHESUS, } *twin brothers, and at-*
DROMIO OF SYRACUSE, } *tendants on the two Antipholuses.*

BALTHAZAR, *a merchant.*
ANGELO, *a goldsmith.*
FIRST MERCHANT, *friend to Antipholus of Syracuse.*

SECOND MERCHANT, *to whom Angelo is a debtor.*
PINCH, *a schoolmaster.*

AEMILIA, *wife to Aegeon, an abbess at Ephesus.*
ADRIANA, *wife to Antipholus of Ephesus.*
LUCIANA, *her sister.*
LUCE, *servant to Adriana.*
A COURTEZAN.

GAOLER, OFFICERS, *and other* ATTENDANTS.

SCENE—*Ephesus.*

ACT I. SCENE I.

A hall in the DUKE'S *palace.*

Enter DUKE, AEGEON, GAOLER, OFFICERS, *and other* ATTENDANTS.

AEGEON.

PROCEED, Solinus, to procure my fall,
And by the doom of death end woes and all.

DUKE OF EPHESUS.

Merchant of Syracusa, plead no more;
I am not partial to infringe our laws:
The enmity and discord which of late
Sprung from the rancorous outrage of your duke
To merchants, our well-dealing countrymen,—
Who, wanting guilders to redeem their lives,
Have seal'd his rigorous statutes with their bloods,
Excludes all pity from our threat'ning looks.
For, since the mortal and intestine jars
'Twixt thy seditious countrymen and us,
It hath in solemn synods been decreed,
Both by the Syracusians and ourselves,
To admit no traffic to our adverse towns:
Nay, more, if any born at Ephesus
Be seen at Syracusian marts and fairs;
Again, if any Syracusian born
Come to the bay of Ephesus, he dies,
His goods confiscate to the duke's dispose;
Unless a thousand marks be levied,
To quit the penalty and to ransom him.
Thy substance, valued at the highest rate,
Cannot amount unto a hundred marks;
Therefore by law thou art condemn'd to die.

AEGEON.

Yet this my comfort,—when your words are done,
My woes end likewise with the evening sun.

DUKE OF EPHESUS.

Well, Syracusian, say, in brief, the cause
Why thou departed'st from thy native home,
And for what cause thou camest to Ephesus.

AEGEON.

A heavier task could not have been imposed
Than I to speak my griefs unspeakable:
Yet, that the world may witness that my end
Was wrought by nature, not by vile offence,
I'll utter what my sorrow gives me leave.
In Syracusa was I born; and wed
Unto a woman, happy but for me,
And by me too, had not our hap been bad.
With her I lived in joy; our wealth increased
By prosperous voyages I often made
To Epidamnum; till my factor's death,
And the great care of goods at random left,
Drew me from kind embracements of my spouse:
From whom my absence was not six months old,
Before herself—almost at fainting under
The pleasing punishment that women bear—
Had made provision for her following me,
And soon and safe arrived where I was.
There had she not been long but she became
A joyful mother of two goodly sons;
And, which was strange, the one so like the other
As could not be distinguish'd but by names.
That very hour, and in the self-same inn,
A meaner woman was delivered
Of such a burden, male twins, both alike:
Those, for their parents were exceeding poor,
I bought, and brought up to attend my sons.
My wife, not meanly proud of two such boys,
Made daily motions for our home return:
Unwilling I agreed. Alas, too soon
We came aboard!
A league from Epidamnum had we sail'd,
Before the always-wind-obeying deep
Gave any tragic instance of our harm:
But longer did we not retain much hope;
For what obscured light the heavens did grant
Did but convey unto our fearful minds
A doubtful warrant of immediate death;
Which though myself would gladly have embraced
Yet the incessant weepings of my wife,
Weeping before for what she saw must come,
And piteous plainings of the pretty babes,
That mourn'd for fashion, ignorant what to fear,
Forced me to seek delays for them and me.
And this it was,—for other means was none:—
The sailors sought for safety by our boat,
And left the ship, then sinking-ripe, to us:
My wife, more careful for the latter-born,
Had fasten'd him unto a small spare mast,
Such as seafaring men provide for storms;
To him one of the other twins was bound,
Whilst I had been like heedful of the other:
The children thus disposed, my wife and I,
Fixing our eyes on whom our care was fixt,
Fasten'd ourselves at either end the mast;
And floating straight, obedient to the stream,
Was carried towards Corinth, as we thought.
At length the sun, gazing upon the earth,

Dispersed those vapours that offended us;
And, by the benefit of his wished light,
The seas waxt calm, and we discovered
Two ships from far making amain to us,
Of Corinth that, of Epidaurus this:
But ere they came,—O, let me say no more!
Gather the sequel by that went before.

DUKE OF EPHESUS.
Nay, forward, old man; do not break off so;
For we may pity, though not pardon thee.

AEGEON.
O, had the gods done so, I had not now
Worthily term'd them merciless to us!
For, ere the ships could meet by twice five leagues,
We were encounter'd by a mighty rock;
Which being violently borne upon,
Our helpful ship was splitted in the midst;
So that, in this unjust divorce of us,
Fortune had left to both of us alike
What to delight in, what to sorrow for.
Her part, poor soul! seeming as burdened
With lesser weight, but not with lesser woe,
Was carried with more speed before the wind;
And in our sight they three were taken up
By fishermen of Corinth, as we thought.
At length, another ship had seized on us;
And, knowing whom it was their hap to save,
Gave healthful welcome to their shipwrackt
    guests;
And would have reft the fishers of their prey,
Had not their bark been very slow of sail,
And therefore homeward did they bend their
    course.—
Thus have you heard me sever'd from my bliss;
That by misfortunes was my life prolong'd,
To tell sad stories of my own mishaps.

DUKE OF EPHESUS.
And, for the sake of them thou sorrowest for,
Do me the favour to dilate at full
What have befall'n of them and thee till now.

AEGEON.
My youngest boy, and yet my eldest care,
At eighteen years became inquisitive
After his brother; and importuned me
That his attendant—so his case was like,
Reft of his brother, but retain'd his name—
Might bear him company in the quest of him:
Whom whilst I labour'd of a love to see,
I hazarded the loss of whom I loved.
Five summers have I spent in furthest Greece,
Roaming clean through the bounds of Asia,
And, coasting homeward, came to Ephesus;
Hopeless to find, yet loth to leave unsought
Or that, or any place that harbours men.
But here must end the story of my life;
And happy were I in my timely death,
Could all my travels warrant me they live.

DUKE OF EPHESUS.
Hapless Aegeon, whom the fates have markt
To bear the extremity of dire mishap!
Now, trust me, were it not against our laws,
Against my crown, my oath, my dignity,—
Which princes, would they, may not disannul,—
My soul should sue as advocate for thee.
But, though thou art adjudged to the death,
And passed sentence may not be recall'd

But to our honour's great disparagement,
Yet will I favour thee in what I can.
Therefore, merchant, I'll limit thee this day
To seek thy life by beneficial help:
Try all the friends thou hast in Ephesus;
Beg thou, or borrow, to make up the sum,
And live; if no, then thou art doom'd to die.—
Gaoler, take him to thy custody.

GAOLER.
I will, my lord.

AEGEON.
Hopeless and helpless doth Aegeon wend,
But to procrastinate his lifeless end.   [Exeunt.

SCENE II.
The Mart.

Enter ANTIPHOLUS OF SYRACUSE, DROMIO
OF SYRACUSE, *and* FIRST MERCHANT.

FIRST MERCHANT.
THEREfore give out you are of Epidamnum,
   Lest that your goods too soon be confiscate.
This very day a Syracusian merchant
Is apprehended for arrival here;
And, not being able to buy out his life,
According to the statute of the town,
Dies ere the weary sun set in the west.
There is your money that I had to keep.

ANTIPHOLUS OF SYRACUSE.
Go bear it to the Centaur, where we host,
And stay there, Dromio, till I come to thee.
Within this hour it will be dinner-time:
Till that, I'll view the manners of the town,
Peruse the traders, gaze upon the buildings,
And then return, and sleep within mine inn;
For with long travel I am stiff and weary.
Get thee away.

DROMIO OF SYRACUSE.
Many a man would take you at your word,
And go indeed, having so good a mean.   [Exit

ANTIPHOLUS OF SYRACUSE.
A trusty villain, sir; that very oft,
When I am dull with care and melancholy,
Lightens my humour with his merry jests.
What, will you walk with me about the town,
And then go to my inn, and dine with me?

FIRST MERCHANT.
I am invited, sir, to certain merchants,
Of whom I hope to make much benefit;
I crave your pardon. Soon at five o'clock,
Please you, I'll meet with you upon the mart,
And afterwards consort you till bed-time:
My present business calls me from you now.

ANTIPHOLUS OF SYRACUSE.
Farewell till then: I will go lose myself,
And wander up and down to view the city.

FIRST MERCHANT.
Sir, I commend you to your own content.   [Exit.

ANTIPHOLUS OF SYRACUSE.
He that commends me to mine own content
Commends me to the thing I cannot get.
I to the world am like a drop of water,
That in the ocean seeks another drop;
Who, falling there to find his fellow forth,
Unseen, inquisitive, confounds himself:
So I, to find a mother and a brother,

In quest of them, unhappy, lose myself.—
Here comes the almanack of my true date.
Enter DROMIO OF EPHESUS.
What now? how chance thou art return'd so
    soon?
DROMIO OF EPHESUS.
Return'd so soon! rather approacht too late:
The capon burns, the pig falls from the spit;
The clock hath strucken twelve upon the bell,—
My mistress made it one upon my cheek:
She is so hot, because the meat is cold;
The meat is cold, because you come not home;
You come not home, because you have no
    stomach;
You have no stomach, having broke your fast;
But we, that know what 'tis to fast and pray,
Are penitent for your default to-day.
ANTIPHOLUS OF SYRACUSE.
Stop in your wind, sir: tell me this, I pray,—
Where have you left the money that I gave you?
DROMIO OF EPHESUS.
O,—sixpence, that I had o' Wednesday last
To pay the saddler for my mistress' crupper:—
The saddler had it, sir; I kept it not.
ANTIPHOLUS OF SYRACUSE.
I am not in a sportive humour now:
Tell me, and dally not, where is the money?
We being strangers here, how darest thou trust
So great a charge from thine own custody?
DROMIO OF EPHESUS.
I pray you, jest, sir, as you sit at dinner:
I from my mistress come to you in post;
If I return, I shall be post indeed,
For she will score your fault upon my pate.
Methinks your maw, like mine, should be your
    clock,
And strike you home without a messenger.
ANTIPHOLUS OF SYRACUSE.
Come, Dromio, come, these jests are out of
    season;
Reserve them till a merrier hour than this.
Where is the gold I gave in charge to thee?
DROMIO OF EPHESUS.
To me, sir! why, you gave no gold to me.
ANTIPHOLUS OF SYRACUSE.
Come on, sir knave, have done your foolishness,
And tell me how thou hast disposed thy charge.
DROMIO OF EPHESUS.
My charge was but to fetch you from the mart
Home to your house, the Phœnix, sir, to dinner:
My mistress and her sister stay for you.
ANTIPHOLUS OF SYRACUSE.
Now, as I am a Christian, answer me,
In what safe place you have bestow'd my money;
Or I shall break that merry sconce of yours,
That stands on tricks when I am undisposed:
Where is the thousand marks thou hadst of me?
DROMIO OF EPHESUS.
I have some marks of yours upon my pate,
Some of my mistress' marks upon my shoulders;
But not a thousand marks between you both.
If I should pay your worship those again,
Perchance you will not bear them patiently.
ANTIPHOLUS OF SYRACUSE.
Thy mistress' marks! what mistress, slave, hast
    thou?

DROMIO OF EPHESUS.
Your worship's wife, my mistress at the Phœnix;
She that doth fast till you come home to dinner,
And prays that you will hie you home to dinner.
ANTIPHOLUS OF SYRACUSE.
What, wilt thou flout me thus unto my face,
Being forbid? There, take you that, sir knave.
                            [*Beating him.*
DROMIO OF EPHESUS.
What mean you, sir? for God's sake, hold your
    hands!
Nay, an you will not, sir, I'll take my heels. [*Exit.*
ANTIPHOLUS OF SYRACUSE.
Upon my life, by some device or other
The villain is o'er-raught of all my money.
They say this town is full of cozenage;
As, nimble jugglers that deceive the eye,
Dark-working sorcerers that change the mind,
Soul-killing witches that deform the body,
Disguised cheaters, prating mountebanks,
And many such-like liberties of sin:
If it prove so, I will be gone the sooner.
I'll to the Centaur, to go seek this slave:
I greatly fear my money is not safe.   [*Exit.*

ACT II. SCENE I.

Before the house of ANTIPHOLUS OF EPHESUS.

Enter ADRIANA *and* LUCIANA.

ADRIANA.

NEITHER my husband nor the slave return'd,
    That in such haste I sent to seek his master!
Sure, Luciana, it is two o'clock.
LUCIANA.
Perhaps some merchant hath invited him,
And from the mart he's somewhere gone to din-
    ner.
Good sister, let us dine, and never fret:
A man is master of his liberty:
Time is their master; and when they see time,
They'll go or come: if so, be patient, sister.
ADRIANA.
Why should their liberty than ours be more?
LUCIANA.
Because their business still lies out o' door.
ADRIANA.
Look, when I serve him so, he takes it ill.
LUCIANA.
O, know he is the bridle of your will.
ADRIANA.
There's none but asses will be bridled so.
LUCIANA.
Why, headstrong liberty is lasht with woe.
There's nothing situate under heaven's eye
But hath his bound, in earth, in sea, in sky:
The beasts, the fishes, and the winged fowls,
Are their males' subjects and at their controls:
Men, more divine, the masters of all these,
Lords of the wide world and wild wat'ry seas,
Indued with intellectual sense and souls,
Of more pre-eminence than fish and fowls,
Are masters to their females and their lords:
Then let your will attend on their accords.
ADRIANA.
This servitude makes you to keep unwed.

LUCIANA.
Not this, but troubles of the marriage-bed.
ADRIANA.
But, were you wedded, you would bear some
sway.
LUCIANA.
Ere I learn love, I'll practise to obey.
ADRIANA.
How if your husband start some other where?
LUCIANA.
Till he come home again, I would forbear.
ADRIANA.
Patience unmoved! no marvel though she pause;
They can be meek that have no other cause.
A wretched soul, bruised with adversity,
We bid be quiet when we hear it cry;
But were we burden'd with like weight of pain,
As much, or more, we should ourselves complain:
So thou, that hast no unkind mate to grieve thee,
With urging helpless patience would relieve me;
But, if thou live to see like right bereft,
This fool-begg'd patience in thee will be left.
LUCIANA.
Well, I will marry one day, but to try.—
Here comes your man; now is your husband nigh.
Enter DROMIO OF EPHESUS.
ADRIANA.
Say, is your tardy master now at hand?
DROMIO OF EPHESUS.
Nay, he's at two hands with me, and that my two
ears can witness.
ADRIANA.
Say, didst thou speak with him? know'st thou his
mind?
DROMIO OF EPHESUS.
Ay, ay, he told his mind upon mine ear:
Beshrew his hand, I scarce could understand it.
LUCIANA.
Spake he so doubtfully, thou couldst not feel his
meaning?
DROMIO OF EPHESUS.
Nay, he struck so plainly, I could too well feel his
blows; and withal so doubtfully, that I could
scarce understand them.
ADRIANA.
But say, I prithee, is he coming home?
It seems he hath great care to please his wife.
DROMIO OF EPHESUS.
Why, mistress, sure my master is horn-mad.
ADRIANA.
Horn-mad, thou villain!
DROMIO OF EPHESUS.
        I mean not cuckold-mad;
But, sure, he is stark mad.
When I desired him to come home to dinner,
He ask'd me for a thousand marks in gold:
' 'Tis dinner-time,' quoth I; 'My gold,' quoth
he:
'Your meat doth burn,' quoth I; 'My gold,'
quoth he:
'Will you come home?' quoth I; 'My gold,'
quoth he;
'Where is the thousand marks I gave thee, vil-
lain?'
'The pig,' quoth I, 'is burn'd;' 'My gold,'
quoth he:

'My mistress, sir,' quoth I; 'Hang up thy mis-
tress!
I know not thy mistress; out on thy mistress!'
LUCIANA.
Quoth who?
DROMIO OF EPHESUS.
Quoth my master: [tress.'
'I know,' quoth he, 'no house, no wife, no mis-
So that my arrant, due unto my tongue,
I thank him, I bear home upon my shoulders;
For, in conclusion, he did beat me there.
ADRIANA.
Go back again, thou slave, and fetch him home.
DROMIO OF EPHESUS.
Go back again, and be new beaten home!
For God's sake, send some other messenger.
ADRIANA.
Back, slave, or I will break thy pate across.
DROMIO OF EPHESUS.
And he will bless that cross with other beating:
Between you I shall have a holy head.
ADRIANA.
Hence, prating peasant! fetch thy master home.
DROMIO OF EPHESUS.
Am I so round with you as you with me,
That like a football you do spurn me thus?
You spurn me hence, and he will spurn me hither:
If I last in this service, you must case me in
leather.   [*Exit.*
LUCIANA.
Fie, how impatience low'reth in your face!
ADRIANA.
His company must do his minions grace,
Whilst I at home starve for a merry look.
Hath homely age th' alluring beauty took
From my poor cheek? then he hath wasted it:
Are my discourses dull? barren my wit?
If voluble and sharp discourse be marr'd,
Unkindness blunts it more than marble hard:
Do their gay vestments his affections bait?
That's not my fault,—he's master of my state:
What ruins are in me that can be found
By him not ruin'd? then is he the ground
Of my defeatures. My decayed fair
A sunny look of his would soon repair:
But, too unruly deer, he breaks the pale,
And feeds from home; poor I am but his stale.
LUCIANA.
Self-harming jealousy,—fie, beat it hence!
ADRIANA.
Unfeeling fools can with such wrongs dispense.
I know his eye doth homage otherwhere;
Or else what lets it but he would be here?
Sister, you know he promised me a chain;—
Would that alone alone he would detain,
So he would keep fair quarter with his bed!
I see the jewel best enamelled
Will lose his beauty; and though gold bides still
The tester's touch, yet often-touching will
Wear gold: and so no man that hath a name,
But falsehood and corruption doth it shame.
Since that my beauty cannot please his eye,
I'll weep what's left away, and weeping die.
LUCIANA.
How many fond fools serve mad jealousy!
        [*Exeunt.*

SCENE II.

The Mart.

Enter ANTIPHOLUS OF SYRACUSE.

ANTIPHOLUS OF SYRACUSE.

THE gold I gave to Dromio is laid up
Safe at the Centaur; and the heedful slave
Is wander'd forth, in care to seek me out.
By computation and mine host's report,
I could not speak with Dromio since at first
I sent him from the mart.—See, here he comes.

Enter DROMIO OF SYRACUSE.

How now, sir! is your merry humour alter'd?
As you love strokes, so jest with me again.
You know no Centaur? you received no gold?
Your mistress sent to have me home to dinner?
My house was at the Phœnix? Wast thou mad,
That thus so madly thou didst answer me?

DROMIO OF SYRACUSE.

What answer, sir? when spake I such a word?

ANTIPHOLUS OF SYRACUSE.

Even now, even here, not half an hour since.

DROMIO OF SYRACUSE.

I did not see you since you sent me hence,
Home to the Centaur, with the gold you gave me.

ANTIPHOLUS OF SYRACUSE.

Villain, thou didst deny the gold's receipt,
And told'st me of a mistress and a dinner;
For which, I hope, thou felt'st I was displeased.

DROMIO OF SYRACUSE.

I am glad to see you in this merry vein:
What means this jest? I pray you, master, tell
me.

ANTIPHOLUS OF SYRACUSE.

Yea, dost thou jeer and flout me in the teeth?
Think'st thou I jest? Hold, take thou that, and
that.   [*Beats* DROMIO.

DROMIO OF SYRACUSE.

Hold, sir, for God's sake! now your jest is earnest:
Upon what bargain do you give it me?

ANTIPHOLUS OF SYRACUSE.

Because that I familiarly sometimes
Do use you for my fool, and chat with you,
Your sauciness will jet upon my love,
And make a common of my serious hours.
When the sun shines let foolish gnats make sport,
But creep in crannies when he hides his beams.
If you will jest with me, know my aspect,
And fashion your demeanour to my looks,
Or I will beat this method in your sconce.

DROMIO OF SYRACUSE.

Sconce call you it? so you would leave battering,
I had rather have it a head: an you use these blows
long, I must get a sconce for my head, and ensconce it too; or else I shall seek my wit in my
shoulders. But, I pray, sir, why am I beaten?

ANTIPHOLUS OF SYRACUSE.

Dost thou not know?

DROMIO OF SYRACUSE.

Nothing, sir, but that I am beaten.

ANTIPHOLUS OF SYRACUSE.

Shall I tell you why?

DROMIO OF SYRACUSE.

Ay, sir, and wherefore; for they say every why
hath a wherefore.

ANTIPHOLUS OF SYRACUSE.

Why, first,—for flouting me; and then where-
For urging it the second time to me.   [fore,—

DROMIO OF SYRACUSE.

Was there ever any man thus beaten out of
season,
When in the why and the wherefore is neither
rime nor reason?
Well, sir, I thank you.

ANTIPHOLUS OF SYRACUSE.

Thank me, sir! for what?

DROMIO OF SYRACUSE.

Marry, sir, for this something that you gave me
for nothing.

ANTIPHOLUS OF SYRACUSE.

I'll make you amends next, to give you nothing
for something. But say, sir, is it dinner-time?

DROMIO OF SYRACUSE.

No, sir: I think the meat wants that I have.

ANTIPHOLUS OF SYRACUSE.

In good time, sir; what's that?

DROMIO OF SYRACUSE.

Basting.

ANTIPHOLUS OF SYRACUSE.

Well, sir, then 'twill be dry.

DROMIO OF SYRACUSE.

If it be, sir, I pray you, eat none of it.

ANTIPHOLUS OF SYRACUSE.

Your reason?

DROMIO OF SYRACUSE.

Lest it make you choleric, and purchase me another dry basting.

ANTIPHOLUS OF SYRACUSE.

Well, sir, learn to jest in good time: there's a time
for all things.

DROMIO OF SYRACUSE.

I durst have denied that, before you were so
choleric.

ANTIPHOLUS OF SYRACUSE.

By what rule, sir?

DROMIO OF SYRACUSE.

Marry, sir, by a rule as plain as the plain bald pate
of father Time himself.

ANTIPHOLUS OF SYRACUSE.

Let's hear it.

DROMIO OF SYRACUSE.

There's no time for a man to recover his hair that
grows bald by nature.

ANTIPHOLUS OF SYRACUSE.

May he not do it by fine and recovery?

DROMIO OF SYRACUSE.

Yes, to pay a fine for a periwig, and recover the
lost hair of another man.

ANTIPHOLUS OF SYRACUSE.

Why is Time such a niggard of hair, being, as it
is, so plentiful an excrement?

DROMIO OF SYRACUSE.

Because it is a blessing that he bestows on beasts
and what he hath scanted men in hair, he hath
given them in wit.

ANTIPHOLUS OF SYRACUSE.

Why, but there's many a man hath more hair than
wit.

DROMIO OF SYRACUSE.

Not a man of those but he hath the wit to lose his
hair.

ANTIPHOLUS OF SYRACUSE.
Why, thou didst conclude hairy men plain-dealers
without wit.
DROMIO OF SYRACUSE.
The plainer dealer, the sooner lost: yet he loseth
it in a kind of jollity.
ANTIPHOLUS OF SYRACUSE.
For what reason?
DROMIO OF SYRACUSE.
For two; and sound ones too.
ANTIPHOLUS OF SYRACUSE.
Nay, not sound, I pray you.
DROMIO OF SYRACUSE.
Sure ones, then.
ANTIPHOLUS OF SYRACUSE.
Nay, not sure, in a thing falsing.
DROMIO OF SYRACUSE.
Certain ones, then.
ANTIPHOLUS OF SYRACUSE.
Name them.
DROMIO OF SYRACUSE.
The one, to save the money that he spends in
tiring; the other, that at dinner they should not
drop in his porridge.
ANTIPHOLUS OF SYRACUSE.
You would all this time have proved there is no
time for all things.
DROMIO OF SYRACUSE.
Marry, and did, sir; namely, no time to recover
hair lost by nature.
ANTIPHOLUS OF SYRACUSE.
But your reason was not substantial, why there is
no time to recover.
DROMIO OF SYRACUSE.
Thus I mend it: Time himself is bald, and there-
fore to the world's end will have bald followers.
ANTIPHOLUS OF SYRACUSE.
I knew 'twould be a bald conclusion:
But, soft! who wafts us yonder?
Enter ADRIANA *and* LUCIANA.
ADRIANA.
Ay, ay, Antipholus, look strange and frown:
Some other mistress hath thy sweet aspects;
I am not Adriana nor thy wife.
The time was once when thou unurged wouldst
vow
That never words were music to thine ear,
That never object pleasing in thine eye,
That never touch well-welcome to thy hand,
That never meat sweet-savour'd in thy taste,
Unless I spake, or look'd, or touch'd, or carved to
thee.
How comes it now, my husband, O, how comes it,
That thou art then estranged from thyself?
Thyself I call it, being strange to me,
That, undividable, incorporate,
Am better than thy dear self's better part.
Ah, do not tear away thyself from me!
For know, my love, as easy mayst thou fall
A drop of water in the breaking gulf,
And take unmingled thence that drop again,
Without addition or diminishing,
As take from me thyself, and not me too.
How dearly would it touch thee to the quick,
Shouldst thou but hear I were licentious,
And that this body, consecrate to thee,

By ruffian lust should be contaminate!
Wouldst thou not spit at me and spurn at me,
And hurl the name of husband in my face,
And tear the stain'd skin off my harlot-brow,
And from my false hand cut the wedding-ring,
And break it with a deep-divorcing vow?
I know thou canst; and therefore see thou do it.
I am possest with an adulterate blot;
My blood is mingled with the grime of lust:
For if we two be one, and thou play false,
I do digest the poison of thy flesh,
Being strumpeted by thy contagion.
Keep, then, fair league and truce with thy true
bed;
I live unstain'd, thou undishonoured.
ANTIPHOLUS OF SYRACUSE.
Plead you to me, fair dame? I know you not:
In Ephesus I am but two hours old,
As strange unto your town as to your talk;
Who, every word by all my wit being scann'd,
Want wit in all one word to understand.
LUCIANA.
Fie, brother! how the world is changed with you!
When were you wont to use my sister thus?
She sent for you by Dromio home to dinner.
ANTIPHOLUS OF SYRACUSE.
By Dromio!
DROMIO OF SYRACUSE.
By me!
ADRIANA.
By thee; and this thou didst return from him,—
That he did buffet thee, and, in his blows,
Denied my house for his, me for his wife.
ANTIPHOLUS OF SYRACUSE.
Did you converse, sir, with this gentlewoman?
What is the course and drift of your compact?
DROMIO OF SYRACUSE.
I, sir! I never saw her till this time.
ANTIPHOLUS OF SYRACUSE.
Villain, thou liest; for even her very words
Didst thou deliver to me on the mart.
DROMIO OF SYRACUSE.
I never spake with her in all my life.
ANTIPHOLUS OF SYRACUSE.
How can she thus, then, call us by our names,
Unless it be by inspiration?
ADRIANA.
How ill agrees it with your gravity
To counterfeit thus grossly with your slave,
Abetting him to thwart me in my mood!
Be it my wrong you are from me exempt,
But wrong not that wrong with a more contempt.
Come, I will fasten on this sleeve of thine:
Thou art an elm, my husband,—I a vine,
Whose weakness, married to thy stronger state,
Makes me with thy strength to communicate:
If aught possess thee from me, it is dross,
Usurping ivy, brier, or idle moss;
Who, all for want of pruning, with intrusion
Infect thy sap, and live on thy confusion.
ANTIPHOLUS OF SYRACUSE [*aside*].
To me she speaks; she moves me for her
theme:
What, was I married to her in my dream?
Or sleep I now, and think I hear all this?
What error drives our eyes and ears amiss?

Until I know this sure uncertainty,
I'll entertain the offer'd fallacy.

LUCIANA.

Dromio, go bid the servants spread for dinner.

DROMIO OF SYRACUSE.

O, for my beads! I cross me for a sinner.
This is the fairy land;—O spite of spites!—
We talk with goblins, owls, and elvish sprites:
If we obey them not, this will ensue,—
They'll suck our breath, or pinch us black and
  blue.

LUCIANA.

Why pratest thou to thyself, and answer'st not?
Dromio, thou drone, thou snail, thou slug, thou
  sot!

DROMIO OF SYRACUSE.

I am transformed, master, am not I?

ANTIPHOLUS OF SYRACUSE.

I think thou art in mind, and so am I.

DROMIO OF SYRACUSE.

Nay, master, both in mind and in my shape.

ANTIPHOLUS OF SYRACUSE.

Thou hast thine own form.

DROMIO OF SYRACUSE.

             No, I am an ape.

LUCIANA.

If thou art changed to aught, 'tis to an ass.

DROMIO OF SYRACUSE.

'Tis true; she rides me, and I long for grass.
'Tis so, I am an ass; else it could never be
But I should know her as well as she knows me.

ADRIANA.

Come, come, no longer will I be a fool,
To put the finger in the eye and weep,
Whilst man and master laugh my woes to
  scorn.—
Come, sir, to dinner.—Dromio, keep the gate.—
Husband, I'll dine above with you to-day,
And shrive you of a thousand idle pranks.—
Sirrah, if any ask you for your master,
Say he dines forth, and let no creature enter.—
Come, sister.—Dromio, play the porter well.

ANTIPHOLUS OF SYRACUSE [aside].

Am I in earth, in heaven, or in hell?
Sleeping or waking? mad or well-advised?
Known unto these, and to myself disguised!
I'll say as they say, and persever so,
And in this mist at all adventures go.

DROMIO OF SYRACUSE.

Master, shall I be porter at the gate?

ADRIANA.

Ay; and let none enter, lest I break your pate.

LUCIANA.

Come, come, Antipholus, we dine too late.

                       [Exeunt.

ACT III. SCENE I.

Before the house of ANTIPHOLUS OF EPHESUS.

Enter ANTIPHOLUS OF EPHESUS, DROMIO OF
EPHESUS, ANGELO, *and* BALTHAZAR.

ANTIPHOLUS OF EPHESUS.

GOOD Signior Angelo, you must excuse us all;
  My wife is shrewish when I keep not hours:
Say that I linger'd with you at your shop
To see the making of her carcanet,

And that to-morrow you will bring it home.
But here's a villain that would face me down
He met me on the mart, and that I beat him,
And charged him with a thousand marks in gold,
And that I did deny my wife and house.—
Thou drunkard, thou, what didst thou mean by
  this?

DROMIO OF EPHESUS.

Say what you will, sir, but I know what I know;
That you beat me at the mart, I have your hand
  to show:
If the skin were parchment, and the blows you
  gave were ink,
Your own handwriting would tell you what I
  think.

ANTIPHOLUS OF EPHESUS.

I think thou art an ass.

DROMIO OF EPHESUS.

           Marry, so it doth appear
By the wrongs I suffer and the blows I bear.
I should kick, being kickt; and, being at that pass,
You would keep from my heels, and beware of an
  ass.

ANTIPHOLUS OF EPHESUS.

You're sad, Signior Balthazar: pray God our
  cheer
May answer my good will and your good welcome
  here!

BALTHAZAR.

I hold your dainties cheap, sir, and your welcome
  dear.

ANTIPHOLUS OF EPHESUS.

O, Signior Balthazar, either at flesh or fish,
A table full of welcome makes scarce one dainty
  dish.

BALTHAZAR.

Good meat, sir, is common; that every churl
  affords.

ANTIPHOLUS OF EPHESUS.

And welcome more common; for that's nothing
  but words.

BALTHAZAR.

Small cheer and great welcome makes a merry
  feast.

ANTIPHOLUS OF EPHESUS.

Ay, to a niggardly host and more sparing guest:
But though my cates be mean, take them in good
  part:
Better cheer may you have, but not with better
  heart.
But, soft! my door is lockt.—Go bid them let us
  in.

DROMIO OF EPHESUS.

Maud, Bridget, Marian, Cicely, Gillian, Ginn!

DROMIO OF SYRACUSE [within].

Mome, malt-horse, capon, coxcomb, idiot,
  patch!
Either get thee from the door, or sit down at the
  hatch.
Dost thou conjure for wenches, that thou call'st
  for such store,
When one is one too many? Go get thee from the
  door.

DROMIO OF EPHESUS.

What patch is made our porter?—My master
  stays in the street.

DROMIO OF SYRACUSE [*within*].
Let him walk from whence he came, lest he catch
cold on's feet.

ANTIPHOLUS OF EPHESUS.
Who talks within there? ho, open the door!

DROMIO OF SYRACUSE [*within*].
Right, sir; I'll tell you when, an you'll tell me
wherefore.

ANTIPHOLUS OF EPHESUS.
Wherefore! for my dinner: I have not dined
to-day.

DROMIO OF SYRACUSE [*within*].
Nor to-day here you must not; come again when
you may.

ANTIPHOLUS OF EPHESUS.
What art thou that keep'st me out from the
house I owe?

DROMIO OF SYRACUSE [*within*].
The porter for this time, sir, and my name is
Dromio.

DROMIO OF EPHESUS.
O villain, thou hast stol'n both mine office and
my name!
The one ne'er got me credit, the other mickle
blame.
If thou hadst been Dromio to-day in my place,
Thou wouldst have changed thy face for a name,
or thy name for an ass.

LUCE *within*].
What a coil is there, Dromio! who are those at
the gate?

DROMIO OF EPHESUS.
Let my master in, Luce.

LUCE [*within*].
         Faith, no; he comes too late;
And so tell your master.

DROMIO OF EPHESUS.
         O Lord, I must laugh!—
Have at you with a proverb;—Shall I set in my
staff?

LUCE [*within*].
Have at you with another; that's, —When? can
you tell?

DROMIO OF SYRACUSE [*within*].
If thy name be call'd Luce,—Luce, thou hast
answer'd him well.

ANTIPHOLUS OF EPHESUS.
Do you hear, you minion? you'll let us in, I hope?

LUCE [*within*].
I thought to have askt you.

DROMIO OF SYRACUSE [*within*].
         And you said no.

DROMIO OF EPHESUS.
So, come, help:—well struck! there was blow for
blow.

ANTIPHOLUS OF EPHESUS.
Thou baggage, let me in.

LUCE [*within*].
         Can you tell for whose sake?

DROMIO OF EPHESUS.
Master, knock the door hard.

LUCE [*within*].
         Let him knock till it ache.

ANTIPHOLUS OF EPHESUS.
You'll cry for this, minion, if I beat the door
down.

LUCE [*within*].
What needs all that, and a pair of stocks in the
town?

ADRIANA [*within*].
Who is that at the door that keeps all this
noise?

DROMIO OF SYRACUSE [*within*].
By my troth, your town is troubled with unruly
boys.

ANTIPHOLUS OF EPHESUS.
Are you there, wife? you might have come
before.

ADRIANA [*within*].
Your wife, sir knave! go get you from the
door.

DROMIO OF EPHESUS.
If you went in pain, master, this knave would go
sore.

ANGELO.
Here is neither cheer, sir, nor welcome: we would
fain have either.

BALTHAZAR.
In debating which was best, we shall part with
neither.

DROMIO OF EPHESUS.
They stand at the door, master; bid them welcome hither.

ANTIPHOLUS OF EPHESUS.
There is something in the wind, that we cannot
get in.

DROMIO OF EPHESUS.
You would say so, master, if your garments were
thin.
Your cake there is warm within; you stand here in
the cold:
It would make a man mad as a buck, to be so
bought and sold.

ANTIPHOLUS OF EPHESUS.
Go fetch me something: I'll break ope the gate.

DROMIO OF SYRACUSE [*within*].
Break any breaking here, and I'll break your
knave's pate.

DROMIO OF EPHESUS.
A man may break a word with you, sir; and words
are but wind;
Ay, and break it in your face, so he break it not
behind.

DROMIO OF SYRACUSE [*within*].
It seems thou want'st breaking: out upon thee,
hind!

DROMIO OF EPHESUS.
Here's too much 'out upon thee!' I pray thee,
let me in.

DROMIO OF SYRACUSE [*within*].
Ay, when fowls have no feathers, and fish have
no fin.

ANTIPHOLUS OF EPHESUS.
Well, I'll break in:—go borrow me a crow.

DROMIO OF EPHESUS.
A crow without feather,—master, mean you so?
For a fish without a fin, there's a fowl without a
feather:
If a crow help us in, sirrah, we'll pluck a crow
together.

ANTIPHOLUS OF EPHESUS.
Go get thee gone; fetch me an iron crow.

BALTHAZAR.

Have patience, sir; O, let it not be so!
Herein you war against your reputation,
And draw within the compass of suspect
Th' unviolated honour of your wife.
Once this,—your long experience of her wisdom,
Her sober virtue, years, and modesty,
Plead on her part some cause to you unknown;
And doubt not, sir, but she will well excuse
Why at this time the doors are made against you.
Be ruled by me: depart in patience,
And let us to the Tiger all to dinner;
And about evening come yourself alone
To know the reason of this strange restraint.
If by strong hand you offer to break in
Now in the stirring passage of the day,
A vulgar comment will be made of it,
And that supposed by the common rout
Against your yet ungalled estimation,
That may with foul intrusion enter in,
And dwell upon your grave when you are dead;
For slander lives upon succession,
For ever housed where it gets possession.

ANTIPHOLUS OF EPHESUS.

You have prevail'd: I will depart in quiet,
And, in despite of mirth, mean to be merry.
I know a wench of excellent discourse,
Pretty and witty; wild, and yet, too, gentle:
There will we dine. This woman that I mean,
My wife—but, I protest, without desert—
Hath oftentimes upbraided me withal:
To her will we to dinner.—Get you home,
And fetch the chain; by this I know 'tis made:
Bring it, I pray you, to the Porpentine;
For there's the house: that chain will I bestow—
Be it for nothing but to spite my wife—
Upon mine hostess there: good sir, make haste.
Since mine own doors refuse to entertain me,
I'll knock elsewhere, to see if they'll disdain me.

ANGELO.

I'll meet you at that place some hour hence.

ANTIPHOLUS OF EPHESUS.

Do so. This jest shall cost me some expense.

[Exeunt.

SCENE II.

The same.

Enter LUCIANA and ANTIPHOLUS OF
SYRACUSE.

LUCIANA.

AND may it be that you have quite forgot
A husband's office? shall, Antipholus,
Even in the spring of love, thy love-springs rot?
Shall love, in building, grow so ruinous?
If you did wed my sister for her wealth,
Then for her wealth's sake use her with more
kindness:
Or if you like elsewhere, do it by stealth;
Muffle your false love with some show of
blindness:
Let not my sister read it in your eye;
Be not thy tongue thy own shame's orator;
Look sweet, speak fair, become disloyalty;
Apparel vice like virtue's harbinger;   [tainted
Bear a fair presence, though your heart be
Teach sin the carriage of a holy saint;

Be secret-false: what need she be acquainted?
What simple thief brags of his own attaint?
'Tis double wrong, to truant with your bed,
And let her read it in thy looks at board:
Shame hath a bastard fame, well managed;
Ill deeds is doubled with an evil word.
Alas, poor women! make us but believe,
Being compact of credit, that you love us;
Though others have the arm, show us the sleeve;
We in your motion turn, and you may move us.
Then, gentle brother, get you in again;
Comfort my sister, cheer her, call her wife:
'Tis holy sport, to be a little vain,
When the sweet breath of flattery conquers
strife.

ANTIPHOLUS OF SYRACUSE.

Sweet mistress,—what your name is else, I know
not,
Nor by what wonder you do hit of mine,—
Less in your knowledge and your grace you show
not
Than our earth's wonder; more than earth div-
ine.
Teach me, dear creature, how to think and speak;
Lay open to my earthy-gross conceit,
Smother'd in errors, feeble, shallow, weak,
The folded meaning of your words' deceit.
Against my soul's pure truth why labour you
To make it wander in an unknown field?
Are you a god? would you create me new?
Transform me, then, and to your power I'll
yield.
But if that I am I, then well I know
Your weeping sister is no wife of mine,
Nor to her bed no homage do I owe:
Far more, far more to you do I decline.
O, train me not, sweet mermaid, with thy note,
To drown me in thy sister's flood of tears:
Sing, siren, for thyself, and I will dote:
Spread o'er the silver waves thy golden hairs,
And as a bed I'll take them, and there lie;
And, in that glorious supposition, think
He gains by death that hath such means to die:
Let Love, being light, be drowned if she sink!

LUCIANA.

What, are you mad, that you do reason so?

ANTIPHOLUS OF SYRACUSE.

Not mad, but mated; how, I do not know.

LUCIANA.

It is a fault that springeth from your eye.

ANTIPHOLUS OF SYRACUSE.

For gazing on your beams, fair sun, being by.

LUCIANA.

Gaze where you should, and that will clear your
sight.

ANTIPHOLUS OF SYRACUSE.

As good to wink, sweet love, as look on night.

LUCIANA.

Why call you me love? call my sister so.

ANTIPHOLUS OF SYRACUSE.

Thy sister's sister.

LUCIANA.

That's my sister.

ANTIPHOLUS OF SYRACUSE.

No;
It is thyself, mine own self's better part,

Mine eye's clear eye, my dear heart's dearer heart,
My food, my fortune, and my sweet hope's aim,
My sole earth's heaven, and my heaven's claim.

LUCIANA.
All this my sister is, or else should be.

ANTIPHOLUS OF SYRACUSE.
Call thyself sister, sweet, for I aim thee.
Thee will I love, and with thee lead my life:
Thou hast no husband yet, nor I no wife.
Give me thy hand.

LUCIANA.
O, soft, sir! hold you still:
I'll fetch my sister, to get her good-will.   [Exit.

Enter DROMIO OF SYRACUSE.

ANTIPHOLUS OF SYRACUSE.
Why, how now, Dromio! where runn'st thou so
    fast?

DROMIO OF SYRACUSE.
Do you know me, sir? am I Dromio? am I your
man? am I myself?

ANTIPHOLUS OF SYRACUSE.
Thou art Dromio, thou art my man, thou art
thyself.

DROMIO OF SYRACUSE.
I am an ass, I am a woman's man, and besides
myself.

ANTIPHOLUS OF SYRACUSE.
What woman's man? and how besides thyself?

DROMIO OF SYRACUSE.
Marry, sir, besides myself, I am due to a woman;
one that claims me, one that haunts me, one that
will have me.

ANTIPHOLUS OF SYRACUSE.
What claim lays she to thee?

DROMIO OF SYRACUSE.
Marry, sir, such claim as you would lay to your
horse; and she would have me as a beast: not that,
I being a beast, she would have me; but that she,
being a very beastly creature, lays claim to me.

ANTIPHOLUS OF SYRACUSE.
What is she?

DROMIO OF SYRACUSE.
A very reverend body; ay, such a one as a man may
not speak of, without he say 'sir-reverence.' I
have but lean luck in the match, and yet is she a
wondrous fat marriage.

ANTIPHOLUS OF SYRACUSE.
How dost thou mean,—a fat marriage?

DROMIO OF SYRACUSE.
Marry, sir, she's the kitchen-wench, and all
grease; and I know not what use to put her to, but
to make a lamp of her, and run from her by her
own light. I warrant, her rags, and the tallow in
them, will burn a Poland winter: if she lives till
doomsday, she'll burn a week longer than the
whole world.

ANTIPHOLUS OF SYRACUSE.
What complexion is she of?

DROMIO OF SYRACUSE.
Swart, like my shoe, but her face nothing like
so clean kept: for why? she sweats; a man may go
over shoes in the grime of it.

ANTIPHOLUS OF SYRACUSE.
That's a fault that water will mend.

DROMIO OF SYRACUSE.
No, sir, 'tis in grain; Noah's flood could not do it.

ANTIPHOLUS OF SYRACUSE.
What's her name?

DROMIO OF SYRACUSE.
Nell, sir; but her name and three quarters, that's
an ell and three quarters, will not measure her
from hip to hip.

ANTIPHOLUS OF SYRACUSE.
Then she bears some breadth?

DROMIO OF SYRACUSE.
No longer from head to foot than from hip to hip:
she is spherical, like a globe; I could find out
countries in her.

ANTIPHOLUS OF SYRACUSE.
In what part of her body stands Ireland?

DROMIO OF SYRACUSE.
Marry, sir, in her buttocks: I found it out by the
bogs.

ANTIPHOLUS OF SYRACUSE.
Where Scotland?

DROMIO OF SYRACUSE.
I found it by the barrenness; hard in the palm of
the hand.

ANTIPHOLUS OF SYRACUSE.
Where France?

DROMIO OF SYRACUSE.
In her forehead; arm'd and reverted, making war
against her heir.

ANTIPHOLUS OF SYRACUSE.
Where England?

DROMIO OF SYRACUSE.
I look'd for the chalky cliffs, but I could find no
whiteness in them; but I guess it stood in her
chin, by the salt rheum that ran between France
and it.

ANTIPHOLUS OF SYRACUSE.
Where Spain?

DROMIO OF SYRACUSE.
Faith, I saw it not; but I felt it hot in her breath.

ANTIPHOLUS OF SYRACUSE.
Where America, the Indies?

DROMIO OF SYRACUSE.
O, sir, upon her nose, all o'er embellish'd with
rubies, carbuncles, sapphires, declining their rich
aspect to the hot breath of Spain; who sent whole
armadoes of caracks to be ballast at her nose.

ANTIPHOLUS OF SYRACUSE.
Where stood Belgia, the Netherlands?

DROMIO OF SYRACUSE.
O, sir, I did not look so low. To conclude, this
drudge, or diviner, laid claim to me; call'd me
Dromio; swore I was assured to her; told me what
privy marks I had about me, as, the mark of my
shoulder, the mole in my neck, the great wart on my
left arm, that I, amazed, ran from her as a witch:
And, I think, if my breast had not been made of
    faith, and my heart of steel,
She had transform'd me to a curtal dog, and made
    me turn i' th' wheel.

ANTIPHOLUS OF SYRACUSE.
Go hie thee presently post to the road:—
An if the wind blow any way from shore,
I will not harbour in this town to-night:—
If any bark put forth, come to the mart,
Where I will walk till thou return to me.
If every one knows us, and we know none,
'Tis time, I think, to trudge, pack, and be gone.

DROMIO OF SYRACUSE.

As from a bear a man would run for life,
So fly I from her that would be my wife.   [*Exit.*

ANTIPHOLUS OF SYRACUSE.

There's none but witches do inhabit here;
And therefore 'tis high time that I were hence.
She that doth call me husband, even my soul
Doth for a wife abhor. But her fair sister,
Possest with such a gentle sovereign grace,
Of such enchanting presence and discourse,
Hath almost made me traitor to myself:
But, lest myself be guilty to self-wrong,
I'll stop mine ears against the mermaid's song.

Enter ANGELO *with the chain.*

ANGELO.

Master Antipholus,—

ANTIPHOLUS OF SYRACUSE.

Ay, that's my name.

ANGELO.

I know it well, sir:—lo, here's the chain.
I thought to have ta'en you at the Porpentine:
The chain unfinish'd made me stay thus long.

ANTIPHOLUS OF SYRACUSE.

What is your will that I shall do with this?

ANGELO.

What please yourself, sir: I have made it for you.

ANTIPHOLUS OF SYRACUSE.

Made it for me, sir! I bespoke it not.

ANGELO.

Not once, nor twice, but twenty times you have.
Go home with it, and please your wife withal;
And soon at supper-time I'll visit you,
And then receive my money for the chain.

ANTIPHOLUS OF SYRACUSE.

I pray you, sir, receive the money now,
For fear you ne'er see chain nor money more.

ANGELO.

You are a merry man, sir: fare you well.   [*Exit.*

ANTIPHOLUS OF SYRACUSE.

What I should think of this, I cannot tell:
But this I think, there's no man is so vain
That would refuse so fair an offer'd chain.
I see a man here needs not live by shifts,
When in the streets he meets such golden gifts.
I'll to the mart, and there for Dromio stay:
If any ship put out, then straight away.   [*Exit.*

ACT IV. SCENE I.

A public place.

Enter SECOND MERCHANT, ANGELO, *and an*
OFFICER.

SECOND MERCHANT:

YOU know since Pentecost the sum is due,
And since I have not much importuned you;
Nor now I had not, but that I am bound
To Persia, and want guilders for my voyage:
Therefore make present satisfaction,
Or I'll attach you by this officer.

ANGELO.

Even just the sum that I do owe to you
Is growing to me by Antipholus;
And in the instant that I met with you
He had of me a chain: at five o'clock
I shall receive the money for the same.

Pleaseth you walk with me down to his house,
I will discharge my bond, and thank you too.

OFFICER.

That labour may you save: see where he comes.

Enter ANTIPHOLUS OF EPHESUS *and* DROMIO
OF EPHESUS *from the* COURTEZAN'S.

ANTIPHOLUS OF EPHESUS.

While I go to the goldsmith's house, go thou
And buy a rope's-end: that will I bestow
Among my wife and her confederates
For locking me out of my doors by day.—
But, soft! I see the goldsmith.—Get thee gone;
Buy thou a rope, and bring it home to me.

DROMIO OF EPHESUS.

I buy a thousand pound a year! I buy a rope!
[*Exit.*

ANTIPHOLUS OF EPHESUS.

A man is well holp up that trusts to you:
You promised your presence and the chain;
But neither chain nor goldsmith came to me.
Belike you thought our love would last too long,
If it were chain'd together, and therefore came
not.

ANGELO.

Saving your merry humour, here's the note
How much your chain weighs to the utmost
carat,
The fineness of the gold, and chargeful fashion,
Which doth amount to three odd ducats more
Than I stand debted to this gentleman:
I pray you, see him presently discharged,
For he is bound to sea, and stays but for it.

ANTIPHOLUS OF EPHESUS.

I am not furnish'd with the present money;
Besides, I have some business in the town.
Good signior, take the stranger to my house,
And with you take the chain, and bid my wife
Disburse the sum on the receipt thereof:
Perchance I will be there as soon as you.

ANGELO.

Then you will bring the chain to her yourself?

ANTIPHOLUS OF EPHESUS.

No; bear it with you, lest I come not time enough.

ANGELO.

Well, sir, I will. Have you the chain about you?

ANTIPHOLUS OF EPHESUS.

An if I have not, sir, I hope you have;
Or else you may return without your money.

ANGELO.

Nay, come, I pray you, sir, give me the chain:
Both wind and tide stays for this gentleman,
And I, to blame, have held him here too long.

ANTIPHOLUS OF EPHESUS.

Good Lord, you use this dalliance to excuse
Your breach of promise to the Porpentine.
I should have chid you for not bringing it,
But, like a shrew, you first begin to brawl.

SECOND MERCHANT.

The hour steals on; I pray you, sir, dispatch.

ANGELO.

You hear how he importunes me;—the chain!

ANTIPHOLUS OF EPHESUS.

Why, give it to my wife, and fetch your money.

ANGELO.

Come, come, you know I gave it you even now.
Either send the chain, or send me by some token.

ANTIPHOLUS OF EPHESUS.
Fie, now you run this humour out of breath.
Come, where's the chain? I pray you, let me see it.
SECOND MERCHANT.
My business cannot brook this dalliance.
Good sir, say whe'r you'll answer me or no:
If not, I'll leave him to the officer.
ANTIPHOLUS OF EPHESUS.
I answer you! what should I answer you?
ANGELO.
The money that you owe me for the chain.
ANTIPHOLUS OF EPHESUS.
I owe you none till I receive the chain.
ANGELO.
You know I gave it you half an hour since.
ANTIPHOLUS OF EPHESUS.
You gave me none: you wrong me much to say so.
ANGELO.
You wrong me more, sir, in denying it:
Consider how it stands upon my credit.
SECOND MERCHANT.
Well, officer, arrest him at my suit.
OFFICER.
I do;—
And charge you in the duke's name to obey me.
ANGELO.
This touches me in reputation.—
Either consent to pay this sum for me,
Or I attach you by this officer.
ANTIPHOLUS OF EPHESUS.
Consent to pay thee that I never had!
Arrest me, foolish fellow, if thou darest.
ANGELO.
Here is thy fee: arrest him, officer.—
I would not spare my brother in this case,
If he should scorn me so apparently.
OFFICER.
I do arrest you, sir: you hear the suit.
ANTIPHOLUS OF EPHESUS.
I do obey thee till I give thee bail.—
But, sirrah, you shall buy this sport as dear
As all the metal in your shop will answer.
ANGELO.
Sir, sir, I shall have law in Ephesus,
To your notorious shame: I doubt it not.
Enter DROMIO OF SYRACUSE *from the Bay.*
DROMIO OF SYRACUSE.
Master, there's a bark of Epidamnum
That stays but till her owner comes aboard,
And then she bears away. Our fraughtage, sir,
I have convey'd aboard; and I have bought
The oil, the balsamum, and aqua-vitæ.
The ship is in her trim; the merry wind
Blows fair from land: they stay for naught at all
But for their owner, master, and yourself.
ANTIPHOLUS OF EPHESUS.
How now! a madman! Why, thou peevish sheep,
What ship of Epidamnum stays for me?
DROMIO OF SYRACUSE.
A ship you sent me to, to hire waftage.
ANTIPHOLUS OF EPHESUS.
Thou drunken slave, I sent thee for a rope,
And told thee to what purpose and what end.
DROMIO OF SYRACUSE.
You sent me for a rope's-end as soon:
You sent me to the bay, sir, for a bark.

ANTIPHOLUS OF EPHESUS.
I will debate this matter at more leisure,
And teach your ears to list me with more heed.
To Adriana, villain, hie thee straight:
Give her this key, and tell her, in the desk
That's cover'd o'er with Turkish tapestry
There is a purse of ducats: let her send it:
Tell her I am arrested in the street,
And that shall bail me: hie thee, slave, be gone.—
On, officer, to prison till it come.
[*Exeunt* SECOND MERCHANT, ANGELO,
OFFICER, *and* ANTIPHOLUS OF EPHE-
SUS.
DROMIO OF SYRACUSE.
To Adriana! that is where we dined,
Where Dowsabel did claim me for her husband:
She is too big, I hope, for me to compass.
Thither I must, although against my will,
For servants must their masters' minds fulfil.
[*Exit.*

SCENE II.

The house of ANTIPHOLUS OF EPHESUS.

Enter ADRIANA *and* LUCIANA.

ADRIANA.
AH, Luciana, did he tempt thee so?
Mightst thou perceive austerely in his eye
That he did plead in earnest, yea or no?
Look'd he or red or pale, or sad or merrily?
What observation madest thou, in this case,
Of his heart's meteors tilting in his face?
LUCIANA.
First he denied you had in him no right.
ADRIANA.
He meant he did me none; the more my spite.
LUCIANA.
Then swore he that he was a stranger here.
ADRIANA.
And true he swore, though yet forsworn he
    were.
LUCIANA.
Then pleaded I for you.
ADRIANA.
              And what said he?
LUCIANA.
That love I begg'd for you he begg'd of me.
ADRIANA.
With what persuasion did he tempt thy love?
LUCIANA.
With words that in an honest suit might move.
First he did praise my beauty, then my speech.
ADRIANA.
Didst speak him fair?
LUCIANA.
              Have patience, I beseech.
ADRIANA.
I cannot, nor I will not, hold me still;
My tongue, though not my heart, shall have his
    will.
He is deformed, crooked, old, and sere,
Ill-faced, worse-bodied, shapeless everywhere;
Vicious, ungentle, foolish, blunt, unkind;
Stigmatical in making, worse in mind.
LUCIANA.
Who would be jealous, then, of such a one?
No evil lost is wail'd when it is gone.

ADRIANA.

Ah, but I think him better than I say,
And yet would herein others' eyes were worse.
Far from her nest the lapwing cries away: [curse.
My heart prays for him, though my tongue do

Enter DROMIO OF SYRACUSE.

DROMIO OF SYRACUSE.

Here, go; the desk, the purse! sweet, now, make
haste.

LUCIANA.

How hast thou lost thy breath?

DROMIO OF SYRACUSE.

By running fast.

ADRIANA.

Where is thy master, Dromio? is he well?

DROMIO OF SYRACUSE.

No, he's in Tartar limbo, worse than hell.
A devil in an everlasting garment hath him;
One whose hard heart is button'd up with steel;
A fiend, a fairy, pitiless and rough;
A wolf, nay, worse,—a fellow all in buff;
A back-friend, a shoulder-clapper, one that
countermands
The passages of alleys, creeks, and narrow lands;
A hound that runs counter, and yet draws dry-
foot well;
One that, before the judgement, carries poor
souls to hell.

ADRIANA.

Why, man, what is the matter?

DROMIO OF SYRACUSE.

I do not know the matter: he is 'rested on the
case.

ADRIANA.

What, is he arrested? tell me at whose suit.

DROMIO OF SYRACUSE.

I know not at whose suit he is arrested well;
But is in a suit of buff which 'rested him, that can
I tell.
Will you send him, mistress, redemption, the
money in his desk?

ADRIANA.

Go fetch it, sister.—This I wonder at,
[*Exit* LUCIANA.
That he, unknown to me, should be in debt.—
Tell me, was he arrested on a band?

DROMIO OF SYRACUSE.

Not on a band, but on a stronger thing,—
A chain, a chain:—do you not hear it ring?

ADRIANA.

What, the chain?

DROMIO OF SYRACUSE.

No, no, the bell:—'tis time that I were gone:
It was two ere I left him, and now the clock
strikes one.

ADRIANA.

The hours come back! that did I never hear.

DROMIO OF SYRACUSE.

O, yes; if any hour meet a sergeant, 'a turns back
for very fear.

ADRIANA.

As if Time were in debt! how fondly dost thou
reason!

DROMIO OF SYRACUSE.

Time is a very bankrout, and owes more than he's
worth to season.

Nay, he's a thief too: have you not heard men say,
That Time comes stealing on by night and day?
If Time be in debt and theft, and a sergeant in
the way,
Hath he not reason to turn back an hour in a
day?

Enter LUCIANA *with the purse.*

ADRIANA.

Go, Dromio; there's the money, bear it straight;
And bring thy master home immediately.
Come, sister: I am prest down with conceit,—
Conceit, my comfort and my injury. [*Exeunt.*

SCENE III.

A public place.

Enter ANTIPHOLUS OF SYRACUSE.

ANTIPHOLUS OF SYRACUSE.

THERE'S not a man I meet but doth salute me
As if I were their well-acquainted friend;
And every one doth call me by my name.
Some tender money to me; some invite me;
Some other give me thanks for kindnesses;
Some offer me commodities to buy;—
Even now a tailor call'd me in his shop,
And show'd me silks that he had bought for me,
And therewithal took measure of my body.
Sure, these are but imaginary wiles,
And Lapland sorcerers inhabit here.

Enter DROMIO OF SYRACUSE.

DROMIO OF SYRACUSE.

Master, here's the gold you sent me for.—What
have you got rid of the picture of old Adam new
apparell'd?

ANTIPHOLUS OF SYRACUSE.

What gold is this? what Adam dost thou mean?

DROMIO OF SYRACUSE.

Not that Adam that kept the Paradise, but that
Adam that keeps the prison: he that goes in the
calf's skin that was kill'd for the Prodigal; he that
came behind you, sir, like an evil angel, and bid
you forsake your liberty.

ANTIPHOLUS OF SYRACUSE.

I understand thee not.

DROMIO OF SYRACUSE.

No? why, 'tis a plain case: he that went, like a
base-viol, in a case of leather; the man, sir, that
when gentlemen are tired, gives them a sob, and
'rests them; he, sir, that takes pity on decay'd
men, and gives them suits of durance; he that
sets up his rest to do more exploits with his mace
than a morris-pike.

ANTIPHOLUS OF SYRACUSE.

What, thou mean'st an officer?

DROMIO OF SYRACUSE.

Ay, sir, the sergeant of the band; he that brings
any man to answer it that breaks his band; one
that thinks a man always going to bed, and says
'God give you good rest!'

ANTIPHOLUS OF SYRACUSE.

Well, sir, there rest in your foolery. Is there any
ship puts forth to-night? may we be gone?

DROMIO OF SYRACUSE.

Why, sir, I brought you word an hour since, that
the bark Expedition put forth to-night; and then
were you hinder'd by the sergeant, to tarry for

the hoy Delay. Here are the angels that you sent
for to deliver you.
ANTIPHOLUS OF SYRACUSE.
The fellow is distract, and so am I;
And here we wander in illusions:
Some blessed power deliver us from hence!
Enter a COURTEZAN.
COURTEZAN.
Well met, well met, Master Antipholus.
I see, sir, you have found the goldsmith now:
Is that the chain you promised me to-day?
ANTIPHOLUS OF SYRACUSE.
Satan, avoid! I charge thee, tempt me not.
DROMIO OF SYRACUSE.
Master, is this Mistress Satan?
ANTIPHOLUS OF SYRACUSE.
It is the devil.
DROMIO OF SYRACUSE.
Nay, she is worse, she is the devil's dam; and here
she comes in the habit of a light wench: and
thereof comes that the wenches say, 'God damn
me;' that's as much as to say, 'God make me a
light wench.' It is written, they appear to men
like angels of light: light is an effect of fire, and
fire will burn; *ergo,* light wenches will burn.
Come not near her.
COURTEZAN.
Your man and you are marvellous merry, sir.
Will you go with me? We'll mend our dinner here.
DROMIO OF SYRACUSE.
Master, if you do, expect spoon-meat; so bespeak
a long spoon.
ANTIPHOLUS OF SYRACUSE.
Why, Dromio?
DROMIO OF SYRACUSE.
Marry, he must have a long spoon that must eat
with the devil.
ANTIPHOLUS OF SYRACUSE.
Avoid, thou fiend! what tell'st thou me of supping?
Thou art, as you are all, a sorceress:
I conjure thee to leave me and be gone.
COURTEZAN.
Give me the ring of mine you had at dinner,
Or, for my diamond, the chain you promised;
And I'll be gone, sir, and not trouble you.
DROMIO OF SYRACUSE.
Some devils ask but the parings of one's nail,
A rush, a hair, a drop of blood, a pin,
A nut, a cherry-stone;
But she, more covetous, would have a chain.
Master, be wise: an if you give it her,
The devil will shake her chain, and fright us with
it.
COURTEZAN.
I pray you, sir, my ring, or else the chain:
I hope you do not mean to cheat me so.
ANTIPHOLUS OF SYRACUSE.
Avaunt, thou witch!—Come, Dromio, let us go.
DROMIO OF SYRACUSE.
'Fly pride,' says the peacock: mistress, that you
know.
    [*Exeunt* ANTIPHOLUS OF SYRACUSE *and*
      DROMIO OF SYRACUSE.
COURTEZAN.
Now, out of doubt Antipholus is mad,
Else would he never so demean himself.

A ring he hath of mine worth forty ducats,
And for the same he promised me a chain:
Both one and other he denies me now.
The reason that I gather he is mad,—
Besides this present instance of his rage,—
Is a mad tale he told to-day at dinner,
Of his own doors being shut against his entrance.
Belike his wife, acquainted with his fits,
On purpose shut the doors against his way.
My way is now to hie home to his house,
And tell his wife that, being lunatic,
He rush'd into my house, and took perforce
My ring away. This course I fittest choose;
For forty ducats is too much to lose.   [*Exit.*

SCENE IV.

A street.

Enter ANTIPHOLUS OF EPHESUS *and the*
OFFICER.
ANTIPHOLUS OF EPHESUS.
FEAR me not, man; I will not break away:
   I'll give thee, ere I leave thee, so much
To warrant thee, as I am 'rested for.   [money,
My wife is in a wayward mood to-day,
And will not lightly trust the messenger:
That I should be attach'd in Ephesus,
I tell you, 'twill sound harshly in her ears.—
Here comes my man; I think he brings the money.
   Enter DROMIO OF EPHESUS *with a rope's-end.*
How now, sir! have you that I sent you for?
DROMIO OF EPHESUS.
Here's that, I warrant you, will pay them all.
ANTIPHOLUS OF EPHESUS.
But where's the money?
DROMIO OF EPHESUS.
Why, sir, I gave the money for the rope.
ANTIPHOLUS OF EPHESUS.
Five hundred ducats, villain, for a rope?
DROMIO OF EPHESUS.
I'll serve you, sir, five hundred at the rate.
ANTIPHOLUS OF EPHESUS.
To what end did I bid thee hie thee home?
DROMIO OF EPHESUS.
To a rope's-end, sir; and to that end am I re-
turn'd.
ANTIPHOLUS OF EPHESUS.
And to that end, sir, I will welcome you.
        [*Beating him.*
OFFICER.
Good sir, be patient.
DROMIO OF EPHESUS.
Nay, 'tis for me to be patient; I am in adversity.
OFFICER.
Good, now, hold thy tongue.
DROMIO OF EPHESUS.
Nay, rather persuade him to hold his hands.
ANTIPHOLUS OF EPHESUS.
Thou whoreson, senseless villain!
DROMIO OF EPHESUS.
I would I were senseless, sir, that I might not feel
your blows.
ANTIPHOLUS OF EPHESUS.
Thou art sensible in nothing but blows, and so is
an ass

DROMIO OF EPHESUS.

I am an ass, indeed; you may prove it by my long
ears.—I have served him from the hour of my
nativity to this instant, and have nothing at his
hands for my service but blows. When I am cold,
he heats me with beating; when I am warm, he
cools me with beating; I am waked with it when
I sleep; raised with it when I sit; driven out of
doors with it when I go from home; welcomed
home with it when I return: nay, I bear it on my
shoulders, as a beggar wont her brat; and, I think,
when he hath lamed me, I shall beg with it from
door to door.

ANTIPHOLUS OF EPHESUS.

Come, go along; my wife is coming yonder.

Enter ADRIANA, LUCIANA, *the* COURTEZAN,
and a schoolmaster call'd PINCH.

DROMIO OF EPHESUS.

Mistress, *respice finem*, respect your end;—or
rather, the prophecy like the parrot, 'Beware the
rope's-end.'

ANTIPHOLUS OF EPHESUS.

Wilt thou still talk?   [*Beating him.*

COURTEZAN.

How say you now? is not your husband mad?

ADRIANA.

His incivility confirms no less.—
Good Doctor Pinch, you are a conjurer;
Establish him in his true sense again,
And I will please you what you will demand.

LUCIANA.

Alas, how fiery and how sharp he looks!

COURTEZAN.

Mark how he trembles in his ecstasy!

PINCH.

Give me your hand, and let me feel your pulse.

ANTIPHOLUS OF EPHESUS.

There is my hand, and let it feel your ear.

      [*Striking him.*

PINCH.

I charge thee, Satan, housed within this man,
To yield possession to my holy prayers,
And to thy state of darkness hie thee straight;
I conjure thee by all the saints in heaven!

ANTIPHOLUS OF EPHESUS.

Peace, doting wizard, peace! I am not mad.

ADRIANA.

O, that thou wert not, poor distressed soul!

ANTIPHOLUS OF EPHESUS.

You minion, you, are these your customers?
Did this companion with the saffron face
Revel and feast it at my house to-day,
Whilst upon me the guilty doors were shut,
And I denied to enter in my house?

ADRIANA.

O husband, God doth know you dined at home;
Where would you had remain'd until this time,
Free from these slanders and this open shame!

ANTIPHOLUS OF EPHESUS.

Dined at home!—Thou villain, what sayest thou?

DROMIO OF EPHESUS.

Sir, sooth to say, you did not dine at home.

ANTIPHOLUS OF EPHESUS.

Were not my doors lockt up, and I shut out?

DROMIO OF EPHESUS.

Perdy, your doors were lockt, and you shut out

ANTIPHOLUS OF EPHESUS.

And did not she herself revile me there?

DROMIO OF EPHESUS.

Sans fable, she herself reviled you there.

ANTIPHOLUS OF EPHESUS.   [me?

Did not her kitchen-maid rail, taunt, and scorn

DROMIO OF EPHESUS.

Certes, she did; the kitchen-vestal scorn'd ye.

ANTIPHOLUS OF EPHESUS.

And did not I in rage depart from thence?

DROMIO OF EPHESUS.

In verity you did;—my bones bear witness,
That since have felt the vigour of his rage.

ADRIANA.

Is't good to soothe him in these contraries?

PINCH.

It is no shame: the fellow finds his vein,
And, yielding to him, humours well his frenzy.

ANTIPHOLUS OF EPHESUS.

Thou hast suborn'd the goldsmith to arrest me.

ADRIANA.

Alas, I sent you money to redeem you,
By Dromio here, who came in haste for it.

DROMIO OF EPHESUS.

Money by me! heart and good-will you might;
But surely, master, not a rag of money.

ANTIPHOLUS OF EPHESUS.

Went'st not thou to her for a purse of ducats?

ADRIANA.

He came to me, and I deliver'd it.

LUCIANA.

And I am witness with her that she did.

DROMIO OF EPHESUS.

God and the rope-maker bear me witness
That I was sent for nothing but a rope!

PINCH [*aside to* ADRIANA].

Mistress, both man and master is possest;
I know it by their pale and deadly looks:
They must be bound, and laid in some dark room.

ANTIPHOLUS OF EPHESUS.

Say, wherefore didst thou lock me forth to-day—
And why dost thou deny the bag of gold?

ADRIANA.

I did not, gentle husband, lock thee forth.

DROMIO OF EPHESUS.

And, gentle master, I received no gold;
But I confess, sir, that we were lockt out.

ADRIANA.

Dissembling villain, thou speak'st false in both.

ANTIPHOLUS OF EPHESUS.

Dissembling harlot, thou art false in all;
And art confederate with a damned pack
To make a loathsome abject scorn of me:
But with these nails I'll pluck out those false eyes
That would behold in me this shameful sport.

ADRIANA.

O, bind him, bind him! let him not come near me

PINCH.

More company!—The fiend is strong within him

LUCIANA.

Ay me, poor man, how pale and wan he looks!

Enter three or four, and offer to bind him; he strives

ANTIPHOLUS OF EPHESUS.

What, will you murder me?—Thou gaoler, thou
I am thy prisoner: wilt thou suffer them
To make a rescue?

OFFICER.
Masters, let him go:
He is my prisoner, and you shall not have him.
PINCH.
Go bind this man, for he is frantic too.
[*They bind* DROMIO OF EPHESUS.
ADRIANA.
What wilt thou do, thou peevish officer?
Hast thou delight to see a wretched man
Do outrage and displeasure to himself?
OFFICER.
He is my prisoner: if I let him go,
The debt he owes will be required of me.
ADRIANA.
I will discharge thee ere I go from thee:
Bear me forthwith unto his creditor,
And, knowing how the debt grows, I will pay
it.—
Good master doctor, see him safe convey'd
Home to my house.—O most unhappy day!
ANTIPHOLUS OF EPHESUS.
O most unhappy strumpet!
DROMIO OF EPHESUS.
Master, I am here enter'd in bond for you.
ANTIPHOLUS OF EPHESUS.
Out on thee, villain! wherefore dost thou mad
me?
DROMIO OF EPHESUS.
Will you be bound for nothing? be mad, good
master; cry, 'The devil!'
LUCIANA.
God help, poor souls, how idly do they talk!
ADRIANA.
Go bear him hence.—Sister, go you with me.
[*Exeunt* PINCH *and* ASSISTANTS, *with*
ANTIPHOLUS OF EPHESUS *and* DRO-
MIO OF EPHESUS.
Say now whose suit is he arrested at?
OFFICER.
One Angelo, a goldsmith: do you know him?
ADRIANA.
I know the man. What is the sum he owes?
OFFICER.
Two hundred ducats.
ADRIANA.
Say, how grows it due?
OFFICER.
Due for a chain your husband had of him.
ADRIANA.
He did bespeak a chain for me, but had it not.
COURTEZAN.
Whenas your husband, all in rage, to-day
Came to my house, and took away my ring,—
The ring I saw upon his finger now,—
Straight after did I meet him with a chain.
ADRIANA.
It may be so, but I did never see it.—
Come, gaoler, bring me where the goldsmith is:
I long to know the truth hereof at large.
Enter ANTIPHOLUS OF SYRACUSE *with his
rapier drawn, and* DROMIO OF SYRACUSE.
LUCIANA.
God, for thy mercy! they are loose again.
ADRIANA.   [help,
And come with naked swords. Let 's call more
To have them bound again.

OFFICER.
Away! they'll kill us.
[*Exeunt* ADRIANA, *&c., as fast as may be,
frighted.*
ANTIPHOLUS OF SYRACUSE.
I see these witches are afraid of swords.
DROMIO OF SYRACUSE.
She that would be your wife now ran from you.
ANTIPHOLUS OF SYRACUSE.
Come to the Centaur; fetch our stuff from thence:
I long that we were safe and sound aboard.
DROMIO OF SYRACUSE.
Faith, stay here this night; they will surely do us
no harm: you saw they speak us fair, give us gold:
methinks they are such a gentle nation, that, but
for the mountain of mad flesh that claims mar-
riage of me, I could find in my heart to stay here
still, and turn witch.
ANTIPHOLUS OF SYRACUSE.
I will not stay to-night for all the town;
Therefore away, to get our stuff aboard. [*Exeunt.*

ACT V. SCENE I.

Before an abbey.

Enter SECOND MERCHANT *and* ANGELO.

ANGELO.
I AM sorry, sir, that I have hinder'd you;
But, I protest, he had the chain of me,
Though most dishonestly he doth deny it.
SECOND MERCHANT.
How is the man esteem'd here in the city?
ANGELO.
Of very reverend reputation, sir,
Of credit infinite, highly beloved,
Second to none that lives here in the city:
His word might bear my wealth at any time.
SECOND MERCHANT.
Speak softly: yonder, as I think, he walks.
Enter ANTIPHOLUS OF SYRACUSE *and* DROMIO
OF SYRACUSE.
ANGELO.
'Tis so; and that self chain about his neck,
Which he forswore most monstrously to have.
Good sir, draw near to me, I'll speak to him.—
Signior Antipholus, I wonder much
That you would put me to this shame and
trouble;
And, not without some scandal to yourself,
With circumstance and oaths so to deny
This chain, which now you wear so openly:
Beside the charge, the shame, imprisonment,
You have done wrong to this my honest friend;
Who, but for staying on our controversy,
Had hoisted sail and put to sea to-day:
This chain you had of me; can you deny it?
ANTIPHOLUS OF SYRACUSE.
I think I had; I never did deny it.
SECOND MERCHANT.
Yes, that you did, sir, and forswore it too.
ANTIPHOLUS OF SYRACUSE.
Who heard me to deny it or forswear it?
SECOND MERCHANT.
These ears of mine, thou know'st, did hear thee:
Fie on thee, wretch! 'tis pity that thou livest
To walk where any honest men resort.

ANTIPHOLUS OF SYRACUSE.

Thou art a villain to impeach me thus:
I'll prove mine honour and mine honesty
Against thee presently, if thou darest stand.

SECOND MERCHANT.

I dare, and do defy thee for a villain. [*They draw.*
Enter ADRIANA, LUCIANA, *the* COURTEZAN,
and others.

ADRIANA.

Hold, hurt him not, for God's sake! he is mad.—
Some get within him, take his sword away:
Bind Dromio too, and bear them to my house.

DROMIO OF SYRACUSE.

Run, master, run; for God's sake, take a house!
This is some priory:—in, or we are spoil'd.

[*Exeunt* ANTIPHOLUS OF SYRACUSE *and*
DROMIO OF SYRACUSE *to the abbey.*
Enter LADY ABBESS.

ABBESS.

Be quiet, people. Wherefore throng you hither?

ADRIANA.

To fetch my poor distracted husband hence.
Let us come in, that we may bind him fast,
And bear him home for his recovery.

ANGELO.

I knew he was not in his perfect wits.

SECOND MERCHANT.

I am sorry now that I did draw on him.

ABBESS.

How long hath this possession held the man?

ADRIANA.

This week he hath been heavy, sour, sad,
And much different from the man he was;
But till this afternoon his passion
Ne'er brake into extremity of rage.

ABBESS.

Hath he not lost much wealth by wrack of sea?
Buried some dear friend? Hath not else his eye
Stray'd his affection in unlawful love,—
A sin prevailing much in youthful men,
Who give their eyes the liberty of gazing?
Which of these sorrows is he subject to?

ADRIANA.

To none of these, except it be the last;
Namely, some love that drew him oft from home.

ABBESS.

You should for that have reprehended him.

ADRIANA.

Why, so I did.

ABBESS.

Ay, but not rough enough.

ADRIANA.

As roughly as my modesty would let me.

ABBESS.

Haply, in private.

ADRIANA.

And in assemblies too.

ABBESS.

Ay, but not enough.

ADRIANA.

It was the copy of our conference:
In bed, he slept not for my urging it;
At board, he fed not for my urging it;
Alone, it was the subject of my theme;
In company I often glanced it;
Still did I tell him it was vile and bad.

ABBESS.

And thereof came it that the man was mad:
The venom-clamours of a jealous woman
Poisons more deadly than a mad-dog's tooth.
It seems his sleeps were hinder'd by thy railing:
And thereof comes it that his head is light.
Thou say'st his meat was sauced with thy up-
braidings:
Unquiet meals make ill digestions,—
Thereof the raging fire of fever bred;
And what's a fever but a fit of madness?
Thou say'st his sports were hinder'd by thy
brawls:
Sweet recreation barr'd, what doth ensue
But moody and dull melancholy,
Kinsman to grim and comfortless despair;
And at her heels a huge infectious troop
Of pale distemperatures and foes to life?
In food, in sport, and life-preserving rest
To be disturb'd, would mad or man or beast:
The consequence is, then, thy jealous fits
Have scared thy husband from the use of wits.

LUCIANA.

She never reprehended him but mildly,
When he demean'd himself rough-rude and
wildly.—
Why bear you these rebukes, and answer not?

ADRIANA.

She did betray me to my own reproof.—
Good people, enter, and lay hold on him.

ABBESS.

No, not a creature enters in my house.

ADRIANA.

Then let your servants bring my husband forth.

ABBESS.

Neither: he took this place for sanctuary,
And it shall privilege him from your hands
Till I have brought him to his wits again,
Or lose my labour in assaying it.

ADRIANA.

I will attend my husband, be his nurse,
Diet his sickness, for it is my office,
And will have no attorney but myself;
And therefore let me have him home with me.

ABBESS.

Be patient; for I will not let him stir
Till I have used the approved means I have,
With wholesome syrups, drugs, and holy prayers
To make of him a formal man again:
It is a branch and parcel of mine oath,
A charitable duty of my order.
Therefore depart, and leave him here with me.

ADRIANA.

I will not hence, and leave my husband here:
And ill it doth beseem your holiness
To separate the husband and the wife.

ABBESS.

Be quiet, and depart: thou shalt not have him.
[*Exit*

LUCIANA.

Complain unto the duke of this indignity.

ADRIANA.

Come, go: I will fall prostrate at his feet,
And never rise until my tears and prayers
Have won his grace to come in person hither,
And take perforce my husband from the abbess.

SECOND MERCHANT.

By this, I think, the dial points at five:
Anon, I'm sure, the duke himself in person
Comes this way to the melancholy vale,
The place of death and sorry execution,
Behind the ditches of the abbey here.

ANGELO.

Upon what cause?

SECOND MERCHANT.

To see a reverend Syracusian merchant,
Who put unluckily into this bay
Against the laws and statutes of this town,
Beheaded publicly for his offence.

ANGELO.

See where they come: we will behold his death.

LUCIANA.

Kneel to the duke before he pass the abbey.

Enter DUKE, *attended;* AEGEON *bareheaded; with
the* HEADSMAN *and other* OFFICERS.

DUKE.

Yet once again proclaim it publicly,
If any friend will pay the sum for him,
He shall not die, so much we tender him.

ADRIANA.

Justice, most sacred duke, against the abbess!

DUKE OF EPHESUS.

She is a virtuous and a reverend lady:
It cannot be that she hath done thee wrong.

ADRIANA.

May it please your grace, Antipholus my hus-
    band,—
Who I mad : lord of me and all I had,
At your important letters,—this ill day
A most outrageous fit of madness took him;
That desp'rately he hurried through the
    street,—
With him his bondman, all as mad as he,—
Doing displeasure to the citizens
By rushing in their houses, bearing thence
Rings, jewels, any thing his rage did like.
Once did I get him bound, and sent him home,
Whilst to take order for the wrongs I went,
That here and there his fury had committed.
Anon, I wot not by what strong escape
He broke from those that had the guard of him;
And both his mad attendant and himself,
Each one with ireful passion, with drawn swords,
Met us again, and, madly bent on us,
Chased us away; till, raising of more aid,
We came again to bind them. Then they fled
Into this abbey, whither we pursued them;
And here the abbess shuts the gates on us,
And will not suffer us to fetch him out,
Nor send him forth, that we may bear him hence.
Therefore, most gracious duke, with thy com-
    mand
Let him be brought forth, and borne hence for
    help.

DUKE OF EPHESUS.

Long since thy husband served me in my wars;
And I to thee engaged a prince's word,
When thou didst make him master of thy bed,
To do him all the grace and good I could.—
Go, some of you, knock at the abbey-gate,
And bid the lady abbess come to me.—
will determine this before I stir.

Enter a SERVANT.

SERVANT.

O mistress, mistress, shift and save yourself!
My master and his man are both broke loose,
Beaten the maids a-row, and bound the doctor,
Whose beard they have singed off with brands or
    fire;
And ever, as it blazed, they threw on him
Great pails of puddled mire to quench the hair:
My master preaches patience to him, and the
    while
His man with scissors nicks him like a fool;
And sure, unless you send some present help,
Between them they will kill the conjurer.

ADRIANA.

Peace, fool! thy master and his man are here;
And that is false thou dost report to us.

SERVANT.

Mistress, upon my life, I tell you true;
I have not breathed almost since I did see it.
He cries for you, and vows, if he can take you,
To scorch your face, and to disfigure you.
    [*Cry within.*
Hark, hark! I hear him, mistress: fly, be gone!

DUKE OF EPHESUS.

Come, stand by me; fear nothing.—Guard with
    halberds!

ADRIANA.

Ay me, it is my husband! Witness you,
That he is borne about invisible:
Even now we housed him in the abbey here;
And now he's there, past thought of human
    reason.

Enter ANTIPHOLUS OF EPHESUS *and* DROMIO
OF EPHESUS.

ANTIPHOLUS OF EPHESUS.

Justice, most gracious duke, O, grant me justice!
Even for the service that long since I did thee,
When I bestrid thee in the wars, and took
Deep scars to save thy life; even for the blood
That then I lost for thee, now grant me justice.

AEGEON.

Unless the fear of death doth make me dote,
I see my son Antipholus, and Dromio.

ANTIPHOLUS OF EPHESUS.

Justice, sweet prince, against that woman there!
She whom thou gavest to me to be my wife,
That hath abused and dishonour'd me
Even in the strength and height of injury:
Beyond imagination is the wrong
That she this day hath shameless thrown on me.

DUKE OF EPHESUS.

Discover how, and thou shalt find me just.

ANTIPHOLUS OF EPHESUS.

This day, great duke, she shut the doors upon
    me,
While she with harlots feasted in my house.

DUKE OF EPHESUS.

A grievous fault.—Say, woman, didst thou so?

ADRIANA.

No, my good lord: myself, he, and my sister,
To-day did dine together. So befall my soul
As this is false he burdens me withal!

LUCIANA.

Ne'er may I look on day, nor sleep on night,
But she tells to your highness simple truth!

ANGELO.

O perjured woman!—They are both forsworn:
In this the madman justly chargeth them.

ANTIPHOLUS OF EPHESUS.

My liege, I am advised what I say;
Neither disturb'd with the effect of wine,
Nor heady-rash, provoked with raging ire,
Albeit my wrongs might make one wiser mad.
This woman lockt me out this day from dinner:
That goldsmith there, were he not pack'd with her,
Could witness it, for he was with me then;
Who parted with me to go fetch a chain,
Promising to bring it to the Porpentine,
Where Balthazar and I did dine together.
Our dinner done, and he not coming thither,
I went to seek him: in the street I met him,
And in his company that gentleman.
There did this perjured goldsmith swear me down
That I this day of him received the chain,
Which, God he knows, I saw not: for the which
He did arrest me with an officer.
I did obey; and sent my peasant home
For certain ducats: he with none return'd.
Then fairly I bespoke the officer
To go in person with me to my house.
By th' way we met
My wife, her sister, and a rabble more
Of vile confederates. Along with them   [villain,
They brought one Pinch, a hungry lean-faced
A mere anatomy, a mountebank,
A threadbare juggler, and a fortune-teller,
A needy, hollow-eyed, sharp-looking wretch,
A living-dead man: this pernicious slave,
Forsooth, took on him as a conjurer;
And, gazing in mine eyes, feeling my pulse,
And with no face, as 'twere, outfacing me,
Cries out, I was possest. Then all together
They fell upon me, bound me, bore me thence,
And in a dark and dankish vault at home
There left me and my man, both bound together;
Till, gnawing with my teeth my bonds in sunder,
I gain'd my freedom, and immediately
Ran hither to your grace; whom I beseech
To give me ample satisfaction
For these deep shames and great indignities.

ANGELO.

My lord, in truth, thus far I witness with him,
That he dined not at home, but was lockt out.

DUKE OF EPHESUS.

But had he such a chain of thee or no?

ANGELO.

He had, my lord: and when he ran in here,
These people saw the chain about his neck.

SECOND MERCHANT.

Besides, I will be sworn these ears of mine
Heard you confess you had the chain of him,
After you first forswore it on the mart:
And thereupon I drew my sword on you;
And then you fled into this abbey here,
From whence, I think, you are come by miracle.

ANTIPHOLUS OF EPHESUS.

I never came within these abbey-walls;
Nor ever didst thou draw thy sword on me:
I never saw the chain, so help me heaven
And this is false you burden me withal!

DUKE OF EPHESUS.

Why, what an intricate impeach is this!
I think you all have drunk of Circe's cup.
If here you housed him, here he would have been;
If he were mad, he would not plead so coldly:—
You say he dined at home; the goldsmith here
Denies that saying.—Sirrah, what say you?

DROMIO OF EPHESUS.

Sir, he dined with her there, at the Porpentine.

COURTEZAN.

He did; and from my finger snatcht that ring.

ANTIPHOLUS OF EPHESUS.

'Tis true, my liege; this ring I had of her.

DUKE OF EPHESUS.

Saw'st thou him enter at the abbey here?

COURTEZAN.

As sure, my liege, as I do see your grace.

DUKE OF EPHESUS.

Why, this is strange.—Go call the abbess
hither.—   [Exit one to the ABBESS.
I think you are all mated or stark mad.

AEGEON.

Most mighty duke, vouchsafe me speak a word:
Haply I see a friend will save my life,
And pay the sum that may deliver me.

DUKE OF EPHESUS.

Speak freely, Syracusian, what thou wilt.

AEGEON.

Is not your name, sir, call'd Antipholus?
And is not that your bondman Dromio?

DROMIO OF EPHESUS.

Within this hour I was his bondman, sir,
But he, I thank him, gnaw'd in two my cords:
Now am I Dromio, and his man unbound.

AEGEON.

I am sure you both of you remember me.

DROMIO OF EPHESUS.

Ourselves we do remember, sir, by you;
For lately we were bound, as you are now.
You are not Pinch's patient, are you, sir?

AEGEON.

Why look you strange on me? you know me
well.

ANTIPHOLUS OF EPHESUS.

I never saw you in my life till now.

AEGEON.

O, grief hath changed me since you saw me
last,
And careful hours with Time's deformed hand
Have written strange defeatures in my face:
But tell me yet, dost thou not know my voice?

ANTIPHOLUS OF EPHESUS.

Neither.

AEGEON.

Dromio, nor thou?

DROMIO OF EPHESUS.

No, trust me, sir, nor I.

AEGEON.

I am sure thou dost.

DROMIO OF EPHESUS.

Ay, sir, but I am sure I do not; and whatsoeve
a man denies, you are now bound to believ
him.

AEGEON.

Not know my voice! O time's extremity,

Hast thou so crack'd and splitted my poor
   tongue
In seven short years, that here my only son
Knows not my feeble key of untuned cares?
Though now this grained face of mine be hid
In sap-consuming winter's drizzled snow,
And all the conduits of my blood froze up,
Yet hath my night of life some memory,
My wasting lamps some fading glimmer left,
My dull deaf ears a little use to hear:
All these old witnesses—I cannot err—
Tell me thou art my son Antipholus.
     ANTIPHOLUS OF EPHESUS.
I never saw my father in my life.
     AEGEON.
But seven years since, in Syracusa, boy,
Thou know'st we parted: but perhaps, my son,
Thou shamest to acknowledge me in misery.
     ANTIPHOLUS OF EPHESUS.
The duke, and all that know me in the city,
Can witness with me that it is not so:
I ne'er saw Syracusa in my life.
     DUKE OF EPHESUS.
I tell thee, Syracusian, twenty years
Have I been patron to Antipholus,
During which time he ne'er saw Syracusa:
I see thy age and dangers make thee dote.
Enter ABBESS, *with* ANTIPHOLUS OF SYRACUSE
    and DROMIO OF SYRACUSE.
     ABBESS.
Most mighty duke, behold a man much wrong'd.
      [*All gather to see them.*
     ADRIANA.
I see two husbands, or mine eyes deceive me.
     DUKE OF EPHESUS.
One of these men is Genius to the other;
And so of these. Which is the natural man,
And which the spirit? who deciphers them?
     DROMIO OF SYRACUSE.
I, sir, am Dromio: command him away.
     DROMIO OF EPHESUS.
I, sir, am Dromio: pray, let me stay.
     ANTIPHOLUS OF SYRACUSE.
Aegeon art thou not? or else his ghost?
     DROMIO OF SYRACUSE.
O, my old master! who hath bound him here?
     ABBESS.
Whoever bound him, I will loose his bonds,
And gain a husband by his liberty.—
Speak, old Aegeon, if thou be'st the man
That hadst a wife once call'd Aemilia,
That bore thee at a burden two fair sons:
O, if thou be'st the same Aegeon, speak,
And speak unto the same Aemilia!
     AEGEON.
If I dream not, thou art Aemilia:
If thou art she, tell me where is that son
That floated with thee on the fatal raft?
     ABBESS.
By men of Epidamnum he and I
And the twin Dromio all were taken up;
But by and by rude fishermen of Corinth
By force took Dromio and my son from them,
And me they left with those of Epidamnum.
What then became of them I cannot tell;
To this fortune that you see me in.

     DUKE OF EPHESUS.
Why, here begins his morning story right:
These two Antipholus', these two so like,
And these two Dromios, one in semblance,—
Besides her urging of her wrack at sea,—
These are the parents to these children,
Which accidentally are met together.—
Antipholus, thou camest from Corinth first?
     ANTIPHOLUS OF SYRACUSE.
No, sir, not I; I came from Syracuse.
     DUKE OF EPHESUS.
Stay, stand apart; I know not which is which.
     ANTIPHOLUS OF EPHESUS.
I came from Corinth, my most gracious lord,—
     DROMIO OF EPHESUS.
And I with him.
     ANTIPHOLUS OF EPHESUS.
Brought to this town by that most famous
   warrior,
Duke Menaphon, your most renowned uncle.
     ADRIANA.
Which of you two did dine with me to-day?
     ANTIPHOLUS OF SYRACUSE.
I, gentle mistress.
     ADRIANA.
      And are not you my husband?
     ANTIPHOLUS OF EPHESUS.
No; I say nay to that.
     ANTIPHOLUS OF SYRACUSE.
And so do I; yet did she call me so:
And this fair gentlewoman, her sister here,
Did call me brother.—[*to* LUCIANA] What I told
   you then,
I hope I shall have leisure to make good;
If this be not a dream I see and hear.
     ANGELO.
That is the chain, sir, which you had of me.
     ANTIPHOLUS OF SYRACUSE.
I think it be, sir; I deny it not.
     ANTIPHOLUS OF EPHESUS.
And you, sir, for this chain arrested me.
     ANGELO.
I think I did, sir; I deny it not.
     ADRIANA.
I sent you money, sir, to be your bail,
By Dromio; but I think he brought it not.
     DROMIO OF EPHESUS.
No, none by me.
     ANTIPHOLUS OF SYRACUSE.
This purse of ducats I received from you,
And Dromio my man did bring them me.
I see we still did meet each other's man;
And I was ta'en for him, and he for me;
And thereupon these errors are arose.
     ANTIPHOLUS OF EPHESUS.
These ducats pawn I for my father here.
     DUKE OF EPHESUS.
It shall not need; thy father hath his life.
     COURTEZAN.
Sir, I must have that diamond from you.
     ANTIPHOLUS OF EPHESUS.
There, take it; and much thanks for my good
   cheer.
     ABBESS.
Renowned duke, vouchsafe to take the pains
To go with us into the abbey here,

And hear at large discoursed all our fortunes;—
And all that are assembled in this place,
That by this sympathized one day's error
Have suffer'd wrong, go keep us company,
And we shall make full satisfaction.—
Thirty-three years have I but gone in travail
Of you, my sons; and, till this present hour,
My heavy burden ne'er delivered.—
The duke, my husband, and my children both,
And you the calendars of their nativity,
Go to a gossip's feast, and joy with me;
After so long grief, such felicity!

           DUKE OF EPHESUS.

With all my heart, I'll gossip at this feast.

         [*Exeunt* DUKE, ABBESS, AEGEON, COUR-
           TEZAN, SECOND MERCHANT, AN-
           GELO, *and* ATTENDANTS.
            DROMIO OF SYRACUSE.

Master, shall I fetch your stuff from shipboard?

           ANTIPHOLUS OF EPHESUS.

Dromio, what stuff of mine hast thou embarkt?

           DROMIO OF SYRACUSE.

Your goods that lay at host, sir, in the Centaur.

           ANTIPHOLUS OF SYRACUSE.

He speaks to me.—I am your master, Dromio:

Come, go with us; we'll look to that anon:
Embrace thy brother there; rejoice with him.

        [*Exeunt* ANTIPHOLUS OF SYRACUSE *and*
          ANTIPHOLUS OF EPHESUS, ADRIANA
          and LUCIANA.
           DROMIO OF SYRACUSE.

There is a fat friend at your master's house,
That kitchen'd me for you to-day at dinner:
She now shall be my sister, not my wife.

           DROMIO OF EPHESUS.

Methinks you are my glass, and not my brother:
I see by you I am a sweet-faced youth.
Will you walk in to see their gossiping?

           DROMIO OF SYRACUSE.

Not I, sir; you are my elder.

           DROMIO OF EPHESUS.

That's a question: how shall we try it?

           DROMIO OF SYRACUSE.

We'll draw cuts for the senior: till then lead thou
   first.

           DROMIO OF EPHESUS.

Nay, then, thus:—
We came into the world like brother and brother;
And now let's go hand in hand, not one before
   another.   [*Exeunt.*

THE TWO GENTLEMEN OF VERONA

DRAMATIS PERSONAE.

DUKE OF MILAN, *father to Silvia.*
VALENTINE, } *the two Gentlemen.*
PROTEUS,
ANTONIO, *father to Proteus.*
THURIO, *a foolish rival to Valentine.*
EGLAMOUR, *agent for Silvia in her escape.*
SPEED, *a clownish servant to Valentine.*
LAUNCE, *the like to Proteus.*
PANTHINO, *servant to Antonio.*

HOST, *where Julia lodges.*
OUTLAWS, *with Valentine.*

JULIA, *beloved of Proteus.*
SILVIA, *beloved of Valentine.*
LUCETTA, *waiting-woman to Julia.*

SERVANTS, MUSICIANS.

SCENE—*Verona; Milan; the frontiers of Mantua.*

ACT I. SCENE I.

Verona. An open place.

Enter VALENTINE *and* PROTEUS.

VALENTINE.

CEASE to persuade, my loving Proteus:
Home-keeping youth have ever homely wits.
Were't not affection chains thy tender days
To the sweet glances of thy honour'd love,
I rather would entreat thy company
To see the wonders of the world abroad,
Than, living dully sluggardized at home,
Wear out thy youth with shapeless idleness.
But since thou lovest, love still, and thrive therein,
Even as I would, when I to love begin.

PROTEUS.

Wilt thou be gone? Sweet Valentine, adieu!
Think on thy Proteus, when thou haply see'st
Some rare note-worthy object in thy travel:
Wish me partaker in thy happiness,   [danger,
When thou dost meet good hap; and in thy
If ever danger do environ thee,
Commend thy grievance to my holy prayers,
For I will be thy beadsman, Valentine.

VALENTINE.

And on a love-book pray for my success?

PROTEUS.

Upon some book I love I'll pray for thee.

VALENTINE.

That's on some shallow story of deep love;
How young Leander cross'd the Hellespont.

PROTEUS.

That's a deep story of a deeper love;
For he was more than over shoes in love.

VALENTINE.

'Tis true; for you are over boots in love,
And yet you never swum the Hellespont.

PROTEUS.

Over the boots! nay, give me not the boots.

VALENTINE.

No, I will not, for it boots thee not.

PROTEUS.

What?

VALENTINE.

To be in love, where scorn is bought with
groans;   [moment's mirth
Coy looks with heart-sore sighs; one fading

With twenty watchful, weary, tedious nights:
If haply won, perhaps a hapless gain;
If lost, why then a grievous labour won;
However, but a folly bought with wit,
Or else a wit by folly vanquished.

PROTEUS.

So, by your circumstance, you call me fool.

VALENTINE.

So, by your circumstance, I fear you'll prove.

PROTEUS.

'Tis love you cavil at: I am not Love.

VALENTINE.

Love is your master, for he masters you:
And he that is so yoked by a fool,
Methinks, should not be chronicled for wise.

PROTEUS.

Yet writers say, as in the sweetest bud
The eating canker dwells, so eating love
Inhabits in the finest wits of all.

VALENTINE.

And writers say, as the most forward bud
Is eaten by the canker ere it blow,
Even so by love the young and tender wit
Is turn'd to folly; blasting in the bud,
Losing his verdure even in the prime,
And all the fair effects of future hopes.
But wherefore waste I time to counsel thee,
That art a votary to fond desire?
Once more adieu! my father at the road
Expects my coming, there to see me shipp'd.

PROTEUS.

And thither will I bring thee, Valentine.

VALENTINE.

Sweet Proteus, no; now let us take our leave.
To Milan let me hear from thee by letters
Of thy success in love, and what news else
Betideth here in absence of thy friend;
And I likewise will visit thee with mine.

PROTEUS.

All happiness bechance to thee in Milan!

VALENTINE.

As much to you at home! and so, farewell.   [*Exit.*

PROTEUS.

He after honour hunts, I after love:
He leaves his friends to dignify them more;
I leave myself, my friends, and all, for love.
Thou, Julia, thou hast metamorphosed me,—

Made me neglect my studies, lose my time,
War with good counsel, set the world at naught;
Made wit with musing weak, heart sick with
  thought.

Enter SPEED.

SPEED.
Sir Proteus, save you! Saw you my master?

PROTEUS.
But now he parted hence, to embark for Milan.

SPEED.
Twenty to one, then, he is shipp'd already,
And I have play'd the sheep in losing him.

PROTEUS.
Indeed, a sheep doth very often stray,
An if the shepherd be awhile away.

SPEED.
You conclude that my master is a shepherd then,
  and I a sheep?

PROTEUS.
I do.

SPEED.
Why, then, my horns are his horns, whether I
  wake or sleep.

PROTEUS.
A silly answer, and fitting well a sheep.

SPEED.
This proves me still a sheep.

PROTEUS.
True; and thy master a shepherd.

SPEED.
Nay, that I can deny by a circumstance.

PROTEUS.
It shall go hard but I'll prove it by another.

SPEED.
The shepherd seeks the sheep, and not the sheep
the shepherd; but I seek my master, and my
master seeks not me: therefore I am no sheep.

PROTEUS.
The sheep for fodder follow the shepherd,
the shepherd for food follows not the sheep;
thou for wages followest thy master, thy master
for wages follows not thee: therefore thou art a
sheep.

SPEED.
Such another proof will make me cry 'baa.'

PROTEUS.
But, dost thou hear? gavest thou my letter to Julia?

SPEED.
Ay, sir: I, a lost mutton, gave your letter to her, a
laced mutton; and she, a laced mutton, gave me, a
lost mutton, nothing for my labour.

PROTEUS.
Here's too small a pasture for such store of muttons.

SPEED.
If the ground be overcharged, you were best stick
her.

PROTEUS.
Nay, in that you are a stray, 'twere best pound you.

SPEED.
Nay, sir, less than a pound shall serve me for
carrying your letter.

PROTEUS.
You mistake; I mean the pound,—a pinfold.

SPEED.
From a pound to a pin? fold it over and over,

'Tis threefold too little for carrying a letter to your
  lover.

PROTEUS.
But what said she?

SPEED [*nodding*].
Ay.

PROTEUS.
Nod, Ay?—why, that's noddy.

SPEED.
You mistook, sir; I say, she did nod: and you ask
me if she did nod; and I say, Ay.

PROTEUS.
And that set together is—noddy.

SPEED.
Now you have taken the pains to set it together
take it for your pains.

PROTEUS.
No, no; you shall have it for bearing the letter.

SPEED.
Well, I perceive I must be fain to bear with you.

PROTEUS.
Why, sir, how do you bear with me?

SPEED.
Marry, sir, the letter very orderly; having nothing
but the word 'noddy' for my pains.

PROTEUS.
Beshrew me, but you have a quick wit.

SPEED.
And yet it cannot overtake your slow purse.

PROTEUS.
Come, come, open the matter in brief; what said
she?

SPEED.
Open your purse, that the money and the
matter may be both at once deliver'd.

PROTEUS.
Well, sir, here is for your pains [*Giving him
money*]. What said she?

SPEED.
Truly, sir, I think you'll hardly win her.

PROTEUS.
Why, couldst thou perceive so much from her?

SPEED.
Sir, I could perceive nothing at all from her; no,
not so much as a ducat for delivering your letter:
and being so hard to me that brought your mind,
I fear she 'll prove as hard to you in telling your
mind. Give her no token but stones; for she's as
hard as steel.

PROTEUS.
What, said she nothing?

SPEED.
No, not so much as 'Take this for thy pains.'
To testify your bounty, I thank you, you have
testern'd me; in requital whereof, henceforth
carry your letters yourself: and so, sir, I'll commend you to my master.

PROTEUS.
Go, go, be gone, to save your ship from wrack,
Which cannot perish having thee aboard,
Being destined to a drier death on shore.
                              [*Exit* SPEED

I must go send some better messenger:
I fear my Julia would not deign my lines,
Receiving them from such a worthless post.
                              [*Exit*

SCENE II.

The same. JULIA'S *garden.*

Enter JULIA *and* LUCETTA.

JULIA.

BUT say, Lucetta, now we are alone,
Wouldst thou, then, counsel me to fall in love?

LUCETTA.

Ay, madam; so you stumble not unheedfully.

JULIA.

Of all the fair resort of gentlemen
That every day with parle encounter me,
In thy opinion which is worthiest love?

LUCETTA.

Please you repeat their names, I'll show my mind
According to my shallow simple skill.

JULIA.

What think'st thou of the fair Sir Eglamour?

LUCETTA.

As of a knight well-spoken, neat, and fine;
But, were I you, he never should be mine.

JULIA.

What think'st thou of the rich Mercatio?

LUCETTA.

Well of his wealth; but of himself, so-so.

JULIA.

What think'st thou of the gentle Proteus?

LUCETTA.

Lord, Lord! to see what folly reigns in us!

JULIA.

How now! what means this passion at his name?

LUCETTA.

Pardon, dear madam: 'tis a passing shame
That I, unworthy body as I am,
Should censure thus on lovely gentlemen.

JULIA.

Why not on Proteus, as of all the rest?

LUCETTA.

Then thus,—of many good I think him best.

JULIA.

Your reason?

LUCETTA.

I have no other but a woman's reason;
I think him so, because I think him so.

JULIA.

And wouldst thou have me cast my love on him?

LUCETTA.

Ay, if you thought your love not cast away.

JULIA.

Why, he, of all the rest, hath never moved me.

LUCETTA.

Yet he, of all the rest, I think, best loves ye.

JULIA.

His little speaking shows his love but small.

LUCETTA.

Fire that's closest kept burns most of all.

JULIA.

They do not love that do not show their love.

LUCETTA.

O, they love least that let men know their love.

JULIA.

would I knew his mind.

LUCETTA.

Peruse this paper, madam.

JULIA [*reads*].

To Julia.—Say, from whom?

LUCETTA.

That the contents will show.

JULIA.

Say, say, who gave it thee?

LUCETTA.

Sir Valentine's page; and sent, I think, from
Proteus.   [way,
He would have given it you; but I, being in the
Did in your name receive it: pardon the fault, I
pray.

JULIA.

Now, by my modesty, a goodly broker!
Dare you presume to harbour wanton lines?
To whisper and conspire against my youth?
Now, trust me, 'tis an office of great worth,
And you an officer fit for the place.
There, take the paper: see it be return'd;
Or else return no more into my sight.

LUCETTA.

To plead for love deserves more fee than hate.

JULIA.

Will ye be gone?

LUCETTA.

That you may ruminate.   [*Exit.*

JULIA.

And yet I would I had o'erlook'd the letter:
It were a shame to call her back again,
And pray her to a fault for which I chid her.
What fool is she, that knows I am a maid,
And would not force the letter to my view,—
Since maids, in modesty, say 'No' to that
Which they would have the profferer construe
'Ay'!
Fie, fie, how wayward is this foolish love,
That, like a testy babe, will scratch the nurse,
And presently, all humbled, kiss the rod!
How churlishly I chid Lucetta hence,
When willingly I would have had her here!
How angerly I taught my brow to frown,
When inward joy enforced my heart to smile!
My penance is, to call Lucetta back,
And ask remission for my folly past.—
What, ho! Lucetta!

Enter LUCETTA.

LUCETTA.

What would your ladyship?

JULIA.

Is 't near dinner-time?

LUCETTA.

I would it were,
That you might kill your stomach on your meat,
And not upon your maid.

JULIA.

What is 't that you took up so gingerly?

LUCETTA.

Nothing.

JULIA.

Why didst thou stoop, then?

LUCETTA.

To take a paper up that I let fall.

JULIA.

And is that paper nothing?

LUCETTA.

Nothing concerning me.

JULIA.

Then let it lie for those that it concerns.

LUCETTA.
Madam, it will not lie where it concerns,
Unless it have a false interpreter.
JULIA.
Some love of yours hath writ to you in rhyme.
LUCETTA.
That I might sing it, madam, to a tune.
Give me a note: your ladyship can set.
JULIA.
As little by such toys as may be possible.
Best sing it to the tune of *Light o' love*.
LUCETTA.
It is too heavy for so light a tune.
JULIA.
Heavy! belike it hath some burden, then?
LUCETTA.
Ay; and melodious were it, would you sing it.
JULIA.
And why not you?
LUCETTA.
            I cannot reach so high.
JULIA.
Let's see your song [*Taking the letter*]. How now,
    minion!
LUCETTA.
Keep tune there still, so you will sing it out:
And yet methinks I do not like this tune.
JULIA.
You do not?
LUCETTA.
            No, madam; 'tis too sharp.
JULIA.
You, minion, are too saucy.
LUCETTA.
            Nay, now you are too flat,
And mar the concord with too harsh a descant:
There wanteth but a mean to fill your song.
JULIA.
The mean is drown'd with your unruly base.
LUCETTA.
Indeed, I bid the base for Proteus.
JULIA.
This babble shall not henceforth trouble me:—
Here is a coil with protestation!—
                    [*Tears the letter.*
Go get you gone, and let the papers lie:
You would be fingering them, to anger me.
LUCETTA.
She makes it strange; but she would be best
    pleased
To be so anger'd with another letter.   [*Exit.*
JULIA.
Nay, would I were so anger'd with the same!
O hateful hands, to tear such loving words!
Injurious wasps, to feed on such sweet honey,
And kill the bees, that yield it, with your stings!
I'll kiss each several paper for amends.
Look, here is ·vrit—'kind Julia:'—unkind Julia!
As in revenge of thy ingratitude,
I throw thy name against the bruising stones,
Trampling contemptuously on thy disdain.
And here is writ—'love-wounded Proteus:'—
Poor wounded name! my bosom, as a bed,
Shall lodge thee, till thy wound be throughly
    heal'd;
And thus I search it with a sovereign kiss.

But twice or thrice was 'Proteus' written down:—
Be calm, good wind, blow not a word away,
Till I have found each letter in the letter,
Except mine own name: that some whirlwind
    bear
Unto a ragged, fearful-hanging rock,
And throw it thence into the raging sea!—
Lo, here in one line is his name twice writ,—
'Poor forlorn Proteus, passionate Proteus,
To the sweet Julia:'—that I'll tear away;—
And yet I will not, sith so prettily
He couples it to his complaining names.
Thus will I fold them one upon another:
Now kiss, embrace, contend, do what you will.
            Enter LUCETTA.
LUCETTA.
Madam,
Dinner is ready, and your father stays.
JULIA.
Well, let us go.
LUCETTA.
What, shall these papers lie like tell-tales here?
JULIA.
If you respect them, best to take them up.
LUCETTA.
Nay, I was taken up for laying them down:
Yet here they shall not lie, for catching cold.
JULIA.
I see you have a month's mind to them.
LUCETTA.
Ay, madam, you may say what sights you see;
I see things too, although you judge I wink.
JULIA.
Come, come; will't please you go?   [*Exeunt.*

SCENE III.

The same. ANTONIO'S *house.*

Enter ANTONIO *and* PANTHINO.

ANTONIO.
TELL me, Panthino, what sad talk was that
    Wherewith my brother held you in the
    cloister?
PANTHINO.
'Twas of his nephew Proteus, your son.
ANTONIO.
Why, what of him?
PANTHINO.
            He wonder'd that your lordship
Would suffer him to spend his youth at home,
While other men, of slender reputation,
Put forth their sons to seek preferment out:
Some to the wars, to try their fortune there;
Some to discover islands far away;
Some to the studious universities.
For any or for all these exercises,
He said that Proteus your son was meet;
And did request me to importune you
To let him spend his time no more at home,
Which would be great impeachment to his
    age,
In having known no travel in his youth.
ANTONIO.
Nor need'st thou much importune me to that
Whereon this month I have been hammering.
I have consider'd well his loss of time,

And how he cannot be a perfect man,
Not being tried and tutor'd in the world:
Experience is by industry achieved,
And perfected by the swift course of time.
Then, tell me, whither were I best to send him?

PANTHINO.

I think your lordship is not ignorant
How his companion, youthful Valentine,
Attends the emperor in his royal court.

ANTONIO.

I know it well.

PANTHINO.

'Twere good, I think, your lordship sent him
  thither:
There shall he practise tilts and tournaments,
Hear sweet discourse, converse with noblemen,
And be in eye of every exercise
Worthy his youth and nobleness of birth.

ANTONIO.

I like thy counsel; well hast thou advised:
And that thou mayst perceive how well I like it,
The execution of it shall make known.
Even with the speediest expedition
I will dispatch him to the emperor's court.

PANTHINO.

To-morrow, may it please you, Don Alphonso,
With other gentlemen of good esteem,
Are journeying to salute the emperor,
And to commend their service to his will.

ANTONIO.

Good company; with them shall Proteus go:
And,—in good time:—now will we break with
  him.

Enter PROTEUS.

PROTEUS.

Sweet love! sweet lines! sweet life!
Here is her hand, the agent of her heart;
Here is her oath for love, her honour's pawn.
O, that our fathers would applaud our loves,
To seal our happiness with their consents!
O heavenly Julia!

ANTONIO.

How now! what letter are you reading there?

PROTEUS.

May 't please your lordship, 'tis a word or two
Of commendations sent from Valentine,
Deliver'd by a friend that came from him.

ANTONIO.

Lend me the letter; let me see what news.

PROTEUS.

There is no news, my lord; but that he writes
How happily he lives, how well beloved,
And daily graced by the emperor;
Wishing me with him, partner of his fortune.

ANTONIO.

And how stand you affected to his wish?

PROTEUS.

As one relying on your lordship's will,
And not depending on his friendly wish.

ANTONIO.

My will is something sorted with his wish.
Muse not that I thus suddenly proceed;
For what I will, I will, and there an end.
I am resolved that thou shalt spend some time
With Valentinus in the emperor's court:
What maintenance he from his friends receives,

Like exhibition thou shalt have from me.
To-morrow be in readiness to go:
Excuse it not, for I am peremptory.

PROTEUS.

My lord, I cannot be so soon provided:
Please you, deliberate a day or two.

ANTONIO.

Look, what thou want'st shall be sent after thee:
No more of stay; to-morrow thou must go.—
Come on, Panthino: you shall be employ'd
To hasten on his expedition.

[Exeunt ANTONIO and PANTHINO.

PROTEUS.

Thus have I shunn'd the fire for fear of burning,
And drench'd me in the sea, where I am drown'd.
I fear'd to show my father Julia's letter,
Lest he should take exceptions to my love;
And with the vantage of mine own excuse
Hath he excepted most against my love.
O, how this spring of love resembleth
  The uncertain glory of an April day,
Which now shows all the beauty of the sun,
  And by and by a cloud takes all away!

Enter PANTHINO.

PANTHINO.

Sir Proteus, your father calls for you:
  He is in haste; therefore, I pray you, go.

PROTEUS.

Why, this it is,—my heart accords thereto,
  And yet a thousand times it answers, No.

[Exeunt.

ACT II. SCENE I.

Milan.   The DUKE'S palace.

Enter VALENTINE and SPEED.

SPEED.

Sir, your glove.

VALENTINE.

Not mine; my gloves are on.

SPEED.

Why, then, this may be yours, for this is but one.

VALENTINE.

Ha, let me see: ay, give it me, it's mine:—
Sweet ornament that decks a thing divine!
Ah, Silvia, Silvia!

SPEED.

Madam Silvia, Madam Silvia!

VALENTINE.

How now, sirrah!

SPEED.

She is not within hearing, sir.

VALENTINE.

Why, sir, who bade you call her?

SPEED.

Your worship, sir; or else I mistook.

VALENTINE.

Well, you'll still be too forward.

SPEED.

And yet I was last chidden for being too slow.

VALENTINE.

Go to, sir: tell me, do you know Madam Silvia?

SPEED.

She that your worship loves?

VALENTINE.

Why, how know you that I am in love?

SPEED.

Marry, by these special marks: first, you have
learn'd, like Sir Proteus, to wreathe your arms,
like a malecontent; to relish a love-song, like a
robin-redbreast; to walk alone, like one that had
the pestilence; to sigh, like a school-boy that had
lost his A B C; to weep, like a young wench that
had buried her grandam; to fast, like one that
takes diet; to watch, like one that fears robbing; to
speak puling, like a beggar at Hallowmas. You
were wont, when you laugh'd, to crow like a cock;
when you walk'd, to walk like one of the lions;
when you fasted, it was presently after dinner;
when you look'd sadly, it was for want of money:
and now you are metamorphosed with a mistress,
that, when I look on you, I can hardly think you
my master.

VALENTINE.

Are all these things perceived in me?

SPEED.

They are all perceived without ye.

VALENTINE.

Without me! they cannot.

SPEED.

Without you! nay, that's certain, for, without you
were so simple, none else would: but you are so
without these follies, that these follies are within
you, and shine through you like the water in an
urinal, that not an eye that sees you but is a
physician to comment on your malady.

VALENTINE.

But tell me, dost thou know my lady Silvia?

SPEED.

She that you gaze on so as she sits at supper?

VALENTINE.

Hast thou observed that? even she I mean.

SPEED.

Why, sir, I know her not.

VALENTINE.

Dost thou know her by my gazing on her, and yet
know'st her not?

SPEED.

Is she not hard-favour'd, sir?

VALENTINE.

Not so fair, boy, as well-favour'd.

SPEED.

Sir, I know that well enough.

VALENTINE.

What dost thou know?

SPEED.

That she is not so fair as, of you, well favour'd.

VALENTINE.

I mean, that her beauty is exquisite, but her
favour infinite.

SPEED.

That's because the one is painted, and the other
out of all count.

VALENTINE.

How painted? and how out of count?

SPEED.

Marry, sir, so painted, to make her fair, that no
man counts of her beauty.

VALENTINE.

How esteem'st thou me? I account of her beauty.

SPEED.

You never saw her since she was deform'd.

VALENTINE.

How long hath she been deform'd?

SPEED.

Ever since you loved her.

VALENTINE.

I have loved her ever since I saw her; and still I
see her beautiful.

SPEED.

If you love her, you cannot see her.

VALENTINE.

Why?

SPEED.

Because Love is blind. O, that you had mine eyes;
or your own eyes had the lights they were wont to
have when you chid at Sir Proteus for going ungarter'd!

VALENTINE.

What should I see then?

SPEED.

Your own present folly, and her passing deformity:
for he, being in love, could not see to garter his
hose; and you, being in love, cannot see to put on
your hose.

VALENTINE.

Belike, boy, then, you are in love; for last morning
you could not see to wipe my shoes.

SPEED.

True, sir; I was in love with my bed: I thank you,
you swinged me for my love, which makes me the
bolder to chide you for yours.

VALENTINE.

In conclusion, I stand affected to her.

SPEED.

I would you were set; so your affection would
cease.

VALENTINE.

Last night she enjoin'd me to write some lines to
one she loves.

SPEED.

And have you?

VALENTINE.

I have.

SPEED.

Are they not lamely writ?

VALENTINE.

No, boy, but as well as I can do them.—Peace!
here she comes.

SPEED [aside].

O excellent motion! O exceeding puppet!   Now
will he interpret to her.

Enter SILVIA.

VALENTINE.

Madam and mistress, a thousand good-morrows!

SPEED [aside].

O, give ye good even! here's a million of
manners.

SILVIA.

Sir Valentine and servant, to you two thousand.

SPEED [aside].

He should give her interest, and she gives it
him.

VALENTINE.

As you enjoin'd me, I have writ your letter
Unto the secret nameless friend of yours;
Which I was much unwilling to proceed in,
But for my duty to your ladyship.

SILVIA.

I thank you, gentle servant: 'tis very clerkly done.

VALENTINE.

Now trust me, madam, it came hardly off;
For, being ignorant to whom it goes,
I writ at random, very doubtfully.

SILVIA.

Perchance you think too much of so much pains?

VALENTINE.

No, madam; so it stead you, I will write,
Please you command, a thousand times as much:
And yet,—

SILVIA.

A pretty period! Well, I guess the sequel;
And yet I will not name it;—and yet I care not;—
And yet take this again;—and yet I thank you;
Meaning henceforth to trouble you no more.

SPEED [aside].

And yet you will; and yet another 'yet.'

VALENTINE.

What means your ladyship? do you not like it?

SILVIA.

Yes, yes; the lines are very quaintly writ:
But since unwillingly, take them again;
Nay, take them.

VALENTINE.

Madam, they are for you.

SILVIA.

Ay, ay, you writ them, sir, at my request;
But I will none of them; they are for you:
I would have had them writ more movingly.

VALENTINE.

Please you, I'll write your ladyship another.

SILVIA.

And when it's writ, for my sake read it over:
And if it please you, so; if not, why, so.

VALENTINE.

If it please me, madam! what then?

SILVIA.

Why, if it please you, take it for your labour:
And so, good morrow, servant.   [Exit.

SPEED.

O jest unseen, inscrutable, invisible,
As a nose on a man's face, or a weathercock on a
    steeple!
My master sues to her; and she hath taught her
    suitor,
He being her pupil, to become her tutor.
O excellent device! was there ever heard a better,
That my master, being scribe, to himself should
    write the letter?

VALENTINE.

How now, sir! what are you reasoning with yourself?

SPEED.

Nay, I was rhyming: 'tis you that have the reason.

VALENTINE.

To do what?

SPEED.

To be a spokesman from Madam Silvia.

VALENTINE.

To whom?

SPEED.

To yourself: why, she woos you by a figure.

VALENTINE.

What figure?

SPEED.

By a letter, I should say.

VALENTINE.

Why, she hath not writ to me?

SPEED.

What need she, when she hath made you write to
yourself? Why, do you not perceive the jest?

VALENTINE.

No, believe me.

SPEED.

No believing you, indeed, sir. But did you perceive her earnest?

VALENTINE.

She gave me none, except an angry word.

SPEED.

Why, she hath given you a letter.

VALENTINE.

That's the letter I writ to her friend.

SPEED.

And that letter hath she deliver'd, and there an
    end.

VALENTINE.

I would it were no worse.

SPEED.

I'll warrant you, 'tis as well:
For often have you writ to her; and she, in
    modesty,
Or else for want of idle time, could not again
    reply;
Or fearing else some messenger that might her
    mind discover,
Herself hath taught her love himself to write unto
    her lover.
All this I speak in print, for in print I found it.
Why muse you, sir? 'tis dinner-time.

VALENTINE.

I have dined.

SPEED.

Ay, but hearken, sir; though the chameleon Love
can feed on the air, I am one that am nourish'd by
my victuals, and would fain have meat. O, be not
like your mistress; be moved, be moved. [Exeunt.

SCENE II.

Verona. JULIA's *garden.*

Enter PROTEUS *and* JULIA.

PROTEUS.

HAVE patience, gentle Julia.

JULIA.

I must, where is no remedy.

PROTEUS.

When possibly I can, I will return.

JULIA.

If you turn not, you will return the sooner.
Keep this remembrance for thy Julia's sake.
                [Gives him a ring.

PROTEUS.

Why, then, we'll make exchange; here, take you
    this.   [Gives her another.

JULIA.

And seal the bargain with a holy kiss.

PROTEUS.

Here is my hand for my true constancy;
And when that hour o'erslips me in the day

Wherein I sigh not, Julia, for thy sake,
The next ensuing hour some foul mischance
Torment me for my love's forgetfulness!
My father stays my coming; answer not;
The tide is now:—nay, not thy tide of tears;
That tide will stay me longer than I should:
Julia, farewell!   [*Exit* JULIA.
    What, gone without a word?
Ay, so true love should do: it cannot speak;
For truth hath better deeds than words to grace
  it.

    Enter PANTHINO.

PANTHINO.

Sir Proteus, you are stay'd for.

        PROTEUS.

Go; I come, I come:—
Alas, this parting strikes poor lovers dumb!
              [*Exeunt.*

SCENE III.

The same. A street.

Enter LAUNCE, *leading his dog.*

LAUNCE.

NAY, 'twill be this hour ere I have done weeping; all the kind of the Launces have this very fault. I have received my proportion, like the prodigious son, and am going with Sir Proteus to the imperial's court. I think Crab my dog be the sourest-natured dog that lives: my mother weeping, my father wailing, my sister crying, our maid howling, our cat wringing her hands, and all our house in a great perplexity, yet did not this cruel-hearted cur shed one tear: he is a stone, a very pebble-stone, and has no more pity in him than a dog: a Jew would have wept to have seen our parting; why, my grandam, having no eyes, look you, wept herself blind at my parting. Nay, I'll show you the manner of it. This shoe is my father;—no, this left shoe is my father;—no, no, this left shoe is my mother;—nay, that cannot be so neither;—yes, it is so, it is so,—it hath the worser sole. This shoe, with the hole in it, is my mother, and this my father; a vengeance on't! there 'tis: now, sir, this staff is my sister; for, look you, she is as white as a lily, and as small as a wand: this hat is Nan, our maid: I am the dog;—no, the dog is himself, and I am the dog,—O, the dog is me, and I am myself; ay, so, so. Now come I to my father; 'Father, your blessing!' now should not the shoe speak a word for weeping: now should I kiss my father; well, he weeps on. Now come I to my mother;—O, that she could speak now like a wood woman!—well, I kiss her; —why, there 'tis; here's my mother's breath up and down. Now come I to my sister: mark the moan she makes. Now the dog all this while sheds not a tear, nor speaks a word: but see how I lay the dust with my tears.

    Enter PANTHINO.

PANTHINO.

Launce, away, away, aboard! thy master is shipp'd, and thou art to post after with oars. What's the matter? why weep'st thou, man? Away, ass! you'll lose the tide, if you tarry any longer.

LAUNCE.

It is no matter if the tied were lost; for it is the unkindest tied that ever any man tied.

PANTHINO.

What's the unkindest tide?

LAUNCE.

Why, he that's tied here,—Crab, my dog.

PANTHINO.

Tut, man, I mean thou'lt lose the flood: and, in losing the flood, lose thy voyage; and, in losing thy voyage, lose thy master; and, in losing thy master, lose thy service; and, in losing thy service,—Why dost thou stop my mouth?

LAUNCE.

For fear thou shouldst lose thy tongue.

PANTHINO.

Where should I lose my tongue?

LAUNCE.

In thy tale.

PANTHINO.

In thy tail!

LAUNCE.

Lose the tide, and the voyage, and the master, and the service, and the tied! Why, man, if the river were dry, I am able to fill it with my tears; if the wind were down, I could drive the boat with my sighs.

PANTHINO.

Come, come away, man; I was sent to call thee.

LAUNCE.

Sir, call me what thou darest.

PANTHINO.

Wilt thou go?

LAUNCE.

Well, I will go.   [*Exeunt.*

SCENE IV.

Milan. The DUKE'S *palace.*

Enter SILVIA, VALENTINE, THURIO, *and* SPEED.

SILVIA.

Servant,—

        VALENTINE.

Mistress?

        SPEED.

Master, Sir Thurio frowns on you.

        VALENTINE.

Ay, boy, it's for love.

        SPEED.

Not of you.

        VALENTINE.

Of my mistress, then.

        SPEED.

'Twere good you knock'd him.

        SILVIA.

Servant, you are sad.

        VALENTINE.

Indeed, madam, I seem so.

        THURIO.

Seem you that you are not?

        VALENTINE.

Haply I do.

        THURIO.

So do counterfeits.

        VALENTINE.

So do you.

THURIO.
What seem I that I am not?
VALENTINE.
Wise.
THURIO.
What instance of the contrary?
VALENTINE.
Your folly.
THURIO.
And how quote you my folly?
VALENTINE.
I quote it in your jerkin.
THURIO.
My jerkin is a doublet.
VALENTINE.
Well, then, I'll double your folly.
THURIO.
How!
SILVIA.
What, angry, Sir Thurio! do you change colour?
VALENTINE.
Give him leave, madam; he is a kind of chameleon.
THURIO.
That hath more mind to feed on your blood than live in your air.
VALENTINE.
You have said, sir.
THURIO.
Ay, sir, and done too, for this time.
VALENTINE.
I know it well, sir; you always end ere you begin.
SILVIA.
A fine volley of words, gentlemen, and quickly shot off.
VALENTINE.
'Tis indeed, madam; we thank the giver.
SILVIA.
Who is that, servant?
VALENTINE.
Yourself, sweet lady; for you gave the fire. Sir Thurio borrows his wit from your ladyship's looks, and spends what he borrows kindly in your company.
THURIO.
Sir, if you spend word for word with me, I shall make your wit bankrupt.
VALENTINE.
I know it well, sir; you have an exchequer of words, and, I think, no other treasure to give your followers,—for it appears, by their bare liveries, that they live by your bare words.
SILVIA.
No more, gentlemen, no more:—here comes my father.

Enter DUKE.

DUKE OF MILAN.
Now, daughter Silvia, you are hard beset.—
Sir Valentine, your father's in good health:
What say you to a letter from your friends
Of much good news?
VALENTINE.
        My lord, I will be thankful
To any happy messenger from thence.
DUKE OF MILAN.
Know ye Don Antonio, your countryman?

VALENTINE.
Ay, my good lord, I know the gentleman
To be of worth and worthy estimation,
And not without desert so well reputed.
DUKE OF MILAN.
Hath he not a son?
VALENTINE.
Ay, my good lord; a son that well deserves
The honour and regard of such a father.
DUKE OF MILAN.
You know him well?
VALENTINE.
I know him as myself; for from our infancy
We have conversed and spent our hours together:
And though myself have been an idle truant,
Omitting the sweet benefit of time
To clothe mine age with angel-like perfection,
Yet hath Sir Proteus, for that's his name,
Made use and fair advantage of his days;
His years but young, but his experience old;
His head unmellow'd, but his judgment ripe;
And, in a word,—for far behind his worth
Comes all the praises that I now bestow,—
He is complete in feature and in mind,
With all good grace to grace a gentleman.
DUKE OF MILAN.
Beshrew me, sir, but if he make this good,
He is as worthy for an empress' love
As meet to be an emperor's counsellor.
Well, sir; this gentleman is come to me,
With commendation from great potentates;
And here he means to spend his time awhile:
I think 'tis no unwelcome news to you.
VALENTINE.
Should I have wish'd a thing, it had been he.
DUKE OF MILAN.
Welcome him, then, according to his worth;
Silvia, I speak to you; and you, Sir Thurio:—
For Valentine, I need not cite him to it:
I will send him hither to you presently.   [*Exit.*
VALENTINE.
This is the gentleman I told your ladyship
Had come along with me, but that his mistress
Did hold his eyes lockt in her crystal looks.
SILVIA.
Belike that now she hath enfranchised them,
Upon some other pawn for fealty.
VALENTINE.
Nay, sure, I think she holds them prisoners still.
SILVIA.
Nay, then, he should be blind; and, being blind,
How could he see his way to seek out you?
VALENTINE.
Why, lady, Love hath twenty pair of eyes.
THURIO.
They say that Love hath not an eye at all.
VALENTINE.
To see such lovers, Thurio, as yourself:
Upon a homely object Love can wink.
SILVIA.
Have done, have done; here comes the gentleman.

Enter PROTEUS.

VALENTINE.
Welcome, dear Proteus!—Mistress, I beseech you,
Confirm his welcome with some special favour.

SILVIA.
His worth is warrant for his welcome hither,
If this be he you oft have wish'd to hear from.
VALENTINE.
Mistress, it is: sweet lady, entertain him
To be my fellow-servant to your ladyship.
SILVIA.
Too low a mistress for so high a servant.
PROTEUS.
Not so, sweet lady; but too mean a servant
To have a look of such a worthy mistress.
VALENTINE.
Leave off discourse of disability:—
Sweet lady, entertain him for your servant.
PROTEUS.
My duty will I boast of, nothing else.
SILVIA.
And duty never yet did want his meed:
Servant, you are welcome to a worthless mistress.
PROTEUS.
I'll die on him that says so, but yourself.
SILVIA.
That you are welcome?
PROTEUS.
That you are worthless.
Enter a SERVANT.
SERVANT.
Madam, my lord your father would speak with
you.
SILVIA.
I wait upon his pleasure.   [*Exit* SERVANT.
Come, Sir Thurio,
Go with me.—Once more, new servant, welcome:
I'll leave you to confer of home affairs;
When you have done, we look to hear from you.
PROTEUS.
We'll both attend upon your ladyship.
[*Exeunt* SILVIA *and* THURIO.
VALENTINE.
Now, tell me, how do all from whence you
came?
PROTEUS.
Your friends are well, and have them much com-
mended.
VALENTINE.
And how do yours?
PROTEUS.
I left them all in health.
VALENTINE.
How does your lady? and how thrives your love?
PROTEUS.
My tales of love were wont to weary you;
I know you joy not in a love-discourse.
VALENTINE.
Ay, Proteus, but that life is alter'd now.
I have done penance for contemning Love,
Whose high imperious thoughts have punish'd
me
With bitter fasts, with penitential groans,
With nightly tears, and daily heart-sore sighs;
For, in revenge of my contempt of love,
Love hath chased sleep from my enthralled
eyes,
And made them watchers of mine own heart's
sorrow.
O gentle Proteus, Love's a mighty lord,

And hath so humbled me, as, I confess,
There is no woe to his correction,
Nor to his service no such joy on earth!
Now, no discourse, except it be of love;
Now can I break my fast, dine, sup, and sleep,
Upon the very naked name of love.
PROTEUS.
Enough; I read your fortune in your eye.
Was this the idol that you worship so?
VALENTINE.
Even she; and is not she a heavenly saint?
PROTEUS.
No; but she is an earthly paragon.
VALENTINE.
Call her divine.
PROTEUS.
I will not flatter her.
VALENTINE.
O, flatter me; for love delights in praises.
PROTEUS.
When I was sick, you gave me bitter pills;
And I must minister the like to you.
VALENTINE.
Then speak the truth by her: if not divine,
Yet let her be a principality,
Sovereign to all the creatures on the earth.
PROTEUS.
Except my mistress.
VALENTINE.
Sweet, except not any;
Except thou wilt except against my love.
PROTEUS.
Have I not reason to prefer mine own?
VALENTINE.
And I will help thee to prefer her too:
She shall be dignified with this high honour,—
To bear my lady's train, lest the base earth
Should from her vesture chance to steal a kiss,
And, of so great a favour growing proud,
Disdain to root the summer-swelling flower,
And make rough winter everlastingly.
PROTEUS.
Why, Valentine, what braggardism is this?
VALENTINE.
Pardon me, Proteus: all I can is nothing
To her, whose worth makes other worthies noth-
ing;
She is alone.
PROTEUS.
Then let her alone.
VALENTINE.
Not for the world: why, man, she is mine own;
And I as rich in having such a jewel
As twenty seas, if all their sand were pearl,
The water nectar, and the rocks pure gold.
Forgive me, that I do not dream on thee,
Because thou see'st me dote upon my love.
My foolish rival, that her father likes
Only for his possessions are so huge,
Is gone with her along; and I must after,
For love, thou know'st, is full of jealousy.
PROTEUS.
But she loves you?
VALENTINE.
Ay, and we are betroth'd: nay, more, our mar-
riage-hour,

With all the cunning manner of our flight,
Determined of; how I must climb her window,
The ladder made of cords; and all the means
Plotted and 'greed on for my happiness.
Good Proteus, go with me to my chamber,
In these affairs to aid me with thy counsel.

PROTEUS.
Go on before; I shall inquire you forth:
I must unto the road, to disembark
Some necessaries that I needs must use;
And then I'll presently attend you.

VALENTINE.
Will you make haste?

PROTEUS.
I will.   [*Exeunt* VALENTINE *and* SPEED.
Even as one heat another heat expels,
Or as one nail by strength drives out another,
So the remembrance of my former love
Is by a newer object quite forgotten.
Is it mine eye, or Valentinus' praise,
Her true perfection, or my false transgression,
That makes me, reasonless, to reason thus?
She's fair; and so is Julia, that I love,—
That I did love, for now my love is thaw'd;
Which, like a waxen image 'gainst a fire,
Bears no impression of the thing it was.
Methinks my zeal to Valentine is cold,
And that I love him not as I was wont:
O, but I love his lady too-too much;
And that's the reason I love him so little.
How shall I dote on her with more advice,
That thus without advice begin to love her!
'Tis but her picture I have yet beheld,
And that hath dazzled my reason's light;
But when I look on her perfections,
There is no reason but I shall be blind.
If I can check my erring love, I will;
If not, to compass her I'll use my skill.   [*Exit.*

SCENE V.

The same.   A street.

Enter SPEED *and* LAUNCE *severally.*

SPEED.
LAUNCE! by mine honesty, welcome to Padua!

LAUNCE.
Forswear not thyself, sweet youth; for I am not
welcome. I reckon this always—that a man is
never undone till he be hang'd; nor never welcome to a place till some certain shot be paid, and
the hostess say, 'Welcome.'

SPEED.
Come on, you madcap, I'll to the alehouse with
you presently; where, for one shot of five pence,
you shalt have five thousand welcomes. But,
sirrah, how did thy master part with Madam
Julia?

LAUNCE.
Marry, after they closed in earnest, they parted
very fairly in jest.

SPEED.
But shall she marry him?

LAUNCE.
No.

SPEED.
How, then? shall he marry her?

LAUNCE.
No, neither.

SPEED.
What, are they broken?

LAUNCE.
No, they are both as whole as a fish.

SPEED.
Why, then, how stands the matter with them?

LAUNCE.
Marry, thus; when it stands well with him, it
stands well with her.

SPEED.
What an ass art thou! I understand thee not.

LAUNCE.
What a block art thou, that thou canst not! My
staff understands me.

SPEED.
What thou say'st?

LAUNCE.
Ay, and what I do too: look thee, I'll but lean, and
my staff understands me.

SPEED.
It stands under thee, indeed.

LAUNCE.
Why, stand-under and under-stand is all one.

SPEED.
But tell me true, will't be a match?

LAUNCE.
Ask my dog: if he say ay, it will; if he say no,
it will; if he shake his tail and say nothing, it
will.

SPEED.
The conclusion is, then, that it will.

LAUNCE.
Thou shalt never get such a secret from me but
by a parable.

SPEED.
'Tis well that I get it so. But, Launce, how
say'st thou, that my master is become a notable
lover?

LAUNCE.
I never knew him otherwise.

SPEED.
Than how?

LAUNCE.
A notable lubber, as thou reportest him to be.

SPEED.
Why, thou whoreson ass, thou mistakest me.

LAUNCE.
Why, fool, I meant not thee; I meant thy master.

SPEED.
I tell thee, my master is become a hot lover.

LAUNCE.
Why, I tell thee, I care not though he burn himself in love. If thou wilt, go with me to the alehouse; if not, thou art an Hebrew, a Jew, and not
worth the name of a Christian.

SPEED.
Why?

LAUNCE.
Because thou hast not so much charity in thee
as to go to the ale with a Christian. Wilt thou
go?

SPEED.
At thy service.   [*Exeunt.*

SCENE VI.

The same.   *The* DUKE'S *palace.*

Enter PROTEUS.

PROTEUS.

To leave my Julia, shall I be forsworn;
  To love fair Silvia, shall I be forsworn;
To wrong my friend, I shall be much forsworn;
And even that power, which gave me first my
    oath,
Provokes me to this threefold perjury:
Love bade me swear, and Love bids me forswear:
O sweet-suggesting Love, if thou hast sinn'd,
Teach me, thy tempted subject, to excuse it!
At first I did adore a twinkling star,
But now I worship a celestial sun:
Unheedful vows may heedfully be broken;
And he wants wit that wants resolved will
To learn his wit t'exchange the bad for better.
Fie, fie, unreverend tongue! to call her bad,
Whose sovereignty so oft thou hast preferr'd
With twenty thousand soul-confirming oaths.
I cannot leave to love, and yet I do;
But there I leave to love where I should love.
Julia I lose, and Valentine I lose:
If I keep them, I needs must lose myself;
If I lose them, thus find I by their loss,—
For Valentine, myself; for Julia, Silvia.
I to myself am dearer than a friend,
For love is still most precious in itself;
And Silvia—witness Heaven, that made her
    fair!—
Shows Julia but a swarthy Ethiop.
I will forget that Julia is alive,
Rememb'ring that my love to her is dead;
And Valentine I'll hold an enemy,
Aiming at Silvia as a sweeter friend.
I cannot now prove constant to myself,
Without some treachery used to Valentine.
This night he meaneth with a corded ladder
To climb celestial Silvia's chamber-window;
Myself in counsel his competitor:
Now presently I'll give her father notice
Of their disguising and pretended flight;
Who, all enraged, will banish Valentine,
For Thurio, he intends, shall wed his daughter:
But, Valentine being gone, I'll quickly cross,
By some sly trick, blunt Thurio's dull proceeding.
Love, lend me wings to make my purpose swift,
As thou hast lent me wit to plot this drift!   [*Exit.*

SCENE VII.

Verona.   JULIA'S *house.*

Enter JULIA *and* LUCETTA.

JULIA.

Counsel, Lucetta; gentle girl, assist me;
  And, even in kind love, I do conjure thee,—
Who art the table wherein all my thoughts
Are visibly character'd and engraved,—
To lesson me; and tell me some good mean,
How, with my honour, I may undertake
A journey to my loving Proteus.

LUCETTA.

Alas, the way is wearisome and long!

JULIA.

A true-devoted pilgrim is not weary
To measure kingdoms with his feeble steps;
Much less shall she that hath Love's wings to fly,
And when the flight is made to one so dear,
Of such divine perfection, as Sir Proteus.

LUCETTA.

Better forbear till Proteus make return.

JULIA.

O, know'st thou not, his looks are my soul's
    food?
Pity the dearth that I have pined in,
By longing for that food so long a time,
Didst thou but know the inly touch of love,
Thou wouldst as soon go kindle fire with snow
As seek to quench the fire of love with words.

LUCETTA.

I do not seek to quench your love's hot fire,
But qualify the fire's extreme rage,
Lest it should burn above the bounds of reason.

JULIA.

The more thou damm'st it up, the more it burns:
The current that with gentle murmur glides,
Thou know'st, being stopp'd, impatiently doth
    rage;
But when his fair course is not hindered,
He makes sweet music with th'enamell'd stones,
Giving a gentle kiss to every sedge
He overtaketh in his pilgrimage;
And so by many winding nooks he strays,
With willing sport, to the wide ocean.
Then let me go, and hinder not my course:
I'll be as patient as a gentle stream,
And make a pastime of each weary step,
Till the last step have brought me to my love;
And there I'll rest, as, after much turmoil,
A blessed soul doth in Elysium.

LUCETTA.

But in what habit will you go along?

JULIA.

Not like a woman; for I would prevent
The loose encounters of lascivious men;
Gentle Lucetta, fit me with such weeds
As may beseem some well-reputed page.

LUCETTA.

Why, then, your ladyship must cut your hair.

JULIA.

No, girl; I'll knit it up in silken strings,
With twenty odd-conceited true-love knots:
To be fantastic may become a youth
Of greater time than I shall show to be.

LUCETTA.

What fashion, madam, shall I make your
    breeches?

JULIA.

That fits as well as—'Tell me, good my lord,
What compass will you wear your farthingale?'
Why, even what fashion thou best likest, Lucetta.

LUCETTA.

You must needs have them with a codpiece,
    madam.

JULIA.

Out, out, Lucetta! that will be ill-favour'd.

LUCETTA.

A round hose, madam, now's not worth a pin,
Unless you have a codpiece to stick pins on.

JULIA.

Lucetta, as thou lovest me, let me have
What thou think'st meet, and is most mannerly.
But tell me, wench, how will the world repute me
For undertaking so unstaid a journey?
I fear me, it will make me scandalized.

LUCETTA.

If you think so, then stay at home, and go not.

JULIA.

Nay, that I will not.

LUCETTA.

Then never dream on infamy, but go.
If Proteus like your journey when you come,
No matter who's displeased when you are gone:
I fear me, he will scarce be pleased withal.

JULIA.

That is the least, Lucetta, of my fear:
A thousand oaths, an ocean of his tears,
And instances of infinite of love,
Warrant me welcome to my Proteus.

LUCETTA.

All these are servants to deceitful men.

JULIA.

Base men, that use them to so base effect!
But truer stars did govern Proteus' birth:
His words are bonds, his oaths are oracles;
His love sincere, his thoughts immaculate;
His tears pure messengers sent from his heart;
His heart as far from fraud as heaven from earth.

LUCETTA.

Pray heaven he prove so, when you come to him!

JULIA.

Now, as thou lovest me, do him not that wrong,
To bear a hard opinion of his truth:
Only deserve my love by loving him;
And presently go with me to my chamber,
To take a note of what I stand in need of,
To furnish me upon my longing journey.
All that is mine I leave at thy dispose,
My goods, my lands, my reputation;
Only, in lieu thereof, dispatch me hence.
Come, answer not, but to it presently;
I am impatient of my tarriance.   [Exeunt.

ACT III. SCENE I.

Milan.   An ante-room in the DUKE'S *palace.*

Enter DUKE, THURIO, *and* PROTEUS.

DUKE OF MILAN.

SIR THURIO, give us leave, I pray, awhile;
We have some secrets to confer about.
                                [Exit THURIO.
Now, tell me, Proteus, what's your will with me?

PROTEUS.

My gracious lord, that which I would discover
The law of friendship bids me to conceal;
But when I call to mind your gracious favours
Done to me, undeserving as I am,
My duty pricks me on to utter that
Which else no worldly good should draw from me.
Know, worthy prince, Sir Valentine, my friend,
This night intends to steal away your daughter;
Myself am one made privy to the plot.
I know you have determined to bestow her
On Thurio, whom your gentle daughter hates;
And should she thus be stol'n away from you,

It would be much vexation to your age.
Thus, for my duty's sake, I rather chose
To cross my friend in his intended drift
Than, by concealing it, heap on your head
A pack of sorrows, which would press you down,
Being unprevented, to your timeless grave.

DUKE OF MILAN.

Proteus, I thank thee for thine honest care;
Which to requite, command me while I live.
This love of theirs myself have often seen,
Haply when they have judged me fast asleep;
And oftentimes have purposed to forbid
Sir Valentine her company and my court:
But, fearing lest my jealous aim might err,
And so, unworthily, disgrace the man,—
A rashness that I ever yet have shunn'd,—
I gave him gentle looks; thereby to find
That which thyself hast now disclosed to me.
And, that thou mayst perceive my fear of this,
Knowing that tender youth is soon suggested,
I nightly lodge her in an upper tower,
The key whereof myself have ever kept;
And thence she cannot be convey'd away.

PROTEUS.

Know, noble lord, they have devised a mean
How he her chamber-window will ascend,
And with a corded ladder fetch her down;
For which the youthful lover now is gone,
And this way comes he with it presently;
Where, if it please you, you may intercept him.
But, good my lord, do it so cunningly
That my discovery be not aimed at;
For love of you, not hate unto my friend,
Hath made me publisher of this pretence.

DUKE OF MILAN.

Upon mine honour, he shall never know
That I had any light from thee of this.

PROTEUS.

Adieu, my lord; Sir Valentine is coming.   [Exit.

Enter VALENTINE.

DUKE OF MILAN.

Sir Valentine, whither away so fast?

VALENTINE.

Please it your grace, there is a messenger
That stays to bear my letters to my friends,
And I am going to deliver them.

DUKE OF MILAN.

Be they of much import?

VALENTINE.

The tenour of them doth but signify
My health, and happy being at your court.

DUKE OF MILAN.

Nay, then, no matter; stay with me awhile;
I am to break with thee of some affairs
That touch me near, wherein thou must be secret.
'Tis not unknown to thee that I have sought
To match my friend Sir Thurio to my daughter.

VALENTINE.

I know it well, my lord; and, sure, the match
Were rich and honourable; besides, the gentleman
Is full of virtue, bounty, worth, and qualities
Beseeming such a wife as your fair daughter:
Cannot your grace win her to fancy him?

DUKE OF MILAN.

No, trust me; she is peevish, sullen, froward,
Proud, disobedient, stubborn, lacking duty;

Neither regarding that she is my child,
Nor fearing me as if I were her father:
And, may I say to thee, this pride of hers,
Upon advice, hath drawn my love from her;
And, where I thought the remnant of mine age
Should have been cherish'd by her child-like
    duty,
I now am full resolved to take a wife,
And turn her out to who will take her in:
Then let her beauty be her wedding-dower;
For me and my possessions she esteems not.

VALENTINE.
What would your grace have me to do in this?

DUKE OF MILAN.
There is a lady of Verona here
Whom I affect; but she is nice and coy,
And naught esteems my aged eloquence:
Now, therefore, would I have thee to my tutor,—
For long agone I have forgot to court;
Besides, the fashion of the time is changed,—
How, and which way, I may bestow myself,
To be regarded in her sun-bright eye.

VALENTINE.
Win her with gifts, if she respect not words:
Dumb jewels often, in their silent kind,
More than quick words, do move a woman's
    mind.

DUKE OF MILAN.
But she did scorn a present that I sent her.

VALENTINE.
A woman sometimes scorns what best contents
    her:
Send her another; never give her o'er;
For scorn at first makes after-love the more.
If she do frown, 'tis not in hate of you,
But rather to beget more love in you:
If she do chide, 'tis not to have you gone;
For why the fools are mad, if left alone.
Take no repulse, whatever she doth say;
For 'get you gone,' she doth not mean 'away!'
Flatter and praise, commend, extol their graces;
Though ne'er so black, say they have angels'
    faces.
That man that hath a tongue, I say, is no man,
If with his tongue he cannot win a woman.

DUKE OF MILAN.
But she I mean is promised by her friends
Unto a youthful gentleman of worth;
And kept severely from resort of men,
That no man hath access by day to her.

VALENTINE.
Why, then, I would resort to her by night.

DUKE OF MILAN.
Ay, but the doors be lockt, and keys kept safe,
That no man hath recourse to her by night.

VALENTINE.
What lets but one may enter at her window?

DUKE OF MILAN.
Her chamber is aloft, far from the ground,
And built so shelving, that one cannot climb it
Without apparent hazard of his life.

VALENTINE.
Why, then, a ladder, quaintly made of cords,
To cast up, with a pair of anchoring hooks,
Would serve to scale another Hero's tower,
So bold Leander would adventure it.

DUKE OF MILAN.
Now, as thou art a gentleman of blood,
Advise me where I may have such a ladder.

VALENTINE.
When would you use it? pray, sir, tell me that.

DUKE OF MILAN.
This very night; for Love is like a child,
That longs for every thing that he can come by.

VALENTINE.
By seven o'clock I'll get you such a ladder.

DUKE OF MILAN.
But, hark thee; I will go to her alone:
How shall I best convey the ladder thither?

VALENTINE.
It will be light, my lord, that you may bear it
Under a cloak that is of any length.

DUKE OF MILAN.
A cloak as long as thine will serve the turn?

VALENTINE.
Ay, my good lord.

DUKE OF MILAN.
                Then let me see thy cloak:
I'll get me one of such another length.

VALENTINE.
Why, any cloak will serve the turn, my lord.

DUKE OF MILAN.
How shall I fashion me to wear a cloak?—
I pray thee, let me feel thy cloak upon me.—
What letter is this same? What's here?—'To
Silvia'!
And here an engine fit for my proceeding!
I'll be so bold to break the seal for once.   [Reads.
    'My thoughts do harbour with my Silvia
        nightly;
        And slaves they are to me, that send them
            flying:
        O, could their master come and go as lightly,
            Himself would lodge where senseless they
            are lying!
    My herald thoughts in thy pure bosom rest
        them;
        While I, their king, that thither them im-
        portune,
    Do curse the grace that with such grace hath
        blest them,
        Because myself do want my servants' for-
        tune:
    I curse myself, for they are sent by me,
    That they should harbour where their lord
        would be.'
What's here?
    'Silvia, this night I will enfranchise thee.'
'Tis so; and here's the ladder for the purpose.
Why, Phaethon,—for thou art Merops' son,—
Wilt thou aspire to guide the heavenly car,
And with thy daring folly burn the world?
Wilt thou reach stars, because they shine on
    thee?
Go, base intruder! overweening slave!
Bestow thy fawning smiles on equal mates;
And think my patience, more than thy desert,
Is privilege for thy departure hence:
Thank me for this, more than for all the favours
Which, all too much, I have bestow'd on thee.
But if thou linger in my territories
Longer than swiftest expedition

Will give thee time to leave our royal court,
By heaven, my wrath shall far exceed the love
I ever bore my daughter or thyself.
Be gone! I will not hear thy vain excuse;
But, as thou lovest thy life, make speed from
    hence.   [*Exit* DUKE.
           VALENTINE.
And why not death, rather than living torment?
To die, is to be banish'd from myself;
And Silvia is myself: banish'd from her,
Is self from self,—a deadly banishment!
What light is light, if Silvia be not seen?
What joy is joy, if Silvia be not by?
Unless it be to think that she is by,
And feed upon the shadow of perfection.
Except I be by Silvia in the night,
There is no music in the nightingale;
Unless I look on Silvia in the day,
There is no day for me to look upon:
She is my essence; and I leave to be,
If I be not by her fair influence
Foster'd, illumined, cherish'd, kept alive.
I fly not death, to fly his deadly doom:
Tarry I here, I but attend on death;
But, fly I hence, I fly away from life.
    Enter PROTEUS *and* LAUNCE.
           PROTEUS.
Run, boy, run, run, and seek him out.
           LAUNCE.
So-ho, so-ho!
           PROTEUS.
What see'st thou?
           LAUNCE.
Him we go to find: there's not a hair on's head
but 'tis a Valentine.
           PROTEUS.
Valentine!
           VALENTINE.
No.
           PROTEUS.
Who then? his spirit?
           VALENTINE.
Neither.
           PROTEUS.
What then?
           VALENTINE.
Nothing.
           LAUNCE.
Can nothing speak? Master, shall I strike?
           PROTEUS.
Who wouldst thou strike?
           LAUNCE.
Nothing.
           PROTEUS.
Villain, forbear.
           LAUNCE.
Why, sir, I'll strike nothing: I pray you,—
           PROTEUS.
Sirrah, I say, forbear.—Friend Valentine, a
    word.
           VALENTINE.
My ears are stopt, and cannot hear good news,
So much of bad already hath possest them.
           PROTEUS.
Then in dumb silence will I bury mine,
For they are harsh, untuneable, and bad.

           VALENTINE.
Is Silvia dead?
           PROTEUS.
No, Valentine.
           VALENTINE.
No Valentine, indeed, for sacred Silvia!—
Hath she forsworn me?
           PROTEUS.
No, Valentine.
           VALENTINE.
No Valentine, if Silvia have forsworn me!—
What is your news?
           LAUNCE.
Sir, there is a proclamation that you are vanish'd.
           PROTEUS.
That thou art banished—O, that's the news!—
From hence, from Silvia, and from me thy friend.
           VALENTINE.
O, I have fed upon this woe already,
And now excess of it will make me surfeit.
Doth Silvia know that I am banished?
           PROTEUS.
Ay, ay; and she hath offer'd to the doom—
Which, unreversed, stands in effectual force—
A sea of melting pearl, which some call tears;
Those at her father's churlish feet she tender'd;
With them, upon her knees, her humble self;
Wringing her hands, whose whiteness so became
    them
As if but now they waxed pale for woe:
But neither bended knees, pure hands held up,
Sad sighs, deep groans, nor silver-shedding tears,
Could penetrate her uncompassionate sire;
But Valentine, if he be ta'en, must die.
Besides, her intercession chafed him so,
When she for thy repeal was suppliant,
That to close prison he commanded her,
With many bitter threats of biding there.
           VALENTINE.
No more; unless the next word that thou speak'st
Have some malignant power upon my life:
If so, I pray thee, breathe it in mine ear,
As ending anthem of my endless dolour.
           PROTEUS.
Cease to lament for that thou canst not help,
And study help for that which thou lament'st.
Time is the nurse and breeder of all good.
Here if thou stay, thou canst not see thy love;
Besides, thy staying will abridge thy life.
Hope is a lover's staff; walk hence with that,
And manage it against despairing thoughts.
Thy letters may be here, though thou art hence;
Which, being writ to me, shall be deliver'd
Even in the milk-white bosom of thy love.
The time now serves not to expostulate:
Come, I'll convey thee through the city-gate;
And, ere I part with thee, confer at large
Of all that may concern thy love-affairs.
As thou lovest Silvia, though not for thyself,
Regard thy danger, and along with me.
           VALENTINE.
I pray thee, Launce, an if thou see'st my boy,
Bid him make haste, and meet me at the north-
    gate.
           PROTEUS.
Go, sirrah, find him out.—Come, Valentine.

VALENTINE.

O my dear Silvia!—Hapless Valentine!

[*Exeunt* VALENTINE *and* PROTEUS.

LAUNCE.

I am but a fool, look you; and yet I have the wit to think my master is a kind of a knave; but that's all one, if he be but one knave. He lives not now 'h it knows me to be in love; yet I am in love; but a team of horse shall not pluck that from me; nor who 'tis I love; and yet 'tis a woman; but what woman, I will not tell myself; and yet 'tis a milk-maid; yet 'tis not a maid, for she hath had gossips; yet 'tis a maid, for she is her master's maid, and serves for wages. She hath more quali-ties than a water-spaniel,—which is much in a bare Christian. [*Pulling out a paper.*] Here is the cate-log of her conditions. [*Reads*] 'Imprimis, She can fetch and carry.' Why, a horse can do no more: nay, a horse cannot fetch, but only carry; therefore is she better than a jade. 'Item, She can milk;' look you, a sweet virtue in a maid with clean hands.

Enter SPEED.

SPEED.

How now, Signior Launce! what news with your mastership?

LAUNCE.

With my master's ship? why, it is at sea.

SPEED.

Well, your old vice still; mistake the word. What news, then, in your paper?

LAUNCE.

The black'st news that ever thou heard'st.

SPEED.

Why, man, how black?

LAUNCE.

Why, as black as ink.

SPEED.

Let me read them.

LAUNCE.

Fie on thee, jolt-head! thou canst not read.

SPEED.

Thou liest; I can.

LAUNCE.

I will try thee. Tell me this: who begot thee?

SPEED.

Marry, the son of my grandfather.

LAUNCE.

O illiterate loiterer! it was the son of thy grandmother: this proves that thou canst not read.

SPEED.

Come, fool, come; try me in thy paper.

LAUNCE.

There; and Saint Nicholas be thy speed!

SPEED [*reads*].

'Imprimis, She can milk.'

LAUNCE.

Ay, that she can.

SPEED.

'Item, She brews good ale.'

LAUNCE.

And thereof comes the proverb,—Blessing of your heart, you brew good ale.

SPEED.

'Item, She can sew.'

LAUNCE.

That's as much as to say, Can she so?

SPEED.

'Item, She can knit.'

LAUNCE.

What need a man care for a stock with a wench, when she can knit him a stock?

SPEED.

'Item, She can wash and scour.'

LAUNCE.

A special virtue; for then she need not be wash'd and scour'd.

SPEED.

'Item, She can spin.'

LAUNCE.

Then may I set the world on wheels, when she can spin for her living.

SPEED.

'Item, She hath many nameless virtues.'

LAUNCE.

That's as much as to say, bastard virtues; that, indeed, know not their fathers, and therefore have no names.

SPEED.

'Here follow her vices.'

LAUNCE.

Close at the heels of her virtues.

SPEED.

'Item, She is not to be kiss'd fasting, in respect of her breath.'

LAUNCE.

Well, that fault may be mended with a breakfast. Read on.

SPEED.

'Item, She hath a sweet mouth.'

LAUNCE.

That makes amends for her sour breath.

SPEED.

'Item, She doth talk in her sleep.'

LAUNCE.

It's no matter for that, so she sleep not in her talk.

SPEED.

'Item, She is slow in words.'

LAUNCE.

O villain, that set this down among her vices! To be slow in words is a woman's only virtue: I pray thee, out with't, and place it for her chief virtue.

SPEED.

'Item, She is proud.'

LAUNCE.

Out with that too; it was Eve's legacy, and cannot be ta'en from her.

SPEED.

'Item, She hath no teeth.'

LAUNCE.

I care not for that neither, because I love crusts.

SPEED.

'Item, she is curst.'

LAUNCE.

Well, the best is, she hath no teeth to bite.

SPEED.

'Item, She will often praise her liquor.'

LAUNCE.

If her liquor be good, she shall: if she will not, I will; for good things should be praised.

SPEED.

'Item, She is too liberal.'

LAUNCE.

Of her tongue she cannot, for that's writ down she is slow of; of her purse she shall not, for that I'll keep shut: now, of another thing she may, and that cannot I help. Well, proceed.

SPEED.

'Item, She hath more hair than wit, and more faults than hairs, and more wealth than faults.'

LAUNCE.

Stop there; I'll have her: she was mine, and not mine, twice or thrice in that last article. Rehearse that once more.

SPEED.

'Item, She hath more hair than wit,'—

LAUNCE.

More hair than wit,—it may be: I'll prove it. The cover of the salt hides the salt, and therefore it is more than the salt; the hair that covers the wit is more than the wit, for the greater hides the less. What's next?

SPEED.

'And more faults than hairs,'—

LAUNCE.

That's monstrous: O, that that were out!

SPEED.

'And more wealth than faults.'

LAUNCE.

Why, that word makes the faults gracious. Well, I'll have her: and if it be a match, as nothing is impossible,—

SPEED.

What then?

LAUNCE.

Why, then will I tell thee—that thy master stays for thee at the north-gate.

SPEED.

For me!

LAUNCE.

For thee! ay; who art thou? he hath stay'd for a better man than thee.

SPEED.

And must I go to him?

LAUNCE.

Thou must run to him, for thou hast stay'd so long, that going will scarce serve the turn.

SPEED.

Why didst not tell me sooner? pox of your love-letters!   [*Exit.*

LAUNCE.

Now will he be swinged for reading my letter,—an unmannerly slave, that will thrust himself into secrets! I'll after, to rejoice in the boy's correction.   [*Exit.*

SCENE II.

The same.   The DUKE'S *palace.*

Enter DUKE *and* THURIO.

DUKE OF MILAN.

SIR Thurio, fear not but that she will love you,
Now Valentine is banish'd from her sight.

THURIO.

Since his exile she hath despised me most,
Forsworn my company, and rail'd at me,
That I am desperate of obtaining her.

DUKE OF MILAN.

This weak impress of love is as a figure
Trenched in ice, which with an hour's heat
Dissolves to water, and doth lose his form.
A little time will melt her frozen thoughts,
And worthless Valentine shall be forgot.

Enter PROTEUS.

How now, Sir Proteus! Is your countryman,
According to our proclamation, gone?

PROTEUS.

Gone, my good lord.

DUKE OF MILAN.

My daughter takes his going grievously.

PROTEUS.

A little time, my lord, will kill that grief.

DUKE OF MILAN.

So I believe; but Thurio thinks not so.
Proteus, the good conceit I hold of thee—
For thou hast shown some sign of good desert—
Makes me the better to confer with thee.

PROTEUS.

Longer than I prove loyal to your grace
Let me not live to look upon your grace.

DUKE OF MILAN.

Thou know'st how willingly I would effect
The match between Sir Thurio and my daughter?

PROTEUS.

I do, my lord.

DUKE OF MILAN.

And also, I think, thou art not ignorant
How she opposes her against my will.

PROTEUS.

She did, my lord, when Valentine was here.

DUKE OF MILAN.

Ay, and perversely she persevers so.
What might we do to make the girl forget
The love of Valentine, and love Sir Thurio?

PROTEUS.

The best way is to slander Valentine
With falsehood, cowardice, and poor descent,—
Three things that women highly hold in hate.

DUKE OF MILAN.

Ay, but she'll think that it is spoke in hate.

PROTEUS.

Ay, if his enemy deliver it:
Therefore it must with circumstance be spoken
By one whom she esteemeth as his friend.

DUKE OF MILAN.

Then you must undertake to slander him.

PROTEUS.

And that, my lord, I shall be loth to do:
'Tis an ill office for a gentleman,
Especially against his very friend.

DUKE OF MILAN.

Where your good word cannot advantage him,
Your slander never can endamage him;
Therefore the office is indifferent,
Being entreated to it by your friend.

PROTEUS.

You have prevail'd, my lord: if I can do it
By aught that I can speak in his dispraise,
She shall not long continue love to him.
But say this weed her love from Valentine,
It follows not that she will love Sir Thurio.

THURIO.

Therefore, as you unwind her love from him,

Lest it should ravel and be good to none,
You must provide to bottom it on me;
Which must be done by praising me as much
As you in worth dispraise Sir Valentine.

DUKE OF MILAN.

And, Proteus, we dare trust you in this kind,
Because we know, on Valentine's report,
You are already Love's firm votary,
And cannot soon revolt and change your mind.
Upon this warrant shall you have access
Where you with Silvia may confer at large;
For she is lumpish, heavy, melancholy,
And, for your friend's sake, will be glad of you;
Where you may temper her, by your persuasion,
To hate young Valentine, and love my friend.

PROTEUS.

As much as I can do, I will effect:—
But you, Sir Thurio, are not sharp enough;
You must lay lime to tangle her desires
By wailful sonnets, whose composed rhymes
Should be full-fraught with serviceable vows.

DUKE OF MILAN.

Ay,
Much is the force of heaven-bred poesy.

PROTEUS.

Say, that upon the altar of her beauty
You sacrifice your tears, your sighs, your heart:
Write till your ink be dry, and with your tears
Moist it again, and frame some feeling line
That may discover such integrity:
For Orpheus' lute was strung with poets' sinews;
Whose golden touch could soften steel and stones,
Make tigers tame, and huge leviathans
Forsake unsounded deeps to dance on sands.
After your dire-lamenting elegies,
Visit by night your lady's chamber-window
With some sweet consort; to their instruments
Tune a deploring dump: the night's dead silence
Will well become such sweet-complaining
grievance.
This, or else nothing, will inherit her.

DUKE OF MILAN.

This discipline shows thou hast been in love.

THURIO.

And thy advice this night I'll put in practice.
Therefore, sweet Proteus, my direction-giver,
Let us into the city presently
To sort some gentlemen well skill'd in music;
I have a sonnet that will serve the turn
To give the onset to thy good advice.

DUKE OF MILAN.

About it, gentlemen.

PROTEUS.

We'll wait upon your grace till after supper,
And afterward determine our proceedings.

DUKE OF MILAN.

Even now about it; I will pardon you.   [Exeunt.

ACT IV.   SCENE I.

A forest.

Enter certain OUTLAWS.

FIRST OUTLAW.

FELLOWS, stand fast; I see a passenger.

SECOND OUTLAW.

If there be ten, shrink not, but down with 'em.

Enter VALENTINE *and* SPEED.

THIRD OUTLAW.

Stand, sir, and throw us that you have about ye:
If not, we'll make you sit, and rifle you.

SPEED.

Sir, we are undone! these are the villains
That all the travellers do fear so much.

VALENTINE.

My friends,—

FIRST OUTLAW.

That's not so, sir,—we are your enemies.

SECOND OUTLAW.

Peace! we'll hear him.

THIRD OUTLAW.

Ay, by my beard, will we; for he is a proper man.

VALENTINE.

Then know that I have little wealth to lose;
A man I am cross'd with adversity:
My riches are these poor habiliments,
Of which if you should here disfurnish me,
You take the sum and substance that I have.

SECOND OUTLAW.

Whither travel you?

VALENTINE.

To Verona.

FIRST OUTLAW.

Whence came you?

VALENTINE.

From Milan.

THIRD OUTLAW.

Have you long sojourn'd there?

VALENTINE.

Some sixteen months; and longer might have
stay'd,
If crooked fortune had not thwarted me.

FIRST OUTLAW.

What, were you banish'd thence?

VALENTINE.

I was.

SECOND OUTLAW.

For what offence?

VALENTINE.

For that which now torments me to rehearse:
I kill'd a man, whose death I much repent;
But yet I slew him manfully in fight,
Without false vantage or base treachery.

FIRST OUTLAW.

Why, ne'er repent it, if it were done so.
But were you banish'd for so small a fault?

VALENTINE.

I was, and held me glad of such a doom.

SECOND OUTLAW.

Have you the tongues?

VALENTINE.

My youthful travel therein made me happy,
Or else I often had been miserable.

THIRD OUTLAW.

By the bare scalp of Robin Hood's fat friar
This fellow were a king for our wild faction!

FIRST OUTLAW.

We'll have him:—sirs, a word.

SPEED.

Master, be one of them; it's an honourable kind
of thievery.

VALENTINE.

Peace, villain!

SECOND OUTLAW.

Tell us this: have you any thing to take to?

VALENTINE.

Nothing but my fortune.

THIRD OUTLAW.

Know, then, that some of us are gentlemen,
Such as the fury of ungovern'd youth
Thrust from the company of awful men:
Myself was from Verona banished
For practising to steal away a lady,
An heir, and near allied unto the duke.

SECOND OUTLAW.

And I from Mantua, for a gentleman,
Who, in my mood, I stabb'd unto the heart.

FIRST OUTLAW.

And I for such-like petty crimes as these.
But to the purpose,—for we cite our faults,
That they may hold excused our lawless lives;
And partly, seeing you are beautified
With goodly shape, and by your own report
A linguist, and a man of such perfection
As we do in our quality much want,—

SECOND OUTLAW.

Indeed, because you are a banish'd man,
Therefore, above the rest, we parley to you:
Are you content to be our general?
To make a virtue of necessity,
And live, as we do, in this wilderness?

THIRD OUTLAW.

What say'st thou? wilt thou be of our consort?
Say ay, and be the captain of us all:
We'll do thee homage and be ruled by thee,
Love thee as our commander and our king.

FIRST OUTLAW.

But if thou scorn our courtesy, thou diest.

SECOND OUTLAW.

Thou shalt not live to brag what we have offer'd.

VALENTINE.

I take your offer, and will live with you,
Provided that you do no outrages
On silly women or poor passengers.

THIRD OUTLAW.

No, we detest such vile base practices.
Come, go with us, we'll bring thee to our crews,
And show thee all the treasure we have got;
Which, with ourselves, all rest at thy dispose.

[Exeunt.

SCENE II.

Milan.   The court of the DUKE'S *palace.*

Enter PROTEUS.

PROTEUS.

ALREADY have I been false to Valentine,
And now I must be as unjust to Thurio.
Under the colour of commending him,
I have access my own love to prefer:
But Silvia is too fair, too true, too holy,
To be corrupted with my worthless gifts.
When I protest true loyalty to her,
She twits me with my falsehood to my friend;
When to her beauty I commend my vows,
She bids me think how I have been forsworn
In breaking faith with Julia whom I loved:
And notwithstanding all her sudden quips,
The least whereof would quell a lover's hope,

Yet, spaniel-like, the more she spurns my love,
The more it grows, and fawneth on her still.
But here comes Thurio: now must we to her
    window,
And give some evening music to her ear.

Enter THURIO *and* MUSICIANS.

THURIO.

How now, Sir Proteus! are you crept before us?

PROTEUS.

Ay, gentle Thurio; for you know that love
Will creep in service where it cannot go.

THURIO.

Ay, but I hope, sir, that you love not here.

PROTEUS.

Sir, but I do; or else I would be hence.

THURIO.

Who? Silvia?

PROTEUS.

Ay, Silvia,—for your sake.

THURIO.

I thank you for your own.—Now, gentlemen,
Let's tune, and to it lustily awhile.

Enter, at a distance, HOST, *and* JULIA *in boy's
    clothes.*

HOST.

Now, my young guest,—methinks you're allicholy: I pray you, why is it?

JULIA.

Marry, mine host, because I cannot be merry.

HOST.

Come, we'll have you merry: I'll bring you where
you shall hear music, and see the gentleman that
you ask'd for.

JULIA.

But shall I hear him speak?

HOST.

Ay, that you shall.

JULIA.

That will be music.

[*Music plays.*

HOST.

Hark, hark!

JULIA.

Is he among these?

HOST.

Ay: but, peace! let's hear 'em.

Song.

Who is Silvia? what is she,
    That all our swains commend her?
Holy, fair, and wise is she;
    The heaven such grace did lend her,
That she might admired be.

Is she kind as she is fair,—
    For beauty lives with kindness?
Love doth to her eyes repair,
    To help him of his blindness;
And, being help'd, inhabits there.

Then to Silvia let us sing,
    That Silvia is excelling;
She excels each mortal thing
    Upon the dull earth dwelling:
To her let us garlands bring.

HOST.
How now! are you sadder than you were before?
How do you, man? the music likes you not.
JULIA.
You mistake; the musician likes me not.
HOST.
Why, my pretty youth?
JULIA.
He plays false, father.
HOST.
How? out of tune on the strings?
JULIA.
Not so; but yet so false that he grieves my very
heart-strings.
HOST.
You have a quick ear.
JULIA.
Ay, I would I were deaf; it makes me have a slow
heart.
HOST.
I perceive you delight not in music.
JULIA.
Not a whit, when it jars so.
HOST.
Hark, what fine change is in the music!
JULIA.
Ay, that change is the spite.
HOST.
You would have them always play but one thing?
JULIA.
I would always have one play but one thing.
But, host, doth this Sir Proteus that we talk on
Often resort unto this gentlewoman?
HOST.
I tell you what Launce, his man, told me,—he
loved her out of all nick.
JULIA.
Where is Launce?
HOST.
Gone to seek his dog; which to-morrow, by his
master's command, he must carry for a present to
his lady.
JULIA.
Peace! stand aside: the company parts.
PROTEUS.
Sir Thurio, fear not you: I will so plead,
That you shall say my cunning drift excels.
THURIO.
Where meet we?
PROTEUS.
At Saint Gregory's well.
THURIO.
                                        Farewell.
[Exeunt THURIO and MUSICIANS.
SILVIA appears above, at her window.
PROTEUS.
Madam, good even to your ladyship.
SILVIA.
I thank you for your music, gentlemen.
Who is that that spake?
PROTEUS.
One, lady, if you knew his pure heart's truth,
You would quickly learn to know him by his
    voice.
SILVIA.
Sir Proteus, as I take it.

PROTEUS.
Sir Proteus, gentle lady, and your servant.
SILVIA.
What is your will?
PROTEUS.
That I may compass yours.
SILVIA.
You have your wish; my will is even this,—
That presently you hie you home to bed.
Thou subtle, perjured, false, disloyal man!
Think'st thou I am so shallow, so conceitless,
To be seduced by thy flattery,
That hast deceived so many with thy vows?
Return, return, and make thy love amends.
For me,—by this pale queen of night I swear,
I am so far from granting thy request,
That I despise thee for thy wrongful suit;
And by and by intend to chide myself
Even for this time I spend in talking to thee.
PROTEUS.
I grant, sweet love, that I did love a lady;
But she is dead.
JULIA [aside].
                        'Twere false, if I should speak it;
For I am sure she is not buried.
SILVIA.
Say that she be; yet Valentine thy friend
Survives; to whom, thyself art witness,
I am betroth'd: and art thou not ashamed
To wrong him with thy importunacy?
PROTEUS.
I likewise hear that Valentine is dead.
SILVIA.
And so suppose am I; for in his grave
Assure thyself my love is buried.
PROTEUS.
Sweet lady, let me rake it from the earth.
SILVIA.
Go to thy lady's grave, and call hers thence;
Or, at the least, in hers sepulchre thine.
JULIA [aside].
He heard not that.
PROTEUS.
Madam, if your heart be so obdurate,
Vouchsafe me yet your picture for my love,
The picture that is hanging in your chamber;
To that I'll speak, to that I'll sigh and weep:
For since the substance of your perfect self
Is else devoted, I am but a shadow;
And to your shadow will I make true love.
JULIA [aside].
If 'twere a substance, you would, sure, deceive
    it,
And make it but a shadow, as I am.
SILVIA.
I am very loth to be your idol, sir;
But since your falsehood shall become you well
To worship shadows and adore false shapes,
Send to me in the morning, and I'll send it:
And so good rest.
PROTEUS.
                        As wretches have o'ernight
That wait for execution in the morn.
[Exeunt PROTEUS, and SILVIA above.
JULIA.
Host, will you go?

HOST.
By my halidom, I was fast asleep.

JULIA.
Pray you, where lies Sir Proteus?

HOST.
Marry, at my house. Trust me, I think 'tis almost day.

JULIA.
Not so; but it hath been the longest night
That e'er I watch'd, and the most heaviest.
[*Exeunt.*

SCENE III.

The same.

Enter EGLAMOUR.

EGLAMOUR.
THIS is the hour that Madam Silvia
Entreated me to call and know her mind:
There's some great matter she'ld employ me in.—
Madam, madam!

SILVIA *above, at her window.*

SILVIA.
Who calls?

EGLAMOUR.
Your servant and your friend;
One that attends your ladyship's command.

SILVIA.
Sir Eglamour, a thousand times good morrow.

EGLAMOUR.
As many, worthy lady, to yourself.
According to your ladyship's impose,
I am thus early come to know what service
It is your pleasure to command me in.

SILVIA.
O Eglamour, thou art a gentleman,
(Think not I flatter, for I swear I do not)
Valiant, wise, remorseful, well accomplish'd:
Thou art not ignorant what dear good will
I bear unto the banish'd Valentine;
Nor how my father would enforce me marry
Vain Thurio, whom my very soul abhors.
Thyself hast loved; and I have heard thee say
No grief did ever come so near thy heart
As when thy lady and thy true love died,
Upon whose grave thou vow'dst pure chastity.
Sir Eglamour, I would to Valentine,
To Mantua, where I hear he makes abode;
And, for the ways are dangerous to pass,
do desire thy worthy company,
Upon whose faith and honour I repose.
Urge not my father's anger, Eglamour,
But think upon my grief.—a lady's grief,—
And on the justice of my flying hence,
To keep me from a most unholy match,
Which heaven and fortune still rewards with plagues.
do desire thee, even from a heart
as full of sorrows as the sea of sands,
To bear me company, and go with me:
If not, to hide what I have said to thee,
That I may venture to depart alone.

EGLAMOUR.
Madam, I pity much your grievances;
Which since I know they virtuously are placed,

I give consent to go along with you;
Recking as little what betideth me
As much I wish all good befortune you.
When will you go?

SILVIA.
This evening coming.

EGLAMOUR.
Where shall I meet you?

SILVIA.
At Friar Patrick's cell,
Where I intend holy confession.

EGLAMOUR.
I will not fail your ladyship. Good morrow,
Gentle lady.

SILVIA.
Good morrow, kind Sir Eglamour.
[*Exeunt* EGLAMOUR, *and* SILVIA *above.*

SCENE IV.

The same.

Enter LAUNCE, *with his Dog.*

LAUNCE.
WHEN a man's servant shall play the cur with
him, look you, it goes hard: one that I
brought up of a puppy; one that I saved from
drowning, when three or four of his blind brothers
and sisters went to it! I have taught him, even as one
would say precisely, 'Thus I would teach a dog.'
I was sent to deliver him as a present to Mistress
Silvia from my master; and I came no sooner into
the dining-chamber, but he steps me to her trencher, and steals her capon's leg: O, 'tis a foul thing
when a cur cannot keep himself in all companies!
I would have, as one should say, one that takes
upon him to be a dog indeed, to be, as it were, a
dog at all things. If I had not had more wit than
he, to take a fault upon me that he did, I think
verily he had been hang'd for't; sure as I live, he
had suffer'd for't; you shall judge He thrusts me
himself into the company of three or four gentlemanlike dogs, under the duke's table: he had not
been there (bless the mark!) a pissing while, but
all the chamber smelt him. 'Out with the dog,'
says one; 'What cur is that?' says another; 'Whip
him out,' says the third; 'Hang him up,' says the
duke. I, having been acquainted with the smell
before, knew it was Crab; and goes me to the fellow that whips the dogs: 'Friend,' quoth I, 'you
mean to whip the dog?' 'Ay, marry, do I,' quoth
he. 'You do him the more wrong,' quoth I;
' 'twas I did the thing you wot of.' He makes me
no more ado, but whips me out of the chamber.
How many masters would do this for his servant?
Nay, I'll be sworn, I have sat in the stocks for
puddings he hath stolen, otherwise he had been
executed; I have stood on the pillory for geese he
hath kill'd, otherwise he had suffer'd for't.—Thou
think'st not of this now! Nay, I remember the
trick you served me when I took my leave of
Madam Silvia; did not I bid thee still mark me,
and do as I do? when didst thou see me heave up
my leg, and make water against a gentlewoman's
farthingale? didst thou ever see me do such a
trick?

Enter PROTEUS, *and* JULIA *in boy's clothes.*

PROTEUS.
Sebastian is thy name? I like thee well,
And will employ thee in some service presently.

JULIA.
In what you please: I will do what I can.

PROTEUS.
I hope thou wilt.—How now, you whoreson peasant!
Where have you been these two days loitering?

LAUNCE.
Marry, sir, I carried Mistress Silvia the dog you
bade me.

PROTEUS.
And what says she to my little jewel?

LAUNCE.
Marry, she says your dog was a cur, and tells you
currish thanks is good enough for such a present.

PROTEUS.
But she received my dog?

LAUNCE.
No, indeed, did she not: here have I brought him
back again.

PROTEUS.
What, didst thou offer her this from me?

LAUNCE.
Ay, sir; the other squirrel was stolen from me by
the hangman boys in the market-place: and then
I offer'd her mine own,—who is a dog as big as
ten of yours, and therefore the gift the greater.

PROTEUS.
Go get thee hence, and find my dog again,
Or ne'er return again into my sight.
Away, I say! stay'st thou to vex me here?
A slave, that still an end turns me to shame!
　　　　　　　　　　　　　　　　　　[*Exit* LAUNCE.
Sebastian, I have entertained thee,
Partly that I have need of such a youth,
That can with some discretion do my business,
For 'tis no trusting to yond foolish lout;
But chiefly for thy face and thy behaviour,
Which—if my augury deceive me not—
Witness good bringing up, fortune, and truth:
Therefore know thou, for this I entertain thee.
Go presently, and take this ring with thee,
Deliver it to Madam Silvia:
She loved me well deliver'd it to me.

JULIA.
It seems you loved not her, to leave her token.
She is dead, belike?

PROTEUS.
　　　　Not so; I think she lives.

JULIA.
Alas!

PROTEUS.
Why dost thou cry, 'Alas'?

JULIA.
　　　　　　　　I cannot choose
But pity her.

PROTEUS.
　　　　Wherefore shouldst thou pity her?

JULIA.
Because methinks that she loved you as well
As you do love your lady Silvia:
She dreams on him that has forgot her love;
You dote on her that cares not for your love.
'Tis pity love should be so contrary;
And thinking on it makes me cry, 'Alas!'

PROTEUS.
Well: give her that ring, and therewithal
This letter:—that's her chamber:—tell my lady
I claim the promise for her heavenly picture.
Your message done, hie home unto my chamber,
Where thou shalt find me, sad and solitary. [*Exit.*

JULIA.
How many women would do such a message?
Alas, poor Proteus! thou hast entertain'd
A fox to be the shepherd of thy lambs:—
Alas, poor fool! why do I pity him,
That with his very heart despiseth me?
Because he loves her, he despiseth me;
Because I love him, I must pity him.
This ring I gave him when he parted from me,
To bind him to remember my good will:
And now am I—unhappy messenger—
To plead for that which I would not obtain;
To carry that which I would have refused;
To praise his faith which I would have dispraised.
I am my master's true-confirmed love;
But cannot be true servant to my master,
Unless I prove false traitor to myself.
Yet will I woo for him; but yet so coldly
As, heaven it knows, I would not have him speed.

Enter SILVIA, *attended.*
Gentlewoman, good day! I pray you, be my mean
To bring me where to speak with Madam Silvia.

SILVIA.
What would you with her, if that I be she?

JULIA.
If you be she, I do entreat your patience
To hear me speak the message I am sent on.

SILVIA.
From whom?

JULIA.
From my master, Sir Proteus, madam.

SILVIA.
O,—he sends you for a picture?

JULIA.
Ay, madam.

SILVIA.
Ursula, bring my picture there.—
Go give your master this: tell him, from me,
One Julia, that his changing thoughts forget,
Would better fit his chamber than this shadow.

JULIA.
Madam, please you peruse this letter:—
Pardon me, madam; I have unadvised
Deliver'd you a paper that I should not:
This is the letter to your ladyship.

SILVIA.
I pray thee, let me look on that again.

JULIA.
It may not be; good madam, pardon me.

SILVIA.
There, hold:—
I will not look upon your master's lines:
I know they are stuft with protestations,
And full of new-found oaths; which he will break
As easily as I do tear his paper.

JULIA.
Madam, he sends your ladyship this ring.

SILVIA.

The more shame for him that he sends it me;
For I have heard him say a thousand times
His Julia gave it him at his departure.
Though his false finger have profaned the ring.
Mine shall not do his Julia so much wrong.

JULIA.

She thanks you.

SILVIA.

What say'st thou?

JULIA.

I thank you, madam, that you tender her.
Poor gentlewoman! my master wrongs her much.

SILVIA.

Dost thou know her?

JULIA.

Almost as well as I do know myself:
To think upon her woes I do protest
That I have wept a hundred several times.

SILVIA.

Belike she thinks that Proteus hath forsook her.

JULIA.

I think she doth; and that's her cause of sorrow.

SILVIA.

Is she not passing fair?

JULIA.

She hath been fairer, madam, than she is:
When she did think my master loved her well,
She, in my judgment, was as fair as you;
But since she did neglect her looking-glass,
And threw her sun-expelling mask away,
The air hath starved the roses in her cheeks,
And pinch'd the lily-tincture of her face,
That now she is become as black as I.

SILVIA.

How tall was she?

JULIA.

About my stature: for, at Pentecost,
When all our pageants of delight were play'd,
Our youth got me to play the woman's part,
And I was trimm'd in Madam Julia's gown;
Which served me as fit, by all men's judgments,
As if the garment had been made for me:
Therefore I know she is about my height.
And at that time I made her weep a-good,
For I did play a lamentable part;
Madam, 'twas Ariadne, passioning
For Theseus' perjury and unjust flight;
Which I so lively acted with my tears,
That my poor mistress, moved therewithal,
Wept bitterly; and, would I might be dead,
If I in thought felt not her very sorrow!

SILVIA.

She is beholding to thee, gentle youth.
Alas, poor lady, desolate and left!
I weep myself to think upon thy words.
Here, youth, there is my purse: I give thee this
For thy sweet mistress' sake, because thou lovest
     her.
Farewell.

JULIA.

And she shall thank you for't, if e'er you know
     her.   [Exit SILVIA, attended.
A virtuous gentlewoman, mild and beautiful!
I hope my master's suit will be but cold,
Since she respects my mistress' love so much.

Alas, how love can trifle with itself!
Here is her picture: let me see; I think,
If I had such a tire, this face of mine
Were full as lovely as is this of hers:
And yet the painter flatter'd her a little,
Unless I flatter with myself too much.
Her hair is auburn, mine is perfect yellow:
If that be all the difference in his love,
I'll get me such a colour'd periwig.
Her eyes are grey as glass; and so are mine:
Ay, but her forehead's low, and mine's as high
What should it be that he respects in her,
But I can make respective in myself,
If this fond Love were not a blinded god?
Come, shadow, come, and take this shadow up,
For 'tis thy rival. O thou senseless form,
Thou shalt be worshipp'd, kiss'd, loved and
     adored!
And, were there sense in his idolatry,
My substance should be statue in thy stead.
I'll use thee kindly for thy mistress' sake,
That used me so; or else, by Jove I vow,
I should have scratch'd out your unseeing eyes,
To make my master out of love with thee! [Exit.

ACT V. SCENE I.

Milan. An abbey.

Enter EGLAMOUR.

EGLAMOUR.

THE sun begins to gild the western sky;
   And now it is about the very hour
That Silvia, at Friar Patrick's cell, should meet
   me.
She will not fail; for lovers break not hours,
Unless it be to come before their time;
So much they spur their expedition.
See where she comes.

Enter SILVIA.

          Lady, a happy evening!

SILVIA.

Amen, amen! Go on, good Eglamour,
Out at the postern by the abbey-wall:
I fear I am attended by some spies.

EGLAMOUR.

Fear not: the forest is not three leagues off;
If we recover that, we are sure enough. [Exeunt.

SCENE II.

The same. The DUKE'S palace.

*Enter THURIO, PROTEUS, and JULIA in boy's
clothes.*

THURIO.

SIR PROTEUS, what says Silvia to my suit?

PROTEUS.

O, sir, I find her milder than she was;
And yet she takes exceptions at your person.

THURIO.

What, that my leg is too long?

PROTEUS.

No; that it is too little.

THURIO.

I'll wear a boot, to make it somewhat rounder.

JULIA [aside].

But love will not be spurr'd to what it loathes.

THURIO.
What says she to my face?
PROTEUS.
She says it is a fair one.
THURIO.
Nay, then, the wanton lies; my face is black.
PROTEUS.
But pearls are fair; and the old saying is,
Black men are pearls in beauteous ladies' eyes.
JULIA [aside].
'Tis true, such pearls as put out ladies' eyes;
For I had rather wink than look on them.
THURIO.
How likes she my discourse?
PROTEUS.
Ill, when you talk of war.
THURIO.
But well, when I discourse of love and peace?
JULIA [aside].
But better, indeed, when you hold your peace.
THURIO.
What says she to my valour?
PROTEUS.
O, sir, she makes no doubt of that.
JULIA [aside].
She needs not, when she knows it cowardice.
THURIO.
What says she to my birth?
PROTEUS.
That you are well derived.
JULIA [aside].
True; from a gentleman to a fool.
THURIO.
Considers she my possessions?
PROTEUS.
O, ay; and pities them.
THURIO.
Wherefore?
JULIA [aside].
That such an ass should owe them.
PROTEUS.
That they are out by lease.
JULIA.
Here comes the duke.
    Enter DUKE OF MILAN.
DUKE OF MILAN.
How now, Sir Proteus! how now, Thurio!
Which of you saw Sir Eglamour of late?
THURIO.
Not I.
PROTEUS.
    Nor I.
DUKE OF MILAN.
Saw you my daughter?
PROTEUS.
                          Neither.
DUKE OF MILAN.
Why, then,
She's fled unto that peasant Valentine;
And Eglamour is in her company.
'Tis true; for Friar Laurence met them both,
As he in penance wander'd through the forest:
Him he knew well; and guess'd that it was she,
But, being mask'd, he was not sure of it:
Besides, she did intend confession
At Patrick's cell this even; and there she was not:

These likelihoods confirm her flight from hence.
Therefore, I pray you, stand not to discourse,
But mount you presently; and meet with me
Upon the rising of the mountain-foot
That leads toward Mantua, whither they are fled:
Dispatch, sweet gentlemen, and follow me.
                                    [Exit.

THURIO.
Why, this it is to be a peevish girl,
That flies her fortune when it follows her.
I'll after, more to be revenged on Eglamour
Than for the love of reckless Silvia.   [Exit.
PROTEUS.
And I will follow, more for Silvia's love
Than hate of Eglamour, that goes with her. [Exit.
JULIA.
And I will follow, more to cross that love
Than hate for Silvia, that is gone for love.   [Exit.

SCENE III.

The forest.

Enter OUTLAWS *with* SILVIA.
FIRST OUTLAW.
COME, come;
    Be patient; we must bring you to our captain.
SILVIA.
A thousand more mischances than this one
Have learn'd me how to brook this patiently.
SECOND OUTLAW.
Come, bring her away.
FIRST OUTLAW.
Where is the gentleman that was with her?
THIRD OUTLAW.
Being nimble-footed, he hath outrun us,
But Moyses and Valerius follow him.
Go thou with her to the west end of the wood;
There is our captain: we'll follow him that's
    fled;
The thicket is beset, he cannot scape.
FIRST OUTLAW.
Come, I must bring you to our captain's cave:
Fear not; he bears an honourable mind,
And will not use a woman lawlessly.
SILVIA.
O Valentine, this I endure for thee!   [Exeunt.

SCENE IV.

Another part of the forest.

Enter VALENTINE.
VALENTINE.
HOW use doth breed a habit in a man!
    This shadowy desert, unfrequented woods,
I better brook than flourishing peopled towns:
Here can I sit alone, unseen of any,
And to the nightingale's complaining notes
Tune my distresses and record my woes.
O thou that dost inhabit in my breast,
Leave not the mansion so long tenantless,
Lest, growing ruinous, the building fall,
And leave no memory of what it was!
Repair me with thy presence, Silvia!
Thou gentle nymph, cherish thy forlorn swain!
                            [Noise within.

What halloing and what stir is this to-day?
These are my mates, that make their wills their
     law,
Have some unhappy passenger in chase:
They love me well; yet I have much to do
To keep them from uncivil outrages.—
Withdraw thee, Valentine: who's this comes here?
                                        [Retires.

Enter PROTEUS, SILVIA, *and* JULIA *in boy's
     clothes.*
                    PROTEUS.
Madam, this service I have done for you,—
Though you respect not aught your servant
     doth,—
To hazard life, and rescue you from him
That would have forced your honour and your
     love:
Vouchsafe me, for my meed, but one fair look;
A smaller boon than this I cannot beg,
And less than this, I am sure, you cannot give.
               VALENTINE [*aside*].
How like a dream is this I see and hear!
Love, lend me patience to forbear awhile.
                    SILVIA.
O miserable, unhappy that I am!
                    PROTEUS.
Unhappy were you, madam, ere I came;
But by my coming I have made you happy.
                    SILVIA.
By thy approach thou makest me most unhappy.
                 JULIA [*aside*].
And me, when he approacheth to your presence.
                    SILVIA.
Had I been seized by a hungry lion,
I would have been a breakfast to the beast,
Rather than have false Proteus rescue me.
O, Heaven be judge how I love Valentine,
Whose life's as tender to me as my soul;
And full as much—for more there cannot be—
I do detest false perjured Proteus!
Therefore be gone, solicit me no more.
                    PROTEUS.
What dangerous action, stood it next to death,
Would I not undergo for one calm look.
O, 'tis the curse in love, and still approved,
When women cannot love where they're beloved!
                    SILVIA.
When Proteus cannot love where he's beloved.
Read over Julia's heart, thy first best love,
For whose dear sake thou didst then rend thy
     faith
Into a thousand oaths; and all those oaths
Descended into perjury, to love me.
Thou hast no faith left now, unless thou'dst
     two,
And that's far worse than none; better have none
Than plural faith, which is too much by one:
Thou counterfeit to thy true friend!
                    PROTEUS.
                              In love
Who respects friend?
                    SILVIA.
          All men but Proteus.
                    PROTEUS.
Nay, if the gentle spirit of moving words
Can no way change you to a milder form,

I'll woo you like a soldier, at arms' end,
And love you 'gainst the nature of love,—force ye.
                    SILVIA.
O heaven!
                    PROTEUS.
I'll force thee yield to my desire.
               VALENTINE [*coming forward*].
Ruffian, let go that rude uncivil touch,—
Thou friend of an ill fashion!
                    PROTEUS.
                         Valentine!
                    VALENTINE.
Thou common friend, that's without faith or love,
For such is a friend now; treacherous man!
Thou hast beguiled my hopes; naught but mine
     eye
Could have persuaded me: now I dare not say
I have one friend alive; thou wouldst disprove me.
Who should be trusted now, when one's right
     hand
Is perjured to the bosom? Proteus,
I am sorry I must never trust thee more,
But count the world a stranger for thy sake.
The private wound is deepest: O time most
     accurst!
'Mongst all foes that a friend should be the worst!
                    PROTEUS.
My shame and guilt confounds me.
Forgive me, Valentine: if hearty sorrow
Be a sufficient ransom for offence,
I tender't here; I do as truly suffer
As e'er I did commit.
                    VALENTINE.
               Then I am paid;
And once again I do receive thee honest.
Who by repentance is not satisfied
Is nor of heaven nor earth; for these are pleased;
By penitence th' Eternal wrath's appeased:
And, that my love may appear plain and free,
All that was mine in Silvia I give thee.
                    JULIA.
O me unhappy!   [*Faints.*
                    PROTEUS.
Look to the boy.
                    VALENTINE.
Why, boy! why, wag! how now! what's the
     matter?
Look up; speak.
                    JULIA.
          O good sir, my master charged me
To deliver a ring to Madam Silvia;
Which, out of my neglect, was never done.
                    PROTEUS.
Where is that ring, boy?
                    JULIA.
          Here 'tis; this is it. [*Gives a ring.*
                    PROTEUS.
How! let me see:—
Why, this is the ring I gave to Julia.
                    JULIA.
O, cry you mercy, sir, I have mistook:
This is the ring you sent to Silvia.
                              [*Shows another ring.*
                    PROTEUS.
But how camest thou by this ring? At my depart
I gave this unto Julia.

JULIA.
And Julia herself did give it me;
And Julia herself hath brought it hither.

PROTEUS.
How! Julia!

JULIA.
Behold her that gave aim to all thy oaths,
And entertain'd 'em deeply in her heart:
How oft hast thou with perjury cleft the root!
O Proteus, let this habit make thee blush!
Be thou ashamed that I have took upon me
Such an immodest raiment,—if shame live
In a disguise of love:
It is the lesser blot, modesty finds,
Women to change their shapes than men their
minds.

PROTEUS.
Than men their minds! 'tis true. O heaven, were
man
But constant, he were perfect! that one error
Fills him with faults; makes him run through all
th' sins:
Inconstancy falls off ere it begins.
What is in Silvia's face, but I may spy
More fresh in Julia's with a constant eye?

VALENTINE.
Come, come, a hand from either:
Let me be blest to make this happy close;
'Twere pity two such friends should be long foes.

PROTEUS.
Bear witness, Heaven, I have my wish for ever.

JULIA.
And I mine.

Enter OUTLAWS, *with* DUKE *and* THURIO.

OUTLAWS.
A prize, a prize, a prize!

VALENTINE.
Forbear, forbear, I say! it is my lord the duke.—
Your grace is welcome to a man disgraced,
Banished Valentine.

DUKE OF MILAN.
Sir Valentine!

THURIO.
Yonder is Silvia; and Silvia's mine.

VALENTINE.
Thurio, give back, or else embrace thy death;
Come not within the measure of my wrath:
Do not name Silvia thine; if once again,
Verona shall not hold thee. Here she stands:
Take but possession of her with a touch;—
I dare thee but to breathe upon my love.

THURIO.
Sir Valentine, I care not for her, I;

I hold him but a fool that will endanger
His body for a girl that loves him not:
I claim her not, and therefore she is thine.

DUKE OF MILAN.
The more degenerate and base art thou,
To make such means for her as thou hast done,
And leave her on such slight conditions.—
Now, by the honour of my ancestry,
I do applaud thy spirit, Valentine,
And think thee worthy of an empress' love:
Know, then, I here forget all former griefs,
Cancel all grudge, repeal thee home again,
Plead a new state in thy unrivall'd merit,
To which I thus subscribe,—Sir Valentine,
Thou art a gentleman, and well derived;
Take thou thy Silvia, for thou hast deserved
her.

VALENTINE.
I thank your grace; the gift hath made me happy.
I now beseech you, for your daughter's sake,
To grant one boon that I shall ask of you.

DUKE OF MILAN.
I grant it, for thine own, whate'er it be.

VALENTINE.
These banish'd men, that I have kept withal,
Are men endued with worthy qualities:
Forgive them what they have committed here,
And let them be recall'd from their exile:
They are reformed, civil, full of good,
And fit for great employment, worthy lord.

DUKE OF MILAN.
Thou hast prevail'd; I pardon them and thee:
Dispose of them as thou know'st their de-
serts.—
Come, let us go: we will include all jars
With triumphs, mirth, and rare solemnity.

VALENTINE.
And, as we walk along, I dare be bold
With our discourse to make your grace to smile.
What think you of this page, my lord?

DUKE OF MILAN.
I think the boy hath grace in him; he blushes.

VALENTINE.
I warrant you, my lord, more grace than boy.

DUKE OF MILAN.
What mean you by that saying?

VALENTINE.
Please you, I'll tell you as we pass along,
That you will wonder what hath fortuned.
Come, Proteus; 'tis your penance but to hear
The story of your loves discovered:
That done, our day of marriage shall be yours;
One feast, one house, one mutual happiness.

[*Exeunt.*

LOVE'S LABOUR'S LOST

DRAMATIS PERSONAE

FERDINAND, *King of Navarre.*
BEROWNE,
LONGAVILLE, }*lords attending on the King.*
DUMAINE,
BOYET, } *lords attending on the Princes of*
MERCADÉ, } *France.*
DON ADRIANO DE ARMADO, *a fantastical Spani-*
ard.
SIR NATHANIEL, *a curate.*
HOLOFERNES, *a schoolmaster.*
DULL, *a constable.*

COSTARD, *a clown.*
MOTH, *page to Armado.*
A FORESTER.

PRINCESS OF FRANCE.
ROSALINE,
MARIA, }*ladies attending on the Princess.*
KATHERINE,
JAQUENETTA, *a country wench.*
LORDS, ATTENDANTS, &c.

SCENE—*Navarre.*

ACT I. SCENE I.

Navarre. A park with a palace in it.
Enter the KING, BEROWNE, LONGAVILLE, *and*
DUMAINE.

KING.

LET fame, that all hunt after in their lives,
   Live register'd upon our brazen tombs,
And then grace us in the disgrace of death;
When, spite of cormorant devouring Time,
Th'endeavour of this present breath may buy
That honour which shall bate his scythe's keen
   edge,
And make us heirs of all eternity.
Therefore, brave conquerors,—for so you are,
That war against your own affections,
And the huge army of the world's desires,—
Our late edict shall strongly stand in force:
Navarre shall be the wonder of the world;
Our court shall be a little Academe,
Still and contemplative in living art.
You three, Berowne, Dumaine, and Longaville,
Have sworn for three years' term to live with me
My fellow-scholars, and to keep those statutes
That are recorded in this schedule here:
Your oaths are pass'd; and now subscribe your
   names,
That his own hand may strike his honour down
That violates the smallest branch herein:
If you are arm'd to do as sworn to do,
Subscribe to your deep oaths, and keep it too.
   LONGAVILLE.
I am resolv'd; 'tis but a three years' fast:
The mind shall banquet, though the body pine:
Fat paunches have lean pates; and dainty bits
Make rich the ribs, but bankrout quite the wits.
   DUMAINE.
My loving lord, Dumaine is mortify'd:
The grosser manner of these world's delights
He throws upon the gross world's baser slaves:
To love, to wealth, to pomp, I pine and die;
With all these living in philosophy.
   BEROWNE.
I can but say their protestation over;
So much, dear liege, I have already sworn,
That is, to live and study here three years.
But there are other strict observances:
As, not to see a woman in that term,—
Which I hope well is not enrolled there;

And one day in a week to touch no food,
And but one meal on every day beside,—
The which I hope is not enrolled there;
And then, to sleep but three hours in the night,
And not be seen to wink of all the day
(When I was wont to think no harm all night,
And make a dark night too of half the day),—
Which I hope well is not enrolled there:
O, these are barren tasks, too hard to keep,—
Not to see ladies, study, fast, not sleep!
   KING.
Your oath is pass'd to pass away from these.
   BEROWNE.
Let me say no, my liege, an if you please:
I only swore to study with your grace,
And stay here in your court for three years'
   space.
   LONGAVILLE.
You swore to that, Berowne, and to the rest.
   BEROWNE.
By yea and nay, sir, then I swore in jest.—
What is the end of study? let me know.
   KING.
Why, that to know, which else we should not
   know.
   BEROWNE.
Things hid and barr'd, you mean, from common
   sense?
   KING.
Ay, that is study's god-like recompense.
   BEROWNE.
Come on, then; I will swear to study so,
To know the thing I am forbid to know
As thus,—to study where I well may dine,
   When I to feast expressly am forbid;
Or study where to meet some mistress fine,
   When mistresses from common sense are hid;
Or, having sworn too hard-a-keeping oath
Study to break it, and not break my troth.
If study's gain be thus, and this be so,
Study knows that which yet it doth not know:
Swear me to this, and I will ne'er say no.
   KING.
These be the stops that hinder study quite,
And train our intellects to vain delight.
   BEROWNE.
Why, all delights are vain; but that most vain,
Which, with pain purchased, doth inherit
   pain:

213

As, painfully to pore upon a book
　To seek the light of truth; while truth the while
Doth falsely blind the eyesight of his look:
　Light, seeking light, doth light of light beguile:
So, ere you find where light in darkness lies,
Your light grows dark by losing of your eyes.
Study me how to please the eye indeed,
　By fixing it upon a fairer eye;
Who dazzling so, that eye shall be his heed,
　And give him light that it was blinded by.
Study is like the heaven's glorious sun,
　That will not be deep-search'd with saucy looks:
Small have continual plodders ever won,
　Save base authority from others' books.
These earthly godfathers of heaven's lights,
　That give a name to every fixed star,
Have no more profit of their shining nights
　Than those that walk and wot not what they
　　are.
Too much to know, is to know naught but fame;
And every godfather can give a name.

KING.
How well he's read, to reason against reading!

DUMAINE.
Proceeded well, to stop all good proceeding!

LONGAVILLE.
He weeds the corn, and still lets grow the weeding.

BEROWNE.
The spring is near, when green geese are a-breed-
　ing.

DUMAINE.
How follows that?

BEROWNE.
Fit in his place and time.

DUMAINE.
In reason nothing.

BEROWNE.
Something, then, in rime.

KING.
Berowne is like an envious-sneaping frost,
　That bites the first-born infants of the spring.

BEROWNE.
Well, say I am; why should proud summer boast,
　Before the birds have any cause to sing?
Why should I joy in an abortive birth?
At Christmas I no more desire a rose
Than wish a snow in May's new-fangled earth;
　But like of each thing that in season grows.
So you—to study now it is too late—
Climb o'er the house to unlock the little gate.

KING.
Well, sit you out: go home, Berowne: adieu.

BEROWNE.
No, my good lord; I have sworn to stay with
　you:
And though I have for barbarism spoke more
　Than for that angel knowledge you can say,
Yet confident I'll keep what I have swore,
　And bide the penance of each three years' day.
Give me the paper,—let me read the same;
And to the strict'st decrees I'll write my name.

KING.
How well this yielding rescues thee from shame!

BEROWNE [reads].
' Item, That no woman shall come within a mile
of my court,'—Hath this been proclaim'd?

LONGAVILLE.
Four days ago.

BEROWNE.
Let's see the penalty.—[reads] ' on pain of losing
her tongue.'—Who devised this penalty?

LONGAVILLE.
Marry, that did I.

BEROWNE.
Sweet lord, and why?

LONGAVILLE.
To fright them hence with that dread penalty.

BEROWNE.
A dangerous law against gentility!
　[Reads] ' Item, If any man be seen to talk with a
woman within the term of three years, he shall en-
dure such public shame as the rest of the court can
possibly devise.'
This article, my liege, yourself must break;
　For well you know here comes in embassy
The French king's daughter with yourself to
　speak,—
　A maid of grace and complete majesty,—
About surrender-up of Aquitaine
　To her decrepit, sick, and bed-rid father:
Therefore this article is made in vain,
　Or vainly comes th'admired princess hither.

KING.
What say you, lords? why, this was quite forgot.

BEROWNE.
So study evermore is overshot:
While it doth study to have what it would,
It doth forget to do the thing it should;
And when it hath the thing it hunteth most,
'Tis won as towns with fire,—so won, so lost.

KING.
We must of force dispense with this decree;
She must lie here on mere necessity.

BEROWNE.
Necessity will make us all forsworn
　Three thousand times within this three years'
　　space;
For every man with his affects is born,
　Not by might master'd, but by special grace:
If I break faith, this word shall speak for me,
I am forsworn on mere necessity.—
So to the laws at large I write my name:
　　　　　　　　　　　　　　　　[Subscribe
And he that breaks them in the least degree
Stands in attainder of eternal shame:
　Suggestions are to other as to me;
But I believe, although I seem so loth,
I am the last that will last keep his oath.
But is there no quick recreation granted?

KING.
Ay, that there is. Our court, you know, is haunte
　With a refined traveller of Spain;
A man in all the world's new fashion planted,
　That hath a mint of phrases in his brain;
One whom the music of his own vain tongue
　Doth ravish like enchanting harmony;
A man of complements, whom right and wrong
　Have chose as umpire of their mutiny:
This child of fancy, that Armado hight,
　For interim to our studies, shall relate,
In high-born words, the worth of many a
　knight

From tawny Spain, lost in the world's de-
bate.
How you delight, my lords, I know not, I;
But, I protest, I love to hear him lie,
And I will use him for my minstrelsy.
BEROWNE.
Armado is a most illustrious wight,
A man of fire-new words, fashion's own knight.
LONGAVILLE.
Costard the swain and he shall be our sport;
And, so to study, three years is but short.
Enter DULL *with a letter, and* COSTARD.
DULL.
Which is the duke's own person?
BEROWNE.
This, fellow: what wouldst?
DULL.
I myself reprehend his own person, for I am his
Grace's tharborough: but I would see his own per-
son in flesh and blood.
BEROWNE.
This is he.
DULL.
Signior Arme—Arme—commends you. There's
villainy abroad: this letter will tell you more.
COSTARD.
Sir, the contempts thereof are as touching me.
KING.
A letter from the magnificent Armado.
BEROWNE.
How low soever the matter, I hope in God for
high words.
LONGAVILLE.
A high hope for a low having: God grant us pa-
ience!
BEROWNE.
To hear? or forbear laughing?
LONGAVILLE.
To hear meekly, sir, and to laugh moderately; or to
forbear both.
BEROWNE.
Well, sir, be it as the style shall give us cause to
climb in the merriness.
COSTARD.
The matter is to me, sir, as concerning Jaque-
etta. The manner of it is, I was taken with the
manner.
BEROWNE.
In what manner?
COSTARD.
In manner and form following, sir; all those three:
I was seen with her in the manor-house, sitting
with her upon the form, and taken following her
into the park; which, put together, is in manner and
form following. Now, sir, for the manner,—it is
the manner of a man to speak to a woman: for the
form,—in some form.
BEROWNE.
For the following, sir?
COSTARD.
As it shall follow in my correction: and God de-
fend the right!
KING.
Will you hear this letter with attention?
BEROWNE.
As we would hear an oracle.

COSTARD.
Such is the simplicity of man to hearken after the
flesh.
KING [*reads*].
Great deputy, the welkin's vicegerent, and sole
dominator of Navarre, my soul's earth's god and
body's fostering patron,—
COSTARD.
Not a word of Costard yet.
KING [*reads*].
So it is,—
COSTARD.
It may be so: but if he says it is so, he is, in telling
true, but so—
KING.
Peace!
COSTARD.
Be to me, and every man that dares not fight!
KING.
No words!
COSTARD.
Of other men's secrets, I beseech you.
KING [*reads*].
So it is, besieged with sable-colour'd me-
lancholy, I did commend the black-oppressing
humour to the most wholesome physic of thy
health-giving air; and, as I am a gentleman, betook myself to walk. The time when? About the
sixth hour; when beasts most graze, birds best
peck, and men sit down to that nourishment which
is call'd supper; so much for the time when. Now
for the ground which; which, I mean, I walkt upon:
it is ycleped thy park. Then for the place where;
where, I mean, I did encounter that obscene and
most preposterous event, that draweth from my
snow-white pen the ebon-colour'd ink, which
here thou viewest, beholdest, surveyest, or seest:
but to the place where,—it standeth north-north-
east and by east from the west corner of thy
curious-knotted garden: there did I see that low-
spirited swain, that base minnow of thy mirth,—
COSTARD.
Me?
KING [*reads*].
that unletter'd small-knowing soul,—
COSTARD.
Me?
KING [*reads*].
that shallow vassal,—
COSTARD.
Still me?
KING [*reads*].
which, as I remember, hight Costard,—
COSTARD.
O, me!
KING [*reads*].
sorted and consorted, contrary to thy estab-
lish'd proclaim'd edict and continent canon,
with—with,—O, with—but with this I passion to
say wherewith,—
COSTARD.
With a wench.
KING [*reads*].
with a child of our grandmother Eve, a fe-
male; or, for thy more sweet understanding, a
woman. Him I—as my ever-esteem'd duty pricks

me on—have sent to thee, to receive the meed of punishment, by thy sweet Grace's officer, Antony Dull; a man of good repute, carriage, bearing, and estimation.

DULL.

Me, an't shall please you; I am Antony Dull.

KING [reads].

For Jaquenetta,—so is the weaker vessel call'd which I apprehended with the aforesaid swain, —I keep her as a vessel of thy law's fury; and shall, at the least of thy sweet notice, bring her to trial. Thine, in all complements of devoted and heart-burning heat of duty,

DON ADRIANO DE ARMADO.

BEROWNE.

This is not so well as I look't for, but the best that ever I heard.

KING.

Ay, the best for the worst.—But, sirrah, what say you to this?

COSTARD.

Sir, I confess the wench.

KING.

Did you hear the proclamation?

COSTARD.

I do confess much of the hearing it, but little of the marking of it.

KING.

It was proclaim'd a year's imprisonment, to be taken with a wench.

COSTARD.

I was taken with none, sir: I was taken with a damsel.

KING.

Well, it was proclaim'd damsel.

COSTARD.

This was no damsel neither, sir; she was a virgin.

KING.

It is so varied too; for it was proclaim'd virgin.

COSTARD.

If it were, I deny her virginity: I was taken with a maid.

KING.

This maid will not serve your turn, sir.

COSTARD.

This maid will serve my turn, sir.

KING.

Sir, I will pronounce your sentence: you shall fast a week with bran and water.

COSTARD.

I had rather pray a month with mutton and porridge.

KING.

And Don Armado shall be your keeper.— My Lord Berowne, see him deliver'd o'er:— And go we, lords, to put in practice that Which each to other hath so strongly sworn.

[Exeunt KING, LONGAVILLE, and DUMAINE.

BEROWNE.

I'll lay my head to any good man's hat, These oaths and laws will prove an idle scorn.— Sirrah, come on.

COSTARD.

I suffer for the truth, sir; for true it is, I was taken with Jaquenetta, and Jaquenetta is a true girl; and

therefore, Welcome the sour cup of prosperity! Affliction may one day smile again; and till then, Sit thee down, sorrow!　　　[Exeunt.

SCENE II.

The same.

Enter ARMADO *and* MOTH, *his Page.*

ARMADO.

BOY, what sign is it when a man of great spirit grows melancholy?

MOTH.

A great sign, sir, that he will look sad.

ARMADO.

Why, sadness is one and the selfsame thing, dear imp.

MOTH.

No, no; O Lord, sir, no.

ARMADO.

How canst thou part sadness and melancholy, my tender juvenal?

MOTH.

By a familiar demonstration of the working, my tough signior.

ARMADO.

Why tough signior? why tough signior?

MOTH.

Why tender juvenal? why tender juvenal?

ARMADO.

I spoke it, tender juvenal, as a congruent epitheton appertaining to thy young days, which we may nominate tender.

MOTH.

And I, tough signior, as an appertinent title to your old time, which we may name tough.

ARMADO.

Pretty and apt.

MOTH.

How mean you, sir? I pretty, and my saying apt? or I apt, and my saying pretty?

ARMADO.

Thou pretty, because little.

MOTH.

Little pretty, because little. Wherefore apt?

ARMADO.

And therefore apt, because quick.

MOTH.

Speak you this in my praise, master?

ARMADO.

In thy condign praise.

MOTH.

I will praise an eel with the same praise.

ARMADO.

What, that an eel is ingenious?

MOTH.

That an eel is quick.

ARMADO.

I do say thou art quick in answers: thou heat'st my blood.

MOTH.

I am answered, sir.

ARMADO.

I love not to be crost.

MOTH [aside].

He speaks the mere contrary,—crosses love not him.

ARMADO.

I have promised to study three years with the duke.

MOTH.

You may do it in an hour, sir.

ARMADO.

Impossible.

MOTH.

How many is one thrice told?

ARMADO.

I am ill at reck'ning,—it fitteth the spirit of a tapster.

MOTH.

You are a gentleman and a gamester, sir.

ARMADO.

I confess both: they are both the varnish of a complete man.

MOTH.

Then, I am sure, you know how much the gross sum of deuce-ace amounts to.

ARMADO.

It doth amount to one more than two.

MOTH.

Which the base vulgar do call three.

ARMADO.

True.

MOTH.

Why, sir, is this such a piece of study? Now here's three studied, ere you'll thrice wink: and how easy it is to put years to the word three, and study three years in two words, the dancing horse will tell you.

ARMADO.

A most fine figure!

MOTH [aside].

To prove you a cipher.

ARMADO.

I will hereupon confess I am in love: and as it is base for a soldier to love, so am I in love with a base wench. If drawing my sword against the humour of affection would deliver me from the reprobate thought of it, I would take Desire prisoner, and ransom him to any French courtier for a new-devised courtesy. I think scorn to sigh: methinks I should outswear Cupid. Comfort me, boy: what great men have been in love?

MOTH.

Hercules, master.

ARMADO.

Most sweet Hercules!—More authority, dear boy, name more; and, sweet my child, let them be men of good repute and carriage.

MOTH.

Samson, master: he was a man of good carriage, great carriage,—for he carried the town-gates on his back like a porter: and he was in love.

ARMADO.

O well-knit Samson! strong-jointed Samson! I do excel thee in my rapier as much as thou didst me in carrying gates. I am in love too:—who was Samson's love, my dear Moth?

MOTH.

A woman, master.

ARMADO.

Of what complexion?

MOTH.

Of all the four, or the three, or the two; or one of the four.

ARMADO.

Tell me precisely of what complexion.

MOTH.

Of the sea-water green, sir.

ARMADO.

Is that one of the four complexions?

MOTH.

As I have read, sir; and the best of them too.

ARMADO.

Green, indeed, is the colour of lovers; but to have a love of that colour, methinks Samson had small reason for it. He surely affected her for her wit.

MOTH.

It was so, sir; for she had a green wit.

ARMADO.

My love is most immaculate white and red.

MOTH.

Most maculate thoughts, master, are maskt under such colours.

ARMADO.

Define, define, well-educated infant.

MOTH.

My father's wit and my mother's tongue assist me!

ARMADO.

Sweet invocation of a child; most pretty and pathetical!

MOTH.

If she be made of white and red,
    Her faults will ne'er be known;
For blushing cheeks by faults are bred,
    And fears by pale white shown:
Then if she fear, or be to blame,
    By this you shall not know;
For still her cheeks possess the same,
    Which native she doth owe.

A dangerous rime, master, against the reason of white and red.

ARMADO.

Is there not a ballad, boy, of the King and the Beggar?

MOTH.

The world was very guilty of such a ballad some three ages since: but, I think, now 'tis not to be found; or, if it were, it would neither serve for the writing nor the tune.

ARMADO.

I will have that subject newly writ o'er, that I may example my digression by some mighty precedent. Boy, I do love that country girl that I took in the park with the rational hind Costard: she deserves well.

MOTH [aside].

To be whipt; and yet a better love than my master

ARMADO.

Sing, boy; my spirit grows heavy in love.

MOTH.

And that's great marvel, loving a light wench.

ARMADO.

I say, sing.

MOTH.

Forbear till this company be past.

Enter DULL, COSTARD, and JAQUENETTA.

DULL.

Sir, the duke's pleasure is, that you keep Costard safe: and you must let him take no delight nor no penance; but a' must fast three days a week. For this damsel, I must keep her at the park: she is allowed for the day-woman. Fare you well.

ARMADO.

I do betray myself with blushing.—Maid,—

JAQUENETTA.

Man.

ARMADO.

I will visit thee at the lodge.

JAQUENETTA.

That's hereby.

ARMADO.

I know where it is situate.

JAQUENETTA.

Lord, how wise you are!

ARMADO.

I will tell thee wonders.

JAQUENETTA.

With that face?

ARMADO.

I love thee.

JAQUENETTA.

So I heard you say.

ARMADO.

And so, farewell.

JAQUENETTA.

Fair weather after you!

DULL.

Come, Jaquenetta, away!

[*Exeunt* DULL *and* JAQUENETTA.

ARMADO.

Villain, thou shalt fast for thy offences ere thou be pardoned.

COSTARD.

Well, sir, I hope, when I do it, I shall do it on a full stomach.

ARMADO.

Thou shalt be heavily punished.

COSTARD.

I am more bound to you than your fellows, for they are but lightly rewarded.

ARMADO.

Take away this villain; shut him up.

MOTH.

Come, you transgressing slave; away!

COSTARD.

Let me not be pent up, sir: I will fast, being loose.

MOTH.

No, sir; that were fast and loose: thou shalt to prison.

COSTARD.

Well, if ever I do see the merry days of desolation that I have seen, some shall see—

MOTH.

What shall some see?

COSTARD.

Nay, nothing, Master Moth, but what they look upon. It is not for prisoners to be too silent in their words; and therefore I will say nothing: I thank God I have as little patience as another man; and therefore I can be quiet.

[*Exeunt* MOTH *and* COSTARD.

ARMADO.

I do affect the very ground, which is base, where her shoe, which is baser, guided by her foot, which is basest, doth tread. I shall be forsworn,—which

is a great argument of falsehood,—if I love. And how can that be true love which is falsely attempted? Love is a familiar; Love is a devil: there is no evil angel but love. Yet was Samson so tempted,—and he had an excellent strength; yet was Solomon so seduced,—and he had a very good wit. Cupid's buttshaft is too hard for Hercules' club; and therefore too much odds for a Spaniard's rapier. The first and second cause will not serve my turn; the passado he respects not, the duello he regards not: his disgrace is to be called boy; but his glory is to subdue men. Adieu, valour! rust, rapier! be still, drum! for your manager is in love; yea, he loveth. Assist me some extemporal god of rime, for I am sure I shall turn sonnet. Devise, wit,—write, pen; for I am for whole volumes in folio.

ACT II. SCENE I.

The same.

Enter the PRINCESS OF FRANCE, ROSALINE, MARIA, KATHARINE, BOYET, LORDS, *and other* ATTENDANTS.

BOYET.

NOW, madam, summon up your dearest spirits:
Consider who the king your father sends;
To whom he sends; and what's his embassy:
Yourself, held precious in the world's esteem,
To parley with the sole inheritor
Of all perfections that a man may owe,
Matchless Navarre; the plea of no less weight
Than Aquitaine,—a dowry for a queen.
Be now as prodigal of all dear grace,
As Nature was in making graces dear,
When she did starve the general world beside,
And prodigally gave them all to you.

PRINCESS.

Good Lord Boyet, my beauty, though but mean,
Needs not the painted flourish of your praise:
Beauty is bought by judgement of the eye,
Not utter'd by base sale of chapmen's tongues:
I am less proud to hear you tell my worth
Than you much willing to be counted wise
In spending your wit in the praise of mine.
But now to task the tasker:—good Boyet,
You are not ignorant, all-telling fame
Doth noise abroad, Navarre hath made a vow,
Till painful study shall outwear three years,
No woman may approach his silent court:
Therefore to's seemeth it a needful course,
Before we enter his forbidden gates,
To know his pleasure; and in that behalf,
Bold of your worthiness, we single you
As our best-moving fair solicitor.
Tell him, the daughter of the King of France,
On serious business, craving quick dispatch,
Importunes personal conference with his Grace:
Haste, signify so much; while we attend,
Like humble-visaged suitors, his high will.

BOYET.

Proud of employment, willingly I go.

PRINCESS.

All pride is willing pride, and yours is so.

[*Exit* BOYET

Who are the votaries, my loving lords,
That are vow-fellows with this virtuous duke?

FIRST LORD.

Lord Longaville is one.

PRINCESS.

         Know you the man?

MARIA.

I know him, madam: at a marriage-feast,
Between Lord Perigort and the beauteous heir
Of Jaques Falconbridge, solemnized
In Normandy, saw I this Longaville:
A man of sovereign parts he is esteem'd;
Well-fitted in arts, glorious in arms:
Nothing becomes him ill that he would well.
The only soil of his fair virtue's gloss—
If virtue's gloss will stain with any soil—
Is a sharp wit match'd with too blunt a will;
Whose edge hath power to cut, whose will still
     wills
It should none spare that come within his power.

PRINCESS.

Some merry mocking lord, belike; is't so?

MARIA.

They say so most that most his humours know.

PRINCESS.

Such short-lived wits do wither as they grow.
Who are the rest?

KATHARINE.

The young Dumaine, a well-accomplisht youth,
Of all that virtue love for virtue loved:
Most power to do most harm, least knowing ill;
For he hath wit to make an ill shape good,
And shape to win grace, though he had no wit.
I saw him at the Duke Alençon's once;
And much too little of that good I saw
Is my report to his great worthiness.

ROSALINE.

Another of these students at that time
Was there with him: if I have heard a truth,
Berowne they call him; but a merrier man,
Within the limit of becoming mirth,
I never spent an hour's talk withal:
His eye begets occasion for his wit;
For every object that the one doth catch,
The other turns to a mirth-moving jest,
Which his fair tongue—conceit's expositor—
Delivers in such apt and gracious words,
That aged ears play truant at his tales,
And younger hearings are quite ravished;
So sweet and voluble is his discourse.

PRINCESS.

God bless my ladies! are they all in love,
That every one her own hath garnished
With such bedecking ornaments of praise?

FIRST LORD.

Here comes Boyet.

Enter BOYET.

PRINCESS.

         Now, what admittance, lord?

BOYET.

Navarre had notice of your fair approach;
And he and his competitors in oath
Were all addrest to meet you, gentle lady,
Before I came. Marry, thus much I have learnt,—
He rather means to lodge you in the field,
Like one that comes here to besiege his court,

Than seek a dispensation for his oath,
To let you enter his unpeopled house.
Here comes Navarre.   [*The Ladies mask.*

Enter KING, LONGAVILLE, DUMAINE,
      BEROWNE, *and* ATTENDANTS.

KING.

Fair princess, welcome to the court of Navarre.

PRINCESS.

'Fair' I give you back again; and 'welcome' I have
not yet: the roof of this court is too high to be
yours; and welcome to the wide fields too base to
be mine.

KING.

You shall be welcome, madam, to my court.

PRINCESS.

I will be welcome, then: conduct me thither.

KING.

Hear me, dear lady,—I have sworn an oath.

PRINCESS.

Our Lady help my lord! he'll be forsworn.

KING.

Not for the world, fair madam, by my will.

PRINCESS.

Why, will shall break it; will, and nothing else.

KING.

Your ladyship is ignorant what it is.

PRINCESS.

Were my lord so, his ignorance were wise,
Where now his knowledge must prove ignorance.
I hear your grace hath sworn-out house-keeping:
'Tis deadly sin to keep that oath, my lord,
And sin to break it.
But pardon me, I am too sudden-bold:
To teach a teacher ill beseemeth me.
Vouchsafe to read the purpose of my coming,
And suddenly resolve me in my suit.

           [*Gives a paper.*

KING.

Madam, I will, if suddenly I may.

PRINCESS.

You will the sooner, that I were away;
For you'll prove perjured, if you make me stay.

BEROWNE.

Did not I dance with you in Brabant once?

ROSALINE.

Did not I dance with you in Brabant once?

BEROWNE.

I know you did.

ROSALINE.

How needless was it, then, to ask the question!

BEROWNE.

You must not be so quick.

ROSALINE.

'Tis 'long of you that spur me with such questions.

BEROWNE.

Your wit's too hot, it speeds too fast, 'twill tire.

ROSALINE.

Not till it leave the rider in the mire.

BEROWNE.

What time o' day?

ROSALINE.

The hour that fools should ask.

BEROWNE.

Now fair befall your mask!

ROSALINE.

Fair fall the face it covers!

BEROWNE.
And send you many lovers!

ROSALINE.
Amen, so you be none.

BEROWNE.
Nay, then will I be gone.

KING.
Madam, your father here doth intimate
The payment of a hundred thousand crowns;
Being but th' one-half of an entire sum
Disbursed by my father in his wars.
But say that he or we—as neither have—
Received that sum, yet there remains unpaid
A hundred thousand more; in surety of the which,
One part of Aquitaine is bound to us,
Although not valued to the money's worth.
If, then, the king your father will restore
But that one-half which is unsatisfied,
We will give up our right in Aquitaine,
And hold fair friendship with his Majesty.
But that, it seems, he little purposeth,
For here he doth demand to have repaid
A hundred thousand crowns; and not demands,
On payment of a hundred thousand crowns,
To have his title live in Aquitaine,
Which we much rather had depart withal,
And have the money by our father lent,
Than Aquitaine so gelded as it is.
Dear princess, were not his requests so far
From reason's yielding, your fair self should make
A yielding, 'gainst some reason, in my breast,
And go well satisfied to France again.

PRINCESS.
You do the king my father too much wrong,
And wrong the reputation of your name,
In so unseeming to confess receipt
Of that which hath so faithfully been paid.

KING.
I do protest I never heard of it;
And if you prove it, I'll repay it back,
Or yield up Aquitaine.

PRINCESS.
          We arrest your word.—
Boyet, you can produce acquittances
For such a sum from special officers
Of Charles his father.

KING.
          Satisfy me so.

BOYET.
So please your grace, the packet is not come,
Where that and other specialties are bound:
To-morrow you shall have a sight of them.

KING.
It shall suffice me: at which interview
All liberal reason I will yield unto.
Meantime receive such welcome at my hand
As honour, without breach of honour, may
Make tender of to thy true worthiness:
You may not come, fair princess, in my gates;
But here without you shall be so received
As you shall deem yourself lodged in my heart,
Though so denied fair harbour in my house.
Your own good thoughts excuse me, and farewell:
To-morrow shall we visit you again.

PRINCESS.
Sweet health and fair desires consort your Grace!

KING.
Thy own wish wish I thee in every place!
              [Exit KING attended.

BEROWNE.
Lady, I will commend you to mine own heart.

ROSALINE.
Pray you, do my commendations; I would be glad
to see it.

BEROWNE.
I would you heard it groan.

ROSALINE.
Is the fool sick?

BEROWNE.
Sick at the heart.

ROSALINE.
Alack, let it blood.

BEROWNE.
Would that do it good?

ROSALINE.
My physic says ay.

BEROWNE.
Will you prick't with your eye?

ROSALINE.
No point, with my knife.

BEROWNE.
Now, God save thy life!

ROSALINE.
And yours from long living!

BEROWNE.
I cannot stay thanksgiving.   [Retiring.

DUMAINE.
Sir, I pray you, a word: what lady is that same?

BOYET.
The heir of Alençon, Katharine her name.

DUMAINE.
A gallant lady. Monsieur, fare you well.   [Exit.

LONGAVILLE.
I beseech you, a word: what is she in the white?

BOYET.
A woman sometimes, an you saw her in the light.

LONGAVILLE.
Perchance light in the light. I desire her name.

BOYET.
She hath but one for herself; to desire that were a
shame.

LONGAVILLE.
Pray you, sir, whose daughter?

BOYET.
Her mother's, I have heard.

LONGAVILLE.
God's blessing on your beard!

BOYET.
Good sir, be not offended.
She is an heir of Falconbridge.

LONGAVILLE.
Nay, my choler is end'd.
She is a most sweet lady.

BOYET.
Not unlike, sir, that may be.
              [Exit LONGAVILLE.

BEROWNE.
What's her name in the cap?

BOYET.
Rosaline, by good hap.

BEROWNE.
Is she wedded or no?

BOYET.
To her will, sir, or so.

BEROWNE.
You are welcome, sir: adieu.

BOYET.
Farewell to me, sir, and welcome to you.

[*Exit* BEROWNE. *Ladies unmask.*

MARIA.
That last is Berowne, the merry madcap lord:
Not a word with him but a jest.

BOYET.
And every jest but a word.

PRINCESS.
It was well done of you to take him at his word.

BOYET.
I was as willing to grapple as he was to board.

MARIA.
Two hot sheeps, marry.

BOYET.
And wherefore not ships?
No sheep, sweet lamb, unless we feed on your
lips.

MARIA.
You sheep, and I pasture: shall that finish the jest?

BOYET.
So you grant pasture for me. [*Offering to kiss her.*

MARIA.
Not so, gentle beast:
My lips are no common, though several they be.

BOYET.
Belonging to whom?

MARIA.
To my fortunes and me.

PRINCESS.
Good wits will be jangling; but, gentles, agree:
This civil war of wits were much better used
On Navarre and his book-men; for here 'tis
abused.

BOYET.
If my observation,—which very seldom lies,—
By the heart's still rhetoric disclosed with eyes,
Deceive me not now, Navarre is infected.

PRINCESS.
With what?

BOYET.
With that which we lovers entitle affected.

PRINCESS.
Your reason?

BOYET.
Why, all his behaviours did make their retire
To the court of his eye, peeping thorough desire:
His heart, like an agate, with your print imprest,
Proud with his form, in his eye pride exprest:
His tongue, all impatient to speak and not see,
Did stumble with haste in his eyesight to be;
All senses to that sense did make their repair,
To feel only looking on fairest of fair:
Methought all his senses were lockt in his eye,
As jewels in crystal for some prince to buy;
Who, tendering their own worth from where they
were glass'd,
Did point you to buy them, along as you pass'd:
His face's own margent did cote such amazes,
That all eyes saw his eyes enchanted with gazes.
I'll give you Aquitaine, and all that is his,
An you give him for my sake but one loving kiss.

PRINCESS.
Come to our pavilion: Boyet is disposed.

BOYET.
But to speak that in words which his eye hath dis-
closed:
I only have made a mouth of his eye,
By adding a tongue which I know will not lie.

ROSALINE.
Thou art an old love-monger, and speakest skilfully.

MARIA.
He is Cupid's grandfather, and learns news of
him.

ROSALINE.
Then was Venus like her mother; for her father is
but grim.

BOYET.
Do you hear, my mad wenches?

MARIA.
No.

BOYET.
What then? do you see?

ROSALINE.
Ay, our way to be gone.

BOYET.
You are too hard for me.

[*Exeunt.*

ACT III. SCENE I.

The same.

Enter ARMADO *and* MOTH.

ARMADO.

WARBLE, child; make passionate my sense
o' hearing.

MOTH.
Concolinel—   [*Singing.*

ARMADO.
Sweet air!—Go, tenderness of years; take this key,
give enlargement to the swain, bring him festi-
nately hither: I must employ him in a letter to my
love.

MOTH.
Master, will you win your love with a French
brawl?

ARMADO.
How meanest thou? brawling in French?

MOTH.
No, my complete master: but to jig off a tune at
the tongue's end, canary to it with your feet, humour it with turning up your eyelids; sigh a note
and sing a note,—sometime through the throat, as
if you swallow'd love with singing love,—sometime through the nose, as if you snuft up love by
smelling love; with your hat penthouse-like, o'er
the shop of your eyes; with your arms crossed on
your thin-belly doublet, like a rabbit on a spit; or
your hands in your pocket, like a man after the old
painting; and keep not too long in one tune, but a
snip and away. These are complements, these are
humours; these betray nice wenches,—that would
be betrayed without these; and make them men of
note—do you note me?—that most are affected to
these.

ARMADO.
How hast thou purchased this experience?

221

MOTH.

By my penny of observation.

ARMADO.

But O,—but O,—

MOTH.

'The hobby-horse is forgot.'

ARMADO.

Call'st thou my love hobby-horse?

MOTH.

No, master; the hobby-horse is but a colt, and your love perhaps a hackney. But have you forgot your love?

ARMADO.

Almost I had.

MOTH.

Negligent student! learn her by heart.

ARMADO.

By heart and in heart, boy.

MOTH.

And out of heart, master: all those three I will prove.

ARMADO.

What wilt thou prove?

MOTH.

A man, if I live;—and this, by, in, and without, upon the instant: by heart you love her, because your heart cannot come by her; in heart you love her, because your heart is in love with her; and out of heart you love her, being out of heart that you cannot enjoy her.

ARMADO.

I am all these three.

MOTH.

And three times as much more,—and yet nothing at all.

ARMADO.

Fetch hither the swain: he must carry me a letter.

MOTH.

A message well sympathized; a horse to be ambassador for an ass.

ARMADO.

Ha, ha! what sayest thou?

MOTH.

Marry, sir, you must send the ass upon the horse, for he is very slow-gaited. But I go.

ARMADO.

The way is but short: away!

MOTH.

As swift as lead, sir.

ARMADO.

Thy meaning, pretty ingenious?
Is not lead a metal heavy, dull, and slow?

MOTH.

Minime, honest master; or rather, master, no.

ARMADO.

I say lead is slow.

MOTH.

    You are too swift, sir, to say so:
Is that lead slow which is fired from a gun?

ARMADO.

Sweet smoke of rhetoric!
He reputes me a cannon, and the bullet, that's he:—
I shoot thee at the swain.

MOTH.

    Thump, then, and I flee.
    [*Exit.*

ARMADO.

A most acute juvenal; voluble and free of grace!—
By thy favour, sweet welkin, I must sigh in thy
   face:—
Most rude melancholy, valour gives thee place.—
My herald is return'd.
       Enter MOTH *with* COSTARD.

MOTH.

A wonder, master! here's a Costard broken in a shin.

ARMADO.

Some enigma, some riddle: come,—thy *l'envoy;*—begin.

COSTARD.

No egma, no riddle, no *l'envoy;* no salve in the mail, sir: O, sir, plantain, a plain plantain! no *l'envoy*, no *l'envoy;* no salve, sir, but a plantain!

ARMADO.

By virtue, thou enforcest laughter; thy silly thought, my spleen: the heaving of my lungs provokes me to ridiculous smiling,—O, pardon me, my stars! Doth the inconsiderate take salve for *l'envoy*, and the word *l'envoy* for a salve?

MOTH.

Do the wise think them other? is not *l'envoy* a salve?

ARMADO.

No, page: it is an epilogue or discourse, to make plain
Some obscure precedence that hath tofore been
   sain.
I will example it:
    The fox, the ape, and the humble-bee,
    Were still at odds, being but three.
There's the moral. Now the *l'envoy*.

MOTH.

I will add the *l'envoy*. Say the moral again.

ARMADO.

    The fox, the ape, and the humble-bee,
    Were still at odds, being but three.

MOTH.

    Until the goose came out of door,
    And stay'd the odds by adding four.
Now will I begin your moral, and do you follow with my *l'envoy*.
    The fox, the ape, and the humble-bee,
    Were still at odds, being but three.

ARMADO.

    Until the goose came out of door,
    Staying the odds by adding four.

MOTH.

A good *l'envoy*, ending in the goose: would you desire more?

COSTARD.

The boy hath sold him a bargain, a goose, that's flat.—
Sir, your pennyworth is good, an your goose be fat.—
To sell a bargain well is as cunning as fast and loose
Let me see—a fat *l'envoy;* ay, that's a fat goose.

ARMADO.

Come hither, come hither. How did this argument begin?

MOTH.

By saying that a Costard was broken in a shin.
Then call'd you for the *l'envoy*.

COSTARD.

True, and I for a plaintain: thus came your argu-
ment in;   [bought;
Then the boy's fat *l'envoy*, the goose that you
And he ended the market.

ARMADO.

But tell me; how was there a Costard broken in a
shin?

MOTH.

I will tell you sensibly.

COSTARD.

Thou hast no feeling of it, Moth: I will speak that
l'envoy:
I, Costard, running out, that was safely within,
Fell over the threshold, and broke my shin.

ARMADO.

We will talk no more of this matter.

COSTARD.

Till there be more matter in the shin.

ARMADO.

Sirrah Costard, I will enfranchise thee.

COSTARD.

O, marry me to one Frances:—I smell some *l'envoy*, some goose, in this.

ARMADO.

By my sweet soul, I mean setting thee at liberty,
enfreedoming thy person: thou wert immured,
restrain'd, captivated, bound.

COSTARD.

True, true; and now you will be my purgation, and
let me loose.

ARMADO.

I give thee thy liberty, set thee from durance; and,
in lieu thereof, impose on thee nothing but this:—
bear this significant [*giving a letter*] to the country
maid Jaquenetta: there is remuneration [*giving
money*]; for the best ward of mine honour is re-
warding my dependents.—Moth, follow.   [*Exit.*

MOTH.

Like the sequel, I.—Signior Costard, adieu.

COSTARD.

My sweet ounce of man's flesh! my incony Jewl!—
                [*Exit* MOTH.
Now will I look to his remuneration. Remuneration! O, that's the Latin word for three farthings:
three farthings — remuneration. — 'What's the
price of this inkle?'—'A penny.'—'No, I'll give
you a remuneration:' why, it carries it.—Remuneration!—why, it is a fairer name than French
crown. I will never buy and sell out of this word.
         Enter BEROWNE.

BEROWNE.

O, my good knave Costard! exceedingly well met.

COSTARD.

Pray you, sir, how much carnation ribbon may a
man buy for a remuneration?

BEROWNE.

What is a remuneration?

COSTARD.

Marry, sir, halfpenny farthing.

BEROWNE.

O, why, then, three-farthing-worth of silk.

COSTARD.

I thank your worship: God be wi' you!

BEROWNE.

O, stay, slave; I must employ thee:

As thou wilt win my favour, good my knave,
Do one thing for me that I shall entreat.

COSTARD.

When would you have it done, sir?

BEROWNE.

O, this afternoon.

COSTARD.

Well, I will do it, sir: fare you well.

BEROWNE.

O, thou knowest not what it is.

COSTARD.

I shall know, sir, when I have done it.

BEROWNE.

Why, villain, thou must know first.

COSTARD.

I will come to your worship to-morrow morning.

BEROWNE.

It must be done this afternoon. Hark, slave, it is
but this:—
The princess comes to hunt here in the park,
And in her train there is a gentle lady;   [name,
When tongues speak sweetly, then they name her
And Rosaline they call her: ask for her;
And to her white hand see thou do commend
This seal'd-up counsel. There's thy guerdon; go.
              [*Giving money.*

COSTARD.

Gardon,—O sweet gardon! better than remuneration; eleven-pence farthing better: most sweet
gardon!—I will do it, sir, in print.—Gardon—remuneration.   [*Exit.*

BEROWNE.

O,—and I, forsooth, in love! I, that have been
   love's whip;
A very beadle to a humorous sigh;
A critic, nay, a night-watch constable;
A domineering pedant o'er the boy,
Than whom no mortal so magnificent!
This wimpled, whining, purblind, wayward boy;
This signior-junior, giant-dwarf, Dan Cupid;
Regent of love-rimes, lord of folded arms,
Th'anointed sovereign of sighs and groans,
Liege of all loiterers and malecontents,
Dread prince of plackets, king of codpieces,
Sole imperator and great general
Of trotting paritors:—O my little heart!—
And I to be a corporal of his field,
And wear his colours like a tumbler's hoop!
What! I love! I sue! I seek a wife!
A woman, that is like a German clock,
Still a-repairing; ever out of frame;
And never going aright, being a watch,
But being watcht that it may still go right!
Nay, to be perjured, which is worst of all;
And, among three, to love the worst of all;
A whitely wanton with a velvet brow,
With two pitch-balls stuck in her face for eyes;
Ay, and, by heaven, one that will do the deed,
Though Argus were her eunuch and her guard:
And I to sigh for her! to watch for her!
To pray for her! Go to; it is a plague
That Cupid will impose for my neglect
Of his almighty dreadful little might.
Well, I will love, write, sigh, pray, sue, and groan:
Some men must love my lady, and some Joan.
              [*Exit.*

ACT IV. SCENE I.

The same.

Enter the PRINCESS, ROSALINE, MARIA,
KATHARINE, BOYET, LORDS, ATTENDANTS,
and a FORESTER.

PRINCESS.

WAS that the king, that spurr'd his horse so
    hard
Against the steep uprising of the hill?

BOYET.

I know not; but I think it was not he.

PRINCESS.

Whoe'er a' was, a' show'd a mounting mind.
Well, lords, to-day we shall have our dispatch:
On Saturday we will return to France.—
Then, forester, my friend, where is the bush
That we must stand and play the murderer in?

FORESTER.

Hereby, upon the edge of yonder coppice;
A stand where you may make the fairest shoot.

PRINCESS.

I thank my beauty, I am fair that shoot,
And thereupon thou speak'st the fairest shoot.

FORESTER.

Pardon me, madam, for I meant not so.

PRINCESS.

What, what? first praise me, and again say no?
O short-lived pride! Not fair? alack for woe!

FORESTER.

Yes, madam, fair.

PRINCESS.

    Nay, never paint me now:
Where fair is not, praise cannot mend the brow.
Here, good my glass, take this for telling true:
    [*Giving him money*
Fair payment for foul words is more than due.

FORESTER.

Nothing but fair is that which you inherit.

PRINCESS.

See, see, my beauty will be saved by merit!
O heresy in fair, fit for these days!
A giving hand, though foul, shall have fair praise.—
But come, the bow:—now mercy goes to kill,
And shooting well is then accounted ill.
Thus will I save my credit in the shoot:
Not wounding, pity would not let me do't;
If wounding, then it was to show my skill,
That more for praise than purpose meant to kill.
And, out of question, so it is sometimes,—
Glory grows guilty of detested crimes,
When, for fame's sake, for praise, an outward
    part,
We bend to that the working of the heart;
As I for praise alone now seek to spill
The poor deer's blood, that my heart means no
    ill.

BOYET.

Do not curst wives hold that self-sovereignty
Only for praise' sake, when they strive to be
Lords o'er their lords?

PRINCESS.

Only for praise: and praise we may afford
To any lady that subdues a lord.

BOYET.

Here comes a member of the commonwealth.

Enter COSTARD.

COSTARD.

God dig-you-den all! Pray you, which is the head
lady?

PRINCESS.

Thou shalt know her, fellow, by the rest that have
no heads.

COSTARD.

Which is the greatest lady, the highest?

PRINCESS.

The thickest and the tallest.

COSTARD.

The thickest and the tallest! it is so; truth is truth.
An your waist, mistress, were as slender as my wit,
One o' these maids' girdles for your waist should
    be fit.   [here.
Are not you the chief woman? you are the thickest

PRINCESS.

What's your will, sir? what's your will?

COSTARD.

I have a letter from Monsieur Berowne to one
    Lady Rosaline.

PRINCESS.

O, thy letter, thy letter! he's a good friend of mine:
Stand aside, good bearer.—Boyet, you can carve;
Break up this capon.

BOYET.

    I am bound to serve.—
This letter is mistook, it importeth none here;
It is writ to Jaquenetta.

PRINCESS.

    We will read it, I swear.
Break the neck of the wax, and every one give ear.

BOYET [*reads*].

By heaven, that thou art fair, is most infallible;
true, that thou art beauteous; truth itself, that
thou art lovely. More fairer than fair, beautiful
than beauteous, truer than truth itself, have commiseration on thy heroical vassal! The magnanimous and most illustrate king Cophetua set eye
upon the pernicious and indubitate beggar Zene-
lophon; and he it was that might rightly say, *Veni,
vidi, vici;* which to annothanize in the vulgar,—O
base and obscure vulgar!—*videlicet,* He came, saw,
and overcame: he came, one; saw, two; overcame,
three. Who came? the king: why did he come? to
see: why did he see? to overcome: to whom came
he? to the beggar: what saw he? the beggar: who
overcame he? the beggar. The conclusion is victory: on whose side? the king's. The captive is enricht: on whose side? the beggar's. The catastrophe is a nuptial: on whose side? the king's,—no, on
both in one, or one in both. I am the king; for so
stands the comparison: thou the beggar; for so witnesseth thy lowliness. Shall I command thy love?
I may: shall I enforce thy love? I could: shall I entreat thy love? I will. What shalt thou exchange for
rags? robes; for tittles? titles; for thyself? me.
Thus, expecting thy reply, I profane my lips on
thy foot, my eyes on thy picture, and my heart on
thy every part.—Thine, in the dearest design of
industry,   DON ADRIANO DE ARMADO.
Thus dost thou hear the Nemean lion roar
  'Gainst thee, thou lamb, that standest as his prey.
Submissive fall his princely feet before,
  And he from forage will incline to play:

But if thou strive, poor soul, what art thou then?
Food for his rage, repasture for his den.
PRINCESS.
What plume of feathers is he that indited this letter?
What vane? what weathercock? did you ever hear
  better?
BOYET.
I am much deceived but I remember the style.
PRINCESS.
Else your memory is bad, going o'er it erewhile.
This Armado is a Spaniard, that keeps here in court;
A phantasm, a Monarcho, and one that makes sport
To the prince and his book-mates.
PRINCESS.
                    Thou fellow, a word:
Who gave thee this letter?
COSTARD.
                    I told you; my lord.
PRINCESS.
To whom shouldst thou give it?
COSTARD.
                    From my lord to my lady.
PRINCESS.
From which lord to which lady?
COSTARD.
From my Lord Berowne, a good master of mine,
To a lady of France that he call'd Rosaline.
PRINCESS.
Thou hast mistaken his letter.—Come, lords,
  away.—
Here, sweet, put up this: 'twill be thine another
  day.   [Exit PRINCESS attended.
BOYET.
Who is the suitor? who is the suitor?
ROSALINE.
                    Shall I teach you to know?
BOYET.
Ay, my continent of beauty.
ROSALINE.
                    Why, she that bears the bow.
Finely put off!
BOYET.
My lady goes to kill horns; but, if thou marry,
Hang me by the neck, if horns that year miscarry.
Finely put on!
ROSALINE.
Well, then, I am the shooter.
BOYET.
                    And who is your deer?
ROSALINE.
If we choose by the horns, yourself: come not near.
Finely put on, indeed!
MARIA.
You still wrangle with her, Boyet, and she strikes
  at the brow.
BOYET.
But she herself is hit lower: have I hit her now?
ROSALINE.
Shall I come upon thee with an old saying, that
was a man when King Pepin of France was a little
boy, as touching the hit it?
BOYET.
So I may answer thee with one as old, that was a
woman when Queen Guinever of Britain was a
little wench, as touching the hit it.

ROSALINE.
Thou canst not hit it, hit it, hit it,
Thou canst not hit it, my good man.
BOYET.
An I cannot, cannot, cannot,
An I cannot, another can.
          [Exeunt ROSALINE and KATHARINE.
COSTARD.
By my troth, most pleasant: how both did fit it!
MARIA.
A mark marvellous well shot, for they both did hit
it.
BOYET.
A mark! O, mark but that mark! A mark, says my
  lady!   [be.
Let the mark have a prick in't, to mete at if it may
MARIA.
Wide o' th' bow-hand! i'faith, your hand is out.
COSTARD.
Indeed, a' must shoot nearer, or he'll ne'er hit the
  clout.
BOYET.
An if my hand be out, then belike your hand is in.
COSTARD.
Then will she get the upshoot by cleaving the pin.
MARIA.
Come, come, you talk greasily; your lips grow foul.
COSTARD.
She's too hard for you at pricks, sir: challenge her
  to bowl.
BOYET.
I fear too much rubbing. Good night, my good owl.
          [Exeunt BOYET and MARIA.
COSTARD.
By my soul, a swain! a most simple clown!
Lord, Lord, how the ladies and I have put him
  down!
O' my troth, most sweet jests! most incony vulgar
  wit!   [were, so fit.
When it comes so smoothly off, so obscenely, as it
Armado o' th' one side;—O, a most dainty man!
To see him walk before a lady and to bear her fan!
To see him kiss his hand! and how most sweetly a'
  will swear!—
And his page o' t'other side, that handful of wit!
Ah, heavens, it is a most pathetical nit!
Sola, sola! [Shout within. Exit COSTARD, running.

SCENE II.

The same.

Enter HOLOFERNES, SIR NATHANIEL, *and*
DULL.

SIR NATHANIEL.
VERY reverend sport, truly; and done in the
testimony of a good conscience.
HOLOFERNES.
The deer was, as you know, *sanguis*,—in blood;
ripe as a pomewater, who now hangeth like a jewel
in the ear of *cœlo*,—the sky, the welkin, the
heaven; and anon falleth like a crab on the face of
terra,—the soil, the land, the earth.
SIR NATHANIEL.
Truly, Master Holofernes, the epithets are sweetly
varied, like a scholar at the least: but, sir, I assure
ye, it was a buck of the first head.

HOLOFERNES.

Sir Nathaniel, *haud credo*.

DULL.

'Twas not a *haud credo;* 'twas a pricket.

HOLOFERNES.

Most barbarous intimation! yet a kind of insinuation, as it were, *in via*, in way, of explication; *facere* as it were, replication, or, rather, *ostentare*, to show, as it were, his inclination,—after his undrest, unpolisht, uneducated, unpruned, untrain'd, or, rather, unletter'd, or, ratherest, unconfirm'd fashion,—to insert again my *haud credo* for a deer.

DULL.

I said the deer was not a *haud credo;* 'twas a pricket.

HOLOFERNES.

Twice-sod simplicity, *bis coctus!*
O thou monster Ignorance, how deformed dost thou look!

SIR NATHANIEL.

Sir, he hath never fed of the dainties that are bred in a book;
he hath not eat paper, as it were; he hath not drunk ink: his intellect is not replenisht; he is only an animal, only sensible in the duller parts:
And such barren plants are set before us, that we thankful should be—
Which we of taste and feeling are—for those parts that do fructify in us more than he.
For as it would ill become me to be vain, indiscreet, or a fool,
So, were there a patch set on learning, to see him in a school: [mind,—
But, *omne bene*, say I; being of an old father's
'Many can brook the weather that love not the wind.'

DULL.

You two are book-men: can you tell by your wit
What was a month old at Cain's birth, that's not five weeks old as yet?

HOLOFERNES.

Dictynna, goodman Dull; Dictynna, goodman Dull.

DULL.

What is Dictynna?

SIR NATHANIEL.

A title to Phœbe, to Luna, to the moon.

HOLOFERNES.

The moon was a month old when Adam was no more,
And raught not to five weeks when he came to fivescore.
Th'allusion holds in the exchange.

DULL.

'Tis true indeed; the collusion holds in the exchange.

HOLOFERNES.

God comfort thy capacity! I say, th'allusion holds in the exchange.

DULL.

And I say, the pollusion holds in the exchange; for the moon is never but a month old: and I say beside, that 'twas a pricket that the princess kill'd.

HOLOFERNES.

Sir Nathaniel, will you hear an extemporal epitaph on the death of the deer? and, to humour the ig-

norant, I have call'd the deer the princess kill'd a pricket.

SIR NATHANIEL.

Perge, good Master Holofernes, *perge:* so it shall please you to abrogate scurrility.

HOLOFERNES.

I will something affect the letter, for it argues facility.

The preyful princess pierced and prickt
   a pretty pleasing pricket;
Some say a sore; but not a sore,
   till now made sore with shooting.
The dogs did yell: put *l* to sore,
   then sorel jumps from thicket;
Or pricket, sore, or else sorel;
   the people fall a-hooting.
If sore be sore, then *l* to sore
   makes fifty sores: O sore *l!*
Of one sore I an hundred make
   by adding but one more *l*.

SIR NATHANIEL.

A rare talent!

DULL [*aside*].

If a talent be a claw, look how he claws him with a talent.

HOLOFERNES.

This is a gift that I have, simple, simple; a foolish extravagant spirit, full of forms, figures, shapes, objects, ideas, apprehensions, motions, revolutions: these are begot in the ventricle of memory, nourisht in the womb of *pia mater*, and deliver'd upon the mellowing of occasion. But the gift is good in those in whom it is acute, and I am thankful for it.

SIR NATHANIEL.

Sir, I praise the Lord for you: and so may my parishioners; for their sons are well tutor'd by you, and their daughters profit very greatly under you: you are a good member of the commonwealth.

HOLOFERNES.

Mehercle, if their sons be ingenious, they shall want no instruction; if their daughters be capable, I will put it to them: but, *vir sapit qui pauca loquitur*. A soul feminine saluteth us.

Enter JAQUENETTA *and* COSTARD.

JAQUENETTA.

God give you good morrow, master person.

HOLOFERNES.

Master person,—*quasi* pers-on. An if one should be pierced, which is the one?

COSTARD.

Marry, master schoolmaster, he that is likest to a hogshead.

HOLOFERNES.

Of piercing a hogshead! a good lustre of conceit in a turf of earth; fire enough for a flint, pearl enough for a swine: 'tis pretty; it is well.

JAQUENETTA.

Good master person, be so good as read me this letter: it was given me by Costard, and sent me from Don Armado: I beseech you, read it.

HOLOFERNES.

Fauste, precor, gelidâ quando pecus omne sub umbrâ Ruminat,—and so forth. Ah, good old Mantuan! I may speak of thee as the traveller doth of Venice;

——*Venetia, Venetia,*
Chi non te vede, non ti pretia.
Old Mantuan, old Mantuan! who understandeth
thee not, loves thee not.—*Ut, re, sol, la, mi, fa.*—
Under pardon, sir, what are the contents? or
rather, as Horace says in his—What, my soul,
verses?

SIR NATHANIEL.

Ay, sir, and very learned.

HOLOFERNES.

Let me hear a staff, a stanze, a verse; *lege, domine.*

SIR NATHANIEL [*reads*].

If love make me forsworn, how shall I swear to
    love?
  Ah, never faith could hold, if not to beauty
    vow'd!
Though to myself forsworn, to thee I'll faithful
    prove;
  Those thoughts to me were oaks, to thee like
    osiers bow'd.
Study his bias leaves, and makes his book thine
    eyes,
  Where all those pleasures live that art would
    comprehend:
If knowledge be the mark, to know thee shall suf-
    fice;
  Well learned is that tongue that well can thee
    commend;
All ignorant that soul that sees thee without won-
    der,—   [mire:
  Which is to me some praise that I thy parts ad-
Thy eye Jove's lightning bears, thy voice his dread-
    ful thunder,
  Which, not to anger bent, is music, and sweet
    fire.
Celestial as thou art, O, pardon love this wrong,
That sings heavens' praise with such an earthly
    tongue.

HOLOFERNES.

You find not the apostrophes, and so miss the accent: let me supervise the canzonet. Here are only
numbers ratified; but, for the elegancy, facility,
and golden cadence of poesy, *caret.* Ovidius Naso
was the man: and why, indeed, Naso, but for smelling out the odoriferous flowers of fancy, the jerks
of invention? *Imitari* is nothing: so doth the hound
his master, the ape his keeper, the tired horse his
rider.—But, damosella virgin, was this directed to
you?

JAQUENETTA.

Ay, sir, from one Monsieur Berowne, one of the
strange queen's lords.

HOLOFERNES.

I will overglance the superscript: 'To the snow-
white hand of the most beauteous Lady Rosaline.'
I will look again on the intellect of the letter, for
the nomination of the party writing to the person
written unto: 'Your ladyship's in all desired employment, Berowne.'—Sir Nathaniel, this Berowne is one of the votaries with the king; and here
he hath framed a letter to a sequent of the stranger
queen's, which accidentally, or by the way of pro-
gression, hath miscarried.—Trip and go, my
sweet; deliver this paper into the royal hand of the
king: it may concern much. Stay not thy compliment; I forgive thy duty: adieu.

JAQUENETTA.

Good Costard, go with me.—Sir, God save your
life!

COSTARD.

Have with thee, my girl.
     [*Exeunt* COSTARD *and* JAQUENETTA.

SIR NATHANIEL.

Sir, you have done this in the fear of God, very
religiously; and, as a certain father saith—

HOLOFERNES.

Sir, tell not me of the father; I do fear colourable
colours. But to return to the verses: did they please
you, Sir Nathaniel?

SIR NATHANIEL.

Marvellous well for the pen.

HOLOFERNES.

I do dine to-day at the father's of a certain pupil of
mine; where, if, before repast, it shall please you
to gratify the table with a grace, I will, on my privilege I have with the parents of the foresaid child
or pupil, undertake your *ben venuto;* where I will
prove those verses to be very unlearned, neither
savouring of poetry, wit, nor invention: I beseech
your society.

SIR NATHANIEL.

And thank you too; for society, saith the text, is the
happiness of life.

HOLOFERNES.

And, certes, the text most infallibly concludes it.—
[*to* DULL] Sir, I do invite you too; you shall not
say me nay: *pauca verba.* Away! the gentles are at
their game, and we will to our recreation.
                              [*Exeunt.*

SCENE III.

The same.

Enter BEROWNE, *with a paper in his hand, alone.*

BEROWNE.

THE king he is hunting the deer; I am coursing
myself: they have pitch'd a toil; I am toiling in
a pitch,—pitch that defiles: defile! a foul word.
Well, Set thee down, sorrow! for so they say the
fool said, and so say I, and I the fool: well proved,
wit! By the Lord, this love is as mad as Ajax: it
kills sheep; it kills me, I a sheep: well proved again
o' my side! I will not love: if I do, hang me; i'faith,
I will not. O, but her eye,—by this light, but for
her eye, I would not love her; yes, for her two eyes.
Well, I do nothing in the world but lie, and lie in
my throat. By heaven, I do love: and it hath taught
me to rime, and to be mallicholy; and here is part
of my rime, and here my mallicholy. Well, she
hath one o' my sonnets already: the clown bore it,
the fool sent it, and the lady hath it: sweet clown,
sweeter fool, sweetest lady! By the world, I would
not care a pin, if the other three were in.—Here
comes one with a paper: God give him grace to
groan!   [*He stands aside.*

The KING *ent'reth.*

KING.

Ay me!

BEROWNE [*aside*].

Shot, by heaven!—Proceed, sweet Cupid: thou
hast thumpt him with thy bird-bolt under the
left pap.—In faith, secrets!

KING [*reads*].
'So sweet a kiss the golden sun gives not
   To those fresh morning drops upon the rose,
As thy eye-beams, when their fresh rays have smot
   The night of dew that on my cheeks down flows:
Nor shines the silver moon one half so bright
   Through the transparent bosom of the deep,
As doth thy face through tears of mine give light;
   Thou shin'st in every tear that I do weep:
No drop but as a coach doth carry thee;
   So ridest thou triumphing in my woe.
Do but behold the tears that swell in me,
   And they thy glory through my grief will show:
But do not love thyself; then thou wilt keep
My tears for glasses, and still make me weep.
O queen of queens! how far dost thou excel,
No thought can think, nor tongue of mortal
   tell.'—
How shall she know my griefs? I'll drop the
   paper:—
Sweet leaves, shade folly.—Who is he comes here?
                    [*Steps aside.*
What, Longaville! and reading! listen, ear.
       BEROWNE [*aside*].
Now, in thy likeness, one more fool appear!
     Enter LONGAVILLE.
       LONGAVILLE.
Ay me, I am forsworn!
       BEROWNE [*aside*].
Why, he comes in like a perjure, wearing papers.
       KING [*aside*].
In love, I hope: sweet fellowship in shame!
       BEROWNE [*aside*].
One drunkard loves another of the name.
       LONGAVILLE.
Am I the first that have been perjured so?
       BEROWNE [*aside*].
I could put thee in comfort,—not by two that I
   know:
Thou makest the triumviry, the corner-cap of
   society,
The shape of Love's Tyburn that hangs up sim-
   plicity.
       LONGAVILLE.
I fear these stubborn lines lack power to move:—
O sweet Maria, empress of my love!—
These numbers will I tear, and write in prose.
       BEROWNE [*aside*].
O, rimes are guards on wanton Cupid's hose:
Disfigure not his shop.
       LONGAVILLE.
       This same shall go.—
                [*Reads.*
Did not the heavenly rhetoric of thine eye,
   'Gainst whom the world can not hold argument,
Persuade my heart to this false perjury?
   Vows for thee broke deserve not punishment.
A woman I forswore; but I will prove,
   Thou being a goddess, I forswore not thee:
My vow was earthly, thou a heavenly love;
   Thy grace being gain'd cures all disgrace in me.
''ows are but breath, and breath a vapour is:
   Then thou, fair sun, which on my earth dost
     shine,
Exhalest this vapour-vow; in thee it is:
   If broken then, it is no fault of mine:

If by me broke, what fool is not so wise
To lose an oath to win a paradise?
       BEROWNE [*aside*].
This is the liver-vein, which makes flesh a
   deity,
A green goose a goddess: pure, pure idolatry,
God amend us, God amend! we are much out o' th'
   way.
       LONGAVILLE.
By whom shall I send this?—Company! stay.
                [*Steps aside.*
       BEROWNE [*aside*].
All hid, all hid, an old infant play.
Like a demigod here sit I in the sky,
And wretched fools' secrets heedfully o'er-eye.
More sacks to the mill! O heavens, I have my
   wish!
     Enter DUMAINE.
Dumaine transform'd! four woodcocks in a
   dish!
       DUMAINE.
O most divine Kate!
       BEROWNE [*aside*].
O most profane coxcomb!
       DUMAINE.
By heaven, the wonder in a mortal eye!
       BEROWNE [*aside*].
By earth she is not, corporal: there you lie.
       DUMAINE.
Her amber hairs for foul hath amber quoted.
       BEROWNE [*aside*].
An amber-colour'd raven was well noted.
       DUMAINE.
As upright as the cedar.
       BEROWNE [*aside*].
          Stoop, I say;
Her shoulder is with child.
       DUMAINE.
           As fair as day.
       BEROWNE [*aside*].
Ay, as some days; but then no sun must shine.
       DUMAINE.
O, that I had my wish!
       LONGAVILLE [*aside*].
          And I had mine!
       KING [*aside*].
And I mine too, good Lord!
       BEROWNE [*aside*].
Amen, so I had mine: is not that a good word?
       DUMAINE.
I would forget her; but a fever she
Reigns in my blood, and will remember'd be.
       BEROWNE [*aside*].
A fever in your blood! why, then incision
Would let her out in saucers: sweet misprision!
       DUMAINE.
Once more I'll read the ode that I have writ.
       BEROWNE [*aside*].
Once more I'll mark how love can vary wit.
       DUMAINE [*reads*].
'On a day—alack the day!—
   Love, whose month is ever May,
   Spied a blossom passing fair
   Playing in the wanton air:
Through the velvet leaves the wind,
   All unseen, can passage find;

That the lover, sick to death,
Wisht himself the heaven's breath.
Air, quoth he, thy cheeks may blow;
Air, would I might triumph so!
But, alack, my hand is sworn
Ne'er to pluck thee from thy thorn;—
Vow, alack, for youth unmeet,
Youth so apt to pluck a sweet!
Do not call it sin in me,
That I am forsworn for thee;
Thou for whom Jove would swear
Juno but an Ethiop were;
And deny himself for Jove,
Turning mortal for thy love.'
This will I send, and something else more plain,
That shall express my true love's fasting pain.
O, would the king, Berowne, and Longaville,
Were lovers too! Ill, to example ill,
Would from my forehead wipe a perjured note;
For none offend where all alike do dote.

LONGAVILLE [advancing].
Dumaine, thy love is far from charity,
That in love's grief desir'st society:
You may look pale, but I should blush, I know,
To be o'erheard and taken napping so.

KING [advancing].
Come, sir, you blush: as his your case is such;
You chide at him, offending twice as much:
You do not love Maria? Longaville
Did never sonnet for her sake compile,
Nor never lay his wreathed arms athwart
His loving bosom, to keep down his heart!
I have been closely shrouded in this bush,
And markt you both, and for you both did blush:
I heard your guilty rimes, observed your fashion,
Saw sighs reek from you, noted well your pas-
sion:
Ay me! says one: O Jove! the other cries;
One her hairs were gold, crystal the other's eyes:
You would for paradise break faith and troth;
[To LONGAVILLE.
And Jove, for your love, would infringe an oath.
[To DUMAINE.
What will Berowne say when that he shall hear
A faith infringed, which such zeal did swear?
How will he scorn! how will he spend his wit!
How will he triumph, leap, and laugh at it!
For all the wealth that ever I did see,
I would not have him know so much by me.

BEROWNE.
Now step I forth to whip hypocrisy. [Advancing.
Ah, good my liege, I pray thee, pardon me!
Good heart, what grace hast thou, thus to reprove
These worms for loving, that art most in love?
Your eyes do make no coaches; in your tears
There is no certain princess that appears;
You'll not be perjured, 'tis a hateful thing;
Tush, none but minstrels like of sonneting!
But are you not ashamed? nay, are you not,
All three of you, to be thus much o'ershot?
You found his mote; the king your mote did see;
But I a beam do find in each of three.
O, what a scene of foolery have I seen,
Of sighs, of groans, of sorrow, and of teen!
O me, with what strict patience have I sat,
To see a king transformed to a gnat!

To see great Hercules whipping a gig,
And profound Solomon to tune a jig,
And Nestor play at push-pin with the boys,
And critic Timon laugh at idle toys!
Where lies thy grief, O tell me, good Dumaine?
And, gentle Longaville, where lies thy pain?
And where my liege's? all about the breast:—
A caudle, ho!

KING.
Too bitter is thy jest.
Are we betray'd thus to thy over-view?

BEROWNE.
Not you to me, but I betray'd by you:
I, that am honest; I, that hold it sin
To break the vow I am engaged in;
I am betray'd, by keeping company
With men like you, men of inconstancy.
When shall you see me write a thing in rime?
Or groan for Joan? or spend a minute's time
In pruning me? When shall you hear that I
Will praise a hand, a foot, a face, an eye,
A gait, a state, a brow, a breast, a waist,
A leg, a limb?—

KING.
Soft! whither away so fast?
A true man or a thief that gallops so?

BEROWNE.
I post from love: good lover, let me go.
Enter JAQUENETTA and COSTARD.

JAQUENETTA.
God bless the king!

KING.
What present hast thou there?

COSTARD.
Some certain treason.

KING.
What makes treason here?

COSTARD.
Nay, it makes nothing, sir.

KING.
If it mar nothing neither,
The treason and you go in peace away together.

JAQUENETTA.
I beseech your Grace, let this letter be read:
Our person misdoubts it; 'twas treason, he said.

KING.
Berowne, read it over.
[Giving him the letter.
Where hadst thou it?

JAQUENETTA.
Of Costard.

KING.
Where hadst thou it?

COSTARD.
Of Dun Adramadio, Dun Adramadio.
[BEROWNE tears the letter.

KING.
How now! what is in you? why dost thou tear it?

BEROWNE.
A toy, my liege, a toy: your Grace needs not fear it.

LONGAVILLE.
It did move him to passion, and therefore let's hear
it.

DUMAINE.
It is Berowne's writing, and here is his name.
[Picking up the pieces.

BEROWNE [to COSTARD].
Ah, you whoreson loggerhead! you were born to
  do me shame.—
Guilty, my lord, guilty! I confess, I confess.
            KING.
What?
            BEROWNE.
      That you three fools lackt me fool to make
  up the mess:
He, he, and you, and you, my liege, and I,
Are pick-purses in love, and we deserve to die.
O, dismiss this audience, and I shall tell you more.
            DUMAINE.
Now the number is even.
            BEROWNE.
            True, true; we are four.
Will these turtles be gone?
            KING.
            Hence, sirs; away!
            COSTARD.
Walk aside the true folk, and let the traitors stay.
     [Exeunt COSTARD and JAQUENETTA.
            BEROWNE.
Sweet lords, sweet lovers, O, let us embrace!
As true we are as flesh and blood can be:
The sea will ebb and flow, heaven show his face;
  Young blood doth not obey an old decree:
We cannot cross the cause why we were born;
Therefore of all hands must we be forsworn.
            KING.
What, did these rent lines show some love of thine?
            BEROWNE.
Did they, quoth you? Who sees the heavenly Rosa-
  line,
That, like a rude and savage man of Inde,
  At the first opening of the gorgeous east,
Bows not his vassal head and strucken blind
  Kisses the base ground with obedient breast?
What peremptory eagle-sighted eye
  Dares look upon the heaven of her brow,
That is not blinded by her majesty?
            KING.
What zeal, what fury hath inspired thee now?
My love, her mistress, is a gracious moon;
  She an attending star, scarce seen a light.
            BEROWNE.
My eyes are then no eyes, nor I Berowne:
  O, but for my love, day would turn to night!
Of all complexions the cull'd sovereignty
  Do meet, as at a fair, in her fair cheek,
Where several worthies make one dignity,
  Where nothing wants that want itself doth seek.
Lend me the flourish of all gentle tongues,—
  Fie, painted rhetoric! O, she needs it not:
To things of sale a seller's praise belongs,
  She passes praise; then praise too short doth blot.
A wither'd hermit, five-score winters worn,
  Might shake off fifty, looking in her eye:
Beauty doth varnish age, as if new-born,
  And gives the crutch the cradle's infancy:
O, 'tis the sun that maketh all things shine.
            KING.
By heaven, thy love is black as ebony.
            BEROWNE.
Is ebony like her? O wood divine!
  A wife of such wood were felicity.

O, who can give an oath? where is a book?
  That I may swear beauty doth beauty lack,
If that she learn not of her eye to look:
  No face is fair that is not full so black.
            KING.
O paradox! Black is the badge of hell,
  The hue of dungeons and the stole of night;
And beauty's crest becomes the heavens well.
            BEROWNE.
Devils soonest tempt, resembling spirits of light.
O, if in black my lady's brows be deckt,
  It mourns that painting and usurping hair
Should ravish doters with a false aspect;
  And therefore is she born to make black fair.
Her favour turns the fashion of the days,
  For native blood is counted painting now;
And therefore red, that would avoid dispraise,
  Paints itself black, to imitate her brow.
            DUMAINE.
To look like her are chimney-sweepers black.
            LONGAVILLE.
And since her time are colliers counted bright.
            KING.
And Ethiopes of their sweet complexion crack.
            DUMAINE.
Dark needs no candles now, for dark is light.
            BEROWNE.
Your mistresses dare never come in rain,
For fear their colours should be washt away.
            KING.
'Twere good, yours did; for, sir, to tell you plain,
I'll find a fairer face not washt to-day.
            BEROWNE.
I'll prove her fair, or talk till doomsday here.
            KING.
No devil will fright thee then so much as she.
            DUMAINE.
I never knew man hold vile stuff so dear.
            LONGAVILLE.
Look, here's thy love: my foot and her face see.
            BEROWNE.
O, if the streets were paved with thine eyes,
Her feet were much too dainty for such tread!
            DUMAINE.
O vile! then, as she goes, what upward lies
The street should see as she walkt overhead.
            KING.
But what of this? are we not all in love?
            BEROWNE.
Nothing so sure; and thereby all forsworn.
            KING.
Then leave this chat; and, good Berowne, now
  prove
Our loving lawful, and our faith not torn.
            DUMAINE.
Ay, marry, there; some flattery for this evil.
            LONGAVILLE.
O, some authority how to proceed;
Some tricks, some quillets, how to cheat the devil.
            DUMAINE.
Some salve for perjury.
            BEROWNE.
            'Tis more than need.
Have at you, then, affection's men-at-arms.
Consider what you first did swear unto,
To fast, to study, and to see no woman;

Flat treason 'gainst the kingly state of youth.
Say, can you fast? your stomachs are too young;
And abstinence engenders maladies.
And where that you have vow'd to study, lords,
In that each of you have forsworn his book,
Can you still dream and pore and thereon look?
For when would you, my lord, or you, or you,
Have found the ground of study's excellence
Without the beauty of a woman's face?
[From women's eyes this doctrine I derive;
They are the ground, the books, the academes
From whence doth spring the true Promethean
    fire.]
Why, universal plodding poisons up
The nimble spirits in the arteries,
As motion and long-during action tires
The sinewy vigour of the traveller.
Now, for not looking on a woman's face,
You have in that forsworn the use of eyes,
And study too, the causer of your vow;
For where is any author in the world
Teaches such beauty as a woman's eye?
Learning is but an adjunct to ourself
And where we are our learning likewise is:
Then when ourselves we see in ladies' eyes,
Do we not likewise see our learning there?
O, we have made a vow to study, lords,
And in that vow we have forsworn our books.
For when would you, my liege, or you, or you,
In leaden contemplation have found out
Such fiery numbers as the prompting eyes
Of beauty's tutors have enrich'd you with?
Other slow arts entirely keep the brain;
And therefore, finding barren practisers,
Scarce show a harvest of their heavy toil:
But love, first learned in a lady's eyes,
Lives not alone immured in the brain;
But, with the motion of all elements,
Courses as swift as thought in every power,
And gives to every power a double power,
Above their functions and their offices.
It adds a precious seeing to the eye;
A lover's eyes will gaze an eagle blind;
A lover's ear will hear the lowest sound,
When the suspicious head of theft is stopt:
Love's feeling is more soft and sensible
Than are the tender horns of cockled snails;
Love's tongue proves dainty Bacchus gross in taste:
For valour, is not Love a Hercules,
Still climbing trees in the Hesperides?
Subtle as Sphinx; as sweet and musical
As bright Apollo's lute, strung with his hair:
And when Love speaks, the voice of all the gods
Make heaven drowsy with the harmony.
Never durst poet touch a pen to write
Until his ink were temper'd with Love's sighs;
O, then his lines would ravish savage ears
And plant in tyrants mild humility.
From women's eyes this doctrine I derive:
They sparkle still the right Promethean fire;
They are the books, the arts, the academes,
That show, contain and nourish all the world:
Else none at all in aught proves excellent.
Then fools you were these women to forswear,
Or keeping what is sworn, you will prove fools.
For wisdom's sake, a word that all men love,

Or for love's sake, a word that loves all men,
Or for men's sake, the authors of these women,
Or women's sake, by whom we men are men,
Let us once lose our oaths to find ourselves,
Or else we lose ourselves to keep our oaths.
It is religion to be thus forsworn,
For charity itself fulfils the law,
And who can sever love from charity?

            KING.
Saint Cupid, then! and, soldiers, to the field!
           BEROWNE.
Advance your standards, and upon them, lords;
Pell-mell, down with them! but be first advised,
In conflict that you get the sun of them.
          LONGAVILLE.
Now to plain-dealing; lay these glozes by:
Shall we resolve to woo these girls of France?
            KING.
And win them too: therefore let us devise
Some entertainment for them in their tents.
           BEROWNE.
First, from the park let us conduct them thither;
Then homeward every man attach the hand
Of his fair mistress: in the afternoon
We will with some strange pastime solace them,
Such as the shortness of the time can shape;
For revels, dances, masks and merry hours
Forerun fair Love, strewing her way with flowers.
            KING.
Away, away! no time shall be omitted
That will betime, and may by us be fitted.
           BEROWNE.
Allons! allons! Sow'd cockle reap'd no corn;
    And justice always whirls in equal measure:
Light wenches may prove plagues to men forsworn;
    If so, our copper buys no better treasure.
                  [*Exeunt.*

ACT V. SCENE I.

The same.

Enter HOLOFERNES, SIR NATHANIEL, *and*
          DULL.

         HOLOFERNES.
SATIS *quod sufficit.*
         SIR NATHANIEL.
I praise God for you, sir: your reasons at dinner
have been sharp and sententious; pleasant without
scurrility, witty without affection, audacious without impudency, learned without opinion, and
strange without heresy. I did converse this quondam day with a companion of the king's, who is
intituled, nominated, or call'd, Don Adriano de
Armado.

         HOLOFERNES.
Novi hominem tanquam te: his humour is lofty, his
discourse peremptory, his tongue filed, his eye
ambitious, his gait majestical, and his general behaviour vain, ridiculous, and thrasonical. He is too
pickt, too spruce, too affected, too odd, as it were,
too peregrinate, as I may call it.
         SIR NATHANIEL
A most singular and choice epithet.
              [*Draws out his table-book.*
         HOLOFERNES.
He draweth out the thread of his verbosity finer

than the staple of his argument. I abhor such fana-
tical phantasms, such insociable and point-device
companions; such rackers of orthography, as to
speak dout, fine, when he should say doubt; det,
when he should pronounce debt,—d, e, b, t, not
d, e, t: he clepeth a calf, cauf; half, hauf; neighbour
vocatur nebour; neigh abbreviated ne. This is abhominable,—which he would call abbominable: it
insinuateth me of insanie: *ne intelligis, domine?* to
make frantic, lunatic.

SIR NATHANIEL.

Laus Deo, bone intelligo.

HOLOFERNES.

Bone?—bone for *bene!* Priscian a little scratcht,
'twill serve.

SIR NATHANIEL.

Videsne quis venit?

HOLOFERNES.

Video, et gaudeo.

Enter ARMADO, MOTH, *and* COSTARD.

ARMADO.

Chirrah!   [*To* MOTH.

HOLOFERNES.

Quare chirrah, not sirrah?

ARMADO.

Men of peace, well encounter'd.

HOLOFERNES.

Most military sir, salutation.

MOTH [*aside to* COSTARD].

They have been at a great feast of languages, and
stolen the scraps.

COSTARD.

O, they have lived long on the alms-basket of
words. I marvel thy master hath not eaten thee
for a word; for thou art not so long by the head as
honorificabilitudinitatibus; thou art easier swallow'd than a flap-dragon.

MOTH.

Peace! the peal begins.

ARMADO [*to* HOLOFERNES].

Monsieur, are you not letter'd?

MOTH.

Yes, yes; he teaches boys the horn-book. What is
a, b, spelt backward, with the horn on his head?

HOLOFERNES.

Ba, *pueritia*, with a horn added.

MOTH.

Ba, most silly sheep with a horn. You hear his
learning.

HOLOFERNES.

Quis, quis, thou consonant?

MOTH.

The last of the five vowels, if You repeat them; or
the fifth, if I.

HOLOFERNES.

I will repeat them,—a, e, i,—

MOTH.

The sheep: the other two concludes it,—o, u.

ARMADO.

Now, by the salt wave of the Mediterraneum, a
sweet touch, a quick venue of wit! snip, snap,
quick and home! it rejoiceth my intellect: true wit!

MOTH.

Offer'd by a child to an old man; which is wit-old.

HOLOFERNES.

What is the figure? what is the figure?

MOTH.

Horns.

HOLOFERNES.

Thou disputes like an infant: go, whip thy gig.

MOTH.

Lend me your horn to make one, and I will whip
about your infamy *circum circa*,—a gig of a cuckold's horn.

COSTARD.

An I had but one penny in the world, thou
shouldst have it to buy gingerbread: hold, there is
the very remuneration I had of thy master, thou
halfpenny purse of wit, thou pigeon-egg of discretion. O, an the heavens were so pleased that thou
wert but my bastard, what a joyful father wouldst
thou make me! Go to; thou hast it *ad dunghill*, at
the fingers' ends, as they say.

HOLOFERNES.

O, I smell false Latin; dunghill for *unguem.*

ARMADO.

Arts-man, *præambula*, we will be singled from the
barbarous. Do you not educate youth at the charge-
house on the top of the mountain?

HOLOFERNES.

Or *mons*, the hill.

ARMADO.

At your sweet pleasure, for the mountain.

HOLOFERNES.

I do, sans question.

ARMADO.

Sir, it is the king's most sweet pleasure and affection to congratulate the princess at her pavilion in
the posteriors of this day, which the rude multitude call the afternoon.

HOLOFERNES.

The posterior of the day, most generous sir, is
liable, congruent and measurable for the afternoon: the word is well cull'd, chose, sweet and apt,
I do assure you, sir, I do assure.

ARMADO.

Sir, the king is a noble gentleman, and my familiar,
I do assure ye, very good friend: for what is inward between us, let it pass. I do beseech thee, remember thy courtesy; I beseech thee, apparel thy
head: and among other importunate and most serious designs, and of great import indeed, too, but
let that pass: for I must tell thee, it will please his
Grace, by the world, sometime to lean upon my
poor shoulder, and with his royal finger, thus,
dally with my excrement, with my mustachio; but,
sweet heart, let that pass. By the world, I recount
no fable: some certain special honours it pleaseth
his greatness to impart to Armado, a soldier, a man
of travel, that hath seen the world; but let that
pass. The very all of all is,—but, sweet heart, I do
implore secrecy,—that the king would have me
present the princess, sweet chuck, with some delightful ostentation o show, or pageant, or antick,
or firework. Now, understanding that the curate
and your sweet self are good at such eruptions and
sudden breaking out of mirth, as it were, I have acquainted you withal, to the end to crave your assistance.

HOLOFERNES.

Sir, you shall present before her the Nine Worthies.
Sir Nathaniel, as concerning some entertainment

of time, some show in the posterior of this day, to
be render'd by our assistance, the king's command, and this most gallant, illustrate, and learned
gentleman, before the princess; I say none so fit as
to present the Nine Worthies.

SIR NATHANIEL.

Where will you find men worthy enough to present them?

HOLOFERNES.

Joshua, yourself; myself or this gallant gentleman,
Judas Maccabæus; this swain, because of his great
limb or joint, shall pass Pompey the Great; the
page, Hercules,—

ARMADO.

Pardon, sir; error: he is not quantity enough for
that Worthy's thumb: he is not so big as the end of
his club.

HOLOFERNES.

Shall I have audience? he shall present Hercules in
minority: his enter and exit shall be strangling a
snake; and I will have an apology for that purpose.

MOTH.

An excellent device! so, if any of the audience hiss,
you may cry, 'Well done, Hercules! now thou
crushest the snake!' that is the way to make an offence gracious, though few have the grace to do it.

ARMADO.

For the rest of the Worthies?—

HOLOFERNES.

I will play three myself.

MOTH.

Thrice-worthy gentleman!

ARMADO.

Shall I tell you a thing?

HOLOFERNES.

We attend.

ARMADO.

We will have, if this fadge not, an antick. I beseech you, follow.

HOLOFERNES.

Via, goodman Dull! thou hast spoken no word all
this while.

DULL.

Nor understood none neither, sir.

HOLOFERNES.

Allons! we will employ thee.

DULL.

I'll make one in a dance, or so; or I will play
On the tabor to the Worthies, and let them dance
the hay.

HOLOFERNES.

Most dull, honest Dull! To our sport, away!

[Exeunt.

SCENE II.

The same. Before the Princess's pavilion.

Enter the PRINCESS, KATHARINE, ROSALINE,
and MARIA.

PRINCESS.

SWEET hearts, we shall be rich ere we depart,
If fairings come thus plentifully in:
A lady wall'd about with diamonds!
Look you what I have from the loving king.

ROSALINE.

Madam, came nothing else along with that?

PRINCESS.

Nothing but this! yes, as much love in rime
As would be cramm'd up in a sheet of paper,
Writ o' both sides the leaf, margent and all,
That he was fain to seal on Cupid's name.

ROSALINE.

That was the way to make his godhead wax,
For he hath been five thousand years a boy.

KATHARINE.

Ay, and a shrewd unhappy gallows too.

ROSALINE.

You'll ne'er be friends with him; a' kill'd your
sister.

KATHARINE.

He made her melancholy, sad, and heavy;
And so she died: had she been light, like you,
Of such a merry, nimble, stirring spirit,
She might ha' been a grandam ere she died:
And so may you; for a light heart lives long.

ROSALINE.

What's your dark meaning, mouse, of this light
word?

KATHARINE.

A light condition in a beauty dark.

ROSALINE.

We need more light to find your meaning out.

KATHARINE.

You'll mar the light by taking it in snuff;
Therefore I'll darkly end the argument.

ROSALINE.

Look, what you do, you do it still i' th' dark.

KATHARINE.

So do not you, for you are a light wench.

ROSALINE.

Indeed I weigh not you, and therefore light.

KATHARINE.

You weigh me not? O, that's you care not for me.

ROSALINE.

Great reason; for 'past cure is still past care.'

PRINCESS.

Well bandied both; a set of wit well play'd.
But, Rosaline, you have a favour too:
Who sent it? and what is it?

ROSALINE.

                I would you knew:
An if my face were but as fair as yours,
My favour were as great; be witness this.
Nay, I have verses too, I thank Berowne:
The numbers true; and, were the numb'ring too,
I were the fairest goddess on the ground:
I am compared to twenty thousand fairs.
O, he hath drawn my picture in his letter!

PRINCESS.

Any thing like?

ROSALINE.

Much in the letters; nothing in the praise.

PRINCESS.

Beauteous as ink; a good conclusion.

KATHARINE.

Fair as a text B in a copy-book.

ROSALINE.

'Ware pencils, ho! let me not die your debtor,
My red dominical, my golden letter:
O that your face were not so full of O's!

PRINCESS.

A pox of that jest! and I beshrew all shrows.

But, Katharine, what was sent to you from fair
  Dumaine?

KATHARINE.
Madam, this glove.

PRINCESS.
        Did he not send you twain?

KATHARINE.
Yes, madam, and moreover
Some thousand verses of a faithful lover,
A huge translation of hypocrisy,
Vilely compiled, profound simplicity.

MARIA.
This and these pearls to me sent Longaville:
The letter is too long by half a mile.

PRINCESS.
I think no less. Dost thou not wish in heart
The chain were longer and the letter short?

MARIA.
Ay, or I would these hands might never part.

PRINCESS.
We are wise girls to mock our lovers so.

ROSALINE.
They are worse fools to purchase mocking so.
That same Berowne I'll torture ere I go:
O that I knew he were but in by th' week!
How I would make him fawn and beg and seek
And wait the season and observe the times,
And spend his prodigal wits in bootless rimes,
And shape his service wholly to my hests,
And make him proud to make me proud that jests!
So pertaunt-like would I o'ersway his state
That he should be my fool and I his fate.

PRINCESS.
None are so surely caught, when they are catcht,
As wit turn'd fool: folly, in wisdom hatcht,
Hath wisdom's warrant and the help of school
And wit's own grace to grace a learned fool.

ROSALINE.
The blood of youth burns not with such excess
As gravity's revolt to wantonness.

MARIA.
Folly in fools bears not so strong a note
As foolery in the wise, when wit doth dote;
Since all the power thereof it doth apply
To prove, by wit, worth in simplicity.

PRINCESS.
Here comes Boyet, and mirth is in his face.

Enter BOYET.

BOYET.
O, I am stabb'd with laughter! Where's her Grace?

PRINCESS.
Thy news, Boyet?

BOYET.
        Prepare, madam, prepare!
Arm, wenches, arm! encounters mounted are
Against your peace: Love doth approach disguised,
Armed in arguments; you'll be surprised:
Muster your wits; stand in your own defence;
Or hide your heads like cowards, and fly hence.

PRINCESS.
Saint Denis to Saint Cupid! What are they
That charge their breath against us? say, scout, say.

BOYET.
Under the cool shade of a sycamore
I thought to close mine eyes some half an hour;
When, lo! to interrupt my purposed rest,

Toward that shade I might behold addrest
The king and his companions: warily
I stole into a neighbour thicket by,
And overheard what you shall overhear;
That, by and by, disguised they will be here.
Their herald is a pretty knavish page,
That well by heart hath conn'd his embassage:
Action and accent did they teach him there;
'Thus must thou speak,' and 'thus thy body bear':
And ever and anon they made a doubt
Presence majestical would put him out;
'For,' quoth the king, 'an angel shalt thou see;
Yet fear not thou, but speak audaciously.'
The boy replied, 'An angel is not evil;
I should have fear'd her had she been a devil.'
With that, all laugh and clapt him on the
  shoulder,
Making the bold wag by their praises bolder:
One rubb'd his elbow thus, and fleer'd and swore
A better speech was never spoke before;
Another, with his finger and his thumb,
Cried, 'Via! we will do't, come what will come;'
The third he caper'd, and cried, 'All goes well;'
The fourth turn'd on the toe, and down he fell.
With that, they all did tumble on the ground,
With such a zealous laughter, so profound,
That in this spleen ridiculous appears,
To check their folly, passion's solemn tears.

PRINCESS.
But what, but what, come they to visit us?

BOYET.
They do, they do; and are apparell'd thus,
Like Muscovites or Russians, as I guess.
Their purpose is to parle, to court and dance;
And every one his love-feat will advance
Unto his several mistress, which they'll know
By favours several which they did bestow.

PRINCESS.
And will they so? the gallants shall be taskt;
For, ladies, we will every one be maskt;
And not a man of them shall have the grace,
Despite of suit, to see a lady's face.
Hold, Rosaline, this favour thou shalt wear,
And then the king will court thee for his dear;
Hold, take thou this, my sweet, and give me thine,
So shall Berowne take me for Rosaline.
And change you favours too; so shall your loves
Woo contrary, deceived by these removes.

ROSALINE.
Come on, then; wear the favours most in sight.

KATHARINE.
But in this changing what is your intent?

PRINCESS.
The effect of my intent is to cross theirs:
They do it but in mocking merriment;
And mock for mock is only my intent.
Their several counsels they unbosom shall
To loves mistook, and so be mockt withal
Upon the next occasion that we meet,
With visages display'd, to talk and greet.

ROSALINE.
But shall we dance, if they desire us to't?

PRINCESS.
No, to the death, we will not move a foot;
Nor to their penn'd speech render we no grace,
But while 'tis spoke each turn away her face.

BOYET.

Why, that contempt will kill the speaker's heart,
And quite divorce his memory from his part.

PRINCESS.

Therefore I do it; and I make no doubt
The rest will ne'er come in, if he be out.
There's no such sport as sport by sport o'erthrown,
To make theirs ours and ours none but our own:
So shall we stay, mocking intended game,
And they, well mockt, depart away with shame.

[*Trumpets sound within.*

BOYET.

The trumpet sounds: be maskt; the maskers come.

[*The Ladies mask.*

Enter BLACKAMOORS *with music;* MOTH *with a
speech; the* KING, BEROWNE, LONGAVILLE, *and*
DUMAINE, *disguised as Russians.*

MOTH.

All hail, the richest beauties on the earth!—

BOYET.

Beauties no richer than rich taffeta.

MOTH.

A holy parcel of the fairest dames

[*The Ladies turn their backs to him.*

That ever turn'd their—backs—to mortal views!

BEROWNE [*aside to* MOTH].

Their eyes, villain, their eyes.

MOTH.

That ever turn'd their eyes to mortal views!—
Out—

BOYET.

True; out indeed.

MOTH.

Out of your favours, heavenly spirits, vouchsafe
Not to behold—

BEROWNE [*aside to* MOTH].

Once to behold, rogue.

MOTH.

Once to behold with your sun-beamed eyes,
——with your sun-beamed eyes—

BOYET.

They will not answer to that epithet;
You were best call it 'daughter-beamed eyes.'

MOTH.

They do not mark me, and that brings me out.

BEROWNE.

Is this your perfectness? be gone, you rogue!

[*Exit* MOTH.

ROSALINE.

What would these strangers? know their minds,
Boyet:
If they do speak our language, 'tis our will
That some plain man recount their purposes:
Know what they would.

BOYET.

What would you with the princess?

BEROWNE.

Nothing but peace and gentle visitation.

ROSALINE.

What would they, say they?

BOYET.

Nothing but peace and gentle visitation.

ROSALINE.

Why, that they have; and bid them so be gone.

BOYET.

She says, you have it, and you may be gone.

KING.

Say to her, we have measured many miles
To tread a measure with her on this grass.

BOYET.

They say, that they have measured many a mile
To tread a measure with you on this grass.

ROSALINE.

It is not so. Ask them how many inches
Is in one mile: if they have measured many,
The measure then of one is easily told.

BOYET.

If to come hither you have measured miles,
And many miles, the princess bids you tell
How many inches doth fill up one mile.

BEROWNE.

Tell her, we measure them by weary steps.

BOYET.

She hears herself.

ROSALINE.

       How many weary steps,
Of many weary miles you have o'ergone,
Are number'd in the travel of one mile?

BEROWNE.

We number nothing that we spend for you:
Our duty is so rich, so infinite,
That we may do it still without accompt.
Vouchsafe to show the sunshine of your face,
That we, like savages, may worship it.

ROSALINE.

My face is but a moon, and clouded too.

KING.

Blessed are clouds, to do as such clouds do!
Vouchsafe, bright moon, and these thy stars, to
shine,
Those clouds removed, upon our watery eyne.

ROSALINE.

O vain petitioner! beg a greater matter;
Thou now requests but moonshine in the water.

KING.

Then, in our measure do but vouchsafe one
change.
Thou bid'st me beg; this begging is not strange.

ROSALINE.

Play, music, then! Nay, you must do it soon.

[*Music plays.*

Not yet! no dance! Thus change I like the moon.

KING.

Will you not dance? How come you thus estranged?

ROSALINE.

You took the moon at full, but now she's changed.

KING.

Yet still she is the moon, and I the man.
The music plays; vouchsafe some motion to it.

ROSALINE.

Our ears vouchsafe it.

KING.

       But your legs should do it.

ROSALINE.

Since you are strangers and come here by
chance,
We'll not be nice: take hands. We will not dance.

KING.

Why take we hands, then?

ROSALINE.

       Only to part friends:
Curtsey, sweet hearts; and so the measure ends.

KING.
More measure of this measure; be not nice.
ROSALINE.
We can afford no more at such a price.
KING.
Price you yourselves: what buys your company?
ROSALINE.
Your absence only.
KING.
That can never be.
ROSALINE.
Then cannot we be bought: and so, adieu;
Twice to your visor, and half once to you.
KING.
If you deny to dance, let's hold more chat.
ROSALINE.
In private, then.
KING.
I am best pleased with that.
[They converse apart.
BEROWNE.
White-handed mistress, one sweet word with thee.
PRINCESS.
Honey, and milk, and sugar; there is three.
BEROWNE.
Nay then, two treys, an if you grow so nice,
Metheglin, wort, and malmsey: well run, dice!
There's half-a-dozen sweets.
PRINCESS.
Seventh sweet, adieu:
Since you can cog, I'll play no more with you.
BEROWNE.
One word in secret.
PRINCESS.
Let it not be sweet.
BEROWNE.
Thou grievest my gall.
PRINCESS.
Gall! bitter.
BEROWNE.
Therefore meet.
[They converse apart.
DUMAINE.
Will you vouchsafe with me to change a word?
MARIA.
Name it.
DUMAINE.
Fair lady,—
MARIA.
Say you so? Fair lord,—
Take that for your fair lady.
DUMAINE.
Please it you,
As much in private, and I'll bid adieu.
[They converse apart.
KATHARINE.
What, was your visard made without a tongue?
LONGAVILLE.
I know the reason, lady, why you ask.
KATHARINE.
O for your reason! quickly, sir; I long.
LONGAVILLE.
You have a double tongue within your mask,
And would afford my speechless visard half.
KATHARINE.
Veal, quoth the Dutchman. Is not 'veal' a calf?

LONGAVILLE.
A calf, fair lady!
KATHARINE.
No, a fair lord calf.
LONGAVILLE.
Let's part the word.
KATHARINE.
No, I'll not be your half:
Take all, and wean it; it may prove an ox.
LONGAVILLE.
Look, how you butt yourself in these sharp mocks!
Will you give horns, chaste lady? do not so.
KATHARINE.
Then die a calf, before your horns do grow.
LONGAVILLE.
One word in private with you, ere I die.
KATHARINE.
Bleat softly then; the butcher hears you cry.
[They converse apart.
BOYET.
The tongues of mocking wenches are as keen
As is the razor's edge invisible,
Cutting a smaller hair than may be seen,
Above the sense of sense; so sensible
Seemeth their conference; their conceits have wings
Fleeter than arrows, bullets, wind, thought, swifter
things.
ROSALINE.
Not one word more, my maids; break off, break off.
BEROWNE.
By heaven, all dry-beaten with pure scoff!
KING.
Farewell, mad wenches; you have simple wits.
PRINCESS.
Twenty adieus, my frozen Muscovits
[Exeunt KING, LORDS, and BLACKAMOORS.
Are these the breed of wits so wonder'd at?
BOYET.
Tapers they are, with your sweet breaths puft out.
ROSALINE.
Well-liking wits they have; gross, gross; fat, fat.
PRINCESS.
O poverty in wit, kingly-poor flout!
Will they not, think you, hang themselves to-night?
Or ever, but in visards, show their faces?
This pert Berowne was out of countenance quite.
ROSALINE.
O, they were all in lamentable cases!
The king was weeping-ripe for a good word.
PRINCESS.
Berowne did swear himself out of all suit.
MARIA.
Dumaine was at my service, and his sword:
No point, quoth I; my servant straight was mute.
KATHARINE.
Lord Longaville said, I came o'er his heart;
And trow you what he call'd me?
PRINCESS.
Qualm, perhaps.
KATHARINE.
Yes, in good faith.
PRINCESS.
Go, sickness as thou art!
ROSALINE.
Well, better wits have worn plain statute-caps.
But will you hear? the king is my love sworn.

PRINCESS.
And quick Berowne hath plighted faith to me.
KATHARINE.
And Longaville was for my service born.
MARIA.
Dumaine is mine, as sure as bark on tree.
BOYET.
Madam, and pretty mistresses, give ear:
Immediately they will again be here
In their own shapes; for it can never be
They will digest this harsh indignity.
PRINCESS.
Will they return?
BOYET.
They will, they will, God knows.
And leap for joy, though they are lame with blows:
Therefore change favours; and, when they repair,
Blow like sweet roses in this summer air.
PRINCESS.
How blow? how blow? speak to be understood.
BOYET.
Fair ladies maskt are roses in their bud;
Dismaskt, their damask sweet commixture shown,
Are angels vailing clouds, or roses blown.
PRINCESS.
Avaunt, perplexity! What shall we do,
If they return in their own shapes to woo?
ROSALINE.
Good madam, if by me you'll be advised,
Let's mock them still, as well known as disguised:
Let us complain to them what fools were here,
Disguised like Muscovites, in shapeless gear;
And wonder what they were and to what end
Their shallow shows and prologue vilely penn'd,
And their rough carriage so ridiculous,
Should be presented at our tent to us.
BOYET.
Ladies, withdraw: the gallants are at hand.
PRINCESS.
Whip to our tents, as roes runs o'er land.
[Exeunt PRINCESS, ROSALINE, KATH-
ARINE, and MARIA.
Enter the KING, BEROWNE, LONGAVILLE, and
DUMAINE, in their proper habits.
KING.
Fair sir, God save you! Where's the princess?
BOYET.
Gone to her tent. Please it your majesty
Command me any service to her thither?
KING.
That she vouchsafe me audience for one word.
BOYET.
I will; and so will she, I know, my lord. [Exit.
BEROWNE.
This fellow pecks up wit as pigeons pease,
And utters it again when God doth please:
He is wit's pedlar, and retails his wares
At wakes and wassails, meetings, markets, fairs;
And we that sell by gross, the Lord doth know,
Have not the grace to grace it with such show.
This gallant pins the wenches on his sleeve;
Had he been Adam, he had tempted Eve;
A' can carve too, and lisp: why, this is he
That kist his hand away in courtesy;
This is the ape of form, monsieur the nice,
That, when he plays at tables, chides the dice

In honourable terms: nay, he can sing
A mean most meanly; and in ushering
Mend him who can: the ladies call him sweet;
The stairs, as he treads on them, kiss his feet:
This is the flower that smiles on every one,
To show his teeth as white as whales bone;
And consciences, that will not die in debt,
Pay him the due of honey-tongued Boyet.
KING.
A blister on his sweet tongue, with my heart,
That put Armado's page out of his part!
BEROWNE.
See where it comes! Behaviour, what wert thou
Till this madman show'd thee? and what art thou
now?
Enter the PRINCESS, usher'd by BOYET; ROSA-
LINE, MARIA, and KATHARINE.
KING.
All hail, sweet madam, and fair time of day!
PRINCESS.
'Fair' in 'all hail' is foul, as I conceive.
KING.
Construe my speeches better, if you may.
PRINCESS.
Then wish me better; I will give you leave.
KING.
We came to visit you, and purpose now
To lead you to our court; vouchsafe it then.
PRINCESS.
This field shall hold me; and so hold your vow:
Nor God, nor I, delights in perjured men.
KING.
Rebuke me not for that which you provoke:
The virtue of your eye must break my oath.
PRINCESS.
You nickname virtue; vice you should have spoke;
For virtue's office never breaks men's troth.
Now by my maiden honour, yet as pure
As the unsullied lily, I protest,
A world of torments though I should endure,
I would not yield to be your house's guest;
So much I hate a breaking cause to be
Of heavenly oaths, vow'd with integrity.
KING.
O, you have lived in desolation here,
Unseen, unvisited, much to our shame.
PRINCESS.
Not so, my lord; it is not so, I swear;
We have had pastimes here and pleasant game:
A mess of Russians left us but of late.
KING.
How, madam! Russians!
PRINCESS.
Ay, in truth, my lord;
Trim gallants, full of courtship and of state.
ROSALINE.
Madam, speak true. It is not so, my lord:
My lady, to the manner of the days,
In courtesy gives undeserving praise.
We four indeed confronted were with four
In Russian habit: here they stay'd an hour,
And talkt apace; and in that hour, my lord,
They did not bless us with one happy word.
I dare not call them fools; but this I think,
When they are thirsty, fools would fain have
drink.

BEROWNE.

This jest is dry to me. Fair gentle sweet,
Your wits makes wise things foolish: when we greet,
With eyes best seeing, heaven's fiery eye,
By light we lose light: your capacity
Is of that nature that to your huge store
Wise things seem foolish and rich things but poor.

ROSALINE.

This proves you wise and rich, for in my eye,—

BEROWNE.

I am a fool, and full of poverty.

ROSALINE.

But that you take what doth to you belong,
It were a fault to snatch words from my tongue.

BEROWNE.

O, I am yours, and all that I possess!

ROSALINE.

All the fool mine?

BEROWNE.

I cannot give you less.

ROSALINE.

Which of the visards was it that you wore?

BEROWNE.

Where? when? what visard? why demand you this?

ROSALINE.

There, then, that visard; that superfluous case
That hid the worse and show'd the better face.

KING.

We are descried; they'll mock us now downright.

DUMAINE.

Let us confess and turn it to a jest.

PRINCESS.

Amazed, my lord? why looks your highness sad?

ROSALINE.

Help, hold his brows! he'll swound! Why look you
pale?
Sea-sick, I think, coming from Muscovy.

BEROWNE.

Thus pour the stars down plagues for perjury.
Can any face of brass hold longer out?
Here stand I, lady: dart thy skill at me;
　Bruise me with scorn, confound me with a flout;
Thrust thy sharp wit quite through my ignorance;
　Cut me to pieces with thy keen conceit;
And I will wish thee never more to dance,
　Nor never more in Russian habit wait.
O, never will I trust to speeches penn'd,
　Nor to the motion of a schoolboy's tongue,
Nor never come in visard to my friend,
　Nor woo in rime, like a blind harper's song!
Taffeta phrases, silken terms precise,
　Three-piled hyperboles, spruce affectation,
Figures pedantical; these summer-flies
　Have blown me full of maggot ostentation:
I do forswear them; and I here protest,
　By this white glove,—how white the hand, God
knows!—
Henceforth my wooing mind shall be exprest
　In russet yeas and honest kersey noes:
And, to begin, wench,—so God help me, la!—
My love to thee is sound, sans crack or flaw.

ROSALINE.

Sans sans, I pray you.

BEROWNE.

　　　　Yet I have a trick
Of the old rage: bear with me, I am sick;

I'll leave it by degrees. Soft, let us see:
Write, 'Lord have mercy on us' on those three;
They are infected; in their hearts it lies;
They have the plague, and caught it of your eyes;
These lords are visited; you are not free,
For the Lord's tokens on you do I see.

PRINCESS.

No, they are free that gave these tokens to us.

BEROWNE.

Our states are forfeit: seek not to undo us.

ROSALINE.

It is not so; for how can this be true,
That you stand forfeit, being those that sue?

BEROWNE.

Peace! for I will not have to do with you.

ROSALINE.

Nor shall not, if I do as I intend.

BEROWNE.

Speak for yourselves; my wit is at an end.

KING.

Teach us, sweet madam, for our rude transgression
Some fair excuse.

PRINCESS.

　　　　The fairest is confession.
Were not you here but even now disguised?

KING.

Madam, I was.

PRINCESS.

　　　　And were you well advised?

KING.

I was, fair madam.

PRINCESS.

　　　　When you then were here,
What did you whisper in your lady's ear?

KING.

That more than all the world I did respect her.

PRINCESS.

When she shall challenge this, you will reject her.

KING.

Upon mine honour, no.

PRINCESS.

　　　　Peace, peace! forbear:
Your oath once broke, you force not to forswear.

KING.

Despise me, when I break this oath of mine.

PRINCESS.

I will: and therefore keep it. Rosaline,
What did the Russian whisper in your ear?

ROSALINE.

Madam, he swore that he did hold me dear
As precious eyesight, and did value me
Above this world; adding thereto, moreover,
That he would wed me, or else die my lover.

PRINCESS.

God give thee joy of him! the noble lord
Most honourably doth uphold his word.

KING.

What mean you, madam? by my life, my troth,
I never swore this lady such an oath.

ROSALINE.

By heaven, you did; and to confirm it plain,
You gave me this: but take it, sir, again.

KING.

My faith and this the princess I did give:
I knew her by this jewel on her sleeve.

PRINCESS.
Pardon me, sir, this jewel did she wear;
And Lord Berowne, I thank him, is my dear.
What, will you have me, or your pearl again?
BEROWNE.
Neither of either; I remit both twain.
I see the trick on't: here was a consent,
Knowing aforehand of our merriment,
To dash it like a Christmas comedy:
Some carry-tale, some please-man, some slight
    zany,
Some mumble-news, some trencher-knight, some
    Dick,
That smiles his cheek in years and knows the trick
To make my lady laugh when she's disposed,
Told our intents before; which once disclosed,
The ladies did change favours: and then we,
Following the signs, woo'd but the sign of she.
Now, to our perjury to add more terror,
We are again forsworn, in will and error.
Much upon this it is: and might not you [to BOYET.
Forestall our sport, to make us thus untrue?
Do not you know my lady's foot by th' squier,
    And laugh upon the apple of her eye?
And stand between her back, sir, and the fire,
    Holding a trencher, jesting merrily?
You put our page out: go, you are allow'd;
Die when you will. a smock shall be your shroud.
You leer upon me, do you? there's an eye
Wounds like a leaden sword.
BOYET.
                    Full merrily
Hath this brave manage, this career, been run.
BEROWNE.
Lo, he is tilting straight! Peace! I have done.
Enter COSTARD.
Welcome, pure wit! thou partest a fair fray.
COSTARD.
O Lord, sir, they would know
Whether the three Worthies shall come in or no.
BEROWNE.
What, are there but three?
COSTARD.
                    No, sir; but it is vara fine,
For every one pursents three.
BEROWNE.
                    And three times thrice is nine.
COSTARD.
Not so, sir; under correction, sir; I hope it is not so.
You cannot beg us, sir, I can assure you, sir; we
    know what we know:
hope, sir, three times thrice, sir,—
BEROWNE.
                    —Is not nine.
COSTARD.
Under correction, sir, we know whereuntil it doth
mount.
BEROWNE.
By Jove, I always took three threes for nine.
COSTARD.
O Lord, sir, it were pity you should get your living
by reck'ning, sir.
BEROWNE.
How much is it?
COSTARD.
O Lord, sir, the parties themselves, the actors, sir,

will show whereuntil it doth amount: for mine
own part, I am, as they say, but to parfect one man
in one poor man, Pompey the Great, sir.
BEROWNE.
Art thou one of the Worthies?
COSTARD.
It pleased them to think me worthy of Pompey the
Great: for mine own part, I know not the degree of
the Worthy, but I am to stand for him.
BEROWNE.
Go, bid them prepare.
COSTARD.
We will turn it finely off, sir; we will take some care.
                                        [Exit.
KING.
Berowne, they will shame us: let them not ap-
proach.
BEROWNE.
We are shame-proof, my lord: and 'tis some policy
To have one show worse than the king's and his
company.
KING.
I say they shall not come.
PRINCESS.
Nay, my good lord, let me o'errule you now;
That sport best pleases that doth least know how:
Where zeal strives to content, and the contents
Dies in the zeal of that which it presents:
Their form confounded makes most form in mirth,
When great things labouring perish in their birth.
BEROWNE.
A right description of our sport, my lord.
Enter ARMADO.
ARMADO.
Anointed, I implore so much expense of thy royal
sweet breath as will utter a brace of words.
    [Converses apart with the KING, and de-
    livers him a paper.
PRINCESS.
Doth this man serve God?
BEROWNE.
Why ask you?
PRINCESS.
A' speaks not like a man of God his making.
ARMADO.
That is all one, my fair, sweet, honey monarch; for,
I protest, the schoolmaster is exceeding fantasti-
cal; too too vain, too too vain: but we will put it, as
they say, to fortune de la guerra. I wish you the
peace of mind, most royal couplement!   [Exit.
KING.
Here is like to be a good presence of Worthies. He
presents Hector of Troy; the swain, Pompey the
Great; the parish curate, Alexander; Armado's
page, Hercules; the pedant, Judas Maccabæus:
And if these four Worthies in their first show
    thrive,
These four will change habits, and present the
    other five.
BEROWNE.
There is five in the first show.
KING.
You are deceived; 'tis not so.
BEROWNE.
The pedant, the braggart, the hedge-priest, the
fool and the boy:—

Abate throw at novum, and the whole world again
Cannot pick out five such, take each one in his vein.
KING.
The ship is under sail, and here she comes amain.
Enter COSTARD, *for* POMPEY.
COSTARD.
I Pompey am,—
BOYET.
You lie, you are not he.
COSTARD.
I Pompey am,—
BOYET.
With libbard's head on knee.
BEROWNE.
Well said, old mocker: I must needs be friends
with thee.
COSTARD.
I Pompey am, Pompey surnamed the Big,—
DUMAINE.
The Great.
COSTARD.
It is 'Great,' sir:—
Pompey surnamed the Great;
That oft in field, with targe and shield, did make
my foe to sweat:
And travelling along this coast, I here am come by
chance,
And lay my arms before the legs of this sweet lass
of France.
If your ladyship would say, 'Thanks, Pompey,' I
had done.
PRINCESS.
Great thanks, great Pompey.
COSTARD.
'Tis not so much worth; but I hope I was perfect:
I made a little fault in 'Great.'
BEROWNE.
My hat to a halfpenny, Pompey proves the best
Worthy.
Enter SIR NATHANIEL, *for* ALEXANDER.
SIR NATHANIEL.
When in the world I lived, I was the world's com-
mander;
By east, west, north, and south, I spread my con-
quering might:
My scutcheon plain declares that I am Alisander,—
BOYET.
Your nose says, no, you are not; for it stands too
right.
BEROWNE.
Your nose smells 'no' in this, most tender-smelling
knight.
PRINCESS.
The conqueror is dismay'd. Proceed, good Alexan-
ander.
SIR NATHANIEL.
When in the world I lived, I was the world's com-
mander.
BOYET.
Most true, 'tis right; you were so, Alisander.
BEROWNE.
Pompey the Great,—
COSTARD.
Your servant, and Costard.
BEROWNE.
Take away the conqueror, take away Alisander.

COSTARD [*to* SIR NATHANIEL].
O, sir, you have overthrown Alisander the conqueror! You will be scraped out of the painted
cloth for this: your lion, that holds his poll-axe
sitting on a close-stool, will be given to Ajax: he
will be the ninth Worthy. A conqueror, and afeard
to speak! run away for shame, Alisander. [SIR
NATHANIEL *retires*.] There, an't shall please
you; a foolish mild man; an honest man, look you,
and soon dasht. He is a marvellous good neighbour, faith, and a very good bowler: but, for Ali-
sander,—alas, you see how 'tis,—a little o'er-
parted. But there are Worthies a-coming will
speak their mind in some other sort.
PRINCESS.
Stand aside, good Pompev.
Enter HOLOFERNES, *for* JUDAS; *and* MOTH, *for*
HERCULES.
HOLOFERNES.
Great Hercules is presented by this imp,
    Whose club kill'd Cerberus, that three-headed
        canis;
And when he was a babe, a child, a shrimp,
    Thus did he strangle serpents in his manus.
Quoniam he seemeth in minority,
Ergo I come with this apology.
—Keep some state in thy exit, and vanish.
[MOTH *retires*.
Judas I am,—
DUMAINE.
A Judas!
HOLOFERNES.
Not Iscariot, sir.
Judas I am, ycliped Maccabæus.
DUMAINE.
Judas Maccabæus clipt is plain Judas.
BEROWNE.
A kissing traitor. How art thou proved Judas?
HOLOFERNES.
Judas I am,—
DUMAINE.
The more shame for you, Judas.
HOLOFERNES.
What mean you, sir?
BOYET.
To make Judas hang himself.
HOLOFERNES.
Begin, sir; you are my elder.
BEROWNE.
Well follow'd: Judas was hang'd on an elder.
HOLOFERNES.
I will not be put out of countenance.
BEROWNE.
Because thou hast no face.
HOLOFERNES.
What is this?
BOYET.
A cittern-head.
DUMAINE.
The head of a bodkin.
BEROWNE.
A Death's face in a ring.
LONGAVILLE.
The face of an old Roman coin, scarce seen.
BOYET.
The pommel of Cæsar's falchion.

DUMAINE.
The carved-bone face on a flask.
BEROWNE.
Saint George's half-cheek in a brooch.
DUMAINE.
Ay, and in a brooch of lead.
BEROWNE.
Ay, and worn in the cap of a tooth-drawer.
And now forward; for we have put thee in coun-
tenance.
HOLOFERNES.
You have put me out of countenance.
BEROWNE.
False; we have given thee faces.
HOLOFERNES.
But you have out-faced them all.
BEROWNE.
An thou wert a lion, we would do so.
BOYET.
Therefore, as he is an ass, let him go.
And so adieu, sweet Jude! nay, why dost thou stay?
DUMAINE.
For the latter end of his name.
BEROWNE.
For the ass to the Jude; give it him:—Jud-as, away!
HOLOFERNES.
This is not generous, not gentle, not humble.
BOYET.
A light for Monsieur Judas! it grows dark, he may
stumble.   [HOLOFERNES retires.
PRINCESS.
Alas, poor Maccabæus, how hath he been baited!
Enter ARMADO, for HECTOR.
BEROWNE.
Hide thy head, Achilles: here comes Hector in
arms.
DUMAINE.
Though my mocks come home by me, I will now
be merry.
KING.
Hector was but a Troyan in respect of this.
BOYET.
But is this Hector?
KING.
I think Hector was not so clean-timber'd.
LONGAVILLE.
His leg is too big for Hector's.
DUMAINE.
More calf, certain.
BOYET.
No; he is best indued in the small.
BEROWNE.
This cannot be Hector.
DUMAINE.
He's a god or a painter; for he makes faces.
ARMADO.
The armipotent Mars, of lances the almighty,
Gave Hector a gift,—
DUMAINE.
A gilt nutmeg.
BEROWNE.
A lemon.
LONGAVILLE.
Stuck with cloves.
DUMAINE.
No, cloven.

ARMADO.
Peace!—
The armipotent Mars, of lances the almighty,
    Gave Hector a gift, the heir of Ilion;
A man so breathed, that certain he would fight; yea
    From morn till night, out of his pavilion.
I am that flower,—
DUMAINE.
That mint.
LONGAVILLE.
                        That columbine.
ARMADO.
Sweet Lord Longaville, rein thy tongue.
LONGAVILLE.
I must rather give it the rein, for it runs against
Hector.
DUMAINE.
Ay, and Hector's a greyhound.
ARMADO.
The sweet war-man is dead and rotten; sweet
chucks, beat not the bones of the buried: when he
breathed, he was a man. But I will forward with
my device. [To the PRINCESS] Sweet royalty, be-
stow on me the sense of hearing.
                        [BEROWNE steps forth.
PRINCESS.
Speak, brave Hector: we are much delighted.
ARMADO.
I do adore thy sweet Grace's slipper.
BOYET [aside to DUMAINE].
Loves her by the foot.
DUMAINE [aside to BOYET].
He may not by the yard.
ARMADO.
This Hector far surmounted Hannibal,—
COSTARD.
The party is gone.
Fellow Hector, she is gone; she is two months on
her way.
ARMADO.
What meanest thou?
COSTARD.
Faith, unless you play the honest Troyan, the poor
wench is cast away; she's quick; the child brags in
her belly already: 'tis yours.
ARMADO.
Dost thou infamonize me among potentates? thou
shalt die.
COSTARD.
Then shall Hector be whipped for Jaquenetta that
is quick by him and hang'd for Pompey that is
dead by him.
DUMAINE.
Most rare Pompey!
BOYET.
Renowned Pompey!
BEROWNE.
Greater than great, great, great, great Pompey!
Pompey the Huge!
DUMAINE.
Hector trembles.
BEROWNE.
Pompey is moved. More Ates, more Ates! stir
them on! stir them on!
DUMAINE.
Hector will challenge him.

BEROWNE.

Ay, if a' have no more man's blood in's belly than will sup a flea.

ARMADO.

By the north pole, I do challenge thee.

COSTARD.

I will not fight with a pole, like a northern man: I'll slash; I'll do it by the sword. I bepray you, let me borrow my arms again.

DUMAINE.

Room for the incensed Worthies!

COSTARD.

I'll do it in my shirt.

DUMAINE.

Most resolute Pompey!

MOTH.

Master, let me take you a button-hole lower. Do you not see Pompey is uncasing for the combat? What mean you? You will lose your reputation.

ARMADO.

Gentlemen and soldiers, pardon me; I will not combat in my shirt.

DUMAINE.

You may not deny it: Pompey hath made the challenge.

ARMADO.

Sweet bloods, I both may and will.

BEROWNE.

What reason have you for't?

ARMADO.

The naked truth of it is, I have no shirt; I go woolward for penance.

BOYET

True, and it was enjoin'd him in Rome for want of linen: since when, I'll be sworn, he wore none but a dishclout of Jaquenetta's, and that a' wears next his heart for a favour.

Enter a Messenger, MONSIEUR MERCADÉ.

MERCADÉ.

God save you, madam!

PRINCESS.

Welcome, Mercadé; But that thou interrupt'st our merriment.

MERCADÉ.

I am sorry, madam; for the news I bring Is heavy in my tongue. The king your father—

PRINCESS.

Dead, for my life!

MERCADÉ.

Even so; my tale is told.

BEROWNE.

Worthies, away! the scene begins to cloud.

ARMADO.

For mine own part, I breathe free breath. I have seen the day of wrong through the little hole of discretion, and I will right myself like a soldier.

[*Exeunt* WORTHIES.

KING.

How fares your majesty?

PRINCESS.

Boyet, prepare; I will away to-night.

KING.

Madam, not so; I do beseech you, stay.

PRINCESS.

Prepare, I say, I thank you, gracious lords, For all your fair endeavours; and entreat,

Out of a new-sad soul, that you vouchsafe
In your rich wisdom to excuse or hide
The liberal opposition of our spirits,
If over-boldly we have borne ourselves
In the converse of breath: your gentleness
Was guilty of it. Farewell, worthy lord!
A heavy heart bears not a humble tongue:
Excuse me so, coming too short of thanks
For my great suit so easily obtain'd.

KING.

The extreme pace of time extremely forms
All causes to the purpose of his speed,
And often at his very loose decides
That which long process could not arbitrate:
And though the mourning brow of progeny
Forbid the smiling courtesy of love
The holy suit which fain it would convince,
Yet, since love's argument was first on foot,
Let not the cloud of sorrow justle it
From what it purposed; since, to wail friends lost
Is not by much so wholesome-profitable
As to rejoice at friends but newly found.

PRINCESS.

I understand you not: my griefs are double.

BEROWNE.

Honest plain words best pierce the ear of grief;
And by these badges understand the king.
For your fair sakes have we neglected time,
Play'd foul play with our oaths: your beauty, ladies,
Hath much deform'd us, fashioning our humours
Even to the opposed end of our intents:
And what in us hath seem'd ridiculous,—
As love is full of unbefitting strains,
All wanton as a child, skipping and vain,
Form'd by the eye and therefore, like the eye,
Full of straying shapes, of habits, and of forms,
Varying in subjects as the eye doth roll
To every varied object in his glance:
Which parti-coated presence of loose love
Put on by us, if, in your heavenly eyes,
Have misbecomed our oaths and gravities,
Those heavenly eyes, that look into these faults,
Suggested us to make. Therefore, ladies,
Our love being yours, the error that love makes
Is likewise yours: we to ourselves prove false,
By being once false for ever to be true
To those that make us both,—fair ladies, you:
And even that falsehood, in itself a sin,
Thus purifies itself and turns to grace.

PRINCESS.

We have received your letters full of love;
Your favours, the ambassadors of love;
And, in our maiden council, rated them
At courtship, pleasant jest and courtesy,
As bombast and as lining to the time:
But more devout than this in our respects
Have we not been; and therefore met your loves
In their own fashion, like a merriment.

DUMAINE.

Our letters, madam, show'd much more than jest.

LONGAVILLE.

So did our looks.

ROSALINE.

We did not cote them so.

KING.
Now, at the latest minute of the hour,
Grant us your loves.
PRINCESS.
                    A time, methinks, too short
To make a world-without-end bargain in.
No, no, my lord, your Grace is perjured much,
Full of dear guiltiness; and therefore this:—
If for my love, as there is no such cause,
You will do aught, this shall you do for me:
Your oath I will not trust; but go with speed
To some forlorn and naked hermitage,
Remote from all the pleasures of the world;
There stay until the twelve celestial signs
Have brought about their annual reckoning.
If this austere insociable life
Change not your offer made in heat of blood;
If frosts and fasts, hard lodging and thin weeds
Nip not the gaudy blossoms of your love,
But that it bear this trial and last love;
Then, at the expiration of the year,
Come challenge me, challenge by these deserts,
And, by this virgin palm now kissing thine,
I will be thine; and till that instant shut
My woeful self up in a mourning house,
Raining the tears of lamentation
For the remembrance of my father's death.
If this thou do deny, let our hands part,
Neither intitled in the other's heart.
KING.
If this, or more than this, I would deny,
   To flatter up these powers of mine with rest,
The sudden hand of death close up mine eye!
   Hence hermit then, my heart is in thy breast.
[BEROWNE.
And what to me, my love? and what to me?
ROSALINE.
You must be purged too, your sins are rackt,
You are attaint with faults and perjury;
Therefore if you my favour mean to get,
A twelvemonth shall you spend, and never rest,
But seek the weary beds of people sick.]
DUMAINE.
But what to me, my love? but what to me?
KATHARINE.
A wife?—A beard, fair health, and honesty;
With three-fold love I wish you all these three.
DUMAINE.
O, shall I say, I thank you, gentle wife?
KATHARINE.
Not so, my lord; a twelvemonth and a day
I'll mark no words that smooth-faced wooers
   say:
Come when the king doth to my lady come;
Then, if I have much love, I'll give you some.
DUMAINE.
I'll serve thee true and faithfully till then.
KATHARINE.
Yet swear not, lest ye be forsworn again.
LONGAVILLE.
What says Maria?
MARIA.
                    At the twelvemonth's end
I'll change my black gown for a faithful friend.
LONGAVILLE.
I'll stay with patience; but the time is long.

MARIA.
The liker you; few taller are so young.
BEROWNE.
Studies my lady? mistress, look on me;
Behold the window of my heart, mine eye,
What humble suit attends thy answer there:
Impose some service on me for thy love.
ROSALINE.
Oft have I heard of you, my Lord Berowne,
Before I saw you; and the world's large tongue
Proclaims you for a man replete with mocks,
Full of comparisons and wounding flouts,
Which you on all estates will execute
That lie within the mercy of your wit.
To weed this wormwood from your fruitful brain,
And therewithal to win me, if you please,
Without the which I am not to be won,
You shall this twelvemonth term from day to day
Visit the speechless sick and still converse
With groaning wretches; and your task shall be,
With all the fierce endeavour of your wit
To enforce the pained impotent to smile.
BEROWNE.
To move wild laughter in the throat of death?
It cannot be; it is impossible:
Mirth cannot move a soul in agony.
ROSALINE.
Why, that's the way to choke a gibing spirit,
Whose influence is begot of that loose grace
Which shallow laughing hearers give to fools:
A jest's prosperity lies in the ear
Of him that hears it, never in the tongue
Of him that makes it: then, if sickly ears,
Deaf'd with the clamours of their own dear groans,
Will hear your idle scorns, continue then,
And I will have you and that fault withal;
But if they will not, throw away that spirit,
And I shall find you empty of that fault,
Right joyful of your reformation.
BEROWNE.
A twelvemonth! well; befall what will befall,
I'll jest a twelvemonth in an hospital.
PRINCESS [to the KING].
Ay, sweet my lord; and so I take my leave.
KING.
No, madam; we will bring you on your way.
BEROWNE.
Our wooing doth not end like an old play;
Jack hath not Jill: these ladies' courtesy
Might well have made our sport a comedy.
KING.
Come, sir, it wants a twelvemonth and a day,
And then 'twill end.
BEROWNE.
                    That's too long for a play.
Enter ARMADO.
ARMADO.
Sweet Majesty, vouchsafe me,—
PRINCESS.
Was not that Hector?
DUMAINE.
The worthy knight of Troy.
ARMADO.
I will kiss thy royal finger, and take leave.
I am a votary; I have vow'd to Jaquenetta to hold
the plough for her sweet love three years. But,

most esteem'd greatness, will you hear the dialogue that the two learned men have compiled in praise of the owl and the cuckoo? it should have follow'd in the end of our show.

KING.

Call them forth quickly; we will do so.

ARMADO.

Holla! approach.

Enter HOLOFERNES, SIR NATHANIEL, MOTH, COSTARD. *and others.*

This side is Hiems, Winter, this Ver, the Spring; the one maintain'd by the owl, the other by the cuckoo. Ver, begin.

The Song.

SPRING.

When daisies pied and violets blue,
　　And lady-smocks all silver-white,
And cuckoo-buds of yellow hue
　　Do paint the meadows with delight,
The cuckoo then on every tree
Mocks married men; for thus sings he,
　　　　Cuckoo;
Cuckoo, cuckoo: O word of fear,
Unpleasing to a married ear!

When shepherds pipe on oaten straws
　　And merry larks are ploughmen's clocks,
When turtles tread, and rooks, and daws,
　　And maidens bleach their summer smocks,

The cuckoo then on every tree,
Mocks married men; for thus sings he,
　　　　Cuckoo;
Cuckoo, cuckoo: O word of fear,
Unpleasing to a married ear!

WINTER.

When icicles hang by the wall,
　　And Dick the shepherd blows his nail,
And Tom bears logs into the hall,
　　And milk comes frozen home in pail,
When blood is nipt and ways be foul,
Then nightly sings the staring owl,
　　　　Tu-whit;
Tu-who, a merry note,
While greasy Joan doth keel the pot.

When all aloud the wind doth blow,
　　And coughing drowns the parson's saw,
And birds sit brooding in the snow,
　　And Marian's nose looks red and raw,
When roasted crabs hiss in the bowl,
Then nightly sings the staring owl,
　　　　Tu-whit;
Tu-who, a merry note,
While greasy Joan doth keel the pot.

ARMADO.

The words of Mercury are harsh after the songs of Apollo. You that way: we this way.　　[*Exeunt.*

ROMEO AND JULIET

DRAMATIS PERSONAE

ESCALUS, *prince of Verona.*
PARIS, *a young nobleman, kinsman to the prince.*
MONTAGUE, ⎰ *heads of two houses at variance with*
CAPULET, ⎱ *each other.*
AN OLD MAN, *of the Capulet family.*
ROMEO, *son to Montague.*
MERCUTIO, *kinsman to the prince, and friend to Romeo.*
BENVOLIO, *nephew to Montague, and friend to Romeo.*
TYBALT, *nephew to Lady Capulet.*
FRIAR LAWRENCE, *a Franciscan.*
FRIAR JOHN, *of the same order.*
BALTHASAR, *servant to Romeo.*

SAMPSON, ⎰ *servants to Capulet.*
GREGORY, ⎱
PETER, *servant to Juliet's nurse.*
ABRAHAM, *servant to Montague.*
AN APOTHECARY.
THREE MUSICIANS.
PAGE *to Paris; another* PAGE; *an* OFFICER.
LADY MONTAGUE, *wife to Montague.*
LADY CAPULET, *wife to Capulet.*
JULIET, *daughter to Capulet.*
NURSE *to Juliet.*

CITIZENS *of Verona;* KINSFOLK *of both houses;* MASKERS, GUARDS, WATCHMEN, *and* ATTENDANTS. CHORUS.

SCENE—*Verona; once, in the fifth act, at Mantua.*

PROLOGUE

Enter CHORUS

CHORUS.

TWO households, both alike in dignity,
 In fair Verona, where we lay our scene,
From ancient grudge break to new mutiny,
 Where civil blood makes civil hands unclean.
From forth the fatal loins of these two foes
 A pair of star-crost lovers take their life;
Whose misadventured piteous overthrows
 Doth with their death bury their parents' strife.
The fearful passage of their death-mark'd love,
 And the continuance of their parents' rage,
Which, but their children's end, naught could re-
Is now the two hours' traffic of our stage; [move,
The which if you with patient ears attend,
What here shall miss, our toil shall strive to mend.
[*Exit.*

ACT I. SCENE 1.

Verona. A public place.

Enter SAMPSON *and* GREGORY, *of the house of* CAPULET, *with swords and bucklers.*

SAMPSON.

GREGORY, o' my word, we'll not carry coals.
 GREGORY.
No, for then we should be colliers.
 SAMPSON.
I mean, an we be in choler, we'll draw.
 GREGORY.
Ay, while you live, draw your neck out o' th' collar.
 SAMPSON.
I strike quickly, being moved.
 GREGORY.
But thou art not quickly moved to strike.
 SAMPSON.
A dog of the house of Montague moves me.
 GREGORY.
To move is to stir; and to be valiant is to stand: therefore, if thou art moved, thou runn'st away.
 SAMPSON.
A dog of that house shall move me to stand: I will take the wall of any man or maid of Montague's.
 GREGORY.
That shows thee a weak slave; for the weakest goes to the wall.

SAMPSON.
'Tis true; and therefore women, being the weaker vessels, are ever thrust to the wall:—therefore I will push Montague's men from the wall, and thrust his maids to the wall.
 GREGORY.
The quarrel is between our masters and us their men.
 SAMPSON.
'Tis all one, I will show myself a tyrant: when I have fought with the men, I will be cruel with the maids, and cut off their heads.
 GREGORY.
The heads of the maids?
 SAMPSON.
Ay, the heads of the maids, or their maidenheads; take it in what sense thou wilt.
 GREGORY.
They must take it in sense that feel it.
 SAMPSON.
Me they shall feel while I am able to stand: and 'tis known I am a pretty piece of flesh.
 GREGORY.
'Tis well thou art not fish; if thou hadst, thou hadst been Poor-John.—Draw thy tool; here comes two of the house of the Montagues.

Enter ABRAHAM *and* BALTHASAR, *two* SERVINGMEN *of the* MONTAGUES.

SAMPSON.
My naked weapon is out: quarrel; I will back thee.
 GREGORY.
How! turn thy back and run?
 SAMPSON.
Fear me not.
 GREGORY.
No, marry; I fear thee!
 SAMPSON.
Let us take the law of our sides; let them begin.
 GREGORY.
I will frown as I pass by; and let them take it as they list.
 SAMPSON.
Nay, as they dare. I will bite my thumb at them; which is a disgrace to them, if they bear it.

ABRAHAM.

Do you bite your thumb at us, sir?

SAMPSON.

I do bite my thumb, sir.

ABRAHAM.

Do you bite your thumb at us, sir?

SAMPSON [aside to GREGORY].

Is the law of our side, if I say ay?

GREGORY [aside to SAMPSON].

No.

SAMPSON.

No, sir, I do not bite my thumb at you, sir; but I bite my thumb, sir.

GREGORY.

Do you quarrel, sir?

ABRAHAM.

Quarrel, sir! no, sir.

SAMPSON.

If you do, sir, I am for you; I serve as good a man as you.

ABRAHAM.

No better.

SAMPSON.

Well, sir.

GREGORY [aside to SAMPSON].

Say 'better': here comes one of my master's kinsmen.

SAMPSON.

Yes, better, sir.

ABRAHAM.

You lie.

SAMPSON.

Draw, if you be men.—Gregory, remember thy swashing blow.   [They fight.

Enter BENVOLIO.

BENVOLIO.

Part, fools!   [Beats down their swords.

Put up your swords; you know not what you do.

Enter TYBALT.

TYBALT.

What, art thou drawn among these heartless hinds?

Turn thee, Benvolio, look upon thy death.

BENVOLIO.

I do but keep the peace: put up thy sword,

Or manage it to part these men with me.

TYBALT.

What, drawn, and talk of peace! I hate the word,

As I hate hell, all Montagues, and thee:

Have at thee, coward!   [They fight.

Enter several of both houses, who join the fray; then
enter three or four CITIZENS with clubs.

CITIZENS.

Clubs, bills, and partisans! strike! beat them down!   [gues!

Down with the Capulets! down with the Monta-

Enter old CAPULET in his gown, and
LADY CAPULET.

CAPULET.

What noise is this?—Give me my long sword, ho!

LADY CAPULET.

A crutch, a crutch!—why call you for a sword?

CAPULET.

My sword. I say!—Old Montague is come,

And flourishes his blade in spite of me.

Enter old MONTAGUE and LADY MONTAGUE.

MONTAGUE.

Thou villain Capulet!—Hold me not, let me go.

LADY MONTAGUE.

Thou shalt not stir one foot to seek a foe.

Enter PRINCE ESCALUS with his TRAIN.

PRINCE ESCALUS.

Rebellious subjects, enemies to peace,

Profaners of this neighbour-stained steel,—

Will they not hear?—what, ho! you men, you beasts,

That quench the fire of your pernicious rage

With purple fountains issuing from your veins,—

On pain of torture, from those bloody hands

Throw your mistemper'd weapons to the ground,

And hear the sentence of your moved prince.

Three civil brawls, bred of an airy word,

By thee, old Capulet, and Montague,

Have thrice disturb'd the quiet of our streets;

And made Verona's ancient citizens

Cast-by their grave beseeming ornaments,

To wield old partisans, in hands as old,

Canker'd with peace, to part your canker'd hate:

If ever you disturb our streets again,

Your lives shall pay the forfeit of the peace.

For this time, all the rest depart away:—

You, Capulet, shall go along with me;—

And, Montague, come you this afternoon,

To know our further pleasure in this case,

To old Freetown, our common judgement-place.—

Once more, on pain of death, all men depart.

[Exeunt all but MONTAGUE, LADY MON-
TAGUE, and BENVOLIO.

MONTAGUE.

Who set this ancient quarrel new abroach?—

Speak, nephew, were you by when it began?

BENVOLIO.

Here were the servants of your adversary,

And yours, close fighting, ere I did approach:

I drew to part them: in the instant came

The fiery Tybalt, with his sword prepared;

Which, as he breathed defiance to my ears,

He swung about his head, and cut the winds,

Who, nothing hurt withal, hist him in scorn:

While we were interchanging thrusts and blows,

Came more and more, and fought on part and part,

Till the prince came, who parted either part.

LADY MONTAGUE.

O, where is Romeo?—saw you him to-day?—

Right glad am I he was not at this fray.

BENVOLIO.

Madam, an hour before the worship sun

Peer'd forth the golden window of the east,

A troubled mind drave me to walk abroad;

Where—underneath the grove of sycamore

That westward rooteth from the city's side—

So early walking did I see your son:

Towards him I made; but he was ware of me,

And stole into the covert of the wood:

I, measuring his affections by my own,

Which then most sought where most might not be found,

Being one too many by my weary self,

Pursued my humour, not pursuing his,

And gladly shunn'd who gladly fled from me.

MONTAGUE.
Many a morning hath he there been seen,
With tears augmenting the fresh morning's dew,
Adding to clouds more clouds with his deep sighs:
But all so soon as the all-cheering sun
Should in the farthest east begin to draw
The shady curtains from Aurora's bed,
Away from light steals home my heavy son,
And private in his chamber pens himself;
Shuts up his windows, locks fair daylight out,
And makes himself an artificial night:
Black and portentous must this humour prove,
Unless good counsel may the cause remove.

BENVOLIO.
My noble uncle, do you know the cause?

MONTAGUE.
I neither know it nor can learn of him.

BENVOLIO.
Have you importuned him by any means?

MONTAGUE.
Both by myself and many other friends:
But he, his own affections' counsellor,
Is to himself,—I will not say how true,—
But to himself so secret and so close,
So far from sounding and discovery,
As is the bud bit with an envious worm,
Ere he can spread his sweet leaves to the air,
Or dedicate his beauty to the sun.
Could we but learn from whence his sorrows
      grow,
We would as willingly give cure as know.
      Enter ROMEO.

BENVOLIO.
See, where he comes: so please you, step aside;
I'll know his grievance, or be much denied.

MONTAGUE.
I would thou wert so happy by thy stay
To hear true shrift.—Come, madam, let's away.
      [*Exeunt* MONTAGUE *and* LADY.

BENVOLIO.
Good morrow, cousin.

ROMEO.
            Is the day so young?

BENVOLIO.
But new struck nine.

ROMEO.
            Ay me! sad hours seem long.
Was that my father that went hence so fast?

BENVOLIO.
It was.—What sadness lengthens Romeo's hours?

ROMEO.
Not having that, which having makes them short.

BENVOLIO.
In love?

ROMEO.
Out—

BENVOLIO.
Of love?

ROMEO.
Out of her favour, where I am in love.

BENVOLIO.
Alas, that love, so gentle in his view,
Should be so tyrannous and rough in proof!

ROMEO.
Alas, that love, whose view is muffled still,
Should, without eyes, see pathways to his will!—

Where shall we dine?—O me!—What fray was
      here?
Yet tell me not, for I have heard it all.
Here's much to do with hate, but more with love:
Why, then, O brawling love! O loving hate!
O any thing, of nothing first create!
O heavy lightness! serious vanity!
Mis-shapen chaos of well-seeming forms!
Feather of lead, bright smoke, cold fire, sick
      health!
Still-waking sleep, that is not what it is!—
This love feel I, that feel no love in this.
Dost thou not laugh?

BENVOLIO.
            No, coz, I rather weep.

ROMEO.
Good heart, at what?

BENVOLIO.
            At thy good heart's oppression.

ROMEO.
Why, such is love's transgression.—
Griefs of mine own lie heavy in my breast;
Which thou wilt propagate, to have it prest
With more of thine: this love, that thou hast
      shown,
Doth add more grief to too much of mine own.
Love is a smoke raised with the fume of sighs;
Being purged, a fire sparkling in lovers' eyes;
Being vext, a sea nourisht with lovers' tears:
What is it else? a madness most discreet,
A choking gall, and a preserving sweet.—
Farewell, my coz.

BENVOLIO.
            Soft! I will go along:
An if you leave me so, you do me wrong.

ROMEO.
Tut, I have lost myself; I am not here;
This is not Romeo, he's some other where.

BENVOLIO.
Tell me in sadness, who is that you love.

ROMEO.
What, shall I groan, and tell thee?

BENVOLIO.
            Groan! why, no;
But sadly tell me who.

ROMEO.
Bid a sick man in sadness make his will,—
Ah, word ill urged to one that is so ill!—
In sadness, cousin, I do love a woman.

BENVOLIO.
I aim'd so near, when I supposed you loved.

ROMEO.
A right good mark-man!—And she's fair I love.

BENVOLIO.
A right fair mark, fair coz, is soonest hit.

ROMEO.
Well, in that hit you miss: she'll not be hit
With Cupid's arrow,—she hath Dian's wit;
And, in strong proof of chastity well arm'd,
From love's weak childish bow she lives un-
      harm'd.
She will not stay the siege of loving terms,
Nor bide th'encounter of assailing eyes,
Nor ope her lap to saint-seducing gold:
O, she is rich in beauty; only poor,
That, when she dies, with beauty dies her store.

BENVOLIO.

Then she hath sworn that she will still live
  chaste?

ROMEO.

She hath, and in that sparing makes huge waste;
For beauty, starved with her severity,
Cuts beauty off from all posterity.
She is too fair, too wise; wisely too fair,
To merit bliss by making me despair:
She hath forsworn to love; and in that vow
Do I live dead that live to tell it now.

BENVOLIO.

Be ruled by me, forget to think of her.

ROMEO.

O, teach me how I should forget to think.

BENVOLIO.

By giving liberty unto thine eyes;
Examine other beauties.

ROMEO.

          'Tis the way
To call hers, exquisite, in question more:
These happy masks that kiss fair ladies' brows,
Being black, put us in mind they hide the fair;
He that is strucken blind cannot forget
The precious treasure of his eyesight lost:
Show me a mistress that is passing fair,
What doth her beauty serve, but as a note
Where I may read who past that passing fair?
Farewell: thou canst not teach me to forget.

BENVOLIO.

I'll pay that doctrine, or else die in debt. [Exeunt.

SCENE II.

Th same. A street.

Enter CAPULET, COUNTY PARIS, *and* SERVANT.

CAPULET.

BUT Montague is bound as well as I,
In penalty alike; and 'tis not hard, I think,
For men so old as we to keep the peace.

PARIS.

Of honourable reckoning are you both;
And pity 'tis you lived at odds so long.
But now, my lord, what say you to my suit?

CAPULET.

But saying o'er what I have said before:
My child is yet a stranger to the world,
She hath not seen the change of fourteen years;
Let two more summers wither in their pride
Ere we may think her ripe to be a bride.

PARIS.

Younger than she are happy mothers made.

CAPULET.

And too soon marr'd are those so early made.
The earth hath swallow'd all my hopes but she,
She is the hopeful lady of my earth:
But woo her, gentle Paris, get her heart,
My will to her consent is but a part;
An she agree, within her scope of choice
Lies my consent and fair-according voice.
This night I hold an old-accustom'd feast,
Whereto I have invited many a guest,
Such as I love; and you, among the store,
One more, most welcome, makes my number
  more.

At my poor house look to behold this night
Earth-treading stars that make dark heaven light:
Such comfort as do lusty young men feel
When well-apparell'd April on the heel
Of limping Winter treads, even such delight
Among fresh female buds shall you this night
Inherit at my house; hear all, all see,
And like her most whose merit most shall be:
Which on more view of many, mine, being one,
May stand in number, though in reckoning none.
Come, go with me.—[*to the* SERVANT, *giving him
  a paper*] Go, sirrah, trudge about
Through fair Verona; find those persons out
Whose names are written there, and to them say,
My house and welcome on their pleasure stay.

        [*Exeunt* CAPULET *and* PARIS.

SERVANT.

Find them out whose names are written here! It
is written that the shoemaker should meddle with
his yard, and the tailor with his last, the fisher
with his pencil, and the painter with his nets; but
I am sent to find those persons whose names are
here writ, and can never find what names the
writing person hath here writ. I must to the
learned:—in good time.

Enter BENVOLIO *and* ROMEO.

BENVOLIO.

Tut, man, one fire burns out another's burning,
  One pain is lessen'd by another's anguish;
Turn giddy, and be holp by backward turning;
  One desperate grief cures with another's lan-
    guish:
Take thou some new infection to thy eye,
And the rank poison of the old will die.

ROMEO.

Your plaintain-leaf is excellent for that.

BENVOLIO.

For what, I pray thee?

ROMEO.

         For your broken shin.

BENVOLIO.

Why, Romeo, art thou mad?

ROMEO.

Not mad, but bound more than a madman is;
Shut up in prison, kept without my food,
Whipt and tormented, and—God-den, good
  fellow.

SERVANT.

God gi' god-den.—I pray, sir, can you read?

ROMEO.

Ay, mine own fortune in my misery.

SERVANT.

Perhaps you have learn'd it without book: but, I
pray, can you read any thing you see?

ROMEO.

Ay, if I know the letters and the language.

SERVANT.

Ye say honestly: rest you merry!

ROMEO.

Stay, fellow; I can read.   [*He reads the paper.*
  'Signior Martino and his wife and daughters;
County Anselme and his beauteous sisters; the
lady widow of Vitruvio; Signior Placentio and his
lovely nieces; Mercutio and his brother Valentine; mine uncle Capulet, his wife, and daughters;
my fair niece Rosaline; Livia; Signior Valentio

and his cousin Tybalt; Lucio and the lively
Helena.'   [*Giving back the paper.*
A fair assembly: whither should they come?

SERVANT.

Up.

ROMEO.

Whither?

SERVANT.

To supper to our house.

ROMEO.

Whose house?

SERVANT.

My master's.

ROMEO.

Indeed, I should have askt you that before.

SERVANT.

Now I'll tell you without asking: my master is the
great rich Capulet; and if you be not of the house
of Montagues, I pray, come and crush a cup of
wine. Rest you merry!   [*Exit.*

BENVOLIO.

At this same ancient feast of Capulet's
Sups the fair Rosaline whom thou so lovest;
With all the admired beauties of Verona:
Go thither; and, with unattainted eye,
Compare her face with some that I shall show,
And I will make thee think thy swan a crow.

ROMEO.

When the devout religion of mine eye
   Maintains such falsehood, then turn tears to
     fires;
And these,—who, often drown'd, could never
     die,—
   Transparent heretics, be burnt for liars!
One fairer than my love! the all-seeing sun
Ne'er saw her match since first the world begun.

BENVOLIO.

Tut, you saw her fair, none else being by,
Herself poised with herself in either eye:
But in that crystal scales let there be weigh'd
Your lady-love against some other maid
That I will show you shining at this feast,
And she shall scant show well that now shows
   best.

ROMEO.

I'll go along, no such sight to be shown,
But to rejoice in splendour of mine own. [*Exeunt.*

SCENE III.

The same.   A room in CAPULET'S *house.*

Enter LADY CAPULET *and* NURSE.

LADY CAPULET.

NURSE, where's my daughter? call her forth
   to me.

NURSE.

Now, by my maidenhead,—at twelve year old,—
I bade her come.   What, lamb! what, lady-bird!
God forbid!—where's this girl?—What, Juliet!

Enter JULIET.

JULIET.

How now! who calls?

NURSE.

Your mother.

JULIET.

Madam, I am here, what is your will?

LADY CAPULET.

This is the matter,—nurse, give leave awhile,
We must talk in secret:—nurse, come back again;
I have remember'd me, thou's hear our council.
Thou know'st my daughter's of a pretty age.

NURSE.

Faith, I can tell her age unto an hour.

LADY CAPULET.

She's not fourteen.

NURSE.

I'll lay fourteen of my teeth,—and yet, to my teen
be it spoken, I have but four,—she's not fourteen. How long is it now to Lammas-tide?

LADY CAPULET.

A fortnight and odd days.

NURSE.

Even or odd, of all days in the year,
Come Lammas-eve at night shall she be fourteen.
Susan and she—God rest all Christian souls!—
Were of an age: well, Susan is with God;
She was too good for me:—but, as I said,
On Lammas-eve at night shall she be fourteen;
That shall she, marry; I remember it well.
'Tis since the earthquake now eleven years;
And she was wean'd,—I never shall forget it,—
Of all the days of the year, upon that day:
For I had then laid wormwood to my dug,
Sitting in the sun under the dove-house wall;
My lord and you were then at Mantua:—
Nay, I do bear a brain:—but, as I said,
When it did taste the wormwood on the nipple
Of my dug, and felt it bitter, pretty fool,
To see it tetchy, and fall out with the dug!
Shake, quoth the dove-house: 'twas no need, I
   trow,
To bid me trudge:
And since that time it is eleven years;
For then she could stand high-lone; nay, by th'
   rood,
She could have run and waddled all about;
For even the day before, she broke her brow:
And then my husband—God be with his soul!
A' was a merry man—took up the child:
'Yea,' quoth he, 'dost thou fall upon thy face?
Thou wilt fall backward when thou hast more wit;
Wilt thou not, Jule?' and, by my holidame,
The pretty wretch left crying, and said 'Ay.'
To see, now, how a jest shall come about!
I warrant, an I should live a thousand years,
I never should forget it: 'Wilt thou not, Jule?'
   quoth he;
And, pretty fool, it stinted, and said 'Ay.'

LADY CAPULET.

Enough of this; I pray thee, hold thy peace.

NURSE.

Yes, madam:—yet I cannot choose but laugh,
To think it should leave crying, and say 'Ay':
And yet, I warrant, it had upon it brow
A bump as big as a young cockerel's stone;
A perilous knock; and it cried bitterly:
'Yea,' quoth my husband, 'fall'st upon thy face?
Thou wilt fall backward when thou comest to
   age;
Wilt thou not, Jule?' it stinted, and said 'Ay.'

JULIA.

And stint thou too, I pray thee, nurse, say I.

NURSE.
Peace, I have done. God mark thee to His grace!
Thou wast the prettiest babe that e'er I nursed;
An I might live to see thee married once,
I have my wish.

LADY CAPULET.
Marry, that 'marry' is the very theme
I came to talk of:—tell me, daughter Juliet,
How stands your disposition to be married?

JULIET.
It is an honour that I dream not of.

NURSE.
An honour! were not I thine only nurse,   [teat.
I would say thou hadst suckt wisdom from thy

LADY CAPULET.
Well, think of marriage now; younger than you,
Here in Verona, ladies of esteem,
Are made already mothers: by my count,
I was your mother much upon these years
That you are now a maid. Thus, then, in brief;—
The valiant Paris seeks you for his love.

NURSE.
A man, young lady! lady, such a man
As all the world—why, he's a man of wax.

LADY CAPULET.
Verona's summer hath not such a flower.

NURSE.
Nay, he's a flower; in faith, a very flower.

LADY CAPULET.
What say you? can you love the gentleman?
This night you shall behold him at our feast;
Read o'er the volume of young Paris' face,
And find delight writ there with beauty's pen
Examine every married lineament,
And see how one another lends content;
And what obscured in this fair volume lies
Find written in the margent of his eyes.
This precious book of love, this unbound lover,
To beautify him only lacks a cover:
The fish lives in the sea; and 'tis much pride
For fair without the fair within to hide:
That book in many's eyes doth share the glory,
That in gold clasps locks in the golden story;
So shall you share all that he doth possess,
By having him, making yourself no less.

NURSE.
No less! nay, bigger; women grow by men.

LADY CAPULET.
Speak briefly, can you like of Paris' love?

JULIET.
I'll look to like, if looking liking move:
But no more deep will I endart mine eye
Than your consent gives strength to make it fly.

Enter a SERVANT.

SERVANT.
Madam, the guests are come, supper served up,
you call'd, my young lady askt for, the nurse
curst in the pantry, and every thing in extremity.
I must hence to wait; I beseech you, follow
straight.

LADY CAPULET.
We follow thee. [*Exit* SERVANT.]—Juliet, the
county stays.

NURSE.
Go, girl, seek happy nights to happy days.

[*Exeunt.*

SCENE IV.

The same. A street.

Enter ROMEO, MERCUTIO, BENVOLIO, *with five
or six other* MASKERS, *and* TORCH-BEARERS.

ROMEO.
WHAT, shall this speech be spoke for our
excuse?
Or shall we on without apology?

BENVOLIO.
The date is out of such prolixity:
We'll have no Cupid hoodwinkt with a scarf,
Bearing a Tartar's painted bow of lath,
Scaring the ladies like a crow-keeper;
Nor no without-book prologue, faintly spoke
After the prompter, for our entrance:
But, let them measure us by what they will,
We'll measure them a measure, and be gone.

ROMEO.
Give me a torch, I am not for this ambling;
Being but heavy, I will bear the light.

MERCUTIO.
Nay, gentle Romeo, we must have you dance.

ROMEO.
Not I, believe me: you have dancing-shoes
With nimble soles: I have a soul of lead,
So stakes me to the ground I cannot move.

MERCUTIO.
You are a lover; borrow Cupid's wings,
And soar with them above a common bound.

ROMEO.
I am too sore enpiercèd with his shaft,
To soar with his light feathers; and so bound,
I cannot bound a pitch above dull woe:
Under love's heavy burden do I sink.

MERCUTIO.
And, to sink in it, should you burden love;
Too great oppression for a tender thing.

ROMEO.
Is love a tender thing? it is too rough,
Too rude, too boisterous, and it pricks like thorn

MERCUTIO.
If love be rough with you, be rough with love;
Prick love for pricking, and you beat love
down.—
Give me a case to put my visage in:
                   [*Putting on a mask.*
A visor for a visor!—what care I
What curious eye doth quote deformities?
Here are the beetle-brows shall blush for me.

BENVOLIO.
Come, knock and enter; and no sooner in,
But every man betake him to his legs.

ROMEO.
A torch for me: let wantons, light of heart,
Tickle the senseless rushes with their heels;
For I am proverb'd with a grandsire phrase,—
I'll be a candle-holder, and look on,—
The game was ne'er so fair, and I am done.

MERCUTIO.
Tut, dun's the mouse, the constable's own word:
If thou art Dun, we'll draw thee from the mire
Of this sir-reverence love, wherein thou stick'st
Up to the ears.—Come, we burn daylight, ho!

ROMEO.
Nay, that's not so.

MERCUTIO.
                  I mean, sir, in delay
We waste our lights in vain, like lamps by day.
Take our good meaning, for our judgement sits
Five times in that, ere once in our five wits.
ROMEO.
And we mean well, in going to this mask;
But 'tis no wit to go.
MERCUTIO.
                Why, may one ask?
ROMEO.
I dreamt a dream to-night.
MERCUTIO.
                  And so did I.
ROMEO.
Well, what was yours?
MERCUTIO.
               That dreamers often lie.
ROMEO.
In bed asleep, while they do dream things true.
MERCUTIO.
O, then, I see Queen Mab hath been with you.
She is the fairies' midwife; and she comes
In shape no bigger than an agate-stone
On the fore-finger of an alderman,
Drawn with a team of little atomies
Athwart men's noses as they lie asleep:
Her wagon-spokes made of long spinners' legs;
The cover, of the wings of grasshoppers;
The traces, of the smallest spider's web;
The collars, of the moonshine's watery beams;
Her whip, of cricket's bone; the lash, of film;
Her wagoner, a small gray-coated gnat,
Not half so big as a round little worm
Prickt from the lazy finger of a maid;
Her chariot is an empty hazel-nut,
Made by the joiner squirrel or old grub,
Time out o' mind the fairies' coachmakers.
And in this state she gallops night by night
Through lovers' brains, and then they dream of
    love;   [straight:
O'er courtiers' knees, that dream on court'sies
O'er lawyers' fingers, who straight dream on fees;
O'er ladies' lips, who straight on kisses dream,—
Which oft the angry Mab with blisters plagues,
Because their breaths with sweetmeats tainted
    are:
Sometime she gallops o'er a courtier's nose,
And then dreams he of smelling out a suit;
And sometime comes she with a tithe-pig's tail
Tickling a parson's nose as 'a lies asleep,
Then dreams he of another benefice:
Sometime she driveth o'er a soldier's neck,
And then dreams he of cutting foreign throats,
Of breaches, ambuscadoes, Spanish blades,
Of healths five-fadom deep; and then anon
Drums in his ear, at which he starts, and wakes;
And, being thus frighted, swears a prayer or two,
And sleeps again. This is that very Mab
That plats the manes of horses in the night;
And bakes the elf-locks in foul sluttish hairs,
Which once untangled, much misfortune bodes:
This is the hag, when maids lie on their backs,
That presses them, and learns them first to bear,
Making them women of good carriage:
This is she—

ROMEO.
Peace, peace, Mercutio, peace!
Thou talk'st of nothing.
MERCUTIO.
               True, I talk of dreams.
Which are the children of an idle brain,
Begot of nothing but vain fantasy;
Which is as thin of substance as the air;
And more inconstant than the wind, who wooes
Even now the frozen bosom of the north,
And, being anger'd, puffs away from thence,
Turning his face to the dew-dropping south.
BENVOLIO.
This wind, you talk of, blows us from ourselves;
Supper is done, and we shall come too late.
ROMEO.
I fear, too early: for my mind misgives
Some consequence, yet hanging in the stars,
Shall bitterly begin his fearful date
With this night's revels; and expire the term
Of a despised life, closed in my breast,
By some vile forfeit of untimely death:
But He, that hath the steerage of my course,
Direct my sail!—On, lusty gentlemen!
BENVOLIO.
Strike, drum.
       [*They march about the stage, and exeunt.*

SCENE V.

The same.   A hall in CAPULET'S *house.*

MUSICIANS *waiting.*   SERVING-MEN *come forth*
with their napkins.

FIRST SERVING-MAN.
WHERE'S Potpan, that he helps not to take
away? he shift a trencher! he scrape a
trencher!
SECOND SERVING-MAN.
When good manners shall lie all in one or two
men's hands, and they unwasht too, 'tis a foul
thing.
FIRST SERVING-MAN.
Away with the joint-stools, remove the court-
cupboard, look to the plate:—good thou, save me
a piece of marchpane; and, as thou lovest me, let
the porter let in Susan Grindstone and Nell.—
Antony and Potpan!
SECOND SERVING-MAN.
Ay, boy, ready.
FIRST SERVING-MAN.
You are lookt for and call'd for, askt for and
sought for, in the great chamber.
THIRD SERVING-MAN.
We cannot be here and there too.—Cheerly,
boys; be brisk awhile, and the longer liver take
all.   [*They retire behind.*
Enter CAPULET, LADY CAPULET, JULIET,
TYBALT, *and others of the house, with the*
GUESTS *and* MASKERS.
CAPULET.
Welcome, gentlemen! ladies that have their toes
Unplagued with corns will have a bout with
    you:—
Ah ha, my mistresses! which of you all
Will now deny to dance? she that makes dainty,

She, I'll swear, hath corns; am I come near ye
  now?—
Welcome, gentlemen! I have seen the day
That I have worn a visor; and could tell
A whispering tale in a fair lady's ear,
Such as would please; 'tis gone, 'tis gone, 'tis
  gone:
You are welcome, gentlemen! Come, musicians,
  play.
A hall, a hall! give room! and foot it, girls.—
               [*Music plays, and they dance.*
More light, you knaves; and turn the tables up,
And quench the fire, the room is grown too
  hot.—
Ah, sirrah, this unlookt-for sport comes well.
Nay, sit, nay, sit, good cousin Capulet;
For you and I are past our dancing days:
How long is 't now since last yourself and I
Were in a mask?

> SECOND CAPULET.
>   By 'r lady, thirty years.

> CAPULET.
What, man! 'tis not so much, 'tis not so much:
'Tis since the nuptial of Lucentio,
Come Pentecost as quickly as it will,
Some five-and-twenty years; and then we maskt.

> SECOND CAPULET.
'Tis more, 'tis more: his son is elder, sir;
His son is thirty.

> CAPULET.
>   Will you tell me that?
His son was but a ward two years ago.

> ROMEO [*to a* SERVANT].
What lady's that, which doth enrich the hand
Of yonder knight?

> SERVANT.
I know not, sir.

> ROMEO.
O, she doth teach the torches to burn bright!
Her beauty hangs upon the cheek of night
Like a rich jewel in an Ethiop's ear;
Beauty too rich for use, for earth too dear!
So shows a snowy dove trooping with crows,
As yonder lady o'er her fellows shows.
The measure done, I'll watch her place of stand,
And, touching hers, make blessed my rude hand.
Did my heart love till now? forswear it, sight!
For I ne'er saw true beauty till this night.

> TYBALT.
This, by his voice, should be a Montague:—
Fetch me my rapier, boy:—what, dares the slave
Come hither, cover'd with an antic face,
To fleer and scorn at our solemnity?
Now, by the stock and honour of my kin,
To strike him dead I hold it not a sin.

> CAPULET.
Why, how now, kinsman! wherefore storm you
  so?

> TYBALT.
Uncle, this is a Montague, our foe;
A villain, that is hither come in spite,
To scorn at our solemnity this night.

> CAPULET.
Young Romeo is it?

> TYBALT.
>   'Tis he, that villain Romeo.

> CAPULET.
Content thee, gentle coz, let him alone,
He bears him like a portly gentleman;
And, to say truth, Verona brags of him
To be a virtuous and well-govern'd youth:
I would not for the wealth of all this town
Here in my house do him disparagement:
Therefore be patient, take no note of him,—
It is my will; the which if thou respect,
Show a fair presence, and put off these frowns,
An ill-beseeming semblance for a feast.

> TYBALT.
It fits, when such a villain is a guest:
I'll not endure him.

> CAPULET.
>   He shall be endured:
What, goodman boy!—I say, he shall;—go to;
Am I the master here, or you? go to.
You'll not endure him!—God shall mend my
  soul,
You'll make a mutiny among my guests!
You will set cock-a-hoop! you'll be the man!

> TYBALT.
Why, uncle, 'tis a shame—

> CAPULET.
>   Go to, go to;
You are a saucy boy:—is't so, indeed?—
This trick may chance to scathe you,—I know
  what:
You must contrary me! marry, 'tis time.—
Well said, my hearts!—You are a princox; go:
Be quiet, or—More light, more light!—For
  shame!
I'll make you quiet: what!—Cheerly, my hearts!

> TYBALT.
Patience perforce with wilful choler meeting
Makes my flesh tremble in their different greet-   [ing.
I will withdraw: but this intrusion shall,
Now seeming sweet, convert to bitter gall.   [*Exit.*

> ROMEO [*to* JULIET].
If I profane with my unworthiest hand
  This holy shrine, the gentle fine is this,—
My lips, two blushing pilgrims, ready stand
  To smooth that rough touch with a tender kiss.

> JULIET.
Good pilgrim, you do wrong your hand too much
  Which mannerly devotion shows in this;
For saints have hands that pilgrims' hands do
  touch,
  And palm to palm is holy palmers' kiss.

> ROMEO.
Have not saints lips, and holy palmers too?

> JULIET.
Ay, pilgrim, lips that they must use in prayer.

> ROMEO.
O, then, dear saint, let lips do what hands do;
They pray; grant thou, lest faith turn to despair.

> JULIET.
Saints do not move, though grant for prayers'
  sake.

> ROMEO.
Then move not, while my prayer's effect I take.
Thus from my lips, by yours, my sin is purged.
                 [*Kissing h*

> JULIET.
Then have my lips the sin that they have took.

ROMEO.
Sin from my lips? O trespass sweetly urged!
Give me my sin again.   [*Kissing her again.*
JULIET.
          You kiss by th' book.
NURSE.
Madam, your mother craves a word with you.
ROMEO.
What is her mother?
NURSE.
          Marry, bachelor,
Her mother is the lady of the house,
And a good lady, and a wise and virtuous:
I nursed her daughter, that you talkt withal;
I tell you, he that can lay hold of her
Shall have the chinks.
ROMEO.
          Is she a Capulet?
O dear account! my life is my foe's debt.
BENVOLIO.
Away, be gone; the sport is at the best.
ROMEO.
Ay, so I fear; the more is my unrest.
CAPULET.
Nay, gentlemen, prepare not to be gone;
We have a trifling foolish banquet towards.—
Is it e'en so? why, then, I thank you all;
I thank you, honest gentlemen; good night.—
More torches here!—Come on, then, let's to bed.
[*to* SECOND CAPULET] Ah, sirrah, by my fay, it
     waxes late:
I'll to my rest.
          [*Exeunt all but* JULIET *and* NURSE.
JULIET.
Come hither, nurse. What is yond gentleman?
NURSE.
The son and heir of old Tiberio.
JULIET.
What's he that now is going out of door?
NURSE.
Marry, that, I think, be young Petruchio.
JULIET.
What's he that follows there, that would not dance?
NURSE.
I know not.
JULIET.
Go, ask his name:—if he be married,
My grave is like to be my wedding-bed.
NURSE.
His name is Romeo, and a Montague;
The only son of your great enemy.
JULIET.
My only love sprung from my only hate!
Too early seen unknown, and known too late!
Prodigious birth of love it is to me,
That I must love a loathed enemy.
NURSE.
What's this? what's this?
JULIET.
          A rime I learn'd even now
Of one I danced withal.
          [*One calls within,* Juliet.
NURSE.
          Anon, anon!—
Come, let's away; the strangers all are gone.
          [*Exeunt.*

ACT II.
PROLOGUE.
Enter CHORUS.
CHORUS.

NOW old desire doth in his death-bed lie,
     And young affection gapes to be his heir;
That fair, for which love groan'd for, and would
     die,
     With tender Juliet matcht, is now not fair.
Now Romeo is beloved, and loves again,
     Alike bewitched by the charm of looks;
But to his foe supposed he must complain,
     And she steal love's sweet bait from fearful
          hooks:
Being held a foe, he may not have access
     To breathe such vows as lovers use to swear;
And she as much in love, her means much less
     To meet her new-beloved any where:
But passion lends them power, time means, to
     meet,
Tempering extremities with extreme sweet.
          [*Exit.*

SCENE I.
Verona. CAPULET'S *orchard.*
Enter ROMEO, *alone.*
ROMEO.

CAN I go forward when my heart is here?
     Turn back, dull earth, and find thy centre out.
          [*He leaps the orchard-wall.*
Enter BENVOLIO *with* MERCUTIO.
BENVOLIO.
Romeo! my cousin Romeo!
MERCUTIO.
          He is wise;
And, on my life, hath stoln him home to bed.
BENVOLIO.
He ran this way, and leapt this orchard-wall:
Call, good Mercutio.
MERCUTIO.
          Nay, I'll conjure too.—
Romeo! humours! madman! passion! lover!
Appear thou in the likeness of a sigh:
Speak but one rime, and I am satisfied;
Cry but 'Ay me!' pronounce but 'love' and
     'dove;'
Speak to my gossip Venus one fair word,
One nickname for her purblind son and heir,
Young Adam Cupid, he that shot so trim,
When King Cophetua loved the beggar-maid!—
He heareth not, he stirreth not, he moveth not;
The ape is dead, and I must conjure him.—
I conjure thee by Rosaline's bright eyes,
By her high forehead and her scarlet lip,
By her fine foot, straight leg, and quivering thigh,
And the demesnes that there adjacent lie,
That in thy likeness thou appear to us!
BENVOLIO.
An if he hear thee, thou wilt anger him.
MERCUTIO.
This cannot anger him: 'twould anger him
To raise a spirit in his mistress' circle
Of some strange nature, letting it there stand
Till she had laid it and conjured it down;
That were some spite: my invocation

Is fair and honest, and, in his mistress' name,
I conjure only but to raise up him.

BENVOLIO.

Come, he hath hid himself among these trees,
To be consorted with the humorous night:
Blind is his love, and best befits the dark.

MERCUTIO.

If love be blind, love cannot hit the mark.
Now will he sit under a medlar-tree,
And wish his mistress were that kind of fruit
As maids call medlars, when they laugh alone.—
O, Romeo, that she were, O, that she were
An open *et-cætera*, thou a poperin pear!
Romeo, good night:—I'll to my truckle-bed;
This field-bed is too cold for me to sleep:
Come, shall we go?

BENVOLIO.

         Go, then; for 'tis in vain
To seek him here that means not to be found.

[*Exeunt.*

ROMEO [*coming forward*].

He jests at scars that never felt a wound.—

[JULIET *appears above at a window.*

But, soft! what light through yonder window
    breaks?
It is the east, and Juliet is the sun!—
Arise, fair sun, and kill the envious moon,
Who is already sick and pale with grief,
That thou her maid art far more fair than she:
Be not her maid, since she is envious;
Her vestal livery is but sick and green,
And none but fools do wear it; cast it off.—
It is my lady; O, it is my love!
O, that she knew she were!—
She speaks, yet she says nothing: what of that?
Her eye discourses; I will answer it.—
I am too bold; 'tis not to me she speaks:
Two of the fairest stars in all the heaven,
Having some business, do entreat her eyes
To twinkle in their spheres till they return.
What if her eyes were there, they in her head?
The brightness of her cheek would shame those
    stars,
As daylight doth a lamp; her eyes in heaven
Would through the airy region stream so bright,
That birds would sing, and think it were not
    night.
See, how she leans her cheek upon her hand!
O, that I were a glove upon that hand,
That I might touch that cheek!

JULIET.

         Ay me!

ROMEO.

         She speaks:—
O, speak again, bright angel! for thou art
As glorious to this night, being o'er my head,
As is a winged messenger of heaven
Unto the white-upturned wondering eyes
Of mortals that fall back to gaze on him
When he bestrides the lazy-pacing clouds
And sails upon the bosom of the air.

JULIET.

O Romeo, Romeo! wherefore art thou Romeo?
Deny thy father, and refuse thy name;
Or, if thou wilt not, be but sworn my love,
And I'll no longer be a Capulet.

ROMEO [*aside*].

Shall I hear more, or shall I speak at this?

JULIET.

'Tis but thy name that is my enemy;—
Thou art thyself though, not a Montague.
What's Montague? it is nor hand, nor foot,
Nor arm, nor face, nor any other part
Belonging to a man. O, be some other name!
What's in a name! that which we call a rose
By any other name would smell as sweet;
So Romeo would, were he not Romeo call'd,
Retain that dear perfection which he owes
Without that title:—Romeo, doff thy name;
And for that name, which is no part of thee,
Take all myself.

ROMEO.

         I take thee at thy word:
Call me but love, and I'll be new baptized;
Henceforth I never will be Romeo.

JULIET.

What man art thou, that, thus bescreen'd in night,
So stumblest on my counsel?

ROMEO.

         By a name
I know not how to tell thee who I am:
My name, dear saint, is hateful to myself,
Because it is an enemy to thee;
Had I it written, I would tear the word.

JULIET.

My ears have not yet drunk a hundred words
Of that tongue's utterance, yet I know the sound:
Art thou not Romeo and a Montague?

ROMEO.

Neither, fair saint, if either thee dislike.

JULIET.

How camest thou hither, tell me, and wherefore?
The orchard-walls are high and hard to climb;
And the place death, considering who thou art,
If any of my kinsmen find thee here.

ROMEO.

With love's light wings did I o'er-perch these
    walls;
For stony limits cannot hold love out:
And what love can do, that dares love attempt;
Therefore thy kinsmen are no let to me.

JULIET.

If they do see thee, they will murder thee.

ROMEO.

Alack, there lies more peril in thine eye
Than twenty of their swords: look thou but sweet,
And I am proof against their enmity.

JULIET.

I would not for the world they saw thee here.

ROMEO.

I have night's cloak to hide me from their sight;
And but thou love me, let them find me here:
My life were better ended by their hate
Than death prorogued, wanting of thy love.

JULIET.

By whose direction found'st thou out this place?

ROMEO.

By love, who first did prompt me to inquire;
He lent me counsel, and I lent him eyes.
I am no pilot; yet, wert thou as far
As that vast shore washt with the furthest sea,
I would adventure for such merchandise.

JULIET.

Thou know'st the mask of night is on my face,
Else would a maiden blush depaint my cheek
For that which thou hast heard me speak to-night.
Fain would I dwell on form, fain, fain deny
What I have spoke: but farewell compliment!
Dost thou love me? I know thou wilt say 'Ay';
And I will take thy word: yet, if thou swear'st,
Thou mayst prove false; at lovers' perjuries,
They say, Jove laughs. O gentle Romeo,
If thou dost love, pronounce it faithfully:
Or if thou think'st I am too quickly won,
I'll frown, and be perverse, and say thee nay,
So thou wilt woo; but else, not for the world.
In truth, fair Montague, I am too fond;
And therefore thou mayst think my haviour light:
But trust me, gentleman, I'll prove more true
Than those that have more cunning to be strange.
I should have been more strange, I must confess,
But that thou overheard'st, ere I was ware,
My true love's passion: therefore pardon me;
And not impute this yielding to light love,
Which the dark night hath so discovered.

ROMEO.

Lady, by yonder blessed moon I swear,
That tips with silver all these fruit-tree tops,—

JULIET.

O, swear not by the moon, th'inconstant moon,
That monthly changes in her circled orb,
Lest that thy love prove likewise variable.

ROMEO.

What shall I swear by?

JULIET.

Do not swear at all;
Or, if thou wilt, swear by thy gracious self,
Which is the god of my idolatry,
And I'll believe thee.

ROMEO.

If my heart's dear love—

JULIET.

Well, do not swear: although I joy in thee,
I have no joy of this contract to-night:
It is too rash, too unadvised, too sudden;
Too like the lightning, which doth cease to be
Ere one can say 'It lightens.' Sweet, good night!
This bud of love, by summer's ripening breath,
May prove a beauteous flower when next we meet.
Good night, good night! as sweet repose and rest
Come to thy heart as that within my breast!

ROMEO.

O, wilt thou leave me so unsatisfied?

JULIET.

What satisfaction canst thou have to-night?

ROMEO.

Th'exchange of thy love's faithful vow for mine.

JULIET.

I gave thee mine before thou didst request it:
And yet I would it were to give again.

ROMEO.

Wouldst thou withdraw it? for what purpose,
love?

JULIET.

But to be frank, and give it thee again.
And yet I wish but for the thing I have:
My bounty is as boundless as the sea,
My love as deep; the more I give to thee,

The more I have, for both are infinite.
I hear some noise within; dear love, adieu!—
         [NURSE call within.
Anon, good nurse!—Sweet Montague, be true.
Stay but a little, I will come again.   [Exit above.

ROMEO.

O blessed, blessed night! I am afeard,
Being in night, all this is but a dream,
Too flattering-sweet to be substantial.

Enter JULIET above.

JULIET.

Three words, dear Romeo, and good night indeed.
If that thy bent of love be honourable,
Thy purpose marriage, send me word to-morrow,
By one that I'll procure to come to thee,
Where and what time thou wilt perform the rite;
And all my fortunes at thy foot I'll lay,
And follow thee my lord throughout the world.

NURSE [within].

Madam!

JULIET.

I come, anon:—But if thou mean'st not well,
I do beseech thee—

NURSE [within].

Madam!

JULIET.

By and by, I come:—
To cease thy suit, and leave me to my grief:
To-morrow will I send.

ROMEO.

So thrive my soul—

JULIET.

A thousand times good night!   [Exit above.

ROMEO.

A thousand times the worse, to want thy light.—
Love goes toward love, as schoolboys from their
    books;
But love from love, toward school with heavy
    looks.   [Retiring.

Enter JULIET again.

JULIET.

Hist! Romeo, hist!—O, for a falconer's voice,
To lure this tassel-gentle back again!
Bondage is hoarse, and may not speak aloud;
Else would I tear the cave where Echo lies,
And make her airy tongue more hoarse than mine,
With repetition of my Romeo's name.
Romeo!

ROMEO.

It is my soul that calls upon my name:
How silver-sweet sound lovers' tongues by night,
Like softest music to attending ears!

JULIET.

Romeo!

ROMEO.

My dear?

JULIET.

At what o'clock to-morrow
Shall I send to thee?

ROMEO.

At the hour of nine.

JULIET.

I will not fail: 'tis twenty years till then.
I have forgot why I did call thee back.

ROMEO.

Let me stand here till thou remember it.

JULIET.

I shall forget, to have thee still stand there,
Remembering how I love thy company.

ROMEO.

And I'll still stay, to have thee still forget,
Forgetting any other home but this.

JULIET.

'Tis almost morning; I would have thee gone,—
And yet no further than a wanton's bird,
Who lets it hop a little from her hand,
Like a poor prisoner in his twisted gyves,
And with a silk thread plucks it back again,
So loving-jealous of his liberty.

ROMEO.

I would I were thy bird.

JULIET.

Sweet, so would I:
Yet I should kill thee with much cherishing.
Good night, good night! parting is such sweet
    sorrow,
That I shall say good night till it be morrow.
                        [*Exit above.*

ROMEO.

Sleep dwell upon thine eyes, peace in thy
    breast!—
Would I were sleep and peace, so sweet to rest!
Hence will I to my ghostly father's cell,
His help to crave, and my dear hap to tell.   [*Exit.*

SCENE II.

The same.   FRIAR LAURENCE'S *cell.*

Enter FRIAR LAURENCE, *alone, with a basket.*

FRIAR LAURENCE.

THE gray-eyed morn smiles on the frowning
    night,
Chequering the eastern clouds with streaks of
    light;
And flecked darkness like a drunkard reels
From forth day's path and Titan's fiery wheels:
Now, ere the sun advance his burning eye,
The day to cheer, and night's dank dew to dry,
I must up-fill this osier-cage of ours
With baleful weeds and precious-juicèd flowers.
The earth, that's nature's mother, is her tomb;
What is her burying grave, that is her womb:
And from her womb children of divers kind
We sucking on her natural bosom find;
Many for many virtues excellent,
None but for some, and yet all different.
O, mickle is the powerful grace that lies
In herbs, plants, stones, and their true qualities:
For naught so vile that on the earth doth live,
But to the earth some special good doth give;
Nor aught so good, but, strain'd from that fair
    use,
Revolts from true birth, stumbling on abuse:
Virtue itself turns vice, being misapplied;
And vice sometime's by action dignified.
Within the infant rind of this small flower
Poison hath residence, and medicine power:
For this, being smelt, with that part cheers each
    part;
Being tasted, slays all senses with the heart.
Two such opposèd kings encamp them still
In man as well as herbs,—grace and rude will;

And where the worser is predominant,
Full soon the canker death eats up that plant.

Enter ROMEO.

ROMEO.

Good morrow, father.

FRIAR LAURENCE.

Benedicite!
What early tongue so sweet saluteth me?—
Young son, it argues a distemper'd head
So soon to bid good morrow to thy bed:
Care keeps his watch in every old man's eye,
And where care lodges sleep will never lie;
But where unbruisèd youth with unstuft brain
Doth couch his limbs, there golden sleep doth
    [reign:
Therefore thy earliness doth me assure
Thou art up-rousèd by some distemperature;
Or if not so, then here I hit it right,—
Our Romeo hath not been in bed to-night.

ROMEO.

That last is true; the sweeter rest was mine.

FRIAR LAURENCE.

God pardon sin! wast thou with Rosaline?

ROMEO.

With Rosaline, my ghostly father? no;
I have forgot that name, and that name's woe.

FRIAR LAURENCE.

That's my good son: but where hast thou been,
    then?

ROMEO.

I'll tell thee, ere thou ask it me agen.
I have been feasting with mine enemy;
Where, on a sudden, one hath wounded me,
That's by me wounded: both our remedies
Within thy help and holy physic lies:
I bear no hatred, blessèd man; for, lo,
My intercession likewise steads my foe.

FRIAR LAURENCE.

Be plain, good son, and homely in thy drift;
Riddling confession finds but riddling shrift.

ROMEO.

Then plainly know my heart's dear love is set
On the fair daughter of rich Capulet:
As mine on hers, so hers is set on mine;
And all combined, save what thou must combine
By holy marriage: when, and where, and how,
We met, we woo'd, and made exchange of vow,
I'll tell thee as we pass; but this I pray,
That thou consent to marry us to-day.

FRIAR LAURENCE.

Holy Saint Francis, what a change is here!
Is Rosaline, whom thou didst love so dear,
So soon forsaken? young men's love, then, lies
Not truly in their hearts, but in their eyes.
Jesu Maria, what a deal of brine
Hath washt thy sallow cheeks for Rosaline!
How much salt water thrown away in waste,
To season love, that of it doth not taste!
The sun not yet thy sighs from heaven clears,
Thy old groans ring yet in mine ancient ears;
Lo, here upon thy cheek the stain doth sit
Of an old tear that is not washt off yet:
If e'er thou wast thyself, and these woes thine,
Thou and these woes were all for Rosaline:
And art thou changed? pronounce this sentence,
    then,—
Women may fall, when there's no strength in men.

ROMEO.

Thou chidd'st me oft for loving Rosaline.

FRIAR LAURENCE.

For doting, not for loving, pupil mine.

ROMEO.

And bad'st me bury love.

FRIAR LAURENCE.

Not in a grave,

To lay one in, another out to have.

ROMEO.

I pray thee, chide not: she whom I love now
Doth grace for grace and love for love allow;
The other did not so.

FRIAR LAURENCE.

O, she knew well

Thy love did read by rote, and could not spell.
But come, young waverer, come, go with me,
In one respect I'll thy assistant be;
For this alliance may so happy prove,
To turn your households' rancour to pure love.

ROMEO.

O, let us hence; I stand on sudden haste.

FRIAR LAURENCE.

Wisely, and slow; they stumble that run fast.

[*Exeunt.*

SCENE III.

A street.

Enter BENVOLIO *and* MERCUTIO.

MERCUTIO.

WHY, where the devil should this Romeo
be?—
Came he not home to-night?

BENVOLIO.

Not to his father's; I spoke with his man.

MERCUTIO.

Ah, that same pale hard-hearted wench, that
Rosaline,
Torments him so, that he will sure run mad.

BENVOLIO.

Tybalt, the kinsman to old Capulet,
Hath sent a letter to his father's house.

MERCUTIO.

A challenge, on my life.

BENVOLIO.

Romeo will answer it.

MERCUTIO.

Any man that can write may answer a letter.

BENVOLIO.

Nay, he will answer the letter's master, how he
dares, being dared.

MERCUTIO.

Alas, poor Romeo, he is already dead! stabb'd
with a white wench's black eye; shot through the
ear with a love-song; the very pin of his heart
cleft with the blind bow-boy's butt-shaft; and is
he a man to encounter Tybalt?

BENVOLIO.

Why, what is Tybalt?

MERCUTIO.

More than prince of cats, I can tell you. O, he is
the courageous captain of complements. He fights
as you sing prick-song, keeps time, distance, and
proportion; rests me his minim rest, one, two, and
the third in your bosom: the very butcher of a
silk button, a duellist, a duellist; a gentleman of

the very first house,—of the first and second
cause: ah, the immortal passado! the punto re-
verso! the hay!—

BENVOLIO.

The what?

MERCUTIO.

The pox of such antic, lisping, affecting fantasti-
coes; these new tuners of accents!—'By Jesu, a
very good blade!—a very tall man!—a very good
whore!'—Why, is not this a lamentable thing,
grandsire, that we should be thus afflicted with
these strange flies, these fashion-mongers, these
pardonnez-mois, who stand so much on the new
form that they cannot sit at ease on the old
bench? O, their *bons*, their *bons !*

BENVOLIO.

Here comes Romeo, here comes Romeo.

MERCUTIO.

Without his roe, like a dried herring:—O flesh,
flesh, how art thou fishified!—Now is he for the
numbers that Petrarch flow'd in; Laura, to his
lady, was but a kitchen-wench,—marry, she had
a better love to be-rime her; Dido, a dowdy;
Cleopatra, a gipsy; Helen and Hero, hildings and
harlots; Thisbe, a gray eye or so, but not to the
purpose:—

Enter ROMEO.

Signior Romeo, *bon jour!* there's a French salutation to your French slop. You gave us the counterfeit fairly last night.

ROMEO.

Good morrow to you both. What counterfeit did
I give you?

MERCUTIO.

The slip, sir, the slip; can you not conceive?

ROMEO.

Pardon, good Mercutio, my business was great;
and in such a case as mine a man may strain
courtesy.

MERCUTIO.

That's as much as to say, Such a case as yours
constrains a man to bow in the hams.

ROMEO.

Meaning, to court'sy.

MERCUTIO.

Thou hast most kindly hit it.

ROMEO.

A most courteous exposition.

MERCUTIO.

Nay, I am the very pink of courtesy.

ROMEO.

Pink for flower.

MERCUTIO.

Right.

ROMEO.

Why, then is my pump well-flower'd.

MERCUTIO.

Well said: follow me this jest now, till thou hast
worn out thy pump; that, when the single sole of
it is worn, the jest may remain, after the wearing,
solely singular.

ROMEO.

O single-soled jest, solely singular for the singleness!

MERCUTIO.

Come between us, good Benvolio, for my wits fail.

ROMEO.

Switch and spurs, switch and spurs; or I'll cry a match.

MERCUTIO.

Nay, if thy wits run the wild-goose chase, I have done; for thou hast more of the wild-goose in one of thy wits than, I am sure, I have in my whole five: was I with you there for the goose?

ROMEO.

Thou wast never with me for any thing when thou wast not there for the goose.

MERCUTIO.

I will bite thee by the ear for that jest.

ROMEO.

Nay, good goose, bite not.

MERCUTIO.

Thy wit is a very bitter sweeting; it is a most sharp sauce.

ROMEO.

And is it not well served in to a sweet goose?

MERCUTIO.

O, here's a wit of cheveril, that stretches from an inch narrow to an ell broad!

ROMEO.

I stretch it out for that word 'broad;' which, added to the goose, proves thee far and wide a broad goose.

MERCUTIO.

Why, is not this better now than groaning for love? now art thou sociable, now art thou Romeo; now art thou what thou art, by art as well as by nature: for this drivelling love is like a great natural, that runs lolling up and down to hide his bauble in a hole.

BENVOLIO.

Stop there, stop there.

MERCUTIO.

Thou desirest me to stop in my tale against the hair.

BENVOLIO.

Thou wouldst else have made thy tale large.

MERCUTIO.

O, thou art deceived; I would have made it short: for I was come to the whole depth of my tale; and meant, indeed, to occupy the argument no longer.

ROMEO.

Here's goodly gear!

Enter NURSE *and her man* PETER.

MERCUTIO.

A sail, a sail, a sail!

BENVOLIO.

Two, two; a shirt and a smock.

NURSE.

Peter!

PETER.

Anon?

NURSE.

My fan, Peter.

MERCUTIO.

Good Peter, to hide her face; for her fan's the fairer face.

NURSE.

God ye good morrow, gentlemen.

MERCUTIO.

God ye good den, fair gentlewoman.

NURSE.

Is it good den?

MERCUTIO.

'Tis no less, I tell you; for the bawdy hand of the dial is now upon the prick of noon.

NURSE.

Out upon you! what a man are you!

ROMEO.

One, gentlewoman, that God hath made, for himself to mar.

NURSE.

By my troth, it is well said;—'for himself to mar,' quoth a'?—Gentlemen, can any of you tell me where I may find the young Romeo?

ROMEO.

I can tell you; but young Romeo will be older when you have found him than he was when you sought him: I am the youngest of that name, for fault of a worse.

NURSE.

You say well.

MERCUTIO.

Yea, is the worst well? very well took, i'faith; wisely, wisely.

NURSE.

If you be he, sir, I desire some confidence with you.

BENVOLIO.

She will indite him to some supper.

MERCUTIO.

A bawd, a bawd, a bawd! So-ho!

ROMEO.

What hast thou found?

MERCUTIO.

No hare, sir; unless a hare, sir, in a Lenten pie, that is something stale and hoar ere it be spent.

[*He walks by them and sings.*

An old hare hoar,
And an old hare hoar,
Is very good meat in Lent:
But a hare that is hoar
Is too much for a score,
When it hoars ere it be spent.—

Romeo, will you come to your father's? we'll to dinner thither.

ROMEO.

I will follow you.

MERCUTIO.

Farewell, ancient lady; farewell,—[*singing*] lady, lady, lady. [*Exeunt* MERCUTIO *and* BENVOLIO.

NURSE.

Marry, farewell!—I pray you, sir, what saucy merchant was this, that was so full of his ropery?

ROMEO.

A gentleman, nurse, that loves to hear himself talk, and will speak more in a minute than he will stand to in a month.

NURSE.

An a' speak any thing against me, I'll take him down, an a' were lustier than he is, and twenty such Jacks; and if I cannot, I'll find those that shall. Scurvy knave! I am none of his flirt-gills; I am none of his skains-mates.—And thou [*she turns to* PETER *her man*] must stand by too, and suffer every knave to use me at his pleasure?

PETER.

I saw no man use you at his pleasure; if I had, my weapon should quickly have been out, I warrant you: I dare draw as soon as another man, if I see occasion in a good quarrel, and the law on my side.

NURSE.

Now, afore God, I am so vext, that every part about me quivers. Scurvy knave!—Pray you, sir, a word: and, as I told you, my young lady bade me inquire you out; what she bade me say, I will keep to myself: but first let me tell ye, if ye should lead her into a fool's-paradise, as they say, it were a very gross kind of behaviour, as they say: for the gentlewoman is young; and therefore, if you should deal double with her, truly it were an ill thing to be offer'd to any gentlewoman, and very weak dealing.

ROMEO.

Nurse, commend me to thy lady and mistress. I protest unto thee—

NURSE.

Good heart, and, i'faith, I will tell her as much: Lord, Lord, she will be a joyful woman.

ROMEO.

What wilt thou tell her, nurse? thou dost not mark me.

NURSE.

I will tell her, sir,—that you do protest; which, as I take it, is a gentlemanlike offer.

ROMEO.

Bid her devise some means to come to shrift
This afternoon;
And there she shall at Friar Laurence' cell
Be shrived and married. Here is for thy pains.

NURSE.

No, truly, sir; not a penny.

ROMEO.

Go to, I say you shall.

NURSE.

This afternoon, sir? well, she shall be there.

ROMEO.

And stay, good nurse, behind the abbey-wall:
Within this hour my man shall be with thee,
And bring thee cords made like a tackled stair;
Which to the high top-gallant of my joy
Must be my convoy in the secret night.
Farewell; be trusty, and I'll quite thy pains:
Farewell; commend me to thy mistress.

NURSE.

Now God in heaven bless thee!—Hark you, sir.

ROMEO.

What say'st thou, my dear nurse?

NURSE.

Is your man secret? Did you ne'er hear say,
Two may keep counsel, putting one away?

ROMEO.

I warrant thee, my man's as true as steel.

NURSE.

Well, sir; my mistress is the sweetest lady—
Lord, Lord! when 'twas a little prating thing,—
O, there is a nobleman in town, one Paris, that would fain lay knife aboard; but she, good soul, had as lief see a toad, a very toad, as see him. I anger her sometimes, and tell her that Paris is the properer man; but, I'll warrant you, when I say

so, she looks as pale as any clout in the versal world. Doth not rosemary and Romeo begin both with a letter?

ROMEO.

Ay, nurse; what of that? both with an R.

NURSE.

Ah, mocker! that's the dog's name; R is for the—
No; I know it begins with some other letter:—
and she hath the prettiest sententious of it, of you and rosemary, that it would do you good to hear it.

ROMEO.

Commend me to thy lady.

NURSE.

Ay, a thousand times. [Exit ROMEO.]—Peter!

PETER.

Anon?

NURSE.

Peter, take my fan, and go before.   [Exeunt.

SCENE IV.

The same.   CAPULET'S orchard.

Enter JULIET.

JULIET.

THE clock struck nine when I did send the nurse;
In half an hour she promised to return.
Perchance she cannot meet him:—that's not so.—
O, she is lame! love's heralds should be thoughts,
Which ten times faster glide than the sun's beams,
Driving back shadows over louring hills:
Therefore do nimble-pinion'd doves draw love,
And therefore hath the wind-swift Cupid wings.
Now is the sun upon the highmost hill
Of this day's journey; and from nine till twelve
Is three long hours,—yet she is not come.
Had she affections and warm youthful blood,
She'ld be as swift in motion as a ball;
My words would bandy her to my sweet love,
And his to me:
But old folks, many feign as they were dead;
Unwieldy, slow, heavy and pale as lead.—
O God, she comes!

Enter NURSE and her man PETER.

O honey nurse, what news?
Hast thou met with him? Send thy man away.

NURSE.

Peter, stay at the gate.   [Exit PETER.

JULIET.

Now, good sweet nurse,—O Lord, why look'st thou sad?
Though news be sad, yet tell them merrily;
If good, thou shamest the music of sweet news
By playing it to me with so sour a face.

NURSE.

I am a-weary, give me leave awhile:—
Fie, how my bones ache! what a jaunt have I had!

JULIET.

I would thou hadst my bones, and I thy news:
Nay, come, I pray thee, speak;—good, good nurse, speak.

NURSE.

Jesu, what haste? can you not stay awhile?
Do you not see that I am out of breath?

JULIET.

How art thou out of breath, when thou hast
  breath
To say to me that thou art out of breath?
The excuse that thou dost make in this delay
Is longer than the tale thou dost excuse.
Is thy news good or bad? answer to that;
Say either, and I'll stay the circumstance:
Let me be satisfied, is't good or bad?

NURSE.

Well, you have made a simple choice; you know
not how to choose a man: Romeo! no, not he;
though his face be better than any man's, yet his
leg excels all men's; and for a hand, and a foot,
and a body,—though they be not to be talkt on,
yet they are past compare: he is not the flower of
courtesy, but, I'll warrant him, as gentle as a
lamb.—Go thy ways, wench; serve God.—What,
have you dined at home?

JULIET.

No, no: but all this did I know before.
What says he of our marriage? what of that?

NURSE.

Lord, how my head aches! what a head have I!
It beats as it would fall in twenty pieces.
My back o' t' other side,—ah, my back, my
  back!—
Beshrew your heart for sending me about,
To catch my death with jauncing up and down!

JULIET.

I'faith, I am sorry that thou art not well.   [love?
Sweet, sweet, sweet nurse, tell me, what says my

NURSE.

Your love says, like an honest gentleman, and a
courteous, and a kind, and a handsome, and, I
warrant, a virtuous,—Where is your mother?

JULIET.

Where is my mother!—why, she is within;
Where should she be? How oddly thou repliest!
'Your love says, like an honest gentleman,—
Where is your mother?'

NURSE.

        O God's lady dear!
Are you so hot? marry, come up, I trow;
Is this the poultice for my aching bones?
Henceforward do your messages yourself.

JULIET.

Here's such a coil!—come, what says Romeo?

NURSE.

Have you got leave to go to shrift to-day?

JULIET.

I have.

NURSE.

Then hie you hence to Friar Laurence' cell;
There stays a husband to make you a wife:
Now comes the wanton blood up in your cheeks,
They'll be in scarlet straight at any news.
Hie you to church; I must another way,
To fetch a ladder, by the which your love
Must climb a bird's-nest soon when it is dark:
I am the drudge, and toil in your delight;
But you shall bear the burden soon at night.
Go; I'll to dinner; hie you to the cell.

JULIET.

Hie to high fortune!—Honest nurse, farewell.
                     [Exeunt.

SCENE V.

FRIAR LAURENCE'S *cell.*

Enter FRIAR LAURENCE *and* ROMEO.

FRIAR LAURENCE.

SO smile the heavens upon this holy act,
  That after-hours with sorrow chide us not!

ROMEO.

Amen, amen! but come what sorrow can,
It cannot countervail the exchange of joy
That one short minute gives me in her sight:
Do thou but close our hands with holy words,
Then love-devouring death do what he dare,—
It is enough I may but call her mine.

FRIAR LAURENCE.

These violent delights have violent ends,
And in their triumph die; like fire and powder,
Which, as they kiss, consume: the sweetest honey
Is loathsome in his own deliciousness,
And in the taste confounds the appetite:
Therefore, love moderately; long love doth so;
Too swift arrives as tardy as too slow.—
Here comes the lady:—O, so light a foot
Will ne'er wear out the everlasting flint:
A lover may bestride the gossamer
That idles in the wanton summer air,
And yet not fall; so light is vanity.

Enter JULIET *somewhat fast, and embraceth*
                     ROMEO.

JULIET.

Good even to my ghostly confessor.

FRIAR LAURENCE.

Romeo shall thank thee, daughter, for us both.

JULIET.

As much to him, else is his thanks too much.

ROMEO.

Ah, Juliet, if the measure of thy joy
Be heapt like mine, and that thy skill be more
To blazon it, then sweeten with thy breath
This neighbour air, and let rich music's tongue
Unfold the imagined happiness that both
Receive in either by this dear encounter.

JULIET.

Conceit, more rich in matter than in words,
Brags of his substance, not of ornament:
They are but beggars that can count their worth;
But my true love is grown to such excess,
I cannot sum up sum of half my wealth.

FRIAR LAURENCE.

Come, come with me, and we will make short
  work;
For, by your leaves, you shall not stay alone
Till holy church incorporate two in one.   [*Exeunt*

ACT III. SCENE I.

Verona.   A public place.

Enter MERCUTIO, BENVOLIO, PAGE, *and*
            SERVANTS.

BENVOLIO.

I PRAY thee, good Mercutio, let's retire:
  The day is hot, the Capulets abroad,
And if we meet, we shall not scape a brawl;
For now, these hot days, is the mad blood
  stirring.

MERCUTIO.

Thou art like one of those fellows that, when he enters the confines of a tavern, claps me his sword upon the table, and says, 'God send me no need of thee!' and, by the operation of the second cup, draws it on the drawer, when, indeed, there is no need.

BENVOLIO.

Am I like such a fellow?

MERCUTIO.

Come, come, thou art as hot a Jack in thy mood as any in Italy; and as soon moved to be moody, and as soon moody to be moved.

BENVOLIO.

And what to?

MERCUTIO.

Nay, an there were two such, we should have none shortly, for one would kill the other. Thou! why, thou wilt quarrel with a man that hath a hair more or a hair less in his beard than thou hast: thou wilt quarrel with a man for cracking nuts, having no other reason but because thou hast hazel eyes;—what eye, but such an eye, would spy out such a quarrel? Thy head is as full of quarrels as an egg is full of meat; and yet thy head hath been beaten as addle as an egg for quarrelling: thou hast quarrell'd with a man for coughing in the street, because he hath waken'd thy dog that hath lain asleep in the sun: didst thou not fall out with a tailor for wearing his new doublet before Easter? with another, for tying his new shoes with old riband? and yet thou wilt tutor me from quarrelling!

BENVOLIO.

An I were so apt to quarrel as thou art, any man should buy the fee-simple of my life for an hour and a quarter.

MERCUTIO.

The fee-simple! O simple!

Enter TYBALT *and others.*

BENVOLIO.

By my head, here come the Capulets.

MERCUTIO.

By my heel, I care not.

TYBALT.

Follow me close, for I will speak to them.—
Gentlemen, good den: a word with one of you.

MERCUTIO.

And but one word with one of us? couple it with something; make it a word and a blow.

TYBALT.

You shall find me apt enough to that, sir, an you will give me occasion.

MERCUTIO.

Could you not take some occasion without giving?

TYBALT.

Mercutio, thou consort'st with Romeo,—

MERCUTIO.

Consort! what, dost thou make us minstrels? an thou make minstrels of us, look to hear nothing but discords: here's my fiddlestick; here's that shall make you dance. Zounds, consort!

BENVOLIO.

We talk here in the public haunt of men:
Either withdraw unto some private place,

And reason coldly of your grievances,
Or else depart; here all eyes gaze on us.

MERCUTIO.

Men's eyes were made to look, and let them gaze;
I will not budge for no man's pleasure, I.

TYBALT.

Well, peace be with you, sir:—here comes my man.

Enter ROMEO.

MERCUTIO.

But I'll be hang'd, sir, if he wear your livery:
Marry, go before to field, he'll be your follower;
Your worship in that sense may call him man.

TYBALT.

Romeo, the hate I bear thee can afford
No better term than this,—thou art a villain.

ROMEO.

Tybalt, the reason that I have to love thee
Doth much excuse the appertaining rage
To such a greeting:—villain am I none:
Therefore farewell; I see thou know'st me not.

TYBALT.

Boy, this shall not excuse the injuries   [draw.
That thou hast done me; therefore turn, and

ROMEO.

I do protest I never injured thee;
But love thee better than thou canst devise,
Till thou shalt know the reason of my love:
And so, good Capulet,—which name I tender
As dearly as my own,—be satisfied.

MERCUTIO.

O calm, dishonourable, vile submission!
Alla stoccata carries it away.—   [*Draws.*
Tybalt, you rat-catcher, will you walk?

TYBALT.

What wouldst thou have with me?

MERCUTIO.

Good king of cats, nothing but one of your nine lives; that I mean to make bold withal, and, as you shall use me hereafter, dry-beat the rest of the eight. Will you pluck your sword out of his pilcher by the ears? make haste, lest mine be about your ears ere it be out.

TYBALT.

I am for you.   [*Drawing.*

ROMEO.

Gentle Mercutio, put thy rapier up.

MERCUTIO.

Come, sir, your passado.   [*They fight.*

ROMEO.

Draw, Benvolio; beat down their weapons.—
Gentlemen, for shame, forbear this outrage!
Tybalt,—Mercutio,—the prince expressly hath
Forbidden bandying in Verona streets:—
Hold, Tybalt!—good Mercutio,—

[TYBALT *under* ROMEO'S *arm thrusts* MERCUTIO, *and flies.*

MERCUTIO.

          I am hurt;—
A plague o' both your houses!—I am sped:—
Is he gone, and hath nothing?

BENVOLIO.

         What, art thou hurt?

MERCUTIO.

Ay, ay, a scratch, a scratch; marry, 'tis enough.
Where is my page?—Go, villain, fetch a surgeon.
         [*Exit* PAGE.

ROMEO.
Courage, man; the hurt cannot be much.
MERCUTIO.
No, 'tis not so deep as a well, nor so wide as a
church-door; but 'tis enough, 'twill serve: ask for
me to-morrow, and you shall find me a grave
man. I am pepper'd, I warrant, for this world:—
a plague o' both your houses!—Zounds, a dog, a
rat, a mouse, a cat, to scratch a man to death! a
braggart, a rogue, a villain, that fights by the book
of arithmetic!—Why, the devil, came you be-
tween us? I was hurt under your arm.
ROMEO.
I thought all for the best.
MERCUTIO.
Help me into some house, Benvolio,
Or I shall faint.—A plague o' both your houses!
They have made worms'-meat of me: I have it,
And soundly too:—your houses!
　　　　　[Exit, led by BENVOLIO and SERVANTS.
ROMEO.
This gentleman, the prince's near ally,
My very friend, hath got his mortal hurt
In my behalf; my reputation stain'd
With Tybalt's slander,—Tybalt, that an hour
Hath been my kinsman:—O sweet Juliet,
Thy beauty hath made me effeminate,
And in my temper soften'd valour's steel!
Enter BENVOLIO.
BENVOLIO.
O Romeo, Romeo, brave Mercutio's dead!
That gallant spirit hath aspired the clouds,
Which too untimely here did scorn the earth.
ROMEO.
This day's black fate on more days doth depend;
This but begins the woe others must end.
Enter TYBALT.
BENVOLIO.
Here comes the furious Tybalt back again.
ROMEO.
Alive, in triumph! and Mercutio slain!
Away to heaven respective lenity,
And fire-eyed fury be my conduct now!
Now, Tybalt, take the 'villain' back again
That late thou gavest me; for Mercutio's soul
Is but a little way above our heads,
Staying for thine to keep him company:
Either thou or I, or both, must go with him.
TYBALT.
Thou, wretched boy, that didst consort him
　　here,
Shalt with him hence.
ROMEO.
　　　　　This shall determine that.
　　　　　[They fight; TYBALT falls.
BENVOLIO.
Romeo, away, be gone!
The citizens are up, and Tybalt slain:—
Stand not amazed:—the prince will doom thee
　　death,
If thou art taken:—hence, be gone, away!
ROMEO.
O, I am fortune's fool!
BENVOLIO.
　　　　　Why dost thou stay?
　　　　　[Exit ROMEO.

Enter CITIZENS and OFFICERS.
FIRST OFFICER.
Which way ran he that kill'd Mercutio?
Tybalt, that murderer, which way ran he?
BENVOLIO.
There lies that Tybalt.
FIRST OFFICER.
　　　　　Up, sir, go with me;
I charge thee in the prince's name, obey.
Enter PRINCE, old MONTAGUE, CAPULET, their
　　WIVES and all.
PRINCE ESCALUS.
Where are the vile beginners of this fray?
BENVOLIO.
O noble prince, I can discover all
The unlucky manage of this fatal brawl:
There lies the man, slain by young Romeo,
That slew thy kinsman, brave Mercutio.
LADY CAPULET.
Tybalt, my cousin! O my brother's child!　　[spilt
O prince! O cousin! husband! O, the blood is
Of my dear kinsman! Prince, as thou art true,
For blood of ours shed blood of Montague.—
O cousin, cousin!
PRINCE ESCALUS.
Benvolio, who began this bloody fray?
BENVOLIO.
Tybalt, here slain, whom Romeo's hand did slay;
Romeo, that spoke him fair, bade him bethink
How nice the quarrel was, and urged withal
Your high displeasure:—all this—uttered
With gentle breath, calm look, knees humbly
　　bow'd—
Could not take truce with the unruly spleen
Of Tybalt deaf to peace, but that he tilts
With piercing steel at bold Mercutio's breast;
Who, all as hot, turns deadly point to point,
And, with a martial scorn, with one hand beats
Cold death aside, and with the other sends
It back to Tybalt, whose dexterity
Retorts it: Romeo he cries aloud,　　[his tongue
'Hold, friends! friends, part!' and, swifter than
His agile arm beats down their fatal points,
And 'twixt them rushes; underneath whose arm
An envious thrust from Tybalt hit the life
Of stout Mercutio, and then Tybalt fled:
But by and by comes back to Romeo,
Who had but newly entertain'd revenge,
And to't they go like lightning; for, ere I
Could draw to part them, was stout Tybalt slain
And, as he fell, did Romeo turn and fly:—
This is the truth, or let Benvolio die.
LADY CAPULET.
He is a kinsman to the Montague,
Affection makes him false, he speaks not true:
Some twenty of them fought in this black strife,
And all those twenty could but kill one life.
I beg for justice, which thou, prince, must give;
Romeo slew Tybalt, Romeo must not live.
PRINCE ESCALUS.
Romeo slew him, he slew Mercutio;
Who now the price of his dear blood doth owe?
MONTAGUE.
Not Romeo, prince, he was Mercutio's friend;
His fault concludes but what the law should end,
The life of Tybalt.

PRINCE ESCALUS.
And for that offence
Immediately we do exile him hence:
I have an interest in your hate's proceeding,
My blood for your rude brawls doth lie a-bleed-
ing;
But I'll amerce you with so strong a fine,
That you shall all repent the loss of mine:
I will be deaf to pleading and excuses;
Nor tears nor prayers shall purchase out abuses,
Therefore use none: let Romeo hence in haste,
Else, when he's found, that hour is his last.
Bear hence this body, and attend our will:
Mercy but murders, pardoning those that kill.
[*Exeunt.*

SCENE II.

The same. CAPULET's *orchard.*

Enter JULIET.

JULIET.
GALLOP apace, you fiery-footed steeds,
Towards Phœbus' lodging: such a wagoner
As Phaethon would whip you to the west,
And bring in cloudy night immediately.
Spread thy close curtain, love-performing night,
That runaway's eyes may wink, and Romeo
Leap to these arms untalkt-of and unseen.
Lovers can see to do their amorous rites
By their own beauties; or, if love be blind,
It best agrees with night.—Come, civil night,
Thou sober-suited matron, all in black,
And learn me how to lose a winning match,
Play'd for a pair of stainless maidenhoods:
Hood my unmann'd blood, bating in my cheeks,
With thy black mantle; till strange love, grown
bold,
Think true love acted simple modesty.
Come, night; come, Romeo; come, thou day in
night;
For thou wilt lie upon the wings of night
Whiter than new snow on a raven's back.—
Come, gentle night,—come, loving, black-brow'd
night,
Give me my Romeo; and, when he shall die,
Take him and cut him out in little stars,
And he will make the face of heaven so fine,
That all the world will be in love with night,
And pay no worship to the garish sun.—
O, I have bought the mansion of a love,
But not possest it; and, though I am sold,
Not yet enjoy'd: so tedious is this day,
As is the night before some festival
To an impatient child that hath new robes
And may not wear them.—O, here comes my
nurse,
And she brings news; and every tongue that
speaks
But Romeo's name speaks heavenly eloquence.
Enter NURSE, *wringing her hands, with the ladder
of cords in her lap.*
Now, nurse, what news? What hast thou there?
the cords
That Romeo bid thee fetch?

NURSE.
Ay, ay, the cords.
[*Throws them down.*

JULIET.
Ay me! what news? why dost thou wring thy
hands?

NURSE.
Ah, well-a-day! he's dead, he's dead, he's dead!
We are undone, lady, we are undone!—
Alack the day!—he's gone, he's kill'd, he's dead!

JULIET.
Can heaven be so envious?

NURSE.
Romeo can,
Though heaven cannot:—O Romeo, Romeo!—
Who ever would have thought it?—Romeo!

JULIET.
What devil art thou, that dost torment me thus?
This torture should be roar'd in dismal hell.
Hath Romeo slain himself? say thou but 'I,'
And that bare vowel 'I' shall poison more
Than the death-darting eye of cockatrice:
I am not I, if there be such an 'I;'
Or those eyes shut, that make thee answer 'I.'
If he be slain, say 'I;' or if not, 'no:'
Brief sounds determine of my weal or woe.

NURSE.
I saw the wound, I saw it with mine eyes,—
God save the mark!—here on his manly breast:
A piteous corse, a bloody piteous corse;
Pale, pale as ashes, all bedaub'd in blood,
All in gore-blood:—I swounded at the sight.

JULIET.
O, break, my heart! poor bankrout, break at
once!
To prison, eyes, ne'er look on liberty!
Vile earth, to earth resign; end motion here;
And thou and Romeo press one heavy bier!

NURSE.
O Tybalt, Tybalt, the best friend I had!
O courteous Tybalt! honest gentleman!
That ever I should live to see thee dead!

JULIET.
What storm is this that blows so contrary?
Is Romeo slaughter'd, and is Tybalt dead?
My dear-loved cousin, and my dearer lord?—
Then, dreadful trumpet, sound the general doom!
For who is living, if those two are gone?

NURSE.
Tybalt is gone, and Romeo banished;
Romeo that kill'd him, he is banished.

JULIET.
O God! did Romeo's hand shed Tybalt's blood?

NURSE.
It did, it did; alas the day, it did!

JULIET.
O serpent heart, hid with a flow'ring face!
Did ever dragon keep so fair a cave?
Beautiful tyrant! fiend angelical!
Dove-feather'd raven! wolvish-ravening lamb!
Despised substance of divinest show!
Just opposite to what thou justly seem'st,
A damned saint, an honourable villain!—
O nature, what hadst thou to do in hell,
When thou didst bower the spirit of a fiend
In mortal paradise of such sweet flesh?
Was ever book containing such vile matter
So fairly bound? O, that deceit should dwell
In such a gorgeous palace!

NURSE.
There's no trust,
No faith, no honesty in men; all perjured,
All forsworn, all naught, all dissemblers.—
Ah, where's my man? give me some *aqua-vitæ*:—
These griefs, these woes, these sorrows make me
old.
Shame come to Romeo!
JULIET.
Blister'd be thy tongue
For such a wish! he was not born to shame:
Upon his brow shame is ashamed to sit;
For 'tis a throne where honour may be crown'd
Sole monarch of the universal earth.
O, what a beast was I to chide at him!
NURSE.
Will you speak well of him that kill'd your cousin?
JULIET.
Shall I speak ill of him that is my husband?
Ah, poor my lord, what tongue shall smooth thy
name,
When I, thy three-hours wife, have mangled it?—
But wherefore, villain, didst thou kill my cousin?
That villain cousin would have kill'd my husband:
Back, foolish tears, back to your native spring;
Your tributary drops belong to woe,
Which you, mistaking, offer up to joy.
My husband lives, that Tybalt would have slain;
And Tybalt's dead, that would have slain my hus-
band:
All this is comfort; wherefore weep I, then ?
Some word there was, worser than Tybalt's death,
That murder'd me: I would forget it fain;
But, O, it presses to my memory,
Like damned guilty deeds to sinners' minds:
'Tybalt is dead, and Romeo—banished;'
That 'banished,' that one word ' banished,'
Hath slain ten thousand Tybalts. Tybalt's death
Was woe enough, if it had ended there:
Or,—if sour woe delights in fellowship,
And needly will be rankt with other griefs,—
Why follow'd not, when she said 'Tybalt's dead,
Thy father, or thy mother, nay, or both,
Which modern lamentation might have moved?
But with a rear-ward following Tybalt's death,
'Romeo is banished,'—to speak that word,
Is father, mother, Tybalt, Romeo, Juliet,
All slain, all dead:—'Romeo is banished,'—
There is no end, no limit, measure, bound,
In that word's death; no words can that woe
sound.—
Where is my father, and my mother, nurse?
NURSE.
Weeping and wailing over Tybalt's corse:
Will you go to them? I will bring you thither.
JULIET.
Wash they his wounds with tears: mine shall be
spent,
When theirs are dry, for Romeo's banishment.
Take up those cords:—poor ropes, you are be-
guiled,
Both you and I; for Romeo is exiled:
He made you for a highway to my bed;
But I, a maid, die maiden-widowed.
Come, cords; come, nurse; I'll to my wedding-bed;
And death, not Romeo, take my maidenhead!

NURSE.
Hie to your chamber: I'll find Romeo
To comfort you:—I wot well where he is.
Hark ye, your Romeo will be here at night:
I'll to him; he is hid at Laurence' cell.
JULIET.
O, find him! give this ring to my true knight,
And bid him come to take his last farewell.
[*Exeunt.*

SCENE III.

FRIAR LAURENCE'S *cell.*

Enter FRIAR LAURENCE.

FRIAR LAURENCE.
ROMEO, come forth; come forth, thou fearful
man:
Affliction is enamour'd of thy parts,
And thou art wedded to calamity.
Enter ROMEO.
ROMEO.
Father, what news? what is the prince's doom?
What sorrow craves acquaintance at my hand,
That I yet know not?
FRIAR LAURENCE.
Too familiar
Is my dear son with such sour company:
I bring thee tidings of the prince's doom.
ROMEO.
What less than doomsday is the prince's doom?
FRIAR LAURENCE.
A gentler judgement—'banisht'—from his lips;
Not body's death, but body's banishment.
ROMEO.
Ha, banishment! be merciful, say 'death;'
For exile hath more terror in his look,
Much more than death: do not say 'banishment.'
FRIAR LAURENCE.
Hence from Verona art thou banished:
Be patient, for the world is broad and wide.
ROMEO.
There is no world without Verona walls,
But purgatory, torture, hell itself.
Hence-banished is banisht from the world,
And world's exile is death:—then ' banished'
Is death mis-term'd: calling death ' banished,'
Thou cutt'st my head off with a golden axe,
And smilest upon the stroke that murders me.
FRIAR LAURENCE.
O deadly sin! O rude unthankfulness!
Thy fault our law calls death; but the kind prince
Taking thy part, hath rusht aside the law,
And turn'd that black word death to banishment:
This is dear mercy, and thou seest it not.
ROMEO.
'Tis torture, and not mercy: heaven is here,
Where Juliet lives; and every cat, and dog,
And little mouse, every unworthy thing,
Live here in heaven, and may look on her;
But Romeo may not:—more validity,
More honourable state, more courtship lives
In carrion-flies than Romeo: they may seize
On the white wonder of dear Juliet's hand,
And steal immortal blessing from her lips;
Who, even in pure and vestal modesty,
Still blush, as thinking their own kisses sin;
But Romeo may not,—he is banished:

This may flies do, when I from this must fly:—
And say'st thou yet, that exile is not death?
Hadst thou no poison mixt, no sharp-ground
  knife,
No sudden mean of death, though ne'er so mean,
But 'banished' to kill me,—'banished'?
O friar, the damned use that word in hell;
Howling attends it: how hast thou the heart,
Being a divine, a ghostly confessor,
A sin-absolver, and my friend profest,
To mangle me with that word 'banished'?
     FRIAR LAURENCE.
Thou fond mad man, hear me a little speak.
     ROMEO.
O, thou wilt speak again of banishment.
     FRIAR LAURENCE.
I'll give thee armour to keep off that word;
Adversity's sweet milk, philosophy,
To comfort thee, though thou art banished.
     ROMEO.
Yet 'banished'?—Hang up philosophy!
Unless philosophy can make a Juliet,
Displant a town, reverse a prince's doom,
It helps not, it prevails not: talk no more.
     FRIAR LAURENCE.
O, then I see that madmen have no ears.
     ROMEO.
How should they, when that wise men have no
  eyes?
     FRIAR LAURENCE.
Let me dispute with thee of thy estate.
     ROMEO.
Thou canst not speak of that thou dost not feel:
Wert thou as young as I, Juliet thy love,
An hour but married, Tybalt murdered,
Doting like me, and like me banished,
Then mightst thou speak, then mightst thou tear
  thy hair,
And fall upon the ground, as I do now,
Taking the measure of an unmade grave.
          [NURSE knocks.
     FRIAR LAURENCE.
Arise; one knocks; good Romeo, hide thyself.
     ROMEO.
Not I; unless the breath of heart-sick groans,
Mist-like, infold me from the search of eyes.
          [She knocks again.
     FRIAR LAURENCE.
Hark, how they knock!—Who's there?—Romeo,
  arise;
Thou wilt be taken.—Stay awhile!—Stand up;
          [Knock.
Run to my study.—By and by!—God's will,
What simpleness is this!—I come, I come!
          [Knock.
Who knocks so hard? whence come you? what's
  your will?
     NURSE [within].
Let me come in, and you shall know my errand;
I come from Lady Juliet.
     FRIAR LAURENCE.
       Welcome, then.
     Enter NURSE.
     NURSE.
O holy friar, O, tell me, holy friar,
Where is my lady's lord, where's Romeo?

     FRIAR LAURENCE.
There on the ground, with his own tears made
  drunk.
     NURSE.
O, he is even in my mistress' case,
Just in her case!
     FRIAR LAURENCE.
       O woeful sympathy!
Piteous predicament!
     NURSE.
       Even so lies she,
Blubbering and weeping, weeping and blubber-
  ing.—
Stand up, stand up; stand, an you be a man:
For Juliet's sake, for her sake, rise and stand,
Why should you fall into so deep an O? [He rises.
     ROMEO.
Nurse!—
     NURSE.
Ah sir! ah sir!—Well, death's the end of all.
     ROMEO.
Spakest thou of Juliet? how is it with her?
Doth she not think me an old murderer,
Now I have stain'd the childhood of our joy
With blood removed but little from her own?
Where is she? and how doth she? and what says
My conceal'd lady to our cancell'd love?
     NURSE.
O, she says nothing, sir, but weeps and weeps;
And now falls on her bed; and then starts up,
And Tybalt calls; and then on Romeo cries,
And then down falls again.
     ROMEO.
         As if that name,
Shot from the deadly level of a gun,
Did murder her; as that name's cursed hand
Murder'd her kinsman.—O, tell me, friar, tell me,
In what vile part of this anatomy
Doth my name lodge? tell me, that I may sack
The hateful mansion.
     [He offers to stab himself, and NURSE
     snatches the dagger away
     FRIAR LAURENCE.
       Hold thy desperate hand:
Art thou a man? thy form cries out thou art:
Thy tears are womanish; thy wild acts denote
The unreasonable fury of a beast:
Unseemly woman in a seeming man!
Or ill-beseeming beast in seeming both!
Thou hast amazed me: by my holy order,
I thought thy disposition better temper'd.
Hast thou slain Tybalt? wilt thou slay thyself?
And slay thy lady that in thy life lives,
By doing damned hate upon thyself?
Why rail'st thou on thy birth, the heaven, and
  earth?   [meet
Since birth, and heaven, and earth, all three do
In thee at once; which thou at once wouldst lose.
Fie, fie, thou shamest thy shape, thy love, thy wit;
Which, like a usurer, abound'st in all,
And usest none in that true use indeed
Which should bedeck thy shape, thy love, thy wit:
Thy noble shape is but a form of wax,
Digressing from the valour of a man;
Thy dear love, sworn, but hollow perjury,
Killing that love which thou hast vow'd to cherish;

Thy wit, that ornament to shape and love,
Mis-shapen in the conduct of them both,
Like powder in a skilless soldier's flask,
Is set a-fire by thine own ignorance,
And thou dismember'd with thine own defence.
What, rouse thee, man! thy Juliet is alive,
For whose dear sake thou wast but lately dead;
There art thou happy: Tybalt would kill thee,
But thou slew'st Tybalt; there art thou happy too:
The law, that threaten'd death, becomes thy friend,
And turns it to exile; there art thou happy:
A pack of blessings lights upon thy back;
Happiness courts thee in her best array;
But, like a misbehaved and sullen wench,
Thou pout'st upon thy fortune and thy love:—
Take heed, take heed, for such die miserable.
Go, get thee to thy love, as was decreed,
Ascend her chamber, hence and comfort her:
But look thou stay not till the watch be set,
For then thou canst not pass to Mantua;
Where thou shalt live, till we can find a time
To blaze your marriage, reconcile your friends,
Beg pardon of the prince, and call thee back
With twenty hundred thousand times more joy
Than thou went'st forth in lamentation.—
Go before, nurse: commend me to thy lady;
And bid her hasten all the house to bed,
Which heavy sorrow makes them apt unto:
Romeo is coming.

NURSE.
O Lord, I could have stay'd here all the night
To hear good counsel: O, what learning is!—
My lord, I'll tell my lady you will come.

ROMEO.
Do so, and bid my sweet prepare to chide.

NURSE.
Here is a ring, sir, that she bade me give you:
[NURSE *offers to go in and turns again.*
Hie you, make haste, for it grows very late. [*Exit.*

ROMEO.
How well my comfort is revived by this!

FRIAR LAURENCE.
Go hence; good night; and here stands all your state:—
Either be gone before the watch be set,
Or by the break of day disguised from hence:
Sojourn in Mantua; I'll find out your man,
And he shall signify from time to time
Every good hap to you that chances here:
Give me thy hand; 'tis late: farewell; good night.

ROMEO.
But that a joy past joy calls out on me,
It were a grief so brief to part with thee:
Farewell. [*Exeunt.*

SCENE IV.

The same. A room in CAPULET'S *house.*

Enter old CAPULET, LADY CAPULET, *and*
COUNTY PARIS.

CAPULET.
THINGS have faln out, sir, so unluckily,
   That we have had no time to move our
    daughter:
Look you, she loved her kinsman Tybalt dearly,

And so did I:—well, we were born to die.
'Tis very late, she'll not come down to-night:
I promise you, but for your company,
I would have been a-bed an hour ago.

PARIS.
These times of woe afford no time to woo.—
Madam, good night: commend me to your daughter.

LADY CAPULET.
I will, and know her mind early to-morrow;
To-night she's mew'd up to her heaviness.
[PARIS *offers to go in and* CAPULET *calls him again.*

CAPULET.
Sir Paris, I will make a desperate tender
Of my child's love: I think she will be ruled
In all respects by me; nay, more, I doubt it not.—
Wife, go you to her ere you go to bed;
Acquaint her here of my son Paris' love;
And bid her, mark you me, on Wednesday next—
But, soft! what day is this?

PARIS.
                 Monday, my lord.

CAPULET.
Monday! ha, ha! Well, Wednesday is too soon,
O' Thursday let it be:—o' Thursday, tell her,
She shall be married to this noble earl.—
Will you be ready? do you like this haste?
We'll keep no great ado,—a friend or two;
For, hark you, Tybalt being slain so late,
It may be thought we held him carelessly,
Being our kinsman, if we revel much:
Therefore we'll have some half-a-dozen friends,
And there an end. But what say you to Thursday?

PARIS.
My lord, I would that Thursday were to-morrow.

CAPULET.
Well, get you gone:—o' Thursday be it, then.—
Go you to Juliet ere you go to bed,
Prepare her, wife, against this wedding-day.—
Farewell, my lord.—Light to my chamber, ho!—
Afore me, it is so very late, that we
May call it early by and by:—good night.
[*Exeunt.*

SCENE V.

JULIET'S *chamber.*
Enter ROMEO *and* JULIET *at the window.*

JULIET.
WILT thou be gone? it is not yet near day:
   It was the nightingale, and not the lark,
That pierced the fearful hollow of thine ear;
Nightly she sings on yond pomegranate-tree:
Believe me, love, it was the nightingale.

ROMEO.
It was the lark, the herald of the morn,
No nightingale: look, love, what envious streaks
Do lace the severing clouds in yonder east:
Night's candles are burnt out, and jocund day
Stands tiptoe on the misty mountain tops.
I must be gone and live, or stay and die.

JULIET.
Yond light is not day-light, I know it, I:
It is some meteor that the sun exhales,
To be to thee this night a torch-bearer,

And light thee on thy way to Mantua:
Therefore stay yet,—thou need'st not to be gone.

ROMEO.

Let me be ta'en, let me be put to death;
I am content, so thou wilt have it so.
I'll say yon gray is not the morning's eye,
'Tis but the pale reflex of Cynthia's brow;
Nor that is not the lark, whose notes do beat
The vaulty heaven so high above our heads:
I have more care to stay than will to go:—
Come, death, and welcome! Juliet wills it so.—
How is't, my soul? let's talk,—it is not day.

JULIET.

It is, it is,—hie hence, be gone, away!
It is the lark that sings so out of tune,
Straining harsh discords and unpleasing sharps.
Some say the lark makes sweet division;
This doth not so, for she divideth us:
Some say the lark and loathed toad change eyes;
O, now I would they had changed voices too!
Since arm from arm that voice doth us affray,
Hunting thee hence with hunt's-up to the day.
O, now be gone; more light and light it grows.

ROMEO.

More light and light,—more dark and dark our
woes!

Enter NURSE.

NURSE.

Madam!

JULIET.

Nurse?

NURSE.

Your lady mother is coming to your chamber:
The day is broke; be wary, look about.   [*Exit.*

JULIET.

Then, window, let day in, and let life out.

ROMEO.

Farewell, farewell! one kiss, and I'll descend.
                          [*He goeth down.*

JULIET.

Art thou gone so? my lord, my love, my friend!
I must hear from thee every day in the hour,
For in a minute there are many days:
O, by this count I shall be much in years
Ere I again behold my Romeo!

ROMEO.

Farewell!
I will omit no opportunity
That may convey my greetings, love, to thee.

JULIET.

O, think'st thou we shall ever meet again?

ROMEO.

I doubt it not; and all these woes shall serve
For sweet discourses in our time to come.

JULIET.

O God, I have an ill-divining soul!
Methinks I see thee, now thou art below,
As one dead in the bottom of a tomb:
Either my eyesight fails, or thou look'st pale.

ROMEO.

And trust me, love, in my eye so do you:
Dry sorrow drinks our blood. Adieu, adieu!
                            [*Exit below.*

JULIET.

O fortune, fortune! all men call thee fickle:
If thou art fickle, what dost thou with him

That s renown'd for faith? Be fickle, fortune;
For then, I hope, thou wilt not keep him long,
But send him back.

LADY CAPULET [*within*].

Ho, daughter! are you up?

JULIET.

Who is't that calls? is it my lady mother?
Is she not down so late, or up so early?
What unaccustom'd cause procures her hither?

Enter LADY CAPULET.

LADY CAPULET.

Why, how now, Juliet!

JULIET.

           Madam, I am not well.

LADY CAPULET.

Evermore weeping for your cousin's death?
What, wilt thou wash him from his grave with
tears?
An if thou couldst, thou couldst not make him
live;
Therefore have done: some grief shows much of
love;
But much of grief shows still some want of wit.

JULIET.

Yet let me weep for such a feeling loss.

LADY CAPULET.

So shall you feel the loss, but not the friend
Which you weep for.

JULIET.

          Feeling so the loss,
I cannot choose but ever weep the friend.

LADY CAPULET.

Well, girl, thou weep'st not so much for his death,
As that the villain lives which slaughter'd him.

JULIET.

What villain, madam?

LADY CAPULET.

          That same villain, Romeo.

JULIET [*aside*].

Villain and he be many miles asunder.—
God pardon him! I do, with all my heart;
And yet no man like he doth grieve my heart.

LADY CAPULET.

That is, because the traitor murderer lives.

JULIET.

Ay, madam, from the reach of these my hands:—
Would none but I might venge my cousin's
death!

LADY CAPULET.

We will have vengeance for it, fear thou not:
Then weep no more. I'll send to one in Mantua,—
Where that same banisht runagate doth live,—
Shall give him such an unaccustom'd dram,
That he shall soon keep Tybalt company:
And then, I hope, thou wilt be satisfied.

JULIET.

Indeed, I never shall be satisfied
With Romeo, till I behold him—dead—
Is my poor heart so for a kinsman vext:
Madam, if you could find out but a man
To bear a poison, I would temper it;
That Romeo should, upon receipt thereof,
Soon sleep in quiet. O, how my heart abhors
To hear him named,—and cannot come to him,
To wreak the love I bore my cousin Tybalt
Upon his body that hath slaughter'd him!

LADY CAPULET.
Find thou the means, and I'll find such a man.
But now I'll tell thee joyful tidings, girl.
JULIET.
And joy comes well in such a needful time:
What are they, I beseech your ladyship?
LADY CAPULET.
Well, well, thou hast a careful father, child;
One who, to put thee from thy heaviness,
Hath sorted out a sudden day of joy,
That thou expect'st not, nor I lookt not for.
JULIET.
Madam, in happy time, what day is that?
LADY CAPULET.
Marry, my child, early next Thursday morn,
The gallant, young, and noble gentleman,
The County Paris, at Saint Peter's Church,
Shall happily make thee there a joyful bride.
JULIET.
Now, by Saint Peter's Church, and Peter too,
He shall not make me there a joyful bride.
I wonder at this haste; that I must wed
Ere he, that should be husband, comes to woo.
I pray you, tell my lord and father, madam,
I will not marry yet; and when I do, I swear
It shall be Romeo, whom you know I hate,
Rather than Paris:—these are news indeed!
LADY CAPULET.
Here comes your father; tell him so yourself,
And see how he will take it at your hands.

Enter CAPULET *and* NURSE.

CAPULET.
When the sun sets, the air doth drizzle dew;
But for the sunset of my brother's son
It rains downright.—
How now! a conduit, girl? what, still in tears?
Evermore show'ring? In one little body
Thou counterfeit'st a bark, a sea, a wind:
For still thy eyes, which I may call the sea,
Do ebb and flow with tears; the bark thy body is,
Sailing in this salt flood; the winds, thy sighs;
Who,—raging with thy tears, and they with
    them,—
Without a sudden calm, will overset
Thy tempest-tossed body.—How now, wife!
Have you deliver'd to her our decree?
LADY CAPULET.
Ay, sir; but she will none, she gives you thanks.
I would the fool were married to her grave!
CAPULET.
Soft! take me with you, take me with you, wife.
How! will she none? doth she not give us thanks?
Is she not proud? doth she not count her blest,
Unworthy as she is, that we have wrought
So worthy a gentleman to be her bridegroom?
JULIET.
Not proud, you have; but thankful, that you have:
Proud can I never be of what I hate;
But thankful even for hate, that is meant love.
CAPULET.
How now, how now, chop-logic! What is this?
'Proud,'—and 'I thank you,'—and 'I thank
    you not;'—
And yet 'not proud:'—mistress minion, you,
Thank me no thankings, nor proud me no
    prouds,

But fettle your fine joints 'gainst Thursday
    next,
To go with Paris to Saint Peter's Church,
Or I will drag thee on a hurdle thither.
Out, you green-sickness carrion! out, you
    baggage!
You tallow-face!
LADY CAPULET.
Fie, fie! what, are you mad?
JULIET.
Good father, I beseech you on my knees,
                                    [*She kneels down.*
Hear me with patience but to speak a word.
CAPULET.
Hang thee, young baggage! disobedient wretch!
I tell thee what,—get thee to church o'
    Thursday,
Or never after look me in the face:
Speak not, reply not, do not answer me;
My fingers itch.—Wife, we scarce thought us
    blest
That God had sent us but this only child;
But now I see this one is one too much,
And that we have a curse in having her:
Out on her, hilding!
NURSE.
                God in heaven bless her!—
You are to blame, my lord, to rate her so.
CAPULET.
And why, my lady wisdom? hold your tongue,
Good prudence; smatter with your gossips, go.
NURSE.
I speak no treason.
CAPULET.
                O, God ye god-den.
NURSE.
May not one speak?
CAPULET.
                Peace, you mumbling fool!
Utter your gravity o'er a gossip's bowl;
For here we need it not.
LADY CAPULET.
                You are too hot.
CAPULET.
God's bread! it makes me mad: day, night, late,
    early,
At home, abroad, alone, in company,
Waking, or sleeping, still my care hath been
To have her matcht: and having now provided
A gentleman of princely parentage,
Of fair demesnes, youthful, and nobly train'd,
Stuft, as they say, with honourable parts,
Proportion'd as one's thought would wish a
    man,—
And then to have a wretched puling fool,
A whining mammet, in her fortune's tender,
To answer—'I'll not wed,—I cannot love,
I am too young,—I pray you, pardon me;'—
But, an you will not wed, I'll pardon you:
Graze where you will, you shall not house with
    me:
Look to't, think on't, I do not use to jest.
Thursday is near; lay hand on heart, advise:
An you be mine, I'll give you to my friend;
An you be not, hang, beg, starve, die in the
    streets,

For, by my soul, I'll ne'er acknowledge thee,
Nor what is mine shall never do thee good:
Trust to't, bethink you; I'll not be forsworn.

                          [*Exit.*

JULIET.

Is there no pity sitting in the clouds,
That sees into the bottom of my grief?
O, sweet my mother, cast me not away!
Delay this marriage for a month, a week;
Or, if you do not, make the bridal bed
In that dim monument where Tybalt lies.

LADY CAPULET.

Talk not to me, for I'll not speak a word:
Do as thou wilt, for I have done with thee.   [*Exit.*

JULIET.

O God!—O nurse, how shall this be prevented?
My husband is on earth, my faith in heaven;
How shall that faith return again to earth,
Unless that husband send it me from heaven
By leaving earth?—comfort me, counsel me.—
Alack, alack, that heaven should practise strata-
    gems
Upon so soft a subject as myself!—
What say'st thou? hast thou not a word of joy?
Some comfort, nurse.

NURSE.

            Faith, here it is. Romeo
Is banished; and all the world to nothing,
That he dares ne'er come back to challenge you;
Or, if he do, it needs must be by stealth.
Then, since the case so stands as now it doth,
    I think it best you married with the county.
O, he's a lovely gentleman!
Romeo's a dishclout to him: an eagle, madam,
Hath not so green, so quick, so fair an eye
As Paris hath. Beshrew my very heart,
I think you are happy in this second match,
For it excels your first; or if it did not,
Your first is dead; or 'twere as good he were,
As living here, and you no use of him.

JULIET.

Speakest thou from thy heart?

NURSE.

And from my soul too; else beshrew them both.

JULIET.

Amen!

NURSE.

What?

JULIET.

Well, thou hast comforted me marvellous
    much.
Go in; and tell my lady I am gone,
Having displeased my father, to Laurence' cell,
To make confession, and to be absolved.

NURSE.

Marry, I will; and this is wisely done.   [*Exit.*

JULIET.

Ancient damnation! O most cursed fiend!
                   [*She looks after* NURSE.
Is it more sin to wish me thus forsworn,
Or to dispraise my lord with that same tongue
Which she hath praised him with above compare
So many thousand times?—Go, counsellor;
Thou and my bosom henceforth shall be twain.—
I'll to the friar, to know his remedy:
If all else fail, myself have power to die.   [*Exit.*

ACT IV. SCENE I.

Verona.   FRIAR LAURENCE'S *cell.*

Enter FRIAR LAURENCE *and* PARIS.

FRIAR LAURENCE.

ON Thursday, sir? the time is very short.

PARIS.

My father Capulet will have it so;
And I am nothing slow to slack his haste.

FRIAR LAURENCE.

You say you do not know the lady's mind:
Uneven is the course; I like it not.

PARIS.

Immoderately she weeps for Tybalt's death,
And therefore have I little talkt of love;
For Venus smiles not in a house of tears.
Now, sir, her father counts it dangerous
That she doth give her sorrow so much sway;
And, in his wisdom, hastes our marriage,
To stop the inundation of her tears;
Which, too much minded by herself alone,
May be put from her by society:
Now do you know the reason of this haste.

FRIAR LAURENCE [*aside*].

I would I knew not why it should be slow'd.—
Look, sir, here comes the lady toward my cell.

Enter JULIET.

PARIS.

Happily met, my lady and my wife!

JULIET.

That may be, sir, when I may be a wife.

PARIS.

That may be must be, love, on Thursday next.

JULIET.

What must be shall be.

FRIAR LAURENCE.

            That's a certain text.

PARIS.

Come you to make confession to this father?

JULIET.

To answer that, were to confess to you.

PARIS.

Do not deny to him that you love me.

JULIET.

I will confess to you that I love him.

PARIS.

So will ye, I am sure, that you love me.

JULIET.

If I do so, it will be of more price,
Being spoke behind your back, than to your
    face.

PARIS.

Poor soul, thy face is much abused with tears.

JULIET.

The tears have got small victory by that;
For it was bad enough before their spite.

PARIS.

Thou wrong'st it, more than tears, with that
    report.

JULIET.

That is no slander, sir, which is a truth;
And what I spake, I spake it to my face.

PARIS.

Thy face is mine, and thou hast slander'd it.

JULIET.

It may be so, for it is not mine own.—

Are you at leisure, holy father, now;
Or shall I come to you at evening mass?
FRIAR LAURENCE.
My leisure serves me, pensive daughter, now.—
My lord, we must entreat the time alone.
PARIS.
God shield I should disturb devotion!—
Juliet, on Thursday early will I rouse ye:
Till then, adieu; and keep this holy kiss.   *[Exit.*
JULIET.
O, shut the door! and when thou hast done so,
Come weep with me; past hope, past cure, past
   help!

FRIAR LAURENCE.
Ah, Juliet, I already know thy grief;
It strains me past the compass of my wits:
I hear thou must, and nothing may prorogue it.
On Thursday next be married to this county.
JULIET.
Tell me not, friar, that thou hear'st of this,
Unless thou tell me how I may prevent it:
If, in thy wisdom, thou canst give no help,
Do thou but call my resolution wise,
And with this knife I'll help it presently.
God join'd my heart and Romeo's, thou our
   hands;
And ere this hand, by thee to Romeo seal'd,
Shall be the label to another deed,
Or my true heart with treacherous revolt
Turn to another, this shall slay them both:
Therefore, out of thy long-experienced time,
Give me some present counsel; or, behold,
'Twixt my extremes and me this bloody knife
Shall play the umpire; arbitrating that
Which the commission of thy years and art
Could to no issue of true honour bring.
Be not so long to speak; I long to die,
If what thou speak'st speak not of remedy.
FRIAR LAURENCE.
Hold, daughter: I do spy a kind of hope,
Which craves as desperate an execution
As that is desperate which we would prevent.
If, rather than to marry County Paris,
Thou hast the strength of will to slay thyself,
Then is it likely thou wilt undertake
A thing like death to chide away this shame,
That copest with death himself to scape from it;
And, if thou darest, I'll give thee remedy.
JULIET.
O, bid me leap, rather than marry Paris,
From off the battlements of yonder tower;
Or walk in thievish ways; or bid me lurk
Where serpents are; chain me with roaring bears;
Or shut me nightly in a charnel-house,
O'er-cover'd quite with dead men's rattling
   bones,
With reeky shanks, and yellow chapless skulls;
Or bid me go into a new-made grave,
And hide me with a dead man in his shroud;
Things that, to hear them told, have made me
   tremble;
And I will do it without fear or doubt,
To live an unstain'd wife to my sweet love.
FRIAR LAURENCE.
Hold, then; go home, be merry, give consent
To marry Paris: Wednesday is to-morrow;

To-morrow night look that thou lie alone,
Let not thy nurse lie with thee in thy chamber:
Take thou this vial, being then in bed,
And this distilled liquor drink thou off:
When, presently, through all thy veins shall run
A cold and drowsy humour; for no pulse
Shall keep his native progress, but surcease:
No warmth, no breath, shall testify thou livest;
The roses in thy lips and cheeks shall fade
To paly ashes; thy eyes' windows fall,
Like death, when he shuts up the day of life;
Each part, deprived of supple government,
Shall, stiff and stark and cold, appear like death:
And in this borrow'd likeness of shrunk death
Thou shalt continue two-and-forty hours,
And then awake as from a pleasant sleep.
Now, when the bridegroom in the morning comes
To rouse thee from thy bed, there art thou dead:
Then, as the manner of our country is,
In thy best robes, uncover'd, on the bier,
Thou shalt be borne to that same ancient vault
Where all the kindred of the Capulets lie.
In the mean time, against thou shalt awake,
Shall Romeo by my letters know our drift;
And hither shall he come: and he and I
Will watch thy waking, and that very night
Shall Romeo bear thee hence to Mantua.
And this shall free thee from this present shame;
If no inconstant toy, nor womanish fear,
Abate thy valour in the acting it.
JULIET.
Give me, give me! O, tell not me of fear!
FRIAR LAURENCE.
Hold; get you gone, be strong and prosperous
In this resolve: I'll send a friar with speed
To Mantua, with my letters to thy lord.
JULIET.
Love give me strength! and strength shall help
   afford.
Farewell, dear father!   *[Exeunt.*

SCENE II.
Hall in CAPULET'S *house.*

Enter CAPULET, LADY CAPULET, NURSE, *and*
SERVING-MEN *two or three.*
CAPULET.
SO many guests invite as here are writ.—
               [Exit FIRST SERVANT.
Sirrah, go hire me twenty cunning cooks.
SECOND SERVING-MAN.
You shall have none ill, sir; for I'll try if they can
lick their fingers.
CAPULET.
How canst thou try them so?
SECOND SERVING-MAN.
Marry, sir, 'tis an ill cook that cannot lick his
own fingers: therefore he that cannot lick his
fingers goes not with me.
CAPULET.
Go, be gone.—   *[Exit* SECOND SERVANT.
We shall be much unfurnish'd for this time.—
What, is my daughter gone to Friar Laurence?
NURSE.
Ay, forsooth.

CAPULET.

Well, he may chance to do some good on her:
A peevish self-will'd harlotry it is.

NURSE.

See where she comes from shrift with merry look.

Enter JULIET.

CAPULET.

How now, my headstrong! where have you been
   gadding?

JULIET.

Where I have learn'd me to repent the sin
Of disobedient opposition
To you and your behests; and am enjoin'd
By holy Laurence to fall prostrate here,
And beg your pardon:—pardon, I beseech you!
Henceforward I am ever ruled by you.

CAPULET.

Send for the county; go tell him of this:
I'll have this knot knit up to-morrow morning.

JULIET.

I met the youthful lord at Laurence' cell;
And gave him what becomed love I might,
Not stepping o'er the bounds of modesty.

CAPULET.

Why, I am glad on't; this is well,—stand up,—
This is as't should be.—Let me see the county;
Ay, marry, go, I say, and fetch him hither.—
Now, afore God, this reverend holy friar,
All our whole city is much bound to him.

JULIET.

Nurse, will you go with me into my closet,
To help me sort such needful ornaments
As you think fit to furnish me to-morrow?

LADY CAPULET.

No, not till Thursday; there is time enough.

CAPULET.

Go, nurse, go with her:—we'll to church to-
   morrow.   [*Exeunt* JULIET *and* NURSE.

LADY CAPULET.

We shall be short in our provision:
'Tis now near night.

CAPULET.

           Tush, I will stir about,
And all things shall be well, I warrant thee, wife:
Go thou to Juliet, help to deck up her;
I'll not to bed to-night;—let me alone;
I'll play the housewife for this once.—What,
   ho!—
They are all forth: well, I will walk myself
To County Paris, to prepare him up
Against to-morrow: my heart is wondrous light,
Since this same wayward girl is so reclaim'd.
                           [*Exeunt.*

SCENE III.

JULIET'S *chamber.*

Enter JULIET *and* NURSE.

JULIET.

AY, those attires are best:—but, gentle nurse,
I pray thee, leave me to myself to-night;
For I have need of many orisons
To move the heavens to smile upon my state,
Which, well thou know'st, is cross and full of sin.

Enter LADY CAPULET.

LADY CAPULET.

What, are you busy, ho? need you my help?

JULIET.

No, madam; we have cull'd such necessaries
As are behoveful for our state to-morrow:
So please you, let me now be left alone,
And let the nurse this night sit up with you;
For, I am sure, you have your hands full all
In this so sudden business.

LADY CAPULET.

                 Good night:
Get thee to bed, and rest; for thou hast need.
   [*Exeunt* LADY CAPULET *and* NURSE.

JULIET.

Farewell!—God knows when we shall meet
   again.
I have a faint cold fear thrills through my veins,
That almost freezes up the heat of life:
I'll call them back again to comfort me;—
Nurse!—What should she do here?
My dismal scene I needs must act alone.—
Come, vial.—
What if this mixture do not work at all?
Must I of force be married to the county?
No, no;—this shall forbid it:—lie thou there.—
                    [*Laying down her dagger.*
What if it be a poison, which the friar
Subtly hath minister'd to have me dead,
Lest in this marriage he should be dishonour'd,
Because he married me before to Romeo?
I fear it is: and yet, methinks, it should not,
For he hath still been tried a holy man:
I will not entertain so bad a thought.—
How if, when I am laid into the tomb,
I wake before the time that Romeo
Come to redeem me? there's a fearful point!
Shall I not, then, be stifled in the vault,
To whose foul mouth no healthsome air breathes
   in,
And there die strangled ere my Romeo comes?
Or, if I live, is it not very like,
The horrible conceit of death and night,
Together with the terror of the place,—
As in a vault, an ancient receptacle,
Where, for this many hundred years, the bones
Of all my buried ancestors are packt;
Where bloody Tybalt, yet but green in earth,
Lies festering in his shroud; where, as they
   say,
At some hours in the night spirits resort;—
Alack, alack, is it not like that I,
So early waking,—what with loathsome smells,
And shrieks like mandrakes' torn out of the
   earth,
That living mortals, hearing them, run mad;—
O, if I wake, shall I not be distraught,
Environed with all these hideous fears?
And madly play with my forefathers' joints?
And pluck the mangled Tybalt from his
   shroud?
And, in this rage, with some great kinsman's
   bone,
As with a club, dash out my desperate brains?—
O, look! methinks I see my cousin's ghost
Seeking out Romeo, that did spit his body
Upon a rapier's point:—stay, Tybalt, stay!—
Romeo, I come! this do I drink to thee.
        [*She falls upon her bed within the curtains.*

271

SCENE IV.

Hall in CAPULET'S *house.*

Enter LADY CAPULET *and* NURSE.

LADY CAPULET.

HOLD, take these keys, and fetch more spices, nurse.

NURSE.

They call for dates and quinces in the pastry.

Enter CAPULET.

CAPULET.

Come, stir, stir, stir! the second cock hath
     crow'd,
The curfew-bell hath rung, 'tis three o'clock:—
Look to the baked meats, good Angelica:
Spare not for cost.

NURSE.

                         Go, you cot-quean, go,
Get you to bed; faith, you'll be sick to-morrow
For this night's watching.

CAPULET.

No, not a whit: what! I have watcht ere now
All night for lesser cause, and ne'er been sick.

LADY CAPULET.

Ay, you have been a mouse-hunt in your time;
But I will watch you from such watching now.

                         [*Exeunt* LADY CAPULET *and* NURSE.

CAPULET.

A jealous-hood, a jealous-hood!

Enter three or four SERVING-MEN *with spits, and*
          logs, and baskets.

                              Now, fellow,
What's there?

FIRST SERVING-MAN.

Things for the cook, sir; but I know not what.

CAPULET.

Make haste, make haste. [*Exit* FIRST SERVING-
MAN.]—Sirrah, fetch drier logs:
Call Peter, he will show thee where they are.

SECOND SERVING-MAN.

I have a head, sir, that will find out logs,
And never trouble Peter for the matter.   [*Exit.*

CAPULET.

Mass, and well said; a merry whoreson, ha!
Thou shalt be logger-head.—Good faith, 'tis day:
The county will be here with music straight,
For so he said he would:—I hear him near.—
                              [*Play music.*
Nurse!—wife!—what, ho!—what, nurse, I say!

Enter NURSE.

Go waken Juliet, go and trim her up:
I'll go and chat with Paris:—hie, make haste,
Make haste; the bridegroom he is come already:
Make haste, I say.   [*Exeunt.*

SCENE V.

JULIET'S *chamber.*

Enter NURSE.

NURSE.

MISTRESS!—what, mistress!—Juliet!—fast,
     I warrant her, she:—
Why, lamb!—why, lady!—fie, you slug-a-bed!—
Why, love, I say!—madam! sweetheart!—why,
     bride!

What, not a word?—you take your pennyworths
     now;
Sleep for a week; for the next night, I warrant,
The County Paris hath set up his rest
That you shall rest but little.—God forgive me,
Marry, and amen, how sound is she asleep!
I must needs wake her.—Madam, madam,
     madam!—
Ay, let the county take you in your bed;
He'll fright you up, i'faith.—Will it not be?
What, drest! and in your clothes! and down
     again!
I must needs wake you:—Lady! lady! lady!—
Alas, alas!—Help, help! my lady's dead!—
O, well-a-day, that ever I was born!—
Some *aqua-vitæ*, ho!—My lord! my lady!

Enter LADY CAPULET.

LADY CAPULET.

What noise is here?

NURSE.

                         O lamentable day!

LADY CAPULET.

What is the matter?

NURSE.

                         Look, look! O heavy day!

LADY CAPULET.

O me, O me!—My child, my only life,
Revive, look up, or I will die with thee!—
Help, help!—call help.

Enter CAPULET.

CAPULET.

For shame, bring Juliet forth; her lord is come.

NURSE.

She's dead, deceased, she's dead; alack the day!

LADY CAPULET.

Alack the day, she's dead, she's dead, she's dead!

CAPULET.

Ha! let me see her:—out, alas! she's cold;
Her blood is settled, and her joints are stiff;
Life and these lips have long been separated:
Death lies on her like an untimely frost
Upon the sweetest flower of all the field.

NURSE.

O lamentable day!

LADY CAPULET.

O woeful time!

CAPULET.

Death, that hath ta'en her hence to make me wail,
Ties up my tongue, and will not let me speak.

Enter FRIAR LAURENCE *and* PARIS, *with*
          MUSICIANS.

FRIAR LAURENCE.

Come, is the bride ready to go to church?

CAPULET.

Ready to go, but never to return:—
O son, the night before thy wedding-day
Hath Death lain with thy wife:—see there she lies,
Flower as she was, deflowered by him.
Death is my son-in-law, Death is my heir;
My daughter he hath wedded: I will die,
And leave him all; life, living, all is Death's.

PARIS.

Have I thought long to see this morning's face,
And doth it give me such a sight as this?

LADY CAPULET.

Accurst, unhappy, wretched, hateful day!

Most miserable hour that e'er time saw
In lasting labour of his pilgrimage!
But one, poor one, one poor and loving child,
But one thing to rejoice and solace in,
And cruel Death hath catcht it from my sight!

NURSE.
O woe! O woeful, woeful, woeful day!
Most lamentable day, most woeful day,
That ever, ever, I did yet behold!
O day! O day! O day! O hateful day!
Never was seen so black a day as this:
O woeful day, O woeful day!

PARIS.
Beguiled, divorced, wronged, spited, slain!
Most detestable Death, by thee beguiled,
By cruel cruel thee quite overthrown!—
O love! O life!—not life, but love in death!

CAPULET.
Despised, distressed, hated, martyr'd, kill'd!—
Uncomfortable time, why camest thou now
To murder, murder our solemnity?—
O child! O child!—my soul, and not my child!—
Dead art thou!—alack, my child is dead;
And with my child my joys are buried!

FRIAR LAURENCE.
Peace, ho, for shame! confusion's cure lives not
In these confusions. Heaven and yourself
Had part in this fair maid; now heaven hath all,
And all the better is it for the maid:
Your part in her you could not keep from death;
But heaven keeps his part in eternal life.
The most you sought was her promotion;
For 'twas your heaven she should be advanced:
And weep ye now, seeing she is advanced
Above the clouds, as high as heaven itself?
O, in this love, you love your child so ill,
That you run mad, seeing that she is well:
She's not well married that lives married long;
But she's best married that dies married young.
Dry up your tears, and stick your rosemary
On this fair corse; and, as the custom is,
In all her best array bear her to church:
For though fond nature bids us all lament,
Yet nature's tears are reason's merriment.

CAPULET.
All things that we ordained festival
Turn from their office to black funeral:
Our instruments to melancholy bells,
Our wedding cheer to a sad burial feast;
Our solemn hymns to sullen dirges change;
Our bridal flowers serve for a burial corse;
And all things change them to the contrary.

FRIAR LAURENCE.
Sir, go you in,—and, madam, go with him;—
And go, Sir Paris;—every one prepare
To follow this fair corse unto her grave:
The heavens do lour upon you for some ill;
Move them no more by crossing their high will.

[They all, but the NURSE and MUSICIANS,
go forth, casting rosemary on her.

FIRST MUSICIAN.
Faith, we may put up our pipes and be gone.

NURSE.
Honest good fellows, ah, put up, put up;
For, well you know, this is a pitiful case.

[Exit.

FIRST MUSICIAN.
Ay, by my troth, the case may be amended.

Enter PETER.

PETER.
Musicians, O, musicians, 'Heart's ease, Heart's
ease:' O, an you will have me live, play 'Heart's
ease.'

FIRST MUSICIAN.
Why 'Heart's ease'?

PETER.
O, musicians, because my heart itself plays 'My
heart is full of woe:' O, play me some merry
dump, to comfort me.

FIRST MUSICIAN.
Not a dump we; 'tis no time to play now.

PETER.
You will not, then?

FIRST MUSICIAN.
No.

PETER.
I will, then, give it you soundly.

FIRST MUSICIAN.
What will you give us?

PETER.
No money, on my faith; but the gleek,—I will
give you the minstrel.

FIRST MUSICIAN.
Then will I give you the serving-creature.

PETER.
Then will I lay the serving-creature's dagger on
your pate. I will carry no crotchets: I'll re you, I'll
fa you; do you note me?

FIRST MUSICIAN.
An you re us and fa us, you note us.

SECOND MUSICIAN.
Pray you, put up your dagger, and put out your
wit.

PETER.
Then have at you with my wit! I will dry-beat
you with an iron wit, and put up my iron dagger.
—Answer me like men:

When griping grief the heart doth wound,
    And doleful dumps the mind oppress,
Then music with her silver sound—

why 'silver sound'? why 'music with her silver
sound'?—What say you, Simon Catling?

FIRST MUSICIAN.
Marry, sir, because silver hath a sweet sound.

PETER.
Pretty!—What say you, Hugh Rebeck?

SECOND MUSICIAN.
I say, 'silver sound,' because musicians sound
for silver.

PETER.
Pretty too!—What say you, James Soundpost?

THIRD MUSICIAN.
Faith, I know not what to say.

PETER.
O, I cry you mercy; you are the singer: I will say
for you. It is 'music with her silver sound,'
because such fellows as you have seldom gold for
sounding:—

Then music with her silver sound
    With speedy help doth lend redress.   [Exit.

FIRST MUSICIAN.
What a pestilent knave is this same!
SECOND MUSICIAN.
Hang him, Jack!—Come, we'll in here; tarry for
the mourners, and stay dinner.   [*Exeunt.*

ACT V. SCENE I.

Mantua. A street.

Enter ROMEO.

ROMEO.
IF I may trust the flattering eye of sleep,
My dreams presage some joyful news at hand:
My bosom's lord sits lightly in his throne;
And all this day an unaccustom'd spirit
Lifts me above the ground with cheerful
    thoughts.
I dreamt my lady came and found me dead,—
Strange dream, that gives a dead man leave to
    think!—
And breathed such life with kisses in my lips,
That I revived, and was an emperor.
Ah me! how sweet is love itself possest,
When but love's shadows are so rich in joy!
    Enter BALTHASAR, *his man, booted.*
News from Verona!—How now, Balthasar!
Dost thou not bring me letters from the friar?
How doth my lady? Is my father well?
How fares my Juliet? that I ask again;
For nothing can be ill, if she be well.
BALTHASAR.
Then she is well, and nothing can be ill:
Her body sleeps in Capels' monument,
And her immortal part with angels lives.
I saw her laid low in her kindred's vault,
And presently took post to tell it you:
O, pardon me for bringing these ill news,
Since you did leave it for my office, sir.
ROMEO.
Is it even so? then I defy you, stars!—
Thou know'st my lodging: get me ink and paper,
And hire post-horses; I will hence to-night.
BALTHASAR.
I do beseech you, sir, have patience:
Your looks are pale and wild, and do import
Some misadventure.
ROMEO.
        Tush, thou art deceived:
Leave me, and do the thing I bid thee do.
Hast thou no letters to me from the friar?
BALTHASAR.
No, my good lord.
ROMEO.
        No matter: get thee gone,
And hire those horses; I'll be with thee straight.
        [*Exit* BALTHASAR.
Well, Juliet, I will lie with thee to-night.
Let's see for means:—O mischief, thou art swift
To enter in the thoughts of desperate men!
I do remember an apothecary,—
And hereabouts he dwells,—which late I noted
In tatter'd weeds, with overwhelming brows,
Culling of simples; meagre were his looks,
Sharp misery had worn him to the bones:
And in his needy shop a tortoise hung,
An alligator stuft, and other skins

Of ill-shaped fishes; and about his shelves
A beggarly account of empty boxes,
Green earthen pots, bladders, and musty seeds,
Remnants of packthread, and old cakes of roses,
Were thinly scatter'd, to make up a show.
Noting this penury, to myself I said,
'An if a man did need a poison now,
Whose sale is present death in Mantua,
Here lives a caitiff wretch would sell it him.'
O, this same thought did but forerun my need;
And this same needy man must sell it me.
As I remember, this should be the house:
Being holiday, the beggar's shop is shut.—
What, ho! apothecary!
        Enter APOTHECARY.
APOTHECARY.
            Who calls so loud?
ROMEO.
Come hither, man.—I see that thou art poor;
Hold, there is forty ducats: let me have
A dram of poison; such soon-speeding gear
As will disperse itself through all the veins,
That the life-weary taker may fall dead;
And that the trunk may be discharged of breath
As violently as hasty powder fired
Doth hurry from the fatal cannon's womb.
APOTHECARY.
Such mortal drugs I have; but Mantua's law
Is death to any he that utters them.
ROMEO.
Art thou so bare and full of wretchedness,
And fear'st to die? famine is in thy cheeks,
Need and oppression starveth in thine eyes,
Contempt and beggary hangs upon thy back,
The world is not thy friend, nor the world's law:
The world affords no law to make thee rich;
Then be not poor, but break it, and take this.
APOTHECARY.
My poverty, but not my will, consents.
ROMEO.
I pay thy poverty, and not thy will.
APOTHECARY.
Put this in any liquid thing you will,
And drink it off; and, if you had the strength
Of twenty men, it would dispatch you straight.
ROMEO.
There is thy gold; worse poison to men's souls,
Doing more murders in this loathsome world,
Than these poor compounds that thou mayst not
    sell:
I sell thee poison: thou hast sold me none.
Farewell: buy food, and get thyself in flesh.—
Come, cordial, and not poison, go with me
To Juliet's grave; for there must I use thee.
        [*Exeunt.*

SCENE II.

Verona. FRIAR LAURENCE'S *cell.*

Enter FRIAR JOHN.

FRIAR JOHN.
HOLY Franciscan friar! brother, ho!
    Enter FRIAR LAURENCE.
FRIAR LAURENCE.
This same should be the voice of Friar John.—
Welcome from Mantua: what says Romeo?
Or, if his mind be writ, give me his letter.

FRIAR JOHN.

Going to find a barefoot brother out,
One of our order, to associate me,
Here in this city visiting the sick,
And finding him, the searchers of the town,
Suspecting that we both were in a house
Where the infectious pestilence did reign,
Seal'd up the doors, and would not let us forth;
So that my speed to Mantua there was stay'd.

FRIAR LAURENCE.

Who bare my letter, then, to Romeo?

FRIAR JOHN.

I could not send it,—here it is again,—
Nor get a messenger to bring it thee,
So fearful were they of infection.

FRIAR LAURENCE.

Unhappy fortune! by my brotherhood,
The letter was not nice, but full of charge
Of dear import; and the neglecting it
May do much danger. Friar John, go hence;
Get me an iron crow, and bring it straight
Unto my cell.

FRIAR JOHN.

Brother, I'll go and bring it thee.   [Exit.

FRIAR LAURENCE.

Now must I to the monument alone;
Within this three hours will fair Juliet wake:
She will beshrew me much that Romeo
Hath had no notice of these accidents;
But I will write again to Mantua,
And keep her at my cell till Romeo come;—
Poor living corse, closed in a dead man's tomb!
          [Exit.

SCENE III.

*The same. A churchyard; in it a monument
belonging to the* CAPULETS.

Enter COUNTY PARIS *and his* PAGE, *with flowers
and sweet water.*

PARIS.

GIVE me thy torch, boy; hence, and stand
aloof:—
Yet put it out, for I would not be seen.
Under yond yew-trees lay thee all along,
Holding thine ear close to the hollow ground;
So shall no foot upon the churchyard tread—
Being loose, unfirm, with digging-up of graves—
But thou shalt hear it: whistle then to me,
As signal that thou hear'st something approach.
Give me those flowers. Do as I bid thee, go.

PAGE [aside].

I am almost afraid to stand alone
Here in the churchyard; yet I will adventure.
          [Retires.

PARIS.

Sweet flower, with flowers thy bridal bed I strew:
          [PARIS strews the tomb with flowers.
O woe, thy canopy is dust and stones!
Which with sweet water nightly I will dew;
Or, wanting that, with tears distill'd by moans:
The obsequies that I for thee will keep,
Nightly shall be to strew thy grave and weep.
          [BOY whistles.
The boy gives warning something doth approach.
What cursed foot wanders this way to-night,

To cross my obsequies and true love's rite?
What, with a torch!—muffle me, night, awhile.
          [Retires.
Enter ROMEO, *and* BALTHASAR *with a torch, a
mattock, and a crow of iron.*

ROMEO.

Give me that mattock and the wrenching-iron.
Hold, take this letter; early in the morning
See thou deliver it to my lord and father.
Give me the light: upon thy life, I charge thee,
Whate'er thou hear'st or seest, stand all aloof,
And do not interrupt me in my course.
Why I descend into this bed of death,
Is partly to behold my lady's face;
But chiefly to take thence from her dead finger
A precious ring,—a ring that I must use
In dear employment: therefore hence, be gone:—
But if thou, jealous, dost return to pry
In what I further shall intend to do,
By heaven, I will tear thee joint by joint,
And strew this hungry churchyard with thy
     limbs:
The time and my intents are savage-wild;
More fierce and more inexorable far
Than empty tigers or the roaring sea.

BALTHASAR.

I will be gone, sir, and not trouble you.

ROMEO.

So shalt thou show me friendship.—Take thou
     that:
Live, and be prosperous: and farewell, good
     fellow.

BALTHASAR [aside].

For all this same, I'll hide me hereabout:
His looks I fear, and his intents I doubt. [Retires.

ROMEO.

Thou detestable maw, thou womb of death,
Gorged with the dearest morsel of the earth,
Thus I enforce thy rotten jaws to open,
          [ROMEO opens the tomb.
And, in despite, I'll cram thee with more food!

PARIS.

This is that banish't haughty Montague
That murder'd my love's cousin,—with which
     grief,
It is supposed, the fair creature died,—
And here is come to do some villainous shame
To the dead bodies: I will apprehend him.—
Stop thy unhallow'd toil, vile Montague!
Can vengeance be pursued further than death?
Condemned villain, I do apprehend thee:
Obey, and go with me; for thou must die.

ROMEO.

I must indeed; and therefore came I hither.—
Good gentle youth, tempt not a desperate man;
Fly hence, and leave me:—think upon these gone;
Let them affright thee.—I beseech thee, youth,
Put not another sin upon my head,
By urging me to fury:—O, be gone!
By heaven, I love thee better than myself;
For I come hither arm'd against myself:
Stay not, be gone;—live, and hereafter say,
A madman's mercy bid thee run away.

PARIS.

I do defy thy conjurations,
And apprehend thee for a felon here.

ROMEO.
Wilt thou provoke me? then have at thee, boy!
                              [*They fight.*
PAGE.
O Lord, they fight! I will go call the watch.
                    [*Exit.—*PARIS *falls.*
PARIS.
O, I am slain!—If thou be merciful,
Open the tomb, lay me with Juliet.
ROMEO.
In faith, I will.—Let me peruse this face:—
Mercutio's kinsman, noble County Paris!—
What said my man, when my betossed soul
Did not attend him as we rode? I think
He told me Paris should have married Juliet:
Said he not so? or did I dream it so?
Or am I mad, hearing him talk of Juliet,
To think it was so?—O, give me thy hand,
One writ with me in sour misfortune's book!
I'll bury thee in a triumphant grave;—
A grave? O, no, a lantern, slaughter'd youth,
For here lies Juliet, and her beauty makes
This vault a feasting presence full of light.
Death, lie thou there, by a dead man interr'd.
                    [*Laying* PARIS *in the tomb.*
How oft when men are at the point of death
Have they been merry? which their keepers call
A lightning before death: O, how may I
Call this a lightning? O my love! my wife!
Death, that hath suckt the honey of thy breath,
Hath had no power yet upon thy beauty:
Thou art not conquer'd; beauty's ensign yet
Is crimson in thy lips and in thy cheeks,
And death's pale flag is not advanced there.
Tybalt, liest thou there in thy bloody sheet?
O, what more favour can I do to thee,
Than with that hand that cut thy youth in twain
To sunder his that was thine enemy?
Forgive me, cousin!—Ah, dear Juliet,
Why art thou yet so fair? shall I believe
That unsubstantial Death is amorous;
And that the lean abhorred monster keeps
Thee here in dark to be his paramour?
For fear of that, I still will stay with thee;
And never from this palace of dim night
Depart again: here, here will I remain
With worms that are thy chamber-maids; O, here
Will I set up my everlasting rest;
And shake the yoke of inauspicious stars
From this world-wearied flesh.—Eyes, look your
    last!
Arms, take your last embrace! and, lips, O you
The doors of breath, seal with a righteous kiss
A dateless bargain to engrossing death!—
Come, bitter conduct, come, unsavoury guide!
Thou desperate pilot, now at once run on
The dashing rocks thy sea-sick weary bark!
Here's to my love! [*drinks*]—O true apothecary!
Thy drugs are quick.—Thus with a kiss I die.
                              [*Dies.*
Enter, at the other end of the churchyard, FRIAR
    LAURENCE, *with a lantern, crow, and spade.*
FRIAR LAURENCE.
Saint Francis be my speed! how oft to-night
Have my old feet stumbled at graves!—Who's
    there?

BALTHASAR.
Here's one, a friend, and one that knows you
    well.
FRIAR LAURENCE.
Bliss be upon you! Tell me, good my friend,
What torch is yond, that vainly lends his light
To grubs and eyeless skulls? as I discern,
It burneth in the Capels' monument.
BALTHASAR.
It doth so, holy sir; and there's my master,
One that you love.
FRIAR LAURENCE.
            Who is it?
BALTHASAR.
                    Romeo.
FRIAR LAURENCE.
How long hath he been there?
BALTHASAR.
                    Full half an hour.
FRIAR LAURENCE.
Go with me to the vault.
BALTHASAR.
                    I dare not, sir:
My master knows not but I am gone hence;
And fearfully did menace me with death,
If I did stay to look on his intents.
FRIAR LAURENCE.
Stay, then; I'll go alone.—Fear comes upon me,
O, much I fear some ill unlucky thing.
BALTHASAR.
As I did sleep under this yew-tree here,
I dreamt my master and another fought,
And that my master slew him.
FRIAR LAURENCE.
                    Romeo!—
Alack, alack, what blood is this, which stains
      [*Stoops and looks on the blood and weapons.*
The stony entrance of this sepulchre?—
What mean these masterless and gory swords
To lie discolour'd by this place of peace?
                              [*Enters the tomb.*
Romeo! O, pale!—Who else? what, Paris too?
And steept in blood?—Ah, what an unkind hour
Is guilty of this lamentable chance!—
The lady stirs.   [JULIET *wakes.*
JULIET.
O comfortable friar! where is my lord?—
I do remember well where I should be,
And there I am: where is my Romeo?
                              [*Noise within.*
FRIAR LAURENCE.
I hear some noise. Lady, come from that nest
Of death, contagion, and unnatural sleep:
A greater power than we can contradict
Hath thwarted our intents: come, come away:
Thy husband in thy bosom there lies dead;
And Paris too: come, I'll dispose of thee
Among a sisterhood of holy nuns:
Stay not to question, for the watch is coming;
Come, go, good Juliet; I dare no longer stay.
                              [*Exit.*
JULIET.
Go, get thee hence, for I will not away.
What's here? a cup, closed in my true love's
    hand?
Poison, I see, hath been his timeless end:—

O churl! drunk all, and left no friendly drop
To help me after?—I will kiss thy lips;
Haply some poison yet doth hang on them,
To make me die with a restorative.   [*Kisses him.*
Thy lips are warm!

FIRST WATCH [*within*].

Lead, boy:—which way?

JULIET.

Yea, noise?—then I'll be brief.—O happy dagger!
     [*Snatching* ROMEO'S *dagger.*
This is thy sheath; there rust, and let me die.
     [*She stabs herself and falls.*
Enter WATCH, *with the* PAGE *of* PARIS.

PAGE.

This is the place; there, where the torch doth
  burn.

FIRST WATCHMAN.

The ground is bloody; search about the church-
Go, some of you, whoe'er you find attach.   [yard:
     [*Exeunt some of the* WATCH.
Pitiful sight! here lies the county slain;—
And Juliet bleeding; warm, and newly dead,
Who here hath lain these two days buried.—
Go, tell the prince,—run to the Capulets,—
Raise up the Montagues,—some others search:—
We see the ground whereon these woes do lie;
But the true ground of all these piteous woes
We cannot without circumstance descry.
Enter some of the WATCH, *with* BALTHASAR.

SECOND WATCHMAN.

Here's Romeo's man; we found him in the
  churchyard.

FIRST WATCHMAN.

Hold him in safety, till the prince come hither.
Enter FRIAR LAURENCE, *and another*
WATCHMAN.

THIRD WATCHMAN.

Here is a friar, that trembles, sighs, and weeps:
We took this mattock and this spade from him,
As he was coming from this churchyard side.

FIRST WATCHMAN.

A great suspicion: stay the friar too.
Enter the PRINCE *and* ATTENDANTS.

PRINCE ESCALUS.

What misadventure is so early up,
That calls our person from our morning rest?
Enter old CAPULET, LADY CAPULET, *and others.*

CAPULET.

What should it be, that they so shriek abroad?

LADY CAPULET.

The people in the street cry 'Romeo,'
Some 'Juliet,' and some 'Paris;' and all run,
With open outcry, toward our monument.

PRINCE ESCALUS.

What fear is this which startles in our ears?

FIRST WATCHMAN.

Sovereign, here lies the County Paris slain;
And Romeo dead; and Juliet, dead before,
Warm, and new kill'd.

PRINCE ESCALUS.

Search, seek, and know how this foul murder
  comes.

FIRST WATCHMAN.

Here is a friar, and slaughter'd Romeo's man;
With instruments upon them, fit to open
These dead men's tombs.

CAPULET.

O heaven!—O wife, look how our daughter bleeds!
This dagger hath mista'en,—for, lo, his house
Is empty on the back of Montague,—
And it mis-sheathed in my daughter's bosom!

LADY CAPULET.

O me! this sight of death is as a bell,
That warns my old age to a sepulchre.
Enter old MONTAGUE *and others.*

PRINCE ESCALUS.

Come, Montague; for thou art early up,
To see thy son and heir more early down.

MONTAGUE.

Alas, my liege, my wife is dead to-night;
Grief of my son's exile hath stopt her breath:
What further woe conspires against mine age?

PRINCE ESCALUS.

Look, and thou shalt see.

MONTAGUE.

O thou untaught! what manners is in this,
To press before thy father to a grave?

PRINCE ESCALUS.

Seal up the mouth of outrage for a while,
Till we can clear these ambiguities,
And know their spring, their head, their true
  descent;
And then will I be general of your woes,
And lead you even to death: meantime forbear,
And let mischance be slave to patience.—
Bring forth the parties of suspicion.

FRIAR LAURENCE.

I am the greatest, able to do least,
Yet most suspected, as the time and place
Doth make against me, of this direful murder;
And here I stand, both to impeach and purge
Myself condemned and myself excused.

PRINCE ESCALUS.

Then say at once what thou dost know in this.

FRIAR LAURENCE.

I will be brief, for my short date of breath
Is not so long as is a tedious tale.
Romeo, there dead, was husband to that Juliet;
And she, there dead, that Romeo's faithful wife:
I married them; and their stoln marriage-day
Was Tybalt's dooms-day, whose untimely death
Banisht the new-made bridegroom from this city;
For whom, and not for Tybalt, Juliet pined.
You, to remove that siege of grief from her,
Betrothed, and would have married her perforce,
To County Paris:—then comes she to me;
And, with wild looks, bid me devise some means
To rid her from this second marriage,
Or in my cell there would she kill herself.
Then gave I her, so tutor'd by my art,
A sleeping potion; which so took effect
As I intended, for it wrought on her
The form of death: meantime I writ to Romeo,
That he should hither come as this dire night,
To help to take her from her borrow'd grave,
Being the time the potion's force should cease.
But he which bore my letter, Friar John,
Was stay'd by accident; and yesternight
Return'd my letter back. Then all alone
At the prefixed hour of her waking,
Came I to take her from her kindred's vault;
Meaning to keep her closely at my cell

Till I conveniently could send to Romeo:
But when I came,—some minute ere the time
Of her awaking,—here untimely lay
The noble Paris and true Romeo dead.
She wakes; and I entreated her come forth,
And bear this work of heaven with patience:
But then a noise did scare me from the tomb;
And she, too desperate, would not go with me,
But, as it seems, did violence on herself.
All this I know; and to the marriage
Her nurse is privy: and, if aught in this
Miscarried by my fault, let my old life
Be sacrificed, some hour before his time,
Unto the rigour of severest law.

PRINCE ESCALUS.
We still have known thee for a holy man.—
Where's Romeo's man? what can he say in this?

BALTHASAR.
I brought my master news of Juliet's death;
And then in post he came from Mantua
To this same place, to this same monument.
This letter he early bid me give his father;
And threaten'd me with death, going in the
   vault,
If I departed not, and left him there.

PRINCE ESCALUS.
Give me the letter,—I will look on it.—
Where is the county's page, that raised the
   watch?—
Sirrah, what made your master in this place?

PAGE.
He came with flowers to strew his lady's grave;
And bid me stand aloof, and so I did:
Anon comes one with light to ope the tomb;

And by and by my master drew on him;
And then I ran away to call the watch.

PRINCE ESCALUS.
This letter doth make good the friar's words,
Their course of love, the tidings of her death:
And here he writes that he did buy a poison
Of a poor pothecary, and therewithal
Came to this vault to die, and lie with Juliet.
Where be these enemies? Capulet, Montague,
See, what a scourge is laid upon your hate,
That heaven finds means to kill your joys with
   love!
And I, for winking at your discords too,
Have lost a brace of kinsmen: all are punisht.

CAPULET.
O brother Montague, give me thy hand:
This is my daughter's jointure, for no more
Can I demand.

MONTAGUE.
          But I can give thee more:
For I will raise her statue in pure gold;
That while Verona by that name is known,
There shall no figure at such rate be set
As that of true and faithful Juliet.

CAPULET.
As rich shall Romeo by his lady lie;
Poor sacrifices of our enmity!

PRINCE ESCALUS.
A glooming peace this morning with it brings;
   The sun, for sorrow, will not show his head:
Go hence, to have more talk of these sad things;
   Some shall be pardon'd, and some punished:
For never was a story of more woe
Than this of Juliet and her Romeo.   [*Exeunt.*

A MIDSUMMER NIGHT'S DREAM

DRAMATIS PERSONAE

THESEUS, *Duke of Athens.*
EGEUS, *father to Hermia.*
LYSANDER, } *in love with Hermia.*
DEMETRIUS, }
PHILOSTRATE, *master of the revels to Theseus.*
QUINCE, *a carpenter.*
SNUG, *a joiner.*
BOTTOM, *a weaver.*
FLUTE, *a bellows-mender.*
SNOUT, *a tinker.*
STARVELING, *a tailor.*

HIPPOLYTA, *queen of the Amazons, betrothed to Theseus.*
HERMIA, *daughter to Egeus, in love with Lysander.*
HELENA, *in love with Demetrius.*

OBERON, *king of the fairies.*
TITANIA, *queen of the fairies.*
PUCK, *or Robin Goodfellow.*
PEAS-BLOSSOM, }
COBWEB, }
MOTH, } *fairies.*
MUSTARD-SEED, }

PYRAMUS, }
THISBE, }
WALL, } *characters in the interlude per-*
MOONSHINE, } *form'd by the Clowns.*
LION, }

Other FAIRIES *attending their* KING *and* QUEEN.
ATTENDANTS *on* THESEUS *and* HIPPOLYTA
SCENE—*Athens, and a wood near it.*

ACT I. SCENE I.

Athens. The palace of THESEUS.

Enter THESEUS, HIPPOLYTA, PHILOSTRATE, *and* ATTENDANTS.

THESEUS.
NOW, fair Hippolyta, our nuptial hour
Draws on apace; four happy days bring in
Another moon: but, O, methinks, how slow
This old moon wanes! she lingers my desires
Like to a step-dame, or a dowager,
Long withering out a young man's revenue.

HIPPOLYTA.
Four days will quickly steep themselves in night;
Four nights will quickly dream away the time;
And then the moon, like to a silver bow
New-bent in heaven, shall behold the night
Of our solemnities.

THESEUS.
Go, Philostrate,
Stir up the Athenian youth to merriments;
Awake the pert and nimble spirit of mirth:
Turn melancholy forth to funerals,—
The pale companion is not for our pomp.
[*Exit* PHILOSTRATE.
Hippolyta, I woo'd thee with my sword,
And won thy love, doing thee injuries;
But I will wed thee in another key,
With pomp, with triumph, and with revelling.
Enter EGEUS *and his daughter* HERMIA,
LYSANDER, *and* DEMETRIUS.

EGEUS.
Happy be Theseus, our renowned duke!

THESEUS.
Thanks, good Egeus: what's the news with thee?

EGEUS.
Full of vexation come I, with complaint
Against my child, my daughter Hermia.
Stand forth, Demetrius. My noble lord,
This man hath my consent to marry her.
Stand forth, Lysander: and, my gracious duke,
This hath bewitch'd the bosom of my child:—
Thou, thou, Lysander, thou hast given her rimes,
And interchanged love-tokens with my child:
Thou hast by moonlight at her window sung,
With feigning voice, verses of feigning love;
And stol'n the impression of her fantasy
With bracelets of thy hair, rings, gauds, conceits,
Knacks, trifles, nosegays, sweetmeats,—messengers
Of strong prevailment in unharden'd youth:
With cunning hast thou filch'd my daughter's heart;
Turn'd her obedience, which is due to me,
To stubborn harshness:—and, my gracious duke,
Be it so she will not here before your Grace
Consent to marry with Demetrius,
I beg the ancient privilege of Athens,—
As she is mine, I may dispose of her:
Which shall be either to this gentleman
Or to her death, according to our law
Immediately provided in that case.

THESEUS.
What say you, Hermia? be advised, fair maid:
To you your father should be as a god;
One that composed your beauties; yea, and one
To whom you are but as a form in wax,
By him imprinted, and within his power
To leave the figure, or disfigure it.
Demetrius is a worthy gentleman.

HERMIA.
So is Lysander.

THESEUS.
In himself he is;
But in this kind, wanting your father's voice,
The other must be held the worthier.

HERMIA.
I would my father lookt but with my eyes.

THESEUS.
Rather your eyes must with his judgement look.
HERMIA.
I do entreat your Grace to pardon me.
I know not by what power I am made bold,
Nor how it may concern my modesty,
In such a presence here to plead my thoughts;
But I beseech your Grace that I may know
The worst that may befall me in this case,
If I refuse to wed Demetrius.
THESEUS.
Either to die the death, or to abjure
For ever the society of men.
Therefore, fair Hermia, question your desires;
Know of your youth, examine well your blood,
Whether, if you yield not to your father's choice,
You can endure the livery of a nun;
For aye to be in shady cloister mew'd,
To live a barren sister all your life,
Chanting faint hymns to the cold fruitless moon.
Thrice-blessed they that master so their blood,
To undergo such maiden pilgrimage;
But earthlier-happy is the rose distill'd
Than that which, withering on the virgin thorn,
Grows, lives, and dies in single blessedness.
HERMIA.
So will I grow, so live, so die, my lord,
Ere I will yield my virgin patent up
Unto his lordship, whose unwished yoke
My soul consents not to give sovereignty.
THESEUS.
Take time to pause; and, by the next new
    moon,—
The sealing-day betwixt my love and me,
For everlasting bond of fellowship,—
Upon that day either prepare to die
For disobedience to your father's will,
Or else to wed Demetrius, as he would;
Or on Diana's altar to protest
For aye austerity and single life.
DEMETRIUS.
Relent, sweet Hermia:—and, Lysander, yield
Thy crazed title to my certain right.
LYSANDER.
You have her father's love, Demetrius;
Let me have Hermia's: do you marry him.
EGEUS.
Scornful Lysander! true, he hath my love,—
And what is mine my love shall render him;
And she is mine,—and all my right of her
I do estate unto Demetrius.
LYSANDER.
I am, my lord, as well derived as he,
As well possest; my love is more than his;
My fortunes every way as fairly rank'd,
If not with vantage, as Demetrius';
And, which is more than all these boasts can be,
I am beloved of beauteous Hermia:
Why should not I, then, prosecute my right?
Demetrius, I'll avouch it to his head,
Made love to Nedar's daughter, Helena,
And won her soul; and she, sweet lady, dotes,
Devoutly dotes, dotes in idolatry,
Upon this spotted and inconstant man.
THESEUS.
I must confess that I have heard so much,

And with Demetrius thought to have spoke
    thereof;
But, being over-full of self-affairs,
My mind did lose it. But, Demetrius, come;
And come, Egeus; you shall go with me,
I have some private schooling for you both.
For you, fair Hermia, look you arm yourself
To fit your fancies to your father's will;
Or else the law of Athens yields you up—
Which by no means we may extenuate—
To death, or to a vow of single life.
Come, my Hippolyta: what cheer, my love?
Demetrius, and Egeus, go along:
I must employ you in some business
Against our nuptial; and confer with you
Of something nearly that concerns yourselves.
EGEUS.
With duty and desire we follow you.
   [*Exeunt* THESEUS, HIPPOLYTA, EGEUS,
        DEMETRIUS, *and* TRAIN.
LYSANDER.
How now, my love! why is your cheek so pale?
How chance the roses there do fade so fast?
HERMIA.
Belike for want of rain, which I could well
Beteem them from the tempest of my eyes.
LYSANDER.
Ay me! for aught that I could ever read,
Could ever hear by tale or history,
The course of true love never did run smooth;
But, either it was different in blood,—
HERMIA.
O cross! too high to be enthrall'd to low!
LYSANDER.
Or else misgraffed in respect of years,—
HERMIA.
O spite! too old to be engaged to young!
LYSANDER.
Or else it stood upon the choice of friends,—
HERMIA.
O hell! to choose love by another's eyes!
LYSANDER.
Or, if there were a sympathy in choice,
War, death, or sickness did lay siege to it,
Making it momentany as a sound,
Swift as a shadow, short as any dream;
Brief as the lightning in the collied night,
That, in a spleen, unfolds both heaven and earth,
And ere a man hath power to say, 'Behold!'
The jaws of darkness do devour it up:
So quick bright things come to confusion.
HERMIA.
If, then, true lovers have been ever crost,
It stands as an edict in destiny:
Then let us teach our trial patience,
Because it is a customary cross,
As due to love as thoughts, and dreams, and sighs
Wishes, and tears, poor fancy's followers.
LYSANDER.
A good persuasion: therefore, hear me, Hermia.
I have a widow aunt, a dowager
Of great revenue, and she hath no child:
From Athens is her house remote seven leagues;
And she respects me as her only son.
There, gentle Hermia, may I marry thee;
And to that place the sharp Athenian law

Cannot pursue us.　If thou lovest me, then,
Steal forth thy father's house to-morrow night;
And in the wood, a league without the town,
Where I did meet thee once with Helena,
To do observance to a morn of May,
There will I stay for thee.

HERMIA.

　　　　　My good Lysander!
I swear to thee, by Cupid's strongest bow,
By his best arrow with the golden head,
By the simplicity of Venus' doves,
By that which knitteth souls and prospers loves,
And by that fire which burn'd the Carthage
　queen,
When the false Troyan under sail was seen;
By all the vows that ever men have broke,
In number more than ever women spoke;—
In that same place thou hast appointed me,
To-morrow truly will I meet with thee.

LYSANDER.

Keep promise, love.　Look, here comes Helena.

Enter HELENA.

HERMIA.

God speed fair Helena! whither away?

HELENA.

Call you me fair? that fair again unsay.
Demetrius loves your fair: O happy fair!
Your eyes are lode-stars; and your tongue's sweet
　air
More tuneable than lark to shepherd's ear,
When wheat is green, when hawthorn buds ap-
　pear.
Sickness is catching: O, were favour so,
Yours would I catch, fair Hermia! ere I go,
My hair should catch your hair, my eye your eye,
My tongue should catch your tongue's sweet
　melody.
Were the world mine, Demetrius being bated,
The rest I'ld give to be to you translated.
O, teach me how you look; and with what art
You sway the motion of Demetrius' heart!

HERMIA.

I frown upon him, yet he loves me still.

HELENA.

O, that your frowns would teach my smiles such
　skill!

HERMIA.

I give him curses, yet he gives me love.

HELENA.

O, that my prayers could such affection move!

HERMIA.

The more I hate, the more he follows me.

HELENA.

The more I love, the more he hateth me.

HERMIA.

His folly, Helena, is no fault of mine.

HELENA.

None, but your beauty: would that fault were
　mine!

HERMIA.

Take comfort: he no more shall see my face;
Lysander and myself will fly this place.
Before the time I did Lysander see,
Seem'd Athens as a paradise to me:
O, then, what graces in my love do dwell,
That he hath turn'd a heaven unto a hell!

LYSANDER.

Helen, to you our minds we will unfold:
To-morrow night, when Phœbe doth behold
Her silver visage in the watery glass,
Decking with liquid pearl the bladed grass,—
A time that lovers' flights doth still conceal,—
Through Athens' gates have we devised to steal.

HERMIA.

And in the wood, where often you and I
Upon faint primrose-beds were wont to lie,
Emptying our bosoms of their counsel sweet,
There my Lysander and myself shall meet;
And thence from Athens turn away our eyes,
To seek new friends and stranger companies.
Farewell, sweet playfellow: pray thou for us;
And good luck grant thee thy Demetrius!—
Keep word, Lysander: we must starve our sight
From lovers' food till morrow deep midnight.

LYSANDER.

I will, my Hermia.　　　　[Exit HERMIA.
　　　　Helena, adieu:
As you on him, Demetrius dote on you!

　　　　　　　　　　　　　　[Exit.

HELENA.

How happy some o'er other-some can be!
Through Athens I am thought as fair as she.
But what of that? Demetrius thinks not so;
He will not know what all but he do know:
And as he errs, doting on Hermia's eyes,
So I, admiring of his qualities.
Things base and vile, holding no quantity,
Love can transpose to form and dignity:
Love looks not with the eyes, but with the mind;
And therefore is wing'd Cupid painted blind:
Nor hath love's mind of any judgement taste;
Wings, and no eyes, figure unheedy haste:
And therefore is Love said to be a child,
Because in choice he is so oft beguiled.
As waggish boys in game themselves forswear,
So the boy Love is perjured every where:
For ere Demetrius lookt on Hermia's eyne,
He hail'd down oaths that he was only mine;
And when this hail some heat from Hermia felt,
So he dissolved, and showers of oaths did melt.
I will go tell him of fair Hermia's flight:
Then to the wood will he to-morrow night
Pursue her; and for this intelligence
If I have thanks, it is a dear expense:
But herein mean I to enrich my pain,
To have his sight thither and back again.　[Exit.

SCENE II.

The same.　A room in QUINCE'S house.

Enter QUINCE the Carpenter, SNUG the Joiner,
　BOTTOM the Weaver, FLUTE the Bellows-
　mender, SNOUT the Tinker, and STARVELING
　the Tailor.

QUINCE.

IS all our company here?

BOTTOM.

You were best to call them generally, man by
man, according to the scrip.

QUINCE.

Here is the scroll of every man's name, which is
thought fit, through all Athens, to play in our

interlude before the duke and the duchess on his wedding-day at night.

BOTTOM.

First, good Peter Quince, say what the play treats on; then read the names of the actors; and so grow to a point.

QUINCE.

Marry, our play is *The most lamentable comedy and most cruel death of Pyramus and Thisby.*

BOTTOM.

A very good piece of work, I assure you, and a merry.—Now, good Peter Quince, call forth your actors by the scroll.—Masters, spread yourselves.

QUINCE.

Answer as I call you.—Nick Bottom the weaver.

BOTTOM.

Ready. Name what part I am for, and proceed.

QUINCE.

You, Nick Bottom, are set down for Pyramus.

BOTTOM.

What is Pyramus? a lover, or a tyrant?

QUINCE.

A lover, that kills himself most gallant for love.

BOTTOM.

That will ask some tears in the true performing of it: if I do it, let the audience look to their eyes; I will move storms, I will condole in some measure. To the rest: yet my chief humour is for a tyrant: I could play Ercles rarely, or a part to tear a cat in, to make all split.

> The raging rocks
> And shivering shocks
> Shall break the locks
>   Of prison-gates;
> And Phibbus' car
> Shall shine from far,
> And make and mar
>   The foolish Fates.

This was lofty!—Now name the rest of the players.—This is Ercles' vein, a tyrant's vein;—a lover is more condoling.

QUINCE.

Francis Flute the bellows-mender.

FLUTE.

Here, Peter Quince.

QUINCE.

You must take Thisby on you.

FLUTE.

What is Thisby? a wandering knight?

QUINCE.

It is the lady that Pyramus must love.

FLUTE.

Nay, faith, let not me play a woman; I have a beard coming.

QUINCE.

That's all one: you shall play it in a mask, and you may speak as small as you will.

BOTTOM.

An I may hide my face, let me play Thisby too: I'll speak in a monstrous little voice;—'Thisne, Thisne,'—'Ah, Pyramus, my lover dear! thy Thisby dear, and lady dear!'

QUINCE.

No, no; you must play Pyramus:—and, Flute, you Thisby.

BOTTOM.

Well, proceed.

QUINCE.

Robin Starveling the tailor.

STARVELING.

Here, Peter Quince.

QUINCE.

Robin Starveling, you must play Thisby's mother. —Tom Snout the tinker.

SNOUT.

Here, Peter Quince.

QUINCE.

You, Pyramus' father; myself, Thisby's father;— Snug the joiner, you, the lion's part:—and, I hope, here is a play fitted.

SNUG.

Have you the lion's part written? pray you, if it be, give it me, for I am slow of study.

QUINCE.

You may do it extempore, for it is nothing but roaring.

BOTTOM.

Let me play the lion too: I will roar, that I will do any man's heart good to hear me; I will roar, that I will make the duke say, 'Let him roar again, let him roar again.'

QUINCE.

An you should do it too terribly, you would fright the duchess and the ladies, that they would shriek; and that were enough to hang us all.

ALL.

That would hang us, every mother's son.

BOTTOM.

I grant you, friends, if you should fright the ladies out of their wits, they would have no more discretion but to hang us: but I will aggravate my voice so, that I will roar you as gently as any sucking dove; I will roar you an 'twere any nightingale.

QUINCE.

You can play no part but Pyramus; for Pyramus is a sweet-faced man; a proper man as one shall see in a summer's day; a most lovely, gentleman-like man: therefore you must needs play Pyramus.

BOTTOM.

Well, I will undertake it. What beard were I best to play it in?

QUINCE.

Why, what you will.

BOTTOM.

I will discharge it in either your straw-colour beard, your orange-tawny beard, your purple-in-grain beard, or your French-crown-colour beard, your perfect yellow.

QUINCE.

Some of your French crowns have no hair at all, and then you will play barefaced.—But, masters, here are your parts: and I am to entreat you, request you, and desire you, to con them by tomorrow night; and meet me in the palace-wood, a mile without the town, by moonlight: there will we rehearse, for if we meet in the city, we shall be dogg'd with company, and our devices known. In the mean time I will draw a bill of properties, such as our play wants. I pray you, fail me not.

BOTTOM.

We will meet; and there we may rehearse most
obscenely and courageously.

QUINCE.

Take pains; be perfit: adieu. At the duke's oak we
meet.

BOTTOM.

Enough; hold, or cut bow-strings.   [*Exeunt.*

ACT II. SCENE I.

A wood near Athens.

Enter a FAIRY *at one door and* PUCK *at another.*

PUCK.

HOW now, spirit! whither wander you?

FAIRY.

Over hill, over dale,
  Thorough bush, thorough brier,
Over park, over pale,
  Thorough flood, thorough fire,
I do wander every where,
Swifter than the moon's sphere;
And I serve the fairy queen,
To dew her orbs upon the green.
The cowslips tall her pensioners be:
In their gold coats spots you see;
Those be rubies, fairy favours,
In those freckles live their savours:
I must go seek some dewdrops here,
And hang a pearl in every cowslip's ear.
Farewell, thou lob of spirits; I'll be gone:
Our queen and all her elves come here anon.

PUCK.

The king doth keep his revels here to-night:
Take heed the queen come not within his sight;
For Oberon is passing fell and wrath,
Because that she, as her attendant, hath
A lovely boy, stol'n from an Indian king;
She never had so sweet a changeling:
And jealous Oberon would have the child
Knight of his train, to trace the forests wild;
But she perforce withholds the loved boy,
Crowns him with flowers, and makes him all her
  joy:
And now they never meet in grove or green,
By fountain clear or spangled starlight sheen,
But they do square, that all their elves, for fear,
Creep into acorn-cups, and hide them there.

FAIRY.

Either I mistake your shape and making quite,
Or else you are that shrewd and knavish sprite
Call'd Robin Goodfellow: are you not he
That frights the maidens of the villagery;
Skim milk, and sometimes labour in the quern,
And bootless make the breathless housewife
  churn;
And sometime make the drink to bear no barm;
Mislead night-wanderers, laughing at their harm?
Those that Hobgoblin call you, and sweet Puck,
You do their work, and they shall have good
  luck:
Are not you he?

PUCK.

Thou speak'st aright;
I am that merry wanderer of the night,
I jest to Oberon, and make him smile,

When I a fat and bean-fed horse beguile,
Neighing in likeness of a filly foal:
And sometime lurk I in a gossip's bowl,
In very likeness of a roasted crab;
And when she drinks, against her lips I bob,
And on her wither'd dewlap pour the ale.
The wisest aunt, telling the saddest tale,
Sometime for three-foot stool mistaketh me;
Then slip I from her bum, down topples she,
And 'tailor' cries, and falls into a cough;
And then the whole quire hold their hips and loff,
And waxen in their mirth, and neeze, and swear
A merrier hour was never wasted there.—
But room, fairy! here comes Oberon.

FAIRY.

And here my mistress,—Would that he were
  gone!

Enter OBERON, *at one door, with his* TRAIN, *and*
TITANIA, *at another, with hers.*

OBERON.

Ill met by moonlight, proud Titania.

TITANIA.

What, jealous Oberon!—Fairies, skip hence:
I have forsworn his bed and company.

OBERON.

Tarry, rash wanton: am not I thy lord?

TITANIA.

Then I must be thy lady: but I know
When thou hast stol'n away from fairy-land,
And in the shape of Corin sat all day,
Playing on pipes of corn, and versing love
To amorous Phyllida. Why art thou here,
Come from the furthest steep of India,
But that, forsooth, the bouncing Amazon,
Your buskin'd mistress and your warrior love,
To Theseus must be wedded? and you come
To give their bed joy and prosperity.

OBERON.

How canst thou thus, for shame, Titania,
Glance at my credit with Hippolyta,
Knowing I know thy love to Theseus?
Didst thou not lead him through the glimmering
  night
From Perigenia, whom he ravished?
And make him with fair Aegle break his faith,
With Ariadne and Antiopa?

TITANIA.

These are the forgeries of jealousy:
And never, since the middle summer's spring,
Met we on hill, in dale, forest, or mead,
By paved fountain or by rushy brook,
Or in the beached margent of the sea,
To dance our ringlets to the whistling wind,
But with thy brawls thou hast disturb'd our sport.
Therefore the winds, piping to us in vain,
As in revenge, have suck'd up from the sea
Contagious fogs; which falling in the land,
Hath every pelting river made so proud,
That they have overborne their continents:
The ox hath therefore stretch'd his yoke in vain,
The ploughman lost his sweat; and the green corn
Hath rotted ere his youth attain'd a beard:
The fold stands empty in the drowned field,
And crows are fatted with the murrion flock;
The nine-men's-morris is fill'd up with mud;
And the quaint mazes in the wanton green,

For lack of tread, are undistinguishable:
The human mortals want their winter cheer;
No night is now with hymn or carol blest:—
Therefore the moon, the governess of floods,
Pale in her anger, washes all the air,
That rheumatic diseases do abound:
And thorough this distemperature we see
The seasons alter: hoary-headed frosts
Fall in the fresh lap of the crimson rose;
And on old Hiems' chin and icy crown
An odorous chaplet of sweet summer buds
Is, as in mockery, set: the spring, the summer,
The childing autumn, angry winter, change
Their wonted liveries; and the mazed world,
By their increase, now knows not which is which:
And this same progeny of evils comes
From our debate, from our dissension;
We are their parents and original.

OBERON.
Do you amend it, then; it lies in you:
Why should Titania cross her Oberon?
I do but beg a little changeling boy,
To be my henchman.

TITANIA.
                    Set your heart at rest:
The fairy-land buys not the child of me.
His mother was a vot'ress of my order:
And, in the spiced Indian air, by night,
Full often hath she gossipt by my side;
And sat with me on Neptune's yellow sands,
Marking th' embarked traders on the flood;
When we have laught to see the sails conceive
And grow big-bellied with the wanton wind;
Which she, with pretty and with swimming gait
Following,—her womb then rich with my young
    squire,—
Would imitate, and sail upon the land,
To fetch me trifles, and return again,
As from a voyage, rich with merchandise.
But she, being mortal, of that boy did die;
And for her sake do I rear up her boy;
And for her sake I will not part with him.

OBERON.
How long within this wood intend you stay?

TITANIA.
Perchance till after Theseus' wedding-day.
If you will patiently dance in our round,
And see our moonlight revels, go with us;
If not, shun me, and I will spare your haunts.

OBERON.
Give me that boy, and I will go with thee.

TITANIA.
Not for thy fairy kingdom.—Fairies, away!
We shall chide downright, if I longer stay.
            [Exit TITANIA with her TRAIN.

OBERON.
Well, go thy way: thou shalt not from this grove
Till I torment thee for this injury.—
My gentle Puck, come hither. Thou remem-
    ber'st
Since once I sat upon a promontory,
And heard a mermaid, on a dolphin's back,
Uttering such dulcet and harmonious breath,
That the rude sea grew civil at her song,
And certain stars shot madly from their spheres,
To hear the sea-maid's music.

PUCK.
            I remember.

OBERON.
That very time I saw—but thou couldst not—
Flying between the cold moon and the earth,
Cupid all arm'd: a certain aim he took
At a fair vestal throned by the west,
And loosed his love-shaft smartly from his bow,
As it should pierce a hundred-thousand hearts:
But I might see young Cupid's fiery shaft
Quencht in the chaste beams of the watery moon,
And the imperial vot'ress passed on,
In maiden meditation, fancy-free,
Yet markt I where the bolt of Cupid fell:
It fell upon a little western flower,
Before milk-white, now purple with love's
    wound,
And maidens call it love-in-idleness.
Fetch me that flower; the herb I shew'd thee once:
The juice of it on sleeping eyelids laid
Will make or man or woman madly dote
Upon the next live creature that it sees.
Fetch me this herb; and be thou here again
Ere the leviathan can swim a league.

PUCK.
I'll put a girdle round about the earth
In forty minutes.   [Exit.

OBERON.
            Having once this juice,
I'll watch Titania when she is asleep,
And drop the liquor of it in her eyes.
The next thing then she waking looks upon,—
Be it on lion, bear, or wolf, or bull,
On meddling monkey or on busy ape,—
She shall pursue it with the soul of love:
And ere I take this charm off from her sight,
As I can take it with another herb,
I'll make her render up her page to me.
But who comes here? I am invisible;
And I will overhear their conference.

Enter DEMETRIUS, HELENA following him.

DEMETRIUS.
I love thee not, therefore pursue me not.
Where is Lysander and fair Hermia?
The one I'll slay, the other slayeth me.
Thou told'st me they were stol'n unto this wood;
And here am I, and wood within this wood,
Because I cannot meet my Hermia.
Hence, get thee gone, and follow me no more.

HELENA.
You draw me, you hard-hearted adamant;
But yet you draw not iron, for my heart
Is true as steel: leave you your power to draw,
And I shall have no power to follow you.

DEMETRIUS.
Do I entice you? do I speak you fair?
Or, rather, do I not in plainest truth
Tell you I do not nor I cannot love you?

HELENA.
And even for that do I love you the more.
I am your spaniel; and, Demetrius,
The more you beat me, I will fawn on you:
Use me but as your spaniel, spurn me, strike me,
Neglect me, lose me; only give me leave,
Unworthy as I am, to follow you.
What worser place can I beg in your love,—

And yet a place of high respect with me,—
Than to be used as you use your dog?
DEMETRIUS.
Tempt not too much the hatred of my spirit;
For I am sick when I do look on thee.
HELENA.
And I am sick when I look not on you.
DEMETRIUS.
You do impeach your modesty too much,
To leave the city, and commit yourself
Into the hands of one that loves you not;
To trust the opportunity of night,
And the ill counsel of a desert place,
With the rich worth of your virginity.
HELENA.
Your virtue is my privilege: for that
It is not night when I do see your face,
Therefore I think I am not in the night;
Nor doth this wood lack worlds of company,
For you in my respect are all the world:
Then how can it be said I am alone,
When all the world is here to look on me?
DEMETRIUS.
I'll run from thee and hide me in the brakes,
And leave thee to the mercy of wild-beasts.
HELENA.
The wildest hath not such a heart as you.
Run when you will, the story shall be changed,—
Apollo flies, and Daphne holds the chase;
The dove pursues the griffin; the mild hind
Makes speed to catch the tiger,—bootless speed,
When cowardice pursues, and valour flies!
DEMETRIUS.
I will not stay thy questions; let me go:
Or, if thou follow me, do not believe
But I shall do thee mischief in the wood.
HELENA.
Ay, in the temple, in the town, the field,
You do me mischief. Fie, Demetrius!
Your wrongs do set a scandal on my sex:
We cannot fight for love, as men may do;
We should be woo'd, and were not made to woo.
I'll follow thee, and make a heaven of hell,
To die upon the hand I love so well.
[Exeunt DEMETRIUS and HELENA.
OBERON.
Fare thee well, nymph: ere he do leave this grove,
Thou shalt fly him, and he shall seek thy love.
Enter PUCK.
Hast thou the flower there? Welcome, wanderer.
PUCK.
Ay, there it is.
OBERON.
I pray thee, give it me.
I know a bank where the wild thyme blows,
Where oxlips and the nodding violet grows;
Quite over-canopied with lush woodbine,
With sweet musk-roses, and with eglantine:
There sleeps Titania sometime of the night,
Lull'd in these flowers with dances and delight;
And there the snake throws her enamell'd skin,
Weed wide enough to wrap a fairy in:
And with the juice of this I'll streak her eyes,
And make her full of hateful fantasies.
Take thou some of it, and seek through this
grove:

A sweet Athenian lady is in love
With a disdainful youth: anoint his eyes;
But do it when the next thing he espies
May be the lady: thou shalt know the man
By the Athenian garments he hath on.
Effect it with some care, that he may prove
More fond on her than she upon her love:
And look thou meet me ere the first cock crow.
PUCK.
Fear not, my lord, your servant shall do so.
[Exeunt.

SCENE II.

Another part of the wood.

Enter TITANIA, *with her* TRAIN.

TITANIA.
COME, now a roundel and a fairy song;
Then, for the third part of a minute, hence;—
Some, to kill cankers in the musk-rose buds;
Some, war with rere-mice for their leathern
wings,
To make my small elves coats; and some, keep
back
The clamorous owl, that nightly hoots and
wonders
At our quaint spirits. Sing me now asleep;
Then to your offices, and let me rest.

Song.
FIRST FAIRY.
You spotted snakes with double tongue,
Thorny hedgehogs, be not seen;
Newts and blind-worms, do no wrong,
Come not near our fairy queen.
Chorus.
Philomel, with melody
Sing in our sweet lullaby;
Lulla, lulla, lullaby; lulla, lulla, lullaby:
Never harm,
Nor spell nor charm,
Come our lovely lady nigh;
So, good night, with lullaby.

SECOND FAIRY.
Weaving spiders, come not here;
Hence, you long-legg'd spinners, hence!
Beetles black, approach not near;
Worm nor snail, do no offence.
Chorus.
Philomel, with melody, &c.

FIRST FAIRY.
Hence, away! now all is well:
One aloof stand sentinel.
[Exeunt FAIRIES. TITANIA *sleeps.*
Enter OBERON.
OBERON.
What thou see'st when thou dost wake,
[Squeezes the flower on TITANIA'S eyelids.
Do it for thy true-love take;
Love and languish for his sake:
Be it ounce, or cat, or bear,
Pard, or boar with bristled hair,
In thy eye that shall appear
When thou wakest, it is thy dear:
Wake when some vile thing is near.   [Exit.

Enter LYSANDER *and* HERMIA.
LYSANDER.
Fair love, you faint with wandering in the
　wood;
And to speak troth, I have forgot our way:
We'll rest us, Hermia, if you think it good,
And tarry for the comfort of the day.
HERMIA.
Be it so, Lysander: find you out a bed;
For I upon this bank will rest my head.
LYSANDER.
One turf shall serve as pillow for us both;
One heart, one bed, two bosoms, and one troth.
HERMIA.
Nay, good Lysander; for my sake, my dear,
Lie further off yet, do not lie so near.
LYSANDER.
O, take the sense, sweet, of my innocence!
Love takes the meaning in love's conference.
I mean, that my heart unto yours is knit,
So that but one heart we can make of it:
Two bosoms interchained with an oath;
So then two bosoms and a single troth.
Then by your side no bed-room me deny;
For lying so, Hermia, I do not lie.
HERMIA.
Lysander riddles very prettily:—
Now much beshrew my manners and my pride,
If Hermia meant to say Lysander lied.
But, gentle friend, for love and courtesy
Lie further off; in human modesty,
Such separation as may well be said
Becomes a virtuous bachelor and a maid,
So far be distant; and, good night, sweet friend:
Thy love ne'er alter till thy sweet life end!
LYSANDER.
Amen, amen, to that fair prayer, say I;
And then end life when I end loyalty!
Here is my bed: sleep give thee all his rest!
HERMIA.
With half that wish the wisher's eyes be prest!
　　　　　　　　　　　　　　[*They sleep.*
Enter PUCK.
PUCK.
Through the forest have I gone,
But Athenian found I none,
On whose eyes I might approve
This flower's force in stirring love.
Night and silence! who is here?
Weeds of Athens he doth wear:
This is he my master said
Despised the Athenian maid;
And here the maiden, sleeping sound,
On the dank and dirty ground:—
Pretty soul! she durst not lie
Near this lack-love, this kill-courtesy.
Churl, upon thy eyes I throw
[*Squeezes the flower on* LYSANDER'S *eyelids.*
All the power this charm doth owe.
When thou wakest, let love forbid
Sleep his seat on thy eyelid:
So awake when I am gone;
For I must now to Oberon. 　　　　[*Exit.*
Enter DEMETRIUS *and* HELENA, *running.*
HELENA.
Stay, though thou kill me, sweet Demetrius.

DEMETRIUS.
I charge thee, hence, and do not haunt me thus.
HELENA.
O, wilt thou darkling leave me? do not so.
DEMETRIUS.
Stay, on thy peril: I alone will go. 　　[*Exit.*
HELENA.
O, I am out of breath in this fond chase!
The more my prayer, the lesser is my grace.
Happy is Hermia, wheresoe'er she lies;
For she hath blessed and attractive eyes.
How came her eyes so bright? Not with salt tears:
If so, my eyes are oftener washt than hers.
No, no, I am as ugly as a bear;
For beasts that meet me run away for fear:
Therefore no marvel though Demetrius
Do, as a monster, fly my presence thus.
What wicked and dissembling glass of mine
Made me compare with Hermia's sphery eyne?—
But who is here?—Lysander! on the ground!
Dead? or asleep?—I see no blood, no wound.—
Lysander, if you live, good sir, awake.
LYSANDER [*starting up*].
And run through fire I will for thy sweet sake.
Transparent Helena! Nature shows art,
That through thy bosom makes me see thy heart.
Where is Demetrius? O, how fit a word
Is that vile name to perish on my sword!
HELENA.
Do not say so, Lysander; say not so.
What though he love your Hermia? Lord, what
　though?
Yet Hermia still loves you: then be content.
LYSANDER.
Content with Hermia! No; I do repent
The tedious minutes I with her have spent.
Not Hermia, but Helena I love:
Who will not change a raven for a dove?
The will of man is by his reason sway'd;
And reason says you are the worthier maid.
Things growing are not ripe until their season:
So I, being young, till now ripe not to reason;
And touching now the point of human skill,
Reason becomes the marshal to my will,
And leads me to your eyes; where I o'erlook
Love's stories, written in Love's richest book.
HELENA.
Wherefore was I to this keen mockery born?
When at your hands did I deserve this scorn?
Is't not enough, is't not enough, young man,
That I did never, no, nor never can,
Deserve a sweet look from Demetrius' eye,
But you must flout my insufficiency? 　　[do,-
Good troth, you do me wrong,—good sooth, you
In such disdainful manner me to woo.
But fare you well: perforce I must confess
I thought you lord of more true gentleness.
O, that a lady, of one man refused,
Should of another therefore be abused! 　　[*Exit*
LYSANDER.
She sees not Hermia.—Hermia, sleep thou there
And never mayst thou come Lysander near!
For, as a surfeit of the sweetest things
The deepest loathing to the stomach brings;
Or, as the heresies that men do leave
Are hated most of those they did deceive;

So thou, my surfeit and my heresy,
Of all be hated, but the most of me!
And, all my powers, address your love and might
To honour Helen, and to be her knight!   [*Exit.*

HERMIA [*awaking*].
Help me, Lysander, help me! do thy best
To pluck this crawling serpent from my breast!
Ay me, for pity!—what a dream was here!
Lysander, look how I do quake with fear:
Methought a serpent eat my heart away,
And you sat smiling at his cruel prey.—
Lysander!—what, removed?—Lysander! lord!—
What, out of hearing? gone? no sound, no word?
Alack, where are you? speak, an if you hear;
Speak, of all loves! I swoon almost with fear.
No?—then I well perceive you are not nigh:
Either death or you I'll find immediately.   [*Exit.*

ACT III. SCENE I.

The wood. TITANIA *lying asleep.*

Enter QUINCE, SNUG, BOTTOM, FLUTE,
SNOUT, *and* STARVELING.

BOTTOM.
ARE we all met?

QUINCE.
Pat, pat; and here's a marvellous convenient
place for our rehearsal. This green plot shall be
our stage, this hawthorn-brake our tiring-house;
and we will do it in action as we will do it before
the duke.

BOTTOM.
Peter Quince,—

QUINCE.
What say'st thou, bully Bottom?

BOTTOM.
There are things in this comedy of *Pyramus and
Thisby* that will never please. First, Pyramus must
draw a sword to kill himself; which the ladies
cannot abide. How answer you that?

SNOUT.
By'r lakin, a parlous fear.

STARVELING.
I believe we must leave the killing out, when all
is done.

BOTTOM.
Not a whit: I have a device to make all well.
Write me a prologue, and let the prologue seem
to say, we will do no harm with our swords, and
that Pyramus is not kill'd indeed; and, for the
more better assurance, tell them that I Pyramus
am not Pyramus, but Bottom the weaver: this
will put them out of fear.

QUINCE.
Well, we will have such a prologue; and it shall
be written in eight and six.

BOTTOM.
No, make it two more: let it be written in eight
and eight.

SNOUT.
Will not the ladies be afeard of the lion?

STARVELING.
I fear it, I promise you.

BOTTOM.
Masters, you ought to consider with yourselves:
to bring in,—God shield us!—a lion among

ladies is a most dreadful thing; for there is not a
more fearful wild-fowl than your lion living; and
we ought to look to't.

SNOUT.
Therefore another prologue must tell he is not
a lion.

BOTTOM.
Nay, you must name his name, and half his face
must be seen through the lion's neck; and he
himself must speak through, saying thus, or to
the same defect,—'Ladies,'—or, 'Fair ladies,—
I would wish you,'—or, 'I would request you,'
—or, 'I would entreat you,—not to fear, not to
tremble: my life for yours. If you think I come
hither as a lion, it were pity of my life: no, I am
no such thing; I am a man as other men are:'—
and there, indeed, let him name his name, and
tell them plainly he is Snug the joiner.

QUINCE.
Well, it shall be so. But there is two hard things,
—that is, to bring the moonlight into a chamber;
for, you know, Pyramus and Thisby meet by
moonlight.

SNUG.
Doth the moon shine that night we play our play?

BOTTOM.
A calendar, a calendar! look in the almanac; find
out moonshine, find out moonshine.

QUINCE.
Yes, it doth shine that night.

BOTTOM.
Why, then may you leave a casement of the great
chamber-window, where we play, open, and the
moon may shine in at the casement.

QUINCE.
Ay; or else one must come in with a bush of
thorns and a lantern, and say he comes to disfigure, or to present, the person of moonshine.
Then, there is another thing: we must have a wall
in the great chamber; for Pyramus and Thisby,
says the story, did talk through the chink of a wall.

SNUG.
You can never bring in a wall.—What say you,
Bottom?

BOTTOM.
Some man or other must present wall: and let
him have some plaster, or some loam, or some
rough-cast about him, to signify wall; and let him
hold his fingers thus, and through that cranny
shall Pyramus and Thisby whisper.

QUINCE.
If that may be, then all is well. Come, sit down,
every mother's son, and rehearse your parts.
Pyramus, you begin: when you have spoken your
speech, enter into that brake;—and so every one
according to his cue.

Enter PUCK *behind.*

PUCK.
What hempen home-spuns have we swaggering
So near the cradle of the fairy queen?   [*here,*
What, a play toward! I'll be an auditor;
An actor too perhaps, if I see cause.

QUINCE.
Speak, Pyramus.—Thisby, stand forth.

BOTTOM.
Thisby, the flowers of odious savours sweet,—

QUINCE.

Odours, odours.

BOTTOM.

——odours savours sweet:
So hath thy breath, my dearest Thisby dear.—
But hark, a voice! stay thou but here awhile,
And by and by I will to thee appear.   [*Exit.*

PUCK [*Aside*].

A stranger Pyramus than e'er play'd here.   [*Exit.*

FLUTE.

Must I speak now?

QUINCE.

Ay, marry, must you; for you must understand
he goes but to see a noise that he heard, and is to
come again.

FLUTE.

Most radiant Pyramus, most lily-white of hue,
Of colour like the red rose on triumphant
     brier,
Most brisky juvenal, and eke most lovely Jew,
     As true as truest horse, that yet would never tire,
I'll meet thee, Pyramus, at Ninny's tomb.

QUINCE.

'Ninus' tomb,' man:—why, you must not speak
that yet; that you answer to Pyramus: you speak
all your part at once, cues and all.—Pyramus
enter: your cue is past; it is, 'never tire.'

FLUTE.

O,—As true as truest horse, that yet would never
tire.

Enter PUCK, *and* BOTTOM *with an ass-head.*

BOTTOM.

If I were fair, Thisby, I were only thine:—

QUINCE.

O monstrous! O strange! we are haunted.—
Pray, masters! fly, masters!—Help!
     [*Exit with* SNUG, FLUTE, SNOUT, *and*
     STARVELING.

PUCK.

I'll follow you, I'll lead you about a round,
     Through bog, through bush, through brake,
          through brier:
Sometime a horse I'll be, sometime a hound,
     A hog, a headless bear, sometime a fire;
And neigh, and bark, and grunt, and roar, and
     burn,
Like horse, hound, hog, bear, fire, at every turn.
     [*Exit.*

BOTTOM.

Why do they run away? this is a knavery of them
to make me afeard.

Enter SNOUT.

SNOUT.

O Bottom, thou art changed! what do I see on
thee?

BOTTOM.

What do you see? you see an ass-head of your
own, do you?   [*Exit* SNOUT.

Enter QUINCE.

QUINCE.

Bless thee, Bottom! bless thee! thou art translated.   [*Exit.*

BOTTOM.

I see their knavery: this is to make an ass of me;
to fright me, if they could. But I will not stir
from this place, do what they can: I will walk up

and down here, and I will sing, that they shall
hear I am not afraid.   [*Sings.*

The ousel-cock so black of hue,
     With orange-tawny bill,
The throstle with his note so true,
     The wren with little quill:—

TITANIA [*awaking*].

What angel wakes me from my flowery bed?

BOTTOM [*sings*].

The finch, the sparrow, and the lark,
     The plain-song cuckoo gray,
Whose note full many a man doth mark,
     And dares not answer nay;—

for, indeed, who would set his wit to so foolish
a bird? who would give a bird the lie, though he
cry 'cuckoo' never so?

TITANIA.

I pray thee, gentle mortal, sing again:
Mine ear is much enamour'd of thy note;
So is mine eye enthralled to thy shape;
And thy fair virtue's force perforce doth move
     me,
On the first view, to say, to swear, I love thee.

BOTTOM.

Methinks, mistress, you should have little reason
for that: and yet, to say the truth, reason and love
keep little company together now-a-days:—the
more the pity that some honest neighbours will
not make them friends. Nay, I can gleek upon
occasion.

TITANIA.

Thou art as wise as thou art beautiful.

BOTTOM.

Not so, neither: but if I had wit enough to get out
of this wood, I have enough to serve mine own
turn.

TITANIA.

Out of this wood do not desire to go:
Thou shalt remain here, whether thou wilt or no.
I am a spirit of no common rate,—
The summer still doth tend upon my state;
And I do love thee: therefore, go with me;
I'll give thee fairies to attend on thee;
And they shall fetch thee jewels from the deep,
And sing, while thou on pressed flowers dost
     sleep:
And I will purge thy mortal grossness so,
That thou shalt like an airy spirit go.—
Peas-blossom! Cobweb! Moth! and Mustard-
     seed!

Enter four FAIRIES.

FIRST FAIRY.

Ready.

SECOND FAIRY.

     And I.

THIRD FAIRY.

And I.

FOURTH FAIRY.

     And I.

ALL.

                    Where shall we go?

TITANIA.

Be kind and courteous to this gentleman,—
Hop in his walks, and gambol in his eyes;
Feed him with apricocks and dewberries,

With purple grapes, green figs, and mulberries;
The honey-bags steal from the humble-bees,
And for night-tapers crop their waxen thighs,
And light them at the fiery glow-worm's eyes,
To have my love to bed and to arise;
And pluck the wings from painted butterflies
To fan the moonbeams from his sleeping eyes:
Nod to him, elves, and do him courtesies.

FIRST FAIRY.

Hail, mortal!

SECOND FAIRY.

Hail!

THIRD FAIRY.

Hail!

FOURTH FAIRY.

Hail!

BOTTOM.

I cry your worships mercy heartily.—I beseech
your worship's name.

COBWEB.

Cobweb.

BOTTOM.

I shall desire you of more acquaintance, good
Master Cobweb: if I cut my finger, I shall make
bold with you.—Your name, honest gentleman?

PEAS-BLOSSOM.

Peas-blossom.

BOTTOM.

I pray you, commend me to Mistress Squash,
your mother, and to Master Peascod, your father.
Good Master Peas-blossom, I shall desire you of
more acquaintance too.—Your name, I beseech
you, sir?

MUSTARD-SEED.

Mustard-seed.

BOTTOM.

Good Master Mustard-seed, I know your
patience well: that same cowardly, giant-like ox-
beef hath devour'd many a gentleman of your
house: I promise you your kindred hath made my
eyes water ere now. I desire you more acquaintance, good Master Mustard-seed.

TITANIA.

Come, wait upon him; lead him to my bower.
The moon methinks looks with a watery eye;
And when she weeps, weeps every little flower,
Lamenting some enforced chastity.
Tie up my love's tongue, bring him silently.

[Exeunt.

SCENE II.

Another part of the wood.

Enter OBERON.

OBERON.

I WONDER if Titania be awaked;
   Then, what it was that next came in her eye,
Which she must dote on in extremity.—
Here comes my messenger.

Enter PUCK.
                        How now, mad spirit!
What night-rule now about this haunted grove?

PUCK.

My mistress with a monster is in love.
Near to her close and consecrated bower,
While she was in her dull and sleeping hour,
A crew of patches, rude mechanicals,

That work for bread upon Athenian stalls,
Were met together to rehearse a play,
Intended for great Theseus' nuptial day.
The shallowest thickskin of that barren sort,
Who Pyramus presented in their sport,
Forsook his scene, and enter'd in a brake:
When I did him at this advantage take,
An ass's nowl I fixed on his head:
Anon his Thisbe must be answered,
And forth my mimic comes. When they him spy,
As wild geese that the creeping fowler eye,
Or russet-pated choughs, many in sort,
Rising and cawing at the gun's report,
Sever themselves, and madly sweep the sky,
So, at his sight, away his fellows fly;
And, at our stamp, here o'er and o'er one falls;
He murder cries, and help from Athens calls.
Their sense thus weak, lost with their fears thus
     strong,
Made senseless things begin to do them wrong;
For briers and thorns at their apparel snatch;
Some, sleeves,—some, hats;—from yielders all
     things catch.
I led them on in this distracted fear,
And left sweet Pyramus translated there:
When in that moment,—so it came to pass,—
Titania waked, and straightway loved an ass.

OBERON.

This falls out better than I could devise.
But hast thou yet latcht the Athenian's eyes
With the love-juice, as I did bid thee do?

PUCK.

I took him sleeping,—that is finisht too,—
And the Athenian woman by his side;
That, when he waked, of force she must be eyed.

Enter HERMIA *and* DEMETRIUS.

OBERON.

Stand close: this is the same Athenian.

PUCK.

This is the woman, but not this the man.

DEMETRIUS.

O, why rebuke you him that loves you so?
Lay breath so bitter on your bitter foe.

HERMIA.

Now I but chide; but I should use thee worse,
For thou, I fear, hast given me cause to curse.
If thou hast slain Lysander in his sleep,
Being o'er shoes in blood, plunge in the deep,
And kill me too.
The sun was not so true unto the day
As he to me: would he have stol'n away
From sleeping Hermia? I'll believe as soon
This whole earth may be bored; and that the
     moon
May through the centre creep, and so displease
Her brother's noontide with th' Antipodes.
It cannot be but thou hast murder'd him;
So should a murderer look,—so dead, so grim.

DEMETRIUS.

So should the murder'd look; and so should I,
Pierced through the heart with your stern cruelty:
Yet you, the murderer, look as bright, as clear,
As yonder Venus in her glimmering sphere.

HERMIA.

What's this to my Lysander? where is he?
Ah, good Demetrius, wilt thou give him me?

DEMETRIUS.
I had rather give his carcass to my hounds.
HERMIA.
Out, dog! out, cur! thou drivest me past the
　　bounds
Of maiden's patience. Hast thou slain him,
　　then?
Henceforth be never number'd among men!
O, once tell true, tell true, even for my sake!
Durst thou have lookt upon him being awake,
And hast thou kill'd him sleeping? O brave
　　touch!
Could not a worm, an adder, do so much?
An adder did it; for with doubler tongue
Than thine, thou serpent, never adder stung.
DEMETRIUS.
You spend your passion on a misprised mood:
I am not guilty of Lysander's blood;
Nor is he dead, for aught that I can tell.
HERMIA.
I pray thee, tell me, then, that he is well.
DEMETRIUS.
An if I could, what should I get therefore?
HERMIA.
A privilege, never to see me more:—
And from thy hated presence part I so:
See me no more, whether he be dead or no. [Exit.
DEMETRIUS.
There is no following her in this fierce vein:
Here therefore for a while I will remain.
So sorrow's heaviness doth heavier grow
For debt that bankrout sleep doth sorrow owe;
Which now in some slight measure it will pay,
If for his tender here I make some stay.
　　　　　　　　　　　　[Lies down and sleeps.
OBERON.
What hast thou done? thou hast mistaken quite,
And laid the love-juice on some true-love's sight:
Of thy misprision must perforce ensue
Some true-love turn'd, and not a false turn'd
　　true.
PUCK.
Then fate o'er-rules; that, one man holding troth,
A million fail, confounding oath on oath.
OBERON.
About the wood go swifter than the wind,
And Helena of Athens look thou find:
All fancy-sick she is, and pale of cheer
With sighs of love, that costs the fresh blood
　　dear:
By some illusion see thou bring her here:
I'll charm his eyes against she do appear.
PUCK.
I go, I go; look how I go,—
Swifter than arrow from the Tartar's bow. [Exit.
OBERON.
　　Flower of this purple dye,
　　Hit with Cupid's archery,
[Squeezes the flower on DEMETRIUS'S eye-
　　lids.
　　Sink in apple of his eye!
　　When his love he doth espy,
　　Let her shine as gloriously
　　As the Venus of the sky.—
　　When thou wakest, if she be by,
　　Beg of her for remedy.

Enter PUCK.
PUCK.
　　Captain of our fairy band,
　　Helena is here at hand;
　　And the youth, mistook by me,
　　Pleading for a lover's fee.
　　Shall we their fond pageant see?
　　Lord, what fools these mortals be!
OBERON.
　　Stand aside: the noise they make
　　Will cause Demetrius to awake.
PUCK.
　　Then will two at once woo one,—
　　That must needs be sport alone;
　　And those things do best please me
　　That befall preposterously.
Enter HELENA and LYSANDER.
LYSANDER.
Why should you think that I should woo in
　　scorn?
Scorn and derision never come in tears:
Look, when I vow, I weep; and vows so born,
　　In their nativity all truth appears.
How can these things in me seem scorn to you,
Bearing the badge of faith, to prove them true?
HELENA.
You do advance your cunning more and more.
　　When truth kills truth, O devilish-holy fray!
These vows are Hermia's: will you give her o'er?
　　Weigh oath with oath, and you will nothing
　　weigh:
Your vows to her and me, put in two scales,
Will even weigh; and both as light as tales.
LYSANDER.
I had no judgement when to her I swore.
HELENA.
Nor none, in my mind, now you give her o'er.
LYSANDER.
Demetrius loves her, and he loves not you.
DEMETRIUS [awaking].
O Helen, goddess, nymph, perfect, divine!
To what, my love, shall I compare thine eyne?
Crystal is muddy. O, how ripe in show
Thy lips, those kissing cherries, tempting grow!
That pure congealed white, high Taurus' snow,
Fann'd with the eastern wind, turns to a crow
When thou hold'st up thy hand: O, let me kiss
This princess of pure white, this seal of bliss!
HELENA.
O spite! O hell! I see you all are bent
To set against me for your merriment:
If you were civil and knew courtesy,
You would not do me thus much injury.
Can you not hate me, as I know you do,
But you must join in souls to mock me too?
If you were men, as men you are in show,
You would not use a gentle lady so;
To vow, and swear, and superpraise my parts,
When I am sure you hate me with your hearts.
You both are rivals, and love Hermia;
And now both rivals, to mock Helena:
A trim exploit, a manly enterprise,
To conjure tears up in a poor maid's eyes
With your derision! none of noble sort
Would so offend a virgin, and extort
A pour soul's patience, all to make you sport.

LYSANDER.

You are unkind, Demetrius; be not so;
For you love Hermia;—this you know I know:
And here, with all good will, with all my heart,
In Hermia's love I yield you up my part;
And yours of Helena to me bequeath,
Whom I do love, and will do to my death.

HELENA.

Never did mockers waste more idle breath.

DEMETRIUS.

Lysander, keep thy Hermia; I will none:
If e'er I loved her, all that love is gone.
My heart to her but as guest-wise sojourn'd,
And now to Helen is it home return'd,
There to remain.

LYSANDER.

Helen, it is not so.

DEMETRIUS.

Disparage not the faith thou dost not know,
Lest, to thy peril, thou aby it dear.—
Look, where thy love comes; yonder is thy dear.

Enter HERMIA.

HERMIA.

Dark night, that from the eye his function takes,
The ear more quick of apprehension makes;
Wherein it doth impair the seeing sense,
It pays the hearing double recompense.—
Thou art not by mine eye, Lysander, found;
Mine ear, I thank it, brought me to thy sound.
But why unkindly didst thou leave me so?

LYSANDER.

Why should he stay, whom love doth press to go?

HERMIA.

What love could press Lysander from my side?

LYSANDER.

Lysander's love, that would not let him bide,—
Fair Helena; who more engilds the night
Than all yon fiery O's and eyes of light.
Why seek'st thou me? could not this make thee
    know,
The hate I bear thee made me leave thee so?

HERMIA.

You speak not as you think: it cannot be.

HELENA.

Lo, she is one of this confederacy!
Now I perceive they have conjoin'd all three
To fashion this false sport in spite of me.
Injurious Hermia! most ungrateful maid!
Have you conspired, have you with these con-
    trived
To bait me with this foul derision?
Is all the counsel that we two have shared,
The sisters' vows, the hours that we have spent,
When we have chid the hasty-footed time
For parting us,—O, and is all forgot?
All school-days' friendship, childhood innocence?
We, Hermia, like two artificial gods,
Have with our needls created both one flower,
Both on one sampler, sitting on one cushion,
Both warbling of one song, both in one key;
As if our hands, our sides, voices, and minds,
Had been incorporate. So we grew together,
Like to a double cherry, seeming parted,
But yet an union in partition;
Two lovely berries moulded on one stem;
So, with two seeming bodies, but one heart;

Two of the first, like coats in heraldry,
Due but to one, and crowned with one crest.
And will you rent our ancient love asunder,
To join with men in scorning your poor friend?
It is not friendly, 'tis not maidenly:
Our sex, as well as I, may chide you for it,
Though I alone do feel the injury.

HERMIA.

I am amazed at your passionate words.
I scorn you not: it seems that you scorn me.

HELENA.

Have you not set Lysander, as in scorn,
To follow me, and praise my eyes and face?
And made your other love, Demetrius—
Who even but now did spurn me with his foot—
To call me goddess, nymph, divine, and rare,
Precious, celestial? Wherefore speaks he this
To her he hates? and wherefore doth Lysander
Deny your love, so rich within his soul,
And tender me, forsooth, affection,
But by your setting on, by your consent?
What though I be not so in grace as you,
So hung upon with love, so fortunate;
But miserable most, to love unloved?
This you should pity rather than despise.

HERMIA.

I understand not what you mean by this.

HELENA.

Ay, do, persever, counterfeit sad looks;
Make mouths upon me when I turn my back;
Wink each at other; hold the sweet jest up:
This sport, well carried, shall be chronicled.
If you have any pity, grace, or manners,
You would not make me such an argument.
But, fare ye well: 'tis partly mine own fault;
Which death or absence soon shall remedy.

LYSANDER.

Stay, gentle Helena; hear my excuse:
My love, my life, my soul, fair Helena!

HELENA.

O excellent!

HERMIA.

Sweet, do not scorn her so.

DEMETRIUS.

If she cannot entreat, I can compel.

LYSANDER.

Thou canst compel no more than she entreat:
Thy threats have no more strength than her
    prayers.—
Helen, I love thee; by my life, I do:
I swear by that which I will lose for thee,
To prove him false that says I love thee not.

DEMETRIUS.

I say I love thee more than he can do.

LYSANDER.

If thou say so, withdraw, and prove it too.

DEMETRIUS.

Quick, come!

HERMIA.

Lysander, whereto tends all this?

LYSANDER.

Away, you Ethiop!

DEMETRIUS.

No, no, sir;
Seem to break loose, take on as you would follow.
But yet come not: you are a tame man, go!

LYSANDER.
Hang off, thou cat, thou burr! vile thing, let
   loose,
Or I will shake thee from me like a serpent!
HERMIA.
Why are you grown so rude? what change is this,
Sweet love?
LYSANDER.
     Thy love! out, tawny Tartar, out!
Out, loathed medicine! O hated potion, hence!
HERMIA.
Do you not jest?
HELENA.
   Yes, sooth; and so do you.
LYSANDER.
Demetrius, I will keep my word with thee.
DEMETRIUS.
I would I had your bond, for I perceive
A weak bond holds you: I'll not trust your word.
LYSANDER.
What, should I hurt her, strike her, kill her dead?
Although I hate her, I'll not harm her so.
HERMIA.
What, can you do me greater harm than hate?
Hate me! wherefore? O me! what news, my love?
Am not I Hermia? are not you Lysander?
I am as fair now as I was erewhile.
Since night you loved me; yet since night you
   left me:
Why, then you left me,—O, the gods forbid!—
In earnest, shall I say?
LYSANDER.
      Ay, by my life;
And never did desire to see thee more.
Therefore be out of hope, of question, doubt;
Be certain, nothing truer; 'tis no jest
That I do hate thee, and love Helena.
HERMIA.
O me!—you juggler! you canker-blossom!
You thief of love! what, have you come by night
And stol'n my love's heart from him?
HELENA.
      Fine, i'faith!
Have you no modesty, no maiden shame,
No touch of bashfulness? What, will you tear
Impatient answers from my gentle tongue?
Fie, fie! you counterfeit, you puppet, you!
HERMIA.
Puppet! why, so; ay, that way goes the game.
Now I perceive that she hath made compare
Between our statures; she hath urged her height;
And with her personage, her tall personage,
Her height, forsooth, she hath prevail'd with him.
And are you grown so high in his esteem,
Because I am so dwarfish and so low?
How low am I, thou painted maypole? speak;
How low am I? I am not yet so low
But that my nails can reach unto thine eyes.
HELENA.
I pray you, though you mock me, gentlemen,
Let her not hurt me: I was never curst;
I have no gift at all in shrewishness;
I am a right maid for my cowardice:
Let her not strike me. You perhaps may think,
Because she is something lower than myself,
That I can match her.

HERMIA.
   Lower! hark, again.
HELENA.
Good Hermia, do not be so bitter with me.
I evermore did love you, Hermia,
Did ever keep your counsels, never wrong'd you;
Save that, in love unto Demetrius,
I told him of your stealth unto this wood,
He follow'd you; for love I follow'd him;
But he hath chid me hence, and threaten'd me
To strike me, spurn me, nay, to kill me too:
And now, so you will let me quiet go,
To Athens will I bear my folly back,
And follow you no further: let me go:
You see how simple and how fond I am.
HERMIA.
Why, get you gone: who is't that hinders you?
HELENA.
A foolish heart, that I leave here behind.
HERMIA.
What, with Lysander?
HELENA.
   With Demetrius.
LYSANDER.
Be not afraid; she shall not harm thee, Helena.
DEMETRIUS.
No, sir, she shall not, though you take her part.
HELENA.
O, when she's angry, she is keen and shrewd!
She was a vixen when she went to school;
And though she be but little, she is fierce.
HERMIA.
Little again! nothing but low and little!—
Why will you suffer her to flout me thus?
Let me come to her.
LYSANDER.
     Get you gone, you dwarf;
You minimus, of hind'ring knot-grass made;
You bead, you acorn.
DEMETRIUS.
     You are too officious
In her behalf that scorns your services.
Let her alone: speak not of Helena;
Take not her part; for, if thou dost intend
Never so little show of love to her,
Thou shalt aby it.
LYSANDER.
   Now she holds me not;
Now follow, if thou darest, to try whose right,
Of thine or mine, is most in Helena.
DEMETRIUS.
Follow! nay, I'll go with thee, cheek by jole.
   [Exeunt LYSANDER and DEMETRIUS.
HERMIA.
You, mistress, all this coil is 'long of you:
Nay, go not back.
HELENA.
   I will not trust you, I,
Nor longer stay in your curst company,
Your hands than mine are quicker for a fray;
My legs are longer though, to run away.   [Exit.
HERMIA.
I am amazed, and know not what to say.   [Exit.
OBERON.
This is thy negligence: still thou mistakest,
Or else committ'st thy knaveries wilfully.

PUCK.
Believe me, king of shadows, I mistook.
Did not you tell me I should know the man
By the Athenian garments he had on?
And so far blameless proves my enterprise,
That I have 'nointed an Athenian's eyes;
And so far am I glad it so did sort,
As this their jangling I esteem a sport.

OBERON.
Thou see'st these lovers seek a place to fight:
Hie therefore, Robin, overcast the night;
The starry welkin cover thou anon
With drooping fog, as black as Acheron;
And lead these testy rivals so astray,
As one come not within another's way.
Like to Lysander sometime frame thy tongue,
Then stir Demetrius up with bitter wrong;
And sometime rail thou like Demetrius;
And from each other look thou lead them thus,
Till o'er their brows death-counterfeiting sleep
With leaden legs and batty wings doth creep:
Then crush this herb into Lysander's eye;
Whose liquor hath this virtuous property,
To take from thence all error with his might,
And make his eyeballs roll with wonted sight.
When they next wake, all this derision
Shall seem a dream and fruitless vision;
And back to Athens shall the lovers wend,
With league whose date till death shall never end.
Whiles I in this affair do thee employ,
I'll to my queen and beg her Indian boy;
And then I will her charmed eye release
From monster's view, and all things shall be
   peace.

PUCK.
My fairy lord, this must be done with haste,
For Night's swift dragons cut the clouds full fast,
And yonder shines Aurora's harbinger;
At whose approach, ghosts, wandering here and
   there,
Troop home to churchyards: damned spirits all,
That in crossways and floods have burial,
Already to their wormy beds are gone;
For fear lest day should look their shames upon,
They wilfully themselves exile from light,
And must for aye consort with black-brow'd
   night.

OBERON.
But we are spirits of another sort:
I with the Morning's love have oft made sport;
And, like a forester, the groves may tread,
Even till the eastern gate, all fiery-red,
Opening on Neptune, with fair blessed beams
Turns into yellow gold his salt green streams.
But, notwithstanding, haste; make no delay:
We may effect this business yet ere day.   [Exit.

PUCK.
Up and down, up and down,
I will lead them up and down:
I am fear'd in field and town:
Goblin, lead them up and down.
Here comes one.

Enter LYSANDER.

LYSANDER.
Where art thou, proud Demetrius? speak thou
now.

PUCK.
Here, villain; drawn and ready. Where art thou?

LYSANDER.
I will be with thee straight.

PUCK.
                    Follow me, then,
To plainer ground.
          [*Exit* LYSANDER, *as following the voice*
          Enter DEMETRIUS.

DEMETRIUS.
          Lysander! speak agen:
Thou runaway, thou coward, art thou fled?
Speak! in some bush? where dost thou hide thy
   head?

PUCK.
Thou coward, art thou bragging to the stars,
Telling the bushes that thou look'st for wars,
And wilt not come? Come, recreant; come, thou
   child;
I'll whip thee with a rod: he is defiled
That draws a sword on thee.

DEMETRIUS.
                    Yea, art thou there?

PUCK.
Follow my voice: we'll try no manhood here.
                                    [*Exeunt.*

Enter LYSANDER.

LYSANDER.
He goes before me and still dares me on:
When I come where he calls, then he is gone.
The villain is much lighter-heel'd than I:
I follow'd fast, but faster he did fly;
That fall'n am I in dark uneven way,
And here will rest me. [*Lies down.*] Come, thou
   gentle day!
For if but once thou show me thy gray light,
I'll find Demetrius, and revenge this spite.
                                    [*Sleeps.*

Enter PUCK *and* DEMETRIUS.

PUCK.
Ho, ho, ho! Coward, why comest thou not?

DEMETRIUS.
Abide me, if thou darest; for well I wot
Thou runn'st before me, shifting every place,
And darest not stand, nor look me in the face.
Where art thou now?

PUCK.
                    Come hither: I am here.

DEMETRIUS.
Nay, then, thou mock'st me. Thou shalt buy this
   dear,
If ever I thy face by daylight see:
Now, go thy way. Faintness constraineth me
To measure out my length on this cold bed.
By day's approach look to be visited.
                    [*Lies down and sleeps.*

Enter HELENA.

HELENA.
O weary night, O long and tedious night,
   Abate thy hours! Shine comforts from the
      east,
That I may back to Athens by daylight,
   From these that my poor company detest:
And sleep, that sometime shuts up sorrow's eye,
Steal me awhile from mine own company.
                    [*Lies down and sleeps.*

PUCK.
Yet but three? Come one more;
Two of both kinds makes up four.
Here she comes, curst and sad:—
Cupid is a knavish lad,
Thus to make poor females mad.
Enter HERMIA.
HERMIA.
Never so weary, never so in woe;
Bedabbled with the dew, and torn with briers;
I can no further crawl, no further go;
My legs can keep no pace with my desires.
Here will I rest me till the break of day.
Heavens shield Lysander, if they mean a fray!
[*Lies down and sleeps.*
PUCK.
On the ground
Sleep sound:
I'll apply
To your eye,
Gentle lover, remedy.
[*Squeezing the herb on* LYSANDER'S *eye-
lids.*
When thou wakest,
Thou takest
True delight
In the sight
Of thy former lady's eye:
And the country proverb known,
That every man should take his own,
In your waking shall be shown:
Jack shall have Jill;
Naught shall go ill;
The man shall have his mare again, and all shall
be well.   [*Exit.*

ACT IV. SCENE I.

The wood. LYSANDER, DEMETRIUS, HELENA,
and HERMIA, *lying asleep.*

Enter TITANIA *and* BOTTOM; PEAS-BLOSSOM,
COBWEB, MOTH, MUSTARD-SEED, *and other*
FAIRIES *attending;* OBERON *behind unseen.*

TITANIA.
COME, sit thee down upon this flowery bed,
While I thy amiable cheeks do coy,
And stick musk-roses in thy sleek smooth head,
And kiss thy fair large ears, my gentle joy.
BOTTOM.
Where's Peas-blossom?
PEAS-BLOSSOM.
Ready.
BOTTOM.
Scratch my head, Peas-blossom.—Where's Mon-
sieur Cobweb?
COBWEB.
Ready.
BOTTOM.
Monsieur Cobweb, good monsieur, get your
weapons in your hand, and kill me a red-hipt
humble-bee on the top of a thistle; and, good
monsieur, bring me the honey-bag. Do not fret
yourself too much in the action, monsieur; and,
good monsieur, have a care the honey-bag break
not; I would be loth to have you overflown with a

honey-bag, signior.—Where's Monsieur Mus-
tard-seed?
MUSTARD-SEED.
Ready.
BOTTOM.
Give me your neif, Monsieur Mustard-seed.
Pray you, leave your courtesy, good monsieur.
MUSTARD-SEED.
What's your will?
BOTTOM.
Nothing, good monsieur, but to help Cavalery
Peas-blossom to scratch. I must to the barber's,
monsieur; for methinks I am marvellous hairy
about the face; and I am such a tender ass, if my
hair do but tickle me, I must scratch.
TITANIA.
What, wilt thou hear some music, my sweet love?
BOTTOM.
I have a reasonable good ear in music: let's have
the tongs and bones.   [*Tongs. Rural music.*
TITANIA.
Or say, sweet love, what thou desirest to eat.
BOTTOM.
Truly, a peck of provender: I could munch your
good dry oats. Methinks I have a great desire to
a bottle of hay: good hay, sweet hay hath no
fellow.
TITANIA.
I have a venturous fairy that shall seek
The squirrel's hoard, and fetch thee hence new
nuts.
BOTTOM.
I had rather have a handful or two of dried peas.
But, I pray you, let none of your people stir me:
I have an exposition of sleep come upon me.
TITANIA.
Sleep thou, and I will wind thee in my arms.—
Fairies, be gone, and be all ways away.—
[*Exeunt* FAIRIES.
So doth the woodbine the sweet honeysuckle
Gently entwist; the female ivy so
Enrings the barky fingers of the elm.
O, how I love thee! how I dote on thee!
[*They sleep.*
Enter PUCK.
OBERON [*advancing*].
Welcome, good Robin. See'st thou this sweet
sight?
Her dotage now I do begin to pity:
For, meeting her of late behind the wood,
Seeking sweet favours for this hateful fool,
I did upbraid her, and fall out with her;
For she his hairy temples then had rounded
With coronet of fresh and fragrant flowers;
And that same dew, which sometime on the buds
Was wont to swell, like round and orient pearls,
Stood now within the pretty flowerets' eyes,
Like tears, that did their own disgrace bewail.
When I had at my pleasure taunted her,
And she in mild terms begg'd my patience,
I then did ask of her her changeling child;
Which straight she gave me, and her fairy sent
To bear him to my bower in fairy-land.
And now I have the boy, I will undo
This hateful imperfection of her eyes:
And, gentle Puck, take this transformed scalp

From off the head of this Athenian swain;
That he, awaking when the other do,
May all to Athens back again repair,
And think no more of this night's accidents,
But as the fierce vexation of a dream.
But first I will release the fairy queen.
      Be as thou wast wont to be;
          [*Touching her eyes with an herb.*
      See as thou wast wont to see:
      Dian's bud o'er Cupid's flower
Hath such force and blessed power.
Now, my Titania: wake you, my sweet queen.
          TITANIA.
My Oberon! what visions have I seen!
Methought I was enamour'd of an ass.
          OBERON.
There lies your love.
          TITANIA.
          How came these things to pass?
O, how mine eyes do loathe his visage now!
          OBERON.
Silence awhile.—Robin, take off this head.—
Titania, music call; and strike more dead
Than common sleep of all these five the sense.
          TITANIA.
Music, ho! music, such as charmeth sleep!
          [*Music, still.*
          PUCK.
Now, when thou wakest, with thine own fool's
    eyes peep.
          OBERON.
Sound, music!—Come, my queen, take hands
    with me,
And rock the ground whereon these sleepers
    be.
Now thou and I are new in amity,
And will to-morrow midnight solemnly
Dance in Duke Theseus' house triumphantly,
And bless it to all fair prosperity:
There shall the pairs of faithful lovers be
Wedded, with Theseus, all in jollity.
          PUCK.
Fairy king, attend, and mark:
I do hear the morning lark.
          OBERON.
Then, my queen, in silence sad,
Trip we after the night's shade:
We the globe can compass soon,
Swifter than the wandering moon.
          TITANIA.
Come, my lord; and in our flight,
Tell me how it came this night
That I sleeping here was found
With these mortals on the ground.
          [*Exeunt. Wind horns.*
Enter THESEUS, HIPPOLYTA, EGEUS, *and*
          TRAIN.
          THESEUS.
Go, one of you, find out the forester;
For now our observation is perform'd;
And since we have the vaward of the day,
My love shall hear the music of my hounds:
Uncouple in the western valley; go:—
Dispatch, I say, and find the forester.—
          [*Exit an* ATTENDANT.
We will, fair queen, up to the mountain's top,

And mark the musical confusion
Of hounds and echo in conjunction.
          HIPPOLYTA.
I was with Hercules and Cadmus once,
When in a wood of Crete they bay'd the bear
With hounds of Sparta: never did I hear
Such gallant chiding; for besides the groves,
The skies, the fountains, every region near
Seem all one mutual cry: I never heard
So musical a discord, such sweet thunder.
          THESEUS.
My hounds are bred out of the Spartan kind,
So flew'd, so sanded; and their heads are hung
With ears that sweep away the morning dew;
Crook-knee'd, and dew-lapt like Thessalian bulls.
Slow in pursuit, but matcht in mouth like bells,
Each under each. A cry more tuneable
Was never holla'd to, nor cheer'd with horn,
In Crete, in Sparta, nor in Thessaly:
Judge when you hear.—But, soft! what nymphs
    are these?
          EGEUS.
My lord, this is my daughter here asleep
And this, Lysander; this Demetrius is;
This Helena, old Nedar's Helena:
I wonder of their being here together.
          THESEUS.
No doubt they rose up early to observe
The rites of May; and, hearing our intent,
Came here in grace of our solemnity.—
But speak, Egeus; is not this the day
That Hermia should give answer of her choice?
          EGEUS.
It is, my lord.
          THESEUS.
Go, bid the huntsmen wake them with their
    horns.
          [*Horns, and they wake. Shout within, and
          they all start up.*
Good morrow, friends.—Saint Valentine is past:
Begin these wood-birds but to couple now?
          LYSANDER.
Pardon, my lord.
          THESEUS.
          I pray you all, stand up.
I know you two are rival enemies:
How comes this gentle concord in the world,
That hatred is so far from jealousy,
To sleep by hate, and fear no enmity?
          LYSANDER.
My lord, I shall reply amazedly,
Half sleep, half waking: but as yet, I swear,
I cannot truly say how I came here;
But, as I think,—for truly would I speak,
And now I do bethink me, so it is,—
I came with Hermia hither: our intent
Was to be gone from Athens, where we might,
Without the peril of the Athenian law,—
          EGEUS.
Enough, enough, my lord; you have enough:
I beg the law, the law, upon his head.—
They would have stol'n away; they would,
    Demetrius,
Thereby to have defeated you and me,
You of your wife, and me of my consent,—
Of my consent that she should be your wife.

DEMETRIUS.

My lord, fair Helen told me of their stealth,
Of this their purpose hither to this wood;
And I in fury hither follow'd them,
Fair Helena in fancy following me.
But, my good lord, I wot not by what power,—
But by some power it is,—my love to Hermia,
Melted as the snow, seems to me now
As the remembrance of an idle gaud,
Which in my childhood I did dote upon;
And all the faith, the virtue of my heart,
The object, and the pleasure of mine eye,
Is only Helena. To her, my lord,
Was I betroth'd ere I saw Hermia:
But, like in sickness, did I loathe this food;
But, as in health, come to my natural taste,
Now do I wish it, love it, long for it,
And will for evermore be true to it.

THESEUS.

Fair lovers, you are fortunately met:
Of this discourse we more will hear anon.—
Egeus, I will overbear your will;
For in the temple, by and by, with us
These couples shall eternally be knit:
And, for the morning now is something worn,
Our purposed hunting shall be set aside.
Away with us to Athens! three and three,
We'll hold a feast in great solemnity.
Come, Hippolyta.

[Exeunt THESEUS, HIPPOLYTA, EGEUS,
and TRAIN.

DEMETRIUS.

These things seem small and undistinguishable,
Like far-off mountains turned into clouds.

HERMIA.

Methinks I see these things with parted eye,
When everything seems double.

HELENA.

So methinks:
And I have found Demetrius like a gemel,
Mine own, and not mine own.

DEMETRIUS.

Are you sure
That we are awake? It seems to me
That yet we sleep, we dream.—Do not you think
The duke was here, and bid us follow him?

HERMIA.

Yea; and my father.

HELENA.

And Hippolyta.

LYSANDER.

And he did bid us follow to the temple.

DEMETRIUS.

Why, then, we are awake: let's follow him;
And, by the way, let us recount our dreams.

[Exeunt.

BOTTOM [awaking].

When my cue comes, call me, and I will answer:
—my next is, 'Most fair Pyramus,'——Heigh-ho!
—Peter Quince! Flute the bellows-mender! Snout
the tinker! Starveling!—God's my life, stol'n
hence, and left me asleep! I have had a most rare
vision. I have had a dream,—past the wit of man
to say what dream it was: man is but an ass, if he
go about to expound this dream. Methought I
was—there is no man can tell what. Methought I

was, and methought I had,—but man is but a
patcht fool, if he will offer to say what methought
I had. The eye of man hath not heard, the ear of
man hath not seen, man's hand is not able to
taste, his tongue to conceive, nor his heart to report, what my dream was. I will get Peter Quince
to write a ballet of this dream: it shall be called
Bottom's Dream, because it hath no bottom; and
I will sing it in the latter end of a play before the
duke: peradventure, to make it the more gracious,
I shall sing it at her death.   [Exit.

SCENE II.

Athens.   A room in QUINCE'S *house.*

Enter QUINCE, FLUTE, SNOUT, *and*
STARVELING.

QUINCE.

HAVE you sent to Bottom's house? is he come
home yet?

STARVELING.

He cannot be heard of. Out of doubt he is transported.

FLUTE.

If he come not, then the play is marr'd: it goes
not forward, doth it?

QUINCE.

It is not possible: you have not a man in all Athens
able to discharge Pyramus but he.

FLUTE.

No, he hath simply the best wit of any handicraft
man in Athens.

QUINCE.

Yea, and the best person too; and he is a very
paramour for a sweet voice.

FLUTE.

You must say paragon: a paramour is, God bless
us, a thing of naught.

Enter SNUG.

SNUG.

Masters, the duke is coming from the temple, and
there is two or three lords and ladies more married: if our sport had gone forward, we had all
been made men.

FLUTE.

O sweet bully Bottom! Thus hath he lost sixpence
a day during his life; he could not have scaped
sixpence a day: an the duke had not given him sixpence a day for playing Pyramus, I'll be hang'd; he
would have deserved it: sixpence a day in Pyramus, or nothing.

Enter BOTTOM.

BOTTOM.

Where are these lads? where are these hearts?

QUINCE.

Bottom!—O most courageous day! O most happy
hour!

BOTTOM.

Masters, I am to discourse wonders: but ask me
not what; for if I tell you, I am no true Athenian.
I will tell you everything, right as it fell out.

QUINCE.

Let us hear, sweet Bottom.

BOTTOM.

Not a word of me. All that I will tell you is, that
the duke hath dined. Get your apparel together,

good strings to your beards, new ribbons to your
pumps; meet presently at the palace; every man
look o'er his part; for the short and the long is,
our play is preferr'd. In any case, let Thisby have
clean linen; and let not him that plays the lion
pare his nails, for they shall hang out for the lion's
claws. And, most dear actors, eat no onions nor
garlic, for we are to utter sweet breath; and I do
not doubt but to hear them say it is a sweet
comedy. No more words: away! go; away!

[Exeunt.

ACT V. SCENE I.

Athens.   *An apartment in the palace of* THESEUS.

Enter THESEUS, HIPPOLYTA, PHILOSTRATE,
LORDS, *and* ATTENDANTS.

HIPPOLYTA.

'TIS strange, my Theseus, that these lovers
  speak of.

THESEUS.

More strange than true: I never may believe
These antick fables nor these fairy toys.
Lovers and madmen have such seething brains,
Such shaping fantasies, that apprehend
More than cool reason ever comprehends.
The lunatic, the lover, and the poet
Are of imagination all compact:—
One sees more devils than vast hell can hold,—
That is, the madman: the lover, all as frantic,
Sees Helen's beauty in a brow of Egypt:
The poet's eye, in a fine frenzy rolling,   [heaven;
Doth glance from heaven to earth, from earth to
And, as imagination bodies forth
The forms of things unknown, the poet's pen
Turns them to shapes, and gives to airy nothing
A local habitation and a name.
Such tricks hath strong imagination,
That, if it would but apprehend some joy,
It comprehends some bringer of that joy;
Or in the night, imagining some fear,
How easy is a bush supposed a bear!

HIPPOLYTA.

But all the story of the night told over,
And all their minds transfigured so together,
More witnesseth than fancy's images,
And grows to something of great constancy;
But, howsoever, strange and admirable.

THESEUS.

Here come the lovers, full of joy and mirth.

Enter LYSANDER, DEMETRIUS, HERMIA, *and*
HELENA.

Joy, gentle friends! joy and fresh days of love
Accompany your hearts!

LYSANDER.

More than to us
Wait in your royal walks, your board, your bed!

THESEUS.

Come now; what masks, what dances shall we
  have,
To wear away this long age of three hours
Between our after-supper and bed-time?
Where is our usual manager of mirth?
What revels are in hand? Is there no play,
To ease the anguish of a torturing hour?
Call Philostrate.

PHILOSTRATE.

Here, mighty Theseus.

THESEUS.

Say, what abridgement have you for this evening?
What mask? what music? How shall we beguile
The lazy time, if not with some delight?

PHILOSTRATE.

There is a brief how many sports are ripe:
Make choice of which your highness will see first.

[*Giving a paper.*

THESEUS [*reads*].

'The battle with the Centaurs, to be sung
By an Athenian eunuch to the harp.'
We'll none of that: that have I told my love,
In glory of my kinsman Hercules.—
[*Reads*] 'The riot of the tipsy Bacchanals,
Tearing the Thracian singer in their rage.'
That is an old device; and it was play'd
When I from Thebes came last a conqueror.—
[*Reads*] 'The thrice-three Muses mourning for the
Of Learning, late deceased in beggary.'   [death
That is some satire, keen and critical,
Not sorting with a nuptial ceremony.—
[*Reads*] 'A tedious brief scene of young Pyramus
And his love Thisbe; very tragical mirth.'
Merry and tragical! tedious and brief!
That is, hot ice and wondrous strange snow.
How shall we find the concord of this discord?

PHILOSTRATE.

A play there is, my lord, some ten words long,
Which is as brief as I have known a play;
But by ten words, my lord, it is too long,
Which makes it tedious; for in all the play
There is not one word apt, one player fitted:
And tragical, my noble lord, it is;
For Pyramus therein doth kill himself.
Which, when I saw rehearsed, I must confess,
Made mine eyes water; but more merry tears
The passion of loud laughter never shed.

THESEUS.

What are they that do play it?

PHILOSTRATE.

Hard-handed men, that work in Athens here,
Which never labour'd in their minds till now;
And now have toil'd their unbreathed memories
With this same play, against your nuptial.

THESEUS.

And we will hear it.

PHILOSTRATE.

No, my noble lord;
It is not for you: I have heard it over,
And it is nothing, nothing in the world;
Unless you can find sport in their intents,
Extremely stretcht and conn'd with cruel pain,
To do you service.

THESEUS.

I will hear that play;
For never any thing can be amiss,
When simpleness and duty tender it.
Go, bring them in:—and take your places, ladies.

[*Exit* PHILOSTRATE.

HIPPOLYTA.

I love not to see wretchedness o'ercharged,
And duty in his service perishing.

THESEUS.

Why, gentle sweet, you shall see no such thing.

HIPPOLYTA.

He says they can do nothing in this kind.

THESEUS.

The kinder we, to give them thanks for nothing.
Our sport shall be to take what they mistake:
And what poor duty cannot do,
Noble respect takes it in might, not merit.
Where I have come, great clerks have purposed
To greet me with premeditated welcomes;
Where I have seen them shiver and look pale,
Make periods in the midst of sentences,
Throttle their practised accent in their fears,
And, in conclusion, dumbly have broke off,
Not paying me a welcome. Trust me, sweet,
Out of this silence yet I pickt a welcome;
And in the modesty of fearful duty
I read as much as from the rattling tongue
Of saucy and audacious eloquence.
Love, therefore, and tongue-tied simplicity,
In least speak most, to my capacity.

Enter PHILOSTRATE.

PHILOSTRATE.

So please your grace, the Prologue is addrest.

THESEUS.

Let him approach.   [*Flourish of trumpets.*

Enter the PROLOGUE.

PROLOGUE.

If we offend, it is with our good will.
   That you should think, we come not to offend,
But with good will. To show our simple skill,
   That is the true beginning of our end.
Consider, then, we come but in despite.
   We do not come as minding to content you,
Our true intent is. All for your delight,
   We are not here. That you should here repent
     you,
The actors are at hand; and, by their show,
You shall know all that you are like to know.

THESEUS.

This fellow doth not stand upon points.

LYSANDER.

He hath rid his prologue like a rough colt; he
knows not the stop. A good moral, my lord: it is
not enough to speak, but to speak true.

HIPPOLYTA.

Indeed he hath play'd on his prologue like a child
on a recorder; a sound, but not in government.

THESEUS.

His speech was like a tangled chain; nothing impair'd, but all disorder'd. Who is next?

Enter PYRAMUS *and* THISBE, WALL, MOON-
SHINE, *and* LION.

PROLOGUE.

Gentles, perchance you wonder at this show;
   But wonder on, till truth make all things plain.
This man is Pyramus, if you would know;
   This beauteous lady, Thisbe is certain.
This man, with lime and rough-cast, doth present
Wall, that vile Wall which did these lovers
     sunder;
And through Wall's chink, poor souls, they are
     content
To whisper; at the which let no man wonder.

This man, with lantern, dog, and bush of thorn,
   Presenteth Moonshine; for, if you will know
By moonshine did these lovers think no scorn
   To meet at Ninus' tomb, there, there to woo.
This grisly beast, which by name Lion hight,
   The trusty Thisbe, coming first by night,
Did scare away, or rather did affright;
   And, as she fled, her mantle she did fall,
   Which Lion vile with bloody mouth did
     stain.
Anon comes Pyramus, sweet youth and tall,
   And finds his trusty Thisbe's mantle slain:
Whereat, with blade, with bloody blameful
     blade,
   He bravely broacht his boiling bloody breast;
And Thisbe, tarrying in mulberry shade,
   His dagger drew, and died. For all the rest,
Let Lion, Moonshine, Wall, and lovers twain,
At large discourse, while here they do remain.

     [*Exeunt* PROLOGUE, PYRAMUS, THISBE,
     LION, *and* MOONSHINE.

THESEUS.

I wonder if the lion be to speak.

DEMETRIUS.

No wonder, my lord: one lion may, when many
asses do.

WALL.

In this same interlude it doth befall
That I, one Snout by name, present a wall;
And such a wall, as I would have you think,
That had in it a crannied hole or chink,
Through which the lovers, Pyramus and Thisbe,
Did whisper often very secretly.
This loam, this rough-cast, and this stone, doth
     show
That I am that same wall; the truth is so:
And this the cranny is, right and sinister,
Through which the fearful lovers are to whisper.

THESEUS.

Would you desire lime and hair to speak better?

DEMETRIUS.

It is the wittiest partition that ever I heard discourse, my lord.

THESEUS.

Pyramus draws near the wall: silence!

Enter PYRAMUS.

PYRAMUS.

O grim-lookt night! O night with hue so black!
   O night, which ever art when day is not!
O night, O night! alack, alack, alack,
   I fear my Thisbe's promise is forgot!—
And thou, O wall, O sweet, O lovely wall,
   That stand'st between her father's ground and
     mine!
Thou wall, O wall, O sweet and lovely wall,
   Show me thy chink, to blink through with mine
     eyne!   [WALL *holds up his fingers.*
Thanks, courteous wall: Jove shield thee well for
     this!
But what see I? No Thisbe do I see.
O wicked wall, through whom I see no bliss!
   Cursed be thy stones for thus deceiving me!'

THESEUS.

The wall, methinks, being sensible, should curse
again.

BOTTOM.

No, in truth, sir, he should not. 'Deceiving me'
is Thisbe's cue: she is to enter now, and I am to
spy her through the wall. You shall see, it will fall
pat as I told you.—Yonder she comes.

Enter THISBE.

THISBE.

O wall, full often hast thou heard my moans,
    For parting my fair Pyramus and me!
My cherry lips have often kist thy stones,
    Thy stones with lime and hair knit up in thee.

PYRAMUS.

I see a voice: now will I to the chink,
To spy an I can hear my Thisbe's face.—
Thisbe!

THISBE.

My love! thou art my love, I think.

PYRAMUS.

Think what thou wilt, I am thy lover's grace;
And, like Limander, am I trusty still.

THISBE.

And I like Helen, till the Fates me kill.

PYRAMUS.

Not Shafalus to Procrus was so true.

THISBE.

As Shafalus to Procrus, I to you.

PYRAMUS.

O, kiss me through the hole of this vile wall!

THISBE.

I kiss the wall's hole, not your lips at all.

PYRAMUS.

Wilt thou at Ninny's tomb meet me straightway?

THISBE.

'Tide life, 'tide death, I come without delay.

[*Exeunt* PYRAMUS *and* THISBE.

WALL.

Thus have I, wall, my part discharged so;
And, being done, thus wall away doth go.   [*Exit.*

THESEUS.

Now is the mural down between the two neighbours.

DEMETRIUS.

No remedy, my lord, when walls are so wilful to
hear without warning.

HIPPOLYTA.

This is the silliest stuff that e'er I heard.

THESEUS.

The best in this kind are but shadows; and the
worst are no worse, if imagination amend them.

HIPPOLYTA.

It must be your imagination then, and not theirs.

THESEUS.

If we imagine no worse of them than they of
themselves, they may pass for excellent men.—
Here come two noble beasts in, a moon and a
lion.

Enter LION *and* MOONSHINE.

LION.

You, ladies, you, whose gentle hearts do fear,
    The smallest monstrous mouse that creeps on
        floor,

May now perchance both quake and tremble here,
    When lion rough in wildest rage doth roar.
Then know that I one Snug the joiner am,
No lion fell, nor else no lion's dam;
For, if I should as lion come in strife
Into this place, 'twere pity on my life.

THESEUS.

A very gentle beast, and of a good conscience.

DEMETRIUS.

The very best at a beast, my lord, that e'er I saw.

LYSANDER.

This lion is a very fox for his valour.

THESEUS.

True; and a goose for his discretion.

DEMETRIUS.

Not so, my lord; for his valour cannot carry his
discretion; and the fox carries the goose.

THESEUS.

His discretion, I am sure, cannot carry his valour;
for the goose carries not the fox. It is well: leave
it to his discretion, and let us listen to the
moon.

MOONSHINE.

This lantern doth the horned moon present;—

DEMETRIUS.

He should have worn the horns on his head.

THESEUS.

He is no crescent, and his horns are invisible
within the circumference.

MOONSHINE.

This lantern doth the horned moon present;
Myself the man-i-th'-moon do seem to be.

THESEUS.

This is the greatest error of all the rest: the man
should be put into the lantern. How is it else the
man-i'-th'-moon?

DEMETRIUS.

He dares not come there for the candle; for, you
see, it is already in snuff.

HIPPOLYTA.

I am a-weary of this moon: would he would
change!

THESEUS.

It appears, by his small light of discretion, that he
is in the wane; but yet, in courtesy, in all reason,
we must stay the time.

LYSANDER.

Proceed, moon.

MOONSHINE.

All that I have to say is, to tell you that the lantern
is the moon; I, the man-i'-th'-moon; this thorn-
bush, my thorn-bush; and this dog, my dog.

DEMETRIUS.

Why, all these should be in the lantern; for all
these are in the moon. But, silence! here comes
Thisbe.

Enter THISBE.

THISBE.

This is old Ninny's tomb. Where is my love?

LION.

O——   [*The* LION *roars;* THISBE *runs off.*

DEMETRIUS.

Well roar'd, lion.

THESEUS.

Well run, Thisbe.

HIPPOLYTA.

Well shone, moon.—Truly, the moon shines with a good grace.

[*The* LION *tears* THISBE'S *mantle, and exit.*

THESEUS.

Well moused, lion.

DEMETRIUS.

And then came Pyramus.

LYSANDER.

And so the lion vanisht.

Enter PYRAMUS.

PYRAMUS.

Sweet moon, I thank thee for thy sunny beams;
I thank thee, moon, for shining now so bright;
For, by thy gracious, golden, glittering streams,
I trust to taste of truest Thisbe's sight.
But stay,—O spite!—
But mark, poor knight,
What dreadful dole is here!
Eyes, do you see?
How can it be?
O dainty duck! O dear!
Thy mantle good,
What, stain'd with blood?
Approach, ye Furies fell!
O Fates, come, come,
Cut thread and thrum;
Quail, crush, conclude, and quell!

THESEUS.

This passion, and the death of a dear friend, would go near to make a man look sad.

HIPPOLYTA.

Beshrew my heart, but I pity the man.

PYRAMUS.

O, wherefore, Nature, didst thou lions frame?
Since lion vile hath here deflower'd my dear:
Which is—no, no—which was the fairest dame
That lived, that loved, that liked, that lookt
with cheer.
Come, tears, confound;
Out, sword, and wound
The pap of Pyramus,—
Ay, that left pap,
Where heart doth hop:—

[*Stabs himself.*

Thus die I, thus, thus, thus.
Now am I dead,
Now am I fled;
My soul is in the sky:
Tongue, lose thy light;
Moon, take thy flight:—

[*Exit* MOONSHINE.

Now die, die, die, die, die.   [*Dies.*

DEMETRIUS.

No die, but an ace, for him; for he is but one.

LYSANDER.

Less than an ace, man; for he is dead; he is nothing.

THESEUS.

With the help of a surgeon he might yet recover; and prove an ass.

HIPPOLYTA.

How chance Moonshine is gone before Thisbe comes back to find her lover?

THESEUS.

She will find him by starlight.—Here she comes, and her passion ends the play.

Enter THISBE.

HIPPOLYTA.

Methinks she should not use a long one for such a Pyramus: I hope she will be brief.

DEMETRIUS.

A mote will turn the balance, which Pyramus, which Thisbe, is the better; he for a man, God warrant us,—she for a woman, God bless us.

LYSANDER.

She hath spied him already with those sweet eyes.

DEMETRIUS.

And thus she moans, *videlicet*:

THISBE.

Asleep, my love?
What, dead, my dove?
O Pyramus, arise!
Speak, speak. Quite dumb?
Dead, dead? A tomb
Must cover thy sweet eyes.
These lily lips,
This cherry nose,
These yellow cowslip cheeks,
Are gone, are gone:
Lovers, make moan:
His eyes were green as leeks.
O Sisters Three,
Come, come to me,
With hands as pale as milk;
Lay them in gore,
Since you have shore
With shears his thread of silk.
Tongue, not a word:
Come, trusty sword;
Come, blade, my breast imbrue;

[*Stabs herself.*

And, farewell, friends,—
Thus Thisbe ends,—
Adieu, adieu, adieu.   [*Dies.*

THESEUS.

Moonshine and Lion are left to bury the dead.

DEMETRIUS.

Ay, and Wall too.

BOTTOM.

No, I assure you; the wall is down that parted their fathers. Will it please you to see the epilogue, or to hear a Bergomask dance between two of our company?

THESEUS.

No epilogue. I pray you; for your play needs no excuse. Never excuse; for when the players are all dead, there need none to be blamed. Marry, if he that writ it had play'd Pyramus and hang'd himself in Thisbe's garter, it would have been a fine tragedy: and so it is, truly; and very notably dis-

charged. But, come, your Bergomask: let your
epilogue alone.   [*A dance.*
The iron tongue of midnight hath told twelve:—
Lovers, to bed; 'tis almost fairy-time.
I fear we shall out-sleep the coming morn,
As much as we this night have overwatcht.
This palpable-gross play hath well beguiled
The heavy gait of night.—Sweet friends, to bed.—
A fortnight hold we this solemnity
In nightly revels and new jollity.

                                [*Exeunt.*

            Enter PUCK.

               PUCK.

Now the hungry lion roars,
    And the wolf behowls the moon;
Whilst the heavy ploughman snores,
    All with weary task fordone.
Now the wasted brands do glow,
    Whilst the screech-owl, screeching loud
Puts the wretch that lies in woe
    In remembrance of a shroud.
Now it is the time of night,
    That the graves, all gaping wide,
Every one lets forth his sprite,
    In the church-way paths to glide:
And we fairies, that do run
    By the triple Hecate's team
From the presence of the sun,
    Following darkness like a dream,
Now are frolic: not a mouse
Shall disturb this hallow'd house:
I am sent, with broom, before,
To sweep the dust behind the door.

    Enter OBERON *and* TITANIA, *with their*
                TRAIN.

              OBERON.

Through the house give glimmering light,
    By the dead and drowsy fire;
Every elf and fairy sprite
    Hop as light as bird from brier;
And this ditty, after me,
Sing, and dance it trippingly.

             TITANIA.

First, rehearse your song by rote,
To each word a warbling note:

Hard in hand, with fairy grace,
Will we sing, and bless this place.

                     [*Song and dance.*

             OBERON.

Now, until the break of day,
Through this house each fairy stray.
To the best bride-bed will we,
Which by us shall blessed be;
And the issue there create
Ever shall be fortunate.
So shall all the couples three
Ever true in loving be;
And the blots of Nature's hand
Shall not in their issue stand;
Never mole, hare-lip, nor scar,
Nor mark prodigious, such as are
Despised in nativity,
Shall upon their children be.
With this field-dew consecrate,
Every fairy take his gait;
And each several chamber bless,
Through this palace, with sweet peace:
Ever shall in safety rest,
And the owner of it blest.
    Trip away;
    Make no stay;
Meet me all by break of day.

    [*Exeunt* OBERON, TITANIA, *and* TRAIN.

              PUCK.

If we shadows have offended,
Think but this, and all is mended,—
That you have but slumber'd here,
While these visions did appear.
And this weak and idle theme,
No more yielding but a dream,
Gentles, do not reprehend:
If you pardon, we will mend.
And, as I am an honest Puck,
If we have unearned luck
Now to 'scape the serpent's tongue,
We will make amends ere long;
Else the Puck a liar call:
So, good night unto you all.
Give me your hands, if we be friends,
And Robin shall restore amends.   [*Exit*

KING JOHN

DRAMATIS PERSONAE

KING JOHN.
PRINCE HENRY, *his son; afterwards King Henry III.*
ARTHUR, *Duke of Bretagne, son to Geffrey, late Duke of Bretagne, the elder brother to King John.*
WILLIAM MARESHALL, *Earl of Pembroke.*
GEFFREY FITZ-PETER, *Earl of Essex, chief-justiciary of England.*
WILLIAM LONGSWORD, *Earl of Salisbury.*
ROBERT BIGOT, *Earl of Norfolk.*
HUBERT DE BURGH, *chamberlain to the King.*
ROBERT FAULCONBRIDGE, *son to Sir Robert Faulconbridge.*
PHILIP FAULCONBRIDGE, *his half-brother, bastard son to King Richard the First.*
JAMES GURNEY, *servant to Lady Faulconbridge.*
PETER *of Pomfret, a prophet.*

PHILIP, *King of France.*
LOUIS, *the Dauphin.*

ARCHDUKE OF AUSTRIA.
CARDINAL PANDULPH, *the Pope's legate.*
MELUN, *a French lord.*
CHATILLON, *ambassador from France to King John.*

ELINOR, *widow of King Henry II. and mother to King John.*
CONSTANCE, *mother to Arthur.*
BLANCH, *daughter to Alphonso, King of Castile, and niece to King John.*
LADY FAULCONBRIDGE, *mother to the Bastard and Robert Faulconbridge.*

LORDS, CITIZENS OF ANGIERS, SHERIFF, HERALDS, OFFICERS, SOLDIERS, MESSENGERS, *and other* ATTENDANTS.

SCENE—*Sometimes in England, and sometimes in France.*

ACT I. SCENE I.

KING JOHN'S *palace.*

Enter KING JOHN, QUEEN ELINOR, PEMBROKE, ESSEX, SALISBURY, *and others, with* CHATILLON.

KING JOHN.

Now, say, Chatillon, what would France with us?

CHATILLON.

Thus, after greeting, speaks the King of France,
In my behaviour, to the majesty,
The borrow'd majesty of England here.

QUEEN ELINOR.

A strange beginning:—borrow'd majesty!

KING JOHN.

Silence, good mother; hear the embassy.

CHATILLON.

Philip of France, in right and true behalf
Of thy deceased brother Geffrey's son,
Arthur Plantagenet, lays most lawful claim
To this fair island and the territories,—
To Ireland, Poictiers, Anjou, Touraine, Maine;
Desiring thee to lay aside the sword
Which sways usurpingly these several titles,
And put the same into young Arthur's hand,
Thy nephew and right royal sovereign.

KING JOHN.

What follows, if we disallow of this?

CHATILLON.

The proud control of fierce and bloody war,
To enforce these rights so forcibly withheld.

KING JOHN.

Here have we war for war, and blood for blood,
Controlment for controlment: so answer France.

CHATILLON.

Then take my king's defiance from my mouth,
The furthest limit of my embassy.

KING JOHN.

Bear mine to him, and so depart in peace:

Be thou as lightning in the eyes of France;
For ere thou canst report I will be there,
The thunder of my cannon shall be heard:
So, hence! Be thou the trumpet of our wrath,
And sullen presage of your own decay.—
An honourable conduct let him have:—
Pembroke, look to't.—Farewell, Chatillon.

[*Exeunt* CHATILLON *and* PEMBROKE.

QUEEN ELINOR.

What now, my son! have I not ever said
How that ambitious Constance would not cease
Till she had kindled France and all the world
Upon the right and party of her son?
This might have been prevented and made whole
With very easy arguments of love;
Which now the manage of two kingdoms must
With fearful bloody issue arbitrate.

KING JOHN.

Our strong possession and our right for us.

QUEEN ELINOR [*aside to* KING JOHN].

Your strong possession much more than your right,
Or else it must go wrong with you and me:
So much my conscience whispers in your ear,
Which none but heaven and you and I shall hear.

Enter a SHERIFF.

ESSEX.

My liege, here is the strangest controversy,
Come from the country to be judged by you,
That e'er I heard: shall I produce the men?

KING JOHN.

Let them approach.— [*Exit* SHERIFF.
Our abbeys and our priories shall pay
This expedition's charge.

Enter SHERIFF, *with* ROBERT FAULCONBRIDGE,
and PHILIP *his bastard brother.*

What men are you?

BASTARD.

Your faithful subject I, a gentleman
Born in Northamptonshire, and eldest son,

As I suppose, to Robert Faulconbridge,
A soldier, by the honour-giving hand
Of Cœur-de-lion knighted in the field.

KING JOHN.

What art thou?

ROBERT FAULCONBRIDGE.

The son and heir to that same Faulconbridge.

KING JOHN.

Is that the elder, and art thou the heir?
You came not of one mother, then, it seems.

BASTARD.

Most certain of one mother, mighty king;
That is well known; and, as I think, one father:
But for the certain knowledge of that truth,
I put you o'er to heaven and to my mother:
Of that I doubt, as all men's children may.

QUEEN ELINOR.

Out on thee, rude man! thou dost shame thy
　　mother
And wound her honour with this diffidence.

BASTARD.

I, madam? no, I have no reason for it,—
That is my brother's plea, and none of mine;
The which if he can prove, a' pops me out
At least from fair five hundred pound a year:
Heaven guard my mother's honour and my land!

KING JOHN.

A good blunt fellow.—Why, being younger born,
Doth he lay claim to thine inheritance?

BASTARD.

I know not why, except to get the land.
But once he slander'd me with bastardy:
But whe'r I be as true begot or no,
That still I lay upon my mother's head;
But, that I am as well begot, my liege,—
Fair fall the bones that took the pains for me!—
Compare our faces, and be judge yourself.
If old Sir Robert did beget us both
And were our father and this son like him,
O old Sir Robert, father, on my knee
I give heaven thanks I was not like to thee!

KING JOHN.

Why, what a madcap hath heaven lent us here!

QUEEN ELINOR.

He hath a trick of Coeur-de-lion's face;
The accent of his tongue affecteth him:
Do you not read some tokens of my son
In the large composition of this man?

KING JOHN.

Mine eye hath well examined his parts,
And finds them perfect Richard.—Sirrah, speak,
What doth move you to claim your brother's land?

BASTARD.

Because he hath a half-face, like my father,
With that half-face would he have all my land:
A half-faced groat five hundred pound a year!

ROBERT FAULCONBRIDGE.

My gracious liege, when that my father lived,
Your brother did employ my father much,—

BASTARD.

Well, sir, by this you cannot get my land:
Your tale must be, how he employ'd my mother.

ROBERT FAULCONBRIDGE.

And once dispatcht him in an embassy
To Germany, there with the emperor
To treat of high affairs touching that time.

Th'advantage of his absence took the king,
And in the meantime sojourn'd at my father's;
Where how he did prevail, I shame to speak,
But truth is truth: large lengths of seas and shores
Between my father and my mother lay,—
As I have heard my father speak himself,—
When this same lusty gentleman was got.
Upon his death-bed he by will bequeath'd
His lands to me; and took it, on his death,
That this, my mother's son, was none of his;
And if he were, he came into the world
Full fourteen weeks before the course of time.
Then, good my liege, let me have what is mine,
My father's land, as was my father's will.

KING JOHN.

Sirrah, your brother is legitimate;
Your father's wife did after wedlock bear him;
And if she did play false, the fault was hers;
Which fault lies on the hazards of all husbands
That marry wives. Tell me, how if my brother,
Who, as you say, took pains to get this son,
Had of your father claim'd this son for his?
In sooth, good friend, your father might have
　　kept
This calf, bred from his cow, from all the world;
In sooth, he might: then, if he were my brother's,
My brother might not claim him; nor your father,
Being none of his, refuse him: this concludes,—
My mother's son did get your father's heir;
Your father's heir must have your father's land.

ROBERT FAULCONBRIDGE.

Shall, then, my father's will be of no force
To dispossess that child which is not his?

BASTARD.

Of no more force to dispossess me, sir,
Than was his will to get me, as I think.

QUEEN ELINOR.

Whether hadst thou rather be a Faulconbridge,
And like thy brother, to enjoy thy land,
Or the reputed son of Cœur-de-lion,
Lord of thy presence, and no land beside?

BASTARD.

Madam, an if my brother had my shape,
And I had his, Sir Robert's his, like him;
And if my legs were two such riding-rods,
My arms such eel-skins stuft; my face so thin,
That in mine ear I durst not stick a rose,
Lest men should say, 'Look, where three-
　　farthings goes!'
And, to his shape, were heir to all this land,—
Would I might never stir from off this place,
I'ld give it every foot to have this face;
I would not be Sir Nob in any case.

QUEEN ELINOR.

I like thee well: wilt thou forsake thy fortune,
Bequeath thy land to him, and follow me?
I am a soldier, and now bound to France.

BASTARD.

Brother, take you my land, I'll take my chance:
Your face hath got five hundred pound a year;
Yet sell your face for five pence, and 'tis dear.—
Madam, I'll follow you unto the death.

QUEEN ELINOR.

Nay, I would have you go before me thither.

BASTARD.

Our country manners give our betters way.

KING JOHN.

What is thy name?

BASTARD.

Philip, my liege,—so is my name begun,—
Philip, good old Sir Robert's wife's eldest son.

KING JOHN.

From henceforth bear his name whose form thou
    bear'st:
Kneel thou down Philip, but rise more great,—
Arise Sir Richard and Plantagenet.

BASTARD.

Brother by the mother's side, give me your hand:
My father gave me honour, yours gave land.—
Now blessed be the hour, by night or day,
When I was got, Sir Robert was away!

QUEEN ELINOR.

The very spirit of Plantagenet!—
I am thy grandam, Richard; call me so.

BASTARD.

Madam, by chance, but not by truth: what
    though?
Something about, a little from the right,
    In at the window, or else o'er the hatch;
Who dares not stir by day must walk by night;
    And have is have, however men do catch;
Near or far off, well won is still well shot;
And I am I, howe'er I was begot.

KING JOHN.

Go, Faulconbridge: now hast thou thy desire;
A landless knight makes thee a landed squire.—
Come, madam,—and come, Richard; we must
    speed
For France, for France; for it is more than need.

BASTARD.

Brother, adieu: good fortune come to thee!
For thou wast got i' th' way of honesty.

                [Exeunt all but BASTARD.

A foot of honour better than I was;
But many a many foot of land the worse.
Well, now can I make any Joan a lady:—
'Good den, Sir Richard:'—'God-a-mercy,
    fellow;'—
And if his name be George, I'll call him Peter;
For new-made honour doth forget men's names,—
'Tis too respective and too sociable
For your conversion. Now your traveller,—
He and his toothpick at my worship's mess;
And when my knightly stomach is sufficed,
Why then I suck my teeth, and catechize
My picked man of countries:—'My dear sir,'
Thus, leaning on mine elbow, I begin,
'I shall beseech you'—that is question now;
And then comes answer like an Absey-book:—
'O sir,' says answer, 'at your best command;
At your employment; at your service, sir:'
'No, sir,' says question, 'I, sweet sir, at yours:'
And so, ere answer knows what question
    would,—
Saving in dialogue of compliment,
And talking of the Alps and Apennines,
The Pyrenean and the river Po,—
It draws toward supper in conclusion so.
But this is worshipful society,
And fits the mounting spirit like myself;
For he is but a bastard to the time,
That doth not smack of observation;

And so am I, whether I smack or no;
And not alone in habit and device,
Exterior form, outward accoutrement,
But from the inward motion to deliver
Sweet, sweet, sweet poison for the age's tooth:
Which, though I will not practise to deceive,
Yet to avoid deceit, I mean to learn;
For it shall strew the footsteps of my rising.—
But who comes in such haste in riding-robes?
What woman-post is this? hath she no husband,
That will take pains to blow a horn before her?

Enter LADY FAULCONBRIDGE *and* JAMES
GURNEY.

O me! it is my mother.—How now, good lady!
What brings you here to court so hastily?

LADY FAULCONBRIDGE.

Where is that slave, thy brother? where is he,
That holds in chase mine honour up and down?

BASTARD.

My brother Robert? old Sir Robert's son?
Colbrand the giant, that same mighty man?
Is it Sir Robert's son that you seek so?

LADY FAULCONBRIDGE.

Sir Robert's son! Ay, thou unreverend boy,
Sir Robert's son: why scorn'st thou at Sir Robert?
He is Sir Robert's son; and so art thou.

BASTARD.

James Gurney, wilt thou give us leave awhile?

JAMES GURNEY.

Good leave, good Philip.

BASTARD.

Philip?—sparrow!—James,
There's toys abroad: anon I'll tell thee more.

                [Exit GURNEY.

Madam, I was not old Sir Robert's son;
Sir Robert might have eat his part in me
Upon Good Friday, and ne'er broke his fast:
Sir Robert could do well: marry, to confess,
Could he get me? Sir Robert could not do it,—
We know his handiwork:—therefore, good
    mother
To whom am I beholding for these limbs?
Sir Robert never holp to make this leg.

LADY FAULCONBRIDGE.

Hast thou conspired with thy brother too,
That for thine own gain shouldst defend mine
    honour?
What means this scorn, thou most untoward
    knave?

BASTARD.

Knight, knight, good mother,—Basilisco-like:
What! I am dubb'd; I have it on my shoulder.
But, mother, I am not Sir Robert's son;
I have disclaim'd Sir Robert and my land;
Legitimation, name, and all is gone:
Then, good my mother, let me know my father,—
Some proper man, I hope: who was it, mother?

LADY FAULCONBRIDGE.

Hast thou denied thyself a Faulconbridge?

BASTARD.

As faithfully as I deny the devil.

LADY FAULCONBRIDGE.

King Richard Coeur-de-lion was thy father:
By long and vehement suit I was seduced
To make room for him in my husband's bed:—
Heaven lay not my transgression to my charge!—

Thou art the issue of my dear offence,
Which was so strongly urged, past my defence.

BASTARD.

Now, by this light, were I to get again,
Madam, I would not wish a better father.
Some sins do bear their privilege on earth,
And so doth yours; your fault was not your folly:
Needs must you lay your heart at his dispose,
Subjected tribute to commanding love,
Against whose fury and unmatched force
The aweless lion could not wage the fight,
Nor keep his princely heart from Richard's hand:
He that perforce robs lions of their hearts
May easily win a woman's. Ay, my mother,
With all my heart I thank thee for my father!
Who lives and dares but say, thou didst not well
When I was got, I'll send his soul to hell.
Come, lady, I will show thee to my kin;
And they shall say, when Richard me begot,
If thou hadst said him nay, it had been sin:
Who says it was, he lies; I say 'twas not.

                           [*Exeunt.*

ACT II. SCENE I.

France. Before the walls of Angiers.

Enter, on one side, PHILIP, *king of France,*
LOUIS, CONSTANCE, ARTHUR, *and* FORCES;
on the other, the ARCHDUKE OF AUSTRIA *and*
FORCES.

KING PHILIP.

BEFORE Angiers well met, brave Austria.—
Arthur, that great forerunner of thy blood,
Richard, that robb'd the lion of his heart,
And fought the holy wars in Palestine,
By this brave duke came early to his grave:
And, for amends to his posterity,
At our importance hither is he come,
To spread his colours, boy, in thy behalf;
And to rebuke the usurpation
Of thy unnatural uncle, English John:
Embrace him, love him, give him welcome hither.

ARTHUR.

God shall forgive you Cœur-de-lion's death
The rather that you give his offspring life,
Shadowing their right under your wings of war:
I give you welcome with a powerless hand,
But with a heart full of unstained love:
Welcome before the gates of Angiers, duke.

KING PHILIP.

A noble boy! Who would not do thee right?

ARCHDUKE OF AUSTRIA.

Upon thy cheek lay I this zealous kiss,
As seal to this indenture of my love;—
That to my home I will no more return,
Till Angiers, and the right thou hast in France,
Together with that pale, that white-faced shore,
Whose foot spurns back the ocean's roaring tides,
And coops from other lands her islanders,—
Even till that England, hedged in with the main,
That water-walled bulwark, still secure
And confident from foreign purposes,—
Even till that utmost corner of the west
Salute thee for her king: till then, fair boy,
Will I not think of home, but follow arms.

CONSTANCE.

O, take his mother's thanks, a widow's thanks,
Till your strong hand shall help to give him
    strength
To make a more requital to your love!

ARCHDUKE OF AUSTRIA.

The peace of heaven is theirs that lift their
    swords
In such a just and charitable war.

KING PHILIP.

Well, then, to work: our cannon shall be bent
Against the brows of this resisting town.—
Call for our chiefest men of discipline,
To cull the plots of best advantages:
We'll lay before this town our royal bones,
Wade to the market-place in Frenchmen's blood,
But we will make it subject to this boy.

CONSTANCE.

Stay for an answer to your embassy,
Lest unadvised you stain your swords with
    blood:
My Lord Chatillon may from England bring
That right in peace, which here we urge in war;
And then we shall repent each drop of blood
That hot rash haste so indirectly shed.

KING PHILIP.

A wonder, lady,—lo, upon thy wish,
Our messenger Chatillon is arrived!

              Enter CHATILLON.

What England says, say briefly, gentle lord;
We coldly pause for thee; Chatillon, speak.

CHATILLON.

Then turn your forces from this paltry siege,
And stir them up against a mightier task.
England, impatient of your just demands,
Hath put himself in arms: the adverse winds,
Whose leisure I have stay'd, have given him
    time
To land his legions all as soon as I;
His marches are expedient to this town,
His forces strong, his soldiers confident.
With him along is come the mother queen,
An Ate, stirring him to blood and strife;
With her her niece, the Lady Blanch of Spain;
With them a bastard of the king's deceased:
And all th' unsettled humours of the land,—
Rash, inconsiderate, fiery voluntaries,
With ladies' faces and fierce dragons' spleens,—
Have sold their fortunes at their native homes,
Bearing their birthrights proudly on their backs,
To make a hazard of new fortunes here:
In brief, a braver choice of dauntless spirits,
Than now the English bottoms have waft o'er,
Did never float upon the swelling tide,
To do offence and scathe in Christendom.
The interruption of their churlish drums
                       [*Drum beats.*
Cuts off more circumstance: they are at hand,
To parley or to fight; therefore prepare.

KING PHILIP.

How much unlookt for is this expedition!

ARCHDUKE OF AUSTRIA.

By how much unexpected, by so much
We must awake endeavour for defence;
For courage mounteth with occasion:
Let them be welcome, then; we are prepared.

Enter KING JOHN, ELINOR, BLANCH, BAS-
TARD, LORDS, *and* FORCES.
KING JOHN.
Peace be to France, if France in peace permit
Our just and lineal entrance to our own!
If not, bleed France, and peace ascend to heaven!
Whiles we, God's wrathful agent, do correct
Their proud contempt that beats His peace to
    heaven.
KING PHILIP.
Peace be to England, if that war return
From France to England, there to live in peace!
England we love; and for that England's sake
With burden of our armour here we sweat.
This toil of ours should be a work of thine;
But thou from loving England art so far,
That thou hast under-wrought his lawful king,
Cut off the sequence of posterity,
Out-faced infant state, and done a rape
Upon the maiden virtue of the crown.
Look here upon thy brother Geffrey's face;—
These eyes, these brows, were moulded out of his:
This little abstract doth contain that large
Which died in Geffrey; and the hand of time
Shall draw this brief into as huge a volume.
That Geffrey was thy elder brother born,
And this his son; England was Geffrey's right,
And this is Geffrey's: in the name of God,
How comes it, then, that thou art call'd a king,
When living blood doth in these temples beat,
Which owe the crown that thou o'ermasterest?
KING JOHN.
From whom hast thou this great commission,
To draw my answer from thy articles?   [France,
KING PHILIP.
From that supernal judge, that stirs good thoughts
In any breast of strong authority,
To look into the blots and stains of right.
That judge hath made me guardian to this boy:
Under whose warrant I impeach thy wrong;
And by whose help I mean to chastise it.
KING JOHN.
Alack, thou dost usurp authority.
KING PHILIP.
Excuse,—it is to beat usurping down.
QUEEN ELINOR.
Who is it thou dost call usurper, France?
CONSTANCE.
Let me make answer;—thy usurping son.
QUEEN ELINOR.
Out, insolent! thy bastard shall be king,
That thou mayst be a queen, and check the world!
CONSTANCE.
My bed was ever to thy son as true
As thine was to thy husband; and this boy
Liker in feature to his father Geffrey
Than thou and John in manners,—being as like
As rain to water, or devil to his dam.
My boy a bastard! By my soul, I think
His father never was so true begot:
It cannot be, an if thou wert his mother.
QUEEN ELINOR.
There's a good mother, boy, that blots thy father.
CONSTANCE.
There's a good grandam, boy, that would blot
    thee.

ARCHDUKE OF AUSTRIA.
Peace!
BASTARD.
    Hear the crier.
ARCHDUKE OF AUSTRIA.
              What the devil art thou?
BASTARD.
One that will play the devil, sir, with you,
An a' may catch your hide and you alone:
You are the hare of whom the proverb goes,
Whose valour plucks dead lions by the beard:
I'll smoke your skin-coat, an I catch you right;
Sirrah, look to't; i'faith, I will, i'faith.
BLANCH.
O, well did he become that lion's robe
That did disrobe the lion of that robe!
BASTARD.
It lies as sightly on the back of him
As great Alcides' shows upon an ass:—
But, ass, I'll take that burden from your back,
Or lay on that shall make your shoulders crack.
ARCHDUKE OF AUSTRIA.
What cracker is this same that deafs our ears
With this abundance of superfluous breath?—
King Philip, determine what we shall do straight.
KING PHILIP.
Women and fools, break off your conference.
King John, this is the very sum of all,—
England and Ireland, Anjou, Touraine, Maine,
In right of Arthur do I claim of thee:
Wilt thou resign them, and lay down thy arms?
KING JOHN.
My life as soon:—I do defy thee, France.—
Arthur of Bretagne, yield thee to my hand;
And, out of my dear love, I'll give thee more
Than e'er the coward hand of France can win:
Submit thee, boy.
QUEEN ELINOR.
           Come to thy grandam, child.
CONSTANCE.
Do, child, go to it grandam, child;
Give grandam kingdom, and it grandam will
Give it a plum, a cherry, and a fig:
There's a good grandam.
ARTHUR.
             Good my mother, peace!
I would that I were low laid in my grave:
I am not worth this coil that's made for me.
QUEEN ELINOR.
His mother shames him so, poor boy, he weeps.
CONSTANCE.
Now shame upon you, whe'r she does or no!
His grandam's wrongs, and not his mother's
    shames,
Draw those heaven-moving pearls from his poor
    eyes,
Which heaven shall take in nature of a fee;
Ay, with these crystal beads heaven shall be
    bribed
To do him justice, and revenge on you.
QUEEN ELINOR.
Thou monstrous slanderer of heaven and earth!
CONSTANCE.
Thou monstrous injurer of heaven and earth!
Call me not slanderer; thou and thine usurp
The dominations, royalties, and rights

Of this oppressed boy: this is thy eld'st son's son,
Infortunate in nothing but in thee:
Thy sins are visited in this   oor child;
The canon of the law is laid on him,
Being but the second generation
Removed from thy sin-conceiving womb.
KING JOHN.
Bedlam, have done.
CONSTANCE.
            I have but this to say,—
That he is not only plagued for her sin,
But God hath made her sin and her the plague
On this removed issue, plagued for her,
And with her plague; her sin his injury,
Her injury the beadle to her sin;
All punisht in the person of this child,
And all for her; a plague upon her!
QUEEN ELINOR.
Thou unadvised scold, I can produce
A will that bars the title of thy son.
CONSTANCE.
Ay, who doubts that? a will! a wicked will;
A woman's will; a canker'd grandam's will!
KING PHILIP.
Peace, lady! pause, or be more temperate:
It ill beseems this presence to cry aim
To these ill-tuned repetitions.—
Some trumpet summon hither to the walls
These men of Angiers: let us hear them speak,
Whose title they admit, Arthur's or John's.
Trumpet sounds.   *Enter* CITIZENS *upon the walls.*
FIRST CITIZEN.
Who is it that hath warn'd us to the walls?
KING PHILIP.
'Tis France, for England.
KING JOHN.
           England, for itself:—
You men of Angiers, and my loving subjects,—
KING PHILIP.
You loving men of Angiers, Arthur's subjects,
Our trumpet call'd you to this gentle parle,—
KING JOHN.
For our advantage; therefore hear us first.
These flags of France, that are advanced here
Before the eye and prospect of your town,
Have hither marcht to your endamagement:
The cannons have their bowels full of wrath,
And ready mounted are they to spit forth
Their iron indignation 'gainst your walls:
All preparation for a bloody siege
And merciless proceeding by these French
Confronts your city's eyes, your winking gates;
And, but for our approach, those sleeping stones,
That as a waist doth girdle you about,
By the compulsion of their ordinance
By this time from their fixed beds of lime
Had been dishabited, and wide havoc made
For bloody power to rush upon your peace.
But, on the sight of us, your lawful king,—
Who painfully, with much expedient march,
Have brought a countercheck before your gates,
To save unscratcht your city's threaten'd
    cheeks,—
Behold, the French, amazed, vouchsafe a parle;
And now, instead of bullets wrapt in fire,
To make a shaking fever in your walls,

They shoot but calm words, folded up in smoke,
To make a faithless error in your ears:
Which trust accordingly, kind citizens,
And let us in, your king; whose labour'd spirits,
Forwearied in this action of swift speed,
Crave harbourage within your city-walls.
KING PHILIP.
When I have said, make answer to us both.
Lo, in this right hand, whose protection
Is most divinely vow'd upon the right
Of him it holds, stands young Plantagenet,
Son to the elder brother of this man,
And king o'er him, and all that he enjoys:
For this down-trodden equity, we tread
In warlike march these greens before your town;
Being no further enemy to you
Than the constraint of hospitable zeal
In the relief of this oppressed child
Religiously provokes. Be pleased, then,
To pay that duty which you truly owe
To him that owes it, namely, this young prince:
And then our arms, like to a muzzled bear,
Save in aspect, hath all offence seal'd up:
Our cannons' malice vainly shall be spent
Against th'invulnerable clouds of heaven;
And with a blessed and unvext retire,
With unhackt swords and helmets all unbruised,
We will bear home that lusty blood again,
Which here we came to spout against your town,
And leave your children, wives, and you in peace.
But if you fondly pass our proffer'd offer,
'Tis not the roundure of your old-faced walls
Can hide you from our messengers of war,
Though all these English, and their discipline,
Were harbour'd in their rude circumference.
Then, tell us, shall your city call us lord,
In that behalf which we have challenged it?
Or shall we give the signal to our rage,
And stalk in blood to our possession?
FIRST CITIZEN.
In brief, we are the king of England's subjects:
For him, and in his right, we hold this town.
KING JOHN.
Acknowledge, then, the king, and let me in.
FIRST CITIZEN.
That can we not; but he that proves the king,
To him will we prove loyal: till that time
Have we ramm'd up our gates against the world.
KING JOHN.
Doth not the crown of England prove the king?
And if not that, I bring you witnesses,
Twice fifteen thousand hearts of England's
    breed,—
BASTARD.
Bastards, and else.
KING JOHN.
To verify our title with their lives.
KING PHILIP.
As many and as well-born bloods as those,—
BASTARD.
Some bastards too.
KING PHILIP.
Stand in his face, to contradict his claim.
FIRST CITIZEN.
Till you compound whose right is worthiest,
We for the worthiest hold the right from both.

KING JOHN.
Then God forgive the sin of all those souls
That to their everlasting residence,
Before the dew of evening fall, shall fleet,
In dreadful trial of our kingdom's king!

KING PHILIP.
Amen, amen!—Mount, chevaliers! to arms!

BASTARD.
Saint George, that swinged the dragon, and e'er
    since
Sits on his horse back at mine hostess' door,
Teach us some fence!—[to AUSTRIA] Sirrah,
    were I at home,
At your den, sirrah, with your lioness,
I'ld set an ox-head to your lion's hide,
And make a monster of you.

ARCHDUKE OF AUSTRIA.
                        Peace! no more.

BASTARD.
O, tremble, for you hear the lion roar!

KING JOHN.
Up higher to the plain; where we'll set forth
In best appointment all our regiments.

BASTARD.
Speed, then, to take advantage of the field.

KING PHILIP.
It shall be so;—[to LOUIS] and at the other hill
Command the rest to stand.—God and our right!
    [Exeunt, severally, the English and French
    KINGS, &c.
    Here, after excursions, enter the HERALD OF
    FRANCE, with trumpets, to the gates.

FRENCH HERALD.
You men of Angiers, open wide your gates,
And let young Arthur, Duke of Bretagne, in,
Who, by the hand of France, this day hath made
Much work for tears in many an English mother,
Whose sons lie scatter'd on the bleeding ground:
Many a widow's husband grovelling lies,
Coldly embracing the discolour'd earth;
And victory, with little loss, doth play
Upon the dancing banners of the French,
Who are at hand, triumphantly display'd,
To enter conquerors, and to proclaim
Arthur of Bretagne England's king and yours.
    Enter ENGLISH HERALD, with trumpet.

ENGLISH HERALD.
Rejoice, you men of Angiers, ring your bells;
King John, your king and England's, doth
    approach,
Commander of this hot malicious day:
Their armours, that marcht hence so silver-
    bright,
Hither return all gilt with Frenchmen's blood;
There stuck no plume in any English crest
That is removed by a staff of France;
Our colours do return in those same hands
That did display them when we first marcht
    forth;
And, like a jolly troop of huntsmen, come
Our lusty English, all with purpled hands,
Dyed in the dying slaughter of their foes:
Open your gates, and give the victors way.

FIRST CITIZEN.
Heralds, from off our towers we might behold,
From first to last, the onset and retire

Of both your armies; whose equality
By our best eyes cannot be censured:
Blood hath bought blood, and blows have
    answer'd blows;
Strength matcht with strength, and power con-
    fronted power:
Both are alike; and both alike we like.
One must prove greatest: while they weight so
    even,
We hold our town for neither; yet for both.
    Enter the two KINGS, with their powers, severally.

KING JOHN.
France, hast thou yet more blood to cast away?
Say, shall the current of our right run on?
Whose passage, vext with thy impediment,
Shall leave his native channel, and o'erswell
With course disturb'd even thy confining shores,
Unless thou let his silver water keep
A peaceful progress to the ocean.

KING PHILIP.
England, thou hast not saved one drop of blood,
In this hot trial, more than we of France;
Rather, lost more: and by this hand I swear,
That sways the earth this climate overlooks,
Before we will lay down our just-borne arms,
We'll put thee down, 'gainst whom these arms
    we bear,
Or add a royal number to the dead,
Gracing the scroll that tells of this war's loss
With slaughter coupled to the name of kings.

BASTARD.
Ha, majesty! how high thy glory towers,
When the rich blood of kings is set on fire!
O, now doth Death line his dead chaps with
    steel;
The swords of soldiers are his teeth, his fangs;
And now he feasts, mousing the flesh of men,
In undetermined differences of kings.—
Why stand these royal fronts amazed thus?
Cry 'havoc,' kings! back to the stained field,
You equal-potent, fiery-kindled spirits!
Then let confusion of one part confirm
The other's peace; till then, blows, blood, and
    death!

KING JOHN.
Whose party do the townsmen yet admit?

KING PHILIP.
Speak, citizens, for England; who's your king?

FIRST CITIZEN.
The king of England, when we know the king.

KING PHILIP.
Know him in us, that here hold up his right.

KING JOHN.
In us, that are our own great deputy,
And bear possession of our person here;
Lord of our presence, Angiers, and of you.

FIRST CITIZEN.
A greater power than we denies all this;
And till it be undoubted, we do lock
Our former scruple in our strong-barr'd gates;
King'd of our fears, until our fears, resolved,
Be by some certain king purged and deposed.

BASTARD.
By heaven, these scroyles of Angiers flout you,
    kings,
And stand securely on their battlements,

As in a theatre, whence they gape and point
At your industrious scenes and acts of death.
Your royal presences be ruled by me:—
Do like the mutines of Jerusalem,
Be friends awhile, and both conjointly bend
Your sharpest deeds of malice on this town:
By east and west let France and England mount
Their battering cannon, charged to the mouths,
Till their soul-fearing clamours have brawl'd
  down
The flinty ribs of this contemptuous city:
I'ld play incessantly upon these jades,
Even till unfenced desolation
Leave them as naked as the vulgar air.
That done, dissever your united strengths,
And part your mingled colours once again;
Turn face to face, and bloody point to point;
Then, in a moment, Fortune shall cull forth
One of one side her happy minion,
To whom in favour she shall give the day,
And kiss him with a glorious victory.
How like you this wild counsel, mighty states?
Smacks it not something of the policy?

         KING JOHN.
Now, by the sky that hangs above our heads,
I like it well.—France, shall we knit our powers,
And lay this Angiers even with the ground;
Then, after, fight who shall be king of it?

         BASTARD.
An if thou hast the mettle of a king,—
Being wrong'd, as we are, by this peevish town,—
Turn thou the mouth of thy artillery,
As we will ours, against these saucy walls;
And when that we have dasht them to the
  ground,
Why, then defy each other, and, pell-mell,
Make work upon ourselves, for heaven or hell.

         KING PHILIP.
Let it be so.—Say, where will you assault?

         KING JOHN.
We from the west will send destruction
Into this city's bosom.

         ARCHDUKE OF AUSTRIA.
I from the north.

         KING PHILIP.
        Our thunder from the south
Shall rain their drift of bullets on this town.

         BASTARD [aside].
O prudent discipline! From north to south,—
Austria and France shoot in each other's mouth:
I'll stir them to it.—Come, away, away!

         FIRST CITIZEN.
Hear us, great kings: vouchsafe awhile to stay,
And I shall show you peace and fair-faced league;
Win you this city without stroke or wound;
Rescue those breathing lives to die in beds,
That here come sacrifices for the field:
Persever not, but hear me, mighty kings.

         KING JOHN.
Speak on, with favour; we are bent to hear.

         FIRST CITIZEN.
That daughter there of Spain, the Lady Blanch,
Is niece to England:—look upon the years
Of Louis the Dauphin and that lovely maid:
If lusty love should go in quest of beauty,
Where should he find it fairer than in Blanch?

If zealous love should go in search of virtue,
Where should he find it purer than in Blanch?
If love ambitious sought a match of birth,
Whose veins bound richer blood than Lady
  Blanch?
Such as she is, in beauty, virtue, birth,
Is the young Dauphin every way complete,—
If not complete, O, say he is not she;
And she again wants nothing, to name want,
If want it be not, that she is not he:
He is the half part of a blessed man,
Left to be finished by such a she;
And she a fair divided excellence,
Whose fulness of perfection lies in him.
O, two such silver currents, when they join,
Do glorify the banks that bound them in;
And two such shores to two such streams made
  one,
Two such controlling bounds shall you be, kings,
To these two princes, if you marry them.
This union shall do more than battery can
To our fast-closed gates; for, at this match,
With swifter spleen than powder can enforce,
The mouth of passage shall we fling wide ope,
And give you entrance: but without this match,
The sea enraged is not half so deaf,
Lions more confident, mountains and rocks
More free from motion; no, not Death himself
In mortal fury half so peremptory,
As we to keep this city.

         BASTARD.
        Here's a stay,
That shakes the rotten carcass of old Death
Out of his rags! Here's a large mouth, indeed,
That spits forth death and mountains, rocks and
  seas;
Talks as familiarly of roaring lions
As maids of thirteen do of puppy-dogs!
What cannoneer begot this lusty blood?
He speaks plain cannon,—fire and smoke and
  bounce;
He gives the bastinado with his tongue:
Our ears are cudgell'd; not a word of his
But buffets better than a fist of France:
Zounds, I was never so bethumpt with words
Since I first call'd my brother's father dad.

      QUEEN ELINOR [aside to KING JOHN].
Son, list to this conjunction, make this match;
Give with our niece a dowry large enough:
For by this knot thou shalt so surely tie
Thy now-unsured assurance to the crown,
That yon green boy shall have no sun to ripe
The bloom that promiseth a mighty fruit.
I see a yielding in the looks of France;
Mark, how they whisper: urge them while their
  souls
Are capable of this ambition,
Lest zeal, now melted by the windy breath
Of soft petitions, pity, and remorse,
Cool and congeal again to what it was.

         FIRST CITIZEN.
Why answer not the double majesties
This friendly treaty of our threaten'd town?

         KING PHILIP.
Speak England first, that hath been forward first
To speak unto this city: what say you?

KING JOHN.
If that the Dauphin there, thy princely son,
Can in this book of beauty read 'I love,'
Her dowry shall weigh equal with a queen:
For Anjou, and fair Touraine, Maine, Poictiers,
And all that we upon this side the sea—
Except this city now by us besieged—
Find liable to our crown and dignity,
Shall gild her bridal bed; and make her rich
In titles, honours, and promotions,
As she in beauty, education, blood,
Holds hand with any princess of the world.

KING PHILIP.
What say'st thou, boy? look in the lady's face.

LOUIS.
I do, my lord; and in her eye I find
A wonder, or a wondrous miracle,
The shadow of myself form'd in her eye;
Which, being but the shadow of your son,
Becomes a sun, and makes your son a shadow:
I do protest I never loved myself,
Till now infixed I beheld myself
Drawn in the flattering table of her eye.
[Whispers with BLANCH.

BASTARD [aside].
Drawn in the flattering table of her eye!—
Hang'd in the frowning wrinkle of her brow!—
And quarter'd in her heart!—he doth espy
Himself love's traitor:—this is pity now,
That, hang'd and drawn and quarter'd, there
In such a love so vile a lout as he. [should be

BLANCH.
My uncle's will in this respect is mine:
If he see aught in you that makes him like,
That any thing he sees, which moves his liking,
I can with ease translate it to my will;
Or if you will, to speak more properly,
I will enforce it easily to my love.
Further I will not flatter you, my lord,
That all I see in you is worthy love,
Than this,—that nothing do I see in you,
Though churlish thoughts themselves should be
    your judge,
That I can find should merit any hate.

KING JOHN.
What say these young ones?—What say you, my
    niece?

BLANCH.
That she is bound in honour still to do
What you in wisdom still vouchsafe to say.

KING JOHN.
Speak then, Prince Dauphin; can you love this
    lady?

LOUIS.
Nay, ask me if I can refrain from love;
For I do love her most unfeignedly.

KING JOHN.
Then do I give Volquessen, Touraine, Maine,
Poictiers, and Anjou, these five provinces,
With her to thee; and this addition more,
Full thirty thousand marks of English coin.—
Philip of France, if thou be pleased withal,
Command thy son and daughter to join hands.

KING PHILIP.
It likes us well.—Young princes, close your
    hands.

ARCHDUKE OF AUSTRIA.
And your lips too; for I am well assured
That I did so when I was first assured.

KING PHILIP.
Now, citizens of Angiers, ope your gates,
Let in that amity which you have made;
For at Saint Mary's chapel presently
The rites of marriage shall be solemnized.—
Is not the Lady Constance in this troop?
I know she is not; for this match made up
Her presence would have interrupted much:
Where is she and her son? tell me, who knows.

LOUIS.
She is sad and passionate at your highness' tent.

KING PHILIP.
And, by my faith, this league that we have made
Will give her sadness very little cure.—
Brother of England, how may we content
This widow lady? In her right we came;
Which we, God knows, have turn'd another way,
To our own vantage.

KING JOHN.
    We will heal up all;
For we'll create young Arthur Duke of Bretagne
And Earl of Richmond; and this rich fair town
We make him lord of.—Call the Lady Constance;
Some speedy messenger bid her repair
To our solemnity:—I trust we shall,
If not fill up the measure of her will,
Yet in some measure satisfy her so
That we shall stop her exclamation.
Go we, as well as haste will suffer us,
To this unlookt-for, unprepared pomp.
[Exeunt all but BASTARD.

BASTARD.
Mad world! mad kings! mad composition!
John, to stop Arthur's title in the whole,
Hath willingly departed with a part;
And France,—whose armour conscience buckled
    on,
Whom zeal and charity brought to the field
As God's own soldier,—rounded in the ear
With that same purpose-changer, that sly devil,
That broker, that still breaks the pate of faith;
That daily break-vow; he that wins of all,
Of kings, of beggars, old men, young men,
    maids,—
Who having no external thing to lose
But the word 'maid,' cheats the poor maid of that,
That smooth-faced gentleman, tickling Com-
    modity,—
Commodity, the bias of the world;
The world, who of itself is peised well,
Made to run even upon even ground,
Till this advantage, this vile-drawing bias,
This sway of motion, this Commodity,
Makes it take head from all indifferency,
From all direction, purpose, course, intent:
And this same bias, this Commodity,
This bawd, this broker, this all-changing word,
Clapt on the outward eye of fickle France,
Hath drawn him from his own determined aid,
From a resolved and honourable war,
To a most base and vile-concluded peace.—
And why rail I on this Commodity?
But for because he hath not woo'd me yet:

Not that I have the power to clutch my hand,
When his fair angels would salute my palm;
But for my hand, as unattempted yet,
Like a poor beggar, raileth on the rich.
Well, whiles I am a beggar, I will rail,
And say, There is no sin but to be rich:
And being rich, my virtue then shall be,
To say, There is no vice but beggary:
Since kings break faith upon commodity,
Gain, be my lord,—for I will worship thee! [*Exit.*

ACT III. SCENE I.

France. The French KING'S *tent.*

Enter CONSTANCE, ARTHUR, *and* SALISBURY.

CONSTANCE.

GONE to be married! gone to swear a peace!
False blood to false blood join'd! gone to be
    friends!
Shall Louis have Blanch? and Blanch those
    provinces?
It is not so; thou hast misspoke, misheard;
Be well advised, tell o'er thy tale again:
It cannot be; thou dost but say 'tis so:
I trust I may not trust thee; for thy word
Is but the vain breath of a common man:
Believe me, I do not believe thee, man;
I have a king's oath to the contrary.
Thou shalt be punisht for thus frighting me,
For I am sick, and capable of fears;
Opprest with wrongs, and therefore full of fears;
A widow, husbandless, subject to fears;
A woman, naturally born to fears;
And though thou now confess thou didst but jest,
With my vext spirits I cannot take a truce,
But they will quake and tremble all this day.
What dost thou mean by shaking of thy head?
Why dost thou look so sadly on my son?
What means that hand upon that breast of thine?
Why holds thine eye that lamentable rheum,
Like a proud river peering o'er his bounds?
Be these sad signs confirmers of thy words?
Then speak again,—not all thy former tale,
But this one word, whether thy tale be true.

EARL OF SALISBURY.

As true as I believe you think them false
That give you cause to prove my saying true.

CONSTANCE.

O, if thou teach me to believe this sorrow,
Teach thou this sorrow how to make me die;
And let belief and life encounter so
As doth the fury of two desperate men,
Which in the very meeting fall and die!—
Louis marry Blanch! O boy, then where art thou?
France friend with England! what becomes of
    me?—
Fellow, be gone: I cannot brook thy sight;
This news hath made thee a most ugly man.

EARL OF SALISBURY.

What other harm have I, good lady, done,
But spoke the harm that is by others done?

CONSTANCE.

Which harm within itself so heinous is,
As it makes harmful all that speak of it.

ARTHUR.

I do beseech you, madam, be content.

CONSTANCE.

If thou, that bidd'st me be content, wert grim,
Ugly, and slanderous to thy mother's womb,
Full of unpleasing blots and sightless stains,
Lame, foolish, crooked, swart, prodigious,
Patcht with foul moles and eye-offending marks,
I would not care, I then would be content;
For then I should not love thee; no, nor thou
Become thy great birth, nor deserve a crown.
But thou art fair; and at thy birth, dear boy,
Nature and Fortune join'd to make thee great:
Of Nature's gifts thou mayst with lilies boast
And with the half-blown rose: but Fortune, O!
She is corrupted, changed, and won from thee;
Sh' adulterates hourly with thine uncle John;
And with her golden hand hath pluckt on
    France
To tread down fair respect of sovereignty,
And made his majesty the bawd to theirs.
France is a bawd to Fortune and King John,
That strumpet Fortune, that usurping John!
Tell me, thou fellow, is not France forsworn?
Envenom him with words: or get thee gone,
And leave those woes alone which I alone
Am bound to under-bear.

EARL OF SALISBURY.

               Pardon me, madam,
I may not go without you to the kings.

CONSTANCE.

Thou mayst, thou shalt; I will not go with thee:
I will instruct my sorrows to be proud;
For grief is proud, and makes his owner stout,
To me, and to the state of my great grief,
Let kings assemble; for my grief's so great,
That no supporter but the huge firm earth
Can hold it up: here I and sorrows sit;
Here is my throne, bid kings come bow to it.
           [*Seats herself on the ground.*

Enter KING JOHN, KING PHILIP, LOUIS,
    BLANCH, ELINOR, BASTARD, AUSTRIA, *and*
    ATTENDANTS.

KING PHILIP.

'Tis true, fair daughter; and this blessed day
Ever in France shall be kept festival;
To solemnize this day the glorious sun
Stays in his course, and plays the alchemist,
Turning with splendour of his precious eye
The meagre cloddy earth to glittering gold:
The yearly course that brings this day about
Shall never see it but a holiday.

CONSTANCE.

A wicked day, and not a holy day!—   [*Rising*
What hath this day deserved? what hath it done,
That it in golden letters should be set
Among the high tides in the calendar?
Nay, rather turn this day out of the week,
This day of shame, oppression, perjury:
Or, if it must stand still, let wives with child
Pray that their burdens may not fall this day,
Lest that their hopes prodigiously be crost:
But on this day let seamen fear no wrack;
No bargains break that are not this day made:
This day, all things begun come to ill end,—
Yes, faith itself to hollow falsehood change!

KING PHILIP.

By heaven, lady, you shall have no cause

To curse the fair proceedings of this day:
Have I not pawn'd to you my majesty?
CONSTANCE.
You have beguiled me with a counterfeit   [tried,
Resembling majesty; which, being toucht and
Proves valueless: you are forsworn, forsworn;
You came in arms to spill mine enemies' blood,
But now in arms you strengthen it with yours:
The grappling vigour and rough frown of war
Is cold in amity and painted peace,
And our oppression hath made up this league.
Arm, arm, you heavens, against these perjured
    kings!
A widow cries; be husband to me, heavens!
Let not the hours of this ungodly day
Wear out the day in peace; but, ere sunset,
Set armed discord 'twixt these perjured kings!
Hear me, O, hear me!
ARCHDUKE OF AUSTRIA.
Lady Constance, peace!
CONSTANCE.
War! war! no peace! peace is to me a war.
O Limoges! O Austria! thou dost shame [coward!
That bloody spoil: thou slave, thou wretch, thou
Thou little valiant, great in villainy!
Thou ever strong upon the stronger side!
Thou Fortune's champion that dost never fight
But when her humorous ladyship is by
To teach thee safety! thou art perjured too,
And sooth'st up greatness. What a fool art thou,
A ramping fool, to brag, and stamp, and swear,
Upon my party! Thou cold-blooded slave,
Hast thou not spoke like thunder on my side?
Been sworn my soldier? bidding me depend
Upon thy stars, thy fortune, and thy strength?
And dost thou now fall over to my foes?
Thou wear a lion's hide! doff it for shame,
And hang a calf's-skin on those recreant limbs.
ARCHDUKE OF AUSTRIA.
O, that a man should speak those words to me!
BASTARD.
And hang a calf's-skin on those recreant limbs.
ARCHDUKE OF AUSTRIA.
Thou darest not say so, villain, for thy life.
BASTARD.
And hang a calf's-skin on those recreant limbs.
KING JOHN.
We like not this; thou dost forget thyself.
KING PHILIP.
Here comes the holy legate of the Pope.
Enter PANDULPH, *attended.*
CARDINAL PANDULPH.
Hail, you anointed deputies of heaven!
To thee, King John, my holy errand is.
I Pandulph, of fair Milan cardinal,
And from Pope Innocent the legate here,
Do in his name religiously demand,
Why thou against the church, our holy mother,
So wilfully dost spurn, and, force perforce,
Keep Stephen Langton, chosen archbishop
Of Canterbury, from that holy see?
This, in our foresaid holy father's name,
Pope Innocent, I do demand of thee.
KING JOHN.
What earthly name to interrogatories
Can task the free breath of a sacred king?

Thou canst not, cardinal, devise a name
So slight, unworthy, and ridiculous,
To charge me to an answer, as the Pope.
Tell him this tale; and from the mouth of England
Add thus much more,—that no Italian priest
Shall tithe or toll in our dominions;
But as we, under heaven, are supreme head,
So, under Him, that great supremacy,
Where we do reign, we will alone uphold,
Without th'assistance of a mortal hand:
So tell the Pope; all reverence set apart
To him and his usurpt authority.
KING PHILIP.
Brother of England, you blaspheme in this.
KING JOHN.
Though you, and all the kings of Christendom,
Are led so grossly by this meddling priest,
Dreading the curse that money may buy out;
And by the merit of vile gold, dross, dust,
Purchase corrupted pardon of a man,
Who in that sale sells pardon from himself;
Though you and all the rest, so grossly led,
This juggling witchcraft with revenue cherish;
Yet I, alone, alone do me oppose
Against the Pope, and count his friends my foes.
CARDINAL PANDULPH.
Then, by the lawful power that I have,
Thou shalt stand cursed and excommunicate:
And blessed shall he be that doth revolt
From his allegiance to an heretic;
And meritorious shall that hand be call'd,
Canonized, and worship as a saint,
That takes away by any secret course
Thy hateful life.
CONSTANCE.
O, lawful let it be
That I have room with Rome to curse awhile!
Good father cardinal, cry thou amen
To my keen curses; for without my wrong
There is no tongue hath power to curse him right.
CARDINAL PANDULPH.
There's law and warrant, lady, for my curse.
CONSTANCE.
And for mine too: when law can do no right,
Let it be lawful that law bar no wrong:
Law cannot give my child his kingdom here;
For he that holds his kingdom holds the law:
Therefore, since law itself is perfect wrong,
How can the law forbid my tongue to curse?
CARDINAL PANDULPH.
Philip of France, on peril of a curse,
Let go the hand of that arch-heretic;
And raise the power of France upon his head,
Unless he do submit himself to Rome.
QUEEN ELINOR.
Look'st thou pale, France? do not let go thy hand
CONSTANCE.
Look to that, devil; lest that France repent,
And by disjoining hands, hell lose a soul.
ARCHDUKE OF AUSTRIA.
King Philip, listen to the cardinal.
BASTARD.
And hang a calf's-skin on his recreant limbs.
ARCHDUKE OF AUSTRIA.
Well, ruffian, I must pocket up these wrongs,
Because—

BASTARD.
Your breeches best may carry them.
KING JOHN.
Philip, what say'st thou to the cardinal?
CONSTANCE.
What should he say, but as the cardinal?
LOUIS.
Bethink you, father; for the difference
Is, purchase of a heavy curse from Rome,
Or the light loss of England for a friend:
Forgo the easier.
BLANCH.
That's the curse of Rome.
CONSTANCE.
O Louis, stand fast! the devil tempts thee here
In likeness of a new untrimmed bride.
BLANCH.
The Lady Constance speaks not from her faith,
But from her need.
CONSTANCE.
O, if thou grant my need,
Which only lives but by the death of faith,
That need must needs infer this principle,—
That faith would live again by death of need!
O, then, tread down my need, and faith mounts
up;
Keep my need up, and faith is trodden down!
KING JOHN.
The king is moved, and answers not to this.
CONSTANCE.
O, be removed from him, and answer well!
ARCHDUKE OF AUSTRIA.
Do so, King Philip; hang no more in doubt.
BASTARD.
Hang nothing but a calf's-skin, most sweet lout.
KING PHILIP.
I am perplext, and know not what to say.
CARDINAL PANDULPH.
What canst thou say but will perplex thee more,
If thou stand excommunicate and cursed?
KING PHILIP.
Good reverend father, make my person yours,
And tell me how you would bestow yourself.
This royal hand and mine are newly knit,
And the conjunction of our inward souls
Married in league, coupled and linkt together
With all religious strength and sacred vows;
The latest breath that gave the sound of words
Was deep-sworn faith, peace, amity, true love
Between our kingdoms and our royal selves;
And even before this truce, but new before,—
No longer than we well could wash our hands,
To clap this royal bargain up of peace,—
Heaven knows, they were besmear'd and over-
stain'd
With slaughter's pencil, where revenge did paint
The fearful difference of incensed kings:
And shall these hands, so lately purged of blood,
So newly join'd in love, so strong in both,
Unyoke this seizure and this kind regreet?
Play fast and loose with faith? so jest with heaven,
Make such unconstant children of ourselves,
As now again to snatch our palm from palm;
Unswear faith sworn; and on the marriage-bed
Of smiling peace to march a bloody host,
And make a riot on the gentle brow

Of true sincerity? O, holy sir,
My reverend father, let it not be so!
Out of your grace devise, ordain, impose
Some gentle order; and then we shall be blest
To do your pleasure, and continue friends.
CARDINAL PANDULPH.
All form is formless, order orderless,
Save what is opposite to England's love.
Therefore, to arms! be champion of our church!
Or let the church, our mother, breathe her
curse,—
A mother's curse,—on her revolting son.
France, thou mayst hold a serpent by the tongue,
A chafed lion by the mortal paw,
A fasting tiger safer by the tooth,   [hold.
Than keep in peace that hand which thou dost
KING PHILIP.
I may disjoin my hand, but not my faith.
CARDINAL PANDULPH.
So makest thou faith an enemy to faith;
And, like a civil war, sett'st oath to oath,
Thy tongue against thy tongue. O, let thy vow
First made to heaven, first be to heaven per-
form'd,—
That is, to be the champion of our church!
What since thou sworest is sworn against thyself,
And may not be performed by thyself:
For that which thou hast sworn to do amiss
Is not amiss when it is truly done;
And being not done, where doing tends to ill,
The truth is then most done, not doing it:
The better act of purposes mistook
Is to mistake again; though indirect,
Yet indirection thereby grows direct,
And falsehood falsehood cures; as fire cools fire
Within the scorched veins of one new-burn'd.
It is religion that doth make vows kept;
But thou hast sworn against religion:
By what thou swear'st against the thing thou
swear'st;
And makest an oath the surety for thy truth
Against an oath: the truth thou art unsure
To swear, swears only not to be forsworn;
Else what a mockery should it be to swear!
But thou dost swear only to be forsworn;
And most forsworn, to keep what thou dost swear.
Therefore thy later vows against thy first
Is in thyself rebellion to thyself;
And better conquest never canst thou make
Than arm thy constant and thy nobler parts
Against these giddy loose suggestions:
Upon which better part our prayers come in,
If thou vouchsafe them; but if not, then know
The peril of our curses light on thee,
So heavy as thou shalt not shake them off,
But in despair die under their black weight.
ARCHDUKE OF AUSTRIA.
Rebellion, flat rebellion!
BASTARD.
Will't not be?
Will not a calf's-skin stop that mouth of thine?
LOUIS.
Father, to arms!
BLANCH.
Upon thy wedding day?
Against the blood that thou hast married?

What, shall our feast be kept with slaughter'd
  men?
Shall braying trumpets and loud churlish
  drums,—
Clamours of hell,—be measures to our pomp?
O husband, hear me!—ay, alack, how new
Is husband in my mouth!—even for that name,
Which till this time my tongue did ne'er pro-
  nounce,
Upon my knee I beg, go not to arms
Against mine uncle.
             CONSTANCE.
             O, upon my knee,
Made hard with kneeling, I do pray to thee,
Thou virtuous Dauphin, alter not the doom
Forethought by heaven!
             BLANCH.
Now shall I see thy love: what motive may
Be stronger with thee than the name of wife?
             CONSTANCE.
That which upholdeth him that thee upholds,
His honour:—O, thine honour, Louis, thine
  honour!
             LOUIS.
I muse your majesty doth seem so cold,
When such profound respects do pull you on.
          CARDINAL PANDULPH.
I will denounce a curse upon his head.
            KING PHILIP.
Thou shalt not need.—England, I will fall from
  thee.
             CONSTANCE.
O fair return of banisht majesty!
           QUEEN ELINOR.
O foul revolt of French inconstancy!
            KING JOHN.
France, thou shalt rue this hour within this hour.
            BASTARD.
Old Time the clock-setter, that bald sexton
  Time,
Is it as he will? well, then, France shall rue.
            BLANCH.
The sun's o'ercast with blood: fair day, adieu!
Which is the side that I must go withal?
I am with both: each army hath a hand;
And in their rage, I having hold of both,
They whirl asunder and dismember me.
Husband, I cannot pray that thou mayst win;
Uncle, I needs must pray that thou mayst lose;
Father, I may not wish the fortune thine;
Grandam, I will not wish thy wishes thrive:
Whoever wins, on that side shall I lose;
Assured loss before the match be play'd.
             LOUIS.
Lady, with me; with me thy fortune lies.
            BLANCH.
There where my fortune lives, there my life dies.
            KING JOHN.
Cousin, go draw our puissance together.
           [Exit BASTARD.
France, I am burn'd up with inflaming wrath;
A rage whose heat hath tl is condition,
That nothing can allay, nothing but blood,—
The blood, the dearest-valued blood of France.
            KING PHILIP.
Thy rage shall burn thee up, and thou shalt turn

To ashes, ere our blood shall quench that fire:
Look to thyself, thou art in jeopardy.
            KING JOHN.
No more than he that threats.—To arms let's hie!
                  [Exeunt.

SCENE II.

The same. Plains near Angiers.

Alarums, excursions. Enter BASTARD, *with*
AUSTRIA'S *head.*

            BASTARD.
NOW, by my life, this day grows wondrous hot;
   Some airy devil hovers in the sky,
And pours down mischief.—Austria's head lie
  there,
While Philip breathes.
    Enter KING JOHN, ARTHUR, *and* HUBERT.
            KING JOHN.
Hubert, keep this boy.—Philip, make up:
My mother is assailed in our tent,
And ta'en, I fear.
             BASTARD.
             My lord, I rescued her;
Her highness is in safety, fear you not:
But on, my liege; for very little pains
Will bring this labour to an happy end.   [Exeunt.

SCENE III.

The same.

Alarums, excursions, retreat. Enter KING JOHN,
ELINOR, ARTHUR, BASTARD, HUBERT, *and*
LORDS.

      KING JOHN [*to* QUEEN ELINOR].
SO shall it be; your Grace shall stay behind,
  So strongly guarded.—[*to* ARTHUR] Cousin,
    look not sad:
Thy grandam loves thee; and thy uncle will
As dear be to thee as thy father was.
            ARTHUR.
O, this will make my mother die with grief!
      KING JOHN [*to* BASTARD].
Cousin, away for England: haste before:
And ere our coming, see thou shake the bags
Of hoarding abbots; their imprison'd angels
Set thou at liberty: the fat ribs of peace
Must by the hungry now be fed upon:
Use our commission in his utmost force.
            BASTARD.
Bell, book, and candle shall not drive me back,
When gold and silver becks me to come on.
I leave your highness.—Grandam, I will pray—
If ever I remember to be holy—
For your fair safety; so, I kiss your hand.
           QUEEN ELINOR.
Farewell, gentle cousin.
            KING JOHN.
             Coz, farewell.
             [Exit BASTARD.
           QUEEN ELINOR.
Come hither, little kinsman; hark, a word.
          [Takes ARTHUR aside
            KING JOHN.
Come hither, Hubert. O my gentle Hubert,
We owe thee much! within this wall of flesh

There is a soul counts thee her creditor,
And with advantage means to pay thy love:
And, my good friend, thy voluntary oath
Lives in this bosom, dearly cherished.
Give me thy hand. I had a thing to say,—
But I will fit it with some better time.
By heaven, Hubert, I am almost ashamed
To say what good respect I have of thee.

HUBERT DE BURGH.
I am much bounden to your majesty.

KING JOHN.
Good friend, thou hast no cause to say so yet:
But thou shalt have; and creep time ne'er so slow,
Yet it shall come for me to do thee good.
I had a thing to say,—but let it go:
The sun is in the heaven, and the proud day,
Attended with the pleasures of the world,
Is all too wanton and too full of gauds
To give me audience:—if the midnight bell
Did, with his iron tongue and brazen mouth,
Sound one into the drowsy ear of night;
If this same were a churchyard where we stand,
And thou possessed with a thousand wrongs;
Or if that surly spirit, melancholy,
Had baked thy blood, and made it heavy-thick,
Which else runs tickling up and down the veins,
Making that idiot, laughter, keep men's eyes,
And strain their cheeks to idle merriment,—
A passion hateful to my purposes;
Or if that thou couldst see me without eyes,
Hear me without thine ears, and make reply
Without a tongue, using conceit alone,
Without eyes, ears, and harmful sound of words;
Then, in despite of brooded watchful day,
I would into thy bosom pour my thoughts:
But, ah, I will not!—yet I love thee well;
And, by my troth, I think thou lovest me well.

HUBERT DE BURGH.
So well, that what you bid me undertake,
Though that my death were adjunct to my act,
By heaven, I would do it.

KING JOHN.
         Do not I know thou wouldst?
Good Hubert, Hubert, Hubert, throw thine eye
On yon young boy: I'll tell thee what, my friend,
He is a very serpent in my way;
And wheresoe'er this foot of mine doth tread,
He lies before me:—dost thou understand me?
Thou art his keeper.

HUBERT DE BURGH.
         And I'll keep him so,
That he shall not offend your majesty.

KING JOHN.
         Death.

HUBERT DE BURGH.
My lord?

KING JOHN.
    A grave.

HUBERT DE BURGH.
    He shall not live.

KING JOHN.
         Enough.
I could be merry now. Hubert, I love thee;
Well, I'll not say what I intend for thee:
Remember.—Madam, fare you well:
I'll send these powers o'er to your majesty.

QUEEN ELINOR.
My blessing go with thee!

KING JOHN.
         For England, cousin, go:
Hubert shall be your man, attend on you
With all true duty.—On toward Calais, ho!
                     [*Exeunt.*

SCENE IV.

The same.   The French KING'S *tent.*

Enter KING PHILIP, LOUIS, PANDULPH, *and*
ATTENDANTS.

KING PHILIP.
SO, by a roaring tempest on the flood,
A whole armado of converted sail
Is scatter'd and disjoin'd from fellowship.

CARDINAL PANDULPH.
Courage and comfort! all shall yet go well.

KING PHILIP.
What can go well, when we have run so ill?
Are we not beaten? Is not Angiers lost?
Arthur ta'en prisoner? divers dear friends slain?
And bloody England into England gone,
O'erbearing interruption, spite of France?

LOUIS.
What he hath won, that hath he fortified:
So hot a speed with such advice disposed,
Such temperate order in so fierce a course,
Doth want example: who hath read or heard
Of any kindred action like to this?

KING PHILIP.
Well could I bear that England had this praise,
So we could find some pattern of our shame.—
Look, who comes here! a grave unto a soul;
Holding th'eternal spirit, against her will,
In the vile prison of afflicted breath.

Enter CONSTANCE.
I prithee, lady, go away with me.

CONSTANCE.
Lo, now! now see the issue of your peace!

KING PHILIP.
Patience, good lady! comfort, gentle Constance!

CONSTANCE.
No, I defy all counsel, all redress,
But that which ends all counsel, true redress,
Death, death:—O amiable lovely death!
Thou odoriferous stench! sound rottenness!
Arise forth from the couch of lasting night,
Thou hate and terror to prosperity,
And I will kiss thy detestable bones;
And put my eyeballs in thy vaulty brows;
And ring these fingers with thy household
    worms;
And stop this gap of breath with fulsome dust;
And be a carrion monster like thyself:
Come, grin on me; and I will think thou smilest,
And buss thee as thy wife! Misery's love,
O, come to me!

KING PHILIP.
         O fair affliction, peace!

CONSTANCE.
No, no, I will not, having breath to cry:
O, that my tongue were in the thunder's mouth!
Then with a passion would I shake the world;
And rouse from sleep that fell anatomy

Which cannot hear a lady's feeble voice,
Which scorns a modern invocation.
> CARDINAL PANDULPH.

Lady, you utter madness, and not sorrow.
> CONSTANCE.

Thou art not holy to belie me so;
I am not mad: this hair I tear is mine;
My name is Constance; I was Geffrey's wife;
Young Arthur is my son, and he is lost:
I am not mad;—I would to heaven I were!
For then 'tis like I should forget myself:
O, if I could, what grief should I forget!—
Preach some philosophy to make me mad,
And thou shalt be canonized, cardinal;
For, being not mad, but sensible of grief,
My reasonable part produces reason
How I may be deliver'd of these woes,
And teaches me to kill or hang myself:
If I were mad, I should forget my son,
Or madly think a babe of clouts were he:
I am not mad; too well, too well I feel
The different plague of each calamity.
> KING PHILIP.

Bind up those tresses.—O, what love I note
In the fair multitude of those her hairs!
Where but by chance a silver drop hath fall'n,
Even to that drop ten thousand wiry friends
Do glue themselves in sociable grief;
Like true, inseparable, faithful loves,
Sticking together in calamity.
> CONSTANCE.

To England, if you will.
> KING PHILIP.
>> Bind up your hairs.
> CONSTANCE.

Yes, that I will; and wherefore will I do it?
I tore them from their bonds, and cried a oud,
'O, that these hands could so redeem my son,
As they have given these hairs their liberty!'
But now I envy at their liberty,
And will again commit them to their bonds,
Because my poor child is a prisoner.—
And, father cardinal, I have heard you say
That we shall see and know our friends in heaven:
If that be true, I shall see my boy again;
For since the birth of Cain, the first male child,
To him that did but yesterday suspire,
There was not such a gracious creature born.
But now will canker-sorrow eat my bud,
And chase the native beauty from his cheek,
And he will look as hollow as a ghost,
As dim and meagre as an ague's fit;
And so he'll die; and, rising so again,
When I shall meet him in the court of heaven
I shall not know him: therefore never, never
Must I behold my pretty Arthur more.
> CARDINAL PANDULPH.

You hold too heinous a respect of grief.
> CONSTANCE.

He talks to me that never had a son.
> KING PHILIP.

You are as fond of grief as of your child.
> CONSTANCE.

Grief fills the room up of my absent child,
Lies in his bed, walks up and down with me,
Puts on his pretty looks, repeats his words,

Remembers me of all his gracious parts,
Stuffs out his vacant garments with his form;
Then have I reason to be fond of grief.
Fare you well: had you such a loss as I,
I could give better comfort than you do.—
I will not keep this form upon my head,
When there is such disorder in my wit.
O Lord! my boy, my Arthur, my fair son!
My life, my joy, my food, my all the world!
My widow-comfort, and my sorrows' cure! *[Exit.*
> KING PHILIP.

I fear some outrage, and I'll follow her.   *[Exit.*
> LOUIS.

There's nothing in this world can make me joy:
Life is as tedious as a twice-told tale
Vexing the dull ear of a drowsy man;
And bitter shame hath spoil'd the sweet world's
      taste,
That it yields naught but shame and bitterness.
> CARDINAL PANDULPH.

Before the curing of a strong disease,
Even in the instant of repair and health,
The fit is strongest; evils that take leave,
On their departure most of all show evil:
What have you lost by losing of this day?
> LOUIS.

All days of glory, joy, and happiness.
> CARDINAL PANDULPH.

If you had won it, certainly you had.
No, no; when Fortune means to men most good,
She looks upon them with a threatening eye.
'Tis strange to think how much King John hath
      lost
In this which he accounts so clearly won:
Are not you grieved that Arthur is his prisoner?
> LOUIS.

As heartily as he is glad he hath him.
> CARDINAL PANDULPH.

Your mind is all as youthful as your blood.
Now hear me speak with a prophetic spirit;
For even the breath of what I mean to speak
Shall blow each dust, each straw, each little rub,
Out of the path which shall directly lead
Thy foot to England's throne; and therefore
      mark.
John hath seized Arthur; and it cannot be,
That, whiles warm life plays in that infant's veins,
The misplaced John should entertain an hour,
One minute, nay, one quiet breath of rest:
A sceptre snatcht with an unruly hand
Must be as boisterously maintain'd as gain'd;
And he that stands upon a slippery place
Makes nice of no vile hold to stay him up:
That John may stand, then Arthur needs must
      fall;
So be it, for it cannot be but so.
> LOUIS.

But what shall I gain by young Arthur's fall?
> CARDINAL PANDULPH.

You, in the right of Lady Blanch your wife,
May then make all the claim that Arthur did.
> LOUIS.

And lose it, life and all, as Arthur did.
> CARDINAL PANDULPH.

How green you are, and fresh in this old world!
John lays you plots; the times conspire with you;

For he that steeps his safety in true blood
Shall find but bloody safety and untrue.
This act, so evilly borne, shall cool the hearts
Of all his people, and freeze up their zeal,
That none so small advantage shall step forth
To check his reign, but they will cherish it;
No natural exhalation in the sky,
No scape of nature, no distemper'd day,
No common wind, no customed event,
But they will pluck away his natural cause,
And call them meteors, prodigies, and signs,
Abortives, presages, and tongues of heaven,
Plainly denouncing vengeance upon John.

LOUIS.

May be he will not touch young Arthur's life,
But hold himself safe in his prisonment.

CARDINAL PANDULPH.

O, sir, when he shall hear of your approach,
If that young Arthur be not gone already,
Even at that news he dies; and then the hearts
Of all his people shall revolt from him,
And kiss the lips of unacquainted change;
And pick strong matter of revolt and wrath
Out of the bloody fingers' ends of John.
Methinks I see this hurly all on foot:
And, O, what better matter breeds for you
Than I have named!—The bastard Faulcon-
  bridge
Is now in England, ransacking the church,
Offending charity: if but a dozen French
Were there in arms, they would be as a call
To train ten thousand English to their side;
Or as a little snow, tumbled about,
Anon becomes a mountain. O noble Dauphin,
Go with me to the king:—'tis wonderful
What may be wrought out of their discontent,
Now that their souls are topful of offence:
For England go:—I will whet on the king.

LOUIS.

Strong reasons make strong actions: let us go:
If you say ay, the king will not say no.   [Exeunt.

ACT IV. SCENE I.

A room in a castle.

Enter HUBERT *and* EXECUTIONERS.

HUBERT DE BURGH.

HEAT me these irons hot; and look thou stand
Within the arras: when I strike my foot
Upon the bosom of the ground, rush forth,
And bind the boy which you shall find with me
Fast to the chair: be heedful: hence, and watch.

FIRST EXECUTIONER.

I hope your warrant will bear out the deed.

HUBERT DE BURGH.

Uncleanly scruples! fear not you: look to't.
      [Exeunt EXECUTIONERS.
Young lad, come forth; I have to say with you.

Enter ARTHUR.

ARTHUR.

Good morrow, Hubert.

HUBERT DE BURGH.

      Good morrow, little prince.

ARTHUR.

As little prince, having so great a title
To be more prince, as may be.—You are sad.

HUBERT DE BURGH.

Indeed, I have been merrier.

ARTHUR.

      Mercy on me!
Methinks no body should be sad but I:
Yet, I remember, when I was in France,
Young gentlemen would be as sad as night,
Only for wantonness. By my christendom,
So I were out of prison, and kept sheep,
I should be as merry as the day is long;
And so I would be here, but that I doubt
My uncle practises more harm to me:
He is afraid of me, and I of him:
Is it my fault that I was Geffrey's son?
No, indeed, is't not; and I would to heaven
I were your son, so you would love me, Hubert.

HUBERT DE BURGH [aside].

If I talk to him, with his innocent prate
He will awake my mercy, which lies dead:
Therefore I will be sudden and dispatch.

ARTHUR.

Are you sick, Hubert? you look pale to-day:
In sooth, I would you were a little sick,
That I might sit all night and watch with you:
I warrant I love you more than you do me.

HUBERT DE BURGH [aside].

His words do take possession of my bosom.—
Read here, young Arthur.   [*Showing a paper.*
    [*Aside*] How now, foolish rheum!
Turning dispiteous torture out of door!
I must be brief, lest resolution drop
Out at mine eyes in tender womanish tears.—
Can you not read it, is it not fair writ?

ARTHUR.

Too fairly, Hubert, for so foul effect:
Must you with hot irons burn out both mine eyes?

HUBERT DE BURGH.

Young boy, I must.

ARTHUR.

      And will you?

HUBERT DE BURGH.

      And I will.

ARTHUR.

Have you the heart? When your head did but
  ache,
I knit my handkercher about your brows,—
The best I had, a princess wrought it me,—
And I did never ask it you again;
And with my hand at midnight held your head;
And like the watchful minutes to the hour,
Still and anon cheer'd up the heavy time,   [grief?'
Saying, 'What lack you?' and, 'Where lies your
Or, 'What good love may I perform for you?'
Many a poor man's son would have lien still,
And ne'er have spoke a loving word to you;
But you at your sick service had a prince.
Nay, you may think my love was crafty love,
And call it cunning:—do, an if you will:
If heaven be pleased that you must use me ill,
Why, then you must.—Will you put out mine
  eyes?
These eyes that never did nor never shall
So much as frown on you?

HUBERT DE BURGH.

      I have sworn to do it;
And with hot irons must I burn them out.

ARTHUR.

Ah, none but in this iron age would do it!
The iron of itself, though heat red-hot,
Approaching near these eyes, would drink my
    tears,
And quench his fiery indignation
Even in the water of mine innocence;
Nay, after that, consume away in rust,
But for containing fire to harm mine eye.
Are you more stubborn-hard than hammer'd
    iron?
An if an angel should have come to me,
And told me Hubert should put out mine eyes,
I would not have believed him,—no tongue but
    Hubert's.

HUBERT DE BURGH.

Come forth!   [*Stamps.*
    Enter EXECUTIONERS, *with cord, irons, &c.*
Do as I bid you do.

ARTHUR.

O, save me, Hubert, save me! my eyes are out
Even with the fierce looks of these bloody men.

HUBERT DE BURGH.

Give me the iron, I say, and bind him here.

ARTHUR.

Alas, what need you be so boisterous-rough?
I will not struggle, I will stand stone-still.
For heaven sake, Hubert, let me not be bound!
Nay, hear me, Hubert!—drive these men away,
And I will sit as quiet as a lamb;
I will not stir, nor wince, nor speak a word,
Nor look upon the iron angerly:
Thrust but these men away, and I'll forgive you,
Whatever torment you do put me to.

HUBERT DE BURGH.

Go, stand within; let me alone with him.

FIRST EXECUTIONER.

I am best pleased to be from such a deed.
             [*Exeunt* EXECUTIONERS.

ARTHUR.

Alas, I then have chid away my friend!
He hath a stern look, but a gentle heart:—
Let him come back, that his compassion may
Give life to yours.

HUBERT DE BURGH.

         Come, boy, prepare yourself.

ARTHUR.

Is there no remedy?

HUBERT DE BURGH.

            None, but to lose your eyes.

ARTHUR.

O heaven!—that there were but a mote in yours,
A grain, a dust, a gnat, a wandering hair,
Any annoyance in that precious sense!
Then, feeling what small things are boisterous
    there,
Your vile intent must needs seem horrible.

HUBERT DE BURGH.

Is this your promise? go to, hold your tongue.

ARTHUR.

Hubert, the utterance of a brace of tongues
Must needs want pleading for a pair of eyes:
Let me not hold my tongue,—let me not, Hubert;
Or, Hubert, if you will, cut out my tongue,
So I may keep my eyes: O, spare mine eyes,
Though to no use but still to look on you!—

Lo, by my troth, the instrument is cold,
And would not harm me.

HUBERT DE BURGH.

            I can heat it, boy.

ARTHUR.

No, in good sooth; the fire is dead with grief,
Being create for comfort, to be used
In undeserved extremes: see else yourself;
There is no malice in this burning coal;
The breath of heaven hath blown his spirit out,
And strew'd repentant ashes on his head.

HUBERT DE BURGH.

But with my breath I can revive it, boy.

ARTHUR.

And if you do, you will but make it blush,
And glow with shame of your proceedings,
    Hubert:
Nay, it perchance will sparkle in your eyes;
And, like a dog that is compell'd to fight,
Snatch at his master that doth tarre him on.
All things that you should use to do me wrong
Deny their office: only you do lack
That mercy which fierce fire and iron extends,
Creatures of note for mercy-lacking uses.

HUBERT DE BURGH.

Well, see to live; I will not touch thine eye
For all the treasure that thine uncle owes:
Yet am I sworn, and I did purpose, boy,
With this same very iron to burn them out.

ARTHUR.

O, now you look like Hubert! all this while
You were disguised.

HUBERT DE BURGH.

         Peace; no more. Adieu.
Your uncle must not know but you are dead;
I'll fill these dogged spies with false reports:
And, pretty child, sleep doubtless and secure
That Hubert, for the wealth of all the world,
Will not offend thee.

ARTHUR.

         O heaven! I thank you, Hubert.

HUBERT DE BURGH.

Silence; no more: go closely in with me:
Much danger do I undergo for thee.   [*Exeunt.*

SCENE II.

KING JOHN'S *palace.*

Enter KING JOHN, PEMBROKE, SALISBURY,
and other LORDS.

KING JOHN.

HERE once again we sit, once again crown'd,
And lookt upon, I hope, with cheerful eyes.

EARL OF PEMBROKE.

This once again, but that your highness pleased,
Was once superfluous: you were crown'd before,
And that high royalty was ne'er pluckt off;
The faiths of men ne'er stained with revolt;
Fresh expectation troubled not the land
With any long'd-for change or better state.

EARL OF SALISBURY.

Therefore, to be possest with double pomp,
To guard a title that was rich before,
To gild refined gold, to paint the lily,
To throw a perfume on the violet,

To smooth the ice, or add another hue
Unto the rainbow, or with taper-light
To seek the beauteous eye of heaven to garnish,
Is wasteful and ridiculous excess.

EARL OF PEMBROKE.
But that your royal pleasure must be done,
This act is as an ancient tale new-told;
And in the last repeating troublesome,
Being urged at a time unseasonable.

EARL OF SALISBURY.
In this, the antique and well-noted face
Of plain old form is much disfigured;
And, like a shifted wind unto a sail,
It makes the course of thoughts to fetch about;
Startles and frights consideration;
Makes sound opinion sick, and truth suspected,
For putting on so new a fashion'd robe.

EARL OF PEMBROKE.
When workmen strive to do better than well,
They do confound their skill in covetousness;
And oftentimes excusing of a fault
Doth make the fault the worse by the excuse,—
As patches set upon a little breach
Discredit more in hiding of the fault
Than did the fault before it was so patcht.

EARL OF SALISBURY.
To this effect, before you were new-crown'd,
We breathed our counsel: but it pleased your
    highness
To overbear it; and we are all well pleased,
Since all and every part of what we would
Doth make a stand at what your highness will.

KING JOHN.
Some reasons of this double coronation
I have possest you with, and think them strong;
And more, more strong, then lesser is my fear,
I shall indue you with: meantime but ask
What you would have reform'd that is not well,
And well shall you perceive how willingly
I will both hear and grant you your requests.

EARL OF PEMBROKE.
Then I—as one that am the tongue of these,
To sound the purposes of all their hearts,
Both for myself and them, but, chief of all,
Your safety, for the which myself and them
Bend their best studies—heartily request
Th'enfranchisement of Arthur; whose restraint
Doth move the murmuring lips of discontent
To break into this dangerous argument,—
If what in rest you have in right you hold,
Why, then your fears—which, as they say, attend
The steps of wrong—should move you to mew up
Your tender kinsman, and to choke his days
With barbarous ignorance, and deny his youth
The rich advantage of good exercise.
That the time's enemies may not have this
To grace occasions, let it be our suit,
That you have bid us ask, his liberty;
Which for our goods we do no further ask
Than whereupon our weal, on you depending,
Counts it your weal he have his liberty.

KING JOHN.
Let it be so: I do commit his youth
To your direction.

Enter HUBERT.

     Hubert, what news with you?

EARL OF PEMBROKE.
This is the man should do the bloody deed;
He show'd his warrant to a friend of mine:
The image of a wicked heinous fault
Lives in his eye; that close aspect of his
Does show the mood of a much-troubled breast;
And I do fearfully believe 'tis done,
What we so fear'd he had a charge to do.

EARL OF SALISBURY.
The colour of the king doth come and go
Between his purpose and his conscience.
Like heralds 'twixt two dreadful battles set:
His passion is so ripe, it needs must break.

EARL OF PEMBROKE.
And when it breaks, I fear will issue thence
The foul corruption of a sweet child's death.

KING JOHN.
We cannot hold mortality's strong hand:—
Good lords, although my will to give is living,
The suit which you demand is gone and dead:
He tells us Arthur is deceased to-night.

EARL OF SALISBURY.
Indeed, we fear'd his sickness was past cure.

EARL OF PEMBROKE.
Indeed, we heard how near his death he was
Before the child himself felt he was sick:
This must be answer'd either here or hence.

KING JOHN.
Why do you bend such solemn brows on me?
Think you I bear the shears of destiny?
Have I commandment on the pulse of life?

EARL OF SALISBURY.
It is apparent foul-play; and 'tis shame
That greatness should so grossly offer it:
So thrive it in your game! and so, farewell.

EARL OF PEMBROKE.
Stay yet, Lord Salisbury; I'll go with thee,
And find th'inheritance of this poor child,
His little kingdom of a forced grave.
That blood which owed the breadth of all this
    isle,
Three foot of it doth hold:—bad world the while!
This must not be thus borne: this will break out
To all our sorrows, and ere long I doubt.

     [*Exeunt* LORDS.

KING JOHN.
They burn in indignation. I repent:
There is no sure foundation set on blood,
No certain life achieved by others' death.—

Enter a MESSENGER.

A fearful eye thou hast: where is that blood
That I have seen inhabit in those cheeks?
So foul a sky clears not without a storm:
Pour down thy weather: how goes all in France?

MESSENGER.
From France to England. Never such a power
For any foreign preparation
Was levied in the body of a land.
The copy of your speed is learn'd by them;
For when you should be told they do prepare,
The tidings comes that they are all arrived.

KING JOHN.
O, where hath our intelligence been drunk?
Where hath it slept? Where is my mother's ear,
That such an army could be drawn in France,
And she not hear of it?

MESSENGER.
My liege, her ear
Is stopt with dust; the first of April died
Your noble mother; and, as I hear, my lord,
The Lady Constance in a frenzy died
Three days before; but this from rumour's tongue
I idly heard; if true or false I know not.

KING JOHN.
Withhold thy speed, dreadful occasion!
O, make a league with me, till I have pleased
My discontented peers! What! mother dead!
How wildly, then, walks my estate in France!—
Under whose conduct came those powers of
France
That thou for truth givest out are landed here?

MESSENGER.
Under the Dauphin.

KING JOHN.
Thou hast made me giddy
With these ill tidings.

Enter BASTARD *and* PETER *of Pomfret.*
Now, what says the world
To your proceedings? do not seek to stuff
My head with more ill news, for it is full.

BASTARD.
But if you be afeard to hear the worst,
Then let the worst, unheard, fall on your head.

KING JOHN.
Bear with me, cousin; for I was amazed
Under the tide: but now I breathe again
Aloft the flood; and can give audience
To any tongue, speak it of what it will.

BASTARD.
How I have sped among the clergy-men,
The sums I have collected shall express.
But as I travell'd hither through the land,
I find the people strangely fantasied;
Possest with rumours, full of idle dreams,
Not knowing what they fear, but full of fear:
And here's a prophet, that I brought with me
From forth the streets of Pomfret, whom I found
With many hundreds treading on his heels;
To whom he sung, in rude harsh-sounding
rimes,
That, ere the next Ascension-day at noon,
Your highness should deliver up your crown.

KING JOHN.
Thou idle dreamer, wherefore didst thou so?

PETER.
Foreknowing that the truth will fall out so.

KING JOHN.
Hubert, away with him; imprison him;
And on that day at noon, whereon he says
I shall yield up my crown, let him be hang'd.
Deliver him to safety; and return,
For I must use thee. [*Exit* HUBERT *with* PETER.
O my gentle cousin,
Hear'st thou the news abroad, who are arrived?

BASTARD.
The French, my lord: men's mouths are full of
it:
Besides, I met Lord Bigot and Lord Salisbury
With eyes as red as new-enkindled fire,
And others more, going to seek the grave
Of Arthur, who, they say, is kill'd to-night
On your suggestion.

KING JOHN.
Gentle kinsman, go,
And thrust thyself into their companies:
I have a way to win their loves again;
Bring them before me.

BASTARD.
I will seek them out.

KING JOHN.
Nay, but make haste; the better foot before.
O, let me have no subject enemies,
When adverse foreigners affright my towns
With dreadful pomp of stout invasion!
Be Mercury, set feathers to thy heels,
And fly like thought from them to me again.

BASTARD.
The spirit of the time shall teach me speed.

KING JOHN.
Spoke like a sprightful noble gentleman.
[*Exit* BASTARD.
Go after him; for he perhaps shall need
Some messenger betwixt me and the peers;
And be thou he.

MESSENGER.
With all my heart, my liege. [*Exit.*

KING JOHN.
My mother dead!

Enter HUBERT.

HUBERT DE BURGH.
My lord, they say five moons were seen to-night;
Four fixed; and the fifth did whirl about
The other four in wondrous motion.

KING JOHN.
Five moons!

HUBERT DE BURGH.
Old men and beldams in the streets
Do prophesy upon it dangerously:
Young Arthur's death is common in their mouths:
And when they talk of him, they shake their
heads,
And whisper one another in the ear;
And he that speaks doth gripe the hearer's wrist;
Whilst he that hears makes fearful action,
With wrinkled brows, with nods, with rolling
eyes.
I saw a smith stand with his hammer, thus,
The whilst his iron did on the anvil cool,
With open mouth swallowing a tailor's news;
Who, with his shears and measure in his hand,
Standing on slippers, which his nimble haste
Had falsely thrust upon contrary feet,
Told of a many thousand warlike French
That were embattailed and rankt in Kent:
Another lean unwasht artificer
Cuts off his tale, and talks of Arthur's death.

KING JOHN.
Why seek'st thou to possess me with these fears?
Why urgest thou so oft young Arthur's death?
Thy hand hath murder'd him: I had a mighty
cause
To wish him dead, but thou hadst none to kill
him.

HUBERT DE BURGH.
No had, my lord! why, did you not provoke me?

KING JOHN.
It is the curse of kings to be attended
By slaves that take their humours for a warrant

To break within the bloody house of life;
And, on the winking of authority,
To understand a law; to know the meaning
Of dangerous majesty, when perchance it frowns
More upon humour than advised respect.

HUBERT DE BURGH.
Here is your hand and seal for what I did.

KING JOHN.
O, when the last account 'twixt heaven and earth
Is to be made, then shall this hand and seal
Witness against us to damnation!
How oft the sight of means to do ill deeds
Make deeds ill done! Hadst not thou been by,
A fellow by the hand of nature markt,
Quoted, and sign'd, to do a deed of shame,
This murder had not come into my mind:
But, taking note of thy abhorr'd aspect,
Finding thee fit for bloody villainy,
Apt, liable to be employ'd in danger,
I faintly broke with thee of Arthur's death;
And thou, to be endeared to a king,
Made it no conscience to destroy a prince.

HUBERT DE BURGH.
My lord,—

KING JOHN.
Hadst thou but shook thy head, or made a pause,
When I spake darkly what I purposed,
Or turn'd an eye of doubt upon my face,
As bid me tell my tale in express words,
Deep shame had struck me dumb, made me
break off,
And those thy fears might have wrought fears in
me:
But thou didst understand me by my signs,
And didst in signs again parley with sin;
Yea, without stop, didst let thy heart consent,
And consequently thy rude hand to act
The deed, which both our tongues held vile to
name.—
Out of my sight, and never see me more!
My nobles leave me; and my state is braved,
Even at my gates, with ranks of foreign powers:
Nay, in the body of this fleshly land,
This kingdom, this confine of blood and breath,
Hostility and civil tumult reigns
Between my conscience and my cousin's death.

HUBERT DE BURGH.
Arm you against your other enemies,
I'll make a peace between your soul and you.
Young Arthur is alive: this hand of mine
Is yet a maiden and an innocent hand,
Not painted with the crimson spots of blood.
Within this bosom never enter'd yet
The dreadful motion of a murderous thought;
And you have slander'd nature in my form,
Which, howsoever rude exteriorly,
Is yet the cover of a fairer mind
Than to be butcher of an innocent child.

KING JOHN.
Doth Arthur live? O, haste thee to the peers,
Throw his report on their incensed rage,
And make them tame to their obedience!
Forgive the comment that my passion made
Upon thy feature; for my rage was blind,
And foul imaginary eyes of blood
Presented thee more hideous than thou art.

O, answer not; but to my closet bring
The angry lords with all expedient haste!
I conjure thee but slowly; run more fast. [Exeunt.

SCENE III.

Before a castle.

Enter ARTHUR *on the walls.*

ARTHUR.
THE wall is high, and yet will I leap down:
Good ground, be pitiful, and hurt me not!
There's few or none do know me: if they did,
This ship-boy's semblance hath disguised me
I am afraid; and yet I'll venture it.   [quite.
If I get down, and do not break my limbs,
I'll find a thousand shifts to get away:
As good to die and go, as die and stay.
                       [Leaps down.
O me! my uncle's spirit is in these stones:
Heaven take my soul, and England keep my
bones!   [Dies.

Enter PEMBROKE, SALISBURY, *and* BIGOT.

EARL OF SALISBURY.
Lords, I will meet him at Saint Edmund's-Bury:
It is our safety, and we must embrace
This gentle offer of the perilous time.

EARL OF PEMBROKE.
Who brought that letter from the cardinal?

EARL OF SALISBURY.
The Count Melun, a noble lord of France;
Whose private with me of the Dauphin's love
Is much more general than these lines import.

ROBERT BIGOT.
To-morrow morning let us meet him, then.

EARL OF SALISBURY.
Or rather then set forward; for 'twill be
Two long days' journey, lords, or e'er we meet.

Enter BASTARD.

BASTARD.
Once more to-day well met, distemper'd lords!
The king by me requests your presence straight.

EARL OF SALISBURY.
The king hath dispossest himself of us:
We will not line his thin bestained cloak
With our pure honours, nor attend the foot
That leaves the print of blood where'er it walks.
Return and tell him so: we know the worst.

BASTARD.
Whate'er you think, good words, I think, were
best.

EARL OF SALISBURY.
Our griefs, and not our manners, reason now.

BASTARD.
But there is little reason in your grief;
Therefore 'twere reason you had manners now.

EARL OF PEMBROKE.
Sir, sir, impatience hath his privilege.

BASTARD.
'Tis true,—to hurt his master, no man else.

EARL OF SALISBURY.
This is the prison:—what is he lies here?
                    [Seeing ARTHUR.

EARL OF PEMBROKE.
O death, made proud with pure and princely
beauty!
The earth had not a hole to hide this deed.

EARL OF SALISBURY.

Murder, as hating what himself hath done,
Doth lay it open to urge on revenge.

ROBERT BIGOT.

Or, when he doom'd this beauty to a grave,
Found it too precious-princely for a grave.

EARL OF SALISBURY.

Sir Richard, what think you? Have you beheld,
Or have you read or heard? or could you think?
Or do you almost think, although you see,
That you do see? could thought, without this
    object,
Form such another? This is the very top,
The height, the crest, or crest unto the crest,
Of murder's arms: this is the bloodiest shame,
The wildest savagery, the vilest stroke,
That ever wall-eyed wrath or staring rage
Presented to the tears of soft remorse.

EARL OF PEMBROKE.

All murders past do stand excused in this:
And this, so sole and so unmatchable,
Shall give a holiness, a purity,
To the yet-unbegotten sin of times;
And prove a deadly bloodshed but a jest,
Exampled by this heinous spectacle.

BASTARD.

It is a damned and a bloody work;
The graceless action of a heavy hand,—
If that it be the work of any hand.

EARL OF SALISBURY.

If that it be the work of any hand!—
We had a kind of light what would ensue:
It is the shameful work of Hubert's hand;
The practice and the purpose of the king:—
From whose obedience I forbid my soul,
Kneeling before this ruin of sweet life,
And breathing to his breathless excellence
The incense of a vow, a holy vow,
Never to taste the pleasures of the world,
Never to be infected with delight,
Nor conversant with ease and idleness,
Till I have set a glory to this hand,
By giving it the worship of revenge.

EARL OF PEMBROKE *and* ROBERT BIGOT.

Our souls religiously confirm thy words.

Enter HUBERT.

HUBERT DE BURGH.

Lords, I am hot with haste in seeking you:
Arthur doth live; the king hath sent for you.

EARL OF SALISBURY.

O, he is bold, and blushes not at death:—
Avaunt, thou hateful villain, get thee gone!

HUBERT DE BURGH.

I am no villain.

EARL OF SALISBURY.

    Must I rob the law?

[*Drawing his sword.*

BASTARD.

Your sword is bright, sir; put it up again.

EARL OF SALISBURY.

Not till I sheathe it in a murderer's skin.

HUBERT DE BURGH.

Stand back, Lord Salisbury,—stand back, I say;
By heaven, I think my sword's as sharp as yours:
I would not have you, lord, forget yourself,
Nor tempt the danger of my true defence;

Lest I, by marking of your rage, forget
Your worth, your greatness, and nobility.

ROBERT BIGOT.

Out, dunghill! darest thou brave a nobleman?

HUBERT DE BURGH.

Not for my life: but yet I dare defend
My innocent life against an emperor.

EARL OF SALISBURY.

Thou art a murderer.

HUBERT DE BURGH.

    Do not prove me so;
Yet I am none: whose tongue soe'er speaks false,
Not truly speaks; who speaks not truly, lies.

EARL OF PEMBROKE.

Cut him to pieces.

BASTARD.

    Keep the peace, I say.

EARL OF SALISBURY.

Stand by, or I shall gall you, Faulconbridge.

BASTARD.

Thou wert better gall the devil, Salisbury:
If thou but frown on me, or stir thy foot,
Or teach thy hasty spleen to do me shame,
I'll strike thee dead. Put up thy sword betime;
Or I'll so maul you and your toasting-iron,
That you shall think the devil is come from hell.

ROBERT BIGOT.

What wilt thou do, renowned Faulconbridge?
Second a villain and a murderer?

HUBERT DE BURGH.

Lord Bigot, I am none.

ROBERT BIGOT.

    Who kill'd this prince?

HUBERT DE BURGH.

'Tis not an hour since I left him well:
I honour'd him, I loved him; and will weep
My date of life out for his sweet life's loss.

EARL OF SALISBURY.

Trust not those cunning waters of his eyes,
For villainy is not without such rheum;
And he, long traded in it, makes it seem
Like rivers of remorse and innocency.
Away with me, all you whose souls abhor
Th'uncleanly savours of a slaughter-house;
For I am stifled with this smell of sin.

ROBERT BIGOT.

Away toward Bury, to the Dauphin there!

EARL OF PEMBROKE.

There, tell the king, he may inquire us out.

[*Exeunt* LORDS.

BASTARD.

Here's a good world!—Knew you of this fair
    work?
Beyond the infinite and boundless reach
Of mercy, if thou didst this deed of death,
Art thou damn'd, Hubert.

HUBERT DE BURGH.

    Do but hear me, sir:—

BASTARD.

Ha! I'll tell thee what;
Thou'rt damn'd as black—nay, nothing is so black;
Thou art more deep damn'd than Prince Lucifer:
There is not yet so ugly a fiend of hell
As thou shalt be, if thou didst kill this child.

HUBERT DE BURGH.

Upon my soul,—

BASTARD.
If thou didst but consent
To this most cruel act, do but despair;
And if thou want'st a cord, the smallest thread
That ever spider twisted from her womb
Will serve to strangle thee; a rush will be a beam
To hang thee on; or wouldst thou drown thyself,
Put but a little water in a spoon,
And it shall be as all the ocean,
Enough to stifle such a villain up.
I do suspect thee very grievously.

HUBERT DE BURGH.
If I in act, consent, or sin of thought,
Be guilty of the stealing that sweet breath
Which was embounded in this beauteous clay,
Let hell want pains enough to torture me!
I left him well.

BASTARD.
Go, bear him in thine arms.—
I am amazed, methinks; and lose my way
Among the thorns and dangers of this world.—
How easy dost thou take all England up!
From forth this morsel of dead royalty,
The life, the right, and truth of all this realm
Is fled to heaven; and England now is left
To tug and scamble, and to part by th' teeth
The unowed interest of proud-swelling state.
Now for the bare-pickt bone of majesty
Doth dogged war bristle his angry crest,
And snarleth in the gentle eyes of peace:
Now powers from home and discontents at home
Meet in one line; and vast confusion waits,
As doth a raven on a sick-fall'n beast,
The imminent decay of wrested pomp.
Now happy he whose cloak and cincture can
Hold out this tempest.—Bear away that child,
And follow me with speed: I'll to the king:
A thousand businesses are brief in hand,
And heaven itself doth frown upon the land.
[Exeunt.

ACT V. SCENE I.

KING JOHN's *palace.*

Enter KING JOHN, PANDULPH *with the crown,
and* ATTENDANTS.

KING JOHN.
THUS have I yielded up into your hand
The circle of my glory.

CARDINAL PANDULPH.
Take again [*Giving back the crown.*
From this my hand, as holding of the Pope
Your sovereign greatness and authority.

KING JOHN.
Now keep your holy word: go meet the French;
And from his holiness use all your power
To stop their marches 'fore we are inflamed.
Our discontented counties do revolt;
Our people quarrel with obedience;
Swearing allegiance and the love of soul
To stranger blood, to foreign royalty.
This inundation of mistemper'd humour
Rests by you only to be qualified:
Then pause not; for the present time's so sick,
That present medicine must be minister'd,
Or overthrow incurable ensues.

CARDINAL PANDULPH.
It was my breath that blew this tempest up,
Upon your stubborn usage of the Pope:
But since you are a gentle convertite,
My tongue shall hush again this storm of war,
And make fair weather in your blustering land.
On this Ascension-day, remember well,
Upon your oath of service to the Pope,
Go I to make the French lay down their arms.
[*Exit.*

KING JOHN.
Is this Ascension-day? Did not the prophet
Say, that before Ascension-day at noon
My crown I should give off? Even so I have:
I did suppose it should be on constraint;
But, heaven be thankt, it is but voluntary.

Enter BASTARD.

BASTARD.
All Kent hath yielded; nothing there holds out
But Dover Castle: London hath received,
Like a kind host, the Dauphin and his powers:
Your nobles will not hear you, but are gone
To offer service to your enemy;
And wild amazement hurries up and down
The little number of your doubtful friends.

KING JOHN.
Would not my lords return to me again,
After they heard young Arthur was alive?

BASTARD.
They found him dead, and cast into the streets;
An empty casket, where the jewel of life
By some damn'd hand was robb'd and ta'en away.

KING JOHN.
That villain Hubert told me he did live.

BASTARD.
So, on my soul, he did, for aught he knew.
But wherefore do you droop? why look you sad?
Be great in act, as you have been in thought;
Let not the world see fear and sad distrust
Govern the motion of a kingly eye:
Be stirring as the time; be fire with fire;
Threaten the threatener, and outface the brow
Of bragging horror: so shall inferior eyes,
That borrow their behaviours from the great,
Grow great by your example, and put on
The dauntless spirit of resolution.
Away, and glister like the god of war,
When he intendeth to become the field:
Show boldness and aspiring confidence.
What, shall they seek the lion in his den,
And fright him there? and make him tremble
　there?
O, let it not be said!—Forage, and run
To meet displeasure further from the doors,
And grapple with him ere he come so nigh.

KING JOHN.
The legate of the Pope hath been with me,
And I have made a happy peace with him;
And he hath promised to dismiss the powers
Led by the Dauphin.

BASTARD.
O inglorious league!
Shall we, upon the footing of our land,
Send fair-play orders, and make compromise,
Insinuation, parley, and base truce,
To arms invasive? shall a beardless boy,

A cocker'd silken wanton, brave our fields,
And flesh his spirit in a warlike soil,
Mocking the air with colours idly spread,
And find no check? Let us, my liege, to arms:
Perchance the cardinal cannot make your peace,
Or if he do, let it at least be said
They saw we had a purpose of defence.

KING JOHN.

Have thou the ordering of this present time.

BASTARD.

Away, then, with good courage! yet, I know,
Our party may well meet a prouder foe.   [*Exeunt.*

SCENE II.

Near St. Edmund's-Bury.   The French camp.

Enter, in arms, LOUIS, SALISBURY, MELUN,
PEMBROKE, BIGOT, *and* SOLDIERS.

LOUIS.

MY Lord Melun, let this be copied out,
And keep it safe for our remembrance:
Return the precedent to these lords again;
That, having our fair order written down,
Both they and we, perusing o'er these notes,
May know wherefore we took the sacrament,
And keep our faiths firm and inviolable.

EARL OF SALISBURY.

Upon our sides it never shall be broken.
And, noble Dauphin, albeit we swear
A voluntary zeal and unurged faith
To your proceedings; yet, believe me, prince,
I am not glad that such a sore of time
Should seek a plaster by contemn'd revolt,
And heal the inveterate canker of one wound
By making many. O, it grieves my soul,
That I must draw this metal from my side
To be a widow-maker! O, and there
Where honourable rescue and defence
Cries out upon the name of Salisbury!
But such is the infection of the time,
That, for the health and physic of our right,
We cannot deal but with the very hand
Of stern injustice and confused wrong.
And is't not pity, O my grieved friends,
That we, the sons and children of this isle,
Were born to see so sad an hour as this;
Wherein we step after a stranger, march
Upon her gentle bosom, and fill up
Her enemies' ranks,—I must withdraw and weep
Upon the spot of this enforced cause,—
To grace the gentry of a land remote,
And follow unacquainted colours here?
What, here? O nation, that thou couldst remove!
That Neptune's arms, who clippeth thee about,
Would bear thee from the knowledge of thyself,
And grapple thee unto a pagan shore;
Where these two Christian armies might combine
The blood of malice in a vein of league,
And not to spend it so unneighbourly!

LOUIS.

A noble temper dost thou show in this;
And great affections wrestling in thy bosom
Do make an earthquake of nobility.
O, what a noble combat hast thou fought
Between compulsion and a brave respect!
Let me wipe off this honourable dew

That silverly doth progress on thy cheeks:
My heart hath melted at a lady's tears,
Being an ordinary inundation;
But this effusion of such manly drops,
This shower, blown up by tempest of the soul,
Startles mine eyes, and makes me more amazed
Than had I seen the vaulty top of heaven
Figured quite o'er with burning meteors.
Lift up thy brow, renowned Salisbury,
And with a great heart heave away this storm:
Commend these waters to those baby eyes
That never saw the giant world enraged;
Nor met with fortune other than at feasts,
Full of warm blood, of mirth, of gossiping.
Come, come; for thou shalt thrust thy hand as deep
Into the purse of rich prosperity
As Louis himself:—so, nobles, shall you all,
That knit your sinews to the strength of mine.—
And even there, methinks, an angel spake:
Look, where the holy legate comes apace,
To give us warrant from the hand of heaven,
And on our actions set the name of right
With holy breath.

Enter PANDULPH, *attended.*

CARDINAL PANDULPH.

Hail, noble Prince of France!
The next is this,—King John hath reconciled
Himself to Rome; his spirit is come in,
That so stood out against the holy church,
The great metropolis and see of Rome:
Therefore thy threatening colours now wind up;
And tame the savage spirit of wild war,
That, like a lion foster'd-up at hand,
It may lie gently at the foot of peace,
And be no further harmful than in show.

LOUIS.

Your Grace shall pardon me, I will not back:
I am too high-born to be propertied,
To be a secondary at control,
Or useful serving-man, and instrument,
To any sovereign state throughout the world.
Your breath first kindled the dead coal of wars
Between this chastised kingdom and myself,
And brought in matter that should feed this fire;
And now 'tis far too huge to be blown out
With that same weak wind which enkindled it.
You taught me how to know the face of right,
Acquainted me with interest to this land,
Yea, thrust this enterprise into my heart;
And come ye now to tell me John hath made
His peace with Rome? What is that peace to me?
I, by the honour of my marriage-bed,
After young Arthur, claim this land for mine;
And, now it is half-conquer'd, must I back
Because that John hath made his peace with Rome?
Am I Rome's slave? What penny hath Rome borne,
What men provided, what munition sent,
To underprop this action? Is't not I
That undergo this charge? who else but I,
And such as to my claim are liable,
Sweat in this business and maintain this war?
Have I not heard these islanders shout out,
Vive le roi! as I have bankt their towns?

Have I not here the best cards for the game,
To win this easy match play'd for a crown?
And shall I now give o'er the yielded set?
No, no, on my soul, it never shall be said.
CARDINAL PANDULPH.
You look but on the outside of this work.
LOUIS.
Outside or inside, I will not return
Till my attempt so much be glorified
As to my ample hope was promised
Before I drew this gallant head of war,
And cull'd these fiery spirits from the world,
To outlook conquest, and to win renown
Even in the jaws of danger and of death.—
　　　　　　　　　　[*Trumpet sounds.*
What lusty trumpet thus doth summon us?
　　　Enter BASTARD, *attended.*
BASTARD.
According to the fair-play of the world,
Let me have audience; I am sent to speak:—
My holy lord of Milan, from the king
I come, to learn how you have dealt for him;
And, as you answer, I do know the scope
And warrant limited unto my tongue.
CARDINAL PANDULPH.
The Dauphin is too wilful-opposite,
And will not temporize with my entreaties;
He flatly says he'll not lay down his arms.
BASTARD.
By all the blood that ever fury breathed, 　[king;
The youth says well.—Now hear our English
For thus his royalty doth speak in me.
He is prepared; and reason too he should:
This apish and unmannerly approach,
This harness'd mask and unadvised revel,
This unhair'd sauciness and boyish troops,
The king doth smile at; and is well prepared
To whip this dwarfish war, these pigmy arms,
From out the circle of his territories. 　　[door,
That hand which had the strength, even at your
To cudgel you, and make you take the hatch;
To dive, like buckets, in concealed wells;
To crouch in litter of your stable planks;
To lie, like pawns, lockt up in chests and trunks;
To hug with swine; to seek sweet safety out
In vaults and prisons; and to thrill and shake
Even at the crying of your nation's crow,
Thinking his voice an armed Englishman;—
Shall that victorious hand be feebled here,
That in your chambers gave you chastisement?
No: know the gallant monarch is in arms;
And, like an eagle o'er his aery, towers,
To souse annoyance that comes near his nest.—
And you degenerate, you ingrate revolts,
You bloody Neroes, ripping up the womb
Of your dear mother England, blush for shame;
For your own ladies and pale-visaged maids,
Like Amazons, come tripping after drums,
Their thimbles into armed gauntlets change,
Their needles to lances, and their gentle hearts
To fierce and bloody inclination.
LOUIS.
There end thy brave, and turn thy face in peace;
We grant thou canst outscold us: fare thee well;
We hold our time too precious to be spent
With such a brabbler.

CARDINAL PANDULPH.
　　　　Give me leave to speak.
BASTARD.
No, I will speak.
LOUIS.
　　　　We will attend to neither.—
Strike up the drums; and let the tongue of war
Plead for our interest and our being here.
BASTARD.
Indeed, your drums, being beaten, will cry out;
And so shall you, being beaten: do but start
An echo with the clamour of thy drum,
And even at hand a drum is ready braced
That shall reverberate all as loud as thine;
Sound but another, and another shall,
As loud as thine, rattle the welkin's ear, 　[hand—
And mock the deep-mouth'd thunder: for at
Not trusting to this halting legate here,
Whom he hath used rather for sport than need—
Is warlike John; and in his forehead sits
A bare-ribb'd death, whose office is this day
To feast upon whole thousands of the French.
LOUIS.
Strike up our drums, to find this danger out.
BASTARD.
And thou shalt find it, Dauphin, do not doubt.
　　　　　　　　　　　　[*Exeunt.*

SCENE III.
The field of battle.

Alarums.　Enter KING JOHN *and* HUBERT.
KING JOHN.
HOW goes the day with us? O, tell me, Hubert.
HUBERT DE BURGH.
Badly, I fear. How fares your majesty?
KING JOHN.
This fever, that hath troubled me so long,
Lies heavy on me;—O, my heart is sick!
　　　Enter a MESSENGER.
MESSENGER.
My lord, your valiant kinsman, Faulconbridge,
Desires your majesty to leave the field,
And send him word by me which way you go.
KING JOHN.
Tell him, toward Swinstead, to the abbey there.
MESSENGER.
Be of good comfort; for the great supply,
That was expected by the Dauphin here,
Are wrackt three nights ago on Goodwin Sands.
This news was brought to Richard but even now:
The French fight coldly, and retire themselves.
KING JOHN.
Ay me, this tyrant fever burns me up,
And will not let me welcome this good news!—
Set on toward Swinstead: to my litter straight;
Weakness possesseth me, and I am faint.
　　　　　　　　　　　　[*Exeunt.*

SCENE IV.
Another part of the field.

Enter SALISBURY, PEMBROKE, *and* BIGOT.
EARL OF SALISBURY.
I DID not think the king so stored with friends.
EARL OF PEMBROKE.
Up once again; put spirit in the French:
If they miscarry, we miscarry too.

EARL OF SALISBURY.

That misbegotten devil, Faulconbridge,
In spite of spite, alone upholds the day.

EARL OF PEMBROKE.

They say King John sore-sick hath left the field.

Enter MELUN, *wounded.*

MELUN.

Lead me to the revolts of England here.

EARL OF SALISBURY.

When we were happy we had other names.

EARL OF PEMBROKE.

It is the Count Melun.

EARL OF SALISBURY.

            Wounded to death.

MELUN.

Fly, noble English, you are bought and sold;
Unthread the rude eye of rebellion,
And welcome home again discarded faith.
Seek out King John, and fall before his feet;
For if the French be lords of this loud day,
He means to recompense the pains you take
By cutting off your heads: thus hath he sworn,
And I with him, and many moe with me,
Upon the altar at Saint Edmund's-Bury;
Even on that altar where we swore to you
Dear amity and everlasting love.

EARL OF SALISBURY.

May this be possible? may this be true?

MELUN.

Have I not hideous death within my view,
Retaining but a quantity of life,
Which bleeds away, even as a form of wax
Resolveth from his figure 'gainst the fire?
What in the world should make me now deceive,
Since I must lose the use of all deceit?
Why should I, then, be false, since it is true
That I must die here, and live hence by truth?
I say again, if Louis do win the day,
He is forsworn, if e'er those eyes of yours
Behold another day break in the east:
But even this night,—whose black contagious
     breath
Already smokes about the burning crest
Of the old, feeble, and day-wearied sun,—
Even this ill night, your breathing shall expire,
Paying the fine of rated treachery
Even with a treacherous fine of all your lives,
If Louis by your assistance win the day.
Commend me to one Hubert, with your king:
The love of him,—and this respect besides,
For that my grandsire was an Englishman,—
Awakes my conscience to confess all this.
In lieu whereof, I pray you, bear me hence
From forth the noise and rumour of the field;
Where I may think the remnant of my thoughts
In peace, and part this body and my soul
With contemplation and devout desires.

EARL OF SALISBURY.

We do believe thee:—and beshrew my soul
But I do love the favour and the form
Of this most fair occasion, by the which
We will untread the steps of damned flight;
And, like a bated and retired flood,
Leaving our rankness and irregular course,
Stoop low within those bounds we have o'er-
     lookt,

And calmly run on in obedience,
Even to our ocean, to our great King John.—
My arm shall give thee help to bear thee hence;
For I do see the cruel pangs of death
Right in thine eye.—Away, my friends! New
     flight;
And happy newness, that intends old right.

[*Exeunt, leading off* MELUN.

SCENE V.

The French camp.

Enter LOUIS *and his* TRAIN.

LOUIS.

THE sun of heaven methought was loth to
     set,
But stay'd, and made the western welkin blush,
When th'English measure backward their own
     ground
In faint retire. O, bravely came we off,
When with a volley of our needless shot,
After such bloody toil, we bid good night;
And wound our tottering colours clearly up,
Last in the field, and almost lords of it!

Enter a MESSENGER.

MESSENGER.

Where is my prince, the Dauphin?

LOUIS.

            Here:—what news?

MESSENGER.

The Count Melun is slain; the English lords,
By his persuasion, are again fall'n off;
And your supply, which you have wisht so long,
Are cast away and sunk on Goodwin Sands.

LOUIS.

Ah, foul shrewd news!—beshrew thy very
     heart!—
I did not think to be so sad to-night
As this hath made me.—Who was he that said
King John did fly an hour or two before
The stumbling night did part our weary powers?

MESSENGER.

Whoever spoke it, it is true, my lord.

LOUIS.

Well; keep good quarter and good care to-night:
The day shall not be up so soon as I,
To try the fair adventure of to-morrow. [*Exeunt.*

SCENE VI.

An open place near Swinstead Abbey.

Enter BASTARD *and* HUBERT, *severally.*

HUBERT DE BURGH.

WHO'S there? speak, ho! speak quickly, or I
     shoot.

BASTARD.

A friend.—What art thou?

HUBERT DE BURGH.

            Of the part of England

BASTARD.

Whither dost thou go?

HUBERT DE BURGH.

What's that to thee? Why may not I demand
Of thine affairs, as well as thou of mine?

BASTARD.

Hubert, I think?

HUBERT DE BURGH.
                 Thou hast a perfect thought:
I will, upon all hazards, well believe   [well.
Thou art my friend, thou know'st my tongue so
Who art thou?

BASTARD.
         Who thou wilt: an if thou please,
Thou mayst befriend me so much as to think
I come one way of the Plantagenets.

HUBERT DE BURGH.
Unkind remembrance! thou and eyeless night
Have done me shame:—brave soldier, pardon me,
That any accent breaking from thy tongue
Should scape the true acquaintance of mine ear.

BASTARD.
Come, come; sans compliment, what news abroad?

HUBERT DE BURGH.
Why, here walk I, in the black brow of night,
To find you out.

BASTARD.
         Brief, then; and what's the news?

HUBERT DE BURGH.
O, my sweet sir, news fitting to the night,—
Black, fearful, comfortless, and horrible.

BASTARD.
Show me the very wound of this ill news:
I am no woman, I'll not swound at it.

HUBERT DE BURGH.
The king, I fear, is poison'd by a monk:
I left him almost speechless; and broke out
To acquaint you with this evil, that you might
The better arm you to the sudden time,
Than if you had at leisure known of this.

BASTARD.
How did he take it? who did taste to him?

HUBERT DE BURGH.
A monk, I tell you; a resolved villain,
Whose bowels suddenly burst out: the king
Yet speaks, and peradventure may recover.

BASTARD.
Who didst thou leave to tend his majesty?

HUBERT DE BURGH.
Why, know you not the lords are all come back,
And brought Prince Henry in their company?
At whose request the king hath pardon'd them,
And they are all about his majesty.

BASTARD.
Withhold thine indignation, mighty heaven,
And tempt us not to bear above our power!—
I'll tell thee, Hubert, half my power this night,
Passing these flats, are taken by the tide,—
These Lincoln Washes have devoured them;
Myself, well-mounted, hardly have escaped.
Away, before! conduct me to the king;
I doubt he will be dead or e'er I come.   [Exeunt.

SCENE VII.

The orchard of Swinstead Abbey.

Enter PRINCE HENRY, SALISBURY, *and* BIGOT.

PRINCE HENRY.
IT is too late: the life of all his blood
Is toucht corruptibly; and his pure brain—
Which some suppose the soul's frail dwelling-
     house—

Doth, by the idle comments that it makes,
Foretell the ending of mortality.
             Enter PEMBROKE.

EARL OF PEMBROKE.
His highness yet doth speak; and holds belief
That, being brought into the open air,
It would allay the burning quality
Of that fell poison which assaileth him.

PRINCE HENRY.
Let him be brought into the orchard here.—
Doth he still rage?   [*Exit* BIGOT.

EARL OF PEMBROKE.
          He is more patient
Than when you left him; even now he sung.

PRINCE HENRY.
O vanity of sickness! fierce extremes
In their continuance will not feel themselves.
Death, having prey'd upon the outward parts,
Leaves them invisible; and his siege is now
Against the mind, the which he pricks and wounds
With many legions of strange fantasies,
Which, in their throng and press to that last hold,
Confound themselves. 'Tis strange that death
     should sing.—
I am the cygnet to this pale faint swan,
Who chants a doleful hymn to his own death,
And from the organ-pipe of frailty sings
His soul and body to their lasting rest.

EARL OF SALISBURY.
Be of good comfort, prince; for you are born
To set a form upon that indigest
Which he hath left so shapeless and so rude.
         KING JOHN *brought in.*

KING JOHN.
Ay, marry, now my soul hath elbow-room;
It would not out at windows nor at doors.
There is so hot a summer in my bosom,
That all my bowels crumble up to dust:
I am a scribbled form, drawn with a pen
Upon a parchment; and against this fire
Do I shrink up.

PRINCE HENRY.
     How fares your majesty?

KING JOHN.
Poison'd,—ill fare;—dead, forsook, cast off:
And none of you will bid the winter come,
To thrust his icy fingers in my maw;
Nor let my kingdom's rivers take their course
Through my burn'd bosom; nor entreat the north
To make his bleak winds kiss my parched lips,
And comfort me with cold:—I do not ask you
     much,
I beg cold comfort; and you are so strait,
And so ingrateful, you deny me that.

PRINCE HENRY.
O, that there were some virtue in my tears,
That might relieve you!

KING JOHN.
           The salt in them is hot.—
Within me is a hell; and there the poison
Is, as a fiend, confined to tyrannize
On unreprievable condemned blood.
           Enter BASTARD.

BASTARD.
O, I am scalded with my violent motion,
And spleen of speed to see your majesty!

KING JOHN.

O cousin, thou art come to set mine eye:
The tackle of my heart is crackt and burn'd;
And all the shrouds, wherewith my life should
    sail,
Are turned to one thread, one little hair:
My heart hath one poor string to stay it by,
Which holds but till thy news be uttered;
And then all this thou see'st is but a clod,
And module of confounded royalty.

BASTARD.

The Dauphin is preparing hitherward,
Where heaven he knows how we shall answer
    him;
For in a night the best part of my power,
As I upon advantage did remove,
Were in the Washes all unwarily
Devoured by the unexpected flood.

        [KING JOHN *dies.*

EARL OF SALISBURY.

You breathe these dead news in as dead an ear.—
My liege! my lord!—but now a king,—now thus.

PRINCE HENRY.

Even so must I run on, and even so stop.
What surety of the world, what hope, what stay,
When this was now a king, and now is clay?

BASTARD.

Art thou gone so? I do but stay behind
To do the office for thee of revenge,
And then my soul shall wait on thee toheaven,
As it on earth hath been thy servant still.—
Now, now, you stars that move in your right
    spheres,
Where be your powers? show now your mended
    faiths;
And instantly return with me again,
To push destruction and perpetual shame
Out of the weak door of our fainting land.
Straight let us seek, or straight we shall be
    sought;
The Dauphin rages at our very heels.

EARL OF SALISBURY.

It seems you know not, then, so much as we:
The Cardinal Pandulph is within at rest,
Who half an hour since came from the Dauphin,

And brings from him such offers of our peace
As we with honour and respect may take,
With purpose presently to leave this war.

BASTARD.

He will the rather do it when he sees
Ourselves well sinewed to our defence.

EARL OF SALISBURY.

Nay, it is in a manner done already;
For many carriages he hath dispatcht
To the sea-side, and put his cause and quarrel
To the disposing of the cardinal:
With whom yourself, myself, and other lords,
If you think meet, this afternoon will post
To consummate this business happily.

BASTARD.

Let it be so:—and you, my noble prince,
With other princes that may best be spared,
Shall wait upon your father's funeral.

PRINCE HENRY.

At Worcester must his body be interr'd;
For so he will'd it.

BASTARD.

        Thither shall it, then:
And happily may your sweet self put on
The lineal state and glory of the land!
To whom, with all submission, on my knee,
I do bequeath my faithful services
And true subjection everlastingly.

EARL OF SALISBURY.

And the like tender of our love we make,
To rest without a spot for evermore.

PRINCE HENRY.

I have a kind soul that would give you thanks,
And knows not how to do it but with tears.

BASTARD.

O, let us pay the time but needful woe,
Since it hath been beforehand with our griefs.—
This England never did, nor never shall,
Lie at the proud foot of a conqueror,
But when it first did help to wound itself.
Now these her princes are come home again,
Come the three corners of the world in arms,
And we shall shock them; naught shall make us
    rue,
If England to itself do rest but true.   [*Exeunt.*

THE TAMING OF THE SHREW

DRAMATIS PERSONAE

A LORD.
CHRISTOPHER SLY, *a tinker.*
HOSTESS, PAGE, PLAYERS,
   HUNTSMEN, *and* SERVANTS.
      } Persons in the Induction.

BAPTISTA, *a rich gentleman of Padua.*
VINCENTIO, *an old gentleman of Pisa.*
LUCENTIO, *son to Vincentio, in love with Bianca.*
PETRUCHIO, *a gentleman of Verona, a suitor to Katharina.*
GREMIO,
HORTENSIO, } *suitors to Bianca.*

TRANIO,
BIONDELLO, } *servants to Lucentio.*
GRUMIO,
CURTIS, } *servants to Petruchio.*
PEDANT.

KATHARINA *the shrew,*
BIANCA, } *daughters to Baptista.*
WIDOW.
TAILOR, HABERDASHER, *and* SERVANTS.

SCENE—*Padua, and sometimes in Petruchio's house in the country.*

INDUCTION. SCENE I.

Before an alehouse on a heath.

Enter HOSTESS *and* SLY.

CHRISTOPHER SLY.
I'LL pheeze you, in faith.

HOSTESS.
A pair of stocks, you rogue!

CHRISTOPHER SLY.
Y'are a baggage: the Slys are no rogues; look in the Chronicles; we came in with Richard Conqueror. Therefore, *paucas pallabris;* let the world slide: sessa!

HOSTESS.
You will not pay for the glasses you have burst?

CHRISTOPHER SLY.
No, not a denier. Go by, Jeronimy; go to thy cold bed, and warm thee.

HOSTESS.
I know my remedy; I must go fetch the third-borough. [*Exit.*

CHRISTOPHER SLY.
Third, or fourth, or fifth borough, I'll answer him by law: I'll not budge an inch, boy: let him come, and kindly.

[*Lies down on the ground and falls asleep.*
Horns winded. Enter a LORD *from hunting, with* HUNTSMEN *and* SERVANTS.

LORD.
Huntsman, I charge thee, tender well my hounds:
Brach Merriman, the poor cur is imbost; [brach.
And couple Clowder with the deep-mouth'd
Saw'st thou not, boy, how Silver made it good
At the hedge-corner, in the coldest fault?
I would not lose the dog for twenty pound.

FIRST HUNTSMAN.
Why, Belman is as good as he, my lord;
He cried upon it at the merest loss,
And twice to-day pickt out the dullest scent:
Trust me, I take him for the better dog.

LORD.
Thou art a fool: if Echo were as fleet,
I would esteem him worth a dozen such.
But sup them well, and look unto them all:
To-morrow I intend to hunt again.

FIRST HUNTSMAN.
I will, my lord.

LORD.
What's here? one dead, or drunk? See, doth he breathe?

SECOND HUNTSMAN.
He breathes, my lord. Were he not warm'd with ale,
This were a bed but cold to sleep so soundly.

LORD.
O monstrous beast! how like a swine he lies!—
Grim death, how foul and loathsome is thine image!—
Sirs, I will practise on this drunken man.
What think you, if he were convey'd to bed,
Wrapt in sweet clothes, rings put upon his fingers,
A most delicious banquet by his bed,
And brave attendants near him when he wakes,—
Would not the beggar then forget himself?

FIRST HUNTSMAN.
Believe me, lord, I think he cannot choose.

SECOND HUNTSMAN.
It would seem strange unto him when he waked.

LORD.
Even as a flattering dream or worthless fancy.
Then take him up, and manage well the jest:—
Carry him gently to my fairest chamber,
And hang it round with all my wanton pictures:
Balm his foul head in warm distilled waters,
And burn sweet wood to make the lodging sweet:
Procure me music ready, when he wakes,
To make a dulcet and a heavenly sound;
And if he chance to speak, be ready straight
And with a low submissive reverence
Say 'What is it your honour will command?'
Let one attend him with a silver basin
Full of rose-water, and bestrew'd with flowers;
Another bear the ewer, the third a diaper,
And say 'Will't please your lordship cool your hands?'
Some one be ready with a costly suit,
And ask him what apparel he will wear;
Another tell him of his hounds and horse,
And that his lady mourns at his disease:

Persuade him that he hath been lunatic;
And when he says he is —, say that he dreams,
For he is nothing but a mighty lord.
This do, and do it kindly, gentle sirs:
It will be pastime passing excellent,
If it be husbanded with modesty.

FIRST HUNTSMAN.
My lord, I warrant you, we'll play our part,
As he shall think, by our true diligence,
He is no less than what we say he is.

LORD.
Take him up gently, and to bed with him;
And each one to his office when he wakes.

[SLY is borne out.   Sound trumpets.
Sirrah, go see what trumpet 'tis that sounds:—
[Exit SERVANT.
Belike, some noble gentleman, that means,
Travelling some journey, to repose him here.—
Enter SERVANT.
How now! who is it?

SERVANT.
An it please your honour,
Players that offer service to your lordship.

LORD.
Bid them come near.
Enter PLAYERS.
Now, fellows, you are welcome.

PLAYERS.
We thank your honour.

LORD.
Do you intend to stay with me to-night?

SECOND PLAYER.
So please your lordship to accept our duty.

LORD.
With all my heart.—This fellow I remember,
Since once he play'd a farmer's eldest son:—
'Twas where you woo'd the gentlewoman so well:
I have forgot your name; but, sure, that part
Was aptly fitted, and naturally perform'd,

FIRST PLAYER.
I think 'twas Soto that your honour means.

LORD.
'Tis very true: thou didst it excellent.—
Well, you are come to me in happy time;
The rather for I have some sport in hand,
Wherein your cunning can assist me much.
There is a lord will hear you play to-night:
But I am doubtful of your modesties;
Lest, over-eying of his odd behaviour,—
For yet his honour never heard a play,—
You break into some merry passion,
And so offend him; for, I tell you, sirs,
If you should smile, he grows impatient.

FIRST PLAYER.
Fear not, my lord: we can contain ourselves,
Were he the veriest antick in the world.

LORD.
Go, sirrah, take them to the buttery,
And give them friendly welcome every one:
Let them want nothing that my house affords.
[Exit one with the PLAYERS.
Sirrah, go you to Barthol'mew my page,
[to another SERVANT.
And see him drest in all suits like a lady:
That done, conduct him to the drunkard's
chamber;

And call him madam, do him obeisance.
Tell him from me,—as he will win my love,—
He bear himself with honourable action,
Such as he hath observed in noble ladies
Unto their lords, by them accomplished:
Such duty to the drunkard let him do,
With soft low tongue and lowly courtesy;
And say, 'What is't your honour will command,
Wherein your lady and your humble wife
May show her duty and make known her love?'
And then,—with kind embracements, tempting
kisses,
And with declining head into his bosom,—
Bid him shed tears, as being overjoy'd
To see her noble lord restored to health,
Who for twice seven years hath esteemed him
No better than a poor and loathsome beggar:
And if the boy have not a woman's gift
To rain a shower of commanded tears,
An onion will do well for such a shift;
Which in a napkin being close convey'd,
Shall in despite enforce a watery eye.
See this dispatcht with all the haste thou canst:
Anon I'll give thee more instructions.
[Exit SERVANT.
I know the boy will well usurp the grace,
Voice, gait, and action of a gentlewoman:
I long to hear him call the drunkard husband;
And how my men will stay themselves from
laughter
When they do homage to this simple peasant.
I'll in to counsel them; haply my presence
May well abate the over-merry spleen
Which otherwise would grow into extremes.
[Exeunt.

SCENE II.

A bedchamber in the LORD'S house.

*Enter aloft the drunkard SLY, with ATTENDANTS;
some with apparel, basin, ewer, and other appur-
tenances; and LORD.*

CHRISTOPHER SLY.
FOR God's sake, a pot of small ale.
FIRST SERVANT.
Will't please your lordship drink a cup of sack?
SECOND SERVANT.
Will't please your honour taste of these conserves?
THIRD SERVANT.
What raiment will your honour wear to-day?
CHRISTOPHER SLY.
I am Christophero Sly; call not me honour nor
lordship: I ne'er drank sack in my life; and if you
give me any conserves, give me conserves of beef:
ne'er ask me what raiment I'll wear; for I have no
more doublets than backs, no more stockings
than legs, nor no more shoes than feet,—nay,
sometime more feet than shoes, or such shoes as
my toes look through the overleather.
LORD.
Heaven cease this idle humour in your honour!
O, that a mighty man, of such descent,
Of such possessions, and so high esteem,
Should be infused with so foul a spirit!
CHRISTOPHER SLY.
What, would you make me mad? Am not I
Christopher Sly, old Sly's son of Burton-heath;

by birth a pedlar, by education a card-maker, by
transmutation a bear-herd, and now by present
profession a tinker? Ask Marian Hacket, the fat
ale-wife of Wincot, if she know me not: if she say
I am not fourteen pence on the score for sheer
ale, score me up for the lying'st knave in Christendom. What! I am not bestraught: here's—

FIRST SERVANT.
O, this it is that makes your lady mourn!

SECOND SERVANT.
O, this it is that makes your servants droop!

LORD.
Hence comes it that your kindred shuns your
    house,
As beaten hence by your strange lunacy.
O noble lord, bethink thee of thy birth;
Call home thy ancient thoughts from banishment,
And banish hence these abject lowly dreams.
Look how thy servants do attend on thee,
Each in his office ready at thy beck.
Wilt thou have music? hark! Apollo plays,
                                        [Music.
And twenty caged nightingales do sing:
Or wilt thou sleep? we'll have thee to a couch
Softer and sweeter than the lustful bed
On purpose trimm'd up for Semiramis.
Say thou wilt walk; we will bestrew the ground:
Or wilt thou ride? thy horses shall be trapt,
Their harness studded all with gold and pearl.
Dost thou love hawking? thou hast hawks will
    soar
Above the morning lark: or wilt thou hunt?
Thy hounds shall make the welkin answer them,
And fetch shrill echoes from the hollow earth.

FIRST SERVANT.
Say thou wilt course; thy greyhounds are as swift
As breathed stags, ay, fleeter than the roe.

SECOND SERVANT.
Dost thou love pictures? we will fetch thee
    straight
Adonis painted by a running brook,
And Cytherea all in sedges hid,
Which seem to move and wanton with her breath,
Even as the waving sedges play with wind.

LORD.
We'll show thee Io as she was a maid,
And how she was beguiled and surprised,
As lively painted as the deed was done.

THIRD SERVANT.
Or Daphne roaming through a thorny wood,
Scratching her legs, that one shall swear she
    bleeds;
And at that sight shall sad Apollo weep,
So workmanly the blood and tears are drawn.

LORD.
Thou art a lord, and nothing but a lord:
Thou hast a lady far more beautiful
Than any woman in this waning age.

FIRST SERVANT.
And, till the tears that she hath shed for thee,
Like envious floods, o'er-run her lovely face,
She was the fairest creature in the world;
And yet she is inferior to none.

CHRISTOPHER SLY.
Am I a lord? and have I such a lady?
Or do I dream? or have I dream'd till now?

I do not sleep: I see, I hear, I speak;
I smell sweet savours, and I feel soft things:—
Upon my life, I am a lord indeed;
And not a tinker, nor Christophero Sly.
Well, bring our lady hither to our sight;
And once again a pot o' th' smallest ale.

SECOND SERVANT.
Will't please your mightiness to wash your
    hands?
    [SERVANTS present a ewer, basin, and napkin.
O, how we joy to see your wit restored!
O, that once more you knew but what you are!
These fifteen years you have been in a dream;
Or when you waked, so waked as if you slept.

CHRISTOPHER SLY.
These fifteen years! by my fay, a goodly nap.
But did I never speak of all that time?

FIRST SERVANT.
O, yes, my lord; but very idle words:
For though you lay here in this goodly chamber,
Yet would you say ye were beaten out of door;
And rail upon the hostess of the house;
And say, you would present her at the leet,
Because she brought stone jugs and no seal'd
    quarts:
Sometimes you would call out for Cicely Hacket.

CHRISTOPHER SLY.
Ay, the woman's maid of the house.

THIRD SERVANT.
Why, sir, you know no house, nor no such maid,
Nor no such men as you have reckon'd up,—
As Stephen Sly, and old John Naps of Greece,
And Peter Turf, and Henry Pimpernell;
And twenty more such names and men as these,
Which never were, nor no man ever saw.

CHRISTOPHER SLY.
Now, Lord be thanked for my good amends!

ALL.
Amen.

CHRISTOPHER SLY.
I thank thee: thou shalt not lose by it.
    Enter the PAGE as a lady, with ATTENDANTS.

PAGE.
How fares my noble lord?

CHRISTOPHER SLY.
Marry, I fare well; for here is cheer enough.
Where is my wife?

PAGE.
Here, noble lord: what is thy will with her?

CHRISTOPHER SLY.
Are you my wife, and will not call me husband?
My men should call me lord: I am your goodman.

PAGE.
My husband and my lord, my lord and husband;
I am your wife in all obedience.

CHRISTOPHER SLY.
I know it well.—What must I call her?

LORD.
Madam.

CHRISTOPHER SLY.
Al'ce madam, or Joan madam?

LORD.
Madam, and nothing else: so lords call ladies.

CHRISTOPHER SLY.
Madam wife, they say that I have dream'd,
And slept above some fifteen year or more.

PAGE.
Ay, and the time seems thirty unto me,
Being all this time abandon'd from your bed.
CHRISTOPHER SLY.
'Tis much.—Servants, leave me and her alone.—
Madam, undress you, and come now to bed.
PAGE.
Thrice-noble lord, let me entreat of you
To pardon me yet for a night or two;
Or, if not so, until the sun be set:
For your physicians have expressly charged,
In peril to incur your former malady,
That I should yet absent me from your bed:
I hope this reason stands for my excuse.
CHRISTOPHER SLY.
Ay, it stands so that I may hardly tarry so long.
But I would be loth to fall into my dreams again:
I will therefore tarry, in despite of the flesh and
the blood.
Enter a MESSENGER.
SERVANT.
Your honour's players, hearing your amendment,
Are come to play a pleasant comedy;
For so your doctors hold it very meet,
Seeing too much sadness hath congeal'd your
blood,
And melancholy is the nurse of frenzy:
Therefore they thought it good you hear a play,
And frame your mind to mirth and merriment,
Which bars a thousand harms and lengthens life.
CHRISTOPHER SLY.
Marry, I will; let them play it. Is not a commonty
a Christmas gambol or a tumbling-trick?
PAGE.
No, my good lord; it is more pleasing stuff.
CHRISTOPHER SLY.
What, household stuff?
PAGE.
It is a kind of history.
CHRISTOPHER SLY.
Well, we'll see't.—Come, madam wife, sit by my
side, and let the world slip: we shall ne'er be
younger.

ACT I. SCENE I.
Padua.   A public place.

Flourish.   Enter LUCENTIO *and his man*
TRANIO.

LUCENTIO.
TRANIO, since, for the great desire I had
To see fair Padua, nursery of arts,
I am arrived for fruitful Lombardy,
The pleasant garden of great Italy;
And, by my father's love and leave, am arm'd
With his good will, and thy good company,
My trusty servant, well approved in all;
Here let us breathe, and haply institute
A course of learning and ingenious studies.
Pisa, renowned for grave citizens,
Gave me my being and my father first,
A merchant of great traffic through the world,
Vincentio, come of the Bentivolii.
Lucentio his son, brought up in Florence,
It shall become, to serve all hopes conceived,
To deck his fortune with his virtuous deeds:

And therefore, Tranio, for the time I study,
Virtue, and that part of philosophy
Will I apply, that treats of happiness
By virtue specially to be achieved.
Tell me thy mind; for I have Pisa left,
And am to Padua come, as he that leaves
A shallow plash, to plunge him in the deep,
And with satiety seeks to quench his thirst.
TRANIO.
Mi perdonate, gentle master mine,
I am in all affected as yourself;
Glad that you thus continue your resolve
To suck the sweets of sweet philosophy.
Only, good master, while we do admire
This virtue and this moral discipline,
Let's be no stoics nor no stocks, I pray;
Or so devote to Aristotle's ethics,
As Ovid be an outcast quite abjured:
Balk logic with acquaintance that you have,
And practise rhetoric in your common talk;
Music and poesy use to quicken you;
The mathematics and the metaphysics,
Fall to them, as you find your stomach serves you;
No profit grows, where is no pleasure ta'en:
In brief, sir, study what you most affect.
LUCENTIO.
Gramercies, Tranio, well dost thou advise.
If, Biondello, thou wert come ashore,
We could at once put us in readiness;
And take a lodging, fit to entertain
Such friends as time in Padua shall beget.
But stay awhile: what company is this?
TRANIO.
Master, some show, to welcome us to town.
Enter BAPTISTA *with his two daughters,* KATHA-
RINA *and* BIANCA; GREMIO, *a pantaloon; and*
HORTENSIO, *suitor to* LIANCA. LUCENTIO
and TRANIO *stand by.*
BAPTISTA.
Gentlemen, importune me no further,
For how I firmly am resolved you know;
That is, not to bestow my youngest daughter
Before I have a husband for the elder:
If either of you both love Katharina,
Because I know you well, and love you well,
Leave shall you have to court her at your pleasure.
GREMIO.
To cart her rather: she's too rough for me.—
There, there, Hortensio, will you any wife?
KATHARINA [*to* BAPTISTA].
I pray you, sir, is it your will
To make a stale of me among these mates?
HORTENSIO.
Mates, maid! how mean you that? no mates for
you,
Unless you were of gentler, milder mould.
KATHARINA.
I'faith, sir, you shall never need to fear:
I wis it is not half way to her heart;
But if it were, doubt not her care should be
To comb your noddle with a three-legg'd stool,
And paint your face, and use you like a fool.
HORTENSIO.
From all such devils, good Lord, deliver us!
GREMIO.
And me too, good Lord!

TRANIO [aside to LUCENTIO].
Hush, master! here's some good pastime toward:
That wench is stark mad, or wonderful froward.
LUCENTIO [aside to TRANIO].
But in the other's silence do I see
Maid's mild behaviour and sobriety.
Peace, Tranio!
TRANIO [aside to LUCENTIO].
Well said, master; mum! and gaze your fill.
BAPTISTA.
Gentlemen, that I may soon make good
What I have said, Bianca, get you in:
And let it not displease thee, good Bianca;
For I will love thee ne'er the less, my girl.
KATHARINA.
A pretty peat! it is best put finger in the eye, an
she knew why.
BIANCA.
Sister, content you in my discontent.—
Sir, to your pleasure humbly I subscribe:
My books and instruments shall be my company,
On them to look, and practise by myself.
LUCENTIO [aside to TRANIO].
Hark, Tranio! thou mayst hear Minerva speak.
HORTENSIO.
Signior Baptista, will you be so strange?
Sorry am I that our good will effects
Bianca's grief.
GREMIO.
Why, will you mew her up,
Signior Baptista, for this fiend of hell,
And make her bear the penance of her tongue?
BAPTISTA.
Gentlemen, content ye; I am resolved:—
Go in, Bianca:—   [Exit BIANCA.
And for I know she taketh most delight
In music, instruments, and poetry,
Schoolmasters will I keep within my house,
Fit to instruct her youth. If you, Hortensio,
Or Signior Gremio, you, know any such,
Prefer them hither; for to cunning men
I will be very kind, and liberal
To mine own children in good bringing-up:
And so, farewell.—Katharina, you may stay;
For I have more to commune with Bianca. [Exit.
KATHARINA.
Why, and I trust I may go too, may I not? What,
shall I be appointed hours; as though, belike, I
knew not what to take, and what to leave, ha?
[Exit.
GREMIO.
You may go to the devil's dam: your gifts are so
good, here's none will hold you.—Our love is not
so great, Hortensio, but we may blow our nails
together, and fast it fairly out: our cake's dough
on both sides. Farewell: yet, for the love I bear
my sweet Bianca, if I can by any means light on a
fit man to teach her that wherein she delights, I
will wish him to her father.
HORTENSIO.
So will I, Signior Gremio: but a word, I pray.
Though the nature of our quarrel yet never
brookt parle, know now, upon advice, it toucheth
us both,—that we may yet again have access to
our fair mistress, and be happy rivals in Bianca's
love,—to labour and effect one thing specially.

GREMIO.
What's that, I pray?
HORTENSIO.
Marry, sir, to get a husband for her sister.
GREMIO.
A husband! a devil.
HORTENSIO.
I say, a husband.
GREMIO.
I say, a devil. Think'st thou, Hortensio, though
her father be very rich, any man is so very a fool
to be married to hell?
HORTENSIO.
Tush, Gremio, though it pass your patience and
mine to endure her loud alarums, why, man, there
be good fellows in the world, an a man could light
on them, would take her with all faults and money
enough.
GREMIO.
I cannot tell; but I had as lief take her dowry with
this condition,—to be whipt at the high-cross
every morning.
HORTENSIO.
Faith, as you say, there's small choice in rotten
apples. But, come; since this bar in law makes us
friends, it shall be so far forth friendly maintain'd,
till by helping Baptista's eldest daughter to a husband, we set his youngest free for a husband, and
then have to't afresh.—Sweet Bianca!—Happy
man be his dole! He that runs fastest gets the
ring. How say you, Signior Gremio?
GREMIO.
I am agreed: and would I had given him the best
horse in Padua to begin his wooing, that would
thoroughly woo her, wed her, and bed her, and
rid the house of her! Come on.
[Exeunt GREMIO and HORTENSIO.
TRANIO.
I pray, sir, tell me,—is it possible
That love should of a sudden take such hold?
LUCENTIO.
O Tranio, till I found it to be true,
I never thought it possible or likely;
But, see! while idly I stood looking on,
I found the effect of love in idleness:
And now in plainness do confess to thee,—
That art to me as secret and as dear
As Anna to the Queen of Carthage was,—
Tranio, I burn, I pine, I perish, Tranio,
If I achieve not this young modest girl.
Counsel me, Tranio, for I know thou canst;
Assist me, Tranio, for I know thou wilt.
TRANIO.
Master, it is no time to chide you now;
Affection is not rated from the heart:
If love have toucht you, naught remains but so,—
Redime te captum quam queas minimo.
LUCENTIO.
Gramercies, lad; go forward; this contents:
The rest will comfort, for thy counsel's sound.
TRANIO.
Master, you lookt so longly on the maid,
Perhaps you markt not what's the pith of all.
LUCENTIO.
O, yes, I saw sweet beauty in her face,
Such as the daughter of Agenor had,

That made great Jove to humble him to her hand,
When with his knees he kist the Cretan strand.
TRANIO.
Saw you no more? markt you not how her sister
Began to scold, and raise up such a storm,
That mortal ears might hardly endure the din?
LUCENTIO.
Tranio, I saw her coral lips to move,
And with her breath she did perfume the air:
Sacred and sweet was all I saw in her.
TRANIO.
Nay, then, 'tis time to stir him from his trance.—
I pray, awake, sir: if you love the maid,
Bend thoughts and wits to achieve her. Thus it
stands:
Her elder sister is so curst and shrewd,
That, till the father rid his hands of her,
Master, your love must live a maid at home;
And therefore has he closely mew'd her up,
Because she will not be annoy'd with suitors.
LUCENTIO.
Ah, Tranio, what a cruel father's he!
But art thou not advised, he took some care
To get her cunning schoolmasters to instruct her?
TRANIO.
Ay, marry, am I, sir; and now 'tis plotted.
LUCENTIO.
I have it, Tranio.
TRANIO.
          Master, for my hand,
Both our inventions meet and jump in one.
LUCENTIO.
Tell me thine first.
TRANIO.
          You will be schoolmaster,
And undertake the teaching of the maid:
That's your device.
LUCENTIO.
          It is: may it be done?
TRANIO.
Not possible; for who shall bear your part,
And be in Padua here Vincentio's son;   [friends;
Keep house, and ply his book; welcome his
Visit his countrymen, and banquet them?
LUCENTIO.
Basta; content thee; for I have it full.
We have not yet been seen in any house;
Nor can we be distinguisht by our faces
For man or master: then it follows thus;—
Thou shalt be master, Tranio, in my stead,
Keep house, and port, and servants, as I should:
I will some other be; some Florentine,
Some Neapolitan, or meaner man of Pisa.
'Tis hatcht, and shall be so:—Tranio, at once
Uncase thee; take my colour'd hat and cloak:
When Biondello comes, he waits on thee;
But I will charm him first to keep his tongue.
TRANIO.
So had you need.   [They exchange habits.
In brief, sir, sith it your pleasure is,
And I am tied to be obedient,—
For so your father charged me at our parting;
'Be serviceable to my son,' quoth he,
Although I think 'twas in another sense,—
I am content to be Lucentio,
Because so well I love Lucentio.

LUCENTIO.
Tranio, be so, because Lucentio loves:
And let me be a slave, t'achieve that maid [eye.—
Whose sudden sight hath thrall'd my wounded
Here comes the rogue.
          Enter BIONDELLO.
          Sirrah, where have you been?
BIONDELLO.
Where have I been! Nay, how now! where are
you? Master, has my fellow Tranio stol'n your
clothes? or you stol'n his? or both? pray, what's
the news?
LUCENTIO.
Sirrah, come hither: 'tis no time to jest,
And therefore frame your manners to the time.
Your fellow Tranio here, to save my life,
Puts my apparel and my countenance on,
And I for my escape have put on his;
For in a quarrel, since I came ashore,
I kill'd a man, and fear I was descried:
Wait you on him, I charge you, as becomes,
While I make way from hence to save my life:
You understand me?
BIONDELLO.
          I, sir! Ne'er a whit.
LUCENTIO.
And not a jot of Tranio in your mouth:
Tranio is changed into Lucentio.
BIONDELLO.
The better for him: would I were so too!
TRANIO.
So could I, faith, boy, to have the next wish after,
That Lucentio indeed had Baptista's youngest
daughter.
But, sirrah,—not for my sake, but your master's,
—I advise   [companies:
You use your manners discreetly in all kind of
When I am alone, why, then I am Tranio;
But in all places else your master Lucentio.
LUCENTIO.
Tranio, let's go:
One thing more rests, that thyself execute,—
To make one among these wooers: if thou ask me
why,—
Sufficeth, my reasons are both good and weighty.
          [Exeunt.
          The Presenters above speak.
FIRST SERVANT.
My lord, you nod; you do not mind the play.
CHRISTOPHER SLY.
Yes, by Saint Anne, do I. A good matter, surely;
comes there any more of it?
PAGE.
My lord, 'tis but begun.
CHRISTOPHER SLY.
'Tis a very excellent piece of work, madam lady;
would 'twere done!   [They sit and mark.

SCENE II.

The same.   Before HORTENSIO'S house.

Enter PETRUCHIO and his man GRUMIO.

PETRUCHIO.
VERONA, for awhile I take my leave,
     To see my friends in Padua; but, of all,
My best beloved and approved friend,

Hortensio; and I trow this is his house.—
Here, sirrah Grumio; knock, I say.

GRUMIO.

Knock, sir! whom should I knock? is there any
man has rebused your worship?

PETRUCHIO.

Villain, I say, knock me here soundly.

GRUMIO.

Knock you here, sir! why, sir, what am I, sir, that
I should knock you here, sir?

PETRUCHIO.

Villain, I say, knock me at this gate,
And rap me well, or I'll knock your knave's pate.

GRUMIO.

My master is grown quarrelsome.—I should
knock you first,
And then I know after who comes by the
worst.

PETRUCHIO.

Will it not be?
Faith, sirrah, an you'll not knock, I'll wring it;
I'll try how you can *sol, fa*, and sing it.

[He wrings him by the ears.

GRUMIO.

Help, masters, help! my master is mad.

PETRUCHIO.

Now, knock when I bid you, sirrah villain!

Enter HORTENSIO.

HORTENSIO.

How now! what's the matter?—My old friend
Grumio! and my good friend Petruchio!—How
do you all at Verona?

PETRUCHIO.

Signior Hortensio, come you to part the fray?
Con tutto il cuore ben trovato, may I say.

HORTENSIO.

*Alla nostra casa ben venuto, molto honorato signor
mio Petruchio.*—
Rise, Grumio, rise: we will compound this quarrel.

GRUMIO [*rising*].

Nay, 'tis no matter, sir, what he 'leges in Latin.—
If this be not a lawful cause for me to leave his
service,—look you, sir,—he bid me knock him and
rap him soundly, sir: well, was it fit for a servant
to use his master so; being perhaps, for aught I
see, two-and-thirty,—a pip out?
Whom would to God I had well knockt at first,
Then had not Grumio come by the worst.

PETRUCHIO.

A senseless villain!—Good Hortensio,
I bade the rascal knock upon your gate,
And could not get him for my heart to do it.

GRUMIO.

Knock at the gate!—O heavens! Spake you not
these words plain,—'Sirrah, knock me here, rap
me here, knock me well, and knock me soundly'?
And come you now with—knocking at the gate?

PETRUCHIO.

Sirrah, be gone, or talk not, I advise you.

HORTENSIO.

Petruchio, patience; I am Grumio's pledge:
Why, this' a heavy chance 'twixt him and you,
Your ancient, trusty, pleasant servant Grumio.
And tell me now, sweet friend, what happy gale
Blows you to Padua here, from old Verona?

PETRUCHIO.

Such wind as scatters young men through the
world,
To seek their fortunes further than at home,
Where small experience grows. But, in a few,
Signior Hortensio, thus it stands with me:—
Antonio, my father, is deceased;
And I have thrust myself into this maze,
Haply to wive and thrive as best I may:
Crowns in my purse I have, and goods at home,
And so am come abroad to see the world.

HORTENSIO.

Petruchio, shall I, then, come roundly to thee,
And wish thee to a shrewd ill-favour'd wife?
Thou'ldst thank me but a little for my counsel:
And yet I'll promise thee she shall be rich,
And very rich: but thou'rt too much my friend,
And I'll not wish thee to her.

PETRUCHIO.

Signior Hortensio, 'twixt such friends as we
Few words suffice; and therefore, if thou know
One rich enough to be Petruchio's wife,—
As wealth is burthen of my wooing dance,—
Be she as foul as was Florentius' love,
As old as Sibyl, and as curst and shrewd
As Socrates' Xantippe, or a worse,
She moves me not, or not removes, at least,
Affection's edge in me, were she as rough
As are the swelling Adriatic seas:
I come to wive it wealthily in Padua;
If wealthily, then happily in Padua.

GRUMIO.

Nay, look you, sir, he tells you flatly what his
mind is: why, give him gold enough and marry
him to a puppet or an aglet-baby; or an old trot
with ne'er a tooth in her head, though she have as
many diseases as two and fifty horses: why, nothing comes amiss, so money comes withal.

HORTENSIO.

Petruchio, since we are stept thus far in,
I will continue that I broacht in jest.
I can, Petruchio, help thee to a wife
With wealth enough, and young and beauteous;
Brought up as best becomes a gentlewoman:
Her only fault—and that is faults enough—
Is, that she is intolerable curst,
And shrewd, and froward; so beyond all measure,
That, were my state far worser than it is,
I would not wed her for a mine of gold.

PETRUCHIO.

Hortensio, peace! thou know'st not gold's effect:
Tell me her father's name, and 'tis enough;
For I will board her, though she chide as loud
As thunder when the clouds in autumn crack.

HORTENSIO.

Her father is Baptista Minola,
An affable and courteous gentleman:
Her name is Katharina Minola,
Renown'd in Padua for her scolding tongue.

PETRUCHIO.

I know her father, though I know not her:
And he knew my deceased father well.
I will not sleep, Hortensio, till I see her;
And therefore let me be thus bold with you
To give you over at this first encounter,
Unless you will accompany me thither.

GRUMIO.

I pray you, sir, let him go while the humour lasts.
O' my word, an she knew him as well as I do, she
would think scolding would do little good upon
him: she may, perhaps, call him half a score
knaves, or so: why, that's nothing; an he begin
once, he'll rail in his rope-tricks. I'll tell you what,
sir,—an she stand him but a little, he will throw a
figure in her face, and so disfigure her with it, that
she shall have no more eyes to see withal than a
cat. You know him not, sir.

HORTENSIO.

Tarry, Petruchio, I must go with thee;
For in Baptista's keep my treasure is:
He hath the jewel of my life in hold,
His youngest daughter, beautiful Bianca;
And her withholds from me and other more,
Suitors to her and rivals in my love;
Supposing it a thing impossible,—
For those defects I have before rehearsed,—
That ever Katharina will be woo'd;
Therefore this order hath Baptista ta'en,
That none shall have access unto Bianca
Till Katharine the curst have got a husband.

GRUMIO.

Katharine the curst!
A title for a maid, of all titles the worst.

HORTENSIO.

Now shall my friend Petruchio do me grace;
And offer me, disguised in sober robes,
To old Baptista as a schoolmaster
Well seen in music, to instruct Bianca;
That so I may, by this device, at least
Have leave and leisure to make love to her,
And unsuspected court her by herself.

GRUMIO.

Here's no knavery! See, to beguile the old folks,
how the young folks lay their heads together!

Enter GREMIO *and* LUCENTIO *disguised.*

Master, master, look about you: who goes there,
ha?

HORTENSIO.

Peace, Grumio! it is the rival of my love.—
Petruchio, stand by awhile.

GRUMIO.

A proper stripling and an amorous!

[They stand aside.

GREMIO.

O, very well; I have perused the note.
Hark you, sir; I'll have them very fairly bound:
All books of love, see that at any hand;
And see you read no other lectures to her:
You understand me:—over and beside
Signior Baptista's liberality,
I'll mend it with a largess:—take your papers too,
And let me have them very well perfumed;
For she is sweeter than perfume itself,
To whom they go to. What will you read to her?

LUCENTIO.

Whate'er I read to her, I'll plead for you
As for my patron,—stand you so assured,—
As firmly as yourself were still in place:
Yea, and perhaps with more successful words
Than you, unless you were a scholar, sir.

GREMIO.

O this learning! what a thing it is!

GRUMIO.

O this woodcock! what an ass it is!

PETRUCHIO.

Peace, sirrah!

HORTENSIO.

Grumio, mum!—*[Coming forward]* God save you,
Signior Gremio!

GREMIO.

And you are well met, Signior Hortensio.
Trow you whither I am going?—To Baptista
Minola.
I promised to inquire carefully
About a schoolmaster for the fair Bianca:
And, by good fortune, I have lighted well
On this young man; for learning and behaviour
Fit for her turn; well read in poetry,
And other books,—good ones, I warrant ye.

HORTENSIO.

'Tis well: and I have met a gentleman
Hath promised me to help me to another,
A fine musician to instruct our mistress;
So shall I no whit be behind in duty
To fair Bianca, so beloved of me.

GREMIO.

Beloved of me,—and that my deeds shall prove.

GRUMIO *[aside]*.

And that his bags shall prove.

HORTENSIO.

Gremio, 'tis now no time to vent our love:
Listen to me; and if you speak me fair,
I'll tell you news indifferent good for either.
Here is a gentleman, whom by chance I met,
Upon agreement from us to his liking,
Will undertake to woo curst Katharine,
Yea, and to marry her, if her dowry please.

GREMIO.

So said, so done, is well:—
Hortensio, have you told him all her faults?

PETRUCHIO.

I know she is an irksome brawling scold:
If that be all, masters, I hear no harm.

GREMIO.

No, say'st me so, friend? What countryman?

PETRUCHIO.

Born in Verona, old Antonio's son:
My father dead, my fortune lives for me;
And I do hope good days and long to see.

GREMIO.

O, sir, such a life, with such a wife, were strange!
But if you have a stomach, to't o' God's name:
You shall have me assisting you in all.
But will you woo this wild-cat?

PETRUCHIO.

Will I live?

GRUMIO.

Will he woo her? ay, or I'll hang her.

PETRUCHIO.

Why came I hither but to that intent?
Think you a little din can daunt mine ears?
Have I not in my time heard lions roar?
Have I not heard the sea, puft up with winds,
Rage like an angry boar chafed with sweat?
Have I not heard great ordnance in the field,
And heaven's artillery thunder in the skies?
Have I not in a pitched battle heard   [clang?
Loud 'larums, neighing steeds, and trumpet's

And do you tell me of a woman's tongue,
That gives not half so great a blow to th'ear
As will a chestnut in a farmer's fire?
Tush, tush! fear boys with bugs.

GRUMIO.

           For he fears none.

GREMIO.

Hortensio, hark:
This gentleman is happily arrived,
My mind presumes, for his own good and ours.

HORTENSIO.

I promised we would be contributors,
And bear his charge of wooing, whatsoe'er.

GREMIO.

And so we will,—provided that he win her.

GRUMIO.

I would I were as sure of a good dinner.

Enter TRANIO *brave, and* BIONDELLO.

TRANIO.

Gentlemen, God save you! If I may be bold,
Tell me, I beseech you, which is the readiest way
To the house of Signior Baptista Minola?

GREMIO.

He that has the two fair daughters,—is't he you
   mean?

TRANIO.

Even he.—Biondello,—

GREMIO.

Hark you, sir; you mean not her to—

TRANIO.

Perhaps, him and her, sir: what have you to do?

PETRUCHIO.

Not her that chides, sir, at any hand, I pray.

TRANIO.

I love no chiders, sir.—Biondello, let's away.

LUCENTIO [*aside*].

Well begun, Tranio.

HORTENSIO.

         Sir, a word ere you go;—
Are you a suitor to the maid you talk of, yea or
   no?

TRANIO.

An if I be, sir, is it any offence?

GREMIO.

No; if without more words you will get you hence.

TRANIO.

Why, sir, I pray, are not the streets as free
For me as for you?

GREMIO.

         But so is not she.

TRANIO.

For what reason, I beseech you?

GREMIO.

        For this reason, if you'll know,—
That she's the choice love of Signior Gremio.

HORTENSIO.

That she's the chosen of Signior Hortensio.

TRANIO.

Softly, my masters! if you be gentlemen,
Do me this right,—hear me with patience.
Baptista is a noble gentleman,
To whom my father is not all unknown;
And, were his daughter fairer than she is,
She may more suitors have, and me for one.
Fair Leda's daughter had a thousand wooers;
Then well one more may fair Bianca have:

And so she shall; Lucentio shall make one,
Though Paris came in hope to speed alone.

GREMIO.

What, this gentleman will out-talk us all!

LUCENTIO.

Sir, give him head: I know he'll prove a jade.

PETRUCHIO.

Hortensio, to what end are all these words?

HORTENSIO.

Sir, let me be so bold as ask you,
Did you yet ever see Baptista's daughter?

TRANIO.

No, sir; but hear I do that he hath two;
The one as famous for a scolding tongue,
As is the other for beauteous modesty.

PETRUCHIO.

Sir, sir, the first's for me; let her go by.

GREMIO.

Yea, leave that labour to great Hercules;
And let it be more than Alcides' twelve.

PETRUCHIO.

Sir, understand you this of me, in sooth:
The youngest daughter, whom you hearken for,
Her father keeps from all access of suitors;
And will not promise her to any man
Until the elder sister first be wed:
The younger then is free, and not before.

TRANIO.

If it be so, sir, that you are the man
Must stead us all, and me amongst the rest;
And if you break the ice, and do this feat,
Achieve the elder, set the younger free
For our access,—whose hap shall be to have her
Will not so graceless be to be ingrate.

HORTENSIO.

Sir, you say well, and well you do conceive;
And since you do profess to be a suitor,
You must, as we do, gratify this gentleman,
To whom we all rest generally beholding.

TRANIO.

Sir, I shall not be slack: in sign whereof,
Please ye we may contrive this afternoon,
And quaff carouses to our mistress' health;
And do as adversaries do in law,—
Strive mightily, but eat and drink as friends.

GRUMIO *and* BIONDELLO.

O excellent motion! Fellows, let's be gone.

HORTENSIO.

The motion's good indeed, and be it so:—
Petruchio, I shall be your *ben venuto.*   [*Exeunt.*

ACT II. SCENE I.

Padua.   A room in BAPTISTA'S *house.*

Enter KATHARINA, *and* BIANCA *with her hands bound.*

BIANCA.

GOOD sister, wrong me not, nor wrong your
   self,
To make a bondmaid and a slave of me;
That I disdain: but for these other gauds,
Unbind my hands, I'll pull them off myself,
Yea, all my raiment, to my petticoat;
Or, what you will command me, will I do.
So well I know my duty to my elders.

KATHARINA.
Of all thy suitors, here I charge thee, tell
Whom thou lovest best: see thou dissemble not.
BIANCA.
Believe me, sister, of all the men alive,
I never yet beheld that special face
Which I could fancy more than any other.
KATHARINA.
Minion, thou liest: is't not Hortensio?
BIANCA.
If you affect him, sister, here I swear
I'll plead for you myself, but you shall have
  him.
KATHARINA.
O, then, belike you fancy riches more:
You will have Gremio to keep you fair.
BIANCA.
Is it for him you do envy me so?
Nay, then, you jest; and now I well perceive
You have but jested with me all this while:
I prithee, sister Kate, untie my hands.
KATHARINA.
If that be jest, then all the rest was so.
                              [Strikes her.
Enter BAPTISTA.
BAPTISTA.
Why, how now, dame! whence grows this inso-
  lence?—
Bianca, stand aside:—poor girl! she weeps:—
Go ply thy needle; meddle not with her.—
For shame, thou hilding of a devilish spirit,
Why dost thou wrong her that did ne'er wrong
  thee?
When did she cross thee with a bitter word?
KATHARINA.
Her silence flouts me, and I'll be revenged.
                         [Flies after BIANCA.
BAPTISTA [holding her back].
What, in my sight?—Bianca, get thee in.
                            [Exit BIANCA.
KATHARINA.
What, will you not suffer me? Nay, now I see
She is your treasure, she must have a husband;
I must dance barefoot on her wedding-day,
And, for your love to her, lead apes in hell.
Talk not to me: I will go sit and weep,
Till I can find occasion of revenge.   [Exit.
BAPTISTA.
Was ever gentleman thus grieved as I?
But who comes here?
Enter GREMIO, with LUCENTIO in the habit of a
  mean man; PETRUCHIO, with HORTENSIO as
  a musician; and TRANIO, with BIONDELLO
  bearing a lute and books.
GREMIO.
Good morrow, neighbour Baptista.
BAPTISTA.
Good morrow, neighbour Gremio.—God save
you, gentlemen!
PETRUCHIO.
And you, good sir! Pray, have you not a daughter
Call'd Katharina, fair and virtuous?
BAPTISTA.
I have a daughter, sir, call'd Katharina.
GREMIO.
You are too blunt: go to it orderly.

PETRUCHIO.
You wrong me, Signior Gremio: give me leave.—
I am a gentleman of Verona, sir,
That, hearing of her beauty and her wit,
Her affability and bashful modesty,
Her wondrous qualities and mild behaviour,
Am bold to show myself a forward guest
Within your house, to make mine eye the witness
Of that report which I so oft have heard.
And, for an entrance to my entertainment,
I do present you with a man of mine,
                      [presenting HORTENSIO.
Cunning in music and the mathematics,
To instruct her fully in those sciences,
Whereof I know she is not ignorant:
Accept of him, or else you do me wrong:
His name is Licio, born in Mantua.
BAPTISTA.
You're welcome, sir; and he, for your good sake.
But for my daughter Katharine,—this I know,
She is not for your turn, the more my grief.
PETRUCHIO.
I see you do not mean to part with her;
Or else you like not of my company.
BAPTISTA.
Mistake me not; I speak but as I find.
Whence are you, sir? what may I call your name?
PETRUCHIO.
Petruchio is my name; Antonio's son,
A man well known throughout all Italy.
BAPTISTA.
I knew him well: you are welcome for his sake.
GREMIO.
Saving your tale, Petruchio, I pray,
Let us, that are poor petitioners, speak too:
Baccare! you are marvellous forward.
PETRUCHIO.   [doing.
O, pardon me, Signior Gremio; I would fain be
GREMIO.
I doubt it not, sir; but you will curse your woo-
  ing.
Neighbour, this is a gift very grateful, I am sure
of it. To express the like kindness myself, that
have been more kindly beholding to you than any,
I freely give unto you this young scholar [present-
ing LUCENTIO], that hath been long studying at
Rheims; as cunning in Greek, Latin, and other
languages, as the other in music and mathematics:
his name is Cambio: pray, accept his service.
BAPTISTA.
A thousand thanks, Signior Gremio.—Welcome,
good Cambio.—But, gentle sir [to TRANIO], me-
thinks you walk like a stranger: may I be so bold
to know the cause of your coming?
TRANIO.
Pardon me, sir, the boldness is mine own;
That, being a stranger in this city here,
Do make myself a suitor to your daughter,
Unto Bianca, fair and virtuous.
Nor is your firm resolve unknown to me,
In the preferment of the eldest sister.
This liberty is all that I request,—
That, upon knowledge of my parentage,
I may have welcome 'mongst the rest that woo,
And free access and favour as the rest:
And, toward the education of your daughters,

I here bestow a simple instrument,
And this small packet of Greek and Latin books:
If you accept them, then their worth is great.
Lucentio is my name.
BAPTISTA.
          Of whence, I pray?
TRANIO.
Of Pisa, sir; son to Vincentio.
BAPTISTA.
A mighty man of Pisa; by report
I know him well: you are very welcome, sir.—
Take you [to HORTENSIO] the lute, and you [to
   LUCENTIO] the set of books;
You shall go see your pupils presently.—
Holla, within!
          Enter a SERVANT.
          Sirrah, lead these gentlemen
To my two daughters; and tell them both
These are their tutors: bid them use them well.
   [Exit SERVANT, with HORTENSIO, LU-
      CENTIO, and BIONDELLO.
We will go walk a little in the orchard,
And then to dinner. You are passing welcome,
And so I pray you all to think yourselves.
PETRUCHIO.
Signior Baptista, my business asketh haste,
And every day I cannot come to woo.
You knew my father well; and in him, me,
Left solely heir to all his lands and goods,
Which I have better'd rather than decreased:
Then tell me,—if I get your daughter's love,
What dowry shall I have with her to wife?
BAPTISTA.
After my death, the one half of my lands,
And in possession twenty thousand crowns.
PETRUCHIO.
And, for that dowry, I'll assure her of
Her widowhood, be it that she survive me,
In all my lands and leases whatsoever:
Let specialties be therefore drawn between us,
That covenants may be kept on either hand.
BAPTISTA.
Ay, when the special thing is well obtain'd,
That is, her love; for that is all in all.
PETRUCHIO.
Why, that is nothing; for I tell you, father,
I am as peremptory as she proud-minded;
And where two raging fires meet together,
They do consume the thing that feeds their fury:
Though little fire grows great with little wind,
Yet extreme gusts will blow out fire and all:
So I to her, and so she yields to me;
For I am rough, and woo not like a babe.
BAPTISTA.
Well mayst thou woo, and happy be thy speed!
But be thou arm'd for some unhappy words.
PETRUCHIO.
Ay, to the proof; as mountains are for winds,
That shakes not, though they blow perpetually.
   Enter HORTENSIO, with his head broke.
BAPTISTA.
How now, my friend! why dost thou look so pale?
HORTENSIO.
For fear, I promise you, if I look pale.
BAPTISTA.
What, will my daughter prove a good musician?

HORTENSIO.
I think she'll sooner prove a soldier:
Iron may hold with her, but never lutes.
BAPTISTA.
Why, then thou canst not break her to the lute?
HORTENSIO.
Why, no; for she hath broke the lute to me.
I did but tell her she mistook her frets,
And bow'd her hand to teach her fingering;
When, with a most impatient devilish spirit,
'Frets call you these?' quoth she; 'I'll fume with
   them:'
And, with that word, she struck me on the head,
And through the instrument my pate made way;
And there I stood amazed for a while,
As on a pillory, looking through the lute;
While she did call me rascal fiddler
And twangling Jack, with twenty such vile terms,
As had she studied to misuse me so.
PETRUCHIO.
Now, by the world, it is a lusty wench;
I love her ten times more than e'er I did:
O, how I long to have some chat with her!
BAPTISTA.
Well, go with me, and be not so discomfited:
Proceed in practice with my younger daughter;
She's apt to learn, and thankful for good turns.
Signior Petruchio, will you go with us,
Or shall I send my daughter Kate to you?
PETRUCHIO.
I pray you do; I will attend her here,—
   [Exeunt BAPTISTA, GREMIO, TRANIO,
      and HORTENSIO.
And woo her with some spirit when she comes.
Say that she rail; why, then, I'll tell her plain,
She sings as sweetly as a nightingale:
Say that she frown; I'll say, she looks as clear
As morning roses newly washt with dew:
Say she be mute and will not speak a word;
Then I'll commend her volubility,
And say she uttereth piercing eloquence:
If she do bid me pack, I'll give her thanks,
As though she bid me stay by her a week:
If she deny to wed, I'll crave the day   [ried.—
When I shall ask the banns, and when be mar-
But here she comes; and now, Petruchio, speak.
   Enter KATHARINA.
Good morrow, Kate; for that's your name, I hear
KATHARINA.
Well have you heard, but something hard of
   hearing:
They call me Katharine that do talk of me.
PETRUCHIO.
You lie, in faith; for you are call'd plain Kate,
And bonny Kate, and sometimes Kate the curst;
But, Kate, the prettiest Kate in Christendom,
Kate of Kate-Hall, my super-dainty Kate,
For dainties are all cates,—and therefore, Kate,
Take this of me, Kate of my consolation;—
Hearing thy mildness praised in every town,
Thy virtues spoke of, and thy beauty sounded,
Yet not so deeply as to thee belongs,—
Myself am moved to woo thee for my wife.
KATHARINA.
Moved! in good time: let him that moved you
   hither

Remove you hence: I knew you at the first,
You were a moveable.

PETRUCHIO.
                     Why, what's a moveable?

KATHARINA.
A joint-stool.

PETRUCHIO.
             Thou hast hit it: come, sit on me.

KATHARINA.
Asses are made to bear, and so are you.

PETRUCHIO.
Women are made to bear, and so are you.

KATHARINA.
No such jade as you, if me you mean.

PETRUCHIO.
Alas, good Kate! I will not burthen thee!
For, knowing thee to be but young and light—

KATHARINA.
Too light for such a swain as you to catch;
And yet as heavy as my weight should be.

PETRUCHIO.
Should be! should—buzz!

KATHARINA.
                Well ta'en, and like a buzzard.

PETRUCHIO.
O slow-wing'd turtle! shall a buzzard take thee?

KATHARINA.
Ay, for a turtle,—as he takes a buzzard.

PETRUCHIO.
Come, come, you wasp; i'faith, you are too angry.

KATHARINA.
If I be waspish, best beware my sting.

PETRUCHIO.
My remedy is then, to pluck it out.

KATHARINA.
Ay, if the fool could find it where it lies.

PETRUCHIO.
Who knows not where a wasp does wear his sting?
In his tail.

KATHARINA.
        In his tongue.

PETRUCHIO.
                 Whose tongue?

KATHARINA.
Yours, if you talk of tails: and so farewell.

PETRUCHIO.
What, with my tongue in your tail? nay, come
    again,
Good Kate; I am a gentleman.

KATHARINA.
               That I'll try.
                 [*She strikes him.*

PETRUCHIO.
I swear I'll cuff you, if you strike again.

KATHARINA.
So may you lose your arms:
If you strike me, you are no gentleman;
And if no gentleman, why, then no arms.

PETRUCHIO.
A herald, Kate? O, put me in thy books!

KATHARINA.
What is your crest? a coxcomb?

PETRUCHIO.
A combless cock, so Kate will be my hen.

KATHARINA.
No cock of mine; you crow too like a craven.

PETRUCHIO.
Nay, come, Kate, come; you must not look so
    sour.

KATHARINA.
It is my fashion when I see a crab.

PETRUCHIO.
Why, here's no crab; and therefore look not sour.

KATHARINA.
There is, there is.

PETRUCHIO.
Then show it me.

KATHARINA.
          Had I a glass, I would.

PETRUCHIO.
What, you mean my face?

KATHARINA.
           Well aim'd of such a young one.

PETRUCHIO.
Now, by Saint George, I am too young for you.

KATHARINA.
Yet you are wither'd.

PETRUCHIO.
          'Tis with cares.

KATHARINA.
                 I care not.

PETRUCHIO.
Nay, hear you, Kate: in sooth, you scape not so.

KATHARINA.
I chafe you, if I tarry: let me go.

PETRUCHIO.
No, not a whit: I find you passing gentle.
'Twas told me you were rough, and coy, and
    sullen,
And now I find report a very liar;
For thou art pleasant, gamesome, passing cour-
    teous;
But slow in speech, yet sweet as spring-time
    flowers:
Thou canst not frown, thou canst not look ask-
    ance,
Nor bite the lip, as angry wenches will;
Nor hast thou pleasure to be cross in talk;
But thou with mildness entertain'st thy wooers,
With gentle conference, soft and affable.
Why does the world report that Kate doth limp?
O slanderous world! Kate, like the hazel-twig,
Is straight and slender; and as brown in hue
As hazel-nuts, and sweeter than the kernels.
O, let me see thee walk: thou dost not halt.

KATHARINA.
Go, fool, and whom thou keep'st command.

PETRUCHIO.
Did ever Dian so become a grove,
As Kate this chamber with her princely gait?
O, be thou Dian, and let her be Kate;
And then let Kate be chaste, and Dian sportful!

KATHARINA.
Where did you study all this goodly speech?

PETRUCHIO.
It is extempore, from my mother-wit.

KATHARINA.
A witty mother! witless else her son.

PETRUCHIO.
Am I not wise?

KATHARINA.
         Yes; keep you warm.

PETRUCHIO.

Marry, so I mean, sweet Katharine, in thy bed:
And therefore, setting all this chat aside,
Thus in plain terms:—your father hath consented
That you shall be my wife; your dowry 'greed on;
And, will you, nill you, I will marry you.
Now, Kate, I am a husband for your turn;
For, by this light, whereby I see thy beauty,—
Thy beauty, that doth make me like thee well,—
Thou must be married to no man but me;
For I am he am born to tame you, Kate,
And bring you from a wild Kate to a Kate
Conformable, as other household Kates.
Here comes your father: never make denial;
I must and will have Katharine to my wife.

Enter BAPTISTA, GREMIO, *and* TRANIO.

BAPTISTA.

Now, Signior Petruchio, how speed you with
My daughter?

PETRUCHIO.

How but well, sir? how but well?
It were impossible I should speed amiss.

BAPTISTA.

Why, how now, daughter Katharine! in your
dumps?

KATHARINA.

Call you me daughter? now, I promise you,
You have show'd a tender fatherly regard,
To wish me wed to one half lunatic;
A mad-cap ruffian and a swearing Jack,
That thinks with oaths to face the matter out.

PETRUCHIO.

Father, 'tis thus:—yourself and all the world,
That talkt of her, have talkt amiss of her:
If she be curst, it is for policy,
For she's not froward, but modest as the dove;
She is not hot, but temperate as the morn;
For patience she will prove a second Grissel,
And Roman Lucrece for her chastity:
And to conclude,—we have 'greed so well to-
gether,
That upon Sunday is the wedding day.

KATHARINA.

I'll see thee hang'd on Sunday first.

GREMIO.

Hark, Petruchio; she says, she'll see thee hang'd
first.

TRANIO.

Is this your speeding? nay, then, good night our
part!

PETRUCHIO.

Be patient, gentlemen; I choose her for myself:
If she and I be pleased, what's that to you?
'Tis bargain'd 'twixt us twain, being alone,
That she shall still be curst in company.
I tell you, 'tis incredible to believe
How much she loves me: O, the kindest Kate!—
She hung about my neck; and kiss on kiss
She vied so fast, protesting oath on oath,
That in a twink she won me to her love.
O, you are novices! 'tis a world to see,
How tame, when men and women are alone,
A meacock wretch can make the curstest
shrew.—
Give me thy hand, Kate: I will unto Venice,
To buy apparel 'gainst the wedding-day.—

Provide the feast, father, and bid the guests;
I will be sure my Katharine shall be fine.

BAPTISTA.

I know not what to say: but give me your hands;
God send you joy, Petruchio! 'tis a match.

GREMIO *and* TRANIO.

Amen, say we: we will be witnesses.

PETRUCHIO.

Father, and wife, and gentlemen, adieu;
I will to Venice; Sunday comes apace:—
We will have rings, and things, and fine array;
And kiss me, Kate; we will be married o'
Sunday.

[*Exeunt* PETRUCHIO *and* KATHARINA
severally.

GREMIO.

Was ever match clapt up so suddenly?

BAPTISTA.

Faith, gentlemen, now I play a merchant's part,
And venture madly on a desperate mart.

TRANIO.

'Twas a commodity lay fretting by you:
'Twill bring you gain, or perish on the seas.

BAPTISTA.

The gain I seek is, quiet in the match.

GREMIO.

No doubt but he hath got a quiet catch.
But now, Baptista, to your younger daughter:
Now is the day we long have looked for:
I am your neighbour, and was suitor first.

TRANIO.

And I am one that love Bianca more
Than words can witness, or your thoughts can
guess.

GREMIO.

Youngling, thou canst not love so dear as I.

TRANIO.

Greybeard, thy love doth freeze.

GREMIO.

But thine doth fry.
Skipper, stand back: 'tis age that nourisheth.

TRANIO.

But youth in ladies' eyes that flourisheth.

BAPTISTA.

Content you, gentlemen: I will compound this
strife:
'Tis deeds must win the prize; and he, of both,
That can assure my daughter greatest dower
Shall have Bianca's love.—
Say, Signior Gremio, what can you assure her?

GREMIO.

First, as you know, my house within the city
Is richly furnished with plate and gold;
Basins and ewers, to lave her dainty hands;
My hangings all of Tyrian tapestry;
In ivory coffers I have stuft my crowns;
In cypress chests my arras-counterpoints,
Costly apparel, tents, and canopies,
Fine linen, Turkey cushions bost with pearl,
Valance of Venice gold in needlework;
Pewter and brass, and all things that belong
To house or housekeeping: then, at my farm
I have a hundred milch-kine to the pail,
Six score fat oxen standing in my stalls;
And all things answerable to this portion.
Myself am struck in years, I must confess;

And if I die to-morrow, this is hers,
If whilst I live she will be only mine.
TRANIO.
That 'only' came well in.—Sir, list to me:
I am my father's heir and only son:
If I may have your daughter to my wife,
I'll leave her houses three or four as good,
Within rich Pisa walls, as any one
Old Signior Gremio has in Padua;
Besides two thousand ducats by the year
Of fruitful land, all which shall be her jointure.—
What, have I pincht you, Signior Gremio?
GREMIO.
Two thousand ducats by the year of land!
My land amounts but to so much in all:
That she shall have: besides an argosy
That now is lying in Marseilles' road.—
What, have I choked you with an argosy?
TRANIO.
Gremio, 'tis known my father hath no less
Than three great argosies; besides two galliasses,
And twelve tight galleys; these I will assure
      her,
And twice as much, whate'er thou offer'st next.
GREMIO.
Nay, I have offer'd all,—I have no more;
And she can have no more than all I have:—
If you like me, she shall have me and mine.
TRANIO.
Why, then, the maid is mine from all the world,
By your firm promise: Gremio is out-vied.
BAPTISTA.
I must confess your offer is the best;
And, let your father make her the assurance,
She is your own; else, you must pardon me:
If you should die before him, where's her
      dower?
TRANIO.
That's but a cavil: he is old, I young.
GREMIO.
And may not young men die, as well as old?
BAPTISTA.
Well, gentlemen,
I am thus resolved:—on Sunday next you know
My daughter Katharine is to be married:
Now, on the Sunday following, shall Bianca
Be bride to you, if you make this assurance;
If not, to Signior Gremio:
And so, I take my leave, and thank you both.
GREMIO.
Adieu, good neighbour.   [Exit BAPTISTA.
            Now I fear thee not:
Sirrah young gamester, your father were a fool
To give thee all, and in his waning age
Set foot under thy table: tut, a toy!
An old Italian fox is not so kind, my boy.   [Exit.
TRANIO.
A vengeance on your crafty wither'd hide!
Yet I have faced it with a card of ten.
'Tis in my head to do my master good:
I see no reason but supposed Lucentio
Must get a father, call'd—supposed Vincentio;
And that's a wonder: fathers commonly
Do get their children; but in this case of wooing,
A child shall get a sire, if I fail not of my cunning.
                                              [Exit.

ACT III. SCENE I.

Padua.   A room in BAPTISTA'S *house.*

Enter LUCENTIO, HORTENSIO, *and* BIANCA.

LUCENTIO.
FIDDLER, forbear; you grow too forward, sir;
   Have you so soon forgot the entertainment
Her sister Katharine welcomed you withal?
HORTENSIO.
But, wrangling pedant, this' the patroness
Of heavenly harmony:
Then give me leave to have prerogative;
And when in music we have spent an hour,
Your lecture shall have leisure for as much.
LUCENTIO.
Preposterous ass, that never read so far
To know the cause why music was ordain'd!
Was it not to refresh the mind of man
After his studies or his usual pain?
Then give me leave to read philosophy,
And while I pause, serve in your harmony.
HORTENSIO.
Sirrah, I will not bear these braves of thine.
BIANCA.
Why, gentlemen, you do me double wrong,
To strive for that which resteth in my choice:
I am no breeching scholar in the schools;
I'll not be tied to hours nor 'pointed times,
But learn my lessons as I please myself.
And, to cut off all strife, here sit we down:—
Take you your instrument, play you the whiles;
His lecture will be done ere you have tuned.
HORTENSIO.
You'll leave his lecture when I am in tune?
      [To BIANCA.   HORTENSIO retires.
LUCENTIO.
That will be never:—tune your instrument.
BIANCA.
Where left we last?
LUCENTIO.
Here, madam:—   [Reads.
      Hac ibat Simois; hic est Sigeia tellus;
      Hic steterat Priami regia celsa senis.
BIANCA.
Conster them.
LUCENTIO.
Hac ibat, as I told you before,—Simois, I am
Lucentio,—hic est, son unto Vincentio of Pisa,—
Sigeia tellus, disguised thus to get your love;—
Hic steterat, and that Lucentio that comes a-woo-
ing,—Priami, is my man Tranio,—regia, bearing
my port,—celsa senis, that we might beguile the
old pantaloon.
HORTENSIO [coming forward].
Madam, my instrument's in tune.
BIANCA.
            Let's hear. [HORTENSIO plays.
O, fie! the treble jars.
LUCENTIO.
            Spit in the hole, man,
And tune again.
BIANCA.
Now let me see if I can conster it:—
Hac ibat Simois, I know you not,—hic est Sigeia
tellus, I trust you not;—Hic steterat Priami, take

heed he hear us not,—*regia*, presume not,—*celsa
senis*, despair not.

HORTENSIO.

Madam, 'tis now in tune.

LUCENTIO.

All but the base.

HORTENSIO.

The base is right; 'tis the base knave that jars.—
[*aside*] How fiery and forward our pedant is!
Now, for my life, the knave doth court my love:
Pedascule, I'll watch you better yet.

BIANCA.

In time I may believe, yet I mistrust.

LUCENTIO.

Mistrust it not; for, sure, Aeacides
Was Ajax,—call'd so from his grandfather.

BIANCA.

I must believe my master; else, I promise you,
I should be arguing still upon that doubt:
But let it rest.—Now, Licio, to you:—
Good masters, take it not unkindly, pray,
That I have been thus pleasant with you both.

HORTENSIO [*to* LUCENTIO].

You may go walk, and give me leave awhile:
My lessons make no music in three parts.

LUCENTIO.

Are you so formal, sir? well, I must wait,
[*aside*] And watch withal; for, but I be deceived,
Our fine musician groweth amorous.

HORTENSIO.

Madam, before you touch the instrument,
To learn the order of my fingering,
I must begin with rudiments of art;
To teach you gamut in a briefer sort,
More pleasant, pithy, and effectual,
Than hath been taught by any of my trade:
And there it is in writing, fairly drawn.

BIANCA.

Why, I am past my gamut long ago.

HORTENSIO.

Yet read the gamut of Hortensio.

BIANCA [*reads*].

  'Gamut I am, the ground of all accord,
    A re, to plead Hortensio's passion;
  B mi, Bianca, take him for thy lord,
    C fa ut, that loves with all affection:
  D sol re, one cliff, two notes have I:
    E la mi, show pity, or I die.'
Call you this gamut? tut, I like it not:
Old fashions please me best; I am not so nice,
To change true rules for old inventions.

Enter a SERVANT.

SERVANT.

Mistress, your father prays you leave your books,
And help to dress your sister's chamber up:
You know to-morrow is the wedding-day.

BIANCA.

Farewell, sweet masters, both; I must be gone.

[*Exeunt* BIANCA *and* SERVANT.

LUCENTIO.

Faith, mistress, then I have no cause to stay.

[*Exit.*

HORTENSIO.

But I have cause to pry into this pedant:
Methinks he looks as though he were in love:—
Yet if thy thoughts, Bianca, be so humble,

To cast thy wandering eyes on every stale,
Seize thee that list: if once I find thee ranging,
Hortensio will be quit with thee by changing.

[*Exit.*

SCENE II.

The same. Before BAPTISTA'S *house.*

Enter BAPTISTA, GREMIO, TRANIO, KATHA-
RINA, BIANCA, LUCENTIO, *and others, with*
ATTENDANTS.

BAPTISTA [*to* TRANIO].

SIGNIOR Lucentio, this is the 'pointed day
That Katharine and Petruchio should be
    married,
And yet we hear not of our son-in-law.
What will be said? what mockery will it be,
To want the bridegroom when the priest attends
To speak the ceremonial rites of marriage!
What says Lucentio to this shame of ours?

KATHARINA.

No shame but mine: I must, forsooth, be forced
To give my hand, opposed against my heart,
Unto a mad-brain rudesby, full of spleen;
Who woo'd in haste, and means to wed at leisure.
I told you, I, he was a frantic fool,
Hiding his bitter jests in blunt behaviour:
And, to be noted for a merry man,
He'll woo a thousand, 'point the day of marriage,
Make feasts, invite friends, and proclaim the
    banns;
Yet never means to wed where he hath woo'd.
Now must the world point at poor Katharine,
And say, 'Lo, there is mad Petruchio's wife,
If it would please him come and marry her!'

TRANIO.

Patience, good Katharine, and Baptista too.
Upon my life, Petruchio means but well,
Whatever fortune stays him from his word:
Though he be blunt, I know him passing wise;
Though he be merry, yet withal he's honest.

KATHARINA.

Would Katharine had never seen him, though!

[*Exit weeping, follow'd by* BIANCA *and others.*

BAPTISTA.

Go, girl; I cannot blame thee now to weep;
For such an injury would vex a saint,
Much more a shrew of thy impatient humour.

Enter BIONDELLO.

BIONDELLO.

Master, master! news, old news and such news as
you never heard of!

BAPTISTA.

Is it new and old too? how may that be?

BIONDELLO.

Why, is it not news, to hear of Petruchio's coming?

BAPTISTA.

Is he come?

BIONDELLO.

Why, no, sir.

BAPTISTA.

What then?

BIONDELLO.

He is coming.

BAPTISTA.

When will he be here?

BIONDELLO.
When he stands where I am, and sees you there.

TRANIO.
But, say, what to thine old news?

BIONDELLO.
Why, Petruchio is coming, in a new hat and an old jerkin; a pair of old breeches, thrice turn'd; a pair of boots that have been candle-cases, one buckled, another laced; an old rusty sword ta'en out of the town-armoury, with a broken hilt, and chapeless; with two broken points: his horse hipt with an old mothy saddle, and stirrups of no kindred; besides, possest with the glanders, and like to mose in the chine; troubled with the lampass, infected with the fashions, full of windgalls, sped with spavins, ray'd with the yellows, past cure of the fives, stark spoil'd with the staggers, begnawn with the bots; sway'd in the back, and shoulder-shotten; near-legg'd before, and with a half-cheekt bit, and a headstall of sheep's leather, which, being restrain'd to keep him from stumbling, hath been often burst, and new-repair'd with knots; one girth six times pieced, and a woman's crupper of velure, which hath two letters for her name fairly set down in studs, and here and there pieced with packthread.

BAPTISTA.
Who comes with him?

BIONDELLO.
O, sir, his lackey, for all the world caparison'd like the horse; with a linen stock on one leg, and a kersey boot-hose on the other, garter'd with a red and blue list; an old hat, and *The Humour of Forty Fancies* prickt in't for a feather: a monster, a very monster in apparel; and not like a Christian footboy or a gentleman's lackey.

TRANIO.
'Tis some odd humour pricks him to this fashion;
Yet oftentimes he goes but mean-apparell'd.

BAPTISTA.
I am glad he's come, howsoe'er he comes.

BIONDELLO.
Why, sir, he comes not.

BAPTISTA.
Didst thou not say he comes?

BIONDELLO.
Who? that Petruchio came?

BAPTISTA.
Ay, that Petruchio came.

BIONDELLO.
No, sir; I say his horse comes, with him on his back.

BAPTISTA.
Why, that's all one.

BIONDELLO.
Nay, by Saint Jamy,
I hold you a penny,
A horse and a man
Is more than one,
And yet not many.

Enter PETRUCHIO *and* GRUMIO.

PETRUCHIO.
Come, where be these gallants? who's at home?

BAPTISTA.
You're welcome, sir.

PETRUCHIO.
And yet I come not well.

BAPTISTA.
And yet you halt not.

TRANIO.
Not so well apparell'd
As I wish you were.

PETRUCHIO.
Were it better, I should rush in thus.
But where is Kate? where is my lovely bride?—
How does my father?—Gentles, methinks you frown:
And wherefore gaze this goodly company,
As if they saw some wondrous monument,
Some comet or unusual prodigy?

BAPTISTA.
Why, sir, you know this is your wedding-day:
First we were sad, fearing you would not come;
Now sadder, that you come so unprovided.
Fie, doff this habit, shame to your estate,
An eye-sore to our solemn festival!

TRANIO.
And tell us, what occasion of import
Hath all so long detain'd you from your wife,
And sent you hither so unlike yourself?

PETRUCHIO.
Tedious it were to tell, and harsh to hear:
Sufficeth, I am come to keep my word,
Though in some part enforced to digress;
Which, at more leisure, I will so excuse
As you shall well be satisfied withal.
But where is Kate? I stay too long from her:
The morning wears, 'tis time we were at church.

TRANIO.
See not your bride in these unreverent robes:
Go to my chamber; put on clothes of mine.

PETRUCHIO.
Not I, believe me: thus I'll visit her.

BAPTISTA.
But thus, I trust, you will not marry her.

PETRUCHIO.
Good sooth, even thus; therefore ha' done with words:
To me she's married, not unto my clothes:
Could I repair what she will wear in me,
As I can change these poor accoutrements,
'Twere well for Kate, and better for myself.
But what a fool am I to chat with you,
When I should bid good morrow to my bride,
And seal the title with a lovely kiss!

[*Exeunt* PETRUCHIO *and* GRUMIO.

TRANIO.
He hath some meaning in his mad attire:
We will persuade him, be it possible,
To put on better ere he go to church.

BAPTISTA.
I'll after him, and see the event of this.

[*Exeunt* BAPTISTA, GREMIO, *and* ATTENDANTS.

TRANIO.
But, sir, to her love concerneth us to add
Her father's liking: which to bring to pass,
As I before imparted to your worship,
I am to get a man,—whate'er he be,
It skills not much, we'll fit him to our turn,—
And he shall be Vincentio of Pisa;
And make assurance here in Padua
Of greater sums than I have promised.

So shall you quietly enjoy your hope,
And marry sweet Bianca with consent.
LUCENTIO.
Were it not that my fellow-schoolmaster
Doth watch Bianca's steps so narrowly,
'Twere good, methinks, to steal our marriage;
Which once perform'd, let all the world say no,
I'll keep mine own, despite of all the world.
TRANIO.
That by degrees we mean to look into,
And watch our vantage in this business:
We'll over-reach the greybeard, Gremio,
The narrow-prying father, Minola,
The quaint musician, amorous Licio;
All for my master's sake, Lucentio.
Enter GREMIO.
Signior Gremio, came you from the church?
GREMIO.
As willingly as e'er I came from school.
TRANIO.
And is the bride and bridegroom coming home?
GREMIO.
A bridegroom say you? 'tis a groom indeed,
A grumbling groom, and that the girl shall
find.
TRANIO.
Curster than she? why, 'tis impossible.
GREMIO.
Why, he's a devil, a devil, a very fiend.
TRANIO.
Why, she's a devil, a devil, the devil's dam.
GREMIO.
Tut, she's a lamb, a dove, a fool to him.
I'll tell you, Sir Lucentio: when the priest
Should ask, if Katharine should be his wife,
'Ay, by gogs-wouns,' quoth he; and swore so
loud,
That, all amazed, the priest let fall the book;
And, as he stoopt again to pick it up,
The mad-brain'd bridegroom took him such a
cuff,
That down fell priest and book, and book and
priest:
'Now take them up,' quoth he, 'if any list.'
TRANIO.
What said the wench when he rose again?
GREMIO.
Trembled and shook; for why he stampt and
swore,
As if the vicar meant to cozen him.
But after many ceremonies done,
He calls for wine: 'A health!' quoth he; as if
He had been aboard, carousing to his mates
After a storm; quaft off the muscadel,
And threw the sops all in the sexton's face;
Having no other reason
But that his beard grew thin and hungerly,
And seem'd to ask him sops as he was drinking.
This done, he took the bride about the neck,
And kist her lips with such a clamorous smack,
That, at the parting, all the church did echo;
And I, seeing this, came thence for very shame;
And after me, I know, the rout is coming.
Such a mad marriage never was before:—
Hark, hark! I hear the minstrels play.
[*Music plays.*

Enter PETRUCHIO, KATHARINA, BIANCA, BAP-
TISTA, GRUMIO; *with* HORTENSIO *and* TRAIN.
PETRUCHIO.
Gentlemen and friends, I thank you for your
pains:
I know you think to dine with me to-day,
And have prepared great store of wedding cheer;
But so it is, my haste doth call me hence,
And therefore here I mean to take my leave.
BAPTISTA.
Is't possible you will away to-night?
PETRUCHIO.
I must away to-day, before night come:
Make it no wonder; if you knew my business,
You would entreat me rather go than stay.
And, honest company, I thank you all,
That have beheld me give away myself
To this most patient, sweet, and virtuous wife:
Dine with my father, drink a health to me;
For I must hence; and farewell to you all.
TRANIO.
Let us entreat you stay till after dinner.
PETRUCHIO.
It may not be.
GREMIO.
Let me entreat you.
PETRUCHIO.
It cannot be.
KATHARINA.
Let me entreat you.
PETRUCHIO.
I am content.
KATHARINA.
Are you content to stay?
PETRUCHIO.
I am content you shall entreat me stay;
But yet not stay, entreat me how you can.
KATHARINA.
Now, if you love me, stay.
PETRUCHIO.
Grumio, my horse.
GRUMIO.
Ay, sir, they be ready: the oats have eaten the
horses.
KATHARINA.
Nay, then,
Do what thou canst, I will not go to-day;
No, nor to-morrow, not till I please myself.
The door is open, sir; there lies your way;
You may be jogging whiles your boots are green;
For me, I'll not be gone till I please myself:
'Tis like you'll prove a jolly surly groom,
That take it on you at the first so roundly.
PETRUCHIO.
O, Kate, content thee; prithee, be not angry.
KATHARINA.
I will be angry: what hast thou to do?—
Father, be quiet: he shall stay my leisure.
GREMIO.
Ay, marry, sir, now it begins to work.
KATHARINA.
Gentlemen, forward to the bridal dinner:
I see a woman may be made a fool,
If she had not a spirit to resist.
PETRUCHIO.
They shall go forward, Kate, at thy command.—

Obey the bride, you that attend on her;
Go to the feast, revel and domineer,
Carouse full measure to her maidenhead,
Be mad and merry,—or go hang yourselves:
But for my bonny Kate, she must with me.
Nay, look not big, nor stamp, nor stare, nor fret;
I will be master of what is mine own:
She is my goods, my chattels; she is my house,
My household-stuff, my field, my barn,
My horse, my ox, my ass, my anything;
And here she stands, touch her whoever dare;
I'll bring mine action on the proudest he
That stops my way in Padua.—Grumio,
Draw forth thy weapon, we are beset with thieves;
Rescue thy mistress, if thou be a man.—   [Kate:
Fear not, sweet wench, they shall not touch thee,
I'll buckler thee against a million.
         [*Exeunt* PETRUCHIO, KATHARINA, *and*
                 GRUMIO.
                 BAPTISTA.
Nay, let them go, a couple of quiet ones.
                 GREMIO.
Went they not quickly, I should die with laughing.
                 TRANIO.
Of all mad matches never was the like.
                 LUCENTIO.
Mistress, what's your opinion of your sister?
                 BIANCA.
That, being mad herself, she's madly mated.
                 GREMIO.
I warrant him, Petruchio is Kated.
                 BAPTISTA.
Neighbours and friends, though bride and bride-
groom wants
For to supply the places at the table,
You know there wants no junkets at the feast.—
Lucentio, you shall supply the bridegroom's
place;
And let Bianca take her sister's room.
                 TRANIO.
Shall sweet Bianca practise how to bride it?
                 BAPTISTA.
She shall, Lucentio.—Come, gentlemen, let's go.
                                         [*Exeunt.*

ACT IV.   SCENE I.

PETRUCHIO'S *country house.*

Enter GRUMIO.

                 GRUMIO.
FIE, fie on all tired jades, on all mad masters, and
all foul ways! Was ever man so beaten? was ever
man so ray'd? was ever man so weary? I am sent
before to make a fire, and they are coming after
to warm them. Now, were not I a little pot, and
soon hot, my very lips might freeze to my teeth,
my tongue to the roof of my mouth, my heart in
my belly, ere I should come by a fire to thaw me:
—but I, with blowing the fire, shall warm myself; for, considering the weather, a taller man
than I will take cold.—Holla, ho! Curtis!
                 Enter CURTIS.
                 CURTIS.
Who is that calls so coldly?
                 GRUMIO.
A piece of ice: if thou doubt it, thou mayst slide

from my shoulder to my heel with no greater a
run but my head and my neck. A fire, good
Curtis.
                 CURTIS.
Is my master and his wife coming, Grumio?
                 GRUMIO.
O, ay, Curtis, ay: and therefore fire, fire; cast on
no water.
                 CURTIS.
Is she so hot a shrew as she's reported?
                 GRUMIO.
She was, good Curtis, before this frost: but, thou
know'st, winter tames man, woman and beast;
for it hath tamed my old master, and my new
mistress, and myself, fellow Curtis.
                 CURTIS.
Away, you three-inch fool! I am no beast.
                 GRUMIO.
Am I but three inches? why, thy horn is a foot;
and so long am I at the least. But wilt thou make
fire, or shall I complain on thee to our mistress,
whose hand—she being now at hand—thou shalt
soon feel, to thy cold comfort, for being slow in
thy hot office?
                 CURTIS.
I prithee, good Grumio, tell me, how goes the
world?
                 GRUMIO.
A cold world, Curtis, in every office but thine;
and therefore fire: do thy duty, and have thy duty;
for my master and mistress are almost frozen to
death.
                 CURTIS.
There's fire ready; and therefore, good Grumio,
the news?
                 GRUMIO.
Why, 'Jack, boy! ho, boy!' and as much news as
wilt thou.
                 CURTIS.
Come, you are so full of cony-catching!—
                 GRUMIO.
Why, therefore fire; for I have caught extreme
cold. Where's the cook? is supper ready, the
house trimm'd, rushes strew'd, cobwebs swept,
the serving-men in their new fustian, their white
stockings, and every officer his wedding-garment
on? Be the jacks fair within, the jills fair without,
the carpets laid, and everything in order?
                 CURTIS.
All ready; and therefore, I pray thee, news?
                 GRUMIO.
First, know, my horse is tired; my master and
mistress fallen out.
                 CURTIS.
How?
                 GRUMIO.
Out of their saddles into the dirt; and thereby
hangs a tale.
                 CURTIS.
Let's ha't, good Grumio.
                 GRUMIO.
Lend thine ear.
                 CURTIS.
Here.
                 GRUMIO.
There.   [*Striking him*

CURTIS.

This is to feel a tale, not to hear a tale.

GRUMIO.

And therefore 'tis call'd a sensible tale: and this cuff was but to knock at your ear, and beseech listening. Now I begin: *Imprimis*, we came down a foul hill, my master riding behind my mistress:—

CURTIS.

Both of one horse?

GRUMIO.

What's that to thee?

CURTIS.

Why, a horse.

GRUMIO.

Tell thou the tale:—but hadst thou not crost me, thou shouldst have heard how her horse fell, and she under her horse; thou shouldst have heard, in how miry a place; how she was bemoil'd; how he left her with the horse upon her; how he beat me because her horse stumbled; how she waded through the dirt to pluck him off me; how he swore; how she pray'd—that never pray'd before; how I cried; how the horses ran away; how her bridle was burst; how I lost my crupper;—with many things of worthy memory, which now shall die in oblivion, and thou return unexperienced to thy grave.

CURTIS.

By this reckoning, he is more shrew than she.

GRUMIO.

Ay; and that thou and the proudest of you all shall find when he comes home. But what talk I of this?—Call forth Nathaniel, Joseph, Nicholas, Philip, Walter, Sugarsop, and the rest: let their heads be slickly comb'd, their blue coats brusht, and their garters of an indifferent knit: let them curtsy with their left legs; and not presume to touch a hair of my master's horse-tail till they kiss their hands. Are they all ready?

CURTIS.

They are.

GRUMIO.

Call them forth.

CURTIS.

Do you hear, ho? you must meet my master, to countenance my mistress!

GRUMIO.

Why, she hath a face of her own.

CURTIS.

Who knows not that?

GRUMIO.

Thou, it seems, that calls for company to countenance her.

CURTIS.

I call them forth to credit her.

GRUMIO.

Why, she comes to borrow nothing of them.

Enter four or five SERVING MEN.

NATHANIEL.

Welcome home, Grumio!

PHILIP.

How now, Grumio!

JOSEPH.

What, Grumio!

NICHOLAS.

Fellow Grumio!

NATHANIEL.

How now, old lad!

GRUMIO.

Welcome, you!—how now, you!—what, you!—fellow, you!—and thus much for greeting. Now, my spruce companions, is all ready, and all things neat?

NATHANIEL.

All things is ready. How near is our master?

GRUMIO.

E'en at hand, alighted by this; and therefore be not—Cock's passion, silence!—I hear my master.

Enter PETRUCHIO *and* KATHARINA.

PETRUCHIO.

Where be these knaves? What, no man at door
To hold my stirrup nor to take my horse!
Where is Nathaniel, Gregory, Philip?—

ALL SERVANTS.

Here, here, sir; here, sir.

PETRUCHIO.

Here, sir! here, sir! here, sir! here, sir!—
You logger-headed and unpolisht grooms!
What, no attendance? no regard? no duty?—
Where is the foolish knave I sent before?

GRUMIO.

Here, sir: as foolish as I was before.

PETRUCHIO.

You peasant swain! you whoreson malt-horse drudge!
Did I not bid thee meet me in the park,
And bring along these rascal knaves with thee?

GRUMIO.

Nathaniel's coat, sir, was not fully made,
And Gabriel's pumps were all unpinkt i' th' heel
There was no link to colour Peter's hat,
And Walter's dagger was not come from sheathing:
There were none fine but Adam, Rafe, and Gregory;
The rest were ragged, old, and beggarly;
Yet, as they are, here are they come to meet you.

PETRUCHIO.

Go, rascals, go, and fetch my supper in.—
    [*Exeunt* SERVANTS.
   [*Sings*] Where is the life that late I led—
Where are those—Sit down, Kate, and welcome.—
Soud, soud, soud, soud!
Enter SERVANTS *with supper.*
Why, when, I say?—Nay, good sweet Kate, be merry.—
Off with my boots, you rogues! you villains, when?
   [*Sings.*] It was the friar of orders grey,
    As he forth walked on his way:—
Out, you rogue! you pluck my foot awry:
Take that, and mend the plucking off the other.—
    [*Strikes him.*
Be merry, Kate.—Some water, here; what, ho!
Where's my spaniel Troilus?—Sirrah, get you hence,
And bid my cousin Ferdinand come hither:—
    [*Exit* SERVANT.
One, Kate, that you must kiss, and be acquainted with.—
Where are my slippers?—Shall I have some water?

Enter one with water.
Come, Kate, and wash, and welcome heartily.—
You whoreson villain! will you let it fall?
                                                   [*Strikes him.*
                    KATHARINA.
Patience, I pray you; 'twas a fault unwilling.
                    PETRUCHIO.
A whoreson, beetle-headed, flap-ear'd knave!—
Come, Kate, sit down; I know you have a
      stomach.
Will you give thanks, sweet Kate; or else shall I?
What's this? mutton?
                    FIRST SERVANT.
                         Ay.
                    PETRUCHIO.
                         Who brought it?
                    PETER.
                                        I.
                    PETRUCHIO.
'Tis burnt; and so is all the meat.
What dogs are these!—Where is the rascal cook?
How durst you, villains, bring it from the dresser,
And serve it thus to me that love it not?
There, take it to you, trenchers, cups, and all:
                    [*Throws the meat, &c., at them.*
You heedless joltheads and unmanner'd slaves!
What, do you grumble? I'll be with you straight.
                                     [*Exeunt* SERVANTS.
                    KATHARINA.
I pray you, husband, be not so disquiet:
The meat was well, if you were so contented.
                    PETRUCHIO.
I tell thee, Kate, 'twas burnt and dried away;
And I expressly am forbid to touch it,
For it engenders choler, planteth anger;
And better 'twere that both of us did fast,—
Since, of ourselves, ourselves are choleric,—
Than feed it with such over-roasted flesh.
Be patient; to-morrow't shall be mended,
And, for this night, we'll fast for company:—
Come, I will bring thee to thy bridal chamber
                                            [*Exeunt.*
        Enter SERVANTS *severally.*
                    NATHANIEL.
Peter, didst ever see the like?
                    PETER.
                         He kills her
In her own humour.
        Enter CURTIS.
                    GRUMIO.
                    Where is he?
                    CURTIS.
                         In her chamber,
Making a sermon of continency to her;
And rails, and swears, and rates, that she, poor
      soul,
Knows not which way to stand, to look, to speak.
And sits as one new-risen from a dream.—
Away, away! for he is coming hither.   [*Exeunt.*
        Enter PETRUCHIO.
                    PETRUCHIO.
Thus have I politicly begun my reign,
And 'tis my hope to end successfully.
My falcon now is sharp, and passing empty;
And, till she stoop, she must not be full-gorged,
For then she never looks upon her lure.

Another way I have to man my haggard,
To make her come, and know her keeper's call,
That is, to watch her, as we watch these kites
That bate, and beat, and will not be obedient.
She eat no meat to-day, nor none shall eat;
Last night she slept not, nor to-night she shall not;
As with the meat, some undeserved fault
I'll find about the making of the bed;
And here I'll fling the pillow, there the bolster,
This way the coverlet, another way the sheets:—
Ay, and amid this hurly, I intend
That all is done in reverent care of her;
And, in conclusion, she shall watch all night:
And, if she chance to nod, I'll rail and brawl,
And with the clamour keep her still awake.
This is a way to kill a wife with kindness;
And thus I'll curb her mad and headstrong
      humour.—
He that knows better how to tame a shrew,
Now let him speak: 'tis charity to shew.   [*Exit.*

                    SCENE II.

        Padua.   Before BAPTISTA'S *house.*

        Enter TRANIO *and* HORTENSIO.

                    TRANIO.
IS'T possible, friend Licio, that Mistress Bianca
    Doth fancy any other but Lucentio?
I tell you, sir, she bears me fair in hand.
                    HORTENSIO.
Sir, to satisfy you in what I have said,
Stand by, and mark the manner of his teaching.
                                     [*They stand aside.*
        Enter BIANCA *and* LUCENTIO.
                    LUCENTIO.
Now, mistress, profit you in what you read?
                    BIANCA.
What, master, read you? first resolve me that.
                    LUCENTIO.
I read that I profess, the Art to Love.
                    BIANCA.
And may you prove, sir, master of your art!
                    LUCENTIO.
While you, sweet dear, prove mistress of my
      heart!   [*They retire.*
                    HORTENSIO.
Quick proceeders, marry! Now, tell me, I pray,
You that durst swear that your mistress Bianca
Loved none in the world so well as Lucentio,—
                    TRANIO.
O despiteful love! unconstant womankind!—
I tell thee, Licio, this is wonderful.
                    HORTENSIO.
Mistake no more: I am not Licio,
Nor a musician, as I seem to be;
But one that scorn to live in this disguise,
For such a one as leaves a gentleman,
And makes a god of such a cullion:
Know, sir, that I am call'd Hortensio.
                    TRANIO.
Signior Hortensio, I have often heard
Of your entire affection to Bianca;
And since mine eyes are witness of her lightness,
I will with you,—if you be so contented,—
Forswear Bianca and her love for ever.

HORTENSIO.

See, how they kiss and court!—Signior Lucentio,
Here is my hand, and here I firmly vow
Never to woo her more; but do forswear her,
As one unworthy all the former favours
That I have fondly flatter'd her withal.

TRANIO.

And here I take the like unfeigned oath,
Never to marry with her though she would
    entreat:
Fie on her! see, how beastly she doth court him!

HORTENSIO.

Would all the world but he had quite forsworn!
For me, that I may surely keep mine oath,
I will be married to a wealthy widow,
Ere three days pass, which hath as long loved me
As I have loved this proud disdainful haggard.
And so farewell, Signior Lucentio.—
Kindness in women, not their beauteous looks,
Shall win my love:—and so, I take my leave,
In resolution as I swore before.

    [*Exit* HORTENSIO; LUCENTIO *and*
      BIANCA *advance.*

TRANIO.

Mistress Bianca, bless you with such grace
As 'longeth to a lover's blessed case!
Nay, I have ta'en you napping, gentle love;
And have forsworn you, with Hortensio.

BIANCA.

Tranio, you jest: but have you both forsworn me?

TRANIO.

Mistress, we have.

LUCENTIO.

    Then we are rid of Licio.

TRANIO.

I'faith, he'll have a lusty widow now,
That shall be woo'd and wedded in a day.

BIANCA.

God give him joy!

TRANIO.

Ay, and he'll tame her.

BIANCA.

      He says so, Tranio.

TRANIO.

Faith, he is gone unto the taming-school.

BIANCA.

The taming-school! what, is there such a place?

TRANIO.

Ay, mistress, and Petruchio is the master;
That teacheth tricks eleven and twenty long,
To tame a shrew, and charm her chattering
    tongue.

    Enter BIONDELLO.

BIONDELLO.

O master, master, I have watcht so long
That I am dog-weary! but at last I spied
An ancient angel coming down the hill,
Will serve the turn.

TRANIO.

    What is he, Biondello?

BIONDELLO.

Master, a mercatante, or a pedant,
I know not what; but formal in apparel,
In gait and countenance surly like a father.

LUCENTIO.

And what of him, Tranio?

TRANIO.

If he be credulous and trust my tale,
I'll make him glad to seem Vincentio;
And give assurance to Baptista Minola,
As if he were the right Vincentio.
Take in your love, and then let me alone.

    [*Exeunt* LUCENTIO *and* BIANCA.
      Enter a PEDANT.

PEDANT.

God save you, sir!

TRANIO.

      And you, sir! you are welcome.
Travel you far on, or are you at the furthest?

PEDANT.

Sir, at the furthest for a week or two:
But then up further, and as far as Rome;
And so to Tripoli, if God lend me life.

TRANIO.

What countryman, I pray?

PEDANT.

        Of Mantua.

TRANIO.

Of Mantua, sir?—marry, God forbid!
And come to Padua, careless of your life?

PEDANT.

My life, sir! how, I pray? for that goes hard.

TRANIO.

'Tis death for any one in Mantua
To come to Padua. Know you not the cause?
Your ships are stay'd at Venice; and the duke—
For private quarrel 'twixt your duke and him—
Hath publisht and proclaim'd it openly:
'Tis marvel, but that you are but newly come,
You might have heard it else proclaim'd about.

PEDANT.

Alas, sir, it is worse for me than so!
For I have bills for money by exchange
From Florence, and must here deliver them.

TRANIO.

Well, sir, to do you courtesy,
This will I do, and this I will advise you:—
First, tell me, have you ever been at Pisa?

PEDANT.

Ay, sir, in Pisa have I often been;
Pisa renowned for grave citizens.

TRANIO.

Among them know you one Vincentio?

PEDANT.

I know him not, but I have heard of him;
A merchant of incomparable wealth.

TRANIO.

He is my father, sir; and, sooth to say,
In countenance somewhat doth resemble you.

BIONDELLO [*aside*].

As much as an apple doth an oyster, and all one

TRANIO.

To save your life in this extremity,
This favour will I do you for his sake;
And think it not the worst of all your fortunes
That you are like to Sir Vincentio.
His name and credit shall you undertake,
And in my house you shall be friendly lodged:—
Look that you take upon you as you should;
You understand me, sir:—so shall you stay
Till you have done your business in the city:
If this be courtesy, sir, accept of it.

PEDANT.

O, sir, I do; and will repute you ever
The patron of my life and liberty.

TRANIO.

Then go with me, to make the matter good.
This, by the way, I let you understand;—
My father is here lookt for every day,
To pass assurance of a dower in marriage
'Twixt me and one Baptista's daughter here:
In all these circumstances I'll instruct you:
Go with me, sir, to clothe you as becomes you.
[Exeunt.

SCENE III.

A room in PETRUCHIO'S *house.*

Enter KATHARINA *and* GRUMIO.

GRUMIO.

NO, no, forsooth; I dare not, for my life.

KATHARINA.

The more my wrong, the more his spite appears:
What, did he marry me to famish me?
Beggars, that come unto my father's door,
Upon entreaty have a present alms;
If not, elsewhere they meet with charity:
But I,—who never knew how to entreat,
Nor never needed that I should entreat,—
Am starved for meat, giddy for lack of sleep;
With oaths kept waking, and with brawling fed:
And that which spites me more than all these
     wants,
He does it under name of perfect love;
As who should say, if I should sleep or eat,
'Twere deadly sickness or else present death.—
I prithee go, and get me some repast;
I care not what, so it be wholesome food.

GRUMIO.

What say you to a neat's foot?

KATHARINA.

'Tis passing good: I prithee let me have it.

GRUMIO.

I fear it is too choleric a meat.
How say you to a fat tripe finely broil'd?

KATHARINA.

I like it well: good Grumio, fetch it me.

GRUMIO.

I cannot tell; I fear 'tis choleric.
What say you to a piece of beef and mustard?

KATHARINA.

A dish that I do love to feed upon.

GRUMIO.

Ay, but the mustard is too hot a little.

KATHARINA.

Why, then the beef, and let the mustard rest.

GRUMIO.

Nay, then I will not: you shall have the mustard,
Or else you get no beef of Grumio.

KATHARINA.

Then both, or one, or any thing thou wilt.

GRUMIO.

Why, then the mustard without the beef.

KATHARINA.

Go, get thee gone, thou false deluding slave,
[Beats him.
That feed'st me with the very name of meat:
Sorrow on thee, and all the pack of you,

That triumph thus upon my misery!
Go, get thee gone, I say.

Enter PETRUCHIO *and* HORTENSIO *with meat.*

PETRUCHIO.

How fares my Kate? What, sweeting, all amort?

HORTENSIO.

Mistress, what cheer?

KATHARINA.

                    Faith, as cold as can be.

PETRUCHIO.

Pluck up thy spirits, look cheerfully upon me.
Here, love; thou see'st how diligent I am
To dress thy meat myself, and bring it thee:
I am sure, sweet Kate, this kindness merits
     thanks.
What, not a word? Nay, then thou lovest it not;
And all my pains is sorted to no proof.—
Here, take away this dish.

KATHARINA.

                    I pray you, let it stand.

PETRUCHIO.

The poorest service is repaid with thanks;
And so shall mine, before you touch the meat.

KATHARINA.

I thank you, sir.

HORTENSIO.

Signior Petruchio, fie! you are to blame.—
Come, Mistress Kate, I'll bear you company.

PETRUCHIO [*aside to* HORTENSIO].

Eat it up all, Hortensio, if thou lovest me.—
[*to* KATHARINA] Much good do it unto thy
     gentle heart!
Kate, eat apace:—and now, my honey love,
Will we return unto thy father's house,
And revel it as bravely as the best,
With silken coats, and caps, and golden rings,
With ruffs, and cuffs, and farthingales, and
     things;
With scarfs, and fans, and double change of
     bravery,
With amber bracelets, beads, and all this
     knavery.
What, hast thou dined? The tailor stays thy
     leisure,
To deck thy body with his ruffling treasure.

Enter TAILOR.

Come, tailor, let us see these ornaments;
Lay forth the gown.

Enter HABERDASHER.

                    What news with you, sir?

HABERDASHER.

Here is the cap your worship did bespeak.

PETRUCHIO.

Why, this was moulded on a porringer;
A velvet dish:—fie, fie! 'tis lewd and filthy:
Why, 'tis a cockle or a walnut-shell,
A knack, a toy, a trick, a baby's cap:
Away with it! come, let me have a bigger.

KATHARINA.

I'll have no bigger: this doth fit the time,
And gentlewomen wear such caps as these.

PETRUCHIO.

When you are gentle, you shall have one too,
And not till then.

HORTENSIO [*aside*].

                    That will not be in haste.

KATHARINA.
Why, sir, I trust I may have leave to speak;
And speak I will; I am no child, no babe:
Your betters have endured me say my mind;
And if you cannot, best you stop your ears.
My tongue will tell the anger of my heart;
Or else my heart, concealing it, will break:
And rather than it shall, I will be free
Even to the uttermost, as I please, in words.
PETRUCHIO.
Why, thou say'st true: it is a paltry cap,
A custard-coffin, a bauble, a silken pie:
I love thee well, in that thou likest it not.
KATHARINA.
Love me or love me not, I like the cap;
And it I will have, or I will have none.
PETRUCHIO.
Thy gown? why, ay:—come, tailor, let us see't.
O, mercy, God! what masking stuff is here?
What's this? a sleeve? 'tis like a demi-cannon:
What, up and down, carved like an apple-tart?
Here's snip, and nip, and cut, and slish, and slash,
Like to a censer in a barber's shop:—
Why, what, o' devil's name, tailor, call'st thou
this?
HORTENSIO [aside].
I see she's like to have neither cap nor gown.
TAILOR.
You bid me make it orderly and well,
According to the fashion and the time.
PETRUCHIO.
Marry, and did; but if you be remember'd,
I did not bid you mar it to the time.
Go, hop me over every kennel home,
For you shall hop without my custom, sir:
I'll none of it: hence! make your best of it.
KATHARINA.
I never saw a better-fashion'd gown,   [able:
More quaint, more pleasing, nor more commend-
Belike you mean to make a puppet of me.
PETRUCHIO.
Why, true; he means to make a puppet of thee.
TAILOR.
She says your worship means to make a puppet
of her.
PETRUCHIO.
O monstrous arrogance! Thou liest, thou thread,
Thou thimble,
Thou yard, three-quarters, half-yard, quarter,
nail!
Thou flea, thou nit, thou winter-cricket thou!—
Braved in mine own house with a skein of thread?
Away, thou rag, thou quantity, thou remnant;
Or I shall so be-mete thee with thy yard,
As thou shalt think on prating whilst thou livest!
I tell thee, I, that thou hast marr'd her gown.
TAILOR.
Your worship is deceived; the gown is made
Just as my master had direction:
Grumio gave order how it should be done.
GRUMIO.
I gave him no order; I gave him the stuff.
TAILOR.
But how did you desire it should be made?
GRUMIO.
Marry, sir, with needle and thread.

TAILOR.
But did you not request to have it cut?
GRUMIO.
Thou hast faced many things;—
TAILOR.
I have.
GRUMIO.
Face not me: thou hast braved many men; brave
not me: I will neither be faced nor braved. I say
unto thee, I bid thy master cut out the gown; but
I did not bid him cut it to pieces: *ergo*, thou liest.
TAILOR.
Why, here is the note of the fashion to testify.
PETRUCHIO.
Read it.
GRUMIO.
The note lies in's throat, if he say I said so.
TAILOR [reads].
Imprimis, a loose-bodied gown:—
GRUMIO.
Master, if ever I said loose-bodied gown, sew me
in the skirts of it, and beat me to death with a
bottom of brown thread: I said a gown.
PETRUCHIO.
Proceed.
TAILOR [reads].
With a small compass cape:—
GRUMIO.
I confess the cape.
TAILOR [reads].
With a trunk sleeve:—
GRUMIO.
I confess two sleeves.
TAILOR [reads].
The sleeves curiously cut.
PETRUCHIO.
Ay, there's the villainy.
GRUMIO.
Error i' th' bill, sir; error i' th' bill.—I com-
manded the sleeves should be cut out, and sew'd
up again, and that I'll prove upon thee, though
thy little finger be arm'd in a thimble.
TAILOR.
This is true that I say; an I had thee in place
where, thou shouldst know it.
GRUMIO.
I am for thee straight: take thou the bill, give me
thy mete-yard, and spare not me.
HORTENSIO.
God-a-mercy, Grumio! then he shall have no
odds.
PETRUCHIO.
Well, sir, in brief, the gown is not for me.
GRUMIO.
You are i' th' right, sir: 'tis for my mistress.
PETRUCHIO.
Go take it up unto thy master's use.
GRUMIO.
Villain, not for thy life: take up my mistress'
gown for thy master's use!
PETRUCHIO.
Why, sir, what's your conceit in that?
GRUMIO.
O, sir, the conceit is deeper than you think for:
Take up my mistress' gown to his master's use!
O, fie, fie, fie!

PETRUCHIO [*aside to* HORTENSIO].
Hortensio, say thou wilt see the tailor paid.—
[*to* TAILOR] Go take it hence; be gone, and say no
more.

HORTENSIO.
Tailor, I'll pay thee for thy gown to-morrow:
Take no unkindness of his hasty words:
Away! I say; commend me to thy master.
[*Exeunt* TAILOR *and* HABERDASHER.

PETRUCHIO.
Well, come, my Kate; we will unto your father's,
Even in these honest mean habiliments:
Our purses shall be proud, our garments poor;
For 'tis the mind that makes the body rich;
And as the sun breaks through the darkest clouds,
So honour peereth in the meanest habit.
What, is the jay more precious than the lark,
Because his feathers are more beautiful?
Or is the adder better than the eel,
Because his painted skin contents the eye?
O, no, good Kate; neither art thou the worse
For this poor furniture and mean array.
If thou account'st it shame, lay it on me;
And therefore frolic: we will hence forthwith,
To feast and sport us at thy father's house.—
Go call my men, and let us straight to him;
And bring our horses unto Long-lane end;
There will we mount, and thither walk on foot.—
Let's see; I think 'tis now some seven o'clock,
And well we may come there by dinner-time.

KATHARINA.
I dare assure you, sir, 'tis almost two;
And 'twill be supper-time ere you come there.

PETRUCHIO.
It shall be seven ere I go to horse:
Look, what I speak, or do, or think to do,
You are still crossing it.—Sirs, let't alone:
I will not go to-day; and ere I do,
It shall be what o'clock I say it is.

HORTENSIO.
Why, so! this gallant will command the sun!
[*Exeunt.*

SCENE IV.

Padua.   Before BAPTISTA'S *house.*

Enter TRANIO, *and the* PEDANT *drest like*
VINCENTIO.

TRANIO.
SIR, this is the house: please it you that I call?
PEDANT.
Ay, what else? and, but I be deceived,
Signior Baptista may remember me,
Near twenty years ago, in Genoa,
Where we were lodgers at the Pegasus.
TRANIO.
'Tis well; and hold your own, in any case,
With such austerity as 'longeth to a father.
PEDANT.
I warrant you. But, sir, here comes your boy;
'Twere good he were school'd.
Enter BIONDELLO.
TRANIO.
Fear you not him.—Sirrah Biondello,
Now do your duty throughly, I advise you:
Imagine 'twere the right Vincentio.

BIONDELLO.
Tut, fear not me.
TRANIO.
But hast thou done thy errand to Baptista?
BIONDELLO.
I told him that your father was at Venice;
And that you lookt for him this day in Padua.
TRANIO.
Thou'rt a tall fellow: hold thee that to drink.
Here comes Baptista:—set your countenance, sir.
Enter BAPTISTA *and* LUCENTIO.
Signior Baptista, you are happily met.—
[*to the* PEDANT] Sir, this is the gentleman I told
you of:
I pray you, stand good father to me now,
Give me Bianca for my patrimony.
PEDANT.
Soft, son!—
Sir, by your leave: having come to Padua
To gather in some debts, my son Lucentio
Made me acquainted with a weighty cause
Of love between your daughter and himself:
And,—for the good report I hear of you,
And for the love he beareth to your daughter,
And she to him,—to stay him not too long,
I am content, in a good father's care,
To have him matcht; and, if you please to like
No worse than I, upon some agreement,
Me shall you find ready and willing
With one consent to have her so bestow'd;
For curious I cannot be with you,
Signior Baptista, of whom I hear so well.
BAPTISTA.
Sir, pardon me in what I have to say:
Your plainness and your shortness please me well.
Right true it is, your son Lucentio here
Doth love my daughter, and she loveth him,
Or both dissemble deeply their affections:
And therefore, if you say no more than this,
That like a father you will deal with him,
And pass my daughter a sufficient dower,
The match is made, and all is done:
Your son shall have my daughter with consent.
TRANIO.
I thank you, sir. Where, then, do you hold best
We be affied, and such assurance ta'en
As shall with either part's agreement stand?
BAPTISTA.
Not in my house, Lucentio; for, you know,
Pitchers have ears, and I have many servants:
Besides, old Gremio is hearkening still;
And happily we might be interrupted.
TRANIO.
Then at my lodging, an it like you:
There doth my father lie; and there, this night,
We'll pass the business privately and well.
Send for your daughter by your servant here;
My boy shall fetch the scrivener presently.
The worst is this,—that at so slender warning,
You are like to have a thin and slender pittance.
BAPTISTA.
It likes me well. Biondello, hie you home,
And bid Bianca make her ready straight;
And, if you will, tell what hath happened—
Lucentio's father is arrived in Padua,
And how she's like to be Lucentio's wife.

BIONDELLO.
I pray the gods she may with all my heart!
TRANIO.
Dally not with the gods, but get thee gone.—
[Exit BIONDELLO.
Signior Baptista, shall I lead the way?
Welcome! one mess is like to be your cheer:
Come, sir; we will better it in Pisa.
BAPTISTA.
I follow you.
[Exeunt TRANIO, PEDANT, and BAPTISTA.
Enter BIONDELLO.
BIONDELLO.
Cambio,—
LUCENTIO.
What say'st thou, Biondello?
BIONDELLO.
You saw my master wink and laugh upon you?
LUCENTIO.
Biondello, what of that?
BIONDELLO.
Faith, nothing; but 'has left me here behind, to
expound the meaning or moral of his signs and
tokens.
LUCENTIO.
I pray thee, moralize them.
BIONDELLO.
Then thus. Baptista is safe, talking with the de-
ceiving father of a deceitful son.
LUCENTIO.
And what of him?
BIONDELLO.
His daughter is to be brought by you to the sup-
per.
LUCENTIO.
And then?
BIONDELLO.
The old priest at Saint Luke's church is at your
command at all hours.
LUCENTIO.
And what of all this?
BIONDELLO.
I cannot tell, except, while they are busied about
a counterfeit assurance, take you assurance of her,
cum privilegio ad imprimendum solum: to th'
church;—take the priest, clerk, and some suffici-
ent honest witnesses:
If this be not that you look for, I have no more to
say,
But bid Bianca farewell for ever and a day.
[Going.
LUCENTIO.
Hear'st thou, Biondello?
BIONDELLO.
I cannot tarry: I knew a wench married in an
afternoon as she went to the garden for parsley to
stuff a rabbit; and so may you, sir: and so, adieu,
sir. My master hath appointed me to go to Saint
Luke's, to bid the priest be ready to come against
you come with your appendix.   [Exit.
LUCENTIO.
I may, and will, if she be so contented:
She will be pleased; then wherefore should I
doubt?
Hap what hap may, I'll roundly go about her:
It shall go hard if Cambio go without her. [Exit.

SCENE V.

A public road.

Enter PETRUCHIO, KATHARINA, *and*
HORTENSIO.

PETRUCHIO.
COME on, o' God's name; once more toward
our father's.
Good Lord, how bright and goodly shines the
moon!
KATHARINA.
The moon! the sun: it is not moonlight now.
PETRUCHIO.
I say it is the moon that shines so bright.
KATHARINA.
I know it is the sun that shines so bright.
PETRUCHIO.
Now, by my mother's son, and that's myself,
It shall be moon, or star, or what I list,
Or e'er I journey to your father's house.—
Go one, and fetch our horses back again.—
Evermore crost and crost; nothing but crost!
HORTENSIO [aside to KATHARINA].
Say as he says, or we shall never go.
KATHARINA.
Forward, I pray, since we have come so far,
And be it moon, or sun, or what you please:
An if you please to call it a rush-candle,
Henceforth I vow it shall be so for me.
PETRUCHIO.
I say it is the moon.
KATHARINA.
        I know it is the moon.
PETRUCHIO.
Nay, then, you lie: it is the blessed sun.
KATHARINA.
Then, God be blest, it is the blessed sun:—
But sun it is not, when you say it is not;
And the moon changes, even as your mind.
What you will have it named, even that it is;
And so it shall be still for Katharine.
HORTENSIO [aside].
Petruchio, go thy ways; the field is won.
PETRUCHIO.
Well, forward, forward! thus the bowl should run,
And not unluckily against the bias.—
But, soft! what company is coming here?
Enter VINCENTIO.
[to VINCENTIO] Good morrow, gentle mistress:
where away?—
Tell me, sweet Kate, and tell me truly too,
Hast thou beheld a fresher gentlewoman?
Such war of white and red within her cheeks!
What stars do spangle heaven with such beauty,
As those two eyes become that heavenly face?—
Fair lovely maid, once more good day to thee.—
Sweet Kate, embrace her for her beauty's sake.
HORTENSIO [aside].
A' will make the man mad, to make a woman of
him.
KATHARINA.
Young budding virgin, fair and fresh and sweet,
Whither away; or where is thy abode?
Happy the parents of so fair a child;
Happier the man whom favourable stars
Allot thee for his lovely bedfellow!

PETRUCHIO.
Why, how now, Kate! I hope thou art not mad:
This is a man, old, wrinkled, faded, wither'd;
And not a maiden, as thou say'st he is.
KATHARINA.
Pardon, old father, my mistaking eyes,
That have been so bedazzled with the sun,
That every thing I look on seemeth green:
Now I perceive thou art a reverend father;
Pardon, I pray thee, for my mad mistaking.
PETRUCHIO.
Do, good old grandsire; and withal make known
Which way thou travellest; if along with us,
We shall be joyful of thy company.
VINCENTIO.
Fair sir, and you my merry mistress,
That with your strange encounter much amazed
   me,
My name is call'd Vincentio; my dwelling Pisa;
And bound I am to Padua; there to visit
A son of mine, which long I have not seen.
PETRUCHIO.
What is his name?
VINCENTIO.
Lucentio, gentle sir.
PETRUCHIO.
Happily met; the happier for thy son.
And now by law, as well as reverend age,
I may entitle thee my loving father:
The sister to my wife, this gentlewoman,
Thy son by this hath married. Wonder not,
Nor be not grieved: she is of good esteem,
Her dowry wealthy, and of worthy birth;
Beside, so qualified as may beseem
The spouse of any noble gentleman.
Let me embrace with old Vincentio:
And wander we to see thy honest son,
Who will of thy arrival be full joyous.
VINCENTIO.
But is this true? or is it else your pleasure,
Like pleasant travellers, to break a jest
Upon the company you overtake?
HORTENSIO.
I do assure thee, father, so it is.
PETRUCHIO.
Come, go along, and see the truth hereof;
For our first merriment hath made thee jealous.
[Exeunt PETRUCHIO, KATHARINA, and
VINCENTIO.
HORTENSIO.
Well, Petruchio, this has put me in heart.
Have to my widow! and if she be froward,
Then hast thou taught Hortensio to be untoward.
[Exit.

ACT V. SCENE I.

Padua.   Before LUCENTIO'S *house.*

Enter BIONDELLO, LUCENTIO, *and* BIANCA;
GREMIO *is out before.*
BIONDELLO.
SOFTLY and swiftly, sir; for the priest is
ready.
LUCENTIO.
I fly, Biondello: but they may chance to need thee
at home; therefore leave us.

BIONDELLO.
Nay, faith, I'll see the church o' your back; and
then come back to my master as soon as I can.
[*Exeunt* LUCENTIO, BIANCA, *and* BION-
DELLO.
GREMIO.
I marvel Cambio comes not all this while.
Enter PETRUCHIO, KATHARINA, VINCENTIO,
GRUMIO, *and* ATTENDANTS.
PETRUCHIO.
Sir, here's the door, this is Lucentio's house:
My father's bears more toward the market-place;
Thither must I; and here I leave you, sir.
VINCENTIO.
You shall not choose but drink before you go:
I think I shall command your welcome here.
And, by all likelihood, some cheer is toward.
[*Knocks.*
GREMIO.
They're busy within; you were best knock louder.
PEDANT *looks out of the window.*
PEDANT.
What's he that knocks as he would beat down the
gate?
VINCENTIO.
Is Signior Lucentio within, sir?
PEDANT.
He's within, sir, but not to be spoken withal.
VINCENTIO.
What if a man bring him a hundred pound or two,
to make merry withal?
PEDANT.
Keep your hundred pounds to yourself: he shall
need none, so long as I live.
PETRUCHIO.
Nay, I told you your son was well beloved in
Padua.—Do you hear, sir?—to leave frivolous
circumstances,—I pray you, tell Signior Lucentio
that his father is come from Pisa, and is here at
the door to speak with him.
PEDANT.
Thou liest: his father is come from Pisa, and here
looking out at the window.
VINCENTIO.
Art thou his father?
PEDANT.
Ay, sir; so his mother says, if I may believe her.
PETRUCHIO [*to* VINCENTIO].
Why, how now, gentleman! why, this is flat
knavery, to take upon you another man's name.
PEDANT.
Lay hands on the villain: I believe a' means to
cozen somebody in this city under my counte-
nance.

Enter BIONDELLO.

BIONDELLO.
I have seen them in the church together: God
send 'em good shipping!—But who is here? mine
old master, Vincentio! now we are undone, and
brought to nothing.
VINCENTIO.
Come hither, crack-hemp.
BIONDELLO.
I hope I may choose, sir.
VINCENTIO.
Come hither, you rogue. What, have you forgot me

BIONDELLO.

Forgot you! no, sir: I could not forget you, for I never saw you before in all my life.

VINCENTIO.

What, you notorious villain, didst thou never see thy master's father, Vincentio?

BIONDELLO.

What, my old worshipful old master? yes, marry, sir: see where he looks out of the window.

VINCENTIO.

Is't so, indeed?   [He beats BIONDELLO.

BIONDELLO.

Help, help, help! here's a madman will murder me.   [Exit.

PEDANT.

Help, son! help, Signior Baptista!

PETRUCHIO.

Prithee, Kate, let's stand aside, and see the end of this controversy.   [They retire.

Enter PEDANT below; BAPTISTA, TRANIO, and SERVANTS.

TRANIO.

Sir, what are you that offer to beat my servant?

VINCENTIO.

What am I, sir! nay, what are you, sir?—O immortal gods! O fine villain! A silken doublet! a velvet hose! a scarlet cloak! and a copatain hat!—O, I am undone! I am undone! while I play the good husband at home, my son and my servant spend all at the university.

TRANIO.

How now! what's the matter?

BAPTISTA.

What, is the man lunatic?

TRANIO.

Sir, you seem a sober ancient gentleman by your habit, but your words show you a madman. Why, sir, what 'cerns it you if I wear pearl and gold? I thank my good father, I am able to maintain it.

VINCENTIO.

Thy father! O villain! he is a sail-maker in Bergamo.

BAPTISTA.

You mistake, sir, you mistake, sir. Pray, what do you think is his name?

VINCENTIO.

His name! as if I knew not his name: I have brought him up ever since he was three years old, and his name is Tranio.

PEDANT.

Away, away, mad ass! his name is Lucentio; and he is mine only son, and heir to the lands of me, Signior Vincentio.

VINCENTIO.

Lucentio! O, he hath murder'd his master!—Lay hold on him, I charge you, in the duke's name.—O, my son, my son!—Tell me, thou villain, where is my son Lucentio?

TRANIO.

Call forth an officer.

SERVANT brings in an OFFICER.

Carry this mad knave to the gaol.—Father Baptista, I charge you see that he be forthcoming.

VINCENTIO.

Carry me to the gaol!

GREMIO.

Stay, officer: he shall not go to prison.

BAPTISTA.

Talk not, Signior Gremio: I say he shall go to prison.

GREMIO.

Take heed, Signior Baptista, lest you be conycatcht in this business: I dare swear this is the right Vincentio.

PEDANT.

Swear, if thou darest.

GREMIO.

Nay, I dare not swear it.

TRANIO.

Then thou wert best say that I am not Lucentio.

GREMIO.

Yes, I know thee to be Signior Lucentio.

BAPTISTA.

Away with the dotard! to the gaol with him!

VINCENTIO.

Thus strangers may be haled and abused:—
O monstrous villainy!

Enter BIONDELLO, with LUCENTIO and BIANCA.

BIONDELLO.

O, we are spoil'd! and yonder he is: deny him, forswear him, or else we are all undone.

LUCENTIO.

Pardon, sweet father.   [Kneeling.

VINCENTIO.

Lives my sweet son?

[Exeunt BIONDELLO, TRANIO, and PEDANT, as fast as may be.

BIANCA.

Pardon, dear father.   [Kneeling.

BAPTISTA.

How hast thou offended?—
Where is Lucentio?

LUCENTIO.

Here's Lucentio,
Right son unto the right Vincentio;
That have by marriage made thy daughter mine,
While counterfeit supposes blear'd thine eyne.

GREMIO.

Here's packing, with a witness, to deceive us all!

VINCENTIO.

Where is that damned villain Tranio,
That faced and braved me in this matter so?

BAPTISTA.

Why, tell me, is not this my Cambio?

BIANCA.

Cambio is changed into Lucentio.

LUCENTIO.

Love wrought these miracles. Bianca's love
Made me exchange my state with Tranio,
While he did bear my countenance in the town,
And happily I have arrived at last
Unto the wished haven of my bliss.
What Tranio did, myself enforced him to;
Then pardon him, sweet father, for my sake.

VINCENTIO.

I'll slit the villain's nose, that would have sent me to the gaol.

BAPTISTA [to LUCENTIO].

But do you hear, sir? have you married my daughter without asking my good-will?

VINCENTIO.
Fear not, Baptista; we will content you, go to: but
I will in, to be revenged for this villainy.   [*Exit.*
BAPTISTA.
And I, to sound the depth of this knavery.   [*Exit.*
LUCENTIO.
Look not pale, Bianca; thy father will not frown.
      [*Exeunt* LUCENTIO *and* BIANCA.
GREMIO.
My cake is dough: but I'll in among the rest;
Out of hope of all, but my share of the feast. [*Exit.*
PETRUCHIO *and* KATHARINA *come forward.*
KATHARINA.
Husband, let's follow, to see the end of this ado.
PETRUCHIO.
First kiss me, Kate, and we will.
KATHARINA.
What, in the midst of the street?
PETRUCHIO.
What, art thou ashamed of me?
KATHARINA.
No, sir, God forbid; but ashamed to kiss.
PETRUCHIO.
Why, then, let's home again: come, sirrah, let's
away.
KATHARINA.
Nay, I will give thee a kiss [*kisses him*]: now, pray
thee, love, stay.
PETRUCHIO.
Is not this well?—Come, my sweet Kate:
Better once than never, for never too late.[*Exeunt.*

SCENE II.

A room in LUCENTIO'S *house.*

Enter BAPTISTA, VINCENTIO, GREMIO, *the*
PEDANT, LUCENTIO, BIANCA, PETRUCHIO,
KATHARINA, HORTENSIO *and* WIDOW, TRA-
NIO, BIONDELLO *and* GRUMIO; *the* SERVING-
MEN *with* TRANIO *bringing in a banquet.*

LUCENTIO.
AT last, though long, our jarring notes agree:
   And time it is, when raging war is done,
To smile at scapes and perils overblown.
My fair Bianca, bid my father welcome,
While I with selfsame kindness welcome thine.
Brother Petruchio, sister Katharina,
And thou, Hortensio, with thy loving widow,—
Feast with the best, and welcome to my house:
My banquet is to close our stomachs up,
After our great good cheer. Pray you, sit down;
For now we sit to chat, as well as eat.
      [*They sit at table.*
PETRUCHIO.
Nothing but sit and sit, and eat and eat!
BAPTISTA.
Padua affords this kindness, son Petruchio.
PETRUCHIO.
Padua affords nothing but what is kind.
HORTENSIO.
For both our sakes, I would that word were true.
PETRUCHIO.
Now, for my life, Hortensio fears his widow.
WIDOW.
Then never trust me, if I be afeard.

PETRUCHIO.
You are very sensible, and yet you miss my sense:
I mean, Hortensio is afeard of you.
WIDOW.
He that is giddy thinks the world turns round.
PETRUCHIO.
Roundly replied.
KATHARINA.
Mistress, how mean you that?
WIDOW.
Thus I conceive by him.
PETRUCHIO.
Conceives by me!—How likes Hortensio that?
HORTENSIO.
My widow says, thus she conceives her tale.
PETRUCHIO.
Very well mended.—Kiss him for that, good
widow.
KATHARINA.
He that is giddy thinks the world turns round:—
I pray you, tell me what you meant by that.
WIDOW.
Your husband, being troubled with a shrew,
Measures my husband's sorrow by his woe:
And now you know my meaning.
KATHARINA.
A very mean meaning.
WIDOW.
            Right, I mean you.
KATHARINA.
And I am mean, indeed, respecting you.
PETRUCHIO.
To her, Kate!
HORTENSIO.
To her, widow!
PETRUCHIO.
A hundred marks, my Kate does put her down.
HORTENSIO.
That's my office.
PETRUCHIO.
Spoke like an officer:—ha' to thee, lad.
      [*Drinks to* HORTENSIO.
BAPTISTA.
How likes Gremio these quick-witted folks?
GREMIO.
Believe me, sir, they butt together well.
BIANCA.
Head and butt! an hasty-witted body
Would say your head and butt were head and
horn.
VINCENTIO.
Ay, mistress bride, hath that awaken'd you?
BIANCA.
Ay, but not frighted me; therefore I'll sleep again.
PETRUCHIO.
Nay, that you shall not: since you have begun,
Have at you for a bitter jest or two!
BIANCA.
Am I your bird? I mean to shift my bush;
And then pursue me as you draw your bow.—
You are welcome all.
      [*Exeunt* BIANCA, KATHARINA, *and* WIDOW.
PETRUCHIO.
She hath prevented me.—Here, Signior Tranio,
This bird you aim'd at, though you hit her not;
Therefore a health to all that shot and mist.

TRANIO.
O, sir, Lucentio slipt me like his greyhound,
Which runs himself, and catches for his master.
PETRUCHIO.
A good swift simile, but something currish.
TRANIO.
'Tis well, sir, that you hunted for yourself:
'Tis thought your deer does hold you at a
    bay.
BAPTISTA.
O, ho, Petruchio! Tranio hits you now.
LUCENTIO.
I thank thee for that gird, good Tranio.
HORTENSIO.
Confess, confess, hath he not hit you here?
PETRUCHIO.
A' has a little gall'd me, I confess;
And, as the jest did glance away from me,
'Tis ten to one it maim'd you two outright.
BAPTISTA.
Now, in good sadness, son Petruchio,
I think thou hast the veriest shrew of all.
PETRUCHIO.
Well, I say no: and therefore, for assurance,
Let's each one send unto his wife;
And he whose wife is most obedient
To come at first when he doth send for her,
Shall win the wager which we will propose.
HORTENSIO.
Content. What is the wager?
LUCENTIO.
                Twenty crowns.
PETRUCHIO.
Twenty crowns!
I'll venture so much of my hawk or hound,
But twenty times so much upon my wife.
LUCENTIO.
A hundred, then.
HORTENSIO.
    Content.
PETRUCHIO.
          A match! 'tis done.
HORTENSIO.
Who shall begin?
LUCENTIO.
That will I.—
Go, Biondello, bid your mistress come to me.
BIONDELLO.
I go.   [Exit.
BAPTISTA.
Son, I'll be your half, Bianca comes.
LUCENTIO.
I'll have no halves; I'll bear it all myself.
Enter BIONDELLO.
How now! what news?
BIONDELLO.
          Sir, my mistress sends you word
That she is busy, and she cannot come.
PETRUCHIO.
How! she is busy, and she cannot come!
Is that an answer?
GREMIO.
         Ay, and a kind one too:
Pray God, sir, your wife send you not a worse.
PETRUCHIO.
I hope, better.

HORTENSIO.
Sirrah Biondello, go and entreat my wife
To come to me forthwith. [Exit BIONDELLO.
PETRUCHIO.
            O, ho! entreat her!
Nay, then she must needs come.
HORTENSIO.
               I am afraid, sir,
Do what you can, yours will not be entreated.
Enter BIONDELLO.
Now, where's my wife?
BIONDELLO.
She says you have some goodly jest in hand:
She will not come; she bids you come to her.
PETRUCHIO.
Worse and worse; she will not come! O vile,
Intolerable, not to be endured!—
Sirrah Grumio, go to your mistress;
Say, I command her come to me.
                      [Exit GRUMIO.
HORTENSIO.
I know her answer.
PETRUCHIO.
    What?
HORTENSIO.
          She will not come.
PETRUCHIO.
The fouler fortune mine, and there an end.
BAPTISTA.
Now, by my holidame, here comes Katharina!
Enter KATHARINA.
KATHARINA.
What is your will, sir, that you send for me?
PETRUCHIO.
Where is your sister, and Hortensio's wife?
KATHARINA.
They sit conferring by the parlour fire.
PETRUCHIO.
Go fetch them hither: if they deny to come,
Swinge me them soundly forth unto their hus-
    bands;
Away, I say, and bring them hither straight.
                [Exit KATHARINA.
LUCENTIO.
Here is a wonder, if you talk of a wonder.
HORTENSIO.
And so it is: I wonder what it bodes.
PETRUCHIO.
Marry, peace it bodes, and love, and quiet
    life,
An awful rule, and right supremacy,
And, to be short, what not that's sweet and
    happy?
BAPTISTA.
Now, fair befall thee good Petruchio!
The wager thou hast won; and I will add
Unto their losses twenty thousand crowns;
Another dowry to another daughter,
For she is changed, as she had never been.
PETRUCHIO.
Nay, I will win my wager better yet,
And show more sign of her obedience,
Her new-built virtue and obedience.
See, where she comes, and brings your froward
    wives
As prisoners to her womanly persuasion.

Enter KATHARINA, *with* BIANCA *and* WIDOW.
Katharine, that cap of yours becomes you not:
Off with that bauble, throw it under foot.
[*She obeys.*

WIDOW.
Lord, let me never have a cause to sigh,
Till I be brought to such a silly pass!
BIANCA.
Fie, what a foolish duty call you this?
LUCENTIO.
I would your duty were as foolish too:
The wisdom of your duty, fair Bianca,
Hath cost me a hundred crowns since supper-
time.

BIANCA.
The more fool you, for laying on my duty.
PETRUCHIO.
Katharine, I charge thee, tell these headstrong
women
What duty they do owe their lords and husbands.
WIDOW.
Come, come, you're mocking: we will have no
telling.
PETRUCHIO.
Come on, I say; and first begin with her.
WIDOW.
She shall not.
PETRUCHIO.
I say she shall:—and first begin with her.
KATHARINA.
Fie, fie! unknit that threatening unkind brow:
And dart not scornful glances from those eyes,
To wound thy lord, thy king, thy governor:
It blots thy beauty, as frosts do bite the meads;
Confounds thy fame, as whirlwinds shake fair
buds;
And in no sense is meet or amiable.
A woman moved is like a fountain troubled,
Muddy, ill-seeming, thick, bereft of beauty;
And while it is so, none so dry or thirsty
Will deign to sip, or touch one drop of it.
Thy husband is thy lord, thy life, thy keeper,
Thy head, thy sovereign; one that cares for thee,
And for thy maintenance commits his body
To painful labour both by sea and land,
To watch the night in storms, the day in cold,
Whilst thou liest warm at home, secure and safe;
And craves no other tribute at thy hands
But love, fair looks, and true obedience,—

Too little payment for so great a debt.
Such duty as the subject owes the prince,
Even such a woman oweth to her husband;
And when she is froward, peevish, sullen, sour,
And not obedient to his honest will,
What is she but a foul contending rebel,
And graceless traitor to her loving lord?
I am ashamed that women are so simple
To offer war, where they should kneel for peace;
Or seek for rule, supremacy, and sway,
When they are bound to serve, love, and obey.
Why are our bodies soft and weak and smooth,
Unapt to toil and trouble in the world,
But that our soft conditions and our hearts
Should well agree with our external parts?
Come, come, you froward and unable worms!
My mind hath been as big as one of yours,
My heart as great; my reason, haply, more,
To bandy word for word and frown for frown:
But now I see our lances are but straws;
Our strength as weak, our weakness past com-
pare,—
That seeming to be most, which we indeed least
are.
Then vail your stomachs, for it is no boot,
And place your hands below your husband's foot:
In token of which duty, if he please,
My hand is ready, may it do him ease.
PETRUCHIO.
Why, there's a wench!—Come on, and kiss me,
Kate.
LUCENTIO.
Well, go thy ways, old lad; for thou shalt ha't.
VINCENTIO.
'Tis a good hearing when children are toward.
LUCENTIO.
But a harsh hearing when women are froward.
PETRUCHIO.
Come, Kate, we'll to bed.—
We three are married, but you two are sped.
'Twas I won the wager, though you hit the white;
[*to* LUCENTIO.
And, being a winner, God give you good night!
[*Exeunt* PETRUCHIO *and* KATHARINA.
HORTENSIO.
Now, go thy ways; thou hast tamed a curst shrow.
LUCENTIO.
'Tis a wonder, by your leave, she will be tamed so.
[*Exeunt.*

KING RICHARD THE SECOND

DRAMATIS PERSONAE

KING RICHARD THE SECOND.
JOHN OF GAUNT, *Duke of Lancaster,*
EDMUND OF LANGLEY, *Duke of York,* } *uncles to the King.*
HENRY, *surnamed* BOLINGBROKE, *Duke of Hereford, son to John of Gaunt; afterwards King Henry IV.*
DUKE OF AUMERLE, *son to the Duke of York.*
THOMAS MOWBRAY, *Duke of Norfolk.*
DUKE OF SURREY.
EARL OF SALISBURY.
LORD BERKLEY.
BUSHY,
BAGOT, } *creatures to King Richard.*
GREEN,
EARL OF NORTHUMBERLAND.
HENRY PERCY, *his son.*

LORD ROSS.
LORD WILLOUGHBY.
LORD FITZWATER.
BISHOP OF CARLISLE.
ABBOT OF WESTMINSTER.
LORD MARSHAL.
SIR STEPHEN SCROOP.
SIR PIERCE OF EXTON.
CAPTAIN OF A BAND OF WELSHMEN.

QUEEN *to King Richard.*
DUCHESS OF YORK.
DUCHESS OF GLOSTER.
LADIES *attending on the Queen.*

LORDS, HERALDS, OFFICERS, SOLDIERS, TWO GARDENERS, KEEPER, MESSENGER, GROOM, *and other* ATTENDANTS.

SCENE—*England and Wales.*

ACT I. SCENE I.

London. KING RICHARD'S *palace.*

Enter KING RICHARD, JOHN OF GAUNT, *with other* NOBLES *and* ATTENDANTS.

KING RICHARD.

OLD John of Gaunt, time-honour'd Lancaster,
Hast thou, according to thy oath and band,
Brought hither Henry Hereford thy bold son,
Here to make good the boisterous late appeal,
Which then our leisure would not let us hear,
Against the duke of Norfolk, Thomas Mowbray?

JOHN OF GAUNT.
I have, my liege.

KING RICHARD.
Tell me, moreover, hast thou sounded him,
If he appeal the duke on ancient malice;
Or worthily, as a good subject should,
On some known ground of treachery in him?

JOHN OF GAUNT.
As near as I could sift him on that argument,—
On some apparent danger seen in him
Aim'd at your highness,—no inveterate malice.

KING RICHARD.
Then call them to our presence: face to face,
And frowning brow to brow, ourselves will hear
Th'accuser and the accused freely speak:—
High-stomach'd are they both, and full of ire,
In rage deaf as the sea, hasty as fire.

Enter BOLINGBROKE *and* NORFOLK.

HENRY BOLINGBROKE.
Many years of happy days befall
My gracious sovereign, my most loving liege!

DUKE OF NORFOLK.
Each day still better other's happiness;
Until the heavens, envying earth's good hap,
Add an immortal title to your crown!

KING RICHARD.
We thank you both: yet one but flatters us,
As well appeareth by the cause you come;
Namely, to appeal each other of high treason.—
Cousin of Hereford, what dost thou object
Against the duke of Norfolk, Thomas Mowbray?

HENRY BOLINGBROKE.
First,—heaven be the record to my speech!—
In the devotion of a subject's love,
Tendering the precious safety of my prince,
And free from other misbegotten hate,
Come I appellant to this princely presence.—
Now, Thomas Mowbray, do I turn to thee,
And mark my greeting well; for what I speak
My body shall make good upon this earth,
Or my divine soul answer it in heaven.
Thou art a traitor and a miscreant,
Too good to be so, and too bad to live,—
Since the more fair and crystal is the sky,
The uglier seem the clouds that in it fly.
Once more, the more to aggravate the note,
With a foul traitor's name stuff I thy throat;
And wish,—so please my sovereign,—ere I move,
What my tongue speaks, my right-drawn sword
    may prove.

DUKE OF NORFOLK.
Let not my cold words here accuse my zeal:
'Tis not the trial of a woman's war,
The bitter clamour of two eager tongues,
Can arbitrate this cause betwixt us twain;
The blood is hot that must be cool'd for this:
Yet can I not of such tame patience boast
As to be husht, and naught at all to say:
First, the fair reverence of your highness curbs
    me
From giving reins and spurs to my free speech;
Which else would post until it had return'd
These terms of treason doubled down his throat.

359

Setting aside his high blood's royalty,
And let him be no kinsman to my liege,
I do defy him, and I spit at him;
Call him a slanderous coward and a villain:
Which to maintain, I would allow him odds;
And meet him, were I tied to run a-foot
Even to the frozen ridges of the Alps,
Or any other ground inhabitable,
Wherever Englishman durst set his foot.
Meantime let this defend my loyalty,—
By all my hopes, most falsely doth he lie.

HENRY BOLINGBROKE.

Pale trembling coward, there I throw my gage,
Disclaiming here the kindred of the king;
And lay aside my high blood's royalty,
Which fear, not reverence, makes thee to except.
If guilty dread have left thee so much strength
As to take up mine honour's pawn, then stoop:
By that and all the rites of knighthood else,
Will I make good against thee, arm to arm,
What I have spoke, or thou canst worse devise.

DUKE OF NORFOLK.

I take it up; and by that sword I swear,
Which gently laid my knighthood on my shoulder,
I'll answer thee in any fair degree,
Or chivalrous design of knightly trial:
And when I mount, alive may I not light,
If I be traitor or unjustly fight!

KING RICHARD.

What doth our cousin lay to Mowbray's charge?
It must be great that can inherit us
So much as of a thought of ill in him.

HENRY BOLINGBROKE.

Look, what I speak, my life shall prove it true:—
That Mowbray hath received eight thousand
    nobles
In name of lendings for your highness' soldiers,
The which he hath detain'd for lewd employ-
    ments,
Like a false traitor and injurious villain.
Besides, I say, and will in battle prove,—
Or here, or elsewhere to the furthest verge
That ever was survey'd by English eye,—
That all the treasons for these eighteen years
Complotted and contrived in this land   [spring.
Fetch from false Mowbray their first head and
Further, I say,—and further will maintain
Upon his bad life to make all this good,—
That he did plot the Duke of Gloster's death,
Suggest his soon-believing adversaries,
And consequently, like a traitor-coward,
Sluiced out his innocent soul through streams of
    blood:
Which blood, like sacrificing Abel's, cries,
Even from the tongueless caverns of the earth,
To me for justice and rough chastisement;
And, by the glorious worth of my descent,
This arm shall do it, or this life be spent.

KING RICHARD

How high a pitch his resolution soars!—
Thomas of Norfolk, what say'st thou to this?

DUKE OF NORFOLK.

O, let my sovereign turn away his face,
And bid his ears a little while be deaf,
Till I have told this slander of his blood,
How God and good men hate so foul a liar!

KING RICHARD.

Mowbray, impartial are our eyes and ears:
Were he my brother, nay, my kingdom's heir,—
As he is but my father's brother's son,—
Now, by my sceptre's awe, I make a vow,
Such neighbour-nearness to our sacred blood
Should nothing privilege him, nor partialize
The unstooping firmness of my upright soul:
He is our subject, Mowbray; so art thou:
Free speech and fearless I to thee allow.

DUKE OF NORFOLK.

Then, Bolingbroke, as low as to thy heart,
Through the false passage of thy throat, thou
    liest!
Three parts of that receipt I had for Calais
Disbursed I duly to his highness' soldiers;
The other part reserved I by consent,
For that my sovereign liege was in my debt
Upon remainder of a dear account,
Since last I went to France to fetch his queen:
Now swallow down that lie.—For Gloster's
    death,—
I slew him not; but, to my own disgrace,
Neglected my sworn duty in that case.—
For you, my noble Lord of Lancaster,
The honourable father to my foe,
Once did I lay an ambush for your life,—
A trespass that doth vex my grieved soul:
But, ere I last received the sacrament,
I did confess it; and exactly begg'd
Your Grace's pardon, and I hope I had it.
This is my fault: as for the rest appeal'd,
It issues from the rancour of a villain,
A recreant and most degenerate traitor:
Which in myself I boldly will defend;
And interchangeably hurl down my gage
Upon this overweening traitor's foot,
To prove myself a loyal gentleman
Even in the best blood chamber'd in his bosom.
In haste whereof, most heartily I pray
Your highness to assign our trial-day.

KING RICHARD.

Wrath-kindled gentlemen, be ruled by me;
Let's purge this choler without letting blood:
This we prescribe, though no physician;
Deep malice makes too deep incision:
Forget, forgive; conclude and be agreed;
Our doctors say this is no month to bleed.—
Good uncle, let this end where it begun;
We'll calm the Duke of Norfolk, you your son.

JOHN OF GAUNT.

To be a make-peace shall become my age:—
Throw down, my son, the Duke of Norfolk's
    gage.

KING RICHARD.

And, Norfolk, throw down his.

JOHN OF GAUNT.

             When, Harry? when?
Obedience bids I should not bid agen.

KING RICHARD.

Norfolk, throw down; we bid; there is no boot.

DUKE OF NORFOLK.

Myself I throw, dread sovereign, at thy foot.
My life thou shalt command, but not my shame:
The one my duty owes; but my fair name—
Despite of death, that lives upon my grave,—

To dark dishonour's use thou shalt not have.
I am disgraced, impeacht, and baffled here;
Pierced to the soul with slander's venom'd spear,
The which no balm can cure but his heart-blood
Which breathed this poison.

KING RICHARD.
              Rage must be withstood:—
Give me his gage:—lions make leopards tame.

DUKE OF NORFOLK.
Yea, but not change his spots: take but my shame,
And I resign my gage. My dear dear lord,
The purest treasure mortal times afford
Is spotless reputation; that away,
Men are but gilded loam or painted clay.
A jewel in a ten-times-barr'd-up chest
Is a bold spirit in a loyal breast.
Mine honour is my life; both grow in one;
Take honour from me, and my life is done:
Then, dear my liege, mine honour let me try;
In that I live, and for that will I die.

KING RICHARD.
Cousin, throw down your gage; do you begin.

HENRY BOLINGBROKE.
O, God defend my soul from such deep sin!
Shall I seem crest-fall'n in my father's sight?
Or with pale beggar-fear impeach my height
Before this outdared dastard? Ere my tongue
Shall wound my honour with such feeble wrong,
Or sound so base a parle, my teeth shall tear
The slavish motive of recanting fear,
And spit it bleeding in his high disgrace,
Where shame doth harbour, even in Mowbray's
     face.   [*Exit* GAUNT.

KING RICHARD.
We were not born to sue, but to command;—
Which since we cannot do to make you friends,
Be ready, as your lives shall answer it,
At Coventry, upon Saint Lambert's day:
There shall your swords and lances arbitrate
The swelling difference of your settled hate:
Since we cannot atone you, we shall see
Justice design the victor's chivalry.—
Lord marshal, command our officers-at-arms
Be ready to direct these home-alarms.   [*Exeunt*.

SCENE II.

The same. A room in the DUKE OF LANCAS-
TER'S *palace*.

Enter GAUNT *and* DUCHESS OF GLOSTER.

JOHN OF GAUNT.
ALAS, the part I had in Woodstock's blood
     Doth more solicit me than your exclaims,
To stir against the butchers of his life!
But since correction lieth in those hands
Which made the fault that we cannot correct,
Put we our quarrel to the will of heaven;
Who, when they see the hours ripe on earth,
Will rain hot vengeance on offenders' heads.

DUCHESS OF GLOSTER.
Finds brotherhood in thee no sharper spur?
Hath love in thy old blood no living fire?
Edward's seven sons, whereof thyself art one,
Were as seven vials of his sacred blood,
Or seven fair branches springing from one root:
Some of those seven are dried by nature's course,

Some of those branches by the Destinies cut;
But Thomas, my dear lord, my life, my Gloster,
One vial full of Edward's sacred blood,
One flourishing branch of his most royal root,
Is crackt, and all the precious liquor spilt,
Is hackt down, and his summer-leaves all faded,
By envy's hand and murder's bloody axe.
Ah, Gaunt, his blood was thine! that bed, that
     womb,
That metal, that self-mould, that fashion'd thee
Made him a man; and though thou livest and
     breathest,
Yet art thou slain in him: thou dost consent
In some large measure to thy father's death,
In that thou seest thy wretched brother die,
Who was the model of thy father's life.
Call it not patience, Gaunt,—it is despair:
In suffering thus thy brother to be slaughter'd,
Thou show'st the naked pathway to thy life,
Teaching stern murder how to butcher thee:
That which in mean men we entitle patience,
Is pale cold cowardice in noble breasts.
What shall I say? to safeguard thine own life,
The best way is to venge my Gloster's death.

JOHN OF GAUNT.
God's is the quarrel; for God's substitute,
His deputy anointed in His sight,
Hath caused his death: the which if wrongfully,
Let heaven revenge; for I may never lift
An angry arm against His minister.

DUCHESS OF GLOSTER.
Where, then, alas, may I complain myself?

JOHN OF GAUNT.
To God, the widow's champion and defence.

DUCHESS OF GLOSTER.
Why, then, I will. Farewell, old Gaunt:
Thou go'st to Coventry, there to behold
Our cousin Hereford and fell Mowbray fight:
O, sit my husband's wrongs on Hereford's spear,
That it may enter butcher Mowbray's breast!
Or, if misfortune miss the first career,
Be Mowbray's sins so heavy in his bosom,
That they may break his foaming courser's back,
And throw the rider headlong in the lists,
A caitiff recreant to my cousin Hereford!
Farewell, old Gaunt: thy sometimes brother's wife
With her companion grief must end her life.

JOHN OF GAUNT.
Sister, farewell; I must to Coventry:
As much good stay with thee as go with me!

DUCHESS OF GLOSTER.
Yet one word more:—grief boundeth where it
     falls,
Not with the empty hollowness, but weight:
I take my leave before I have begun;
For sorrow ends not when it seemeth done.
Commend me to my brother, Edmund York.
Lo, this is all:—nay, yet depart not so;
Though this be all, do not so quickly go;
I shall remember more. Bid him—ah, what?—
With all good speed at Plashy visit me.
Alack, and what shall good old York there see,
But empty lodgings and unfurnisht walls,
Unpeopled offices, untrodden stones?   [roans?
And what cheer there for welcome, but my
Therefore commend me; let him not come there,

To seek out sorrow that dwells every where.
Desolate, desolate, will I hence and die:
The last leave of thee takes my weeping eye.

[*Exeunt.*

SCENE III.

Gosford Green, near Coventry.

Lists set out, and a throne; with ATTENDANTS.
Enter the LORD MARSHAL *and* AUMERLE.

LORD MARSHAL.

MY Lord Aumerle, is Harry Hereford arm'd?

DUKE OF AUMERLE.

Yea, at all points; and longs to enter in.

LORD MARSHAL.

The Duke of Norfolk, sprightfully and bold,
Stays but the summons of the appellant's trumpet.

DUKE OF AUMERLE.

Why, then, the champions are prepared, and stay
For nothing but his majesty's approach.

The trumpets sound, and the KING *enters with his
nobles,* GAUNT, BUSHY, BAGOT, GREEN, *and
others. When they are set, enter the* DUKE OF
NORFOLK *in arms, defendant, with a* HERALD.

KING RICHARD.

Marshal, demand of yonder champion
The cause of his arrival here in arms:
Ask him his name; and orderly proceed
To swear him in the justice of his cause.

LORD MARSHAL.

In God's name and the king's, say who thou art,
And why thou comest thus knightly clad in arms;
Against what man thou comest, and what thy
quarrel:
Speak truly, on thy knighthood and thy oath;
As so defend thee heaven and thy valour!

DUKE OF NORFOLK.

My name is Thomas Mowbray, duke of Norfolk;
Who hither come engaged by my oath,—
Which God defend a knight should violate!—
Both to defend my loyalty and truth
To God, my king, and my succeeding issue,
Against the Duke of Hereford that appeals me;
And, by the grace of God and this mine arm,
To prove him, in defending of myself,
A traitor to my God, my king, and me:
And as I truly fight, defend me heaven!

The trumpets sound. Enter BOLINGBROKE, *appellant, in armour, with a* HERALD.

KING RICHARD.

Marshal, ask yonder knight in arms,
Both who he is, and why he cometh hither
Thus plated in habiliments of war;
And formally, according to our law,
Depose him in the justice of his cause.

LORD MARSHAL.

What is thy name? and wherefore comest thou
hither,
Before King Richard in his royal lists?
Against whom comest thou? and what's thy
quarrel?
Speak like a true knight, so defend thee heaven!

HENRY BOLINGBROKE.

Harry of Hereford, Lancaster, and Derby,
Am I; who ready here do stand in arms,
To prove, by God's grace, and my body's valour,

In lists, on Thomas Mowbray, duke of Norfolk,
That he is a traitor, foul and dangerous,
To God of heaven, King Richard, and to me:
And as I truly fight, defend me heaven!

LORD MARSHAL.

On pain of death, no person be so bold
Or daring-hardy as to touch the lists,
Except the marshal and such officers
Appointed to direct these fair designs.

HENRY BOLINGBROKE.

Lord marshal, let me kiss my sovereign's hand,
And bow my knee before his majesty:
For Mowbray and myself are like two men
That vow a long and weary pilgrimage;
Then let us take a ceremonious leave
And loving farewell of our several friends.

LORD MARSHAL.

The appellant in all duty greets your highness,
And craves to kiss your hand and take his leave.

KING RICHARD.

We will descend and fold him in our arms.—
Cousin of Hereford, as thy cause is right,
So be thy fortune in this royal fight!
Farewell, my blood; which if to-day thou shed,
Lament we may, but not revenge thee dead.

HENRY BOLINGBROKE.

O, let no noble eye profane a tear
For me, if I be gored with Mowbray's spear:
As confident as is the falcon's flight
Against a bird, do I with Mowbray fight.—
[*to* LORD MARSHAL] My loving lord, I take my
leave of you;—
Of you, my noble cousin, Lord Aumerle;
Not sick, although I have to do with death,
But lusty, young, and cheerly drawing breath.—
Lo, as at English feasts, so I regreet
The daintiest last, to make the end most sweet:
[*to* GAUNT] O thou, the earthly author of my
blood,—
Whose youthful spirit, in me regenerate,
Doth with a twofold vigour lift me up
To reach at victory above my head,—
Add proof unto mine armour with thy prayers;
And with thy blessings steel my lance's point,
That it may enter Mowbray's waxen coat,
And furbish new the name of John o' Gaunt,
Even in the lusty haviour of his son.

JOHN OF GAUNT.

God in thy good cause make thee prosperous!
Be swift like lightning in the execution;
And let thy blows, doubly redoubled,
Fall like amazing thunder on the casque
Of thy adverse pernicious enemy:
Rouse up thy youthful blood, be valiant and live.

HENRY BOLINGBROKE.

Mine innocency and Saint George to thrive!

DUKE OF NORFOLK.

However God or fortune cast my lot,
There lives or dies, true to King Richard's throne,
A loyal, just, and upright gentleman:
Never did captive with a freer heart
Cast off his chains of bondage, and embrace
His golden uncontroll'd enfranchisement,
More than my dancing soul doth celebrate
This feast of battle with mine adversary —
Most mighty liege, and my companion peers,

Take from my mouth the wish of happy years:
As gentle and as jocund as to jest
Go I to fight: truth hath a quiet breast.
KING RICHARD.
Farewell, my lord: securely I espy
Virtue with valour couched in thine eye.—
Order the trial, marshal, and begin.
LORD MARSHAL.
Harry of Hereford, Lancaster, and Derby,
Receive thy lance; and God defend the right!
HENRY BOLINGBROKE.
Strong as a tower in hope, I cry amen.
LORD MARSHAL [to an OFFICER].
Go bear this lance to Thomas, duke of Norfolk.
FIRST HERALD.
Harry of Hereford, Lancaster, and Derby,
Stands here for God, his sovereign, and himself,
On pain to be found false and recreant,
To prove the duke of Norfolk, Thomas Mowbray,
A traitor to his God, his king, and him;
And dares him to set forward to the fight.
SECOND HERALD.
Here standeth Thomas Mowbray, duke of
   Norfolk,
On pain to be found false and recreant,
Both to defend himself, and to approve
Henry of Hereford, Lancaster, and Derby,
To God, his sovereign, and to him disloyal;
Courageously, and with a free desire,
Attending but the signal to begin.
LORD MARSHAL.
Sound, trumpets; and set forward, combatants.
[A charge sounded.
Stay, the king hath thrown his warder down.
KING RICHARD.
Let them lay by their helmets and their spears,
And both return back to their chairs again:—
Withdraw with us:—and let the trumpets sound
While we return these dukes what we decree.—
[A long flourish.
Draw near,
And list what with our council we have done.
For that our kingdom's earth should not be soil'd
With that dear blood which it hath fostered;
And for our eyes do hate the dire aspect
Of civil wounds plough'd up with neighbours'
   sword;
And for we think the eagle-winged pride
Of sky-aspiring and ambitious thoughts,
With rival-hating envy, set on you
To wake our peace, which in our country's cradle
Draws the sweet infant breath of gentle sleep;
Which so roused up with boisterous untuned
   drums,
With harsh-resounding trumpets' dreadful bray,
And grating shock of wrathful iron arms,
Migh from our quiet confines fright fair peace,
And make us wade even in our kindred's blood;—
Therefore we banish you our territories;—
You, cousin Hereford, upon pain of life,
Till twice five summers have enrich'd our fields,
Shall not regreet our fair dominions,
But tread the stranger paths of banishment.
HENRY BOLINGBROKE.
Your will be done: this must my comfort be,—
That sun that warms you here shall shine on me;

And those his golden beams to you here lent
Shall point on me and gild my banishment.
KING RICHARD.
Norfolk, for thee remains a heavier doom,
Which I with some unwillingness pronounce:
The sly slow hours shall not determinate
The dateless limit of thy dear exile;—
The hopeless word of 'never to return'
Breathe I against thee, upon pain of life.
DUKE OF NORFOLK.
A heavy sentence, my most sovereign liege,
And all unlookt-for from your highness' mouth:
A dearer merit, not so deep a maim
As to be cast forth in the common air,
Have I deserved at your highness' hands.
The language I have learn'd these forty years,
My native English, now I must forgo:
And now my tongue's use is to me no more
Than an unstringed viol or a harp;
Or like a cunning instrument cased up,
Or, being open, put into his hands
That knows no touch to tune the harmony:
Within my mouth you have engaol'd my tongue,
Doubly portcullised with my teeth and lips;
And dull, unfeeling, barren ignorance
Is made my gaoler to attend on me.
I am too old to fawn upon a nurse,
Too far in years to be a pupil now:
What is thy sentence, then, but speechless
   death,
Which robs my tongue from breathing native
   breath?
KING RICHARD.
It boots thee not to be compassionate:
After our sentence plaining comes too late.
DUKE OF NORFOLK.
Then thus I turn me from my country's light,
To dwell in solemn shades of endless night.
KING RICHARD.
Return again, and take an oath with thee.
Lay on our royal sword your banisht hands;
Swear by the duty that you owe to God,—
Our part therein we banish with yourselves,—
To keep the oath that we administer:—
You never shall—so help you truth and God!—
Embrace each other's love in banishment;
Nor never look upon each other's face;
Nor never write, regreet, nor reconcile
This louring tempest of your home-bred
   hate;
Nor never by advised purpose meet
To plot, contrive, or complot any ill
'Gainst us, our state, our subjects, or our land
HENRY BOLINGBROKE.
I swear.
DUKE OF NORFOLK.
And I, to keep all this.
HENRY BOLINGBROKE.
Norfolk, so far as to mine enemy;—
By this time, had the king permitted us,
One of our souls had wander'd in the air,
Banisht this frail sepulchre of our flesh,
As now our flesh is banisht from this land:
Confess thy treasons, ere thou fly the realm;
Since thou hast far to go, bear not along
The clogging burden of a guilty soul.

DUKE OF NORFOLK.

No, Bolingbroke: if ever I were traitor,
My name be blotted from the book of life,
And I from heaven banisht, as from hence!
But what thou art, God, thou, and I do know;
And all too soon, I fear, the king shall rue.—
Farewell, my liege.—Now no way can I stray:
Save back to England, all the world's my way.

[Exit.

KING RICHARD.

Uncle, even in the glasses of thine eyes
I see thy grieved heart: thy sad aspect
Hath from the number of his banisht years
Pluckt four away.—[to BOLINGBROKE] Six
   frozen winters spent,
Return with welcome home from banishment.

HENRY BOLINGBROKE.

How long a time lies in one little word!
Four lagging winters and four wanton springs
End in a word: such is the breath of kings.

JOHN OF GAUNT.

I thank my liege, that in regard of me
He shortens four years of my son's exile:
But little vantage shall I reap thereby;
For, ere the six years that he hath to spend
Can change their moons and bring their times
   about,
My oil-dried lamp and time-bewasted light
Shall be extinct with age and endless night;
My inch of taper will be burnt and done,
And blindfold death not let me see my son.

KING RICHARD.

Why, uncle, thou hast many years to live.

JOHN OF GAUNT.

But not a minute, king, that thou canst give:
Shorten my days thou canst with sullen sorrow,
And pluck nights from me, but not lend a
   morrow;
Thou canst help time to furrow me with age,
But stop no wrinkle in his pilgrimage;
Thy word is current with him for my death,
But dead, thy kingdom cannot buy my breath.

KING RICHARD.

Thy son is banisht upon good advice,
Whereto thy tongue a party-verdict gave:
Why at our justice seem'st thou, then, to lour?

JOHN OF GAUNT.

Things sweet to taste prove in digestion sour.
You urged me as a judge; but I had rather
You would have bid me argue like a father.
O, had it been a stranger, not my child,   [mild:
To smooth his fault I should have been more
A partial slander sought I to avoid,
And in the sentence my own life destroy'd.
Alas, I lookt when some of you should say,
I was too strict to make mine own away;
But you gave leave to my unwilling tongue
Against my will to do myself this wrong.

KING RICHARD.

Cousin, farewell;—and, uncle, bid him so:
Six years we banish him, and he shall go.

[Flourish.   Exeunt KING RICHARD and
   TRAIN.

DUKE OF AUMERLE.

Cousin, farewell: what presence must not know,
From where you do remain let paper show.

LORD MARSHAL.

My lord, no leave take I; for I will ride,
As far as land will let me, by your side.

JOHN OF GAUNT.

O, to what purpose dost thou hoard thy words,
That thou return'st no greeting to thy friends?

HENRY BOLINGBROKE.

I have too few to take my leave of you,
When the tongue's office should be prodigal
To breathe th'abundant dolour of the heart.

JOHN OF GAUNT.

Thy grief is but thy absence for a time.

HENRY BOLINGBROKE.

Joy absent, grief is present for that time.

JOHN OF GAUNT.

What is six winters? they are quickly gone.

HENRY BOLINGBROKE.

To men in joy; but grief makes one hour ten.

JOHN OF GAUNT.

Call it a travel that thou takest for pleasure.

HENRY BOLINGBROKE.

My heart will sigh when I miscall it so,
Which finds it an enforced pilgrimage.

JOHN OF GAUNT.

The sullen passage of thy weary steps
Esteem as foil, wherein thou art to set
The precious jewel of thy home-return.

HENRY BOLINGBROKE.

Nay, rather, every tedious stride I make
Will but remember me what deal of world
I wander from the jewels that I love.
Must I not serve a long apprenticehood
To foreign passages; and in the end,
Having my freedom, boast of nothing else
But that I was a journeyman to grief?

JOHN OF GAUNT.

All places that the eye of heaven visits
Are to a wise man ports and happy havens.
Teach thy necessity to reason thus;
There is no virtue like necessity.
Think not the king did banish thee,
But thou the king; woe doth the heavier sit,
Where it perceives it is but faintly borne.
Go say, I sent thee forth to purchase honour,
And not, the king exiled thee; or suppose
Devouring pestilence hangs in our air,
And thou art flying to a fresher clime:
Look, what thy soul holds dear, imagine it
To lie that way thou go'st, not whence thou
   comest:
Suppose the singing-birds musicians,
The grass whereon thou tread'st the presence
   strew'd,
The flowers fair ladies, and thy steps no more
Than a delightful measure or a dance;
For gnarling sorrow hath less power to bite
The man that mocks at it and sets it light.

HENRY BOLINGBROKE.

O, who can hold a fire in his hand
By thinking on the frosty Caucasus?
Or cloy the hungry edge of appetite
By bare imagination of a feast?
Or wallow naked in December snow
By thinking on fantastic summer's heat?
O, no! the apprehension of the good
Gives but the greater feeling to the worse:

Fell sorrow's tooth doth never rankle more
Than when he bites, but lanceth not the sore.
JOHN OF GAUNT.
Come, come, my son, I'll bring thee on thy way:
Had I thy youth and cause, I would not stay.
HENRY BOLINGBROKE.
Then, England's ground, farewell; sweet soil,
adieu;
My mother, and my nurse, that bears me yet!
Where'er I wander, boast of this I can.—
Though banist, yet a true-born Englishman.
[*Exeunt.*

SCENE IV.

The court.

Enter, from one side, KING RICHARD, BAGOT,
and GREEN; *from the other,* AUMERLE.

KING RICHARD.
WE did observe.—Cousin Aumerle,
How far brought you high Hereford on his
way?
DUKE OF AUMERLE.
I brought high Hereford, if you call him so,
But to the next highway, and there I left him.
KING RICHARD.
And say, what store of parting tears were shed?
DUKE OF AUMERLE.
Faith, none for me; except the north-east wind,
Which then blew bitterly against our faces,
Awaked the sleeping rheum, and so by chance
Did grace our hollow parting with a tear.
KING RICHARD.
What said our cousin when you parted with him?
DUKE OF AUMERLE.
'Farewell;'
And, for my heart disdained that my tongue
Should so profane the word, that taught me craft
To counterfeit oppression of such grief,
That words seem'd buried in my sorrow's grave.
Marry, would the word 'farewell' have lengthen'd
hours,
And added years to his short banishment,
He should have had a volume of 'farewells;'
But since it would not, he had none of me.
KING RICHARD.
He is our cousin, cousin; but 'tis doubt,
When time shall call him home from banishment,
Whether our kinsman come to see his friends,
Ourself, and Bushy, Bagot here, and Green,
Observed his courtship to the common people;
How he did seem to dive into their hearts
With humble and familiar courtesy;
What reverence he did throw away on slaves;
Wooing poor craftsmen with the craft of smiles,
And patient underbearing of his fortune,
As 'twere to banish their affects with him.
Off goes his bonnet to an oyster-wench;
A brace of draymen bid God speed him well,
And had the tribute of his supple knee,
With 'Thanks, my countrymen, my loving
friends;'
As were our England in reversion his,
And he our subjects' next degree in hope.
GREEN.
Well, he is gone; and with him go these thoughts.
Now for the rebels which stand out in Ireland,—

Expedient manage must be made, my liege,
Ere further leisure yield them further means
For their advantage and your highness' loss.
KING RICHARD.
We will ourself in person to this war:
And, for our coffers, with too great a court
And liberal largess, are grown somewhat light,
We are enforced to farm our royal realm;
The revenue whereof shall furnish us
For our affairs in hand. If that come short,
Our substitutes at home shall have blank charters;
Whereto, when they shall know what men are
rich,
They shall subscribe them for large sums of gold,
And send them after to supply our wants;
For we will make for Ireland presently.
Enter BUSHY.
Bushy, what news?
BUSHY.
Old John of Gaunt is grievous sick, my lord,
Suddenly taken; and hath sent post-haste
To entreat your majesty to visit him.
KING RICHARD.
Where lies he?
BUSHY.
At Ely-house.
KING RICHARD.
Now put it, God, in the physician's mind
To help him to his grave immediately!
The lining of his coffers shall make coats
To deck our soldiers for these Irish wars.—
Come, gentlemen, let's all go visit him:
Pray God we may make haste, and come too late!
ALL.
Amen.   [*Exeunt.*

ACT II. SCENE I.

London.   A room in Ely-house.

Enter GAUNT *sick, with the* DUKE OF YORK
and others.

JOHN OF GAUNT.
WILL the king come, that I may breathe my
last
In wholesome counsel to his unstaid youth?
DUKE OF YORK.
Vex not yourself, nor strive not with your breath;
For all in vain comes counsel to his ear.
JOHN OF GAUNT.
O, but they say the tongues of dying men
Enforce attention like deep harmony:
Where words are scarce, they are seldom spent
in vain;
For they breathe truth that breathe their words in
pain.
He that no more must say is listen'd more
Than they whom youth and ease have taught to
gloze;
More are men's ends markt than their lives
before:
The setting sun, and music at the close,
As the last taste of sweets, is sweetest last,
Writ in remembrance more than things long past:
Though Richard my life's counsel would not hear,
My death's sad tale may yet undeaf his ear.

DUKE OF YORK.

No; it is stopt with other flattering sounds,
As, praises of his state: then there are found
Lascivious metres, to whose venom sound
The open ear of youth doth always listen;
Report of fashions in proud Italy,
Whose manners still our tardy apish nation
Limps after in base imitation.
Where doth the world thrust forth a vanity,—
So it be new, there's no respect how vile,—
That is not quickly buzz'd into his ears?
Then all too late comes counsel to be heard,
Where will doth mutiny with wit's regard.
Direct not him, whose way himself will choose:
'Tis breath thou lack'st, and that breath wilt thou
    lose.

JOHN OF GAUNT.

Methinks I am a prophet new-inspired,
And thus, expiring, do foretell of him:
His rash fierce blaze of riot cannot last,
For violent fires soon burn out themselves;
Small showers last long, but sudden storms are
    short;
He tires betimes that spurs too fast betimes;
With eager feeding food doth choke the feeder:
Light vanity, insatiate cormorant,
Consuming means, soon preys upon itself.
This royal throne of kings, this scepter'd isle,
This earth of majesty, this seat of Mars,
This other Eden, demi-Paradise;
This fortress built by Nature for herself
Against infection and the hand of war;
This happy breed of men, this little world;
This precious stone set in the silver sea,
Which serves it in the office of a wall,
Or as a moat defensive to a house,
Against the envy of less happier lands;
This blessed plot, this earth, this realm, this
    England,
This nurse, this teeming womb of royal kings,
Fear'd by their breed, and famous by their
    birth,
Renowned for their deeds as far from home,—
For Christian service and true chivalry,—
As is the sepulchre, in stubborn Jewry,
Of the world's ransom, blessed Mary's Son;—
This land of such dear souls, this dear dear land,
Dear for her reputation through the world,
Is now leased out—I die pronouncing it—
Like to a tenement or pelting farm:
England, bound in with the triumphant sea,
Whose rocky shore beats back the envious siege
Of watery Neptune, is now bound in with shame,
With inky blots, and rotten parchment bonds:
That England, that was wont to conquer others,
Hath made a shameful conquest of itself.
Ah, would the scandal vanish with my life,
How happy then were my ensuing death!

Enter KING RICHARD *and* QUEEN, AUMERLE,
    BUSHY, GREEN, BAGOT, ROSS, *and* WIL-
    LOUGHBY.

DUKE OF YORK.

The king is come: deal mildly with his youth;
For young hot colts being raged do rage the more.

QUEEN.

How fares our noble uncle, Lancaster?

KING RICHARD.

What comfort, man? how is 't with aged Gaunt?

JOHN OF GAUNT.

O, how that name befits my composition!
Old Gaunt, indeed; and gaunt in being old:
Within me grief hath kept a tedious fast;
And who abstains from meat, that is not gaunt?
For sleeping England long time have I watcht;
Watching breeds leanness, leanness is all gaunt:
The pleasure that some fathers feed upon,
Is my strict fast,—I mean, my children's looks;
And therein fasting, hast thou made me gaunt:
Gaunt am I for the grave, gaunt as a grave,
Whose hollow womb inherits naught but bones.

KING RICHARD.

Can sick men play so nicely with their names?

JOHN OF GAUNT.

No, misery makes sport to mock itself:
Since thou dost seek to kill my name in me,
I mock my name, great king, to flatter thee.

KING RICHARD.

Should dying men flatter with those that live?

JOHN OF GAUNT.

No, no, men living flatter those that die.

KING RICHARD.

Thou, now a-dying, say'st thou flatter'st me.

JOHN OF GAUNT.

O, no! thou diest, though I the sicker be.

KING RICHARD.

I am in health, I breathe, and see thee ill.

JOHN OF GAUNT.

Now, He that made me knows I see thee ill;
Ill in myself to see, and in thee seeing ill.
Thy death-bed is no lesser than thy land,
Wherein thou liest in reputation sick;
And thou, too careless patient as thou art,
Committ'st thy 'nointed body to the cure
Of those physicians that first wounded thee:
A thousand flatterers sit within thy crown,
Whose compass is no bigger than thy head;
And yet, incaged in so small a verge,
The waste is no whit lesser than thy land.
O, had thy grandsire, with a prophet's eye,
Seen how his son's son should destroy his sons,
From forth thy reach he would have laid thy
    shame,
Deposing thee before thou wert possest,
Which art possest now to depose thyself.
Why, cousin, wert thou regent of the world,
It were a shame to let this land by lease;
But for thy world enjoying but this land,
Is it not more than shame to shame it so?
Landlord of England art thou now, not king:
Thy state of law is bond-slave to the law;
And thou—

KING RICHARD.
                   A lunatic lean-witted fool,
Presuming on an ague's privilege,
Darest with thy frozen admonition
Make pale our cheek, chasing the royal blood
With fury from his native residence.
Now, by my seat's right royal majesty,
Wert thou not brother to great Edward's son,
This tongue that runs so roundly in thy head
Should run thy head from thy unreverent
    shoulders.

JOHN OF GAUNT.

O, spare me not, my brother Edward's son,
For that I was his father Edward's son;—
That blood already, like the pelican,
Hast thou tapt out, and drunkenly caroused:
My brother Gloster, plain well-meaning soul,—
Whom fair befall in heaven 'mongst happy
    souls!—
May be a precedent and witness good
That thou respect'st not spilling Edward's
    blood:
Join with the present sickness that I have;
And thy unkindness be like crooked age,
To crop at once a too-long wither'd flower.
Live in thy shame, but die not shame with thee!—
These words hereafter thy tormentors be!—
Convey me to my bed, then to my grave:
Love they to live that love and honour have.
            [Exit, borne out by his ATTENDANTS.

KING RICHARD.

And let them die that age and sullens have;
For both hast thou, and both become the grave.

DUKE OF YORK.

I do beseech your majesty, impute his words
To wayward sickliness and age in him:
He loves you, on my life, and holds you dear
As Harry, duke of Hereford, were he here.

KING RICHARD.

Right, you say true: as Hereford's love, so his;
As theirs, so mine; and all be as it is.

            Enter NORTHUMBERLAND.

EARL OF NORTHUMBERLAND.

My liege, old Gaunt commends him to your
    majesty.

KING RICHARD.

What says he?

EARL OF NORTHUMBERLAND.

            Nay, nothing; all is said:
His tongue is now a stringless instrument;
Words, life, and all, old Lancaster hath spent.

DUKE OF YORK.

Be York the next that must be bankrupt so!
Though death be poor, it ends a mortal woe.

KING RICHARD.

The ripest fruit first falls, and so doth he;
His time is spent, our pilgrimage must be:
So much for that.—Now for our Irish wars:
We must supplant these rough rug-headed kerns,
Which live like venom, where no venom else
But only they have privilege to live.
And for these great affairs do ask some charge,
Towards our assistance we do seize to us
The plate, coin, revenues, and movables,
Whereof our uncle Gaunt did stand possest.

DUKE OF YORK.

How long shall I be patient? ah, how long
Shall tender duty make me suffer wrong?
Not Gloster's death, nor Hereford's banishment,
Not Gaunt's rebukes, nor England's private
    wrongs,
Nor the prevention of poor Bolingbroke
About his marriage, nor my own disgrace,
Have ever made me sour my patient cheek,
Or bend one wrinkle on my sovereign's face.
I am the last of noble Edward's sons,
Of whom thy father, Prince of Wales, was first:

In war was never lion raged more fierce,
In peace was never gentle lamb more mild,
Than was that young and princely gentleman.
His face thou hast, for even so lookt he,
Accomplisht with the number of thy hours;
But when he frown'd, it was against the French,
And not against his friends: his noble hand
Did win what he did spend, and spent not that
Which his triumphant father's hand had won:
His hands were guilty of no kindred's blood,
But bloody with the enemies of his kin.
O Richard! York is too far gone with grief,
Or else he never would compare between.

KING RICHARD.

Why, uncle, what's the matter?

DUKE OF YORK.

                        O my liege,
Pardon me, if you please; if not, I, pleased
Not to be pardon'd, am content withal.
Seek you to seize, and gripe into your hands,
The royalties and rights of banisht Hereford?
Is not Gaunt dead? and doth not Hereford live?
Was not Gaunt just? and is not Harry true?
Did not the one deserve to have an heir?
Is not his heir a well-deserving son?
Take Hereford's rights away, and take from
    Time
His charters and his customary rights;
Let not to-morrow, then, ensue to-day;
Be not thyself,—for how art thou a king
But by fair sequence and succession?
Now, afore God,—God forbid I say true!—
If you do wrongfully seize Hereford's rights,
Call in the letters-patents that he hath
By his attorneys-general to sue
His livery, and deny his offer'd homage,
You pluck a thousand dangers on your head,
You lose a thousand well-disposed hearts,
And prick my tender patience to those thoughts
Which honour and allegiance cannot think.

KING RICHARD.

Think what you will, we seize into our hands
His plate, his goods, his money, and his lands.

DUKE OF YORK.

I'll not be by the while: my liege, farewell:
What will ensue hereof, there's none can tell;
But by bad courses may be understood
That their events can never fall out good.   [Exit

KING RICHARD.

Go, Bushy, to the Earl of Wiltshire straight:
Bid him repair to us to Ely-house
To see this business. To-morrow next
We will for Ireland; and 'tis time, I trow:
And we create, in absence of ourself,
Our uncle York lord governor of England;
For he is just, and always loved us well.—
Come on, our queen: to-morrow must we part;
Be merry, for our time of stay is short.

        [Flourish. Exeunt KING, QUEEN, AU-
            MERLE, BUSHY, GREEN, and BAGOT

EARL OF NORTHUMBERLAND.

Well, lords, the Duke of Lancaster is dead.

LORD ROSS.

And living too; for now his son is duke.

LORD WILLOUGHBY.

Barely in title, not in revenues.

EARL OF NORTHUMBERLAND.
Richly in both, if justice had her right.
LORD ROSS.
My heart is great; but it must break with silence,
Ere't be disburden'd with a liberal tongue.
EARL OF NORTHUMBERLAND.
Nay, speak thy mind; and let him ne'er speak more
That speaks thy words again to do thee harm!
LORD WILLOUGHBY.
Tends that thou wouldst speak to the Duke of Hereford?
If it be so, out with it boldly, man;
Quick is mine ear to hear of good towards him.
LORD ROSS.
No good at all, that I can do for him;
Unless you call it good to pity him,
Bereft and gelded of his patrimony.
EARL OF NORTHUMBERLAND.
Now, afore God, 'tis shame such wrongs are borne
In him, a royal prince, and many moe
Of noble blood in this declining land.
The king is not himself, but basely led
By flatterers; and what they will inform,
Merely in hate, 'gainst any of us all,
That will the king severely prosecute
'Gainst us, our lives, our children, and our heirs.
LORD ROSS.
The commons hath he pill'd with grievous taxes,
And quite lost their hearts: the nobles hath he fined
For ancient quarrels, and quite lost their hearts.
LORD WILLOUGHBY.
And daily new exactions are devised,—
As blanks, benevolences, and I wot not what:
But what, o' God's name, doth become of this?
EARL OF NORTHUMBERLAND.
Wars have not wasted it, for warr'd he hath not,
But basely yielded upon compromise
That which his ancestors achieved with blows:
More hath he spent in peace than they in wars.
LORD ROSS.
The Earl of Wiltshire hath the realm in farm.
LORD WILLOUGHBY.
The king's grown bankrout, like a broken man.
EARL OF NORTHUMBERLAND.
Reproach and dissolution hangeth over him.
LORD ROSS.
He hath not money for these Irish wars,
His burdenous taxations notwithstanding,
But by the robbing of the banisht duke.
EARL OF NORTHUMBERLAND.
His noble kinsman:—most degenerate king!
But, lords, we hear this fearful tempest sing,
Yet seek no shelter to avoid the storm;
We see the wind sit sore upon our sails,
And yet we strike not, but securely perish.
LORD ROSS.
We see the very wrack that we must suffer;
And unavoided is the danger now,
For suffering so the causes of our wrack.
EARL OF NORTHUMBERLAND.
Not so; even through the hollow eyes of death
I spy life peering; but I dare not say
How near the tidings of our comfort is.

LORD WILLOUGHBY.
Nay, let us share thy thoughts, as thou dost ours.
LORD ROSS.
Be confident to speak, Northumberland:
We three are but thyself; and, speaking so,
Thy words are but as thoughts; therefore, be bold.
EARL OF NORTHUMBERLAND.
Then thus:—I have from Port le Blanc, a bay
In Brittany, received intelligence
That Harry, Duke of Hereford, Rainold, Lord Cobham,

.   .   .   .   .

That late broke from the Duke of Exeter,
His brother, Archbishop late of Canterbury,
Sir Thomas Erpingham, Sir John Ramston,
Sir John Norbery, Sir Robert Waterton, and
Francis Quoint,—
All these well furnisht by the Duke of Bretagne,
With eight tall ships, three thousand men of war,
Are making hither with all due expedience,
And shortly mean to touch our northern shore:
Perhaps they had ere this, but that they stay
The first departing of the king for Ireland.
If, then, we shall shake off our slavish yoke,
Imp out our drooping country's broken wing,
Redeem from broking pawn the blemisht crown,
Wipe off the dust that hides our sceptre's gilt,
And make high majesty look like itself,
Away with me in post to Ravenspurg;
But if you faint, as fearing to do so,
Stay, and be secret, and myself will go.
LORD ROSS.
To horse, to horse! urge doubts to them that fear.
LORD WILLOUGHBY.
Hold out my horse, and I will first be there.
[*Exeunt.*

SCENE II.

The Court.

Enter QUEEN, BUSHY, *and* BAGOT.

BUSHY.
MADAM, your majesty is too much sad:
You promised, when you parted with the king,
To lay aside life-harming heaviness,
And entertain a cheerful disposition.
QUEEN.
To please the king, I did; to please myself,
I cannot do it; yet I know no cause
Why I should welcome such a guest as grief,
Save bidding farewell to so sweet a guest
As my sweet Richard: yet, again, methinks
Some unborn sorrow, ripe in fortune's womb,
Is coming towards me; and my inward soul
With nothing trembles: at something it grieves,
More than with parting from my lord the king.
BUSHY.
Each substance of a grief hath twenty shadows,
Which shows like grief itself, but is not so;
For sorrow's eye, glazed with blinding tears,
Divides one thing entire to many objects;
Like perspectives, which rightly gazed upon,
Show nothing but confusion,—eyed awry,
Distinguish form: so your sweet majesty,
Looking awry upon your lord's departure,
Find shapes of grief, more than himself, to wail;

Which, lookt on as it is, is naught but shadows
Of what it is not. Then, thrice-gracious queen,
More than your lord's departure weep not,—
   more's not seen;
Or if it be, 'tis with false sorrow's eye,
Which for things true weeps things imaginary.
> QUEEN.

It may be so; but yet my inward soul
Persuades me it is otherwise: howe'er it be,
I cannot but be sad; so heavy sad,
As, though, on thinking, on no thought I think,
Makes me with heavy nothing faint and shrink.
> BUSHY.

'Tis nothing but conceit, my gracious lady.
> QUEEN.

'Tis nothing less: conceit is still derived
From some forefather grief; mine is not so,
For nothing hath begot my something grief;
Or something hath the nothing that I grieve:
'Tis in reversion that I do possess;
But what it is, that is not yet known; what
I cannot name; 'tis nameless woe, I wot.
> *Enter* GREEN.
> GREEN.

God save your majesty! and well met, gentlemen:
I hope the king is not yet shipt for Ireland.
> QUEEN.

Why hopest thou so? 'tis better hope he is;
For his designs crave haste, his haste good hope:
Then wherefore dost thou hope he is not shipt?
> GREEN.

That he, our hope, might have retired his power,
And driven into despair an enemy's hope,
Who strongly hath set footing in this land:
The banisht Bolingbroke repeals himself,
And with uplifted arms is safe arrived
At Ravenspurg.
> QUEEN.
> Now God in heaven forbid!
> GREEN.

Ah madam, 'tis too true: and that is worse,
The Lord Northumberland, his son young Henry
   Percy,
The Lords of Ross, Beaumond, and Willoughby,
With all their powerful friends, are fled to him.
> BUSHY.

Why have you not proclaim'd Northumberland
And all the rest revolted faction traitors?
> GREEN.

We have: whereupon the Earl of Worcester
Hath broke his staff, resign'd his stewardship,
And all the household servants fled with him
To Bolingbroke.
> QUEEN.

So, Green, thou art the midwife to my woe,
And Bolingbroke my sorrow's dismal heir:
Now hath my soul brought forth her prodigy;
And I, a gasping new-deliver'd mother,
Have woe to woe, sorrow to sorrow join'd.
> BUSHY.

Despair not, madam.
> QUEEN.
> Who shall hinder me?

I will despair, and be at enmity
With cozening hope,—he is a flatterer,
A parasite, a keeper-back of death,

Who gently would dissolve the bands of life,
Which false hope lingers in extremity.
> GREEN.

Here comes the Duke of York.
> QUEEN.

With signs of war about his aged neck:
O, full of careful business are his looks!
> *Enter* YORK.

Uncle, for God's sake, speak comfortable words.
> DUKE OF YORK.

Should I do so, I should belie my thoughts:
Comfort's in heaven; and we are on the earth,
Where nothing lives but crosses, cares, and grief.
Your husband, he is gone to save far off,
Whilst others come to make him lose at home:
Here am I left to underprop his land,
Who, weak with age, cannot support myself:
Now comes the sick hour that his surfeit made;
Now shall he try his friends that flatter'd him.
> *Enter a* SERVANT.
> SERVANT.

My lord, your son was gone before I came.
> DUKE OF YORK.

He was?—Why, so!—go all which way it will!—
The nobles they are fled, the commons they are
   cold,
And will, I fear, revolt on Hereford's side.—
Sirrah, get thee to Plashy, to my sister Gloster;
Bid her send me presently a thousand pound:—
Hold, take my ring.
> SERVANT.

My lord, I had forgot to tell your lordship,
To-day, as I came by, I called there;—
But I shall grieve you to report the rest.
> DUKE OF YORK.

What is it, knave?
> SERVANT.

An hour before I came, the duchess died.
> DUKE OF YORK.

God for his mercy! what a tide of woes
Comes rushing on this woful land at once!
I know not what to do.—I would to God,—
So my untruth had not provoked him to it,—
The king had cut off my head with my
   brother's.—
What, are there no posts dispatcht for Ire-
   land?—
How shall we do for money for these wars?—
Come, sister,—cousin, I would say,—pray, par-
   don me.—
Go, fellow, get thee home, provide some carts,
And bring away the armour that is there.
>   [*Exit* SERVANT.

Gentlemen, will you go muster men? If I
Know how or which way to order these affairs,
Thus disorderly thrust into my hands,
Never believe me. Both are my kinsmen:—
Th'one is my sovereign, whom both my oath
And duty bids defend; th'other, again,
Is my kinsman, whom the king hath wrong'd,
Whom conscience and my kindred bids to right.
Well, somewhat we must do.—Come, cousin, I'll
Dispose of you.—Gentlemen, go muster up your
   men,
And meet me presently at Berkley.
I should to Plashy too;—

But time will not permit:—all is uneven,
And every thing is left at six and seven.
                    [*Exeunt* YORK *and* QUEEN.
                    BUSHY.
The wind sits fair for news to go to Ireland,
But none returns. For us to levy power
Proportionable to the enemy
Is all unpossible.
                    GREEN.
Besides, our nearness to the king in love
Is near the hate of those love not the king.
                    BAGOT.
And that's the wavering commons: for their love
Lies in their purses; and whoso empties them,
By so much fills their hearts with deadly hate.
                    BUSHY.
Wherein the king stands generally condemn'd.
                    BAGOT.
If judgement lie in them, then so do we,
Because we ever have been near the king.
                    GREEN.
Well, I will for refuge straight to Bristol-castle:
The Earl of Wiltshire is already there.
                    BUSHY.
Thither will I with you; for little office
The hateful commons will perform for us,
Except like curs to tear us all to pieces.—
Will you go along with us?
                    BAGOT.
No; I will to Ireland to his majesty.
Farewell: if heart's presages be not vain,
We three here part that ne'er shall meet again.
                    BUSHY.
That's as York thrives to beat back Bolingbroke.
                    GREEN.
Alas, poor duke! the task he undertakes
Is numbering sands, and drinking oceans dry:
Where one on his side fights, thousands will fly.
Farewell at once,—for once, for all, and ever.
                    BUSHY.
Well, we may meet again.
                    BAGOT.
                    I fear me, never.
                            [*Exeunt.*

SCENE III.

The wilds in Glostershire.

Enter BOLINGBROKE *and* NORTHUMBER-
LAND, *with* FORCES.

                    HENRY BOLINGBROKE.
HOW far is it, my lord, to Berkley now?
                    EARL OF NORTHUMBERLAND.
Believe me, noble lord,
I am a stranger here in Glostershire:
These high wild hills and rough uneven ways
Draw out our miles, and make them wearisome;
And yet your fair discourse hath been as sugar,
Making the hard way sweet and delectable.
But I bethink me what a weary way
From Ravenspurg to Cotswold will be found
In Ross and Willoughby, wanting your company,
Which, I protest, hath very much beguiled
The tediousness and process of my travel:
But theirs is sweeten'd with the hope to have
The present benefit which I possess;
And hope to joy is little less in joy

Than hope enjoy'd: by this the weary lords
Shall make their way seem short; as mine hath
    done
By sight of what I have, your noble company.
                    HENRY BOLINGBROKE.
Of much less value is my company
Than your good words.—But who comes here?
                    EARL OF NORTHUMBERLAND.
It is my son, young Harry Percy,
Sent from my brother Worcester, whencesoever.
                    Enter PERCY.
Harry, how fares your uncle?
                    HENRY PERCY.
I had thought, my lord, to have learn'd his health
    of you.
                    EARL OF NORTHUMBERLAND.
Why, is he not with the queen?
                    HENRY PERCY.
No, my good lord; he hath forsook the court,
Broken his staff of office, and dispersed
The household of the king.
                    EARL OF NORTHUMBERLAND.
                    What was his reason?
He was not so resolved when last we spake to-
    gether.
                    HENRY PERCY.
Because your lordship was proclaimed traitor.
But he, my lord, is gone to Ravenspurg,
To offer service to the Duke of Hereford;
And sent me over by Berkley, to discover
What power the Duke of York had levied there;
Then with directions to repair to Ravenspurg.
                    EARL OF NORTHUMBERLAND.
Have you forgot the Duke of Hereford, boy?
                    HENRY PERCY.
No, my good lord; for that is not forgot
Which ne'er I did remember: to my knowledge,
I never in my life did look on him.
                    EARL OF NORTHUMBERLAND.
Then learn to know him now; this is the duke.
                    HENRY PERCY.
My gracious lord, I tender you my service,
Such as it is, being tender, raw, and young;
Which elder days shall ripen, and confirm
To more approved service and desert.
                    HENRY BOLINGBROKE.
I thank thee, gentle Percy; and be sure
I count myself in nothing else so happy
As in a soul remembering my good friends;
And, as my fortune ripens with thy love,
It shall be still thy true love's recompense:
My heart this covenant makes, my hand thus seals
    it.
                    EARL OF NORTHUMBERLAND.
How far is it to Berkley? and what stir
Keeps good old York there with his men of war?
                    HENRY PERCY.
There stands the castle, by yond tuft of trees,
Mann'd with three hundred men, as I have
    heard;
And in it are the Lords of York, Berkley, and
    Seymour,—
None else of name and noble estimate.
                    EARL OF NORTHUMBERLAND.
Here come the Lords of Ross and Willoughby,
Bloody with spurring, fiery-red with haste.

Enter ROSS *and* WILLOUGHBY.
HENRY BOLINGBROKE.
Welcome, my lords. I wot your love pursues
A banisht traitor: all my treasury
Is yet but unfelt thanks, which, more enrich'd,
Shall be your love and labour's recompense.
LORD ROSS.
Your presence makes us rich, most noble lord.
LORD WILLOUGHBY.
And far surmounts our labour to attain it.
HENRY BOLINGBROKE.
Evermore thanks, the exchequer of the poor;
Which, till my infant fortune comes to years,
Stands for my bounty.—But who comes here?
EARL OF NORTHUMBERLAND.
It is my Lord of Berkley, as I guess.
Enter BERKLEY.
LORD BERKLEY.
My Lord of Hereford, my message is to you.
HENRY BOLINGBROKE.
My lord, my answer is—'to Lancaster;'
And I am come to seek that name in England;
And I must find that title in your tongue,
B< for. I make reply to aught you say.
LORD BERKLEY.
Mistake me not, my lord; 'tis not my meaning
To raze one title of your honour out:—
To you, m.y lord, I come,—what lord you will,—
From the most gracious regent of this land,
The Duke of York, to know what pricks you on
To take advantage of the absent time,
And fright our native peace with self-born arms.
HENRY BOLINGBROKE.
I shall not need transport my words by you;
Here comes his Grace in person.
Enter YORK *attended.*
     My noble uncle! [*Kneels.*
DUKE OF YORK.
Show me thy humble heart, and not thy knee,
Whose duty is deceivable and false.
HENRY BOLINGBROKE.
My gracious uncle!
DUKE OF YORK.
Tut, tut!
Grace me no grace, nor uncle me no uncle:
I am no traitor's uncle; and that word 'grace'
In an ungracious mouth is but profane.
Why have those banisht and forbidden legs
Dared once to touch a dust of England's ground?
But, then, more 'why?'—why have they dared to
So many miles upon her peaceful bosom, [march
Frighting her pale-faced villages with war
And ostentation of despised arms?
Comest thou because th' anointed king is hence?
Why, foolish boy, the king is left behind,
And in my loyal bosom lies his power.
Were I but now the lord of such hot youth
As when brave Gaunt thy father, and myself,
Rescued the Black Prince, that young Mars of men,
From forth the ranks of many thousand French,
O, then, how quickly should this arm of mine,
Now prisoner to the palsy, chastise thee,
And minister correction to thy fault!
HENRY BOLINGBROKE.
My gracious uncle, let me know my fault;
On what condition stands it and wherein?

DUKE OF YORK.
Even in condition of the worst degree,—
In gross rebellion and detested treason:
Thou art a banisht man; and here art come
Before the expiration of thy time,
In braving arms against thy sovereign.
HENRY BOLINGBROKE.
As I was banisht, I was banisht Hereford;
But as I come, I come for Lancaster.
And, noble uncle, I beseech your Grace
Look on my wrongs with an indifferent eye:
You are my father, for methinks in you
I see old Gaunt alive; O, then, my father,
Will you permit that I shall stand condemn'd
A wandering vagabond; my rights and royalties
Pluckt from my arms perforce, and given away
To upstart unthrifts? Wherefore was I born?
If that my cousin king be King of England,
It must be granted I am Duke of Lancaster.
You have a son, Aumerle, my noble cousin;
Had you first died, and he been thus trod down,
He should have found his uncle Gaunt a father,
To rouse his wrongs, and chase them to the bay.
I am denied to sue my livery here,
And yet my letters-patents give me leave:
My father's goods are all distrain'd and sold;
And these and all are all amiss employ'd.
What would you have me do? I am a subject,
And I challenge law: attorneys are denied me;
And therefore personally I lay my claim
To my inheritance of free descent.
EARL OF NORTHUMBERLAND.
The noble duke hath been too much abused.
LORD ROSS.
It stands your Grace upon to do him right.
LORD WILLOUGHBY.
Base men by his endowments are made great.
DUKE OF YORK.
My lords of England, let me tell you this:—
I have had feeling of my cousin's wrongs,
And labour'd all I could to do him right;
But in this kind to come, in braving arms,
Be his own carver, and cut out his way,
To find out right with wrong,—it may not be;
And you that do abet him in this kind
Cherish rebellion and are rebels all.
EARL OF NORTHUMBERLAND.
The noble duke hath sworn his coming is
But for his own; and for the right of that
We all have strongly sworn to give him aid;
And let him ne'er see joy that breaks that oath!
DUKE OF YORK.
Well, well, I see the issue of these arms;
I cannot mend it, I must needs confess,
Because my power is weak and all ill left:
But if I could, by Him that gave me life,
I would attach you all, and make you stoop
Unto the sovereign mercy of the king;
But since I cannot, be it known to you
I do remain as neuter. So, fare you well;—
Unless you please to enter in the castle,
And there repose you for this night.
HENRY BOLINGBROKE.
An offer, uncle, that we will accept:
But we must win your Grace to go with us
To Bristol-castle, which they say is held

By Bushy, Bagot, and their complices,
The caterpillars of the commonwealth,
Which I have sworn to weed and pluck away.

DUKE OF YORK.

It may be I will go with you:—but yet I'll pause;
For I am loth to break our country's laws.
Nor friends nor foes, to me welcome you are:
Things past redress are now with me past care.

[*Exeunt.*

SCENE IV.

A camp in Wales.

Enter SALISBURY *and a* CAPTAIN.

CAPTAIN.

MY Lord of Salisbury, we have stay'd ten days,
And hardly kept our countrymen together,
And yet we hear no tidings from the king;
Therefore we will disperse ourselves: farewell.

EARL OF SALISBURY.

Stay yet another day, thou trusty Welshman:
The king reposeth all his confidence in thee.

CAPTAIN.

'Tis thought the king is dead; we will not stay.
The bay-trees in our country all are wither'd,
And meteors fright the fixed stars of heaven;
The pale-faced moon looks bloody on the earth,
And leant-lookt prophets whisper fearful change;
Rich men look sad, and ruffians dance and
  leap,—
The one in fear to lose what they enjoy,
The other to enjoy by rage and war:
These signs forerun the death or fall of kings.—
Farewell: our countrymen are gone and fled,
As well assured Richard their king is dead. [*Exit.*

EARL OF SALISBURY.

Ah, Richard, with the eyes of heavy mind,
I see thy glory, like a shooting star,
Fall to the base earth from the firmament!
Thy sun sets weeping in the lowly west,
Witnessing storms to come, woe, and unrest:
Thy friends are fled, to wait upon thy foes;
And crossly to thy good all fortune goes.   [*Exit.*

ACT III.   SCENE I.

BOLINGBROKE'S *camp at Bristol.*

Enter BOLINGBROKE, YORK, NORTHUMBER-
LAND, PERCY, WILLOUGHBY, *with* BUSHY
and GREEN, *prisoners.*

HENRY BOLINGBROKE.

BRING forth these men.
  Bushy and Green, I will not vex your souls—
Since presently your souls must part your
  bodies—
With too much urging your pernicious lives,
For 'twere no charity; yet, to wash your blood
From off my hands, here, in the view of men,
I will unfold some causes of your deaths.
You have misled a prince, a royal king,
A happy gentleman in blood and lineaments,
By you unhappied and disfigured clean:
You have in manner with your sinful hours
Made a divorce betwixt his queen and him;
Broke the possession of a royal bed,
And stain'd the beauty of a fair queen's cheeks

With tears drawn from her eyes by your foul
  wrongs.
Myself,—a prince by fortune of my birth,
Near to the king in blood, and near in love
Till you did make him misinterpret me,—
Have stoopt my neck under your injuries,
And sigh'd my English breath in foreign clouds,
Eating the bitter bread of banishment;
Whilst you have fed upon my signories,
Disparkt my parks, and fell'd my forest-woods,
From my own windows torn my household coat,
Razed out my imprese, leaving me no sign,
Save men's opinions and my living blood,
To show the world I am a gentleman.
This and much more, much more than twice all
  this,
Condemns you to the death.—See them deliver'd
  over
To execution and the hand of death.

BUSHY.

More welcome is the stroke of death to me
Than Bolingbroke to England.—Lords, farewell.

GREEN.

My comfort is, that heaven will take our souls,
And plague injustice with the pains of hell.

HENRY BOLINGBROKE.

My Lord Northumberland, see them dispatcht.
  [*Exeunt* NORTHUMBERLAND *and others,*
    with the PRISONERS.
Uncle, you say the queen is at your house;
For God's sake, fairly let her be entreated:
Tell her I send to her my kind commends;
Take special care my greetings be deliver'd.

DUKE OF YORK.

A gentleman of mine I have dispatcht
With letters of your love to her at large.

HENRY BOLINGBROKE.

Thanks, gentle uncle.—Come, lords, away,
To fight with Glendower and his complices:
Awhile to work, and after holiday.   [*Exeunt.*

SCENE II.

The coast of Wales.   A castle in view.

Drums: flourish and colours.   Enter KING RICH-
ARD, *the* BISHOP OF CARLISLE, AUMERLE
and SOLDIERS.

KING RICHARD.

BARKLOUGHLY-castle call they this at
  hand?

DUKE OF AUMERLE.

Yea, my lord. How brooks your Grace the air,
After your late tossing on the breaking seas?

KING RICHARD.

Needs must I like it well: I weep for joy
To stand upon my kingdom once again.—
Dear earth, I do salute thee with my hand,
Though rebels wound thee with their horses'
  hoofs:
As a long-parted mother with her child
Plays fondly with her tears and smiles in meeting
So, weeping, smiling, greet I thee, my earth,
And do thee favours with my royal hands.
Feed not thy sovereign's foe, my gentle earth,
Nor with thy sweets comfort his ravenous sense;
But let thy spiders, that suck up thy venom,

And heavy-gaited toads, lie in their way,
Doing annoyance to the treacherous feet
Which with usurping steps do trample thee:
Yield stinging nettles to mine enemies;
And when they from thy bosom pluck a flower,
Guard it, I pray thee, with a lurking adder,
Whose double tongue may with a mortal touch
Throw death upon thy sovereign's enemies.—
Mock not my senseless conjuration, lords:
This earth shall have a feeling, and these stones
Prove armed soldiers, ere her native king
Shall falter under foul rebellion's arms.

BISHOP OF CARLISLE.

Fear not, my lord: that Power that made you
   king
Hath power to keep you king in spite of all.
The means that heaven yields must be embraced,
And not neglected; else, if heaven would,
And we will not, heaven's offer we refuse,
The proffer'd means of succour and redress.

DUKE OF AUMERLE.

He means, my lord, that we are too remiss;
Whilst Bolingbroke, through our security,
Grows strong and great in substance and in
   friends.

KING RICHARD.

Discomfortable cousin! know'st thou not
That when the searching eye of heaven is hid
Behind the globe, that lights the lower world,
Then thieves and robbers range abroad unseen,
In murders and in outrage, boldly here;
But when, from under this terrestrial ball,
He fires the proud tops of the eastern pines,
And darts his light through every guilty hole,
Then murders, treasons, and detested sins,
The cloak of night being pluckt from off their
   backs,
Stand bare and naked, trembling at themselves?
So when this thief, this traitor, Bolingbroke,—
Who all this while hath revell'd in the night,
Whilst we were wandering with the Antipodes,—
Shall see us rising in our throne, the east,
His treasons will sit blushing in his face,
Not able to endure the sight of day,
But self-affrighted tremble at his sin.
Not all the water in the rough rude sea
Can wash the balm from an anointed king;
The breath of worldly men cannot depose
The deputy elected by the Lord:
For every man that Bolingbroke hath prest
To lift shrewd steel against our golden crown,
God for his Richard hath in heavenly pay
A glorious angel: then, if angels fight,
Weak men must fall; for heaven still guards the
   right.

Enter SALISBURY.

Welcome, my lord: how far off lies your power?

EARL OF SALISBURY.

Not near nor further off, my gracious lord,
Than this weak arm: discomfort guides my
   tongue,
And bids me speak of nothing but despair.
One day too late, I fear me, noble lord,
Hath clouded all thy happy days on earth:
O, call back yesterday, bid time return,
And thou shalt have twelve thousand fighting men!

To-day, to-day, unhappy day, too late,
O'erthrows thy joys, friends, fortune, and thy
   state;
For all the Welshmen, hearing thou wert dead,
Are gone to Bolingbroke, dispersed and fled.

DUKE OF AUMERLE.

Comfort, my liege: why looks your Grace so pale?

KING RICHARD.

But now the blood of twenty thousand men
Did triumph in my face, and they are fled;
And, till so much blood thither come agen,
Have I not reason to look pale and dead?
All souls that will be safe, fly from my side;
For time hath set a blot upon my pride.

DUKE OF AUMERLE.

Comfort, my liege; remember who you are.

KING RICHARD.

I had forgot myself: am I not king?
Awake, thou coward majesty! thou sleepest.
Is not the king's name twenty thousand names?
Arm, arm, my name! a puny subject strikes
At thy great glory.—Look not to the ground,
Ye favourites of a king: are we not high?
High be our thoughts: I know my uncle York
Hath power enough to serve our turn.—
But who comes here?

Enter SCROOP.

SIR STEPHEN SCROOP.

More health and happiness betide my liege
Than can my care-tuned tongue deliver him!

KING RICHARD.

Mine ear is open and my heart prepared:
The worst is worldly loss thou canst unfold.
Say, is my kingdom lost? why, 'twas my care;
And what loss is it to be rid of care?
Strives Bolingbroke to be as great as we?
Greater he shall not be; if he serve God,
We'll serve Him too, and be his fellow so:
Revolt our subjects? that we cannot mend;
They break their faith to God as well as us:
Cry woe, destruction, ruin, loss, decay;
The worst is death, and death will have his day.

SIR STEPHEN SCROOP.

Glad am I that your highness is so arm'd
To bear the tidings of calamity.
Like an unseasonable stormy day,
Which makes the silver rivers drown their shores,
As if the world were all dissolved to tears;
So high above his limits swel's the rage
Of Bolingbroke, covering your fearful land
With hard bright steel, and hearts harder than
   steel.
White-beards have arm'd their thin and hairless
   scalps
Against thy majesty; boys with women's voices
Strive to speak big, and clap their female joints
In stiff unwieldy arms against thy crown;
The very beadsmen learn to bend their bows
Of double-fatal yew against thy state;
Yea, distaff-women manage rusty bills
Against thy seat: both young and old rebel,
And all goes worse than I have power to tell.

KING RICHARD.

Too well, too well thou tell'st a tale so ill.
Where is the Earl of Wiltshire? where is Bagot?
What is become of Bushy? where is Green?

That they have let the dangerous enemy
Measure our confines with such peaceful steps?
If we prevail, their heads shall pay for it:
I warrant they have made peace with Boling-
broke.

SIR STEPHEN SCROOP.

Peace have they made with him, indeed, my lord.

KING RICHARD.

O villains, vipers, damn'd without redemption!
Dogs, easily won to fawn on any man!
Snakes, in my heart-blood warm'd, that sting my
heart!
Three Judases, each one thrice worse than Judas!
Would they make peace? terrible hell make war
Upon their spotted souls for this offence!

SIR STEPHEN SCROOP.

Sweet love, I see, changing his property,
Turns to the sourest and most deadly hate:—
Again uncurse their souls; their peace is made
With heads: and not with hands: those whom you
curse
Have felt the worst of death's destroying wound,
And lie full low, graved in the hollow ground.

DUKE OF AUMERLE.

Is Bushy, Green, and the Earl of Wiltshire dead?

SIR STEPHEN SCROOP.

Ay, all of them at Bristol lost their heads.

DUKE OF AUMERLE.

Where is the duke my father with his power?

KING RICHARD.

No matter where;—of comfort no man speak:
Let's talk of graves, of worms, and epitaphs;
Make dust our paper, and with rainy eyes
Write sorrow on the bosom of the earth.
Let's choose executors, and talk of wills:
And yet not so,—for what can we bequeath,
Save our deposed bodies to the ground?
Our lands, our lives, and all are Bolingbroke's,
And nothing can we call our own but death,
And that small model of the barren earth
Which serves as paste and cover to our bones.
For God's sake, let us sit upon the ground,
And tell sad stories of the death of kings:—
How some have been deposed; some slain in war;
Some haunted by the ghosts they have deposed;
Some poison'd by their wives; some sleeping
kill'd;
All murder'd:—for within the hollow crown
That rounds the mortal temples of a king
Keeps Death his court; and there the antick sits,
Scoffing his state, and grinning at his pomp;
Allowing him a breath, a little scene,
To monarchize, be fear'd, and kill with looks;
Infusing him with self and vain conceit,—
As if this flesh, which walls about our life,
Were brass impregnable; and humour'd thus,
Comes at the last, and with a little pin
Bores through his castle-wall, and—farewell
king!
Cover your heads, and mock not flesh and blood
With solemn reverence; throw away respect,
Tradition, form, and ceremonious duty;
For you have but mistook me all this while:
I live with bread like you, feel want,
Taste grief, need friends:—subjected thus,
How can you say to me, I am a king?

BISHOP OF CARLISLE.

My lord, wise men ne'er sit and wail their woes,
But presently prevent the ways to wail.
To fear the foe, since fear oppresseth strength,
Gives, in your weakness, strength unto your foe,
And so your follies fight against yourself.
Fear, and be slain; no worse can come to fight:
And fight and die is death destroying death;
Where fearing dying pays death servile breath.

DUKE OF AUMERLE.

My father hath a power; inquire of him;
And learn to make a body of a limb.

KING RICHARD.

Thou chidest me well:—proud Bolingbroke, I
come
To change blows with thee for our day of doom.
This ague-fit of fear is over-blown;
An easy task it is to win our own.—
Say, Scroop, where lies our uncle with his power?
Speak sweetly, man, although thy looks be sour.

SIR STEPHEN SCROOP.

Men judge by the complexion of the sky
The state and inclination of the day;
So may you by my dull and heavy eye,
My tongue hath but a heavier tale to say.
I play the torturer, by small and small
To lengthen out the worst that must be spoken:—
Your uncle York is join'd with Bolingbroke,
And all your northern castles yielded up,
And all your southern gentlemen in arms
Upon his party.

KING RICHARD.

Thou hast said enough.—
[to AUMERLE] Beshrew thee, cousin, which didst
lead me forth
Of that sweet way I was in to despair!
What say you now? what comfort have we now?
By heaven, I'll hate him everlastingly
That bids me be of comfort any more.
Go to Flint-castle: there I'll pine away;
A king, woe's slave, shall kingly woe obey.
That power I have, discharge; and let them go
To ear the land that hath some hope to grow,
For I have none:—let no man speak again
To alter this, for counsel is but vain.

DUKE OF AUMERLE.

My liege, one word.

KING RICHARD.

He does me double wrong
That wounds me with the flatteries of his tongue.
Discharge my followers: let them hence away,
From Richard's night to Bolingbroke's fair day.

[Exeunt.

SCENE III.

Wales.   Before Flint-castle.

Enter, with drums and colours, BOLINGBROKE,
YORK, NORTHUMBERLAND, *and* FORCES.

HENRY BOLINGBROKE.

SO that by this intelligence we learn
The Welshmen are dispersed; and Salisbury
Is gone to meet the king, who lately landed
With some few private friends upon this coast.

EARL OF NORTHUMBERLAND.

The news is very fair and good, my lord:
Richard not far from hence hath hid his head.

DUKE OF YORK.

It would beseem the Lord Northumberland
To say 'King Richard:'—alack the heavy day
When such a sacred king should hide his head!

EARL OF NORTHUMBERLAND.

Your Grace mistakes; only to be brief,
Left I his title out.

DUKE OF YORK.

The time hath been,
Would you have been so brief with him, he would
Have been so brief with you, to shorten you,
For taking so the head, your whole head's length.

HENRY BOLINGBROKE.

Mistake not, uncle, further than you should.

DUKE OF YORK.

Take not, good cousin, further than you should,
Lest you mistake: the heavens are over our heads.

HENRY BOLINGBROKE.

I know it, uncle; and oppose not myself
Against their will.—But who comes here?

Enter PERCY.

Welcome, Harry: what, will not this castle yield?

HENRY PERCY.

The castle royally is mann'd, my lord,
Against thy entrance.

HENRY BOLINGBROKE.

Royally!
Why, it contains no king?

HENRY PERCY.

Yes, my good lord,
It doth contain a king; King Richard lies
Within the limits of yon lime and stone:
And with him are the Lord Aumerle, Lord Salis-
bury,
Sir Stephen Scroop; besides a clergyman
Of holy reverence; who I cannot learn.

EARL OF NORTHUMBERLAND.

O, belike it is the Bishop of Carlisle.

HENRY BOLINGBROKE.

[*to* NORTHUMBERLAND] Noble lord,
Go to the rude ribs of that ancient castle;
Through brazen trumpet send the breath of
parley
Into his ruin'd ears, and thus deliver:—
Henry Bolingbroke
On both his knees doth kiss King Richard's hand,
And sends allegiance and true faith of heart
To his most royal person; hither come
Even at his feet to lay my arms and power,
Provided that my banishment repeal'd
And lands restored again be freely granted:
If not, I'll use th' advantage of my power,
And lay the summer's dust with showers of blood
Rain'd from the wounds of slaughter'd English-
men:
The which, how far off from the mind of Boling-
broke
It is, such crimson tempest should bedrench
The fresh green lap of fair King Richard's land,
My stooping duty tenderly shall show.
Go, signify as much, while here we march
Upon the grassy carpet of this plain.
Let's march without the noise of threatening
drum,
That from this castle's totter'd battlements
Our fair appointments may be well perused.

Methinks King Richard and myself should meet
With no less terror than the elements
Of fire and water, when their thundering shock
At meeting tears the cloudy cheeks of heaven.
Be he the fire, I'll be the yielding water:
The rage be his, while on the earth I rain
My waters,—on the earth and not on him.
March on, and mark King Richard how he looks.

Parle without, and answer within. Then a flourish.
Enter, on the walls, KING RICHARD, *the*
BISHOP OF CARLISLE, AUMERLE, SCROOP,
and SALISBURY.

DUKE OF YORK.

See, see, King Richard doth himself appear,
As doth the blushing discontented sun
From out the fiery portal of the east,
When he perceives the envious clouds are bent
To dim his glory, and to stain the track
Of his bright passage to the occident.
Yet looks he like a king: behold, his eye,
As bright as is the eagle's, lightens forth
Controlling majesty:—alack, alack, for woe,
That any harm should stain so fair a show!

KING RICHARD [*to* NORTHUMBERLAND].

We are amazed; and thus long have we stood
To watch the fearful bending of thy knee,
Because we thought ourself thy lawful king:
And if we be, how dare thy joints forget
To pay their awful duty to our presence?
If we be not, show us the hand of God
That hath dismist us from our stewardship;
For well we know, no hand of blood and bone
Can gripe the sacred handle of our sceptre,
Unless he do profane, steal, or usurp.
And though you think that all, as you have done,
Have torn their souls by turning them from us,
And we are barren and bereft of friends;
Yet know,—my master, God omnipotent,
Is mustering in his clouds, on our behalf,
Armies of pestilence; and they shall strike
Your children yet unborn and unbegot,
That lift your vassal hands against my head,
And threat the glory of my precious crown.
Tell Bolingbroke,—for yond methinks he
stands,—
That every stride he makes upon my land
Is dangerous treason: he is come to ope
The purple testament of bleeding war;
But ere the crown he looks for live in peace,
Ten thousand bloody crowns of mothers' sons
Shall ill become the flower of England's face,
Change the complexion of her maid-pale peace
To scarlet indignation, and bedew
Her pastures' grass with faithful English blood.

EARL OF NORTHUMBERLAND.

The king of heaven forbid our lord the king
Should so with civil and uncivil arms
Be rusht upon! Thy thrice-noble cousin
Harry Bolingbroke doth humbly kiss thy hand;
And by the honourable tomb he swears
That stands upon your royal grandsire's bones,
And by the royalties of both your bloods,—
Currents that spring from one most gracious
head,—
And by the buried hand of warlike Gaunt,
And by the worth and honour of himself,

Comprising all that may be sworn or said,—
His coming hither hath no further scope
Than for his lineal royalties, and to beg
Enfranchisement immediate on his knees:
Which on thy royal party granted once,
His glittering arms he will commend to rust,
His barbed steeds to stables, and his heart
To faithful service of your majesty.
This swears he, as he is a prince, is just;
And, as I am a gentleman, I credit him.

KING RICHARD.
Northumberland, say thus the king returns:—
His noble cousin is right welcome hither;
And all the number of his fair demands
Shall be accomplisht without contradiction:
With all the gracious utterance thou hast
Speak to his gentle hearing kind commends.—
[to AUMERLE] We do debase ourself, cousin, do we not,
To look so poorly, and to speak so fair?
Shall we call back Northumberland, and send
Defiance to the traitor, and so die?

DUKE OF AUMERLE.
No, good my lord; let's fight with gentle words
Till time lend friends, and friends their helpful swords.

KING RICHARD.
O God, O God! that e'er this tongue of mine,
That laid the sentence of dread banishment
On yond proud man, should take it off again
With words of sooth! O, that I were as great
As is my grief, or lesser than my name!
Or that I could forget what I have been!
Or not remember what I must be now!
Swell'st thou, proud heart? I'll give thee scope to beat,
Since foes have scope to beat both thee and me.

DUKE OF AUMERLE.
Northumberland comes back from Bolingbroke.

KING RICHARD.
What must the king do now? must he submit?
The king shall do it: must he be deposed?
The king shall be contented: must he lose
The name of king? o' God's name, let it go:
I'll give my jewels for a set of beads,
My gorgeous palace for a hermitage,
My gay apparel for an almsman's gown,
My figured goblets for a dish of wood,
My sceptre for a palmer's walking-staff,
My subjects for a pair of carved saints,
And my large kingdom for a little grave,
A little little grave, an obscure grave;—
Or I'll be buried in the king's highway,
Some way of common trade, where subjects' feet
May hourly trample on their sovereign's head;
For on my heart they tread now whilst I live;
And buried once, why not upon my head?—
Aumerle, thou weep'st,—my tender-hearted cousin!
We'll make foul weather with despised tears;
Our sighs and they shall lodge the summer corn,
And make a dearth in this revolting land.
Or shall we play the wantons with our woes,
And make some pretty match with shedding tears?
As thus;—to drop them still upon one place,

Till they have fretted us a pair of graves
Within the earth; and, therein laid,—'There lies
Two kinsmen digg'd their graves with weeping eyes.'
Would not this ill do well?—Well, well, I see
I talk but idly, and you laugh at me.—
Most mighty prince, my Lord Northumberland,
What says King Bolingbroke? will his majesty
Give Richard leave to live till Richard die?
You make a leg, and Bolingbroke says ay.

EARL OF NORTHUMBERLAND.
My lord, in the base court he doth attend
To speak with you;—may it please you to come down.

KING RICHARD.
Down, down I come; like glistering Phaëton,
Wanting the manage of unruly jades.
In the base court? Base court, where kings grow base,
To come at traitors' calls, and do them grace.
In the base court? Come down? Down, court!
down, king!
For night-owls shriek where mounting larks should sing.   [Exeunt above.

HENRY BOLINGBROKE.
What says his majesty?

EARL OF NORTHUMBERLAND.
                Sorrow and grief of heart
Makes him speak fondly, like a frantic man:
Yet he is come.

Enter KING RICHARD *attended, below.*

HENRY BOLINGBROKE.
Stand all apart,
And show fair duty to his majesty.—
My gracious lord,—   [Kneeling.

KING RICHARD.
Fair cousin, you debase your princely knee
To make the base earth proud with kissing it:
Me rather had my heart might feel your love
Than my unpleased eye see your courtesy.
Up, cousin, up;—your heart is up, I know.
Thus high at least [touching his own head], although your knee be low.

HENRY BOLINGBROKE.
My gracious lord, I come but for mine own.

KING RICHARD.
Your own is yours, and I am yours, and all.

HENRY BOLINGBROKE.
So far be mine, my most redoubted lord,
As my true service shall deserve your love.

KING RICHARD.
Well you deserve:—they well deserve to have,
That know the strong'st and surest way to get.—
Uncle, give me your hand: nay, dry your eyes;
Tears show their love, but want their remedies.—
Cousin, I am too young to be your father,
Though you are old enough to be my heir.
What you will have, I'll give, and willing too;
For do we must what force will have us do.—
Set on towards London:—cousin, is it so?

HENRY BOLINGBROKE.
Yea, my good lord.

KING RICHARD.
          Then I must not say no.
    [Flourish.   Exeunt.

SCENE IV.

Langley. The DUKE OF YORK'S *garden.*

Enter the QUEEN *and two* LADIES.

QUEEN.

WHAT sport shall we devise here in this
　　garden,
To drive away the heavy thought of care?

FIRST LADY.

Madam, we'll play at bowls.

QUEEN.

'Twill make me think the world is full of rubs,
And that my fortune runs against the bias.

FIRST LADY.

Madame, we'll dance.

QUEEN.

My leg can　ep no measure in delight,
When my poor heart no measure keeps in grief:
Therefore, no dancing, girl; some other sport.

FIRST LADY.

Madam, we'll tell tales.

QUEEN.

Of sorrow of or joy?

FIRST LADY.

　　　　　　Of either, madam.

QUEEN.

Of neither, girl;
For if of joy, being altogether wanting,
It doth remember me the more of sorrow;
Or if of grief, being altogether had,
It adds more sorrow to my want of joy:
For what I have, I need not to repeat;
And what I want, it boots not to complain.

FIRST LADY.

Madam, I'll sing.

QUEEN.

　　　　　'Tis well that thou hast cause;
But thou shouldst please me better, wouldst thou
　　weep.

FIRST LADY.

I could weep, madam, would it do you good.

QUEEN.

And I could weep, would weeping do me good,
And never borrow any tear of thee.—
But stay, here come the gardeners:
Let's step into the shadow of these trees.
My wretchedness unto a row of pins,
They'll talk of state; for every one doth so
Against a change: woe is forerun with woe.

[QUEEN *and* LADIES *retire.*

Enter a GARDENER *and two* SERVANTS.

GARDENER.

Go, bind thou up yon dangling apricocks,
Which, like unruly children, make their sire
Stoop with oppression of their prodigal weight:
Give some supportance to the bending twigs.—
Go thou, and, like an executioner,
Cut off the heads of too-fast-growing sprays,
That look too lofty in our commonwealth:
All must be even in our government.—
You thus employ'd, I will go root away
The noisome weeds, that without profit suck
The soil's fertility from wholesome flowers.

FIRST SERVANT.

Why should we, in the compass of a pale,
Keep law and form and due proportion,

Showing, as in a model, our firm estate,
When our sea-walled garden, the whole land,
Is full of weeds; her fairest flowers choked up,
Her fruit-trees all unpruned, her hedges ruin'd,
Her knots disorder'd, and her wholesome herbs
Swarming with caterpillars?

GARDENER.

　　　　　　　Hold thy peace:—
He that hath suffer'd this disorder'd spring
Hath now himself met with the fall of leaf:
The weeds that his broad-spreading leaves did
　　shelter,
That seem'd in eating him to hold him up,
Are pluckt up root and all by Bolingbroke,—
I mean the Earl of Wiltshire, Bushy, Green.

FIRST SERVANT.

What, are they dead?

GARDENER.

　　　　　　They are; and Bolingbroke
Hath seized the wasteful king.—O, what pity is it
That he had not so trimm'd and drest his land
As we this garden! We at time of year
Do wound the bark, the skin of our fruit-trees,
Lest, being over-proud in sap and blood,
With too much riches it confound itself:
Had he done so to great and growing men,
They might have lived to bear, and he to taste
Their fruits of duty. All superfluous branches
We lop away, that bearing boughs may live:
Had he done so, himself had borne the crown,
Which waste of idle hours hath quite thrown
　　down.

FIRST SERVANT.

What, think you, then, the king shall be deposed?

GARDENER.

Deprest he is already; and deposed
'Tis doubt he will be: letters came last night
To a dear friend of the good Duke of York's,
That tell black tidings.

QUEEN.

O, I am prest to death through want of speak-
　　ing!—　　　　　[*Comes forward with* LADIES.
Thou, old Adam's likeness, set to dress this
　　garden,
How dares thy harsh rude tongue sound this un-
　　pleasing news?
What Eve, what serpent, hath suggested thee
To make a second fall of cursed man?
Why dost thou say King Richard is deposed?
Darest thou, thou little better thing than earth,
Divine his downfall? Say, where, when, and how,
Camest thou by this ill tidings? speak, thou
　　wretch.

GARDENER.

Pardon me, madam: little joy have I
To breathe this news: yet what I say is true.
King Richard, he is in the mighty hold
Of Bolingbroke: their fortunes both are weigh'd:
In your lord's scale is nothing but himself,
And some few vanities that make him light;
But in the balance of great Bolingbroke,
Besides himself, are all the English peers,
And with that odds he weighs King Richard
　　down.
Post you to London, and you will find it so;
I speak no more than every man doth know.

QUEEN.

Nimble mischance, that art so light of foot,
Doth not thy embassage belong to me,
And am I last that knows it? O, thou think'st
To serve me last, that I may longest keep
Thy sorrow in my breast.—Come, ladies, go,
To meet at London London's king in woe.—
What, was I born to this, that my sad look
Should grace the triumph of great Bolingbroke?
Gardener, for telling me this news of woe,
Pray God the plants thou graft'st may never
    grow.   [*Exeunt* QUEEN *and* LADIES.

GARDENER.

Poor queen! so that thy state might be no worse,
I would my skill were subject to thy curse.—
Here did she fall a tear; here, in this place,
I'll set a bank of rue, sour herb of grace:
Rue, even for ruth, here shortly shall be seen,
In the remembrance of a weeping queen.
                            [*Exeunt.*

ACT IV. SCENE I.

Westminster Hall.

Enter as to the Parliament BOLINGBROKE, AU-
MERLE, NORTHUMBERLAND, PERCY, FITZ-
WATER, SURREY, *another* LORD, *the* BISHOP
OF CARLISLE, *the* ABBOT OF WESTMINSTER,
and ATTENDANTS. HERALD, OFFICERS, *and*
BAGOT.

HENRY BOLINGBROKE.

CALL forth Bagot.
    Now, Bagot, freely speak thy mind;
What dost thou know of noble Gloster's death;
Who wrought it with the king, and who per-
    form'd
The bloody office of his timeless end.

BAGOT.

Then set before my face the Lord Aumerle.

HENRY BOLINGBROKE.

Cousin, stand forth, and look upon that man.

BAGOT.

My Lord Aumerle, I know your daring tongue
Scorns to unsay what once it hath deliver'd.
In that dead time when Gloster's death was
    plotted,
I heard you say,—'Is not my arm of length,
That reacheth from the restful English court
As far as Calais, to my uncle's head?'
Amongst much other talk, that very time,
I heard you say that you had rather refuse
The offer of an hundred thousand crowns
Than Bolingbroke's return to England;
Adding withal, how blest this land would be
In this your cousin's death.

DUKE OF AUMERLE.

                    Princes, and noble lords,
What answer shall I make to this base man?
Shall I so much dishonour my fair stars,
On equal terms to give him chastisement?
Either I must, or have mine honour soil'd
With the attainder of his slanderous lips.—
There is my gage, the manual seal of death,
That marks thee out for hell: I say, thou liest,
And will maintain what thou hast said is false

In thy heart-blood, though being all too base
To stain the temper of my knightly sword.

HENRY BOLINGBROKE.

Bagot, forbear; thou shalt not take it up.

DUKE OF AUMERLE.

Excepting one, I would he were the best
In all this presence that hath moved me so.

LORD FITZWATER.

If that thy valour stand on sympathy,
There is my gage, Aumerle, in gage to thine:
By that fair sun which shows me where thou
    stand'st,
I heard thee say, and vauntingly thou spakest it
That thou wert cause of noble Gloster's death.
If thou deny'st it twenty times, thou liest;
And I will turn thy falsehood to thy heart,
Where it was forged, with my rapier's point.

DUKE OF AUMERLE.

Thou darest not, coward, live to see that day.

LORD FITZWATER.

Now, by my soul, I would it were this hour.

DUKE OF AUMERLE.

Fitzwater, thou art damn'd to hell for this.

HENRY PERCY.

Aumerle, thou liest; his honour is as true
In this appeal as thou art all unjust;
And that thou art so, there I throw my gage,
To prove it on thee to th' extremest point
Of mortal breathing: seize it, if thou darest.

DUKE OF AUMERLE.

And if I do not, may my hands rot off,
And never brandish more revengeful steel
Over the glittering helmet of my foe!

ANOTHER LORD.

I task the earth to the like, forsworn Aumerle;
And spur thee on with full as many lies
As may be holla'd in thy treacherous ear
From sun to sun: there is my honour's pawn;
Engage it to the trial, if thou darest.

DUKE OF AUMERLE.

Who sets me else? by heaven, I'll throw at all:
I have a thousand spirits in one breast,
To answer twenty thousand such as you.

DUKE OF SURREY.

My Lord Fitzwater, I do remember well
The very time Aumerle and you did talk.

LORD FITZWATER.

'Tis very true: you were in presence then;
And you can witness with me this is true.

DUKE OF SURREY.

As false, by heaven, as heaven itself is true.

LORD FITZWATER.

Surrey, thou liest.

DUKE OF SURREY.

                Dishonourable boy!
That lie shall lie so heavy on my sword,
That it shall render vengeance and revenge
Till thou the lie-giver and that lie do lie
In earth as quiet as thy father's skull:
In proof whereof, there is my honour's pawn;
Engage it to the trial, if thou darest.

LORD FITZWATER.

How fondly dost thou spur a forward horse!
If I dare eat, or drink, or breathe, or live,
I dare meet Surrey in a wilderness,
And spit upon him, whilst I say he lies,

And lies, and lies: there is my bond of faith,
To tie thee to my strong correction.—
As I intend to thrive in this new world,
Aumerle is guilty of my true appeal:
Besides, I heard the banisht Norfolk say,
That thou, Aumerle, didst send two of thy men
To execute the noble duke at Calais.

DUKE OF AUMERLE.

Some honest Christian trust me with a gage,
That Norfolk lies: here do I throw down this,
If he may be repeal'd, to try his honour.

HENRY BOLINGBROKE.

These differences shall all rest under gage
Till Norfolk be repeal'd: repeal'd he shall be,
And, though mine enemy, restored again
To all his lands and signories: when he's return'd,
Against Aumerle we will enforce his trial.

BISHOP OF CARLISLE.

That honourable day shall ne'er be seen.
Many a time hath banisht Norfolk fought
For Jesu Christ in glorious Christian field,
Streaming the ensign of the Christian cross
Against black pagans, Turks, and Saracens;
And toil'd with works of war, retired himself
To Italy; and there, at Venice, gave
His body to that pleasant country's earth,
And his pure soul unto his captain Christ,
Under whose colours he had fought so long.

HENRY BOLINGBROKE.

Why, bishop, is Norfolk dead?

BISHOP OF CARLISLE.

As surely as I live, my lord.

HENRY BOLINGBROKE.

Sweet peace conduct his sweet soul to the bosom
Of good old Abraham!—Lords appellants,
Your differences shall all rest under gage
Till we assign you to your days of trial.

Enter YORK, *attended.*

DUKE OF YORK.

Great Duke of Lancaster, I come to thee
From plume-pluckt Richard; who with willing
    soul
Adopts thee heir, and his high sceptre yields
To the possession of thy royal hand:
Ascend his throne, descending now from him,—
And long live Henry, fourth of that name!

HENRY BOLINGBROKE.

In God's name, I'll ascend the regal throne.

BISHOP OF CARLISLE.

Marry, God forbid!—
Worst in this royal presence may I speak,
Yet best beseeming me to speak the truth.
Would God that any in this noble presence
Were enough noble to be upright judge
Of noble Richard! then true noblesse would
Learn him forbearance from so foul a wrong.
What subject can give sentence on his king?
And who sits here that is not Richard's subject?
Thieves are not judged but they are by to hear,
Although apparent guilt be seen in them;
And shall the figure of God's majesty,
His captain, steward, deputy elect,
Anointed, crowned, planted many years,
Be judged by subject and inferior breath,
And he himself not present? O, forfend it, God,
That in a Christian climate, souls refined

Should show so heinous, black, obscene a deed!
I speak to subjects, and a subject speaks,
Stirr'd up by God, thus boldly for his king.
My Lord of Hereford here, whom you call king,
Is a foul traitor to proud Hereford's king;
And if you crown him, let me prophesy,—
The blood of English shall manure the ground,
And future ages groan for this foul act;
Peace shall go sleep with Turks and infidels,
And in this seat of peace tumultuous wars
Shall kin with kin and kind with kind confound;
Disorder, horror, fear, and mutiny,
Shall here inhabit, and this land be call'd
The field of Golgotha and dead men's skulls.
O, if you raise this house against this house,
It will the wofullest division prove
That ever fell upon this cursed earth.
Prevent, resist it, let it not be so,
Lest child, child's children cry against you 'woe!'

EARL OF NORTHUMBERLAND.

Well have you argued, sir; and, for your pains,
Of capital treason we arrest you here.—
My Lord of Westminster, be it your charge
To keep him safely till his day of trial.—   [suit.
May it please you, lords, to grant the commons'

HENRY BOLINGBROKE.

Fetch hither Richard, that in common view
He may surrender; so we shall proceed
Without suspicion.

DUKE OF YORK.

               I will be his conduct.   [*Exit.*

HENRY BOLINGBROKE.

Lords, you that here are under our arrest,
Procure your sureties for your days of answer.—
Little are we beholding to your love,
                              [*to* CARLISLE.
And little lookt for at your helping hands.

Enter YORK, *with* KING RICHARD, *and*
        OFFICERS *bearing the crown, &c.*

KING RICHARD.

Alack, why am I sent for to a king,
Before I have shook off the regal thoughts
Wherewith I reign'd? I hardly yet have learn'd
To insinuate, flatter, bow, and bend my knee:
Give sorrow leave awhile to tutor me
To this submission. Yet I well remember
The favours of these men: were they not mine?
Did they not sometime cry, 'All hail!' to me?
So Judas did to Christ: but he, in twelve,
Found truth in all but one; I, in twelve thousand,
    none.
God save the king!—Will no man say amen?
Am I both priest and clerk? well then, amen.
God save the king! although I be not he;
And yet, amen, if heaven do think him me.—
To do what service am I sent for hither?

DUKE OF YORK.

To do that office of thine own good will
Which tired majesty did make thee offer,—
The resignation of thy state and crown
To Henry Bolingbroke.

KING RICHARD.

Give me the crown.—Here, cousin, seize the
    crown;
Here, cousin:
On this side my hand, and on that side yours.

Now is this golden crown like a deep well
That owes two buckets, filling one another;
The emptier ever dancing in the air,
The other down, unseen, and full of water:
That bucket down and full of tears am I,
Drinking my griefs, whilst you mount up on high.

HENRY BOLINGBROKE.
I thought you had been willing to resign.

KING RICHARD.
My crown I am; but still my griefs are mine:
You may my glories and my state depose,
But not my griefs; still am I king of those.

HENRY BOLINGBROKE.
Part of your cares you give me with your crown.

KING RICHARD.
Your cares set up do not pluck my cares down.
My care is, loss of care, by old care done;
Your care is, gain of care, by new care won:
The cares I give, I have, though given away;
They tend the crown, yet still with me they stay.

HENRY BOLINGBROKE.
Are you contented to resign the crown?

KING RICHARD.
Ay, no;—no, ay; for I must nothing be;
Therefore no no, for I resign to thee.
Now mark me, how I will undo myself:—
I give this heavy weight from off my head,
And this unwieldy sceptre from my hand,
The pride of kingly sway from out my heart;
With mine own tears I wash away my balm,
With mine own hands I give away my crown,
With mine own tongue deny my sacred state,
With mine own breath release all duty's rites:
All pomp and majesty I do forswear;
My manors, rents, revenues I forgo;
My acts, decrees, and statutes I deny:
God pardon all oaths that are broke to me!
God keep all vows unbroke that swear to thee!
Make me, that nothing have, with nothing
    grieved,
And thou with all pleased, that hast all achieved!
Long mayst thou live in Richard's seat to sit,
And soon lie Richard in an earthy pit!
God save King Henry, unking'd Richard says,
And send him many years of sunshine days!—
What more remains?

EARL OF NORTHUMBERLAND.
                No more, but that you read
                    [Offering a paper.
These accusations, and these grievous crimes
Committed by your person and your followers
Against the state and profit of this land;
That, by confessing them, the souls of men
May deem that you are worthily deposed.

KING RICHARD.
Must I do so? and must I ravel out
My weaved-up follies? Gentle Northumberland,
If thy offences were upon record,
Would it not shame thee in so fair a troop
To read a lecture of them? If thou wouldst,
There shouldst thou find one heinous article,—
Containing the deposing of a king,
And cracking the strong warrant of an oath,—
Markt with a blot, damn'd in the book of
    heaven:—
Nay, all of you that stand and look upon,

Whilst that my wretchedness doth bait myself,—
Though some of you, with Pilate, wash your
    hands,
Showing an outward pity; yet you Pilates
Have here deliver'd me to my sour cross,
And water cannot wash away your sin.

EARL OF NORTHUMBERLAND.
My lord, dispatch; read o'er these articles.

KING RICHARD.
Mine eyes are full of tears, I cannot see:
And yet salt water blinds them not so much
But they can see a sort of traitors here.
Nay, if I turn mine eyes upon myself,
I find myself a traitor with the rest;
For I have given here my soul's consent
T'undeck the pompous body of a king;
Made glory base, and sovereignty a slave,
Proud majesty a subject, state a peasant.

EARL OF NORTHUMBERLAND.
My lord,—

KING RICHARD.
No lord of thine, thou haught-insulting man,
Nor no man's lord; I have no name, no title,—
No, not that name was given me at the font,—
But 'tis usurpt:—alack the heavy day,
That I have worn so many winters out,
And know not now what name to call myself!
O, that I were a mockery-king of snow,
Standing before the sun of Bolingbroke,
To melt myself away in water-drops!—
Good king,—great king,—and yet not greatly
    good,—
An if my word be sterling yet in England,
Let it command a mirror hither straight,
That it may show me what a face I have,
Since it is bankrupt of his majesty.

HENRY BOLINGBROKE.
Go, some of you, and fetch a looking-glass.
                        [Exit an ATTENDANT.

EARL OF NORTHUMBERLAND.
Read o'er this paper while the glass doth come.

KING RICHARD.
Fiend, thou torment'st me ere I come to hell!

HENRY BOLINGBROKE.
Urge it no more, my Lord Northumberland.

EARL OF NORTHUMBERLAND.
The commons will not, then, be satisfied.

KING RICHARD.
They shall be satisfied: I'll read enough,
When I do see the very book indeed
Where all my sins are writ, and that's myself.
                Enter ATTENDANT *with a glass.*
Give me the glass, and therein will I read.—
No deeper wrinkles yet? hath sorrow struck
So many blows upon this face of mine,
And made no deeper wounds!—O flattering glass,
Like to my followers in prosperity,
Thou dost beguile me! Was this face the face
That every day under his household roof
Did keep ten thousand men? was this the face
That, like the sun, did make beholders wink?
Was this the face that faced so many follies,
And was at last out-faced by Bolingbroke?
A brittle glory shineth in this face:
As brittle as the glory is the face;
                [*Dashes the glass against the groun*

For there it is, crackt in a hundred shivers.—
Mark, silent king, the moral of this sport,—
How soon my sorrow hath destroy'd my face.
    HENRY BOLINGBROKE.
The shadow of your sorrow hath destroy'd
The shadow of your face.
    KING RICHARD.
         Say that again.
The shadow of my sorrow? ha! let 's see:—
'Tis very true, my grief lies all within;
And these external manners of lament
Are merely shadows to the unseen grief
That swells with silence in the tortured soul;
There lies the substance: and I thank thee, king,
For thy great bounty, that not only givest
Me cause to wail, but teachest me the way
How to lament the cause. I'll beg one boon,
And then be gone and trouble you no more.
Shall I obtain it?
    HENRY BOLINGBROKE.
         Name it, fair cousin.
    KING HENRY.
Fair cousin! I am greater than a king:
For when I was a king, my flatterers
Were then but subjects; being now a subject,
I have a king here to my flatterer.
Being so great, I have no need to beg.
    HENRY BOLINGBROKE.
Yet ask.
    KING RICHARD.
And shall I have?
    HENRY BOLINGBROKE.
You shall.
    KING RICHARD.
Then give me leave to go.
    HENRY BOLINGBROKE.
Whither?
    KING RICHARD.
Whither you will, so I were from your sights.
    HENRY BOLINGBROKE.
Go, some of you convey him to the Tower.
    KING RICHARD.
O, good! convey?—conveyers are you all,
That rise thus nimbly by a true king's fall.
    [Exeunt KING RICHARD, some LORDS,
        and a GUARD.
    HENRY BOLINGBROKE.
On Wednesday next we solemnly set down
Our coronation: lords, prepare yourselves.
    [Exeunt all except the BISHOP OF CAR-
    LISLE, the ABBOT OF WESTMINSTER,
    and AUMERLE.
    ABBOT OF WESTMINSTER.
A woful pageant have we here beheld.
    BISHOP OF CARLISLE.
The woe's to come; the children yet unborn
Shall feel this day as sharp to them as thorn.
    DUKE OF AUMERLE.
You holy clergymen, is there no plot
To rid the realm of this pernicious blot?
    ABBOT OF WESTMINSTER.
My lord,
Before I freely speak my mind herein,
You shall not only take the sacrament
To bury mine intents, but also to effect
Whatever I shall happen to devise.—

I see your brows are full of discontent,
Your hearts of sorrow, and your eyes of tears:
Come home with me to supper: I will lay
A plot shall show us all a merry day.   [Exeunt

ACT V.   SCENE I.

London.   A street leading to the Tower.

Enter QUEEN *and* LADIES.

    QUEEN.
THIS way the king will come; this is the way
  To Julius Caesar's ill-erected tower,
To whose flint bosom my condemned lord
Is doom'd a prisoner by proud Bolingbroke:
Here let us rest, if this rebellious earth
Have any resting for her true king's queen.—
But soft, but see, or rather do not see,
My fair rose wither: yet look up, behold,
That you in pity may dissolve to dew,
And wash him fresh again with true-love tears.
    Enter KING RICHARD *and* GUARDS.
Ah, thou, the model where old Troy did stand,
Thou map of honour, thou King Richard's tomb,
And not King Richard; thou most beauteous inn,
Why should hard-favour'd grief be lodged in
    thee,
When triumph is become an alehouse guest?
    KING RICHARD.
Join not with grief, fair woman, do not so,
To make my end too sudden: learn, good soul,
To think our former state a happy dream;
From which awaked, the truth of what we are
Shows us but this: I am sworn brother, sweet,
To grim Necessity; and he and I
Will keep a league till death. Hie thee to France,
And cloister thee in some religious house:
Our holy lives must win a new world's crown,
Which our profane hours here have stricken
    down.
    QUEEN.
What, is my Richard both in shape and mind
Transform'd and weaken'd? hath Bolingbroke
    deposed
Thine intellect? hath he been in thy heart?
The lion dying thrusteth forth his paw,
And wounds the earth, if nothing else, with rage
To be o'erpower'd; and wilt thou, pupil-like,
Take thy correction mildly, kiss the rod,
And fawn on rage with base humility,
Which art a lion and a king of beasts?
    KING RICHARD.
A king of beasts, indeed; if aught but beasts,
I had been still a happy king of men.
Good sometime queen, prepare thee hence for
    France:
Think I am dead; and that even here thou takest,
As from my death-bed, thy last living leave.
In winter's tedious nights sit by the fire
With good old folks, and let them tell thee tales
Of woful ages long ago betid;
And ere thou bid good night, to quit their griefs
Tell thou the lamentable tale of me,
And send the hearers weeping to their beds:
For why the senseless brands will sympathize
The heavy accent of thy moving tongue,
And in compassion weep the fire out;

And some will mourn in ashes, some coal-black,
For the deposing of a rightful king.

Enter NORTHUMBERLAND *attended.*

EARL OF NORTHUMBERLAND.

My lord, the mind of Bolingbroke is changed;
You must to Pomfret, not unto the Tower.—
And, madam, there is order ta'en for you;
With all swift speed you must away to France.

KING RICHARD.

Northumberland, thou ladder wherewithal
The mounting Bolingbroke ascends my throne,
The time shall not be many hours of age
More than it is, ere foul sin gathering head
Shall break into corruption: thou shalt think,
Though he divide the realm, and give thee half,
It is too little, helping him to all;
And he shall think, that thou, which know'st the way
To plant unrightful kings, wilt know again,
Being ne'er so little urged, another way
To pluck him headlong from the usurped throne.
The love of wicked friends converts to fear;
That fear to hate; and hate turns one or both
To worthy danger and deserved death.

EARL OF NORTHUMBERLAND.

My guilt be on my head, and there an end.
Take leave, and part; for you must part forthwith.

KING RICHARD.

Doubly divorced!—Bad men, you violate
A twofold marriage,—'twixt my crown and me,
And then betwixt me and my married wife.—
Let me unkiss the oath 'twixt thee and me;
And yet not so, for with a kiss 'twas made.—
Part us, Northumberland; I towards the north,
Where shivering cold and sickness pines the clime;
My wife to France,—from whence, set forth in pomp,
She came adorned hither like sweet May,
Sent back to Hallowmas or short'st of day.

QUEEN.

And must we be divided? must we part?

KING RICHARD.

Ay, hand from hand, my love, and heart from heart.

QUEEN.

Banish us both, and send the king with me.

EARL OF NORTHUMBERLAND.

That were some love, but little policy.

QUEEN.

Then whither he goes, thither let me go.

KING RICHARD.

So two, together weeping, make one woe.
Weep thou for me in France, I for thee here;
Better far off than, near, be ne'er the near.
Go, count thy way with sighs; I, mine with groans.

QUEEN.

So longest way shall have the longest moans.

KING RICHARD.

Twice for one step I'll groan, the way being short,
And piece the way out with a heavy heart.
Come, come, in wooing sorrow let's be brief,
Since, wedding it, there is such length in grief:

One kiss shall stop our mouths, and dumbly part;
Thus give I mine, and thus take I thy heart.

[*They kiss.*

QUEEN.

Give me mine own again; 'twere no good part
To take on me to keep and kill thy heart.

[*They kiss again.*

So, now I have mine own again, be gone,
That I may strive to kill it with a groan.

KING RICHARD.

We make woe wanton with this fond delay:
Once more, adieu; the rest let sorrow say.

[*Exeunt.*

SCENE II.

The DUKE OF YORK'S *palace.*

Enter YORK *and his* DUCHESS.

DUCHESS OF YORK.

MY lord, you told me you would tell the rest,
When weeping made you break the story off
Of our two cousins coming into London.

DUKE OF YORK.

Where did I leave?

DUCHESS OF YORK.

At that sad stop, my lord,
Where rude misgovern'd hands from windows' tops
Threw dust and rubbish on King Richard's head.

DUKE OF YORK.

Then, as I said, the duke, great Bolingbroke,—
Mounted upon a hot and fiery steed,
Which his aspiring rider seem'd to know,—
With slow but stately pace kept on his course,
While all tongues cried, 'God save thee, Bolingbroke!'
You would have thought the very windows spake,
So many greedy looks of young and old
Through casements darted their desiring eyes
Upon his visage; and that all the walls
With painted imagery had said at once,
'Jesu preserve thee! welcome, Bolingbroke!'
Whilst he, from one side to the other turning,
Bareheaded, lower than his proud steed's neck,
Bespake them thus,—'I thank you, countrymen:'
And thus still doing, thus he past along.

DUCHESS OF YORK.

Alack, poor Richard! where rode he the whilst?

DUKE OF YORK.

As in a theatre, the eyes of men,
After a well-graced actor leaves the stage,
Are idly bent on him that enters next,
Thinking his prattle to be tedious;
Even so, or with much more contempt, men's eyes
Did scowl on gentle Richard; no man cried, 'God save him!'
No joyful tongue gave him his welcome home:
But dust was thrown upon his sacred head;
Which with such gentle sorrow he shook off,—
His face still combating with tears and smiles,
The badges of his grief and patience,—
That had not God, for some strong purpose, steel'd
The hearts of men, they must perforce have melted,

And barbarism itself have pitied him.
But heaven hath a hand in these events,
To whose high will we bound our calm contents.
To Bolingbroke are we sworn subjects now,
Whose state and honour I for aye allow.
DUCHESS OF YORK.
Here comes my son Aumerle.
DUKE OF YORK.
                    Aumerle that was;
But that is lost for being Richard's friend,
And, madam, you must call him Rutland now:
I am in parliament pledge for his truth
And lasting fealty to the new-made king.
Enter AUMERLE.
DUCHESS OF YORK.
Welcome, my son: who are the violets now
That strew the green lap of the new-come
    spring?
DUKE OF AUMERLE.
Madam, I know not, nor I greatly care not:
God knows I had as lief be none as one.
DUKE OF YORK.
Well, bear you well in this new spring of time,
Lest you be cropt before you come to prime.
What news from Oxford?—hold those justs and
    triumphs?
DUKE OF AUMERLE.
For aught I know, my lord, they do.
DUKE OF YORK.
You will be there, I know.
DUKE OF AUMERLE.
If God prevent not, I do purpose so.
DUKE OF YORK.
What seal is that that hangs without thy bosom?
Yea, look'st thou pale? let me see the writing.
DUKE OF AUMERLE.
My lord, 'tis nothing.
DUKE OF YORK.
             No matter, then, who see it:
I will be satisfied; let me see the writing.
DUKE OF AUMERLE.
I do beseech your Grace to pardon me:
It is a matter of small consequence,
Which for some reasons I would not have seen.
DUKE OF YORK.
Which for some reasons, sir, I mean to see.
I fear, I fear,—
DUCHESS OF YORK.
          What should you fear?
'Tis nothing but some band that he is enter'd
    into
For gay apparel 'gainst the triumph-day.
DUKE OF YORK.
Bound to himself! what doth he with a bond
That he is bound to? Wife, thou art a fool.—
Boy, let me see the writing.
DUKE OF AUMERLE.
I do beseech you, pardon me; I may not show it.
DUKE OF YORK.
I will be satisfied: let me see 't, I say.
    [*He plucks it out of his bosom and reads it.*
Treason! foul treason!—Villain! traitor! slave!
DUCHESS OF YORK.
What is the matter, my lord!
DUKE OF YORK.
Ho! who is within there? ho!

Enter a SERVANT.
                 Saddle my horse.—
God for his mercy, what treachery is here!
DUCHESS OF YORK.
Why, what is it, my lord?
DUKE OF YORK.
Give me my boots, I say; saddle my horse,—
                [*Exit* SERVANT.
Now, by mine honour, by my life, by my troth,
I will appeach the villain.
DUCHESS OF YORK.
              What is the matter?
DUKE OF YORK.
Peace, foolish woman.
DUCHESS OF YORK.
I will not peace.—What is the matter, Aumerle?
DUKE OF AUMERLE.
Good mother, be content; it is no more
Than my poor life must answer.
DUCHESS OF YORK.
               Thy life answer!
DUKE OF YORK.
Bring me my boots:—I will unto the king.
His MAN *enters with his boots.*
DUCHESS OF YORK.
Strike him, Aumerle.—Poor boy, thou art
    amazed.—
Hence, villain! never more come in my sight.
DUKE OF YORK.
Give me my boots, I say.
DUCHESS OF YORK.
Why, York, what wilt thou do?
Wilt thou not hide the trespass of thine own?
Have we more sons? or are we like to have?
Is not my teeming date drunk up with time?
And wilt thou pluck my fair son from mine age,
And rob me of a happy mother's name?
Is he not like thee? is he not thine own?
DUKE OF YORK.
Thou fond mad woman,
Wilt thou conceal this dark conspiracy?
A dozen of them here have ta'en the sacrament,
And interchangeably set down their hands,
To kill the king at Oxford.
DUCHESS OF YORK.
           He shall be none;
We'll keep him here: then what is that to him?
DUKE OF YORK.
Away, fond woman! were he twenty times my son,
I would appeach him.
DUCHESS OF YORK.
          Hadst thou groan'd for him
As I have done, thou wouldst be more pitiful.
But now I know thy mind; thou dost suspect
That I have been disloyal to thy bed,
And that he is a bastard, not thy son:
Sweet York, sweet husband, be not of that mind:
He is as like thee as a man may be,
Not like to me, nor any of my kin,
And yet I love him.
DUKE OF YORK.
         Make way, unruly woman!
                      [*Exit.*
DUCHESS OF YORK.
After, Aumerle, mount thee upon his horse;
Spur post, and get before him to the king,

And beg thy pardon ere he do accuse thee.
I'll not be long behind; though I be old,
I doubt not but to ride as fast as York;
And never will I rise up from the ground
Till Bolingbroke have pardon'd thee. Away, be
    gone!   [*Exeunt.*

SCENE III.

Windsor Castle.

Enter BOLINGBROKE, PERCY, *and other* LORDS.

HENRY BOLINGBROKE.

CAN no man tell me of my unthrifty son?
   'Tis full three months since I did see him
last:—
If any plague hang over us, 'tis he.
I would to God, my lords, he might be found:
Inquire at London, 'mongst the taverns there,
For there, they say, he daily doth frequent,
With unrestrained loose companions,—
Even such, they say, as stand in narrow lanes,
And beat our watch, and rob our passengers;
While he, young wanton and effeminate boy,
Takes on the point of honour to support
So dissolute a crew.

HENRY PERCY.

My lord, some two days since I saw the prince,
And told him of those triumphs held at Oxford.

HENRY BOLINGBROKE.

And what said the gallant?

HENRY PERCY.

His answer was,—he would unto the stews,
And from the common'st creature pluck a glove,
And wear it as a favour; and with that
He would unhorse the lustiest challenger.

HENRY BOLINGBROKE.

As dissolute as desperate; yet through both
I see some sparkles of a better hope,
Which elder days may happily bring forth.—
But who comes here?

Enter AUMERLE, *hastily.*

DUKE OF AUMERLE.

           Where is the king?

HENRY BOLINGBROKE.

                  What means
Our cousin, that he stares and looks so wildly?

DUKE OF AUMERLE.

God save your Grace! I do beseech your maj-
    esty,
To have some conference with your Grace alone.

HENRY BOLINGBROKE.

Withdraw yourselves, and leave us here alone.
        [*Exeunt* PERCY *and* LORDS.
What is the matter with our cousin now?

DUKE OF AUMERLE.

For ever may my knees grow to the earth,
                [*Kneels.*
My tongue cleave to my roof within my mouth,
Unless a pardon ere I rise or speak.

HENRY BOLINGBROKE.

Intended or committed was this fault?
If on the first, how heinous e'er it be,
To win thy after-love I pardon thee.

DUKE OF AUMERLE.

Then give me leave that I may turn the key,
That no man enter till my tale be done.

HENRY BOLINGBROKE.

Have thy desire.

DUKE OF YORK [*within*].

My liege, beware; look to thyself;
Thou hast a traitor in thy presence there.

HENRY BOLINGBROKE.

Villain, I'll make thee safe.   [*Drawing.*

DUKE OF AUMERLE.

Stay thy revengeful hand; thou hast no cause to
    fear.

DUKE OF YORK [*within*].

Open the door, secure, foolhardy king:
Shall I, for love, speak treason to thy face?
Open the door, or I will break it open.

Enter YORK.

HENRY BOLINGBROKE.

What is the matter, uncle? speak;
Recover breath; tell us how near is danger,
That we may arm us to encounter it.

DUKE OF YORK.

Peruse this writing here, and thou shalt know
The treason that my haste forbids me show.

DUKE OF AUMERLE.

Remember, as thou read'st, thy promise past:
I do repent me; read not my name there;
My heart is not confederate with my hand.

DUKE OF YORK.

It was, villain, ere thy hand did set it down.—
I tore it from the traitor's bosom, king;
Fear, and not love, begets his penitence:
Forget to pity him, lest thy pity prove
A serpent that will sting thee to the heart.

HENRY BOLINGBROKE.

O heinous, strong, and bold conspiracy!—
O loyal father of a treacherous son!
Thou sheer, immaculate, and silver fountain,
From whence this stream through muddy
    passages
Hath held his current, and defiled himself!
Thy overflow of good converts to bad;
And thy abundant goodness shall excuse
This deadly blot in thy digressing son.

DUKE OF YORK.

So shall my virtue be his vice's bawd;
And he shall spend mine honour with his
    shame,
As thriftless sons their scraping fathers' gold.
Mine honour lives when his dishonour dies,
Or my shamed life in his dishonour lies:
Thou kill'st me in his life; giving him breath,
The traitor lives, the true man's put to death.

DUCHESS OF YORK [*within*].

What ho, my liege! for God's sake, let me in.

HENRY BOLINGBROKE.

What shrill-voiced suppliant makes this eager
    cry?

DUCHESS OF YORK [*within*].

A woman, and thy aunt, great king; 'tis I.
Speak with me, pity me, open the door:
A beggar begs that never begg'd before.

HENRY BOLINGBROKE.

Our scene is alter'd from a serious thing,
And now changed to 'The Beggar and the
    King.'—
My dangerous cousin, let your mother in:
I know she is come to pray for your foul sin.

DUKE OF YORK.
If thou do pardon, whosoever pray,
More sins, for this forgiveness, prosper may.
This fester'd joint cut off, the rest rest sound;
This let alone will all the rest confound.
          Enter DUCHESS.
DUCHESS OF YORK.
O king, believe not this hard-hearted man!
Love, loving not itself, none other can.
          DUKE OF YORK.
Thou frantic woman, what dost thou make here?
Shall thy old dugs once more a traitor rear?
          DUCHESS OF YORK.
Sweet York, be patient.—Hear me, gentle liege.
                              [*Kneels.*
          HENRY BOLINGBROKE.
Rise up, good aunt.
          DUCHESS OF YORK.
                    Not yet, I thee beseech:
For ever will I walk upon my knees,
And never see day that the happy sees,
Till thou give joy; until thou bid me joy,
By pardoning Rutland, my transgressing boy.
          DUKE OF AUMERLE.
Unto my mother's prayers I bend my knee.
                              [*Kneels.*
          DUKE OF YORK.
Against them both my true joints bended be.
                              [*Kneels.*
Ill mayst thou thrive, if thou grant any grace!
          DUCHESS OF YORK.
Pleads he in earnest? look upon his face;
His eyes do drop no tears, his prayers are in jest;
His words come from his mouth, ours from our
          breast:
He prays but faintly, and would be denied;
We pray with heart and soul, and all beside:
His weary joints would gladly rise, I know;
Our knees shall kneel till to the ground they grow:
His prayers are full of false hypocrisy;
Ours of true zeal and deep integrity.
Our prayers do out-pray his; then let them have
That mercy which true prayer ought to have.
          HENRY BOLINGBROKE.
Good aunt, stand up.
          DUCHESS OF YORK.
                    Nay, do not say 'stand up;'
But 'pardon' first, and afterwards 'stand up.'
An if I were thy nurse, thy tongue to teach,
'Pardon' should be the first word of thy speech.
I never long'd to hear a word till now;
Say 'pardon' king; let pity teach thee how:
The word is short, but not so short as sweet;
No word like 'pardon' for kings' mouths so meet.
          DUKE OF YORK.
Speak it in French, king; say, *pardonne moi.*
          DUCHESS OF YORK.
Dost thou teach pardon pardon to destroy?
Ah, my sour husband, my hard-hearted lord,
That sett'st the word itself against the word!—
Speak 'pardon' as 'tis current in our land;
The chopping French we do not understand.
Thine eye begins to speak, set thy tongue there:
Or in thy piteous heart plant thou thine ear;
That hearing how our plaints and prayers do
Pity may move thee 'pardon' to rehearse. [pierce,

          HENRY BOLINGBROKE.
Good aunt, stand up.
          DUCHESS OF YORK.
                    I do not sue to stand;
Pardon is all the suit I have in hand.
          HENRY BOLINGBROKE.
I pardon him, as God shall pardon me.
          DUCHESS OF YORK.
O happy vantage of a kneeling knee!
Yet am I sick for fear: speak it again;
Twice saying 'pardon' doth not pardon twain,
But makes one pardon strong.
          HENRY BOLINGBROKE.
                    With all my heart
I pardon him.
          DUCHESS OF YORK.
          A god on earth thou art.
          HENRY BOLINGBROKE.
But for our trusty brother-in-law, and the abbot,
With all the rest of that consorted crew,
Destruction straight shall dog them at the heels.—
Good uncle, help to order several powers
To Oxford, or where'er these traitors are:
They shall not live within this world, I swear,
But I will have them, if I once know where.
Uncle, farewell:—and, cousin too, adieu:
Your mother well hath pray'd, and prove you
          true.
          DUCHESS OF YORK.
Come, my old son:—I pray God make thee new.
                              [*Exeunt.*

SCENE IV.

The same.

Enter SIR PIERCE OF EXTON *and a* SERVANT.

          SIR PIERCE OF EXTON.
DIDST thou not mark the king, what words he
          spake,—
'Have I no friend will rid me of this living fear?'
Was it not so?
          SERVANT.
          Those were his very words.
          SIR PIERCE OF EXTON.
'Have I no friend?' quoth he: he spake it twice,
And urged it twice together,—did he not?
          SERVANT.
He did.
          SIR PIERCE OF EXTON.
And speaking it, he wistly lookt on me;
As who should say,—'I would thou wert the man
That would divorce this terror from my heart,'—
Meaning the king at Pomfret. Come, let's go:
I am the king's friend, and will rid his foe.
                              [*Exeunt.*

SCENE V.

Pomfret Castle.

Enter KING RICHARD.

          KING RICHARD.
I HAVE been studying how I may compare
This prison where I live unto the world:
And, for because the world is populous,
And here is not a creature but myself,
I cannot do it; —yet I'll hammer it out.
My brain I'll prove the female to my soul,

My soul the father: and these two beget
A generation of still-breeding thoughts,
And these same thoughts people this little world;
In humours like the people of this world,
For no thought is contented. The better sort,—
As thoughts of things divine,—are intermixt
With scruples, and do set the word itself
Against the word:
As thus, 'Come, little ones;' and then again,
'It is as hard to come as for a camel
To thread the postern of a small needle's eye.'
Thoughts tending to ambition, they do plot
Unlikely wonders; how these vain weak nails
May tear a passage through the flinty rib
Of this hard world, my ragged prison-walls;
And, for they cannot, die in their own pride.
Thoughts tending to content flatter themselves
That they are not the first of fortune's slaves,
Nor shall not be the last; like silly beggars,
Who, sitting in the stocks, refuge their shame,
That many have and others must sit there;
And in this thought they find a kind of ease,
Bearing their own misfortunes on the back
Of such as have before endured the like.
Thus play I, in one person, many people,
And none contented: sometimes am I king;
Then treason makes me wish myself a beggar,
And so I am: then crushing penury
Persuades me I was better when a king;
Then am I king'd again: and by and by
Think that I am unking'd by Bolingbroke,
And straight am nothing:—but whate'er I be,
Nor I, nor any man that but man is,
With nothing shall be pleased, till he be eased
With being nothing.—Music do I hear? [Music.
Ha, ha! keep time:—how sour sweet music is,
When time is broke and no proportion kept!
So is it in the music of men's lives.
And here have I the daintiness of ear
To check time broke in a disorder'd string;
But, for the concord of my state and time,
Had not an ear to hear my true time broke.
I wasted time, and now doth time waste me;
For now hath time made me his numbering
    clock;
My thoughts are minutes; and with sighs the—
    jar
Their watches to mine eyes, the outward watch,
Whereto my finger, like a dial's point,
Is pointing still, in cleansing them from tears:
Now, sir, the sound that tells what hour it is,
Are clamorous groans, which strike upon my
    heart,
Which is the bell: so sighs and tears and groans
Show minutes, times, and hours:—but my time
Runs posting on in Bolingbroke's proud joy,
While I stand fooling here, his Jack o' th' clock.
This music mads me; let it sound no more;
For though it have holp madmen to their wits,
In me it seems it will make wise men mad.
Yet, blessing on his heart that gives it me!
For 'tis a sign of love; and love to Richard
Is a strange brooch in this all-hating world.
          Enter GROOM.
                    GROOM.
Hail, royal prince!

                    KING RICHARD.
    Thanks, noble peer;
The cheapest of us is ten groats too dear.
What art thou? and how comest thou hither,
Where no man never comes, but that sad dog
That brings me food to make misfortune live?
                    GROOM.
I was a poor groom of thy stable, king,   [York,
When thou wert king; who, travelling towards
With much ado at length have gotten leave
To look upon my sometimes royal master's face.
O, how it yearn'd my heart, when I beheld,
In London streets, that coronation-day,
When Bolingbroke rode on roan Barbary,—
That horse that thou so often hast bestrid,
That horse that I so carefully have drest!
                    KING RICHARD.
Rode he on Barbary? Tell me, gentle friend,
How went he under him?
                    GROOM.
So proudly as if he disdain'd the ground.
                    KING RICHARD.
So proud that Bolingbroke was on his back!
That jade hath eat bread from my royal hand;
This hand hath made him proud with clapping
    him.
Would he not stumble? would he not fall down,—
Since pride must have a fall,—and break the neck
Of that proud man that did usurp his back?
Forgiveness, horse! why do I rail on thee,
Since thou, created to be awed by man,
Wast born to bear? I was not made a horse;
And yet I bear a burden like an ass,
Spur-gall'd and tired by jauncing Bolingbroke.
          Enter KEEPER, *with a dish.*
          KEEPER [*to the* GROOM].
Fellow, give place; here is no longer stay.
                    KING RICHARD.
If thou love me, 'tis time thou wert away.
                    GROOM.
What my tongue dares not, that my heart shall
    say.   [*Exit.*
                    KEEPER.
My lord, will't please you to fall to?
                    KING RICHARD.
Taste of it first, as thou art wont to do.
                    KEEPER.
My lord, I dare not. Sir Pierce of Exton,
Who lately came from th' king, commands the
    contrary.
                    KING RICHARD.
The devil take Henry of Lancaster and thee!
Patience is stale, and I am weary of it.
                    [*Beats the* KEEPER.
                    KEEPER.
Help, help, help!
     Enter SIR PIERCE OF EXTON *and* SERVANTS,
                    arm'd.
                    KING RICHARD.
How now! what means death in this rude assault?
Villain, thy own hand yields thy death's instru-
    ment.
     [*Snatching a weapon, and killing a* SERVANT.
Go thou, and fill another room in hell.
     [*He kills another* SERVANT. *Then* EXTON
                    strikes him down.

That hand shall burn in never-quenching fire
That staggers thus my person.—Exton, thy fierce
    hand
Hath with the king's blood stain'd the king's own
    land.
Mount, mount, my soul! thy seat is up on high;
Whilst my gross flesh sinks downward, here to
    die.   [Dies.
              SIR PIERCE OF EXTON.
As full of valour as of royal blood:
Both have I spilt;—O, would the deed were
    good!
For now the devil, that told me I did well,
Says that this deed is chronicled in hell.
This dead king to the living king I'll bear:—
Take hence the rest, and give them burial here.
                                          [Exeunt.

              SCENE VI.
              Windsor Castle.

Flourish. Enter BOLINGBROKE, YORK, LORDS,
    and ATTENDANTS.

              HENRY BOLINGBROKE.
KIND uncle York, the latest news we hear
    Is that the rebels have consumed with fire
Our town of Cicester in Glostershire;
But whether they be ta'en or slain we hear not.
              Enter NORTHUMBERLAND.
Welcome, my lord: what is the news?
              EARL OF NORTHUMBERLAND.
First, to thy sacred state wish I all happiness.
The next news is, I have to London sent
The heads of Oxford, Salisbury, Blunt, and
    Kent:
The manner of their taking may appear
At large discoursed in this paper here.
              HENRY BOLINGBROKE.
We thank thee, gentle Percy, for thy pains;
And to thy worth will add right worthy gains.
              Enter FITZWATER.
              LORD FITZWATER.
My lord, I have from Oxford sent to London
The heads of Brocas and Sir Bennet Seely,
Two of the dangerous consorted traitors
That sought at Oxford thy dire overthrow.

              HENRY BOLINGBROKE.
Thy pains, Fitzwater, shall not be forgot;
Right noble is thy merit, well I wot.
    Enter PERCY, with the BISHOP OF CARLISLE.
              HENRY PERCY.
The grand conspirator, Abbot of Westminster,
With clog of conscience and sour melancholy,
Hath yielded up his body to the grave;
But here is Carlisle living, to abide
Thy kingly doom and sentence of his pride.
              HENRY BOLINGBROKE.
Carlisle, this is your doom:—
Choose out some secret place, some reverend
    room,
More than thou hast, and with it joy thy life;
So, as thou livest in peace, die free from strife:
For though mine enemy thou hast ever been,
High sparks of honour in thee have I seen.
    Enter SIR PIERCE OF EXTON, with a coffin.
              SIR PIERCE OF EXTON.
Great king, within this coffin I present
Thy buried fear: herein all breathless lies
The mightiest of thy greatest enemies,
Richard of Bourdeaux, by me hither brought.
              HENRY BOLINGBROKE.
Exton, I thank thee not; for thou hast wrought
A deed of slander, with thy fatal hand,
Upon my head and all this famous land.
              SIR PIERCE OF EXTON.
From your own mouth, my lord, did I this deed.
              HENRY BOLINGBROKE.
They love not poison that do poison need,
Nor do I thee: though I did wish him dead,
I hate the murderer, love him murdered.
The guilt of conscience take thou for thy labour,
But neither my good word nor princely favour:
With Cain go wander through the shades of
    night,
And never show thy head by day nor light.—
Lords, I protest, my soul is full of woe
That blood should sprinkle me to make me grow:
Come, mourn with me for that I do lament,
And put on sullen black incontinent:
I'll make a voyage to the Holy Land,
To wash this blood off from my guilty hand:—
March sadly after; grace my mournings here,
In weeping after this untimely bier.   [Exeunt.

THE MERCHANT OF VENICE

DRAMATIS PERSONAE

DUKE OF VENICE.
PRINCE OF MOROCCO, *suitors to Portia.*
PRINCE OF ARRAGON,
ANTONIO, *a merchant of Venice.*
BASSANIO, *his kinsman and friend.*
SOLANIO,
SALARINO, *friends to Antonio and Bassanio.*
GRATIANO,
LORENZO, *in love with Jessica.*
SHYLOCK, *a rich Jew.*
TUBAL, *a Jew, his friend.*
LAUNCELOT GOBBO, *a clown, servant to Shylock.*
OLD GOBBO, *father to Launcelot.*

LEONARDO, *servant to Bassanio.*
BALTHAZAR, *servants to Portia.*
STEPHANO,
PORTIA, *a rich heiress.*
NERISSA, *her waiting-maid.*
JESSICA, *daughter to Shylock.*

MAGNIFICOES OF VENICE, OFFICERS OF THE COURT OF JUSTICE, GAOLER, SERVANTS, *and other* ATTENDANTS.

SCENE—*Partly at Venice, and partly at Belmont, the seat of Portia, on the Continent.*

ACT I. SCENE I.

Venice. A street.

Enter ANTONIO, SALARINO, *and* SOLANIO.

ANTONIO.

IN sooth, I know not why I am so sad:
It wearies me; you say it wearies you;
But how I caught it, found it, or came by it,
What stuff 'tis made of, whereof it is born,
I am to learn;
And such a want-wit sadness makes of me,
That I have much ado to know myself.

SALARINO.

Your mind is tossing on the ocean;
There, where your argosies with portly sail,—
Like signiors and rich burghers of the flood,
Or, as it were, the pageants of the sea,—
Do overpeer the petty traffickers,
That curtsey to them, do them reverence,
As they fly by them with their woven wings.

SOLANIO.

Believe me, sir, had I such venture forth,
The better part of my affections would
Be with my hopes abroad. I should be still
Plucking the grass, to know where sits the wind;
Peering in maps for ports, and piers, and roads;
And every object that might make me fear
Misfortune to my ventures, out of doubt
Would make me sad.

SALARINO.

My wind, cooling my broth.
Would blow me to an ague, when I thought
What harm a wind too great might do at sea.
I should not see the sandy hour-glass run,
But I should think of shallows and of flats;
And see my wealthy Andrew dockt in sand,
Vailing her high-top lower than her ribs,
To kiss her burial. Should I go to church,
And see the holy edifice of stone,
And not bethink me straight of dangerous rocks,
Which touching but my gentle vessel's side,
Would scatter all her spices on the stream;
Enrobe the roaring waters with my silks;

And, in a word, but even now worth this,
And now worth nothing? Shall I have the thought
To think on this; and shall I lack the thought,
That such a thing bechanced would make me sad?
But tell not me; I know Antonio
Is sad to think upon his merchandise.

ANTONIO.

Believe me, no: I think my fortune for it,
My ventures are not in one bottom trusted,
Nor to one place; nor is my whole estate
Upon the fortune of this present year:
Therefore my merchandise makes me not sad.

SALARINO.

Why, then you are in love.

ANTONIO.

Fie, fie

SALARINO.

Not in love neither? Then let's say you're sad,
Because you are not merry: and 'twere as easy
For you to laugh, and leap, and say you are merry,
Because you are not sad. Now, by two-headed Janus,
Nature hath framed strange fellows in her time:
Some that will evermore peep through their eyes,
And laugh, like parrots, at a bag-piper;
And other of such vinegar aspect,
That they'll not show their teeth in way of smile,
Though Nestor swear the jest be laughable.

SOLANIO.

Here comes Bassanio, your most noble kinsman,
Gratiano, and Lorenzo. Fare ye well:
We leave you now with better company.

SALARINO.

I would have stay'd till I had made you merry,
If worthier friends had not prevented me.

ANTONIO.

Your worth is very dear in my regard.
I take it, your own business calls on you,
And you embrace th' occasion to depart.

Enter BASSANIO, LORENZO, *and* GRATIANO.

SALARINO.

Good morrow, my good lords.

BASSANIO.

Good signiors both, when shall we laugh? say,
    when?
You grow exceeding strange: must it be so?

SALARINO.

We'll make our leisures to attend on yours.

[*Exeunt* SALARINO *and* SOLANIO.

LORENZO.

My Lord Bassanio, since you have found Antonio,
We two will leave you: but, at dinner-time,
I pray you, have in mind where we must meet.

BASSANIO.

I will not fail you.

GRATIANO.

You look not well, Signior Antonio;
You have too much respect upon the world:
They lose it that do buy it with much care:
Believe me, you are marvellously changed.

ANTONIO.

I hold the world but as the world, Gratiano;
A stage, where every man must play a part,
And mine a sad one.

GRATIANO.

Let me play the fool:
With mirth and laughter let old wrinkles come;
And let my liver rather heat with wine
Than my heart cool with mortifying groans.
Why should a man, whose blood is warm within,
Sit like his grandsire cut in alabaster?
Sleep when he wakes? and creep into the jaun-
    dice
By being peevish? I tell thee what, Antonio,—
I love thee, and it is my love that speaks,—
There are a sort of men, whose visages
Do cream and mantle like a standing pond;
And do a wilful stillness entertain,
With purpose to be drest in an opinion
Of wisdom, gravity, profound conceit;
As who should say, 'I am Sir Oracle,
And when I ope my lips, let no dog bark!'
O my Antonio, I do know of these,
That therefore only are reputed wise
For saying nothing; when, I am very sure,
If they should speak, would almost damn those
    ears,
Which, hearing them, would call their brothers
    fools.
I'll tell thee more of this another time:
But fish not, with this melancholy bait,
For this fool-gudgeon, this opinion.—
Come, good Lorenzo.—Fare ye well awhile:
I'll end my exhortation after dinner.

LORENZO.

Well, we will leave you, then, till dinner-time:
I must be one of these same dumb wise men,
For Gratiano never lets me speak.

GRATIANO.

Well, keep me company but two years moe,
Thou shalt not know the sound of thine own
    tongue.

ANTONIO.

Farewell: I'll grow a talker for this gear.

GRATIANO.

Thanks, i'faith; for silence is only commendable
In a neat's tongue dried, and a maid not vendible.

[*Exeunt* GRATIANO *and* LORENZO.

ANTONIO.

Is that any thing now?

BASSANIO.

Gratiano speaks an infinite deal of nothing, more
than any man in all Venice. His reasons are as two
grains of wheat hid in two bushels of chaff: you
shall seek all day ere you find them; and when you
have them, they are not worth the search.

ANTONIO.

Well; tell me now, what lady is the same
To whom you swore a secret pilgrimage,
That you to-day promised to tell me of?

BASSANIO.

'Tis not unknown to you, Antonio,
How much I have disabled mine estate,
By something showing a more swelling port
Than my faint means would grant continuance:
Nor do I now make moan to be abridged
From such a noble rate; but my chief care
Is, to come fairly off from the great debts,
Wherein my time, something too prodigal,
Hath left me gaged. To you, Antonio,
I owe the most, in money and in love;
And from your love I have a warranty
To unburden all my plots and purposes
How to get clear of all the debts I owe.

ANTONIO.

I pray you, good Bassanio, let me know it;
And if it stand, as you yourself still do,
Within the eye of honour, be assured
My purse, my person, my extremest means,
Lie all unlockt to your occasions.

BASSANIO.

In my school-days, when I had lost one shaft,
I shot his fellow of the selfsame flight
The selfsame way with more advised watch,
To find the other forth; and by advent'ring both,
I oft found both: I urge this childhood proof,
Because what follows is pure innocence.
I owe you much; and, like a wilful youth,
That which I owe is lost: but if you please
To shoot another arrow that self way
Which you did shoot the first, I do not doubt,
As I will watch the aim, or to find both,
Or bring your latter hazard back again,
And thankfully rest debtor for the first.

ANTONIO.

You know me well; and herein spend but time
To wind about my love with circumstance;
And out of doubt you do me now more wrong
In making question of my uttermost,
Than if you had made waste of all I have:
Then do but say to me what I should do,
That in your knowledge may by me be done,
And I am prest unto it: therefore, speak.

BASSANIO.

In Belmont is a lady richly left;
And she is fair, and, fairer than that word,
Of wondrous virtues: sometimes from her eyes
I did receive fair speechless messages:
Her name is Portia; nothing undervalued
To Cato's daughter, Brutus' Portia:
Nor is the wide world ignorant of her worth;
For the four winds blow in from every coast
Renowned suitors: and her sunny locks
Hang on her temples like a golden fleece;

Which makes her seat of Belmont Colchos' strond,
And many Jasons come in quest of her.
O my Antonio, had I but the means
To hold a rival place with one of them,
I have a mind presages me such thrift,
That I should questionless be fortunate!

ANTONIO.

Thou know'st that all my fortunes are at sea;
Neither have I money, nor commodity
To raise a present sum: therefore, go forth;
Try what my credit can in Venice do:
That shall be rackt, even to the uttermost,
To furnish thee to Belmont, to fair Portia.
Go, presently inquire, and so will I,
Where money is; and I no question make,
To have it of my trust, or for my sake.　[Exeunt.

SCENE II.

Belmont. A room in PORTIA'S house.

Enter PORTIA and NERISSA.

PORTIA.

BY my troth, Nerissa, my little body is aweary
of this great world.

NERISSA.

You would be, sweet madam, if your miseries
were in the same abundance as your good fortunes are: and yet, for aught I see, they are as sick
that surfeit with too much, as they that starve
with nothing. It is no mean happiness, therefore,
to be seated in the mean: superfluity comes sooner
by white hairs; but competency lives longer.

PORTIA.

Good sentences, and well pronounced.

NERISSA.

They would be better, if well follow'd.

PORTIA.

If to do were as easy as to know what were good
to do, chapels had been churches, and poor men's
cottages princes' palaces. It is a good divine that
follows his own instructions: I can easier teach
twenty what were good to be done, than be one of
the twenty to follow mine own teaching. The
brain may devise laws for the blood; but a hot
temper leaps o'er a cold decree: such a hare is
madness the youth, to skip o'er the meshes of
good-counsel the cripple. But this reasoning is
not in the fashion to choose me a husband:—O
me, the word 'choose'! I may neither choose who
I would, nor refuse who I dislike; so is the will of
a living daughter curb'd by the will of a dead
father.—Is it not hard, Nerissa, that I cannot
choose one, nor refuse none?

NERISSA.

Your father was ever virtuous; and holy men, at
their death, have good inspirations: therefore, the
lottery, that he hath devised in these three chests
of gold, silver, and lead,—whereof who chooses
his meaning chooses you,—will, no doubt, never
be chosen by any rightly, but one who shall rightly
love. But what warmth is there in your affection
towards any of these princely suitors that are
already come?

PORTIA.

I pray thee, over-name them; and as thou namest

them, I will describe them; and, according to my
description, level at my affection.

NERISSA.

First, there is the Neapolitan prince.

PORTIA.

Ay, that's a colt indeed, for he doth nothing but
talk of his horse; and he makes it a great appro-
priation to his own good parts, that he can shoe
him himself. I am much afeard my lady his
mother play'd false with a smith.

NERISSA.

Then there is the County Palatine.

PORTIA.

He doth nothing but frown; as who should say,
'An you will not have me, choose:' he hears merry
tales, and smiles not: I fear he will prove the
weeping philosopher when he grows old, being so
full of unmannerly sadness in his youth. I had
rather be married to a Death's-head with a bone
in his mouth than to either of these:—God defend
me from these two!

NERISSA.

How say you by the French lord, Monsieur Le
Bon?

PORTIA.

God made him, and therefore let him pass for a
man. In truth, I know it is a sin to be a mocker:
but, he!—why, he hath a horse better than the
Neapolitan's; a better bad habit of frowning than
the Count Palatine: he is every man in no man; if
a throstle sing, he falls straight a-capering; he will
fence with his own shadow: if I should marry him,
I should marry twenty husbands. If he would
despise me, I would forgive him; for if he love me
to madness, I shall never requite him.

NERISSA.

What say you, then, to Falconbridge, the young
baron of England?

PORTIA.

You know I say nothing to him: for he understands not me, nor I him: he hath neither Latin,
French, nor Italian; and you will come into the
court and swear that I have a poor pennyworth in
the English. He is a proper man's picture; but,
alas, who can converse with a dumb-show? How
oddly he is suited! I think he bought his doublet
in Italy, his round hose in France, his bonnet in
Germany, and his behaviour every where.

NERISSA.

What think you of the Scottish lord, his neighbour?

PORTIA.

That he hath a neighbourly charity in him; for he
borrow'd a box of the ear of the Englishman, and
swore he would pay him again when he was able:
I think the Frenchman became his surety, and
seal'd under for another.

NERISSA.

How like you the young German, the Duke of
Saxony's nephew?

PORTIA.

Very vilely in the morning, when he is sober; and
most vilely in the afternoon, when he is drunk:
when he is best, he is a little worse than a man;
and when he is worst, he is little better than a
beast. An the worst fall that ever fell, I hope I
shall make shift to go without him.

NERISSA.

If he should offer to choose, and choose the right casket, you should refuse to perform your father's will, if you should refuse to accept him.

PORTIA.

Therefore, for fear of the worst, I pray thee, set a deep glass of Rhenish wine on the contrary casket; for, if the devil be within, and that temptation without, I know he will choose it. I will do any thing, Nerissa, ere I will be married to a sponge.

NERISSA.

You need not fear, lady, the having any of these lords: they have acquainted me with their determinations; which is, indeed, to return to their home, and to trouble you with no more suit, unless you may be won by some other sort than your father's imposition, depending on the caskets.

PORTIA.

If I live to be as old as Sibylla, I will die as chaste as Diana, unless I be obtain'd by the manner of my father's will. I am glad this parcel of wooers are so reasonable; for there is not one among them but I dote on his very absence; and I pray God grant them a fair departure.

NERISSA.

Do you not remember, lady, in your father's time, a Venetian, a scholar and a soldier, that came hither in company of the Marquis of Montferrat?

PORTIA.

Yes, yes, it was Bassanio: as I think, so was he call'd.

NERISSA.

True, madam: he, of all the men that ever my foolish eyes lookt upon, was the best deserving a fair lady.

PORTIA.

I remember him well; and I remember him worthy of thy praise.

Enter a SERVANT.

How now! what news?

SERVANT.

The four strangers seek for you, madam, to take their leave: and there is a forerunner come from a fifth, the Prince of Morocco; who brings word, the prince his master will be here to-night.

PORTIA.

If a could bid the fifth welcome with so good a heart as I can bid the other four farewell, I should be glad of his approach: if he have the condition of a saint and the complexion of a devil, I had rather he should shrive me than wive me. Come, Nerissa.—Sirrah, go before.— Whiles we shut the gates upon one wooer, another knocks at the door.   [*Exeunt.*

SCENE III.

Venice.   A public place.

Enter BASSANIO *with* SHYLOCK *the Jew.*

SHYLOCK.

THREE thousand ducats,—well.

BASSANIO.

Ay, sir, for three months.

SHYLOCK.

For three months,—well.

BASSANIO.

For the which, as I told you, Antonio shall be bound.

SHYLOCK.

Antonio shall become bound,—well.

BASSANIO.

May you stead me? will you pleasure me? shall I know your answer?

SHYLOCK.

Three thousand ducats for three months, and Antonio bound.

BASSANIO.

Your answer to that.

SHYLOCK.

Antonio is a good man.

BASSANIO.

Have you heard any imputation to the contrary?

SHYLOCK.

Ho, no, no, no, no;—my meaning, in saying he is a good man is to have you understand me that he is sufficient. Yet his means are in supposition: he hath an argosy bound to Tripolis, another to the Indies; I understand, moreover, upon the Rialto, he hath a third at Mexico, a fourth for England, —and other ventures he hath, squander'd abroad. But ships are but boards, sailors but men: there be land-rats and water-rats, water-thieves and land-thieves, I mean pirates; and then there is the peril of waters, winds, and rocks. The man is, notwithstanding, sufficient:—three thousand ducats: —I think I may take his bond.

BASSANIO.

Be assured you may.

SHYLOCK.

I will be assured I may; and, that I may be assured, I will bethink me. May I speak with Antonio?

BASSANIO.

If it please you to dine with us.

SHYLOCK.

Yes, to smell pork; to eat of the habitation which your prophet the Nazarite conjured the devil into. I will buy with you, sell with you, talk with you, walk with you, and so following; but I will not eat with you, drink with you, nor pray with you. What news on the Rialto?—Who is he comes here?

Enter ANTONIO.

BASSANIO.

This is Signior Antonio.

SHYLOCK [*aside*].

How like a fawning publican he looks!
I hate him for he is a Christian!
But more, for that, in low simplicity,
He lends out money gratis, and brings down
The rate of usance here with us in Venice.
If I can catch him once upon the hip,
I will feed fat the ancient grudge I bear him.
He hates our sacred nation; and he rails,
Even there where merchants most do congregate,
On me, my bargains, and my well-won thrift,
Which he calls interest. Cursed be my tribe,
If I forgive him!

BASSANIO.
Shylock, do you hear?
SHYLOCK.
I am debating of my present store;
And, by the near guess of my memory,
I cannot instantly raise up the gross
Of full three thousand ducats. What of that?
Tubal, a wealthy Hebrew of my tribe,
Will furnish me. But soft! how many months
Do you desire?—Rest you fair, good signior;
                                        [to ANTONIO.
Your worship was the last man in our mouths.
ANTONIO.
Shylock, although I neither lend nor borrow
By taking nor by giving of excess,
Yet, to supply the ripe wants of my friend,
I'll break a custom.—Is he yet possest
How much ye would?
SHYLOCK.
                Ay, ay, three thousand ducats.
ANTONIO.
And for three months.
SHYLOCK.
I had forgot,—three months, you told me so.
Well, then, your bond; and let me see,—but hear
you;
Methought you said you neither lend nor borrow
Upon advantage.
ANTONIO.
                I do never use it.
SHYLOCK.
When Jacob grazed his uncle Laban's sheep,—
This Jacob from our holy Abram was
(As his wise mother wrought in his behalf)
The third possessor; ay, he was the third,—
ANTONIO.
And what of him? did he take interest?
SHYLOCK.
No, not take interest; not as you would say,
Directly interest: mark what Jacob did.
When Laban and himself were compromised
That all the eanlings which were streakt and pied
Should fall as Jacob's hire, the ewes, being rank,
In th' end of autumn turned to the rams;
And when the work of generation was
Between these woolly breeders in the act,
The skilful shepherd peel'd me certain wands,
And, in the doing of the deed of kind,
He stuck them up before the fulsome ewes,
Who, then conceiving, did in eaning time
Fall parti-colour'd lambs, and those were Jacob's.
This was a way to thrive, and he was blest:
And thrift is blessing, if men steal it not.
ANTONIO.
This was a venture, sir, that Jacob served for;
A thing not in his power to bring to pass,
But sway'd and fashion'd by the hand of heaven.
Was this inserted to make interest good?
Or is your gold and silver ewes and rams?
SHYLOCK.
I cannot tell: I make it breed as fast:—
But note me, signior.
ANTONIO.
                Mark you this, Bassanio,
The devil can cite Scripture for his purpose.
An evil soul, producing holy witness,

Is like a villain with a smiling cheek;
A goodly apple rotten at the heart:
O, what a goodly outside falsehood hath!
SHYLOCK.
Three thousand ducats,—'tis a good round sum.
Three months from twelve,—then, let me see, the
rate—
ANTONIO.
Well, Shylock, shall we be beholden to you?
SHYLOCK.
Signior Antonio, many a time and oft,
In the Rialto, you have rated me
About my moneys and my usances:
Still have I borne it with a patient shrug;
For sufferance is the badge of all our tribe:
You call me misbeliever, cut-throat dog,
And spit upon my Jewish gaberdine,
And all for use of that which is mine own.
Well, then, it now appears you need my help:
Go to, then; you come to me, and you say,
'Shylock, we would have moneys:'—you say so;
You, that did void your rheum upon my beard,
And foot me as you spurn a stranger cur
Over your threshold: moneys is your suit.
What should I say to you? Should I not say,
'Hath a dog money? is it possible
A cur can lend three thousand ducats?' or
Shall I bend low, and in a bondman's key,
With bated breath and whispering humbleness,
Say this,—
'Fair sir, you spit on me on Wednesday last;
You spurn'd me such a day; another time
You call'd me dog; and for these courtesies
I'll lend you thus much moneys'?
ANTONIO.
I am as like to call thee so again,
To spit on thee again, to spurn thee too.
If thou wilt lend this money, lend it not
As to thy friends—for when did friendship take
A breed for barren metal of his friend?—
But lend it rather to thine enemy;
Who if he break, thou mayst with better face
Exact the penalty.
SHYLOCK.
                Why, look you, how you storm!
I would be friends with you, and have your love,
Forget the shames that you have stain'd me
with,
Supply your present wants, and take no doit
Of usance for my moneys,
And you'll not hear me: this is kind I offer.
BASSANIO
This were kindness.
SHYLOCK.
                This kindness will I show:—
Go with me to a notary, seal me there
Your single bond; and, in a merry sport,
If you repay me not on such a day,
In such a place, such sum or sums as are
Exprest in the condition, let the forfeit
Be nominated for an equal pound
Of your fair flesh, to be cut off and taken
In what part of your body pleaseth me.
ANTONIO.
Content, i'faith: I'll seal to such a bond,
And say there is much kindness in the Jew.

BASSANIO.

You shall not seal to such a bond for me:
I'll rather dwell in my necessity.

ANTONIO.

Why, fear not, man; I will not forfeit it:
Within these two months, that's a month before
This bond expires, I do expect return
Of thrice three times the value of this bond.

SHYLOCK.

O father Abram, what these Christians are,
Whose own hard dealings teaches them suspect
The thoughts of others!—Pray you, tell me this;
If he should break his day, what should I gain
By the exaction of the forfeiture?
A pound of man's flesh taken from a man
Is not so estimable, profitable neither,
As flesh of muttons, beefs, or goats. I say,
To buy his favour, I extend this friendship:
If he will take it, so; if not, adieu;
And, for my love, I pray you wrong me not.

ANTONIO.

Yes, Shylock, I will seal unto this bond.

SHYLOCK.

Then meet me forthwith at the notary's,—
Give him direction for this merry bond;
And I will go and purse the ducats straight;
See to my house, left in the fearful guard
Of an unthrifty knave; and presently
I will be with you.

ANTONIO.

Hie thee, gentle Jew.
           [*Exit* SHYLOCK.
The Hebrew will turn Christian: he grows kind.

BASSANIO.

I like not fair terms and a villain's mind.

ANTONIO.

Come on: in this there can be no dismay;
My ships come home a month before the day.
           [*Exeunt.*

ACT II. SCENE I.

Belmont. A room in PORTIA'S *house.*

Enter the PRINCE OF MOROCCO, *a tawny Moor
all in white, and three or four* FOLLOWERS *accordingly, with* PORTIA, NERISSA, *and their*
TRAIN. *Flourish of cornets.*

PRINCE OF MOROCCO.

MISLIKE me not for my complexion,
    The shadow'd livery of the burnisht sun,
To whom I am a neighbour and near bred.
Bring me the fairest creature northward born,
Where Phœbus' fire scarce thaws the icicles,
And let us make incision for your love,
To prove whose blood is reddest, his or mine.
I tell thee, lady, this aspect of mine
Hath fear'd the valiant: by my love, I swear
The best-regarded virgins of our clime
Hath loved it too: I would not change this hue,
Except to steal your thoughts, my gentle queen.

PORTIA.

In terms of choice I am not solely led
By nice direction of a maiden's eyes;
Besides, the lottery of my destiny
Bars me the right of voluntary choosing:
But, if my father had not scanted me,

And hedg'd me by his will, to yield myself
His wife who wins me by that means I told you,
Yourself, renowned prince, then stood as fair
As any comer I have lookt on yet
For my affection.

PRINCE OF MOROCCO.

        Even for that I thank you:
Therefore, I pray you, lead me to the caskets,
To try my fortune. By this scimitar,
That slew the Sophy and a Persian prince
That won three fields of Sultan Solyman,
I would outstare the sternest eyes that look,
Outbrave the heart most daring on the earth,
Pluck the young sucking-cubs from the she-bear,
Yea, mock the lion when he roars for prey,
To win thee, lady. But, alas the while!
If Hercules and Lichas play at dice
Which is the better man, the greater throw
May turn by fortune from the weaker hand:
So is Alcides beaten by his page;
And so may I, blind Fortune leading me,
Miss that which one unworthier may attain,
And die with grieving.

PORTIA.

        You must take your chance;
And either not attempt to choose at all,
Or swear before you choose,—if you choose
    wrong,
Never to speak to lady afterward
In way of marriage: therefore be advised.

PRINCE OF MOROCCO.

Nor will not. Come, bring me unto my chance.

PORTIA.

First, forward to the temple: after dinner
Your hazard shall be made.

PRINCE OF MOROCCO.

        Good fortune, then!
To make me blest or cursed'st among men.
           [*Cornets, and exeunt.*

SCENE II.

Venice. A street.

Enter LAUNCELOT *the Clown, alone.*

LAUNCELOT GOBBO.

CERTAINLY my conscience will serve me to
run from this Jew my master. The fiend is at
mine elbow, and tempts me, saying to me, 'Gobbo, Launcelot Gobbo, good Launcelot,' or 'good
Gobbo,' or 'good Launcelot Gobbo, use your
legs, take the start, run away.' My conscience
says, 'No; take heed, honest Launcelot; take heed,
honest Gobbo,' or, as aforesaid, 'honest Launcelot Gobbo; do not run; scorn running with thy
heels.' Well, the most courageous fiend bids me
pack: '*Via!*' says the fiend, 'away!' says the fiend;
'for the heavens, rouse up a brave mind,' says the
fiend, 'and run.' Well, my conscience, hanging
about the neck of my heart, says very wisely to
me, 'My honest friend Launcelot, being an honest
man's son,'—or rather an honest woman's son;—
for, indeed, my father did something smack,
something grow to,—he had a kind of taste;—
well, my conscience says, 'Launcelot, budge not.'
'Budge,' says the fiend. 'Budge not,' says my conscience. 'Conscience,' say I, 'you counsel well;

'fiend,' say I, 'you counsel well:' to be ruled by my conscience, I should stay with the Jew my master, who—God bless the mark!—is a kind of devil; and, to run away from the Jew, I should be ruled by the fiend, who, saving your reverence, is the devil himself. Certainly the Jew is the very devil incarnal; and, in my conscience, my conscience is but a kind of hard conscience, to offer to counsel me to stay with the Jew. The fiend gives the more friendly counsel: I will run, fiend; my heels are at your command; I will run.

Enter OLD GOBBO, *with a basket.*

OLD GOBBO.

Master young man, you, I pray you, which is the way to master Jew's?

LAUNCELOT GOBBO [*aside*].

O heavens, this is my true-begotten father! who, being more than sand-blind, high-gravel-blind, knows me not:—I will try confusions with him.

OLD GOBBO.

Master young gentleman, I pray you, which is the way to master Jew's?

LAUNCELOT GOBBO.

Turn up on your right hand at the next turning, but, at the next turning of all, on your left; marry, at the very next turning, turn of no hand, but turn down indirectly to the Jew's house.

OLD GOBBO.

By God's sonties, 'twill be a hard way to hit. Can you tell me whether one Launcelot, that dwells with him, dwell with him or no?

LAUNCELOT GOBBO.

Talk you of young Master Launcelot?—[*aside*] Mark me now; now will I raise the waters.—Talk you of young Master Launcelot?

OLD GOBBO.

No master, sir, but a poor man's son: his father, though I say it, is an honest exceeding poor man, and, God be thankt, well to live.

LAUNCELOT GOBBO.

Well, let his father be what a' will, we talk of young Master Launcelot.

OLD GOBBO.

Your worship's friend, and Launcelot, sir.

LAUNCELOT GOBBO.

But, I pray you, *ergo*, old man, *ergo*, I beseech you, talk you of young Master Launcelot?

OLD GOBBO.

Of Launcelot, an't please your mastership.

LAUNCELOT GOBBO.

Ergo, Master Launcelot. Talk not of Master Launcelot, father; for the young gentleman—according to Fates and Destinies, and such odd sayings, the Sisters Three, and such branches of learning—is, indeed, deceased; or, as you would say in plain terms, gone to heaven.

OLD GOBBO.

Marry, God forbid! the boy was the very staff of my age, my very prop.

LAUNCELOT GOBBO.

Do I look like a cudgel or a hovel-post, a staff, or a prop?—Do you know me, father?

OLD GOBBO.

Alack the day, I know you not, young gentleman: but, I pray you, tell me, is my boy—God rest his soul!—alive or dead?

LAUNCELOT GOBBO.

Do you not know me, father?

OLD GOBBO.

Alack, sir, I am sand-blind; I know you not.

LAUNCELOT GOBBO.

Nay, indeed, if you had your eyes, you might fail of the knowing me: it is a wise father that knows his own child. Well, old man, I will tell you news of your son: give me your blessing [*kneels*]: truth will come to light; murder cannot be hid long,—a man's son may; but, in the end, truth will out.

OLD GOBBO.

Pray you, sir, stand up: I am sure you are not Launcelot, my boy.

LAUNCELOT GOBBO.

Pray you, let's have no more fooling about it, but give me your blessing: I am Launcelot, your boy that was, your son that is, your child that shall be.

OLD GOBBO.

I cannot think you are my son.

LAUNCELOT GOBBO.

I know not what I shall think of that: but I am Launcelot, the Jew's man; and I am sure Margery your wife is my mother.

OLD GOBBO.

Her name is Margery, indeed: I'll be sworn, if thou be Launcelot, thou art mine own flesh and blood. Lord worship might he be! what a beard hast thou got! thou hast got more hair on thy chin than Dobbin my fill-horse has on his tail.

LAUNCELOT GOBBO [*rising*].

It should seem, then, that Dobbin's tail grows backward; I am sure he had more hair of his tail than I have of my face when I last saw him.

OLD GOBBO.

Lord, how art thou changed! How dost thou and thy master agree? I have brought him a present. How 'gree you now?

LAUNCELOT GOBBO.

Well, well: but, for mine own part, as I have set up my rest to run away, so I will not rest till I have run some ground. My master's a very Jew: give him a present! give him a halter: I am famisht in his service; you may tell every finger I have with my ribs. Father, I am glad you are come: give me your present to one Master Bassanio, who, indeed, gives rare new liveries: if I serve not him, I will run as far as God has any ground.—O rare fortune! here comes the man:—to him, father; for I am a Jew, if I serve the Jew any longer.

Enter BASSANIO, *with* LEONARDO *and a* FOLLOWER *or two.*

BASSANIO.

You may do so;—but let it be so hasted, that supper be ready at the furthest by five of the clock. See these letters deliver'd; put the liveries to making; and desire Gratiano to come anon to my lodging.   [*Exit a* SERVANT.

LAUNCELOT GOBBO.

To him, father.

OLD GOBBO.

God bless your worship!

BASSANIO.

Gramercy: wouldst thou aught with me?

OLD GOBBO.

Here's my son, sir, a poor boy,—

LAUNCELOT GOBBO.

Not a poor boy, sir, but the rich Jew's man; that would, sir,—as my father shall specify,—

OLD GOBBO.

He hath a great infection, sir, as one would say, to serve,—

LAUNCELOT GOBBO.

Indeed, the short and the long is, I serve the Jew, and have a desire,—as my father shall specify,—

OLD GOBBO.

His master and he—saving your worship's reverence—are scarce cater-cousins,—

LAUNCELOT GOBBO.

To be brief, the very truth is, that the Jew having done me wrong, doth cause me,—as my father, being, I hope, an old man, shall frutify unto you,—

OLD GOBBO.

I have here a dish of doves that I would bestow upon your worship; and my suit is,—

LAUNCELOT GOBBO.

In very brief, the suit is impertinent to myself, as your worship shall know by this honest old man; and, though I say it, though old man, yet poor man, my father.

BASSANIO.

One speak for both.—What would you?

LAUNCELOT GOBBO.

Serve you, sir.

OLD GOBBO.

That is the very defect of the matter, sir.

BASSANIO.

I know thee well; thou hast obtain'd thy suit:
Shylock thy master spoke with me this day,
And hath preferr'd thee,—if it be preferment
To leave a rich Jew's service, to become
The follower of so poor a gentleman.

LAUNCELOT GOBBO.

The old proverb is very well parted between my master Shylock and you, sir: you have the grace of God, sir, and he hath enough.

BASSANIO.

Thou speak'st it well.—Go, father, with thy son.—
Take leave of thy old master, and inquire
My lodging out.—Give him a livery
More guarded than his fellows': see it done.

LAUNCELOT GOBBO.

Father, in.—I cannot get a service, no;—I have ne'er a tongue in my head.—Well [looking on his palm], if any man in Italy have a fairer table, which doth offer to swear upon a book, I shall have good fortune!—Go to, here's a simple line of life! here's a small trifle of wives! alas, fifteen wives is nothing! eleven widows and nine maids is a simple coming-in for one man; and then to scape drowning thrice, and to be in peril of my life with the edge of a feather-bed,—here are simple scapes! Well, if Fortune be a woman, she's a good wench for this gear.—Father, come; I'll take my leave of the Jew in the twinkling of an eye. [Exeunt LAUNCELOT and OLD GOBBO.

BASSANIO.

I pray thee, good Leonardo, think on this:
These things being bought and orderly bestow'd,
Return in haste, for I do feast to-night
My best-esteem'd acquaintance: hie thee, go.

LEONARDO.

My best endeavours shall be done herein.

Enter GRATIANO.

GRATIANO.

Where's your master?

LEONARDO.

Yonder, sir, he walks. [Exit.

GRATIANO.

Signior Bassanio,—

BASSANIO.

Gratiano!

GRATIANO.

I have a suit to you.

BASSANIO.

You have obtain'd it.

GRATIANO.

You must not deny me: I must go with you to Belmont.

BASSANIO.

Why, then you must. But hear thee, Gratiano:
Thou art too wild, too rude, and bold of voice,—
Parts that become thee happily enough,
And in such eyes as ours appear not faults;
But where thou art not known, why, there they show
Something too liberal. Prithee, take pain
To allay with some cold drops of modesty
Thy skipping spirit; lest, through thy wild behaviour,
I be misconstred in the place I go to,
And lose my hopes.

GRATIANO.

Signior Bassanio, hear me:
If I do not put on a sober habit,
Talk with respect, and swear but now and then,
Wear prayer-books in my pocket, look demurely;
Nay, more, while grace is saying, hood mine eyes
Thus with my hat, and sigh, and say amen;
Use all the observance of civility,
Like one well studied in a sad ostent
To please his grandam,—never trust me more.

BASSANIO.

Well, we shall see your bearing.

GRATIANO.

Nay, but I bar to-night: you shall not gauge me
By what we do to-night.

BASSANIO.

No, that were pity:
I would entreat you rather to put on
Your boldest suit of mirth, for we have friends
That purpose merriment. But fare ye well:
I have some business.

GRATIANO.

And I must to Lorenzo and the rest:
But we will visit you at supper-time. [Exeunt.

SCENE III.

The same.   A room in SHYLOCK'S house.

Enter JESSICA AND LAUNCELOT.

JESSICA.

I AM sorry thou wilt leave my father so:
Our house is hell: and thou, a merry devil,
Didst rob it of some taste of tediousness.

But fare thee well; there is a ducat for thee:
And, Launcelot, soon at supper shalt thou see
Lorenzo, who is thy new master's guest:
Give him this letter; do it secretly;—
And so farewell: I would not have my father
See me in talk with thee.

LAUNCELOT GOBBO.
Adieu; tears exhibit my tongue. Most beautiful
pagan, most sweet Jew! if a Christian did not
play the knave and get thee, I am much deceived.
But, adieu: these foolish drops do something
drown my manly spirit: adieu.

JESSICA.
Farewell, good Launcelot.— [Exit LAUNCELOT.
Alack, what heinous sin is it in me
To be ashamed to be my father's child!
But though I am a daughter to his blood,
I am not to his manners. O Lorenzo,
If thou keep promise, I shall end this strife,—
Become a Christian, and thy loving wife!   [Exit.

SCENE IV.

The same.   A street.

Enter GRATIANO, LORENZO, SALARINO, *and*
SOLANIO.

LORENZO.
NAY, we will slink away in supper-time,
Disguise us at my lodging, and return
All in an hour.

GRATIANO.
We have not made good preparation.

SALARINO.
We have not spoke us yet of torch-bearers.

SOLANIO.
'Tis vile, unless it may be quaintly order'd,
And better in my mind not undertook.

LORENZO.
'Tis now but four o'clock: we have two hours
To furnish us.

Enter LAUNCELOT, *with a letter.*
Friend Launcelot, what's the news?

LAUNCELOT GOBBO.
An it shall please you to break up this, it shall
seem to signify.

LORENZO.
I know the hand: in faith, 'tis a fair hand;
And whiter than the paper it writ on
Is the fair hand that writ.

GRATIANO.
Love-news, in faith.

LAUNCELOT GOBBO.
By your leave, sir.

LORENZO.
Whither goest thou?

LAUNCELOT GOBBO.
Marry, sir, to bid my old master the Jew to sup
to-night with my new master the Christian.

LORENZO.
Hold here, take this [*gives money*]:—tell gentle
Jessica
I will not fail her; speak it privately; go.—
[*Exit* LAUNCELOT.
Gentlemen, will you prepare you for this mask
to-night?
I am provided of a torch-bearer.

SALARINO.
Ay, marry, I'll be gone about it straight.

SOLANIO.
And so will I.

LORENZO.
Meet me and Gratiano
At Gratiano's lodging some hour hence.

SALARINO.
'Tis good we do so.
[*Exeunt* SALARINO *and* SOLANIO.

GRATIANO.
Was not that letter from fair Jessica?

LORENZO.
I must needs tell thee all. She hath directed
How I shall take her from her father's house;
What gold and jewels she is furnish'd with;
What page's suit she hath in readiness.
If e'er the Jew her father come to heaven,
It will be for his gentle daughter's sake:
And never dare misfortune cross her foot,
Unless she do it under this excuse,—
That she is issue to a faithless Jew,—
Come, go with me: peruse this as thou goest:
Fair Jessica shall be my torch-bearer.   [*Exeunt.*

SCENE V.

The same.   Before SHYLOCK'S *house.*

Enter SHYLOCK *and* LAUNCELOT.

SHYLOCK.
WELL, thou shalt see, thy eyes shall be thy
judge,
The difference of old Shylock and Bassanio:—
What, Jessica!—thou shalt not gormandize,
As thou hast done with me;—what, Jessica!—
And sleep and snore, and rend apparel out;—
Why, Jessica, I say!

LAUNCELOT GOBBO.
Why, Jessica!

SHYLOCK.
Who bids thee call? I do not bid thee call.

LAUNCELOT GOBBO.
Your worship was wont to tell me that I could do
nothing without bidding.

Enter JESSICA.

JESSICA.
Call you? what is your will?

SHYLOCK.
I am bid forth to supper, Jessica:
There are my keys.—But wherefore should I go?
I am not bid for love; they flatter me:
But yet I'll go in hate, to feed upon
The prodigal Christian.—Jessica, my girl,
Look to my house.—I am right loth to go:
There is some ill a-brewing towards my rest,
For I did dream of money-bags to-night.

LAUNCELOT GOBBO.
I beseech you, sir, go: my young master doth expect your reproach.

SHYLOCK.
So do I his.

LAUNCELOT GOBBO.
And they have conspired together,—I will not
say you shall see a mask; but if you do, then it was
not for nothing that my nose fell a-bleeding on
Black-Monday last at six o'clock i' th' morning,

falling out that year on Ash-Wednesday was four year, in th' afternoon.

SHYLOCK.

What, are there masks?—Hear you me, Jessica:
Lock up my doors; and when you hear the drum,
And the vile squealing of the wry-neckt fife,
Clamber not you up to the casements then,
Nor thrust your head into the public street,
To gaze on Christian fools with varnisht faces;
But stop my house's ears, I mean my casements:
Let not the sound of shallow foppery enter
My sober house.—By Jacob's staff, I swear
I have no mind of feasting forth to-night:
But I will go.—Go you before me, sirrah;
Say I will come.

LAUNCELOT GOBBO.
I will go before, sir.—
Mistress, look out at window for all this;
There will come a Christian by
Will be worth a Jewess' eye.   *[Exit.*

SHYLOCK.

What says that fool of Hagar's offspring, ha?

JESSICA.

His words were, 'Farewell, mistress;' nothing else.

SHYLOCK.

The patch is kind enough; but a huge feeder,
Snail-slow in profit, and he sleeps by day
More than the wild-cat: drones hive not with me;
Therefore I part with him; and part with him
To one that I would have him help to waste
His borrow'd purse.—Well, Jessica, go in:
Perhaps I will return immediately:
Do as I bid you; shut doors after you:
Fast bind, fast find,—
A proverb never stale in thrifty mind.   *[Exit.*

JESSICA.

Farewell; and if my fortune be not crost,
I have a father, you a daughter, lost.   *[Exit.*

Enter the Maskers GRATIANO *and* SALARINO.

GRATIANO.

This is the pent-house under which Lorenzo
Desired us to make stand.

SALARINO.
His hour is almost past.

GRATIANO.

And it is marvel he out-dwells his hour,
For lovers ever run before the clock.

SALARINO.

O, ten times faster Venus' pigeons fly
To seal love's bonds new-made than they are wont
To keep obliged faith unforfeited!

GRATIANO.

That ever holds: who riseth from a feast
With that keen appetite that he sits down?
Where is the horse that doth untread again
His tedious measures with the unbated fire
That he did pace them first? All things that are,
Are with more spirit chased than enjoy'd.
How like a younker or a prodigal
The scarfed bark puts from her native bay,
Hugg'd and embraced by the strumpet wind!
How like a prodigal doth she return,
With over-weather'd ribs, and ragged sails,
Lean, rent, and beggar'd by the strumpet wind!

SALARINO.

Here comes Lorenzo:—more of this hereafter.

Enter LORENZO.

LORENZO.

Sweet friends, your patience for my long abode;
Not I, but my affairs, have made you wait:
When you shall please to play the thieves for wives,
I'll watch as long for you then.—Approach;
Here dwells my father Jew.—Ho! who's within?

Enter JESSICA, *above, in boy's clothes.*

JESSICA.

Who are you? Tell me, for more certainty,
Albeit I'll swear that I do know your tongue.

LORENZO.

Lorenzo, and thy love.

JESSICA.

Lorenzo, certain; and my love, indeed,—
For who love I so much? And now who knows
But you, Lorenzo, whether I am yours?

LORENZO.

Heaven and thy thoughts are witness that thou art.

JESSICA.

Here, catch this casket; it is worth the pains.
I am glad 'tis night, you do not look on me,
For I am much ashamed of my exchange:
But love is blind, and lovers cannot see
The pretty follies that themselves commit;
For if they could, Cupid himself would blush
To see me thus transformed to a boy.

LORENZO.

Descend, for you must be my torch-bearer.

JESSICA.

What, must I hold a candle to my shames?
They in themselves, good sooth, are too-too light.
Why, 'tis an office of discovery, love;
And I should be obscured.

LORENZO.
So are you, sweet,
Even in the lovely garnish of a boy.
But come at once;
For the close night doth play the runaway,
And we are stay'd for at Bassanio's feast.

JESSICA.

I will make fast the doors, and gild myself
With some moe ducats, and be with you straight.
    [Exit above.

GRATIANO.

Now, by my hood, a Gentile, and no Jew.

LORENZO.

Beshrew me but I love her heartily;
For she is wise, if I can judge of her;
And fair she is, if that mine eyes be true;
And true she is, as she hath proved herself;
And therefore, like herself, wise, fair, and true,
Shall she be placed in my constant soul.

Enter JESSICA, *below.*

What, art thou come?—On, gentlemen; away!
Our masking mates by this time for us stay.
    [Exit with JESSICA *and* SALARINO.

Enter ANTONIO.

ANTONIO.

Who's there?

GRATIANO.

Signior Antonio!

ANTONIO.

Fie, fie, Gratiano! where are all the rest?
'Tis nine o'clock; our friends all stay for you.
No mask to-night: the wind is come about;
Bassanio presently will go aboard:
I have sent twenty out to seek for you.

GRATIANO.

I am glad on't: I desire no more delight
Than to be under sail and gone to-night. [*Exeunt.*

SCENE VI.

Belmont.   *A room in* PORTIA'S *house.*

Enter PORTIA, *with the* PRINCE OF MOROCCO,
and their TRAINS.   *Flourish cornets.*

PORTIA.

GO draw aside the curtains, and discover
The several caskets to this noble prince.—
Now make your choice.

PRINCE OF MOROCCO.

The first, of gold, which this inscription bears,—
'Who chooseth me shall gain what many men
   desire;'
The second, silver, which this promise carries,—
'Who chooseth me shall get as much as he de-
   serves;'
This third, dull lead, with warning all as blunt,—
'Who chooseth me must give and hazard all he
   hath.'—
How shall I know if I do choose the right?

PORTIA.

The one of them contains my picture, prince:
If you choose that, then I am yours withal.

PRINCE OF MOROCCO.

Some god direct my judgement! Let me see;
I will survey the inscriptions back again.
What says this leaden casket?
'Who chooseth me must give and hazard all he
   hath.'
Must give,—for what? for lead? hazard for lead?
This casket threatens: men that hazard all
Do it in hope of fair advantages:
A golden mind stoops not to shows of dross;
I'll then nor give nor hazard aught for lead.
What says the silver, with her virgin hue?
'Who chooseth me shall get as much as he de-
   serves.'
As much as he deserves!—Pause there, Morocco,
And weigh thy value with an even hand:
If thou be'st rated by thy estimation,
Thou dost deserve enough; and yet enough
May not extend so far as to the lady:
And yet to be afeard of my deserving,
Were but a weak disabling of myself.
As much as I deserve!—Why, that's the lady:
I do in birth deserve her, and in fortunes,
In graces, and in qualities of breeding;
But more than these, in love I do deserve.
What if I stray'd no further, but chose here?—
Let's see once more this saying graved in gold:
'Who chooseth me shall gain what many men
   desire.'
Why, that's the lady; all the world desires her;
From the four corners of the earth they come,
To kiss this shrine, this mortal-breathing saint:
The Hyrcanian deserts and the vasty wilds

Of wide Arabia are as throughfares now
For princes to come view fair Portia:
The watery kingdom, whose ambitious head
Spits in the face of heaven, is no bar
To stop the foreign spirits; but they come,
As o'er a brook, to see fair Portia.
One of these three contains her heavenly picture.
Is't like that lead contains her? 'Twere damnation
To think so base a thought: it were too gross
To rib her cerecloth in the obscure grave.
Or shall I think in silver she's immured,
Being ten times undervalued to tried gold?
O sinful thought! Never so rich a gem
Was set in worse than gold. They have in England
A coin that bears the figure of an angel
Stamped in gold,—but that's insculpt upon;
But here an angel in a golden bed
Lies all within.—Deliver me the key:
Here do I choose, and thrive I as I may!

PORTIA.

There, take it, prince; and if my form lie there,
Then I am yours.   [*He opens the golden casket.*

PRINCE OF MOROCCO.

        O hell! what have we here?
A carrion Death, within whose empty eye
There is a written scroll! I'll read the writing.

   All that glisters is not gold,—
   Often have you heard that told:
   Many a man his life hath sold
   But my outside to behold:
   Gilded tombs do worms infold.
   Had you been as wise as bold,
   Young in limbs, in judgement old,
   Your answer had not been inscroll'd:
   Fare you well; your suit is cold.

Cold, indeed; and labour lost:
   Then, farewell, heat; and welcome, frost!—
Portia, adieu. I have too grieved a heart
To take a tedious leave: thus losers part.

       [*Exit with his* TRAIN.   *Cornets.*

PORTIA.

A gentle riddance.—Draw the curtains, go.—
Let all of his complexion choose me so.   [*Exeunt.*

SCENE VII.

Venice.   A street.

Enter SALARINO *and* SOLANIO.

SALARINO.

WHY, man, I saw Bassanio under sail:
With him is Gratiano gone along;
And in their ship I am sure Lorenzo is not.

SOLANIO.

The villain Jew with outcries raised the duke;
Who went with him to search Bassanio's ship.

SALARINO.

He came too late, the ship was under sail:
But there the duke was given to understand
That in a gondola were seen together
Lorenzo and his amorous Jessica:
Besides, Antonio certified the duke
They were not with Bassanio in his ship.

SOLANIO.

I never heard a passion so confused,
So strange, outrageous, and so variable,

As the dog Jew did utter in the streets:
'My daughter!—O my ducats!—O my daughter!
Fled with a Christian!—O my Christian ducats!—
Justice! the law! my ducats, and my daughter!
A sealed bag, two sealed bags of ducats,
Of double ducats, stol'n from me by my daughter!
And jewels,—two stones, two rich and precious
     stones,
Stol'n by my daughter!—Justice! find the girl!
She hath the stones upon her, and the ducats!'
                    SALARINO.
Why, all the boys in Venice follow him,
Crying,—his stones, his daughter, and his ducats.
                    SOLANIO.
Let good Antonio look he keep his day,
Or he shall pay for this.
                    SALARINO.
                    Marry, well remember'd,
I reason'd with a Frenchman yesterday,
Who told me,—in the narrow seas that part
The French and English, there miscarried
A vessel of our country richly fraught:
I thought upon Antonio when he told me;
And wisht in silence that it were not his.
                    SOLANIO.
You were best to tell Antonio what you hear;
Yet do not suddenly, for it may grieve him.
                    SALARINO.
A kinder gentleman treads not the earth.
I saw Bassanio and Antonio part:
Bassanio told him he would make some speed
Of his return: he answer'd, 'Do not so,—
Slubber not business for my sake, Bassanio,
But stay the very riping of the time;
And for the Jew's bond which he hath of me,
Let it not enter in your mind of love:
Be merry; and employ your chiefest thoughts
To courtship, and such fair ostents of love
As shall conveniently become you there:'
And even there, his eye being big with tears,
Turning his face, he put his hand behind him,
And with affection wondrous sensible
He wrung Bassanio's hand; and so they parted.
                    SOLANIO.
I think he only loves the world for him.
I pray thee, let us go and find him out,
And quicken his embraced heaviness
With some delight or other.
                    SALARINO.
                    Do we so.   [*Exeunt.*

SCENE VIII.

Belmont.   A room in PORTIA'S *house.*

Enter NERISSA *and a* SERVITOR.

                    NERISSA.
QUICK, quick, I pray thee; draw the curtain
     straight:
The Prince of Arragon hath ta'en his oath,
And comes to his election presently.

Enter PRINCE OF ARRAGON, *his* TRAIN, *and*
     PORTIA.   *Flourish cornets.*
                    PORTIA.
Behold, there stand the caskets, noble prince:
If you choose that wherein I am contain'd,

Straight shall our nuptial rites be solemnized:
But if you fail, without more speech, my lord,
You must be gone from hence immediately.
                    PRINCE OF ARRAGON.
I am enjoin'd by oath to observe three things:—
First, never to unfold to any one
Which casket 'twas I chose; next, if I fail
Of the right casket, never in my life
To woo a maid in way of marriage; lastly,
If I do fail in fortune of my choice,
Immediately to leave you and be gone.
                    PORTIA.
To these injunctions every one doth swear
That comes to hazard for my worthless self.
                    PRINCE OF ARRAGON.
And so have I addrest me.   Fortune now
To my heart's hope!—Gold, silver, and base lead.
'Who chooseth me must give and hazard all he
     hath.'
You shall look fairer, ere I give or hazard.
What says the golden chest? ha! let me see:
'Who chooseth me shall gain what many men
     desire.'
What many men desire!—that many may be
     meant
By the fool multitude, that choose by show,
Not learning more than the fond eye doth teach;
Which pries not to th' interior, but, like the
     martlet,
Builds in the weather on the outward wall,
Even in the force and road of casualty.
I will not choose what many men desire,
Because I will not jump with common spirits,
And rank me with the barbarous multitudes.
Why, then to thee, thou silver treasure-house;
Tell me once more what title thou dost bear:
'Who chooseth me shall get as much as he de-
     serves:'
And well said too; for who shall go about
To cozen fortune, and be honourable
Without the stamp of merit? Let none presume
To wear an undeserved dignity.
O, that estates, degrees, and offices,
Were not derived corruptly! and that clear honour
Were purchased by the merit of the wearer!
How many then should cover that stand bare!
How many be commanded that command!
How much low peasantry would then be glean'd
From the true seed of honour! and how much
     honour
Pickt from the chaff and ruin of the times,
To be new-varnisht! Well, but to my choice:
'Who chooseth me shall get as much as he de-
     serves.'
I will assume desert.—Give me a key for this,
And instantly unlock my fortunes here.
                    [*He opens the silver casket.*
                    PORTIA [*aside*].
Too long a pause for that which you find here.
                    PRINCE OF ARRAGON.
What's here? the portrait of a blinking idiot,
Presenting me a schedule! I will read it.
How much unlike art thou to Portia!
How much unlike my hopes and my deservings!
'Who chooseth me shall have as much as he de
     serves.'

Did I deserve no more than a fool's head?
Is that my prize? are my deserts no better?
PORTIA.
To offend, and judge, are distinct offices,
And of opposed natures.
PRINCE OF ARRAGON.
                    What is here?

The fire seven times tried this:
Seven times tried that judgement is,
That did never choose amiss.
Some there be that shadows kiss;
Such have but a shadow's bliss.
There be fools alive, I wis,
Silver'd o'er; and so was this.
Take what wife you will to bed,
I will ever be your head:
So be gone; you are sped.

Still more fool I shall appear
By the time I linger here:
With one fool's head I came to woo,
But I go away with two.—
Sweet, adieu. I'll keep my oath,
Patiently to bear my wroth.

[*Exit with his* TRAIN.
PORTIA.
Thus hath the candle singed the moth.
O, these deliberate fools! when they do choose,
They have the wisdom by their wit to lose.
NERISSA.
The ancient saying is no heresy,—
Hanging and wiving goes by destiny.
PORTIA.
Come, draw the curtain, Nerissa.
Enter a SERVANT.
SERVANT.
Where is my lady?
PORTIA.
                Here: what would my lord?
SERVANT.
Madam, there is alighted at your gate
A young Venetian, one that comes before
To signify th' approaching of his lord;
From whom he bringeth sensible regreets,
To wit, besides commends and courteous breath,
Gifts of rich value. Yet I have not seen
So likely an ambassador of love:
A day in April never came so sweet,
To show how costly summer was at hand,
As this fore-spurrer comes before his lord.
PORTIA.
No more, I pray thee: I am half afeard
Thou wilt say anon he is some kin to thee,
Thou spend'st such high-day wit in praising
Come, come, Nerissa; for I long to see   [him.—
Quick Cupid's post that comes so mannerly.
NERISSA.
Bassanio, lord Love, if thy will it be!   [*Exeunt.*

ACT III.   SCENE I.
Venice.   A street.
Enter SOLANIO *and* SALARINO.
SOLANIO.
NOW, what news on the Rialto?
SOLANIO.
Why, yet it lives there uncheckt, that Antonio

hath a ship of rich lading wrackt on the narrow
seas; the Goodwins, I think they call the place; a
very dangerous flat and fatal, where the carcasses
of many a tall ship lie buried, as they say, if my
gossip Report be an honest woman of her word.
SOLANIO.
I would she were as lying a gossip in that as ever
knapt ginger, or made her neighbours believe she
wept for the death of a third husband. But it is
true,—without any slips of prolixity, or crossing
the plain highway of talk,—that the good Antonio, the honest Antonio,——O, that I had a
title good enough to keep his name company!—
SALARINO.
Come, the full stop.
SOLANIO.
Ha,—what sayest thou?—Why, the end is, he hath
lost a ship.
SALARINO.
I would it might prove the end of his losses.
SOLANIO.
Let me say amen betimes, lest the devil cross my
prayer,—for here he comes in the likeness of a Jew.
Enter SHYLOCK.
How now, Shylock! what news among the mer-
chants?
SHYLOCK.
You knew, none so well, none so well as you, of my
daughter's flight.
SALARINO.
That's certain: I, for my part, knew the tailor that
made the wings she flew withal.
SOLANIO.
And Shylock, for his own part, knew the bird was
fledged; and then it is the complexion of them all
to leave the dam.
SHYLOCK.
She is damn'd for it.
SALARINO.
That's certain, if the devil may be her judge.
SHYLOCK.
My own flesh and blood to rebel!
SOLANIO.
Out upon it, old carrion! rebels it at these years?
SHYLOCK.
I say my daughter is my flesh and blood.
SALARINO.
There is more difference between thy flesh and
hers than between jet and ivory; more between
your bloods than there is between red wine and
rhenish.—But tell us, do you hear whether An-
tonio have had any loss at sea or no?
SHYLOCK.
There I have another bad match: a bankrout, a
prodigal, who dare scarce show his head on the
Rialto;—a beggar, that was used to come so smug
upon the mart;—let him look to his bond; he was
wont to call me usurer;—let him look to his bond:
he was wont to lend money for a Christian courtesy:—let him look to his bond.
SALARINO.
Why, I am sure, if he forfeit, thou wilt not take
his flesh: what's that good for?
SHYLOCK.
To bait fish withal: if it will feed nothing else, it
will feed my revenge. He hath disgraced me, and

hinder'd me half a million; laught at my losses, mockt at my gains, scorn'd my nation, thwarted my bargains, cooled my friends, heated mine enemies: and what's his reason? I am a Jew. Hath not a Jew eyes? hath not a Jew hands, organs, dimensions, senses, affections, passions? fed with the same food, hurt with the same weapons, subject to the same diseases, heal'd by the same means, warm'd and cool'd by the same winter and summer, as a Christian is? If you prick us, do we not bleed? if you tickle us, do we not laugh? if you poison us, do we not die? and if you wrong us, shall we not revenge? if we are like you in the rest, we will resemble you in that. If a Jew wrong a Christian, what is his humility? revenge: if a Christian wrong a Jew, what should his sufferance be by Christian example? why, revenge. The villainy you teach me, I will execute; and it shall go hard but I will better the instruction.

Enter a SERVANT *from* ANTONIO.

SERVANT.

Gentlemen, my master Antonio is at his house, and desires to speak with you both.

SALARINO.

We have been up and down to seek him.

SOLANIO.

Here comes another of the tribe: a third cannot be matcht, unless the devil himself turn Jew.

[*Exeunt* SOLANIO, SALARINO, *and* SERVANT.

Enter TUBAL.

SHYLOCK.

How now, Tubal! what news from Genoa? hast thou found my daughter?

TUBAL.

I often came where I did hear of her, but cannot find her.

SHYLOCK.

Why, there, there, there, there! a diamond gone, cost me two thousand ducats in Frankfort! The curse never fell upon our nation till now; I never felt it till now:—two thousand ducats in that; and other precious, precious jewels.—I would my daughter were dead at my foot, and the jewels in her ear! would she were hearsed at my foot, and the ducats in her coffin! No news of them?—Why, so:—and I know not what's spent in the search: why, thou, loss upon loss! the thief gone with so much, and so much to find the thief; and no satisfaction, no revenge: nor no ill luck stirring but what lights on my shoulders; no sighs but of my breathing; no tears but of my shedding.

TUBAL.

Yes, other men have ill luck too: Antonio, as I heard in Genoa,—

SHYLOCK.

What, what, what? ill luck, ill luck?

TUBAL.

Hath an argosy cast away, coming from Tripolis.

SHYLOCK.

I thank God, I thank God!—Is't true, is't true?

TUBAL.

I spoke with some of the sailors that escaped the wrack.

SHYLOCK.

I thank thee, good Tubal:—good news, good news! ha, ha!—where? in Genoa?

TUBAL.

Your daughter spent in Genoa, as I heard, one night fourscore ducats.

SHYLOCK.

Thou stick'st a dagger in me:—I shall never see my gold again: fourscore ducats at a sitting! fourscore ducats!

TUBAL.

There came divers of Antonio's creditors in my company to Venice, that swear he cannot choose but break.

SHYLOCK.

I am very glad of it:—I'll plague him; I'll torture him:—I am glad on't.

TUBAL.

One of them show'd me a ring that he had of your daughter for a monkey.

SHYLOCK.

Out upon her! Thou torturest me, Tubal: it was my turquoise; I had it of Leah when I was a bachelor: I would not have given it for a wilderness of monkeys.

TUBAL.

But Antonio is certainly undone.

SHYLOCK.

Nay, that's true, that's very true. Go, Tubal, fee me an officer; bespeak him a fortnight before. I will have the heart of him, if he forfeit; for, were he out of Venice, I can make what merchandise I will. Go, Tubal, and meet me at our synagogue; go, good Tubal; at our synagogue, Tubal.

[*Exeunt.*

SCENE II.

Belmont.   A room in PORTIA'S *house.*

Enter BASSANIO, PORTIA, GRATIANO, NERISSA, *and all their* TRAIN.

PORTIA.

I PRAY you, tarry: pause a day or two
Before you hazard; for, in choosing wrong,
I lose your company: therefore, forbear awhile.
There's something tells me—but it is not love—
I would not lose you; and you know yourself,
Hate counsels not in such a quality.
But lest you should not understand me well,—
And yet a maiden hath no tongue but thought,—
I would detain you here some month or two
Before you venture for me. I could teach you
How to choose right, but then I am forsworn;
So will I never be: so may you miss me;
But if you do, you'll make me wish a sin,
That I had been forsworn. Beshrew your eyes,
They have o'erlookt me, and divided me;
One half of me is yours, the other half yours,—
Mine own, I would say; but if mine, then yours,
And so all yours! O, these naughty times
Put bars between the owners and their rights!
And so, though yours, not yours.—Prove it so,
Let fortune go to hell for it,—not I.
I speak too long; but 'tis to peize the time,
To eke it, and to draw it out in length,
To stay you from election.

BASSIANO.

Let me choose;
For, as I am, I live upon the rack.

PORTIA.

Upon the rack, Bassanio! then confess
What treason there is mingled with your love.

BASSANIO.

None but that ugly treason of mistrust,
Which makes me fear the enjoying of my love:
There may as well be amity and league
'Tween snow and fire, as treason and my love.

PORTIA.

Ay, but I fear you speak upon the rack,
Where men enforced do speak any thing.

BASSANIO.

Promise me life, and I'll confess the truth.

PORTIA.

Well then, confess, and live.

BASSANIO.

　　　　　　　　　　'Confess,' and 'love,'
Had been the very sum of my confession:
O happy torment, when my torturer
Doth teach me answers for deliverance!
But let me to my fortune and the caskets.

PORTIA.

Away, then! I am lockt in one of them:
If you do love me, you will find me out.—
Nerissa, and the rest, stand all aloof.—
Let music sound while he doth make his choice;
Then, if he lose, he makes a swan-like end,
Fading in music: that the comparison　　[stream
May stand more proper, my eye shall be the
And watery death-bed for him. He may win;
And what is music then? then music is
Even as the flourish when true subjects bow
To a new-crowned monarch: such it is
As are those dulcet sounds in break of day
That creep into the dreaming bridegroom's ear,
And summon him to marriage.—Now he goes,
With no less presence, but with much more love,
Than young Alcides, when he did redeem
The virgin tribute paid by howling Troy
To the sea-monster: I stand for sacrifice;
The rest aloof are the Dardanian wives,
With bleared visages, come forth to view
The issue of th' exploit. Go, Hercules!
Live thou, I live:—with much much more dismay
I view the fight then thou that makest the fray.
Here music.—A Song, the whilst BASSANIO *comments on the caskets to himself.*

Tell me where is fancy bred,
Or in the heart or in the head?
How begot, how nourished?
　　Reply, reply.
It is engender'd in the eyes,
With gazing fed; and fancy dies
In the cradle where it lies.
　　Let us all ring fancy's knell;
　　I'll begin it,—Ding, dong, bell.
All. Ding, dong, bell.

BASSANIO.

So may the outward shows be least themselves:
The world is still deceived with ornament.
In law, what plea so tainted and corrupt,
But, being season'd with a gracious voice,
Obscures the show of evil? In religion,
What damned error, but some sober brow
Will bless it, and approve it with a text,
Hiding the grossness with fair ornament?
There is no vice so simple, but assumes
Some mark of virtue on his outward parts:
How many cowards, whose hearts are all as false
As stairs of sand, wear yet upon their chins
The beards of Hercules and frowning Mars;
Who, inward searcht, have livers white as milk;
And these assume but valour's excrement
To render them redoubted! Look on beauty,
And you shall see 'tis purchased by the weight;
Which therein works a miracle in nature,
Making them lightest that wear most of it:
So are those crisped snaky golden locks,
Which make such wanton gambols with the wind,
Upon supposed fairness, often known
To be the dowry of a second head,
The skull that bred them in the sepulchre.
Thus ornament is but the guiled shore
To a most dangerous sea; the beauteous scarf
Veiling an Indian beauty; in a word,
The seeming truth which cunning times put on
To entrap the wisest. Therefore, thou gaudy
　　gold,
Hard food for Midas, I will none of thee;
Nor none of thee, thou stale and common drudge
'Tween man and man: but thou, thou meagre
　　lead,　　　　　　　　　　　　　　　[aught,
Which rather threatenest than dost promise
Thy paleness moves me more than eloquence;
And here choose I:—joy be the consequence!

PORTIA [*aside*].

How all the other passions fleet to air,—
As doubtful thoughts, and rash-embraced despair,
And shuddering fear, and green-eyed jealousy!
O love, be moderate; allay thy ecstasy;
In measure rain thy joy; scant this excess!
I feel too much thy blessing : make it less,
For fear I surfeit!

BASSANIO.

　　　　　　What find I here?
　　　　　　　[*Opening the leaden casket.*
Fair Portia's counterfeit! What demi-god
Hath come so near creation? Move these eyes?
Or whether, riding on the balls of mine,
Seem they in motion? Here are sever'd lips,
Parted with sugar breath: so sweet a bar
Should sunder such sweet friends. Here in her
　　hairs
The painter plays the spider; and hath woven
A golden mesh t'entrap the hearts of men,
Faster than gnats in cobwebs: but her eyes,—
How could he see to do them? having made one,
Methinks it should have power to steal both his,
And leave itself unfurnisht. Yet look, how far
The substance of my praise doth wrong this
　　shadow
In underprizing it, so far this shadow
Doth limp behind the substance.—Here's the
　　scroll,
The continent and summary of my fortune.

You that choose not by the view,
Chance as fair, and choose as true!
Since this fortune falls to you,
Be content, and seek no new.
If you be well pleased with this,

And hold your fortune for your bliss,
Turn you where your lady is,
And claim her with a loving kiss.

A gentle scroll.—Fair lady, by your leave;
                      [*Kissing her.*
I come by note, to give and to receive.
Like one of two contending in a prize,
That thinks he hath done well in people's eyes,
Hearing applause and universal shout,
Giddy in spirit, still gazing in a doubt
Whether those peals of praise be his or no;
So, thrice-fair lady, stand I, even so;
As doubtful whether what I see be true,
Until confirm'd, sign'd, ratified by you.

                PORTIA.
You see me, Lord Bassanio, where I stand,
Such as I am: though for myself alone
I would not be ambitious in my wish,
To wish myself much better; yet for you
I would be trebled twenty times myself;
A thousand times more fair, ten thousand times
    more rich;
That, only to stand high in your account,
I might in virtues, beauties, livings, friends,
Exceed account: but the full sum of me
Is sum of nothing; which, to term in gross,
Is an unlesson'd girl, unschool'd, unpractised:
Happy in this, she is not yet so old
But she may learn; happier than this,
She is not bred so dull but she can learn;
Happiest of all is that her gentle spirit
Commits itself to yours to be directed,
As from her lord, her governor, her king.
Myself and what is mine to you and yours
Is now converted: but now I was the lord
Of this fair mansion, master of my servants,
Queen o'er myself; and even now, but now,
This house, these servants, and this same myself,
Are yours, my lord: I give them with this ring;
Which when you part from, lose, or give away,
Let it presage the ruin of your love,
And be my vantage to exclaim on you.

              BASSANIO.
Madam, you have bereft me of all words,
Only my blood speaks to you in my veins:
And there is such confusion in my powers,
As, after some oration fairly spoke
By a beloved prince, there doth appear
Among the buzzing pleased multitude;
Where every something, being blent together,
Turns to a wild of nothing, save of joy,
Exprest and not exprest. But when this ring
Parts from this finger, then parts life from hence:
O, then be bold to say Bassanio's dead!

              NERISSA.
My lord and lady, it is now our time,
That have stood by, and seen our wishes prosper,
To cry, good joy:—good joy, my lord and lady!

             GRATIANO.
My Lord Bassanio and my gentle lady,
    wish you all the joy that you can wish;
For I am sure you can wish none from me:
And, when your honours mean to solemnize
The bargain of your faith, I do beseech you,
Even at that time I may be married too.

             BASSANIO.
With all my heart, so thou canst get a wife.

             GRATIANO.
I thank your lordship, you have got me one.
My eyes, my lord, can look as swift as yours:
You saw the mistress, I beheld the maid;
You loved, I loved; for intermission
No more pertains to me, my lord, than you.
Your fortune stood upon the caskets there;
And so did mine too, as the matter falls;
For wooing here, until I sweat again,
And swearing, till my very roof was dry
With oaths of love, at last,—if promise last,—
I got a promise of this fair one here,
To have her love, provided that your fortune
Achieved her mistress.

             PORTIA.
            Is this true, Nerissa?

             NERISSA.
Madam, it is, so you stand pleased withal.

             BASSANIO.
And do you, Gratiano, mean good faith?

             GRATIANO.
Yes, faith, my lord.

             BASSANIO.
Our feast shall be much honour'd in your marriage.

             GRATIANO.
We'll play with them the first boy for a thousand
ducats.

             NERISSA.
What, and stake down?

             GRATIANO.
No; we shall ne'er win at that sport, and stake
down.—
But who comes here? Lorenzo and his infidel?
What, and my old Venetian friend Solanio?

     Enter LORENZO, JESSICA, *and* SOLANIO.

             BASSANIO.
Lorenzo and Solanio, welcome hither;
If that the youth of my new interest here
Have power to bid you welcome.—By your
    leave,
I bid my very friends and countrymen,
Sweet Portia, welcome.

             PORTIA.
            So do I, my lord;
They are entirely welcome.

             LORENZO.
I thank your honour.—For my part, my lord,
My purpose was not to have seen you here;
But meeting with Solanio by the way,
He did entreat me, past all saying nay,
To come with him along.

             SOLANIO.
            I did, my lord;
And I have reason for't. Signior Antonio
Commends him to you. [*Gives* BASSANIO *a letter.*

             BASSANIO.
            Ere I ope his letter,
I pray you, tell me how my good friend doth.

             SOLANIO.
Not sick, my lord, unless it be in mind;
Not well, unless in mind: his letter there
Will show you his estate.

             [BASSANIO *reads the letter.*

GRATIANO.
Nerissa, cheer yon stranger; bid her welcome.—
Your hand, Solanio: what's the news from
    Venice?
How doth that royal merchant, good Antonio?
I know he will be glad of our success;
We are the Jasons, we have won the fleece.

SOLANIO.
I would you had won the fleece that he hath lost!

PORTIA.
There are some shrewd contents in yon same
    paper,
That steals the colour from Bassanio's cheek:
Some dear friend dead; else nothing in the world
Could turn so much the constitution
Of any constant man. What, worse and worse!—
With leave, Bassanio; I am half yourself,
And I must freely have the half of any thing
That this same paper brings you.

BASSANIO.
                    O sweet Portia,
Here are a few of the unpleasant'st words
That ever blotted paper! Gentle lady,
When I did first impart my love to you,
I freely told you, all the wealth I had
Ran in my veins,—I was a gentleman;
And then I told you true: and yet, dear lady,
Rating myself at nothing, you shall see
How much I was a braggart. When I told you
My state was nothing, I should then have told you
That I was worse than nothing; for, indeed,
I have engaged myself to a dear friend,
Engaged my friend to his mere enemy,
To feed my means. Here is a letter, lady,—
The paper as the body of my friend,
And every word in it a gaping wound,
Issuing life-blood.—But is it true, Solanio?
Have all his ventures fail'd? What, not one hit?
From Tripolis, from Mexico, and England,
From Lisbon, Barbary, and India?
And not one vessel scape the dreadful touch
Of merchant-marring rocks?

SOLANIO.
                    Not one, my lord.
Besides, it should appear, that if he had
The present money to discharge the Jew,
He would not take it. Never did I know
A creature, that did bear the shape of man,
So keen and greedy to confound a man;
He plies the duke at morning and at night;
And doth impeach the freedom of the state,
If they deny him justice: twenty merchants,
The duke himself, and the magnificoes
Of greatest port, have all persuaded with him;
But none can drive him from the envious plea
Of forfeiture, of justice, and his bond.

JESSICA.
When I was with him, I have heard him swear,
To Tubal and to Chus, his countrymen,
That he would rather have Antonio's flesh
Than twenty times the value of the sum
That he did owe him: and I know, my lord,
If law, authority, and power deny not,
It will go hard with poor Antonio.

PORTIA.
Is it your dear friend that is thus in trouble?

BASSANIO.
The dearest friend to me, the kindest man,
The best-condition'd and unwearied spirit
In doing courtesies; and one in whom
The ancient Roman honour more appears
Than any that draws breath in Italy.

PORTIA.
What sum owes he the Jew?

BASSANIO.
For me three thousand ducats.

PORTIA.
                    What, no more?
Pay him six thousand, and deface the bond;
Double six thousand, and then treble that,
Before a friend of this description
Shall lose a hair through Bassanio's fault.
First go with me to church and call me wife,
And then away to Venice to your friend;
For never shall you lie by Portia's side
With an unquiet soul. You shall have gold
To pay the petty debt twenty times over:
When it is paid, bring your true friend along.
My maid Nerissa and myself meantime
Will live as maids and widows. Come, away!
For you shall hence upon your wedding-day:
Bid your friends welcome, show a merry cheer:
Since you are dear-bought, I will love you dear.—
But let me hear the letter of your friend.

BASSANIO [reads].
Sweet Bassanio, my ships have all miscarried,
my creditors grow cruel, my estate is very low,
my bond to the Jew is forfeit; and since in paying
it, it is impossible I should live, all debts are
clear'd between you and I, if I might but see you
at my death. Notwithstanding, use your pleasure:
if your love do not persuade you to come, let not
my letter.

PORTIA.
O love, dispatch all business, and be gone!

BASSANIO.
Since I have your good leave to go away,
    I will make haste: but, till I come again,
No bed shall e'er be guilty of my stay,
    No rest be interposer 'twixt us twain.   [Exeunt.

SCENE III.
Venice.   A street.

Enter SHYLOCK, SALARINO, ANTONIO, and
GAOLER.

SHYLOCK.
GAOLER, look to him:—tell not me of
    mercy;—
This is the fool that lent out money gratis:—
Gaoler, look to him.

ANTONIO.
                    Hear me yet, good Shylock.

SHYLOCK.
I'll have my bond; speak not against my bond:
I have sworn an oath that I will have my bond.
Thou call'dst me dog before thou hadst a cause;
But, since I am a dog, beware my fangs:
The duke shall grant me justice.—I do wonder,
Thou naughty gaoler, that thou art so fond
To come abroad with him at his request.

ANTONIO.
I pray thee, hear me speak.
SHYLOCK.
I'll have my bond; I will not hear thee speak:
I'll have my bond; and therefore speak no more.
I'll not be made a soft and dull-eyed fool,
To shake the head, relent, and sigh, and yield
To Christian intercessors. Follow not;
I'll have no speaking: I will have my bond. [*Exit.*
SALARINO.
It is the most impenetrable cur
That ever kept with men.
ANTONIO.
Let him alone:
I'll follow him no more with bootless prayers.
He seeks my life; his reason well I know:
I oft deliver'd from his forfeitures
Many that have at times made moan to me;
Therefore he hates me.
SALARINO.
I am sure the duke
Will never grant this forfeiture to hold.
ANTONIO.
The duke cannot deny the course of law;
For the commodity that strangers have
With us in Venice, if it be denied,
Will much impeach the justice of the state;
Since that the trade and profit of the city
Consisteth of all nations. Therefore, go:
These griefs and losses have so bated me,
That I shall hardly spare a pound of flesh
To-morrow to my bloody creditor.—
Well, gaoler, on.—Pray God, Bassanio come
To see me pay his debt,—and then I care not!
[*Exeunt.*

SCENE IV.

Belmont.   A room in PORTIA'S *house.*

Enter PORTIA, NERISSA, LORENZO, JESSICA,
and BALTHAZAR, *a man of* PORTIA'S.

LORENZO.
MADAM, although I speak it in your presence,
You have a noble and a true conceit
Of god-like amity; which appears most strongly
In bearing thus the absence of your lord.
But if you knew to whom you show this honour,
How true a gentleman you sen i relief,
How dear a lover of my lord your husband,
I know you would be prouder of the work
Than customary bounty can enforce you.
PORTIA.
I never did repent for doing good,
Nor shall not now: for in companions
That do converse and waste the time together,
Whose souls do bear an egal yoke of love,
There must be needs a like proportion
Of lineaments, of manners, and of spirit;
Which makes me think that this Antonio,
Being the bosom lover of my lord,
Must needs be like my lord. If it be so,
How little is the cost I have bestow'd
In purchasing the semblance of my soul
From out the state of hellish cruelty!
This comes too near the praising of myself;
Therefore no more of it: hear other things.—

Lorenzo, I commit into your hands
The husbandry and manage of my house
Until my lord's return: for mine own part,
I have toward heaven breathed a secret vow
To live in prayer and contemplation,
Only attended by Nerissa here,
Until her husband and my lord's return:
There is a monastery two miles off;
And there will we abide. I do desire you
Not to deny this imposition;
The which my love and some necessity
Now lays upon you.
LORENZO.
Madam, with all my heart;
I shall obey you in all fair commands.
PORTIA.
My people do already know my mind,
And will acknowledge you and Jessica
In place of Lord Bassanio and myself.
So fare you well, till we shall meet again.
LORENZO.
Fair thoughts and happy hours attend on you!
JESSICA.
I wish your ladyship all heart's content.
PORTIA.
I thank you for your wish, and am well pleased
To wish it back on you: fare you well, Jessica.
[*Exeunt* JESSICA *and* LORENZO.
Now, Balthazar,
As I have ever found thee honest-true,
So let me find thee still. Take this same letter,
And use thou all the endeavour of a man
In speed to Padua: see thou render this
Into my cousin's hand, Doctor Bellario;
And, look, what notes and garments he doth give
      thee,
Bring them, I pray thee, with imagined speed
Unto the tranect, to the common ferry
Which trades to Venice. Waste no time in words,
But get thee gone: I shall be there before thee.
BALTHAZAR.
Madam, I go with all convenient speed.   [*Exit.*
PORTIA.
Come on, Nerissa; I have work in hand
That you yet know not of: we'll see our husbands
Before they think of us.
NERISSA.
Shall they see us?
PORTIA.
They shall, Nerissa; but in such a habit,
That they shall think we are accomplished
With that we lack. I'll hold thee any wager,
When we are both accoutred like young men,
I'll prove the prettier fellow of the two,
And wear my dagger with the braver grace;
And speak between the change of man and boy
With a reed voice; and turn two mincing steps
Into a manly stride; and speak of frays,
Like a fine-bragging youth; and tell quaint lies,
How honourable ladies sought my love,
Which I denying, they fell sick and died,—
I could not do withal;—then I'll repent,
And wish, for all that, that I had not kill'd them:
And twenty of these puny lies I'll tell;
That men shall swear I have discontinued school
Above a twelvemonth:—I have within my mind

405

A thousand raw tricks of these bragging Jacks,
Which I will practise.

NERISSA.
           Why, shall we turn to men?

PORTIA.
Fie, what a question's that,
If thou wert near a lewd interpreter!
But come, I'll tell thee all my whole device
When I am in my coach, which stays for us
At the park-gate; and therefore haste away,
For we must measure twenty miles to-day.

                          [*Exeunt.*

SCENE V.

The same.   A garden.

Enter LAUNCELOT *and* JESSICA.

LAUNCELOT.
YES, truly; for, look you, the sins of the father
are to be laid upon the children: therefore,
I promise ye, I fear you. I was always plain with
you, and so now I speak my agitation of the matter: therefore be o' good cheer; for, truly, I think
you are damn'd. There is but one hope in it that
can do you any good; and that is but a kind of
bastard hope neither.

JESSICA.
And what hope is that, I pray thee?

LAUNCELOT.
Marry, you may partly hope that your father got
you not,—that you are not the Jew's daughter.

JESSICA.
That were a kind of bastard hope, indeed: so
the sins of my mother should be visited upon
me.

LAUNCELOT.
Truly, then, I fear you are damn'd both by father
and mother: thus when I shun Scylla, your father,
I fall into Charybdis, your mother: well, you are
gone both ways.

JESSICA.
I shall be saved by my husband; he hath made me
a Christian.

LAUNCELOT.
Truly, the more to blame he: we were Christians
enow before; e'en as many as could well live, one
by another. This making of Christians will raise
the price of hogs: if we grow all to be pork-eaters,
we shall not shortly have a rasher on the coals for
money.

JESSICA.
I'll tell my husband, Launcelot, what you say:
here he comes.

Enter LORENZO.

LORENZO.
I shall grow jealous of you shortly, Launcelot, if
you thus get my wife into corners.

JESSICA.
Nay, you need not fear us, Lorenzo: Launcelot
and I are out. He tells me flatly, there's no mercy
for me in heaven, because I am a Jew's daughter:
and he says, you are no good member of the
commonwealth; for, in converting Jews to Christians, you raise the price of pork.

LORENZO.
I shall answer that better to the commonwealth

than you can the getting up of the negro's belly:
the Moor's with child by you, Launcelot.

LAUNCELOT.
It is much that the Moor should be more than
reason: but if she be less than an honest woman,
she is indeed more than I took her for.

LORENZO.
How every fool can play upon the word! I think
the best grace of wit will shortly turn into silence,
and discourse grow commendable in none only
but parrots.—Go in, sirrah; bid them prepare for
dinner.

LAUNCELOT.
That's done, sir; they have all stomachs.

LORENZO.
Goodly Lord, what a wit-snapper are you! then
bid them prepare dinner.

LAUNCELOT.
That is done too, sir; only 'cover' is the word.

LORENZO.
Will you cover, then, sir?

LAUNCELOT.
Not so, sir, neither; I know my duty.

LORENZO.
Yet more quarrelling with occasion! Wilt thou
show the whole wealth of thy wit in an instant? I
pray thee, understand a plain man in his plain
meaning: go to thy fellows, bid them cover the
table, serve in the meat, and we will come in to
dinner.

LAUNCELOT.
For the table, sir, it shall be served in; for the
meat, sir, it shall be cover'd; for your coming in
to dinner, sir, why, let it be as humours and conceits shall govern.   [*Exit.*

LORENZO.
O dear discretion, how his words are suited!
The fool hath planted in his memory
An army of good words; and I do know
A many fools, that stand in better place,
Garnisht like him, that for a tricksy word
Defy the matter.—How cheer'st thou, Jessica?
And now, good sweet, say thy opinion,—
How dost thou like the Lord Bassanio's wife?

JESSICA.
Past all expressing. It is very meet
The Lord Bassanio live an upright life;
For, having such a blessing in his lady,
He finds the joys of heaven here on earth;
And if on earth he do not mean it, then
In reason he should never come to heaven.
Why, if two gods should play some heavenly
    match,
And on the wager lay two earthly women,
And Portia one, there must be something else
Pawn'd with the other; for the poor rude world
Hath not her fellow.

LORENZO.
          Even such a husband
Hast thou of me as she is for a wife.

JESSICA.
Nay, but ask my opinion too of that.

LORENZO.
I will anon: first, let us go to dinner.

JESSICA.
Nay, let me praise you while I have a stomach.

LORENZO.

No, prithee, let it serve for table-talk;
Then, howsoe'er thou speak'st, 'mong other
    things
I shall digest it.

JESSICA.

Well, I'll set you forth.   [Exeunt.

ACT IV. SCENE I.

Venice.   A court of justice.

Enter the DUKE, *the* MAGNIFICOES, ANTONIO,
    BASSANIO, GRATIANO, SOLANIO, SALARINO,
    and others.

DUKE OF VENICE.

WHAT, is Antonio here?

ANTONIO.

Ready, so please your Grace.

DUKE OF VENICE.

I am sorry for thee: thou art come to answer
A stony adversary, an inhuman wretch
Uncapable of pity, void and empty
From any dram of mercy.

ANTONIO.

                    I have heard
Your Grace hath ta'en great pains to qualify
His rigorous course; but since he stands obdurate,
And that no lawful means can carry me
Out of his envy's reach, I do oppose
My patience to his fury; and am arm'd
To suffer, with a quietness of spirit,
The very tyranny and rage of his.

DUKE OF VENICE.

Go one, and call the Jew into the court.

SOLANIO.

He's ready at the door: he comes, my lord.

Enter SHYLOCK.

DUKE OF VENICE.

Make room, and let him stand before our face.—
Shylock, the world thinks, and I think so too,
That thou but lead'st this fashion of thy malice
To the last hour of act; and then 'tis thought
Thou'lt show thy mercy and remorse more
    strange
Than is thy strange apparent cruelty;
And where thou now exact'st the penalty,—
Which is a pound of this poor merchant's flesh,—
Thou wilt not only loose the forfeiture,
But, toucht with human gentleness and love,
Forgive a moiety of the principal;
Glancing an eye of pity on his losses,
That have of late so huddled on his back,
Enow to press a royal merchant down,
And pluck commiseration of his state
From brassy bosoms and rough hearts of flint,
From stubborn Turks and Tartars, never train'd
To offices of tender courtesy.
We all expect a gentle answer, Jew.

SHYLOCK.

I have possest your Grace of what I purpose;
And by our holy Sabbath have I sworn
To have the due and forfeit of my bond:
If you deny it, let the danger light
Upon your charter and your city's freedom.
You'll ask me, why I rather choose to have
A weight of carrion-flesh than to receive

Three thousand ducats: I'll not answer that;
But say it is my humour: is it answer'd?
What if my house be troubled with a rat,
And I be pleased to give ten thousand ducats
To have it baned! What, are you answer'd yet?
Some men there are love not a gaping pig;
Some, that are mad if they behold a cat;
And others, when the bag-pipe sings i' th' nose,
Cannot contain their urine: for affection,
Mistress of passion, sways it to the mood
Of what it likes or loathes. Now, for your answer:
As there is no firm reason to be render'd,
Why he cannot abide a gaping pig;
Why he, a harmless necessary cat;
Why he, a woollen bag-pipe,—but of force
Must yield to such inevitable shame
As to offend himself, being offended;
So can I give no reason, nor I will not,
More than a lodged hate and a certain loathing
I bear Antonio, that I follow thus
A losing suit against him. Are you answer'd?

BASSANIO.

This is no answer, thou unfeeling man,
To excuse the current of thy cruelty.

SHYLOCK.

I am not bound to please thee with my answer.

BASSANIO.

Do all men kill the things they do not love?

SHYLOCK.

Hates any man the thing he would not kill?

BASSANIO.

Every offence is not a hate at first.

SHYLOCK.

What, would'st thou have a serpent sting thee
    twice?

ANTONIO.

I pray you, think you question with the Jew:
You may as well go stand upon the beach,
And bid the main flood bate his usual height;
You may as well use question with the wolf,
Why he hath made the ewe bleat for the lamb;
You may as well forbid the mountain pines
To wag their high tops, and to make no noise,
When they are fretten with the gusts of heaven;
You may as well do any thing most hard,
As seek to soften that,—than which what's
    harder?—
His Jewish heart:—therefore, I do beseech you,
Make no more offers, use no further means,
But, with all brief and plain conveniency,
Let me have judgement, and the Jew his will.

BASSANIO.

For thy three thousand ducats here is six.

SHYLOCK.

If every ducat in six thousand ducats
Were in six parts, and every part a ducat,
I would not draw them,—I would have my bond.

DUKE OF VENICE.

How shalt thou hope for mercy, rendering none?

SHYLOCK.

What judgement shall I dread, doing no wrong?
You have among you many a purchased slave,
Which, like your asses and your dogs and mules.
You use in abject and in slavish parts,
Because you bought them:—shall I say to you,
Let them be free, marry them to your heirs?

Why sweat they under burdens? let their beds
Be made as soft as yours, and let their palates
Be season'd with such viands? You will answer,
The slaves are ours:—so do I answer you:
The pound of flesh, which I demand of him,
Is dearly bought, 'tis mine, and I will have it.
If you deny me, fie upon your law!
There is no force in the decrees of Venice.
I stand for judgment: answer.—shall I have it?

DUKE OF VENICE.
Upon my power I may dismiss this court,
Unless Bellario, a learned doctor,
Whom I have sent for to determine this,
Come here to-day.

SOLANIO.
My lord, here stays without
A messenger with letters from the doctor,
New come from Padua.

DUKE OF VENICE.
Bring us the letters; call the messenger.

BASSANIO.
Good cheer, Antonio! What, man, courage yet
The Jew shall have my flesh, blood, bones, and all,
Ere thou shalt lose for me one drop of blood.

ANTONIO.
I am a tainted wether of the flock,
Meetest for death: the weakest kind of fruit
Drops earliest to the ground; and so let me:
You cannot better be employ'd, Bassanio,
Than to live still, and write mine epitaph.

Enter NERISSA, *dressed like a lawyer's clerk.*

DUKE OF VENICE.
Came you from Padua, from Bellario?

NERISSA.
From both, my lord. Bellario greets your Grace.
[*Presents a letter.*

BASSANIO.
Why dost thou whet thy knife so earnestly?

SHYLOCK.
To cut the forfeiture from that bankrout there.

GRATIANO.
Not on thy sole, but on thy soul, harsh Jew,
Thou makest thy knife keen; but no metal can,
No, not the hangman's axe, bear half the keenness
Of thy sharp envy. Can no prayers pierce thee?

SHYLOCK.
No, none that thou hast wit enough to make.

GRATIANO.
O, be thou damn'd, inexecrable dog!
And for thy life let justice be accused.
Thou almost makest me waver in my faith,
To hold opinion with Pythagoras,
That souls of animals infuse themselves
Into the trunks of men: thy currish spirit
Govern'd a wolf, who, hang'd for human slaughter,
Even from the gallows did his fell soul fleet,
And, whilst thou lay'st in thy unhallow'd dam,
Infused itself in thee; for thy desires
Are wolvish, bloody, starved, and ravenous.

SHYLOCK.
Till thou canst rail the seal from off my bond,
Thou but offend'st thy lungs to speak so loud:
Repair thy wit, good youth, or it will fall
To cureless ruin.—I stand here for law.

DUKE OF VENICE.
This letter from Bellario doth commend
A young and learned doctor to our court.—
Where is he?

NERISSA.
He attendeth here hard by,
To know your answer, whether you'll admit him.

DUKE OF VENICE.
With all my heart.—Some three or four of you
Go give him courteous conduct to this place.—
Meantime the court shall hear Bellario's letter.

CLERK [*reads*].
Your Grace shall understand, that at the receipt
of your letter I am very sick: but in the instant
that your messenger came, in loving visitation
was with me a young doctor of Rome; his name is
Balthazar. I acquainted him with the cause in
controversy between the Jew and Antonio the
merchant: we turn'd o'er many books together: he
is furnisht with my opinion; which, better'd with
his own learning,—the greatness whereof I cannot enough commend,—comes with him, at my
importunity, to fill up your Grace's request in my
stead. I beseech you, let his lack of years be no
impediment to let him lack a reverend estimation;
for I never knew so young a body with so old a
head. I leave him to your gracious acceptance,
whose trial shall better publish his commendation.

DUKE OF VENICE.
You hear the learn'd Bellario, what he writes:
And here, I take it, is the doctor come.

Enter PORTIA *for* BALTHAZAR.

Give me your hand. Come you from old Bellario?

PORTIA.
I did, my lord.

DUKE OF VENICE.
You are welcome: take your place.
Are you acquainted with the difference
That holds this present question in the court?

PORTIA.
I am informed throughly of the cause.—
Which is the merchant here, and which the Jew?

DUKE OF VENICE.
Antonio and old Shylock, both stand forth.

PORTIA.
Is your name Shylock?

SHYLOCK.
Shylock is my name.

PORTIA.
Of a strange nature is the suit you follow;
Yet in such rule, that the Venetian law
Cannot impugn you as you do proceed.—
You stand within his danger, do you not?

ANTONIO.
Ay, so he says.

PORTIA.
Do you confess the bond?

ANTONIO.
I do.

PORTIA.
Then must the Jew be merciful.

SHYLOCK.
On what compulsion must I? tell me that.

PORTIA.
The quality of mercy is not strain'd,—
It droppeth as the gentle rain from heaven

Upon the place beneath: it is twice blest,—
It blesseth him that gives, and him that takes:
'Tis mightiest in the mightiest: it becomes
The throned monarch better than his crown;
His sceptre shows the force of temporal power,
The attribute to awe and majesty,
Wherein doth sit the dread and fear of kings;
But mercy is above this sceptred sway,—
It is enthroned in the hearts of kings,
It is an attribute to God himself;
And earthly power doth then show likest God's
When mercy seasons justice. Therefore, Jew,
Though justice be thy plea, consider this,—
That, in the course of justice, none of us
Should see salvation: we do pray for mercy;
And that same prayer doth teach us all to render
The deeds of mercy. I have spoke thus much
To mitigate the justice of thy plea;
Which if thou follow, this strict court of Venice
Must needs give sentence 'gainst the merchant
    there.

SHYLOCK.
My deeds upon my head! I crave the law,
The penalty and forfeit of my bond.

PORTIA.
Is he not able to discharge the money?

BASSANIO.
Yes, here I tender it for him in the court;
Yea, thrice the sum: if that will not suffice,
I will be bound to pay it ten times o'er,
On forfeit of my hands, my head, my heart:
If this will not suffice, it must appear
That malice bears down truth. And I beseech you,
Wrest once the law to your authority:
To do a great right, do a little wrong;
And curb this cruel devil of his will.

PORTIA.
It must not be; there is no power in Venice
Can alter a decree established:
'Twill be recorded for a precedent;
And many an error, by the same example,
Will rush into the state: it cannot be.

SHYLOCK.
A Daniel come to judgement! yea, a Daniel!—
O wise young judge, how I do honour thee!

PORTIA.
I pray you, let me look upon the bond.

SHYLOCK.
Here 'tis, most reverend doctor, here it is.

PORTIA.
Shylock, there's thrice thy money offer'd thee.

SHYLOCK.
An oath, an oath, I have an oath in heaven:
Shall I lay perjury upon my soul?
No, not for Venice.

PORTIA.
            Why, this bond is forfeit;
And lawfully by this the Jew may claim
A pound of flesh, to be by him cut off
Nearest the merchant's heart.—Be merciful:
Take thrice thy money; bid me tear the bond.

SHYLOCK.
When it is paid according to the tenour.—
It doth appear you are a worthy judge;
You know the law, your exposition
Hath been most sound: I charge you by the law,

Whereof you are a well-deserving pillar,
Proceed to judgement: by my soul I swear
There is no power in the tongue of man
To alter me: I stay here on my bond.

ANTONIO.
Most heartily I do beseech the court
To give the judgement.

PORTIA.
            Why then, thus it is:—
You must prepare your bosom for his knife.

SHYLOCK.
O noble judge! O excellent young man!

PORTIA.
For the intent and purpose of the law
Hath full relation to the penalty,
Which here appeareth due upon the bond.

SHYLOCK.
'Tis very true: O wise and upright judge!
How much more elder art thou than thy looks!

PORTIA.
Therefore lay bare your bosom.

SHYLOCK.
                        Ay, his breast:
So says the bond:—doth it not, noble judge?—
Nearest his heart: those are the very words.

PORTIA.
It is so. Are there balance here to weigh
The flesh?

SHYLOCK.
I have them ready.

PORTIA.
Have by some surgeon, Shylock, on your charge,
To stop his wounds, lest he do bleed to death.

SHYLOCK.
Is it so nominated in the bond?

PORTIA.
It is not so exprest: but what of that?
'Twere good you do so much for charity.

SHYLOCK.
I cannot find it; 'tis not in the bond.

PORTIA.
You, merchant, have you any thing to say?

ANTONIO.
But little: I am arm'd and well prepared.—
Give me your hand, Bassanio: fare you well!
Grieve not that I am fall'n to this for you;
For herein Fortune shows herself more kind
Than is her custom: it is still her use
To let the wretched man outlive his wealth,
To view with hollow eye and wrinkled brow
An age of poverty; from which lingering penance
Of such a misery doth she cut me off.
Commend me to your honourable wife:
Tell her the process of Antonio's end;
Say how I loved you, speak me fair in death;
And, when the tale is told, bid her be judge
Whether Bassanio had not once a love.
Repent but you that you shall lose your friend,
And he repents not that he pays your debt;
For, if the Jew do cut but deep enough,
I'll pay it presently with all my heart.

BASSANIO.
Antonio, I am married to a wife
Which is as dear to me as life itself;
But life itself, my wife, and all the world,
Are not with me esteem'd above thy life:

I would lose all, ay, sacrifice them all
Here to this devil, to deliver you.
             PORTIA.
Your wife would give you little thanks for that,
If she were by, to hear you make the offer.
             GRATIANO.
I have a wife, whom, I protest, I love:
I would she were in heaven, so she could
Entreat some power to change this currish Jew.
             NERISSA.
'Tis well you offer it behind her back;
The wish would make else an unquiet house.
        SHYLOCK [aside].
These be the Christian husbands! I have a
    daughter;
Would any of the stock of Barabbas
Had been her husband rather than a Christian!—
We trifle time: I pray thee, pursue sentence.
             PORTIA.
A pound of that same merchant's flesh is thine:
The court awards it, and the law doth give it.
             SHYLOCK.
Most rightful judge!
             PORTIA.
And you must cut this flesh from off his breast:
The law allows it, and the court awards it.
             SHYLOCK.
Most learned judge!—A sentence! come, prepare!
             PORTIA.
Tarry a little; there is something else.
This bond doth give thee here no jot of blood,—
The words expressly are, 'a pound of flesh':
Take then thy bond, take thou thy pound of flesh;
But, in the cutting it, if thou dost shed
One drop of Christian blood, thy lands and goods
Are, by the laws of Venice, confiscate
Unto the state of Venice.
             GRATIANO.
O upright judge!—Mark, Jew:—O learned judge!
             SHYLOCK.
Is that the law?
             PORTIA.
           Thyself shalt see the act:
For, as thou urgest justice, be assured
Thou shalt have justice, more than thou desirest.
             GRATIANO.
O learned judge!—Mark, Jew:—a learned judge!
             SHYLOCK.
I take his offer, then;— pay the bond thrice,
And let the Christian go.
             BASSANIO.
           Here is the money.
             PORTIA.
Soft!
The Jew shall have all justice;—soft! no haste:—
He shall have nothing but the penalty.
             GRATIANO.
O Jew! an upright judge, a learned judge!
             PORTIA.
Therefore prepare thee to cut off the flesh.
Shed thou no blood; nor cut thou less nor more
But just a pound of flesh: if thou cutt'st more
Or less than a just pound,—be it but so much
As makes it light or heavy in the substance,
Or the division of the twentieth part
Of one poor scruple, nay, if the scale do turn

But in the estimation of a hair,—
Thou diest, and all thy goods are confiscate.
             GRATIANO.
A second Daniel, a Daniel, Jew!
Now, infidel, I have you on the hip.
             PORTIA.
Why doth the Jew pause? take thy forfeiture.
             SHYLOCK.
Give me my principal, and let me go.
             BASSANIO.
I have it ready for thee; here it is.
             PORTIA.
He hath refused it in the open court:
He shall have merely justice and his bond.
             GRATIANO.
A Daniel, still say I, a second Daniel!—
I thank thee, Jew, for teaching me that word.
             SHYLOCK.
Shall I not have barely my principal?
             PORTIA.
Thou shalt have nothing but the forfeiture,
To be so taken at thy peril, Jew.
             SHYLOCK.
Why, then the devil give him good of it!
I'll stay no longer question.
             PORTIA.
                 Tarry, Jew:
The law hath yet another hold on you.
It is enacted in the laws of Venice,—
If it be proved against an alien
That by direct or indirect attempts
He seek the life of any citizen,
The party 'gainst the which he doth contrive
Shall seize one half his goods; the other half
Comes to the privy coffer of the state;
And the offender's life lies in the mercy
Of the duke only, 'gainst all other voice.
In which predicament, I say, thou stand'st;
For it appears, by manifest proceeding,
That indirectly, and directly too,
Thou hast contrived against the very life
Of the defendant; and thou hast incurr'd
The danger formerly by me rehearsed.
Down, therefore, and beg mercy of the duke.
             GRATIANO.
Beg that thou mayst have leave to hang thyself:
And yet, thy wealth being forfeit to the state,
Thou hast not left the value of a cord;   [charge.
Therefore thou must be hang'd at the state's
           DUKE OF VENICE.
That thou shalt see the difference of our spirits,
I pardon thee thy life before thou ask it:
For half thy wealth, it is Antonio's;
The other half comes to the general state,
Which humbleness may drive unto a fine.
             PORTIA.
Ay, for the state,—not for Antonio.
             SHYLOCK.
Nay, take my life and all; pardon not that:
You take my house, when you do take the prop
That doth sustain my house; you take my life,
When you do take the means whereby I live.
             PORTIA.
What mercy can you render him, Antonio?
             GRATIANO.
A halter gratis; nothing else, for God's sake.

ANTONIO.

So please my lord the duke and all the court
To quit the fine for one half of his goods,
I am content; so he will let me have
The other half in use, to render it,
Upon his death, unto the gentleman
That lately stole his daughter:
Two things provided more,—that, for this
  favour,
He presently become a Christian;
The other, that he do record a gift,
Here in the court, of all he dies possest,
Unto his son Lorenzo and his daughter.

DUKE OF VENICE.

He shall do this; or else I do recant
The pardon that I late pronounced here.

PORTIA.

Art thou contented, Jew? what dost thou say?

SHYLOCK.

I am content.

PORTIA.

    Clerk, draw a deed of gift.

SHYLOCK.

I pray you, give me leave to go from hence;
I am not well: send the deed after me,
And I will sign it.

DUKE OF VENICE.

        Get thee gone, but do it.

GRATIANO.

In christening shalt thou have two godfathers:
Had I been judge, thou shouldst have had ten
  more,
To bring thee to the gallows, not the font.
                    [*Exit* SHYLOCK.

DUKE OF VENICE.

Sir, I entreat you home with me to dinner.

PORTIA.

I humbly do desire your Grace of pardon:
I must away this night toward Padua,
And it is meet I presently set forth.

DUKE OF VENICE.

I am sorry that your leisure serves you not.—
Antonio, gratify this gentleman;
For, in my mind, you are much bound to him.
          [*Exeunt* DUKE *and his* TRAIN.

BASSANIO.

Most worthy gentleman, I and my friend
Have by your wisdom been this day acquitted
Of grievous penalties; in lieu whereof
Three thousand ducats, due unto the Jew,
We freely cope your courteous pains withal.

ANTONIO.

And stand indebted, over and above,
In love and service to you evermore.

PORTIA.

He is well paid that is well satisfied;
And I, delivering you, am satisfied,
And therein do account myself well paid:
My mind was never yet more mercenary.
I pray you, know me when we meet again:
I wish you well, and so I take my leave.

BASSANIO.

Dear sir, of force I must attempt you further:
Take some remembrance of us, as a tribute,
Not as a fee: grant me two things, I pray you,—
Not to deny me, and to pardon me.

PORTIA.

You press me far, and therefore I will yield.
[*to* ANTONIO] Give me your gloves, I'll wear
  them for your sake;
[*to* BASSANIO] And, for your love, I'll take this
  ring from you:—
Do not draw back your hand; I'll take no more;
And you in love shall not deny me this.

BASSANIO.

This ring, good sir,—alas, it is a trifle!
I will not shame myself to give you this.

PORTIA.

I will have nothing else but only this;
And now methinks I have a mind to it.

BASSANIO.

There's more depends on this than on the value,
The dearest ring in Venice will I give you,
And find it out by proclamation:
Only for this, I pray you, pardon me.

PORTIA.

I see, sir, you are liberal in offers:
You taught me first to beg; and now methinks
You teach me how a beggar should be answer'd.

BASSANIO.

Good sir, this ring was given me by my wife;
And, when she put it on, she made me vow
That I should neither sell nor give nor lose it.

PORTIA.

That 'scuse serves many men to save their gifts.
An if your wife be not a mad-woman,
And know how well I have deserved this ring,
She would not hold out enemy for ever
For giving it to me. Well, peace be with you!
         [*Exeunt* PORTIA *and* NERISSA.

ANTONIO.

My Lord Bassanio, let him have the ring:
Let his deservings, and my love withal,
Be valued 'gainst your wife's commandment.

BASSANIO.

Go, Gratiano, run and overtake him;
Give him this ring; and bring him, if thou canst,
Unto Antonio's house: away! make haste.
                   [*Exit* GRATIANO.
Come, you and I will thither presently;
And in the morning early will we both
Fly toward Belmont: come, Antonio.   [*Exeunt.*

SCENE II.

The same. A street.

Enter PORTIA *and* NERISSA.

PORTIA.

INQUIRE the Jew's house out, give him this
  deed,
And let him sign it: we'll away to-night,
And be a day before our husbands home:
This deed will be well welcome to Lorenzo.

Enter GRATIANO.

GRATIANO.

Fair sir, you are well o'erta'en:
My Lord Bassanio, upon more advice,
Hath sent you here this ring; and doth entreat
Your company at dinner.

PORTIA.

           That cannot be:
His ring I do accept most thankfully;

And so, I pray you, tell him: furthermore,
I pray you, show my youth old Shylock's house.
GRATIANO.
That will I do.
NERISSA.
      Sir, I would speak with you.—
to PORTIA] I'll see if I can get my husband's
   ring,
Which I did make him swear to keep for ever.
PORTIA [to NERISSA].
Thou mayst, I warrant. We shall have old swear-
   ing
That they did give the rings away to men;
But we'll outface them, and outswear them too.—
Away! make haste: thou know'st where I will
   tarry.
NERISSA.
Come, good sir, will you show me to this house?
                         [Exeunt.

ACT V.   SCENE I.

Belmont.   Avenue to PORTIA'S *house.*

Enter LORENZO *and* JESSICA.

LORENZO.
THE moon shines bright:—in such a night
   as this,
When the sweet wind did gently kiss the trees,
And they did make no noise,—in such a night
Troilus methinks mounted the Troyan walls,
And sigh'd his soul toward the Grecian tents,
Where Cressid lay that night.
JESSICA.
          In such a night
Did Thisbe fearfully o'ertrip the dew,
And saw the lion's shadow ere himself,
And ran dismay'd away.
LORENZO.
          In such a night
Stood Dido with a willow in her hand
Upon the wild sea-banks, and waft her love
To come again to Carthage.
JESSICA.
          In such a night
Medea gather'd the enchanted herbs
That did renew old Aeson.
LORENZO.
          In such a night
Did Jessica steal from the wealthy Jew,
And with an unthrift love did run from Venice
As far as Belmont.
JESSICA.
          In such a night
Did young Lorenzo swear he loved her well,
Stealing her soul with many vows of faith,
And ne'er a true one.
LORENZO.
          In such a night
Did pretty Jessica, like a little shrew,
Slander her love, and he forgave it her.
JESSICA.
I would out-night you, did no body come:
But, hark, I hear the footing of a man.
Enter STEPHANO.
LORENZO.
Who comse so fast in silence of the night?

STEPHANO.
A friend.
LORENZO.
A friend! what friend? your name, I pray you,
   friend?
STEPHANO.
Stephano is my name; and I bring word
My mistress will before the break of day
Be here at Belmont: she doth stray about
By holy crosses, where she kneels and prays
For happy wedlock hours.
LORENZO.
              Who comes with her?
STEPHANO.
None but a holy hermit and her maid.
I pray you, is my master yet return'd?
LORENZO.
He is not, nor we have not heard from him.—
But go we in, I pray thee, Jessica,
And ceremoniously let us prepare
Some welcome for the mistress of the house.
Enter LAUNCELOT.
LAUNCELOT GOBBO.
Sola, sola! wo ha, ho! sola, sola!
LORENZO.
Who calls?
LAUNCELOT GOBBO.
Sola!—did you see Master Lorenzo? Master
Lorenzo!—sola, sola!
LORENZO.
Leave hollaing, man:—here.
LAUNCELOT GOBBO.
Sola!—where? where?
LORENZO.
Here.
LAUNCELOT GOBBO.
Tell him there's a post come from my master,
with his horn full of good news: my master will be
here ere morning.   [Exit.
LORENZO.
Sweet soul, let's in, and there expect their com-
   ing.
And yet no matter:—why should we go in ?—
My friend Stephano, signify, I pray you,
Within the house, your mistress is at hand;
And bring your music forth into the air.
                  [Exit STEPHANO.
How sweet the moonlight sleeps upon this bank!
Here will we sit, and let the sounds of music
Creep in our ears: soft stillness and the night
Become the touches of sweet harmony.
Sit, Jessica. Look, how the floor of heaven
Is thick inlaid with patines of bright gold:
There's not the smallest orb which thou be-
   hold'st
But in his motion like an angel sings,
Still quiring to the young-eyed cherubins,—
Such harmony is in immortal souls;
But whilst this muddy vesture of decay
Doth grossly close it in, we cannot hear it.
Enter MUSICIANS.
Come, ho, and wake Diana with a hymn!
With sweetest touches pierce your mistress' ear,
And draw her home with music.   [Music plays.
JESSICA.
I am never merry when I hear sweet music.

LORENZO.
The reason is, your spirits are attentive:
For do but note a wild and wanton herd,
Or race of youthful and unhandled colts,
Fetching mad bounds, bellowing, and neighing loud,
Which is the hot condition of their blood;
If they but hear perchance a trumpet sound,
Or any air of music touch their ears,
You shall perceive them make a mutual stand,
Their savage eyes turn'd to a modest gaze,
By the sweet power of music: therefore the poet
Did feign that Orpheus drew trees, stones, and floods;
Since naught so stockish, hard, and full of rage,
But music for the time doth change his nature.
The man that hath no music in himself,
Nor is not moved with concord of sweet sounds,
Is fit for treasons, stratagems, and spoils;
The motions of his spirit are dull as night,
And his affections dark as Erebus:
Let no such man be trusted.—Mark the music.
Enter PORTIA *and* NERISSA.
PORTIA.
That light we see is burning in my hall.
How far that little candle throws his beams!
So shines a good deed in a naughty world.
NERISSA.
When the moon shone, we did not see the candle.
PORTIA.
So doth the greater glory dim the less:
A substitute shines brightly as a king,
Until a king be by; and then his state
Empties itself, as doth an inland brook
Into the main of waters.—Music! hark!
NERISSA.
It is your music, madam, of the house.
PORTIA.
Nothing is good, I see, without respect:
Methinks it sounds much sweeter than by day.
NERISSA.
Silence bestows that virtue on it, madam.
PORTIA.
The crow doth sing as sweetly as the lark,
When neither is attended; and I think
The nightingale, if she should sing by day,
When every goose is cackling, would be thought
No better a musician than the wren.
How many things by season season'd are
To their right praise and true perfection!—
Peace, ho! the moon sleeps with Endymion,
And would not be awaked. [*Music ceases.*
LORENZO.
That is the voice,
Or I am much deceived, of Portia.
PORTIA.
He knows me, as the blind man knows the cuckoo,
By the bad voice.
LORENZO.
Dear lady, welcome home.
PORTIA.
We have been praying for our husbands' health,
Which speed, we hope, the better for our words.
Are they return'd?
LORENZO.
Madam, they are not yet;

But there is come a messenger before,
To signify their coming.
PORTIA.
Go in, Nerissa;
Give orders to my servants that they take
No note at all of our being absent hence;—
Nor you, Lorenzo;—Jessica, nor you
[*A tucket sound.*
LORENZO.
Your husband is at hand; I hear his trumpet:
We are no tell-tales, madam; fear you not.
PORTIA.
This night methinks is but the daylight sick;
It looks a little paler: 'tis a day,
Such as the day is when the sun is hid.
Enter BASSANIO, ANTONIO, GRATIANO, *and their* FOLLOWERS.
BASSANIO.
We should hold day with the Antipodes,
If you would walk in absence of the sun.
PORTIA.
Let me give light, but let me not be light;
For a light wife doth make a heavy husband,
And never be Bassanio so for me: [lord
But God sort all!—You're welcome home, my
BASSANIO.
I thank you, madam. Give welcome to my friend
This is the man, this is Antonio,
To whom I am so infinitely bound.
PORTIA.
You should in all sense be much bound to him,
For, as I hear, he was much bound for you.
ANTONIO.
No more than I am well acquitted of.
PORTIA.
Sir, you are very welcome to our house:
It must appear in other ways than words,
Therefore I scant this breathing courtesy.
GRATIANO [*to* NERISSA].
By yonder moon I swear you do me wrong;
In faith, I gave it to the judge's clerk:
Would he were gelt that had it, for my part,
Since you do take it, love, so much at heart.
PORTIA.
A quarrel, ho, already! what's the matter?
GRATIANO.
About a hoop of gold, a paltry ring
That she did give to me; whose posy was
For all the world like cutler's poetry
Upon a knife, 'Love me, and leave me not.'
NERISSA.
What talk you of the posy or the value?
You swore to me, when I did give it you,
That you would wear it till your hour of death;
And that it should lie with you in your grave:
Though not for me, yet for your vehement oaths,
You should have been respective, and have kept it.
Gave it a judge's clerk! no, God's my judge,
The clerk will ne'er wear hair on's face that had it.
GRATIANO.
He will, an if he live to be a man.
NERISSA.
Ay, if a woman live to be a man.
GRATIANO.
Now, by this hand, I gave it to a youth,—
A kind of boy; a little scrubbed boy,

No higher than thyself, the judge's clerk;
A prating boy, that begg'd it as a fee:
I could not for my heart deny it him.
PORTIA.
You were to blame,—I must be plain with you,—
To part so slightly with your wife's first gift;
A thing stuck on with oaths upon your finger,
And so riveted with faith unto your flesh.
I gave my love a ring, and made him swear
Never to part with it; and here he stands,—
I dare be sworn for him, he would not leave it,
Nor pluck it from his finger, for the wealth
That the world masters. Now, in faith, Gratiano,
You give your wife too unkind a cause of grief:
An 'twere to me, I should be mad at it.
BASSANIO [aside].
Why, I were best to cut my left hand off,
And swear I lost the ring defending it.
GRATIANO.
My Lord Bassanio gave his ring away
Unto the judge that begg'd it, and indeed
Deserved it too; and then the boy, his clerk,
That took some pains in writing, he begg'd mine:
And neither man nor master would take aught
But the two rings.
PORTIA.
What ring gave you, my lord?
Not that, I hope, which you received of me.
BASSANIO.
If I could add a lie unto a fault,
I would deny it; but you see my finger
Hath not the ring upon it,—it is gone.
PORTIA.
Even so void is your false heart of truth.
By heaven, I will ne'er come in your bed
Until I see the ring.
NERISSA.
Nor I in yours
Till I again see mine.
BASSANIO.
Sweet Portia,
If you did know to whom I gave the ring,
If you did know for whom I gave the ring,
And would conceive for what I gave the ring,
And how unwillingly I left the ring,
When naught would be accepted but the ring,
You would abate the strength of your displeasure.
PORTIA.
If you had known the virtue of the ring,
Or half her worthiness that gave the ring,
Or your own honour to contain the ring,
You would not then have parted with the ring.
What man is there so much unreasonable,
If you had pleased to have defended it
With any terms of zeal, wanted the modesty
To urge the thing held as a ceremony?
Nerissa teaches me what to believe:
I'll die for't but some woman had the ring.
BASSANIO.
No, by my honour, madam, by my soul,
No woman had it, but a civil doctor,
Which did refuse three thousand ducats of me,
And begg'd the ring; the which I did deny him,
And suffer'd him to go displeased away;
Even he that did uphold the very life
Of my dear friend. What should I say, sweet lady?

I was enforced to send it after him:
I was beset with shame and courtesy;
My honour would not let ingratitude
So much besmear it. Pardon me, good lady;
For, by these blessed candles of the night,
Had you been there, I think, you would have
begg'd
The ring of me to give the worthy doctor.
PORTIA.
Let not that doctor e'er come near my house:
Since he hath got the jewel that I loved,
And that which you did swear to keep for me,
I will become as liberal as you;
I'll not deny him any thing I have,
No, not my body nor my husband's bed:
Know him I shall, I am well sure of it:
Lie not a night from home; watch me like Argus:
If you do not, if I be left alone,
Now, by mine honour, which is yet mine own,
I'll have that doctor for my bedfellow.
NERISSA.
And I his clerk; therefore be well advised
How you do leave me to mine own protection.
GRATIANO.
Well, do you so: let not me take him, then;
For if I do, I'll mar the young clerk's pen.
ANTONIO.
I am the unhappy subject of these quarrels.
PORTIA.
Sir, grieve not you; you are welcome notwith-
standing.
BASSANIO.
Portia, forgive me this enforced wrong;
And, in the hearing of these many friends,
I swear to thee, even by thine own fair eyes,
Wherein I see myself,—
PORTIA.
Mark you but that!
In both my eyes he doubly sees himself;
In each eye, one:—swear by your double self,
And there's an oath of credit.
BASSANIO.
Nay, but hear me:
Pardon this fault, and by my soul I swear
I never more will break an oath with thee.
ANTONIO.
I once did lend my body for his wealth;
Which, but for him that had your husband's
ring,
Had quite miscarried: I dare be bound again,
My soul upon the forfeit, that your lord
Will never more break faith advisedly.
PORTIA.
Then you shall be his surety. Give him this;
And bid him keep it better than the other.
ANTONIO.
Here, Lord Bassanio; swear to keep this ring.
BASSANIO.
By heaven, it is the same I gave the doctor!
PORTIA.
I had it of him: pardon me, Bassanio;
For, by this ring, the doctor lay with me.
NERISSA.
And pardon me, my gentle Gratiano;
For that same scrubbed boy, the doctor's clerk,
In lieu of this, last night did lie with me.

GRATIANO.
Why, this is like the mending of highways
In summer, where the ways are fair enough:
What, are we cuckolds ere we have deserved it?

PORTIA.
Speak not so grossly.—You are all amazed:
Here is a letter, read it at your leisure;
It comes from Padua, from Bellario:
There you shall find that Portia was the doctor;
Nerissa there her clerk: Lorenzo here
Shall witness I set forth as soon as you,
And even but now return'd; I have not yet
Enter'd my house.—Antonio, you are welcome;
And I have better news in store for you
Than you expect: unseal this letter soon;
There you shall find three of your argosies
Are richly come to harbour suddenly:
You shall not know by what strange accident
I chanced on this letter.

ANTONIO.
        I am dumb.

BASSANIO.
Were you the doctor, and I knew you not?

GRATIANO.
Were you the clerk that is to make me cuckold?

NERISSA.
Ay, but the clerk that never means to do it,
Unless he live until he be a man.

BASSANIO.
Sweet doctor, you shall be my bedfellow:
When I am absent, then lie with my wife.

ANTONIO.
Sweet lady, you have given me life and living;
For here I read for certain that my ships
Are safely come to road.

PORTIA.
        How now, Lorenzo!
My clerk hath some good comforts too for you.

NERISSA.
Ay, and I'll give them him without a fee.—
There do I give to you and Jessica,
From the rich Jew, a special deed of gift,
After his death, of all he dies possest of.

LORENZO.
Fair ladies, you drop manna in the way
Of starved people.

PORTIA.
        It is almost morning,
And yet I am sure you are not satisfied
Of these events at full. Let us go in;
And charge us there upon inter'gatories,
And we will answer all things faithfully.

GRATIANO.
Let it be so: the first inter'gatory
That my Nerissa shall be sworn on is,
Whether till the next night she had rather
    stay,
Or go to bed now, being two hours to day:
But were the day come, I should wish it dark,
That I were couching with the doctor's clerk.
Well, while I live I'll fear no other thing
So sore as keeping safe Nerissa's ring.   [*Exeunt.*

THE FIRST PART OF
KING HENRY THE FOURTH

DRAMATIS PERSONAE

KING HENRY THE FOURTH.
HENRY, *Prince of Wales,*
PRINCE JOHN *of Lancaster,* } *sons to the King.*
EARL OF WESTMORELAND.
SIR WALTER BLUNT.
THOMAS PERCY, *Earl of Worcester.*
HENRY PERCY, *Earl of Northumberland.*
HENRY PERCY, *surnamed* HOTSPUR, *his son.*
EDMUND MORTIMER, *Earl of March.*
SCROOP, *Archbishop of York.*
ARCHIBALD, *Earl of Douglas.*
OWEN GLENDOWER.
SIR RICHARD VERNON.
SIR JOHN FALSTAFF.
SIR MICHAEL, *a friend to the Archbishop of York.*

POINTZ.
GADSHILL.
PETO.
BARDOLPH.

LADY PERCY, *wife to Hotspur, and sister to Mortimer.*
LADY MORTIMER, *daughter to Glendower, and wife to Mortimer.*
MISTRESS QUICKLY, *hostess of a tavern in Eastcheap.*

LORDS, OFFICERS, SHERIFF, VINTNER, CHAMBERLAIN, DRAWERS, TWO CARRIERS, TRAVELLERS, *and* ATTENDANTS.

SCENE—*England.*

ACT I. SCENE I.
London.   The palace.

Enter KING HENRY, WESTMORELAND, SIR WALTER BLUNT, *and others.*

KING HENRY.

SO shaken as we are, so wan with care,
Find we a time for frighted peace to pant,
And breathe short-winded accents of new broils
To be commenced in stronds afar remote.
No more the thirsty entrance of this soil
Shall daub her lips with her own children's blood;
No more shall trenching war channel her fields,
Nor bruise her flowerets with the armed hoofs
Of hostile paces: those opposed eyes,
Which, like the meteors of a troubled heaven,
All of one nature, of one substance bred,
Did lately meet in the intestine shock
And furious close of civil butchery,
Shall now, in mutual well-beseeming ranks,
March all one way, and be no more opposed
Against acquaintance, kindred, and allies:
The edge of war, like an ill-sheathed knife,
No more shall cut his master. Therefore, friends,
As far as to the sepulchre of Christ,—
Whose soldier now, under whose blessed cross
We are impressed and engaged to fight,—
Forthwith a power of English shall we levy;
Whose arms were moulded in their mothers'
To chase these pagans in those holy fields [womb
Over whose acres walkt those blessed feet
Which fourteen hundred years ago were nail'd
For our advantage on the bitter cross.
But this our purpose now is twelve month old,
And bootless 'tis to tell you we will go:
Therefore we meet not now.—Then let me hear
Of you, my gentle cousin Westmoreland,
What yesternight our council did decree
In forwarding this dear expedience.

EARL OF WESTMORELAND.

My liege, this haste was hot in question,
And many limits of the charge set down

But yesternight: when, all athwart, there came
A post from Wales loaden with heavy news;
Whose worst was,—that the noble Mortimer,
Leading the men of Herefordshire to fight
Against the irregular and wild Glendower,
Was by the rude hands of that Welshman taken,
A thousand of his people butchered;
Upon whose dead corpse there was such misuse,
Such beastly, shameless transformation,
By those Welshwomen done, as may not be
Without much shame re-told or spoken of.

KING HENRY.

It seems, then, that the tidings of this broil
Brake off our business for the Holy Land.

EARL OF WESTMORELAND.

This, matcht with other, did, my gracious lord;
For more uneven and unwelcome news
Came from the north, and thus it did import:
On Holy-rood day, the gallant Hotspur there,
Young Harry Percy, and brave Archibald,
That ever-valiant and approved Scot,
At Holmedon met,
Where they did spend a sad and bloody hour;
As by discharge of their artillery,
And shape of likelihood, the news was told;
For he that brought them, in the very heat
And pride of their contention did take horse,
Uncertain of the issue any way.

KING HENRY.

Here is a dear, a true industrious friend,
Sir Walter Blunt, new lighted from his horse,
Stain'd with the variation of each soil
Betwixt that Holmedon and this seat of ours;
And he hath brought us smooth and welcome news.
The Earl of Douglas is discomfited;
Ten thousand bold Scots, two-and-twenty knights,
Balk'd in their own blood, did Sir Walter see
On Holmedon's plains: of prisoners, Hotspur took
Mordake the Earl of Fife, and eldest son

To beaten Douglas; and the Earl of Athol,
Of Murray, Angus, and Menteith:
And is not this an honourable spoil,
A gallant prize? ha, cousin, is it not?

EARL OF WESTMORELAND.

In faith,
It is a conquest for a prince to boast of.

KING HENRY.

Yea, there thou makest me sad, and makest me sin
In envy that my Lord Northumberland
Should be the father to so blest a son,—
A son who is the theme of honour's tongue;
Amongst a grove, the very straightest plant;
Who is sweet Fortune's minion and her pride:
Whilst I, by looking on the praise of him,
See riot and dishonour stain the brow
Of my young Harry. O, that it could be proved
That some night-tripping fairy had exchanged
In cradle-clothes our children where they lay,
And call'd mine Percy, his Plantagenet!
Then would I have his Harry, and he mine:
But let him from my thoughts.—What think you,
      coz,
Of this young Percy's pride? the prisoners,
Which he in this adventure hath surprised,
To his own use he keeps; and sends me word
I shall have none but Mordake Earl of Fife.

EARL OF WESTMORELAND.

This is his uncle's teaching, this is Worcester,
Malevolent to you in all aspects;
Which makes him prune himself, and bristle up
The crest of youth against your dignity.

KING HENRY.

But I have sent for him to answer this;
And for this cause awhile we must neglect
Our holy purpose to Jerusalem.
Cousin, on Wednesday next our council we
Will hold at Windsor,—so inform the lords:
But come yourself with speed to us again;
For more is to be said and to be done
Than out of anger can be uttered.

EARL OF WESTMORELAND.

I will, my liege.   [Exeunt.

SCENE II.

London.   A tavern.

Enter PRINCE HENRY and FALSTAFF.

SIR JOHN FALSTAFF.

NOW, Hal, what time of day is it, lad?

PRINCE HENRY.

Thou art so fat-witted, with drinking of old sack,
and unbuttoning thee after supper, and sleeping
upon benches after noon, that thou hast forgotten
to demand that truly which thou wouldst truly
know What a devil hast thou to do with the time
of the day? unless hours were cups of sack, and
minutes capons, and clocks the tongues of bawds,
and dials the signs of leaping-houses, and the
blessed sun himself a fair hot wench in flame-
colour'd taffeta,—I see no reason why thou
shouldst be so superfluous to demand the time of
the day.

SIR JOHN FALSTAFF.

Indeed, you come near me now, Hal; for we that
take purses go by the moon and the seven stars,

and not by Phœbus, he, 'that wandering knight
so fair.' And, I prithee, sweet wag, when thou art
king,—as, God save thy Grace,—majesty I should
say, for grace thou wilt have none,—

PRINCE HENRY.

What, none?

SIR JOHN FALSTAFF.

No, by my troth,—not so much as will serve to be
prologue to an egg and butter.

PRINCE HENRY.

Well, how then? come, roundly, roundly.

SIR JOHN FALSTAFF.

Marry, then, sweet wag, when thou art king, let
not us that are squires of the night's body be
call'd thieves of the day's beauty: let us be Diana's
foresters, gentlemen of the shade, minions of the
moon; and let men say we be men of good government, being govern'd, as the sea is, by our noble
and chaste mistress the moon, under whose countenance we steal.

PRINCE HENRY.

Thou say'st well, and it holds well too; for the
fortune of us that are the moon's men doth ebb
and flow like the sea, being govern'd, as the sea is,
by the moon. As, for proof, now: a purse of gold
most resolutely snatcht on Monday night, and
most dissolutely spent on Tuesday morning; got
with swearing 'lay by,' and spent with crying
'bring in;' now in as low an ebb as the foot of the
ladder, and by and by in as high a flow as the
ridge of the gallows.

SIR JOHN FALSTAFF.

By the Lord, thou say'st true, lad. And is not my
hostess of the tavern a most sweet wench?

PRINCE HENRY.

As the honey of Hybla, my old lad of the castle.
And is not a buff jerkin a most sweet robe of
durance?

SIR JOHN FALSTAFF.

How now, how now, mad wag! what, in thy quips
and thy quiddities? what a plague have I to do
with a buff jerkin?

PRINCE HENRY.

Why, what a pox have I to do with my hostess of
the tavern?

SIR JOHN FALSTAFF.

Well, thou hast call'd her to a reckoning many a
time and oft.

PRINCE HENRY.

Did I ever call for thee to pay thy part?

SIR JOHN FALSTAFF.

No; I'll give thee thy due, thou hast paid all there.

PRINCE HENRY.

Yea, and elsewhere, so far as my coin would
stretch; and where it would not, I have used my
credit.

SIR JOHN FALSTAFF.

Yea, and so used it, that, were it not here apparent
that thou art heir apparent—But, I prithee,
sweet wag, shall there be gallows standing in
England when thou art king? and resolution thus
fobb'd as it is with the rusty curb of old father
antick the law? Do not thou, when thou art king,
hang a thief.

PRINCE HENRY.

No; thou shalt.

SIR JOHN FALSTAFF.
Shall I? O rare! By the Lord, I'll be a brave judge.

PRINCE HENRY.
Thou judgest false already: I mean, thou shalt have the hanging of the thieves, and so become a rare hangman.

SIR JOHN FALSTAFF.
Well, Hal, well; and in some sort it jumps with my humour as well as waiting in the court, I can tell you.

PRINCE HENRY.
For obtaining of suits?

SIR JOHN FALSTAFF.
Yea, for obtaining of suits, whereof the hangman hath no lean wardrobe. 'Sblood, I am as melancholy as a gib-cat or a lugg'd bear.

PRINCE HENRY.
Or an old lion, or a lover's lute.

SIR JOHN FALSTAFF.
Yea, or the drone of a Lincolnshire bagpipe.

PRINCE HENRY.
What say'st thou to a hare, or the melancholy of Moor-ditch?

SIR JOHN FALSTAFF.
Thou hast the most unsavoury similes, and art, indeed, the most comparative, rascalliest,—sweet young prince. But, Hal, I prithee, trouble me no more with vanity. I would to God thou and I knew where a commodity of good names were to be bought. An old lord of the council rated me the other day in the street about you, sir,—but I markt him not; and yet he talkt very wisely,—but I regarded him not; and yet he talkt wisely, and in the street too.

PRINCE HENRY.
Thou didst well; for wisdom cries out in the streets, and no man regards it.

SIR JOHN FALSTAFF.
O, thou hast damnable iteration, and art, indeed, able to corrupt a saint. Thou hast done much harm upon me, Hal,—God forgive thee for it! Before I knew thee, Hal, I knew nothing; and now am I, if a man should speak truly, little better than one of the wicked. I must give over this life, and I will give it over; by the Lord, an I do not, I am a villain: I'll be damn'd for never a king's son in Christendom.

PRINCE HENRY.
Where shall we take a purse to-morrow, Jack?

SIR JOHN FALSTAFF.
Zounds, where thou wilt, lad; I'll make one: an I do not, call me villain, and baffle me.

PRINCE HENRY.
I see a good amendment of life in thee,—from praying to purse-taking.

Enter POINTZ.

SIR JOHN FALSTAFF.
Why, Hal, 'tis my vocation, Hal; 'tis no sin for a man to labour in his vocation.—Pointz!—Now shall we know if Gadshill have set a match.—O, if men were to be saved by merit, what hole in hell were hot enough for him? This is the most omnipotent villain that ever cried 'stand' to a true man.

PRINCE HENRY.
Good morrow, Ned.

POINTZ.
Good morrow, sweet Hal.—What says Monsieur Remorse? what says Sir John Sack-and-sugar? Jack, how agrees the devil and thee about thy soul, that thou soldest him on Good-Friday last for a cup of Madeira and a cold capon's leg?

PRINCE HENRY.
Sir John stands to his word,—the devil shall have his bargain; for he was never yet a breaker of proverbs,—he will give the devil his due.

POINTZ.
Then art thou damn'd for keeping thy word with the devil.

PRINCE HENRY.
Else he had been damn'd for cozening the devil.

POINTZ.
But, my lads, my lads, to-morrow morning, by four o'clock, early at Gadshill! there are pilgrims going to Canterbury with rich offerings, and traders riding to London with fat purses: I have vizards for you all; you have horses for yourselves: Gadshill lies to-night in Rochester: I have bespoke supper to-morrow night in Eastcheap: we may do it as secure as sleep. If you will go, I will stuff your purses full of crowns; if you will not, tarry at home and be hang'd.

SIR JOHN FALSTAFF.
Hear ye, Yedward; if I tarry at home and go not, I'll hang you for going.

POINTZ.
You will, chops?

SIR JOHN FALSTAFF.
Hal, wilt thou make one?

PRINCE HENRY.
Who, I rob? I a thief? not I, by my faith.

SIR JOHN FALSTAFF.
There's neither honesty, manhood, nor good fellowship in thee, nor thou camest not of the blood royal, if thou darest not stand for ten shillings.

PRINCE HENRY.
Well, then, once in my days I'll be a madcap.

SIR JOHN FALSTAFF.
Why, that's well said.

PRINCE HENRY.
Well, come what will, I'll tarry at home.

SIR JOHN FALSTAFF.
By the Lord, I'll be a traitor, then, when thou art king.

PRINCE HENRY.
I care not.

POINTZ.
Sir John, I prithee, leave the prince and me alone: I will lay him down such reasons for this adventure, that he shall go.

SIR JOHN FALSTAFF.
Well, God give thee the spirit of persuasion, and him the ears of profiting, that what thou speakest may move, and what he hears may be believed, that the true prince may, for recreation sake, prove a false thief; for the poor abuses of the time want countenance. Farewell: you shall find me in Eastcheap.

PRINCE HENRY.
Farewell, thou latter spring! farewell, All-hallown summer!   [*Exit* FALSTAFF

POINTZ.

Now, my good sweet honey lord, ride with us to-morrow: I have a jest to execute that I cannot manage alone. Falstaff, Bardolph, Peto, and Gadshill, shall rob those men that we have already waylaid; yourself and I will not be there; and when they have the booty, if you and I do not rob them, cut this head from my shoulders.

PRINCE HENRY.

But how shall we part with them in setting forth?

POINTZ.

Why, we will set forth before or after them, and appoint them a place of meeting, wherein it is at our pleasure to fail; and then will they adventure upon the exploit themselves; which they shall have no sooner achieved but we'll set upon them.

PRINCE HENRY.

Yea, but 'tis like that they will know us by our horses, by our habits, and by every other appointment, to be ourselves.

POINTZ.

Tut! our horses they shall not see,—I'll tie them in the wood; our vizards we will change, after we leave them; and, sirrah, I have cases of buckram for the nonce, to immask our noted outward garments.

PRINCE HENRY.

Yea, but I doubt they will be too hard for us.

POINTZ.

Well, for two of them, I know them to be as true-bred cowards as ever turn'd back; and for the third, if he fight longer than he sees reason, I'll forswear arms. The virtue of this jest will be, the incomprehensible lies that this same fat rogue will tell us when we meet at supper: how thirty, at least, he fought with; what wards, what blows, what extremities he endured; and in the reproof of this lies the jest.

PRINCE HENRY.

Well, I'll go with thee: provide us all things necessary, and meet me to night in Eastcheap; there I'll sup. Farewell.

POINTZ.

Farewell, my lord.   [Exit.

PRINCE HENRY.

I know you all, and will awhile uphold
The unyoked humour of your idleness:
Yet herein will I imitate the sun,
Who doth permit the base contagious clouds
To smother up his beauty from the world,
That, when he please again to be himself,
Being wanted, he may be more wonder'd at,
By breaking through the foul and ugly mists
Of vapours that did seem to strangle him.
If all the year were playing holidays,
To sport would be as tedious as to work;
But when they seldom come, they wisht for
    come,
And nothing pleaseth but rare accidents.
So, when this loose behaviour I throw off,
And pay the debt I never promised,
By how much better than my word I am,
By so much shall I falsify men's hopes;
And, like bright metal on a sullen ground,
My reformation, glittering o'er my fault,
Shall show more goodly and attract more eyes

Than that which hath no foil to set it off.
I'll so offend, to make offence a skill;
Redeeming time, when men think least I will.
                                                   [Exit.

SCENE III.

London.   The palace.

Enter KING HENRY, NORTHUMBERLAND, WOR-
CESTER, HOTSPUR, SIR WALTER BLUNT, *and*
others.

KING HENRY.

MY blood hath been too cold and temperate,
    Unapt to stir at these indignities,
And you have found me; for accordingly
You tread upon my patience: but be sure
I will from henceforth rather be myself,
Mighty and to be fear'd, than my condition;
Which hath been smooth as oil, soft as young
    down,
And therefore lost that title of respect
Which the proud soul ne'er pays but to the
    proud.

EARL OF WORCESTER.

Our house, my sovereign liege, little deserves
The scourge of greatness to be used on it;
And that same greatness too which our own hands
Have holp to make so portly.

EARL OF NORTHUMBERLAND.

My lord,—

KING HENRY.

Worcester, get thee gone; for I do see
Danger and disobedience in thine eye:
O, sir, your presence is too bold and peremptory,
And majesty might never yet endure
The moody frontier of a servant brow.
You have good leave to leave us: when we need
Your use and counsel, we shall send for you.
                           [Exit WORCESTER.
[to NORTHUMBERLAND] You were about to
    speak.

EARL OF NORTHUMBERLAND.

                               Yea, my good lord.
Those prisoners in your highness' name de-
    manded,
Which Harry Percy here at Holmedon took,
Were, as he says, not with such strength denied
As is deliver'd to your majesty:
Either envy, therefore, or misprision
Is guilty of this fault, and not my son.

HOTSPUR.

My liege, I did deny no prisoners.
But I remember, when the fight was done,
When I was dry with rage and extreme toil,
Breathless and faint, leaning upon my sword,
Came there a certain lord, neat, and trimly drest,
Fresh as a bridegroom; and his chin new reapt
Show'd like a stubble-land at harvest-home;
He was perfumed like a milliner;
And 'twixt his finger and his thumb he held
A pouncet-box, which ever and anon
He gave his nose, and took't away again;—
Who therewith angry, when it next came there,
Took it in snuff:—and still he smiled and talkt;
And as the soldiers bore dead bodies by,
He call'd them untaught knaves, unmannerly,
To bring a slovenly unhandsome corse

Betwixt the wind and his nobility.
With many holiday and lady terms
He question'd me; amongst the rest, demanded
My prisoners in your majesty's behalf.
I then, all smarting with my wounds being cold,
To be so pester'd with a popinjay,
Out of my grief and my impatience,
Answer'd neglectingly, I know not what,—
He should, or he should not; for he made me mad
To see him shine so brisk, and smell so sweet,
And talk so like a waiting-gentlewoman
Of guns and drums and wounds,—God save the
    mark!—
And telling me the sovereign'st thing on earth
Was parmaceti for an inward bruise;
And that it was great pity, so it was,
This villainous salt-petre should be digg'd
Out of the bowels of the harmless earth,
Which many a good tall fellow had destroy'd
So cowardly; and but for these vile guns,
He would himself have been a soldier.
This bald unjointed chat of his, my lord,
I answer'd indirectly, as I said;
And I beseech you, let not his report
Come current for an accusation
Betwixt my love and your high majesty.
                    SIR WALTER BLUNT.
The circumstance consider'd, good my lord,
Whate'er Lord Harry Percy then had said
To such a person, and in such a place,
At such a time, with all the rest re-told,
May reasonably die, and never rise
To do him wrong, or any way impeach
What then he said, so he unsay it now.
                    KING HENRY.
Why, yet he doth deny his prisoners,
But with proviso and exception,—
That we at our own charge shall ransom straight
His brother-in-law, the foolish Mortimer;
Who, on my soul, hath wilfully betray'd
The lives of those that he did lead to fight
Against the great magician, damn'd Glendower,
Whose daughter, as we hear, that Earl of March
Hath lately married. Shall our coffers, then,
Be emptied to redeem a traitor home?
Shall we buy treason, and indent with fears,
When they have lost and forfeited themselves?
No, on the barren mountains let him starve;
For I shall never hold that man my friend
Whose tongue shall ask me for one penny cost
To ransom home revolted Mortimer.
                    HOTSPUR.
Revolted Mortimer!
He never did fall off, my sovereign liege,
But by the chance of war:—to prove that true
Needs no more but one tongue for all those
    wounds,
Those mouthed wounds, which valiantly he took,
When on the gentle Severn's sedgy bank,
In single opposition, hand to hand,
He did confound the best part of an hour
In changing hardiment with great Glendower:
Three times they breathed, and three times did
    they drink,
Upon agreement, of swift Severn's flood;
Who then, affrighted with their bloody looks,

Ran fearfully among the trembling reeds,
And hid his crisp head in the hollow bank
Blood-stained with these valiant combatants.
Never did base and rotten policy
Colour her working with such deadly wounds;
Nor never could the noble Mortimer
Receive so many, and all willingly:
Then let him not be slander'd with revolt.
                    KING HENRY.
Thou dost belie him, Percy, thou dost belie him;
He never did encounter with Glendower:
I tell thee,
He durst as well have met the devil alone
As Owen Glendower for an enemy.
Art thou not ashamed? But, sirrah, henceforth
Let me not hear you speak of Mortimer:
Send me your prisoners with the speediest means,
Or you shall hear in such a kind from me
As will displease you.—My Lord Northumber-
    land,
We license your departure with your son.—
Send us your prisoners, or you will hear of it.
    [Exeunt KING HENRY, BLUNT, and TRAIN.
                    HOTSPUR.
An if the devil come and roar for them,
I will not send them:—I will after straight
And tell him so: for I will ease my heart,
Albeit I make a hazard of my head.
                    EARL OF NORTHUMBERLAND.
What, drunk with choler? stay, and pause awhile:
Here comes your uncle.
                    Enter WORCESTER.
                    HOTSPUR.
                        Speak of Mortimer!
Zounds, I will speak of him; and let my soul
Want mercy, if I do not join with him:
Yea, on his part I'll empty all these veins,
And shed my dear blood drop by drop i' th' dust,
But I will lift the down-trod Mortimer
As high i' th' air as this unthankful king,
As this ingrate and canker'd Bolingbroke.
                    EARL OF NORTHUMBERLAND.
[to WORCESTER] Brother, the king hath made
    your nephew mad.
                    EARL OF WORCESTER.
Who struck this heat up after I was gone?
                    HOTSPUR.
He will, forsooth, have all my prisoners;
And when I urged the ransom once again
Of my wife's brother, then his cheek lookt pale,
And on my face he turn'd an eye of death,
Trembling even at the name of Mortimer.
                    EARL OF WORCESTER.
I cannot blame him: was not he proclaim'd
By Richard that dead is the next of blood?
                    EARL OF NORTHUMBERLAND.
He was; I heard the proclamation:
And then it was when the unhappy king—
Whose wrongs in us God pardon!—did set forth
Upon his Irish expedition;
From whence he intercepted did return
To be deposed, and shortly murdered.
                    EARL OF WORCESTER.
And for whose death we in the world's wide
    mouth
Live scandalized and foully spoken of.

HOTSPUR.
But, soft, I pray you; did King Richard then
Proclaim my brother Edmund Mortimer
Heir to the crown?
EARL OF NORTHUMBERLAND.
         He did; myself did hear it.
HOTSPUR.
Nay, then I cannot blame his cousin king,
That wisht him on the barren mountains starve.
But shall it be, that you, that set the crown
Upon the head of this forgetful man,
And for his sake wear the detested blot
Of murderous subornation,—shall it be,
That you a world of curses undergo,
Being the agents, or base second means,
The cords, the ladder, or the hangman rather?—
O, pardon me, that I descend so low,
To show the line and the predicament
Wherein you range under this subtle king;—
Shall it, for shame, be spoken in these days,
Or fill up chronicles in time to come,
That men of your nobility and power
Did gage them both in an unjust behalf,—
As both of you, God pardon it! have done,—
To put down Richard, that sweet lovely rose,
And plant this thorn, this canker, Bolingbroke?
And shall it, in more shame, be further spoken,
That you are fool'd, discarded, and shook off
By him for whom these shames ye underwent?
No; yet time serves, wherein you may redeem
Your banisht honours, and restore yourselves
Into the good thoughts of the world again;
Revenge the jeering and disdain'd contempt
Of this proud king, who studies day and night
To answer all the debt he owes to you
Even with the bloody payment of your deaths:
Therefore, I say,—
EARL OF WORCESTER.
      Peace, cousin, say no more:
And now I will unclasp a secret book,
And to your quick-conceiving discontents
I'll read you matter deep and dangerous;
As full of peril and adventurous spirit
As to o'er-walk a current roaring loud
On the unsteadfast footing of a spear.
HOTSPUR.
If he fall in, good night!—or sink or swim:—
Send danger from the east unto the west,
So honour cross it from the north to south,
And let them grapple:—O, the blood more stirs
To rouse a lion than to start a hare!
EARL OF NORTHUMBERLAND.
Imagination of some great exploit
Drives him beyond the bounds of patience.
HOTSPUR.
By heaven, methinks it were an easy leap,
To pluck bright honour from the pale-faced
    moon;
Or dive into the bottom of the deep,
Where fadom-line could never touch the ground,
And pluck up drowned honour by the locks;
So he that doth redeem her thence might wear
Without corrival all her dignities:
But out upon this half-faced fellowship!
EARL OF WORCESTER.
He apprehends a world of figures here,

But not the form of what he should attend.—
Good cousin, give me audience for a while.
HOTSPUR.
I cry you mercy.
EARL OF WORCESTER.
      Those same noble Scots
That are your prisoners,—
HOTSPUR.
          I'll keep them all;
By God, he shall not have a Scot of them;
No, if a Scot would save his soul, he shall not:
I'll keep them, by this hand.
EARL OF WORCESTER.
         You start away,
And lend no ear unto my purposes.—
Those prisoners you shall keep.
HOTSPUR.
        Nay, I will; that's flat:—
He said he would not ransom Mortimer;
Forbad my tongue to speak of Mortimer;
But I will find him when he lies asleep,
And in his ear I'll holla 'Mortimer!'
Nay, I'll have a starling shall be taught to speak
Nothing but 'Mortimer,' and give it him,
To keep his anger still in motion.
EARL OF WORCESTER.
Hear you, cousin; a word.
HOTSPUR.
All studies here I solemnly defy,
Save how to gall and pinch this Bolingbroke:
And that same sword-and-buckler Prince of
    Wales,—
But that I think his father loves him not,
And would be glad he met with some mischance,
I would have him poison'd with a pot of ale.
EARL OF WORCESTER.
Farewell, kinsman: I'll talk to you
When you are better temper'd to attend.
EARL OF NORTHUMBERLAND.
Why, what a wasp-stung and impatient fool
Art thou to break into this woman's mood,
Tying thine ear to no tongue but thine own!
HOTSPUR.
Why, look you, I am whipt and scourged with
    rods,
Nettled, and stung with pismires, when I hear
Of this vile politician, Bolingbroke.
In Richard's time,—what do you call the
    place?—
A plague upon 't—it is in Glostershire;—
'Twas where the madcap duke his uncle kept,—
His uncle York;—where I first bow'd my knee
Unto this king of smiles, this Bolingbroke,—
'Sblood !—
When you and he came back from Ravenspurg.
EARL OF NORTHUMBERLAND.
At Berkley-castle.
HOTSPUR.
You say true:—
Why, what a candy deal of courtesy
This fawning greyhound then did proffer me!
Look, 'when his infant fortune came to age,'
And, 'gentle Harry Percy,' and, 'kind cousin,'—
O, the devil take such cozeners!—God forgive
    me!—
Good uncle, tell your tale; I have done.

EARL OF WORCESTER.
Nay, if you have not, to it again;
We will stay your leisure.
HOTSPUR.
I have done, i' faith.
EARL OF WORCESTER.
Then once more to your Scottish prisoners.
Deliver them up without their ransom straight,
And make the Douglas' son your only mean
For powers in Scotland; which, for divers reasons
Which I shall send you written, be assured,
Will easily be granted—. [to NORTHUMBER-
LAND] You, my lord,
Your son in Scotland being thus employ'd,
Shall secretly into the bosom creep
Of that same noble prelate, well beloved,
The archbishop.
HOTSPUR.
Of York, is it not?
EARL OF WORCESTER.
True; who bears hard
His brother's death at Bristol, the Lord Scroop.
I speak not this in estimation,
As what I think might be, but what I know
Is ruminated, plotted, and set down,
And only stays but to behold the face
Of that occasion that shall bring it on.
HOTSPUR.
I smell it: upon my life, it will do well.
EARL OF NORTHUMBERLAND.
Before the game is a-foot, thou still lett'st slip.
HOTSPUR.
Why, it cannot choose but be a noble plot:—
And then the power of Scotland and of York,—
To join with Mortimer, ha?
EARL OF WORCESTER.
And so they shall.
HOTSPUR.
In faith, it is exceedingly well aim'd.
EARL OF WORCESTER.
And 'tis no little reason bids us speed,
To save our heads by raising of a head;
For, bear ourselves as even as we can,
The king will always think him in our debt,
And think we think ourselves unsatisfied,
Till he hath found a time to pay us home:
And see already how he doth begin
To make us strangers to his looks of love.
HOTSPUR.
He does, he does; we'll be revenged on him.
EARL OF WORCESTER.
Cousin, farewell:—no further go in this
Than I by letters shall direct your course.
When time is ripe,—which will be suddenly,—
I'll steal to Glendower and Lord Mortimer;
Where you and Douglas, and our powers at once,
As I will fashion it, shall happily meet,
To bear our fortunes in our own strong arms,
Which now we hold at much uncertainty.
EARL OF NORTHUMBERLAND.
Farewell, good brother: we shall thrive, I trust.
HOTSPUR.
Uncle, adieu:—O, let the hours be short,
Till fields and blows and groans applaud our
sport!   [Exeunt.

ACT II. SCENE I.

Rochester.   An inn-yard.

Enter a CARRIER *with a lantern in his hand.*

FIRST CARRIER.

HEIGH-HO! an't be not four by the day, I'll
be hang'd: Charles' wain is over the new
chimney, and yet our horse not packt.—What,
ostler!
OSTLER [*within*].
Anon, anon.
FIRST CARRIER.
I prithee, Tom, beat Cut's saddle, put a few
flocks in the point; poor jade is wrung in the
withers out of all cess.
Enter another CARRIER.
SECOND CARRIER.
Peas and beans are as dank here as a dog, and that is
the next way to give poor jades the bots: this house
is turn'd upside down since Robin ostler died.
FIRST CARRIER.
Poor fellow! never joy'd since the price of oats
rose; it was the death of him.
SECOND CARRIER.
I think this be the most villainous house in all
London road for fleas: I am stung like a tench.
FIRST CARRIER.
Like a tench! by the mass, there is ne'er a king
christen could be better bit than I have been since
the first cock.
SECOND CARRIER.
Why, they will allow us ne'er a jordan, and then
we leak in the chimney; and your chamber-lie
breeds fleas like a loach.
FIRST CARRIER.
What, ostler! come away, and be hang'd! come
away.
SECOND CARRIER.
I have a gammon of bacon and two razes of gin-
ger, to be deliver'd as far as Charing-cross.
FIRST CARRIER.
God's body, the turkeys in my pannier are quite
starved.—What, ostler!—A plague on thee! hast
thou never an eye in thy head? canst not hear? An
'twere not as good a deed as drink, to break the
pate on thee, I am a very villain.—Come, and be
hang'd!—hast no faith in thee?
Enter GADSHILL.
GADSHILL.
Good morrow, carriers. What's o'clock?
FIRST CARRIER.
I think it be two o'clock.
GADSHILL.
I prithee, lend me thy lantern, to see my gelding
in the stable.
FIRST CARRIER.
Nay, by God, soft; I know a trick worth two of
that, i' faith.
GADSHILL.
I pray thee, lend me thine.
SECOND CARRIER.
Ay, when? canst tell?—Lend me thy lantern,
quoth a?—marry, I'll see thee hang'd first.
GADSHILL.
Sirrah carrier, what time do you mean to come to
London?

SECOND CARRIER.

Time enough to go to bed with a candle, I warrant thee.—Come, neighbour Mugs, we'll call up the gentlemen: they will along with company, for they have great charge. *[Exeunt* CARRIERS.

GADSHILL.

What, ho! chamberlain!

CHAMBERLAIN *[within]*.

At hand, quoth pick-purse.

GADSHILL.

That's even as fair as—at hand, quoth the chamberlain; for thou variest no more from picking of purses than giving direction doth from labouring; thou lay'st the plot how.

Enter CHAMBERLAIN.

CHAMBERLAIN.

Good morrow, Master Gadshill. It holds current that I told you yesternight:—there's a franklin in the wild of Kent hath brought three hundred marks with him in gold: I heard him tell it to one of his company last night at supper; a kind of auditor; one that hath abundance of charge too, God knows what. They are up already, and call for eggs and butter; they will away presently.

GADSHILL.

Sirrah, if they meet not with Saint Nicholas' clerks, I'll give thee this neck.

CHAMBERLAIN.

No, I'll none of it: I prithee, keep that for the hangman; for I know thou worship'st Saint Nicholas as truly as a man of falsehood may.

GADSHILL.

What talkest thou to me of the hangman? if I hang, I'll make a fat pair of gallows; for if I hang, old Sir John hangs with me, and thou know'st he's no starveling! Tut! there are other Trojans that thou dream'st not of, the which, for sport sake, are content to do the profession some grace; that would, if matters should be lookt into, for their own credit sake, make all whole. I am join'd with no foot land-rakers, no long-staff sixpenny strikers, none of these mad mustachio purple-hued malt-worms; but with nobility and tranquillity, burgomasters and great oneyers, such as can hold in, such as will strike sooner than speak, and speak sooner than drink, and drink sooner than pray: and yet, zounds, I lie; for they pray continually to their saint, the commonwealth; or, rather, not pray to her, but prey on her,—for they ride up and down on her, and make her their boots.

CHAMBERLAIN.

What, the commonwealth their boots? will she hold out water in foul way?

GADSHILL.

She will, she will; justice hath liquor'd her. We steal as in a castle, cock-sure; we have the receipt of fern-seed,—we walk invisible.

CHAMBERLAIN.

Nay, by my faith, I think you are more beholding to the night than to fern-seed for your walking invisible.

GADSHILL.

Give me thy hand: thou shalt have a share in our purchase, as I am a true man.

CHAMBERLAIN.

Nay, rather let me have it, as you are a false thief.

GADSHILL.

Go to; *homo* is a common name to all men. Bid the ostler bring my gelding out of the stable. Farewell, you muddy knave. *[Exeunt.*

SCENE II.

The road by Gadshill.

Enter PRINCE HENRY *and* POINTZ; BARDOLPH *and* PETO *at some distance.*

POINTZ.

COME, shelter, shelter: I have removed Falstaff's horse, and he frets like a gumm'd velvet.

PRINCE HENRY.

Stand close. *[They retire.*

Enter FALSTAFF.

SIR JOHN FALSTAFF.

Pointz! Pointz, and be hang'd! Pointz!

PRINCE HENRY *[coming forward]*.

Peace, ye fat-kidney'd rascal! what a brawling dost thou keep!

SIR JOHN FALSTAFF.

Where's Pointz, Hal?

PRINCE HENRY.

He is walkt up to the top of the hill: I'll go seek him. *[Retires.*

SIR JOHN FALSTAFF.

I am accurst to rob in that thief's company: the rascal hath removed my horse, and tied him I know not where. If I travel but four foot by the squier further a-foot, I shall break my wind. Well, I doubt not but to die a fair death for all this, if I scape hanging for killing that rogue. I have forsworn his company hourly any time this two-and-twenty year, and yet I am bewitcht with the rogue's company. If the rascal have not given me medicines to make me love him, I'll be hang'd; it could not be else; I have drunk medicines.—Pointz!—Hal!—a plague upon you both!—Bardolph!—Peto!—I'll starve, ere I'll rob a foot further. An 'twere not as good a deed as drink, to turn true man, and to leave these rogues, I am the veriest varlet that ever chew'd with a tooth. Eight yards of uneven ground is threescore and ten miles a-foot with me; and the stony-hearted villains know it well enough: a plague upon't, when thieves cannot be true one to another! *[They whistle.]* Whew!—A plague upon you all! Give me my horse, you rogues; give me my horse, and be hang'd!

PRINCE HENRY *[coming forward]*.

Peace, ye fat-guts! lie down; lay thine ear close to the ground, and list if thou canst hear the tread of travellers.

SIR JOHN FALSTAFF.

Have you any levers to lift me up again, being down? 'Sblood, I'll not bear mine own flesh so far a-foot again for all the coin in thy father's exchequer. What a plague mean ye to colt me thus?

PRINCE HENRY.

Thou liest; thou art not colted, thou art uncolted.

SIR JOHN FALSTAFF.

I prithee, good Prince Hal, help me to my horse, good king's son.

PRINCE HENRY.
Out, ye rogue! shall I be your ostler?
SIR JOHN FALSTAFF.
Go, hang thyself in thine own heir-apparent
garters! If I be ta'en, I'll peach for this. An I
have not ballads made on you all, and sung to
filthy tunes, let a cup of sack be my poison:—
when a jest is so forward, and a-foot too!—I hate
it.
Enter GADSHILL.
GADSHILL.
Stand!
SIR JOHN FALSTAFF.
So I do, against my will.
POINTZ.
O, 'tis our setter: I know his voice.
[*Coming forward with* BARDOLPH *and*
PETO.
BARDOLPH.
What news?
GADSHILL.
Case ye, case ye; on with your vizards: there's
money of the king's coming down the hill; 'tis
going to the king's exchequer.
SIR JOHN FALSTAFF.
You lie, ye rogue; 'tis going to the king's tavern.
GADSHILL.
There's enough to make us all.
SIR JOHN FALSTAFF.
To be hang'd.
PRINCE HENRY.
Sirs, you four shall front them in the narrow lane;
Ned Pointz and I will walk lower: if they scape
from your encounter, then they light on us.
PETO.
How many be there of them?
GADSHILL.
Some eight or ten.
SIR JOHN FALSTAFF.
Zounds, will they not rob us?
PRINCE HENRY.
What, a coward, Sir John Paunch?
SIR JOHN FALSTAFF.
Indeed, I am not John of Gaunt, your grand-
father; but yet no coward, Hal.
PRINCE HENRY.
Well, we leave that to the proof.
POINTZ.
Sirrah Jack, thy horse stands behind the hedge:
when thou need'st him, there thou shalt find him.
Farewell, and stand fast.
SIR JOHN FALSTAFF.
Now cannot I strike him, if I should be hang'd.
PRINCE HENRY [*aside to* POINTZ].
Ned, where are our disguises?
POINTZ [*aside to* PRINCE HENRY].
Here, hard by: stand close.
[*Exeunt* PRINCE HENRY *and* POINTZ.
SIR JOHN FALSTAFF.
Now, my masters, happy man be his dole, say I:
every man to his business.
Enter TRAVELLERS.
FIRST TRAVELLER.
Come, neighbour: the boy shall lead our horses
down the hill; we'll walk a-foot awhile, and ease
our legs.

THIEVES.
Stand!
TRAVELLERS.
Jesus bless us!
SIR JOHN FALSTAFF.
Strike; down with them; cut the villains' throats:
—ah, whoreson caterpillars! bacon-fed knaves!
they hate us youth:—down with them; fleece
them.
TRAVELLERS.
O, we are undone, both we and ours for ever!
SIR JOHN FALSTAFF.
Hang ye, gorbellied knaves, are ye undone? No,
ye fat chuffs; I would your store were here! On,
bacons, on! What, ye knaves! young men must
live. You are grand-jurors, are ye? we'll jure ye,
i' faith.
[*Here they rob them and bind them. Exeunt.*
Enter PRINCE HENRY *and* POINTZ *disguised.*
PRINCE HENRY.
The thieves have bound the true men. Now
could thou and I rob the thieves, and go merrily
to London, it would be argument for a week,
laughter for a month, and a good jest for ever.
POINTZ.
Stand close: I hear them coming.   [*They retire.*
Enter THIEVES *again.*
SIR JOHN FALSTAFF.
Come, my masters, let us share, and then to horse
before day. An the Prince and Pointz be not two
arrant cowards, there's no equity stirring: there's
no more valour in that Pointz than in a wild-duck.
PRINCE HENRY.
Your money!
POINTZ.
Villains!
[*As they are sharing, the* PRINCE *and*
POINTZ *set upon them. They all run
away, and* FALSTAFF *after a blow or two
runs away too, leaving the booty behind
them.*
PRINCE HENRY.
Got with much ease. Now merrily to horse:
The thieves are scatter'd, and possest with fear
So strongly that they dare not meet each other;
Each takes his fellow for an officer.
Away, good Ned. Falstaff sweats to death,
And lards the lean earth as he walks along:
Were't not for laughing, I should pity him.
POINTZ.
How the rogue roar'd!   [*Exeunt.*

SCENE III.
Warkworth Castle.

Enter HOTSPUR *solus, reading a letter.*
HOTSPUR.
'BUT, for mine own part, my lord, I could
be well contented to be there, in respect
of the love I bear your house.'—He could be contented,—why is he not, then? In respect of the
love he bears our house:—he shows in this, he
loves his own barn better than he loves our house.
Let me see some more. 'The purpose you undertake is dangerous:'—why, that's certain: 'tis dangerous to take a cold, to sleep, to drink; but I tell

you, my lord fool, out of this nettle, danger, we pluck this flower, safety. 'The purpose you undertake is dangerous; the friends you have named uncertain; the time 'tself unsorted; and your whole plot too light for the counterpoise of so great an opposition.'—Say you so, say you so? I say unto you again, you are a shallow, cowardly hind, and you lie. What a lack-brain is this! By the Lord, our plot is a good plot as ever was laid; our friends true and constant: a good plot, good friends, and full of expectation; an excellent plot, very good friends. What a frosty-spirited rogue is this! Why, my Lord of York commends the plot and the general course of the action. Zounds, an I were now by this rascal, I could brain him with his lady's fan. Is there not my father, my uncle, and myself? Lord Edmund Mortimer, my Lord of York, and Owen Glendower? is there not, besides, the Douglas? have I not all their letters to meet me in arms by the ninth of the next month? and are they not some of them set forward already? What a pagan rascal is this! an infidel! Ha! you shall see now, in very sincerity of fear and cold heart, will he to the king, and lay open all our proceedings. O, I could divide myself, and go to buffets, for moving such a dish of skim milk with so honourable an action! Hang him! let him tell the king: we are prepared. I will set forward to-night.

Enter LADY PERCY.

How now, Kate! I must leave you within these two hours.

LADY PERCY.

O, my good lord, why are you thus alone?
For what offence have I this fortnight been
A banisht woman from my Harry's bed?
Tell me, sweet lord, what is't that takes from thee
Thy stomach, pleasure, and thy golden sleep?
Why dost thou bend thine eyes upon the earth,
And start so often when thou sitt'st alone?
Why hast thou lost the fresh blood in thy cheeks;
And given my treasures and my rights of thee
To thick-eyed musing and curst melancholy?
In thy faint slumbers I by thee have watcht,
And heard thee murmur tales of iron wars;
Speak terms of manage to thy bounding steed;
Cry, 'Courage! to the field!'—and thou hast talkt
Of sallies and retires, of trenches, tents,
Of palisadoes, frontiers, parapets,
Of basilisks, of cannon, culverin,
Of prisoners' ransom, and of soldiers slain,
And all the currents of a heady fight.
Thy spirit within thee hath been so at war,
And thus hath so bestirr'd thee in thy sleep,
That beads of sweat have stood upon thy brow,
Like bubbles in a late-disturbed stream;
And in thy face strange motions have appear'd,
Such as we see when men restrain their breath
On some great sudden hest. O, what portents are these?
Some heavy business hath my lord in hand,
And I must know it, else he loves me not.

HOTSPUR.

What, ho!

Enter a SERVANT.

Is Gilliams with the packet gone?

SERVANT.

He is, my lord, an hour ago.

HOTSPUR.

Hath Butler brought those horses from the sheriff?

SERVANT.

One horse, my lord, he brought even now.

HOTSPUR.

What horse? a roan, a crop-ear, is it not?

SERVANT.

It is, my lord.

HOTSPUR.

That roan shall be my throne.
Well, I will back him straight: O *esperance!*—
Bid Butler lead him forth into the park.

[*Exit* SERVANT.

LADY PERCY.

But hear you, my lord.

HOTSPUR.

What say'st thou, my lady?

LADY PERCY.

What is it carries you away?

HOTSPUR.

Why, my horse,
My love,—my horse.

LADY PERCY.

Out, you mad-headed ape!
A weasel hath not such a deal of spleen
As you are tost with. In faith,
I'll know your business, Harry,—that I will.
I fear my brother Mortimer doth stir
About his title, and hath sent for you
To line his enterprise: but if you go,—

HOTSPUR.

So far a-foot, I shall be weary, love.

LADY PERCY.

Come, come, you paraquito, answer me
Directly unto this question that I ask:
In faith, I'll break thy little finger, Harry,
An if thou wilt not tell me all things true.

HOTSPUR.

Away, away, you trifler!—Love?—I love thee not,
I care not for thee, Kate: this is no world
To play with mammets and to tilt with lips:
We must have bloody noses and crackt crowns,
And pass them current too.—God's me, my horse!—
What say'st thou, Kate? what wouldst thou have with me?

LADY PERCY.

Do you not love me? do you not, indeed?
Well, do not, then; for since you love me not,
I will not love myself. Do you not love me?
Nay, tell me if you speak in jest or no.

HOTSPUR.

Come, wilt thou see me ride?
And when I am o' horseback, I will swear
I love thee infinitely. But hark you, Kate;
I must not have you henceforth question me
Whither I go, nor reason whereabout:
Whither I must, I must; and, to conclude,
This evening must I leave you, gentle Kate.
I know you wise; but yet no further wise

Than Harry Percy's wife: constant you are;
But yet a woman: and for secrecy,
No lady closer; for I well believe
Thou wilt not utter what thou dost not know,—
And so far will I trust thee, gentle Kate.

LADY PERCY.
How! so far?

HOTSPUR.
Not an inch further. But hark you, Kate:
Whither I go, thither shall you go too;
To-day will I set forth, to-morrow you.—
Will this content you, Kate?

LADY PERCY.
It must of force.
[Exeunt.

SCENE IV.

Eastcheap.   The Boar's-Head Tavern.

Enter PRINCE HENRY.

PRINCE HENRY.
NED, prithee, come out of that fat room, and lend me thy hand to laugh a little.

Enter POINTZ.

POINTZ.
Where hast been, Hal?

PRINCE HENRY.
With three or four loggerheads amongst three or fourscore hogsheads. I have sounded the very base-string of humility. Sirrah, I am sworn brother to a leash of drawers; and can tell them all by their christen names, as,—Tom, Dick, and Francis. They take it already upon their salvation, that though I be but Prince of Wales, yet I am the king of courtesy; and tell me flatly I am no proud Jack, like Falstaff, but a Corinthian, a lad of mettle, a good boy, by the Lord, so they call me, and when I am king of England, I shall command all the good lads in Eastcheap. They call drinking deep, dyeing scarlet; and when you breathe in your watering, they cry 'hem!' and bid you play it off. To conclude, I am so good a proficient in one quarter of an hour, that I can drink with any tinker in his own language during my life. I tell thee, Ned, thou hast lost much honour, that thou wert not with me in this action. But, sweet Ned,—to sweeten which name of Ned, I give thee this pennyworth of sugar, clapt even now into my hand by an under-skinker, one that never spake other English in his life than 'Eight shillings and sixpence,' and 'You are welcome,' with this shrill addition, 'Anon, anon, sir! Score a pint of bastard in the Half-moon,' or so:—but, Ned, to drive away the time till Falstaff come, I prithee, do thou stand in some by-room, while I question my puny drawer to what end he gave me the sugar; and do thou never leave calling 'Francis,' that his tale to me may be nothing but 'anon.' Step aside, and I'll show thee a precedent.
[Exit POINTZ.

Francis!

POINTZ [within].

PRINCE HENRY.
Thou art perfect.

POINTZ [within].
Francis!

Enter FRANCIS.

FRANCIS.
Anon, anon, sir.—Look down into the Pomgarnet, Ralph.

PRINCE HENRY.
Come hither, Francis.

FRANCIS.
My lord?

PRINCE HENRY.
How long hast thou to serve, Francis?

FRANCIS.
Forsooth, five years, and as much as to—

POINTZ [within].
Francis!

FRANCIS.
Anon, anon, sir.

PRINCE HENRY.
Five years! by'r lady, a long lease for the clinking of pewter. But, Francis, darest thou be so valiant as to play the coward with thy indenture and show it a fair pair of heels and run from it?

FRANCIS.
O Lord, sir, I'll be sworn upon all the books in England, I could find in my heart—

POINTZ [within].
Francis!

FRANCIS.
Anon, anon, sir.

PRINCE HENRY.
How old art thou, Francis?

FRANCIS.
Let me see,—about Michaelmas next I shall be—

POINTZ [within].
Francis!

FRANCIS.
Anon, sir.—Pray you, stay a little, my lord.

PRINCE HENRY.
Nay, but hark you, Francis: for the sugar thou gavest me,—'twas a pennyworth, was't not?—

FRANCIS.
O Lord, sir, I would it had been two!

PRINCE HENRY.
I will give thee for it a thousand pound: ask me when thou wilt, and thou shalt have it.

POINTZ [within].
Francis!

FRANCIS.
Anon, anon.

PRINCE HENRY.
Anon, Francis? No, Francis; but to-morrow, Francis; or, Francis, o' Thursday; or, indeed, Francis, when thou wilt. But, Francis,—

FRANCIS.
My lord?

PRINCE HENRY.
Wilt thou rob this leathern-jerkin, crystal-button, nott-pated, agate-ring, puke-stocking, caddisgarter, smooth-tongue, Spanish-pouch,—

FRANCIS.
O Lord, sir, what do you mean?

PRINCE HENRY.
Why, then, your brown bastard is your only drink; for, look you, Francis, your white canvas doublet will sully: in Barbary, sir, it cannot come to so much.

FRANCIS.

What, sir?

POINTZ [*within*].

Francis!

PRINCE HENRY.

Away, you rogue! dost thou not hear them call?
[*Here they both call him; the* DRAWER *stands
amazed, not knowing which way to go.*
Enter VINTNER.

VINTNER.

What, stand'st thou still, and hear'st such a calling? Look to the guests within. [*Exit* FRANCIS.]
My lord, old Sir John, with half-a-dozen more,
are at the door: shall I let them in?

PRINCE HENRY.

Let them alone awhile, and then open the door.
[*Exit* VINTNER.] Pointz!
Enter POINTZ.

POINTZ.

Anon, anon, sir.

PRINCE HENRY.

Sirrah, Falstaff and the rest of the thieves are at
the door: shall we be merry?

POINTZ.

As merry as crickets, my lad. But hark ye; what
cunning match have you made with this jest of
the drawer? come, what's the issue?

PRINCE HENRY.

I am now of all humours that have show'd themselves humours since the old days of goodman Adam to the pupil age of this present
twelve o'clock at midnight. — What's o'clock,
Francis?

FRANCIS [*within*].

Anon, anon, sir.

PRINCE HENRY.

That ever this fellow should have fewer words
than a parrot, and yet the son of a woman! His industry is up-stairs and down-stairs; his eloquence
the parcel of a reckoning. I am not yet of Percy's
mind, the Hotspur of the north; he that kills me
some six or seven dozen of Scots at a breakfast,
washes his hands, and says to his wife, "Fie upon
this quiet life! I want work.' 'O my sweet Harry,'
says she, 'how many hast thou kill'd to-day?'
'Give my roan horse a drench,' says he, and answers, 'Some fourteen,' an hour after,—'a trifle, a
trifle.' I prithee, call in Falstaff: I'll play Percy,
and that damn'd brawn shall play Dame Mortimer his wife. 'Rivo,' says the drunkard. Call in
ribs, call in tallow.
Enter FALSTAFF, GADSHILL, BARDOLPH, *and*
PETO; *followed by* FRANCIS *with wine.*

POINTZ.

Welcome, Jack: where hast thou been?

SIR JOHN FALSTAFF.

A plague of all cowards, I say, and a vengeance
too! marry, and amen!—Give me a cup of sack,
boy.—Ere I lead this life long, I'll sew netherstocks, and mend them and foot them too. A
plague of all cowards!—Give me a cup of
sack, rogue.—Is there no virtue extant?
[*Drinks.*

PRINCE HENRY.

Didst thou never see Titan kiss a dish of butter
(pitiful-hearted Titan!) that melted at the sweet
tale of the sun! if thou didst, then behold that
compound.

SIR JOHN FALSTAFF.

You rogue, here's lime in this sack too: there is
nothing but roguery to be found in villainous
man: yet a coward is worse than a cup of sack with
lime in it,—a villainous coward.—Go thy ways,
old Jack; die when thou wilt, if manhood, good
manhood, be not forgot upon the face of the
earth, then am I a shotten herring. There lives
not three good men unhang'd in England; and
one of them is fat, and grows old: God help the
while! a bad world, I say. I would I were a
weaver; I could sing psalms or any thing. A
plague of all cowards! I say still.

PRINCE HENRY.

How now, wool-sack! what mutter you?

SIR JOHN FALSTAFF.

A king's son! If I do not beat thee out of thy
kingdom with a dagger of lath, and drive all thy
subjects afore thee like a flock of wild-geese, I'll
never wear hair on my face more. You Prince of
Wales!

PRINCE HENRY.

Why, you whoreson round man, what's the
matter?

SIR JOHN FALSTAFF.

Are not you a coward? answer me to that:—and
Pointz there?

POINTZ.

Zounds, ye fat paunch, an ye call me coward, by
the Lord, I'll stab thee.

SIR JOHN FALSTAFF.

I call thee coward! I'll see thee damn'd ere I call
thee coward: but I would give a thousand pound,
I could run as fast as thou canst. You are straight
enough in the shoulders,—you care not who sees
your back: call you that backing of your friends?
A plague upon such backing! give me them that
will face me.—Give me a cup of sack:—I am a
rogue, if I drunk to-day.

PRINCE HENRY.

O villain! thy lips are scarce wiped since thou
drunk'st last.

SIR JOHN FALSTAFF.

All's one for that. A plague of all cowards! still
say I.   [*Drinks.*

PRINCE HENRY.

What's the matter?

SIR JOHN FALSTAFF.

What's the matter! there be four of us here have
ta'en a thousand pound this day morning.

PRINCE HENRY.

Where is it, Jack? where is it?

SIR JOHN FALSTAFF.

Where is it! taken from us it is: a hundred upon
poor four of us.

PRINCE HENRY.

What, a hundred, man?

SIR JOHN FALSTAFF.

I am a rogue, if I were not at half-sword with a
dozen of them two hours together. I have scaped
by miracle. I am eight times thrust through the
doublet, four through the hose; my buckler cut
through and through; my sword hackt like a handsaw,—*ecce signum!* I never dealt better since I was

a man: all would not do. A plague of all cowards!
—Let them speak: if they speak more or less than
truth, they are villains and the sons of darkness.

PRINCE HENRY.
Speak, sirs; how was it?

GADSHILL.
We four set upon some dozen,—

SIR JOHN FALSTAFF.
Sixteen at least, my lord.

GADSHILL.
And bound them.

PETO.
No, no, they were not bound.

SIR JOHN FALSTAFF.
You rogue, they were bound, every man of them;
or I am a Jew else, an Ebrew Jew.

GADSHILL.
As we were sharing, some six or seven fresh men
set upon us,—

SIR JOHN FALSTAFF.
And unbound the rest, and then come in the
other.

PRINCE HENRY.
What, fought you with them all?

SIR JOHN FALSTAFF.
All! I know not what you call all; but if I fought
not with fifty of them, I am a bunch of radish: if
there were not two or three and fifty upon poor
old Jack, then am I no two-legg'd creature.

PRINCE HENRY.
Pray God you have not murder'd some of them.

SIR JOHN FALSTAFF.
Nay, that's past praying for: I have pepper'd two
of them; two I am sure I have paid,—two rogues
in buckram suits. I tell thee what, Hal,—if I tell
thee a lie, spit in my face, call me horse. Thou
knowest my old ward;—here I lay, and thus I
bore my point. Four rogues in buckram let drive
at me,—

PRINCE HENRY.
What, four? thou saidst but two even now.

SIR JOHN FALSTAFF.
Four, Hal; I told thee four.

POINTZ.
Ay, ay, he said four.

SIR JOHN FALSTAFF.
These four came all a-front, and mainly thrust at
me. I made me no more ado but took all their
seven points in my target, thus.

PRINCE HENRY.
Seven? why, there were but four even now.

SIR JOHN FALSTAFF.
In buckram?

POINTZ.
Ay, four, in buckram suits.

SIR JOHN FALSTAFF.
Seven, by these hilts, or I am a villain else.

PRINCE HENRY.
Prithee, let him alone; we shall have more anon.

SIR JOHN FALSTAFF.
Dost thou hear me, Hal?

PRINCE HENRY.
Ay, and mark thee too, Jack.

SIR JOHN FALSTAFF.
Do so, for it is worth the listening to.   These nine
in buckram that I told thee of,—

PRINCE HENRY.
So, two more already.

SIR JOHN FALSTAFF.
Their points being broken,—

POINTZ.
Down fell their hose.

SIR JOHN FALSTAFF.
Began to give me ground: but I follow'd me close,
came in foot and hand; and with a thought seven
of the eleven I paid.

PRINCE HENRY.
O monstrous! eleven buckram men grown out of
two!

SIR JOHN FALSTAFF.
But, as the devil would have it, three misbegotten
knaves in Kendal green came at my back and let
drive at me;—for it was so dark, Hal, that thou
couldst not see thy hand.

PRINCE HENRY.
These lies are like their father that begets them,—
gross as a mountain, open, palpable. Why, thou
clay-brain'd guts, thou nott-pated fool, thou
whoreson, obscene, greasy tallow-keech,—

SIR JOHN FALSTAFF.
What, art thou mad? art thou mad? is not the
truth the truth?

PRINCE HENRY.
Why, how couldst thou know these men in
Kendal green, when it was so dark thou couldst
not see thy hand? come, tell us your reason: what
say'st thou to this?

POINTZ.
Come, your reason, Jack, your reason.

SIR JOHN FALSTAFF.
What, upon compulsion? Zounds, an I were at
the strappado, or all the racks in the world, I
would not tell you on compulsion. Give you a
reason on compulsion! if reasons were as plentiful
as blackberries, I would give no man a reason
upon compulsion, I.

PRINCE HENRY.
I'll be no longer guilty of this sin; this sanguine
coward, this bed-presser, this horse-back-
breaker, this huge hill of flesh,—

SIR JOHN FALSTAFF.
Away, you starveling, you eel-skin, you dried
neat's-tongue, you bull's-pizzle, you stock-fish,—
O, for breath to utter what is like thee!—you
tailor's-yard, you sheath, you bow-case, you vile
standing-tuck,—

PRINCE HENRY.
Well, breathe awhile, and then to it again: and
when thou hast tired thyself in base comparisons,
hear me speak but this.

POINTZ.
Mark, Jack.

PRINCE HENRY.
We two saw you four set on four and bound
them, and were masters of their wealth.—Mark
now, how a plain tale shall put you down.—Then
did we two set on you four; and, with a word, out-
faced you from your prize, and have it; yea, and
can show it you here in the house:—and, Falstaff,
you carried your guts away as nimbly, with as
quick dexterity, and roar'd for mercy, and still
ran and roar'd, as ever I heard bull-calf. What a

slave art thou, to hack thy sword as thou hast done, and then say it was in fight! What trick, what device, what starting-hole, canst thou now find out to hide thee from this open and apparent shame?

POINTZ.

Come, let's hear, Jack; what trick hast thou now?

SIR JOHN FALSTAFF.

By the Lord, I knew ye as well as he that made ye. Why, hear you, my masters: was it for me to kill the heir-apparent? should I turn upon the true prince? why, thou knowest I am as valiant as Hercules: but beware instinct; the lion will not touch the true prince. Instinct is a great matter; I was a coward on instinct. I shall think the better of myself and thee during my life; I for a valiant lion, and thou for a true prince. But, by the Lord, lads, I am glad you have the money.—Hostess, clap-to the doors [to HOSTESS within]:—watch to-night, pray to-morrow.—Gallants, lads, boys, hearts of gold, all the titles of good fellowship come to you! What, shall we be merry? shall we have a play extempore?

PRINCE HENRY.

Content;—and the argument shall be thy running away.

SIR JOHN FALSTAFF.

Ah, no more of that, Hal, an thou lovest me!

Enter HOSTESS.

HOSTESS.

O Jesu, my lord the prince,—

PRINCE HENRY.

How now, my lady the hostess! what say'st thou to me?

HOSTESS.

Marry, my lord, there is a nobleman of the court at door would speak with you: he says he comes from your father.

PRINCE HENRY.

Give him as much as will make him a royal man, and send him back again to my mother.

SIR JOHN FALSTAFF.

What manner of man is he?

HOSTESS.

An old man.

SIR JOHN FALSTAFF.

What doth gravity out of his bed at midnight?—Shall I give him his answer?

PRINCE HENRY.

Prithee, do, Jack.

SIR JOHN FALSTAFF.

Faith, and I'll send him packing.   [*Exit.*

PRINCE HENRY.

Now, sirs:—by'r lady, you fought fair;—so did you, Peto;—so did you, Bardolph: you are lions too, you ran away upon instinct, you will not touch the true prince; no,—fie!

BARDOLPH.

Faith, I ran when I saw others run.

PRINCE HENRY.

Faith, tell me now in earnest, how came Falstaff's sword so hackt?

PETO.

Why, he hackt it with his dagger; and said he would swear truth out of England, but he would make you believe it was done in fight; and persuaded us to do the like.

BARDOLPH.

Yea, and to tickle our noses with spear-grass to make them bleed; and then to beslubber our garments with it, and swear it was the blood of true men. I did that I did not this seven year before,—I blusht to hear his monstrous devices.

PRINCE HENRY.

O villain, thou stolest a cup of sack eighteen years ago, and wert taken with the manner, and ever since thou hast blusht extempore. Thou hadst fire and sword on thy side, and yet thou ran'st away: what instinct hadst thou for it?

BARDOLPH.

My lord, do you see these meteors? do you behold these exhalations?

PRINCE HENRY.

I do.

BARDOLPH.

What think you they portend?

PRINCE HENRY.

Hot livers and cold purses.

BARDOLPH.

Choler, my lord, if rightly taken.

PRINCE HENRY.

No, if rightly taken, halter.—Here comes lean Jack, here comes bare-bone.

Enter FALSTAFF.

How now, my sweet creature of bombast! How long is't ago, Jack, since thou saw'st thine own knee?

SIR JOHN FALSTAFF.

My own knee! when I was about thy years, Hal, I was not an eagle's talon in the waist; I could have crept into any alderman's thumb-ring: a plague of sighing and grief! it blows a man up like a bladder.—There's villainous news abroad: here was Sir John Bracy from your father; you must to the court in the morning. That same mad fellow of the north, Percy; and he of Wales, that gave Amaimon the bastinado, and made Lucifer cuckold, and swore the devil his true liegeman upon the cross of a Welsh hook,—what, a plague, call you him?—

POINTZ.

O, Glendower.

SIR JOHN FALSTAFF.

Owen, Owen,—the same; and his son-in-law, Mortimer; and old Northumberland; and that sprightly Scot of Scots, Douglas, that runs o' horseback up a hill perpendicular,—

PRINCE HENRY.

He that rides at high speed and with his pistol kills a sparrow flying.

SIR JOHN FALSTAFF.

You have hit it.

PRINCE HENRY.

So did he never the sparrow.

SIR JOHN FALSTAFF.

Well, that rascal hath good mettle in him; he will not run.

PRINCE HENRY.

Why, what a rascal art thou, then, to praise him so for running!

SIR JOHN FALSTAFF.

O' horseback, ye cuckoo; but a-foot he will not budge a foot.

PRINCE HENRY.

Yes, Jack, upon instinct.

SIR JOHN FALSTAFF.

I grant ye, upon instinct.—Well, he is there too, and one Mordake, and a thousand blue-caps more: Worcester is stolen away to-night; thy father's beard is turn'd white with the news: you may buy land now as cheap as stinking mackerel.

PRINCE HENRY.

Why, then, it is like, if there come a hot June, and this civil buffeting hold, we shall buy maidenheads as they buy hob-nails, by the hundreds.

SIR JOHN FALSTAFF.

By the mass, lad, thou say'st true; it is like we shall have good trading that way.—But tell me, Hal, art thou not horrible afeard? thou being heir-apparent, could the world pick thee out three such enemies again as that fiend Douglas, that spirit Percy, and that devil Glendower? art thou not horribly afraid? doth not thy blood thrill at it?

PRINCE HENRY.

Not a whit, i'faith; I lack some of thy instinct.

SIR JOHN FALSTAFF.

Well, thou wilt be horribly chid to-morrow when thou comest to thy father: if thou love me, practise an answer.

PRINCE HENRY.

Do thou stand for my father, and examine me upon the particulars of my life.

SIR JOHN FALSTAFF.

Shall I? content:—this chair shall be my state, this dagger my sceptre, and this cushion my crown.

PRINCE HENRY.

Thy state is taken for a joint-stool, thy golden sceptre for a leaden dagger, and thy precious rich crown for a pitiful bald crown!

SIR JOHN FALSTAFF.

Well, an the fire of grace be not quite out of thee, now shalt thou be moved.—Give me a cup of sack to make my eyes look red, that it may be thought I have wept; for I must speak in passion, and I will do it in King Cambyses' vein.

[Drinks.

PRINCE HENRY.

Well, here is my leg.

SIR JOHN FALSTAFF.

And here is my speech.—Stand aside, nobility.

HOSTESS.

O Jesu, this is excellent sport, i' faith!

SIR JOHN FALSTAFF.

Weep not, sweet queen; for trickling tears are vain.

HOSTESS.

O, the father, how he holds his countenance!

SIR JOHN FALSTAFF.

For God's sake, lords, convey my tristful queen; For tears do stop the flood-gates of her eyes.

HOSTESS.

O Jesu, he doth it as like one of these harlotry players as ever I see!

SIR JOHN FALSTAFF.

Peace, good pint-pot; peace, good tickle-brain.—

Harry, I do not only marvel where thou spendest thy time, but also how thou art accompanied: for though the camomile, the more it is trodden on, the faster it grows, yet youth, the more it is wasted, the sooner it wears. That thou art my son, I have partly thy mother's word, partly my own opinion; but chiefly a villainous trick of thine eye, and a foolish hanging of thy nether lip, that doth warrant me. If, then, thou be son to me, here lies the point;—why, being son to me, art thou so pointed at? Shall the blessed sun of heaven prove a micher, and eat blackberries? a question not to be askt. Shall the son of England prove a thief, and take purses? a question to be askt. There is a thing, Harry, which thou hast often heard of, and it is known to many in our land by the name of pitch: this pitch, as ancient writers do report, doth defile; so doth the company thou keepest: for, Harry, now I do not speak to thee in drink, but in tears; not in pleasure, but in passion; not in words only, but in woes also:— and yet there is a virtuous man whom I have often noted in thy company, but I know not his name.

PRINCE HENRY.

What manner of man, an it like your majesty?

SIR JOHN FALSTAFF.

A goodly portly man, i' faith, and a corpulent; of a cheerful look, a pleasing eye, and a most noble carriage; and, as I think, his age some fifty, or, by'r lady, inclining to three-score; and now I remember me, his name is Falstaff: if that man should be lewdly given, he deceiveth me; for, Harry, I see virtue in his looks. If, then, the tree may be known by the fruit, as the fruit by the tree, then, peremptorily I speak it, there is virtue in that Falstaff: him keep with, the rest banish. And tell me now, thou naughty varlet, tell me where hast thou been this month?

PRINCE HENRY.

Dost thou speak like a king? Do thou stand for me, and I'll play my father.

SIR JOHN FALSTAFF.

Depose me? if thou dost it half so gravely, so majestically, both in word and matter, hang me up by the heels for a rabbit-sucker or a poulter's hare.

PRINCE HENRY.

Well, here I am set.

SIR JOHN FALSTAFF.

And here I stand:—judge, my masters.

PRINCE HENRY.

Now, Harry, whence come you?

SIR JOHN FALSTAFF.

My noble lord, from Eastcheap.

PRINCE HENRY.

The complaints I hear of thee are grievous.

SIR JOHN FALSTAFF.

'Sblood, my lord, they are false:—nay, I'll tickle ye for a young prince, i' faith.

PRINCE HENRY.

Swearest thou, ungracious boy? henceforth ne'er look on me. Thou art violently carried away from grace: there is a devil haunts thee, in the likeness of an old fat man,—a tun of man is thy companion. Why dost thou converse with that trunk of humours, that bolting-hutch of beastliness, that swoll'n parcel of dropsies, that huge bombard of sack, that stuft cloakbag of guts, that roasted Manningtree ox with the pudding in his belly, that reverend vice, that gray iniquity, that father ruffian, that vanity in years? Wherein is he good, but to taste sack and drink it? wherein neat and cleanly, but to carve a capon and eat it? wherein cunning, but in craft? wherein crafty, but in villainy? wherein villainous, but in all things? wherein worthy, but in nothing?

SIR JOHN FALSTAFF.

I would your Grace would take me with you: whom means your Grace?

PRINCE HENRY.

That villainous abominable misleader of youth, Falstaff, that old white-bearded Satan.

SIR JOHN FALSTAFF.

My lord, the man I know.

PRINCE HENRY.

I know thou dost.

SIR JOHN FALSTAFF.

But to say I know more harm in him than in myself, were to say more than I know. That he is old,—the more the pity,—his white hairs do witness it; but that he is—saving your reverence —a whoremaster, that I utterly deny. If sack and sugar be a fault, God help the wicked! if to be old and merry be a sin, then many an old host that I know is damn'd: if to be fat be to be hated, then Pharaoh's lean kine are to be loved. No, my good lord; banish Peto, banish Bardolph, banish Pointz: but, for sweet Jack Falstaff, kind Jack Falstaff, true Jack Falstaff, valiant Jack Falstaff, and therefore more valiant, being, as he is, old Jack Falstaff, banish not him thy Harry's company, banish not him thy Harry's company:— banish plump Jack, and banish all the world.

PRINCE HENRY.

I do, I will.   [A knocking heard.

[Exeunt HOSTESS, FRANCIS, and BAR-
DOLPH.
Enter BARDOLPH, running.

BARDOLPH.

O, my lord, my lord! the sheriff with a most monstrous watch is at the door.

SIR JOHN FALSTAFF.

Out, ye rogue!—Play out the play: I have much to say in the behalf of that Falstaff.

Enter HOSTESS, hastily.

HOSTESS.

O Jesu, my lord, my lord,—

PRINCE HENRY.

Heigh, heigh! the devil rides upon a fiddlestick: what's the matter?

HOSTESS.

The sheriff and all the watch are at the door: they are come to search the house. Shall I let them in?

SIR JOHN FALSTAFF.

Dost thou hear, Hal? never call a true piece of gold a counterfeit: thou art essentially mad, without seeming so.

PRINCE HENRY.

And thou a natural coward, without instinct.

SIR JOHN FALSTAFF.

I deny your major: if you will deny the sheriff, so; if not, let him enter: if I become not a cart as well

as another man, a plague on my bringing up! I hope I shall as soon be strangled with a halter as another.

PRINCE HENRY.

Go, hide thee behind the arras:—the rest walk up above. Now, my masters, for a true face and good conscience.

SIR JOHN FALSTAFF.

Both which I have had; but their date is out, and therefore I'll hide me.

PRINCE HENRY.

Call in the sheriff.

[Exeunt all except the PRINCE and POINTZ.
Enter SHERIFF and CARRIER.

Now, master sheriff, what's your will with me?

SHERIFF.

First, pardon me, my lord. A hue and cry
Hath follow'd certain men unto this house.

PRINCE HENRY.

What men?

SHERIFF.

One of them is well known, my gracious lord,
A gross fat man.

CARRIER.

As fat as butter.

PRINCE HENRY.

The man, I do assure you, is not here;
For I myself at this time have employ'd him.
And, sheriff, I will engage my word to thee,
That I will, by to-morrow dinner-time,
Send him to answer thee, or any man,
For any thing he shall be charged withal:
And so, let me entreat you leave the house.

SHERIFF.

I will, my lord. There are two gentlemen
Have in this robbery lost three hundred marks.

PRINCE HENRY.

It may be so: if he have robb'd these men,
He shall be answerable; and so, farewell.

SHERIFF.

Good night, my noble lord.

PRINCE HENRY.

I think it is good morrow, is it not?

SHERIFF.

Indeed, my lord, I think it be two o'clock.

[Exeunt SHERIFF and CARRIER.

PRINCE HENRY.

This oily rascal is known as well as Paul's.
Go, call him forth.

POINTZ.

Falstaff!—fast asleep behind the arras, and snorting like a horse.

PRINCE HENRY.

Hark, how hard he fetches breath. Search his pockets. [He searcheth his pockets and findeth certain papers.] What hast thou found?

POINTZ.

Nothing but papers, my lord.

PRINCE HENRY.

Let's see what they be: read them.

POINTZ [reads].

Item, A capon,	.	.	.	2s. 2d.
Item, Sauce,	.	.	.	4d.
Item, Sack, two gallons,	.	.	5s. 8d.
Item, Anchovies and sack after supper,			2s. 6d.
Item, Bread,	.	.	.	ob.

PRINCE HENRY.

O monstrous! but one half-pennyworth of bread
to this intolerable deal of sack!—What there is
else, keep close; we'll read it at more advantage:
there let him sleep till day. I'll to the court in the
morning. We must all to the wars, and thy place
shall be honourable. I'll procure this fat rogue a
charge of foot; and I know his death will be a
march of twelve-score. The money shall be paid
back again with advantage. Be with me betimes
in the morning; and so, good morrow, Pointz.

POINTZ.

Good morrow, good my lord.   [*Exeunt.*

ACT III. SCENE I.

Bangor.   The Archdeacon's house.

Enter HOTSPUR, WORCESTER, MORTIMER,
and GLENDOWER.

EDMUND MORTIMER.

THESE promises are fair, the parties sure,
And our induction full of prosperous hope.

HOTSPUR.

Lord Mortimer,—and cousin Glendower,—
Will you sit down?—
And uncle Worcester:—a plague upon it!
I have forgot the map.

OWEN GLENDOWER.

No, here it is.
Sit, cousin Percy;—sit, good cousin Hotspur,
For by that name as oft as Lancaster
Doth speak of you, his cheek looks pale, and with
A rising sigh he wisheth you in heaven.

HOTSPUR.

And you in hell, as oft as he hears Owen Glendower spoke of.

OWEN GLENDOWER.

I cannot blame him: at my nativity
The front of heaven was full of fiery shapes,
Of burning cressets; and at my birth
The frame and huge foundation of the earth
Shaked like a coward.

HOTSPUR.

Why, so it would have done at the same season, if
your mother's cat had but kitten'd, though yourself had never been born.

OWEN GLENDOWER.

I say the earth did shake when I was born.

HOTSPUR.

And I say the earth was not of my mind,
If you suppose as fearing you it shook.

OWEN GLENDOWER.

The heavens were all on fire, the earth did
  tremble.

HOTSPUR.

O, then the earth shook to see the heavens on fire,
And not in fear of your nativity.
Diseased nature oftentimes breaks forth
In strange eruptions; oft the teeming earth
Is with a kind of colic pincht and vext
By the imprisoning of unruly wind
Within her womb; which, for enlargement
  striving,
Shakes the old beldam earth, and topples down
Steeples and moss-grown towers. At your birth

Our grandam earth, having this distemperature,
In passion shook.

OWEN GLENDOWER.

Cousin, of many men
I do not bear these crossings. Give me leave
To tell you once again, that at my birth
The front of heaven was full of fiery shapes;
The goats ran from the mountains, and the herds
Were strangely clamorous to the frighted fields.
These signs have markt me extraordinary;
And all the courses of my life do show
I am not in the roll of common men.
Where is he living,—clipt in with the sea
That chides the banks of England, Scotland,
  Wales,—
Which calls me pupil, or hath read to me?
And bring him out that is but woman's son
Can trace me in the tedious ways of art,
And hold me pace in deep experiments.

HOTSPUR.

I think there is no man speaks better Welsh.—
I'll to dinner.

EDMUND MORTIMER.

Peace, cousin Percy; you will make him mad.

OWEN GLENDOWER.

I can call spirits from the vasty deep.

HOTSPUR.

Why, so can I, or so can any man;
But will they come when you do call for them?

OWEN GLENDOWER.

Why, I can teach you, cousin, to command
The devil.

HOTSPUR.

And I can teach thee, coz, to shame the devil
By telling truth: tell truth, and shame the devil.—
If thou have power to raise him, bring him
  hither,
And I'll be sworn I have power to shame him
  hence.
O, while you live, tell truth, and shame the devil!

EDMUND MORTIMER.

Come, come, no more of this unprofitable chat.

OWEN GLENDOWER.

Three times hath Henry Bolingbroke made head
Against my power; thrice from the banks of Wye
And sandy-bottom'd Severn have I sent him
Bootless home and weather-beaten back.

HOTSPUR.

Home without boots, and in foul weather too!
How scapes he agues, in the devil's name?

OWEN GLENDOWER.

Come, here's the map: shall we divide our right
According to our threefold order ta'en?

EDMUND MORTIMER.

The archdeacon hath divided it
Into three limits very equally:—
England, from Trent and Severn hitherto,
By south and east is to my part assign'd:
All westward, Wales beyond the Severn shore,
And all the fertile land within that bound,
To Owen Glendower:—and, dear coz, to you
The remnant northward, lying off from Trent.
And our indentures tripartite are drawn;
Which being sealed interchangeably,—
A business that this night may execute,—
To-morrow, cousin Percy, you, and I,

And my good Lord of Worcester, will set forth
To meet your father and the Scottish power,
As is appointed us, at Shrewsbury.
My father Glendower is not ready yet,
Nor shall we need his help these fourteen days:—
[to GLENDOWER] Within that space you may have
    drawn together   [men.
Your tenants, friends, and neighbouring gentle-
             OWEN GLENDOWER.
A shorter time shall send me to you, lords:
And in my conduct shall your ladies come;
From whom you now must steal, and take no
    leave,
For there will be a world of water shed
Upon the parting of your wives and you.
             HOTSPUR.
Methinks my moiety, north from Burton here,
In quantity equals not one of yours:
See how this river comes me cranking in,
And cuts me from the best of all my land
A huge half-moon, a monstrous cantle out.
I'll have the current in this place damm'd up;
And here the smug and silver Trent shall run
In a new channel, fair and evenly:
It shall not wind with such a deep indent,
To rob me of so rich a bottom here.
             OWEN GLENDOWER.
Not wind? it shall, it must; you see it doth.
             EDMUND MORTIMER.
Yea, but
Mark how he bears his course, and runs me up
With like advantage on the other side;
Gelding the opposed continent as much
As on the other side it takes from you.
             EARL OF WORCESTER.
Yea, but a little charge will trench him here,
And on this north side win this cape of land;
And then he runs straight and even.
             HOTSPUR.
I'll have it so: a little charge will do it.
             OWEN GLENDOWER.
I'll not have it alter'd.
             HOTSPUR.
             Will not you?
             OWEN GLENDOWER.
No, nor you shall not.
             HOTSPUR.
             Who shall say me nay?
             OWEN GLENDOWER.
Why, that will I.
             HOTSPUR.
             Let me not understand you, then;
Speak it in Welsh.
             OWEN GLENDOWER.
I can speak English, lord, as well as you;
For I was train'd up in the English court;
Where, being but young, I framed to the harp
Many an English ditty lovely well,
And gave the tongue a helpful ornament,—
A virtue that was never seen in you.
             HOTSPUR.
Marry, and I am glad of it with all my heart:
I had rather be a kitten, and cry mew,
Than one of these same metre ballet-mongers;
I had rather hear a brazen canstick turn'd,
Or a dry wheel grate on the axletree;

And that would set my teeth nothing on edge,
Nothing so much as mincing poetry:—
'Tis like the forced gait of a shuffling nag.
             OWEN GLENDOWER.
Come, you shall have Trent turn'd.
             HOTSPUR.
I do not care: I'll give thrice so much land
To any well-deserving friend;
But in the way of bargain, mark ye me,
I'll cavil on the ninth part of a hair.
Are the indentures drawn? shall we be gone?
             OWEN GLENDOWER.
The moon shines fair; you may away by night:
I'll in and haste the writer, and withal
Break with your wives of your departure hence:
I am afraid my daughter will run mad,
So much she doteth on her Mortimer.   [Exit.
             EDMUND MORTIMER.
Fie, cousin Percy! how you cross my father!
             HOTSPUR.
I cannot choose: sometime he angers me
With telling me of the moldwarp and the ant,
Of the dreamer Merlin and his prophecies,
And of a dragon and a finless fish,
A clip-wing'd griffin and a moulten raven,
A couching lion and a ramping cat,
And such a deal of skimble-skamble stuff
As puts me from my faith. I tell you what,—
He held me last night at least nine hours
In reckoning up the several devils' names
That were his lackeys: I cried 'hum,' and 'well,
    go to,'
But markt him not a word. O, he is as tedious
As a tired horse, a railing wife;
Worse than a smoky house:—I had rather live
With cheese and garlic in a windmill, far,
Than feed on cates and have him talk to me
In any summer-house in Christendom.
             EDMUND MORTIMER.
In faith, he is a worthy gentleman;
Exceedingly well-read, and profited
In strange concealments; valiant as a lion,
And wondrous affable, and as bountiful
As mines of India. Shall I tell you, cousin?
He holds your temper in a high respect,
And curbs himself even of his natural scope
When you do cross his humour; faith, he does:
I warrant you, that man is not alive
Might so have tempted him as you have done,
Without the taste of danger and reproof:
But do not use it oft, let me entreat you.
             EARL OF WORCESTER.
In faith, my lord, you are too wilful-blame;
And since your coming hither have done enough
To put him quite beside his patience.
You must needs learn, lord, to amend this fault:
Though sometimes it show greatness, courage,
    blood,—
And that's the dearest grace it renders you,—
Yet oftentimes it doth present harsh rage,
Defect of manners, want of government,
Pride, haughtiness, opinion, and disdain:
The least of which haunting a nobleman
Loseth men's hearts, and leaves behind a stain
Upon the beauty of all parts besides,
Beguiling them of commendation.

HOTSPUR.

Well, I am school'd: good manners be your speed!
Here come our wives, and let us take our leave.

Enter GLENDOWER, *with the* LADIES.

EDMUND MORTIMER.

This is the deadly spite that angers me,—
My wife can speak no English, I no Welsh.

OWEN GLENDOWER.

My daughter weeps: she will not part with you;
She'll be a soldier too, she'll to the wars.

EDMUND MORTIMER.

Good father, tell her that she and my aunt Percy
Shall follow in your conduct speedily.

[GLENDOWER *speaks to her in Welsh, and
she answers him in the same.*

OWEN GLENDOWER.

She is desperate here; a peevish self-will'd harlotry, one that no persuasion can do good upon.

[*The* LADY *speaks in Welsh.*

EDMUND MORTIMER.

I understand thy looks: that pretty Welsh
Which thou pour'st down from these swelling
  heavens
I am too perfect in; and, but for shame,
In such a parley should I answer thee.

[*The* LADY *speaks again in Welsh.*

I understand thy kisses, and thou mine,
And that's a feeling disputation:
But I will never be a truant, love,
Till I have learn'd thy language; for thy tongue
Makes Welsh as sweet as ditties highly penn'd,
Sung by a fair queen in a summer's bower,
With ravishing division, to her lute.

OWEN GLENDOWER.

Nay, if you melt, then will she run quite mad.

[*The* LADY *speaks again in Welsh.*

EDMUND MORTIMER.

O, I am ignorance itself in this!

OWEN GLENDOWER.

She bids you on the wanton rushes lay you down,
And rest your gentle head upon her lap,
And she will sing the song that pleaseth you,
And on your eyelids crown the god of sleep,
Charming your blood with pleasing heaviness;
Making such difference 'twixt wake and sleep,
As is the difference betwixt day and night,
The hour before the heavenly-harness'd team
Begins his golden progress in the east.

EDMUND MORTIMER.

With all my heart I'll sit and hear her sing:
By that time will our book, I think, be drawn.

OWEN GLENDOWER.

Do so;
And those musicians that shall play to you
Hang in the air a thousand leagues from hence;
And straight they shall be here: sit, and attend.

HOTSPUR.

Come, Kate, thou art perfect in lying down:
come, quick, quick, that I may lay my head in thy
lap.

LADY PERCY.

Go, ye giddy goose.   [*The music plays.*

HOTSPUR.

Now I perceive the devil understands Welsh;
And 'tis no marvel he is so humorous.
By 'r lady, he is a good musician.

LADY PERCY.

Then should you be nothing but musical; for you
are altogether govern'd by humours. Lie still, ye
thief, and hear the lady sing in Welsh.

HOTSPUR.

I had rather hear Lady, my brach, howl in Irish.

LADY PERCY.

Wouldst thou have thy head broken?

HOTSPUR.

No.

LADY PERCY.

Then be still.

HOTSPUR.

Neither; 'tis a woman's fault.

LADY PERCY.

Now God help thee!

HOTSPUR.

To the Welsh lady's bed.

LADY PERCY.

What's that?

HOTSPUR.

Peace! she sings.

[*Here the* LADY *sings a Welsh song.*

Come, Kate, I'll have your song too.

LADY PERCY.

Not mine, in good sooth.

HOTSPUR.

Not yours, in good sooth! Heart! you swear like a
comfit-maker's wife. 'Not you, in good sooth;' and
'as true as I live;' and 'as God shall mend me;' and
'as sure as day;'
And givest such sarcenet surety for thy oaths,
As if thou never walk'st further than Finsbury.
Swear me, Kate, like a lady as thou art,
A good mouth-filling oath; and leave 'in sooth,'
And such protest of pepper-gingerbread,
To velvet-guards and Sunday-citizens.
Come, sing.

LADY PERCY.

I will not sing.

HOTSPUR.

'Tis the next way to turn tailor, or be redbreast
teacher. An the indentures be drawn, I'll away
within these two hours; and so, come in when ye
will.   [*Exit.*

OWEN GLENDOWER.

Come, come, Lord Mortimer; you are as slow
As hot Lord Percy is on fire to go.
By this our book is drawn; we'll but seal, and then
To horse immediately.

EDMUND MORTIMER.

               With all my heart. [*Exeunt.*

SCENE II.

London.   The palace.

Enter KING HENRY, PRINCE HENRY, *and*
LORDS.

KING HENRY.

LORDS, give us leave; the Prince of Wales
  and I
Must have some private conference: but be near
  at hand,
For we shall presently have need of you.

[*Exeunt* LORDS

I know not whether God will have it so,
For some displeasing service I have done,
That, in his secret doom, out of my blood
He'll breed revengement and a scourge for me;
But thou dost, in thy passages of life,
Make me believe that thou art only markt
For the hot vengeance and the rod of heaven
To punish my mistreadings. Tell me else,
Could such inordinate and low desires,
Such poor, such base, such lewd, such mean at-
   tempts,
Such barren pleasures, rude society,
As thou art matcht withal and grafted to,
Accompany the greatness of thy blood,
And hold their level with thy princely heart?

PRINCE HENRY.

So please your majesty, I would I could
Quit all offences with as clear excuse
As well as I am doubtless I can purge
Myself of many I am charged withal
Yet such extenuation let me beg,
As, in reproof of many tales devised,—
Which oft the ear of greatness needs must hear,—
By smiling pick-thanks and base news-mongers,
I may, for some things true, wherein my youth
Hath faulty wander'd and irregular,
Find pardon on my true submission.

KING HENRY.

God pardon thee!—yet let me wonder, Harry,
At thy affections, which do hold a wing
Quite from the flight of all thy ancestors.
Thy place in council thou hast rudely lost,
Which by thy younger brother is supplied;
And art almost an alien to the hearts
Of all the court and princes of my blood:
The hope and expectation of thy time
Is ruin'd; and the soul of every man
Prophetically do forethink thy fall.
Had I so lavish of my presence been,
So common-hackney'd in the eyes of men,
So stale and cheap to vulgar company,—
Opinion, that did help me to the crown,
Had still kept loyal to possession,
And left me in reputeless banishment,
A fellow of no mark nor likelihood.
By being seldom seen, I could not stir
But, like a comet, I was wonder'd at;
That men would tell their children, 'This is he;'
Others would say, 'Where, which is Bolingbroke?'
And then I stole all courtesy from heaven,
And drest myself in such humility
That I did pluck allegiance from men's hearts,
Loud shouts and salutations from their mouths,
Even in the presence of the crowned king.
Thus did I keep my person fresh and new;
My presence, like a robe pontifical,
Ne'er seen but wonder'd at: and so my state,
Seldom but sumptuous, show'd like a feast,
And won by rareness such solemnity.
The skipping king, he ambled up and down
With shallow jesters and rash bavin wits,
Soon kindled and soon burnt; carded his state;
Mingled his royalty with capering fools;
Had his great name profaned with their scorns,
And gave his countenance, against his name,
To laugh at gibing boys, and stand the push

Of every beardless vain comparative;
Grew a companion to the common streets,
Enfeoft himself to popularity;
That, being daily swallow'd by men's eyes,
They surfeited with honey, and began
To loathe the taste of sweetness, whereof a little
More than a little is by much too much.
So, when he had occasion to be seen,
He was but as the cuckoo is in June,
Heard, not regarded,—seen, but with such eyes
As, sick and blunted with community,
Afford no extraordinary gaze,
Such as is bent on sun-like majesty
When it shines seldom in admiring eyes;
But rather drowzed, and hung their eyelids down,
Slept in his face and render'd such aspect
As cloudy men use to their adversaries,
Being with his presence glutted, gorged, and full.
And in that very line, Harry, stand'st thou;
For thou hast lost thy princely privilege
With vile participation: not an eye
But is a-weary of thy common sight,
Save mine, which hath desired to see thee more;
Which now doth that I would not have it do,—
Make blind itself with foolish tenderness.

PRINCE HENRY.

I shall hereafter, my thrice-gracious lord,
Be more myself.

KING HENRY.

          For all the world,
As thou art to this hour, was Richard then
When I from France set foot at Ravenspurg;
And even as I was then is Percy now.
Now, by my sceptre, and my soul to boot,
He hath more worthy interest to the state
Than thou, the shadow of succession;
For, of no right, nor colour like to right,
He doth fill fields with harness in the realm;
Turns head against the lion's armed jaws;
And, being no more in debt to years than thou,
Leads ancient lords and reverend bishops on
To bloody battles and to bruising arms.
What never-dying honour hath he got
Against renowned Douglas! whose high deeds,
Whose hot incursions, and great name in arms,
Holds from all soldiers chief majority
And military title capital
Through all the kingdoms that acknowledge
   Christ:
Thrice hath this Hotspur, Mars in swathling·
   clothes,
This infant warrior, in his enterprises
Discomfited great Douglas: ta'en him once,
Enlarged him, and made a friend of him,
To fill the mouth of deep defiance up,
And shake the peace and safety of our throne.
And what say you to this? Percy, Northumber-
   land,
The Archbishop's Grace of York, Douglas, Mor-
   timer,
Capitulate against us, and are up.
But wherefore do I tell these news to thee?
Why, Harry, do I tell thee of my foes,
Which art my near'st and dearest enemy?
Thou that art like enough,—through vassal fear,
Base inclination, and the start of spleen,—

435

To fight against me under Percy's pay,
To dog his heels, and court'sy at his frowns,
To show how much thou art degenerate.
PRINCE HENRY.
Do not think so; you shall not find it so:
And God forgive them that so much have sway'd
Your majesty's good thoughts away from me!
I will redeem all this on Percy's head,
And, in the closing of some glorious day,
Be bold to tell you that I am your son;
When I will wear a garment all of blood,
And stain my favours in a bloody mask,
Which, washt away, shall scour my shame with
it:
And that shall be the day, whene'er it lights,
That this same child of honour and renown,
This gallant Hotspur, this all-praised knight,
And your unthought-of Harry, chance to meet.
For every honour sitting on his helm,
Would they were multitudes, and on my head
My shames redoubled! for the time will come,
That I shall make this northern youth exchange
His glorious deeds for my indignities.
Percy is but my factor, good my lord,
To engross up glorious deeds on my behalf;
And I will call him to so strict account,
That he shall render every glory up,
Yea, even the slightest worship of his time,
Or I will tear the reckoning from his heart.
This, in the name of God, I promise here:
The which if He be pleased I shall perform,
I do beseech your majesty, may salve
The long-grown wounds of my intemperance:
If not, the end of life cancels all bands;
And I will die a hundred thousand deaths
Ere break the smallest parcel of this vow.
KING HENRY.
A hundred thousand rebels die in this:—
Thou shalt have charge and sovereign trust
herein.
Enter SIR WALTER BLUNT.
How now, good Blunt! thy looks are full of
speed.
SIR WALTER BLUNT.
So hath the business that I come to speak of.
Lord Mortimer of Scotland hath sent word
That Douglas and the English rebels met
The eleventh of this month at Shrewsbury:
A mighty and a fearful head they are,
If promises be kept on every hand,
As ever offer'd foul play in a state.
KING HENRY.
The Earl of Westmoreland set forth to-day;
With him my son, Lord John of Lancaster
For this advertisement is five days old:—
On Wednesday next, Harry, you shall set for-
ward;
On Thursday we ourselves will march:
Our meeting is Bridgenorth: and, Harry, you
Shall march through Glostershire; by which ac-
count,
Our business valued, some twelve days hence
Our general forces at Bridgenorth shall meet.
Our hands are full of business: let's away;
Advantage feeds him fat, while men delay.
[*Exeunt.*

SCENE III.

Eastcheap.   The Boar's-Head Tavern.

Enter FALSTAFF *and* BARDOLPH.

SIR JOHN FALSTAFF.

BARDOLPH, am I not fall'n away vilely since
this last action? do I not bate? do I not
dwindle? Why, my skin hangs about me like an
old lady's loose gown; I am wither'd like an old
apple-john. Well, I'll repent, and that suddenly,
while I am in some liking; I shall be out of heart
shortly, and then I shall have no strength to repent. An I have not forgotten what the inside of a
church is made of, I am a peppercorn, a brewer's
horse: the inside of a church! Company, villainous
company, hath been the spoil of me.
BARDOLPH.
Sir John, you are so fretful, you cannot live long.
SIR JOHN FALSTAFF.
Why, there is it:—come, sing me a bawdy song;
make me merry. I was as virtuously given as a
gentleman need to be; virtuous enough; swore
little; diced not above seven times a week; went to
a bawdy-house not above once in a quarter—of
an hour; paid money that I borrow'd—three or
four times; lived well, and in good compass: and
now I live out of all order, out of all compass.
BARDOLPH.
Why, you are so fat, Sir John, that you must
needs be out of all compass,—out of all reasonable compass, Sir John.
SIR JOHN FALSTAFF.
Do thou amend thy face, and I'll amend my life:
thou art our admiral, thou bearest the lantern in
the poop,—but 'tis in the nose of thee; thou art
the Knight of the Burning Lamp.
BARDOLPH.
Why, Sir John, my face does you no harm.
SIR JOHN FALSTAFF.
No, I'll be sworn; I make as good use of it as
many a man doth of a death's-head or a *memento
mori:* I never see thy face but I think upon hell-
fire, and Dives that lived in purple; for there he
is in his robes, burning, burning. If thou wert any
way given to virtue, I would swear by thy face;
my oath should be, 'By this fire, that's God's
angel:' but thou art altogether given over; and
wert indeed, but for the light in thy face, the son
of utter darkness. When thou ran'st up Gadshill
in the night to catch my horse, if I did not think
thou hadst been an *ignis fatuus* or a ball of wildfire, there's no purchase in money. O, thou art a
perpetual triumph, an everlasting bonfire-light!
Thou hast saved me a thousand marks in links and
torches, walking with thee in the night betwixt
tavern and tavern: but the sack that thou hast
drunk me would have bought me lights as good
cheap at the dearest chandler's in Europe. I have
maintain'd that salamander of yours with fire any
time this two-and-thirty years; God reward me
for it!
BARDOLPH.
'Sblood, I would my face were in your belly!
SIR JOHN FALSTAFF.
God-a-mercy! so should I be sure to be heart-
burn'd.

Enter HOSTESS.

How now, Dame Partlet the hen! have you inquired yet who pickt my pocket?

HOSTESS.

Why, Sir John, what do you think, Sir John? do you think I keep thieves in my house? I have searcht, I have inquired, so has my husband, man by man, boy by boy, servant by servant: the tithe of a hair was never lost in my house before.

SIR JOHN FALSTAFF.

Ye lie, hostess: Bardolph was shaved, and lost many a hair; and I'll be sworn my pocket was pickt. Go to, you are a woman, go.

HOSTESS.

Who, I? no; I defy thee: God's light, I was never call'd so in mine own house before.

SIR JOHN FALSTAFF.

Go to, I know you well enough.

HOSTESS.

No, Sir John; you do not know me, Sir John. I know you, Sir John: you owe me money, Sir John; and now you pick a quarrel to beguile me of it: I bought you a dozen of shirts to your back.

SIR JOHN FALSTAFF.

Dowlas, filthy dowlas: I have given them away to bakers' wives, and they have made bolters of them.

HOSTESS.

Now, as I am a true woman, holland of eight shillings an ell. You owe money here besides, Sir John, for your diet and by-drinkings, and money lent you, four-and-twenty pound.

SIR JOHN FALSTAFF.

He had his part of it; let him pay.

HOSTESS.

He? alas, he is poor; he hath nothing.

SIR JOHN FALSTAFF.

How! poor? look upon his face; what call you rich? let them coin his nose, let them coin his cheeks: I'll not pay a denier. What, will you make a younker of me? shall I not take mine ease in mine inn, but I shall have my pocket pickt? I have lost a seal-ring of my grandfather's worth forty mark.

HOSTESS.

O Jesu, I have heard the prince tell him, I know not how oft, that that ring was copper!

SIR JOHN FALSTAFF.

How! the prince is a Jack, a sneak-cup: 'sblood, an he were here, I would cudgel him like a dog, if he would say so.

Enter the PRINCE *and* POINTZ, *marching, and* FALSTAFF *meets them, playing on his truncheon like a fife.*

How now, lad! is the wind in that door, i' faith? must we all march?

BARDOLPH.

Yea, two and two, Newgate-fashion.

HOSTESS.

My lord, I pray you, hear me.

PRINCE HENRY.

What say'st thou, Mistress Quickly! How doth thy husband? I love him well; he is an honest man.

HOSTESS.

Good my lord, hear me.

SIR JOHN FALSTAFF.

Prithee, let her alone, and list to me.

PRINCE HENRY.

What say'st thou, Jack?

SIR JOHN FALSTAFF.

The other night I fell asleep here behind the arras, and had my pocket pickt: this house is turn'd bawdy-house; they pick pockets.

PRINCE HENRY.

What didst thou lose, Jack?

SIR JOHN FALSTAFF.

Wilt thou believe me, Hal? three or four bonds of forty pound a-piece, and a seal-ring of my grandfather's.

PRINCE HENRY.

A trifle, some eight-penny matter.

HOSTESS.

So I told him, my lord; and I said I heard your Grace say so: and, my lord, he speaks most vilely of you, like a foul-mouth'd man as he is; and said he would cudgel you.

PRINCE HENRY.

What! he did not?

HOSTESS.

There's neither faith, truth, nor womanhood in me else.

SIR JOHN FALSTAFF.

There's no more faith in thee than in a stew'd prune; nor no more truth in thee than in a drawn fox; and for womanhood, Maid Marian may be the deputy's wife of the ward to thee. Go, you thing, go.

HOSTESS.

Say, what thing? what thing?

SIR JOHN FALSTAFF.

What thing! why, a thing to thank God on.

HOSTESS.

I am no thing to thank God on, I would thou shouldst know it; I am an honest man's wife: and, setting thy knighthood aside, thou art a knave to call me so.

SIR JOHN FALSTAFF.

Setting thy womanhood aside, thou art a beast to say otherwise.

HOSTESS.

Say, what beast, thou knave, thou?

SIR JOHN FALSTAFF.

What beast! why, an otter.

PRINCE HENRY.

An otter, Sir John! why an otter?

SIR JOHN FALSTAFF.

Why, she's neither fish nor flesh; a man knows not where to have her.

HOSTESS.

Thou art an unjust man in saying so: thou or any man knows where to have me, thou knave, thou!

PRINCE HENRY.

Thou say'st true, hostess; and he slanders thee most grossly.

HOSTESS.

So he doth you, my lord; and said this other day you ought him a thousand pound.

PRINCE HENRY.

Sirrah, do I owe you a thousand pound?

SIR JOHN FALSTAFF.

A thousand pound, Hal! a million: thy love is worth a million; thou owest me thy love.

HOSTESS.

Nay, my lord, he call'd you Jack, and said he would cudgel you.

SIR JOHN FALSTAFF.

Did I, Bardolph?

BARDOLPH.

Indeed, Sir John, you said so.

SIR JOHN FALSTAFF.

Yea,—if he said my ring was copper.

PRINCE HENRY.

I say 'tis copper: darest thou be as good as thy word now?

SIR JOHN FALSTAFF.

Why, Hal, thou know'st, as thou art but man, I dare; but as thou art prince, I fear thee as I fear the roaring of the lion's whelp.

PRINCE HENRY.

And why not as the lion?

SIR JOHN FALSTAFF.

The king himself is to be fear'd as the lion: dost thou think I'll fear thee as I fear thy father? nay, an I do, I pray God my girdle break.

PRINCE HENRY.

O, if it should, how would thy guts fall about thy knees! But, sirrah, there's no room for faith, truth, nor honesty in this bosom of thine,—it is all fill'd up with guts and midriff. Charge an honest woman with picking thy pocket! why, thou whoreson, impudent, embost rascal, if there were anything in thy pocket but tavern-reckonings, memorandums of bawdy-houses, and one poor pennyworth of sugar-candy to make thee long-winded,—if thy pocket were enricht with any other injuries but these, I am a villain: and yet you will stand to it; you will not pocket-up wrong: art thou not ashamed?

SIR JOHN FALSTAFF.

Dost thou hear, Hal? thou know'st in the state of innocency Adam fell; and what should poor Jack Falstaff do in the days of villainy? Thou seest I have more flesh than another man; and therefore more frailty. You confess, then, you pickt my pocket?

PRINCE HENRY.

It appears so by the story.

SIR JOHN FALSTAFF.

Hostess, I forgive thee: go, make ready breakfast; love thy husband, look to thy servants, cherish thy guests: thou shalt find me tractable to any honest reason; thou seest I am pacified still.— Nay, prithee, be gone. [Exit Hostess.] Now, Hal, to the news at court: for the robbery, lad,—how is that answer'd?

PRINCE HENRY.

O, my sweet beef, I must still be good angel to thee:—the money is paid back again.

SIR JOHN FALSTAFF.

O, I do not like that paying back; 'tis a double labour.

PRINCE HENRY.

I am good friends with my father, and may do any thing.

SIR JOHN FALSTAFF.

Rob me the exchequer the first thing thou dost, and do it with unwasht hands too.

BARDOLPH.

Do, my lord.

PRINCE HENRY.

I have procured thee, Jack, a charge of foot.

SIR JOHN FALSTAFF.

I would it had been of horse. Where shall I find one that can steal well? O, for a fine thief, of the age of two-and-twenty or thereabouts! I am hein-ously unprovided. Well, God be thankt for these rebels,—they offend none but the virtuous: I laud them, I praise them.

PRINCE HENRY.

Bardolph,—

BARDOLPH.

My lord?

PRINCE HENRY.

Go bear this letter to Lord John of Lancaster, to my brother John; this to my Lord of Westmore-land. [Exit BARDOLPH.] Go, Pointz, to horse, to horse; for thou and I have thirty miles to ride yet ere dinner-time. [Exit POINTZ.] Jack, meet me to-morrow in the Temple-hall at two o'clock in the afternoon:

There shalt thou know thy charge; and there re-
ceive
Money and order for their furniture.
The land is burning; Percy stands on high;
And either we or they must lower lie.   [Exit.

SIR JOHN FALSTAFF.

Rare words! brave world!—Hostess, my breakfast; come:—
O, I could wish this tavern were my drum! [Exit.

ACT IV. SCENE I.

The rebel camp near Shrewsbury.

Enter HOTSPUR, WORCESTER, *and* DOUGLAS.

HOTSPUR.

WELL said, my noble Scot: if speaking truth
In this fine age were not thought flattery,
Such attribution should the Douglas have,
As not a soldier of this season's stamp
Should go so general current through the world.
By God, I cannot flatter; I defy
The tongues of soothers; but a braver place
In my heart's love hath no man than yourself:
Nay, task me to my word; approve me, lord.

EARL OF DOUGLAS.

Thou art the king of honour:
No man so potent breathes upon the ground
But I will beard him.

HOTSPUR.

Do so, and 'tis well.—

Enter a MESSENGER *with letters.*

What letters hast thou there?—I can but thank
you.

MESSENGER.

These letters come from your father.

HOTSPUR.

Letters from him! why comes he not himself?

MESSENGER.

He cannot come, my lord; he is grievous sick.

HOTSPUR.

Zounds! how has he the leisure to be sick
In such a justling time? Who leads his power?
Under whose government come they along?

MESSENGER.
His letters bear his mind, not I, my lord.
EARL OF WORCESTER.
I prithee, tell me, doth he keep his bed?
MESSENGER.
He did, my lord, four days ere I set forth;
And at the time of my departure thence
He was much fear'd by his physicians.
EARL OF WORCESTER.
I would the state of time had first been whole
Ere he by sickness had been visited:
His health was never better worth than now.
HOTSPUR.
Sick now! droop now! this sickness doth infect
The very life-blood of our enterprise;
'Tis catching hither, even to our camp.—
He writes me here, that inward sickness,—
And that his friends by deputation could not
So soon be drawn; nor did he think it meet
To lay so dangerous and dear a trust
On any soul removed, but on his own.
Yet doth he give us bold advertisement,
That with our small conjunction we should on,
To see how fortune is disposed to us;
For, as he writes, there is no quailing now,
Because the king is certainly possest
Of all our purposes. What say you to it?
EARL OF WORCESTER.
Your father's sickness is a maim to us.
HOTSPUR.
A perilous gash, a very limb lopt off:—
And yet, in faith, it is not; his present want
Seems more than we shall find it:—were it good
To set the exact wealth of all our states
All at one cast? to set so rich a main
On the nice hazard of one doubtful hour?
It were not good; for therein should we read
The very bottom and the soul of hope,
The very list, the very utmost bound
Of all our fortunes.
EARL OF DOUGLAS.
         Faith, and so we should;
Where now remains a sweet reversion;
We may boldly spend upon the hope of what
Is to come in:
A comfort of retirement lives in this.
HOTSPUR.
A rendezvous, a home to fly unto,
If that the devil and mischance look big
Upon the maidenhead of our affairs.
EARL OF WORCESTER.
But yet I would your father had been here.
The quality and hair of our attempt
Brooks no division: it will be thought
By some, that know not why he is away,
That wisdom, loyalty, and mere dislike
Of our proceedings, kept the earl from hence:
And think how such an apprehension
May turn the tide of fearful faction,
And breed a kind of question in our cause;
For well you know we of the offering side
Must keep aloof from strict arbitrement,
And stop all sight-holes, every loop from
   whence
The eye of reason may pry in upon us:
This absence of your father's draws a curtain,

That shows the ignorant a kind of fear
Before not dreamt of.
HOTSPUR.
         You strain too far.
I, rather, of his absence make this use:—
It lends a lustre and more great opinion,
A larger dare to our great enterprise,
Than if the earl were here; for men must think,
If we, without his help, can make a head
To push against a kingdom, with his help
We shall o'erturn it topsy-turvy down.—
Yet all goes well, yet all our joints are whole.
EARL OF DOUGLAS.
As heart can think: there is not such a word
Spoke of in Scotland as this term of fear.
Enter SIR RICHARD VERNON.
HOTSPUR.
My cousin Vernon! welcome, by my soul.
SIR RICHARD VERNON.
Pray God my news be worth a welcome, lord.
The Earl of Westmoreland, seven thousand
   strong,
Is marching hitherwards; with him Prince John.
HOTSPUR.
No harm:—what more?
SIR RICHARD VERNON.
         And further, I have learn'd,
The king himself in person is set forth,
Or hitherwards intended speedily,
With strong and mighty preparation.
HOTSPUR.
He shall be welcome too. Where is his son,
The nimble-footed madcap Prince of Wales,
And his comrades, that daft the world aside,
And bid it pass?
SIR RICHARD VERNON.
         All furnisht, all in arms;
All plumed like estridges that wing the wind;
Bated like eagles having lately bathed;
Glittering in golden coats, like images;
As full of spirit as the month of May,
And gorgeous as the sun at midsummer;
Wanton as youthful goats, wild as young bulls.
I saw young Harry,—with his beaver on,
His cuisses on his thighs, gallantly arm'd,—
Rise from the ground like feather'd Mercury,
And vaulted with such ease into his seat,
As if an angel dropt down from the clouds,
To turn and wind a fiery Pegasus,
And witch the world with noble horsemanship.
HOTSPUR.
No more, no more: worse than the sun in March,
This praise doth nourish agues. Let them come;
They come like sacrifices in their trim,
And to the fire-eyed maid of smoky war,
All hot and bleeding, will we offer them:
The mailed Mars shall on his altar sit
Up to the ears in blood. I am on fire
To hear this rich reprisal is so nigh,
And yet not ours.—Come, let me taste my horse,
Who is to bear me, like a thunderbolt,
Against the bosom of the Prince of Wales :
Harry to Harry shall, hot horse to horse,
Meet, and ne'er part till one drop down a
   corse.—
O, that Glendower were come!

SIR RICHARD VERNON.
                    There is more news:
I learn'd in Worcester, as I rode along,
He cannot draw his power this fourteen days.
                    EARL OF DOUGLAS.
That's the worst tidings that I hear of yet.
                    EARL OF WORCESTER.
Ay, by my faith, that bears a frosty sound.
                    HOTSPUR.
What may the king's whole battle reach unto?
                    SIR RICHARD VERNON.
To thirty thousand.
                    HOTSPUR.
                    Forty let it be:
My father and Glendower being both away,
The powers of us may serve so great a day.
Come, let us take a muster speedily:
Doomsday is near; die all, die merrily.
                    EARL OF DOUGLAS.
Talk not of dying: I am out of fear
Of death or death's hand for this one half-year.
                                        [*Exeunt.*

SCENE II.

A public road near Coventry.

Enter FALSTAFF *and* BARDOLPH.

SIR JOHN FALSTAFF.

BARDOLPH, get thee before to Coventry;
fill me a bottle of sack: our soldiers shall
march through; we'll to Sutton-Co'fil' to-night.
                    BARDOLPH.
Will you give me money, captain?
                    SIR JOHN FALSTAFF.
Lay out, lay out.
                    BARDOLPH.
This bottle makes an angel.
                    SIR JOHN FALSTAFF.
An if it do, take it for thy labour; and if it make
twenty, take them all; I'll answer the coinage.
Bid my lieutenant Peto meet me at town's end.
                    BARDOLPH.
I will, captain: farewell.   [*Exit.*
                    SIR JOHN FALSTAFF.
If I be not ashamed of my soldiers, I am a soused
gurnet. I have misused the king's press damnably.
I have got, in exchange of a hundred and fifty
soldiers, three hundred and odd pounds. I press
me none but good householders, yeomen's sons;
inquire me out contracted bachelors, such as had
been askt twice on the banns; such a commodity
of warm slaves as had as lieve hear the devil as a
drum; such as fear the report of a caliver worse
than a struck fowl or a hurt wild-duck. I prest me
none but such toasts-and-butter, with hearts in
their bellies no bigger than pins'-heads, and they
have bought out their services; and now my whole
charge consists of ancients, corporals, lieutenants,
gentlemen of companies, slaves as ragged as
Lazarus in the painted cloth, where the glutton's
dogs lickt his sores; and such as, indeed, were
never soldiers, but discarded unjust serving-men,
younger sons to younger brothers, revolted tapsters, and ostlers trade-fall'n; the cankers of a
calm world and a long peace; ten times more dishonourable ragged than an old-faced ancient: and

such have I, to fill up the rooms of them that have
bought out their services, that you would think
that I had a hundred and fifty tatter'd prodigals
lately come from swine-keeping, from eating
draff and husks. A mad fellow met me on the way,
and told me I had unloaded all the gibbets, and
prest the dead bodies. No eye hath seen such
scarecrows. I'll not march through Coventry
with them, that's flat:—nay, and the villains
march wide betwixt the legs, as if they had gyves
on; for, indeed, I had the most of them out of
prison. There's but a shirt and a half in all my
company; and the half-shirt is two napkins tackt
together and thrown over the shoulders like a
herald's coat without sleeves; and the shirt, to say
the truth, stolen from my host at Saint Albans,
or the red-nose innkeeper of Daventry. But that's
all one; they'll find linen enough on every hedge.

Enter the PRINCE *and* WESTMORELAND.

                    PRINCE HENRY.
How now, blown Jack! how now, quilt!
                    SIR JOHN FALSTAFF.
What, Hal! how now, mad wag! what a devil dost
thou in Warwickshire?—My good Lord of Westmoreland, I cry you mercy: I thought your honour
had already been at Shrewsbury.
                    EARL OF WESTMORELAND.
Faith, Sir John, 'tis more than time that I were
there, and you too; but my powers are there already. The king, I can tell you, looks for us all:
we must away all night.
                    SIR JOHN FALSTAFF.
Tut, never fear me: I am as vigilant as a cat to
steal cream.
                    PRINCE HENRY.
I think, to steal cream, indeed; for thy theft hath
already made thee butter. But tell me, Jack,
whose fellows are these that come after?
                    SIR JOHN FALSTAFF.
Mine, Hal, mine.
                    PRINCE HENRY.
I did never see such pitiful rascals.
                    SIR JOHN FALSTAFF.
Tut, tut; good enough to toss; food for powder,
food for powder; they'll fill a pit as well as better:
tush, man, mortal men, mortal men.
                    EARL OF WESTMORELAND.
Ay, but, Sir John, methinks they are exceeding
poor and bare,—too beggarly.
                    SIR JOHN FALSTAFF.
Faith, for their poverty, I know not where they
had that; and for their bareness, I am sure they
never learn'd that of me.
                    PRINCE HENRY.
No, I'll be sworn; unless you call three fingers on
the ribs bare. But, sirrah, make haste: Percy is al-
ready in the field.   [*Exit.*
                    SIR JOHN FALSTAFF.
What, is the king encampt?
                    EARL OF WESTMORELAND.
He is, Sir John: I fear we shall stay too long.[*Exit*
                    SIR JOHN FALSTAFF.
Well,
To the latter end of a fray and the beginning of a
    feast
Fits a dull fighter and a keen guest.   [*Exit.*

SCENE III.

The rebel camp near Shrewsbury.

Enter HOTSPUR, WORCESTER, DOUGLAS, *and* VERNON.

HOTSPUR.

WE'LL fight with him to-night.

EARL OF WORCESTER.

It may not be.

EARL OF DOUGLAS.

You give him, then, advantage.

SIR RICHARD VERNON.

Not a whit.

HOTSPUR.

Why say you so? looks he not for supply?

SIR RICHARD VERNON.

So do we.

HOTSPUR.

His is certain, ours is doubtful.

EARL OF WORCESTER.

Good cousin, be advised; stir not to-night.

SIR RICHARD VERNON.

Do not, my lord.

EARL OF DOUGLAS.

You do not counsel well:
You speak it out of fear and cold heart.

SIR RICHARD VERNON.

Do me no slander, Douglas: by my life,—
And I dare well maintain it with my life,—
If well-respected honour bid me on,
I hold as little counsel with weak fear
As you, my lord, or any Scot that this day lives:—
Let it be seen to-morrow in the battle
Which of us fears.

EARL OF DOUGLAS.

Yea, or to-night.

SIR RICHARD VERNON.

Content.

HOTSPUR.

To-night, say I.

SIR RICHARD VERNON.

Come, come, it may not be. I wonder much,
Being men of such great leading as you are,
That you foresee not what impediments
Drag back our expedition: certain horse
Of my cousin Vernon's are not yet come up:
Your uncle Worcester's horse came but to-day;
And now their pride and mettle is asleep,
Their courage with hard labour tame and dull,
That not a horse is half the half of himself.

HOTSPUR.

So are the horses of the enemy
In general, journey-bated and brought low:
The better part of ours are full of rest.

EARL OF WORCESTER.

The number of the king exceedeth ours:
For God's sake, cousin, stay till all come in.

[*The trumpet sounds a parley.*

Enter SIR WALTER BLUNT.

SIR WALTER BLUNT.

I come with gracious offers from the king,
If you vouchsafe me hearing and respect.

HOTSPUR.

Welcome, Sir Walter Blunt; and would to God
You were of our determination!
Some of us love you well; and even those some

Envy your great deservings and good name,
Because you are not of our quality,
But stand against us like an enemy.

SIR WALTER BLUNT.

And God defend but still I should stand so,
So long as out of limit and true rule
You stand against anointed majesty!
But, to my charge!—The king hath sent to know
The nature of your griefs; and whereupon
You conjure from the breast of civil peace
Such bold hostility, teaching his duteous land
Audacious cruelty. If that the king
Have any way your good deserts forgot,
Which he confesseth to be manifold,
He bids you name your griefs; and with all speed
You shall have your desires with interest,
And pardon absolute for yourself and these
Herein misled by your suggestion.

HOTSPUR.

The king is kind; and well we know the king
Knows at what time to promise, when to pay.
My father and my uncle and myself
Did give him that same royalty he wears;
And when he was not six-and-twenty strong,
Sick in the world's regard, wretched and low,
A poor unminded outlaw sneaking home,
My father gave him welcome to the shore;
And when he heard him swear and vow to God,
He came but to be Duke of Lancaster,
To sue his livery and beg his peace,
With tears of innocency and terms of zeal,—
My father, in kind heart and pity moved,
Swore him assistance, and perform'd it too.
Now, when the lords and barons of the realm
Perceived Northumberland did lean to him,
The more and less came in with cap and knee;
Met him in boroughs, cities, villages,
Attended him on bridges, stood in lanes,
Laid gifts before him, proffer'd him their oaths,
Gave him their heirs as pages, follow'd him
Even at the heels in golden multitudes.
He presently,—as greatness knows itself,—
Steps me a little higher than his vow
Made to my father, while his blood was poor,
Upon the naked shore at Ravenspurg;
And now, forsooth, takes on him to reform
Some certain edicts and some strait decrees
That lie too heavy on the commonwealth;
Cries out upon abuses, seems to weep
Over his country's wrongs; and, by this face,
This seeming brow of justice, did he win
The hearts of all that he did angle for:
Proceeded further; cut me off the heads
Of all the favourites, that the absent king
In deputation left behind him here
When he was personal in the Irish war.

SIR WALTER BLUNT.

Tut, I came not to hear this.

HOTSPUR.

Then to the point.

In short time after, he deposed the king;
Soon after that, deprived him of his life;
And, in the neck of that, taskt the whole state:
To make that worse, suffer'd his kinsman
March,—
Who is, if every owner were well placed,

441

Indeed his king,—to be engaged in Wales,
There without ransom to lie forfeited;
Disgraced me in my happy victories,
Sought to entrap me by intelligence;
Rated my uncle from the council-board;
In rage dismiss'd my father from the court;
Broke oath on oath, committed wrong on wrong;
And, in conclusion, drove us to seek out
This head of safety; and withal to pry
Into his title, the which we find
Too indirect for long continuance.

SIR WALTER BLUNT.
Shall I return this answer to the king?

HOTSPUR.
Not so, Sir Walter: we'll withdraw awhile.
Go to the king; and let there be impawn'd
Some surety for a safe return again,
And in the morning early shall mine uncle
Bring him our purposes: and so, farewell.

SIR WALTER BLUNT.
I would you would accept of grace and love.

HOTSPUR.
And may be so we shall.

SIR WALTER BLUNT.
Pray God you do.
[Exeunt.

SCENE IV.

York.   The ARCHBISHOP'S palace.

Enter the ARCHBISHOP OF YORK and
SIR MICHAEL.

ARCHBISHOP OF YORK.
HIE, good Sir Michael; bear this sealed brief
With winged haste to the lord marshal;
This to my cousin Scroop; and all the rest
To whom they are directed. If you knew   [haste.
How much they do import, you would make

SIR MICHAEL.
My good lord,
I guess their tenour.

ARCHBISHOP OF YORK.
Like enough you do.
To-morrow, good Sir Michael, is a day
Wherein the fortune of ten thousand men
Must bide the touch; for, sir, at Shrewsbury,
As I am truly given to understand,
The king, with mighty and quick-raised power,
Meets with Lord Harry: and, I fear, Sir Michael,
What with the sickness of Northumberland,
Whose power was in the first proportion,
And what with Owen Glendower's absence
   thence,
Who with them was a rated sinew too,
And comes not in, o'er-ruled by prophecies,—
I fear the power of Percy is too weak
To wage an instant trial with the king.

SIR MICHAEL.
Why, my good lord, you need not fear;
There is Douglas and Lord Mortimer.

ARCHBISHOP OF YORK.
No, Mortimer is not there.

SIR MICHAEL.
But there is Mordake, Vernon, Lord Harry Percy,
And there is my Lord of Worcester; and a head
Of gallant warriors, noble gentlemen.

ARCHBISHOP OF YORK.
And so there is: but yet the king hath drawn
The special head of all the land together;—
The Prince of Wales, Lord John of Lancaster,
The noble Westmoreland, and warlike Blunt;
And many moe corrivals and dear men
Of estimation and command in arms.

SIR MICHAEL.
Doubt not, my lord, they shall be well opposed.

ARCHBISHOP OF YORK.
I hope no less, yet needful 'tis to fear;
And, to prevent the worst, Sir Michael, speed:
For if Lord Percy thrive not, ere the king
Dismiss his power, he means to visit us,
For he hath heard of our confederacy,—
And 'tis but wisdom to make strong against
   him:
Therefore make haste. I must go write again
To other friends; and so, farewell, Sir Michael.
[Exeunt.

ACT V.   SCENE I.

The KING'S camp near Shrewsbury.

Enter the KING, PRINCE OF WALES, LORD
JOHN OF LANCASTER, SIR WALTER BLUNT,
and FALSTAFF.

KING HENRY.
HOW bloodily the sun begins to peer
Above yon busky hill! the day looks pale
At his distemperature.

PRINCE HENRY.
The southern wind
Doth play the trumpet to his purposes;
And by his hollow whistling in the leaves
Foretells a tempest and a blustering day.

KING HENRY.
Then with the losers let it sympathise,
For nothing can seem foul to those that win.
[The trumpet sounds.
Enter WORCESTER and VERNON.
How now, my Lord of Worcester! 'tis not well
That you and I should meet upon such terms
As now we meet. You have deceived our trust;
And made us doff our easy robes of peace,
To crush our old limbs in ungentle steel:
This is not well, my lord, this is not well.
What say you to it? will you again unknit
This churlish knot of all-abhorred war?
And move in that obedient orb again
Where you did give a fair and natural light;
And be no more an exhaled meteor,
A prodigy of fear, and a portent
Of broached mischief to the unborn times?

EARL OF WORCESTER.
Hear me, my liege:
For mine own part, I could be well content
To entertain the lag-end of my life
With quiet hours; for, I do protest,
I have not sought the day of this dislike.

KING HENRY.
You have not sought it! how comes it, then?

SIR JOHN FALSTAFF.
Rebellion lay in his way, and he found it.

PRINCE HENRY.
Peace, chewet, peace!

EARL OF WORCESTER.

It pleased your majesty to turn your looks
Of favour from myself and all our house;
And yet I must remember you, my lord,
We were the first and dearest of your friends.
For you my staff of office did I break
In Richard's time; and posted day and night
To meet you on the way, and kiss your hand,
When yet you were in place and in account
Nothing so strong and fortunate as I.
It was myself, my brother, and his son,
That brought you home, and boldly did out-
    dare
The dangers of the time. You swore to us,
And you did swear that oath at Doncaster,
That you did nothing purpose 'gainst the state;
Nor claim no further than your new-fall'n
    right,
The seat of Gaunt, dukedom of Lancaster:
To this we swore our aid. But in short space
It rain'd down fortune showering on your
    head;
And such a flood of greatness fell on you,—
What with our help, what with the absent
    king,
What with the injuries of a wanton time,
The seeming sufferances that you had borne,
And the contrarious winds that held the king
So long in his unlucky Irish wars
That all in England did repute him dead,—
And from this swarm of fair advantages
You took occasion to be quickly woo'd
To gripe the general sway into your hand;
Forgot your oath to us at Doncaster;
And, being fed by us, you used us so
As that ungentle gull, the cuckoo's bird,
Useth the sparrow,—did oppress our nest;
Grew by our feeding to so great a bulk,
That even our love durst not come near your
    sight
For fear of swallowing; but with nimble wing
We were enforced, for safety sake, to fly
Out of your sight, and raise this present head:
Whereby we stand opposed by such means
As you yourself have forged against yourself,
By unkind usage, dangerous countenance,
And violation of all faith and troth
Sworn to us in your younger enterprise.

KING HENRY.

These things, indeed, you have articulate,
Proclaim'd at market-crosses, read in churches,
To face the garment of rebellion
With some fine colour that may please the eye
Of fickle changelings and poor discontents,
Which gape and rub the elbow at the news
Of hurlyburly innovation:
And never yet did insurrection want
Such water-colours to impaint his cause;
Nor moody beggars, starving for a time
Of pellmell havoc and confusion.

PRINCE HENRY.

In both our armies there is many a soul
Shall pay full dearly for this encounter,
If once they join in trial. Tell your nephew,
The Prince of Wales doth join with all the
    world

In praise of Henry Percy: by my hopes,
This present enterprise set off his head,
I do not think a braver gentleman,
More active-valiant or more valiant-young,
More daring or more bold, is now alive
To grace this latter age with noble deeds.
For my part, I may speak it to my shame,
I have a truant been to chivalry;
And so I hear he doth account me too:
Yet this before my father's majesty,—
I am content that he shall take the odds
Of his great name and estimation,
And will, to save the blood on either side,
Try fortune with him in a single fight.

KING HENRY.

And, Prince of Wales, so dare we venture thee,
Albeit considerations infinite
Do make against it.—No, good Worcester,
    no,
We love our people well; even those we love
That are misled upon your cousin's part;
And, will they take the offer of our grace,
Both he, and they, and you, yea, every man
Shall be my friend again, and I'll be his:
So tell your cousin, and bring me word
What he will do: but if he will not yield,
Rebuke and dread correction wait on us,
And they shall do their office So, be gone;
We will not now be troubled with reply:
We offer fair; take it advisedly.

[*Exeunt* WORCESTER *and* VERNON.

PRINCE HENRY.

It will not be accepted, on my life:
The Douglas and the Hotspur both together
Are confident against the world in arms.

KING HENRY.

Hence, therefore, every leader to his charge;
For, on their answer, will we set on them:
And God befriend us, as our cause is just!

[*Exeunt* KING, BLUNT, *and* PRINCE JOHN.

SIR JOHN FALSTAFF.

Hal, if thou see me down in the battle, and bestride me, so; 'tis a point of friendship.

PRINCE HENRY.

Nothing but a colossus can do thee that friendship. Say thy prayers, and farewell.

SIR JOHN FALSTAFF.

I would 'twere bedtime, Hal, and all well.

PRINCE HENRY.

Why, thou owest God a death.   [*Exit.*

SIR JOHN FALSTAFF.

'Tis not due yet; I would be loth to pay him before his day. What need I be so forward with him
that calls not on me? Well, 'tis no matter; honour
pricks me on. Yea, but how if honour prick me
off when I come on? how then? Can honour set to
a leg? no: or an arm? no: or take away the grief of
a wound? no. Honour hath no skill in surgery,
then? no. What is honour? a word. What is that
word honour? air. A trim reckoning!—Who hath
it? he that died o' Wednesday. Doth he feel it? no.
Doth he hear it? no. 'Tis insensible, then? yea, to
the dead. But will it not live with the living? no.
Why? detraction will not suffer it. Therefore I'll
none of it: honour is a mere scutcheon:—and so
ends my catechism.   [*Exit.*

SCENE II.

The rebel camp.

Enter WORCESTER *and* VERNON.

EARL OF WORCESTER.

O, NO, my nephew must not know Sir Richard,
The liberal and kind offer of the king.

SIR RICHARD VERNON.

'Twere best he did.

EARL OF WORCESTER.

Then are we all undone.
It is not possible, it cannot be,
The king should keep his word in loving us;
He will suspect us still, and find a time
To punish this offence in other faults:
Suspicion all our lives shall be stuck full of
    eyes;
For treason is but trusted like the fox,
Who, ne'er so tame, so cherisht, and lockt up,
Will have a wild trick of his ancestors.
Look how we can, or sad or merrily,
Interpretation will misquote our looks;
And we shall feed like oxen at a stall,
The better cherisht, still the nearer death.
My nephew's trespass may be well forgot —
It hath the excuse of youth and heat of blood;
And an adopted name of privilege,—
A hare-brain'd Hotspur, govern'd by a spleen:
All his offences live upon my head
And on his father's: we did train him on;
And, his corruption being ta'en from us,
We, as the spring of all, shall pay for all.
Therefore, good cousin, let not Harry know,
In any case, the offer of the king.

SIR RICHARD VERNON.

Deliver what you will, I'll say 'tis so.
Here comes your cousin.

Enter HOTSPUR *and* DOUGLAS; OFFICERS *and*
    SOLDIERS *behind.*

HOTSPUR.

My uncle is return'd:—
Deliver up, my Lord of Westmoreland.—
Uncle, what news?

EARL OF WORCESTER.

The king will bid you battle presently.

EARL OF DOUGLAS.

Defy him by the Lord of Westmoreland.

HOTSPUR.

Lord Douglas, go you and tell him so.

EARL OF DOUGLAS.

Marry, and shall, and very willingly.   [*Exit.*

EARL OF WORCESTER.

There is no seeming mercy in the king.

HOTSPUR.

Did you beg any? God forbid!

EARL OF WORCESTER.

I told him gently of our grievances,
Of his oath-breaking; which he mended thus,
By now forswearing that he is forsworn:
He calls us rebels, traitors; and will scourge
With haughty arms this hateful name in us.

Enter DOUGLAS.

EARL OF DOUGLAS.

Arm, gentlemen; to arms! for I have thrown
A brave defiance in King Henry's teeth,
And Westmoreland, that was engaged, did bear it;
Which cannot choose but bring him quickly on.

EARL OF WORCESTER.

The Prince of Wales stept forth before the king,
And, nephew challenged you to single fight.

HOTSPUR.

O, would the quarrel lay upon our heads;
And that no man might draw short breath to-day
But I and Harry Monmouth! Tell me, tell me,
How show'd his tasking? seem'd it in contempt?

SIR RICHARD VERNON.

No, by my soul; I never in my life
Did hear a challenge urged more modestly,
Unless a brother should a brother dare
To gentle exercise and proof of arms.
He gave you all the duties of a man;
Trimm'd up your praises with a princely tongue;
Spoke your deservings like a chronicle;
Making you ever better than his praise,
By still dispraising praise valued with you:
And, which became him like a prince indeed,
He made a blushing cital of himself;
And chid his truant youth with such a grace,
As if he master'd there a double spirit,
Of teaching and of learning instantly.
There did he pause: but let me tell the world,—
If he outlive the envy of this day,
England did never owe so sweet a hope,
So much misconstrued in his wantonness.

HOTSPUR.

Cousin, I think thou art enamoured
On his follies: never did I hear
Of any prince so wild a libertine.
But be he as he will, yet once ere night
I will embrace him with a soldier's arm,
That he shall shrink under my courtesy.—
Arm, arm with speed:—and, fellows, soldiers,
    friends,
Better consider what you have to do
Than I, that have not well the gift of tongue,
Can lift your blood up with persuasion.

Enter a MESSENGER.

MESSENGER.

My lord, here are letters for you.

HOTSPUR.

I cannot read them now.—
O gentlemen, the time of life is short!
To spend that shortness basely were too long,
If life did ride upon a dial's point,
Still ending at the arrival of an hour.
An if we live, we live to tread on kings;
If die, brave death, when princes die with us!
Now, for our consciences,—the arms are fair,
When the intent of bearing them is just.

Enter another MESSENGER.

MESSENGER.

My lord, prepare; the king comes on apace.

HOTSPUR.

I thank him, that he cuts me from my tale,
For I profess not talking; only this,—
Let each man do his best: and here draw I
A sword, whose temper I intend to stain
With the best blood that I can meet withal
In the adventure of this perilous day.
Now,—*Esperance!*—Percy!—and set on.—
Sound all the lofty instruments of war,

And by that music let us all embrace;
For, heaven to earth, some of us never shall
A second time do such a courtesy.
          [*The trumpets sound.   They embrace, and exeunt.*

SCENE III.

Plain between the camps.

The KING *enters with his Power.   Alarum to the battle.   Then enter* DOUGLAS *and* SIR WALTER BLUNT.

SIR WALTER BLUNT.

WHAT is thy name, that in the battle thus
          Thou crossest me? what honour dost thou seek
Upon my head?

EARL OF DOUGLAS.
                    Know, then, my name is Douglas;
And I do haunt thee in the battle thus
Because some tell me that thou art a king.

SIR WALTER BLUNT.
They tell thee true.

EARL OF DOUGLAS.
The Lord of Stafford dear to-day hath bought
Thy likeness; for, instead of thee, King Harry,
This sword hath ended him: so shall it thee,
Unless thou yield thee as my prisoner.

SIR WALTER BLUNT.
I was not born a yielder, thou proud Scot;
And thou shalt find a king that will revenge
Lord Stafford's death.
          [*They fight,* DOUGLAS *kills* BLUNT.
          Enter HOTSPUR.

HOTSPUR.
O Douglas, hadst thou fought at Holmedon thus,
I never had triumpht upon a Scot.

EARL OF DOUGLAS.
All's done, all's won; here breathless lies the king.

HOTSPUR.
Where?

EARL OF DOUGLAS.
Here.

HOTSPUR.
This, Douglas? no; I know this face full well:
A gallant knight he was, his name was Blunt;
Semblably furnisht like the king himself.

EARL OF DOUGLAS.
A fool go with thy soul, whither it goes!
A borrow'd title hast thou bought too dear:
Why didst thou tell me that thou wert a king?

HOTSPUR.
The king hath many masking in his coats.

EARL OF DOUGLAS.
Now, by my sword, I will kill all his coats;
I'll murder all his wardrobe piece by piece,
Until I meet the king.

HOTSPUR.
                    Up, and away!
Our soldiers stand full fairly for the day.
          [*Exeunt.*
Alarum.   Enter FALSTAFF *solus.*

SIR JOHN FALSTAFF.
Though I could scape shot-free at London, I fear
the shot here; here's no scoring but upon the
pate.—Soft! who are you? Sir Walter Blunt:—

there's honour for you! here's no vanity!—I am
as hot as molten lead, and as heavy too: God
keep lead out of me! I need no more weight than
mine own bowels.—I have led my ragamuffins
where they are pepper'd: there's but three of my
hundred and fifty left alive; and they are for the
town's end,—to beg during life.—But who comes
here?

Enter PRINCE HENRY.

PRINCE HENRY.
What, stand'st thou idle here? lend me thy sword:
Many a nobleman lies stark and stiff
Under the hoofs of vaunting enemies,
Whose deaths are yet unrevenged:
I prithee, lend me thy sword.

SIR JOHN FALSTAFF.
O Hal, I prithee, give me leave to breathe awhile.
—Turk Gregory never did such deeds in arms as
I have done this day. I have paid Percy, I have
made him sure.

PRINCE HENRY.
He is, indeed; and living to kill thee. I prithee,
lend me thy sword.

SIR JOHN FALSTAFF.
Nay, before God, Hal, if Percy be alive, thou
gett'st not my sword; but take my pistol, if thou
wilt.

PRINCE HENRY.
Give it me: what, is it in the case?

SIR JOHN FALSTAFF.
Ay, Hal. 'Tis hot, 'tis hot: there's that will sack a
city.   [*The* PRINCE *draws it out, and finds it to be a bottle of sack.*

PRINCE HENRY.
What, is it a time to jest and dally now?
          [*He throws the bottle at him.   Exit.*

SIR JOHN FALSTAFF.
Well, if Percy be alive, I'll pierce him. If he do
come in my way, so; if he do not, if I come in his
willingly, let him make a carbonado of me. I like
not such grinning honour as Sir Walter hath: give
me life; which if I can save, so; if not, honour
comes unlookt for, and there's an end.   [*Exit.*

SCENE IV.

Another part of the field.

Alarum.   Excursions.   Enter KING, *the* PRINCE, LORD JOHN OF LANCASTER, *and* WESTMORE-LAND.

KING HENRY.

I PRITHEE,
          Harry, withdraw thyself; thou bleed'st too much.—
Lord John of Lancaster, go you with him.

PRINCE JOHN.
Not I, my lord, unless I did bleed too.

PRINCE HENRY.
I beseech your majesty, make up,
Lest your retirement do amaze your friends.

KING HENRY.
I will do so.—
My Lord of Westmoreland, lead him to his tent.

EARL OF WESTMORELAND.
Come, my lord, I will lead you to your tent.

PRINCE HENRY.
Lead me, my lord? I do not need your help:
And God forbid. a shallow scratch should drive
The Prince of Wales from such a field as this,
Where stain'd nobility lies trodden on,
And rebels' arms triumph in massacres!
PRINCE JOHN.
We breathe too long:—come, cousin Westmore-
land,
Our duty this way lies; for God's sake, come.
[*Exeunt* PRINCE JOHN *and* WESTMORE-
LAND.
PRINCE HENRY.
By God, thou hast deceived me, Lancaster;
I did not think thee lord of such a spirit:
Before, I loved thee as a brother, John;
But now, I do respect thee as my soul.
KING HENRY.
I saw him hold Lord Percy at the point
With lustier maintenance than I did look for
Of such an ungrown warrior.
PRINCE HENRY.
                    O, this boy
Lends mettle to us all!   [*Exit*.
Enter DOUGLAS.
EARL OF DOUGLAS.
Another king! they grow like Hydra's heads:
I am the Douglas, fatal to all those
That wear those colours on them:—what art thou,
That counterfeit'st the person of a king?
KING HENRY.
The king himself; who, Douglas, grieves at heart,
So many of his shadows thou hast met,
And not the very king. I have two boys
Seek Percy and thyself about the field:
But, seeing thou fall'st on me so luckily,
I will assay thee: so, defend thyself.
EARL OF DOUGLAS.
I fear thou art another counterfeit;
And yet, in faith, thou bear'st thee like a king:
But mine I am sure thou art, whoe'er thou be,
And thus I win thee.
[*They fight; the* KING *being in danger, enter*
PRINCE OF WALES.
PRINCE HENRY.
Hold up thy head, vile Scot, or thou art like
Never to hold it up again! the spirits
Of valiant Shirley, Stafford, Blunt, are in my
arms:
It is the Prince of Wales that threatens thee;
Who never promiseth but he means to pay.
[*They fight;* DOUGLAS *flies*.
Cheerly, my lord: how fares your Grace?—
Sir Nicholas Gawsey hath for succour sent,
And so hath Clifton: I'll to Clifton straight.
KING HENRY.
Stay, and breathe awhile:—
Thou hast redeem'd thy lost opinion;
And show'd thou makest some tender of my life,
In this fair rescue thou hast brought to me.
PRINCE HENRY.
O God, they did me too much injury
That ever said I hearken'd for your death!
If it were so, I might have let alone
The insulting hand of Douglas over you,
Which would have been as speedy in your end

As all the poisonous potions in the world,
And saved the treacherous labour of your son.
KING HENRY.
Make up to Clifton: I'll to Sir Nicholas Gawsey.
[*Exit*.
Enter HOTSPUR.
HOTSPUR.
If I mistake not, thou art Harry Monmouth.
PRINCE HENRY.
Thou speak'st as if I would deny my name.
HOTSPUR.
My name is Harry Percy.
PRINCE HENRY.
                    Why, then I see
A very valiant rebel of the name.
I am the Prince of Wales; and think not, Percy,
To share with me in glory any more:
Two stars keep not their motion in one sphere;
Nor can one England brook a double reign,
Of Harry Percy and the Prince of Wales.
HOTSPUR.
Nor shall it, Harry, for the hour is come
To end the one of us; and would to God
Thy name in arms were now as great as mine!
PRINCE HENRY.
I'll make it greater ere I part from thee;
And all the budding honours on thy crest
I'll crop, to make a garland for my head.
HOTSPUR.
I can no longer brook thy vanities.   [*They fight*.
Enter FALSTAFF.
SIR JOHN FALSTAFF.
Well said, Hal! to it, Hal!—Nay, you shall find no
boy's play here, I can tell you.
Enter DOUGLAS; *he fights with* FALSTAFF, *who
falls down as if he were dead, and exit* DOUGLAS.
The PRINCE *killeth* PERCY.
HOTSPUR.
O Harry, thou hast robb'd me of my youth!
I better brook the loss of brittle life
Than those proud titles thou hast won of me;
They wound my thoughts worse than thy sword
my flesh:—
But thought's the slave of life, and life time's fool;
And time, that takes survey of all the world,
Must have a stop. O, I could prophesy,
But that the earthy and cold hand of death
Lies on my tongue:—no, Percy, thou art dust,
And food for—   [*Dies*.
PRINCE HENRY.
For worms, brave Percy: fare thee well, great
heart!—
Ill-weaved ambition, how much art thou shrunk!
When that this body did contain a spirit,
A kingdom for it was too small a bound;
But now two paces of the vilest earth
Is room enough:—this earth that bears thee
dead
Bears not alive so stout a gentleman.
If thou wert sensible of courtesy,
I should not make so dear a show of zeal:—
But let my favours hide thy mangled face;
And, even in thy behalf, I'll thank myself
For doing these fair rites of tenderness.
Adieu, and take thy praise with thee to heaven!
Thy ignomy sleep with thee in the grave,

But not remember'd in thy epitaph!—
                    [*He spieth* FALSTAFF *on the ground.*
What, old acquaintance! could not all this flesh
Keep in a little life? Poor Jack, farewell!
I could have better spared a better man:
O, I should have a heavy miss of thee,
If I were much in love with vanity!
Death hath not struck so fat a deer to-day,
Though many dearer, in this bloody fray.
Embowell'd will I see thee by and by:
Till then in blood by noble Percy lie.   [*Exit.*
                    [FALSTAFF *riseth up.*
              SIR JOHN FALSTAFF.
Embowell'd! if thou embowel me to-day, I'll give
you leave to powder me and eat me too to-mor-
row. 'Sblood, 'twas time to counterfeit, or that
hot termagant Scot had paid me scot and lot too.
Counterfeit? I lie, I am no counterfeit: to die, is to
be a counterfeit; for he is but the counterfeit of a
man who hath not the life of a man: but to counterfeit dying, when a man thereby liveth, is to be
no counterfeit, but the true and perfect image of
life indeed. The better part of valour is discretion;
in the which better part I have saved my life.
Zounds, I am afraid of this gunpowder Percy,
though he be dead: how, if he should counterfeit
too, and rise? by my faith, I am afraid he would
prove the better counterfeit. Therefore I'll make
him sure; yea, and I'll swear I kill'd him. Why
may not he rise as well as I? Nothing confutes me
but eyes, and nobody sees me. Therefore, sirrah
[*stabbing him*], with a new wound in your thigh,
come you along with me.
              [*He takes up* HOTSPUR *on his back.*
Enter the PRINCE OF WALES *and* LORD JOHN
              OF LANCASTER.
              PRINCE HENRY.
Come, brother John; full bravely hast thou flesht
Thy maiden sword.
              LORD JOHN OF LANCASTER.
                    But, soft! whom have we here?
Did you not tell me this fat man was dead?
              PRINCE HENRY.
I did; I saw him dead,
Breathless and bleeding on the ground.—
Art thou alive? or is it fantasy
That plays upon our eyesight? I prithee, speak;
We will not trust our eyes without our ears:—
Thou art not what thou seem'st.
              SIR JOHN FALSTAFF.
No, that's certain; I am not a double man: but if
I be not Jack Falstaff, then am I a Jack. There is
Percy [*throwing the body down*]: if your father will
do me any honour, so; if not, let him kill the next
Percy himself. I look to be either earl or duke, I
can assure you.
              PRINCE HENRY.
Why, Percy I kill'd myself, and saw thee dead.
              SIR JOHN FALSTAFF.
Didst thou?—Lord, Lord, how this world is given
to lying!—I grant you I was down and out of
breath; and so was he: but we rose both at an instant, and fought a long hour by Shrewsbury
clock. If I may be believed, so; if not, let them
that should reward valour bear the sin upon their
own heads. I'll take it upon my death, I gave him

this wound in the thigh: if the man were alive,
and would deny it, zounds, I would make him eat
a piece of my sword.
              LORD JOHN OF LANCASTER.
This is the strangest tale that e'er I heard.
              PRINCE HENRY.
This is the strangest fellow, brother John.—
Come, bring your luggage nobly on your back:
For my part, if a lie may do thee grace,
I'll gild it with the happiest terms I have.
                    [*A retreat is sounded.*
The trumpet sounds retreat; the day is ours.
Come, brother, let's to the highest of the field,
To see what friends are living, who are dead.
                    [*Exeunt* PRINCES.
              SIR JOHN FALSTAFF.
I'll follow, as they say, for reward. He that re-
wards me, God reward him! If I do grow great,
I'll grow less; for I'll purge, and leave sack, and
live cleanly as a nobleman should do.
                    [*Exit, bearing off the body.*

              SCENE V.

              Another part of the field.

The trumpets sound.   Enter the KING, PRINCE
    OF WALES, LORD JOHN OF LANCASTER,
    WESTMORELAND, *and others, with* WORCES-
    TER *and* VERNON *prisoners.*

              KING HENRY.
THUS ever did rebellion find rebuke.—
    Ill-spirited Worcester! did we not send grace,
Pardon, and terms of love to all of you?
And wouldst thou turn our offers contrary?
Misuse the tenour of thy kinsman's trust?
Three knights upon our party slain to-day,
A noble earl, and many a creature else,
Had been alive this hour,
If, like a Christian, thou hadst truly borne
Betwixt our armies true intelligence.
              EARL OF WORCESTER.
What I have done my safety urged me to;
And I embrace this fortune patiently,
Since not to be avoided it falls on me.
              KING HENRY.
Bear Worcester to the death, and Vernon too:
Other offenders we will pause upon.—
              [*Exeunt* WORCESTER *and* VERNON, *guarded.*
How goes the field?
              PRINCE HENRY.
The noble Scot, Lord Douglas, when he saw
The fortune of the day quite turn'd from him,
The noble Percy slain, and all his men
Upon the foot of fear,—fled with the rest;
And falling from a hill, he was so bruised
That the pursuers took him. At my tent
The Douglas is; and I beseech your Grace
I may dispose of him.
              KING HENRY.
                    With all my heart.
              PRINCE HENRY.
Then, brother John of Lancaster, to you
This honourable bounty shall belong:
Go to the Douglas, and deliver him

Up to his pleasure, ransomless and free;
His valour, shown upon our crests to-day,
Hath taught us how to cherish such high deeds
Even in the bosom of our adversaries.

       LORD JOHN OF LANCASTER.

I thank your Grace for this high courtesy
Which I shall give away immediately.

       KING HENRY.

Then this remains,—that we divide our
  power.—
You, son John, and my cousin Westmoreland,
Towards York shall bend you with your dearest
  speed,
To meet Northumberland and the prelate Scroop,
Who, as we hear, are busily in arms:
Myself,—and you, son Harry,—will towards
  Wales,
To fight with Glendower and the Earl of March.
Rebellion in this land shall lose his sway,
Meeting the check of such another day:
And since this business so fair is done,
Let us not leave till all our own be won.   [*Exeunt.*

THE SECOND PART OF
KING HENRY THE FOURTH

DRAMATIS PERSONAE

RUMOUR, *the Presenter.*
KING HENRY THE FOURTH.
PRINCE HENRY, *afterwards crown'd* KING
  HENRY THE FIFTH.
PRINCE JOHN of Lan-
  caster,
HUMPHREY of Gloster,
THOMAS of Clarence, } *Sons to Henry the Fourth and Brethren to Henry the Fifth.*
NORTHUMBERLAND,
THE ARCHBISHOP OF
  YORK,
MOWBRAY,
HASTINGS,
LORD BARDOLPH,
TRAVERS,
MORTON,
COLEVILE, } *Opposites to the King. Henry the Fourth.*
WARWICK,
WESTMORELAND,
SURREY,
GOWER,
HARCOURT,
BLUNT, } *Of the King's Priory.*
LORD CHIEF JUSTICE,

POINTZ,
FALSTAFF,
BARDOLPH,
PISTOL,
PETO,
PAGE,
A SERVANT *of the Chief Justice.*
SHALLOW,
SILENCE, } *both Country Justices.*
DAVY, *servant to Shallow.*
FANG *and* SNARE, *two Sergeants.*
MOULDY,
SHADOW,
WART,
FEEBLE,
BULLCALF, } *Recruits.*
DRAWERS. BEADLES. GROOMS. PORTER.

NORTHUMBERLAND'S WIFE.
PERCY'S WIDOW.
HOSTESS QUICKLY.
DOLL TEARSHEET.
EPILOGUE.

SCENE—*England.*

INDUCTION.

Warkworth. Before the castle.

Enter RUMOUR, *painted full of tongues.*

RUMOUR.

OPEN your ears; for which of you will stop
The vent of hearing when loud Rumour
    speaks?
I, from the orient to the drooping west,
Making the wind my post-horse, still unfold
The acts commenced on this ball of earth:
Upon my tongues continual slanders ride,
The which in every language I pronounce,
Stuffing the ears of men with false reports.
I speak of peace, while covert enmity,
Under the smile of safety, wounds the world:
And who but Rumour, who but only I,
Make fearful musters and prepared defence,
Whilst the big year, swoln with some other grief,
Is thought with child by the stern tyrant war,
And no such matter? Rumour is a pipe
Blown by surmises, jealousies, conjectures;
And of so easy and so plain a stop,
That the blunt monster with uncounted heads,
The still-discordant wavering multitude,
Can play upon it. But what need I thus
My well-known body to anatomise
Among my household? Why is Rumour here?
I run before King Harry's victory;
Who, in a bloody field by Shrewsbury,
Hath beaten down young Hotspur and his troops,
Quenching the flame of bold rebellion
Even with the rebels' blood. But what mean I
To speak so true at first? my office is
To noise abroad, that Harry Monmouth fell
Under the wrath of noble Hotspur's sword;
And that the king before the Douglas' rage
Stoopt his anointed head as low as death.
This have I rumour'd through the peasant towns
Between that royal field of Shrewsbury
And this worm-eaten hold of ragged stone,
Where Hotspur's father, old Northumberland,
Lies crafty-sick: the posts come tiring on,
And not a man of them brings other news
Than they have learn'd of me: from Rumour's
    tongues
They bring smooth comforts false, worse than
    true wrongs.   [*Exit.*

ACT I. SCENE I.

The same.

Enter LORD BARDOLPH; *the* PORTER *at the gate.*

LORD BARDOLPH.

WHO keeps the gate here, ho? Where is the
earl?

PORTER.

What shall I say you are?

LORD BARDOLPH.

                 Tell thou the earl
That the Lord Bardolph doth attend him here.

PORTER.

His lordship is walkt forth into the orchard:

Please it your honour, knock but at the gate,
And he himself will answer.

LORD BARDOLPH.
Here comes the earl.
[*Exit* PORTER.

Enter NORTHUMBERLAND.

NORTHUMBERLAND.
What news, Lord Bardolph? every minute now
Should be the father of some stratagem:
The times are wild; contention, like a horse
Full of high feeding, madly hath broke loose,
And bears down all before him.

LORD BARDOLPH.
Noble earl,
I bring you certain news from Shrewsbury.

NORTHUMBERLAND.
Good, an God will!

LORD BARDOLPH.
As good as heart can wish:—
The king is almost wounded to the death;
And, in the fortune of my lord your son,
Prince Harry slain outright; and both the Blunts
Kill'd by the hand of Douglas; young Prince John
And Westmoreland and Stafford fled the field;
And Harry Monmouth's brawn, the hulk Sir
    John,
Is prisoner to your son: O, such a day,
So fought, so follow'd, and so fairly won,
Came not till now to dignify the times,
Since Cæsar's fortunes !

NORTHUMBERLAND.
How is this derived?
Saw you the field? came you from Shrewsbury?

LORD BARDOLPH.
I spake with one, my lord, that came from thence,
A gentleman well bred and of good name,
That freely render'd me these news for true.

NORTHUMBERLAND.
Here comes my servant Travers, whom I sent
On Tuesday last to listen after news.

LORD BARDOLPH.
My lord, I over-rode him on the way;
And he is furnisht with no certainties
More than he haply may retail from me.

Enter TRAVERS.

NORTHUMBERLAND.
Now, Travers, what good tidings comes with you?

TRAVERS.
My lord, Sir John Umfrevile turn'd me back
With joyful tidings; and, being better horsed,
Out-rode me. After him came spurring hard
A gentleman, almost forspent with speed,
That stopt by me to breathe his bloodied horse.
He askt the way to Chester; and of him
I did demand what news from Shrewsbury:
He told me that rebellion had ill luck,
And that young Harry Percy's spur was cold.
With that, he gave his able horse the head,
And, bending forward, struck his armed heels
Against the panting sides of his poor jade
Up to the rowel-head; and starting so,
He seem'd in running to devour the way,
Staying no longer question.

NORTHUMBERLAND.
Ha!—Again:
Said he young Harry Percy's spur was cold?

Of Hotspur, Coldspur? that rebellion
Had met ill luck?

LORD BARDOLPH.
My lord, I'll tell you what;
If my young lord your son have not the day,
Upon mine honour, for a silken point
I'll give my barony: ne'er talk of it.

NORTHUMBERLAND.
Why should the gentleman that rode by Travers
Give, then, such instances of loss?

LORD BARDOLPH.
Who, he?
He was some hilding fellow, that had stoln
The horse he rode on; and, upon my life,
Spoke at a venture.—Look, here comes more
    news.

Enter MORTON.

NORTHUMBERLAND.
Yea, this man's brow, like to a title-leaf,
Foretells the nature of a tragic volume:
So looks the strond whereon the imperious flood
Hath left a witness'd usurpation.—
Say, Morton, didst thou come from Shrewsbury?

MORTON.
I ran from Shrewsbury, my noble lord;
Where hateful death put on his ugliest mask
To fright our party.

NORTHUMBERLAND.
How doth my son and brother?
Thou tremblest; and the whiteness in thy cheek
Is apter than thy tongue to tell thy errand.
Even such a man, so faint, so spiritless,
So dull, so dead in look, so woe-begone,
Drew Priam's curtain in the dead of night,
And would have told him half his Troy was
    burnt;
But Priam found the fire ere he his tongue,
And I my Percy's death ere thou report'st it.
This thou wouldst say, 'Your son did thus and
    thus;
Your brother thus; so fought the noble Douglas;'
Stopping my greedy ear with their bold deeds:
But in the end, to stop my ear indeed,
Thou hast a sigh to blow away this praise,
Ending with 'Brother, son, and all are dead.'

MORTON.
Douglas is living, and your brother, yet;
But, for my lord your son,—

NORTHUMBERLAND.
Why, he is dead.
See what a ready tongue suspicion hath!
He that but fears the thing he would not know
Hath by instinct knowledge from others' eyes,
That what he fear'd is chanced. Yet speak,
    Morton;
Tell thou thy earl his divination lies,
And I will take it as a sweet disgrace,
And make thee rich for doing me such wrong.

MORTON.
You are too great to be by me gainsaid:
Your spirit is too true, your fears too certain.

NORTHUMBERLAND.
Yet, for all this, say not that Percy's dead.
I see a strange confession in thine eye:
Thou shakest thy head, and hold'st it fear or sin
To speak a truth. If he be slain, say so;

The tongue offends not that reports his death:
And he doth sin that doth belie the dead;
Not he which says the dead is not alive.
Yet the first bringer of unwelcome news
Hath but a losing office; and his tongue
Sounds ever after as a sullen bell,
Remember'd tolling a departing friend.

LORD BARDOLPH.
I cannot think, my lord, your son is dead.

MORTON.
I am sorry I should force you to believe
That which I would to God I had not seen;
But these mine eyes saw him in bloody state,
Rendering faint quittance, wearied and out-
breathed,
To Harry Monmouth; whose swift wrath beat
down
The never-daunted Percy to the earth,
From whence with life he never more sprung up.
In few, his death—whose spirit lent a fire
Even to the dullest peasant in his camp—
Being bruited once, took fire and heat away
From the best-temper'd courage in his troops;
For from his metal was his party steel'd;
Which once in him abated, all the rest
Turn'd on themselves, like dull and heavy lead:
And as the thing that's heavy in itself,
Upon enforcement flies with greatest speed,
So did our men, heavy in Hotspur's loss,
Lend to this weight such lightness with their fear,
That arrows fled not swifter toward their aim
Than did our soldiers, aiming at their safety,
Fly from the field. Then was that noble Wor-
cester
Too soon ta'en prisoner; and that furious Scot,
The bloody Douglas, whose well-labouring sword
Had three times slain th'appearance of the king,
Gan vail his stomach, and did grace the shame
Of those that turn'd their backs; and in his flight,
Stumbling in fear, was took. The sum of all
Is, that the king hath won; and hath sent out
A speedy power to encounter you, my lord,
Under the conduct of young Lancaster
And Westmoreland. This is the news at full.

NORTHUMBERLAND.
For this I shall have time enough to mourn.
In poison there is physic; and these news,
Having been well, that would have made me sick,
Being sick, have in some measure made me well:
And as the wretch, whose fever-weaken'd joints,
Like strengthless hinges, buckle under life,
Impatient of his fit, breaks like a fire
Out of his keeper's arms; even so my limbs,
Weaken'd with grief, being now enraged with
grief,
Are thrice themselves. Hence, therefore, thou
nice crutch!
A scaly gauntlet now, with joints of steel,
Must glove this hand: and hence, thou sickly
quoif!
Thou art a guard too wanton for the head
Which princes, flesht with conquest, aim to hit.
Now bind my brows with iron; and approach
The ragged'st hour that time and spite dare bring
To frown upon th'enraged Northumberland!
Let heaven kiss earth! now let not Nature's hand

Keep the wild flood confined! let order die!
And let this world no longer be a stage
To feed contention in a lingering act;
But let one spirit of the first-born Cain
Reign in all bosoms, that, each heart being set
On bloody courses, the rude scene may end,
And darkness be the burier of the dead!

TRAVERS.
This strained passion doth you wrong, my lord.

LORD BARDOLPH.
Sweet earl, divorce not wisdom from your honour.

MORTON.
The lives of all your loving complices
Lean on your health; the which, if you give o'er
To stormy passion, must perforce decay.
You cast th'event of war, my noble lord,
And summ'd the account of chance, before you
said,
'Let us make head.' It was your presurmise
That, in the dole of blows, your son might drop;
You knew he walkt o'er perils on an edge,
More likely to fall in than to get o'er;
You were advised his flesh was capable
Of wounds and scars, and that his forward spirit
Would lift him where most trade of danger
ranged:
Yet did you say, 'Go forth;' and none of this,
Though strongly apprehended, could restrain
The stiff-borne action: what hath, then, befaln,
Or what hath this bold enterprise brought forth,
More than that being which was like to be?

LORD BARDOLPH.
We all that are engaged to this loss
Knew that we ventured on such dangerous seas,
That if we wrought out life, 'twas ten to one;
And yet we ventured, for the gain proposed
Choked the respect of likely peril fear'd;
And since we are o'erset, venture again.
Come, we will all put forth, body and goods.

MORTON.
'Tis more than time: and, my most noble lord,
I hear for certain, and do speak the truth,
The gentle Archbishop of York is up
With well-appointed powers: he is a man
Who with a double surety binds his followers.
My lord your son had only but the corpse,
But shadows and the shows of men, to fight;
For that same word, rebellion, did divide
The action of their bodies from their souls;
And they did fight with queasiness, constrain'd,
As men drink potions; that their weapons only
Seem'd on our side, but, for their spirits and
souls,
This word, rebellion, it had froze them up,
As fish are in a pond. But now the bishop
Turns insurrection to religion:
Supposed sincere and holy in his thoughts,
He's follow'd both with body and with mind;
And doth enlarge his rising with the blood
Of fair King Richard, scraped from Pomfret
stones;
Derives from heaven his quarrel and his cause;
Tells them he doth bestride a bleeding land,
Gasping for life under great Bolingbroke;
And more and less do flock to follow him.

NORTHUMBERLAND.
I knew of this before, but, to speak truth,
This present grief had wiped it from my mind.
Go in with me; and counsel every man
The aptest way for safety and revenge:
Get posts and letters, and make friends with
  speed,—
Never so few, and never yet more need. [*Exeunt.*

SCENE II.

London.   A street.

Enter FALSTAFF, *with his* PAGE *bearing his
sword and buckler.*

FALSTAFF.
SIRRAH, you giant, what says the doctor to
my water?

PAGE.
He said, sir, the water itself was a good healthy
water; but, for the party that owed it, he might
have moe diseases than he knew for.

FALSTAFF.
Men of all sorts take a pride to gird at me: the
brain of this foolish-compounded clay, man, is
not able to invent any thing that tends to laughter,
more than I invent or is invented on me: I am not
only witty in myself, but the cause that wit is in
other men. I do here walk before thee like a sow
that hath overwhelm'd all her litter but one. If the
prince put thee into my service for any other
reason than to set me off, why then I have no
judgement. Thou whoreson mandrake, thou art
fitter to be worn in my cap than to wait at my
heels. I was never mann'd with an agate till now:
but I will inset you neither in gold nor silver, but
in vile apparel, and send you back again to your
master, for a jewel,— the juvenal, the prince your
master, whose chin is not yet fledged. I will sooner
have a beard grow in the palm of my hand than
he shall get one on his cheek; and yet he will not
stick to say his face is a face-royal: God may
finish it when he will, 'tis not a hair amiss yet: he
may keep it still at a face-royal, for a barber shall
never earn sixpence out of it; and yet he'll be
crowing as if he had writ man ever since his father
was a bachelor. He may keep his own grace, but
he's almost out of mine, I can assure him.—
What said Master Dombledon about the satin for
my short cloak and my slops?

PAGE.
He said, sir, you should procure him better assurance than Bardolph: he would not take his bond
and yours; he liked not the security.

FALSTAFF.
Let him be damn'd, like the glutton! pray God
his tongue be hotter!—A whoreson Achitophel! a
rascally yea-forsooth knave! to bear a gentleman
in hand, and then stand upon security!—The
whoreson smooth-pates do now wear nothing but
high shoes, and bunches of keys at their girdles;
and if a man is through with them in honest
taking-up, then they must stand upon security. I
had as lief they would put ratsbane in my mouth
as offer to stop it with security. I lookt a' should
have sent me two-and-twenty yards of satin, as I
am a true knight, and he sends me security. Well,

he may sleep in security; for he hath the horn of
abundance, and the lightness of his wife shines
through it: and yet cannot he see, though he
have his own lantern to light him.—Where's
Bardolph?

PAGE.
He's gone into Smithfield to buy your worship a
horse.

FALSTAFF.
I bought him in Paul's, and he'll buy me a horse
in Smithfield: an I could get me but a wife in
the stews, I were mann'd, horsed, and wived.

PAGE.
Sir, here comes the nobleman that committed the
prince for striking him about Bardolph.

FALSTAFF.
Wait close; I will not see him.
Enter the LORD CHIEF JUSTICE *and* SERVANT.

LORD CHIEF JUSTICE.
What's he that goes there?

SERVANT.
Falstaff, an't please your lordship.

LORD CHIEF JUSTICE.
He that was in question for the robbery?

SERVANT.
He, my lord: but he hath since done good service
at Shrewsbury; and, as I hear, is now going with
some charge to the Lord John of Lancaster.

LORD CHIEF JUSTICE.
What, to York? Call him back again.

SERVANT.
Sir John Falstaff!

FALSTAFF.
Boy, tell him I am deaf.

PAGE.
You must speak louder; my master is deaf.

LORD CHIEF JUSTICE.
I am sure he is, to the hearing of any thing good.
—Go, pluck him by the elbow; I must speak with
him.

SERVANT.
Sir John,—

FALSTAFF.
What! a young knave, and begging! Is there not
wars? is there not employment? doth not the king
lack subjects? do not the rebels need soldiers?
Though it be a shame to be on any side but one,
it is worse shame to beg than to be on the worst
side, were it worse than the name of rebellion can
tell how to make it.

SERVANT.
You mistake me, sir.

FALSTAFF.
Why, sir, did I say you were an honest man? setting my knighthood and my soldiership aside, I
had lied in my throat, if I had said so.

SERVANT.
I pray you, sir, then set your knighthood and your
soldiership aside; and give me leave to tell you,
you lie in your throat, if you say I am any other
than an honest man.

FALSTAFF.
I give thee leave to tell me so! I lay aside that
which grows to me! If thou gett'st any leave of
me, hang me; if thou takest leave, thou wert better
be hang'd. You hunt-counter: hence! avaunt!

SERVANT.

Sir, my lord would speak with you.

LORD CHIEF JUSTICE.

Sir John Falstaff, a word with you.

FALSTAFF.

My good lord!—God give your lordship good time of day. I am glad to see your lordship abroad: I heard say your lordship was sick: I hope your lordship goes abroad by advice. Your lordship, though not clean past your youth, hath yet some smack of age in you, some relish of the saltness of time; and I most humbly beseech your lordship to have a reverend care of your health.

LORD CHIEF JUSTICE.

Sir John, I sent for you before your expedition to Shrewsbury.

FALSTAFF.

An't please your lordship, I hear his majesty is return'd with some discomfort from Wales.

LORD CHIEF JUSTICE.

I talk not of his majesty:—you would not come when I sent for you.

FALSTAFF.

And I hear, moreover, his highness is faln into this same whoreson apoplexy.

LORD CHIEF JUSTICE.

Well, God mend him!—I pray you, let me speak with you.

FALSTAFF.

This apoplexy is, as I take it, a kind of lethargy, an't please your lordship; a kind of sleeping in the blood, a whoreson tingling.

LORD CHIEF JUSTICE.

What tell you me of it? be it as it is.

FALSTAFF.

It hath its original from much grief, from study, and perturbation of the brain: I have read the cause of his effects in Galen: it is a kind of deafness.

LORD CHIEF JUSTICE.

I think you are faln into the disease; for you hear not what I say to you.

FALSTAFF.

Very well, my lord, very well: rather, an't please you, it is the disease of not listening, the malady of not marking, that I am troubled withal.

LORD CHIEF JUSTICE.

To punish you by the heels would amend the attention of your ears; and I care not if I do become your physician.

FALSTAFF.

I am as poor as Job, my lord, but not so patient: your lordship may minister the potion of imprisonment to me in respect of poverty; but how I should be your patient to follow your prescriptions, the wise may make some dram of a scruple, or, indeed, a scruple itself.

LORD CHIEF JUSTICE.

I sent for you, when there were matters against you for your life, to come speak with me.

FALSTAFF.

As I was then advised by my learned counsel in the laws of this land-service, I did not come.

LORD CHIEF JUSTICE.

Well, the truth is, Sir John, you live in great infamy.

FALSTAFF.

He that buckles him in my belt cannot live in less.

LORD CHIEF JUSTICE.

Your means are very slender, and your waste is great.

FALSTAFF.

I would it were otherwise; I would my means were greater, and my waist slenderer.

LORD CHIEF JUSTICE.

You have misled the youthful prince.

FALSTAFF.

The young prince hath misled me: I am the fellow with the great belly, and he my dog.

LORD CHIEF JUSTICE.

Well, I am loth to gall a new-heal'd wound: your day's service at Shrewsbury hath a little gilded over your night's exploit on Gadshill: you may thank the unquiet time for your quiet o'er-posting that action.

FALSTAFF.

My lord,—

LORD CHIEF JUSTICE.

But since all is well, keep it so: wake not a sleeping wolf.

FALSTAFF.

To wake a wolf is as bad as to smell a fox.

LORD CHIEF JUSTICE.

What! you are as a candle, the better part burnt out.

FALSTAFF.

A wassail candle, my lord; all tallow: if I did say of wax, my growth would approve the truth.

LORD CHIEF JUSTICE.

There is not a white hair on your face but should have his effect of gravity.

FALSTAFF.

His effect of gravy, gravy, gravy.

LORD CHIEF JUSTICE.

You follow the young prince up and down, like his ill angel.

FALSTAFF.

Not so, my lord; your ill angel is light; but I hope he that looks upon me will take me without weighing: and yet, in some respects, I grant, I cannot go:—I cannot tell. Virtue is of so little regard in these costermonger times, that true valour is turn'd bear-herd: pregnancy is made a tapster, and hath his quick wit wasted in giving reckonings: all the other gifts appertinent to man, as the malice of this age shapes them, are not worth a gooseberry. You that are old consider not the capacities of us that are young; you measure the heat of our livers with the bitterness of your galls: and we that are in the vaward of our youth, I must confess, are wags too.

LORD CHIEF JUSTICE.

Do you set down your name in the scroll of youth, that are written down old with all the characters of age? Have you not a moist eye? a dry hand? a yellow cheek? a white beard? a decreasing leg? an increasing belly? is not your voice broken? your wind short? your chin double? your wit single? and every part about you blasted with antiquity? and will you yet call yourself young? Fie, fie, fie, Sir John!

FALSTAFF.

My lord, I was born about three of the clock in the afternoon, with a white head and something a round belly. For my voice,—I have lost it with hallooing, and singing of anthems. To approve my youth further, I will not: the truth is, I am only old in judgement and understanding; and he that will caper with me for a thousand marks, let him lend me the money, and have at him. For the box of th'ear that the prince gave you,—he gave it like a rude prince, and you took it like a sensible lord. I have checkt him for it; and the young lion repents,—marry, not in ashes and sackcloth, but in new silk and old sack.

LORD CHIEF JUSTICE.

Well, God send the prince a better companion!

FALSTAFF.

God send the companion a better prince! I cannot rid my hands of him.

LORD CHIEF JUSTICE.

Well, the king hath sever'd you and Prince Harry: I hear you are going with Lord John of Lancaster against the Archbishop and the Earl of Northumberland.

FALSTAFF.

Yea; I thank your pretty sweet wit for it. But look you pray, all you that kiss my lady Peace at home, that our armies join not in a hot day; for, by the Lord, I take but two shirts out with me, and I mean not to sweat extraordinarily: if it be a hot day, an I brandish any thing but a bottle, I would I might never spit white again. There is not a dangerous action can peep out his head, but I am thrust upon it: well, I cannot last ever: but it was alway yet the trick of our English nation, if they have a good thing, to make it too common. If ye will needs say I am an old man, you should give me rest. I would to God, my name were not so terrible to the enemy as it is: I were better to be eaten to death with a rust than to be scour'd to nothing with perpetual motion.

LORD CHIEF JUSTICE.

Well, be honest, be honest; and God bless your expedition!

FALSTAFF.

Will your lordship lend me a thousand pound to furnish me forth?

LORD CHIEF JUSTICE.

Not a penny, not a penny; you are too impatient to bear crosses. Fare you well: commend me to my cousin Westmoreland.

[Exeunt CHIEF JUSTICE and SERVANT.

FALSTAFF.

If I do, fillip me with a three-man beetle.— A man can no more separate age and covetousness than a' can part young limbs and lechery: but the gout galls the one, and the pox pinches the other; and so both the degrees prevent my curses.—Boy!

PAGE.

Sir?

FALSTAFF.

What money is in my purse?

PAGE.

Seven groats and two pence.

FALSTAFF.

I can get no remedy against this consumption of the purse: borrowing only lingers and lingers it out, but the disease is incurable.—Go bear this letter to my Lord of Lancaster; this to the prince; this to the Earl of Westmoreland; and this to old Mistress Ursula, whom I have weekly sworn to marry since I perceived the first white hair on my chin. About it: you know where to find me. [Exit PAGE.] A pox of this gout! or, a gout of this pox! for the one or the other plays the rogue with my great toe. 'Tis no matter if I do halt; I have the wars for my colour, and my pension shall seem the more reasonable. A good wit will make use of any thing: I will turn diseases to commodity.

[Exit.

SCENE III.

York.   The ARCHBISHOP'S *palace.*

Enter the ARCHBISHOP, HASTINGS, MOWBRAY, *and* LORD BARDOLPH.

ARCHBISHOP OF YORK.

THUS have you heard our cause and know our means;

And, my most noble friends, I pray you all
Speak plainly your opinions of our hopes:—
And first, lord marshal, what say you to it?

MOWBRAY.

I well allow the occasion of our arms;
But gladly would be better satisfied
How, in our means, we should advance ourselves
To look with forehead bold and big enough
Upon the power and puissance of the king.

HASTINGS.

Our present musters grow upon the file
To five-and-twenty thousand men of choice;
And our supplies live largely in the hope
Of great Northumberland, whose bosom burns
With an incensed fire of injuries.

LORD BARDOLPH.

The question, then, Lord Hastings, standeth thus;—
Whether our present five-and-twenty thousand
May hold up head without Northumberland?

HASTINGS.

With him, we may.

LORD BARDOLPH.

Yea, marry, there's the point:
But if without him we be thought too feeble,
My judgement is, we should not step too far
Till we had his assistance by the hand;
For, in a theme so bloody-faced as this,
Conjecture, expectation, and surmise
Of aids incertain should not be admitted.

ARCHBISHOP OF YORK.

'Tis very true, Lord Bardolph; for, indeed,
It was young Hotspur's case at Shrewsbury.

LORD BARDOLPH.

It was, my lord; who lined himself with hope,
Eating the air on promise of supply,
Flattering himself with project of a power
Much smaller than the smallest of his thoughts:
And so, with great imagination,
Proper to madmen, led his powers to death,
And, winking, leapt into destruction.

HASTINGS.

But, by your leave, it never yet did hurt
To lay down likelihoods and forms of hope.

LORD BARDOLPH.
Yes, if this present quality of war;—
Indeed, the instant action—a cause on foot—
Lives so in hope, as in an early spring
We see th'appearing buds; which to prove fruit,
Hope gives not so much warrant, as despair
That frosts will bite them. When we mean to
    build,
We first survey the plot, then draw the model;
And when we see the figure of the house.
Then must we rate the cost of the ere. tion;
Which if we find outweighs ability,
What do we then but draw anew the model
In fewer offices, or at last desist
To build at all? Much more, in this great work—
Which is almost to pluck a kingdom down,
And set another up—should we survey
The plot of situation and the model,
Consent upon a sure foundation,
Question surveyors, know our own estate,
How able such a work to undergo,
To weigh against his opposite; or else
We fortify in paper and in figures,
Using the names of men instead of men:
Like one that draws the model of a house
Beycnd his power to build it; who, half through,
Gives o'er, and leaves his part-created cost
A naked subject to the weeping clouds,
And waste for churlish winter's tyranny.
                HASTINGS.
Grant that our hopes—yet likely of fair birth—
Should be still-born, and that we now possest
The utmost man of expectation;
I think we are a body strong enough,
Even as we are, to equal with the king.
            LORD BARDOLPH.
What, is the king but five-and-twenty thousand?
                HASTINGS.
To us no more; nay, not so much, Lord Bardolph.
For his divisions, as the times do brawl,
Are in three heads: one power against the French,
And one against Glendower; perforce a third
Must take up us: so is the unfirm king
In three divided; and his coffers sound
With hollow poverty and emptiness.
          ARCHBISHOP OF YORK.
That he should draw his several strengths to-
    gether,
And come against us in full puissance,
Need not be dreaded.
                HASTINGS.
            If he should do so,
He leaves his back unarm'd, the French and Welsh
Baying him at the heels: never fear that.
            LORD BARDOLPH.
Who is it like should lead his forces hither?
                HASTINGS.
The Duke of Lancaster and Westmoreland;
Against the Welsh, himself and Harry Mon-
    mouth:
But who is substituted 'gainst the French,
I have no certain notice.
          ARCHBISHOP OF YORK.
            Let us on,
And publish the occasion of our arms.
The commonwealth is sick of their own choice;

Their over-greedy love hath surfeited:
An habitation giddy and unsure
Hath he that buildeth on the vulgar heart.
O thou fond many! with what loud applause
Didst thou beat heaven with blessing Boling-
    broke,
Before he was what thou wouldst have him be!
And being now trimm'd in thine own desires,
Thou, beastly feeder, art so full of him,
That thou provokest thyself to cast him up.
So, so, thou common dog, didst thou disgorge
Thy glutton bosom of the royal Richard;
And now thou wouldst eat thy dead vomit up,
And howl'st to find it. What trust is in these
    times?
They that, when Richard lived, would have him
    die,
Are now become enamour'd on his grave:
Thou, that threw'st dust upon his goodly head
When through proud London he came sighing on
After th'admired heels of Bolingbroke,
Cry'st now, 'O earth, yield us that king again,
And take thou this!' O thoughts of men accurst!
Past, and to come, seems best; things present,
    worst.
                MOWBRAY.
Shall we go draw our numbers, and set on?
                HASTINGS.
We are time's subjects, and time bids be gone.
                                    [Exeunt.

ACT II. SCENE I.

London.   A street.

Enter HOSTESS, FANG *and his* BOY *with her,
and* SNARE *following.*

                HOSTESS.
MASTER Fang, have you enter'd the exion?
                FANG.
It is enter'd.
                HOSTESS.
Where's your yeoman? Is't a lusty yeoman? will
a' stand to't?
                FANG.
Sirrah, where's Snare?
                HOSTESS.
O Lord, ay! good Master Snare.
                SNARE.
Here, here.
                FANG.
Snare, we must arrest Sir John Falstaff.
                HOSTESS.
Yes, good Master Snare; I have enter'd him and
all.
                SNARE.
It may chance cost some of us our lives, for he
will stab.
                HOSTESS.
Alas the day! take heed of him; he stabb'd me in
mine own house, and that most beastly: in good
faith, a' cares not what mischief he doth, if his
weapon be out: he will foin like any devil; he will
spare neither man, woman, nor child.
                FANG.
If I can close with him, I care not for his thrust.
                HOSTESS.
No, nor I neither: I'll be at your elbow.

FANG.

An I but fist him once; an a' come but within my vice,—

HOSTESS.

I am undone by his going; I warrant you, he's an infinitive thing upon my score:—good Master Fang, hold him sure;—good Master Snare, let him not scape. A' comes continuantly to Pie-corner—saving your manhoods—to buy a saddle; and he is indited to dinner to the Lubber's-head in Lumbert-street, to Master Smooth's the silk-man: I pray ye, since my exion is enter'd, and my case so openly known to the world, let him be brought in to his answer. A hundred mark is a long one for a poor lone woman to bear: and I have borne, and borne, and borne; and have been fubb'd off, and fubb'd off, and fubb'd off, from this day to that day, that it is a shame to be thought on. There is no honesty in such dealing; unless a woman should be made an ass and a beast, to bear every knave's wrong.—Yonder he comes; and that arrant malmsey-nose knave Bardolph with him. Do your offices, do your offices, Master Fang and Master Snare; do me, do me, do me your offices.

Enter FALSTAFF, PAGE, *and* BARDOLPH.

FALSTAFF.

How now! whose mare's dead? what's the matter?

FANG.

Sir John, I arrest you at the suit of Mistress Quickly.

FALSTAFF.

Away, varlets!—Draw, Bardolph: cut me off the villain's head; throw the quean in the channel.

HOSTESS.

Throw me in the channel! I'll throw thee in the channel. Wilt thou? wilt thou? thou bastardly rogue!—Murder, murder! Ah, thou honey-suckle villain! wilt thou kill God's officers and the king's? Ah, thou honey-seed rogue! thou art a honey-seed, a man-queller, and a woman-queller.

FALSTAFF.

Keep them off, Bardolph.

FANG.

A rescue! a rescue!

HOSTESS.

Good people, bring a rescue or two.—Thou wo't, wo't thou? thou wo't, wo't ta? do, do, thou rogue! do, thou hemp-seed!

FALSTAFF.

Away, you scullion! you rampallian! you fusti-larian! I'll tickle your catastrophe.

Enter the LORD CHIEF JUSTICE, *and his men.*

LORD CHIEF JUSTICE.

What is the matter? keep the peace here, ho!

HOSTESS.

Good my lord, be good to me! I beseech you, stand to me!

LORD CHIEF JUSTICE

How now, Sir John! what are you brawling here? Doth this become your place, your time, and busi-ness? You should have been well on your way to York.— Stand from him, fellow: wherefore hang'st upon him?

HOSTESS.

O my most worshipful lord, an't please your Grace, I am a poor widow of Eastcheap, and he is arrested at my suit.

LORD CHIEF JUSTICE.

For what sum?

HOSTESS.

It is more than for some, my lord; it is for all,— all I have. He hath eaten me out of house and home; he hath put all my substance into that fat belly of his:—but I will have some of it out again, or I will ride thee o' nights like the mare.

FALSTAFF.

I think I am as like to ride the mare, if I have any vantage of ground to get up.

LORD CHIEF JUSTICE.

How comes this, Sir John? Fie! what man of good temper would endure this tempest of exclama-tion? Are you not ashamed to enforce a poor widow to so rough a course to come by her own?

FALSTAFF.

What is the gross sum that I owe thee?

HOSTESS.

Marry, if thou wert an honest man, thyself and the money too. Thou didst swear to me upon a parcel-gilt goblet, sitting in my Dolphin-cham-ber, at the round table, by a sea-coal fire, upon Wednesday in Wheeson-week, when the prince broke thy head for liking his father to a singing-man of Windsor,—thou didst swear to me then, as I was washing thy wound, to marry me, and make me my lady thy wife. Canst thou deny it? Did not goodwife Keech, the butcher's wife, come in then, and call me gossip Quickly? coming in to borrow a mess of vinegar; telling us she had a good dish of prawns; whereby thou didst desire to eat some; whereby I told thee they were ill for a green wound? And didst thou not, when she was gone down stairs, desire me to be no more so familiarity with such poor people; saying that ere long they should call me madam? And didst thou not kiss me, and bid me fetch thee thirty shillings? I put thee now to thy book-oath: deny it, if thou canst.

FALSTAFF.

My lord, this is a poor mad soul; and she says, up and down the town, that her eldest son is like you: she hath been in good case, and the truth is, poverty hath distracted her. But for these fool-ish officers, I beseech you I may have redress against them.

LORD CHIEF JUSTICE.

Sir John, Sir John, I am well acquainted with your manner of wrenching the true cause the false way. It is not a confident brow, nor the throng of words that come with such more than impudent sauciness from you, can thrust me from a level consideration: you have, as it appears to me, practised upon the easy-yielding spirit of this woman, and made her serve your uses both in purse and in person.

HOSTESS.

Yea, in truth, my lord.

LORD CHIEF JUSTICE.

Pray thee, peace.—Pay her the debt you owe her, and unpay the villainy you have done her: the one you may do with sterling money, and the other with current repentance.

FALSTAFF.

My lord, I will not undergo this sneap without reply. You call honourable boldness impudent sauciness: if a man will make court'sy, and say nothing, he is virtuous:—no, my lord, my humble duty remember'd, I will not be your suitor. I say to you, I do desire deliverance from these officers, being upon hasty employment in the king's affairs.

LORD CHIEF JUSTICE.

You speak as having power to do wrong: but answer in the effect of your reputation, and satisfy the poor woman.

FALSTAFF.

Come hither, hostess.   [Takes her aside.

Enter GOWER.

LORD CHIEF JUSTICE.

Now, Master Gower, what news?

GOWER.

The king, my lord, and Harry Prince of Wales Are near at hand: the rest the paper tells.

[Gives a letter.

FALSTAFF.

As I am a gentleman,—

HOSTESS.

Faith, you said so before.

FALSTAFF.

As I am a gentleman:—come, no more words of it.

HOSTESS.

By this heavenly ground I tread on, I must be fain to pawn both my plate and the tapestry of my dining-chambers.

FALSTAFF.

Glasses, glasses, is the only drinking: and for thy walls,—a pretty slight drollery, or the story of the Prodigal, or the German Hunting in water-work, is worth a thousand of these bed-hangings and these fly bitten tapestries. Let it be ten pound, if thou canst. Come, an 'twere not for thy humours, there's not a better wench in England. Go, wash thy face, and draw the action. Come, thou must not be in this humour with me; dost not know me? come, come, I know thou wast set on to this.

HOSTESS.

Pray thee, Sir John, let it be but twenty nobles: i' faith, I am loth to pawn my plate, so God save me, la.

FALSTAFF.

Let it alone; I'll make other shift: you'll be a fool still.

HOSTESS.

Well, you shall have it, though I pawn my gown. I hope you'll come to supper. You'll pay me all together?

FALSTAFF.

Will I live?—[To BARDOLPH] Go, with her, with her; hook on, hook on.

HOSTESS.

Will you have Doll Tearsheet meet you at supper?

FALSTAFF.

No more words; let's have her.

[Exeunt HOSTESS, BARDOLPH, OFFICERS, and BOY.

LORD CHIEF JUSTICE.

I have heard better news.

FALSTAFF.

What's the news, my lord?

LORD CHIEF JUSTICE.

Where lay the king last night?

GOWER.

At Basingstoke, my lord.

FALSTAFF.

I hope, my lord, all's well: what is the news, my lord?

LORD CHIEF JUSTICE.

Come all his forces back?

GOWER.

No; fifteen hundred foot, five hundred horse, Are marcht up to my Lord of Lancaster, Against Northumberland and the Archbishop.

FALSTAFF.

Comes the king back from Wales, my noble lord?

LORD CHIEF JUSTICE.

You shall have letters of me presently: Come, go along with me, good Master Gower.

FALSTAFF.

My lord!

LORD CHIEF JUSTICE.

What's the matter?

FALSTAFF.

Master Gower, shall I entreat you with me to dinner?

GOWER.

I must wait upon my good lord here,—I thank you, good Sir John.

LORD CHIEF JUSTICE.

Sir John, you loiter here too long, being you are to take soldiers up in counties as you go.

FALSTAFF.

Will you sup with me, Master Gower?

LORD CHIEF JUSTICE.

What foolish master taught you these manners, Sir John?

FALSTAFF.

Master Gower, if they become me not, he was a fool that taught them me.—This is the right fencing grace, my lord; tap for tap, and so part fair.

LORD CHIEF JUSTICE.

Now, the Lord lighten thee! thou art a great fool.

[Exeunt.

SCENE II.

London.   Another Street.

Enter PRINCE HENRY and POINTZ.

PRINCE HENRY.

BEFORE God, I am exceeding weary.

POINTZ.

Is't come to that? I had thought weariness durst not have attach'd one of so high blood.

PRINCE HENRY.

Faith, it does me; though it discolours the complexion of my greatness to acknowledge it. Doth it not show vilely in me to desire small beer?

POINTZ.

Why, a prince should not be so loosely studied as to remember so weak a composition.

PRINCE HENRY.

Belike, then, my appetite was not princely got; for, by my troth, I do now remember the poor creature, small beer. But, indeed, these humble considerations make me out of love with my greatness. What a disgrace is it to me to remember thy name! or to know thy face to-morrow! or to take note how many pair of silk stockings thou hast, viz. these, and those that were thy peach-colour'd ones! or to bear the inventory of thy shirts, as, one for superfluity, and one other for use!—but that the tennis-court-keeper knows better than I; for it is a low ebb of linen with thee when thou keepest not racket there; as thou hast not done a great while, because the rest of thy low-countries have made a shift to eat up thy holland: and God knows whether those that bawl out of the ruins of thy linen shall inherit his kingdom: but the midwives say the children are not in the fault; whereupon the world increases, and kindreds are mightily strengthen'd.

POINTZ.

How ill it follows, after you have labour'd so hard, you should talk so idly! Tell me, how many good young princes would do so, their fathers being so sick as yours at this time is?

PRINCE HENRY.

Shall I tell thee one thing, Pointz?

POINTZ.

Yes, faith; and let it be an excellent good thing.

PRINCE HENRY.

It shall serve among wits of no higher breeding than thine.

POINTZ.

Go to; I stand the push of your one thing that you will tell.

PRINCE HENRY.

Marry, I tell thee,—it is not meet that I should be sad, now my father is sick: albeit I could tell to thee,—as to one it pleases me, for fault of a better, to call my friend,—I could be sad, and sad indeed too.

POINTZ.

Very hardly upon such a subject.

PRINCE HENRY.

By this hand, thou think'st me as far in the devil's book as thou and Falstaff for obduracy and persistency: let the end try the man. But I tell thee, my heart bleeds inwardly that my father is so sick: and keeping such vile company as thou art hath in reason taken from me all ostentation of sorrow.

POINTZ.

The reason?

PRINCE HENRY.

What wouldst thou think of me, if I should weep?

POINTZ.

I would think thee a most princely hypocrite.

PRINCE HENRY.

It would be every man's thought; and thou art a blessed fellow to think as every man thinks: never a man's thought in the world keeps the road-way better than thine: every man would think me an hypocrite indeed. And what accites your most worshipful thought to think so?

POINTZ.

Why, because you have been so lewd, and so much engraft to Falstaff.

PRINCE HENRY.

And to thee.

POINTZ.

By this light, I am well spoke on; I can hear it with mine own ears: the worst that they can say of me is, that I am a second brother, and that I am a proper fellow of my hands; and those two things, I confess, I cannot help.—By the mass, here comes Bardolph.

PRINCE HENRY.

And the boy that I gave Falstaff: a' had him from me Christian; and look, if the fat villain have not transform'd him ape.

Enter BARDOLPH *and* PAGE.

BARDOLPH.

God save your Grace!

PRINCE HENRY.

And yours, most noble Bardolph!

BARDOLPH [*to the* PAGE].

Come, you virtuous ass, you bashful fool, must you be blushing? wherefore blush you now? What a maidenly man-at-arms are you become! Is't such a matter to get a pottle-pot's maidenhead?

PAGE.

A' calls me e'en now, my lord, through a red lattice, and I could discern no part of his face from the window: at last I spied his eyes; and methought he had made two holes in the alewife's new petticoat, and so peept through.

PRINCE HENRY.

Hath not the boy profited?

BARDOLPH.

Away, you whoreson upright rabbit, away!

PAGE.

Away, you rascally Althæa's dream, away!

PRINCE HENRY.

Instruct us, boy; what dream, boy?

PAGE.

Marry, my lord, Althæa dream'd she was deliver'd of a firebrand; and therefore I call him her dream.

PRINCE HENRY.

A crown's worth of good interpretation:—there 'tis, boy.   [*Gives money.*

POINTZ.

O, that this good blossom could be kept from cankers!—Well, there is sixpence to preserve thee.   [*Gives money.*

BARDOLPH.

An you do not make him hang'd among you, the gallows shall have wrong.

PRINCE HENRY.

And how doth thy master, Bardolph?

BARDOLPH.

Well, my lord. He heard of your Grace's coming to town; there's a letter for you.   [*Gives a letter.*

POINTZ.

Deliver'd with good respect.—And how doth the martlemas, your master?

BARDOLPH.

In bodily health, sir.

POINTZ.

Marry, the immortal part needs a physician; but that moves not him: though that be sick, it dies not.

PRINCE HENRY.

I do allow this wen to be as familiar with me as my dog: and he holds his place; for look you how he writes.

POINTZ [reads].

'John Falstaff, knight,'—every man must know
that, as oft as he has occasion to name himself:
even like those that are kin to the king; for they
never prick their finger but they say, 'There's
some of the king's blood spilt.' 'How comes
that?' says he, that takes upon him not to conceive. The answer is as ready as a borrower's cap,
'I am the king's poor cousin, sir.'

PRINCE HENRY.

Nay, they will be kin to us, or they will fetch it
from Japhet. But to the letter:—

POINTZ [reads].

'Sir John Falstaff, knight, to the son of the king,
nearest his father, Harry Prince of Wales, greeting.'—Why, this is a certificate.

PRINCE HENRY.

Peace!

POINTZ [reads].

'I will imitate the honourable Roman in brevity:'
—sure he means brevity in breath, short-winded.
—'I commend me to thee, I commend thee, and I
leave thee. Be not too familiar with Pointz; for he
misuses thy favours so much, that he swears thou
art to marry his sister Nell. Repent at idle times
as thou may'st; and so, farewell.

> 'Thine, by yea and no (which is as much as
> to say, as thou usest him), JACK FAL-
> STAFF with my familiars, JOHN with my
> brothers and sisters, and SIR JOHN with
> all Europe.'

My lord, I'll steep this letter in sack, and make
him eat it.

PRINCE HENRY.

That's to make him eat twenty of his words. But do
you use me thus, Ned? must I marry your sister?

POINTZ.

God send the wench no worse fortune! but I
never said so.

PRINCE HENRY.

Well, thus we play the fools with the time; and
the spirits of the wise sit in the clouds and mock
us.—Is your master here in London?

BARDOLPH.

Yes, my lord.

PRINCE HENRY.

Where sups he? doth the old boar feed in the old
frank?

BARDOLPH.

At the old place, my lord,—in Eastcheap.

PRINCE HENRY.

What company?

PAGE.

Ephesians, my lord,—of the old church.

PRINCE HENRY.

Sup any women with him?

PAGE.

None, my lord, but old Mistress Quickly and
Mistress Doll Tearsheet.

PRINCE HENRY.

What pagan may that be?

PAGE.

A proper gentlewoman, sir, and a kinswoman of
my master's.

PRINCE HENRY.

Even such kin as the parish heifers are to the
town bull.—Shall we steal upon them, Ned, at
supper?

POINTZ.

I am your shadow, my lord; I'll follow you.

PRINCE HENRY.

Sirrah, you boy,—and Bardolph,—no word to
your master that I am yet come to town: there's
for your silence.   [Gives money.

BARDOLPH.

I have no tongue, sir.

PAGE.

And for mine, sir,—I will govern it.

PRINCE HENRY.

Fare you well; go. [Exeunt BARDOLPH and
PAGE.]—This Doll Tearsheet should be some
road.

POINTZ.

I warrant you, as common as the way between
Saint Alban's and London.

PRINCE HENRY.

How might we see Falstaff bestow himself to-
night in his true colours, and not ourselves be
seen?

POINTZ.

Put on two leathern jerkins and aprons, and wait
upon him at his table as drawers.

PRINCE HENRY.

From a god to a bull? a heavy descension! it was
Jove's case. From a prince to a prentice? a low
transformation! that shall be mine; for in every
thing the purpose must weigh with the folly.
Follow me, Ned.   [Exeunt.

SCENE III.

Warkworth.   Before the castle.

Enter NORTHUMBERLAND, LADY NORTHUM-
BERLAND, *and* LADY PERCY.

NORTHUMBERLAND.

I PRAY thee, loving wife, and gentle daughter,
  Give even way unto my rough affairs:
Put not you on the visage of the times,
And be, like them, to Percy troublesome.

LADY NORTHUMBERLAND.

I have given over, I will speak no more:
Do what you will; your wisdom be your guide.

NORTHUMBERLAND.

Alas, sweet wife, my honour is at pawn;
And, but my going, nothing can redeem it.

LADY PERCY.

O, yet, for God's sake, go not to these wars!
The time was, father, that you broke your word,
When you were more endear'd to it than now;
When your own Percy, when my heart's dear
    Harry,
Threw many a northward look to see his father
Bring up his powers; but he did long in vain.
Who then persuaded you to stay at home?
There were two honours lost,—yours and your
    son's.
For yours,—the God of heaven brighten it!
For his,—it stuck upon him, as the sun
In the gray vault of heaven; and by his light
Did all the chivalry of England move
To do brave acts: he was, indeed, the glass
Wherein the noble youth did dress themselves:

He had no legs tht practised not his gait;
And speaking thick, which nature made his
  blemish,
Became the accents of the valiant;
For those th at could spea'k low and tardily
Would turn their own perfection to abuse,
To seem like him: so that in speech, in gait,
In diet, in affections of delight,
In military rules, humours of blood,
He was the mark and glass, copy and book,
That fashion'd others. And him,—O wondrous
  him!
O miracle of men!—him did you leave—
Second to none, unseconded by you—
To look upon the hideous god of war
In disadvantage; to abide a field
'Where nothing but the sound of Hotspur's name
Did seem defensible:—so you left him.
Never, O never, do his ghost the wrong
To hold your honour more precise and nice
With others than with him! let them alone:
The marshal and the archbishop are strong:
Had my sweet Harry had but half their numbers,
To-day might I, hanging on Hotspur's neck,
Have talkt of Monmouth's grave.

NORTHUMBERLAND.
                      Beshrew your heart,
Fair daughter, you do draw my spirits from me
With new lamenting ancient oversights.
But I must go, and meet with danger there;
Or it will seek me in another place,
And find me worse provided.

LADY NORTHUMBERLAND.
                      O, fly to Scotland,
Till that the nobles and the armed commons
Have of their puissance made a little taste.

LADY PERCY.
If they get ground and vantage of the king,
Then join you with them, like a rib of steel,
To make strength stronger; but, for all our loves,
First let them try themselves. So did your son;
He was so suffer'd: so came I a widow;
And never shall have length of life enough
To rain upon remembrance with mine eyes,
That it may grow and sprout as high as heaven,
For recordation to my noble husband.

NORTHUMBERLAND.
Come, come, go in with me. 'Tis with my mind
As with the tide swell'd up unto his height,
That makes a still-stand, running neither way:
Fain would I go to meet the archbishop,
But many thousand reasons hold me back.
I will resolve for Scotland: there am I,
Till time and vantage crave my company.
                              [Exeunt.

SCENE IV.

London.   The Boar's-Head Tavern in Eastcheap.

Enter two DRAWERS.

FIRST DRAWER.
WHAT the devil hast thou brought there?
  apple-johns? thou know'st Sir John cannot
endure an apple-john.

SECOND DRAWER.
Mass, thou say'st true. The prince once set a dish
of apple-johns before him, and told him there
were five more Sir Johns; and, putting off his hat,
said, 'I will now take my leave of these six dry,
round, old, wither'd knights.' It anger'd him to
the heart: but he hath forgot that.

FIRST DRAWER.
Why, then, cover, and set them down: and see if
thou canst find out Sneak's noise; Mistress Tearsheet would fain hear some music. Dispatch:—
the room where they supt is too hot; they'll come
in straight.

SECOND DRAWER.
Sirrah, here will be the prince and Master Pointz
anon; and they will put on two of our jerkins and
aprons; and Sir John must not know of it: Bardolph hath brought word.

FIRST DRAWER.
By the mass, here will be old utis: it will be an
excellent stratagem.

SECOND DRAWER.
I'll see if I can find out Sneak.   [Exit.
    Enter HOSTESS and DOLL TEARSHEET.

HOSTESS.
I'faith, sweetheart, methinks now you are in an
excellent good temperality: your pulsidge beats
as extraordinarily as heart would desire; and your
colour, I warrant you, is as red as any rose, in
good truth, la: but, i'faith, you have drunk too
much canaries; and that's a marvellous searching
wine, and it perfumes the blood ere one can say
'What's this?'—How do you now?

DOLL TEARSHEET.
Better than I was:—hem.

HOSTESS.
Why, that's well said; a good heart's worth gold.
—Lo, here comes Sir John.
        Enter FALSTAFF.

FALSTAFF [singing].
'When Arthur first in court'—Empty the jordan.
[Exit FIRST DRAWER.]—[singing] 'And was a
worthy king.'—How now, Mistress Doll!

HOSTESS.
Sick of a calm; yea, good faith.

FALSTAFF.
So is all her sect; an they be once in a calm, they
are sick.

DOLL TEARSHEET.
You muddy rascal, is that all the comfort you give
me?

FALSTAFF.
You make fat rascals, Mistress Doll.

DOLL TEARSHEET.
I make them! gluttony and diseases make them; I
make them not.

FALSTAFF.
If the cook help to make the gluttony, you help to
make the diseases, Doll; we catch of you, Doll,
we catch of you; grant that, my poor virtue, grant
that.

DOLL TEARSHEET.
Yea, joy,—our chains and our jewels.

FALSTAFF.
'Your brooches, pearls, and ouches:'—for to
serve bravely is to come halting off, you know: to
come off the breach with his pike bent bravely, and to
surgery bravely; to venture upon the charged
chambers bravely,—

DOLL TEARSHEET.

Hang yourself, you muddy conger, hang yourself!

HOSTESS.

By my troth, this is the old fashion; you two never meet but you fall to some discord: you are both, i' good truth, as rheumatic as two dry toasts; you cannot one bear with another's confirmities. What the good-year! one must bear, and that must be you [to DOLL TEARSHEET]: you are the weaker vessel, as they say, the emptier vessel.

DOLL TEARSHEET.

Can a weak empty vessel bear such a huge full hogshead? there's a whole merchant's venture of Bourdeaux stuff in him; you have not seen a hulk better stuft in the hold.—Come, I'll be friends with thee, Jack: thou art going to the wars; and whether I shall ever see thee again or no, there is nobody cares.

Enter FIRST DRAWER.

FIRST DRAWER.

Sir, Ancient Pistol's below, and would speak with you.

DOLL TEARSHEET.

Hang him, swaggering rascal! let him not come hither: it is the foul-mouth'd'st rogue in England.

HOSTESS.

If he swagger, let him not come here: no, by my faith; I must live among my neighbours; I'll no swaggerers: I am in good name and fame with the very best:—shut the door;—there comes no swaggerers here: I have not lived all this while, to have ʼwaggering now:—shut the door, I pray you.

FALSTAFF.

Dost thou hear, hostess?—

HOSTESS.

Pray ye, pacify yourself, Sir John: there comes no swaggerers here.

FALSTAFF.

Dost thou hear? it is mine ancient.

HOSTESS.

Tilly-fally, Sir John, ne'er tell me: your ancient swaggerer comes not in my doors. I was before Master Tisick, the deputy, t'other day; and, as he said to me, 'twas no longer ago than Wednesday last, 'I' good faith, neighbour Quickly,' says he;— Master Dumbe, our minister, was by then;— 'neighbour Quickly,' says he, 'receive those that are civil; for,' saith he, 'you are in an ill name:' —now a' said so, I can tell whereupon; 'for,' says he, 'you are an honest woman, and well thought on; therefore take heed what guests you receive: receive,' says he, 'no swaggering companions.' There comes none here: you would bless you to hear what he said: no, I'll no swaggerers.

FALSTAFF.

He's no swaggerer, hostess; a tame cheater, i' faith; you may stroke him as gently as a puppy greyhound; he'll not swagger with a Barbary hen, if her feathers turn back in any show of resistance. —Call him up, drawer. [*Exit* FIRST DRAWER.

HOSTESS.

Cheater, call you him? I will bar no honest man my house, nor no cheater: but I do not love swaggering; by my troth, I am the worse when one says 'swagger': feel, masters, how I shake; look you, I warrant you.

DOLL TEARSHEET.

So you do, hostess.

HOSTESS.

Do I? yea, in very truth, do I, an 'twere an aspen-leaf: I cannot abide swaggerers.

Enter PISTOL, BARDOLPH, *and* PAGE.

PISTOL.

God save you, Sir John!

FALSTAFF.

Welcome, Ancient Pistol. Here, Pistol, I charge you with a cup of sack: do you discharge upon mine hostess.

PISTOL.

I will discharge upon her, Sir John, with two bullets.

FALSTAFF.

She is pistol-proof, sir; you shall hardly offend her.

HOSTESS.

Come, I'll drink no proofs nor no bullets: I'll drink no more than will do me good, for no man's pleasure, I.

PISTOL.

Then to you, Mistress Dorothy; I will charge you.

DOLL TEARSHEET.

Charge me! I scorn you, scurvy companion. What! you poor, base, rascally, cheating, lack-linen mate! Away, you mouldy rogue, away! I am meat for your master.

PISTOL.

I know you, Mistress Dorothy.

DOLL TEARSHEET.

Away, you cut-purse rascal! you filthy bung, away! by this wine, I'll thrust my knife in your mouldy chaps, an you play the saucy cuttle with me. Away, you bottle-ale rascal! you basket-hilt stale juggler, you!—Since when, I pray you, sir? —God's light, with two points on your shoulder? much!

PISTOL.

God let me not live, but I will murder your ruff for this.

FALSTAFF.

No more, Pistol; I would not have you go off here: discharge yourself of our company, Pistol.

HOSTESS.

No, good Captain Pistol; not here, sweet captain.

DOLL TEARSHEET.

Captain! thou abominable damn'd cheater, art thou not ashamed to be call'd captain? An captains were of my mind, they would truncheon you out, for taking their names upon you before you have earn'd them. You a captain! you slave, for what? for tearing a poor whore's ruff in a bawdy-house!—He a captain! hang him, rogue! he lives upon mouldy stew'd prunes and dried cakes. A captain! God's light, these villains will make the word as odious as the word 'occupy;' which was an excellent good word before it was ill sorted: therefore captains had need look to't.

BARDOLPH.

Pray thee, go down, good ancient.

FALSTAFF.

Hark thee hither, Mistress Doll.

PISTOL.

Not I: I tell thee what, Corporal Bardolph,—I could tear her: I'll be revenged of her.

PAGE.

Pray thee, go down.

PISTOL.

I'll see her damned first;—to Pluto's damned
lake, by this hand, to the infernal deep, with
Erebus and tortures vile also. Hold hook and line,
say I. Down, down, dogs! down, faitors! Have we
not Hiren here?

HOSTESS.

Good Captain Peesel, be quiet; 'tis very late, i'
faith: I beseek you now, aggravate your choler.

PISTOL.

These be good humours, indeed! Shall pack-
horses,
And hollow pamper'd jades of Asia,
Which cannot go but thirty mile a-day,
Compare with Cæsars, and with Cannibals,
And Trojan Greeks? nay, rather damn them with
King Cerberus; and let the welkin roar.
Shall we fall foul for toys?

HOSTESS.

By my troth, captain, these are very bitter words.

BARDOLPH.

Be gone, good ancient: this will grow to a brawl
anon.

PISTOL.

Die men like dogs! give crowns like pins! Have
we not Hiren here?

HOSTESS.

O' my word, captain, there's none such here.
What the good-year! do you think I would deny
her? For God's sake, be quiet.

PISTOL.

Then feed, and be fat, my fair Calipolis.
Come, give's some sack.
Si fortune me tormente, sperato me contento.—
Fear we broadsides? no, let the fiend give fire:
Give me some sack:—and, sweetheart, lie thou
there.   [*Laying down his sword.*
Come we to full points here, and are etceteras
nothing?

FALSTAFF.

Pistol, I would be quiet.

PISTOL.

Sweet knight, I kiss thy neif: what! we have seen
the seven stars.

DOLL TEARSHEET.

For God's sake, thrust him down stairs: I cannot
endure such a fustian rascal.

PISTOL.

Thrust him down stairs! know we not Galloway
nags?

FALSTAFF.

Quoit him down, Bardolph, like a shove-groat
shilling: nay, an a' do nothing but speak nothing,
a' shall be nothing here.

BARDOLPH.

Come, get you down stairs.

PISTOL.

What! shall we have incision? shall we imbrue?—
                    [*Snatching up his sword.*
Then death rock me asleep, abridge my doleful
days!
Why, then, let grievous, ghastly, gaping wounds
Untwine the Sisters Three! Come, Atropos, I
say!

HOSTESS.

Here's goodly stuff toward!

FALSTAFF.

Give me my rapier, boy.

DOLL TEARSHEET.

I pray thee, Jack, I pray thee, do not draw.

FALSTAFF.

Get you down stairs.
                    [*Drawing, and driving* PISTOL *out.*

HOSTESS.

Here's a goodly tumult! I'll forswear keeping
house, afore I'll be in these tirrits and frights.
So; murder, I warrant now.—Alas, alas! put up
your naked weapons, put up your naked weapons.
                    [*Exeunt* PISTOL *and* BARDOLPH.

DOLL TEARSHEET.

I pray thee, Jack, be quiet; the rascal's gone. Ah,
you whoreson little valiant villain, you!

HOSTESS.

Are you not hurt i' th' groin? methought a' made
a shrewd thrust at your belly.

Enter BARDOLPH.

FALSTAFF.

Have you turn'd him out o' doors?

BARDOLPH.

Yes, sir. The rascal's drunk; you have hurt him,
sir, i' th' shoulder.

FALSTAFF.

A rascal! to brave me!

DOLL TEARSHEET.

Ah, you sweet little rogue, you! Alas, poor ape,
how thou sweat'st! come, let me wipe thy face;
come on, you whoreson chops:—ah, rogue! i'
faith, I love thee: thou art as valorous as Hector
of Troy, worth five of Agamemnon, and ten times
better than the Nine Worthies: ah, villain!

FALSTAFF.

A rascally slave! I will toss the rogue in a blanket.

DOLL TEARSHEET.

Do, an thou darest for thy heart: an thou dost,
I'll canvass thee between a pair of sheets.

Enter MUSICIANS.

PAGE.

The music is come, sir.

FALSTAFF.

Let them play:—play, sirs.—Sit on my knee,
Doll. [*Music.*] A rascal bragging slave! the rogue
fled from me like quicksilver.

DOLL TEARSHEET.

I'faith, and thou followdst him like a church.
Thou whoreson little tidy Bartholomew boar-pig,
when wilt thou leave fighting o' days and foining
o' nights, and begin to patch up thine old body
for heaven?

Enter, behind, PRINCE HENRY *and* POINTZ *disguised as* DRAWERS.

FALSTAFF.

Peace, good Doll! do not speak like a death's-
head; do not bid me remember mine end.

DOLL TEARSHEET.

Sirrah, what humour's the prince of?

FALSTAFF.

A good shallow young fellow: a' would have made
a good pantler, a' would ha' chipt bread well.

DOLL TEARSHEET.

They say Pointz has a good wit.

FALSTAFF.

He a good wit? hang him, baboon! his wit's as thick as Tewkesbury mustard; there's no more conceit in him than is in a mallet.

DOLL TEARSHEET.

Why does the prince love him so, then?

FALSTAFF.

Because their legs are both of a bigness; and a' plays at quoits well; and eats conger and fennel; and drinks off candles' ends for flap-dragons; and rides the wild-mare with the boys; and jumps upon joint-stools; and swears with a good grace; and wears his boots very smooth, like unto the sign of the leg; and breeds no bate with telling of discreet stories; and such other gambol faculties a' has, that show a weak mind and an able body, for the which the prince admits him: for the prince himself is such another; the weight of a hair will turn the scales between their avoirdupois.

PRINCE HENRY.

Would not this nave of a wheel have his ears cut off?

POINTZ.

Let's beat him before his whore.

PRINCE HENRY.

Look, whether the wither'd elder hath not his poll claw'd like a parrot.

POINTZ.

Is it not strange that desire should so many years outlive performance?

FALSTAFF.

Kiss me, Doll.

PRINCE HENRY.

Saturn and Venus this year in conjunction! what says the almanac to that?

POINTZ.

And, look, whether the fiery Trigon, his man, be not lisping to his master's own tables, his notebook, his counsel-keeper.

FALSTAFF.

Thou dost give me flattering busses.

DOLL TEARSHEET.

By my troth, I kiss thee with a most constant heart.

FALSTAFF.

I am old, I am old.

DOLL TEARSHEET.

I love thee better than I love e'er a scurvy young boy of them all.

FALSTAFF.

What stuff wilt have a kirtle of? I shall receive money o' Thursday: shalt have a cap to-morrow. A merry song, come: it grows late; we'll to bed. Thou'lt forget me when I am gone.

DOLL TEARSHEET.

By my troth, thou'lt set me a-weeping, an thou say'st so: prove that ever I dress myself handsome till thy return:—well, hearken the end.

FALSTAFF.

Some sack, Francis.

PRINCE HENRY and POINTZ.

Anon, anon, sir.   [Advancing.

FALSTAFF.

Ha! a bastard son of the king's?—And art not thou Pointz his brother?

PRINCE HENRY.

Why, thou globe of sinful continents, what a life dost thou lead!

FALSTAFF.

A better than thou: I am a gentleman; thou art a drawer.

PRINCE HENRY.

Very true, sir; and I come to draw you out by the ears.

HOSTESS.

O, the Lord preserve thy good Grace! by my troth, welcome to London. Now, the Lord bless that sweet face of thine! O Jesu, are you come from Wales?

FALSTAFF.

Thou whoreson mad compound of majesty,—by this light flesh and corrupt blood, thou art welcome.

[Leaning his hand upon DOLL TEARSHEET.

DOLL TEARSHEET.

How, you fat fool! I scorn you.

POINTZ.

My lord, he will drive you out of your revenge, and turn all to a merriment, if you take not the heat.

PRINCE HENRY.

You whoreson candle-mine, you, how vilely did you speak of me even now before this honest, virtuous, civil gentlewoman!

HOSTESS.

God's blessing of your good heart! and so she is, by my troth.

FALSTAFF.

Didst thou hear me?

PRINCE HENRY.

Yea; and you knew me, as you did when you ran away by Gadshill: you knew I was at your back, and spoke it on purpose to try my patience.

FALSTAFF.

No, no, no; not so; I did not think thou wast within hearing.

PRINCE HENRY.

I shall drive you, then, to confess the wilful abuse; and then I know how to handle you.

FALSTAFF.

No abuse, Hal, o' mine honour; no abuse.

PRINCE HENRY.

Not,—to dispraise me, and call me pantler, and bread-chipper, and I know not what!

FALSTAFF.

No abuse, Hal!

POINTZ.

No abuse!

FALSTAFF.

No abuse, Ned, i' th' world; honest Ned, none. I dispraised him before the wicked, that the wicked might not fall in love with him;—in which doing, I have done the part of a careful friend and a true subject, and thy father is to give me thanks for it. No abuse, Hal;—none, Ned, none;—no, faith, boys, none.

PRINCE HENRY.

See now, whether pure fear and entire cowardice doth not make thee wrong this virtuous gentlewoman to close with us. Is she of the wicked? is thine hostess here of the wicked? or is thy boy of the wicked? or honest Bardolph, whose zeal burns in his nose, of the wicked?

POINTZ.

Answer, thou dead elm, answer.

FALSTAFF.

The fiend hath prickt down Bardolph irrecoverable; and his face is Lucifer's privy-kitchen, where he doth nothing but roast malt-worms. For the boy,—there is a good angel about him; but the devil outbids him too.

PRINCE HENRY.

For the women?

FALSTAFF.

For one of them,—she is in hell already, and burns, poor soul! For the other,—I owe her money; and whether she be damn'd for that, I know not.

HOSTESS.

No, I warrant you.

FALSTAFF.

No, I think thou art not; I think thou art quit for that. Marry, there is another indictment upon thee, for suffering flesh to be eaten in thy house, contrary to the law; for the which I think thou wilt howl.

HOSTESS.

All victuallers do so: what's a joint of mutton or two in a whole Lent?

PRINCE HENRY.

You, gentlewoman,—

DOLL TEARSHEET.

What says your Grace?

FALSTAFF.

His grace says that which his flesh rebels against.

[Knocking within.

HOSTESS.

Who knocks so loud at door?—Look to the door there, Francis.

Enter PETO.

PRINCE HENRY.

Peto, how now! what news?

PETO.

The king your father is at Westminster;
And there are twenty weak and wearied posts
Come from the north: and, as I came along,
I met and overtook a dozen captains,
Bare-headed, sweating, knocking at the taverns,
And asking every one for Sir John Falstaff.

PRINCE HENRY.

By heaven, Pointz, I feel me much to blame,
So idly to profane the precious time;
When tempest of commotion, like the south,
Borne with black vapour, doth begin to melt,
And drop upon our bare unarmed heads.   [night.
Give me my sword and cloak.—Falstaff, good-

[Exeunt PRINCE HENRY, POINTZ, PETO,
and BARDOLPH.

FALSTAFF.

Now comes in the sweetest morsel of the night, and we must hence, and leave it unpickt. [Knocking within.] More knocking at the door!

Enter BARDOLPH.

How now! what's the matter?

BARDOLPH.

You must away to court, sir, presently;
A dozen captains stay at door for you.

FALSTAFF [to the PAGE].

Pay the musicians, sirrah.—Farewell, hostess;—farewell, Doll.—You see, my good wenches, how men of merit are sought after: the undeserver may sleep, when the man of action is call'd on. Farewell, good wenches: if I be not sent away post, I will see you again ere I go.

DOLL TEARSHEET.

I cannot speak;—if my heart be not ready to burst,—well, sweet Jack, have a care of thyself.

FALSTAFF.

Farewell, farewell.

[Exeunt FALSTAFF and BARDOLPH.

HOSTESS.

Well, fare thee well: I have known thee these twenty-nine years, come peascod-time; but an honester and truer-hearted man,—well, fare thee well.

BARDOLPH [within].

Mistress Tearsheet!

HOSTESS.

What's the matter?

BARDOLPH [within].

Bid Mistress Tearsheet come to my master.

HOSTESS.

O, run, Doll, run; run, good Doll: come [she comes blubber'd]; yea, will you come, Doll?

[Exeunt.

ACT III. SCENE I.

Westminster.   A room in the palace.

Enter KING HENRY *in his nightgown, with a*
PAGE.

KING HENRY.

GO call the Earls of Surrey and of Warwick;
But, ere they come, bid them o'er-read these letters,
And well consider of them: make good speed.

[Exit PAGE.

How many thousand of my poorest subjects
Are at this hour asleep!—O sleep, O gentle sleep,
Nature's soft nurse, how have I frighted thee,
That thou no more wilt weigh my eyelids down,
And steep my senses in forgetfulness?
Why rather, sleep, liest thou in smoky cribs,
Upon uneasy pallets stretching thee,
And husht with buzzing night-flies to thy slumber,
Than in the perfumed chambers of the great,
Under the canopies of costly state,
And lull'd with sound of sweetest melody?
O thou dull god, why liest thou with the vile
In loathsome beds, and leavest the kingly couch
A watch-case or a common 'larum-bell?
Wilt thou upon the high and giddy mast
Seal up the ship-boy's eyes, and rock his brains
In cradle of the rude imperious surge,
And in the visitation of the winds,
Who take the ruffian billows by the top,
Curling their monstrous heads, and hanging them
With deafening clamour in the slippery shrouds,
That, with the hurly, death itself awakes?—
Canst thou, O partial sleep, give thy repose
To the wet sea-boy in an hour so rude;
And in the calmest and most stillest night,

With all appliances and means to boot,
Deny it to a king? Then, happy low, lie down!
Uneasy lies the head that wears a crown.

Enter WARWICK *and* SURREY.

WARWICK.

Many good morrows to your majesty!

KING HENRY.

Is it good morrow, lords?

WARWICK.

'Tis one o'clock, and past.

KING HENRY.

Why, then, good morrow to you all, my lords.
Have you read o'er the letters that I sent you?

WARWICK.

We have, my liege.

KING HENRY.

Then you perceive the body of our kingdom
How foul it is; what rank diseases grow,
And with what danger, near the heart of it.

WARWICK.

It is but as a body yet distemper'd;
Which to his former strength may be restored
With good advice and little medicine:
My Lord Northumberland will soon be cool'd.

KING HENRY.

O God! that one might read the book of fate,
And see the revolution of the times
Make mountains level, and the continent,
Weary of solid firmness, melt itself
Into the sea! and, other times, to see
The beachy girdle of the ocean
Too wide for Neptune's hips; how chances mock,
And changes fill the cup of alteration
With divers liquors! O, if this were seen,
The happiest youth,—viewing his progress
    through,
What perils past, what crosses to ensue,—
Would shut the book, and sit him down and die.
'Tis not ten years gone   [friends,
Since Richard and Northumberland, great
Did feast together, and in two years after
Were they at wars: it is but eight years since
This Percy was the man nearest my soul;
Who like a brother toil'd in my affairs,
And laid his love and life under my foot;
Yea, for my sake, even to the eyes of Richard
Gave him defiance. But which of you was by—
[*to* WARWICK] You, cousin Nevil, as I may re-
    member—
When Richard,—with his eye brimful of tears,
Then checkt and rated by Northumberland,—
Did speak these words, now proved a prophecy?
'Northumberland, thou ladder by the which
My cousin Bolingbroke ascends my throne,'—
Though then, God knows, I had no such intent,
But that necessity so bow'd the state,
That I and greatness were compell'd to kiss:—
'The time shall come,' thus did he follow it,
'The time will come, that foul sin, gathering
    head,
Shall break into corruption:'—so went on,
Foretelling this same time's condition,
And the division of our amity.

WARWICK.

There is a history in all men's lives,
Figuring the nature of the times deceased;
The which observed, a man may prophesy,
With a near aim, of the main chance of things
As yet not come to life, which in their seeds
And weak beginnings lie intreasured.
Such things become the hatch and brood of time;
And, by the necessary form of this,
King Richard might create a perfect guess,
That great Northumberland, then false to him,
Would of that seed grow to a greater falseness;
Which should not find a ground to root upon,
Unless on you.

KING HENRY.

    Are these things, then, necessities?
Then let us meet them like necessities;—
And that same word even now cries out on us:
They say the bishop and Northumberland
Are fifty thousand strong.

WARWICK.

    It cannot be, my lord;
Rumour doth double, like the voice and echo,
The numbers of the fear'd. Please it your Grace
To go to bed. Upon my soul, my lord,
The powers that you already have sent forth
Shall bring this prize in very easily.
To comfort you the more, I have received
A certain instance that Glendower is dead.
Your majesty hath been this fortnight ill;
And these unseason'd hours perforce must add
Unto your sickness.

KING HENRY.

    I will take your counsel:
And were these inward wars once out of hand,
We would, dear lords, unto the Holy Land.

[*Exeunt.*

SCENE II.

Glostershire.   *Court before* JUSTICE
SHALLOW'S *house.*

Enter SHALLOW *and* SILENCE; MOULDY,
SHADOW, WART, FEEBLE, BULLCALF, *and*
SERVANTS, *behind.*

SHALLOW.

COME on, come on, come on, sir; give me
your hand, sir, give me your hand, sir: an
early stirrer, by the rood! And how doth my good
cousin Silence?

SILENCE.

Good morrow, good cousin Shallow.

SHALLOW.

And how doth my good cousin, your bedfellow?
and your fairest daughter and mine, my god-
daughter Ellen?

SILENCE.

Alas, a black ousel, cousin Shallow!

SHALLOW.

By yea and nay, sir, I dare say my cousin William
is become a good scholar: he is at Oxford still, is
he not?

SILENCE.

Indeed, sir, to my cost.

SHALLOW.

A' must, then, to the inns o' court shortly: I was
once of Clement's-inn, where I think they will
talk of mad Shallow yet.

SILENCE.

You were call'd 'lusty Shallow' then, cousin.

SHALLOW.

By the mass, I was call'd any thing; and I would have done any thing indeed too, and roundly too. There was I, and little John Doit of Staffordshire, and black George Barnes, and Francis Pickbone, and Will Squele a Cotsall man,—you had not four such swinge-bucklers in all the inns o' court again: and, I may say to you, we knew where the bona-robas were, and had the best of them all at commandment. Then was Jack Falstaff, now Sir John, a boy, and page to Thomas Mowbray, duke of Norfolk.

SILENCE.

This Sir John, cousin, that comes hither anon about soldiers?

SHALLOW.

The same Sir John, the very same. I see him break Skogan's head at the court-gate, when a' was a crack not thus high: and the very same day did I fight with one Sampson Stockfish, a fruiterer, behind Gray's-inn. Jesu, Jesu, the mad days that I have spent! and to see how many of my old acquaintance are dead!

SILENCE.

We shall all follow, cousin.

SHALLOW.

Certain, 'tis certain; very sure, very sure: death, as the Psalmist saith, is certain to all; all shall die.—How a good yoke of bullocks at Stamford fair?

SILENCE.

Truly, cousin, I was not there.

SHALLOW.

Death is certain.—Is old Double of your town living yet?

SILENCE.

Dead, sir.

SHALLOW.

Jesu, Jesu, dead!—a' drew a good bow;—and dead!—a' shot a fine shoot:—John o' Gaunt loved him well, and betted much money on his head. Dead!—a' would have clapt i' th' clout at twelve score; and carried you a forehand shaft a fourteen and fourteen and a half, that it would have done a man's heart good to see.—How a score of ewes now?

SILENCE.

Thereafter as they be: a score of good ewes may be worth ten pounds.

SHALLOW.

And is old Double dead?

SILENCE.

Here come two of Sir John Falstaff's men, as I think.

Enter BARDOLPH *and one with him.*

BARDOLPH.

Good morrow, honest gentlemen: I beseech you, which is Justice Shallow?

SHALLOW.

I am Robert Shallow, sir; a poor esquire of this county, and one of the king's justices of the peace: what is your good pleasure with me?

BARDOLPH.

My captain, sir, commends him to you; my captain, Sir John Falstaff,—a tall gentleman, by heaven, and a most gallant leader.

SHALLOW.

He greets me well, sir. I knew him a good back-sword man. How doth the good knight? may I ask how my lady his wife doth?

BARDOLPH.

Sir, pardon; a soldier is better accommodated than with a wife.

SHALLOW.

It is well said, in faith, sir; and it is well said indeed too. Better accommodated!—it is good; yea, indeed, is it: good phrases are surely, and ever were, very commendable. Accommodated!—it comes of *accommodo:* very good; a good phrase.

BARDOLPH.

Pardon, sir; I have heard the word. Phrase call you it? by this good day, I know not the phrase; but I will maintain the word with my sword to be a soldier-like word, and a word of exceeding good command, by heaven. Accommodated; that is, when a man is, as they say, accommodated; or when a man is, being, whereby a' may be thought to be accommodated; which is an excellent thing.

SHALLOW.

It is very just.—Look, here comes good Sir John.

Enter FALSTAFF.

Give me your good hand, give me your worship's good hand: by my troth, you like well, and bear your years very well: welcome, good Sir John.

FALSTAFF.

I am glad to see you well, good Master Robert Shallow:—Master Surecard, as I think?

SHALLOW.

No, Sir John; it is my cousin Silence, in commission with me.

FALSTAFF.

Good Master Silence, it well befits you should be of the peace.

SILENCE.

Your good worship is welcome.

FALSTAFF.

Fie! this is hot weather, gentlemen. Have you provided me here half a dozen sufficient men?

SHALLOW.

Marry, have we, sir. Will you sit?

FALSTAFF.

Let me see them, I beseech you.

SHALLOW.

Where's the roll? where's the roll? where's the roll?—Let me see, let me see, let me see. So, so, so, so, so, so, so: yea, marry, sir:—Ralph Mouldy! —let them appear as I call; let them do so, let them do so.—Let me see; where is Mouldy?

MOULDY.

Here, an't please you.

SHALLOW.

What think you, Sir John? a good-limb'd fellow; young, strong, and of good friends.

FALSTAFF.

Is thy name Mouldy?

MOULDY.

Yea, an't please you.

FALSTAFF.

'Tis the more time thou wert used.

SHALLOW.

Ha, ha, ha! most excellent, i'faith! things that are

mouldy lack use: very singular good!—in faith,
well said, Sir John; very well said.

FALSTAFF [*to* SHALLOW].
Prick him.

MOULDY.
I was prickt well enough before, an you could
have let me alone: my old dame will be undone
now, for one to do her husbandry and her drud-
gery: you need not to have prickt me; there are
other men fitter to go out than I.

FALSTAFF.
Go to: peace, Mouldy; you shall go. Mouldy, it is
time you were spent.

MOULDY.
Spent!

SHALLOW.
Peace, fellow, peace; stand aside: know you where
you are?—For th'other, Sir John:—let me see;—
Simon Shadow!

FALSTAFF.
Yea, marry, let me have him to sit under: he's like
to be a cold soldier.

SHALLOW.
Where's Shadow?

SHADOW.
Here, sir.

FALSTAFF.
Shadow, whose son art thou?

SHADOW.
My mother's son, sir.

FALSTAFF.
Thy mother's son! like enough; and thy father's
shadow: so the son of the female is the shadow of
the male: it is often so, indeed; but much of the
father's substance!

SHALLOW.
Do you like him, Sir John?

FALSTAFF.
Shadow will serve for summer,—prick him; for
we have a number of shadows to fill up the mus-
ter-book.

SHALLOW.
Thomas Wart!

FALSTAFF.
Where's he?

WART.
Here, sir.

FALSTAFF.
Is thy name Wart?

WART.
Yea, sir.

FALSTAFF.
Thou art a very ragged wart.

SHALLOW.
Shall I prick him, Sir John?

FALSTAFF.
It were superfluous; for his apparel is built upon
his back, and the whole frame stands upon pins:
prick him no more.

SHALLOW.
Ha, ha, ha!—you can do it, sir; you can do it: I
commend you well—Francis Feeble!

FEEBLE.
Here, sir.

FALSTAFF.
What trade art thou, Feeble?

FEEBLE.
A woman's tailor, sir.

SHALLOW.
Shall I prick him, sir?

FALSTAFF.
You may: but if he had been a man's tailor, he'ld
ha' prickt you.—Wilt thou make as many holes in
an enemy's battle as thou hast done in a woman's
petticoat?

FEEBLE.
I will do my good will, sir; you can have no more.

FALSTAFF.
Well said, good woman's tailor! well said, courageous Feeble! thou wilt be as valiant as the
wrathful dove or most magnanimous mouse.—
Prick the woman's tailor well, Master Shallow;
deep, Master Shallow.

FEEBLE.
I would Wart might have gone, sir.

FALSTAFF.
I would thou wert a man's tailor, that thou
mightst mend him, and make him fit to go. I cannot put him to a private soldier, that is the leader
of so many thousands: let that suffice, most
forcible Feeble.

FEEBLE.
It shall suffice, sir.

FALSTAFF.
I am bound to thee, reverend Feeble.—Who is
next?

SHALLOW.
Peter Bullcalf o' th' green!

FALSTAFF.
Yea, marry, let's see Bullcalf.

BULLCALF.
Here, sir.

FALSTAFF.
'Fore God, a likely fellow!—Come, prick me
Bullcalf till he roar again.

BULLCALF.
O Lord! good my lord captain,—

FALSTAFF.
What, dost thou roar before thou art prickt?

BULLCALF.
O Lord, sir! I am a diseased man.

FALSTAFF.
What disease hast thou?

BULLCALF.
A whoreson cold, sir,—a cough, sir,—which I
caught with ringing in the king's affairs upon his
coronation-day, sir.

FALSTAFF.
Come, thou shalt go to the wars in a gown; we will
have away thy cold; and I will take such order,
that thy friends shall ring for thee.—Is here all?

SHALLOW.
Here is two more call'd than your number; you
must have but four here, sir:—and so, I pray you,
go in with me to dinner.

FALSTAFF.
Come, I will go drink with you, but I cannot
tarry dinner. I am glad to see you, by my troth,
Master Shallow.

SHALLOW.
O, Sir John, do you remember since we lay all
night in the windmill in Saint George's field?

FALSTAFF.

No more of that, good Master Shallow, no more of that.

SHALLOW.

Ha, 'twas a merry night. And is Jane Nightwork alive?

FALSTAFF.

She lives, Master Shallow.

SHALLOW.

She never could away with me.

FALSTAFF.

Never, never; she would always say she could not abide Master Shallow.

SHALLOW.

By the mass, I could anger her to the heart. She was then a bona-roba. Doth she hold her own well?

FALSTAFF.

Old, old, Master Shallow.

SHALLOW.

Nay, she must be old; she cannot choose but be old; certain she's old; and had Robin Nightwork by old Nightwork before I came to Clement's-inn.

SILENCE.

That's fifty-five year ago.

SHALLOW.

Ha, cousin Silence, that thou hadst seen that that this knight and I have seen!—Ha, Sir John, said I well?

FALSTAFF.

We have heard the chimes at midnight, Master Shallow.

SHALLOW.

That we have, that we have, that we have; in faith, Sir John, we have: our watch-word was, 'Hem, boys!'—Come, let's to dinner; come, let's to dinner:—Jesus, the days that we have seen!—come, come.

[Exeunt FALSTAFF, SHALLOW, and SILENCE.

BULLCALF.

Good master corporate Bardolph, stand my friend; and here's four Harry ten shillings in French crowns for you. In very truth, sir, I had as lief be hang'd, sir, as go: and yet, for mine own part, sir, I do not care; but rather, because I am unwilling, and, for mine own part, have a desire to stay with my friends; else, sir, I did not care, for mine own part, so much.

BARDOLPH.

Go to; stand aside.

MOULDY.

And, good master corporal captain, for my old dame's sake, stand my friend: she has nobody to do any thing about her when I am gone; and she is old, and cannot help herself: you shall have forty, sir.

BARDOLPH.

Go to; stand aside.

FEEBLE.

By my troth, I care not; a man can die but once;—we owe God a death: I'll ne'er bear a base mind: an't be my destiny, so; an't be not, so: no man's too good to serve's prince; and let it go which way it will, he that dies this year is quit for the next.

BARDOLPH.

Well said; thou'rt a good fellow.

FEEBLE.

Faith, I'll bear no base mind.

Enter FALSTAFF, SHALLOW, and SILENCE.

FALSTAFF.

Come, sir, which men shall I have?

SHALLOW.

Four of which you please.

BARDOLPH.

Sir, a word with you:—I have three pound to free Mouldy and Bullcalf.

FALSTAFF.

Go to; well.

SHALLOW.

Come, Sir John, which four will you have?

FALSTAFF.

Do you choose for me.

SHALLOW.

Marry, then,—Mouldy, Bullcalf, Feeble, and Shadow.

FALSTAFF.

Mouldy and Bullcalf:—for you, Mouldy, stay at home till you are past service:—and for your part, Bullcalf, grow till you come unto it:—I will none of you.

SHALLOW.

Sir John, Sir John, do not yourself wrong: they are your likeliest men, and I would have you served with the best.

FALSTAFF.

Will you tell me, Master Shallow, how to choose a man? Care I for the limb, the thews, the stature, bulk, and big assemblance of a man! Give me the spirit, Master Shallow.—Here's Wart;—you see what a ragged appearance it is: a' shall charge you, and discharge you, with the motion of a pewterer's hammer; come off, and on, swifter than he that gibbets-on the brewer's bucket. And this same half-faced fellow, Shadow,—give me this man: he presents no mark to the enemy,—the foeman may with as great aim level at the edge of a penknife. And, for a retreat,—how swiftly will this Feeble, the woman's tailor, run off! O, give me the spare men, and spare me the great ones.—Put me a caliver into Wart's hand, Bardolph.

BARDOLPH.

Hold, Wart, traverse; thus, thus, thus.

FALSTAFF.

Come, manage me your caliver. So:—very well —go to:—very good:—exceeding good.—O, give me always a little, lean, old, chapt, bald shot.— Well said, i'faith, Wart: thou'rt a good scab; hold, there's a tester for thee.

SHALLOW.

He is not his craft's-master; he doth not do it right. I remember at Mile-end Green,—when I lay at Clement's-inn,—I was then Sir Dagonet in Arthur's show,—there was a little quiver fellow, and a' would manage you his piece thus; and a' would about and about, and come you in and come you in: 'rah, tah, tah,' would a' say; 'bounce' would a' say; and away again would a' go, and again would a' come:—I shall ne'er see such a fellow.

FALSTAFF.

These fellows will do well, Master Shallow.—
God keep you, Master Silence: I will not use
many words with you.—Fare you well, gentlemen
both: I thank you: I must a dozen mile to-night.
—Bardolph, give the soldiers coats.

SHALLOW.

Sir John, the Lord bless you! God prosper your
affairs! God send us peace! As you return, visit
our house; let our old acquaintance be renew'd:
peradventure I will with ye to the court.

FALSTAFF.

'Fore God, I would you would, Master Shallow.

SHALLOW.

Go to; I have spoke at a word; God keep you.

FALSTAFF.

Fare you well, gentle gentlemen. [*Exeunt* SHAL-
LOW *and* SILENCE.] On, Bardolph; lead the men
away. [*Exeunt* BARDOLPH, RECRUITS, &c.] As I
return, I will fetch off these justices: I do see the
bottom of Justice Shallow. Lord, Lord, how subject we old men are to this vice of lying! This
same starved justice hath done nothing but prate
to me of the wildness of his youth, and the feats
he hath done about Turnbull-street; and every
third word a lie, duer paid to the hearer than the
Turk's tribute. I do remember him at Clement's-
inn, like a man made after supper of a cheese-
paring: when a' was naked, he was, for all the
world, like a forkt radish, with a head fantastically
carved upon it with a knife; a' was so forlorn, that
his dimensions to any thick sight were invisible:
a' was the very genius of famine; yet lecherous as
a monkey, and the whores call'd him mandrake:
a' came ever in the rearward of the fashion; and
sung those tunes to the overscutcht huswives that
he heard the carmen whistle, and sware they were
his Fancies or his Good-nights. And now is this
Vice's dagger become a squire, and talks as familiarly of John o' Gaunt as if he had been sworn
brother to him; and I'll be sworn a' ne'er saw him
but once in the Tilt-yard; and then he burst his
head for crowding among the marshal's men. I
saw it, and told John o' Gaunt he beat his own
name; for you might have thrust him and all his
apparel into an eel-skin; the case of a treble haut-
boy was a mansion for him, a court:—and now
has he land and beefs. Well, I'll be acquainted
with him, if I return; and it shall go hard but I'll
make him a philosopher's two stones to me: if the
young dace be a bait for the old pike, I see no
reason, in the law of nature, but I may snap at
him. Let time shape, and there an end. [*Exit.*

ACT IV. SCENE I.

Yorkshire. Gaultree Forest.

Enter the ARCHBISHOP OF YORK, MOWBRAY,
HASTINGS, *and others.*

ARCHBISHOP OF YORK.

WHAT is this forest call'd?

HASTINGS.

'Tis Gaultree Forest, an't shall please your
Grace.

ARCHBISHOP OF YORK.

Here stand, my lords; and send discoverers forth
To know the numbers of our enemies.

HASTINGS.

We have sent forth already.

ARCHBISHOP OF YORK.

'Tis well done.
My friends and brethren in these great affairs,
I must acquaint you that I have received
New-dated letters from Northumberland;
Their cold intent, tenour, and substance, thus:—
Here doth he wish his person, with such powers
As might hold sortance with his quality,
The which he could not levy; whereupon
He is retired, to ripe his growing fortunes,
To Scotland; and concludes in hearty prayers
That your attempts may overlive the hazard
And fearful meeting of their opposite.

MOWBRAY.

Thus do the hopes we have in him touch ground,
And dash themselves to pieces.

Enter a MESSENGER.

HASTINGS.

Now, what news?

MESSENGER.

West of this forest, scarcely off a mile,
In goodly form comes on the enemy,
And, by the ground they hide, I judge their
number
Upon or near the rate of thirty thousand.

MOWBRAY.

The just proportion that we gave them out.
Let us sway on, and face them in the field.

ARCHBISHOP OF YORK.

What well-appointed leader fronts us here?

MOWBRAY.

I think it is my Lord of Westmoreland.

Enter WESTMORELAND.

WESTMORELAND.

Health and fair greeting from our general,
The prince, Lord John and Duke of Lancaster.

ARCHBISHOP OF YORK.

Say on, my Lord of Westmoreland, in peace:
What doth concern your coming?

WESTMORELAND.

Then, my lord,
Unto your Grace do I in chief address
The substance of my speech. If that rebellion
Came like itself, in base and abject routs,
Led on by heady youth, guarded with rags,
And countenanced by boys and beggary,—
I say, if damn'd commotion so appear'd,
In his true, native, and most proper shape,
You, reverend father, and these noble lords,
Had not been here, to dress the ugly form
Of base and bloody insurrection
With your fair honours. You, lord archbishop,—
Whose see is by a civil peace maintain'd;
Whose beard the silver hand of peace hath toucht;
Whose learning and good letters peace hath tu-
tor'd;
Whose white investments figure innocence,
The dove and very blessed spirit of peace,—
Wherefore do you so ill translate yourself
Out of the speech of peace, that bears such grace,
Into the harsh and boisterous tongue of war;

Turning your books to greaves, your ink to blood,
Your pens to lances, and your tongue divine
To a loud trumpet and a point of war?
ARCHBISHOP OF YORK.
Wherefore do I this?—so the question stands.
Briefly to this end:—we are all diseased;
And with our surfeiting and wanton hours
Have brought ourselves into a burning fever,
And we must bleed for it: of which disease
Our late king, Richard, being infected, died.
But, my most noble Lord of Westmoreland,
I take not on me here as a physician;
Nor do I, as an enemy to peace,
Troop in the throngs of military men;
But, rather, show awhile like fearful war,
To diet rank minds sick of happiness,
And purge th'obstructions which begin to stop
Our very veins of life. Hear me more plainly.
I have in equal balance justly weigh'd
What wrongs our arms may do, what wrongs we
   suffer,
And find our griefs heavier than our offences.
We see which way the stream of time doth run,
And are enforced from our most quiet sphere
By the rough torrent of occasion;
And have the summary of all our griefs,
When time shall serve, to show in articles;
Which long ere this we offer'd to the king,
And might by no suit gain our audience:
When we are wrong'd, and would unfold our
   griefs,
We are denied access unto his person
Even by those men that most have done us wrong.
The dangers of the days but newly gone,
Whose memory is written on the earth
With yet-appearing blood, and the examples
Of every minute's instance, present now,
Have put us in these ill-beseeming arms;
Not to break peace, or any branch of it,
But to establish here a peace indeed,
Concurring both in name and quality.
WESTMORELAND.
When ever yet was your appeal denied?
Wherein have you been galled by the king?
What peer hath been suborn'd to grate on you;—
That you should seal this lawless bloody book
Of forged rebellion with a seal divine,
And consecrate commotion's bitter edge?
ARCHBISHOP OF YORK.
My brother general, the commonwealth,
To brother born an household cruelty,
I make my quarrel in particular.
WESTMORELAND.
There is no need of any such redress;
Or if there were, it not belongs to you.
MOWBRAY.
Why not to him in part, and to us all
That feel the bruises of the days before,
And suffer the condition of these times
To lay a heavy and unequal hand
Upon our honours?
WESTMORELAND.
        O, my good Lord Mowbray,
Construe the times to their necessities,
And you shall say indeed, it is the time,
And not the king, that doth you injuries.

Yet, for your part, it not appears to me,
Either from the king, or in the present time,
That you should have an inch of any ground
To build a grief on: were you not restored
To all the Duke of Norfolk's signiories,
Your noble and right-well-remember'd father's?
MOWBRAY.
What thing, in honour, had my father lost,
That need to be revived and breathed in me?
The king, that loved him, as the state stood then,
Was, force perforce, compell'd to banish him:
And then that Henry Bolingbroke and he—
Being mounted and both roused in their seats,
Their neighing coursers daring of the spur,
Their armed staves in charge, their beavers
   down,
Their eyes of fire sparkling through sights of steel,
And the loud trumpet blowing them together,—
Then, then, when there was nothing could have
   stay'd
My father from the breast of Bolingbroke,
O, when the king did throw his warder down,
His own life hung upon the staff he threw:
Then threw he down himself, and all their lives
That by indictment and by dint of sword
Have since miscarried under Bolingbroke.
WESTMORELAND.
You speak, Lord Mowbray, now you know not
   what.
The Earl of Hereford was reputed then
In England the most valiant gentleman:
Who knows on whom fortune would then have
   smiled?
But if your father had been victor there,
He ne'er had borne it out of Coventry:
For all the country, in a general voice,
Cried hate upon him; and all their prayers and
   love
Were set on Hereford, whom they doted on,
And blest and graced indeed, more than the king.
But this is mere digression from my purpose.—
Here come I from our princely general
To know your griefs; to tell you from his Grace
That he will give you audience; and wherein
It shall appear that your demands are just,
You shall enjoy them,—every thing set off
That might so much as think you enemies.
MOWBRAY.
But he hath forced us to compel this offer;
And it proceeds from policy, not love.
WESTMORELAND.
Mowbray, you overween to take it so;
This offer comes from mercy, not from fear:
For, lo! within a ken our army lies;
Upon mine honour, all too confident
To give admittance to a thought of fear.
Our battle is more full of names than yours,
Our men more perfect in the use of arms,
Our armour all as strong, our cause the best;
Then reason will our hearts should be as good:
Say you not, then, our offer is compell'd.
MOWBRAY.
Well, by my will we shall admit no parley.
WESTMORELAND.
That argues but the shame of your offence:
A rotten case abides no handling.

470

HASTINGS.
Hath the Prince John a full commission,
In very ample virtue of his father,
To hear and absolutely to determine
Of what conditions we shall stand upon?
WESTMORELAND.
That is intended in the general's name:
I muse you make so slight a question.
ARCHBISHOP OF YORK.
Then take, my Lord of Westmoreland, this
schedule,
For this contains our general grievances:
Each several article herein redrest,
All members of our cause, both here and hence,
That are insinew'd to this action,
Acquitted by a true substantial form
And present execution of our wills
To us and to our purposes consign'd,—
We come within our awful banks again,
And knit our powers to the arm of peace.
WESTMORELAND.
This will I show the general. Please you, lords,
In sight of both our battles we may meet;
And either end in peace,—which God so
frame!—
Or to the place of difference call the swords
Which must decide it.
ARCHBISHOP OF YORK.
My lord, we will do so.
[Exit WESTMORELAND.
MOWBRAY.
There is a thing within my bosom tells me
That no conditions of our peace can stand.
HASTINGS.
Fear you not that: if we can make our peace
Upon such large terms and so absolute
As our conditions shall consist upon,
Our peace shall stand as firm as rocky mountains.
MOWBRAY.
Yea, but our valuation shall be such,
That every slight and false-derived cause,
Yea, every idle, nice, and wanton reason
Shall to the king taste of this action;
That, were our royal faiths martyrs in love,
We shall be winnow'd with so rough a wind,
That even our corn shall seem as light as chaff,
And good from bad find no partition.
ARCHBISHOP OF YORK.
No, no, my lord. Note this,—the king is weary
Of dainty and such picking grievances:
For he hath found, to end one doubt by death
Revives two greater in the heirs of life;
And therefore will he wipe his tables clean,
And keep no tell-tale to his memory,
That may repeat and history his loss
To new remembrance: for full well he knows
He cannot so precisely weed this land
As his misdoubts present occasion:
His foes are so enrooted with his friends,
That, plucking to unfix an enemy,
He doth unfasten so and shake a friend.
So that this land, like an offensive wife
That hath enraged him on to offer strokes,
As he is striking, holds his infant up,
And hangs resolved correction in the arm
That was uprear'd to execution.

HASTINGS.
Besides, the king hath wasted all his rods
On late offenders, that he now doth lack
The very instruments of chastisement:
So that his power, like to a fangless lion,
May offer, but not hold.
ARCHBISHOP OF YORK.
'Tis very true:
And therefore be assured, my good lord marshal,
If we do now make our atonement well,
Our peace will, like a broken limb united,
Grow stronger for the breaking.
MOWBRAY.
Be it so.
Here is return'd my Lord of Westmoreland.
Enter WESTMORELAND.
WESTMORELAND.
The prince is here at hand: pleaseth your lordship
To meet his Grace just distance 'tween our
armies.
MOWBRAY.
Your Grace of York, in God's name, then, set
forward.
ARCHBISHOP OF YORK.
Before, and greet his Grace:—my lord, we come.
[Exeunt.

SCENE II.
Another part of the forest.

Enter, from one side, MOWBRAY, *the* ARCH-
BISHOP, HASTINGS, *and others; from the
other side,* PRINCE JOHN OF LANCASTER,
WESTMORELAND, OFFICERS, *and* ATTEND-
ANTS.

PRINCE JOHN OF LANCASTER.
YOU are well encounter'd here, my cousin
Mowbray:—
Good day to you, gentle lord archbishop;—
And so to you, Lord Hastings,—and to all.—
My Lord of York, it better show'd with you,
When that your flock, assembled by the bell,
Encircled you to hear with reverence
Your exposition on the holy text,
Than now to see you here an iron man,
Cheering a rout of rebels with your drum,
Turning the word to sword, and life to death.
That man that sits within a monarch's heart,
And ripens in the sunshine of his favour,
Would he abuse the countenance of the king,
Alack, what mischiefs might he set abroach,
In shadow of such greatness! With you, lord
bishop,
It is even so. Who hath not heard it spoken,
How deep you were within the books of God?
To us the speaker in his parliament;
To us th' imagined voice of God himself;
The very opener and intelligencer
Between the grace, the sanctities of heaven
And our dull workings. O, who shall believe,
But you misuse the reverence of your place,
Employ the countenance and grace of heaven,
As a false favourite doth his prince's name,
In deeds dishonourable ? You have ta'en up,
Under the counterfeited zeal of God,
The subjects of his substitute, my father,

And both against the peace of heaven and him
Have here up-swarm'd them.
ARCHBISHOP OF YORK.
Good my Lord of Lancaster,
I am not here against your father's peace;
But, as I told my Lord of Westmoreland,
The time misorder'd doth, in common sense,
Crowd us and crush us to this monstrous form,
To hold our safety up. I sent your Grace
The parcels and particulars of our grief,—
The which hath been with scorn shoved from
the court,—
Whereon this Hydra son of war is born;
Whose dangerous eyes may well be charm'd
asleep
With grant of our most just and right desires,
And true obedience, of this madness cured,
Stoop tamely to the foot of majesty.
MOWBRAY.
If not, we ready are to try our fortunes
To the last man.

HASTINGS.
And though we here fall down,
We have supplies to second our attempt:
If they miscarry, theirs shall second them;
And so success of mischief shall be born,
And heir from heir shall hold this quarrel up,
Whiles England shall have generation.
PRINCE JOHN OF LANCASTER.
You are too shallow, Hastings, much too shallow,
To sound the bottom of the after-times.
WESTMORELAND.
Pleaseth your Grace to answer them directly,
How far-forth you do like their articles.
PRINCE JOHN OF LANCASTER.
I like them all, and do allow them well;
And swear here, by the honour of my blood,
My father's purposes have been mistook;
And some about him have too lavishly
Wrested his meaning and authority.—
My lord, these griefs shall be with speed re-
drest;
Upon my soul, they shall. If this may please you,
Discharge your powers unto their several
counties,
As we will ours: and here, between the armies,
Let's drink together friendly and embrace,
That all their eyes may bear those tokens home
Of our restored love and amity.
ARCHBISHOP OF YORK.
I take your princely word for these redresses.
PRINCE JOHN OF LANCASTER.
I give it you, and will maintain my word:
And thereupon I drink unto your Grace. [*Drinks.*
HASTINGS [*to an* OFFICER].
Go, captain, and deliver to the army
This news of peace: let them have pay, and part:
I know it will well please them. Hie thee, captain.
[*Exit* OFFICER.
ARCHBISHOP OF YORK.
To you, my noble Lord of Westmoreland.
[*Drinks.*
WESTMORELAND.
I pledge your Grace [*Drinks*]; and, if you knew
what pains
I have bestow'd to breed this present peace,

You would drink freely: but my love to ye
Shall show itself more openly hereafter.
ARCHBISHOP OF YORK.
I do not doubt you.
WESTMORELAND.
I am glad of it.—
Health to my lord and gentle cousin, Mowbray.
[*Drinks.*
MOWBRAY.
You wish me health in very happy season;
For I am, on the sudden, something ill.
ARCHBISHOP OF YORK.
Against ill chances men are ever merry;
But heaviness foreruns the good event.
WESTMORELAND.
Therefore be merry, coz; since sudden sorrow
Serves to say thus, 'Some good thing comes to-
morrow.'
ARCHBISHOP OF YORK.
Believe me, I am passing light in spirit.
MOWBRAY.
So much the worse, if your own rule be true.
[*Shouts within.*
The word of peace is render'd: hark, how they
shout!
MOWBRAY.
This had been cheerful after victory.
ARCHBISHOP OF YORK.
A peace is of the nature of a conquest;
For then both parties nobly are subdued,
And neither party loser.
PRINCE JOHN OF LANCASTER.
Go, my lord,
And let our army be discharged too.
[*Exit* WESTMORELAND.
And, good my lord, so please you, let our trains
March by us, that we may peruse the men
We should have coped withal.
ARCHBISHOP OF YORK.
Go, good Lord Hastings,
And, ere they be dismiss'd, let them march by.
[*Exit* HASTINGS.
PRINCE JOHN OF LANCASTER.
I trust, lords, we shall lie to-night together.
Enter WESTMORELAND.
Now, cousin, wherefore stands our army still?
WESTMORELAND.
The leaders, having charge from you to stand,
Will not go off until they hear you speak.
PRINCE JOHN OF LANCASTER.
They know their duties.
Enter HASTINGS.
HASTINGS.
My lord, our army is dispersed already:
Like youthful steers unyoked, they take their
courses
East, west, north, south; or, like a school broke
up,
Each hurries toward his home and sporting-
place.
WESTMORELAND.
Good tidings, my Lord Hastings; for the which
I do arrest thee, traitor, of high treason:—
And you, lord archbishop,—and you, Lord
Mowbray,—
Of capital treason I attach you both.

MOWBRAY.
Is this proceeding just and honourable?
WESTMORELAND.
Is your assembly so?
ARCHBISHOP OF YORK.
Will you thus break your faith!
PRINCE JOHN OF LANCASTER.
I pawn'd thee none:
I promised you redress of these same grievances
Whereof you did complain; which, by mine
honour,
I will perform with a most Christian care.
But for you, rebels,—look to taste the due
Meet for rebellion and such acts as yours.
Most shallowly did you these arms commence,
Fondly brought here, and foolishly sent hence.—
Strike up our drums, pursue the scatter'd stray:
God, and not we, hath safely fought to-day.—
Some guard these traitors to the block of death,
Treason's true bed and yielder-up of breath.
[*Exeunt.*

SCENE III.

Another part of the forest.

Alarums: excursions. Enter FALSTAFF *and*
COLEVILE, *meeting.*

WHAT'S your name, sir? of what condition
are you, and of what place, I pray?
COLEVILE.
I am a knight, sir; and my name is Colevile of the
dale.
FALSTAFF.
Well, then, Colevile is your name, a knight is
your degree, and your place the dale: Colevile
shall be still your name, a traitor your degree, and
the dungeon your place,—a dale deep enough; so
shall you be still Colevile of the dale.
COLEVILE.
Are not you Sir John Falstaff?
FALSTAFF.
As good a man as he, sir, whoe'er I am. Do ye
yield, sir? or shall I sweat for you? If I do sweat,
they are the drops of thy lovers, and they weep
for thy death: therefore rouse up fear and trembling, and do observance to my mercy.
COLEVILE.
I think you are Sir John Falstaff; and in that
thought yield me.
FALSTAFF.
I have a whole school of tongues in this belly of
mine; and not a tongue of them all speaks any
other word but my name. An I had but a belly of
any indifferency, I were simply the most active
fellow in Europe: my womb, my womb, my
womb, undoes me.—Here comes our general.
Enter PRINCE JOHN OF LANCASTER, WEST-
MORELAND, BLUNT, *and others.*
PRINCE JOHN OF LANCASTER.
The heat is past; follow no further now:—
Call in the powers, good cousin Westmoreland.
[*Exit* WESTMORELAND.
Now, Falstaff, where have you been all this
while?
When every thing is ended, then you come:

These tardy tricks of yours will, on my life,
One time or other break some gallows' back.
FALSTAFF.
I would be sorry, my lord, but it should be thus:
I never knew yet but rebuke and check was the
reward of valour. Do you think me a swallow,
an arrow, or a bullet? have I, in my poor and
old motion, the expedition of thought? I have
speeded hither with the very extremest inch of
possibility; I have founder'd nine-score and odd
posts: and here, travel-tainted as I am, have, in
my pure and immaculate valour, taken Sir John
Colevile of the dale, a most furious knight and
valorous enemy. But what of that? he saw me,
and yielded; that I may justly say with the hook-
nosed fellow of Rome,—I came, saw, and overcame.
PRINCE JOHN OF LANCASTER.
It was more of his courtesy than your deserving.
FALSTAFF.
I know not:—here he is, and here I yield him:
and I beseech your Grace, let it be bookt with
the rest of this day's deeds; or, by the Lord, I will
have it in a particular ballad else, with mine own
picture on the top of it, Colevile kissing my foot:
to the which course if I be enforced, if you do
not all show like gilt twopences to me, and I, in
the clear sky of fame, o'ershine you as much as
the full moon doth the cinders of the element,
which show like pins' heads to her, believe not
the word of the noble: therefore let me have right,
and let desert mount.
PRINCE JOHN OF LANCASTER.
Thine's too heavy to mount.
FALSTAFF.
Let it shine, then.
PRINCE JOHN OF LANCASTER.
Thine's too thick to shine.
FALSTAFF.
Let it do something, my good lord, that may do
me good, and call it what you will.
PRINCE JOHN OF LANCASTER.
Is thy name Colevile?
COLEVILE.
It is, my lord.
PRINCE JOHN OF LANCASTER.
A famous rebel art thou, Colevile.
FALSTAFF.
And a famous true subject took him.
COLEVILE.
I am, my lord, but as my betters are,
That led me hither: had they been ruled by me,
You should have won them dearer than you
have.
FALSTAFF.
I know not how they sold themselves: but thou,
like a kind fellow, gavest thyself away gratis; and
I thank thee for thee.
Enter WESTMORELAND.
PRINCE JOHN OF LANCASTER.
Now, have you left pursuit?
WESTMORELAND.
Retreat is made, and execution stay'd.
PRINCE JOHN OF LANCASTER.
Send Colevile, with his confederates,
To York, to present execution:—

Blunt, lead him hence; and see you guard him
  sure.
  [*Exeunt* BLUNT *and others with* COLEVILE.
And now dispatch we toward the court, my
  lords:
I hear the king my father is sore sick:
Our news shall go before us to his majesty,—
Which, cousin, you shall bear,—to comfort him;
And we with sober speed will follow you.
  PRINCE JOHN OF LANCASTER.
My lord, I beseech you, give me leave to go
Through Glostershire: and, when you come to
  court,
Stand my good lord, pray, in your good report.
  PRINCE JOHN OF LANCASTER.
Fare you well, Falstaff: I, in my condition,
Shall better speak of you than you deserve.
  [*Exeunt all except* FALSTAFF.
  FALSTAFF.
I would you had but the wit: 'twere better than
your dukedom.—Good faith, this same young
sober-blooded boy doth not love me; nor a man
cannot make him laugh;—but that's no marvel,
he drinks no wine. There's never none of these
demure boys come to any proof; for thin drink
doth so over-cool their blood, and making many
fish-meals, that they fall into a kind of male
green-sickness; and then, when they marry, they
get wenches: they are generally fools and cowards;
—which some of us should be too, but for in-
flammation. A good sherris-sack hath a twofold
operation in it. It ascends me into the brain; dries
me there all the foolish and dull and crudy vapours
which environ it; makes it apprehensive, quick,
forgetive, full of nimble, fiery, and delectable
shapes; which, deliver'd o'er to the voice, the
tongue, which is the birth, becomes excellent wit.
The second property of your excellent sherris is,
the warming of the blood; which, before cold and
settled, left the liver white and pale, which is
the badge of pusillanimity and cowardice; but
the sherris warms it, and makes it course from the
inwards to the parts extreme: it illumineth the
face, which, as a beacon, gives warning to all
the rest of this little kingdom, man, to arm; and
then the vital commoners and inland petty spirits
muster me all to their captain, the heart, who,
great and puft up with this retinue, doth any deed
of courage: and this valour comes of sherris. So
that skill in the weapon is nothing without sack,
for that sets it a-work; and learning, a mere hoard
of gold kept by a devil, till sack commences it,
and sets it in act and use. Hereof comes it, that
Prince Harry is valiant; for the cold blood he did
naturally inherit of his father, he hath, like lean,
sterile, and bare land, manured, husbanded, and
till'd, with excellent endeavour of drinking good
and good store of fertile sherris, that he is become
very hot and valiant. If I had a thousand sons,
the first humane principle I would teach them
should be,—to forswear thin potations, and to
addict themselves to sack.
  Enter BARDOLPH.
How now, Bardolph!
  BARDOLPH.
The army is discharged all, and gone.

  FALSTAFF.
Let them go. I'll through Glostershire; and there
will I visit Master Robert Shallow, esquire: I have
him already tempering between my finger and my
thumb, and shortly will I seal with him. Come
away. [*Exeunt.*

SCENE IV.

Westminster. The Jerusalem Chamber.

Enter the KING, THOMAS DUKE OF CLARENCE,
  HUMPHREY OF GLOSTER, WARWICK, *and*
  others.

  KING HENRY.
NOW, lords, if God doth give successful end
  To this debate that bleedeth at our doors,
We will our youth lead on to higher fields,
And draw no swords but what are sanctified.
Our navy is addrest, our power collected,
Our substitutes in absence well invested,
And every thing lies level to our wish:
Only, we want a little personal strength;
And pause us, till these rebels, now afoot,
Come underneath the yoke of government.
  WARWICK.
Both which we doubt not but your majesty
Shall soon enjoy.
  KING HENRY.
  Humphrey, my son of Gloster,
Where is the prince your brother?
  GLOSTER.
I think he's gone to hunt, my lord, at Windsor.
  KING HENRY.
And how accompanied?
  GLOSTER.
  I do not know, my lord.
  KING HENRY.
Is not his brother, Thomas of Clarence, with
  him?
  GLOSTER.
No, my good lord; he is in presence here.
  CLARENCE.
What would my lord and father?
  KING HENRY.
Nothing but well to thee, Thomas of Clarence.
How chance thou art not with the prince thy
  brother?
He loves thee, and thou dost neglect him,
  Thomas;
Thou hast a better place in his affection
Than all thy brothers: cherish it, my boy;
And noble offices thou mayst effect
Of mediation, after I am dead,
Between his greatness and thy other brethren:
Therefore omit him not; blunt not his love,
Nor lose the good advantage of his grace
By seeming cold or careless of his will;
For he is gracious, if he be observed:
He hath a tear for pity, and a hand
Open as day for melting charity:
Yet notwithstanding, being incensed, he's flint;
As humorous as winter, and as sudden
As flaws congealed in the spring of day.
His temper, therefore, must be well observed:
Chide him for faults, and do it reverently,
When you perceive his blood inclined to mirth;

But, being moody, give him line and scope,
Till that his passions, like a whale on ground,
Confound themselves with working. Learn this,
   Thomas,
And thou shalt prove a shelter to thy friends;
A hoop of gold to bind thy brothers in,
That the united vessel of their blood,
Mingled with venom of suggestion—
As, force perforce, the age will pour it in—
Shall never leak, though it do work as strong
As aconitum or rash gunpowder.

CLARENCE.
I shall observe him with all care and love.

KING HENRY.
Why art thou not at Windsor with him, Thomas?

CLARENCE.
He is not there to-day; he dines in London.

KING HENRY.
And how accompanied? canst thou tell that?

CLARENCE.
With Pointz, and other his continual followers.

KING HENRY.
Most subject is the fattest soil to weeds;
And he, the noble image of my youth,
Is overspread with them: therefore my grief
Stretches itself beyond the hour of death:
The blood weeps from my heart, when I do shape,
In forms imaginary, th'unguided days
And rotten times that you shall look upon
When I am sleeping with my ancestors.
For when his headstrong riot hath no curb,
When rage and hot blood are his counsellors,
When means and lavish manners meet together,
O, with what wings shall his affections fly
Towards fronting peril and opposed decay!

WARWICK.
My gracious lord, you look beyond him quite:
The prince but studies his companions, [guage,
Like a strange tongue; wherein, to gain the lan-
'Tis needful that the most immodest word
Be lookt upon and learn'd; which once attain'd
Your highness knows, comes to no further use
But to be known and hated. So, like gross terms,
The prince will, in the perfectness of time,
Cast off his followers; and their memory
Shall as a pattern or a measure live,
By which his grace must mete the lives of others,
Turning past evils to advantages.

KING HENRY.
'Tis seldom when the bee doth leave her comb
In the dead carrion.

Enter WESTMORELAND.
        Who's here? Westmoreland?

WESTMORELAND.
Health to my sovereign, and new happiness
Added to that that I am to deliver!
Prince John, your son, doth kiss your Grace's
   hand:
Mowbray, the Bishop Scroop, Hastings, and all,
Are brought to the correction of your law;
There is not now a rebel's sword unsheathed,
But Peace puts forth her olive every where:
The manner how this action hath been borne,
Here at more leisure may your highness read,
With every course in his particular.
                       [Giving packet.

KING HENRY.
O Westmoreland, thou art a summer bird,
Which ever in the haunch of winter sings
The lifting-up of day.—Look, here's more news.

Enter HARCOURT.

HARCOURT.
From enemies heaven keep your majesty;
And, when they stand against you, may they fall
As those that I am come to tell you of!
The Earl Northumberland and the Lord Bardolph,
With a great power of English and of Scots,
Are by the shrieve of Yorkshire overthrown:
The manner and true order of the fight,
This packet, please it you, contains at large.
                       [Giving packet.

KING HENRY.
And wherefore should these good news make me
   sick?
Will Fortune never come with both hands full,
But write her fair words still in foulest letters?
She either gives a stomach, and no food,—
Such are the poor, in health; or else a feast,
And takes away the stomach,—such are the rich,
That have abundance, and enjoy it not.
I should rejoice now at this happy news;
And now my sight fails, and my brain is giddy:—
O me! come near me; now I am much ill.
                       [Falls back.

GLOSTER.
Comfort, your majesty!

CLARENCE.
        O my royal father!

WESTMORELAND.
My sovereign lord, cheer up yourself, look up.

WARWICK.
Be patient, princes; you do know, these fits
Are with his highness very ordinary.
Stand from him, give him air; he'll straight be
   well.

CLARENCE.
No, no, he cannot long hold out these pangs:
Th'incessant care and labour of his mind
Hath wrought the mure, that should confine it in,
So thin that life looks through and will break out.

GLOSTER.
The people fear me; for they do observe
Unfather'd heirs and loathly births of nature:
The seasons change their manners, as the year
Had found some months asleep, and leapt them
   over.

CLARENCE.
The river hath thrice flow'd, no ebb between;
And the old folk, time's doting chronicles,
Say it did so a little time before
That our great-grandsire, Edward, sick'd and
   died.

WARWICK.
Speak lower, princes, for the king recovers.

GLOSTER.
This apoplex will certain be his end.

KING HENRY.
I pray you, take me up, and bear me hence
Into some other chamber: softly, pray.
    [They lay the KING *on a bed in an inner
     room.*
Let there be no noise made, my gentle friends;

Unless some dull and favourable hand
Will whisper music to my weary spirit.
WARWICK.
Call for the music in the other room.
KING HENRY.
Set me the crown upon my pillow here.
CLARENCE.
His eye is hollow, and he changes much.
WARWICK.
Less noise, less noise!
Enter PRINCE HENRY.
PRINCE HENRY.
Who saw the Duke of Clarence?
CLARENCE.
I am here, brother, full of heaviness.
PRINCE HENRY.
How now! rain within doors, and none abroad!
How doth the king?
GLOSTER.
Exceeding ill.
PRINCE HENRY.
Heard he
The good news yet? tell it him.
GLOSTER.
He alter'd much
Upon the hearing it.
PRINCE HENRY.
If he be sick with joy, he'll recover without physic.
WARWICK.
Not so much noise, my lords:—sweet prince,
  speak low;
The king your father is disposed to sleep.
CLARENCE.
Let us withdraw into the other room.
WARWICK.
Will't please your Grace to go along with us?
PRINCE HENRY.
No; I will sit and watch here by the king.
        [*Exeunt all except* PRINCE HENRY.
Why doth the crown lie there upon his pillow,
Being so troublesome a bedfellow?
O polisht perturbation! golden care!
That keep'st the ports of slumber open wide
To many a watchful night!—sleep with it now!
Yet not so sound and half so deeply sweet
As he whose brow with homely biggen bound
Snores out the watch of night. O majesty!
When thou dost pinch thy bearer, thou dost sit
Like a rich armour worn in heat of day,
That scalds with safety. By his gates of breath
There lies a downy feather which stirs not:
Did he suspire, that light and weightless down
Perforce must move.—My gracious lord! my
  father!—
This sleep is sound indeed; this is a sleep,
That from this golden rigol hath divorced
So many English kings. Thy due from me
Is tears and heavy sorrows of the blood,
Which nature, love, and filial tenderness,
Shall, O dear father, pay thee plenteously:
My due from thee is this imperial crown,
Which, as immediate from thy place and blood,
Derives itself to me. Lo, here it sits,—
        [*Putting it on his head.*
Which God shall guard: and put the world's
  whole strength

Into one giant arm, it shall not force
This lineal honour from me: this from thee
Will I to mine leave, as 'tis left to me.   [*Exit.*
KING HENRY.
Warwick! Gloster! Clarence!
        Enter WARWICK *and the rest.*
CLARENCE.
Doth the king call?
WARWICK.
What would your majesty? how fares your Grace?
KING HENRY.
Why did you leave me here alone, my lords?
CLARENCE.
We left the prince my brother here, my liege,
Who undertook to sit and watch by you.
KING HENRY.
The Prince of Wales! Where is he? let me see him:
He is not here.
WARWICK.
This door is open; he is gone this way.
GLOSTER.
He came not through the chamber where we
  stay'd.
KING HENRY.
Where is the crown? who took it from my pillow?
WARWICK.
When we withdrew, my liege, we left it here.
KING HENRY.
The prince hath ta'en it hence:—go, seek him
  out.
Is he so hasty, that he doth suppose
My sleep my death?—
Find him, my Lord of Warwick; chide him hither.
        [*Exit* WARWICK.
This part of his conjoins with my disease,
And helps to end me.—See, sons, what things you
  are!
How quickly nature falls into revolt
When gold becomes her object!
For this the foolish over-careful fathers
Have broke their sleeps with thought, their brains
  with care,
Their bones with industry;
For this they have engrossed and piled up
The canker'd heaps of strange-achieved gold;
For this they have been thoughtful to invest
Their sons with arts and martial exercises:
When, like the bee, culling from every flower
The virtuous sweets,
Our thighs packt with wax, our mouths with
  honey,
We bring it to the hive; and, like the bees,
Are murder'd for our pains. This bitter taste
Yield his engrossments to the ending father.
        Enter WARWICK.
Now, where is he that will not stay so long
Till his friend sickness hath determined me?
WARWICK.
My lord, I found the prince in the next room,
Washing with kindly tears his gentle cheeks;
With such a deep demeanour in great sorrow,
That tyranny, which never quaff'd but blood,
Would, by beholding him, have washt his knife
With gentle eye-drops. He is coming hither.
KING HENRY.
But wherefore did he take away the crown?

Enter PRINCE HENRY.

Lo, where he comes.—Come hither to me,
   Harry.—
Depart the chamber, leave us here alone.
       [*Exeunt all except* KING HENRY *and*
       PRINCE HENRY.

PRINCE HENRY.

I never thought to hear you speak again.

KING HENRY.

Thy wish was father, Harry, to that thought:
I stay too long by thee, I weary thee.
Dost thou so hunger for mine empty chair,
That thou wilt needs invest thee with my honours
Before thy hour be ripe? O foolish youth!
Thou seek'st the greatness that will overwhelm
   thee.
Stay but a little; for my cloud of dignity
Is held from falling with so weak a wind
That it will quickly drop: my day is dim.
Thou hast stoln that which, after some few
   hours,
Were thine without offence; and at my death
Thou hast seal'd up my expectation:
Thy life did manifest thou loved'st me not,
And thou wilt have me die assured of it.
Thou hidest a thousand daggers in thy thoughts,
Which thou hast whetted on thy stony heart,
To stab at half an hour of my life.
What! canst thou not forbear me half an hour?
Then, get thee gone, and dig my grave thyself;
And bid the merry bells ring to thine ear,
That thou art crowned, not that I am dead.
Let all the tears that should bedew my hearse
Be drops of balm to sanctify thy head:
Only compound me with forgotten dust;
Give that which gave thee life unto the worms.
Pluck down my officers, break my decrees;
For now a time is come to mock at form:—
Harry the Fifth is crown'd:—up, vanity!
Down, royal state! all you sage counsellors, hence!
And to the English court assemble now,
From every region, apes of idleness!
Now, neighbour confines, purge you of your
   scum:
Have you a ruffian that will swear, drink, dance,
Revel the night, rob, murder, and commit
The oldest sins the newest kind of ways?
Be happy, he will trouble you no more;
England shall double-gild his treble guilt,—
England shall give him office, honour, might;
For the Fifth Harry from curb'd licence plucks
The muzzle of restraint, and the wild dog
Shall flesh his tooth in every innocent.
O my poor kingdom, sick with civil blows!
When that my care could not withhold thy riots,
What wilt thou do when riot is thy care?
O, thou wilt be a wilderness again,
Peopled with wolves, thy old inhabitants!

PRINCE HENRY.

O, pardon me, my liege! but for my tears,
       [*Kneeling.*
The moist impediments unto my speech,
I had forestall'd this dear and deep rebuke,
Ere you with grief had spoke, and I had heard
The course of it so far. There is your crown;
And He that wears the crown immortally

Long guard it yours! If I affect it more
Than as your honour and as your renown,
Let me no more from this obedience rise,—
Which my most inward true and duteous spirit
Teacheth,—this prostrate and exterior bending!
God witness with me, when I here came in,
       [*Rising.*
And found no course of breath within your
   majesty,
How cold it struck my heart! If I do feign,
O, let me in my present wildness die,
And never live to show th'incredulous world
The noble change that I have purposed!
Coming to look on you, thinking you dead,—
And dead almost, my liege, to think you were,—
I spake unto this crown as having sense,
And thus upbraided it: 'The care on thee depend-
   ing
Hath fed upon the body of my father;
Therefore, thou, best of gold, art worst of gold:
Other, less fine in carat, is more precious,
Preserving life in medicine potable;
But thou, most fine, most honour'd, most re-
   nown'd,
Hast eat thy bearer up.' Thus, my most royal
   liege,
Accusing it, I put it on my head,
To try with it—as with an enemy
That had before my face murder'd my father—
The quarrel of a true inheritor.
But if it did infect my blood with joy,
Or swell my thoughts to any strain of pride;
If any rebel or vain spirit of mine
Did with the least affection of a welcome
Give entertainment to the might of it,—
Let God for ever keep it from my head,
And make me as the poorest vassal is,
That doth with awe and terror kneel to it!

KING HENRY.

O my son,
God put it in thy mind to take it hence,
That thou mightst win the more thy father's love,
Pleading so wisely in excuse of it!
Come hither, Harry, sit thou by my bed;
And hear, I think, the very latest counsel
That ever I shall breathe. God knows, my son,
By what by-paths and indirect crookt ways
I met this crown; and I myself know well
How troublesome it sat upon my head:
To thee it shall descend with better quiet,
Better opinion, better confirmation;
For all the soil of the achievement goes
With me into the earth. It seem'd in me
But as an honour snatcht with boisterous hand;
And I had many living to upbraid
My gain of it by their assistances;
Which daily grew to quarrel and to bloodshed,
Wounding supposed peace: all these bold fears
Thou see'st with peril I have answered;
For all my reign hath been but as a scene
Acting that argument: and now my death
Changes the mode; for what in me was purchased,
Falls upon thee in a more fairer sort;
So thou the garland wear'st successively.
Yet, though thou stand'st more sure than I could
   do,

Thou art not firm enough, since griefs are green;
And all my foes, which thou must make thy
   friends,
Have but their stings and teeth newly ta'en out;
By whose fell working I was first advanced,
And by whose power I well might lodge a fear
To be again displaced: which to avoid,
I cut some off, and had a purpose now
To lead out many to the Holy Land,
Lest rest and lying still might make them look
Too near unto my state. Therefore, my Harry,
Be it thy course to busy giddy minds   [out,
With foreign quarrels; that action, hence borne
May waste the memory of the former days.
More would I, but my lungs are wasted so
That strength of speech is utterly denied me.
How I came by the crown, O God forgive;
And grant it may with thee in true peace live!

PRINCE HENRY.
My gracious liege,
You won it, wore it, kept it, gave it me;
Then plain and right must my possession be:
Which I with more than with a common pain
'Gainst all the world will rightfully maintain.

KING HENRY.
Look, look, here comes my John of Lancaster.

Enter PRINCE JOHN OF LANCASTER, WAR-
WICK, LORDS, *and others.*

PRINCE JOHN OF LANCASTER.
Health, peace, and happiness to my royal father!

KING HENRY.
Thou bring'st me happiness and peace, son John;
But health, alack, with youthful wings is flown
From this bare wither'd trunk: upon thy sight
My worldly business makes a period.—
Where is my Lord of Warwick?

PRINCE HENRY.
My Lord of Warwick!

KING HENRY.
Doth any name particular belong
Unto the lodging where I first did swoon?

WARWICK.
'Tis call'd Jerusalem, my noble lord.

KING HENRY.
Laud be to God!—even there my life must end.
It hath been prophesied to me many years,
I should not die but in Jerusalem;
Which vainly I supposed the Holy Land:—
But bear me to that chamber; there I'll lie;
In that Jerusalem shall Harry die.   [*Exeunt.*

ACT V. SCENE I.

Glostershire. SHALLOW'S *house.*

Enter SHALLOW, FALSTAFF, BARDOLPH, *and*
PAGE.

SHALLOW.
BY cock and pie, sir, you shall not away to-night.
—What, Davy, I say!

FALSTAFF.
You must excuse me, Master Robert Shallow.

SHALLOW.
I will not excuse you; you shall not be excused;
excuses shall not be admitted; there is no excuse
shall serve; you shall not be excused.—Why,
Davy!

Enter DAVY.

DAVY.
Here, sir.

SHALLOW.
Davy, Davy, Davy, Davy,—let me see, Davy; let
me see, Davy; let me see:—yea, marry, William
cook, bid him come hither.—Sir John, you shall
not be excused.

DAVY.
Marry, sir, thus; those precepts cannot be served:
and again, sir,—shall we sow the headland with
wheat?

SHALLOW.
With red wheat, Davy. But for William cook:—
are there no young pigeons?

DAVY.
Yes, sir.—Here is now the smith's note for shoe-
ing and plough-irons.

SHALLOW.
Let it be cast, and paid.—Sir John, you shall not
be excused.

DAVY.
Now, sir, a new link to the bucket must needs be
had:—and, sir, do you mean to stop any of
William's wages, about the sack he lost the other
day at Hinckley fair?

SHALLOW.
A' shall answer it.—Some pigeons, Davy, a
couple of short-legg'd hens, a joint of mutton, and
any pretty little tiny kickshaws, tell William cook.

DAVY.
Doth the man of war stay all night, sir?

SHALLOW.
Yea, Davy. I will use him well: a friend i'th'
court is better than a penny in purse. Use his men
well, Davy; for they are arrant knaves, and will
backbite.

DAVY.
No worse than they are backbitten, sir; for they
have marvellous foul linen.

SHALLOW.
Well conceited, Davy:—about thy business, Davy.

DAVY.
I beseech you, sir, to countenance William Visor
of Woncot against Clement Perkes o'th' hill.

SHALLOW.
There is many complaints, Davy, against that
Visor: that Visor is an arrant knave, on my know-
ledge.

DAVY.
I grant your worship that he is a knave, sir; but
yet, God forbid, sir, but a knave should have
some countenance at his friend's request. An
honest man, sir, is able to speak for himself, when
a knave is not. I have served your worship truly,
sir, this eight years; and if I cannot once or twice
in a quarter bear out a knave against an honest
man, I have but a very little credit with your worship. The knave is mine honest friend, sir; therefore, I beseech your worship, let him be countenanced.

SHALLOW.
Go to; I say he shall have no wrong. Look about,
Davy. [*Exit* DAVY.] Where are you, Sir John?
Come, come, come, off with your boots.—Give
me your hand, Master Bardolph.

BARDOLPH.
I am glad to see your worship.

SHALLOW.
I thank thee with all my heart, kind Master Bardolph:—[to the PAGE] and welcome, my tall fellow.—Come, Sir John.

FALSTAFF.
I'll follow you, good Master Robert Shallow. [Exit SHALLOW.] Bardolph, look to our horses. [Exeunt BARDOLPH and PAGE.] If I were saw'd into quantities, I should make four dozen of such bearded hermits'-staves as Master Shallow. It is a wonderful thing to see the semblable coherence of his men's spirits and his: they, by observing of him, do bear themselves like foolish justices; he, by conversing with them, is turn'd into a justice-like serving-man: their spirits are so married in conjunction with the participation of society, that they flock together in consent, like so many wild-geese. If I had a suit to Master Shallow, I would humour his men with the imputation of being near their master: if to his men, I would curry with Master Shallow, that no man could better command his servants. It is certain that either wise bearing or ignorant carriage is caught, as men take diseases, one of another: therefore let men take heed of their company. I will devise matter enough out of this Shallow to keep Prince Harry in continual laughter the wearing-out of six fashions,—which is four terms, or two actions, —and a' shall laugh without intervallums. O, it is much that a lie with a slight oath, and a jest with a sad brow, will do with a fellow that never had the ache in his shoulders! O, you shall see him laugh till his face be like a wet cloak ill laid up!

SHALLOW [within].
Sir John!

FALSTAFF.
I come, Master Shallow; I come, Master Shallow.
[Exit.

SCENE II.

Westminster.   The palace.

Enter WARWICK and the LORD CHIEF JUSTICE, meeting.

WARWICK.
HOW now, my lord chief justice! whither away?

LORD CHIEF JUSTICE.
How doth the king?

WARWICK.
Exceeding well; his cares are now all ended.

LORD CHIEF JUSTICE.
I hope, not dead.

WARWICK.
He's walkt the way of nature;
And, to our purposes, he lives no more.

LORD CHIEF JUSTICE.
I would his majesty had call'd me with him:
The service that I truly did his life
Hath left me open to all injuries.

WARWICK.
Indeed I think the young king loves you not.

LORD CHIEF JUSTICE.
I know he doth not; and do arm myself

To welcome the condition of the time;
Which cannot look more hideously upon me
Than I have drawn it in my fantasy.

WARWICK.
Here come the heavy issue of dead Harry:
O, that the living Harry had the temper
Of him, the worst of these three gentlemen!
How many nobles then should hold their places,
That must strike sail to spirits of vile sort!

LORD CHIEF JUSTICE.
O God, I fear all will be overturn'd!

Enter JOHN OF LANCASTER, CLARENCE,
GLOSTER, WESTMORELAND, and others.

PRINCE JOHN OF LANCASTER.
Good morrow, cousin Warwick, good morrow.

GLOSTER and CLARENCE.
Good morrow, cousin.

PRINCE JOHN OF LANCASTER.
We meet like men that had forgot to speak.

WARWICK.
We do remember; but our argument
Is all too heavy to admit much talk.

PRINCE JOHN OF LANCASTER.
Well, peace be with him that hath made us heavy!

LORD CHIEF JUSTICE.
Peace be with us, lest we be heavier!

GLOSTER.
O, good my lord, you've lost a friend indeed;
And I dare swear you borrow not that face
Of seeming sorrow,—it is sure your own.

PRINCE JOHN OF LANCASTER.
Though no man be assured what grace to find,
You stand in coldest expectation:
I am the sorrier; would 'twere otherwise.

CLARENCE.
Well, you must now speak Sir John Falstaff fair;
Which swims against your stream of quality.

LORD CHIEF JUSTICE.
Sweet princes, what I did, I did in honour,
Led by th'impartial conduct of my soul;
And never shall you see that I will beg
A ragged and forestall'd remission.
If truth and upright innocency fail me,
I'll to the king my master that is dead,
And tell him who hath sent me after him.

WARWICK.
Here comes the prince.

Enter KING HENRY THE FIFTH, attended.

LORD CHIEF JUSTICE.
Good morrow; and God save your majesty!

KING HENRY THE FIFTH.
This new and gorgeous garment, majesty,
Sits not so easy on me as you think.—
Brothers, you mix your sadness with some fear:
This is the English, not the Turkish court;
Not Amurath an Amurath succeeds,
But Harry Harry. Yet be sad, good brothers,
For, by my faith, it very well becomes you:
Sorrow so royally in you appears,
That I will deeply put the fashion on,
And wear it in my heart: why, then, be sad;
But entertain no more of it, good brothers,
Than a joint burden laid upon us all.
For me, by heaven, I bid you be assured,
I'll be your father and your brother too;
Let me but bear your love, I'll bear your cares:

Yet weep that Harry's dead; and so will I;
But Harry lives, that shall convert those tears,
By number, into hours of happiness.

CLARENCE, PRINCE JOHN OF LANCASTER,
and GLOSTER.

We hope no other from your majesty.

KING HENRY THE FIFTH.

You all look strangely on me:—and you most;
                    [To the CHIEF JUSTICE.
You are, I think, assured I love you not.

LORD CHIEF JUSTICE.

I am assured, if I be measured rightly,
Your majesty hath no just cause to hate me.

KING HENRY THE FIFTH.

No!
How might a prince of my great hopes forget
So great indignities you laid upon me?
What! rate, rebuke, and roughly send to prison
Th'immediate heir of England? Was this easy?
May this be washt in Lethe and forgotten?

LORD CHIEF JUSTICE.

I then did use the person of your father;
The image of his power lay then in me:
And in th'administration of his law,
Whiles I was busy for the commonwealth,
Your highness pleased to forget my place,
The majesty and power of law and justice,
The image of the king whom I presented,
And struck me in my very seat of judgement;
Whereon, as an offender to your father,
I gave bold way to my authority,
And did commit you. If the deed were ill,
Be you contented, wearing now the garland,
To have a son set your decrees at naught,
To pluck down justice from your awful bench,
To trip the course of law, and blunt the sword
That guards the peace and safety of your person;
Nay, more, to spurn at your most royal image,
And mock your workings in a second body.
Question your royal thoughts, make the case
    yours;
Be now the father, and propose a son;
Hear your own dignity so much profaned,
See your most dreadful laws so loosely slighted,
Behold yourself so by a son disdain'd;
And then imagine me taking your part,
And, in your power, soft silencing your son:
After this cold considerance, sentence me;
And, as you are a king, speak in your state
What I have done that misbecame my place,
My person, or my liege's sovereignty.

KING HENRY THE FIFTH.

You are right, justice, and you weigh this well;
Therefore still bear the balance and the sword:
And I do wish your honours may increase,
Till you do live to see a son of mine
Offend you, and obey you, as I did.
So shall I live to speak my father's words:
'Happy am I, that have a man so bold
That dares do justice on my proper son;
And not less happy, having such a son
That would deliver up his greatness so
Into the hands of justice.'—You did commit me:
For which, I do commit into your hand
Th'unstained sword that you have used to bear;
With this remembrance,—that you use the same

With the like bold, just, and impartial spirit
As you have done 'gainst me. There is my hand.
You shall be as a father to my youth:
My voice shall sound as you do prompt mine
    ear;
And I will stoop and humble my intents
To your well-practised wise directions.—
And, princes all, believe me, I beseech you;—
My father is gone wild into his grave,
For in his tomb lie my affections;
And with his spirit sadly I survive,
To mock the expectation of the world,
To frustrate prophecies, and to raze out
Rotten opinion, who hath writ me down
After my seeming. The tide of blood in me
Hath proudly flow'd in vanity till now:
Now doth it turn, and ebb back to the sea,
Where it shall mingle with the state of floods,
And flow henceforth in formal majesty.
Now call we our high court of parliament:
And let us choose such limbs of noble counsel,
That the great body of our state may go
In equal rank with the best-govern'd nation;
That war, or peace, or both at once, may be
As things acquainted and familiar to us;
In which you, father, shall have foremost hand.
Our coronation done, we will accite,
As I before remember'd, all our state:
And, God consigning to my good intents,
No prince nor peer shall have just cause to say,
God shorten Harry's happy life one day! [Exeunt.

SCENE III.

Glostershire. SHALLOW'S *orchard.*

Enter FALSTAFF, SHALLOW, SILENCE, BAR-
DOLPH, *the* PAGE, *and* DAVY.

SHALLOW.

NAY, you shall see my orchard, where, in an
arbour, we will eat a last year's pippin of
my own graffing, with a dish of caraways, and so
forth:—come, cousin Silence:—and then to bed.

FALSTAFF.

'Fore God, you have here a goodly dwelling and
a rich.

SHALLOW.

Barren, barren, barren; beggars all, beggars all,
Sir John:—marry, good air.—Spread, Davy;
spread, Davy: well said, Davy.

FALSTAFF.

This Davy serves you for good uses; he is your
serving-man and your husband.

SHALLOW.

A good varlet, a good varlet, a very good varlet,
Sir John:—by the mass, I have drunk too much
sack at supper:—a good varlet. Now sit down,
now sit down:—come, cousin.

SILENCE.

Ah, sirrah! quoth-a,—we shall
                                    [*Singing*
  Do nothing but eat, and make good cheer,
    And praise God for the merry year;
  When flesh is cheap and females dear,
    And lusty lads roam here and there
        So merrily,
  And ever among so merrily.

FALSTAFF.
There's a merry heart!—Good Master Silence, I'll give you a health for that anon.

SHALLOW.
Give Master Bardolph some wine, Davy.

DAVY.
Sweet sir, sit; I'll be with you anon; most sweet sir, sit.—Master page, good master page, sit.—Proface! What you want in meat, we'll have in drink: but you must bear;—the heart's all.
[Exit.

SHALLOW.
Be merry, Master Bardolph;—and, my little soldier there, be merry.

SILENCE [singing].
Be merry, be merry, my wife has all;
For women are shrews, both short and tall:
'Tis merry in hall when beards wag all,
    And welcome merry Shrove-tide.
Be merry, be merry.

FALSTAFF.
I did not think Master Silence had been a man of this mettle.

SILENCE.
Who, I? I have been merry twice and once ere now.

Enter DAVY.

DAVY.
There's a dish of leather-coats for you.
[Setting them before BARDOLPH.

SHALLOW.
Davy,—

DAVY.
Your worship?—[to BARDOLPH] I'll be with you straight.—A cup of wine, sir?

SILENCE [singing].
A cup of wine that's brisk and fine,
And drink unto the leman mine;
    And a merry heart lives long-a.

FALSTAFF.
Well said, Master Silence. .

SILENCE.
And we shall be merry;—now comes in the sweet o' th' night.

FALSTAFF.
Health and long life to you, Master Silence!

SILENCE [singing].
Fill the cup, and let it come;
I'll pledge you a mile to the bottom.

SHALLOW.
Honest Bardolph, welcome: if thou want'st any thing, and wilt not call, beshrew thy heart.—[to the PAGE] Welcome, my little tiny thief, and welcome indeed too.—I'll drink to Master Bardolph, and to all the cavaleroes about London.

DAVY.
I hope to see London once ere I die.

BARDOLPH.
An I might see you there, Davy,—

SHALLOW.
By the mass, you'll crack a quart together,—ha! will you not, Master Bardolph?

BARDOLPH.
Yea, sir, in a pottle-pot.

SHALLOW.
By God's liggens, I thank thee:—the knave will

stick by thee, I can assure thee that: a' will not out; he is true bred.

BARDOLPH.
And I'll stick by him, sir.

SHALLOW.
Why, there spoke a king. Lack nothing: be merry.
[Knocking within.] Look who's at door there, ho! who knocks?
[Exit DAVY.

FALSTAFF.
Why, now you have done me right.
[To SILENCE, who has drunk a bumper.

SILENCE [singing].
Do me right,
And dub me knight:
    Samingo.
Is't not so?

FALSTAFF.
'Tis so.

SILENCE.
Is't so? Why, then, say an old man can do somewhat.

Enter DAVY.

DAVY.
An't please your worship, there's one Pistol come from the court with news.

FALSTAFF.
From the court! let him come in.

Enter PISTOL.

How now, Pistol!

PISTOL.
Sir John, God save you!

FALSTAFF.
What wind blew you hither, Pistol?

PISTOL.
Not the ill wind which blows no man to good.—Sweet knight, thou art now one of the greatest men in the realm.

SILENCE.
By'r lady, I think a' be, but goodman Puff of Barson.

PISTOL.
Puff!
Puff in thy teeth, most recreant coward base!—
Sir John, I am thy Pistol and thy friend,
And helter-skelter have I rode to thee;
And tidings do I bring, and lucky joys,
And golden times, and happy news of price.

FALSTAFF.
I pray thee, now, deliver them like a man of this world.

PISTOL.
A foutre for the world and worldlings base!
I speak of Africa and golden joys.

FALSTAFF.
O base Assyrian knight, what is thy news?
Let King Cophetua know the truth thereof.

SILENCE [singing].
And Robin Hood, Scarlet, and John.

PISTOL.
Shall dunghill curs confront the Helicons?
And shall good news be baffled?
Then, Pistol, lay thy head in Furies' lap.

SHALLOW.
Honest gentleman, I know not your breeding.

PISTOL.
Why, then, lament therefore.

SHALLOW.

Give me pardon, sir:—if, sir, you come with news from the court, I take it there's but two ways,—either to utter them, or to conceal them. I am, sir, under the king, in some authority.

PISTOL.

Under which king, Besonian? speak, or die.

SHALLOW.

Under King Harry.

PISTOL.

Harry the Fourth? or Fifth?

SHALLOW.

Harry the Fourth.

PISTOL.

A foutre for thine office!—
Sir John, thy tender lambkin now is king;
Harry the Fifth's the man. I speak the truth:
When Pistol lies, do this; and fig me, like
The bragging Spaniard.

FALSTAFF.

What, is the old king dead?

PISTOL.

As nail in door: the things I speak are just.

FALSTAFF.

Away, Bardolph! saddle my horse.—Master Robert Shallow, choose what office thou wilt in the land, 'tis thine.—Pistol, I will double-charge thee with dignities.

BARDOLPH.

O joyful day!—
I would not take a knighthood for my fortune.

PISTOL.

What, I do bring good news?

FALSTAFF.

Carry Master Silence to bed.—Master Shallow, my Lord Shallow, be what thou wilt; I am fortune's steward. Get on thy boots: we'll ride all night.—O sweet Pistol!—Away, Bardolph! [*Exit* BARDOLPH.]—Come, Pistol, utter more to me; and, withal, devise something to do thyself good. —Boot, boot, Master Shallow! I know the young king is sick for me. Let us take any man's horses; the laws of England are at my commandment. Blessed are they that have been my friends; and woe to my lord chief justice!

PISTOL.

Let vultures vile seize on his lungs also!
'Where is the life that late I led?' say they:
Why, here it is;—welcome this pleasant day!
[*Exeunt.*

SCENE IV.

London. A street.

Enter HOSTESS QUICKLY, DOLL TEARSHEET, *and* BEADLES.

HOSTESS.

NO, thou arrant knave: I would to God that I might die, that I might have thee hang'd: thou hast drawn my shoulder out of joint.

FIRST BEADLE.

The constables have deliver'd her over to me; and she shall have whipping-cheer enough, I warrant her: there hath been a man or two lately kill'd about her.

DOLL TEARSHEET.

Nut-hook, nut-hook, you lie. Come on; I'll tell

thee what, thou damn'd tripe-visaged rascal, an the child I go with do miscarry, thou wert better thou hadst struck thy mother, thou paper-faced villain.

HOSTESS.

O the Lord, that Sir John were come! he would make this a bloody day to somebody. But I pray God the fruit of her womb miscarry!

FIRST BEADLE.

If it do, you shall have a dozen of cushions again; you have but eleven now. Come, I charge you both go with me; for the man is dead that you and Pistol beat amongst you.

DOLL TEARSHEET.

I'll tell thee what, thou thin man in a censer, I will have you as soundly swinged for this,—you blue-bottle rogue, you filthy famisht correctioner, if you be not swinged, I'll forswear half-kirtles.

FIRST BEADLE.

Come, come, you she knight-errant, come.

HOSTESS.

O God, that right should thus overcome might! Well, of sufferance comes ease.

DOLL TEARSHEET.

Come, you rogue, come; bring me to a justice.

HOSTESS.

Ay, come, you starved bloodhound.

DOLL TEARSHEET.

Goodman death, goodman bones!

HOSTESS.

Thou atomy, thou!

DOLL TEARSHEET.

Come, you thin thing; come, you rascal.

FIRST BEADLE.

Very well. [*Exeunt.*

SCENE V.

A public place near Westminster Abbey.

Enter two GROOMS, *strewing rushes.*

FIRST GROOM.

MORE rushes, more rushes.

SECOND GROOM.

The trumpets have sounded twice.

FIRST GROOM.

'Twill be two o'clock ere they come from th coronation. Dispatch, dispatch. [*Exeun*

Enter FALSTAFF, SHALLOW, PISTOL, BARDOLPH, *and* PAGE.

FALSTAFF.

Stand here by me, Master Robert Shallow; I wi make the king do you grace: I will leer upon hi as a' comes by; and do but mark the countenanc that he will give me.

PISTOL.

God bless thy lungs, good knight.

FALSTAFF.

Come here, Pistol; stand behind me!—[*to* SHA LOW] O, if I had had time to have made ne liveries, I would have bestow'd the thousa pound I borrow'd of you. But 'tis no matter; th poor show doth better: this doth infer the zea had to see him;—

SHALLOW.

It doth so.

FALSTAFF.
It shows my earnestness of affection,—
SHALLOW.
It doth so.
FALSTAFF.
My devotion,—
SHALLOW.
It doth, it doth, it doth.
FALSTAFF.
As it were, to ride day and night; and not to de-
liberate, not to remember, not to have patience to
shift me,—
SHALLOW.
It is best, certain.
FALSTAFF.
But to stand stain'd with travel, and sweating
with desire to see him; thinking of nothing else,
putting all affairs else in oblivion, as if there were
nothing else to be done but to see him.
PISTOL.
'Tis *semper idem*, for *obsque hoc nihil est:* 'tis all in
every part.
SHALLOW.
'Tis so, indeed.
PISTOL.
My knight, I will inflame thy noble liver,
And make thee rage.
Thy Doll, and Helen of thy noble thoughts,
Is in base durance and contagious prison;
Haled thither
By most mechanical and dirty hand:—
Rouse up revenge from ebon den with fell Alec-
to's snake,
For Doll is in. Pistol speaks naught but truth.
FALSTAFF.
I will deliver her.
[*Shouts within, and the trumpets sound.*
PISTOL.
There roar'd the sea, and trumpet-clangor
sounds.
Enter the KING *and his* TRAIN, *the* LORD
CHIEF JUSTICE *among them.*
FALSTAFF.
God save thy Grace, King Hal! my royal Hal!
PISTOL.
The heavens thee guard and keep, most royal imp
of fame!
FALSTAFF.
God save thee, my sweet boy!
KING HENRY THE FIFTH.
My lord chief justice, speak to that vain man.
LORD CHIEF JUSTICE.
Have you your wits? know you what 'tis you
speak?
FALSTAFF.
My king! my Jove! I speak to thee, my heart!
KING HENRY THE FIFTH.
I know thee not, old man: fall to thy prayers;
How ill white hairs become a fool and jester!
I have long dream'd of such a kind of man,
So surfeit-swell'd, so old, and so profane;
But, being awaked, I do despise my dream.
Make less thy body hence, and more thy grace;
Leave gormandizing; know the grave doth gape
For thee thrice wider than for other men.—
Reply not to me with a fool-born jest:

Presume not that I am the thing I was;
For God doth know, so shall the world perceive,
That I have turn'd away my former self;
So will I those that kept me company.
When thou dost hear I am as I have been,
Approach me, and thou shalt be as thou wast,
The tutor and the feeder of my riots:
Till then, I banish thee, on pain of death,—
As I have done the rest of my misleaders,—
Not to come near our person by ten mile.
For competence of life I will allow you,
That lack of means enforce you not to evil:
And, as we hear you do reform yourselves,
We will, according to your strength and quali-
ties,
Give you advancement.—Be it your charge, my
lord,
To see perform'd the tenour of our word.—
Set on.   [*Exeunt* KING *and his* TRAIN.
FALSTAFF.
Master Shallow, I owe you a thousand pound.
SHALLOW.
Yea, marry, Sir John; which I beseech you to let
me have home with me.
FALSTAFF.
That can hardly be, Master Shallow. Do not you
grieve at this; I shall be sent for in private to him:
look you, he must seem thus to the world: fear
not your advancements; I will be the man yet that
shall make you great.
SHALLOW.
I cannot well perceive how,—unless you should
give me your doublet, and stuff me out with
straw. I beseech you, good Sir John, let me have
five hundred of my thousand.
FALSTAFF.
Sir, I will be as good as my word: this that you
heard was but a colour.
SHALLOW.
A colour that I fear you will die in, Sir John.
FALSTAFF.
Fear no colours: go with me to dinner:—come,
Lieutenant Pistol;—come, Bardolph:—I shall be
sent for soon at night.
Enter PRINCE JOHN OF LANCASTER, *the* LORD
CHIEF JUSTICE, OFFICERS, *&c.*
LORD CHIEF JUSTICE.
Go, carry Sir John Falstaff to the Fleet;
Take all his company along with him.
FALSTAFF.
My lord, my lord,—
LORD CHIEF JUSTICE.
I cannot now speak: I will hear you soon.—
Take them away.
PISTOL.
Si fortuna me tormenta, spero contenta.
[*Exeunt all but* PRINCE JOHN *and* CHIEF
JUSTICE.
PRINCE JOHN OF LANCASTER.
I like this fair proceeding of the king's:
He hath intent his wonted followers
Shall all be very well provided for;
But all are banisht till their conversations
Appear more wise and modest to the world.
LORD CHIEF JUSTICE.
And so they are.

PRINCE JOHN OF LANCASTER.
The king hath call'd his parliament, my lord.
LORD CHIEF JUSTICE.
He hath.
PRINCE JOHN OF LANCASTER.
I will lay odds that, ere this year expire,
We bear our civil swords and native fire
As far as France: I heard a bird so sing,
Whose music, to my thinking, pleased the king.
Come, will you hence?   [*Exeunt.*

EPILOGUE.

Spoken by a DANCER.

FIRST my fear; then my court'sy; last my speech.
My fear is, your displeasure; my court'sy,
my duty; and my speech, to beg your pardons.
If you look for a good speech now, you undo me:
for what I have to say is of mine own making; and
what indeed I should say will, I doubt, prove
mine own marring. But to the purpose, and so to
the venture.—Be it known to you,—as it is very
well,—I was lately here in the end of a displeasing play, to pray your patience for it, and to
promise you a better. I meant, indeed, to pay you
with this; which, if, like an ill venture, it come
unluckily home, I break, and you, my gentle
creditors, lose. Here I promised you I would be,
and here I commit my body to your mercies: bate
me some, and I will pay you some, and, as most
debtors do, promise you infinitely.

If my tongue cannot entreat you to acquit me,
will you command me to use my legs? and yet
that were but light payment,—to dance out of
your debt. But a good conscience will make any
possible satisfaction, and so would I. All the
gentlewomen here have forgiven me: if the
gentlemen will not, then the gentlemen do not
agree with the gentlewomen, which was never
seen before in such an assembly.

One word more, I beseech you. If you be not
too much cloy'd with fat meat, our humble
author will continue the story, with Sir John in
it, and make you merry with fair Katharine of
France: where, for any thing I know, Falstaff
shall die of a sweat, unless already a' be kill'd
with your hard opinions; for Oldcastle died a
martyr, and this is not the man. My tongue is
weary; when my legs are too, I will bid you good
night; and so kneel down before you;—but, indeed, to pray for the queen.

KING HENRY THE FIFTH

DRAMATIS PERSONAE

KING HENRY THE FIFTH.
DUKE OF GLOSTER, } *brothers to the King.*
DUKE OF BEDFORD, }
DUKE OF EXETER, *uncle to the King.*
DUKE OF YORK, *cousin to the King.*
EARL OF SALISBURY.
EARL OF WESTMORELAND.
EARL OF WARWICK.
ARCHBISHOP OF CANTERBURY.
BISHOP OF ELY.
EARL OF CAMBRIDGE.
LORD SCROOP.
SIR THOMAS GREY.
SIR THOMAS ERPINGHAM, GOWER, FLUELLEN,
   MACMORRIS, JAMY, *officers in King Henry's
   army.*
JOHN BATES, ALEXANDER COURT, MICHAEL
   WILLIAMS, *soldiers in the same.*
PISTOL.
NYM.
BARDOLPH.
BOY.
A HERALD.

CHARLES THE SIXTH, *King of France.*
LOUIS, *the Dauphin.*
DUKE OF BURGUNDY.
DUKE OF ORLEANS.
DUKE OF BOURBON.
THE CONSTABLE OF FRANCE.
RAMBURES, GRANDPRÉ, *French lords.*
GOVERNOR OF HARFLEUR.
MONTJOY, *a French herald.*
AMBASSADORS *to the King of England.*

ISABEL, *Queen of France.*
KATHARINE, *daughter to Charles and Isabel.*
ALICE, *a lady attending on her.*
HOSTESS *of a tavern in Eastcheap (formerly
   Mistress Quickly, and now married to Pistol).*

LORDS, LADIES, OFFICERS, SOLDIERS,
CITIZENS, MESSENGERS, *and* ATTENDANTS.

CHORUS.

SCENE—*England; afterwards France.*

PROLOGUE.

Enter CHORUS.

CHORUS.

O FOR a Muse of fire, that would ascend
   The brightest heaven of invention,—
A kingdom for a stage, princes to act,
And monarchs to behold the swelling scene!
Then should the warlike Harry, like himself,
Assume the port of Mars; and at his heels,
Leasht-in like hounds, should famine, sword, and
   fire,
Crouch for employment. But pardon, gentles all,
The flat unraised spirits that have dared
On this unworthy scaffold to bring forth
So great an object: can this cockpit hold
The vasty fields of France? or may we cram
Within this wooden O the very casques
That did affright the air at Agincourt?
O, pardon! since a crooked figure may
Attest in little place a million;
And let us, ciphers to this great accompt,
On your imaginary forces work.
Suppose within the girdle of these walls
Are now confined two mighty monarchies,
Whose high-upreared and abutting fronts
The perilous narrow ocean parts asunder:
Piece-out our imperfections with your thoughts;
Into a thousand parts divide one man,
And make imaginary puissance;
Think, when we talk of horses, that you see them
Printing their proud hoofs i'th'receiving earth;—
For 'tis your thoughts that now must deck our
   kings,
Carry them here and there; jumping o'er times,
Turning th'accomplishment of many years
Into an hour-glass: for the which supply,
Admit me Chorus to this history;
Who, prologue-like, your humble patience pray,
Gently to hear, kindly to judge, our play.   [*Exit.*

ACT I. SCENE I.

London.   An ante-chamber in the KING'S
palace.

Enter the ARCHBISHOP OF CANTERBURY
and the BISHOP OF ELY.

ARCHBISHOP OF CANTERBURY.

MY lord, I'll tell you,—that self bill is
   urged,
Which in th'eleventh year of the last king's
   reign
Was like, and had indeed against us past,
But that the scambling and unquiet time
Did push it out of further question.

BISHOP OF ELY.

But how, my lord, shall we resist it now?

ARCHBISHOP OF CANTERBURY.

It must be thought on. If it pass against us,
We lose the better half of our possession;
For all the temporal lands, which men devout
By testament have given to the church,
Would they strip from us; being valued thus,—
As much as would maintain, to the king's honour,
Full fifteen earls and fifteen hundred knights,
Six thousand and two hundred good esquires;
And, to relief of lazars and weak age,
Of indigent faint souls past corporal toil,
A hundred almshouses right well supplied;
And to the coffers of the king, beside,
A thousand pounds by th'year: thus runs the bill.

BISHOP OF ELY.

This would drink deep.

485

ARCHBISHOP OF CANTERBURY.
        'Twould drink the cup and all.
          BISHOP OF ELY.
But what prevention?
      ARCHBISHOP OF CANTERBURY.
The king is full of grace and fair regard.
          BISHOP OF ELY.
And a true lover of the holy church.
      ARCHBISHOP OF CANTERBURY.
The courses of his youth promised it not.
The breath no sooner left his father's body,
But that his wildness, mortified in him,
Seem'd to die too; yea, at that very moment,
Consideration, like an angel, came,
And whipt th'offending Adam out of him,
Leaving his body as a paradise,
T'envelop and contain celestial spirits.
Never was such a sudden scholar made;
Never came reformation in a flood,
With such a heady current, scouring faults;
Nor never Hydra-headed wilfulness
So soon did lose his seat, and all at once,
As in this king.
          BISHOP OF ELY.
        We are blessed in the change.
      ARCHBISHOP OF CANTERBURY.
Hear him but reason in divinity,
And, all-admiring, with an inward wish
You would desire the king were made a prelate:
Hear him debate of commonwealth affairs,
You would say it hath been all-in-all his study:
List his discourse of war, and you shall hear
A fearful battle render'd you in music:
Turn him to any cause of policy,
The Gordian knot of it he will unloose,
Familiar as his garter:—that, when he speaks,
The air, a charter'd libertine, is still,
And the mute wonder lurketh in men's ears,
To steal his sweet and honey'd sentences;
So that the art and practic part of life
Must be the mistress to this theoric:
Which is a wonder how his Grace should glean
   it,
Since his addiction was to courses vain;
His companies unletter'd, rude, and shallow;
His hours fill'd up with riots, banquets, sports;
And never noted in him any study,
Any retirement, any sequestration
From open haunts and popularity.
          BISHOP OF ELY.
The strawberry grows underneath the nettle,
And wholesome berries thrive and ripen best
Neighbour'd by fruit of baser quality:
And so the prince obscured his contemplation
Under the veil of wildness; which, no doubt,
Grew like the summer grass, fastest by night,
Unseen, yet crescive in his faculty.
      ARCHBISHOP OF CANTERBURY.
It must be so; for miracles are ceased;
And therefore we must needs admit the means
How things are perfected.
          BISHOP OF ELY.
               But, my good lord,
How now for mitigation of this bill
Urged by the commons? Doth his majesty
Incline to it, or no?

ARCHBISHOP OF CANTERBURY.
          He seems indifferent;
Or, rather, swaying more upon our part
Than cherishing th'exhibiters against us:
For I have made an offer to his majesty,—
Upon our spiritual convocation,
And in regard of causes now in hand,
Which I have open'd to his Grace at large,
As touching France,—to give a greater sum
Than ever at one time the clergy yet
Did to his predecessors part withal.
          BISHOP OF ELY.
How did this offer seem received, my lord?
      ARCHBISHOP OF CANTERBURY.
With good acceptance of his majesty;
Save that there was not time enough to hear—
As, I perceived, his Grace would fain have done—
The severals and unhidden passages
Of his true titles to some certain dukedoms,
And, generally, to the crown and seat of France,
Derived from Edward, his great-grandfather.
          BISHOP OF ELY.
What was th'impediment that broke this off?
      ARCHBISHOP OF CANTERBURY.
The French ambassador upon that instant
Craved audience;—and the hour, I think, is come
To give him hearing: is it four o'clock?
          BISHOP OF ELY.
It is.
      ARCHBISHOP OF CANTERBURY.
Then go we in, to know his embassy;
Which I could, with a ready guess, declare,
Before the Frenchman speak a word of it.
          BISHOP OF ELY.
I'll wait upon you; and I long to hear it.
                    [*Exeunt.*

SCENE II.

The same.   The Presence-chamber.

Enter KING HENRY, GLOSTER, BEDFORD,
   EXETER, WARWICK, WESTMORELAND, *and*
   ATTENDANTS.

            KING HENRY.
WHERE is my gracious Lord of Canterbury?
          DUKE OF EXETER.
Not here in presence.
          KING HENRY.
          Send for him, good uncle.
        EARL OF WESTMORELAND.
Shall we call in th'ambassador, my liege?
            KING HENRY.
Not yet, my cousin: we would be resolved,
Before we hear him, of some things of weight,
That task our thoughts, concerning us and
   France.
Enter the ARCHBISHOP OF CANTERBURY *and*
   the BISHOP OF ELY.
      ARCHBISHOP OF CANTERBURY.
God and his angels guard your sacred throne,
And make you long become it!
            KING HENRY.
                  Sure, we thank you.
My learned lord, we pray you to proceed,
And justly and religiously unfold
Why the law Salique, that they have in France,
Or should, or should not, bar us in our claim:

And God forbid, my dear and faithful lord,
That you should fashion, wrest, or bow your
   reading,
Or nicely charge your understanding soul
With opening titles miscreate, whose right
Suits not in native colours with the truth;
For God doth know how many, now in health,
Shall drop their blood in approbation
Of what your reverence shall incite us to.
Therefore take heed how you impawn our person,
How you awake the sleeping sword of war:
We charge you, in the name of God, take heed;
For never two such kingdoms did contend
Without much fall of blood; whose guiltless drops
Are every one a woe, a sore complaint
'Gainst him whose wrongs give edge unto the
   swords
That make such waste in brief mortality.
Under this conjuration, speak, my lord;
For we will hear, note, and believe in heart
That what you speak is in your conscience washt
As pure as sin with baptism.

ARCHBISHOP OF CANTERBURY.
Then hear me, gracious sovereign,—and you
   peers,
That owe yourselves, your lives, and services
To this imperial throne.—There is no bar
To make against your highness' claim to France
But this, which they produce from Pharamond,—
In terram Salicam mulieres ne succedant,
'No woman shall succeed in Salique land:'
Which Salique land the French unjustly gloze
To be the realm of France, and Pharamond
The founder of this law and female bar.
Yet their own authors faithfully affirm
That the land Salique is in Germany,
Between the floods of Sala and of Elbe;
Where Charles the Great, having subdued the
   Saxons,
There left behind and settled certain French;
Who, holding in disdain the German women
For some dishonest manners of their life,
Establisht then this law,—to wit, no female
Should be inheritrix in Salique land:
Which Salique, as I said, 'twixt Elbe and Sala,
Is at this day in Germany call'd Meisen.
Then doth it well appear, the Salique law
Was not devised for the realm of France:
Nor did the French possess the Salique land
Until four hundred one and twenty years
After defunction of King Pharamond,
Idly supposed the founder of this law;
Who died within the year of our redemption
Four hundred twenty-six; and Charles the Great
Subdued the Saxons, and did seat the French
Beyond the river Sala, in the year
Eight hundred five. Besides, their writers say,
King Pepin, which deposed Childeric,
Did, as heir general, being descended
Of Blithild, which was daughter to King Clothair,
Make claim and title to the crown of France.
Hugh Capet also,—who usurpt the crown
Of Charles the duke of Lorraine, sole heir male
Of the true line and stock of Charles the Great,—
To find his title with some shows of truth,
Though, in pure truth, it was corrupt and naught,

Convey'd himself as heir to th'Lady Lingar
Daughter to Charlemain, who was the son
To Louis the emperor, and Louis the son
Of Charles the Great. Also King Louis the
   Tenth,
Who was sole heir to the usurper Capet,
Could not keep quiet in his conscience,
Wearing the crown of France, till satisfied
That fair Queen Isabel, his grandmother,
Was lineal of the Lady Ermengare,
Daughter to Charles the foresaid duke of Lor-
   raine:
By the which marriage the line of Charles the
   Great
Was re-united to the crown of France.
So that, as clear as is the summer's sun,
King Pepin's title, and Hugh Capet's claim,
King Louis his satisfaction, all appear
To hold in right and title of the female:
So do the kings of France unto this day;
Howbeit they would hold up this Salique law
To bar your highness claiming from the female;
And rather choose to hide them in a net
Than amply to imbar their crooked titles
Usurpt from you and your progenitors.

KING HENRY.
May I with right and conscience make this
   claim?

ARCHBISHOP OF CANTERBURY.
The sin upon my head, dread sovereign!
For in the Book of Numbers is it writ,—
When the man dies, let the inheritance
Descend unto the daughter. Gracious lord,
Stand for your own; unwind your bloody flag;
Look back into your mighty ancestors:
Go, my dread lord, to your great-grandsire's
   tomb,
From whom you claim; invoke his warlike spirit,
And your great-uncle's, Edward the Black
   Prince,
Who on the French ground play'd a tragedy,
Making defeat on the full power of France,
Whiles his most mighty father on a hill
Stood smiling to behold his lion's whelp
Forage in blood of French nobility.
O noble English, that could entertain
With half their forces the full pride of France,
And let another half stand laughing by,
All out of work and cold for action!

BISHOP OF ELY.
Awake remembrance of these valiant dead,
And with your puissant arm renew their feats:
You are their heir; you sit upon their throne;
The blood and courage that renowned them
Runs in your veins; and my thrice-puissant liege
Is in the very May-morn of his youth,
Ripe for exploits and mighty enterprises.

DUKE OF EXETER.
Your brother kings and monarchs of the earth
Do all expect that you should rouse yourself,
As did the former lions of your blood.

EARL OF WESTMORELAND.
They know your Grace hath cause and means
   and might;
So hath your highness; never king of England
Had nobles richer and more loyal subjects,

Whose hearts have left their bodies here in
  England,
And lie pavilion'd in the fields of France.
ARCHBISHOP OF CANTERBURY.
O, let their bodies follow, my dear liege,
With blood and sword and fire to win your right:
In aid whereof we of the spirituality
Will raise your highness such a mighty sum
As never did the clergy at one time
Bring in to any of your ancestors.
KING HENRY.
We must not only arm t'invade the French,
But lay down our proportions to defend
Against the Scot, who will make road upon us
With all advantages.
ARCHBISHOP OF CANTERBURY.
They of those marches, gracious sovereign,
Shall be a wall sufficient to defend
Our inland from the pilfering borderers.
KING HENRY.
We do not mean the coursing snatchers only,
But fear the main intendment of the Scot,
Who hath been still a giddy neighbour to us;
For you shall read that my great-grandfather
Never went with his forces into France,
But that the Scot on his unfurnish'd kingdom
Came pouring, like the tide into a breach,
With ample and brim fullness of his force;
Galling the gleaned land with hot assays,
Girding with grievous siege castles and towns;
That England, being empty of defence,
Hath shook and trembled at th'ill neighbourhood.
ARCHBISHOP OF CANTERBURY.
She hath been then more fear'd than harm'd, my
  liege;
For hear her but exampled by herself:—
When all her chivalry hath been in France,
And she a mourning widow of her nobles,
She hath herself not only well defended
But taken, and impounded as a stray,
The King of Scots; whom she did send to France,
To fill King Edward's fame with prisoner kings,
And make her chronicle as rich with praise
As is the ooze and bottom of the sea
With sunken wrack and sumless treasuries.
EARL OF WESTMORELAND.
But there's a saying, very old and true,—
    'If that you will France win,
      Then with Scotland first begin:'
For once the eagle England being in prey,
To her unguarded nest the weasel Scot
Comes sneaking, and so sucks her princely eggs;
Playing the mouse in absence of the cat,
To spoil and havoc more than she can eat.
DUKE OF EXETER.
It follows, then, the cat must stay at home:
Yet that is but a curst necessity,
Since we have locks to safeguard necessaries,
And pretty traps to catch the petty thieves.
While that the armed hand doth fight abroad,
Th'advised head defends itself at home;
For government, though high, and low, and
  lower,
Put into parts, doth keep in one concent,
Congreeing in a full and natural close,
Like music.

ARCHBISHOP OF CANTERBURY.
    True: therefore doth heaven divide
The state of man in divers functions,
Setting endeavour in continual motion;
To which is fixed, as an aim or butt,
Obedience: for so work the honey-bees,
Creatures that, by a rule in nature, teach
The art of order to a peopled kingdom.
They have a king, and officers of sorts:
Where some, like magistrates, correct at home;
Others, like merchants, venture trade abroad;
Others, like soldiers, armed in their stings,
Make boot upon the summer's velvet buds;
Which pillage they with merry march bring
  home
To the tent-royal of their emperor:
Who, busied in his majesty, surveys
The singing masons building roofs of gold;
The civil citizens kneading-up the honey;
The poor mechanic porters crowding in
Their heavy burdens at his narrow gate;
The sad-eyed justice, with his surly hum,
Delivering o'er to executors pale
The lazy yawning drone. I this infer,—
That many things, having full reference
To one concent, may work contrariously:
As many arrows, loosed several ways,
Fly to one mark;
As many several ways meet in one town;
As many fresh streams run in one self sea;
As many lines close in the dial's centre;
So may a thousand actions, once afoot,
End in one purpose, and be all well borne
Without defeat. Therefore to France, my liege.
Divide your happy England into four;
Whereof take you one quarter into France,
And you withal shall make all Gallia shake.
If we, with thrice such powers left at home,
Cannot defend our own doors from the dog,
Let us be worried, and our nation lose
The name of hardiness and policy.
KING HENRY.
Call in the messengers sent from the Dauphin.
      [Exeunt some ATTENDANTS.
Now are we well resolved; and, by God's help,
And yours, the noble sinews of our power,
France being ours, we'll bend it to our awe,
Or break it all to pieces: or there we'll sit,
Ruling in large and ample empery
O'er France and all her almost kingly dukedoms,
Or lay these bones in an unworthy urn,
Tombless, with no remembrance over them:
Either our history shall with full mouth
Speak freely of our acts, or else our grave,
Like Turkish mute, shall have a tongueless
  mouth,
Not worshipt with a waxen epitaph.
      Enter AMBASSADORS of France, attended.
Now are we well prepared to know the pleasure
Of our fair cousin Dauphin; for we hear
Your greeting is from him, not from the king.
FIRST AMBASSADOR.
May't please your majesty to give us leave
Freely to render what we have in charge;
Or shall we sparingly show you far off
The Dauphin's meaning and our embassy?

KING HENRY.
We are no tyrant, but a Christian king;
Unto whose grace our passion is as subject
As are our wretches fetter'd in our prisons:
Therefore with frank and with uncurbed plain-
　　ness
Tell us the Dauphin's mind.
　　　　　FIRST AMBASSADOR.
　　　　　　　　Thus, then, in few.
Your highness, lately sending into France,
Did claim some certain dukedoms, in the right
Of your great predecessor, King Edward the
　　Third.
In answer of which claim, the prince our master
Says, that you savour too much of your youth;
And bids you be advised, there's naught in
　　France
That can be with a nimble galliard won;—
You cannot revel into dukedoms there.
He therefore sends you, meeter for your spirit,
This tun of treasure; and, in lieu of this,
Desires you let the dukedoms that you claim
Hear no more of you. This the Dauphin speaks.
　　　　　KING HENRY.
What treasure, uncle?
　　　　　DUKE OF EXETER.
　　　　　　　Tennis-balls, my liege.
　　　　　KING HENRY.
We are glad the Dauphin is so pleasant with us;
His present and your pains we thank you for:
When we have matcht our rackets to these balls,
We will, in France, by God's grace, play a set
Shall strike his father's crown into the hazard.
Tell him he hath made a match with such a
　　wrangler
That all the courts of France will be disturb'd
With chases. And we understand him well,
How he comes o'er us with our wilder days,
Not measuring what use we made of them.
We never valued this poor seat of England;
And therefore, living hence, did give ourself
To barbarous licence; as 'tis ever common
That men are merriest when they are from home.
But tell the Dauphin, I will keep my state,
Be like a king, and show my sail of greatness,
When I do rouse me in my throne of France:
For that I have laid by my majesty,
And plodded like a man for working-days;
But I will rise there with so full a glory,
That I will dazzle all the eyes of France,
Yea, strike the Dauphin blind to look on us.
And tell the pleasant prince, this mock of his
Hath turn'd his balls to gun-stones; and his soul
Shall stand sore charged for the wasteful ven-
　　geance
That shall fly with them: for many a thousand
　　widows
Shall this his mock mock out of their dear hus-
　　bands;
Mock mothers from their sons, mock castles
　　down;
And some are yet ungotten and unborn
That shall have cause to curse the Dauphin's
　　scorn.
But this lies all within the will of God,
To whom I do appeal; and in whose name,

Tell you the Dauphin, I am coming on,
To venge me as I may, and to put forth
My rightful hand in a well-hallow'd cause.
So, get you hence in peace; and tell the Dauphin,
His jest will savour but of shallow wit,
When thousands weep, more than did laugh at
　　it.—
Convey them with safe conduct.—Fare you well.
　　　　　　　[Exeunt AMBASSADORS.
　　　　　DUKE OF EXETER.
This was a merry message.
　　　　　KING HENRY.
We hope to make the sender blush at it.
Therefore, my lords, omit no happy hour
That may give furtherance to our expedition;
For we have now no thought in us but France,
Save those to God, that run before our business.
Therefore let our proportions for these wars
Be soon collected, and all things thought upon
That may with reasonable swiftness add
More feathers to our wings; for, God before,
We'll chide this Dauphin at his father's door.
Therefore let every man now task his thought,
That this fair action may on foot be brought.
　　　　　　[Flourish. Exeunt.

ACT II.
PROLOGUE.
Enter CHORUS.
CHORUS.

NOW all the youth of England are on fire,
　　And silken dalliance in the wardrobe lies:
Now thrive the armourers, and honour's thought
Reigns solely in the breast of every man:
They sell the pasture now to buy the horse;
Following the mirror of all Christian kings,
With winged heels, as English Mercuries.
For now sits Expectation in the air,
And hides a sword from hilts unto the point
With crowns imperial, crowns, and coronets,
Promised to Harry and his followers.
The French, advised by good intelligence
Of this most dreadful preparation,
Shake in their fear; and with pale policy
Seek to divert the English purposes.
O England!—model to thy inward greatness,
Like little body with a mighty heart,—
What mightst thou do, that honour would thee
　　do,
Were all thy children kind and natural!
But see thy fault! France hath in thee found out
A nest of hollow bosoms, which he fills
With treacherous crowns; and three corrupted
　　men,—
One, Richard earl of Cambridge; and the second,
Henry Lord Scroop of Masham; and the third,
Sir Thomas Grey, knight, of Northumberland,—
Have, for the gilt of France—O guilt indeed!—
Confirm'd conspiracy with fearful France;
And by their hands this grace of kings must die,
If hell and treason hold their promises,
Ere he take ship for France, and in Southampton.
Linger your patience on; and we'll digest
Th'abuse of distance; force a play.
The sum is paid; the traitors are agreed;

The king is set from London; and the scene
Is now transported, gentles, to Southampton,—
There is the playhouse now, there must you sit:
And thence to France shall we convey you safe,
And bring you back, charming the narrow seas
To give you gentle pass; for, if we may,
We'll not offend one stomach with our play.
But, till the king come forth, and not till then,
Unto Southampton do we shift our scene.   [*Exit.*

SCENE I.

London. Before the Boar's Head Tavern, Eastcheap.

Enter CORPORAL NYM *and* LIEUTENANT BARDOLPH.

BARDOLPH.

WELL met, Corporal Nym.

NYM.

Good morrow, Lieutenant Bardolph.

BARDOLPH.

What, are Ancient Pistol and you friends yet?

NYM.

For my part, I care not: I say little; but when time shall serve, there shall be smites;—but that shall be as it may. I dare not fight; but I will wink, and hold out mine iron: it is a simple one; but what though? it will toast cheese, and it will endure cold as another man's sword will: and there's the humour of it.

BARDOLPH.

I will bestow a breakfast to make you friends; and we'll be all three sworn brothers to France: let's be so, good Corporal Nym.

NYM.

Faith, I will live so long as I may, that's the certain of it; and when I cannot live any longer, I will do as I may: that is my rest, that is the rendezvous of it.

BARDOLPH.

It is certain, corporal, that he is married to Nell Quickly: and, certainly, she did you wrong; for you were troth-plight to her.

NYM.

I cannot tell:—things must be as they may: men may sleep, and they may have their throats about them at that time; and, some say, knives have edges. It must be as it may: though patience be a tired mare, yet she will plod. There must be conclusions. Well, I cannot tell.

BARDOLPH.

Here comes Ancient Pistol and his wife:—good corporal, be patient here.

Enter PISTOL *and* HOSTESS.

How now, mine host Pistol!

PISTOL.

Base tike, call'st thou me host?
Now, by this hand, I swear, I scorn the term;
Nor shall my Nell keep lodgers.

HOSTESS.

No, by my troth, not long; for we cannot lodge and board a dozen or fourteen gentlewomen that live honestly by the prick of their needles, but it will be thought we keep a bawdy-house straight. [NYM *and* PISTOL *draw.*] O well-a-day, Lady, if he be not drawn now! We shall see wilful adultery and murder committed.

BARDOLPH.

Good lieutenant,—good corporal,—offer nothing here.

NYM.

Pish!

PISTOL.

Pish for thee, Iceland dog! thou prick-ear'd cur of Iceland!

HOSTESS.

Good Corporal Nym, show thy valour, and put up your sword.

NYM.

Will you shog off? I would have you *solus*.

PISTOL.

Solus, egregious dog? O viper vile!
The *solus* in thy most mervailous face;
The *solus* in thy teeth, and in thy throat,
And in thy hateful lungs, yea, in thy maw, perdy,
And, which is worse, within thy nasty mouth!
I do retort the *solus* in thy bowels;
For I can take, and Pistol's cock is up,
And flashing fire will follow.

NYM.

I am not Barbason; you cannot conjure me. I have an humour to knock you indifferently well. If you grow foul with me, Pistol, I will scour you with my rapier, as I may, in fair terms: if you would walk off, I would prick your guts a little, in good terms, as I may: and that's the humour of it.

PISTOL.

O braggart vile, and damned furious wight!
The grave doth gape, and doting death is near;
Therefore exhale.

BARDOLPH.

Hear me, hear me what I say:—he that strikes the first stroke, I'll run him up to the hilts, as I am a soldier.   [*Draws.*

PISTOL.

An oath of mickle might; and fury shall abate.—
Give me thy fist, thy fore-foot to me give:
Thy spirits are most tall.

[*They sheath their swords.*

NYM.

I will cut thy throat, one time or other, in fair terms: that is the humour of it.

PISTOL.

Couple a gorge!
That is the word. I thee defy again.
O hound of Crete, think'st thou my spouse to get?
No; to the spital go,
And from the powdering-tub of infamy
Fetch forth the lazar kite of Cressid's kind,
Doll Tearsheet she by name, and her espouse:
I have, and I will hold, the *quondam* Quickly
For the only she; and—*pauca*, there's enough.
Go to.

Enter BOY.

BOY.

Mine host Pistol, you must come to my master,—and you, hostess:—he is very sick, and would to bed.—Good Bardolph, put thy face between his sheets, and do the office of a warming-pan.—Faith, he's very ill.

BARDOLPH.

Away, you rogue!

HOSTESS.

By my troth, he'll yield the crow a pudding one of these days: the king has kill'd his heart.—Good husband, come home presently.

[*Exeunt* HOSTESS *and* BOY.

BARDOLPH.

Come, shall I make you two friends? We must to France together: why the devil should we keep knives to cut one another's throats?

PISTOL.

Let floods o'erswell, and fiends for food howl on!

NYM.

You'll pay me the eight shillings I won of you at betting?

PISTOL.

Base is the slave that pays.

NYM.

That now I will have: that's the humour of it.

PISTOL.

As manhood shall compound: push home.

[*They draw.*

BARDOLPH.

By this sword, he that makes the first thrust, I'll kill him; by this sword, I will.   [*Draws.*

PISTOL.

Sword is an oath, and oaths must have their course.

BARDOLPH.

Corporal Nym, an thou wilt be friends, be friends: an thou wilt not, why, then be enemies with me too. Prithee, put up.

NYM.

I shall have my eight shillings I won of you at betting?

PISTOL.

A noble shalt thou have, and present pay;
And liquor likewise will I give to thee,
And friendship shall combine and brotherhood;
I'll live by Nym, and Nym shall live by me;—
Is not this just?—for I shall sutler be
Unto the camp, and profits will accrue.
Give me thy hand.   [*They sheathe their swords.*

NYM.

I shall have my noble?

PISTOL.

In cash most justly paid.

NYM.

Well, then, that's the humour of it.

Enter HOSTESS.

HOSTESS.

As ever you came of women, come in quickly to Sir John. Ah, poor heart! he is so shaked of a burning quotidian tertian, that it is most lamentable to behold. Sweet men, come to him.

NYM.

The king hath run bad humours on the knight, that's the even of it.

PISTOL.

Nym, thou hast spoke the right;
His heart is fracted and corroborate.

NYM.

The king is a good king: but it must be as it may; he passes some humours and careers.

PISTOL.

Let us condole the knight; for, lambkins, we will live.   [*Exeunt.*

SCENE II.

Southampton. A council-chamber.

Enter EXETER, BEDFORD, *and* WESTMORE-
LAND.

DUKE OF BEDFORD.

'FORE God, his Grace is bold, to trust these traitors.

DUKE OF EXETER.

They shall be apprehended by and by.

EARL OF WESTMORELAND.

How smooth and even they do bear themselves!
As if allegiance in their bosoms sat,
Crowned with faith and constant loyalty.

DUKE OF BEDFORD.

The king hath note of all that they intend,
By interception which they dream not of.

DUKE OF EXETER.

Nay, but the man that was his bedfellow,
Whom he hath dull'd and cloy'd with gracious favours,
That he should, for a foreign purse, so sell
His sovereign's life to death and treachery!

Trumpets sound. Enter KING HENRY, CAM-
BRIDGE, SCROOP, GREY, LORDS, *and* ATTEN-
DANTS.

KING HENRY.

Now sits the wind fair, and we will aboard.
My Lord of Cambridge,—and my kind Lord of Masham,—
And you, my gentle knight,—give me your thoughts:
Think you not that the powers we bear with us
Will cut their passage through the force of France,
Doing the execution and the act
For which we have in head assembled them?

LORD SCROOP.

No doubt, my liege, if each man do his best.

KING HENRY.

I doubt not that; since we are well persuaded
We carry not a heart with us from hence
That grows not in a fair consent with ours,
Nor leave not one behind that doth not wish
Success and conquest to attend on us.

EARL OF CAMBRIDGE.

Never was monarch better fear'd and loved
Than is your majesty: there's not, I think, a subject
That sits in heart-grief and uneasiness
Under the sweet shade of your government.

SIR THOMAS GREY.

True: those that were your father's enemies
Have steept their galls in honey, and do serve you
With hearts create of duty and of zeal.

KING HENRY.

We therefore have great cause of thankfulness;
And shall forget the office of our hand,
Sooner than quittance of desert and merit
According to the weight and worthiness.

LORD SCROOP.

So service shall with steeled sinews toil,
And labour shall refresh itself with hope,
To do your Grace incessant services.

KING HENRY.
We judge no less.—Uncle of Exeter,
Enlarge the man committed yesterday,
That rail'd against our person: we consider
It was excess of wine that set him on;
And, on his more advice, we pardon him.

LORD SCROOP.
That's mercy, but too much security:
Let him be punisht, sovereign; lest example
Breed, by his sufferance, more of such a kind.

KING HENRY.
O, let us yet be merciful.

EARL OF CAMBRIDGE.
So may your highness, and yet punish too.

SIR THOMAS GREY.
Sir, you show great mercy, if you give him life,
After the taste of much correction.

KING HENRY.
Alas, your too much love and care of me
Are heavy orisons 'gainst this poor wretch!
If little faults, proceeding on distemper,
Shall not be winkt at, how shall we stretch our
    eye
When capital crimes, chew'd, swallow'd, and
    digested,
Appear before us?—We'll yet enlarge that man,
Though Cambridge, Scroop, and Grey, in their
    dear care
And tender preservation of our person,
Would have him punisht. And now to our French
    causes:
Who are the late commissioners?

EARL OF CAMBRIDGE.
I one, my lord:
Your highness bade me ask for it to-day.

LORD SCROOP.
So did you me, my liege.

SIR THOMAS GREY.
And me, my royal sovereign.

KING HENRY.
Then, Richard earl of Cambridge, there is
    yours;—
There yours, Lord Scroop of Masham;—and, sir
    knight,
Grey of Northumberland, this same is yours:—
Read them; and know, I know your worthiness.—
My Lord of Westmoreland, and uncle Exeter,
We will aboard to-night.—Why, how now, gentle-
    men!
What see you in those papers, that you lose
So much complexion?—Look ye, how they
    change!
Their cheeks are paper.—Why, what read you
    there,
That hath so cowarded and chased your blood
Out of appearance?

EARL OF CAMBRIDGE.
            I do confess my fault;
And do submit me to your highness' mercy.

SIR THOMAS GREY and LORD SCROOP.
To which we all appeal.

KING HENRY.
The mercy that was quick in us but late,
By your own counsel is supprest and kill'd:
You must not dare, for shame, to talk of mercy;
For your own reasons turn into your bosoms,

As dogs upon their masters, worrying you.—
See you, my princes and my noble peers, [here,—
These English monsters! My Lord of Cambridge
You know how apt our love was to accord
To furnish him with all appertinents
Belonging to his honour; and this man
Hath, for a few light crowns, lightly conspired,
And sworn unto the practices of France,
To kill us here in Hampton: to the which
This knight, no less for bounty bound to us
Than Cambridge is, hath likewise sworn.—But, O,
What shall I say to thee, Lord Scroop? thou cruel,
Ingrateful, savage, and inhuman creature!
Thou that didst bear the key of all my counsels,
That knew'st the very bottom of my soul,
That almost mightst have coin'd me into gold,
Wouldst thou have practised on me for thy use,—
May it be possible, that foreign hire
Could out of thee extract one spark of evil
That might annoy my finger? 'tis so strange,
That, though the truth of it stands off as gross
As black from white, my eye will scarcely see it.
Treason and murder ever kept together,
As two yoke-devils sworn to either's purpose,
Working so grossly in a natural cause,
That admiration did not whoop at them:
But thou, 'gainst all proportion, didst bring in
Wonder to wait on treason and on murder:
And whatsoever cunning fiend it was
That wrought upon thee so preposterously,
Hath got the voice in hell for excellence:
And other devils, that suggest by treasons,
Do botch and bungle up damnation
With patches, colours, and with forms being fetcht
From glistering semblances of piety;
But he that temper'd thee bade thee stand up,
Gave thee no instance why thou shouldst do
    treason,
Unless to dub thee with the name of traitor.
If that same demon that hath gull'd thee thus
Should with his lion-gait walk the whole world,
He might return to vasty Tartar back,
And tell the legions, 'I can never win
A soul so easy as that Englishman's.'
O, how hast thou with jealousy infected
The sweetness of affiance! Show men dutiful?
Why, so didst thou: seem they grave and learned?
Why, so didst thou: come they of noble family?
Why, so didst thou: seem they religious?
Why, so didst thou: or are they spare in diet;
Free from gross passion, or of mirth or anger;
Constant in spirit, not swerving with the blood;
Garnisht and deckt in modest complement;
Not working with the eye without the ear,
And but in purged judgement trusting neither?
Such and so finely bolted didst thou seem:
And thus thy fall hath left a kind of blot,
To mark the full-fraught man and best indued
With some suspicion. I will weep for thee;
For this revolt of thine, methinks, is like
Another fall of man.—Their faults are open:
Arrest them to the answer of the law;—
And God acquit them of their practices!

DUKE OF EXETER.
I arrest thee of high treason, by the name of
Richard earl of Cambridge.

I arrest thee of high treason, by the name of
Henry Lord Scroop of Masham.
I arrest thee of high treason, by the name of
Thomas Grey, knight, of Northumberland.

LORD SCROOP.

Our purposes God justly hath discover'd;
And I repent my fault more than my death;
Which I beseech your highness to forgive,
Although my body pay the price of it.

EARL OF CAMBRIDGE.

For me,—the gold of France did not seduce;
Although I did admit it as a motive
The sooner to effect what I intended:
But God be thanked for prevention;
Which I in sufferance heartily will rejoice,
Beseeching God and you to pardon me.

SIR THOMAS GREY.

Never did faithful subject more rejoice
At the discovery of most dangerous treason
Than I do at this hour joy o'er myself,
Prevented from a damned enterprise:
My fault, but not my body, pardon, sovereign.

KING HENRY.

God quit you in his mercy! Hear your sentence.
You have conspired against our royal person,
Join'd with an enemy proclaim'd, and from his
   coffers
Received the golden earnest of our death;
Wherein you would have sold your king to
His princes and his peers to servitude, [slaughter,
His subjects to oppression and contempt,
And his whole kingdom into desolation.
Touching our person, seek we no revenge;
But we our kingdom's safety must so tender,
Whose ruin you have sought, that to her laws
We do deliver you. Get you, therefore, hence,
Poor miserable wretches, to your death:
The taste whereof, God of his mercy give
You patience to endure, and true repentance
Of all your dear offences!—Bear them hence.

   [*Exeunt* CAMBRIDGE, SCROOP, *and* GREY,
      guarded.

Now, lords, for France; the enterprise whereof
Shall be to you as us like glorious.
We doubt not of a fair and lucky war,
Since God so graciously hath brought to light
This dangerous treason, lurking in our way
To hinder our beginnings; we doubt not now
But every rub is smoothed on our way.
Then, forth, dear countrymen: let us deliver
Our puissance into the hand of God,
Putting it straight in expedition.
Cheerly to sea; the signs of war advance:
No king of England, if not king of France.
                      [*Exeunt.*

SCENE III.

*London. Before the Boar's-Head Tavern,
Eastcheap.*

Enter PISTOL, HOSTESS, NYM, BARDOLPH,
and BOY.

HOSTESS.

PRITHEE, honey-sweet husband, let me
bring thee to Staines.

PISTOL.

No; for my manly heart doth yearn.—

Bardolph, be blithe;—Nym, rouse thy vaunting
   veins;—
Boy, bristle thy courage up;—for Falstaff he is
   dead,
And we must yearn therefore.

BARDOLPH.

Would I were with him, wheresome'er he is,
either in heaven or in hell!

HOSTESS.

Nay, sure, he's not in hell: he's in Arthur's
bosom, if ever man went to Arthur's bosom. A'
made a finer end, and went away, an it had been
any christom child; a' parted ev'n just between
twelve and one, ev'n at the turning o' th' tide: for
after I saw him fumble with the sheets, and play
with flowers, and smile upon his fingers' ends, I
knew there was but one way; for his nose was as
sharp as a pen, and a' babbled of green fields.
'How now, Sir John!' quoth I: ' what, man! be o'
good cheer.' So a' cried out 'God, God, God!'
three or four times. Now I, to comfort him, bid
him a' should not think of God; I hoped there
was no need to trouble himself with any such
thoughts yet. So a' bade me lay more clothes on
his feet: I put my hand into the bed and felt them,
and they were as cold as any stone; then I felt to
his knees, and they were as cold as any stone; and
so upward and upward, and all was as cold as any
stone.

NYM.

They say he cried out of sack.

HOSTESS.

Ay, that a' did.

BARDOLPH.

And of women.

HOSTESS

Nay, that a' did not.

BOY.

Yes, that a' did; and said they were devils incarnate.

HOSTESS.

A' could never abide carnation; 'twas a colour he
never liked.

BOY.

A' said once, the devil would have him about
women.

HOSTESS.

A' did in some sort, indeed, handle women; but
then he was rheumatic, and talkt of the whore of
Babylon.

BOY.

Do you not remember, a' saw a flea stick upon
Bardolph's nose, and a' said it was a black soul
burning in hell-fire?

BARDOLPH.

Well, the fuel is gone that maintain'd that fire:
that's all the riches I got in his service.

NYM.

Shall we shog? the king will be gone from Southampton.

PISTOL.

Come, let's away.—My love, give me thy lips.
Look to my chattels and my movables:
Let senses rule; the word is 'Pitch and pay;'
Trust none;
For oaths are straws, men's faiths are wafer-cakes,

And hold-fast is the only dog, my duck:
Therefore, *caveto* be thy counsellor.
Go, clear thy crystals.—Yoke-fellows in arms,
Let us to France; like horse-leeches, my boys,
To suck, to suck, the very blood to suck!

BOY.

And that's but unwholesome food, they say.

PISTOL.

Touch her soft mouth, and march.

BARDOLPH.

Farewell, hostess.   [*Kissing her.*

NYM.

I cannot kiss, that is the humour of it; but, adieu.

PISTOL.

Let housewifery appear: keep close, I thee command.

HOSTESS.

Farewell; adieu.   [*Exeunt.*

SCENE IV.

France. A room in the French KING'S *palace.*

Flourish. Enter the French KING, *the* DAUPHIN,
the DUKE OF BURGUNDY, *the* CONSTABLE,
and others.

FRENCH KING.

THUS comes the English with full power upon
     us;
And more than carefully it us concerns
To answer royally in our defences.
Therefore the Dukes of Berri and of Bretagne,
Of Brabant and of Orleans, shall make forth,—
And you, Prince Dauphin,—with all swift dispatch,
To line and new repair our towns of war
With men of courage and with means defendant;
For England his approaches makes as fierce
As waters to the sucking of a gulf.
It fits us, then, to be as provident
As fear may teach us, out of late examples
Left by the fatal and neglected English
Upon our fields.

DAUPHIN.

              My most redoubted father,
It is most meet we arm us 'gainst the foe;
For peace itself should not so dull a kingdom,
Though war nor no known quarrel were in question,
But that defences, musters, preparations,
Should be maintain'd, assembled, and collected,
As were a war in expectation.
Therefore, I say 'tis meet we all go forth
To view the sick and feeble parts of France:
And let us do it with no show of fear;
No, with no more than if we heard that England
Were busied with a Whitsun morris-dance:
For, my good liege, she is so idly king'd,
He sceptre so fantastically borne
By a vain, giddy, shallow, humorous youth,
That fear attends her not.

CONSTABLE OF FRANCE.

                    O peace, Prince Dauphin!
You are too much mistaken in this king:
Question your Grace the late ambassadors,—
With what great state he heard their embassy,
How well supplied with noble counsellors,

How modest in exception, and withal
How terrible in constant resolution,—
And you shall find his vanities forespent
Were but the outside of the Roman Brutus,
Covering discretion with a coat of folly;
As gardeners do with ordure hide those roots
That shall first spring and be most delicate.

DAUPHIN.

Well, 'tis not so, my lord high-constable;
But though we think it so, it is no matter:
In cases of defence 'tis best to weigh
The enemy more mighty than he seems:
So the proportions of defence are fill'd;
Which, of a weak and niggardly projection,
Doth, like a miser, spoil his coat with scanting
A little cloth.

FRENCH KING.

          Think we King Harry strong;
And princes, look you strongly arm to meet him.
The kindred of him hath been flesht upon us;
And he is bred out of that bloody strain
That haunted us in our familiar paths:
Witness our too-much memorable shame
When Cressy battle fatally was struck,
And all our princes captived by the hand
Of that black name, Edward, Black Prince of
     Wales;
Whiles that his mountain sire,—on mountain
     standing,
Up in the air, crown'd with the golden sun,—
Saw his heroical seed, and smiled to see him,
Mangle the work of nature, and deface
The patterns that by God and by French fathers
Had twenty years been made. This is a stem
Of that victorious stock; and let us fear
The native mightiness and fate of him.

Enter a MESSENGER.

MESSENGER.

Ambassadors from Harry king of England
Do crave admittance to your majesty.

FRENCH KING.

We'll give them present audience. Go, and bring
them.
            [*Exeunt* MESSENGER *and certain* LORDS.
You see this chase is hotly follow'd, friends.

DAUPHIN.

Turn head, and stop pursuit; for coward dogs
Most spend their mouths, when what they seem
     to threaten
Runs far before them. Good my sovereign,
Take up the English short; and let them know
Of what a monarchy you are the head:
Self-love, my liege, is not so vile a sin
As self-neglecting.

Enter LORDS, *with* EXETER *and* TRAIN.

FRENCH KING.

              From our brother England?

DUKE OF EXETER.

From him; and thus he greets your majesty.
He wills you, in the name of God Almighty,
That you divest yourself, and lay apart
The borrow'd glories, that, by gift of heaven,
By law of nature and of nations, 'longs
To him and to his heirs; namely, the crown,
And all wide-stretched honours that pertain,
By custom and the ordinance of times,

Unto the crown of France. That you may know
'Tis no sinister nor no awkward claim,
Pickt from the worm-holes of long-vanisht days,
Nor from the dust of old oblivion raked,
He sends you this most memorable line,
                   [*Gives a paper.*
In every branch truly demonstrative;
Willing you overlook this pedigree:
And when you find him evenly derived
From his most famed of famous ancestors,
Edward the Third, he bids you then resign
Your crown and kingdom, indirectly held
From him the native and true challenger.

FRENCH KING.

Or else what follows?

DUKE OF EXETER.

Bloody constraint; for if you hide the crown
Even in your hearts, there will he rake for it:
Therefore in fierce tempest is he coming,
In thunder and in earthquake, like a Jove,
That, if requiring fail, he will compel;
And bids you, in the bowels of the Lord,
Deliver up the crown; and to take mercy
On the poor souls for whom this hungry war
Opens his vasty jaws: and on your head
Turns he the widows' tears, the orphans' cries,
The dead men's blood, the pining maidens'
     groans,
For husbands, fathers, and betrothed lovers,
That shall be swallow'd in this controversy.
This is his claim, his threatening, and my message;
Unless the Dauphin be in presence here,
To whom expressly I bring greeting too.

FRENCH KING.

For us, we will consider of this further:
To-morrow shall you bear our full intent
Back to our brother England.

DAUPHIN.

               For the Dauphin,
I stand here for him: what to him from England?

DUKE OF EXETER.

Scorn and defiance; slight regard, contempt,
And any thing that may not misbecome
The mighty sender, doth he prize you at.
Thus says my king: an if your father's highness
Do not, in grant of all demands at large,
Sweeten the bitter mock you sent his majesty,
He'll call you to so hot an answer of it,
That caves and womby vaultages of France
Shall chide your trespass, and return your mock
In second accent of his ordnance.

DAUPHIN.

Say, if my father render fair return,
It is against my will; for I desire
Nothing but odds with England: to that end,
As matching to his youth and vanity,
I did present him with the Paris balls.

DUKE OF EXETER.

He'll make your Paris Louvre shake for it,
Were it the mistress-court of mighty Europe:
And, be assured, you'll find a difference,
As we, his subjects, have in wonder found,
Between the promise of his greener days
And these he masters now: now he weighs time,
Even to the utmost grain:—that you shall read
In your own losses, if he stay in France.

FRENCH KING.

To-morrow shall you know our mind at full.

DUKE OF EXETER.

Dispatch us with all speed, lest that our king
Come here himself to question our delay;
For he is footed in this land already.

FRENCH KING.

You shall be soon dispatcht with fair conditions
A night is but small breath and little pause
To answer matters of this consequence.
                   [*Flourish. Exeunt.*

ACT III.
PROLOGUE.

Enter CHORUS.

CHORUS.

THUS with imagined wing our swift scene flies,
    In motion of no less celerity
Than that of thought. Suppose that you have seen
The well-appointed king at Hampton pier
Embark his royalty; and his brave fleet
With silken streamers the young Phœbus fanning:
Play with your fancies; and in them behold
Upon the hempen tackle ship-boys climbing;
Hear the shrill whistle which doth order give
To sounds confused; behold the threaden sails,
Borne with th'invisible and creeping wind,
Draw the huge bottoms through the furrow'd sea,
Breasting the lofty surge: O, do but think
You stand upon the rivage, and behold
A city on th'inconstant billows dancing;
For so appears this fleet majestical,
Holding due course to Harfleur. Follow, follow!
Grapple your minds to sternage of this navy;
And leave your England, as dead midnight still,
Guarded with grandsires, babies, and old women,
Either past, or not arrived to, pith and puissance;
For who is he, whose chin is but enricht
With one appearing hair, that will not follow
These cull'd and choice-drawn cavaliers to
     France?
Work, work your thoughts, and therein see a siege;
Behold the ordnance on their carriages,
With fatal mouths gaping on girded Harfleur.
Suppose th'ambassador from the French comes
     back;
Tells Harry that the king doth offer him
Katharine his daughter; and with her, to dowry,
Some petty and unprofitable dukedoms.
The offer likes not: and the nimble gunner
With linstock now the devilish cannon touches,
         [*Alarum, and chambers go off, within.*
And down goes all before them. Still be kind,
And eke out our performance with your mind.
                       [*Exit.*

SCENE I.

France. Before Harfleur.

Alarums. Ente KING HENRY, EXETER, BED-
FORD, GLOSTER, *and* SOLDIERS, *with scaling-
ladders.*

KING HENRY.

ONCE more unto the breach, dear friends,
    once more;
Or close the wall up with our English dead!

In peace there's nothing so becomes a man
As modest stillness and humility:
But when the blast of war blows in our ears,
Then imitate the action of the tiger;
Stiffen the sinews, summon up the blood,
Disguise fair nature with hard-favour'd rage:
Then lend the eye a terrible aspect;
Let it pry through the portage of the head
Like the brass cannon; let the brow o'erwhelm it
As fearfully as doth a galled rock
O'erhang and jutty his confounded base,
Swill'd with the wild and wasteful ocean.
Now set the teeth, and stretch the nostril wide;
Hold hard the breath, and bend up every spirit
To his full height!—On, on, you noble English,
Whose blood is fet from fathers of war-proof!—
Fathers that, like so many Alexanders,
Have in these parts from morn till even fought,
And sheathed their swords for lack of argu-
　　ment:—
Dishonour not your mothers; now attest
That those whom you call'd fathers did beget
　　you!
Be copy now to men of grosser blood,
And teach them how to war!—And you, good
　　yeomen,
Whose limbs were made in England, show us here
The mettle of your pasture; let us swear
That you are worth your breeding: which I doubt
　　not;
For there is none of you so mean and base,
That hath not noble lustre in your eyes.
I see you stand like greyhounds in the slips,
Straining upon the start. The game's afoot:
Follow your spirit; and, upon this charge,
Cry 'God for Harry, England, and Saint George!'
　　[Exeunt. Alarum, and chambers go off, within.

SCENE II.

The same.

Enter NYM, BARDOLPH, PISTOL, *and* BOY.

BARDOLPH.

ON, on, on, on, on! to the breach, to the
breach!

NYM.

Pray thee, corporal, stay: the knocks are too hot;
and, for mine own part, I have not a case of lives:
the humour of it is too hot, that is the very plain-
song of it.

PISTOL.

The plain-song is most just; for humours do a-
bound;
Knocks go and come; God's vassals drop and die;
　　And sword and shield,
　　In bloody field,
Doth win immortal fame.

BOY.

Would I were in an alehouse in London! I would
give all my fame for a pot of ale and safety.

PISTOL.

And I:
　　If wishes would prevail with me,
　　My purpose should not fail with me,
　　But thither would I hie.

BOY.

　　As duly, but not as truly,
　　As bird doth sing on bough.
　　　Enter FLUELLEN.

FLUELLEN.

Got's plood!—Up to the preaches, you rascals!
will you not up to the preaches?
　　　　[Driving them forward.

PISTOL.

Be merciful, great duke, to men of mould!
Abate thy rage, abate thy manly rage!
Abate thy rage, great duke!
Good bawcock, bate thy rage! use lenity, sweet
　　chuck!

NYM.

These be good humours!—your honour runs bad
humours.
　　[Exeunt NYM, BARDOLPH, *and* PISTOL
　　　driven in by FLUELLEN.

BOY.

As young as I am, I have observed these three
swashers. I am boy to them all three: but all they
three, though they would serve me, could not be
man to me; for, indeed, three such antics do not
amount to a man. For Bardolph,—he is white-
liver'd and red-faced; by the means whereof a'
faces it out, but fights not. For Pistol,—he hath a
killing tongue and a quiet sword; by the means
whereof a' breaks words, and keeps whole
weapons. For Nym,—he hath heard that men of
few words are the best men; and therefore he
scorns to say his prayers, lest a' should be thought
a coward: but his few bad words are matcht with
as few good deeds; for a' never broke any man's
head but his own, and that was against a post
when he was drunk. They will steal any thing, and
call it purchase. Bardolph stole a lute-case, bore
it twelve leagues, and sold it for three-half-pence.
Nym and Bardolph are sworn brothers in filching; and in Calais they stole a fire-shovel: I knew
by that piece of service the men would carry coals.
They would have me as familiar with men's
pockets as their gloves or their handkerchers:
which makes much against my manhood, if I
should take from another's pocket to put into
mine; for it is plain pocketing-up of wrongs. I
must leave them, and seek some better service:
their villainy goes against my weak stomach, and
therefore I must cast it up.　　　　[Exit.
　　Enter FLUELLEN, GOWER *following*.

GOWER.

Captain Fluellen, you must come presently to the
mines; the Duke of Gloster would speak with you.

FLUELLEN.

To the mines! tell you the duke, it is not so goot to
come to the mines; for, look you, the mines is not
according to the disciplines of the war: the con-
cavities of it is not sufficient; for, look you, th'athversary—you may discuss unto the duke, look
you—is digt himself four yard under the counter-
mines: by Cheshu, I think a' will plow up all, if
there is not petter directions.

GOWER.

The Duke of Gloster, to whom the order of the
siege is given, is altogether directed by an Irishman,—a very valiant gentleman, i'faith.

FLUELLEN.
It is Captain Macmorris, is it not?

GOWER.
I think it be.

FLUELLEN.
By Cheshu, he is an ass, as in the 'orld: I will verify as much in his peard: he has no more directions in the true disciplines of the wars, look you, of the Roman disciplines, than is a puppy-dog.

GOWER.
Here a' comes; and the Scots captain, Captain Jamy, with him.

FLUELLEN.
Captain Jamy is a marvellous falorous gentleman, that is certain; and of great expedition and knowledge in th'auncient wars, upon my particular knowledge of his directions: by Cheshu, he will maintain his argument as well as any military man in the 'orld, in the disciplines of the pristine wars of the Romans.

Enter MACMORRIS and JAMY.

JAMY.
I say gude-day, Captain Fluellen.

FLUELLEN.
Got-den to your worship, goot Captain Jamy.

GOWER.
How now, Captain Macmorris! have you quit the mines? have the pioners given o'er?

MACMORRIS.
By Chrish, la, tish ill done; the work ish give over, the trompet sound the retreat. By my hand, I swear, and my father's soul, the work ish ill done; it ish give over: I would have blow'd up the town, so Chrish save me, la, in an hour: O, tish ill done, tish ill done; by my hand, tish ill done!

FLUELLEN.
Captain Macmorris, I peseech you now, will you voutsafe me, look you, a few disputations with you, as partly touching or concerning the disciplines of the war, the Roman wars, in the way of argument, look you, and friendly communication; partly to satisfy my opinion, and partly for the satisfaction, look you, of my mind, as touching the direction of the military discipline; that is the point.

JAMY.
It sall be vary gude, gude feith, gude captains baith: and I sall quit you with gude leve, as I may pick occasion; that sall I, marry.

MACMORRIS.
It is no time to discourse, so Chrish save me: the day is hot, and the weather, and the wars, and the king, and the dukes: it is no time to discourse. The town is beseecht, and the trompet call us to the breach; and we talk, and, be Chrish, do nothing: 'tis shame for us all: so God sa' me, 'tis shame to stand still; it is shame, by my hand: and there is throats to be cut, and works to be done; and there ish nothing done, so Chrish sa' me, la.

JAMY.
By the mess, ere theise eyes of mine take themselves to slomber, ay'll de gude service, or ay'll lig i'th' grund for it; ay, or go to death; and ay'll pay't as valorously as I may, that sall I suerly do, that is the breff and the long. Marry, I wad full fain heard some question 'tween you tway.

FLUELLEN.
Captain Macmorris, I think, look you, under your correction, there is not many of your nation—

MACMORRIS.
Of my nation! What ish my nation? Ish a villain, and a bastard, and a knave, and a rascal. What ish my nation? Who talks of my nation?

FLUELLEN.
Look you, if you take the matter otherwise than is meant, Captain Macmorris, peradventure I shall think you do not use me with that affability as in discretion you ought to use me, look you; being as goot a man as yourself, both in the disciplines of war, and in the derivation of my birth, and in other particularities.

MACMORRIS.
I do not know you so good a man as myself: so Chrish save me, I will cut off your head.

GOWER.
Gentlemen both, you will mistake each other.

JAMY.
A! that's a foul fault. 　　　　[A parley sounded.

GOWER.
The town sounds a parley.

FLUELLEN.
Captain Macmorris, when there is more petter opportunity to be required, look you, I will be so pold as to tell you I know the disciplines of war; and there is an end. 　　　　[Exeunt.

SCENE III.

The same.

The GOVERNOR *and some* CITIZENS *on the walls; the English forces below. Enter* KING HENRY *and his* TRAIN *before the Gates.*

KING HENRY.
HOW yet resolves the governor of the town?
This is the latest parle we will admit:
Therefore, to our best mercy give yourselves;
Or, like to men proud of destruction,
Defy us to our worst: for, as I am a soldier,
A name that, in my thoughts, becomes me best,
If I begin the battery once again,
I will not leave the half-achieved Harfleur
Till in her ashes she lie buried.
The gates of mercy shall be all shut up;
And the flesht soldier,—rough and hard of heart,—
In liberty of bloody hand shall range
With conscience wide as hell; mowing like grass
Your fresh-fair virgins and your flowering infants.
What is it then to me, if impious war,—
Array'd in flames, like to the prince of fiends,—
Do, with his smircht complexion, all fell feats
Enlinkt to waste and desolation?
What is't to me, when you yourselves are cause,
If your pure maidens fall into the hand
Of hot and forcing violation?
What rein can hold licentious wickedness
When down the hill he holds his fierce career?
We may as bootless spend our vain command
Upon th'enraged soldiers in their spoil,
As send precepts to the leviathan
To come ashore. Therefore, you men of Harfleur
Take pity of your town and of your people,

Whiles yet my soldiers are in my command;
Whiles yet the cool and temperate wind of grace
O'erblows the filthy and contagious clouds
Of heady murder, spoil, and villainy.
If not, why, in a moment, look to see
The blind and bloody soldier with foul hand
Defile the locks of your shrill-shrieking daughters;
Your fathers taken by the silver beards,
And their most reverend heads dasht to the walls;
Your naked infants spitted upon pikes,
Whiles the mad mothers with their howls confused
Do break the clouds, as did the wives of Jewry
At Herod's bloody-hunting slaughtermen.
What say you? will you yield, and this avoid?
Or, guilty in defence, be thus destroy'd?

GOVERNOR OF HARFLEUR.
Our expectation hath this day an end:
The Dauphin, whom of succour we entreated,
Returns us, that his powers are yet not ready
To raise so great a siege. Therefore, dread king,
We yield our town and lives to thy soft mercy.
Enter our gates; dispose of us and ours;
For we no longer are defensible.

KING HENRY.
Open your gates.—Come, uncle Exeter,
Go you and enter Harfleur; there remain,
And fortify it strongly 'gainst the French:
Use mercy to them all. For us, dear uncle,—
The winter coming on, and sickness growing
Upon our soldiers,—we will retire to Calais.
To-night in Harfleur will we be your guest;
To-morrow for the march are we addrest.

[*Flourish, and enter the town.*

SCENE IV.

The French KING'S *palace.*

Enter KATHARINE *and* ALICE.

KATHARINE.
A LICE, *tu as été en Angleterre, et tu parles
bien le langage.*

ALICE.
Un peu, madame.

KATHARINE.
*Je te prie m'enseignez; il faut que j'apprenne à
parler. Comment appelez-vous la main en Anglois?*

ALICE.
La main? elle est appelée de hand.

KATHARINE.
De hand. *Et les doigts?*

ALICE.
*Les doigts? ma foi, j'oublie les doigts; mais je me
souviendrai. Les doigts? je pense qu'ils sont appelés*
de fingres; *oui*, de fingres.

KATHARINE.
La main, de hand; *les doigts*, de fingres. *Je pense
que je suis le bon écolier; j'ai gagné deux mots
d'Anglois vitement. Comment appelez-vous les
ongles?*

ALICE.
Les ongles? nous les appelons de nails.

KATHARINE.
De nails. *Ecoutez; dites-moi, si je parle bien: de
hand, de fingres, et* de nails.

ALICE.
C'est bien dit, madame; il est fort bon Anglois.

KATHARINE.
Dites-moi l'Anglois pour le bras.

ALICE.
De arm, *madame.*

KATHARINE.
Et le coude?

ALICE.
D'elbow.

KATHARINE.
D'elbow. *Je m'en fais la répétition de tous les mots
que vous m'avez appris dès à présent.*

ALICE.
Il est trop difficile, madame, comme je pense.

KATHARINE.
Excusez-moi, Alice; *écoutez:* d'hand, de fingres,
de nails, d'arm, de bilbow.

ALICE.
D'elbow, *madame.*

KATHARINE.
O Seigneur Dieu, je m'en oublie! d'elbow. *Comment appelez-vous le col?*

ALICE.
De neck, *madame.*

KATHARINE.
De nick. *Et le menton?*

ALICE.
De chin.

KATHARINE.
De sin. *Le col*, de nick; *le menton*, de sin.

ALICE.
*Oui. Sauf votre honneur, en vérité, vous prononcez
les mots aussi droit que les natifs d'Angleterre.*

KATHARINE.
*Je ne doute point d'apprendre, par la grace de Dieu,
et en peu de temps.*

ALICE.
N'avez-vous pas déjà oublié ce que je vous ai enseigné?

KATHARINE.
Non, je réciterai à vous promptement: d'hand, de
fingres, de mails,—

ALICE.
De nails, *madame.*

KATHARINE.
De nails, de arm, de ilbow.

ALICE.
Sauf votre honneur, d'elbow.

KATHARINE.
Ainsi dis-je; d'elbow, de nick, *et* de sin. *Comment
appelez-vous le pied et la robe?*

ALICE.
De foot, *madame; et* de coun.

KATHARINE.
De foot *et* de coun! *O Seigneur Dieu! ce sont mots
de son mauvais, corruptible, gros, et impudique, et
non pour les dames d'honneur d'user: je ne voudrais
prononcer ces mots devant les seigneurs de France
pour tout le monde. Foh!* le foot *et le* coun! *Néanmoins, je réciterai une autre fois ma leçon ensemble:*
d'hand, de fingres, de nails, d'arm, d'elbow, de
nick, de sin, de foot, de coun.

ALICE.
Excellent, madame!

KATHARINE.
C'est assez pour une fois: allons-nous à diner.

[*Exeunt.*

SCENE V.

The same.

Enter the KING OF FRANCE, *the* DAUPHIN, BOURBON, *the* CONSTABLE OF FRANCE, *and others.*

FRENCH KING.

'TIS certain he hath past the river Somme.
THE CONSTABLE OF FRANCE.
And if he be not fought withal, my lord,
Let us not live in France; let us quit all,
And give our vineyards to a barbarous people.
DAUPHIN.
O Dieu vivant! shall a few sprays of us,
The emptying of our fathers' luxury,
Our scions, put in wild and savage stock,
Spirt up so suddenly into the clouds,
And overlook their grafters?
DUKE OF BOURBON.
Normans, but bastard Normans, Norman bastards!
Mort de ma vie! if they march along
Unfought withal, but I will sell my dukedom,
To buy a slobbery and a dirty farm
In that nook-shotten isle of Albion.
THE CONSTABLE OF FRANCE.
Dieu de batailles! where have they this mettle?
Is not their climate foggy, raw, and dull;
On whom, as in despite, the sun looks pale,
Killing their fruit with frowns? Can sodden water,
A drench for sur-rein'd jades, their barley-broth,
Decoct their cold blood to such valiant heat?
And shall our quick blood, spirited with wine,
Seem frosty? O, for honour of our land,
Let us not hang like roping icicles
Upon our houses' thatch, whiles a more frosty people
Sweat drops of gallant youth in our rich fields,—
Poor we may call them in their native lords!
DAUPHIN.
By faith and honour,
Our madams mock at us, and plainly say
Our mettle is bred out, and they will give
Their bodies to the lust of English youth
To new-store France with bastard warriors.
DUKE OF BOURBON.
They bid us to the English dancing-schools,
And teach lavoltas high and swift corantos;
Saying our grace is only in our heels,
And that we are most lofty runaways.
FRENCH KING.
Where is Montjoy the herald? speed him hence;
Let him greet England with our sharp defiance.—
Up, princes! and, with spirit of honour edged
More sharper than your swords, hie to the field:
Charles Delabreth, high-Constable of France;
You Dukes of Orleans, Bourbon, and of Berri,
Alençon, Brabant, Bar, and Burgundy;
Jaques Chatillon, Rambures, Vaudemont,
Beaumont, Grandpré, Roussi, and Fauconberg,
Foix, Lestrale, Bouciqualt, and Charolois;
High dukes, great princes, barons, lords, and knights,
For your great seats now quit you of great shames.
Bar Harry England, that sweeps through our land

With pennons painted in the blood of Harfleur:
Rush on his host, as doth the melted snow
Upon the valleys, whose low vassal seat
The Alps doth spit and void his rheum upon:
Go down upon him,—you have power enough,—
And in a captive chariot into Rouen
Bring him our prisoner.
THE CONSTABLE OF FRANCE.
                          This becomes the great.
Sorry am I his numbers are so few,
His soldiers sick, and famisht in their march;
For I am sure, when he shall see our army,
He'll drop his heart into the sink of fear,
And for achievement offer us his ransom.
FRENCH KING.
Therefore, lord Constable, haste on Montjoy;
And let him say to England, that we send
To know what willing ransom he will give.—
Prince Dauphin, you shall stay with us in Rouen.
DAUPHIN.
Not so, I do beseech your majesty.
FRENCH KING.
Be patient; for you shall remain with us.
Now forth, lord Constable, and princes all,
And quickly bring us word of England's fall.
                                          [*Exeunt*

SCENE VI.

The English camp in Picardy.

Enter GOWER *and* FLUELLEN, *meeting.*

GOWER.

HOW now, Captain Fluellen! come you from the bridge?
FLUELLEN.
I assure you, there is very excellent services committed at the pridge.
GOWER.
Is the Duke of Exeter safe?
FLUELLEN.
The Duke of Exeter is as magnanimous as Agamemnon; and a man that I love and honour with my soul, and my heart, and my duty, and my life, and my living, and my uttermost power: he is not —Got be praised and plest!—any hurt in the 'orld; but keeps the pridge most valiantly, with excellent discipline. There is an auncient there at the pridge,—I think in my very conscience he is as valiant a man as Mark Antony; and he is a man of no estimation in the 'orld; but I did see him do gallant service.
GOWER.
What do you call him?
FLUELLEN.
He is called Auncient Pistol.
GOWER.
I know him not.
FLUELLEN.
Here is the man.
Enter PISTOL.
PISTOL.
Captain, I thee beseech to do me favours:
The Duke of Exeter doth love thee well.
FLUELLEN.
Ay, I praise Got; and I have merited some love at his hands.

PISTOL.

Bardolph, a soldier, firm and sound of heart,
And of buxom valour, hath, by cruel fate,
And giddy Fortune's furious fickle wheel,—
That goddess blind,
That stands upon the rolling restless stone,—

FLUELLEN.

By your patience, Auncient Pistol. Fortune is
painted plind, with a muffler afore her eyes, to
signify to you that Fortune is plind; and she is
painted also with a wheel, to signify to you, which
is the moral of it, that she is turning, and inconstant, and mutability, and variation: and her foot,
look you, is fixt upon a spherical stone, which
rolls, and rolls, and rolls:—in good truth, the poet
makes a most excellent description of it: Fortune
is an excellent moral.

PISTOL.

Fortune is Bardolph's foe, and frowns on him;
For he hath stoln a pax, and hanged must a'
be,—
A damned death!
Let gallows gape for dog; let man go free,
And let not hemp his windpipe suffocate:
But Exeter hath given the doom of death
For pax of little price.
Therefore, go speak,—the duke will hear thy
voice;
And let not Bardolph's vital thread be cut
With edge of penny cord and vile reproach:
Speak, captain, for his life, and I will thee re-
quite.

FLUELLEN.

Auncient Pistol, I do partly understand your
meaning.

PISTOL.

Why, then, rejoice therefore.

FLUELLEN.

Certainly, auncient, it is not a thing to rejoice at:
for if, look you, he were my prother, I would desire the duke to use his goot pleasure, and put him
to execution; for discipline ought to be used.

PISTOL.

Die and be damn'd! and figo for thy friendship!

FLUELLEN.

It is well.

PISTOL.

The fig of Spain!　　　　　　　　[Exit.

FLUELLEN.

Very goot.

GOWER.

Why, this is an arrant counterfeit rascal; I remember him now; a bawd, a cutpurse.

FLUELLEN.

I'll assure you, a' utter'd as prave 'ords at the
pridge as you shall see in a summer's day. But it
is very well; what he has spoke to me, that is well,
I warrant you, when time is serve.

GOWER.

Why, 'tis a gull, a fool, a rogue, that now and then
goes to the wars, to grace himself, at his return
into London, under the form of a soldier. And
such fellows are perfect in the great commanders'
names: and they will learn you by rote where services were done;—at such and such a sconce, at
such a breach, at such a convoy; who came off

bravely, who was shot, who disgraced, what terms
the enemy stood on; and this they con perfectly
in the phrase of war, which they trick up with
new-turn'd oaths: and what a beard of the
general's cut, and a horrid suit of the camp, will
do among foaming bottles and ale-washt wits, is
wonderful to be thought on. But you must learn
to know such slanders of the age, or else you may
be marvellously mistook.

FLUELLEN.

I tell you what, Captain Gower;—I do perceive
he is not the man that he would gladly make show
to the 'orld he is: if I find a hole in his coat, I will
tell him my mind. [Drum within.] Hark you, the
king is coming; and I must speak with him from
the pridge.

Drum and colours.　　Enter KING HENRY, GLOS-
TER, and his poor SOLDIERS.

Got pless your majesty!

KING HENRY.

How now, Fluellen! camest thou from the
bridge?

FLUELLEN.

Ay, so please your majesty. The Duke of Exeter
has very gallantly maintain'd the pridge: the
French is gone off, look you; and there is gallant
and most prave passages: marry, th'athversary
was have possession of the pridge; but he is enforced to retire, and the Duke of Exeter is master
of the pridge: I can tell your majesty, the duke is
a prave man.

KING HENRY.

What men have you lost, Fluellen?

FLUELLEN.

The perdition of th'athversary hath been very
great, reasonable great: marry, for my part, I
think the duke hath lost never a man, but one
that is like to be executed for robbing a church,—
one Bardolph, if your majesty know the man: his
face is all bubukles, and whelks, and knobs, and
flames o' fire: and his lips plows at his nose, and
it is like a coal of fire, sometimes plue and sometimes red; but his nose is executed, and his fire's
out.

KING HENRY.

We would have all such offenders so cut off:—
and we give express charge that, in our marches
through the country, there be nothing compell'd
from the villages, nothing taken but paid for,
none of the French upbraided or abused in disdainful language; for when lenity and cruelty play
for a kingdom, the gentler gamester is the soonest
winner.

Tucket.　Enter MONTJOY.

MONTJOY.

You know me by my habit.

KING HENRY.

Well, then, I know thee: what shall I know of thee?

MONTJOY.

My master's mind.

KING HENRY.

Unfold it.

MONTJOY.

Thus says my king:—Say thou to Harry of
England: Though we seem'd dead, we did but
sleep; advantage is a better soldier than rashness.

Tell him, we could have rebuked him at Harfleur,
but that we thought not good to bruise an injury
till it were full ripe:—now we speak upon our
cue, and our voice is imperial: England shall repent his folly, see his weakness, and admire our
sufferance. Bid him, therefore, consider of his
ransom; which must proportion the losses we
have borne, the subjects we have lost, the disgrace we have digested; which, in weight to re-
answer, his pettiness would bow under. For our
losses, his exchequer is too poor; for th'effusion
of our blood, the muster of his kingdom too faint
a number; and for our disgrace, his own person,
kneeling at our feet, but a weak and worthless
satisfaction. To this add defiance: and tell him,
for conclusion, he hath betray'd his followers,
whose condemnation is pronounced. So far my
king and master; so much my office.

KING HENRY.
What is thy name? I know thy quality.

MONTJOY.
Montjoy.

KING HENRY.
Thou dost thy office fairly. Turn thee back,
And tell thy king,—I do not seek him now;
But could be willing to march on to Calais
Without impeachment: for, to say the sooth,—
Though 'tis no wisdom to confess so much
Unto an enemy of craft and vantage,—
My people are with sickness much enfeebled;
My numbers lessen'd; and those few I have,
Almost no better than so many French;
Who when they were in health, I tell thee, herald,
I thought upon one pair of English legs
Did march three Frenchmen.—Yet, forgive me,
    God,
That I do brag thus!—this your air of France
Hath blown that vice in me; I must repent.
Go, therefore, tell thy master here I am;
My ransom is this frail and worthless trunk;
My army but a weak and sickly guard:
Yet, God before, tell him we will come on,
Though France himself, and such another
    neighbour,
Stand in our way. There's for thy labour, Mont-
    joy.   [Gives a purse.
Go, bid thy master well advise himself:
If we may pass, we will; if we be hinder'd,
We shall your tawny ground with your red blood
Discolour: and so, Montjoy, fare you well.
The sum of all our answer is but this:
We would not seek a battle, as we are;
Nor, as we are, we say, we will not shun it:
So tell your master.

MONTJOY.
I shall deliver so. Thanks to your highness.
    [Exit.

DUKE OF GLOSTER.
I hope they will not come upon us now.

KING HENRY.
We are in God's hand, brother, not in theirs.
March to the bridge; it now draws toward
    night:—
Beyond the river we'll encamp ourselves;
And on to-morrow bid them march away.
    [Exeunt.

SCENE VII.

The French camp near Agincourt.

Enter the CONSTABLE OF FRANCE, the LORD
RAMBURES, ORLEANS, the DAUPHIN, and
others.

THE CONSTABLE OF FRANCE.
Tut! I have the best armour of the world.—
Would it were day!

DUKE OF ORLEANS.
You have an excellent armour; but let my horse
have his due.

THE CONSTABLE OF FRANCE.
It is the best horse of Europe.

DUKE OF ORLEANS.
Will it never be morning?

DAUPHIN.
My Lord of Orleans, and my lord high-Constable, you talk of horse and armour?

DUKE OF ORLEANS.
You are as well provided of both as any prince in
the world.

DAUPHIN.
What a long night is this!—I will not change my
horse with any that treads but on four pasterns.
Ça, ha! he bounds from the earth, as if his entrails were hairs; le cheval volant, the Pegasus, qui
a les narines de feu! When I bestride him, I soar,
I am a hawk: he trots the air; the earth sings when
he touches it; the basest horn of his hoof is more
musical than the pipe of Hermes.

DUKE OF ORLEANS.
He's of the colour of the nutmeg.

DAUPHIN.
And of the heat of the ginger. It is a beast for
Perseus: he is pure air and fire; and the dull elements of earth and water never appear in him, but
only in patient stillness while his rider mounts
him: he is, indeed, a horse; and all other jades you
may call beasts.

THE CONSTABLE OF FRANCE.
Indeed, my lord, it is a most absolute and excellent horse.

DAUPHIN.
It is the prince of palfreys; his neigh is like the
bidding of a monarch, and his countenance enforces homage.

DUKE OF ORLEANS.
No more, cousin.

DAUPHIN.
Nay, the man hath no wit that cannot, from the
rising of the lark to the lodging of the lamb, vary
deserved praise on my palfrey: it is a theme as
fluent as the sea; turn the sands into eloquent
tongues, and my horse is argument for them all:
'tis a subject for a sovereign to reason on, and for
a sovereign's sovereign to ride on; and for the
world, familiar to us and unknown, to lay apart
their particular functions, and wonder at him.
I once writ a sonnet in his praise, and began
thus: 'Wonder of nature,'—

DUKE OF ORLEANS.
I have heard a sonnet begin so to one's mistress.

DAUPHIN.
Then did they imitate that which I composed to
my courser; for my horse is my mistress.

DUKE OF ORLEANS.
Your mistress bears well.

DAUPHIN.
Me well; which is the prescript praise and perfection of a good and particular mistress.

THE CONSTABLE OF FRANCE.
Ma foi, methought yesterday your mistress shrewdly shook your back.

DAUPHIN.
So, perhaps, did yours.

THE CONSTABLE OF FRANCE.
Mine was not bridled.

DAUPHIN.
O, then, belike she was old and gentle; and you rode, like a kern of Ireland, your French hose off, and in your strait strossers.

THE CONSTABLE OF FRANCE.
You have good judgement in horsemanship.

DAUPHIN.
Be warn'd by me, then: they that ride so, and ride not warily, fall into foul bogs. I had rather have my horse to my mistress.

THE CONSTABLE OF FRANCE.
I had as lief have my mistress a jade.

DAUPHIN.
I tell thee, constable, my mistress wears her own hair.

THE CONSTABLE OF FRANCE.
I could make as true a boast as that, if I had a sow to my mistress.

DAUPHIN.
Le chien est retourné à son propre vomissement, et la truie lavée au bourbier: thou makest use of any thing.

THE CONSTABLE OF FRANCE.
Yet do I not use my horse for my mistress; or any such proverb, so little kin to the purpose.

RAMBURES.
My lord constable, the armour that I saw in your tent to-night,—are those stars or suns upon it?

THE CONSTABLE OF FRANCE.
Stars, my lord.

DAUPHIN.
Some of them will fall to-morrow, I hope.

THE CONSTABLE OF FRANCE.
And yet my sky shall not want.

DAUPHIN.
That may be, for you bear a many superfluously, and 'twere more honour some were away.

THE CONSTABLE OF FRANCE.
Even as your horse bears your praises; who would trot as well, were some of your brags dismounted.

DAUPHIN.
Would I were able to load him with his desert!—Will it never be day?—I will trot to-morrow a mile, and my way shall be paved with English faces.

THE CONSTABLE OF FRANCE.
I will not say so, for fear I should be faced out of my way: but I would it were morning; for I would fain be about the ears of the English.

RAMBURES.
Who will go to hazard with me for twenty prisoners?

THE CONSTABLE OF FRANCE.
You must first go yourself to hazard, ere you have them.

DAUPHIN.
'Tis midnight; I'll go arm myself.   [*Exit.*

DUKE OF ORLEANS.
The Dauphin longs for morning.

RAMBURES.
He longs to eat the English.

THE CONSTABLE OF FRANCE.
I think he will eat all he kills.

DUKE OF ORLEANS.
By the white hand of my lady, he's a gallant prince.

THE CONSTABLE OF FRANCE.
Swear by her foot, that she may tread out the oath.

DUKE OF ORLEANS.
He is, simply, the most active gentleman of France.

THE CONSTABLE OF FRANCE.
Doing is activity: and he will still be doing.

DUKE OF ORLEANS.
He never did harm, that I heard of.

THE CONSTABLE OF FRANCE.
Nor will do none to-morrow: he will keep that good name still.

DUKE OF ORLEANS.
I know him to be valiant.

THE CONSTABLE OF FRANCE.
I was told that by one that knows him better than you.

DUKE OF ORLEANS.
What's he?

THE CONSTABLE OF FRANCE.
Marry, he told me so himself; and he said he cared not who knew it.

DUKE OF ORLEANS.
He needs not; it is no hidden virtue in him.

THE CONSTABLE OF FRANCE.
By my faith, sir, but it is; never any body saw it but his lackey: 'tis a hooded valour; and when it appears, it will bate.

DUKE OF ORLEANS.
Ill-will never said well.

THE CONSTABLE OF FRANCE.
I will cap that proverb with—There is flattery in friendship.

DUKE OF ORLEANS.
And I will take up that with—Give the devil his due.

THE CONSTABLE OF FRANCE.
Well placed: there stands your friend for the devil: have at the very eye of that proverb, with—A pox of the devil.

DUKE OF ORLEANS.
You are the better by proverbs, by how much—A fool's bolt is soon shot.

THE CONSTABLE OF FRANCE.
You have shot over.

DUKE OF ORLEANS.
'Tis not the first time you were overshot.

Enter a MESSENGER.

MESSENGER.
My lord high-Constable, the English lie within fifteen hundred paces of your tents.

THE CONSTABLE OF FRANCE.
Who hath measured the ground?

MESSENGER.
The Lord Grandpré.

THE CONSTABLE OF FRANCE.
A valiant and most expert gentleman.—Would it
were day!—Alas, poor Harry of England! he longs
not for the dawning, as we do.

DUKE OF ORLEANS.
What a wretched and peevish fellow is this King
of England, to mope with his fat-brain'd followers
so far out of his knowledge!

THE CONSTABLE OF FRANCE.
If the English had any apprehension, they would
run away.

DUKE OF ORLEANS.
That they lack; for if their heads had any intellectual armour, they could never wear such heavy
head-pieces.

RAMBURES.
That island of England breeds very valiant
creatures; their mastiffs are of unmatchable
courage.

DUKE OF ORLEANS.
Foolish curs, that run winking into the mouth of
a Russian bear, and have their heads crusht like
rotten apples! You may as well say, that's a valiant
flea that dare eat his breakfast on the lip of a lion.

THE CONSTABLE OF FRANCE.
Just, just; and the men do sympathize with the
mastiffs in robustious and rough coming-on, leaving their wits with their wives: and then give them
great meals of beef, and iron and steel, they will
eat like wolves, and fight like devils.

DUKE OF ORLEANS.
Ay, but these English are shrewdly out of beef.

THE CONSTABLE OF FRANCE.
Then shall we find to-morrow they have only
stomachs to eat, and none to fight. Now is it time
to arm; come, shall we about it?

DUKE OF ORLEANS.
It is now two o'clock: but, let me see,—by ten
We shall have each a hundred Englishmen.

[Exeunt.

ACT IV.
PROLOGUE.

Enter CHORUS.

CHORUS.
NOW entertain conjecture of a time
When creeping murmur and the poring dark
Fills the wide vessel of the universe.
From camp to camp, through the foul womb of
night,
The hum of either army stilly sounds,
That the fixt sentinels almost receive
The secret whispers of each other's watch:
Fire answers fire; and through their paly flames
Each battle sees the other's umber'd face:
Steed threatens steed, in high and boastful neighs
Piercing the night's dull ear; and from the tents,
The armourers, accomplishing the knights,
With busy hammers closing rivets up,
Give dreadful note of preparation:
The country cocks do crow, the clocks do toll,
And the third hour of drowsy morning name.
Proud of their numbers, and secure in soul,
The confident and over-lusty French
Do the low-rated English play at dice;

And chide the cripple tardy-gaited night,
Who, like a foul and ugly witch, doth limp
So tediously away. The poor condemned English,
Like sacrifices, by their watchful fires
Sit patiently, and inly ruminate
The morning's danger; and their gesture sad
Investing lank-lean cheeks, and war-worn coats,
Presenteth them unto the gazing moon
So many horrid ghosts. O, now, who will behold
The royal captain of this ruin'd band
Walking from watch to watch, from tent to tent,
Let him cry, 'Praise and glory on his head!'
For forth he goes and visits all his host;
Bids them good morrow with a modest smile,
And calls them brothers, friends, and country-
men.
Upon his royal face there is no note
How dread an army hath enrounded him;
Nor doth he dedicate one jot of colour
Unto the weary and all-watched night;
But freshly looks, and over-bears attaint
With cheerful semblance and sweet majesty;
That every wretch, pining and pale before,
Beholding him, plucks comfort from his looks:
A largess universal, like the sun,
His liberal eye doth give to every one,
Thawing cold fear. Then, mean and gentle all,
Behold, as may unworthiness define,
A little touch of Harry in the night:
And so our scene must to the battle fly;
Where—O for pity!—we shall much disgrace
With four or five most vile and ragged foils,
Right ill-disposed, in brawl ridiculous,
The name of Agincourt. Yet, sit and see;
Minding true things by what their mockeries be.

[Exit.

SCENE I.
The English camp at Agincourt.

Enter KING HENRY, BEDFORD, *and* GLOSTER.

KING HENRY.
GLOSTER, 'tis true that we are in great dan-
ger;
The greater therefore should our courage be.—
Good morrow, brother Bedford.—God Al-
mighty!
There is some soul of goodness in things evil,
Would men observingly distil it out;
For our bad neighbour makes us early stirrers,
Which is both healthful and good husbandry:
Besides, they are our outward consciences,
And preachers to us all; admonishing
That we should dress us fairly for our end.
Thus may we gather honey from the weed,
And make a moral of the devil himself.

Enter ERPINGHAM.
Good morrow, old Sir Thomas Erpingham:
A good soft pillow for that good white head
Were better than a churlish turf of France.

SIR THOMAS ERPINGHAM.
Not so, my liege: this lodging likes me better,
Since I may say, 'Now lie I like a king.'

KING HENRY.
'Tis good for men to love their present pains
Upon example; so the spirit is eased:

And when the mind is quicken'd, out of doubt
The organs, though defunct and dead before,
Break up their drowsy grave, and newly move
With casted slough and fresh legerity.
Lend me thy cloak, Sir Thomas.—Brothers both,
Commend me to the princes in our camp;
Do my good morrow to them; and anon
Desire them all to my pavilion.

DUKE OF GLOSTER.

We shall, my liege.

SIR THOMAS ERPINGHAM.

Shall I attend your Grace?

KING HENRY.

     No, my good knight;
Go with my brothers to my lords of England:
I and my bosom must debate awhile,
And then I would no other company.

SIR THOMAS ERPINGHAM.

The Lord in heaven bless thee, noble Harry!

[Exeunt GLOSTER, BEDFORD, and
ERPINGHAM.

KING HENRY.

God-a-mercy, old heart! thou speak'st cheerfully.

Enter PISTOL.

PISTOL.

Qui va là?

KING HENRY.

A friend.

PISTOL.

Discuss unto me; art thou officer?
Or art thou base, common, and popular?

KING HENRY.

I am a gentleman of a company.

PISTOL.

Trail'st thou the puissant pike?

KING HENRY.

Even so. What are you?

PISTOL.

As good a gentleman as the emperor.

KING HENRY.

Then you are a better than the king.

PISTOL.

The king's a bawcock, and a heart of gold,
A lad of life, an imp of fame;
Of parents good, of fist most valiant:
I kiss his dirty shoe, and from heart-string
I love the lovely bully.—What is thy name?

KING HENRY.

Harry le Roy.

PISTOL.

Le Roy!
A Cornish name: art thou of Cornish crew?

KING HENRY.

No, I am a Welshman.

PISTOL.

Know'st thou Fluellen?

KING HENRY.

Yes.

PISTOL.

Tell him, I'll knock his leek about his pate
Upon Saint Davy's day.

KING HENRY.

Do not you wear your dagger in your cap that
day, lest he knock that about yours.

PISTOL.

Art thou his friend?

KING HENRY.

And his kinsman too.

PISTOL.

The figo for thee, then!

KING HENRY.

I thank you: God be with you!

PISTOL.

My name is Pistol call'd.   [Exit.

KING HENRY.

It sorts well with your fierceness.

Enter FLUELLEN and GOWER, severally.

GOWER.

Captain Fluellen!

FLUELLEN.

So! in the name of Cheshu Christ, speak lower. It
is the greatest admiration in the universal 'orld,
when the true and auncient prerogatifs and laws
of the wars is not kept: if you would take the
pains but to examine the wars of Pompey the
Great, you shall find, I warrant you, that there is
no tiddle-taddle nor pibble-pabble in Pompey's
camp; I warrant you, you shall find the ceremonies of the wars, and the cares of it, and the
forms of it, and the sobriety of it, and the modesty
of it, to be otherwise.

GOWER.

Why, the enemy is loud; you heard him all night.

FLUELLEN.

If the enemy is an ass, and a fool, and a prating
coxcomb, is it meet, think you, that we should
also, look you, be an ass, and a fool, and a prating
coxcomb,—in your own conscience, now?

GOWER.

I will speak lower.

FLUELLEN.

I pray you, and peseech you, that you will.

[Exeunt GOWER and FLUELLEN.

KING HENRY.

Though it appear a little out of fashion,
There is much care and valour in this Welshman.

Enter three SOLDIERS, JOHN BATES, ALEXAN-
DER COURT, and MICHAEL WILLIAMS.

ALEXANDER COURT.

Brother John Bates, is not that the morning
which breaks yonder?

JOHN BATES.

I think it be: but we have no great cause to desire
the approach of day.

MICHAEL WILLIAMS.

We see yonder the beginning of the day, but I
think we shall never see the end of it.—Who goes
there?

KING HENRY.

A friend.

MICHAEL WILLIAMS.

Under what captain serve you?

KING HENRY.

Under Sir Thomas Erpingham.

MICHAEL WILLIAMS.

A good old commander and a most kind gentleman: I pray you, what thinks he of our estate?

KING HENRY.

Even as men wrackt upon a sand, that look to be
washt off the next tide.

JOHN BATES.

He hath not told his thought to the king?

KING HENRY.

No; nor it is meet he should. For, though I speak it to you, I think the king is but a man, as I am: the violet smells to him as it doth to me; the element shows to him as it doth to me; all his senses have but human conditions: his ceremonies laid by, in his nakedness he appears but a man; and though his affections are higher mounted than ours, yet, when they stoop, they stoop with the like wing. Therefore when he sees reason of fears, as we do, his fears, out of doubt, be of the same relish as ours are: yet, in reason, no man should possess him with any appearance of fear, lest he, by showing it, should dishearten his army.

JOHN BATES.

He may show what outward courage he will; but I believe, as cold a night as 'tis, he could wish himself in Thames up to the neck;—and so I would he were, and I by him, at all adventures, so we were quit here.

KING HENRY.

By my troth, I will speak my conscience of the king: I think he would not wish himself any where but where he is.

JOHN BATES.

Then I would he were here alone; so should he be sure to be ransom'd, and a many poor men's lives saved.

KING HENRY.

I dare say you love him not so ill, to wish him here alone, howsoever you speak this, to feel other men's minds: methinks I could not die any where so contented as in the king's company,—his cause being just, and his quarrel honourable.

MICHAEL WILLIAMS.

That's more than we know.

JOHN BATES.

Ay, or more than we should seek after; for we know enough, if we know we are the king's subjects: if his cause be wrong, our obedience to the king wipes the crime of it out of us.

MICHAEL WILLIAMS.

But if the cause be not good, the king himself hath a heavy reckoning to make, when all those legs and arms and heads, chopt off in battle, shall join together at the latter day, and cry all, 'We died at such a place;' some swearing; some crying for a surgeon; some, upon their wives left poor behind them; some, upon the debts they owe; some, upon their children rawly left. I am afeard there are few die well that die in battle, for how can they charitably dispose of any thing, when blood is their argument? Now, if these men do not die well, it will be a black matter for the king that led them to it; who to disobey were against all proportion of subjection.

KING HENRY.

So, if a son, that is by his father sent about merchandise, do sinfully miscarry upon the sea, the imputation of his wickedness, by your rule, should be imposed upon his father that sent him: or if a servant, under his master's command transporting a sum of money, be assail'd by robbers, and die in many irreconciled iniquities, you may call the business of the master the author of the servant's damnation:—but this is not so: the king is not bound to answer the particular endings of his soldiers, the father of his son, nor the master of his servant; for they purpose not their death, when they purpose their services. Besides, there is no king, be his cause never so spotless, if it come to the arbitrement of swords, can try it out with all unspotted soldiers: some peradventure have on them the guilt of premeditated and contrived murder; some, of beguiling virgins with the broken seals of perjury; some, making the wars their bulwark, that have before gored the gentle bosom of peace with pillage and robbery. Now, if these men have defeated the law and outrun native punishment, though they can outstrip men, they have no wings to fly from God: war is His beadle, war is His vengeance; so that here men are punisht for before-breach of the king's laws in now the king's quarrel: where they fear'd the death, they have borne life away; and where they would be safe, they perish: then if they die unprovided, no more is the king guilty of their damnation, than he was before guilty of those impieties for the which they are now visited. Every subject's duty is the king's; but every subject's soul is his own. Therefore should every soldier in the wars do as every sick man in his bed,—wash every mote out of his conscience: and dying so, death is to him advantage; or not dying, the time was blessedly lost wherein such preparation was gain'd: and in him that escapes, it were not sin to think that, making God so free an offer, He let him outlive that day to see His greatness, and to teach others how they should prepare.

MICHAEL WILLIAMS.

'Tis certain, every man that dies ill, the ill upon his own head,—the king is not to answer it.

JOHN BATES.

I do not desire he should answer for me; and yet I determine to fight lustily for him.

KING HENRY.

I myself heard the king say he would not be ransom'd.

MICHAEL WILLIAMS.

Ay, he said so, to make us fight cheerfully: but when our throats are cut, he may be ransom'd, and we ne'er the wiser.

KING HENRY.

If I live to see it, I will never trust his word after.

MICHAEL WILLIAMS.

'Mass, you'll pay him then! That's a perilous shot out of an elder-gun, that a poor and a private displeasure can do against a monarch! you may as well go about to turn the sun to ice with fanning in his face with a peacock's feather. You'll never trust his word after! come, 'tis a foolish saying.

KING HENRY.

Your reproof is something too round: I should be angry with you, if the time were convenient.

MICHAEL WILLIAMS.

Let it be a quarrel between us, if you live.

KING HENRY.

I embrace it.

MICHAEL WILLIAMS.

How shall I know thee again?

KING HENRY.

Give me any gage of thine, and I will wear it in

my bonnet: then, if ever thou darest acknowledge
it, I will make it my quarrel.

MICHAEL WILLIAMS.

Here's my glove: give me another of thine.

KING HENRY.

There.

MICHAEL WILLIAMS.

This will I also wear in my cap: if ever thou come to
me and say, after to-morrow, 'This is my glove,'
by this hand, I will take thee a box on the ear.

KING HENRY.

If ever I live to see it, I will challenge it.

MICHAEL WILLIAMS.

Thou darest as well be hang'd.

KING HENRY.

Well, I will do it, though I take thee in the king's
company.

MICHAEL WILLIAMS.

Keep thy word: fare thee well.

JOHN BATES.

Be friends, you English fools, be friends: we have
French quarrels enow, if you could tell how to
reckon.

KING HENRY.

Indeed, the French may lay twenty French
crowns to one, they will beat us; for they bear
them on their shoulders: but it is no English
treason to cut French crowns; and to-morrow the
king himself will be a clipper. [*Exeunt* SOLDIERS.
Upon the king!—let us our lives, our souls,
Our debts, our careful wives,
Our children, and our sins, lay on the king!
We must bear all. O hard condition,
Twin-born with greatness, subject to the breath
Of every fool, whose sense no more can feel
But his own wringing!
What infinite heart's-ease must kings neglect,
That private men enjoy!
And what have kings, that privates have not too,
Save ceremony,—save general ceremony?
And what art thou, thou idol ceremony?
What kind of god art thou, that suffer'st more
Of mortal griefs than do thy worshippers?
What are thy rents? what are thy comings-in?
O ceremony, show me but thy worth!
What is thy soul, O adoration?
Art thou aught else but place, degree, and form,
Creating awe and fear in other men?
Wherein thou art less happy being fear'd
Than they in fearing.
What drink'st thou oft, instead of homage sweet,
But poison'd flattery? O, be sick, great greatness,
And bid thy ceremony give thee cure!
Think'st thou the fiery fever will go out
With titles blown from adulation?
Will it give place to flexure and low bending?
Canst thou, when thou command'st the beggar's
    knee,
Command the health of it? No, thou proud dream,
That play'st so subtly with a king's repose:
I am a king that find thee; and I know
'Tis not the balm, the sceptre, and the ball,
The sword, the mace, the crown imperial,
The intertissued robe of gold and pearl,
The farced title running 'fore the king,
The throne he sits on, nor the tide of pomp

That beats upon the high shore of this world,—
No, not all these, thrice-gorgeous ceremony,
Not all these, laid in bed majestical,
Can sleep so soundly as the wretched slave,
Who, with a body fill'd and vacant mind,
Gets him to rest, cramm'd with distressful bread;
Never sees horrid night, the child of hell;
But, like a lackey, from the rise to set,
Sweats in the eye of Phœbus, and all night
Sleeps in Elysium; next day, after dawn,
Doth rise, and help Hyperion to his horse;
And follows so the ever-running year,
With profitable labour, to his grave:
And, but for ceremony, such a wretch,
Winding up days with toil and nights with sleep,
Had the fore-hand and vantage of a king.
The slave, a member of the country's peace,
Enjoys it; but in gross brain little wots
What watch the king keeps to maintain the peace,
Whose hours the peasant best advantages.

Enter ERPINGHAM.

SIR THOMAS ERPINGHAM.

My lord, your nobles, jealous of your absence,
Seek through your camp to find you.

KING HENRY.

                Good old knight,
Collect them all together at my tent:
I'll be before thee.

SIR THOMAS ERPINGHAM.

          I shall do't, my lord.   [*Exit.*

KING HENRY.

O God of battles! steel my soldiers' hearts;
Possess them not with fear; take from them now
The sense of reckoning, if th'opposed numbers
Pluck their hearts from them!—Not to-day, O
    Lord,
O, not to-day, think not upon the fault
My father made in compassing the crown!
I Richard's body have interred new;
And on it have bestow'd more contrite tears
Than from it issued forced drops of blood:
Five hundred poor I have in yearly pay,
Who twice a-day their wither'd hands hold up
Toward heaven, to pardon blood; and I have built
Two chantries, where the sad and solemn priests
Sing still for Richard's soul. More will I do;
Though all that I can do is nothing worth,
Since that my penitence comes after all,
Imploring pardon.

Enter GLOSTER.

DUKE OF GLOSTER.

My liege!

KING HENRY.

        My brother Gloster's voice?—Ay;
I know thy errand, I will go with thee:—
The day, my friends, and all things stay for me.

                       [*Exeunt.*

SCENE II.

The French camp.

Enter the DAUPHIN, ORLEANS, RAMBURES,
and others.

DUKE OF ORLEANS.

THE sun doth gild our armour; up, my lords!

DAUPHIN.

Montez à cheval!—My horse! *varlet, laquais!* ha!

DUKE OF ORLEANS.

O brave spirit!

DAUPHIN.

Via!—les eaux et la terre,—

DUKE OF ORLEANS.

Rien puis? l'air et le feu,—

DAUPHIN.

Ciel! cousin Orleans.

Enter CONSTABLE.

Now, my lord Constable!

THE CONSTABLE OF FRANCE.

Hark, how our steeds for present service neigh!

DAUPHIN.

Mount them, and make incision in their hides,
That their hot blood may spin in English eyes,
And dout them with superfluous courage, ha!

RAMBURES.

What, will you have them weep our horses' blood?
How shall we, then, behold their natural tears?

Enter a MESSENGER.

MESSENGER.

The English are embattled, you French peers.

THE CONSTABLE OF FRANCE.

To horse, you gallant princes! straight to horse!
Do but behold yond poor and starved band,
And your fair show shall suck away their souls,
Leaving them but the shales and husks of men.
There is not work enough for all our hands;
Scarce blood enough in all their sickly veins
To give each naked curtle-axe a stain,
That our French gallants shall to-day draw out,
And sheathe for lack of sport: let us but blow on
them,
The vapour of our valour will o'erturn them.
'Tis positive 'gainst all exceptions, lords,
That our superfluous lackeys and our peasants,—
Who in unnecessary action swarm
About our squares of battle,—were enow
To purge this field of such a hilding foe;
Though we upon this mountain's basis by
Took stand for idle speculation,—
But that our honour must not. What's to say?
A very little little let us do,
And all is done. Then let the trumpets sound
The tucket-sonance and the note to mount:
For our approach shall so much dare the field,
That England shall couch down in fear, and yield.

Enter GRANDPRÉ.

GRANDPRÉ.

Why do you stay so long, my lords of France?
Yond island carrions, desperate of their bones,
Ill-favouredly become the morning field:
Their ragged curtains poorly are let loose,
And our air shakes them passing scornfully:
Big Mars seems bankrout in their beggar'd host,
And faintly through a rusty beaver peeps:
The horsemen sit like fixed candlesticks,
With torch-staves in their hand; and their poor
jades
Lob down their heads, dropping the hides and
hips,
The gum down-roping from their pale-dead eyes,
And in their pale dull mouths the gimmal-bit
Lies foul with chew'd grass, still and motionless;
And their executors, the knavish crows,
Fly o'er them, all impatient for their hour.

Description cannot suit itself in words
To demonstrate the life of such a battle
In life so lifeless as it shows itself.

THE CONSTABLE OF FRANCE.

They have said their prayers, and they stay for
death.

DAUPHIN.

Shall we go send them dinners and fresh suits,
And give their fasting horses provender,
And after fight with them?

THE CONSTABLE OF FRANCE.

I stay but for my guidon:—to the field!—
I will the banner from a trumpet take,
And use it for my haste. Come, come, away!
The sun is high, and we outwear the day.

[*Exeunt.*

SCENE III.

The English camp.

Enter GLOSTER, BEDFORD, EXETER, ERPING-
HAM, *with all his host;* SALISBURY, *and* WEST-
MORELAND.

DUKE OF GLOSTER.

WHERE is the king?

DUKE OF BEDFORD.

The king himself is rode to view the battle.

EARL OF WESTMORELAND.

Of fighting-men they have full three-score thousand.

DUKE OF EXETER.

There's five to one; besides, they all are fresh.

EARL OF SALISBURY.

God's arm strike with us! 'tis a fearful odds.
God b' wi' you, princes all; I'll to my charge:
If we no more meet till we meet in heaven,
Then, joyfully,—my noble Lord of Bedford,—
My dear Lord Gloster,—and my good Lord
Exeter,—
And my kind kinsman,—warriors all, adieu!

DUKE OF BEDFORD.

Farewell, good Salisbury; and good luck go with
thee!

DUKE OF EXETER.

Farewell, kind lord; fight valiantly to-day:
And yet I do thee wrong to mind thee of it,
For thou art framed of the firm truth of valour.

[*Exit* SALISBURY.

DUKE OF BEDFORD.

He is as full of valour as of kindness;
Princely in both.

Enter KING HENRY.

EARL OF WESTMORELAND.

　　　　　O, that we now had here
But one ten thousand of those men in England
That do no work to-day!

KING HENRY.

　　　　　　　What's he that wishes so?
My cousin Westmoreland?—No, my fair cousin:
If we are markt to die, we are enow
To do our country loss; and if to live,
The fewer men, the greater share of honour.
God's will! I pray thee, wish not one man more.
By Jove, I am not covetous for gold;
Nor care I who doth feed upon my cost;
It yearns me not if men my garments wear;

Such outward things dwell not in my desires:
But if it be a sin to covet honour,
I am the most offending soul alive.
No, faith, my coz, wish not a man from England:
God's peace! I would not lose so great an honour,
As one man more, methinks, would share from me,
For the best hope I have. O, do not wish one more!
Rather proclaim it, Westmoreland, through my host,
That he which hath no stomach to this fight,
Let him depart; his passport shall be made,
And crowns for convoy put into his purse:
We would not die in that man's company
That fears his fellowship to die with us.
This day is call'd the feast of Crispian:
He that outlives this day, and comes safe home,
Will stand a tip-toe when this day is named,
And rouse him at the name of Crispian.
He that shall live this day, and see old age,
Will yearly on the vigil feast his neighbours,
And say, 'To-morrow is Saint Crispian:'
Then will he strip his sleeve and show his scars,
And say, 'These wounds I had on Crispin's day.'
Old men forget; yet all shall be forgot,
But he'll remember with advantages
What feats he did that day: then shall our names,
Familiar in their mouths as household words,—
Harry the king, Bedford and Exeter,
Warwick and Talbot, Salisbury and Gloster,—
Be in their flowing cups freshly remember'd.
This story shall the good man teach his son;
And Crispin Crispian shall ne'er go by,
From this day to the ending of the world,
But we in it shall be remembered,—
We few, we happy few, we band of brothers;
For he to-day that sheds his blood with me
Shall be my brother; be he ne'er so vile,
This day shall gentle his condition:
And gentlemen in England now a-bed
Shall think themselves accurst they were not here;
And hold their manhoods cheap whiles any speaks
That fought with us upon Saint Crispin's day.

Enter SALISBURY.

EARL OF SALISBURY.
My sovereign lord, bestow yourself with speed:
The French are bravely in their battles set,
And will with all expedience charge on us.

KING HENRY.
All things are ready, if our minds be so.

EARL OF WESTMORELAND.
Perish the man whose mind is backward now!

KING HENRY.
Thou dost not wish more help from England, coz?

EARL OF WESTMORELAND.
God's will! my liege, would you and I alone,
Without more help, might fight this battle out!

KING HENRY.
Why, now thou hast unwisht five thousand men;
Which likes me better than to wish us one.—
You know your places: God be with you all!

Tucket. Enter MONTJOY.

MONTJOY.
Once more I come to know of thee, King Harry,
If for thy ransom thou wilt now compound,

Before thy most assured overthrow:
For certainly thou art so near the gulf,
Thou needs must be englutted. Besides, in mercy,
The Constable desires thee thou wilt mind
Thy followers of repentance; that their souls
May make a peaceful and a sweet retire
From off these fields, where, wretches, their poor bodies
Must lie and fester.

KING HENRY.
Who hath sent thee now?

MONTJOY.
The Constable of France.

KING HENRY.
I pray thee, bear my former answer back:
Bid them achieve me, and then sell my bones.
Good God! why should they mock poor fellows thus?
The man that once did sell the lion's skin
While the beast lived, was kill'd with hunting him.
A many of our bodies shall no doubt
Find native graves; upon the which, I trust,
Shall witness live in brass of this day's work:
And those that leave their valiant bones in France,
Dying like men, though buried in your dunghills,
They shall be famed; for there the sun shall greet them,
And draw their honours reeking up to heaven;
Leaving their earthly parts to choke your clime,
The smell whereof shall breed a plague in France.
Mark, then, abounding valour in our English;
That, being dead, like to the bullet's grazing,
Break out into a second course of mischief,
Killing in relapse of mortality.
Let me speak proudly:—tell the Constable
We are but warriors for the working-day;
Our gayness and our gilt are all besmircht
With rainy marching in the painful field;
There's not a piece of feather in our host,—
Good argument, I hope, we will not fly,—
And time hath worn us into slovenry:
But, by the mass, our hearts are in the trim;
And my poor soldiers tell me, yet ere night
They'll be in fresher robes; or they will pluck
The gay new coats o'er the French soldiers' heads,
And turn them out of service. If they do this,—
As, if God please, they shall,—my ransom then
Will soon be levied. Herald, save thou thy labour;
Come thou no more for ransom, gentle herald:
They shall have none, I swear, but these my joints,—
Which if they have as I will leave 'em them,
Shall yield them little, tell the Constable.

MONTJOY.
I shall, King Harry. And so, fare thee well:
Thou never shalt hear herald any more.   [*Exit.*

KING HENRY.
I fear thou'lt once more come again for ransom.

Enter YORK.

DUKE OF YORK.
My lord, most humbly on my knee I beg
The leading of the vaward.

KING HENRY.

Take it, brave York.—Now, soldiers, march
    away:—
And how thou pleasest, God, dispose the day!
                        [*Exeunt.*

SCENE IV.

The field of battle.

Alarum: excursions. Enter PISTOL, *French*
SOLDIER, *and* BOY.

PISTOL.

YIELD, cur!

FRENCH SOLDIER.

*Je pense que vous êtes le gentilhomme de bonne
qualité.*

PISTOL.

Qualtitie calmie custure me! Art thou a gentleman?
what is thy name? discuss.

FRENCH SOLDIER.

O Seigneur Dieu!

PISTOL.

O, Signieur Dew should be a gentleman:—
Perpend my words, O Signieur Dew, and
    mark;—
O Signieur Dew, thou diest on point of fox,
Except, O signieur, thou do give to me
Egregious ransom.

FRENCH SOLDIER.

O, prenez miséricorde! ayez pitié de moy!

PISTOL.

Moy shall not serve; I will have forty moys;
Or I will fetch thy rim out at thy throat
In drops of crimson blood.

FRENCH SOLDIER.

Est-il impossible d'échapper la force de ton bras?

PISTOL.

Brass, cur!
Thou damned and luxurious mountain-goat,
Offer'st me brass?

FRENCH SOLDIER.

O, pardonnez-moy!

PISTOL.

Say'st thou me so? is that a ton of moys?—
Come hither, boy: ask me this slave in French
What is his name.

BOY.

Écoutez: comment êtes-vous appelé?

FRENCH SOLDIER.

Monsieur le Fer.

BOY.

He says his name is Master Fer.

PISTOL.

Master Fer! I'll fer him, and firk him, and ferret
him:—discuss the same in French unto him.

BOY.

I do not know the French for fer, and ferret, and
firk.

PISTOL.

Bid him prepare; for I will cut his throat.

FRENCH SOLDIER.

Que dit-il, monsieur?

BOY.

*Il me commande de vous dire que vous faites vous
prêt; car ce soldat ici est disposé tout à cette heure de
couper votre gorge.*

PISTOL.

Owy, cuppele gorge, permafoy,
Peasant, unless thou give me crowns, brave
    crowns;
Or mangled shalt thou be by this my sword.

FRENCH SOLDIER.

*O, je vous supplie, pour l'amour de Dieu, me par-
donner! Je suis gentilhomme de bonne maison: gar-
dez ma vie, et je vous donnerai deux cents écus.*

PISTOL.

What are his words?

BOY.

He prays you to save his life: he is a gentleman of
a good house; and for his ransom he will give you
two hundred crowns.

PISTOL.

Tell him my fury shall abate, and I
The crowns will take.

FRENCH SOLDIER.

Petit monsieur, que dit-il?

BOY.

*Encore qu'il est contre son jurement de pardonner
aucun prisonnier, néanmoins, pour les écus que vous
l'avez promis, il est content de vous donner la liberté,
le franchisement.*

FRENCH SOLDIER.

*Sur mes genoux je vous donne mille remercîmens; et
je m'estime heureux que je suis tombé entre les mains
d'un chevalier, je pense, le plus brave, vaillant, et
très distingué seigneur d'Angleterre.*

PISTOL.

Expound unto me, boy.

BOY.

He gives you, upon his knees, a thousand thanks;
and he esteems himself happy that he hath faln
into the hands of one, as he thinks, the most brave,
valorous, and thrice-worthy signieur of England.

PISTOL.

As I suck blood, I will some mercy show.—Follow me, cur.   [*Exit.*

BOY.

Suivez-vous le grand capitaine. [*Exit* FRENCH
SOLDIER.] I did never know so full a voice issue
from so empty a heart: but the saying is true,—
The empty vessel makes the greatest sound. Bardolph and Nym had ten times more valour than
this roaring devil i'th'old play, that every one
may pare his nails with a wooden dagger; and
they are both hang'd; and so would this be, if he
durst steal any thing adventurously. I must stay
with the lackeys, with the luggage of our camp:
the French might have a good prey of us, if he
knew of it; for there is none to guard it but boys.
                        [*Exit.*

SCENE V.

Another part of the field.

Enter CONSTABLE, ORLEANS, BOURBON,
DAUPHIN, RAMBURES, *and others.*

THE CONSTABLE OF FRANCE.

O DIABLE!

DUKE OF ORLEANS.

O Seigneur!—le jour est perdu, tout est perdu!

DAUPHIN.

Mort de ma vie! all is confounded, all!

Reproach and everlasting shame
Sit mocking in our plumes.—*O méchante for-*
tune!—
Do not run away.   [*A short alarum.*
          THE CONSTABLE OF FRANCE.
          Why, all our ranks are broke.
          DAUPHIN.
O perdurable shame!—let's stab ourselves.
Be these the wretches that we play'd at dice for?
          DUKE OF ORLEANS.
Is this the king we sent to for his ransom?
          DUKE OF BOURBON.
Shame, and eternal shame, nothing but shame!
Let's die in honour: once more back again;
And he that will not follow Bourbon now,
Let him go hence, and with his cap in hand,
Like a base pandar, hold the chamber-door
Whilst by a slave, no gentler than my dog,
His fairest daughter is contaminate.
          THE CONSTABLE OF FRANCE.
Disorder, that hath spoil'd us, friend us now!
Let us on heaps go offer up our lives.
          DUKE OF ORLEANS.
We are enow, yet living in the field,
To smother up the English in our throngs,
If any order might be thought upon.
          DUKE OF BOURBON.
The devil take order now! I'll to the throng:
Let life be short; else shame will be too long.
                              [*Exeunt.*

SCENE VI.

Another part of the field.

Alarum.   Enter KING HENRY *and* FORCES,
EXETER, *and others.*

          KING HENRY.
WELL have we done, thrice-valiant country-
          men:
But all's not done; yet keep the French the field.
          DUKE OF EXETER.
The Duke of York commends him to your ma-
jesty.
          KING HENRY.
Lives he, good uncle? thrice within this hour
I saw him down; thrice up again, and fighting;
From helmet to the spur all blood he was.
          DUKE OF EXETER.
In which array, brave soldier, doth he lie,
Larding the plain; and by his bloody side,
Yoke-fellow to his honour-owing wounds,
The noble Earl of Suffolk also lies.
Suffolk first died: and York, all haggled over,
Comes to him, where in gore he lay insteep,
And takes him by the beard; kisses the gashes
That bloodily did yawn upon his face;
And cries aloud, 'Tarry, dear cousin Suffolk!
My soul shall thine keep company to heaven;
Tarry, sweet soul, for mine, then fly abreast;
As in this glorious and well-foughten field
We kept together in our chivalry!'
Upon these words I came, and cheer'd him up:
He smiled me in the face, raught me his hand,
And, with a feeble gripe, says, 'Dear my lord,
Commend my service to my sovereign.'
So did he turn, and over Suffolk's neck

He threw his wounded arm, and kist his lips;
And so, espoused to death, with blood he seal'd
A testament of noble-ending love.
The pretty and sweet manner of it forced
Those waters from me which I would have stopt;
But I had not so much of man in me,
And all my mother came into mine eyes,
And gave me up to tears.
          KING HENRY.
                    I blame you not;
For, hearing this, I must perforce compound
With mistful eyes, or they will issue too.—
                              [*Alarum*
But, hark! what new alarum is this same?—
The French have reinforced their scatter'd
     men:—
Then every soldier kill his prisoners;
Give the word through.   [*Exeunt.*

SCENE VII.

Another part of the field.

Enter FLUELLEN *and* GOWER.

          FLUELLEN.
KILL the poys and the luggage! 'tis expressly
     against the law of arms: 'tis as arrant a piece
of knavery, mark you now, as can be offert; in
your conscience, now, is it not?
          GOWER.
'Tis certain there's not a boy left alive; and the
cowardly rascals that ran from the battle ha' done
this slaughter: besides, they have burn'd and
carried away all that was in the king's tent; wherefore the king, most worthily, hath caused every
soldier to cut his prisoner's throat.   O, 'tis a gallant king!
          FLUELLEN.
Ay, he was porn at Monmouth, Captain Gower.
What call you the town's name where Alexander
the Pig was porn?
          GOWER.
Alexander the Great.
          FLUELLEN.
Why, I pray you, is not pig great? the pig, or the
great, or the mighty, or the huge, or the magnanimous, are all one reckonings, save the phrase is a
little variations.
          GOWER.
I think Alexander the Great was born in Macedon:
his father was call'd Philip of Macedon, as I take
it.
          FLUELLEN.
I think it is in Macedon where Alexander is porn.
I tell you, captain, if you look in the maps of the
'orld, I warrant you sall find, in the comparisons
between Macedon and Monmouth, that the situ-
ations, look you, is both alike. There is a river in
Macedon; and there is also moreover a river at
Monmouth: it is called Wye at Monmouth; but
it is out of my prains what is the name of the
other river; but 'tis all one, 'tis alike as my fingers
is to my fingers, and there is salmons in both. If
you mark Alexander's life well, Harry of Monmouth's life is come after it indifferent well; for
there is figures in all things. Alexander,—Got

knows, and you know,—in his rages, and his furies, and his wraths, and his cholers, and his moods, and his displeasures, and his indignations, and also being a little intoxicates in his prains, did, in his ales and his angers, look you, kill his pest friend, Cleitus.

GOWER.

Our king is not like him in that: he never kill'd any of his friends.

FLUELLEN.

It is not well done, mark you now, to take the tales out of my mouth, ere it is made and finisht. I speak but in the figures and comparisons of it: as Alexander kill'd his friend Cleitus, being in his ales and his cups; so also Harry Monmouth, being in his right wits and his goot judgements, turn'd away the fat knight with the great-pelly doublet: he was full of jests, and gipes, and knaveries, and mocks; I have forgot his name.

GOWER.

Sir John Falstaff.

FLUELLEN.

That is he:—I'll tell you there is goot men porn at Monmouth.

GOWER.

Here comes his majesty.

Alarum. Enter KING HENRY *and* FORCES; WARWICK, GLOSTER, EXETER, *and others.*

KING HENRY.

I was not angry since I came to France
Until this instant.—Take a trumpet, herald;
Ride thou unto the horsemen on yond hill:
If they will fight with us, bid them come down,
Or void the field; they do offend our sight:
If they'll do neither, we will come to them,
And make them skirr away, as swift as stones
Enforced from the old Assyrian slings:
Besides, we'll cut the throats of those we have;
And not a man of them that we shall take
Shall taste our mercy:—go, and tell them so.

DUKE OF EXETER.

Here comes the herald of the French, my liege.

DUKE OF GLOSTER.

His eyes are humbler than they used to be.

Enter MONTJOY.

KING HENRY.

How now! what means this, herald? know'st thou not
That I have fined these bones of mine for ransom?
Comest thou again for ransom?

MONTJOY.

No, great king:
I come to thee for charitable licence
That we may wander o'er this bloody field
To look our dead, and then to bury them;
To sort our nobles from our common men;
For many of our princes—woe the while—
Lie drown'd and soakt in mercenary blood;
So do our vulgar drench their peasant limbs
In blood of princes; and their wounded steeds
Fret fetlock deep in gore, and with wild rage
Yerk out their armed heels at their dead masters,
Killing them twice. O, give us leave, great king,
To view the field in safety, and dispose
Of their dead bodies!

KING HENRY.

I tell thee truly, herald,
I know not if the day be ours or no;
For yet a many of your horsemen peer
And gallop o'er the field.

MONTJOY.

The day is yours.

KING HENRY.

Praised be God, and not our strength, for it!—
What is this castle call'd that stands hard by?

MONTJOY.

They call it Agincourt.

KING HENRY.

Then call we this the field of Agincourt,
Fought on the day of Crispin Crispianus.

FLUELLEN.

Your grandfather of famous memory, an't please your majesty, and your great-uncle Edward the Plack Prince of Wales, as I have read in the chronicles, fought a most prave pattle here in France.

KING HENRY.

They did, Fluellen.

FLUELLEN.

Your majesty says very true: if your majesties is remember'd of it, the Welshmen did goot service in a garden where leeks did grow, wearing leeks in their Monmouth caps; which, your majesty knows, to this hour is an honourable padge of the service; and I do pelieve your majesty takes no scorn to wear the leek upon Saint Tavy's day.

KING HENRY.

I wear it for a memorable honour;
For I am Welsh, you know, good countryman.

FLUELLEN.

All the water in Wye cannot wash your majesty's Welsh plood out of your pody, I can tell you that: Got pless it, and preserve it, as long as it pleases his grace, and his majesty too!

KING HENRY.

Thanks, good my countryman.

FLUELLEN.

By Cheshu, I am your majesty's countryman, I care not who know it; I will confess it to all the 'orld: I need not to be ashamed of your majesty, praised be Got, so long as your majesty is an honest man.

KING HENRY.

God keep me so!—Our heralds go with him:
Bring me just notice of the numbers dead
On both our parts.—Call yonder fellow hither.

[*Points to* WILLIAMS.   *Exeunt* HERALDS *with* MONTJOY.

DUKE OF EXETER.

Soldier, you must come to the king.

KING HENRY.

Soldier, why wear'st thou that glove in thy cap?

MICHAEL WILLIAMS.

An't please your majesty, 'tis the gage of one that I should fight withal, if he be alive.

KING HENRY.

An Englishman?

MICHAEL WILLIAMS.

An't please your majesty, a rascal that swagger'd with me last night; who, if alive, and ever dare to challenge this glove, I have sworn to take him a box o'th'ear: or if I can see my glove in his cap, which he swore, as he was a soldier, he would wear if alive, I will strike it out soundly.

KING HENRY.

What think you, Captain Fluellen? is it fit this soldier keep his oath?

FLUELLEN.

He is a craven and a villain else, an't please your majesty, in my conscience.

KING HENRY.

It may be his enemy is a gentleman of great sort, quite from the answer of his degree.

FLUELLEN.

Though he be as goot a gentleman as the tevil is, as Lucifer and Belzebub himself, it is necessary, look your Grace, that he keep his vow and his oath: if he be perjured, see you now, his reputation is as arrant a villain and a Jack-sauce, as ever his plack shoe trod upon Got's ground and his earth, in my conscience, la.

KING HENRY.

Then keep thy vow, sirrah, when thou meet'st the fellow.

MICHAEL WILLIAMS.

So I will, my liege, as I live.

KING HENRY.

Who servest thou under?

MICHAEL WILLIAMS.

Under Captain Gower, my liege.

FLUELLEN.

Gower is a goot captain, and is goot knowledge and literatured in the wars.

KING HENRY.

Call him hither to me, soldier.

MICHAEL WILLIAMS.

I will, my liege.   [Exit.

KING HENRY.

Here, Fluellen; wear thou this favour for me, and stick it in thy cap: when Alençon and myself were down together, I pluckt this glove from his helm: if any man challenge this, he is a friend to Alençon, and an enemy to our person; if thou encounter any such, apprehend him, an thou dost me love.

FLUELLEN.

Your Grace does me as great honours as can be desired in the hearts of his subjects: I would fain see the man, that has but two legs, that shall find himself aggriefed at this glove; that is all; but I would fain see it once, an please Got of his grace that I might see.

KING HENRY.

Know'st thou Gower?

FLUELLEN.

He is my dear friend, an please you.

KING HENRY.

Pray thee, go seek him, and bring him to my tent.

FLUELLEN.

I will fetch him.

KING HENRY.

My Lord of Warwick, and my brother Gloster,
Follow Fluellen closely at the heels:
The glove which I have given him for a favour
May haply purchase him a box o'th'ear;
It is the soldier's; I, by bargain, should
Wear it myself. Follow, good cousin Warwick:
If that the soldier strike him,—as I judge

By his blunt bearing, he will keep his word,—
Some sudden mischief may arise of it;
For I do know Fluellen valiant,
And, toucht with choler, hot as gunpowder,
And quickly will return an injury:
Follow, and see there be no harm between them.—
Go you with me, uncle of Exeter.   [Exeunt.

SCENE VIII.

Before KING HENRY'S *pavilion.*

Enter GOWER *and* WILLIAMS.

MICHAEL WILLIAMS.

I WARRANT it is to knight you, captain.

Enter FLUELLEN.

FLUELLEN.

Got's will and his pleasure, captain, I peseech you now, come apace to the king: there is more goot toward you peradventure than is in your knowledge to dream of.

MICHAEL WILLIAMS.

Sir, know you this glove?

FLUELLEN.

Know the glove! I know the glove is a glove.

MICHAEL WILLIAMS.

I know this; and thus I challenge it. [*Strikes him.*

FLUELLEN.

'Splood, an arrant traitor as any's in the universal 'orld, or in France, or in England!

GOWER.

How now, sir! you villain!

MICHAEL WILLIAMS.

Do you think I'll be forsworn?

FLUELLEN.

Stand away, Captain Gower; I will give treason his payment into plows, I warrant you.

MICHAEL WILLIAMS.

I am no traitor.

FLUELLEN.

That's a lie in thy throat.—I charge you in his majesty's name, apprehend him: he's a friend of the Duke Alençon's.

Enter WARWICK *and* GLOSTER.

EARL OF WARWICK.

How now, how now! what's the matter?

FLUELLEN.

My Lord of Warwick, here is—praised be Got for it!—a most contagious treason come to light, look you, as you shall desire in a summer's day.— Here is his majesty.

Enter KING HENRY *and* EXETER.

KING HENRY.

How now! what's the matter?

FLUELLEN.

My liege, here is a villain and a traitor, that, look your Grace, has struck the glove which your majesty is take out of the helmet of Alençon.

MICHAEL WILLIAMS.

My liege, this was my glove; here is the fellow of it; and he that I gave it to in change promised to wear it in his cap: I promised to strike him, if he did: I met this man with my glove in his cap, and I have been as good as my word.

FLUELLEN.

Your majesty hear now, saving your majesty's manhood, what an arrant, rascally, beggarly, lousy

knave it is: I hope your majesty is pear me testimony, and witness, and will avouchment, that
this is the glove of Alençon, that your majesty is
give me, in your conscience, now.

KING HENRY.

Give me thy glove, soldier: look, here is the
fellow of it.
'Twas I, indeed, thou promised'st to strike;
And thou hast given me most bitter terms.

FLUELLEN.

An please your majesty, let his neck answer for it,
if there is any martial law in the 'orld.

KING HENRY.

How canst thou make me satisfaction?

MICHAEL WILLIAMS.

All offences, my liege, come from the heart: never
came any from mine that might offend your majesty.

KING HENRY.

It was ourself thou didst abuse.

MICHAEL WILLIAMS.

Your majesty came not like yourself: you appear'd to me but as a common man; witness the
night, your garments, your lowliness; and what
your highness suffer'd under that shape, I beseech you take it for your own fault, and not
mine: for had you been as I took you for, I made
no offence; therefore, I beseech your highness,
pardon me.

KING HENRY.

Here, uncle Exeter, fill this glove with crowns,
And give it to this fellow.—Keep it, fellow;
And wear it for an honour in thy cap
Till I do challenge it.—Give him the crowns:—
And, captain, you must needs be friends with him.

FLUELLEN.

By this day and this light, the fellow has mettle
enough in his pelly.—Hold, there is twelve pence
for you; and I pray you to serve Got, and keep you
out of prawls, and prabbles, and quarrels, and
dissensions, and, I warrant you, it is the petter
for you.

MICHAEL WILLIAMS.

I will none of your money.

FLUELLEN.

It is with a goot will; I can tell you, it will serve
you to mend your shoes: come, wherefore should
you be so pashful? your shoes is not so goot: 'tis
a goot silling, I warrant you, or I will change it.

Enter an English HERALD.

KING HENRY.

Now, herald,—are the dead number'd?

HERALD.

Here is the number of the slaughter'd French.
                          [*Delivers a paper.*

KING HENRY.

What prisoners of good sort are taken, uncle?

DUKE OF EXETER.

Charles duke of Orleans, nephew to the king;
John duke of Bourbon, and Lord Bouciqualt:
Of other lords and barons, knights and squires,
Full fifteen hundred, besides common men.

KING HENRY.

This note doth tell me of ten thousand French
That in the field lie slain: of princes, in this
number,

And nobles bearing banners, there lie dead
One hundred twenty-six: added to these,
Of knights, esquires, and gallant gentlemen,
Eight thousand and four hundred; of the which,
Five hundred were but yesterday dubb'd knights:
So that, in these ten thousand they have lost,
There are but sixteen hundred mercenaries;
The rest are princes, barons, lords, knights,
    squires,
And gentlemen of blood and quality.
The names of those their nobles that lie dead,—
Charles Delabreth, high-Constable of France;
Jaques of Chatillon, admiral of France;
The master of the cross-bows, Lord Rambures;
Great-master of France, the brave Sir Guiscard
    Dauphin;
John duke of Alençon; Antony duke of Brabant,
The brother to the Duke of Burgundy;
And Edward duke of Bar: of lusty earls,
Grandpré and Roussi, Fauconberg and Foix,
Beaumont and Marle, Vaudemont and Lestrale.
Here was a royal fellowship of death!—
Where is the number of our English dead?—
           [HERALD *presents another paper.*
Edward the duke of York, the Earl of Suffolk,
Sir Richard Ketly, Davy Gam, esquire;
None else of name; and of all other men
But five and twenty.—O God, Thy arm was here;
And not to us, but to Thy arm alone,
Ascribe we all!—When, without stratagem,
But in plain shock and even play of battle,
Was ever known so great and little loss
On one part and on th'other?—Take it, God,
For it is only Thine!

DUKE OF EXETER.

        'Tis wonderful!

KING HENRY.

Come, go we in procession to the village:
And be it death proclaimed through our host
To boast of this, or take that praise from God
Which is His only.

FLUELLEN.

Is it not lawful, an please your majesty, to tell how
many is kill'd?

KING HENRY.

Yes, captain; but with this acknowledgement,
That God fought for us.

FLUELLEN.

Yes, my conscience, He did us great goot.

KING HENRY.

Do we all holy rites:
Let there be sung *Non nobis* and *Te Deum.*
The dead with charity enclosed in clay,
We'll then to Calais; and to England then;
Where ne'er from France arrived more happy
   men.   [*Exeunt*

ACT V.

PROLOGUE.

Enter CHORUS.

CHORUS.

VOUCHSAFE to those that have not read the
     story,
That I may prompt them: and of such as have,
I humbly pray them to admit th'excuse

Of time, of numbers, and due course of things,
Which cannot in their huge and proper life
Be here presented. Now we bear the king
Towards Calais: grant him there; there seen,
Heave him away upon your winged thoughts
Athwart the sea. Behold, the English beach
Pales in the flood with men, with wives, and boys,
Whose shouts and claps out-voice the deep-
    mouth'd sea,
Which, like a mighty whiffler 'fore the king,
Seems to prepare his way: so let him land;
And solemnly see him set on to London.
So swift a pace hath thought, that even now
You may imagine him upon Blackheath;
Where that his lords desire him to have borne
His bruised helmet and his bended sword
Before him through the city: he forbids it,
Being free from vainness and self-glorious pride;
Giving full trophy, signal, and ostent,
Quite from himself to God. But now behold,
In the quick forge and working-house of thought,
How London doth pour out her citizens!
The mayor, and all his brethen, in best sort,—
Like to the senators of th'antique Rome,
With the plebeians swarming at their heels,—
Go forth, and fetch their conquering Cæsar in:
As, by a lower but loving likelihood,
Were now the general of our gracious empress—
As in good time he may—from Ireland coming,
Bringing rebellion broached on his sword,
How many would the peaceful city quit,
To welcome him! much more, and much more
    cause,
Did they this Harry. Now in London place him;—
As yet the lamentation of the French
Invites the King of England's stay at home;—
The emperor coming in behalf of France,
To order peace between them;—and omit
All the occurrences, whatever chanced,
Till Harry's back-return again to France:
There must we bring him; and myself have play'd
The interim, by remembering you 'tis past.
Then brook abridgement; and your eyes advance,
After your thoughts, straight back again to France.
                                        [*Exit.*

SCENE I.

France. The English camp.

Enter FLUELLEN *and* GOWER.

GOWER.

NAY, that's right; but why wear you your
leek to-day? Saint Davy's day is past.
            FLUELLEN.
There is occasions and causes why and wherefore in all things: I will tell you, asse my friend,
Captain Gower:—the rascally, scald, peggarly,
lousy, pragging knave, Pistol,—which you and
yourself, and all the 'orld, know to be no petter
than a fellow, look you now, of no merits,—he is
come to me, and prings me pread and salt yesterday, look you, and pid me eat my leek: it was in a
place where I could not preed no contention with
him; but I will be so pold as to wear it in my cap
till I see him once again, and then I will tell him a
little piece of my desires.

GOWER.
Why, here he comes, swelling like a turkeycock.
            FLUELLEN.
'Tis no matter for his swellings nor his turkey-
cocks.

Enter PISTOL.

Got pless you, Auncient Pistol! you scurvy, lousy
knave, Got pless you!

            PISTOL.
Ha! art thou bedlam? dost thou thirst, base Tro-
jan,
To have me fold up Parca's fatal web?
Hence! I am qualmish at the smell of leek.

            FLUELLEN.
I peseech you heartily, scurvy, lousy knave, at
my desires, and my requests, and my petitions, to
eat, look you, this leek: because, look you, you do
not love it, nor your affections, and your appetites,
and your disgestions, does not agree with it, I
would desire you to eat it.

            PISTOL.
Not for Cadwallader and all his goats.
            FLUELLEN.
There is one goat for you. [*Strikes him.*] Will you
be so goot, scald knave, as eat it?

            PISTOL.
Base Trojan, thou shalt die.
            FLUELLEN.
You say very true, scald knave,—when Got's will
is: I will desire you to live in the mean time, and
eat your victuals: come, there is sauce for it.
[*Strikes him again.*] You call'd me yesterday
mountain-squire; but I will make you to-day a
squire of low degree. I pray you, fall to: if you can
mock a leek, you can eat a leek.

            GOWER.
Enough, captain: you have astonisht him.
            FLUELLEN.
I say, I will make him eat some part of my leek,
or I will peat his pate four days.—Pite, I pray you;
it is goot for your green wound and your ploody
coxcomb.

            PISTOL.
Must I bite?

            FLUELLEN.
Yes, certainly, and out of doubt, and out of question too, and ambiguities.

            PISTOL.
By this leek, I will most horribly revenge:
I eat and eat, I swear—

            FLUELLEN.
Eat, I pray you: will you have some more sauce to
your leek? there is not enough leek to swear by.

            PISTOL.
Quiet thy cudgel; thou dost see I eat.
            FLUELLEN.
Much goot do you, scald knave, heartily. Nay,
pray you, throw none away; the skin is goot for
your proken coxcomb. When you take occasions
to see leeks hereafter, I pray you, mock at 'em;
that is all.

            PISTOL.
Good.

            FLUELLEN.
Ay, leeks is goot:—hold you, there is a groat to
heal your pate.

PISTOL.

Me a groat!

FLUELLEN.

Yes, verily and in truth, you shall take it; or I
have another leek in my pocket, which you shall
eat.

PISTOL.

I take thy groat in earnest of revenge.

FLUELLEN.

If I owe you any thing, I will pay you in cudgels;
you shall be a woodmonger, and buy nothing of
me but cudgels. Got b' wi' you, and keep you.
and heal your pate.   [*Exit.*

PISTOL.

All hell shall stir for this.

GOWER.

Go, go; you are a counterfeit cowardly knave.
Will you mock at an ancient tradition,—begun
upon an honourable respect, and worn as a memorable trophy of predeceased valour,—and dare
not avouch in your deeds any of your words? I
have seen you gleeking and galling at this gentleman twice or thrice. You thought, because he
could not speak English in the native garb, he
could not therefore handle an English cudgel: you
find it otherwise; and henceforth let a Welsh correction teach you a good English condition. Fare
ye well.   [*Exit.*

PISTOL.

Doth Fortune play the huswife with me now?
News have I, that my Nell is dead i'th'spital
Of malady of France;
And there my rendezvous is quite cut off.
Old I do wax; and from my weary limbs
Honour is cudgell'd. Well, bawd will I turn,
And something lean to cutpurse of quick hand.
To England will I steal, and there I'll steal:
And patches will I get unto these scars,
And swear I got them in the Gallia wars.   [*Exit.*

SCENE II.

France. The French KING'S *palace.*

Enter, at one door, KING HENRY, BEDFORD,
GLOSTER, EXETER, WARWICK, WESTMORE-
LAND, *and other* LORDS; *at another, the*
French KING, QUEEN ISABEL, *the* PRINCESS
KATHARINE, ALICE, *other* LADIES, *and*
LORDS; *the* DUKE OF BURGUNDY, *and his*
TRAIN.

KING HENRY.

PEACE to this meeting, wherefore we are met!
Unto our brother France, and to our sister,
Health and fair time of day;—joy and good wishes
To our most fair and princely cousin Katharine;—
And. as a branch and member of this royalty,
By whom this great assembly is contrived,
We do salute you, Duke of Burgundy;—
And, princes French, and peers, health to you all!

FRENCH KING.

Right joyous are we to behold your face,
Most worthy brother England; fairly met:—
So are you, princes English, every one.

QUEEN ISABEL.

So happy be the issue, brother England,
Of this good day and of this gracious meeting,

As we are now glad to behold your eyes;
Yours eyes, which hitherto have borne in them
Against the French, that met them in their bent,
The fatal balls of murdering basilisks:
The venom of such looks, we fairly hope,
Have lost their quality; and that this day
Shall change all griefs and quarrels into love.

KING HENRY.

To cry amen to that, thus we appear.

QUEEN ISABEL.

You English princes all, I do salute you.

DUKE OF BURGUNDY.

My duty to you both, on equal love,
Great Kings of France and England! That I
   have labour'd,
With all my wits, my pains, and strong endea-
   vours,
To bring your most imperial majesties
Unto this bar and royal interview,
Your mightiness on both parts best can witness.
Since, then, my office hath so far prevail'd,
That, face to face and royal eye to eye,
You have congreeted, let it not disgrace me,
If I demand, before this royal view,
What rub or what impediment there is,
Why that the naked, poor, and mangled Peace,
Dear nurse of arts, plenties, and joyful births,
Should not, in this best garden of the world,
Our fertile France, put up her lovely visage?
Alas, she hath from France too long been chased!
And all her husbandry doth lie on heaps,
Corrupting in its own fertility.
Her vine, the merry cheerer of the heart,
Unpruned dies; her hedges even-pleacht,
Like prisoners wildly overgrown with hair,
Put forth disorder'd twigs; her fallow leas
The darnel, hemlock, and rank fumitory,
Do root upon, while that the coulter rusts,
That should deracinate such savagery;
The even mead, that erst brought sweetly forth
The freckled cowslip, burnet, and green clover,
Wanting the scythe, all uncorrected, rank,
Conceives by idleness, and nothing teems
But hateful docks, rough thistles, kecksies, burs,
Losing both beauty and utility.
And as our vineyards, fallows, meads, and hedges,
Defective in their natures, grow to wildness,
Even so our houses, and ourselves and children,
Have lost, or do not learn for want of time,
The sciences that should become our country;
But grow, like savages,—as soldiers will,
That nothing do but meditate on blood,—
To swearing, and stern looks, diffused attire,
And every thing that seems unnatural.
Which to reduce into our former favour,
You are assembled: and my speech entreats
That I may know the let, why gentle Peace
Should not expel these inconveniences,
And bless us with her former qualities.

KING HENRY.

If, Duke of Burgundy, you would the peace,
Whose want gives growth to th'imperfections
Which you have cited, you must buy that peace
With full accord to all our just demands;
Whose tenours and particular effects
You have, enscheduled briefly, in your hands.

DUKE OF BURGUNDY.
The king hath heard them; to the which as yet
There is no answer made.

KING HENRY.
         Well, then, the peace,
Which you before so urged, lies in his answer.

FRENCH KING.
I have but with a cursorary eye
O'erglanced the articles: pleaseth your Grace
To appoint some of your council presently
To sit with us once more, with better heed
To re-survey them, we will suddenly
Pass our accept and peremptory answer.

KING HENRY.
Brother, we shall.—Go, uncle Exeter,— [ter,—
And brother Clarence,—and you, brother Glos-
Warwick,—and Huntingdon,—go with the king;
And take with you free power to ratify,
Augment, or alter, as your wisdoms best
Shall see advantageable for our dignity,
Any thing in or out of our demands;
And we'll consign thereto.—Will you, fair sister,
Go with the princes, or stay here with us?

QUEEN ISABEL.
Our gracious brother, I will go with them:
Haply a woman's voice may do some good,
When articles too nicely urged be stood on.

KING HENRY.
Yet leave our cousin Katharine here with us:
She is our capital demand, comprised
Within the fore-rank of our articles.

QUEEN ISABEL.
She hath good leave.

    [*Exeunt all except* KING HENRY, KATH-
    ARINE, *and* ALICE.

KING HENRY.
        Fair Katharine, and most fair!
Will you vouchsafe to teach a soldier terms
Such as will enter at a lady's ear,
And plead his love-suit to her gentle heart?

KATHARINE.
Your majesty shall mock at me; I cannot speak
your England.

KING HENRY.
O fair Katharine, if you will love me soundly with
your French heart, I will be glad to hear you confess it brokenly with your English tongue. Do
you like me, Kate?

KATHARINE.
Pardonnez-moi, I cannot tell vat is 'like me.'

KING HENRY.
An angel is like you, Kate, and you are like an
angel.

KATHARINE.
Que dit-il? que je suis semblable à les anges?

ALICE.
Oui, vraiment, sauf votre grace, ainsi dit-il.

KING HENRY.
I said so, dear Katharine; and I must not blush to
affirm it.

KATHARINE.
*O bon Dieu! les langues des hommes sont pleines de
tromperies.*

KING HENRY.
What says she, fair one? that the tongues of men
are full of deceits?

ALICE.
Oui, dat de tongues of de mans is be full of deceits
—dat is de princess.

KING HENRY.
The princess is the better Englishwoman. I'faith,
Kate, my wooing is fit for thy understanding:
I am glad thou canst speak no better English; for,
if thou couldst, thou wouldst find me such a plain
king, that thou wouldst think I had sold my farm
to buy my crown. I know no ways to mince it in
love, but directly to say, 'I love you:' then, if you
urge me further than to say, 'Do you in faith?'
I wear out my suit. Give me your answer; i'faith,
do; and so clap hands and a bargain: how say you,
lady?

KATHARINE.
Sauf votre honneur, me understand vell.

KING HENRY.
Marry, if you would put me to verses or to dance
for your sake, Kate, why, you undid me: for the
one, I have neither words nor measure; and for
the other, I have no strength in measure, yet a
reasonable measure in strength. If I could win a
lady at leap-frog, or by vaulting into my saddle
with my armour on my back, under the correction
of bragging be it spoken, I should quickly leap into a wife. Or if I might buffet for my love, or
bound my horse for her favours, I could lay on
like a butcher, and sit like a jack-an-apes, never
off. But, before God, Kate, I cannot look greenly,
nor gasp out my eloquence, nor I have no cunning in protestation; only downright oaths, which
I never use till urged, nor never break for urging.
If thou canst love a fellow of this temper, Kate,
whose face is not worth sun-burning, that never
looks in his glass for love of any thing he sees
there,—let thine eye be thy cook. I speak to thee
plain soldier: if thou canst love me for this, take
me; if not, to say to thee that I shall die, is true,—
but for thy love, by the Lord, no; yet I love thee
too. And while thou livest, dear Kate, take a fellow of plain and uncoin'd constancy; for he perforce must do thee right, because he hath not the
gift to woo in other places: for these fellows of infinite tongue, that can rime themselves into ladies'
favours, they do always reason themselves out
again. What! a speaker is but a prater; a rime is
but a ballad. A good leg will fall; a straight back
will stoop; a black beard will turn white; a curl'd
pate will grow bald; a fair face will wither; a full
eye will wax hollow: but a good heart, Kate, is the
sun and the moon; or, rather, the sun, and not the
moon,—for it shines bright, and never changes,
but keeps his course truly. If thou would have
such a one, take me: and take me, take a soldier;
take a soldier, take a king: and what say'st thou,
then, to my love? speak, my fair, and fairly, I pray
thee.

KATHARINE.
Is it possible dat I sould love de enemy of France?

KING HENRY.
No; it is not possible you should love the enemy
of France, Kate: but, in loving me, you should
love the friend of France; for I love France so well,
that I will not part with a village of it; I will have
it all mine: and, Kate, when France is mine and

I am yours, then yours is France and you are mine.

KATHARINE.

I cannot tell vat is dat.

KING HENRY.

No, Kate? I will tell thee in French; which I am sure will hang upon my tongue like a new-married wife about her husband's neck, hardly to be shook off. *Je quand sur le possession de France, et quand vous avez le possession de moi,*—let me see, what then? Saint Denis be my speed!—*donc votre est France et vous êtes mienne.* It is as easy for me, Kate, to conquer the kingdom, as to speak so much more French: I shall never move thee in French, unless it be to laugh at me.

KATHARINE.

Sauf votre honneur, le Français que vous parlez, il est meilleur que l'Anglais lequel je parle.

KING HENRY.

No, faith, is't not, Kate: but thy speaking of my tongue, and I thine, most truly-falsely, must needs be granted to be much at one. But, Kate, dost thou understand thus much English,—Canst thou love me?

KATHARINE.

I cannot tell.

KING HENRY.

Can any of your neighbours tell, Kate? I'll ask them. Come, I know thou lovest me: and at night, when you come into your closet, you'll question this gentlewoman about me; and I know, Kate, you will to her dispraise those parts in me that you love with your heart: but, good Kate, mock me mercifully; the rather, gentle princess, because I love thee cruelly. If ever thou beest mine, Kate, —as I have a saving faith within me tells me thou shalt,—I get thee with scambling, and thou must therefore needs prove a good soldier-breeder: shall not thou and I, between Saint Denis and Saint George, compound a boy, half French, half English, that shall go to Constantinople and take the Turk by the beard? shall we not? what say'st thou, my fair flower-de-luce?

KATHARINE.

I do not know dat.

KING HENRY.

No; 'tis hereafter to know, but now to promise: do but now promise, Kate, you will endeavour for your French part of such a boy; and for my English moiety take the word of a king and a bachelor. How answer you, *la plus belle Katharine du monde, mon très-chère et devin déesse?*

KATHARINE.

Your majestee ave *fausse* French enough to deceive de most *sage demoiselle* dat is *en France.*

KING HENRY.

Now, fie upon my false French! By mine honour, in true English, I love thee, Kate: by which honour I dare not swear thou lovest me; yet my blood begins to flatter me that thou dost, notwithstanding the poor and untempering effect of my visage. Now, beshrew my father's ambition! he was thinking of civil wars when he got me: therefore was I created with a stubborn outside, with an aspect of iron, that, when I come to woo ladies, I fright them. But, in faith, Kate, the elder I wax, the better I shall appear: my comfort is, that old age, that ill layer-up of beauty, can do no more spoil upon my face: thou hast me, if thou hast me, at the worst; and thou shalt wear me, if thou wear me, better and better:—and therefore tell me, most fair Katharine, will you have me? Put off your maiden blushes; avouch the thoughts of your heart with the looks of an empress; take me by the hand, and say, 'Harry of England, I am thine:' which word thou shalt no sooner bless mine ear withal, but I will tell thee aloud, 'England is thine, Ireland is thine, France is thine, and Henry Plantagenet is thine;' who, though I speak it before his face, if he be not fellow with the best king, thou shalt find the best king of good fellows. Come, your answer in broken music,—for thy voice is music, and thy English broken; therefore, queen of all Katharines, break thy mind to me in broken English,—wilt thou have me?

KATHARINE.

Dat is as it sall please de *roi mon père.*

KING HENRY.

Nay, it will please him well, Kate,—it shall please him, Kate.

KATHARINE.

Den it sall also content me.

KING HENRY.

Upon that I kiss your hand, and I call you my queen.

KATHARINE.

Laissez, mon seigneur, laissez, laissez: ma foi, je ne veux point que vous abaissiez votre grandeur en baisant la main d'une votre indigne serviteur; excusez-moi, je vous supplie, mon très-puissant seigneur.

KING HENRY.

Then I will kiss your lips, Kate.

KATHARINE.

Les dames et demoiselles pour être baisées devant leur noces, il n'est pas la coutume de France.

KING HENRY.

Madam my interpreter, what says she?

ALICE.

Dat it is not be de fashion *pour les* ladies of France,—I cannot tell vat is *baiser en* Anglish.

KING HENRY.

To kiss.

ALICE.

Your majestee *entendre* bettre *que moi.*

KING HENRY.

It is not a fashion for the maids in France to kiss before they are married, would she say?

ALICE.

Oui, vraiment.

KING HENRY.

O Kate, nice customs court'sy to great kings. Dear Kate, you and I cannot be confined within the weak list of a country's fashion: we are the makers of manners, Kate; and the liberty that follows our places stops the mouth of all find-faults, —as I will do yours for upholding the nice fashion of your country in denying me a kiss: therefore, patiently and yielding. [*Kissing her.*] You have witchcraft in your lips, Kate: there is more eloquence in a sugar touch of them than in the tongues of the French council; and they should sooner persuade Harry of England than a general petition of monarchs.—Here comes your father.

Enter the French KING *and* QUEEN, BURGUNDY, BEDFORD, GLOSTER, EXETER, WESTMORELAND, WARWICK, &c.

DUKE OF BURGUNDY.

God save your majesty! my royal cousin,
Teach you our princess English?

KING HENRY.

I would have her learn, my fair cousin, how perfectly I love her; and that is good English.

DUKE OF BURGUNDY.

Is she not apt?

KING HENRY.

Our tongue is rough, coz, and my condition is not smooth; so that, having neither the voice nor the heart of flattery about me, I cannot so conjure up the spirit of love in her, that he will appear in his true likeness.

DUKE OF BURGUNDY.

Pardon the frankness of my mirth, if I answer you for that. If you would conjure in her, you must make a circle; if conjure up love in her in his true likeness, he must appear naked and blind. Can you blame her, then, being a maid yet rosed-over with the virgin crimson of modesty, if she deny the appearance of a naked blind boy in her naked seeing self? It were, my lord, a hard condition for a maid to consign to.

KING HENRY.

Yet they do wink and yield,—as love is blind and enforces.

DUKE OF BURGUNDY.

They are then excused, my lord, when they see not what they do.

KING HENRY.

Then, good my lord, teach your cousin to consent winking.

DUKE OF BURGUNDY.

I will wink on her to consent, my lord, if you will teach her to know my meaning: for maids, well summer'd and warm kept, are like flies at Bartholomew-tide, blind, though they have their eyes; and then they will endure handling, which before would not abide looking on.

KING HENRY.

This moral ties me over to time and a hot summer; and so I shall catch the fly, your cousin, in the latter end, and she must be blind too.

DUKE OF BURGUNDY.

As love is, my lord, before it loves.

KING HENRY.

It is so: and you may, some of you, thank love for my blindness, who cannot see many a fair French city for one fair French maid that stands in my way.

FRENCH KING.

Yes, my lord, you see them perspectively, the cities turn'd into a maid; for they are all girdled with maiden walls that war hath never enter'd.

KING HENRY.

Shall Kate be my wife?

FRENCH KING.

So please you.

KING HENRY.

I am content; so the maiden cities you talk of may wait on her: so the maid that stood in the way for my wish shall show me the way to my will.

FRENCH KING.

We have consented to all terms of reason.

KING HENRY.

Is't so, my lords of England?

EARL OF WESTMORELAND.

The king hath granted every article:—
His daughter first; and then, in sequel, all,
According to their firm proposed natures.

DUKE OF EXETER.

Only, he hath not yet subscribed this:
Where your majesty demands, that the King of France, having any occasion to write for matter of grant, shall name your highness in this form and with this addition, in French, *Notre très-cher fils Henri, roi d'Angleterre, héritier de France;* and thus in Latin, *Præclarissimus filius noster Henricus, rex Angliæ, et hæres Franciæ.*

FRENCH KING.

Nor this I have not, brother, so denied,
But your request shall make me let it pass.

KING HENRY.

I pray you, then, in love and dear alliance,
Let that one article rank with the rest;
And thereupon give me your daughter.

FRENCH KING.

Take her, fair son; and from her blood raise up
Issue to me; that the contending kingdoms
Of France and England, whose very shores look
    pale
With envy of each other's happiness,
May cease their hatred; and this dear conjunction
Plant neighbourhood and Christian-like accord
In their sweet bosoms, that never war advance
His bleeding sword 'twixt England and fair
    France.

ALL.

Amen!

KING HENRY.

Now, welcome, Kate;—and bear me witness all,
That here I kiss her as my sovereign queen.

[*Flourish.*

QUEEN ISABEL.

God, the best maker of all marriages,
Combine your hearts in one, your realms in one!
As man and wife, being two, are one in love,
So be there 'twixt your kingdoms such a spousal,
That never may ill office, or fell jealousy,
Which troubles oft the bed of blessed marriage,
Thrust in between the paction of these kingdoms,
To make divorce of their incorporate league;
That English may as French, French Englishmen,
Receive each other!—God speak this Amen!

ALL.

Amen!

KING HENRY.

Prepare we for our marriage:—on which day,
My lord of Burgundy, we'll take your oath,
And all the peers', for surety of our leagues.
Then shall I swear to Kate, and you to me;
And may our oaths well kept and prosperous be!

[*Sennet. Exeunt.*

EPILOGUE.

Enter CHORUS.

CHORUS.

Thus far, with rough and all unable pen,
  Our bending author hath pursued the story;
In little room confining mighty men,
  Mangling by starts the full course of their
    glory.
Small time, but in that small, most greatly liv'd
  This star of England: fortune made his sword;
By which the world's best garden he achieved,
  And of it left his son imperial lord.
Henry the Sixth, in infant bands crown'd king
  Of France and England, did this king suc-
    ceed;
Whose state so many had the managing,
  That they lost France, and made his England
    bleed:
Which oft our stage hath shown; and for their
  sake,
  In your fair minds let this acceptance take.
                                        [*Exit*

MUCH ADO ABOUT NOTHING

DRAMATIS PERSONAE

DON PEDRO, *prince of Arragon.*
DON JOHN, *his bastard brother.*
CLAUDIO, *a young lord of Florence.*
BENEDICK, *a young lord of Padua.*
LEONATO, *governor of Messina.*
ANTONIO, *his brother.*
BALTHAZAR, *attendant on Don Pedro.*
BORACHIO, ⎫
CONRADE, ⎬ *followers of Don John.*
FRIAR FRANCIS.

DOGBERRY, *a constable.*
VERGES, *a headborough.*
A SEXTON.
A BOY.
HERO, *daughter to Leonato.*
BEATRICE, *niece to Leonato.*
MARGARET, ⎫
URSULA, ⎬ *gentlewomen attending on Hero.*

MESSENGERS, WATCH, ATTENDANTS, &c.

SCENE—*Messina.*

ACT I. SCENE I.

Before LEONATO'S *house.*

Enter LEONATO, HERO, *and* BEATRICE, *with
a* MESSENGER.

LEONATO.

I LEARN in this letter that Don Pedro of
Arragon comes this night to Messina.

MESSENGER.

He is very near by this: he was not three leagues
off when I left him.

LEONATO.

How many gentlemen have you lost in this action?

MESSENGER.

But few of any sort, and none of name.

LEONATO.

A victory is twice itself when the achiever brings
home full numbers. I find here that Don Pedro
hath bestow'd much honour on a young Florentine called Claudio.

MESSENGER.

Much deserved on his part, and equally remember'd by Don Pedro. He hath borne himself beyond the promise of his age; doing, in the figure
of a lamb, the feats of a lion: he hath, indeed,
better better'd expectation than you must expect
of me to tell you how.

LEONATO.

He hath an uncle here in Messina will be very
much glad of it.

MESSENGER.

I have already deliver'd him letters, and there
appears much joy in him; even so much, that joy
could not show itself modest enough without a
badge of bitterness.

LEONATO.

Did he break out into tears?

MESSENGER.

In great measure.

LEONATO.

A kind overflow of kindness: there are no faces
truer than those that are so wash'd. How much
better is it to weep at joy than to joy at weeping!

BEATRICE.

I pray you, is Signior Mountanto return'd from
the wars or no?

MESSENGER.

I know none of that name, lady: there was none
such in the army of any sort.

LEONATO.

What is he that you ask for, niece?

HERO.

My cousin means Signior Benedick of Padua.

MESSENGER.

O, he's return'd; and as pleasant as ever he was.

BEATRICE.

He set up his bills here in Messina, and challenged Cupid at the flight; and my uncle's fool,
reading the challenge, subscribed for Cupid, and
challenged him at the birdbolt.—I pray you, how
many hath he kill'd and eaten in these wars? But
how many hath he kill'd? for, indeed, I promised
to eat all of his killing.

LEONATO.

Faith, niece, you tax Signior Benedick too much;
but he'll be meet with you, I doubt it not.

MESSENGER.

He hath done good service, lady, in these wars.

BEATRICE.

You had musty victual, and he hath holp to eat
it: he's a very valiant trencher-man; he hath an
excellent stomach.

MESSENGER.

And a good soldier too, lady.

BEATRICE.

And a good soldier to a lady:—but what is he to
a lord?

MESSENGER.

A lord to a lord, a man to a man; stuft with all
honourable virtues.

BEATRICE.

It is so, indeed; he is no less than a stuft man: but
for the stuffing,—well, we are all mortal.

LEONATO.

You must not, sir, mistake my niece. There is a
kind of merry war betwixt Signior Benedick and
her: they never meet but there's a skirmish of wit
bewteen them.

BEATRICE.

Alas, he gets nothing by that! In our last conflict
four of his five wits went halting off, and now is
the whole man govern'd with one: so that if he

have wit enough to keep himself warm, let him bear it for a difference between himself and his horse; for it is all the wealth that he hath left, to be known a reasonable creature.—Who is his companion now? He hath every month a new sworn brother.

MESSENGER.

Is't possible?

BEATRICE.

Very easily possible: he wears his faith but as the fashion of his hat; it ever changes with the next block.

MESSENGER.

I see, lady, the gentleman is not in your books.

BEATRICE.

No; an he were, I would burn my study. But, I pray you, who is his companion? Is there no young squarer now that will make a voyage with him to the devil?

MESSENGER.

He is most in the company of the right noble Claudio.

BEATRICE.

O Lord, he will hang upon him like a disease: he is sooner caught than the pestilence, and the taker runs presently mad. God help the noble Claudio! if he have caught the Benedick, it will cost him a thousand pound ere a' be cured.

MESSENGER.

I will hold friends with you, lady.

BEATRICE.

Do, good friend.

LEONATO.

You will never run mad, niece.

BEATRICE.

No, not till a hot January.

MESSENGER.

Don Pedro is approach'd.

Enter DON PEDRO, DON JOHN, CLAUDIO, BENEDICK, *and* BALTHAZAR.

DON PEDRO.

Good Signior Leonato, you are come to meet your trouble: the fashion of the world is to avoid cost, and you encounter it.

LEONATO.

Never came trouble to my house in the likeness of your grace: for trouble being gone, comfort should remain; but when you depart from me, sorrow abides, and happiness takes his leave.

DON PEDRO.

You embrace your charge too willingly.—I think this is your daughter.

LEONATO.

Her mother hath many times told me so.

BENEDICK.

Were you in doubt, sir, that you askt her?

LEONATO.

Signior Benedick, no; for then were you a child.

DON PEDRO.

You have it full, Benedick: we may guess by this what you are, being a man.—Truly, the lady fathers herself.—Be happy, lady; for you are like an honourable father.

BENEDICK.

If Signior Leonato be her father, she would not

have his head on her shoulders for all Messina, as like him as she is.

BEATRICE.

I wonder that you will still be talking, Signior Benedick: nobody marks you.

BENEDICK.

What, my dear Lady Disdain! are you yet living?

BEATRICE.

Is it possible disdain should die while she hath such meet food to feed it as Signior Benedick? Courtesy itself must convert to disdain, if you come in her presence.

BENEDICK.

Then is courtesy a turncoat.—But it is certain I am loved of all ladies, only you excepted: and I would I could find it in my heart that I had not a hard heart; for, truly, I love none.

BEATRICE.

A dear happiness to women: they would else have been troubled with a pernicious suitor. I thank God and my cold blood, I am of your humour for that: I had rather hear my dog bark at a crow than a man swear he loves me.

BENEDICK.

God keep your ladyship still in that mind! so some gentleman or other shall scape a predestinate scratcht face.

BEATRICE.

Scratching could not make it worse, an 'twere such a face as yours were.

BENEDICK.

Well, you are a rare parrot-teacher.

BEATRICE.

A bird of my tongue is better than a beast of yours.

BENEDICK.

I would my horse had the speed of your tongue, and so good a continuer. But keep your way, i' God's name; I have done.

BEATRICE.

You always end with a jade's trick: I know you of old.

DON PEDRO.

This is the sum of all: Leonato,—Signior Claudio and Signior Benedick,—my dear friend Leonato hath invited you all. I tell him we shall stay here at the least a month; and he heartily prays some occasion may detain us longer: I dare swear he is no hypocrite, but prays from his heart.

LEONATO.

If you swear, my lord, you shall not be forsworn. —Let me bid you welcome, my lord: being reconciled to the prince your brother, I owe you all duty.

DON JOHN.

I thank you: I am not of many words, but I thank you.

LEONATO.

Please it your Grace lead on?

DON PEDRO.

Your hand, Leonato; we will go together.

[*Exeunt all except* BENEDICK *and* CLAUDIO.

CLAUDIO.

Benedick, didst thou note the daughter of Signior Leonato?

BENEDICK.

I noted her not; but I lookt on her.

CLAUDIO.

Is she not a modest young lady?

BENEDICK.

Do you question me, as an honest man should do, for my simple true judgement, or would you have me speak after my custom, as being a profest tyrant to their sex?

CLAUDIO.

No; I pray thee speak in sober judgement.

BENEDICK.

Why, i'faith, methinks she's too low for a high praise, too brown for a fair praise, and too little for a great praise: only this commendation I can afford her,—that were she other than she is, she were unhandsome; and being no other but as she is, I do not like her.

CLAUDIO.

Thou think'st I am in sport: I pray thee tell me truly how thou likest her.

BENEDICK.

Would you buy her, that you inquire after her?

CLAUDIO.

Can the world buy such a jewel?

BENEDICK.

Yea, and a case to put it into. But speak you this with a sad brow? or do you play the flouting Jack, to tell us Cupid is a good hare-finder, and Vulcan a rare carpenter? Come, in what key shall a man take you, to go in the song?

CLAUDIO.

In mine eye she is the sweetest lady that ever I lookt on.

BENEDICK.

I can see yet without spectacles, and I see no such matter: there's her cousin, an she were not possest with a fury, exceeds her as much in beauty as the first of May doth the last of December. But I hope you have no intent to turn husband, have you?

CLAUDIO.

I would scarce trust myself, though I had sworn the contrary, if Hero would be my wife.

BENEDICK.

Is't come to this? In faith, hath not the world one man but he will wear his cap with suspicion? Shall I never see a bachelor of threescore again? Go to, i'faith; an thou wilt needs thrust thy neck into a yoke, wear the print of it, and sigh away Sundays. Look; Don Pedro is return'd to seek you.

Enter DON PEDRO.

DON PEDRO.

What secret hath held you here, that you follow'd not to Leonato's?

BENEDICK.

I would your Grace would constrain me to tell.

DON PEDRO.

I charge thee on thy allegiance.

BENEDICK.

You hear, Count Claudio: I can be secret as a dumb man, I would have you think so; but on my allegiance,—mark you this, on my allegiance.— He is in love. With who?—now that is your Grace's part.—Mark how short his answer is;— With Hero, Leonato's short daughter.

CLAUDIO.

If this were so, so were it utter'd.

BENEDICK.

Like the old tale, my lord: 'it is not so, nor 'twas not so; but indeed, God forbid it should be so.'

CLAUDIO.

If my passion change not shortly, God forbid it should be otherwise.

DON PEDRO.

Amen, if you love her; for the lady is very well worthy.

CLAUDIO.

You speak this to fetch me in, my lord.

DON PEDRO.

By my troth, I speak my thought.

CLAUDIO.

And, in faith, my lord, I spoke mine.

BENEDICK.

And, by my two faiths and troths, my lord, I spoke mine.

CLAUDIO.

That I love her, I feel.

DON PEDRO.

That she is worthy, I know.

BENEDICK.

That I neither feel how she should be loved, nor know how she should be worthy, is the opinion that fire cannot melt out of me: I will die in it at the stake.

DON PEDRO.

Thou wast ever an obstinate heretic in the despite of beauty.

CLAUDIO.

And never could maintain his part but in the force of his will.

BENEDICK.

That a woman conceived me, I thank her; that she brought me up, I likewise give her most humble thanks: but that I will have a recheat winded in my forehead, or hang my bugle in an invisible baldrick, all women shall pardon me. Because I will not do them the wrong to mistrust any, I will do myself the right to trust none; and the fine is (for the which I may go the finer), I will live a bachelor.

DON PEDRO.

I shall see thee, ere I die, look pale with love.

BENEDICK.

With anger, with sickness, or with hunger, my lord; not with love: prove that ever I lose more blood with love than I will get again with drinking, pick out mine eyes with a ballet-maker's pen, and hang me up at the door of a brothel-house for the sign of blind Cupid.

DON PEDRO.

Well, if ever thou dost fall from this faith, thou wilt prove a notable argument.

BENEDICK.

If I do, hang me in a bottle like a cat, and shoot at me; and he that hits me, let him be clapt on the shoulder, and called Adam.

DON PEDRO.

Well, as time shall try:

'In time the savage bull doth bear the yoke.'

BENEDICK.

The savage bull may; but if ever the sensible Benedick bear it, pluck off the bull's horns, and set them in my forehead; and let me be vilely

painted; and in such great letters as they write,
'Here is good horse to hire,' let them signify
under my sign, 'Here you may see Benedick the
married man.'

CLAUDIO.
If this should ever happen, thou wouldst be horn-mad.

DON PEDRO.
Nay, if Cupid have not spent all his quiver in
Venice, thou wilt quake for this shortly.

BENEDICK.
I look for an earthquake too, then.

DON PEDRO.
Well, you will temporize with the hours. In the
meantime, good Signior Benedick, repair to
Leonato's: commend me to him, and tell him I
will not fail him at supper; for indeed he hath
made great preparation.

BENEDICK.
I have almost matter enough in me for such an
embassage; and so I commit you,—

CLAUDIO.
To the tuition of God: From my house (if I had
it),—

DON PEDRO.
The sixth of July: Your loving friend, Benedick.

BENEDICK.
Nay, mock not, mock not. The body of your discourse is sometime guarded with fragments, and
the guards are but slightly basted on neither: ere
you flout old ends any further, examine your conscience: and so I leave you.　　　　　[Exit.

CLAUDIO.
My liege, your highness now may do me good.

DON PEDRO.
My love is thine to teach: teach it but how,
And thou shalt see how apt it is to learn
Any hard lesson that may do thee good.

CLAUDIO.
Hath Leonato any son, my lord?

DON PEDRO.
No child but Hero; she's his only heir.
Dost thou affect her, Claudio?

CLAUDIO.
　　　　　　　O, my lord,
When you went onward on this ended action,
I lookt upon her with a soldier's eye,
That liked, but had a rougher task in hand
Than to drive liking to the name of love:
But now I am return'd, and that war-thoughts
Have left their places vacant, in their rooms
Come thronging soft and delicate desires,
All prompting me how fair young Hero is,
Saying, I liked her ere I went to wars.

DON PEDRO.
Thou wilt be like a lover presently
And tire the hearer with a book of words.
If thou dost love fair Hero, cherish it;
And I will break with her and with her father,
And thou shalt have her. Was't not to this end
That thou began'st to twist so fine a story?

CLAUDIO.
How sweetly you do minister to love,
That know love's grief by his complexion!
But lest my liking might too sudden seem,
I would have salved it with a longer treatise.

DON PEDRO.
What need the bridge much broader than the
flood?
The fairest grant is the necessity.
Look, what will serve is fit: 'tis once, thou lovest;
And I will fit thee with the remedy.
I know we shall have revelling to-night:
I will assume thy part in some disguise,
And tell fair Hero I am Claudio;
And in her bosom I'll unclasp my heart,
And take her hearing prisoner with the force
And strong encounter of my amorous tale:
Then after to her father will I break;
And the conclusion is, she shall be thine.
In practice let us put it presently.　　[Exeunt.

SCENE II.
A room in LEONATO'S house.
Enter, severally, LEONATO and ANTONIO.

LEONATO.
HOW now, brother! Where is my cousin,
your son? hath he provided this music?

ANTONIO.
He is very busy about it. But, brother, I can tell
you strange news, that you yet dreamt not of.

LEONATO.
Are they good?

ANTONIO.
As the event stamps them: but they have a good
cover; they show well outward. The prince and
Count Claudio, walking in a thick-pleacht alley
in my orchard, were thus much overheard by a
man of mine: the prince discover'd to Claudio
that he loved my niece your daughter, and meant
to acknowledge it this night in a dance; and if he
found her accordant, he meant to take the present time by the top, and instantly break with you
of it.

LEONATO.
Hath the fellow any wit that told you this?

ANTONIO.
A good sharp fellow: I will send for him; and
question him yourself.

LEONATO.
No, no; we will hold it as a dream till it appear
itself: but I will acquaint my daughter withal,
that she may be the better prepared for an
answer, if peradventure this be true. Go you and
tell her of it.—[Exit ANTONIO.—Several persons
cross the stage.] Cousins, you know what you have
to do.—O, I cry you mercy, friend; go you with
me, and I will use your skill.—Good cousin, have
a care this busy time.　　　　　[Exit.

SCENE III.
Another room in LEONATO'S house.
Enter DON JOHN and CONRADE.

CONRADE.
WHAT the good-year, my lord! why are you
thus out of measure sad?

DON JOHN.
There is no measure in the occasion that breeds
it; therefore the sadness is without limit.

CONRADE.
You should hear reason.

DON JOHN.
And when I have heard it, what blessing bringeth it?

CONRADE.
If not a present remedy, yet a patient sufferance.

DON JOHN.
I wonder that thou, being (as thou say'st thou art) born under Saturn, goest about to apply a moral medicine to a mortifying mischief. I cannot hide what I am: I must be sad when I have cause, and smile at no man's jests; eat when I have stomach, and wait for no man's leisure; sleep when I am drowsy, and tend on no man's business; laugh when I am merry, and claw no man in his humour.

CONRADE.
Yea, but you must not make the full show of this till you may do it without controlment. You have of late stood out against your brother, and he hath ta'en you newly into his grace; where it is impossible you should take true root but by the fair weather that you make yourself: it is needful that you frame the season for your own harvest.

DON JOHN.
I had rather be a canker in a hedge than a rose in his grace; and it better fits my blood to be disdain'd of all than to fashion a carriage to rob love from any: in this, though I cannot be said to be a flattering honest man, it must not be denied but I am a plain-dealing villain. I am trusted with a muzzle, and enfranchised with a clog; therefore I have decreed not to sing in my cage. If I had my mouth, I would bite; if I had my liberty, I would do my liking: in the mean time let me be that I am, and seek not to alter me.

CONRADE.
Can you make no use of your discontent?

DON JOHN.
I make all use of it, for I use it only.—Who comes here?

Enter BORACHIO.
What news, Borachio?

BORACHIO.
I came yonder from a great supper: the prince your brother is royally entertain'd by Leonato; and I can give you intelligence of an intended marriage.

DON JOHN.
Will it serve for any model to build mischief on? What is he for a fool that betroths himself to unquietness?

BORACHIO.
Marry, it is your brother's right hand.

DON JOHN.
Who, the most exquisite Claudio?

Even he.

DON JOHN.
A proper squire! And who, and who? which way looks he?

BORACHIO.
Marry, on Hero, the daughter and heir of Leonato.

DON JOHN.
A very forward March-chick! How came you to this?

BORACHIO.
Being entertain'd for a perfumer, as I was smoking a musty room, comes me the prince and Claudio, hand in hand, in sad conference: I whipt me behind the arras; and there heard it agreed upon, that the prince should woo Hero for himself, and having obtain'd her, give her to Count Claudio.

DON JOHN.
Come, come, let us thither: this may prove food to my displeasure. That young start-up hath all the glory of my overthrow: if I can cross him any way, I bless myself every way. You are both sure, and will assist me?

CONRADE.
To the death, my lord.

DON JOHN.
Let us to the great supper: their cheer is the greater that I am subdued. Would the cook were of my mind!—Shall we go prove what's to be done?

BORACHIO.
We'll wait upon your lordship.   [*Exeunt.*

ACT II. SCENE I.
A hall in LEONATO'S *house.*

Enter LEONATO, ANTONIO, HERO, BEATRICE, *and others.*

LEONATO.
WAS not Count John here at supper?

ANTONIO.
I saw him not.

BEATRICE.
How tartly that gentleman looks! I never can see him but I am heart-burn'd an hour after.

HERO.
He is of a very melancholy disposition.

BEATRICE.
He were an excellent man that were made just in the midway between him and Benedick: the one is too like an image, and says nothing; and the other too like my lady's eldest son, evermore tattling.

LEONATO.
Then half Signior Benedick's tongue in Count John's mouth, and half Count John's melancholy in Signior Benedick's face,—

BEATRICE.
With a good leg and a good foot, uncle, and money enough in his purse, such a man would win any woman in the world,—if a' could get her good-will.

LEONATO.
By my troth, niece, thou wilt never get thee a husband, if thou be so shrewd of thy tongue.

ANTONIO.
In faith, she's too curst.

BEATRICE.
Too curst is more than curst: I shall lessen God's sending that way; for it is said, 'God sends a curst cow short horns;' but to a cow too curst he sends none.

LEONATO.

So, by being too curst, God will send you no horns.

BEATRICE.

Just, if he send me no husband; for the which blessing I am at him upon my knees every morning and evening. Lord, I could not endure a husband with a beard on his face: I had rather lie in the woollen.

LEONATO.

You may light on a husband that hath no beard.

BEATRICE.

What should I do with him? dress him in my apparel, and make him my waiting-gentlewoman? He that hath a beard is more than a youth; and he that hath no beard is less than a man: and he that is more than a youth is not for me; and he that is less than a man, I am not for him: therefore I will even take sixpence in earnest of the bear-ward, and lead his apes into hell.

LEONATO.

Well, then, go you into hell?

BEATRICE.

No; but to the gate; and there will the devil meet me, like an old cuckold, with horns on his head, and say, 'Get you to heaven, Beatrice, get you to heaven; here's no place for you maids:' so deliver I up my apes, and away to Saint Peter for the heavens; he shows me where the bachelors sit, and there live we as merry as the day is long.

ANTONIO.

Well, niece [to HERO], I trust you will be ruled by your father.

BEATRICE.

Yes, faith; it is my cousin's duty to make curtsey, and say, 'Father, as it please you:'—but yet for all that, cousin, let him be a handsome fellow, or else make another curtsey, and say, 'Father, as it please me.'

LEONATO.

Well, niece, I hope to see you one day fitted with a husband.

BEATRICE.

Not till God make men of some other metal than earth. Would it not grieve a woman to be over-master'd with a piece of valiant dust? to make an account of her life to a clod of wayward marl? No, uncle, I'll none: Adam's sons are my brethren; and, truly, I hold it a sin to match in my kindred.

LEONATO.

Daughter, remember what I told you: if the prince do solicit you in that kind, you know your answer.

BEATRICE.

The fault will be in the music, cousin, if you be not wooed in good time: if the prince be too important, tell him there is measure in every thing, and so dance out the answer. For, hear me, Hero:—wooing, wedding, and repenting, is as a Scotch jig, a measure, and a cinque-pace: the first suit is hot and hasty, like a Scotch jig, and full as fantastical; the wedding, mannerly-modest, as a measure, full of state and ancientry; and then comes repentance, and, with his bad legs, falls into the cinque-pace faster and faster, till he sink into his grave.

LEONATO.

Cousin, you apprehend passing shrewdly.

BEATRICE.

I have a good eye, uncle; I can see a church by daylight.

LEONATO.

The revellers are ent'ring, brother: make good room.

Enter DON PEDRO, CLAUDIO, BENEDICK, BAL-
THAZAR, DON JOHN, BORACHIO, MARGARET,
URSULA, *and others, maskt; with a drum.*

DON PEDRO.

Lady, will you walk about with your friend?

HERO.

So you walk softly, and look sweetly, and say nothing, I am yours for the walk; and especially when I walk away.

DON PEDRO.

With me in your company?

HERO.

I may say so, when I please.

DON PEDRO.

And when please you to say so?

HERO.

When I like your favour; for God defend the lute should be like the case!

DON PEDRO.

My visor is Philemon's roof; within the house is Jove.

HERO.

Why, then, your visor should be thatcht.

DON PEDRO.

Speak low, if you speak love.

[*Takes her aside.*

BALTHAZAR.

Well, I would you did like me.

MARGARET.

So would not I, for your own sake; for I have many ill qualities.

BALTHAZAR.

Which is one?

MARGARET.

I say my prayers aloud.

BALTHAZAR.

I love you the better: the hearers may cry, Amen.

MARGARET.

God match me with a good dancer!

BALTHAZAR.

Amen.

MARGARET.

And God keep him out of my sight when the dance is done!—Answer, clerk.

BALTHAZAR.

No more words: the clerk is answer'd.

URSULA.

I know you well enough; you are Signior Antonio.

ANTONIO.

At a word, I am not.

URSULA.

I know you by the waggling of your head.

ANTONIO.

To tell you true, I counterfeit him.

URSULA.

You could never do him so ill-well, unless you were the very man. Here's his dry hand up and down: you are he, you are he.

ANTONIO.

At a word, I am not.

URSULA.

Come, come, do you think I do not know you by your excellent wit? can virtue hide itself? Go to, mum, you are he: graces will appear, and there's an end.

BEATRICE.

Will you not tell me who told you so?

BENEDICK.

No, you shall pardon me.

BEATRICE.

Nor will you not tell me who you are?

BENEDICK.

Not now.

BEATRICE.

That I was disdainful, and that I had my good wit out of the *Hundred Merry Tales:*—well, this was Signior Benedick that said so.

BENEDICK.

What's he?

BEATRICE.

I am sure you know him well enough.

BENEDICK.

Not I, believe me.

BEATRICE.

Did he never make you laugh?

BENEDICK.

I pray you, what is he?

BEATRICE.

Why, he is the prince's jester: a very dull fool; only his gift is in devising impossible slanders: none but libertines delight in him; and the commendation is not in his wit, but in his villainy; for he both pleases men and angers them, and then they laugh at him and beat him. I am sure he is in the fleet: I would he had boarded me.

BENEDICK.

When I know the gentleman, I'll tell him what you say.

BEATRICE.

Do, do: he'll but break a comparison or two on me; which, peradventure, not markt, or not laugh'd at, strikes him into melancholy; and then there's a partridge wing saved, for the fool will eat no supper that night. [*Music within.*] We must follow the leaders.

BENEDICK.

In every good thing.

BEATRICE.

Nay, if they lead to any ill, I will leave them at the next turning.

[*Music. Dance. Then exeunt all except* DON JOHN, BORACHIO, *and* CLAUDIO.

DON JOHN.

Sure my brother is amorous on Hero, and hath withdrawn her father to break with him about it. The ladies follow her, and but one visor remains.

BORACHIO.

And that is Claudio: I know him by his bearing.

DON JOHN.

Are not you Signior Benedick?

CLAUDIO.

You know me well; I am he.

DON JOHN.

Signior, you are very near my brother in his love:

he is enamour'd on Hero; I pray you, dissuade him from her, she is no equal for his birth: you may do the part of an honest man in it.

CLAUDIO.

How know you he loves her?

DON JOHN.

I heard him swear his affection.

BORACHIO.

So did I too; and he swore he would marry her to-night.

DON JOHN.

Come, let us to the banquet.

[*Exeunt* DON JOHN *and* BORACHIO.

CLAUDIO.

Thus answer I in name of Benedick,
But hear these ill news with the ears of Claudio.
'Tis certain so;—the prince wooes for himself.
Friendship is constant in all other things
Save in the office and affairs of love:
Therefore all hearts in love use their own tongues;
Let every eye negotiate for itself,
And trust no agent; for beauty is a witch,
Against whose charms faith melteth into blood.
This is an accident of hourly proof,
Which I mistrusted not. Farewell, therefore,
  Hero!

Enter BENEDICK.

BENEDICK.

Count Claudio?

CLAUDIO.

Yea, the same.

BENEDICK.

Come, will you go with me?

CLAUDIO.

Whither?

BENEDICK.

Even to the next willow, about your own business, county. What fashion will you wear the garland of? about your neck, like an usurer's chain? or under your arm, like a lieutenant's scarf? You must wear it one way, for the prince hath got your Hero.

CLAUDIO.

I wish him joy of her.

BENEDICK.

Why, that's spoken like an honest drovier: so they sell bullocks. But did you think the prince would have served you thus?

CLAUDIO.

I pray you, leave me.

BENEDICK.

Ho! now you strike like the blind man: 'twas the boy that stole your meat, and you'll beat the post.

CLAUDIO.

If it will not be, I'll leave you.   [*Exit.*

BENEDICK.

Alas, poor hurt fowl! now will he creep into sedges.—But, that my Lady Beatrice should know me, and not know me! The prince's fool!— Ha! it may be I go under that title because I am merry.—Yea, but so I am apt to do myself wrong; I am not so reputed: it is the base thought, bitter disposition, of Beatrice that puts the world into her person, and so gives me out. Well, I'll be revenged as I may.

Enter DON PEDRO.

DON PEDRO.

Now, signior, where's the count? did you see him?

BENEDICK.

Troth, my lord, I have play'd the part of Lady Fame. I found him here as melancholy as a lodge in a warren: I told him, and I think I told him true, that your grace had got the good-will of this young lady; and I offer'd him my company to a willow-tree, either to make him a garland, as being forsaken, or to bind him up a rod, as being worthy to be whipt.

DON PEDRO.

To be whipt! What's his fault?

BENEDICK.

The flat transgression of a school-boy, who, being overjoy'd with finding a bird's-nest, shows it his companion, and he steals it.

DON PEDRO.

Wilt thou make a trust a transgression? The transgression is in the stealer.

BENEDICK.

Yet it had not been amiss the rod had been made, and the garland too; for the garland he might have worn himself, and the rod he might have bestow'd on you, who, as I take it, have stolen his bird's-nest.

DON PEDRO.

I will but teach them to sing, and restore them to the owner.

BENEDICK.

If their singing answer your saying, by my faith, you say honestly.

DON PEDRO.

The Lady Beatrice hath a quarrel to you: the gentleman that danced with her told her she is much wrong'd by you.

BENEDICK.

O, she misused me past the endurance of a block! an oak but with one green leaf on it would have answer'd her; my very visor began to assume life and scold with her. She told me,—not thinking I had been myself,—that I was the prince's jester, and that I was duller than a great thaw; huddling jest upon jest with such impossible conveyance upon me that I stood like a man at a mark, with a whole army shooting at me. She speaks poniards, and every word stabs: if her breath were as terrible as her terminations, there were no living near her; she would infect to the north star. I would not marry her, though she were endow'd with all that Adam had left him before he transgrest: she would have made Hercules have turn'd spit, yea, and have cleft his club to make the fire too. Come, talk not of her: you shall find her the infernal Ate in good apparel. I would to God some scholar would conjure her; for certainly, while she is here, a man may live as quiet in hell as in a sanctuary; and people sin upon purpose, because they would go thither; so, indeed, all disquiet, horror, and perturbation follow her.

DON PEDRO.

Look, here she comes.

Enter CLAUDIO, BEATRICE, HERO, & LEONATO.

BENEDICK.

Will your grace command me any service to the world's end? I will go on the slightest errand now to the Antipodes that you can devise to send me on; I will fetch you a toothpicker now from the furthest inch of Asia; bring you the length of Prester John's foot; fetch you a hair off the great Cham's beard; do you any embassage to the Pigmies;—rather than hold three words' conference with this harpy. You have no employment for me?

DON PEDRO.

None, but to desire your good company.

BENEDICK.

O God, sir, here's a dish I love not: I cannot endure my Lady Tongue.   [*Exit.*

DON PEDRO.

Come, lady, come; you have lost the heart of Signior Benedick.

BEATRICE.

Indeed, my lord, he lent it me awhile; and I gave him use for it,—a double heart for his single one: marry, once before he won it of me with false dice, therefore your grace may well say I have lost it.

DON PEDRO.

You have put him down, lady, you have put him down.

BEATRICE.

So I would not he should do me, my lord, lest I should prove the mother of fools.—I have brought Count Claudio, whom you sent me to seek.

DON PEDRO.

Why, how now, count! wherefore are you sad?

CLAUDIO.

Not sad, my lord.

DON PEDRO.

How then? sick?

CLAUDIO.

Neither, my lord.

BEATRICE.

The count is neither sad, nor sick, nor merry, nor well; but civil, count,—civil as an orange, and something of that jealous complexion.

DON PEDRO.

I'faith, lady, I think your blazon to be true; though, I'll be sworn, if he be so, his conceit is false.—Here, Claudio, I have woo'd in thy name, and fair Hero is won: I have broke with her father, and, his good-will obtain'd, name the day of marriage, and God give thee joy!

LEONATO.

Count, take of me my daughter, and with her my fortunes: his grace hath made the match, and all grace say Amen to it!

BEATRICE.

Speak, count, 'tis your cue.

CLAUDIO.

Silence is the perfectest herald of joy: I were but little happy, if I could say how much.—Lady, as you are mine, I am yours: I give away myself for you, and dote upon the exchange.

BEATRICE.

Speak, cousin; or, if you cannot, stop his mouth with a kiss, and let not him speak neither.

DON PEDRO.

In faith, lady, you have a merry heart.

BEATRICE.

Yea, my lord; I thank it, poor fool, it keeps on the windy side of care.—My cousin tells him in his ear that he is in her heart.

CLAUDIO.

And so she doth, cousin.

BEATRICE.

Good Lord, for alliance!—Thus goes every one to the world but I, and I am sun-burn'd; I may sit in a corner, and cry heigh-ho for a husband!

DON PEDRO.

Lady Beatrice, I will get you one.

BEATRICE.

I would rather have one of your father's getting. Hath your grace ne'er a brother like you? Your father got excellent husbands, if a maid could come by them.

DON PEDRO.

Will you have me, lady?

BEATRICE.

No, my lord, unless I might have another for working-days: your grace is too costly to wear every day. But, I beseech your grace, pardon me: I was born to speak all mirth and no matter.

DON PEDRO.

Your silence most offends me, and to be merry best becomes you; for, out of question, you were born in a merry hour.

BEATRICE.

No, sure, my lord, my mother cried; but then there was a star danced, and under that was I born.—Cousins, God give you joy!

LEONATO.

Niece, will you look to those things I told you of?

BEATRICE.

I cry you mercy, uncle.—By your grace's pardon.

[_Exit._

DON PEDRO.

By my troth, a pleasant-spirited lady.

LEONATO.

There's little of the melancholy element in her, my lord: she is never sad but when she sleeps; and not ever sad then; for I have heard my daughter say, she hath often dreamt of unhappiness, and waked herself with laughing.

DON PEDRO.

She cannot endure to hear tell of a husband.

LEONATO.

O, by no means: she mocks all her wooers out of suit.

DON PEDRO.

She were an excellent wife for Benedick.

LEONATO.

O Lord, my lord, if they were but a week married, they would talk themselves mad!

DON PEDRO.

County Claudio, when mean you to go to church?

CLAUDIO.

To-morrow, my lord: time goes on crutches till love have all his rites.

LEONATO.

Not till Monday, my dear son, which is hence a just seven-night; and a time too brief, too, to have all things answer my mind.

DON PEDRO.

Come, you shake the head at so long a breathing: but, I warrant thee, Claudio, the time shall not go dully by us. I will, in the interim, undertake one of Hercules' labours; which is, to bring Signior Benedick and the Lady Beatrice into a mountain of affection the one with the other. I would fain have it a match; and I doubt not but to fashion it, if you three will but minister such assistance as I shall give you direction.

LEONATO.

My lord, I am for you, though it cost me ten nights' watchings.

CLAUDIO.

And I, my lord.

DON PEDRO.

And you too, gentle Hero?

HERO.

I will do any modest office, my lord, to help my cousin to a good husband.

DON PEDRO.

And Benedick is not the unhopefullest husband that I know. Thus far can I praise him; he is of a noble strain, of approved valour, and confirm'd honesty. I will teach you how to humour your cousin, that she shall fall in love with Benedick;— and I, with your two helps, will so practise on Benedick, that, in despite of his quick wit and his queasy stomach, he shall fall in love with Beatrice. If we can do this, Cupid is no longer an archer: his glory shall be ours, for we are the only love-gods. Go in with me, and I will tell you my drift.

[_Exeunt._

SCENE II.

Another room in LEONATO'S _house._

Enter DON JOHN _and_ BORACHIO.

DON JOHN.

IT is so; the Count Claudio shall marry the daughter of Leonato.

BORACHIO.

Yea, my lord; but I can cross it.

DON JOHN.

Any bar, any cross, any impediment will be medicinable to me: I am sick in displeasure to him; and whatsoever comes athwart his affection ranges evenly with mine. How canst thou cross this marriage?

BORACHIO.

Not honestly, my lord; but so covertly that no dishonesty shall appear in me.

DON JOHN.

Show me briefly how.

BORACHIO.

I think I told your lordship, a year since, how much I am in the favour of Margaret, the waiting-gentlewoman to Hero.

DON JOHN.

I remember.

BORACHIO.

I can, at any unseasonable instant of the night, appoint her to look out at her lady's chamber-window.

DON JOHN.

What life is in that, to be the death of this marriage?

BORACHIO.

The poison of that lies in you to temper. Go you to the prince your brother; spare not to tell him that he hath wrong'd his honour in marrying the renown'd Claudio (whose estimation do you mightily hold up) to a contaminated stale, such a one as Hero.

DON JOHN.
What proof shall I make of that?

BORACHIO.
Proof enough to misuse the prince, to vex Claudio, to undo Hero, and kill Leonato. Look you for any other issue?

DON JOHN.
Only to despite them, I will endeavour any thing.

BORACHIO.
Go, then; find me a meet hour to draw Don Pedro and the Count Claudio alone: tell them that you know that Hero loves me; intend a kind of zeal both to the prince and Claudio, as,—in love of your brother's honour, who hath made this match, and his friend's reputation, who is thus like to be cozen'd with the semblance of a maid,—that you have discover'd thus. They will scarcely believe this without trial: offer them instances; which shall bear no less likelihood than to see me at her chamber-window; hear me call Margaret, Hero; hear Margaret term me Claudio; and bring them to see this the very night before the intended wedding,—for in the mean time I will so fashion the matter that Hero shall be absent, and there shall appear such seeming truth of Hero's disloyalty, that jealousy shall be call'd assurance, and all the preparation overthrown.

DON JOHN.
Grow this to what adverse issue it can, I will put it in practice. Be cunning in the working this, and thy fee is a thousand ducats.

BORACHIO.
Be you constant in the accusation, and my cunning shall not shame me.

DON JOHN.
I will presently go learn their day of marriage.
[Exeunt.

SCENE III.

LEONATO's *orchard.*

Enter BENEDICK *alone.*

BENEDICK.

Boy,—

Enter BOY.

BOY.
Signior?

BENEDICK.
In my chamber-window lies a book: bring it hither to me in the orchard.

BOY.
I am here already, sir.

BENEDICK.
I know that; but I would have thee hence, and here again. [*Exit* BOY.]—I do much wonder that one man, seeing how much another man is a fool when he dedicates his behaviours to love, will, after he hath laught at such shallow follies in others, become the argument of his own scorn by falling in love: and such a man is Claudio. I have known when there was no music with him but the drum and the fife; and now had he rather hear the tabor and the pipe: I have known when he would have walkt ten mile a-foot to see a good armour; and now will he lie ten nights awake, carving the fashion of a new doublet. He was wont to speak plain and to the purpose, like an honest man and a soldier; and now is he turn'd orthography; his words are a very fantastical banquet,—just so many strange dishes. May I be so converted, and see with these eyes? I cannot tell; I think not: I will not be sworn but love may transform me to an oyster; but I'll take my oath on it, till he have made an oyster of me, he shall never make me such a fool. One woman is fair,—yet I am well; another is wise,—yet I am well; another virtuous,—yet I am well: but till all graces be in one woman, one woman shall not come in my grace. Rich she shall be, that's certain; wise, or I'll none; virtuous, or I'll never cheapen her; fair, or I'll never look on her; mild or come not near me; noble, or not I for an angel; of good discourse, an excellent musician, and her hair shall be of what colour it please God.—Ha, the prince and Monsieur Love! I will hide me in the arbour. [*Withdraws into the arbour.*

Enter DON PEDRO, CLAUDIO, LEONATO, BALTHAZAR, *and* MUSICIANS.

DON PEDRO.
Come, shall we hear this music?

CLAUDIO.
Yea, my good lord.—How still the evening is,
As husht on purpose to grace harmony!

DON PEDRO.
See you where Benedick hath hid himself?

CLAUDIO.
O, very well, my lord: the music ended,
We'll fit the kid-fox with a pennyworth.

DON PEDRO.
Come, Balthazar, we'll hear that song again.

BALTHAZAR.
O, good my lord, tax not so bad a voice
To slander music any more than once.

DON PEDRO.
It is the witness still of excellency
To put a strange face on his own perfection:—
I pray thee, sing, and let me woo no more.

BALTHAZAR.
Because you talk of wooing, I will sing;
Since many a wooer doth commence his suit
To her he thinks not worthy; yet he wooes,
Yet will he swear he loves.

DON PEDRO.
Nay, pray thee, come;
Or, if thou wilt hold longer argument,
Do it in notes.

BALTHAZAR.
Note this before my notes,—
There's not a note of mine that's worth the noting.

DON PEDRO.
Why, these are very crotchets that he speaks;
Note notes, forsooth, and nothing! [*Music.*

BENEDICK [*aside*].
Now, 'Divine air!' now is his soul ravisht!—Is it not strange that sheeps' guts should hale souls out of men's bodies?—Well, a horn for my money, when all's done.

BALTHAZAR *sings.*
Sigh no more, ladies, sigh no more,
  Men were deceivers ever;
One foot in sea, and one on shore;
  To one thing constant never:
    Then sigh not so,
    But let them go,
And be you blithe and bonny;
  Converting all your sounds of woe
    Into Hey nonny, nonny.

Sing no more ditties, sing no moe
  Of dumps so dull and heavy;
The fraud of men was ever so,
  Since summer first was leavy.
    Then sigh not so, &c.

DON PEDRO.
By my troth, a good song.

BALTHAZAR.
And an ill singer, my lord.

DON PEDRO.
Ha, no, no, faith; thou sing'st well enough for a shift.

BENEDICK [*aside*].
An he had been a dog that should have howl'd thus, they would have hang'd him: and I pray God his bad voice bode no mischief! I had as lief have heard the night-raven, come what plague could have come after it.

DON PEDRO.
Yea, marry, dost thou hear, Balthazar? I pray thee, get us some excellent music; for to-morrow night we would have it at the Lady Hero's chamber-window.

BALTHAZAR.
The best I can, my lord.

DON PEDRO.
Do so: farewell. [*Exeunt* BALTHAZAR *and* MUSICIANS.]—Come hither, Leonato. What was it you told me of to-day,—that your niece Beatrice was in love with Signior Benedick?

CLAUDIO.
O, ay:—stalk on, stalk on; the fowl sits [*aside to* PEDRO].—I did never think that lady would have loved any man.

LEONATO.
No, nor I neither; but most wonderful that she should so dote on Signior Benedick, whom she hath in all outward behaviours seem'd ever to abhor.

BENEDICK [*aside*].
Is't possible? Sits the wind in that corner?

LEONATO.
By my troth, my lord, I cannot tell what to think of it: but that she loves him with an enraged affection,—it is past the infinite of thought.

DON PEDRO.
May be she doth but counterfeit.

CLAUDIO.
Faith, like enough.

LEONATO.
O God, counterfeit! There was never counterfeit of passion came so near the life of passion as she discovers it.

DON PEDRO.
Why, what effects of passion shows she?

CLAUDIO [*aside*].
Bait the hook well; this fish will bite.

LEONATO.
What effects, my lord!—She will sit you,—you heard my daughter tell you how.

CLAUDIO.
She did, indeed.

DON PEDRO.
How, how, I pray you? You amaze me: I would have thought her spirit had been invincible against all assaults of affection.

LEONATO.
I would have sworn it had, my lord; especially against Benedick.

BENEDICK [*aside*].
I should think this a gull, but that the white-bearded fellow speaks it: knavery cannot, sure, hide himself in such reverence.

CLAUDIO [*aside*].
He hath ta'en th'infection: hold it up.

DON PEDRO.
Hath she made her affection known to Benedick?

LEONATO.
No; and swears she never will: that's her torment.

CLAUDIO.
'Tis true, indeed; so your daughter says: 'Shall I,' says she, 'that have so oft encounter'd him with scorn, write to him that I love him?'

LEONATO.
This says she now when she is beginning to write to him; for she'll be up twenty times a night; and there will she sit in her smock till she have writ a sheet of paper:—my daughter tells us all.

CLAUDIO.
Now you talk of a sheet of paper, I remember a pretty jest your daughter told us of.

LEONATO.
O,—when she had writ it, and was reading it over, she found Benedick and Beatrice between the sheet?—

CLAUDIO.
That.

LEONATO.
O, she tore the letter into a thousand halfpence; rail'd at herself, that she should be so immodest to write to one that she knew would flout her: 'I measure him,' says she, 'by my own spirit; for I should flout him, if he writ to me; yea, though I love him, I should.'

CLAUDIO.
Then down upon her knees she falls, weeps, sobs, beats her heart, tears her hair, prays, curses;—'O sweet Benedick! God give me patience!'

LEONATO.
She doth indeed; my daughter says so: and the ecstasy hath so much overborne her, that my daughter is sometime afeard she will do a desperate outrage to herself: it is very true.

DON PEDRO.
It were good that Benedick knew of it by some other, if she will not discover it.

CLAUDIO.
To what end? He would but make a sport of it, and torment the poor lady worse.

DON PEDRO.

An he should, it were an alms to hang him. She's an excellent-sweet lady; and, out of all suspicion, she is virtuous.

CLAUDIO.

And she is exceeding wise.

DON PEDRO.

In everything but in loving Benedick.

LEONATO.

O, my lord, wisdom and blood combating in so tender a body, we have ten proofs to one that blood hath the victory. I am sorry for her, as I have just cause, being her uncle and her guardian.

DON PEDRO.

I would she had bestow'd this dotage on me: I would have daff'd all other respects, and made her half myself. I pray you, tell Benedick of it, and hear what he will say.

LEONATO.

Were it good, think you?

CLAUDIO.

Hero thinks surely she will die; for she says she will die, if he love her not; and she will die, ere she make her love known; and she will die, if he woo her, rather than she will bate one breath of her accustom'd crossness.

DON PEDRO.

She doth well: if she should make tender of her love, 'tis very possible he'll scorn it; for the man, as you know all, hath a contemptible spirit.

CLAUDIO.

He is a very proper man.

DON PEDRO.

He hath indeed a good outward happiness.

CLAUDIO.

'Fore God, and in my mind, very wise.

DON PEDRO.

He doth indeed show some sparks that are like wit.

LEONATO.

And I take him to be valiant.

DON PEDRO.

As Hector, I assure you: and in the managing of quarrels you may say he is wise; for either he avoids them with great discretion, or undertakes them with a most Christian-like fear.

LEONATO.

If he do fear God, a' must necessarily keep the peace: if he break the peace, he ought to enter into a quarrel with fear and trembling.

DON PEDRO.

And so will he do; for the man doth fear God, howsoever it seems not in him by some large jests he will make. Well, I am sorry for your niece. Shall we go seek Benedick, and tell him of her love?

CLAUDIO.

Never tell him, my lord: let her wear it out with good counsel.

LEONATO.

Nay, that's impossible: she may wear her heart out first.

DON PEDRO.

Well, we will hear further of it by your daughter: let it cool the while. I love Benedick well; and I could wish he would modestly examine himself, to see how much he is unworthy so good a lady.

LEONATO.

My lord, will you walk? dinner is ready.

CLAUDIO [aside].

If he do not dote on her upon this, I will never trust my expectation.

DON PEDRO [aside].

Let there be the same net spread for her: and that must your daughter and her gentlewomen carry. The sport will be, when they hold one an opinion of another's dotage, and no such matter: that's the scene that I would see, which will be merely a dumb-show. Let us send her to call him in to dinner.

[Exeunt DON PEDRO, CLAUDIO, and LEONATO.

BENEDICK [coming forward].

This can be no trick: the conference was sadly borne. They have the truth of this from Hero. They seem to pity the lady: it seems her affections have their full bent. Love me! why, it must be requited. I hear how I am censured: they say I will bear myself proudly, if I perceive the love come from her; they say too that she will rather die than give any sign of affection.—I did never think to marry:—I must not seem proud:—happy are they that hear their detractions, and can put them to mending. They say the lady is fair,—'tis a truth, I can bear them witness; and virtuous,—'tis so, I cannot reprove it; and wise, but for loving me,—by my troth, it is no addition to her wit, nor no great argument of her folly, for I will be horribly in love with her. I may chance have some odd quirks and remnants of wit broken on me, because I have rail'd so long against marriage: but doth not the appetite alter? a man loves the meat in his youth that he cannot endure in his age. Shall quips and sentences, and these paper-bullets of the brain, awe a man from the career of his humour? no, the world must be peopled. When I said I would die a bachelor, I did not think I should live till I were married.—Here comes Beatrice. By this day, she's a fair lady: I do spy some marks of love in her.

Enter BEATRICE.

BEATRICE.

Against my will I am sent to bid you come in to dinner.

BENEDICK.

Fair Beatrice, I thank you for your pains.

BEATRICE.

I took no more pains for those thanks than you take pains to thank me: if it had been painful, I would not have come.

BENEDICK.

You take pleasure, then, in the message?

BEATRICE.

Yea, just so much as you may take upon a knife's point, and choke a daw withal.—You have no stomach, signior: fare you well. [Exit.

BENEDICK.

Ha! 'Against my will I am sent to bid you come in to dinner,'—there's a double meaning in that. 'I took no more pains for those thanks than you took pains to thank me,'—that's as much as to say,

Any pains that I take for you is as easy as thanks.
—If I do not take pity of her, I am a villain; if I
do not love her, I am a Jew. I will go get her
picture.   [*Exit.*

ACT III.   SCENE I.

LEONATO'S *orchard.*

Enter HERO *and two gentlewomen,* MARGARET
and URSULA.

HERO.

GOOD Margaret, run thee to the parlour;
There shalt thou find my cousin Beatrice
Proposing with the prince and Claudio:
Whisper her ear, and tell her, I and Ursula
Walk in the orchard, and our whole discourse
Is all of her; say that thou overheard'st us;
And bid her steal into the pleached bower,
Where honeysuckles, ripen'd by the sun,
Forbid the sun to enter;—like favourites,
Made proud by princes, that advance their pride
Against that power that bred it:—there will she
    hide her,
To listen our purpose. This is thy office:
Bear thee well in it, and leave us alone.

MARGARET.

I'll make her come, I warrant you, presently.
                                         [*Exit.*

HERO.

Now, Ursula, when Beatrice doth come,
As we do trace this alley up and down,
Our talk must only be of Benedick.
When I do name him, let it be thy part
To praise him more than ever man did merit:
My talk to thee must be, how Benedick
Is sick in love with Beatrice. Of this matter
Is little Cupid's crafty arrow made,
That only wounds by hearsay. Now begin;

Enter BEATRICE, *behind.*

For look where Beatrice, like a lapwing, runs
Close by the ground, to hear our conference.

URSULA.

The pleasant'st angling is to see the fish
Cut with her golden oars the silver stream,
And greedily devour the treacherous bait:
So angle we for Beatrice; who even now
Is couched in the woodbine coverture.
Fear you not my part of the dialogue.

HERO.

Then go we near her, that her ear lose nothing
Of the false-sweet bait that we lay for it.—
                       [*They advance to the bower.*
No, truly, Ursula, she's too disdainful;
I know her spirits are as coy and wild
As haggards of the rock.

URSULA.

            But are you sure
That Benedick loves Beatrice so entirely?

HERO.

So says the prince and my new-trothed lord.

URSULA.

And did they bid you tell her of it, madam?

HERO.

They did entreat me to acquaint her of it;
But I persuaded them, if they loved Benedick,

To wish him wrestle with affection,
And never to let Beatrice know of it.

URSULA.

Why did you so? Doth not the gentleman
Deserve as full as fortunate a bed
As ever Beatrice shall couch upon?

HERO.

O god of love! I know he doth deserve
As much as may be yielded to a man:
But Nature never framed a woman's heart
Of prouder stuff than that of Beatrice;
Disdain and scorn ride sparkling in her eyes,
Misprising what they look on; and her wit
Values itself so highly, that to her
All matter else seems weak: she cannot love,
Nor take no shape nor project of affection,
She is so self-endear'd.

URSULA.

            Sure, I think so;
And therefore certainly it were not good
She knew his love, lest she make sport at it.

HERO.

Why, you speak truth. I never yet saw man,
How wise, how noble, young, how rarely-featured,
But she would spell him backward: if fair-faced,
She'd swear the gentleman should be her sister;
If black, why, Nature, drawing of an antic,
Made a foul blot; if tall, a lance ill-headed;
If low, an agate very vilely cut;
If speaking, why, a vane blown with all winds;
If silent, why, a block moved with none.
So turns she every man the wrong side out;
And never gives to truth and virtue that
Which simpleness and merit purchaseth.

URSULA.

Sure, sure, such carping is not commendable.

HERO.

No, not to be so odd, and from all fashions,
As Beatrice is, cannot be commendable:
But who dare tell her so? If I should speak,   [me
She would mock me into air; O, she would laugh
Out of myself, press me to death with wit!
Therefore let Benedick, like cover'd fire,
Consume away in sighs, waste inwardly:
It were a better death than die with mocks,
Which is as bad as die with tickling.

URSULA.

Yet tell her of it: hear what she will say.

HERO.

No; rather I will go to Benedick,
And counsel him to fight against his passion.
And, truly, I'll devise some honest slanders
To stain my cousin with: one doth not know
How much an ill word may empoison liking.

URSULA.

O, do not do your cousin such a wrong!
She cannot be so much without true judgement
(Having so swift and excellent a wit
As she is prized to have) as to refuse
So rare a gentleman as Signior Benedick.

HERO.

He is the only man of Italy,
Always excepted my dear Claudio.

URSULA.

I pray you, be not angry with me, madam,
Speaking my fancy: Signior Benedick,

For shape, for bearing, argument, and valour,
Goes foremost in report through Italy.
HERO.
Indeed, he hath an excellent good name.
URSULA.
His excellence did earn it, ere he had it.—
When are you married, madam?
HERO.
Why, every day, to-morrow. Come, go in:
I'll show thee some attires; and have thy counsel
Which is the best to furnish me to-morrow.
URSULA [aside].
She's limed, I warrant you: we have caught her,
      madam.
HERO [aside].
If it prove so, then loving goes by haps:
Some Cupid kills with arrows, some with traps.
                    [Exeunt HERO and URSULA.
BEATRICE [coming forward].
What fire is in mine ears? Can this be true?
      Stand I condemn'd for pride and scorn so
            much?
Contempt, farewell! and maiden pride, adieu!
      No glory lives behind the back of such.
And, Benedick, love on; I will requite thee,
      Taming my wild heart to thy loving hand:
If thou dost love, my kindness shall incite thee
      To bind our loves up in a holy band;
For others say, thou dost deserve, and I
Believe it better than reportingly.   [Exit.

SCENE II.

A room in LEONATO'S *house.*

Enter DON PEDRO, CLAUDIO, BENEDICK, *and*
LEONATO.

DON PEDRO.
I DO but stay till your marriage be consummate, and then go I toward Arragon.
CLAUDIO.
I'll bring you thither, my lord, if you'll vouchsafe me.
DON PEDRO.
Nay, that would be as great a soil in the new gloss
of your marriage, as to show a child his new coat,
and forbid him to wear it. I will only be bold with
Benedick for his company; for, from the crown of
his head to the sole of his foot, he is all mirth: he
hath twice or thrice cut Cupid's bow-string, and
the little hangman dare not shoot at him; he hath
a heart as sound as a bell, and his tongue is the
clapper,—for what his heart thinks, his tongue
speaks.
BENEDICK.
Gallants, I am not as I have been.
LEONATO.
So say I: methinks you are sadder.
CLAUDIO.
I hope he be in love.
DON PEDRO.
Hang him, truant! there's no true drop of blood
in him, to be truly toucht with love: if he be sad,
he wants money.
BENEDICK.
I have the toothache.

DON PEDRO.
Draw it.
BENEDICK.
Hang it!
CLAUDIO.
You must hang it first, and draw it afterwards.
DON PEDRO.
What! sigh for the toothache?
LEONATO.
Where is but a humour or a worm?
BENEDICK.
Well, every one can master a grief but he that has
it.
CLAUDIO.
Yet say I he is in love.
DON PEDRO.
There is no appearance of fancy in him, unless it
be a fancy that he hath to strange disguises; as, to
be a Dutchman to-day, a Frenchman to-morrow;
or in the shape of two countries at once, as, a
German from the waist downward, all slops, and
a Spaniard from the hip upward, no doublet. Un-
less he have a fancy to this foolery, as it appears
he hath, he is no fool for fancy, as you would have
it appear he is.
CLAUDIO.
If he be not in love with some woman, there is no
believing old signs: a' brushes his hat o' morn-
ings; what should that bode?
DON PEDRO.
Hath any man seen him at the barber's?
CLAUDIO.
No, but the barber's man hath been seen with
him; and the old ornament of his cheek hath al-
ready stuft tennis-balls.
LEONATO.
Indeed, he looks younger than he did, by the loss
of a beard.
DON PEDRO.
Nay, a' rubs himself with civet: can you smell him
out by that?
CLAUDIO.
That's as much as to say, the sweet youth's in love.
DON PEDRO.
The greatest note of it is his melancholy.
CLAUDIO.
And when was he wont to wash his face?
DON PEDRO.
Yea, or to paint himself? for the which, I hear
what they say of him.
CLAUDIO.
Nay, but his jesting spirit; which is now crept
into a lute-string, and new-govern'd by stops.
DON PEDRO.
Indeed, that tells a heavy tale for him. Conclude,
conclude he is in love.
CLAUDIO.
Nay, but I know who loves him.
DON PEDRO.
That would I know too: I warrant, one that
knows him not.
CLAUDIO.
Yes, and his ill conditions; and, in despite of all,
dies for him.
DON PEDRO.
She shall be buried with her face upwards.

BENEDICK.

Yet is this no charm for the toothache.—Old signior, walk aside with me: I have studied eight or nine wise words to speak to you, which these hobby-horses must not hear.

[*Exeunt* BENEDICK *and* LEONATO.

DON PEDRO.

For my life, to break with him about Beatrice.

CLAUDIO.

'Tis even so. Hero and Margaret have by this play'd their parts with Beatrice; and then the two bears will not bite one another when they meet.

Enter DON JOHN.

DON JOHN.

My lord and brother, God save you!

DON PEDRO.

Good den, brother.

DON JOHN.

If your leisure served, I would speak with you.

DON PEDRO.

In private?

DON JOHN.

If it please you: yet Count Claudio may hear: for what I would speak of concerns him.

DON PEDRO.

What's the matter?

DON JOHN [*to* CLAUDIO].

Means your lordship to be married to-morrow?

DON PEDRO.

You know he does.

DON JOHN.

I know not that, when he knows what I know.

CLAUDIO.

If there be any impediment, I pray you discover it.

DON JOHN.

You may think I love you not: let that appear hereafter, and aim better at me by that I now will manifest. For my brother, I think he holds you well; and in dearness of heart hath holp to effect your ensuing marriage,—surely suit ill spent and labour ill bestow'd.

DON PEDRO.

Why, what's the matter?

DON JOHN.

I came hither to tell you; and, circumstances shorten'd (for she hath been too long a talking of), the lady is disloyal.

CLAUDIO.

Who, Hero?

DON JOHN.

Even she; Leonato's Hero, your Hero, every man's Hero.

CLAUDIO.

Disloyal!

DON JOHN.

The word is too good to paint out her wickedness; I could say she were worse: think you of a worse title, and I will fit her to it. Wonder not till further warrant: go but with me to-night, you shall see her chamber-window enter'd, even the night before her wedding-day: if you love her then, to-morrow wed her; but it would better fit your honour to change your mind.

CLAUDIO.

May this be so?

DON PEDRO.

I will not think it.

DON JOHN.

If you dare not trust that you see, confess ro: that you know: if you will follow me, I will show you enough; and when you have seen more, and heard more, proceed accordingly.

CLAUDIO.

If I see anything to-night why I should not m r y her to-morrow, in the congregation, where I should wed her, there will I shame her.

DON PEDRO.

And, as I woo'd for thee to obtain her, I will join thee to disgrace her.

DON JOHN.

I will disparage her no further till you are my witnesses: bear it coldly but till midnight, and let the issue show itself.

DON PEDRO.

O day untowardly turn'd!

CLAUDIO.

O mischief strangely thwarting!

DON JOHN.

O plague right well prevented! so will you say when you have seen the sequel.   [*Exeunt.*

SCENE III.

A street.

Enter DOGBERRY *and his compartner* VERGES, *with the* WATCH.

DOGBERRY.

ARE you good men and true?

VERGES.

Yea, or else it were pity but they should suffer salvation, body and soul.

DOGBERRY.

Nay, that were a punishment too good for them, if they should have any allegiance in them, being chosen for the prince's watch.

VERGES.

Well, give them their charge, neighbour Dogberry.

DOGBERRY.

First, who think you the most desartless man to be constable?

FIRST WATCHMAN.

Hugh Oatcake, sir, or George Seacoal; for they can write and read.

DOGBERRY.

Come hither, neighbour Seacoal. God hath blest you with a good name; to be a well-favour'd man is the gift of fortune; but to write and read comes by nature.

SECOND WATCHMAN.

Both which, master constable,—

DOGBERRY.

You have: I knew it would be your answer. Well, for your favour, sir, why, give God thanks, and make no boast of it; and for your writing and reading, let that appear when there is no need of such vanity. You are thought here to be the most senseless and fit man for the constable of the watch; therefore bear you the lantern. This is your charge:—you shall comprehend all vagrom men; you are to bid any man stand, in the prince's name.

SECOND WATCHMAN.
How if a' will not stand?

DOGBERRY.
Why, then, take no note of him, but let him go; and presently call the rest of the watch together, and thank God you are rid of a knave.

VERGES.
If he will not stand when he is bidden, he is none of the prince's subjects.

DOGBERRY.
True, and they are to meddle with none but the prince's subjects.—You shall also make no noise in the streets; for for the watch to babble and talk is most tolerable and not to be endured.

SECOND WATCHMAN.
We will rather sleep than talk: we know what belongs to a watch.

DOGBERRY.
Why, you speak like an ancient and most quiet watchman; for I cannot see how sleeping should offend: only, have a care that your bills be not stolen.—Well, you are to call at all the ale-houses, and bid those that are drunk get them to bed.

SECOND WATCHMAN.
How if they will not?

DOGBERRY.
Why, then, let them alone till they are sober: if they make you not then the better answer, you may say they are not the men you took them for.

SECOND WATCHMAN.
Well, sir.

DOGBERRY.
If you meet a thief, you may suspect him, by virtue of your office, to be no true man; and, for such kind of men, the less you meddle or make with them, why, the more is for your honesty.

SECOND WATCHMAN.
If we know him to be a thief, shall we not lay hands on him?

DOGBERRY.
Truly, by your office, you may; but I think they that touch pitch will be defiled: the most peaceable way for you, if you do take a thief, is to let him show himself what he is, and steal out of your company.

VERGES.
You have been always call'd a merciful man, partner.

DOGBERRY.
Truly, I would not hang a dog by my will, much more a man who hath any honesty in him.

VERGES.
If you hear a child cry in the night, you must call to the nurse and bid her still it.

SECOND WATCHMAN.
How if the nurse be asleep and will not hear us?

DOGBERRY.
Why, then, depart in peace, and let the child wake her with crying; for the ewe that will not hear her lamb when it baes will never answer a calf when he bleats.

VERGES.
'Tis very true.

DOGBERRY.
This is the end of the charge:—you, constable, are to present the prince's own person: if you meet the prince in the night, you may stay him.

VERGES.
Nay, by'r lady, that I think a' cannot.

DOGBERRY.
Five shillings to one on't, with any man that knows the statues, he may stay him: marry, not without the prince be willing; for, indeed, the watch ought to offend no man; and it is an offence to stay a man against his will.

VERGES.
By'r lady, I think it be so.

DOGBERRY.
Ha, ah-ha! Well, masters, good night: an there be any matter of weight chances, call up me: keep your fellows' counsels and your own; and good night.—Come, neighbour.

FIRST WATCHMAN.
Well, masters, we hear our charge: let us go sit here upon the church-bench till two, and then all to bed.

DOGBERRY.
One word more, honest neighbours. I pray you, watch about Signior Leonato's door; for the wedding being there to-morrow, there is a great coil to-night. Adieu: be vigitant, I beseech you.

[*Exeunt* DOGBERRY *and* VERGES.
Enter BORACHIO *and* CONRADE.

BORACHIO.
What, Conrade!—

FIRST WATCHMAN [*aside*].
Peace! stir not.

BORACHIO.
Conrade, I say!—

CONRADE.
Here, man; I am at thy elbow.

BORACHIO.
Mass, and my elbow itcht; I thought there would a scab follow.

CONRADE.
I will owe thee an answer for that: and now forward with thy tale.

BORACHIO.
Stand thee close, then, under this pent-house, for it drizzles rain; and I will, like a true drunkard, utter all to thee.

FIRST WATCHMAN [*aside*].
Some treason, masters: yet stand close.

BORACHIO.
Therefore know I have earn'd of Don John a thousand ducats.

CONRADE.
Is it possible that any villainy should be so dear?

BORACHIO.
Thou shouldst rather ask, if it were possible any villainy should be so rich; for when rich villains have need of poor ones, poor ones may make what price they will.

CONRADE.
I wonder at it.

BORACHIO.
That shows thou art unconfirm'd. Thou knowest that the fashion of a doublet, or a hat, or a cloak, is nothing to a man.

CONRADE.
Yes, it is apparel.

BORACHIO.

I mean, the fashion.

CONRADE.

Yes, the fashion is the fashion.

BORACHIO.

Tush! I may as well say the fool's the fool. But seest thou not what a deform'd thief this fashion is?

FIRST WATCHMAN [aside].

I know that Deform'd; a' has been a vile thief this seven year; a' goes up and down like a gentleman: I remember his name.

BORACHIO.

Didst thou not hear somebody?

CONRADE.

No; 'twas the vane on the house.

BORACHIO.

Seest thou not, I say, what a deform'd thief this fashion is? how giddily 'a turns about all the hot bloods between fourteen and five-and-thirty? sometimes fashioning them like Pharaoh's soldiers in the reechy painting, sometime like god Bel's priests in the old church-window, sometime like the shaven Hercules in the smircht worm-eaten tapestry, where his codpiece seems as massy as his club?

CONRADE.

All this I see; and I see that the fashion wears out more apparel than the man. But art not thou thyself giddy with the fashion too, that thou hast shifted out of thy tale into telling me of the fashion?

BORACHIO.

Not so, neither: but know that I have to-night woo'd Margaret, the Lady Hero's gentlewoman, by the name of Hero: she leans me out at her mistress' chamber-window, bids me a thousand times good night,—I tell this tale vilely:—I should first tell thee how the prince, Claudio, and my master, planted and placed and possest by my master Don John, saw afar off in the orchard this amiable encounter.

CONRADE.

And thought they Margaret was Hero?

BORACHIO.

Two of them did, the prince and Claudio; but the devil my master knew she was Margaret; and partly by his oaths, which first possest them, partly by the dark night, which did deceive them, but chiefly by my villainy, which did confirm any slander that Don John had made, away went Claudio enraged; swore he would meet her, as he was appointed, next morning at the temple, and there, before the whole congregation, shame her with what he saw o'ernight, and send her home again without a husband.

FIRST WATCHMAN.

We charge you, in the prince's name, stand!

SECOND WATCHMAN.

Call up the right master constable. We have here recover'd the most dangerous piece of lechery that ever was known in the commonwealth.

FIRST WATCHMAN.

And one Deform'd is one of them: I know him; a' wears a lock.

CONRADE.

Masters, masters,—

SECOND WATCHMAN.

You'll be made bring Deform'd forth, I warrant you.

CONRADE.

Masters,—

FIRST WATCHMAN.

Never speak: we charge you let us obey you to go with us.

BORACHIO.

We are like to prove a goodly commodity, being taken up of these men's bills.

CONRADE.

A commodity in question, I warrant you.—Come, we'll obey you.   [Exeunt.

SCENE IV.

A room in LEONATO'S *house.*

Enter HERO, MARGARET, *and* URSULA.

HERO.

GOOD Ursula, wake my cousin Beatrice, and desire her to rise.

URSULA.

I will, lady.

HERO.

And bid her come hither.

URSULA.

Well.   [Exit.

MARGARET.

Troth, I think your other rabato were better.

HERO.

No, pray thee, good Meg, I'll wear this.

MARGARET.

By my troth, 's not so good; and I warrant your cousin will say so.

HERO.

My cousin's a fool, and thou art another: I'll wear none but this.

MARGARET.

I like the new tire within excellently, if the hair were a thought browner; and your gown's a most rare fashion, i'faith. I saw the Duchess of Milan's gown that they praise so.

HERO.

O, that exceeds, they say.

MARGARET.

By my troth, 's but a night-gown in respect of yours,—cloth-o'-gold, and cuts, and laced with silver, set with pearls, down sleeves, side sleeves, and skirts round underborne with a bluish tinsel: but for a fine, quaint, graceful, and excellent fashion, yours is worth ten on't.

HERO.

God give me joy to wear it! for my heart is exceeding heavy.

MARGARET.

'Twill be heavier soon by the weight of a man.

HERO.

Fie upon thee! art not ashamed?

MARGARET.

Of what, lady? of speaking honourably? Is not marriage honourable in a beggar? Is not your lord honourable without marriage? I think you would have me say, 'saving your reverence, a husband'; an bad thinking do not wrest true speaking, I'll offend nobody: is there any harm in 'the heavier for a husband'? None, I think, an it be the right husband and the right wife; otherwise 'tis light, and not heavy: ask my Lady Beatrice else; here she comes.

Enter BEATRICE.

HERO.

Good morrow, coz.

BEATRICE.

Good morrow, sweet Hero.

HERO.

Why, how now! do you speak in the sick tune?

BEATRICE.

I am out of all other tune, methinks.

MARGARET.

Clap's into *Light o' love*; that goes without a burden: do you sing it, and I'll dance it.

BEATRICE.

Ye light o' love, with your heels!—then, if your husband have stables enough, you'll see he shall lack no barns.

MARGARET.

O illegitimate construction! I scorn that with my heels.

BEATRICE.

'Tis almost five o'clock, cousin; 'tis time you were ready.—By my troth, I am exceeding ill:—heigh-ho!

MARGARET.

For a hawk, a horse, or a husband?

BEATRICE.

For the letter that begins them all, H.

MARGARET.

Well, an you be not turn'd Turk, there's no more sailing by the star.

BEATRICE.

What means the fool, trow?

MARGARET.

Nothing I; but God send every one their heart's desire!

HERO.

These gloves the Count sent me; they are an excellent perfume.

BEATRICE.

I am stuft, cousin; I cannot smell.

MARGARET.

A maid, and stuft! there's goodly catching of cold.

BEATRICE.

O, God help me! God help me! how long have you profest apprehension?

MARGARET.

Ever since you left it. Doth not my wit become me rarely?

BEATRICE.

It is not seen enough; you should wear it in your cap.—By my troth, I am sick.

MARGARET.

Get you some of this distill'd Carduus Benedictus, and lay it to your heart: it is the only thing for a qualm.

HERO.

There thou prick'st her with a thistle.

BEATRICE.

Benedictus! why Benedictus? you have some moral in this Benedictus.

MARGARET.

Moral! no, by my troth, I have no moral meaning; I meant, plain holy-thistle. You may think per-

chance that I think you are in love: nay, by'r lady, I am not such a fool to think what I list; nor I list not to think what I can; nor, indeed, I cannot think, if I would think my heart out of thinking, that you are in love, or that you will be in love, or that you can be in love. Yet Benedick was such another, and now is he become a man: he swore he would never marry; and yet now, in despite of his heart, he eats his meat without grudging: and how you may be converted, I know not; but methinks you look with your eyes as other women do.

BEATRICE.

What pace is this that thy tongue keeps?

MARGARET.

Not a false gallop.

Enter URSULA.

URSULA.

Madam, withdraw: the prince, the count, Signior Benedick, Don John, and all the gallants of the town, are come to fetch you to church.

HERO.

Help to dress me, good coz, good Meg, good Ursula.   [*Exeunt.*

SCENE V.

Another room in LEONATO'S *house.*

Enter LEONATO, *with the* CONSTABLE DOG-BERRY *and the* HEADBOROUGH VERGES.

LEONATO.

WHAT would you with me, honest neighbour?

DOGBERRY.

Marry, sir, I would have some confidence with you that decerns you nearly.

LEONATO.

Brief, I pray you; for you see it is a busy time with me.

DOGBERRY.

Marry, this it is, sir,—

VERGES.

Yes, in truth it is, sir.

LEONATO.

What is it, my good friends?

DOGBERRY.

Goodman Verges, sir, speaks a little off the matter: an old man, sir, and his wits are not so blunt as, God help, I would desire they were; but, in faith, honest as the skin between his brows.

VERGES.

Yes, I thank God I am as honest as any man living that is an old man and no honester than I.

DOGBERRY.

Comparisons are odorous: *palabras*, neighbour Verges.

LEONATO.

Neighbours, you are tedious.

DOGBERRY.

It pleases your worship to say so, but we are the poor duke's officers; but truly, for mine own part, if I were as tedious as a king, I could find in my heart to bestow it all of your worship.

LEONATO.

All thy tediousness on me, ha!

DOGBERRY.

Yea, an 'twere a thousand pound more than 'tis;

for I hear as good exclamation on your worship
as of any man in the city; and though I be but a
poor man, I am glad to hear it.

VERGES.

And so am I.

LEONATO.

I would fain know what you have to say.

VERGES.

Marry, sir, our watch to-night, excepting your
worship's presence, ha' ta'en a couple of as arrant
knaves as any in Messina.

DOGBERRY.

A good old man, sir; he will be talking: as they
say, When the age is in, the wit is out: God help
us! it is a world to see!—Well said, i'faith, neighbour Verges:—well, God's a good man; an two
men ride of a horse, one must ride behind.—An
honest soul, i'faith, sir; by my troth, he is, as ever
broke bread: but God is to be worshipt: all men
are not alike,—alas, good neighbour!

LEONATO.

Indeed, neighbour, he comes too short of you.

DOGBERRY.

Gifts that God gives.

LEONATO.

I must leave you.

DOGBERRY.

One word, sir: our watch, sir, have indeed compre-
hended two aspicious persons, and we would have
them this morning examined before your worship.

LEONATO.

Take their examination yourself, and bring it me:
I am now in great haste, as it may appear unto you.

DOGBERRY.

It shall be suffigance.

LEONATO.

Drink some wine ere you go: fare you well.

Enter a MESSENGER.

MESSENGER.

My lord, they stay for you to give your daughter
to her husband.

LEONATO.

I'll wait upon them: I am ready.

[*Exeunt* LEONATO *and* MESSENGER.

DOGBERRY.

Go, good partner, go, get you to Francis Seacoal;
bid him bring his pen and inkhorn to the gaol: we
are now to examination these men.

VERGES.

And we must do it wisely.

DOGBERRY.

We will spare for no wit, I warrant you; here's
that shall drive some of them to a non-come; only
get the learned writer to set down our excommu-
nication, and meet me at the gaol.   [*Exeunt.*

ACT IV. SCENE I.

A church.

Enter DON PEDRO, DON JOHN, LEONATO,
    FRIAR FRANCIS, CLAUDIO, BENEDICK,
    HERO, BEATRICE, *and* ATTENDANTS.

LEONATO.

COME, Friar Francis, be brief; only to the
plain form of marriage, and you shall recount their particular duties afterwards.

FRIAR FRANCIS.

You come hither, my lord, to marry this lady?

CLAUDIO.

No.

LEONATO.

To be married to her:—friar, you come to marry
her.

FRIAR FRANCIS.

Lady, you come hither to be married to this
count?

HERO.

I do.

FRIAR FRANCIS.

If either of you know any inward impediment
why you should not be conjoin'd, I charge you,
on your souls, to utter it.

CLAUDIO.

Know you any, Hero?

HERO.

None, my lord.

FRIAR FRANCIS.

Know you any, count?

LEONATO.

I dare make his answer,—none.

CLAUDIO.

O, what men dare do! what men may do! what
men daily do, not knowing what they do!

BENEDICK.

How now! interjections? Why, then, some be of
laughing, as, Ah, ha, he!

CLAUDIO.

Stand thee by, friar.—Father, by your leave:
Will you with free and unconstrained soul
Give me this maid, your daughter?

LEONATO.

As freely, son, as God did give her me.

CLAUDIO.

And what have I to give you back, whose worth
May counterpoise this rich and precious gift?

DON PEDRO.

Nothing, unless you render her again.

CLAUDIO.

Sweet prince, you learn me noble thankful-
    ness.—
There, Leonato, take her back again:
Give not this rotten orange to your friend;
She's but the sign and semblance of her
    honour.—
Behold how like a maid she blushes here!
O, what authority and show of truth
Can cunning sin cover itself withal!
Comes not that blood as modest evidence
To witness simple virtue? Would you not swear,
All you that see her, that she were a maid,
By these exterior shows? But she is none:
She knows the heat of a luxurious bed;
Her blush is guiltiness, not modesty.

LEONATO.

What do you mean, my lord?

CLAUDIO.

Not to be married, not to knit my soul
To an approved wanton.

LEONATO.

Dear my lord, if you, in your own proof,
Have vanquisht the resistance of her youth,
And made defeat of her virginity,—

CLAUDIO.

I know what you would say: if I have known her,
You will say she did embrace me as a husband,
And so extenuate the 'forehand sin:
No, Leonato,
I never tempted her with word too large;
But, as a brother to his sister, show'd
Bashful sincerity and comely love.

HERO.

And seem'd I ever otherwise to you?

CLAUDIO.

Out on thee, seeming! I will write against it:
You seem to me as Dian in her orb,
As chaste as is the bud ere it be blown;
But you are more intemperate in your blood
Than Venus, or those pamper'd animals
That rage in savage sensuality.

HERO.

Is my lord well, that he doth speak so wide?

CLAUDIO.

Sweet prince, why speak not you?

DON PEDRO.

           What should I speak?
I stand dishonour'd, that have gone about
To link my dear friend to a common stale.

LEONATO.

Are these things spoken? or do I but dream?

DON JOHN.

Sir, they are spoken, and these things are true.

BENEDICK.

This looks not like a nuptial.

HERO.

           True!—O God!

CLAUDIO.

Leonato, stand I here?
Is this the prince? is this the prince's brother?
Is this face Hero's? are our eyes our own?

LEONATO.

All this is so: but what of this, my lord?

CLAUDIO.

Let me but move one question to your daughter;
And, by that fatherly and kindly power
That you have in her, bid her answer truly.

LEONATO.

I charge thee do so, as thou art my child.

HERO.

O, God defend me! how am I beset!—
What kind of catechising call you this?

CLAUDIO.

To make you answer truly to your name.

HERO.

Is it not Hero? Who can blot that name
With any just reproach?

CLAUDIO.

           Marry, that can Hero;
Hero itself can blot out Hero's virtue.
What man was he talkt with you yesternight
Out at your window betwixt twelve and one?
Now, if you are a maid, answer to this.

HERO.

I talkt with no man at that hour, my lord.

DON PEDRO.

Why, then are you no maiden.—Leonato,
I am sorry you must hear: upon mine honour,
Myself, my brother, and this grieved count
Did see her, hear her, at that hour last night

Talk with a ruffian at her chamber-window;
Who hath indeed, most like a liberal villain,
Confest the vile encounters they have had
A thousand times in secret.

DON JOHN.

Fie, fie! they are not to be named, my lord,
Not to be spoke of;
There is not chastity enough in language,
Without offence to utter them.—Thus, pretty
    lady,
I am sorry for thy much misgovernment.

CLAUDIO.

O Hero, what a Hero hadst thou been,
If half thy outward graces had been placed
About thy thoughts and counsels of thy heart!
But fare thee well, most foul, most fair! farewell,
Thou pure impiety and impious purity!
For thee I'll lock up all the gates of love,
And on my eyelids shall conjecture hang,
To turn all beauty into thoughts of harm,
And never shall it more be gracious.

LEONATO.

Hath no man's dagger here a point for me?

                     [HERO *swoons.*

BEATRICE.

Why, how now, cousin! wherefore sink you down?

DON JOHN.

Come, let us go. These things, come thus to light,
Smother her spirits up.

     [*Exeunt* DON PEDRO, DON JOHN, CLAU-
        DIO, *and* ATTENDANTS.

BENEDICK.

How doth the lady?

BEATRICE.

           Dead, I think:—help, uncle:—
Hero! why, Hero!—uncle!—Signior Benedick!—
    friar!

LEONATO.

O Fate, take not away thy heavy hand!
Death is the fairest cover for her shame
That may be wisht for.

BEATRICE.

           How now, cousin Hero!

FRIAR FRANCIS.

Have comfort, lady.

LEONATO.

Dost thou look up?

FRIAR FRANCIS.

           Yea, wherefore should she not?

LEONATO.

Wherefore! Why, doth not every earthly thing
Cry shame upon her? Could she here deny
The story that is printed in her blood?—
Do not live, Hero; do not ope thine eyes:
For, did I think thou wouldst not quickly die,
Thought I thy spirits were stronger than thy
    shames,
Myself would, on the rearward of reproaches,
Strike at thy life. Grieved I, I had but one?
Chid I for that at frugal nature's frame?
O, one too much by thee! Why had I one?
Why ever wast thou lovely in my eyes?
Why had I not with charitable hand
Took up a beggar's issue at my gates,
Who smirched thus and mired with infamy,
I might have said, 'No part of it is mine;

This shame derives itself from unknown loins'?
But mine, and mine I loved, and mine I praised,
And mine that I was proud on; mine so much
That I myself was to myself not mine,
Valuing of her; why, she—O, she is fall'n
Into a pit of ink, that the wide sea
Hath drops too few to wash her clean again,
And salt too little which may season give
To her foul-tainted flesh!

BENEDICK.
                    Sir, sir, be patient.
For my part, I am so attired in wonder,
I know not what to say.

BEATRICE.
O, on my soul, my cousin is belied!

BENEDICK.
Lady, were you her bedfellow last night?

BEATRICE.
No, truly, not; although, until last night,
I have this twelvemonth been her bedfellow.

LEONATO.
Confirm'd, confirm'd! O, that is stronger made
Which was before barr'd up with ribs of iron!
Would the two princes lie? and Claudio lie,
Who loved her so, that, speaking of her foul-
        ness,
Washt it with tears? Hence from her! let her die.

FRIAR FRANCIS.
Hear me a little;
For I have only been silent so long,
And given way unto this course of fortune,
By noting of the lady: I have markt
A thousand blushing apparitions
To start into her face; a thousand innocent
        shames
In angel whiteness beat away those blushes;
And in her eye there hath appear'd a fire,
To burn the errors that these princes hold
Against her maiden truth. Call me a fool;
Trust not my reading nor my observations,
Which with experimental seal doth warrant
The tenour of my book; trust not my age,
My reverence, calling, nor divinity,
If this sweet lady lie not guiltless here
Under some biting error.

LEONATO.
                    Friar, it cannot be.
Thou see'st that all the grace that she hath left
Is that she will not add to her damnation
A sin of perjury; she not denies it:
Why seek'st thou, then, to cover with excuse
That which appears in proper nakedness?

FRIAR FRANCIS.
Lady, what man is he you are accused of?

HERO.
They know that do accuse me; I know none:
If I know more of any man alive
Than that which maiden modesty doth warrant,
Let all my sins lack mercy!—O my father,
Prove you that any man with me conversed
At hours unmeet, or that I yesternight
Maintain'd the change of words with any crea-
        ture,
Refuse me, hate me, torture me to death!

FRIAR FRANCIS.
There is some strange misprision in the princes.

BENEDICK.
Two of them have the very bent of honour;
And if their wisdoms be misled in this,
The practice of it lives in John the bastard,
Whose spirits toil in frame of villainies.

LEONATO.
I know not. If they speak but truth of her,
These hands shall tear her; if they wrong her
        honour,
The proudest of them shall well hear of it.
Time hath not yet so dried this blood of mine,
Nor age so eat up my invention,
Nor fortune made such havoc of my means,
Nor my bad life reft me so much of friends,
But they shall find, awaked in such a kind,
Both strength of limb and policy of mind,
Ability in means and choice of friends,
To quit me of them throughly.

FRIAR FRANCIS.
                    Pause awhile,
And let my counsel sway you in this case.
Your daughter here the princes left for dead,
Let her awhile be secretly kept in,
And publish it that she is dead indeed;
Maintain a mourning ostentation,
And on your family's old monument
Hang mournful epitaphs, and do all rites
That appertain unto a burial.

LEONATO.
What shall become of this? what will this do?

FRIAR FRANCIS.
Marry, this, well carried, shall on her behalf
Change slander to remorse;—that is some good:
But not for that dream I on this strange course,
But on this travail look for greater birth.
She dying, as it must be so maintain'd,
Upon the instant that she was accused,
Shall be lamented, pitied, and excused
Of every hearer: for it so falls out,
That what we have we prize not to the worth
Whiles we enjoy it; but being lackt and lost,
Why, then we rack the value, then we find
The virtue that possession would not show us
Whiles it was ours. So will it fare with Claudio:
When he shall hear she died upon his words,
Th'idea of her life shall sweetly creep
Into his study of imagination;
And every lovely organ of her life
Shall come apparell'd in more precious habit,
More moving-delicate and full of life,
Into the eye and prospect of his soul,
Than when she lived indeed; then shall he
        mourn
(If ever love had interest in his liver),
And wish he had not so accused her,—
No, though he thought his accusation true.
Let this be so, and doubt not but success
Will fashion the event in better shape
Than I can lay it down in likelihood.
But if all aim but this be levell'd false,
The supposition of the lady's death
Will quench the wonder of her infamy:
And if it sort not well, you may conceal her
(As best befits her wounded reputation)
In some reclusive and religious life,
Out of all eyes, tongues, minds, and injuries.

BENEDICK.
Signior Leonato, let the friar advise you:
And though you know my inwardness and love
Is very much unto the prince and Claudio,
Yet, by mine honour, I will deal in this
As secretly and justly as your soul
Should with your body.

LEONATO.
                    Being that I flow in grief,
The smallest twine may lead me.

FRIAR FRANCIS.
'Tis well consented: presently away;   [cure.—
    For to strange sores strangely they strain the
Come, lady, die to live: this wedding-day [endure.
    Perhaps is but prolong'd: have patience and
                [*Exeunt* FRIAR FRANCIS, HERO, *and*
LEONATO.

BENEDICK.
Lady Beatrice, have you wept all this while?

BEATRICE.
Yea, and I will weep a while longer.

BENEDICK.
I will not desire that.

BEATRICE.
You have no reason; I do it freely.

BENEDICK.
Surely I do believe your fair cousin is wrong'd.

BEATRICE.
Ah, how much might the man deserve of me that
would right her!

BENEDICK.
Is there any way to show such friendship?

BEATRICE.
A very even way, but no such friend.

BENEDICK.
May a man do it?

BEATRICE.
It is a man's office, but not yours.

BENEDICK.
I do love nothing in the world so well as you: is
not that strange?

BEATRICE.
As strange as the thing I know not. It were as
possible for me to say I loved nothing so well as
you: but believe me not; and yet I lie not; I confess nothing, nor I deny nothing.—I am sorry for
my cousin.

BENEDICK.
By my sword, Beatrice, thou lovest me.

BEATRICE.
Do not swear by it, and eat it.

BENEDICK.
I will swear by it that you love me; and I will
make him eat it that says I love not you.

BEATRICE.
Will you not eat your word?

BENEDICK.
With no sauce that can be devised to it. I protest
I love thee.

BEATRICE.
Why, then, God forgive me!

BENEDICK.
What offence, sweet Beatrice?

BEATRICE.
You have stay'd me in a happy hour: I was about
to protest I loved you.

BENEDICK.
And do it with all thy heart.

BEATRICE.
I love you with so much of my heart, that none is
left to protest.

BENEDICK.
Come, bid me do any thing for thee.

BEATRICE.
Kill Claudio.

BENEDICK.
Ha! not for the wide world.

BEATRICE.
You kill me to deny it.   Farewell.

BENEDICK.
Tarry, sweet Beatrice.

BEATRICE.
I am gone, though I am here:—there is no love in
you:—nay, I pray you, let me go.

BENEDICK.
Beatrice,—

BEATRICE.
In faith, I will go.

BENEDICK.
We'll be friends first.

BEATRICE.
You dare easier be friends with me than fight with
mine enemy.

BENEDICK.
Is Claudio thine enemy?

BEATRICE.
Is he not approved in the height a villain, that
hath slander'd, scorn'd, dishonour'd my kinswoman?—O that I were a man!—What, bear her
in hand until they come to take hands; and then,
with public accusation, uncover'd slander, un-
mitigated rancour,—O God, that I were a man! I
would eat his heart in the market-place.

BENEDICK.
Hear me, Beatrice,—

BEATRICE.
Talk with a man out at a window!—a proper saying!

BENEDICK.
Nay, but, Beatrice,—

BEATRICE.
Sweet Hero!—she is wrong'd, she is slander'd,
she is undone.

BENEDICK.
Beat—

BEATRICE.
Princes and counties! Surely, a princely testimony, a goodly count, Count Comfect; a sweet
gallant, surely! O that I were a man for his sake!
or that I had any friend would be a man for my
sake! But manhood is melted into curtsies, valour
into compliment, and men are only turn'd into
tongue, and trim ones too: he is now as valiant as
Hercules that only tells a lie, and swears it.—I
cannot be a man with wishing, therefore I will
die a woman with grieving.

BENEDICK.
Tarry, good Beatrice. By this hand, I love
thee.

BEATRICE.
Use it for my love some other way than swearing
by it.

BENEDICK.
Think you in your soul the Count Claudio hath wrong'd Hero?

BEATRICE.
Yea, as sure as I have a thought or a soul.

BENEDICK.
Enough, I am engaged; I will challenge him. I will kiss your hand, and so I leave you. By this hand, Claudio shall render me a dear account. As you hear of me, so think of me. Go, comfort your cousin: I must say she is dead: and so, farewell.
[*Exeunt.*

SCENE II.

A prison.

Enter DOGBERRY *and* VERGES, *and* SEXTON, *in gowns; and the* WATCH, *with* CONRADE *and* BORACHIO.

DOGBERRY.
IS our whole dissembly appear'd?

VERGES.
O, a stool and a cushion for the sexton.

SEXTON.
Which be the malefactors?

DOGBERRY.
Marry, that am I and my partner.

VERGES.
Nay, that's certain; we have the exhibition to examine.

SEXTON.
But which are the offenders that are to be examined? let them come before master constable.

DOGBERRY.
Yea, marry, let them come before me.—What is your name, friend?

BORACHIO.
Borachio.

DOGBERRY.
Pray, write down—Borachio.—Yours, sirrah?

CONRADE.
I am a gentleman, sir, and my name is Conrade.

DOGBERRY.
Write down—master gentleman Conrade.—Masters, do you serve God?

CONRADE *and* BORACHIO.
Yea, sir, we hope.

DOGBERRY.
Write down—that they hope they serve God:—and write God first; for God defend but God should go before such villains!—Masters, it is proved already that you are little better than false knaves; and it will go near to be thought so shortly. How answer you for yourselves?

CONRADE.
Marry, sir, we say we are none.

DOGBERRY.
A marvellous witty fellow, I assure you; but I will go about with him.—Come you hither, sirrah: a word in your ear, sir; I say to you, it is thought you are false knaves.

BORACHIO.
Sir, I say to you we are none.

DOGBERRY.
Well, stand aside.—'Fore God, they are both in a tale. Have you writ down—that they are none?

SEXTON.
Master constable, you go not the way to examine: you must call forth the watch that are their accusers.

DOGBERRY.
Yea, marry, that's the eftest way.—Let the watch come forth.—Masters, I charge you, in the prince's name, accuse these men.

FIRST WATCHMAN.
This man said, sir, that Don John, the prince's brother, was a villain.

DOGBERRY.
Write down—Prince John a villain.—Why, this is flat perjury, to call a prince's brother villain.

BORACHIO.
Master constable,—

DOGBERRY.
Pray thee, fellow, peace: I do not like thy look, I promise thee.

SEXTON.
What heard you him say else?

SECOND WATCHMAN.
Marry, that he had received a thousand ducats of Don John for accusing the Lady Hero wrongfully.

DOGBERRY.
Flat burglary as ever was committed.

VERGES.
Yea, by th'mass, that it is.

SEXTON.
What else, fellow?

FIRST WATCHMAN.
And that Count Claudio did mean, upon his words, to disgrace Hero before the whole assembly, and not marry her.

DOGBERRY.
O villain! thou wilt be condemn'd into everlasting redemption for this.

SEXTON.
What else?

SECOND WATCHMAN.
This is all.

SEXTON.
And this is more, masters, than you can deny. Prince John is this morning secretly stolen away; Hero was in this manner accused, in this very manner refused, and upon the grief of this suddenly died.—Master constable, let these men be bound, and brought to Leonato's: I will go before and show him their examination.   [*Exit.*

DOGBERRY.
Come, let them be opinion'd.

VERGES.
Let them be in the hands—

CONRADE.
Off, coxcomb!

DOGBERRY.
God's my life, where's the sexton? let him write down—the prince's officer, coxcomb.—Come, bind them.—Thou naughty varlet!

CONRADE.
Away! you are an ass, you are an ass.

DOGBERRY.
Dost thou not suspect my place? dost thou not suspect my years?—O that he were here to write me down an ass!—but, masters, remember that I

am an ass; though it be not written down, yet forget not that I am an ass.—No, thou villain, thou art full of piety, as shall be proved upon thee by good witness. I am a wise fellow; and, which is more, an officer; and, which is more, a householder; and, which is more, as pretty a piece of flesh as any in Messina; and one that knows the law, go to; and a rich fellow enough. go to; find a fellow that hath had losses; and one that hath two gowns, and every thing handsome about him.—Bring him away.—O that I had been writ down an ass!

[*Exeunt.*

ACT V. SCENE I.

Before LEONATO'S *house.*

Enter LEONATO *and his brother* ANTONIO.

ANTONIO.

IF you go on thus, you will kill yourself;
And 'tis not wisdom thus to second grief
Against yourself.

LEONATO.

        I pray thee, cease thy counsel,
Which falls into mine ears as profitless
As water in a sieve· give not me counsel;
Nor let no comforter delight mine ear
But such a one whose wrongs do suit with mine.
Bring me a father that so loved his child,
Whose joy of her is overwhelm'd like mine,
And bid him speak of patience;
Measure his woe the length and breadth of mine,
And let it answer every strain for strain,
As thus for thus, and such a grief for such,
In every lineament, branch, shape. and form:
If such a one will smile, and stroke his beard,
Bid sorrow wag, cry 'hem' when he should groan,
Patch grief with proverbs, make misfortune drunk
With candle-wasters,—bring him yet to me,
And I of him will gather patience.
But there is no such man: for, brother, men
Can counsel and speak comfort to that grief
Which they themselves not feel; but, tasting it,
Their counsel turns to passion, which before
Would give preceptial medicine to rage,
Fetter strong madness in a silken thread,
Charm ache with air, and agony with words:
No, no, 'tis all men's office to speak patience
To those that wring under the load of sorrow,
But no man's virtue nor sufficiency
To be so moral when he shall endure
The like himself. Therefore give me no counsel:
My griefs cry louder than advertisement.

ANTONIO.

Therein do men from children nothing differ.

LEONATO.

I pray thee, peace,—I will be flesh and blood;
For there was never yet philosopher
That could endure the toothache patiently,
However they have writ the style of gods,
And made a push at chance and sufferance.

ANTONIO.

Yet bend not all the harm upon yourself;
Make those that do offend you suffer too.

LEONATO.

There thou speak'st reason: nay, I will do so.
My soul doth tell me Hero is belied;

And that shall Claudio know; so shall the prince,
And all of them that thus dishonour her.

ANTONIO.

Here comes the prince and Claudio hastily.

Enter DON PEDRO *and* CLAUDIO.

DON PEDRO.

Good den, good den.

CLAUDIO.

        Good day to both of you.

LEONATO.

Hear you, my lords,—

DON PEDRO.

        We have some haste, Leonato.

LEONATO.

Some haste, my lord!—well, fare you well, my lord:—
Are you so hasty now?—well, all is one.

DON PEDRO.

Nay, do not quarrel with us, good old man.

ANTONIO.

If he could right himself with quarrelling,
Some of us would lie low.

CLAUDIO.

        Who wrongs him?

LEONATO.

Marry, thou dost wrong me; thou dissembler, thou:—
Nay, never lay thy hand upon thy sword;
I fear thee not.

CLAUDIO.

        Marry, beshrew my hand,
If it should give your age such cause of fear:
In faith, my hand meant nothing to my sword.

LEONATO.

Tush, tush, man; never fleer and jest at me:
I speak not like a dotard nor a fool,
As, under privilege of age, to brag
What I have done, being young, or what would do,
Were I not old.   Know, Claudio, to thy head,
Thou hast so wrong'd mine innocent child and me,
That I am forced to lay my reverence by,
And, with grey hairs and bruise of many days,
Do challenge thee to trial of a man.
I say thou hast belied mine innocent child;
Thy slander hath gone through and through her heart,
And she lies buried with her ancestors,—
O, in a tomb where never scandal slept,
Save this of hers, framed by thy villainy!

CLAUDIO.

My villainy!

LEONATO.

        Thine, Claudio; thine, I say.

DON PEDRO.

You say not right, old man.

LEONATO.

        My lord, my lord,
I'll prove it on his body, if he dare,
Despite his nice fence and his active practice,
His May of youth and bloom of lustihood.

CLAUDIO.

Away! I will not have to do with you.

LEONATO.

Canst thou so daff me? Thou hast kill'd my child.
If thou kill'st me, boy, thou shalt kill a man.

ANTONIO.

He shall kill two of us, and men indeed:
But that's no matter; let him kill one first;—
Win me and wear me,—let him answer me.—
Come, follow me, boy; come, sir boy, come, fol-
  low me:
Sir boy, I'll whip you from your foining fence;
Nay, as I am a gentleman, I will.

LEONATO.

Brother,—

ANTONIO.

Content yourself. God knows I loved my niece;
And she is dead, slander'd to death by villains,
That dare as well answer a man indeed
As I dare take a serpent by the tongue;
Boys, apes, braggarts, Jacks, milksops!

LEONATO.

                    Brother Antony,—

ANTONIO.

Hold you content. What, man! I know them, yea,
And what they weigh, even to the utmost
  scruple,—
Scrambling, out-facing, fashion-mong'ring boys,
That lie, and cog, and flout, deprave, and slander,
Go antickly, show outward hideousness,
And speak off half a dozen dangerous words,
How they might hurt their enemies, if they durst;
And this is all.

LEONATO.

But, brother Antony,—

ANTONIO.

                    Come, 'tis no matter:
Do not you meddle; let me deal in this.

DON PEDRO.

Gentlemen both, we will not wake your patience.
My heart is sorry for your daughter's death:
But, on my honour, she was charged with nothing
But what was true, and very full of proof.

LEONATO.

My lord, my lord,—

DON PEDRO.

              I will not hear you.

LEONATO.

                              No?—

Come, brother, away.—I will be heard.

ANTONIO.

                          And shall,
Or some of us will smart for't.

            [Exeunt LEONATO and ANTONIO.

DON PEDRO.

See, see; here comes the man we went to seek.

            Enter BENEDICT.

CLAUDIO.

Now, signior, what news?

BENEDICK.

Good day, my lord.

DON PEDRO.

Welcome, signior: you are almost come to part
almost a fray.

CLAUDIO.

We had like to have had our two noses snapt off
with two old men without teeth.

DON PEDRO.

Leonato and his brother. What think'st thou?
Had we fought, I doubt we should have been too
young for them.

BENEDICK.

In a false quarrel there is no true valour. I came
to seek you both.

CLAUDIO.

We have been up and down to seek thee; for we
are high-proof melancholy, and would fain have it
beaten away. Wilt thou use thy wit?

BENEDICK.

It is in my scabbard: shall I draw it?

DON PEDRO.

Dost thou wear thy wit by thy side?

CLAUDIO.

Never any did so, though very many have been
beside their wit.—I will bid thee draw, as we do
the minstrels; draw, to pleasure us.

DON PEDRO.

As I am an honest man, he looks pale.—Art thou
sick, or angry?

CLAUDIO.

What, courage, man! What though care kill'd a
cat, thou hast mettle enough in thee to kill care.

BENEDICK.

Sir, I shall meet your wit in the career, an you
charge it against me. I pray you choose another
subject.

CLAUDIO.

Nay, then, give him another staff: this last was
broke cross.

DON PEDRO.

By this light, he changes more and more: I think
he be angry indeed.

CLAUDIO.

If he be, he knows how to turn his girdle.

BENEDICK.

Shall I speak a word in your ear?

CLAUDIO.

God bless me from a challenge!

BENEDICK.

You are a villain;—I jest not:—I will make it good
how you dare, with what you dare, and when you
dare.—Do me right, or I will protest your
cowardice. You have kill'd a sweet lady, and her
death shall fall heavy on you. Let me hear from
you.

CLAUDIO.

Well, I will meet you, so I may have good cheer.

DON PEDRO.

What, a feast? a feast?

CLAUDIO.

I'faith, I thank him; he hath bid me to a calf's-
head and a capon; the which if I do not carve
most curiously, say my knife's naught.—Shall I
not find a woodcock too?

BENEDICT.

Sir, your wit ambles well; it goes easily.

DON PEDRO.

I'll tell thee how Beatrice praised thy wit the
other day. I said, thou hadst a fine wit: ' True,'
says she, 'a fine little one.' 'No,' said I, 'a great
wit:' 'Right,' says she, 'a great gross one.' 'Nay,'
said I, 'a good wit:' 'Just,' said she, 'it hurts nobody.' 'Nay,' said I, 'the gentleman is wise:'
'Certain,' said she, 'a wise gentleman.' 'Nay,' said
I, 'he hath the tongues:' 'That I believe,' said she,
'for he swore a thing to me on Monday night,
which he forswore on Tuesday morning; there's

a double tongue; there's two tongues.' Thus did she, an hour together, trans-shape thy particular virtues: yet at last she concluded with a sigh, thou wast the properest man in Italy.

CLAUDIO.

For the which she wept heartily, and said she cared not.

DON PEDRO.

Yea, that she did; but yet, for all that, an if she did not hate him deadly, she would love him dearly:—the old man's daughter told us all.

CLAUDIO.

All, all; and, moreover, God saw him when he was hid in the garden.

DON PEDRO.

But when shall we set the savage bull's horns on the sensible Benedick's head?

CLAUDIO.

Yea, and text underneath, 'Here dwells Benedick, the married man'?

BENEDICK.

Fare you well, boy: you know my mind. I will leave you now to your gossip-like humour: you break jests as braggarts do their blades, which, God be thank'd, hurt not.—My lord, for your many courtesies I thank you: I must discontinue your company: your brother the bastard is fled from Messina: you have among you kill'd a sweet and innocent lady. For my Lord Lackbeard there, he and I shall meet: and till then peace be with him.   [Exit.

DON PEDRO.

He is in earnest.

CLAUDIO.

In most profound earnest; and, I'll warrant you, for the love of Beatrice.

DON PEDRO.

And hath challenged thee.

CLAUDIO.

Most sincerely.

DON PEDRO.

What a pretty thing man is when he goes in his doublet and hose, and leaves off his wit!

CLAUDIO.

He is then a giant to an ape: but then is an ape a doctor to such a man.

DON PEDRO.

But, soft you, let me be: pluck up, my heart, and be sad! Did he not say, my brother was fled?
Enter DOGBERRY and VERGES, and the WATCH, with CONRADE and BORACHIO.

DOGBERRY.

Come, you, sir: if justice cannot tame you, she shall ne'er weigh more reasons in her balance: nay, an you be a cursing hypocrite once, you must be lookt to.

DON PEDRO.

How now! two of my brother's men bound! Borachio one!

CLAUDIO.

Hearken after their offence, my lord.

DON PEDRO.

Officers, what offence have these men done?

DOGBERRY.

Marry, sir, they have committed false report; moreover, they have spoken untruths; second-

arily, they are slanders; sixth and lastly, they have belied a lady; thirdly, thay have verified unjust things; and, to conclude, they are lying knaves.

DON PEDRO.

First, I ask thee what they have done; thirdly, I ask thee what's their offence; sixth and lastly, why they are committed: and, to conclude, what you lay to their charge.

CLAUDIO.

Rightly reason'd, and in his own division; and, by my troth, there's one meaning well suited.

DON PEDRO.

Who have you offended, masters, that you are thus bound to your answer? this learned constable is too cunning to be understood: what's your offence?

BORACHIO.

Sweet prince, let me go no further to mine answer: do you hear me, and let this count kill me. I have deceived even your very eyes: what your wisdoms could not discover, these shallow fools have brought to light; who, in the night, overheard me confessing to this man, how Don John your brother incensed me to slander the Lady Hero; how you were brought into the orchard, and saw me court Margaret in Hero's garments; how you disgraced her, when you should marry her: my villainy they have upon record; which I had rather seal with my death than repeat over to my shame. The lady is dead upon mine and my master's false accusation; and, briefly, I desire nothing but the reward of a villain.

DON PEDRO.

Runs not this speech like iron through your blood?

CLAUDIO.

I have drunk poison whiles he utter'd it.

DON PEDRO.

But did my brother set thee on to this?

BORACHIO.

Yea, and paid me richly for the practice of it.

DON PEDRO.

He is composed and framed of treachery: And fled he is upon this villainy.

CLAUDIO.

Sweet Hero! now thy image doth appear In the rare semblance that I loved it first.

DOGBERRY.

Come, bring away the plaintiffs: by this time our sexton hath reform'd Signior Leonato of the matter: and, masters, do not forget to specify, when time and place shall serve, that I am an ass.

VERGES.

Here, here comes master Signior Leonato, and the sexton too.
Enter LEONATO and ANTONIO, with the SEXTON.

LEONATO.

Which is the villain? let me see his eyes, That, when I note another man like him, I may avoid him: which of these is he?

BORACHIO.

If you would know your wronger, look on me.

LEONATO.

Art thou the slave that with thy breath hast kill'd Mine innocent child?

BORACHIO.
Yea, even I alone.
LEONATO.
No, not so, villain; thou beliest thyself:
Here stand a pair of honourable men,
A third is fled, that had a hand in it.—
I thank you, princes, for my daughter's death:
Record it with your high and worthy deeds;
'Twas bravely done, if you bethink you of it.
CLAUDIO.
I know not how to pray your patience;
Yet I must speak. Choose your revenge your-
self;
Impose me to what penance your invention
Can lay upon my sin: yet sinn'd I not
But in mistaking.
DON PEDRO.
By my soul, nor I:
And yet, to satisfy this good old man,
I would bend under any heavy weight
That he'll enjoin me to.
LEONATO.
I cannot bid you bid my daughter live,—
That were impossible: but, I pray you both,
Possess the people in Messina here
How innocent she died; and if your love
Can labour aught in sad invention,
Hang her an epitaph upon her tomb,
And sing it to her bones,—sing it to-night:—
To-morrow morning come you to my house;
And since you could not be my son-in-law,
Be yet my nephew: my brother hath a daughter,
Almost the copy of my child that's dead,
And she alone is heir to both of us:
Give her the right you should have given her
cousin,
And so dies my revenge.
CLAUDIO.
O noble sir,
Your over-kindness doth wring tears from me!
I do embrace your offer; and dispose
For henceforth of poor Claudio.
LEONATO.
To-morrow, then, I will expect your coming;
To-night I take my leave.—This naughty man
Shall face to face be brought to Margaret,
Who I believe was packt in all this wrong,
Hired to it by your brother.
BORACHIO.
No, by my soul, she was not;
Nor knew not what she did when she spoke to me;
But always hath been just and virtuous
In any thing that I do know by her.
DOGBERRY.
Moreover, sir (which indeed is not under white
and black), this plaintiff here, the offender, did
call me ass: I beseech you, let it be remember'd
in his punishment. And also, the watch heard
them talk of one Deform'd: they say he wears a
key in his ear, and a lock hanging by it; and bor-
rows money in God's name,—the which he hath
used so long and never paid, that now men grow
hard-hearted, and will lend nothing for God's
sake: pray you, examine him upon that point.
LEONATO.
I thank thee for thy care and honest pains.

DOGBERRY.
Your worship speaks like a most thankful and
reverend youth; and I praise God for you.
LEONATO.
There's for thy pains.
DOGBERRY.
God save the foundation!
LEONATO.
Go, I discharge thee of thy prisoner, and I thank
thee.
DOGBERRY.
I leave an arrant knave with your worship; which
I beseech your worship to correct yourself, for
the example of others. God keep your worship! I
wish your worship well; God restore you to
health! I humbly give you leave to depart; and if
a merry meeting may be wisht, God prohibit it!
—Come, neighbour.
[Exeunt DOGBERRY and VERGES.
LEONATO.
Until to-morrow morning, lords, farewell.
ANTONIO.
Farewell, my lords: we look for you to-morrow.
DON PEDRO.
We will not fail.
CLAUDIO.
To-night I'll mourn with Hero.
[Exeunt DON PEDRO and CLAUDIO.
LEONATO [to the WATCH].
Bring you these fellows on. We'll talk with Mar-
garet,
How her acquaintance grew with this lewd fellow.
[Exeunt severally.

SCENE II.

LEONATO'S garden.

Enter, severally, BENEDICK and MARGARET.

BENEDICK.
PRAY thee, sweet Mistress Margaret, deserve
well at my hands by helping me to the speech of
Beatrice.
MARGARET.
Will you, then, write me a sonnet in praise of my
beauty?
BENEDICK.
In so high a style, Margaret, that no man living
shall come over it; for, in most comely truth, thou
deservest it.
MARGARET.
To have no man come over me! why, shall I al-
ways keep below stairs?
BENEDICK.
Thy wit is as quick as the greyhound's mouth,—
it catches.
MARGARET.
And yours as blunt as the fencer's foils, which
hit, but hurt not.
BENEDICK.
A most manly wit, Margaret; it will not hurt a
woman: and so, I pray thee, call Beatrice: I give
thee the bucklers.
MARGARET.
Give us the swords; we have bucklers of our
own.

BENEDICK.

If you use them, Margaret, you must put in the pikes with a vice; and they are dangerous weapons for maids.

MARGARET.

Well, I will call Beatrice to you, who I think hath legs.

BENEDICK.

And therefore will come.   [*Exit* MARGARET.
                                                    [*He sings.*

The god of love,
That sits above,
And knows me, and knows me,
How pitiful I deserve,—

I mean in singing; but in loving,—Leander the good swimmer, Troilus the first employer of pandars, and a whole book full of these quondam carpet-mongers, whose names yet run smoothly in the even road of a blank verse,—why, they were never so truly turn'd over and over as my poor self in love. Marry, I cannot show it in rime; I have tried: I can find out no rime to 'lady' but 'baby,'—an innocent rime; for 'scorn,' 'horn,'—a hard rime; for 'school,' 'fool,'—a babbling rime; very ominous endings: no, I was not born under a riming planet, nor I cannot woo in festival terms.
                         Enter BEATRICE.

Sweet Beatrice, wouldst thou come when I call'd thee?

BEATRICE.

Yea, signior, and depart when you bid me.

BENEDICK.

O, stay but till then!

BEATRICE.

'Then' is spoken; fare you well now:—and yet, ere I go, let me go with that I came; which is, with knowing what hath past between you and Claudio.

BENEDICK.

Only foul words; and thereupon I will kiss thee.

BEATRICE.

Foul words is but foul wind, and foul wind is but foul breath, and foul breath is noisome; therefore I will depart unkist.

BENEDICK.

Thou hast frighted the word out of his right sense, so forcible is thy wit. But I must tell thee plainly, Claudio undergoes my challenge; and either I must shortly hear from him, or I will subscribe him a coward. And, I pray thee now, tell me for which of my bad parts didst thou first fall in love with me?

BEATRICE.

For them all together; which maintain'd so politic a state of evil, that they will not admit any good part to intermingle with them. But for which of my good parts did you first suffer love for me?

BENEDICK.

Suffer love,—a good epithet! I do suffer love indeed, for I love thee against my will.

BEATRICE.

In spite of your heart, I think; alas, poor heart! If you spite it for my sake, I will spite it for yours; for I will never love that which my friend hates.

BENEDICK.

Thou and I are too wise to woo peaceably.

BEATRICE.

It appears not in this confession: there's not one wise man among twenty that will praise himself.

BENEDICK.

An old, an old instance, Beatrice, that lived in the time of good neighbours. If a man do not erect in this age his own tomb ere he dies, he shall live no longer in monument than the bell rings and the widow weeps.

BEATRICE.

And how long is that, think you?

BENEDICK.

Question:—why, an hour in clamour, and a quarter in rheum: therefore is it most expedient for the wise, if Don Worm, his conscience, find no impediment to the contrary, to be the trumpet of his own virtues, as I am to myself. So much for praising myself, who, I myself will bear witness, is praiseworthy: and now tell me, how doth your cousin?

BEATRICE.

Very ill.

BENEDICK.

And how do you?

BEATRICE.

Very ill too.

BENEDICK.

Serve God, love me, and mend. There will I leave you too, for here comes one in haste.
                         Enter URSULA.

URSULA.

Madam, you must come to your uncle. Yonder's old coil at home: it is proved my Lady Hero hath been falsely accused, the prince and Claudio mightily abused; and Don John is the author of all, who is fled and gone. Will you come presently?

BEATRICE.

Will you go hear this news, signior?

BENEDICK.

I will live in thy heart, die in thy lap, and be buried in thy eyes; and moreover I will go with thee to thy uncle's.   [*Exeunt.*

SCENE III.

A church.

Enter DON PEDRO, CLAUDIO, *and three or four
with tapers.*

CLAUDIO.

IS this the monument of Leonato?

ATTENDANT.

It is, my lord.

CLAUDIO [*reads from a scroll*].

Done to death by slanderous tongues
    Was the Hero that here lies;
Death, in guerdon of her wrongs,
    Gives her fame which never dies.
So the life that died with shame
Lives in death with glorious fame.
Hang thou there upon the tomb,
Praising her when I am dumb.—

Now, music, sound, and sing your solemn hymn

Song.

Pardon, goddess of the night,
Those that slew thy virgin knight;
For the which, with songs of woe,
Round about her tomb they go.
    Midnight, assist our moan;
    Help us to sigh and groan,
        Heavily, heavily;
Graves, yawn, and yield your dead,
Till death be uttered,
        Heavily, heavily.

CLAUDIO.

Now, unto thy bones good night!—
Yearly will I do this rite.

DON PEDRO.

Good morrow, masters; put your torches out:
    The wolves have prey'd; and look, the gentle
    day.
Before the wheels of Phœbus, round about
    Dapples the drowsy east with spots of grey.
Thanks to you all, and leave us: fare you well.

CLAUDIO.

Good morrow, masters: each his several way.

DON PEDRO.

Come, let us hence, and put on other weeds;
    And then to Leonato's we will go.

CLAUDIO.

And Hymen now with luckier issue speed's
    Than this for whom we render'd up this woe!
                                        [*Exeunt.*

SCENE IV.

A room in LEONATO'S *house.*

Enter LEONATO, ANTONIO, BENEDICK, BEA-
TRICE, MARGARET, URSULA, FRIAR FRANCIS,
and HERO.

FRIAR FRANCIS.

DID I not tell you she was innocent?

LEONATO.

So are the prince and Claudio, who accused her
Upon the error that you heard debated:
But Margaret was in some fault for this,
Although against her will, as it appears
In the true course of all the question.

ANTONIO.

Well, I am glad that all things sort so well.

BENEDICK.

And so am I, being else by faith enforced
To call young Claudio to a reckoning for it.

LEONATO.

Well, daughter, and you gentlewomen all,
Withdraw into a chamber by yourselves,
And when I send for you, come hither maskt:
The prince and Claudio promised by this hour
To visit me.—You know your office, brother:
                                    [*Exeunt* LADIES.
You must be father to your brother's daughter,
And give her to young Claudio.

ANTONIO.

Which I will do with confirm'd countenance.

BENEDICK.

Friar, I must entreat your pains, I think.

FRIAR FRANCIS.

To do what, signior?

BENEDICK.

To bind me, or undo me; one of them.—

Signior Leonato, truth it is, good signior,
Your niece regards me with an eye of favour.

LEONATO.

That eye my daughter lent her: 'tis most true.

BENEDICK.

And I do with an eye of love requite her.

LEONATO.

The sight whereof I think you had from me,
From Claudio, and the prince: but what's your
    will?

BENEDICK.

Your answer, sir, is enigmatical:
But, for my will, my will is, your good-will
May stand with ours, this day to be conjoin'd
In the state of honourable marriage:—
In which, good friar, I shall desire your help.

LEONATO.

My heart is with your liking.

FRIAR FRANCIS.

                                And my help.—
Here comes the prince and Claudio.
        Enter DON PEDRO *and* CLAUDIO, *with*
                        ATTENDANTS.

DON PEDRO.

Good morrow to this fair assembly.

LEONATO.

Good morrow, prince; good morrow, Claudio:
We here attend you. Are you yet determined
To-day to marry with my brother's daughter?

CLAUDIO.

I'll hold my mind, were she an Ethiop.

LEONATO.

Call her forth, brother; here's the friar ready.
                                    [*Exit* ANTONIO.

DON PEDRO.

Good morrow, Benedick. Why, what's the mat-
    ter,
That you have such a February face,
So full of frost, of storm, and cloudiness?

CLAUDIO.

I think he thinks upon the savage bull.—
Tush, fear not, man; we'll tip thy horns with gold,
And all Europa shall rejoice at thee;
As once Europa did at lusty Jove,
When he would play the noble beast in love.

BENEDICK.

Bull Jove, sir, had an amiable low;
And some such strange bull leapt your father's
    cow,
And got a calf in that same noble feat
Much like to you, for you have just his bleat.

CLAUDIO.

For this I owe you: here come other reck'nings.
        Enter ANTONIO, *with the* LADIES *maskt.*
Which is the lady I must seize upon?

ANTONIO.

This same is she, and I do give you her.

CLAUDIO.

Why, then she's mine.—Sweet, let me see your
    face.

LEONATO.

No, that you shall not, till you take her hand
Before this friar, and swear to marry her.

CLAUDIO.

Give me your hand before this holy friar:
I am your husband, if you like of me.

HERO.
And when I lived, I was your other wife:
[*Unmasking.*
And when you loved, you were my other hus-
band.

CLAUDIO.
Another Hero!

HERO.
Nothing certainer:
One Hero died defiled; but I do live,
And surely as I live, I am a maid.

DON PEDRO.
The former Hero! Hero that is dead!

LEONATO.
She died, my lord, but whiles her slander lived.

FRIAR FRANCIS.
All this amazement can I qualify;
When after that the holy rites are ended,
I'll tell you largely of fair Hero's death:
Meantime let wonder seem familiar,
And to the chapel let us presently.

BENEDICK.
Soft and fair, friar.—Which is Beatrice?

BEATRICE [*unmasking*].
I answer to that name. What is your will?

BENEDICK.
Do not you love me?

BEATRICE.
Why, no; no more than reason.

BENEDICK.
Why, then your uncle, and the prince, and Clau-
dio
Have been deceived; for they swore you did.

BEATRICE.
Do not you love me?

BENEDICK.
Troth, no; no more than reason.

BEATRICE.
Why, then my cousin, Margaret, and Ursula
Are much deceived; for they did swear you did.

BENEDICK.
They swore that you were almost sick for me.

BEATRICE.
They swore that you were well-nigh dead for me.

BENEDICK.
'Tis no such matter.—Then you do not love me?

BEATRICE.
No, truly, but in friendly recompense.

LEONATO.
Come, cousin, I am sure you love the gentleman.

CLAUDIO.
And I'll be sworn upon't that he loves her;
For here's a paper, written in his hand,
A halting sonnet of his own pure brain,
Fashion'd to Beatrice.

HERO.
And here's another,
Writ in my cousin's hand, stol'n from her pocket,
Containing her affection unto Benedick.

BENEDICK.
A miracle! here's our own hands against our
hearts.—Come, I will have thee; but, by this
light, I take thee for pity.

BEATRICE.
I would not deny you;—but, by this good day, I
yield upon great persuasion; and partly to save
your life, for I was told you were in a consumption.

BENEDICK.
Peace! I will stop your mouth.   [*Kissing her.*

DON PEDRO.
How dost thou, Benedick, the married man?

BENEDICK.
I'll tell thee what, prince; a college of wit-crackers
cannot flout me out of my humour. Dost thou
think I care for a satire or an epigram? No: if a
man will be beaten with brains, a' shall wear nothing handsome about him. In brief, since I do
purpose to marry, I will think nothing to any
purpose that the world can say against it; and
therefore never flout at me for what I have said
against it; for man is a giddy thing, and this is my
conclusion.—For thy part, Claudio, I did think
to have beaten thee; but in that thou art like to be
my kinsman, live unbruised, and love my cousin.

CLAUDIO.
I had well hoped thou wouldst have denied Beatrice, that I might have cudgell'd thee out of thy
single life, to make thee a double-dealer; which,
out of question, thou wilt be, if my cousin do not
look exceeding narrowly to thee.

BENEDICK.
Come, come, we are friends.—Let's have a dance
ere we are married, that we may lighten our own
hearts and our wives' heels.

LEONATO.
We'll have dancing afterward.

BENEDICK.
First, of my word; therefore play, music!—
Prince, thou art sad; get thee a wife, get thee a
wife: there is no staff more reverend than one tipt
with horn.

Enter a MESSENGER.

MESSENGER.
My lord, your brother John is ta'en in flight,
And brought with armed men back to Messina.

BENEDICK.
Think not on him till to-morrow: I'll devise thee
brave punishments for him —Strike up, pipers!
[*Dance. Exeunt.*

THE MERRY WIVES OF WINDSOR

DRAMATIS PERSONAE

SIR JOHN FALSTAFF.
FENTON, *a gentleman.*
SHALLOW, *a country justice.*
SLENDER, *cousin to Shallow.*
FORD
PAGE } *two gentlemen dwelling at Windsor.*
WILLIAM PAGE, *a boy, son to Page.*
SIR HUGH EVANS, *a Welsh parson.*
DOCTOR CAIUS, *a French physician.*
HOST OF THE GARTER INN.
BARDOLPH,
PISTOL, } *followers of Falstaff.*
NYM,

ROBIN, *page to Falstaff.*
SIMPLE, *servant to Slender.*
RUGBY, *servant to Doctor Caius.*

MISTRESS FORD.
MISTRESS PAGE.
ANNE PAGE, *her daughter.*
MISTRESS QUICKLY, *servant to Doctor Caius.*

SERVANTS *to Page, Ford, &c.*

SCENE—*Windsor, and the neighbourhood.*

ACT I. SCENE I.

Windsor. Before PAGE'S *house.*

Enter JUSTICE SHALLOW, SLENDER, *and* SIR HUGH EVANS.

SHALLOW.

SIR HUGH, persuade me not; I will make a Star-Chamber matter of it: if he were twenty Sir John Falstaffs, he shall not abuse Robert Shallow, esquire.

SLENDER.
In the county of Gloster, justice of peace and *coram.*

SHALLOW.
Ay, cousin Slender, and *cust-alorum.*

SLENDER.
Ay, and *rato-lorum* too; and a gentleman born, master parson; who writes himself *armigero,*—in any bill, warrant, quittance, or obligation, *armigero.*

SHALLOW.
Ay, that I do; and have done any time these three hundred years.

SLENDER.
All his successors gone before him hath done't; and all his ancestors that come after him may: they may give the dozen white luces in their coat.

SHALLOW.
It is an old coat.

SIR HUGH EVANS.
The dozen white louses do become an old coat well; it agrees well, passant; it is a familiar beast to man, and signifies—love.

SHALLOW.
The luce is the fresh fish; the salt fish is an old coat.

SLENDER.
I may quarter, coz?

SHALLOW.
You may, by marrying.

SIR HUGH EVANS.
It is marring indeed, if he quarter it.

SHALLOW.
Not a whit.

SIR HUGH EVANS.
Yes, py'r lady; if he has a quarter of your coat, there is but three skirts for yourself, in my simple conjectures: but that is all one. If Sir John Falstaff have committed disparagements unto you, I am of the church, and will be glad to do my benevolence to make atonements and compremises between you.

SHALLOW.
The Council shall hear it; it is a riot.

SIR HUGH EVANS.
It is not meet the Council hear a riot; there is no fear of Got in a riot: the Council, look you, shall desire to hear the fear of Got, and not to hear a riot; take your vizaments in that.

SHALLOW.
Ha! o' my life, if I were young again, the sword should end it.

SIR HUGH EVANS.
It is petter that friends is the sword, and end it: and there is also another device in my prain, which peradventure prings goot discretions with it:—there is Anne Page, which is daughter to Master George Page, which is pretty virginity.

SLENDER.
Mistress Anne Page! She has brown hair, and speaks small like a woman.

SIR HUGH EVANS.
It is that fery person for all the orld, as just as you will desire; and seven hundred pounds of moneys, and gold, and silver, is her grandsire upon his death's-bed (Got deliver to a joyful resurrections!) give, when she is able to overtake seventeen years old. It were a goot motion if we leave our pribbles and prabbles, and desire a marriage between Master Abraham and Mistress Anne Page.

SHALLOW.
Did her grandsire leave her seven hundred pound?

SIR HUGH EVANS.
Ay, and her father is make her a petter penny.

SHALLOW.
I know the young gentlewoman; she has good gifts.

SIR HUGH EVANS.
Seven hundred pounds and possibilities is goot gifts.

SHALLOW.
Well, let us see honest Master Page. Is Falstaff there?

SIR HUGH EVANS.
Shall I tell you a lie? I do despise a liar as I do despise one that is false, or as I despise one that is not true. The knight, Sir John, is there; and, I beseech you, be ruled by your well-willers. I will peat the door for Master Page. [Knocks.] What, ho! Got pless your house here!

PAGE [within].
Who's there?

SIR HUGH EVANS.
Here is Got's plessing, and your friend, and Justice Shallow; and here young Master Slender, that peradventures shall tell you another tale, if matters grow to your likings.

Enter PAGE.

PAGE.
I am glad to see your worships well. I thank you for my venison, Master Shallow.

SHALLOW.
Master Page, I am glad to see you: much good do it your good heart! I wish'd your venison better; it was ill kill'd.—How doth good Mistress Page?— and I thank you always with my heart, la; with my heart.

PAGE.
Sir, I thank you.

SHALLOW.
Sir, I thank you; by yea and no, I do.

PAGE.
I am glad to see you, good Master Slender.

SLENDER.
How does your fallow greyhound, sir? I heard say he was outrun on Cotsall.

PAGE.
It could not be judged, sir.

SLENDER.
You'll not confess, you'll not confess.

SHALLOW.
That he will not.—'Tis your fault, 'tis your fault:—'tis a good dog.

PAGE.
A cur, sir.

SHALLOW.
Sir, he's a good dog, and a fair dog: can there be more said? he is good and fair.—Is Sir John Falstaff here?

PAGE.
Sir, he is within; and I would I could do a good office between you.

SIR HUGH EVANS.
It is spoke as a Christians ought to speak.

SHALLOW.
He hath wrong'd me, Master Page.

PAGE.
Sir, he doth in some sort confess it.

SHALLOW.
If it be confess'd, it is not redress'd: is not that so, Master Page? He hath wrong'd me; indeed he hath;—at a word, he hath;—believe me; Robert Shallow, esquire, saith he is wrong'd.

PAGE.
Here comes Sir John.

Enter SIR JOHN FALSTAFF, BARDOLPH, NYM, and PISTOL.

SIR JOHN FALSTAFF.
Now, Master Shallow,—you'll complain of me to the king?

SHALLOW.
Knight, you have beaten my men, killed my deer, and broke open my lodge.

SIR JOHN FALSTAFF.
But not kiss'd your keeper's daughter?

SHALLOW.
Tut, a pin! this shall be answer'd.

SIR JOHN FALSTAFF.
I will answer it straight; I have done all this:— that is now answer'd.

SHALLOW.
The Council shall know this.

SIR JOHN FALSTAFF.
'Twere better for you if it were known in counsel: you'll be laugh'd at.

SIR HUGH EVANS.
Pauca verba, Sir John, goot worts.

SIR JOHN FALSTAFF.
Good worts! good cabbage.—Slender, I broke your head: what matter have you against me?

SLENDER.
Marry, sir, I have matter in my head against you: and against your cony-catching rascals, Bardolph, Nym, and Pistol; they carried me to the tavern and made me drunk, and afterward picked my pocket.

BARDOLPH.
You Banbury cheese!

SLENDER.
Ay, it is no matter.

PISTOL.
How now, Mephostophilus!

SLENDER.
Ay, it is no matter.

NYM.
Slice, I say! pauca, pauca; slice! that's my humour.

SLENDER.
Where's Simple, my man?—can you tell, cousin?

SIR HUGH EVANS.
Peace, I pray you.—Now let us understand. There is three umpires in this matter, as I understand; that is, Master Page, fidelicet Master Page; and there is myself, fidelicet myself; and the three party is, lastly and finally, mine host of the Garter.

PAGE.
We three, to hear it and end it between them.

SIR HUGH EVANS.
Fery goot: I will make a prief of it in my note-book; and we will afterwards ork upon the cause with as great discreetly as we can.

SIR JOHN FALSTAFF.
Pistol,—

PISTOL.
He hears with ears.

SIR HUGH EVANS.
The tevil and his tam! what phrase is this, 'He hears with ear'? why, it is affectations.

SIR JOHN FALSTAFF.
Pistol, did you pick Master Slender's purse?

SLENDER.

Ay, by these gloves, did he—or I would I might never come in mine own great chamber again else —of seven groats in mill-sixpences, and two Edward shovel-boards, that cost me two shilling and two pence a-piece of Yead Miller, by these gloves.

SIR JOHN FALSTAFF.

Is this true, Pistol?

SIR HUGH EVANS.

No; it is false, if it is a pick-purse.

PISTOL.

Ha, thou mountain-foreigner!—Sir John and master mine,
I combat challenge of this latten bilbo.—
Word of denial in thy labras here;
Word of denial:—froth and scum, thou liest!

SLENDER.

By these gloves, then, 'twas he.

NYM.

Be avised, sir, and pass good humours: I will say 'marry trap' with you, if you run the nuthook's humour on me; that is the very note of it.

SLENDER.

By this hat, then, he in the red face had it; for though I cannot remember what I did when you made me drunk, yet I am not altogether an ass.

SIR JOHN FALSTAFF.

What say you, Scarlet and John?

BARDOLPH.

Why, sir, for my part, I say the gentleman had drunk himself out of his five sentences,—

SIR HUGH EVANS.

It is his five senses: fie, what the ignorance is!

BARDOLPH.

And being fap, sir, was, as they say, cashiered; and so conclusions passed the careires.

SLENDER.

Ay, you spake in Latin then too; but 'tis no matter: I'll ne'er be drunk whilst I live again, but in honest, civil, godly company, for this trick: if I be drunk, I'll be drunk with those that have the fear of God, and not with drunken knaves.

SIR HUGH EVANS.

So Got udge me, that is a virtuous mind.

SIR JOHN FALSTAFF.

You hear all these matters denied, gentlemen; you hear it.

Enter ANNE PAGE, with wine; MISTRESS FORD and MISTRESS PAGE.

PAGE.

Nay, daughter, carry the wine in; we'll drink within.   [Exit ANNE PAGE.

SLENDER.

O heaven! this is Mistress Anne Page.

PAGE.

How now, Mistress Ford!

SIR JOHN FALSTAFF.

Mistress Ford, by my troth, you are very well met: by your leave, good mistress.   [Kisses her.

PAGE.

Wife, bid these gentlemen welcome,—Come, we have a hot venison-pasty to dinner: come, gentlemen, I hope we shall drink down all unkindness.

[Exeunt all except SHALLOW, SLENDER, and EVANS.

SLENDER.

I had rather than forty shillings I had my Book of Songs and Sonnets here.

Enter SIMPLE.

How now, Simple! where have you been? I must wait on myself, must I? You have not the Book of Riddles about you, have you?

SIMPLE.

Book of Riddles! why, did you not lend it to Alice Shortcake upon All-hallowmas last, a fortnight afore Michaelmas?

SHALLOW.

Come, coz; come, coz; we stay for you. A word with you, coz; marry, this, coz;—there is, as 'twere, a tender, a kind of tender, made afar off by Sir Hugh here. Do you understand me?

SLENDER.

Ay, sir, you shall find me reasonable; if it be so, I shall do that that is reason.

SHALLOW.

Nay, but understand me.

SLENDER.

So I do, sir.

SIR HUGH EVANS.

Give ear to his motions, Master Slender: I will description the matter to you, if you be capacity of it.

SLENDER.

Nay, I will do as my cousin Shallow says: I pray you, pardon me; he's a justice of peace in his country, simple though I stand here.

SIR HUGH EVANS.

But that is not the question: the question is concerning your marriage.

SHALLOW.

Ay, there's the point, sir.

SIR HUGH EVANS.

Marry, is it; the very point of it; to Mistress Anne Page.

SLENDER.

Why, if it be so, I will marry her upon any reasonable demands.

SIR HUGH EVANS.

But can you affection the oman? Let us command to know that of your mouth or of your lips; for divers philosophers hold that the lips is parcel of the mouth. Therefore, precisely, can you carry your good will to the maid?

SHALLOW.

Cousin Abraham Slender, can you love her?

SLENDER.

I hope, sir, I will do as it shall become one that would do reason.

SIR HUGH EVANS.

Nay, Got's lords and his ladies, you must speak positable, if you can carry her your desires towards her.

SHALLOW.

That you must. Will you, upon good dowry, marry her?

SLENDER.

I will do a greater thing than that, upon your request, cousin, in any reason.

SHALLOW.

Nay. conceive me, conceive me, sweet coz: what I do is to pleasure you, coz. Can you love the maid?

SLENDER.

I will marry her, sir, at your request: but if there be no great love in the beginning, yet heaven may decrease it upon better acquaintance, when we are married and have more occasion to know one another; I hope, upon familiarity will grow more contempt: but if you say, 'marry her,' I will marry her; that I am freely dissolved, and dissolutely.

SIR HUGH EVANS.

It is a fery discretion answer; save the faul is in the ort 'dissolutely:' the ort is, according to our meaning, 'resolutely:'—his meaning is goot.

SHALLOW.

Ay, I think my cousin meant well.

SLENDER.

Ay, or else I would I might be hang'd, la.

SHALLOW.

Here comes fair Mistress Anne.

Enter ANNE PAGE.

Would I were young for your sake, Mistress Anne!

ANNE PAGE.

The dinner is on the table; my father desires your worships' company.

SHALLOW.

I will wait on him, fair Mistress Anne.

SIR HUGH EVANS.

Od's plessed will! I will not be absence at the grace.   [*Exeunt* SHALLOW *and* EVANS.

ANNE PAGE.

Will't please your worship to come in, sir?

SLENDER.

No, I thank you, forsooth, heartily; I am very well.

ANNE PAGE.

The dinner attends you, sir.

SLENDER.

I am not a-hungry, I thank you, forsooth.—Go, sirrah, for all you are my man, go wait upon my cousin Shallow. [*Exit* SIMPLE.] A justice of peace sometime may be beholding to his friend for a man.—I keep but three men and a boy yet, till my mother be dead: but what though? yet I live like a poor gentleman born.

ANNE PAGE.

I may not go in without your worship: they will not sit till you come.

SLENDER.

I'faith, I'll eat nothing; I thank you as much as though I did.

ANNE PAGE.

I pray you, sir, walk in.

SLENDER.

I had rather walk here, I thank you. I bruised my shin th'other day with playing at sword and dagger with a master of fence,—three veneys for a dish of stew'd prunes; and, by my troth, I cannot abide the smell of hot meat since.—Why do your dogs bark so? be there bears i'th'town?

ANNE PAGE.

I think there are, sir; I heard them talk'd of.

SLENDER.

I love the sport well; but I shall as soon quarrel at it as any man in England. You are afraid, if you see the bear loose, are you not?

ANNE PAGE.

Ay, indeed, sir.

SLENDER.

That's meat and drink to me, now. I have seen Sackerson loose twenty times, and have taken him by the chain; but, I warrant you, the women have so cried and shriek'd at it, that it pass'd:—but women, indeed, cannot abide 'em; they are very ill-favour'd rough things.

Enter PAGE.

PAGE.

Come, gentle Master Slender, come; we stay for you.

SLENDER.

I'll eat nothing, I thank you, sir.

PAGE.

By cock and pie, you shall not choose, sir: come, come.

SLENDER.

Nay, pray you, lead the way.

PAGE.

Come on, sir.

SLENDER.

Mistress Anne, yourself shall go first.

ANNE PAGE.

Not I, sir; pray you, keep on.

SLENDER.

Truly, I will not go first; truly, la; I will not do you that wrong.

ANNE PAGE.

I pray you, sir.

SLENDER.

I'll rather be unmannerly than troublesome. You do yourself wrong, indeed, la.   [*Exeunt.*

SCENE II.

The same.

Enter SIR HUGH EVANS *and* SIMPLE.

SIR HUGH EVANS.

GO your ways, and ask of Doctor Caius' house which is the way: and there dwells one Mistress Quickly, which is in the manner of his nurse, or his try nurse, or his cook, or his laundry, his washer, and his wringer.

SIMPLE.

Well, sir.

SIR HUGH EVANS.

Nay, it is petter yet.—Give her this letter; for it is a oman that altogether's acquaintance with Mistress Anne Page: and the letter is, to desire and require her to solicit your master's desires to Mistress Anne Page. I pray you, be gone: I will make an end of my dinner; there's pippins and seese to come.   [*Exeunt.*

SCENE III.

A room in the Garter Inn.

Enter FALSTAFF, HOST, BARDOLPH, NYM, PISTOL, *and* ROBIN.

SIR JOHN FALSTAFF.

MINE host of the Garter,—

HOST.

What says my bully-rook? speak scholarly and wisely.

SIR JOHN FALSTAFF.

Truly, mine host, I must turn away some of my followers.

HOST.

Discard, bully Hercules; cashier: let them wag; trot, trot.

SIR JOHN FALSTAFF.

I sit at ten pounds a-week.

HOST.

Thou'rt an emperor, Cæsar, Keisar, and Pheezar. I will entertain Bardolph; he shall draw, he shall tap: said I well, bully Hector?

SIR JOHN FALSTAFF.

Do so, good mine host.

HOST.

I have spoke; let him follow.—Let me see thee froth and lime: I am at a word; follow.   [Exit.

SIR JOHN FALSTAFF.

Bardolph, follow him. A tapster is a good trade: an old cloak makes a new jerkin; a wither'd serving-man a fresh tapster. Go; adieu.

BARDOLPH.

It is a life that I have desired: I will thrive.

PISTOL.

O base Hungarian wight! wilt thou the spigot wield?   [Exit BARDOLPH.

NYM.

He was gotten in drink: is not the humour conceited? His mind is not heroic, and there's the humour of it.

SIR JOHN FALSTAFF.

I am glad I am so acquit of this tinder-box: his thefts were too open; his filching was like an unskilful singer,—he kept not time.

NYM.

The good humour is to steal at a minim's rest.

PISTOL.

'Convey' the wise it call. 'Steal'! foh! a fico for the phrase!

SIR JOHN FALSTAFF.

Well, sirs, I am almost out at heels.

PISTOL.

Why, then, let kibes ensue.

SIR JOHN FALSTAFF.

There is no remedy; I must cony-catch; I must shift.

PISTOL.

Young ravens must have food.

SIR JOHN FALSTAFF.

Which of you know Ford of this town?

PISTOL.

I ken the wight: he is of substance good.

SIR JOHN FALSTAFF.

My honest lads, I will tell you what I am about.

PISTOL.

Two yards, and more.

SIR JOHN FALSTAFF.

No quips now, Pistol:—indeed, I am in the waist two yards about; but I am now about no waste; I am about thrift. Briefly, I do mean to make love to Ford's wife: I spy entertainment in her; she discourses, she carves, she gives the leer of invitation: I can construe the action of her familiar style; and the hardest voice of her behaviour, to be English'd rightly, is, 'I am Sir John Falstaff's.'

PISTOL.

He hath studied her well, and translated her well, —out of honesty into English.

NYM.

The anchor is deep: will that humour pass?

SIR JOHN FALSTAFF.

Now, the report goes she has all the rule of her husband's purse:—he hath a legion of angels.

PISTOL.

As many devils entertain; and, 'To her, boy,' say I.

NYM.

The humour rises; it is good: humour me the angels.

SIR JOHN FALSTAFF.

I have writ me here a letter to her: and here another to Page's wife, who even now gave me good eyes too, examined my parts with most judicious œilliades; sometimes the beam of her view gilded my foot, sometimes my portly belly.

PISTOL.

Then did the sun on dunghill shine.

NYM.

I thank thee for that humour.

SIR JOHN FALSTAFF.

O, she did so course o'er my exteriors with such a greedy intention, that the appetite of her eye did seem to scorch me up like a burning-glass! Here's another letter to her: she bears the purse too; she is a region in Guiana, all gold and bounty. I will be cheaters to them both, and they shall be exchequers to me; they shall be my East and West Indies, and I will trade to them both. Go bear thou this letter to Mistress Page; and thou this to Mistress Ford: we will thrive, lads, we will thrive.

PISTOL.

Shall I Sir Pandarus of Troy become,
And by my side wear steel? then, Lucifer take all!

NYM.

I will run no base humour: here, take the humour-letter: I will keep the haviour of reputation.

SIR JOHN FALSTAFF [to ROBIN].

Hold, sirrah, bear you these letters tightly;
Sail like my pinnace to these golden shores.—
Rogues, hence, avaunt! vanish like hailstones, go;
Trudge, plod away o'th'hoof; seek shelter, pack!
Falstaff will learn the humour of the age,
French thrift, you rogues; myself and skirted page.

[Exeunt FALSTAFF and ROBIN.

PISTOL.

Let vultures gripe thy guts! for gourd and fullam holds,
And high and low beguiles the rich and poor:
Tester I'll have in pouch when thou shalt lack,
Base Phrygian Turk !

NYM.

I have operations in my head, which be humours of revenge.

PISTOL.

Wilt thou revenge?

NYM.

By welkin and her star!

PISTOL.

With wit or steel?

NYM.

With both the humours, I:
I will discuss the humour of this love to Page.

PISTOL.

And I to Ford shall eke unfold
    How Falstaff, varlet vile,
His dove will prove, his gold will hold,
    And his soft couch defile.

NYM.

My humour shall not cool: I will incense Page to
deal with poison; I will possess him with yellow-
ness, for the revolt of mien is dangerous: that is
my true humour.

PISTOL.

Thou art the Mars of malecontents: I second
thee; troop on.   [*Exeunt.*

SCENE IV.

A room in DOCTOR CAIUS'S *house.*

Enter MISTRESS QUICKLY *and* SIMPLE.

MISTRESS QUICKLY.

WHAT, John Rugby!
        Enter RUGBY.
I pray thee, go to the casement, and see if you
can see my master, Master Doctor Caius, coming. If he do, i'faith, and find any body in the
house, here will be an old abusing of God's
patience and the king's English.

RUGBY.

I'll go watch.

MISTRESS QUICKLY.

Go; and we'll have a posset for't soon at night, in
faith, at the latter end of a sea-coal fire. [*Exit*
RUGBY.] An honest, willing, kind fellow, as ever
servant shall come in house withal; and, I warrant you, no tell-tale nor no breed-bate: his worst
fault is, that he is given to prayer; he is something peevish that way: but nobody but has his
fault;—but let that pass.—Peter Simple you say
your name is?

SIMPLE.

Ay, for fault of a better.

MISTRESS QUICKLY.

And Master Slender's your master?

SIMPLE.

Ay, forsooth.

MISTRESS QUICKLY.

Does he not wear a great round beard, like a
glover's paring-knife?

SIMPLE.

No, forsooth: he hath but a little wee face, with a
little yellow beard,—a Cain-colour'd beard.

MISTRESS QUICKLY.

A softly-sprighted man, is he not?

SIMPLE.

Ay, forsooth: but he is as tall a man of his hands as
any is between this and his head; he hath fought
with a warrener.

MISTRESS QUICKLY.

How say you?—O, I should remember him: does
he not hold up his head, as it were, and strut in
his gait?

SIMPLE.

Yes, indeed, does he.

MISTRESS QUICKLY.

Well, heaven send Anne Page no worse fortune!
Tell Master Parson Evans I will do what I can
for your master: Anne is a good girl, and I wish—

Enter RUGBY.

RUGBY.

Out, alas! here comes my master.

MISTRESS QUICKLY.

We shall all be shent. [*Exit* RUGBY.]—Run in
here, good young man; go into this closet:—he
will not stay long. [*Shuts* SIMPLE *in the closet.*]—
What, John Rugby! John! what, John, I say! Go,
John, go inquire for my master; I doubt he be not
well, that he comes not home.   [*Sings.*
    And down, down, adown-a, &c.

Enter DOCTOR CAIUS.

DOCTOR CAIUS.

Vat is you sing? I do not like dese toys. Pray you,
go and vetch me in my closet *un boitier vert,*—a
box, a green-a box: do intend vat I speak? a
green-a box.

MISTRESS QUICKLY.

Ay, forsooth; I'll fetch it you.—[*aside*] I am glad
he went not in himself: if he had found the young
man, he would have been horn-mad.

DOCTOR CAIUS.

*Fe, fe, fe, fe! ma foi, il fait fort chaud. Je m'en vais
à la cour,—la grande affaire.*

MISTRESS QUICKLY.

Is it this, sir?

DOCTOR CAIUS.

Oui; mette le au mon pocket: *dépêche,* quickly.—
Vere is dat knave Rugby?

MISTRESS QUICKLY.

What, John Rugby! John!

Enter RUGBY.

RUGBY.

Here, sir.

DOCTOR CAIUS.

You are John Rugby, and you are Jack Rugby.
Come, take-a your rapier, and come after my heel
to de court.

RUGBY.

'Tis ready, sir, here in the porch.

DOCTOR CAIUS.

By my trot, I tarry too long.—Od's me! *Qu'ai-
j'oublié!* dere is some simples in my closet, dat I
vill not for de varld I shall leave behind.

MISTRESS QUICKLY.

Ay me, he'll find the young man there, and be
mad!

DOCTOR CAIUS.

O *diable, diable!* vat is in my closet? Villain!
larron! [*Pulling* SIMPLE *out.*]—Rugby, my rapier!

MISTRESS QUICKLY.

Good master, be content.

DOCTOR CAIUS.

Verefore shall I be content-a?

MISTRESS QUICKLY.

The young man is an honest man.

DOCTOR CAIUS.

Vat shall de honest man do in my closet? dere is
no honest man dat shall come in my closet.

MISTRESS QUICKLY.

I beseech you, be not so phlegmatic. Hear the
truth of it: he came of an errand to me from
Parson Hugh.

DOCTOR CAIUS.

Vell.

SIMPLE.

Ay, forsooth; to desire her to—

MISTRESS QUICKLY.

Peace, I pray you.

DOCTOR CAIUS.

Peace-a your tongue.—Speak-a your tale.

SIMPLE.

To desire this honest gentlewoman, your maid, to
speak a good word to Mistress Anne Page for my
master in the way of marriage.

MISTRESS QUICKLY.

This is all, indeed, la; but I'll ne'er put my finger
in the fire, and need not.

DOCTOR CAIUS.

Sir Hugh send-a you?—Rugby, *baille* me some
paper.—Tarry you a little-a while.   [*Writes.*

MISTRESS QUICKLY.

I am glad he is so quiet: if he had been throughly
moved, you should have heard him so loud and
so melancholy.—But notwithstanding, man, I'll
do you your master what good I can: and the very
yea and the no is, the French doctor, my master,
—I may call him my master, look you, for I keep
his house; and I wash, wring, brew, bake, scour,
dress meat and drink, make the beds, and do all
myself,—

SIMPLE.

'Tis a great charge to come under one body's hand.

MISTRESS QUICKLY.

Are you avised o' that? you shall find it a great
charge: and to be up early and down late;—but
notwithstanding, to tell you in your ear,—I
would have no words of it,—my master himself is
in love with Mistress Anne Page: but notwithstanding that, I know Anne's mind,—that's
neither here nor there.

DOCTOR CAIUS.

You jack'nape,—give-a dis letter to Sir Hugh; by
gar, it is a shallenge: I vill cut his troat in de park;
and I vill teach a scurvy jack-a-nape priest to
meddle or make:—you may be gone; it is not
good you tarry here:—by gar, I vill cut all his two
stones; by gar, he shall not have a stone to trow
at his dog.   [*Exit* SIMPLE.

MISTRESS QUICKLY.

Alas, he speaks but for his friend.

DOCTOR CAIUS.

It is no matter-a ver dat:—do not you tell-a me
dat I shall have Anne Page for myself?—by gar, I
vill kill de Jack priest; and I have appointed mine
host of de Jarteer to measure our weapon:—by
gar, I vill myself have Anne Page.

MISTRESS QUICKLY.

Sir, the maid loves you, and all shall be well. We
must give folks leave to prate: what, the good-jer!

DOCTOR CAIUS.

Rugby, come to de court vit me.—By gar, if I
have not Anne Page, I shall turn your head out of
my door.—Follow my heels, Rugby.

[*Exeunt* CAIUS *and* RUGBY.

MISTRESS QUICKLY.

You shall have An fool's-head of your own. No, I
know Anne's mind for that: never a woman in
Windsor knows more of Anne's mind than I do;
nor can do more than I do with her, I thank
heaven.

FENTON [*within*].

Who's within there? ho!

MISTRESS QUICKLY.

Who's there, I trow? Come near the house, I
pray you.

Enter FENTON.

FENTON.

How now, good woman! how dost thou?

MISTRESS QUICKLY.

The better that it pleases your good worship to
ask.

FENTON.

What news? how does pretty Mistress Anne?

MISTRESS QUICKLY.

In truth, sir, and she is pretty, and honest, and
gentle; and one that is your friend, I can tell you
that by the way; I praise heaven for it.

FENTON.

Shall I do any good, think'st thou? shall I not
lose my suit?

MISTRESS QUICKLY.

Troth, sir, all is in his hands above: but notwithstanding, Master Fenton, I'll be sworn on a book,
she loves you.—Have not your worship a wart
above your eye?

FENTON.

Yes, marry, have I; what of that?

MISTRESS QUICKLY.

Well, thereby hangs a tale:—good faith, it is such
another Nan;—but, I detest, an honest maid as
ever broke bread:—we had an hour's talk of that
wart:—I shall never laugh but in that maid's
company!—But, indeed, she is given too much to
allicholy and musing: but for you—well, go to.

FENTON.

Well, I shall see her to-day. Hold, there's money
for thee; let me have thy voice in my behalf: if
thou see'st her before me, commend me.

MISTRESS QUICKLY.

Will I? i'faith, that we will; and I will tell your
worship more of the wart the next time we have
confidence; and of other wooers.

FENTON.

Well, farewell; I am in great haste now.

MISTRESS QUICKLY.

Farewell to your worship. [*Exit* FENTON.] Truly,
an honest gentleman: but Anne loves him not;
for I know Anne's mind as well as another does.
—Out upon't! what have I forgot?   [*Exit.*

ACT II. SCENE I.

Before PAGE'S *house.*

Enter MISTRESS PAGE, *with a letter.*

MISTRESS PAGE.

WHAT, have I scaped love-letters in the
holiday-time of my beauty, and am I now
a subject for them? Let me see.   [*Reads.*
Ask me no reason why I love you; for though
Love use Reason for his physician, he admits him
not for his counsellor. You are not young, no
more am I; go to, then, there's sympathy: you are
merry, so am I; ha, ha! then there's more sympathy: you love sack, and so do I; would you desire better sympathy? Let it suffice thee, Mistress
Page,—at the least, if the love of soldier can suf-

fice,—that I love thee. I will not say, pity me,—
'tis not a soldier-like phrase; but I say, love me.
By me,
>Thine own true knight,
>By day or night,
>Or any kind of light,
>With all his might
>For thee to fight,   JOHN FALSTAFF.

What a Herod of Jewry is this!—O wicked, wicked
world!—one that is well-nigh worn to pieces with
age to show himself a young gallant! What an un-
weigh'd behaviour hath this Flemish drunkard
pick'd—with the devil's name—out of my conversation, that he dares in this manner assay me?
Why, he hath not been thrice in my company!—
What should I say to him?—I was then frugal of
my mirth:—Heaven forgive me!—Why, I'll exhibit a bill in the parliament for the putting-down
of fat men. How shall I be revenged on him? for
revenged I will be, as sure as his guts are made of
puddings.

Enter MISTRESS FORD.

MISTRESS FORD.
Mistress Page! trust me, I was going to your house.

MISTRESS PAGE.
And, trust me, I was coming to you. You look
very ill.

MISTRESS FORD.
Nay, I'll ne'er believe that; I have to show to the
contrary.

MISTRESS PAGE.
Faith, but you do, in my mind.

MISTRESS FORD.
Well, I do, then; yet, I say, I could show you to
the contrary. O Mistress Page, give me some
counsel!

MISTRESS PAGE.
What's the matter, woman?

MISTRESS FORD.
O woman, if it were not for one trifling respect, I
could come to such honour!

MISTRESS PAGE.
Hang the trifle, woman! take the honour. What is
it?—dispense with trifles;—what is it?

MISTRESS FORD.
If I would but go to hell for an eternal moment
or so, I could be knighted.

MISTRESS PAGE.
What? thou liest!—Sir Alice Ford! These knights
will hack; and so thou shouldst not alter the
article of thy gentry.

MISTRESS FORD.
We burn daylight:—here, read, read; perceive
how I might be knighted.—I shall think the
worse of fat men, as long as I have an eye to make
difference of men's liking: and yet he would not
swear; praised women's modesty; and gave such
orderly and well-behaved reproof to all uncome-
liness, that I would have sworn his disposition
would have gone to the truth of his words; but
they do no more adhere and keep place together
than the Hundredth Psalm to the tune of *Green
sleeves.* What tempest, I trow, threw this whale,
with so many tuns of oil in his belly, ashore at
Windsor? How shall I be revenged on him? I
think the best way were to entertain him with

hope, till the wicked fire of lust have melted
him in his own grease.—Did you ever hear the
like?

MISTRESS PAGE.
Letter for letter, but that the name of Page and
Ford differs!—To thy great comfort in this
mystery of ill opinions, here's the twin-brother of
thy letter: but let thine inherit first; for, I protest, mine never shall. I warrant he hath a
thousand of these letters, writ with blank space
for different names,—sure, more,—and these are
of the second edition: he will print them, out of
doubt; for he cares not what he puts into the
press, when he would put us two. I had rather be
a giantess, and lie under Mount Pelion. Well, I
will find you twenty lascivious turtles, ere one
chaste man.

MISTRESS FORD.
Why, this is the very same; the very hand, the
very words. What doth he think of us?

MISTRESS PAGE.
Nay, I know not: it makes me almost ready to
wrangle with mine own honesty. I'll entertain
myself like one that I am not acquainted withal;
for, sure, unless he know some strain in me, that
I know not myself, he would never have boarded
me in this fury.

MISTRESS FORD.
Boarding, call you it? I'll be sure to keep him
above deck.

MISTRESS PAGE.
So will I: if he come under my hatches, I'll never
to sea again. Let's be revenged on him: let's
appoint him a meeting; give him a show of comfort in his suit; and lead him on with a fine-baited
delay, till he hath pawn'd his horses to mine host
of the Garter.

MISTRESS FORD.
Nay, I will consent to act any villainy against
him, that may not sully the chariness of our
honesty. O, that my husband saw this letter! it
would give eternal food to his jealousy.

MISTRESS PAGE.
Why, look where he comes;—and my good man,
too: he's as far from jealousy as I am from giving
him cause; and that, I hope, is an unmeasurable
distance.

MISTRESS FORD.
You are the happier woman.

MISTRESS PAGE.
Let's consult together against this greasy knight.
Come hither.   [*They retire.*

Enter FORD, PISTOL, PAGE, *and* NYM.

FORD.
Well, I hope it be not so.

PISTOL.
Hope is a curtal dog in some affairs:
Sir John affects thy wife.

FORD.
Why, sir, my wife is not young.

PISTOL.
He woos both high and low, both rich and poor,
Both young and old, one with another, Ford;
He loves the gallimaufry: Ford, perpend.

FORD.
Love my wife!

PISTOL.

With liver burning hot. Prevent, or go thou,
Like Sir Actæon he, with Ringwood at thy
   heels:—
O, odious is the name!

FORD.

What name, sir?

PISTOL.

The horn, I say. Farewell.
Take heed; have open eye; for thieves do foot by
   night:
Take heed, ere summer comes, or cuckoo-birds
   do sing.—
Away, Sir Corporal Nym!—
Believe it, Page; he speaks sense.   [Exit.

FORD.

I will be patient; I will find out this.

NYM [to PAGE].

And this is true; I like not the humour of lying.
He hath wrong'd me in some humours: I should
have borne the humour'd letter to her; but I have
a sword, and it shall bite upon my necessity. He
loves your wife; there's the short and the long.
My name is Corporal Nym; I speak, and I
avouch 'tis true: my name is Nym, and Falstaff
loves your wife.—Adieu. I love not the humour
of bread and cheese; and there's the humour of it.
Adieu.   [Exit.

PAGE.

'The humour of it,' quoth a'! here's a fellow
frights humour out of his wits.

FORD.

I will seek out Falstaff.

PAGE.

I never heard such a drawling, affecting rogue.

FORD.

If I do find it:—well.

PAGE.

I will not believe such a Cataian, though the
priest o'th'town commended him for a true man.

FORD.

'Twas a good sensible fellow:—well.

[MISTRESS PAGE and MISTRESS FORD
   come forward.

PAGE.

How now, Meg!

MISTRESS PAGE.

Whither go you, George?—Hark you.

MISTRESS FORD.

How now, sweet Frank! why art thou melancholy?

FORD.

I melancholy! I am not melancholy.—Get you
home, go.

MISTRESS FORD.

Faith, thou hast some crotchets in thy head now.
—Will you go, Mistress Page?

MISTRESS PAGE.

Have with you.—You'll come to dinner, George?
—[Aside to MISTRESS FORD] Look who comes
yonder: she shall be our messenger to this paltry
knight.

MISTRESS FORD [aside to MISTRESS PAGE].

Trust me, I thought on her: she'll fit it.

Enter MISTRESS QUICKLY.

MISTRESS PAGE.

You are come to see my daughter Anne?

MISTRESS QUICKLY.

Ay, forsooth; and, I pray, how does good Mistress
Anne?

MISTRESS PAGE.

Go in with us and see: we have an hour's talk
with you.

[Exeunt MISTRESS PAGE, MISTRESS
   FORD, and MISTRESS QUICKLY.

PAGE.

How now, Master Ford!

FORD.

You heard what this knave told me, did you not?

PAGE.

Yes: and you heard what the other told me?

FORD.

Do you think there is truth in them?

PAGE.

Hang 'em, slaves! I do not think the knight would
offer it: but these that accuse him in his intent towards our wives are a yoke of his discarded men;
very rogues, now they be out of service.

FORD.

Were they his men?

PAGE.

Marry, were they.

FORD.

I like it never the better for that.—Does he lie at
the Garter?

PAGE.

Ay, marry, does he. If he should intend this
voyage toward my wife, I would turn her loose to
him; and what he gets more of her than sharp
words, let it lie on my head.

FORD.

I do not misdoubt my wife; but I would be loth
to turn them together. A man may be too confident: I would have nothing lie on my head: I
cannot be thus satisfied.

PAGE.

Look where my ranting host of the Garter comes:
there is either liquor in his pate, or money in his
purse, when he looks so merrily.

Enter HOST.

How now, mine host!

HOST.

How now, bully-rook! thou'rt a gentleman.—
Cavalero-justice, I say!

Enter SHALLOW.

SHALLOW.

I follow, mine host, I follow.—Good even and
twenty, good Master Page! Master Page, will you
go with us? we have sport in hand.

HOST.

Tell him, cavalero-justice; tell him, bully-rook.

SHALLOW.

Sir, there is a fray to be fought between Sir Hugh
the Welsh priest and Caius the French doctor.

FORD.

Good mine host o'th'Garter, a word with you.

HOST.

What say'st thou, my bully-rook?

[They go aside.

SHALLOW [to PAGE].

Will you go with us to behold it? My merry host
hath had the measuring of their weapons; and, I
think, hath appointed them contrary places; for,

believe me, I hear the parson is no jester. Hark, I will tell you what our sport shall be.

[*They go aside.*

HOST.

Hast thou no suit against my knight, my guest-cavalier?

FORD.

None, I protest: but I'll give you a pottle of burnt sack to give me recourse to him, and tell him my name is Brook, only for a jest.

HOST.

My hand, bully; thou shalt have egress and regress;—said I well?—and thy name shall be Brook. It is a merry knight.—Will you go, mynheers?

SHALLOW.

Have with you, mine host.

PAGE.

I have heard the Frenchman hath good skill in his rapier.

SHALLOW.

Tut, sir, I could have told you more. In these times you stand on distance, your passes, stoccadoes, and I know not what: 'tis the heart, Master Page; 'tis here, 'tis here. I have seen the time, with my long sword I would have made you four tall fellows skip like rats.

HOST.

Here, boys, here, here! shall we wag?

PAGE.

Have with you.—I had rather hear them scold than fight. [*Exeunt* HOST, SHALLOW, *and* PAGE.

FORD.

Though Page be a secure fool, and stands so firmly on his wife's frailty, yet I cannot put off my opinion so easily: she was in his company at Page's house; and what they made there, I know not. Well, I will look further into't: and I have a disguise to sound Falstaff. If I find her honest, I lose not my labour, if she be otherwise, 'tis labour well bestow'd. [*Exit.*

SCENE II.

A room in the Garter Inn.

Enter FALSTAFF *and* PISTOL.

SIR JOHN FALSTAFF.

I WILL not lend thee a penny.

PISTOL.

Why, then the world's mine oyster,
Which I with sword will open.—
I will retort the sum in equipage.

SIR JOHN FALSTAFF.

Not a penny. I have been content, sir, you should lay my countenance to pawn: I have grated upon my good friends for three reprieves for you and your coach-fellow Nym; or else you had look'd through the grate, like a geminy of baboons. I am damn'd in hell for swearing to gentlemen my friends you were good soldiers and tall fellows; and when Mistress Bridget lost the handle of her fan, I took't upon mine honour thou hadst it not.

PISTOL.

Didst not thou share? hadst thou not fifteen pence?

SIR JOHN FALSTAFF.

Reason, you rogue, reason: think'st thou I'll endanger my soul gratis? At a word, hang no more about me, I am no gibbet for you:—go:—a short knife and a throng;—to your manor of Pickthatch, go.—You'll not bear a letter for me, you rogue!—you stand upon your honour!—Why, thou unconfinable baseness, it is as much as I can do to keep the terms of my honour precise; I, I, I myself sometimes, leaving the fear of God on the left hand, and hiding mine honour in my necessity, am fain to shuffle, to hedge, and to lurch; and yet you, rogue, will ensconce your rags, your cat-a-mountain looks, your red-lattice phrases, and your bold-beating oaths, under the shelter of your honour! You will not do it, you!

PISTOL.

I do relent:—what would thou more of man?

SIR JOHN FALSTAFF.

Well, go to, away, no more!

Enter ROBIN.

ROBIN.

Sir, here's a woman would speak with you.

SIR JOHN FALSTAFF.

Let her approach.

Enter MISTRESS QUICKLY.

MISTRESS QUICKLY.

Give your worship good morrow.

SIR JOHN FALSTAFF.

Good morrow, good wife.

MISTRESS QUICKLY.

Not so, an't please your worship.

SIR JOHN FALSTAFF.

Good maid, then.

MISTRESS QUICKLY.

I'll be sworn;
As my mother was, the first hour I was born.

SIR JOHN FALSTAFF.

I do believe the swearer. What with me?

MISTRESS QUICKLY.

Shall I vouchsafe your worship a word or two?

SIR JOHN FALSTAFF.

Two thousand, fair woman: and I'll vouchsafe thee the hearing.

MISTRESS QUICKLY.

There is one Mistress Ford, sir:—I pray, come a little nearer this ways:—I myself dwell with Master Doctor Caius,—

SIR JOHN FALSTAFF.

Well, on: Mistress Ford, you say,—

MISTRESS QUICKLY.

Your worship says very true:—I pray your worship, come a little nearer this ways.

SIR JOHN FALSTAFF.

I warrant thee, nobody hears;—mine own people, mine own people.

MISTRESS QUICKLY.

Are they so? God bless them, and make them his servants!

SIR JOHN FALSTAFF.

Well, Mistress Ford;—what of her?

MISTRESS QUICKLY.

Why, sir, she's a good creature.—Lord, Lord! your worship's a wanton! Well, heaven forgive you, and all of us, I pray!—

SIR JOHN FALSTAFF.
Mistress Ford;—come, Mistress Ford,—
MISTRESS QUICKLY.
Marry, this is the short and the long of it; you
have brought her into such a canaries as 'tis wonderful. The best courtier of them all, when the
court lay at Windsor, could never have brought
her to such a canary. Yet there has been knights,
and lords, and gentlemen, with their coaches; I
warrant you, coach after coach, letter after letter,
gift after gift; smelling so sweetly—all musk—
and so rushling, I warrant you, in silk and gold;
and in such alligant terms; and in such wine and
sugar of the best and the fairest, that would have
won any woman's heart; and, I warrant you, they
could never get an eye-wink of her:—I had myself twenty angels given me this morning; but I
defy all angels—in any such sort, as they say—
but in the way of honesty:—and, I warrant you,
they could never get her so much as sip on a cup
with the proudest of them all: and yet there has
been earls, nay, which is more, pensioners; but, I
warrant you, all is one with her.
SIR JOHN FALSTAFF.
But what says she to me? be brief, my good she-
Mercury.
MISTRESS QUICKLY.
Marry, she hath received your letter; for the
which she thanks you a thousand times: and she
gives you to notify, that her husband will be absence from his house between ten and eleven.
SIR JOHN FALSTAFF.
Ten and eleven?
MISTRESS QUICKLY.
Ay, forsooth; and then you may come and see the
picture, she says, that you wot of;—Master Ford,
her husband, will be from home. Alas, the sweet
woman leads an ill life with him! he's a very
jealousy man: she leads a very frampold life with
him, good heart.
SIR JOHN FALSTAFF.
Ten and eleven:—woman, commend me to her; I
will not fail her.
MISTRESS QUICKLY.
Why, you say well. But I have another messenger
to your worship. Mistress Page hath her hearty
commendations to you, too:—and let me tell you
in your ear, she's as fartuous a civil modest wife,
and one, I tell you, that will not miss you morning
nor evening prayer, as any is in Windsor, whoe'er
be the other:—and she bade me tell your worship
that her husband is seldom from home; but, she
hopes, there will come a time. I never knew a
woman so dote upon a man: surely, I think you
have charms, la; yes, in truth.
SIR JOHN FALSTAFF.
Not I, I assure thee: setting the attraction of my
good parts aside, I have no other charms. .
MISTRESS QUICKLY.
Blessing on your heart for't!
SIR JOHN FALSTAFF.
But, I pray thee, tell me this,—has Ford's wife and
Page's wife acquainted each other how they love me?
MISTRESS QUICKLY.
That were a jest indeed!—they have not so little
grace, I hope:—that were a trick indeed!—But

Mistress Page would desire you to send her your
little page, of all loves: her husband has a marvellous infection to the little page; and, truly, Master
Page is an honest man. Never a wife in Windsor
leads a better life than she does: do what she will,
say what she will, take all, pay all, go to bed when
she list, rise when she list, all is as she will: and,
truly, she deserves it; for if there be a kind woman
in Windsor, she is one. You must send her your
page; no remedy.
SIR JOHN FALSTAFF.
Why, I will.
MISTRESS QUICKLY.
Nay, but do so, then: and, look you, he may come
and go between you both; and, in any case, have
a nay-word, that you may know one another's
mind, and the boy never need to understand any
thing; for 'tis not good that children should know
any wickedness: old folks, you know, have discretion, as they say, and know the world.
SIR JOHN FALSTAFF.
Fare thee well: commend me to them both:
there's my purse; I am yet thy debtor.—Boy, go
along with this woman. [Exeunt MISTRESS
QUICKLY and ROBIN.]—This news distracts me!
PISTOL.
This punk is one of Cupid's carriers:—
Clap on more sails; pursue; up with your fights;
Give fire; she is my prize, or ocean whelm them
all!   [Exit.
SIR JOHN FALSTAFF.
Say'st thou so, old Jack? go thy ways: I'll make
more of thy old body than I have done. Will they
yet look after thee? Wilt thou, after the expense of
so much money, be now a gainer? Good body, I
thank thee. Let them say 'tis grossly done; so it be
fairly done, no matter.
Enter BARDOLPH, with a cup of sack.
BARDOLPH.
Sir John, there's one Master Brook below would
fain speak with you, and be acquainted with you;
and hath sent your worship a morning's draught
of sack.
SIR JOHN FALSTAFF.
Brook is his name?
BARDOLPH.
Ay, sir.
SIR JOHN FALSTAFF.
Call him in. [Exit BARDOLPH.] Such Brooks are
welcome to me, that o'erflow such liquor.—Ah,
ha! Mistress Ford and Mistress Page, have I en-
compass'd you? go to; via!
Enter BARDOLPH, with FORD disguised.
FORD.
'Bless you, sir!
SIR JOHN FALSTAFF.
And you, sir! Would you speak with me?
FORD.
I make bold to press with so little preparation
upon you.
SIR JOHN FALSTAFF.
You're welcome. What's your will?—Give us
leave, drawer.   [Exit BARDOLPH.
FORD.
Sir, I am a gentleman that have spent much; my
name is Brook.

SIR JOHN FALSTAFF.

Good Master Brook, I desire more acquaintance of you.

FORD.

Good Sir John, I sue for yours: not to charge you; for I must let you understand I think myself in better plight for a lender than you are: the which hath something embolden'd me to this unseason'd intrusion; for they say, if money go before, all ways do lie open.

SIR JOHN FALSTAFF.

Money is a good soldier, sir, and will on.

FORD.

Troth, and I have a bag of money here troubles me: if you will help to bear it, Sir John, take all, or half, for easing me of the carriage.

SIR JOHN FALSTAFF.

Sir, I know not how I may deserve to be your porter.

FORD.

I will tell you, sir, if you will give me the hearing.

SIR JOHN FALSTAFF.

Speak, good Master Brook: I shall be glad to be your servant.

FORD.

Sir, I hear you are a scholar,—I will be brief with you;—and you have been a man long known to me, though I had never so good means, as desire, to make myself acquainted with you. I shall discover a thing to you, wherein I must very much lay open mine own imperfection: but, good Sir John, as you have one eye upon my follies, as you hear them unfolded, turn another into the register of your own; that I may pass with a reproof the easier, sith you yourself know how easy it is to be such an offender.

SIR JOHN FALSTAFF.

Very well, sir; proceed.

FORD.

There is a gentlewoman in this town, her husband's name is Ford.

SIR JOHN FALSTAFF.

Well, sir.

FORD.

I have long loved her, and, I protest to you, bestow'd much on her: follow'd her with a doting observance; engross'd opportunities to meet her; fee'd every slight occasion that could but niggardly give me sight of her; not only bought many presents to give her, but have given largely to many to know what she would have given; briefly, I have pursued her as love hath pursued me; which hath been on the wing of all occasions. But whatsoever I have merited, either in my mind or in my means, meed, I am sure, I have received none; unless experience be a jewel: that I have purchased at an infinite rate; and that hath taught me to say this:

Love like a shadow flies when substance love pursues;

Pursuing that that flies, and flying what pursues.

SIR JOHN FALSTAFF.

Have you received no promise of satisfaction at her hands?

FORD.

Never.

SIR JOHN FALSTAFF

Have you importuned her to such a purpose?

FORD.

Never.

SIR JOHN FALSTAFF.

Of what quality was your love, then?

FORD.

Like a fair house built on another man's ground; so that I have lost my edifice by mistaking the place where I erected it.

SIR JOHN FALSTAFF.

To what purpose have you unfolded this to me?

FORD.

When I have told you that, I have told you all. Some say, that though she appear honest to me, yet in other places she enlargeth her mirth so far that there is shrewd construction made of her. Now, Sir John, here is the heart of my purpose: you are a gentleman of excellent breeding, admirable discourse, of great admittance, authentic in your place and person, generally allow'd for your many war-like, court-like, and learned preparations,—

SIR JOHN FALSTAFF.

O, sir!

FORD.

Believe it, for you know it.—There is money; spend it, spend it; spend more; spend all I have; only give me so much of your time in exchange of it, as to lay an amiable siege to the honesty of this Ford's wife: use your art of wooing; win her to consent to you: if any man may, you may as soon as any.

SIR JOHN FALSTAFF.

Would it apply well to the vehemency of your affection, that I should win what you would enjoy? Methinks you prescribe to yourself very preposterously.

FORD.

O, understand my drift. She dwells so securely on the excellency of her honour, that the folly of my soul dares not present itself: she is too bright to be look'd against. Now, could I come to her with any detection in my hand, my desires had instance and argument to commend themselves: I could drive her then from the ward of her purity, her reputation, her marriage-vow, and a thousand other her defences, which now are too-too strongly embattled against me. What say you to't, Sir John?

SIR JOHN FALSTAFF.

Master Brook, I will first make bold with your money; next, give me your hand; and last, as I am a gentleman, you shall, if you will, enjoy Ford's wife.

FORD.

O good sir!

SIR JOHN FALSTAFF.

Master Brook, I say you shall.

FORD.

Want no money, Sir John; you shall want none.

SIR JOHN FALSTAFF.

Want no Mistress Ford, Master Brook; you shall want none. I shall be with her—I may tell you—by her own appointment; even as you came in to me, her assistant, or go-between, parted from me:

I say I shall be with her between ten and eleven; for at that time the jealous rascally knave her husband will be forth. Come you to me at night; you shall know how I speed.

FORD.

I am blest in your acquaintance. Do you know Ford, sir?

SIR JOHN FALSTAFF.

Hang him, poor cuckoldy knave! I know him not:—yet I wrong him to call him poor; they say the jealous wittolly knave hath masses of money; for the which his wife seems to me well-favour'd. I will use her as the key of the cuckoldly rogue's coffer; and there's my harvest-home.

FORD.

I would you knew Ford, sir, that you might avoid him, if you saw him.

SIR JOHN FALSTAFF.

Hang him, mechanical salt-butter rogue! I will stare him out of his wits; I will awe him with my cudgel,—it shall hang like a meteor o'er the cuckold's horns. Master Brook, thou shalt know I will predominate over the peasant, and thou shalt lie with his wife.—Come to me soon at night:—Ford's a knave, and I will aggravate his style; thou, Master Brook, shalt know him for knave and cuckold:—come to me soon at night.

[Exit.

FORD.

What a damn'd Epicurean rascal is this!—My heart is ready to crack with impatience.—Who says this is improvident jealousy? my wife hath sent to him, the hour is fixt, the match is made. Would any man have thought this?—See the hell of having a false woman! My bed shall be abused, my coffers ransack'd, my reputation gnawn at; and I shall not only receive this villainous wrong, but stand under the adoption of abominable terms, and by him that does me this wrong. Terms! names!—Amaimon sounds well; Lucifer, well; Barbason, well; yet they are devils' additions, the names of fiends: but cuckold! wittol!—Cuckold! the devil himself hath not such a name. Page is an ass, a secure ass: he will trust his wife; he will not be jealous. I will rather trust a Fleming with my butter, Parson Hugh the Welshman with my cheese, an Irishman with my aquavitæ bottle, or a thief to walk my ambling gelding, than my wife with herself: then she plots, then she ruminates, then she devises; and what they think in their hearts they may effect, they will break their hearts but they will effect. Heaven be praised for my jealousy!—Eleven o'clock the hour:—I will prevent this, detect my wife, be revenged on Falstaff, and laugh at Page. I will about it; better three hours too soon than a minute too late, Fie, fie, fie! cuckold! cuckold! cuckold! [Exit.

SCENE III.

A field near Windsor.

Enter CAIUS *and* RUGBY.

DOCTOR CAIUS.

JACK RUGBY,—

RUGBY.

Sir?

DOCTOR CAIUS.

Vat is de clock, Jack?

RUGBY.

'Tis past the hour, sir, that Sir Hugh promised to meet.

DOCTOR CAIUS.

By gar, he has save his soul, dat he is no come; he has pray his Pible vell, dat he is no come: by gar, Jack Rugby, he is dead already, if he be come.

RUGBY.

He is wise, sir; he knew your worship would kill him, if he came.

DOCTOR CAIUS.

By gar, de herring is no dead so as I vill kill him. Take your rapier, Jack; I vill tell you how I vill kill him.

RUGBY.

Alas, sir, I cannot fence.

DOCTOR CAIUS.

Villainy, take your rapier.

RUGBY.

Forbear; here's company.

Enter HOST, SHALLOW, SLENDER, *and* PAGE.

HOST.

'Bless thee, bully doctor!

SHALLOW.

'Save you, Master Doctor Caius!

PAGE.

Now, good master doctor!

SLENDER.

'Give you good morrow, sir.

DOCTOR CAIUS.

Vat be all you, one, two, tree, four, come for?

HOST.

To see thee fight, to see thee foin, to see thee traverse; to see thee here, to see thee there; to see thee pass thy punto, thy stock, thy reverse, thy distance, thy montant. Is he dead, my Ethiopian? is he dead, my Francisco? ha, bully! What says my Aesculapius? my Galen? my heart of elder? ha! is he dead, bully-stale? is he dead?

DOCTOR CAIUS.

By gar, he is de coward Jack priest of de vorld; he is not show his face.

HOST.

Thou art a Castilian, King Urinal! Hector of Greece, my boy!

DOCTOR CAIUS.

I pray you, bear vitness that me have stay six or seven, two, tree hours for him, and he is no come.

SHALLOW.

He is the wiser man, master doctor: he is a curer of souls, and you a curer of bodies; if you should fight, you go against the hair of your professions.—Is it not true, Master Page?

PAGE.

Master Shallow, you have yourself been a great fighter, though now a man of peace.

SHALLOW.

Bodikins, Master Page, though I now be old, and of the peace, if I see a sword out, my finger itches to make one. Though we are justices, and doctors, and churchmen, Master Page, we have some salt of our youth in us; we are the sons of women, Master Page.

PAGE.
'Tis true, Master Shallow.

SHALLOW.
It will be found so, Master Page.—Master Doctor Caius, I am come to fetch you home. I am sworn of the peace: you have show'd yourself a wise physician, and Sir Hugh hath shown himself a wise and patient churchman. You must go with me, master doctor.

HOST.
Pardon, guest-justice.—A word, Monsieur Mockwater.

DOCTOR CAIUS.
Mock-vater! vat is dat?

HOST.
Mock-water, in our English tongue, is valour, bully.

DOCTOR CAIUS.
By gar, den, I have as mush mock-water as de Englishman.—Scurvy jack-dog priest! by gar, me vill cut his ears.

HOST.
He will clapper-claw thee tightly, bully.

DOCTOR CAIUS.
Clapper-de-claw! vat is dat?

HOST.
That is, he will make thee amends.

DOCTOR CAIUS.
By gar, me do look he shall clapper-de-claw me; for, by gar, me vill have it.

HOST.
And I will provoke him to't, or let him wag.

DOCTOR CAIUS.
Me tank you for dat.

HOST.
And, moreover, bully,—But first, master guest, and Master Page, and eke Cavalero Slender, go you through the town to Frogmore.
[Aside to them.

PAGE.
Sir Hugh is there, is he?

HOST.
He is there: see what humour he is in; and I will bring the doctor about by the fields. Will it do well?

SHALLOW.
We will do it.

PAGE, SHALLOW, and SLENDER.
Adieu, good master doctor.
[Exeunt PAGE, SHALLOW, and SLENDER.

DOCTOR CAIUS.
By gar, me vill kill de priest; for he speak for a jack-an-ape to Anne Page.

HOST.
Let him die: sheathe thy impatience, throw cold water on thy choler: go about the fields with me through Frogmore: I will bring thee where Mistress Anne Page is, at a farm-house a-feasting; and thou shalt woo her. Cried I aim? said I well?

DOCTOR CAIUS.
By gar, me dank you vor dat: by gar, I love you; and I shall procure-a you de good guest, de earl, de knight, de lords, de gentlemen, my patients.

HOST.
For the which I will be thy adversary toward Anne Page. Said I well?

DOCTOR CAIUS.
By gar, 'tis good; vell said.

HOST.
Let us wag, then.

DOCTOR CAIUS.
Come at my heels, Jack Rugby.   [Exeunt.

ACT III. SCENE I.

A field near Frogmore.

Enter SIR HUGH EVANS and SIMPLE.

SIR HUGH EVANS.
I PRAY you now, good Master Slender's servingman, and friend Simple by your name, which way have you look'd for Master Caius, that calls himself doctor of physic?

SIMPLE.
Marry, sir, the pittie-ward, the park-ward, every way; old Windsor way, and every way but the town way.

SIR HUGH EVANS.
I most fehemently desire you you will also look that way.

SIMPLE.
I will, sir.   [Retires.

SIR HUGH EVANS.
Pless my soul, how full of cholers I am, and trempling of mind!—I shall be glad if he have deceived me:—how melancholies I am!—I will knog his urinals about his knave's costard when I have goot opportunities for the ork:—Pless my soul!—   [Sings.
To shallow rivers, to whose falls
Melodious birds sing madrigals;
There will we make our peds of roses,
And a thousand fragrant posies.
To shallow—
Mercy on me! I have a great dispositions to cry.—   [Sings.
Melodious birds sing madrigals;—
Whenas I sat in Pabylon,—
And a thousand vagram posies.
To shallow, &c.

SIMPLE [coming forward].
Yonder he is coming, this way, Sir Hugh.

SIR HUGH EVANS.
He's welcome.—   [Sings.
To shallow rivers, to whose falls—
Heaven prosper the right!—What weapons is he?

SIMPLE.
No weapons, sir. There comes my master, Master Shallow, and another gentleman, from Frogmore, over the stile, this way.

SIR HUGH EVANS.
Pray you, give me my gown; or else keep it in your arms.

Enter PAGE, SHALLOW, and SLENDER.

SHALLOW.
How now, master parson! Good morrow, good Sir Hugh. Keep a gamester from the dice, and a good student from his book, and it is wonderful.

SLENDER [aside].
Ah, sweet Anne Page!

PAGE.
'Save you, good Sir Hugh!

SIR HUGH EVANS.
'Pless you from his mercy sake, all of you!

SHALLOW.
What, the sword and the word! do you study them both, master parson?

PAGE.
And youthful still, in your doublet and hose this raw rheumatic day?

SIR HUGH EVANS.
There is reasons and causes for it.

PAGE.
We are come to you to do a good office, master parson.

SIR HUGH EVANS.
Fery well: what is it?

PAGE.
Yonder is a most reverend gentleman, who, be-like having received wrong by some person, is at most odds with his own gravity and patience that ever you saw.

SHALLOW.
I have lived fourscore years and upward; I never heard a man of his place, gravity, and learning, so wide of his own respect.

What is he?

SIR HUGH EVANS.

PAGE.
I think you know him; Master Doctor Caius, the renown'd French physician.

SIR HUGH EVANS.
Got's will, and his passion of my heart! I had as lief you would tell me of a mess of porridge.

Why?

PAGE.

SIR HUGH EVANS.
He has no more knowledge in Hibbocrates and Galen,—and he is a knave besides; a cowardly knave as you would desires to be acquainted withal.

PAGE.
I warrant you, he's the man should fight with him.

SLENDER [aside].
O sweet Anne Page!

SHALLOW.
It appears so, by his weapons.—Keep them asunder:—here comes Doctor Caius.

Enter HOST, CAIUS, and RUGBY.

PAGE.
Nay, good master parson, keep in your weapon.

SHALLOW.
So do you, good master doctor.

HOST.
Disarm them, and let them question: let them keep their limbs whole, and hack our English.

DOCTOR CAIUS.
I pray you, let-a me speak a word vit your ear. Verefore vill you not meet-a me?

SIR HUGH EVANS [aside to CAIUS].
Pray you, use your patience: in goot time.

DOCTOR CAIUS.
By gar, you are de coward, de Jack dog, John ape.

SIR HUGH EVANS [aside to CAIUS].
Pray you, let us not be laughing-stogs to other men's humours; I desire you in friendship, and I will one way or other make you amends.—[aloud]

I will knog your urinals about your knave's cogs-comb for missing your meetings and appointments.

DOCTOR CAIUS.
Diable!—Jack Rugby,—mine host de Jarteer,—have I not stay for him to kill him? have I not, at de place I did appoint?

SIR HUGH EVANS.
As I am a Christians soul, now, look you, this is the place appointed: I'll be judgement by mine host of the Garter.

HOST.
Peace, I say, Gallia and Guallia, French and Welsh, soul-curer and body-curer!

DOCTOR CAIUS.
Ay, dat is very good; excellent.

HOST.
Peace, I say! hear mine host of the Garter. Am I politic? am I subtle? am I a Machivell? Shall I lose my doctor? no; he gives me the potions and the motions. Shall I lose my parson, my priest, my Sir Hugh? no; he gives me the proverbs and the noverbs.—Give me thy hand, terrestrial; so. —Give me thy hand, celestial; so.—Boys of art, I have deceived you both; I have directed you to wrong places: your hearts are mighty, your skins are whole, and let burnt sack be the issue.—Come, lay their swords to pawn.—Follow me, lads of peace; follow, follow, follow.

SHALLOW.
Trust me, a mad host.—Follow, gentlemen, follow.

SLENDER [aside].
O sweet Anne Page!

[Exeunt SHALLOW, SLENDER, PAGE, and HOST.

DOCTOR CAIUS.
Ha, do I perceive dat? have you make-a de sot of us, ha, ha?

SIR HUGH EVANS.
This is well; he has made us his vlouting stog.—I desire you that we may be friends; and let us knog our prains together to be revenge on this same scall, scurvy, cogging companion; the host of the Garter.

DOCTOR CAIUS.
By gar, vit all my heart. He promise to bring me vere is Anne Page; by gar, he deceive me too.

SIR HUGH EVANS.
Well, I will smite his noddles. Pray you, follow.

[Exeunt.

SCENE II.

The street, in Windsor.

Enter MISTRESS PAGE and ROBIN.

MISTRESS PAGE.
NAY, keep your way, little gallant; you were wont to be a follower, but now you are a leader. Whether had you rather lead mine eyes, or eye your master's heels?

ROBIN.
I had rather, forsooth, go before you like a man than follow him like a dwarf.

MISTRESS PAGE.
O, you are a flattering boy: now I see you'll be a courtier.

Enter FORD.

FORD.

Well met, Mistress Page. Whither go you?

MISTRESS PAGE.

Truly, sir, to see your wife. Is she at home?

FORD.

Ay, and as idle as she may hang together, for want of company. I think, if your husbands were dead, you two would marry.

MISTRESS PAGE.

Be sure of that,—two other husbands.

FORD.

Where had you this pretty weathercock?

MISTRESS PAGE.

I cannot tell what the dickens his name is my husband had him of.—What do you call your knight's name, sirrah?

ROBIN.

Sir John Falstaff.

FORD.

Sir John Falstaff!

MISTRESS PAGE.

He, he; I can never hit on's name.—There is such a league between my good man and he!—Is your wife at home indeed?

FORD.

Indeed she is.

MISTRESS PAGE.

By your leave, sir: I am sick till I see her.

[*Exeunt* MISTRESS PAGE *and* ROBIN.

FORD.

Has Page any brains? hath he any eyes? hath he any thinking? Sure, they sleep; he hath no use of them. Why, this boy will carry a letter twenty mile, as easy as a cannon will shoot point-blank twelve score. He pieces out his wife's inclination; he gives her folly motion and advantage: and now she's going to my wife, and Falstaff's boy with her:—a man may hear this shower sing in the wind:—and Falstaff's boy with her!—Good plots! —they are laid; and our revolted wives share damnation together. Well; I will take him, then torture my wife, pluck the borrow'd veil of modesty from the so seeming Mistress Page, divulge Page himself for a secure and wilful Actæon; and to these violent proceedings all my neighbours shall cry aim. [*Clock strikes.*] The clock gives me my cue, and my assurance bids me search: there I shall find Falstaff: I shall be rather praised for this than mock'd; for it is as positive as the earth is firm that Falstaff is there: I will go.

Enter PAGE, SHALLOW, SLENDER, HOST, SIR HUGH EVANS, CAIUS, *and* RUGBY.

SHALLOW, PAGE, &C.

Well met, Master Ford.

FORD.

Trust me, a good knot: I have good cheer at home; and I pray you all, go with me.

SHALLOW.

I must excuse myself, Master Ford.

SLENDER.

And so must I, sir: we have appointed to dine with Mistress Anne, and I would not break with her for more money than I'll speak of.

SHALLOW.

We have linger'd about a match between Anne

Page and my cousin Slender, and this day we shall have our answer.

SLENDER.

I hope I have your good will, father Page.

PAGE.

You have, Master Slender; I stand wholly for you:—but my wife, master doctor, is for you altogether.

DOCTOR CAIUS.

Ay, by gar; and de maid is love-a me; my nursh-a Quickly tell me so mush.

HOST.

What say you to young Master Fenton? he capers, he dances, he has eyes of youth, he writes verses, he speaks holiday, he smells April and May: he will carry't, he will carry't; 'tis in his buttons; he will carry't.

PAGE.

Not by my consent, I promise you. The gentleman is of no having: he kept company with the wild prince and Pointz; he is of too high a region; he knows too much. No, he shall not knit a knot in his fortunes with the finger of my substance: if he take her, let him take her simply; the wealth I have waits on my consent, and my consent goes not that way.

FORD.

I beseech you heartily, some of you go home with me to dinner: besides your cheer, you shall have sport; I will show you a monster.—Master doctor, you shall go;—so shall you, Master Page;—and you, Sir Hugh.

SHALLOW.

Well, fare you well: we shall have the freer wooing at Master Page's.

[*Exeunt* SHALLOW *and* SLENDER.

DOCTOR CAIUS.

Go home, John Rugby; I come anon.

[*Exit* RUGBY.

HOST.

Farewell, my hearts: I will to my honest knight Falstaff, and drink canary with him. [*Exit.*

FORD [*aside*].

I think I shall drink in pipe-wine first with him; I'll make him dance.—Will you go, gentles?

ALL.

Have with you to see this monster. [*Exeunt.*

SCENE III.

A room in FORD'S *house.*

Enter MISTRESS FORD *and* MISTRESS PAGE.

MISTRESS FORD.

WHAT, John! What, Robert!

MISTRESS PAGE.

Quickly, quickly:—is the buck-basket—

MISTRESS FORD.

I warrant.—What, Robin, I say!

Enter SERVANTS *with a basket.*

MISTRESS PAGE.

Come, come, come.

MISTRESS FORD.

Here, set it down.

MISTRESS PAGE.

Give your men the charge: we must be brief.

MISTRESS FORD.

Marry, as I told you before, John and Robert, be ready here hard by in the brew-house; and when I suddenly call you, come forth, and, without any pause or staggering, take this basket on your shoulders: that done, trudge with it in all haste, and carry it among the whitsters in Datchet-mead, and there empty it in the muddy ditch close by the Thames side.

MISTRESS PAGE.

You will do it?

MISTRESS FORD.

I ha' told them over and over; they lack no direction.—Be gone, and come when you are called.   [Exeunt SERVANTS.

MISTRESS PAGE.

Here comes little Robin.

Enter ROBIN.

MISTRESS FORD.

How now, my eyas-musket! what news with you?

ROBIN.

My master, Sir John, is come in at your back-door, Mistress Ford, and requests your company.

MISTRESS PAGE.

You little Jack-a-Lent, have you been true to us?

ROBIN.

Ay, I'll be sworn. My master knows not of your being here, and hath threaten'd to put me into everlasting liberty, if I tell you of it; for he swears he'll turn me away.

MISTRESS PAGE.

Thou'rt a good boy: this secrecy of thine shall be a tailor to thee, and shall make thee a new doublet and hose.—I'll go hide me.

MISTRESS FORD.

Do so.—Go tell thy master I am alone.—Mistress Page, remember you your cue.

[Exit ROBIN.

MISTRESS PAGE.

I warrant thee; if I do not act it, hiss me.   [Exit.

MISTRESS FORD.

Go to, then: we'll use this unwholesome humidity, this gross watery pumpion; we'll teach him to know turtles from jays.

Enter FALSTAFF.

SIR JOHN FALSTAFF.

Have I caught thee, my heavenly jewel? Why, now let me die, for I have lived long enough; this is the period of my ambition: O this blessed hour!

MISTRESS FORD.

O sweet Sir John!

SIR JOHN FALSTAFF.

Mistress Ford, I cannot cog, I cannot prate, Mistress Ford. Now shall I sin in my wish,—I would thy husband were dead; I'll speak it before the best lord,—I would make thee my lady.

MISTRESS FORD.

I your lady, Sir John! alas, I should be a pitiful lady!

SIR JOHN FALSTAFF.

Let the court of France show me such another. I see how thine eye would emulate the diamond: thou hast the right arch'd beauty of the brow that becomes the ship-tire, the tire-valiant, or any tire of Venetian admittance.

MISTRESS FORD.

A plain kerchief, Sir John: my brows become nothing else; nor that well neither.

SIR JOHN FALSTAFF.

By the Lord, thou art a traitor to say so: thou wouldst make an absolute courtier; and the firm fixture of thy foot would give an excellent motion to thy gait in a semi-circled farthingale. I see what thou wert, if Fortune thy foe were not, Nature thy friend. Come, thou canst not hide it.

MISTRESS FORD.

Believe me, there's no such thing in me.

SIR JOHN FALSTAFF.

What made me love thee? let that persuade thee there's something extraordinary in thee. Come, I cannot cog, and say thou art this and that, like a many of these lisping hawthorn-buds, that come like women in men's apparel, and smell like Bucklersbury in simple-time; I cannot: but I love thee; none but thee; and thou deservest it.

MISTRESS FORD.

Do not betray me, sir. I fear you love Mistress Page.

SIR JOHN FALSTAFF.

Thou mightst as well say I love to walk by the Counter-gate, which is as hateful to me as the reek of a lime-kiln.

MISTRESS FORD.

Well, heaven knows how I love you; and you shall one day find it.

SIR JOHN FALSTAFF.

Keep in that mind; I'll deserve it.

MISTRESS FORD.

Nay, I must tell you, so you do; or else I could not be in that mind.

ROBIN [within].

Mistress Ford, Mistress Ford! here's Mistress Page at the door, sweating, and blowing, and looking wildly, and would needs speak with you presently.

SIR JOHN FALSTAFF.

She shall not see me: I will ensconce me behind the arras.

MISTRESS FORD.

Pray you, do so: she's a very tattling woman.

[FALSTAFF hides himself behind the arras.

Enter MISTRESS PAGE and ROBIN.

What's the matter? how now!

MISTRESS PAGE.

O Mistress Ford, what have you done? You're shamed, you're overthrown, you're undone for ever!

MISTRESS FORD.

What's the matter, good Mistress Page?

MISTRESS PAGE.

O well-a-day, Mistress Ford! having an honest man to your husband, to give him such cause of suspicion!

MISTRESS FORD.

What cause of suspicion?

MISTRESS PAGE.

What cause of suspicion! Out upon you! how am I mistook in you!

MISTRESS FORD.

Why, alas, what's the matter?

MISTRESS PAGE.

Your husband's coming hither, woman, with all the officers in Windsor, to search for a gentleman that he says is here now in the house, by your consent, to take an ill advantage of his absence: you are undone.

MISTRESS FORD.

'Tis not so, I hope.

MISTRESS PAGE.

Pray heaven it be not so, that you have such a man here! but 'tis most certain your husband's coming, with half Windsor at his heels, to search for such a one. I come before to tell you. If you know yourself clear, why, I am glad of it; but if you have a friend here, convey, convey him out. Be not amazed; call all your senses to you; defend your reputation, or bid farewell to your good life for ever.

MISTRESS FORD.

What shall I do?—There is a gentleman my dear friend; and I fear not mine own shame so much as his peril! I had rather than a thousand pound he were out of the house.

MISTRESS PAGE.

For shame! never stand 'you had rather' and 'you had rather:' your husband's here at hand; bethink you of some conveyance: in the house you cannot hide him.—O, how have you deceived me!—Look, here is a basket: if he be of any reasonable stature, he may creep in here; and throw foul linen upon him, as if it were going to bucking: or, —it is whiting-time,—send him by your two men to Datchet-mead.

MISTRESS FORD.

He's too big to go in there. What shall I do?

Enter FALSTAFF.

SIR JOHN FALSTAFF.

Let me see't, let me see't, O, let me see't!—I'll in, I'll in:—follow your friend's counsel:—I'll in.

MISTRESS PAGE.

What, Sir John Falstaff! Are these your letters, knight?

SIR JOHN FALSTAFF [*aside to* MISTRESS PAGE].

I love thee, and none but thee:—[*aloud*] help me away: let me creep in here. I'll never—

[*Goes into the basket; they cover him with foul linen.*

MISTRESS PAGE.

Help to cover your master, boy.—Call your men, Mistress Ford.—You dissembling knight!

[*Exit* ROBIN.

MISTRESS FORD.

What, John! Robert! John!

Enter SERVANTS.

Go take up these clothes here quickly:—where's the cowl-staff? look, how you drumble!—carry them to the laundress in Datchet-mead; quickly, come.

Enter FORD, PAGE, CAIUS, *and* SIR HUGH EVANS.

FORD.

Pray you, come near: if I suspect without cause, why then make sport at me; then let me be your jest; I deserve it.—How now! whither bear you this?

SERVANTS.

To the laundress, forsooth.

MISTRESS FORD.

Why, what have you to do whither they bear it? You were best meddle with buck-washing.

FORD.

Buck!—I would I could wash myself of the buck! —Buck, buck, buck! Ay, buck; I warrant you, buck; and of the season too, it shall appear. [*Exeunt* SERVANTS *with the basket.*]—Gentlemen, I have dream'd to-night; I'll tell you my dream. Here, here, here be my keys: ascend my chambers; search, seek, find out: I'll warrant we'll unkennel the fox.—Let me stop this way first [*Locks the door*].—So, now uncape.

PAGE.

Good Master Ford, be contented: you wrong yourself too much.

FORD.

True, Master Page.—Up, gentlemen; you shall see sport anon: follow me, gentlemen. [*Exit.*

SIR HUGH EVANS.

This is fery fantastical humours and jealousies.

DOCTOR CAIUS.

By gar, 'tis no de fashion of France; it is not jealous in France.

PAGE.

Nay, follow him, gentlemen; see the issue of his search.

[*Exeunt* PAGE, CAIUS, *and* EVANS.

MISTRESS PAGE.

Is there not a double excellency in this?

MISTRESS FORD.

I know not which pleases me better, that my husband is deceived, or Sir John.

MISTRESS PAGE.

What a taking was he in when your husband asked what was in the basket!

MISTRESS FORD.

I am half afraid he will have need of washing; so throwing him into the water will do him a benefit.

MISTRESS PAGE.

Hang him, dishonest rascal! I would all of the same strain were in the same distress.

MISTRESS FORD.

I think my husband hath some special suspicion of Falstaff's being here; for I never saw him so gross in his jealousy till now.

MISTRESS PAGE.

I will lay a plot to try that; and we will yet have more tricks with Falstaff; his dissolute disease will scarce obey this medicine.

MISTRESS FORD.

Shall we send that foolish carrion Mistress Quickly to him, and excuse his throwing into the water; and give him another hope, to betray him to another punishment?

MISTRESS PAGE.

We will do it: let him be sent for to-morrow eight o'clock, to have amends.

Enter FORD, PAGE, CAIUS, *and* SIR HUGH EVANS.

FORD.

I cannot find him: may be the knave bragg'd of that he could not compass.

MISTRESS PAGE [*aside to* MISTRESS FORD].
Heard you that?
MISTRESS FORD [*aside to* MISTRESS PAGE].
Ay, ay, peace.—You use me well, Master Ford,
do you?
FORD.
Ay, I do so.
MISTRESS FORD.
Heaven make you better than your thoughts!
FORD.
Amen!
MISTRESS PAGE.
You do yourself mighty wrong, Master Ford.
FORD.
Ay, ay; I must bear it.
SIR HUGH EVANS.
If there be any pody in the house, and in the
chambers, and in the coffers, and in the presses,
heaven forgive my sins at the day of judg-
ment!
DOCTOR CAIUS.
By gar, nor I too: dere is no bodies.
PAGE.
Fie, fie, Master Ford! are you not ashamed? What
spirit, what devil suggests this imagination? I
would not ha' your distemper in this kind for the
wealth of Windsor Castle.
FORD.
'Tis my fault, Master Page: I suffer for it.
SIR HUGH EVANS.
You suffer for a pad conscience: your wife is as
honest a omans as I will desires among five
thousand, and five hundred too.
DOCTOR CAIUS.
By gar, I see 'tis an honest woman.
FORD.
Well;—I promised you a dinner:—come, come,
walk in the Park: I pray you, pardon me; I will
hereafter make known to you why I have done
this.—Come, wife;—come, Mistress Page.—I
pray you, pardon me; pray heartily, pardon
me.
PAGE.
Let's go in, gentleman; but, trust me, we'll mock
him. I do invite you to-morrow morning to my
house to breakfast; after, we'll a-birding together;
I have a fine hawk for the bush. Shall it be
so?
FORD.
Any thing.
SIR HUGH EVANS.
If there is one, I shall make two in the company.
DOCTOR CAIUS.
If dere be one or two, I shall make-a de turd.
SIR HUGH EVANS.
In your teeth: for shame!
FORD.
Pray you, go, Master Page.
SIR HUGH EVANS.
I pray you now, remembrance to-morrow on the
lousy knave, mine host.
DOCTOR CAIUS.
Dat is good; by gar, vit all my heart.
SIR HUGH EVANS.
A lousy knave, to have his gibes and his mock-
eries!　　　　　　　　　　　　　　　[*Exeunt.*

SCENE IV.
A room in PAGE'S *house.*
Enter FENTON *and* ANNE PAGE.

FENTON.
I SEE I cannot get thy father's love;
Therefore no more turn me to him, sweet Nan.
ANNE PAGE.
Alas, how then?
FENTON.
Why, thou must be thyself.
He doth object I am too great of birth;
And that, my state being gall'd with my expense,
I seek to heal it only by his wealth:
Besides these, other bars he lays before me,—
My riots past, my wild societies;
And tells me 'tis a thing impossible
I should love thee but as a property.
ANNE PAGE.
May be he tells you true.
FENTON.
No, heaven so speed me in my time to come!
Albeit, I will confess, thy father's wealth
Was the first motive that I woo'd thee, Anne:
Yet, wooing thee, I found thee of more value
Than stamps in gold or sums in sealed bags;
And 'tis the very riches of thyself
That now I aim at.
ANNE PAGE.
　　　　　　　Gentle Master Fenton,
Yet seek my father's love; still seek it, sir:
If opportunity and humblest suit
Cannot attain it, why, then—Hark you hither.
　　　　　　　　　　[*They converse apart.*
Enter SHALLOW, SLENDER, *and* MISTRESS
QUICKLY.
SHALLOW.
Break their talk, Mistress Quickly: my kinsman
shall speak for himself.
SLENDER.
I'll make a shaft or a bolt on't: slid, 'tis but ven-
turing.
SHALLOW.
Be not dismay'd.
SLENDER.
No, she shall not dismay me: I care not for that,
—but that I am afeard.
MISTRESS QUICKLY.
Hark ye: Master Slender would speak a word
with you.
ANNE PAGE.
I come to him.—[*aside*] This is my father's
choice.
O, what a world of vile ill-favour'd faults
Looks handsome in three hundred pounds a-year!
MISTRESS QUICKLY.
And how does good Master Fenton? Pray you, a
word with you.
SHALLOW.
She's coming; to her, coz. O boy, thou hadst a
father!
SLENDER.
I had a father, Mistress Anne;—my uncle can tell
you good jests of him.—Pray you, uncle, tell
Mistress Anne the jest, how my father stole two
geese out of a pen, good uncle.

SHALLOW.

Mistress Anne, my cousin loves you.

SLENDER.

Ay, that I do; as well as I love any woman in Glostershire.

SHALLOW.

He will maintain you like a gentlewoman.

SLENDER.

Ay, that I will, come cut and long-tail, under the degree of a squire.

SHALLOW.

He will make you a hundred and fifty pounds jointure.

ANNE PAGE.

Good Master Shallow, let him woo for himself.

SHALLOW.

Marry, I thank you for it; I thank you for that good comfort.—She calls you, coz: I'll leave you.

ANNE PAGE.

Now, Master Slender,—

SLENDER.

Now, good Mistress Anne,—

ANNE PAGE.

What is your will?

SLENDER.

My will! od's heartlings, that's a pretty jest indeed! I ne'er made my will yet, I thank heaven; I am not such a sickly creature, I give heaven praise.

ANNE PAGE.

I mean, Master Slender, what would you with me?

SLENDER.

Truly, for mine own part, I would little or nothing with you. Your father and my uncle hath made motions: if it be my luck, so; if not, happy man be his dole! They can tell you how things go better than I can: you may ask your father; here he comes.

Enter PAGE *and* MISTRESS PAGE.

PAGE.

Now, Master Slender:—love him, daughter Anne.—

Why, how now! what does Master Fenton here? You wrong me, sir, thus still to haunt my house: I told you, sir, my daughter is disposed of.

FENTON.

Nay, Master Page, be not impatient.

MISTRESS PAGE.

Good Master Fenton, come not to my child.

PAGE.

She is no match for you.

FENTON.

Sir, will you hear me?

PAGE.

No, good Master Fenton.— Come, Master Shallow; come, son Slender; in.— Knowing my mind, you wrong me, Master Fenton.

[*Exeunt* PAGE, SHALLOW, *and* SLENDER.

MISTRESS QUICKLY.

Speak to Mistress Page.

FENTON.

Good Mistress Page, for that I love your daughter In such a righteous fashion as I do,

Perforce, against all checks, rebukes, and manners, I must advance the colours of my love, And not retire: let me have your good will.

ANNE PAGE.

Good mother, do not marry me to yond fool.

MISTRESS PAGE.

I mean it not; I seek you a better husband.

MISTRESS QUICKLY.

That's my master, master doctor.

ANNE PAGE.

Alas, I had rather be set quick i'th'earth, And bowl'd to death with turnips!

MISTRESS PAGE.

Come, trouble not yourself.—Good Master Fenton, I will not be your friend nor enemy: My daughter will I question how she loves you, And as I find her, so am I affected. Till then farewell, sir: she must needs go in; Her father will be angry.

FENTON.

Farewell, gentle mistress.—Farewell, Nan.

[*Exeunt* MISTRESS PAGE *and* ANNE PAGE.

MISTRESS QUICKLY.

This is my doing now:—'Nay,' said I, 'will you cast away your child on a fool and a physician? Look on Master Fenton:'—this is my doing.

FENTON.

I thank thee; and I pray thee, once to-night Give my sweet Nan this ring: there's for thy pains.

MISTRESS QUICKLY.

Now heaven send thee good fortune! [*Exit* FENTON.] A kind heart he hath: a woman would run through fire and water for such a kind heart. But yet I would my master had Mistress Anne; or I would Master Slender had her; or, in sooth, I would Master Fenton had her: I will do what I can for them all three; for so I have promised, and I'll be as good as my word; but speciously for Master Fenton. Well, I must of another errand to Sir John Falstaff from my two mistresses: what a beast am I to slack it! [*Exit.*

SCENE V.

A room in the Garter Inn.

Enter FALSTAFF *and* BARDOLPH.

SIR JOHN FALSTAFF.

BARDOLPH, I say,—

BARDOLPH.

Here, sir.

SIR JOHN FALSTAFF.

Go fetch me a quart of sack; put a toast in't. [*Exit* BARDOLPH.] Have I lived to be carried in a basket, like a barrow of butcher's offal, and to be thrown in the Thames? Well, if I be served such another trick, I'll have my brains ta'en out, and butter'd, and give them to a dog for a new-year's gift. The rogues slighted me into the river with as little remorse as they would have drown'd a bitch's blind puppies, fifteen i'th'litter: and you may know by my size that I have a kind of alacrity in sinking; if the bottom were as deep as hell, I should down. I had been drown'd, but that the shore was shelvy and shallow,—a death that I abhor; for the water swells a man; and what a thing should I have been when I had been swell'd! I should have been a mountain of mummy.

Enter BARDOLPH *with sack.*

BARDOLPH.

Here's Mistress Quickly, sir, to speak with you.

SIR JOHN FALSTAFF.

Come, let me pour in some sack to the Thames water; for my belly's as cold as if I had swallow'd snowballs for pills to cool the reins. Call her in.

BARDOLPH.

Come in, woman!

Enter MISTRESS QUICKLY.

MISTRESS QUICKLY.

By your leave; I cry you mercy:—give your worship good morrow.

SIR JOHN FALSTAFF.

Take away these chalices. Go brew me a pottle of sack finely.

BARDOLPH.

With eggs, sir?

SIR JOHN FALSTAFF.

Simple of itself; I'll no pullet-sperm in my brewage. [*Exit* BARDOLPH.] How now!

MISTRESS QUICKLY.

Marry, sir, I come to your worship from Mistress Ford.

SIR JOHN FALSTAFF.

Mistress Ford! I have had ford enough; I was thrown into the ford; I have my belly full of ford.

MISTRESS QUICKLY.

Alas the day! good heart, that was not her fault: she does so take on with her men; they mistook their erection.

SIR JOHN FALSTAFF.

So did I mine, to build upon a foolish woman's promise.

MISTRESS QUICKLY.

Well, she laments, sir, for it, that it would yearn your heart to see it. Her husband goes this morning a-birding; she desires you once more to come to her between eight and nine: I must carry her word quickly: she'll make you amends, I warrant you.

SIR JOHN FALSTAFF.

Well, I will visit her: tell her so; and bid her think what a man is: let her consider his frailty, and then judge of my merit.

MISTRESS QUICKLY.

I will tell her.

SIR JOHN FALSTAFF.

Do so. Between nine and ten, say'st thou?

MISTRESS QUICKLY.

Eight and nine, sir.

SIR JOHN FALSTAFF.

Well, be gone: I will not miss her.

MISTRESS QUICKLY.

Peace be with you, sir.   [*Exit.*

SIR JOHN FALSTAFF.

I marvel I hear not of Master Brook; he sent me word to stay within: I like his money well.—O, here he comes.

Enter FORD *disguised.*

FORD.

Bless you, sir!

SIR JOHN FALSTAFF.

Now, Master Brook,—you come to know what hath pass'd between me and Ford's wife?

FORD.

That, indeed, Sir John, is my business.

SIR JOHN FALSTAFF.

Master Brook, I will not lie to you: I was at her house the hour she appointed me.

FORD.

And how sped you, sir?

SIR JOHN FALSTAFF.

Very ill-favour'dly, Master Brook.

FORD.

How so, sir? Did she change her determination?

SIR JOHN FALSTAFF.

No, Master Brook; but the peaking cornuto her husband, Master Brook, dwelling in a continual 'larum of jealousy, comes me in the instant of our encounter, after we had embraced, kiss'd, protested, and, as it were, spoke the prologue of our comedy; and at his heels a rabble of his companions, thither provoked and instigated by his distemper, and, forsooth, to search his house for his wife's love.

FORD.

What, while you were there?

SIR JOHN FALSTAFF.

While I was there.

FORD.

And did he search for you, and could not find you?

SIR JOHN FALSTAFF.

You shall hear. As good luck would have it, comes in one Mistress Page; gives intelligence of Ford's approach; and, in her invention and Ford's wife's distraction, they convey'd me into a buck-basket.

FORD.

A buck-basket!

SIR JOHN FALSTAFF.

By the Lord, a buck-basket!—ramm'd me in with foul shirts and smocks, socks, foul stockings, greasy napkins; that, Master Brook, there was the rankest compound of villainous smell that ever offended nostril.

FORD.

And how long lay you there?

SIR JOHN FALSTAFF.

Nay, you shall hear, Master Brook, what I have suffer'd to bring this woman to evil for your good. Being thus cramm'd in the basket, a couple of Ford's knaves, his hinds, were call'd forth by their mistress to carry me in the name of foul clothes to Datchet-lane: they took me on their shoulders; met the jealous knave their master in the door, who asked them once or twice what they had in their basket: I quaked for fear, lest the lunatic knave would have search'd it; but fate, ordaining he should be a cuckold, held his hand. Well: on went he for a search, and away went I for foul clothes. But mark the sequel, Master Brook: I suffer'd the pangs of three several deaths; first, an intolerable fright, to be detected with a jealous rotten bell-wether; next, to be compass'd, like a good bilbo, in the circumference of a peck, hilt to point, heel to head; and then, to be stopt in, like a strong distillation, with stinking clothes that fretted in their own grease: think of that,—a man of my kidney,—think of that,—that am as subject to heat as butter; a man of cont.nual dissolution and thaw;—it was a miracle to scape suffocation. And in the height of this bath, when I was more than half stew'd in grease, like a Dutch dish, to be thrown into the Thames, and cool'd, glowing hot, in that surge, like a horse-shoe; think of that,—hissing hot,—think of that, Master Brook.

FORD.

In good sadness, sir, I am sorry that for my sake you have suffer'd all this. My suit, then, is desperate; you'll undertake her no more?

SIR JOHN FALSTAFF.

Master Brook, I will be thrown into Etna, as I have been into Thames, ere I will leave her thus. Her husband is this morning gone a-birding: I have received from her another embassy of meeting; 'twixt eight and nine is the hour, Master Brook.

FORD.

'Tis past eight already, sir.

SIR JOHN FALSTAFF.

Is it? I will then address me to my appointment. Come to me at your convenient leisure, and you shall know how I speed; and the conclusion shall be crown'd with your enjoying her. Adieu. You shall have her, Master Brook; Master Brook, you shall cuckold Ford. [*Exit.*

FORD.

Hum,—ha! is this a vision? is this a dream? do I sleep? Master Ford, awake! awake, Master Ford! there's a hole made in your best coat, Master Ford. This 'tis to be married! this 'tis to have linen and buck-baskets!—Well, I will proclaim myself what I am: I will now take the lecher; he is at my house; he cannot scape me; 'tis impossible he should; he cannot creep into a halfpenny purse, nor into a pepper-box: but, lest the devil that guides him should aid him, I will search impossible places. Though what I am I cannot avoid, yet to be what I would not shall not make me tame: if I have horns to make one mad, let the proverb go with me,—I'll be horn-mad. [*Exit.*

ACT IV. SCENE I.

The street.

Enter MISTRESS PAGE, MISTRESS QUICKLY, *and* WILLIAM.

MISTRESS PAGE.

IS he at Master Ford's already, think'st thou?

MISTRESS QUICKLY.

Sure he is by this, or will be presently: but, truly, he is very courageous mad about his throwing into the water. Mistress Ford desires you to come suddenly.

MISTRESS PAGE.

I'll be with her by and by; I'll but bring my young man here to school. Look, where his master comes: 'tis a playing-day, I see.

Enter SIR HUGH EVANS.

How now, Sir Hugh! no school to-day?

SIR HUGH EVANS.

No; Master Slender is let the boys leave to play.

MISTRESS QUICKLY.

Blessing of his heart!

MISTRESS PAGE.

Sir Hugh, my husband says my son profits nothing in the world at his book. I pray you, ask him some questions in his accidence.

SIR HUGH EVANS.

Come hither, William; hold up your head; come.

MISTRESS PAGE.

Come on, sirrah; hold up your head; answer your master, be not afraid.

SIR HUGH EVANS.

William, how many numbers is in nouns?

WILLIAM PAGE.

Two.

MISTRESS QUICKLY.

Truly, I thought there had been one number more, because they say, Od's-nouns.

SIR HUGH EVANS.

Peace your tattlings.—What is *fair*, William?

WILLIAM PAGE.

Pulcher.

MISTRESS QUICKLY.

Polecats! there are fairer things than polecats, sure.

SIR HUGH EVANS.

You are a very simplicity oman: I pray you, peace.—What is *lapis*, William?

WILLIAM PAGE.

A stone.

SIR HUGH EVANS.

And what is a stone, William?

WILLIAM PAGE.

A pebble.

SIR HUGH EVANS.

No, it is *lapis:* I pray you, remember in your prain.

WILLIAM PAGE.

Lapis.

SIR HUGH EVANS.

That is a good William. What is he, William, that does lend articles?

WILLIAM PAGE.

Articles are borrowed of the pronoun, and be thus declined, *Singulariter, nominativo, hic, hæc, hoc.*

SIR HUGH EVANS.

Nominativo, hig, hag, hog;—pray you, mark: *genitivo, hujus.* Well, what is your accusative case?

WILLIAM PAGE.

Accusativo, hinc.

SIR HUGH EVANS.

I pray you, have your remembrance, child; *accusativo, hung, hang, hog.*

MISTRESS QUICKLY.

Hang-hog is Latin for bacon, I warrant you.

SIR HUGH EVANS.

Leave your prabbles, oman.—What is the focative case, William?

WILLIAM PAGE.

O,—vocativo, O.

SIR HUGH EVANS.

Remember, William; focative is *caret.*

MISTRESS QUICKLY.

And that's a good root.

SIR HUGH EVANS.

Oman, forbear.

MISTRESS PAGE.

Peace!

SIR HUGH EVANS.

What is your genitive case plural, William?

WILLIAM PAGE.

Genitive case!

SIR HUGH EVANS.

Ay.

WILLIAM PAGE.

Genitivo,—horum, harum, horum.

MISTRESS QUICKLY.

Vengeance of Jenny's case! fie on her!—never name her, child, if she be a whore.

SIR HUGH EVANS.

For shame, oman.

MISTRESS QUICKLY.

You do ill to teach the child such words:—he teaches him to hick and to hack, which they'll do fast enough of themselves, and to call whorum:—fie upon you!

SIR HUGH EVANS.

Oman, art thou lunatics? hast thou no understandings for thy cases, and the numbers of the genders? Thou art as foolish Christian creatures as I would desires.

MISTRESS PAGE.

Prithee, hold thy peace.

SIR HUGH EVANS.

Show me now, William, some declensions of your pronouns.

WILLIAM PAGE.

Forsooth, I have forgot.

SIR HUGH EVANS.

It is *qui, quæ, quod:* if you forget your *quies,* your *quæs,* and your *quods,* you must be preeches. Go your ways, and play; go.

MISTRESS PAGE.

He is a better scholar than I thought he was.

SIR HUGH EVANS.

He is a good sprag memory. Farewell, Mistress Page.

MISTRESS PAGE.

Adieu, good Sir Hugh. [*Exit* EVANS.]—Get you home, boy.—Come, we stay too long.   [*Exeunt.*

SCENE II.

A room in FORD'S *house.*

Enter FALSTAFF *and* MISTRESS FORD.

SIR JOHN FALSTAFF.

MISTRESS FORD, your sorrow hath eaten up my sufferance. I see you are obsequious in your love, and I profess requital to a hair's breadth; not only, Mistress Ford, in the simple office of love, but in all the accoutrement, complement, and ceremony of it. But are you sure of your husband now?

MISTRESS FORD.

He's a-birding, sweet Sir John.

MISTRESS PAGE [*within*].

What, ho, gossip Ford! what, ho!

MISTRESS FORD.

Step into the chamber, Sir John.

[*Exit* FALSTAFF.

Enter MISTRESS PAGE.

MISTRESS PAGE.

How now, sweetheart! who's at home besides yourself?

MISTRESS FORD.

Why, none but mine own people.

MISTRESS PAGE.

Indeed!

MISTRESS FORD.

No, certainly.—[*Aside to her*] Speak louder.

MISTRESS PAGE.

Truly, I am so glad you have nobody here.

MISTRESS FORD.

Why?

MISTRESS PAGE.

Why, woman, your husband is in his old lunes again: he so takes on yonder with my husband; so rails against all married mankind; so curses all Eve's daughters, of what complexion soever; and so buffets himself on the forehead, crying, ' Peer out, peer out!' that any madness I ever yet beheld seem'd but tameness, civility, and patience, to this his distemper he is in now: I am glad the fat knight is not here.

MISTRESS FORD.

Why, does he talk of him?

MISTRESS PAGE.

Of none but him; and swears he was carried out, the last time he search'd for him, in a basket; protests to my husband he is now here; and hath drawn him and the rest of their company from their sport, to make another experiment of his suspicion: but I am glad the knight is not here; now he shall see his own foolery.

MISTRESS FORD.

How near is he, Mistress Page?

MISTRESS PAGE.

Hard by; at street end; he will be here anon.

MISTRESS FORD.

I am undone!—the knight is here.

MISTRESS PAGE.

Why, then, you are utterly shamed, and he's but a dead man. What a woman are you!—Away with him, away with him! better shame than murder.

MISTRESS FORD.

Which way should he go? how should I bestow him? Shall I put him into the basket again?

Enter FALSTAFF.

SIR JOHN FALSTAFF.

No, I'll come no more i'th'basket. May I not go out ere he come?

MISTRESS PAGE.

Alas, three of Master Ford's brothers watch the door with pistols, that none shall issue out; otherwise you might slip away ere he came. But what make you here?

SIR JOHN FALSTAFF.

What shall I do?—I'll creep up into the chimney.

MISTRESS FORD.

There they always use to discharge their birding-pieces.

MISTRESS PAGE.

Creep into the kiln-hole.

SIR JOHN FALSTAFF.

Where is it?

MISTRESS FORD.

He will seek there, on my word. Neither press, coffer, chest, trunk, well, vault, but he hath an abstract for the remembrance of such places, and goes to them by his note: there is no hiding you in the house.

SIR JOHN FALSTAFF.

I'll go out, then.

MISTRESS PAGE.

If you go out in your own semblance, you die, Sir John. Unless you go out disguised,—

MISTRESS FORD.

How might we disguise him?

MISTRESS PAGE.

Alas the day, I know not! There is no woman's gown big enough for him; otherwise he might put on a hat, a muffler, and a kerchief, and so escape.

SIR JOHN FALSTAFF.

Good hearts, devise something: any extremity rather than a mischief.

MISTRESS FORD.

My maid's aunt, the fat woman of Brainford, has a gown above.

MISTRESS PAGE.

On my word, it will serve him; she's as big as he is: and there's her thrumm'd hat, and her muffler too.—Run up, Sir John.

MISTRESS FORD.

Go, go, sweet Sir John: Mistress Page and I will look some linen for your head.

MISTRESS PAGE.

Quick, quick! we'll come dress you straight: put on the gown the while.   [Exit FALSTAFF.

MISTRESS FORD.

I would my husband would meet him in this shape: he cannot abide the old woman of Brainford; he swears she's a witch; forbade her my house, and hath threaten'd to beat her.

MISTRESS PAGE.

Heaven guide him to thy husband's cudgel, and the devil guide his cudgel afterwards!

MISTRESS FORD.

But is my husband coming?

MISTRESS PAGE.

Ay, in good sadness, is he; and talks of the basket too, howsoever he hath had intelligence.

MISTRESS FORD.

We'll try that; for I'll appoint my men to carry the basket again, to meet him at the door with it, as they did last time.

MISTRESS PAGE.

Nay, but he'll be here presently: let's go dress him like the witch of Brainford.

MISTRESS FORD.

I'll first direct my men what they shall do with the basket. Go up; I'll bring linen for him straight.   [Exit.

MISTRESS PAGE.

Hang him, dishonest varlet! we cannot misuse him enough.

We'll leave a proof, by that which we will do,
Wives may be merry, and yet honest too:
We do not act that often jest and laugh;
'Tis old, but true,—Still swine eats all the draff.
          [Exit.

Enter MISTRESS FORD with two SERVANTS.

MISTRESS FORD.

Go, sirs, take the basket again on your shoulders: your master is hard at door; if he bid you set it down, obey him: quickly, dispatch.   [Exit.

FIRST SERVANT.

Come, come, take it up.

SECOND SERVANT.

Pray heaven it be not full of knight again.

FIRST SERVANT.

I hope not; I had as lief bear so much lead.

Enter FORD, PAGE, SHALLOW, CAIUS, and SIR HUGH EVANS.

FORD.

Ay, but if it prove true, Master Page, have you any way then to unfool me again?—Set down the basket, villain!—Somebody call my wife.—You, youth in a basket, come out here!—O you pandarly rascals! there's a knot, a ging, a pack, a conspiracy against me: now shall the devil be shamed.—What, wife, I say! come, come forth! behold what honest clothes you send forth to bleaching!

MISTRESS PAGE.

Why, this passes! Master Ford, you are not to go loose any longer; you must be pinion'd.

SIR HUGH EVANS.

Why, this is lunatics! this is mad as a mad dog!

SHALLOW.

Indeed, Master Ford, this is not well; indeed.

FORD.

So say I too, sir.

Enter MISTRESS FORD.

Come hither, Mistress Ford; Mistress Ford, the honest woman, the modest wife, the virtuous creature, that hath the jealous fool to her husband! —I suspect without cause, mistress, do I?

MISTRESS FORD.

Heaven be my witness you do, if you suspect me in any dishonesty.

FORD.

Well said, brazen-face! hold it out.—Come forth, sirrah!   [Pulling the clothes out of the basket.

PAGE.

This passes!

MISTRESS FORD.

Are you not ashamed? let the clothes alone.

FORD.

I shall find you anon.

SIR HUGH EVANS.

'Tis unreasonable! Will you take up your wife's clothes? Come away.

FORD.

Empty the basket, I say!

MISTRESS FORD.

Why, man, why,—

FORD.

Master Page, as I am a man, there was one convey'd out of my house yesterday in this basket: why may not he be there again? In my house I am sure he is: my intelligence is true; my jealousy is reasonable.—Pluck me out all the linen.

MISTRESS FORD.

If you find a man there, he shall die a flea's death.

PAGE.

Here's no man.

SHALLOW.

By my fidelity, this is not well, Master Ford; this wrongs you.

SIR HUGH EVANS.

Master Ford, you must pray, and not follow the imaginations of your own heart: this is jealousies.

FORD.
Well, he's not here I seek for.

PAGE.
No, nor nowhere else but in your brain.

FORD.
Help to search my house this one time. If I find not what I seek, show no colour for my extremity; let me for ever be your table-sport; let them say of me, 'As jealous as Ford, that search'd a hollow walnut for his wife's leman.' Satisfy me once more; once more search with me.

MISTRESS FORD.
What, ho, Mistress Page! come you and the old woman down; my husband will come into the chamber.

FORD.
Old woman! what old woman's that?

MISTRESS FORD.
Why it is my maid's aunt of Brainford.

FORD.
A witch, a quean, an old cozening quean! Have I not forbid her my house? She comes of errands, does she? We are simple men; we do not know what's brought to pass under the profession of fortune-telling. She works by charms, by spells, by th'figure; and such daubery as this is beyond our element; we know nothing.—Come down, you witch, you hag, you; come down, I say!

MISTRESS FORD.
Nay, good, sweet husband,—Good gentlemen, let him not strike the old woman.

Enter FALSTAFF *in woman's clothes, led by* MISTRESS PAGE.

MISTRESS PAGE.
Come, Mother Prat; come, give me your hand.

FORD.
I'll prat her.—[*Beating him*] Out of my door, you witch, you rag, you baggage, you polecat, you ronyon! out, out! I'll conjure you, I'll fortune-tell you.   [*Exit* FALSTAFF.

MISTRESS PAGE.
Are you not ashamed? I think you have kill'd the poor woman.

MISTRESS FORD.
Nay, he will do it.—'Tis a goodly credit for you.

FORD.
Hang her, witch!

SIR HUGH EVANS.
By yea and no, I think the oman is a witch indeed: I like not when a oman has a great peard: I spy a great peard under her muffler.

FORD.
Will you follow, gentlemen? I beseech you, follow; see but the issue of my jealousy: if I cry out thus upon no trail, never trust me when I open again.

PAGE.
Let's obey his humour a little further: come, gentlemen.

[*Exeunt* FORD, PAGE, SHALLOW, CAIUS, *and* EVANS.

MISTRESS PAGE.
Trust me, he beat him most pitifully.

MISTRESS FORD.
Nay, by th'mass, that he did not; he beat him most unpitifully methought.

MISTRESS PAGE.
I'll have the cudgel hallow'd, and hung o'er the altar; it hath done meritorious service.

MISTRESS FORD.
What think you? may we, with the warrant of womanhood and the witness of a good conscience, pursue him with any further revenge?

MISTRESS PAGE.
The spirit of wantonness is, sure, scared out of him: if the devil have him not in fee-simple, with fine and recovery, he will never, I think, in the way of waste, attempt us again.

MISTRESS FORD.
Shall we tell our husbands how we have served him?

MISTRESS PAGE.
Yes, by all means; if it be but to scrape the figures out of your husband's brains. If they can find in their hearts the poor unvirtuous fat knight shall be any further afflicted, we two will still be the ministers.

MISTRESS FORD.
I'll warrant they'll have him publicly shamed: and methinks there would be no period to the jest, should he not be publicly shamed.

MISTRESS PAGE.
Come, to the forge with it, then; shape it: I would not have things cool.   [*Exeunt.*

SCENE III.

A room in the Garter Inn.

Enter HOST *and* BARDOLPH.

BARDOLPH.
SIR, the Germans desire to have three of your horses: the duke himself will be to-morrow at court, and they are going to meet him.

HOST.
What duke should that be comes so secretly? I hear not of him in the court. Let me speak with the gentlemen: they speak English?

BARDOLPH.
Ay, sir; I'll call them to you.

HOST.
They shall have my horses; but I'll make them pay; I'll sauce them: they have had my house a week at command; I have turn'd away my other guests: they must come off; I'll sauce them. Come.
[*Exeunt*

SCENE IV.

A room in FORD'S *house.*

Enter PAGE, FORD, MISTRESS PAGE, MISTRESS FORD, *and* SIR HUGH EVANS.

SIR HUGH EVANS.
'TIS one of the best discretions of a oman as ever I did look upon.

PAGE.
And did he send you both these letters at an instant?

MISTRESS PAGE.
Within a quarter of an hour.

FORD.
Pardon me, wife. Henceforth do what thou wilt; I rather will suspect the sun with cold

Than thee with wantonness: now doth thy hon-
our stand
In him that was of late an heretic.
As firm as faith.

PAGE.
'Tis well, 'tis well; no more:
Be not as extreme in submission
As in offence.
But let our plot go forward: let our wives
Yet once again, to make us public sport,
Appoint a meeting with this old fat fellow,
Where we may take him, and disgrace him for it.

FORD.
There is no better way than that they spoke of.

PAGE.
How! to send him word they'll meet him in the
Park at midnight? Fie, fie! he'll never come.

SIR HUGH EVANS.
You say he has been thrown in the rivers; and has
been grievously peaten, as an old oman: methinks
there should be terrors in him that he should not
come; methinks his flesh is punish'd, he shall have
no desires.

PAGE.
So think I too.

MISTRESS FORD.
Devise but how you'll use him when he comes,
And let us two devise to bring him thither.

MISTRESS PAGE.
There is an old tale goes that Herne the Hunter,
Sometime a keeper here in Windsor forest,
Doth all the winter-time, at still midnight,
Walk round about an oak, with great ragg'd horns;
And there he blasts the tree, and takes the cattle,
And makes milch-kine yield blood, and shakes a
chain
In a most hideous and dreadful manner:
You have heard of such a spirit; and well you
know
The superstitious idle-headed eld
Received, and did deliver to our age,
This tale of Herne the hunter for a truth.

PAGE.
Why, yet there want not many that do fear
In deep of night to walk by this Herne's oak:
But what of this?

MISTRESS FORD.
Marry, this is our device;
That Falstaff at that oak shall meet with us,
Disguised like Herne, with huge horns on his
head.

PAGE.
Well, let it not be doubted but he'll come:
And in this shape when you have brought him
thither,
What shall be done with him? what is your plot?

MISTRESS PAGE.
That likewise have we thought upon, and thus:
Nan Page my daughter, and my little son,
And three or four more of their growth, we'll
dress
Like urchins, ouphs, and fairies, green and white,
With rounds of waxen tapers on their heads,
And rattles in their hands: upon a sudden,
As Falstaff, she, and I, are newly met,
Let them from forth a sawpit rush at once

With some diffused song: upon their sight,
We two in great amazedness will fly;
Then let them all encircle him about.
And, fairy-like, to-pinch the unclean knight;
And ask him why, that hour of fairy revel,
In their so sacred paths he dares to tread
In shape profane.

MISTRESS FORD.
And till he tell the truth,
Let the supposed fairies pinch him sound,
And burn him with their tapers.

MISTRESS PAGE.
The truth being known,
We'll all present ourselves, dis-horn the spirit,
And mock him home to Windsor.

FORD.
The children must
Be practised well to this, or they'll ne'er do't.

SIR HUGH EVANS.
I will teach the children their behaviours; and I
will be like a jack-an-apes also, to burn the knight
with my taber.

FORD.
That will be excellent.   I'll go buy them vizards.

MISTRESS PAGE.
My Nan shall be the queen of all the fairies,
Finely attired in a robe of white.

PAGE.
That silk will I go buy:—[aside] and in that time
Shall Master Slender steal my Nan away,
And marry her at Eton.—Go send to Falstaff
straight.

FORD.
Nay, I'll to him again in name of Brook:
He'll tell me all his purpose: sure, he'll come.

MISTRESS PAGE.
Fear not you that. Go get us properties
And tricking for our fairies.

SIR HUGH EVANS.
Let us about it: it is admirable pleasures and fery
honest knaveries.

[Exeunt PAGE, FORD, and EVANS.

MISTRESS PAGE.
Go, Mistress Ford,
Send quickly to Sir John, to know his mind.

[Exit MISTRESS FORD.
I'll to the doctor: he hath my good will,
And none but he, to marry with Nan Page.
That Slender, though well landed, is an idiot;
And he my husband best of all affects.
The doctor is well money'd, and his friends
Potent at court: he, none but he, shall have her,
Though twenty thousand worthier come to crave
her.

[Exit.

SCENE V.

A room in the Garter Inn.

Enter HOST and SIMPLE.

HOST.
WHAT wouldst thou have, boor? what, thickskin? speak, breathe, discuss; brief, short,
quick, snap.

SIMPLE.
Marry, sir, I come to speak with Sir John Falstaff
from Master Slender.

HOST.

There's his chamber, his house, his castle, his standing-bed, and truckle-bed; 'tis painted about with the story of the Prodigal, fresh and new. Go knock and call; he'll speak like an Anthropophaginian unto thee: knock, I say.

SIMPLE.

There's an old woman, a fat woman, gone up into his chamber: I'll be so bold as stay, sir, till she come down; I come to speak with her, indeed.

HOST.

Ha! a fat woman! the knight may be robb'd: I'll call.—Bully knight! bully Sir John! speak from thy lungs military: art thou there? it is thine host, thine Ephesian, calls.

SIR JOHN FALSTAFF [above].

How now, mine host!

HOST.

Here's a Bohemian-Tartar tarries the coming down of thy fat woman. Let her descend, bully, let her descend; my chambers are honourable: fie! privacy? fie!

Enter FALSTAFF.

SIR JOHN FALSTAFF.

There was, mine host, an old fat woman even now with me; but she's gone.

SIMPLE.

Pray you, sir, was't not the wise-woman of Brainford?

SIR JOHN FALSTAFF.

Ay, marry, was it, mussel-shell: what would you with her?

SIMPLE.

My master, sir, Master Slender, sent to her, seeing her go through the streets, to know, sir, whether one Nym, sir, that beguiled him of a chain, had the chain or no.

SIR JOHN FALSTAFF.

I spake with the old woman about it.

SIMPLE.

And what says she, I pray, sir?

SIR JOHN FALSTAFF.

Marry, she says that the very same man that beguiled Master Slender of his chain cozen'd him of it.

SIMPLE.

I would I could have spoken with the woman herself; I had other things to have spoken with her too from him.

SIR JOHN FALSTAFF.

What are they? let us know.

HOST.

Ay, come; quick.

SIMPLE.

I may not conceal them, sir.

HOST.

Conceal them, or thou diest.

SIMPLE.

Why, sir, they were nothing but about Mistress Anne Page; to know if it were my master's fortune to have her or no.

SIR JOHN FALSTAFF.

'Tis, 'tis his fortune.

SIMPLE.

What, sir?

SIR JOHN FALSTAFF.

To have her,—or no. Go; say the woman told me so.

SIMPLE.

May I be bold to say so, sir?

SIR JOHN FALSTAFF.

Ay, sir Tike!—who more bold?

SIMPLE.

I thank your worship: I shall make my master glad with these tidings.   [*Exit.*

HOST.

Thou art clerkly, thou art clerkly, Sir John. Was there a wise woman with thee?

SIR JOHN FALSTAFF.

Ay, that there was, mine host; one that hath taught me more wit than ever I learn'd before in my life; and I paid nothing for it neither, but was paid for my learning.

Enter BARDOLPH.

BARDOLPH.

Out, alas, sir! cozenage, mere cozenage!

HOST.

Where be my horses? speak well of them, varletto.

BARDOLPH.

Run away with the cozeners: for so soon as I came beyond Eton, they threw me off, from behind one of them, in a slough of mire; and set spurs and away, like three German devils, three Dr. Faustuses.

HOST.

They are gone but to meet the duke, villain: do not say they be fled; Germans are honest men.

Enter SIR HUGH EVANS.

SIR HUGH EVANS.

Where is mine host?

HOST.

What is the matter, sir?

SIR HUGH EVANS.

Have a care of your entertainments: there is a friend of mine come to town, tells me there is three cozen-germans that has cozen'd all the hosts of Readins, of Maidenhead, of Colebrook, of horses and money. I tell you for good will, look you: you are wise, and full of gibes and vloutingstogs, and 'tis not convenient you should be cozen'd. Fare you well.   [*Exit.*

Enter DOCTOR CAIUS.

DOCTOR CAIUS.

Vere is mine host de Jarteer?

HOST.

Here, master doctor, in perplexity and doubtful dilemma.

DOCTOR CAIUS.

I cannot tell vat is dat: but it is tell-a me dat you make grand preparation for a duke de Jamany: by my trot, dere is no duke dat de court is know to come. I tell you for good vill: adieu.   [*Exit.*

HOST.

Hue and cry, villain, go!—Assist me, knight.—I am undone!—Fly, run, hue and cry, villain!—I am undone!   [*Exeunt* HOST *and* BARDOLPH.

SIR JOHN FALSTAFF.

I would all the world might be cozen'd; for I have been cozen'd and beaten too. If it should come to the ear of the court, how I have been transform'd, and how my transformation hath been wash'd and cudgell'd, they would melt me out of my fat drop by drop, and liquor fishermen's boots with me: I warrant they would whip me with their fine wits till I were as crest-fallen as a dried pear. I never prosper'd since I forswore myself at primero. Well, if my wind were but long enough to say my prayers, I would repent.

    Enter MISTRESS QUICKLY.

Now, whence come you?

      MISTRESS QUICKLY.

From the two parties, forsooth.

      SIR JOHN FALSTAFF.

The devil take one party, and his dam the other! and so they shall be both bestow'd. I have suffer'd more for their sakes, more than the villainous inconstancy of man's disposition is able to bear.

      MISTRESS QUICKLY.

And have not they suffer'd? Yes, I warrant; speciously one of them; Mistress Ford, good heart, is beaten black and blue, that you cannot see a white spot about her.

      SIR JOHN FALSTAFF.

What tell'st thou me of black and blue? I was beaten myself into all the colours of the rainbow; and I was like to be apprehended for the witch of Brainford: but that my admirable dexterity of wit, my counterfeiting the action of an old woman, deliver'd me, the knave constable had set me i' th' stocks, i' th' common stocks, for a witch.

      MISTRESS QUICKLY.

Sir, let me speak with you in your chamber: you shall hear how things go; and, I warrant, to your content. Here is a letter will say somewhat. Good hearts, what ado here is to bring you together! Sure, one of you does not serve heaven well, that you are so cross'd.

      SIR JOHN FALSTAFF.

Come up into my chamber.   [*Exeunt.*

SCENE VI.

Another room in the Garter Inn.

Enter FENTON *and* HOST.

      HOST.

MASTER FENTON, talk not to me; my mind is heavy: I will give over all.

      FENTON.

Yet hear me speak. Assist me in my purpose, And, as I am a gentleman, I'll give thee A hundred pound in gold more than your loss.

      HOST.

I will hear you, Master Fenton; and I will at the least keep your counsel.

      FENTON.

From time to time I have acquainted you With the dear love I bear to fair Anne Page; Who mutually hath answer'd my affection, So far forth as herself might be her chooser, Even to my wish: I have a letter from her Of such contents as you will wonder at; The mirth whereof so larded with my matter, That neither singly can be manifested Without the show of both;—wherein fat Falstaff Hath a great scene: the image of the jest I'll show you here at large. Hark, good mine host.

To-night at Herne's oak, just 'twixt twelve and one, Must my sweet Nan present the Fairy Queen; The purpose why, is here: in which disguise, While other jests are something rank on foot, Her father hath commanded her to slip Away with Slender, and with him at Eton Immediately to marry: she hath consented: Now, sir, Her mother, even strong against that match, And firm for Doctor Caius, hath appointed That he shall likewise shuffle her away, While other sports are tasking of their minds, And at the deanery, where a priest attends, Straight marry her: to this her mother's plot She, seemingly obedient, likewise hath Made promise to the doctor.—Now, thus it rests: Her father means she shall be all in white; And in that habit, when Slender sees his time To take her by the hand, and bid her go, She shall go with him: her mother hath intended, The better to denote her to the doctor,— For they must all be mask'd and vizarded,— That quaint in green she shall be loose enrobed, With ribands pendent, flaring 'bout her head; And when the doctor spies his vantage ripe, To pinch her by the hand, and, on that token, The maid hath given consent to go with him.

      HOST.

Which means she to deceive, father or mother?

      FENTON.

Both, my good host, to go along with me: And here it rests,—that you'll procure the vicar To stay for me at church 'twixt twelve and one, And, in the lawful name of marrying, To give our hearts united ceremony.

      HOST.

Well, husband your device; I'll to the vicar: Bring you the maid, you shall not lack a priest.

      FENTON.

So shall I evermore be bound to thee; Besides, I'll make a present recompense.   [*Exeunt.*

ACT V. SCENE I.

A room in the Garter Inn.

Enter FALSTAFF *and* MISTRESS QUICKLY.

      SIR JOHN FALSTAFF.

PRITHEE, no more prattling; go:—I'll hold. This is the third time; I hope good luck lies in odd numbers. Away! go. They say there is divinity in odd numbers, either in nativity, chance, or death. Away!

      MISTRESS QUICKLY.

I'll provide you a chain; and I'll do what I can to get you a pair of horns.

      SIR JOHN FALSTAFF.

Away, I say; time wears: hold up your head, and mince.   [*Exit* MISTRESS QUICKLY.

      Enter FORD *disguised.*

How now, Master Brook! Master Brook, the matter will be known to-night, or never. Be you in the Park about midnight, at Herne's oak, and you shall see wonders.

FORD.

Went you not to her yesterday, sir, as you told me you had appointed?

SIR JOHN FALSTAFF.

I went to her, Master Brook, as you see, like a poor old man: but I came from her, Master Brook, like a poor old woman. That same knave Ford, her husband, hath the finest mad devil of jealousy in him, Master Brook, that ever govern'd frenzy:—I will tell you:—he beat me grievously, in the shape of a woman; for in the shape of man, Master Brook, I fear not Goliath with a weaver's beam; because I know also life is a shuttle. I am in haste; go along with me: I'll tell you all, Master Brook. Since I pluck'd geese, play'd truant, and whipp'd top, I knew not what 'twas to be beaten till lately. Follow me: I'll tell you strange things of this knave Ford; on whom to-night I will be revenged, and I will deliver his wife into your hand. Follow:—strange things in hand, Master Brook:—follow.　　　　　　　[*Exeunt.*

SCENE II.

Windsor Park.

Enter PAGE, SHALLOW, *and* SLENDER.

PAGE.

COME, come; we'll couch i'th'castle-ditch till we see the light of our fairies.—Remember, son Slender, my daughter.

SLENDER.

Ay, forsooth; I have spoke with her, and we have a nay-word how to know one another: I come to her in white, and cry 'mum;' she cries 'budget;' and by that we know one another.

SHALLOW.

That's good too; but what needs either your 'mum' or her 'budget'? the white will decipher her well enough.—It hath struck ten o'clock.

PAGE.

The night is dark; light and spirits will become it well. Heaven prosper our sport! No man means evil but the devil, and we shall know him by his horns. Let's away; follow me.　　　[*Exeunt.*

SCENE III.

A street leading to the Park.

Enter MISTRESS PAGE, MISTRESS FORD, *and* DOCTOR CAIUS.

MISTRESS PAGE.

MASTER doctor, my daughter is in green: when you see your time, take her by the hand, away with her to the deanery, and dispatch it quickly. Go before into the Park: we two must go together.

DOCTOR CAIUS.

I know vat I have to do. Adieu.

MISTRESS PAGE.

Fare you well, sir. [*Exit* CAIUS.]—My husband will not rejoice so much at the abuse of Falstaff as he will chafe at the doctor's marrying my daughter: but 'tis no matter; better a little chiding than a great deal of heart-break.

MISTRESS FORD.

Where is Nan now and her troop of fairies? and the Welsh devil Hugh?

MISTRESS PAGE.

They are all couch'd in a pit hard by Herne's oak, with obscured lights; which, at the very instant of Falstaff's and our meeting, they will at once display to the night.

MISTRESS FORD.

That cannot choose but amaze him.

MISTRESS PAGE.

If he be not amazed, he will be mock'd; if he be amazed, he will every way be mock'd.

MISTRESS FORD.

We'll betray him finely.

MISTRESS PAGE.

Against such lewdsters and their lechery
Those that betray them do no treachery.

MISTRESS FORD.

The hour draws on. To the oak, to the oak!

[*Exeunt.*

SCENE IV.

Windsor Park.

Enter SIR HUGH EVANS *disguised as a Satyr,
with* ANNE PAGE *and others as Fairies.*

SIR HUGH EVANS.

TRIB, trib, fairies; come; and remember your parts: be pold, I pray you; follow me into the pit; and when I give the watch-ords, do as I pid you: come, come; trib, trib.　[*Exeunt.*

SCENE V.

Another part of the Park.

Enter FALSTAFF, *with a buck's head upon him.*

SIR JOHN FALSTAFF.

THE Windsor bell hath struck twelve; the minute draws on. Now, the hot-blooded gods assist me!—Remember, Jove, thou wast a bull for thy Europa; love set on thy horns:—O powerful love! that, in some respects, makes a beast a man; in some other, a man a beast.—You were also, Jupiter, a swan for the love of Leda:—O omnipotent love! how near the god drew to the complexion of a goose!—A fault done first in the form of a beast; —O Jove, a beastly fault! and then another fault in the semblance of a fowl;—think on't, Jove; a foul fault! When gods have hot backs, what shall poor men do? For me, I am here a Windsor stag; and the fattest, I think, i'th'forest.—Send me a cool rut-time, Jove, or who can blame me to piss my tallow?—Who comes here? my doe?

Enter MISTRESS FORD *and* MISTRESS PAGE.

MISTRESS FORD.

Sir John! art thou there, my deer? my male deer?

SIR JOHN FALSTAFF.

My doe with the black scut!—Let the sky rain potatoes; let it thunder to the tune of *Green sleeves*, hail kissing-comfits, and snow eryngoes; let there come a tempest of provocation, I will shelter me here.　　　　　　　　[*Embracing her.*

MISTRESS FORD.

Mistress Page is come with me, sweetheart.

SIR JOHN FALSTAFF.

Divide me like a bribe-buck, each a haunch: I will keep my sides to myself, my shoulders for the fellow of this walk, and my horns I bequeath your husbands. Am I a woodman, ha? Speak I like Herne the hunter?—Why, now is Cupid a child of conscience; he makes restitution. As I am a true spirit, welcome!   [*Noise of horns within.*

MISTRESS PAGE.

Alas, what noise?

MISTRESS FORD.

Heaven forgive our sins!

SIR JOHN FALSTAFF.

What should this be?

MISTRESS FORD *and* MISTRESS PAGE.

Away, away!   [*They run off.*

SIR JOHN FALSTAFF.

I think the devil will not have me damn'd, lest the oil that's in me should set hell on fire; he would never else cross me thus.

Enter SIR HUGH EVANS *as a Satyr,* PISTOL *as Hobgoblin,* ANNE PAGE *as Fairy Queen, and others as fairies.*

ANNE PAGE.

Fairies, black, gray, green, and white,
You moonshine revellers, and shades of night,
You orphan heirs of fixed destiny,
Attend your office and your quality.—
Crier Hobgoblin, make the fairy oyes.

PISTOL.

Elves, list your names; silence, you airy toys.
Cricket, to Windsor chimneys shalt thou leap:
Where fires thou find'st unraked and hearths unswept,
There pinch the maids as blue as bilberry:
Our radiant queen hates sluts and sluttery.

SIR JOHN FALSTAFF.

They are fairies; he that speaks to them shall die:
I'll wink and couch: no man their works must eye.
    [*Lies down upon his face.*

SIR HUGH EVANS.

Where's Pead?—Go you, and where you find a maid
That, ere she sleep, has thrice her prayers said,
Raise up the organs of her fantasy,
Sleep she as sound as careless infancy:
But those as sleep and think not on their sins,
Pinch them, arms, legs, backs, shoulders, sides, and shins.

ANNE PAGE.

About, about;
Search Windsor Castle, elves, within and out:
Strew good luck, ouphs, on every sacred room;
That it may stand till the perpetual doom,
In site as wholesome as in state 'tis fit,
Worthy the owner, and the owner it.
The several chairs of order look you scour
With juice of balm and every precious flower:
Each fair instalment, coat, and several crest,
With loyal blazon, evermore be blest!
And nightly, meadow-fairies, look you sing,
Like to the Garter's compass, in a ring:
Th' expressure that it bears, green let it be,
More fertile-fresh than all the field to see;
And *Honi soit qui mal y pense* write

In emerald tufts, flowers purple, blue, and white;
Like sapphire, pearl, and rich embroidery,
Buckled below fair knighthood's bending knee:—
Fairies use flowers for their charactery.
Away; disperse: but till 'tis one o'clock,
Our dance of custom round about the oak
Of Herne the hunter let us not forget.

SIR HUGH EVANS.

Pray you, lock hand in hand; yourselves in order set;
And twenty glow-worms shall our lanterns be,
To guide our measure round about the tree.—
But stay; I smell a man of middle-earth.

SIR JOHN FALSTAFF.

Heavens defend me from that Welsh fairy, lest he transform me to a piece of cheese!

PISTOL.

Vile worm, thou wast o'erlook'd even in thy birth.

ANNE PAGE.

With trial-fire touch me his finger-end:
If he be chaste, the flame will back descend,
And turn him to no pain; but if he start,
It is the flesh of a corrupted heart.

PISTOL.

A trial, come.

SIR HUGH EVANS.

Come, will this wood take fire?
    [*They put the tapers to his fingers and he starts.*

SIR JOHN FALSTAFF.

O, O, O!

ANNE PAGE.

Corrupt, corrupt, and tainted in desire!—
About him, fairies; sing a scornful rhyme;
And, as you trip, still pinch him to your time.

SIR HUGH EVANS.

It is right; indeed he is full of lecheries and iniquity.

Song.

Fie on sinful fantasy!
Fie on lust and luxury!
Lust is but a bloody fire,
Kindled with unchaste desire,
Fed in heart; whose flames aspire,
As thoughts do blow them, higher and higher.
Pinch him, fairies, mutually;
Pinch him for his villainy;
Pinch him, and burn him, and turn him about,
Till candles and starlight and moonshine be out.

Here they pinch him and sing about him, and the DOCTOR *comes one way, and steals away a Boy in green;* SLENDER *another way, and takes off a Boy in white; and* FENTON *steals* ANNE PAGE. *A noise of hunting is made within. All the Fairies run away.* FALSTAFF *pulls off his buck's head, and rises.*

Enter PAGE, FORD, MISTRESS PAGE, *and* MISTRESS FORD.

PAGE.

Nay, do not fly; I think we have watch'd you now:
Will none but Herne the hunter serve your turn?

MISTRESS PAGE.

I pray you, come, hold up the jest no higher.—
Now, good Sir John, how like you Windsor wives?—
See you these, husband? do not these fair yokes
Become the forest better than the town?

FORD.

Now, sir, who's a cuckold now?—Master Brook, Falstaff's a knave, a cuckoldly knave; here are his horns, Master Brook: and, Master Brook, he hath enjoy'd nothing of Ford's but his buck-basket, his cudgel, and twenty pounds of money, which must be paid to Master Brook; his horses are arrested for it, Master Brook.

MISTRESS FORD.

Sir John, we have had ill luck; we could never meet. I will never take you for my love again; but I will always count you my deer.

SIR JOHN FALSTAFF.

I do begin to perceive that I am made an ass.

FORD.

Ay, and an ox too: both the proofs are extant.

SIR JOHN FALSTAFF.

And these are not fairies? I was three or four times in the thought they were not fairies: and yet the guiltiness of my mind, the sudden surprise of my powers, drove the grossness of the foppery into a received belief, in despite of the teeth of all rhyme and reason, that they were fairies. See now how wit may be made a Jack-a-Lent, when 'tis upon ill employment!

SIR HUGH EVANS.

Sir John Falstaff, serve Got, and leave your desires, and fairies will not pinse you.

FORD.

Well said, fairy Hugh.

SIR HUGH EVANS.

And leave you your jealousies too, I pray you.

FORD.

I will never mistrust my wife again, till thou art able to woo her in good English.

SIR JOHN FALSTAFF.

Have I laid my brain in the sun, and dried it, that it wants matter to prevent so gross o'er-reaching as this? Am I ridden with a Welsh goat too? shall I have a coxcomb of frize? 'Tis time I were choked with a piece of toasted cheese.

SIR HUGH EVANS.

Seese is not to give putter; your pelly is all putter.

SIR JOHN FALSTAFF.

'Seese' and 'putter'! have I lived to stand at the taunt of one that makes fritters of English? This is enough to be the decay of lust and late-walking through the realm.

MISTRESS PAGE.

Why, Sir John, do you think, though we would have thrust virtue out of our hearts by the head and shoulders, and have given ourselves without scruple to hell, that ever the devil could have made you our delight?

FORD.

What, a hodge-pudding? a bag of flax?

MISTRESS PAGE.

A puff'd man?

FORD.

Old, cold, wither'd, and of intolerable entrails?

FORD.

And one that is as slanderous as Satan?

PAGE.

And as poor as Job?

FORD.

And as wicked as his wife?

SIR HUGH EVANS.

And given to fornications, and to taverns, and sack, and wine, and metheglins, and to drinkings, and swearings and starings, pribbles and prabbles?

SIR JOHN FALSTAFF.

Well, I am your theme: you have the start of me; I am dejected; I am not able to answer the Welsh flannel; ignorance itself is a plummet o'er me: use me as you will.

FORD.

Marry, sir, we'll bring you to Windsor, to one Master Brook, that you have cozen'd of money, to whom you should have been a pandar: over and above that you have suffer'd, I think to repay that money will be a biting affliction.

MISTRESS FORD.

Nay, husband, let that go to make amends; Forgive that sum, and so we'll all be friends.

FORD.

Well, here is my hand; all's forgiven at last.

PAGE.

Yet be cheerful, knight: thou shalt eat a posset to-night at my house; where I will desire thee to laugh at my wife, that now laughs at thee: tell her Master Slender hath married her daughter.

MISTRESS PAGE [aside].

Doctors doubt that: if Anne Page be my daughter, she is, by this, Doctor Caius' wife.

Enter SLENDER.

SLENDER.

Whoa, ho! ho, father Page!

PAGE.

Son, how now! how now, son! have you dispatch'd?

SLENDER.

Dispatch'd!—I'll make the best in Glostershire know on't; would I were hang'd, la, else!

PAGE.

Of what, son?

SLENDER.

I came yonder at Eton to marry Mistress Anne Page, and she's a great lubberly boy. If it had not been i'th'church, I would have swinged him, or he should have swinged me. If I did not think it had been Anne Page, would I might never stir!—and 'tis a postmaster's boy.

PAGE.

Upon my life, then, you took the wrong.

SLENDER.

What need you tell me that? I think so, when I took a boy for a girl. If I had been married to him, for all he was in woman's apparel, I would not have had him.

PAGE.

Why, this is your own folly. Did not I tell you how you should know my daughter by her garments?

SLENDER.

I went to her in white, and cried 'mum,' and she cried 'budget,' as Anne and I had appointed; and yet it was not Anne, but a postmaster's boy.

SIR HUGH EVANS.

Jeshu, Master Slender! cannot you see but marry boys?

PAGE.

O, I am vext at heart! what shall I do?

MISTRESS PAGE.
Good George, be not angry: I knew of your purpose; turn'd my daughter into green; and, indeed, she is now with the doctor at the deanery, and there married.

Enter CAIUS.

DOCTOR CAIUS.
Vere is Mistress Page? By gar, I am cozen'd: I ha' married *un garçon*, a boy; *un paysan*, by gar, a boy; it is not Anne Page: by gar, I am cozen'd.

MISTRESS PAGE.
Why, did you take her in green?

DOCTOR CAIUS.
Ay, by gar, and 'tis a boy: by gar, I'll raise all Windsor. 　　　　　　　　　　　　　　[*Exit.*

FORD.
This is strange. Who hath got the right Anne?

PAGE.
My heart misgives me:—here comes Master Fenton.

Enter FENTON *and* ANNE PAGE.
How now, Master Fenton!

ANNE PAGE.
Pardon, good father!—good my mother, pardon!

PAGE.
Now, mistress,—how chance you went not with Master Slender?

MISTRESS PAGE.
Why went you not with master doctor, maid?

FENTON.
You do amaze her: hear the truth of it.
You would have married her most shamefully,
Where there was no proportion held in love.
The truth is, she and I, long since contracted,

Are now so sure that nothing can dissolve us.
Th' offence is holy that she hath committed,
And this deceit loses the name of craft,
Of disobedience, or unduteous title,
Since therein she doth evitate and shun
A thousand irreligious cursed hours,
Which forced marriage would have brought upon
　her.

FORD.
Stand not amazed: here is no remedy:
In love the heavens themselves do guide the
　state;
Money buys lands, and wives are sold by fate.

SIR JOHN FALSTAFF.
I am glad, though you have ta'en a special stand
to strike at me, that your arrow hath glanced.

PAGE.
Well, what remedy?—Fenton, heaven give thee
　joy!—
What cannot be eschew'd must be embraced.

SIR JOHN FALSTAFF.
When night-dogs run, all sorts of deer are chased.

SIR HUGH EVANS.
I will also dance and eat plums at your weddings.

MISTRESS PAGE.
Well, I will muse no further.—Master Fenton,
Heaven give you many, many merry days!—
Good husband, let us every one go home,
And laugh this sport o'er by a country fire;
Sir John and all.

FORD.
　　　　　　　Let it be so.—Sir John,
To Master Brook you yet shall hold your word;
For he to-night shall lie with Mistress Ford.
　　　　　　　　　　　　　　[*Exeunt.*

JULIUS CAESAR

DRAMATIS PERSONAE

JULIUS CAESAR.
OCTAVIUS CAESAR,
MARCUS ANTONIUS,
M. AEMILIUS LEPIDUS,
} *triumvirs after the death of Julius Caesar.*

CICERO,
PUBLIUS,
POPILIUS LENA,
} *senators.*

MARCUS BRUTUS,
CASSIUS,
CASCA,
TREBONIUS,
LIGARIUS,
DECIUS BRUTUS,
METELLUS CIMBER,
CINNA,
} *conspirators against Julius Caesar.*

FLAVIUS *and* MARULLUS, *tribunes.*
ARTEMIDORUS, *a sophist of Cnidos.*
A SOOTHSAYER.
CINNA, *a poet.*
ANOTHER POET.

LUCILIUS,
TITINIUS,
MESSALA,
YOUNG CATO,
VOLUMNIUS,
} *friends to Brutus and Cassius.*

VARRO,
CLITUS,
CLAUDIUS,
STRATO,
LUCIUS,
DARDANIUS,
} *servants to Brutus.*

PINDARUS, *servant to Cassius.*

CALPHURNIA, *wife to Cæsar.*
PORTIA, *wife to* BRUTUS.

SENATORS, CITIZENS, GUARDS, ATTENDANTS, &c.

SCENE—*During a great part of the play at Rome; afterwards near Sardis, and near Philippi.*

ACT I. SCENE I.

Rome. A street.

Enter FLAVIUS, MARULLUS, *and certain* COMMONERS *over the stage.*

FLAVIUS.

HENCE! home, you idle creatures, get you home:
Is this a holiday? what! know you not,
Being mechanical, you ought not walk
Upon a labouring day without the sign
Of your profession?—Speak, what trade art thou?

FIRST CITIZEN.
Why, sir, a carpenter.

MARULLUS.
Where is thy leather apron and thy rule?
What dost thou with thy best apparel on?—
You, sir, what trade are you?

SECOND CITIZEN.
Truly, sir, in respect of a fine workman, I am but, as you would say, a cobbler.

MARULLUS.
But what trade art thou? answer me directly.

SECOND CITIZEN.
A trade, sir, that I hope I may use with a safe conscience; which is, indeed, sir, a mender of bad soles.

MARULLUS.
What trade, thou knave? thou naughty knave, what trade?

SECOND CITIZEN.
Nay, I beseech you, sir, be not out with me: yet if you be out, sir, I can mend you.

MARULLUS.
What meanest thou by that? mend me, thou saucy fellow!

SECOND CITIZEN.
Why, sir, cobble you.

FLAVIUS.
Thou art a cobbler, art thou?

SECOND CITIZEN.
Truly, sir, all that I live by is with the awl: I meddle with no tradesman's matters, nor women's matters, but with awl. I am, indeed, sir, a surgeon to old shoes; when they are in great danger, I recover them. As proper men as ever trod upon neats-leather have gone upon my handiwork.

FLAVIUS.
But wherefore art not in thy shop to-day?
Why dost thou lead these men about the streets?

SECOND CITIZEN.
Truly, sir, to wear out their shoes, to get myself into more work. But, indeed, sir, we make holiday, to see Cæsar, and to rejoice in his triumph.

MARULLUS.
Wherefore rejoice? What conquest brings he home?
What tributaries follow him to Rome,
To grace in captive bonds his chariot-wheels?
You blocks, you stones, you worse than senseless things!
O you hard hearts, you cruel men of Rome,
Knew you not Pompey? Many a time and oft
Have you climb'd up to walls and battlements,
To towers and windows, yea, to chimney-tops,
Your infants in your arms, and there have sat
The live-long day, with patient expectation,
To see great Pompey pass the streets of Rome:
And when you saw his chariot but appear,
Have you not made an universal shout,
That Tiber trembled underneath her banks,
To hear the replication of your sounds
Made in her concave shores?
And do you now put on your best attire?
And do you now cull out a holiday?
And do you now strew flowers in his way
That comes in triumph over Pompey's blood?
Be gone!
Run to your houses, fall upon your knees,

Pray to the gods to intermit the plague
That needs must light on this ingratitude.
               FLAVIUS.
Go, go, good countrymen, and, for this fault,
Assemble all the poor men of your sort;
Draw them to Tiber banks, and weep your tears
Into the channel, till the lowest stream
Do kiss the most exalted shores of all.
               [*Exeunt all the* COMMONERS.
See, whe'r their basest metal be not moved!
They vanish tongue-tied in their guiltiness.
Go you down that way towards the Capitol;
This way will I: disrobe the images,
If you do find them deckt with ceremonies.
               MARULLUS.
May we do so?
You know it is the feast of Lupercal.
               FLAVIUS.
It is no matter; let no images
Be hung with Cæsar's trophies. I'll about,
And drive away the vulgar from the streets:
So do you too, where you perceive them thick.
These growing feathers pluckt from Cæsar's wing
Will make him fly an ordinary pitch;
Who else would soar above the view of men,
And keep us all in servile fearfulness.   [*Exeunt.*

SCENE II.

The same.   A public place.

Enter CAESAR; ANTONY, *for the course;* CAL-
PHURNIA, PORTIA, DECIUS, CICERO, BRUTUS,
CASSIUS, & CASCA; *a great crowd following,
among them a* SOOTHSAYER.
               JULIUS CAESAR.
CALPHURNIA,—
               CASCA.
Peace, ho! Cæsar speaks. [*Music ceases.*
               JULIUS CAESAR.
               Calphurnia,—
               CALPHURNIA.
Here, my lord.
               JULIUS CAESAR.
Stand you directly in Antonius' way,
When he doth run his course.—Antonius,—
               MARCUS ANTONIUS.
Cæsar, my lord?
               JULIUS CAESAR.
Forget not, in your speed, Antonius,
To touch Calphurnia; for our elders say,
The barren, touched in this holy chase,
Shake off their sterile curse.
               MARCUS ANTONIUS.
               I shall remember:
When Cæsar says 'Do this,' it is perform'd.
               JULIUS CAESAR.
Set on; and leave no ceremony out.   [*Music.*
               SOOTHSAYER.
Cæsar!
               JULIUS CAESAR.
Ha! who calls?
               CASCA.
Bid every noise be still:—peace yet again!
               [*Music ceases.*
               JULIUS CAESAR.
Who is it in the press that calls on me?

I hear a tongue, shriller than all the music,
Cry 'Cæsar.' Speak; Cæsar is turn'd to hear.
               SOOTHSAYER.
Beware the ides of March.
               JULIUS CAESAR.
               What man is that?
               MARCUS BRUTUS.
A soothsayer bids you beware the ides of March.
               JULIUS CAESAR.
Set him before me; let me see his face.
               CASSIUS.
Fellow, come from the throng; look upon Cæsar.
               JULIUS CAESAR.
What say'st thou to me now? speak once again.
               SOOTHSAYER.
Beware the ides of March.
               JULIUS CAESAR.
He is a dreamer; let us leave him:—pass.
      [*Sennet.   Exeunt all but* BRUTUS *and* CASSIUS.
               CASSIUS.
Will you go see the order of the course?
               MARCUS BRUTUS.
Not I.
               CASSIUS.
I pray you, do.
               MARCUS BRUTUS.
I am not gamesome: I do lack some part
Of that quick spirit that is in Antony.
Let me not hinder, Cassius, your desires;
I'll leave you.
               CASSIUS.
Brutus, I do observe you now of late:
I have not from your eyes that gentleness
And show of love as I was wont to have:
You bear too stubborn and too strange a hand
Over your friend that loves you.
               MARCUS BRUTUS.
               Cassius,
Be not deceived: if I have veil'd my look,
I turn the trouble of my countenance
Merely upon myself. Vexed I am,
Of late, with passions of some difference,
Conceptions only proper to myself,
Which give some soil, perhaps, to my behaviours;
But let not therefore my good friends be grieved,—
Among which number, Cassius, be you one,—
Nor construe any further my neglect,
Than that poor Brutus, with himself at war,
Forgets the shows of love to other men.
               CASSIUS.
Then, Brutus, I have much mistook your passion;
By means whereof this breast of mine hath
   buried
Thoughts of great value, worthy cogitations.
Tell me, good Brutus, can you see your face?
               MARCUS BRUTUS.
No, Cassius; for the eye sees not itself
But by reflection from some other thing.
               CASSIUS.
'Tis just:
And it is very much lamented, Brutus,
That you have no such mirrors as will turn
Your hidden worthiness into your eye,
That you might see your shadow. I have heard,
Where many of the best respect in Rome,—
Except immortal Cæsar,—speaking of Brutus,

And groaning underneath this age's yoke,
Have wisht that noble Brutus had his eyes.

MARCUS BRUTUS.

Into what dangers would you lead me, Cassius,
That you would have me seek into myself
For that which is not in me?

CASSIUS.

Therefore, good Brutus, be prepared to hear:
And, since you know you cannot see yourself
So well as by reflection, I, your glass,
Will modestly discover to yourself
That of yourself which you yet know not of.
And be not jealous on me, gentle Brutus:
Were I a common laughter, or did use
To stale with ordinary oaths my love
To every new protester; if you know
That I do fawn on men, and hug them hard,
And after scandal them; or if you know
That I profess myself in banqueting
To all the rout, then hold me dangerous.

[*Flourish and shout.*

MARCUS BRUTUS.

What means this shouting? I do fear, the people
Choose Cæsar for their king.

CASSIUS.

              Ay, do you fear it?
Then must I think you would not have it so.

MARCUS BRUTUS.

I would not, Cassius; yet I love him well.—
But wherefore do you hold me here so long?
What is it that you would impart to me?
If it be aught toward the general good,
Set honour in one eye, and death i'th'other,
And I will look on both indifferently;
For, let the gods so speed me as I love
The name of honour more than I fear death.

CASSIUS.

I know that virtue to be in you, Brutus,
As well as I do know your outward favour.
Well, honour is the subject of my story.—
I cannot tell what you and other men
Think of this life; but, for my single self,
I had as lief not be as live to be
In awe of such a thing as I myself.
I was born free as Cæsar; so were you:
We both have fed as well; and we can both
Endure the winter's cold as well as he:
For once, upon a raw and gusty day,
The troubled Tiber chafing with her shores,
Cæsar said to me, 'Darest thou, Cassius, now
Leap in with me into this angry flood,
And swim to yonder point?' Upon the word,
Accoutred as I was, I plunged in,
And bade him follow: so, indeed, he did.
The torrent roar'd; and we did buffet it
With lusty sinews, throwing it aside
And stemming it with hearts of controversy:
But ere we could arrive the point proposed,
Cæsar cried, 'Help me, Cassius, or I sink!'
I, as Aeneas, our great ancestor,
Did from the flames of Troy upon his shoulder
The old Anchises bear, so from the waves of Tiber
Did I the tired Cæsar: and this man
Is now become a god; and Cassius is
A wretched creature, and must bend his body,
If Cæsar carelessly but nod on him.

He had a fever when he was in Spain,
And, when the fit was on him, I did mark
How he did shake: 'tis true, this god did shake:
His coward lips did from their colour fly;
And that same eye, whose bend doth awe the
    world,
Did lose his lustre: I did hear him groan:
Ay, and that tongue of his, that bade the Romans
Mark him, and write his speeches in their books,
Alas, it cried, 'Give me some drink, Titinius,'
As a sick girl. Ye gods, it doth amaze me,
A man of such a feeble temper should
So get the start of the majestic world,
And bear the palm alone.   [*Flourish and shout.*

MARCUS BRUTUS.

Another general shout!
I do believe that these applauses are
For some new honours that are heapt on Cæsar.

CASSIUS.

Why, man, he doth bestride the narrow world
Like a Colossus; and we petty men
Walk under his huge legs, and peep about
To find ourselves dishonourable graves.
Men at some time are masters of their fates:
The fault, dear Brutus, is not in our stars,
But in ourselves, that we are underlings.
Brutus, and Cæsar: what should be in that Cæsar?
Why should that name be sounded more than
    yours?
Write them together, yours is as fair a name;
Sound them, it doth become the mouth as well;
Weigh them, it is as heavy; conjure with 'em,
Brutus will start a spirit as soon as Cæsar.
Now, in the names of all the gods at once,
Upon what meat doth this our Cæsar feed,
That he is grown so great? Age, thou art shamed!
Rome, thou hast lost the breed of noble bloods!
When went there by an age, since the great flood,
But it was famed with more than with one man?
When could they say, till now, that talkt of Rome,
That her wide walls encompast but one man?
Now is it Rome indeed, and room enough,
When there is in it but one only man.
O, you and I have heard our fathers say,
There was a Brutus once that would have brookt
Th'eternal devil to keep his state in Rome
As easily as a king.

MARCUS BRUTUS.

That you do love me, I am nothing jealous;
What you would work me to, I have some aim:
How I have thought of this, and of these times,
I shall recount hereafter; for this present,
I would not, so with love I might entreat you,
Be any further moved. What you have said,
I will consider; what you have to say,
I will with patience hear; and find a time
Both meet to hear and answer such high things.
Till then, my noble friend, chew upon this;
Brutus had rather be a villager
Than to repute himself a son of Rome
Under these hard conditions as this time
Is like to lay upon us.

CASSIUS.

              I am glad
That my weak words have struck but thus much
Of fire from Brutus.   [show

MARCUS BRUTUS.

The games are done, and Cæsar is returning.

CASSIUS.

As they pass by, pluck Casca by the sleeve;
And he will, after his sour fashion, tell you
What hath proceeded worthy note to-day.

Enter CAESAR *and his* TRAIN.

MARCUS BRUTUS.

I will do so:—but, look you, Cassius,
The angry spot doth glow on Cæsar's brow,
And all the rest look like a chidden train:
Calphurnia's cheek is pale; and Cicero
Looks with such ferret and such fiery eyes
As we have seen him in the Capitol,
Being crost in conference by some senator.

CASSIUS.

Casca will tell us what the matter is.

JULIUS CAESAR.

Antonius,—

MARCUS ANTONIUS.

Cæsar?

JULIUS CAESAR.

Let me have men about me that are fat;
Sleek-headed men, and such as sleep o' nights:
Yond Cassius has a lean and hungry look;
He thinks too much: such men are dangerous.

MARCUS ANTONIUS.

Fear him not, Cæsar; he's not dangerous;
He is a noble Roman, and well given.

JULIUS CAESAR.

Would he were fatter!—but I fear him not:
Yet if my name were liable to fear,
I do not know the man I should avoid
So soon as that spare Cassius. He reads much;
He is a great observer, and he looks
Quite through the deeds of men: he loves no
    plays,
As thou dost, Antony; he hears no music:
Seldom he smiles; and smiles in such a sort
As if he mockt himself, and scorn'd his spirit
That could be moved to smile at any thing.
Such men as he be never at heart's ease
Whiles they behold a greater than themselves;
And therefore are they very dangerous.
I rather tell thee what is to be fear'd
Than what I fear,—for always I am Cæsar.
Come on my right hand, for this ear is deaf,
And tell me truly what thou think'st of him.

[*Exeunt* CAESAR *and all his* TRAIN *but*
CASCA.

CASCA.

You pull'd me by the cloak; would you speak with
    me?

MARCUS BRUTUS.

Ay, Casca; tell us what hath chanced to-day,
That Cæsar looks so sad.

CASCA.

Why, you were with him, were you not?

MARCUS BRUTUS.

I should not, then, ask Casca what had chanced.

CASCA.

Why, there was a crown offer'd him; and being
offer'd him, he put it by with the back of his hand,
thus; and then the people fell a-shouting.

MARCUS BRUTUS.

What was the second noise for?

CASCA.

Why, for that too.

CASSIUS.

They shouted thrice: what was the last cry for?

CASCA.

Why, for that too.

MARCUS BRUTUS.

Was the crown offer'd him thrice?

CASCA.

Ay, marry, was't, and he put it by thrice, every
time gentler than other; and at every putting-by
mine honest neighbours shouted.

CASSIUS.

Who offer'd him the crown?

CASCA.

Why, Antony.

MARCUS BRUTUS.

Tell us the manner of it, gentle Casca.

CASCA.

I can as well be hang'd as tell the manner of it: it
was mere foolery; I did not mark it. I saw Mark
Antony offer him a crown;—yet 'twas not a crown
neither, 'twas one of these coronets;—and, as I
told you, he put it by once: but, for all that, to my
thinking, he would fain have had it. Then he offer'd it to him again; then he put it by again: but,
to my thinking, he was very loth to lay his fingers
off it. And then he offer'd it the third time; he put
it the third time by; and still as he refused it, the
rabblement shouted, and clapt their chopt hands,
and threw up their sweaty nightcaps, and utter'd
such a deal of stinking breath because Cæsar
r. fused the crown, that it had almost choked
Cæsar; for he swounded, and fell down at it: and
for my own part, I durst not laugh, for fear of
opening my lips and receiving the bad air.

CASSIUS.

But, soft, I pray you: what, did Cæsar swound?

CASCA.

He fell down in the market-place, and foam'd at
mouth, and was speechless.

MARCUS BRUTUS.

'Tis very like; —he hath the falling-sickness.

CASSIUS.

No, Cæsar hath it not: but you, and I,
And honest Casca, we have the falling-sickness.

CASCA.

I know not what you mean by that; but, I am sure,
Cæsar fell down. If the tag-rag people did not
clap him and hiss him, according as he pleased
and displeased them, as they use to do the players
in the theatre, I am no true man.

MARCUS BRUTUS.

What said he when he came unto himself?

CASCA.

Marry, before he fell down, when he perceived
the common herd was glad he refused the crown,
he pluckt me ope his doublet, and offer'd them
his throat to cut:—an I had been a man of any occupation, if I would not have taken him at a word,
I would I might go to hell among the rogues:—
and so he fell. When he came to himself again, he
said, if he had done or said any thing amiss, he
desired their worships to think it was his infirmity. Three or four wenches, where I stood,
cried, 'Alas, good soul!' and forgave him with all

their hearts: but there's no heed to be taken of
them; if Cæsar had stabb'd their mothers, they
would have done no less.

MARCUS BRUTUS.
And after that, he came, thus sad, away?

CASCA.
Ay.

CASSIUS.
Did Cicero say any thing?

CASCA.
Ay, he spoke Greek.

CASSIUS.
To what effect?

CASCA.
Nay, an I tell you that, I'll ne'er look you i'th'
face again: but those that understood him smiled
at one another, and shook their heads; but, for
mine own part, it was Greek to me. I could tell
you more news too: Marullus and Flavius, for
pulling scarfs off Cæsar's images, are put to silence.
Fare you well. There was more foolery yet, if I
could remember it.

CASSIUS.
Will you sup with me to-night, Casca?

CASCA.
No, I am promised forth.

CASSIUS.
Will you dine with me to-morrow?

CASCA.
Ay, if I be alive, and your mind hold, and your
dinner worth the eating.

CASSIUS.
Good; I will expect you.

CASCA.
Do so: farewell, both.   [*Exit.*

MARCUS BRUTUS.
What a blunt fellow is this grown to be!
He was quick mettle when he went to school.

CASSIUS.
So is he now, in execution
Of any bold or noble enterprise,
However he puts on this tardy form.
This rudeness is a source to his good wit,
Which gives men stomach to digest his words
With better appetite.

MARCUS BRUTUS.
And so it is. For this time I will leave you:
To-morrow, if you please to speak with me,
I will come home to you; or, if you will,
Come home to me, and I will wait for you.

CASSIUS.
I will do so:—till then, think of the world.
      [*Exit* BRUTUS.
Well Brutus, thou art noble; yet, I see,
Thy honourable mettle may be wrought
From that it is disposed: therefore 'tis meet
That noble minds keep ever with their likes;
For who so firm that cannot be seduced?
Cæsar doth bear me hard; but he loves Brutus:
If I were Brutus now, and he were Cassius,
He should not humour me. I will this night,
In several hands, in at his windows throw,
As if they came from several citizens,
Writings, all tending to the great opinion
That Rome holds of his name; wherein obscurely
Cæsar's ambition shall be glanced at:

And, after this, let Cæsar seat him sure;
For we will shake him, or worse days endure.
      [*Exit.*

SCENE III.

The same. A street.

Thunder and lightning. Enter, from opposite sides,
CASCA, *with his sword drawn, and* CICERO.

CICERO.
GOOD even, Casca: brought you Cæsar home?
Why are you breathless? and why stare you
so?

CASCA.
Are not you moved, when all the sway of earth
Shakes like a thing unfirm? O Cicero,
I have seen tempests, when the scolding winds
Have rived the knotty oaks; and I have seen
Th'ambitious ocean swell and rage and foam,
To be exalted with the threat'ning clouds:
But never till to-night, never till now,
Did I go through a tempest dropping fire.
Either there is a civil strife in heaven;
Or else the world, too saucy with the gods,
Incenses them to send destruction.

CICERO.
Why, saw you any thing more wonderful?

CASCA.
A common slave—you know him well by sight—
Held up his left hand, which did flame and burn
Like twenty torches join'd; and yet his hand,
Not sensible of fire, remain'd unscorcht.
Besides,—I ha' not since put up my sword,—
Against the Capitol I met a lion,
Who glared upon me, and went surly by,
Without annoying me: and there were drawn
Upon a heap a hundred ghastly women,
Transformed with their fear; who swore they saw
Men, all in fire, walk up and down the streets.
And yesterday the bird of night did sit
Even at noonday upon the market-place,
Hooting and shrieking. When these prodigies
Do so conjointly meet, let not men say,
'These are their reasons,—they are natural;'
For, I believe, they are portentous things
Unto the climate that they point upon.

CICERO.
Indeed, it is a strange-disposed time:
But men may construe things after their fashion,
Clean from the purpose of the things themselves.
Comes Cæsar to the Capitol to-morrow?

CASCA.
He doth; for he did bid Antonius
Send word to you he would be there to-morrow.

CICERO.
Good night, then, Casca: this disturbed sky
Is not to walk in.

CASCA.
Farewell, Cicero.
      [*Exit* CICERO.
Enter CASSIUS.

CASSIUS.
Who's there?

CASCA.
A Roman.

CASSIUS.
Casca, by your voice.

CASCA.

Your ear is good. Cassius, what night is this!

CASSIUS.

A very pleasing night to honest men.

CASCA.

Who ever knew the heavens menace so?

CASSIUS.

Those that have known the earth so full of faults.
For my part, I have walkt about the streets,
Submitting me unto the perilous night;
And, thus unbraced, Casca, as you see,
Have bared my bosom to the thunder-stone:
And when the cross blue lightning seem'd to open
The breast of heaven, I did present myself
Even in the aim and very flash of it.

CASCA.

But wherefore did you so much tempt the
   heavens?
It is the part of men to fear and tremble,
When the most mighty gods by tokens send
Such dreadful heralds to astonish us.

CASSIUS.

You are dull, Casca; and those sparks of life
That should be in a Roman you do want,
Or else you use not. You look pale, and gaze,
And put on fear, and cast yourself in wonder,
To see the strange impatience of the heavens:
But if you would consider the true cause
Why all these fires, why all these gliding ghosts,
Why birds and beasts from quality and kind—
Why old men, fools, and children calculate;
Why all these things change from their ordinance,
Their natures, and pre-formed faculties,
To monstrous quality;—why, you shall find
That heaven hath infused them with these spirits,
To make them instruments of fear and warning
Unto some monstrous state.
Now could I, Casca, name to thee a man
Most like this dreadful night,
That thunders, lightens, opens graves, and roars
As doth the lion in the Capitol, —
A man no mightier than thyself or me
In personal action; yet prodigious grown,
And fearful, as these strange eruptions are.

CASCA.

'Tis Cæsar that you mean; is it not, Cassius?

CASSIUS.

Let it be who it is; for Romans now
Have thews and limbs like to their ancestors;
But, woe the while! our fathers' minds are dead,
And we are govern'd with our mothers' spirits;
Our yoke and sufferance show us womanish.

CASCA.

Indeed, they say the senators to-morrow
Mean to establish Cæsar as a king;
And he shall wear his crown by sea and land,
In every place, save here in Italy.

CASSIUS.

I know where I will wear this dagger, then;
Cassius from bondage will deliver Cassius:
Therein, ye gods, you make the weak most
   strong;
Therein, ye gods, you tyrants do defeat:
Nor stony tower, nor walls of beaten brass
Nor airless dungeon, nor strong links of iron,
Can be retentive to the strength of spirit;

But life, being weary of these worldly bars,
Never lacks power to dismiss itself.
If I know this, know all the world besides,
That part of tyranny that I do bear
I can shake off at pleasure.   [Thunder still.

CASCA.

          So can I:
So every bondman in his own hand bears
The power to cancel his captivity.

CASSIUS.

And why should Cæsar be a tyrant, then?
Poor man! I know he would not be a wolf,
But that he sees the Romans are but sheep:
He were no lion, were not Romans hinds.
Those that with haste will make a mighty fire
Begin it with weak straws: what trash is Rome,
What rubbish, and what offal, when it serves
For the base matter to illuminate
So vile a thing as Cæsar! But, O grief,
Where hast thou led me? I perhaps speak this
Before a willing bondman: then I know
My answer must be made; but I am arm'd,
And dangers are to me indifferent.

CASCA.

You speak to Casca; and to such a man
That is no fleering tell-tale. Hold, my hand:
Be factious for redress of all these griefs;
And I will set this foot of mine as far
As who goes farthest.

CASSIUS.

          There's a bargain made.
Now know you, Casca, I have moved already
Some certain of the noblest-minded Romans
To undergo with me an enterprise
Of honourable-dangerous consequence;
And I do know, by this, they stay for me
In Pompey's porch: for now, this fearful night,
There is no stir or walking in the streets;
And the complexion of the element
In's favour's like the work we have in hand,
Most bloody, fiery and most terrible.

CASCA.

Stand close awhile, for here comes one in haste.

CASSIUS.

'Tis Cinna,—I do know him by his gait;
He is a friend.

Enter CINNA.
          Cinna, where haste you so?

CINNA.

To find out you. Who's that? Metellus Cimber?

CASSIUS.

No, it is Casca; one incorporate
To our attempts. Am I not stay'd for, Cinna?

CINNA.

I am glad on't. What a fearful night is this!
There's two or three of us have seen strange
   sights.

CASSIUS.

Am I not stay'd for? tell me.

CINNA.

          Yes, you are.—
O Cassius, if you could
But win the noble Brutus to our party—

CASSIUS.

Be you content: good Cinna, take this paper,
And look you lay it in the prætor's chair,

Where Brutus may but find it; and throw this
In at his window; set this up with wax
Upon old Brutus' statue: all this done,
Repair to Pompey's porch, where you shall find us.
Is Decius Brutus and Trebonius there?

CINNA.

All but Metellus Cimber; and he's gone
To seek you at your house. Well, I will hie,
And so bestow these papers as you bade me.

CASSIUS.

That done, repair to Pompey's theatre.

                 [*Exit* CINNA.

Come, Casca, you and I will yet, ere day,
See Brutus at his house: three parts of him
Is ours already; and the man entire,
Upon the next encounter, yields him ours.

CASCA.

O, he sits high in all the people's hearts:
And that which would appear offence in us,
His countenance, like richest alchemy,
Will change to virtue and to worthiness.

CASSIUS.

Him, and his worth, and our great need of him,
You have right well conceited. Let us go,
For it is after midnight; and, ere day,
We will awake him, and be sure of him.   [*Exeunt.*

ACT II. SCENE I.

Rome. BRUTUS' *orchard.*

Enter MARCUS BRUTUS.

MARCUS BRUTUS.

WHAT, Lucius, ho!—
     I cannot, by the progress of the stars,
Give guess how near to day.—Lucius, I say!—
I would it were my fault to sleep so soundly.—
When, Lucius, when? awake, I say! what, Lucius!

Enter LUCIUS.

LUCIUS.

Call'd you, my lord?

MARCUS BRUTUS.

Get me a taper in my study, Lucius:
When it is lighted, come and call me here.

LUCIUS.

I will, my lord.   [*Exit.*

MARCUS BRUTUS.

It must be by his death: and, for my part,
I know no personal cause to spurn at him,
But for the general. He would be crown'd:—
How that might change his nature, there's the
     question:
It is the bright day that brings forth the adder;
And that craves wary walking. Crown him?—
     that;—
And then, I grant, we put a sting in him,
That at his will he may do danger with.
Th'abuse of greatness is, when it disjoins
Remorse from power: and, to speak truth of Cæsar,
I have not known when his affections sway'd
More than his reason. But 'tis a common proof,
That lowliness is young ambition's ladder,
Whereto the climber-upward turns his face;
But when he once attains the upmost round,
He then unto the ladder turns his back,
Looks in the clouds, scorning the base degrees

By which he did ascend: so Cæsar may;
Then, lest he may, prevent. And, since the
     quarrel
Will bear no colour for the thing he is,
Fashion it thus; that what he is, augmented,
Would run to these and these extremities:
And therefore think him as a serpent's egg,
Which, hatcht, would, as his kind, grow mischiev-
     ous;
And kill him in the shell.

Enter LUCIUS.

LUCIUS.

The taper burneth in your closet, sir.
Searching the window for a flint, I found
               [*Gives him the letter.*
This paper, thus seal'd up; and, I am sure,
It did not lie there when I went to bed.

MARCUS BRUTUS.

Get you to bed again; it is not day.
Is not to-morrow, boy, the ides of March?

LUCIUS.

I know not, sir.

MARCUS BRUTUS.

Look in the calendar, and bring me word.

LUCIUS.

I will, sir.   [*Exit.*

MARCUS BRUTUS.

The exhalations, whizzing in the air,
Give so much light, that I may read by them.
             [*Opens the letter and reads.*
'Brutus, thou sleep'st; awake, and see thyself.
Shall Rome, &c. Speak, strike, redress!'—
' Brutus, thou sleep'st: awake!'—
Such instigations have been often dropt
Where I have took them up.
' Shall Rome, &c.' Thus must I piece it out;
Shall Rome stand under one man's awe? What,
     Rome?
My ancestors did from the streets of Rome
The Tarquin drive, when he was call'd a king.
' Speak, strike, redress!'—Am I entreated
To speak and strike? O Rome, I make thee
     promise,
If the redress will follow, thou receivest
Thy full petition at the hand of Brutus!

Enter LUCIUS.

LUCIUS.

Sir, March is wasted fifteen days. [*Knock within.*

MARCUS BRUTUS.

'Tis good. Go to the gate; somebody knocks,
                 [*Exit* LUCIUS.
Since Cassius first did whet me against Cæsar,
I have not slept.
Between the acting of a dreadful thing
And the first motion, all the interim is
Like a phantasma or a hideous dream:
The Genius and the mortal instruments
Are then in council; and the state of man,
Like to a little kingdom, suffers then
The nature of an insurrection.

Enter LUCIUS.

LUCIUS.

Sir, 'tis your brother Cassius at the door,
Who doth desire to see you.

MARCUS BRUTUS.

                Is he alone?

LUCIUS.
No, sir, there are moe with him.
MARCUS BRUTUS.
Do you know them?
LUCIUS.
No, sir; their hats are pluckt about their ears,
And half their faces buried in their cloaks,
That by no means I may discover them
By any mark of favour.
MARCUS BRUTUS.
Let 'em enter.
[*Exit* LUCIUS.
They are the faction. O conspiracy,
Shamest thou to show thy dangerous brow by
night,
When evils are most free? O, then, by day
Where wilt thou find a cavern dark enough
To mask thy monstrous visage? Seek none, con-
spiracy;
Hide it in smiles and affability:
For if thou put thy native semblance on,
Not Erebus itself were dim enough
To hide thee from prevention.
Enter the Conspirators, CASSIUS, CASCA, DECIUS,
CINNA, METELLUS CIMBER, *and* TREBONIUS.
CASSIUS.
I think we are too bold upon your rest:
Good morrow, Brutus; do we trouble you?
MARCUS BRUTUS.
I have been up this hour; awake all night.
Know I these men that come along with you?
CASSIUS.
Yes, every man of them; and no man here
But honours you; and every one doth wish
You had but that opinion of yourself
Which every noble Roman bears of you—
This is Trebonius.
MARCUS BRUTUS.
He is welcome hither.
CASSIUS.
This, Decius Brutus.
MARCUS BRUTUS.
He is welcome too.
CASSIUS.
This, Casca; this, Cinna; and this, Metellus Cim-
ber.
MARCUS BRUTUS.
They are all welcome.—
What watchful cares do interpose themselves
Betwixt your eyes and night?
CASSIUS.
Shall I entreat a word? [*They whisper.*
DECIUS BRUTUS.
Here lies the east: doth not the day break here?
CASCA.
No.
CINNA.
O, pardon, sir, it doth; and yon gray lines
That fret the clouds are messengers of day.
CASCA.
You shall confess that you are both deceived.
Here, as I point my sword, the sun arises;
Which is a great way growing on the south,
Weighing the youthful season of the year.
Some two months hence, up higher toward the
north

He first presents his fire; and the high east
Stands, as the Capitol, directly here.
MARCUS BRUTUS.
Give me your hands all over, one by one.
CASSIUS.
And let us swear our resolution.
MARCUS BRUTUS.
No, not an oath: if not the face of men,
The sufferance of our souls, the time's abuse,—
If these be motives weak, break off betimes,
And every man hence to his idle bed;
So let high-sighted tyranny range on,
Till each man drop by lottery. But if these,
As I am sure they do, bear fire enough
To kindle cowards, and to steel with valour
The melting spirits of women; then, countrymen,
What need we any spur, but our own cause,
To prick us to redress? what other bond
Than secret Romans, that have spoke the word,
And will not palter? and what other oath
Than honesty to honesty engaged,
That this shall be, or we will fall for it?
Swear priests, and cowards, and men cautelous,
Old feeble carrions, and such suffering souls
That welcome wrongs; unto bad causes swear
Such creatures as men doubt: but do not stain
The even virtue of our enterprise,
Nor th'insuppressive mettle of our spirits,
To think that or our cause or our performance
Did need an oath; when every drop of blood
That every Roman bears, and nobly bears,
Is guilty of a several bastardy,
If he do break the smallest particle
Of any promise that hath past from him.
CASSIUS.
But what of Cicero? shall we sound him?
I think he will stand very strong with us.
CASCA.
Let us not leave him out.
CINNA.
No, by no means.
METELLUS CIMBER.
O, let us have him; for his silver hairs
Will purchase us a good opinion,
And buy men's voices to commend our deeds:
It shall be said, his judgement ruled our hands;
Our youths and wildness shall no whit appear,
But all be buried in his gravity.
MARCUS BRUTUS.
O, name him not: let us not break with him;
For he will never follow any thing
That other men begin.
CASSIUS.
Then leave him out.
CASCA.
Indeed he is not fit.
DECIUS BRUTUS.
Shall no man else be toucht but only Cæsar?
CASSIUS.
Decius, well urged:—I think it is not meet,
Mark Antony, so well beloved of Cæsar,
Should outlive Cæsar: we shall find of him
A shrewd contriver; and, you know, his means,
If he improve them, may well stretch so far
As to annoy us all: which to prevent,
Let Antony and Cæsar fall together.

MARCUS BRUTUS.
Our course will seem too bloody, Caius Cassius,
To cut the head off, and then hack the limbs,—
Like wrath in death, and envy afterwards;
For Antony is but a limb of Cæsar:
Let's be sacrificers, but not butchers, Caius.
We all stand up against the spirit of Cæsar;
And in the spirit of men there is no blood:
O, that we, then, could come by Cæsar's spirit,
And not dismember Cæsar! But, alas,
Cæsar must bleed for it! And, gentle friends,
Let's kill him boldly, but not wrathfully;
Let's carve him as a dish fit for the gods,
Not hew him as a carcass fit for hounds:
And let our hearts, as subtle masters do,
Stir up their servants to an act of rage,
And after seem to chide 'em. This shall make
Our purpose necessary, and not envious:
Which so appearing to the common eyes,
We shall be call'd purgers, not murderers.
And for Mark Antony, think not of him;
For he can do no more than Cæsar's arm
When Cæsar's head is off.

CASSIUS.
                    Yet I fear him;
For in the ingrafted love he bears to Cæsar—

MARCUS BRUTUS.
Alas, good Cassius, do not think of him:
If he love Cæsar, all that he can do
Is to himself,—take thought, and die for Cæsar:
And that were much he should; for he is given
To sports, to wildness, and much company.

TREBONIUS.
There is no fear in him; let him not die;
For he will live, and laugh at this hereafter.
                                [*Clock strikes.*

MARCUS BRUTUS.
Peace! count the clock.

CASSIUS.
                    The clock hath stricken three.

TREBONIUS.
'Tis time to part.

CASSIUS.
                    But it is doubtful yet,
Whether Cæsar will come forth to-day or no;
For he is superstitious grown of late;
Quite from the main opinion he held once
Of fantasy, of dreams, and ceremonies:
It may be, these apparent prodigies,
The unaccustom'd terror of this night,
And the persuasion of his augurers,
May hold him from the Capitol to-day.

DECIUS BRUTUS.
Never fear that: if he be so resolved,
I can o'ersway him; for he loves to hear
That unicorns may be betray'd with trees,
And bears with glasses, elephants with holes,
Lions with toils, and men with flatterers:
But when I tell him he hates flatterers,
He says he does,—being then most flattered.
Let me work;
For I can give his humour the true bent,
And I will bring him to the Capitol.

CASSIUS.
Nay, we will all of us be there to fetch him.

MARCUS BRUTUS.
By the eighth hour: is that the uttermost?

CINNA.
Be that the uttermost, and fail not then.

METELLUS CIMBER.
Caius Ligarius doth bear Cæsar hard,
Who rated him for speaking well of Pompey:
I wonder none of you have thought of him.

MARCUS BRUTUS.
Now, good Metellus, go along by him:
He loves me well, and I have given him reasons;
Send him but hither, and I'll fashion him.

CASSIUS.
The morning comes upon's: we'll leave you,
      Brutus:—
And, friends, disperse yourselves; but all remember
What you have said, and show yourselves true
      Romans.

MARCUS BRUTUS.
Good gentlemen, look fresh and merrily;
Let not our looks put on our purposes;
But bear it as our Roman actors do,
With untired spirits and formal constancy:
And so, good morrow to you every one.
                [*Exeunt all but* BRUTUS.
Boy! Lucius!—Fast asleep? It is no matter;
Enjoy the honey-heavy dew of slumber:
Thou hast no figures nor no fantasies,
Which busy care draws in the brains of men;
Therefore thou sleep'st so sound.

                    Enter PORTIA.

PORTIA.
                    Brutus, my lord!

MARCUS BRUTUS.
Portia, what mean you? wherefore rise you now?
It is not for your health thus to commit
Your weak condition to the raw-cold morning.

PORTIA.
Nor for yours neither. Y' have ungently, Brutus,
Stole from my bed: and yesternight, at supper,
You suddenly arose, and walkt about,
Musing and sighing, with your arms across;
And when I askt you what the matter was,
You stared upon me with ungentle looks:
I urged you further; then you scratcht your
      head,
And too impatiently stampt with your foot:
Yet I insisted, yet you answer'd not;
But, with an angry wafture of your hand,
Gave sign for me to leave you: so I did;
Fearing to strengthen that impatience
Which seem'd too much enkindled; and withal
Hoping it was but an effect of humour,
Which sometime hath his hour with every man.
It will not let you eat, nor talk, nor sleep;
And, could it work so much upon your shape,
As it hath much prevail'd on your condition,
I should not know you, Brutus. Dear my lord,
Make me acquainted with your cause of grief.

MARCUS BRUTUS.
I am not well in health, and that is all.

PORTIA.
Brutus is wise, and, were he not in health,
He would embrace the means to come by it.

MARCUS BRUTUS.
Why, so I do.—Good Portia, go to bed.

PORTIA.

Is Brutus sick,—and is it physical
To walk unbraced, and suck up the humours
Of the dank morning? What, is Brutus sick,—
And will he steal out of his wholesome bed,
To dare the vile contagion of the night,
And tempt the rheumy and unpurged air
To add unto his sickness? No, my Brutus;
You have some sick offence within your mind,
Which, by the right and virtue of my place,
I ought to know of: and, upon my knees,
I charm you, by my once-commended beauty,
By all your vows of love, and that great vow
Which did incorporate and make us one,
That you unfold to me, yourself, your half,
Why you are heavy; and what men to-night
Have had resort to you,—for here have been
Some six or seven, who did hide their faces
Even from darkness.

MARCUS BRUTUS.
                    Kneel not, gentle Portia.

PORTIA.

I should not need, if you were gentle Brutus.
Within the bond of marriage, tell me, Brutus,
Is it excepted I should know no secrets
That appertain to you? Am I yourself
But, as it were, in sort or limitation,—
To keep with you at meals, comfort your bed,
And talk to you sometimes? Dwell I but in the
Of your good pleasure? If it be no more, [suburbs
Portia is Brutus' harlot, not his wife.

MARCUS BRUTUS.

You are my true and honourable wife;
As dear to me as are the ruddy drops
That visit my sad heart.

PORTIA.

If this were true, then should I know this secret.
I grant I am a woman; but withal
A woman that Lord Brutus took to wife:
I grant I am a woman; but withal
A woman well-reputed,—Cato's daughter.
Think you I am no stronger than my sex,
Being so father'd and so husbanded?
Tell me your counsels; I will not disclose 'em:
I have made strong proof of my constancy,
Giving myself a voluntary wound
Here, in the thigh: can I bear that with patience,
And not my husband's secrets?

MARCUS BRUTUS.
                    O ye gods,
Render me worthy of this noble wife!   [Knock.
Hark, hark! one knocks: Portia, go in awhile;
And by and by thy bosom shall partake
The secrets of my heart:
All my engagements I will construe to thee,
All the charactery of my sad brows:—
Leave me with haste. [Exit PORTIA.]—Lucius,
    who's that knocks?

Enter LUCIUS with LIGARIUS.

LUCIUS.

Here is a sick man that would speak with you.

MARCUS BRUTUS.

Caius Ligarius, that Metellus spake of.—
Boy, stand aside.—Caius Ligarius,—how!

LIGARIUS.

Vouchsafe good-morrow from a feeble tongue.

MARCUS BRUTUS.

O, what a time have you chose out, brave Caius,
To wear a kerchief! Would you were not sick!

LIGARIUS.

I am not sick, if Brutus have in hand
Any exploit worthy the name of honour.

MARCUS BRUTUS.

Such an exploit have I in hand, Ligarius,
Had you a healthful ear to hear of it.

LIGARIUS.

By all the gods that Romans bow before,
I here discard my sickness! Soul of Rome!
Brave son, derived from honourable loins!
Thou, like an exorcist, hast conjured up
My mortified spirit. Now bid me run,
And I will strive with things impossible;
Yea, get the better of them. What's to do?

MARCUS BRUTUS.

A piece of work that will make sick men whole.

LIGARIUS.

But are not some whole that we must make sick?

MARCUS BRUTUS.

That must we also. What it is, my Caius,
I shall unfold to thee, as we are going
To whom it must be done.

LIGARIUS.
                    Set on your foot;
And, with a heart new-fired, I follow you,
To do I know not what: but it sufficeth
That Brutus leads me on.

MARCUS BRUTUS.
                    Follow me, then.   [Exeunt.

SCENE II.

The same. A hall in CAESAR'S *palace.*

Thunder and lightning. Enter JULIUS CAESAR, *in
his nightgown.*

JULIUS CAESAR.

NOR heaven nor earth have been at peace to-
    night:
Thrice hath Calphurnia in her sleep cried out,
'Help, ho! they murder Cæsar!'—Who's within?

Enter a SERVANT.

SERVANT.

My lord?

JULIUS CAESAR.

Go bid the priests do present sacrifice,
And bring me their opinions of success.

SERVANT.

I will, my lord.   [Exit.

Enter CALPHURNIA.

CALPHURNIA.

What mean you, Cæsar? think you to walk forth?
You shall not stir out of your house to-day.

JULIUS CAESAR.

Cæsar shall forth: the things that threaten'd me
Ne'er lookt but on my back; when they shall see
The face of Cæsar, they are vanished.

CALPHURNIA.

Cæsar, I never stood on ceremonies,
Yet now they fright me. There is one within,
Besides the things that we have heard and seen,
Recounts most horrid sights seen by the watch.
A lioness hath whelped in the streets;

And graves have yawn'd, and yielded up their
   dead;
Fierce fiery warriors fight upon the clouds,
In ranks and squadrons and right form of war,
Which drizzled blood upon the Capitol;
The noise of battle hurtled in the air,
Horses did neigh, and dying men did groan;
And ghosts did shriek and squeal about the streets.
O Cæsar, these things are beyond all use,
And I do fear them!

JULIUS CAESAR.
           What can be avoided
Whose end is purposed by the mighty gods?
Yet Cæsar shall go forth; for these predictions
Are to the world in general as to Cæsar.

CALPHURNIA.
When beggars die, there are no comets seen;
The heavens themselves blaze forth the death of
   princes.

JULIUS CAESAR.
Cowards die many times before their deaths;
The valiant never taste of death but once.
Of all the wonders that I yet have heard,
It seems to me most strange that men should
   fear;
Seeing that death, a necessary end,
Will come when it will come.
      Enter SERVANT.
          What say the augurers?

SERVANT.
They would not have you to stir forth to-day.
Plucking the entrails of an offering forth,
They could not find a heart within the beast.

JULIUS CAESAR.
The gods do this in shame of cowardice:
Cæsar should be a beast without a heart,
If he should stay at home to-day for fear.
No, Cæsar shall not: danger knows full well
That Cæsar is more dangerous than he:
We are two lions litter'd in one day,
And I the elder and more terrible:—
And Cæsar shall go forth.

CALPHURNIA.
          Alas, my lord,
Your wisdom is consumed in confidence.
Do not go forth to-day: call it my fear
That keeps you in the house, and not your own.
We'll send Mark Antony to the senate-house;
And he shall say you are not well to-day:
Let me, upon my knee, prevail in this.

JULIUS CAESAR.
Mark Antony shall say I am not well;
And, for thy humour, I will stay at home.
      Enter DECIUS.
Here's Decius Brutus, he shall tell them so.

DECIUS BRUTUS.
Cæsar, all hail! good morrow, worthy Cæsar:
I come to fetch you to the senate-house.

JULIUS CAESAR.
And you are come in very happy time,
To bear my greeting to the senators,
And tell them that I will not come to-day:
Cannot, is false; and that I dare not, falser:
I will not come to-day,—tell them so, Decius.

CALPHURNIA.
Say he is sick.

JULIUS CAESAR.
        Shall Cæsar send a lie?
Have I in conquest stretcht mine arm so far
To be afeard to tell graybeards the truth?
Decius, go tell them Cæsar will not come.

DECIUS BRUTUS.
Most mighty Cæsar, let me know some cause,
Lest I be laught at when I tell them so.

JULIUS CAESAR.
The cause is in my will,—I will not come;
That is enough to satisfy the senate.
But, for your private satisfaction,
Because I love you, I will let you know,—
Calphurnia here, my wife, stays me at home:
She dreamt to-night she saw my statua,
Which, like a fountain with an hundred spouts,
Did run pure blood; and many lusty Romans
Came smiling, and did bathe their hands in it:
And these does she apply for warnings and por-
   tents
And evils imminent; and on her knee
Hath begg'd that I will stay at home to-day.

DECIUS BRUTUS.
This dream is all amiss interpreted;
It was a vision fair and fortunate:
Your statue spouting blood in many pipes,
In which so many smiling Romans bathed,
Signifies that from you great Rome shall suck
Reviving blood; and that great men shall press
For tinctures, stains, relics, and recognizance.
This by Calphurnia's dream is signified.

JULIUS CAESAR.
And this way have you well expounded it.

DECIUS BRUTUS.
I have, when you have heard what I can say:
And know it now,—the senate have concluded
To give, this day, a crown to mighty Cæsar.
If you shall send them word you will not come,
Their minds may change. Besides, it were a
   mock
Apt to be render'd, for some one to say,
'Break up the senate till another time,
When Cæsar's wife shall meet with better
   dreams.'
If Cæsar hide himself, shall they not whisper,
'Lo, Cæsar is afraid'?
Pardon me, Cæsar; for my dear dear love
To your proceeding bids me tell you this;
And reason to my love is liable.

JULIUS CAESAR.
How foolish do your fears seem now, Calphur-
   nia!
I am ashamed I did yield to them.—
Give me my robe, for I will go:—
  Enter PUBLIUS, BRUTUS, LIGARIUS, METEL-
    LUS, CASCA, TREBONIUS, *and* CINNA.
And look where Publius is come to fetch me.

PUBLIUS.
Good morrow, Cæsar.

JULIUS CAESAR.
         Welcome, Publius.—
What, Brutus, are you stirr'd so early too?—
Good morrow, Casca.—Caius Ligarius,
Cæsar was ne'er so much your enemy
As that same ague which hath made you lean.—
What is't o'clock?

DECIUS BRUTUS.
Cæsar, 'tis strucken eight.
JULIUS CAESAR.
I thank you for your pains and courtesy.
Enter ANTONY.
See! Antony, that revels long o' nights,
Is notwithstanding up.—Good morrow, Antony.
MARCUS ANTONIUS.
So to most noble Cæsar.
JULIUS CAESAR.
Bid them prepare within:—
I am to blame to be thus waited for.—
Now, Cinna:—now, Metellus:—what, Trebonius!
I have an hour's talk in store for you;
Remember that you call on me to-day:
Be near me, that I may remember you.
TREBONIUS.
Cæsar, I will:—[*aside*] and so near will I be,
That your best friends shall wish I had been fur-
ther.
JULIUS CAESAR.
Good friends, go in, and taste some wine with
me;
And we, like friends, will straightway go together.
DECIUS BRUTUS [*aside*].
That every like is not the same, O Cæsar,
The heart of Brutus yearns to think upon!
[*Exeunt.*

SCENE III.

The same. A street near the Capitol.

Enter ARTEMIDORUS, *reading a paper.*

ARTEMIDORUS.
'CAESAR, beware of Brutus; take heed of
Cassius; come not near Casca; have an eye to
Cinna; trust not Trebonius; mark well Metellus
Cimber; Decius Brutus loves thee not: thou hast
wrong'd Caius Ligarius. There is but one mind in
all these men, and it is bent against Cæsar. If
thou beest not immortal, look about you: security
gives way to conspiracy. The mighty gods defend
thee! Thy lover,
ARTEMIDORUS.'
Here will I stand till Cæsar pass along,
And as a suitor will I give him this.
My heart laments that virtue cannot live
Out of the teeth of emulation.
If thou read this, O Cæsar, thou mayst live;
If not, the Fates with traitors do contrive.   [*Exit.*

SCENE IV.

*The same. Another part of the same street, before
the house of* BRUTUS.

Enter PORTIA *and* LUCIUS.

PORTIA.
I PRITHEE, boy, run to the senate-house;
Stay not to answer me, but get thee gone:
Why dost thou stay?
LUCIUS.
To know my errand, madam.
PORTIA.
I would have had thee there, and here again,
Ere I can tell thee what thou shouldst do there.—

[*aside*] O constancy, be strong upon my side,
Set a huge mountain 'tween my heart and
tongue!
I have a man's mind, but a woman's might.
How hard it is for women to keep counsel!—
Art thou here yet?
LUCIUS.
Madam, what should I do?
Run to the Capitol, and nothing else?
And so return to you, and nothing else?
PORTIA.
Yes, bring me word, boy, if thy lord look well,
For he went sickly forth: and take good note
What Cæsar doth, what suitors press to him.
Hark, boy! what noise is that?
LUCIUS.
I hear none, madam.
PORTIA.
Prithee, listen well:
I heard a bustling rumour, like a fray,
And the wind brings it from the Capitol.
LUCIUS.
Sooth, madam, I hear nothing.
Enter the SOOTHSAYER.
PORTIA.
Come hither, fellow: which way hast thou been?
SOOTHSAYER.
At mine own house, good lady.
PORTIA.
What is 't o'clock?
SOOTHSAYER.
About the ninth hour, lady.
PORTIA.
Is Cæsar yet gone to the Capitol?
SOOTHSAYER.
Madam, not yet: I go to take my stand,
To see him pass on to the Capitol.
PORTIA.
Thou hast some suit to Cæsar, hast thou not?
SOOTHSAYER.
That I have, lady: if it will please Cæsar
To be so good to Cæsar as to hear me,
I shall beseech him to befriend himself.
PORTIA.
Why, know'st thou any harm's intended towards
him?
SOOTHSAYER.
None that I know will be, much that I fear may
chance.
Good morrow to you.—Here the street is
narrow:
The throng that follows Cæsar at the heels,
Of senators, of prætors, common suitors,
Will crowd a feeble man almost to death:
I'll get me to a place more void, and there
Speak to great Cæsar as he comes along.   [*Exit.*
PORTIA.
I must go in.—[*Aside*] Ay me, how weak a thing
The heart of woman is! O Brutus,
The heavens speed thee in thine enterprise!—
Sure, the boy heard me.—Brutus hath a suit
That Cæsar will not grant.—O, I grow faint.—
Run, Lucius, and commend me to my lord;
Say I am merry: come to me again,
And bring me word what he doth say to thee.
[*Exeunt severally.*

ACT III. SCENE I.

Rome.   Before the Capitol; the SENATE *sitting.*

A crowd of people; among them ARTEMIDORUS *and the* SOOTHSAYER. *Flourish. Enter* CAESAR, BRUTUS, CASSIUS, CASCA, DECIUS, METELLUS, TREBONIUS, CINNA, ANTONY, LEPIDUS, POPILIUS, PUBLIUS, *and others.*

JULIUS CAESAR.

THE ides of March are come.

SOOTHSAYER.

Ay, Cæsar; but not gone.

ARTEMIDORUS.

Hail, Cæsar! read this schedule.

DECIUS BRUTUS.

Trebonius doth desire you to o'er-read,
At your best leisure, this his humble suit.

ARTEMIDORUS.

O Cæsar, read mine first; for mine's a suit
That touches Cæsar nearer; read it, great Cæsar.

JULIUS CAESAR.

What touches us ourself, shall be last served.

ARTEMIDORUS.

Delay not, Cæsar; read it instantly.

JULIUS CAESAR.

What, is the fellow mad?

PUBLIUS.

Sirrah, give place.

CASSIUS.

What, urge you your petitions in the street?
Come to the Capitol.

CAESAR *enters the Capitol, the rest following.*
All the SENATORS *rise.*

POPILIUS LENA.

I wish your enterprise to-day may thrive.

CASSIUS.

What enterprise, Popilius?

POPILIUS LENA.

Fare you well. [*Advances to* CAESAR.

MARCUS BRUTUS.

What said Popilius Lena?

CASSIUS.

He wisht to-day our enterprise might thrive.
I fear our purpose is discovered.

MARCUS BRUTUS.

Look, how he makes to Cæsar: mark him.

CASSIUS.

Casca,
Be sudden, for we fear prevention.—
Brutus, what shall be done? If this be known,
Cassius or Cæsar never shall turn back,
For I will slay myself.

MARCUS BRUTUS.

Cassius, be constant:
Popilius Lena speaks not of our purpose;
For, look, he smiles, and Cæsar doth not change.

CASSIUS.

Trebonius knows his time; for, look you, Brutus,
He draws Mark Antony out of the way.

[*Exeunt* ANTONY *and* TREBONIUS. CAESAR
and the SENATORS *take their seats.*

DECIUS BRUTUS.

Where is Metellus Cimber? Let him go,
And presently prefer his suit to Cæsar.

MARCUS BRUTUS.

He is addrest: press near and second him.

CINNA.

Casca, you are the first that rears your hand.

JULIUS CAESAR.

Are we all ready? What is now amiss
That Cæsar and his senate must redress?

METELLUS CIMBER.

Most high, most mighty, and most puissant
Cæsar,
Metellus Cimber throws before thy seat
An humble heart,—   [*Kneeling.*

JULIUS CAESAR.

I must prevent thee, Cimber.
These couchings and these lowly courtesies
Might fire the blood of ordinary men,
And turn pre-ordinance and first decree
Into the law of children. Be not fond,
To think that Cæsar bears such rebel blood
That will be thaw'd from the true quality
With that which melteth fools; I mean, sweet
words,
Low-crooked curt'sies, and base spaniel-fawn-
ing.
Thy brother by decree is banished:
If thou dost bend, and pray, and fawn for him,
I spurn thee like a cur out of my way.
Know, Cæsar doth not wrong; nor without cause
Will he be satisfied.

METELLUS CIMBER.

Is there no voice more worthy than my own,
To sound more sweetly in great Cæsar's ear
For the repealing of my banisht brother?

MARCUS BRUTUS.

I kiss thy hand, but not in flattery, Cæsar;
Desiring thee that Publius Cimber may
Have an immediate freedom of repeal.

JULIUS CAESAR.

What, Brutus!

CASSIUS.

Pardon, Cæsar; Cæsar, pardon:
As low as to thy foot doth Cassius fall,
To beg enfranchisement for Publius Cimber.

JULIUS CAESAR.

I could be well moved, if I were as you;
If I could pray to move, prayers would move me:
But I am constant as the northern star,
Of whose true-fixt and resting quality
There is no fellow in the firmament.
The skies are painted with unnumber'd sparks,
They are all fire, and every one doth shine;
But there's but one in all doth hold his place:
So in the world,—'tis furnisht well with men,
And men are flesh and blood, and apprehensive;
Yet in the number I do know but one
That unassailable holds on his rank,
Unshaked of motion: and that I am he,
Let me a little show it, even in this,—
That I was constant Cimber should be banisht,
And constant do remain to keep him so.

CINNA.

O Cæsar,—

JULIUS CAESAR.

Hence! wilt thou lift up Olympus?

DECIUS BRUTUS.

Great Cæsar,—

JULIUS CAESAR.

Doth not Brutus bootless kneel?

CASCA.
Speak, hands, for me! 　　　[*They stab* CAESAR.
JULIUS CAESAR.
Et tu, Brute?—Then fall, Cæsar! 　　　[*Dies.*
CINNA.
Liberty! Freedom! Tyranny is dead!—
Run hence, proclaim, cry it about the streets.
CASSIUS.
Some to the common pulpits, and cry out,
'Liberty, freedom, and enfranchisement!'
MARCUS BRUTUS.
People, and senators, be not affrighted;
Fly not; stand still:—ambition's debt is paid.
CASCA.
Go to the pulpit, Brutus.
DECIUS BRUTUS.
And Cassius too.
MARCUS BRUTUS.
Where's Publius?
CINNA.
Here, quite confounded with this mutiny.
METELLUS CIMBER.
Stand fast together, lest some friend of Cæsar's
Should chance—
MARCUS BRUTUS.
Talk not of standing.—Publius, good cheer;
There is no harm intended to your person,
Nor to no Roman else: so tell them, Publius.
CASSIUS.
And leave us, Publius; lest that the people,
Rushing on us, should do your age some mischief.
MARCUS BRUTUS.
Do so:—and let no man abide this deed,
But we the doers.
Enter TREBONIUS.
CASSIUS.
Where is Antony?
TREBONIUS.
Fled to his house amazed:
Men, wives, and children stare, cry out, and run
As it were doomsday.
MARCUS BRUTUS.
Fates, we will know your pleasures:—
That we shall die, we know; 'tis but the time,
And drawing days out, that men stand upon.
CASSIUS.
Why, he that cuts off twenty years of life
Cuts off so many years of fearing death.
MARCUS BRUTUS.
Grant that, and then is death a benefit:
So are we Cæsar's friends, that have abridged
His time of fearing death.—Stoop, Romans,
　　stoop,
And let us bathe our hands in Cæsar's blood
Up to the elbows, and besmear our swords:
Then walk we forth, even to the market-place,
And, waving our red weapons o'er our heads,
Let's all cry, 'Peace, freedom, and liberty!'
CASSIUS.
Stoop then, and wash.—How many ages hence
Shall this our lofty scene be acted over
In states unborn and accents yet unknown!
MARCUS BRUTUS.
How many times shall Cæsar bleed in sport,
That now on Pompey's basis lies along
No worthier than the dust!

CASSIUS.
So oft as that shall be,
So often shall the knot of us be call'd
The men that gave their country liberty.
DECIUS BRUTUS.
What, shall we forth?
CASSIUS.
Ay, every man away:
Brutus shall lead; and we will grace his heels
With the most boldest and best hearts of Rome.
MARCUS BRUTUS.
Soft! who comes here!
Enter a SERVANT.
A friend of Antony's.
SERVANT.
Thus, Brutus, did my master bid me kneel;
Thus did Mark Antony bid me fall down;
And, being prostrate, thus he bade me say:—
Brutus is noble, wise, valiant, and honest;
Cæsar was mighty, bold, royal, and loving:
Say I love Brutus, and I honour him;
Say I fear'd Cæsar, honour'd him, and loved him.
If Brutus will vouchsafe that Antony
May safely come to him, and be resolved
How Cæsar hath deserved to lie in death,
Mark Antony shall not love Cæsar dead
So well as Brutus living; but will follow
The fortunes and affairs of noble Brutus
Thorough the hazards of this untrod state
With all true faith. So says my master Antony.
MARCUS BRUTUS.
Thy master is a wise and valiant Roman;
I never thought him worse.
Tell him, so please him come unto this place,
He shall be satisfied; and, by my honour,
Depart untouch'd.
SERVANT.
I'll fetch him presently. 　　　[*Exit.*
MARCUS BRUTUS.
I know that we shall have him well to friend.
CASSIUS.
I wish we may: but yet have I a mind
That fears him much; and my misgiving still
Falls shrewdly to the purpose.
MARCUS BRUTUS.
But here comes Antony.
Enter ANTONY.
Welcome, Mark Antony.
MARCUS ANTONIUS.
O mighty Cæsar! dost thou lie so low?
Are all thy conquests, glories, triumphs, spoils,
Shrunk to this little measure? Fare thee well.—
I know not, gentlemen, what you intend,
Who else must be let blood, who else is rank:
If I myself, there is no hour so fit
As Cæsar's death's hour: nor no instrument
Of half that worth as those your swords, made rich
With the most noble blood of all this world.
I do beseech ye, if you bear me hard,
Now, whilst your purpled hands do reek and
　　smoke,
Fulfil your pleasure. Live a thousand years,
I shall not find myself so apt to die:
No place will please me so, no mean of death
As here by Cæsar, and by you cut off,
The choice and master spirits of this age.

MARCUS BRUTUS.

O Antony, beg not your death of us.
Though now we must appear bloody and cruel,
As, by our hands and this our present act,
You see we do; yet see you but our hands,
And this the bleeding business they have done:
Our hearts you see not,—they are pitiful;
And pity to the general wrong of Rome—
As fire drives out fire, so pity pity—
Hath done this deed on Cæsar. For your part,
To you our swords have leaden points, Mark
   Antony,
Our arms no strength of malice; and our hearts,
Of brothers' temper, do receive you in
With all kind love, good thoughts, and reverence.

CASSIUS.

Your voice shall be as strong as any man's
In the disposing of new dignities.

MARCUS BRUTUS.

Only be patient till we have appeased
The multitude, beside themselves with fear,
And then we will de iver you the cause,
Why I, that did love Cæsar when I struck him,
Have thus proceeded.

MARCUS ANTONIUS.

        I doubt not of your wisdom.
Let each man render me his bloody hand:
First, Marcus Brutus, will I shake with you:—
Next, Caius Cassius, do I take your hand;—
Now, Decius Brutus, yours;—now yours, Metel-
   lus;
Yours, Cinna;—and, my valiant Casca, yours;—
Though last, not least in love, yours, good Tre-
   bonius.
Gentlemen all,—alas, what shall I say?
My credit now stands on such slippery ground,
That one of two bad ways you must conceit me,
Either a coward or a flatterer.—
That I did love thee, Cæsar, O, 'tis true:
If, then, thy spirit look upon us now,
Shall it not grieve thee dearer than thy death,
To see thy Antony making his peace,
Shaking the bloody fingers of thy foes,
Most noble! in the presence of thy corse?
Had I as many eyes as thou hast wounds,
Weeping as fast as they stream forth thy blood,
It would become me better than to close
In terms of friendship with thine enemies. [hart;
Pardon me, Julius!—Here wast thou bay'd, brave
Here didst thou fall; and here thy hunters stand,
Sign'd in thy spoil, and crimson'd in thy lethe.—
O world, thou wast the forest to this hart;
And this, indeed, O world, the heart of thee.—
How like a deer, strucken by many princes,
Dost thou here lie!

CASSIUS.

Mark Antony,—

MARCUS ANTONIUS.

        Pardon me, Caius Cassius:
The enemies of Cæsar shall say this;
Then, in a friend, it is cold modesty.

CASSIUS.

I blame you not for praising Cæsar so;
But what compact mean you to have with us?
Will you be prickt in number of our friends;
Or shall we on, and not depend on you?

MARCUS ANTONIUS.

Therefore I took your hands; but was, indeed,
Sway'd from the point, by looking down on
   Cæsar.
Friends am I with you all, and love you all;
Upon this hope, that you shall give me reasons
Why and wherein Cæsar was dangerous.

MARCUS BRUTUS.

Or else were this a savage spectacle:
Our reasons are so full of good regard,
That were you, Antony, the son of Cæsar,
You should be satisfied.

MARCUS ANTONIUS.

        That's all I seek:
And am moreover suitor that I may
Produce his body to the market-place;
And in the pulpit, as becomes a friend,
Speak in the order of his funeral.

MARCUS BRUTUS.

You shall, Mark Antony.

CASSIUS.

        Brutus, a word with you.
[aside to BRUTUS] You know not what you do: do
   not consent
That Antony speak in his funeral:
Know you how much the people may be moved
By that which he will utter?

MARCUS BRUTUS [aside to CASSIUS].

        By your pardon;—
I will myself into the pulpit first,
And show the reason of our Cæsar's death:
What Antony shall speak, I will protest
He speaks by leave and by permission;
And that we are contented Cæsar shall
Have all true rites and lawful ceremonies.
It shall advantage more than do us wrong.

CASSIUS [aside to MARCUS BRUTUS].

I know not what may fall; I like it not.

MARCUS BRUTUS.

Mark Antony, here, take you Cæsar's body.
You shall not in your funeral speech blame us,
But speak all good you can devise of Cæsar;
And say you do't by our permission;
Else shall you not have any hand at all
About his funeral: and you shall speak
In the same pulpit whereto I am going,
After my speech is ended.

MARCUS ANTONIUS.

        Be it so;
I do desire no more.

MARCUS BRUTUS.

Prepare the body, then, and follow us.
        [Exeunt all but ANTONY.

MARCUS ANTONIUS.

O, pardon me, thou bleeding piece of earth,
That I am meek and gentle with these butchers!
Thou art the ruins of the noblest man
That ever lived in the tide of times.
Woe to the hand that shed this costly blood!
Over thy wounds now do I prophesy,—
Which, like dumb mouths, do ope their ruby lips,
To beg the voice and utterance of my tongue,—
A curse shall light upon the limbs of men;
Domestic fury and fierce civil strife
Shall cumber all the parts of Italy;
Blood and destruction shall be so in use,

And dreadful objects so familiar,
That mothers shall but smile when they behold
Their infants quarter'd with the hands of war;
All pity choked with custom of fell deeds:
And Cæsar's spirit, ranging for revenge,
With Ate by his side come hot from hell,
Shall in these confines with a monarch's voice
Cry 'Havoc,' and let slip the dogs of war;
That this foul deed shall smell above the earth
With carrion men, groaning for burial.
                    Enter OCTAVIUS' SERVANT.
You serve Octavius Cæsar, do you not?
                    SERVANT.
I do, Mark Antony.
                    MARCUS ANTONIUS.
Cæsar did write for him to come to Rome.
                    SERVANT.
He did receive his letters, and is coming;
And bid me say to you by word of mouth—
O Cæsar!—   [*Seeing the body.*
                    MARCUS ANTONIUS.
Thy heart is big, get thee apart and weep.
Passion, I see, is catching; for mine eyes,
Seeing those beads of sorrow stand in thine,
Begin to water. Is thy master coming?
                    SERVANT.
He lies to-night within seven leagues of Rome.
                    MARCUS ANTONIUS.
Post back with speed, and tell him what hath
    chanced:
Here is a mourning Rome, a dangerous Rome,
No Rome of safety for Octavius yet;
Hie hence, and tell him so. Yet, stay awhile;
Thou shalt not back till I have borne this corse
Into the market-place: there shall I try,
In my oration, how the people take
The cruel issue of these bloody men;
According to the which, thou shalt discourse
To young Octavius of the state of things.
Lend me your hand.
                    [*Exeunt with* CAESAR'S *body.*

SCENE II.

The same.   The Forum.
Enter BRUTUS *and* CASSIUS, *and a throng of*
CITIZENS.
                    CITIZENS.
WE will be satisfied; let us be satisfied.
                    MARCUS BRUTUS.
Then follow me, and give me audience, friends.
Cassius, go you into the other street,
And part the numbers.
Those that will hear me speak, let 'em stay here;
Those that will follow Cassius, go with him;
And public reasons shall be rendered
Of Cæsar's death.
                    FIRST CITIZEN.
            I will hear Brutus speak.
                    SECOND CITIZEN.
I will hear Cassius; and compare their reasons,
When severally we hear them rendered.
            [*Exit* CASSIUS, *with some of the* CITIZENS.
            BRUTUS *goes into the pulpit.*
                    THIRD CITIZEN.
The noble Brutus is ascended: silence!

                    MARCUS BRUTUS.
Be patient till the last.
Romans, countrymen, and lovers! hear me for my
cause; and be silent, that you may hear: believe
me for mine honour; and have respect to mine
honour, that you may believe: censure me in your
wisdom; and awake your senses, that you may the
better judge. If there be any in this assembly, any
dear friend of Cæsar's, to him I say, that Brutus'
love to Cæsar was no less than his. If, then, that
friend demand why Brutus rose against Cæsar,
this is my answer,—Not that I loved Cæsar less,
but that I loved Rome more. Had you rather
Cæsar were living, and die all slaves, than that
Cæsar were dead, to live all free men? As Cæsar
loved me, I weep for him; as he was fortunate, I
rejoice at it; as he was valiant, I honour him: but,
as he was ambitious, I slew him. There is tears
for his love; joy for his fortune; honour for his
valour; and death for his ambition. Who is here
so base that would be a bondman? If any, speak;
for him have I offended. Who is here so rude that
would not be a Roman? If any, speak; for him
have I offended. Who is here so vile that will not
love his country? If any, speak; for him have I
offended. I pause for a reply.
                    CITIZENS.
None, Brutus, none.
                    MARCUS BRUTUS.
Then none have I offended. I have done no more
to Cæsar than you shall do to Brutus. The question of his death is enroll'd in the Capitol; his
glory not extenuated, wherein he was worthy; nor
his offences enforced, for which he suffer'd death.
Here comes his body, mourn'd by Mark Antony:
                    Enter ANTONY *with* CÆSAR'S *body.*
who, though he had no hand in his death, shall
receive the benefit of his dying, a place in the
commonwealth; as which of you shall not? With
this I depart,—that, as I slew my best lover for
the good of Rome, I have the same dagger for
myself, when it shall please my country to need
my death.
                    CITIZENS.
Live, Brutus! live, live!
                    FIRST CITIZEN.
Bring him with triumph home unto his house.
                    SECOND CITIZEN.
Give him a statue with his ancestors.
                    THIRD CITIZEN.
Let him be Cæsar.
                    FOURTH CITIZEN.
                    Cæsar's better parts
Shall be crown'd in Brutus.
                    FIRST CITIZEN.
We'll bring him to his house with shouts and
    clamours.
                    MARCUS BRUTUS.
My countrymen,—
                    SECOND CITIZEN.
                    Peace, silence! Brutus speaks.
                    FIRST CITIZEN.
Peace, ho!
                    MARCUS BRUTUS.
Good countrymen, let me depart alone,
And, for my sake, stay here with Antony:

Do grace to Cæsar's corpse, and grace his speech
Tending to Cæsar's glories; which Mark Antony,
By our permission, is allow'd to make.
I do entreat you, not a man depart,
Save I alone, till Antony have spoke.   [*Exit.*
FIRST CITIZEN.
Stay, ho! and let us hear Mark Antony.
THIRD CITIZEN.
Let him go up into the public chair;
We'll hear him.—Noble Antony, go up.
MARCUS ANTONIUS.
For Brutus' sake, I am beholding to you.
[*Goes up.*
FOURTH CITIZEN.
What does he say of Brutus?
THIRD CITIZEN.
He says, for Brutus' sake,
He finds himself beholding to us all.
FOURTH CITIZEN.
'Twere best he speak no harm of Brutus here.
FIRST CITIZEN.
This Cæsar was a tyrant.
THIRD CITIZEN.
Nay, that's certain:
We are blest that Rome is rid of him.
SECOND CITIZEN.
Peace! let us hear what Antony can say.
MARCUS ANTONIUS.
You gentle Romans,—
CITIZENS.
Peace, ho! let us hear him.
MARCUS ANTONIUS.
Friends, Romans, countrymen, lend me your
ears;
I come to bury Cæsar, not to praise him.
The evil that men do lives after them;
The good is oft interred with their bones;
So let it be with Cæsar. The noble Brutus
Hath told you Cæsar was ambitious:
If it were so, it was a grievous fault;
And grievously hath Cæsar answer'd it.
Here, under leave of Brutus and the rest,—
For Brutus is an honourable man;
So are they all, all honourable men,—
Come I to speak in Cæsar's funeral.
He was my friend, faithful and just to me:
But Brutus says he was ambitious;
And Brutus is an honourable man.
He hath brought many captives home to Rome,
Whose ransoms did the general coffers fill:
Did this in Cæsar seem ambitious?
When that the poor have cried, Cæsar hath wept:
Ambition should be made of sterner stuff:
Yet Brutus says he was ambitious;
And Brutus is an honourable man.
You all did see that on the Lupercal
I thrice presented him a kingly crown,
Which he did thrice refuse: was this ambition?
Yet Brutus says he was ambitious;
And, sure, he is an honourable man.
I speak not to disprove what Brutus spoke,
But here I am to speak what I do know.
You all did love him once,—not without cause:
What cause withholds you, then, to mourn for
him?
O judgement, thou art fled to brutish beasts,

And men have lost their reason!—Bear with me;
My heart is in the coffin there with Cæsar,
And I must pause till it come back to me.
FIRST CITIZEN.
Methinks there is much reason in his sayings.
SECOND CITIZEN.
If thou consider rightly of the matter,
Cæsar has had great wrong.
THIRD CITIZEN.
Has he, masters?
I fear there will a worse come in his place.
FOURTH CITIZEN.
Markt ye his words? He would not take the
crown;
Therefore 'tis certain he was not ambitious.
FIRST CITIZEN.
If it be found so, some will dear abide it.
SECOND CITIZEN.
Poor soul! his eyes are red as fire with weeping.
THIRD CITIZEN.
There's not a nobler man in Rome than Antony.
FOURTH CITIZEN.
Now mark him, he begins again to speak.
MARCUS ANTONIUS.
But yesterday the word of Cæsar might
Have stood against the world: now lies he there,
And none so poor to do him reverence.
O masters, if I were disposed to stir
Your hearts and minds to mutiny and rage,
I should do Brutus wrong, and Cassius wrong,
Who, you all know, are honourable men:
I will not do them wrong; I rather choose
To wrong the dead, to wrong myself, and you,
Than I will wrong such honourable men.
But here's a parchment with the seal of Cæsar,—
I found it in his closet,—'tis his will:
Let but the commons hear this testament,—
Which, pardon me, I do not mean to read,—
And they would go and kiss dead Cæsar's wounds,
And dip their napkins in his sacred blood;
Yea, beg a hair of him for memory,
And, dying, mention it within their wills,
Bequeathing it, as a rich legacy,
Unto their issue.
FOURTH CITIZEN.
We'll hear the will: read it, Mark Antony.
CITIZENS.
The will, the will! we will hear Cæsar's will.
MARCUS ANTONIUS.
Have patience, gentle friends, I must not read it;
It is not meet you know how Cæsar loved you.
You are not wood, you are not stones, but men;
And, being men, hearing the will of Cæsar,
It will inflame you, it will make you mad:
'Tis good you know not that you are his heirs;
For, if you should, O, what would come of it!
FOURTH CITIZEN.
Read the will: we'll hear it, Antony;
You shall read us the will,—Cæsar's will.
MARCUS ANTONIUS.
Will you be patient? will you stay awhile?
I have o'ershot myself to tell you of it:
I fear I wrong the honourable men
Whose daggers have stabb'd Cæsar; I do fear it.
FOURTH CITIZEN.
They were traitors: honourable men!

CITIZENS.
The will! the testament!

SECOND CITIZEN.
They were villains, murderers: the will! read the will.

MARCUS ANTONIUS.
You will compel me, then, to read the will?
Then make a ring about the corpse of Cæsar,
And let me show you him that made the will.
Shall I descend? and will you give me leave?

CITIZENS.
Come down.

SECOND CITIZEN.
Descend.

THIRD CITIZEN.
You shall have leave.   [ANTONY *comes down.*

FOURTH CITIZEN.
A ring; stand round.

FIRST CITIZEN.
Stand from the hearse, stand from the body.

SECOND CITIZEN.
Room for Antony,—most noble Antony.

MARCUS ANTONIUS.
Nay, press not so upon me; stand far off.

CITIZENS.
Stand back; room; bear back.

MARCUS ANTONIUS.
If you have tears, prepare to shed them now.
You all do know this mantle: I remember
The first time ever Cæsar put it on;
'Twas on a summer's evening, in his tent,
That day he overcame the Nervii:—
Look, in this place ran Cassius' dagger through:
See what a rent the envious Casca made:
Through this the well-beloved Brutus stabb'd;
And, as he pluckt his cursed steel away,
Mark how the blood of Cæsar follow'd it,
As rushing out of doors, to be resolved
If Brutus so unkindly knockt, or no;
For Brutus, as you know, was Cæsar's angel:
Judge, O you gods, how dearly Cæsar loved him!
This was the most unkindest cut of all;
For when the noble Cæsar saw him stab,
Ingratitude, more strong than traitors' arms,
Quite vanquisht him: then burst his mighty heart;
And, in his mantle muffling up his face,
Even at the base of Pompey's statua,
Which all the while ran blood, great Cæsar fell.
O, what a fall was there, my countrymen!
Then I, and you, and all of us fell down,
Whilst bloody treason flourisht over us.
O, now you weep; and, I perceive, you feel
The dint of pity: these are gracious drops.
Kind souls, what, weep you when you but behold
Our Cæsar's vesture wounded? Look you here,
Here is himself, marr'd, as you see, with traitors.

FIRST CITIZEN.
O piteous spectacle!

SECOND CITIZEN.
O noble Cæsar!

THIRD CITIZEN.
O woeful day!

FOURTH CITIZEN.
O traitors, villains!

FIRST CITIZEN.
O most bloody sight!

SECOND CITIZEN.
We will be revenged.

CITIZENS.
Revenge,—about,—seek,—burn,—fire,—kill,—
slay,—let not a traitor live!

MARCUS ANTONIUS.
Stay, countrymen.

FIRST CITIZEN.
Peace there! hear the noble Antony.

SECOND CITIZEN.
We'll hear him, we'll follow him, we'll die with him.

MARCUS ANTONIUS.
Good friends, sweet friends, let me not stir you up
To such a sudden flood of mutiny.
They that have done this deed are honourable;—
What private griefs they have, alas, I know not,
That made them do it;—they are wise and honourable,
And will, no doubt, with reasons answer you.
I come not, friends, to steal away your hearts:
I am no orator, as Brutus is;
But, as you know me all, a plain blunt man,
That love my friend; and that they know full well
That gave me public leave to speak of him:
For I have neither wit, nor words, nor worth,
Action, nor utterance, nor the power of speech,
To stir men's blood: I only speak right on;
I tell you that which you yourselves do know;
Show you sweet Cæsar's wounds, poor poor dumb mouths,
And bid them speak for me: but were I Brutus,
And Brutus Antony, there were an Antony
Would ruffle up your spirits, and put a tongue
In every wound of Cæsar, that should move
The stones of Rome to rise and mutiny.

CITIZENS.
We'll mutiny.

FIRST CITIZEN.
We'll burn the house of Brutus.

THIRD CITIZEN.
Away, then! come, seek the conspirators.

MARCUS ANTONIUS.
Yet hear me, countrymen; yet hear me speak.

CITIZENS.
Peace, ho! hear Antony,—most noble Antony.

MARCUS ANTONIUS.
Why, friends, you go to do you know not what:
Wherein hath Cæsar thus deserved your loves?
Alas, you know not,—I must tell you, then:—
You have forgot the will I told you of.

CITIZENS.
Most true; the will:—let's stay and hear the will.

MARCUS ANTONIUS.
Here is the will, and under Cæsar's seal:—
To every Roman citizen he gives,
To every several man, seventy-five drachmas.

SECOND CITIZEN.
Most noble Cæsar!—we'll revenge his death.

THIRD CITIZEN.
O royal Cæsar!

MARCUS ANTONIUS.
Hear me with patience.

CITIZENS.
Peace, ho!

MARCUS ANTONIUS.
Moreover, he hath left you all his walks,
His private arbours, and new-planted orchards,
On this side Tiber; he hath left them you,
And to your heirs for ever,—common pleasures,
To walk abroad, and recreate yourselves.
Here was a Cæsar! when comes such another?
          FIRST CITIZEN.
Never, never.—Come, away, away!
We'll burn his body in the holy place,
And with the brands fire the traitors' houses.
Take up the body.
          SECOND CITIZEN.
Go fetch fire.
          THIRD CITIZEN.
Pluck down benches.
          FOURTH CITIZEN.
Pluck down forms, windows, any thing.
      [*Exeunt* CITIZENS *with the body.*
          MARCUS ANTONIUS.
Now let it work:—mischief, thou art afoot,
Take thou what course thou wilt!
          Enter SERVANT.
                How now, fellow!
          SERVANT.
Sir, Octavius is already come to Rome.
          MARCUS ANTONIUS.
Where is he?
          SERVANT.
He and Lepidus are at Cæsar's house.
          MARCUS ANTONIUS.
And thither will I straight to visit him:
He comes upon a wish. Fortune is merry,
And in this mood will give us any thing.
          SERVANT.
I heard him say, Brutus and Cassius
Are rid like madmen through the gates of Rome.
          MARCUS ANTONIUS.
Belike they had some notice of the people
How I had moved them. Bring me to Octavius.
                    [*Exeunt.*

SCENE III.
The same. A street.

Enter CINNA *the poet, and after him the* CITIZENS.
          CINNA.
I DREAMT to-night that I did feast with Cæsar,
  And things unlucky charge my fantasy:
I have no will to wander forth of doors,
Yet something leads me forth.
          FIRST CITIZEN.
What is your name?
          SECOND CITIZEN.
Whither are you going?
          THIRD CITIZEN.
Where do you dwell?
          FOURTH CITIZEN.
Are you a married man or a bachelor?
          SECOND CITIZEN.
Answer every man directly.
          FIRST CITIZEN.
Ay, and briefly.
          FOURTH CITIZEN.
Ay, and wisely.
          THIRD CITIZEN.
Ay, and truly, you were best.

          CINNA.
What is my name? Whither am I going? Where
do I dwell? Am I a married man or a bachelor?
Then, to answer every man directly and briefly,
wisely and truly:—wisely I say, I am a bachelor.
          SECOND CITIZEN.
That's as much as to say, they are fools that
marry:—you'll bear me a bang for that, I fear.
Proceed; directly.
          CINNA.
Directly, I am going to Cæsar's funeral.
          FIRST CITIZEN.
As a friend or an enemy?
          CINNA.
As a friend.
          SECOND CITIZEN.
That matter is answer'd directly.
          FOURTH CITIZEN.
For your dwelling,—briefly.
          CINNA.
Briefly, I dwell by the Capitol.
          THIRD CITIZEN.
Your name, sir, truly.
          CINNA.
Truly, my name is Cinna.
          FIRST CITIZEN.
Tear him to pieces; he's a conspirator.
          CINNA.
I am Cinna the poet, I am Cinna the poet.
          FOURTH CITIZEN.
Tear him for his bad verses, tear him for his bad
verses.
          CINNA.
I am not Cinna the conspirator.
          FOURTH CITIZEN.
Is is no matter, his name's Cinna; pluck but his
name out of his heart, and turn him going.
          THIRD CITIZEN.
Tear him, tear him! Come, brands, ho! fire-
brands: to Brutus', to Cassius'; burn all: some to
Decius' house, and some to Casca's; some to
Ligarius': away, go!   [*Exeunt.*

ACT IV. SCENE I.
Rome. A room in ANTONY'S *house.*

ANTONY, OCTAVIUS, *and* LEPIDUS, *seated
          at a table.*
          MARCUS ANTONIUS.
THESE many, then, shall die; their names are
  prickt.
          OCTAVIUS CAESAR.
Your brother too must die; consent you, Lepidus?
          AEMILIUS LEPIDUS.
I do consent,—
          OCTAVIUS CAESAR.
          Prick him down, Antony.
          AEMILIUS LEPIDUS.
Upon condition Publius shall not live,
Who is your sister's son, Mark Antony.
          MARCUS ANTONIUS.
He shall not live; look, with a spot I damn him.
But, Lepidus, go you to Cæsar's house;
Fetch the will hither, and we shall determine
How to cut off some charge in legacies.

AEMILIUS LEPIDUS.
What, shall I find you here?
OCTAVIUS CAESAR.
Or here, or at
The Capitol.   [*Exit* LEPIDUS.
MARCUS ANTONIUS.
This is a slight unmeritable man,
Meet to be sent on errands: is it fit,
The threefold world divided, he should stand
One of the three to share it?
OCTAVIUS CAESAR.
So you thought him;
And took his voice who should be prickt to die,
In our black sentence and proscription.
MARCUS ANTONIUS.
Octavius, I have seen more days than you:
And though we lay these honours on this man,
To ease ourselves of divers slanderous loads,
He shall but bear them as the ass bears gold,
To groan and sweat under the business,
Either led or driven, as we point the way;
And having brought our treasure where we will,
Then take we down his load, and turn him off,
Like to the empty ass, to shake his ears,
And graze in commons.
OCTAVIUS CAESAR.
You may do your will:
But he's a tried and valiant soldier.
MARCUS ANTONIUS.
So is my horse, Octavius; and for that
I do appoint him store of provender:
It is a creature that I teach to fight,
To wind, to stop, to run directly on,—
His corporal motion govern'd by my spirit.
And, in some taste, is Lepidus but so;
He must be taught, and train'd, and bid go forth;—
A barren-spirited fellow; one that feeds
On abject orts and imitations,
Which, out of use and staled by other men,
Begin his fashion: do not talk of him
But as a property. And now, Octavius,
Listen great things:—Brutus and Cassius
Are levying powers: we must straight make head:
Therefore let our alliance be combined,
Our best friends made, and our best means
    stretcht out;
And let us presently go sit in council,
How covert matters may be best disclosed,
And open perils surest answered.
OCTAVIUS CAESAR.
Let us do so: for we are at the stake,
And bay'd about with many enemies;
And some that smile have in their hearts, I fear,
Millions of mischiefs.   [*Exeunt.*

SCENE II.

Before BRUTUS' *tent, in the camp near Sardis.*

Drum. Enter BRUTUS, LUCILIUS, LUCIUS, *and
   the* ARMY; TITINIUS *and* PINDARUS *meet
   them.*
MARCUS BRUTUS.
STAND, ho!
LUCILIUS.
Give the word, ho! and stand.

MARCUS BRUTUS.
What now, Lucilius! is Cassius near?
LUCILIUS.
He is at hand; and Pindarus is come
To do you salutation from his master.
MARCUS BRUTUS.
He greets me well.—Your master, Pindarus,
In his own change, or by ill officers,
Hath given me some worthy cause to wish
Things done, undone: but, if he be at hand,
I shall be satisfied.
PINDARUS.
I do not doubt
But that my noble master will appear
Such as he is, full of regard and honour.
MARCUS BRUTUS.
He is not doubted.—A word, Lucilius;
How he received you, let me be resolved.
LUCILIUS.
With courtesy and with respect enough;
But not with such familiar instances,
Nor with such free and friendly conference,
As he hath used of old.
MARCUS BRUTUS.
Thou hast described
A hot friend cooling: ever note, Lucilius,
When love begins to sicken and decay,
It useth an enforced ceremony.
There are no tricks in plain and simple faith:
But hollow men, like horses hot at hand,
Make gallant show and promise of their mettle;
But when they should endure the bloody spur,
They fall their crests, and, like deceitful jades,
Sink in the trial. Comes his army on?
LUCILIUS.
They mean this night in Sardis to be quarter'd;
The greater part, the horse in general,
Are come with Cassius.   [*Low march within.*
MARCUS BRUTUS.
Hark! he is arrived:—
March gently on to meet him.
Enter CASSIUS *and his* POWERS.
CASSIUS.
Stand, ho!
MARCUS BRUTUS.
Stand, ho! Speak the word along.
FIRST SOLDIER.
Stand!
SECOND SOLDIER.
Stand!
THIRD SOLDIER.
Stand!
CASSIUS.
Most noble brother, you have done me wrong.
MARCUS BRUTUS.
Judge me, you gods! wrong I mine enemies?
And if not so, how should I wrong a brother?
CASSIUS.
Brutus, this sober form of yours hides wrongs;
And when you do them—
MARCUS BRUTUS.
Cassius, be content;
Speak your griefs softly,—I do know you well:—
Before the eyes of both our armies here,
Which should perceive nothing but love from us,
Let us not wrangle: bid them move away;

Then in my tent, Cassius, enlarge your griefs,
And I will give you audience.
CASSIUS.
Pindarus,
Bid our commanders lead their charges off
A little from this ground.
MARCUS BRUTUS.
Lucilius, do you the like; and let no man
Come to our tent till we have done our conference.
Let Lucius and Titinius guard our door. [*Exeunt.*

SCENE III.

Within the tent of BRUTUS.

Enter BRUTUS *and* CASSIUS.

CASSIUS.

T HAT you have wrong'd me doth appear in
this:
You have condemn'd and noted Lucius Pella
For taking bribes here of the Sardians;
Wherein my letters, praying on his side,
Because I knew the man, were slighted off.
MARCUS BRUTUS.
You wrong'd yourself to write in such a case.
CASSIUS.
In such a time as this it is not meet
That every nice offence should bear his comment.
MARCUS BRUTUS.
Let me tell you, Cassius, you yourself
Are much condemn'd to have an itching palm;
To sell and mart your offices for gold
To undeservers.
CASSIUS.
I an itching palm!
You know that you are Brutus that speaks this,
Or, by the gods, this speech were else your last.
MARCUS BRUTUS.
The name of Cassius honours this corruption,
And chastisement doth therefore hide his head.
CASSIUS.
Chastisement!
MARCUS BRUTUS.
Remember March, the ides of March remember:
Did not great Julius bleed for justice' sake?
What villain toucht his body, that did stab,
And not for justice? What, shall one of us,
That struck the foremost man of all this world
But for supporting robbers, shall we now
Contaminate our fingers with base bribes,
And sell the mighty space of our large honours
For so much trash as may be grasped thus?—
I had rather be a dog, and bay the moon,
Than such a Roman.
CASSIUS.
Brutus, bay not me,—
I'll not endure it: you forget yourself,
To hedge me in; I am a soldier, I,
Older in practice, abler than yourself
To make conditions.
MARCUS BRUTUS.
Go to; you are not, Cassius.
CASSIUS.
I am.
MARCUS BRUTUS.
I say you are not.

CASSIUS.
Urge me no more, I shall forget myself;
Have mind upon your health, tempt me no fur-
ther.
MARCUS BRUTUS.
Away, slight man!
CASSIUS.
Is't possible?
MARCUS BRUTUS.
Hear me, for I will speak.
Must I give way and room to your rash choler?
Shall I be frighted when a madman stares?
CASSIUS.
O ye gods, ye gods! must I endure all this?
MARCUS BRUTUS.
All this! ay, more: fret till your proud heart break;
Go show your slaves how choleric you are,
And make your bondmen tremble. Must I budge?
Must I observe you? must I stand and crouch
Under your testy humour? By the gods,
You shall digest the venom of your spleen,
Though it do split you; for, from this day forth,
I'll use you for my mirth, yea, for my laughter,
When you are waspish.
CASSIUS.
Is it come to this?
MARCUS BRUTUS.
You say you are a better soldier:
Let it appear so; make your vaunting true,
And it shall please me well: for mine own part,
I shall be glad to learn of noble men.
CASSIUS.
You wrong me every way; you wrong me,
Brutus;
I said, an elder soldier, not a better:
Did I say 'better'?
MARCUS BRUTUS.
If you did, I care not.
CASSIUS.
When Cæsar lived he durst not thus have moved
me.
MARCUS BRUTUS.
Peace, peace! you durst not so have tempted him.
CASSIUS.
I durst not!
MARCUS BRUTUS.
No.
CASSIUS.
What, durst not tempt him!
MARCUS BRUTUS.
For your life you durst not.
CASSIUS.
Do not presume too much upon my love;
I may do that I shall be sorry for.
MARCUS BRUTUS.
You have done that you should be sorry for.
There is no terror, Cassius, in your threats;
For I am arm'd so strong in honesty,
That they pass by me as the idle wind,
Which I respect not. I did send to you
For certain sums of gold, which you denied me;—
For I can raise no money by vile means:
By heaven, I had rather coin my heart,
And drop my blood for drachmas, than to wring
From the hard hands of peasants their vile trash
By any indirection;—I did send

To you for gold to pay my legions,
Which you denied me: was that done like Cassius?
Should I have answer'd Caius Cassius so?
When Marcus Brutus grows so covetous,
To lock such rascal counters from his friends,
Be ready, gods, with all your thunderbolts;
Dash him to pieces!

CASSIUS.
I denied you not.

MARCUS BRUTUS.
You did.

CASSIUS.
I did not:—he was but a fool that brought
My answer back.—Brutus hath rived my heart:
A friend should bear his friend's infirmities,
But Brutus makes mine greater than they are.

MARCUS BRUTUS.
I do not, till you practise them on me.

CASSIUS.
You love me not.

MARCUS BRUTUS.
I do not like your faults.

CASSIUS.
A friendly eye could never see such faults.

MARCUS BRUTUS.
A flatterer's would not, though they do appear
As huge as high Olympus.

CASSIUS.
Come, Antony, and young Octavius, come,
Revenge yourselves alone on Cassius,
For Cassius is a-weary of the world;
Hated by one he loves; braved by his brother;
Checkt like a bondman; all his faults observed,
Set in a note-book, learn'd, and conn'd by rote,
To cast into my teeth. O, I could weep
My spirit from mine eyes!—There is my dagger,
And here my naked breast; within, a heart
Dearer than Pluto's mine, richer than gold:
If that thou be'st a Roman, take it forth;
I, that denied thee gold, will give my heart:
Strike, as thou didst at Cæsar; for, I know,
When thou didst hate him worst, thou lovedst
    him better
Than ever thou lovedst Cassius.

MARCUS BRUTUS.
Sheathe your dagger:
Be angry when you will, it shall have scope;
Do what you will, dishonour shall be humour.
O Cassius, you are yoked with a lamb
That carries anger as the flint bears fire;
Who, much enforced, shows a hasty spark,
And straight is cold again.

CASSIUS.
Hath Cassius lived
To be but mirth and laughter to his Brutus,
When grief, and blood ill-temper'd, vexeth him?

MARCUS BRUTUS.
When I spoke that, I was ill-temper'd too.

CASSIUS.
Do you confess so much? Give me your hand.

MARCUS BRUTUS.
And my heart too.

CASSIUS.
O Brutus,—

MARCUS BRUTUS.
What's the matter?

CASSIUS.
Have not you love enough to bear with me,
When that rash humour which my mother gave
    me
Makes me forgetful?

MARCUS BRUTUS.
Yes, Cassius; and, from henceforth,
When you are over-earnest with your Brutus,
He'll think your mother chides, and leave you so.

POET [within].
Let me go in to see the generals;
There is some grudge between 'em, 'tis not meet
They be alone.

LUCILIUS [within].
You shall not come to them.

POET [within].
Nothing but death shall stay me.
Enter POET, follow'd by LUCILIUS, TITINIUS,
    and LUCIUS.

CASSIUS.
How now! what's the matter?

POET.
For shame, you generals! what do you mean?
Love, and be friends, as two such men should be;
For I have seen more years, I'm sure, than ye.

CASSIUS.
Ha, ha! how vilely doth this cynic rime!

MARCUS BRUTUS.
Get you hence, sirrah; saucy fellow, hence!

CASSIUS.
Bear with him, Brutus; 'tis his fashion.

MARCUS BRUTUS.
I'll know his humour, when he knows his time:
What should the wars do with these jigging
    fools?—
Companion, hence!

CASSIUS.
Away, away, be gone!
[Exit POET.

MARCUS BRUTUS.
Lucilius and Titinius, bid the commanders
Prepare to lodge their companies to-night.

CASSIUS.
And come yourselves, and bring Messala with
    you
Immediately to us.
[Exeunt LUCILIUS and TITINIUS.

MARCUS BRUTUS.
Lucius, a bowl of wine!

CASSIUS.
I did not think you could have been so angry.

MARCUS BRUTUS.
O Cassius, I am sick of many griefs.

CASSIUS.
Of your philosophy you make no use,
If you give place to accidental evils.

MARCUS BRUTUS.
No man bears sorrow better:—Portia is dead.

CASSIUS.
Ha! Portia!

MARCUS BRUTUS.
She is dead.

CASSIUS.
How scaped I killing when I crost you so?—
O insupportable and touching loss!—
Upon what sickness?

MARCUS BRUTUS.
        Impatient of my absence,
And grief that young Octavius with Mark Antony
Have made themselves so strong;—for with her
    death
That tidings came;—with this she fell distract,
And, her attendants absent, swallow'd fire.
CASSIUS.
And died so?

MARCUS BRUTUS.
      Even so.
CASSIUS.
        O ye immortal gods!
Enter LUCIUS, *with wine and taper.*
MARCUS BRUTUS.
Speak no more of her.—Give me a bowl of
    wine.—
In this I bury all unkindness, Cassius.   [*Drinks.*
CASSIUS.
My heart is thirsty for that noble pledge.—
Fill, Lucius, till the wine o'erswell the cup;
I cannot drink too much of Brutus' love. [*Drinks.*
MARCUS BRUTUS.
Come in, Titinius!   [*Exit* LUCIUS.
Enter TITINIUS, *with* MESSALA.
        Welcome, good Messala.—
Now sit we close about this taper here,
And call in question our necessities.
CASSIUS.
Portia, art thou gone?
MARCUS BRUTUS.
        No more, I pray you.—
Messala, I have here received letters,
That young Octavius and Mark Antony
Come down upon us with a mighty power,
Bending their expedition toward Philippi.
MESSALA.
Myself have letters of the selfsame tenour.
MARCUS BRUTUS.
With what addition?
MESSALA.
That by proscription and bills of outlawry,
Octavius, Antony, and Lepidus,
Have put to death an hundred senators.
MARCUS BRUTUS.
Therein our letters do not well agree;
Mine speak of seventy senators that died
By their proscriptions, Cicero being one.
CASSIUS.
Cicero one!
MESSALA.
      Cicero is dead,
And by that order of proscription.—
Had you your letters from your wife, my lord?
MARCUS BRUTUS.
No, Messala.
MESSALA.
Nor nothing in your letters writ of her?
MARCUS BRUTUS.
Nothing, Messala.
MESSALA.
      That, methinks, is strange.
MARCUS BRUTUS.
Why ask you? hear you aught of her in yours?
MESSALA.
No, my lord.

MARCUS BRUTUS.
Now, as you are a Roman, tell me true.
MESSALA.
Then like a Roman bear the truth I tell:
For certain she is dead, and by strange manner.
MARCUS BRUTUS.
Why, farewell, Portia.—We must die, Messala:
With meditating that she must die once,
I have the patience to endure it now.
MESSALA.
Even so great men great losses should endure.
CASSIUS.
I have as much of this in art as you,
But yet my nature could not bear it so.
MARCUS BRUTUS.
Well, to our work alive. What do you think
Of marching to Philippi presently?
CASSIUS.
I do not think it good.
MARCUS BRUTUS.
        Your reason?
CASSIUS.
            This it is:—
'Tis better that the enemy seek us:
So shall he waste his means, weary his soldiers,
Doing himself offence; whilst we, lying still,
Are full of rest, defence, and nimbleness.
MARCUS BRUTUS.
Good reasons must, of force, give place to better.
The people 'twixt Philippi and this ground
Do stand but in a forced affection;
For they have grudged us contribution:
The enemy, marching along by them,
By them shall make a fuller number up,
Come on refresht, new-added, and encouraged;
From which advantage shall we cut him off,
If at Philippi we do face him there,
These people at our back.
CASSIUS.
        Hear me, good brother.
MARCUS BRUTUS.
Under your pardon.—You must note beside,
That we have tried the utmost of our friends,
Our legions are brim-full, our cause is ripe:
The enemy increaseth every day;
We, at the height, are ready to decline.
There is a tide in the affairs of men,
Which, taken at the flood, leads on to fortune;
Omitted, all the voyage of their life
Is bound in shallows and in miseries.
On such a full sea are we now afloat;
And we must take the current when it serves,
Or lose our ventures.
CASSIUS.
        Then, with your will, go on,
We'll along ourselves, and meet them at Philippi.
MARCUS BRUTUS.
The deep of night is crept upon our talk,
And nature must obey necessity;
Which we will niggard with a little rest.
There is no more to say?
CASSIUS.
        No more. Good night:
Early to-morrow will we rise, and hence.
MARCUS BRUTUS.
Lucius, my gown!—Farewell, good Messala:—

Good night, Titinius:—noble, noble Cassius,
Good night, and good repose.
CASSIUS.
O my dear brother!
This was an ill beginning of the night:
Never come such division 'tween our souls!
Let it not, Brutus.
MARCUS BRUTUS.
Every thing is well.
CASSIUS.
Good night, my lord.
MARCUS BRUTUS.
Good night, good brother.
TITINIUS AND MESSALA.
Good night, Lord Brutus.
MARCUS BRUTUS.
Farewell, every one.
[*Exeunt* CASSIUS, TITINIUS, *and* MESSALA.
Enter LUCIUS, *with the gown.*
Give me the gown. Where is thy instrument?
LUCIUS.
Here in the tent.
MARCUS BRUTUS.
What, thou speak'st drowsily?
Poor knave, I blame thee not; thou art o'er-
  watcht.
Call Claudius and some other of my men;
I'll have them sleep on cushions in my tent.
LUCIUS.
Varro and Claudius!
Enter VARRO *and* CLAUDIUS.
VARRO.
Calls my lord?
MARCUS BRUTUS.
I pray you, sirs, lie in my tent and sleep;
It may be I shall raise you by and by
On business to my brother Cassius.
VARRO.
So please you, we will stand and watch your
  pleasure.
MARCUS BRUTUS.
I will not have it so: lie down, good sirs;
It may be I shall otherwise bethink me.—
Look, Lucius, here's the book I sought for so;
I put it in the pocket of my gown.
[VARRO *and* CLAUDIUS *lie down.*
LUCIUS.
I was sure your lordship did not give it me.
MARCUS BRUTUS.
Bear with me, good boy, I am much forgetful.
Canst thou hold up thy heavy eyes awhile,
And touch thy instrument a strain or two?
LUCIUS.
Ay, my lord, an't please you.
MARCUS BRUTUS.
It does, my boy:
I trouble thee too much, but thou art willing.
LUCIUS.
It is my duty, sir.
MARCUS BRUTUS.
I should not urge thy duty past thy might;
I know young bloods look for a time of rest.
LUCIUS.
I have slept, my lord, already.
MARCUS BRUTUS.
It was well done; and thou shalt sleep again;

I will not hold thee long: if I do live,
I will be good to thee.   [*Music, and a song.*
This is a sleepy tune:—O murderous slumber,
Lay'st thou thy leaden mace upon my boy,
That plays thee music?—Gentle knave, good
  night:
I will not do thee so much wrong to wake thee:
If thou dost nod, thou break'st thy instrument;
I'll take it from thee; and, good boy, good night.—
Let me see, let me see;—is not the leaf turn'd
  down
Where I left reading? Here it is, I think.
Enter the GHOST OF CAESAR.
How ill this taper burns!—Ha! who comes here?
I think it is the weakness of mine eyes
That shapes this monstrous apparition.
It comes upon me.—Art thou any thing?
Art thou some god, some angel, or some devil,
That makest my blood cold, and my hair to stare?
Speak to me what thou art.
GHOST OF CAESAR.
Thy evil spirit, Brutus.
MARCUS BRUTUS.
Why comest thou?
GHOST OF CAESAR.
To tell thee thou shalt see me at Philippi.
MARCUS BRUTUS.
Well; then I shall see thee again?
GHOST OF CAESAR.
Ay, at Philippi.
MARCUS BRUTUS.
Why, I will see thee at Philippi, then.
[GHOST *vanishes.*
Now I have taken heart thou vanishest:
Ill spirit, I would hold more talk with thee.—
Boy, Lucius!—Varro! Claudius!—Sirs, awake!—
Claudius!
LUCIUS.
The strings, my lord, are false.
MARCUS BRUTUS.
He thinks he still is at his instrument.—
Lucius, awake!
LUCIUS.
My lord?
MARCUS BRUTUS.
Didst thou dream, Lucius, that thou so criedst
  out?
LUCIUS.
My lord, I do not know that I did cry.
MARCUS BRUTUS.
Yes, that thou didst: didst thou see any thing?
LUCIUS.
Nothing, my lord.
MARCUS BRUTUS.
Sleep again, Lucius.—Sirrah Claudius!—
[*to* VARRO] Fellow thou, awake!
VARRO.
My lord?
CLAUDIUS.
My lord?
MARCUS BRUTUS.
Why did you so cry out, sirs, in your sleep?
VARRO AND CLAUDIUS.
Did we, my lord?
MARCUS BRUTUS.
Ay: saw you any thing?

VARRO.

No, my lord, I saw nothing.

CLAUDIUS.

Nor I, myl ord.

MARCUS BRUTUS.

Go and commend me to my brother Cassius;
Bid him set on his powers betimes before,
And we will follow.

VARRO AND CLAUDIUS.

It shall be done, my lord.

[Exeunt.

ACT V. SCENE I.

The plains of Philippi.

Enter OCTAVIUS, ANTONY, *and their* ARMY.

OCTAVIUS CAESAR.

NOW, Antony, our hopes are answered:
You said the enemy would not come down,
But keep the hills and upper regions:
It proves not so; their battles are at hand;
They mean to warn us at Philippi here,
Answering before we do demand of them.

MARCUS ANTONIUS.

Tut, I am in their bosoms, and I know
Wherefore they do it: they could be content
To visit other places; and come down
With fearful bravery, thinking by this face
To fasten in our thoughts that they have courage;
But 'tis not so.

Enter a MESSENGER.

MESSENGER.

Prepare you, generals:
The enemy comes on in gallant show;
Their bloody sign of battle is hung out,
And something to be done immediately.

MARCUS ANTONIUS.

Octavius, lead your battle softly on,
Upon the left hand of the even field.

OCTAVIUS CAESAR.

Upon the right hand I; keep thou the left.

MARCUS ANTONIUS.

Why do you cross me in this exigent?

OCTAVIUS CAESAR.

I do not cross you; but I will do so. [March.
Drum. *Enter* BRUTUS, CASSIUS, *and their*
ARMY; LUCILIUS, TITINIUS, MESSALA, *and
others.*

MARCUS BRUTUS.

They stand, and would have parley.

CASSIUS.

Stand fast, Titinius: we must out and talk.

OCTAVIUS CAESAR.

Mark Antony, shall we give sign of battle?

MARCUS ANTONIUS.

No, Caesar, we will answer on their charge.
Make forth; the generals would have some
    words.

OCTAVIUS CAESAR.

Stir not until the signal.

MARCUS BRUTUS.

Words before blows:—is it so, countrymen?

OCTAVIUS CAESAR.

Not that we love words better, as you do.

MARCUS BRUTUS.

Good words are better than bad strokes, Octavius.

MARCUS ANTONIUS.

In your bad strokes, Brutus, you give good words;
Witness the hole you made in Caesar's heart,
Crying, 'Long live! hail, Caesar!'

CASSIUS.

Antony,
The posture of your blows are yet unknown;
But for your words, they rob the Hybla bees,
And leave them honeyless.

MARCUS ANTONIUS.

Not stingless too.

MARCUS BRUTUS.

O, yes, and soundless, too;
For you have stoln their buzzing, Antony,
And very wisely threat before you sting.

MARCUS ANTONIUS.

Villains, you did not so, when your vile daggers
Hackt one another in the sides of Caesar:
You show'd your teeth like apes, and fawn'd like
    hounds,
And bow'd like bondmen, kissing Caesar's feet;
Whilst damned Casca, like a cur, behind
Struck Caesar on the neck. O you flatterers!

CASSIUS.

Flatterers!—Now, Brutus, thank yourself:
This tongue had not offended so to-day,
If Cassius might have ruled.

OCTAVIUS CAESAR.

Come, come, the cause: if arguing make us sweat,
The proof of it will turn to redder drops.
Look,—
I draw a sword against conspirators;
When think you that the sword goes up again?—
Never, till Caesar's three-and-thirty wounds
Be well avenged; or till another Caesar
Have added slaughter to the words of traitors.

MARCUS BRUTUS.

Caesar, thou canst not die by traitors' hands,
Unless thou bring'st them with thee.

OCTAVIUS CAESAR.

So I hope;
I was not born to die on Brutus' sword.

MARCUS BRUTUS.

O, if thou wert the noblest of thy strain, [able.
Young man, thou couldst not die more honour-

CASSIUS.

A peevish schoolboy, worthless of such honour,
Join'd with a masker and a reveller!

MARCUS ANTONIUS.

Old Cassius still!

OCTAVIUS CAESAR.

Come, Antony; away!—
Defiance, traitors, hurl we in your teeth:
If you dare fight to-day, come to the field;
If not, when you have stomachs.

[Exeunt OCTAVIUS, ANTONY, *and their* ARMY

CASSIUS.

Why, now, blow wind, swell billow, and swim
    bark!
The storm is up, and all is on the hazard.

MARCUS BRUTUS.

Ho,
Lucilius! hark; a word with you.

LUCILIUS.

My lord?

[BRUTUS *and* LUCILIUS *converse apart.*

CASSIUS.

Messala,—

MESSALA.

What says my general?

CASSIUS.

Messala,

This is my birth-day; as this very day
Was Cassius born. Give me thy hand, Messala:
Be thou my witness that, against my will,
As Pompey was, am I compell'd to set
Upon one battle all our liberties.
You know that I held Epicurus strong,
And his opinion: now I change my mind,
And partly credit things that do presage.
Coming from Sardis, on our former ensign
Two mighty eagles fell; and there they percht,
Gorging and feeding from our soldiers' hands;
Who to Philippi here consorted us:
This morning are they fled away and gone;
And in their steads do ravens, crows, and kites,
Fly o'er our heads, and downward look on us,
As we were sickly prey: their shadows seem
A canopy most fatal, under which
Our army lies, ready to give up the ghost.

MESSALA.

Believe not so.

CASSIUS.

I but believe it partly;
For I am fresh of spirit, and resolved
To meet all perils very constantly.

MARCUS BRUTUS.

Even so, Lucilius.

CASSIUS.

Now, most noble Brutus,
The gods to-day stand friendly, that we may,
Lovers in peace, lead on our days to age!
But, since the affairs of men rest still incertain,
Let's reason with the worst that may befall.
If we do lose this battle, then is this
The very last time we shall speak together:
What are you, then, determined to do?

MARCUS BRUTUS.

Even by the rule of that philosophy
By which I did blame Cato for the death
Which he did give himself:—I know not how,
But I do find it cowardly and vile,
For fear of what might fall, so to prevent
The time of life:—arming myself with patience
To stay the providence of some high powers
That govern us below.

CASSIUS.

Then, if we lose this battle,
You are contented to be led in triumph
Thorough the streets of Rome?

MARCUS BRUTUS.

No, Cassius, no: think not, thou noble Roman,
That ever Brutus will go bound to Rome;
He bears too great a mind. But this same day
Must end that work the ides of March begun;
And whether we shall meet again I know not.
Therefore our everlasting farewell take:—
For ever, and for ever, farewell, Cassius!
If we do meet again, why, we shall smile;
If not, why, then, this parting was well made.

CASSIUS.

For ever, and for ever, farewell, Brutus!
If we do meet again, we'll smile indeed;
If not, 'tis true this parting was well made.

MARCUS BRUTUS.

Why, then, lead on.—O, that a man might know
The end of this day's business ere it come!
But it sufficeth that the day will end,
And then the end is known.—Come, ho! away!

[Exeunt.

SCENE II.

The same.　The field of battle.

Alarums.　Enter BRUTUS *and* MESSALA.

MARCUS BRUTUS.

RIDE, ride, Messala, ride, and give these bills
Unto the legions on the other side:
Let them set on at once; for I perceive
But cold demeanour in Octavius' wing,
And sudden push gives them the overthrow.
Ride, ride, Messala: let them all come down.

[Exeunt.

SCENE III.

The same.　Another part of the field.

Alarums.　Enter CASSIUS *and* TITINIUS.

CASSIUS.

O LOOK, Titinius, look, the villains fly!
Myself have to mine own turn'd enemy:
This ensign here of mine was turning back;
I slew the coward, and did take it from him.

TITINIUS.

O Cassius, Brutus gave the word too early;
Who, having some advantage on Octavius,
Took it too eagerly: his soldiers fell to spoil,
Whilst we by Antony are all enclosed.

Enter PINDARUS.

PINDARUS.

Fly further off, my lord, fly further off;
Mark Antony is in your tents, my lord:
Fly, therefore, noble Cassius, fly far off.

CASSIUS.

This hill is far enough.—Look, look, Titinius;
Are those my tents where I perceive the fire?

TITINIUS.

They are, my lord.

CASSIUS.

Titinius, if thou lovest me,
Mount thou my horse, and hide thy spurs in him,
Till he have brought thee up to yonder troops,
And here again; that I may rest assured
Whether yond troops are friend or enemy.

TITINIUS.

I will be here again, even with a thought.　[Exit.

CASSIUS.

Go, Pindarus, get higher on that hill;
My sight was ever thick; regard Titinius,
And tell me what thou notest about the field.—

[PINDARUS goes up.

This day I breathed first: time is come round,
And where I did begin, there shall I end;
My life is run his compass.—Sirrah, what news?

PINDARUS [above].

O my lord!

CASSIUS.

What news?

PINDARUS [above].

Titinius is enclosed round about

With horsemen, that make to him on the spur;—
Yet he spurs on.—Now they are almost on him;—
Now, Titinius!—
Now some light: O, he lights too: he's ta'en; [*shout*]
    and, hark!
They shout for joy.

CASSIUS.
                Come down, behold no more.—
O, coward that I am, to live so long,
To see my best friend ta'en before my face!
PINDARUS *descends.*
Come hither, sirrah:
In Parthia did I take thee prisoner;
And then I swore thee, saving of thy life,
That whatsoever I did bid thee do,
Thou shouldst attempt it. Come now, keep thine
    oath;
Now be a freeman; and, with this good sword,
That ran through Cæsar's bowels, search this
    bosom.
Stand not to answer: here, take thou the hilts;
And, when my face is cover'd, as 'tis now,
Guide thou the sword.—Cæsar, thou art revenged,
Even with the sword that kill'd thee.   [*Dies.*
PINDARUS.
So, I am free; yet would not so have been,
Durst I have done my will. O Cassius!
Far from this country Pindarus shall run,
Where never Roman shall take note of him. [*Exit.*
Enter TITINIUS *with* MESSALA.
MESSALA.
It is but change, Titinius; for Octavius
Is overthrown by noble Brutus' power,
As Cassius' legions are by Antony.
TITINIUS.
These tidings will well comfort Cassius.
MESSALA.
Where did you leave him?
TITINIUS.
                All disconsolate,
With Pindarus his bondman, on this hill.
MESSALA.
Is not that he that lies upon the ground?
TITINIUS.
He lies not like the living. O my heart!
MESSALA.
Is not that he?
TITINIUS.
                No, this was he, Messala,
But Cassius is no more.—O setting sun,
As in thy red rays thou dost sink to night,
So in his red blood Cassius' day is set,—
The sun of Rome is set! Our day is gone;   [done!
Clouds, dews, and dangers come; our deeds are
Mistrust of my success hath done this deed.
MESSALA.
Mistrust of good success hath done this deed.
O hateful Error, Melancholy's child,
Why dost thou show to the apt thoughts of men
The things that are not? O Error, soon conceived,
Thou never comest unto a happy birth,
But kill'st the mother that engender'd thee!
TITINIUS.
What, Pindarus! where art thou, Pindarus?
MESSALA.
Seek him, Titinius, whilst I go to meet

The noble Brutus, thrusting this report
Into his ears: I may say, thrusting it;
For piercing steel, and darts envenomed,
Shall be as welcome to the ears of Brutus
As tidings of this sight.
TITINIUS.
                Hie you, Messala,
And I will seek for Pindarus the while.
                        [*Exit* MESSALA.
Why didst thou send me forth, brave Cassius?
Did I not meet thy friends? and did not they
Put on my brows this wreath of victory,
And bid me give it thee? Didst thou not hear
    their shouts?
Alas, thou hast misconstrued every thing!
But, hold thee, take this garland on thy brow;
Thy Brutus bid me give it thee, and I
Will do his bidding.—Brutus, come apace,
And see how I regarded Caius Cassius.—
By your leave, gods:—this is a Roman's part:
Come, Cassius' sword, and find Titinius' heart.
                                [*Dies.*
Alarums.   Enter MESSALA, *with* BRUTUS, *young*
    CATO, STRATO, VOLUMNIUS, *and* LUCILIUS.
MARCUS BRUTUS.
Where, where, Messala, doth his body lie?
MESSALA.
Lo, yonder; and Titinius mourning it.
MARCUS BRUTUS.
Titinius' face is upward.
YOUNG CATO.
                He is slain.
MARCUS BRUTUS.
O Julius Cæsar, thou art mighty yet!
Thy spirit walks abroad, and turns our swords
In our own proper entrails.   [*Low alarums.*
YOUNG CATO.
                Brave Titinius!
Look, whe'r he have not crown'd dead Cassius!
MARCUS BRUTUS.
Are yet two Romans living such as these?—
The last of all the Romans, fare thee well!
It is impossible that ever Rome
Should breed thy fellow.—Friends, I owe more
    tears
To this dead man than you shall see me pay.—
I shall find time, Cassius, I shall find time.—
Come, therefore, and to Thasos send his body:
His funerals shall not be in our camp,
Lest it discomfort us.—Lucilius, come;—
And come, young Cato;—let us to the field.—
Labeo and Flavius, set our battles on:—
'Tis three o'clock; and, Romans, yet ere night
We shall try fortune in a second fight.   [*Exeunt.*

SCENE IV.
The same.   Another part of the field.

Alarum.   Enter, fighting, SOLDIERS *of both
    armies; then* BRUTUS, YOUNG CATO, LUCIL-
    IUS, *and others.*
MARCUS BRUTUS.
YET, countrymen, O, yet hold up your heads!
YOUNG CATO.
What bastard doth not? Who will go with me?
I will proclaim my name about the field:—

I am the son of Marcus Cato, ho!
A foe to tyrants, and my country's friend;
I am the son of Marcus Cato, ho!
MARCUS BRUTUS.
And I am Brutus, Marcus Brutus, I;
Brutus, my country's friend; know me for Brutus!
[*Exit.*
LUCILIUS.
O young and noble Cato, art thou down?
Why, now thou diest as bravely as Titinius;
And mayst be honour'd, being Cato's son.
FIRST SOLDIER.
Yield, or thou diest.
LUCILIUS.
            Only I yield to die:
There is so much that thou wilt kill me straight;
            [*Offering money.*
Kill Brutus, and be honour'd in his death.
FIRST SOLDIER.
We must not.—A noble prisoner!
SECOND SOLDIER.
Room, ho! Tell Antony, Brutus is ta'en.
FIRST SOLDIER.
I'll tell the news:—here comes the general.
Enter ANTONY.
Brutus is ta'en, Brutus is ta'en, my lord.
MARCUS ANTONIUS.
Where is he?
LUCILIUS.
Safe, Antony; Brutus is safe enough:
I dare assure thee that no enemy
Shall ever take alive the noble Brutus:
The gods defend him from so great a shame!
When you do find him, or alive or dead,
He will be found like Brutus, like himself.
MARCUS ANTONIUS.
This is not Brutus, friend; but, I assure you,
A prize no less in worth: keep this man safe,
Give him all kindness: I had rather have
Such men my friends than enemies. Go on,
And see whe'r Brutus be alive or dead;
And bring us word unto Octavius' tent
How every thing is chanced.   [*Exeunt.*

SCENE V.

The same.   Another part of the field.

Enter BRUTUS, DARDANIUS, CLITUS, STRATO, *and* VOLUMNIUS.

MARCUS BRUTUS.
COME, poor remains of friends, rest on this rock.
CLITUS.
Statilius show'd the torch-light; but, my lord,
He came not back: he is or ta'en or slain.
MARCUS BRUTUS.
Sit thee down, Clitus: slaying is the word;
It is a deed in fashion. Hark thee, Clitus.
            [*Whispers him.*
CLITUS.
What, I, my lord? No, not for all the world.
MARCUS BRUTUS.
Peace, then, no words.
CLITUS.
            I'll rather kill myself.

MARCUS BRUTUS.
Hark thee, Dardanius.   [*Whispers him.*
DARDANIUS.
            Shall I do such a deed?
CLITUS.
O Dardanius!
DARDANIUS.
O Clitus!
CLITUS.
What ill request did Brutus make to thee?
DARDANIUS.
To kill him, Clitus. Look, he meditates.
CLITUS.
Now is that noble vessel full of grief,
That it runs over even at his eyes.
MARCUS BRUTUS.
Come hither, good Volumnius; list a word.
VOLUMNIUS.
What says my lord?
MARCUS BRUTUS.
            Why, this, Volumnius:
The ghost of Cæsar hath appear'd to me
Two several times by night,—at Sardis once,
And, this last night, here in Philippi fields:
I know my hour is come.
VOLUMNIUS.
            Not so, my lord.
MARCUS BRUTUS.
Nay, I am sure it is, Volumnius.
Thou seest the world, Volumnius, how it goes;
Our enemies have beat us to the pit: [*Low alarums*
It is more worthy to leap in ourselves,
Than tarry till they push us. Good Volumnius,
Thou know'st that we two went to school together:
Even for that our love of old, I prithee,
Hold thou my sword-hilts, whilst I run on it.
VOLUMNIUS.
That's not an office for a friend, my lord.
            [*Alarum still.*
CLITUS.
Fly, fly, my lord; there is no tarrying here.
MARCUS BRUTUS.
Farewell to you;—and you;—and you, Volumnius.—
Strato, thou hast been all this while asleep;
Farewell to thee too, Strato.—Countrymen,
My heart doth joy, that yet, in all my life,
I found no man but he was true to me.
I shall have glory by this losing day,
More than Octavius and Mark Antony
By this vile conquest shall attain unto.
So, fare you well at once; for Brutus' tongue
Hath almost ended his life's history:
Night hangs upon mine eyes; my bones would rest,
That have but labour'd to attain this hour.
            [*Alarums. Cry within,* 'Fly, fly, fly!'
CLITUS.
Fly, my lord, fly.
MARCUS BRUTUS.
            Hence! I will follow.
            [*Exeunt* CLITUS, DARDANIUS, *and* VOLUMNIUS.
I prithee, Strato, stay thou by thy lord:
Thou art a fellow of a good respect;

609

Thy life hath had some smatch of honour in it:
Hold, then, my sword, and turn away thy face,
While I do run upon it. Wilt thou, Strato?
STRATO.
Give me your hand first: fare you well, my lord.
MARCUS BRUTUS.
Farewell, good Strato.—Cæsar, now be still:
I kill'd not thee with half so good a will.
[*He runs on his sword, and dies.*
Alarums. Retreat. Enter OCTAVIUS, ANTONY,
MESSALA, LUCILIUS, *and the* ARMY.
OCTAVIUS CAESAR.
What man is that?
MESSALA.
My master's man.—Strato, where is thy master?
STRATO.
Free from the bondage you are in, Messala:
The conquerors can but make a fire of him;
For Brutus only overcame himself,
And no man else hath honour by his death.
LUCILIUS.
So Brutus should be found.—I thank thee,
    Brutus,
That thou hast proved Lucilius' saying true.
OCTAVIUS CAESAR.
All that served Brutus, I will entertain them.—
Fellow, wilt thou bestow thy time with me?

STRATO.
Ay, if Messala will prefer me to you.
OCTAVIUS CAESAR.
Do so, good Messala.
MESSALA.
How died my master, Strato?
STRATO.
I held the sword, and he did run on it.
MESSALA.
Octavius, then take him to follow thee,
That did the latest service to my master.
MARCUS ANTONIUS.
This was the noblest Roman of them all:
All the conspirators, save only he,
Did that they did in envy of great Cæsar;
He only, in a general honest thought,
And common good to all, made one of them.
His life was gentle; and the elements
So mixt in him, that Nature might stand up
And say to all the world, 'This was a man!'
OCTAVIUS CAESAR.
According to his virtue let us use him,
With all respect and rites of burial.
Within my tent his bones to-night shall lie,
Most like a soldier, order'd honourably.—
So, call the field to rest: and let's away,
To part the glories of this happy day.   [*Exeunt.*

AS YOU LIKE IT

DRAMATIS PERSONAE

DUKE, *living in banishment.*
FREDERICK, *his brother, and usurper of his dominions.*
AMIENS, JAQUES, } *lords attending on the banisht Duke.*
LE BEAU, *a courtier attending on Frederick.*
CHARLES, *wrestler to Frederick.*
OLIVER, JAQUES, ORLANDO, } *sons of Sir Rowland de Boys.*
ADAM, DENIS, } *servants to Oliver.*
TOUCHSTONE, *a clown.*
SIR OLIVER MARTEXT, *a vicar.*

CORIN, SILVIUS, } *shepherds.*
WILLIAM, *a country fellow, in love with Audrey.*
A person representing HYMEN.

ROSALIND, *daughter to the banisht Duke.*
CELIA, *daughter to Frederick.*
PHEBE, *a shepherdess.*
AUDREY, *a country wench.*

LORDS, PAGES, *and* ATTENDANTS, *&c.*

SCENE—*Oliver's house; Duke Frederick's court; and the Forest of Arden.*

ACT I. SCENE I.

Orchard of OLIVER'S *house.*

Enter ORLANDO *and* ADAM.

ORLANDO.

AS I remember, Adam, it was upon this fashion bequeath'd me by will but poor a thousand crowns, and, as thou say'st, charged my brother, on his blessing, to breed me well: and there begins my sadness. My brother Jacques he keeps at school, and report speaks goldenly of his profit: for my part, he keeps me rustically at home, or, to speak more properly, stays me here at home unkept; for call you that keeping for a gentleman of my birth, that differs not from the stalling of an ox? His horses are bred better; for, besides that they are fair with their feeding, they are taught their manage, and to that end riders dearly hired: but I, his brother, gain nothing under him but growth; for the which his animals on his dunghills are as much bound to him as I. Besides this nothing that he so plentifully gives me, the something that nature gave me his countenance seems to take from me: he lets me feed with his hinds, bars me the place of a brother, and, as much as in him lies, mines my gentility with my education. This is it, Adam, that grieves me; and the spirit of my father, which I think is within me, begins to mutiny against this servitude: I will no longer endure it, though yet I know no wise remedy how to avoid it.

ADAM.

Yonder comes my master, your brother.

ORLANDO.

Go apart, Adam, and thou shalt hear how he will shake me up.

Enter OLIVER.

OLIVER.

Now, sir! what make you here?

ORLANDO.

Nothing: I am not taught to make anything.

OLIVER.

What mar you then, sir?

ORLANDO.

Marry, sir, I am helping you to mar that which God made, a poor unworthy brother of yours, with idleness.

OLIVER.

Marry, sir, be better employ'd, and be naught awhile.

ORLANDO.

Shall I keep your hogs, and eat husks with them? What prodigal's portion have I spent that I should come to such penury?

OLIVER.

Know you where you are, sir?

ORLANDO.

O, sir, very well: here in your orchard.

OLIVER.

Know you before whom, sir?

ORLANDO.

Ay, better than him I am before knows me. I know you are my eldest brother; and, in the gentle condition of blood, you should so know me. The courtesy of nations allows you my better, in that you are the first-born; but the same tradition takes not away my blood, were there twenty brothers betwixt us: I have as much of my father in me as you; albeit, I confess, your coming before me is nearer to his reverence.

OLIVER.

What, boy!

ORLANDO.

Come, come, elder brother, you are too young in this.

OLIVER.

Wilt thou lay hands on me, villain?

ORLANDO.

I am no villain; I am the youngest son of Sir Rowland de Boys; he was my father, and he is thrice a villain that says such a father begot villains. Wert thou not my brother, I would not take this hand from thy throat t ll this other had pull'd out thy tongue for saying so; thou hast rail'd on thyself.

ADAM.

Sweet masters, be patient: for your father's remembrance, be at accord.

OLIVER.

Let me go, I say.

ORLANDO.

I will not, till I please: you shall hear me. My father charged you in his will to give me good education: you have train'd me like a peasant, obscuring and hiding from me all gentleman-like qualities. The spirit of my father grows strong in me, and I will no longer endure it: therefore allow me such exercises as may become a gentleman, or give me the poor allottery my father left me by testament; with that I will go buy my fortunes.

OLIVER.

And what wilt thou do? beg, when that is spent? Well, sir, get you in: I will not long be troubled with you; you shall have some part of your will: I pray you, leave me.

ORLANDO.

I will no further offend you than becomes me for my good.

OLIVER.

Get you with him, you old dog.

ADAM.

Is 'old dog' my reward? Most true, I have lost my teeth in your service.—God be with my old master! he would not have spoke such a word.

[Exeunt ORLANDO and ADAM.

OLIVER.

Is it even so? begin you to grow upon me? I will physic your rankness, and yet give no thousand crowns neither.—Holla, Denis!

Enter DENIS.

DENIS.

Calls your worship?

OLIVER.

Was not Charles, the duke's wrestler, here to speak with me?

DENIS.

So please you, he is here at the door, and importunes access to you.

OLIVER.

Call him in. [Exit DENIS.] 'Twill be a good way; and to-morrow the wrestling is.

Enter CHARLES.

CHARLES.

Good morrow to your worship.

OLIVER.

Good morrow, Monsieur Charles.—What's the new news at the new court?

CHARLES.

There's no news at the court, sir, but the old news: that is, the old duke is banisht by his younger brother the new duke; and three or four loving lords have put themselves into voluntary exile with him, whose lands and revenues enrich the new duke; therefore he gives them good leave to wander.

OLIVER.

Can you tell if Rosalind, the duke's daughter, be banisht with her father?

CHARLES.

O, no; for the duke's daughter, her cousin, so loves her, being ever from their cradles bred together, that she would have follow'd her exile, or have died to stay behind her. She is at the court, and no less beloved of her uncle than his own daughter; and never two ladies loved as they do.

OLIVER.

Where will the old duke live?

CHARLES.

They say he is already in the forest of Arden, and a many merry men with him; and there they live like the old Robin Hood of England: they say many young gentlemen flock to him every day, and fleet the time carelessly, as they did in the golden world.

OLIVER.

What, you wrestle to-morrow before the new duke?

CHARLES.

Marry, do I, sir; and I came to acquaint you with a matter. I am given, sir, secretly to understand that your younger brother Orlando hath a disposition to come in disguised against me to try a fall. To-morrow, sir, I wrestle for my credit; and he that escapes me without some broken limb shall acquit him well. Your brother is but young and tender; and, for your love, I would be loth to foil him, as I must, for my own honour, if he come in: therefore, out of my love to you, I came hither to acquaint you withal, that either you might stay him from his intendment or brook such disgrace well as he shall run into, in that it is a thing of his own search and altogether against my will.

OLIVER.

Charles, I thank thee for thy love to me, which thou shalt find I will most kindly requite. I had myself notice of my brother's purpose herein, and have by underhand means labour'd to dissuade him from it; but he is resolute. I'll tell thee, Charles: it is the stubbornest young fellow of France; full of ambition, an envious emulator of every man's good parts, a secret and villainous contriver against me his natural brother: therefore use thy discretion; I had as lief thou didst break his neck as his finger. And thou wert best look to't; for if thou dost him any slight disgrace, or if he do not mightily grace himself on thee, he will practise against thee by poison, entrap thee by some treacherous device, and never leave thee till he hath ta'en thy life by some indirect means or other; for, I assure thee, and almost with tears I speak it, there is not one so young and so villainous this day living. I speak but brotherly of him; but should I anatomize him to thee as he is, I must blush and weep, and thou must look pale and wonder.

CHARLES.

I am heartily glad I came hither to you. If he come to-morrow, I'll give him his payment: if ever he go alone again, I'll never wrestle for prize more: and so, God keep your worship!

OLIVER.

Farewell, good Charles. [Exit CHARLES.] Now will I stir this gamester: I hope I shall see an end of him; for my soul, yet I know not why, hates nothing more than he. Yet he's gentle; never school'd, and yet learned; full of noble device; of all sorts enchantingly beloved; and, indeed, so much in the heart of the world, and especially of my own people, who best know him, that I am altogether misprised: but it shall not be so long;

this wrestler shall clear all: nothing remains but that I kindle the boy thither; which now I'll go about.   [*Exit.*

SCENE II.

Lawn before the DUKE'S *palace.*

Enter ROSALIND *and* CELIA.

CELIA.

I PRAY thee, Rosalind, sweet my coz, be merry.

ROSALIND.

Dear Celia, I show more mirth than I am mistress of; and would you yet I were merrier? Unless you could teach me to forget a banisht father, you must not learn me how to remember any extraordinary pleasure.

CELIA.

Herein I see thou lovest me not with the full weight that I love thee. If my uncle, thy banisht father, had banisht thy uncle, the duke my father, so thou hadst been still with me, I could have taught my love to take thy father for mine: so wouldst thou, if the truth of thy love to me were so righteously temper'd as mine is to thee.

ROSALIND.

Well, I will forget the condition of my estate, to rejoice in yours.

CELIA.

You know my father hath no child but I, nor none is like to have: and, truly, when he dies, thou shalt be his heir; for what he hath taken away from thy father perforce, I will render thee again in affection; by mine honour, I will; and when I break that oath, let me turn monster: therefore, my sweet Rose, my dear Rose, be merry.

ROSALIND.

From henceforth I will, coz, and devise sports. Let me see; what think you of falling in love?

CELIA.

Marry, I prithee, do, to make sport withal: but love no man in good earnest; nor no further in sport neither than with safety of a pure blush thou mayst in honour come off again.

ROSALIND.

What shall be our sport, then?

CELIA.

Let us sit and mock the good housewife Fortune from her wheel, that her gifts may henceforth be bestow'd equally.

ROSALIND.

I would we could do so; for her benefits are mightily misplaced; and the bountiful blind woman doth most mistake in her gifts to women.

CELIA.

'Tis true; for those that she makes fair, she scarce makes honest; and those that she makes honest, she makes very ill-favour'dly.

ROSALIND.

Nay, now thou goest from Fortune's office to Nature's: Fortune reigns in gifts of the world, not in the lineaments of Nature.

Enter TOUCHSTONE.

CELIA.

No? when Nature hath made a fair creature, may she not by Fortune fall into the fire? Though Nature hath given us wit to flout at Fortune, hath not Fortune sent in this fool to cut off the argument?

ROSALIND.

Indeed, there is Fortune too hard for Nature, when Fortune makes Nature's natural the cutter-off of Nature's wit.

CELIA.

Peradventure this is not Fortune's work neither, but Nature's; who perceiveth our natural wits too dull to reason of such goddesses and hath sent this natural for our whetstone; for always the dulness of the fool is the whetstone of the wits.— How now, wit! whither wander you?

TOUCHSTONE.

Mistress, you must come away to your father.

CELIA.

Were you made the messenger?

TOUCHSTONE.

No, by mine honour; but I was bid to come for you.

ROSALIND.

Where learn'd you that oath, fool?

TOUCHSTONE.

Of a certain knight that swore by his honour they were good pancakes, and swore by his honour the mustard was naught: now I'll stand to it, the pancakes were naught, and the mustard was good; and yet was not the knight forsworn.

CELIA.

How prove you that, in the great heap of your knowledge?

ROSALIND.

Ay, marry, now unmuzzle your wisdom.

TOUCHSTONE.

Stand you both forth now: stroke your chins, and swear by your beards that I am a knave.

CELIA.

By our beards, if we had them, thou art.

TOUCHSTONE.

By my knavery, if I had it, then I were; but if you swear by that that is not, you are not forsworn: no more was this knight, swearing by his honour, for he never had any; or if he had, he had sworn it away before ever he saw those pancakes or that mustard.

CELIA.

Prithee, who is't that thou mean'st?

TOUCHSTONE.

One that old Frederick, your father, loves.

CELIA.

My father's love is enough to honour him enough: speak no more of him; you'll be whipt for taxation one of these days.

TOUCHSTONE.

The more pity, that fools may not speak wisely what wise men do foolishly.

CELIA.

By my troth, thou sayest true; for since the little wit that fools have was silenced, the little foolery that wise men have makes a great show.—Here comes Monsieur Le Beau.

ROSALIND.

With his mouth full of news.

CELIA.

Which he will put on us, as pigeons feed their young.

ROSALIND.

Then shall we be news-cramm'd.

CELIA.

All the better; we shall be the more marketable.

Enter LE BEAU.

Bon jour, Monsieur Le Beau: what's the news?

LE BEAU.

Fair princess, you have lost much good sport.

CELIA.

Sport! of what colour!

LE BEAU.

What colour, madam! how shall I answer you?

ROSALIND.

As wit and fortune will.

TOUCHSTONE.

Or as the Destinies decrees.

CELIA.

Well said: that was laid on with a trowel.

TOUCHSTONE.

Nay, if I keep not my rank,—

ROSALIND.

Thou losest thy old smell.

LE BEAU.

You amaze me, ladies: I would have told you of good wrestling, which you have lost the sight of.

ROSALIND.

Yet tell us the manner of the wrestling.

LE BEAU.

I will tell you the beginning; and, if it please your ladyships, you may see the end; for the best is yet to do; and here, where you are, they are coming to perform it.

CELIA.

Well,—the beginning, that is dead and buried.

LE BEAU.

There comes an old man and his three sons,—

CELIA.

I could match this beginning with an old tale.

LE BEAU.

Three proper young men, of excellent growth and presence.

ROSALIND.

With bills on their necks, 'Be it known unto all men by these presents.'

LE BEAU.

The eldest of the three wrestled with Charles, the duke's wrestler; which Charles in a moment threw him, and broke three of his ribs, that there is little hope of life in him: so he served the second, and so the third. Yonder they lie; the poor old man, their father, making such pitiful dole over them, that all the beholders take his part with weeping.

ROSALIND.

Alas!

TOUCHSTONE.

But what is the sport, monsieur, that the ladies have lost?

LE BEAU.

Why, this that I speak of.

TOUCHSTONE.

Thus men may grow wiser every day! it is the first time that ever I heard breaking of ribs was sport for ladies.

CELIA.

Or I, I promise thee.

ROSALIND.

But is there any else longs to see this broken music in his sides? is there yet another dotes upon rib-breaking?—Shall we see this wrestling, cousin?

LE BEAU.

You must, if you stay here; for here is the place appointed for the wrestling, and they are ready to perform it.

CELIA.

Yonder, sure, they are coming: let us now stay and see it.

Flourish. Enter DUKE FREDERICK, LORDS, OR-LANDO, CHARLES, *and* ATTENDANTS.

DUKE FREDERICK.

Come on: since the youth will not be entreated, his own peril on his forwardness.

ROSALIND.

Is yonder the man?

LE BEAU.

Even he, madam.

CELIA.

Alas, he is too young! yet he looks successfully.

DUKE FREDERICK.

How now, daughter, and cousin! are you crept hither to see the wrestling?

ROSALIND.

Ay, my liege, so please you give us leave.

DUKE FREDERICK.

You will take little delight in it, I can tell you, there is such odds in the men. In pity of the challenger's youth, I would fain dissuade him, but he will not be entreated. Speak to him, ladies; see if you can move him.

CELIA.

Call him hither, good Monsieur Le Beau.

DUKE FREDERICK.

Do so: I'll not be by.

LE BEAU.

Monsieur the challenger, the princess calls for you.

ORLANDO.

I attend them with all respect and duty.

ROSALIND.

Young man, have you challenged Charles the wrestler?

ORLANDO.

No, fair princess; he is the general challenger: I come but in, as others do, to try with him the strength of my youth.

CELIA.

Young gentleman, your spirits are too bold for your years. You have seen cruel proof of this man's strength: if you saw yourself with your eyes, or knew yourself with your judgement, the fear of your adventure would counsel you to a more equal enterprise. We pray you, for your own sake, to embrace your own safety, and give over this attempt.

ROSALIND.

Do, young sir; your reputation shall not therefore be misprised: we will make it our suit to the duke that the wrestling might not go forward.

ORLANDO.

I beseech you, punish me not with your hard thoughts: wherein I confess me much guilty, to deny so fair and excellent ladies any thing. But

let your fair eyes and gentle wishes go with me
to my trial; wherein if I be foil'd, there is but one
shamed that was never gracious; if kill'd, but one
dead that is willing to be so: I shall do my friends
no wrong, for I have none to lament me; the
world no injury, for in it I have nothing; only in
the world I fill up a place, which may be better
supplied when I have made it empty.

ROSALIND.
The little strength that I have, I would it were
with you.

CELIA.
And mine, to eke out hers.

ROSALIND.
Fare you well: pray heaven I be deceived in you!

CELIA.
Your heart's desires be with you!

CHARLES.
Come, where is this young gallant that is so desirous to lie with his mother earth?

ORLANDO.
Ready, sir; but his will hath in it a more modest
working.

DUKE FREDERICK.
You shall try but one fall.

CHARLES.
No, I warrant your grace, you shall not entreat
him to a second, that have so mightily persuaded
him from a first.

ORLANDO.
An you mean to mock me after, you should not
have mockt me before: but come your ways.

ROSALIND.
Now Hercules be thy speed, young man!

CELIA.
I would I were invisible, to catch the strong
fellow by the leg.   [Wrestle.

ROSALIND.
O excellent young man!

CELIA.
If I had a thunderbolt in mine eye, I can tell who
should down.   [Shout. CHARLES is thrown.

DUKE FREDERICK.
No more, no more.

ORLANDO.
Yes, I beseech your Grace: I am not yet well
breath'd.

DUKE FREDERICK.
How dost thou, Charles?

LE BEAU.
He cannot speak, my lord.

DUKE FREDERICK.
Bear him away. What is thy name, young man?

ORLANDO.
Orlando, my liege; the youngest son of Sir Rowland de Boys.

DUKE FREDERICK.
I would thou hadst been son to some man else:
The world esteem'd thy father honourable,
But I did find him still mine enemy: [deed,
Thou shouldst have better pleased me with this
Hadst thou descended from another house.
But fare thee well; thou art a gallant youth:
I would thou hadst told me of another father.
        [Exeunt DUKE FREDERICK, TRAIN, and
                LE BEAU.

CELIA.
Were I my father, coz, would I do this?

ORLANDO.
I am more proud to be Sir Rowland's son,
His youngest son;—and would not change that
        calling,
To be adopted heir to Frederick.

ROSALIND.
My father loved Sir Rowland as his soul,
And all the world was of my father's mind:
Had I before known this young man his son,
I should have given him tears unto entreaties,
Ere he should thus have ventured.

CELIA.
                                Gentle cousin,
Let us go thank him and encourage him:
My father's rough and envious disposition
Sticks me at heart.—Sir, you have well deserved:
If you do keep your promises in love
But justly, as you have exceeded all promise,
Your mistress shall be happy.

ROSALIND.
                                Gentleman,
        [Giving him a chain from her neck.
Wear this for me, one out of suits with fortune,
That would give more, but that her hand lacks
        means.
—Shall we go, coz?

CELIA.
        Ay.—Fare you well, fair gentleman.

ORLANDO.
Can I not say, I thank you? My better parts   [up
Are all thrown down, and that which here stands
Is but a quintain, a mere lifeless block.

ROSALIND.
He calls us back: my pride fell with my fortunes;
I'll ask him what he would.—Did you call, sir?—
Sir, you have wrestled well, and overthrown
More than your enemies.

CELIA.
                        Will you go, coz?

ROSALIND.
Have with you.—Fare you well.
        [Exeunt ROSALIND and CELIA.

ORLANDO.
What passion hangs these weights upon my
        tongue?
I cannot speak to her, yet she urged conference.
O poor Orlando, thou art overthrown!
Or Charles or something weaker masters thee.
                Enter LE BEAU.

LE BEAU
Good sir, I do in friendship counsel you
To leave this place. Albeit you have deserved
High commendation, true applause and love,
Yet such is now the duke's condition
That he misconsters all that you have done.
The duke is humorous: what he is, indeed,
More suits you to conceive than I to speak of.

ORLANDO.
I thank you, sir: and, pray you. tell me this,—
Which of the two was daughter of the duke,
That here was at the wrestling?

LE BEAU.
Neither his daughter, if we judge by manners;
But yet, indeed, the smaller is his daughter:

The other is daughter to the banisht duke,
And here detain'd by her usurping uncle,
To keep his daughter company: whose loves
Are dearer than the natural bond of sisters.
But I can tell you that of late this duke
Hath ta'en displeasure 'gainst his gentle niece,
Grounded upon no other argument
But that the people praise her for her virtues
And pity her for her good father's sake;
And, on my life, his malice 'gainst the lady
Will suddenly break forth.—Sir, fare you well:
Hereafter, in a better world than this,
I shall desire more love and knowledge of you.

ORLANDO.

I rest much bounden to you: fare you well.

[*Exit* LE BEAU.

Thus must I from the smoke into the smother;
From tyrant duke unto a tyrant brother:—
But heavenly Rosalind!   [*Exit.*

SCENE III.

A room in the palace.

Enter CELIA *and* ROSALIND.

WHY, cousin; why, Rosalind;—Cupid have
mercy!—not a word?

ROSALIND.

Not one to throw at a dog.

CELIA.

No, thy words are too precious to be cast away
upon curs; throw some of them at me; come, lame
me with reasons.

ROSALIND.

Then there were two cousins laid up; when the
one should be lamed with reasons, and the other
mad without any.

CELIA.

But is all this for your father?

ROSALIND.

No, some of it is for my father's child. O, how
full of briers is this working-day world!

CELIA.

They are but burs, cousin, thrown upon thee in
holiday foolery: if we walk not in the trodden
paths, our very petticoats will catch them.

ROSALIND.

I could shake them off my coat: these burs are in
my heart.

CELIA.

Hem them away.

ROSALIND.

I would try, if I could cry 'hem,' and have him.

CELIA.

Come, come, wrestle with thy affections.

ROSALIND.

O, they take the part of a better wrestler than myself!

CELIA.

O, a good wish upon you! you will try in time,
in despite of a fall.—But, turning these jests out
of service, let us talk in good earnest: is it possible,
on such a sudden, you should fall into so strong a
liking with old Sir Rowland's youngest son?

ROSALIND.

The duke my father loved his father dearly.

CELIA.

Doth it therefore ensue that you should love his
son dearly? By this kind of chase, I should hate
him, for my father hated his father dearly; yet I
hate not Orlando.

ROSALIND.

No, faith, hate him not, for my sake.

CELIA.

Why should I? doth he not deserve well?

ROSALIND.

Let me love him for that; and do you love him
because I do.—Look, here comes the duke.

CELIA.

With his eyes full of anger.

Enter DUKE FREDERICK, *with* LORDS.

DUKE FREDERICK.

Mistress, dispatch you with your safest haste,
And get you from our court.

ROSALIND.

          Me, uncle?

DUKE FREDERICK.

          You, cousin:
Within these ten days if that thou be'st found
So near our public court as twenty miles,
Thou diest for it.

ROSALIND.

          I do beseech your Grace,
Let me the knowledge of my fault bear with me:
If with myself I hold intelligence,
Or have acquaintance with mine own desires;
If that I do not dream, or be not frantic,
As I do trust I am not,—then, dear uncle,
Never so much as in a thought unborn
Did I offend your highness.

DUKE FREDERICK.

          Thus do all traitors:
If their purgation did consist in words,
They are as innocent as grace itself:
Let it suffice thee that I trust thee not.

ROSALIND.

Yet your mistrust cannot make me a traitor:
Tell me whereon the likelihood depends.

DUKE FREDERICK.

Thou art thy father's daughter; there's enough.

ROSALIND.

So was I when your highness took his dukedom;
So was I when your highness banisht him:
Treason is not inherited, my lord;
Or, if we did derive it from our friends,
What's that to me? my father was no traitor:
Then, good my liege, mistake me not so much
To think my poverty is treacherous.

CELIA.

Dear sovereign, hear me speak.

DUKE FREDERICK.

Ay, Celia; we stay'd her for your sake,
Else had she with her father ranged along.

CELIA.

I did not then entreat to have her stay;
It was your pleasure and your own remorse:
I was too young that time to value her;
But now I know her: if she be a traitor,
Why, so am I; we still have slept together,
Rose at an instant, learn'd, play'd, eat together;
And wheresoe'er we went, like Juno's swans,
Still we went coupled and inseparable.

DUKE FREDERICK.
She is too subtle for thee; and her smoothness,
Her very silence and her patience
Speak to the people, and they pity her.
Thou art a fool: she robs thee of thy name;
And thou wilt show more bright and seem more
    virtuous
When she is gone. Then open not thy lips:
Firm and irrevocable is my doom
Which I have pass'd upon her;—she is banisht.
CELIA.
Pronounce that sentence then on me, my liege:
I cannot live out of her company.
DUKE FREDERICK.
You are a fool.—You, niece, provide yourself:
If you outstay the time, upon mine honour,
And in the greatness of my word, you die.
    [Exeunt DUKE FREDERICK and LORDS.
CELIA.
O my poor Rosalind! whither wilt thou go?
Wilt thou change fathers? I will give thee mine.
I charge thee, be not thou more grieved than I am.
ROSALIND.
I have more cause.
CELIA.
    Thou hast not, cousin;
Prithee, be cheerful: know'st thou not, the duke
Hath banisht me, his daughter?
ROSALIND.
        That he hath not.
CELIA.
No, hath not? Rosalind lacks then the love
Which teacheth me that thou and I am one:
Shall we be sunder'd? shall we part, sweet girl?
No: let my father seek another heir.
Therefore devise with me how we may fly,
Whither to go and what to bear with us;
And do not seek to take the charge upon you,
To bear your griefs yourself and leave me out:
For, by this heaven, now at our sorrows pale,
Say what thou canst, I'll go along with thee.
ROSALIND.
Why, whither shall we go?
CELIA.
To seek my uncle in the forest of Arden.
ROSALIND.
Alas, what danger will it be to us,
Maids as we are, to travel forth so far!
Beauty provoketh thieves sooner than gold.
CELIA.
I'll put myself in poor and mean attire,
And with a kind of umber smirch my face;
The like do you: so shall we pass along
And never stir assailants.
ROSALIND.
        Were it not better,
Because that I am more than common tall,
That I did suit me all points like a man?
A gallant curtle-axe upon my thigh,
A boar-spear in my hand; and—in my heart
Lie there what hidden woman's fear there will—
We'll have a swashing and a martial outside;
As many other mannish cowards have
That do outface it with their semblances.
CELIA.
What shall I call thee when thou art a man?

ROSALIND.
I'll have no worse a name than Jove's own page;
And therefore look you call me Ganymede.
But what will you be call'd?
CELIA.
Something that hath a reference to my state;
No longer Celia, but Aliena.
ROSALIND.
But, cousin, what if we assay'd to steal
The clownish fool out of your father's court?
Would he not be a comfort to our travel?
CELIA.
He'll go along o'er the wide world with me;
Leave me alone to woo him. Let's away,
And get our jewels and our wealth together;
Devise the fittest time and safest way
To hide us from pursuit that will be made
After my flight. Now go we in content,
To liberty, and not to banishment.   [Exeunt.

ACT II. SCENE I.

The Forest of Arden.

Enter DUKE SENIOR, AMIENS, *and two or three*
    LORDS, *like foresters.*

DUKE SENIOR.
NOW, my co-mates and brothers in exile,
    Hath not old custom made this life more
        sweet
Than that of painted pomp? Are not these woods
More free from peril than the envious court?
Here feel we but the penalty of Adam,
The seasons' difference; as the icy fang
And churlish chiding of the winter's wind,
Which, when it bites and blows upon my body,
Even till I shrink with cold, I smile, and say
'This is no flattery; these are counsellors
That feelingly persuade me what I am.'
Sweet are the uses of adversity;
Which, like the toad, ugly and venomous,
Wears yet a precious jewel in his head;
And this our life, exempt from public haunt,
Finds tongues in trees, books in the running
    brooks,
Sermons in stones, and good in every thing:
I would not change it.
AMIENS.
        Happy is your Grace,
That can translate the stubbornness of fortune
Into so quiet and so sweet a style.
DUKE SENIOR.
Come, shall we go and kill us venison?
And yet it irks me the poor dappled fools,
Being native burghers of this desert city,
Should in their own confines with forked heads
Have their round haunches gored.
FIRST LORD.
        Indeed, my lord,
The melancholy Jaques grieves at that;
And, in that kind, swears you do more usurp
Than doth your brother that hath banisht you.
To-day my Lord of Amiens and myself
Did steal behind him, as he lay along
Under an oak, whose antique root peeps out
Upon the brook that brawls along this wood;

To the which place a poor sequester'd stag,
That from the hunter's aim had ta'en a hurt,
Did come to languish; and, indeed, my lord,
The wretched animal heaved forth such groans,
That their discharge did stretch his leathern coat
Almost to bursting; and the big round tears
Coursed one another down his innocent nose
In piteous chase: and thus the hairy fool,
Much marked of the melancholy Jaques,
Stood on th'extremest verge of the swift brook,
Augmenting it with tears.

DUKE SENIOR.
           But what said Jaques?
Did he not moralise this spectacle?

FIRST LORD.
O, yes, into a thousand similes.
First, for his weeping into the needless stream;
'Poor deer,' quoth he, 'thou makest a testament
As worldlings do, giving thy sum of more
To that which had too much:' then, being there
    alone,
Left and abandon'd of his velvet friends;
''Tis right,' quoth he; 'thus misery doth part
The flux of company:' anon, a careless herd,
Full of the pasture, jumps along by him,
And never stays to greet him; 'Ay,' quoth Jaques,
'Sweep on, you fat and greasy citizens;
'Tis just the fashion: wherefore do you look
Upon that poor and broken bankrupt there?'
Thus most invectively he pierceth through
The body of the country, city, court,
Yea, and of this our life: swearing that we
Are mere usurpers, tyrants, and what's worse,
To fright the animals, and to kill them up,
In their assign'd and native dwelling-place.

DUKE SENIOR.
And did you leave him in this contemplation?

SECOND LORD.
We did, my lord, weeping and commenting
Upon the sobbing deer.

DUKE SENIOR.
           Show me the place:
I love to cope him in these sullen fits,
For then he's full of matter.

FIRST LORD.
I'll bring you to him straight.   [*Exeunt.*

SCENE II.

A room in the palace.

Enter DUKE FREDERICK, *with* LORDS.

DUKE FREDERICK.
CAN it be possible that no man saw them?
It cannot be: some villains of my court
Are of consent and sufferance in this.

FIRST LORD.
I cannot hear of any that did see her.
The ladies, her attendants of her chamber,
Saw her a-bed; and, in the morning early,
They found the bed untreasured of their mistress.

SECOND LORD.
My lord, the roynish clown, at whom so oft
Your Grace was wont to laugh, is also missing.
Hesperia, the princess' gentlewoman,
Confesses that she secretly o'erheard

Your daughter and her cousin much commend
The parts and graces of the wrestler
That did but lately foil the sinewy Charles;
And she believes, wherever they are gone,
That youth is surely in their company.

DUKE FREDERICK.
Send to his brother's; fetch that gallant hither:
If he be absent, bring his brother to me;
I'll make him find him: do this suddenly;
And let not search and inquisition quail
To bring again these foolish runaways.   [*Exeunt.*

SCENE III.

Before OLIVER'S *house.*

Enter ORLANDO *and* ADAM, *meeting.*

ORLANDO.
WHO'S there?

ADAM.
What, my young master? O my gentle master!
O my sweet master! O you memory
Of old Sir Rowland! why, what make you here?
Why are you virtuous? why do people love you?
And wherefore are you gentle, strong, and
    valiant?
Why would you be so fond to overcome
The bony priser of the humorous duke?
Your praise is come too swiftly home before you.
Know you not, master, to some kind of men
Their graces serve them but as enemies?
No more do yours: your virtues, gentle master,
Are sanctified and holy traitors to you.
O, what a world is this, when what is comely
Envenoms him that bears it!

ORLANDO.
Why, what's the matter?

ADAM.
           O, unhappy youth!
Come not within these doors; within this roof
The enemy of all your graces lives:
Your brother—no, no brother; yet the son—
Yet not the son, I will not call him son
Of him I was about to call his father—
Hath heard your praises; and this night he means
To burn the lodging where you use to lie,
And you within it: if he fail of that,
He will have other means to cut you off:
I overheard him and his practices.
This is no place; this house is but a butchery:
Abhor it, fear it, do not enter it.

ORLANDO.
Why, whither, Adam, wouldst thou have me go?

ADAM.
No matter whither, so you come not here.

ORLANDO.
What, wouldst thou have me go and beg my food?
Or with a base and boisterous sword enforce
A thievish living on the common road?
This I must do, or know not what to do:
Yet this I will not do, do how I can;
I rather will subject me to the malice
Of a diverted blood and bloody brother.

ADAM.
But do not so. I have five hundred crowns,
The thrifty hire I saved under your father,

Which I did store to be my foster-nurse
When service should in my old limbs lie lame
And unregarded age in corners thrown:
Take that; and He that doth the ravens feed,
Yea, providently caters for the sparrow,
Be comfort to my age! Here is the gold;
All this I give you. Let me be your servant:
Though I look old, yet I am strong and lusty:
For in my youth I never did apply
Hot and rebellious liquors in my blood,
Nor did not with unbashful forehead woo
The means of weakness and debility;
Therefore my age is as a lusty winter,
Frosty, but kindly: let me go with you;
I'll do the service of a younger man
In all your business and necessities.

ORLANDO.

O good old man, how well in thee appears
The constant service of the antique world,
When service sweat for duty, not for meed!
Thou art not for the fashion of these times,
Where none will sweat but for promotion,
And having that, do choke their service up
Even with the having: it is not so with thee.
But, poor old man, thou prunest a rotten tree,
That cannot so much as a blossom yield
In lieu of all thy pains and husbandry.
But come thy ways: we'll go along together;
And ere we have thy youthful wages spent,
We'll light upon some settled low content.

ADAM.

Master, go on, and I will follow thee,
To the last gasp, with truth and loyalty.
From seventeen years till now almost fourscore
Here lived I, but now live here no more.
At seventeen years many their fortunes seek;
But at fourscore it is too late a week:
Yet fortune cannot recompense me better
Than to die well and not my master's debtor.
[Exeunt.

SCENE IV.

The Forest of Arden.

Enter ROSALIND for GANYMEDE, CELIA for
ALIENA, and TOUCHSTONE.

ROSALIND.

O JUPITER, how weary are my spirits!

TOUCHSTONE.

I care not for my spirits, if my legs were not
weary.

ROSALIND.

I could find in my heart to disgrace my man's apparel and to cry like a woman; but I must comfort
the weaker vessel, as doublet and hose ought to
show itself courageous to petticoat: therefore,
courage, good Aliena!

CELIA.

I pray you, bear with me; I cannot go no further.

TOUCHSTONE.

For my part, I had rather bear with you than
bear you; yet I should bear no cross, if I did
bear you, for I think you have no money in your
purse.

ROSALIND.

Well, this is the forest of Arden.

TOUCHSTONE.

Ay, now am I in Arden; the more fool I; when I
was at home, I was in a better place: but travellers
must be content.

ROSALIND.

Ay, be so, good Touchstone.
Enter CORIN and SILVIUS.
Look you, who comes here; a young man and an
old in solemn talk.

CORIN.

That is the way to make her scorn you still.

SILVIUS.

O Corin, that thou knew'st how I do love her!

CORIN.

I partly guess; for I have loved ere now.

SILVIUS.

No, Corin, being old, thou canst not guess;
Though in thy youth thou wast as true a lover
As ever sigh'd upon a midnight pillow:
But if thy love were ever like to mine,—
As sure I think did never man love so,—
How many actions most ridiculous
Hast thou been drawn to by thy fantasy?

CORIN.

Into a thousand that I have forgotten.

SILVIUS.

O, thou didst then never love so heartily!
If thou remember'st not the slightest folly
That ever love did make thee run into,
Thou hast not loved:
Or if thou hast not sat as I do now,
Wearing thy hearer in thy mistress' praise,
Thou hast not loved:
Or if thou hast not broke from company
Abruptly, as my passion now makes me,
Thou hast not loved.
O Phebe, Phebe, Phebe!   [Exit.

ROSALIND.

Alas, poor shepherd! searching of thy wound, I
have by hard adventure found mine own.

TOUCHSTONE.

And I mine. I remember, when I was in love I
broke my sword upon a stone, and bid him take
that for coming a-night to Jane Smile: and I remember the kissing of her batlet, and the cow's
dugs that her pretty chopt hands had milkt: and I
remember the wooing of a peascod instead of her;
from whom I took two cods, and, giving her them
again, said with weeping tears, 'Wear these for
my sake.' We that are true lovers run into strange
capers; but as all is mortal in nature, so is all
nature in love mortal in folly.

ROSALIND.

Thou speak'st wiser than thou art ware of.

TOUCHSTONE.

Nay, I shall ne'er be ware of mine own wit till I
break my shins against it.

ROSALIND.

Jove, Jove! this shepherd's passion
Is much upon my fashion.

TOUCHSTONE.

And mine; but it grows something stale with me.

CELIA.

I pray you, one of you question yond man,
If he for gold will give us any food:
I faint almost to death.

TOUCHSTONE.
Holla, you clown!

ROSALIND.
Peace, fool: he's not thy kinsman.

CORIN.
Who calls?

TOUCHSTONE.
Your betters, sir.

CORIN.
Else are they very wretched.

ROSALIND.
Peace, I say.—Good even to you, friend.

CORIN.
And to you, gentle sir, and to you all.

ROSALIND.
I prithee, shepherd, if that love or gold
Can in this desert place buy entertainment,
Bring us where we may rest ourselves and feed:
Here's a young maid with travel much opprest,
And faints for succour.

CORIN.
Fair sir, I pity her,
And wish, for her sake more than for mine own,
My fortunes were more able to relieve her;
But I am shepherd to another man
And do not shear the fleeces that I graze:
My master is of churlish disposition,
And little recks to find the way to heaven
By doing deeds of hospitality:
Besides, his cote, his flocks, and bounds of feed,
Are now on sale; and at our sheepcote now,
By reason of his absence, there is nothing
That you will feed on; but what is, come see,
And in my voice most welcome shall you be.

ROSALIND.
What is he that shall buy his flock and pasture?

CORIN.
That young swain that you saw here but erewhile,
That little cares for buying any thing.

ROSALIND.
I pray thee, if it stand with honesty,
Buy thou the cottage, pasture, and the flock,
And thou shalt have to pay for it of us.

CELIA.
And we will mend thy wages. I like this place,
And willingly could waste my time in it.

CORIN.
Assuredly the thing is to be sold:
Go with me: if you like, upon report,
The soil, the profit, and this kind of life,
I will your very faithful feeder be,
And buy it with your gold right suddenly.

[*Exeunt.*

SCENE V.

The forest.

Enter AMIENS, JAQUES, *and others.*

AMIENS [*sings*].

UNDER the greenwood tree
Who loves to lie with me,
And turn his merry note
Unto the sweet bird's throat,
Come hither, come hither, come hither:
Here shall he see
No enemy
But winter and rough weather.

JAQUES.
More, more, I prithee, more.

AMIENS.
It will make you melancholy, Monsieur Jaques.

JAQUES.
I thank it. More, I prithee, more. I can suck melancholy out of a song, as a weasel sucks eggs. More, I prithee, more.

AMIENS.
My voice is ragged: I know I cannot please you.

JAQUES.
I do not desire you to please me; I do desire you to sing. Come, more; another stanzo: call you 'em stanzos?

AMIENS.
What you will, Monsieur Jaques.

JAQUES.
Nay, I care not for their names; they owe me nothing. Will you sing?

AMIENS.
More at your request than to please myself.

JAQUES.
Well, then, if ever I thank any man, I'll thank you: but that they call compliment is like th' encounter of two dog-apes; and when a man thanks me heartily, methinks I have given him a penny and he renders me the beggarly thanks. Come, sing; and you that will not, hold your tongues.

AMIENS.
Well, I'll end the song.—Sirs, cover the while; the duke will drink under this tree.—He hath been all this day to look you.

JAQUES.
And I have been all this day to avoid him. He is too disputable for my company: I think of as many matters as he; but I give heaven thanks, and make no boast of them. Come, warble, come.

Song.

Who doth ambition shun   [*All together here.*
And loves to live i'th'sun,
Seeking the food he eats
And pleased with what he gets,
Come hither, come hither, come hither:
Here shall he see
No enemy
But winter and rough weather.

JAQUES.
I'll give you a verse to this note, that I made yesterday in despite of my invention.

AMIENS.
And I'll sing it.

JAQUES.
Thus it goes:—

If it do come to pass
That any man turn ass,
Leaving his wealth and ease,
A stubborn will to please,
Ducdame, ducdame, ducdame:
Here shall he see
Gross fools as he,
An if he will come to me.

AMIENS.
What's that 'ducdame'?

JAQUES.
'Tis a Greek invocation, to call fools into a circle.
I'll go sleep, if I can; if I cannot, I'll rail against
all the first-born of Egypt.

AMIENS.
And I'll go seek the duke: his banquet is prepared.   [*Exeunt severally.*

SCENE VI.

The forest.

Enter ORLANDO *and* ADAM.

ADAM.
DEAR master, I can go no further: O, I die
for food! Here lie I down, and measure out
my grave. Farewell, kind master.

ORLANDO.
Why, how now, Adam! no greater heart in thee?
Live a little; comfort a little; cheer thyself a little.
If this uncouth forest yield any thing savage, I
will either be food for it or bring it for food to
thee. Thy conceit is nearer death than thy powers.
For my sake be comfortable; hold death awhile at
the arm's end: I will here be with thee presently;
and if I bring thee not something to eat, I will
give thee leave to die: but if thou diest before I
come, thou art a mocker of my labour. Well said!
thou look'st cheerly; and I'll be with thee quickly.
Yet thou liest in the bleak air: come, I will bear
thee to some shelter; and thou shalt not die for
lack of a dinner, if there live any thing in this
desert. Cheerly, good Adam!   [*Exeunt.*

SCENE VII.

The forest.   A table set out.

Enter DUKE SENIOR, AMIENS, *and* LORDS *ike*
OUTLAWS.

DUKE SENIOR.
I THINK he be transform'd into a beast;
For I can no where find him like a man.

FIRST LORD.
My lord, he is but even now gone hence:
Here was he merry, hearing of a song.

DUKE SENIOR.
If he, compact of jars, grow musical,
We shall have shortly discord in the spheres.
Go, seek him: tell him I would speak with him.

Enter JAQUES.

FIRST LORD.
He saves my labour by his own approach.

DUKE SENIOR.
Why, how now, monsieur! what a life is this,
That your poor friends must woo your company!
What, you look merrily!

JAQUES.
A fool, a fool! I met a fool i'th'forest,
A motley fool; a miserable world!
As I do live by food, I met a fool;
Who laid him down and baskt him in the sun,
And rail'd on Lady Fortune in good terms,
In good set terms, and yet a motley fool.
'Good morrow, fool,' quoth I. 'No, sir,' quoth he,
'Call me not fool till heaven hath sent me fortune:'
And then he drew a dial from his poke,

And, looking on it with lack-lustre eye,
Says very wisely, 'It is ten o'clock:
Thus we may see,' quoth he, 'how the world wags:
'Tis but an hour ago since it was nine,
And after one hour more 'twill be eleven;
And so, from hour to hour, we ripe and ripe,
And then, from hour to hour, we rot and rot;
And thereby hangs a tale.' When I did hear
The motley fool thus moral on the time,
My lungs began to crow like chanticleer,
That fools should be so deep-contemplative;
And I did laugh sans intermission
An hour by his dial. O noble fool!
A worthy fool! Motley's the only wear.

DUKE SENIOR.
What fool is this?

JAQUES.
O worthy fool! One that hath been a courtier;
And says, if ladies be but young and fair,
They have the gift to know it: and in his brain,—
Which is as dry as the remainder biscuit
After a voyage,—he hath strange places cramm'd
With observation, the which he vents
In mangled forms.—O, that I were a fool!
I am ambitious for a motley coat.

DUKE SENIOR.
Thou shalt have one.

JAQUES.
                    It is my only suit;
Provided that you weed your better judgements
Of all opinion that grows rank in them
That I am wise. I must have liberty
Withal, as large a charter as the wind,
To blow on whom I please; for so fools have:
And they that are most galled with my folly,
They most must laugh. And why, sir, must they
          so?
The 'why' is plain as way to parish church:
He that a fool doth very wisely hit
Doth very foolishly, although he smart,
Not to seem senseless of the bob: if not,
The wise man's folly is anatomized
Even by the squandering glances of the fool.
Invest me in my motley; give me leave
To speak my mind, and I will through and through
Cleanse the foul body of th'infected world,
If they will patiently receive my medicine.

DUKE SENIOR.
Fie on thee! I can tell what thou wouldst do.

JAQUES.
What, for a counter, would I do but good?

DUKE SENIOR.
Most mischievous foul sin, in chiding sin:
For thou thyself hast been a libertine,
As sensual as the brutish sting itself;
And all th'imbossed sores and headed evils,
That thou with license of free foot hast caught,
Wouldst thou disgorge into the general world.

JAQUES.
Why, who cries out on pride,
That can therein tax any private party?
Doth it not flow as hugely as the sea,
Till that the weary very means do ebb?
What woman in the city do I name,
When that I say the city-woman bears
The cost of princes on unworthy shoulders?

Who can come in and say that I mean her,
When such a one as she such is her neighbour?
Or what is he of basest function,
That says his bravery is not on my cost,
Thinking that I mean him, but therein suits
His folly to the mettle of my speech?
There then; how then? what then? Let me see
    wherein
My tongue hath wrong'd him: if it do him right,
Then he hath wrong'd himself; if he be free,
Why, then my taxing like a wild-goose flies,
Unclaim'd of any man.—But who comes here?
   Enter ORLANDO, *with his sword drawn.*
         ORLANDO.
Forbear, and eat no more!
         JAQUES.
         Why, I have eat none yet.
         ORLANDO.
Nor shalt not, till necessity be served.
         JAQUES.
Of what kind should this cock come of?
         DUKE SENIOR.
Art thou thus bolden'd, man, by thy distress,
Or else a rude despiser of good manners,
That in civility thou seem'st so empty?
         ORLANDO.
You touch'd my vein at first: the thorny point
Of bare distress hath ta'en from me the show
Of smooth civility: yet am I inland bred,
And know some nurture. But forbear, I say:
He dies that touches any of this fruit
Till I and my affairs are answered.
         JAQUES.
An you will not be answer'd with reason, I must
die.
         DUKE SENIOR.
What would you have? Your gentleness shall
    force
More than your force move us to gentleness.
         ORLANDO.
I almost die for food; and let me have it.
         DUKE SENIOR.
Sit down and feed, and welcome to our table.
         ORLANDO.
Speak you so gently? Pardon me, I pray you:
I thought that all things had been savage here;
And therefore put I on the countenance
Of stern commandment. But whate'er you are,
That in this desert inaccessible,
Under the shade of melancholy boughs,
Lose and neglect the creeping hours of time;
If ever you have lookt on better days,
If ever been where bells have knoll'd to church,
If ever sat at any good man's feast,
If ever from your eyelids wiped a tear,
And know what 'tis to pity and be pitied,—
Let gentleness my strong enforcement be:
In the which hope I blush, and hide my sword.
         DUKE SENIOR.
True is it that we have seen better days,
And have with holy bell been knoll'd to church,
And sat at good men's feasts, and wiped our eyes
Of drops that sacred pity hath engender'd:
And therefore sit you down in gentleness,
And take upon command what help we have,
That to your wanting may be minister'd

         ORLANDO.
Then but forbear your food a little while,
Whiles, like a doe, I go to find my fawn,
And give it food. There is an old poor man,
Who after me hath many a weary step
Limpt in pure love: till he be first sufficed,—
Opprest with two weak evils, age and hunger,—
I will not touch a bit.
         DUKE SENIOR.
         Go find him out,
And we will nothing waste till you return.
         ORLANDO.
I thank ye; and be blest for your good comfort!
                    [*Exit.*
         DUKE SENIOR.
Thou seest we are not all alone unhappy:
This wide and universal theatre
Presents more woeful pageants than the scene
Wherein we play in.
         JAQUES.
         All the world's a stage,
And all the men and women merely players:
They have their exits and their entrances;
And one man in his time plays many parts,
His acts being seven ages. As, first the infant,
Mewling and puking in the nurse's arms.
And then the whining schoolboy, with his satchel
And shining morning face, creeping like snail
Unwillingly to school. And then the lover,
Sighing like furnace, with a woeful ballad
Made to his mistress' eyebrow. Then the soldier,
Full of strange oaths, and bearded like the pard,
Jealous in honour, sudden and quick in quarrel,
Seeking the bubble reputation   [tice,
Even in the cannon's mouth. And then the jus-
In fair round belly with good capon lined,
With eyes severe and beard of formal cut,
Full of wise saws and modern instances;
And so he plays his part. The sixth age shifts
Into the lean and slipper'd pantaloon,
With spectacles on nose and pouch on side;
His youthful hose, well saved, a world too wide
For his shrunk shank; and his big manly voice,
Turning again toward childish treble, pipes
And whistles in his sound. Last scene of all,
That ends this strange eventful history,
Is second childishness and mere oblivion,
Sans teeth, sans eyes, sans taste, sans every
    thing.
   Enter ORLANDO, *with* ADAM.
         DUKE SENIOR.
Welcome. Set down your venerable burthen,
And let him feed.
         ORLANDO.
I thank you most for him.
         ADAM.
         So had you need:—
I scarce can speak to thank you for myself.
         DUKE SENIOR.
Welcome; fall to: I will not trouble you
As yet, to question you about your fortunes.—
Give us some music; and, good cousin, sing.
         AMIENS.
    Blow, blow, thou winter wind,
      Thou art not so unkind
        As man's ingratitude;

Thy tooth is not so keen,
Because thou art not seen,
   Although thy breath be rude.
Heigh-ho! sing, heigh-ho! unto the green holly:
Most friendship is feigning, most loving mere
      folly:
   Then, heigh-ho, the holly!
   This life is most jolly.

Freeze, freeze, thou bitter sky,
That dost not bite so nigh
   As benefits forgot:
Though thou the waters warp,
Thy sting is not so sharp
   As friend remember'd not.
Heigh-ho! sing, heigh-ho! etc.

DUKE SENIOR.
If that you were the good Sir Rowland's son,
As you have whisper'd faithfully you were,
And as mine eye doth his effigies witness
Most truly limn'd and living in your face,—
Be truly welcome hither: I am the duke,
That loved your father: the residue of your for-
   tune,
Go to my cave and tell me. Good old man,
Thou art right welcome as thy master is.—
Support him by the arm.—Give me your hand,
And let me all your fortunes understand. [Exeunt.

ACT III. SCENE I.
A room in the palace.

Enter DUKE FREDERICK, LORDS, *and*
OLIVER.

DUKE FREDERICK.
NOT see him since? Sir, sir, that cannot be:
But were I not the better part made mercy,
I should not seek an absent argument
Of my revenge, thou present. But look to it:
Find out thy brother, wheresoe'er he is;
Seek him with candle; bring him dead or living
Within this twelvemonth, or turn thou no more
To seek a living in our territory.
Thy lands, and all things that thou dost call thine
Worth seizure, do we seize into our hands,
Till thou canst quit thee by thy brother's mouth
Of what we think against thee.

OLIVER.
O, that your highness knew my heart in this!
I never loved my brother in my life.

DUKE FREDERICK.
More villain thou.—Well, push him out of doors;
And let my officers of such a nature
Make an extent upon his house and lands:
Do this expediently, and turn him going.
                      [Exeunt.

SCENE II.
The forest.

Enter ORLANDO, *with a paper.*

ORLANDO.
HANG there, my verse, in witness of my love:
And thou, thrice-crowned queen of night,
   survey

With thy chaste eye, from thy pale sphere above,
   Thy huntress' name, that my full life doth sway.
O Rosalind! these trees shall be my books,
   And in their barks my thoughts I'll character;
That every eye, which in this forest looks,
   Shall see thy virtue witness'd every where.
Run, run, Orlando; carve on every tree
The fair, the chaste, and unexpressive she. [Exit.

Enter CORIN *and* TOUCHSTONE.

CORIN.
And how like you this shepherd's life, Master
Touchstone?

TOUCHSTONE.
Truly, shepherd, in respect of itself, it is a good
life; but in respect that it is a shepherd's life, it is
naught. In respect that it is solitary, I like it very
well; but in respect that it is private, it is a very
vile life. Now, in respect it is in the fields, it
pleaseth me well; but in respect it is not in the
court, it is tedious. As it is a spare life, look you,
it fits my humour well; but as there is no more
plenty in it, it goes much against my stomach.
Hast any philosophy in thee, shepherd?

CORIN.
No more but that I know the more one sickens the
worse at ease he is; and that he that wants money,
means, and content, is without three good friends;
that the property of rain is to wet, and fire to
burn; that good pasture makes fat sheep; and that
a great cause of the night is lack of the sun; that
he that hath learn'd no wit by nature nor art may
complain of good breeding, or comes of a very
dull kindred.

TOUCHSTONE.
Such a one is a natural philosopher. Wast ever in
court, shepherd?

CORIN.
No, truly.

TOUCHSTONE.
Then thou art damn'd.

CORIN.
Nay, I hope,—

TOUCHSTONE.
Truly, thou art damn'd; like an ill-roasted egg, all
on one side.

CORIN.
For not being at court? Your reason.

TOUCHSTONE.
Why, if thou never wast at court, thou never
saw'st good manners; if thou never saw'st good
manners, then thy manners must be wicked; and
wickedness is sin, and sin is damnation. Thou art
in a parlous state, shepherd.

CORIN.
Not a whit, Touchstone: those that are good
manners at the court, are as ridiculous in the
country as the behaviour of the country is most
mockable at the court. You told me you salute not
at the court, but you kiss your hands: that courtesy would be uncleanly, if courtiers were
shepherds.

TOUCHSTONE.
Instance, briefly; come, instance.

CORIN.
Why, we are still handling our ewes; and their
fells, you know, are greasy.

TOUCHSTONE.

Why, do not your courtier's hands sweat? and is not the grease of a mutton as wholesome as the sweat of a man? Shallow, shallow. A better instance, I say; come.

CORIN.

Besides, our hands are hard.

TOUCHSTONE.

Your lips will feel them the sooner. Shallow again. A more sounder instance, come.

CORIN.

And they are often tarr'd over with the surgery of our sheep; and would you have us kiss tar? The courtier's hands are perfumed with civet.

TOUCHSTONE.

Most shallow man! thou worms-meat, in respect of a good piece of flesh, indeed!—Learn of the wise, and perpend: civet is of a baser birth than tar,—the very uncleanly flux of a cat. Mend the instance, shepherd.

CORIN.

You have too courtly a wit for me: I'll rest.

TOUCHSTONE.

Wilt thou rest damn'd? God help thee, shallow man! God make incision in thee! thou art raw.

CORIN.

Sir, I am a true labourer: I earn that I eat, get that I wear; owe no man hate, envy no man's happiness; glad of other men's good, content with my harm; and the greatest of my pride is, to see my ewes graze and my lambs suck.

TOUCHSTONE.

That is another simple sin in you; to bring the ewes and the rams together, and to offer to get your living by the copulation of cattle; to be bawd to a bell-wether; and to betray a she-lamb of a twelvemonth to a crooked-pated, old, cuckoldly ram, out of all reasonable match. If thou be'st not damn'd for this, the devil himself will have no shepherds; I cannot see else how thou shouldst scape.

CORIN.

Here comes young Master Ganymede, my new mistress's brother.

Enter ROSALIND, *with a paper, reading.*

ROSALIND.

From the east to western Ind,
No jewel is like Rosalind.
Her worth, being mounted on the wind,
Through all the world bears Rosalind.
All the pictures fairest lined
Are but black to Rosalind.
Let no face be kept in mind
But the fair of Rosalind.

TOUCHSTONE.

I'll rime you so eight years together, dinners and suppers and sleeping-hours excepted: it is the right butter-women's rank to market.

ROSALIND.

Out, fool!

TOUCHSTONE.

For a taste:

If a hart do lack a hind,
Let him seek out Rosalind.
If the cat will after kind,
So be sure will Rosalind.

Winter garments must be lined,
So must slender Rosalind.
They that reap must sheaf and bind;
Then to cart with Rosalind.
Sweetest nut hath sourest rind,
Such a nut is Rosalind.
He that sweetest rose will find,
Must find love's prick and Rosalind.

This is the very false gallop of verses: why do you infect yourself with them?

ROSALIND.

Peace, you dull fool! I found them on a tree.

TOUCHSTONE.

Truly, the tree yields bad fruit.

ROSALIND.

I'll graff it with you, and then I shall graff it with a medlar: then it will be the earliest fruit i'th'country; for you'll be rotten ere you be half ripe, and that's the right virtue of the medlar.

TOUCHSTONE.

You have said; but whether wisely or no, let the forest judge.

Enter CELIA, *with a writing.*

ROSALIND.

Peace!
Here comes my sister, reading: stand aside.

CELIA [*reads*].

Why should this a desert be?
For it is unpeopled? No;
Tongues I'll hang on every tree,
That shall civil sayings show:
Some, how brief the life of man
Runs his erring pilgrimage,
That the stretching of a span
Buckles in his sum of age;
Some, of violated vows
'Twixt the souls of friend and friend:
But upon the fairest boughs,
Or at every sentence end,
Will I Rosalinda write;
Teaching all that read to know
The quintessence of every sprite
Heaven would in little show.
Therefore Heaven Nature charged
That one body should be fill'd
With all graces wide-enlarged:
Nature presently distill'd
Helen's cheek, but not her heart;
Cleopatra's majesty;
Atalanta's better part;
Sad Lucretia's modesty.
Thus Rosalind of many parts
By heavenly synod was devised;
Of many faces, eyes, and hearts,
To have the touches dearest prized.
Heaven would that she these gifts should have,
And I to live and die her slave.

ROSALIND.

O most gentle pulpiter!—what tedious homily of love have you wearied your parishioners withal, and never cried, 'Have patience, good people!'

CELIA.

How now! back, friends:—shepherd, go off a little:—go with him, sirrah.

TOUCHSTONE.

Come, shepherd, let us make an honourable retreat; though not with bag and baggage, yet with scrip and scrippage.

[*Exeunt* CORIN *and* TOUCHSTONE.

CELIA.

Didst thou hear these verses?

ROSALIND.

O, yes, I heard them all, and more too; for some of them had in them more feet than the verses would bear.

CELIA.

That's no matter: the feet might bear the verses.

ROSALIND.

Ay, but the feet were lame, and could not bear themselves without the verse, and therefore stood lamely in the verse.

CELIA.

But didst thou hear without wondering how thy name should be hang'd and carved upon these trees?

ROSALIND.

I was seven of the nine days out of the wonder before you came; for look here what I found on a palm-tree:—I was never so berimed since Pythagoras' time, that I was an Irish rat, which I can hardly remember.

CELIA.

Trow you who hath done this?

ROSALIND.

Is it a man?

CELIA.

And a chain, that you once wore, about his neck. Change you colour?

ROSALIND.

I prithee, who?

CELIA.

O Lord, Lord! it is a hard matter for friends to meet; but mountains may be removed with earthquakes, and so encounter.

ROSALIND.

Nay, but who is it?

CELIA.

Is it possible?

ROSALIND.

Nay, I prithee now with most petitionary vehemence, tell me who it is.

CELIA.

O wonderful, wonderful, and most wonderful wonderful! and yet again wonderful, and after that, out of all whooping!

ROSALIND.

Good my complexion! dost thou think, though I am caparison'd like a man, I have a doublet and hose in my disposition? One inch of delay more is a South-sea of discovery; I prithee, tell me who is it quickly, and speak apace. I would thou couldst stammer, that thou mightest pour this conceal'd man out of thy mouth, as wine comes out of a narrow-mouth'd bottle,—either too much at once, or none at all. I prithee, take the cork out of thy mouth, that I may drink thy tidings.

CELIA.

So you may put a man in your belly.

ROSALIND.

Is he of God's making? What manner of man? Is his head worth a hat, or his chin worth a beard?

CELIA.

Nay, he hath but a little beard.

ROSALIND.

Why, God will send more, if the man will be thankful: let me stay the growth of his beard, if thou delay me not the knowledge of his chin.

CELIA.

It is young Orlando, that tript up the wrestler's heels and your heart both in an instant.

ROSALIND.

Nay, but the devil take mocking: speak, sad brow and true maid.

CELIA.

I'faith, coz, 'tis he.

ROSALIND.

Orlando?

CELIA.

Orlando.

ROSALIND.

Alas the day! what shall I do with my doublet and hose?—What did he when thou saw'st him? What said he? How lookt he? Wherein went he? What makes he here? Did he ask for me? Where remains he? How parted he with thee? and when shalt thou see him again? Answer me in one word.

CELIA.

You must borrow me Gargantua's mouth first: 'tis a word too great for any mouth of this age's size. To say ay and no to these particulars is more than to answer in a catechism.

ROSALIND.

But doth he know that I am in this forest, and in man's apparel? Looks he as freshly as he did the day he wrestled?

CELIA.

It is as easy to count atomies as to resolve the propositions of a lover:—but take a taste of my finding him, and relish it with good observance. I found him under a tree, like a dropt acorn.

ROSALIND.

It may well be call'd Jove's tree, when it drops forth such fruit.

CELIA.

Give me audience, good madam.

ROSALIND.

Proceed.

CELIA.

There lay he, stretcht along, like a wounded knight.

ROSALIND.

Though it be pity to see such a sight, it well becomes the ground.

CELIA.

Cry, holla! to thy tongue, I prithee; it curvets unseasonably. He was furnisht like a hunter.

ROSALIND.

O, ominous, he comes to kill my heart.

CELIA.

I would sing my song without a burthen: thou bring'st me out of tune.

ROSALIND.
Do you not know I am a woman? when I think, I
must speak. Sweet, say on.

CELIA.
You bring me out.—Soft! comes he not here?

ROSALIND.
'Tis he: slink by, and note him.
[CELIA *and* ROSALIND *retire.*
Enter ORLANDO *and* JAQUES.

JAQUES.
I thank you for your company; but, good faith, I
had as lief have been myself alone.

ORLANDO.
And so had I; but yet, for fashion sake,
I thank you too for your society.

JAQUES.
God b'wi'you! let's meet as little as we can.

ORLANDO.
I do desire we may be better strangers.

JAQUES.
I pray you, mar no more trees with writing love-
songs in their barks.

ORLANDO.
I pray you, mar no moe of my verses with reading
them ill-favour'dly.

JAQUES.
Rosalind is your love's name?

ORLANDO.
Yes, just.

JAQUES.
I do not like her name.

ORLANDO.
There was no thought of pleasing you when she
was christen'd.

JAQUES.
What stature is she of?

ORLANDO.
Just as high as my heart.

JAQUES.
You are full of pretty answers. Have you not been
acquainted with goldsmiths' wives, and conn'd
them out of rings?

ORLANDO.
Not so; but I answer you right painted cloth, from
whence you have studied your questions.

JAQUES.
You have a nimble wit: I think 'twas made of
Atalanta's heels. Will you sit down with me? and
we two will rail against our mistress the world and
all our misery.

ORLANDO.
I will chide no breather in the world but myself,
against whom I know most faults.

JAQUES.
The worst fault you have is to be in love.

ORLANDO.
'Tis a fault I will not change for your best virtue.
I am weary of you.

JAQUES.
By my troth, I was seeking for a fool when I found
you.

ORLANDO.
He is drown'd in the brook: look but in, and you
shall see him.

JAQUES.
There I shall see mine own figure.

ORLANDO.
Which I take to be either a fool or a cipher.

JAQUES.
I'll tarry no longer with you: farewell, good Signior Love.

ORLANDO.
I am glad of your departure: adieu, good Monsieur Melancholy.
[*Exit* JAQUES. CELIA *and* ROSALIND
come forward.

ROSALIND [*aside to* CELIA].
I will speak to him like a saucy lackey, and under
that habit play the knave with him.—Do you
hear, forester?

ORLANDO.
Very well: what would you?

ROSALIND.
I pray you, what is't o'clock?

ORLANDO.
You should ask me, what time o'day: there's no
clock in the forest.

ROSALIND.
Then there is no true lover in the forest; else
sighing every minute, and groaning every hour,
would detect the lazy foot of Time as well as a
clock.

ORLANDO.
And why not the swift foot of Time? had not that
been as proper?

ROSALIND.
By no means, sir. Time travels in divers paces
with divers persons: I'll tell you who Time
ambles withal, who Time trots withal, who Time
gallops withal, and who he stands still withal.

ORLANDO.
I prithee, who doth he trot withal?

ROSALIND.
Marry, he trots hard with a young maid between
the contract of her marriage and the day it is
solemnized: if the interim be but a se'nnight,
Time's pace is so hard that it seems the length
of seven year.

ORLANDO.
Who ambles Time withal?

ROSALIND.
With a priest that lacks Latin, and a rich man
that hath not the gout; for the one sleeps easily,
because he cannot study; and the other lives
merrily, because he feels no pain: the one lacking
the burthen of lean and wasteful learning; the
other knowing no burthen of heavy tedious
penury: these Time ambles withal.

ORLANDO.
Who doth he gallop withal?

ROSALIND.
With a thief to the gallows; for though he go as
softly as foot can fall, he thinks himself too soon
there.

ORLANDO.
Who stays it still withal?

ROSALIND.
With lawyers in the vacation; for they sleep between term and term, and then they perceive not
how Time moves.

ORLANDO.
Where dwell you, pretty youth?

ROSALIND.
With this shepherdess, my sister; here in the skirts of the forest, like fringe upon a petticoat.

ORLANDO.
Are you native of this place?

ROSALIND.
As the cony, that you see dwell where she is kindled.

ORLANDO.
Your accent is something finer than you could purchase in so removed a dwelling.

ROSALIND.
I have been told so of many: but indeed an old religious uncle of mine taught me to speak, who was in his youth an inland man; one that knew courtship too well, for there he fell in love. I have heard him read many lectures against it; and I thank God I am not a woman, to be toucht with so many giddy offences as he hath generally taxt their whole sex withal.

ORLANDO.
Can you remember any of the principal evils that he laid to the charge of women?

ROSALIND.
There were none principal: they were all like one another as half-pence are; every one fault seeming monstrous till his fellow-fault came to match it.

ORLANDO.
I prithee, recount some of them.

ROSALIND.
No, I will not cast away my physic but on those that are sick. There is a man haunts the forest, that abuses our young plants with carving Rosalind on their barks; hangs odes upon hawthorns, and elegies on brambles; all, forsooth, deifying the name of Rosalind: if I could meet that fancy-monger, I would give him some good counsel, for he seems to have the quotidian of love upon him.

ORLANDO.
I am he that is so love-shaked: I pray you, tell me your remedy.

ROSALIND.
There is none of my uncle's marks upon you: he taught me how to know a man in love; in which cage of rushes I am sure you are not prisoner.

ORLANDO.
What were his marks?

ROSALIND.
A lean cheek,—which you have not; a blue eye and sunken,—which you have not; an unquestionable spirit,—which you have not; a beard neglected,—which you have not;—but I pardon you for that; for simply your having in beard is a younger brother's revenue:—then your hose should be ungarter'd, your bonnet unbanded, your sleeve unbutton'd, your shoe untied, and every thing about you demonstrating a careless desolation;—but you are no such man,—you are rather point-devise in your accoutrements, as loving yourself than seeming the lover of any other.

ORLANDO.
Fair youth, I would I could make thee believe I love.

ROSALIND.
Me believe it! you may as soon make her that you love believe it; which, I warrant, she is apter to do than to confess she does: that is one of the points in the which women still give the lie to their consciences. But, in good sooth, are you he that hangs the verses on the trees, wherein Rosalind is so admired?

ORLANDO.
I swear to thee, youth, by the white hand of Rosalind, I am that he, that unfortunate he.

ROSALIND.
But are you so much in love as your rimes speak?

ORLANDO.
Neither rime nor reason can express how much.

ROSALIND.
Love is merely a madness; and, I tell you, deserves as well a dark house and a whip as madmen do: and the reason why they are not so punisht and cured is, that the lunacy is so ordinary, that the whippers are in love too. Yet I profess curing it by counsel.

ORLANDO.
Did you ever cure any so?

ROSALIND.
Yes, one; and in this manner. He was to imagine me his love, his mistress; and I set him every day to woo me: at which time would I, being but a moonish youth, grieve, be effeminate, changeable, longing, and liking; proud, fantastical, apish, shallow, inconstant, full of tears, full of smiles; for every passion something, and for no passion truly any thing, as boys and women are for the most part cattle of this colour: would now like him, now loathe him; then entertain him, then forswear him; now weep for him, then spit at him; that I drave my suitor from his mad humour of love to a loving humour of madness; which was, to forswear the full stream of the world, and to live in a nook merely monastic. And thus I cured him; and this way will I take upon me to wash your liver as clean as a sound sheep's heart, that there shall not be one spot of love in't.

ORLANDO.
I would not be cured, youth.

ROSALIND.
I would cure you, if you would but call me Rosalind, and come every day to my cote and woo me.

ORLANDO.
Now, by the faith of my love, I will: tell me where it is.

ROSALIND.
Go with me to it, and I'll show it you: and, by the way, you shall tell me where in the forest you live. Will you go?

ORLANDO.
With all my heart, good youth.

ROSALIND.
Nay, you must call me Rosalind.—Come, sister, will you go?   [Exeunt.

SCENE III.

The forest.

Enter TOUCHSTONE *and* AUDREY; JAQUES *behind.*

TOUCHSTONE.
COME apace, good Audrey: I will fetch up your goats, Audrey. And how, Audrey? am I the man yet? doth my simple feature content you?

AUDREY.

Your features! Lord warrant us! what features?

TOUCHSTONE.

I am here with thee and thy goats, as the most capricious poet, honest Ovid, was among the Goths.

JAQUES [aside].

O knowledge ill-inhabited,—worse than Jove in a thatcht house!

TOUCHSTONE.

When a man's verses cannot be understood, nor a man's good wit seconded with the forward child Understanding, it strikes a man more dead than a great reckoning in a little room.—Truly, I would the gods had made thee poetical.

AUDREY.

I do not know what 'poetical' is: is it honest in deed and word? is it a true thing?

TOUCHSTONE.

No, truly; for the truest poetry is the most feigning; and lovers are given to poetry; and what they swear in poetry may be said as lovers they do feign.

AUDREY.

Do you wish, then, that the gods had made me poetical?

TOUCHSTONE.

I do, truly; for thou swear'st to me thou art honest: now, if thou wert a poet, I might have some hope thou didst feign.

AUDREY.

Would you not have me honest?

TOUCHSTONE.

No, truly, unless thou wert hard-favour'd; for honesty coupled to beauty is to have honey a sauce to sugar.

JAQUES [aside].

A material fool!

AUDREY.

Well, I am not fair; and therefore I pray the gods make me honest.

TOUCHSTONE.

Truly, and to cast away honesty upon a foul slut, were to put good meat into an unclean dish.

AUDREY.

I am not a slut, though I thank the gods I am foul.

TOUCHSTONE.

Well, praised be the gods for thy foulness! sluttishness may come hereafter. But be it as it may be, I will marry thee: and to that end I have been with Sir Oliver Martext, the vicar of the next village; who hath promised to meet me in this place of the forest, and to couple us.

JAQUES [aside].

I would fain see this meeting.

AUDREY.

Well, the gods give us joy!

TOUCHSTONE.

Amen. A man may, if he were of a fearful heart, stagger in this attempt; for here we have no temple but the wood, no assembly but hornbeasts. But what though? Courage! As horns are odious, they are necessary. It is said, ' Many a man knows no end of his goods:' right; many a man has good horns, and knows no end of them. Well, that is the dowry of his wife; 'tis none of his own getting. Horns? even so; poor men alone?

No, no; the noblest deer hath them as huge as the rascal. Is the single man therefore blessed? No: as a wall'd town is more worthier than a village, so is the forehead of a married man more honourable than the bare brow of a bachelor; and by how much defence is better than no skill, by so much is a horn more precious than to want.—Here comes Sir Oliver.

Enter SIR OLIVER MARTEXT.

Sir Oliver Martext, you are well met: will you dispatch us here under this tree, or shall we go with you to your chapel?

SIR OLIVER MARTEXT.

Is there none here to give the woman?

TOUCHSTONE.

I will not take her on gift of any man.

SIR OLIVER MARTEXT.

Truly, she must be given, or the marriage is not lawful.

JAQUES [coming forward].

Proceed, proceed: I'll give her.

TOUCHSTONE.

Good even, good Master What-ye-call't: how do you, sir? You are very well met: God ild you for your last company: I am very glad to see you:—even a toy in hand here, sir:—nay, pray be cover'd.

JAQUES.

Will you be married, motley?

TOUCHSTONE.

As the ox hath his bow, sir, the horse his curb, and the falcon her bells, so man hath his desires; and as pigeons bill, so wedlock would be nibbling.

JAQUES.

And will you, being a man of your breeding, be married under a bush like a beggar? Get you to church and have a good priest that can tell you what marriage is: this fellow will but join you together as they join wainscot; then one of you will prove a shrunk panel, and like green timber warp, warp.

TOUCHSTONE [aside].

I am not in the mind but I were better to be married of him than of another: for he is not like to marry me well; and not being well married, it will be a good excuse for me hereafter to leave my wife.

JAQUES.

Go thou with me, and let me counsel thee.

TOUCHSTONE.

Come, sweet Audrey:

We must be married, or we must live in bawdry.—

Farewell, good Master Oliver:—not,

O sweet Oliver,
O brave Oliver,
Leave me not behind thee;—

but,

Wind away,
Be gone, I say,
I will not to wedding with thee.

[*Exeunt* JAQUES, TOUCHSTONE, *and* AUDREY.

SIR OLIVER MARTEXT.

'Tis no matter: ne'er a fantastical knave of them all shall flout me out of my calling. [*Exit.*

SCENE IV.

The forest.

Enter ROSALIND *and* CELIA.

ROSALIND.

NEVER talk to me; I will weep.

CELIA.

Do, I prithee; but yet have the grace to consider that tears do not become a man.

ROSALIND.

But have I not cause to weep?

CELIA.

As good cause as one would desire: therefore weep.

ROSALIND.

His very hair is of the dissembling colour.

CELIA.

Something browner than Judas's: marry, his kisses are Judas's own children.

ROSALIND.

I'faith, his hair is of a good colour.

CELIA.

An excellent colour: your chestnut was ever the only colour.

ROSALIND.

And his kissing is as full of sanctity as the touch of holy bread.

CELIA.

He hath bought a pair of cast lips of Diana: a nun of winter's sisterhood kisses not more religiously; the very ice of chastity is in them.

ROSALIND.

But why did he swear he would come this morning, and comes not?

CELIA.

Nay, certainly, there is no truth in him.

ROSALIND.

Do you think so?

CELIA.

Yes; I think he is not a pick-purse nor a horse-stealer; but for his verity in love, I do think him as concave as a cover'd goblet or a worm-eaten nut.

ROSALIND.

Not true in love?

CELIA.

Yes, when he is in; but I think he is not in.

ROSALIND.

You have heard him swear downright he was.

CELIA.

'Was' is not 'is:' besides, the oath of a lover is no stronger than the word of a tapster; they are both the confirmers of false reckonings. He attends here in the forest on the duke your father.

ROSALIND.

I met the duke yesterday, and had much question with him: he askt me, of what parentage I was; I told him, of as good as he; so he laught, and let me go. But what talk we of fathers, when there is such a man as Orlando?

CELIA.

O, that's a brave man! he writes brave verses, speaks brave words, swears brave oaths, and breaks them bravely, quite traverse, athwart the heart of his lover; as a puisny tilter, that spurs his horse but on one side, breaks his staff like a noble goose: but all's brave that youth mounts and folly guides.—Who comes here?

Enter CORIN.

CORIN.

Mistress and master, you have oft inquired
After the shepherd that complain'd of love,
Who you saw sitting by me on the turf,
Praising the proud disdainful shepherdess
That was his mistress.

CELIA.

    Well, and what of him?

CORIN.

If you will see a pageant truly play'd,
Between the pale complexion of true love
And the red glow of scorn and proud disdain,
Go hence a little, and I shall conduct you,
If you will mark it.

ROSALIND.

    O, come, let us remove:
The sight of lovers feedeth those in love.—
Bring us to this sight, and you shall say
I'll prove a busy actor in their play.   [*Exeunt.*

SCENE V.

The forest.

Enter SILVIUS *and* PHEBE.

SILVIUS.

SWEET Phebe, do not scorn me; do not, Phebe:
Say that you love me not; but say not so
In bitterness. The common executioner,
Whose heart th'accustom'd sight of death makes
  hard,
Falls not the axe upon the humbled neck
But first begs pardon: will you sterner be
Than he that dies and lives by bloody drops?

Enter ROSALIND *and* CELIA; CORIN *behind.*

PHEBE.

I would not be thy executioner:
I fly thee, for I would not injure thee.
Thou tell'st me there is murder in mine eye:
'Tis pretty, sure, and very probable,
That eyes that are the frail'st and softest things,
Who shut their coward gates on atomies—
Should be call'd tyrants, butchers, murderers!
Now I do frown on thee with all my heart;
And, if mine eyes can wound, now let them kill
  thee:
Now counterfeit to swoon; why, now fall down;
Or, if thou canst not, O, for shame, for shame,
Lie not, to say mine eyes are murderers!
Now show the wound mine eye hath made in
  thee:
Scratch thee but with a pin, and there remains
Some scar of it; lean but upon a rush,
The cicatrice and capable impressure
Thy palm some moment keeps: but now mine
  eyes,
Which I have darted at thee, hurt thee not;
Nor, I am sure, there is no force in eyes
That can do hurt.

SILVIUS.

    O dear Phebe,
If ever—as that ever may be near—
You meet in some fresh cheek the power of fancy,
Then shall you know the wounds invisible
That love's keen arrows make.

PHEBE.

                      But, till that time,
Come not thou near me: and, when that time
  comes,
Afflict me with thy mocks, pity me not;
As, till that time, I shall not pity thee.

        ROSALIND [*coming forward*].

And why, I pray you? Who might be your
  mother,
That you insult, exult, and all at once,
Over the wretched? What though you have no
  beauty,—
As, by my faith, I see no more in you
Than without candle may go dark to bed,—
Must you be therefore proud and pitiless?
Why, what means this? Why do you look on me?
I see no more in you than in the ordinary
Of nature's sale-work:—'Od's my little life,
I think she means to tangle my eyes too!—
No, faith, proud mistress, hope not after it:
'Tis not your inky brows, your black-silk hair,
Your bugle eyeballs, nor your cheek of cream,
That can entame my spirits to your worship.—
You foolish shepherd, wherefore do you follow
  her,
Like foggy south, puffing with wind and rain?
You are a thousand times a properer man
Than she a woman: 'tis such fools as you
That makes the world full of ill-favour'd children:
'Tis not her glass, but you, that flatters her;
And out of you she sees herself more proper
Than any of her lineaments can show her.—
But, mistress, know yourself: down on your knees,
And thank heaven, fasting, for a good man's love:
For I must tell you friendly in your ear,—
Sell when you can: you are not for all markets:
Cry the man mercy; love him; take his offer.
Foul is most foul, being foul to be a scoffer.—
So, take her to thee, shepherd:—fare you well.

             PHEBE.

Sweet youth, I pray you, chide a year together:
I had rather hear you chide than this man woo.

          ROSALIND.

He's fall'n in love with her foulness, and she'll
fall in love with my anger:—if it be so, as fast as
she answers thee with frowning looks, I'll sauce
her with bitter words.—Why look you so upon me?

             PHEBE.

For no ill will I bear you.

          ROSALIND.

I pray you, do not fall in love with me,
For I am falser than vows made in wine:
Besides, I like you not.—If you will know my
  house,
'Tis at the tuft of olives here hard by.—
Will you go, sister?—Shepherd, ply her hard.—
Come, sister.—Shepherdess, look on him better,
And be not proud: though all the world could see,
None could be so abused in sight as he.—
Come, to our flock.

      [*Exeunt* ROSALIND, CELIA, *and* CORIN.

             PHEBE.

Dead shepherd, now I find thy saw of might,—
'Who ever loved that loved not at first sight?'

           SILVIUS.

Sweet Phebe,—

             PHEBE.

Ha, what say'st thou, Silvius?

           SILVIUS.

Sweet Phebe, pity me.

             PHEBE.

Why, I am sorry for thee, gentle Silvius.

           SILVIUS.

Wherever sorrow is, relief would be:
If you do sorrow at my grief in love,
By giving love, your sorrow and my grief
Were both extermined.

             PHEBE.

Thou hast my love: is not that neighbourly?

           SILVIUS.

I would have you.

             PHEBE.

          Why, that were covetousness.
Silvius, the time was, that I hated thee;
And yet it is not that I bear thee love:
But since that thou canst talk of love so well,
Thy company, which erst was irksome to me,
I will endure; and I'll employ thee too:
But do not look for further recompense
Than thine own gladness that thou art employ'd.

          SILVIUS.

So holy and so perfect is my love,
And I in such a poverty of grace,
That I shall think it a most plenteous crop
To glean the broken ears after the man
That the main harvest reaps: loose now and then
A scatter'd smile, and that I'll live upon.

             PHEBE.

Know'st thou the youth that spoke to me erewhile?

           SILVIUS.

Not very well, but I have met him oft;
And he hath bought the cottage and the bounds
That the old carlot once was master of.

             PHEBE.

Think not I love him, though I ask for him;
'Tis but a peevish boy:—yet he talks well;—
But what care I for words? yet words do well,
When he that speaks them pleases those that hear.
It is a pretty youth:—not very pretty:—
But, sure, he's proud; and yet his pride becomes
  him:
He'll make a proper man: the best thing in him
Is his complexion; and faster than his tongue
Did make offence, his eye did heal it up.
He is not very tall; yet for his years he's tall:
His leg is but so-so; and yet 'tis well:
There was a pretty redness in his lip,
A little riper and more lusty red
Than that mixt in his cheek; 'twas just the differ-
  ence
Betwixt the constant red and mingled damask.
There be some women, Silvius, had they markt
  him
In parcels as I did, would have gone near
To fall in love with him: but, for my part,
I love him not, nor hate him not; and yet
I have more cause to hate him than to love him:
For what had he to do to chide at me?
He said mine eyes were black, and my hair black;
And, now I am remember'd, scorn'd at me:
I marvel why I answer'd not again:

But that's all one: omittance is no quittance.
I'll write to him a very taunting letter,
And thou shalt bear it; wilt thou, Silvius?
                    SILVIUS.
Phebe, with all my heart.
                    PHEBE.
                         I'll write it straight;
The matter's in my head and in my heart:
I will be bitter with him and passing short.
Go with me, Silvius.   [*Exeunt.*

ACT IV. SCENE I.
The forest.

Enter ROSALIND, CELIA, *and* JAQUES.
                    JAQUES.
I PRITHEE, pretty youth, let me be better acquainted with thee.
                    ROSALIND.
They say you are a melancholy fellow.
                    JAQUES.
I am so; I do love it better than laughing.
                    ROSALIND.
Those that are in extremity of either are abominable fellows, and betray themselves to every modern censure worse than drunkards.
                    JAQUES.
Why, 'tis good to be sad and say nothing.
                    ROSALIND.
Why, then 'tis good to be a post.
                    JAQUES.
I have neither the scholar's melancholy, which is emulation; nor the musician's, which is fantastical; nor the courtier's, which is proud; nor the soldier's, which is ambitious; nor the lawyer's, which is politic; nor the lady's, which is nice; nor the lover's, which is all these;—but it is a melancholy of mine own, compounded of many simples, extracted from many objects, and, indeed, the sundry contemplation of my travels, which, by often rumination, wraps me in a most humorous sadness.
                    ROSALIND.
A traveller! By my faith, you have great reason to be sad: I fear you have sold your own lands, to see other men's; then, to have seen much, and to have nothing, is to have rich eyes and poor hands.
                    JAQUES.
Yes, I have gain'd my experience.
                    ROSALIND.
And your experience makes you sad: I had rather have a fool to make me merry than experience to make me sad; and to travel for it too!
Enter ORLANDO.
                    ORLANDO.
Good day and happiness, dear Rosalind!
                    JAQUES.
Nay, then, God b'wi'you, an you talk in blank verse!   [*Exit.*
                    ROSALIND.
Farewell, Monsieur Traveller: look you lisp, and wear strange suits; disable all the benefits of your own country; be out of love with your nativity, and almost chide God for making you that countenance you are; or I will scarce think you have

swam in a gondola. Why, how now, Orlando! where have you been all this while? You a lover! —An you serve me such another trick, never come in my sight more.
                    ORLANDO.
My fair Rosalind, I come within an hour of my promise.
                    ROSALIND.
Break an hour's promise in love! He that will divide a minute into a thousand parts, and break but a part of the thousandth part of a minute in the affairs of love, it may be said of him, that Cupid hath clapt him o'th'shoulder, but I'll warrant him heart-whole.
                    ORLANDO.
Pardon me, dear Rosalind.
                    ROSALIND.
Nay, an you be so tardy, come no more in my sight: I had as lief be woo'd of a snail.
                    ORLANDO.
Of a snail!
                    ROSALIND.
Ay, of a snail; for though he comes slowly, he carries his house on his head,—a better jointure, I think, than you make a woman: besides, he brings his destiny with him.
                    ORLANDO.
What's that?
                    ROSALIND.
Why, horns; which such as you are fain to be beholding to your wives for: but he comes arm'd in his fortune, and prevents the slander of his wife.
                    ORLANDO.
Virtue is no horn-maker; and my Rosalind is virtuous.
                    ROSALIND.
And I am your Rosalind.
                    CELIA.
It pleases him to call you so; but he hath a Rosalind of a better leer than you.
                    ROSALIND.
Come, woo me, woo me; for now I am in a holiday humour, and like enough to consent.—What would you say to me now, an I were your very very Rosalind?
                    ORLANDO.
I would kiss before I spoke.
                    ROSALIND.
Nay, you were better speak first; and when you were gravell'd for lack of matter, you might take occasion to kiss. Very good orators, when they are out, they will spit; and for lovers, lacking (God warn us!) matter, the cleanliest shift is to kiss.
                    ORLANDO.
How if the kiss be denied?
                    ROSALIND.
Then she puts you to entreaty, and there begins new matter.
                    ORLANDO.
Who could be out, being before his beloved mistress?
                    ROSALIND.
Marry, that should you, if I were your mistress; or I should think my honesty ranker than my wit.
                    ORLANDO.
What, of my suit?

ROSALIND.

Not out of your apparel, and yet out of your suit. Am not I your Rosalind?

ORLANDO.

I take some joy to say you are, because I would be talking of her.

ROSALIND.

Well, in her person, I say,—I will not have you.

ORLANDO.

Then, in mine own person, I die.

ROSALIND.

No, faith, die by attorney. The poor world is almost six thousand years old, and in all this time there was not any man died in his own person, *videlicet*, in a love-cause. Troilus had his brains dasht out with a Grecian club; yet he did what he could to die before; and he is one of the patterns of love. Leander, he would have lived many a fair year, though Hero had turn'd nun, if it had not been for a hot midsummer night; for, good youth, he went but forth to wash him in the Hellespont, and, being taken with the cramp, was drown'd: and the foolish chroniclers of that age found it was —Hero of Sestos. But these are all lies: men have died from time to time, and worms have eaten them, but not for love.

ORLANDO.

I would not have my right Rosalind of this mind; for, I protest, her frown might kill me.

ROSALIND.

By this hand, it will not kill a fly. But come, now I will be your Rosalind in a more coming-on disposition; and ask me what you will, I will grant it.

ORLANDO.

Then love me, Rosalind.

ROSALIND.

Yes, faith, will I, Fridays and Saturdays and all.

ORLANDO.

And wilt thou have me?

ROSALIND.

Ay, and twenty such.

ORLANDO.

What sayest thou?

ROSALIND.

Are you not good?

ORLANDO.

I hope so.

ROSALIND.

Why, then, can one desire too much of a good thing?—Come, sister, you shall be the priest, and marry us.—Give me your hand, Orlando.—What do you say, sister?

ORLANDO.

Pray thee, marry us.

CELIA.

I cannot say the words.

ROSALIND.

You must begin,—'Will you, Orlando,'—

CELIA.

Go to.—Will you, Orlando, have to wife this Rosalind?

ORLANDO.

I will.

ROSALIND.

Ay, but when?

ORLANDO.

Why now; as fast as she can marry us.

ROSALIND.

Then you must say,—'I take thee, Rosalind, for wife.'

ORLANDO.

I take thee, Rosalind, for wife.

ROSALIND.

I might ask you for your commission; but,—I do take thee, Orlando, for my husband:—there's a girl goes before the priest; and, certainly, a woman's thought runs before her actions.

ORLANDO.

So do all thoughts,—they are wing'd.

ROSALIND.

Now tell me how long you would have her, after you have possest her.

ORLANDO.

For ever and a day.

ROSALIND.

Say a day, without the ever. No, no, Orlando; men are April when they woo, December when they wed: maids are May when they are maids, but the sky changes when they are wives. I will be more jealous of thee than a Barbary cock-pigeon over his hen; more clamorous than a parrot against rain; more new-fangled than an ape; more giddy in my desires than a monkey: I will weep for nothing, like Diana in the fountain, and I will do that when you are disposed to be merry; I will laugh like a hyen, and that when thou art inclined to weep.

ORLANDO.

But will my Rosalind do so?

ROSALIND.

By my life, she will do as I do.

ORLANDO.

O, but she is wise.

ROSALIND.

Or else she could not have the wit to do this: the wiser, the waywarder: make the doors upon a woman's wit, and it will out at the casement; shut that, and 'twill out at the key-hole; stop that, 'twill fly with the smoke out at the chimney.

ORLANDO.

A man that had a wife with such a wit, he might say,—'Wit, whither wilt?'

ROSALIND.

Nay, you might keep that check for it till you met your wife's wit going to your neighbour's bed.

ORLANDO.

And what wit could wit have to excuse that?

ROSALIND.

Marry, to say,—she came to seek you there. You shall never take her without her answer, unless you take her without her tongue. O, that woman that cannot make her fault her husband's occasion, let her never nurse her child herself, for she will breed it like a fool!

ORLANDO.

For these two hours, Rosalind, I will leave thee.

ROSALIND.

Alas, dear love, I cannot lack thee two hours!

ORLANDO.

I must attend the duke at dinner: by two o'clock I will be with thee again.

ROSALIND.

Ay, go your ways, go your ways;—I knew what you would prove: my friends told me as much, and I thought no less:—that flattering tongue of yours won me:—'tis but one cast away, and so,—come, death!—Two o'clock is your hour?

ORLANDO.

Ay, sweet Rosalind.

ROSALIND.

By my troth, and in good earnest, and so God mend me, and by all pretty oaths that are not dangerous, if you break one jot of your promise, or come one minute behind your hour, I will think you the most pathetical break-promise, and the most hollow lover, and the most unworthy of her you call Rosalind, that may be chosen out of the gross band of the unfaithful: therefore beware my censure, and keep your promise.

ORLANDO.

With no less religion than if thou wert indeed my Rosalind: so, adieu.

ROSALIND.

Well, Time is the old justice that examines all such offenders, and let Time try: adieu.

[Exit ORLANDO.

CELIA.

You have simply misused our sex in your love-prate: we must have your doublet and hose pluckt over your head, and show the world what the bird hath done to her own nest.

ROSALIND.

O coz, coz, coz, my pretty little coz, that thou didst know how many fathom deep I am in love! But it cannot be sounded: my affection hath an unknown bottom, like the bay of Portugal.

CELIA.

Or rather, bottomless; that as fast as you pour affection in, it runs out.

ROSALIND.

No, that same wicked bastard of Venus, that was begot of thought, conceived of spleen, and born of madness; that blind rascally boy, that abuses every one's eyes, because his own are out, let him be judge how deep I am in love:—I'll tell thee, Aliena, I cannot be out of the sight of Orlando; I'll go find a shadow, and sigh till he come.

CELIA.

And I'll sleep.

[Exeunt.

SCENE II.

The forest.

Enter JAQUES, LORDS, *and* FORESTERS.

JAQUES.

WHICH is he that kill'd the deer?

A LORD.

Sir, it was I.

JAQUES.

Let's present him to the duke, like a Roman conqueror; and it would do well to set the deer's horns upon his head, for a branch of victory.—Have you no song, forester, for this purpose?

FORESTER.

Yes, sir.

JAQUES.

Sing it: 'tis no matter how it be in tune, so it make noise enough.

Song.

What shall he have that kill'd the deer?
His leather skin and horns to wear.
Then sing him home!
[The rest shall bear this burthen.
Take thou no scorn to wear the horn;
It was a crest ere thou wast born;
    Thy father's father wore it,
    And thy father bore it:
The horn, the horn, the lusty horn
Is not a thing to laugh to scorn.   *[Exeunt.*

SCENE III.

The forest.

Enter ROSALIND AND CELIA.

ROSALIND.

HOW say you now? Is it not past two o'clock? and here much Orlando!

CELIA.

I warrant you, with pure love and troubled brain, he hath ta'en his bow and arrows, and is gone forth—to sleep. Look, who comes here.

Enter SILVIUS.

SILVIUS.

My errand is to you, fair youth;—
My gentle Phebe bid me give you this:
        [gives a letter.
I know not the contents; but, as I guess
By the stern brow and waspish action
Which she did use as she was writing of it,
It bears an angry tenour: pardon me,
I am but as a guiltless messenger.

ROSALIND.

Patience herself would startle at this letter,
And play the swaggerer; bear this, bear all:
She says I am not fair; that I lack manners;
She calls me proud; and that she could not love
  me,
Were man as rare as phœnix. 'Od's my will!
Her love is not the hare that I do hunt:
Why writes she so to me?—Well, shepherd, well,
This is a letter of your own device.

SILVIUS.

No, I protest, I know not the contents:
Phebe did write it.

ROSALIND.

        Come, come, you are a fool,
And turn'd into the extremity of love.
I saw her hand: she has a leathern hand,
A freestone-colour'd hand: I verily did think
That her old gloves were on, but 'twas her hands:
She has a housewife's hand; but that's no matter:
I say, she never did invent this letter;
This is a man's invention, and his hand.

SILVIUS.

Sure, it is hers.

ROSALIND.

Why, 'tis a boisterous and a cruel style,
A style for challengers; why, she defies me,
Like Turk to Christian: women's gentle brain
Could not drop forth such giant-rude invention,

Such Ethiop words, blacker in their effect
Than in their countenance.—Will you hear the
  letter?

SILVIUS.
So please you, for I never heard it yet;
Yet heard too much of Phebe's cruelty.

ROSALIND.
She Phebes me: mark how the tyrant writes.
  [*Reads*] Art thou god to shepherd turn'd,
       That a maiden's heart hath burn'd?—
Can a woman rail thus?

SILVIUS.
Call you this railing?

ROSALIND [*reads*].
  Why, thy godhead laid apart,
  Warr'st thou with a woman's heart?—
Did you ever hear such railing?—
  Whiles the eye of man did woo me,
  That could do no vengeance to me.—
Meaning me a beast.—
  If the scorn of your bright eyne
  Have power to raise such love in mine,
  Alack, in me what strange effect
  Would they work in mild aspect!
  Whiles you chid me, I did love;
  How, then, might your prayers move!
  He that brings this love to thee
  Little knows this love in me:
  And by him seal up thy mind;
  Whether that thy youth and kind
  Will the faithful offer take
  Of me, and all that I can make;
  Or else by him my love deny,
  And then I'll study how to die.

SILVIUS.
Call you this chiding?

CELIA.
Alas, poor shepherd!

ROSALIND.
Do you pity him? no, he deserves no pity. Wilt
thou love such a woman? What, to make thee an
instrument, and play false strains upon thee! not
to be endured! Well, go your way to her, for I see
love hath made thee a tame snake, and say this to
her:—that if she love me, I charge her to love
thee; if she will not, I will never have her, unless
thou entreat for her.—If you be a true lover,
hence, and not a word; for here comes more company.   [*Exit* SILVIUS.

Enter OLIVER.

OLIVER.
Good morrow, fair ones: pray you, if you know,
Where in the purlieus of this forest stands
A sheep-cote fenced about with olive-trees?

CELIA.
West of this place, down in the neighbour bot-
  tom:
The rank of osiers, by the murmuring stream,
Left on your right hand, brings you to the place.
But at this hour the house doth keep itself;
There's none within.

OLIVER.
If that an eye may profit by a tongue,
Then should I know you by description;
Such garments and such years:—'The boy is fair,
Of female favour, and bestows himself

Like a ripe sister: the woman low,
And browner than her brother.' Are not you
The owners of the house I did inquire for?

CELIA.
It is no boast, being askt, to say we are.

OLIVER.
Orlando doth commend him to you both;
And to that youth he calls his Rosalind
He sends this bloody napkin;—are you he?

ROSALIND.
I am: what must we understand by this?

OLIVER.
Some of my shame; if you will know of me
What man I am, and how, and why, and where
This handkercher was stain'd.

CELIA.
               I pray you, tell it.

OLIVER.
When last the young Orlando parted from you,
He left a promise to return again
Within an hour; and, pacing through the forest,
Chewing the food of sweet and bitter fancy,
Lo, what befell! he threw his eye aside,
And, mark, what object did present itself:
Under an oak, whose boughs were moss'd with
  age,
And high top bald with dry antiquity,
A wretched ragged man, o'ergrown with hair,
Lay sleeping on his back: about his neck
A green and gilded snake had wreath'd itself,
Who with her head, nimble in threats, approacht
The opening of his mouth; but suddenly,
Seeing Orlando, it unlinkt itself,
And with indented glides did slip away
Into a bush: under which bush's shade
A lioness, with udders all drawn dry,
Lay couching, head on ground, with catlike
  watch,
When that the sleeping man should stir; for 'tis
The royal disposition of that beast
To prey on nothing that doth seem as dead:
This seen, Orlando did approach the man,
And found it was his brother, his elder brother.

CELIA.
O, I have heard him speak of that same brother;
And he did render him the most unnatural
That lived 'mongst men.

OLIVER.
          And well he might so do,
For well I know he was unnatural.

ROSALIND.
But, to Orlando:—did he leave him there,
Food to the suckt and hungry lioness?

OLIVER.
Twice did he turn his back, and purposed so;
But kindness, nobler ever than revenge,
And nature, stronger than his just occasion,
Made him give battle to the lioness,
Who quickly fell before him: in which hurtling
From miserable slumber I awaked.

CELIA.
Are you his brother?

ROSALIND.
         Was't you he rescued?

CELIA.
Was't you that did so oft contrive to kill him?

OLIVER.
'Twas I: but 'tis not I: I do not shame
To tell you what I was, since my conversion
So sweetly tastes, being the thing I am.

ROSALIND.
But, for the bloody napkin?—

OLIVER.
By and by.
When from the first to last, betwixt us two,
Tears our recountments had most kindly bathed,
As how I came into that desert place;—
In brief, he led me to the gentle duke,
Who gave me fresh array and entertainment,
Committing me unto my brother's love;
Who led me instantly unto his cave,
There stript himself, and here upon his arm
The lioness had torn some flesh away,
Which all this while had bled; and now he fainted,
And cried, in fainting, upon Rosalind.
Brief, I recover'd him, bound up his wound;
And, after some small space, being strong at
   heart,
He sent me hither, stranger as I am,
To tell this story, that you might excuse
His broken promise, and to give this napkin,
Dyed in his blood, unto the shepherd youth
That he in sport doth call his Rosalind.

CELIA.
Why, how now, Ganymede! sweet Ganymede!
              [ROSALIND *faints*.

OLIVER.
Many will swoon when they do look on blood.

CELIA.
There is more in it.—Cousin Ganymede!

OLIVER.
Look, he recovers.

ROSALIND.
I would I were at home.

CELIA.
We'll lead you thither.—
I pray you, will you take him by the arm?

OLIVER.
Be of good cheer, youth:—you a man? you lack a
man's heart.

ROSALIND.
I do so, I confess it! Ah, sirrah, a body would
think this was well counterfeited! I pray you, tell
your brother how well I counterfeited.—Heigh-ho!

OLIVER.
This was not counterfeit: there is too great testimony in your complexion, that it was a passion of
earnest.

ROSALIND.
Counterfeit, I assure you.

OLIVER.
Well, then, take a good heart, and counterfeit to
be a man.

ROSALIND.
So I do: but, i'faith, I should have been a woman
by right.

CELIA.
Come, you look paler and paler: pray you, draw
homewards.—Good sir, go with us.

OLIVER.
That will I, for I must bear answer back
How you excuse my brother, Rosalind.

ROSALIND.
I shall devise something: but, I pray you, commend my counterfeiting to him:—will you go?
              [*Exeunt.*

ACT V. SCENE I.

The forest.

Enter TOUCHSTONE *and* AUDREY.

TOUCHSTONE.
WE shall find a time, Audrey; patience, gentle
Audrey.

AUDREY.
Faith, the priest was good enough, for all the old
gentleman's saying.

TOUCHSTONE.
A most wicked Sir Oliver, Audrey, a most vile
Martext. But, Audrey, there is a youth here in the
forest lays claim to you.

AUDREY.
Ay, I know who 'tis: he hath no interest in me in
the world: here comes the man you mean.

TOUCHSTONE.
It is meat and drink to me to see a clown: by my
troth, we that have good wits have much to
answer for; we shall be flouting; we cannot hold.

Enter WILLIAM.

WILLIAM.
Good even, Audrey.

AUDREY.
God ye good even, William.

WILLIAM.
And good even to you, sir.

TOUCHSTONE.
Good even, gentle friend. Cover thy head, cover
thy head; nay, prithee, be cover'd. How old are
you, friend?

WILLIAM.
Five and twenty, sir.

TOUCHSTONE.
A ripe age. Is thy name William?

WILLIAM.
William, sir.

TOUCHSTONE.
A fair name. Wast born i'th'forest here?

WILLIAM.
Ay, sir, I thank God.

TOUCHSTONE.
Thank God;—a good answer. Art rich?

WILLIAM.
Faith, sir, so-so.

TOUCHSTONE.
So-so is good, very good, very excellent good:—
and yet it is not; it is but so-so. Art thou wise?

WILLIAM.
Ay, sir, I have a pretty wit.

TOUCHSTONE.
Why, thou say'st well. I do now remember a saying, 'The fool doth think he is wise; but the wise
man knows himself to be a fool.' The heathen
philosopher, when he had a desire to eat a grape,
would open his lips when he put it into his mouth;
meaning thereby, that grapes were made to eat,
and lips to open. You do love this maid?

WILLIAM.
I do, sir.

TOUCHSTONE.

Give me your hand. Art thou learned?

WILLIAM.

No, sir.

TOUCHSTONE.

Then learn this of me:—to have, is to have; for it is a figure in rhetoric, that drink, being pour'd out of a cup into a glass, by filling the one doth empty the other; for all your writers do consent that *ipse* is he: now, you are not *ipse*, for I am he.

WILLIAM.

Which he, sir?

TOUCHSTONE.

He, sir, that must marry this woman. Therefore, you clown, abandon,—which is in the vulgar leave,—the society,—which in the boorish is company,—of this female,—which in the common is woman; which together is, abandon the society of this female, or, clown, thou perishest; or, to thy better understanding, diest; or (to wit) I kill thee, make thee away, translate thy life into death, thy liberty into bondage: I will deal in poison with thee, or in bastinado, or in steel; I will bandy with thee in faction; I will o'er-run thee with policy; I will kill thee a hundred and fifty ways: therefore tremble, and depart.

AUDREY.

Do, good William.

WILLIAM.

God rest you merry, sir.   [*Exit.*

Enter CORIN.

CORIN.

Our master and mistress seek you; come, away, away!

TOUCHSTONE.

Trip, Audrey, trip, Audrey.—I attend, I attend.
    [*Exeunt.*

SCENE II.

The forest.

Enter ORLANDO *and* OLIVER.

ORLANDO.

IS'T possible that, on so little acquaintance, you should like her? that, but seeing, you should love her? and, loving, woo? and, wooing, she should grant? and will you persever to enjoy her?

OLIVER.

Neither call the giddiness of it in question, the poverty of her, the small acquaintance, my sudden wooing, nor her sudden consenting; but say with me, I love Aliena; say with her, that she loves me; consent with both, that we may enjoy each other: it shall be to your good; for my father's house, and all the revenue that was old Sir Rowland's, will I estate upon you, and here live and die a shepherd.

ORLANDO.

You have my consent. Let your wedding be to-morrow: thither will I invite the duke, and all's contented followers. Go you and prepare Aliena; for, look you, here comes my Rosalind.

Enter ROSALIND.

ROSALIND.

God save you, brother.

OLIVER.

And you, fair sister.   [*Exit.*

ROSALIND.

O, my dear Orlando, how it grieves me to see thee wear thy heart in a scarf!

ORLANDO.

It is my arm.

ROSALIND.

I thought thy heart had been wounded with the claws of a lion.

ORLANDO.

Wounded it is, but with the eyes of a lady.

ROSALIND.

Did your brother tell you how I counterfeited to swoon when he show'd me your handkercher?

ORLANDO.

Ay, and greater wonders than that.

ROSALIND.

O, I know where you are:—nay, 'tis true: there was never any thing so sudden, but the fight of two rams, and Cæsar's thrasonical brag of—'I came, saw, and overcame:' for your brother and my sister no sooner met, but they lookt; no sooner lookt, but they loved; no sooner loved, but they sigh'd; no sooner sigh'd, but they askt one another the reason; no sooner knew the reason, but they sought the remedy: and in these degrees have they made a pair of stairs to marriage, which they will climb incontinent, or else be incontinent before marriage: they are in the very wrath of love, and they will together; clubs cannot part them.

ORLANDO.

They shall be married to-morrow; and I will bid the duke to the nuptial. But, O, how bitter a thing it is to look into happiness through another man's eyes! By so much the more shall I to-morrow be at the height of heart-heaviness, by how much I shall think my brother happy in having what he wishes for.

ROSALIND.

Why, then, to-morrow I cannot serve your turn for Rosalind?

ORLANDO.

I can live no longer by thinking.

ROSALIND.

I will weary you, then, no longer with idle talking. Know of me, then—for now I speak to some purpose,—that I know you are a gentleman of good conceit: I speak not this, that you should bear a good opinion of my knowledge, insomuch I say I know you are; neither do I labour for a greater esteem than may in some little measure draw a belief from you, to do yourself good, and not to grace me. Believe, then, if you please, that I can do strange things: I have, since I was three year old, conversed with a magician, most profound in his art, and yet not damnable. If you do love Rosalind so near the heart as your gesture cries it out, when your brother marries Aliena, shall you marry her: I know into what straits of fortune she is driven; and it is not impossible to me, if it appear not inconvenient to you, to set her before your eyes to-morrow human as she is, and without any danger.

ORLANDO.

Speak'st thou in sober meanings?

ROSALIND.

By my life I do; which I tender dearly, though I say I am a magician. Therefore, put you in your best array, bid your friends; for if you will be married to-morrow,you shall; and to Rosalind, if you will.—Look, here comes a lover of mine, and a lover of hers.

Enter SILVIUS *and* PHEBE.

PHEBE.

Youth, you have done me much ungentleness,
To show the letter that I writ to you.

ROSALIND.

I care not, if I have: it is my study
To seem despiteful and ungentle to you:
You are there follow'd by a faithful shepherd;
Look upon him, love him; he worships you.

PHEBE.

Good shepherd, tell this youth what 'tis to love.

SILVIUS.

It is to be all made of sighs and tears;—
And so am I for Phebe.

PHEBE.

And I for Ganymede.

ORLANDO.

And I for Rosalind.

ROSALIND.

And I for no woman.

SILVIUS.

It is to be all made of faith and service;—
And so am I for Phebe.

PHEBE.

And I for Ganymede.

ORLANDO.

And I for Rosalind.

ROSALIND.

And I for no woman.

SILVIUS.

It is to be all made of fantasy,
All made of passion, and all made of wishes;
All adoration, duty, and observance,
All humbleness, all patience, and impatience,
All purity, all trial, all deservings;—
And so am I for Phebe.

PHEBE.

And so am I for Ganymede.

ORLANDO.

And so am I for Rosalind.

ROSALIND.

And so am I for no woman.

PHEBE [*to* ROSALIND].

If this be so, why blame you me to love you?

SILVIUS [*to* PHEBE]

If this be so, why blame you me to love you?

ORLANDO.

If this be so, why blame you me to love you?

ROSALIND.

Who do you speak to,—'Why blame you me to love you?'

ORLANDO.

To her that is not here, not doth not hear.

ROSALIND.

Pray you, no more of this; 'tis like the howling of Irish wolves against the moon.—I will help you [*to* SILVIUS], if I can:—I would love you [*to* PHEBE], if I could.—To-morrow meet me all to-gether.—I will marry you [*to* PHEBE], if ever I marry woman, and I'll be married to-morrow;—I will satisfy you [*to* ORLANDO], if ever I satisfy man and you shall be married to-morrow:—I will content you [*to* SILVIUS], if what pleases you contents you. and you shall be married to-morrow.—As you [*to* ORLANDO] love Rosalind, meet:—as you [*to* SILVIUS] love Phebe, meet: and as I love no woman, I'll meet.—So, fare you well: I have left you commands.

SILVIUS.

I'll not fail, if I live.

PHEBE.

Nor I.

ORLANDO.

Nor I.   [*Exeunt.*

SCENE III.

The forest.

Enter TOUCHSTONE *and* AUDREY.

TOUCHSTONE.

TO-MORROW is the joyful day, Audrey; to-morrow will we be married.

AUDREY.

I do desire it with all my heart; and I hope it is no dishonest desire, to desire to be a woman of the world. Here come two of the banisht duke's pages.

Enter two PAGES.

FIRST PAGE.

Well met, honest gentleman.

TOUCHSTONE.

By my troth, well met. Come, sit, sit, and a song.

SECOND PAGE.

We are for you: sit i'th'middle.

FIRST PAGE.

Shall we clap into't roundly, without hawking, or spitting, or saying we are hoarse, which are the only prologues to a bad voice?

SECOND PAGE.

I'faith, i'faith; and both in a tune, like two gipsies on a horse.

Song.

It was a lover and his lass,
    With a hey, and a ho, and a hey nonino,
That o'er the green corn-field did pass
    In spring-time, the only pretty ring-time,
When birds do sing, hey ding a ding, ding:
Sweet lovers love the spring.

Between the acres of the rye,
    With a hey, and a ho, and a hey nonino,
These pretty country-folks would lie
    In spring-time, &c.

This carol they began that hour,
    With a hey, and a ho, and a hey nonino,
How that a life was but a flower
    In spring-time, &c.

And therefore take the present time,
    With a hey, and a ho, and a hey nonino;
For love is crowned with the prime
    In spring-time, &c.

TOUCHSTONE.

Truly, young gentlemen, though there was no great matter in the ditty, yet the note was very untuneable.

FIRST PAGE.

You are deceived, sir: we kept time, we lost not our time.

TOUCHSTONE.

By my troth, yes; I count it but time lost to hear such a foolish song. God b'wi'you; and God mend your voices!—Come, Audrey.   [*Exeunt.*

SCENE IV.

The forest.

Enter DUKE SENIOR, AMIENS, JAQUES, ORLANDO, OLIVER, *and* CELIA.

DUKE SENIOR.

DOST thou believe, Orlando, that the boy
Can do all this that he hath promised?

ORLANDO.

I sometimes do believe, and sometimes do not;
As those that fear,—they hope, and know they fear.

Enter ROSALIND, SILVIUS, *and* PHEBE.

ROSALIND.

Patience once more, whiles our compact is urged;—
You say, if I bring in your Rosalind, [*to the* DUKE.
You will bestow her on Orlando here?

DUKE SENIOR.

That would I, had I kingdoms to give with her.

ROSALIND [*to* ORLANDO].

And you say, you will have her, when I bring her?

ORLANDO.

That would I, were I of all kingdoms king.

ROSALIND [*to* PHEBE].

You say, you'll marry me, if I be willing?

PHEBE.

That will I, should I die the hour after.

ROSALIND.

But if you do refuse to marry me,
You'll give yourself to this most faithful shepherd?

PHEBE.

So is the bargain.

ROSALIND [*to* SILVIUS].

You say, that you'll have Phebe, if she will?

SILVIUS.

Though to have her and death were both one thing.

ROSALIND.

I have promised to make this matter even.
Keep you your word, O duke, to give your daughter;—
You yours, Orlando, to receive his daughter:—
Keep your word, Phebe, that you'll marry me,
Or else, refusing me, to wed this shepherd:—
Keep your word, Silvius, that you'll marry her,
If she refuse me:—and from hence I go,
To make these doubts all even.

    [*Exeunt* ROSALIND *and* CELIA.

DUKE SENIOR.

I do remember in this shepherd boy
Some lively touches of my daughter's favour.

ORLANDO.

My lord, the first time that I ever saw him
Methought he was a brother to your daughter:
But, my good lord, this boy is forest-born,
And hath been tutor'd in the rudiments
Of many desperate studies by his uncle,
Whom he reports to be a great magician,
Obscured in the circle of this forest.

JAQUES.

There is, sure, another flood toward, and these couples are coming to the ark. Here comes a pair of very strange beasts, which in all tongues are call'd fools.

Enter TOUCHSTONE *and* AUDREY.

TOUCHSTONE.

Salutation and greeting to you all!

JAQUES.

Good my lord, bid him welcome: this is the motley-minded gentleman that I have so often met in the forest: he hath been a courtier, he swears.

TOUCHSTONE.

If any man doubt that, let him put me to my purgation. I have trod a measure; I have flatter'd a lady; I have been politic with my friend, smooth with mine enemy; I have undone three tailors; I have had four quarrels, and like to have fought one.

JAQUES.

And how was that ta'en up?

TOUCHSTONE.

Faith, we met, and found the quarrel was upon the seventh cause.

JAQUES.

How seventh cause?—Good my lord, like this fellow.

DUKE SENIOR.

I like him very well.

TOUCHSTONE.

God ild you, sir; I desire you of the like. I press in here, sir, amongst the rest of the country copulatives, to swear and to forswear; according as marriage binds and blood breaks:—a poor virgin, sir, an ill-favour'd thing, sir, but mine own; a poor humour of mine, sir, to take that that no man else will: rich honesty dwells like a miser, sir, in a poor house; as your pearl in your foul oyster.

DUKE SENIOR.

By my faith, he is very swift and sententious.

TOUCHSTONE.

According to the fool's bolt, sir, and such dulcet diseases.

JAQUES.

But, for the seventh cause; how did you find the quarrel on the seventh cause?

TOUCHSTONE.

Upon a lie seven times removed:—bear your body more seeming, Audrey:—as thus, sir. I did dislike the cut of a certain courtier's beard: he sent me word, if I said his beard was not cut well, he was in the mind it was: this is call'd the Retort Courteous. If I sent him word again it was not well cut, he would send me word he cut it to please himself: this is call'd the Quip Modest. If again it was not well cut, he disabled my judgement: this is call'd the Reply Churlish. If again it was not well cut, he would answer I spake not true: this is call'd the Reproof Valiant. If again it was not well cut, he would say I lie: this is call'd the Counter-check Quarrelsome: and so to the Lie Circumstantial and the Lie Direct.

JAQUES.

And how oft did you say his beard was not well cut?

TOUCHSTONE.

I durst go no further than the Lie Circumstantial, nor he durst not give me the Lie Direct; and so we measured swords, and parted.

JAQUES.

Can you nominate in order now the degrees of the lie?

TOUCHSTONE.

O sir, we quarrel in print, by the book; as you have books for good manners: I will name you the degrees. The first, the Retort Courteous; the second, the Quip Modest; the third, the Reply Churlish; the fourth, the Reproof Valiant; the fifth, the Countercheck Quarrelsome; the sixth, the Lie with Circumstance; the seventh, the Lie Direct. All these you may avoid, but the Lie Direct; and you may avoid that too with an 'if.' I knew when seven justices could not take up a quarrel; but when the parties were met themselves, one of them thought but of an 'if,' as, 'If you said so, then I said so;' and they shook hands, and swore brothers. Your 'if' is the only peacemaker; much virtue in 'if.'

JAQUES.

Is not this a rare fellow, my lord? he's as good at any thing, and yet a fool.

DUKE SENIOR.

He uses his folly like a stalking-horse, and under the presentation of that he shoots his wit.

Enter HYMEN *leading* ROSALIND *in woman's clothes, and* CELIA. *Still music.*

HYMEN.

Then is there mirth in heaven,
When earthly things made even
    Atone together.
Good duke, receive thy daughter:
Hymen from heaven brought her,
    Yea, brought her hither,
That thou mightst join her hand with his
Whose heart within her bosom is.

ROSALIND [*to* DUKE SENIOR].

To you I give myself, for I am yours.—
[*to* ORLANDO]. To you I give myself, for I am yours.

DUKE SENIOR.

If there be truth in sight, you are my daughter.

ORLANDO.

If there be truth in sight, you are my Rosalind.

PHEBE.

If sight and shape be true,
Why, then,—my love adieu!

ROSALIND [*to* DUKE SENIOR].

I'll have no father, if you be not he:—

[*to* ORLANDO]. I'll have no husband, if you be not he:—
[*to* PHEBE]. Nor ne'er wed woman, if you be not she.

HYMEN.

Peace, ho! I bar confusion:
'Tis I must make conclusion
    Of these most strange events:
Here's eight that must take hands
To join in Hymen's bands,
    If truth holds true contents.
You and you no cross shall part:—
        [*to* ORLANDO *and* ROSALIND.
You and you are heart in heart:—
        [*to* OLIVER *and* CELIA.
You to his love must accord,   [*to* PHEBE.
Or have a woman to your lord:—
You and you are sure together,
      [*to* TOUCHSTONE *and* AUDREY.
As the winter to foul weather.
Whiles a wedlock-hymn we sing,
Feed yourselves with questioning;
That reason wonder may diminish,
How thus we met, and these things finish.

Song.

Wedding is great Juno's crown:
    O blessed bond of board and bed!
'Tis Hymen peoples every town;
    High wedlock, then, be honoured:
Honour, high honour, and renown,
To Hymen, god of every town!

DUKE SENIOR.

O my dear niece, welcome thou art to me,
Even daughter-welcome, in no less degree!

PHEBE [*to* SILVIUS].

I will not eat my word, now thou art mine;
Thy faith my fancy to thee doth combine.

Enter JAQUES DE BOYS.

JAQUES DE BOYS.

Let me have audience for a word or two:
I am the second son of old Sir Rowland,
That bring these tidings to this fair assembly.—
Duke Frederick, hearing how that every day
Men of great worth resorted to this forest,
Addrest a mighty power; which were on foot,
In his own conduct, purposely to take
His brother here, and put him to the sword:
And to the skirts of this wild wood he came;
Where meeting with an old religious man,
After some question with him, was converted
Both from his enterprise and from the world;
His crown bequeathing to his banisht brother,
And all their lands restored to them again
That were with him exiled. This to be true,
I do engage my life.

DUKE SENIOR.

        Welcome, young man;
Thou offer'st fairly to thy brothers' wedding:
To one, his lands withheld; and to the other,
A land itself at large, a potent dukedom.
First, in this forest, let us do those ends
That here were well begun and well begot:
And after, every of this happy number,
That have endured shrewd days and nights with us,

Shall share the good of our returned fortune,
According to the measure of their states.
Meantime forget this new-fall'n dignity,
And fall into our rustic revelry.—
Play, music!—and you, brides and bridegrooms
    all,
With measure heap'd in joy, to th'measures fall.

JAQUES.

Sir, by your patience.—If I heard you rightly,
The duke hath put on a religious life,
And thrown into neglect the pompous court?

JAQUES DE BOYS.

He hath.

JAQUES.

To him will I: out of these convertites
There is much matter to be heard and learn'd.—
You [to DUKE SENIOR] to your former honour I
    bequeath;
Your patience and your virtue well deserve it:—
You [to ORLANDO] to a love that your true faith
    doth merit:—
You [to OLIVER] to your land, and love, and great
    allies:—
You [to SILVIUS] to a long and well-deserved
    bed:—
And you [to TOUCHSTONE] to wrangling; for thy
    loving voyage
Is but for two months victuall'd.—So, to your
    pleasures:
I am for other than for dancing measures.

DUKE SENIOR.

Stay, Jaques, stay.

JAQUES.

To see no pastime I:—what you would have
I'll stay to know at your abandon'd cave.   [Exit.

DUKE SENIOR.

Proceed, proceed: we will begin these rites,
As we do trust they'll end, in true delights.

                                        [A dance.

EPILOGUE.

ROSALIND.

IT is not the fashion to see the lady the epilogue;
but it is no more unhandsome than to see the lord
the prologue. If it be true that good wine needs no
bush, 'tis true that a good play needs no epilogue:
yet to good wine they do use good bushes; and
good plays prove the better by the help of good
epilogues. What a case am I in, then, that am
neither a good epilogue, nor cannot insinuate with
you in the behalf of a good play! I am not furnisht
like a beggar, therefore to beg will not become
me: my way is, to conjure you; and I'll begin with
the women. I charge you, O women, for the love
you bear to men, to like as much of this play as
please you: and I charge you, O men, for the love
you bear to women (as I perceive by your simpering, none of you hates them), that between you
and the women the play may please. If I were a
woman, I would kiss as many of you as had beards
that pleased me, complexions that liked me, and
breaths that I defied not: and, I am sure, as many
as have good beards, or good faces, or sweet
breaths, will, for my kind offer, when I make
curtsy, bid me farewell.   [Exeunt.

TWELFTH NIGHT; OR, WHAT YOU WILL

DRAMATIS PERSONAE

ORSINO, *Duke of Illyria.*
SEBASTIAN, *a young gentleman.*
ANTONIO, *a sea captain, friend to Sebastian.*
A SEA CAPTAIN, *friend to Viola.*
VALENTINE, } *gentlemen attending on the Duke.*
CURIO,
SIR TOBY BELCH, *uncle to Olivia.*
SIR ANDREW AGUECHEEK.
MALVOLIO, *steward to Olivia.*

FABIAN, } *servants to Olivia.*
CLOWN,
OLIVIA.
VIOLA, *sister to Sebastian.*
MARIA, *Olivia's woman.*

LORDS, *a* PRIEST, SAILORS, OFFICERS,
MUSICIANS, *and* ATTENDANTS.

SCENE—*A city in Illyria, and the sea-coast near it.*

ACT I. SCENE I.

The DUKE'S *palace.*

Enter DUKE, LORDS, *and* CURIO; MUSICIANS *attending.*

DUKE OF ILLYRIA.

IF music be the food of love, play on;
Give me excess of it, that, surfeiting,
The appetite may sicken, and so die.—
That strain again!—it had a dying fall:
O, it came o'er my ear like the sweet sound,
That breathes upon a bank of violets,
Stealing and giving odour!—Enough; no more;
'Tis not so sweet now as it was before.
O spirit of love, how quick and fresh art thou!
That, notwithstanding thy capacity
Receiveth as the sea, naught enters there,
Of what validity and pitch soe'er,
But falls into abatement and low price,
Even in a minute! so full of shapes is fancy,
That it alone is high-fantastical.

CURIO.

Will you go hunt, my lord?

DUKE OF ILLYRIA.

What, Curio?

CURIO.

The hart.

DUKE OF ILLYRIA.

Why, so I do, the noblest that I have:
O, when mine eyes did see Olivia first,
Methought she purged the air of pestilence!
That instant was I turn'd into a hart;
And my desires, like fell and cruel hounds,
E'er since pursue me.

Enter VALENTINE.

How now! what news from her?

VALENTINE.

So please my lord, I might not be admitted;
But from her handmaid do return this answer:
The element itself, till seven years hence,
Shall not behold her face at ample view;
But, like a cloistress, she will veiled walk,
And water once a day her chamber round
With eye-offending brine: all this to season

A brother's dead love, which she would keep fresh
And lasting in her sad remembrance.

DUKE OF ILLYRIA.

O, she that hath a heart of that fine frame
To pay this debt of love but to a brother,
How will she love, when the rich golden shaft
Hath kill'd the flock of all affections else
That live in her; when liver, brain, and heart,
These sovereign thrones, are all supplied, and
fill'd
Her sweet perfections with one self king!—
Away before me to sweet beds of flowers:
Love-thoughts lie rich when canopied with
bowers.   [*Exeunt.*

SCENE II.

The sea-coast.

Enter VIOLA, CAPTAIN, *and* SAILORS.

VIOLA.

WHAT country, friends, is this?

CAPTAIN.

This is Illyria, lady.

VIOLA.

And what should I do in Illyria?
My brother he is in Elysium.
Perchance he is not drown'd:—what think you,
sailors?

CAPTAIN.

It is perchance that you yourself were saved.

VIOLA.

O my poor brother! and so perchance may he be.

CAPTAIN.

True, madam; and, to comfort you with chance,
Assure yourself, after our ship did split,
When you, and those poor number saved with
you,
Hung on our driving boat, I saw your brother,
Most provident in peril, bind himself—
Courage and hope both teaching him the prac-
tice—
To a strong mast that lived upon the sea;
Where, like Arion on the dolphin's back,
I saw him hold acquaintance with the waves
So long as I could see.

VIOLA.

For saying so, there's gold:
Mine own escape unfoldeth to my hope,
Whereto thy speech serves for authority,
The like of him. Know'st thou this country?

CAPTAIN.

Ay, madam, well; for I was bred and born
Not three hours' travel from this very place.

VIOLA.

Who governs here?

CAPTAIN.

A noble duke, in nature as in name.

VIOLA.

What is his name?

CAPTAIN.

Orsino.

VIOLA.

Orsino! I have heard my father name him:
He was a bachelor then.

CAPTAIN.

And so is now, or was so very late;
For but a month ago I went from hence,
And then 'twas fresh in murmur,—as, you know,
What great ones do, the less will prattle of,—
That he did seek the love of fair Olivia.

VIOLA.

What's she?

CAPTAIN.

A virtuous maid, the daughter of a count
That died some twelvemonth since; then leaving
　　her
In the protection of his son, her brother,
Who shortly also died: for whose dear loss,
They say, she hath abjured the company
And sight of men.

VIOLA.

O, that I served that lady,
And might not be deliver'd to the world,
Till I had made mine own occasion mellow,
What my estate is!

CAPTAIN.

That were hard to compass;
Because she will admit no kind of suit,
No, not the duke's.

VIOLA.

There is a fair behaviour in thee, captain;
And though that nature with a beauteous wall
Doth oft close in pollution, yet of thee
I will believe thou hast a mind that suits
With this thy fair and outward character.
I prithee,—and I'll pay thee bounteously,—
Conceal me what I am; and be my aid
For such disguise as haply shall become
The form of my intent. I'll serve this duke:
Thou shalt present me as an eunuch to him:
It may be worth thy pains; for I can sing,
And speak to him in many sorts of music,
That will allow me very worth his service.
What else may hap, to time I will commit;
Only shape thou thy silence to my wit.

CAPTAIN.

Be you his eunuch, and your mute I'll be:
When my tongue blabs, then let mine eyes not
　　see.

VIOLA.

I thank thee: lead me on.　　　　　　［Exeunt.

SCENE III.

Olivia's house.

Enter SIR TOBY BELCH *and* MARIA.

SIR TOBY BELCH.

WHAT a plague means my niece, to take the
death of her brother thus? I am sure care's
an enemy to life.

MARIA.

By my troth, Sir Toby, you must come in earlier
o'nights: your cousin, my lady, takes great exceptions to your ill hours.

SIR TOBY BELCH.

Why, let her except before excepted.

MARIA.

Ay, but you must confine yourself within the
modest limits of order.

SIR TOBY BELCH.

Confine! I'll confine myself no finer than I am:
these clothes are good enough to drink in; and so
be these boots too,—an they be not, let them hang
themselves in their own straps.

MARIA.

That quaffing and drinking will undo you: I
heard my lady talk of it yesterday; and of a foolish
knight that you brought in one night here to be
her wooer.

SIR TOBY BELCH.

Who, Sir Andrew Aguecheek?

MARIA.

Ay, he.

SIR TOBY BELCH.

He's as tall a man as any's in Illyria.

MARIA.

What's that to th'purpose?

SIR TOBY BELCH.

Why, he has three thousand ducats a year.

MARIA.

Ay, but he'll have but a year in all these ducats:
he's a very fool and a prodigal.

SIR TOBY BELCH.

Fie, that you'll say so! he plays o'th'viol-de-gam-
boys, and speaks three or four languages word for
word without book, and hath all the good gifts of
nature.

MARIA.

He hath, indeed, almost natural: for, besides
that he's a fool, he's a great quarreller; and, but
that he hath the gift of a coward to allay the
gust he hath in quarrelling, 'tis thought among
the prudent he would quickly have the gift of a
grave.

SIR TOBY BELCH.

By this hand, they are scoundrels and substractors
that say so of him. Who are they?

MARIA.

They that add, moreover, he's drunk nightly in
your company.

SIR TOBY BELCH.

With drinking healths to my niece: I'll drink to
her as long as there is a passage in my throat
and drink in Illyria: he's a coward and a coistrel
that will not drink to my niece till his brains
turn o'th'toe like a parish-top. What, wench!
Castiliano volto; for here comes Sir Andrew
Agueface.

Enter SIR ANDREW AGUECHEEK.

SIR ANDREW AGUECHEEK.
Sir Toby Belch,—how now, Sir Toby Belch!

SIR TOBY BELCH.
Sweet Sir Andrew!

SIR ANDREW AGUECHEEK.
Bless you, fair shrew.

MARIA.
And you too, sir.

SIR TOBY BELCH.
Accost, Sir Andrew, accost.

SIR ANDREW AGUECHEEK.
What's that?

SIR TOBY BELCH.
My niece's chambermaid.

SIR ANDREW AGUECHEEK.
Good Mistress Accost, I desire better acquaintance.

MARIA.
My name is Mary, sir.

SIR ANDREW AGUECHEEK.
Good Mistress Mary Accost,—

SIR TOBY BELCH.
You mistake, knight: 'accost' is front her, board her, woo her, assail her.

SIR ANDREW AGUECHEEK.
By my troth, I would not undertake her in this company. Is that the meaning of 'accost'?

MARIA.
Fare you well, gentlemen.

SIR TOBY BELCH.
An thou let part so, Sir Andrew, would thou mightst never draw sword again.

SIR ANDREW AGUECHEEK.
An you part so, mistress, I would I might never draw sword again. Fair lady, do you think you have fools in hand?

MARIA.
Sir, I have not you by th'hand.

SIR ANDREW AGUECHEEK.
Marry, but you shall have; and here's my hand.

MARIA.
Now, sir, thought is free: I pray you, bring your hand to th'buttery-bar, and let it drink.

SIR ANDREW AGUECHEEK.
Wherefore, sweet-heart? what's your metaphor?

MARIA.
It's dry, sir.

SIR ANDREW AGUECHEEK.
Why, I think so: I am not such an ass but I can keep my hand dry. But what's your jest?

MARIA.
A dry jest, sir.

SIR ANDREW AGUECHEEK.
Are you full of them?

MARIA.
Ay, sir, I have them at my fingers' ends: marry, now I let go your hand, I am barren.   [*Exit.*

SIR TOBY BELCH.
O knight, thou lack'st a cup of canary: when did I see thee so put down?

SIR ANDREW AGUECHEEK.
Never in your life, I think; unless you see canary put me down. Methinks sometimes I have no more wit than a Christian or an ordinary man has:

but I am a great eater of beef, and I believe that does harm to my wit.

SIR TOBY BELCH.
No question.

SIR ANDREW AGUECHEEK.
An I thought that, I'ld forswear it. I'll ride home to-morrow, Sir Toby.

SIR TOBY BELCH.
Pourquoi, my dear knight?

SIR ANDREW AGUECHEEK.
What is *pourquoi?* do or not do? I would I had bestow'd that time in the tongues that I have in fencing, dancing, and bear-baiting: O, had I but follow'd the arts!

SIR TOBY BELCH.
Then hadst thou had an excellent head of hair.

SIR ANDREW AGUECHEEK.
Why, would that have mended my hair?

SIR TOBY BELCH.
Past question; for thou seest it will not curl by nature.

SIR ANDREW AGUECHEEK.
But it becomes me well enough, does't not?

SIR TOBY BELCH.
Excellent; it hangs like flax on a distaff; and I hope to see a housewife take thee between her legs and spin it off.

SIR ANDREW AGUECHEEK.
Faith, I'll home to-morrow, Sir Toby: your niece will not be seen; or if she be, it's four to one she'll none of me: the count himself here hard by woos her.

SIR TOBY BELCH.
She'll none o'th'count: she'll not match above her degree, neither in estate, years, nor wit; I have heard her swear't. Tut, there's life in't, man.

SIR ANDREW AGUECHEEK.
I'll stay a month longer. I am a fellow o'th' strangest mind i'th'world; I delight in masks and revels sometimes altogether.

SIR TOBY BELCH.
Art thou good at these kickshawses, knight?

SIR ANDREW AGUECHEEK.
As any man in Illyria, whatsoever he be, under the degree of my betters; and yet I will not compare with a nobleman.

SIR TOBY BELCH.
What is thy excellence in a galliard, knight?

SIR ANDREW AGUECHEEK.
Faith, I can cut a caper.

SIR TOBY BELCH.
And I can cut the mutton to't.

SIR ANDREW AGUECHEEK.
And I think I have the back-trick simply as strong as any man in Illyria.

SIR TOBY BELCH.
Wherefore are these things hid? wherefore have these gifts a curtain before 'em? are they like to take dust, like Mistress Mall's picture? why dost thou not go to church in a galliard, and come home in a coranto? My very walk should be a jig; I would not so much as make water but in a sink-a-pace. What dost thou mean? is it a world to hide virtues in? I did think, by the excellent constitution of thy leg, it was form'd under the star of a galliard.

SIR ANDREW AGUECHEEK.

Ay, 'tis strong, and it does indifferent well in a
flame-colour'd stock. Shall we set about some
revels?

SIR TOBY BELCH.

What shall we do else? were we not born under
Taurus?

SIR ANDREW AGUECHEEK.

Taurus! that's sides and heart.

SIR TOBY BELCH.

No, sir; it is legs and thighs. Let me see thee
caper [SIR ANDREW dances]: ha! higher: ha, ha!
excellent!   [Exeunt.

SCENE IV.

The Duke's palace.

Enter VALENTINE, *and* VIOLA *in man's attire.*

VALENTINE.

IF the duke continue these favours towards you,
Cesario, you are like to be much advanced: he
hath known you but three days, and already you
are no stranger.

VIOLA.

You either fear his humour or my negligence,
that you call in question the continuance of his
love: is he inconstant, sir, in his favours?

VALENTINE.

No, believe me.

VIOLA.

I thank you. Here comes the count.

Enter DUKE, CURIO, *and* ATTENDANTS.

DUKE OF ILLYRIA.

Who saw Cesario, ho?

VIOLA.

On your attendance, my lord; here.

DUKE OF ILLYRIA.

Stand you awhile aloof.—Cesario,
Thou know'st no less but all; I have unclaspt
To thee the book even of my secret soul:
Therefore, good youth, address thy gait unto her,
Be not denied access, stand at her doors,
And tell them, there thy fixed foot shall grow
Till thou have audience.

VIOLA.

         Sure, my noble lord,
If she be so abandon'd to her sorrow
As it is spoke, she never will admit me.

DUKE OF ILLYRIA.

Be clamorous, and leap all civil bounds,
Rather than make unprofited return.

VIOLA.

Say I do speak with her, my lord, what then?

DUKE OF ILLYRIA.

O, then unfold the passion of my love,
Surprise her with discourse of my dear faith!
It shall become thee well to act my woes;
She will attend it better in thy youth
Than in a nuncio of more grave aspect.

VIOLA.

I think not so, my lord.

DUKE OF ILLYRIA.

         Dear lad, believe it;
For they shall yet belie thy happy years,
That say thou art a man: Diana's lip
Is not more smooth and rubious; thy small pipe

Is as the maiden's organ, shrill and sound;
And all is semblative a woman's part.
I know thy constellation is right apt
For this affair:—some four or five attend him;
All, if you will; for I myself am best
When least in company:—prosper well in this,
And thou shalt live as freely as thy lord,
To call his fortunes thine.

VIOLA.

         I'll do my best
To woo your lady:—[aside] yet, a barful strife!
Whoe'er I woo, myself would be his wife.

                    [Exeunt.

SCENE V.

OLIVIA'S *house.*

Enter MARIA *and* CLOWN.

MARIA.

NAY, either tell me where thou hast been, or
I will not open my lips so wide as a bristle
may enter in way of thy excuse: my lady will hang
thee for thy absence.

CLOWN.

Let her hang me: he that is well hang'd in this
world need to fear no colours.

MARIA.

Make that good.

CLOWN.

He shall see none to fear.

MARIA.

A good lenten answer: I can tell thee where that
saying was born, of,—I fear no colours.

CLOWN.

Where, good Mistress Mary?

MARIA.

In the wars; and that may you be bold to say in
your foolery.

CLOWN.

Well, God give them wisdom that have it; and
those that are fools, let them use their talents.

MARIA.

Yet you will be hang'd for being so long absent;
or, to be turn'd away,—is not that as good as a
hanging to you?

CLOWN.

Many a good hanging prevents a bad marriage;
and, for turning away, let summer bear it out.

MARIA.

You are resolute, then?

CLOWN.

Not so, neither; but I am resolved on two points.

MARIA.

That if one break, the other will hold; or, if both
break, your gaskins fall.

CLOWN.

Apt, in good faith; very apt. Well, go thy way; if
Sir Toby would leave drinking, thou wert as
witty a piece of Eve's flesh as any in Illyria.

MARIA.

Peace, you rogue, no more o'that. Here comes
my lady: make your excuse wisely, you were best.

                    [Exit.

CLOWN.

Wit, an't be thy will, put me into good fooling!
Those wits, that think they have thee, do very oft

prove fools; and I, that am sure I lack thee, may pass for a wise man: for what says Quinapalus? 'Better a witty fool than a foolish wit.'

Enter LADY OLIVIA *with* MALVOLIO.

God bless thee, lady!

OLIVIA.

Take the fool away.

CLOWN.

Do you not hear, fellows? Take away the lady.

OLIVIA.

Go to, y'are a dry fool: I'll no more of you: besides, you grow dishonest.

CLOWN.

Two faults, madonna, that drink and good counsel will amend: for give the dry fool drink, then is the fool not dry: bid the dishonest man mend himself; if he mend, he is no longer dishonest: if he cannot, let the botcher mend him: any thing that's mended is but patcht: virtue that transgresses is but patcht with sin; and sin that amends is but patcht with virtue: if that this simple syllogism will serve, so; if it will not, what remedy? As there is no true cuckold but calamity, so beauty's a flower.—The lady bade take away the fool; therefore, I say again, take her away.

OLIVIA.

Sir, I bade them take away you.

CLOWN.

Misprision in the highest degree!—Lady, *cucullus non facit monachum;* that's as much to say as, I wear not motley in my brain. Good madonna, give me leave to prove you a fool.

OLIVIA.

Can you do it?

CLOWN.

Dexteriously, good madonna.

OLIVIA.

Make your proof.

CLOWN.

I must catechize you for it, madonna: good my mouse of virtue, answer me.

OLIVIA.

Well, sir, for want of other idleness, I'll bide your proof.

CLOWN.

Good madonna, why mourn'st thou?

OLIVIA.

Good fool, for my brother's death.

CLOWN.

I think his soul is in hell, madonna.

OLIVIA.

I know his soul is in heaven, fool.

CLOWN.

The more fool, madonna, to mourn for your brother's soul being in heaven.—Take away the fool, gentlemen.

OLIVIA.

What think you of this fool, Malvolio? doth he not mend?

MALVOLIO.

Yes, and shall do till the pangs of death shake him: infirmity, that decays the wise, doth ever make the better fool.

CLOWN.

God send you, sir, a speedy infirmity, for the better increasing your folly! Sir Toby will be

sworn that I am no fox; but he will not pass his word for twopence that you are no fool.

OLIVIA.

How say you to that, Malvolio?

MALVOLIO.

I marvel your ladyship takes delight in such a barren rascal: I saw him put down the other day with an ordinary fool, that has no more brain than a stone. Look you now, he's out of his guard already; unless you laugh and minister occasion to him, he is gagg'd. I protest, I take these wise men, that crow so at these set kind of fools, no better than the fools' zanies.

OLIVIA.

O, you are sick of self-love, Malvolio, and taste with a distemper'd appetite. To be generous, guiltless, and of free disposition, is to take those things for bird-bolts that you deem cannonbullets: there is no slander in an allow'd fool, though he do nothing but rail; nor no railing in a known discreet man, though he do nothing but reprove.

CLOWN.

Now Mercury endue thee with leasing, for thou speak'st well of fools!

Enter MARIA.

MARIA.

Madam, there is at the gate a young gentleman much desires to speak with you.

OLIVIA.

From the Count Orsino, is it?

MARIA.

I know not, madam: 'tis a fair young man, and well attended.

OLIVIA.

Who of my people hold him in delay?

MARIA.

Sir Toby, madam, your kinsman.

OLIVIA.

Fetch him off, I pray you; he speaks nothing but madman: fie on him! [*Exit* MARIA.] Go you, Malvolio: if it be a suit from the count, I am sick, or not at home; what you will, to dismiss it. [*Exit* MALVOLIO.] Now you see, sir, how your fooling grows old, and people dislike it.

CLOWN.

Thou hast spoke for us, madonna, as if thy eldest son should be a fool; whose skull Jove cram with brains! for—here he comes—one of thy kin has a most weak *pia mater*.

Enter SIR TOBY.

OLIVIA.

By mine honour, half drunk.—What is he at the gate, cousin?

SIR TOBY BELCH.

A gentleman.

OLIVIA.

A gentleman! what gentleman?

SIR TOBY BELCH.

'Tis a gentleman here—a plague o'these pickleherring!—How now, sot!

CLOWN.

Good Sir Toby!—

OLIVIA.

Cousin, cousin, how have you come so early by this lethargy?

SIR TOBY BELCH.

Lechery! I defy lechery. There's one at the gate.

OLIVIA.

Ay, marry, what is he?

SIR TOBY BELCH.

Let him be the devil, an he will, I care not: give me faith, say I. Well, it's all one.　　　[Exit.

OLIVIA.

What's a drunken man like, fool?

CLOWN.

Like a drown'd man, a fool, and a madman: one draught above heat makes him a fool; the second mads him; and a third drowns him.

OLIVIA.

Go thou and seek the crowner, and let him sit o' my coz; for he's in the third degree of drink,— he's drown'd: go, look after him.

CLOWN.

He is but mad yet, madonna; and the fool shall look to the madman.　　　[Exit.

Enter MALVOLIO.

MALVOLIO.

Madam, yond young fellow swears he will speak with you. I told him you were sick; he takes on him to understand so much, and therefore comes to speak with you: I told him you were asleep; he seems to have a foreknowledge of that too, and therefore comes to speak with you. What is to be said to him, lady? he's fortified against any denial.

OLIVIA.

Tell him he shall not speak with me.

MALVOLIO.

Has been told so; and he says, he'll stand at your door like a sheriff's post, and be the supporter to a bench, but he'll speak with you.

OLIVIA.

What kind o' man is he?

MALVOLIO.

Why, of mankind.

OLIVIA.

What manner of man?

MALVOLIO.

Of very ill manner; he'll speak with you, will you or no.

OLIVIA.

Of what personage and years is he?

MALVOLIO.

Not yet old enough for a man, nor young enough for a boy; as a squash is before 'tis a peascod, or a codling when 'tis almost an apple: 'tis with him e'en standing water, between boy and man. He is very well-favour'd, and he speaks very shrewishly; one would think his mother's milk were scarce out of him.

OLIVIA.

Let him approach: call in my gentlewoman.

MALVOLIO.

Gentlewoman, my lady calls.　　　[Exit.

Enter MARIA.

OLIVIA.

Give me my veil: come, throw it o'er my face. We'll once more hear Orsino's embassy.

Enter VIOLA.

VIOLA.

The honourable lady of the house, which is she?

OLIVIA.

Speak to me; I shall answer for her. Your will?

VIOLA.

Most radiant, exquisite, and unmatchable beauty, —I pray you, tell me if this be the lady of the house, for I never saw her: I would be loth to cast away my speech; for, besides that it is excellently well penn'd, I have taken great pains to con it. Good beauties, let me sustain no scorn; I am very comptible, even to the least sinister usage.

OLIVIA.

Whence came you, sir?

VIOLA.

I can say little more than I have studied, and that question's out of my part. Good gentle one, give me modest assurance if you be the lady of the house, that I may proceed in my speech.

OLIVIA.

Are you a comedian?

VIOLA.

No, my profound heart: and yet, by the very fangs of malice I swear I am not that I play. Are you the lady of the house?

OLIVIA.

If I do not usurp myself, I am.

VIOLA.

Most certain, if you are she, you do usurp yourself; for, what is yours to bestow is not yours to reserve. But this is from my commission: I will on with my speech in your praise, and then show you the heart of my message.

OLIVIA.

Come to what is important in't: I forgive you the praise.

VIOLA.

Alas, I took great pains to study it, and 'tis poetical.

OLIVIA.

It is the more like to be feign'd: I pray you, keep it in. I heard you were saucy at my gates; and allow'd your approach rather to wonder at you than to hear you. If you be mad, be gone; if you have reason, be brief: 'tis not that time of moon with me to make one in so skipping a dialogue.

MALVOLIO.

Will you hoist sail, sir? here lies your way.

VIOLA.

No, good swabber; I am to hull here a little longer. Some mollification for your giant, sweet lady. Tell me your mind: I am a messenger.

OLIVIA.

Sure, you have some hideous matter to deliver, when the courtesy of it is so fearful. Speak your office.

VIOLA.

It alone concerns your ear. I bring no overture of war, no taxation of homage: I hold the olive in my hand; my words are as full of peace as matter.

OLIVIA.

Yet you began rudely. What are you? what would you?

VIOLA.

The rudeness that hath appear'd in me have I learn'd from my entertainment. What I am, and what I would, are as secret as maidenhead: to your ears, divinity; to any other's, profanation.

OLIVIA.

Give us the place alone: we will hear this divinity.
[*Exit* MARIA.] Now, sir, what is your text?

VIOLA.

Most sweet lady,—

OLIVIA.

A comfortable doctrine, and much may be said of
it. Where lies your text?

VIOLA.

In Orsino's bosom.

OLIVIA.

In his bosom! In what chapter of his bosom?

VIOLA.

To answer by the method, in the first of his
heart.

OLIVIA.

O, I have read it: it is heresy. Have you no more
to say?

VIOLA.

Good madam, let me see your face.

OLIVIA.

Have you any commission from your lord to negotiate with my face? You are now out of your
text: but we will draw the curtain, and show you
the picture. Look you, sir, such a one I was, this
presents: is't not well done?　　　　[*Unveiling*.

VIOLA.

Excellently done, if God did all.

OLIVIA.

'Tis in grain, sir; 'twill endure wind and weather.

VIOLA.

'Tis beauty truly blent, whose red and white
Nature's own sweet and cunning hand laid on:
Lady, you are the cruell'st she alive,
If you will lead these graces to the grave,
And leave the world no copy.

OLIVIA.

O, sir, I will not be so hard-hearted; I will give
out divers schedules of my beauty: it shall be in-
ventoried, and every particle and utensil labell'd
to my will:—as, item, two lips, indifferent red;
item, two gray eyes, with lids to them; item, one
neck, one chin, and so forth. Were you sent
hither to 'praise me?

VIOLA.

I see you what you are,—you are too proud;
But, if you were the devil, you are fair.
My lord and master loves you: O, such love
Could be but recompensed, though you were
crown'd
The nonpareil of beauty!

OLIVIA.

How does he love me?

VIOLA.

With adorations, with fertile tears,
With groans that thunder love, with sighs of
fire.

OLIVIA.

Your lord does know my mind; I cannot love
him:
Yet I suppose him virtuous, know him noble,
Of great estate, of fresh and stainless youth;
In voices well divulged, free, learn'd, and valiant;
And, in dimension and the shape of nature,
A gracious person: but yet I cannot love him;
He might have took his answer long ago.

VIOLA.

If I did love you in my master's flame,
With such a suffering, such a deadly life,
In your denial I would find no sense;
I would not understand it.

OLIVIA.

Why, what would you?

VIOLA.

Make me a willow cabin at your gate,
And call upon my soul within the house;
Write loyal cantons of contemned love,
And sing them loud even in the dead of night;
Holla your name to the reverberate hills,
And make the babbling gossip of the air
Cry out, 'Olivia!' O, you should not rest
Between the elements of air and earth,
But you should pity me!

OLIVIA.

You might do much. What is your parentage?

VIOLA.

Above my fortunes, yet my state is well:
I am a gentleman.

OLIVIA.

Get you to your lord;
I cannot love him: let him send no more;
Unless, perchance, you come to me again,
To tell me how he takes it. Fare you well:
I thank you for your pains: spend this for me.

VIOLA.

I am no fee'd post, lady; keep your purse:
My master, not myself, lacks recompense.
Love make his heart of flint, that you shall love;
And let your fervour, like my master's, be
Placed in contempt! Farewell, fair cruelty. [*Exit*.

OLIVIA.

'What is your parentage?'
'Above my fortunes, yet my state is well:
I am a gentleman.' I'll be sworn thou art;
Thy tongue, thy face, thy limbs, actions, and
spirit,
Do give thee fivefold blazon:—not too fast;—
Soft, soft!—
Unless the master were the man.—How now!
Even so quickly may one catch the plague?
Methinks I feel this youth's perfections
With an invisible and subtle stealth
To creep in at mine eyes. Well, let it be.—
What, ho, Malvolio!

Enter MALVOLIO.

MALVOLIO.

Here, madam, at your service.

OLIVIA.

Run after that same peevish messenger,
The county's man: he left this ring behind him,
Would I or not: tell him I'll none of it.
Desire him not to flatter with his lord,
Nor hold him up with hopes; I am not for him:
If that the youth will come this way to-morrow,
I'll give him reasons for't. Hie thee, Malvolio.

MALVOLIO.

Madam, I will.　　　　　　　　　　　[*Exit*.

OLIVIA.

I do I know not what; and fear to find
Mine eye too great a flatterer for my mind.
Fate, show thy force: ourselves we do not owe;
What is decreed must be,—and be this so! [*Exit*.

ACT II. SCENE I.

The sea-coast.

Enter ANTONIO *and* SEBASTIAN.

ANTONIO.

WILL you stay no longer? nor will you not
that I go with you?

SEBASTIAN.

By your patience, no. My stars shine darkly over
me: the malignancy of my fate might perhaps distemper yours; therefore I shall crave of you your
leave that I may bear my evils alone: it were a bad
recompense for your love, to lay any of them on
you.

ANTONIO.

Let me yet know of you whither you are bound.

SEBASTIAN.

No, sooth, sir: my determinate voyage is mere extravagancy. But I perceive in you so excellent a
touch of modesty, that you will not extort from
me what I am willing to keep in; therefore it
charges me in manners the rather to express myself. You must know of me, then, Antonio, my
name is Sebastian, which I call'd Roderigo. My
father was that Sebastian of Messaline, whom I
know you have heard of. He left behind him myself and a sister, both born in an hour: if the
heavens had been pleased, would we had so
ended! but you, sir, alter'd that; for some hour
before you took me from the breach of the sea
was my sister drown'd.

ANTONIO.

Alas the day!

SEBASTIAN.

A lady, sir, though it was said she much
resembled me, was yet of many accounted
beautiful: but, though I could not, with such
estimable wonder, overfar believe that, yet
thus far I will boldly publish her,—she bore
a mind that envy could not but call fair. She
is drown'd already, sir, with salt water, though
I seem to drown her remembrance again with
more.

ANTONIO.

Pardon me, sir, your bad entertainment.

SEBASTIAN.

O good Antonio, forgive me your trouble!

ANTONIO.

If you will not murder me for my love, let me be
your servant.

SEBASTIAN.

If you will not undo what you have done, that is,
kill him whom you have recover'd, desire it not.
Fare ye well at once: my bosom is full of kindness;
and I am yet so near the manners of my mother,
that, upon the least occasion more, mine eyes
will tell tales of me. I am bound to the Count
Orsino's court: farewell.   [*Exit.*

ANTONIO.

The gentleness of all the gods go with thee!
I have many enemies in Orsino's court,
Else would I very shortly see thee there:
But, come what may, I do adore thee so,
That danger shall seem sport, and I will go.

[*Exit.*

SCENE II.

A street.

Enter VIOLA, MALVOLIO *following.*

MALVOLIO.

WERE not you even now with the Countess
Olivia?

VIOLA.

Even now, sir; on a moderate pace I have since
arrived but hither.

MALVOLIO.

She returns this ring to you, sir: you might have
saved me my pains, to have taken it away yourself. She adds, moreover, that you should put
your lord into a desperate assurance she will none
of him: and one thing more, that you be never so
hardy to come again in his affairs, unless it be to
report your lord's taking of this. Receive it so.

VIOLA.

She took no ring of me;—I'll none of it.

MALVOLIO.

Come, sir, you peevishly threw it to her; and her
will is, it should be so return'd: if it be worth
stooping for, there it lies in your eye; if not, be it
his that finds it.   [*Exit.*

VIOLA.

I left no ring with her: what means this lady?
Fortune forbid, my outside have not charm'd
her!
She made good view of me; indeed, so much,
That, sure, methought, her eyes had lost her
tongue,
For she did speak in starts distractedly.
She loves me, sure; the cunning of her passion
Invites me in this churlish messenger.
None of my lord's ring! why, he sent her none.
I am the man: if it be so, as 'tis,
Poor lady, she were better love a dream.
Disguise, I see, thou art a wickedness,
Wherein the pregnant enemy does much.
How easy is it for the proper-false
In women's waxen hearts to set their forms!
Alas, our frailty is the cause, not we!
For such as we are made of, such we be.
How will this fadge? my master loves her dearly;
And I, poor monster, fond as much on him;
And she, mistaken, seems to dote on me.
What will become of this? As I am man,
My state is desperate for my master's love;
As I am woman,—now, alas the day!—
What thriftless sighs shall poor Olivia breathe!
O Time, thou must untangle this, not I;
It is too hard a knot for me t'untie!   [*Exit.*

SCENE III.

Olivia's house.

Enter SIR TOBY *and* SIR ANDREW.

SIR TOBY BELCH.

APPROACH, Sir Andrew: not to be a-bed
after midnight is to be up betimes; and *dilu-
culo surgere*, thou know'st,—

SIR ANDREW AGUECHEEK.

Nay, by my troth, I know not: but I know, to be
up late is to be up late.

SIR TOBY BELCH.

A false conclusion: I hate it as an unfill'd can. To be up after midnight, and to go to bed then, is early: so that to go to bed after midnight is to go to bed betimes. Does not our life consist of the four elements?

SIR ANDREW AGUECHEEK.

Faith, so they say; but, I think, it rather consists of eating and drinking.

SIR TOBY BELCH.

Th'art a scholar: let us therefore eat and drink.— Marian, I say! a stoup of wine!

SIR ANDREW AGUECHEEK.

Here comes the fool, i'faith.

Enter CLOWN.

CLOWN.

How now, my hearts! did you never see the picture of We Three?

SIR TOBY BELCH.

Welcome, ass. Now let's have a catch.

SIR ANDREW AGUECHEEK.

By my troth, the fool has an excellent breast. I had rather than forty shillings I had such a leg, and so sweet a breath to sing, as the fool has. In sooth, thou wast in very gracious fooling last night, when thou spokest of Pigrogromitus, of the Vapians passing the equinoctial of Queubus: 'twas very good, i'faith. I sent thee sixpence for thy leman: hadst it?

CLOWN.

I did impeticos thy gratillity; for Malvolio's nose is no whipstock; my lady has a white hand, and the Myrmidons are no bottle-ale houses.

SIR ANDREW AGUECHEEK.

Excellent! why, this is the best fooling, when all is done. Now, a song.

SIR TOBY BELCH.

Come on; there is sixpence for you: let's have a song.

SIR ANDREW AGUECHEEK.

There's a testril of me too; if one knight give a—

CLOWN.

Would you have a love-song, or a song of good life?

SIR TOBY BELCH.

A love-song, a love-song.

SIR ANDREW AGUECHEEK.

Ay, ay: I care not for good life.

CLOWN [*sings*].

O mistress mine, where are you roaming?
O, stay and hear; your true-love's coming,
   That can sing both high and low:
Trip no further, pretty sweeting;
Journeys end in lovers' meeting,
   Every wise man's son doth know.

SIR ANDREW AGUECHEEK.

Excellent good, i'faith.

SIR TOBY BELCH.

Good, good.

CLOWN.

What is love? 'tis not hereafter;
Present mirth hath present laughter;
   What's to come is still unsure:
In delay there lies no plenty;
Then come kiss me, sweet-and-twenty,
   Youth's a stuff will not endure.

SIR ANDREW AGUECHEEK.

A mellifluous voice, as I am true knight.

SIR TOBY BELCH.

A contagious breath.

SIR ANDREW AGUECHEEK.

Very sweet and contagious, i'faith.

SIR TOBY BELCH.

To hear by the nose, it is dulcet in contagion. But shall we make the welkin dance indeed? shall we rouse the night-owl in a catch that will draw three souls out of one weaver? shall we do that?

SIR ANDREW AGUECHEEK.

An you love me, let's do't: I am dog at a catch.

CLOWN.

By'r lady, sir, and some dogs will catch well.

SIR ANDREW AGUECHEEK.

Most certain. Let our catch be, 'Thou knave.'

CLOWN.

'Hold thy peace, thou knave,' knight? I shall be constrain'd in't to call thee knave, knight.

SIR ANDREW AGUECHEEK.

'Tis not the first time I have constrain'd one to call me knave. Begin, fool: it begins, 'Hold thy peace.'

CLOWN.

I shall never begin, if I hold my peace.

SIR ANDREW AGUECHEEK.

Good, i'faith. Come, begin.   [*Catch sung.*

Enter MARIA.

MARIA.

What a caterwauling do you keep here! If my lady have not call'd up her steward Malvolio, and bid him turn you out of doors, never trust me.

SIR TOBY BELCH.

My lady's a Cataian, we are politicians, Malvolio's a Peg-a-Ramsey, and 'Three merry men be we.' Am not I consanguineous? am I not of her blood? Tilly-vally, lady! [*Sings*] 'There dwelt a man in Babylon, lady, lady!'

CLOWN.

Beshrew me, the knight's in admirable fooling.

SIR ANDREW AGUECHEEK.

Ay, he does well enough if he be disposed, and so do I too: he does it with a better grace, but I do it more natural.

SIR TOBY BELCH.

'O, the twelfth day of December,—'

MARIA.

For the love o' God, peace!

Enter MALVOLIO.

MALVOLIO.

My masters, are you mad? or what are you? Have you no wit, manners, nor honesty, but to gabble like tinkers at this time of night? Do ye make an ale-house of my lady's house, that ye squeak out your cosiers' catches without any mitigation or remorse of voice? Is there no respect of place, persons, nor time, in you?

SIR TOBY BELCH.

We did keep time, sir, in our catches. Sneck-up!

MALVOLIO.

Sir Toby, I must be round with you. My lady bade me tell you, that, though she harbours you as her kinsman, she's nothing allied to your disorders. If you can separate yourself and your misdemeanours, you are welcome to the house; if not, an it would please you to take leave of her, she is very willing to bid you farewell.

SIR TOBY BELCH.

'Farewell, dear heart, since I must needs be gone.'

MARIA.

Nay, good Sir Toby.

CLOWN.

'His eyes do show his days are almost done.'

MALVOLIO.

Is't even so?

SIR TOBY BELCH.

'But I will never die.'

CLOWN.

Sir Toby, there you lie.

MALVOLIO.

This is much credit to you.

SIR TOBY BELCH.

'Shall I bid him go?'

CLOWN.

'What an if you do?'

SIR TOBY BELCH.

'Shall I bid him go, and spare not?'

CLOWN.

'O, no, no, no, no, you dare not.'

SIR TOBY BELCH.

Out o'time, sir? ye lie.—Art any more than a steward? Dost thou think, because thou art virtuous, there shall be no more cakes and ale?

CLOWN.

Yes, by Saint Anne; and ginger shall be hot i'th' mouth too.

SIR TOBY BELCH.

Th'art i'th'right.—Go, sir, rub your chain with crumbs.—A stoup of wine, Maria!

MALVOLIO.

Mistress Mary, if you prized my lady's favour at any thing more than contempt, you would not give means for this uncivil rule: she shall know of it, by this hand.   [Exit.

MARIA.

Go shake your ears.

SIR ANDREW AGUECHEEK.

'Twere as good a deed as to drink when a man's a-hungry, to challenge him the field, and then to break promise with him, and make a fool of him.

SIR TOBY BELCH.

Do't, knight: I'll write thee a challenge; or I'll deliver thy indignation to him by word of mouth.

MARIA.

Sweet Sir Toby, be patient for to-night; since the youth of the count's was to-day with my lady, she is much out of quiet. For Monsieur Malvolio, let me alone with him: if I do not gull him into a nayword, and make him a common recreation, do not think I have wit enough to lie straight in my bed: I know I can do it.

SIR TOBY BELCH.

Possess us, possess us; tell us something of him.

MARIA.

Marry, sir, sometimes he is a kind of puritan.

SIR ANDREW AGUECHEEK.

O, if I thought that, I'ld beat him like a dog!

SIR TOBY BELCH.

What, for being a puritan? thy exquisite reason, dear knight?

SIR ANDREW AGUECHEEK.

I have no exquisite reason for't, but I have reason good enough.

MARIA.

The devil a puritan that he is, or any thing constantly, but a time-pleaser; an affection'd ass, that cons state without book, and utters it by great swarths: the best persuaded of himself, so cramm'd, as he thinks, with excellencies, that it is his grounds of faith that all that look on him love him; and on that vice in him will my revenge find notable cause to work.

SIR TOBY BELCH.

What wilt thou do?

MARIA.

I will drop in his way some obscure epistles of love; wherein, by the colour of his beard, the shape of his leg, the manner of his gait, the expressure of his eye, forehead, and complexion, he shall find himself most feelingly personated: I can write very like my lady, your niece; on a forgotten matter we can hardly make distinction of our hands.

SIR TOBY BELCH.

Excellent! I smell a device.

SIR ANDREW AGUECHEEK.

I have't in my nose too.

SIR TOBY BELCH.

He shall think, by the letters that thou wilt drop, that they come from my niece, and that she's in love with him.

MARIA.

My purpose is, indeed, a horse of that colour.

SIR TOBY BELCH.

And your horse now would make him an ass.

MARIA.

Ass, I doubt not.

SIR ANDREW AGUECHEEK.

O, 'twill be admirable!

MARIA.

Sport royal, I warrant you: I know my physic will work with him. I will plant you two, and let the fool make a third, where he shall find the letter: observe his construction of it. For this night, to bed, and dream on the event. Farewell.

SIR TOBY BELCH.

Good night, Penthesilea.   [Exit MARIA.

SIR ANDREW AGUECHEEK.

Before me, she's a good wench.

SIR TOBY BELCH.

She's a beagle, true-bred, and one that adores me: what o'that?

SIR ANDREW AGUECHEEK.

I was adored once too.

SIR TOBY BELCH.

Let's to bed, knight.—Thou hadst need send for more money.

SIR ANDREW AGUECHEEK.

If I cannot recover your niece, I am a foul way out.

SIR TOBY BELCH.

Send for money, knight: if thou hast her not i'th' end, call me cut.

SIR ANDREW AGUECHEEK.

If I do not, never trust me, take it how you will.

SIR TOBY BELCH.

Come, come; I'll go burn some sack; 'tis too late
to go to bed now: come, knight; come, knight.
                                        [*Exeunt.*

SCENE IV.

The DUKE'S *palace.*

Enter DUKE, VIOLA, CURIO, *and others.*

DUKE OF ILLYRIA.

GIVE me some music:—now, good morrow,
friends:—
Now, good Cesario, but that piece of song,
That old and antique song we heard last night:
Methought it did relieve my passion much,
More than light airs and recollected terms
Of these most brisk and giddy-paced times:—
Come, but one verse.

CURIO.

He is not here, so please your lordship, that should
sing it.

DUKE OF ILLYRIA.

Who was it?

CURIO.

Feste, the jester, my lord; a fool that the Lady
Olivia's father took much delight in: he is about
the house.

DUKE OF ILLYRIA.

Seek him out: and play the tune the while.
                        [*Exit* CURIO.   *Music plays.*
Come hither, boy: if ever thou shalt love,
In the sweet pangs of it remember me;
For such as I am all true lovers are,
Unstaid and skittish in all motions else,
Save in the constant image of the creature
That is beloved.—How dost thou like this tune?

VIOLA.

It gives a very echo to the seat
Where Love is throned.

DUKE OF ILLYRIA.

          Thou dost speak masterly:
My life upon't, young though thou art, thine eye
Hath stay'd upon some favour that it loves;—
Hath it not, boy?

VIOLA.

          A little, by your favour.

DUKE OF ILLYRIA.

What kind of woman is't?

VIOLA.

          Of your complexion.

DUKE OF ILLYRIA.

She is not worth thee, then.   What years, i'faith?

VIOLA.

About your years, my lord.

DUKE OF ILLYRIA.

Too old, by heaven: let still the woman take
An elder than herself; so wears she to him,
So sways she level in her husband's heart:
For, boy, however we do praise ourselves,
Our fancies are more giddy and unfirm,
More longing, wavering, sooner lost and worn,
Than women's are.

VIOLA.

          I think it well, my lord.

DUKE OF ILLYRIA.

Then let thy love be younger than thyself,
Or thy affection cannot hold the bent;

For women are as roses, whose fair flower
Being once display'd, doth fall that very hour.

VIOLA.

And so they are: alas, that they are so,—
To die, even when they to perfection grow!

Enter CURIO *and* CLOWN.

DUKE OF ILLYRIA.

O, fellow, come, the song we had last night.—
Mark it, Cesario; it is old and plain:
The spinsters and the knitters in the sun,
And the free maids that weave their thread with
bones,
Do use to chant it: it is silly sooth,
And dallies with the innocence of love,
Like the old age.

CLOWN.

Are you ready, sir?

DUKE OF ILLYRIA.

Ay; prithee, sing.   [*Music.*

CLOWN.

Come away, come away, death,
    And in sad cypress let me be laid;
Fly away, fly away, breath;
    I am slain by a fair cruel maid.
My shroud of white, stuck all with yew,
    O, prepare it!
My part of death, no one so true
    Did share it.

Not a flower, not a flower sweet,
    On my black coffin let there be strown;
Not a friend, not a friend greet
    My poor corpse, where my bones shall be
thrown:
A thousand thousand sighs to save,
    Lay me, O, where
Sad true lover never find my grave,
    To weep there!

DUKE OF ILLYRIA.

There's for thy pains.

CLOWN.

No pains, sir; I take pleasure in singing, sir.

DUKE OF ILLYRIA.

I'll pay thy pleasure, then.

CLOWN.

Truly, sir, and pleasure will be paid, one time or
another.

DUKE OF ILLYRIA.

Give me now leave to leave thee.

CLOWN.

Now, the melancholy god protect thee; and the
tailor make thy doublet of changeable taffeta, for
thy mind is a very opal! I would have men of such
constancy put to sea, that their business might be
every thing, and their intent every where; for
that's it that always makes a good voyage of nothing. Farewell.   [*Exit.*

DUKE OF ILLYRIA.

Let all the rest give place.
          [*Exeunt* CURIO *and* ATTENDANTS.
                    Once more, Cesario,
Get thee to yond same sovereign cruelty:
Tell her, my love, more noble than the world,
Prizes not quantity of dirty lands;
The parts that Fortune hath bestow'd upon her,
Tell her, I hold as giddily as Fortune;

But 'tis that miracle and queen of gems,
That nature pranks her in, attracts my soul.
VIOLA.
But if she cannot love you, sir?
DUKE OF ILLYRIA.
I cannot be so answer'd.
VIOLA.
         Sooth, but you must.
Say that some lady—as, perhaps, there is—
Hath for your love as great a pang of heart
As you have for Olivia: you cannot love her;
You tell her so; must she not, then, be answer'd?
DUKE OF ILLYRIA.
There is no woman's sides
Can bide the beating of so strong a passion
As love doth give my heart; no woman's heart
So big, to hold so much; they lack retention.
Alas, their love may be call'd appetite,—
No motion of the liver, but the palate,—
That suffer surfeit, cloyment, and revolt;
But mine is all as hungry as the sea,
And can digest as much: make no compare
Between that love a woman can bear me
And that I owe Olivia.
VIOLA.
         Ay, but I know,—
DUKE OF ILLYRIA.
What dost thou know?
VIOLA.
Too well what love women to men may owe:
In faith, they are as true of heart as we.
My father had a daughter loved a man,
As it might be, perhaps, were I a woman,
I should your lordship.
DUKE OF ILLYRIA.
         And what's her history?
VIOLA.
A blank, my lord. She never told her love,
But let concealment, like a worm i'th'bud,
Feed on her damask cheek: she pined in thought;
And, with a green and yellow melancholy,
She sat like Patience on a monument,
Smiling at grief. Was not this love indeed?
We men may say more, swear more: but, indeed,
Our shows are more than will; for still we prove
Much in our vows, but little in our love.
DUKE OF ILLYRIA.
But died thy sister of her love, my boy?
VIOLA.
I am all the daughters of my father's house,
And all the brothers too;—and yet I know not.—
Sir, shall I to this lady?
DUKE OF ILLYRIA.
         Ay, that's the theme.
To her in haste; give her this jewel; say,
My love can give no place, bide no denay.
                     [*Exeunt.*

SCENE V.

OLIVIA'S *garden.*

Enter SIR TOBY, SIR ANDREW, *and* FABIAN.

SIR TOBY BELCH.
COME thy ways, Signior Fabian.
FABIAN.
Nay, I'll come: if I lose a scruple of this sport, let
me be boil'd to death with melancholy.

SIR TOBY BELCH.
Wouldst thou not be glad to have the nig-
gardly rascally sheep-biter come by some notable
shame?
FABIAN.
I would exult, man: you know he brought me
out o'favour with my lady about a bear-baiting
here.
SIR TOBY BELCH.
To anger him, we'll have the bear again; and we
will fool him black and blue:—shall we not, Sir
Andrew?
SIR ANDREW AGUECHEEK.
An we do not, it is pity of our lives.
SIR TOBY BELCH.
Here comes the little villain.
            Enter MARIA.
How now, my metal of India!
MARIA.
Get ye all three into the box-tree: Malvolio's coming down this walk: he has been yonder i'the sun
practising behaviour to his own shadow this half-
hour: observe him, for the love of mockery; for I
know this letter will make a contemplative idiot of
him. Close, in the name of jesting! Lie thou there
[*throws down a letter*]; for here comes the trout that
must be caught with tickling.   [*Exit.*
         Enter MALVOLIO.
MALVOLIO.
'Tis but fortune; all is fortune. Maria once told
me she did affect me: and I have heard herself
come thus near, that, should she fancy, it should
be one of my complexion. Besides, she uses me
with a more exalted respect than any one else that
follows her. What should I think on't?
SIR TOBY BELCH.
Here's an overweening rogue!
FABIAN.
O, peace! Contemplation makes a rare turkey-
cock of him: how he jets under his advanced
plumes!
SIR ANDREW AGUECHEEK.
'Slight, I could so beat the rogue!
SIR TOBY BELCH.
Peace, I say.
MALVOLIO.
To be Count Malvolio,—
SIR TOBY BELCH.
Ah, rogue!
SIR ANDREW AGUECHEEK.
Pistol him, pistol him.
SIR TOBY BELCH.
Peace, peace!
MALVOLIO.
There is example for't; the lady of the Strachy
married the yeoman of the wardrobe.
SIR ANDREW AGUECHEEK.
Fie on him, Jezebel!
FABIAN.
O, peace! now he's deeply in: look how imagina-
tion blows him.
MALVOLIO.
Having been three months married to her, sitting
in my state,—
SIR TOBY BELCH.
O, for a stone-bow, to hit him in the eye!

MALVOLIO.

Calling my officers about me, in my brancht velvet gown; having come from a day-bed, where I have left Olivia sleeping,—

SIR TOBY BELCH.

Fire and brimstone!

FABIAN.

O, peace, peace!

MALVOLIO.

And then to have the humour of state; and after a demure travel of regard,—telling them I know my place, as I would they should do theirs,—to ask for my kinsman Toby,—

SIR TOBY BELCH.

Bolts and shackles!

FABIAN.

O, peace, peace, peace! now, now.

MALVOLIO.

Seven of my people, with an obedient start, make out for him: I frown the while; and perchance wind up my watch, or play with some rich jewel. Toby approaches; court'sies there to me,—

SIR TOBY BELCH.

Shall this fellow live?

FABIAN.

Though our silence be drawn from us with cars, yet peace.

MALVOLIO.

I extend my hand to him thus, quenching my familiar smile with an austere regard of control,—

SIR TOBY BELCH.

And does not Toby take you a blow o'the lips, then?

MALVOLIO.

Saying, 'Cousin Toby, my fortunes having cast me on your niece, give me this prerogative of speech,'—

SIR TOBY BELCH.

What, what?

MALVOLIO.

'You must amend your drunkenness.'

SIR TOBY BELCH.

Out, scab!

FABIAN.

Nay, patience, or we break the sinews of our plot.

MALVOLIO.

'Besides, you waste the treasure of your time with a foolish knight,'—

SIR ANDREW AGUECHEEK.

That's me, I warrant you.

MALVOLIO.

'One Sir Andrew,'—

SIR ANDREW AGUECHEEK.

I knew 'twas I; for many do call me fool.

MALVOLIO.

What employment have we here?

[Taking up the letter.

FABIAN.

Now is the woodcock near the gin.

SIR TOBY BELCH.

O, peace! and the spirit of humours intimate reading aloud to him!

MALVOLIO.

By my life, this is my lady's hand: these be her very C's, her U's, and her T's; and thus makes she

her great P's. It is, in contempt of question, her hand.

SIR ANDREW AGUECHEEK.

Her C's, her U's, and her T's: why that?

MALVOLIO [*reads*].

To the unknown beloved, this, and my good wishes: her very phrases!—By your leave, wax.— Soft!—and the impressure her Lucrece, with which she uses to seal: 'tis my lady. To whom should this be?

FABIAN.

This wins him, liver and all.

MALVOLIO [*reads*].

    Jove knows I love:
      But who?
    Lips, do not move;
    No man must know.

'No man must know.'—What follows? the numbers alter'd!—'No man must know:'—if this should be thee, Malvolio?

SIR TOBY BELCH.

Marry, hang thee, brock!

MALVOLIO [*reads*].

    I may command where I adore;
    But silence, like a Lucrece knife,
    With bloodless stroke my heart doth gore:
    M, O, A, I, doth sway my life.

FABIAN.

A fustian riddle!

SIR TOBY BELCH.

Excellent wench, say I.

MALVOLIO.

'M, O, A, I, doth sway my life.'—Nay, but first, let me see,—let me see,—let me see.

FABIAN.

What dish o'poison has she drest him!

SIR TOBY BELCH.

And with what wing the staniel checks at it!

MALVOLIO.

'I may command where I adore.' Why, she may command me: I serve her; she is my lady. Why, this is evident to any formal capacity; there is no obstruction in this:—and the end,—what should that alphabetical position portend? if I could make that resemble something in me,—Softly!— M, O, A, I,—

SIR TOBY BELCH.

O, ay, make up that:—he is now at a cold scent.

FABIAN.

Sowter will cry upon't, for all this, though it be as rank as a fox.

MALVOLIO.

M,—Malvolio;—M,—why, that begins my name.

FABIAN.

Did not I say he would work it out? the cur is excellent at faults.

MALVOLIO.

M,—but then there is no consonancy in the sequel; that suffers under probation: A should follow, but O does.

FABIAN.

And O shall end, I hope.

SIR TOBY BELCH.

Ay, or I'll cudgel him, and make him cry O!

MALVOLIO.

And then I comes behind.

FABIAN.

Ay, an you had any eye behind you, you might see more detraction at your heels than fortunes before you.

MALVOLIO.

M, O, A, I;—this simulation is not as the former: —and yet, to crush this a little, it would bow to me, for every one of these letters are in my name. Soft! here follows prose.—[reads] If this fall into thy hand, revolve. In my stars I am above thee; but be not afraid of greatness: some are born great, some achieve greatness, and some have greatness thrust upon 'em. Thy Fates open their hands; let thy blood and spirit embrace them: and, to inure thyself to what thou art like to be, cast thy humble slough, and appear fresh. Be opposite with a kinsman, surly with servants; let thy tongue tang arguments of state; put thyself into the trick of singularity: she thus advises thee that sighs for thee. Remember who commended thy yellow stockings, and wisht to see thee ever cross-garter'd: I say, remember. Go to, thou art made, if thou desirest to be so; if not, let me see thee a steward still, the fellow of servants, and not worthy to touch Fortune's fingers. Farewell. She that would alter services with thee,

THE FORTUNATE-UNHAPPY.

Daylight and champain discovers not more: this is open. I will be proud, I will read politic authors, I will baffle Sir Toby, I will wash off gross acquaintance, I will be point-devise the very man. I do not now fool myself, to let imagination jade me; for every reason excites to this, that my lady loves me. She did commend my yellow stockings of late, she did praise my leg being cross-garter'd; and in this she manifests herself to my love, and, with a kind of injunction, drives me to these habits of her liking. I thank my stars, I am happy. I will be strange, stout, in yellow stockings, and cross-garter'd, even with the swiftness of putting on. Jove and my stars be praised!—Here is yet a postscript. [reads] 'Thou canst not choose but know who I am. If thou entertain'st my love, let it appear in thy smiling: thy smiles become thee well; therefore in my presence still smile, dear my sweet, I prithee.' Jove, I thank thee.—I will smile; I will do every thing that thou wilt have me. [Exit.

FABIAN.

I will not give my part of this sport for a pension of thousands to be paid from the Sophy.

SIR TOBY BELCH.

I could marry this wench for this device,—

SIR ANDREW AGUECHEEK.

So could I too.

SIR TOBY BELCH.

And ask no other dowry with her but such another jest.

SIR ANDREW AGUECHEEK.

Nor I neither.

FABIAN.

Here comes my noble gull-catcher.

Enter MARIA.

SIR TOBY BELCH.

Wilt thou set thy foot o'my neck?

SIR ANDREW AGUECHEEK.

Or o'mine either?

SIR TOBY BELCH.

Shall I play my freedom at tray-trip, and become thy bond-slave?

SIR ANDREW AGUECHEEK.

I'faith, or I either?

SIR TOBY BELCH.

Why, thou hast put him in such a dream, that, when the image of it leaves him, he must run mad.

MARIA.

Nay, but say true; does it work upon him?

SIR TOBY BELCH.

Like aqua-vitæ with a midwife.

MARIA.

If you will then see the fruits of the sport, mark his first approach before my lady: he will come to her in yellow stockings, and 'tis a colour she abhors, and cross-garter'd, a fashion she detests; and he will smile upon her, which will now be so unsuitable to her disposition, being addicted to a melancholy as she is, that it cannot but turn him into a notable contempt. If you will see it, follow me.

SIR TOBY BELCH.

To the gates of Tartar, thou most excellent devil of wit!

SIR ANDREW AGUECHEEK.

I'll make one too. [Exeunt.

ACT III. SCENE I.

OLIVIA'S *garden*.

Enter VIOLA, *and* CLOWN *with a tabor*.

VIOLA.

SAVE thee, friend, and thy music! dost thou live by thy tabor?

CLOWN.

No, sir, I live by the church.

VIOLA.

Art thou a churchman?

CLOWN.

No such matter, sir: I do live by the church; for I do live at my house, and my house doth stand by the church.

VIOLA.

So thou mayst say, the king lies by a beggar, if a beggar dwell near him; or, the church stands by thy tabor, if thy tabor stand by the church.

CLOWN.

You have said, sir.—To see this age!—A sentence is but a cheveril glove to a good wit: how quickly the wrong side may be turn'd outward!

VIOLA.

Nay, that's certain; they that dally nicely with words may quickly make them wanton.

CLOWN.

I would, therefore, my sister had had no name, sir.

VIOLA.

Why, man?

CLOWN.

Why, sir, her name's a word; and to dally with that word might make my sister wanton. But, indeed, words are very rascals, since bonds disgraced them.

VIOLA.
Thy reason, man?

CLOWN.
Troth, sir, I can yield you none without words; and words are grown so false, I am loth to prove reason with them.

VIOLA.
I warrant thou art a merry fellow, and carest for nothing.

CLOWN.
Not so, sir; I do care for something; but in my conscience, sir, I do not care for you: if that be to care for nothing, sir, I would it would make you invisible.

VIOLA.
Art not thou the Lady Olivia's fool?

CLOWN.
No, indeed, sir; the Lady Olivia has no folly: she will keep no fool, sir, till she be married; and fools are as like husbands as pilchers are to herrings,—the husband's the bigger: I am, indeed, not her fool, but her corrupter of words.

VIOLA.
I saw thee late at the Count Orsino's.

CLOWN.
Foolery, sir, does walk about the orb like the sun, it shines every where. I would be sorry, sir, but the fool should be as oft with your master as with my mistress: I think I saw your wisdom there.

VIOLA.
Nay, an thou pass upon me, I'll no more with thee. Hold, there's expenses for thee.

CLOWN.
Now Jove, in his next commodity of hair, send thee a beard!

VIOLA.
By my troth, I'll tell thee, I am almost sick for one; though I would not have it grow on my chin. Is thy lady within?

CLOWN.
Would not a pair of these have bred, sir?

VIOLA.
Yes, being kept together and put to use.

CLOWN.
I would play Lord Pandarus of Phrygia, sir, to bring a Cressida to this Troilus.

VIOLA.
I understand you, sir; 'tis well begg'd.

CLOWN.
The matter, I hope, is not great, sir, begging but a beggar: Cressida was a beggar. My lady is within, sir. I will conster to them whence you come; who you are, and what you would, are out of my welkin,—I might say element, but the word is over-worn. [*Exit.*

VIOLA.
This fellow is wise enough to play the fool;
And to do that well craves a kind of wit:
He must observe their mood on whom he jests,
The quality of persons, and the time;
Not, like the haggard, check at every feather
That comes before his eye. This is a practice
As full of labour as a wise man's art:
For folly, that he wisely shows, is fit;
But wise men, folly-fall'n, quite taint their wit.

Enter SIR TOBY *and* SIR ANDREW.

SIR TOBY BELCH.
Save you, gentleman!

VIOLA.
And you, sir.

SIR ANDREW AGUECHEEK.
Dieu vous garde, monsieur.

VIOLA.
Et vous aussi; votre serviteur.

SIR ANDREW AGUECHEEK.
I hope, sir, you are; and I am yours.

SIR TOBY BELCH.
Will you encounter the house? my niece is desirous you should enter, if your trade be to her.

VIOLA.
I am bound to your niece, sir; I mean, she is the list of my voyage.

SIR TOBY BELCH.
Taste your legs, sir; put them to motion.

VIOLA.
My legs do better understand me, sir, than I understand what you mean by bidding me taste my legs.

SIR TOBY BELCH.
I mean, to go, sir, to enter.

VIOLA.
I will answer you with gait and entrance:—but we are prevented.

Enter OLIVIA *and* MARIA.
Most excellent accomplisht lady, the heavens rain odours on you!

SIR ANDREW AGUECHEEK [*aside*].
That youth's a rare courtier: 'Rain odours:'—well.

VIOLA.
My matter hath no voice, lady, but to your own most pregnant and vouchsafed ear.

SIR ANDREW AGUECHEEK [*aside*].
'Odours,' 'pregnant,' and 'vouchsafed:'—I'll get 'em all three all ready.

OLIVIA.
Let the garden-door be shut, and leave me to my hearing. [*Exeunt* SIR TOBY, SIR ANDREW, *and* MARIA.] Give me your hand, sir.

VIOLA.
My duty, madam, and most humble service.

OLIVIA.
What is your name?

VIOLA.
Cesario is your servant's name, fair princess.

OLIVIA.
My servant, sir! 'Twas never merry world
Since lowly feigning was call'd compliment:
Y'are servant to the Count Orsino, youth.

VIOLA.
And he is yours, and his must needs be yours:
Your servant's servant is your servant, madam.

OLIVIA.
For him, I think not on him: for his thoughts,
Would they were blanks, rather than fill'd with me!

VIOLA.
Madam, I come to whet your gentle thoughts
On his behalf:—

OLIVIA.
　　　　O, by your leave, I pray you,—
I bade you never speak again of him:

But, would you undertake another suit,
I had rather hear you to solicit that
Than music from the spheres.
            VIOLA.
                   Dear lady,—
            OLIVIA.
Give me leave, beseech you. I did send,
After the last enchantment you did here,
A ring in chase of you: so did I abuse
Myself, my servant, and, I fear me, you:
Under your hard construction must I sit,
To force that on you, in a shameful cunning,
Which you knew none of yours: what might you
    think?
Have you not set mine honour at the stake,
And baited it with all th'unmuzzled thoughts
That tyrannous heart can think? To one of your
    receiving
Enough is shown: a cypress, not a bosom,
Hides my poor heart. So, let me hear you speak.
            VIOLA.
I pity you.
            OLIVIA.
       That's a degree to love.
            VIOLA.
No, not a grise; for 'tis a vulgar proof,
That very oft we pity enemies.
            OLIVIA.
Why, then, methinks 'tis time to smile again.
O world, how apt the poor are to be proud!
If one should be a prey, how much the better
To fall before the lion than the wolf!
                  [Clock strikes.
The clock upbraids me with the waste of time.—
Be not afraid, good youth, I will not have you:
And yet, when wit and youth is come to harvest,
Your wife is like to reap a proper man:
There lies your way, due west.
            VIOLA.
               Then westward-ho!—
Grace and good disposition attend your ladyship!
You'll nothing, madam, to my lord by me?
            OLIVIA.
Stay:
I prithee, tell me what thou think'st of me.
            VIOLA.
That you do think you are not what you are.
            OLIVIA.
If I think so, I think the same of you.
            VIOLA.
Then think you right: I am not what I am.
            OLIVIA.
I would you were as I would have you be!
            VIOLA.
Would it be better, madam, than I am,
I wish it might; for now I am your fool.
            OLIVIA.
O, what a deal of scorn looks beautiful
In the contempt and anger of his lip!
A murderous guilt shows not itself more soon
Than love that would seem hid: love's night is
    noon.
Cesario, by the roses of the spring,
By maidhood, honour, truth, and every thing,
I love thee so, that, maugre all thy pride,
Nor wit nor reason can my passion hide.

Do not extort thy reasons from this clause,
For that I woo, thou therefore hast no cause;
But, rather, reason thus with reason fetter,—
Love sought is good, but given unsought is better.
            VIOLA.
By innocence I swear, and by my youth,
I have one heart, one bosom, and one truth,—
And that no woman has; nor never none
Shall mistress be of it, save I alone.
And so adieu, good madam: never more
Will I my master's tears to you deplore.
            OLIVIA.
Yet come again; for thou perhaps mayst move
That heart, which now abhors, to like his love.
                  [Exeunt.

SCENE II.

OLIVIA'S *house.*

Enter SIR TOBY, SIR ANDREW, *and* FABIAN.

        SIR ANDREW AGUECHEEK.
N O, faith, I'll not stay a jot longer.
           SIR TOBY BELCH.
Thy reason, dear venom; give thy reason.
           FABIAN.
You must needs yield your reason, Sir Andrew.
        SIR ANDREW AGUECHEEK.
Marry, I saw your niece do more favours to the
count's serving-man than ever she bestow'd upon
me; I saw't i'th'orchard.
           SIR TOBY BELCH.
Did she see thee the while, old boy? tell me that.
        SIR ANDREW AGUECHEEK.
As plain as I see you now.
           FABIAN.
This was a great argument of love in her toward
you.
        SIR ANDREW AGUECHEEK.
'Slight, will you make an ass o'me?
           FABIAN.
I will prove it legitimate, sir, upon the oaths of
judgement and reason.
           SIR TOBY BELCH.
And they have been grand-jurymen since before
Noah was a sailor.
           FABIAN.
She did show favour to the youth in your sight
only to exasperate you, to awake your dormouse
valour, to put fire in your heart, and brimstone
in your liver. You should then have accosted her;
and with some excellent jests, fire-new from the
mint, you should have bang'd the youth into
dumbness. This was lookt for at your hand, and
this was balkt: the double gilt of this opportunity
you let time wash off, and you are now sail'd into
the north of my lady's opinion; where you will
hang like an icicle on a Dutchman's beard, unless
you do redeem it by some laudable attempt either
of valour or policy.
        SIR ANDREW AGUECHEEK.
An't be any way, it must be with valour; for
policy I hate: I had as lief be a Brownist as a politician.
           SIR TOBY BELCH.
Why, then, build me thy fortunes upon the basis
of valour. Challenge me the count's youth to fight

with him; hurt him in eleven places: my niece shall take note of it; and assure thyself, there is no love-broker in the world can more prevail in man's commendation with woman than report of valour.

FABIAN.

There is no way but this, Sir Andrew.

SIR ANDREW AGUECHEEK.

Will either of you bear me a challenge to him?

SIR TOBY BELCH.

Go, write it in a martial hand; be curst and brief; it is no matter how witty, so it be eloquent and full of invention: taunt him with the license of ink: if thou 'thou'st' him some thrice, it shall not be amiss; and as many lies as will lie in thy sheet of paper, although the sheet were big enough for the bed of Ware in England, set 'em down: go, about it. Let there be gall enough in thy ink, though thou write with a goose-pen, no matter: about it.

SIR ANDREW AGUECHEEK.

Where shall I find you?

SIR TOBY BELCH.

We'll call thee at the *cubiculo:* go.

[*Exit* SIR ANDREW.

FABIAN.

This is a dear manakin to you, Sir Toby.

SIR TOBY BELCH.

I have been dear to him, lad,—some two thousand strong, or so.

FABIAN.

We shall have a rare letter from him: but you'll not deliver't?

SIR TOBY BELCH.

Never trust me, then; and by all means stir on the youth to an answer. I think oxen and wainropes cannot hale them together. For Andrew, if he were open'd, and you find so much blood in his liver as will clog the foot of a flea, I'll eat the rest of th'anatomy.

FABIAN.

And his opposite, the youth, bears in his visage no great presage of cruelty.

SIR TOBY BELCH.

Look, where the youngest wren of nine comes.

Enter MARIA.

MARIA.

If you desire the spleen, and will laugh your-selves into stitches, follow me. Yond gull Malvo-lio is turn'd heathen, a very renegado; for there is no Christian, that means to be saved by believing rightly, can ever believe such impossible passages of grossness. He's in yellow stockings.

SIR TOBY BELCH.

And cross-garter'd?

MARIA.

Most villainously; like a pedant that keeps a school i'th'church.—I have dogg'd him, like his mur-derer. He does obey every point of the letter that I dropt to betray him: he does smile his face into more lines than is in the new map, with the aug-mentation of the Indies: you have not seen such a thing as 'tis; I can hardly forbear hurling things at him. I know my lady will strike him: if she do, he'll smile, and take't for a great favour.

SIR TOBY BELCH.

Come, bring us, bring us where he is.　　[*Exeunt.*

SCENE III.

A street.

Enter SEBASTIAN *and* ANTONIO.

SEBASTIAN.

I WOULD not, by my will, have troubled you;
But, since you make your pleasure of your pains,
I will no further chide you.

ANTONIO.

I could not stay behind you: my desire,
More sharp than filed steel, did spur me forth;
And not all love to see you,—though so much
As might have drawn me to a longer voyage,—
But jealousy what might befall your travel,
Being skilless in these parts; which to a stranger,
Unguided and unfriended, often prove
Rough and unhospitable: my willing love,
The rather by these arguments of fear,
Set forth in your pursuit.

SEBASTIAN.

　　　　　　My kind Antonio,
I can no other answer make, but thanks,
And thanks, and ever; oft good turns
Are shuffled off with such uncurrent pay:
But, were my worth, as is my conscience, firm,
You should find better deal'ng. What's to do?
Shall we go see the reliques of this town?

ANTONIO.

To-morrow, sir; best first go see your lodging.

SEBASTIAN.

I am not weary, and 'tis long to night:
I pray you, let us satisfy our eyes
With the memorials and the things of fame
That do renown this city.

ANTONIO.

　　　　　　Would you'ld pardon me;
I do not without danger walk these streets:
Once, in a sea-fight, 'gainst the count his galleys
I did some service; of such note, indeed,
That, were I ta'en here, it would scarce be
　　answer'd.

SEBASTIAN.

Belike you slew great number of his people?

ANTONIO.

Th'offence is not of such a bloody nature;
Albeit the quality of the time and quarrel
Might well have given us bloody argument.
It might have since been answer'd in repaying
What we took from them; which, for traffic's sake,
Most of our city did: only myself stood out;
For which, if I be lapsed in this place,
I shall pay dear.

SEBASTIAN.

　　　　　Do not, then, walk too open.

ANTONIO.

It doth not fit me. Hold, sir, here's my purse.
In the south suburbs, at the Elephant,
Is best to lodge: I will bespeak our diet,　　[ledge
Whiles you beguile the time and feed your know-
With viewing of the town: there shall you have me.

SEBASTIAN.

Why I your purse?

ANTONIO.

Hap'ly your eye shall light upon some toy
You have desire to purchase; and your store,
I think, is not for idle markets, sir.

SEBASTIAN.
I'll be your purse-bearer, and leave you for
An hour.

ANTONIO.
To th'Elephant.

SEBASTIAN.
I do remember.
[*Exeunt.*

SCENE IV.

OLIVIA'S *garden.*

Enter OLIVIA *and* MARIA.

OLIVIA.
I HAVE sent after him: he says he'll come;—
How shall I feast him? what bestow of him?
For youth is bought more oft than begg'd or bor-
I speak too loud.—   [row'd.
Where is Malvolio?—he is sad and civil,
And suits well for a servant with my fortunes:—
Where is Malvolio?

MARIA.
He's coming, madam; but in very strange manner. He is, sure, possest, madam.

OLIVIA.
Why, what's the matter? does he rave?

MARIA.
No, madam, he does nothing but smile: your
ladyship were best to have some guard about you,
if he come; for, sure, the man is tainted in's wits.

OLIVIA.
Go call him hither. [*Exit* MARIA.] I am as mad as
he,
If sad and merry madness equal be.

Enter MARIA, *with* MALVOLIO.
How now, Malvolio!

MALVOLIO.
Sweet lady, ho, ho.   [*Smiles fantastically.*

OLIVIA.
Smilest thou?
I sent for thee upon a sad occasion.

MALVOLIO.
Sad, lady! I could be sad: this does make some
obstruction in the blood, this cross-gartering; but
what of that? if it please the eye of one, it is with
me as the very true sonnet is, 'Please one, and
please all.'

OLIVIA.
Why, how dost thou, man? what is the matter
with thee?

MALVOLIO.
Not black in my mind, though yellow in my legs.
It did come to his hands, and commands shall be
executed: I think we do know the sweet Roman
hand.

OLIVIA.
Wilt thou go to bed, Malvolio?

MALVOLIO.
To bed! ay, sweet-heart; and I'll come to thee.

OLIVIA.
God comfort thee! Why dost thou smile so, and
kiss thy hand so oft?

MARIA.
How do you, Malvolio?

MALVOLIO.
At your request! yes: nightingales answer daws.

MARIA.
Why appear you with this ridiculous boldness
before my lady?

MALVOLIO.
'Be not afraid of greatness:'—'twas well writ.

OLIVIA.
What mean'st thou by that, Malvolio?

MALVOLIO.
'Some are born great,'—

OLIVIA.
Ha!

MALVOLIO.
'Some achieve greatness,'—

OLIVIA.
What say'st thou?

MALVOLIO.
'And some have greatness thrust upon them.'

OLIVIA.
Heaven restore thee!

MALVOLIO.
'Remember who commended thy yellow stockings,'—

OLIVIA.
Thy yellow stockings!

MALVOLIO.
'And wisht to see thee cross-garter'd.'

OLIVIA.
Cross-garter'd!

MALVOLIO.
Go to, thou art made, if thou desirest to be so;'—

OLIVIA.
Am I made?

MALVOLIO.
'If not, let me see thee a servant still.'

OLIVIA.
Why, this is very midsummer madness.

Enter a SERVANT.

SERVANT.
Madam, the young gentleman of the Count Orsino's is return'd: I could hardly entreat him back:
he attends your ladyship's pleasure.

OLIVIA.
I'll come to him. [*Exit* SERVANT.] Good Maria,
let this fellow be lookt to. Where's my cousin
Toby? Let some of my people have a special care
of him: I would not have him miscarry for the
half of my dowry.   [*Exeunt* OLIVIA *and* MARIA.

MALVOLIO.
O, ho! do you come near me now? no worse man
than Sir Toby to look to me? This concurs directly with the letter: she sends him on purpose, that
I may appear stubborn to him; for she incites me
to that in the letter. 'Cast thy humble slough,' says
she; 'be opposite with a kinsman, surly with servants; let thy tongue tang with arguments of
state; put thyself into the trick of singularity;'—
and, consequently, sets down the manner how; as,
a sad face, a reverend carriage, a slow tongue, in
the habit of some sir of note, and so forth. I have
limed her; but it is Joves's doing, and Jove make
me thankful! And, when she went away now,
'Let this fellow be lookt to:' fellow! not Malvolio,
nor after my degree, but fellow. Why, every
thing adheres together, that no dram of a scruple,
no scruple of a scruple, no obstacle, no incredulous or unsafe circumstance—What can be said?

Nothing, that can be, can come between me and the full prospect of my hopes. Well, Jove, not I, is the doer of this, and he is to be thankt.

Enter MARIA *with* SIR TOBY *and* FABIAN.

SIR TOBY BELCH.
Which way is he, in the name of sanctity? If all the devils of hell be drawn in little, and Legion himself possess him, yet I'll speak to him.

FABIAN.
Here he is, here he is.—How is't with you, sir? how is't with you, man?

MALVOLIO.
Go off; I discard you: let me enjoy my private: go off.

MARIA.
Lo, how hollow the fiend speaks within him; did not I tell you?—Sir Toby, my lady prays you to have a care of him.

MALVOLIO.
Ah, ha! does she so?

SIR TOBY BELCH.
Go to, go to; peace, peace; we must deal gently with him: let me alone.—How do you, Malvolio? how is't with you? What, man! defy the devil: consider, he's an enemy to mankind.

MALVOLIO.
Do you know what you say?

MARIA.
La you, an you speak ill of the devil, how he takes it at heart! Pray God, he be not bewitcht!

FABIAN.
Carry his water to th'wise woman.

MARIA.
Marry, and it shall be done to-morrow morning, if I live. My lady would not lose him for more than I'll say.

MALVOLIO.
How now, mistress!

MARIA.
O Lord!

SIR TOBY BELCH.
Prithee, hold thy peace; this is not the way: do you not see you move him? let me alone with him.

FABIAN.
No way but gentleness; gently, gently: the fiend is rough, and will not be roughly used.

SIR TOBY BELCH.
Why, how now, my bawcock! how dost thou, chuck?

MALVOLIO.
Sir!

SIR TOBY BELCH.
Ay, Biddy, come with me. What, man! 'tis not for gravity to play at cherry-pit with Satan: hang him, foul collier!

MARIA.
Get him to say his prayers; good Sir Toby, get him to pray.

MALVOLIO.
My prayers, minx!

MARIA.
No, I warrant you, he will not hear of godliness.

MALVOLIO.
Go, hang yourselves all! you are idle shallow things: I am not of your element: you shall know more hereafter. [*Exit.*

SIR TOBY BELCH.
Is't possible?

FABIAN.
If this were play'd upon a stage now, I could condemn it as an improbable fiction.

SIR TOBY BELCH.
His very genius hath taken the infection of the device, man.

MARIA.
Nay, pursue him now, lest the device take air, and taint.

FABIAN.
Why, we shall make him mad indeed.

MARIA.
The house will be the quieter.

SIR TOBY BELCH.
Come, we'll have him in a dark room and bound. My niece is already in the belief that he's mad; we may carry it thus, for our pleasure and his penance, till our very pastime, tired out of breath, prompt us to have mercy on him: at which time we will bring the device to the bar, and crown thee for a finder of madmen.—But see, but see.

FABIAN.
More matter for a May morning.

Enter SIR ANDREW.

SIR ANDREW AGUECHEEK.
Here's the challenge, read it: I warrant there's vinegar and pepper in't.

FABIAN.
Is't so saucy?

SIR ANDREW AGUECHEEK.
Ay, is't, I warrant him: do but read.

SIR TOBY BELCH.
Give me. [*reads*] Youth, whatsoever thou art, thou art but a scurvy fellow.

FABIAN.
Good, and valiant.

SIR TOBY BELCH [*reads*].
Wonder not, nor admire not in thy mind, why I do call thee so, for I will show thee no reason for't.

FABIAN.
A good note: that keeps you from the blow of the law.

SIR TOBY BELCH [*reads*].
Thou comest to the Lady Olivia, and in my sight she uses thee kindly: but thou liest in thy throat; that is not the matter I challenge thee for.

FABIAN.
Very brief, and to exceeding good sense—less.

SIR TOBY BELCH [*reads*].
I will waylay thee going home; where if it be thy chance to kill me,—

FABIAN.
Good.

SIR TOBY BELCH [*reads*].
Thou kill'st me like a rogue and a villain.

FABIAN.
Still you keep o'th'windy side of the law: good.

SIR TOBY BELCH [*reads*].
Fare thee well; and God have mercy upon one of our souls! He may have mercy upon mine; but my hope is better, and so look to thyself. Thy friend, as thou usest him, and thy sworn enemy,

ANDREW AGUECHEEK.

If this letter move him not, his legs cannot: I'll give't him.

MARIA.

You may have very fit occasion for't: he is now in some commerce with my lady, and will by and by depart.

SIR TOBY BELCH.

Go, Sir Andrew; scout me for him at the corner of the orchard, like a bum-baily: so soon as ever thou seest him, draw; and, as thou draw'st, swear horrible; for it comes to pass oft, that a terrible oath, with a swaggering accent sharply twang'd off, gives manhood more approbation then ever proof itself would have earn'd him. Away!

SIR ANDREW AGUECHEEK.

Nay, let me alone for swearing.   [Exit.

SIR TOBY BELCH.

Now will not I deliver his letter: for the behaviour of the young gentleman gives him out to be of good capacity and breeding: his employment between his lord and my niece confirms no less: therefore this letter, being so excellently ignorant, will breed no terror in the youth: he will find it comes from a clodpole. But, sir, I will deliver his challenge by word of mouth; set upon Aguecheek a notable report of valour; and drive the gentleman—as I know his youth will aptly receive it—into a most hideous opinion of his rage, skill, fury, and impetuosity. This will so fright them both, that they will kill one another by the look, like cockatrices.

FABIAN.

Here he comes with your niece: give them way till he take leave, and presently after him.

SIR TOBY BELCH.

I will meditate the while upon some horrid message for a challenge.

  [Exeunt SIR TOBY, FABIAN, and MARIA.
  Enter OLIVIA, with VIOLA.

OLIVIA.

I have said too much unto a heart of stone,
And laid mine honour too unchary out:
There's something in me that reproves my fault;
But such a headstrong potent fault it is,
That it but mocks reproof.

VIOLA.

With the same 'haviour that your passion bears,
Goes on my master's griefs.

OLIVIA.

Here, wear this jewel for me, 'tis my picture:
Refuse it not: it hath no tongue to vex you:
And, I beseech you, come again to-morrow.
What shall you ask of me that I'll deny,
That honour saved may upon asking give?

VIOLA.

Nothing but this,—your true love for my master.

OLIVIA.

How with mine honour may I give him that
Which I have given to you?

VIOLA.

    I will acquit you.

OLIVIA.

Well, come again to-morrow; fare thee well:
A fiend like thee might bear my soul to hell.

  [Exit.

Enter SIR TOBY *and* FABIAN.

SIR TOBY BELCH.

Gentleman, God save thee!

VIOLA.

And you, sir.

SIR TOBY BELCH.

That defence thou hast, betake thee to't: of what nature the wrongs are thou hast done him, I know not: but thy intercepter, full of despite, bloody as the hunter, attends thee at the orchard-end: dismount thy tuck, be yare in thy preparation; for thy assailant is quick, skilful, and deadly.

VIOLA.

You mistake, sir; I am sure no man hath any quarrel to me: my remembrance is very free and clear from any image of offence done to any man.

SIR TOBY BELCH.

You'll find it otherwise, I assure you: therefore, if you hold your life at any price, betake you to your guard; for your opposite hath in him what youth, strength, skill, and wrath can furnish man withal.

VIOLA.

I pray you, sir, what is he?

SIR TOBY BELCH.

He is knight, dubb'd with unhatcht rapier and on carpet consideration; but he is a devil in private brawl: souls and bodies hath he divorced three; and his incensement at this moment is so implacable, that satisfaction can be none but by pangs of death and sepulchre: hob-nob is his word; give't or take't.

VIOLA.

I will return again into the house, and desire some conduct of the lady. I am no fighter. I have heard of some kind of men that put quarrels purposely on others, to taste their valour; belike this is a man of that quirk.

SIR TOBY BELCH.

Sir, no; his indignation derives itself out of a very competent injury: therefore, get you on, and give him his desire. Back you shall not to the house, unless you undertake that with me which with as much safety you might answer him: therefore, on, or strip your sword stark naked; for meddle you must, that's certain, or forswear to wear iron about you.

VIOLA.

This is as uncivil as strange. I beseech you, do me this courteous office, as to know of the knight what my offence to him is: it is something of my negligence, nothing of my purpose.

SIR TOBY BELCH.

I will do so.—Signior Fabian, stay you by this gentleman till my return.   [Exit.

VIOLA.

Pray you, sir, do you know of this matter?

FABIAN.

I know the knight is incensed against you, even to a mortal arbitrement; but nothing of the circumstance more.

VIOLA.

I beseech you, what manner of man is he?

FABIAN.

Nothing of that wonderful promise, to read him by his form, as you are like to find him in the proof of his valour. He is, indeed, sir, the most skilful, bloody, and fatal opposite that you could possibly have found in any part of Illyria. Will you walk towards him? I will make your peace with him, if I can.

VIOLA.

I shall be much bound to you for't: I am one that had rather go with sir priest than sir knight: I care not who knows so much of my mettle.   [Exeunt.

Enter SIR TOBY and SIR ANDREW.

SIR TOBY BELCH.

Why, man, he's a very devil; I have not seen such a firago. I had a pass with him, rapier, scabbard, and all, and he gives me the stuck-in with such a mortal motion, that it is inevitable; and on the answer, he pays you as surely as your feet hit the ground they step on: they say he has been fencer to the Sophy.

SIR ANDREW AGUECHEEK.

Pox on't, I'll not meddle with him.

SIR TOBY BELCH.

Ay, but he will not now be pacified: Fabian can scarce hold him yonder.

SIR ANDREW AGUECHEEK.

Plague on't, an I thought he had been valiant and so cunning in fence, I'ld have seen him damn'd ere I'ld have challenged him. Let him let the matter slip, and I'll give him my horse, gray Capulet.

SIR TOBY BELCH.

I'll make the motion: stand here, make a good show on't: this shall end without the perdition of souls.—[aside] Marry, I'll ride your horse as well as I ride you.

Enter FABIAN and VIOLA.

[to FABIAN] I have his horse to take up the quarrel: I have persuaded him the youth's a devil.

FABIAN.

He is as horribly conceited of him; and pants and looks pale, as if a bear were at his heels.

SIR TOBY BELCH [to VIOLA].

There's no remedy, sir; he will fight with you for's oath-sake: marry, he hath better bethought him of his quarrel, and he finds that now scarce to be worth talking of: therefore draw, for the supportance of his vow; he protests he will not hurt you.

VIOLA [aside].

Pray God defend me! A little thing would make me tell them how much I lack of a man.

FABIAN.

Give ground, if you see him furious.

SIR TOBY BELCH.

Come, Sir Andrew, there's no remedy; the gentleman will, for his honour's sake, have one bout with you; he cannot by the duello avoid it: but he has promised me, as he is a gentleman and a soldier, he will not hurt you. Come on, to't.

SIR ANDREW AGUECHEEK.

Pray God, he keep his oath!   [Draws.

VIOLA.

I do assure you, 'tis against my will.   [Draws.

Enter ANTONIO.

ANTONIO.

Put up your sword. If this young gentleman Have done offence, I take the fault on me: If you offend him, I for him defy you.

SIR TOBY BELCH.

You, sir! why, what are you?

ANTONIO [drawing].

One, sir, that for his love dares yet do more Than you have heard him brag to you he will.

SIR TOBY BELCH.

Nay, if you be an undertaker, I am for you.

[Draws.

FABIAN.

O good Sir Toby, hold! here come the officers.

SIR TOBY BELCH [to ANTONIO].

I'll be with you anon.

VIOLA [to SIR ANDREW].

Pray, sir, put your sword up, if you please.

SIR ANDREW AGUECHEEK.

Marry, will I, sir; and, for that I promised you, I'll be as good as my word: he will bear you easily, and reins well.

Enter OFFICERS.

FIRST OFFICER.

This is the man; do thy office.

SECOND OFFICER.

Antonio, I arrest thee at the suit of Count Orsino

ANTONIO.

You do mistake me, sir.

FIRST OFFICER.

No, sir, no jot; I know your favour well, Though now you have no sea-cap on your head.— Take him away: he knows I know him well.

ANTONIO.

I must obey. [to VIOLA] This comes with seeking you:
But there's no remedy; I shall answer it.
What will you do, now my necessity
Makes me to ask you for my purse? It grieves me
Much more for what I cannot do for you
Than what befalls myself. You stand amazed;
But be of comfort.

SECOND OFFICER.

Come sir, away.

ANTONIO.

I must entreat of you some of that money.

VIOLA.

What money, sir?
For the fair kindness you have show'd me here,
And, part, being prompted by your present
Out of my lean and low ability   [trouble,
I'll lend you something: my having is not much;
I'll make division of my present with you:
Hold, there's half my coffer.

ANTONIO.

    Will you deny me now?
Is't possible that my deserts to you
Can lack persuasion? Do not tempt my misery,
Lest that it make me so unsound a man
As to upbraid you with those kindnesses
That I have done for you.

VIOLA.

    I know of none;
Nor know I you by voice or any feature:
I hate ingratitude more in a man
Than lying, vainness, babbling, drunkenness,
Or any taint of vice whose strong corruption
Inhabits our frail blood.

ANTONIO.

    O heavens themselves!

SECOND OFFICER.
Come, sir, I pray you, go.
ANTONIO.
Let me speak a little. This youth that you see here
I snatcht one half out of the jaws of death,
Relieved him with such sanctity of love,
And to his image, which methought did promise
Most venerable worth, did I devotion.
FIRST OFFICER.
What's that to us? The time goes by: away!
ANTONIO.
But, O, how vile an idol proves this god!
Thou hast, Sebastian, done good feature shame.
In nature there's no blemish but the mind;
None can be call'd deform'd but the unkind:
Virtue is beauty: but the beauteous evil
Are empty trunks, o'erflourisht by the devil.
FIRST OFFICER.
The man grows mad: away with him!—come,
   come, sir.
ANTONIO.
Lead me on.   [*Exit with* OFFICERS.
VIOLA.
Methinks his words do from such passion fly,
That he believes himself: so do not I.
Prove true, imagination, O, prove true,
That I, dear brother, be now ta'en for you!
SIR TOBY BELCH.
Come hither, knight; come hither, Fabian: we'll
whisper o'er a couplet or two of most sage saws.
VIOLA.
He named Sebastian: I my brother know
Yet living in my glass; even such, and so,
In favour was my brother; and he went
Still in this fashion, colour, ornament,—
For him I imitate: O, if it prove,
Tempests are kind, and salt waves fresh in love!
                      [*Exit.*
SIR TOBY BELCH.
A very dishonest paltry boy, and more a coward
than a hare: his dishonesty appears in leaving his
friend here in necessity, and denying him; and for
his cowardship, ask Fabian.
FABIAN.
A coward, a most devout coward, religious in it.
SIR ANDREW AGUECHEEK.
'Slid, I'll after him again, and beat him.
SIR TOBY BELCH.
Do; cuff him soundly, but never draw thy sword.
SIR ANDREW AGUECHEEK.
An I do not,—   [*Exit.*
FABIAN.
Come, let's see the event.
SIR TOBY BELCH.
I dare lay any money 'twill be nothing yet.
                      [*Exeunt.*

ACT IV. SCENE I.

Before OLIVIA'S *house.*

Enter SEBASTIAN *and* CLOWN.

CLOWN.
WILL you make me believe that I am not
   sent for you?
SEBASTIAN.
Go to, go to, thou art a foolish fellow:
Let me be clear of thee.

CLOWN.
Well held out, i'faith! No, I do not know you; nor
I am not sent to you by my lady, to bid you come
speak with her; nor your name is not Master
Cesario; nor this is not my nose neither. Nothing
that is so is so.
SEBASTIAN.
I prithee, vent thy folly somewhere else;
Thou know'st not me.
CLOWN.
Vent my folly! he has heard that word of some
great man, and now applies it to a fool: vent my
folly! I am afraid this great lubber, the world, will
prove a cockney.—I prithee, now, ungird thy
strangeness, and tell me what I shall vent to my
lady: shall I vent to her that thou art coming?
SEBASTIAN.
I prithee, foolish Greek, depart from me:
There's money for thee: if you tarry longer,
I shall give worse payment.
CLOWN.
By my troth, thou hast an open hand.—These
wise men, that give fools money, get themselves a
good report after fourteen years' purchase.

Enter SIR ANDREW.

SIR ANDREW AGUECHEEK.
Now, sir, have I met you again? there's for you.
                [*Striking* SEBASTIAN.
SEBASTIAN.
Why, there's for thee, and there, and there!
                [*Beating* SIR ANDREW.
Are all the people mad?

Enter SIR TOBY *and* FABIAN.

SIR TOBY BELCH.
Hold, sir, or I'll throw your dagger o'er the house.
CLOWN.
This will I tell my lady straight: I would not be in
some of your coats for twopence.   [*Exit.*
SIR TOBY BELCH.
Come on, sir; hold.
SIR ANDREW AGUECHEEK.
Nay, let him alone: I'll go another way to work
with him; I'll have an action of battery against
him, if there be any law in Illyria: though I struck
him first, yet it's no matter for that.
SEBASTIAN.
Let go thy hand.
SIR TOBY BELCH.
Come, sir, I will not let you go. Come, my young
soldier, put up your iron: you are well flesht; come
on.
SEBASTIAN.
I will be free from thee. What wouldst thou now?
If thou darest tempt me further, draw thy sword.
                      [*Draws.*
SIR TOBY BELCH.
What, what? Nay, then I must have an ounce or
two of this malapert blood from you.   [*Draws.*

Enter OLIVIA.

OLIVIA.
Hold, Toby; on thy life, I charge thee, hold!
SIR TOBY BELCH.
Madam!
OLIVIA.
Will it be ever thus? Ungracious wretch,
Fit for the mountains and the barbarous caves,

Where manners ne'er were preacht! out of my
    sight!—
Be not offended, dear Cesario.—
Rudesby, be gone!

    [*Exeunt* SIR TOBY, SIR ANDREW, *and*
      FABIAN.
                  I prithee, gentle friend,
Let thy fair wisdom, not thy passion, sway
In this uncivil and unjust extent
Against thy peace. Go with me to my house;
And hear thou there how many fruitless pranks
This ruffian hath botcht up, that thou thereby
Mayst smile at this: thou shalt not choose but go:
Do not deny. Beshrew his soul for me,
He started one poor heart of mine in thee.

             SEBASTIAN.
What relish is in this? how runs the stream?
Or I am mad, or else this is a dream:
I et fancy still my sense in Lethe steep;
If it be thus to dream, still let me sleep!

             OLIVIA.
Nay, come, I prithee: would thou'ldst be ruled by
    me!

             SEBASTIAN.
Madam, I will.

             OLIVIA.
O, say so, and so be !   [*Exeunt.*

SCENE II.

OLIVIA'S *house.*

Enter MARIA *and* CLOWN.

             MARIA.

NAY, I prithee, put on this gown and this
beard; make him believe thou art Sir Topas
the curate: do it quickly; I'll call Sir Toby the
whilst.   [*Exit.*

             CLOWN.
Well, I'll put it on, and I will dissemble myself
in't; and I would I were the first that ever dissembled in such a gown. I am not tall enough to become the function well; nor lean enough to be
thought a good student: but to be said an honest
man and a good housekeeper, goes as fairly as to
say a careful man and a great scholar. The competitors enter.

    Enter SIR TOBY *and* MARIA.

          SIR TOBY BELCH.
Jove bless thee, master parson.

             CLOWN.
Bonos dies, Sir Toby: for, as the old hermit of
Prague, that never saw pen and ink, very wittily
said to a niece of King Gorboduc, 'That that is
is;' so I, being master parson, am master parson;
for, what is that but that, and is but is?

          SIR TOBY BELCH.
To him, Sir Topas.

             CLOWN.
What, ho, I say,—peace in this prison!

          SIR TOBY BELCH.
The knave counterfeits well; a good knave.

        MALVOLIO [*within*].
Who calls there?

             CLOWN.
Sir Topas the curate, who comes to visit Malvolio
the lunatic.

             MALVOLIO.
Sir Topas, Sir Topas, good Sir Topas, go to my
lady.

             CLOWN.
Out, hyperbolical fiend! how vexest thou this
man! talkest thou nothing but of ladies?

          SIR TOBY BELCH.
Well said, master parson.

             MALVOLIO.
Sir Topas, never was man thus wrong'd: good Sir
Topas, do not think I am mad: they have laid me
here in hideous darkness.

             CLOWN.
Fie, thou dishonest Satan! I call thee by the most
modest terms; for I am one of those gentle ones
that will use the devil himself with courtesy: say'st
thou that house is dark?

             MALVOLIO.
As hell, Sir Topas.

             CLOWN.
Why, it hath bay windows transparent as barri-
cadoes, and the clearstories toward the south-
north are as lustrous as ebony; and yet complainest
thou of obstruction?

             MALVOLIO.
I am not mad, Sir Topas: I say to you, this house
is dark.

             CLOWN.
Madman, thou errest: I say, there is no darkness
but ignorance; in which thou art more puzzled
than the Egyptians in their fog.

             MALVOLIO.
I say, this house is as dark as ignorance, though
ignorance were as dark as hell; and I say, there
was never man thus abused. I am no more mad
than you are: make the trial of it in any constant
question.

             CLOWN.
What is the opinion of Pythagoras concerning
wildfowl?

             MALVOLIO.
That the soul of our grandam might haply inhabit a bird.

             CLOWN.
What think'st thou of his opinion?

             MALVOLIO.
I think nobly of the soul, and no way approve his
opinion.

             CLOWN.
Fare thee well. Remain thou still in darkness: thou
shalt hold the opinion of Pythagoras ere I will allow of thy wits; and fear to kill a woodcock, lest
thou dispossess the soul of thy grandam. Fare
thee well.

             MALVOLIO.
Sir Topas, Sir Topas,—

          SIR TOBY BELCH.
My most exquisite Sir Topas!

             CLOWN.
Nay, I am for all waters.

             MARIA.
Thou mightst have done this without thy beard
and gown: he sees thee not.

          SIR TOBY BELCH.
To him in thine own voice, and bring me word
how thou find'st him: I would we were well rid of

this knavery. If he may be conveniently deliver'd, I would he were; for I am now so far in offence with my niece, that I cannot pursue with any safety this sport to the upshot. Come by and by to my chamber.   [*Exeunt* SIR TOBY *and* MARIA.

CLOWN [*singing*].
Hey, Robin, jolly Robin,
     Tell me how thy lady does.

MALVOLIO.
Fool,—

CLOWN.
'My lady is unkind, perdy.'

MALVOLIO.
Fool,—

CLOWN.
'Alas, why is she so?'

MALVOLIO.
Fool, I say,—

CLOWN.
'She loves another'—Who calls, ha?

MALVOLIO.
Good fool, as ever thou wilt deserve well at my hand, help me to a candle, and pen, ink, and paper: as I am a gentleman, I will live to be thankful to thee for't.

CLOWN.
Master Malvolio!

MALVOLIO.
Ay, good fool.

CLOWN.
Alas, sir, how fell you besides your five wits?

MALVOLIO.
Fool, there was never man so notoriously abused: I am as well in my wits, fool, as thou art.

CLOWN.
But as well? then you are mad indeed, if you be no better in your wits than a fool.

MALVOLIO.
They have here propertied me; keep me in darkness, send ministers to me, asses, and do all they can to face me out of my wits.

CLOWN.
Advise you what you say; the minister is here.— Malvolio, Malvolio, thy wits the heavens restore! endeavour thyself to sleep, and leave thy vain bibble-babble.

MALVOLIO.
Sir Topas,—

CLOWN.
Maintain no words with him, good fellow.—Who, I, sir? not I, sir. God b'wi'you, good Sir Topas! —Marry, amen.—I will, sir, I will.

MALVOLIO.
Fool, fool, fool, I say,—

CLOWN.
Alas, sir, be patient. What say you, sir? I am shent for speaking to you.

MALVOLIO.
Good fool, help me to some light and some paper: I tell thee, I am as well in my wits as any man in Illyria.

CLOWN.
Well-a-day, that you were, sir!

MALVOLIO.
By this hand, I am. Good fool, some ink, paper, and light; and convey what I will set down to my lady: it shall advantage thee more than ever the bearing of letter did.

CLOWN.
I will help you to't. But tell me true, are you not mad indeed? or do you but counterfeit?

MALVOLIO.
Believe me, I am not; I tell thee true.

CLOWN.
Nay, I'll ne'er believe a madman till I see his brains. I will fetch you light, and paper, and ink.

MALVOLIO.
Fool, I'll requite it in the highest degree: I prithee, be gone.

CLOWN [*singing*].
     I am gone, sir;
          And anon, sir,
     I'll be with you again,
          In a trice,
          Like to the old Vice,
     Your need to sustain;
     Who, with dagger of lath,
     In his rage and his wrath,
          Cries, ah, ha! to the devil:
     Like a mad lad,
     Pare thy nails, dad;
          Adieu, goodman devil.   [*Exit.*

SCENE III.

OLIVIA'S *garden.*

Enter SEBASTIAN.

SEBASTIAN.
THIS is the air; that is the glorious sun;
     This pearl she gave me, I do feel't and see't:
And though 'tis wonder that enwraps me thus,
Yet 'tis not madness. Where's Antonio, then?
I could not find him at the Elephant:
Yet there he was; and there I found this credit,
That he did range the town to seek me out.
His counsel now might do me golden service;
For though my soul disputes well with my sense,
That this may be some error, but no madness,
Yet doth this accident and flood of fortune
So far exceed all instance, all discourse,
That I am ready to distrust mine eyes,
And wrangle with my reason, that persuades me
To any other trust but that I am mad
Or else the lady's mad; yet, if 'twere so,
She could not sway her house, command her fol-
     lowers,
Take and give back affairs, and their dispatch,
With such a smooth, discreet, and stable bearing,
As I perceive she does: there's something in't
That is deceivable. But here the lady comes.

Enter OLIVIA *and a* PRIEST.

OLIVIA.
Blame not this haste of mine. If you mean well,
Now go with me and with this holy man
Into the chantry by: there, before him,
And underneath that consecrated roof,
Plight me the full assurance of your faith;
That my most jealous and too doubtful soul
May live at peace: he shall conceal it,
Whiles you are willing it shall come to note,
What time we will our celebration keep
According to my birth.—What do you say?

SEBASTIAN.
I'll follow this good man, and go with you;
And, having sworn truth, ever will be true.

OLIVIA.
Then lead the way, good father; and heavens so
  shine,
That they may fairly note this act of mine!
                                    [*Exeunt.*

ACT V. SCENE I.

Before OLIVIA'S *house.*

Enter CLOWN *and* FABIAN.

FABIAN.
NOW, as thou lovest me, let me see his letter.

CLOWN.
Good Master Fabian, grant me another request.

FABIAN.
Any thing.

CLOWN.
Do not desire to see this letter.

FABIAN.
This is, to give a dog, and in recompense desire
my dog again.

Enter DUKE, VIOLA, CURIO, *and* ATTEN-
DANTS.

DUKE OF ILLYRIA.
Belong you to the Lady Olivia, friends?

CLOWN.
Ay, sir; we are some of her trappings.

DUKE OF ILLYRIA.
I know thee well: how dost thou, my good fellow?

CLOWN.
Truly, sir, the better for my foes, and the worse
for my friends.

DUKE OF ILLYRIA.
Just the contrary; the better for thy friends.

CLOWN.
No, sir, the worse.

DUKE OF ILLYRIA.
How can that be?

CLOWN.
Marry, sir, they praise me, and make an ass of me;
now my foes tell me plainly I am an ass: so that
by my foes, sir, I profit in the knowledge of myself; and by my friends I am abused: so that,
conclusions to be as kisses, if your four nega-
tives make your two affirmatives, why, then,
the worse for my friends, and the better for my
foes.

DUKE OF ILLYRIA.
Why, this is excellent.

CLOWN.
By my troth, sir, no; though it please you to be
one of my friends.

DUKE OF ILLYRIA.
Thou shalt not be the worse for me: there's gold.
                                [*Gives money.*

CLOWN.
But that it would be double-dealing, sir, I would
you could make it another.

DUKE OF ILLYRIA.
O, you give me ill counsel.

CLOWN.
Put your grace in your pocket, sir, for this once,
and let your flesh and blood obey it.

DUKE OF ILLYRIA.
Well, I will be so much a sinner to be a double-
dealer: there's another.   [*Gives money.*

CLOWN.
Primo, secundo, tertio, is a good play; and the old
saying is, the third pays for all: the *triplex,* sir, is
a good tripping measure; or the bells of Saint
Bennet, sir, may put you in mind,—one, two,
three.

DUKE OF ILLYRIA.
You can fool no more money out of me at this
throw: if you will let your lady know I am here to
speak with her, and bring her along with you, it
may awake my bounty further.

CLOWN.
Marry, sir, lullaby to your bounty till I come
again.   I go, sir; but I would not have you to
think that my desire of having is the sin of covetousness: but, as you say, sir, let your bounty take
a nap, I will awake it anon.   [*Exit.*

VIOLA.
Here comes the man, sir, that did rescue me.

Enter OFFICERS, *with* ANTONIO.

DUKE OF ILLYRIA.
That face of his I do remember well;
Yet, when I saw it last, it was besmear'd
As black as Vulcan in the smoke of war:
A bawbling vessel was he captain of,
For shallow draught and bulk unprizable;
With which such scatheful grapple did he make
With the most noble bottom of our fleet,
That very envy and the tongue of loss
Cried fame and honour on him.—What's the mat-
  ter?

FIRST OFFICER.
Orsino, this is that Antonio
That took the Phœnix and her fraught from
  Candy;
And this is he that did the Tiger board,
When your young nephew Titus lost his leg:
Here in the streets, desperate of shame and state,
In private brabble did we apprehend him.

VIOLA.
He did me kindness, sir; drew on my side;
But, in conclusion, put strange speech upon me,—
I know not what 'twas but distraction.

DUKE OF ILLYRIA.
Notable pirate! thou salt-water thief!
What foolish boldness brought thee to their
  mercies,
Whom thou, in terms so bloody and so dear,
Hast made thine enemies?

ANTONIO.
                          Orsino, noble sir,
Be pleased that I shake off these names you give
  me:
Antonio never yet was thief or pirate,
Though, I confess, on base and ground enough,
Orsino's enemy. A witchcraft drew me hither:
That most ingrateful boy there by your side,
From the rude sea's enraged and foamy mouth
Did I redeem; a wreck past hope he was:
His life I gave him, and did thereto add
My love, without retention or restraint,
All his in dedication; for his sake
Did I expose myself, pure for his love,

Into the danger of this adverse town;
Drew to defend him when he was beset:
Where being apprehended, his false cunning,
Not meaning to partake with me in danger,
Taught him to face me out of his acquaintance,
And grew a twenty-years-removed thing
While one would wink; denied me mine own
　　purse,
Which I had recommended to his use
Not half an hour before.
　　　　　　　　　　　VIOLA.
　　　　　　　　How can this be?
　　　　　DUKE OF ILLYRIA.
When came he to this town?
　　　　　ANTONIO.
To-day, my lord: and for three months before—
No interim, not a minute's vacancy—
Both day and night did we keep company.
　　　　　DUKE OF ILLYRIA.
Here comes the countess: now heaven walks on
　　earth.—
But for thee, fellow; fellow, thy words are mad-
　　ness:
Three months this youth hath tended upon me;
But more of that anon. Take him aside.
　　　Enter OLIVIA and ATTENDANTS.
　　　　　　OLIVIA.
What would my lord, but that he may not have,
Wherein Olivia may seem serviceable?—
Cesario, you do not keep promise with me.
　　　　　　VIOLA.
Madam!
　　　　　DUKE OF ILLYRIA.
Gracious Olivia,—
　　　　　　OLIVIA.
What do you say, Cesario? Good my lord,—
　　　　　　VIOLA.
My lord would speak; my duty hushes me.
　　　　　　OLIVIA.
If it be aught to the old tune, my lord,
It is as fat and fulsome to mine ear
As howling after music.
　　　　　DUKE OF ILLYRIA.
　　　　　　Still so cruel?
　　　　　　OLIVIA.
Still so constant, lord.
　　　　　DUKE OF ILLYRIA.
What, to perverseness? you uncivil lady,
To whose ingrate and unauspicious altars
My soul the faithfull'st offerings hath breathed out
That e'er devotion tender'd! What shall I do?
　　　　　　OLIVIA.
Even what it please my lord, that shall become him.
　　　　　DUKE OF ILLYRIA.
Why should I not, had I the heart to do it,
Like to th'Egyptian thief at point of death,
Kill what I love? a savage jealousy
That sometimes savours nobly.—But hear me
　　this:
Since you to non-regardance cast my faith,
And that I partly know the instrument
That screws me from my true place in your
　　favour,
Live you, the marble-breasted tyrant, still;
But this your minion, whom I know you love,
And whom, by heaven I swear, I tender dearly,

Him will I tear out of that cruel eye,
Where he sits crowned in his master's spite.—
Come, boy, with me; my thoughts are ripe in
　　mischief:
I'll sacrifice the lamb that I do love,
To spite a raven's heart within a dove.
　　　　　　VIOLA.
And I, most jocund, apt, and willingly,
To do you rest, a thousand deaths would die.
　　　　　　OLIVIA.
Where goes Cesario?
　　　　　　VIOLA.
　　　　　　After him I love
More than I love these eyes, more than my life,
More, by all mores, than e'er I shall love wife.
If I do feign, you witnesses above
Punish my life for tainting of my love!
　　　　　　OLIVIA.
Ay me, detested! how am I beguiled!
　　　　　　VIOLA.
Who does beguile you? who does do you wrong?
　　　　　　OLIVIA.
Hast thou forgot thyself? is it so long?
Call forth the holy father. [Exit an ATTENDANT
　　　　　DUKE OF ILLYRIA.
　　　　　　Come, away! [to VIOLA
　　　　　　OLIVIA.
Whither, my lord?—Cesario, husband, stay.
　　　　　DUKE OF ILLYRIA.
Husband!
　　　　　　OLIVIA.
　　　　Ay, husband: can he that deny?
　　　　　DUKE OF ILLYRIA.
Her husband, sirrah!
　　　　　　VIOLA.
　　　　　　No, my lord, not I.
　　　　　　OLIVIA.
Alas, it is the baseness of thy fear
That makes thee strangle thy propriety:
Fear not, Cesario; take thy fortunes up;
Be that thou know'st thou art, and then thou art
As great as that thou fear'st.
　　　Enter ATTENDANT, with PRIEST.
　　　　　　O, welcome, father!
Father, I charge thee, by thy reverence,
Here to unfold—though lately we intended
To keep in darkness what occasion now
Reveals before 'tis ripe—what thou dost know
Hath newly past between this youth and me.
　　　　　　PRIEST.
A contract of eternal bond of love,
Confirm'd by mutual joinder of your hands,
Attested by the holy close of lips,
Strengthen'd by interchangement of your rings;
And all the ceremony of this compact
Seal'd in my function, by my testimony:
Since when, my watch hath told me, toward my
　　grave
I have travell'd but two hours.
　　　　　DUKE OF ILLYRIA.
O thou dissembling cub! what wilt thou be
When time hath sow'd a grizzle on thy case?
Or will not else thy craft so quickly grow,
That thine own trip shall be thine overthrow?
Farewell, and take her; but direct thy feet
Where thou and I henceforth may never meet.

VIOLA.
My lord, I do protest,—
OLIVIA.
          O, do not swear!
Hold little faith, though thou hast too much fear.
Enter SIR ANDREW.
SIR ANDREW AGUECHEEK.
For the love of God, a surgeon! send one presently
to Sir Toby.
OLIVIA.
What's the matter?
SIR ANDREW AGUECHEEK.
'Has broke my head across, and has given Sir
Toby a bloody coxcomb too: for the love of God,
your help! I had rather than forty pound I were
at home.
OLIVIA.
Who has done this, Sir Andrew?
SIR ANDREW AGUECHEEK.
The count's gentleman, one Cesario: we took him
for a coward, but he's the very devil incardinate.
DUKE OF ILLYRIA.
My gentleman Cesario?
SIR ANDREW AGUECHEEK.
'Od's lifelings, here he is!—You broke my head
for nothing; and that that I did, I was set on to
do't by Sir Toby.
VIOLA.
Why do you speak to me? I never hurt you:
You drew your sword upon me without cause;
But I bespake you fair, and hurt you not.
SIR ANDREW AGUECHEEK.
If a bloody coxcomb be a hurt, you have hurt me:
I think you set nothing by a bloody coxcomb.—
Here comes Sir Toby halting; you shall hear
more: but if he had not been in drink, he would
have tickled you othergates than he did.
Enter SIR TOBY *and* CLOWN.
DUKE OF ILLYRIA.
How now, gentleman! how is't with you?
SIR TOBY BELCH.
That's all one: has hurt me, and there's the end
on't.—Sot, didst see Dick surgeon, sot?
CLOWN.
O, he's drunk, Sir Toby, an hour agone; his eyes
were set at eight i'th'morning.
SIR TOBY BELCH.
Then he's a rogue and a passy-measures pavin: I
hate a drunken rogue.
OLIVIA.
Away with him! Who hath made this havoc with
them?
SIR ANDREW AGUECHEEK.
I'll help you, Sir Toby, because we'll be drest to-
gether.
SIR TOBY BELCH.
Will you help? an ass-head and a coxcomb and a
knave, a thin-faced knave, a gull?
OLIVIA.
Get him to bed, and let his hurt be lookt to.
[*Exeunt* CLOWN, FABIAN, SIR TOBY, *and*
SIR ANDREW.
Enter SEBASTIAN.
SEBASTIAN.
I am sorry, madam, I have hurt your kinsman;
But, had it been the brother of my blood,

I must have done no less with wit and safety.
You throw a strange regard upon me, and by that
I do perceive it hath offended you:
Pardon me, sweet one, even for the vows
We made each other but so late ago.
DUKE OF ILLYRIA.
One face, one voice, one habit, and two persons,—
A natural perspective, that is and is not!
SEBASTIAN.
Antonio, O my dear Antonio!
How have the hours rackt and tortured me,
Since I have lost thee!
ANTONIO.
Sebastian are you?
SEBASTIAN.
         Fear'st thou that, Antonio?
ANTONIO.
How have you made division of yourself?
An apple, cleft in two, is not more twin
Than these two creatures. Which is Sebastian?
OLIVIA.
Most wonderful!
SEBASTIAN.
Do I stand there? I never had a brother;
Nor can there be that deity in my nature,
Of here and every where. I had a sister,
Whom the blind waves and surges have de-
     vour'd.—
Of charity, what kin are you to me?   [*to* VIOLA.
What countryman? what name? what parentage?
VIOLA.
Of Messaline: Sebastian was my father;
Such a Sebastian was my brother too,
So went he suited to his watery tomb:
If spirits can assume both form and suit,
You come to fright us.
SEBASTIAN.
        A spirit I am indeed;
But am in that dimension grossly clad,
Which from the womb I did participate.
Were you a woman, as the rest goes even,
I should my tears let fall upon your cheek,
And say, 'Thrice-welcome, drowned Viola!'
VIOLA.
My father had a mole upon his brow,—
SEBASTIAN.
And so had mine.
VIOLA.
And died that day when Viola from her birth
Had number'd thirteen years.
SEBASTIAN.
O, that record is lively in my soul!
He finished, indeed, his mortal act
That day that made my sister thirteen years.
VIOLA.
If nothing lets to make us happy both
But this my masculine usurpt attire,
Do not embrace me till each circumstance
Of place, time, fortune, do cohere and jump,
That I am Viola: which to confirm,
I'll bring you to a captain in this town,
Where lie my maiden weeds; by whose gentle
     help
I was preserved to serve this noble count.
All the occurrence of my fortune since
Hath been between this lady and this lord.

SEBASTIAN [to OLIVIA].
So comes it, lady, you have been mistook:
But nature to her bias drew in that.
You would have been contracted to a maid;
Nor are you therein, by my life, deceived,—
You are betrothed both to a maid and man.

DUKE OF ILLYRIA.
Be not amazed; right noble is his blood.—
If this be so, as yet the glass seems true,
I shall have share in this most happy wrack.—
[to VIOLA] Boy, thou hast said to me a thousand
   times
Thou never shouldst love woman like to me.

VIOLA.
And all those sayings will I over-swear;
And all those swearings keep as true in soul
As doth that orbed continent the fire
That severs day from night.

DUKE OF ILLYRIA.
          Give me thy hand;
And let me see thee in thy woman's weeds.

VIOLA.
The captain that did bring me first on shore
Hath my maid's garments: he, upon some action,
Is now in durance, at Malvolio's suit,
A gentleman and follower of my lady's.

OLIVIA.
He shall enlarge him:—fetch Malvolio hither:—
And yet, alas, now I remember me,
They say, poor gentlemen, he's much distract.
Enter CLOWN *with a letter, and* FABIAN.
A most extracting frenzy of mine own
From my remembrance clearly banisht his.—
How does he, sirrah?

CLOWN.
Truly, madam, he holds Beelzebub at the stave's
end as well as a man in his case may do: has here
writ a letter to you; I should have given't you to-
day morning, but as a madman's epistles are no
gospels, so it skills not much when they are deliver'd.

OLIVIA.
Open't, and read it.

CLOWN.
Look, then, to be well edified when the fool
delivers the madman. [*reads*] By the Lord,
madam,—

OLIVIA.
How now! art thou mad?

CLOWN.
No, madam, I do but read madness: an your ladyship will have it as it ought to be, you must allow
vox.

OLIVIA.
Prithee, read i'thy right wits.

CLOWN.
So I do, madonna; but to read his right wits is to
read thus: therefore perpend, my princess, and
give ear.

OLIVIA.
Read it you, sirrah.   [*to* FABIAN.
FABIAN [*reads*].
By the Lord, madam, you wrong me, and the
world shall know it: though you have put me into
darkness, and given your drunken cousin rule
over me, yet have I the benefit of my senses as

well as your ladyship. I have your own letter that
induced me to the semblance I put on; with the
which I doubt not but to do myself much right, or
you much shame. Think of me as you please. I
leave my duty a little unthought of, and speak
out of my injury.
    THE MADLY-USED MALVOLIO.

OLIVIA.
Did he write this?

CLOWN.
Ay, madam.

DUKE OF ILLYRIA.
This savours not much of distraction.

OLIVIA.
See him deliver'd, Fabian; bring him hither.
                  [*Exit* FABIAN.
My lord, so please you, these things further
   thought on,
To think me as well a sister as a wife,
One day shall crown th'alliance on't, so please
   you,
Here at my house, and at my proper cost.

DUKE OF ILLYRIA.
Madam, I am most apt t'embrace your offer.—
[*to* VIOLA] Your master quits you; and, for your
   service done him,
So much against the mettle of your sex,
So far beneath your soft and tender breeding,
And since you call'd me master for so long,
Here is my hand: you shall from this time be
Your master's mistress.

OLIVIA.
        A sister!—you are she.
Enter FABIAN, *with* MALVOLIO.

DUKE OF ILLYRIA.
Is this the madman?

OLIVIA.
        Ay, my lord, this same.—
How now, Malvolio!

MALVOLIO!
        Madam, you have done me wron
Notorious wrong.

OLIVIA.
      Have I, Malvolio? no.

MALVOLIO.
Lady, you have. Pray you, peruse that letter:
You must not now deny it is your hand,—
Write from it, if you can, in hand or phrase;
Or say 'tis not your seal, not your invention:
You can say none of this: well, grant it, then,
And tell me, in the modesty of honour,
Why you have given me such clear lights of
   favour,
Bade me come smiling and cross-garter'd to you,
To put on yellow stockings, and to frown
Upon Sir Toby and the lighter people;
And, acting this in an obedient hope,
Why have you suffer'd me to be imprison'd,
Kept in a dark house, visited by the priest,
And made the most notorious geck and gull
That e'er invention play'd on? tell me why.

OLIVIA.
Alas, Malvolio, this is not my writing,
Though, I confess, much like the character:
But, out of question, 'tis Maria's hand.
And now I do bethink me, it was she

First told me thou wast mad: thou camest in
   smiling,
And in such forms which here were presupposed
Upon thee in the letter. Prithee, be content:
This practice hath most shrewdly past upon thee;
But, when we know the grounds and authors of it,
Thou shalt be both the plaintiff and the judge
Of thine own cause.

FABIAN.
        Good madam, hear me speak:
And let no quarrel nor no brawl to come
Taint the condition of this present hour,
Which I have wonder'd at. In hope it shall not,
Most freely I confess, myself and Toby
Set this device against Malvolio here,
Upon some stubborn and uncourteous parts
We had conceived in him: Maria writ
The letter at Sir Toby's great importance;
In recompense whereof he hath married her.
How with a sportful malice it was follow'd,
May rather pluck on laughter than revenge;
If that the injuries be justly weigh'd
That have on both sides past.

OLIVIA.
Alas, poor fool, how have they baffled thee!

CLOWN.
Why, 'some are born great, some achieve greatness, and some have greatness thrown upon them.' I was one, sir, in this interlude,—one Sir Topas, sir; but that's all one.—'By the Lord, fool, I am not mad;'—but do you remember? 'Madam, why laugh you at such a barren rascal? an you smile not, he's gagg'd:' and thus the whirligig of time brings in his revenges.

MALVOLIO.
I'll be revenged on the whole pack of you. [*Exit.*

OLIVIA.
He hath been most notoriously abused.

DUKE OF ILLYRIA.
Pursue him, and entreat him to a peace:—
He hath not told us of the captain yet:
When that is known, and golden time convents,
A solemn combination shall be made
Of our dear souls. Meantime, sweet sister,
We will not part from hence.—Cesario, come;
For so you shall be, while you are a man;
But when in other habits you are seen,
Orsino's mistress and his fancy's queen.
        [*Exeunt all, except* CLOWN.

CLOWN [*sings*].
When that I was and a little tiny boy,
  With hey, ho, the wind and the rain,
A foolish thing was but a toy,
  For the rain it raineth every day.

But when I came to man's estate,
  With hey, ho, the wind and the rain,
'Gainst knaves and thieves men shut their gate,
  For the rain it raineth every day.

But when I came, alas! to wive,
  With hey, ho, the wind and the rain,
By swaggering could I never thrive,
  For the rain it raineth every day.

But when I came unto my beds,
  With hey, ho, the wind and the rain,
With toss-pots still had drunken heads,
  For the rain it raineth every day.

A great while ago the world begun,
  With hey, ho, the wind and the rain:—
But that's all one, our play is done,
  And we'll strive to please you every day.
        [*Exit.*

HAMLET
PRINCE OF DENMARK

DRAMATIS PERSONAE

CLAUDIUS, *King of Denmark.*
HAMLET, *son to the late, and nephew to the present king.*
POLONIUS, *lord chamberlain.*
HORATIO, *friend to Hamlet.*
LAERTES, *son to Polonius.*
VOLTIMAND,
CORNELIUS,
ROSENCRANTZ,
GUILDENSTERN, } *courtiers.*
OSRIC,
A GENTLEMAN,
A PRIEST.
MARCELLUS, } *officers.*
BERNARDO,
FRANCISCO, *a soldier.*

REYNALDO, *servant to Polonius.*
PLAYERS.
TWO CLOWNS, *grave-diggers.*
FORTINBRAS, *Prince of Norway.*
A CAPTAIN.
ENGLISH AMBASSADORS.

GERTRUDE, *Queen of Denmark, and mother to Hamlet.*
OPHELIA, *daughter to Polonius.*

LORDS, LADIES, OFFICERS, SOLDIERS, SAILORS, MESSENGERS, *and other* ATTENDANTS.

GHOST *of Hamlet's father.*

SCENE—*Denmark.*

ACT I. SCENE I.

Elsinore. A platform before the castle.

FRANCISCO *at his post. Enter to him* BERNARDO.

BERNARDO.

WHO'S there?

FRANCISCO.
Nay, answer me: stand, and unfold yourself.

BERNARDO.
Long live the king!

FRANCISCO.
Bernardo?

BERNARDO.
He.

FRANCISCO.
You come most carefully upon your hour.

BERNARDO.
'Tis now struck twelve; get thee to bed, Francisco.

FRANCISCO.
For this relief much thanks: 'tis bitter cold,
And I am sick at heart.

BERNARDO.
Have you had quiet guard?

FRANCISCO.
Not a mouse stirring.

BERNARDO.
Well, good night.
If you do meet Horatio and Marcellus,
The rivals of my watch, bid them make haste.

FRANCISCO.
I think I hear them.—Stand, ho! Who is there?
Enter HORATIO *and* MARCELLUS.

HORATIO.
Friends to this ground.

MARCELLUS.
And liegemen to the Dane.

FRANCISCO.
Give you good night.

MARCELLUS.
O, farewell, honest soldier:
Who hath relieved you?

FRANCISCO.
Bernardo has my place.
Give you good night. [*Exit.*

MARCELLUS.
Holla! Bernardo!

BERNARDO.
Say,—
What, is Horatio there?

HORATIO.
A piece of him.

BERNARDO.
Welcome, Horatio:—welcome, good Marcellus.

MARCELLUS.
What, has this thing appear'd again to-night?

BERNARDO.
I have seen nothing.

MARCELLUS.
Horatio says 'tis but our fantasy,
And will not let belief take hold of him
Touching this dreaded sight, twice seen of us:
Therefore I have entreated him along
With us to watch the minutes of this night;
That, if again this apparition come,
He may approve our eyes, and speak to it.

HORATIO.
Tush, tush, 'twill not appear.

BERNARDO.
Sit down awhile;
And let us once again assail your ears,
That are so fortified against our story,
What we two nights have seen.

HORATIO.
Well, sit we down,
And let us hear Bernardo speak of this.

BERNARDO.
Last night of all,
When yond same star that's westward from the pole

Had made his course t'illume that part of heaven
Where now it burns, Marcellus and myself,
The bell then beating one,—

MARCELLUS.
Peace, break thee off; look, where it comes again!

Enter GHOST.

BERNARDO.
In the same figure, like the king that's dead.

MARCELLUS.
Thou art a scholar; speak to it, Horatio.

BERNARDO.
Looks it not like the king? mark it, Horatio.

HORATIO.
Most like:—it harrows me with fear and wonder.

BERNARDO.
It would be spoke to.

MARCELLUS.
Question it, Horatio.

HORATIO.
What art thou, that usurp'st this time of night,
Together with that fair and warlike form
In which the majesty of buried Denmark
Did sometimes march? by heaven I charge thee,
    speak!

MARCELLUS.
It is offended.

BERNARDO.
See, it stalks away!

HORATIO.
Stay! speak, speak! I charge thee, speak!

[*Exit* GHOST.

MARCELLUS.
'Tis gone, and will not answer.

BERNARDO.
How now, Horatio! you tremble, and look pale:
Is not this something more than fantasy?
What think you on't?

HORATIO.
Before my God, I might not this believe
Without the sensible and true avouch
Of mine own eyes.

MARCELLUS.
Is it not like the king?

HORATIO.
As thou art to thyself:
Such was the very armour he had on
When he th'ambitious Norway combated;
So frown'd he once, when, in an angry parle,
He smote the sledded Polacks on the ice.
'Tis strange.

MARCELLUS.
Thus twice before, and jump at this dead hour,
With martial stalk hath he gone by our watch.

HORATIO.
In what particular thought to work I know not;
But, in the gross and scope of my opinion,
This bodes some strange eruption to our state.

MARCELLUS.
Good now, sit down, and tell me, he that knows,
Why this same strict and most observant watch
So nightly toils the subject of the land;
And why such daily cast of brazen cannon,
And foreign mart for implements of war;
Why such impress of shipwrights, whose sore task
Does not divide the Sunday from the week;
What might be toward, that this sweaty haste

Doth make the night joint-labourer with the day:
Who is't that can inform me?

HORATIO.
That can I;
At least, the whisper goes so. Our last king,
Whose image even but now appear'd to us,
Was, as you know, by Fortinbras of Norway,
Thereto prickt on by a most emulate pride,
Dared to the combat; in which our valiant Ham-
    let—
For so this side of our known world esteem'd
    him—
Did slay this Fortinbras; who, by a seal'd compact,
Well ratified by law and heraldry,
Did forfeit, with his life, all those his lands
Which he stood seized of to the conqueror:
Against the which, a moiety competent
Was gaged by our king; which had return'd
To the inheritance of Fortinbras,
Had he been vanquisher; as, by the same cov'nant,
And carriage of the article design'd,
His fell to Hamlet. Now, sir, young Fortinbras,
Of unimproved mettle hot and full,
Hath in the skirts of Norway, here and there,
Sharkt up a list of lawless resolutes,
For food and diet, to some enterprise
That hath a stomach in't: which is no other—
As it doth well appear unto our state—
But to recover of us, by strong hand
And terms compulsative, those foresaid lands
So by his father lost: and this, I take it,
Is the main motive of our preparations,
The source of this our watch, and the chief head
Of this post-haste and romage in the land.

BERNARDO.
I think it be no other but e'en so:
Well may it sort, that this portentous figure
Comes armed through our watch; so like the king
That was and is the question of these wars.

HORATIO.
A mote it is to trouble the mind's eye.
In the most high and palmy state of Rome,
A little ere the mightiest Julius fell,
The graves stood tenantless, and the sheeted dead
Did squeak and gibber in the Roman streets:
As, stars with trains of fire, and dews of blood,
Disasters in the sun; and the moist star,
Upon whose influence Neptune's empire stands,
Was sick almost to doomsday with eclipse:
And even the like precurse of fierce events—
As harbingers preceding still the fates,
And prologue to the omen coming on—
Have heaven and earth together demonstrated
Unto our climatures and countrymen.—
But, soft, behold! lo, where it comes again!

Enter GHOST *again.*
I'll cross it, though it blast me.—Stay, illusion!
If thou hast any sound, or use of voice,
Speak to me:
If there be any good thing to be done,
That may to thee do ease, and grace to me,
Speak to me:
If thou art privy to thy country's fate,
Which, happily, foreknowing may avoid,
O, speak!
Or if thou hast uphoarded in thy life

Extorted treasure in the womb of earth,
For which, they say, you spirits oft walk in death,
                              [*Cock crows.*
Speak of it:—stay, and speak!—Stop it, Marcellus.
                    MARCELLUS.
Shall I strike at it with my partisan?
                    HORATIO.
Do, if it will not stand.
                    BERNARDO.
                         'Tis here!
                    HORATIO.
                              'Tis here!
                    MARCELLUS.
'Tis gone!   [*Exit* GHOST.
We do it wrong, being so majestical,
To offer it the show of violence;
For it is, as the air, invulnerable,
And our vain blows malicious mockery.
                    BERNARDO.
It was about to speak when the cock crew.
                    HORATIO.
And then it started like a guilty thing
Upon a fearful summons. I have heard,
The cock, that is the trumpet to the morn,
Doth with his lofty and shrill-sounding throat
Awake the god of day; and at his warning,
Whether in sea or fire, in earth or air,
Th'extravagant and erring spirit hies
To his confine: and of the truth herein
This present object made probation.
                    MARCELLUS.
It faded on the crowing of the cock.
Some say, that ever 'gainst that season comes
Wherein our Saviour's birth is celebrated,
The bird of dawning singeth all night long:
And then, they say, no spirit dare stir abroad;
The nights are wholesome; then no planets strike,
No fairy takes, nor witch hath power to charm;
So hallow'd and so gracious is the time.
                    HORATIO.
So have I heard, and do in part believe it.
But, look, the morn, in russet mantle clad,
Walks o'er the dew of yon high eastern hill:
Break we our watch up: and, by my advice,
Let us impart what we have seen to-night
Unto young Hamlet; for, upon my life,
This spirit, dumb to us, will speak to him:
Do you consent we shall acquaint him with it,
As needful in our loves, fitting our duty?
                    MARCELLUS.
Let's do't, I pray; and I this morning know
Where we shall find him most convenient.
                              [*Exeunt.*

SCENE II.

A room of state in the castle.

Enter the KING, QUEEN, HAMLET, POLONIUS,
LAERTES, VOLTIMAND, CORNELIUS, LORDS,
and ATTENDANTS.
                    KING.
THOUGH yet of Hamlet our dear brother's
    death
The memory be green; and that it us befitted
To bear our hearts in grief, and our whole king-
    dom

To be contracted in one brow of woe;
Yet so far hath discretion fought with nature,
That we with wisest sorrow think on him,
Together with remembrance of ourselves.
Therefore our sometime sister, now our queen,
Th'imperial jointress of this warlike state,
Have we, as 'twere with a defeated joy,—
With one auspicious, and one dropping eye,
With mirth in funeral, and with dirge in marriage,
In equal scale weighing delight and dole,—
Taken to wife: nor have we herein barr'd
Your better wisdoms, which have freely gone
With this affair along:—for all, our thanks.
Now follows, that you know, young Fortinbras,
Holding a weak supposal of our worth,
Or thinking by our late dear brother's death
Our state to be disjoint and out of frame,
Colleagued with the dream of his advantage,—
He hath not fail'd to pester us with message,
Importing the surrender of those lands
Lost by his father, with all bands of law,
To our most valiant brother. So much for him.—
Now for ourself, and for this time of meeting:
Thus much the business is:—we have here writ
To Norway, uncle of young Fortinbras,—
Who, impotent and bed-rid, scarcely hears
Of this his nephew's purpose,—to suppress
His further gait herein; in that the levies,
The lists, and full proportions, are all made
Out of his subject:—and we here dispatch
You, good Cornelius, and you, Voltimand,
For bearers of this greeting to old Norway;
Giving to you no further personal power
To business with the king, more than the scope
Of these delated articles allow.
Farewell; and let your haste commend your duty.
          CORNELIUS *and* VOLTIMAND.
In that and all things will we show our duty.
                    KING.
We doubt it nothing: heartily farewell.
          [*Exeunt* VOLTIMAND *and* CORNELIUS.
And now, Laertes, what's the news with you?
You told us of some suit; what is't, Laertes?
You cannot speak of reason to the Dane,
And lose your voice: what would'st thou beg,
    Laertes,
That shall not be my offer, not thy asking?
The head is not more native to the heart,
The hand more instrumental to the mouth,
Than is the throne of Denmark to thy father.
What wouldst thou have, Laertes?
                    LAERTES.
                         Dread my lord,
Your leave and favour to return to France;
From whence though willingly I came to Den-
    mark,
To show my duty in your coronation;
Yet now, I must confess, that duty done,
My thoughts and wishes bend again toward
    France,
And bow them to your gracious leave and pardon.
                    KING.
Have you your father's leave? What says Polonius?
                    POLONIUS.
He hath, my lord, wrung from me my slow leave
By laboursome petition; and, at last,

Upon his will I seal'd my hard consent:
I do beseech you, give him leave to go.
    KING.
Take thy fair hour, Laertes; time be thine,
And thy best graces spend it at thy will!—
But now, my cousin Hamlet, and my son,—
    HAMLET [aside].
A little more than kin, and less than kind.
    KING.
How is it that the clouds still hang on you?
    HAMLET.
Not so, my lord; I am too much i'th'sun.
    QUEEN.
Good Hamlet, cast thy nighted colour off,
And let thine eye look like a friend on Denmark.
Do not for ever with thy vailed lids
Seek for thy noble father in the dust:
Thou know'st 'tis common,—all that live must
    die,
Passing through nature to eternity.
    HAMLET.
Ay, madam, it is common.
    QUEEN.
    If it be,
Why seems it so particular with thee?
    HAMLET.
Seems, madam! nay, it is; I know not 'seems.'
'Tis not alone my inky cloak, good mother,
Nor customary suits of solemn black,
Nor windy suspiration of forced breath,
No, nor the fruitful river in the eye,
Nor the dejected haviour of the visage,
Together with all forms, moods, shows of grief,
That can denote me truly: these, indeed, seem,
For they are actions that a man might play:
But I have that within which passeth show;
These but the trappings and the suits of woe.
    KING.
'Tis sweet and commendable in your nature,
    Hamlet,
To give these mourning duties to your father:
But, you must know, your father lost a father;
That father lost, lost his; and the survivor bound,
In filial obligation, for some term
To do obsequious sorrow: but to persever
In obstinate condolement, is a course
Of impious stubbornness; 'tis unmanly grief:
It shows a will most incorrect to heaven;
A heart unfortified, a mind impatient;
An understanding simple and unschool'd:
For what we know must be, and is as common
As any the most vulgar thing to sense,
Why should we, in our peevish opposition,
Take it to heart? Fie! 'tis a fault to heaven,
A fault against the dead, a fault to nature,
To reason most absurd; whose common theme
Is death of fathers, and who still hath cried,
From the first corse till he that died to-day,
'This must be so.' We pray you, throw to earth
This unprevailing woe; and think of us
As of a father: for let the world take note,
You are the most immediate to our throne;
And with no less nobility of love
Than that which dearest father bears his son,
Do I impart toward you. For your intent
In going back to school in Wittenberg,

It is most retrograde to our desire:
And we beseech you, bend you to remain
Here, in the cheer and comfort of our eye,
Our chiefest courtier, cousin, and our son.
    QUEEN.
Let not thy mother lose her prayers, Hamlet:
I pray thee, stay with us; go not to Wittenberg.
    HAMLET.
I shall in all my best obey you, madam.
    KING.
Why, 'tis a loving and a fair reply:
Be as ourself in Denmark.—Madam, come;
This gentle and unforced accord of Hamlet
Sits smiling to my heart: in grace whereof,
No jocund health that Denmark drinks to-day,
But the great cannon to the clouds shall tell;
And the king's rouse the heaven shall bruit again,
Re-speaking earthly thunder. Come away.
    [Exeunt all but HAMLET.
    HAMLET.
O, that this too too solid flesh would melt,
Thaw, and resolve itself into a dew!
Or that the Everlasting had not fixt
His canon 'gainst self-slaughter! O God! God!
How weary, stale, flat, and unprofitable
Seem to me all the uses of this world!
Fie on't! O, fie! 'tis an unweeded garden,
That grows to seed; things rank and gross in
    nature
Possess it merely. That it should come to this!
But two months dead!—nay, not so much, not
    two:
So excellent a king; that was, to this,
Hyperion to a satyr: so loving to my mother,
That he might not beteem the winds of heaven
Visit her face too roughly. Heaven and earth!
Must I remember? why, she would hang on him,
As if increase of appetite had grown
By what it fed on: and yet, within a month,—
Let me not think on't,—Frailty, thy name is
    woman!—
A little month; or e'er those shoes were old
With which she follow'd my poor father's body,
Like Niobe, all tears;—why she, even she—
O God! a beast, that wants discourse of reason,
Would have mourn'd longer—married with my
    uncle,
My father's brother; but no more like my father
Than I to Hercules: within a month;
Ere yet the salt of most unrighteous tears
Had left the flushing in her galled eyes,
She married:—O, most wicked speed, to post
With such dexterity to incestuous sheets!
It is not nor it cannot come to good:
But break, my heart,—for I must hold my tongue!
Enter HORATIO, MARCELLUS, and BERNARDO.
    HORATIO.
Hail to your lordship!
    HAMLET.
    I am glad to see you well:
Horatio,—or I do forget myself.
    HORATIO.
The same, my lord, and your poor servant ever.
    HAMLET.
Sir, my good friend; I'll change that name with
    you:

And what make you from Wittenberg, Horatio?—
Marcellus?
>MARCELLUS.
My good lord,—
>HAMLET.
I am very glad to see you.—Good even, sir.—
But what, in faith, make you from Wittenberg?
>HORATIO.
A truant disposition, good my lord.
>HAMLET.
I would not hear your enemy say so;
Nor shall you do mine ear that violence
To make it truster of your own report
Against yourself: I know you are no truant.
But what is your affair in Elsinore?
We'll teach you to drink deep ere you depart.
>HORATIO.
My lord, I came to see your father's funeral.
>HAMLET.
I pray thee, do not mock me, fellow-student;
I think it was to see my mother's wedding.
>HORATIO.
Indeed, my lord, it follow'd hard upon.
>HAMLET.
Thrift, thrift, Horatio! the funeral baked meats
Did coldly furnish forth the marriage tables.
Would I had met my dearest foe in heaven
Or ever I had seen that day, Horatio!—
My father,—methinks I see my father.
>HORATIO.
O, where, my lord?
>HAMLET.
>In my mind's eye, Horatio.
>HORATIO.
I saw him once; he was a goodly king.
>HAMLET.
He was a man, take him for all in all,
I shall not look upon his like again.
>HORATIO.
My lord, I think I saw him yesternight.
>HAMLET.
Saw? who?
>HORATIO.
My lord, the king your father.
>HAMLET.
>The king my father!
>HORATIO.
Season your admiration for a while
With an attent ear; till I may deliver,
Upon the witness of these gentlemen,
This marvel to you.
>HAMLET.
>For God's love, let me hear.
>HORATIO.
Two nights together had these gentlemen,
Marcellus and Bernardo, on their watch,
In the dead vast and middle of the night,
Been thus encounter'd. A figure like your father,
Armed at point, exactly, cap-a-pe,
Appears before them, and with solemn march
Goes slowly and stately by them: thrice he walkt
By their opprest and fear-surprised eyes,
Within his truncheon's length; whilst they, dis-
    till'd
Almost to jelly with the act of fear,
Stand dumb, and speak not to him. This to me

In dreadful secrecy impart they did;
And I with them the third night kept the watch:
Where, as they had deliver'd, both in time,
Form of the thing, each word made true and good,
The apparition comes: I knew your father;
These hands are not more like.
>HAMLET.
>But where was this?
>MARCELLUS.
My lord, upon the platform where we watcht.
>HAMLET.
Did you not speak to it?
>HORATIO.
>My lord, I did;
But answer made it none: yet once methought
It lifted up its head, and did address
Itself to motion, like as it would speak:
But even then the morning cock crew loud;
And at the sound it shrunk in haste away,
And vanisht from our sight.
>HAMLET.
>'Tis very strange.
>HORATIO.
As I do live, my honour'd lord, 'tis true;
And we did think it writ down in our duty
To let you know of it.
>HAMLET.
Indeed, indeed, sirs, but this troubles me.
Hold you the watch to-night?
>MARCELLUS AND BERNARDO.
>We do, my lord.
>HAMLET.
Arm'd, say you?
>MARCELLUS AND BERNARDO.
Arm'd, my lord.
>HAMLET.
From top to toe?
>MARCELLUS AND BERNARDO.
>My lord, from head to foot.
>HAMLET.
Then saw you not his face?
>HORATIO.
O, yes, my lord; he wore his beaver up.
>HAMLET.
What, lookt he frowningly?
>HORATIO.
A countenance more in sorrow than in anger.
>HAMLET.
Pale or red?
>HORATIO.
Nay, very pale.
>HAMLET.
>And fixt his eyes upon you?
>HORATIO.
Most constantly.
>HAMLET.
>I would I had been there.
>HORATIO.
It would have much amazed you.
>HAMLET.
Very like, very like. Stay'd it long?
>HORATIO.
While one with moderate haste might tell a
    hundred.
>MARCELLUS AND BERNARDO.
Longer, longer.

HORATIO.

Not when I saw't.

HAMLET.

His beard was grizzled,—no?

HORATIO.

It was, as I have seen it in his life,
A sable silver'd.

HAMLET.

I will watch to-night;
Perchance 'twill walk again.

HORATIO.

I warrant it will.

HAMLET.

If it assume my noble father's person,
I'll speak to it, though hell itself should gape,
And bid me hold my peace. I pray you all,
If you have hitherto conceal'd this sight,
Let it be tenable in your silence still;
And whatsoever else shall hap to-night,
Give it an understanding, but no tongue:
I will requite your loves. So, fare you well:
Upon the platform, 'twixt eleven and twelve,
I'll visit you.

ALL.

Our duty to your honour.

HAMLET.

Your loves, as mine to you: farewell.
　　　　　　　　　[Exeunt all but HAMLET.
My father's spirit in arms! all is not well;
I doubt some foul play: would the night were
　　come!
Till then sit still, my soul: foul deeds will rise,
Though all the earth o'erwhelm them, to men's
　　eyes. 　　　　　　　　　　　　　[Exit.

SCENE III.

A room in POLONIUS' house.

Enter LAERTES and OPHELIA.

LAERTES.

MY necessaries are embarkt: farewell:
And, sister, as the winds give benefit,
And convoy is assistant, do not sleep,
But let me hear from you.

OPHELIA.

Do you doubt that?

LAERTES.

For Hamlet, and the trifling of his favour,
Hold it a fashion, and a toy in blood;
A violet in the youth of primy nature,
Forward, not permanent, sweet, not lasting,
The perfume and suppliance of a minute;
No more.

OPHELIA.

No more but so?

LAERTES.

Think it no more:
For nature, crescent, does not grow alone
In thews and bulk; but, as this temple waxes,
The inward service of the mind and soul
Grows wide withal. Perhaps he loves you now;
And now no soil nor cautel doth besmirch
The virtue of his will: but you must fear,
His greatness weigh'd, his will is not his own;
For he himself is subject to his birth:
He may not, as unvalued persons do,

Carve for himself; for on his choice depends
The safety and health of this whole state;
And therefore must his choice be circumscribed
Unto the voice and yielding of that body,
Whereof he is the head. Then if he says he loves
　　you,
It fits your wisdom so far to believe it,
As he in his particular act and place
May give his saying deed; which is no further
Than the main voice of Denmark goes withal.
Then weigh what loss your honour may sustain,
If with too credent ear you list his songs,
Or lose your heart; or your chaste treasure open
To his unmaster'd importunity.
Fear it, Ophelia, fear it, my dear sister;
And keep you in the rear of your affection,
Out of the shot and danger of desire.
The chariest maid is prodigal enough,
If she unmask her beauty to the moon:
Virtue itself scapes not calumnious strokes:
The canker galls the infants of the spring,
Too oft before their buttons be disclosed;
And in the morn and liquid dew of youth
Contagious blastments are most imminent.
Be wary, then; best safety lies in fear:
Youth to itself rebels, though none else near.

OPHELIA.

I shall th'effect of this good lesson keep,
As watchman to my heart. But, good my brother,
Do not, as some ungracious pastors do,
Show me the steep and thorny way to heaven;
Whilst, like a puft and reckless libertine,
Himself the primrose path of dalliance treads,
And recks not his own rede.

LAERTES.

O, fear me not.
I stay too long:—but here my father comes.
　　　　　　　　Enter POLONIUS.
A double blessing is a double grace;
Occasion smiles upon a second leave.

POLONIUS.

Yet here, Laertes! aboard, aboard, for shame!
The wind sits in the shoulder of your sail,
And you are stay'd for. There,—my blessing with
　　thee! 　　　[*Laying his hand on LAERTES' head.*
And these few precepts in thy memory
See thou character. Give thy thoughts no tongue,
Nor any unproportion'd thought his act.
Be thou familiar, but by no means vulgar.
The friends thou hast, and their adoption tried,
Grapple them to thy soul with hoops of steel;
But do not dull thy palm with entertainment
Of each new-hatcht, unfledged comrade. Beware
Of entrance to a quarrel; but being in,
Bear't, that th'opposed may beware of thee.
Give every man thine ear, but few thy voice:
Take each man's censure, but reserve thy judge-
　　ment.
Costly thy habit as thy purse can buy,
But not exprest in fancy; rich, not gaudy:
For the apparel oft proclaims the man;
And they in France of the best rank and station
Are most select and generous, chief in that.
Neither a borrower nor a lender be:
For loan oft loses both itself and friend;
And borrowing dulls the edge of husbandry.

This above all,—to thine own self be true;
And it must follow, as the night the day,
Thou canst not then be false to any man.
Farewell: my blessing season this in thee!
LAERTES.
Most humbly do I take my leave, my lord.
POLONIUS.
The time invites you; go, your servants tend.
LAERTES.
Farewell, Ophelia; and remember well
What I have said to you.
OPHELIA.
　　　　　　'Tis in my memory lockt,
And you yourself shall keep the key of it.
LAERTES.
Farewell.　　　　　　　　　　　　[Exit.
POLONIUS.
What is't, Ophelia, he hath said to you?
OPHELIA.
So please you, something touching the Lord
　Hamlet.
POLONIUS.
Marry, well bethought:
'Tis told me, he hath very oft of late
Given private time to you; and you yourself
Have of your audience been most free and boun-
　teous:
If it be so,—as so 'tis put on me,
And that in way of caution,—I must tell you,
You do not understand yourself so clearly
As it behoves my daughter and your honour.
What is between you? give me up the truth.
OPHELIA.
He hath, my lord, of late made many tenders
Of his affection to me.
POLONIUS.
Affection! pooh! you speak like a green girl,
Unsifted in such perilous circumstance.
Do you believe his tenders, as you call them?
OPHELIA.
I do not know, my lord, what I should think.
POLONIUS.
Marry, I'll teach you: think yourself a baby;
That you have ta'en these tenders for true pay,
Which are not sterling. Tender yourself more
　dearly;
Or—not to crack the wind of the poor phrase,
Running it thus—you'll tender me a fool.
OPHELIA.
My lord, he hath importuned me with love
In honourable fashion.
POLONIUS.
Ay, fashion you may call't; go to, go to.
OPHELIA.
And hath given countenance to his speech, my
　lord,
With almost all the holy vows of heaven.
POLONIUS.
Ay, springes to catch woodcocks. I do know,
When the blood burns, how prodigal the soul
Lends the tongue vows: these blazes, daughter,
Giving more light than heat,—extinct in both,
Even in their promise, as it is a-making,—
You must not take for fire. From this time
Be somewhat scanter of your maiden presence;
Set your entreatments at a higher rate

Than a command to parley. For Lord Hamlet,
Believe so much in him, that he is young;
And with a larger tether may he walk
Than may be given you: in few, Ophelia,
Do not believe his vows; for they are brokers,—
Not of that dye which their investments show,
But mere implorators of unholy suits,
Breathing like sanctified and pious bawds,
The better to beguile. This is for all,—
I would not, in plain terms, from this time forth,
Have you so slander any moment leisure
As to give words or talk with the Lord Hamlet.
Look to't, I charge you: come your ways.
OPHELIA.
I shall obey, my lord.　　　　　　[Exeunt.

SCENE IV.
The platform before the castle.
Enter HAMLET, HORATIO, and MARCELLUS.
HAMLET.
THE air bites shrewdly; it is very cold.
HORATIO.
It is a nipping and an eager air.
HAMLET.
What hour now?
HORATIO.
　　　　　I think it lacks of twelve.
MARCELLUS.
No, it is struck.
HORATIO.
Indeed? I heard it not: then it draws near the
　season
Wherein the spirit held his wont to walk.
　　　[A flourish of trumpets, and ordnance shot
　　　　off, within.
What does this mean, my lord?
HAMLET.
The king doth wake to-night, and takes his rouse,
Keeps wassail, and the swaggering up-spring
　reels;
And, as he drains his draughts of Rhenish down,
The kettle-drum and trumpet thus bray out
The triumph of his pledge.
HORATIO.
　　　　　　Is it a custom?
HAMLET.
Ay, marry, is't:
But to my mind,—though I am native here,
And to the manner born,—it is a custom
More honour'd in the breach than the observance.
This heavy-headed revel east and west
Makes us traduced and taxt of other nations:
They clepe us drunkards, and with swinish
　phrase
Soil our addition; and, indeed, it takes
From our achievements, though perform'd at
　height,
The pith and marrow of our attribute.
So, oft it chances in particular men,
That, for some vicious mole of nature in them,
As, in their birth,—wherein they are not guilty,
Since nature cannot choose his origin,—
By the o'ergrowth of some complexion,
Oft breaking down the pales and forts of reason;

Or by some habit, that too much o'er-leavens
The form of plausive manners;—that these men,—
Carrying, I say, the stamp of one defect,
Being nature's livery, or fortune's star,—
Their virtues else—be they as pure as grace,
As infinite as man may undergo—
Shall in the general censure take corruption
From that particular fault: the dram of eale
Doth all the noble substance of a doubt
To his own scandal.

HORATIO.
    Look, my lord, it comes!
Enter GHOST.

HAMLET.
Angels and ministers of grace defend us!—
Be thou a spirit of health or goblin damn'd,
Bring with thee airs from heaven or blasts from
    hell,
Be thy intents wicked or charitable,
Thou comest in such a questionable shape,
That I will speak to thee: I'll call thee Hamlet,
King, father, royal Dane: O, answer me!
Let me not burst in ignorance; but tell
Why thy canonized bones, hearsed in death,
Have burst their cerements; why the sepulchre,
Wherein we saw thee quietly inurn'd,
Hath oped his ponderous and marble jaws
To cast thee up again! What may this mean,
That thou, dead corse, again, in complete steel,
Revisit'st thus the glimpses of the moon,
Making night hideous; and we fools of nature
So horridly to shake our disposition
With thoughts beyond the reaches of our souls?
Say, why is this? wherefore? what should we do?
    [GHOST *beckons* HAMLET.

HORATIO.
It beckons you to go away with it,
As if it some impartment did desire
To you alone.

MARCELLUS.
    Look, with what courteous action
It waves you to a more removed ground:
But do not go with it.

HORATIO.
    No, by no means.

HAMLET.
It will not speak; then I will follow it.

HORATIO.
Do not, my lord.

HAMLET.
    Why, what should be the fear?
I do not set my life at a pin's fee;
And for my soul, what can it do to that,
Being a thing immortal as itself?
It waves me forth again;—I'll follow it.

HORATIO.
What if it tempt you toward the flood, my lord,
Or to the dreadful summit of the cliff
That beetles o'er his base into the sea,
And there assume some other horrible form,
Which might deprive your sovereignty of reason,
And draw you into madness? think of it:
The very place puts toys of desperation,
Without more motive, into every brain,
That looks so many fathoms to the sea,
And hears it roar beneath.

HAMLET.
    It waves me still.—
Go on; I'll follow thee.

MARCELLUS.
You shall not go, my lord.

HAMLET.
    Hold off your hands.

HORATIO.
Be ruled; you shall not go.

HAMLET.
    My fate cries out,
And makes each petty artery in this body
As hardy as the Nemean lion's nerve.—
Still am I call'd:—unhand me, gentlemen;—
By heaven, I'll make a ghost of him that lets me:—
I say, away!—Go on; I'll follow thee.
    [*Exeunt* GHOST *and* HAMLET.

HORATIO.
He waxes desperate with imagination.

MARCELLUS.
Let's follow; 'tis not fit thus to obey him.

HORATIO.
Have after.—To what issue will this come?

MARCELLUS.
Something is rotten in the state of Denmark.

HORATIO.
Heaven will direct it.

MARCELLUS.
    Nay, let's follow him.
    [*Exeunt.*

SCENE V.

Another part of the platform.

Enter GHOST *and* HAMLET.

HAMLET.
WHERE wilt thou lead me? speak; I'll go no
    further.

GHOST.
Mark me.

HAMLET.
    I will.

GHOST.
    My hour is almost come,
When I to sulphurous and tormenting flames
Must render up myself.

HAMLET.
    Alas, poor ghost!

GHOST.
Pity me not, but lend thy serious hearing
To what I shall unfold.

HAMLET.
    Speak; I am bound to hear.

GHOST.
So art thou to revenge, when thou shalt hear.

HAMLET.
What?

GHOST.
I am thy father's spirit;
Doom'd for a certain term to walk the night,
And for the day confined to fast in fires,
Till the foul crimes done in my days of nature
Are burnt and purged away. But that I am forbid
To tell the secrets of my prison-house,
I could a tale unfold, whose lightest word
Would harrow up thy soul; freeze thy young blood;

Make thy two eyes, like stars, start from their
    spheres;
Thy knotted and combined locks to part,
And each particular hair to stand an end,
Like quills upon the fretful porpentine:
But this eternal blazon must not be
To ears of flesh and blood.—List, list, O, list!—
If thou didst ever thy dear father love,—
HAMLET.
O God!
GHOST.
Revenge his foul and most unnatural murder.
HAMLET.
Murder!
GHOST.
Murder most foul, as in the best it is;
But this most foul, strange, and unnatural.
HAMLET.
Haste me to know't, that I, with wings as swift
As meditation or the thoughts of love,
May sweep to my revenge.
GHOST.
              I find thee apt;
And duller shouldst thou be than the fat weed
That roots itself in ease on Lethe wharf,
Wouldst thou not stir in this. Now, Hamlet,
    hear:
'Tis given out that, sleeping in my orchard,
A serpent stung me; so the whole ear of Denmark
Is by a forged process of my death
Rankly abused: but know, thou noble youth,
The serpent that did sting thy father's life
Now wears his crown.
HAMLET.
            O my prophetic soul!
My uncle!
GHOST.
Ay, that incestuous, that adulterate beast,
With witchcraft of his wit, with traitorous gifts,—
O wicked wit and gifts, that have the power
So to seduce!—won to his shameful lust
The will of my most seeming-virtuous queen:
O Hamlet, what a falling-off was there!
From me, whose love was of that dignity,
That it went hand in hand even with the vow
I made to her in marriage; and to decline
Upon a wretch, whose natural gifts were poor
To those of mine!
But virtue, as it never will be moved,
Though lewdness court it in a shape of heaven;
So lust, though to a radiant angel linkt,
Will sate itself in a celestial bed,
And prey on garbage.
But, soft! methinks I scent the morning air;
Brief let me be.—Sleeping within my orchard,
My custom always in the afternoon,
Upon my secure hour thy uncle stole,
With juice of cursed hebenon in a vial,
And in the porches of mine ears did pour
The leperous distilment; whose effect
Holds such an enmity with blood of man,
That, swift as quicksilver, it courses through
The natural gates and alleys of the body;
And, with a sudden vigour, it doth posset
And curd, like eager droppings into milk,
The thin and wholesome blood: so did it mine;

And a most instant tetter barkt about,
Most lazar-like, with vile and loathsome crust
All my smooth body.
Thus was I, sleeping, by a brother's hand
Of life, of crown, of queen, at once dispatcht:
Cut off even in the blossoms of my sin,
Unhousell'd, disappointed, unaneled;
No reckoning made, but sent to my account
With all my imperfections on my head:
O, horrible! O, horrible! most horrible!
If thou hast nature in thee, bear it not;
Let not the royal bed of Denmark be
A couch for luxury and damned incest.
But, howsoever thou pursuest this act,
Taint not thy mind, nor let thy soul contrive
Against thy mother aught: leave her to heaven,
And to those thorns that in her bosom lodge
To prick and sting her. Fare thee well at once!
The glow-worm shows the matin to be near,
And 'gins to pale his uneffectual fire:
Adieu, adieu, adieu! remember me.   [*Exit.*
HAMLET.
O all you host of heaven! O earth! what else?
And shall I couple hell?—O, fie!—Hold, hold, my
    heart;
And you, my sinews, grow not instant old,
But bear me stiffly up.—Remember thee!
Ay, thou poor ghost, while memory holds a seat
In this distracted globe. Remember thee!
Yea, from the table of my memory
I'll wipe away all trivial fond records,
All saws of books, all forms, all pressures past,
That youth and observation copied there;
And thy commandment all alone shall live
Within the book and volume of my brain,
Unmixt with baser matter: yes, by heaven!—
O most pernicious woman!
O villain, villain, smiling, damned villain!
My tables,—meet it is I set it down,
That one may smile, and smile, and be a villain;
At least I'm sure it may be so in Denmark:
[*Writing.*
So, uncle, there you are. Now to my word;
It is, 'Adieu, adieu! remember me:'
I have sworn't.
HORATIO [*within*].
My lord, my lord,—
MARCELLUS [*within*].
            Lord Hamlet,—
HORATIO [*within*].
                Heaven secure him!
HAMLET.
So be it!
HORATIO [*within*].
Illo, ho, ho, my lord!
HAMLET.
Hillo, ho, ho, boy! come, bird, come.
Enter HORATIO *and* MARCELLUS.
MARCELLUS.
How is't, my noble lord?
HORATIO.
            What news, my lord?
HAMLET.
O, wonderful!
HORATIO.
Good my lord, tell it.

678

HAMLET.

No; you will reveal it.

HORATIO.

Not I, my lord, by heaven.

MARCELLUS.

Nor I, my lord.

HAMLET.

How say you, then; would heart of man once
think it?—

But you'll be secret?

HORATIO and MARCELLUS.

Ay, by heaven, my lord.

HAMLET.

There's ne'er a villain dwelling in all Denmark
But he's an arrant knave.

HORATIO.

There needs no ghost, my lord, come from the
To tell us this.   [grave

HAMLET.

Why, right; you are i'th'right;
And so, without more circumstance at all,
I hold it fit that we shake hands and part:
You, as your business and desire shall point you,—
For every man hath business and desire,
Such as it is;—and for mine own poor part,
Look you, I'll go pray.

HORATIO.

These are but wild and whirling words, my lord.

HAMLET.

I'm sorry they offend you, heartily;
Yes, faith, heartily.

HORATIO.

There's no offence, my lord.

HAMLET.

Yes, by Saint Patrick, but there is, Horatio,
And much offence too. Touching this vision
here,—

It is an honest ghost, that let me tell you:
For your desire to know what is between us,
O'ermaster't as you may. And now, good friends,
As you are friends, scholars, and soldiers,
Give me one poor request.

HORATIO.

What is't, my lord? we will.

HAMLET.

Never make known what you have seen to-night.

HORATIO and MARCELLUS.

My lord, we will not.

HAMLET.

Nay, but swear't.

HORATIO.

In faith,

My lord, not I.

MARCELLUS.

Nor I, my lord, in faith.

HAMLET.

Upon my sword.

MARCELLUS.

We have sworn, my lord, already.

HAMLET.

Indeed, upon my sword, indeed.

GHOST [cries under the stage].

Swear.

HAMLET.

Ah, ha, boy! say'st thou so? art thou there, true-
penny?—

Come on,—you hear this fellow in the cellarage,—
Consent to swear.

HORATIO.

Propose the oath, my lord.

HAMLET.

Never to speak of this that you have seen,
Swear by my sword.

GHOST [beneath].

Swear.

HAMLET.

Hic et ubique? then we'll shift our ground.—
Come hither, gentlemen,
And lay your hands again upon my sword:
Never to speak of this that you have heard,
Swear by my sword.

GHOST [beneath].

Swear.

HAMLET.

Well said, old mole! canst work i'th'earth so fast?
A worthy pioneer!—Once more remove, good
friends.

HORATIO.

O day and night, but this is wondrous strange!

HAMLET.

And therefore as a stranger give it welcome.
There are more things in heaven and earth,
Horatio,
Than are dreamt of in your philosophy.
But come;—
Here, as before, never, so help you mercy,
How strange or odd soe'er I bear myself,—
As I, perchance, hereafter shall think meet
To put an antic disposition on,—
That you, at such times seeing me, never shall,
With arms encumber'd thus, or this head-shake,
Or by pronouncing of some doubtful phrase,
As 'Well, well, we know,' or 'We could, an if we
would,'
Or 'If we list to speak,' or 'There be, an if they
might,'
Or such ambiguous giving out, to note
That you know aught of me:—this not to do,
So grace and mercy at your most need help you,
Swear.

GHOST [beneath].

Swear.

HAMLET.

Rest, rest, perturbed spirit!—So, gentlemen,
With all my love I do commend me to you:
And what so poor a man as Hamlet is
May do t'express his love and friending to you,
God willing, shall not lack. Let us go in together;
And still your fingers on your lips, I pray.
The time is out of joint:—O cursed spite,
That ever I was born to set it right!—
Nay, come, let's go together.   [Exeunt.

ACT II. SCENE I.

Elsinore.   A room in POLONIUS' house.

Enter POLONIUS and REYNALDO.

POLONIUS.

GIVE him this money and these notes, Reynaldo.

REYNALDO.

I will, my lord.

POLONIUS.
You shall do marvellous wisely, good Reynaldo,
Before you visit him, to make inquiry
Of his behaviour.
REYNALDO.
My lord, I did intend it.
POLONIUS.
Marry, well said; very well said. Look you, sir,
Inquire me first what Danskers are in Paris;
And how, and who, what means, and where they
    keep,
What company, at what expense; and finding,
By this encompassment and drift of question,
That they do know my son, come you more
    nearer
Than your particular demands will touch it:
Take you, as 'twere, some distant knowledge of
    him;
As thus, 'I know his father and his friends,
And in part him;'—do you mark this, Reynaldo?
REYNALDO.
Ay, very well, my lord.
POLONIUS.
'And in part him;—but,' you may say, 'not well:
But, if't be he I mean, he's very wild;
Addicted so and so;'—and there put on him
What forgeries you please; marry, none so rank
As may dishonour him; take heed of that;
But, sir, such wanton, wild, and usual slips
As are companions noted and most known
To youth and liberty.
REYNALDO.
As gaming, my lord.
POLONIUS.
Ay, or drinking, fencing, swearing,
Quarrelling, drabbing:—you may go so far.
REYNALDO.
My lord, that would dishonour him.
POLONIUS.
Faith, no; as you may season it in the charge.
You must not put another scandal on him,
That he is open to incontinency;
That's not my meaning: but breathe his faults so
    quaintly,
That they may seem the taints of liberty;
The flash and outbreak of a fiery mind;
A savageness in unreclaimed blood,
Of general assault.
REYNALDO.
But, my good lord,—
POLONIUS.
Wherefore should you do this?
REYNALDO.
Ay, my lord,
I would know that.
POLONIUS.
Marry, sir, here's my drift;
And, I believe, it is a fetch of warrant:
You laying these slight sullies on my son,
As 'twere a thing a little soil'd i'th'working,
Mark you,
Your party in converse, him you would sound,
Having ever seen in the prenominate crimes
The youth you breathe of guilty, be assured
He closes with you in this consequence;
'Good sir,' or so; or 'friend,' or 'gentleman,'—

According to the phrase, or the addition,
Of man and country.
REYNALDO.
Very good, my lord.
POLONIUS.
And then, sir, does he this,—he does—What was
I about to say?—By the mass, I was about to say
something:—where did I leave?
REYNALDO.
At 'closes in the consequence,' at 'friend or so,'
and 'gentleman.'
POLONIUS.
At 'closes in the consequence,'—ay, marry;
He closes with you thus: 'I know the gentleman;
I saw him yesterday, or t'other day,
Or then, or then; with such, or such; and, as you
    say,
There was a' gaming; there o'ertook in's rouse;
There falling out at tennis:' or perchance,
'I saw him enter such a house of sale,'—
Videlicet, a brothel,—or so forth.—
See you now;
Your bait of falsehood takes this carp of truth:
And thus do we of wisdom and of reach,
With windlasses and with assays of bias,
By indirections find directions out:
So, by my former lecture and advice,
Shall you my son. You have me, have you not?
REYNALDO.
My lord, I have.
POLONIUS.
God be wi' ye! fare ye well.
REYNALDO.
Good my lord!
POLONIUS.
Observe his inclination in yourself.
REYNALDO.
I shall, my lord.
POLONIUS.
And let him ply his music.
REYNALDO.
Well, my lord.
POLONIUS.
Farewell!   [Exit REYNALDO.
Enter OPHELIA.
How now, Ophelia! what's the matter?
OPHELIA.
O, my lord, my lord, I have been so affrighted!
POLONIUS.
With what, i'th'name of God?
OPHELIA.
My lord, as I was sewing in my chamber,
Lord Hamlet,—with his doublet all unbraced;
No hat upon his head; his stockings foul'd,
Ungarter'd, and down-gyved to his ancle;
Pale as his shirt; his knees knocking each other;
And with a look so piteous in purport
As if he had been loosed out of hell
To speak of horrors.—he comes before me.
POLONIUS.
Mad for thy love?
OPHELIA.
My lord, I do not know;
But, truly, I do fear it.
POLONIUS.
What said he?

OPHELIA.

He took me by the wrist, and held me hard;
Then goes he to the length of all his arm;
And, with his other hand thus o'er his brow,
He falls to such perusal of my face
As he would draw it. Long stay'd he so;
At last,—a little shaking of mine arm,
And thrice his head thus waving up and down,—
He raised a sigh so piteous and profound,
That it did seem to shatter all his bulk,
And end his being: that done, he lets me go:
And, with his head over his shoulder turn'd,
He seem'd to find his way without his eyes;
For out o' doors he went without their help,
And, to the last, bended their light on me.

POLONIUS.

Come, go with me: I will go seek the king.
This is the very ecstasy of love;
Whose violent property fordoes itself,
And leads the will to desperate undertakings,
As oft as any passion under heaven
That does afflict our natures. I am sorry,—
What, have you given him any hard words of
  late?

OPHELIA.

No. my good lord; but, as you did command,
I did repel his letters, and denied
His access to me.

POLONIUS.

        That hath made him mad.—
I am sorry that with better heed and judgement
I had not quoted him: I fear'd he did but trifle,
Ar d meant to wrack thee; but, beshrew my
  jealousy!
It seems it is as proper to our age
To cast beyond ourselves in our opinions,
As it is common for the younger sort
To lack discretion. Come, go we to the king:
This must be known; which, being kept close,
  might move
More grief to hide than hate to utter love.
Come.   *[Exeunt.*

SCENE II.

A room in the castle.

Enter KING, QUEEN, ROSENCRANTZ, GUILDEN-
STERN, *and* ATTENDANTS.

KING.

WELCOME, dear Rosencrantz and Guilden-
  stern!
Moreover that we much did long to see you,
The need we have to use you did provoke
Our hasty sending. Something have you heard
Of Hamlet's transformation; so call it,
Since nor th'exterior nor the inward man
Resembles that it was. What it should be,
More than his father's death, that thus hath put
  him
So much from th'understanding of himself,
I cannot dream of: I entreat you both,
That, being of so young days brought up with
  him,
And sith so neighbour'd to his youth and haviour,
That you vouchsafe your rest here in our court
Some little time: so by your companies

To draw him on to pleasures, and to gather,
So much as from occasion you may glean,
Whether aught, to us unknown, afflicts him thus,
That, open'd, lies within our remedy.

QUEEN.

Good gentlemen, he hath much talkt of you;
And sure I am two men there are not living
To whom he more adheres. If it will please you
To show us so much gentry and good will
As to expend your time with us awhile,
For the supply and profit of our hope,
Your visitation shall receive such thanks
As fits a king's remembrance.

ROSENCRANTZ.

                 Both your majesties
Might, by the sovereign power you have of us,
Put your dread pleasures more into command
Than to entreaty.

GUILDENSTERN.

            But we both obey,
And here give up ourselves, in the full bent,
To lay our service freely at your feet,
To be commanded.

KING.

Thanks, Rosencrantz and gentle Guildenstern.

QUEEN.

Thanks, Guildenstern and gentle Rosencrantz:
And I beseech you instantly to visit
My too-much-changed son.—Go, some of you,
And bring these gentlemen where Hamlet is.

GUILDENSTERN.

Heavens make our presence and our practices
Pleasant and helpful to him!

QUEEN.

             Ay, amen!
[Exeunt ROSENCRANTZ, GUILDEN-
STERN, *and some* ATTENDANTS.
Enter POLONIUS.

POLONIUS.

Th'ambassadors from Norway, my good lord,
Are joyfully return'd.

KING.

Thou still hast been the father of good news.

POLONIUS.

Have I, my lord? Assure you, my good liege,
I hold my duty, as I hold my soul,
Both to my God and to my gracious king:
And I do think—or else this brain of mine
Hunts not the trail of policy so sure
As it hath used to do—that I have found
The very cause of Hamlet's lunacy.

KING.

O, speak of that; that do I long to hear.

POLONIUS.

Give first admittance to th'ambassadors;
My news shall be the fruit to that great feast.

KING.

Thyself do grace to them, and bring them in.
                      [Exit POLONIUS.
He tells me, my dear Gertrude, he hath found
The head and source of all your son's distemper.

QUEEN.

I doubt it is no other but the main,—
His father's death, and our o'erhasty marriage.

KING.

Well, we shall sift him.

Enter POLONIUS, *with* VOLTIMAND *and*
CORNELIUS.
　　　　　　　　Welcome, my good friends!
Say, Voltimand, what from our brother Norway?
　　　　　　VOLTIMAND.
Most fair return of greetings and desires.
Upon our first, he sent out to suppress
His nephew's levies; which to him appear'd
To be a preparation 'gainst the Polack;
But, better lookt into, he truly found
It was against your highness: whereat grieved,—
That so his sickness, age, and impotence,
Was falsely borne in hand,—sends out arrests
On Fortinbras; which he, in brief, obeys;
Receives rebuke from Norway; and, in fine,
Makes vow before his uncle never more
To give th'assay of arms against your majesty.
Whereon old Norway, overcome with joy,
Gives him three thousand crowns in annual fee;
And his commission to employ these soldiers,
So levied as before, against the Polack:
With an entreaty, herein further shown,
　　　　　　　　　　　[*Gives a paper.*
That it might please you to give quiet pass
Through your dominions for this enterprise,
On such regards of safety and allowance
As therein are set down.
　　　　　　KING.
　　　　　　　　　　It likes us well;
And at our more consider'd time we'll read,
Answer, and think upon this business.
Meantime we thank you for your well-took
　labour:
Go to your rest; at night we'll feast together:
Most welcome home!
　　　[*Exeunt* VOLTIMAND *and* CORNELIUS.
　　　　　　POLONIUS.
　　　　　　This business is well ended.—
My liege, and madam,—to expostulate
What majesty should be, what duty is,
Why day is day, night night, and time is time,
Were nothing but to waste night, day, and time.
Therefore, since brevity is the soul of wit,
And tediousness the limbs and outward flour-
　ishes,
I will be brief:—your noble son is mad:
Mad call I it; for, to define true madness,
What is't but to be nothing else but mad?
But let that go.
　　　　　　QUEEN.
　　　　More matter, with less art.
　　　　　　POLONIUS.
Madam, I swear I use no art at all.
That he is mad, 'tis true: 'tis true, 'tis pity,
And pity 'tis 'tis true· a foolish figure;
But farewell it, for I will use no art.
Mad let us grant him, then: and now remains
That we find out the cause of this effect,—
Or rather say, the cause of this defect,
For this effect defective comes by cause:
Thus it remains, and the remainder thus.
Perpend.
I have a daughter.—have whilst she is mine,—
Who, in her duty and obedience, mark,
Hath given me this: now gather, and surmise.
　　　　　　　　　　　　[*Reads.*

To the celestial and my soul's idol, the most beau-
tified Ophelia,—
That's an ill phrase, a vile phrase,—'beautified' is
a vile phrase: but you shall hear. Thus:　[*Reads.*
In her excellent white bosom, these, &c.—
　　　　　　QUEEN.
Came this from Hamlet to her?
　　　　　　POLONIUS.
Good madam, stay awhile; I will be faithful.
　　　　　　　　　　　　[*Reads.*
　　Doubt thou the stars are fire;
　　　Doubt that the sun doth move;
　　　Doubt truth to be a liar;
　　　But never doubt I love.
O dear Ophelia, I am ill at these numbers; I
have not art to reckon my groans: but that I love
thee best, O most best, believe it. Adieu.
　　Thine evermore, most dear lady, whilst
　　　this machine is to him,　　HAMLET.
This, in obedience, hath my daughter shown me:
And more above, hath his solicitings,
As they fell out by time, by means, and place,
All given to mine ear.
　　　　　　KING.
　　　　　　　But how hath she
Receiv'd his love?
　　　　　　POLONIUS.
　　　　What do you think of me?
　　　　　　KING.
As of a man faithful and honourable.
　　　　　　POLONIUS.
I would fain prove so. But what might you think,
When I had seen this hot love on the wing,—
As I perceived it, I must tell you that,
Before my daughter told me,—what might you,
Or my dear majesty your queen here, think,
If I had play'd the desk or table-book;
Or given my heart a winking, mute and dumb;
Or lookt upon this love with idle sight;—
What might you think? No, I went round to work,
And my young mistress thus I did bespeak:
'Lord Hamlet is a prince, out of thy star;
This must not be:' and then I prescripts gave her,
That she should lock herself from his resort,
Admit no messengers, receive no tokens.
Which done, she took the fruits of my advice;
And he, repulsed,—a short tale to make,—
Fell into a sadness; then into a fast;
Thence to a watch; thence into a weakness;
Thence to a lightness; and, by this declension,
Into the madness wherein now he raves,
And all we mourn for.
　　　　　　KING.
　　　　　　Do you think 'tis this?
　　　　　　QUEEN.
It may be, very like.
　　　　　　POLONIUS.
Hath there been such a time—I'ld fain know
　that—
That I have positively said ''Tis so,'
When it proved otherwise?
　　　　　　KING.
　　　　　　　Not that I know.
POLONIUS [*pointing to his head and shoulder*].
Take this from this, if this be otherwise:
If circumstances lead me, I will find

Where truth is hid, though it were hid indeed
Within the centre.

KING.
How may we try it further?

POLONIUS.
You know, sometimes he walks four hours together
Here in the lobby.

QUEEN.
So he does, indeed.

POLONIUS.
At such a time I'll loose my daughter to him:
Be you and I behind an arras then;
Mark the encounter: if he love her not,
And be not from his reason faln thereon,
Let me be no assistant for a state,
But keep a farm and carters.

KING.
We will try it.

QUEEN.
But, look, where sadly the poor wretch comes
  reading.

POLONIUS.
Away, I do beseech you, both away:
I'll board him presently:—O, give me leave.
    [*Exeunt* KING, QUEEN, *and* ATTENDANTS.
    Enter HAMLET, *reading on a book.*
How does my good Lord Hamlet?

HAMLET.
Well, God-a-mercy.

POLONIUS.
Do you know me, my lord?

HAMLET.
Excellent well; you are a fishmonger.

POLONIUS.
Not I, my lord.

HAMLET.
Then I would you were so honest a man.

POLONIUS.
Honest, my lord!

HAMLET.
Ay, sir; to be honest, as this world goes, is to be
one man pickt out of ten thousand.

POLONIUS.
That's very true, my lord.

HAMLET.
For if the sun breed maggots in a dead dog, being
a god kissing carrion,—Have you a daughter?

POLONIUS.
I have, my lord.

HAMLET.
Let her not walk i' th' sun: conception is a blessing; but not as your daughter may conceive:—
friend, look to't.

POLONIUS [*aside*].
How say you by that? Still harping on my
daughter:—yet he knew me not at first; he said I
was a fishmonger: he is far gone, far gone: and
truly in my youth I suffer'd much extremity for
love; very near this. I'll speak to him again.—
What do you read, my lord?

HAMLET.
Words, words, words.

POLONIUS.
What is the matter, my lord?

HAMLET.
Between who?

POLONIUS.
I mean, the matter that you read, my lord.

HAMLET.
Slanders, sir: for the satirical rogue says here,
that old men have gray beards; that their faces are
wrinkled; their eyes purging thick amber and
plum-tree gum; and that they have a plentiful lack
of wit, together with most weak hams: all which,
sir, though I most powerfully and potently believe, yet I hold it not honesty to have it thus set
down; for yourself, sir, shall grow old as I am, if,
like a crab, you could go backward.

POLONIUS [*aside*].
Though this be madness, yet there is method in't.
—Will you walk out of the air, my lord?

HAMLET.
Into my grave?

POLONIUS.
Indeed, that is out o' th' air.—[*aside*] How pregnant sometimes his replies are! a happiness that
often madness hits on, which reason and sanity
could not so prosperously be deliver'd of. I will
leave him, and suddenly contrive the means of
meeting between him and my daughter.—My
honourable lord, I will most humbly take my
leave of you.

HAMLET.
You cannot, sir, take from me any thing that I
will more willingly part withal.—except my life,
except my life, except my life.

POLONIUS.
Fare you well, my lord.

HAMLET.
These tedious old fools!
    Enter ROSENCRANTZ *and* GUILDENSTERN.

POLONIUS.
You go to seeek the Lord Hamlet; there he is.

ROSENCRANTZ [*to* POLONIUS].
God save you, sir!   [*Exit* POLONIUS.

GUILDENSTERN.
My honour'd lord!

ROSENCRANTZ.
My most dear lord!

HAMLET.
My excellent good friends! How dost thou, Guildenstern? Ah, Rosencrantz! Good lads, how do ye
both?

ROSENCRANTZ.
As the indifferent children of the earth.

GUILDENSTERN.
Happy, in that we are not overhappy;
On Fortune's cap we are not the very button.

HAMLET.
Nor the soles of her shoe?

ROSENCRANTZ.
Neither, my lord.

HAMLET.
Then you live about her waist, or in the middle of
her favours?

GUILDENSTERN.
Faith, her privates we.

HAMLET.
In the secret parts of Fortune? O, most true; she
is a strumpet. What's the news?

ROSENCRANTZ.
None, my lord, but that the world's grown honest.

HAMLET.

Then is doomsday near: but your news is not true. Let me question more in particular: what have you, my good friends, deserved at the hands of Fortune, that she sends you to prison hither?

GUILDENSTERN.

Prison, my lord!

HAMLET.

Denmark's a prison.

ROSENCRANTZ.

Then is the world one.

HAMLET.

A goodly one; in which there are many confines, wards, and dungeons, Denmark being one o'th' worst.

ROSENCRANTZ.

We think not so, my lord.

HAMLET.

Why, then, 'tis none to you: for there is nothing either good or bad, but thinking makes it so: to me it is a prison.

ROSENCRANTZ.

Why, then, your ambition makes it one; 'tis too narrow for your mind.

HAMLET.

O God, I could be bounded in a nut-shell, and count myself a king of infinite space, were it not that I have bad dreams.

GUILDENSTERN.

Which dreams, indeed, are ambition; for the very substance of the ambitious is merely the shadow of a dream.

HAMLET.

A dream itself is but a shadow.

ROSENCRANTZ.

Truly, and I hold ambition of so airy and light a quality, that it is but a shadow's shadow.

HAMLET.

Then are our beggars bodies, and our monarchs and outstretcht heroes the beggars' shadows. Shall we to th'court? for, by my fay, I cannot reason.

ROSENCRANTZ and GUILDENSTERN.

We'll wait upon you.

HAMLET.

No such matter: I will not sort you with the rest of my servants; for, to speak to you like an honest man, I am most dreadfully attended. But, in the beaten way of friendship, what make you at Elsinore?

ROSENCRANTZ.

To visit you, my lord; no other occasion.

HAMLET.

Beggar that I am, I am even poor in thanks; but I thank you: and sure, dear friends, my thanks are too dear a halfpenny. Were you not sent for? Is it your own inclining? Is it a free visitation? Come, deal justly with me: come, come; nay, speak.

GUILDENSTERN.

What should we say, my lord?

HAMLET.

Why, any thing—but to the purpose. You were sent for; and there is a kind of confession in your looks, which your modesties have not craft enough to colour: I know the good king and queen have sent for you.

ROSENCRANTZ.

To what end, my lord?

HAMLET.

That you must teach me. But let me conjure you, by the rights of our fellowship, by the consonancy of our youth, by the obligation of our ever-preserved love, and by what more dear a better proposer could charge you withal, be even and direct with me, whether you were sent for, or no.

ROSENCRANTZ [aside to GUILDENSTERN].

What say you?

HAMLET [aside].

Nay, then, I have an eye of you.—If you love me, hold not off.

GUILDENSTERN.

My lord, we were sent for.

HAMLET.

I will tell you why; so shall my anticipation prevent your discovery, and your secrecy to the king and queen moult no feather. I have of late—but wherefore I know not—lost all my mirth, forgone all custom of exercises; and, indeed, it goes so heavily with my disposition that this goodly frame, the earth, seems to me a sterile promontory; this most excellent canopy, the air, look you, this brave o'erhanging firmament, this majestical roof fretted with golden fire,—why, it appears no other thing to me than a foul and pestilent congregation of vapours. What a piece of work is man! how noble in reason! how infinite in faculty! in form and moving how express and admirable! in action how like an angel! in apprehension how like a god! the beauty of the world! the paragon of animals! And yet, to me, what is this quintessence of dust? man delights not me; no, nor woman neither, though by your smiling you seem to say so.

ROSENCRANTZ.

My lord, there was no such stuff in my thoughts.

HAMLET.

Why did you laugh, then, when I said 'man delights not me'?

ROSENCRANTZ.

To think, my lord, if you delight not in man, what lenten entertainment the players shall receive from you: we coted them on the way; and hither are they coming, to offer you service.

HAMLET.

He that plays the king shall be welcome,—his majesty shall have tribute of me; the adventurous knight shall use his foil and target; the lover shall not sigh gratis; the humorous man shall end his part in peace; the clown shall make those laugh whose lungs are tickle o'th'sere; and the lady shall say her mind freely, or the blank verse shall halt for't.—What players are they?

ROSENCRANTZ.

Even those you were wont to take such delight in, the tragedians of the city.

HAMLET.

How chances it they travel? their residence, both in reputation and profit, was better both ways.

ROSENCRANTZ.

I think their inhibition comes by the means of the late innovation.

HAMLET.

Do they hold the same estimation they did when I was in the city? are they so follow'd?

ROSENCRANTZ.

No, indeed, they are not.

HAMLET.

How comes it? do they grow rusty?

ROSENCRANTZ.

Nay, their endeavour keeps in the wonted pace: but there is, sir, an aery of children, little eyases, that cry out on the top of question, and are most tyrannically clapt for't: these are now the fashion; and so berattle the common stages,—so they call them,—that many wearing rapiers are afraid of goose-quills, and dare scarce come thither.

HAMLET.

What, are they children? who maintains 'em? how are they escoted? Will they pursue the quality no longer than they can sing? will they not say afterwards, if they should grow themselves to common players,—as it is most like, if their means are no better,—their writers do them wrong, to make them exclaim against their own succession?

ROSENCRANTZ.

Faith, there has been much to do on both sides; and the nation holds it no sin to tarre them to controversy; there was, for a while, no money bid for argument, unless the poet and the player went to cuffs in the question.

HAMLET.

Is't possible?

GUILDENSTERN.

O, there has been much throwing about of brains.

HAMLET.

Do the boys carry it away?

ROSENCRANTZ.

Ay, that they do, my lord; Hercules and his load too.

HAMLET.

It is not very strange; for my uncle is king of Denmark, and those that would make mows at him while my father lived, give twenty, forty, fifty, an hundred ducats a-piece for his picture in little. 'Sblood, there is something in this more than natural, if philosophy could find it out.

[Flourish of trumpets within.

GUILDENSTERN.

There are the players.

HAMLET.

Gentlemen, you are welcome to Elsinore. Your hands, come: the appurtenance of welcome is fashion and ceremony: let me comply with you in this garb; lest my extent to the players, which, I tell you, must show fairly outward, should more appear like entertainment than yours. You are welcome: but my uncle-father and aunt-mother are deceived.

GUILDENSTERN.

In what, my dear lord?

HAMLET.

I am but mad north-north-west: when the wind is southerly I know a hawk from a hand-saw.

Enter POLONIUS.

POLONIUS.

Well be with you, gentlemen!

HAMLET.

Hark you, Guildenstern;—and you too;—at each ear a hearer: that great baby you see there is not yet out of his swaddling-clouts.

ROSENCRANTZ.

Happily he's the second time come to them; for they say an old man is twice a child.

HAMLET.

I will prophesy he comes to tell me of the players; mark it.—You say right, sir: o' Monday morning; 'twas then, indeed.

POLONIUS.

My lord, I have news to tell you.

HAMLET.

My lord, I have news to tell you. When Roscius was an actor in Rome,—

POLONIUS.

The actors are come hither, my lord.

HAMLET.

Buz, buz!

POLONIUS.

Upon mine honour,—

HAMLET.

Then came each actor on his ass,—

POLONIUS.

The best actors in the world, either for tragedy, comedy, history, pastoral, pastoral-comical, historical-pastoral, tragical-historical, tragical-comical-historical-pastoral, scene individable, or poem unlimited: Seneca cannot be too heavy, nor Plautus too light. For the law of writ and the liberty, these are the only men.

HAMLET.

O Jephthah, judge of Israel, what a treasure hadst thou!

POLONIUS.

What a treasure had he, my lord?

HAMLET.

Why,

   'One fair daughter, and no more,
     The which he loved passing well.'

POLONIUS [aside].

Still on my daughter.

HAMLET.

Am I not i'th'right, old Jephthah?

POLONIUS.

If you call me Jephthah, my lord, I have a daughter that I love passing well.

HAMLET.

Nay, that follows not.

POLONIUS.

What follows, then, my lord?

HAMLET.

Why,

   'As by lot, God wot,'

and then, you know,

   'It came to pass, as most like it was,'—

the first row of the pious chanson will show you more; for look, where my abridgement comes.

Enter four or five PLAYERS.

You are welcome, masters; welcome, all; I am glad to see thee well; welcome, good friends.—O, my old friend! Why, thy face is valanced since I saw thee last; comest thou to beard me in Denmark?—What, my young lady and mistress! By'r lady, your ladyship is nearer to heaven than when

I saw you last by the altitude of a chopine. Pray God, your voice, like a piece of uncurrent gold, be not crackt within the ring.—Masters, you are all welcome. We'll e'en to't like French falconers, fly at any thing we see: we'll have a speech straight: come, give us a taste of your quality; come, a passionate speech.

FIRST PLAYER.

What speech, my good lord?

HAMLET.

I heard thee speak me a speech once,—but it was never acted; or, if it was, not above once; for the play, I remember, pleased not the million; 'twas caviare to the general: but it was—as I received it, and others, whose judgements in such matters cried in the top of mine—an excellent play, well digested in the scenes, set down with as much modesty as cunning. I remember, one said there were no sallets in the lines to make the matter savoury, nor no matter in the phrase that might indict the author of affection: but call'd it an honest method, as wholesome as sweet, and by very much more handsome than fine. One speech in it I chiefly loved: 'twas Aeneas' tale to Dido; and thereabout of it especially where he speaks of Priam's slaughter: if it live in your memory, begin at this line;—let me see, let me see;

'The rugged Pyrrhus, like th'Hyrcanian beast,'
—'tis not so:—it begins with Pyrrhus;

'The rugged Pyrrhus,—he whose sable arms,
Black as his purpose, did the night resemble
When he lay couched in the ominous horse,—
Hath now this dread and black complexion smear'd
With heraldry more dismal; head to foot
Now is he total gules; horridly trickt
With blood of fathers, mothers, daughters, sons,
Baked and impasted with the parching streets,
That lend a tyrannous and damned light
To their vile murders: roasted in wrath and fire,
And thus o'er-sized with coagulate gore,
With eyes like carbuncles, the hellish Pyrrhus
Old grandsire Priam seeks.'—

So, proceed you.

POLONIUS.

'Fore God, my lord, well spoken, with good accent and good discretion.

FIRST PLAYER.

'Anon he finds him
Striking too short at Greeks; his antique sword,
Rebellious to his arm, lies where it falls,
Repugnant to command: unequal matcht,
Pyrrhus at Priam drives; in rage strikes wide;
But with the whiff and wind of his fell sword
Th'unnerved father falls. Then senseless Ilium,
Seeming to feel this blow, with flaming top
Stoops to his base; and with a hideous crash
Takes prisoner Pyrrhus' ear: for, lo! his sword,
Which was declining on the milky head
Of reverend Priam, seem'd i'th'air to stick:
So, as a painted tyrant, Pyrrhus stood;
And, like a neutral to his will and matter,
Did nothing.
But, as we often see, against some storm,

A silence in the heavens, the rack stand still,
The bold winds speechless, and the orb below
As hush as death, anon the dreadful thunder
Doth rend the region; so, after Pyrrhus' pause,
Aroused vengeance sets him new a-work;
And never did the Cyclops' hammers fall
On Mars his armour, forged for proof eterne,
With less remorse than Pyrrhus' bleeding sword
Now falls on Priam.—
Out, out, thou strumpet, Fortune! All you gods,
In general synod, take away her power;
Break all the spokes and fellies from her wheel,
And bowl the round nave down the hill of heaven,
As low as to the fiends!'

POLONIUS.

This is too long.

HAMLET.

It shall to th'barber's, with your beard.—Prithee, say on:—he's for a jig or a tale of bawdry, or he sleeps:—say on: come to Hecuba.

FIRST PLAYER.

'But who, O, who had seen the mobled queen—'

HAMLET.

'The mobled queen'?

POLONIUS.

That's good; 'mobled queen' is good.

FIRST PLAYER.

'Run barefoot up and down, threat'ning the flames
With bisson rheum; a clout upon that head
Where late the diadem stood; and for a robe,
About her lank and all o'er-teemed loins,
A blanket, in th'alarm of fear caught up;—
Who this had seen, with tongue in venom steept,
'Gainst Fortune's state would treason have pronounced:
But if the gods themselves did see her then,
When she saw Pyrrhus make malicious sport
In mincing with his sword her husband's limbs,
The instant burst of clamour that she made—
Unless things mortal move them not at all—
Would have made milch the burning eyes of heaven,
And passion in the gods.'

POLONIUS.

Look, whe'r he has not turn'd his colour, and has tears in's eyes.—Pray you, no more.

HAMLET.

'Tis well; I'll have thee speak out the rest soon.—Good my lord, will you see the players well bestow'd? Do you hear, let them be well used; for they are the abstract and brief chronicles of the time: after your death you were better have a bad epitaph than their ill report while you live.

POLONIUS.

My lord, I will use them according to their desert.

HAMLET.

God's bodykins, man, better: use every man after his desert, and who should scape whipping? Use them after your own honour and dignity: the less they deserve, the more merit is in your bounty. Take them in.

POLONIUS.

Come, sirs.

HAMLET.

Follow him, friends: we'll hear a play to-morrow. [*Exit* POLONIUS *with all the* PLAYERS *but the First.*] Dost thou hear me, old friend; can you play the Murder of Gonzago?

FIRST PLAYER.

Ay, my lord.

HAMLET.

We'll ha't to-morrow night. You could, for a need, study a speech of some dozen or sixteen lines, which I would set down and insert in't, could you not?

FIRST PLAYER.

Ay, my lord.

HAMLET.

Very well.—Follow that lord; and look you mock him not. [*Exit* FIRST PLAYER.] My good friends, I'll leave you till night: you are welcome to Elsinore.

ROSENCRANTZ.

Good my lord!

HAMLET.

Ay, so, God be wi' ye! [*Exeunt* ROSENCRANTZ *and* GUILDENSTERN.] Now I am alone.
O, what a rogue and peasant slave am I!
Is it not monstrous, that this player here,
But in a fiction, in a dream of passion,
Could force his soul so to his own conceit,
That, from her working, all his visage wann'd;
Tears in his eyes, distraction in's aspect,
A broken voice, and his whole function suiting
With forms to his conceit? and all for nothing!
For Hecuba!
What's Hecuba to him, or he to Hecuba,
That he should weep for her? What would he do,
Had he the motive and the cue for passion
That I have? He would drown the stage with tears,
And cleave the general ear with horrid speech;
Make mad the guilty, and appal the free,
Confound the ignorant; and amaze, indeed,
The very faculties of eyes and ears.
Yet I,
A dull and muddy-mettled rascal, peak,
Like John-a-dreams, unpregnant of my cause,
And can say nothing; no, not for a king,
Upon whose property and most dear life
A damn'd defeat was made. Am I a coward?
Who calls me villain? breaks my pate across?
Plucks off my beard, and blows it in my face?
Tweaks me by th'nose? gives me the lie i'th' throat,
As deep as to the lungs? who does me this, ha?
'Swounds, I should take it: for it cannot be
But I am pigeon-liver'd, and lack gall
To make oppression bitter; or, ere this,
I should have fatted all the region kites
With this slave's offal:—bloody, bawdy villain!
Remorseless, treacherous, lecherous, kindless villain!
O, vengeance!
Why, what an ass am I! This is most brave,
That I, the son of a dear father murder'd,

Prompted to my revenge by heaven and hell,
Must, like a whore, unpack my heart with words,
And fall a-cursing, like a very drab,
A scullion!
Fie upon't! foh!—About, my brain! I have heard
That guilty creatures sitting at a play
Have by the very cunning of the scene
Been struck so to the soul, that presently
They have proclaim'd their malefactions;
For murder, though it have no tongue, will speak
With most miraculous organ. I'll have these players
Play something like the murder of my father
Before mine uncle: I'll observe his looks;
I'll tent him to the quick: if he but blench,
I know my course. The spirit that I have seen
May be the devil: and the devil hath power
T'assume a pleasing shape; yea, and perhaps
Out of my weakness and my melancholy,
As he is very potent with such spirits,
Abuses me to damn me: I'll have grounds
More relative than this:—the play's the thing
Wherein I'll catch the conscience of the king.
[*Exit.*

ACT III. SCENE I.

Elsinore.   A room in the castle.

Enter KING, QUEEN, POLONIUS, OPHELIA, ROSENCRANTZ, *and* GUILDENSTERN.

KING.

AND can you, by no drift of circumstance,
Get from him why he puts on this confusion,
Grating so harshly all his days of quiet
With turbulent and dangerous lunacy?

ROSENCRANTZ.

He does confess he feels himself distracted;
But from what cause he will by no means speak.

GUILDENSTERN.

Nor do we find him forward to be sounded;
But, with a crafty madness, keeps aloof,
When we would bring him on to some confession
Of his true state.

QUEEN.

Did he receive you well?

ROSENCRANTZ.

Most like a gentleman.

GUILDENSTERN.

But with much forcing of his disposition.

ROSENCRANTZ.

Niggard of question; but, of our demands,
Most free in his reply.

QUEEN.

Did you assay him
To any pastime?

ROSENCRANTZ.

Madam, it so fell out, that certain players
We o'er-raught on the way: of these we told him;
And there did seem in him a kind of joy
To hear of it: they are about the court;
And, as I think, they have already order
This night to play before him.

POLONIUS.

'Tis most true:
And he beseecht me to entreat your majesties
To hear and see the matter.

KING.
With all my heart; and it doth much content me
To hear him so inclined.—
Good gentlemen, give him a further edge,
And drive his purpose on to these delights.

ROSENCRANTZ.
We shall, my lord.
    [*Exeunt* ROSENCRANTZ *and* GUILDEN-
    STERN.

KING.
        Sweet Gertrude, leave us too;
For we have closely sent for Hamlet hither,
That he, as 'twere by accident, may here
Affront Ophelia;
Her father and myself—lawful espials—
Will so bestow ourselves that, seeing, unseen,
We may of their encounter frankly judge;
And gather by him, as he is behaved,
If't be th'affliction of his love or no
That thus he suffers for.

QUEEN.
        I shall obey you:—
And for your part, Ophelia, I do wish
That your good beauties be the happy cause
Of Hamlet's wildness: so shall I hope your
    virtues
Will bring him to his wonted way again,
To both your honours.

OPHELIA.
        Madam, I wish it may.
    [*Exit* QUEEN.

POLONIUS.
Ophelia, walk you here.—Gracious, so please you,
We will bestow ourselves.—[*to* OPHELIA] Read
    on this book;
That show of such an exercise may colour
Your loneliness.—We are oft to blame in this,—
'Tis too much proved,—that with devotion's
    visage
And pious action we do sugar o'er
The devil himself.

KING [*aside*].
        O, 'tis too true!
How smart a lash that speech doth give my con-
    science!
The harlot's cheek, beautied with plastering art,
Is not more ugly to the thing that helps it
Than is my deed to my most painted word:
O heavy burden!

POLONIUS.
I hear him coming: let's withdraw, my lord.
    [*Exeunt* KING *and* POLONIUS.
    Enter HAMLET.

HAMLET.
To be, or not to be,—that is the question:—
Whether 'tis nobler in the mind to suffer
The slings and arrows of outrageous fortune,
Or to take arms against a sea of troubles,
And by opposing end them?—To die,—to sleep,—
No more; and by a sleep to say we end
The heart-ache, and the thousand natural shocks
That flesh is heir to, 'tis a consummation
Devoutly to be wisht. To die,—to sleep;—
To sleep! perchance to dream: ay, there's the rub;
For in that sleep of death what dreams may come,
When we have shuffled off this mortal coil,

Must give us pause: there's the respect
That makes calamity of so long life;
For who would bear the whips and scorns of time,
The oppressor's wrong, the proud man's con-
    tumely,
The pangs of despised love, the law's delay,
The insolence of office, and the spurns
That patient merit of the unworthy takes,
When he himself might his quietus make
With a bare bodkin? who would fardels bear,
To grunt and sweat under a weary life,
But that the dread of something after death,—
The undiscover'd country, from whose bourn
No traveller returns,—puzzles the will,
And makes us rather bear those ills we have
Than fly to others that we know not of?
Thus conscience does make cowards of us all;
And thus the native hue of resolution
Is sicklied o'er with the pale cast of thought;
And enterprises of great pith and moment,
With this regard, their currents turn awry,
And lose the name of action.—Soft you now!
The fair Ophelia!—Nymph, in thy orisons
Be all my sins remember'd.

OPHELIA.
        Good my lord,
How does your honour for this many a day?

HAMLET.
I humbly thank you; well, well, well.

OPHELIA.
My lord, I have remembrances of yours,
That I have longed long to re-deliver;
I pray you, now receive them.

HAMLET.
        No, not I;
I never gave you aught.

OPHELIA.
My honour'd lord, you know right well you did;
And, with them, words of so sweet breath com-
    posed
As made the things more rich: their perfume lost,
Take these again; for to the noble mind
Rich gifts wax poor when givers prove unkind.
There, my lord.

HAMLET.
Ha, ha! are you honest?

OPHELIA.
        My lord?

HAMLET.
Are you fair?

OPHELIA.
What means your lordship?

HAMLET.
That if you be honest and fair, your honesty
should admit no discourse to your beauty.

OPHELIA.
Could beauty, my lord, have better commerce
than with honesty?

HAMLET.
Ay, truly; for the power of beauty will sooner
transform honesty from what it is to a bawd than
the force of honesty can translate beauty into his
likeness: this was sometime a paradox, but now
the time gives it proof. I did love you once.

OPHELIA.
Indeed, my lord, you made me believe so.

HAMLET.

You should not have believed me; for virtue cannot so inoculate our old stock, but we shall relish of it: I loved you not.

OPHELIA.

I was the more deceived.

HAMLET.

Get thee to a nunnery: why wouldst thou be a breeder of sinners? I am myself indifferent honest: but yet I could accuse me of such things, that it were better my mother had not borne me: I am very proud, revengeful, ambitious; with more offences at my beck than I have thoughts to put them in, imagination to give them shape, or time to act them in. What should such fellows as I do crawling between earth and heaven? We are arrant knaves, all; believe none of us. Go thy ways to a nunnery. Where's your father?

OPHELIA.

At home, my lord.

HAMLET.

Let the doors be shut upon him, that he may play the fool no where but in's own house. Farewell.

OPHELIA.

O, help him, you sweet heavens!

HAMLET.

If thou dost marry, I'll give thee this plague for thy dowry,—be thou as chaste as ice, as pure as snow, thou shalt not escape calumny. Get thee to a nunnery, go: farewell. Or, if thou wilt needs marry, marry a fool; for wise men know well enough what monsters you make of them. To a nunnery, go; and quickly too. Farewell.

OPHELIA.

O heavenly powers, restore him!

HAMLET.

I have heard of your paintings too, well enough; God has given you one face, and you make yourselves another: you jig, you amble, and you lisp, and nickname God's creatures, and make your wantonness your ignorance. Go to, I'll no more on't; it hath made me mad. I say, we will have no more marriages: those that are married already, all but one, shall live; the rest shall keep as they are. To a nunnery, go.   [Exit.

OPHELIA.

O, what a noble mind is here o'erthrown!
The courtier's, soldier's, scholar's eye, tongue, sword;
Th'expectancy and rose of the fair state,
The glass of fashion and the mould of form,
Th'observ'd of all observers,—quite, quite down!
And I, of ladies most deject and wretched,
That suckt the honey of his music vows,
Now see that noble and most sovereign reason,
Like sweet bells jangled, out of tune and harsh;
That unmatcht form and feature of blown youth
Blasted with ecstasy: O, woe is me
T'have seen what I have seen, see what I see!

Enter KING *and* POLONIUS.

KING.

Love! his affections do not that way tend;
Nor what he spake, though it lackt form a little,
Was not like madness. There's something in his soul

O'er which his melancholy sits on brood;
And I do doubt the hatch and the disclose
Will be some danger: which for to prevent,
I have in quick determination
Thus set it down:—he shall with speed to England,
For the demand of our neglected tribute:
Haply, the seas, and countries different,
With variable objects, shall expel
This something-settled matter in his heart;
Whereon his brains still beating puts him thus
From fashion of himself. What think you on't?

POLONIUS.

It shall do well: but yet do I believe
The origin and commencement of his grief
Sprung from neglected love.—How now, Ophelia!
You need not tell us what Lord Hamlet said;
We heard it all.—My lord, do as you please;
But, if you hold it fit, after the play,
Let his queen mother all alone entreat him
To show his grief: let her be round with him;
And I'll be placed, so please you, in the ear
Of all their conference. If she find him not,
To England send him; or confine him where
Your wisdom best shall think.

KING.

         It shall be so:
Madness in great ones must not unwatcht go.

     [Exeunt.

SCENE II.

A hall in the castle.

Enter HAMLET *and two or three of the*
PLAYERS.

HAMLET.

SPEAK the speech, I pray you, as I pronounced it to you, trippingly on the tongue: but if you mouth it, as many of your players do, I had as lief the town-crier spoke my lines. Nor do not saw the air too much with your hand, thus; but use all gently: for in the very torrent, tempest, and, as I may say, the whirlwind of passion, you must acquire and beget a temperance that may give it smoothness. O, it offends me to the soul to hear a robustious periwig-pated fellow tear a passion to tatters, to very rags, to split the ears of the groundlings, who, for the most part, are capable of nothing but inexplicable dumb-shows and noise: I would have such a fellow whipt for o'erdoing Termagant; it out-herods Herod: pray you, avoid it.

FIRST PLAYER.

I warrant your honour.

HAMLET.

Be not too tame neither, but let your own discretion be your tutor: suit the action to the word, the word to the action; with this special observance, that you o'erstep not the modesty of nature: for any thing so overdone is from the purpose of playing, whose end, both at the first and now, was and is, to hold, as 'twere, the mirror up to nature; to show virtue her own feature, scorn her own image, and the very age and body of the time his form and pressure. Now, this overdone, or

come tardy off, though it make the unskilful
laugh, cannot but make the judicious grieve; the
censure of the which one must, in your allowance,
o'erweigh a whole theatre of others. O, there be
players that I have seen play,—and heard others
praise, and that highly,—not to speak it pro-
fanely, that, neither having the accent of Christians, nor the gait of Christian, pagan, nor man,
have so strutted and bellow'd, that I have thought
some of nature's journeymen had made them,
and not made them well, they imitated humanity
so abominably.

FIRST PLAYER.

I hope we have reform'd that indifferently with
us, sir.

HAMLET.

O, reform it altogether. And let those that play
your clowns speak no more than is set down for
them: for there be of them that will themselves
laugh, to set on some quantity of barren spectators to laugh too; though, in the mean time, some
necessary question of the play be then to be consider'd; that's villainous, and shows a most pitiful
ambition in the fool that uses it. Go, make you
ready.   [Exeunt PLAYERS.

Enter POLONIUS, ROSENCRANTZ, and
GUILDENSTERN.

How now, my lord! will the king hear this piece
of work?

POLONIUS.

And the queen too, and that presently.

HAMLET.

Bid the players make haste.   [Exit POLONIUS.
Will you two help to hasten them?

ROSENCRANTZ and GUILDENSTERN.

We will, my lord.

[Exeunt ROSENCRANTZ and GUILDEN-
STERN.

HAMLET.

What, ho, Horatio!

Enter HORATIO.

HORATIO.

Here, sweet lord, at your service.

HAMLET.

Horatio, thou art e'en as just a man
As e'er my conversation coped withal.

HORATIO.

O, my dear lord,—

HAMLET.

                          Nay, do not think I flatter;
For what advancement may I hope from thee,
That no revenue hast, but thy good spirits,
To feed and clothe thee? Why should the poor be
    flatter'd?
No, let the candied tongue lick absurd pomp;
And crook the pregnant hinges of the knee
Where thrift may follow fawning. Dost thou
    hear?
Since my dear soul was mistress of her choice,
And could of men distinguish, her election
Hath seal'd thee for herself: for thou hast been
As one, in suffering all, that suffers nothing;
A man that fortune's buffets and rewards
Hast ta'en with equal thanks: and blest are those
Whose blood and judgement are so well com-
    mingled,

That they are not a pipe for fortune's finger
To sound what stop she please. Give me that
    man
That is not passion's slave, and I will wear him
In my heart's core, ay, in my heart of heart,
As I do thee.—Something too much of this.—
There is a play to-night before the king;
One scene of it comes near the circumstance
Which I have told thee of my father's death:
I prithee, when thou seest that act a-foot,
Even with the very comment of thy soul
Observe my uncle: if his occulted guilt
Do not itself unkennel in one speech,
It is a damned ghost that we have seen;
And my imaginations are as foul
As Vulcan's stithy. Give him heedful note:
For I mine eyes will rivet to his face;
And, after, we will both our judgements join
In censure of his seeming.

HORATIO.

                          Well, my lord:
If he steal aught the whilst this play is playing,
And scape detecting, I will pay the theft.

HAMLET.

They're coming to the play; I must be idle:
Get you a place.
Danish march. A flourish. Enter KING, QUEEN,
    POLONIUS, OPHELIA, ROSENCRANTZ,
    GUILDENSTERN, and other LORDS attendant,
    with the GUARD carrying torches.

KING.

How fares our cousin Hamlet?

HAMLET.

Excellent, i'faith; of the chameleon's dish: I eat
the air, promise-cramm'd: you cannot feed capons
so.

KING.

I have nothing with this answer, Hamlet; these
words are not mine.

HAMLET.

No, nor mine now.—[to POLONIUS] My lord,
you play'd once i' th' university, you say?

POLONIUS.

That did I, my lord; and was accounted a good
actor.

HAMLET.

And what did you enact?

POLONIUS.

I did enact Julius Cæsar: I was kill'd i'th'Capitol; Brutus kill'd me.

HAMLET.

It was a brute part of him to kill so capital a calf
there.—Be the players ready?

ROSENCRANTZ.

Ay, my lord; they stay upon your patience.

QUEEN.

Come hither, my dear Hamlet, sit by me.

HAMLET.

No, good mother; here's metal more attractive.

POLONIUS [to the KING].

O, ho! do you mark that?

HAMLET.

Lady, shall I lie in your lap?

[Lying down at OPHELIA's feet.

OPHELIA.

No, my lord.

HAMLET.
I mean, my head upon your lap?
OPHELIA.
Ay, my lord.
HAMLET.
Do you think I meant country matters?
OPHELIA.
I think nothing, my lord.
HAMLET.
That's a fair thought to lie between maids' legs.
OPHELIA.
What is, my lord?
HAMLET.
Nothing.
OPHELIA.
You are merry, my lord.
HAMLET.
Who, I?
OPHELIA.
Ay, my lord.
HAMLET.
O God, your only jig-maker. What should a man
do but be merry? for, look you, how cheerfully
my mother looks, and my father died within's
two hours.
OPHELIA.
Nay, 'tis twice two months, my lord.
HAMLET.
So long? Nay, then, let the devil wear black, for
I'll have a suit of sables. O heavens! die two
months ago, and not forgotten yet? Then there's
hope a great man's memory may outlive his life
half a year: but, by'r lady, he must build churches,
then; or else shall he suffer not thinking on, with
the hobby-horse, whose epitaph is, 'For, O, for, O,
the hobby-horse is forgot.'
    Hautboys play. The dumb-show enters.
Enter a KING *and a* QUEEN *very lovingly; the*
QUEEN *embracing him, and he her. She kneels,
and makes show of protestation unto him. He
takes her up, and declines his head upon her neck;
lays him down upon a bank of flowers: she, seeing
him asleep, leaves him. Anon comes in a fellow,
takes off his crown, kisses it, and pours poison in
the* KING'S *ears, and exit. The* QUEEN *returns;
finds the* KING *dead, and makes passionate
action. The* POISONER, *with some two or three*
MUTES, *comes in again, seeming to lament with
her. The dead body is carried away. The*
POISONER *wooes the* QUEEN *with gifts: she
seems loth and unwilling awhile, but in the end
accepts his love.*   [*Exeunt.*
OPHELIA.
What means this, my lord?
HAMLET.
Marry, this is miching mallecho; it means mis-
chief.
OPHELIA.
Belike this show imports the argument of the
play.
    Enter PROLOGUE.
HAMLET.
We shall know by this fellow: the players cannot
keep counsel: they'll tell all.
OPHELIA.
Will he tell us what this show meant?

HAMLET.
Ay, or any show that you'll show him: be not you
ashamed to show, he'll not shame to tell you what
it means.
OPHELIA.
You are naught, you are naught: I'll mark the
play.
PROLOGUE.
    For us, and for our tragedy,
    Here stooping to your clemency,
    We beg your hearing patiently.   [*Exit.*
HAMLET.
Is this a prologue, or the posy of a ring?
OPHELIA.
'Tis brief, my lord.
HAMLET.
As woman's love.
    Enter two PLAYERS, KING *and* QUEEN.
PLAYER KING.
Full thirty times hath Phœbus' cart gone round
Neptune's salt wash and Tellus' orbed ground,
And thirty dozen moons with borrow'd sheen
About the world have times twelve thirties been,
Since love our hearts, and Hymen did our hands,
Unite commutual in most sacred bands.
PLAYER QUEEN.
So many journeys may the sun and moon
Make us again count o'er ere love be done!
But, woe is me, you are so sick of late,
So far from cheer and from your former state,
That I distrust you. Yet, though I distrust,
Discomfort you, my lord, it nothing must:
For women's fear and love hold quantity;
In neither aught, or in extremity.
Now, what my love is, proof hath made you
    know;
And as my love is sized, my fear is so:
Where love is great, the littlest doubts are fear;
Where little fears grow great, great love grows
    there.
PLAYER KING.
Faith, I must leave thee, love, and shortly too;
My operant powers their functions leave to do:
And thou shalt live in this fair world behind,
Honour'd, beloved; and haply one as kind
For husband shalt thou—
PLAYER QUEEN.
            O, confound the rest!
Such love must needs be treason in my breast:
In second husband let me be accurst!
None wed the second but who kill'd the first.
HAMLET [*aside*].
Wormwood, wormwood.
PLAYER QUEEN.
The instances that second marriage move
Are base respects of thrift, but none of love:
A second time I kill my husband dead
When second husband kisses me in bed.
PLAYER KING.
I do believe you think what now you speak;
But what we do determine oft we break.
Purpose is but the slave to memory;
Of violent birth, but poor validity;
Which now, like fruit unripe, sticks on the tree;
But fall, unshaken, when they mellow be.
Most necessary 'tis that we forget

To pay ourselves what to ourselves is debt:
What to ourselves in passion we propose,
The passion ending, doth the purpose lose.
The violence of either grief or joy
Their own enactures with themselves destroy:
Where joy most revels, grief doth most lament;
Grief joys, joy grieves, on slender accident.
This world is not for aye; nor 'tis not strange
That even our loves should with our fortunes
    change;
For 'tis a question left us yet to prove,
Whether love lead fortune, or else fortune love.
The great man down, you mark his favourite flies;
The poor advanced makes friends of enemies.
And hitherto doth love on fortune tend:
For who not needs shall never lack a friend;
And who in want a hollow friend doth try,
Directly seasons him his enemy.
But, orderly to end where I begun,—
Our wills and fates do so contrary run,
That our devices still are overthrown;
Our thoughts are ours, their ends none of our
    own:
So think thou wilt no second husband wed;
But die thy thoughts when thy first lord is dead.

PLAYER QUEEN.
Nor earth to me give food, nor heaven light!
Sport and repose lock from me day and night!
To desperation turn my trust and hope!
An anchor's cheer in prison be my scope!
Each opposite that blanks the face of joy
Meet what I would have well, and it destroy!
Both here and hence pursue me lasting strife,
If, once a widow, ever I be wife!

HAMLET.
If she should break it now!

PLAYER KING.
'Tis deeply sworn. Sweet, leave me here awhile;
My spirits grow dull, and fain I would beguile
The tedious day with sleep.   [Sleeps.

PLAYER QUEEN.
    Sleep rock thy brain;
And never come mischance between us twain!
    [Exit.

HAMLET.
Madam, how like you this play?

QUEEN.
The lady doth protest too much, methinks.

HAMLET.
O, but she'll keep her word.

KING.
Have you heard the argument? Is there no offence
in't?

HAMLET.
No, no, they do but jest, poison in jest; no offence
i'th'world.

KING.
What do you call the play?

HAMLET.
The Mouse-trap. Marry, how? Tropically. This
play is the image of a murder done in Vienna:
Gonzago is the duke's name; his wife, Baptista:
you shall see anon; 'tis a knavish piece of work:
but what o'that? your majesty, and we that have
free souls, it touches us not: let the gall'd jade
wince, our withers are unwrung.

Enter PLAYER, as LUCIANUS.
This is one Lucianus, nephew to the king.

OPHELIA.
You are as good as a chorus, my lord.

HAMLET.
I could interpret between you and your love, if I
could see the puppets dallying.

OPHELIA.
You are keen, my lord, you are keen.

HAMLET.
It would cost you a groaning to take off my edge.

OPHELIA.
Still better, and worse.

HAMLET.
So you mistake your husbands.—Begin, murderer;
pox, leave thy damnable faces, and begin. Come:
—the croaking raven doth bellow for revenge.

LUCIANUS.
Thoughts black, hands apt, drugs fit, and time
    agreeing;
Confederate season, else no creature seeing;
Thou mixture rank, of midnight weeds collected,
With Hecate's ban thrice blasted, thrice infected,
Thy natural magic and dire property,
On wholesome life usurp immediately.
    [Pours the poison in his ears.

HAMLET.
He poisons him i'th'garden for's estate. His
name's Gonzago: the story is extant, and writ in
choice Italian: you shall see anon how the murderer gets the love of Gonzago's wife.

OPHELIA.
The king rises.

HAMLET.
What, frighted with false fire!

QUEEN.
How fares my lord?

POLONIUS.
Give o'er the play.

KING.
Give me some light:—away!

ALL.
Lights, lights, lights.
    [Exeunt all but HAMLET and HORATIO.

HAMLET.
Why, let the stricken deer go weep,
    The hart ungalled play;
For some must watch, while some must sleep:
    So runs the world away.—
Would not this, sir, and a forest of feathers,—if the
rest of my fortunes turn Turk with me,—with
two Provincial roses on my razed shoes, get me a
fellowship in a cry of players, sir?

HORATIO.
Half a share.

HAMLET.
A whole one, I.
    For thou dost know, O Damon dear,
    This realm dismantled was
    Of Jove himself; and now reigns here
    A very, very—pajock.

HORATIO.
You might have rimed.

HAMLET.
O good Horatio, I'll take the ghost's word for a
thousand pound. Didst perceive?

HORATIO.

Very well, my lord.

HAMLET.

Upon the talk of the poisoning,—

HORATIO.

I did very well note him.

HAMLET.

Ah, ha!—Come, some music! come, the recorders!—

For if the king like not the comedy,

Why, then, belike,—he likes it not, perdy.—

Come, some music!

Enter ROSENCRANTZ *and* GUILDENSTERN.

GUILDENSTERN.

Good my lord, vouchsafe me a word with you.

HAMLET.

Sir, a whole history.

GUILDENSTERN.

The king, sir,—

HAMLET.

Ay, sir, what of him?

GUILDENSTERN.

Is, in his retirement, marvellous distemper'd.

HAMLET.

With drink, sir?

GUILDENSTERN.

No, my lord, with choler.

HAMLET.

Your wisdom should show itself more richer to
signify this to his doctor; for, for me to put him
to his purgation would perhaps plunge him into
far more choler.

GUILDENSTERN.

Good my lord, put your discourse into some
frame, and start not so wildly from my affair.

HAMLET.

I am tame, sir:—pronounce.

GUILDENSTERN.

The queen, your mother, in most great affliction
of spirit, hath sent me to you.

HAMLET.

You are welcome.

GUILDENSTERN.

Nay, good my lord, this courtesy is not of the
right breed. If it shall please you to make me a
wholesome answer, I will do your mother's commandment: if not, your pardon and my return
shall be the end of the business.

HAMLET.

Sir, I cannot.

GUILDENSTERN.

What, my lord?

HAMLET.

Make you a wholesome answer; my wit's diseased: but, sir, such answer as I can make, you
shall command; or, rather, as you say, my mother:
therefore no more, but to the matter: my mother,
you say,—

ROSENCRANTZ.

Then thus she says; your behaviour hath struck
her into amazement and admiration.

HAMLET.

O wonderful son, that can so astonish a mother!
—But is there no sequel at the heels of this
mother's admiration? impart.

ROSENCRANTZ.

She desires to speak with you in her closet, ere you
go to bed.

HAMLET.

We shall obey, were she ten times our mother.
Have you any further trade with us?

ROSENCRANTZ.

My lord, you once did love me.

HAMLET.

And do still, by these pickers and stealers.

ROSENCRANTZ.

Good my lord, what is your cause of distemper?
you do, surely, bar the door upon your own
liberty, if you deny your griefs to your friend.

HAMLET.

Sir, I lack advancement.

ROSENCRANTZ.

How can that be, when you have the voice of the
king himself for your succession in Denmark?

HAMLET.

Ay, sir, but 'While the grass grows,'—the proverb is something musty.

Enter PLAYERS *with recorders.*

O, the recorders:—let me see one.—To withdraw
with you:—why do you go about to recover the
wind of me, as if you would drive me into a toil?

GUILDENSTERN.

O, my lord, if my duty be too bold, my love is too
unmannerly.

HAMLET.

I do not well understand that. Will you play upon
this pipe?

GUILDENSTERN.

My lord, I cannot.

HAMLET.

I pray you.

GUILDENSTERN.

Believe me, I cannot.

HAMLET.

I do beseech you.

GUILDENSTERN.

I know no touch of it, my lord.

HAMLET.

'Tis as easy as lying: govern these ventages with
your finger and thumb, give it breath with your
mouth, and it will discourse most eloquent music.
Look you, these are the stops.

GUILDENSTERN.

But these cannot I command to any utterance of
harmony; I have not the skill.

HAMLET.

Why, look you now, how unworthy a thing you
make of me! You would play upon me; you would
seem to know my stops; you would pluck out the
heart of my mystery; you would sound me from
my lowest note to the top of my compass: and
there is much music, excellent voice, in this little
organ; yet cannot you make it speak. 'Sblood, do
you think I am easier to be play'd on than a pipe?
Call me what instrument you will, though you can
fret me, you cannot play upon me.

Enter POLONIUS.

God bless you, sir!

POLONIUS.

My lord, the queen would speak with you, and
presently.

HAMLET.
Do you see yonder cloud that's almost in shape of
a camel?

POLONIUS.
By th'mass, and 'tis like a camel, indeed.

HAMLET.
Methinks it is like a weasel.

POLONIUS.
It is backt like a weasel.

HAMLET.
Or like a whale?

POLONIUS.
Very like a whale.

HAMLET.
Then will I come to my mother by and by.—They
fool me to the top of my bent.—I will come by
and by.

POLONIUS.
I will say so.

HAMLET.
By and by is easily said. [*Exit* POLONIUS.]—
Leave me, friends.
     [*Exeunt* ROSENCRANTZ, GUILDENSTERN,
       HORATIO, *and* PLAYERS.
'Tis now the very witching time of night,
When churchyards yawn, and hell itself breathes
    out
Contagion to this world: now could I drink hot
    blood,
And do such bitter business as the day
Would quake to look on. Soft! now to my
    mother.—
    heart, lose not thy nature; let not ever
The soul of Nero enter this firm bosom:
Let me be cruel, not unnatural:
I will speak daggers to her, but use none;
My tongue and soul in this be hypocrites,—
How in my words soever she be shent,
To give them seals never, my soul, consent! [*Exit.*

SCENE III.

A room in the castle.

Enter KING, ROSENCRANTZ, *and*
GUILDENSTERN.

KING.
I LIKE him not; nor stands it safe with us
To let his madness range. Therefore prepare
    you;
I your commission will forthwith dispatch,
And he to England shall along with you:
The terms of our estate may not endure
Hazard so dangerous as doth hourly grow
Out of his lunacies.

GUILDENSTERN.
       We will ourselves provide:
Most holy and religious fear it is
To keep those many many bodies safe
That live and feed upon your majesty.

ROSENCRANTZ.
The single and peculiar life is bound,
With all the strength and armour of the mind,
To keep itself from noyance; but much more
That spirit upon whose weal depends and rests
The lives of many. The cease of majesty

Dies not alone; but, like a gulf, doth draw
What's near it with it: 'tis a massy wheel,
Fixt on the summit of the highest mount,
To whose huge spokes ten thousand lesser things
Are mortised and adjoin'd; which, when it falls,
Each small annexment, petty consequence,
Attends the boisterous ruin. Ne'er alone
Did the king sigh, but with a general groan.

KING.
Arm you, I pray you, to this speedy voyage;
For we will fetters put upon this fear,
Which now goes too free-footed.

ROSENCRANTZ *and* GUILDENSTERN.
       We will haste us.
    [*Exeunt* ROSENCRANTZ *and* GUILDENSTERN.
       Enter POLONIUS.

POLONIUS.
My lord, he's going to his mother's closet:
Behind the arras I'll convey myself,
To hear the process; I'll warrant she'll tax him
    home:
And, as you said, and wisely was it said,
'Tis meet that some more audience than a
    mother,
Since nature makes them partial, should o'erhear
The speech, of vantage. Fare you well, my liege:
I'll call upon you ere you go to bed,
And tell you what I know.

KING.
       Thanks, dear my lord.
       [*Exit* POLONIUS.
O, my offence is rank, it smells to heaven;
It hath the primal eldest curse upon't,—
A brother's murder!—Pray can I not,
Though inclination be as sharp as will:
My stronger guilt defeats my strong intent;
And, like a man to double business bound,
I stand in pause where I shall first begin,
And both neglect. What if this cursed hand
Were thicker than itself with brother's blood,
Is there not rain enough in the sweet heavens
To wash it white as snow? Whereto serves mercy
But to confront the visage of offence?
And what's in prayer but this twofold force,—
To be forestalled ere we come to fall,
Or pardon'd being down? Then I'll look up;
My fault is past. But, O, what form of prayer
Can serve my turn? 'Forgive me my foul
    murder'?—
That cannot be; since I am still possest
Of those effects for which I did the murder,—
My crown, mine own ambition, and my queen.
May one be pardon'd, and retain th'offence?
In the corrupted currents of this world
Offence's gilded hand may shove by justice;
And oft 'tis seen the wicked prize itself
Buys out the law: but 'tis not so above;
There is no shuffling,—there the action lies
In his true nature; and we ourselves compell'd,
Even to the teeth and forehead of our faults,
To give in evidence. What then? what rests?
Try what repentance can: what can it not?
Yet what can it when one can not repent?
O wretched state! O bosom black as death!
O limed soul, that, struggling to be free,
Art more engaged! Help, angels! Make assay:

Bow, stubborn knees; and, heart with strings of
  steel,
Be soft as sinews of the new-born babe!
All may be well.   [*Retires and kneels.*
      Enter HAMLET.
      HAMLET.
Now might I do it pat, now he is praying;
And now I'll do't:—and so he goes to heaven;
And so am I revenged:—that would be scann'd:
A villain kills my father; and, for that,
I, his sole son, do this same villain send
To heaven.
O, this is hire and salary, not revenge.
He took my father grossly, full of bread;
With all his crimes broad blown, as flush as May;
And how his audit stands who knows save
  heaven?
But, in our circumstance and course of thought,
'Tis heavy with him: and am I, then, revenged,
To take him in the purging of his soul,
When he is fit and season'd for his passage?
No.
Up, sword; and know thou a more horrid hent:
When he is drunk, asleep, or in his rage;
Or in th'incestuous pleasure of his bed;
At gaming, swearing; or about some act
That has no relish of salvation in't;—
Then trip him, that his heels may kick at heaven;
And that his soul may be as damn'd and black
As hell, whereto it goes. My mother stays:
This physic but prolongs thy sickly days.   [*Exit.*
      KING [*rising*].
My words fly up, my thoughts remain below:
Words without thoughts never to heaven go.
                                          [*Exit.*

      SCENE IV.
      The Queen's closet.
      Enter QUEEN *and* POLONIUS.
      POLONIUS.
HE will come straight. Look you lay home to
  him:
Tell him his pranks have been too broad to bear
  with,
And that your Grace hath screen'd and stood
  between
Much heat and him. I'll sconce me even here.
Pray you, be round with him.
      HAMLET [*within*].
Mother, mother, mother!
      QUEEN.
I'll warrant you; fear me not:—withdraw,
I hear him coming.
      [POLONIUS *goes behind the arras.*
      Enter HAMLET.
      HAMLET.
Now, mother, what's the matter?
      QUEEN.
Hamlet, thou hast thy father much offended.
      HAMLET.
Mother, you have my father much offended.
      QUEEN.
Come, come, you answer with an idle tongue.
      HAMLET.
Go, go, you question with a wicked tongue.

      QUEEN.
Why, how now, Hamlet!
      HAMLET.
            What's the matter now?
      QUEEN.
Have you forgot me?
      HAMLET.
            No, by the rood, not so:
You are the queen, your husband's brother's wife;
And—would it were not so!—you are my mother.
      QUEEN.
Nay, then, I'll set those to you that can speak.
      HAMLET.
Come, come, and sit you down; you shall not
  budge;
You go not till I set you up a glass
Where you may see the inmost part of you.
      QUEEN.
What wilt thou do? thou wilt not murder me?—
Help, help, ho!
      POLONIUS [*behind*].
What, ho! help, help, help!
      HAMLET [*drawing*].
How now! a rat? Dead for a ducat, dead!
            [*Makes a pass through the arras.*
      POLONIUS [*behind*].
O, I am slain!   [*Falls and dies.*
      QUEEN.
O me, what hast thou done?
      HAMLET.
Nay, I know not: is it the king?
      QUEEN.
O, what a rash and bloody deed is this!
      HAMLET.
A bloody deed!—almost as bad, good mother,
As kill a king, and marry with his brother.
      QUEEN.
As kill a king!
      HAMLET.
            Ay, lady, 'twas my word.—
            [*Lifts up the arras, and sees* POLONIUS.
Thou wretched, rash, intruding fool, farewell!
I took thee for thy better: take thy fortune;
Thou find'st to be too busy is some danger.—
Leave wringing of your hands: peace; sit you
  down,
And let me wring your heart: for so I shall,
If it be made of penetrable stuff;
If damned custom have not brazed it so,
That it is proof and bulwark against sense.
      QUEEN.
What have I done, that thou darest wag thy tongue
In noise so rude against me?
      HAMLET.
            Such an act
That blurs the grace and blush of modesty;
Calls virtue hypocrite; takes off the rose
From the fair forehead of an innocent love,
And sets a blister there; makes marriage-vows
As false as dicers' oaths: O, such a deed
As from the body of contraction plucks
The very soul; and sweet religion makes
A rhapsody of words: heaven's face doth glow;
Yea, this solidity and compound mass,
With tristful visage, as against the doom,
Is thought-sick at the act.

QUEEN.
　　　　　　　　Ay me, what act,
That roars so loud, and thunders in the index?
HAMLET.
Look here, upon this picture, and on this,
The counterfeit presentment of two brothers.
See, what a grace was seated on this brow;
Hyperion's curls; the front of Jove himself;
An eye like Mars, to threaten and command;
A station like the herald Mercury
New-lighted on a heaven-kissing hill;
A combination and a form indeed,
Where every god did seem to set his seal,
To give the world assurance of a man:
This was your husband.—Look you now, what
　　follows:
Here is your husband; like a mildew'd ear,
Blasting his wholesome brother. Have you eyes?
Could you on this fair mountain leave to feed,
And batten on this moor? Ha! have you eyes?
You cannot call it love; for at your age
The hey-day in the blood is tame, it's humble,
And waits upon the judgement: and what judge-
　　ment
Would step from this to this? Sense, sure, you have,
Else could you not have motion: but, sure, that
　　sense
Is apoplext: for madness would not err;
Nor sense to ecstasy was ne'er so thrall'd
But it reserved some quantity of choice,
To serve in such a difference. What devil was't
That thus hath cozen'd you at hoodman-blind?
Eyes without feeling, feeling without sight,
Ears without hands or eyes, smelling sans all,
Or but a sickly part of one true sense
Could not so mope.
O shame! where is thy blush? Rebellious hell,
If thou canst mutine in a matron's bones,
To flaming youth let virtue be as wax,
And melt in her own fire: proclaim no shame
When the compulsive ardour gives the charge,
Since frost itself as actively doth burn,
And reason pandars will.
QUEEN.
　　　　　　O Hamlet, speak no more:
Thou turn'st mine eyes into my very soul;
And there I see such black and grained spots
As will not leave their tinct.
HAMLET.
　　　　　　　Nay, but to live
In the rank sweat of an enseamed bed,
Stew'd in corruption, honeying and making love
Over the nasty sty,—
QUEEN.
　　　　　O, speak to me no more;
These words, like daggers, enter in mine ears;
No more, sweet Hamlet!
HAMLET.
　　　　　　A murderer and a villain;
A slave that is not twentieth part the tithe
Of your precedent lord; a vice of kings;
A cutpurse of the empire and the rule,
That from a shelf the precious diadem stole,
And put it in his pocket!
QUEEN.
　　　　　No more!

HAMLET.
A king of shreds and patches,—
　　　　　　　Enter GHOST.
Save me, and hover o'er me with your wings,
You heavenly guards!—What would your graci-
　　ous figure?
QUEEN.
Alas, he's mad!
HAMLET.
Do you not come your tardy son to chide,
That, lapsed in time and passion, lets go by
Th'important acting of your dread command?
O, say!
GHOST.
Do not forget: this visitation
Is but to whet thy almost blunted purpose.
But, look, amazement on thy mother sits:
O, step between her and her fighting soul,—
Conceit in weakest bodies strongest works,—
Speak to her, Hamlet.
HAMLET.
　　　　　　How is it with you, lady?
QUEEN.
Alas, how is't with you,
That you do bend your eye on vacancy,
And with th'incorporal air do hold discourse?
Forth at your eyes your spirits wildly peep;
And, as the sleeping soldiers in th'alarm,
Your bedded hair, like life in excrements,
Start up, and stand an end. O gentle son,
Upon the heat and flame of thy distemper
Sprinkle cool patience. Whereon do you look?
HAMLET.
On him, on him! Look you, how pale he glares!
His form and cause conjoin'd, preaching to stones,
Would make them capable.—Do not look upon me;
Lest with this piteous action you convert
My stern effects: then what I have to do
Will want true colour; tears perchance for blood.
QUEEN.
To whom do you speak this?
HAMLET.
　　　　　　Do you see nothing there?
QUEEN.
Nothing at all; yet all that is I see.
HAMLET.
Nor did you nothing hear?
QUEEN.
　　　　　No, nothing but ourselves.
HAMLET.
Why, look you there! look, how it steals away!
My father, in his habit as he lived!
Look, where he goes, even now, out at the portal!
　　　　　　　　　　　　[*Exit* GHOST.
QUEEN.
This is the very coinage of your brain:
This bodiless creation ecstasy
Is very cunning in.
HAMLET.
　　　　Ecstasy!
My pulse, as yours, doth temperately keep time,
And makes as healthful music: it is not madness
That I have utter'd: bring me to the test,
And I the matter will re-word; which madness
Would gambol from. Mother, for love of grace,
Lay not that flattering unction to your soul,

That not your trespass, but my madness speaks:
It will but skin and film the ulcerous place,
Whilst rank corruption, mining all within,
Infects unseen. Confess yourself to heaven;
Repent what's past; avoid what is to come;
And do not spread the compost on the weeds,
To make them ranker. Forgive me this my virtue;
For in the fatness of these pursy times
Virtue itself of vice must pardon beg,
Yea, curb and woo for leave to do him good.

QUEEN.

O Hamlet, thou hast cleft my heart in twain.

HAMLET.

O, throw away the worser part of it,
And live the purer with the other half.
Good night: but go not to my uncle's bed;
Assume a virtue, if you have it not.
That monster, custom, who all sense doth eat,
Of habits devil, is angel yet in this,
That to the use of actions fair and good
He likewise gives a frock or livery,
That aptly is put on. Refrain to-night;
And that shall lend a kind of easiness
To the next abstinence: the next more easy;
For use almost can change the stamp of nature,
And either master the devil, or throw him out
With wondrous potency. Once more, good night:
And when you are desirous to be blest,
I'll blessing beg of you.—For this same lord,
                    [*Pointing to* POLONIUS.
I do repent: but heaven hath pleased it so,
To punish me with this, and this with me,
That I must be their scourge and minister.
I will bestow him, and will answer well
The death I gave him. So, again, good night.—
I must be cruel, only to be kind:
Thus bad begins, and worse remains behind.—
One word more, good lady.

QUEEN.

                    What shall I do?

HAMLET.

Not this, by no means, that I bid you do:
Let the bloat king tempt you again to bed;
Pinch wanton on your cheek; call you his mouse;
And let him, for a pair of reechy kisses,
Or paddling in your neck with his damn'd fingers,
Make you to ravel all this matter out,
That I essentially am not in madness,
But mad in craft. 'Twere good you let him know;
For who, that's but a queen, fair, sober, wise,
Would from a paddock, from a bat, a gib,
Such dear concernings hide? who would do so?
No, in despite of sense and secrecy,
Unpeg the basket on the house's top,
Let the birds fly, and, like the famous ape,
To try conclusions, in the basket creep,
And break your own neck down.

QUEEN.

Be thou assured, if words be made of breath
And breath of life, I have no life to breathe
What thou hast said to me.

HAMLET.

I must to England; you know that?

QUEEN.

                    Alack,
I had forgot: 'tis so concluded on.

HAMLET.

There's letters seal'd: and my two school-
    fellows,—
Whom I will trust as I will adders fang'd,—
They bear the mandate; they must sweep my way,
And marshal me to knavery. Let it work;
For 'tis the sport to have the enginer
Hoist with his own petar: and 't shall go hard
But I will delve one yard below their mines,
And blow them at the moon: O, 'tis most sweet
When in one line two crafts directly meet.—
This man shall set me packing:
I'll lug the guts into the neighbour room.—
Mother, good night.—Indeed, this counsellor
Is now most still, most secret, and most grave,
Who was in life a foolish prating knave.
Come, sir, to draw toward an end with you.—
Good night, mother.

        [*Exeunt severally;* HAMLET *tugging in*
        POLONIUS.

ACT IV. SCENE I.

A room in the castle.

Enter KING, QUEEN, ROSENCRANTZ, *and*
    and GUILDENSTERN.

KING.

THERE'S matter in these sighs, these pro-
    found heaves:
You must translate: 'tis fit we understand them.
Where is your son?

QUEEN.

Bestow this place on us a little while.

    [*Exeunt* ROSENCRANTZ *and* GUILDENSTERN.

Ah, my good lord, what have I seen to-night!

KING.

What, Gertrude? How does Hamlet?

QUEEN.

Mad as the sea and wind, when both contend
Which is the mightier: in his lawless fit,
Behind the arras hearing something stir,
Whips out his rapier, cries 'A rat, a rat!'
And, in this brainish apprehension, kills
The unseen good old man.

KING.

                    O heavy deed!
It had been so with us, had we been there:
His liberty is full of threats to all;
To you yourself, to us, to every one.
Alas, how shall this bloody deed be answer'd?
It will be laid to us, whose providence
Should have kept short, restrain'd, and out of
    haunt
This mad young man: but so much was our love,
We would not understand what was most fit;
But, like the owner of a foul disease,
To keep it from divulging, let it feed
Even on the pith of life. Where is he gone?

QUEEN.

To draw apart the body he hath kill'd:
O'er whom his very madness, like some ore
Among a mineral of metals base,
Shows itself pure; he weeps for what is done.

KING.

O Gertrude, come away!
The sun no sooner shall the mountains touch,

But we will ship him hence: and this vile deed
We must, with all our majesty and skill,
Both countenance and excuse.—Ho, Guilden-
    stern!
    Enter ROSENCRANTZ *and* GUILDENSTERN.
Friends both, go join you with some further aid:
Hamlet in madness hath Polonius slain,
And from his mother's closet hath he dragg'd him:
Go seek him out; speak fair, and bring the body
Into the chapel. I pray you, haste in this.
    [*Exeunt* ROSENCRANTZ *and* GUILDEN-
        STERN.
Come, Gertrude, we'll call up our wisest friends;
And let them know both what we mean to do,
And what's untimely done: so, haply, slander—
Whose whisper o'er the world's diameter,
As level as the cannon to his blank,
Transports his poison'd shot—may miss our
    name,
And hit the woundless air.—O, come away!
My soul is full of discord and dismay.   [*Exeunt.*

SCENE II.

Another room in the castle.

Enter HAMLET.

HAMLET.

SAFELY stow'd.
    ROSENCRANTZ *and* GUILDENSTERN
        [*within*].
Hamlet! Lord Hamlet!
    HAMLET.
What noise? who calls on Hamlet? O, here they
come.
    Enter ROSENCRANTZ *and* GUILDENSTERN.
    ROSENCRANTZ.
What have you done, my lord, with the dead
    body?
    HAMLET.
Compounded it with dust, whereto 'tis kin.
    ROSENCRANTZ.
Tell us where 'tis; that we may take it thence,
And bear it to the chapel.
    HAMLET.
Do not believe it.
    ROSENCRANTZ.
Believe what?
    HAMLET.
That I can keep your counsel, and not mine own.
Besides, to be demanded of a sponge!—what rep-
lication should be made by the son of a king?
    ROSENCRANTZ.
Take you me for a sponge, my lord?
    HAMLET.
Ay, sir; that soaks up the king's countenance, his
rewards, his authorities. But such officers do the
king best service in the end: he keeps them, like
an ape, in the corner of his jaw; first mouth'd, to
be last swallow'd: when he needs what you have
glean'd, it is but squeezing you, and, sponge, you
shall be dry again.
    ROSENCRANTZ.
I understand you not, my lord.
    HAMLET.
I am glad of it: a knavish speech sleeps in a foolish
ear.

    ROSENCRANTZ.
My lord, you must tell us where the body is, and
go with us to the king.
    HAMLET.
The body is with the king, but the king is not with
the body. The king is a thing—
    GUILDENSTERN.
A thing, my lord?
    HAMLET.
Of nothing: bring me to him. Hide fox, and all
after.   [*Exeunt.*

SCENE III.

Another room in the castle.

Enter KING, *attended.*

KING.

I HAVE sent to seek him, and to find the body.
  How dangerous is it that this man goes loose!
Yet must not we put the strong law on him:
He's loved of the distracted multitude,
Who like not in their judgement, but their eyes;
And where 'tis so, th'offender's scourge is
    weigh'd,
But never the offence. To bear all smooth and
    even,
This sudden sending him away must seem
Deliberate pause: diseases desperate grown
By desperate appliance are relieved,
Or not at all.
    Enter ROSENCRANTZ.
    How now! what hath befaln?
    ROSENCRANTZ.
Where the dead body is bestow'd, my lord,
We cannot get from him.
    KING.
        But where is he?
    ROSENCRANTZ.
Without, my lord; guarded, to know your
    pleasure.
    KING.
Bring him before us.
    ROSENCRANTZ.
Ho, Guildenstern! bring in my lord.
    Enter HAMLET *and* GUILDENSTERN.
    KING.
Now, Hamlet, where's Polonius?
    HAMLET.
At supper.
    KING.
At supper! where?
    HAMLET.
Not where he eats, but where he is eaten: a certain
convocation of politic worms are e'en at him.
Your worm is your only emperor for diet: we fat
all creatures else to fat us, and we fat ourselves for
maggots: your fat king and your lean beggar is but
variable service,—two dishes, but to one table:
that's the end.
    KING.
Alas, alas!
    HAMLET.
A man may fish with the worm that hath eat of a
king, and eat of the fish that hath fed of that worm.
    KING.
What dost thou mean by this?

HAMLET.

Nothing but to show you how a king may go a progress through the guts of a beggar.

KING.

Where is Polonius?

HAMLET.

In heaven; send thither to see: if your messenger find him not there, seek him i'th'other place yourself. But, indeed, if you find him not within this month, you shall nose him as you go up the stairs into the lobby.

KING.

Go seek him there.   [*To some* ATTENDANTS.

HAMLET.

He will stay till ye come. [*Exeunt* ATTENDANTS.

KING.

Hamlet, this deed, for thine especial safety,—
Which we do tender, as we dearly grieve   [hence
For that which thou hast done,—must send thee
With fiery quickness: therefore prepare thyself;
The bark is ready, and the wind at help,
Th'associates tend, and every thing is bent
For England.

HAMLET.

For England!

KING.

Ay, Hamlet.

HAMLET.

Good.

KING.

So is it, if thou knew'st our purposes.

HAMLET.

I see a cherub that sees them.—But, come; for England!—Farewell, dear mother.

KING.

Thy loving father, Hamlet.

HAMLET.

My mother: father and mother is man and wife;
man and wife is one flesh; and so, my mother.—
Come, for England!   [*Exit.*

KING.

Follow him at foot; tempt him with speed aboard;
Delay it not; I'll have him hence to-night:
Away! for every thing is seal'd and done
That else leans on th'affair: pray you, make haste.
   [*Exeunt* ROSENCRANTZ *and* GUILDENSTERN.
And, England, if my love thou hold'st at aught,—
As my great power thereof may give thee sense,
Since yet thy cicatrice looks raw and red
After the Danish sword, and thy free awe
Pays homage to us,—thou mayst not coldly set
Our sovereign process; which imports at full,
By letters conjuring to that effect,
The present death of Hamlet. Do it, England;
For like the hectic in my blood he rages,
And thou must cure me: till I know 'tis done,
Howe'er my haps, my joys were ne'er begun.
                [*Exit.*

SCENE IV.

A plain in Denmark.

Enter FORTINBRAS *with his* ARMY *over the stage.*

FORTINBRAS.

GO, captain, from me greet the Danish king;
Tell him that, by his license, Fortinbras
Claims the conveyance of a promised march

Over his kingdom. You know the rendezvous.
If that his majesty would aught with us,
We shall express our duty in his eye;
And let him know so.

CAPTAIN.

I will do't, my lord.

FORTINBRAS.

Go softly on.   [*Exeunt all but* CAPTAIN.
Enter HAMLET, ROSENCRANTZ, GUILDEN-
STERN, *and others.*

HAMLET.

Good sir, whose powers are these?

CAPTAIN.

They are of Norway, sir.

HAMLET.

How purposed, sir, I pray you?

CAPTAIN.

Against some part of Poland.

HAMLET.

Who commands them, sir?

CAPTAIN.

The nephew to old Norway, Fortinbras.

HAMLET.

Goes it against the main of Poland, sir,
Or for some frontier?

CAPTAIN.

Truly to speak, sir, and with no addition,
We go to gain a little patch of ground
That hath in it no profit but the name.
To pay five ducats, five, I would not farm it;
Nor will it yield to Norway or the Pole
A ranker rate, should it be sold in fee.

HAMLET.

Why, then, the Polack never will defend it.

CAPTAIN.

Yes, it is already garrison'd.

HAMLET.

Two thousand souls and twenty thousand ducats
Will not debate the question of this straw:
This is th'imposthume of much wealth and peace,
That inward breaks, and shows no cause without
Why the man dies.—I humbly thank you, sir.

CAPTAIN.

God be wi' you, sir.   [*Exit.*

ROSENCRANTZ.

Will't please you go, my lord?

HAMLET.

I'll be with you straight. Go a little before.
            [*Exeunt all but* HAMLET
How all occasions do inform against me,
And spur my dull revenge! What is a man,
If his chief good and market of his time
Be but to sleep and feed? a beast, no more.
Sure, he that made us with such large discourse,
Looking before and after, gave us not
That capability and godlike reason
To fust in us unused. Now, whether it be
Bestial oblivion, or some craven scruple
Of thinking too precisely on th'event,—
A thought which, quarter'd, hath but one part wisdom
And ever three parts coward,—I do not know
Why yet I live to say 'This thing's to do;'
Sith I have cause, and will, and strength, and means
To do't. Examples, gross as earth, exhort me:

Witness this army, of such mass and charge,
Led by a delicate and tender prince;
Whose spirit, with divine ambition puft,
Makes mouths at the invisible event;
Exposing what is mortal and unsure
To all that fortune, death, and danger dare,
Even for an egg-shell. Rightly to be great
Is not to stir without great argument,
But greatly to find quarrel in a straw
When honour's at the stake. How stand I, then,
That have a father kill'd, a mother stain'd,
Excitements of my reason and my blood,
And let all sleep? while, to my shame, I see
The imminent death of twenty thousand men,
That for a fantasy and trick of fame
Go to their graves like beds; fight for a plot
Whereon the numbers cannot try the cause,
Which is not tomb enough and continent
To hide the slain?—O, from this time forth,
My thoughts be bloody, or be nothing worth!
                              [*Exit.*

SCENE V.

Elsinore. A room in the castle.

Enter QUEEN *and* HORATIO.

QUEEN.
I WILL not speak with her.
              HORATIO.
She is importunate, indeed distract;
Her mood will needs be pitied.
              QUEEN.
                What would she have?
              HORATIO.
She speaks much of her father; says she hears
There's tricks i'th'world; and hems, and beats her
    heart;
Spurns enviously at straws; speaks things in doubt,
That carry but half sense: her speech is nothing,
Yet the unshaped use of it doth move
The hearers to collection; they aim at it,
And botch the words up fit to their own thoughts;
Which, as her winks and nods and gestures yield
    them,
Indeed would make one think there might be
    thought,
Though nothing sure, yet much unhappily.
'Twere good she were spoken with; for she may
    strew
Dangerous conjectures in ill-breeding minds.
              QUEEN.
Let her come in.   [*Exit* HORATIO.
To my sick soul, as sin's true nature is,
Each toy seems prologue to some great amiss:
So full of artless jealousy is guilt,
It spills itself in fearing to be spilt.
     Enter HORATIO, *with* OPHELIA *distracted.*
              OPHELIA.
Where is the beauteous majesty of Denmark?
              QUEEN.
How now, Ophelia!
             OPHELIA [*sings*].
How should I your true-love know
      From another one?
By his cockle hat and staff,
      And his sandal shoon.

              QUEEN.
Alas, sweet lady, what imports this song?
             OPHELIA.
Say you? nay, pray you, mark.   [*Sings.*
      He is dead and gone, lady,
      He is dead and gone;
      At his head a grass-green turf,
      At his heels a stone.
              QUEEN.
Nay, but, Ophelia,—
             OPHELIA.
Pray you, mark.   [*Sings.*
      White his shroud as the mountain snow,
          Enter KING.
              QUEEN.
Alas, look here, my lord.
           OPHELIA [*sings*].
      Larded with sweet flowers;
      Which bewept to the grave did go
      With true-love showers.
              KING.
How do you, pretty lady?
             OPHELIA.
Well, God 'ild you! They say the owl was a
baker's daughter. Lord, we know what we are,
but know not what we may be. God be at your
table!
              KING.
Conceit upon her father.
             OPHELIA.
Pray you, let's have no words of this; but when
they ask you what it means, say you this: [*Sings.*
      To-morrow is Saint Valentine's day,
      All in the morning betime,
      And I a maid at your window,
      To be your Valentine.
      Then up he rose, and donn'd his clothes,
      And dupt the chamber-door;
      Let in the maid, that out a maid
      Never departed more.
              KING.
Pretty Ophelia!
             OPHELIA.
Indeed, la, without an oath, I'll make an end on't:
                              [*Sings.*
      By Gis and by Saint Charity,
      Alack, and fie for shame!
      Young men will do't, if they come to't;
      By cock, they are to blame.
      Quoth she, before you tumbled me,
      You promised me to wed.
He answers:
      So would I ha' done, by yonder sun,
      An thou hadst not come to my bed.
              KING.
How long hath she been thus?
             OPHELIA.
I hope all will be well. We must be patient: but
I cannot choose but weep, to think they should
lay him i'th'cold ground. My brother shall know
of it: and so I thank you for your good counsel.—
Come, my coach!—Good night, ladies; good
night, sweet ladies; good night, good night. [*Exit.*
              KING.
Follow her close; give her good watch, I pray you.
                         [*Exit* HORATIO.

O, this is the poison of deep grief; it springs
All from her father's death. O Gertrude, Gertrude,
When sorrows come, they come not single spies,
But in battalions! First, her father slain:
Next, your son gone; and he most violent author
Of his own just remove: the people muddied,
Thick and unwholesome in their thoughts and
 whispers,
For good Polonius' death; and we have done but
 greenly,
In hugger-mugger to inter him: poor Ophelia
Divided from herself and her fair judgement,
Without the which we are pictures, or mere beasts:
Last, and as much containing as all these,
Her brother is in secret come from France;
Feeds on his wonder, keep himself in clouds,
And wants not buzzers to infect his ear
With pestilent speeches of his father's death;
Wherein necessity, of matter beggar'd,
Will nothing stick our person to arraign
In ear and ear. O my dear Gertrude, this,
Like to a murdering-piece, in many places
Gives me superfluous death. [*A noise within.*

      QUEEN.
     Alack, what noise is this?
      KING.
Where are my Switzers? Let them guard the door.
    Enter a GENTLEMAN.
What is the matter?
     GENTLEMAN.
    Save yourself, my lord:
The ocean, overpeering of his list,
Eats not the flats with more impetuous haste
Than young Laertes, in a riotous head,
O'erbears your officers. The rabble call him lord;
And, as the world were now but to begin,
Antiquity forgot, custom not known,
The ratifiers and props of every word,
They cry, 'Choose we; Laertes shall be king!'
Caps, hands, and tongues applaud it to the clouds,
'Laertes shall be king, Laertes king!'
     QUEEN.
How cheerfully on the false trail they cry!
O, this is counter, you false Danish dogs!
     KING.
The doors are broke.   [*Noise within.*
 Enter LAERTES, *arm'd;* DANES *following.*
     LAERTES.
Where is this king?—Sirs, stand you all without.
     DANES.
No, let's come in.
     LAERTES.
   I pray you, give me leave.
     DANES.
We will, we will. [*They retire without the door.*
     LAERTES.
I thank you:—keep the door.—O thou vile king,
Give me my father!
     QUEEN.
   Calmly, good Laertes.
     LAERTES.
That drop of blood that's calm proclaims me
 bastard;
Cries cuckold to my father; brands the harlot
Even here, between the chaste unsmirched brow
Of my true mother.

     KING.
    What is the cause, Laertes,
That thy rebellion looks so giant-like?—
Let him go, Gertrude; do not fear our person:
There's such divinity doth hedge a king,
That treason can but peep to what it would,
Acts little of his will.—Tell me, Laertes,
Why thou art thus incensed:—let him go, Ger-
 trude:—
Speak, man.
     LAERTES.
Where is my father?
     KING.
    Dead.
     QUEEN.
    But not by him.
     KING.
Let him demand his fill.
     LAERTES.
How came he dead? I'll not be juggled with:
To hell, allegiance! vows, to the blackest devil!
Conscience and grace, to the profoundest pit!
I dare damnation:—to this point I stand,—
That both the worlds I give to negligence,
Let come what comes; only I'll be revenged
Most throughly for my father.
     KING.
    Who shall stay you?
     LAERTES.
My will, not all the world:
And for my means, I'll husband them so well,
They shall go far with little.
     KING.
    Good Laertes,
If you desire to know the certainty
Of your dear father's death, is't writ in your re-
 venge,
That, swoopstake, you will draw both friend and
 foe,
Winner and loser?
     LAERTES.
None but his enemies.
     KING.
    Will you know them, then?
     LAERTES.
To his good friends thus wide I'll ope my arms,
And, like the kind life-rendering pelican,
Repast them with my blood.
     KING.
    Why, now you speak
Like a good child and a true gentleman.
That I am guiltless of your father's death,
And am most sensibly in grief for it,
It shall as level to your judgement 'pear
As day does to your eye.
     DANES [*within*].
    Let her come in.
     LAERTES.
How now! what noise is that?
    Enter OPHELIA.
O heat, dry up my brains! tears seven-times salt,
Burn out the sense and virtue of mine eye!—
By heaven, thy madness shall be paid by weight,
Till our scale turn the beam. O rose of May!
Dear maid, kind sister, sweet Ophelia!—
O heavens! is't possible a young maid's wits

Should be as mortal as an old man's life?
Nature is fine in love; and, where 'tis fine,
It sends some precious instance of itself
After the thing it loves.

OPHELIA [*sings*].
    They bore him barefaced on the bier;
    Hey non nonny, nonny, hey nonny;
    And in his grave rain'd many a tear,—
Fare you well, my dove!

LAERTES.
Hadst thou thy wits, and didst persuade revenge,
It could not move thus.

OPHELIA.
You must sing, 'Down a-down, an you call him
a-down-a.' O, how the wheel becomes it! It is the
false steward, that stole his master's daughter.

LAERTES.
This nothing's more than matter.

OPHELIA.
There's rosemary, that's for remembrance; pray
you, love, remember: and there is pansies, that's
for thoughts.

LAERTES.
A document in madness,—thoughts and remembrance fitted.

OPHELIA.
There's fennel for you, and columbines:—there's
rue for you; and here's some for me:—we may
call it herb-grace o' Sundays:—O, you must wear
your rue with a difference.—There's a daisy:—I
would give you some violets, but they wither'd
all when my father died:—they say he made a
good end,—   [*Sings.*
    For bonny sweet Robin is all my joy,—

LAERTES.
Thought and affliction, passion, hell itself,
She turns to favour and to prettiness.

OPHELIA [*sings*].
    And will a' not come again?
    And will a' not come again?
      No, no, he is dead:
      Go to thy death-bed:
    He never will come again.

    His beard was as white as snow,
    All flaxen was his poll:
      He is gone, he is gone,
      And we cast away moan:
    God ha' mercy on his soul!
And of all Christian souls, I pray God.—God be
wi' you.   [*Exit.*

LAERTES.
Do you see this, O God?

KING.
Laertes, I must commune with your grief,
Or you deny me right. Go but apart,
Make choice of whom your wisest friends you
    will,
And they shall hear and judge 'twixt you and me:
If by direct or by collateral hand
They find us toucht, we will our kingdom give,
Our crown, our life, and all that we call ours,
To you in satisfaction; but if not,
Be you content to lend your patience to us,
And we shall jointly labour with your soul
To give it due content.

LAERTES.
    Let this be so;
His means of death, his obscure burial,—
No trophy, sword, nor hatchment o'er his bones,
No noble rite nor formal ostentation,—
Cry to be heard, as 'twere from heaven to earth,
That I must call't in question.

KING.
    So you shall;
And where th'offence is let the great axe fall.
I pray you, go with me.   [*Exeunt.*

SCENE VI.

Another room in the castle.

Enter HORATIO *and a* SERVANT.

HORATIO.
WHAT are they that would speak with me?

SERVANT.
Seafaring men, sir: they say they have letters for you.

HORATIO.
Let them come in.—   [*Exit* SERVANT.
I do not know from what part of the world
I should be greeted, if not from Lord Hamlet.

Enter SAILORS.

FIRST SAILOR.
God bless you, sir.

HORATIO.
Let Him bless thee too.

FIRST SAILOR.
He shall, sir, an't please Him. There's a letter
for you, sir,—it comes from the ambassador that
was bound for England,—if your name be Horatio, as I am let to know it is.

HORATIO [*reads*].
Horatio, when thou shalt have overlookt this,
give these fellows some means to the king: they
have letters for him. Ere we were two days old at
sea, a pirate of very warlike appointment gave us
chase. Finding ourselves too slow of sail, we put
on a compell'd valour; and in the grapple I boarded them: on the instant they got clear of our ship;
so I alone became their prisoner. They have dealt
with me like thieves of mercy: but they knew
what they did; I am to do a good turn for them.
Let the king have the letters I have sent; and repair thou to me with as much speed as thou
wouldest fly death. I have words to speak in thine
ear will make thee dumb; yet are they much too
light for the bore of the matter. These good fellows will bring thee where I am. Rosencrantz and
Guildenstern hold their course for England: of
them I have much to tell thee. Farewell.

    He that thou knowest thine, HAMLET.
Come, I will make you way for these your letters;
And do't the speedier, that you may direct me
To him from whom you brought them.   [*Exeunt.*

SCENE VII.

Another room in the castle.

Enter KING *and* LAERTES.

KING.
NOW must your conscience my acquittance
    seal,
And you must put me in your heart for friend,

Sith you have heard, and with a knowing ear,
That he which hath your noble father slain
Pursued my life.

LAERTES.
It well appears:—but tell me
Why you proceeded not against these feats,
So crimeful and so capital in nature,
As by your safety, wisdom, all things else,
You mainly were stirr'd up.

KING.
O, for two special reasons;
Which may to you, perhaps, seem much un-
sinew'd,
But yet to me th' are strong. The queen his mother
Lives almost by his looks; and for myself,—
My virtue or my plague, be it either which,—
She's so conjunctive to my life and soul,
That, as the star moves not but in his sphere,
I could not but by her. The other motive,
Why to a public count I might not go,
Is the great love the general gender bear him;
Who, dipping all his faults in their affection,
Would, like the spring that turneth wood to stone,
Convert his gyves to graces; so that my arrows,
Too slightly timber'd for so loud a wind,
Would have reverted to my bow again,
And not where I had aim'd them.

LAERTES.
And so have I a noble father lost;
A sister driven into desperate terms,—
Whose worth, if praises may go back again,
Stood challenger on mount of all the age
For her perfections:—but my revenge will come.

KING.
Break not your sleeps for that: you must not think
That we are made of stuff so flat and dull,
That we can let our beard be shook with danger,
And think it pastime. You shortly shall hear more:
I loved your father, and we love ourself;
And that, I hope, will teach you to imagine—
Enter a MESSENGER.
How now! what news?

MESSENGER.
Letters, my lord, from Hamlet:
This to your majesty; this to the queen.

KING.
From Hamlet! who brought them?

MESSENGER.
Sailors, my lord, they say; I saw them not:
They were given me by Claudio,—he received
them
Of him that brought them.

KING.
Laertes, you shall hear them.—
Leave us.   [*Exit* MESSENGER.
[*Reads*] High and mighty,—You shall know I am
set naked on your kingdom. To-morrow shall I
beg leave to see your kingly eyes: when I shall,
first asking your pardon thereunto, recount the
occasion of my sudden and more strange return.
HAMLET.
What should this mean? Are all the rest come
back?
Or is it some abuse, and no such thing?

LAERTES.
Know you the hand?

KING.
'Tis Hamlet's character:—'Naked,'—
And in a postscript here, he says, 'alone.'
Can you advise me?

LAERTES.
I'm lost in it, my lord. But let him come;
It warms the very sickness in my heart,
That I shall live and tell him to his teeth,
'Thus diddest thou.'

KING.
If it be so, Laertes,—
As how should it be so? how otherwise?—
Will you be ruled by me?

LAERTES.
Ay, my lord;
So you will not o'errule me to a peace.

KING.
To thine own peace. If he be now return'd,—
As checking at his voyage, and that he means
No more to undertake it,—I will work him
To an exploit, now ripe in my device,
Under the which he shall not choose but fall:
And for his death no wind of blame shall breathe;
But even his mother shall uncharge the practice,
And call it accident.

LAERTES.
My lord, I will be ruled;
The rather, if you could devise it so,
That I might be the organ.

KING.
It falls right.
You have been talkt of since your travel much,
And that in Hamlet's hearing, for a quality
Wherein, they say, you shine: your sum of parts
Did not together pluck such envy from him,
As did that one; and that, in my regard,
Of the unworthiest siege.

LAERTES.
What part is that, my lord?

KING.
A very riband in the cap of youth,
Yet needful too; for youth no less becomes
The light and careless livery that it wears
Than settled age his sables and his weeds,
Importing health and graveness.—Two months
since,
Here was a gentleman of Normandy,—
I've seen myself, and served against, the French,
And they can well on horseback: but this gallant
Had witchcraft in't; he grew unto his seat;
And to such wondrous doing brought his horse,
As he had been incorpsed and demi-natured
With the brave beast: so far he topt my thought,
That I, in forgery of shapes and tricks,
Come short of what he did.

LAERTES.
A Norman was't?

KING.
A Norman.

LAERTES.
Upon my life, Lamond.

KING.
The very same.

LAERTES.
I know him well: he is the brooch, indeed,
And gem of all the nation.

KING.
He made confession of you;
And gave you such a masterly report,
For art and exercise in your defence,
And for your rapier most especially,
That he cried out, 'twould be a sight indeed,
If one could match you: the scrimers of their nation,
He swore, had neither motion, guard, nor eye,
If you opposed them. Sir, this report of his
Did Hamlet so envenom with his envy,
That he could nothing do but wish and beg
Your sudden coming o'er, to play with him.
Now, out of this,—

LAERTES.
　　　　What out of this, my lord?
KING.
Laertes, was your father dear to you?
Or are you like the painting of a sorrow,
A face without a heart?

LAERTES.
　　　　　　Why ask you this?
KING.
Not that I think you did not love your father;
But that I know love is begun by time;
And that I see, in passages of proof,
Time qualifies the spark and fire of it.
There lives within the very flame of love
A kind of wick or snuff that will abate it;
And nothing is at a like goodness still;
For goodness, growing to a plurisy,
Dies in his own too-much: that we would do,
We should do when we would; for this 'would'
　changes,
And hath abatements and delays as many
As there are tongues, are hands, are accidents;
And then this 'should' is like a spendthrift sigh,
That hurts by easing. But, to th'quick o'th'
　ulcer:—
Hamlet comes back: what would you undertake,
To show yourself your father's son in deed
More than in words?

LAERTES.
　　　　To cut his throat i'th'church.
KING.
No place, indeed, should murder sanctuarize;
Revenge should have no bounds. But, good
　Laertes,
Will you do this, keep close within your chamber.
Hamlet return'd shall know you are come home:
We'll put on those shall praise your excellence,
And set a double varnish on the fame
The Frenchman gave you; bring you, in fine,
　together,
And wager on your heads: he, being remiss,
Most generous, and free from all contriving,
Will not peruse the foils; so that, with ease,
Or with a little shuffling, you may choose
A sword unbated, and, in a pass of practice,
Requite him for your father.

LAERTES.
　　　　　　I will do't:
And for that purpose I'll anoint my sword.
I bought an unction of a mountebank,
So mortal, that but dip a knife in it,
Where it draws blood no cataplasm so rare,
Collected from all simples that have virtue

Under the moon, can save the thing from death
That is but scratch't withal: I'll touch my point
With this contagion, that, if I gall him slightly,
It may be death.

KING.
　　　　Let's further think of this;
Weigh what convenience both of time and means
May fit us to our shape: if this should fail,
And that our drift look through our bad per-
　formance,
'Twere better not assay'd: therefore this project
Should have a back or second, that might hold,
If this should blast in proof. Soft!—let me see:—
We'll make a solemn wager on your cunnings,—
I ha't:
When in your motion you are hot and dry,—
As make your bouts more violent to that end,—
And that he calls for drink, I'll have prepared him
A chalice for the nonce; whereon but sipping,
If he by chance escape your venom'd stuck,
Our purpose may hold there. But stay! what
　noise?—

Enter QUEEN.
How now, sweet queen!

QUEEN.
One woe doth tread upon another's heel,
So fast they follow:—your sister's drown'd,
　Laertes.

LAERTES.
Drown'd! O, where?

QUEEN.
There is a willow grows aslant a brook,
That shows his hoar leaves in the glassy stream;
There with fantastic garlands did she come
Of crow-flowers, nettles, daisies, and long purples
That liberal shepherds give a grosser name,
But our cold maids do dead men's fingers call them:
There, on the pendent boughs her coronet weeds
Clambering to hang, an envious sliver broke;
When down her weedy trophies and herself
Fell in the weeping brook. Her clothes spread wide,
And, mermaid-like, awhile they bore her up;
Which time she chanted snatches of old tunes,
As one incapable of her own distress,
Or like a creature native and indued
Unto that element: but long it could not be
Till that her garments, heavy with their drink,
Pull'd the poor wretch from her melodious lay
To muddy death.

LAERTES.
　　　　Alas, then, she is drown'd?
QUEEN.
Drown'd, drown'd.

LAERTES.
Too much of water hast thou, poor Ophelia,
And therefore I forbid my tears: but yet
It is our trick; nature her custom holds,
Let shame say what it will: when these are gone,
The woman will be out.—Adieu, my lord:
I have a speech of fire, that fain would blaze,
But that this folly douts it. 　　　　[*Exit.*
KING.
　　　　　　Let's follow, Gertrude:
How much I had to do to calm his rage!
Now fear I this will give it start again;
Therefore let's follow. 　　　　　　[*Exeunt.*

ACT V. SCENE I.

Elsinore.　A churchyard.

Enter two CLOWNS, *with spades, &c.*

FIRST CLOWN.

IS she to be buried in Christian burial that wilfully seeks her own salvation?

SECOND CLOWN.

I tell thee she is; and therefore make her grave straight: the crowner hath sat on her, and finds it Christian burial.

FIRST CLOWN.

How can that be, unless she drown'd herself in her own defence?

SECOND CLOWN.

Why, 'tis found so.

FIRST CLOWN.

It must be *se offendendo;* it cannot be else. For here lies the point: if I drown myself wittingly, it argues an act: and an act hath three branches; it is, to act, to do, to perform: argal, she drown'd herself wittingly.

SECOND CLOWN.

Nay, but hear you, goodman delver,—

FIRST CLOWN.

Give me leave. Here lies the water; good: here stands the man; good: if the man go to this water and drown himself, it is, will he, nill he, he goes,—mark you that; but if the water come to him and drown him, he drowns not himself: argal, he that is not guilty of his own death shortens not his own life.

SECOND CLOWN.

But is this law?

FIRST CLOWN.

Ay, marry, is't; crowner's quest-law.

SECOND CLOWN.

Will you ha' the truth on't? If this had not been a gentlewoman, she should have been buried out o'Christian burial.

FIRST CLOWN.

Why, there thou sayst: and the more pity that great folk should have countenance in this world to drown or hang themselves, more than their even Christian.—Come, my spade. There is no ancient gentlemen but gardeners, ditchers, and grave-makers: they hold up Adam's profession.

SECOND CLOWN.

Was he a gentleman?

FIRST CLOWN.

A' was the first that ever bore arms.

SECOND CLOWN.

Why, he had none.

FIRST CLOWN.

What, art a heathen? How dost thou understand the Scripture? The Scripture says, Adam digg'd: could he dig without arms? I'll put another question to thee: if thou answerest me not to the purpose, confess thyself—

SECOND CLOWN.

Go to.

FIRST CLOWN.

What is he that builds stronger than either the mason, the shipwright, or the carpenter?

SECOND CLOWN.

The gallows-maker; for that frame outlives a thousand tenants.

FIRST CLOWN.

I like thy wit well, in good faith: the gallows does well; but how does it well? it does well to those that do ill: now, thou dost ill to say the gallows is built stronger than the church: argal, the gallows may do well to thee. To't again, come.

SECOND CLOWN.

'Who builds stronger than a mason, a shipwright, or a carpenter?'

FIRST CLOWN.

Ay, tell me that, and unyoke.

SECOND CLOWN.

Marry, now I can tell.

FIRST CLOWN.

To't.

SECOND CLOWN.

Mass, I cannot tell.

Enter HAMLET *and* HORATIO, *afar off.*

FIRST CLOWN.

Cudgel thy brains no more about it, for your dull ass will not mend his pace with beating; and when you are askt this question next, say 'a grave-maker:' the houses that he makes lasts till dooms-day. Go, get thee to Yaughan; fetch me a stoop of liquor.　　　　[*Exit* SECOND CLOWN.

[*He digs, and sings.*

In youth, when I did love, did love,
　　Methought it was very sweet,
To contract, O, the time, for, ah, my behove,
　　O, methought there was nothing meet.

HAMLET.

Has this fellow no feeling of his business, that he sings at grave-making?

HORATIO.

Custom hath made it in him a property of easiness.

HAMLET.

'Tis e'en so: the hand of little employment hath the daintier sense.

FIRST CLOWN [*sings*].

But age, with his stealing steps,
　　Hath claw'd me in his clutch,
And hath shipt me intil the land,
　　As if I had never been such.
　　　　　　[*Throws up a skull.*

HAMLET.

That skull had a tongue in it, and could sing once: how the knave jowls it to the ground, as if it were Cain's jaw-bone, that did the first murder! It might be the pate of a politician, which this ass now o'er-reaches; one that would circumvent God, might it not?

HORATIO.

It might, my lord.

HAMLET.

Or of a courtier; which could say 'Good morrow, sweet lord! How dost thou, good lord?' This might be my lord such-a-one, that praised my lord such-a-one's horse, when he meant to beg it,—might it not?

HORATIO.

Ay, my lord.

HAMLET.

Why, e'en so: and now my Lady Worm's; chapless, and knockt about the mazard with a sexton's
spade: here's fine revolution, an we had the trick
to see't. Did these bones cost no more the breeding, but to play at loggats with 'em? mine ache to
think on't.

FIRST CLOWN [sings].

A pickaxe, and a spade, a spade,
     For and a shrouding-sheet:
O, a pit of clay for to be made
     For such a guest is meet.

             [Throws up another skull.

HAMLET.

There's another: why may not that be the skull
of a lawyer? Where be his quiddits now, his
quillets, his cases, his tenures, and his tricks? why
does he suffer this rude knave now to knock him
about the sconce with a dirty shovel, and will not
tell him of his action of battery? Hum! This
fellow might be in's time a great buyer of land,
with his statutes, his recognizances, his fines, his
double vouchers, his recoveries: is this the fine
of his fines, and the recovery of his recoveries, to
have his fine pate full of fine dirt? will his vouchers
vouch him no more of his purchases, and double
ones too, than the length and breadth of a pair of
indentures? The very conveyances of his lands
will hardly lie in this box; and must the inheritor
himself have no more, ha?

HORATIO.

Not a jot more, my lord.

HAMLET.

Is not parchment made of sheep-skins?

HORATIO.

Ay, my lord, and of calf-skins too.

HAMLET.

They are sheep and calves which seek out assurance in that. I will speak to this fellow.—Whose
grave's this, sirrah?

FIRST CLOWN.

Mine, sir.—   [Sings.
    O, a pit of clay for to be made
       For such a guest is meet.

HAMLET.

I think it be thine, indeed; for thou liest in't.

FIRST CLOWN.

You lie out on't, sir, and therefore it is not yours:
for my part, I do not lie in't, and yet it is mine.

HAMLET.

Thou dost lie in't, to be in't, and say it is thine:
'tis for the dead, not for the quick; therefore thou
liest.

FIRST CLOWN.

'Tis a quick lie, sir; 'twill away again, from me to
you.

HAMLET.

What man dost thou dig it for?

FIRST CLOWN.

For no man, sir.

HAMLET.

What woman, then?

FIRST CLOWN.

For none, neither.

HAMLET.

Who is to be buried in't?

FIRST CLOWN.

One that was a woman, sir; but, rest her soul,
she's dead.

HAMLET.

How absolute the knave is! we must speak by the
card, or equivocation will undo us. By the Lord,
Horatio, this three years I have taken note of it;
the age is grown so pickt, that the toe of the
peasant comes so near the heel of the courtier, he
galls his kibe.—How long hast thou been a grave-
maker?

FIRST CLOWN.

Of all the days i'th'year, I came to't that day
that our last king Hamlet o'ercame Fortinbras.

HAMLET.

How long is that since?

FIRST CLOWN.

Cannot you tell that? every fool can tell that: it
was that very day that young Hamlet was born,—
he that is mad, and sent into England.

HAMLET.

Ay, marry, why was he sent into England?

FIRST CLOWN.

Why, because a' was mad: a' shall recover his wits
there; or, if a' do not, 'tis no great matter there.

HAMLET.

Why?

FIRST CLOWN.

'Twill not be seen in him there; there the men
are as mad as he.

HAMLET.

How came he mad?

FIRST CLOWN.

Very strangely, they say.

HAMLET.

How strangely?

FIRST CLOWN.

Faith, e'en with losing his wits.

HAMLET.

Upon what ground?

FIRST CLOWN.

Why, here in Denmark: I have been sexton here,
man and boy, thirty years.

HAMLET.

How long will a man lie i'th'earth ere he rot?

FIRST CLOWN.

I'faith, if a' be not rotten before a' die,—as we
have many pocky corses now-a-days that will
scarce hold the laying in,—a' will last you some
eight year or nine year: a tanner will last you nine
year.

HAMLET.

Why he more than another?

FIRST CLOWN.

Why, sir, his hide is so tann'd with his trade that
a' will keep out water a great while; and your
water is a sore decayer of your whoreson dead
body. Here's a skull now hath lain you i'th'
earth three-and-twenty years.

HAMLET.

Whose was it?

FIRST CLOWN.

A whoreson mad fellow's it was: whose do you
think it was?

HAMLET.

Nay, I know not.

FIRST CLOWN.

A pestilence on him for a mad rogue! a' pour'd a
flagon of Rhenish on my head once. This same
skull, sir, was Yorick's skull, the king's jester.

HAMLET.

This?

FIRST CLOWN.

E'en that.

HAMLET.

Let me see. [*Takes the skull.*]—Alas, poor Yorick!
—I knew him, Horatio: a fellow of infinite jest,
of most excellent fancy: he hath borne me on his
back a thousand times; and now, how abhorred
in my imagination it is! my gorge rises at it. Here
hung those lips that I have kist I know not how
oft. Where be your gibes now? your gambols?
your songs? your flashes of merriment, that were
wont to set the table on a roar? Not one now, to
mock your own grinning? quite chop-fal'n? Now
get you to my lady's chamber, and tell her, let
her paint an inch thick, to this favour she must
come; make her laugh at that.—Prithee, Horatio,
tell me one thing.

HORATIO.

What's that, my lord?

HAMLET.

Dost thou think Alexander lookt o' this fashion i'
th'earth?

HORATIO.

E'en so.

HAMLET.

And smelt so? pah!   [*Puts down the skull.*

HORATIO.

E'en so, my lord.

HAMLET.

To what base uses we may return, Horatio! Why
may not imagination trace the noble dust of
Alexander till he find it stopping a bung-hole?

HORATIO.

'Twere to consider too curiously, to consider so.

HAMLET.

No, faith, not a jot; but to follow him thither with
modesty enough, and likelihood to lead it: as
thus; Alexander died, Alexander was buried,
Alexander returneth into dust; the dust is earth:
of earth we make loam; and why of that loam
whereto he was converted might they not stop a
beer-barrel?

Imperious Cæsar, dead and turn'd to clay,
Might stop a hole to keep the wind away;
O, that that earth which kept the world in awe
Should patch a wall t'expel the winter's flaw!—
But soft! but soft! aside:—here comes the king,

Enter KING, QUEEN, LAERTES *and the Corse;*
PRIESTS *and* LORDS *attendant.*

The queen, the courtiers: who is that they follow?
And with such maimed rites? This doth betoken
The corse they follow did with desperate hand
Fordo its own life: 'twas of some estate.
Couch we awhile, and mark.

[*Retiring with* HORATIO.

LAERTES.

What ceremony else?

HAMLET.

That is Laertes,
A very noble youth: mark.

LAERTES.

What ceremony else?

FIRST PRIEST.

Her obsequies have been as far enlarged
As we have warrantise: her death was doubtful;
And, but that great command o'ersways the order,
She should in ground unsanctified have lodged
Till the last trumpet; for charitable prayers,
Shards, flints, and pebbles should be thrown on
her:
Yet here she is allow'd her virgin crants,
Her maiden strewments, and the bringing home
Of bell and burial.

LAERTES.

Must there no more be done?

FIRST PRIEST.

No more be done:
We should profane the service of the dead
To sing a requiem, and such rest to her
As to peace-parted souls.

LAERTES.

Lay her i'th'earth;—
And from her fair and unpolluted flesh
May violets spring!—I tell thee, churlish priest,
A ministering angel shall my sister be,
When thou liest howling.

HAMLET.

What, the fair Ophelia!

QUEEN.

Sweets to the sweet: farewell! [*Scattering flowers.*
I hoped thou shouldst have been my Hamlet's
wife;
I thought thy bride-bed to have deckt, sweet
maid,
And not have strew'd thy grave.

LAERTES.

O, treble woe
Fall ten times treble on that cursed head
Whose wicked deed thy most ingenious sense
Depriv'd thee of!—Hold off the earth awhile,
Till I have caught her once more in mine arms:

[*Leaps into the grave.*

Now pile your dust upon the quick and dead,
Till of this flat a mountain you have made
T'o'ertop old Pelion or the skyish head
Of blue Olympus.

HAMLET [*advancing*].

What is he whose grief
Bears such an emphasis; whose phrase of sorrow
Conjures the wandering stars, and makes them
stand
Like wonder-wounded hearers? This is I,
Hamlet the Dane.   [*Leaps into the grave.*

LAERTES.

The devil take thy soul!

[*Grappling with him.*

HAMLET.

Thou pray'st not well.
I prithee, take thy fingers from my throat;
For, though I am not splenitive and rash,
Yet have I something in me dangerous,
Which let thy wisdom fear: hold off thy hand!

KING.

Pluck them asunder.

QUEEN.

Hamlet, Hamlet!

ALL.

Gentlemen,—

HORATIO.

Good my lord, be quiet.

[*The* ATTENDANTS *part them, and they come out of the grave.*

HAMLET.

Why, I will fight with him upon this theme
Until my eyelids will no longer wag.

QUEEN.

O my son, what theme?

HAMLET.

I loved Ophelia: forty thousand brothers
Could not, with all their quantity of love,
Make up my sum.—What wilt thou do for her?

KING.

O, he is mad, Laertes.

QUEEN.

For love of God, forbear him.

HAMLET.

'Swounds, show me what thou'lt do:
Woo't weep? woo't fight? woo't fast? woo't tear
thyself?
Woo't drink up eisel? eat a crocodile?
I'll do't.—Dost thou come here to whine?
To outface me with leaping in her grave?
Be buried quick with her, and so will I:
And if thou prate of mountains, let them throw
Millions of acres on us, till our ground,
Singeing his pate against the burning zone,
Make Ossa like a wart! Nay, an thou'lt mouth,
I'll rant as well as thou.

QUEEN.

This is mere madness:
And thus awhile the fit will work on him;
Anon, as patient as the female dove
When that her golden couplets are disclosed,
His silence will sit drooping.

HAMLET.

Hear you, sir;
What is the reason that you use me thus?
I loved you ever: but it is no matter;
Let Hercules himself do what he may,
The cat will mew, and dog will have his day. [*Exit.*

KING.

I pray you, good Horatio, wait upon him.—

[*Exit* HORATIO.

[*to* LAERTES] Strengthen your patience in our
last night's speech;
We'll put the matter to the present push.—
Good Gertrude, set some watch over your son.—
This grave shall have a living monument:
An hour of quiet shortly shall we see;
Till then, in patience our proceeding be.

[*Exeunt.*

SCENE II.

A hall in the castle.

Enter HAMLET *and* HORATIO.

HAMLET.

SO much for this, sir: now shall you see the
other;—
You do remember all the circumstance?

HORATIO.

Remember it, my lord!

HAMLET.

Sir, in my heart there was a kind of fighting,
That would not let me sleep: methought I lay
Worse than the mutines in the bilboes. Rashly,
And praised be rashness for it, let us know,
Our indiscretion sometime serves us well,
When our deep plots do pall: and that should
learn us
There's a divinity that shapes our ends,
Rough-hew them how we will,—

HORATIO.

That is most certain.

HAMLET.

Up from my cabin,
My sea-gown scarft about me, in the dark
Groped I to find out them: had my desire;
Finger'd their packet; and, in fine, withdrew
To mine own room again: making so bold,
My fears forgetting manners, to unseal
Their grand commission; where I found,
Horatio,—
O royal knavery!—an exact command,—
Larded with many several sorts of reasons,
Importing Denmark's health, and England's too,
With, ho! such bugs and goblins in my life,—
That, on the supervise, no leisure bated,
No, not to stay the grinding of the axe,
My head should be struck off.

HORATIO.

Is't possible?

HAMLET.

Here's the commission: read it at more leisure.
But wilt thou hear me how I did proceed?

HORATIO.

I beseech you.

HAMLET.

Being thus be-netted round with villainies,—
Ere I could make a prologue to my brains,
They had begun the play,—I sat me down;
Devised a new commission; wrote it fair:—
I once did hold it, as our statists do,
A baseness to write fair, and labour'd much
How to forget that learning; but, sir, now
It did me yeoman's service:—wilt thou know
The effect of what I wrote?

HORATIO.

Ay, good my lord.

HAMLET.

An earnest conjuration from the king,—
As England was his faithful tributary;
As love between them like the palm might
flourish;
As peace should still her wheaten garland wear,
And stand a comma 'tween their amities;
And many such-like *As*-es of great charge,—
That, on the view and knowing of these contents,
Without debatement further, more or less,
He should the bearers put to sudden death,
Not shriving-time allow'd.

HORATIO.

How was this seal'd?

HAMLET.

Why, even in that was heaven ordinant.
I had my father's signet in my purse,
Which was the model of that Danish seal;
Folded the writ up in the form of th'other;

Subscribed it; gave't th'impression; placed it
safely,
The changeling never known. Now, the next
day
Was our sea-fight; and what to this was sequent
Thou know'st already.

HORATIO.
So Guildenstern and Rosencrantz go to't.

HAMLET.
Why, man, they did make love to this employ-
ment;
They are not near my conscience; their defeat
Does by their own insinuation grow:
'Tis dangerous when the baser nature comes
Between the pass and fell incensed points
Of mighty opposites.

HORATIO.
         Why, what a king is this!

HAMLET.
Does it not, thinks't thee, stand me now upon,—
He that hath kill'd my king, and whored my
mother;
Popt in between th'election and my hopes;
Thrown out his angle for my proper life,
And with such cozenage,—is't not perfect con-
science
To quit him with this arm? and is't not to be
damn'd
To let this canker of our nature come
In further evil?

HORATIO.
It must be shortly known to him from England
What is the issue of the business there.

HAMLET.
It will be short: the interim is mine;
And a man's life's no more than to say 'one.'
But I am very sorry, good Horatio,
That to Laertes I forgot myself;
For, by the image of my cause, I see
The portraiture of his: I'll court his favours:
But, sure, the bravery of his grief did put me
Into a towering passion.

HORATIO.
         Peace! who comes here?
Enter OSRIC.

OSRIC.
Your lordship is right welcome back to Denmark.

HAMLET.
I humbly thank you, sir.—[*aside to* HORATIO]
Dost know this water-fly?

HORATIO [*aside to* HAMLET].
No, my good lord.

HAMLET [*aside to* HORATIO].
Thy state is the more gracious; for 'tis a vice to
know him. He hath much land, and fertile: let a
beast be lord of beasts, and his crib shall stand at
the king's mess: 'tis a chough; but, as I say,
spacious in the possession of dirt.

OSRIC.
Sweet lord, if your lordship were at leisure, I
should impart a thing to you from his majesty.

HAMLET.
I will receive it, sir, with all diligence of spirit.
Put your bonnet to his right use; 'tis for the head.

OSRIC.
I thank your lordship, it is very hot.

HAMLET.
No, believe me, 'tis very cold; the wind is
northerly.

OSRIC.
It is indifferent cold, my lord, indeed.

HAMLET.
But yet methinks it is very sultry and hot for my
complexion.

OSRIC.
Exceedingly, my lord; it is very sultry,—as
'twere,—I cannot tell how.—But, my lord, his
majesty bade me signify to you, that he has laid a
great wager on your head: sir, this is the matter,—

HAMLET.
I beseech you, remember—
     [HAMLET *moves him to put on his hat.*

OSRIC.
Nay, good my lord: for mine ease, in good faith.
Sir, here is newly come to court Laertes; believe
me, an absolute gentleman, full of most excellent
differences, of very soft society and great showing: indeed, to speak feelingly of him, he is the
card or calendar of gentry, for you shall find in
him the continent of what part a gentleman would
see.

HAMLET.
Sir, his definement suffers no perdition in you;—
though, I know, to divide him inventorially would
dizzy the arithmetic of memory, and yet but yaw
neither, in respect of his quick sail. But, in the
verity of extolment, I take him to be a soul of
great article; and his infusion of such dearth and
rareness, as, to make true diction of him, his
semblable is his mirror; and who else would trace
him, his umbrage, nothing more.

OSRIC.
Your lordship speaks most infallibly of him.

HAMLET.
The concernancy, sir? why do we wrap the gentleman in our more rawer breath?

OSRIC.
Sir?

HORATIO.
Is't not possible to understand in another tongue?
You will do't, sir, really.

HAMLET.
What imports the nomination of this gentleman?

OSRIC.
Of Laertes?

HORATIO [*aside to* HAMLET].
His purse is empty already: all's golden words
are spent.

HAMLET.
Of him, sir.

OSRIC.
I know you are not ignorant—

HAMLET.
I would you did, sir; yet, in faith, if you did, it
would not much approve me:—well, sir.

OSRIC.
You are not ignorant of what excellence Laertes
is—

HAMLET.
I dare not confess that, lest I should compare
with him in excellence; but, to know a man well,
were to know himself.

OSRIC.

I mean, sir, for his weapon; but in the imputation laid on him by them, in his meed he's unfellow'd.

HAMLET.

What's his weapon?

OSRIC.

Rapier and dagger.

HAMLET.

That's two of his weapons: but, well.

OSRIC.

The king, sir, hath wager'd with him six Barbary horses: against the which he has imponed, as I take it, six French rapiers and poniards, with their assigns, as girdle, hangers, and so: three of the carriages, in faith, are very dear to fancy, very responsive to the hilts, most delicate carriages, and of very liberal conceit.

HAMLET.

What call you the carriages?

HORATIO [aside to HAMLET].

I knew you must be edified by the margent ere you had done.

OSRIC.

The carriages, sir, are the hangers.

HAMLET.

The phrase would be more german to the matter, if we could carry cannon by our sides: I would it might be hangers till then. But, on: six Barbary horses against six French swords, their assigns, and three liberal-conceited carriages; that's the French bet against the Danish. Why is this 'imponed,' as you call it?

OSRIC.

The king, sir, hath laid, that in a dozen passes between yourself and him, he shall not exceed you three hits: he hath laid on twelve for nine; and it would come to immediate trial, if your lordship would vouchsafe the answer.

HAMLET.

How if I answer no?

OSRIC.

I mean, my lord, the opposition of your person in trial.

HAMLET.

Sir, I will walk here in the hall: if it please his majesty, 'tis the breathing time of day with me; let the foils be brought, the gentleman willing, and the king hold his purpose, I will win for him an I can; if not, I will gain nothing but my shame and the odd hits.

OSRIC.

Shall I re-deliver you e'en so?

HAMLET.

To this effect, sir; after what flourish your nature will.

OSRIC.

I commend my duty to your lordship.

HAMLET.

Yours, yours. [Exit OSRIC.]—He does well to commend it himself; there are no tongues else for's turn.

HORATIO.

This lapwing runs away with the shell on his head.

HAMLET.

He did comply with his dug, before he suckt it. Thus has he—and many more of the same bevy

that I know the drossy age dotes on—only got the tune of the time, and outward habit of encounter; a kind of yesty collection, which carries them through and through the most fann'd and winnow'd opinions; and do but blow them to their trial, the bubbles are out.

Enter a LORD.

LORD.

My lord, his majesty commended him to you by young Osric, who brings back to him, that you attend him in the hall: he sends to know if your pleasure hold to play with Laertes, or that you will take longer time.

HAMLET.

I am constant to my purposes; they follow the king's pleasure: if his fitness speaks, mine is ready; now or whensoever, provided I be so able as now.

LORD.

The king and queen and all are coming down.

HAMLET.

In happy time.

LORD.

The queen desires you to use some gentle entertainment to Laertes before you fall to play.

HAMLET.

She well instructs me.   [Exit LORD.

HORATIO.

You will lose this wager, my lord.

HAMLET.

I do not think so; since he went into France, I have been in continual practice; I shall win at the odds. But thou wouldst not think how ill all's here about my heart: but it is no matter.

HORATIO.

Nay, good my lord,—

HAMLET.

It is but foolery; but it is such a kind of gain-giving as would perhaps trouble a woman.

HORATIO.

If your mind dislike any thing, obey it: I will forestall their repair hither, and say you are not fit.

HAMLET.

Not a whit, we defy augury: there's a special providence in the fall of a sparrow. If it be now, 'tis not to come; if it be not to come, it will be now; if it be not now, yet it will come: the readiness is all: since no man knows aught of what he leaves, what is't to leave betimes? Let be.

Enter KING, QUEEN, LAERTES, LORDS, OSRIC, and ATTENDANTS with foils and gauntlets: a table and flagons of wine on it.

KING.

Come, Hamlet, come, and take this hand from me.

[The KING puts LAERTES' hand into HAMLET'S.

HAMLET.

Give me your pardon, sir: I've done you wrong;
But pardon't, as you are a gentleman.
This presence knows,
And you must needs have heard, how I am punisht
With sore distraction. What I have done,
That might your nature, honour, and exception
Roughly awake, I here proclaim was madness.
Was't Hamlet wrong'd Laertes? Never Hamlet:
If Hamlet from himself be ta'en away,

And when he's not himself does wrong Laertes,
Then Hamlet does it not, Hamlet denies it.
Who does it, then? His madness: if't be so,
Hamlet is of the faction that is wrong'd;
His madness is poor Hamlet's enemy.
Sir, in this audience,
Let my disclaiming from a purposed evil
Free me so far in your most generous thoughts,
That I have shot mine arrow o'er the house,
And hurt my brother.
　　　　　　　LAERTES.
　　　　　　　I am satisfied in nature,
Whose motive, in this case, should stir me most
To my revenge: but in my terms of honour
I stand aloof; and will no reconcilement
Till by some elder masters, of known honour,
I have a voice and precedent of peace,
To keep my name ungored. But till that time
I do receive your offer'd love like love,
And will not wrong it.
　　　　　　HAMLET.
　　　　　　　I embrace it freely;
And will this brother's wager frankly play.—
Give us the foils.—Come on.
　　　　　　LAERTES.
　　　　　　　Come, one for me.
　　　　　　HAMLET.
I'll be your foil, Laertes: in mine ignorance
Your skill shall, like a star i'th'darkest night,
Stick fiery off indeed.
　　　　　　LAERTES.
　　　　　　You mock me, sir.
　　　　　　HAMLET.
No, by this hand.
　　　　　　KING.
Give them the foils, young Osric.—Cousin Hamlet,
You know the wager?
　　　　　　HAMLET.
　　　　　　　Very well, my lord;
Your Grace hath laid the odds o'th'weaker side.
　　　　　　KING.
I do not fear it; I have seen you both:
But since he is better'd, we have therefore odds.
　　　　　　LAERTES.
This is too heavy, let me see another.
　　　　　　HAMLET.
This likes me well. These foils have all a length?
　　　　　　　　　　[They prepare to play.
　　　　　　OSRIC.
Ay, my good lord.
　　　　　　KING.
Set me the stoops of wine upon that table.—
If Hamlet give the first or second hit,
Or quit in answer of the third exchange,
Let all the battlements their ordnance fire;
The king shall drink to Hamlet's better breath;
And in the cup an union shall he throw,
Richer than that which four successive kings
In Denmark's crown have worn. Give me the cups;
And let the kettle to the trumpet speak,
The trumpet to the cannoneer without,
The cannons to the heavens, the heaven to earth,
'Now the king drinks to Hamlet.'—Come, begin;
And you, the judges, bear a wary eye.

　　　　　　HAMLET.
Come on, sir.
　　　　　　LAERTES.
　　　　　Come, my lord.　　　　　[They play.
　　　　　　HAMLET.
　　　　　　　　One.
　　　　　　LAERTES.
　　　　　　　　　No.
　　　　　　HAMLET.
　　　　　　　　　　Judgement.
　　　　　　OSRIC.
A hit, a very palpable hit.
　　　　　　LAERTES.
　　　　　　　Well;—again.
　　　　　　KING.
Stay; give me drink.—Hamlet, this pearl is
　　thine;
Here's to thy health.
　　　　　　[Trumpets sound, and shot goes off.
　　　　　　　Give him the cup.
　　　　　　HAMLET.
I'll play this bout first; set it by awhile.—
Come.—[They play.] Another hit; what say you?
　　　　　　LAERTES.
A touch, a touch, I do confess.
　　　　　　KING.
Our son shall win.
　　　　　　QUEEN.
　　　　　He's fat, and scant of breath.
Here, Hamlet, take my napkin, rub thy brows:
The queen carouses to thy fortune, Hamlet.
　　　　　　HAMLET.
Good madam!
　　　　　　KING.
　　　　Gertrude, do not drink.
　　　　　　QUEEN.
I will, my lord; I pray you, pardon me.　　[Drinks.
　　　　　　KING [aside].
It is the poison'd cup; it is too late.
　　　　　　HAMLET.
I dare not drink yet, madam; by and by.
　　　　　　QUEEN.
Come, let me wipe thy face.
　　　　　　LAERTES.
My lord, I'll hit him now.
　　　　　　KING.
　　　　　　　I do not think't.
　　　　　　LAERTES [aside].
And yet 'tis almost 'gainst my conscience.
　　　　　　HAMLET.
Come, for the third, Laertes: you but dally;
I pray you, pass with your best violence
I am afeared you make a wanton of me.
　　　　　　LAERTES.
Say you so? come on.　　　　　[They play.
　　　　　　OSRIC.
Nothing, neither way.
　　　　　　LAERTES.
Have at you now!
　　　　[LAERTES wounds HAMLET; then, in scuf-
　　　　fling they change rapiers, and HAMLET
　　　　wounds LAERTES.
　　　　　　KING.
　　　　Part them; they are incensed.
　　　　　　HAMLET.
Nay, come, again.　　　　　[The QUEEN falls.

OSRIC.
Look to the queen there, ho!
HORATIO.
They bleed on both sides.—How is it, my lord?
OSRIC.
How is't, Laertes?
LAERTES.
Why, as a woodcock to mine own springe, Osric;
I am justly kill'd with mine own treachery.
HAMLET.
How does the queen?
KING.
She swounds to see them bleed.
QUEEN.
No, no, the drink, the drink,—O my dear Hamlet,—
The drink, the drink!—I am poison'd.   [Dies.
HAMLET.
O villainy!—Ho! let the door be lockt:
Treachery! seek it out.   [LAERTES falls.
LAERTES.
It is here, Hamlet: Hamlet, thou art slain;
No medicine in the world can do thee good,
In thee there is not half an hour of life;
The treacherous instrument is in thy hand,
Unbated and envenom'd: the foul practice
Hath turn'd itself on me; lo, here I lie,
Never to rise again: thy mother's poison'd:—
I can no more:—the king, the king's to blame.
HAMLET.
The point envenom'd too!—
Then, venom, to thy work.   [Stabs the KING.
ALL.
Treason! treason!
KING.
O, yet defend me, friends; I am but hurt.
HAMLET.
Here, thou incestuous, murderous, damned Dane,
Drink off this potion:—is thy union here?
Follow my mother.   [KING dies.
LAERTES.
He is justly served;
It is a poison temper'd by himself.—
Exchange forgiveness with me, noble Hamlet:
Mine and my father's death come not upon thee.
Nor thine on me!   [Dies.
HAMLET.
Heaven make thee free of it! I follow thee.—
I am dead, Horatio.—Wretched queen, adieu!—
You that look pale and tremble at this chance,
That are but mutes or audience to this act,
Had I but time,—as this fell sergeant, death,
Is strict in his arrest,—O, I could tell you,—
But let it be.—Horatio, I am dead;
Thou livest; report me and my cause aright
To the unsatisfied.
HORATIO.
Never believe it:
I am more an antique Roman than a Dane:
Here's yet some liquor left.
HAMLET.
As th'art a man,
Give me the cup: let go; by heaven, I'll have't.
O good Horatio, what a wounded name,
Things standing thus unknown, shall live behind
me!

If thou didst ever hold me in thy heart,
Absent thee from felicity awhile,
And in this harsh world draw thy breath in pain,
To tell my story.   [March afar off, and shot within.
What warlike noise is this?
OSRIC.
Young Fortinbras, with conquest come from Poland,
To the ambassadors of England gives
This warlike volley.
HAMLET.
O, I die, Horatio;
The potent poison quite o'er-crows my spirit:
I cannot live to hear the news from England;
But I do prophesy th'election lights
On Fortinbras: he has my dying voice;
So tell him, with the occurrents, more and less,
Which have solicited—the rest is silence.   [Dies.
HORATIO.
Now cracks a noble heart.—good night, sweet prince;
And flights of angels sing thee to thy rest!—
Why does the drum come hither?   [March within.
Enter FORTINBRAS and the English AMBASSADORS, with drum, colours, and ATTENDANTS.
FORTINBRAS.
Where is this sight?
HORATIO.
What is it ye would see?
If aught of woe or wonder, cease your search.
FORTINBRAS.
This quarry cries on havoc.—O proud Death,
What feast is toward in thine eternal cell,
That thou so many princes at a shot
So bloodily hast struck?
FIRST AMBASSADOR.
The sight is dismal;
And our affairs from England come too late:
The ears are senseless that should give us hearing,
To tell him his commandment is fulfill'd,
That Rosencrantz and Guildenstern are dead:
Where should we have our thanks?
HORATIO.
Not from his mouth.
Had it th'ability of life to thank you:
He never gave commandment for their death.
But since, so jump upon this bloody question,
You from the Polack wars, and you from England,
Are here arrived, give order that these bodies
High on a stage be placed to the view;
And let me speak to th'yet unknowing world
How these things came about: so shall you hear
Of carnal, bloody, and unnatural acts;
Of accidental judgements, casual slaughters;
Of deaths put on by cunning and forced cause;
And, in this upshot, purposes mistook
Faln on the inventors' heads: all this can I
Truly deliver.
FORTINBRAS.
Let us haste to hear it,
And call the noblest to the audience.
For me, with sorrow I embrace my fortune:
I have some rights of memory in this kingdom,
Which now to claim my vantage doth invite me.

HORATIO.
Of that I shall have also cause to speak,
And from his mouth whose voice will draw on
more:
But let this same be presently perform'd,
Even while men's minds are wild; lest more mis-
chance,
On plots and errors, happen.
FORTINBRAS.
Let four captains
Bear Hamlet, like a soldier, to the stage;

For he was likely, had he been put on,
To have proved most royally: and, for his pas-
sage,
The soldiers' music and the rites of war
Speak loudly for him.—
Take up the bodies:—such a sight as this
Becomes the field, but here shows much amiss.—
Go, bid the soldiers shoot.
[*A dead march. Exeunt, bearing off the dead
bodies; after which a peal of ordnance is
shot off.*

TROILUS AND CRESSIDA

DRAMATIS PERSONAE

PRIAM, *King of Troy.*
HECTOR,
TROILUS,
PARIS, } *his sons.*
DEIPHOBUS,
HELENUS,
MARGARELON, *a bastard son of Priam.*
AENEAS,
ANTENOR, } *Trojan commanders.*
CALCHAS, *a Trojan priest, taking part with the Greeks.*
PANDARUS, *uncle to Cressida.*
AGAMEMNON, *the Grecian general.*
MENELAUS, *his brother.*
ACHILLES,
AJAX, } *Grecian commanders.*
ULYSSES,

NESTOR,
DIOMEDES, } *Grecian commanders.*
PATROCLUS,
THERSITES, *a deform'd and scurrilous Grecian.*
ALEXANDER, *servant to Cressida.*
SERVANT *to Troilus.*
SERVANT *to Paris.*
SERVANT *to Diomedes.*

HELEN, *wife to Menelaus.*
ANDROMACHE, *wife to Hector.*
CASSANDRA, *daughter of Priam; a prophetess.*
CRESSIDA, *daughter of Calchas.*

TROJAN *and* GREEK SOLDIERS, *and* ATTEN-DANTS.

SCENE—*Troy, and the Grecian camp before it.*

PROLOGUE.

IN Troy, there lies the scene. From isles of
Greece
The princes orgulous, their high blood chafed,
Have to the port of Athens sent their ships,
Fraught with the ministers and instruments
Of cruel war: sixty and nine, that wore
Their crownets regal, from th'Athenian bay
Put forth toward Phrygia: and their vow is made
To ransack Troy; within whose strong immures
The ravisht Helen, Menelaus' queen,
With wanton Paris sleeps; and that's the quarrel.
To Tenedos they come;
And the deep-drawing barks do there disgorge
Their warlike fraughtage: now on Dardan plains
The fresh and yet unbruised Greeks do pitch
Their brave pavilions: Priam's six-gated city,
Dardan, and Tymbria, Helias, Chetas, Troien,
And Antenorides, with massy staples,
And corresponsive and fulfilling bolts,
Sperr up the sons of Troy.
Now expectation, tickling skittish spirits,
On one and other side, Trojan and Greek,
Sets all on hazard: and hither am I come
A prologue arm'd,—but not in confidence
Of author's pen or actor's voice; but suited
In like conditions as our argument,—
To tell you, fair beholders, that our play
Leaps o'er the vaunt and firstlings of those broils,
Beginning in the middle; starting thence away
To what may be digested in a play.
Like, or find fault; do as your pleasures are;
Now good or bad, 'tis but the chance of war.

ACT I. SCENE I.

Troy. Before PRIAM'S *palace.*

Enter PANDARUS *and* TROILUS.

TROILUS.

CALL here my varlet; I'll unarm again:
Why should I war without the walls of Troy,
That find such cruel battle here within?

Each Trojan that is master of his heart,
Let him to field; Troilus, alas, hath none!

PANDARUS.

Will this gear ne'er be mended?

TROILUS.

The Greeks are strong, and skilful to their
strength,
Fierce to their skill, and to their fierceness valiant;
But I am weaker than a woman's tear,
Tamer than sleep, fonder than ignorance,
Less valiant than the virgin in the night,
And skilless as unpractised infancy.

PANDARUS.

Well, I have told you enough of this: for my part,
I'll not meddle nor make no further. He that will
have a cake out of the wheat must needs tarry the
grinding.

TROILUS.

Have I not tarried?

PANDARUS.

Ay, the grinding; but you must tarry the bolting.

TROILUS.

Have I not tarried?

PANDARUS.

Ay, the bolting; but you must tarry the leavening.

TROILUS.

Still have I tarried.

PANDARUS.

Ay, to the leavening; but here's yet in the word
'hereafter' the kneading, the making of the cake,
the heating of the oven, and the baking; nay, you
must stay the cooling too, or you may chance to
burn your lips.

TROILUS.

Patience herself, what goddess e'er she be,
Doth lesser blench at sufferance than I do.
At Priam's royal table do I sit;
And when fair Cressid comes into my thoughts,—
So, traitor!—'when she comes!'—When is she
thence?

PANDARUS.

Well, she lookt yesternight fairer than ever I saw
her look, or any woman else.

TROILUS.

I was about to tell thee,—when my heart,
As wedged with a sigh, would rive in twain;
Lest Hector or my father should perceive me,—
I have—as when the sun doth light a storm—
Buried this sigh in wrinkle of a smile:
But sorrow, that is coucht in seeming gladness,
Is like that mirth fate turns to sudden sadness.

PANDARUS.

An her hair were not somewhat darker than
Helen's,—well, go to,—there were no more comparison between the women,—but, for my part,
she is my kinswoman; I would not, as they term
it, praise her,—but I would somebody had heard
her talk yesterday, as I did. I will not dispraise
your sister Cassandra's wit; but—

TROILUS.

O Pandarus! I tell thee, Pandarus,—
When I do tell thee, there my hopes lie drown'd,
Reply not in how many fadoms deep
They lie indrencht. I tell thee, I am mad
In Cressid's love: thou answer'st, 'she is fair;'
Pour'st in the open ulcer of my heart
Her eyes, her hair, her cheek, her gait, her voice;
Handlest in thy discourse, O, that her hand,
In whose comparison all whites are ink,
Writing their own reproach; to whose soft seizure
The cygnet's down is harsh, and spirit of sense
Hard as the palm of ploughman!—this thou tell'st
   me,
As true thou tell'st me, when I say I love her;
But, saying thus, instead of oil and balm,
Thou lay'st in every gash that love hath given me
The knife that made it.

PANDARUS.

I speak no more than truth.

TROILUS.

Thou dost not speak so much.

PANDARUS.

Faith, I'll not meddle in't. Let her be as she is: if
she be fair, 'tis the better for her; an she be not,
she has the mends in her own hands.

TROILUS.

Good Pandarus,—how now, Pandarus!

PANDARUS.

I have had my labour for my travail; ill-thought
on of her, and ill-thought on of you: gone between and between, but small thanks for my
labour.

TROILUS.

What, art thou angry, Pandarus? what, with me?

PANDARUS.

Because she's kin to me, therefore she's not so
fair as Helen: an she were not kin to me, she would
be as fair on Friday as Helen is on Sunday. But
what care I? I care not an she were a black-a-moor;
'tis all one to me.

TROILUS.

Say I she is not fair?

PANDARUS.

I do not care whether you do or no. She's a fool to
stay behind her father; let her to the Greeks; and
so I'll tell her the next time I see her: for my part,
I'll meddle nor make no more i'th'matter.

TROILUS.

Pandarus,—

PANDARUS.

Not I.

TROILUS.

Sweet Pandarus,—

PANDARUS.

Pray you, speak no more to me: I will leave all as I
found it, and there an end.

[Exit PANDARUS. Sound alarum.

TROILUS.

Peace, you ungracious clamours! peace, rude
   sounds!
Fools on both sides! Helen must needs be fair,
When with your blood you daily paint her thus.
I cannot fight upon this argument;
It is too starved a subject for my sword.
But Pandarus,—O gods, how do you plague me!
I cannot come to Cressid but by Pandar;
And he's as tetchy to be woo'd to woo,
As she is stubborn-chaste against all suit.
Tell me, Apollo, for thy Daphne's love,
What Cressid is, what Pandar, and what we?
Her bed is India; there she lies, a pearl:
Between our Ilium and where she resides,
Let it be call'd the wild and wandering flood.
Ourself the merchant; and this sailing Pandar,
Our doubtful hope, our convoy, and our bark.

Alarum. Enter AENEAS.

AENEAS.

How now, Prince Troilus! wherefore not a-field?

TROILUS.

Because not there: this woman's answer sorts,
For womanish it is to be from thence.
What news, Aeneas, from the field to-day?

AENEAS.

That Paris is returned home, and hurt.

TROILUS.

By whom, Aeneas?

AENEAS.

Troilus, by Menelaus.

TROILUS.

Let Paris bleed; 'tis but a scar to scorn;
Paris is gored with Menelaus' horn.   [*Alarum.*

AENEAS.

Hark, what good sport is out of town to-day!

TROILUS.

Better at home, if 'would I might' were 'may.'—
But to the sport abroad:—are you bound thither?

AENEAS.

In all swift haste.

TROILUS.

Come, go we, then, together.   [*Exeunt*

SCENE II.

The same. A street.

Enter CRESSIDA *and* ALEXANDER *her* MAN.

CRESSIDA.

WHO were those went by?

ALEXANDER.

Queen Hecuba and Helen

CRESSIDA.

And whither go they?

ALEXANDER.

Up to the eastern tower,
Whose height commands as subject all the vale,

To see the battle. Hector, whose patience
Is, as a virtue, fixt, to-day was moved:
He chid Andromache, and struck his armourer;
And, like as there were husbandry in war,
Before the sun rose, he was harnest light,
And to the field goes he; where every flower
Did, as a prophet, weep what it foresaw
In Hector's wrath.

CRESSIDA.
    What was his cause of anger?

ALEXANDER.
The noise goes, this: there is among the Greeks
A lord of Trojan blood, nephew to Hector;
They call him Ajax.

CRESSIDA.
    Good; and what of him?

ALEXANDER.
They say he is a very man *per se*,
And stands alone.

CRESSIDA.
So do all men,—unless they are drunk, sick, or
have no legs.

ALEXANDER.
This man, lady, hath robb'd many beasts of their
particular additions; he is as valiant as the lion,
churlish as the bear, slow as the elephant: a man
into whom nature hath so crowded humours, that
his valour is crusht into folly, his folly sauced
with discretion: there is no man hath a virtue that
he hath not a glimpse of; nor any man an attaint
but he carries some stain of it: he is melancholy
without cause, and merry against the hair: he hath
the joints of every thing; but every thing so out of
joint, that he is a gouty Briareus, many hands and
no use; or purblind Argus, all eyes and no sight.

CRESSIDA.
But how should this man, that makes me smile,
make Hector angry?

ALEXANDER.
They say he yesterday coped Hector in the battle,
and struck him down; the disdain and shame
whereof hath ever since kept Hector fasting and
waking.

CRESSIDA.
Who comes here?

ALEXANDER.
Madam, your uncle Pandarus.

Enter PANDARUS.

CRESSIDA.
Hector's a gallant man.

ALEXANDER.
As may be in the world, lady.

PANDARUS.
What's that? what's that?

CRESSIDA.
Good morrow, uncle Pandarus.

PANDARUS.
Good morrow, cousin Cressid: what do you talk
of?—Good morrow, Alexander.—How do you,
cousin? When were you at Ilium?

CRESSIDA.
This morning, uncle.

PANDARUS.
What were you talking of when I came? Was
Hector arm'd and gone, ere·ye came to Ilium?
Helen was not up, was she?

CRESSIDA.
Hector was gone; but Helen was not up.

PANDARUS.
E'en so: Hector was stirring early.

CRESSIDA.
That were we talking of, and of his anger.

PANDARUS.
Was he angry?

CRESSIDA.
So he says here.

PANDARUS.
True, he was so; I know the cause too; he'll lay
about him to-day, I can tell them that: and there's
Troilus will not come far behind him; let them
take heed of Troilus, I can tell them that too.

CRESSIDA.
What, is he angry too?

PANDARUS.
Who, Troilus? Troilus is the better man of the
two.

CRESSIDA.
O Jupiter! there's no comparison.

PANDARUS.
What, not between Troilus and Hector? Do you
know a man if you see him?

CRESSIDA.
Ay, if I ever saw him before, and knew him.

PANDARUS.
Well, I say Troilus is Troilus.

CRESSIDA.
Then you say as I say; for, I am sure, he is not
Hector.

PANDARUS.
No, nor Hector is not Troilus in some degrees.

CRESSIDA.
'Tis just to each of them; he is himself.

PANDARUS.
Himself! Alas, poor Troilus! I would he were,—

CRESSIDA.
So he is.

PANDARUS.
Condition, I had gone barefoot to India.

CRESSIDA.
He is not Hector.

PANDARUS.
Himself! no, he's not himself:—would a' were
himself! Well, the gods are above; time must
friend or end: well, Troilus, well,—I would my
heart were in her body!—No, Hector is not a better man than Troilus.

CRESSIDA.
Excuse me.

PANDARUS.
He is elder.

CRESSIDA.
Pardon me, pardon me.

PANDARUS.
Th'other's not come to't; you shall tell me another tale, when th'other's come to't. Hector
shall not have his wit this year,—

CRESSIDA.
He shall not need it, if he have his own.

PANDARUS.
Nor his qualities,—

CRESSIDA.
No matter.

PANDARUS.

Nor his beauty.

CRESSIDA.

'Twould not become him,—his own's better.

PANDARUS.

You have no judgement, niece: Helen herself swore th'other day, that Troilus, for a brown favour—for so 'tis, I must confess,—not brown neither,—

CRESSIDA.

No, but brown.

PANDARUS.

Faith, to say truth, brown and not brown.

CRESSIDA.

To say the truth, true and not true.

PANDARUS.

She praised his complexion above Paris.

CRESSIDA.

Why, Paris hath colour enough.

PANDARUS.

So he has.

CRESSIDA.

Then Troilus should have too much: if she praised him above, his complexion is higher than his; he having colour enough, and the other higher, is too flaming a praise for a good complexion. I had as lief Helen's golden tongue had commended Troilus for a copper nose.

PANDARUS.

I swear to you, I think Helen loves him better than Paris.

CRESSIDA.

Then she's a merry Greek indeed.

PANDARUS.

Nay, I am sure she does. She came to him th' other day into the compass window,—and, you know, he has not past three or four hairs on his chin—

CRESSIDA.

Indeed, a tapster's arithmetic may soon bring his particulars therein to a total.

PANDARUS.

Why, he is very young: and yet will he, within three pound, lift as much as his brother Hector.

CRESSIDA.

Is he so young a man, and so old a lifter?

PANDARUS.

But, to prove to you that Helen loves him,—she came, and puts me her white hand to his cloven chin—

CRESSIDA.

Juno have mercy! how came it cloven?

PANDARUS.

Why, you know, 'tis dimpled: I think his smiling becomes him better than any man in all Phrygia.

CRESSIDA.

O, he smiles valiantly.

PANDARUS.

Does he not?

CRESSIDA.

O yes, an 'twere a cloud in autumn.

PANDARUS.

Why, go to, then:—but to prove to you that Helen loves Troilus,—

CRESSIDA.

Troilus will stand to the proof, if you'll prove it so.

PANDARUS.

Troilus! why, he esteems her no more than I esteem an addle egg.

CRESSIDA.

If you love an addle egg as well as you love an idle head, you would eat chickens i'th'shell.

PANDARUS.

I cannot choose but laugh, to think how she tickled his chin;—indeed, she has a marvellous white hand, I must needs confess,—

CRESSIDA.

Without the rack.

PANDARUS.

And she takes upon her to spy a white hair on his chin.

CRESSIDA.

Alas, poor chin! many a wart is richer.

PANDARUS.

But there was such laughing!—Queen Hecuba laught, that her eyes ran o'er,—

CRESSIDA.

With mill-stones.

PANDARUS.

And Cassandra laught,—

CRESSIDA.

But there was more temperate fire under the pot of her eyes:—did her eyes run o'er too?

PANDARUS.

And Hector laught.

CRESSIDA.

At what was all this laughing?

PANDARUS.

Marry, at the white hair that Helen spied on Troilus' chin.

CRESSIDA.

An't had been a green hair, I should have laught too.

PANDARUS.

They laught not so much at the hair as at his pretty answer.

CRESSIDA.

What was his answer?

PANDARUS.

Quoth she, 'Here's but one and fifty hairs on your chin, and one of them is white.'

CRESSIDA.

This is her question.

PANDARUS.

That's true; make no question of that. 'One and fifty hairs,' quoth he, 'and one white: that white hair is my father, and all the rest are his sons.' 'Jupiter!' quoth she, 'which of these hairs is Paris my husband?' 'The forkt one,' quoth he; 'pluck't out, and give it him.' But there was such laughing! and Helen so blusht, and Paris so chafed, and all the rest so laught, that it past.

CRESSIDA.

So let it now; for it has been a great while going by.

PANDARUS.

Well, cousin, I told you a thing yesterday; think on't.

CRESSIDA.

So I do.

PANDARUS.

I'll be sworn 'tis true; he will weep you, an 'twere a man born in April.

CRESSIDA.

And I'll spring up in his tears, an 'twere a nettle against May.   [*A retreat sounded.*

PANDARUS.

Hark! they are coming from the field: shall we stand up here, and see them as they pass toward Ilium? good niece, do,—sweet niece Cressida.

CRESSIDA.

At your pleasure.

PANDARUS.

Here, here, here's an excellent place; here we may see most bravely: I'll tell you them all by their names as they pass by; but mark Troilus above the rest.

CRESSIDA.

Speak not so loud.

AENEAS *passes.*

PANDARUS.

That's Aeneas: is not that a brave man? he's one of the flowers of Troy, I can tell you: but mark Troilus; you shall see anon.

ANTENOR *passes.*

CRESSIDA.

Who's that?

PANDARUS.

That's Antenor: he has a shrewd wit, I can tell you; and he's a man good enough: he's one o'th' soundest judgements in Troy, whosoever, and a proper man of person.—When comes Troilus?— I'll show you Troilus anon: if he see me, you shall see him nod at me.

CRESSIDA.

Will he give you the nod?

PANDARUS.

You shall see.

CRESSIDA.

If he do, the rich shall have more.

HECTOR *passes.*

PANDARUS.

That's Hector, that, that, look you, that; there's a fellow!—Go thy way, Hector!—There's a brave man, niece.—O brave Hector!—Look how he looks! there's a countenance! is't not a brave man?

CRESSIDA.

O, a brave man!

PANDARUS.

Is a' not? it does a man's heart good:—look you what hacks are on his helmet! look you yonder, do you see? look you there: there's no jesting; there's laying on, take't off who will, as they say: there be hacks!

CRESSIDA.

Be those with swords?

PANDARUS.

Swords! any thing, he cares not; an the devil come to him, it's all one: by God's lid, it does one's heart good.—Yonder comes Paris, yonder comes Paris:

PARIS *passes.*

look ye yonder, niece; is't not a gallant man too, is't not?—Why, this is brave now.—Who said he came hurt home to-day? he's not hurt: why, this will do Helen's heart good now, ha!—Would I could see Troilus now!—You shall see Troilus anon.

HELENUS *passes.*

CRESSIDA.

Who's that?

PANDARUS.

That's Helenus:—I marvel where Troilus is:— that's Helenus:—I think he went not forth to-day:—that's Helenus.

CRESSIDA.

Can Helenus fight, uncle?

PANDARUS.

Helenus! no; yes, he'll fight indifferent well.—I marvel where Troilus is.—Hark! do you not hear the people cry 'Troilus'?—Helenus is a priest.

CRESSIDA.

What sneaking fellow comes yonder?

TROILUS *passes.*

PANDARUS.

Where? yonder? that's Deiphobus': tis Troilus! there's a man, niece! Hem! Brave Troilus! the prince of chivalry!

CRESSIDA.

Peace, for shame, peace!

PANDARUS.

Mark him; note him:—O brave Troilus!—look well upon him, niece: look you how his sword is bloodied, and his helm more hackt than Hector's; and how he looks, and how he goes!—O admirable youth! he ne'er saw three-and-twenty.—Go thy way, Troilus, go thy way!—Had I a sister were a grace, or a daughter a goddess, he should take his choice. O admirable man! Paris?—Paris is dirt to him; and, I warrant, Helen, to change, would give an eye to boot.

CRESSIDA.

Here come more.

COMMON SOLDIERS *pass.*

PANDARUS.

Asses, fools, dolts! chaff and bran, chaff and bran! porridge after meat!—I could live and die i'th' eyes of Troilus.—Ne'er look, ne'er look; the eagles are gone: crows and daws, crows and daws! —I had rather be such a man as Troilus than Agamemnon and all Greece.

CRESSIDA.

There is among the Greeks Achilles,—a better man than Troilus.

PANDARUS.

Achilles! a drayman, a porter, a very camel.

CRESSIDA.

Well, well.

PANDARUS.

Well, well!—Why, have you any discretion? have you any eyes? do you know what a man is? Is not birth, beauty, good shape, discourse, manhood, learning, gentleness, virtue, youth, liberality, and such like, the spice and salt that season a man?

CRESSIDA.

Ay, a minced man: and then to be baked with no date in the pie,—for then the man's date's out.

PANDARUS.

You are such a woman! one knows not at what ward you lie.

CRESSIDA.

Upon my back, to defend my belly; upon my wit, to defend my wiles; upon my secrecy, to defend mine honesty; my mask, to defend my beauty;

and you, to defend all these: and at all these wards I lie, at a thousand watches.

PANDARUS.

Say one of your watches.

CRESSIDA.

Nay, I'll watch you for that; and that's one of the chiefest of them too: if I cannot ward what I would not have hit, I can watch you for telling how I took the blow; unless it swell past hiding, and then it's past watching.

PANDARUS.

You are such another!

Enter TROILUS' BOY.

BOY.

Sir, my lord would instantly speak with you.

PANDARUS.

Where?

BOY.

At your own house; there he unarms him.

PANDARUS.

Good boy, tell him I come. [*Exit* BOY.] I doubt he be hurt.—Fare ye well, good niece.

CRESSIDA.

Adieu, uncle.

PANDARUS.

I'll be with you, niece, by and by.

CRESSIDA.

To bring, uncle.

PANDARUS.

Ay, a token from Troilus.

CRESSIDA.

By the same token—you are a bawd.

[*Exit* PANDARUS.

Words, vows, gifts, tears, and love's full sacrifice,
He offers in another's enterprise:
But more in Troilus thousand-fold I see
Than in the glass of Pandar's praise may be;
Yet hold I off. Women are angels, wooing:
Things won are done: joy's soul lies in the doing:
That she beloved knows naught that knows not this,—
Men prize the thing ungain'd more than it is:
That she was never yet that ever knew
Love got so sweet as when desire did sue:
Therefore this maxim out of love, I teach,—
Achievement is command; ungain'd, beseech:
Then, though my heart's content firm love doth bear,
Nothing of that shall from mine eyes appear.

[*Exeunt.*

SCENE III.

The Grecian camp. Before AGAMEMNON'S *tent.*

Sennet. Enter AGAMEMNON, NESTOR, ULYSSES, MENELAUS, *with others.*

AGAMEMNON.

PRINCES,
What grief hath set the jaundice on your cheeks?
The ample proposition that hope makes
In all designs begun on earth below
Fails in the promised largeness: checks and disasters
Grow in the veins of actions highest rear'd;

As knots, by the conflux of meeting sap,
Infect the sound pine, and divert his grain
Tortive and errant from his course of growth.
Nor, princes, is it matter new to us,
That we come short of our suppose so far,
That, after seven years' siege, yet Troy walls stand;
Sith every action that hath gone before,
Whereof we have record, trial did draw
Bias and thwart, not answering the aim,
And that unbodied figure of the thought
That gave't surmised shape. Why, then, you princes,
Do you with cheeks abasht behold our works,
And call them shames, which are, indeed, naught else
But the protractive trials of great Jove
To find persistive constancy in men?
The fineness of which metal is not found
In fortune's love; for then the bold and coward,
The wise and fool, the artist and unread,
The hard and soft, seem all affined and kin:
But, in the wind and tempest of her frown,
Distinction, with a broad and powerful fan,
Puffing at all, winnows the light away;
And what hath mass or matter, by itself
Lies rich in virtue and unmingled.

NESTOR.

With due observance of thy godlike seat,
Great Agamemnon, Nestor shall apply
Thy latest words. In the reproof of chance
Lies the true proof of men: the sea being smooth,
How many shallow bauble boats dare sail
Upon her patient breast, making their way
With those of nobler bulk!
But let the ruffian Boreas once enrage
The gentle Thetis, and, anon, behold
The strong-ribb'd bark through liquid mountains cut,
Bounding between the two moist elements,
Like Perseus' horse: where's then the saucy boat,
Whose weak untimber'd sides but even now
Co-rivall'd greatness? either to harbour fled,
Or made a toast for Neptune. Even so
Doth valour's show and valour's worth divide
In storms of fortune: for in her ray and brightness
The herd hath more annoyance by the breese
Than by the tiger; but when the splitting wind
Makes flexible the knees of knotted oaks,
And flies fled under shade, why, then the thing of courage,
As roused with rage, with rage doth sympathize,
And with an accent tuned in selfsame key
Returns to chiding fortune.

ULYSSES.

Agamemnon,—
Thou great commander, nerve and bone of Greece,
Heart of our numbers, soul and only spirit,
In whom the tempers and the minds of all
Should be shut up,—hear what Ulysses speaks.
Besides the applause and approbation
The which—[*to* AGAMEMNON] most mighty for thy place and sway,—
[*to* NESTOR] And thou most reverend for thy stretcht-out life—

I give to both your speeches,—which were such
As Agamemnon and the hand of Greece
Should hold up high in brass; and such again
As venerable Nestor, hatcht in silver,
Should with a bond of air—strong as the axletree
On which heaven rides—knit all the Greekish ears
To his experienced tongue,—yet let it please
  both,
Though great and wise, to hear Ulysses speak.

AGAMEMNON.

Speak, Prince of Ithaca; and be't of less expect
That matter needless, of importless burden,
Divide thy lips, than we are confident,
When rank Thersites opes his mastic jaws,
We shall hear music, wit, and oracle.

ULYSSES.

Troy, yet upon his basis, had been down,
And the great Hector's sword had lackt a master,
But for these instances.
The specialty of rule hath been neglected:
And, look, how many Grecian tents do stand
Hollow upon this plain, so many hollow factions.
When that the general is not like the hive,
To whom the foragers shall all repair,
What honey is expected? Degree being vizarded,
Th'unworthiest shows as fairly in the mask.
The heavens themselves, the planets, and this
  centre,
Observe degree, priority, and place,
Insisture, course, proportion, season, form,
Office, and custom, in all line of order:
And therefore is the glorious planet Sol
In noble eminence enthroned and sphered
Amidst the other; whose med'cinable eye
Corrects the ill aspects of planets evil,
And posts, like the commandment of a king,
Sans check, to good and bad: but when the
  planets,
In evil mixture, to disorder wander,
What plagues, and what portents, what mutiny,
What raging of the sea, shaking of earth,
Commotion in the winds, frights, changes, hor-
  rors,
Divert and crack, rend and deracinate
The unity and married calm of states
Quite from their fixure! O, when degree is
  shaked,
Which is the ladder to all high designs,
The enterprise is sick! How could communities,
Degrees in schools, and brotherhoods in cities,
Peaceful commerce from dividable shores,
The primogenity and due of birth,
Prerogative of age, crowns, sceptres, laurels,
But by degree, stand in authentic place?
Take but degree away, untune that string,
And, hark, what discord follows! each thing meets
In mere oppugnancy: the bounded waters
Should lift their bosoms higher than the shores,
And make a sop of all this solid globe:
Strength should be lord of imbecility,
And the rude son should strike his father dead:
Force should be right; or rather, right and
  wrong—
Between whose endless jar justice resides—
Should lose their names, and so should justice
  too.

Then every thing includes itself in power,
Power into will, will into appetite;
And appetite, an universal wolf,
So doubly seconded with will and power,
Must make perforce an universal prey,
And last eat up himself. Great Agamemnon,
This chaos, when degree is suffocate,
Follows the choking.
And this neglection of degree it is
That by a pace goes backward, with a purpose
It hath to climb. The general's disdain'd
By him one step below; he, by the next;
That next, by him beneath: so every step,
Exampled by the first pace that is sick
Of his superior, grows to an envious fever
Of pale and bloodless emulation:
And 'tis this fever that keeps Troy on foot,
Not her own sinews. To end a tale of length,
Troy in our weakness stands, not in her strength.

NESTOR.

Mose wisely hath Ulysses here discover'd
The fever whereof all our power is sick.

AGAMEMNON.

The nature of the sickness found, Ulysses,
What is the remedy?

ULYSSES.

The great Achilles,—whom opinion crowns
The sinew and the forehand of our host,—
Having his ear full of his airy fame,
Grows dainty of his worth, and in his tent
Lies mocking our designs: with him, Patroclus,
Upon a lazy bed, the livelong day
Breaks scurril jests;
And with ridiculous and awkward action—
Which, slanderer, he imitation calls—
He pageants us. Sometime, great Agamemnon,
Thy topless deputation he puts on;
And, like a strutting player,—whose conceit
Lies in his hamstring, and doth think it rich
To hear the wooden dialogue and sound
'Twixt his stretcht footing and the scaffoldage,—
Such to-be-pitied and o'er-wrested seeming
He acts thy greatness in: and when he speaks,
'Tis like a chime a-mending; with terms un-
  squared,
Which, from the tongue of roaring Typhon dropt,
Would seem hyperboles. At this fusty stuff
The large Achilles, on his prest bed lolling,
From his deep chest laughs out a loud applause;
Cries, 'Excellent! 'tis Agamemnon just.
Now play me Nestor; hem, and stroke thy beard,
As he being drest to some oration.'
That's done;—as near as the extremest ends
Of parallels; as like as Vulcan and his wife:
Yet god Achilles still cries, 'Excellent!
'Tis Nestor right. Now play him me, Patroclus,
Arming to answer in a night-alarm.'
And then, forsooth, the faint defects of age
Must be the scene of mirth; to cough and spit,
And, with a palsy fumbling on his gorget,
Shake in and out the rivet:—and at this sport
Sir Valour dies; cries, 'O, enough, Patroclus;
Or give me ribs of steel! I shall split all
In pleasure of my spleen.' And in this fashion,
All our abilities, gifts, natures, shapes,
Severals and generals of grace exact,

Achievements, plots, orders, preventions,
Excitements to the field, or speech for truce,
Success or loss, what is or is not, serves
As stuff for these two to make paradoxes.
NESTOR.
And in the imitation of these twain—
Who, as Ulysses says, opinion crowns
With an imperial voice—many are infect.
Ajax is grown self-will'd; and bears his head
In such a rein, in full as proud a pace
As broad Achilles; keeps his tent like him;
Makes factious feasts; rails on our state of war,
Bold as an oracle; and sets Thersites—
A slave whose gall coins slanders like a mint—
To match us in comparisons with dirt,
To weaken and discredit our exposure,
How rank soever rounded in with danger.
ULYSSES.
They tax our policy, and call it cowardice;
Count wisdom as no member of the war;
Forestall prescience, and esteem no act
But that of hand: the still and mental parts,
That do contrive how many hands shall strike,
When fitness calls them on; and know, by
    measure
Of their observant toil, the enemies' weight,—
Why, this hath not a finger's dignity:
They call this bed-work, mappery, closet-war;
So that the ram that batters down the wall,
For the great swing and rudeness of his poise,
They place before his hand that made the engine,
Or those that with the fineness of their souls
By reason guide his execution.
NESTOR.
Let this be granted, and Achilles' horse
Makes many Thetis' sons.   [Tucket.
AGAMEMNON.
What trumpet? look, Menelaus.
MENELAUS.
From Troy.
Enter AENEAS.
AGAMEMNON.
What would you 'fore our tent?
AENEAS.
Is this great Agamemnon's tent, I pray you?
AGAMEMNON.
Even this.
AENEAS.
May one, that is a herald and a prince,
Do a fair message to his kingly ears?
AGAMEMNON.
With surety stronger than Achilles' arm
'Fore all the Greekish heads, which with one
    voice
Call Agamemnon head and general.
AENEAS.
Fair leave and large security. How may
A stranger to those most imperial looks
Know them from eyes of other mortals?
AGAMEMNON.
                                How?
AENEAS.
Ay;
I ask, that I might waken reverence,
And bid the cheek be ready with a blush
Modest as morning when she coldly eyes

The youthful Phœbus:
Which is that god in office, guiding men?
Which is the high and mighty Agamemnon?
AGAMEMNON.
This Trojan scorns us; or the men of Troy
Are ceremonious courtiers.
AENEAS.
Courtiers as free, as debonair, unarm'd,
As bending angels; that's their fame in peace:
But when they would seem soldiers, they have
    galls,
Good arms, strong joints, true swords; and,
    Jove's accord,
Nothing so full of heart. But peace, Aeneas,
Peace, Trojan; lay thy finger on thy lips!
The worthiness of praise distains his worth,
If that the praised himself bring the praise forth:
But what the repining enemy commends,
That breath fame blows; that praise, sole pure,
    transcends.
AGAMEMNON.
Sir, you of Troy, call you yourself Aeneas?
AENEAS.
Ay, Greek, that is my name.
AGAMEMNON.
What's your affair, I pray you?
AENEAS.
Sir, pardon; 'tis for Agamemnon's ears.
AGAMEMNON.
He hears naught privately that comes from Troy.
AENEAS.
Nor I from Troy come not to whisper him:
I bring a trumpet to awake his ear;
To set his sense on the attentive bent,
And then to speak.
AGAMEMNON.
                Speak frankly as the wind;
It is not Agamemnon's sleeping hour:
That thou shalt know, Trojan, he is awake,
He tells thee so himself.
AENEAS.
                Trumpet, blow loud,
Send thy brass voice through all these lazy tents;
And every Greek of mettle, let him know,
What Troy means fairly shall be spoke aloud.
                    [Trumpet sounds.
We have, great Agamemnon, here in Troy
A prince call'd Hector,—Priam is his father,—
Who in this dull and long-continued truce
Is rusty grown: he bade me take a trumpet,
And to this purpose speak. Kings, princes, lords!
If there be one among the fair'st of Greece
That holds his honour higher than his ease;
That seeks his praise more than he fears his peril;
That knows his valour, and knows not his fear;
That loves his mistress more than in confession
With truant vows to her own lips he loves,
And dare avow her beauty and her worth
In other arms than hers,—to him this challenge.
Hector, in view of Trojans and of Greeks,
Shall make it good, or do his best to do it,
He hath a lady, wiser, fairer, truer,
Than ever Greek did compass in his arms;
And will to-morrow with his trumpet call
Midway between your tents and walls of Troy,
To rouse a Grecian that is true in love:

If any come, Hector shall honour him;
If none, he'll say in Troy when he retires,
The Grecian dames are sunburnt, and not worth
The splinter of a lance. Even so much.

AGAMEMNON.
This shall be told our lovers, Lord Aeneas;
If none of them have soul in such a kind,
We left them all at home: but we are soldiers;
And may that soldier a mere recreant prove,
That means not, hath not, or is not in love!
If then one is, or hath, or means to be,
That one meets Hector; if none else, I am he.

NESTOR.
Tell him of Nestor, one that was a man
When Hector's grandsire suckt: he is old now;
But if there be not in our Grecian host
One noble man that hath one spark of fire,
To answer for his love, tell him from me,—
I'll hide my silver beard in a gold beaver,
And in my vantbrace put this wither'd brawn;
And, meeting him, will tell him that my lady
Was fairer than his grandam, and as chaste
As may be in the world; his youth in flood,
I'll prove this truth with my three drops of blood.

AENEAS.
Now heavens forbid such scarcity of youth!

ULYSSES.
Amen.

AGAMEMNON.
Fair Lord Aeneas, let me touch your hand;
To our pavilion shall I lead you, sir.
Achilles shall have word of this intent;
So shall each lord of Greece, from tent to tent:
Yourself shall feast with us before you go,
And find the welcome of a noble foe.

[*Exeunt all but* ULYSSES *and* NESTOR.

ULYSSES.
Nestor,—

NESTOR.
What says Ulysses?

ULYSSES.
I have a young conception in my brain;
Be you my time to bring it to some shape.

NESTOR.
What is't?

ULYSSES.
This 'tis:—
Blunt wedges rive hard knots: the seeded pride
That hath to this maturity blown up
In rank Achilles must or now be cropt,
Or, shedding, breed a nursery of like evil,
To overbulk us all.

NESTOR.
Well, and how?

ULYSSES.
This challenge that the gallant Hector sends,
However it is spread in general name,
Relates in purpose only to Achilles.

NESTOR.
The purpose is perspicuous even as substance
Whose grossness little characters sum up:
And, in the publication, make no strain,
But that Achilles, were his brain as barren
As banks of Libya,—though, Apollo knows,
'Tis dry enough,—will, with great speed of judge-
ment,

Ay, with celerity, find Hector's purpose
Pointing on him.

ULYSSES.
And wake him to the answer, think you?

NESTOR.
Yes,
It is most meet: who may you else oppose,
That can from Hector bring his honour off,
If not Achilles? Though't be a sportful combat,
Yet in the trial much opinion dwells;
For here the Trojans taste our dear'st repute
With their finest palate: and trust to me, Ulysses,
Our imputation shall be oddly poised
In this wild action; for the success,
Although particular, shall give a scantling
Of good or bad unto the general;
And in such indexes, although small pricks
To their subsequent volumes, there is seen
The baby figure of the giant mass
Of things to come at large. It is supposed,
He that meets Hector issues from our choice:
And choice, being mutual act of all our souls,
Makes merit her election; and doth boil,
As 'twere from forth us all, a man distill'd
Out of our virtues; who miscarrying,   [part,
What heart receives from hence the conquering
To steel a strong opinion to themselves?
Which entertain'd, limbs are his instruments,
In no less working than are swords and bows
Directive by the limbs.

ULYSSES.
Give pardon to my speech;—
Therefore 'tis meet Achilles meet not Hector.
Let us, like merchants, show our foulest wares,
And think, perchance, they'll sell; if not,
The lustre of the better yet to show,
Shall show the better. Do not, then, consent
That ever Hector and Achilles meet;
For both our honour and our shame in this
Are dogg'd with two strange followers.

NESTOR.
I see them not with my old eyes: what are they?

ULYSSES.
What glory our Achilles shares from Hector,
Were he not proud, we all should share with him:
But he already is too insolent;
And we were better parch in Afric sun
Than in the pride and salt scorn of his eyes,
Should he scape Hector fair: if he were foil'd,
Why, then we did our main opinion crush
In taint of our best man. No, make a lottery;
And, by device, let blockish Ajax draw
The sort of fight with Hector: among ourselves
Give him allowance as the worthier man;
For that will physic the great Myrmidon
Who broils in loud applause, and make him fall
His crest that prouder than blue Iris bends.
If the dull brainless Ajax come safe off,
We'll dress him up in voices: if he fail,
Yet go we under our opinion still
That we have better men. But, hit or miss,
Our project's life this shape of sense assumes,—
Ajax employ'd plucks down Achilles' plumes.

NESTOR.
Ulysses,
Now I begin to relish thy advice;

And I will give a taste of it forthwith
To Agamemnon: go we to him straight.
Two curs shall tame each other: pride alone
Must tarre the mastiffs on, as 'twere their bone.
[*Exeunt.*

ACT II. SCENE I.

A part of the Grecian camp.

Enter AJAX *and* THERSITES.

AJAX.

THERSITES,—

THERSITES.

Agamemnon,—how if he had boils,—full, all
over, generally?—

AJAX.

Thersites,—

THERSITES.

And those boils did run?—Say so,—did not the
general run then? were not that a botchy core?—

AJAX.

Dog,—

THERSITES.

Then would come some matter from him; I see
none now.

AJAX.

Thou bitch-wolf's son, canst thou not hear? Feel,
then.   [*Strikes him.*

THERSITES.

The plague of Greece upon thee, thou mongrel
beef-witted lord!

AJAX.

Speak, then, thou vinewedst leaven, speak: I will
beat thee into handsomeness.

THERSITES.

I shall sooner rail thee into wit and holiness: but,
I think, thy horse will sooner con an oration than
thou learn a prayer without book. Thou canst
strike, canst thou? a red murrain o' thy jade's
tricks!

AJAX.

Toadstool, learn me the proclamation.

THERSITES.

Dost thou think I have no sense, thou strikest me
thus?

AJAX.

The proclamation!

THERSITES.

Thou art proclaim'd a fool, I think.

AJAX.

Do not, porpentine, do not: my fingers itch.

THERSITES.

I would thou didst itch from head to foot, and I
had the scratching of thee; I would make thee
the loathsom'st scab in Greece. When thou art
forth in the incursions, thou strikest as slow as
another.

AJAX.

I say, the proclamation!

THERSITES.

Thou grumblest and railest every hour on
Achilles; and thou art as full of envy at his greatness as Cerberus is at Proserpina's beauty, ay,
that thou bark'st at him.

AJAX.

Mistress Thersites!

THERSITES.

Thou shouldst strike him.

AJAX.

Cobloaf!

THERSITES.

He would pun thee into shivers with his fist, as a
sailor breaks a biscuit.

AJAX.

You whoreson cur!   [*Beating him.*

THERSITES.

Do, do.

AJAX.

Thou stool for a witch!

THERSITES.

Ay, do, do; thou sodden-witted lord! thou hast no
more brain than I have in mine elbows; an as-
sinego may tutor thee: thou scurvy-valiant ass!
thou art here but to thrash Trojans; and thou art
bought and sold among those of any wit, like a
barbarian slave. If thou use to beat me, I will
begin at thy heel, and tell what thou art by inches,
thou thing of no bowels, thou!

AJAX.

You dog!

THERSITES.

You scurvy lord!

AJAX.

You cur!   [*Beating him.*

THERSITES.

Mars his idiot! do, rudeness, do, camel; do, do.

Enter ACHILLES *and* PATROCLUS.

ACHILLES.

Why, how now, Ajax! wherefore do you thus?—
How now, Thersites! what's the matter, man?

THERSITES.

You see him there, do you?

ACHILLES.

Ay, what's the matter?

THERSITES.

Nay, look upon him.

ACHILLES.

So I do: what's the matter?

THERSITES.

Nay, but regard him well.

ACHILLES.

Well! why, so I do.

THERSITES.

But yet you look not well upon him; for, whosoever you take him to be, he is Ajax.

ACHILLES.

I know that, fool.

THERSITES.

Ay, but that fool knows not himself.

AJAX.

Therefore I beat thee.

THERSITES.

Lo, lo, lo, lo, what modicums of wit he utters! his
evasions have ears thus long. I have bobb'd his
brain more than he has beat my bones: I will buy
nine sparrows for a penny, and his *pia mater* is not
worth the ninth part of a sparrow. This lord,
Achilles, Ajax,—who wears his wit in his belly,
and his guts in his head,—I'll tell you what I say
of him.

ACHILLES.

What?

THERSITES.

I say, this Ajax—

[AJAX *offers to beat him,* ACHILLES *interposes.*

ACHILLES.

Nay, good Ajax.

THERSITES.

Has not so much wit—

ACHILLES.

Nay, I must hold you.

THERSITES.

As will stop the eye of Helen's needle, for whom
he comes to fight.

ACHILLES.

Peace, fool!

THERSITES.

I would have peace and quietness, but the fool
will not: he there; that he; look you there.

AJAX.

O thou damn'd cur! I shall—

ACHILLES.

Will you set your wit to a fool's?

THERSITES.

No, I warrant you; for a fool's will shame it.

PATROCLUS.

Good words, Thersites.

ACHILLES.

What's the quarrel?

AJAX.

I bade the vile owl go learn me the tenour of the
proclamation, and he rails upon me.

THERSITES.

I serve thee not.

AJAX.

Well, go to, go to.

THERSITES.

I serve here voluntary.

ACHILLES.

Your last service was sufferance, 'twas not voluntary,—no man is beaten voluntary: Ajax was here
the voluntary, and you as under an impress.

THERSITES.

E'en so; a great deal of your wit, too, lies in your
sinews, or else there be liars. Hector shall have a
great catch, if he knock out either of your brains:
a' were as good crack a fusty nut with no kernel.

ACHILLES.

What, with me too, Thersites?

THERSITES.

There's Ulysses and old Nestor—whose wit was
mouldy ere your grandsires had nails on their
toes—yoke you like draught-oxen, and make you
plough up the wars.

ACHILLES.

What, what?

THERSITES.

Yes, good sooth: to, Achilles! to, Ajax! to!

AJAX.

I shall cut out your tongue.

THERSITES.

'Tis no matter; I shall speak as much as thou
afterwards.

PATROCLUS.

No more words, Thersites; peace!

THERSITES.

I will hold my peace when Achilles' brach bids
me, shall I?

ACHILLES.

There's for you, Patroclus.

THERSITES.

I will see you hang'd, like clotpoles, ere I come
any more to your tents: I will keep where there is
wit stirring, and leave the faction of fools.   [*Exit.*

PATROCLUS.

A good riddance.

ACHILLES.

Marry, this, sir, is proclaim'd through all our
host:—

That Hector, by the fifth hour of the sun,
Will, with a trumpet, 'twixt our tents and Troy,
To-morrow morning call some knight to arms
That hath a stomach; and such a one that dare
Maintain—I know not what; 'tis trash. Farewell.

AJAX.

Farewell. Who shall answer him?

ACHILLES.

I know not,—'tis put to lottery; otherwise
He knew his man.

[*Exeunt* ACHILLES *and* PATROCLUS.

AJAX.

O, meaning you.—I will go learn more of it.

[*Exit.*

SCENE II.

Troy. PRIAM'S *palace.*

Enter PRIAM, HECTOR, TROILUS, PARIS,
and HELENUS.

PRIAM.

AFTER so many hours, lives, speeches spent,
Thus once again says Nestor from the
   Greeks:—
'Deliver Helen, and all damage else—
As honour, loss of time, travail, expense,
Wounds, friends, and what else dear that is con-
  sumed
In hot digestion of this cormorant war—
Shall be struck off:'—Hector, what say you to't?

HECTOR.

Though no man lesser fears the Greeks than I
As far as toucheth my particular,
Yet, dread Priam,
There is no lady of more softer bowels,
More spongy to suck in the sense of fear,
More ready to cry out 'Who knows what follows?'
Than Hector is: the wound of peace is surety,
Surety secure; but modest doubt is call'd
The beacon of the wise, the tent that searches
To th'bottom of the worst. Let Helen go:
Since the first sword was drawn about this ques-
  tion,
Every tithe soul, 'mongst many thousand dismes,
Hath been as dear as Helen,—I mean, of ours:
If we have lost so many tenths of ours,
To guard a thing not ours nor worth to us,
Had it our name, the value of one ten,—
What merit's in that reason which denies
The yielding of her up?

TROILUS.

          Fie, fie, my brother!
Weigh you the worth and honour of a king,
So great as our dread father, in a scale
Of common ounces? will you with counters sum

The past-proportion of his infinite?
And buckle in a waist most fathomless
With spans and inches so diminutive
As fears and reasons? fie, for godly shame!

HELENUS.

No marvel, though you bite so sharp at reasons,
You are so empty of them. Should not our father
Bear the great sway of his affairs with reasons,
Because your speech hath none that tells him so?

TROILUS.

You are for dreams and slumbers, brother priest;
You fur your gloves with reason. Here are your
  reasons:
You know an enemy intends you harm;
You know a sword employ'd is perilous,
And reason flies the object of all harm:
Who marvels, then, when Helenus beholds
A Grecian and his sword, if he do set
The very wings of reason to his heels,
And fly like chidden Mercury from Jove,
Or like a star disorb'd? Nay, if we talk of reason,
Let's shut our gates, and sleep: manhood and
  honour
Should have hare-hearts, would they but fat their
  thoughts
With this cramm'd reason: reason and respect
Make livers pale, and lustihood deject.

HECTOR.

Brother, she is not worth what she doth cost
The holding.

TROILUS.
        What is aught, but as 'tis valued?

HECTOR.

But value dwells not in particular will;
It holds his estimate and dignity
As well therein 'tis precious of itself
As in the prizer: 'tis mad idolatry
To make the service greater than the god;
And the will dotes, that is attributive
To what infectiously itself affects,
Without some image of th'affected merit.

TROILUS.

I take to-day a wife, and my election
Is led on in the conduct of my will;
My will enkindled by mine eyes and ears,
Two traded pilots 'twixt the dangerous shores
Of will and judgement: how may I avoid,
Although my will distaste what it elected,
The wife I chose? there can be no evasion
To blench from this, and to stand firm by honour:
We turn not back the silks upon the merchant
When we have soil'd them; nor the remainder
  viands
We do not throw in unrespective sieve
Because we now are full. It was thought meet
Paris should do some vengeance on the Greeks:
Your breath of full consent bellied his sails;
The seas and winds, old wranglers, took a truce,
And did him service: he touch'd the ports desired;
And, for an old aunt whom the Greeks held cap-
  tive,
He brought a Grecian queen, whose youth and
  freshness
Wrinkles Apollo's, and makes stale the morning.
Why keep we her? the Grecians keep our aunt:
Is she worth keeping? why, she is a pearl,

Whose price hath launcht above a thousand ships,
And turn'd crown'd kings to merchants.
If you'll avouch 'twas wisdom Paris went,—
As you must needs, for you all cried, 'Go, go;'
If you'll confess he brought home noble prize.—
As you must needs, for you all clapt your hands,
And cried, 'Inestimable!'—why do you now
The issue of your proper wisdoms rate,
And do a deed that fortune never did,—
Beggar the estimation which you prized
Richer than sea and land? O, theft most base,
That we have stoln what we do fear to keep!
But, thieves, unworthy of a thing so stoln,
That in their country did them that disgrace
We fear to warrant in our native place!

CASSANDRA [within].

Cry, Trojans, cry!

PRIAM.
        What noise? what shriek is this?

TROILUS.

'Tis our mad sister, I do know her voice.

CASSANDRA [within].

Cry, Trojans!

HECTOR.

It is Cassandra.

Enter CASSANDRA, *raving, with her hair
about her ears.*

CASSANDRA.

Cry, Trojans, cry! lend me ten thousand eyes,
And I will fill them with prophetic tears.

HECTOR.

Peace, sister, peace!

CASSANDRA.

Virgins and boys, mid-age and wrinkled eld,
Soft infancy, that nothing canst but cry,
Add to my clamours! let us pay betimes
A moiety of that mass of moan to come.
Cry, Trojans, cry! practise your eyes with tears!
Troy must not be, nor goodly Ilion stand;
Our firebrand brother, Paris, burns us all.
Cry, Trojans, cry! a Helen and a woe!
Cry, cry! Troy burns, or else let Helen go. [*Exit.*

HECTOR.

Now, youthful Troilus, do not these high strains
Of divination in our sister work
Some touches of remorse? or is your blood
So madly hot, that no discourse of reason,
Nor fear of bad success in a bad cause,
Can qualify the same?

TROILUS.
        Why, brother Hector,
We may not think the justness of each act
Such and no other than event doth form it;
Nor once deject the courage of our minds,
Because Cassandra's mad: her brain-sick rap-
  tures
Cannot distaste the goodness of a quarrel
Which hath our several honours all engaged
To make it gracious. For my private part,
I am no more touch'd than all Priam's sons:
And Jove forbid there should be done amongst us
Such things as might offend the weakest spleen
To fight for and maintain!

PARIS.

Else might the world convince of levity
As well my undertakings as your counsels:

But I attest the gods, your full consent
Gave wings to my propension, and cut off
All fears attending on so dire a project.
For what, alas, can these my single arms?
What propugnation is in one man's valour,
To stand the push and enmity of those
This quarrel would excite? Yet, I protest,
Were I alone to pass the difficulties,
And had as ample power as I have will,
Paris should ne'er retract what he hath done,
Nor faint in the pursuit.

PRIAM.
                         Paris, you speak
Like one besotted on your sweet delights:
You have the honey still, but these the gall;
So to be valiant is no praise at all.

PARIS.
Sir, I propose not merely to myself
The pleasures such a beauty brings with it;
But I would have the soil of her fair rape
Wiped off, in honourable keeping her.
What treason were it to the ransackt queen,
Disgrace to your great worths, and shame to me,
Now to deliver her possession up
On terms of base compulsion! Can it be
That so degenerate a strain as this
Should once set footing in your generous bosoms?
There's not the meanest spirit on our party
Without a heart to dare, or sword to draw,
When Helen is defended; nor none so noble
Whose life were ill bestow'd, or death unfamed,
Where Helen is the subject: then, I say,
Well may we fight for her, whom, we know well,
The world's large spaces cannot parallel.

HECTOR.
Paris and Troilus, you have both said well;
And on the cause and question now in hand
Have glozed, but superficially; not much
Unlike young men, whom Aristotle thought
Unfit to hear moral philosophy:
The reasons you allege do more conduce
To the hot passion of distemper'd blood
Than to make up a free determination
'Twixt right and wrong; for pleasure and revenge
Have ears more deaf than adders to the voice
Of any true decision. Nature craves
All dues be render'd to their owners: now,
What nearer debt in all humanity
Than wife is to the husband? If this law
Of nature be corrupted through affection,
And that great minds, of partial indulgence
To their benumbed wills, resist the same,
There is a law in each well-order'd nation
To curb those raging appetites that are
Most disobedient and refractory.
If Helen, then, be wife to Sparta's king,—
As it is known she is,—these moral laws
Of nature and of nations speak aloud
To have her back return'd: thus to persist
In doing wrong extenuates not wrong,
But makes it much more heavy. Hector's opinion
Is this, in way of truth: yet, ne'ertheless,
My spritely brethren, I propend to you
In resolution to keep Helen still;
For 'tis a cause that hath no mean dependance
Upon our joint and several dignities.

TROILUS.
Why, there you toucht the life of our design:
Were it not glory that we more affected
Than the performance of our heaving spleens,
I would not wish a drop of Trojan blood
Spent more in her defence. But, worthy Hector,
She is a theme of honour and renown;
A spur to valiant and magnanimous deeds;
Whose present courage may beat down our foes,
And fame in time to come canonize us:
For, I presume, brave Hector would not lose
So rich advantage of a promised glory,
As smiles upon the forehead of this action,
For the wide world's revenue.

HECTOR.
                         I am yours,
You valiant offspring of great Priamus.—
I have a roisting challenge sent amongst
The dull and factious nobles of the Greeks
Will strike amazement to their drowsy spirits:
I was advertised their great general slept,
Whilst emulation in the army crept:
This, I presume, will wake him.   [Exeunt.

SCENE III.
The Grecian camp.   Before ACHILLES' tent.
Enter THERSITES.

THERSITES.
HOW now, Thersites! what, lost in the labyrinth of thy fury! Shall the elephant Ajax
carry it thus? he beats me, and I rail at him: O,
worthy satisfaction! would it were otherwise; that
I could beat him, whilst he rail'd at me: 'sfoot, I'll
learn to conjure and raise devils, but I'll see some
issue of my spiteful execrations. Then there's
Achilles,—a rare enginer. If Troy be not taken
till these two undermine it, the walls will stand
till they fall of themselves. O thou great thunder-
darter of Olympus, forget that thou art Jove, the
king of gods; and, Mercury, lose all the serpentine
craft of thy caduceus; if ye take not that little little
less-than-little wit from them that they have!
which short-arm'd ignorance itself knows is so
abundant scarce, it will not in circumvention deliver a fly from a spider, without drawing their
massy irons and cutting the web. After this, the
vengeance on the whole camp! or, rather, the
Neapolitan bone-ache! for that, methinks, is the
curse dependant on those that war for a placket.
I have said my prayers; and devil Envy say
Amen.—What, ho! my Lord Achilles!
Enter PATROCLUS.

PATROCLUS.
Who's there? Thersites! Good Thersites, come in
and rail.

THERSITES.
If I could ha' remember'd a gilt counterfeit, thou
wouldst not have slipt out of my contemplation:
but it is no matter; thyself upon thyself! The
common curse of mankind, folly and ignorance,
be thine in great revenue! heaven bless thee from
a tutor, and discipline come not near thee! Let
thy blood be thy direction till thy death! then
if she that lays thee out says thou art a fair

corse, I'll be sworn and sworn upon't she never shrouded any but lazars. Amen.—Where's Achilles?

PATROCLUS.

What, art thou devout? wast thou in prayer?

THERSITES.

Ay; the heavens hear me!

Enter ACHILLES.

ACHILLES.

Who's there?

PATROCLUS.

Thersites, my lord.

ACHILLES.

Where, where?—Art thou come? why, my cheese, my digestion, why hast thou not served thyself in to my table so many meals? Come,—what's Agamemnon?

THERSITES.

Thy commander, Achilles.—Then tell me, Patroclus, what's Achilles?

PATROCLUS.

Thy lord, Thersites: then tell me, I pray thee, what's thyself?

THERSITES.

Thy knower, Patroclus: then tell me, Patroclus, what art thou?

PATROCLUS.

Thou mayst tell that know'st.

ACHILLES.

O, tell, tell.

THERSITES.

I'll decline the whole question. Agamemnon commands Achilles; Achilles is my lord; I am Patroclus' knower; and Patroclus is a fool.

PATROCLUS.

You rascal!

THERSITES.

Peace, fool! I have not done.

ACHILLES.

He is a privileged man.—Proceed, Thersites.

THERSITES.

Agamemnon is a fool; Achilles is a fool; Thersites is a fool; and, as aforesaid, Patroclus is a fool.

ACHILLES.

Derive this; come.

THERSITES.

Agamemnon is a fool to offer to command Achilles; Achilles is a fool to be commanded of Agamemnon; Thersites is a fool to serve such a fool; and Patroclus is a fool positive.

PATROCLUS.

Why am I a fool?

THERSITES.

Make that demand to the Creator. It suffices me thou art.—Look you, who comes here?

ACHILLES.

Patroclus, I'll speak with nobody.—Come in with me, Thersites.   [*Exit.*

THERSITES.

Here is such patchery, such juggling, and such knavery! all the argument is a cuckold and a whore; a good quarrel to draw emulous factions and bleed to death upon. Now, the dry serpigo on the subject! and war and lechery confound all!

[*Exit.*

Enter AGAMEMNON, ULYSSES, NESTOR, DIOMEDES, *and* AJAX.

AGAMEMNON.

Where is Achilles?

PATROCLUS.

Within his tent: but ill-disposed, my lord.

AGAMEMNON.

Let it be known to him that we are here.
He shent our messengers; and we lay by
Our appertainments, visiting of him:
Let him be told so; lest perchance he think
We dare not move the question of our place,
Or know not what we are.

PATROCLUS.

         I shall say so to him.   [*Exit.*

ULYSSES.

We saw him at the opening of his tent:
He is not sick.

AJAX.

Yes, lion-sick, sick of proud heart: you may call it melancholy, if you will favour the man; but, by my head, 'tis pride: but why, why? let him show us the cause.—A word, my lord.

[*Takes* AGAMEMNON *aside.*

NESTOR.

What moves Ajax thus to bay at him?

ULYSSES.

Achilles hath inveigled his fool from him.

NESTOR.

Who, Thersites?

ULYSSES.

He.

NESTOR.

Then will Ajax lack matter, if he have lost his argument.

ULYSSES.

No, you see, he is his argument that has his argument,—Achilles.

NESTOR.

All the better; their fraction is more our wish than their faction: but it was a strong composure a fool could disunite.

ULYSSES.

The amity that wisdom knits not, folly may easily untie.—Here comes Patroclus.

NESTOR.

No Achilles with him.

ULYSSES.

The elephant hath joints, but none for courtesy: his legs are legs for necessity, not for flexure.

Enter PATROCLUS.

PATROCLUS.

Achilles bids me say, he is much sorry,
If any thing more than your sport and pleasure
Did move your greatness and this noble state
To call upon him; he hopes it is no other
But for your health and your digestion sake,—
An after-dinner's breath.

AGAMEMNON.

         Hear you, Patroclus:—
We are too well acquainted with these answers:
But his evasion, wing'd thus swift with scorn,
Cannot outfly our apprehensions.
Much attribute he hath; and much the reason
Why we ascribe it to him: yet all his virtues,
Not virtuously on his own part beheld,

Do in our eyes begin to lose their gloss;
Yea, like fair fruit in an unwholesome dish,
Are like to rot untasted. Go and tell him,
We come to speak with him; and you shall not sin,
If you do say we think him over-proud
And under-honest; in self-assumption greater
Than in the note of judgement; and worthier than
    himself
Here tend the savage strangeness he puts on,
Disguise the holy strength of their command,
And underwrite in an observing kind
His humorous predominance; yea, watch
His pettish lunes, his ebbs, his flows, as if
The passage and whole carriage of this action
Rode on his tide. Go tell him this; and add,
That if he overhold his price so much,
We'll none of him; but let him, like an engine
Not portable, lie under this report,—
'Bring action hither, this cannot go to war:
A stirring dwarf we do allowance give
Before a sleeping giant:'—tell him so.

           PATROCLUS.
I shall; and bring his answer presently.   [*Exit.*

           AGAMEMNON.
In second voice we'll not be satisfied;
We come to speak with him.—Ulysses, enter you.
                    [*Exit* ULYSSES.

           AJAX.
What is he more than another?

           AGAMEMNON.
No more than what he thinks he is.

           AJAX.
Is he so much? Do you not think he thinks himself a better man than I am?

           AGAMEMNON.
No question.

           AJAX.
Will you subscribe his thought, and say he is?

           AGAMEMNON.
No, noble Ajax; you are as strong, as valiant, as wise, no less noble, much more gentle, and altogether more tractable.

           AJAX.
Why should a man be proud? How doth pride grow? I know not what pride is.

           AGAMEMNON.
Your mind is the clearer, Ajax, and your virtues the fairer. He that is proud eats up himself; pride is his own glass, his own trumpet, his own chronicle; and whatever praises itself but in the deed, devours the deed in the praise.

           AJAX.
I do hate a proud man, as I hate the engendering of toads.

           NESTOR [*aside*].
Yet he loves himself: is't not strange?
           Enter ULYSSES.

           ULYSSES.
Achilles will not to the field to-morrow.

           AGAMEMNON.
What's his excuse?

           ULYSSES.
           He doth rely on none;
But carries on the stream of his dispose,
Without observance or respect of any,
In will peculiar and in self-admission.

           AGAMEMNON.
Why will he not, upon our fair request,
Untent his person, and share the air with us?

           ULYSSES.
Things small as nothing, for request's sake only,
He makes important: possest he is with greatness;
And speaks not to himself, but with a pride
That quarrels at self-breath: imagined worth
Holds in his blood such swoln and hot discourse,
That 'twixt his mental and his active parts
Kingdom'd Achilles in commotion rages,
And batters down himself: what should I say?
He is so plaguy proud, that the death-tokens of it
Cry 'No recovery.'

           AGAMEMNON.
           Let Ajax go to him.—
Dear lord, go you and greet him in his tent:
'Tis said he holds you well; and will be led,
At your request, a little from himself.

           ULYSSES.
O Agamemnon, let it not be so!
We'll consecrate the steps that Ajax makes
When they go from Achilles: shall the proud
    lord,
That bastes his arrogance with his own seam,
And never suffers matter of the world
Enter his thoughts, save such as doth revolve
And ruminate himself,—shall he be worship
Of that we hold an idol more than he?
No, this thrice-worthy and right-valiant lord
Must not so stale his palm, nobly acquired;
Nor, by my will, assubjugate his merit,
As amply titled as Achilles is,
By going to Achilles:
That were to enlard his fat-already pride,
And add more coals to Cancer when he burns
With entertaining great Hyperion.
This lord go to him! Jupiter forbid;
And say in thunder, 'Achilles go to him.'

           NESTOR [*aside*].
O, this is well; he rubs the vein of him.

           DIOMEDES [*aside*].
And how his silence drinks up this applause

           AJAX.
If I go to him, with my armed fist
I'll pash him o'er the face.

           AGAMEMNON.
O, no, you shall not go.

           AJAX.
An a' be proud with me, I'll pheeze his pride:
Let me go to him.

           ULYSSES.
Not for the worth that hangs upon our quarrel.

           AJAX.
A paltry, insolent fellow!

           NESTOR [*aside*].
How he describes himself!

           AJAX.
Can he not be sociable?

           ULYSSES [*aside*].
The raven chides blackness.

           AJAX.
I'll let his humours blood.

           AGAMEMNON [*aside*].
He will be the physician that should be the patient.

AJAX.
An all men were o' my mind,—
ULYSSES [*aside*].
Wit would be out of fashion.
AJAX.
A' should not bear it so, a' should eat swords
first: shall pride carry it?
NESTOR [*aside*].
An 'twould, you'ld carry half.
ULYSSES [*aside*].
A' would have ten shares.
AJAX.
I will knead him; I'll make him supple.
NESTOR [*aside*].
He's not yet through warm: force him with
praises: pour in, pour in; his ambition is dry.
ULYSSES [*to* AGAMEMNON].
My lord, you feed too much on this dislike.
NESTOR.
Our noble general, do not do so.
DIOMEDES.
You must prepare to fight without Achilles.
ULYSSES.
Why, 'tis this naming of him does him harm.
Here is a man—but 'tis before his face;
I will be silent.
NESTOR.
Wherefore should you so?
He is not emulous, as Achilles is.
ULYSSES.
Know the whole world, he is as valiant.
AJAX.
A whoreson dog, that shall palter thus with us!
Would he were a Trojan!
NESTOR.
What a vice were it in Ajax now,—
ULYSSES.
If he were proud,—
DIOMEDES.
Or covetous of praise,—
ULYSSES.
Ay, or surly borne,—
DIOMEDES.
Or strange, or self-affected!
ULYSSES.
Thank the heavens, lord, thou art of sweet com-
posure;
Praise him that got thee, she that gave thee suck:
Famed be thy tutor, and thy parts of nature
Thrice-famed, beyond all erudition:
But he that disciplined thy arms to fight,
Let Mars divide eternity in twain,
And give him half: and, for thy vigour,
Bull-bearing Milo his addition yield
To sinewy Ajax. I will not praise thy wisdom,
Which, like a bourn, a pale, a shore, confines
Thy spacious and dilated parts: here's Nestor,—
Instructed by the antiquary times,
He must, he is, he cannot but be wise:—
But pardon, father Nestor, were your days
As green as Ajax', and your brain so temper'd,
You should not have the eminence of him,
But be as Ajax.
AJAX.
Shall I call you father?

NESTOR.
Ay, my good son.
DIOMEDES.
Be ruled by him, Lord Ajax.
ULYSSES.
There is no tarrying here; the hart Achilles
Keeps thicket. Please it our great general
To call together all his state of war;
Fresh kings are come to Troy: to-morrow
We must with all our main of power stand fast:
And here's a lord,—come knights from east to
west,
And cull their flower, Ajax shall cope the best.
AGAMEMNON.
Go we to council. Let Achilles sleep:
Light boats sail swift, though greater hulks draw
deep. [*Exeunt.*

ACT III. SCENE I.

Troy. PRIAM'S *palace.*

Enter PANDARUS *and a* SERVANT.

PANDARUS.
FRIEND, you,—pray you, a word: do not you
follow the young Lord Paris?
SERVANT.
Ay, sir, when he goes before me.
PANDARUS.
You depend upon him, I mean?
SERVANT.
Sir, I do depend upon the Lord.
PANDARUS.
You depend upon a noble gentleman; I must
needs praise him.
SERVANT.
The Lord be praised!
PANDARUS.
You know me, do you not?
SERVANT.
Faith, sir, superficially.
PANDARUS.
Friend, know me better, I am the Lord Pandarus.
SERVANT.
I hope I shall know your honour better.
PANDARUS.
I do desire it.
SERVANT.
You are in the state of grace.
PANDARUS.
Grace! not so, friend; honour and lordship are
my titles. [*Music sounds within.*]—What music is
this?
SERVANT.
I do but partly know, sir: it is music in parts.
PANDARUS.
Know you the musicians?
SERVANT.
Wholly, sir.
PANDARUS.
Who play they to?
SERVANT.
To the hearers, sir.
PANDARUS.
At whose pleasure, friend?
SERVANT.
At mine, sir, and theirs that love music.

PANDARUS.
Command, I mean, friend.

SERVANT.
Who shall I command, sir?

PANDARUS.
Friend, we understand not one another: I am too courtly, and thou art too cunning. At whose request do these men play?

SERVANT.
That's to't, indeed, sir: marry, sir, at the request of Paris my lord, who's there in person; with him, the mortal Venus, the heart-blood of beauty, love's invisible soul,—

PANDARUS.
Who, my cousin Cressida?

SERVANT.
No, sir, Helen: could you not find out that by her attributes?

PANDARUS.
It should seem, fellow, that thou hast not seen the Lady Cressida. I come to speak with Paris from the Prince Troilus: I will make a complimental assault upon him, for my business seethes.

SERVANT.
Sodden business! there's a stew'd phrase indeed!

Enter PARIS *and* HELEN, *attended.*

PANDARUS.
Fair be to you, my lord, and to all this fair company! fair desires, in all fair measure, fairly guide them!—especially to you, fair queen! fair thoughts be your fair pillow!

HELEN.
Dear lord, you are full of fair words.

PANDARUS.
You speak your fair pleasure, sweet queen.—Fair prince, here is good broken music.

PARIS.
You have broke it, cousin: and, by my life, you shall make it whole again; you shall piece it out with a piece of your performance.—Nell, he is full of harmony.

PANDARUS.
Truly, lady, no.

HELEN.
O, sir,—

PANDARUS.
Rude, in sooth; in good sooth, very rude.

PARIS.
Well said, my lord! well, you say so in fits.

PANDARUS.
I have business to my lord, dear queen.—My lord, will you vouchsafe me a word?

HELEN.
Nay, this shall not hedge us out: we'll hear you sing, certainly.

PANDARUS.
Well, sweet queen, you are pleasant with me.— But, marry, thus, my lord,—My dear lord, and most esteem'd friend, your brother Troilus,—

HELEN.
My Lord Pandarus; honey-sweet lord,—

PANDARUS.
Go to, sweet queen, go to:—commends himself most affectionately to you,—

HELEN.
You shall not bob us out of our melody: if you do, our melancholy upon your head!

PANDARUS.
Sweet queen, sweet queen; that's a sweet queen, i'faith,—

HELEN.
And to make a sweet lady sad is a sour offence. Nay, that shall not serve your turn; that shall it not, in truth, la. Nay, I care not for such words; no, no.

PANDARUS.
And, my lord, he desires you, that if the king call for him at supper, you will make his excuse.

HELEN.
My Lord Pandarus,—

PANDARUS.
What says my sweet queen,—my very very sweet queen?

PARIS.
What exploit's in hand? where sups he to-night?

HELEN.
Nay, but, my lord,—

PANDARUS.
What says my sweet queen?—My cousin will fall out with you. You must not know where he sups.

PARIS.
I'll lay my life, with my disposer Cressida.

PANDARUS.
No, no, no such matter; you are wide: come, your disposer is sick.

PARIS.
Well, I'll make excuse.

PANDARUS.
Ay, good my lord. Why should you say Cressida? no, your poor disposer's sick.

PARIS.
I spy.

PANDARUS.
You spy! what do you spy?—Come, give me an instrument.—Now, sweet queen.

HELEN.
Why, this is kindly done.

PANDARUS.
My niece is horribly in love with a thing you have, sweet queen.

HELEN.
She shall have it, my lord, if it be not my lord Paris.

PANDARUS.
He! no, she'll none of him; they two are twa

HELEN.
Falling in, after falling out, may make them three.

PANDARUS.
Come, come, I'll hear no more of this; I'll sing you a song now.

HELEN.
Ay, ay, prithee now. By my troth, sweet lord, thou hast a fine forehead.

PANDARUS.
Ay, you may, you may.

HELEN.
Let thy song be love: this love will undo us all. O Cupid, Cupid, Cupid!

PANDARUS.
Love! ay, that it shall, i'faith.

PARIS.
Ay, good now, love, love, nothing but love.
PANDARUS.
In good troth, it begins so.   [*Sings.*
    Love, love, nothing but love, still more!
        For, O, love's bow
        Shoots buck and doe:
        The shaft confounds,
        Not that it wounds,
    But tickles still the sore.
    These lovers cry—Oh! oh! they die!
        Yet that which seems the wound to kill
    Doth turn oh! oh! to ha! ha! he!
        So dying love lives still:
    Oh! oh! a while, but ha! ha! ha!
    Oh! oh! groans out for ha! ha! ha!
Heigh-ho!
HELEN.
In love, i'faith, to the very tip of the nose.
PARIS.
He eats nothing but doves, love; and that breeds
hot blood, and hot blood begets hot thoughts,
and hot thoughts beget hot deeds, and hot deeds
is love.
PANDARUS.
Is this the generation of love? hot blood, hot
thoughts, and hot deeds? Why, they are vipers:
is love a generation of vipers?—Sweet lord, who's
a-field to-day?
PARIS.
Hector, Deiphobus, Helenus, Antenor, and all
the gallantry of Troy: I would fain have arm'd
to-day, but my Nell would not have it so. How
chance my brother Troilus went not?
HELEN.
He hangs the lip at something:—you know all,
Lord Pandarus.
PANDARUS.
Not I, honey-sweet queen.—I long to hear how
they sped to-day.—You'll remember your
brother's excuse?
PARIS.
To a hair.
PANDARUS.
Farewell, sweet queen.
HELEN.
Commend me to your niece.
PANDARUS.
I will, sweet queen.   [*Exit.*
        [*Sound a retreat.*
PARIS.
They're come from field: let us to Priam's hall,
To greet the warriors. Sweet Helen, I must woo
    you
To help unarm our Hector: his stubborn buckles,
With these your white enchanting fingers toucht,
Shall more obey than to the edge of steel
Or force of Greekish sinews; you shall do more
Than all the island kings,—disarm great Hector.
HELEN.
'Twill make us proud to be his servant, Paris;
Yea, what he shall receive of us in duty
Gives us more palm in beauty than we have,
Yea, overshines ourself.
PARIS.
Sweet, above thought I love thee.   [*Exeunt.*

SCENE II.

PANDARUS' orchard.

Enter PANDARUS *and* TROILUS' BOY, *meeting.*

PANDARUS.
HOW now! where's thy master? at my cousin
    Cressida's?
BOY.
No, sir; he stays for you to conduct him thither.
PANDARUS.
O, here he comes.
        Enter TROILUS.
How now, how now!
TROILUS.
Sirrah, walk off.   [*Exit* BOY.
PANDARUS.
Have you seen my cousin?
TROILUS.
No, Pandarus: I stalk about her door,
Like a strange soul upon the Stygian banks
Staying for waftage. O, be thou my Charon,
And give me swift transportance to those fields
Where I may wallow in the lily-beds
Proposed for the deserver! O gentle Pandarus,
From Cupid's shoulder pluck his painted wings,
And fly with me to Cressid!
PANDARUS.
Walk here i'th'orchard, I'll bring her straight.
        [*Exit.*
TROILUS.
I am giddy; expectation whirls me round.
Th'imaginary relish is so sweet
That it enchants my sense: what will it be,
When that the watery palate tastes indeed
Love's thrice-repured nectar? death, I fear me;
Swooning destruction; or some joy too fine,
Too subtle-potent, tuned too sharp in sweetness,
For the capacity of my ruder powers:
I fear it much; and I do fear besides,
That I shall lose distinction in my joys;
As doth a battle, when they charge on heaps
The enemy flying.
        Enter PANDARUS.
PANDARUS.
She's making her ready, she'll come straight: you
must be witty now. She does so blush, and
fetches her wind so short, as if she were fray'd
with a sprite: I'll fetch her. It is the prettiest vil-
lain: she fetches her breath as short as a new-ta'en
sparrow.   [*Exit.*
TROILUS.
Even such a passion doth embrace my bosom:
My heart beats thicker than a feverous pulse;
And all my powers do their bestowing lose,
Like vassalage at unawares encountering
The eye of majesty.
        Enter PANDARUS *with* CRESSIDA.
PANDARUS.
Come, come, what need you blush? shame's a
baby.—Here she is now: swear the oaths now to
her that you have sworn to me.—What, are you
gone again? you must be watcht ere you be made
tame, must you? Come your ways, come your
ways: an you draw backward, we'll put you i'th'
fills. Why do you not speak to her? Come, draw
this curtain, and let's see your picture. Alas the

day, how loth you are to offend daylight! an 'twere dark, you'ld close sooner. So, so; rub on, and kiss the mistress. How now! a kiss in fee-farm! build there, carpenter; the air is sweet. Nay, you shall fight your hearts out ere I part you. The falcon as the tercel, for all the ducks i'th'river: go to, go to.

TROILUS.
You have bereft me of all words, lady.

PANDARUS.
Words pay no debts, give her deeds: but she'll bereave you o'th'deeds too, if she call your activity in question. What, billing again? Here's —'In witness whereof the parties interchange-ably'—Come in, come in: I'll go get a fire.   [Exit.

CRESSIDA.
Will you walk in, my lord?

TROILUS.
O Cressida, how often have I wisht me thus!

CRESSIDA.
Wisht, my lord!—The gods grant—O my lord!

TROILUS.
What should they grant? what makes this pretty abruption? What too curious dreg espies my sweet lady in the fountain of our love?

CRESSIDA.
More dregs than water, if my fears have eyes.

TROILUS.
Fears make devils of cherubins; they never see truly.

CRESSIDA.
Blind fear, that seeing reason leads, finds safer footing than blind reason stumbling without fear: to fear the worst oft cures the worst.

TROILUS.
O, let my lady apprehend no fear: in all Cupid's pageant there is presented no monster.

CRESSIDA.
Nor nothing monstrous neither?

TROILUS.
Nothing, but our undertakings; when we vow to weep seas, live in fire, eat rocks, tame tigers; thinking it harder for our mistress to devise im-position enough than for us to undergo any diffi-culty imposed. This is the monstruosity in love, lady,—that the will is infinite, and the execution confined; that the desire is boundless, and the act a slave to limit.

CRESSIDA.
They say, all lovers swear more performance than they are able, and yet reserve an ability that they never perform; vowing more than the perfection of ten, and discharging less than the tenth part of one. They that have the voice of lions and the act of hares, are they not monsters?

TROILUS.
Are there such? such are not we: praise us as we are tasted, allow us as we prove; our head shall go bare till merit crown it: no perfection in re-version shall have a praise in present: we will not name desert before his birth; and, being born, his addition shall be humble. Few words to fair faith: Troilus shall be such to Cressid as what envy can say worst shall be a mock for his truth, and what truth can speak truest not truer than Troilus.

CRESSIDA.
Will you walk in, my lord?
      Enter PANDARUS.

PANDARUS.
What, blushing still? have you not done talking yet?

CRESSIDA.
Well, uncle, what folly I commit, I dedicate to you.

PANDARUS.
I thank you for that: if my lord get a boy of you, you'll give him me. Be true to my lord: if he flinch, chide me for it.

TROILUS.
You know now your hostages; your uncle's word and my firm faith.

PANDARUS.
Nay, I'll give my word for her too: our kindred, though they be long ere they are wooed, they are constant being won: they are burs, I can tell you; they'll stick where they are thrown.

CRESSIDA.
Boldness comes to me now, and brings me
      heart:—
Prince Troilus, I have loved you night and day
For many weary months.

TROILUS.
Why was my Cressid, then, so hard to win?

CRESSIDA.
Hard to seem won: but I was won, my lord,
With the first glance that ever—pardon me—
If I confess much, you will play the tyrant.
I love you now; but not, till now, so much
But I might master it:—in faith, I lie;
My thoughts were like unbridled children,
      grown
Too headstrong for their mother:—see, we fools!
Why have I blabb'd? who shall be true to us
When we are so unsecret to ourselves?—
But, though I loved you well, I woo'd you not;
And yet, good faith, I wisht myself a man,
Or that we women had men's head privilege
Of speaking first. Sweet, bid me hold my tongue;
For, in this rapture, I shall surely speak
The thing I shall repent. See, see, your silence,
Cunning in dumbness, from my weakness draws
My very soul of counsel!—stop my mouth.

TROILUS.
And shall, albeit sweet music issues thence.
                              [Kisses her.

PANDARUS.
Pretty, i'faith.

CRESSIDA.
My lord, I do beseech you, pardon me;
'Twas not my purpose thus to beg a kiss:
I am ashamed;—O heavens! what have I done?
For this time will I take my leave, my lord.

TROILUS.
Your leave, sweet Cressid!

PANDARUS.
Leave! an you take leave till to-morrow morn-ing,—

CRESSIDA.
Pray you, content you.

TROILUS.
      What offends you, lady?

CRESSIDA.
Sir, mine own comp ny.

TROILUS.
            You cannot shun
Yourself.

CRESSIDA.
         Let me go and try:
I have a kind of self resides with you;
But an unkind self, that itself will leave,
To be another's fool. I would be gone:—
Where is my wit? I know not what I speak.

TROILUS.
Well know they what they speak that speak so
    wisely.

CRESSIDA.
Perchance, my lord, I show'd more craft than
    love;
And fell so roundly to a large confession,
To angle for your thoughts: but you are wise;
Or else you love not; for to be wise and love
Exceeds man's might; that dwells with gods above.

TROILUS.
O, that I thought it could be in a woman—
As, if it can, I will presume in you—
To feed for aye her lamp and flames of love;
To keep her constancy in plight and youth,
Outliving beauty's outward, with a mind
That doth renew swifter than blood decays!
Or, that persuasion could but thus convince me,—
That my integrity and truth to you
Might be affronted with the match and weight
Of such a winnow'd purity in love;
How were I then uplifted! but, alas!
I am as true as truth's simplicity,
And simpler than the infancy of truth.

CRESSIDA.
In that I'll war with you.

TROILUS.
           O virtuous fight,
When right with right wars who shall be most
    right!
True swains in love shall, in the world to come,
Approve their truths by Troilus: when their
    rimes,
Full of protest, of oath, and big compare,
Want similes, truth tired with iteration,—
As true as steel, as plantage to the moon,
As sun to day, as turtle to her mate,
As iron to adamant, as earth to th'centre,—
Yet, after all comparisons of truth,
As truth's authentic author to be cited,
'As true as Troilus' shall crown up the verse,
And sanctify the numbers.

CRESSIDA.
         Prophet may you be!
If I be false, or swerve a hair from truth,
When time is old and hath forgot itself,
When waterdrops have worn the stones of Troy,
And blind oblivion swallow'd cities up,
And mighty states characterless are grated
To dusty nothing; yet let memory,
From false to false, amor g false maids in love,
Upbraid my falsehood! when they've said 'as false
As air, as water, wind, or sandy earth,
As fox to lamb, or wolf to heifer's calf,
Pard to the hind, or stepdame to her son,'—

'Yea,' let them say, to stick the heart of falsehood,
'As false as Cressid.'

PANDARUS.
Go to, a bargain made: seal it, seal it; I'll be the
witness. Here I hold your hand; here my cousin's.
If ever you prove false one to another, since I
have taken such pains to bring you together, let
all pitiful goers-between be call'd to the world's
end after my name; call them all Pandars; let all
inconstant men be Troiluses, all false women
Cressids, and all brokers-between Pandars! say,
amen.

TROILUS.
Amen.

CRESSIDA.
Amen.

PANDARUS.
Amen. Whereupon I will show you a chamber
with a bed; which bed, because it shall not speak
of your pretty encounters, press it to death: away!
And Cupid grant all tongue-tied maidens here
Bed, chamber, Pandar to provide this gear!
                       [*Exeunt.*

SCENE III.
The Grecian camp.

Flourish.   *Enter* AGAMEMNON, ULYSSES,
    DIOMEDES, NESTOR, AJAX, MENELAUS, *and*
    CALCHAS.

CALCHAS.
NOW, princes, for the service I have done you
    Th'advantage of the time prompts me aloud
To call for recompense. Appear it to your mind
That, through the sight I bear in things to love,
I have abandon'd Troy, left my possession,
Incurr'd a traitor's name; exposed myself,
From certain and possest conveniences,
To doubtful fortunes; sequest'ring from me all
That time, acquaintance, custom, and condition,
Made tame and most familiar to my nature;
And here, to do you service, am become
As new into the world, strange, unacquainted:
I do beseech you, as in way of taste,
To give me now a little benefit,
Out of those many register'd in promise,
Which, you say, live to come in my behalf.

AGAMEMNON.
What wouldst thou of us, Trojan? make demand.

CALCHAS.
You have a Trojan prisoner, call'd Antenor,
Yesterday took: Troy holds him very dear.
Oft have you—often have you thanks therefore—
Desired my Cressid in right great exchange,
Whom Troy hath still denied: but this Antenor,
I know, is such a wrest in their affairs,
That their negotiations all must slack,
Wanting his manage; and they will almost
Give us a prince of blood, a son of Priam,
In change of him: let him be sent, great princes,
And he shall buy my daughter; and her presence
Shall quite strike off all service I have done,
In most accepted pay.

AGAMEMNON.
          Let Diomedes bear him,
And bring us Cressid hither: Calchas shall have

What he requests of us.—Good Diomed,
Furnish you fairly for this interchange:
Withal, bring word if Hector will to-morrow
Be answer'd in his challenge: Ajax is ready.

DIOMEDES.
This shall I undertake; and 'tis a burden
Which I am proud to bear.

[*Exeunt* DIOMEDES *and* CALCHAS.
Enter ACHILLES *and* PATROCLUS, *before their tent.*

ULYSSES.
Achilles stands i'th'entrance of his tent:—
Please it our general to pass strangely by him,
As if he were forgot; and, princes all,
Lay negligent and loose regard upon him:
I will come last. 'Tis like he'll question me
Why such unplausive eyes are bent on him:
If so, I have derision medicinable,
To use between your strangeness and his pride,
Which his own will shall have desire to drink:
It may do good: pride hath no other glass
To show itself but pride; for supple knees
Feed arrogance, and are the proud man's fees.

AGAMEMNON.
We'll execute your purpose, and put on
A form of strangeness as we pass along:—
So do each lord; and either greet him not,
Or else disdainfully, which shall shake him more
Than if not lookt on. I will lead the way.

ACHILLES.
What, comes the general to speak with me?
You know my mind, I'll fight no more 'gainst
   Troy.

AGAMEMNON.
What says Achilles? would he aught with us?

NESTOR.
Would you, my lord, aught with the general?

ACHILLES.
No.

NESTOR.
Nothing, my lord.

AGAMEMNON.
The better.

[*Exeunt* AGAMEMNON *and* NESTOR.

ACHILLES.
Good day, good day.

MENELAUS.
How do you? how do you?   [*Exit.*

ACHILLES.
What, does the cuckold scorn me?

AJAX.
How now, Patroclus!

ACHILLES.
Good morrow, Ajax.

AJAX.
Ha!

ACHILLES.
Good morrow.

AJAX.
Ay, and good next day too.   [*Exit.*

ACHILLES.
What mean these fellows? Know they not
   Achilles?

PATROCLUS.
They pass by strangely: they were used to bend,
To send their smiles before them to Achilles;

To come as humbly as they use to creep
To holy altars.

ACHILLES.
What, am I poor of late?
'Tis certain, greatness, once faln out with fortune,
Must fall out with men too: what the declined is,
He shall as soon read in the eyes of others
As feel in his own fall; for men, like butterflies,
Show not their mealy wings but to the summer;
And not a man, for being simply man,
Hath any honour, but honour for those honours
That are without him, as place, riches, favour,
Prizes of accident as oft as merit:
Which when they fall, as being slippery standers,
The love that lean'd on them as slippery too,
Do one pluck down another, and together
Die in the fall. But 'tis not so with me:
Fortune and I are friends: I do enjoy
At ample point all that I did possess,
Save these men's looks; who do, methinks, find
   out
Something not worth in me such rich beholding
As they have often given. Here is Ulysses:
I'll interrupt his reading.—
How now, Ulysses!

ULYSSES.
Now, great Thetis' son!

ACHILLES.
What are you reading?

ULYSSES.
A strange fellow here
Writes me, 'That man—how dearly ever parted,
How much in having, or without or in—
Cannot make boast to have that which he hath,
Nor feels not what he owes, but by reflection;
As when his virtues shining upon others
Heat them, and they retort that heat again
To the first giver.'

ACHILLES.
This is not strange, Ulysses.
The beauty that is borne here in the face
The bearer knows not, but commends itself
To others' eyes: nor doth the eye itself,
That most pure spirit of sense, behold itself,
Not going from itself; but eye to eye opposed
Salutes each other with each other's form:
For speculation turns not to itself,
Till it hath travell'd, and is mirror'd there
Where it may see itself. This is not strange at all.

ULYSSES.
I do not strain at the position,—
It is familiar,—but at the author's drift;
Who, in his circumstance, expressly proves
That no man is the lord of any thing,
Though in and of him there be much consisting,
Till he communicate his parts to others;
Nor doth he of himself know them for aught
Till he behold them formed in th'applause
Where they're extended; who, like an arch,
   reverb'rates
The voice again; or, like a gate of steel
Fronting the sun, receives and renders back
His figure and his heat. I was much rapt in this;
And apprehended here immediately
The unknown Ajax.
Heavens, what a man is there! a very horse;

That has he knows not what. Nature, what things
   there are,
Most abject in regard, and dear in use!
What things again most dear in the esteem,
And poor in worth! Now shall we see to-morrow—
An act that very chance doth throw upon him—
Ajax renown'd. O heavens, what some men do,
While some men leave to do!
How some men creep in skittish Fortune's hall,
Whiles others play the idiots in her eyes!
How one man eats into another's pride,
While pride is fasting in his wantonness!
To see these Grecian lords!—why, even already
They clap the lubber Ajax on the shoulder,
As if his foot were on brave Hector's breast,
And great Troy shrieking.

ACHILLES.
I do believe it; for they past by me
As misers do by beggars,—neither gave to me
Good word nor look: what, are my deeds forgot?

ULYSSES.
Time hath, my lord, a wallet at his back,
Wherein he puts alms for oblivion,
A great-sized monster of ingratitudes:
Those scraps are good deeds past; which are de-
   vour'd
As fast as they are made, forgot as soon
As done: perseverance, dear my lord,
Keeps honour bright: to have done, is to hang
Quite out of fashion, like a rusty mail
In monumental mockery. Take the instant way;
For honour travels in a strait so narrow,
Where one but goes abreast: keep, then, the path;
For emulation hath a thousand sons,
That one by one pursue: if you give way,
Or hedge aside from the direct forthright,
Like to an enter'd tide, they all rush by,
And leave you hindmost;
Or, like a gallant horse faln in first rank,
Lie there for pavement to the abject rear,
O'er-run and trampled on: then what they do in
   present,
Though less than yours in past, must o'ertop
   yours;
For time is like a fashionable host,
That slightly shakes his parting guest by th'hand,
And with his arms outstretcht, as he would fly,
Grasps-in the comer: welcome ever smiles,
And farewell goes out sighing. O, let not virtue
   seek
Remuneration for the thing it was;
For beauty, wit,
High birth, vigour of bone, desert in service,
Love, friendship, charity, are subjects all
To envious and calumniating time.
One touch of nature makes the whole world kin,—
That all, with one consent, praise new-born
   gawds,
Though they are made and moulded of things
   past,
And give to dust, that is a little gilt,
More laud than gilt o'er-dusted.
The present eye praises the present object:
Then marvel not, thou great and complete man,
That all the Greeks begin to worship Ajax;
Since things in motion sooner catch the eye

Than what not stirs. The cry went once on thee,
And still it might, and yet it may again,
If thou wouldst not entomb thyself alive,
And case thy reputation in thy tent;
Whose glorious deeds, but in these fields of late,
Made emulous missions 'mongst the gods them-
   selves,
And drave great Mars to faction.

ACHILLES.
                Of this my privacy
I have strong reasons.

ULYSSES.
              But 'gainst your privacy
The reasons are more potent and heroical:
'Tis known, Achilles, that you are in love
With one of Priam's daughters.

ACHILLES.
                    Ha! known!

ULYSSES.
Is that a wonder?
The providence that's in a watchful state
Knows almost every grain of Pluto's gold;
Finds bottom in th'uncomprehensive deeps;
Keeps place with thought, and almost, like the
   gods,
Does thoughts unveil in their dumb cradles.
There is a mystery—with whom relation
Durst never meddle—in the soul of state;
Which hath an operation more divine
Than breath or pen can give expressure to:
All the commerce that you have had with Troy
As perfectly is ours as yours, my lord;
And better would it fit Achilles much
To throw down Hector than Polyxena:
But it must grieve young Pyrrhus now at home,
When fame shall in our islands sound her trump,
And all the Greekish girls shall tripping sing,
'Great Hector's sister did Achilles win;
But our great Ajax bravely beat down him.'
Farewell, my lord: I as your lover speak;
The fool slides o'er the ice that you should break.
                               [*Exit.*

PATROCLUS.
To this effect, Achilles, have I moved you:
A woman impudent and mannish grown
Is not more loath'd than an effeminate man
In time of action. I stand condemn'd for this;
They think, my little stomach to the war,
And your great love to me, restrains you thus:
Sweet, rouse yourself; and the weak wanton Cupid
Shall from your neck unloose his amorous fold,
And, like a dew-drop from the lion's mane,
Be shook to air.

ACHILLES.
        Shall Ajax fight with Hector?

PATROCLUS.
Ay, and perhaps receive much honour by him.

ACHILLES.
I see my reputation is at stake;
My fame is shrewdly gored.

PATROCLUS.
                O, then, beware;
Those wounds heal ill that men do give them-
   selves:
Omission to do what is necessary
Seals a commission to a blank of danger;

And danger, like an ague, subtly taints
Even then when we sit idly in the sun.

ACHILLES.

Go call Thersites hither, sweet Patroclus:
I'll send the fool to Ajax, and desire him
T'invite the Trojan lords after the combat
To see us here unarm'd: I have a woman's longing,
An appetite that I am sick withal,
To see great Hector in his weeds of peace;
To talk with him, and to behold his visage,
Even to my full of view.—A labour saved!

Enter THERSITES.

THERSITES.

A wonder!

ACHILLES.

What?

THERSITES.

Ajax goes up and down the field, asking for himself.

ACHILLES.

How so?

THERSITES.

He must fight singly to-morrow with Hector; and
is so prophetically proud of an heroical cudgelling
that he raves in saying nothing.

ACHILLES.

How can that be?

THERSITES.

Why, he stalks up and down like a peacock,—a
stride and a stand: ruminates like an hostess that
hath no arithmetic but her brain to set down her
reckoning: bites his lip with a politic regard, as
who should say 'There were wit in this head, an
'twould out;' and so there is; but it lies as coldly
in him as fire in a flint, which will not show without knocking. The man's undone for ever; for
if Hector break not his neck i'th'combat, he'll
break't himself in vainglory. He knows me not:
I said, 'Good morrow, Ajax;' and he replies,
'Thanks, Agamemnon.' What think you of this
man, that takes me for the general? He's grown
a very land-fish, languageless, a monster. A
plague of opinion! a man may wear it on both
sides, like a leather jerkin.

ACHILLES.

Thou must be my ambassador to him, Thersites.

THERSITES.

Who, I? why, he'll answer nobody; he professes
not answering: speaking is for beggars; he wears
his tongue in's arms. I will put on his presence:
let Patroclus make demands to me, you shall see
the pageant of Ajax.

ACHILLES.

To him, Patroclus: tell him,—I humbly desire
the valiant Ajax to invite the most valorous
Hector to come unarm'd to my tent; and to procure safe-conduct for his person of the magnanimous and most illustrious six-or-seven-times-
honour'd captain-general of the Grecian army,
Agamemnon, et cetera. Do this.

PATROCLUS.

Jove bless great Ajax!

THERSITES.

Hum!

PATROCLUS.

I come from the worthy Achilles,—

THERSITES.

Ha!

PATROCLUS.

Who most humbly desires you to invite Hector to
his tent,—

THERSITES.

Hum!

PATROCLUS.

And to procure safe-conduct from Agamemnon.

THERSITES.

Agamemnon!

PATROCLUS.

Ay, my lord.

THERSITES.

Ha!

PATROCLUS.

What say you to't?

THERSITES.

God b'wi'you, with all my heart.

PATROCLUS.

Your answer, sir.

THERSITES.

If to-morrow be a fair day, by eleven o'clock it
will go one way or other: howsoever, he shall pay
for me ere he has me.

PATROCLUS.

Your answer, sir.

THERSITES.

Fare you well, with all my heart.

ACHILLES.

Why, but he is not in this tune, is he?

THERSITES.

No, but he's out o' tune thus. What music will be
in him when Hector has knockt out his brains,
I know not; but, I am sure, none,—unless
the fiddler Apollo get his sinews to make catlings on.

ACHILLES.

Come, thou shalt bear a letter to him straight.

THERSITES.

Let me bear another to his horse; for that's the
more capable creature.

ACHILLES.

My mind is troubled, like a fountain stirr'd;
And I myself see not the bottom of it.

[*Exeunt* ACHILLES *and* PATROCLUS.

THERSITES.

Would the fountain of your mind were clear again,
that I might water an ass at it! I had rather be a
tick in a sheep than such a valiant ignorance.

[*Exit.*

ACT IV. SCENE I.

Troy. A street.

Enter, at one door, AENEAS, *and* SERVANT *with a
torch; at another,* PARIS, DEIPHOBUS, AN-
TENOR, DIOMEDES *the Grecian, and others,
with torches.*

PARIS.

SEE, ho! who is that there?

DEIPHOBUS.

It is the Lord Aeneas.

AENEAS.

Is the prince there in person?—
Had I so good occasion to lie long

As you, Prince Paris, nothing but heavenly busi-
ness
Should rob my bed-mate of my company.
DIOMEDES.
That's my mind too.—Good morrow, Lord
Aeneas.
PARIS.
A valiant Greek, Aeneas,—take his hand,—
Witness the process of your speech, wherein
You told how Diomed, a whole week by days,
Did haunt you in the field.
AENEAS.
Health to you, valiant sir,
During all question of the gentle truce;
But when I meet you arm'd, as black defiance
As heart can think or courage execute.
DIOMEDES.
The one and other Diomed embraces.
Our bloods are now in calm; and, so long, health;
But when contention and occasion meet,
By Jove, I'll play the hunter for thy life
With all my force, pursuit, and policy.
AENEAS.
And thou shalt hunt a lion, that will fly
With his face backward.—In humane gentleness,
Welcome to Troy! now, by Anchises' life,
Welcome, indeed! By Venus' hand I swear
No man alive can love in such a sort
The thing he means to kill more excellently.
DIOMEDES.
We sympathize:—Jove, let Aeneas live,
If to my sword his fate be not the glory,
A thousand complete courses of the sun!
But, in mine emulous honour, let him die,
With every joint a wound, and that to-morrow!
AENEAS.
We know each other well.
DIOMEDES.
We do; and long to know each other worse.
PARIS.
This is the most despiteful gentle greeting,
The noblest hateful love, that e'er I heard of.—
What business, lord, so early?
AENEAS.
I was sent for to the king; but why, I know not.
PARIS.
His purpose meets you: 'twas to bring this Greek
To Calchas' house; and there to render him,
For the enfreed Antenor, the fair Cressid:
Let's have your company; or, if you please,
Haste there before us: I constantly do think—
Or, rather, call my thought a certain knowledge—
My brother Troilus lodges there to-night:
Rouse him, and give him note of our approach,
With the whole quality wherefore: I fear
We shall be much unwelcome.
AENEAS.
That I assure you:
Troilus had rather Troy were borne to Greece
Than Cressid borne from Troy.
PARIS.
There is no help;
The bitter disposition of the time
Will have it so. On, lord; we'll follow you.
AENEAS.
Good morrow, all.   [*Exit with* SERVANT.

PARIS.
And tell me, noble Diomed,—faith, tell me
true,
Even in the soul of sound good-fellowship,—
Who, in your thoughts, merits fair Helen best,
Myself or Menelaus?
DIOMEDES.
Both alike:
He merits well to have her, that doth seek her,
Not making any scruple of her soilure,
With such a hell of pain and world of charge;
And you as well to keep her, that defend her,
Not palating the taste of her dishonour,
With such a costly loss of wealth and friends:
He, like a puling cuckold, would drink up
The lees and dregs of a flat tamed piece;
You, like a lecher, out of whorish loins
Are pleased to breed out your inheritors:
Both merits poised, each weighs nor less nor
more;
But he as he, the heavier for a whore.
PARIS.
You are too bitter to your countrywoman.
DIOMEDES.
She's bitter to her country: hear me, Paris:—
For every false drop in her bawdy veins
A Grecian's life hath sunk; for every scruple
Of her contaminated carrion weight
A Trojan hath been slain; since she could speak,
She hath not given so many good words breath
As for her Greeks and Trojans suffer'd death.
PARIS.
Fair Diomed, you do as chapmen do,
Dispraise the thing that you desire to buy:
But we in silence hold this virtue well,—
We'll not commend what we intend not sell.
Here lies our way.   [*Exeunt.*

SCENE II.
Court of PANDARUS' *house.*
Enter TROILUS *and* CRESSIDA.
TROILUS.
DEAR, trouble not yourself: the morn is cold.
CRESSIDA.
Then, sweet my lord, I'll call mine uncle down;
He shall unbolt the gates.
TROILUS.
Trouble him not;
To bed, to bed: sleep kill those pretty eyes,
And give as soft attachment to thy senses
As infants' empty of all thought!
CRESSIDA.
Good morrow, then.
TROILUS.
I prithee now, to bed.
CRESSIDA.
Are you a-weary of me?
TROILUS.
O Cressida! but that the busy day,
Waked by the lark, hath roused the ribald crows,
And dreaming night will hide our joys no longer,
I would not from thee.
CRESSIDA.
Night hath been too brief.

TROILUS.

Beshrew the witch! with venomous wights she stays
As tediously as hell; but flies the grasps of love
With wings more momentary-swift than thought.
You will catch cold, and curse me.

CRESSIDA.

　　　　　　　　　Prithee, tarry;—
You men will never tarry.—
O foolish Cressid!—I might have still held off,
And then you would have tarried.—Hark! there's
　one up.

PANDARUS [within].

What, 's all the doors open here?

TROILUS.

It is your uncle.

CRESSIDA.

A pestilence on him! now will he be mocking:
I shall have such a life!

Enter PANDARUS.

PANDARUS.

How now, how now! how go maidenheads?—
Here, you maid! where's my cousin Cressid?

CRESSIDA.

Go hang yourself, you naughty mocking uncle!
You bring me to do—and then you flout me too.

PANDARUS.

To do what? to do what?—let her say what:—
what have I brought you to do?

CRESSIDA.

Come, come, beshrew your heart! you'll ne'er be
　good,
Nor suffer others.

PANDARUS.

Ha, ha! Alas, poor wretch! ah, poor capocchia!
hast not slept to-night? would he not—a naughty
man—let it sleep? a bugbear take him!

CRESSIDA.

Did not I tell you?—would he were knockt i'th'
　head!—　　　　　　　　　[One knocks.
Who's that at door? good uncle, go and see.—
My lord, come you again into my chamber:
You smile and mock me, as if I meant naughtily.

TROILUS.

Ha, ha!

CRESSIDA.

Come, you are deceived, I think of no such
　thing.—　　　　　　　　　[Knock.
How earnestly they knock!—Pray you, come in:
I would not for half Troy have you seen here.
　　　　　　　　[Exeunt TROILUS and CRESSIDA.

PANDARUS.

Who's there? what's the matter? will you beat
down the door? How now! what's the matter?

Enter AENEAS.

AENEAS.

Good morrow, lord, good morrow.

PANDARUS.

Who's there? my Lord Aeneas! By my troth,
I knew you not: what news with you so early?

AENEAS.

Is not Prince Troilus here?

PANDARUS.

Here! what should he do here?

AENEAS.

Come, he is here, my lord; do not deny him:
It doth import him much to speak with me.

PANDARUS.

Is he here, say you? 'tis more than I know, I'll be
sworn:—for my own part, I came in late. What
should he do here?

AENEAS.

Who!—nay, then:—come, come, you'll do him
wrong ere you're ware: you'll be so true to him to
be false to him: do not you know of him, but yet
go fetch him hither; go.

Enter TROILUS.

TROILUS.

How now! what's the matter?

AENEAS.

My lord, I scarce have leisure to salute you,
My matter is so rash: there is at hand
Paris your brother, and Deiphobus,
The Grecian Diomed, and our Antenor
Deliver'd to us; and for him forthwith,
Ere the first sacrifice, within this hour,
We must give up to Diomedes' hand
The Lady Cressida.

TROILUS.

　　　　　Is it so concluded?

AENEAS.

By Priam and the general state of Troy:
They are at hand, and ready to effect it.

TROILUS.

How my achievements mock me!—
I will go meet them: and, my Lord Aeneas,
We met by chance; you did not find me here.

AENEAS.

Good, good, my lord; the secrets of nature
Have not more gift in taciturnity.
　　　　　　　[Exeunt TROILUS and AENEAS.

PANDARUS.

Is't possible? no sooner got but lost? The devil
take Antenor! the young prince will go mad: a
plague upon Antenor! I would they had broke's
neck!

Enter CRESSIDA.

CRESSIDA.

How now! what's the matter? who was here?

PANDARUS.

Ah, ah!

CRESSIDA.

Why sigh you so profoundly? where's my
lord? gone! Tell me, sweet uncle, what's the
matter?

PANDARUS.

Would I were as deep under the earth as I am
above!

CRESSIDA.

O the gods!—what's the matter?

PANDARUS.

Prithee, get thee in: would thou hadst ne'er been
born! I knew thou wouldst be his death:—O, poor
gentleman!—A plague upon Antenor!

CRESSIDA.

Good uncle, I beseech you, on my knees I beseech you, what's the matter?

PANDARUS.

Thou must be gone, wench, thou must be gone;
thou art changed for Antenor: thou must to
thy father, and be gone from Troilus: 'twill
be his death; 'twill be his bane; he cannot
bear it.

CRESSIDA.
O you immortal gods!—I will not go.
PANDARUS.
Thou must.
CRESSIDA.
I will not, uncle: I have forgot my father;
I know no touch of consanguinity;
No kin, no love, no blood, no soul so near me
As the sweet Troilus.—O you gods divine,
Make Cressid's name the very crown of falsehood,
If ever she leave Troilus! Time, force, and death,
Do to this body what extremes you can;
But the strong base and building of my love
Is as the very centre of the earth,
Drawing all things to it.—I'll go in and weep,—
PANDARUS.
Do, do.
CRESSIDA.
Tear my bright hair, and scratch my praised
  cheeks;
Crack my clear voice with sobs, and break my
  heart
With sounding 'Troilus.' I will not go from Troy.
                              [Exeunt.

SCENE III.

Before PANDARUS' *house.*

Enter PARIS, TROILUS, AENEAS, DEIPHOBUS,
    ANTENOR, *and* DIOMEDES.

PARIS.
IT is great morning; and the hour prefixt
  Of her delivery to this valiant Greek
Comes fast upon:—good my brother Troilus,
Tell you the lady what she is to do,
And haste her to the purpose.
TROILUS.
                    Walk into her house;
I'll bring her to the Grecian presently:
And to his hand when I deliver her,
Think it an altar, and thy brother Troilus
A priest, there offering to it his own heart. [*Exit.*
PARIS.
I know what 'tis to love;
And would, as I shall pity, I could help!—
Please you walk in, my lords.   [*Exeunt.*

SCENE IV.

A room in PANDARUS' *house.*

Enter PANDARUS *and* CRESSIDA.

PANDARUS.
BE moderate, be moderate.
CRESSIDA.
Why tell you me of moderation?
The grief is fine, full, perfect, that I taste,
And violenteth in a sense as strong
As that which causeth it: how can I moderate it?
If I could temporize with my affection,
Or brew it to a weak and colder palate,
The like allayment could I give my grief:
My love admits no qualifying dross;
No more my grief, in such a precious loss.
PANDARUS.
Here, here, here he comes.

Enter TROILUS.

Ah, sweet ducks!
CRESSIDA.
O Troilus! Troilus!   [*Embracing him.*
PANDARUS.
What a pair of spectacles is here! Let me embrace
too. 'O heart,' as the goodly saying is,
    '——O heart, O heavy heart,
    Why sigh'st thou without breaking?'
where he answers again,
    'Because thou canst not ease thy smart
    By friendship nor by speaking.'
There was never a truer rime. Let us cast
away nothing, for we may live to have need of
such a verse: we see it, we see it.—How now,
lambs!
TROILUS.
Cressid, I love thee in so strain'd a purity,
That the blest gods, as angry with my fancy,
More bright in zeal than the devotion which
Cold lips blow to their deities, take thee from
  me.
CRESSIDA.
Have the gods envy?
PANDARUS.
Ay, ay, ay, ay; 'tis too plain a case.
CRESSIDA.
And is it true that I must go from Troy?
TROILUS.
A hateful truth.
CRESSIDA.
            What, and from Troilus too?
TROILUS.
From Troy and Troilus.
CRESSIDA.
                Is it possible?
TROILUS.
And suddenly; where injury of chance
Puts back leave-taking, justles roughly by
All time of pause, rudely beguiles our lips
Of all rejoindure, forcibly prevents
Our lockt embrasures, strangles our dear vows
Even in the birth of our own labouring breath:
We two, that with so many thousand sighs
Did buy each other, must poorly sell ourselves
With the rude brevity and discharge of one.
Injurious time now, with a robber's haste,
Crams his rich thievery up, he knows not how:
As many farewells as be stars in heaven,
With distinct breath and consign'd kisses to them,
He fumbles up into a loose adieu;
And scants us with a single famisht kiss,
Distasted with the salt of broken tears.
AENEAS [*within*].
My lord, is the lady ready?
TROILUS.
Hark! you are call'd: some say the Genius so
Cries 'Come!' to him that instantly must die.—
Bid them have patience; she shall come anon.
PANDARUS.
Where are my tears? rain, to lay this wind, or my
heart will be blown up by the root.   [*Exit.*
CRESSIDA.
I must, then, to the Grecians?
TROILUS.
                    No remedy.

CRESSIDA.
A woful Cressid 'mongst the merry Greeks!
When shall we see again?
TROILUS.
Hear me, my love: be thou but true of heart,—
CRESSIDA.
I true! how now! what wicked deem is this?
TROILUS.
Nay, we must use expostulation kindly,
For it is parting from us:
I speak not 'be thou true,' as fearing thee;
For I will throw my glove to Death himself,
That there's no maculation in thy heart:
But 'be thou true,' say I, to fashion in
My sequent protestation; be thou true,
And I will see thee.
CRESSIDA.
O, you shall be exposed, my lord, to dangers
As infinite as imminent! but I'll be true.
TROILUS.
And I'll grow friend with danger. Wear this
sleeve.
CRESSIDA.
And you this glove. When shall I see you?
TROILUS.
I will corrupt the Grecian sentinels,
To give thee nightly visitation.
But yet, be true.
CRESSIDA.
O heavens!—'be true' again!
TROILUS.
Hear why I speak it, love:
The Grecian youths are full of quality;
They're loving, well composed with gifts of nature,
And swelling o'er with arts and exercise:
How novelty may move, and parts with person,
Alas, a kind of godly jealousy—
Which, I beseech you, call a virtuous sin—
Makes me afeard.
CRESSIDA.
O heavens! you love me not.
TROILUS.
Die I a villain, then!
In this I do not call your faith in question
So mainly as my merit: I cannot sing,
Nor heel the high lavolt, nor sweeten talk,
Nor play at subtle games; fair virtues all,
To which the Grecians are most prompt and preg-
nant:
But I can tell, that in each grace of these
There lurks a still and dumb-discoursive devil
That tempts most cunningly: but be not tempted.
CRESSIDA.
Do you think I will?
TROILUS.
No.
But something may be done that we will not:
And sometimes we are devils to ourselves,
When we will tempt the frailty of our powers,
Presuming on their changeful potency.
AENEAS [within].
Nay, good my lord,—
TROILUS.
Come, kiss; and let us part.
PARIS [within].
Brother Troilus!

TROILUS.
Good brother, come you hither;
And bring Aeneas and the Grecian with you.
CRESSIDA.
My lord, will you be true?
TROILUS.
Who, I? alas, it is my vice, my fault:
Whiles others fish with craft for great opinion,
I with great truth catch mere simplicity;
Whilst some with cunning gild their copper
crowns,
With truth and plainness I do wear mine bare.
Fear not my truth: the moral of my wit
Is 'plain and true;' there's all the reach of it.
Enter AENEAS, PARIS, ANTENOR, DEIPHO-
BUS, and DIOMEDES.
Welcome, Sir Diomed! here is the lady
Which for Antenor we deliver you:
At the port, lord, I'll give her to thy hand;
And by the way possess thee what she is.
Entreat her fair; and, by my soul, fair Greek,
If e'er thou stand at mercy of my sword,
Name Cressid, and thy life shall be as safe
As Priam is in Ilion.
DIOMEDES.
Fair Lady Cressid,
So please you, save the thanks this prince ex-
pects:
The lustre in your eye, heaven in your cheek,
Pleads your fair usage; and to Diomed
You shall be mistress, and command him wholly.
TROILUS.
Grecian, thou dost not use me courteously,
To shame the zeal of my petition to thee
In praising her: I tell thee, lord of Greece,
She is as far high-soaring o'er thy praises
As thou unworthy to be call'd her servant.
I charge thee use her well, even for my charge;
For, by the dreadful Pluto, if thou dost not,
Though the great bulk Achilles be thy guard,
I'll cut thy throat.
DIOMEDES.
O, be not moved, Prince Troilus:
Let me be privileged by my place and message
To be a speaker free; when I am hence,
I'll answer to my lust: and know you, lord,
I'll nothing do on charge: to her own worth
She shall be prized; but that you say, 'Be't so,'
I'll speak it in my spirit and honour, 'No.'
TROILUS.
Come, to the port.—I'll tell thee, Diomed,
This brave shall oft make thee to hide thy head.—
Lady, give me your hand; and, as we walk,
To our own selves bend we our needful talk.
[Exeunt TROILUS, CRESSIDA, and DIO-
MEDES. Sound trumpet.
PARIS.
Hark! Hector's trumpet.
AENEAS.
How have we spent this morning!
The prince must think me tardy and remiss,
That swore to ride before him to the field.
PARIS.
'Tis Troilus' fault: come, come, to field with him
DEIPHOBUS.
Let us make ready straight.

AENEAS.

Yea, with a bridegroom's fresh alacrity,
Let us address to tend on Hector's heels:
The glory of our Troy doth this day lie
On his fair worth and single chivalry.   [*Exeunt.*

SCENE V.

The Grecian camp. Lists set out.

Enter AJAX, *arm'd;* AGAMEMNON, ACHILLES,
PATROCLUS, MENELAUS, ULYSSES, NESTOR,
and others.

AGAMEMNON.

HERE art thou in appointment fresh and fair,
Anticipating time with starting courage.
Give with thy trumpet a loud note to Troy,
Thou dreadful Ajax; that the appalled air
May pierce the head of the great combatant,
And hale him hither.

AJAX.

Thou, trumpet, there's my purse.
Now crack thy lungs, and split thy brazen pipe:
Blow, villain, till thy sphered bias cheek
Outswell the colic of puft Aquilon:
Come, stretch thy chest, and let thy eyes spout
    blood;
Thou blow'st for Hector.   [*Trumpet sounds.*

ULYSSES.

No trumpet answers.

ACHILLES.

'Tis but early days.

AGAMEMNON.

Is not yond Diomed, with Calchas' daughter?

ULYSSES.

'Tis he, I ken the manner of his gait;
He rises on the toe: that spirit of his
In aspiration lifts him from the earth.

Enter DIOMEDES *with* CRESSIDA.

AGAMEMNON.

Is this the Lady Cressid?

DIOMEDES.

Even she.

AGAMEMNON.

Most dearly welcome to the Greeks, sweet lady.
    [*Kisses her.*

NESTOR.

Our general doth salute you with a kiss.

ULYSSES.

Yet is the kindness but particular;
'Twere better she were kist in general.

NESTOR.

And very courtly counsel: I'll begin.—
    [*Kisses her.*
So much for Nestor.

ACHILLES.

I'll take that winter from your lips, fair lady:
    [*Kisses her.*
Achilles bids you welcome.

MENELAUS.

I had good argument for kissing once.

PATROCLUS.

But that's no argument for kissing now;
For thus popt Paris in his hardiment,
And parted thus you and your argument.
    [*Kisses her.*

ULYSSES.

O deadly gall, and theme of all our scorns!
For which we lose our heads to gild his horns.

PATROCLUS.

The first was Menelaus' kiss;—this, mine:
    [*Kisses her again.*
Patroclus kisses you.

MENELAUS.

O, this is trim!

PATROCLUS.

Paris and I kiss evermore for him.

MENELAUS.

I'll have my kiss, sir.—Lady, by your leave.

CRESSIDA.

In kissing, do you render or receive?

MENELAUS.

Both take and give.

CRESSIDA.

I'll make my match to live,
The kiss you take is better than you give;
Therefore no kiss.

MENELAUS.

I'll give you boot, I'll give you three for one.

CRESSIDA.

You're an odd man; give even, or give none.

MENELAUS.

An odd man, lady! every man is odd.

CRESSIDA.

No, Paris is not; for you know 'tis true
That you are odd, and he is even with you.

MENELAUS.

You fillip me o' th' head.

CRESSIDA.

No, I'll be sworn.

ULYSSES.

It were no match, your nail against his horn.—
May I, sweet lady, beg a kiss of you?

CRESSIDA.

You may.

ULYSSES.

I do desire it.

CRESSIDA.

Why, beg, then.

ULYSSES.

Why, then, for Venus' sake, give me a kiss,
When Helen is a maid again, and his.

CRESSIDA.

I am your debtor, claim it when 'tis due.

ULYSSES.

Never's my day, and then a kiss of you.

DIOMEDES.

Lady, a word:—I'll bring you to your father.
    [*Exit with* CRESSIDA.

NESTOR.

A woman of quick sense.

ULYSSES.

Fie, fie upon her!
There's language in her eye, her cheek, her lip,
Nay, her foot speaks; her wanton spirits look out
At every joint and motive of her body.
O, these encounterers, so glib of tongue,
That give a coasting welcome ere it comes,
And wide unclasp the tables of their thoughts
To every ticklish reader! set them down
For sluttish spoils of opportunity
And daughters of the game.   [*Trumpet within.*

ALL.
The Trojans' trumpet.

AGAMEMNON.

Yonder comes the troop.

Flourish. Enter all of Troy; HECTOR, AENEAS,
TROILUS, *and* ATTENDANTS.

AENEAS.
Hail, all the state of Greece! what shall be done
To him that victory commands? or do you purpose
A victor shall be known? will you the knights
Shall to the edge of all extremity
Pursue each other; or shall be divided
By any voice or order of the field?
Hector bade ask.

AGAMEMNON.

Which way would Hector have it?

AENEAS.
He cares not; he'll obey conditions.

ACHILLES.
'Tis done like Hector; but securely done,
A little proudly, and great deal misprizing
The knight opposed.

AENEAS.

If not Achilles, sir,
What is your name?

ACHILLES.

If not Achilles, nothing.

AENEAS.
Therefore Achilles: but whate'er, know this:—
In the extremity of great and little,
Valour and pride excel themselves in Hector;
The one almost as infinite as all,
The other blank as nothing. Weigh him well,
And that which looks like pride is courtesy.
This Ajax is half made of Hector's blood:
In love whereof half Hector stays at home;
Half heart, half hand, half Hector comes to seek
This blended knight, half Trojan and half Greek.

ACHILLES.
A maiden battle, then?—O, I perceive you.

Enter DIOMEDES.

AGAMEMNON.
Here is Sir Diomed.—Go, gentle knight,
Stand by our Ajax: as you and Lord Aeneas
Consent upon the order of their fight,
So be it; either to the uttermost,
Or else a breath: the combatants being kin
Half stints their strife before their strokes begin.

[AJAX *and* HECTOR *enter the lists.*

ULYSSES.
They are opposed already.

AGAMEMNON.
What Trojan is that same that looks so heavy?

ULYSSES.
The youngest son of Priam, a true knight;
Not yet mature, yet matchless: firm of word;
Speaking in deeds, and deedless in his tongue;
Not soon provoked, nor being provoked soon
   calm'd:
His heart and hand both open and both free;
For what he has he gives, what thinks he shows;
Yet gives he not till judgement guide his bounty,
Nor dignifies an impair thought with breath:
Manly as Hector, but more dangerous;
For Hector, in his blaze of wrath, subscribes
To tender objects; but he, in heat of action,

Is more vindicative than jealous love:
They call him Troilus; and on him erect
A second hope, as fairly built as Hector.
Thus says Aeneas; one that knows the youth
Even to his inches, and with private soul
Did in great Ilion thus translate him to me.

[*Alarum.* HECTOR *and* AJAX *fight.*

AGAMEMNON.
They are in action.

NESTOR.
Now, Ajax, hold thine own!

TROILUS.

Hector, thou sleep'st;
Awake thee!

AGAMEMNON.
His blows are well disposed:—there, Ajax!

DIOMEDES.
You must no more.   [*Trumpets cease.*

AENEAS.
Princes, enough, so please you.

AJAX.
I am not warm yet; let us fight again.

DIOMEDES.
As Hector pleases.

HECTOR.

Why, then will I no more:—
Thou art, great lord, my father's sister's son,
A cousin-german to great Priam's seed;
The obligation of our blood forbids
A gory emulation 'twixt us twain:
Were thy commixtion Greek and Trojan so
That thou couldst say, 'This hand is Grecian all,
And this is Trojan; the sinews of this leg
All Greek, and this all Troy; my mother's blood
Runs on the dexter cheek, and this sinister
Bounds in my father's;' by Jove multipotent,
Thou shouldst not bear from me a Greekish
   member
Wherein my sword had not impressure made
Of our rank feud: but the just gods gainsay
That any drop thou borrow'dst from thy mother,
My sacred aunt, should by my mortal sword
Be drained! Let me embrace thee, Ajax:
By him that thunders, thou hast lusty arms;
Hector would have them fall upon him thus:
Cousin, all honour to thee!

AJAX.

I thank thee, Hector:
Thou art too gentle and too free a man:
I came to kill thee, cousin, and bear hence
A great addition earned in thy death.

HECTOR.
Not Neoptolemus so mirable—
On whose bright crest Fame with her loud'st oyes
Cries 'This is he'—could promise to himself
A thought of added honour torn from Hector.

AENEAS.
There is expectance here from both the sides,
What further you will do.

HECTOR.

We'll answer it;
The issue is embracement:—Ajax, farewell.

AJAX.
If I might in entreaties find success—
As seld I have the chance—I would desire
My famous cousin to our Grecian tents.

DIOMEDES.
'Tis Agamemnon's wish; and great Achilles
Doth long to see unarm'd the valiant Hector.
HECTOR.
Aeneas, call my brother Troilus to me:
And signify this loving interview
To the expecters of our Trojan part;
Desire them home.—Give me thy hand, my
     cousin;
I will go eat with thee, and see your knights.
     AGAMEMNON and the rest come forward.
AJAX.
Great Agamemnon comes to meet us here.
HECTOR.
The worthiest of them tell me name by name;
But for Achilles, mine own searching eyes
Shall find him by his large and portly size.
AGAMEMNON.
Worthy of arms! as welcome as to one
That would be rid of such an enemy;
But that's no welcome: understand more clear,
What's past and what's to come is strew'd with
     husks
And formless ruin of oblivion;
But in this extant moment, faith and troth,
Strain'd purely from all hollow bias-drawing,
Bids thee, with most divine integrity,
From heart of very heart, great Hector, welcome.
HECTOR.
I thank thee, most imperious Agamemnon.
AGAMEMNON [to TROILUS].
My well-famed lord of Troy, no less to you.
MENELAUS.
Let me confirm my princely brother's greeting;—
You brace of warlike brothers, welcome hither.
HECTOR.
Who must we answer?
AENEAS.
          The noble Menelaus.
HECTOR.
O, you, my lord? by Mars his gauntlet, thanks!
Mock not, that I affect th'untraded oath;
Your quondam wife swears still by Venus' glove:
She's well, but bade me not commend her to you.
MENELAUS.
Name her not now, sir; she's a deadly theme.
HECTOR.
O, pardon; I offend.
NESTOR.
I have, thou gallant Trojan, seen thee oft,
Labouring for destiny, make cruel way
Through ranks of Greekish youth; and I have
     seen thee,
As hot as Perseus, spur thy Phrygian steed,
Despising many forfeits and subduements,
When thou hast hung thy advanced sword i'th'air,
Not letting it decline on the declined;
That I have said to some my standers-by,
'Lo, Jupiter is yonder, dealing life!'
And I have seen thee pause and take thy breath,
When that a ring of Greeks have hemm'd thee in,
Like an Olympian wrestling: this have I seen;
But this thy countenance, still lockt in steel,
I never saw till now. I knew thy grandsire,
And once fought with him: he was a soldier good;
But, by great Mars, the captain of us all,

Never like thee. Let an old man embrace thee;
And, worthy warrior, welcome to our tents.
AENEAS.
'Tis the old Nestor.
HECTOR.
Let me embrace thee. good old chronicle,
That hast so long walkt hand in hand with time:—
Most reverend Nestor, I am glad to clasp thee.
NESTOR.
I would my arms could match thee in contention,
As they contend with thee in courtesy.
HECTOR.
I would they could.
NESTOR.
Ha!
By this white beard, I'ld fight with thee to-
     morrow:—
Well, welcome, welcome!—I have seen the time—
ULYSSES.
I wonder now how yonder city stands
When we have here her base and pillar by us.
HECTOR.
I know your favour, Lord Ulysses, well.
Ah, sir, there's many a Greek and Trojan dead,
Since first I saw yourself and Diomed
In Ilion, on your Greekish embassy.
ULYSSES.
Sir, I foretold you then what would ensue:
My prophecy is but half his journey yet;
For yonder walls, that pertly front your town,
Yond towers, whose wanton tops do buss the
Must kiss their own feet.   [clouds,
HECTOR.
          I must not believe you:
There they stand yet; and modestly I think,
The fall of every Phrygian stone will cost
A drop of Grecian blood: the end crowns all;
And that old common arbitrator, Time,
Will one day end it.
ULYSSES.
          So to him we leave it.
Most gentle and most valiant Hector, welcome:
After the general, I beseech you next
To feast with me, and see me at my tent.
ACHILLES.
I shall forestall thee, Lord Ulysses, thou!—
Now, Hector, I have fed mine eyes on thee;
I have with exact view perused thee, Hector,
And quoted joint by joint.
HECTOR.
          Is this Achilles?
ACHILLES.
I am Achilles.
HECTOR.
Stand fair, I pray thee: let me look on thee.
ACHILLES.
Behold thy fill.
HECTOR.
          Nay, I have done already.
ACHILLES.
Thou art too brief: I will the second time,
As I would buy thee, view thee limb by limb.
HECTOR.
O, like a book of sport thou'lt read me o'er;
But there's more in me than thou understand'st
Why dost thou so oppress me with thine eye?

ACHILLES.

Tell me, you heavens, in which part of his body
Shall I destroy him? whether there, or there, or
there?
That I may give the local wound a name,
And make distinct the very breach whereout
Hector's great spirit flew: answer me, heavens!

HECTOR.

It would discredit the blest gods, proud man,
To answer such a question: stand again:
Think'st thou to catch my life so pleasantly
As to prenominate in nice conjecture
Where thou wilt hit me dead?

ACHILLES.

I tell thee, yea.

HECTOR.

Wert thou the oracle to tell me so,
I'ld not believe thee. Henceforth guard thee well;
For I'll not kill thee there, not there, nor there;
But, by the forge that stithied Mars his helm,
I'll kill thee every where, yea, o'er and o'er.—
You wisest Grecians, pardon me this brag,
His insolence draws folly from my lips;
But I'll endeavour deeds to match these words,
Or may I never—

AJAX.

Do not chafe thee, cousin:—
And you, Achilles, let these threats alone,
Till accident or purpose bring you to't:
You may have every day enough of Hector,
If you have stomach; the general state, I fear,
Can scarce entreat you to be odd with him.

HECTOR.

I pray you, let us see you in the field:
We have had pelting wars, since you refused
The Grecians' cause.

ACHILLES.

Dost thou entreat me, Hector?
To-morrow do I meet thee, fell as death;
To-night all friends.

HECTOR.

Thy hand upon that match.

AGAMEMNON.

First, all you peers of Greece, go to my tent;
There in the full convive we: afterwards,
As Hector's leisure and your bounties shall
Concur together, severally entreat him.—
Beat loud the tabourines, let the trumpets blow,
That this great soldier may his welcome know.

[Exeunt all but TROILUS and ULYSSES.

TROILUS.

My Lord Ulysses, tell me, I beseech you,
In what place of the field doth Calchas keep?

ULYSSES.

At Menelaus' tent, most princely Troilus:
There Diomed doth feast with him to-night;
Who neither looks upon the heaven nor earth,
But gives all gaze and bent of amorous view
On the fair Cressid.

TROILUS.

Shall I, sweet lord, be bound to you so much,
After we part from Agamemnon's tent,
To bring me thither?

ULYSSES.

You shall command me, sir.
As gentle tell me, of what honour was

This Cressida in Troy? Had she no lover there
That wails her absence?

TROILUS.

O, sir, to such as boasting show their scars
A mock is due. Will you walk on, my lord?
She was beloved, she loved; she is, and doth:
But still sweet love is food for fortune's tooth.

[Exeunt.

ACT V. SCENE I.

The Grecian camp. Before ACHILLES' *tent.*

Enter ACHILLES *and* PATROCLUS.

ACHILLES.

I'LL heat his blood with Greekish wine to-night,
Which with my scimitar I'll cool to-morrow.—
Patroclus, let us feast him to the height.

PATROCLUS.

Here comes Thersites.

Enter THERSITES.

ACHILLES.

How now, thou core of envy!
Thou crusty batch of nature, what's the news?

THERSITES.

Why, thou picture of what thou seem'st, and idol
of idiot-worshippers, here's a letter for thee.

ACHILLES.

From whence, fragment?

THERSITES.

Why, thou full dish of fool, from Troy.

PATROCLUS.

Who keeps the tent now?

THERSITES.

The surgeon's box, or the patient's wound.

PATROCLUS.

Well said, adversity! and what need these tricks?

THERSITES.

Prithee, be silent, boy; I profit not by thy talk:
thou art thought to be Achilles' male varlet.

PATROCLUS.

Male varlet, you rogue! what's that?

THERSITES.

Why, his masculine whore. Now, the rotten diseases of the south, the guts-griping, ruptures,
catarrhs, loads o'gravel i'th'back, lethargies,
cold palsies, raw eyes, dirt-rotten livers, wheezing
lungs, bladders full of imposthume, sciaticas,
limekilns i'th'palm, incurable bone-ache, and the
rivell'd fee-simple of the tetter, take and take
again such preposterous discoveries!

PATROCLUS.

Why, thou damnable box of envy, thou, what
mean'st thou to curse thus?

THERSITES.

Do I curse thee?

PATROCLUS.

Why, no, you ruinous butt; you whoreson indis-
tinguishable cur, no.

THERSITES.

No! why art thou, then, exasperate, thou idle im-
material skein of sleave-silk, thou green sarcenet
flap for a sore eye, thou tassel of a prodigal's
purse, thou? Ah, how the poor world is pester'd
with such waterflies,—diminutives of nature!

PATROCLUS.

Out, gall!

THERSITES.

Finch-egg!

ACHILLES.

My sweet Patroclus, I am thwarted quite
From my great purpose in to-morrow's battle.
Here is a letter from Queen Hecuba;
A token from her daughter, my fair love;
Both taxing me and gaging me to keep
An oath that I have sworn. I will not break it:
Fall Greeks; fail fame; honour or go or stay;
My major vow lies here, this I'll obey.
Come, come, Thersites, help to trim my tent;
This night in banqueting must all be spent.—
Away, Patroclus!

[Exeunt ACHILLES and PATROCLUS.

THERSITES.

With too much blood and too little brain, these
two may run mad; but, if with too much brain and
too little blood they do, I'll be a curer of madmen.
Here's Agamemnon,—an honest fellow enough,
and one that loves quails: but he has not so much
brain as ear-wax: and the goodly transformation
of Jupiter there, his brother, the bull,—the primi-
tive statue, and oblique memorial of cuckolds; a
thrifty shoeing-horn in a chain, hanging at his
brother's leg,—to what form, but that he is,
should wit larded with malice, and malice forced
with wit, turn him to? To an ass, were nothing;
he is both ass and ox: to an ox, were nothing; he is
both ox and ass. To be a dog, a mule, a cat, a
fitchew, a toad, a lizard, an owl, a puttock, or a
herring without a roe, I would not care; but to
be Menelaus!—I would conspire against destiny.
Ask me not what I would be, if I were not Thersites; for I care not to be the louse of a lazar,
so I were not Menelaus.—Hoyday! spirits and
fires!

Enter HECTOR, TROILUS, AJAX, AGAMEMNON,
ULYSSES, NESTOR, MENELAUS, DIOMEDES,
with lights.

AGAMEMNON.

We go wrong, we go wrong.

AJAX.
                    No, yonder 'tis;
There, where we see the lights.

HECTOR.
                    I trouble you.

AJAX.

No, not a whit.

ULYSSES.

Here comes himself to guide you.
Enter ACHILLES.

ACHILLES.

Welcome, brave Hector; welcome, princes all.

AGAMEMNON.

So now, fair Prince of Troy, I bid good night.
Ajax commands the guard to tend on you.

HECTOR.

Thanks and good night to the Greeks' general.

MENELAUS.

Good night, my lord.

HECTOR.
          Good night, sweet Lord Menelaus.

THERSITES.

Sweet draught: sweet, quoth a'! sweet sink, sweet
sewer.

ACHILLES.

Good night and welcome, both at once, to those
That go or tarry.

AGAMEMNON.

Good night.
          [Exeunt AGAMEMNON and MENELAUS.

ACHILLES.

Old Nestor tarries; and you too, Diomed,
Keep Hector company an hour or two.

DIOMEDES.

I cannot, lord; I have important business,   [tor.
The tide whereof is now.—Good night, great Hec-

HECTOR.

Give me your hand.

ULYSSES [aside to TROILUS].

Follow his torch; he goes to Calchas' tent:
I'll keep you company.

TROILUS [aside to ULYSSES].

Sweet sir, you honour me.

HECTOR.

And so, good night.
          [Exit DIOMEDES; ULYSSES and TROILUS
          following.

ACHILLES.
          Come, come, enter my tent.
          [Exeunt ACHILLES, HECTOR, AJAX, and
          NESTOR.

THERSITES.

That same Diomed's a false-hearted rogue, a most
unjust knave; I will no more trust him when he
leers than I will a serpent when he hisses: he will
spend his mouth, and promise, like Brabbler the
hound; but when he performs, astronomers foretell it; it is prodigious, there will come some
change; the sun borrows of the moon, when Diomed keeps his word. I will rather leave to see
Hector than not to dog him: they say he keeps a
Trojan drab, and uses the traitor Calchas' tent:
I'll after.—Nothing but lechery! all incontinent
varlets!   [Exit.

SCENE II.

The same. Before CALCHAS' tent.

Enter DIOMEDES.

DIOMEDES.

WHAT, are you up here, ho? speak.

CALCHAS [within].

Who calls?

DIOMEDES.

Diomed.—Calchas, I think. Where's your daughter?

CALCHAS [within].

She comes to you.
          Enter TROILUS and ULYSSES, at a distance;
          after them THERSITES.

ULYSSES.

Stand where the torch may not discover us.
          Enter CRESSIDA.

TROILUS.

Cressid comes forth to him.

DIOMEDES.
                    How now, my charge!

CRESSIDA.

Now, my sweet guardian!—Hark, a word with you.
                              [Whispers.

TROILUS.
Yea, so familiar!

ULYSSES.
She will sing any man at first sight.

THERSITES.
And any man may sing her, if he can take her cliff: she's noted.

DIOMEDES.
Will you remember?

CRESSIDA.
Remember! yes.

DIOMEDES.
Nay, but do, then;
And let your mind be coupled with your words.

TROILUS.
What should she remember?

ULYSSES.
List.

CRESSIDA.
Sweet honey Greek, tempt me no more to folly.

THERSITES.
Roguery!

DIOMEDES.
Nay, then,—

CRESSIDA.
I'll tell you what,—

DIOMEDES.
Foh, foh! come, tell a pin: you are forsworn.

CRESSIDA.
In faith, I cannot: what would you have me do?

THERSITES.
A juggling trick,—to be secretly open.

DIOMEDES.
What did you swear you would bestow on me?

CRESSIDA.
I prithee, do not hold me to mine oath;
Bid me do any thing but that, sweet Greek.

DIOMEDES.
Good night.

TROILUS.
Hold, patience!

ULYSSES.
How now, Trojan!

CRESSIDA.
Diomed,—

DIOMEDES.
No, no, good night: I'll be your fool no more.

TROILUS.
Thy better must.

CRESSIDA.
Hark, one word in your ear.

TROILUS.
O plague and madness!

ULYSSES.
You are moved, prince; let us depart, I pray you,
Lest your displeasure should enlarge itself
To wrathful terms: this place is dangerous;
The time right deadly; I beseech you, go.

TROILUS.
Behold, I pray you!

ULYSSES.
          Nay, good my lord, go off:
You flow to great distraction; come, my lord.

TROILUS.
I pray thee, stay.

ULYSSES.
You have not patience; come.

TROILUS.
I pray you, stay; by hell and all hell's torments,
I will not speak a word!

DIOMEDES.
          And so, good night.

CRESSIDA.
Nay, but you part in anger.

TROILUS.
          Doth that grieve thee?
O wither'd truth!

ULYSSES.
Why, how now, lord!

TROILUS.
          By Jove,
I will be patient.

CRESSIDA.
          Guardian!—why, Greek!

DIOMEDES.
Foh, foh! adieu; you palter.

CRESSIDA.
In faith, I do not: come hither once again.

ULYSSES.
You shake, my lord, at something: will you go?
You will break out.

TROILUS.
          She strokes his cheek!

ULYSSES.
          Come, come.

TROILUS.
Nay, stay; by Jove, I will not speak a word:
There is between my will and all offences
A guard of patience:—stay a little while.

THERSITES.
How the devil luxury, with his fat rump and potato-finger, tickles these together! Fry, lechery, fry!

DIOMEDES.
But will you, then?

CRESSIDA.
In faith, I will, la; never trust me else.

DIOMEDES.
Give me some token for the surety of it.

CRESSIDA.
I'll fetch you one.   [Exit.

ULYSSES.
You have sworn patience.

TROILUS.
          Fear me not, sweet lord;
I will not be myself, nor have cognition
Of what I feel: I am all patience.

Enter CRESSIDA.

THERSITES.
Now the pledge; now, now, now!

CRESSIDA.
Here, Diomed, keep this sleeve.

TROILUS.
O beauty! where is thy faith?

ULYSSES.
          My lord,—

TROILUS.
I will be patient; outwardly I will.

CRESSIDA.
You look upon that sleeve; behold it well.—
He loved me—O false wench!—Give't me again.

DIOMEDES.
Whose was't?
CRESSIDA.
It is no matter, now I have't again.
I will not meet with you to-morrow night:
I prithee, Diomed, visit me no more.
THERSITES.
Now she sharpens:—well said, whetstone!
DIOMEDES.
I shall have it.
CRESSIDA.
What, this?
DIOMEDES.
Ay, that.
CRESSIDA.
O, all you gods!—O pretty, pretty pledge!
Thy master now lies thinking in his bed
Of thee and me: and sighs, and takes my glove,
And gives memorial dainty kisses to it,
As I kiss thee.—Nay, do not snatch it from me;
He that takes that doth take my heart withal.
DIOMEDES.
I had your heart before, this follows it.
TROILUS.
I did swear patience.
CRESSIDA.
You shall not have it, Diomed; faith, you shall
not;
I'll give you something else.
DIOMEDES.
I will have this: whose was it?
CRESSIDA.
It is no matter.
DIOMEDES.
Come, tell me whose it was.
CRESSIDA.
'Twas one's that loved me better than you will.
But, now you have it, take it.
DIOMEDES.
Whose was it?
CRESSIDA.
By all Diana's waiting-women yond,
And by herself, I will not tell you whose.
DIOMEDES.
To-morrow will I wear it on my helm;
And grieve his spirit that dares not challenge it.
TROILUS.
Wert thou the devil, and worest it on thy horn,
It should be challenged.
CRESSIDA.
Well, well, 'tis done, 'tis past;—and yet it is not;
I will not keep my word,
DIOMEDES.
Why, then, farewell;
Thou never shalt mock Diomed again.
CRESSIDA.
You shall not go:—one cannot speak a word,
But it straight starts you.
DIOMEDES.
I do not like this fooling.
THERSITES.
Nor I, by Pluto: but that that likes not you pleases
me best.
DIOMEDES.
What, shall I come? the hour?

CRESSIDA.
Ay, come:—O Jove!—do come:—I shall be
plagued.
DIOMEDES.
Farewell till then.
CRESSIDA.
Good night: I prithee, come.
Exit DIOMEDES.
Troilus, farewell! one eye yet looks on thee;
But with my heart the other eye doth see.
Ah, poor our sex! this fault in us I find,
The error of our eye directs our mind:
What error leads must err; O, then conclude
Minds sway'd by eyes are full of turpitude. [*Exit.*
THERSITES.
A proof of strength she could not publish more,
Unless she said 'My mind is now turn'd whore.'
ULYSSES.
All's done, my lord.
TROILUS.
It is.
ULYSSES.
Why stay we, then?
TROILUS.
To make a recordation to my soul
Of every syllable that here was spoke.
But if I tell how these two did co-act,
Shall I not lie in publishing a truth?
Sith yet there is a credence in my heart,
An esperance so obstinately strong,
That doth invert th'attest of eyes and ears;
As if those organs had deceptious functions,
Created only to calumniate.
Was Cressid here?
ULYSSES.
I cannot conjure, Trojan.
TROILUS.
She was not, sure.
ULYSSES.
Most sure she was.
TROILUS.
Why, my negation hath no taste of madness.
ULYSSES.
Nor mine, my lord: Cressid was here but now.
TROILUS.
Let it not be believed for womanhood!
Think, we had mothers; do not give advantage
To stubborn critics,—apt, without a theme,
For depravation,—to square the general sex
By Cressid's rule: rather think this not Cressid.
ULYSSES.
What hath she done, prince, that can soil our
mothers?
TROILUS.
Nothing at all, unless that this were she.
THERSITES.
Will he swagger himself out on's own eyes?
TROILUS.
This she? no, this is Diomed's Cressida:
If beauty have a soul, this is not she;
If souls guide vows, if vows be sanctimonies,
If sanctimony be the gods' delight,
If there be rule in unity itself,
This is not she. O madness of discourse,
That cause sets up with and against itself!
Bi-fold authority! where reason can revolt

Without perdition, and loss assume all reason
Without revolt: this is, and is not, Cressid!
Within my soul there doth conduce a fight
Of this strange nature, that a thing inseparate
Divides more wider than the sky and earth;
And yet the spacious breadth of this division
Admits no orifex for a point, as subtle
As Ariachne's broken woof, to enter.
Instance, O instance! strong as Pluto's gates;
Cressid is mine, tied with the bonds of heaven:
Instance, O instance! strong as heaven itself;
The bonds of heaven are slipt, dissolved, and
　　loosed;
And with another knot, five-finger-tied,
The fractions of her faith, orts of her love,
The fragments, scraps, the bits, and greasy
　　relics
Of her o'er-eaten faith, are bound to Diomed.

ULYSSES.

May worthy Troilus be half attacht
With that which here his passion doth express?

TROILUS.

Ay, Greek, and that shall be divulged well
In characters as red as Mars his heart
Inflamed with Venus; never did young man
　　fancy
With so eternal and so fixt a soul.
Hark, Greek:—as much as I do Cressid love,
So much by weight hate I her Diomed:
That sleeve is mine that he'll bear on his helm;
Were it a casque composed by Vulcan's skill,
My sword should bite it: not the dreadful spout,
Which shipmen do the hurricano call,
Constringed in mass by the almighty sun,
Shall dizzy with more clamour Neptune's ear
In his descent than shall my prompted sword
Falling on Diomed.

THERSITES.

He'll tickle it for his concupy.

TROILUS.

O Cressid! O false Cressid! false, false, false!
Let all untruths stand by thy stained name,
And they'll seem glorious.

ULYSSES.

　　　　　　　　O, contain yourself;
Your passion draws ears hither.

Enter AENEAS.

AENEAS.

I have been seeking you this hour, my lord:
Hector, by this, is arming him in Troy;
Ajax, your guard, stays to conduct you home.

TROILUS.

Have with you, prince.—My courteous lord,
　　adieu.—
Farewell, revolted fair!—and, Diomed,
Stand fast, and wear a castle on thy head!

ULYSSES.

I'll bring you to the gates.

TROILUS.

Accept distracted thanks.

[Exeunt TROILUS, AENEAS, and ULYSSES.

THERSITES.

Would I could meet that rogue Diomed! I would
croak like a raven; I would bode, I would bode.
Patroclus will give me any thing for the intelligence of this whore: the parrot will not do more

for an almond than he for a commodious drab.
Lechery, lechery; still, wars and lechery; nothing
else holds fashion: a burning devil take them!

[Exit.

SCENE III.

Troy. Before PRIAM'S palace.

Enter HECTOR and ANDROMACHE.

ANDROMACHE.

WHEN was my lord so much ungently tem-
　　per'd,
To stop his ears against admonishment?
Unarm, unarm, and do not fight to-day.

HECTOR.

You train me to offend you; get you in:
By all the everlasting gods, I'll go!

ANDROMACHE.

My dreams will, sure, prove ominous to the day.

HECTOR.

No more, I say.

Enter CASSANDRA.

CASSANDRA.

　　　　　　Where is my brother Hector?

ANDROMACHE.

Here, sister; arm'd, and bloody in intent.
Consort with me in loud and dear petition,
Pursue we him on knees; for I have dream'd
Of bloody turbulence, and this whole night
Hath nothing been but shapes and forms of
　　slaughter.

CASSANDRA.

O, 'tis true.

HECTOR.

　　　　　Ho! bid my trumpet sound!

CASSANDRA.

No notes of sally, for the heavens, sweet brother.

HECTOR.

Be gone, I say: the gods have heard me swear.

CASSANDRA.

The gods are deaf to hot and peevish vows:
They are polluted offerings, more abhorr'd
Than spotted livers in the sacrifice.

ANDROMACHE.

O, be persuaded! do not count it holy
To hurt by being just: it is as lawful,
For we would give much, to use violent thefts,
And rob in the behalf of charity.

CASSANDRA.

It is the purpose that makes strong the vow;
But vows to every purpose must not hold:
Unarm, sweet Hector.

HECTOR.

　　　　　　　Hold you still, I say;
Mine honour keeps the weather of my fate:
Life every man holds dear; but the brave man
Holds honour far more precious-dear than life.

Enter TROILUS.

How now, young man! mean'st thou to fight to-
　　day?

ANDROMACHE.

Cassandra, call my father to persuade.

[Exit CASSANDRA.

HECTOR.

No, faith, young Troilus; doff thy harness, youth;
I am to-day i'th'vein of chivalry:

Let grow thy sinews till their knots be strong,
And tempt not yet the brushes of the war.
Unarm thee, go; and doubt thou not, brave boy,
I'll stand to-day for thee, and me, and Troy.

TROILUS.
Brother, you have a vice of mercy in you,
Which better fits a lion than a man.

HECTOR.
What vice is that, good Troilus? chide me for it.

TROILUS.
When many times the captive Grecian falls,
Even in the fan and wind of your fair sword,
You bid them rise, and live.

HECTOR.
O, 'tis fair play.

TROILUS.
Fool's play, by heaven, Hector.

HECTOR.
How now! how now!

TROILUS.
For th'love of all the gods,
Let's leave the hermit pity with our mothers;
And when we have our armours buckled on,
The venom'd vengeance ride upon our swords,
Spur them to ruthful work, rein them from ruth.

HECTOR.
Fie, savage, fie!

TROILUS.
Hector, then 'tis wars.

HECTOR.
Troilus, I would not have you fight to-day.

TROILUS.
Who should withhold me?
Not fate, obedience, nor the hand of Mars
Beckoning with fiery truncheon my retire;
Not Priamus and Hecuba on knees,
Their eyes o'ergalled with recourse of tears;
Nor you, my brother, with your true sword
    drawn,
Opposed to hinder me, should stop my way,
But by my ruin.

Enter CASSANDRA *with* PRIAM.

CASSANDRA.
Lay hold upon him, Priam, hold him fast:
He is thy crutch; now if thou lose thy stay,
Thou on him leaning, and all Troy on thee,
Fall all together.

PRIAM.
Come, Hector, come, go back:
Thy wife hath dream'd; thy mother hath had
    visions;
Cassandra doth foresee; and I myself
Am like a prophet suddenly enrapt,
To tell thee that this day is ominous:
Therefore, come back.

HECTOR.
Aeneas is a-field;
And I do stand engaged to many Greeks,
Even in the faith of valour, to appear
This morning to them.

PRIAM.
Ay, but thou shalt not go.

HECTOR.
I must not break my faith.
You know me dutiful; therefore, dear sir,
Let me not shame respect; but give me leave

To take that course by your consent and voice,
Which you do here forbid me, royal Priam.

CASSANDRA.
O Priam, yield not to him!

ANDROMACHE.
Do not, dear father.

HECTOR.
Andromache, I am offended with you:
Upon the love you bear me, get you in.
        [*Exit* ANDROMACHE.

TROILUS.
This foolish, dreaming, superstitious girl
Makes all these bodements.

CASSANDRA.
O, farewell, dear Hector!
Look, how thou diest! look, how thy eye turns
    pale!
Look, how thy wounds do bleed at many vents!
Hark, how Troy roars! how Hecuba cries out!
How poor Andromache shrills her dolours forth!
Behold distraction, frenzy, and amazement,
Like witless anticks, one another meet,
And all cry 'Hector! Hector's dead!' O Hector!

TROILUS.
Away! away!

CASSANDRA.
Farewell:—yet, soft!—Hector, I take my leave:
Thou dost thyself and all our Troy deceive.
        [*Exit.*

HECTOR.
You are amazed, my liege, at her exclaim:
Go in, and cheer the town: we'll forth, and fight;
Do deeds worth praise, and tell you them at night.

PRIAM.
Farewell: the gods with safety stand about thee!
  [*Exeunt severally* PRIAM *and* HECTOR. *Alarum.*

TROILUS.
They are at it, hark!—Proud Diomed, believe,
I come to lose my arm, or win my sleeve.

Enter PANDARUS.

PANDARUS.
Do you hear, my lord? do you hear?

TROILUS.
What now?

PANDARUS.
Here's a letter come from yond poor girl.

TROILUS.
Let me read.

PANDARUS.
A whoreson tisick, a whoreson rascally tisick so
troubles me, and the foolish fortune of this girl;
and what one thing, what another, that I shall
leave you one o'th's days: and I have a rheum in
mine eyes too; and such an ache in my bones, that,
unless a man were curst, I cannot tell what to
think on't.—What says she there?

TROILUS.
Words, words, mere words, no matter from the
    heart;
Th'effect doth operate another way.—
        [*Tearing the letter.*
Go, wind, to wind, there turn and change to-
    gether.—
My love with words and errors still she feeds;
But edifies another with her deeds.
        [*Exeunt severally.*

SCENE IV.

Plains between Troy and the Grecian camp.

Alarums: excursions. Enter THERSITES.

THERSITES.

NOW they are clapper-clawing one another; I'll go look on. That dissembling abominable varlet, Diomed, has got that same scurvy doting foolish young knave's sleeve of Troy there in his helm: I would fain see them meet; that that same young Trojan ass, that loves the whore there, might send that Greekish whore-masterly villain, with the sleeve, back to the dissembling luxurious drab of a sleeveless errand. O'th't'other side, the policy of those crafty swearing rascals—that stale old mouse-eaten dry cheese, Nestor, and that same-dog-fox, Ulysses—is not proved worth a black-berry:—they set me up, in policy, that mongrel cur, Ajax, against that dog of as bad a kind, Achilles: and now is the cur Ajax prouder than the cur Achilles, and will not arm to-day; where-upon the Grecians begin to proclaim barbarism, and policy grows into an ill opinion.—Soft! here comes sleeve, and t'other.

Enter DIOMEDES *and* TROILUS.

TROILUS.

Fly not: for shouldst thou take the river Styx, I would swim after.

DIOMEDES.

Thou dost miscall retire: I do not fly; but advantageous care Withdrew me from the odds of multitude: Have at thee!

THERSITES.

Hold thy whore, Grecian! now for thy whore, Trojan!—now the sleeve! now the sleeve!

[*Exeunt* TROILUS *and* DIOMEDES, *fighting.*

Enter HECTOR.

HECTOR.

What art thou, Greek? art thou for Hector's match?

Art thou of blood and honour?

THERSITES.

No, no,—I am a rascal; a scurvy railing knave; a very filthy rogue.

HECTOR.

I do believe thee;—live.   [*Exit.*

THERSITES.

God-a-mercy, that thou wilt believe me; but a plague break thy neck for frighting me!—What's become of the wenching rogues? I think they have swallow'd one another: I would laugh at that miracle:—yet, in a sort, lechery eats itself. I'll seek them.   [*Exit.*

SCENE V.

Another part of the plains.

Enter DIOMEDES *and* SERVANT.

DIOMEDES.

GO, go, my servant, take thou Troilus' horse; Present the fair steed to my lady Cressid: Fellow, commend my service to her beauty; Tell her I have chastised the amorous Trojan, And am her knight by proof.

SERVANT.

I go, my lord. [*Exit.*

Enter AGAMEMNON.

AGAMEMNON.

Renew, renew! The fierce Polydamas Hath beat down Menon: bastard Margarelon Hath Doreus prisoner, And stands colossus-wise, waving his beam, Upon the pashed corses of the kings Epistrophus and Cedius: Polyxenes is slain; Amphimachus and Thoas deadly hurt; Patroclus ta'en or slain; and Palamedes Sore hurt and bruised: the dreadful Sagittary Appals our numbers;—haste we, Diomed, To reinforcement, or we perish all.

Enter NESTOR.

NESTOR.

Go, bear Patroclus' body to Achilles; And bid the snail-paced Ajax arm for shame.— There is a thousand Hectors in the field: Now here he fights on Galathe his horse, And there lacks work; anon he's there afoot, And there they fly or die, like scaled sculls Before the belching whale; then is he yonder, And there the strawy Greeks, ripe for his edge, Fall down before him, like the mower's swath: Here, there, and every where, he leaves and takes; Dexterity so obeying appetite, That what he will he does; and does so much, That proof is call'd impossibility.

Enter ULYSSES.

ULYSSES.

O, courage, courage, princes! great Achilles Is arming, weeping, cursing, vowing vengeance: Patroclus' wounds have roused his drowsy blood, Together with his mangled Myrmidons, That noseless, handless, hackt and chipt, come to him, Crying on Hector. Ajax hath lost a friend, And foams at mouth, and he is arm'd and at it, Roaring for Troilus; who hath done to-day Mad and fantastic execution; Engaging and redeeming of himself, With such a careless force and forceless care, As if that luck, in very spite of cunning, Bade him win all.

Enter AJAX.

AJAX.

Troilus! thou coward Troilus!   [*Exit.*

DIOMEDES.

Ay, there, there.

NESTOR.

So, so, we draw together.

Enter ACHILLES.

ACHILLES.

Where is this Hector?— Come, come, thou boy-queller, show thy face; Know what it is to meet Achilles angry:— Hector! where's Hector? I will none but Hector.

[*Exeunt.*

SCENE VI.

Another part of the plains.

Enter AJAX.

AJAX.

TROILUS, thou coward Troilus, show thy head!

Enter DIOMEDES.

DIOMEDES.

Troilus, I say! where's Troilus?

AJAX.
                        What wouldst thou?
DIOMEDES.
I would correct him.
                        AJAX.
Were I the general, thou shouldst have my office
Ere that correction.—Troilus, I say! what, Troilus!
                Enter TROILUS.
                TROILUS.
O traitor Diomed!—turn thy false face, thou
        traitor,
And pay thy life thou owest me for my horse!
                DIOMEDES.
Ha, art thou there?
                AJAX.
I'll fight with him alone: stand, Diomed.
                DIOMEDES.
He is my prize; I will not look upon.
                TROILUS.
Come, both you cogging Greeks; have at you both!
                [Exeunt, fighting.
                Enter HECTOR.
                HECTOR.
Yea, Troilus? O, well fought, my youngest brother!
                Enter ACHILLES.
                ACHILLES.
Now do I see thee, ha!—have at thee, Hector!
                HECTOR.
Pause, if thou wilt.
                ACHILLES.
I do disdain thy courtesy, proud Trojan:
Be happy that my arms are out of use:
My rest and negligence befriend thee now,
But thou anon shalt hear of me again;
Till when, go seek thy fortune.   *[Exit.*
                HECTOR.
                        Fare thee well:—
I would have been much more a fresher man,
Had I expected thee.
                Enter TROILUS.
                        How now, my brother!
                TROILUS.
Ajax hath ta'en Aeneas: shall it be?
No, by the flame of yonder glorious heaven,
He shall not carry him; I'll be ta'en too,
Or bring him off:—fate, hear me what I say!
I reck not though I end my life to-day.   *[Exit.*
        Enter one in sumptuous armour.
                HECTOR.
Stand, stand, thou Greek; thou art a goodly
        mark:—
No? wilt thou not?—I like thy armour well;
I'll frush it, and unlock the rivets all,
But I'll be master of it:—wilt thou not, beast,
        abide?
Why then, fly on, I'll hunt thee for thy hide.
                [Exeunt.

SCENE VII.

Another part of the plains.

Enter ACHILLES *with* MYRMIDONS.
                ACHILLES.
COME here about me, you my Myrmidons;
        Mark what I say. Attend me where I wheel:
Strike not a stroke, but keep yourselves in breath:

And when I have the bloody Hector found,
Empale him with your weapons round about;
In fellest manner execute your arms.
Follow me, sirs, and my proceedings eye:—
It is decreed Hector the great must die.   *[Exeunt.*
        Enter MENELAUS *and* PARIS, *fighting;*
                then THERSITES.
                THERSITES.
The cuckold and the cuckold-maker are at it.—
Now, bull! now, dog! 'Loo, Paris, 'loo! now my
double-henn'd sparrow! 'loo, Paris, 'loo!—The
bull has the game:—ware horns, ho!
        [Exeunt PARIS *and* MENELAUS.
        Enter MARGARELON.
                MARGARELON.
Turn, slave, and fight.
                THERSITES.
What art thou?
                MARGARELON.
A bastard son of Priam's.
                THERSITES.
I am a bastard too; I love bastards: I am a bastard
begot, bastard instructed, bastard in mind, bastard in valour, in every thing illegitimate. One
bear will not bite another, and wherefore should
one bastard? Take heed, the quarrel's most ominous to us: if the son of a whore fight for a whore,
he tempts judgement: farewell, bastard.   *[Exit.*
                MARGARELON.
The devil take thee, coward!   *[Exit.*

SCENE VIII.

Another part of the plains.

Enter HECTOR.
                HECTOR.
MOST putrefied core, so fair without,
        Thy goodly armour thus hath cost thy life.
Now is my day's work done; I'll take good breath:
Rest, sword; thou hast thy fill of blood and death.
        *[Puts off his helmet, and hangs his shield be-
                hind him.*
        Enter ACHILLES *and* MYRMIDONS.
                ACHILLES.
Look, Hector, how the sun begins to set;
How ugly night comes breathing at his heels:
Even with the vail and darkening of the sun,
To close the day up, Hector's life is done.
                HECTOR.
I am unarm'd; forgo this vantage, Greek.
                ACHILLES.
Strike, fellows, strike; this is the man I seek.
                        *[*HECTOR *falls.*
So, Ilion, fall thou next! now, Troy, sink down!
Here lies thy heart, thy sinews, and thy bone.—
On, Myrmidons; and cry you all amain,
'Achilles hath the mighty Hector slain.'—
                        [A retreat sounded.
Hark! a retire upon our Grecian part.
                MYRMIDONS.
The Trojan trumpets sound the like, my lord.
                ACHILLES.
The dragon wing of night o'erspreads the earth,
And, stickler-like, the armies separates.
My half-supt sword, that frankly would have fed,

Pleased with this dainty bait, thus goes to bed.
                    [*Sheathes his sword.*
Come, tie his body to my horse's tail;
Along the field I will the Trojan trail.   [*Exeunt.*

SCENE IX.

Another part of the plains.

Enter AGAMEMNON, AJAX, MENELAUS, NESTOR,
DIOMEDES, *and the rest, marching. Shouts within.*

AGAMEMNON.

HARK! hark! what shout is that?
                    NESTOR.
Peace, drums!
[*within*] Achilles! Achilles! Hector's slain! Achilles!
                    DIOMEDES.
The bruit is, Hector's slain, and by Achilles.
                    AJAX.
If it be so, yet bragless let it be;
Great Hector was a man as good as he.
                    AGAMEMNON.
March patiently along:—let one be sent
To pray Achilles see us at our tent.—
If in his death the gods have us befriended,
Great Troy is ours, and our sharp wars are ended.
                    [*Exeunt, marching.*

SCENE X.

Another part of the plains.

Enter AENEAS, PARIS, ANTENOR, *and*
DEIPHOBUS.

AENEAS.

STAND, ho! yet are we masters of the field:
Never go home; here starve we out the night.
                    Enter TROILUS.
                    TROILUS.
Hector is slain.
                    ALL.
Hector!—the gods forbid!
                    TROILUS.
He's dead; and at the murderer's horse's tail,
In beastly sort, dragg'd through the shameful
  field.—
Frown on, you heavens, effect your rage with
  speed!
Sit, gods, upon your thrones, and smile at Troy!
I say, at once let your brief plagues be mercy,
And linger not our sure destructions on!
                    AENEAS.
My lord, you do discomfort all the host.
                    TROILUS.
You understand me not that tell me so:
I do not speak of flight, of fear, of death;

But dare all imminence that gods and men
Address their dangers in. Hector is gone:
Who shall tell Priam so, or Hecuba?
Let him that will a screech-owl aye be call'd,
Go into Troy, and say there 'Hector's dead:'
There is a word will Priam turn to stone;
Make wells and Niobes of the maids and wives,
Cold statues of the youth; and, in a word,
Scare Troy out of itself. But, march away:
Hector is dead; there is no more to say.
Stay yet.—You vile abominable tents,
Thus proudly pight upon our Phrygian plains,
Let Titan rise as early as he dare,
I'll through and through you!—and, thou great-
  sized coward,
No space of earth shall sunder our two hates:
I'll haunt thee like a wicked conscience still,
That mouldeth goblins swift as frenzy's
  thoughts.—
Strike a free march to Troy!—with comfort go:
Hope of revenge shall hide our inward woe.
          [*Exeunt* AENEAS *and* TROJANS.
    As TROILUS *is going out, enter, from the other
          side,* PANDARUS.
                    PANDARUS.
But hear you, hear you!
                    TROILUS.
Hence, broker-lackey! ignomy and shame
Pursue thy life, and live aye with thy name! [*Exit.*
                    PANDARUS.
A goodly medicine for my aching bones!—O
world! world! world! thus is the poor agent de-
spised! O traders and bawds, how earnestly are
you set a-work, and how ill requited! why should
our endeavour be so loved, and the performance
so loathed? what verse for it? what instance for it?
—Let me see:—
    Full merrily the humble-bee doth sing,
      Till he hath lost his honey and his sting;
    And being once subdued in armed tail,
      Sweet honey and sweet notes together fail.—
Good traders in the flesh, set this in your painted
cloths.
As many as be here of Pandar's hall,
Your eyes, half out, weep out at Pandar's fall;
Or if you cannot weep, yet give some groans,
Though not for me, yet for your aching bones.
Brethren and sisters of the hold-door trade,
Some two months hence my will shall here be
  made:
It should be now, but that my fear is this,—
Some galled goose of Winchester would hiss:
Till then I'll sweat, and seek about for eases;
And at that time bequeath you my diseases. [*Exit.*

ALL'S WELL THAT ENDS WELL

DRAMATIS PERSONAE

KING OF FRANCE.
DUKE OF FLORENCE.
BERTRAM, *Count of Rousillon.*
LAFEU, *an old lord.*
PAROLLES, *a follower of Bertram.*
Several young French LORDS, *who serve with Bertram in the Florentine war.*
STEWARD, \ *servants to the Countess of*
LAVACHE, *a Clown,* / *Rousillon.*
A PAGE.

COUNTESS OF ROUSILLON, *mother to Bertram.*
HELENA, *a gentlewoman protected by the Countess.*
A WIDOW *of Florence.*
DIANA, *her daughter.*
VIOLENTA, \ *neighbours and friends to the Widow.*
MARIANA, /

LORDS ATTENDING ON THE KING; OFFICERS, SOLDIERS, &c., FRENCH AND FLORENTINE.

SCENE—*Rousillon; Paris; Florence; Marseilles.*

ACT I. SCENE I.

Rousillon. A hall in the house of the COUNTESS.

Enter BERTRAM, *the* COUNTESS OF ROUSILLON, HELENA, *and* LAFEU, *all in black.*

COUNTESS.

IN delivering my son from me, I bury a second husband.

BERTRAM.

And I, in going, madam, weep o'er my father's death anew; but I must attend his majesty's command, to whom I am now in ward, evermore in subjection.

LAFEU.

You shall find of the king a husband, madam;—you, sir, a father: he that so generally is at all times good, must of necessity hold his virtue to you; whose worthiness would stir it up where it wanted, rather than lack it where there is such abundance.

COUNTESS.

What hope is there of his majesty's amendment?

LAFEU.

He hath abandon'd his physicians, madam; under whose practices he hath persecuted time with hope; and finds no other advantage in the process but only the losing of hope by time.

COUNTESS.

This young gentlewoman had a father,—O, that 'had'! how sad a passage 'tis!—whose skill was almost as great as his honesty; had it stretcht so far, would have made nature immortal, and death should have play for lack of work. Would, for the king's sake, he were living! I think it would be the death of the king's disease.

LAFEU.

How call'd you the man you speak of, madam?

COUNTESS.

He was famous, sir, in his profession, and it was his great right to be so,—Gerard de Narbon.

LAFEU.

He was excellent indeed, madam: the king very lately spoke of him admiringly and mourningly: he was skilful enough to have lived still, if knowledge could be set up against mortality.

BERTRAM.

What is it, my good lord, the king languishes of?

LAFEU.

A fistula, my lord.

BERTRAM.

I heard not of it before.

LAFEU.

I would it were not notorious.—Was this gentlewoman the daughter of Gerard de Narbon?

COUNTESS.

His sole child, my lord; and bequeath'd to my overlooking. I have those hopes of her good that her education promises: her dispositions she inherits, which makes fair gifts fairer; for where an unclean mind carries virtuous qualities, there commendations go with pity,—they are virtues and traitors too: in her they are the better for their simpleness; she derives her honesty, and achieves her goodness.

LAFEU.

Your commendations, madam, get from her **tears.**

COUNTESS.

'Tis the best brine a maiden can season her praise in. The remembrance of her father never approaches her heart but the tyranny of her sorrows takes all livelihood from her cheek.—No more of this, Helena,—go to, no more; lest it be rather thought you affect a sorrow than to have—

HELENA.

I do affect a sorrow, indeed; but I have it too.

LAFEU.

Moderate lamentation is the right of the dead; excessive grief the enemy of the living.

COUNTESS.

If the living be enemy to the grief, the **excess** makes it soon mortal.

LAFEU.

How understand we that?

BERTRAM.

Madam, I desire your holy wishes.

COUNTESS.

Be thou blest, Bertram! and succeed thy father
In manners, as in shape! thy blood and virtue
Contend for empire in thee, and thy goodness
Share with thy birthright! Love all, trust a few,
Do wrong to none; be able for thine enemy
Rather in power than use, and keep thy friend
Under thy own life's key; be checkt for silence,
But never taxt for speech. What heaven more will,
That thee may furnish, and my prayers pluck down,
Fall on thy head!—Farewell, my lord:

'Tis an unseason'd courtier; good my lord,
Advise him.

LAFEU.
He cannot want the best
That shall attend his love.

COUNTESS.
Heaven bless him!—Farewell, Bertram.   [*Exit.*
BERTRAM [*to* HELENA].
The best wishes that can be forged in your
thoughts be servants to you! Be comfortable to
my mother, your mistress, and make much of her.

LAFEU.
Farewell, pretty lady: you must hold the credit of
your father.   [*Exeunt* BERTRAM *and* LAFEU.

HELENA.
O, were that all! I think not on my father;
And these great tears grace his remembrance more
Than those I shed for him. What was he like?
I have forgot him: my imagination
Carries no favour in't but Bertram's.
I am undone: there is no living, none,
If Bertram be away. 'Twere all one
That I should love a bright particular star
And think to wed it, he is so above me:
In his bright radiance and collateral light
Must I be comforted, not in his sphere.
The ambition in my love thus plagues itself:
The hind that would be mated by the lion
Must die for love. 'Twas pretty, though a plague,
To see him every hour; to sit and draw
His arched brows, his hawking eye, his curls,
In our heart's table,—heart too capable
Of every line and trick of his sweet favour:
But now he's gone, and my idolatrous fancy
Must sanctify his reliques.—Who comes here?
One that goes with him: I love him for his sake;
And yet I know him a notorious liar,
Think him a great way fool, solely a coward;
Yet these fixt evils sit so fit in him,
That they take place, when virtue's steely bones
Look bleak i'th'cold wind: withal, full oft we see
Cold wisdom waiting on superfluous folly.

Enter PAROLLES.
PAROLLES.
Save you, fair queen!

HELENA.
And you, monarch!

PAROLLES.
No.

HELENA.
And no.

PAROLLES.
Are you meditating on virginity?

HELENA.
Ay. You have some stain of soldier in you: let me
ask you a question. Man is enemy to virginity;
how may we barricado it against him?

PAROLLES.
Keep him out.

HELENA.
But he assails; and our virginity, though valiant in
the defence, yet is weak: unfold to us some warlike resistance.

PAROLLES.
There is none: man, sitting down before you, will
undermine you, and blow you up.

HELENA.
Bless our poor virginity from underminers and
blowers-up!—Is there no military policy, how
virgins might blow up men?

PAROLLES.
Virginity being blown down, man will quicklier
be blown up: marry, in blowing him down again,
with the breach yourselves made, you lose your
city. It is not politic in the commonwealth of
nature to preserve virginity. Loss of virginity is
rational increase; and there was never virgin got
till virginity was first lost. That you were made of,
is metal to make virgins. Virginity, by being once
lost, may be ten times found; by being ever kept,
it is ever lost: 'tis too cold a companion; away
with't!

HELENA.
I will stand for't a little, though therefore I die a
virgin.

PAROLLES.
There's little can be said in't; 'tis against the rule
of nature. To speak on the part of virginity, is to
accuse your mothers; which is most infallible disobedience. He that hangs himself is a virgin: virginity murders itself; and should be buried in
highways, out of all sanctified limit, as a desperate
offendress against nature. Virginity breeds mites,
much like a cheese; consumes itself to the very
paring, and so dies with feeding his own stomach.
Besides, virginity is peevish, proud, idle, made of
self-love, which is the most inhibited sin in the
canon. Keep it not; you cannot choose but lose
by't: out with't! within ten year it will make itself
ten, which is a goodly increase; and the principal
itself not much the worse: away with't!

HELENA.
How might one do, sir, to lose it to her own
liking?

PAROLLES.
Let me see: marry, ill, to like him that ne'er it
likes. 'Tis a commodity will lose the gloss with
lying; the longer kept, the less worth: off with't
while 'tis vendible; answer the time of request.
Virginity, like an old courtier, wears her cap out
of fashion; richly suited, but unsuitable: just like
the brooch and the toothpick, which wear not
now. Your date is better in your pie and your
porridge than in your cheek: and your virginity,
your old virginity, is like one of our French
wither'd pears,—it looks ill, it eats dryly; marry,
'tis a wither'd pear; it was formerly better; marry,
yet, 'tis a wither'd pear: will you any thing with it?

HELENA.
Not my virginity yet. . . .
There shall your master have a thousand loves,
A mother, and a mistress, and a friend,
A phœnix, captain, and an enemy,
A guide, a goddess, and a sovereign,
A counsellor, a traitress, and a dear;
His humble ambition, proud humility,
His jarring concord, and his discord dulcet,
His faith, his sweet disaster; with a world
Of pretty, fond, adoptious christendoms,
That blinking Cupid gossips. Now shall he—
I know not what he shall:—God send him well!—
The court's a learning-place;—and he is one—

PAROLLES.
What one, i'faith?

HELENA.
That I wish well.—'Tis pity—

PAROLLES.
What's pity?

HELENA.
That wishing well had not a body in't,
Which might be felt; that we, the poorer born,
Whose baser stars do shut us up in wishes,
Might with effects of them follow our friends,
And show what we alone must think; which never
Returns us thanks.

Enter a PAGE.

PAGE.
Monsieur Parolles, my lord calls for you. [*Exit.*

PAROLLES.
Little Helen, farewell: if I can remember thee, I
will think of thee at court.

HELENA.
Monsieur Parolles, you were born under a charitable star.

PAROLLES.
Under Mars, I.

HELENA.
I especially think, under Mars.

PAROLLES.
Why under Mars?

HELENA.
The wars have so kept you under, that you must
needs be born under Mars.

PAROLLES.
When he was predominant.

HELENA.
When he was retrograde, I think, rather.

PAROLLES.
Why think you so?

HELENA.
You go so much backward when you fight.

PAROLLES.
That's for advantage.

HELENA.
So is running away, when fear proposes the safety:
but the composition, that your valour and fear
makes in you, is a virtue of a good wing, and I
like the wear well.

PAROLLES.
I am so full of businesses, I cannot answer thee
acutely. I will return perfect courtier; in the
which, my instruction shall serve to naturalize
thee, so thou wilt be capable of a courtier's
counsel, and understand what advice shall thrust
upon thee; else thou diest in thine unthankfulness, and thine ignorance makes thee away: farewell. When thou hast leisure, say thy prayers;
when thou hast none, remember thy friends: get
thee a good husband, and use him as he uses thee:
so, farewell.   [*Exit.*

HELENA.
Our remedies oft in ourselves do lie,
Which we ascribe to heaven: the fated sky
Gives us free scope; only doth backward pull
Our slow designs when we ourselves are dull.
What power is it which mounts my love so high;
That makes me see, and cannot feed mine eye?
The mightiest space in fortune nature brings

To join like likes and kiss like native things.
Impossible be strange attempts to those
That weigh their pains in sense; and do suppose
What hath not been can't be: who ever strove
To show her merit, that did miss her love?
The king's disease,—my project may deceive me,
But my intents are fixt, and will not leave me.
                                                [*Exit.*

SCENE II.

Paris.   A room in the KING'S *palace.*

Flourish of cornets.   Enter the KING OF FRANCE
with letters, and divers ATTENDANTS.

KING.
THE Florentines and Senoys are by th' ears;
Have fought with equal fortune, and continue
A braving war.

FIRST LORD.
So 'tis reported, sir.

KING.
Nay, 'tis most credible; we here receive it
A certainty, vouch'd from our cousin Austria,
With caution, that the Florentine will move us
For speedy aid; wherein our dearest friend
Prejudicates the business, and would seem
To have us make denial.

FIRST LORD.
His love and wisdom,
Approved so to your majesty, may plead
For amplest credence.

KING.
He hath arm'd our answer,
And Florence is denied before he comes:
Yet, for our gentlemen that mean to see
The Tuscan service, freely have they leave
To stand on either part.

SECOND LORD.
It well may serve
A nursery to our gentry, who are sick
For breathing and exploit.

KING.
What's he comes here?

Enter BERTRAM, LAFEU, *and* PAROLLES.

FIRST LORD.
It is the Count Rousillon, my good lord,
Young Bertram.

KING.
Youth, thou bear'st thy father's face;
Frank nature, rather curious than in haste,
Hath well composed thee. Thy father's moral
parts
Mayst thou inherit too! Welcome to Paris.

BERTRAM.
My thanks and duty are your majesty's.

KING.
I would I had that corporal soundness now
As when thy father and myself in friendship
First tried our soldiership! He did look far
Into the service of the time, and was
Discipled of the bravest: he lasted long;
But on us both did haggish age steal on,
And wore us out of act. It much repairs me
To talk of your good father. In his youth
He had the wit, which I can well observe
To-day in our young lords; but they may jest,
Till their own scorn return to them unnoted,

Ere they can hide their levity in honour
So like a courtier: contempt nor bitterness
Were in his pride, or sharpness; if they were,
His equal had awaked them; and his honour,
Clock to itself, knew the true minute when
Exception bid him speak, and at this time
His tongue obey'd his hand: who were below him
He used as creatures of another place;
And bow'd his eminent top to their low ranks,
Making them proud of his humility,
In their poor praise he humbled. Such a man
Might be a copy to these younger times;
Which, follow'd well, would demonstrate them now
But goers backward.

BERTRAM.
           His good remembrance, sir,
Lies richer in your thoughts than on his tomb;
So in approof lives not his epitaph
As in your royal speech.

KING.
Would I were with him! He would always say,—
Methinks I hear him now; his plausive words
He scatter'd not in ears, but grafted them,
To grow there, and to bear,—'Let me not live,'—
Thus his good melancholy oft began,
On the catastrophe and heel of pastime,
When it was out,—'Let me not live,' quoth he,
'After my flame lacks oil, to be the snuff
Of younger spirits, whose apprehensive senses
All but new things disdain; whose judgements are
Mere fathers of their garments; whose constancies
Expire before their fashions:'—this he wisht:
I, after him, do after him wish too,
Since I nor wax nor honey can bring home,
I quickly were dissolved from my hive,
To give some labourer room.

SECOND LORD.
           You are loved, sir;
They that least lend it you shall lack you first.

KING.
I fill a place, I know't.—How long is't, count,
Since the physician at your father's died?
He was much famed.

BERTRAM.
           Some six months since, my lord.

KING.
If he were living, I would try him yet;—
Lend me an arm;—the rest have worn me out
With several applications:—nature and sickness
Debate it at their leisure. Welcome, count;
My son's no dearer.

BERTRAM.
Thank your majesty.
[Exeunt. Flourish.

SCENE III.

Rousillon.   A room in the house of the COUNTESS.

Enter COUNTESS, STEWARD, and CLOWN.

COUNTESS.
I WILL now hear: what say you of this gentle-woman?

STEWARD.
Madam, the care I have had to even your content,
I wish might be found in the calendar of my

past endeavours; for then we wound our modesty,
and make foul the clearness of our deservings,
when of ourselves we publish them.

COUNTESS.
What does this knave here? Get you gone, sirrah:
the complaints I have heard of you I do not all
believe: 'tis my slowness that I do not; for I know
you lack not folly to commit them, and have
ability enough to make such knaveries yours.

CLOWN.
'Tis not unknown to you, madam, I am a poor
fellow.

COUNTESS.
Well, sir.

CLOWN.
No, madam, 'tis not so well that I am poor;
though many of the rich are damn'd: but, if I
may have your ladyship's good-will to go to the
world, Isbel your woman and I will do as we may.

COUNTESS.
Wilt thou needs be a beggar?

CLOWN.
I do beg your good-will in this case.

COUNTESS.
In what case?

CLOWN.
In Isbel's case and mine own. Service is no heritage: and I think I shall never have the blessing
of God till I have issue o' my body; for they say
barns are blessings.

COUNTESS.
Tell me thy reason why thou wilt marry.

CLOWN.
My poor body, madam, requires it: I am driven
on by the flesh; and he must needs go that the
devil drives.

COUNTESS.
Is this all your worship's reason?

CLOWN.
Faith, madam, I have other holy reasons, such as
they are.

COUNTESS.
May the world know them?

CLOWN.
I have been, madam, a wicked creature, as you
and all flesh and blood are; and, indeed, I do
marry that I may repent.

COUNTESS.
Thy marriage,—sooner than thy wickedness.

CLOWN.
I am out o' friends, madam; and I hope to have
friends for my wife's sake.

COUNTESS.
Such friends are thine enemies, knave.

CLOWN.
Y'are shallow, madam; e'en great friends; for the
knaves come to do that for me, which I am
a-weary of. He that ears my land spares my team,
and gives me leave to in the crop; if I be his
cuckold, he's my drudge: he that comforts my
wife is the cherisher of my flesh and blood; he
that cherishes my flesh and blood loves my flesh
and blood; he that loves my flesh and blood is my
friend: ergo, he that kisses my wife is my friend.
If men could be contented to be what they are,
there were no fear in marriage; for young Char-

bon the puritan and old Poysam the papist, how-some'er their hearts are sever'd in religion, their heads are both one,—they may jowl horns together, like any deer i'th'herd.

COUNTESS.

Wilt thou ever be a foul-mouth'd and calumnious knave?

CLOWN.

A prophet I, madam; and I speak the truth the next way:

For I the ballad will repeat,
    Which men full true shall find;
Your marriage comes by destiny,
    Your cuckoo sings by kind.

COUNTESS.

Get you gone, sir; I'll talk with you more anon.

STEWARD.

May it please you, madam, that he bid Helen come to you: of her I am to speak.

COUNTESS.

Sirrah, tell my gentlewoman I would speak with her; Helen I mean.

CLOWN.

Was this fair face the cause, quoth she,
    Why the Grecians sacked Troy?
Fond done, done fond,
    Was this King Priam's joy?
With that she sighed as she stood,
With that she sighed as she stood,
    And gave this sentence then;
Among nine bad if one be good,
Among nine bad if one be good,
    There's yet one good in ten.

COUNTESS.

What, one good in ten? you corrupt the song, sirrah.

CLOWN.

One good woman in ten, madam; which is a purifying o'th'song: would God would serve the world so all the year! we'ld find no fault with the tithe-woman, if I were the parson: one in ten, quoth a'! an we might have a good woman born but 'fore every blazing star, or at an earthquake, 'twould mend the lottery well: a man may draw his heart out, ere a' pluck one.

COUNTESS.

You'll begone, sir knave, and do as I command you?

CLOWN.

That man should be at woman's command, and yet no hurt done!—Though honesty be no puritan, yet it will do no hurt; it will wear the surplice of humility over the black gown of a big heart.— I am going, forsooth: the business is for Helen to come hither.   [Exit.

COUNTESS.

Well, now.

STEWARD.

I know, madam, you love your gentlewoman entirely.

COUNTESS.

Faith, I do: her father bequeath'd her to me; and she herself, without other advantage, may lawfully make title to as much love as she finds: there is more owing her than is paid; and more shall be paid her than she'll demand.

STEWARD.

Madam, I was very late more near her than I think she wisht me: alone she was, and did communicate to herself her own words to her own ears; she thought, I dare vow for her, they toucht not any stranger sense. Her matter was, she loved your son: Fortune, she said, was no goddess, that had put such difference betwixt their two estates; Love no god, that would not extend his might, only where qualities were level; Dian no queen of virgins, that would suffer her poor knight surprised, without rescue in the first assault, or ransom afterward. This she deliver'd in the most bitter touch of sorrow that e'er I heard virgin exclaim in: which I held my duty speedily to acquaint you withal; sithence, in the loss that may happen, it concerns you something to know it.

COUNTESS.

You have discharged this honestly; keep it to yourself: many likelihoods inform'd me of this before, which hung so tottering in the balance, that I could neither believe nor misdoubt. Pray you, leave me: stall this in your bosom, and I thank you for your honest care: I will speak with you further anon.   [Exit STEWARD.

Even so it was with me when I was young:
    If we are nature's, these are ours; this thorn
Doth to our rose of youth rightly belong;
    Our blood to us, this to our blood is born;
It is the show and seal of nature's truth,
Where love's strong passion is imprest in youth:
By our remembrances of days foregone,
Such were our faults; nor then we thought them
    none.

Enter HELENA.

Her eye is sick on't: I observe her now.

HELENA.

What is your pleasure, madam?

COUNTESS.

                    You know, Helen,
I am a mother to you.

HELENA.

Mine honourable mistress,

COUNTESS.

                    Nay, a mother:
Why not a mother? When I said a mother,
Methought you saw a serpent: what's in 'mother,'
That you start at it? I say, I am your mother;
And put you in the catalogue of those
That were enwombed mine: 'tis often seen
Adoption strives with nature; and choice breeds
A native slip to us from foreign seeds:
You ne'er opprest me with a mother's groan,
Yet I express to you a mother's care:—
God's mercy, maiden! does it curd thy blood,
To say, I am thy mother? What's the matter,
That this distemper'd messenger of wet,
The many-colour'd Iris, rounds thine eye?
Why,—that you are my daughter?

HELENA.

                        That I am not.

COUNTESS.

I say, I am your mother.

HELENA.

                    Pardon, madam;
The Count Rousillon cannot be my brother:

I am from humble, he from honour'd name;
No note upon my parents, his all noble:
My master, my dear lord he is; and I
His servant live, and will his vassal die:
He must not be my brother.
COUNTESS.
                    Nor I your mother?
HELENA.
You are my mother, madam; would you were—
So that my lord your son were not my brother—
Indeed my mother!—or were you both our
    mothers,
I care no more for than I do for heaven,
So I were not his sister. Can't no other,
But I your daughter, he must be my brother?
COUNTESS.
Yes, Helen, you might be my daughter-in-law:
God shield, you mean it not! 'daughter' and
    'mother'
So strive upon your pulse. What, pale again?
My fear hath catcht your fondness: now I see
The mystery of your loneliness, and find
Your salt tears' head: now to all sense 'tis gross
You love my son; invention is ashamed,
Against the proclamation of thy passion,
To say thou dost not: therefore tell me true;
But tell me then, 'tis so;—for, look, thy cheeks
Confess it, th'one to th'other; and thine eyes
See it so grossly shown in thy behaviours,
That in their kind they speak it: only sin
And hellish obstinacy tie thy tongue,
That truth should be suspected. Speak, is't so?
If it be so, you have wound a goodly clew;
If it be not, forswear't: howe'er, I charge thee,
As heaven shall work in me for thine avail,
To tell me truly.
HELENA.
            Good madam, pardon me!
COUNTESS.
Do you love my son?
HELENA.
            Your pardon, noble mistress!
COUNTESS.
Love you my son?
HELENA.
            Do not you love him, madam?
COUNTESS.
Go not about; my love hath in't a bond,
Whereof the world takes note: come, come, dis-
    close
The state of your affection; for your passions
Have to the full appeacht.
HELENA.
            Then, I confess,
Here on my knee, before high heaven and you,
That before you, and next unto high heaven,
I love your son:—
My friends were poor, but honest; so's my love:
Be not offended; for it hurts not him,
That he is loved of me: I follow him not
By any token of presumptuous suit;
Nor would I have him till I do deserve him;
Yet never know how that desert should be.
I know I love in vain, strive against hope;
Yet in this captious and intenible sieve
I still pour in the waters of my love,

And lack not to lose still: thus, Indian-like,
Religious in mine error, I adore
The sun, that looks upon his worshipper,
But knows of him no more. My dearest madam,
Let not your hate encounter with my love,
For loving where you do: but, if yourself,
Whose aged honour cites a virtuous youth,
Did ever, in so true a flame of liking,
Wish chastely, and love dearly, that your Dian
Was both herself and Love; O, then, give pity
To her, whose state is such, that cannot choose
But lend and give, where she is sure to lose;
That seeks not to find that her search implies,
But, riddle-like, lives sweetly where she dies!
COUNTESS.
Had you not lately an intent,—speak truly,—
To go to Paris?
HELENA.
            Madam, I had.
COUNTESS.
                        Wherefore?
Tell true.
HELENA.
I will tell truth; by grace itself, I swear.
You know my father left me some prescriptions
Of rare and proved effects, such as his reading
And manifest experience had collected
For general sovereignty; and that he will'd me
In heedfull'st reservation to bestow them,
As notes, whose faculties inclusive were,
More than they were in note: amongst the rest,
There is a remedy, approved, set down,
To cure the desperate languishings whereof
The king is render'd lost.
COUNTESS.
            This was your motive
For Paris, was it? speak.
HELENA.
My lord your son made me to think of this;
Else Paris, and the medicine, and the king,
Had from the conversation of my thoughts
Haply been absent then.
COUNTESS.
            But think you, Helen,
If you should tender your supposed aid,
He would receive it? he and his physicians
Are of a mind; he, that they cannot help him;
They, that they cannot help: how shall they credit
A poor unlearned virgin, when the schools,
Embowell'd of their doctrine, have left off
The danger to itself?
HELENA.
            There's something hints,
More than my father's skill, which was the
    greatest
Of his profession, that his good receipt
Shall, for my legacy, be sanctified
By th'luckiest stars in heaven: and, would your
    honour
But give me leave to try success, I'ld venture
This well-lost life of mine on his Grace's cure
By such a day and hour.
COUNTESS.
            Dost thou believe't?
HELENA.
Ay, madam, knowingly.

COUNTESS.

Why, Helen, thou shalt have my leave, and love,
Means, and attendants, and my loving greetings
To those of mine in court: I'll stay at home,
And pray God's blessing into thy attempt:
Be gone to-morrow; and be sure of this,
What I can help thee to, thou shalt not miss.
                                              [*Exeunt.*

ACT II. SCENE I.

Paris.   A room in the KING'S *palace.*

Enter the KING, *with divers young* LORDS, *taking
leave for the Florentine war;* BERTRAM, PAR-
OLLES, *and* ATTENDANTS. *Flourish of cornets.*

                    KING.

FAREWELL, young lords; these warlike prin-
     ciples
Do not throw from you: and you, my lords, fare-
     well:
Share the advice betwixt you; if both gain, all
The gift doth stretch itself as 'tis received,
And is enough for both.
                    FIRST LORD.
                         'Tis our hope, sir,
After well-enter'd soldiers, to return
And find your Grace in health.
                    KING.
No, no, it cannot be; and yet my heart
Will not confess he owes the malady
That doth my life besiege. Farewell, young lords;
Whether I live or die, be you the sons
Of worthy Frenchmen: let higher Italy—
Those lated that inherit but the fall
Of the last monarchy—see that you come
Not to woo honour, but to wed it; when
The bravest questant shrinks, find what you seek,
That fame may cry you loud: I say, farewell.
                    SECOND LORD.
Health, at your bidding, serve your majesty!
                    KING.
Those girls of Italy, take heed of them:
They say, our French lack language to deny,
If they demand: beware of being captives,
Before you serve.
                    BOTH LORDS.
              Our hearts receive your warnings.
                    KING.
Farewell.—Come hither to me. [*Exit, attended.*
                    FIRST LORD.
O my sweet lord, that you will stay behind us!
                    PAROLLES.
'Tis not his fault, the spark.
                    SECOND LORD.
                         O, 'tis brave wars!
                    PAROLLES.
Most admirable: I have seen those wars.
                    BERTRAM.
I am commanded here, and kept a coil with
'Too young,' and 'the next year,' and ''tis too
     early.'
                    PAROLLES.
An thy mind stand to't, boy, steal away bravely.
                    BERTRAM.
I shall stay here the forehorse to a smock,
Creaking my shoes on the plain masonry,

Till honour be bought up, and no sword worn
But one to dance with! By heaven, I'll steal
     away.
                    FIRST LORD.
There's honour in the theft.
                    PAROLLES.
                         Commit it, count.
                    SECOND LORD.
I am your accessary; and so, farewell.
                    BERTRAM.
I grow to you, and our parting is a tortured body.
                    FIRST LORD.
Farewell, captain.
                    SECOND LORD.
Sweet Monsieur Parolles!
                    PAROLLES.
Noble heroes, my sword and yours are kin. Good
sparks and lustrous, a word, good metals:—you
shall find in the regiment of the Spinii one Cap-
tain Spurio, with his cicatrice, an emblem of war,
here on his sinister cheek; it was this very sword
entrencht it: say to him, I live; and observe his
reports for me.
                    SECOND LORD.
We shall, noble captain.
                    PAROLLES.
Mars dote on you for his novices!
                                        [*Exeunt* LORDS.
What will ye do?
                    BERTRAM.
Stay; the king!
     Enter KING; BERTRAM & PAROLLES *retire.*
                    PAROLLES.
Use a more spacious ceremony to the noble lords;
you have restrain'd yourself within the list of too
cold an adieu: be more expressive to them: for
they wear themselves in the cap of the time, there
do muster true gait, eat, speak, and move under
the influence of the most received star; and though
the devil lead the measure, such are to be follow'd: after them, and take a more dilated farewell.
                    BERTRAM.
And I will do so.
                    PAROLLES.
Worthy fellows; and like to prove most sinewy
sword-men. [*Exeunt* BERTRAM *and* PAROLLES.
                    Enter LAFEU.
                    LAFEU [*kneeling*].
Pardon, my lord, for me and for my tidings.
                    KING.
I'll fee thee to stand up.
                    LAFEU [*rising*].
Then here's a man stands that has brought his
     pardon.
I would you had kneel'd, my lord, to ask me
     mercy;
And that, at my bidding, you could so stand up.
                    KING.
I would I had; so I had broke thy pate,
And askt thee mercy for't.
                    LAFEU.
Good faith, across: but, my good lord, 'tis thus;
Will you be cured of your infirmity?
                    KING.
No.

759

LAFEU.

O, will you eat no grapes, my royal fox?
Yes, but you will my noble grapes, an if
My royal fox could reach them: I have seen a
    medicine
That's able to breathe life into a stone,
Quicken a rock, and make you dance canary
With sprightly fire and motion; whose simple touch
Is powerful to araise King Pepin, nay,
To give great Charlemain a pen in's hand,
And write to her a love-line.

KING.

What 'her' is this?

LAFEU.

Why, doctor she: my lord, there's one arrived,
If you will see her:—now, by my faith and honour,
If seriously I may convey my thoughts
In this my light deliverance, I have spoke
With one that, in her sex, her years, profession,
Wisdom, and constancy, hath amazed me more
Than I dare blame my weakness: will you see her,—
For that is her demand,—and know her business?
That done, laugh well at me.

KING.

Now, good Lafeu,
Bring in the admiration; that we with thee
May spend our wonder too, or take off thine
By wondering how thou took'st it.

LAFEU.

Nay, I'll fit you,
And not be all day neither.   [Exit.

KING.

Thus he his special nothing ever prologues.

Enter LAFEU, with HELENA.

LAFEU.

Nay, come your ways.

KING.

This haste hath wings indeed.

LAFEU.

Nay, come your ways;
This is his majesty, say your mind to him:
A traitor you do look like; but such traitors
His majesty seldom fears: I am Cressid's uncle,
That dare leave two together; fare you well.
                                               [Exit.

KING.

Now, fair one, does your business follow us?

HELENA.

Ay, my good lord.
Gerard de Narbon was my father; one,
In what he did profess, well found.

KING.

I knew him.

HELENA.

The rather will I spare my praises towards him;
Knowing him is enough. On's bed of death
Many receipts he gave me; chiefly one,
Which, as the dearest issue of his practice,
And of his old experience th'only darling,
He bade me store up, as a triple eye,
Safer than mine own two, more dear: I have so:
And, hearing your high majesty is toucht
With that malignant cause, wherein the honour
Of my dear father's gift stands chief in power,
I come to tender it, and my appliance,
With all bound humbleness.

KING.

We thank you, maiden;
But may not be so credulous of cure,
When our most learned doctors leave us, and
The congregated college have concluded
That labouring art can never ransom nature
From her inaidable state,—I say we must not
So stain our judgement, or corrupt our hope,
To prostitute our past-cure malady
To empirics; or to dissever so
Our great self and our credit, to esteem
A senseless help, when help past sense we deem.

HELENA.

My duty, then, shall pay me for my pains:
I will no more enforce mine office on you;
Humbly entreating from your royal thoughts
A modest one, to bear me back again.

KING.

I cannot give thee less, to be call'd grateful:
Thou thought'st to help me; and such thanks I
    give
As one near death to those that wish him live:
But, what at full I know, thou know'st no part;
I knowing all my peril, thou no art.

HELENA.

What I can do can do no hurt to try,
Since you set up your rest 'gainst remedy.
He that of greatest works is finisher,
Oft does them by the weakest minister:
So holy writ in babes hath judgement shown,
When judges have been babes; great floods have
    flown
From simple sources; and great seas have dried,
When miracles have by the greatest been denied.
Oft expectation fails, and most oft there
Where most it promises; and oft it hits
Where hope is coldest, and despair most fits.

KING.

I must not hear thee; fare thee well, kind maid;
Thy pains, not used, must by thyself be paid:
Proffers not took reap thanks for their reward.

HELENA.

Inspired merit so by breath is barr'd:
It is not so with Him that all things knows,
As 'tis with us that square our guess by shows;
But most it is presumption in us when
The help of heaven we count the act of men.
Dear sir, to my endeavours give consent;
Of heaven, not me, make an experiment.
I am not an impostor, that proclaim
Myself against the level of mine aim;
But know I think, and think I know most sure,
My art is not past power, nor you past cure.

KING.

Art thou so confident? within what space
Hopest thou my cure?

HELENA.

The great'st grace lending grace,
Ere twice the horses of the sun shall bring
Their fiery torcher his diurnal ring;
Ere twice in murk and occidental damp
Moist Hesperus hath quencht his sleepy lamp;
Or four and twenty times the pilot's glass
Hath told the thievish minutes how they pass;
What is infirm from your sound parts shall fly,
Health shall live free, and sickness freely die.

KING.
Upon thy certainty and confidence
What darest thou venture?
HELENA.
                    Tax of impudence,—
A strumpet's boldness, a divulged shame,—
Traduced by odious ballads; my maiden's name
Sear'd otherwise; nay, worse, if worse, extended
With vilest torture let my life be ended.
KING.
Methinks in thee some blessed spirit doth speak,
His powerful sound within an organ weak:
And what impossibility would slay
In common sense, sense saves another way.
Thy life is dear; for all, that life can rate
Worth name of life, in thee hath estimate,—
Youth, beauty, wisdom, courage, all
That happiness and prime can happy call:
Thou this to hazard, needs must intimate
Skill infinite or monstrous desperate.
Sweet practiser, thy physic I will try,
That ministers thine own death, if I die.
HELENA.
If I break time, or flinch in property
Of what I spoke, unpitied let me die,
And well deserved: not helping, death's my fee;
But, if I help, what do you promise me?
KING.
Make thy demand.
HELENA.
                    But will you make it even?
KING.
Ay, by my sceptre and my hopes of heaven.
HELENA.
Then shalt thou give me with thy kingly hand
What husband in thy power I will command:
Exempted be from me the arrogance
To choose from forth the royal blood of France,
My low and humble name to propagate
With any branch or image of thy state;
But such a one, thy vassal, whom I know
Is free for me to ask, thee to bestow.
KING.
Here is my hand; the premises observed,
Thy will by my performance shall be served:
So make the choice of thy own time; for I,
Thy resolved patient, on thee still rely.
More should I question thee, and more I must,—
Though more to know could not be more to
                    trust,—
From whence thou camest, how tended on: but rest
Unquestion'd welcome, and undoubted blest.—
Give me some help here, ho!—If thou proceed
As high as word, my deed shall match thy deed.
                    [Flourish. Exeunt.

SCENE II.

Rousillon. A room in the house of the COUNTESS.

Enter COUNTESS *and* CLOWN.

COUNTESS.
COME on, sir; I shall now put you to the
height of your breeding.
CLOWN.
I will show myself highly fed and lowly taught: I
know my business is but to the court.

COUNTESS.
To the court! why, what place make you special,
when you put off that with such contempt? But
to the court!
CLOWN.
Truly, madam, if God have lent a man any manners, he may easily put it off at court: he that cannot make a leg, put off's cap, kiss his hand, and
say nothing, has neither leg, hands, lip, nor cap;
and, indeed, such a fellow, to say precisely, were
not for the court: but, for me, I have an answer
will serve all men.
COUNTESS.
Marry, that's a bountiful answer that fits all questions.
CLOWN.
It is like a barber's chair, that fits all buttocks,—
the pin-buttock, the quatch-buttock, the brawn-
buttock, or any buttock.
COUNTESS.
Will your answer serve fit to all questions?
CLOWN.
As fit as ten groats is for the hand of an attorney,
as your French crown for your taffeta punk, as
Tib's rush for Tom's forefinger, as a pancake for
Shrove-Tuesday, a morris for May-day, as the
nail to his hole, the cuckold to his horn, as a
scolding quean to a wrangling knave, as the nun's
lip to the friar's mouth, nay, as the pudding to his
skin.
COUNTESS.
Have you, I say, an answer of such fitness for all
questions?
CLOWN.
From below your duke to beneath your constable,
it will fit any question.
COUNTESS.
It must be an answer of most monstrous size that
must fit all demands.
CLOWN.
But a trifle neither, in good faith, if the learned
should speak truth of it: here it is, and all that
belongs to't. Ask me if I am a courtier: it shall do
you no harm to learn.
COUNTESS.
To be young again, if we could:—I will be a fool
in question, hoping to be the wiser by your
answer. I pray you, sir, are you a courtier?
CLOWN.
'O Lord, sir!'—there's a simple putting off.—
More, more, a hundred of them.
COUNTESS.
Sir, I am a poor friend of yours that loves you.
CLOWN.
'O Lord, sir!'—Thick, thick, spare not me.
COUNTESS.
I think, sir, you can eat none of this homely meat.
CLOWN.
'O Lord, sir!'—Nay, put me to't, I warrant you.
COUNTESS.
You were lately whipt, sir, as I think.
CLOWN.
'O Lord, sir!'—Spare not me.
COUNTESS.
Do you cry, 'O Lord, sir!' at your whipping, and
'Spare me not '? Indeed, your 'O Lord, sir!' is

very sequent to your whipping: you would answer
very well to a whipping, if you were but bound
to't.

CLOWN.

I ne'er had worse luck in my life in my 'O Lord,
sir!' I see things may serve long, but not serve
ever.

COUNTESS.

I play the noble housewife with the time,
To entertain it so merrily with a fool.

CLOWN.

'O Lord, sir!'—why, there't serves well again.

COUNTESS.

An end, sir: to your business. Give Helen this,
And urge her to a present answer back:
Commend me to my kinsmen and my son:
This is not much.

CLOWN.

Not much commendation to them.

COUNTESS.

Not much employment for you: you understand
me?

CLOWN.

Most fruitfully: I am there before my legs.

COUNTESS.

Haste you again.   [*Exeunt severally.*

SCENE III.

Paris.   A room in the KING'S *palace.*

Enter LAFEU *and* PAROLLES.

LAFEU.

THEY say miracles are past; and we have our
philosophical persons, to make modern and
familiar, things supernatural and causeless. Hence
is it that we make trifles of terrors; ensconcing ourselves into seeming knowledge, when we should
submit ourselves to an unknown fear. Why, 'tis
the rarest argument of wonder that hath shot out
in our latter times.

PAROLLES.

And so 'tis.

LAFEU.

To be relinquisht of the artists,—

PAROLLES.

So I say.

LAFEU.

Both of Galen and Paracelsus, of all the learned
and authentic fellows,—

PAROLLES.

Right; so I say.

LAFEU.

That gave him out incurable,—

PAROLLES.

Why, there 'tis; so say I too.

LAFEU.

Not to be helpt,—

PAROLLES.

Right; as 'twere, a man assured of a—

LAFEU.

Uncertain life, and sure death.

PAROLLES.

Just, you say well; so would I have said.

LAFEU.

I may truly say, it is a novelty to the world.

PAROLLES.

It is, indeed: if you will have it in showing, you
shall read it in—What do ye call there?—

LAFEU.

A showing of a heavenly effect in an earthly actor.

PAROLLES.

That's it I would have said, the very same.

LAFEU.

Why, your dolphin is not lustier: 'fore me, I
speak in respect—

PAROLLES.

Nay, 'tis strange, 'tis very strange, that is the
brief and the tedious of it; and he's of a most
facinerious spirit that will not acknowledge it to
be the—

LAFEU.

Very hand of heaven—

PAROLLES.

Ay, so I say.

LAFEU.

In a most weak and debile minister great power,
great transcendence: which should, indeed, give
us a further use to be made than alone the recovery of the king.

PAROLLES.

As to be—

LAFEU.

Generally thankful.

PAROLLES.

I would have said it; you say well.—Here comes
the king.

Enter KING, HELENA, *and* ATTENDANTS.

LAFEU.

Lustig, as the Dutchman says: I'll like a maid the
better, whilst I have a tooth in my head: why, he's
able to lead her a coranto.

PAROLLES.

Mort du vinaigre! is not this Helen?

LAFEU.

'Fore God, I think so.

KING.

Go, call before me all the lords in court.—
                            [*Exit an* ATTENDANT.
Sit, my preserver, by thy patient's side;
And with this healthful hand, whose banisht
    sense
Thou hast repeal'd, a second time receive
The confirmation of my promised gift,
Which but attends thy naming.

Enter three or four LORDS *and* BERTRAM.

Fair maid, send forth thine eye: this youthful
    parcel
Of noble bachelors stand at my bestowing,
O'er whom both sovereign power and father's
    voice
I have to use: thy frank election make;
Thou hast power to choose, and they none to
    forsake.

HELENA.

To each of you one fair and virtuous mistress
Fall, when Love please!—marry, to each, but
    one!

LAFEU.

I'ld give bay curtal and his furniture,
My mouth no more were broken than these boys',
And writ as little beard.

KING.
        Peruse them well:
Not one of these but had a noble father.
HELENA.
Gentlemen,
Heaven hath, through me, restored the king to
  health.
ALL.
We understand it, and thank heaven for you.
HELENA.
I am a simple maid; and therein wealthiest,
That I protest I simply am a maid.—
Please it your majesty, I have done already:
The blushes in my cheeks thus whisper me,
'We blush that thou shouldst choose; but, be
  refused,
Let the white death sit on thy cheek for ever;
We'll ne'er come there again.'
KING.
            Make choice; and, see,
Who shuns thy love shuns all his love in me.
HELENA.
Now, Dian, from thy altar do I fly;
And to imperial Love, that god most high,
Do my sighs stream.—[to FIRST LORD] Sir, will
  you hear my suit?
FIRST LORD.
And grant it.
HELENA.
      Thanks, sir; all the rest is mute.
LAFEU.
I had rather be in this choice than throw ames-ace
for my life.
HELENA [to SECOND LORD].
The honour, sir, that flames in your fair eyes,
Before I speak, too threateningly replies:
Love make your fortunes twenty times above
Her that so wishes and her humble love!
SECOND LORD.
No better, if you please.
HELENA.
          My wish receive,
Which great Love grant! and so, I take my leave.
LAFEU.
Do all they deny her? An they were sons of mine,
I'ld have them whipt; or I would send them to the
Turk, to make eunuchs of.
HELENA [to THIRD LORD].
Be not afraid that I your hand should take;
I'll never do you wrong for your own sake:
Blessing upon your vows! and in your bed
Find fairer fortune, if you ever wed!
LAFEU.
These boys are boys of ice, they'll none have her:
sure, they are bastards to the English; the French
ne'er got 'em.
HELENA [to FOURTH LORD].
You are too young, too happy, and too good,
To make yourself a son out of my blood.
FOURTH LORD.
Fair one, I think not so.
LAFEU.
There's one grape yet,—I am sure thy father
drunk wine:—but if thou be'st not an ass, I
am a youth of fourteen; I have known thee
already.

HELENA [to BERTRAM].
I dare not say I take you; but I give
Me and my service, ever whilst I live,
Into your guiding power.—This is the man.
KING.
Why, then, young Bertram, take her; she's thy wife.
BERTRAM.
My wife, my liege! I shall beseech your highness,
In such a business give me leave to use
The help of mine own eyes.
KING.
           Know'st thou not, Bertram,
What she has done for me?
BERTRAM.
             Yes, my good lord;
But never hope to know why I should marry her.
KING.
Thou know'st she has raised me from my sickly
  bed.
BERTRAM.
But follows it, my lord, to bring me down
Must answer for your raising? I know her well:
She had her breeding at my father's charge.
A poor physician's daughter my wife!—Disdain
Rather corrupt me ever!
KING.
'Tis only title thou disdain'st in her, the which
I can build up. Strange is it that our bloods,
Of colour, weight, and heat, pour'd all together,
Would quite confound distinction, yet stand off
In differences so mighty. If she be
All that is virtuous,—save what thou dislikest,
A poor physician's daughter,—thou dislikest
Of virtue for the name: but do not so:
From lowest place when virtuous things proceed,
The place is dignified by th'doer's deed:
Where great additions swell's, and virtue none,
It is a dropsied honour: good alone
Is good without a name; vileness is so:
The property by what it is should go,
Not by the title. She is young, wise, fair;
In these to nature she's immediate heir;
And these breed honour: that is honour's scorn,
Which challenges itself as honour's born,
And is not like the sire: honours thrive,
When rather from our acts we them derive
Than our foregoers: the mere word's a slave,
Debosht on every tomb, on every grave
A lying trophy; and as oft is dumb
Where dust and damn'd oblivion is the tomb
Of honour'd bones indeed. What should be said?
If thou canst like this creature as a maid,
I can create the rest: virtue and she
Is her own dower; honour and wealth from me.
BERTRAM.
I cannot love her, nor will strive to do't.
KING.
Thou wrong'st thyself, if thou shouldst strive to
  choose.
HELENA.
That you are well restored, my lord, I'm glad:
Let the rest go.
KING.
My honour's at the stake; which to defeat,
I must produce my power. Here, take her hand,
Proud scornful boy, unworthy this good gift;

That dost in vile misprision shackle up
My love and her desert; that canst not dream,
We, poising us in her defective scale,
Shall weigh thee to the beam; that wilt not know,
It is in us to plant thine honour where
We please to have it grow. Check thy contempt:
Obey our will, which travails in thy good:
Believe not thy disdain, but presently
Do thine own fortunes that obedient right
Which both thy duty owes and our power claims;
Or I will throw thee from my care for ever
Into the staggers and the careless lapse
Of youth and ignorance; both my revenge and hate
Loosing upon thee, in the name of justice,
Without all terms of pity. Speak; thine answer.

BERTRAM.
Pardon, my gracious lord; for I submit
My fancy to your eyes: when I consider
What great creation and what dole of honour
Flies where you bid it, I find that she, which late
Was in my nobler thoughts most base, is now
The praised of the king; who, so ennobled,
Is, as 'twere, born so.

KING.
                    Take her by the hand,
And tell her she is thine: to whom I promise
A counterpoise; if not to thy estate,
A balance more replete.

BERTRAM.
                    I take her hand.

KING.
Good fortune and the favour of the king
Smile upon this contract; whose ceremony
Shall seem expedient on the now-born brief,
And be perform'd to-night: the solemn feast
Shall more attend upon the coming space,
Expecting absent friends. As thou lovest her,
Thy love's to me religious; else, does err.

[*Exeunt all but* LAFEU *and* PAROLLES.

LAFEU.
Do you hear, monsieur? a word with you.

PAROLLES.
Your pleasure, sir?

LAFEU.
Your lord and master did well to make his recantation.

PAROLLES.
Recantation!—My lord! my master!

LAFEU.
Ay; is it not a language I speak?

PAROLLES.
A most harsh one, and not to be understood without bloody succeeding. My master!

LAFEU.
Are you companion to the Count Rousillon?

PAROLLES.
To any count,—to all counts,—to what is man.

LAFEU.
To what is count's man: count's master is of another style.

PAROLLES.
You are too old, sir; let it satisfy you, you are too
old.

LAFEU.
I must tell thee, sirrah, I write man; to which title
age cannot bring thee.

PAROLLES.
What I dare too well do, I dare not do.

LAFEU.
I did think thee, for two ordinaries, to be a pretty
wise fellow; thou didst make tolerable vent of thy
travel; it might pass: yet the scarfs and the ban-
nerets about thee did manifoldly dissuade me
from believing thee a vessel of too great a burthen.
I have now found thee; when I lose thee again, I
care not: yet art thou good for nothing but taking
up; and that thou'rt scarce worth.

PAROLLES.
Hadst thou not the privilege of antiquity upon
thee,—

LAFEU.
Do not plunge thyself too far in anger, lest thou
hasten thy trial; which if—Lord have mercy on
thee for a hen! So, my good window of lattice,
fare thee well: thy casement I need not open, for
I look through thee. Give me thy hand.

PAROLLES.
My lord, you give me most egregious indignity.

LAFEU.
Ay, with all my heart; and thou art worthy of it.

PAROLLES.
I have not, my lord, deserved it.

LAFEU.
Yes, good faith, every dram of it; and I will not
bate thee a scruple.

PAROLLES.
Well, I shall be wiser—

LAFEU.
Ev'n as soon as thou canst, for thou hast to pull
at a smack o'th'contrary. If ever thou be'st
bound in thy scarf and beaten, thou shalt find
what it is to be proud of thy bondage. I have a
desire to hold my acquaintance with thee, or
rather my knowledge, that I may say, in the default, he is a man I know.

PAROLLES.
My lord, you do me most insupportable vexation.

LAFEU.
I would it were hell-pains for thy sake, and my
poor doing eternal: for doing I am past; as I will
by thee, in what motion age will give me leave.

[*Exit.*

PAROLLES.
Well, thou hast a son shall take this disgrace off
me; scurvy, old, filthy, scurvy lord!—Well, I must
be patient; there is no fettering of authority. I'll
beat him, by my life, if I can meet him with any
convenience, an he were double and double a
lord. I'll have no more pity of his age than I
would have of—I'll beat him, an if I could but
meet him again.

Enter LAFEU.

LAFEU.
Sirrah, your lord and master's married; there's
news for you: you have a new mistress.

PAROLLES.
I most unfeignedly beseech your lordship to
make some reservation of your wrongs: he is my
good lord; whom I serve above is my master.

LAFEU.
Who? God?

PAROLLES.

Ay, sir.

LAFEU.

The devil it is that's thy master. Why dost thou garter up thy arms o' this fashion? dost make hose of thy sleeves? do other servants so? Thou wert best set thy lower part where thy nose stands. By mine honour, if I were but two hours younger, I'ld beat thee: methinks't, thou art a general offence, and every man should beat thee: I think thou wast created for men to breathe themselves upon thee.

PAROLLES.

This is hard and undeserved measure, my lord.

LAFEU.

Go to, sir; you were beaten in Italy for picking a kernel out of a pomegranate; you are a vagabond, and no true traveller: you are more saucy with lords and honourable personages than the herald-ry of your birth and virtue gives you commission. You are not worth another word, else I'ld call you knave. I leave you.   [Exit.

PAROLLES.

Good, very good; it is so then:—good, very good; let it be conceal'd awhile.

Enter BERTRAM.

BERTRAM.

Undone, and forfeited to cares for ever!

PAROLLES.

What's the matter, sweet-heart?

BERTRAM.

Although before the solemn priest I have sworn, I will not bed her.

PAROLLES.

What, what, sweet-heart?

BERTRAM.

O, my Parolles, they have married me!— I'll to the Tuscan wars, and never bed her.

PAROLLES.

France is a dog-hole, and it no more merits The tread of a man's foot: to th'wars!

BERTRAM.

There's letters from my mother: what th'import is, I know not yet.

PAROLLES.

Ay, that would be known. To th'wars, my boy, to th'wars!

He wears his honour in a box unseen, That hugs his kicky-wicky here at home, Spending his manly marrow in her arms, Which should sustain the bound and high curvet Of Mars's fiery steed. To other regions! France is a stable; we that dwell in't jades; Therefore, to th'wars!

BERTRAM.

It shall be so: I'll send her to my house, Acquaint my mother with my hate to her, And wherefore I am fled; write to the king That which I durst not speak: his present gift Shall furnish me to those Italian fields, Where noble fellows strike: war is no strife To the dark house and the detested wife.

PAROLLES.

Will this capriccio hold in thee, art sure?

BERTRAM.

Go with me to my chamber, and advise me.

I'll send her straight away: to-morrow I'll to the wars, she to her single sorrow.

PAROLLES.

Why, these balls bound; there's noise in it.— 'Tis hard: A young man married is a man that's marr'd: Therefore, away, and leave her; bravely go: The king has done you wrong; but, hush, 'tis so.

[Exeunt.

SCENE IV.

Paris.   The KING'S *palace.*

Enter HELENA *and* CLOWN.

HELENA.

MY mother greets me kindly: is she well?

CLOWN.

She is not well; but yet she has her health: she's very merry; but yet she is not well: but thanks be given, she's very well, and wants nothing i'th' world; but yet she is not well.

HELENA.

If she be very well, what does she ail, that she's not very well?

CLOWN.

Truly, she's very well indeed, but for two things.

HELENA.

What two things?

CLOWN.

One, that she's not in heaven, whither God send her quickly! the other, that she's in earth, from whence God send her quickly!

Enter PAROLLES.

PAROLLES.

Bless you, my fortunate lady!

HELENA.

I hope, sir, I have your good will to have mine own good fortunes.

PAROLLES.

You had my prayers to lead them on; and to keep them on, have them still.—O, my knave,—how does my old lady?

CLOWN.

So that you had her wrinkles, and I her money, I would she did as you say.

PAROLLES.

Why, I say nothing.

CLOWN.

Marry, you are the wiser man; for many a man's tongue shakes out his master's undoing: to say nothing, to do nothing, to know nothing, and to have nothing, is to be a great part of your title; which is within a very little of nothing.

PAROLLES.

Away! th'art a knave.

CLOWN.

You should have said, sir, before a knave th'art a knave; that's, before me th'art a knave: this had been truth, sir.

PAROLLES.

Go to, thou art a witty fool; I have found thee.

CLOWN.

Did you find me in yourself, sir? or were you taught to find me? The search, sir, was profitable; and much fool may you find in you, even to the world's pleasure and the increase of laughter.

PAROLLES.
A good knave, i'faith, and well fed.—
Madam, my lord will go away to-night;
A very serious business calls on him.
The great prerogative and rite of love,
Which, as your due, time claims, he does acknow-
ledge;
But puts it off by a compell'd restraint;
Whose want, and whose delay, is strew'd with
sweets,
Which they distil now in the curbed time,
To make the coming hour o'erflow with joy,
And pleasure drown the brim.
HELENA.
What's his will else?
PAROLLES.
That you will take your instant leave o'th'king,
And make this haste as your own good proceed-
ing,
Strengthen'd with what apology you think
May make it probable need.
HELENA.
What more commands he?
PAROLLES.
That, having this obtain'd, you presently
Attend his further pleasure.
HELENA.
In every thing I wait upon his will.
PAROLLES.
I shall report it so.
HELENA.
I pray you. [*Exit* PAROLLES.]
Come, sirrah.   [*Exeunt.*

SCENE V.

Paris.   The KING'S *palace.*

Enter LAFEU *and* BERTRAM.

LAFEU.
BUT I hope your lordship thinks not him a
soldier.
BERTRAM.
Yes, my lord, and of very valiant approof.
LAFEU.
You have it from his own deliverance.
BERTRAM.
And by other warranted testimony.
LAFEU.
Then my dial goes not true: I took this lark for a
bunting.
BERTRAM.
I do assure you, my lord, he is very great in
knowledge, and accordingly valiant.
LAFEU.
I have, then, sinn'd against his experience, and
transgrest against his valour; and my state that
way is dangerous, since I cannot yet find in my
heart to repent. Here he comes: I pray you, make
us friends; I will pursue the amity.
Enter PAROLLES.
PAROLLES [*to* BERTRAM].
These things shall be done, sir.
LAFEU.
Pray you, sir, who's his tailor?
PAROLLES.
Sir?

LAFEU.
O, I know him well, I, sir; he, sir, 's a good work-
man, a very good tailor.
BERTRAM [*aside to* PAROLLES].
Is she gone to the king?
PAROLLES [*aside to* BERTRAM].
She is.
BERTRAM [*aside to* PAROLLES].
Will she away to-night?
PAROLLES [*aside to* BERTRAM].
As you'll have her.
BERTRAM [*aside to* PAROLLES].
I've writ my letters, casketed my treasure,
Given order for our horses; and to-night,
When I should take possession of the bride,
End ere I do begin.
LAFEU.
A good traveller is something at the latter end of
a dinner; but one that lies three-thirds, and uses a
known truth to pass a thousand nothings with,
should be once heard, and thrice beaten.—God
save you, captain.
BERTRAM.
Is there any unkindness between my lord and
you, monsieur?
PAROLLES.
I know not how I have deserved to run into my
lord's displeasure.
LAFEU.
You have made shift to run into't, boots and
spurs and all, like him that leapt into the custard;
and out of it you'll run again, rather than suffer
question for your residence.
BERTRAM.
It may be you have mistaken him, my lord.
LAFEU.
And shall do so ever, though I took him at's
prayers. Fare you well, my lord; and believe this
of me, there can be no kernel in this light nut; the
soul of this man is his clothes: trust him not in
matter of heavy consequence; I have kept of them
tame, and know their natures.—Farewell, mon-
sieur: I have spoken better of you than you have
worth or wit to deserve at my hand; but we must
do good against evil.   [*Exit.*
PAROLLES.
An idle lord, I swear.
BERTRAM.
I think so.
PAROLLES.
Why, do you not know him?
BERTRAM.
Yes, I do know him well; and common speech
Gives him a worthy pass.—Here comes my clog.
Enter HELENA.
HELENA.
I have, sir, as I was commanded from you,
Spoke with the king, and have procured his leave
For present parting; only, he desires
Some private speech with you.
BERTRAM.
I shall obey his will.
You must not marvel, Helen, at my course,
Which holds not colour with the time, nor does
The ministration and required office
On my particular. Prepared I was not

For such a business; therefore am I found
So much unsettled: this drives me to entreat you,
That presently you take your way for home,
And rather muse than ask why I entreat you;
For my respects are better than they seem,
And my appointments have in them a need
Greater than shows itself, at the first view,
To you that know them not. This to my mother:
                              [*Giving a letter.*
'Twill be two days ere I shall see you; so,
I leave you to your wisdom.

HELENA.
                    Sir, I can nothing say,
But that I am your most obedient servant.

BERTRAM.
Come, come, no more of that.

HELENA.
                    And ever shall
With true observance seek to eke out that
Wherein toward me my homely stars have fail'd
To equal my good fortune.

BERTRAM.
                    Let that go:
My haste is very great: farewell, hie home.

HELENA.
Pray, sir, your pardon.

BERTRAM.
                    Well, what would you say?

HELENA.
I am not worthy of the wealth I owe;
Nor dare I say 'tis mine,—and yet it is;
But, like a timorous thief, most fain would steal
What law does vouch mine own.

BERTRAM.
                    What would you have?

HELENA.
Something; and scarce so much:—nothing, in-
deed.—
I would not tell you what I would, my lord:—
Faith, yes;—
Strangers and foes do sunder, and not kiss.

BERTRAM.
I pray you, stay not, but in haste to horse.

HELENA.
I shall not break your bidding, good my lord.

BERTRAM.
Where are my other men, monsieur?—Farewell.
                              [*Exit* HELENA.
Go thou toward home; where I will never come,
Whilst I can shake my sword, or hear the drum.—
Away, and for our flight.

PAROLLES.
                    Bravely, coragio!
                              [*Exeunt.*

ACT III. SCENE I.

Florence.   A room in the DUKE'S *palace.*

Flourish.   Enter the DUKE OF FLORENCE, *two*
French LORDS *and a troop of* SOLDIERS.

DUKE.
SO that, from point to point, now have you
heard
The fundamental reasons of this war;
Whose great decision hath much blood let forth,
And more thirsts after.

FIRST LORD.
                    Holy seems the quarrel
Upon your Grace's part; black and fearful
On the opposer.

DUKE.
Therefore we marvel much our cousin France
Would, in so just a business, shut his bosom
Against our borrowing prayers.

SECOND LORD.
                    Good my lord,
The reasons of our state I cannot yield,
But like a common and an outward man,
That the great figure of a council frames
By self-unable motion: therefore dare not
Say what I think of it, since I have found
Myself in my incertain grounds to fail
As often as I guest.

DUKE.
Be it his pleasure.

SECOND LORD.
But I am sure the younger of our nation,
That surfeit on their ease, will day by day
Come here for physic.

DUKE.
                    Welcome shall they be;
And all the honours that can fly from us
Shall on them settle. You know your places well;
When better fall, for your avails they fell:
To-morrow to the field.   [*Flourish.   Exeunt.*

SCENE II.

Rousillon.   A room in the house of the COUNTESS.

Enter COUNTESS *and* CLOWN.

COUNTESS.
IT hath happen'd all as I would have had it,
save that he comes not along with her.

CLOWN.
By my troth, I take my young lord to be a very
melancholy man.

COUNTESS.
By what observance, I pray you?

CLOWN.
Why, he will look upon his boot, and sing; mend
the ruff, and sing; ask questions, and sing; pick
his teeth, and sing. I know a man that had this
trick of melancholy sold a goodly manor for a
song.

COUNTESS.
Let me see what he writes, and when he means to
come.   [*Opening a letter.*

CLOWN.
I have no mind to Isbel, since I was at court: our
old ling and our Isbels o'th'country are nothing
like your old ling and your Isbels o'th'court: the
brains of my Cupid's knockt out; and I begin to
love, as an old man loves money, with no stomach.

COUNTESS.
What have we here?

CLOWN.
E'en that you have there.   [*Exit.*

COUNTESS [*reads*].
I have sent you a daughter-in-law: she hath recover'd the king, and undone me. I have wedded
her, not bedded her; and sworn to make the 'not'

eternal. You shall hear I am run away: know it before the report come. If there be breadth enough in the world, I will hold a long distance. My duty to you. Your unfortunate son,

BERTRAM.

This is not well, rash and unbridled boy,
To fly the favours of so good a king;
To pluck his indignation on thy head
By the misprising of a maid too virtuous
For the contempt of empire.

Enter CLOWN.

CLOWN.

O madam, yonder is heavy news within between two soldiers and my young lady!

COUNTESS.

What is the matter?

CLOWN.

Nay, there is some comfort in the news, some comfort; your son will not be kill'd so soon as I thought he would.

COUNTESS.

Why should he be kill'd?

CLOWN.

So say I, madam, if he run away, as I hear he does: the danger is in standing to't; that's the loss of men, though it be the getting of children. Here they come will tell you more: for my part, I only hear your son was run away. [*Exit.*

Enter HELENA *and two* GENTLEMEN.

FIRST GENTLEMAN.

Save you, good madam.

HELENA.

Madam, my lord is gone, for ever gone.

SECOND GENTLEMAN.

Do not say so.

COUNTESS.

Think upon patience.—Pray you, gentlemen,—
I have felt so many quirks of joy and grief,
That the first face of neither, on the start,
Can woman me unto't:—where is my son, I pray
   you?

SECOND GENTLEMAN.

Madam, he's gone to serve the Duke of Florence:
We met him thitherward; for thence we came,
And, after some dispatch in hand at court,
Thither we bend again.

HELENA.

Look on his letter, madam; here's my passport.
[*Reads*] When thou canst get the ring upon my finger which never shall come off, and show me a child begotten of thy body that I am father to, then call me husband: but in such a 'then' I write a 'never.'
This is a dreadful sentence.

COUNTESS.

Brought you this letter, gentlemen?

FIRST GENTLEMAN.

Ay, madam;
And, for the contents' sake, are sorry for our pains.

COUNTESS.

I prithee, lady, have a better cheer;
If thou engrossest all the griefs are thine,
Thou robb'st me of a moiety: he was my son;
But I do wash his name out of my blood,
And thou art all my child.—Towards Florence is he?

SECOND GENTLEMAN.

Ay, madam.

COUNTESS.

And to be a soldier?

SECOND GENTLEMAN.

Such is his noble purpose: and, believe't,
The duke will lay upon him all the honour
That good convenience claims.

COUNTESS.

Return you thither?

FIRST GENTLEMAN.

Ay, madam, with the swiftest wing of speed.

HELENA [*reads*].

'Till I have no wife, I have nothing in France.'
'Tis bitter.

COUNTESS.

Find you that there?

HELENA.

Ay, madam.

FIRST GENTLEMAN.

'Tis but the boldness of his hand, haply, which his heart was not consenting to.

COUNTESS.

Nothing in France, until he have no wife!
There's nothing here that is too good for him,
But only she; and she deserves a lord,
That twenty such rude boys might tend upon,
And call her hourly mistress.—Who was with him?

FIRST GENTLEMAN.

A servant only, and a gentleman
Which I have sometime known.

COUNTESS.

Parolles, was't not?

FIRST GENTLEMAN.

Ay, my good lady, he.

COUNTESS.

A very tainted fellow, and full of wickedness.
My son corrupts a well-derived nature
With his inducement.

FIRST GENTLEMAN.

Indeed, good lady,
The fellow has a deal of that too much,
Which holds him much to have.

COUNTESS.

Y'are welcome, gentlemen.
I will entreat you, when you see my son,
To tell him that his sword can never win
The honour that he loses: more I'll entreat you
Written to bear along.

SECOND GENTLEMAN.

We serve you, madam,
In that and all your worthiest affairs.

COUNTESS.

Not so, but as we change our courtesies.
Will you draw near?

[*Exeunt* COUNTESS *and* GENTLEMEN.

HELENA.

'Till I have no wife, I have nothing in France.'
Nothing in France, until he has no wife!
Thou shalt have none, Rousillon, none in France;
Then hast thou all again. Poor lord! is't I
That chase thee from thy country, and expose
Those tender limbs of thine to the event
Of the none-sparing war? and is it I
That drive thee from the sportive court, where thou

Wast shot at with fair eyes, to be the mark
Of smoky muskets? O you leaden messengers,
That ride upon the violent speed of fire,
Fly with false aim; move the still-piecing air,
That sings with piercing; do not touch my lord!
Whoever shoots at him, I set him there;
Whoever charges on his forward breast,
I am the caitiff that do hold him to't;
And, though I kill him not, I am the cause
His death was so effected: better 'twere
I met the ravin lion when he roar'd
With sharp constraint of hunger; better 'twere
That all the miseries which nature owes
Were mine at once. No, come thou home, Rousil-
Whence honour but of danger wins a scar,   [lon,
As oft it loses all: I will be gone;
My being here it is that holds thee hence:
Shall I stay here to do't? no, no, although
The air of paradise did fan the house,
The angels officed all: I will be gone,
That pitiful rumour may report my flight,
To consolate thine ear. Come, night; end, day!
For with the dark, poor thief, I'll steal away.
                                                [Exit.

SCENE III.

Florence.   Before the DUKE'S *palace.*

Flourish.   Enter the DUKE OF FLORENCE,
BERTRAM, PAROLLES, SOLDIERS, *Drum,
and Trumpets.*

DUKE.

THE general of our horse thou art; and we,
    Great in our hope, lay our best love and
        credence
Upon thy promising fortune.

BERTRAM.
                            Sir, it is
A charge too heavy for my strength; but yet
We'll strive to bear it, for your worthy sake,
To th'extreme edge of hazard.

DUKE.
                            Then go thou forth;
And Fortune play upon thy prosperous helm,
As thy auspicious mistress!

BERTRAM.
                        This very day,
Great Mars, I put myself into thy file:
Make me but like my thoughts, and I shall prove
A lover of thy drum, hater of love.   [*Exeunt.*

SCENE IV.

Rousillon.   A room in the house of the COUNTESS.

Enter COUNTESS *and* STEWARD.

COUNTESS.

ALAS! and would you take the letter of her?
    Might you not know she would do as she
        has done,
By sending me a letter? Read it again.

STEWARD [*reads*].
I am Saint Jaques' pilgrim, thither gone:
    Ambitious love hath so in me offended,
That barefoot plod I the cold ground upon,
    With sainted vow my faults to have amended.
Write, write, that from the bloody course of war
    My dearest master, your dear son, may hie:

Bless him at home in peace, whilst I from far
    His name with zealous fervour sanctify:
His taken labours bid him me forgive;
    I, his despiteful Juno, sent him forth
From courtly friends, with camping foes to live,
    Where death and danger dogs the heels of
        worth:
He is too good and fair for death and me;
Whom I myself embrace, to set him free.

COUNTESS.
Ah, what sharp stings are in her mildest words!—
Rinaldo, you did never lack advice so much,
As letting her pass so: had I spoke with her,
I could have well diverted her intents,
Which thus she hath prevented.

STEWARD.
                            Pardon me, madam:
If I had given you this at over-night,
She might have been o'erta'en; and yet she writes,
Pursuit would be but vain.

COUNTESS.
                        What angel shall
Bless this unworthy husband? he cannot thrive,
Unless her prayers, whom heaven delights to hear,
And loves to grant, reprieve him from the wrath
Of greatest justice.—Write, write, Rinaldo,
To this unworthy husband of his wife;
Let every word weigh heavy of her worth,
That he does weigh too light: my greatest grief,
Though little he do feel it, set down sharply.
Dispatch the most convenient messenger:—
When haply he shall hear that she is gone,
He will return; and hope I may that she,
Hearing so much, will speed her foot again,
Led hither by pure love: which of them both
Is dearest to me, I have no skill in sense
To make distinction:—provide this messenger:—
My heart is heavy and mine age is weak:
Grief would have tears, and sorrow bids me speak.
                                        [*Exeunt.*

SCENE V.

Without the walls of Florence.   A tucket afar off.

Enter an old WIDOW *of Florence,* DIANA, VIO-
LENTA, MARIANA, *with other* CITIZENS.

WIDOW.

NAY, come; for if they do approach the city,
    we shall lose all the sight.

DIANA.
They say the French count has done most honourable service.

WIDOW.
It is reported that he has taken their greatest
commander; and that with his own hand he slew
the duke's brother. [*Tucket.*] We have lost our
labour; they are gone a contrary way: hark! you
may know by their trumpets.

MARIANA.
Come, let's return again, and suffice ourselves
with the report of it. Well, Diana, take heed of
this French earl: the honour of a maid is her name;
and no legacy is so rich as honesty.

WIDOW.
I have told my neighbour how you have been
solicited by a gentleman his companion.

MARIANA.

I know that knave; hang him! one Parolles: a filthy officer he is in those suggestions for the young earl.—Beware of them, Diana; their promises, enticements, oaths, tokens, and all these engines of lust, are not the things they go under: many a maid hath been seduced by them; and the misery is, example, that so terrible shows in the wrack of maidenhood, cannot for all that dissuade succession, but that they are limed with the twigs that threaten them. I hope I need not to advise you further; but I hope your own grace will keep you where you are, though there were no further danger known but the modesty which is so lost.

DIANA.

You shall not need to fear me.

WIDOW.

I hope so.—Look, here comes a pilgrim: I know she will lie at my house; thither they send one another: I'll question her.

Enter HELENA, *in the dress of a pilgrim.*

God save you, pilgrim! whither are you bound?

HELENA.

To Saint Jaques le Grand.
Where do the palmers lodge, I do beseech you?

WIDOW.

At the Saint Francis here, beside the port.

HELENA.

Is this the way?

WIDOW.

Ay, marry, is't.—Hark you! they come this way.—   [*A march afar off.*
If you will tarry, holy pilgrim,
But till the troops come by,
I will conduct you where you shall be lodged;
The rather, for I think I know your hostess
As ample as myself.

HELENA.

Is it yourself?

WIDOW.

If you shall please so, pilgrim.

HELENA.

I thank you, and will stay upon your leisure.

WIDOW.

You came, I think, from France?

HELENA.

I did so.

WIDOW.

Here you shall see a countryman of yours
That has done worthy service.

HELENA.

His name, I pray you.

DIANA.

The Count Rousillon: know you such a one?

HELENA.

But by the ear, that hears most nobly of him:
His face I know not.

DIANA.

Whatsome'er he is,
He's bravely taken here. He stole from France,
As 'tis reported, for the king had married him
Against his liking: think you it is so?

HELENA.

Ay, surely, mere the truth: I know his lady.

DIANA.

There is a gentleman that serves the count
Reports but coarsely of her.

HELENA.

What's his name?

DIANA.

Monsieur Parolles.

HELENA.

O, I believe with him,
In argument of praise, or to the worth
Of the great count himself, she is too mean
To have her name repeated: all her deserving
Is a reserved honesty, and that
I have not heard examined.

DIANA.

Alas, poor lady!
'Tis a hard bondage to become the wife
Of a detesting lord.

WIDOW.

I write good creature; wheresoe'er she is,
Her heart weighs sadly: this young maid might do her
A shrewd turn, if she pleased.

HELENA.

How do you mean?
May be the amorous count solicits her
In the unlawful purpose.

WIDOW.

He does indeed;
And brokes with all that can in such a suit
Corrupt the tender honour of a maid:
But she is arm'd for him, and keeps her guard
In honestest defence.

MARIANA.

The gods forbid else!

WIDOW.

So, now they come:—

Drum and Colours.

Enter BERTRAM, PAROLLES, *and the whole army.*

That is Antonio, the duke's eldest son;
That, Escalus.

HELENA.

Which is the Frenchman?

DIANA.

He;
That with the plume: 'tis a most gallant fellow.
I would he loved his wife: if he were honester,
He were much goodlier: is't not a handsome gentleman?

HELENA.

I like him well.

DIANA.

'Tis pity he is not honest: yond's that same knave
That leads him to these passes: were I his lady,
I would poison that vile rascal.

HELENA.

Which is he?

DIANA.

That jack-an-apes with scarfs: why is he melancholy?

HELENA.

Perchance he's hurt i'the battle.

PAROLLES.

Lose our drum! well.

MARIANA.
He's shrewdly vext at something: look, he has
  spied us.
WIDOW.
Marry, hang you!
MARIANA.
And your courtesy, for a ring-carrier!
  [*Exeunt* BERTRAM, PAROLLES, &c.
WIDOW.
The troop is past. Come pilgrim, I will bring you
Where you shall host: of enjoin'd penitents
There's four or five, to Great Saint Jaques bound,
Already at my house.
HELENA.
              I humbly thank you:
Please it this matron and this gentle maid
To eat with us to-night, the charge and thanking
Shall be for me; and, to requite you further,
I will bestow some precepts of this virgin
Worthy the note.
BOTH.
  We'll take your offer kindly. [*Exeunt.*

SCENE VI.

Camp before Florence.

Enter BERTRAM *and the two French* LORDS.

FIRST LORD.
NAY, good my lord, put him to't; let him have
  his way.
SECOND LORD.
If your lordship find him not a hilding, hold me
no more in your respect.
FIRST LORD.
On my life, my lord, a bubble.
BERTRAM.
Do you think I am so far deceived in him?
FIRST LORD.
Believe it, my lord, in mine own direct know-
ledge, without any malice, but to speak of him as
my kinsman, he's a most notable coward, an in-
finite and endless liar, an hourly promise-breaker,
the owner of no one good quality worthy your
lordship's entertainment.
SECOND LORD.
It were fit you knew him; lest, reposing too far
in his virtue, which he hath not, he might at
some great and trusty business, in a main danger,
fail you.
BERTRAM.
I would I knew in what particular action to try
him.
SECOND LORD.
None better than to let him fetch off his drum,
which you hear him so confidently undertake to do.
FIRST LORD.
I, with a troop of Florentines, will suddenly surprise him; such I will have, whom, I am sure, he
knows not from the enemy: we will bind and
hoodwink him so, that he shall suppose no other
but that he is carried into the leaguer of the adversaries, when we bring him to our own tents.
Be but your lordship present at his examination:
if he do not, for the promise of his life, and in the
highest compulsion of base fear, offer to betray
you, and deliver all the intelligence in his power

against you, and that with the divine forfeit of his
soul upon oath, never trust my judgement in any
thing.
SECOND LORD.
O, for the love of laughter, let him fetch off his
drum; he says he has a stratagem for't: when your
lordship sees the bottom of his success in't, and
to what metal this counterfeit lump of ore will be
melted, if you give him not John Drum's entertainment, your inclining cannot be removed.—
Here he comes.
FIRST LORD.
O, for the love of laughter, hinder not the humour
of his design: let him fetch off his drum in any
hand.

Enter PAROLLES.

BERTRAM.
How now, monsieur! this drum sticks sorely in
your disposition.
SECOND LORD.
A pox on't, let it go; 'tis but a drum.
PAROLLES.
But a drum! is't but a drum? A drum so lost!—
There was excellent command,—to charge in with
our horse upon our own wings, and to rend our
own soldiers!
SECOND LORD.
That was not to be blamed in the command of the
service: it was a disaster of war that Cæsar him-
self could not have prevented, if he had been there
to command.
BERTRAM.
Well, we cannot greatly condemn our success:
some dishonour we had in the loss of that drum;
but it is not to be recover'd.
PAROLLES.
It might have been recover'd.
BERTRAM.
It might; but it is not now.
PAROLLES.
It is to be recover'd: but that the merit of service
is seldom attributed to the true and exact per-
former, I would have that drum or another, or *hic
jacet.*
BERTRAM.
Why, if you have a stomach, to't: monsieur, if you
think your mystery in stratagem can bring this
instrument of honour again into his native quar-
ter, be magnanimous in the enterprise, and go on;
I will grace the attempt for a worthy exploit: if
you speed well in it, the duke shall both speak of
it, and extend to you what further becomes his
greatness, even to the utmost syllable of your
worthiness.
PAROLLES.
By the hand of a soldier, I will undertake it.
BERTRAM.
But you must not now slumber in it.
PAROLLES.
I'll about it this evening: and I will presently pen
down my dilemmas, encourage myself in my
certainty, put myself in my mortal preparation;
and, by midnight, look to hear further from me.
BERTRAM.
May I be bold to acquaint his Grace you are gone
about it?

PAROLLES.
I know not what the success will be, my lord; but
the attempt I vow.

BERTRAM.
I know th'art valiant; and, to the possibility of thy
soldiership, will subscribe for thee. Farewell.

PAROLLES.
I love not many words.   [Exit.

FIRST LORD.
No more than a fish loves water.—Is not this a
strange fellow, my lord, that so confidently seems
to undertake this business, which he knows is not
to be done; damns himself to do, and dares better
be damn'd than to do't?

SECOND LORD.
You do not know him, my lord, as we do: certain
it is, that he will steal himself into a man's favour,
and for a week escape a great deal of discoveries; but
when you find him out, you have him ever after.

BERTRAM.
Why, do you think he will make no deed at all of
this, that so seriously he does address himself unto?

FIRST LORD.
None in the world; but return with an invention,
and clap upon you two or thee probable lies: but
we have almost embost him,—you shall see his
fall to-night; for indeed he is not for your lordship's respect.

SECOND LORD.
We'll make you some sport with the fox, ere we
case him. He was first smoked by the old Lord
Lafeu: when his disguise and he is parted, tell me
what a sprat you shall find him: which you shall
see this very night.

FIRST LORD.
I must go look my twigs: he shall be caught.

BERTRAM.
Your brother, he shall go along with me.

FIRST LORD.
As't please your lordship: I'll leave you   [Exit.

BERTRAM.
Now will I lead you to the house, and show you
The lass I spoke of.

SECOND LORD.
                    But you say she's honest.

BERTRAM.
That's all the fault: I spoke with her but once,
And found her wondrous cold; but I sent to her,
By this same coxcomb that we have i'the wind,
Tokens and letters which she did re-send;
And this is all I have done. She's a fair creature:
Will you go see her?

SECOND LORD.
                    With all my heart, my lord.
                                        [Exeunt.

SCENE VII.

Florence.   A room in the WIDOW's house.

Enter HELENA and WIDOW.

HELENA.
IF you misdoubt me that I am not she,
I know not how I shall assure you further,
But I shall lose the grounds I work upon.

WIDOW.
Though my estate be fall'n, I was well born,
Nothing acquainted with these businesses:

And would not put my reputation now
In any staining act.

HELENA.
                    Nor would I wish you.
First, give me trust, the count he is my husband,
And what to your sworn counsel I have spoken
Is so from word to word; and then you cannot,
By the good aid that I of you shall borrow,
Err in bestowing it.

WIDOW.
                    I should believe you;
For you have show'd me that which well approves
Y'are great in fortune.

HELENA.
                    Take this purse of gold,
And let me buy your friendly help thus far,
Which I will over-pay and pay again,   [daughter,
When I have found it. The count he woos your
Lays down his wanton siege before her beauty,
Resolved to carry her: let her, in fine, consent,
As we'll direct her how 'tis best to bear it;
Now his impatient blood will naught deny
That she'll demand: a ring the county wears,
That downward hath succeeded in his house
From son to son, some four or five descents
Since the first father wore it: this ring he holds
In most rich choice; yet, in his idle fire,
To buy his will, it would not seem too dear,
Howe'er repented after.

WIDOW.
                    Now I see
The bottom of your purpose.

HELENA.
You see it lawful, then: it is no more,
But that your daughter, ere she seems as won,
Desires this ring; appoints him an encounter;
In fine, delivers me to fill the time,
Herself most chastely absent: after this,
To marry her, I'll add three thousand crowns
To what is past already.

WIDOW.
                    I have yielded:
Instruct my daughter how she shall persever,
That time and place with this deceit so lawful
May prove coherent. Every night he comes
With music of all sorts, and songs composed
To her unworthiness: it nothing steads us
To chide him from our eaves; for he persists,
As if his life lay on't.

HELENA.
                    Why, then, to-night
Let us assay our plot; which, if it speed,
Is wicked meaning in a lawful deed,
And lawful meaning in unlawful act;
Where both not sin, and yet a sinful fact:
But let's about it.   [Exeunt.

ACT IV. SCENE I.

Without the Florentine camp.

Enter First French LORD, with five or six other
SOLDIERS, in ambush.

FIRST LORD.
HE can come no other way but by this hedge-
corner. When you sally upon him, speak what
terrible language you will,—though you understand it not yourselves, no matter; for we must not

seem to understand him, unless some one among us, whom we must produce for an interpreter.

FIRST SOLDIER.
Good captain, let me be th'interpreter.

FIRST LORD.
Art not acquainted with him? knows he not thy voice?

FIRST SOLDIER.
No, sir, I warrant you.

FIRST LORD.
But what linsey-woolsey hast thou to speak to us again?

FIRST SOLDIER.
E'en such as you speak to me.

FIRST LORD.
He must think us some band of strangers i'the adversary's entertainment. Now, he hath a smack of all neighbouring languages; therefore we must every one be a man of his own fancy, not to know what we speak one to another; so we seem to know, is to know straight our purpose: choughs' language, gabble enough, and good enough. As for you, interpreter, you must seem very politic. —But couch, ho! here he comes,—to beguile two hours in a sleep, and then to return and swear the lies he forges.

Enter PAROLLES.

PAROLLES.
Ten o'clock: within these three hours 'twill be time enough to go home. What shall I say I have done? It must be a very plausive invention that carries it: they begin to smoke me; and disgraces have of late knockt too often at my door. I find my tongue is too foolhardy; but my heart hath the fear of Mars before it and of his creatures, not daring the reports of my tongue.

FIRST LORD [*aside*].
This is the first truth that e'er thine own tongue was guilty of.

PAROLLES.
What the devil should move me to undertake the recovery of this drum, being not ignorant of the impossibility, and knowing I had no such purpose? I must give myself some hurts, and say I got them in exploit: yet slight ones will not carry it; they will say, 'Came you off with so little?' and great ones I dare not give. Wherefore, what's the instance? Tongue, I must put you into a butter-woman's mouth, and buy myself another of Bajazet's mule, if you prattle me into these perils.

FIRST LORD [*aside*].
Is it possible he should know what he is, and be that he is?

PAROLLES.
I would the cutting of my garments would serve the turn, or the breaking of my Spanish sword.

FIRST LORD [*aside*].
We cannot afford you so.

PAROLLES.
Or the baring of my beard; and to say it was in stratagem.

FIRST LORD [*aside*].
'Twould not do.

PRAOLLES.
Or to drown my clothes, and say I was stript—

FIRST LORD [*aside*].
Hardly serve.

PAROLLES.
Though I swore I leapt from the window of the citadel—

FIRST LORD [*aside*].
How deep?

PAROLLES.
Thirty fadom.

FIRST LORD [*aside*].
Three great oaths would scarce make that be believed.

PAROLLES.
I would I had any drum of the enemy's: I would swear I recover'd it.

FIRST LORD [*aside*].
You shall hear one anon.   [*Alarum within.*

PAROLLES.
A drum now of the enemy's!

FIRST LORD.
Throca movousus, cargo, cargo, cargo.

ALL.
Cargo, cargo, cargo, villianda par corbo, cargo.

PAROLLES.
O, ransom, ransom!—do not hide mine eyes.
        [*They seize and blindfold him.*

FIRST SOLDIER.
Boskos thromuldo boskos.

PAROLLES.
I know you are the Muskos' regiment;
And I shall lose my life for want of language:
If there be here German, or Dane, low Dutch,
Italian, or French, let him speak to me; I'll
Discover that which shall undo the Florentine.

FIRST SOLDIER.
Boskos vauvado:—
I understand thee, and can speak thy tongue:—
Kerelybonto:—sir,
Betake thee to thy faith, for seventeen poniards
Are at thy bosom.

PAROLLES.
        O!

FIRST SOLDIER.
        O, pray, pray, pray!—
Manka revania dulche.

FIRST LORD.
Oscorbidulchos volivorco.

FIRST SOLDIER.
The general is content to spare thee yet;
And, hoodwinkt as thou art, will lead thee on
To gather from thee: haply thou mayst inform
Something to save thy life.

PAROLLES.
        O, let me live!
And all the secrets of our camp I'll show,
Their force, their purposes; nay, I'll speak that
Which you will wonder at.

FIRST SOLDIER.
        But wilt thou faithfully?

PAROLLES.
If I do not, damn me.

FIRST SOLDIER.
        Acordo linta:—
Come on; thou art granted space.
        [*Exit, with* PAROLLES *guarded.   A short alarum within.*

FIRST LORD.
Go, tell the Count Rousillon, and my brother,
We have caught the woodcock, and will keep him
    muffled
Till we do hear from them.
            SECOND SOLDIER.
                    Captain, I will.
            FIRST LORD.
A' will betray us all unto ourselves:—
Inform 'em that.
            SECOND SOLDIER.
                So I will, sir.
            FIRST LORD.
Till then I'll keep him dark and safely lockt.
                            [Exeunt.

SCENE II.

Florence.   A room in the WIDOW'S *house.*

Enter BERTRAM *and* DIANA.

            BERTRAM.

THEY told me that your name was Fonti-
    bell.
            DIANA.
No, my good lord, Diana.
            BERTRAM.
                Titled goddess;
And worth it, with addition! But, fair soul,
In your fine frame hath love no quality?
If the quick fire of youth light not your mind,
You are no maiden, but a monument:
When you are dead, you should be such a one
As you are now, for you are cold and stern;
And now you should be as your mother was
When your sweet self was got.
            DIANA.
She then was honest.
            BERTRAM.
                So should you be.
            DIANA.
                        No:
My mother did but duty; such, my lord,
As you owe to your wife.
            BERTRAM.
                No more o'that,—
I prithee, do not strive against my vows:
I was compell'd to her; but I love thee
By love's own sweet constraint, and will for ever
Do thee all rights of service.
            DIANA.
                    Ay, so you serve us
Till we serve you; but when you have our roses,
You barely leave our thorns to prick ourselves,
And mock us with our bareness.
            BERTRAM.
                How have I sworn!
            DIANA.
'Tis not the many oaths that makes the truth,
But the plain single vow that is vow'd true.
What is not holy, that we swear not by,
But take the High'st to witness: then, pray you,
    tell me,
If I should swear by Jove's great attributes,
I loved you dearly, would you believe my oaths,
When I did love you ill? this has no holding,
To swear by him whom I protest to love,

That I will work against him. Therefore your
    oaths
Are words and poor conditions; but unseal'd;
At least in my opinion.
            BERTRAM.
                Change it, change it;
Be not so holy-cruel: love is holy;
And my integrity ne'er knew the crafts
That you do charge men with. Stand no more off,
But give thyself unto my sick desires,
Who then recover: say thou art mine, and ever
My love as it begins shall so persever.
            DIANA.
I see that men make ropes in such a scarr,
That we'll forsake ourselves. Give me that ring.
            BERTRAM.
I'll lend it thee, my dear; but have no power
To give it from me.
            DIANA.
                Will you not, my lord?
            BERTRAM.
It is an honour 'longing to our house,
Bequeathed down from many ancestors;
Which were the greatest obloquy i'the world
In me to lose.
            DIANA.
                Mine honour's such a ring:
My chastity's the jewel of our house,
Bequeathed down from many ancestors;
Which were the greatest obloquy i'the world
In me to lose: thus your own proper wisdom
Brings in the champion honour on my part,
Against your vain assault.
            BERTRAM.
                Here, take my ring:
My house, mine honour, yea, my life, be thine,
And I'll be bid by thee.
            DIANA.
When midnight comes, knock at my chamber-
    window:
I'll order take my mother shall not hear.
Now will I charge you in the band of truth,
When you have conquer'd my yet maiden bed,
Remain there but an hour, nor speak to me:
My reasons are most strong; and you shall know
    them
When back again this ring shall be deliver'd:
And on your finger, in the night, I'll put
Another ring, that what in time proceeds
May token to the future our past deeds.
Adieu, till then; then fail not. You have won
A wife of me, though there my hope be done.
            BERTRAM.
A heaven on earth I have won by wooing thee.
                            [Exit.
            DIANA.
For which live long to thank both heaven and me!
You may so in the end.—
My mother told me just how he would woo,
As if she sat in's heart; she says all men
Have the like oaths: he has sworn to marry me
When his wife's dead; therefore I'll lie with him
When I am buried. Since Frenchmen are so braid,
Marry that will, I live and die a maid:
Only, in this disguise, I think't no sin
To cozen him that would unjustly win.   [Exit.

SCENE III.

The Florentine camp.

Enter the two French LORDS *and some two or three* SOLDIERS.

FIRST LORD.

YOU have not given him his mother's letter?

SECOND LORD.

I have deliver'd it an hour since: there is something in't that stings his nature; for, on the reading it, he changed almost into another man.

FIRST LORD.

He has much worthy blame laid upon him for shaking off so good a wife and so sweet a lady.

SECOND LORD.

Especially he hath incurr'd the everlasting displeasure of the king, who had even tuned his bounty to sing happiness to him. I will tell you a thing, but you shall let it dwell darkly with you.

FIRST LORD.

When you have spoken it, 'tis dead, and I am the grave of it.

SECOND LORD.

He hath perverted a young gentlewoman here in Florence, of a most chaste renown; and this night he fleshes his will in the spoil of her honour: he hath given her his monumental ring, and thinks himself made in the unchaste composition.

FIRST LORD.

Now, God delay our rebellion! as we are ourselves, what things are we!

SECOND LORD.

Merely our own traitors. And as in the common course of all treasons, we still see them reveal themselves, till they attain to their abhorr'd ends, so he that in this action contrives against his own nobility, in his proper stream o'erflows himself.

FIRST LORD.

Is it not meant damnable in us, to be trumpeters of our unlawful intents? We shall not, then, have his company to-night?

SECOND LORD.

Not till after midnight; for he is dieted to his hour.

FIRST LORD.

That approaches apace: I would gladly have him see his company anatomized, that he might take a measure of his own judgements, wherein so curiously he had set this counterfeit.

SECOND LORD.

We will not meddle with him till he come; for his presence must be the whip of the other.

FIRST LORD.

In the mean time, what hear you of these wars?

SECOND LORD.

I hear there is an overture of peace.

FIRST LORD.

Nay, I assure you, a peace concluded.

SECOND LORD.

What will Count Rousillon do then? will he travel higher, or return again into France?

FIRST LORD.

I perceive, by this demand, you are not altogether of his council.

SECOND LORD.

Let it be forbid, sir! so should I be a great deal of his act.

FIRST LORD.

Sir, his wife, some two months since, fled from his house; her pretence is a pilgrimage to Saint Jaques le Grand; which holy undertaking, with most austere sanctimony, she accomplisht; and, there residing, the tenderness of her nature became as a prey to her grief; in fine, made a groan of her last breath; and now she sings in heaven.

SECOND LORD.

How is this justified?

FIRST LORD.

The stronger part of it by her own letters, which make her story true, even to the point of her death: her death itself, which could not be her office to say is come, was faithfully confirm'd by the rector of the place.

SECOND LORD.

Hath the count all this intelligence?

FIRST LORD.

Ay, and the particular confirmations, point from point, to the full arming of the verity.

SECOND LORD.

I am heartily sorry that he'll be glad of this.

FIRST LORD.

How mightily sometimes we make us comforts of our losses!

SECOND LORD.

And how mightily some other times we drown our gain in tears! The great dignity that his valour hath here acquired for him shall at home be encounter'd with a shame as ample.

FIRST LORD.

The web of our life is of a mingled yarn, good and ill together: our virtues would be proud, if our faults whipt them not: and our crimes would despair, if they were not cherish'd by our virtues.

Enter a MESSENGER.

How now! where's your master?

MESSENGER.

He met the duke in the street, sir, of whom he hath taken a solemn leave: his lordship will next morning for France. The duke hath offer'd him letters of commendations to the king.   [*Exit.*

SECOND LORD.

They shall be no more than needful there, if they were more than they can commend.

FIRST LORD.

They cannot be too sweet for the king's tartness. Here's his lordship now.

Enter BERTRAM.

How now, my lord! is't not after midnight?

BERTRAM.

I have to-night dispatcht sixteen businesses, a month's length a-piece, by an abstract of success: I have congied with the duke, done my adieu with his nearest; buried a wife, mourn'd for her; writ to my lady mother I am returning; entertain'd my convoy; and between these main parcels of dispatch, effected many nicer needs: the last was the greatest, but that I have not ended yet.

SECOND LORD.

If the business be of any difficulty, and this morning your departure hence, it requires haste of your lordship.

BERTRAM.

I mean, the business is not ended, as fearing to hear of it hereafter. But shall we have this dialogue between the fool and the soldier?—Come, bring forth this counterfeit module, has deceived me, like a double-meaning prophesier.

SECOND LORD.

Bring him forth [*Exeunt* SOLDIERS]:—has sat i'the stocks all night, poor gallant knave.

BERTRAM.

No matter; his heels have deserved it, in usurping his spurs so long. How does he carry himself?

SECOND LORD.

I have told your lordship already,—the stocks carry him. But, to answer you as you would be understood; he weeps like a wench that had shed her milk: he hath confest himself to Morgan, whom he supposes to be a friar, from the time of his remembrance to this very instant disaster of his setting i'the stocks: and what think you he hath confest?

BFRTRAM.

Nothing of me, has a'?

SECOND LORD.

His confession is taken, and it shall be read to his face: if your lordship be in't, as I believe you are, you must have the patience to hear it.

Enter SOLDIERS *with* PAROLLES *muffled.*

BERTRAM.

A plague upon him! muffled! he can say nothing of me.

FIRST LORD.

Hush, hush! Hoodman comes.—*Portotartarossa.*

FIRST SOLDIER.

He calls for the tortures: what will you say without 'em?

PAROLLES.

I will confess what I know without constraint: if ye pinch me like a pasty, I can say no more.

FIRST SOLDIER.

Bosko chimurcho.

FIRST LORD.

Boblibindo chicurmurco.

FIRST SOLDIER.

You are a merciful general.—Our general bids you answer to what I shall ask you out of a note.

PAROLLES.

And truly, as I hope to live.

FIRST SOLDIER [*reads*].

'First demand of him how many horse the duke is strong.' What say you to that?

PAROLLES.

Five or six thousand; but very weak and unserviceable: the troops are all scatter'd, and the commanders very poor rogues, upon my reputation and credit, and as I hope to live.

FIRST SOLDIER.

Shall I set down your answer so?

PAROLLES.

Do: I'll take the sacrament on't, how and which way you will.

BERTRAM.

All's one to him. What a past-saving slave is this!

FIRST LORD.

Y'are deceived, my lord: this is Monsieur Parolles, the gallant militarist,—that was his own phrase,

—that had the whole theoric of war in the knot of his scarf, and the practice in the chape of his dagger.

SECOND LORD.

I will never trust a man again for keeping his sword clean; nor believe he can have every thing in him by wearing his apparel neatly.

FIRST SOLDIER.

Well, that's set down.

PAROLLES.

Five or six thousand horse, I said,—I will say true,—or thereabouts, set down,—for I'll speak truth.

FIRST LORD.

He's very near the truth in this.

BERTRAM.

But I con him no thanks for't, in the nature he delivers it.

PAROLLES.

Poor rogues, I pray you, say.

FIRST SOLDIER.

Well, that's set down.

PAROLLES.

I humbly thank you, sir. A truth's a truth,—the rogues are marvellous poor.

FIRST SOLDIER [*reads*].

'Demand of him, of what strength they are afoot.' What say you to that?

PAROLLES.

By my troth, sir, if I were to live but this present hour, I will tell true. Let me see: Spurio, a hundred and fifty; Sebastian, so many; Corambus, so many; Jaques, so many; Guiltian, Cosmo, Lodowick, and Gratii, two hundred fifty each; mine own company, Chitopher, Vaumond, Bentii, two hundred fifty each: so that the muster-file, rotten and sound, upon my life, amounts not to fifteen thousand poll; half of the which dare not shake the snow from off their cassocks, lest they shake themselves to pieces.

BERTRAM.

What shall be done to him?

FIRST LORD.

Nothing, but let him have thanks.—Demand of him my condition, and what credit I have with the duke.

FIRST SOLDIER.

Well, that's set down. [*Reads*] 'You shall demand of him, whether one Captain Dumain be i'the camp, a Frenchman; what his reputation is with the duke; what his valour, honesty, and expertness in wars; or whether he thinks it were not possible, with well-weighing sums of gold, to corrupt him to a revolt.' What say you to this? what do you know of it?

PAROLLES.

I beseech you, let me answer to the particular of the inter'gatories: demand them singly.

FIRST SOLDIER.

Do you know this Captain Dumain?

PAROLLES.

I know him: a' was a botcher's 'prentice in Paris, from whence he was whipt for getting the shrieve's fool with child,—a dumb innocent, that could not say him nay.

[FIRST LORD *lifts up his hand in anger.*

BERTRAM.
Nay, by your leave, hold your hands; though I
know his brains are forfeit to the next tile that
falls.

FIRST SOLDIER.
Well, is this captain in the Duke of Florence's
camp?

PAROLLES.
Upon my knowledge, he is, and lousy.

FIRST LORD.
Nay, look not so upon me; we shall hear of your
lordship anon.

FIRST SOLDIER.
What is his reputation with the duke?

PAROLLES.
The duke knows him for no other but a poor
officer of mine; and writ to me this other day to
turn him out o'the band: I think I have his letter
in my pocket.

FIRST SOLDIER.
Marry, we'll search.

PAROLLES.
In good sadness, I do not know; either it is there,
or it is upon a file, with the duke's other letters, in
my tent.

FIRST SOLDIER.
Here 'tis; here's a paper: shall I read it to
you?

PAROLLES.
I do not know if it be it or no.

BERTRAM.
Our interpreter does it well.

FIRST LORD.
Excellently.

FIRST SOLDIER [reads].
Dian, the count's a fool, and full of gold,—

PAROLLES.
That is not the duke's letter, sir; that is an advertisement to a proper maid in Florence, one Diana,
to take heed of the allurement of one Count
Rousillon, a foolish idle boy, but, for all that, very
ruttish: I pray you, sir, put it up again.

FIRST SOLDIER.
Nay, I'll read it first, by your favour.

PAROLLES.
My meaning in't, I protest, was very honest in
the behalf of the maid; for I knew the young
count to be a dangerous and lascivious boy, who
is a whale to virginity, and devours up all the fry
it finds.

BERTRAM.
Damnable both-sides rogue!

FIRST SOLDIER [reads].
When he swears oaths, bid him drop gold, and
    take it;
After he scores, he never pays the score:
Half won is match well made; match, and well
    make it;
He ne'er pays after-debts, take it before;
And say a soldier, Dian, told thee this,
Men are to mell with, boys are but to kiss:
For count of this, the count's a fool, I know it,
Who pays before, but not when he does owe it.

Thine, as he vow'd to thee in thine ear,
                                    PAROLLES.

BERTRAM.
He shall be whipt through the army, with this
rime in's forehead.

SECOND LORD.
This is your devoted friend, sir, the manifold
linguist and the armipotent soldier.

BERTRAM.
I could endure any thing before but a cat, and
now he's a cat to me.

FIRST SOLDIER.
I perceive, sir, by our general's looks, we shall be
fain to hang you.

PAROLLES.
My life, sir, in any case: not that I am afraid to
die; but that, my offences being many, I would
repent out the remainder of nature: let me live,
sir, in a dungeon, i'the stocks, or any where, so
I may live.

FIRST SOLDIER.
We'll see what may be done, so you confess freely;
therefore, once more to this Captain Dumain: you
have answer'd to his reputation with the duke,
and to his valour: what is his honesty?

PAROLLES.
He will steal, sir, an egg out of a cloister: for rapes
and ravishments he parallels Nessus: he professes
not keeping of oaths; in breaking 'em he is stronger than Hercules: he will lie, sir, with such volubility, that you would think truth were a fool:
drunkenness is his best virtue, for he will be
swine-drunk; and in his sleep he does little harm,
save to his bed-clothes about him; but they know
his conditions, and lay him in straw. I have but
little more to say, sir, of his honesty: he has every
thing that an honest man should not have; what
an honest man should have, he has nothing.

FIRST LORD.
I begin to love him for this.

BERTRAM.
For this description of thine honesty? A pox upon
him for me, he's more and more a cat.

FIRST SOLDIER.
What say you to his expertness in war?

PAROLLES.
Faith, sir, has led the drum before the English
tragedians,—to belie him, I will not,—and more
of his soldiership I know not; except, in that
country he had the honour to be the officer at a
place there called Mile-end, to instruct for the
doubling of files: I would do the man what honour
I can, but of this I am not certain.

FIRST LORD.
He hath out-villain'd villainy so far, that the rarity
redeems him.

BERTRAM.
A pox on him, he's a cat still.

FIRST SOLDIER.
His qualities being at this poor price, I need not
to ask you if gold will corrupt him to revolt.

PAROLLES.
Sir, for a cardecu he will sell the fee-simple of his
salvation, the inheritance of it; and cut th'entail
from all remainders, and a perpetual succession
for it perpetually.

FIRST SOLDIER.
What's his brother, the other Captain Dumain?

SECOND LORD.

Why does he ask him of me?

FIRST SOLDIER.

What's he?

PAROLLES.

E'en a crow o'the same nest; not altogether so great as the first in goodness, but greater a great deal in evil: he excels his brother for a coward, yet his brother is reputed one of the best that is: in a retreat he outruns any lackey; marry, in coming on he has the cramp.

FIRST SOLDIER.

If your life be saved, will you undertake to betray the Florentine?

PAROLLES.

Ay, and the captain of his horse, Count Rousillon.

FIRST SOLDIER.

I'll whisper with the general, and know his pleasure.

PAROLLES [aside].

I'll no more drumming; a plague of all drums! Only to seem to deserve well, and to beguile the supposition of that lascivious young boy the count, have I run into this danger: yet who would have suspected an ambush where I was taken?

FIRST SOLDIER.

There is no remedy, sir, but you must die: the general says, you that have so traitorously discover'd the secrets of your army, and made such pestiferous reports of men very nobly held, can serve the world for no honest use; therefore you must die.—Come, headsman, off with his head.

PAROLLES.

O Lord, sir, let me live, or let me see my death!

FIRST SOLDIER.

That shall you, and take your leave of all your friends. [Unmuffling him.
So, look about you: know you any here?

BERTRAM.

Good morrow, noble captain.

SECOND LORD.

God bless you, Captain Parolles.

FIRST LORD.

God save you, noble captain.

SECOND LORD.

Captain, what greeting will you to my Lord Lafeu? I am for France.

FIRST LORD.

Good captain, will you give me a copy of the sonnet you writ to Diana in behalf of the Count Rousillon? an I were not a very coward, I'ld compel it of you; but fare you well.

[Exeunt BERTRAM and LORDS.

FIRST SOLDIER.

You are undone, captain; all but your scarf, that has a knot on't yet.

PAROLLES.

Who cannot be crusht with a plot?

FIRST SOLDIER.

If you could find out a country where but women were that had received so much shame, you might begin an impudent nation. Fare ye well, sir; I am for France too: we shall speak of you there.

[Exit with SOLDIERS.

PAROLLES.

Yet am I thankful: if my heart were great,

'Twould burst at this. Captain I'll be no more;
But I will eat and drink, and sleep as soft
As captain shall: simply the thing I am
Shall make me live. Who knows himself a brag-
    gart,
Let him fear this; for it will come to pass,
That every braggart shall be found an ass.
Rust, sword! cool, blushes! and, Parolles, live
Safest in shame! being fool'd, by foolery thrive!
There's place and means for every man alive.
I'll after them. [Exit.

SCENE IV.

Florence. A room in the WIDOW'S *house.*

Enter HELENA, WIDOW, *and* DIANA.

HELENA.

THAT you may well perceive I have not
   wrong'd you,
One of the greatest in the Christian world
Shall be my surety; 'fore whose throne 'tis need-
    ful,
Ere I can perfect mine intents, to kneel:
Time was, I did him a desired office,
Dear almost as his life; which gratitude
Through flinty Tartar's bosom would peep forth,
And answer, thanks: I duly am inform'd
His Grace is at Marseilles; to which place
We have convenient convoy. You must know,
I am supposed dead: the army breaking,
My husband hies him home; where, heaven aid-
    ing,
And by the leave of my good lord the king,
We'll be before our welcome.

WIDOW.

          Gentle madam,
You never had a servant to whose trust
Your business was more welcome.

HELENA.

           Nor you, mistress,
Ever a friend whose thoughts more truly labour
To recompense your love: doubt not but heaven
Hath brought me up to be your daughter's dower,
As it hath fated her to be my motive
And helper to a husband. But, O strange men!
That can such sweet use make of what they hate,
When saucy trusting of the cozen'd thoughts
Defiles the pitchy night! so lust doth play
With what it loathes, for that which is away:
But more of this hereafter.—You, Diana,
Under my poor instructions yet must suffer
Something in my behalf.

DIANA.

          Let death and honesty
Go with your impositions, I am yours
Upon your will to suffer.

HELENA.

           Yet, I pray you:
But, with the word, the time will bring on sum-
    mer,
When briers shall have leaves as well as thorns,
And be as sweet as sharp. We must away;
Our wagon is prepared, and time revives us:
All's Well that Ends Well: still the fine's the crown;
Whate'er the course, the end is the renown.

[Exeunt.

SCENE V.

Rousillon.   A room in the house of the COUNTESS.

Enter COUNTESS, LAFEU, *and* CLOWN.

LAFEU.

NO, no, no, your son was misled with a snipt-taffeta fellow there, whose villainous saffron would have made all the unbaked and doughy youth of a nation in his colour: your daughter-in-law had been alive at this hour, and your son here at home, more advanced by the king than by that red-tail'd humble-bee I speak of.

COUNTESS.

I would he had not known him! it was the death of the most virtuous gentlewoman that ever nature had praise for creating: if she had partaken of my flesh, and cost me the dearest groans of a mother, I could not have owed her a more rooted love.

LAFEU.

'Twas a good lady, 'twas a good lady: we may pick a thousand sallets ere we light on such another herb.

CLOWN.

Indeed, sir, she was the sweet marjoram of the sallet, or rather, the herb of grace.

LAFEU.

They are not sallet-herbs, you knave; they are nose-herbs.

CLOWN.

I am no great Nebuchadnezzar, sir; I have not much skill in grass.

LAFEU.

Whether dost thou profess thyself,—a knave or a fool?

CLOWN.

A fool, sir, at a woman's service, and a knave at a man's.

LAFEU.

Your distinction?

CLOWN.

I would cozen the man of his wife, and do his service.

LAFEU.

So you were a knave at his service, indeed.

CLOWN.

And I would give his wife my bauble, sir, to do her service.

LAFEU.

I will subscribe for thee, thou art both knave and fool.

CLOWN.

At your service.

LAFEU.

No, no, no.

CLOWN.

Why, sir, if I cannot serve you, I can serve as great a prince as you are.

LAFEU.

Who's that? a Frenchman?

CLOWN.

Faith, sir, a' has an English name; but his phisnomy is more hotter in France than there.

LAFEU.

What prince is that?

CLOWN.

The black prince, sir; *alias*, the prince of darkness; *alias*, the devil.

LAFEU.

Hold thee, there's my purse: I give thee not this to suggest thee from thy master thou talk'st of; serve him still.

CLOWN.

I am a woodland fellow, sir, that always loved a great fire; and the master I speak of ever keeps a good fire. But, sure, he is the prince of the world; let his nobility remain in's court. I am for the house with the narrow gate, which I take to be too little for pomp to enter: some that humble themselves may; but the many will be too chill and tender, and they'll be for the flowery way that leads to the broad gate and the great fire.

LAFEU.

Go thy ways, I begin to be a-weary of thee; and I tell thee so before, because I would not fall out with thee. Go thy ways: let my horses be well lookt to, without any tricks.

CLOWN.

If I put any tricks upon 'em, sir, they shall be jades' tricks; which are their own right by the law of nature.   [*Exit.*

LAFEU.

A shrewd knave and an unhappy.

COUNTESS.

So he is. My lord that's gone made himself much sport out of him: by his authority he remains here, which he thinks is a patent for his sauciness; and, indeed, he has no pace, but runs where he will.

LAFEU.

I like him well; 'tis not amiss. And I was about to tell you, since I heard of the good lady's death, and that my lord your son was upon his return home, I moved the king my master to speak in the behalf of my daughter; which, in the minority of them both, his majesty, out of a self-gracious remembrance, did first propose; his highness hath promised me to do it: and, to stop up the displeasure he hath conceived against your son, there is no fitter matter. How does your ladyship like it?

COUNTESS.

With very much content, my lord; and I wish it happily effected.

LAFEU.

His highness comes post from Marseilles, of as able body as when he number'd thirty: he will be here to-morrow, or I am deceived by him that in such intelligence hath seldom fail'd.

COUNTESS.

It rejoices me, that I hope I shall see him ere I die. I have letters that my son will be here to-night: I shall beseech your lordship to remain with me till they meet together.

LAFEU.

Madam, I was thinking with what manners I might safely be admitted.

COUNTESS.

You need but plead your honourable privilege.

LAFEU.

Lady, of that I have made a bold charter; but, I thank my God, it holds yet.

Enter CLOWN.

CLOWN.

O madam, yonder's my lord your son with a patch
of velvet on's face: whether there be a scar under't
or no, the velvet knows: but 'tis a goodly patch of
velvet: his left cheek is a cheek of two pile and a
half, but his right cheek is worn bare.

LAFEU.

A scar nobly got, or a noble scar, is a good livery
of honour; so belike is that.

CLOWN.

But it is your carbonadoed face.

LAFEU.

Let us go see your son, I pray you: I long to talk
with the young noble soldier.

CLOWN.

Faith, there's a dozen of 'em, with delicate fine
hats, and most courteous feathers, which bow the
head and nod at every man.   [*Exeunt.*

ACT V. SCENE I.

Marseilles. A street.

Enter HELENA, WIDOW, *and* DIANA, *with
two* ATTENDANTS.

HELENA.

BUT this exceeding posting day and night
Must wear your spirits low; we cannot help it:
But, since you have made the days and nights as
    one,
To wear your gentle limbs in my affairs,
Be bold you do so grow in my requital
As nothing can unroot you.—In happy time;—

Enter a GENTLE ASTRINGER.

This man may help me to his majesty's ear,
If he would spend his power.—God save you, sir.

GENTLE ASTRINGER.

And you.

HELENA.

Sir, I have seen you in the court of France.

GENTLE ASTRINGER.

I have been sometimes there.

HELENA.

I do presume, sir, that you are not fall'n
From the report that goes upon your goodness;
And therefore, goaded with most sharp occasions,
Which lay nice manners by, I put you to
The use of your own virtues; for the which
I shall continue thankful.

GENTLE ASTRINGER.

    What's your will?

HELENA.

That it will please you
To give this poor petition to the king;
And aid me with that store of power you have
To come into his presence.

GENTLE ASTRINGER.

The king's not here.

HELENA.

Not here, sir!

GENTLE ASTRINGER.

    Not, indeed:
He hence removed last night, and with more
    haste
Than is his use.

WIDOW.

Lord, how we lose our pains!

HELENA.

All's Well that Ends Well yet,
Though time seem so adverse and means unfit.—
I do beseech you, whither is he gone?

GENTLE ASTRINGER.

Marry, as I take it, to Rousillon;
Whither I am going.

HELENA.

    I do beseech you, sir,
Since you are like to see the king before me,
Commend the paper to his gracious hand;
Which, I presume, shall render you no blame,
But rather make you thank your pains for it.
I will come after you with what good speed
Our means will make us means.

GENTLE ASTRINGER.

    This I'll do for you.

HELENA.

And you shall find yourself to be well thankt,
Whate'er falls more.—We must to horse again:—
Go, go, provide.   [*Exeunt.*

SCENE II.

Rousillon. Before the house of the COUNTESS.

Enter CLOWN *and* PAROLLES.

PAROLLES.

GOOD Monsieur Lavache, give my Lord
Lafeu this letter: I have ere now, sir, been
better known to you, when I have held familiarity
with fresher clothes; but I am now, sir, muddied
in Fortune's mood, and smell somewhat strong of
her strong displeasure.

CLOWN.

Truly, Fortune's displeasure is but sluttish, if it
smell so strongly as thou speak'st of: I will henceforth eat no fish of Fortune's buttering. Prithee,
allow the wind.

PAROLLES.

Nay, you need not to stop your nose, sir; I spake
but by a metaphor.

CLOWN.

Indeed, sir, if your metaphor stink, I will stop my
nose; or against any man's metaphor. Prithee, get
thee further.

PAROLLES.

Pray you, sir, deliver me this paper.

CLOWN.

Foh, prithee, stand away: a paper from Fortune's
close-stool to give to a nobleman! Look, here he
comes himself.

Enter LAFEU.

Here is a pur of Fortune's, sir, or of Fortune's
cat,—but not a musk-cat,—that has fall'n into the
unclean fishpond of her displeasure, and, as he
says, is muddied withal: pray you, sir, use the
carp as you may: for he looks like a poor, decay'd,
ingenious, foolish, rascally knave. I do pity his
distress in my similes of comfort, and leave him
to your lordship.   [*Exit.*

PAROLLES.

My lord, I am a man whom Fortune hath cruelly
scratcht.

LAFEU.

And what would you have me to do? 'tis too late
to pare her nails now. Wherein have you play'd
the knave with Fortune, that she should scratch
you, who of herself is a good lady, and would not
have knaves thrive long under her? There's a
cardecu for you: let the justices make you and
Fortune friends; I am for other business.

PAROLLES.

I beseech your honour to hear me one single
word.

LAFEU.

You beg a single penny more: come, you shall
ha't; save your word.

PAROLLES.

My name, my good lord, is Parolles.

LAFEU.

You beg more than 'word,' then.—Cox my passion! give me your hand:—how does your drum?

PAROLLES.

O my good lord, you were the first that found me!

LAFEU.

Was I, in sooth? and I was the first that lost thee.

PAROLLES.

It lies in you, my lord, to bring me in some grace,
for you did bring me out.

LAFEU.

Out upon thee, knave! dost thou put upon me at
once both the office of God and the devil? one
brings thee in grace, and the other brings thee
out. [*Trumpets sound.*] The king's coming; I know
by his trumpets.—Sirrah, inquire further after
me; I had talk of you last night: though you are a
fool and a knave, you shall eat; go to, follow.

PAROLLES.

I praise God for you.   [*Exeunt.*

SCENE III.

The same. A room in the house of the COUNTESS.

Flourish. Enter KING, COUNTESS, LAFEU, *the
two French* LORDS, GENTLEMEN, GUARDS,
&c.

KING.

WE lost a jewel of her; and our esteem
Was made much poorer by it: but your son,
As mad in folly, lackt the sense to know
Her estimation home.

COUNTESS.

          'Tis past, my liege;
And I beseech your majesty to make it
Natural rebellion, done i'the blaze of youth;
When oil and fire, too strong for reason's force,
O'erbears it, and burns on.

KING.

          My honour'd lady,
I have forgiven and forgotten all;
Though my revenges were high-bent upon him,
And watcht the time to shoot.

LAFEU.

          This I must say,—
But first I beg my pardon,—the young lord
Did to his majesty, his mother, and his lady,
Offence of mighty note: but to himself
The greatest wrong of all: he lost a wife,
Whose beauty did astonish the survey

Of richest eyes; whose words all ears took captive;
Whose dear perfection hearts that scorn'd to serve
Humbly call'd mistress.

KING.

          Praising what is lost
Makes the remembrance dear. Well, call him
hither;
We are reconciled, and the first view shall kill
All repetition:—let him not ask our pardon;
The nature of his great offence is dead,
And deeper than oblivion we do bury
Th'incensing reliques of it: let him approach,
A stranger, no offender; and inform him
So 'tis our will he should.

FIRST GENTLEMAN.

          I shall, my liege.   [*Exit.*

KING.

What says he to your daughter? have you spoke?

LAFEU.

All that he is hath reference to your highness.

KING.

Then shall we have a match. I have letters sent me
That sets him high in fame.

Enter BERTRAM, *with* FIRST GENTLEMAN.

LAFEU.

          He looks well on't.

KING.

I am not a day of season,
For thou mayst see a sunshine and a hail
In me at once: but to the brightest beams
Distracted clouds give way; so stand thou forth,
The time is fair again.

BERTRAM.

          My high-repented blames,
Dear sovereign, pardon to me.

KING.

          All is whole;
Not one word more of the consumed time.
Let's take the instant by the forward top;
For we are old, and on our quick'st decrees
Th'inaudible and noiseless foot of Time
Steals ere we can effect them. You remember
The daughter of this lord?

BERTRAM.

          Admiringly, my liege: at first
I stuck my choice upon her, ere my heart
Durst make too bold a herald of my tongue:
Where the impression of mine eye infixing,
Contempt his scornful perspective did lend me,
Which warpt the line of every other favour;
Scorn'd a fair colour, or exprest it stol'n;
Extended or contracted all proportions
To a most hideous object: thence it came
That she whom all men praised, and whom myself,
Since I have lost, have loved, was in mine eye
The dust that did offend it.

KING.

          Well excused:
That thou didst love her, strikes some scores away
From the great compt: but love that comes too
late,
Like a remorseful pardon slowly carried,
To the great sender turns a sour offence,
Crying, 'That's good that's gone.' Our rasher
faults
Make trivial price of serious things we have,

Not knowing them until we know their grave:
Oft our displeasures, to ourselves unjust,
Destroy our friends, and after weep their dust:
Our old love waking cries to see what's done,
While shameful hate sleeps out the afternoon.
Be this sweet Helen's knell, and now forget her.
Send forth your amorous token for fair Maudlin:
The main consents are had; and here we'll stay
To see our widower's second marriage-day.

COUNTESS.

Which better than the first, O dear heaven, bless!
Or, ere they meet, in me, O nature, cesse!

LAFEU.

Come on, my son, in whom my house's name
Must be digested, give a favour from you,
To sparkle in the spirits of my daughter,
That she may quickly come.—
    [BERTRAM *gives a ring to* LAFEU.
            By my old beard,
And every hair that's on't, Helen, that's dead,
Was a sweet creature: such a ring as this,
The last that e'er I took her leave at court,
I saw upon her finger.

BERTRAM.

           Hers it was not.

KING.

Now, pray you, let me see it; for mine eye,
While I was speaking, oft was fasten'd to't.—
This ring was mine, and when I gave it Helen,
I bade her, if her fortunes ever stood
Necessitied to help, that by this token
I would relieve her. Had you that craft, to reave her
Of what should stead her most?

BERTRAM.

          My gracious sovereign,
Howe'er it pleases you to take it so,
The ring was never hers.

COUNTESS.

         Son, on my life,
I have seen her wear it; and she reckon'd it
At her life's rate.

LAFEU.

    I am sure I saw her wear it.

BERTRAM.

You are deceived, my lord; she never saw it:
In Florence was it from a casement thrown me,
Wrapt in a paper, which contain'd the name
Of her that threw it: noble she was, and thought
I stood engaged: but when I had subscribed
To mine own fortune, and inform'd her fully
I could not answer in that course of honour
As she had made the overture, she ceased
In heavy satisfaction, and would never
Receive the ring again.

KING.

         Plutus himself,
That knows the tinct and multiplying medicine,
Hath not in nature's mystery more science
Than I have in this ring: 'twas mine, 'twas Helen's,
Whoever gave it you. Then, if you know
That you are well acquainted with yourself,
Confess 'twas hers, and by what rough enforce-
    ment
You got it from her: she call'd the saints to surety
That she would never put it from her finger,
Unless she gave it to yourself in bed,—

Where you have never come,—or sent it us
Upon her great disaster.

BERTRAM.

        She never saw it.

KING.

Thou speak'st it falsely, as I love mine honour;
And makest conjectural fears to come into me,
Which I would fain shut out. If it should prove
That thou art so inhuman,—'twill not prove so;—
And yet I know not:—thou didst hate her deadly,
And she is dead, which nothing, but to close
Her eyes myself, could win me to believe,
More than to see this ring.—Take him away.—
           [*Guards seize* BERTRAM.
My fore-past proofs, howe'er the matter fall,
Shall tax my fears of little vanity,
Having vainly fear'd too little.—Away with him!—
We'll sift this matter further.

BERTRAM.

         If you shall prove
This ring was ever hers, you shall as easy
Prove that I husbanded her bed in Florence,
Where yet she never was.   [*Exit, guarded.*

KING.

I am wrapt in dismal thinkings.

Enter a GENTLE ASTRINGER.

GENTLE ASTRINGER.

        Gracious sovereign,
Whether I have been to blame or no, I know not:
Here's a petition from a Florentine,
Who hath for four or five removes come short
To tender it herself. I undertook it,
Vanquisht thereto by the fair grace and speech
Of the poor suppliant, who by this, I know,
Is here attending: her business looks in her
With an importing visage; and she told me,
In a sweet verbal brief, it did concern
Your highness with herself.

KING [*reads*].

Upon his many protestations to marry me when
his wife was dead, I blush to say it, he won me.
Now is the Count Rousillon a widower: his vows
are forfeited to me, and my honour's paid to him.
He stole from Florence, taking no leave, and I
follow him to his country for justice: grant it me,
O king! in you it best lies; otherwise a seducer
flourishes, and a poor maid is undone.
               DIANA CAPULET.

LAFEU.

I will buy me a son-in-law in a fair, and toll: for
this, I'll none of him.

KING.

The heavens have thought well on thee, Lafeu,
To bring forth this discov'ry.—Seek these suit-
    ors.—
Go speedily and bring again the count.
  [*Exeunt* GENTLEMAN *and some* ATTENDANTS.
I am afeared the life of Helen, lady,
Was foully snatcht.

COUNTESS.

    Now, justice on the doers!

Enter BERTRAM, *guarded.*

KING.

I wonder, sir, sith wives are monsters to you,
And that you fly them as you swear them lordship,
Yet you desire to marry.

Enter GENTLEMAN, *with* WIDOW *and* DIANA.
                          What woman's that?
DIANA.
I am, my lord, a wretched Florentine,
Derived from the ancient Capulet:
My suit, as I do understand, you know,
And therefore know how far I may be pitied.
WIDOW.
I am her mother, sir, whose age and honour
Both suffer under this complaint we bring;
And both shall cease, without your remedy.
KING.
Come hither, count: do you know these women?
BERTRAM.
My lord, I neither can nor will deny
But that I know them: do they charge me further?
DIANA.
Why do you look so strange upon your wife?
BERTRAM.
She's none of mine, my lord.
DIANA.
                          If you shall marry,
You give away this hand, and that is mine;
You give away heaven's vows, and those are
    mine;
You give away myself, which is known mine;
For I by vow am so embodied yours,
That she which marries you must marry me,—
Either both or none.
LAFEU [*to* BERTRAM].
Your reputation comes too short for my daughter;
you are no husband for her.
BERTRAM.
My lord, this is a fond and desperate creature,
Whom sometime I have laught with: let your
    highness
Lay a more noble thought upon mine honour
Than for to think that I would sink it here.
KING.
Sir, for my thoughts, you have them ill to friend
Till your deeds gain them: fairer prove your hon-
    our
Than in my thought it lies!
DIANA.
                          Good my lord,
Ask him upon his oath, if he does think
He had not my virginity.
KING.
What say'st thou to her?
BERTRAM.
                          She's impudent, my lord,
And was a common gamester to the camp.
DIANA.
He does me wrong, my lord; if I were so,
He might have bought me at a common price:
Do not believe him: O, behold this ring,
Whose high respect and rich validity
Did lack a parallel; yet, for all that,
He gave it to a commoner o'the camp,
If I be one.
COUNTESS.
He blushes, and 'tis his:
Of six preceding ancestors, that gem,
Conferr'd by testament to the sequent issue,
Hath it been owed and worn. This is his wife;
That ring's a thousand proofs.

KING.
                          Methought you said
You saw one here in court could witness it.
DIANA.
I did, my lord, but loth am to produce
So bad an instrument: his name's Parolles.
LAFEU.
I saw the man to-day, if man he be.
KING.
Find him, and bring him hither.
                          [*Exit an* ATTENDANT.
BERTRAM.
                          What of him?
He's quoted for a most perfidious slave,
With all the spots o'the world taxt and debosht;
Whose nature sickens but to speak a truth.
Am I or that or this for what he'll utter,
That will speak any thing?
KING.
                          She hath that ring of yours.
BERTRAM.
I think she has: certain it is I liked her,
And boarded her i'the wanton way of youth:
She knew her distance, and did angle for me,
Madding my eagerness with her restraint,
As all impediments in fancy's course
Are motives of more fancy; and, in fine,
Her infinite cunning, with her modern grace,
Subdued me to her rate: she got the ring;
And I had that which any inferior might
At market-price have bought.
DIANA.
                          I must be patient:
You, that turn'd off a first so noble wife,
May justly diet me. I pray you yet,—
Since you lack virtue, I will lose a husband,—
Send for your ring, I will return it home,
And give me mine again.
BERTRAM.
                          I have it not.
KING.
What ring was yours, I pray you?
DIANA.
                          Sir, much like
The same upon your finger.
KING.
Know you this ring? this ring was his of late.
DIANA.
And this was it I gave him, being a-bed.
KING.
The story, then, goes false, you threw it him
Out of a casement.
DIANA.
                          I have spoke the truth.
BERTRAM.
My lord, I do confess the ring was hers.
KING.
You boggle shrewdly, every feather starts you.—
    Enter PAROLLES, *with* ATTENDANT.
Is this the man you speak of?
DIANA.
                          Ay, my lord.
KING.
Tell me, sirrah,—but tell me true, I charge
    you,
Not fearing the displeasure of your master,

Which, on your just proceeding, I'll keep off,—
By him and by this woman here what know you?

PAROLLES.

So please your majesty, my master hath been an
honourable gentleman: tricks he hath had in him,
which gentlemen have.

KING.

Come, come, to the purpose: did he love this
woman?

PAROLLES.

Faith, sir, he did love her; but how?

KING.

How, I pray you?

PAROLLES.

He did love her, sir, as a gentleman loves a
woman.

KING.

How is that?

PAROLLES.

He loved her, sir, and loved her not.

KING.

As thou art a knave, and no knave.—What an
equivocal companion is this!

PAROLLES.

I am a poor man, and at your majesty's command.

LAFEU.

He's a good drum, my lord, but a naughty orator.

DIANA.

Do you know he promised me marriage?

PAROLLES.

Faith, I know more than I'll speak.

KING.

But wilt thou not speak all thou know'st?

PAROLLES.

Yes, so please your majesty. I did go between
them, as I said; but more than that, he loved her,
—for, indeed, he was mad for her, and talkt of
Satan, and of Limbo, and of Furies, and I know
not what: yet I was in that credit with them at
that time, that I knew of their going to bed; and
of other motions, as promising her marriage, and
things which would derive me ill will to speak of;
therefore I will not speak what I know.

KING.

Thou hast spoken all already, unless thou canst
say they are married; but thou art too fine in thy
evidence; therefore stand aside.—
This ring, you say, was yours?

DIANA.

Ay, my good lord.

KING.

Where did you buy it? or who gave it you?

DIANA.

It was not given me, not I did not buy it.

KING.

Who lent it you?

DIANA.

It was not lent me neither.

KING.

Where did you find it, then?

DIANA.

I found it not.

KING.

If it were yours by none of all these ways,
How could you give it him?

DIANA.

I never gave it him.

LAFEU.

This woman's an easy glove, my lord; she goes off
and on at pleasure.

KING.

This ring was mine; I gave it his first wife.

DIANA.

It might be yours or hers, for aught I know.

KING.

Take her away; I do not like her now;
To prison with her: and away with him.—
Unless thou tell'st me where thou hadst this ring,
Thou diest within this hour.

DIANA.

I'll never tell you.

KING.

Take her away.

DIANA.

I'll put in bail, my liege.

KING.

I think thee now some common customer.

DIANA.

By Jove, if ever I knew man, 'twas you.

KING.

Wherefore hast thou accused him all this while?

DIANA.

Because he's guilty, and he is not guilty:
He knows I am no maid, and he'll swear to't;
I'll swear I am a maid, and he knows not.
Great king, I am no strumpet, by my life;
I'm either maid, or else this old man's wife.
                    [Pointing to LAFEU.

KING.

She does abuse our ears: to prison with her.

DIANA.

Good mother, fetch my bail.—Stay, royal sir:
                    [Exit WIDOW.
The jeweller that owes the ring is sent for,
And he shall surety me. But for this lord,
Who hath abused me, as he knows himself,
Though yet he never harm'd me, here I quit him:
He knows himself my bed he hath defiled;
And at that time he got his wife with child:
Dead though she be, she feels her young one
    kick:
So there's my riddle,—One that's dead is quick:
And now behold the meaning.

Enter WIDOW, with HELENA.

KING.

                    Is there no exorcist
Beguiles the truer office of mine eyes?
Is't real that I see?

HELENA.

                    No, my good lord;
'Tis but the shadow of a wife you see,
The name, and not the thing.

BERTRAM.

                    Both, both:—O, pardon!

HELENA.

O my good lord, when I was like this maid,
I found you wondrous kind. There is your ring;
And, look you, here's your letter; this it says:
'When from my finger you can get this ring,
And are by me with child, &c.' This is done:
Will you be mine, now you are doubly won?

BERTRAM.
If, she, my liege, can make me know this clearly,
I'll love her dearly, ever, ever dearly.
HELENA.
If it appear not plain, and prove untrue,
Deadly divorce step between me and you!—
O my dear mother, do I see you living?
LAFEU.
Mine eyes smell onions; I shall weep anon:—
[to PAROLLES] Good Tom Drum, lend me a
handkercher: so, I thank thee: wait on me home,
I'll make sport with thee: let thy courtesies alone,
they are scurvy ones.
KING.
Let us from point to point this story know,
To make the even truth in pleasure flow.—
[to DIANA] If thou be'st yet a fresh uncropped
flower,

Choose thou thy husband, and I'll pay thy
dower;
For I can guess that, by thy honest aid,
Thou kept'st a wife herself, thyself a maid.—
Of that, and all the progress, more and less,
Resolvedly more leisure shall express:
All yet seems well; and if it end so meet,
The bitter past, more welcome is the sweet.
[Flourish.

EPILOGUE.
Spoken by the KING.
The king's a beggar, now the play is done:
All is well ended, if this suit be won,
That you express content; which we will pay,
With strife to please you, day exceeding day:
Ours be your patience then, and yours our
parts;
Your gentle hands lend us, and take our hearts.
[Exeunt.

MEASURE FOR MEASURE

DRAMATIS PERSONAE

VINCENTIO, *the Duke.*
ANGELO, *the Deputy.*
ESCALUS, *an ancient Lord.*
CLAUDIO, *a young Gentleman.*
LUCIO, *a Fantastic.*
TWO OTHER LIKE GENTLEMEN.
PROVOST.
THOMAS, } *Two Friars.*
PETER,
A JUSTICE.
VARRIUS.
ELBOW, *a simple Constable.*
FROTH, *a foolish Gentleman.*

POMPEY, *servant to Mistress Overdone.*
ABHORSON, *an Executioner.*
BARNARDINE, *a dissolute Prisoner.*

ISABELLA, *sister to Claudio.*
MARIANA, *betrothed to Angelo.*
JULIET, *beloved of Claudio.*
FRANCISCA, *a Nun.*
MISTRESS OVERDONE, *a Bawd.*

LORDS, OFFICERS, CITIZENS, BOY, *and*
ATTENDANTS.

SCENE—*Vienna.*

ACT I. SCENE I.

An apartment in the DUKE'S *palace.*

Enter DUKE, ESCALUS, LORDS, & ATTENDANTS.

DUKE.

Escalus,—

ESCALUS.
My lord?

DUKE.
Of government the properties to unfold,
Would seem in me t'affect speech and discourse;
Since I am put to know that your own science
Exceeds, in that, the lists of all advice
My strength can give you: then no more remains
But that to your sufficiency . . . . .
. . . . as your worth is able,
And let them work. The nature of our people,
Our city's institutions, and the terms
For common justice, you're as pregnant in
As art and practice has enriched any
That we remember. There is our commission,
From which we would not have you warp.—Call
   hither,
I say, bid come before us Angelo.
                          [*Exit an* ATTENDANT.
What figure of us think you he will bear?
For, you must know, we have with special soul
Elected him our absence to supply;
Lent him our terror, dress'd him with our love,
And given his deputation all the organs
Of our own power: what think you of it?

ESCALUS.
If any in Vienna be of worth
To undergo such ample grace and honour,
It is Lord Angelo.

DUKE.
   Look where he comes.

Enter ANGELO.

ANGELO.
Always obedient to your grace's will,
I come to know your pleasure.

DUKE.
                          Angelo,
There is a kind of character in thy life,
That to th'observer doth thy history
Fully unfold. Thyself and thy belongings

Are not thine own so proper, as to waste
Thyself upon thy virtues, they on thee.
Heaven doth with us as we with torches do,
Not light them for themselves; for if our virtues
Did not go forth of us, 'twere all alike
As if we had them not. Spirits are not finely
   touch'd
But to fine issues; nor Nature never lends
The smallest scruple of her excellence
But, like a thrifty goddess, she determines
Herself the glory of a creditor,
Both thanks and use. But I do bend my speech
To one that can my part in him advertise;
Hold, therefore, Angelo:—
In our remove be thou at full ourself;
Mortality and mercy in Vienna
Live in thy tongue and heart: old Escalus,
Though first in question, is thy secondary:—
Take thy commission.

ANGELO.
                  Now, good my lord,
Let there be some more test made of my metal,
Before so noble and so great a figure
Be stamp'd upon it.

DUKE.
                  No more evasion:
We have with a leaven'd and prepared choice
Proceeded to you; therefore take your honours.
Our haste from hence is of so quick condition,
That it prefers itself and leaves unquestion'd
Matters of needful value. We shall write to you,
As time and our concernings shall importune,
How it goes with us; and do look to know
What doth befall you here. So, fare you well:
To th'hopeful execution do I leave you
Of your commissions.

ANGELO.
                  Yet, give leave, my lord,
That we may bring you something on the way.

DUKE.
My haste may not admit it;
Nor need you, on mine honour, have to do
With any scruple: your scope is as mine own,
So to enforce or qualify the laws
As to your soul seems good. Give me your hand:
I'll privily away. I love the people,

786

But do not like to stage me to their eyes:
Though it do well, I do not relish well
Their loud applause and Aves vehement;
Nor do I think the man of safe discretion
That does affect it. Once more, fare you well.

ANGELO.
The heavens give safety to your purposes!—

ESCALUS.
Lead forth and bring you back in happiness!

DUKE.
I thank you. Fare you well.   [Exit.

ESCALUS.
I shall desire you, sir, to give me leave
To have free speech with you; and it concerns
    me
To look into the bottom of my place:
A power I have, but of what strength and nature
I am not yet instructed.

ANGELO.
'Tis so with me. Let us withdraw together,
And we may soon our satisfaction have
Touching that point.

ESCALUS.
         I'll wait upon your honour.
         [Exeunt.

SCENE II.

A street.

Enter LUCIO *and two other* GENTLEMEN.

LUCIO.
IF the duke, with the other dukes, come not to
composition with the King of Hungary, why,
then, all the dukes fall upon the king.

FIRST GENTLEMAN.
Heaven grant us its peace, but not the King of
Hungary's!

SECOND GENTLEMAN.
Amen.

LUCIO.
Thou concludest like the sanctimonious pirate,
that went to sea with the Ten Commandments,
but scraped one out of the table.

SECOND GENTLEMAN.
'Thou shalt not steal'?

LUCIO.
Ay, that he razed.

FIRST GENTLEMAN.
Why, 'twas a commandment to command the
captain and all the rest from their functions: they
put forth to steal. There's not a soldier of us all,
that, in the thanksgiving before meat, do relish the
petition well that prays for peace.

SECOND GENTLEMAN.
I never heard any soldier dislike it.

LUCIO.
I believe thee; for I think thou never wast where
grace was said.

SECOND GENTLEMAN.
No? a dozen times at least.

FIRST GENTLEMAN.
What, in metre?

LUCIO.
In any proportion or in any language.

FIRST GENTLEMAN.
I think, or in any religion.

LUCIO.
Ay, why not? Grace is grace, despite of all controversy: as, for example,—thou thyself art a
wicked villain, despite of all grace.

FIRST GENTLEMAN.
Well, there went but a pair of shears between
us.

LUCIO.
I grant; as there may between the lists and the
velvet. Thou art the list.

FIRST GENTLEMAN.
And thou the velvet: thou art good velvet; thou'rt
a three-piled piece, I warrant thee: I had as lief be
a list of an English kersey, as be piled, as thou art
piled, for a French velvet. Do I speak feelingly
now?

LUCIO.
I think thou dost; and, indeed, with most painful
feeling of thy speech, I will, out of thine own
confession, learn to begin thy health; but, whilst
I live, forget to drink after thee.

FIRST GENTLEMAN.
I think I have done myself wrong, have I not?

SECOND GENTLEMAN.
Yes, that thou hast, whether thou art tainted or
free.

LUCIO.
Behold, behold, where Madam Mitigation comes!

FIRST GENTLEMAN.
I have purchased as many diseases under her roof
as come to—

SECOND GENTLEMAN.
To what, I pray?

FIRST GENTLEMAN.
Judge.

SECOND GENTLEMAN.
To three thousand dolours a year.

FIRST GENTLEMAN.
Ay, and more.

LUCIO.
A French crown more.

FIRST GENTLEMAN.
Thou art always figuring diseases in me; but thou
art full of error,—I am sound.

LUCIO.
Nay, not as one would say, healthy; but so sound
as things that are hollow: thy bones are hollow;
impiety has made a feast of thee.

Enter MISTRESS OVERDONE.

FIRST GENTLEMAN.
How now! which of your hips has the most profound sciatica?

MISTRESS OVERDONE.
Well, well; there's one yonder arrested and
carried to prison was worth five thousand of
you all.

SECOND GENTLEMAN.
Who's that, I pray thee?

MISTRESS OVERDONE.
Marry, sir, that's Claudio, Signior Claudio.

FIRST GENTLEMAN.
Claudio to prison! 'tis not so.

MISTRESS OVERDONE.
Nay, but I know 'tis so: I saw him arrested; saw
him carried away; and, which is more, within
these three days his head to be chopp'd off.

LUCIO.

But, after all this fooling, I would not have it so. Art thou sure of this?

MISTRESS OVERDONE.

I am too sure of it: and it is for getting Madam Julietta with child.

LUCIO.

Believe me, this may be: he promised to meet me two hours since, and he was ever precise in promise-keeping.

SECOND GENTLEMAN.

Besides, you know, it draws something near to the speech we had to such a purpose.

FIRST GENTLEMAN.

But, most of all, agreeing with the proclamation.

LUCIO.

Away! let's go learn the truth of it.

[Exeunt LUCIO and GENTLEMEN.

MISTRESS OVERDONE.

Thus, what with the war, what with the sweat, what with the gallows, and what with poverty, I am custom-shrunk.

Enter POMPEY.

How now! What's the news with you?

POMPEY.

Yonder man is carried to prison.

MISTRESS OVERDONE.

Well: what has he done?

POMPEY.

A woman.

MISTRESS OVERDONE.

But what's his offence?

POMPEY.

Groping for trouts in a peculiar river.

MISTRESS OVERDONE.

What, is there a maid with child by him?

POMPEY.

No, but there's a woman with maid by him. You have not heard of the proclamation, have you?

MISTRESS OVERDONE.

What proclamation, man?

POMPEY.

All houses in the suburbs of Vienna must be pluck'd down.

MISTRESS OVERDONE.

And what shall become of those in the city?

POMPEY.

They shall stand for seed: they had gone down too, but that a wise burgher put in for them.

MISTRESS OVERDONE.

But shall all our houses of resort in the suburbs be pull'd down?

POMPEY.

To the ground, mistress.

MISTRESS OVERDONE.

Why, here's a change indeed in the commonwealth! What shall become of me?

POMPEY.

Come; fear not you: good counsellors lack no clients: though you change your place, you need not change your trade; I'll be your tapster still. Courage! there will be pity taken on you: you that have worn your eyes almost out in the service, you will be consider'd.

MISTRESS OVERDONE.

What's to do here, Thomas Tapster? let's withdraw.

POMPEY.

Here comes Signior Claudio, led by the provost to prison; and there's Madam Juliet. [Exeunt

Enter PROVOST, CLAUDIO, JULIET, and OFFICERS.

CLAUDIO.

Fellow, why dost thou show me thus to th'world? Bear me to prison, where I am committed.

PROVOST.

I do it not in evil disposition, But from Lord Angelo by special charge.

CLAUDIO.

Thus can the demigod Authority Make us pay down for our offence by weight.— The words of heaven;—on whom it will, it will; On whom it will not, so; yet still 'tis just.

Enter LUCIO and two GENTLEMEN.

LUCIO.

Why, how now, Claudio! whence comes this restraint?

CLAUDIO.

From too much liberty, my Lucio, liberty: As surfeit is the father of much fast, So every scope by the immoderate use Turns to restraint. Our natures do pursue, Like rats that ravin down their proper bane, A thirsty evil; and when we drink we die.

LUCIO.

If I could speak so wisely under an arrest, I would send for certain of my creditors: and yet, to say the truth, I had as lief have the foppery of freedom as the morality of imprisonment.—What's thy offence, Claudio?

CLAUDIO.

What but to speak of would offend again.

LUCIO.

What, is't murder?

CLAUDIO.

No.

LUCIO.

Lechery?

CLAUDIO.

Call it so.

PROVOST.

Away, sir! you must go.

CLAUDIO.

One word, good friend.—Lucio, a word with you.

[Takes him aside.

LUCIO.

A hundred, if they'll do you any good.— Is lechery so look'd after?

CLAUDIO.

Thus stands it with me:—upon a true contract I got possession of Julietta's bed: You know the lady; she is fast my wife, Save that we do the denunciation lack Of outward order: this we came not to, Only for propagation of a dower Remaining in the coffer of her friends; From whom we thought it meet to hide our love Till time had made them for us. But it chances The stealth of our most mutual entertainment With character too gross is writ on Juliet.

LUCIO.

With child, perhaps?

CLAUDIO.

Unhappily, even so.

And the new deputy now for the duke,—
Whether it be the fault and glimpse of newness,
Or whether that the body public be
A horse whereon the governor doth ride,
Who, newly in the seat, that it may know
He can command, lets it straight feel the spur;
Whether the tyranny be in his place,
Or in his eminence that fills it up,
I stagger in:—but this new governor
Awakes me all the enrolled penalties
Which have, like unscour'd armour, hung by the
    wall
So long, that nineteen zodiacs have gone round,
And none of them been worn; and, for a name,
Now puts the drowsy and neglected act
Freshly on me:—'tis surely for a name.

LUCIO.

I warrant it is: and thy head stands so tickle on thy
shoulders, that a milkmaid, if she be in love, may
sigh it off. Send after the duke, and appeal to him.

CLAUDIO.

I have done so, but he's not to be found.
I prithee, Lucio, do me this kind service:—
This day my sister should the cloister enter.
And there receive her approbation:
Acquaint her with the danger of my state;
Implore her, in my voice, that she make friends
To the strict deputy; bid herself assay him:
I have great hope in that; for in her youth
There is a prone and speechless dialect,
Such as move men; beside, she hath prosperous art
When she will play with reason and discourse,
And well she can persuade.

LUCIO.

I pray she may; as well for the encouragement of
the like, which else would stand under grievous
imposition, as for the enjoying of thy life, who I
would be sorry should be thus foolishly lost at a
game of tick-tack. I'll to her.

CLAUDIO.

I thank you, good friend Lucio.

LUCIO.

Within two hours.

CLAUDIO.

Come, officer, away! [*Exeunt.*

SCENE III.

A monastery.

Enter DUKE *and* FRIAR THOMAS.

DUKE.

NO, holy father; throw away that thought;
    Believe not that the dribbling dart of love
Can pierce a complete bosom. Why I desire thee
To give me secret harbour, hath a purpose
More grave and wrinkled than the aims and ends
Of burning youth.

FRIAR THOMAS.

May your grace speak of it?

DUKE.

My holy sir, none better knows than you
How I have ever loved the life removed;

And held in idle price to haunt assemblies,
Where youth, and cost, and witless bravery keeps.
I have deliver'd to Lord Angelo—
A man of stricture and firm abstinence—
My absolute power and place here in Vienna,
And he supposes me travell'd to Poland;
For so I have strew'd it in the common ear,
And so it is received. Now, pious sir,
You will demand of me why I do this?

FRIAR THOMAS.

Gladly, my lord.

DUKE.

We have strict statutes and most biting laws,—
The needful bits and curbs to headstrong wills,—
Which for this fourteen years we have let slip;
Even like an o'ergrown lion in a cave,
That goes not out to prey. Now, as fond fathers,
Having bound up the threat'ning twigs of birch,
Only to stick it in their children's sight
For terror, not to use, in time the rod
Becomes more mock'd than fear'd; so our decrees,
Dead to infliction, to themselves are dead;
And liberty plucks justice by the nose;
The baby beats the nurse, and quite athwart
Goes all decorum.

FRIAR THOMAS.

It rested in your grace
To unloose this tied-up justice when you pleased:
And it in you more dreadful would have seem'd
Than in Lord Angelo.

DUKE.

I do fear, too dreadful:
Sith 'twas my fault to give the people scope,
'Twould be my tyranny to strike and gall them
For what I bid them do: for we bid this be done,
When evil deeds have their permissive pass,
And not the punishment. Therefore, indeed, my
    father,
I have on Angelo imposed the office,
Who may, in th'ambush of my name, strike
    home;
And yet my nature never in the fight
To do it slander. And to behold his sway,
I will, as 'twere a brother of your order,
Visit both prince and people: therefore, I prithee,
Supply me with the habit, and instruct me
How I may formally in person bear me
Like a true friar. Moe reasons for this action
At our more leisure shall I render you;
Only, this one:—Lord Angelo is precise;
Stands at a guard with envy; scarce confesses
That his blood flows, or that his appetite
Is more to bread than stone: hence shall we see,
If power change purpose, what our seemers be.
[*Exeunt.*

SCENE IV.

A nunnery.

Enter ISABELLA *and* FRANCISCA, *a* NUN.

ISABELLA.

AND have you nuns no further privileges?

FRANCISCA.

Are not these large enough?

ISABELLA.

Yes, truly: I speak not as desiring more;

But rather wishing a more strict restraint
Upon the sisterhood, the votarists of Saint
  Clare.

LUCIO [*within*].
Ho! Peace be in this place!

ISABELLA.
             Who's that which calls?

FRANCISCA.
It is a man's voice. Gentle Isabella,
Turn you the key, and know his business of him;
You may, I may not; you are yet unsworn.
When you have vow'd, you must not speak with
  men
But in the presence of the prioress:
Then, if you speak, you must not show your face;
Or, if you show your face, you must not speak.
He calls again; I pray you, answer him.   [*Exit*.

ISABELLA.
Peace and prosperity! Who is't that calls?

Enter LUCIO.

LUCIO.
Hail, virgin, if you be, as those cheek-roses
Proclaim you are no less! Can you so stead me
As bring me to the sight of Isabella,
A novice of this place, and the fair sister
To her unhappy brother Claudio?

ISABELLA.
Why 'her unhappy brother'? let me ask;
The rather, for I now must make you know
I am that Isabella and his sister.

LUCIO.
Gentle and fair, your brother kindly greets you:
Not to be weary with you, he's in prison.

ISABELLA.
Woe me! for what?

LUCIO.
For that which, if myself might be his judge,
He should receive his punishment in thanks:
He hath got his friend with child.

ISABELLA.
Sir, make me not your story.

LUCIO.
                'Tis true.
I would not—though 'tis my familiar sin
With maids to seem the lapwing, and to jest,
Tongue far from heart—play with all virgins so:
I hold you as a thing ensky'd and sainted;
By your renouncement, an immortal spirit;
And to be talk'd with in sincerity,
As with a saint.

ISABELLA.
You do blaspheme the good in mocking me.

LUCIO.
Do not believe it. Fewness and truth, 'tis thus:—
Your brother and his lover have embraced:
As those that feed grow full; as blossoming-time,
That from the seedness the bare fallow brings
To teeming foison; even so her plenteous womb
Expresseth his full tilth and husbandry.

ISABELLA.
Some one with child by him?—My cousin Juliet?

LUCIO.
Is she your cousin?

ISABELLA.
Adoptedly; as school-maids change their names
By vain, though apt, affection.

LUCIO.
               She it is.

ISABELLA.
O, let him marry her.

LUCIO.
             This is the point.
The duke is very strangely gone from hence;
Bore many gentlemen, myself being one,
In hand, and hope of action: but we do learn
By those that know the very nerves of state,
His givings-out were of an infinite distance
From his true-meant design. Upon his place,
And with full line of his authority,
Governs Lord Angelo; a man whose blood
Is very snow-broth; one who never feels
The wanton stings and motions of the sense,
But doth rebate and blunt his natural edge
With profits of the mind, study and fast.
He—to give fear to use and liberty,
Which have for long run by the hideous law,
As mice by lions—hath pick'd out an act,
Under whose heavy sense your brother's life
Falls into forfeit: he arrests him on it;
And follows close the rigour of the statute,
To make him an example. All hope is gone,
Unless you have the grace by your fair prayer
To soften Angelo: and that's my pith
Of business 'twixt you and your poor brother.

ISABELLA.
Doth he so seek his life?

LUCIO.
              Has censured him
Already; and, as I hear, the provost hath
A warrant for his execution.

ISABELLA.
Alas, what poor ability's in me
To do him good!

LUCIO.
           Assay the power you have.

ISABELLA.
My power! Alas, I doubt,—

LUCIO.
            Our doubts are traitors
And make us lose the good we oft might win
By fearing to attempt. Go to Lord Angelo,
And let him learn to know, when maidens
  sue,
Men give like gods; but when they weep and
  kneel,
All their petitions are as freely theirs
As they themselves would owe them.

ISABELLA.
I'll see what I can do.

LUCIO.
           But speedily.

ISABELLA.
I will about it straight;
No longer staying but to give the mother
Notice of my affair. I humbly thank you:
Commend me to my brother: soon at night
I'll send him certain word of my success.

LUCIO.
I take my leave of you.

ISABELLA.
          Good sir, adieu.   [*Exeunt*.

ACT II. SCENE I.

A hall in ANGELO'S *house.*

Enter ANGELO, ESCALUS, *a* JUSTICE, PROVOST, OFFICERS, *and other* ATTENDANTS.

ANGELO.

WE must not make a scarecrow of the law,
  Setting it up to fear the birds of prey,
And let it keep one shape, till custom make it
Their perch, and not their terror.

ESCALUS.
                            Ay, but yet
Let us be keen, and rather cut a little,
Than fall, and bruise to death. Alas, this gentleman,
Whom I would save, had a most noble father!
Let but your honour know,—
Whom I believe to be most strait in virtue,—
That, in the working of your own affections,
Had time cohered with place, or place with wishing,
Or that the resolute acting of your blood
Could have attain'd th'effect of your own purpose,
Whether you had not sometime in your life
Err'd in this point which now you censure him,
And pull'd the law upon you.

ANGELO.
'Tis one thing to be tempted, Escalus,
Another thing to fall. I not deny,
The jury, passing on the prisoner's life,
May in the sworn twelve have a thief or two
Guiltier than him they try. What's open made to justice,
That justice seizes: what know the laws
That thieves do pass on thieves? 'Tis very pregnant,
The jewel that we find, we stoop and take't,
Because we see it; but what we do not see
We tread upon, and never think of it.
You may not so extenuate his offence
For I have had such faults; but rather tell me,
When I, that censure him, do so offend,
Let mine own judgement pattern out my death,
And nothing come in partial. Sir, he must die.

ESCALUS.
Be it as your wisdom will.

ANGELO.
                    Where is the provost?

PROVOST.
Here, if it like your honour.

ANGELO.
                    See that Claudio
Be executed by nine to-morrow morning:
Bring him his confessor, let him be prepared;
For that's the utmost of his pilgrimage.
                            [*Exit* PROVOST.

ESCALUS [*aside*].
Well, heaven forgive him! and forgive us all!
Some rise by sin, and some by virtue fall;
Some run from brakes of vice, and answer none;
And some condemned for a fault alone.

Enter ELBOW, *and* OFFICERS *with* FROTH *and*
POMPEY.

ELBOW.
Come, bring them away: if these be good people
in a commonweal that do nothing but use their abuses in common houses, I know no law: bring them away.

ANGELO.
How now, sir! What's your name? and what's the matter?

ELBOW.
If it please your honour, I am the poor duke's constable, and my name is Elbow: I do lean upon justice, sir, and do bring in here before your good honour two notorious benefactors.

ANGELO.
Benefactors! Well; what benefactors are they? are they not malefactors?

ELBOW.
If it please your honour, I know not well what they are: but precise villains they are, that I am sure of; and void of all profanation in the world that good Christians ought to have.

ESCALUS.
This comes off well; here's a wise officer.

ANGELO.
Go to:—what quality are they of? Elbow is your name? why dost thou not speak, Elbow?

POMPEY.
He cannot, sir; he's out at elbow.

ANGELO.
What are you, sir?

ELBOW.
He, sir! a tapster, sir; parcel-bawd; one that serves a bad woman; whose house, sir, was, as they say, pluck'd down in the suburbs; and now she professes a hot-house, which, I think, is a very ill house too.

ESCALUS.
How know you that?

ELBOW.
My wife, sir, whom I detest before heaven and your honour,—

ESCALUS.
How! thy wife!

ELBOW.
Ay, sir,—whom, I thank heaven, is an honest woman,—

ESCALUS.
Dost thou detest her therefore?

ELBOW.
I say, sir, I will detest myself also, as well as she, that this house, if it be not a bawd's house, it is pity of her life, for it is a naughty house.

ESCALUS.
How dost thou know that, constable?

ELBOW.
Marry, sir, by my wife; who, if she had been a woman cardinally given, might have been accused in fornication, adultery, and all uncleanliness there.

ESCALUS.
By the woman's means?

ELBOW.
Ay, sir, by Mistress Overdone's means: but as she spit in his face, so she defied him.

POMPEY.
Sir, if it please your honour, this is not so.

ELBOW.
Prove it before these varlets here, thou honourable man; prove it.

ESCALUS [*to* ANGELO].

Do you hear how he misplaces?

POMPEY.

Sir, she came in great with child; and longing—saving your honour's reverence—for stew'd prunes. Sir, we had but two in the house, which at that very distant time stood, as it were, in a fruit-dish, a dish of some three-pence;—your honours have seen such dishes; they are not China dishes, but very good dishes,—

ESCALUS.

Go to, go to: no matter for the dish, sir.

POMPEY.

No, indeed, sir, not of a pin; you are therein in the right:—but to the point. As I say, this Mistress Elbow, being, as I say, with child, and being great-bellied, and longing, as I said, for prunes; and having but two in the dish, as I said, Master Froth here, this very man, having eaten the rest, as I said, and, as I say, paying for them very honestly;—for, as you know, Master Froth, I could not give you three-pence again,—

FROTH.

No, indeed.

POMPEY.

Very well;—you being then, if you be re-member'd, cracking the stones of the aforesaid prunes,—

FROTH.

Ay, so I did indeed.

POMPEY.

Why, very well;—I telling you then, if you be remember'd, that such a one and such a one were past cure of the thing you wot of, unless they kept very good diet, as I told you,—

FROTH.

All this is true.

POMPEY.

Why, very well, then,—

ESCALUS.

Come, you are a tedious fool: to the purpose. What was done to Elbow's wife, that he hath cause to complain of? Come me to what was done to her.

POMPEY.

Sir, your honour cannot come to that yet.

ESCALUS.

No, sir, nor I mean it not.

POMPEY.

Sir, but you shall come to it, by your honour's leave. And, I beseech you, look into Master Froth here, sir; a man of fourscore pound a year; whose father died at Hallowmas:—was't not at Hallowmas, Master Froth?—

FROTH.

All-hallond eve.

POMPEY.

Why, very well; I hope here be truths. He, sir, sitting, as I say, in a lower chair, sir;—'twas in the Bunch of Grapes, where, indeed, you have a delight to sit, have you not?—

FROTH.

I have so; because it is an open room, and good for winter.

POMPEY.

Why, very well, then; I hope here be truths.

ANGELO.

This will last out a night in Russia,

When nights are longest there: I'll take my leave,

And leave you to the hearing of the cause;

Hoping you'll find good cause to whip them all.

ESCALUS.

I think no less. Good morrow to your lordship.

[*Exit* ANGELO.

Now, sir, come on: what was done to Elbow's wife, once more?

POMPEY.

Once, sir! there was nothing done to her once.

ELBOW.

I beseech you, sir, ask him what this man did to my wife.

POMPEY.

I beseech your honour, ask me.

ESCALUS.

Well, sir; what did this gentleman to her?

POMPEY.

I beseech you, sir, look in this gentleman's face. —Good Master Froth, look upon his honour; 'tis for a good purpose.—Doth your honour mark his face?

ESCALUS.

Ay, sir, very well.

POMPEY.

Nay, I beseech you, mark it well.

ESCALUS.

Well, I do so.

POMPEY.

Doth your honour see any harm in his face?

ESCALUS.

Why, no.

POMPEY.

I'll be supposed upon a book, his face is the worst thing about him. Good, then; if his face be the worst thing about him, how could Master Froth do the constable's wife any harm? I would know that of your honour.

ESCALUS.

He's in the right.—Constable, what say you to it?

ELBOW.

First, an it like you, the house is a respected house; next, this is a respected fellow; and his mistress is a respected woman.

POMPEY.

By this hand, sir, his wife is a more respected person than any of us all.

ELBOW.

Varlet, thou liest; thou liest, wicked varlet! the time is yet to come, that she was ever respected with man, woman, or child.

POMPEY.

Sir, she was respected with him before he married with her.

ESCALUS.

Which is the wiser here? Justice or Iniquity?—Is this true?

ELBOW.

O thou caitiff! O thou varlet! O thou wicked Hannibal! I respected with her before I was married to her!—If ever I was respected with her, or she with me, let not your worship think me the poor duke's officer.—Prove this, thou wicked Hanniba', or I'll have mine action of battery on thee.

ESCALUS.

If he took you a box o'th'ear, you might have your action of slander too.

ELBOW.

Marry, I thank your good worship for it.—What is't your worship's pleasure I shall do with this wicked caitiff?

ESCALUS.

Truly, officer, because he hath some offences in him that thou wouldst discover if thou couldst, let him continue in his courses till thou know'st what they are.

ELBOW.

Marry, I thank your worship for it.—Thou seest, thou wicked varlet, now, what's come upon thee: thou art to continue now, thou varlet; thou art to continue.

ESCALUS [to FROTH].

Where were you born, friend?

FROTH.

Here in Vienna, sir.

ESCALUS.

Are you of fourscore pounds a year?

FROTH.

Yes, an't please you, sir.

ESCALUS.

So.—[to POMPEY] What trade are you of, sir?

POMPEY.

A tapster; a poor widow's tapster.

ESCALUS.

Your mistress' name?

POMPEY.

Mistress Overdone.

ESCALUS.

Hath she had any more than one husband?

POMPEY.

Nine, sir; Overdone by the last.

ESCALUS.

Nine!—Come hither to me, Master Froth. Master Froth, I would not have you acquainted with tapsters: they will draw you, Master Froth, and you will hang them. Get you gone, and let me hear no more of you.

FROTH.

I thank your worship. For mine own part, I never come into any room in a taphouse, but I am drawn in.

ESCALUS.

Well, no more of it, Master Froth: farewell. [Exit FROTH.] Come you hither to me, master tapster. What's your name, master tapster?

POMPEY.

Pompey.

ESCALUS.

What else?

POMPEY.

Bum, sir.

ESCALUS.

Troth, and your bum is the greatest thing about you; so that, in the beastliest sense, you are Pompey the Great. Pompey, you are partly a bawd, Pompey, howsoever you colour it in being a tapster. Are you not? come, tell me true: it shall be the better for you.

POMPEY.

Truly, sir, I am a poor fellow that would live.

ESCALUS.

How would you live, Pompey? by being a bawd? What do you think of the trade, Pompey? is it a lawful trade?

POMPEY.

If the law would allow it, sir.

ESCALUS.

But the law will not allow it, Pompey; nor it shall not be allow'd in Vienna.

POMPEY.

Does your worship mean to geld and splay all the youth of the city?

ESCALUS.

No, Pompey.

POMPEY.

Truly, sir, in my poor opinion, they will to't, then. If your worship will take order for the drabs and the knaves, you need not to fear the bawds.

ESCALUS.

There is pretty orders beginning, I can tell you: it is but heading and hanging.

POMPEY.

If you head and hang all that offend that way but for ten year together, you'll be glad to give out a commission for more heads: if this law hold in Vienna ten year, I'll rent the fairest house in it after three-pence a bay: if you live to see this come to pass, say Pompey told you so.

ESCALUS.

Thank you, good Pompey; and, in requital of your prophecy, hark you:—I advise you, let me not find you before me again upon any complaint whatsoever; no, not for dwelling where you do: if I do, Pompey, I shall beat you to your tent, and prove a shrewd Cæsar to you; in plain dealing, Pompey, I shall have you whipt: so, for this time, Pompey, fare you well.

POMPEY.

I thank your worship for your good counsel.— [aside] But I shall follow it as the flesh and fortune shall better determine.

Whip me? No, no; let carman whip his jade:
The valiant's heart's not whipt out of his trade.
[Exit.

ESCALUS.

Come hither to me, Master Elbow; come hither, master constable. How long have you been in this place of constable?

ELBOW.

Seven year and a half, sir.

ESCALUS.

I thought, by your readiness in the office, you had continued in it some time. You say, seven years together?

ELBOW.

And a half, sir.

ESCALUS.

Alas, it hath been great pains to you! They do you wrong to put you so oft upon't: are there not men in your ward sufficient to serve it?

ELBOW.

Faith, sir, few of any wit in such matters: as they are chosen, they are glad to choose me for them; I do it for some piece of money, and go through with all.

ESCALUS.
Look you bring me in the names of some six or
seven, the most sufficient of your parish.
ELBOW.
To your worship's house, sir?
ESCALUS.
To my house. Fare you well.   [*Exit* ELBOW.
What's o'clock, think you?
JUSTICE.
Eleven, sir.
ESCALUS.
I pray you home to dinner with me.
JUSTICE.
I humbly thank you.
ESCALUS.
It grieves me for the death of Claudio;
But there's no remedy.
JUSTICE.
Lord Angelo is severe.
ESCALUS.
    It is but needful:
Mercy is not itself, that oft looks so;
Pardon is still the nurse of second woe:
But yet,—poor Claudio!—There is no remedy.—
Come, sir.   [*Exeunt.*

SCENE II.
Another room in the same.
Enter PROVOST *and a* SERVANT.
SERVANT.
HE'S hearing of a cause; he will come straight:
I'll tell him of you.
PROVOST.
    Pray you, do. [*Exit* SERVANT.] I'll know
His pleasure; may be he will relent. Alas,
He hath but as offended in a dream!
All sects, all ages smack of this vice; and he
To die for't!
Enter ANGELO.
ANGELO.
Now, what's the matter, provost?
PROVOST.
Is it your will Claudio shall die to-morrow?
ANGELO.
Did not I tell thee yea? hadst thou not order?
Why dost thou ask again?
PROVOST.
    Lest I might be too rash:
Under your good correction, I have seen,
When, after execution, judgement hath
Repented o'er his doom.
ANGELO.
    Go to; let that be mine:
Do you your office, or give up your place,
And you shall well be spared.
PROVOST.
    I crave your honour's pardon.—
What shall be done, sir, with the groaning Juliet?
She's very near her hour.
ANGELO.
    Dispose of her
To some more fitter place; and that with speed.
Enter SERVANT.
SERVANT.
Here is the sister of the man condemn'd
Desires access to you.

ANGELO.
    Hath he a sister?
PROVOST.
Ay, my good lord; a very virtuous maid,
And to be shortly of a sisterhood,
If not already.
ANGELO.
    Well, let her be admitted. [*Exit* SERVANT.
See you the fornicatress be removed:
Let her have needful, but not lavish, means;
There shall be order for't.
Enter ISABELLA *and* LUCIO.
PROVOST.
    'Save your honour!
ANGELO.
Stay a little while.—[*to* ISABELLA.] You're wel-
come: what's your will?
ISABELLA.
I am a woeful suitor to your honour,
Please but your honour hear me.
ANGELO.
    Well; what's your suit?
ISABELLA.
There is a vice that most I do abhor,
And most desire should meet the blow of justice;
For which I would not plead, but that I must;
For which I must not plead, but that I am
At war 'twixt *will* and *will not*.
ANGELO.
    Well; the matter?
ISABELLA.
I have a brother is condemn'd to die:
I do beseech you, let it be his fault,
And not my brother.
PROVOST [*aside*].
    Heaven give thee moving graces!
ANGELO.
Condemn the fault, and not the actor of it?
Why, every fault's condemn'd ere it be done:
Mine were the very cipher of a function,
To fine the faults, whose fine stands in record,
And let go by the actor.
ISABELLA.
    O just but severe law!
I had a brother, then.—Heaven keep your honour!
LUCIO [*aside to* ISABELLA].
Give't not o'er so: to him again, entreat him;
Kneel down before him, hang upon his gown:
You are too cold; if you should need a pin,
You could not with more tame a tongue desire it:
To him, I say.
ISABELLA.
Must he needs die?
ANGELO.
    Maiden, no remedy.
ISABELLA.
Yes; I do think that you might pardon him,
And neither heaven nor man grieve at the mercy.
ANGELO.
I will not do't.
ISABELLA.
    But can you, if you would?
ANGELO.
Look, what I will not, that I cannot do.
ISABELLA.
But might you do't, and do the world no wrong,

If so your heart were touch'd with that remorse
As mine is to him.

ANGELO.
He's sentenced; 'tis too late.

LUCIO [*aside to* ISABELLA].
You are too cold.

ISABELLA.
Too late! why, no; I, that do speak a word,
May call it back again. Well, believe this,
No ceremony that to great ones 'longs,
Not the king's crown nor the deputed sword,
The marshal's truncheon nor the judge's robe,
Become them with one half so good a grace
As mercy does.
If he had been as you, and you as he,
You would have slipp'd like him; but he, like you,
Would not have been so stern.

ANGELO.
Pray you, be gone.

ISABELLA.
I would to heaven I had your potency,
And you were Isabel! should it then be thus?
No; I would tell what 'twere to be a judge,
And what a prisoner.

LUCIO [*aside to* ISABELLA].
Ay, touch him; there's the vein.

ANGELO.
Your brother is a forfeit of the law,
And you but waste your words.

ISABELLA.
Alas, alas!
Why, all the souls that were were forfeit once;
And He that might the vantage best have took
Found out the remedy. How would you be,
If He, which is the top of judgement, should
But judge you as you are? O, think on that;
And mercy then will breathe within your lips,
Like man new-made.

ANGELO.
Be you content, fair maid;
It is the law, not I, condemn your brother:
Were he my kinsman, brother, or my son,
It should be thus with him:—he must die to-
morrow.

ISABELLA.
To-morrow! O, that's sudden! Spare him, spare
him!—
He's not prepared for death. Even for our kitch-
ens
We kill the fowl of season: shall we serve heaven
With less respect than we do minister
To our gross selves? Good, good my lord, bethink
you;
Who is it that hath died for this offence?
There's many have committed it.

LUCIO [*aside to* ISABELLA].
Ay, well said.

ANGELO.
The law hath not been dead, though it hath slept:
Those many had not dared to do that evil,
If that the first that did th'edict infringe
Had answer'd for his deed: now 'tis awake,
Takes note of what is done; and, like a prophet,
Looks in a glass, that shows what future evils,—
Either new, or by remissness new-conceived,
And so in progress to be hatch'd and born,—

Are now to have no successive degrees,
But, ere they live, to end.

ISABELLA.
Yet show some pity.

ANGELO.
I show it most of all when I show justice;
For then I pity those I do not know,
Which a dismiss'd offence would after gall;
And do him right that, answering one foul wrong
Lives not to act another. Be satisfied;
Your brother dies to-morrow; be content.

ISABELLA.
So you must be the first that gives this sentence,
And he that suffers. O, it is excellent
To have a giant's strength; but it is tyrannous
To use it like a giant.

LUCIO [*aside to* ISABELLA].
That's well said.

ISABELLA.
Could great men thunder
As Jove himself does, Jove would ne'er be quiet,
For every pelting, petty officer
Would use his heaven for thunder. Nothing but
thunder!
Merciful Heaven,
Thou rather with thy sharp and sulphurous bolt
Splitt'st the unwedgeable and gnarled oak
Than the soft myrtle: but man, proud man,
Drest in a little brief authority,—
Most ignorant of what he's most assured,
His glassy essence,—like an angry ape,
Plays such fantastic tricks before high heaven
As make the angels weep; who, with our spleens,
Would all themselves laugh mortal.

LUCIO [*aside to* ISABELLA].
O, to him, to him, wench! he will relent;
He's coming; I perceive't.

PROVOST [*aside*].
Pray heaven she win him!

ISABELLA.
We cannot weigh our brother with ourself:
Great men may jest with saints; 'tis wit in them,
But in the less foul profanation.

LUCIO [*aside to* ISABELLA].
Thou'rt i'the right, girl; more o' that.

ISABELLA.
That in the captain's but a choleric word,
Which in the soldier is flat blasphemy.

LUCIO [*aside to* ISABELLA].
Art avised o' that? more on't.

ANGELO.
Why do you put these sayings upon me?

ISABELLA.
Because authority, though it err like others,
Hath yet a kind of medicine in itself,
That skins the vice o'the top. Go to your bosom;
Knock there, and ask your heart what it doth
know
That's like my brother's fault: if it confess
A natural guiltiness such as is his,
Let it not sound a thought upon your tongue
Against my brother's life.

ANGELO [*aside*].
She speaks, and 'tis
Such sense, that my sense breeds with't.—Fare
you well.

ISABELLA.
Gentle my lord, turn back.
ANGELO.
I will bethink me: come again to-morrow.
ISABELLA.
Hark how I'll bribe you: good my lord, turn back.
ANGELO.
How! bribe me!
ISABELLA.
Ay, with such gifts that heaven shall share with
you.
LUCIO [aside to ISABELLA].
You had marr'd all else.
ISABELLA.
Not with fond shekels of the tested gold,
Or stones, whose rates are either rich or poor
As fancy values them; but with true prayers,
That shall be up at heaven and enter there
Ere sun-rise,—prayers from preserved souls,
From fasting maids, whose minds are dedicate
To nothing temporal.
ANGELO.
Well; come to me to-morrow.
LUCIO [aside to ISABELLA].
Go to; 'tis well; away!
ISABELLA.
Heaven keep your honour safe!
ANGELO [aside].
Amen; for I
Am that way going to temptation,
Where prayers cross.
ISABELLA.
At what hour to-morrow
Shall I attend your lordship?
ANGELO.
At any time 'fore noon?
ISABELLA.
Save you honour!
[Exeunt ISABELLA, LUCIO, and PROVOST.
ANGELO.
From thee,—even from thy virtue!—
What's this, what's this? Is this her fault or mine?
The tempter or the tempted, who sins most, ha?
Not she; nor doth she tempt: but it is I
That, lying by the violet in the sun,
Do as the carrion does, not as the flower,
Corrupt with virtuous season. Can it be
That modesty may more betray our sense
Than woman's lightness? Having waste ground
enough,
Shall we desire to raze the sanctuary,
And pitch our evils there? O, fie, fie, fie!
What dost thou, or what art thou, Angelo?
Dost thou desire her foully for those things
That make her good? O, let her brother live:
Thieves for their robbery have authority
When judges steal themselves. What, do I love
her,
That I desire to hear her speak again,
And feast upon her eyes? What is't I dream on?
O cunning enemy, that, to catch a saint,
With saints dost bait thy hook! Most dangerous
Is that temptation that doth goad us on
To sin in loving virtue: never could the strumpet,
With all her double vigour, art and nature,
Once stir my temper; but this virtuous maid

Subdues me quite:—ever till now,
When men were fond, I smiled, and wonder'd
how.   [Exit.

SCENE III.
A prison.

Enter, severally, DUKE *disguised as a friar, and*
PROVOST.

DUKE.
HAIL to you, provost!—so I think you are.
PROVOST.
I am the provost. What's your will, good friar?
DUKE.
Bound by my charity and my blest order,
I come to visit the afflicted spirits
Here in the prison. Do me the common right
To let me see them, and to make me know
The nature of their crimes, that I may minister
To them accordingly.
PROVOST.
I would do more than that, if more were needful.
Look, here comes one,—a gentlewoman of mine,
Who, falling in the flaws of her own youth,
Hath blister'd her report: she is with child;
And he that got it, sentenced,— a young man
More fit to do another such offence
Than die for this.
Enter JULIET.
DUKE.
When must he die?
PROVOST.
As I do think, to-morrow.—
[to JULIET.] I have provided for you: stay awhile,
And you shall be conducted.
DUKE.
Repent you, fair one, of the sin you carry?
JULIET.
I do; and bear the shame most patiently.
DUKE.
I'll teach you how you shall arraign your con-
science,
And try your penitence, if it be sound,
Or hollowly put on.
JULIET.
I'll gladly learn.
DUKE.
Love you the man that wrong'd you?
JULIET.
Yes, as I love the woman that wrong'd him.
DUKE.
So, then, it seems your most offenceful act
Was mutually committed?
JULIET.
Mutually.
DUKE.
Then was your sin of heavier kind than his.
JULIET.
I do confess it, and repent it, father.
DUKE.
'Tis meet so, daughter: but lest you do repent,
As that the sin hath brought you to this shame,—
Which sorrow is always toward ourselves, not
heaven,
Showing we would not spare heaven as we love it,
But as we stand in fear,—

JULIET.
I do repent me, as it is an evil,
And take the shame with joy.
DUKE.
There rest.
Your partner, as I hear, must die to-morrow,
And I am going with instruction to him.
Grace go with you! *Benedicite!*   [*Exit.*
JULIET.
Must die to-morrow! O injurious law,
That respites me a life, whose very comfort
Is still a dying horror!
PROVOST.
'Tis pity of him.   [*Exeunt.*

SCENE IV.

ANGELO'S *house.*

Enter ANGELO.

ANGELO.

WHEN I would pray and think, I think and
pray
To several subjects. Heaven hath my empty
words;
Whilst my invention, hearing not my tongue,
Anchors on Isabel: Heaven in my mouth,
As if I did but only chew his name;
And in my heart the strong and swelling evil
Of my conception. The state, whereon I studied,
Is like a good thing, being often read,
Grown sear'd and tedious; yea, my gravity,
Wherein—let no man hear me—I take pride,
Could I with boot change for an idle plume,
Which the air beats for vain. O place, O form,
How often dost thou with thy case, thy habit,
Wrench awe from fools, and tie the wiser souls
To thy false seeming! Blood, thou art blood:
Let's write good angel on the devil's horn,
'Tis not the devil's crest.

Enter SERVANT.

How now! who's there?
SERVANT.
One Isabel, a sister,
Desires access to you.
ANGELO.
Teach her the way.
[*Exit* SERVANT.
O heavens!
Why does my blood thus muster to my heart,
Making both it unable for itself,
And dispossessing all my other parts
Of necessary fitness?
So play the foolish throngs with one that swoons;
Come all to help him, and so stop the air
By which he should revive: and even so
The general, subject to a well-wish'd king,
Quit their own part, and in obsequious fondness
Crowd to his presence, where their untaught love
Must needs appear offence.

Enter ISABELLA.

How now, fair maid!
ISABELLA.
I am come to know your pleasure.
ANGELO.
That you might know it, would much better please
me

Than to demand what 'tis. Your brother cannot
live.
ISABELLA.
Even so.—Heaven keep your honour!   [*Retiring.*
ANGELO.
Yet may he live awhile; and, it may be,
As long as you or I: yet he must die.
ISABELLA.
Under your sentence?
ANGELO.
Yea.
ISABELLA.
When, I beseech you? that in his reprieve,
Longer or shorter, he may be so fitted
That his soul sicken not.
ANGELO.
Ha! fie, these filthy vices! It were as good
To pardon him that hath from nature stol'n
A man already made, as to remit
Their saucy sweetness that do coin heaven's
image
In stamps that are forbid: 'tis all as easy
Falsely to take away a life true made,
As to put metal in restrained means
To make a false one.
ISABELLA.
'Tis set down so in heaven, but not in earth.
ANGELO.
Say you so? then I shall pose you quickly.
Which had you rather,—that the most just law
Now took your brother's life; or, to redeem him,
Give up your body to such sweet uncleanness
As she that he hath stain'd?
ISABELLA.
Sir, believe this,
I had rather give my body than my soul.
ANGELO.
I talk not of your soul: our compell'd sins
Stand more for number than accompt.
ISABELLA.
How say you
ANGELO.
Nay, I'll not warrant that; for I can speak
Against the thing I say. Answer to this:—
I, now the voice of the recorded law,
Pronounce a sentence on your brother's life:
Might there not be a charity in sin
To save this brother's life?
ISABELLA.
Please you to do't,
I'll take it as a peril to my soul,
It is no sin at all, but charity.
ANGELO.
Pleased you to do't at peril of your soul,
Were equal poise of sin and charity.
ISABELLA.
That I do beg his life, if it be sin,
Heaven let me bear it! you granting of my suit,
If that be sin, I'll make it my morn-prayer
To have it added to the faults of mine,
And nothing of your answer.
ANGELO.
Nay, but hear me.
Your sense pursues not mine: either you are ig-
norant,
Or seem so, craftily; and that's not good.

ISABELLA.
Let me be ignorant, and in nothing good,
But graciously to know I am no better.

ANGELO.
Thus wisdom wishes to appear most bright
When it doth tax itself; as these black masks
Proclaim an enshield beauty ten times louder
Than beauty could, display'd.—But mark me;
To be received plain, I'll speak more gross:
Your brother is to die.

ISABELLA.
So.

ANGELO.
And his offence is so, as it appears,
Accountant to the law upon that pain.

ISABELLA.
True.

ANGELO.
Admit no other way to save his life,—
As I subscribe not that, nor any other,
But in the toss of question,—that you, his sister,
Finding yourself desired of such a person,
Whose credit with the judge, or own great place,
Could fetch your brother from the manacles
Of the all-bridling law; and that there were
No earthly mean to save him, but that either
You must lay down the treasures of your body
To this supposed, or else to let him suffer;
What would you do?

ISABELLA.
As much for my poor brother as myself:
That is, were I under the terms of death,
Th'impression of keen whips I'ld wear as rubies,
And strip myself to death, as to a bed
That longing have been sick for, ere I'ld yield
My body up to shame.

ANGELO.
                    Then must
Your brother die.

ISABELLA.
                And 'twere the cheaper way:
Better it were a brother died at once,
Than that a sister, by redeeming him,
Should die for ever.

ANGELO.
Were not you, then, as cruel as the sentence
That you have slander'd so?

ISABELLA.
Ignomy in ransom, and free pardon,
Are of two houses: lawful mercy
Is nothing kin to foul redemption.

ANGELO.
You seem'd of late to make the law a tyrant;
And rather proved the sliding of your brother
A merriment than a vice.

ISABELLA.
O, pardon me, my lord; it oft falls out,   [mean:
To have what we would have, we speak not what we
I something do excuse the thing I hate,
For his advantage that I dearly love.

ANGELO.
We are all frail.

ISABELLA.
                Else let my brother die,
If not a feodary, but only he,
Owe and succeed this weakness.

ANGELO.
                    Nay, women are frail too.

ISABELLA.
Ay, as the glasses where they view themselves;
Which are as easy broke as they make forms.
Women!—Help heaven! men their creation mar
In profiting by them. Nay, call us ten times
    frail;
For we are soft as our complexions are,
And credulous to false prints.

ANGELO.
                I think it well:
And from this testimony of your own sex,—
Since, I suppose, we are made to be no stronger
Than faults may shake our frames,—let me be
    bold;—
I do arrest your words. Be that you are,
That is, a woman; if you be more, you're none;
If you be one,—as you are well exprest
By all external warrants,—show it now,
By putting on the destined livery.

ISABELLA.
I have no tongue but one: gentle my lord,
Let me entreat you speak the former language.

ANGELO.
Plainly conceive, I love you.

ISABELLA.
My brother did love Juliet; and you tell me
That he shall die for't.

ANGELO.
He shall not, Isabel, if you give me love.

ISABELLA.
I know your virtue hath a licence in't,
Which seems a little fouler than it is,
To pluck on others.

ANGELO.
                Believe me, on mine honour,
My words express my purpose.

ISABELLA.
Ha! little honour to be much believed,
And most pernicious purpose!—Seeming, seem-
    ing!—
I will proclaim thee, Angelo; look for't:
Sign me a present pardon for my brother,
Or with an outstretch'd throat I'll tell the world
Aloud what man thou art.

ANGELO.
                Who will believe thee, Isabel?
My unsoil'd name, th'austereness of my life,
My vouch against you, and my place i'the state,
Will so your accusation overweigh,
That you shall stifle in your own report,
And smell of calumny. I have begun;
And now I give my sensual race the rein:
Fit thy consent to my sharp appetite;
Lay by all nicety and prolixious blushes,
That banish what they sue for; redeem thy
    brother
By yielding up thy body to my will;
Or else he must not only die the death,
But thy unkindness shall his death draw out
To lingering sufferance. Answer me to-morrow,
Or, by the affection that now guides me most,
I'll prove a tyrant to him. As for you,
Say what you can, my false o'erweighs your true.
                                            [Exit.

ISABELLA.
To whom should I complain? Did I tell this,
Who would believe me? O perilous mouths,
That bear in them one and the self-same tongue,
Either of condemnation or approof;
Bidding the law make court'sy to their will;
Hooking both right and wrong to the appetite,
To follow as it draws! I'll to my brother:
Though he hath fall'n by prompture of the blood,
Yet hath he in him such a mind of honour,
That, had he twenty heads to tender down
On twenty bloody blocks, he'ld yield them up,
Before his sister should her body stoop
To such abhorred pollution.
Then, Isabel, live chaste, and, brother, die:
More than our brother is our chastity.
I'll tell him yet of Angelo's request,
And fit his mind to death, for his soul's rest.
       [*Exit.*

ACT III. SCENE I.

The prison.

Enter DUKE *disguised as before,* CLAUDIO, *and*
PROVOST.

DUKE.
SO, then, you hope of pardon from Lord Angelo?
            CLAUDIO.
The miserable have no other medicine
But only hope:
I have hope to live, and am prepared to die.
            DUKE.
Be absolute for death; either death or life
Shall thereby be the sweeter. Reason thus with
    life:—
If I do lose thee, I do lose a thing
That none but fools would keep: a breath thou art,
Servile to all the skyey influences
That do this habitation, where thou keep'st,
Hourly afflict: merely, thou art death's fool;
For him thou labour'st by thy flight to shun,
And yet runn'st toward him still. Thou art not
    noble;
For all th'accommodations that thou bear'st
Are nursed by baseness. Thou'rt by no means
    valiant;
For thou dost fear the soft and tender fork
Of a poor worm. Thy best of rest is sleep,
And that thou oft provokest; yet grossly fear'st
Thy death, which is no more. Thou art not
    thyself;
For thou exists on many a thousand grains
That issue out of dust. Happy thou art not;
For what thou hast not, still thou strivest to get,
And what thou hast, forgett'st. Thou art not
    certain;
For thy complexion shifts to strange affects,
After the moon. If thou art rich, thou'rt poor;
For, like an ass whose back with ingots bows,
Thou bear'st thy heavy riches but a journey,
And death unloads thee. Friend hast thou none;
For thine own bowels, which do call thee sire,
The mere effusions of thy proper loins,
Do curse the gout, serpigo, and the rheum,
For ending thee no sooner. Thou hast nor youth
    nor age,

But, as it were, an after-dinner's sleep,
Dreaming on both; for all thy blessed youth
Becomes as aged, and doth beg the alms
Of palsied eld; and when thou art old and rich,
Thou hast neither heat, affection, limb, nor
    beauty,
To make thy riches pleasant. What's yet in this
That bears the name of life? Yet in this life
Lie hid moe thousand deaths: yet death we fear,
That makes these odds all even.
            CLAUDIO.
                I humbly thank you.
To sue to live, I find I seek to die;
And, seeking death, find life: let it come on.
            ISABELLA [*within*].
What, ho! Peace here; grace and good company!
            PROVOST.
Who's there? come in: the wish deserves a wel-
    come.
            DUKE.
Dear sir, ere long I'll visit you again.
            CLAUDIO.
Most holy sir, I thank you.
            Enter ISABELLA.
            ISABELLA.
My business is a word or two with Claudio.
            PROVOST.
And very welcome.—Look, signior, here's your
    sister.
            DUKE.
Provost, a word with you.
            PROVOST.
                As many as you please.
            DUKE.
Bring me to hear them speak, where I may be
    conceal'd.   [*Exeunt* DUKE *and* PROVOST.
            CLAUDIO.
Now, sister, what's the comfort?
            ISABELLA.
                Why,
As all comforts are; most good, most good in-
    deed.
Lord Angelo, having affairs to heaven,
Intends you for his swift ambassador,
Where you shall be an everlasting leiger:
Therefore your best appointment make with
    speed;
To-morrow you set on.
            CLAUDIO.
                Is there no remedy?
            ISABELLA.
None, but such remedy as, to save a head,
To cleave a heart in twain.
            CLAUDIO.
                But is there any?
            ISABELLA.
Yes, brother, you may live:
There is a devilish mercy in the judge,
If you'll implore it, that will free your life,
But fetter you till death.
            CLAUDIO.
                Perpetual durance?
            ISABELLA.
Ay, just; perpetual durance,—a restraint,
Though all the world's vastidity you had,
To a determined scope.

CLAUDIO.
But in what nature?
ISABELLA.
In such a one as, you consenting to't,
Would bark your honour from that trunk you bear,
And leave you naked.
CLAUDIO.
Let me know the point.
ISABELLA.
O, I do fear thee, Claudio; and I quake,
Lest thou a feverous life shouldst entertain,
And six or seven winters more respect
Than a perpetual honour. Darest thou die?
The sense of death is most in apprehension;
And the poor beetle that we tread upon,
In corporal sufferance finds a pang as great
As when a giant dies.
CLAUDIO.
Why give you me this shame?
Think you I can a resolution fetch
From flowery tenderness? If I must die,
I will encounter darkness as a bride,
And hug it in mine arms.
ISABELLA.
There spake my brother; there my father's grave
Did utter forth a voice! Yes, thou must die:
Thou art too noble to conserve a life
In base appliances. This outward-sainted
          deputy—
Whose settled visage and deliberate word
Nips yo ith i'the head, and follies doth emmew
As falcon doth the fowl—is yet a devil;
His filth within being cast, he would appear
A pond as deep as hell.
CLAUDIO.
The priestly Angelo?
ISABELLA.
O, 'tis the cunning livery of hell,
The damned'st body to invest and cover
In priestly guards! Dost thou think, Claudio?—
If I would yield him my virginity,
Thou mightst be freed.
CLAUDIO.
O heavens! it cannot be.
ISABELLA.
Yes, he would give't thee, from this rank offence,
So to offend him still. This night's the time
That I should do what I abhor to name,
Or else thou diest to-morrow.
CLAUDIO.
Thou shalt not do't.
ISABELLA.
O, were it but my life,
I'd throw it down for your deliverance
As frankly as a pin.
CLAUDIO.
Thanks, dear Isabel.
ISABELLA.
Be ready, Claudio, for your death to-morrow.
CLAUDIO.
Yes.—Has he affections in him,
That thus can make him bite the law by the nose,
When he would force it? Sure, it is no sin;
Or of the deadly seven it is the least.
ISABELLA.
Which is the least?

CLAUDIO.
If it were damnable, he being so wise,
Why would he for the momentary trick
Be perdurably fined?—O Isobel!
ISABELLA.
What says my brother?
CLAUDIO.
Death is a fearful thing.
ISABELLA.
And shamed life a hateful.
CLAUDIO.
Ay, but to die, and go we know not where;
To lie in cold obstruction, and to rot;
This sensible warm motion to become
A kneaded clod; and the delighted spirit
To bathe in fiery floods, or to reside
In thrilling region of thick-ribbed ice;
To be imprison'd in the viewless winds,
And blown with restless violence round about
The pendent world; or to be worse than worst
Of those that lawless and incertain thought
Imagine howling!—'tis too horrible!
The weariest and most loathed worldly life
That age, ache, penury, and imprisonment
Can lay on nature, is a paradise
To what we fear of death.
ISABELLA.
Alas, alas!
CLAUDIO.
Sweet sister, let me live:
What sin you do to save a brother's life,
Nature dispenses with the deed so far
That it becomes a virtue.
ISABELLA.
O you beast!
O faithless coward! O dishonest wretch!
Wilt thou be made a man out of my vice?
Is't not a kind of incest, to take life
From thine own sister's shame? What should I
          think?
Heaven shield my mother play'd my father fair?
For such a warped slip of wilderness
Ne'er issued from his blood. Take my defiance;
Die, perish! might but my bending down
Reprieve thee from thy fate, it should proceed:
I'll pray a thousand prayers for thy death,—
No word to save thee.
CLAUDIO.
Nay, hear me, Isabel.
ISABELLA.
O, fie, fie, fie!
Thy sin's not accidental, but a trade.
Mercy to thee would prove itself a bawd:
'Tis best that thou diest quickly.   [Going.
CLAUDIO.
O, hear me, Isabella!
Enter DUKE.
DUKE.
Vouchsafe a word, young sister, but one word.
ISABELLA.
What is your will?
DUKE.
Might you dispense with your leisure, I would
by and by have some speech with you: the satis-
faction I would require is likewise your own
benefit.

ISABELLA.

I have no superfluous leisure; my stay must be stolen out of other affairs; but I will attend you awhile.

DUKE.

Son, I have overheard what hath pass'd between you and your sister. Angelo had never the purpose to corrupt her; only he hath made an assay of her virtue to practise his judgement with the disposition of natures: she, having the truth of honour in her, hath made him that gracious denial which he is most glad to receive. I am confessor to Angelo, and I know this to be true; therefore prepare yourself to death: do not satisfy your resolution with hopes that are fallible: to-morrow you must die; go to your knees, and make ready.

CLAUDIO.

Let me ask my sister pardon. I am so out of love with life, that I will sue to be rid of it.

DUKE.

Hold you there: farewell. [*Exit* CLAUDIO.] Provost, a word with you!

Enter PROVOST.

PROVOST.

What's your will, father?

DUKE.

That now you are come, you will be gone. Leave me awhile with the maid: my mind promises with my habit no loss shall touch her by my company.

PROVOST.

In good time.   [*Exit.*

DUKE.

The hand that hath made you fair hath made you good: the goodness that is cheap in beauty makes beauty brief in goodness; but grace, being the soul of your complexion, shall keep the body of it ever fair. The assault that Angelo hath made to you, fortune hath convey'd to my understanding; and, but that frailty hath examples for his falling, I should wonder at Angelo. How will you do to content this substitute, and to save your brother?

ISABELLA.

I am now going to resolve him, I had rather my brother die by the law than my son should be unlawfully born. But, O, how much is the good duke deceived in Angelo! If ever he return, and I can speak to him, I will open my lips in vain, or discover his government.

DUKE.

That shall not be much amiss: yet, as the matter now stands, he will avoid your accusation,—he made trial of you only. Therefore fasten your ear on my advisings: to the love I have in doing good a remedy presents itself. I do make myself believe that you may most uprighteously do a poor wrong'd lady a merited benefit; redeem your brother from the angry law; do no stain to your own gracious person; and much please the absent duke, if peradventure he shall ever return to have hearing of this business.

ISABELLA.

Let me hear you speak further. I have spirit to do any thing that appears not foul in the truth of my spirit.

DUKE.

Virtue is bold, and goodness never fearful. Have you not heard speak of Mariana, the sister of Frederick the great soldier who miscarried at sea?

ISABELLA.

I have heard of the lady, and good words went with her name.

DUKE.

She should this Angelo have married; was affianced to her by oath, and the nuptial appointed: between which time of the contract and limit of the solemnity, her brother Frederick was wrackt at sea, having in that perish'd vessel the dowry of his sister. But mark how heavily this befell to the poor gentlewoman: there she lost a noble and renown'd brother, in his love toward her ever most kind and natural; with him, the portion and sinew of her fortune, her marriage-dowry; with both, her combinate husband, this well-seeming Angelo.

ISABELLA.

Can this be so? did Angelo so leave her?

DUKE.

Left her in her tears, and dried not one of them with his comfort; swallow'd his vows whole, pretending in her discoveries of dishonour: in few, bestow'd her on her own lamentation, which she yet wears for his sake; and he, a marble to her tears, is wash'd with them, but relents not.

ISABELLA.

What a merit were it in death to take this poor maid from the world! What corruption in this life, that it will let this man live!—But how out of this can she avail?

DUKE.

It is a rupture that you may easily heal: and the cure of it not only saves your brother, but keeps you from dishonour in doing it.

ISABELLA.

Show me how, good father.

DUKE.

This forenamed maid hath yet in her the continuance of her first affection: his unjust unkindness, that in all reason should have quench'd her love, hath, like an impediment in the current, made it more violent and unruly. Go you to Angelo; answer his requiring with a plausible obedience; agree with his demands to the point; only refer yourself to this advantage,—first, that your stay with him may not be long; that the time may have all shadow and silence in it; and the place answer to convenience. This being granted in course—and now follows all—we shall advise this wrong'd maid to stead up your appointment, go in your place; if the encounter acknowledge itself hereafter, it may compel him to her recompense: and here, by this, is your brother saved, your honour untainted, the poor Mariana advantaged, and the corrupt deputy scaled. The maid will I frame and make fit for his attempt. If you think well to carry this as you may, the doubleness of the benefit defends the deceit from reproof. What think you of it?

ISABELLA.

The image of it gives me content already; and I trust it will grow to a most prosperous perfection.

DUKE.

It lies much in your holding up. Haste you
speedily to Angelo: if for this night he entreat you
to his bed, give him promise of satisfaction. I will
presently to Saint Luke's: there, at the moated
grange, resides this dejected Mariana. At that
place call upon me; and dispatch with Angelo,
that it may be quickly.

ISABELLA.

I thank you for this comfort. Fare you well, good
father.   [*Exeunt.*

SCENE II.

The street before the prison.

Enter DUKE *disguised as before; to him,* ELBOW
and OFFICERS *with* POMPEY.

ELBOW.

NAY, if there be no remedy for it, but that you
will needs buy and sell men and women like
beasts, we shall have all the world drink brown
and white bastard.

DUKE.

O heavens! what stuff is here?

POMPEY.

'Twas never merry world since, of two usuries,
the merriest was put down, and the worser allowed by order of law a furr'd gown to keep him
warm; and furr'd with fox and lamb-skins too, to
signify, that craft, being richer than innocency,
stands for the facing.

ELBOW.

Come your way, sir.—'Bless you, good father
friar.

DUKE.

And you, good brother father. What offence hath
this man made you, sir?

ELBOW.

Marry, sir, he hath offended the law: and, sir, we
take him to be a thief too, sir; for we have found
upon him, sir, a strange picklock, which we have
sent to the deputy.

DUKE.

Fie, sirrah! a bawd, a wicked bawd!
The evil that thou causest to be done,
That is thy means to live. Do thou but think
What 'tis to cram a maw or clothe a back
From such a filthy vice: say to thyself,—
From their abominable and beastly touches
I drink, I eat, array myself, and live.
Canst thou believe thy living is a life,
So stinkingly depending? Go mend, go mend.

POMPEY.

Indeed, it does stink in some sort, sir; but yet, sir,
I would prove—

DUKE.

Nay, if the devil have given thee proofs for sin,
Thou wilt prove his.—Take him to prison,
    officer:
Correction and instruction must both work
Ere this rude beast will profit.

ELBOW.

He must before the deputy, sir; he has given him
warning: the deputy cannot abide a whoremaster:
if he be a whoremonger, and comes before him,
he were as good go a mile on his errand.

DUKE.

That we were all, as some would seem to be,
From our faults, or faults from seeming, free!

ELBOW.

His neck will come to your waist,—a cord, sir.

POMPEY.

I spy comfort; I cry, bail! Here's a gentleman and
a friend of mine.

Enter LUCIO.

LUCIO.

How now, noble Pompey! What, at the wheels of
Cæsar! art thou led in triumph? What, is there
none of Pygmalion's images, newly-made woman,
to be had now, for putting the hand in the pocket
and extracting it clutch'd? What reply, ha? What
say'st thou to this tune, matter, and method? Is't
not drown'd i'the last rain, ha? What say'st thou,
Trot? Is the world as it was, man? Which is the
way? Is it sad, and few words? or how? The trick
of it?

DUKE.

Still thus, and thus; still worse!

LUCIO.

How doth my dear morsel, thy mistress? Procures
she still, ha?

POMPEY.

Troth, sir, she hath eaten up all her beef, and she
is herself in the tub.

LUCIO.

Why, 'tis good; it is the right of it; it must be so:
ever your fresh whore and your powder'd bawd:
an unshunn'd consequence; it must be so. Art
going to prison, Pompey?

POMPEY.

Yes, faith, sir.

LUCIO.

Why, 'tis not amiss, Pompey. Farewell: go, say I
sent thee thither. For debt, Pompey? or how?

ELBOW.

For being a bawd, for being a bawd.

LUCIO.

Well, then, imprison him: if imprisonment be the
due of a bawd, why, 'tis his right: bawd is he
doubtless, and of antiquity too; bawd-born.—
Farewell, good Pompey. Commend me to the
prison, Pompey: you will turn good husband now,
Pompey; you will keep the house.

POMPEY.

I hope, sir, your good worship will be my bail.

LUCIO.

No, indeed, will I not, Pompey; it is not the wear.
I will pray, Pompey, to increase your bondage:
if you take it not patiently, why, your mettle
is the more. Adieu, trusty Pompey.—Bless you,
friar.

DUKE.

And you.

LUCIO.

Does Bridget paint still, Pompey, ha?

ELBOW.

Come your ways, sir; come.

POMPEY.

You will not bail me, then, sir?

LUCIO.

Then, Pompey, nor now.—What news abroad,
friar, what news?

ELBOW.

Come your ways, sir; come.

LUCIO.

Go,—to kennel, Pompey, go. [*Exeunt* ELBOW *and* OFFICERS *with* POMPEY.] What news, friar, of the duke?

DUKE.

I know none. Can you tell me of any?

LUCIO.

Some say he is with the Emperor of Russia; other some, he is in Rome: but where is he, think you?

DUKE.

I know not where; but wheresoever, I wish him well.

LUCIO.

It was a mad fantastical trick of him to steal from the state, and usurp the beggary he was never born to. Lord Angelo dukes it well in his absence; he puts transgression to't.

DUKE.

He does well in't.

LUCIO.

A little more lenity to lechery would do no harm in him: something too crabb'd that way, friar.

DUKE.

It is too general a vice, and severity must cure it.

LUCIO.

Yes, in good sooth, the vice is of a great kindred; it is well allied; but it is impossible to extirp it quite, friar, till eating and drinking be put down. They say this Angelo was not made by man and woman, after the downright way of creation: is it true, think you?

DUKE.

How should he be made, then?

LUCIO.

Some report a sea-maid spawn'd him; some, that he was begot between two stock-fishes. But it is certain, that, when he makes water, his urine is congeal'd ice; that I know to be true: and he is a motion ungenerative; that's infallible.

DUKE.

You are pleasant, sir, and speak apace.

LUCIO.

Why, what a ruthless thing is this in him, for the rebellion of a codpiece to take away the life of a man! Would the duke that is absent have done this? Ere he would have hang'd a man for the getting a hundred bastards, he would have paid for the nursing a thousand: he had some feeling of the sport; he knew the service, and that instructed him to mercy.

DUKE.

I never heard the absent duke much detected for women; he was not inclined that way.

LUCIO.

O, sir, you are deceived.

DUKE.

'Tis not possible.

LUCIO.

Who, not the duke? yes, your beggar of fifty; and his use was to put a ducat in her clack-dish: the duke had crotchets in him. He would be drunk too; that let me inform you.

DUKE.

You do him wrong, surely.

LUCIO.

Sir, I was an inward of his. A sly fellow was the duke: and I believe I know the cause of his withdrawing.

DUKE.

What, I prithee, might be the cause?

LUCIO.

No,—pardon; 'tis a secret must be lockt within the teeth and the lips: but this I can let you understand,—the greater file of the subject held the duke to be wise.

DUKE.

Wise! why, no question but he was.

LUCIO.

A very superficial, ignorant, unweighing fellow.

DUKE.

Either this is envy in you, folly, or mistaking: the very stream of his life and the business he hath helm'd must, upon a warranted need, give him a better proclamation. Let him be but testimonied in his own bringings-forth, and he shall appear to the envious a scholar, a statesman, and a soldier. Therefore you speak unskilfully; or if your knowledge be more, it is much darken'd in your malice.

LUCIO.

Sir, I know him, and I love him.

DUKE.

Love talks with better knowledge, and knowledge with dearer love.

LUCIO.

Come, sir, I know what I know.

DUKE.

I can hardly believe that, since you know not what you speak. But, if ever the duke return,—as our prayers are he may,—let me desire you to make your answer before him. If it be honest you have spoke, you have courage to maintain it: I am bound to call upon you; and, I pray you, your name?

LUCIO.

Sir, my name is Lucio; well known to the duke.

DUKE.

He shall know you better, sir, if I may live to report you.

LUCIO.

I fear you not.

DUKE.

O, you hope the duke will return no more; or you imagine me too unhurtful an opposite. But, indeed, I can do you little harm; you'll forswear this again.

LUCIO.

I'll be hang'd first: thou art deceived in me, friar. But no more of this. Canst thou tell if Claudio die to-morrow or no?

DUKE.

Why should he die, sir?

LUCIO.

Why, for filling a bottle with a tun-dish. I would the duke we talk of were return'd again: this ungenitured agent will unpeople the province with continency; sparrows must not build in his house-eaves, because they are lecherous. The duke yet would have dark deeds darkly answer'd; he would never bring them to light: would he were return'd! Marry, this Claudio is condemn'd for un-trussing. Farewell, good friar: I prithee, pray for me. The duke, I say to thee again, would eat mutton on Fridays. He's now past it; yet, and I say to thee, he would mouth with a beggar, though she smelt brown bread and garlick: say that I said so. Farewell.   [*Exit.*

DUKE.
No might nor greatness in mortality
Can censure scape; back-wounding calumny
The whitest virtue strikes. What king so strong
Can tie the gall up in the slanderous tongue?—
But who comes here?—
      Enter ESCALUS, PROVOST, *and* OFFICERS
            with MISTRESS OVERDONE.

ESCALUS.
Go; away with her to prison!

MISTRESS OVERDONE.
Good my lord, be good to me; your honour is accounted a merciful man; good my lord.

ESCALUS.
Double and treble admonition, and still forfeit in the same kind? This would make mercy swear and play the tyrant.

PROVOST.
A bawd of eleven years' continuance, may it please your honour.

MISTRESS OVERDONE.
My lord, this is one Lucio's information against me. Mistress Kate Keep-down was with child by him in the duke's time; he promised her marriage: his child is a year and a quarter old, come Philip and Jacob: I have kept it myself; and see how he goes about to abuse me!

ESCALUS.
That fellow is a fellow of much license:—let him be call'd before us.—Away with her to prison!—Go to; no more words. [*Exeunt* OFFICERS *with* MISTRESS OVERDONE.] Provost, my brother Angelo will not be alter'd; Claudio must die to-morrow: let him be furnish'd with divines, and have all charitable preparation. If my brother wrought by my pity, it should not be so with him.

PROVOST.
So please you, this friar hath been with him, and advised him for the entertainment of death.

ESCALUS.
Good even, good father.

DUKE.
Bliss and goodness on you!

ESCALUS.
Of whence are you?

DUKE.
Not of this country, though my chance is now
To use it for my time: I am a brother
Of gracious order, late come from the See
In special business from his holiness.

ESCALUS.
What news abroad i' the world?

DUKE.
None, but that there is so great a fever on good-ness, that the dissolution of it must cure it: novelty is only in request; and it is as dangerous to be aged in any kind of course, as it is virtuous to be constant in any undertaking: there is scarce truth enough alive to make societies secure; but security enough to make fellowships accurst: —much upon this riddle runs the wisdom of the world. This news is old enough, yet it is every day's news. I pray you, sir, of what disposition was the duke?

ESCALUS.
One that, above all other strifes, contended es-pecially to know himself.

DUKE.
What pleasure was he given to?

ESCALUS.
Rather rejoicing to see another merry, than merry at any thing which profest to make him rejoice: a gentleman of all temperance. But leave we him to his events, with a prayer they may prove pros-perous; and let me desire to know how you find Claudio prepared. I am made to understand that you have lent him visitation.

DUKE.
He professes to have received no sinister measure from his judge, but most willingly humbles him-self to the determination of justice: yet had he framed to himself, by the instruction of his frailty, many deceiving promises of life; which I, by my good leisure, have discredited to him, and now is he resolved to die.

ESCALUS.
You have paid the heavens your function, and the prisoner the very debt of your calling. I have labour'd for the poor gentleman to the extremest shore of my modesty: but my brother justice have I found so severe, that he hath forced me to tell him he is indeed Justice.

DUKE.
If his own life answer the straitness of his pro-ceeding, it shall become him well; wherein if he chance to fail, he hath sentenced him-self.

ESCALUS.
I am going to visit the prisoner. Fare you well.

DUKE.
Peace be with you!
            [*Exeunt* ESCALUS *and* PROVOST.
He who the sword of heaven will bear
Should be as holy as severe;
Pattern in himself to know,
Grace to stand, and virtue go;
More nor less to others paying
Than by self-offences weighing.
Shame to him whose cruel striking
Kills for faults of his own liking!
Twice treble shame on Angelo,
To weed my vice, and let his grow!
O, what may man within him hide,
Though angel on the outward side!
How may likeness wade in crimes,
Making practice on the times,
To draw with idle spiders' strings
Most ponderous and substantial things!
Craft against vice I must apply:
With Angelo to-night shall lie
His old betrothed but despised;
So disguise shall, by the disguised,
Pay with falsehood false exacting,
And perform an old contracting.   [*Exit.*

ACT IV. SCENE I.

The Moated Grange.

Enter MARIANA; *a* BOY *singing.*

Song.

TAKE, O take those lips away,
   That so sweetly were forsworn;
And those eyes, the break of day,
   Lights that do mislead the morn:
But my kisses bring again, bring again;
Seals of love, but seal'd in vain, seal'd in vain.

MARIANA.

Break off thy song, and haste thee quick away:
Here comes a man of comfort, whose advice
Hath often still'd my brawling discontent.
                       [Exit BOY.

Enter DUKE *disguised as before.*

I cry you mercy, sir; and well could wish
You had not found me here so musical:
Let me excuse me, and believe me so,—
My mirth it much displeased, but pleased my woe.

DUKE.

'Tis good; though music oft hath such a charm
To make bad good, and good provoke to harm.—
I pray you, tell me, hath anybody inquired for me
here to-day? much upon this time have I promised here to meet.

MARIANA.

You have not been inquired after: I have sat here
all day.

DUKE.

I do constantly believe you.—The time is come
even now. I shall crave your forbearance a little:
may be I will call upon you anon, for some advantage to yourself.

MARIANA.

I am always bound to you.   *[Exit.*

Enter ISABELLA.

DUKE.

Very well met, and welcome.
What is the news from this good deputy?

ISABELLA.

He hath a garden circummured with brick,
Whose western side is with a vineyard back'd;
And to that vineyard is a planched gate,
That makes his opening with this bigger key:
This other doth command a little door
Which from the vineyard to the garden leads;
There have I made my promise
Upon the heavy middle of the night
To call upon him.

DUKE.

But shall you on your knowledge find this way?

ISABELLA.

I have ta'en a due and wary note upon't:
With whispering and most guilty diligence,
In action all of precept, he did show me
The way twice o'er.

DUKE.

        Are there no other tokens
Between you 'greed concerning her observance?

ISABELLA.

No, none, but only a repair i'the dark;
And that I have possest him my most stay
Can be but brief; for I have made him know
I have a servant comes with me along,

That stays upon me; whose persuasion is
I come about my brother.

DUKE.

        'Tis well borne up.
I have not yet made known to Mariana
A word of this.—What, ho! within! come forth!

Enter MARIANA.

I pray you, be acquainted with this maid;
She comes to do you good.

ISABELLA.

        I do desire the like.

DUKE.

Do you persuade yourself that I respect you?

MARIANA.

Good friar, I know you do, and have found it.

DUKE.

Take, then, this your companion by the hand,
Who hath a story ready for your ear.
I shall attend your leisure: but make haste;
The vaporous night approaches.

MARIANA.

        Will't please you walk aside?
    [Exeunt MARIANA *and* ISABELLA.

DUKE.

O place and greatness, millions of false eyes
Are stuck upon thee! volumes of report
Run with these false and most contrarious quests
Upon thy doings! thousand escapes of wit
Make thee the father of their idle dream,
And rack thee in their fancies!

Enter MARIANA *and* ISABELLA.

        Welcome! How agreed?

ISABELLA.

She'll take the enterprise upon her, father,
If you advise it.

DUKE.

        It is not my consent,
But my entreaty too.

ISABELLA.

        Little have you to say
When you depart from him, but, soft and low,
'Remember now my brother.'

MARIANA.

        Fear me not.

DUKE.

Nor, gentle daughter, fear you not at all.
He is your husband on a pre-contract:
To bring you thus together, 'tis no sin,
Sith that the justice of your title to him
Doth flourish the deceit. Come, let us go:
Our corn's to reap, for yet our tilth's to sow.
                [Exeunt.

SCENE II.

The prison.

Enter PROVOST *and* POMPEY.

PROVOST.

COME hither, sirrah. Can you cut off a man's
head?

POMPEY.

If the man be a bachelor, sir, I can; but if he be a
married man, he's his wife's head, and I can
never cut off a woman's head.

PROVOST.

Come, sir, leave me your snatches, and yield me
a direct answer. To-morrow morning are to die

Claudio and Barnardine. Here is in our prison a common executioner, who in his office lacks a helper: if you will take it on you to assist him, it shall redeem you from your gyves; if not, you shall have your full time of imprisonment, and your deliverance with an unpitied whipping, for you have been a notorious bawd.

POMPEY.

Sir, I have been an unlawful bawd time out of mind; but yet I will be content to be a lawful hangman. I would be glad to receive some instruction from my fellow partner.

PROVOST.

What, ho, Abhorson! Where's Abhorson, there?
Enter ABHORSON.

ABHORSON.

Do you call, sir?

PROVOST.

Sirrah, here's a fellow will help you to-morrow in your execution. If you think it meet, compound with him by the year, and let him abide here with you; if not, use him for the present, and dismiss him. He cannot plead his estimation with you; he hath been a bawd.

ABHORSON.

A bawd, sir! fie upon him! he will discredit our mystery.

PROVOST.

Go to, sir; you weigh equally; a feather will turn the scale. 　　　　　　　　　　　　[*Exit.*

POMPEY.

Pray, sir, by your good favour,—for surely, sir, a good favour you have, but that you have a hanging look,—do you call, sir, your occupation a mystery?

ABHORSON.

Ay, sir; a mystery.

POMPEY.

Painting, sir, I have heard say, is a mystery; and your whores, sir, being members of my occupation, using painting, do prove my occupation a mystery: but what mystery there should be in hanging, if I should be hang'd, I cannot imagine.

ABHORSON.

Sir, it is a mystery.

POMPEY.

Proof?

ABHORSON.

Every true man's apparel fits your thief: if it be too little for your thief, your true man thinks it big enough; if it be too big for your thief, your thief thinks it little enough: so every true man's apparel fits your thief. 　　　　　
Enter PROVOST.

PROVOST.

Are you agreed?

POMPEY.

Sir, I will serve him; for I do find your hangman is a more penitent trade than your bawd,—he doth oftener ask forgiveness.

PROVOST.

You, sirrah, provide your block and your axe to-morrow four o'clock.

ABHORSON.

Come on, bawd; I will instruct thee in my trade; follow.

POMPEY.

I do desire to learn, sir: and I hope, if you have occasion to use me for your own turn, you shall find me yare; for, truly, sir, for your kindness I owe you a good turn.

PROVOST.

Call hither Barnardine and Claudio:
　　　　[*Exeunt* POMPEY *and* ABHORSON.
Th'one has my pity; not a jot the other,
Being a murderer, though he were my brother.
　　　　　　Enter CLAUDIO.
Look, here's the warrant, Claudio, for thy death:
'Tis now dead midnight, and by eight to-morrow
Thou must be made immortal. Where's Barnardine?

CLAUDIO.

As fast lockt up in sleep as guiltless labour,
When it lies starkly in the traveller's bones:
He will not wake.

PROVOST.

　　　　　Who can do good on him?
Well, go, prepare thyself. [*Knocking within.*] But, hark, what noise?—
Heaven give your spirits comfort! [*Exit* CLAUDIO.] By and by!—
I hope it is some pardon or reprieve
For the most gentle Claudio.
　　　Enter DUKE *disguised as before.*
　　　　　　　　　　Welcome, father.

DUKE.

The best and wholesom'st spirits of the night
Envelop you, good provost! Who call'd here of late?

PROVOST.

None, since the curfew rung.

DUKE.

Not Isabel?

PROVOST.

　　　No.

DUKE.

　　　　They will, then, ere't be long.

PROVOST.

What comfort is for Claudio?

DUKE.

There's some in hope.

PROVOST.

　　　　　It is a bitter deputy.

DUKE.

Not so, not so; his life is parallel'd
Even with the stroke and line of his great justice:
He doth with holy abstinence subdue
That in himself which he spurs on his power
To qualify in others: were he meal'd with that
Which he corrects, then were he tyrannous;
But this being so, he's just. 　　　[*Knocking within.*
　　　　　Now are they come.
　　　　　　　　　[*Exit* PROVOST.
This is a gentle provost: seldom, when
The steeled gaoler is the friend of men.
　　　　　　　　　[*Knocking within.*
How now! what noise? That spirit's possest with haste
That wounds th'unresisting postern with these 　　[strokes.
　　　　　Enter PROVOST.

PROVOST.

There he must stay until the officer
Arise to let him in: he is call'd up.

DUKE.
Have you no countermand for Claudio yet,
But he must die to-morrow?
PROVOST.
            None, sir, none.
DUKE.
As near the dawning, provost, as it is,
You shall hear more ere morning.
PROVOST.
            Happily
You something know; yet I believe there comes
No countermand; no such example have we:
Besides, upon the very siege of justice
Lord Angelo hath to the public ear
Profest the contrary.
      Enter a MESSENGER.
          This is his lordship's man.
DUKE.
And here comes Claudio's pardon.
      MESSENGER [*giving a paper*].
My lord hath sent you this note; and by me
this further charge,—that you swerve not from
the smallest article of it, neither in time, matter,
or other circumstance. Good morrow; for, as I
take it, it is almost day.
PROVOST.
I shall obey him.   [*Exit* MESSENGER.
      DUKE [*aside*].
This is his pardon, purchased by such sin
For which the pardoner himself is in.
Hence hath offence his quick celerity,
When it is borne in high authority:
When vice makes mercy, mercy's so extended,
That for the fault's love is th'offender friended.—
Now, sir, what news?
PROVOST.
I told you: Lord Angelo, belike thinking me re-
miss in mine office, awakens me with this un-
wonted putting-on; methinks strangely, for he
hath not used it before.
DUKE.
Pray you, let's hear.
      PROVOST [*reads*].
Whatsoever you may hear to the contrary, let
Claudio be executed by four of the clock; and in
the afternoon Barnardine: for my better satisfac-
tion, let me have Claudio's head sent me by five.
Let this be duly perform'd; with a thought that
more depends on it than we must yet deliver.
Thus fail not to do your office, as you will answer
it at your peril.
What say you to this, sir?
DUKE.
What is that Barnardine who is to be executed in
th'afternoon?
PROVOST.
A Bohemian born, but here nursed up and bred;
one that is a prisoner nine years old.
DUKE.
How came it that the absent duke had not either
deliver'd him to his liberty or executed him? I
have heard it was ever his manner to do so.
PROVOST.
His friends still wrought reprieves for him: and,
indeed, his fact, till now in the government of
Lord Angelo, came not to an undoubtful proof.

DUKE.
It is now apparent?
PROVOST.
Most manifest, and not denied by himself.
DUKE.
Hath he borne himself penitently in prison? How
seems he to be touch'd?
PROVOST.
A man that apprehends death no more dreadfully
but as a drunken sleep; careless, reckless, and
fearless of what's past, present, or to come; in-
sensible of mortality, and desperately mortal.
DUKE.
He wants advice.
PROVOST.
He will hear none: he hath evermore had the
liberty of the prison; give him leave to escape
hence, he would not: drunk many times a day, if
not many days entirely drunk. We have very oft
awaked him, as if to carry him to execution, and
show'd him a seeming warrant for it: it hath not
moved him at all.
DUKE.
More of him anon. There is written in your brow,
provost, honesty and constancy: if I read it not
truly, my ancient skill beguiles me; but, in the
boldness of my cunning, I will lay myself in
hazard. Claudio, whom here you have warrant to
execute, is no greater forfeit to the law than
Angelo, who hath sentenced him. To make
you understand this in a manifested effect, I
crave but four days' respite; for the which you
are to do me both a present and a dangerous
courtesy.
PROVOST.
Pray, sir, in what?
DUKE.
In the delaying death.
PROVOST.
Alack, how may I do it,—having the hour limited,
and an express command, under penalty, to
deliver his head in the view of Angelo? I may
make my case as Claudio's, to cross this in the
smallest.
DUKE.
By the vow of mine order I warrant you, if my instructions may be your guide. Let this Barnadine
be this morning executed, and his head borne to
Angelo.
PROVOST.
Angelo hath seen them both, and will discover the
favour.
DUKE.
O, death's a great disguiser; and you may add to
it. Shave the head and tie the beard; and say it
was the desire of the penitent to be so bared be-
fore his death: you know the course is common.
If any thing fall to you upon this, more than
thanks and good fortune, by the saint whom I
profess, I will plead against it with my life.
PROVOST.
Pardon me, good father; it is against my oath.
DUKE.
Were you sworn to the duke, or to the deputy?
PROVOST.
To him, and to his substitutes.

DUKE.

You will think you have made no offence, if the duke avouch the justice of your dealing?

PROVOST.

But what likelihood is in that?

DUKE.

Not a resemblance, but a certainty. Yet since I see you fearful that neither my coat, integrity, nor persuasion can with ease attempt you, I will go further than I meant, to pluck all fears out of you. Look you, sir, here is the hand and seal of the duke: you know the character, I doubt not; and the signet is not strange to you.

PROVOST.

I know them both.

DUKE.

The contents of this is the return of the duke: you shall anon over-read it at your pleasure; where you shall find, within these two days he will be here. This is a thing that Angelo knows not; for he this very day receives letters of strange tenour; perchance of the duke's death; perchance entering into some monastery; but, by chance, nothing of what is writ. Look, th'unfolding star calls up the shepherd. Put not yourself into amazement how these things should be: all difficulties are but easy when they are known. Call your executioner, and off with Barnardine's head: I will give him a present shrift, and advise him for a better place. Yet you are amazed; but this shall absolutely resolve you. Come away; it is almost clear dawn.

[*Exeunt.*

SCENE III.

Another room in the same.

Enter POMPEY.

POMPEY.

I AM as well acquainted here as I was in our house of profession: one would think it were Mistress Overdone's own house, for here be many of her old customers. First, here's young Master Rash; he's in for a commodity of brown paper and old ginger, nine-score and seventeen pounds; of which he made five marks, ready money; marry, then ginger was not much in request, for the old women were all dead. Then is there here one Master Caper, at the suit of Master Three-pile the mercer, for some four suits of peach-colour'd satin, which now peaches him a beggar. Then have we here young Dizzy, and young Master Deep-vow, and Master Copper-spur, and Master Starve-lackey, the rapier-and-dagger-man, and young Drop-heir that kill'd lusty Pudding, and Master Forthright the tilter, and brave Master Shoe-tie the great traveller, and wild Half-can that stabb'd Pots, and, I think, forty more, all great doers in our trade, and are now 'for the Lord's sake.'

Enter ABHORSON.

ABHORSON.

Sirrah, bring Barnardine hither.

POMPEY.

Master Barnardine! you must rise and be hang'd, Master Barnardine!

ABHORSON.

What, ho, Barnardine!

BARNARDINE [*within*].

A pox o' your throats! Who makes that noise there? Who are you?

POMPEY.

Your friends, sir; the hangman. You must be so good, sir, to rise and be put to death.

BARNARDINE [*within*].

Away, you rogue, away! I am sleepy.

ABHORSON.

Tell him he must awake, and that quickly too.

POMPEY.

Pray, Master Barnardine, awake till you are executed, and sleep afterwards.

ABHORSON.

Go in to him, and fetch him out.

POMPEY.

He is coming, sir, he is coming; I hear his straw rustle.

ABHORSON.

Is the axe upon the block, sirrah?

POMPEY.

Very ready, sir.

Enter BARNARDINE.

BARNARDINE.

How now, Abhorson! what's the news with you?

ABHORSON.

Truly, sir, I would desire you to clap into your prayers; for, look you, the warrant's come.

BARNARDINE.

You rogue, I have been drinking all night; I am not fitted for't.

POMPEY.

O, the better, sir; for he that drinks all night, and is hang'd betimes in the morning, may sleep the sounder all the next day.

ABHORSON.

Look you, sir; here comes your ghostly father: do we jest now, think you?

Enter DUKE *disguised as before.*

DUKE.

Sir, induced by my charity, and hearing how hastily you are to depart, I am come to advise you, comfort you, and pray with you.

BARNARDINE.

Friar, not I: I have been drinking hard all night, and I will have more time to prepare me, or they shall beat out my brains with billets: I will not consent to die this day, that's certain.

DUKE.

O, sir, you must: and therefore I beseech you Look forward on the journey you shall go.

BARNARDINE.

I swear I will not die to-day for any man's persuasion.

DUKE.

But hear you,—

BARNARDINE.

Not a word: if you have anything to say to me, come to my ward; from thence will not I to-day.

[*Exit.*

DUKE.

Unfit to live or die: O gravel heart!—
After him, fellows; bring him to the block.

[*Exeunt* ABHORSON *and* POMPEY.

Enter PROVOST.

PROVOST.

Now, sir, how do you find the prisoner?

DUKE.

A creature unprepared, unmeet for death;
And to transport him in the mind he is
Were damnable.

PROVOST.

Here in the prison, father,
There died this morning of a cruel fever
One Ragozine, a most notorious pirate,
A man of Claudio's years: his beard and head
Just of his colour. What if we do omit
This reprobate till he were well inclined;
And satisfy the deputy with the visage
Of Ragozine, more like to Claudio?

DUKE.

O, 'tis an accident that heaven provides!
Dispatch it presently; the hour draws on
Prefixt by Angelo: see this be done,
And sent according to command; whiles I
Persuade this rude wretch willingly to die.

PROVOST.

This shall be done, good father, presently.
But Barnardine must die this afternoon:
And how shall we continue Claudio,
To save me from the danger that might come
If he were known alive?

DUKE.

Let this be done,—put them in secret holds,
Both Barnardine and Claudio:
Ere twice the sun hath made his journal greeting
To th'under generation, you shall find
Your safety manifested.

PROVOST.

I am your free dependant.

DUKE.

Quick, dispatch,
And send the head to Angelo. [*Exit* PROVOST.
Now will I write letters to Angelo,—
The provost, he shall bear them,—whose contents
Shall witness to him I am near at home,
And that, by great injunctions, I am bound
To enter publicly: him I'll desire
To meet me at the consecrated fount,
A league below the city: and from thence,
By cold gradation and well-balanced form,
We shall proceed with Angelo.

Enter PROVOST *with* RAGOZINE'S *head*.

PROVOST.

Here is the head; I'll carry it myself.

DUKE.

Convenient is it. Make a swift return;
For I would commune with you of such things
That want no ear but yours.

PROVOST.

I'll make all speed. [*Exit.*

ISABELLA [*within*].

Peace, ho, be here!

DUKE.

The tongue of Isabel. She's come to know
If yet her brother's pardon be come hither:
But I will keep her ignorant of her good,
To make her heavenly comforts of despair,
When it is least expected.

Enter ISABELLA.

ISABELLA.

Ho, by your leave!

DUKE.

Good morning to you, fair and gracious daughter.

ISABELLA.

The better, given by so holy a man.
Hath yet the deputy sent my brother's pardon?

DUKE.

He hath released him, Isabel, from the world:
His head is off, and sent to Angelo.

ISABELLA.

Nay, but it is not so.

DUKE.

It is no other: show your wisdom, daughter,
In your close patience.

ISABELLA.

O, I will to him and pluck out his eyes!

DUKE.

You shall not be admitted to his sight.

ISABELLA.

Unhappy Claudio! wretched Isabel!
Injurious world! most damned Angelo!

DUKE.

This nor hurts him nor profits you a jot;
Forbear it therefore; give your cause to heaven.
Mark what I say, which you shall find
By every syllable a faithful verity:
The duke comes home to-morrow;—nay, dry
    your eyes;
One of our covent, and his confessor,
Gives me this instance: already he hath carried
Notice to Escalus and Angelo;
Who do prepare to meet him at the gates,
There to give up their power. If you can, pace
    your wisdom
In that good path that I would wish it go;
And you shall have your bosom on this wretch,
Grace of the duke, revenges to your heart,
And general honour.

ISABELLA.

I am directed by you.

DUKE.

This letter, then, to Friar Peter give;
'Tis that he sent me of the duke's return:
Say, by this token, I desire his company
At Mariana's house to-night. Her cause and yours
I'll perfect him withal; and he shall bring you
Before the duke; and to the head of Angelo
Accuse him home and home. For my poor self,
I am combined by a sacred vow,
And shall be absent. Wend you with this letter:
Command these fretting waters from your eyes
With a light heart; trust not my holy order,
If I pervert your course.—Who's here?

Enter LUCIO.

LUCIO.

Good even, friar: where's the provost?

DUKE.

Not within, sir.

LUCIO.

O pretty Isabella, I am pale at mine heart to see
thine eyes so red: thou must be patient. I am fain
to dine and sup with water and bran; I dare not
for my head fill my belly; one fruitful meal would
set me to't. But they say the duke will be here to-

morrow. By my troth, Isabel, I loved thy brother:
if the old fantastical duke of dark corners had
been at home, he had lived.   [*Exit* ISABELLA.

DUKE.

Sir, the duke is marvellous little beholding to
your reports; but the best is, he lives not in them.

LUCIO.

Friar, thou know'st not the duke so well as I do:
he's a better woodman than thou takest him for.

DUKE.

Well, you'll answer this one day. Fare ye well.

LUCIO.

Nay, tarry; I'll go along with thee: I can tell thee
pretty tales of the duke.

DUKE.

You have told me too many of him already, sir, if
they be true; if not true, none were enough.

LUCIO.

I was once before him for getting a wench with
child.

DUKE.

Did you such a thing?

LUCIO.

Yes, marry, did I: but I was fain to forswear it;
they would else have married me to the rotten
medlar.

DUKE.

Sir, your company is fairer than honest. Rest you
well.

LUCIO.

By my troth, I'll go with thee to the lane's end:
if bawdy talk offend you, we'll have very little of
it. Nay, friar, I am a kind of burr; I shall stick.
          [*Exeunt.*

SCENE IV.

ANGELO'S *house.*

Enter ANGELO *and* ESCALUS.

ESCALUS.

EVERY letter he hath writ hath disvouch'd
other.

ANGELO.

In most uneven and distracted manner. His
actions show much like to madness: pray heaven
his wisdom be not tainted! And why meet him at
the gates, and redeliver our authorities there?

ESCALUS.

I guess not.

ANGELO.

And why should we proclaim it in an hour before
his entering, that if any crave redress of injustice, they should exhibit their petitions in the
street?

ESCALUS.

He shows his reason for that;—to have a dispatch
of complaints, and to deliver us from devices
hereafter, which shall then have no power to stand
against us.

ANGELO.

Well, I beseech you, let it be proclaim'd:
Betimes i'the morn I'll call you at your house:
Give notice to such men of sort and suit
As are to meet him.

ESCALUS.

I shall, sir. Fare you well.

ANGELO.

Good night.   [*Exit* ESCALUS.
This deed unshapes me quite, makes me un-
    pregnant,
And dull to all proceedings. A deflower'd maid!
And by an eminent body that enforced
The law against it! But that her tender shame
Will not proclaim against her maiden loss,
How might she tongue me! Yet reason dares her
    no;
For my authority bears a credent bulk,
That no particular scandal once can touch
But it confounds the breather. He should have
    lived,
Save that his riotous youth, with dangerous sense,
Might in the times to come have ta'en revenge,
By so receiving a dishonour'd life
With ransom of such shame. Would yet he had
    lived!
Alack, when once our grace we have forgot,
Nothing goes right,—we would, and we would
    not!   [*Exit.*

SCENE V.

Fields without the town.

Enter DUKE *in his own habit, and* FRIAR PETER.

DUKE.

THESE letters at fit time deliver me:
          [*Giving letters.*
The provost knows our purpose and our plot.
The matter being afoot, keep your instruction,
And hold you ever to our special drift;
Though sometimes you do blench from this to that,
As cause doth minister. Go call at Flavius' house,
And tell him where I stay: give the like notice
To Valentinus, Rowland, and to Crassus,
And bid them bring the trumpets to the gate;
But send me Flavius first.

FRIAR PETER.

          It shall be speeded well. [*Exit.*

Enter VARRIUS.

DUKE.

I thank thee, Varrius; thou hast made good haste:
Come, we will walk. There's other of our friends
Will greet us here anon, my gentle Varrius.

          [*Exeunt.*

SCENE VI.

Street near the city-gate.

Enter ISABELLA *and* MARIANA.

ISABELLA.

TO speak so indirectly I am loth:
    I would say the truth; but to accuse him so,
That is your part: yet I am advised to do it;
He says, to vailful purpose.

MARIANA.

          Be ruled by him.

ISABELLA.

Besides, he tells me that, if peradventure
He speak against me on the adverse side,
I should not think it strange; for 'tis a physic
That's bitter to sweet end.

MARIANA.

I would Friar Peter,—

ISABELLA.
O, peace! the friar is come.

Enter FRIAR PETER.

FRIAR PETER.
Come, I have found you out a stand most fit,
Where you may have such vantage on the duke,
He shall not pass you. Twice have the trumpets
  sounded;
The generous and gravest citizens
Have hent the gates, and very near upon
The duke is ent'ring: therefore, hence, away!
                            [*Exeunt.*

ACT V. SCENE I.

A public place near the city-gate.

MARIANA *veiled,* ISABELLA, *and* FRIAR PETER
at their stand. Enter *at opposite doors,* DUKE *in
his own habit,* VARRIUS, LORDS; ANGELO,
ESCALUS, LUCIO, PROVOST, OFFICERS, *and*
CITIZENS.

DUKE.
MY very worthy cousin, fairly met:—
  Our old and faithful friend, we are glad to
  see you.

ANGELO *and* ESCALUS.
Happy return be to your royal grace!

DUKE.
Many and hearty thankings to you both.
We have made inquiry of you; and we hear
Such goodness of your justice, that our soul
Cannot but yield you forth to public thanks,
Forerunning more requital.

ANGELO.
You make my bonds still greater.

DUKE.
O, your desert speaks loud; and I should wrong it,
To lock it in the wards of covert bosom,
When it deserves, with characters of brass,
A forted residence 'gainst the tooth of time
And razure of oblivion. Give me your hand,
And let the subject see, to make them know
That outward courtesies would fain proclaim
Favours that keep within.—Come, Escalus;
You must walk by us on our other hand:—
And good supporters are you.

FRIAR PETER *and* ISABELLA *come forward.*

FRIAR PETER.
Now is your time: speak loud, and kneel before him.

ISABELLA.
Justice, O royal duke! Vail your regard
Upon a wrong'd, I would fain have said, a maid!
O worthy prince, dishonour not your eye
By throwing it on any other object
Till you have heard me in my true complaint,
And given me justice, justice, justice, justice!

DUKE.
Relate your wrongs; in what? by whom? be brief.
Here is Lord Angelo shall give you justice.
Reveal yourself to him.

ISABELLA.
O worthy duke,
You bid me seek redemption of the devil:
Hear me yourself; for that which I must speak
Must either punish me, not being believed,
Or wring redress from you: hear me, O, hear me,
  here!

ANGELO.
My lord, her wits, I fear me, are not firm:
She hath been a suitor to me for her brother
Cut off by course of justice,—

ISABELLA.
By course of justice!

ANGELO.
And she will speak most bitterly and strange.

ISABELLA.
Most strange, but yet most truly, will I speak:
That Angelo's forsworn; is it not strange?
That Angelo's a murderer; is't not strange?
That Angelo is an adulterous thief,
An hypocrite, a virgin-violator;
Is it not strange and strange?

DUKE.
Nay, it is ten times strange.

ISABELLA.
It is not truer he is Angelo
Than this is all as true as it is strange:
Nay, it is ten times true; for truth is truth
To th'end of reck'ning.

DUKE.
Away with her!—Poor soul,
She speaks this in th'infirmity of sense.

ISABELLA.
O prince, I conjure thee, as thou believest
There is another comfort than this world,
That thou neglect me not, with that opinion
That I am touch'd with madness! Make not im-
  possible
That which but seems unlike: 'tis not impos-
  sible
But one, the wicked'st caitiff on the ground,
May seem as shy, as grave, as just, as absolute
As Angelo; even so may Angelo,
In all his dressings, charants, titles, forms,
Be an arch-villain; believe it, royal prince:
If he be less, he's nothing; but he's more,
Had I more name for badness.

DUKE.
By mine honesty,
If she be mad,—as I believe no other,—
Her madness hath the oddest frame of sense,
Such a dependency of thing on thing,
As e'er I heard in madness.

ISABELLA.
O gracious duke,
Harp not on that; nor do not banish reason
For inequality; but let your reason serve
To make the truth appear where it seems hid,
And hide the false seems true.

DUKE.
Many that are not mad
Have, sure, more lack of reason.—What would
  you say?

ISABELLA.
I am the sister of one Claudio,
Condemn'd upon the act of fornication
To lose his head; condemn'd by Angelo:
I, in probation of a sisterhood,
Was sent to by my brother; one Lucio
As then the messenger,—

LUCIO.
That's I, an't like your grace:
I came to her from Claudio, and desired her

To try her gracious fortune with Lord Angelo
For her poor brother's pardon.

ISABELLA.
　　　　　　　　That's he indeed.

DUKE.
You were not bid to speak.

LUCIO.
　　　　　　　　No, my good lord;
Nor wish'd to hold my peace.

DUKE.
　　　　　　　　I wish you now, then;
Pray you, take note of it: and when you have
A business for yourself, pray heaven you then
Be perfect.

LUCIO.
I warrant your honour.

DUKE.
The warrant's for yourself; take heed to't.

ISABELLA.
This gentleman told somewhat of my tale,—

LUCIO.
Right.

DUKE.
It may be right; but you are i'the wrong
To speak before your time.—Proceed.

ISABELLA.
　　　　　　　　　　　I went
To this pernicious caitiff deputy,—

DUKE.
That's somewhat madly spoken.

ISABELLA.
　　　　　　　　Pardon it;
The phrase is to the matter.

DUKE.
Mended again. The matter;—proceed.

ISABELLA.
In brief,—to set the needless process by,
How I persuaded, how I pray'd, and kneel'd,
How he refell'd me, and how I replied,—
For this was of much length,—the vile conclusion
I now begin with grief and shame to utter;
He would not, but by gift of my chaste body
To his concupiscible intemperate lust,
Release my brother; and, after much debatement,
My sisterly remorse confutes mine honour,
And I did yield to him; but the next morn betimes,
His purpose surfeiting, he sends a warrant
For my poor brother's head.

DUKE.
　　　　　　　　This is most likely!

ISABELLA.
O, that it were as like as it is true!

DUKE.
By heaven, fond wretch, thou know'st not what
　　thou speak'st.
Or else thou art suborn'd against his honour
In hateful practice. First, his integrity
Stands without blemish. Next, it imports no
　　reason
That with such vehemency he should pursue
Faults proper to himself: if he had so offended,
He would have weigh'd thy brother by himself,
And not have cut him off. Some one hath set you
　　on:
Confess the truth, and say by whose advice
Thou camest here to complain.

ISABELLA.
　　　　　　　　　　And is this all?
Then, O you blessed ministers above,
Keep me in patience, and with ripen'd time
Unfold the evil which is here wrapt up
In countenance!—Heaven shield your grace from
　　woe,
As I, thus wrong'd, hence unbelieved go!

DUKE.
I know you'ld fain be gone.—An officer!
To prison with her!—Shall we thus permit
A blasting and a scandalous breath to fall
On him so near us? This needs must be a prac-
　　tice.—
Who knew of your intent and coming hither?

ISABELLA.
One that I would were here, Friar Lodowick.

DUKE.
A ghostly father, belike.—Who knows that
　　Lodowick?

LUCIO.
My lord, I know him; 'tis a meddling friar;
I do not like the man: had he been lay, my lord,
For certain words he spake against your grace
In your retirement, I had swinged him soundly.

DUKE.
Words against me! this' a good friar, belike!
And to set on this wretched woman here
Against our substitute!—Let this friar be found.

LUCIO.
But yesternight, my lord, she and that friar,
I saw them at the prison: a saucy friar,
A very scurvy fellow.

FRIAR PETER.
　　　　　　　　Bless'd be your royal grace!
I have stood by, my lord, and I have heard
Your royal ear abused. First, hath this woman
Most wrongfully accused your substitute,
Who is as free from touch or soil with her
As she from one ungot.

DUKE.
　　　　　　　　We did believe no less.
Know you that Friar Lodowick that she speaks of?

FRIAR PETER.
I know him for a man divine and holy;
Not scurvy, nor a temporary meddler,
As he's reported by this gentleman;
And, on my trus , a man that never yet
Did, as he vouch :s, misreport your grace.

LUCIO.
My lord, most villainously; believe it.

FRIAR PETER.
Well, he in time may come to clear himself;
But at this instant he is sick, my lord,
Of a strange fever. Upon his mere request,—
Being come to knowledge that there was complaint
Intended 'gainst Lord Angelo,—came I hither,
To speak, as from his mouth, what he doth know
Is true and false; and what he, with his oath
And all probation, will make up full clear,
Whensoever he's convented. First, for this
　　woman,—
To justify this worthy nobleman,
So vulgarly and personally accused,—
Her shall you hear disproved to her eyes,
Till she herself confess it.

DUKE.
Good friar, let's hear it.
[ISABELLA *is carried off guarded; and* MARI-
ANA *comes forward.*
Do you not smile at this, Lord Angelo?—
O heaven, the vanity of wretched fools!—
Give us some seats.—Come, cousin Angelo;
In this I'll be impartial; be you judge
Of your own cause.—Is this the witness, friar?
First, let her show her face, and after speak.

MARIANA.
Pardon, my lord; I will not show my face
Until my husband bid me.

DUKE.
What, are you married?

MARIANA.
No, my lord.

DUKE.
Are you a maid?

MARIANA.
No, my lord.

DUKE.
A widow, then?

MARIANA.
Neither, my lord.

DUKE.
Why, you are nothing, then:—neither maid,
widow, nor wife?

LUCIO.
My lord, she may be a punk; for many of them are
neither maid, widow, nor wife.

DUKE.
Silence that fellow: I would he had some cause
To prattle for himself.

LUCIO.
Well, my lord.

MARIANA.
My lord, I do confess I ne'er was married;
And I confess, besides, I am no maid: [not
I've known my husband: yet my husband knows
That ever he knew me.

LUCIO.
He was drunk, then, my lord: it can be no better.

DUKE.
For the benefit of silence, would thou wert so too!

LUCIO.
Well, my lord.

DUKE.
This is no witness for Lord Angelo.

MARIANA.
Now I come to't, my lord:
She that accuses him of fornication,
In self-same manner doth accuse my husband;
And charges him, my lord, with such a time
When I'll depose I had him in mine arms
With all th'effect of love.

ANGELO.
Charges she moe than me?

MARIANA.
Not that I know.

DUKE.
No? you say your husband.

MARIANA.
Why, just, my lord, and that is Angelo,
Who thinks he knows that he ne'er knew my body,
But knows he thinks that he knows Isabel's.

ANGELO.
This is a strange abuse.—Let's see thy face.

MARIANA.
My husband bids me; now I will unmask.
This is that face, thou cruel Angelo,   [*Unveiling.*
Which once thou sworest was worth the looking on;
This is the hand which, with a vow'd contract,
Was fast belockt in thine; this is the body
That took away the match from Isabel,
And did supply thee at thy garden-house
In her imagined person.

DUKE.
Know you this woman?

LUCIO.
Carnally, she says.

DUKE.
Sirrah, no more!

LUCIO.
Enough, my lord.

ANGELO.
My lord, I must confess I know this woman:
And five years since there was some speech of
    marriage
Betwixt myself and her; which was broke off,
Partly for that her promised proportions
Came short of composition; but in chief
For that her reputation was disvalued
In levity: since which time of five years
I never spake with her, saw her, nor heard from
    her,
Upon my faith and honour.

MARIANA.
Noble prince,
As there comes light from heaven and words from
    breath,
As there is sense in truth and truth in virtue,
I am affianced this man's wife as strongly
As words could make up vows: and, my good lord,
But Tuesday night last gone, in's garden-house,
He knew me as a wife. As this is true,
Let me in safety raise me from my knees;
Or else for ever be confixed here,
A marble monument!

ANGELO.
I did but smile till now;
Now, good my lord, give me the scope of justice;
My patience here is touch'd. I do perceive
These poor informal women are no more
But instruments of some more mightier member
That sets them on: let me have way, my lord,
To find this practice out.

DUKE.
Ay, with my heart;
And punish them to your height of pleasure.—
Thou foolish friar; and thou pernicious woman,
Compact with her that's gone, think'st thou thy
    oaths,
Though they would swear down each particular
    saint,
Were testimonies against his worth and credit,
That's seal'd in approbation?—You, Lord Esca-
    lus,
Sit with my cousin; lend him your kind pains
To find out this abuse, whence 'tis derived.—
There is another friar that set them on;
Let him be sent for.

FRIAR PETER.
Would he were here, my lord! for he, indeed,
Hath set the women on to this complaint:
Your provost knows the place where he abides,
And he may fetch him.

DUKE.
Go do it instantly. [*Exit* PROVOST.
And you, my noble and well-warranted cousin,
Whom it concerns to hear this matter forth,
Do with your injuries as seems you best,
In any chastisement: I for a while will leave you;
But stir not till you have well determined
Upon these slanderers.

ESCALUS.
My lord, we'll do it throughly.   [*Exit* DUKE.
Signior Lucio, did not you say you knew that
Friar Lodowick to be a dishonest person?

LUCIO.
Cucullus non facit monachum: honest in nothing
but in his clothes; and one that hath spoke most
villainous speeches of the duke.

ESCALUS.
We shall entreat you to abide here till he come,
and enforce them against him: we shall find this
friar a notable fellow.

LUCIO.
As any in Vienna, on my word.

ESCALUS.
Call that same Isabel here once again: I would
speak with her. [*Exit an* ATTENDANT.]—Pray
you, my lord, give me leave to question; you shall
see how I'll handle her.

LUCIO.
Not better than he, by her own report.

ESCALUS.
Say you?

LUCIO.
Marry, sir, I think, if you handled her privately,
she would sooner confess: perchance, publicly,
she'll be ashamed.

ESCALUS.
I will go darkly to work with her.

LUCIO.
That's the way; for women are light at midnight.
Enter OFFICERS *with* ISABELLA.

ESCALUS [*to* ISABELLA].
Come on, mistress: here's a gentlewoman denies
all that you have said.

LUCIO.
My lord, here comes the rascal I spoke of; here
with the provost.

ESCALUS.
In very good time:—speak not you to him till we
call upon you.

LUCIO.
Mum.
Enter DUKE *disguised as a friar, and* PROVOST.

ESCALUS.
Come, sir: did you set these women on to slander
Lord Angelo? they have confess'd you did.

DUKE.
'Tis false.

ESCALUS.
How! know you where you are?

DUKE.
Respect to your great place! and let the devil

Be sometime honour'd for his burning throne!—
Where is the duke? 'tis he should hear me speak.

ESCALUS.
The duke's in us; and we will hear you speak:
Look you speak justly.

DUKE.
Boldly, at least.—But, O, poor souls,
Come you to seek the lamb here of the fox?
Good night to your redress! Is the duke gone?
Then is your cause gone too. The duke's unjust,
Thus to retort your manifest appeal,
And put your trial in the villain's mouth
Which here you come to accuse.

LUCIO.
This is the rascal; this is he I spoke of.

ESCALUS.
Why, thou unreverend and unhallow'd friar,
Is't not enough thou hast suborn'd these women
To accuse this worthy man, but, in foul mouth,
And in the witness of his proper ear,
To call him villain? and then to glance from him
To th'duke himself, to tax him with injustice?—
Take him hence; to th'rack with him!—We'll
    touse you
Joint by joint, but we will know his purpose.—
What, 'unjust'?

DUKE.
Be not so hot; the duke
Dare no more stretch this finger of mine than he
Dare rack his own: his subject am I not,
Nor here provincial. My business in this state
Made me a looker-on here in Vienna,
Where I have seen corruption boil and bubble
Till it o'er-run the stew; laws for all faults,
But faults so countenanced, that the strong statutes
Stand like the forfeits in a barber's shop,
As much in mock as mark.

ESCALUS.
Slander to th'state!—Away with him to prison!

ANGELO.
What can you vouch against him, Signior Lucio?
Is this the man that you did tell us of?

LUCIO.
'Tis he, my lord.—Come hither, goodman bald-
pate: do you know me?

DUKE.
I remember you, sir, by the sound of your voice:
I met you at the prison, in the absence of the duke.

LUCIO.
O, did you so? And do you remember what you
said of the duke?

DUKE.
Most notedly, sir.

LUCIO.
Do you so, sir? And was the duke a fleshmonger,
a fool, and a coward, as you then reported him to
be?

DUKE.
You must, sir, change persons with me, ere you
make that my report; you, indeed, spoke so of
him; and much more, much worse.

LUCIO.
O thou damnable fellow! Did not I pluck thee by
the nose for thy speeches?

DUKE.
I protest I love the duke as I love myself.

ANGELO.

Hark, how the villain would close now, after his treasonable abuses!

ESCALUS.

Such a fellow is not to be talk'd withal.—Away with him to prison!—Where is the provost?— Away with him to prison! lay bolts enough upon him: let him speak no more.—Away with those giglots too, and with the other confederate companion!

DUKE [to the PROVOST].

Stay, sir; stay awhile;

ANGELO.

What, resists he?—Help him, Lucio.

LUCIO.

Come, sir; come, sir; come sir, foh, sir! Why, you bald-pated, lying rascal, you must be hooded, must you? Show your knave's visage, with a pox to you! show your sheep-biting face, and be hang'd an hour! Will't not off?

[Pulls off the friar's hood, and discovers the DUKE.

DUKE.

Thou art the first knave that e'er madest a duke.— First, provost, let me bail these gentle three.— [to LUCIO] Sneak not away, sir; for the friar and you
Must have a word anon.—Lay hold on him.

LUCIO.

This may prove worse than hanging.

DUKE [to ESCALUS].

What you have spoke I pardon: sit you down: We'll borrow place of him.—[to ANGELO] Sir, by your leave.
Hast thou or word, or wit, or impudence, That yet can do thee office? If thou hast, Rely upon it till my tale be heard, And hold no longer out.

ANGELO.

O my dread lord, I should be guiltier than my guiltiness, To think I can be undiscernible, When I perceive your grace, like power divine, Hath look'd upon my passes. Then, good prince, No longer session hold upon my shame, But let my trial be mine own confession: Immediate sentence then, and sequent death, Is all the grace I beg.

DUKE.

Come hither, Mariana.— Say, wast thou e'er contracted to this woman?

ANGELO.

I was, my lord.

DUKE.

Go take her hence, and marry her instantly.— Do you the office, friar; which consummate, Return him here again.—Go with him, provost.

[Exeunt ANGELO, MARIANA, FRIAR PETER, and PROVOST.

ESCALUS.

My lord, I am more amazed at his dishonour Than at the strangeness of it.

DUKE.

Come hither, Isabel. Your friar is now your prince: as I was then Advertising and holy to your business,

Not changing heart with habit, I am still Attorney'd at your service.

ISABELLA.

O, give me pardon, That I, your vassal, have employ'd and pain'd Your unknown sovereignty!

DUKE.

You are pardon'd, Isabel: And now, dear maid, be you as free to us. Your brother's death, I know, sits at your heart; And you may marvel why I obscured myself, Labouring to save his life, and would not rather Make rash remonstrance of my hidden power Than let him so be lost. O most kind maid, It was the swift celerity of his death, Which I did think with slower foot came on, That brain'd my purpose:—but peace be with him!
That life is better life, past fearing death, Than that which lives to fear: make it your comfort, So happy is your brother.

ISABELLA.

I do, my lord.

Enter ANGELO, MARIANA, FRIAR PETER, and PROVOST.

DUKE.

For this new-married man, approaching here, Whose salt imagination yet hath wrong'd Your well-defended honour, you must pardon For Mariana's sake: but as he adjudged your brother,—
Being criminal, in double violation Of sacred chastity, and of promise-breach Thereon dependent, for your brother's life,— The very mercy of the law cries out Most audible, even from his proper tongue, 'An Angelo for Claudio, death for death!' Haste still pays haste, and leisure answers leisure; Like doth quit like, and Measure still for Measure. Then, Angelo, thy fault thus manifested,— Which, though thou wouldst deny, denies thee vantage,—
We do condemn thee to the very block Where Claudio stoop'd to death, and with like haste.—
Away with him!

MARIANA.

O my most gracious lord, I hope you will not mock me with a husband.

DUKE.

It is your husband mock'd you with a husband. Consenting to the safeguard of your honour, I thought your marriage fit; else imputation, For that he knew you, might reproach your life, And choke your good to come; for his possessions, Although by confiscation they are ours, We do instate and widow you withal, To buy you a better husband.

MARIANA.

O my dear lord, I crave no other, nor no better man.

DUKE.

Never crave him; we are definitive.

MARIANA.

Gentle my liege,—   [Kneeling.

DUKE.
You do but lose your labour.—
Away with him to death!—[to LUCIO] Now, sir, to
　you.

MARIANA.
O my good lord!—Sweet Isabel, take my part;
Lend me your knees, and all my life to come
I'll lend you all my life to do you service.

DUKE.
Against all sense you do importune her:
Should she kneel down in mercy of this fact,
Her brother's ghost his paved bed would break,
And take her hence in horror.

MARIANA.
　　　　　　　　　　　Isabel,
Sweet Isabel, do yet but kneel by me;
Hold up your hands, say nothing,—I'll speak
　all.
They say, best men are moulded out of faults;
And, for the most, become much more the
　better
For being a little bad: so may my husband.
O Isabel, will you not lend a knee?

DUKE.
He dies for Claudio's death.

ISABELLA.
　　　　　Most bounteous sir, [Kneeling.
Look, if it please you, on this man condemn'd,
As if my brother lived: I partly think
A due sincerity govern'd his deeds,
Till he did look on me: since it is so,
Let him not die. My brother had but justice,
In that he did the thing for which he died:
For Angelo,
His act did not o'ertake his bad intent;
And must be buried but as an intent
That perish'd by the way: thoughts are no sub-
　jects,
Intents but merely thoughts.

MARIANA.
　　　　　　　Merely, my lord.

DUKE.
Your suit's unprofitable; stand up, I say.—
I have bethought me of another fault.—
Provost, how came it Claudio was beheaded
At an unusual hour?

PROVOST.
　　　　It was commanded so.

DUKE.
Had you a special warrant for the deed?

PROVOST.
No, my good lord; it was by private message.

DUKE.
For which I do discharge you of your office:
Give up your keys.

PROVOST.
　　　　　Pardon me, noble lord:
I thought it was a fault, but knew it not;
Yet did repent me, after more advice:
For testimony whereof, one in the prison,
That should by private order else have died,
I have reserved alive.

DUKE.
What's he?

PROVOST.
His name is Barnardine.

DUKE.
I would thou hadst done so by Claudio.—
Go fetch him hither; let me look upon him.
　　　　　　　　　　[Exit PROVOST.

ESCALUS.
I am sorry, one so learned and so wise
As you, Lord Angelo, have still appear'd,
Should slip so grossly, both in the heat of blood,
And lack of temper'd judgement afterward.

ANGELO.
I am sorry that such sorrow I procure:
And so deep sticks it in my penitent heart,
That I crave death more willingly than mercy;
'Tis my deserving, and I do entreat it.

Enter PROVOST, with BARNARDINE, CLAUDIO
　　　muffled, and JULIET.

DUKE.
Which is that Barnardine?

PROVOST.
　　　　　　This, my lord.

DUKE.
There was a friar told me of this man.—
Sirrah, thou art said to have a stubborn soul,
That apprehends no further than this world,
And squarest thy life according. Thou'rt con-
　demn'd:
But, for those earthly faults, I quit them all;
And pray thee take this mercy to provide
For better times to come.—Friar, advise him;
I leave him to your hand.—What muffled fellow's
　that?

PROVOST.
This is another prisoner that I saved,
Who should have died when Claudio lost his head;
As like almost to Claudio as himself.
　　　　　　　　[Unmuffles CLAUDIO.

DUKE [to ISABELLA].
If he be like your brother, for his sake
Is he pardon'd; and, for your lovely sake,
Give me your hand, and say you will be mine,
He is my brother too: but fitter time for that.
By this Lord Angelo perceives he's safe;
Methinks I see a quick'ning in his eye.—
Well, Angelo, your evil quits you well:
Look that you love your wife; her worth worth
　yours.—
I find an apt remission in myself;
And yet here's one in place I cannot pardon.—
[to LUCIO] You, sirrah, that knew me for a fool, a
　coward,
One all of luxury, an ass, a madman;
Wherein have I so deserved of you,
That you extol me thus?

LUCIO.
Faith, my lord, I spoke it but according to the
trick. If you will hang me for it, you may; but
I had rather it would please you I might be
whipt.

DUKE.
Whipt first, sir, and hang'd after.—
Proclaim it, provost, round about the city,
If any woman wrong'd by this lewd fellow,—
As I have heard him swear himself there's one
Whom he begot with child,—let her appear,
And he shall marry her: the nuptial finish'd,
Let him be whipt and hang'd.

LUCIO.

I beseech your highness, do not marry me to a
whore! Your highness said even now, I made you
a duke: good my lord, do not recompense me in
making me a cuckold.

DUKE.

Upon mine honour, thou shalt marry her.
Thy slanders I forgive; and therewithal
Remit thy other forfeits.—Take him to prison;
And see our pleasure herein executed.

LUCIO.

Marrying a punk, my lord, is pressing to death,
whipping, and hanging.

DUKE.

Slandering a prince deserves it.—

[Exeunt OFFICERS with LUCIO.

She, Claudio, that you wrong'd, look you restore.—

Joy to you, Mariana!—Love her, Angelo:
I have confess'd her, and I know her virtue.—
Thanks, good friend Escalus, for thy much good-
    ness:
There's more behind that is more gratulate.—
Thanks, provost, for thy care and secrecy:
We shall employ thee in a worthier place.—
Forgive him, Angelo, that brought you home
The head of Ragozine for Claudio's:
Th'offence pardons itself.—Dear Isabel,
I have a motion much imports your good;
Whereto if you'll a willing ear incline,
What's mine is yours, and what is yours is
    mine.—
So, bring us to our palace; where we'll show
What's yet behind, that's meet you all should
    know.   [Exeunt.

OTHELLO,
THE MOOR OF VENICE

DRAMATIS PERSONAE

DUKE OF VENICE.
BRABANTIO, *a senator.*
OTHER SENATORS.
GRATIANO, *brother to Brabantio.*
LODOVICO, *kinsman to Brabantio.*
OTHELLO, *a noble Moor in the service of the Venetian state.*
CASSIO, *his lieutenant.*
IAGO, *his ancient.*
RODERIGO, *a Venetian gentleman.*

MONTANO, *Othello's predecessor in the government of Cyprus.*
CLOWN, *servant to Othello.*

DESDEMONA, *daughter to Brabantio and wife to Othello.*
EMILIA, *wife to Iago.*
BIANCA, *mistress to Cassio.*

SAILOR, MESSENGER, HERALD, OFFICERS, GENTLEMEN, MUSICIANS, *and* ATTENDANTS.

SCENE—*Venice: a seaport in Cyprus.*

ACT I. SCENE I.

Venice. A street.

Enter RODERIGO *and* IAGO.

RODERIGO.

TUSH, never tell me; I take it much unkindly
That thou, Iago, who hast had my purse
As if the strings were thine, shouldst know of this,—

IAGO.
'Sblood, but you will not hear me:—
If ever I did dream of such a matter,
Abhor me.

RODERIGO.
Thou told'st me thou didst hold him in thy hate.
IAGO.
Despise me, if I do not. Three great ones of the city,
In personal suit to make me his lieutenant,
Off-capt to him:—and, by the faith of man,
I know my price, I am worth no worse a place:—
But he, as loving his own pride and purposes,
Evades them, with a bombast circumstance
Horribly stuft with epithets of war;
And, in conclusion,
Nonsuits my mediators; for, 'Certes,' says he,
'I have already chose my officer.'
And what was he?
Forsooth, a great arithmetician,
One Michael Cassio, a Florentine,
A fellow almost damn'd in a fair wife;
That never set a squadron in the field,
Nor the division of a battle knows
More than a spinster; unless the bookish theoric,
Wherein the toged consuls can propose
As masterly as he: mere prattle, without practice,
Is all his soldiership. But he, sir, had th'election:
And I—of whom his eyes had seen the proof
At Rhodes, at Cyprus, and on other grounds
Christian and heathen—must be be-lee'd and calm'd
By debitor and creditor; this counter-caster,
He, in good time, must his lieutenant be,
And I—God bless the mark!—his Moorship's ancient.

RODERIGO.
By heaven, I rather would have been his hangman.
IAGO.
Why, there's no remedy; 'tis the curse of service,
Preferment goes by letter and affection,
And not by old gradation, where each second
Stood heir to th' first. Now, sir, be judge yourself,
Whether I in any just term am affined
To love the Moor.

RODERIGO.
I would not follow him, then.
IAGO.
O, sir, content you;
I follow him to serve my turn upon him:
We cannot all be masters, nor all masters
Cannot be truly follow'd. You shall mark
Many a duteous and knee-crooking knave,
That, doting on his own obsequious bondage,
Wears out his time, much like his master's ass,
For naught but provender; and, when he's old, cashier'd:
Whip me such honest knaves. Others there are,
Who, trimm'd in forms and visages of duty,
Keep yet their hearts attending on themselves;
And, throwing but shows of service on their lords,
Do well thrive by them, and, when they have lined their coats,
Do themselves homage: these fellows have some soul;
And such a one do I profess myself.
For, sir,
It is as sure as you are Roderigo,
Were I the Moor, I would not be Iago:
In following him, I follow but myself;
Heaven is my judge, not I for love and duty,
But seeming so, for my peculiar end:
For when my outward action doth demonstrate
The native act and figure of my heart
In compliment extern, 'tis not long after
But I will wear my heart upon my sleeve
For daws to peck at: I am not what I am.
RODERIGO.
What a full fortune does the thick-lips owe,
If he can carry't thus!

IAGO.
Call up her father,
Rouse him:—make after him, poison his delight,
Proclaim him in the streets; incense her kinsmen:
And though he in a fertile climate dwell,
Plague him with flies; though that his joy be joy,
Yet throw such changes of vexation on't,
As it may lose some colour.

RODERIGO.
Here is her father's house; I'll call aloud.

IAGO.
Do; with like timorous accent and dire yell
As when, by night and negligence, the fire
Is spied in populous cities.

RODERIGO.
What, ho, Brabantio! Signior Brabantio, ho!

IAGO.
Awake! what, ho, Brabantio! thieves! thieves!
thieves!
Look to your house, your daughter, and your
bags!
Thieves! thieves!

BRABANTIO *appears above, at a window.*

BRABANTIO.
What is the reason of this terrible summons?
What is the matter there?

RODERIGO.
Signior, is all your family within?

IAGO.
Are your doors lockt?

BRABANTIO.
Why, wherefore ask you this?

IAGO.
Zounds, sir, y'are robb'd; for shame, put on your
gown;
Your heart is burst, you have lost half your soul;
Even now, now, very now, an old black ram
Is tupping your white ewe. Arise, arise;
Awake the snorting citizens with the bell,
Or else the devil will make a grandsire of you:
Arise, I say.

BRABANTIO.
What, have you lost your wits?

RODERIGO.
Most reverend signior, do you know my voice?

BRABANTIO.
Not I: what are you?

RODERIGO.
My name is Roderigo.

BRABANTIO.
The worser welcome:
I have charged thee not to haunt about my doors:
In honest plainness thou hast heard me say
My daughter is not for thee; and now, in mad-
ness,
Being full of supper and distempering draughts,
Upon malicious bravery, dost thou come
To start my quiet;—

RODERIGO.
Sir, sir, sir,—

BRABANTIO.
But thou must needs be sure
My spirit and my place have in them power
To make this bitter to thee.

RODERIGO.
Patience, good sir.

BRABANTIO.
What tell'st thou me of robbing? this is Venice;
My house is not a grange.

RODERIGO.
Most grave Brabantio,
In simple and pure soul I come to you.

IAGO.
Zounds, sir, you are one of those that will not
serve God, if the devil bid you. Because we come
to do you service, and you think we are ruffians,
you'll have your daughter cover'd with a Barbary
horse; you'll have your nephews neigh to you;
you'll have coursers for cousins, and gennets for
germans.

BRABANTIO.
What profane wretch art thou?

IAGO.
I am one, sir, that comes to tell you your daughter
and the Moor are now making the beast with two
backs.

BRABANTIO.
Thou art a villain.

IAGO.
You are—a senator.

BRABANTIO.
This thou shalt answer: I know thee, Roderigo.

RODERIGO.
Sir, I will answer any thing. But, I beseech you,
If't be your pleasure and most wise consent,
As partly I find it is, that your fair daughter,
At this odd-even and dull watch o'the night,
Transported, with no worse nor better guard
But with a knave of common hire, a gondolier,
To the gross clasps of a lascivious Moor,—
If this be known to you, and your allowance,
We then have done you bold and saucy wrongs;
But, if you know not this, my manners tell me
We have your wrong rebuke. Do not believe
That, from the sense of all civility,
I thus would play and trifle with your reverence:
Your daughter,—if you have not given her leave,—
I say again, hath made a gross revolt;
Tying her duty, beauty, wit, and fortunes,
In an extravagant and wheeling stranger
Of here and every where. Straight satisfy your-
self:
If she be in her chamber or your house,
Let loose on me the justice of the state
For thus deluding you.

BRABANTIO.
Strike on the tinder, ho!
Give me a taper!—call up all my people!—
This accident is not unlike my dream:
Belief of it oppresses me already.—
Light, I say! light!   [*Exit above.*

IAGO.
Farewell; for I must leave you:
It seems not meet, nor wholesome to my place,
To be produced—as, if I stay, I shall—
Against the Moor: for, I do know, the state,
However this may gall him with some check,
Cannot with safety cast him; for he's embarkt
With such loud reason to the Cyprus wars,
Which even now stand in act, that, for their souls,
Another of his fadom they have none
To lead their business: in which regard,

Though I do hate him as I do hell-pains,
Yet, for necessity of present life,
I must show out a flag and sign of love,
Which is indeed but sign. That you shall surely
   find him,
Lead to the Sagittary the raised search;
And there will I be with him. So, farewell. [*Exit.*
  Enter, below, BRABANTIO, *with* SERVANTS
    and torches.
        BRABANTIO.
It is too true an evil: gone she is;
And what's to come of my despised time
Is naught but bitterness.—Now, Roderigo,
Where didst thou see her?—O unhappy girl!—.
With the Moor, say'st thou?—Who would be a
   father!—
How didst thou know 'twas she?—O, she de-
   ceives me
Past thought!—What said she to you?—Get more
   tapers;
Raise all my kindred.—Are they married, think
   you?
        RODERIGO.
Truly, I think they are.
        BRABANTIO.
O heaven!—How got she out?—O treason of the
   blood!—
Fathers, from hence trust not your daughters'
   minds
By what you see them act.—Is there not charms
By which the property of youth and maidhood
May be abused? Have you not read, Roderigo,
Of some such thing?
        RODERIGO.
       Yes, sir, I have indeed.
        BRABANTIO.
Call up my brother.—O, would you had had her!—
Some one way, some another.—Do you know
Where we may apprehend her and the Moor?
        RODERIGO.
I think I can discover him, if you please
To get good guard, and go along with me.
        BRABANTIO.
Pray you, lead on. At every house I'll call;
I may command at most.—Get weapons, ho!
And raise some special officers of night.—
On, good Roderigo;—I'll deserve your pains.
                  [*Exeunt.*

SCENE II.

Another street.

Enter OTHELLO, IAGO, *and* ATTENDANTS
   with torches.

        IAGO.
THOUGH in the trade of war I have slain men,
  Yet do I hold it very stuff o' the conscience
To do no contrived murder: I lack iniquity
Sometimes to do me service: nine or ten times
I had thought t'have yerkt him here under the
   ribs.
        OTHELLO.
'Tis better as it is.
        IAGO.
       Nay, but he prated,
And spoke such scurvy and provoking terms

Against your honour,
That, with the little godliness I have,
I did full hard forbear him. But, I pray you, sir,
Are you fast married? Be assured of this,
That the magnifico is much beloved;
And hath, in his effect, a voice potential
As double as the duke's: he will divorce you;
Or put upon you what restraint and grievance
The law—with all his might t'enforce it on—
Will give him cable.
        OTHELLO.
       Let him do his spite:
My services which I have done the signiory
Shall out-tongue his complaints. 'Tis yet to
   know,—
Which, when I know that boasting is an honour,
I shall promulgate,—I fetch my life and being
From men of royal siege; and my demerits
May speak, unbonneted, to as proud a fortune
As this that I have reacht: for know, Iago,
But that I love the gentle Desdemona,
I would not my unhoused free condition
Put into circumscription and confine
For the sea's worth. But, look! what lights come
   yond?
        IAGO.
Those are the raised father and his friends:
You were best go in.
        OTHELLO.
       Not I; I must be found:
My parts, my title, and my perfect soul
Shall manifest me rightly. Is it they?
        IAGO.
By Janus, I think no.
  Enter CASSIO, *and certain* OFFICERS *with*
    torches.
        OTHELLO.
The servants of the duke, and my lieutenant.—
The goodness of the night upon you, friends!
What is the news?
        CASSIO.
       The duke does greet you, general,
And he requires your haste-post-haste appearance
Even on the instant.
        OTHELLO.
       What is the matter, think you?
        CASSIO.
Something from Cyprus, as I may divine:
It is a business of some heat: the galleys
Have sent a dozen sequent messengers
This very night at one another's heels;
And many of the consuls, raised and met,
Are at the duke's already: you have been hotly
   call'd for;
When, being not at your lodging to be found,
The senate hath sent about three several quests
To search you out.
        OTHELLO.
       'Tis well I am found by you.
I will but spend a word here in the house,
And go with you.   [*Exit.*
        CASSIO.
       Ancient, what makes he here?
        IAGO.
Faith, he to-night hath boarded a land carack:
If it prove lawful prize, he's made for ever.

CASSIO.
I do not understand.

IAGO.
      He's married.

CASSIO.
              To who?

Enter OTHELLO.

IAGO.
Marry, to—Come, captain, will you go?

OTHELLO.
              Have with you.

CASSIO.
Here comes another troop to seek for you.

IAGO.
It is Brabantio:—general, be advised;
He comes to bad intent.

Enter BRABANTIO, RODERIGO, *and* OFFICERS
with torches and weapons.

OTHELLO.
      Holla! stand there!

RODERIGO.
Signior, it is the Moor.

BRABANTIO.
      Down with him, thief!
    [*They draw on both sides.*

IAGO.
You, Roderigo! come, sir, I am for you.

OTHELLO.
Keep up your bright swords, for the dew will rust
   them.—
Good signior, you shall more command with
   years
Than with your weapons.

BRABANTIO.
O thou foul thief, where hast thou stow'd my
   daughter?
Damn'd as thou art, thou hast enchanted her;
For I'll refer me to all things of sense,
If she in chains of magic were not bound,
Whether a maid so tender, fair, and happy,
So opposite to marriage that she shunn'd
The wealthy curled darlings of our nation,
Would ever have, t'incur a general mock,
Run from her guardage to the sooty bosom
Of such a thing as thou,—to fear, not to delight.
Judge me the world, if 'tis not gross in sense
That thou hast practised on her with foul
   charms;
Abused her delicate youth with drugs or minerals
That weaken motion:—I'll have't disputed on;
'Tis probable, and palpable to thinking.
I therefore apprehend and do attach thee
For an abuser of the world, a practiser
Of arts inhibited and out of warrant.—
Lay hold upon him: if he do resist,
Subdue him at his peril.

OTHELLO.
          Hold your hands,
Both you of my inclining, and the rest:
Were it my cue to fight, I should have known it
Without a prompter.—Where will you that I go
To answer this your charge?

BRABANTIO.
         To prison; till fit time
Of law, and course of direct session,
Call thee to answer.

OTHELLO.
      What if I do obey?
How may the duke be therewith satisfied,
Whose messengers are here about my side,
Upon some present business of the state
To bring me to him?

FIRST OFFICER.
      'Tis true, most worthy signior;
The duke's in council, and your noble self,
I am sure, is sent for.

BRABANTIO.
      How! the duke in council!
In this time of the night!—Bring him away;
Mine's not an idle cause: the duke himself,
Or any of my brothers of the state,
Cannot but feel this wrong as 'twere their own;
For if such actions may have passage free,
Bond-slaves and pagans shall our statesmen be.
                 [*Exeunt.*

SCENE III.

A council-chamber.

The DUKE *and* SENATORS *sitting at a table;*
OFFICERS *attending.*

DUKE.
THERE is no composition in these news
   That gives them credit.

FIRST SENATOR.
      Indeed, they are disproportion'd;
My letters say a hundred and seven galleys.

DUKE.
And mine, a hundred and forty.

SECOND SENATOR.
         And mine, two hundred:
But though they jump not on a just account,—
As in these cases, where the aim reports,
'Tis oft with difference,—yet do they all confirm
A Turkish fleet, and bearing up to Cyprus.

DUKE.
Nay, it is possible enough to judgement:
I do not so secure me in the error,
But the main article I do approve
In fearful sense.

SAILOR [*within*].
What, ho! what, ho! what, ho!

FIRST OFFICER.
A messenger from the galleys.

Enter a SAILOR.

DUKE.
      Now, what's the business?

SAILOR.
The Turkish preparation makes for Rhodes;
So was I bid report here to the state
By Signior Angelo.

DUKE.
How say you by this change?

FIRST SENATOR.
         This cannot be,
By no assay of reason: 'tis a pageant,
To keep us in false gaze. When we consider
Th'importancy of Cyprus to the Turk;
And let ourselves again but understand,
That as it more concerns the Turk than Rhodes,
So may he with more facile question bear it,
For that it stands not in such warlike brace,

But altogether lacks th'abilities
That Rhodes is drest in:—if we make thought of
   this,
We must not think the Turk is so unskilful
To leave that latest which concerns him first,
Neglecting an attempt of ease and gain,
To wake and wage a danger profitless.

DUKE.
Nay, in all confidence, he's not for Rhodes.

FIRST OFFICER.
Here is more news.

Enter a MESSENGER.

MESSENGER.
The Ottomites, reverend and gracious,
Steering with due course toward the isle of Rhodes,
Have there injointed them with an after fleet.

FIRST SENATOR.
Ay, so I thought. How many, as you guess?

MESSENGER.
Of thirty sail: and now they do re-stem
Their backward course, bearing with frank ap-
   pearance
Their purposes toward Cyprus.—Signior Mon-
   tano,
Your trusty and most valiant servitor,
With his free duty recommends you thus,
And prays you to believe him.

DUKE.
'Tis certain, then, for Cyprus.—
Marcus Luccicos, is not he in town?

FIRST SENATOR.
He's now in Florence.

DUKE.
Write from us to him; post-post-haste dispatch.

FIRST SENATOR.
Here comes Brabantio and the valiant Moor.

Enter BRABANTIO, OTHELLO, IAGO,
RODERIGO, *and* OFFICERS.

DUKE.
Valiant Othello, we must straight employ you
Against the general enemy Ottoman.—
[*to* BRABANTIO] I did not see you; welcome,
   gentle signior;
We lackt your counsel and your help to-night.

BRABANTIO.
So did I yours. Good your Grace, pardon me;
Neither my place, nor aught I heard of business,
Hath raised me from my bed; nor doth the general
   care
Take hold on me; for my particular grief
Is of so flood-gate and o'erbearing nature
That it engluts and swallows other sorrows,
And it is still itself.

DUKE.
Why, what's the matter?

BRABANTIO.
My daughter! O, my daughter!

DUKE *and* SENATOR.
Dead?

BRABANTIO.
Ay, to me;
She is abused, stoln from me, and corrupted
By spells and medicines bought of mountebanks;
For nature so preposterously to err,
Being not deficient, blind, or lame of sense,
Sans witchcraft could not.

DUKE.
Whoe'er he be that, in this foul proceeding,
Hath thus beguiled your daughter of herself,
And you of her, the bloody book of law
You shall yourself read in the bitter letter
After your own sense; yea, though our proper son
Stood in your action.

BRABANTIO.
Humbly I thank your Grace.
Here is the man, this Moor; whom now, it seems,
Your special mandate, for the state-affairs,
Hath hither brought.

DUKE *and* SENATOR.
We are very sorry for't.

DUKE [*to* OTHELLO].
What, in your own part, can you say to this?

BRABANTIO.
Nothing, but this is so.

OTHELLO.
Most potent, grave, and reverend signiors,
My very noble and approved good masters,
That I have ta'en away this old man's daughter,
It is most true; true, I have married her:
The very head and front of my offending
Hath this extent, no more. Rude am I in my
   speech,
And little blest with the soft phrase of peace;
For since these arms of mine had seven years' pith,
Till now some nine moons wasted, they have used
Their dearest action in the tented field;
And little of this great world can I speak,
More than pertains to feats of broil and battle;
And therefore little shall I grace my cause
In speaking for myself. Yet, by your gracious
   patience,
I will a round unvarnisht tale deliver
Of my whole course of love; what drugs, what
   charms,
What conjuration, and what mighty magic,—
For such proceeding I am charged withal,—
I won his daughter.

BRABANTIO.
A maiden never bold;
Of spirit so still and quiet, that her motion
Blusht at herself; and she—in spite of nature,
Of years, of country, credit, every thing—
To fall in love with what she fear'd to look on!
It is a judgement maim'd and most imperfect,
That will confess perfection so could err
Against all rules of nature; and must be driven
To find out practices of cunning hell,
Why this should be. I therefore vouch again,
That with some mixtures powerful o'er the blood,
Or with some dram conjured to this effect,
He wrought upon her.

DUKE.
To vouch this, is no proof,
Without more wider and more overt test
Than these thin habits and poor likelihoods
Of modern seeming do prefer against him.

FIRST SENATOR.
But, Othello, speak:
Did you by indirect and forced courses
Subdue and poison this young maid's affections?
Or came it by request, and such fair question
As soul to soul affordeth?

OTHELLO.
                    I do beseech you,
Send for the lady to the Sagittary,
And let her speak of me before her father:
If you do find me foul in her report,
The trust, the office, I do hold of you,
Not only take away, but let your sentence
Even fall upon my life.

DUKE.
            Fetch Desdemona hither.

OTHELLO.
Ancient, conduct them, you best know the
    place.—   [*Exeunt* IAGO *and* ATTENDANTS.
And, till she come, as truly as to heaven
I do confess the vices of my blood,
So justly to your grave ears I'll present
How I did thrive in this fair lady's love,
And she in mine.

DUKE.
Say it, Othello.

OTHELLO.
Her father loved me; oft invited me;
Still question'd me the story of my life,
From year to year,—the battles, sieges, fortunes,
That I have past.
I ran it through, even from my boyish days
To the very moment that he bade me tell it:
Wherein I spake of most disastrous chances,
Of moving accidents by flood and field;
Of hair-breadth scapes i'th'imminent deadly
    breach;
Of being taken by the insolent foe,
And sold to slavery; of my redemption thence,
And portance in my travel's history:
Wherein of antres vast and deserts idle,
Rough quarries, rocks, and hills whose heads
    touch heaven,
It was my hint to speak,—such was the process;
And of the Cannibals that each other eat,
The Anthropophagi, and men whose heads
Do grow beneath their shoulders. This to hear
Would Desdemona seriously incline:
But still the house-affairs would draw her thence;
Which ever as she could with haste dispatch,
She'ld come again, and with a greedy ear
Devour up my discourse:—which I observing,
Took once a pliant hour; and found good means
To draw from her a prayer of earnest heart
That I would all my pilgrimage dilate,
Whereof by parcels she had something heard,
But not intentively: I did consent;
And often did beguile her of her tears,
When I did speak of some distressful stroke
That my youth suffer'd. My story being done,
She gave me for my pains a world of sighs:
She swore,—in faith, 'twas strange, 'twas passing
    strange;
'Twas pitiful, 'twas wondrous pitiful:
She wisht she had not heard it: yet she wisht
That heaven had made her such a man: she thankt
    me;
And bade me, if I had a friend that loved her,
I should but teach him how to tell my story,
And that would woo her. Upon this hint I spake:
She loved me for the dangers I had past;
And I loved her that she did pity them.

This only is the witchcraft I have used:—
Here comes the lady; let her witness it.

        Enter DESDEMONA *with* IAGO *and*
                    ATTENDANTS.

DUKE.
I think this tale would win my daughter too.—
Good Brabantio,
Take up this mangled matter at the best:
Men do their broken weapons rather use
Than their bare hands.

BRABANTIO.
            I pray you, hear her speak:
If she confess that she was half the wooer,
Destruction on my head, if my bad blame
Light on the man!—Come hither, gentle mistress:
Do you perceive in all this noble company
Where most you owe obedience?

DESDEMONA.
                    My noble father,
I do perceive here a divided duty:
To you I am bound for life and education;
My life and education both do learn me
How to respect you; you are the lord of duty,—
I am hitherto your daughter: but here's my
    husband;
And so much duty as my mother show'd
To you, preferring you before her father,
So much I challenge that I may profess
Due to the Moor my lord.

BRABANTIO.
            God be wi' you! I have done.
Please it your Grace, on to the state-affairs:
I had rather to adopt a child than get it.—
Come hither, Moor:
I here do give thee that with all my heart
Which, but thou hast already, with all my heart
I would keep from thee.—For your sake, jewel,
I am glad at soul I have no other child;
For thy escape would teach me tyranny,
To hang clogs on them.—I have done, my lord.

DUKE.
Let me speak like yourself; and lay a sentence,
Which, as a grise or step, may help these lovers
Into your favour.
When remedies are past, the griefs are ended
By seeing the worst, which late on hopes de-
    pended.
To mourn a mischief that is past and gone
Is the next way to draw new mischief on.
What cannot be preserved when fortune takes,
Patience her injury a mockery makes.
The robb'd that smiles steals something from the
    thief;
He robs himself that spends a bootless grief.

BRABANTIO.
So let the Turk of Cyprus us beguile;
We lose it not, so long as we can smile.
He bears the sentence well that nothing bears
But the free comfort which from thence he hears:
But he bears both the sentence and the sorrow
That to pay grief must of poor patience borrow.
These sentences, to sugar, or to gall,
Being strong on both sides, are equivocal:
But words are words; I never yet did hear
That the bruised heart was pierced through the
    ear.—

I humbly beseech you, proceed to th'affairs of
    state.
               DUKE.
The Turk with a most mighty preparation makes
for Cyprus:—Othello, the fortitude of the place
is best known to you; and though we have there a
substitute of most allow'd sufficiency, yet opinion,
a sovereign mistress of effects, throws a more
safer voice on you: you must therefore be content
to slubber the gloss of your new fortunes with
this more stubborn and boisterous expedition.
              OTHELLO.
The tyrant custom, most grave senators,
Hath made the flinty and steel couch of war
My thrice-driven bed of down: I do agnize
A natural and prompt alacrity
I find in hardness; and do undertake
This present war against the Ottomites.
Most humbly, therefore, bending to your state,
I crave fit disposition for my wife;
Due reference of place and exhibition;
With such accommodation and besort
As levels with her breeding.
              DUKE.
                    If you please,
Be't at her father's.
            BRABANTIO.
              I'll not have it so.
              OTHELLO.
Nor I.
             DESDEMONA.
              Nor I; I would not there reside,
To put my father in impatient thoughts
By being in his eye. Most gracious duke,
To my unfolding lend your prosperous ear;
And let me find a charter in your voice,
T'assist my simpleness.
              DUKE.
What would you, Desdemona?
             DESDEMONA.
That I did love the Moor to live with him,
My downright violence and storm of fortunes
May trumpet to the world: my heart's subdued
Even to the very quality of my lord:
I saw Othello's visage in his mind;
And to his honours and his valiant parts
Did I my soul and fortunes consecrate.
So that, dear lords, if I be left behind,
A moth of peace, and he go to the war,
The rites for which I love him are bereft me,
And I a heavy interim shall support
By his dear absence. Let me go with him.
              OTHELLO.
Your voices, lords: beseech you, let her will
Have a free way.
Vouch with me, heaven, I therefore beg it not,
To please the palate of my appetite;
Nor to comply with heat—the young affects
In me defunct—and proper satisfaction;
But to be free and bounteous to her mind:
And heaven defend your good souls, that you
    think
I will your serious and great business scant
For she is with me: no, when light-wing'd toys
Of feather'd Cupid seel with wanton dullness
My speculative and officed instruments,

That my disports corrupt and taint my business,
Let housewives make a skillet of my helm,
And all indign and base adversities
Make head against my estimation!
              DUKE.
Be it as you shall privately determine,
Either for her stay or going: th'affair cries haste,
And speed must answer it.
          FIRST SENATOR.
You must away to-night.
              OTHELLO.
                With all my heart.
              DUKE.
At nine i'the morning here we'll meet again.—
Othello, leave some officer behind,
And he shall our commission bring to you;
With such things else of quality and respect
As doth import you.
              OTHELLO.
          So please your Grace, my ancient;
A man he is of honesty and trust:
To his conveyance I assign my wife,
With what else needful your good Grace shall
    think
To be sent after me.
              DUKE.
              Let it be so.—
Good night to every one.—[to BRABANTIO] And,
    noble signior,
If virtue no delighted beauty lack,
Your son-in-law is far more fair than black.
          FIRST SENATOR.
Adieu, brave Moor: use Desdemona well.
           BRABANTIO.
Look to her, Moor, if thou hast eyes to see:
She has deceived her father, and may thee.
        [*Exeunt* DUKE, SENATORS, OFFICERS, *&c.*
              OTHELLO.
My life upon her faith!—Honest Iago,
My Desdemona must I leave to thee:
I prithee, let thy wife attend on her;
And bring them after in the best advantage.—
Come, Desdemona; I have but an hour
Of love, of worldly matters and direction,
To spend with thee: we must obey the time.
        [*Exeunt* OTHELLO *and* DESDEMONA.
             RODERIGO.
Iago,—
               IAGO.
What say'st thou, noble heart?
             RODERIGO.
What will I do, think'st thou?
               IAGO.
Why, go to bed, and sleep.
             RODERIGO.
I will incontinently drown myself.
               IAGO.
If thou dost, I shall never love thee after. Why,
thou silly gentleman!
             RODERIGO.
It is silliness to live when to live is torment; and
then have we a prescription to die when death is
our physician.
               IAGO.
O villainous! I have lookt upon the world for four
times seven years; and since I could distinguish

betwixt a benefit and an injury, I never found man that knew how to love himself. Ere I would say, I would drown myself for the love of a guinea-hen, I would change my humanity with a baboon.

RODERIGO.

What should I do? I confess it is my shame to be so fond; but it is not in my virtue to amend it.

IAGO.

Virtue! a fig! 'tis in ourselves that we are thus or thus. Our bodies are gardens; to the which our wills are gardeners: so that if we will plant nettles, or sow lettuce; set hyssop, and weed-up thyme; supply it with one gender of herbs, or distract it with many; either to have it sterile with idleness, or manured with industry; why, the power and corrigible authority of this lies in our wills. If the balance of our lives had not one scale of reason to poise another of sensuality, the blood and baseness of our natures would conduct us to most preposterous conclusions: but we have reason to cool our raging motions, our carnal stings, our unbitted lusts; whereof I take this that you call love to be a sect or scion.

RODERIGO.

It cannot be.

IAGO.

It is merely a lust of the blood and a permission of the will. Come, be a man: drown thyself! drown cats and blind puppies. I have profest me thy friend, and I confess me knit to thy deserving with cables of perdurable toughness; I could never better stead thee than now. Put money in thy purse; follow thou the wars; defeat thy favour with an usurpt beard; I say, put money in thy purse. It cannot be that Desdemona should long continue her love to the Moor,—put money in thy purse,—nor he his to her: it was a violent commencement, and thou shalt see an answerable sequestration;—put but money in thy purse.— These Moors are changeable in their wills:—fill thy purse with money:—the food that to him now is as luscious as locusts shall be to him shortly as bitter as coloquintida. She must change for youth; when she is sated with his body, she will find the error of her choice: she must have change, she must: therefore put money in thy purse.—If thou wilt needs damn thyself, do it a more delicate way than drowning. Make all the money thou canst: if sanctimony and a frail vow betwixt an erring barbarian and a supersubtle Venetian be not too hard for my wits and all the tribe of hell, thou shalt enjoy her; therefore make money. A pox of drowning thyself! it is clean out of the way: seek thou rather to be hang'd in compassing thy joy than to be drown'd and go without her.

RODERIGO.

Wilt thou be fast to my hopes, if I depend on the issue?

IAGO.

Thou art sure of me:—go, make money:—I have told thee often, and I re-tell thee again and again, I hate the Moor: my cause is hearted: thine hath no less reason. Let us be conjunctive in our revenge against him: if thou canst cuckold him, thou dost thyself a pleasure, me a sport. There are many events in the womb of time, which will be deliver'd. Traverse; go; provide thy money. We will have more of this to-morrow. Adieu.

RODERIGO.

Where shall we meet i'the morning.

IAGO.

At my lodging.

RODERIGO.

I'll be with thee betimes.

IAGO.

Go to; farewell. Do you hear, Roderigo?

RODERIGO.

What say you?

IAGO.

No more of drowning, do you hear?

RODERIGO.

I am changed: I'll go sell all my land.

IAGO.

Go to; farewell! put money in your purse.

[Exit RODERIGO.

Thus do I ever make my fool my purse;
For I mine own gain'd knowledge should profane,
If I would time expend with such a snipe,
But for my sport and profit. I hate the Moor;
And it is thought abroad, that 'twixt my sheets
'Has done my office: I know not if't be true;
But I, for mere suspicion in that kind,
Will do as if for surety. He holds me well;
The better shall my purpose work on him.
Cassio's a proper man: let me see now;
To get his place, and to plume up my will
In double knavery—How, how?—Let's see:—
After some time, to abuse Othello's ear
That he is too familiar with his wife:—
He hath a person, and a smooth dispose,
To be suspected; framed to make women false.
The Moor is of a free and open nature,
That thinks men honest that but seem to be so;
And will as tenderly be led by th' nose
As asses are.
I have't;—it is engender'd:—hell and night
Must bring this monstrous birth to the world's
    light.   [Exit.

ACT II. SCENE I.

A seaport town in Cyprus.   An open place near the Quay.

Enter MONTANO *and two* GENTLEMEN.

MONTANO.

WHAT from the cape can you discern at sea?

FIRST GENTLEMAN.

Nothing at all: it is a high-wrought flood;
I cannot 'twixt the heaven and the main
Descry a sail.

MONTANO.

Methinks the wind hath spoke aloud at land;
A fuller blast ne'er shook our battlements:
If it hath ruffian'd so upon the sea,
What ribs of oak, when mountains melt on them,
Can hold the mortise? What shall we hear of this?

SECOND GENTLEMAN.

A segregation of the Turkish fleet:
For do but stand upon the foaming shore,
The chiding billow seems to pelt the clouds;

The wind-shaked surge, with high and mon-
　strous mane,
Seems to cast water on the burning bear,
And quench the guards of th'ever-fixed pole:
I never did like molestation view
On the enchafed flood.
　　　　　　　MONTANO.
　　　　　　　　If that the Turkish fleet
Be not enshelter'd and embay'd, they are
　drown'd;
It is impossible they bear it out.
　　　　Enter a third GENTLEMAN.
　　　　THIRD GENTLEMAN.
News, lads! our wars are done.
The desperate tempest hath so bang'd the Turks,
That their designment halts: a noble ship of
　Venice
Hath seen a grievous wrack and sufferance
On most part of their fleet.
　　　　　　　MONTANO.
How! is this true?
　　　　THIRD GENTLEMAN.
　　　　　　The ship is here put in,
A Veronesa; Michael Cassio,
Lieutenant to the warlike Moor Othello,
Is come on shore: the Moor himself's at sea,
And is in full commission here for Cyprus.
　　　　　　　MONTANO.
I am glad on't; 'tis a worthy governor.
　　　　THIRD GENTLEMAN.
But this same Cassio, though he speak of comfort
Touching the Turkish loss, yet he looks sadly,
And prays the Moor be safe; for they were parted
With foul and violent tempest.
　　　　　　　MONTANO.
　　　　　　　　Pray heaven he be;
For I have served him, and the man commands
Like a full soldier. Let's to the seaside, ho!
As well to see the vessel that's come in
As to throw out our eyes for brave Othello,
Even till we make the main and th'aerial blue
An indistinct regard.
　　　　THIRD GENTLEMAN.
　　　　　　Come, let's do so;
For every minute is expectancy
Of more arrivance.
　　　　Enter CASSIO.
　　　　　　CASSIO.
Thanks, you the valiant of this warlike isle,
That so approve the Moor! O, let the heavens
Give him defence against the elements,
For I have lost him on a dangerous sea!
　　　　　　MONTANO.
Is he well shipt?
　　　　　　CASSIO.
His bark is stoutly timber'd, and his pilot
Of very expert and approved allowance;
Therefore my hopes, not surfeited to death,
Stand in bold cure.
　　　[*within*]　　　A sail, a sail, a sail!
　　　　Enter a fourth GENTLEMAN.
　　　　　　CASSIO.
What noise?
　　　　FOURTH GENTLEMAN.
The town is empty; on the brow o'the sea
Stand ranks of people, and they cry 'A sail!'

　　　　　　CASSIO.
My hopes do shape him for the governor.
　　　　　　　　　　　[*Guns within.*
　　　　SECOND GENTLEMAN.
They do discharge their shot of courtesy:
Our friends at least.
　　　　　　CASSIO.
　　　　　　I pray you, sir, go forth,
And give us truth who 'tis that is arrived.
　　　　SECOND GENTLEMAN.
I shall.　　　　　　　　　　　[*Exit.*
　　　　　　MONTANO.
But, good lieutenant, is your general wived?
　　　　　　CASSIO.
Most fortunately: he hath achieved a maid
That paragons description and wild fame;
One that excels the quirks of blazoning pens,
And in th' essential vesture of creation
Does tire the ingener.
　　　　Enter second GENTLEMAN.
　　　　　　How now! who has put in?
　　　　SECOND GENTLEMAN.
'Tis one Iago, ancient to the general.
　　　　　　CASSIO.
'Has had most favourable and happy speed:
Tempests themselves, high seas, and howling
　winds,
The gutter'd rocks, and congregated sands,—
Traitors ensteep'd to clog the guiltless keel,—
As having sense of beauty, do omit
Their mortal natures, letting go safely by
The divine Desdemona.
　　　　　　MONTANO.
　　　　　　What is she?
　　　　　　CASSIO.
She that I spake of, our great captain's captain,
Left in the conduct of the bold Iago;
Whose footing here anticipates our thoughts
A se'nnight's speed.—Great Jove, Othello guard,
And swell his sail with thine own powerful breath,
That he may bless this bay with his tall ship,
Make love's quick pants in Desdemona's arms,
Give renew'd fire to our extinct spirits,
And bring all Cyprus comfort!—O, behold,
　　　Enter DESDEMONA, EMILIA, IAGO,
　　　　RODERIGO, *and* ATTENDANTS.
The riches of the ship is come on shore!
Ye men of Cyprus, let her have your knees.—
Hail to thee, lady! and the grace of heaven
Before, behind thee, and on every hand,
Enwheel thee round!
　　　　　　DESDEMONA.
　　　　　　I thank you, valiant Cassio.
What tidings can you tell me of my lord?
　　　　　　CASSIO.
He is not yet arrived: nor know I aught
But that he's well, and will be shortly here.
　　　　　　DESDEMONA.
O, but I fear—How lost you company?
　　　　　　CASSIO.
The great contention of the sea and skies
Parted our fellowship:—but, hark! a sail.
　　　[*within*] A sail, a sail!　　　　[*Guns within.*
　　　　SECOND GENTLEMAN.
They give their greeting to the citadel:
This likewise is a friend.

CASSIO.
See for the news.—
[*Exit* GENTLEMAN.
Good ancient, you are welcome:—[*to* EMILIA]
  welcome, mistress:—
Let it not gall your patience, good Iago,
That I extend my manners; 'tis my breeding
That gives me this bold show of courtesy.
[*Kissing her.*

IAGO.
Sir, would she give you so much of her lips
As of her tongue she oft bestows on me,
You'ld have enough.

DESDEMONA.
Alas, she has no speech.

IAGO.
In faith, too much;
I find it still, when I have list to sleep:
Marry, before your ladyship, I grant,
She puts her tongue a little in her heart,
And chides with thinking.

EMILIA.
You have little cause to say so.

IAGO.
Come on, come on; you are pictures out of doors,
Bells in your parlours, wild-cats in your kitchens,
Saints in your injuries, devils being offended,
Players in your housewifery, and housewives in
  your beds.

DESDEMONA.
O, fie upon thee, slanderer!

IAGO.
Nay, it is true, or else I am a Turk:
You rise to play, and go to bed to work.

EMILIA.
You shall not write my praise.

IAGO.
No, let me not.

DESDEMONA.
What wouldst thou write of me, if thou shouldst
  praise me?

IAGO.
O gentle lady, do not put me to't;
For I am nothing, if not critical.

DESDEMONA.
Come on, assay.—There's one gone to the harbour?

IAGO.
Ay, madam.

DESDEMONA.
I am not merry; but I do beguile
The thing I am, by seeming otherwise.—
Come, how wouldst thou praise me?

IAGO.
I am about it; but, indeed, my invention
Comes from my pate as birdlime does from
  frize,—
It plucks out brains and all: but my Muse labours,
And thus she is deliver'd.
If she be fair and wise,—fairness and wit,
The one's for use, the other useth it.

DESDEMONA.
Well praised! How if she be black and witty?

IAGO.
If she be black, and thereto have a wit,
She'll find a white that shall her blackness hit.

DESDEMONA.
Worse and worse.

EMILIA.
How if fair and foolish?

IAGO.
She never yet was foolish that was fair;
For even her folly helpt her to an heir.

DESDEMONA.
These are old fond paradoxes to make fools laugh
i'th'alehouse. What miserable praise hast thou
for her that's foul and foolish?

IAGO.
There's none so foul, and foolish thereunto,
But does foul pranks which fair and wise ones do.

DESDEMONA.
O heavy ignorance!—thou praisest the worst best.
But what praise couldst thou bestow on a deserving woman indeed,—one that, in the authority of
her merit, did justly put on the vouch of very
malice itself?

IAGO.
She that was ever fair, and never proud;
Had tongue at will, and yet was never loud;
Never lackt gold, and yet went never gay;
Fled from her wish, and yet said 'Now I may;'
She that, being anger'd, her revenge being nigh,
Bade her wrong stay, and her displeasure fly;
She that in wisdom never was so frail
To change the cod's head for the salmon's tail;
She that could think, and ne'er disclose her mind;
See suitors following, and not look behind;
She was a wight, if ever such wight were,—

DESDEMONA.
To do what?

IAGO.
To suckle fools and chronicle small beer.

DESDEMONA.
O most lame and impotent conclusion!—Do not
learn of him, Emilia, though he be thy husband.
—How say you, Cassio? is he not a most profane
and liberal counsellor?

CASSIO.
He speaks home, madam: you may relish him
more in the soldier than in the scholar.

IAGO [*aside*].
He takes her by the palm: ay, well said, whisper:
with as little a web as this will I ensnare as great
a fly as Cassio. Ay, smile upon her, do; I will gyve
thee in thine own courtship. You say true; 'tis so,
indeed; if such tricks as these strip you out of
your lieutenantry, it had been better you had not
kist your three fingers so oft, which now again
you are most apt to play the sir in. Very good;
well kist! an excellent courtesy! 'tis so, indeed.
Yet again your fingers to your lips? would they
were clyster-pipes for your sake! [*Trumpet within*]
—The Moor! I know his trumpet.

CASSIO.
'Tis truly so.

DESDEMONA.
Let's meet him, and receive him.

CASSIO.
Lo, where he comes!
Enter OTHELLO *and* ATTENDANTS.

OTHELLO.
O my fair warrior!

DESDEMONA.
My dear Othello!
OTHELLO.
It gives me wonder great as my content
To see you here before me. O my soul's joy!
If after every tempest come such calms,
May the winds blow till they have waken'd death!
And let the labouring bark climb hills of seas
Olympus-high, and duck again as low
As hell's from heaven! If it were now to die,
'Twere now to be most happy; for, I fear,
My soul hath her content so absolute,
That not another comfort like to this
Succeeds in unknown fate.
DESDEMONA.
The heavens forbid
But that our loves and comforts should increase,
Even as our days do grow!
OTHELLO.
Amen to that, sweet powers!
I cannot speak enough of this content;
It stops me here; it is too much of joy:
And this, and this, the greatest discords be
[Kissing her.
That e'er our hearts shall make!
IAGO [aside].
O, you are well tuned now!
But I'll set down the pegs that make this music,
As honest as I am.
OTHELLO.
Come, let us to the castle.—
News, friends; our wars are done, the Turks are
drown'd.
How does my old acquaintance of this isle?—
Honey, you shall be well desired in Cyprus,
I have found great love amongst them. O my sweet,
I prattle out of fashion, and I dote
In mine own comforts.—I prithee, good Iago,
Go to the bay and disembark my coffers:
Bring thou the master to the citadel;
He is a good one, and his worthiness
Does challenge much respect.—Come, Desde-
mona,
Once more well met at Cyprus.
[Exeunt OTHELLO, DESDEMONA, and
ATTENDANTS.
IAGO.
Do thou meet me presently at the harbour. Come
hither. If thou be'st valiant,—as, they say, base
men being in love have then a nobility in their
natures more than is native to them,—list me.
The lieutenant to-night watches on the court-of-
guard:—first, I must tell thee this—Desdemona
is directly in love with him.
RODERIGO.
With him! why, 'tis not possible.
IAGO.
Lay thy finger thus, and let thy soul be instructed.
Mark me with what violence she first loved the
Moor, but for bragging, and telling her fantastical
lies: and will she love him still for prating? let not
thy discreet heart think it. Her eye must be fed;
and what delight shall she have to look on the
devil? When the blood is made dull with the act
of sport, there should be—again to inflame it,
and to give satiety a fresh appetite—loveliness in

favour, sympathy in ears, manners, and beauties;
all which the Moor is defective in: now, for want
of these required conveniences, her delicate tenderness will find itself abused, begin to heave the
gorge, disrelish and abhor the Moor; very nature
will instruct her in it, and compel her to some
second choice. Now, sir, this granted,—as it is a
most pregnant and unforced position,—who
stands so eminent in the degree of this fortune as
Cassio does? a knave very voluble; no further con-
scionable than in putting on the mere form of
civil and humane seeming, for the better compassing of his salt and most hidden loose affection? why, none; why, none: a slipper and subtle
knave; a finder of occasions; that has an eye can
stamp and counterfeit advantages, though true
advantage never present itself: a devilish knave!
Besides, the knave is handsome, young, and hath
all those requisites in him that folly and green
minds look after: a pestilent complete knave; and
the woman hath found him already.
RODERIGO.
I cannot believe that in her; she's full of most
blest condition.
IAGO.
Blest fig's-end! the wine she drinks is made of
grapes: if she had been blest, she would never
have loved the Moor: blest pudding! Didst thou
not see her paddle with the palm of his hand?
didst not mark that?
RODERIGO.
Yes, that I did; but that was but courtesy.
IAGO.
Lechery, by this hand; an index and obscure prologue to the history of lust and foul thoughts.
They met so near with their lips, that their
breaths embraced together. Villainous thoughts,
Roderigo! when these mutualities so marshal the
way, hard at hand comes the master and main
exercise, the incorporate conclusion: pish!—But,
sir, be you ruled by me: I have brought you from
Venice. Watch you to-night; for the command,
I'll lay't upon you: Cassio knows you not:—I'll
not be far from you: do you find some occasion to
anger Cassio, either by speaking too loud, or
tainting his discipline; or from what other course
you please, which the time shall more favourably
minister.
RODERIGO.
Well.
IAGO.
Sir, he is rash, and very sudden in choler, and
haply may strike at you: provoke him, that he
may; for even out of that will I cause these of
Cyprus to mutiny; whose qualification shall come
into no true taste again but by the displanting of
Cassio. So shall you have a shorter journey to
your desires, by the means I shall then have to
prefer them; and the impediment most profitably
removed, without the which there were no ex-
pectation of our prosperity.
RODERIGO.
I will do this, if I can bring it to any opportunity.
IAGO.
I warrant thee. Meet me by and by at the citadel:
I must fetch his necessaries ashore. Farewell.

RODERIGO.

Adieu.   [*Exit.*

IAGO.

That Cassio loves her, I do well believe it;
That she loves him, 'tis apt, and of great credit:
The Moor—howbeit that I endure him not—
Is of a constant, loving, noble nature;
And I dare think he'll prove to Desdemona
A most dear husband. Now, I do love her too;
Not out of absolute lust,—though peradventure
I stand accountant for as great a sin,—
But partly led to diet my revenge,
For that I do suspect the lusty Moor
Hath leapt into my seat: the thought whereof
Doth, like a poisonous mineral, gnaw my inwards;
And nothing can or shall content my soul
Till I am even'd with him, wife for wife;
Or failing so, yet that I put the Moor
At least into a jealousy so strong
That judgement cannot cure. Which thing to do,
If this poor trash of Venice, whom I trash
For his quick hunting, stand the putting on,
I'll have our Michael Cassio on the hip;
Abuse him to the Moor in the rank garb,—
For I fear Cassio with my night-cap too;
Make the Moor thank me, love me, and reward
     me,
For making him egregiously an ass,
And practising upon his peace and quiet
Even to madness. 'Tis here, but yet confused:
Knavery's plain face is never seen till used. [*Exit.*

SCENE II.

A street.

Enter OTHELLO'S HERALD *with a proclamation;*
PEOPLE *following.*

HERALD.

IT is Othello's pleasure, our noble and valiant
general, that, upon certain tidings now arrived,
importing the mere perdition of the Turkish
fleet, every man put himself into triumph; some
to dance, some to make bonfires, each man to
what sport and revels his addiction leads him:
for, besides these beneficial news, it is the celebration of his nuptial:—so much was his pleasure
should be proclaim'd. All offices are open; and
there is full liberty of feasting from this present
hour of five till the bell have told eleven. Heaven
bless the isle of Cyprus and our noble general
Othello!   [*Exeunt.*

SCENE III.

A hall in the castle.

Enter OTHELLO, DESDEMONA, CASSIO, *and*
ATTENDANTS.

OTHELLO.

GOOD Michael, look you to the guard to-night:
Let's teach ourselves that honourable stop,
Not to outsport discretion.

CASSIO.

Iago hath direction what to do;
But, notwithstanding, with my personal eye
Will I look to't.

OTHELLO.

Iago is most honest.
Michael, good night: to-morrow with your earliest
Let me have speech with you.—[*to* DESDEMONA]
     Come, my dear love,—
The purchase made, the fruits are to ensue;
That profit's yet to come 'twixt me and you.—
Good night.
         [*Exeunt* OTHELLO, DESDEMONA, *and*
            ATTENDANTS.
            Enter IAGO.

CASSIO.

Welcome, Iago; we must to the watch.

IAGO.

Not this hour, lieutenant; 'tis not yet ten o'the
clock. Our general cast us thus early for the love
of his Desdemona; who let us not therefore blame;
he hath not yet made wanton the night with her;
and she is sport for Jove.

CASSIO.

She's a most exquisite lady.

IAGO.

And, I'll warrant her, full of game.

CASSIO.

Indeed, she's a most fresh and delicate creature.

IAGO.

What an eye she has! methinks it sounds a parley
to provocation.

CASSIO.

An inviting eye; and yet methinks right modest.

IAGO.

And when she speaks, is it not an alarum to love?

CASSIO.

She is, indeed, perfection.

IAGO.

Well, happiness to their sheets! Come, lieutenant,
I have a stoop of wine; and here without are a
brace of Cyprus gallants that would fain have a
measure to the health of black Othello.

CASSIO.

Not to-night, good Iago: I have very poor and
unhappy brains for drinking: I could well wish
courtesy would invent some other custom of
entertainment.

IAGO.

O, they are our friends; but one cup: I'll drink for
you.

CASSIO.

I have drunk but one cup to-night, and that was
craftily qualified too, and, behold, what innovation it makes here: I am unfortunate in the infirmity, and dare not task my weakness with any
more.

IAGO.

What, man! 'tis a night of revels: the gallants
desire it.

CASSIO.

Where are they?

IAGO.

Here at the door; I pray you, call them in.

CASSIO.

I'll do't; but it dislikes me.   [*Exit.*

IAGO.

If I can fasten but one cup upon him,
With that which he hath drunk to-night already,
He'll be as full of quarrel and offence

As my young mistress' dog. Now, my sick fool
  Roderigo,
Whom love hath turn'd almost the wrong side out,
To Desdemona hath to-night caroused
Potations pottle-deep; and he's to watch:
Three lads of Cyprus—noble swelling spirits,
That hold their honours in a wary distance,
The very elements of this warlike isle—
Have I to-night fluster'd with flowing cups,
And they watch too. Now, 'mongst this flock of
  drunkards
Am I to put our Cassio in some action
That may offend the isle:—but here they come:
If consequence do but approve my dream,
My boat sails freely, both with wind and stream.
  Enter CASSIO, MONTANO, *and* GENTLEMEN;
      SERVANTS *following with wine.*

CASSIO.
'Fore God, they have given me a rouse already.

MONTANO.
Good faith, a little one; not past a pint, as I am a
soldier.

IAGO.
Some wine, ho!   [*Sings.*
    And let me the canakin clink, clink;
    And let me the canakin clink;
      A soldier's a man;
      A life's but a span;
    Why, then, let a soldier drink.
Some wine, boys!

CASSIO.
'Fore God, an excellent song.

IAGO.
I learn'd it in England, where, indeed, they are
most potent in potting: your Dane, your German,
and your swag-bellied Hollander,—Drink, ho!—
are nothing to your English.

CASSIO.
Is your Englishman so expert in his drinking?

IAGO.
Why, he drinks you, with facility, your Dane
dead drunk; he sweats not to overthrow your
Almain; he gives your Hollander a vomit, ere the
next pottle can be fill'd.

CASSIO.
To the health of our general!

MONTANO.
I am for it, lieutenant; and I'll do you justice.

IAGO.
O sweet England!   [*Sings*
    King Stephen was a worthy peer,
      His breeches cost him but a crown;
    He held them sixpence all too dear,
      With that he call'd the tailor lown.

    He was a wight of high renown,
      And thou art but of low degree:
    'Tis pride that pulls the country down;
      Then take thine auld cloak about thee.
Some wine, ho!

CASSIO.
Why, this is a more exquisite song than the other.

IAGO.
Will you hear't again?

CASSIO.
No; for I hold him to be unworthy of his place
that does those things.—Well,—God's above all;

and there be souls must be saved, and there be
souls must not be saved.

IAGO.
It's true, good lieutenant.

CASSIO.
For mine own part,—no offence to the general,
nor any man of quality,—I hope to be saved.

IAGO.
And so do I too, lieutenant.

CASSIO.
Ay, but, by your leave, not before me; the lieutenant is to be saved before the ancient. Let's
have no more of this; let's to our affairs.—God
forgive us our sins!—Gentlemen, let's look to our
business. Do not think, gentlemen, I am drunk:
this is my ancient;—This is my right hand, and
this is my left:—I am not drunk now; I can stand
well enough, and speak well enough.

ALL.
Excellent well.

CASSIO.
Why, very well, then; you must not think, then,
that I am drunk.   [*Exit.*

MONTANO.
To the platform, masters; come, let's set the
watch.

IAGO.
You see this fellow that is gone before;—
He is a soldier fit to stand by Cæsar
And give direction: and do but see his vice;
'Tis to his virtue a just equinox,
The one as long as th'other: 'tis pity of him.
I fear the trust Othello puts him in,
On some odd time of his infirmity,
Will shake this island.

MONTANO.
            But is he often thus?

IAGO.
'Tis evermore the prologue to his sleep:
He'll watch the horologe a double set,
If drink rock not his cradle.

MONTANO.
            It were well
The general were put in mind of it.
Perhaps he sees it not; or his good nature
Prizes the virtue that appears in Cassio,
And looks not on his evils: is not this true?
         Enter RODERIGO.

IAGO [*aside to* RODERIGO].
How now, Roderigo!
I pray you, after the lieutenant; go.
              [*Exit* RODERIGO.

MONTANO.
And 'tis great pity that the noble Moor
Should hazard such a place as his own second
With one of an ingraft infirmity:
It were an honest action to say
So to the Moor.

IAGO.
         Not I, for this fair island:
I do love Cassio well; and would do much
To cure him of this evil—But, hark! what noise?
        [*Cry within,*—'Help! help!'
    Enter CASSIO, *driving in* RODERIGO.

CASSIO.
Zounds, you rogue! you rascal!

MONTANO.
What's the matter, lieutenant?

CASSIO.
A knave teach me my duty! but I'll beat the knave
into a twiggen bottle.

RODERIGO.
Beat me!

CASSIO.
Dost thou prate, rogue? [*Striking* RODERIGO.

MONTANO.
Nay, good lieutenant; I pray you, sir, hold your
hand.

CASSIO.
Let me go, sir, or I'll knock you o'er the mazard.

MONTANO.
Come, come, you're drunk.

CASSIO.
Drunk!   [*They fight.*

IAGO [*aside to* RODERIGO].
Away, I say, go out; and cry a mutiny!
            [*Exit* RODERIGO.
Nay, good lieutenant,—God's will, gentlemen;—
Help, ho!—Lieutenant,—sir,—Montano,—sir;—
Help, masters!—Here's a goodly watch indeed!
            [*Bell rings.*
Who's that which rings the bell?—Diablo, ho!
The town will rise: God's will, lieutenant, hold;
You will be shamed for ever.

Enter OTHELLO *and* ATTENDANTS.

OTHELLO.
            What is the matter here?

MONTANO.
Zounds, I bleed still; I am hurt to the death.
            [*Faints.*

OTHELLO.
Hold, for your lives!

IAGO.
Hold, ho! Lieutenant,—sir,—Montano,—gentle-
men,—
Have you forgot all sense of place and duty?
Hold! the general speaks to you; hold, hold, for
shame!

OTHELLO.
Why, how now, ho! from whence ariseth this?
Are we turn'd Turks, and to ourselves do that
Which heaven hath forbid the Ottomites?
For Christian shame, put by this barbarous brawl:
He that stirs next to carve for his own rage,
Holds his soul light; he dies upon his motion.—
Silence that dreadful bell! it frights the isle
From her propriety.—What is the matter,
masters?—
Honest Iago, that look'st dead with grieving,
Speak, who began this? on thy love, I charge thee.

IAGO.
I do not know:—friends all but now, even now,
In quarter, and in terms like bride and groom
Devesting them for bed; and then, but now—
As if some planet had unwitted men—
Swords out, and tilting one at other's breast,
In opposition bloody. I cannot speak
Any beginning to this peevish odds;
And would in action glorious I had lost
Those legs that brought me to a part of it!

OTHELLO.
How comes it, Michael, you are thus forgot?

CASSIO.
I pray you, pardon me; I cannot speak.

OTHELLO.
Worthy Montano, you were wont be civil;
The gravity and stillness of your youth
The world hath noted, and your name is great
In mouths of wisest censure: what's the matter,
That you unlace your reputation thus,
And spend your rich opinion for the name
Of a night-brawler? give me answer to it.

MONTANO.
Worthy Othello, I am hurt to danger:
Your officer, Iago, can inform you—
While I spare speech, which something now
offends me—
Of all that I do know: nor know I aught
By me that's said or done amiss this night;
Unless self-charity be sometimes a vice,
And to defend ourselves it be a sin
When violence assails us.

OTHELLO.
            Now, by heaven,
My blood begins my safer guides to rule;
And passion, having my best judgement collied,
Assays to lead the way:—if I once stir,
Or do but lift this arm, the best of you
Shall sink in my rebuke. Give me to know
How this foul rout began, who set it on;
And he that is approved in this offence,
Though he had twinn'd with me, both at a birth,
Shall lose me.—What! in a town of war,
Yet wild, the people's hearts brimful of fear,
To manage private and domestic quarrel,
In night, and on the court and guard of safety!
'Tis monstrous.—Iago, who began't?

MONTANO.
If partially affined, or leagued in office,
Thou dost deliver more or less than truth,
Thou art no soldier.

IAGO.
            Touch me not so near:
I had rather have this tongue cut from my mouth
Than it should do offence to Michael Cassio;
Yet, I persuade myself, to speak the truth
Shall nothing wrong him.—Thus it is, general.
Montano and myself being in speech,
There comes a fellow crying out for help;
And Cassio following him with determined
sword
To execute upon him. Sir, this gentleman
Steps in to Cassio, and entreats his pause:
Myself the crying fellow did pursue,
Lest by his clamour—as it so fell out—
The town might fall in fright: he, swift of foot,
Outran my purpose; and I return'd the rather
For that I heard the clink and fall of swords,
And Cassio high in oath; which till to-night
I ne'er might say before. When I came back,—
For this was brief,—I found them close together,
At blow and thrust; even as again they were
When you yourself did part them.
More of this matter cannot I report:—
But men are men; the best sometimes forget:—
Though Cassio did some little wrong to him,—
As men in rage strike those that wish them best,—
Yet, surely, Cassio, I believe, received

From him that fled some strange indignity,
Which patience could not pass.

OTHELLO.

                I know, Iago,
Thy honesty and love doth mince this matter,
Making it light to Cassio. —Cassio, I love thee;
But never more be officer of mine.—

Enter DESDEMONA, *attended.*

Look, if my gentle love be not raised up!—
I'll make thee an example.

DESDEMONA.

                What's the matter?

OTHELLO.

All's well now, sweeting; come away to bed.—
Sir, for your hurts, myself will be your surgeon:
Lead him off.   [*Exeunt some with* MONTANO.
Iago, look with care about the town,
And silence those whom this vile brawl distracted.—
Come, Desdemona: 'tis the soldiers' life
To have their balmy slumbers waked with strife.

        [*Exeunt all but* IAGO *and* CASSIO.

IAGO.

What, are you hurt, lieutenant?

CASSIO.

Ay, past all surgery.

IAGO.

Marry, heaven forbid!

CASSIO.

Reputation, reputation, reputation! O, I have lost
my reputation! I have lost the immortal part of
myself, and what remains is bestial.—My reputation, Iago, my reputation!

IAGO.

As I am an honest man, I thought you had received some bodily wound; there is more sense in
that than in reputation. Reputation is an idle and
most false imposition; oft got without merit, and
lost without deserving: you have lost no reputation at all, unless you repute yourself such a loser.
What, man! there are ways to recover the general
again: you are but now cast in his mood, a punishment more in policy than in malice, even so as
one would beat his offenceless dog to affright
an imperious lion: sue to him again, and he's
yours.

CASSIO.

I will rather sue to be despised than to deceive so
good a commander with so slight, so drunken,
and so indiscreet an officer. Drunk? and speak
parrot? and squabble? swagger? swear? and discourse fustian with one's own shadow?—O thou
invisible spirit of wine, if thou hast no name to be
known by, let us call thee devil!

IAGO.

What was he that you follow'd with your sword?
What had he done to you?

CASSIO.

I know not.

IAGO.

Is't possible?

CASSIO.

I remember a mass of things, but nothing distinctly; a quarrel, but nothing wherefore.—O
God, that men should put an enemy in their
mouths to steal away their brains! that we should,

with joy, pleasance, revel, and applause, transform ourselves into beasts!

IAGO.

Why, but you are now well enough: how came
you thus recover'd?

CASSIO.

It hath pleased the devil drunkenness to give
place to the devil wrath: one unperfectness shows
me another, to make me frankly despise myself.

IAGO.

Come, you are too severe a moraler: as the time,
the place, and the condition of this country stands,
I could heartily wish this had not befaln; but,
since it is as it is, mend it for your own good.

CASSIO.

I will ask him for my place again,—he shall tell
me I am a drunkard! Had I as many mouths as
Hydra, such an answer would stop them all. To
be now a sensible man, by and by a fool, and
presently a beast! O strange!—Every inordinate
cup is unblest, and the ingredient is a devil.

IAGO.

Come, come, good wine is a good familiar creature, if it be well used: exclaim no more against
it. And, good lieutenant, I think you think I love
you.

CASSIO.

I have well approved it, sir.—I drunk!

IAGO.

You or any man living may be drunk at a time,
man. I'll tell you what you shall do. Our general's
wife is now the general;—I may say so in this
respect, for that he hath devoted and given up
himself to the contemplation, mark, and denotement of her parts and graces:—confess yourself
freely to her; importune her help to put you in
your place again: she is of so free, so kind, so apt,
so blessed a disposition, she holds it a vice in her
goodness not to do more than she is requested:
this broken joint between you and her husband
entreat her to splinter; and, my fortunes against
any lay worth naming, this crack of your love
shall grow stronger than it was before.

CASSIO.

You advise me well.

IAGO.

I protest, in the sincerity of love and honest kindness.

CASSIO.

I think it freely; and betimes in the morning I
will beseech the virtuous Desdemona to undertake for me: I am desperate of my fortunes if they
check me here.

IAGO.

You are in the right. Good night, lieutenant; I
must to the watch.

CASSIO.

Good night, honest Iago.   [*Exit.*

IAGO.

And what's he, then, that says I play the villain?
When this advice is free I give and honest,
Probal to thinking, and, indeed, the course
To win the Moor again? For 'tis most easy
Th'inclining Desdemona to subdue
In any honest suit: she's framed as fruitful
As the free elements. And then for her

To win the Moor,—were't to renounce his bap-
   tism,
All seals and symbols of redeemed sin,
His soul is so enfetter'd to her love,
That she may make, unmake, do what she list,
Even as her appetite shall play the god
With his weak function. How am I, then, a villain
To counsel Cassio to this parallel course,
Directly to his good? Divinity of hell!
When devils will the blackest sins put on,
They do suggest at first with heavenly shows,
As I do now: for whiles this honest fool
Plies Desdemona to repair his fortunes,
And she for him pleads strongly to the Moor,
I'll pour this pestilence into his ear,—
That she repeals him for her body's lust;
And by how much she strives to do him good,
She shall undo her credit with the Moor.
So will I turn her virtue into pitch;
And out of her own goodness make the net
That shall enmesh them all.

    Enter RODERIGO.
             How, now, Roderigo!
          RODERIGO.
I do follow here in the chase, not like a hound
that hunts, but one that fills up the cry. My
money is almost spent; I have been to-night ex-
ceedingly well cudgell'd; and I think the issue
will be—I shall have so much experience for my
pains; and so, with no money at all, and a little
more wit, return again to Venice.
          IAGO.
How poor are they that have not patience!
What wound did ever heal but by degrees?
Thou know'st we work by wit, and not by witch-
   craft;
And wit depends on dilatory time.
Does't not go well? Cassio hath beaten thee,
And thou, by that small hurt, hast cashier'd
   Cassio:
Though other things grow fair against the sun,
Yet fruits that blossom first will first be ripe:
Content thyself awhile.—By th'mass, 'tis morn-
   ing;
Pleasure and action make the hours seem short.—
Retire thee; go where thou art billeted:
Away, I say; thou shalt know more hereafter:
Nay, get thee gone. [*Exit* RODERIGO.] Two
   things are to be done,—
My wife must move for Cassio to her mistress;
I'll set her on;
Myself the while to draw the Moor apart,
And bring him jump when he may Cassio find
Soliciting his wife:—ay, that's the way;
Dull not device by coldness and delay.   [*Exit.*

ACT III. SCENE I.

Cyprus. Before the castle.

Enter CASSIO *and some* MUSICIANS.
          CASSIO.
MASTERS, play here,—I will content your
   pains,—
Something that's brief; and bid 'Good morrow,
   general.'   [*Music.*

    Enter CLOWN.
          CLOWN.
Why, masters, have your instruments been in
Naples, that they speak i'th'nose thus?
     FIRST MUSICIAN.
How, sir, how!
          CLOWN.
Are these, I pray you, wind-instruments?
     FIRST MUSICIAN.
Ay, marry, are they, sir.
          CLOWN.
O, thereby hangs a tail.
     FIRST MUSICIAN.
Whereby hangs a tale, sir?
          CLOWN.
Marry, sir, by many a wind-instrument that I
know. But, masters, here's money for you: and
the general so likes your music, that he de-
sires you, of all loves, to make no more noise
with it.
     FIRST MUSICIAN.
Well, sir, we will not.
          CLOWN.
If you have any music that may not be heard, to't
again: but, as they say, to hear music the general
does not greatly care.
     FIRST MUSICIAN.
We have none such, sir.
          CLOWN.
Then put up your pipes in your bag, for I'll away:
go; vanish into air; away!   [*Exeunt* MUSICIANS.
          CASSIO.
Dost thou hear, my honest friend?
          CLOWN.
No, I hear not your honest friend; I hear you.
          CASSIO.
Prithee, keep up thy quillets. There's a poor piece
of gold for thee: if the gentlewoman that attends
the general's wife be stirring, tell her there's one
Cassio entreats her a little favour of speech: wilt
thou do this?
          CLOWN.
She is stirring, sir: if she will stir hither, I shall
seem to notify unto her.
          CASSIO.
Do, good my friend.   [*Exit* CLOWN.
    Enter IAGO.
       In happy time, Iago.
          IAGO.
You have not been a-bed, then?
          CASSIO.
Why, no; the day had broke
Before we parted. I have made bold, Iago,
To send in to your wife: my suit to her
Is, that she will to virtuous Desdemona
Procure me some access.
          IAGO.
         I'll send her to you presently;
And I'll devise a mean to draw the Moor
Out of the way, that your converse and business
May be more free.
          CASSIO.
I humbly thank you for't. [*Exit* IAGO.] I never
   knew
A Florentine more kind and honest.

Enter EMILIA.

EMILIA.

Good morrow, good lieutenant: I am sorry
For your displeasure; but all will sure be well.
The general and his wife are talking of it;
And she speaks for you stoutly: the Moor replies,
That he you hurt is of great fame in Cyprus
And great affinity, and that in wholesome wisdom
He might not but refuse you; but he protests he
    loves you,
And needs no other suitor but his likings
To take the safest occasion by the front
To bring you in again.

CASSIO.

    Yet, I beseech you,—
If you think fit, or that it may be done,—
Give me advantage of some brief discourse
With Desdemona alone.

EMILIA.

    Pray you, come in:
I will bestow you where you shall have time
To speak your bosom freely.

CASSIO.

I am much bound to you. [*Exeunt.*

SCENE II.

A room in the castle.

Enter OTHELLO, IAGO, *and* GENTLEMEN.

OTHELLO.

THESE letters give, Iago, to the pilot;
    And, by him, do my duties to the senate:
That done, I will be walking on the works;
Repair there to me.

IAGO.

    Well, my good lord, I'll do't.

OTHELLO.

This fortification, gentlemen,—shall we see't?

GENTLEMAN.

We'll wait upon your lordship. [*Exeunt.*

SCENE III.

The garden of the castle.

Enter DESDEMONA, CASSIO, *and* EMILIA.

DESDEMONA.

BE thou assured, good Cassio, I will do
    All my abilities in thy behalf.

EMILIA.

Good madam, do: I warrant it grieves my hus-
    band,
As if the case were his.

DESDEMONA.

O, that's an honest fellow.—Do not doubt, Cas-
    sio,
But I will have my lord and you again
As friendly as you were.

CASSIO.

    Bounteous madam,
Whatever shall become of Michael Cassio,
He's never any thing but your true servant.

DESDEMONA.

I know't,—I thank you. You do love my lord:
You have known him long; and be you well as-
    sured

He shall in strangeness stand no further off
Than in a politic distance.

CASSIO.

    Ay, but, lady,
That policy may either last so long,
Or feed upon such nice and waterish diet,
Or breed itself so out of circumstance,
That, I being absent, and my place supplied,
My general will forget my love and service.

DESDEMONA.

Do not doubt that; before Emilia here
I give thee warrant of thy place: assure thee,
If I do vow a friendship, I'll perform it
To the last article: my lord shall never rest;
I'll watch him tame, and talk him out of patience;
His bed shall seem a school, his board a shrift;
I'll intermingle every thing he does
With Cassio's suit: therefore be merry, Cassio;
For thy solicitor shall rather die
Than give thy cause away.

EMILIA.

Madam, here comes my lord.

CASSIO.

Madam, I'll take my leave.

DESDEMONA.

Why, stay, and hear me speak.

CASSIO.

Madam, not now: I am very ill at ease,
Unfit for mine own purposes.

DESDEMONA.

Well, do your discretion.   [*Exit* CASSIO.

Enter OTHELLO *and* IAGO.

IAGO.

Ha! I like not that.

OTHELLO.

    What dost thou say?

IAGO.

Nothing, my lord: or if—I know not what.

OTHELLO.

Was not that Cassio parted from my wife?

IAGO.

Cassio, my lord! No, sure, I cannot think it,
That he would steal away so guilty-like,
Seeing you coming.

OTHELLO.

    I do believe 'twas he.

DESDEMONA.

How now, my lord!
I have been talking with a suitor here,
A man that languishes in your displeasure.

OTHELLO.

Who is't you mean?

DESDEMONA.

Why, your lieutenant, Cassio. Good my lord,
If I have any grace or power to move you,
His present reconciliation take;
For if he be not one that truly loves you,
That errs in ignorance, and not in cunning,
I have no judgement in an honest face:
I prithee, call him back.

OTHELLO.

    Went he hence now?

DESDEMONA.

Ay, sooth; so humbled,
That he hath left part of his grief with me,
To suffer with him. Good love, call him back.

OTHELLO.
Not now, sweet Desdemona; some other time.
DESDEMONA.
But shall't be shortly?
OTHELLO.
The sooner, sweet, for you.
DESDEMONA.
Shall't be to-night at supper?
OTHELLO.
No, not to-night.
DESDEMONA.
To-morrow dinner, then?
OTHELLO.
I shall not dine at home;
I meet the captains at the citadel.
DESDEMONA.
Why, then, to-morrow night; or Tuesday morn;
On Tuesday noon, or night; on Wednesday
morn:—
I prithee, name the time; but let it not
Exceed three days: in faith, he's penitent;
And yet his trespass, in our common reason,—
Save that, they say, the wars must make examples
Out of their best,—is not almost a fault
T'incur a private check. When shall he come?
Tell me, Othello: I wonder in my soul,
What you would ask me, that I should deny,
Or stand so mammering on. What! Michael Cas-
sio,
That came a-wooing with you; and so many a time,
When I have spoke of you dispraisingly,
Hath ta'en your part; to have so much to do
To bring him in! Trust me, I could do much—
OTHELLO.
Prithee, no more: let him come when he will;
I will deny thee nothing.
DESDEMONA.
Why, this is not a boon;
'Tis as I should entreat you wear your gloves,
Or feed on nourishing dishes, or keep you warm,
Or sue to you to do a peculiar profit
To your own person: nay, when I have a suit
Wherein I mean to touch your love indeed,
It shall be full of poise and difficult weight,
And fearful to be granted.
OTHELLO.
I will deny thee nothing:
Whereon, I do beseech thee, grant me this,
To leave me but a little to myself.
DESDEMONA.
Shall I deny you? no: farewell, my lord.
OTHELLO.
Farewell, my Desdemona: I'll come to thee
straight.
DESDEMONA.
Emilia, come.—Be as your fancies teach you;
Whate'er you be, I am obedient.
[Exit, with EMILIA.
OTHELLO.
Excellent wretch! Perdition catch my soul,
But I do love thee! and when I love thee not,
Chaos is come again.
IAGO.
My noble lord,—
OTHELLO.
What dost thou say, Iago?

IAGO.
Did Michael Cassio, when you woo'd my lady,
Know of your love?
OTHELLO.
He did, from first to last: why dost thou ask?
IAGO.
But for a satisfaction of my thought;
No further harm.
OTHELLO.
Why of thy thought, Iago?
IAGO.
I did not think he had been acquainted with her.
OTHELLO.
O, yes; and went between us very oft.
IAGO.
Indeed!
OTHELLO.
Indeed! ay, indeed:—discern'st thou aught in
that?
Is he not honest?
IAGO.
Honest, my lord!
OTHELLO.
Honest! ay, honest.
IAGO.
My lord, for aught I know.
OTHELLO.
What dost thou think?
IAGO.
Think, my lord!
OTHELLO.
Think, my lord!
By heaven, he echoes me,
As if there were some monster in his thought
Too hideous to be shown.—Thou dost mean
something:
I heard thee say even now, thou likedst not that,
When Cassio left my wife: what didst not like?
And when I told thee he was of my counsel
In my whole course of wooing, thou criedst 'In-
deed!'
And didst contract and purse thy brow together,
As if thou then hadst shut up in thy brain
Some horrible conceit: if thou dost love me,
Show me thy thought.
IAGO.
My lord, you know I love you.
OTHELLO.
I think thou dost;
And, for I know thou'rt full of love and honesty,
And weigh'st thy words before thou givest them
breath,
Therefore these stops of thine fright me the more:
For such things in a false disloyal knave
Are tricks of custom; but in a man that's just
They're close delations, working from the heart,
That passion cannot rule.
IAGO.
For Michael Cassio,
I dare be sworn I think that he is honest.
OTHELLO.
I think so too.
IAGO.
Men should be what they seem;
Or those that be not, would they might seem
none!

OTHELLO.
Certain, men should be what they seem.
IAGO.
Why, then, I think Cassio's an honest man.
OTHELLO.
Nay, yet there's more in this:
I prithee, speak to me as to thy thinkings,
As thou dost ruminate; and give thy worst of
   thoughts
The worst of words.
IAGO.
        Good my lord, pardon me:
Though I am bound to every act of duty,
I am not bound to that all slaves are free to.
Utter my thoughts? Why, say they are vile and
   false,—
As where's that palace whereinto foul things
Sometimes intrude not? who has a breast so pure,
But some uncleanly apprehensions
Keep leets and law-days, and in session sit
With meditations lawful?
OTHELLO.
Thou dost conspire against thy friend, Iago,
If thou but think'st him wrong'd, and makest his
   ear
A stranger to thy thoughts.
IAGO.
        I do beseech you—
Though I perchance am vicious in my guess,
As, I confess, it is my nature's plague
To spy into abuses, and oft my jealousy
Shapes faults that are not—that your wisdom yet,
From one that so imperfectly conceits,
Would take no notice; nor build yourself a trouble
Out of his scattering and unsure observance:—
It were not for your quiet nor your good,
Nor for my manhood, honesty, or wisdom,
To let you know my thoughts.
OTHELLO.
        What dost thou mean?
IAGO.
Good name in man and woman, dear my lord,
Is the immediate jewel of their souls:
Who steals my purse steals trash; 'tis something,
   nothing;
'Twas mine, 'tis his, and has been slave to thou-
   sands;
But he that filches from me my good name
Robs me of that which not enriches him,
And makes me poor indeed.
OTHELLO.
By heaven, I'll know thy thoughts!
IAGO.
You cannot, if my heart were in your hand;
Nor shall not, whilst 'tis in my custody.
OTHELLO.
Ha!
IAGO.
O, beware, my lord, of jealousy;
It is the green-eyed monster, which doth mock
The meat it feeds on: that cuckold lives in bliss
Who, certain of his fate, loves not his wronger;
But, O, what damned minutes tells he o'er
Who dotes, yet doubts, suspects, yet strongly loves!
OTHELLO.
O misery!

IAGO.
Poor and content is rich, and rich enough;
But riches fineless is as poor as winter
To him that ever fears he shall be poor:—
Good heaven, the souls of all my tribe defend
From jealousy!
OTHELLO.
        Why, why is this?
Think'st thou I'ld make a life of jealousy,
To follow still the changes of the moon
With fresh suspicions? No; to be once in doubt
Is once to be resolved: exchange me for a goat,
When I shall turn the business of my soul
To such exsufflicate and blown surmises,
Matching thy inference. 'Tis not to make me
   jealous
To say my wife is fair, feeds well, loves company,
Is free of speech, sings, plays, and dances well;
Where virtue is, these are more virtuous:
Nor from mine own weak merits will I draw
The smallest fear or doubt of her revolt;
For she had eyes, and chose me. No, Iago;
I'll see before I doubt; when I doubt, prove;
And, on the proof, there is no more but this,—
Away at once with love or jealousy!
IAGO.
I am glad of it; for now I shall have reason
To show the love and duty that I bear you
With franker spirit: therefore, as I am bound,
Receive it from me:—I speak not yet of proof.
Look to your wife; observe her well with Cassio;
Wear your eye thus, not jealous nor secure:
I would not have your free and noble nature,
Out of self-bounty, be abused; look to't:
I know our country disposition well;
In Venice they do let heaven see the pranks
They dare not show their husbands; their best
   conscience
Is—not to leave undone, but keep unknown.
OTHELLO.
Dost thou say so?
IAGO.
She did deceive her father, marrying you;
And when she seem'd to shake and fear your looks,
She loved them most.
OTHELLO.
        And so she did.
IAGO.
        Why, go to, then;
She that, so young, could give out such a seeming,
To seel her father's eyes up close as oak—
He thought 'twas witchcraft:—but I am much to
   blame;
I humbly do beseech you of your pardon
For too much loving you.
OTHELLO.
        I am bound to thee for ever.
IAGO.
I see this hath a little dasht your spirits.
OTHELLO.
Not a jot, not a jot.
IAGO.
        I'faith, I fear it has.
I hope you will consider what is spoke
Comes from my love;—but I do see y'are
   moved:—

OTHELLO

I am to pray you not to strain my speech
To grosser issues nor to larger reach
Than to suspicion.
                    OTHELLO.
I will not.
                    IAGO.
                  Should you do so, my lord,
My speech should fall into such vile success
As my thoughts aim not at. Cassio's my worthy
    friend:—
My lord, I see y'are moved.
                    OTHELLO.
                        No, not much moved:—
I do not think but Desdemona's honest.
                    IAGO.
Long live she so! and long live you to think so!
                    OTHELLO.
And yet, how nature erring from itself,—
                    IAGO.
Ay, there's the point:—as—to be bold with you—
Not to affect many proposed matches
Of her own clime, complexion, and degree,
Whereto we see in all things nature tends,—
Foh! one may smell in such, a will most rank,
Foul disproportion, thoughts unnatural:—
But pardon me: I do not in position
Distinctly speak of her; though I may fear
Her will, recoiling to her better judgement,
May fall to match you with her country forms,
And happily repent.
                    OTHELLO.
                  Farewell, farewell:
If more thou dost perceive, let me know more;
Set on thy wife to observe: leave me, Iago.
                    IAGO.
My lord, I take my leave.   [Going.
                    OTHELLO.
Why did I marry?—This honest creature doubt-
    less
Sees and knows more, much more, than he un-
    folds.
                    IAGO.
My lord, I would I might entreat your honour
                              [Returning.
To scan this thing no further; leave it to time:
Although 'tis fit that Cassio have his place,—
For, sure, he fills it up with great ability,—
Yet, if you please to hold him off awhile,
You shall by that perceive him and his means:
Note if your lady strain his entertainment
With any strong or vehement importunity;
Much will be seen in that. In the mean time
Let me be thought too busy in my fears,—
As worthy cause I have to fear I am,—
And hold her free, I do beseech your honour.
                    OTHELLO.
Fear not my government.
                    IAGO.
I once more take my leave.   [Exit.
                    OTHELLO.
This fellow's of exceeding honesty,
And knows all qualities, with a learned spirit,
Of human dealings. If I do prove her haggard,
Though that her jesses were my dear heart-
    strings,
I'ld whistle her off, and let her down the wind,

To prey at fortune. Haply, for I am black,
And have not those soft parts of conversation
That chamberers have; or, for I am declined
Into the vale of years,—yet that's not much;—
She's gone; I am abused; and my relief
Must be to loathe her. O curse of marriage,
That we can call these delicate creatures ours,
And not their appetites! I had rather be a toad,
And live upon the vapour of a dungeon,
Than keep a corner in the thing I love
For others' uses. Yet, 'tis the plague of great ones;
Prerogatived are they less than the base;
'Tis destiny unshunnable, like death:
Even then this forked plague is fated to us
When we do quicken.—Desdemona comes:
If she be false, O, then heaven mocks itself!—
I'll not believe't.
        Enter DESDEMONA and EMILIA.
                    DESDEMONA.
                  How now, my dear Othello!
Your dinner, and the generous islanders
By you invited, do attend your presence.
                    OTHELLO.
I am to blame.
                    DESDEMONA.
                  Why do you speak so faintly?
Are you not well?
                    OTHELLO.
I have a pain upon my forehead here.
                    DESDEMONA.
Faith, that's with watching; 'twill away again:
Let me but bind it hard, within this hour
It will be well.
                    OTHELLO.
                  Your napkin is too little;
[He puts the handkerchief from him; and she
    drops it.
Let it alone. Come, I'll go in with you.
                    DESDEMONA.
I am very sorry that you are not well.
        [Exeunt OTHELLO and DESDEMONA.
                    EMILIA.
I am glad I have found this napkin:
This was her first remembrance from the Moor:
My wayward husband hath a hundred times
Woo'd me to steal it; but she so loves the token,—
For he conjured her she should ever keep it,—
That she reserves it evermore about her
To kiss and talk to. I'll have the work ta'en out,
And give't Iago:
What he will do with it heaven knows, not I;
I nothing but to please his fantasy.
                    Enter IAGO.
                    IAGO.
How now! what do you here alone?
                    EMILIA.
Do not you chide; I have a thing for you.
                    IAGO.
A thing for me!—it is a common thing—
                    EMILIA.
Ha!
                    IAGO.
To have a foolish wife.
                    EMILIA.
O, is that all? What will you give me now
For that same handkerchief?

IAGO.
                       What handkerchief?

EMILIA.
What handkerchief!
Why, that the Moor first gave to Desdemona;
That which so often you did bid me steal.

IAGO.
Hast stoln it from her?

EMILIA.
No, faith; she let it drop by negligence,
And, to th'advantage, I, being here, took't up.
Look, here it is.

IAGO.
      ·   A good wench; give it me.

EMILIA.
What will you do with't, that you have been so earnest
To have me filch it?

IAGO.
      Why, what's that to you? [*Snatching it.*

EMILIA.
If't be not for some purpose of import,
Give't me again: poor lady, she'll run mad
When she shall lack it.

IAGO.
Be not acknown on't; I have use for it.
Go, leave me.   [*Exit* EMILIA.
I will in Cassio's lodging lose this napkin,
And let him find it. Trifles light as air
Are to the jealous confirmations strong
As proofs of holy writ: this may do something.
The Moor already changes with my poison:—
Dangerous conceits are, in their natures, poisons,
Which at the first are scarce found to distaste,
But, with a little act upon the blood,
Burn like the mines of sulphur.—I did say so:—
Look, where he comes! Not poppy, nor mandragora,
Nor all the drowsy syrups of the world,
Shall ever medicine thee to that sweet sleep
Which thou owedst yesterday.

Enter OTHELLO.

OTHELLO.
                  Ha! ha! false to me?

IAGO.
Why, how now, general! no more of that.

OTHELLO.
Avaunt! be gone! thou hast set me on the rack:—
I swear 'tis better to be much abused
Than but to know't a little.

IAGO.
               How now, my lord!

OTHELLO.
What sense had I of her stoln hours of lust?
I saw't not, thought it not, it harm'd not me:
I slept the next night well, was free and merry;
I found not Cassio's kisses on her lips:
He that is robb'd, not wanting what is stoln,
Let him not know't, and he's not robb'd at all.

IAGO.
I am sorry to hear this.

OTHELLO.
I had been happy, if the general camp,
Pioners and all, had tasted her sweet body,
So I had nothing known. O, now, for ever
Farewell the tranquil mind! farewell content!
Farewell the plumed troop, and the big wars,
That make ambition virtue! O, farewell!
Farewell the neighing steed, and the shrill trump,
The spirit-stirring drum, th'ear-piercing fife,
The royal banner, and all quality,
Pride, pomp, and circumstance of glorious war!
And, O you mortal engines, whose rude throats
Th'immortal Jove's dread clamours counterfeit,
Farewell! Othello's occupation's gone!

IAGO.
Is't possible, my lord?

OTHELLO.
Villain, be sure thou prove my love a whore,—
Be sure of it; give me the ocular proof;
Or, by the worth of man's eternal soul,
Thou hadst been better have been born a dog
Than answer my waked wrath!

IAGO.
                   Is't come to this?

OTHELLO.
Make me to see't; or, at the least, so prove it,
That the probation bear no hinge nor loop
To hang a doubt on; or woe upon thy life!

IAGO.
My noble lord,—

OTHELLO.
If thou dost slander her, and torture me,
Never pray more; abandon all remorse;
On horror's head horrors accumulate;
Do deeds to make heaven weep, all earth amazed;
For nothing canst thou to damnation add
Greater than that.

IAGO.
      O grace! O heaven forgive me!
Are you a man? have you a soul or sense?—
God be wi'you! take mine office.—O wretched fool,
That livest to make thine honesty a vice!—
O monstrous world! Take note, take note, O world,
To be direct and honest is not safe.—
I thank you for this profit; and from hence
I'll love no friend, sith love breeds such offence.

OTHELLO.
Nay, stay:—thou shouldst be honest.

IAGO.
I should be wise; for honesty's a fool,
And loses that it works for.

OTHELLO.
              By the world,
I think my wife be honest, and think she is not;
I think that thou art just, and think thou art not:
I'll have some proof: her name, that was as fresh
As Dian's visage, is now begrimed and black
As mine own face.—If there be cords or knives,
Poison, or fire, or suffocating streams,
I'll not endure it.—Would I were satisfied!

IAGO.
I see, sir, you are eaten up with passion:
I do repent me that I put it to you.
You would be satisfied?

OTHELLO.
             Would! nay, I will.

IAGO.
And may: but, how? how satisfied, my lord?
Would you, the supervisor, grossly gape on,—
Behold her topt?

OTHELLO.
Death and damnation! O!
IAGO.
It were a tedious difficulty, I think,
To bring them to that prospect: damn them, then,
If ever mortal eyes do see them bolster
More than their own! What then? how then?
What shall I say? Where's satisfaction?
It is impossible you should see this,
Were they as prime as goats, as hot as monkeys,
As salt as wolves in pride, and fools as gross
As ignorance made drunk. But yet, I say,
If imputation and strong circumstances—
Which lead directly to the door of truth—
Will give you satisfaction, you may have't.
OTHELLO.
Give me a living reason she's disloyal.
IAGO.
I do not like the office:
But, sith I am enter'd in this cause so far,—
Prickt to't by foolish honesty and love,—
I will go on. I lay with Cassio lately;
And, being troubled with a raging tooth,
I could not sleep.
There are a kind of men so loose of soul
That in their sleeps will mutter their affairs;
One of this kind is Cassio:
In sleep I heard him say, 'Sweet Desdemona,
Let us be wary, let us hide our loves;'
And then, sir, would he gripe and wring my hand,
Cry 'O sweet creature!' and then kiss me hard,
As if he pluckt up kisses by the roots
That grew upon my lips: then laid his leg
Over my thigh, and sigh'd, and kist; and then
Cried 'Cursed fate that gave thee to the Moor!'
OTHELLO.
O monstrous! monstrous!
IAGO.
Nay, this was but his dream.
OTHELLO.
But this denoted a foregone conclusion:
'Tis a shrewd doubt, though it be but a dream.
IAGO.
And this may help to thicken other proofs
That do demonstrate thinly.
OTHELLO.
I'll tear her all to pieces.
IAGO.
Nay, but be wise: yet we see nothing done;
She may be honest yet. Tell me but this,—
Have you not sometimes seen a handkerchief
Spotted with strawberries in your wife's hand?
OTHELLO.
I gave her such a one; 'twas my first gift.
IAGO.
I know not that: but such a handkerchief—
I am sure it was your wife's—did I to-day
See Cassio wipe his beard with.
OTHELLO.
If it be that,—
IAGO.
If it be that, or any that was hers,
It speaks against her with the other proofs.
OTHELLO.
O, that the slave had forty thousand lives,—
One is too poor, too weak for my revenge!

Now do I see 'tis true.—Look here, Iago;
All my fond love thus do I blow to heaven:
'Tis gone.—
Arise, black vengeance, from the hollow hell!
Yield up, O love, thy crown and hearted throne
To tyrannous hate! Swell, bosom, with thy
　　fraught,
For 'tis of aspics' tongues!
IAGO.
Yet be content.
OTHELLO.
O, blood, blood, blood!
IAGO.
Patience, I say; your mind perhaps may change.
OTHELLO.
Never, Iago. Like to the Pontic sea,
Whose icy current and compulsive course
Ne'er feels retiring ebb, but keeps due on
To the Propontic and the Hellespont;
Even so my bloody thoughts, with violent pace,
Shall ne'er look back, ne'er ebb to humble love,
Till that a capable and wide revenge
Swallow them up.—Now, by yond marble heaven,
In the due reverence of a sacred vow　　　[Kneels.
I here engage my words.
IAGO.
Do not rise yet.—　[Kneels.
Witness, you ever-burning lights above,
You elements that clip us round about,—
Witness that here Iago doth give up
The execution of his wit, hands, heart,
To wrong'd Othello's service! Let him command,
And to obey shall be in me remorse,
What bloody business ever.　　　[They rise.
OTHELLO.
I greet thy love,
Not with vain thanks, but with acceptance boun-
　　teous,
And will upon the instant put thee to't:
Within these three days let me hear thee say
That Cassio's not alive.
IAGO.
My friend is dead; 'tis done at your request:
But let her live.
OTHELLO.
Damn her, lewd minx! O, damn her!
Come, go with me apart; I will withdraw,
To furnish me with some swift means of death
For the fair devil. Now art thou my lieutenant.
IAGO.
I am your own for ever.　　　[Exeunt.

SCENE IV.

Before the castle.

Enter DESDEMONA, EMILIA, *and* CLOWN.

DESDEMONA.
DO you know, sirrah, where Lieutenant Cassio
lies?
CLOWN.
I dare not say he lies any where.
DESDEMONA.
Why, man?
CLOWN.
He's a soldier; and for one to say a soldier lies, is
stabbing.

DESDEMONA.
Go to: where lodges he?
CLOWN.
To tell you where he lodges, is to tell you where I lie.
DESDEMONA.
Can any thing be made of this?
CLOWN.
I know not where he lodges; and for me to devise a lodging, and say he lies here or he lies there, were to lie in mine own throat.
DESDEMONA.
Can you inquire him out, and be edified by report?
CLOWN.
I will catechize the world for him; that is, make questions, and by them answer.
DESDEMONA.
Seek him, bid him come hither: tell him I have moved my lord on his behalf, and hope all will be well.
CLOWN.
To do this is within the compass of man's wit; and therefore I will attempt the doing it.   [Exit.
DESDEMONA.
Where should I lose that handkerchief, Emilia?
EMILIA.
I know not, madam.
DESDEMONA.
Believe me, I had rather have lost my purse
Full of crusadoes: and, but my noble Moor
Is true of mind, and made of no such baseness
As jealous creatures are, it were enough
To put him to ill thinking.
EMILIA.
Is he not jealous?
DESDEMONA.
Who, he? I think the sun where he was born
Drew all such humours from him.
EMILIA.
Look, where he comes.
DESDEMONA.
I will not leave him now till Cassio
Be call'd to him.
Enter OTHELLO.
How is't with you, my lord?
OTHELLO.
Well, my good lady.—[aside] O, hardness to dissemble!—
How do you, Desdemona?
DESDEMONA.
Well, my good lord.
OTHELLO.
Give me your hand: this hand is moist, my lady.
DESDEMONA.
It yet hath felt no age nor known no sorrow.
OTHELLO.
This argues fruitfulness and liberal heart:—
Hot, hot, and moist: this hand of yours requires
A sequester from liberty, fasting and prayer,
Much castigation, exercise devout;
For here's a young and sweating devil here,
That commonly rebels. 'Tis a good hand,
A frank one.
DESDEMONA.
You may, indeed, say so;
For 'twas that hand that gave away my heart.

OTHELLO.
A liberal hand: the hearts of old gave hands;
But our new heraldry is hands, not hearts.
DESDEMONA.
I cannot speak of this. Come now, your promise.
OTHELLO.
What promise, chuck?
DESDEMONA.
I have sent to bid Cassio come speak with you.
OTHELLO.
I have a salt and sorry rheum offends me;
Lend me thy handkerchief.
DESDEMONA.
Here, my lord.
OTHELLO.
That which I gave you.
DESDEMONA.
I have it not about me.
OTHELLO.
Not?
DESDEMONA.
No, indeed, my lord.
OTHELLO.
That is a fault.
That handkerchief
Did an Egyptian to my mother give;
She was a charmer, and could almost read   [it,
The thoughts of people: she told her, while she kept
'Twould make her amiable, and subdue my father
Entirely to her love; but if she lost it,
Or made a gift of it, my father's eye   [hunt
Should hold her loathed, and his spirits should
After new fancies: she, dying, gave it me;
And bid me, when my fate would have me wive,
To give it her. I did so: and take heed on't;
Make it a darling like your precious eye;
To lose't or give't away were such perdition
As nothing else could match.
DESDEMONA.
Is't possible?
OTHELLO.
'Tis true: there's magic in the web of it:
A sibyl, that had number'd in the world
The sun to course two hundred compasses,
In her prophetic fury sew'd the work;
The worms were hallow'd that did breed the silk;
And it was dyed in mummy which the skilful
Conserved of maidens' hearts.
DESDEMONA.
Indeed! is't true?
OTHELLO.
Most veritable; therefore look to't well.
DESDEMONA.
Then would to God that I had never seen't!
OTHELLO.
Ha! wherefore?
DESDEMONA.
Why do you speak so startingly and rash?
OTHELLO.
Is't lost? is't gone? speak; is't out o'the way?
DESDEMONA.
Heaven bless us!
OTHELLO.
Say you?
DESDEMONA.
It is not lost; but what an if it were?

OTHELLO.

How!

DESDEMONA.

I say, it is not lost.

OTHELLO.
Fetch't, let me see't.

DESDEMONA.

Why, so I can, sir, but I will not now.
This is a trick to put me from my suit:
Pray you, let Cassio be received again.

OTHELLO.

Fetch me the handkerchief: my mind misgives.

DESDEMONA.

Come, come;
You'll never meet a more sufficient man.

OTHELLO.

The handkerchief!

DESDEMONA.
I pray, talk me of Cassio.

OTHELLO.

The handkerchief!

DESDEMONA.
A man that all his time
Hath founded his good fortunes on your love,
Shared dangers with you,—

OTHELLO.

The handkerchief!

DESDEMONA.

In sooth, you are to blame.

OTHELLO.

Away!   [Exit.

EMILIA.

Is not this man jealous?

DESDEMONA.

I ne'er saw this before.
Sure, there's some wonder in this handkerchief:
I am most unhappy in the loss of it.

EMILIA.

'Tis not a year or two shows us a man:
They are all but stomachs, and we all but food;
They eat us hungerly, and when they are full,
They belch us.—Look you,—Cassio and my hus-
band.

Enter CASSIO and IAGO.

IAGO.

There is no other way; 'tis she must do't:
And, lo, the happiness! go, and importune her.

DESDEMONA.

How now, good Cassio! what's the news with you?

CASSIO.

Madam, my former suit: I do beseech you
That by your virtuous means I may again
Exist, and be a member of his love
Whom I with all the office of my heart
Entirely honour: I would not be delay'd.
If my offence be of such mortal kind
That nor my service past, nor present sorrows,
Nor purposed merit in futurity,
Can ransom me into his love again,
But to know so must be my benefit;
So shall I clothe me in a forced content,
And shut myself up in some other course,
To fortune's alms.

DESDEMONA.
Alas, thrice-gentle Cassio!
My advocation is not now in tune;

My lord is not my lord; nor should I know him,
Were he in favour as in humour alter'd.
So help me every spirit sanctified,
As I have spoken for you all my best,
And stood within the blank of his displeasure
For my free speech! You must awhile be patient:
What I can do I will; and more I will
Than for myself I dare: let that suffice you.

IAGO.

Is my lord angry?

EMILIA.
He went hence but now,
And certainly in strange unquietness.

IAGO.

Can he be angry? I have seen the cannon,
When it hath blown his ranks into the air,
And, like the devil, from his very arm
Puft his own brother;—and can he be angry?
Something of moment, then: I will go meet him:
There's matter in't indeed, if he be angry.

DESDEMONA.

I prithee, do so.   [Exit IAGO.
Something, sure, of state,—
Either from Venice, or some unhatcht practice
Made demonstrable here in Cyprus to him,—
Hath puddled his clear spirit; and in such cases
Men's natures wrangle with inferior things,
Though great ones are their object. 'Tis even so;
For let our fingers ache, and it indues
Our other healthful members even to that sense
Of pain: nay, we must think men are not gods,
Nor of them look for such observancy
As fits the bridal.—Beshrew me much, Emilia,
I was—unhandsome warrior as I am—
Arraigning his unkindness with my soul;
But now I find I had suborn'd the witness,
And he's indicted falsely.

EMILIA.

Pray heaven it be state-matters, as you think,
And no conception nor no jealous toy
Concerning you.

DESDEMONA.

Alas the day, I never gave him cause!

EMILIA.

But jealous souls will not be answer'd so;
They are not ever jealous for the cause,
But jealous for they're jealous: it is a monster
Begot upon itself, born on itself.

DESDEMONA.

Heaven keep that monster from Othello's mind!

EMILIA.

Lady, amen.

DESDEMONA.

I will go seek him.—Cassio, walk hereabout:
If I do find him fit, I'll move your suit,
And seek to effect it to my uttermost.

CASSIO.

I humbly thank your ladyship.
[Exeunt DESDEMONA and EMILIA.
Enter BIANCA.

BIANCA.

Save you, friend Cassio!

CASSIO.
What make you from home?
How is it with you, my most fair Bianca?
I'faith, sweet love, I was coming to your house.

BIANCA.
And I was going to your lodging, Cassio.
What, keep a week away? seven days and nights?
Eight score eight hours? and lovers' absent hours,
More tedious than the dial eight score times?
O weary reckoning!

CASSIO.
　　　　　Pardon me, Bianca:
I have this while with leaden thoughts been
　　prest;
But I shall, in a more continuate time,
Strike off this score of absence. Sweet Bianca,
　　　[*Giving her* DESDEMONA'*s handkerchief.*
Take me this work out.

BIANCA.
　　　　　O Cassio, whence came this?
This is some token from a newer friend:
To the felt absence now I feel a cause:
Is't come to this? Well, well.

CASSIO.
　　　　　Go to, woman!
Throw your vile guesses in the devil's teeth,
From whence you have them. You are jealous
　　now
That this is from some mistress, some remem-
　　brance:
No, in good troth, Bianca.

BIANCA.
　　　　　Why, whose is it?

CASSIO.
I know not neither: I found it in my chamber.
I like the work well: ere it be demanded,—
As like enough it will,—I'd have it copied:
Take it, and do't; and leave me for this time.

BIANCA.
Leave you! wherefore?

CASSIO.
I do attend here on the general;
And think it no addition, nor my wish,
To have him see me woman'd.

BIANCA.
　　　　　Why, I pray you?

CASSIO.
Not that I love you not.

BIANCA.
　　　　　But that you do not love me.
I pray you, bring me on the way a little;
And say if I shall see you soon at night.

CASSIO.
'Tis but a little way that I can bring you;
For I attend here: but I'll see you soon.

BIANCA.
'Tis very good; I must be circumstanced.
　　　　　　　　　　　　[*Exeunt.*

ACT IV. SCENE I.

Cyprus.   Before the castle.

Enter OTHELLO *and* IAGO.

IAGO.
WILL you think so?

OTHELLO.
　　　　　Think so, Iago!

IAGO.
　　　　　　　　　What,
To kiss in private?

OTHELLO.
　　　　　An unauthorized kiss.

IAGO.
Or to be naked with her friend in bed
An hour or more, not meaning any harm?

OTHELLO.
Naked in bed, Iago, and not mean harm!
It is hypocrisy against the devil:
They that mean virtuously and yet do so,
The devil their virtue tempts, and they tempt
　　heaven.

IAGO.
So they do nothing, 'tis a venial slip:
But if I give my wife a handkerchief,—

OTHELLO.
What then?

IAGO.
Why, then, 'tis hers, my lord; and, being hers,
She may, I think, bestow't on any man.

OTHELLO.
She is protectress of her honour too:
May she give that?

IAGO.
Her honour is an essence that's not seen;
They have it very oft that have it not:
But, for the handkerchief,—

OTHELLO.
By heaven, I would most gladly have forgot
　　it:—
Thou said'st,—O, it comes o'er my memory,
As doth the raven o'er the infected house,
Boding to all,—he had my handkerchief.

IAGO.
Ay, what of that?

OTHELLO.
　　　　　That's not so good now.

IAGO.
　　　　　　　　　What,
If I had said I had seen him do you wrong?
Or heard him say,—as knaves be such abroad,
Who having, by their own importunate suit,
Or voluntary dotage of some mistress,
Convinced or supplied them, cannot choose
But they must blab—

OTHELLO.
　　　　　Hath he said any thing?

IAGO.
He hath, my lord; but be you well assured,
No more than he'll unswear.

OTHELLO.
　　　　　　　　　What hath he said?

IAGO.
Faith, that he did—I know not what he did.

OTHELLO.
What? what?

IAGO.
Lie—

OTHELLO.
　　　　　With her?

IAGO.
　　　　　With her, on her; what you will.

OTHELLO.
Lie with her! lie on her!—We say lie on her, when
they belie her.—Lie with her! that's fulsome.—
Handkerchief—confessions—handkerchief!—To
confess, and be hang'd for his labour;—first, to be

hang'd, and then to confess.—I tremble at it.
Nature would not invest herself in such shadowing passion without some instruction. It is not
words that shake me thus:—pish!—noses, ears,
and lips.—Is't possible?—Confess—handkerchief!—O devil!—   [*Falls in a trance.*

IAGO.

Work on,
My medicine, work! Thus credulous fools are
   caught;
And many worthy and chaste dames even thus,
All guiltless, meet reproach.—What, ho! my
   lord!
My lord, I say! Othello!

Enter CASSIO.
                How now, Cassio!

CASSIO.

What's the matter?

IAGO.

My lord is faln into an epilepsy:
This is his second fit; he had one yesterday.

CASSIO.

Rub him about the temples.

IAGO.
                  No, forbear;
The lethargy must have his quiet course:
If not, he foams at mouth, and by and by
Breaks out to savage madness. Look, he stirs:
Do you withdraw yourself a little while,
He will recover straight: when he is gone,
I would on great occasion speak with you.
                    [*Exit* CASSIO.
How is it, general? have you not hurt your head?

OTHELLO.

Dost thou mock me?

IAGO.
            I mock you! no, by heaven.
Would you would bear your fortune like a man!

OTHELLO.

A horned man's a monster and a beast.

IAGO.

There's many a beast, then, in a populous city,
And many a civil monster.

OTHELLO.

Did he confess it?

IAGO.

Good sir, be a man;
Think every bearded fellow that's but yoked
May draw with you: there's millions now alive
That nightly lie in those unproper beds
Which they dare swear peculiar: your case is
   better.
O, 'tis the spite of hell, the fiend's arch-mock,
To lip a wanton in a secure couch,
And to suppose her chaste! No, let me know;
And knowing what I am, I know what she shall
   be.

OTHELLO.

O, thou art wise; 'tis certain.

IAGO.
              Stand you awhile apart;
Confine yourself but in a patient list.
Whilst you were here o'erwhelmed with your
   grief,—
A passion most unfitting such a man,—
Cassio came hither: I shifted him away,

And laid good 'scuse upon your ecstasy;
Bade him anon return, and here speak with me;
The which he promised. Do but encave your-
   self,
And mark the fleers, the gibes, and notable
   scorns,
That dwell in every region of his face;
For I will make him tell the tale anew,—
Where, how, how oft, how long ago, and when
He hath, and is again to cope your wife:
I say, but mark his gesture. Marry, patience;
Or I shall say y'are all in all in spleen,
And nothing of a man.

OTHELLO.
             Dost thou hear, Iago?
I will be found most cunning in my patience;
But—dost thou hear?—most bloody.

IAGO.
                That's not amiss;
But yet keep time in all. Will you withdraw?
               [OTHELLO *retires.*
Now will I question Cassio of Bianca,
A housewife that, by selling her desires,
Buys herself bread and clothes: it is a creature
That dotes on Cassio,—as 'tis the strumpet's
   plague
To beguile many and be beguiled by one:—
He, when he hears of her, cannot refrain
From the excess of laughter:—here he comes:—
As he shall smile, Othello shall go mad;
And his unbookish jealousy must construe
Poor Cassio's smiles, gestures, and light be-
   haviour,
Quite in the wrong.

Enter CASSIO.
           How do you now, lieutenant?

CASSIO.

The worser that you give me the addition
Whose want even kills me.

IAGO.

Ply Desdemona well, and you are sure on't.
Now, if this suit lay in Bianca's power,
               [*Speaking lower.*
How quickly should you speed!

CASSIO.
              Alas, poor caitiff!

OTHELLO [*aside*].

Look, how he laughs already!

IAGO.

I never knew a woman love man so.

CASSIO.

Alas, poor rogue! I think, i'faith, she loves me.

OTHELLO [*aside*].

Now he denies it faintly, and laughs it out.

IAGO.

Do you hear, Cassio?

OTHELLO [*aside*].
           Now he importunes him
To tell it o'er:—go to; well said, well said.

IAGO.

She gives it out that you shall marry her:
Do you intend it?

CASSIO.

Ha, ha, ha!

OTHELLO [*aside*].

Do you triumph, Roman? do you triumph?

CASSIO.
I marry her!—what, a customer! Prithee, bear some charity to my wit; do not think it so unwholesome:—ha, ha, ha!

OTHELLO [aside].
So, so, so, so:—they laugh that win.

IAGO.
Faith, the cry goes that you shall marry her.

CASSIO.
Prithee, say true.

IAGO.
I am a very villain else.

OTHELLO [aside].
Have you scored me? Well.

CASSIO.
This is the monkey's own giving out: she is persuaded I will marry her, out of her own love and flattery, not out of my promise.

OTHELLO [aside].
Iago beckons me; now he begins the story.

CASSIO.
She was here even now; she haunts me in every place. I was, the other day, talking on the sea-bank with certain Venetians; and thither comes the bauble, and by this hand she falls me thus about my neck,—

OTHELLO [aside].
Crying 'O dear Cassio!' as it were: his gesture imports it.

CASSIO.
So hangs, and lolls, and weeps upon me; so hales and pulls me:—ha, ha, ha!

OTHELLO [aside].
Now he tells how she pluckt him to my chamber. O, I see that nose of yours, but not that dog I shall throw it to.

CASSIO.
Well, I must leave her company.

IAGO.
Before me! look, where she comes.

CASSIO.
'Tis such another fitchew! marry, a perfumed one.
Enter BIANCA.
What do you mean by this haunting of me?

BIANCA.
Let the devil and his dam haunt you! What did you mean by that same handkerchief you gave me even now? I was a fine fool to take it. I must take out the work?—A likely piece of work, that you should find it in your chamber, and not know who left it there! This is some minx's token, and I must take out the work? There,—give it your hobby-horse: wheresoever you had it, I'll take out no work on't.

CASSIO.
How now, my sweet Bianca! how now! how now!

OTHELLO [aside].
By heaven, that should be my handkerchief!

BIANCA.
An you'll come to supper to-night, you may; an you will not, come when you are next prepared for.   [Exit.

IAGO.
After her, after her.

CASSIO.
Faith, I must; she'll rail i'the street else.

IAGO.
Will you sup there?

CASSIO.
Faith, I intend so.

IAGO.
Well, I may chance to see you; for I would very fain speak with you.

CASSIO.
Prithee, come; will you?

IAGO.
Go to; say no more.   [Exit CASSIO.

OTHELLO [coming forward].
How shall I murder him, Iago?

IAGO.
Did you perceive how he laught at his vice?

OTHELLO.
O Iago!

IAGO.
And did you see the handkerchief?

OTHELLO.
Was that mine?

IAGO.
Yours, by this hand: and to see how he prizes the foolish woman your wife! she gave it him, and he hath given it his whore.

OTHELLO.
I would have him nine years a-killing. A fine woman! a fair woman! a sweet woman!

IAGO.
Nay, you must forget that.

OTHELLO.
Ay, let her rot, and perish, and be damn'd to-night; for she shall not live: no, my heart is turn'd to stone; I strike it, and it hurts my hand.—O, the world hath not a sweeter creature: she might lie by an emperor's side, and command him tasks.

IAGO.
Nay, that's not your way.

OTHELLO.
Hang her! I do but say what she is:—so delicate with her needle!—an admirable musician! O, she will sing the savageness out of a bear!—of so high and plenteous wit and invention!—

IAGO.
She's the worse for all this.

OTHELLO.
O, a thousand thousand times:—and then, of so gentle a condition!

IAGO.
Ay, too gentle.

OTHELLO.
Nay, that's certain:—but yet the pity of it, Iago! O Iago, the pity of it, Iago!

IAGO.
If you are so fond over her iniquity, give her patent to offend; for, if it touch not you, it comes near nobody.

OTHELLO.
I will chop her into messes:—cuckold me!

IAGO.
O, 'tis foul in her.

OTHELLO.
With mine officer!

IAGO.
That's fouler.

OTHELLO.

Get me some poison, Iago; this night:—I'll not
expostulate with her, lest her body and beauty
unprovide my mind again:—this night, Iago.

IAGO.

Do it not with poison, strangle her in her bed,
even the bed she hath contaminated.

OTHELLO.

Good, good: the justice of it pleases: very good.

IAGO.

And for Cassio,—let me be his undertaker: you
shall hear more by midnight.

OTHELLO.

Excellent good. [*A trumpet within.*] What trumpet
is that same?

IAGO.

Something from Venice, sure. 'Tis Lodovico
Come from the duke: and, see, your wife is with him.

Enter LODOVICO, DESDEMONA, *and*
ATTENDANTS.

LODOVICO.

Save you, worthy general!

OTHELLO.

          With all my heart, sir.

LODOVICO.

The duke and senators of Venice greet you.
          [*Gives him a packet.*

OTHELLO.

I kiss the instrument of their pleasures.
          [*Opens the packet, and reads.*

DESDEMONA.

And what's the news, good cousin Lodovico?

IAGO.

I am very glad to see you, signior;
Welcome to Cyprus.

LODOVICO.

I thank you. How does Lieutenant Cassio?

IAGO.

Lives, sir.

DESDEMONA.

Cousin, there's faln between him and my lord
An unkind breach: but you shall make all well.

OTHELLO.

Are you sure of that?

DESDEMONA.

My lord?

OTHELLO [*reads*].

This fail you not to do, as you will—

LODOVICO.

He did not call: he's busy in the paper.
Is there division 'twixt my lord and Cassio?

DESDEMONA.

A most unhappy one: I would do much
T'atone them, for the love I bear to Cassio.

OTHELLO.

Fire and brimstone!

DESDEMONA.

          My lord?

OTHELLO.

          Are you wise?

DESDEMONA.

What, is he angry?

LODOVICO.

          May be the letter moved him;
For, as I think, they do command him home,
Deputing Cassio in his government.

DESDEMONA.

Trust me, I am glad on't.

OTHELLO.

          Indeed!

DESDEMONA.

          My lord?

OTHELLO.

I am glad to see you mad.

DESDEMONA.

          Why, sweet Othello,—

OTHELLO.

Devil!   [*Striking her.*

DESDEMONA.

I have not deserved this.

LODOVICO.

My lord, this would not be believed in Venice,
Though I should swear I saw't: 'tis very much:
Make her amends; she weeps.

OTHELLO.

          O devil, devil!
If that the earth could teem with woman's tears,
Each drop she falls would prove a crocodile.—
Out of my sight!

DESDEMONA.

          I will not stay to offend you.
          [*Going.*

LODOVICO.

Truly, an obedient lady:—
I do beseech your lordship, call her back.

OTHELLO.

Mistress!

DESDEMONA.

          My lord?

OTHELLO.

          What would you with her, sir?

LODOVICO.

Who, I, my lord?

OTHELLO.

Ay; you did wish that I would make her turn:
Sir, she can turn, and turn, and yet go on,
And turn again; and she can weep, sir, weep;
And she's obedient, as you say,—obedient,—
Very obedient.—Proceed you in your tears.—
Concerning this, sir,—O well-painted passion!—
I am commanded home.—Get you away;
I'll send for you anon.—Sir, I obey the mandate,
And will return to Venice.—Hence, avaunt!
          [*Exit* DESDEMONA.
Cassio shall have my place. And, sir, to-night
I do entreat that we may sup together:
You are welcome, sir, to Cyprus.—Goats and
monkeys!   [*Exit.*

LODOVICO.

Is this the noble Moor whom our full senate
Call all-in-all sufficient?—Is this the nature
Whom passion could not shake? whose solid virtue
The shot of accident, nor dart of chance,
Could neither graze nor pierce?

IAGO.

          He is much changed.

LODOVICO.

Are his wits safe? is he not light of brain?

IAGO.

He's that he is: I may not breathe my censure.
What he might be,—if, what he might, he is not,—
I would to heaven he were!

LODOVICO.
                What, strike his wife!
IAGO.
Faith, that was not so well; yet would I knew
That stroke would prove the worst!
LODOVICO.
                   Is it his use?
Or did the letters work upon his blood,
And new-create this fault?
IAGO.
                 Alas, alas!
It is not honesty in me to speak
What I have seen and know. You shall observe
    him;
And his own courses will denote him so,
That I may save my speech: do but go after,
And mark how he continues.
LODOVICO.
I am sorry that I am deceived in him.   [*Exeunt.*

SCENE II.

A room in the castle.
Enter OTHELLO *and* EMILIA.
OTHELLO.
YOU have seen nothing, then?
EMILIA.
Nor ever heard, nor ever did suspect.
OTHELLO.
Yes, you have seen Cassio and she together.
EMILIA.
But then I saw no harm, and then I heard
Each syllable that breath made up between them.
OTHELLO.
What, did they never whisper?
EMILIA.
                 Never, my lord.
OTHELLO.
Nor send you out o'th'way?
EMILIA.
Never.
OTHELLO.
To fetch her fan, her gloves, her mask, nor noth-
    ing?
EMILIA.
Never, my lord.
OTHELLO.
That's strange.
EMILIA.
I durst, my lord, to wager she is honest,
Lay down my soul at stake: if you think other,
Remove your thought,—it doth abuse your bosom.
If any wretch have put this in your head,
Let heaven requite it with the serpent's curse!
For, if she be not honest, chaste, and true,
There's no man happy; the purest of their wives
Is foul as slander.
OTHELLO.
          Bid her come hither:—go.
                     [*Exit* EMILIA.
She says enough;—yet she's a simple bawd
That cannot say as much. This is a subtle whore,
A closet-lock-and-key of villainous secrets:
And yet she'll kneel and pray; I have seen her
    do't.

Enter DESDEMONA *with* EMILIA.
DESDEMONA.
My lord, what is your will?
OTHELLO.
           Pray, chuck, come hither.
DESDEMONA.
What is your pleasure?
OTHELLO.
            Let me see your eyes;
Look in my face.
DESDEMONA.
        What horrible fancy's this?
OTHELLO [*to* EMILIA].
Some of your function, mistress;
Leave procreants alone, and shut the door;
Cough, or cry 'hem,' if any body come:
Your mystery, your mystery;—nay, dispatch.
                     [*Exit* EMILIA.
DESDEMONA.
Upon my knees, what doth your speech import?
I understand a fury in your words,
But not the words.
OTHELLO.
Why, what art thou?
DESDEMONA.
          Your wife, my lord; your true
And loyal wife.
OTHELLO.
       Come, swear it, damn thyself;
Lest, being like one of heaven, the devils them-
    selves
Should fear to seize thee: therefore be double-
    damn'd,—
Swear thou art honest.
DESDEMONA.
         Heaven doth truly know it.
OTHELLO.
Heaven truly knows that thou art false as hell.
DESDEMONA.
To whom, my lord? with whom? how am I false?
OTHELLO.
Ah, Desdemona!—away! away! away!
DESDEMONA.
Alas the heavy day!—Why do you weep?
Am I the motive of these tears, my lord?
If haply you my father do suspect
An instrument of this your calling back,
Lay not your blame on me: if you have lost
    him,
Why, I have lost him too.
OTHELLO.
            Had it pleased heaven
To try me with affliction; had they rain'd
All kinds of sores and shames on my bare head;
Steep'd me in poverty to the very lips;
Given to captivity me and my utmost hopes;
I should have found in some place of my soul
A drop of patience: but, alas, to make me
A fixed figure for the time of scorn
To point his slow unmoving finger at!—
Yet could I bear that too; well, very well:
But there, where I have garner'd up my heart,
Where either I must live, or bear no life,—
The fountain from the which my current runs,
Or else dries up; to be discarded thence!
Or keep it as a cistern for foul toads

To knot and gender in!—turn thy complexion
    there,
Patience, thou young and rose-lipt cherubin,—
Ay, there, look grim as hell!
            DESDEMONA.
I hope my noble lord esteems me honest.
            OTHELLO.
O, ay; as summer flies are in the shambles,
That quicken even with blowing. O thou weed,
Who art so lovely fair, and smell'st so sweet,
That the sense aches at thee,—would thou hadst
    ne'er been born!
            DESDEMONA.
Alas, what ignorant sin have I committed?
            OTHELLO.
Was this fair paper, this most goodly book,
Made to write 'whore' upon? What committed!
Committed!—O thou public commoner!
I should make very forges of my cheeks,
That would to cinders burn up modesty,
Did I but speak thy deeds.—What committed!
Heaven stops the nose at it, and the moon winks;
The bawdy wind, that kisses all it meets,
Is husht within the hollow mine of earth,
And will not hear it.—What committed!—
Impudent strumpet!
            DESDEMONA.
            By heaven, you do me wrong.
            OTHELLO.
Are not you a strumpet?
            DESDEMONA.
            No, as I am a Christian:
If to preserve this vessel for my lord
From any other foul unlawful touch,
Be not to be a strumpet, I am none.
            OTHELLO.
What, not a whore?
            DESDEMONA.
            No, as I shall be saved.
            OTHELLO.
Is't possible?
            DESDEMONA.
O, heaven forgive us!
            OTHELLO.
            I cry you mercy, then:
I took you for that cunning whore of Venice
That married with Othello.—You, mistress,
That have the office opposite to Saint Peter,
And keep the gate of hell!
            Enter EMILIA.
            You, you, ay, you!
We have done our course; there's money for your
    pains:
I pray you, turn the key, and keep our counsel.
                        [*Exit.*
            EMILIA.
Alas, what does this gentleman conceive?—
How do you, madam? how do you, my good lady?
            DESDEMONA.
Faith, half asleep.
            EMILIA.
Good madam, what's the matter with my lord?
            DESDEMONA.
With who?
            EMILIA.
Why, with my lord, madam.

            DESDEMONA.
Who is thy lord?
            EMILIA.
He that is yours, sweet lady.
            DESDEMONA.
I have none: do not talk to me, Emilia;
I cannot weep; nor answer have I none,
But what should go by water. Prithee, to-night
Lay on my bed my wedding-sheets,—remem-
    ber;—
And call thy husband hither.
            EMILIA.
            Here's a change indeed! [*Exit.*
            DESDEMONA.
'Tis meet I should be used so, very meet.
How have I been behaved, that he might stick
The small'st opinion on my least misuse?
      Enter EMILIA *with* IAGO.
            IAGO.
What is your pleasure, madam? How is't with you?
            DESDEMONA.
I cannot tell. Those that do teach young babes
Do it with gentle means and easy tasks:
He might have chid me so; for, in good faith,
I am a child to chiding.
            IAGO.
            What's the matter, lady?
            EMILIA.
Alas, Iago, my lord hath so bewhored her,
Thrown such despite and heavy terms upon her,
As true hearts cannot bear.
            DESDEMONA.
Am I that name, Iago?
            IAGO.
            What name, fair lady?
            DESDEMONA.
Such as she says my lord did say I was.
            EMILIA.
He call'd her whore: a beggar in his drink
Could not have laid such terms upon his callet.
            IAGO.
Why did he so?
            DESDEMONA.
I do not know; I am sure I am none such.
            IAGO.
Do not weep, do not weep:—alas the day!
            EMILIA.
Hath she forsook so many noble matches,
Her father, and her country, and her friends,
To be call'd whore? would it not make one weep?
            DESDEMONA.
It is my wretched fortune.
            IAGO.
            Beshrew him for't!
How comes this trick upon him?
            DESDEMONA.
            Nay, heaven doth know.
            EMILIA.
I will be hang'd, if some eternal villain,
Some busy and insinuating rogue,
Some cogging, cozening slave, to get some office,
Have not devised this slander; I'll be hang'd else.
            IAGO.
Fie, there is no such man; it is impossible.
            DESDEMONA.
If any such there be, heaven pardon him!

EMILIA.
A halter pardon him! and hell gnaw his bones!
Why should he call her whore? who keeps her
   company?
What place? what time? what form? what likeli-
   hood?
The Moor's abused by some most villainous
   knave,
Some base notorious knave, some scurvy fel-
   low:—
O heaven, that such companions thou'ldst unfold,
And put in every honest hand a whip
To lash the rascals naked through the world
Even from the east to th'west!

IAGO.
             Speak within door.

EMILIA.
O, fie upon them! Some such squire he was
That turn'd your wit the seamy side without,
And made you to suspect me with the Moor.

IAGO.
You are a fool; go to.

DESDEMONA.
          O good Iago,
What shall I do to win my lord again?
Good friend, go to him; for, by this light of
   heaven,
I know not how I lost him. Here I kneel:—
If e'er my will did trespass 'gainst his love,
Either in discourse of thought or actual deed;
Or that mine eyes, mine ears, or any sense,
Delighted them in any other form;
Or that I do not yet, and ever did,
And ever will—though he do shake me off
To beggarly divorcement—love him dearly,
Comfort forswear me! Unkindness may do much;
And his unkindness may defeat my life,
But never taint my love. I cannot say 'whore,'—
It does abhor me now I speak the word;
To do the act that might the addition earn
Not the world's mass of vanity could make me.

IAGO.
I pray you, be content: 'tis but his humour:
The business of the state does him offence,
And he does chide with you.

DESDEMONA.
If 'twere no other,—

IAGO.
       'Tis but so, I warrant. [*Trumpets within.*
Hark, how these instruments summon to supper!
The messengers of Venice stay the meat:
Go in, and weep not; all things shall be well.
      [*Exeunt* DESDEMONA *and* EMILIA.
        Enter RODERIGO.
How now, Roderigo!

RODERIGO.
I do not find that thou deal'st justly with me.

IAGO.
What in the contrary?

RODERIGO.
Every day thou daff'st me with some device, Iago;
and rather, as it seems to me now, keep'st from
me all conveniency than suppliest me with the
least advantage of hope. I will, indeed, no longer
endure it; nor am I yet persuaded to put up in
peace what already I have foolishly suffer'd.

IAGO.
Will you hear me, Roderigo?

RODERIGO.
Faith, I have heard too much; for your words and
performances are no kin together.

IAGO.
You charge me most unjustly.

RODERIGO.
With naught but truth. I have wasted myself out
of my means. The jewels you have had from me
to deliver to Desdemona would half have corrupted a votarist: you have told me she hath received them, and return'd me expectations and
comforts of sudden respect and acquaintance; but
I find none.

IAGO.
Well; go to; very well.

RODERIGO.
Very well! go to! I cannot go to, man; nor 'tis not
very well: nay, I think it is scurvy, and begin to
find myself fopt in it.

IAGO.
Very well.

RODERIGO.
I tell you 'tis not very well. I will make myself
known to Desdemona: if she will return me my
jewels, I will give over my suit, and repent my
unlawful solicitation; if not, assure yourself I will
seek satisfaction of you.

IAGO.
You have said now.

RODERIGO.
Ay, and said nothing but what I protest intendment of doing.

IAGO.
Why, now I see there's mettle in thee; and even
from this instant do build on thee a better opinion
than ever before. Give me thy hand, Roderigo:
thou hast taken against me a most just exception;
but yet, I protest, I have dealt most directly in
thy affair.

RODERIGO.
It hath not appear'd.

IAGO.
I grant, indeed, it hath not appear'd; and your
suspicion is not without wit and judgement. But,
Roderigo, if thou hast that in thee indeed, which
I have greater reason to believe now than ever,—
I mean purpose, courage, and valour,—this night
show it: if thou the next night following enjoy not
Desdemona, take me from this world with
treachery, and devise engines for my life.

RODERIGO.
Well, what is it? is it within reason and compass?

IAGO.
Sir, there is especial commission come from
Venice to depute Cassio in Othello's place.

RODERIGO.
Is that true? why, then Othello and Desdemona
return again to Venice.

IAGO.
O, no; he goes into Mauritania, and takes away
with him the fair Desdemona, unless his abode be
linger'd here by some accident: wherein none can
be so determinate as the removing of Cassio.

RODERIGO.
How do you mean, removing of him?
IAGO.
Why, by making him uncapable of Othello's place,—knocking out his brains.
RODERIGO.
And that you would have me to do?
IAGO.
Ay, if you dare do yourself a profit and a right. He sups to-night with a harlotry, and thither will I go to him:—he knows not yet of his honourable fortune. If you will watch his going thence,—which I will fashion to fall out between twelve and one,—you may take him at your pleasure: I will be near to second your attempt, and he shall fall between us. Come, stand not amazed at it, but go along with me; I will show you such a necessity in his death, that you shall think yourself bound to put it on him. It is now high supper-time, and the night grows to waste: about it.
RODERIGO.
I will hear further reason for this.
IAGO.
And you shall be satisfied.　　　　[Exeunt.

SCENE III.

Another room in the castle.

Enter OTHELLO, LODOVICO, DESDEMONA, EMILIA, *and* ATTENDANTS.

LODOVICO.
I DO beseech you, sir, trouble yourself no further.
OTHELLO.
O, pardon me; 'twill do me good to walk.
LODOVICO.
Madam, good night; I humbly thank your lady-ship.
DESDEMONA.
Your honour is most welcome.
OTHELLO.
　　　　　　　　　　Will you walk, sir?
O,—Desdemona,—
DESDEMONA.
My lord?
OTHELLO.
Get you to bed on th'instant; I will be return'd forthwith: dismiss your attendant there: look't be done.
DESDEMONA.
I will, my lord.
　　　　[Exeunt OTHELLO, LODOVICO, and AT-
　　　　TENDANTS.
EMILIA.
How goes it now? he looks gentler than he did.
DESDEMONA.
He says he will return incontinent:
He hath commanded me to go to bed,
And bade me to dismiss you.
EMILIA.
　　　　　　　　Dismiss me!
DESDEMONA.
It was his bidding; therefore, good Emilia,
Give me my nightly wearing, and adieu:
We must not now displease him.

EMILIA.
I would you had never seen him!
DESDEMONA.
So would not I: my love doth so approve him,
That even his stubbornness, his checks, his frowns,—
Prithee, unpin me,—have grace and favour in them.
EMILIA.
I have laid those sheets you bade me on the bed.
DESDEMONA.
All's one.—Good faith, how foolish are our minds!—
If I do die before thee, prithee, shroud me
In one of those same sheets.
EMILIA.
　　　　　　　Come, come, you talk.
DESDEMONA.
My mother had a maid call'd Barbara:
She was in love; and he she loved proved mad,
And did forsake her: she had a song of 'willow;'
An old thing 'twas, but it exprest her fortune,
And she died singing it: that song to-night
Will not go from my mind; I have much to do,
But to go hang my head all at one side,
And sing it like poor Barbara.—Prithee, dispatch.
EMILIA.
Shall I go fetch your night-gown?
DESDEMONA.
　　　　　　　　No, unpin me here.—
This Lodovico is a proper man.
EMILIA.
A very handsome man.
DESDEMONA.
He speaks well.
EMILIA.
I know a lady in Venice would have walkt bare-foot to Palestine for a touch of his nether lip.
DESDEMONA [*singing*].
　　The poor soul sat sighing by a sycamore tree,
　　　Sing all a green willow;
　　Her hand on her bosom, her head on her knee,
　　　Sing willow, willow, willow:
　　The fresh streams ran by her, and murmur'd her moans;
　　　Sing willow, willow, willow;
　　Her salt tears fell from her, and soften'd the stones;—
Lay by these:—
　　　Sing willow, willow, willow;
Prithee, hie thee; he'll come anon:—
　　Sing all a green willow must be my garland.
　Let nobody blame him; his scorn I approve,—
Nay, that's not next.—Hark! who is't that knocks?
EMILIA.
It is the wind.
DESDEMONA.
　　I call'd my love false love; but what said he then?
　　　Sing willow, willow, willow;
　　If I court moe women, you'll couch with moe men.—
So, get thee gone; good night. Mine eyes do itch;
Doth that bode weeping?
EMILIA.
　　　　　　'Tis neither here nor there.

DESDEMONA.

I have heard it said so.—O, these men, these men!—
Dost thou in conscience think,—tell me, Emilia,—
That there be women do abuse their husbands
In such gross kind?

EMILIA.

There be some such, no question.

DESDEMONA.

Wouldst thou do such a deed for all the world?

EMILIA.

Why, would not you?

DESDEMONA.

No, by this heavenly light!

EMILIA.

Nor I neither by this heavenly light; I might do't
as well i'th'dark.

DESDEMONA.

Wouldst thou do such a deed for all the world?

EMILIA.

The world is a huge thing: it is a great price for a
small vice.

DESDEMONA.

In troth, I think thou wouldst not.

EMILIA.

In troth, I think I should; and undo't when I had
done. Marry, I would not do such a thing for a
joint-ring, nor for measures of lawn, nor for
gowns, petticoats, nor caps, nor any petty exhibition; but, for the whole world,—why, who
would not make her husband a cuckold to make
him a monarch? I should venture purgatory for't.

DESDEMONA.

Beshrew me, if I would do such a wrong
For the whole world.

EMILIA.

Why, the wrong is but a wrong i'th'world; and
having the world for your labour, 'tis a wrong in
your own world, and you might quickly make it
right.

DESDEMONA.

I do not think there is any such woman.

EMILIA.

Yes, a dozen; and as many to th'vantage as would
store the world they play'd for.
But I do think it is their husbands' faults
If wives do fall: say that they slack their duties,
And pour our treasures into foreign laps;
Or else break out in peevish jealousies,
Throwing restraint upon us; or say they strike us,
Or scant our former having in despite;
Why, we have galls; and though we have some
grace,
Yet have we some revenge. Let husbands know
Their wives have sense like them: they see, and
smell,
And have their palates both for sweet and sour,
As husbands have. What is it that they do
When they change us for others? Is it sport?
I think it is: and doth affection breed it?
I think it doth: is't frailty that thus errs?
It is so too:—and have not we affections,
Desires for sport, and frailty, as men have?
Then let them use us well: else let them know,
The ills we do, their ills instruct us so.

DESDEMONA.

Good night, good night: heaven me such usage
send,
Not to pick bad from bad, but by bad mend!

[Exeunt.

ACT V. SCENE I.

Cyprus.   A street.

Enter IAGO *and* RODERIGO.

IAGO.

HERE, stand behind this bulk; straight will he
come:
Wear thy good rapier bare, and put it home:
Quick, quick; fear nothing; I'll be at thy elbow:
It makes us, or it mars us; think on that,
And fix most firm thy resolution.

RODERIGO.

Be near at hand; I may miscarry in't.

IAGO.

Here, at thy hand: be bold, and take thy stand.

[Retires to a little distance.

RODERIGO.

I have no great devotion to the deed;
And yet he hath given me satisfying reasons:—
'Tis but a man gone:—forth, my sword; he dies.

[Goes to his stand.

IAGO.

I have rubb'd this young quat almost to the sense,
And he grows angry. Now, whether he kill Cassio,
Or Cassio him, or each do kill the other,
Every way makes my gain: live Roderigo,
He calls me to a restitution large
Of gold and jewels that I bobb'd from him,
As gifts to Desdemona;
It must not be: if Cassio do remain,
He hath a daily beauty in his life
That makes me ugly; and, besides, the Moor
May unfold me to him; there stand I in much
peril:
No, he must die. But so: I hear him coming.

Enter CASSIO.

RODERIGO.

I know his gait, 'tis he.—Villain, thou diest!

[Makes a pass at CASSIO.

CASSIO.

That thrust had been mine enemy indeed,
But that my coat is better than thou know'st:
I will make proof of thine.

[Draws, and wounds RODERIGO.

RODERIGO.

O, I am slain!

[IAGO cuts CASSIO behind in the leg, and
exit.

CASSIO.

I am maim'd for ever.—Help, ho! murder! murder!   [Falls.

Enter OTHELLO, *at some distance.*

OTHELLO.

The voice of Cassio:—Iago keeps his word.

RODERIGO.

O, villain that I am!

OTHELLO.

It is even so.

CASSIO.

O, help, ho! light! a surgeon!

OTHELLO.

'Tis he:—O brave Iago, honest and just,
That hast such noble sense of thy friend's wrong!
Thou teachest me:—Minion, your dear lies dead,
And your unblest fate hies: strumpet, I come!
Forth of my heart those charms, thine eyes, are
   blotted;
Thy bed lust-stain'd shall with lust's blood be
   spotted.   [*Exit.*

Enter LODOVICO *and* GRATIANO.

CASSIO.

What, ho! no watch? no passage? murder! murder!

GRATIANO.

'Tis some mischance; the cry is very direful.

CASSIO.

O, help!

LODOVICO.

Hark!

RODERIGO.

O wretched villain!

LODOVICO.

Two or three groan:—it is a heavy night:
These may be counterfeits: let's think't unsafe
To come in to the cry without more help.

RODERIGO.

Nobody come? then shall I bleed to death.

LODOVICO.

Hark!

GRATIANO.

Here's one comes in his shirt, with light and
   weapons.
            Enter IAGO, *with a light.*

IAGO.

Who's there? whose noise is this that cries on
   murder?

LODOVICO.

We do not know.

IAGO.

Did not you hear a cry?

CASSIO.

Here, here! for heaven's sake, help me!

IAGO.

What's the matter?

GRATIANO.

This is Othello's ancient, as I take it.

LODOVICO.

The same indeed; a very valiant fellow.

IAGO.

What are you here that cry so grievously?

CASSIO.

Iago? O, I am spoil'd, undone by villains!
Give me some help.

IAGO.

O me, lieutenant! what villains have done this?

CASSIO.

I think that one of them is hereabout,
And cannot make away.

IAGO.

O treacherous villains!—
What are you there? come in, and give some
   help.
        [*To* LODOVICO *and* GRATIANO.

RODERIGO.

O, help me here!

CASSIO.

That's one of them.

IAGO.

O murderous slave! O villain!
            [*Stabs* RODERIGO.

RODERIGO.

O damn'd Iago! O inhuman dog!

IAGO.

Kill men i'th'dark!—Where be these bloody
   thieves?—
How silent is this town!—Ho! murder! murder!—
What may you be? are you of good or evil?

LODOVICO.

As you shall prove us, praise us.

IAGO.

Signior Lodovico?

LODOVICO.

He, sir.

IAGO.

I cry you mercy. Here's Cassio hurt by villains.

GRATIANO.

Cassio!

IAGO.

How is't, brother?

CASSIO.

My leg is cut in two.

IAGO.

Marry, heaven forbid!—
Light, gentlemen:—I'll bind it with my shirt.
           Enter BIANCA.

BIANCA.

What is the matter, ho? who is't that cried?

IAGO.

Who is't that cried!

BIANCA.

O my dear Cassio! my sweet Cassio!
O Cassio, Cassio, Cassio!

IAGO.

O notable strumpet!—Cassio, may you suspect
Who they should be that have thus mangled you?

CASSIO.

No.

GRATIANO.

I am sorry to find you thus: I have been to seek you.

IAGO.

Lend me a garter:—so.—O, for a chair,
To bear him easily hence!

BIANCA.

Alas, he faints!—O Cassio, Cassio, Cassio!

IAGO.

Gentlemen all, I do suspect this trash
To be a party in this injury.—
Patience awhile, good Cassio.—Come, come;
Lend me a light.—Know we this face or no?
Alas, my friend and my dear countryman
Roderigo? no:—yes, sure; O heaven! Roderigo.

GRATIANO.

What, of Venice?

IAGO.

Even he, sir: did you know him?

GRATIANO.

Know him! ay.

IAGO.

Signior Gratiano? I cry you gentle pardon;
These bloody accidents must excuse my manners,
That so neglected you.

GRATIANO.

I am glad to see you.

IAGO.

How do you, Cassio?—O, a chair, a chair!

GRATIANO.

Roderigo!

IAGO.

He, he, 'tis he.—[*a chair brought in.*] O, that's well said;—the chair:—
Some good man bear him carefully from hence;
I'll fetch the general's surgeon.—[*to* BIANCA] For you, mistress,   [Cassio,
Save you your labour.—He that lies slain here,
Was my dear friend: what malice was between you?

CASSIO.

None in the world; nor do I know the man.

IAGO [*to* BIANCA].

What, look you pale?—O, bear him out o'th'air.—
      [CASSIO *and* RODERIGO *are borne off.*
Stay you, good gentlemen.—Look you pale, mistress?—
Do you perceive the gastness of her eye?—
Nay, if you stare, we shall hear more anon.—
Behold her well; I pray you, look upon her:
Do you see, gentlemen? nay, guiltiness will speak,
Though tongues were out of use.

Enter EMILIA.

EMILIA.

'Las, what's the matter? what's the matter, husband?

IAGO.

Cassio hath here been set on in the dark
By Roderigo, and fellows that are scaped:
He's almost slain, and Roderigo dead.

EMILIA.

Alas, good gentleman! alas, good Cassio!

IAGO.

This is the fruit of whoring.—Prithee, Emilia,
Go know of Cassio where he supt to-night.—
[*to* BIANCA] What, do you shake at that?

BIANCA.

He supt at my house; but I therefore shake not.

IAGO.

O, did he so? I charge you, go with me.

EMILIA.

Fie, fie upon thee, strumpet!

BIANCA.

I am no strumpet; but of life as honest
As you that thus abuse me.

EMILIA.

      As I! foh! fie upon thee!

IAGO.

Kind gentlemen, let's go see poor Cassio drest.—
[*to* BIANCA] Come, mistress, you must tell's
Emilia, run you to the citadel,   [another tale.—
And tell my lord and lady what hath hapt.—
Will you go on afore?—[*aside*] This is the night
That either makes me or fordoes me quite.

      [*Exeunt.*

SCENE II.

A bedchamber in the castle: DESDEMONA *in bed asleep; a light burning.*

Enter OTHELLO.

OTHELLO.

IT is the cause, it is the cause, my soul,—
Let me not name it to you, you chaste stars!
It is the cause.—Yet I'll not shed her blood;

Nor scar that whiter skin of hers than snow,
And smooth as monumental alabaster.
Yet she must die, else she'll betray more men.—
Put out the light, and then put out the light:
If I quench thee, thou flaming minister,
I can again thy former light restore,
Should I repent me:—but once put out thy light,
Thou cunning'st pattern of excelling nature,
I know not where is that Promethean heat
That can thy light relume. When I have pluckt the rose,
I cannot give it vital growth again,
It needs must wither:—I'll smell it on the tree.—
      [*Kissing her.*
O balmy breath, that dost almost persuade
Justice to break her sword!—One more, one more:—
Be thus when thou art dead, and I will kill thee,
And love thee after:—one more, and this the last:
So sweet was ne'er so fatal. I must weep,
But they are cruel tears: this sorrow's heavenly;
It strikes where it doth love.—She wakes.

DESDEMONA.

Who's there? Othello?

OTHELLO.

      Ay, Desdemona.

DESDEMONA.

Will you come to bed, my lord?

OTHELLO.

Have you pray'd to-night, Desdemona?

DESDEMONA.

      Ay, my lord.

OTHELLO.

If you bethink yourself of any crime
Unreconciled as yet to heaven and grace,
Solicit for it straight.

DESDEMONA.

Alack, my lord, what may you mean by that?

OTHELLO.

Well, do it, and be brief; I will walk by:
I would not kill thy unprepared spirit;
No,—heaven forfend!—I would not kill thy soul.

DESDEMONA.

Talk you of killing?

OTHELLO.

Ay, I do.

DESDEMONA.

Then heaven have mercy on me!

OTHELLO.

Amen, with all my heart!

DESDEMONA.

If you say so, I hope you will not kill me.

OTHELLO.

Hum!

DESDEMONA.

And yet I fear you; for you are fatal then
When your eyes roll so: why I should fear I know not,
Since guiltiness I know not; but yet I feel I fear.

OTHELLO.

Think on thy sins.

DESDEMONA.

      They are loves I bear to you.

OTHELLO.

Ay, and for that thou diest.

DESDEMONA.
That death's unnatural that kills for loving.—
Alas, why gnaw you so your nether lip?
Some bloody passion shakes your very frame:
These are portents; but yet I hope, I hope,
They do not point on me.

OTHELLO.
                   Peace, and be still!

DESDEMONA.
I will so. What's the matter?

OTHELLO.
That handkerchief which I so loved and gave thee
Thou gavest to Cassio.

DESDEMONA.
                No, by my life and soul!
Send for the man, and ask him.

OTHELLO.
                  Sweet soul, take heed,
Take heed of perjury; thou art on thy death-bed.

DESDEMONA.
Ay, but not yet to die.

OTHELLO.
                 Yes, presently:
Therefore confess thee freely of thy sin;
For to deny each article with oath
Cannot remove nor choke the strong conception
That I do groan withal. Thou art to die.

DESDEMONA.
Then Lord have mercy on me!

OTHELLO.
                I say, amen.

DESDEMONA.
And have you mercy too!—I never did
Offend you in my life; never loved Cassio
But with such general warranty of heaven
As I might love; I never gave him token.

OTHELLO.
By heaven, I saw my handkerchief in's hand.
O perjured woman! thou dost stone my heart,
And makest me call what I intend to do
A murder, which I thought a sacrifice!
I saw the handkerchief.

DESDEMONA.
             He found it, then;
I never gave it him:—send for him hither;
Let him confess a truth.

OTHELLO.
              He hath confest.

DESDEMONA.
What, my lord?

OTHELLO.
That he hath used thee.

DESDEMONA.
             How? unlawfully?

OTHELLO.
                      Ay.

DESDEMONA.
He will not say so.

OTHELLO.
          No, his mouth is stopt;
Honest Iago hath ta'en order for't.

DESDEMONA.
O, my fear interprets:—what, is he dead?

OTHELLO.
Had all his hairs been lives, my great revenge
Had stomach for them all.

DESDEMONA.
Alas, he is betray'd, and I undone!

OTHELLO.
Out, strumpet! weep'st thou for him to my face?

DESDEMONA.
O, banish me, my lord, but kill me not!

OTHELLO.
Down, strumpet!

DESDEMONA.
Kill me to-morrow; let me live to-night!

OTHELLO.
Nay, if you strive,—

DESDEMONA.
But half an hour!

OTHELLO.
             Being done, there is no pause.

DESDEMONA.
But while I say one prayer!

OTHELLO.
              It is too late. [*Smothers her.*

EMILIA [*at the door*].
My lord, my lord! what, ho! my lord, my lord!

OTHELLO.
What noise is this?—Not dead? not yet quite
    dead?
I that am cruel am yet merciful;
I would not have thee linger in thy pain:—
So, so.

EMILIA [*within*].
What, ho! my lord, my lord!

OTHELLO.
                Who's there?

EMILIA [*within*].
O, good my lord, I would speak a word with you!

OTHELLO.
Yes: 'tis Emilia:—by and by.—She's dead.—
'Tis like she comes to speak of Cassio's death;
The noise was high.—Ha! no more moving?
Still as the grave.—Shall she come in? were't
    good?—
I think she stirs again:—no.—What's best to do?
If she come in, she'll sure speak to my wife:
My wife! my wife! what wife! I have no wife.
O, insupportable! O heavy hour!
Methinks it should be now a huge eclipse
Of sun and moon, and that th'affrighted globe
Should yawn at alteration.

EMILIA [*within*].
               I do beseech you
That I may speak with you, O, good my lord!

OTHELLO.
I had forgot thee: O, come in, Emilia:—
Soft,—by and by:—let me the curtains draw.—
Where art thou?   [*Opens the door.*

Enter EMILIA.
          What's the matter with thee now?

EMILIA.
O, my good lord, yonder's foul murders done!

OTHELLO.
What, now?

EMILIA.
But now, my lord.

OTHELLO.
It is the very error of the moon;
She comes more near the earth than she was wont,
And makes men mad.

EMILIA.
Cassio, my lord, hath kill'd a young Venetian
Call'd Roderigo.
OTHELLO.
Roderigo kill'd!
And Cassio kill'd!
EMILIA.
No, Cassio is not kill'd.
OTHELLO.
Not Cassio kill'd! then murder's out of tune,
And sweet revenge grows harsh.
DESDEMONA.
O falsely, falsely murder'd!
EMILIA.
Alas, what cry is that?
OTHELLO.
That! what?
EMILIA.
Out, and alas! that was my lady's voice.—
Help! help, ho! help!—O lady, speak again!
Sweet Desdemona! O sweet mistress, speak!
DESDEMONA.
A guiltless death I die.
EMILIA.
O, who hath done
This deed?
DESDEMONA.
Nobody,—I myself. Farewell:
Commend me to my kind lord: O, farewell! [Dies.
OTHELLO.
Why, how should she be murder'd?
EMILIA.
Alas, who knows?
OTHELLO.
You heard her say herself, it was not I.
EMILIA.
She said so: I must needs report the truth.
OTHELLO.
She's, like a liar, gone to burning hell:
'Twas I that kill'd her.
EMILIA.
O, the more angel she,
And you the blacker devil!
OTHELLO.
She turn'd to folly, and she was a whore.
EMILIA.
Thou dost belie her, and thou art a devil.
OTHELLO.
She was false as water.
EMILIA.
Thou art rash as fire, to say
That she was false: O, she was heavenly true!
OTHELLO.
Cassio did top her; ask thy husband else.
O, I were damn'd beneath all depth in hell,
But that I did proceed upon just grounds
To this extremity. Thy husband knew it all.
EMILIA.
My husband!
OTHELLO.
Thy husband.
EMILIA.
That she was false to wedlock?
OTHELLO.
Ay, with Cassio. Nay, had she been true,
If heaven would make me such another world

Of one entire and perfect chrysolite,
I'ld not have sold her for it.
EMILIA.
My husband!
OTHELLO.
Ay, 'twas he that told me first:
An honest man he is, and hates the slime
That sticks on filthy deeds.
EMILIA.
My husband!
OTHELLO.
What needs this iterance, woman? I say thy hus-
band.
EMILIA.
O mistress, villainy hath made mocks with love!—
My husband say that she was false!
OTHELLO.
He, woman:
I say thy husband: dost understand the word?
My friend, thy husband, honest, honest Iago.
EMILIA.
If he say so, may his pernicious soul
Rot half a grain a day! he lies to th'heart:
She was too fond of her most filthy bargain.
OTHELLO.
Ha!
EMILIA.
Do thy worst:
This deed of thine is no more worthy heaven
Than thou wast worthy her.
OTHELLO.
Peace, you were best.
EMILIA.
Thou hast not half that power to do me harm
As I have to be hurt. O gull! O dolt!
As ignorant as dirt! thou hast done a deed—
I care not for thy sword; I'll make thee known,
Though I lost twenty lives.—Help! help, ho! help!
The Moor hath kill'd my mistress! Murder! mur-
der!
Enter MONTANO, GRATIANO, and IAGO.
MONTANO.
What is the matter?—How now, general!
EMILIA.
O, are you come, Iago? you have done well,
That men must lay their murders on your neck.
GRATIANO.
What is the matter?
EMILIA.
Disprove this villain, if thou be'st a man:
He says thou told'st him that his wife was false:
I know thou didst not, thou'rt not such a villain:
Speak, for my heart is full.
IAGO.
I told him what I thought; and told no more
Than what he found himself was apt and true.
EMILIA.
But did you ever tell him she was false?
IAGO.
I did.
EMILIA.
You told a lie; an odious, damned lie;
Upon my soul, a lie; a wicked lie:—
She false with Cassio!—did you say with Cassio?
IAGO.
With Cassio, mistress. Go to, charm your tongue.

EMILIA.
I will not charm my tongue; I am bound to speak:
My mistress here lies murder'd in her bed,—
ALL.
O heavens forfend!
EMILIA.
And your reports have set the murder on.
OTHELLO.
Nay, stare not, masters: it is true, indeed.
GRATIANO.
'Tis a strange truth.
MONTANO.
O monstrous act!
EMILIA.
Villainy, villainy, villainy!
I think upon't,—I think,—I smell't;—O vil-
lainy!—
I thought so then;—I'll kill myself for grief:—
O villainy, villainy!
IAGO.
What, are you mad? I charge you, get you home.
EMILIA.
Good gentlemen, let me have leave to speak:
'Tis proper I obey him, but not now.—
Perchance, Iago, I will ne'er go home.
OTHELLO.
O! O! O!   [Falling on the bed.
EMILIA.
Nay, lay thee down and roar;
For thou hast kill'd the sweetest innocent
That e'er did lift up eye.
OTHELLO.
O, she was foul!— [Rising.
I scarce did know you, uncle: there lies your niece,
Whose breath, indeed, these hands have newly
I know this act shows horrible and grim.   [stopt:
GRATIANO.
Poor Desdemona! I am glad thy father's dead:
Thy match was mortal to him, and pure grief
Shore his old thread in twain: did he live now,
This sight would make him do a desperate turn,
Yea, curse his better angel from his side,
And fall to reprobance.
OTHELLO.
'Tis pitiful; but yet Iago knows
That she with Cassio hath the act of shame
A thousand times committed; Cassio confest it:
And she did gratify his amorous works
With that recognizance and pledge of love
Which I first gave her; I saw it in his hand:
It was a handkerchief, an antique token
My father gave my mother.
EMILIA.
O heaven! O heavenly powers!
IAGO.
Come, hold your peace.
EMILIA.
'Twill out, 'twill out:—I peace!
No, I will speak as liberal as the north:
Let heaven and men and devils, let them all,
All, all, cry shame against me, yet I'll speak.
IAGO.
Be wise, and get you home.
EMILIA.
I will not.
[IAGO offers to stab EMILIA.

GRATIANO.
          Fie!
Your sword upon a woman?
EMILIA.
O thou dull Moor! that handkerchief thou speak'st
of
I found by fortune, and did give my husband;
For often, with a solemn earnestness—
More than, indeed, belong'd to such a trifle—
He begg'd of me to steal it.
IAGO.
          Villainous whore!
EMILIA.
She give it Cassio! no, alas, I found it,
And I did give't my husband.
IAGO.
          Filth, thou liest!
EMILIA.
By heaven, I do not, I do not, gentlemen.—
O murderous coxcomb! what should such a fool
Do with so good a wife!
OTHELLO.
         Are there no stones in heaven
But what serve for the thunder?—Precious vil-
lain!
    [He runs at IAGO: IAGO stabs EMILIA,
    and exit.
GRATIANO.
The woman falls; sure, he hath kill'd his wife.
EMILIA.
Ay, ay:—O, lay me by my mistress' side.
GRATIANO.
He's gone, but his wife's kill'd.
MONTANO.
'Tis a notorious villain. Take you this weapon,
Which I have here recover'd from the Moor:
Come, guard the door without; let him not pass,
But kill him rather. I'll after that same villain,
For 'tis a damned slave.
    [Exeunt MONTANO and GRATIANO.
OTHELLO.
         I am not valiant neither,
But every puny whipster gets my sword:—
But why should honour outlive honesty?
Let it go all.
EMILIA.
         What did thy song bode, lady?
Hark, canst thou hear me? I will play the swan,
And die in music:—'Willow, willow, willow.—'
          [Singing.
Moor, she was chaste; she loved thee, cruel Moor;
So come my soul to bliss as I speak true;
So speaking as I think, I die,—I die.   [Dies.
OTHELLO.
I have another weapon in this chamber;
It is a sword of Spain, the ice-brook's temper:—
O, here it is.—Uncle, I must come forth.
GRATIANO [within].
If thou attempt it, it will cost thee dear:
Thou hast no weapon, and perforce must suffer.
OTHELLO.
Look in upon me, then, and speak with me,
Or, naked as I am, I will assault thee.
    Enter GRATIANO.
GRATIANO.
What is the matter?

OTHELLO.
                Behold, I have a weapon;
A better never did itself sustain
Upon a soldier's thigh: I have seen the day
That, with this little arm and this good sword,
I have made my way through more impediments
Than twenty times your stop:—but, O vain
      boast!
Who can control his fate? 'tis not so now.—
Be not afraid, though you do see me weapon'd;
Here is my journey's end, here is my butt,
And very sea-mark of my utmost sail.
Do you go back dismay'd? 'tis a lost fear;
Man but a rush against Othello's breast,
And he retires:—where should Othello go?—
Now, how dost thou look now? O ill-starr'd
      wench!
Pale as thy smock! when we shall meet at compt,
This look of thine will hurl my soul from heaven,
And fiends will snatch at it. Cold, cold, my girl!
Even like thy chastity.—
O cursed, cursed slave!—Whip me, ye devils,
From the possession of this heavenly sight!
Blow me about in winds! roast me in sulphur!—
Wash me in steep-down gulfs of liquid fire!—
O Desdemona! Desdemona! dead!
O! O! O!

Enter LODOVICO, MONTANO, CASSIO *carried in
a chair, and* OFFICERS *with* IAGO, *prisoner.*

LODOVICO.
Where is this rash and most unfortunate man?
                OTHELLO.
That's he that was Othello;—here I am.
                LODOVICO.
Where is that viper? bring the villain forth.
                OTHELLO.
I look down towards his feet,—but that's a fable.
If that thou be'st a devil, I cannot kill thee.
                                [*Wounds* IAGO.
                LODOVICO.
Wrench his sword from him.
                                [OTHELLO *is disarm'd.*
                IAGO.
                I bleed, sir; but not kill'd.
                OTHELLO.
I am not sorry neither: I'ld have thee live;
For, in my sense, 'tis happiness to die.
                LODOVICO.
O thou Othello, that wert once so good,
Faln in the practice of a damned slave,
What shall be said to thee?
                OTHELLO.
                Why, any thing:
An honourable murderer, if you will;
For naught I did in hate, but all in honour.
                LODOVICO.
This wretch hath part confest his villainy:
Did you and he consent in Cassio's death?
                OTHELLO.
Ay.
                CASSIO.
Dear general, I never gave you cause.
                OTHELLO.
I do believe it, and I ask your pardon.
Will you, I pray, demand that demi-devil
Why he hath thus ensnared my soul and body?

IAGO.
Demand me nothing: what you know, you know:
From this time forth I never will speak word.
                LODOVICO.
What, not to pray?
                GRATIANO.
                Torments will ope your lips.
                OTHELLO.
Well, thou dost best.
                LODOVICO.
Sir, you shall understand what hath befaln,
Which, as I think, you know not. Here is a letter
Found in the pocket of the slain Roderigo;
And here another: the one of them imports
The death of Cassio to be undertook
By Roderigo.
                OTHELLO.
O villain!
                CASSIO.
        Most heathenish and most gross!
                LODOVICO.
Now here's another discontented paper,
Found in his pocket too; and this, it seems,
Roderigo meant t'have sent this damned villain;
But that, belike, Iago in the interim
Came in and satisfied him.
                OTHELLO.
                O the pernicious caitiff!—
How came you, Cassio, by that handkerchief
That was my wife's?
                CASSIO.
                I found it in my chamber:
And he himself confest but even now
That there he dropt it for a special purpose
Which wrought to his desire.
                OTHELLO.
                O fool! fool! fool!
                CASSIO.
There is besides in Roderigo's letter,—
How he upbraids Iago, that he made him
Brave me upon the watch; whereon it came
That I was cast: and even but now he spake,
After long seeming dead,—Iago hurt him,
Iago set him on.
                LODOVICO.
You must forsake this room, and go with us:
Your power and your command is taken off,
And Cassio rules in Cyprus. For this slave,
If there be any cunning cruelty
Than can torment him much and hold him long,
It shall be his. You shall close prisoner rest,
Till that the nature of your fault be known
To the Venetian state.—Come, bring away.
                OTHELLO.
Soft you; a word or two before you go.
I have done the state some service, and they
      know't;—
No more of that.—I pray you, in your letters,
When you shall these unlucky deeds relate,
Speak of me as I am; nothing extenuate,
Nor set down aught in malice: then must you
      speak
Of one that loved not wisely, but too well;
Of one not easily jealous, but, being wrought,
Perplext in the extreme; of one whose hand,
Like the base Indian, threw a pearl away

Richer than all his tribe; of one whose subdued
Albeit unused to the melting mood,   [eyes,
Drop tears as fast as the Arabian trees
Their medicinable gum. Set you down this;
And say besides, that in Aleppo once,
Where a malignant and a turban'd Turk
Beat a Venetian and traduced the state,
I took by th'throat the circumcised dog,
And smote him—thus.   [*He stabs himself.*
                    LODOVICO.
O bloody period!
                    GRATIANO.
          All that's spoke is marr'd.
                    OTHELLO.
I kist thee ere I kill'd thee: no way but this,
               [*Falling upon* DESDEMONA.

Killing myself, to die upon a kiss.   [*Dies.*
                    CASSIO.
This did I fear, but thought he had no weapon;
For he was great of heart.
               LODOVICO [*to* IAGO].
                         O Spartan dog,
More fell than anguish, hunger, or the sea!
Look on the tragic loading of this bed;
This is thy work: the object poisons sight;
Let it be hid. Gratiano, keep the house,
And seize upon the fortunes of the Moor,
For they succeed on you. To you, lord governor,
Remains the censure of this hellish villain;
The time, the place, the torture. O, enforce it!
Myself will straight aboard, and to the state
This heavy act with heavy heart relate.   [*Exeunt.*

MACBETH

DRAMATIS PERSONAE

DUNCAN, *king of Scotland.*
MALCOLM,
DONALBAIN, } *his sons.*
MACBETH,
BANQUO, } *generals of the King's army.*
MACDUFF,
LENNOX,
ROSS,
MENTEITH, } *noblemen of Scotland.*
ANGUS,
CAITHNESS,
FLEANCE, *son to Banquo.*
SIWARD, *earl of Northumberland, general of the English forces.*
YOUNG SIWARD, *his son.*
SEYTON, *an officer attending on Macbeth.*
BOY, *son to Macduff.*
AN ENGLISH DOCTOR.

A SCOTCH DOCTOR.
A SERGEANT.
A PORTER.
AN OLD MAN.

LADY MACBETH.
LADY MACDUFF.
GENTLEWOMAN *attending on Lady Macbeth.*

HECATE.
THREE WITCHES.
APPARITIONS.

LORDS, GENTLEMEN, OFFICERS, SOLDIERS, MURDERERS, ATTENDANTS, *and* MESSENGERS.

SCENE—*in the end of the fourth Act in England; through the rest of the play in Scotland.*

ACT I. SCENE I.

An open place.

Thunder and lightning. Enter three WITCHES.

FIRST WITCH.
WHEN shall we three meet again
In thunder, lightning, or in rain?
SECOND WITCH.
When the hurlyburly's done,
When the battle's lost and won.
THIRD WITCH.
That will be ere the set of sun.
FIRST WITCH.
Where the place?
SECOND WITCH.
Upon the heath.
THIRD WITCH.
There to meet with Macbeth.
FIRST WITCH.
I come, Graymalkin!
SECOND WITCH.
Paddock calls:—anon!
ALL.
Fair is foul, and foul is fair:
Hover through the fog and filthy air.   [*Exeunt.*

SCENE II.

A camp near Forres.

Alarum within. Enter DUNCAN, MALCOLM, DONALBAIN, LENNOX, *with* ATTENDANTS, *meeting a bleeding* SERGEANT.

DUNCAN.
WHAT bloody man is that? He can report,
As seemeth by his plight, of the revolt
The newest state.
MALCOLM.
This is the sergeant,
Who, like a good and hardy soldier, fought
'Gainst my captivity.—Hail, brave friend!
Say to the king thy knowledge of the broil
As thou didst leave it.

SERGEANT.
Doubtful it stood;
As two spent swimmers, that do cling together
And choke their art. The merciless Macdonwald—
Worthy to be a rebel, for, to that,
The multiplying villainies of nature
Do swarm upon him—from the western isles
Of kerns and gallowglasses is supplied;
And fortune, on his damned quarrel smiling,
Show'd like a rebel's whore: but all's too weak;
For brave Macbeth,—well he deserves that
name,—
Disdaining fortune, with his brandisht steel,
Which smoked with bloody execution,
Like valour's minion,
Carved out his passage till he faced the slave;
Which ne'er shook hands, nor bade farewell to him,
Till he unseam'd him from the nave to th'chops,
And fixt his head upon our battlements.
DUNCAN.
O valiant cousin! worthy gentleman!
SERGEANT.
As whence the sun 'gins his reflection
Shipwracking storms and direful thunders break;
So from that spring, whence comfort seem'd to
come,
Discomfort swells. Mark, king of Scotland, mark:
No sooner justice had, with valour arm'd,
Compell'd these skipping kerns to trust their heels,
But the Norweyan lord, surveying vantage,
With furbisht arms and new supplies of men,
Began a fresh assault.
DUNCAN.
Dismay'd not this
Our captains, Macbeth and Banquo?
SERGEANT.
Yes;
As sparrows eagles, or the hare the lion.
If I say sooth, I must report they were
As cannons overcharged with double cracks;
So they
Doubly redoubled strokes upon the foe:

Except they meant to bathe in reeking wounds,
Or memorize another Golgotha,
I cannot tell:—
But I am faint, my gashes cry for help.
           DUNCAN.
So well thy words become thee as thy wounds;
They smack of honour both.—Go get him sur-
    geons.   [*Exit* SERGEANT, *attended.*
Who comes here?
           Enter ROSS.
           MALCOLM.
         The worthy thane of Ross.
           LENNOX.
What haste looks through his eyes! So should he
    look
That seems to speak things strange.
           ROSS.
                God save the king!
           DUNCAN.
Whence camest thou, worthy thane?
           ROSS.
              From Fife, great king;
Where the Norweyan banners flout the sky
And fan our people cold. Norway himself,
With terrible numbers,
Assisted by that most disloyal traitor
The thane of Cawdor, began a dismal conflict;
Till that Bellona's bridegroom, lapt in proof,
Confronted him with self-comparisons,
Point against point rebellious, arm 'gainst arm,
Curbing his lavish spirit: and, to conclude,
The victory fell on us.
           DUNCAN.
         Great happiness!
           ROSS.
That now
Sweno, the Norways' king, craves composition;
Nor would we deign him burial of his men
Till he disbursed, at Saint Colme's-inch,
Ten thousand dollars to our general use.
           DUNCAN.
No more that thane of Cawdor shall deceive
Our bosom interest:—go pronounce his present
    death,
And with his former title greet Macbeth.
           ROSS.
I'll see it done.
           DUNCAN.
What he hath lost noble Macbeth hath won.
                  [*Exeunt.*

SCENE III.

A heath.

Thunder. Enter the three WITCHES.
           FIRST WITCH.
WHERE hast thou been, sister?
           SECOND WITCH.
Killing swine.
           THIRD WITCH.
Sister, where thou?
           FIRST WITCH.
A sailor's wife had chestnuts in her lap,
And muncht, and muncht, and muncht:—
'Give me,' quoth I:
Aroint thee, witch!' the rump-fed ronyon cries.

Her husband's to Aleppo gone, master o'th'Tiger:
But in a sieve I'll thither sail,
And, like a rat without a tail,
I'll do, I'll do, and I'll do.
           SECOND WITCH.
I'll give thee a wind.
           FIRST WITCH.
Th'art kind.
           THIRD WITCH.
And I another.
           FIRST WITCH.
I myself have all the other;
And the very ports they blow,
All the quarters that they know
I'th'shipman's card.
I will drain him dry as hay:
Sleep shall neither night nor day
Hang upon his pent-house lid;
He shall live a man forbid:
Weary se'nnights nine times nine
Shall he dwindle, peak, and pine:
Though his bark cannot be lost,
Yet it shall be tempest-tost.—
Look what I have.
           SECOND WITCH.
Show me, show me.
           FIRST WITCH.
Here I have a pilot's thumb,
Wrackt as homeward he did come.   [*Drum within.*
           THIRD WITCH.
A drum, a drum!
Macbeth doth come.
           ALL.
The weird sisters, hand in hand,
Posters of the sea and land,
Thus do go about, about:
Thrice to thine, and thrice to mine,
And thrice again, to make up nine:—
Peace!—the charm's wound up.
      Enter MACBETH *and* BANQUO; SOLDIERS *at*
              some distance.
           MACBETH.
So foul and fair a day I have not seen.
           BANQUO.
How far is't call'd to Forres?—What are these
So wither'd, and so wild in their attire,
That look not like th'inhabitants o'th'earth,
And yet are on't?—Live you? or are you aught
That man may question? You seem to under-
    stand me,
By each at once her choppy finger laying
Upon her skinny lips:—you should be women,
And yet your beards forbid me to interpret
That you are so.
           MACBETH.
      Speak, if you can;—what are you?
           FIRST WITCH.
All hail, Macbeth! hail to thee, thane of Glamis!
           SECOND WITCH.
All hail, Macbeth! hail to thee, thane of Cawdor!
           THIRD WITCH.
All hail, Macbeth, that shalt be king hereafter !
           BANQUO.
Good sir, why do you start; and seem to fear
Things that do sound so fair?—I'th'name of
    truth,

Are ye fantastical, or that indeed
Which outwardly ye show? My noble partner
You greet with present grace, and great prediction
Of noble having and of royal hope,
That he seems rapt withal:—to me you speak not:
If you can look into the seeds of time,
And say which grain will grow, and which will
     not,
Speak, then, to me, who neither beg nor fear
Your favours nor your hate.

FIRST WITCH.
Hail!

SECOND WITCH.
Hail!

THIRD WITCH.
Hail!

FIRST WITCH.
Lesser than Macbeth, and greater.

SECOND WITCH.
Not so happy, yet much happier.

THIRD WITCH.
Thou shalt get kings, though thou be none:
So, all hail, Macbeth and Banquo!

FIRST WITCH.
Banquo and Macbeth, all hail!

MACBETH.
Stay, you imperfect speakers, tell me more:
By Sinel's death I know I am thane of Glamis;
But how of Cawdor? the thane of Cawdor lives,
A prosperous gentleman; and to be king
Stands not within the prospect of belief,
No more than to be Cawdor. Say from whence
You owe this strange intelligence? or why
Upon this blasted heath you stop our way
With such prophetic greeting? Speak, I charge
     you.   [WITCHES *vanish.*

BANQUO.
The earth hath bubbles, as the water has,
And these are of them:—whither are they vanisht?

MACBETH.
Into the air; and what seem'd corporal melted
As breath into the wind.—Would they had
     stay'd!

BANQUO.
Were such things here as we do speak about?
Or have we eaten on the insane root
That takes the reason prisoner?

MACBETH.
Your children shall be kings.

BANQUO.
                    You shall be king.

MACBETH.
And thane of Cawdor too,—went it not so?

BANQUO.
To th'selfsame tune and words.—Who's here?

Enter ROSS *and* ANGUS.

ROSS.
The king hath happily received, Macbeth,
The news of thy success: and when he reads
Thy personal venture in the rebels' fight,
His wonders and his praises do contend
Which should be thine or his: silenced with that,
In viewing o'er the rest o'th'selfsame day,
He finds thee in the stout Norweyan ranks,
Nothing afeard of what thyself didst make,
Strange images of death. As thick as hail

Came post with post; and every one did bear
Thy praises in his kingdom's great defence,
And pour'd them down before him.

ANGUS.
                    We are sent
To give thee, from our royal master, thanks;
Only to herald thee into his sight, not pay thee.

ROSS.
And, for an earnest of a greater honour,
He bade me, from him, call thee thane of Caw-
     dor:
In which addition, hail, most worthy thane!
For it is thine.

BANQUO [*aside*].
What, can the devil speak true?

MACBETH.
The thane of Cawdor lives: why do you dress me
In borrow'd robes?

ANGUS.
                    Who was the thane lives yet;
But under heavy judgement bears that life
Which he deserves to lose. Whether he was com-
     bined
With those of Norway, or did line the rebel
With hidden help and vantage, or that with both
He labour'd in his country's wrack, I know not;
But treasons capital, confest and proved,
Have overthrown him.

MACBETH [*aside*].
                    Glamis, and thane of Cawdor!
The greatest is behind.—[*to* ROSS *and* ANGUS]
     Thanks for your pains.—
[*aside to* BANQUO] Do you not hope your children
     shall be kings,
When those that gave the thane of Cawdor to me
Promised no less to them?

BANQUO [*aside to* MACBETH].
                    That, trusted home,
Might yet enkindle you unto the crown,
Besides the thane of Cawdor. But 'tis strange:
And oftentimes, to win us to our harm,
The instruments of darkness tell us truths,
Win us with honest trifles, to betray's
In deepest consequence.—
Cousins, a word, I pray you.

MACBETH [*aside*].
                    Two truths are told,
As happy prologues to the swelling act
Of the imperial theme.—I thank you, gentle-
     men.—
[*aside*] This supernatural soliciting
Cannot be ill, cannot be good:—if ill,
Why hath it given me earnest of success,
Commencing in a truth? I am thane of Cawdor:
If good, why do I yield to that suggestion
Whose horrid image doth unfix my hair,
And make my seated heart knock at my ribs,
Against the use of nature? Present fears
Are less than horrible imaginings:
My thought, whose murder yet is but fantas-
     tical,
Shakes so my single state of man, that function
Is smother'd in surmise; and nothing is
But what is not.

BANQUO.
Look, how our partner's rapt.

MACBETH [*aside*].
If chance will have me king, why, chance may
  crown me,
Without my stir.
          BANQUO.
              New honours come upon him,
Like our strange garments, cleave not to their
  mould
But with the aid of use.
          MACBETH [*aside*].
          Come what come may,
Time and the hour runs through the roughest day.
          BANQUO.
Worthy Macbeth, we stay upon your leisure.
          MACBETH.
Give me your favour:—my dull brain was wrought
With things forgotten. Kind gentlemen, your
  pains
Are register'd where every day I turn
The leaf to read them.—Let us toward the king.—
[*aside to* BANQUO] Think upon what hath chanced;
  and, at more time,
The interim having weigh'd it, let us speak
Our free hearts each to other.
          BANQUO [*aside to* MACBETH].
              Very gladly.
          MACBETH [*aside to* BANQUO].
Till then, enough.—Come, friends.   [*Exeunt*.

SCENE IV.

Forres. A room in the palace.

Flourish. Enter DUNCAN, MALCOLM, DONAL-
BAIN, LENNOX, *and* ATTENDANTS.

          DUNCAN.
IS execution done on Cawdor? Are not
  Those in commission yet return'd?
          MALCOLM.
              My liege,
They are not yet come back. But I have spoke
With one that saw him die: who did report,
That very frankly he confest his treasons;
Implored your highness' pardon; and set forth
A deep repentance: nothing in his life
Became him like the leaving it; he died
As one that had been studied in his death
To throw away the dearest thing he owed,
As 'twere a careless trifle.
          DUNCAN.
              There's no art
To find the mind's construction in the face:
He was a gentleman on whom I built
An absolute trust.
Enter MACBETH, BANQUO, ROSS, *and* ANGUS.
          O worthiest cousin!
The sin of my ingratitude even now
Was heavy on me: thou art so far before,
That swiftest wing of recompense is slow
To overtake thee. Would thou hadst less deserved,
That the proportion both of thanks and payment
Might have been mine! only I have left to say,
More is thy due than more than all can pay.
          MACBETH.
The service and the loyalty I owe,
In doing it, pays itself. Your highness' part

Is to receive our duties; and our duties
Are to your throne and state children and ser-
  vants;
Which do but what they should by doing every
  thing
Safe toward your love and honour.
          DUNCAN.
              Welcome hither:
I have begun to plant thee, and will labour
To make thee full of growing.—Noble Banquo,
That hast no less deserved, nor must be known
No less to have done so; let me infold thee
And hold thee to my heart.
          BANQUO.
              There if I grow,
The harvest is your own.
          DUNCAN.
              My plenteous joys,
Wanton in fulness, seek to hide themselves
In drops of sorrow.—Sons, kinsmen, thanes,
And you whose places are the nearest, know,
We will establish our estate upon
Our eldest, Malcolm; whom we name hereafter
The Prince of Cumberland: which honour must
Not unaccompanied invest him only,
But signs of nobleness, like stars, shall shine
On all deservers.—From hence to Inverness,
And bind us further to you.
          MACBETH.
The rest is labour, which is not used for you:
I'll be myself the harbinger, and make joyful
The hearing of my wife with your approach:
So, humbly take my leave.
          DUNCAN.
              My worthy Cawdor!
          MACBETH [*aside*].
The Prince of Cumberland! that is a step
On which I must fall down, or else o'erleap,
For in my way it lies. Stars, hide your fires;
Let not light see my black and deep desires:
The eye wink at the hand; yet let that be,
Which the eye fears, when it is done, to see. [*Exit*.
          DUNCAN.
True, worthy Banquo,—he is full so valiant;
And in his commendations I am fed,—
It is a banquet to me. Let's after him,
Whose care is gone before to bid us welcome:
It is a peerless kinsman.   [*Flourish. Exeunt*.

SCENE V.

Inverness. A room in MACBETH'S *castle.*

Enter LADY MACBETH *alone, with a letter.*

          LADY MACBETH.
'THEY met me in the day of success; and I
  have learn'd by the perfect'st report, they
have more in them than mortal knowledge. When
I burnt in desire to question them further, they
made themselves air, into which they vanisht.
Whiles I stood rapt in the wonder of it, came
missives from the king, who all-hail'd me "Thane
of Cawdor;" by which title, before, these weird
sisters saluted me, and referr'd me to the coming
on of time, with "Hail, king that shalt be!" This
have I thought good to deliver thee, my dearest

partner of greatness, that thou mightst not lose
the dues of rejoicing, by being ignorant of what
greatness is promised thee. Lay it to thy heart,
and farewell.'
Glamis thou art, and Cawdor; and shalt be
What thou art promised: yet do I fear thy nature;
It is too full o'th'milk of human kindness
To catch the nearest way: thou wouldst be great;
Art not without ambition; but without
The illness should attend it: what thou wouldst
   highly,
That wouldst thou holily; wouldst not play false,
And yet wouldst wrongly win: thou'ldst have,
   great Glamis,
That which cries 'Thus thou must do, if thou
   have it;
And that which rather thou dost fear to do
Than wishest should be undone.' Hie thee hither,
That I may pour my spirits in thine ear;
And chastise with the valour of my tongue
All that impedes thee from the golden round,
Which fate and metaphysical aid doth seem
To have thee crown'd withal.

Enter a MESSENGER.
                What is your tidings?
MESSENGER.
The king comes here to-night.
    LADY MACBETH.
              Thou'rt mad to say it:
Is not thy master with him? who, were't so,
Would have inform'd for preparation.
    MESSENGER.
So please you, it is true:—our thane is coming:
One of my fellows had the speed of him;
Who, almost dead for breath, had scarcely more
Than would make up his message.
    LADY MACBETH.
              Give him tending;
He brings great news.   [*Exit* MESSENGER.
          The raven himself is hoarse
That croaks the fatal entrance of Duncan
Under my battlements. Come, you spirits
That tend on mortal thoughts, unsex me here;
And fill me, from the crown to the toe, top-full
Of direst cruelty! make thick my blood,
Stop up th'access and passage to remorse,
That no compunctious visitings of nature
Shake my fell purpose, nor keep peace between
Th'effect and it! Come to my woman's breasts,
And take my milk for gall, you murd'ring minis-
   ters,
Wherever in your sightless substances
You wait on nature's mischief! Come, thick night,
And pall thee in the dunnest smoke of hell,
That my keen knife see not the wound it makes,
Nor heaven peep through the blanket of the dark,
To cry 'Hold, hold!'
    Enter MACBETH.
          Great Glamis! worthy Cawdor!
Greater than both, by the all-hail hereafter!
Thy letters have transported me beyond
This ignorant present, and I feel now
The future in the instant.
    MACBETH.
             My dearest love,
Duncan comes here to-night.

    LADY MACBETH.
             And when goes hence?
    MACBETH.
To-morrow, as he purposes.
    LADY MACBETH.
              O, never
Shall sun that morrow see!
Your face, my thane, is as a book where men
May read strange matters:—to beguile the time,
Look like the time; bear welcome in your eye,
Your hand, your tongue: look like the innocent
   flower,
But be the serpent under't. He that's coming
Must be provided for: and you shall put
This night's great business into my dispatch;
Which shall to all our nights and days to come
Give solely sovereign sway and masterdom.
    MACBETH.
We will speak further.
    LADY MACBETH.
             Only look up clear;
To alter favour ever is to fear:
Leave all the rest to me.   [*Exeunt.*

SCENE VI.

The same. Before MACBETH'S *castle.*

Hautboys and torches. Enter DUNCAN, MALCOLM,
  DONALBAIN, BANQUO, LENNOX, MACDUFF,
  ROSS, ANGUS, *and* ATTENDANTS.

    DUNCAN.
THIS castle hath a pleasant seat; the air
Nimbly and sweetly recommends itself
Unto our gentle senses.
    BANQUO.
            This guest of summer,
The temple-haunting martlet, does approve,
By his lov'd mansionry, that the heavens' breath
Smells wooingly here: no jutty, frieze,
Buttress, nor coign of vantage, but this bird
Hath made his pendent bed and procreant cradle:
Where they most breed and haunt, I have observed
The air is delicate.
    Enter LADY MACBETH.
    DUNCAN.
        See, see, our honour'd hostess!—
The love that follows us sometime is our trouble,
Which still we thank as love. Herein I teach you
Now you shall bid God 'ild us for your pains,
And thank us for your trouble.
    LADY MACBETH.
            All our service
In every point twice done, and then done double,
Were poor and single business to contend
Against those honours deep and broad wherewith
Your majesty loads our house: for those of old,
And the late dignities heapt up to them,
We rest your hermits.
    DUNCAN.
         Where's the thane of Cawdor?
We coursed him at the heels, and had a purpose
To be his purveyor: but he rides well;
And his great love, sharp as his spur, hath holp him
To his home before us. Fair and noble hostess,
We are your guest to-night.

LADY MACBETH.
                              Your servants ever
Have theirs, themselves, and what is theirs, in
    compt,
To make their audit at your highness' pleasure,
Still to return your own.
                    DUNCAN.
                              Give me your hand;
Conduct me to mine host: we love him highly,
And shall continue our graces towards him.
By your leave, hostess.   [Exeunt.

SCENE VII.

The same. A lobby in MACBETH'S *castle.*

Hautboys and torches. Enter a SEWER, *and divers*
SERVANTS *with dishes and service, over the
stage. Then enter* MACBETH.

                    MACBETH.
IF it were done—when 'tis done—then 'twere
   well
It were done quickly: if th'assassination
Could trammel up the consequence, and catch,
With his surcease, success; that but this blow
Might be the be-all and the end-all here,
But here, upon this bank and shoal of time,
We'ld jump the life to come. But in these cases
We still have judgement here; that we but teach
Bloody instructions, which, being taught, return
To plague th'inventor: this even-handed justice
Commends th'ingredients of our poison'd
    chalice
To our own lips. He's here in double trust:
First, as I am his kinsman and his subject,
Strong both against the deed; then, as his host,
Who should against his murderer shut the door,
Not bear the knife myself. Besides, this Duncan
Hath borne his faculties so meek, hath been
So clear in his great office, that his virtues
Will plead like angels, trumpet-tongued, against
The deep damnation of his taking-off;
And pity, like a naked new-born babe,
Striding the blast, or heaven's cherubin, horsed
Upon the sightless couriers of the air,
Shall blow the horrid deed in every eye,
That tears shall drown the wind,—I have no
    spur
To prick the sides of my intent, but only
Vaulting ambition, which o'erleaps itself,
And falls on th'other.
                  Enter LADY MACBETH.
                   How now! what news?
                LADY MACBETH.
He has almost supt: why have you left the cham-
ber?
                    MACBETH.
Hath he askt for me?
                LADY MACBETH.
                   Know you not he has?
                    MACBETH.
We will proceed no further in this business:
He hath honour'd me of late; and I have bought
Golden opinions from all sorts of people,
Which would be worn now in their newest gloss,
Not cast aside so soon.

                LADY MACBETH.
                              Was the hope drunk
Wherein you drest yourself? hath it slept since?
And wakes it now, to look so green and pale
At what it did so freely? From this time
Such I account thy love. Art thou afeard
To be the same in thine own act and valour
As thou art in desire? Wouldst thou have that
Which thou esteem'st the ornament of life,
And live a coward in thine own esteem,
Letting 'I dare not' wait upon 'I would,'
Like the poor cat i'th'adage?
                    MACBETH.
                              Prithee, peace:
I dare do all that may become a man;
Who dares do more is none.
                LADY MACBETH.
                              What beast was't, then,
That made you break this enterprise to me?
When you durst do it, then you were a man;
And, to be more than what you were, you would
Be so much more the man. Nor time nor place
Did then adhere, and yet you would make both:
They have made themselves, and that their fitness
    now
Does unmake you. I have given suck, and know
How tender 'tis to love the babe that milks me:
I would, while it was smiling in my face,
Have pluckt my nipple from his boneless gums,
And dasht the brains out, had I so sworn as you
Have done to this.
                    MACBETH.
                   If we should fail?
                LADY MACBETH.
                              We fail:
But screw your courage to the sticking-place,
And we'll not fail. When Duncan is asleep,—
Whereto the rather shall his day's hard journey
Soundly invite him,—his two chamberlains
Will I with wine and wassail so convince,
That memory, the warder of the brain,
Shall be a fume, and the receipt of reason
A limbeck only: when in swinish sleep
Their drenched natures lie as in a death,
What cannot you and I perform upon
Th'unguarded Duncan? what not put upon
His spongy officers, who shall bear the guilt
Of our great quell?
                    MACBETH.
                              Bring forth men-children only;
For thy undaunted mettle should compose
Nothing but males. Will it not be received,
When we have markt with blood those sleepy
    two
Of his own chamber, and used their very daggers,
That they have done't?
                LADY MACBETH.
                              Who dares receive it other,
As we shall make our griefs and clamour roar
Upon his death?
                    MACBETH.
                              I am settled, and bend up
Each corporal agent to this terrible feat.
Away, and mock the time with fairest show:
False face must hide what the false heart doth
    know.   [Exeunt.

ACT II. SCENE I.

Inverness.　Court of MACBETH'S *castle.*

Enter BANQUO, *and* FLEANCE *with a torch
before him.*

BANQUO.

HOW goes the night, boy?

FLEANCE.

The moon is down; I have not heard the clock.

BANQUO.

And she goes down at twelve.

FLEANCE.

I take't, 'tis later, sir.

BANQUO.

Hold, take my sword:—there's husbandry in
　heaven,
Their candles are all out:—take thee that too.—
A heavy summons lies like lead upon me,
And yet I would not sleep:—merciful powers,
Restrain in me the cursed thoughts that nature
Gives way to in repose!—Give me my sword.—
Who's there?

Enter MACBETH, *and a* SERVANT *with a
torch.*

MACBETH.

A friend.

BANQUO.

What, sir, not yet at rest? The king's a-bed:
He hath been in unusual pleasure, and
Sent forth great largess to your officers:
This diamond he greets your wife withal,
By the name of most kind hostess; and shut up
In measureless content.

MACBETH.

Being unprepared,
Our will became the servant to defect;
Which else should free have wrought.

BANQUO.

All's well.—
I dreamt last night of the three weird sisters:
To you they have show'd some truth.

MACBETH.

I think not of them:
Yet, when we can entreat an hour to serve,
We would spend it in some words upon that busi-
　ness,
If you would grant the time.

BANQUO.

At your kind'st leisure.

MACBETH.

If you shall cleave to my consent,—when 'tis,
It shall make honour for you.

BANQUO.

So I lose none
In seeking to augment it, but still keep
My bosom franchised, and allegiance clear,
I shall be counsell'd.

MACBETH.

Good repose the while!

BANQUO.

Thanks, sir: the like to you!

[Exeunt BANQUO *and* FLEANCE.

MACBETH.

Go bid thy mistress, when my drink is ready,
She strike upon the bell. Get thee to bed.

[Exit SERVANT.

Is this a dagger which I see before me,
The handle toward my hand? Come, let me clutch
　thee:—
I have thee not, and yet I see thee still.
Art thou not, fatal vision, sensible
To feeling as to sight? or art thou but
A dagger of the mind, a false creation,
Proceeding from the heat-oppressed brain?
I see thee yet, in form as palpable
As this which now I draw.
Thou marshall'st me the way that I was going;
And such an instrument I was to use.
Mine eyes are made the fools o'th'other senses,
Or else worth all the rest: I see thee still;
And on thy blade and dudgeon gouts of blood,
Which was not so before.—There's no such thing:
It is the bloody business which informs
Thus to mine eyes.—Now o'er the one half-world
Nature seems dead, and wicked dreams abuse
The curtain'd sleep; now witchcraft celebrates
Pale Hecate's offerings; and wither'd murder,
Alarum'd by his sentinel, the wolf,
Whose howl's his watch, thus with his stealthy
　pace,
With Tarquin's ravishing strides, towards his
　design
Moves like a ghost.—Thou sure and firm-set
　earth,
Hear not my steps, which way they walk, for fear
Thy very stones prate of my whereabout,
And take the present horror from the time,
Which now suits with it.—Whiles I threat, he
　lives:
Words to the heat of deeds too cold breath gives.

[A bell rings.

I go, and it is done; the bell invites me.
Hear it not, Duncan; for it is a knell
That summons thee to heaven or to hell.　　*[Exit.*

SCENE II.

The same.

Enter LADY MACBETH.

LADY MACBETH.

THAT which hath made them drunk hath made
　me bold;
What hath quencht them hath given me fire.—
Hark!—Peace!
It was the owl that shriekt, the fatal bellman,
Which gives the stern'st good-night.—He is
　about it:
The doors are open; and the surfeited grooms
Do mock their charge with snores: I have drugg'd
　their possets,
That death and nature do contend about them,
Whether they live or die.

MACBETH *[within].*

Who's there? what, ho!

LADY MACBETH.

Alack, I am afraid they have awaked,
And 'tis not done:—th'attempt, and not the
　deed,
Confounds us.—Hark!—I laid their daggers ready;
He could not miss 'em.—Had he not resembled
My father as he slept, I had done't.—My husband!

Enter MACBETH.

MACBETH.

I have done the deed.—Didst thou not hear a noise?

LADY MACBETH.

I heard the owl scream and the crickets cry.
Did not you speak?

MACBETH.

When?

LADY MACBETH.

Now.

MACBETH.

As I descended?

LADY MACBETH.

Ay.

MACBETH.

Hark!—
Who lies i'th'second chamber?

LADY MACBETH.

Donalbain.

MACBETH.

This is a sorry sight. [*Looking on his hands.*

LADY MACBETH.

A foolish thought, to say a sorry sight.

MACBETH.

There's one did laugh in's sleep, and one cried
'Murder!'
That they did wake each other: I stood and heard
them:
But they did say their prayers, and addrest them
Again to sleep.

LADY MACBETH.

There are two lodged together.

MACBETH.

One cried 'God bless us!' and 'Amen!' the other;
As they had seen me, with these hangman's
hands.
Listening their fear, I could not say 'Amen!'
When they did say 'God bless us!'

LADY MACBETH.

Consider it not so deeply.

MACBETH.

But wherefore could not I pronounce 'Amen'?
I had most need of blessing, and 'Amen'
Stuck in my throat.

LADY MACBETH.

These deeds must not be thought
After these ways; so, it will make us mad.

MACBETH.

Methought I heard a voice cry 'Sleep no more!
Macbeth does murder sleep,'—the innocent sleep,
Sleep that knits up the ravell'd sleave of care,
The death of each day's life, sore labour's bath,
Balm of hurt minds, great nature's second course,
Chief nourisher in life's feast,—

LADY MACBETH.

What do you mean?

MACBETH.

Still it cried 'Sleep no more!' to all the house:
'Glamis hath murder'd sleep, and therefore
Cawdor
Shall sleep no more,—Macbeth shall sleep no
more!'

LADY MACBETH.

Who was it that thus cried? Why, worthy thane,
You do unbend your noble strength, to think

So brainsickly of things.—Go get some water,
And wash this filthy witness from your hand.—
Why did you bring these daggers from the place?
They must lie there: go carry them, and smear
The sleepy grooms with blood.

MACBETH.

I'll go no more:
I am afraid to think what I have done;
Look on't again I dare not.

LADY MACBETH.

Infirm of purpose!
Give me the daggers: the sleeping and the dead
Are but as pictures: 'tis the eye of childhood
That fears a painted devil. If he do bleed,
I'll gild the faces of the grooms withal;
For it must seem their guilt. [*Exit. Knock within.*

MACBETH.

Whence is that knocking?
How is't with me, when every noise appals me?
What hands are here? ha! they pluck out mine
eyes!
Will all great Neptune's ocean wash this blood
Clean from my hand? No; this my hand will
rather
The multitudinous seas incarnadine,
Making the green one red.

Enter LADY MACBETH.

LADY MACBETH.

My hands are of your colour; but I shame
To wear a heart so white. [*knock.*] I hear a
knocking
At the south entry:—retire we to our chamber:
A little water clears us of this deed:
How easy is it, then! Your constancy
Hath left you unattended.—[*knock.*] Hark! more
knocking:
Get on your nightgown, lest occasion call us,
And show us to be watchers:—be not lost
So poorly in your thoughts.

MACBETH.

To know my deed, 'twere best not know myself.
[*Knock.*
Wake Duncan with thy knocking! I would thou
couldst!   [*Exeunt.*

SCENE III.

The same.

Enter a PORTER. *Knocking within.*

PORTER.

HERE'S a knocking indeed! If a man were porter of hell-gate, he should have old turning
the key.—[*knock.*] Knock, knock, knock! Who's
there, i'th'name of Belzebub? Here's a farmer that
hang'd himself on th'expectation of plenty: come
in time; have napkins enow about you; here you'll
sweat for't. [*knock.*] Knock, knock! Who's there,
i'th'other devil's name? Faith, here's an equivocator that could swear in both the scales against
either scale; who committed treason enough for
God's sake, yet could not equivocate to heaven:
O, come in, equivocator.—[*knock.*] Knock,
knock, knock! Who's there? Faith, here's an
English tailor come hither, for stealing out of a
French hose: come in, tailor; here you may roast
your goose.—[*knock.*] Knock, knock; never at

quiet! What are you?—But this place is too cold for hell. I'll devil-porter it no further: I had thought to have let in some of all professions, that go the primrose way to th'everlasting bonfire. —[_knock._] Anon, anon! I pray you, remember the porter.   [_Opens the gate._

Enter MACDUFF _and_ LENNOX.

MACDUFF.
Was it so late, friend, ere you went to bed,
That you do lie so late?

PORTER.
Faith, sir, we were carousing till the second cock: and drink, sir, is a great provoker of three things.

MACDUFF.
What three things does drink especially provoke?

PORTER.
Marry, sir, nose-painting, sleep, and urine. Lechery, sir, it provokes, and unprovokes; it provokes the desire, but it takes away the performance: therefore, much drink may be said to be an equivocator with lechery: it makes him, and it mars him; it sets him on, and it takes him off; it persuades him, and disheartens him; makes him stand to, and not stand to; in conclusion, equivocates him in a sleep, and, giving him the lie, leaves him.

MACDUFF.
I believe drink gave thee the lie last night.

PORTER.
That it did, sir, i'the very throat on me: but I requited him for his lie; and, I think, being too strong for him, though he took up my legs sometime, yet I made a shift to cast him.

MACDUFF.
Is thy master stirring?—
Our knocking has awaked him; here he comes.

Enter MACBETH.

LENNOX.
Good morrow, noble sir.

MACBETH.
    Good morrow, both.

MACDUFF.
Is the king stirring, worthy thane?

MACBETH.
    Not yet.

MACDUFF.
He did command me to call timely on him:
I have almost slipt the hour.

MACBETH.
    I'll bring you to him.

MACDUFF.
I know this is a joyful trouble to you;
But yet 'tis one.

MACBETH.
The labour we delight in physics pain.
This is the door.

MACDUFF.
    I'll make so bold to call,
For 'tis my limited service.   [_Exit._

LENNOX.
Goes the king hence to-day?

MACBETH.
    He does: he did appoint so.

LENNOX.
The night has been unruly: where we lay,
Our chimneys were blown down; and, as they say,

Lamentings heard i'th'air; strange screams of death;
And prophesying, with accents terrible,
Of dire combustion and confused events
New hatcht to th'woeful time: the obscure bird
Clamour'd the livelong night: some say, the earth
Was feverous and did shake.

MACBETH.
    'Twas a rough night.

LENNOX.
My young remembrance cannot parallel
A fellow to it.

Enter MACDUFF.

MACDUFF.
O horror, horror, horror! Tongue nor heart
Cannot conceive nor name thee!

MACBETH _and_ LENNOX.
What's the matter?

MACDUFF.
Confusion now hath made his masterpiece!
Most sacrilegious murder hath broke ope
The Lord's anointed temple, and stole thence
The life o'th'building!

MACBETH.
    What is't you say? the life?

LENNOX.
Mean you his majesty?

MACDUFF.
Approach the chamber, and destroy your sight
With a new Gorgon:—do not bid me speak;
See, and then speak yourselves.

    [_Exeunt_ MACBETH _and_ LENNOX.
    Awake, awake!—
Ring the alarum-bell:—murder and treason!—
Banquo and Donalbain! Malcolm! awake!
Shake off this downy sleep, death's counterfeit,
And look on death itself! up, up, and see
The great doom's image! Malcolm! Banquo!
As from your graves rise up, and walk like sprites,
To countenance this horror!   [_Bell rings._

Enter LADY MACBETH.

LADY MACBETH.
    What's the business,
That such a hideous trumpet calls to parley
The sleepers of the house? speak, speak!

MACDUFF.
    O gentle lady,
'Tis not for you to hear what I can speak:
The repetition, in a woman's ear,
Would murder as it fell.

Enter BANQUO.

    O Banquo, Banquo,
Our royal master's murder'd!

LADY MACBETH.
    Woe, alas!
What, in our house?

BANQUO.
    Too cruel any where.—
Dear Duff, I prithee, contradict thyself,
And say it is not so.

Enter MACBETH, LENNOX, _and_ ROSS.

MACBETH.
Had I but died an hour before this chance,
I had lived a blessed time; for, from this instant,
There's nothing serious in mortality:

All is but toys: renown and grace is dead;
The wine of life is drawn, and the mere lees
Is left this vault to brag of.
>   *Enter* MALCOLM *and* DONALBAIN.
>   DONALBAIN.
What is amiss?
>   MACBETH.
>   You are, and do not know't:
The spring, the head, the fountain of your blood
Is stopt,—the very source of it is stopt.
>   MACDUFF.
Your royal father's murder'd.
>   MALCOLM.
>   O, by whom?
>   LENNOX.
Those of his chamber, as it seem'd, had done't:
Their hands and faces were all badged with blood;
So were their daggers, which, unwiped, we found
Upon their pillows:
They stared, and were distracted; no man's life
Was to be trusted with them.
>   MACBETH.
O, yet I do repent me of my fury,
That I did kill them.
>   MACDUFF.
>   Wherefore did you so?
>   MACBETH.
Who can be wise, amazed, temperate and furious,
Loyal and neutral, in a moment? No man:
The expedition of my violent love
Outrun the pauser, reason. Here lay Duncan,
His silver skin laced with his golden blood;
And his gasht stabs lookt like a breach in nature
For ruin's wasteful entrance: there, the mur-
>   derers,
Steept in the colours of their trade, their daggers
Unmannerly breecht with gore: who could refrain,
That had a heart to love, and in that heart
Courage to make's love known?
>   LADY MACBETH.
>   Help me hence, ho!
>   MACDUFF.
Look to the lady.
>   MALCOLM [*aside to* DONALBAIN].
>   Why do we hold our tongues,
That most may claim this argument for ours?
>   DONALBAIN [*aside to* MALCOLM].
What should be spoken here, where our fate,
Hid in an auger-hole, may rush, and seize us?
Let's away;
Our tears are not yet brew'd.
>   MALCOLM [*aside to* DONALBAIN].
>   Nor our strong sorrow
Upon the foot of motion.
>   BANQUO.
>   Look to the lady:—
>   [LADY MACBETH *is carried out.*
And when we have our naked frailties hid,
That suffer in exposure, let us meet,
And question this most bloody piece of work,
To know it further. Fears and scruples shake us:
In the great hand of God I stand; and thence
Against the undivulged pretence I fight
Of treasonous malice.
>   MACDUFF.
>   And so do I.

>   ALL.
>   So all.
>   MACBETH.
Let's briefly put on manly readiness,
And meet i'th'hall together.
>   ALL.
>   Well contented.
>   [*Exeunt all but* MALCOLM *and* DONALBAIN.
>   MALCOLM.
What will you do? Let's not consort with them:
To show an unfelt sorrow is an office
Which the false man does easy. I'll to England.
>   DONALBAIN.
To Ireland I; our separated fortune
Shall keep us both the safer: where we are,
There's daggers in men's smiles: the near in blood,
The nearer bloody.
>   MALCOLM.
>   This murderous shaft that's shot
Hath not yet lighted; and our safest way
Is to avoid the aim. Therefore, to horse;
And let us not be dainty of leave-taking,
But shift away: there's warrant in that theft
Which steals itself, when there's no mercy left.
>   [*Exeunt.*

SCENE IV.

Without MACBETH'S *castle.*

Enter ROSS *and an* OLD MAN.

>   OLD MAN.
THREESCORE and ten I can remember well:
      Within the volume of which time I have seen
Hours dreadful and things strange; but this sore
>   night
Hath trifled former knowings.
>   ROSS.
>   Ha, good father,
Thou seest, the heavens, as troubled with man's
>   act,
Threatens his bloody stage: by th'clock 'tis day,
And yet dark night strangles the travelling lamp:
Is't night's predominance, or the day's shame,
That darkness does the face of earth entomb,
When living light should kiss it?
>   OLD MAN.
>   'Tis unnatural,
Even like the deed that's done. On Tuesday last,
A falcon, towering in her pride of place,
Was by a mousing owl hawkt at and kill'd.
>   ROSS.
And Duncan's horses,—a thing most strange and
>   certain,—
Beauteous and swift, the minions of their race,
Turn'd wild in nature, broke their stalls, flung out,
Contending 'gainst obedience, as they would
>   make
War with mankind.
>   OLD MAN.
>   'Tis said they eat each other.
>   ROSS.
They did so,—to th'amazement of mine eyes,
That lookt upon't.—Here comes the good Mac-
>   duff.
>   *Enter* MACDUFF.
How goes the world, sir, now?

MACDUFF.
                    Why, see you not?
ROSS.
Is't known who did this more than bloody deed?
MACDUFF.
Those that Macbeth hath slain.
ROSS.
                              Alas, the day!
What good could they pretend?
MACDUFF.
                    They were suborn'd:
Malcolm and Donalbain, the king's two sons,
Are stoln away and fled; which puts upon them
Suspicion of the deed.
ROSS.
                    'Gainst nature still:
Thriftless ambition, that wilt ravin up
Thine own life's means!—Then 'tis most like
The sovereignty will fall upon Macbeth.
MACDUFF.
He is already named; and gone to Scone
To be invested.
ROSS.
          Where is Duncan's body?
MACDUFF.
Carried to the Colme-kill,
The sacred storehouse of his predecessors,
And guardian of their bones.
ROSS.
               Will you to Scone?
MACDUFF.
No, cousin, I'll to Fife.
ROSS.
          Well, I will thither.
MACDUFF.
Well, may you see things well done there,—
adieu,—
Lest our old robes sit easier than our new!
ROSS.
Farewell, father.
OLD MAN.
God's benison go with you; and with those
That would make good of bad, and friends of
     foes!   [Exeunt.

ACT III. SCENE I.

Forres.   The palace.

Enter BANQUO.

BANQUO.

THOU hast it now,—king, Cawdor, Glamis,
     all,
As the weird women promised; and, I fear,
Thou play'dst most foully for't: yet it was said
It should not stand in thy posterity;
But that myself should be the root and father
Of many kings. If there come truth from them,—
As upon thee, Macbeth, their speeches shine,—
Why, by the verities on thee made good,
May they not be my oracles as well,
And set me up in hope? But, hush; no more.
Sennet sounded.   Enter MACBETH, *as king;* LADY
     MACBETH, *as queen;* LENNOX, ROSS, LORDS,
     LADIES, *and* ATTENDANTS.
MACBETH.
Here's our chief guest.

LADY MACBETH.
               If he had been forgotten,
It had been as a gap in our great feast,
And all-thing unbecoming.
MACBETH.
To-night we hold a solemn supper, sir,
And I'll request your presence.
BANQUO.
                    Let your highness
Command upon me; to the which my duties
Are with a most indissoluble tie
For ever knit.
MACBETH.
Ride you this afternoon?
BANQUO.
               Ay, my good lord.
MACBETH.
We should have else desired your good advice—
Which still hath been both grave and pros-
     perous—
In this day's council; but we'll take't to-morrow.
Is't far you ride?
BANQUO.
          As far, my lord, as will fill up the time
'Twixt this and supper: go not my horse the better,
I must become a borrower of the night
For a dark hour or twain.
MACBETH.
               Fail not our feast.
BANQUO.
My lord, I will not.
MACBETH.
We hear, our bloody cousins are bestow'd
In England and in Ireland; not confessing
Their cruel parricide, filling their hearers
With strange invention: but of that to-morrow;
When therewithal we shall have cause of state
Craving us jointly. Hie you to horse: adieu,
Till you return at night. Goes Fleance with you?
BANQUO.
Ay, my good lord: our time does call upon's.
MACBETH.
I wish your horses swift and sure of foot;
And so I do commend you to their backs.
Farewell.   [Exit BANQUO.
Let every man be master of his time
Till seven at night; to make society
The sweeter welcome, we will keep ourself
Till supper-time alone: while then, God be with
     you!
[Exeunt all but MACBETH and an ATTENDANT.
Sirrah, a word with you: attend those men
Our pleasure?
ATTENDANT.
They are, my lord, without the palace-gate.
MACBETH.
Bring them before us.   [Exit ATTENDANT.
               To be thus is nothing;
But to be safely thus.—Our fears in Banquo
Stick deep; and in his royalty of nature
Reigns that which would be fear'd; 'tis much he
     dares;
And, to that dauntless temper of his mind,
He hath a wisdom that doth guide his valour
To act in safety. There is none but he
Whose being I do fear: and, under him,

My Genius is rebuked; as, it is said,
Mark Antony's was by Cæsar. He chid the sisters,
When first they put the name of king upon me,
And bade them speak to him; then, prophet-like,
They hail'd him father to a line of kings:
Upon my head they placed a fruitless crown,
And put a barren sceptre in my gripe,
Thence to be wrencht with an unlineal hand,
No son of mine succeeding. If't be so,
For Banquo's issue have I filed my mind;
For them the gracious Duncan have I murder'd;
Put rancours in the vessel of my peace
Only for them; and mine eternal jewel
Given to the common enemy of man,
To make them kings, the seed of Banquo kings!
Rather than so, come, fate, into the list,
And champion me to th'utterance!—Who's there?
　　Enter ATTENDANT, *with two* MURDERERS.
Now go to the door, and stay there till we call.
　　　　　　　　　　　[*Exit* ATTENDANT.
Was it not yesterday we spoke together?
　　　　　　FIRST MURDERER.
It was, so please your highness.
　　　　　　MACBETH.
　　　　　　　　　　Well then, now
Have you consider'd of my speeches? Know
That it was he, in the times past, which held you
So under fortune; which you thought had been
Our innocent self: this I made good to you
In our last conference, past in probation with you,
How you were borne in hand, how crost, the in-
　　strument,
Who wrought with them, and all things else that
To half a soul and to a notion crazed　　[might
Say 'Thus did Banquo.'
　　　　　　FIRST MURDERER.
　　　　　　　　You made it known to us.
　　　　　　MACBETH.
I did so; and went further, which is now
Our point of second meeting. Do you find
Your patience so predominant in your nature,
That you can let this go? Are you so gospell'd,
To pray for this good man and for his issue,
Whose heavy hand hath bow'd you to the grave,
And beggar'd yours for ever?
　　　　　　FIRST MURDERER.
　　　　　　　　We are men, my liege.
　　　　　　MACBETH.
Ay, in the catalogue ye go for men;
As hounds, and greyhounds, mongrels, spaniels,
　　curs,
Shoughs, water-rugs, and demi-wolves, are clept
All by the name of dogs: the valued file
Distinguishes the swift, the slow, the subtle,
The housekeeper, the hunter, every one
According to the gift which bounteous nature
Hath in him closed; whereby he does receive
Particular addition, from the bill
That writes them all alike: and so of men.
Now, if you have a station in the file,
Not i'th'worst rank of manhood, say't;
And I will put that business in your bosoms,
Whose execution takes your enemy off;
Grapples you to the heart and love of us,
Who wear our health but sickly in his life,
Which in his death were perfect.

　　　　　　SECOND MURDERER.
　　　　　　　　I am one, my liege,
Whom the vile blows and buffets of the world
Hath so incensed, that I am reckless what
I do to spite the world.
　　　　　　FIRST MURDERER.
　　　　　　　　And I another,
So weary with disasters, tugg'd with fortune,
That I would set my life on any chance,
To mend it, or be rid on't.
　　　　　　MACBETH.
　　　　　　　　Both of you
Know Banquo was your enemy.
　　　　　　BOTH MURDERERS.
　　　　　　　　　　True, my lord.
　　　　　　MACBETH.
So is he mine; and in such bloody distance,
That every minute of his being thrusts
Against my near'st of life: and though I could
With barefaced power sweep him from my sight,
And bid my will avouch it, yet I must not,
For certain friends that are both his and mine,
Whose loves I may not drop, but wail his fall
Who I myself struck down: and thence it is,
That I to your assistance do make love;
Masking the business from the common eye
For sundry weighty reasons.
　　　　　　SECOND MURDERER.
　　　　　　　　We shall, my lord,
Perform what you command us.
　　　　　　FIRST MURDERER.
　　　　　　　　Though our lives—
　　　　　　MACBETH.
Your spirits shine through you. Within this hour
　　at most,
I will advise you where to plant yourselves;
Acquaint you with the perfect spy o'th'time,
The moment on't; for't must be done to-night,
And something from the palace; always thought
That I require a clearness: and with him—
To leave no rubs nor botches in the work—
Fleance his son, that keeps him company,
Whose absence is no less material to me
Than is his father's, must embrace the fate
Of that dark hour. Resolve yourselves apart:
I'll come to you anon.
　　　　　　BOTH MURDERERS.
　　　　　　　　We are resolved, my lord.
　　　　　　MACBETH.
I'll call upon you straight: abide within.
　　　　　　　　[*Exeunt* MURDERERS.
It is concluded:—Banquo, thy soul's flight,
If it find heaven, must find it out to-night.　[*Exit*

SCENE II.

The palace.

Enter LADY MACBETH *and a* SERVANT.

　　　　　　LADY MACBETH.
IS Banquo gone from court?
　　　　　　SERVANT.
Ay, madam, but returns again to-night.
　　　　　　LADY MACBETH.
Say to the king, I would attend his leisure
For a few words.

SERVANT.
Madam, I will.   [*Exit.*
LADY MACBETH.
                    Naught's had, all's spent,
Where our desire is got without content:
'Tis safer to be that which we destroy,
Than, by destruction, dwell in doubtful joy.
                    Enter MACBETH.
How now, my lord! why do you keep alone,
Of sorriest fancies your companions making;
Using those thoughts which should indeed have
    died
With them they think on? Things without all
    remedy
Should be without regard: what's done is done.
MACBETH.
We have scotcht the snake, not kill'd it:
She'll close, and be herself; whilst our poor malice
Remains in danger of her former tooth.
But let the frame of things disjoint, both the
    worlds suffer,
Ere we will eat our meal in fear, and sleep
In the affliction of these terrible dreams
That shake us nightly: better be with the dead,
Whom we, to gain our peace, have sent to peace,
Than on the torture of the mind to lie
In restless ecstasy. Duncan is in his grave;
After life's fitful fever he sleeps well;
Treason has done his worst: nor steel, nor poison,
Malice domestic, foreign levy, nothing,
Can touch him further.
LADY MACBETH.
                    Come on; gentle my lord,
Sleek o'er your rugged looks; be bright and jovial
Among your guests to-night.
MACBETH.
                    So shall I, love;
And so, I pray, be you: let your remembrance
Apply to Banquo; present him eminence, both
With eye and tongue: unsafe the while that we
Must lave our honours in these flattering streams;
And make our faces vizards to our hearts,
Disguising what they are.
LADY MACBETH.
                    You must leave this.
MACBETH.
O, full of scorpions is my mind, dear wife!
Thou know'st that Banquo and his Fleance live.
LADY MACBETH.
But in them nature's copy's not eterne.
MACBETH.
There's comfort yet; they are assailable;
Then be thou jocund: ere the bat hath flown
His cloister'd flight; ere, to black Hecate's sum-
    mons,
The shard-borne beetle with his drowsy hums
Hath rung night's yawning peal, there shall be
    done
A deed of dreadful note.
LADY MACBETH.
                    What's to be done?
MACBETH.
Be innocent of the knowledge, dearest chuck,
Till thou applaud the deed.—Come, seeling night,
Scarf up the tender eye of pitiful day;
And with thy bloody and invisible hand

Cancel and tear to pieces that great bond
Which keeps me pale!—Light thickens; and the
    crow
Makes wing to th'rooky wood:
Good things of day begin to droop and drowse;
Whiles night's black agents to their preys do
    rouse.—
Thou marvell'st at my words: but hold thee still;
Things bad begun make strong themselves by ill:
So, prithee, go with me.   [*Exeunt.*

SCENE III.

A park, with a gate leading to the palace.

Enter three MURDERERS.

FIRST MURDERER.

BUT who did bid thee join with us?
THIRD MURDERER.
                    Macbeth.
SECOND MURDERER.
He needs not our mistrust; since he delivers
Our offices, and what we have to do,
To the direction just.
FIRST MURDERER.
                    Then stand with us.
The west yet glimmers with some streaks of day:
Now spurs the lated traveller apace
To gain the timely inn; and near approaches
The subject of our watch.
THIRD MURDERER.
                    Hark! I hear horses.
BANQUO [*within*].
Give us a light there, ho!
SECOND MURDERER.
                    Then 'tis he: the rest
That are within the note of expectation
Already are i'th'court.
FIRST MURDERER.
                    His horses go about.
THIRD MURDERER.
Almost a mile: but he does usually,
So all men do, from hence to th'palace-gate
Make it their walk.
SECOND MURDERER.
                    A light, a light!
THIRD MURDERER.
                    'Tis he.
FIRST MURDERER.
Stand to't.
                    Enter BANQUO, *and* FLEANCE *with a torch.*
BANQUO.
It will be rain to-night.
FIRST MURDERER.
                    Let it come down.
                    [*They assault* BANQUO.
BANQUO.
O, treachery!—Fly, good Fleance, fly, fly, fly!
Thou mayst revenge.—O slave!
                    [*Dies.* FLEANCE *escapes.*
THIRD MURDERER.
Who did strike out the light?
FIRST MURDERER.
                    Was't not the way?
THIRD MURDERER.
There's but one down; the son is fled.

SECOND MURDERER.
                 We have lost
Best half of our affair.
           FIRST MURDERER.
Well, let's away, and say how much is done.
                       [*Exeunt.*

SCENE IV.

A room of state in the palace.

Banquet prepared. Enter MACBETH, LADY MAC-
BETH, ROSS, LENNOX, LORDS, *and* ATTEN-
DANTS.

           MACBETH.
YOU know your own degrees, sit down: at first
And last the hearty welcome.
           LORDS.
               Thanks to your majesty.
           MACBETH.
Ourself will mingle with society,
And play the humble host.
Our hostess keeps her state; but, in best time,
We will require her welcome.
           LADY MACBETH.
Pronounce it for me, sir, to all our friends;
For my heart speaks they are welcome.
           MACBETH.
See, they encounter thee with their hearts'
     thanks.—
Both sides are even: here I'll sit i'th'midst:
      Enter first MURDERER *to the door.*
Be large in mirth; anon we'll drink a measure
The table round.—There's blood upon thy face.
           MURDERER.
'Tis Banquo's, then.
           MACBETH.
'Tis better thee without than he within.
Is he dispatcht?
           MURDERER.
My lord, his throat is cut; that I did for him.
           MACBETH.
Thou art the best o'th'cut-throats: yet he's good
That did the like for Fleance: if thou didst it,
Thou art the nonpareil.
           MURDERER.
               Most royal sir,
Fleance is scaped.
           MACBETH.
Then comes my fit again: I had else been perfect;
Whole as the marble, founded as the rock;
As broad and general as the casing air:
But now I am cabin'd, cribb'd, confined, bound
     in
To saucy doubts and fears. But Banquo's safe?
           MURDERER.
Ay, my good lord: safe in a ditch he bides,
With twenty trenched gashes on his head;
The least a death to nature.
           MACBETH.
               Thanks for that:
There the grown serpent lies; the worm, that's
     fled,
Hath nature that in time will venom breed,
No teeth for th'present.—Get thee gone: to-mor-
     row
We'll hear ourselves again.   [*Exit* MURDERER.

           LADY MACBETH.
             My royal lord,
You do not give the cheer: the feast is sold
That is not often voucht, while 'tis a-making,
'Tis given with welcome: to feed were best at
     home;
From thence the sauce to meat is ceremony;
Meeting were bare without it.
           MACBETH.
               Sweet remembrancer!—
Now, good digestion wait on appetite,
And health to both!
           LENNOX.
           May't please your highness sit.
      Enter the GHOST *of* BANQUO, *and sits in*
         MACBETH'S *place.*
           MACBETH.
Here had we now our country's honour rooft,
Were the graced person of our Banquo present;
Who may I rather challenge for unkindness
Than pity for mischance!
           ROSS.
              His absence, sir,
Lays blame upon his promise. Please't your high-
     ness
To grace us with your royal company.
           MACBETH.
The table's full.
           LENNOX.
           Here is a place reserved, sir.
           MACBETH.
Where?
           LENNOX.
Here, my good lord. What is't that moves your
     highness?
           MACBETH.
Which of you have done this?
           LORDS.
             What, my good lord?
           MACBETH.
Thou canst not say I did it: never shake
Thy gory locks at me.
           ROSS.
Gentlemen, rise; his highness is not well.
           LADY MACBETH.
Sit, worthy friends:—my lord is often thus,
And hath been from his youth: pray you, keep
     seat;
The fit is momentary; upon a thought
He will again be well: if much you note him,
You shall offend him, and extend his passion:
Feed, and regard him not.—Are you a man?
           MACBETH.
Ay, and a bold one, that dare look on that
Which might appal the devil.
           LADY MACBETH.
             O proper stuff!
This is the very painting of your fear:
This is the air-drawn dagger which, you said,
Led you to Duncan. O, these flaws and starts,
Impostors to true fear, would well become
A woman's story at a winter's fire,
Authoriz'd by her grandam. Shame itself!
Why do you make such faces? When all's done,
You look but on a stool.

MACBETH.
Prithee, see there! behold! look! lo! how say you?—
Why, what care I? If thou canst nod, speak too.—
If charnel-houses and our graves must send
Those that we bury back, our monuments
Shall be the maws of kites.　　[GHOST *disappears.*
LADY MACBETH.
　　　　　　What, quite unmann'd in folly?
MACBETH.
If I stand here, I saw him.
LADY MACBETH.
　　　　　　Fie, for shame!
MACBETH.
Blood hath been shed ere now, i'th'olden time,
Ere human statute purged the gentle weal;
Ay, and since too, murders have been perform'd
Too terrible for the ear: the time has been,
That, when the brains were out, the man would die,
And there an end; but now they rise again,
With twenty mortal murders on their crowns,
And push us from our stools: this is more strange
Than such a murder is.
LADY MACBETH.
　　　　　　My worthy lord,
Your noble friends do lack you.
MACBETH.
　　　　　　I do forget:—
Do not muse at me, my most worthy friends;
I have a strange infirmity, which is nothing　[all;
To those that know me. Come, love and health to
Then I'll sit down.—Give me some wine, fill full.—
I drink to th'general joy o'the whole table,
And to our dear friend Banquo, whom we miss;
Would he were here! to all, and him, we thirst,
And all to all.
LORDS.
Our duties, and the pledge.
Enter GHOST.
MACBETH.
Avaunt! and quit my sight! let the earth hide thee!
Thy bones are marrowless, thy blood is cold;
Thou hast no speculation in those eyes
Which thou dost glare with!
LADY MACBETH.
　　　　　　Think of this, good peers,
But as a thing of custom: 'tis no other;
Only it spoils the pleasure of the time.
MACBETH.
What man dare, I dare:
Approach thou like the rugged Russian bear,
The arm'd rhinoceros, or the Hyrcan tiger;
Take any shape but that, and my firm nerves
Shall never tremble: or be alive again,
And dare me to the desert with thy sword;
If trembling I inhibit then, protest me
The baby of a girl. Hence, horrible shadow!
Unreal mockery, hence!　　[GHOST *vanishes.*
　　　　　　Why, so;—being gone,
I am a man again.—Pray you, sit still.
LADY MACBETH.
You have displaced the mirth, broke the good
　　meeting,
With most admired disorder.
MACBETH.
　　　　　　Can such things be,
And overcome us like a summer's cloud,

Without our special wonder? You make me
　　strange
Even to the disposition that I owe,
When now I think you can behold such sights,
And keep the natural ruby of your cheeks,
When mine is blancht with fear.
ROSS.
　　　　　　What sights, my lord?
LADY MACBETH.
I pray you, speak not; he grows worse and worse;
Question enrages him: at once, good night:—
Stand not upon the order of your going,
But go at once.
LENNOX.
　　　　　　Good night; and better health
Attend his majesty!
LADY MACBETH.
　　　　　　A kind good night to all!
[*Exeunt all but* MACBETH *and* LADY MACBETH.
MACBETH.
It will have blood; they say blood will have blood:
Stones have been known to move, and trees to
　　speak;
Augurs, and understood relations have
By maggot-pies and choughs and rooks brought
　　forth
The secret'st man of blood.—What is the night?
LADY MACBETH.
Almost at odds with morning, which is which.
MACBETH.
How say'st thou, that Macduff denies his person
At our great bidding?
LADY MACBETH.
　　　　　　Did you send to him, sir?
MACBETH.
I hear it by the way; but I will send:
There's not a one of them but in his house
I keep a servant fee'd. I will to-morrow,
And betimes I will, to the weird sisters go:
More shall they speak; for now I am bent to know,
By the worst means, the worst. For mine own
　　good,
All causes shall give way: I am in blood
Stept in so far, that, should I wade no more,
Returning were as tedious as go o'er:
Strange things I have in head, that will to hand;
Which must be acted ere they may be scann'd.
LADY MACBETH.
You lack the season of all natures, sleep.
MACBETH.
Come, we'll to sleep. My strange and self-abuse
Is the initiate fear, that wants hard use:—
We are yet but young in deed.　　[*Exeunt.*

SCENE V.

A heath.

Thunder.　Enter the three WITCHES, *meeting*
HECATE.

FIRST WITCH.
WHY, how now, Hecate! you look angerly.
HECATE.
Have I not reason, beldams as you are,
Saucy and overbold? How did you dare
To trade and traffic with Macbeth

In riddles and affairs of death;
And I, the mistress of your charms,
The close contriver of all harms,
Was never call'd to bear my part,
Or show the glory of our art?
And, which is worse, all you have done
Hath been but for a wayward son,
Spiteful and wrathful; who, as others do,
Loves for his own ends, not for you.
But make amends now: get you gone,
And at the pit of Acheron
Meet me i'the morning: thither he
Will come to know his destiny:
Your vessels and your spells provide,
Your charms, and every thing beside.
I am for the air; this night I'll spend
Unto a dismal and a fatal end:
Great business must be wrought ere noon:
Upon the corner of the moon
There hangs a vaporous drop profound;
I'll catch it ere it come to ground:
And that, distill'd by magic sleights,
Shall raise such artificial sprites,
As, by the strength of their illusion,
Shall draw him on to his confusion:
He shall spurn fate, scorn death, and bear
His hopes 'bove wisdom, grace, and fear:
And you all know security
Is mortals' chiefest enemy.

        [*Music and a song within,* 'Come away,
          come away,' *&c.*
Hark! I am call'd; my little spirit, see,
Sits in a foggy cloud, and stays for me.   [*Exit.*
          FIRST WITCH.
Come, let's make haste; she'll soon be back again.
                             [*Exeunt.*

SCENE VI.

Forres. A room in the palace.

Enter LENNOX *and another* LORD.

          LENNOX.
MY former speeches have but hit your
   thoughts,
Which can interpret further: only, I say,
Things have been strangely borne. The gracious
   Duncan
Was pitied of Macbeth:—marry, he was dead:—
And the right-valiant Banquo walkt too late;
Whom, you may say, if't please you, Fleance
   kill'd,
For Fleance fled: men must not walk too late.
Who cannot want the thought, how monstrous
It was for Malcolm and for Donalbain
To kill their gracious father? damned fact!
How it did grieve Macbeth! did he not straight,
In pious rage, the two delinquents tear,
That were the slaves of drink and thralls of sleep?
Was not that nobly done? Ay, and wisely too;
For 'twould have anger'd any heart alive
To hear the men deny't. So that, I say,
He has borne all things well: and I do think
That, had he Duncan's sons under his key,—
As, an't please heaven, he shall not,—they should
   find
What 'twere to kill a father; so should Fleance.

But, peace!—for from broad words, and 'cause he
His presence at the tyrant's feast, I hear,   [fail'd
Macduff lives in disgrace: sir, can you tell
Where he bestows himself?
          LORD.
             The son of Duncan,
From whom this tyrant holds the due of birth,
Lives in the English court; and is received
Of the most pious Edward with such grace,
That the malevolence of fortune nothing
Takes from his high respect: thither Macduff
Is gone to pray the holy king, upon his aid
To wake Northumberland and warlike Siward:
That, by the help of these—with Him above
To ratify the work—we may again
Give to our tables meat, sleep to our nights;
Free from our feasts and banquets bloody knives;
Do faithful homage, and receive free honours;—
All which we pine for now: and this report
Hath so exasperate the king, that he
Prepares for some attempt of war.
          LENNOX.
           Sent he to Macduff?
          LORD.
He did: and with an absolute 'Sir, not I,'
The cloudy messenger turns me his back,
And hums, as who should say, 'You'll rue the
   time
That clogs me with this answer.'
          LENNOX.
           And that well might
Advise him to a caution, to hold what distance
His wisdom can provide. Some holy angel
Fly to the court of England, and unfold
His message ere he come; that a swift blessing
May soon return to this our suffering country
Under a hand accurst!
          LORD.
          I'll send my prayers with him.
                         [*Exeunt.*

ACT IV. SCENE I.

A cavern. In the middle, a cauldron boiling.

Thunder. Enter the three WITCHES.

          FIRST WITCH.
THRICE the brinded cat hath mew'd.
          SECOND WITCH.
Thrice and once the hedge-pig whined.
          THIRD WITCH.
Harpier cries:—'tis time, 'tis time.
          FIRST WITCH.
Round about the caldron go;
In the poison'd entrails throw.—
Toad, that under cold stone
Days and nights has thirty-one
Swelter'd venom sleeping got,
Boil thou first i'the charmed pot.
          ALL.
Double, double toil and trouble;
Fire, burn; and, caldron, bubble.
          SECOND WITCH.
Fillet of a fenny snake,
In the caldron boil and bake;
Eye of newt, and toe of frog,
Wool of bat, and tongue of dog,

Adder's fork, and blind-worm's sting,
Lizard's leg, and howlet's wing,—
For a charm of powerful trouble,
Like a hell-broth boil and bubble.
ALL.
Double, double toil and trouble;
Fire, burn; and, caldron, bubble.
THIRD WITCH.
Scale of dragon; tooth of wolf;
Witches' mummy; maw and gulf
Of the ravin'd salt-sea shark;
Root of hemlock digg'd i'the dark;
Liver of blaspheming Jew;
Gall of goat; and slips of yew
Sliver'd in the moon's eclipse;
Nose of Turk, and Tartar's lips;
Finger of birth-strangled babe
Ditch-deliver'd by a drab,—
Make the gruel thick and slab:
Add thereto a tiger's chaudron,
For th'ingredients of our caldron.
ALL.
Double, double toil and trouble;
Fire, burn; and, caldron, bubble.
SECOND WITCH.
Cool it with a baboon's blood,
Then the charm is firm and good.
Enter HECATE.
HECATE.
O, well done! I commend your pains;
And every one shall share i'the gains:
And now about the caldron sing,
Like elves and fairies in a ring,
Enchanting all that you put in.
[*Music and a song*, 'Black Spirits,' &c.
[*Exit* HECATE.
SECOND WITCH.
By the pricking of my thumbs,
Something wicked this way comes:—
Open, locks,
Whoever knocks!
Enter MACBETH.
MACBETH.
How now, you secret, black, and midnight hags!
What is't you do?
ALL.
A deed without a name.
MACBETH.
I conjure you, by that which you profess,—
Howe'er you come to know it,—answer me:
Though you untie the winds, and let them fight
Against the churches; though the yesty waves
Confound and swallow navigation up;
Though bladed corn be lodged, and trees blown
    down;
Though castles topple on their warders' heads;
Though palaces and pyramids do slope
Their heads to their foundations; though the
    treasure
Of nature's germens tumble all together,
Even till destruction sicken,—answer me
To what I ask you.
FIRST WITCH.
Speak.
SECOND WITCH.
Demand.

THIRD WITCH.
                    We'll answer.
FIRST WITCH.
Say, if th'hadst rather hear it from our mouths,
Or from our masters?
MACBETH.
                Call 'em, let me see 'em.
FIRST WITCH.
Pour in sow's blood, that hath eaten
Her nine farrow; grease that's sweaten
From the murderer's gibbet throw
Into the flame.
ALL.
        Come, high or low;
Thyself and office deftly show!
Thunder.   FIRST APPARITION: *an arm'd Head.*
MACBETH.
Tell me, thou unknown power,—
FIRST WITCH.
                        He knows thy thought:
Hear his speech, but say thou naught.
FIRST APPARITION.
Macbeth! Macbeth! Macbeth! beware Macduff;
Beware the thane of Fife.—Dismiss me:—
    enough.   [*Descends.*
MACBETH.
Whate'er thou art, for thy good caution, thanks;
Thou hast harpt my fear aright:—but one word
    more,—
FIRST WITCH.
He will not be commanded: here's another,
More potent than the first.
Thunder. SECOND APPARITION: *a bloody Child.*
SECOND APPARITION.
Macbeth! Macbeth! Macbeth!—
MACBETH.
Had I three ears, I'ld hear thee.
SECOND APPARITION.
Be bloody, bold, and resolute; laugh to scorn
The power of man, for none of woman born
Shall harm Macbeth.   [*Descends.*
MACBETH.
Then live, Macduff: what need I fear of thee?
But yet I'll make assurance double sure,
And take a bond of fate: thou shalt not live;
That I may tell pale-hearted fear it lies,
And sleep in spite of thunder.
Thunder. THIRD APPARITION: *a Child crown'd,
            with a tree in his hand.*
                        What is this,
That rises like the issue of a king,
And wears upon his baby-brow the round
And top of sovereignty?
ALL.
            Listen, but speak not to't.
THIRD APPARITION.
Be lion-mettled, proud; and take no care
Who chafes, who frets, or where conspirers are:
Macbeth shall never vanquish'd be, until
Great Birnam wood to high Dunsinane hill
Shall come against him.   [*Descends.*
MACBETH.
                    That will never be:
Who can impress the forest; bid the tree
Unfix his earth-bound root? Sweet bodements!
    good!

Rebellion's head, rise never, till the wood
Of Birnam rise, and our high-placed Macbeth
Shall live the lease of nature, pay his breath
To time and mortal custom.—Yet my heart
Throbs to know one thing: tell me,—if your art
Can tell so much,—shall Banquo's issue ever
Reign in this kingdom?
                    ALL.
                Seek to know no more.
            MACBETH.
I will be satisfied: deny me this,
And an eternal curse fall on you! Let me know:—
Why sinks that caldron? and what noise is this?
                            [Hautboys.
            FIRST WITCH.
Show!
            SECOND WITCH.
Show!
            THIRD WITCH.
Show!
                    ALL.
Show his eyes, and grieve his heart;
Come like shadows, so depart!
    A show of eight KINGS, *the last with a glass in
        his hand;* BANQUO'S GHOST *following.*
            MACBETH.
Thou art too like the spirit of Banquo; down!
Thy crown does sear mine eyeballs:—and thy hair,
Thou other gold-bound brow, is like the first:—
A third is like the former.—Filthy hags!
Why do you show me this?—A fourth?—Start,
    eyes!—
What, will the line stretch out to th'crack of
    doom?—
Another yet?—A seventh?—I'll see no more:—
And yet the eighth appears, who bears a glass
Which shows me many more; and some I see
That twofold balls and treble sceptres carry:
Horrible sight!—Now I see 'tis true;
For the blood-bolter'd Banquo smiles upon me,
And points at them for his.—What, is this so?
            FIRST WITCH.
Ay, sir, all this is so:—but why
Stands Macbeth thus amazedly?—
Come, sisters, cheer we up his sprites,
And show the best of our delights:
I'll charm the air to give a sound,
While you perform your antic round;
That this great king may kindly say
Our duties did his welcome pay.
        [*Music. The* WITCHES *dance, and vanish.*
            MACBETH.
Where are they? Gone?—Let this pernicious hour
Stand aye accursed in the calendar!—
Come in, without there!
            Enter LENNOX.
            LENNOX.
                What's your Grace's will?
            MACBETH.
Saw you the weird sisters?
            LENNOX.
                No, my lord.
            MACBETH.
Came they not by you?
            LENNOX.
                No, indeed, my lord.

            MACBETH.
Infected be the air whereon they ride;
And damn'd all those that trust them!—I did hear
The galloping of horse: who was't came by?
            LENNOX.
'Tis two or three, my lord, that bring you word
Macduff is fled to England.
            MACBETH.
                Fled to England!
            LENNOX.
Ay, my good lord.
            MACBETH.
Time, thou anticipatest my dread exploits:
The flighty purpose never is o'ertook
Unless the deed go with it: from this moment
The very firstlings of my heart shall be
The firstlings of my hand. And even now,
To crown my thoughts with acts, be it thought
    and done:
The castle of Macduff I will surprise;
Seize upon Fife; give to the edge o'th'sword
His wife, his babes, and all unfortunate souls
That trace him in his line. No boasting like a
    fool;
This deed I'll do before this purpose cool:
But no more sights!—Where are these gentlemen?
Come, bring me where they are.   [*Exeunt.*

            SCENE II.
    Fife.   A room in MACDUFF'S *castle.*
    Enter LADY MACDUFF, *her* SON, *and* ROSS.
            LADY MACDUFF.
WHAT had he done, to make him fly the land?
            ROSS.
You must have patience, madam.
            LADY MACDUFF.
                He had none:
His flight was madness: when our actions do not,
Our fears do make us traitors.
            ROSS.
                You know not
Whether it was his wisdom or his fear.
            LADY MACDUFF.
Wisdom! to leave his wife, to leave his babes,
His mansion, and his titles, in a place
From whence himself does fly? He loves us not;
He wants the natural touch: for the poor wren,
The most diminutive of birds, will fight,
Her young ones in her nest, against the owl.
All is the fear, and nothing is the love;
As little is the wisdom, where the flight
So runs against all reason.
            ROSS.
                My dearest coz,
I pray you, school yourself: but for your husband,
He is noble, wise, judicious, and best knows
The fits o'th'season. I dare not speak much
    further:
But cruel are the times, when we are traitors,
And do not know ourselves; when we hold ru-
    mour
From what we fear, yet know not what we fear,
But float upon a wild and violent sea
Each way and move.—I take my leave of you:

Shall not be long but I'll be here again:
Things at the worst will cease, or else climb up-
　　ward
To what they were before.—My pretty cousin,
Blessing upon you!
　　　　　　LADY MACDUFF.
Father'd he is, and yet he's fatherless.
　　　　　　　ROSS.
I am so much a fool, should I stay longer,
It would be my disgrace and your discomfort:
I take my leave at once.　　　　　　[Exit.
　　　　　　LADY MACDUFF.
　　　　　　　Sirrah, your father's dead:
And what will you do now? How will you live?
　　　　　　　SON.
As birds do, mother.
　　　　　　LADY MACDUFF.
　　　　　　　What, with worms and flies?
　　　　　　　SON.
With what I get, I mean; and so do they.
　　　　　　LADY MACDUFF.
Poor bird! thou'ldst never fear the net nor lime,
The pitfall nor the gin.
　　　　　　　SON.
Why should I, mother? Poor birds they are not
　　set for.
My father is not dead, for all your saying.
　　　　　　LADY MACDUFF.
Yes, he is dead: how wilt thou do for a father?
　　　　　　　SON.
Nay, how will you do for a husband?
　　　　　　LADY MACDUFF.
Why, I can buy me twenty at any market.
　　　　　　　SON.
Then you'll buy 'em to sell again.
　　　　　　LADY MACDUFF.
Thou speak'st with all thy wit; and yet, i'faith,
With wit enough for thee.
　　　　　　　SON.
Was my father a traitor, mother?
　　　　　　LADY MACDUFF.
Ay, that he was.
　　　　　　　SON.
What is a traitor?
　　　　　　LADY MACDUFF.
Why, one that swears and lies.
　　　　　　　SON.
And be all traitors that do so?
　　　　　　LADY MACDUFF.
Every one that does so is a traitor, and must be
hang'd.
　　　　　　　SON.
And must they all be hang'd that swear and lie?
　　　　　　LADY MACDUFF.
Every one.
　　　　　　　SON.
Who must hang them?
　　　　　　LADY MACDUFF.
Why, the honest men.
　　　　　　　SON.
Then the liars and swearers are fools; for there
are liars and swearers enow to beat the honest
men, and hang up them.
　　　　　　LADY MACDUFF.
Now, God help thee, poor monkey! But how wilt
thou do for a father?

　　　　　　　SON.
If he were dead, you'ld weep for him: if you
would not, it were a good sign that I should
quickly have a new father.
　　　　　　LADY MACDUFF.
Poor prattler, how thou talk'st!
　　　　　Enter a MESSENGER.
　　　　　　MESSENGER.
Bless you, fair dame! I am not to you known,
Though in your state of honour I am perfect.
I doubt some danger does approach you nearly:
If you will take a homely man's advice,
Be not found here; hence, with your little ones.
To fright you thus, methinks, I am too savage;
To do worse to you were fell cruelty,
Which is too nigh your person. Heaven preserve
　　you!
I dare abide no longer.　　　　　　[Exit.
　　　　　　LADY MACDUFF.
　　　　　　　Whither should I fly?
I have done no harm. But I remember now
I am in this earthly world; where to do harm
Is often laudable; to do good, sometime
Accounted dangerous folly: why then, alas,
Do I put up that womanly defence,
To say I have done no harm?
　　　　　Enter MURDERERS.
　　　　　　　What are these faces?
　　　　　FIRST MURDERER.
Where is your husband?
　　　　　　LADY MACDUFF.
I hope, in no place so unsanctified
Where such as thou mayst find him.
　　　　　FIRST MURDERER.
　　　　　　　He's a traitor!
　　　　　　　SON.
Thou liest, thou shag-hair'd villain!
　　　　　FIRST MURDERER.
　　　　　　What, you egg! [Stabbing him.
Young fry of treachery!
　　　　　　　SON.
　　　　　　He has kill'd me, mother:
Run away, I pray you!　　　　　　[Dies.
　[Exit LADY MACDUFF, crying 'Murder!'
　　and pursued by the MURDERERS.

　　　　　　SCENE III.

England.　　Before the KING'S palace.

　Enter MALCOLM and MACDUFF.

　　　　　　MALCOLM.
LET us seek out some desolate shade, and there
　　Weep our sad bosoms empty.
　　　　　　MACDUFF.
　　　　　　　Let us rather
Hold fast the mortal sword; and, like good men,
Bestride our down-faln birthdom: each new morn
New widows howl; new orphans cry; new sorrows
Strike heaven on the face, that it resounds
As if it felt with Scotland, and yell'd out
Like syllable of dolour.
　　　　　　MALCOLM.
　　　　　　　What I believe, I'll wail;
What know, believe; and what I can redress,
As I shall find the time to friend, I will.

What you have spoke, it may be so perchance.
This tyrant, whose sole name blisters our tongues,
Was once thought honest: you have loved him
　　well;
He hath not toucht you yet. I am young; but
　　something
You may deserve of him through me, and wis-
　　dom
To offer up a weak, poor, innocent lamb
T'appease an angry god.
　　　　　　MACDUFF.
I am not treacherous.
　　　　　　MALCOLM.
　　　　　　　　　But Macbeth is.
A good and virtuous nature may recoil
In an imperial charge. But I shall crave your par-
　　don;
That which you are, my thoughts cannot trans-
　　pose:
Angels are bright still, though the brightest fell:
Though all things foul would wear the brows of
　　grace,
Yet grace must still look so.
　　　　　　MACDUFF.
　　　　　　　　I have lost my hopes.
　　　　　　MALCOLM.
Perchance even there where I did find my doubts.
Why in that rawness left you wife and child,
Those precious motives, those strong knots of
　　love,
Without leave-taking?—I pray you,
Let not my jealousies be your dishonours,
But mine own safeties:—you may be rightly just,
Whatever I shall think.
　　　　　　MACDUFF.
　　　　　　　Bleed, bleed, poor country!
Great tyranny, lay thou thy basis sure,
For goodness dare not check thee! wear thou thy
　　wrongs,
Thy title is affeer'd!—Fare thee well, lord:
I would not be the villain that thou think'st
For the whole space that's in the tyrant's grasp,
And the rich East to boot.
　　　　　　MALCOLM.
　　　　　　　　Be not offended:
I speak not as in absolute fear of you.
I think our country sinks beneath the yoke;
It weeps, it bleeds; and each new day a gash
Is added to her wounds: I think, withal,
There would be hands uplifted in my right;
And here, from gracious England, have I offer
Of goodly thousands: but, for all this
When I shall tread upon the tyrant's head,
Or wear it on my sword, yet my poor country
Shall have more vices than it had before;
More suffer, and more sundry ways than ever,
By him that shall succeed.
　　　　　　MACDUFF.
　　　　　　　What should he be?
　　　　　　MALCOLM.
It is myself I mean: in whom I know
All the particulars of vice so grafted,
That, when they shall be open'd, black Macbeth
Will seem as pure as snow; and the poor state
Esteem him as a lamb, being compared
With my confineless harms.

　　　　　　MACDUFF.
　　　　　　　Not in the legions
Of horrid hell can come a devil more damn'd
In evils to top Macbeth.
　　　　　　MALCOLM.
　　　　　　I grant him bloody,
Luxurious, avaricious, false, deceitful,
Sudden, malicious, smacking of every sin
That has a name: but there's no bottom, none,
In my voluptuousness: your wives, your daugh-
　　ters,
Your matrons, and your maids, could not fill up
The cistern of my lust; and my desire
All continent impediments would o'erbear,
That did oppose my will: better Macbeth
Than such an one to reign.
　　　　　　MACDUFF.
　　　　　　　Boundless intemperance
In nature is a tyranny; it hath been
Th'untimely emptying of the happy throne,
And fall of many kings. But fear not yet
To take upon you what is yours: you may
Convey your pleasures in a spacious plenty,
And yet seem cold, the time you may so hoodwink.
We have willing dames enough; there cannot be
That vulture in you, to devour so many
As will to greatness dedicate themselves,
Finding it so inclined.
　　　　　　MALCOLM.
　　　　　　With this, there grows,
In my most ill-composed affection, such
A stanchless avarice, that, were I king,
I should cut off the nobles for their lands;
Desire his jewels, and this other's house:
And my more-having would be as a sauce
To make me hunger more; that I should forge
Quarrels unjust against the good and loyal,
Destroying them for wealth.
　　　　　　MACDUFF.
　　　　　　　This avarice
Sticks deeper; grows with more pernicious root
Than summer-seeming lust; and it hath been
The sword of our slain kings: yet do not fear;
Scotland hath foisons to fill up your will,
Of your mere own: all these are portable,
With other graces weigh'd.
　　　　　　MALCOLM.
But I have none: the king-becoming graces,
As justice, verity, temperance, stableness,
Bounty, perseverance, mercy, lowliness,
Devotion, patience, courage, fortitude,
I have no relish of them; but abound
In the division of each several crime,
Acting it many ways. Nay, had I power, I should
Pour the sweet milk of concord into hell,
Uproar the universal peace, confound
All unity on earth.
　　　　　　MACDUFF.
　　　　　　O Scotland, Scotland!
　　　　　　MALCOLM.
If such a one be fit to govern, speak:
I am as I have spoken.
　　　　　　MACDUFF.
　　　　　　Fit to govern!
No, not to live.—O nation miserable,
With an untitled tyrant bloody-sceptred,

When shalt thou see thy wholesome days again,
Since that the truest issue of thy throne
By his own interdiction stands accurst,
And does blaspheme his breed?—Thy royal father
Was a most sainted king: the queen that bore
      thee,
Oftener upon her knees than on her feet,
Died every day she lived. Fare thee well!
These evils thou repeat'st upon thyself
Hath banisht me from Scotland.—O my breast,
Thy hope ends here!

             MALCOLM.
                 Macduff, this noble passion,
Child of integrity, hath from my soul
Wiped the black scruples, reconciled my thoughts
To thy good truth and honour. Devilish Macbeth
By many of these trains hath sought to win me
Into his power; and modest wisdom plucks me
From over-credulous haste: but God above
Deal between thee and me! for even now
I put myself to thy direction, and
Unspeak mine own detraction; here abjure
The taints and blames I laid upon myself,
For strangers to my nature. I am yet
Unknown to woman; never was forsworn;
Scarcely have coveted what was mine own;
At no time broke my faith; would not betray
The devil to his fellow; and delight
No less in truth than life: my first false speaking
Was this upon myself:—what I am truly,
Is thine, and my poor country's, to command:—
Whither, indeed, before thy here-approach,
Old Siward, with ten thousand warlike men,
Already at a point, was setting forth:
Now we'll together; and the chance of goodness
Be like our warranted quarrel! Why are you silent?

             MACDUFF.
Such welcome and unwelcome things at once
'Tis hard to reconcile.

        Enter a DOCTOR.
             MALCOLM.
Well; more anon.—Comes the king forth, I pray
      you?

             DOCTOR.
Ay, sir; there are a crew of wretched souls
That stay his cure: their malady convinces
The great assay of art; but, at his touch,
Such sanctity hath heaven given his hand,
They presently amend.

             MALCOLM.
      I thank you, doctor. [*Exit* DOCTOR.
             MACDUFF.
What's the disease he means?

             MALCOLM.
                  'Tis call'd the evil:
A most miraculous work in this good king;
Which often, since my here-remain in England,
I have seen him do. How he solicits heaven,
Himself best knows: but strangely-visited people,
All swoln and ulcerous, pitiful to the eye,
The mere despair of surgery, he cures;
Hanging a golden stamp about their necks,
Put on with holy prayers: and 'tis spoken,
To the succeeding royalty he leaves
The healing benediction. With this strange virtue,
He hath a heavenly gift of prophecy;

And sundry blessings hang about his throne,
That speak him full of grace.

             MACDUFF.
                 See, who comes here?
             MALCOLM.
My countryman; but yet I know him not.
        Enter ROSS.
             MACDUFF.
My ever-gentle cousin, welcome hither.
             MALCOLM.
I know him now:—good God, betimes remove
The means that makes us strangers!
             ROSS.
                           Sir, amen.
             MACDUFF.
Stands Scotland where it did?
             ROSS.
                    Alas, poor country,—
Almost afraid to know itself! It cannot
Be call'd our mother, but our grave: where noth-
      ing,
But who knows nothing, is once seen to smile;
Where sighs, and groans, and shrieks that rent the
      air,
Are made, not markt; where violent sorrow seems
A modern ecstasy: the dead man's knell
Is there scarce askt for who; and good men's lives
Expire before the flowers in their caps,
Dying or e'er they sicken.
             MACDUFF.
                 O, relation
Too nice, and yet too true!
             MALCOLM.
                    What's the newest grief?
             ROSS.
That of an hour's age doth hiss the speaker;
Each minute teems a new one.
             MACDUFF.
                      How does my wife?
             ROSS.
Why, well.
             MACDUFF.
             And all my children?
             ROSS.
                    Well too.
             MACDUFF.
The tyrant has not batter'd at their peace?
             ROSS.
No; they were well at peace when I did leave 'em.
             MACDUFF.
Be not a niggard of your speech: how goes't?
             ROSS.
When I came hither to transport the tidings,
Which I have heavily borne, there ran a rumour
Of many worthy fellows that were out;
Which was to my belief witness'd the rather,
For that I saw the tyrant's power a-foot:
Now is the time of help; your eye in Scotland
Would create soldiers, make our women fight,
To doff their dire distresses.
             MALCOLM.
                  Be't their comfort
We are coming thither: gracious England hath
Lent us good Siward and ten thousand men;
An older and a better soldier none
That Christendom gives out.

ROSS.
Would I could answer
This comfort with the like! But I have words
That would be howl'd out in the desert air,
Where hearing should not latch them.
MACDUFF.
What concern they?
The general cause? or is it a fee-grief
Due to some single breast?
ROSS.
No mind that's honest
But in it shares some woe; though the main part
Pertains to you alone.
MACDUFF.
If it be mine,
Keep it not from me, quickly let me have it.
ROSS.
Let not your ears despise my tongue for ever,
Which shall possess them with the heaviest
sound
That ever yet they heard.
MACDUFF.
Hum! I guess at it.
ROSS.
Your castle is surprised; your wife and babes
Savagely slaughter'd: to relate the manner,
Were, on the quarry of these murder'd deer,
To add the death of you.
MALCOLM.
Merciful heaven!—
What, man! ne'er pull your hat upon your brows;
Give sorrow words: the grief that does not speak
Whispers the o'er-fraught heart, and bids it
break.
MACDUFF.
My children too?
ROSS.
Wife, children, servants, all
That could be found.
MACDUFF.
And I must be from thence!—
My wife kill'd too?
ROSS.
I have said.
MALCOLM.
Be comforted:
Let's make us medicines of our great revenge,
To cure this deadly grief.
MACDUFF.
He has no children.—All my pretty ones?
Did you say all?—O hell-kite!—All?
What, all my pretty chickens and their dam
At one fell swoop?
MALCOLM.
Dispute it like a man.
MACDUFF.
I shall do so;
But I must also feel it as a man:
I cannot but remember such things were,
That were most precious to me.—Did heaven look
on,
And would not take their part? Sinful Macduff,
They were all struck for thee! naught that I am,
Not for their own demerits, but for mine,
Fell slaughter on their souls: heaven rest them
now!

MALCOLM.
Be this the whetstone of your sword: let grief
Convert to anger; blunt not the heart, enrage it.
MACDUFF.
O, I could play the woman with mine eyes,
And braggart with my tongue!—But, gentle
heavens,
Cut short all intermission; front to front
Bring thou this fiend of Scotland and myself;
Within my sword's length set him; if he scape,
Heaven forgive him too!
MALCOLM.
This tune goes manly.
Come, go we to the king; our power is ready;
Our lack is nothing but our leave: Macbeth
Is ripe for shaking, and the powers above
Put on their instruments. Receive what cheer you
may:
The night is long that never finds the day.
[Exeunt.

ACT V. SCENE I.

Dunsinane. A room in the castle.

Enter a DOCTOR OF PHYSIC *and a* WAITING-
GENTLEWOMAN.

DOCTOR.
I HAVE two nights watcht with you, but can
perceive no truth in your report. When was it
she last walkt?
GENTLEWOMAN.
Since his majesty went into the field, I have seen
her rise from her bed, throw her nightgown upon
her, unlock her closet, take forth paper, fold it,
write upon't, read it, afterwards seal it, and again
return to bed; yet all this while in a most fast
sleep.
DOCTOR.
A great perturbation in nature,—to receive at
once the benefit of sleep, and do the effects of
watching!—In this slumbery agitation, besides
her walking and other actual performances, what,
at any time, have you heard her say?
GENTLEWOMAN.
That, sir, which I will not report after her.
DOCTOR.
You may to me; and 'tis most meet you should.
GENTLEWOMAN.
Neither to you nor any one; having no witness to
confirm my speech.—Lo you, here she comes!
Enter LADY MACBETH, *with a taper.*
This is her very guise; and, upon my life, fast
asleep.
Observe her; stand close.
DOCTOR.
How came she by that light?
GENTLEWOMAN.
Why, it stood by her: she has light by her con-
tinually; 'tis her command.
DOCTOR.
You see, her eyes are open.
GENTLEWOMAN.
Ay, but their sense are shut.
DOCTOR.
What is it she does now? Look, how she rubs her
hands.

GENTLEWOMAN.

It is an accustom'd action with her, to seem thus washing her hands: I have known her continue in this a quarter of an hour.

LADY MACBETH.

Yet here's a spot.

DOCTOR.

Hark! she speaks: I will set down what comes from her, to satisfy my remembrance the more strongly.

LADY MACBETH.

Out, damned spot! out, I say!—One, two; why, then 'tis time to do't.—Hell is murky!—Fie, my lord, fie! a soldier, and afeard? What need we fear who knows it, when none can call our power to account?—Yet who would have thought the old man to have had so much blood in him?

DOCTOR.

Do you mark that?

LADY MACBETH.

The thane of Fife had a wife; where is she now?— What, will these hands ne'er be clean?—No more o'that, my lord, no more o'that: you mar all with this starting.

DOCTOR.

Go to, go to; you have known what you should not.

GENTLEWOMAN.

She has spoke what she should not, I am sure of that: heaven knows what she has known.

LADY MACBETH.

Here's the smell of the blood still: all the perfumes of Arabia will not sweeten this little hand. Oh, oh, oh!

DOCTOR.

What a sigh is there! The heart is sorely charged.

GENTLEWOMAN.

I would not have such a heart in my bosom for the dignity of the whole body.

DOCTOR.

Well, well, well,—

GENTLEWOMAN.

Pray God it be, sir.

DOCTOR.

This disease is beyond my practice: yet I have known those which have walkt in their sleep who have died holily in their beds.

LADY MACBETH.

Wash your hands, put on your nightgown; look not so pale:—I tell you yet again, Banquo's buried; he cannot come out on's grave.

DOCTOR.

Even so?

LADY MACBETH.

To bed, to bed; there's knocking at the gate: come, come, come, come, give me your hand: what's done cannot be undone: to bed, to bed, to bed. [Exit.

DOCTOR.

Will she go now to bed?

GENTLEWOMAN.

Directly.

DOCTOR.

Foul whisperings are abroad: unnatural deeds Do breed unnatural troubles: infected minds To their deaf pillows will discharge their secrets:

More needs she the divine than the physician:— God, God forgive us all!—Look after her; Remove from her the means of all annoyance, And still keep eyes upon her:—so, good night: My mind she has mated, and amazed my sight: I think, but dare not speak.

GENTLEWOMAN.

Good night, good doctor. [Exeunt.

SCENE II.

The country near Dunsinane.

Drum and colours. Enter MENTEITH, CAITHNESS, ANGUS, LENNOX, *and* SOLDIERS.

MENTEITH.

THE English power is near, led on by Malcolm, His uncle Siward, and the good Macduff: Revenges burn in them; for their dear causes Would to the bleeding and the grim alarm Excite the mortified man.

ANGUS.

                 Near Birnam wood Shall we well meet them; that way are they coming.

CAITHNESS.

Who knows if Donalbain be with his brother?

LENNOX.

For certain, sir, he is not: I have a file Of all the gentry: there is Siward's son, And many unrough youths, that even now Protest their first of manhood.

MENTEITH.

                 What does the tyrant?

CAITHNESS.

Great Dunsinane he strongly fortifies: Some say he's mad; others, that lesser hate him, Do call it valiant fury: but, for certain, He cannot buckle his distemper'd cause Within the belt of rule.

ANGUS.

                 Now does he feel His secret murders sticking on his hands; Now minutely revolts upbraid his faith-breach Those he commands move only in command, Nothing in love: now does he feel his title Hang loose about him, like a giant's robe Upon a dwarfish thief.

MENTEITH.

                 Who, then, shall blame His pester'd senses to recoil and start, When all that is within him does condemn Itself for being there?

CAITHNESS.

                 Well, march we on, To give obedience where 'tis truly owed: Meet we the medicine of the sickly weal; And with him pour we in our country's purge Each drop of us.

LENNOX.

                 Or so much as it needs, To dew the sovereign flower, and drown the weeds. Make we our march towards Birnam.

                 [Exeunt, marching.

SCENE III.

Dunsinane.　A room in the castle.

Enter MACBETH, DOCTOR, *and* ATTENDANTS.

MACBETH.

BRING me no more reports; let them fly all:
Till Birnam wood remove to Dunsinane,
I cannot taint with fear. What's the boy Malcolm?
Was he not born of woman? The spirits that know
All mortal consequences have pronounced me thus,
'Fear not, Macbeth; no man that's born of woman
Shall e'er have power upon thee.'—Then fly,
　false thanes,
And mingle with the English epicures:
The mind I sway by and the heart I bear
Shall never sag with doubt nor shake with fear.

Enter A SERVANT.

The devil damn thee black, thou cream-faced loon!
Where gott'st thou that goose look?

SERVANT.

There is ten thousand—

MACBETH.

　　　　　Geese, villain?

SERVANT.

　　　　　　　　Soldiers, sir.

MACBETH.

Go prick thy face, and over-red thy fear,
Thou lily-liver'd boy. What soldiers, patch?
Death of thy soul! those linen cheeks of thine
Are counsellors to fear. What soldiers, whey-face?

SERVANT.

The English force, so please you.

MACBETH.

Take thy face hence.　　　[*Exit* SERVANT.
　　　　Seyton!—I am sick at heart,
When I behold—Seyton, I say!—This push
Will chair me ever, or dis-seat me now.
I have lived long enough: my way of life
Is faln into the sear, the yellow leaf;
And that which should accompany old age,
As honour, love, obedience, troops of friends,
I must not look to have; but, in their stead,
Curses not loud but deep, mouth-honour, breath,
Which the poor heart would fain deny, and dare
Seyton!　　　　　　　　　[not.—

Enter SEYTON.

SEYTON.

What is your gracious pleasure?

MACBETH.

　　　　　　　What news more?

SEYTON.

All is confirm'd, my lord, which was reported.

MACBETH.

I'll fight, till from my bones my flesh be hackt.
Give me my armour.

SEYTON.

　　　　'Tis not needed yet.

MACBETH.

I'll put it on.—
Send out moe horses, skirr the country round;
Hang those that talk of fear.—Give me mine
How does your patient, doctor?　　　[armour.—

DOCTOR.

　　　　　Not so sick, my lord,
As she is troubled with thick-coming fancies,
That keep her from her rest.

MACBETH.

　　　　　　　Cure her of that:
Canst thou not minister to a mind diseased;
Pluck from the memory a rooted sorrow;
Raze out the written troubles of the brain;
And with some sweet oblivious antidote
Cleanse the stuft bosom of that perilous stuff
Which weighs upon the heart?

DOCTOR.

　　　　　　　Therein the patient
Must minister to himself.

MACBETH.

Throw physic to the dogs,—I'll none of it.—
Come, put mine armour on; give me my staff:—
Seyton, send out.—Doctor, the thanes fly from
　me.—
Come, sir, dispatch.—If thou couldst, doctor, cast
The water of my land, find her disease,
And purge it to a sound and pristine health,
I would applaud thee to the very echo,
That should applaud again.—Pull't off, I say.—
What rhubarb, senna, or what purgative drug,
Would scour these English hence? Hear'st thou of
　them?

DOCTOR.

Ay, my good lord; your royal preparation
Makes us hear something.

MACBETH.

　　　　　　　Bring it after me.—
I will not be afraid of death and bane,
Till Birnam forest come to Dunsinane.
　　　　　　[*Exeunt all but* DOCTOR.

DOCTOR.

Were I from Dunsinane away and clear,
Profit again should hardly draw me here.　　[*Exit.*

SCENE IV.

Country near Dunsinane: a wood in view.

Drum and colours.　Enter MALCOLM, OLD SI-
WARD *and* YOUNG SIWARD, MACDUFF, MEN-
TEITH, CAITHNESS, ANGUS, LENNOX, ROSS,
and SOLDIERS, *marching.*

MALCOLM.

COUSINS, I hope the days are near at hand
That chambers will be safe.

MENTEITH.

　　　　　　We doubt it nothing.

SIWARD.

What wood is this before us?

MENTEITH.

　　　　　　The wood of Birnam.

MALCOLM.

Let every soldier hew him down a bough,
And bear't before him: thereby shall we shadow
The numbers of our host, and make discovery
Err in report of us.

SOLDIERS.

It shall be done.

SIWARD.

We learn no other but the confident tyrant
Keeps still in Dunsinane, and will endure
Our setting down before't.

MALCOLM.

　　　　　　'Tis his main hope:
For where there is advantage to be ta'en,

Both more and less have given him the revolt;
And none serve with him but constrained things,
Whose hearts are absent too.

MACDUFF.
                 Let our just censures
Attend the true event, and put we on
Industrious soldiership.

SIWARD.
                 The time approaches
That will with due decision make us know
What we shall say we have, and what we owe.
Thoughts speculative their unsure hopes relate;
But certain issue strokes must arbitrate:
Towards which advance the war.

                 [Exeunt, marching.

SCENE V.

Dunsinane. Within the castle.

Enter MACBETH, SEYTON, *and* SOLDIERS,
with drum and colours.

MACBETH.

HANG out our banners on the outward walls;
   The cry is still, 'They come:' our castle's
       strength
Will laugh a siege to scorn: here let them lie
Till famine and the ague eat them up:
Were they not forced with those that should be
       ours,
We might have met them dareful, beard to beard,
And beat them backward home.
           [A cry within of women.
                What is that noise?

SEYTON.
It is the cry of women, my good lord.   *[Exit.*

MACBETH.
I have almost forgot the taste of fears:
The time has been, my senses would have cool'd
To hear a night-shriek; and my fell of hair
Would at a dismal treatise rouse and stir
As life were in't: I have supt full with horrors;
Direness, familiar to my slaughterous thoughts,
Cannot once start me.
         Enter SEYTON.
             Wherefore was that cry?

SEYTON.
The queen, my lord, is dead.

MACBETH.
She should have died hereafter;
There would have been a time for such a word.—
To-morrow, and to-morrow, and to-morrow,
Creeps in this petty pace from day to day,
To the last syllable of recorded time;
And all our yesterdays have lighted fools
The way to dusty death. Out, out, brief candle!
Life's but a walking shadow; a poor player,
That struts and frets his hour upon the stage,
And then is heard no more: it is a tale
Told by an idiot, full of sound and fury,
Signifying nothing.
         Enter a MESSENGER.
Thou comest to use thy tongue; thy story quickly.

MESSENGER.
Gracious my lord,
I should report that which I say I saw,
But know not how to do it.

MACBETH.
               Well, say, sir.

MESSENGER.
As I did stand my watch upon the hill,
I lookt toward Birnam, and anon, methought,
The wood began to move.

MACBETH.
               Liar and slave!

MESSENGER.
Let me endure your wrath, if't be not so:
Within this three mile may you see it coming;
I say, a moving grove.

MACBETH.
             If thou speak'st false,
Upon the next tree shalt thou hang alive,
Till famine cling thee: if thy speech be sooth,
I care not if thou dost for me as much.—
I pull in resolution; and begin
To doubt th'equivocation of the fiend,
That lies like truth: 'Fear not, till Birnam wood
Do come to Dunsinane;'—and now a wood
Comes toward Dunsinane.—Arm, arm, and out!
If this which he avouches does appear,
There is nor flying hence nor tarrying here.
I 'gin to be a-weary of the sun,
And wish th'estate o'th'world were now undone.—
Ring the alarum-bell!—Blow, wind! come, wrack!
At least we'll die with harness on our back.
                 [Exeunt.

SCENE VI.

The same. A plain before the castle.

Drum and colours. Enter MALCOLM, OLD SI-
WARD, MACDUFF, *&c., and their* ARMY *with
boughs.*

MALCOLM.

NOW near enough; your leafy screens throw
   down,
And show like those you are.—You, worthy uncle,
Shall, with my cousin, your right-noble son,
Lead our first battle: worthy Macduff and we
Shall take upon's what else remains to do,
According to our order.

SIWARD.
               Fare you well.—
Do we but find the tyrant's power to-night,
Let us be beaten, if we cannot fight.

MACDUFF.
Make all our trumpets speak; give them all breath,
Those clamorous harbingers of blood and death.
                 [Exeunt.

SCENE VII.

The same. Another part of the plain.

Alarums. Enter MACBETH.

MACBETH.

THEY have tied me to a stake; I cannot fly,
   But, bear-like, I must fight the course —
       What's he
That was not born of woman? Such a one
Am I to fear, or none.
         Enter YOUNG SIWARD.

YOUNG SIWARD.
What is thy name?

MACBETH.
Thou'lt be afraid to hear it.
YOUNG SIWARD.
No; though thou call'st thyself a hotter name
Than any is in hell.
MACBETH.
My name's Macbeth.
YOUNG SIWARD.
The devil himself could not pronounce a title
More hateful to mine ear.
MACBETH.
No, nor more fearful.
YOUNG SIWARD.
Thou liest, abhorred tyrant; with my sword
I'll prove the lie thou speak'st.
[*They fight, and* YOUNG SIWARD *is slain.*
MACBETH.
Thou wast born of woman.—
But swords I smile at, weapons laugh to scorn,
Brandisht by man that's of a woman born. [*Exit.*
Alarums. Enter MACDUFF.
MACDUFF.
That way the noise is.—Tyrant, show thy face!
If thou be'st slain and with no stroke of mine,
My wife and children's ghosts will haunt me still.
I cannot strike at wretched kerns, whose arms
Are hired to bear their staves: either thou, Mac-
beth,
Or else my sword, with an unbatter'd edge,
I sheathe again undeeded. There thou shouldst be;
By this great clatter, one of greatest note
Seems bruited:—let me find him, fortune!
And more I beg not.   [*Exit. Alarum.*
Enter MALCOLM *and* OLD SIWARD.
SIWARD.
This way, my lord;—the castle's gently render'd:
The tyrant's people on both sides do fight;
The noble thanes do bravely in the war:
The day almost itself professes yours,
And little is to do.
MALCOLM.
We have met with foes
That strike beside us.
SIWARD.
Enter, sir, the castle. [*Exeunt. Alarum.*

SCENE VIII.

The same.   Another part of the plain.

Enter MACBETH.

MACBETH.
WHY should I play the Roman fool, and die
On mine own sword? whiles I see lives, the
Do better upon them.   [*gashes*
Enter MACDUFF.
MACDUFF.
Turn, hell-hound, turn!
MACBETH.
Of all men else I have avoided thee:
But get thee back; my soul is too much charged
With blood of thine already.
MACDUFF.
I have no words,—
My voice is in my sword; thou bloodier villain
Than terms can give thee out!
[*They fight. Alarum.*

MACBETH.
Thou losest labour:
As easy mayst thou the intrenchant air
With thy keen sword impress, as make me bleed:
Let fall thy blade on vulnerable crests;
I bear a charmed life, which must not yield
To one of woman born.
MACDUFF.
Despair thy charm;
And let the angel whom thou still hast served
Tell thee, Macduff was from his mother's womb
Untimely ript.
MACBETH.
Accursed be that tongue that tells me so,
For it hath cow'd my better part of man!
And be these juggling fiends no more believed,
That palter with us in a double sense;
That keep the word of promise to our ear,
And break it to our hope!—I'll not fight with
thee.
MACDUFF.
Then yield thee, coward,
And live to be the show and gaze o'th'time:
We'll have thee, as our rarer monsters are,
Painted upon a pole, and underwrit
'Here may you see the tyrant.'
MACBETH.
I will not yield,
To kiss the ground before young Malcolm's feet,
And to be baited with the rabble's curse.
Though Birnam wood be come to Dunsinane,
And thou opposed, being of no woman born,
Yet I will try the last:—before my body
I throw my warlike shield: lay on, Macduff;
And damn'd be him that first cries 'Hold,
enough!'   [*Exeunt, fighting.*
Retreat.   Flourish.   Enter, with drum and colours,
MALCOLM, OLD SIWARD, ROSS, THANES,
and SOLDIERS.
MALCOLM.
I would the friends we miss were safe arrived.
SIWARD.
Some must go off: and yet, by these I see,
So great a day as this is cheaply bought.
MALCOLM.
Macduff is missing, and your noble son.
ROSS.
Your son, my lord, has paid a soldier's debt:
He only lived but till he was a man;
The which no sooner had his prowess confirm'd
In the unshrinking station where he fought,
But like a man he died.
SIWARD.
Then he is dead?
ROSS.
Ay, and brought off the field: your cause of sor-
row
Must not be measured by his worth, for then
It hath no end.
SIWARD.
Had he his hurts before?
ROSS.
Ay, on the front.
SIWARD.
Why then, God's soldier be he!
Had I as many sons as I have hairs,

I would not wish them to a fairer death:
And so, his knell is knoll'd.

MALCOLM.
                    He's worth more sorrow,
And that I'll spend for him.

SIWARD.
                    He's worth no more:
They say he parted well, and paid his score:
And so, God be with him!—Here comes newer
comfort.

Enter MACDUFF, *with* MACBETH'S *head.*

MACDUFF.
Hail, king! for so thou art: behold, where stands
Th'usurper's cursed head: the time is free:
I see thee compast with thy kingdom's pearl,
That speak my salutation in their minds;
Whose voices I desire aloud with mine,—
Hail, King of Scotland!

ALL.
Hail, King of Scotland! [*Flourish.*

MALCOLM.
We shall not spend a large expense of time
Before we reckon with your several loves,
And make us even with you. My thanes and kins-
men,
Henceforth be earls,—the first that ever Scot-
land
In such an honour named. What's more to do,
Which would be planted newly with the time,—
As calling home our exiled friends abroad,
That fled the snares of watchful tyranny;
Producing forth the cruel ministers
Of this dead butcher, and his fiend-like queen,—
Who, as 'tis thought, by self and violent hands
Took off her life;—this, and what needful else
That calls upon us, by the grace of Grace,
We will perform in measure, time, and place:
So, thanks to all at once and to each one,
Whom we invite to see us crown'd at Scone.
                    [*Flourish. Exeunt.*

KING LEAR

DRAMATIS PERSONAE

LEAR, *King of Britain.*
KING OF FRANCE.
DUKE OF BURGUNDY.
DUKE OF CORNWALL.
DUKE OF ALBANY.
EARL OF KENT.
EARL OF GLOSTER.
EDGAR, *son to Gloster.*
EDMUND, *bastard son to Gloster.*
CURAN, *a courtier.*
OSWALD, *steward to Goneril.*
OLD MAN, *tenant to Gloster.*
DOCTOR.

FOOL.
AN OFFICER, *employ'd by Edmund.*
GENTLEMAN, *attendant on Cordelia.*
A HERALD.
SERVANTS *to Cornwall.*

GONERIL,
REGAN, } *daughters to Lear.*
CORDELIA,

KNIGHTS *attending on Lear,* OFFICERS, MES-
SENGERS, SOLDIERS, *and* ATTENDANTS.

SCENE—*Britain.*

ACT I. SCENE I.

KING LEAR'S *palace.*

Enter KENT, GLOSTER, *and* EDMUND.

EARL OF KENT.
I THOUGHT the king had more affected the
Duke of Albany than Cornwall.
EARL OF GLOSTER.
It did always seem so to us: but now, in the divi-
sion of the kingdom, it appears not which of the
dukes he values most; for equalities are so
weigh'd, that curiosity in neither can make choice
of either's moiety.
EARL OF KENT.
Is not this your son, my lord?
EARL OF GLOSTER.
His breeding, sir, hath been at my charge: I have
so often blusht to acknowledge him, that now I
am brazed to't.
EARL OF KENT.
I cannot conceive you.
EARL OF GLOSTER.
Sir, this young fellow's mother could: whereupon
she grew round-womb'd, and had, indeed, sir, a
son for her cradle ere she had a husband for her
bed. Do you smell a fault?
EARL OF KENT.
I cannot wish the fault undone, the issue of it
being so proper.
EARL OF GLOSTER.
But I have a son, sir, by order of law, some year
elder than this, who yet is no dearer in my ac-
count: though this knave came something saucily
into the world before he was sent for, yet was his
mother fair; there was good sport at his making,
and the whoreson must be acknowledged.—Do
you know this noble gentleman, Edmund?
EDMUND.
No, my lord.
EARL OF GLOSTER.
My Lord of Kent: remember him hereafter as my
honourable friend.
EDMUND.
My services to your lordship.
EARL OF KENT.
I must love you, and sue to know you better.

EDMUND.
Sir, I shall study deserving.
EARL OF GLOSTER.
He hath been out nine years, and away he shall
again.—The king is coming.
Sennet. Enter one bearing a coronet, KING LEAR,
CORNWALL, ALBANY, GONERIL, REGAN,
CORDELIA, *and* ATTENDANTS.
KING LEAR.
Attend the Lords of France and Burgundy,
Gloster.
EARL OF GLOSTER.
I shall, my liege.
[*Exeunt* GLOSTER *and* EDMUND.
KING LEAR.
Meantime we shall express our darker purpose.
Give me the map there. Know we have divided
In three our kingdom: and 'tis our fast intent
To shake all cares and business from our age;
Conferring them on younger strengths, while we
Unburden'd crawl toward death.—Our son of
Cornwall,
And you, our no less loving son of Albany,
We have this hour a constant will to publish
Our daughters' several dowers, that future strife
May be prevented now. The princes, France and
Burgundy,
Great rivals in our youngest daughter's love,
Long in our court have made their amorous
sojourn,
And here are to be answer'd. Tell me, my
daughters,—
Since now we will divest us both of rule,
Interest of territory, cares of state,—
Which of you shall we say doth love us most?
That our largest bounty may extend
Where nature doth with merit challenge. Goneril,
Our eldest-born, speak first.
GONERIL.
Sir, I love you more than words can wield the
matter;
Dearer than eyesight, space, and liberty;
Beyond what can be valued, rich or rare;
No less than life, with grace, health, beauty,
honour;
As much as child e'er loved, or father found;

A love that makes breath poor, and speech unable;
Beyond all manner of so much I love you.
                CORDELIA [*aside*].
What shall Cordelia do? Love, and be silent.
                KING LEAR.
Of all these bounds, even from this line to this,
With shadowy forests and with champains richt,
With plenteous rivers and wide-skirted meads,
We make thee lady: to thine and Albany's issue
Be this perpetual. What says our second daughter,
Our dearest Regan, wife to Cornwall? Speak.
                REGAN.
I am made of that self metal as my sister,
And prize me at her worth. In my true heart
I find she names my very deed of love;
Only she comes too short,—that I profess
Myself an enemy to all other joys,
Which the most precious square of sense pos-
    sesses;
And find I am alone felicitate
In your dear highness' love.
                CORDELIA [*aside*].
                    Then poor Cordelia!
And yet not so; since, I am sure, my love's
More richer than my tongue.
                KING LEAR.
To thee and thine hereditary ever
Remain this ample third of our fair kingdom;
No less in space, validity, and pleasure,
Than that conferr'd on Goneril.—Now, our joy,
Although our last, not least; to whose young
    love
The vines of France and milk of Burgundy
Strive to be interest; what can you say to draw
A third more opulent than your sisters? Speak.
                CORDELIA.
Nothing, my lord.
                KING LEAR.
Nothing!
                CORDELIA.
Nothing.
                KING LEAR.
Nothing will come of nothing: speak again.
                CORDELIA.
Unhappy that I am, I cannot heave
My heart into my mouth: I love your majesty
According to my bond; nor more nor less.
                KING LEAR.
How, how, Cordelia! mend your speech a little,
Lest it may mar your fortunes.
                CORDELIA.
                    Good my lord,
You have begot me, bred me, loved me: I
Return those duties back as are right fit,
Obey you, love you, and most honour you.
Why have my sisters husbands, if they say
They love you all? Haply, when I shall wed,
That lord whose hand must take my plight shall
    carry
Half my love with him, half my care and duty:
Sure, I shall never marry like my sisters,
To love my father all.
                KING LEAR.
But goes thy heart with this?
                CORDELIA.
                    Ay, good my lord.

                KING LEAR.
So young, and so untender?
                CORDELIA.
So young, my lord, and true.
                KING LEAR.
Let it be so,—thy truth, then, be thy dower:
For, by the sacred radiance of the sun,
The mysteries of Hecate, and the night;
By all the operation of the orbs
From whom we do exist, and cease to be;
Here I disclaim all my paternal care,
Propinquity and property of blood,
And as a stranger to my heart and me
Hold thee, from this, for ever. The barbarous
    Scythian,
Or he that makes his generation messes
To gorge his appetite, shall to my bosom
Be as well neighbour'd, pitied, and relieved,
As thou my sometime daughter.
                EARL OF KENT.
                    Good my liege,—
                KING LEAR.
Peace, Kent!
Come not between the dragon and his wrath.—
I loved her most, and thought to set my rest
On her kind nursery.—Hence, and avoid my
    sight!—
So be my grave my peace, as here I give
Her father's heart from her!—Call France;—who
    stirs?
Call Burgundy.—Cornwall and Albany,
With my two daughters' dowers digest this third:
Let pride, which she calls plainness, marry her.
I do invest you jointly in my power,
Pre-eminence, and all the large effects
That troop with majesty.—Ourself, by monthly
    course,
With reservation of an hundred knights,
By you to be sustain'd, shall our abode
Make with you by due turns. Only we still retain
The name, and all the additions to a king;
The sway, revenue, execution of the rest,
Beloved sons, be yours: which to confirm,
This coronet part betwixt you. [*Giving the crown.*
                EARL OF KENT.
                    Royal Lear,
Whom I have ever honour'd as my king,
Loved as my father, as my master follow'd,
As my great patron thought on in my prayers,—
                KING LEAR.
The bow is bent and drawn, make from the shaft.
                EARL OF KENT.
Let it fall rather, though the fork invade
The region of my heart: be Kent unmannerly,
When Lear is mad. What wouldst thou do, old
    man?
Think'st thou that duty shall have dread to speak,
When power to flattery bows? To plainness
    honour's bound,
When majesty falls to folly. Reverse thy doom;
And, in thy best consideration, check
This hideous rashness: answer my life my judge-
    ment,
Thy youngest daughter does not love thee least;
Nor are those empty-hearted whose low sound
Reverbs no hollowness.

KING LEAR.
Kent, on thy life, no more.
EARL OF KENT.
My life I never held but as a pawn
To wage against thine enemies; nor fear to lose it,
Thy safety being the motive.
KING LEAR.
Out of my sight!
EARL OF KENT.
See better, Lear; and let me still remain
The true blank of thine eye.
KING LEAR.
Now, by Apollo,—
EARL OF KENT.
Now, by Apollo, king,
Thou swear'st thy gods in vain.
KING LEAR.
O, vassal! miscreant!
[Laying his hand on his sword.
DUKES OF ALBANY and CORNWALL.
Dear sir, forbear.
EARL OF KENT.
Do;
Kill thy physician, and the fee bestow
Upon the foul disease. Revoke thy doom;
Or, whilst I can vent clamour from my throat,
I'll tell thee thou dost evil.
KING LEAR.
Hear me, recreant!
On thine allegiance, hear me!
Since thou hast sought to make us break our
vow,
Which we durst never yet, and with strain'd
pride
To come between our sentence and our power,
Which nor our nature nor our place can bear,
Our potency made good, take thy reward.
Five days we do allot thee, for provision
To shield thee from diseases of the world;
And, on the sixth, to turn thy hated back
Upon our kingdom: if, on the tenth day follow-
ing,
Thy banisht trunk be found in our dominions,
The moment is thy death. Away! by Jupiter,
This shall not be revoked.
EARL OF KENT.
Fare thee well, king: sith thus thou wilt appear,
Freedom lives hence, and banishment is here.
[to CORDELIA] The gods to their dear shelter
take thee, maid,
That justly think'st, and hast most rightly said!
[to REGAN and GONERIL] And your large
speeches may your deeds approve,
That good effects may spring from words of love.
Thus Kent, O princes, bids you all adieu;
He'll shape his old course in a country new. [Exit.
Flourish. Enter GLOSTER, with FRANCE,
BURGUNDY, and ATTENDANTS.
EARL OF GLOSTER.
Here's France and Burgundy, my noble lord.
KING LEAR.
My Lord of Burgundy,
We first address towards you, who with this king
Hath rivall'd for our daughter, what, in the least,
Will you require in present dower with her,
Or cease your quest of love?

DUKE OF BURGUNDY.
Most royal majesty,
I crave no more than hath your highness offer'd,
Nor will you tender less.
KING LEAR.
Right noble Burgundy,
When she was dear to us, we did hold her so;
But now her price is faln. Sir, there she stands:
If aught within that little-seeming substance,
Or all of it, with our displeasure pieced,
And nothing more, may fitly like your Grace,
She's there, and she is yours.
DUKE OF BURGUNDY.
I know no answer.
KING LEAR.
Will you, with those infirmities she owes,
Unfriended, new-adopted to our hate,
Dower'd with our curse, and stranger'd with our
oath,
Take her, or leave her?
DUKE OF BURGUNDY.
Pardon me, royal sir;
Election makes not up on such conditions.
KING LEAR.
Then leave her, sir; for, by the power that made
me,
I tell you all her wealth.—[to FRANCE] For you,
great king,
I would not from your love make such a stray,
To match you where I hate; therefore beseech you
T'avert your liking a more worthier way
Than on a wretch whom nature is ashamed
Almost t'acknowledge hers.
KING OF FRANCE.
This is most strange,
That she, that even but now was your best object,
The argument of your praise, balm of your age,
Most best, most dearest, should in this trice of
time
Commit a thing so monstrous, to dismantle
So many folds of favour. Sure, her offence
Must be of such unnatural degree,
That monsters it, or your fore-vouch'd affection
Faln into taint: which to believe of her,
Must be a faith that reason without miracle
Should never plant in me.
CORDELIA.
I yet beseech your majesty,—
If for I want that glib and oily art,
To speak and purpose not; since what I well in-
tend,
I'll do't before I speak,—that you make known
It is no vicious blot, murder, or foulness,
No unchaste action, or dishonour'd step,
That hath deprived me of your grace and favour;
But even for want of that for which I am richer,—
A still-soliciting eye, and such a tongue
As I am glad I have not, though not to have it
Hath lost me in your liking.
KING LEAR.
Better thou
Hadst not been born than not t'have pleased me
better.
KING OF FRANCE.
Is it but this? a tardiness in nature
Which often leaves the history unspoke

That it intends to do? My Lord of Burgundy,
What say you to the lady? Love's not love
When it is mingled with regards that stand
Aloof from the entire point. Will you have her?
She is herself a dowry.
DUKE OF BURGUNDY.
Royal Lear,
Give but that portion which yourself proposed,
And here I take Cordelia by the hand,
Duchess of Burgundy.
KING LEAR.
Nothing: I have sworn; I am firm.
DUKE OF BURGUNDY.
I am sorry, then, you have so lost a father
That you must lose a husband.
CORDELIA.
Peace be with Burgundy!
Since that respects of fortune are his love,
I shall not be his wife.
KING OF FRANCE.
Fairest Cordelia, that art most rich, being poor;
Most choice, forsaken; and most loved, despised!
Thee and thy virtues here I seize upon:
Be it lawful I take up what's cast away.
Gods, gods! 'tis strange that from their cold'st
   neglect
My love should kindle to inflamed respect.—
Thy dowerless daughter, king, thrown to my
   chance,
Is queen of us, of ours, and our fair France:
Not all the dukes of waterish Burgundy
Can buy this unprized precious maid of me.—
Bid them farewell, Cordelia, though unkind:
Thou losest here, a better where to find.
KING LEAR.
Thou hast her, France: let her be thine; for we
Have no such daughter, nor shall ever see
That face of hers again:—Therefore be gone
Without our grace, our love, our benison.—
Come, noble Burgundy.
   [*Flourish. Exeunt* LEAR, BURGUNDY,
     CORNWALL, ALBANY, GLOSTER *and*
     ATTENDANTS.
KING OF FRANCE.
Bid farewell to your sisters.
CORDELIA.
The jewels of our father, with washt eyes
Cordelia leaves you: I know you what you are;
And, like a sister, am most loth to call   [father:
Your faults as they are named. Love well our
To your professed bosoms I commit him:
But yet, alas, stood I within his grace,
I would prefer him to a better place.
So, farewell to you both.
REGAN.
Prescribe not us our duties.
GONERIL.
Let your study
Be to content your lord, who hath received you
At fortune's alms. You have obedience scanted,
And well are worth the want that you have
   wanted.
CORDELIA.
Time shall unfold what pleated cunning hides:
Who covers faults, at last shame them derides.
Well may you prosper!

KING OF FRANCE.
Come, my fair Cordelia.
   [*Exeunt* FRANCE *and* CORDELIA.
GONERIL.
Sister, it is not a little I have to say of what most
nearly appertains to us both. I think our father
will hence to-night.
REGAN.
That's most certain, and with you; next month
with us.
GONERIL.
You see how full of changes his age is; the observation we have made of it hath not been little:
he always loved our sister most; and with what
poor judgement he hath now cast her off appears
too grossly.
REGAN.
'Tis the infirmity of his age: yet he hath ever but
slenderly known himself.
GONERIL.
The best and soundest of his time hath been but
rash; then must we look to receive from his age,
not alone the imperfections of long-ingrafted condition, but therewithal the unruly waywardness
that infirm and choleric years bring with them.
REGAN.
Such unconstant starts are we like to have from
him as this of Kent's banishment.
GONERIL.
There is further compliment of leave-taking between France and him. Pray you, let's hit together: if our father carry authority with such
dispositions as he bears, this last surrender of his
will but offend us.
REGAN.
We shall further think on't.
GONERIL.
We must do something, and i'the heat.   [*Exeunt.*

SCENE II.
The EARL OF GLOSTER'S *castle.*
Enter EDMUND, *with a letter.*
EDMUND.
THOU, nature, art my goddess; to thy law
  My services are bound. Wherefore should I
Stand in the plague of custom, and permit
The curiosity of nations to deprive me,
For that I am some twelve or fourteen moon-
   shines
Lag of a brother? Why bastard? wherefore base?
When my dimensions are as well compact,
My mind as generous, and my shape as true,
As honest madam's issue? Why brand they us
With base? with baseness? bastardy? base, base?
Who, in the lusty stealth of nature, take
More composition and fierce quality
Than doth, within a dull, stale, tired bed,
Go to th'creating a whole tribe of fops,
Got 'tween asleep and wake?—Well, then,
Legitimate Edgar, I must have your land:
Our father's love is to the bastard Edmund
As to th'legitimate: fine word,—legitimate!
Well, my legitimate, if this letter speed,
And my invention thrive, Edmund the base

Shall top th'legitimate—I grow; I prosper:—
Now, gods, stand up for bastards!

Enter GLOSTER.

EARL OF GLOSTER.

Kent banisht thus! and France in choler parted!
And the king gone to-night! subscribed his
   power!
Confined to exhibition! All this done
Upon the gad!—Edmund, how now! what news?

EDMUND.

So please your lordship, none.

[Putting up the letter.

EARL OF GLOSTER.

Why so earnestly seek you to put up that letter?

EDMUND.

I know no news, my lord.

EARL OF GLOSTER.

What paper were you reading?

EDMUND.

Nothing, my lord.

EARL OF GLOSTER.

No? What needed, then, that terrible dispatch of
it into your pocket? the quality of nothing hath
not such need to hide itself. Let's see: come, if it
be nothing, I shall not need spectacles.

EDMUND.

I beseech you, sir, pardon me: it is a letter from
my brother, that I have not all o'er-read; and for
so much as I have perused, I find it not fit for
your o'er-looking.

EARL OF GLOSTER.

Give me the letter, sir.

EDMUND.

I shall offend, either to detain or give it. The contents, as in part I understand them, are to blame.

EARL OF GLOSTER

Let's see, let's see.

EDMUND.

I hope, for my brother's justification, he wrote
this but as an essay or taste of my virtue.

EARL OF GLOSTER [*reads*].

This policy and reverence of age makes the
world bitter to the best of our times; keeps our
fortunes from us till our oldness cannot relish
them. I begin to find an idle and fond bondage in
the oppression of aged tyranny; who sways, not
as it hath power, but as it is suffer'd. Come to me,
that of this I may speak more. If our father would
sleep till I waked him, you should enjoy half his
revenue for ever, and live the beloved of your
brother,   EDGAR.
Hum—conspiracy!—'Sleep till I waked him, you
should enjoy half his revenue!'—My son Edgar!
Had he a hand to write this? a heart and brain to
breed it in?—When came this to you? who
brought it?

EDMUND.

It was not brought me, my lord,—there's the cunning of it; I found it thrown in at the casement of
my closet.

EARL OF GLOSTER.

You know the character to be your brother's?

EDMUND.

If the matter were good, my lord, I durst swear it
were his; but, in respect of that, I would fain think
it were not.

EARL OF GLOSTER.

It is his.

EDMUND.

It is his hand, my lord; but I hope his heart is not
in the contents.

EARL OF GLOSTER.

Has he never before sounded you in this business?

EDMUND.

Never, my lord: but I have heard him oft maintain it to be fit, that, sons at perfect age, and
fathers declining, the father should be as ward to
the son, and the son manage his revenue.

EARL OF GLOSTER.

O villain, villain!—His very opinion in the letter!
—Abhorred villain! Unnatural, detested, brutish
villain! worse than brutish!—Go, sirrah, seek
him; I'll apprehend him:—abominable villain!
—Where is he?

EDMUND.

I do not well know, my lord. If it shall please you
to suspend your indignation against my brother
till you can derive from him better testimony of
his intent, you shall run a certain course; where,
if you violently proceed against him, mistaking
his purpose, it would make a great gap in your
own honour, and shake in pieces the heart of his
obedience. I dare pawn down my life for him,
that he hath writ this to feel my affection to your
honour, and to no other pretence of danger.

EARL OF GLOSTER.

Think you so?

EDMUND.

If your honour judge it meet, I will place you
where you shall hear us confer of this, and by an
auricular assurance have your satisfaction; and that
without any further delay than this very evening.

EARL OF GLOSTER.

He cannot be such a monster—

EDMUND.

Nor is not, sure.

EARL OF GLOSTER.

To his father, that so tenderly and entirely loves
him.—Heaven and earth!—Edmund, seek him
out; wind me into him, I pray you: frame the
business after your own wisdom. I would unstate
myself, to be in a due resolution.

EDMUND.

I will seek him, sir, presently; convey the business
as I shall find means, and acquaint you withal.

EARL OF GLOSTER.

These late eclipses in the sun and moon portend
no good to us: though the wisdom of nature can
reason it thus and thus, yet nature finds itself
scourged by the sequent effects: love cools, friendship falls off, brothers divide: in cities, mutinies,
in countries, discord; in palaces, treason; and the
bond crackt 'twixt son and father. This villain of
mine comes under the prediction; there's son
against father: the king falls from bias of nature;
there's father against child. We have seen the best
of our time: machinations, hollowness, treachery,
and all ruinous disorders, follow us disquietly to
our graves.—Find out this villain, Edmund; it
shall lose thee nothing; do it carefully.—And the
noble and true-hearted Kent banisht! his offence,
honesty!—'Tis strange.   *[Exit.*

EDMUND.

This is the excellent foppery of the world, that, when we are sick in fortune,—often the surfeit of our own behaviour,—we make guilty of our disasters the sun, the moon, and the stars: as if we were villains by necessity; fools by heavenly compulsion; knaves, thieves, and treachers, by spherical predominance; drunkards, liars, and adulterers, by an enforced obedience of planetary influence; and all that we are evil in, by a divine thrusting on: an admirable evasion of whoremaster man, to lay his goatish disposition to the charge of a star! My father compounded with my mother under the dragon's tail; and my nativity was under *ursa major*; so that it follows, I am rough and lecherous.—Fut, I should have been that I am, had the maidenliest star in the firmament twinkled on my bastardizing.—Edgar! pat he comes like the catastrophe of the old comedy: my cue is villainous melancholy, with a sigh like Tom o'Bedlam.

Enter EDGAR.

O, these eclipses do portend these divisions! fa, sol, la, mi.

EDGAR.

How now, brother Edmund! what serious contemplation are you in?

EDMUND.

I am thinking, brother, of a prediction I read this other day, what should follow these eclipses.

EDGAR.

Do you busy yourself with that?

EDMUND.

I promise you, the effects he writes of succeed unhappily; as of unnaturalness between the child and the parent; death, dearth, dissolutions of ancient amities; divisions in state, menaces and maledictions against king and nobles; needless diffidences, banishment of friends, dissipation of cohorts, nuptial breaches, and I know not what.

EDGAR.

How long have you been a sectary astronomical?

EDMUND.

Come, come; when saw you my father last?

EDGAR.

The night gone by.

EDMUND.

Spake you with him?

EDGAR.

Ay, two hours together.

EDMUND.

Parted you in good terms? Found you no displeasure in him by word nor countenance?

EDGAR.

None at all.

EDMUND.

Bethink yourself wherein you may have offended him: and at my entreaty forbear his presence till some little time hath qualified the heat of his displeasure; which at this instant so rageth in him, that with the mischief of your person it would scarcely allay.

EDGAR.

Some villain hath done me wrong.

EDMUND.

That's my fear. I pray you, have a continent forbearance till the speed of his rage goes slower; and, as I say, retire with me to my lodging, from whence I will fitly bring you to hear my lord speak: pray you, go; there's my key:—if you do stir abroad, go arm'd.

EDGAR.

Arm'd, brother!

EDMUND.

Brother, I advise you to the best; I am no honest man if there be any good meaning toward you: I have told you what I have seen and heard; but faintly, nothing like the image and horror of it: pray you, away.

EDGAR.

Shall I hear from you anon?

EDMUND.

I do serve you in this business.   [*Exit* EDGAR.

A credulous father! and a brother noble,
Whose nature is so far from doing harms,
That he suspects none; on whose foolish honesty
My practices ride easy!—I see the business.—
Let me, if not by birth, have lands by wit:
All with me's meet that I can fashion fit.   [*Exit.*

SCENE III.

The DUKE OF ALBANY'S *palace.*

Enter GONERIL *and* OSWALD, *her steward.*

GONERIL.

DID my father strike my gentleman for chiding of his fool?

OSWALD.

Ay, madam.

GONERIL.

By day and night, he wrongs me; every hour
He flashes into one gross crime or other,
That sets us all at odds: I'll not endure it:
His knights grow riotous, and himself upbraids us
On every trifle.—When he returns from hunting,
I will not speak with him; say I am sick:—
If you come slack of former services,
You shall do well; the fault of it I'll answer
                 [*Horns within.*

OSWALD.

He's coming, madam; I hear him.

GONERIL.

Put on what weary negligence you please,
You and your fellows; I'ld have it come to question:
If he distaste it, let him to my sister,
Whose mind and mine, I know, in that are one,
Not to be over-ruled. Idle old man,
That still would manage those authorities
That he hath given away!—Now, by my life,
Old fools are babes again; and must be used
With checks as flatteries, when they are seen abused.
Remember what I have said.

OSWALD.

            Very well, madam.

GONERIL.

And let his knights have colder looks among you;
What grows of it, no matter; advise your fellows so:

I would breed from hence occasions, and I shall,
That I may speak:—I'll write straight to my sister,
To hold my very course.—Prepare for dinner.
                          [*Exeunt.*

SCENE IV.
A hall in the same.
Enter KENT, *disguised.*
EARL OF KENT.
IF but as well I other accents borrow,
That can my speech defuse, my good intent
May carry through itself to that full issue
For which I razed my likeness.—Now, banisht Kent,
If thou canst serve where thou dost stand con-
    demn'd,
So may it come, thy master, whom thou lovest,
Shall find thee full of labours.
    Horns within. Enter LEAR, KNIGHTS, *and*
    ATTENDANTS.
KING LEAR.
Let me not stay a jot for dinner; go get it ready.
                          [*Exit an* ATTENDANT.
How now! what art thou?
EARL OF KENT.
A man, sir.
KING LEAR.
What dost thou profess? What wouldst thou with us?
EARL OF KENT.
I do profess to be no less than I seem; to serve him truly that will put me in trust; to love him that is honest; to converse with him that is wise, and says little; to fear judgement; to fight when I cannot choose; and to eat no fish.
KING LEAR.
What art thou?
EARL OF KENT.
A very honest-hearted fellow, and as poor as the king.
KING LEAR.
If thou be as poor for a subject as he is for a king, thou art poor enough. What wouldst thou?
EARL OF KENT.
Service.
KING LEAR.
Who wouldst thou serve?
EARL OF KENT.
You.
KING LEAR.
Dost thou know me, fellow?
EARL OF KENT.
No, sir; but you have that in your countenance which I would fain call master.
KING LEAR.
What's that?
EARL OF KENT.
Authority.
KING LEAR.
What services canst thou do?
EARL OF KENT.
I can keep honest counsel, ride, run, mar a curious tale in telling it, and deliver a plain message bluntly: that which ordinary men are fit for, I am qualified in; and the best of me is diligence.

KING LEAR.
How old art thou?
EARL OF KENT.
Not so young, sir, to love a woman for singing, nor so old to dote on her for any thing: I have years on my back forty-eight.
KING LEAR.
Follow me; thou shalt serve me: if I like thee no worse after dinner, I will not part from thee yet. —Dinner, ho, dinner!—Where's my knave? my fool?—Go you, and call my fool hither.
                          [*Exit an* ATTENDANT.
    Enter OSWALD.
You, you, sirrah, where's my daughter?
OSWALD.
So please you,—   [*Exit.*
KING LEAR.
What says the fellow there? Call the clotpoll back.
[*Exit a* KNIGHT.]—Where's my fool, ho?—I think the world's asleep.
    Enter KNIGHT.
How now! where's that mongrel?
KNIGHT.
He says, my lord, your daughter is not well.
KING LEAR.
Why came not the slave back to me when I call'd him?
KNIGHT.
Sir, he answer'd me in the roundest manner, he would not.
KING LEAR.
He would not!
KNIGHT.
My lord, I know not what the matter is; but, to my judgement, your highness is not entertain'd with that ceremonious affection as you were wont; there's a great abatement of kindness appears as well in the general dependants as in the duke him-self also and your daughter.
KING LEAR.
Ha! say'st thou so?
KNIGHT.
I beseech you, pardon me, my lord, if I be mis-taken; for my duty cannot be silent when I think your highness wrong'd.
KING LEAR.
Thou but rememberest me of mine own concep-tion: I have perceived a most faint neglect of late; which I have rather blamed as mine own jealous curiosity than as a very pretence and purpose of unkindness: I will look further into't. — But where's my fool? I have not seen him this two days.
KNIGHT.
Since my young lady's going into France, sir, the fool hath much pined away.
KING LEAR.
No more of that; I have noted it well.—Go you, and tell my daughter I would speak with her.
[*Exit an* ATTENDANT.]—Go you, call hither my fool.   [*Exit an* ATTENDANT.
    Enter OSWALD.
O, you sir, you, come you hither, sir: who am I, sir?
OSWALD.
My lady's father.

KING LEAR.

'My lady's father!' my lord's knave: you whoreson dog! you slave! you cur!

OSWALD.

I am none of these, my lord; I beseech your pardon.

KING LEAR.

Do you bandy looks with me, you rascal?

[Striking him.

OSWALD.

I'll not be struck, my lord.

EARL OF KENT.

Nor tript neither, you base football player.

[Tripping up his heels.

KING LEAR.

I thank thee, fellow; thou servest me, and I'll love thee.

EARL OF KENT.

Come, sir, arise, away! I'll teach you differences: away, away! If you will measure your lubber's length again, tarry: but away! go to; have you wisdom? so.   [Pushes OSWALD out.

KING LEAR.

Now, my friendly knave, I thank thee: there's earnest of thy service.   [Giving KENT money.

Enter FOOL.

FOOL.

Let me hire him too:—here's my coxcomb.

[Offering KENT his cap.

KING LEAR.

How now, my pretty knave! how dost thou?

FOOL.

Sirrah, you were best take my coxcomb.

EARL OF KENT.

Why, fool?

FOOL.

Why, for taking one's part that's out of favour: nay, an thou canst not smile as the wind sits, thou'lt catch cold shortly: there, take my coxcomb: why, this fellow hath banisht two on's daughters, and did the third a blessing against his will; if thou follow him, thou must needs wear my coxcomb.—How now, nuncle! Would I had two coxcombs and two daughters!

KING LEAR.

Why, my boy?

FOOL.

If I gave them all my living, I'd keep my coxcombs myself. There's mine; beg another of thy daughters.

KING LEAR.

Take heed, sirrah,—the whip.

FOOL.

Truth's a dog must to kennel; he must be whipt out, when Lady the brach may stand by the fire and stink.

KING LEAR.

A pestilent gall to me!

FOOL.

Sirrah, I'll teach thee a speech.

KING LEAR.

Do.

FOOL.

Mark it, nuncle;
   Have more than thou showest,
   Speak less than thou knowest,

Lend less than thou owest,
Ride more than thou goest,
Learn more than thou trowest,
Set less than thou throwest;
Leave thy drink and thy whore,
   And keep in-a-door,
   And thou shalt have more
Than two tens to a score.

EARL OF KENT.

This is nothing, fool.

FOOL.

Then 'tis like the breath of an unfee'd lawyer,—you gave me nothing for't.—Can you make no use of nothing, nuncle?

KING LEAR.

Why, no, boy; nothing can be made out of nothing.

FOOL [to EARL OF KENT].

Prithee, tell him, so much the rent of his land comes to: he will not believe a fool.

KING LEAR.

A bitter fool!

FOOL.

Dost thou know the difference, my boy, between a bitter fool and a sweet fool?

KING LEAR.

No, lad; teach me.

FOOL.

   That lord that counsell'd thee
      To give away thy land,
   Come place him here by me,—
      Do thou for him stand:
   The sweet and bitter fool
      Will presently appear;
   The one in motley here,
      The other found out there.

KING LEAR.

Dost thou call me fool, boy?

FOOL.

All thy other titles thou hast given away; that thou wast born with.

EARL OF KENT.

This is not altogether fool, my lord.

FOOL.

No, faith, lords and great men will not let me; if I had a monopoly out, they would have part on't: and ladies too, they will not let me have all fool to myself; they'll be snatching.—Give me an egg, nuncle, and I'll give thee two crowns.

KING LEAR.

What two crowns shall they be?

FOOL.

Why, after I have cut the egg i'th'middle, and eat up the meat, the two crowns of the egg. When thou clovest thy crown i'th'middle, and gavest away both parts, thou borest thine ass on thy back o'er the dirt: thou hadst little wit in thy bald crown, when thou gavest thy golden one away. If I speak like myself in this, let him be whipt that first finds it so.   [Singing.

   Fools had ne'er less grace in a year;
      For wise men are grown foppish,
   And know not how their wits to wear,
      Their manners are so apish.

KING LEAR.

When were you wont to be so full of songs, sirrah?

FOOL.

I have used it, nuncle, ever since thou madest thy
daughters thy mothers: for when thou gavest
them the rod, and putt'st down thine own
breeches,   [*Singing.*

    Then they for sudden joy did weep,
      And I for sorrow sung,
    That such a king should play bo-peep,
      And go the fools among.

Prithee, nuncle, keep a schoolmaster that can
teach thy fool to lie: I would fain learn to lie.

KING LEAR.

An you lie, sirrah, we'll have you whipt.

FOOL.

I marvel what kin thou and thy daughters are:
they'll have me whipt for speaking true, thou'lt
have me whipt for lying; and sometimes I am
whipt for holding my peace. I had rather be any
kind o'thing than a fool: and yet I would not be
thee, nuncle; thou hast pared thy wit o'both
sides, and left nothing i'th'middle:—here comes
one o'th'parings.

Enter GONERIL.

KING LEAR.

How now, daughter! what makes that frontlet on?
Methinks you are too much of late i'th'frown.

FOOL.

Thou wast a pretty fellow when thou hadst no
need to care for her frowning; now thou art an O
without a figure: I am better than thou art now; I
am a fool, thou art nothing.—[*to* GONERIL] Yes,
forsooth, I will hold my tongue; so your face bids
me, though you say nothing.

    Mum, mum:
    He that keeps nor crust nor crum,
      Weary of all, shall want some.—

That's a sheal'd peascod.   [*Pointing to* LEAR.

GONERIL.

Not only, sir, this your all-licensed fool,
But other of your insolent retinue
Do hourly carp and quarrel; breaking forth
In rank and not-to-be-endured riots. Sir,
I had thought, by making this well known unto
    you,
To have found a safe redress; but now grow
    fearful,
By what yourself too late have spoke and done,
That you protect this course, and put it on
By your allowance; which if you should, the fault
Would not scape censure, nor the redresses sleep,
Which, in the tender of a wholesome weal,
Might in their working do you that offence,
Which else were shame, that then necessity
Will call discreet proceeding.

FOOL.

For, you trow, nuncle,
    The hedge-sparrow fed the cuckoo so long,
    That it had its head bit off by its young.
So, out went the candle, and we were left dark-
    ling.

KING LEAR.

Are you our daughter?

GONERIL.

Come, sir,
I would you would make use of that good wisdom
Whereof I know you are fraught; and put away

These dispositions, that of late transform you
From what you rightly are.

FOOL.

May not an ass know when the cart draws the
horse?—Whoop, Jug! I love thee.

KING LEAR.

Doth any here know me?—Why, this is not Lear:
Doth Lear walk thus? speak thus? Where are his
    eyes?
Either his notion weakens, or his discernings
Are lethargied—Ha! waking? 'tis not so.—
Who is it that can tell me who I am?—

FOOL.

Lear's shadow.

KING LEAR.

I would learn that; for, by the marks of sove-
    reignty,
Knowledge, and reason, I should be false-per-
    suaded
I had daughters.

FOOL.

Which they will make an obedient father.

KING LEAR.

Your name, fair gentlewoman?

GONERIL.

This admiration, sir, is much o'th'savour
Of other your new pranks. I do beseech you
To understand my purposes aright:
As you are old and reverend, should be wise.
Here do you keep a hundred knights and squires;
Men so disorder'd, so debosht, and bold,
That this our court, infected with their manners,
Shows like a riotous inn: epicurism and lust
Makes it more like a tavern or a brothel
Than a graced palace. The shame itself doth
    speak
For instant remedy: be, then, desired
By her, that else will take the thing she begs,
A little to disquantity your train;
And the remainder, that shall still depend,
To be such men as may besort your age,
Which know themselves and you.

KING LEAR.

                Darkness and devils!—
Saddle my horses; call my train together.—
Degenerate bastard! I'll not trouble thee:
Yet have I left a daughter.

GONERIL.

You strike my people; and your disorder'd rabble
Make servants of their betters.

Enter ALBANY.

KING LEAR.

Woe, that too late repents,—[*to* ALBANY] O, sir,
    are you come?
Is it your will? Speak, sir.—Prepare my horses.—
Ingratitude, thou marble-hearted fiend,
More hideous when thou show'st thee in a child
Than the sea-monster!

DUKE OF ALBANY.

            Pray, sir, be patient.

KING LEAR [*to* GONERIL].

Detested kite! thou liest:
My train are men of choice and rarest parts,
That all particulars of duty know,
And in the most exact regard support
The worships of their name.—O most small fault,

How ugly didst thou in Cordelia show!
Which, like an engine, wrencht my frame of
   nature
From the fixt place; drew from my heart all love,
And added to the gall. O Lear, Lear, Lear!
Beat at this gate, that let thy folly in,
                            [Striking his head.
And thy dear judgement out!—Go, go, my people.

DUKE OF ALBANY.
My lord, I am guiltless, as I am ignorant
Of what hath moved you.

KING LEAR.
                It may be so, my lord.—
Hear, nature, hear; dear goddess, hear!
Suspend thy purpose, if thou didst intend
To make this creature fruitful!
Into her womb convey sterility!
Dry up in her the organs of increase;
And from her derogate body never spring
A babe to honour her! If she must teem,
Create her child of spleen; that it may live,
And be a thwart disnatured torment to her!
Let it stamp wrinkles in her brow of youth;
With cadent tears fret channels in her cheeks;
Turn all her mother's pains and benefits
To laughter and contempt,—that she may feel
How sharper than a serpent's tooth it is
To have a thankless child!—Away, away!   *[Exit.*

DUKE OF ALBANY.
Now, gods that we adore, whereof comes this?

GONERIL.
Never afflict yourself to know the cause;
But let his disposition have that scope
That dotage gives it.
             Enter LEAR.

KING LEAR.
What, fifty of my followers at a clap!
Within a fortnight!

DUKE OF ALBANY.
            What's the matter, sir?

KING LEAR.
I'll tell thee.—*[to* GONERIL] Life and death! I am
   ashamed
That thou hast power to shake my manhood thus;
That these hot tears, which break from me per-
   force,
Should make thee worth them.—Blasts and fogs
   upon thee!
Th'untented woundings of a father's curse
Pierce every sense about thee!—Old fond eyes,
Beweep this cause again, I'll pluck ye out,
And cast you, with the waters that you lose,
To temper clay.—Yea, is it come to this?
Let it be so:—I have another daughter,
Who, I am sure, is kind and comfortable:
When she shall hear this of thee, with her nails
She'll flay thy wolvish visage. Thou shalt find
That I'll resume the shape which thou dost think
I have cast off for ever; thou shalt, I warrant
   thee.
    [Exeunt LEAR, KENT, *and* ATTENDANTS.

GONERIL.
Do you mark that, my lord?

DUKE OF ALBANY.
I cannot be so partial, Goneril,
To the great love I bear you,—

GONERIL.
Pray you, content.—What, Oswald, ho!—
[to the FOOL] You, sir, more knave than fool, after
   your master.

FOOL.
Nuncle Lear, nuncle Lear, tarry, and take the
fool with thee.—
       A fox, when one has caught her,
       And such a daughter,
       Should sure to the slaughter,
       If my cap would buy a halter:
       So the fool follows after.   *[Exit.*

GONERIL.
This man hath had good counsel:—a hundred
   knights!
'Tis politic and safe to let him keep   [dream,
At point a hundred knights: yes, that, on every
Each buzz, each fancy, each complaint, dislike,
He may enguard his dotage with their powers,
And hold our lives in mercy.—Oswald, I say!—

DUKE OF ALBANY.
Well, you may fear too far.

GONERIL.
           Safer than trust too far:
Let me still take away the harms I fear,
Not fear still to be taken: I know his heart.
What he hath utter'd I have writ my sister:
If she sustain him and his hundred knights,
When I have show'd th'unfitness,—
          Enter OSWALD.
               How now, Oswald!
What, have you writ that letter to my sister?

OSWALD.
Ay, madam.

GONERIL.
Take you some company, and away to horse:
Inform her full of my particular fear;
And thereto add such reasons of your own
As may compact it more. Get you gone;
And hasten your return. [*Exit* OSWALD.] No, no,
   my lord,
This milky gentleness and course of yours,
Though I condemn not, yet, under pardon,
You are much more attaskt for want of wisdom
Than praised for harmful mildness.

DUKE OF ALBANY.
How far your eyes may pierce I cannot tell:
Striving to better, oft we mar what's well.

GONERIL.
Nay, then—

DUKE OF ALBANY.
Well, well; the event.   *[Exeunt.*

SCENE V.
Court before the same.

Enter LEAR, KENT, *and* FOOL.

KING LEAR.
GO you before to Gloster with these letters.
Acquaint my daughter no further with any
thing you know than comes from her demand out
of the letter. If your diligence be not speedy, I
shall be there afore you.

EARL OF KENT.
I will not sleep, my lord, till I have deliver'd
your letter.   *[Exit.*

FOOL.

If a man's brains were in's heels, were't not in danger of kibes?

KING LEAR.

Ay, boy.

FOOL.

Then, I prithee, be merry; thy wit shall ne'er go slip-shod.

KING LEAR.

Ha, ha, ha!

FOOL.

Shalt see thy other daughter will use thee kindly; for though she's as like this as a crab's like an apple, yet I can tell what I can tell.

KING LEAR.

What canst tell, boy?

FOOL.

She will taste as like this as a crab does to a crab. Thou canst tell why one's nose stands i'th'middle on's face?

KING LEAR.

No.

FOOL.

Why, to keep one's eyes of either side's nose; that what a man cannot smell out, he may spy into.

KING LEAR.

I did her wrong—

FOOL.

Canst tell how an oyster makes his shell?

KING LEAR.

No.

FOOL.

Nor I neither; but I can tell why a snail has a house.

KING LEAR.

Why?

FOOL.

Why, to put's head in; not to give it away to his daughters, and leave his horns without a case.

KING LEAR.

I will forget my nature.—So kind a father!—Be my horses ready?

FOOL.

Thy asses are gone about 'em. The reason why the seven stars are no more than seven is a pretty reason.

KING LEAR.

Because they are not eight?

FOOL.

Yes, indeed: thou wouldst make a good fool.

KING LEAR.

To take't again perforce!—Monster ingratitude!

FOOL.

If thou wert my fool, nuncle, I'ld have thee beaten for being old before thy time.

KING LEAR.

How's that?

FOOL.

Thou shouldst not have been old till thou hadst been wise.

KING LEAR.

O, let me not be mad, not mad, sweet heaven! Keep me in temper: I would not be mad!

Enter GENTLEMAN.

How now! are the horses ready?

GENTLEMAN.

Ready, my lord.

KING LEAR.

Come, boy.

FOOL.

She that's a maid now, and laughs at my departure,
Shall not be a maid long, unless things be cut shorter.   [*Exeunt.*

ACT II. SCENE I.

A court within the castle of the EARL OF GLOSTER.

Enter EDMUND *and* CURAN, *meeting.*

EDMUND.

SAVE thee, Curan.

CURAN.

And you, sir. I have been with your father, and given him notice that the Duke of Cornwall and Regan his duchess will be here with him this night.

EDMUND.

How comes that?

CURAN.

Nay, I know not.—You have heard of the news abroad,—I mean the whisper'd ones, for they are yet but ear-kissing arguments?

EDMUND.

Not I: pray you, what are they?

CURAN.

Have you heard of no likely wars toward 'twixt the Dukes of Cornwall and Albany?

EDMUND.

Not a word.

CURAN.

You may do, then, in time. Fare you well, sir.
                                        [*Exit.*

EDMUND.

The duke be here to-night? The better! best!
This weaves itself perforce into my business.
My father hath set guard to take my brother;
And I have one thing, of a queasy question,
Which I must act:—briefness and fortune, work!—
Brother, a word;—descend:—brother, I say!

Enter EDGAR.

My father watches:—O sir, fly this place;
Intelligence is given where you are hid;
You have now the good advantage of the night:—
Have you not spoken 'gainst the Duke of Cornwall?
He's coming hither; now, i'th'night, i'th'haste,
And Regan with him: have you nothing said
Upon his party 'gainst the Duke of Albany?
Advise yourself.

EDGAR.

I am sure on't, not a word.

EDMUND.

I hear my father coming:—pardon me;
In cunning I must draw my sword upon you:—
Draw: seem to defend yourself: now quit you well.—
Yield:—come before my father.—Light, ho, here!
Fly, brother.—Torches, torches!—So, farewell.
                                [*Exit* EDGAR.

Some blood drawn on me would beget opinion
　　　　　　[*Wounds his arm.*
Of my more fierce endeavour: I have seen drunk-
ards
Do more than this in sport.—Father, father!—
Stop, stop!—No help?

Enter GLOSTER, *and* SERVANTS *with torches.*

EARL OF GLOSTER.
　　　　Now, Edmund, where's the villain?
EDMUND.
Here stood he in the dark, his sharp sword out,
Mumbling of wicked charms, conjuring the moon
To stand's auspicious mistress,—
EARL OF GLOSTER.
　　　　　　　　But where is he?
EDMUND.
Look, sir, I bleed.
EARL OF GLOSTER.
　　　　　Where is the villain, Edmund?
EDMUND.
Fled this way, sir. When by no means he could—
EARL OF GLOSTER.
Pursue him, ho!—Go after. [*Exeunt some* SER-
VANTS.]—By no means what?
EDMUND.
Persuade me to the murder of your lordship;
But that I told him the revenging gods
'Gainst parricides did all their thunders bend;
Spoke with how manifold and strong a bond
The child was bound to th'father;—sir, in fine,
Seeing how loathly opposite I stood
To his unnatural purpose, in fell motion,
With his prepared sword he charges home
My unprovided body, lanced mine arm:
But when he saw my best alarum'd spirits,
Bold in the quarrel's right, roused to th'encoun-
ter,
Or whether gasted by the noise I made,
Full suddenly he fled.
EARL OF GLOSTER.
　　　　Let him fly far:
Not in this land shall he remain uncaught;
And found—dispatch. The noble duke my
master,
My worthy arch and patron, comes to-night:
By his authority I will proclaim it,
That he which finds him shall deserve our
thanks,
Bringing the murderous coward to the stake;
He that conceals him, death.
EDMUND.
When I dissuaded him from his intent,
And found him pight to do it, with curst speech
I threaten'd to discover him: he replied,
'Thou unpossessing bastard! dost thou think,
If I would stand against thee, would the reposal
Of any trust, virtue, or worth, in thee
Make thy words faith'd? No: what I should
deny,—
As this I would; ay, though thou didst produce
My very character,—I'ld turn it all
To thy suggestion, plot, and damned practice:
And thou must make a dullard of the world,
If they not thought the profits of my death
Were very pregnant and potential spurs
To make thee seek it.'

EARL OF GLOSTER.
　　　　　Strong and fasten'd villain!
Would he deny his letter?—I never got him.—
　　　　　　[*Tucket within.*
Hark, the duke's trumpets! I know not why he
comes.—
All ports I'll bar; the villain shall not scape;
The duke must grant me that: besides, his picture
I will send far and near, that all the kingdom
May have due note of him; and of my land,
Loyal and natural boy, I'll work the means
To make thee capable.

Enter CORNWALL, REGAN, *and* ATTENDANTS.

DUKE OF CORNWALL.
How now, my noble friend! since I came hither,—
Which I can call but now,—I have heard strange
news.
REGAN.
If it be true, all vengeance comes too short
Which can pursue th' offender. How dost, my
lord?
EARL OF GLOSTER.
O madam, my old heart is crackt, is crackt!
REGAN.
What, did my father's godson seek your life?
He whom my father named? your Edgar?
DUKE OF GLOSTER.
O lady, lady, shame would have it hid!
REGAN.
Was he not companion with the riotous knights
That tend upon my father?
EARL OF GLOSTER.
I know not, madam:—'tis too bad, too bad.
EDMUND.
Yes, madam, he was of that consort.
REGAN.
No marvel, then, though he were ill affected:
'Tis they have put him on the old man's death,
To have th'expense and waste of his revenues.
I have this present evening from my sister
Been well inform'd of them; and with such
cautions,
That if they come to sojourn at my house,
I'll not be there.
DUKE OF CORNWALL.
　　　　Nor I, assure thee, Regan.—
Edmund, I hear that you have shown your father
A child-like office.
EDMUND.
　　　　'Twas my duty, sir.
EARL OF GLOSTER.
He did bewray his practice: and received
This hurt you see, striving to apprehend him.
DUKE OF CORNWALL.
Is he pursued?
EARL OF GLOSTER.
　　　　Ay, my good lord.
DUKE OF CORNWALL.
If he be taken, he shall never more
Be fear'd of doing harm: make your own purpose,
How in my strength you please.—For you,
Edmund,
Whose virtue and obedience doth this instant
So much commend itself, you shall be ours:
Nature of such deep trust we shall much need;
You we first seize on.

EDMUND.
I shall serve you, sir,
Truly, however else.
EARL OF GLOSTER.
For him I thank your Grace.
DUKE OF CORNWALL.
You know not why we came to visit you,—
REGAN.
Thus out of season, threading dark-eyed night:
Occasions, noble Gloster, of some poise,
Wherein we must have use of your advice:—
Our father he hath writ, so hath our sister,
Of differences, which I best thought it fit
To answer from our home; the several messengers
From hence attend dispatch. Our good old friend,
Lay comforts to your bosom; and bestow
Your needful counsel to our business,
Which craves the instant use.
EARL OF GLOSTER.
I serve you, madam:
Your Graces are right welcome.   [*Exeunt.*

SCENE II.

Before GLOSTER'S *castle.*

Enter KENT *and* OSWALD, *severally.*

OSWALD.
GOOD dawning to thee, friend: art of this house?
EARL OF KENT.
Ay.
OSWALD.
Where may we set our horses?
EARL OF KENT.
I'the mire.
OSWALD.
Prithee, if thou lovest me, tell me.
EARL OF KENT.
I love thee not.
OSWALD.
Why, then, I care not for thee.
EARL OF KENT.
If I had thee in Lipsbury pinfold, I would make
thee care for me.
OSWALD.
Why dost thou use me thus? I know thee not.
EARL OF KENT.
Fellow, I know thee.
OSWALD.
What dost thou know me for?
EARL OF KENT.
A knave; a rascal; an eater of broken meats; a
base, proud, shallow, beggarly, three-suited,
hundred-pound, filthy, worsted-stocking knave;
a lily-liver'd, action-taking, whoreson, glass-
gazing, superserviceable, finical rogue; one-
trunk-inheriting slave; one that wouldst be a
bawd in way of good service, and art nothing but
the composition of a knave, beggar, coward,
pandar, and the son and heir of a mongrel bitch:
one whom I will beat into clamorous whining, if
thou deniest the least syllable of thy addition.
OSWALD.
Why, what a monstrous fellow art thou, thus to
rail on one that is neither known of thee nor
knows thee!

EARL OF KENT.
What a brazen-faced varlet art thou, to deny thou
knowest me! Is it two days since I tript up thy
heels, and beat thee, before the king? Draw, you
rogue: for, though it be night, yet the moon
shines; I'll make a sop o'the moonshine of you:
draw, you whoreson cullionly barbermonger,
draw.   [*Drawing his sword.*
OSWALD.
Away! I have nothing to do with thee.
EARL OF KENT.
Draw, you rascal: you come with letters against
the king; and take Vanity the puppet's part against
the royalty of her father: draw, you rogue, or I'll
so carbonado your shanks:—draw, you rascal;
come your ways.
OSWALD.
Help, ho! murder! help!
EARL OF KENT.
Strike, you slave; stand, rogue, stand; you neat
slave, strike.   [*Beating him.*
OSWALD.
Help, ho! murder! murder!
Enter EDMUND, *with his rapier drawn.*
EDMUND.
How now! What's the matter?   [*Parts them.*
EARL OF KENT.
With you, goodman boy, an you please: come,
I'll flesh you; come on, young master.
Enter CORNWALL, REGAN, GLOSTER, *and*
SERVANTS.
EARL OF GLOSTER.
Weapons! arms! What's the matter here?
DUKE OF CORNWALL.
Keep peace, upon your lives;
He dies that strikes again. What is the matter?
REGAN.
The messengers from our sister and the king.
DUKE OF CORNWALL.
What is your difference? speak.
OSWALD.
I am scarce in breath, my lord.
EARL OF KENT.
No marvel, you have so bestirr'd your valour.
You cowardly rascal, nature disclaims in thee: a
tailor made thee.
DUKE OF CORNWALL.
Thou art a strange fellow: a tailor make a man?
EARL OF KENT.
Ay, a tailor, sir: a stone-cutter or a painter could
not have made him so ill, though they had been
but two hours at the trade.
DUKE OF CORNWALL.
Speak yet, how grew your quarrel?
OSWALD.
This ancient ruffian, sir, whose life I have spared
at suit of his gray beard,—
EARL OF KENT.
Thou whoreson zed! thou unnecessary letter!—
My lord, if you will give me leave, I will tread
this unbolted villain into mortar, and daub the
wall of a jakes with him.—'Spare my gray beard,'
you wagtail?
DUKE OF CORNWALL.
Peace, sirrah!
You beastly knave, know you no reverence?

EARL OF KENT.
Yes, sir; but anger hath a privilege.

DUKE OF CORNWALL.
Why art thou angry?

EARL OF KENT.
That such a slave as this should wear a sword,
Who wears no honesty. Such smiling rogues as
these,
Like rats, oft bite the holy cords a-twain
Which are too intrinse t'unloose; smooth every
passion
That in the natures of their lords rebel,
Bring oil to fire, snow to their colder moods;
Renege, affirm, and turn their halcyon beaks
With every gale and vary of their masters,
Knowing naught, like dogs, but following.—
A plague upon your epileptic visage!
Smile you my speeches, as I were a fool?
Goose, if I had you upon Sarum plain,
I'ld drive ye cackling home to Camelot.

DUKE OF CORNWALL.
What, art thou mad, old fellow?

EARL OF GLOSTER.
How fell you out? say that.

EARL OF KENT.
No contraries hold more antipathy
Than I and such a knave.

DUKE OF CORNWALL.
Why dost thou call him knave? What's his
offence?

EARL OF KENT.
His countenance likes me not.

DUKE OF CORNWALL.
No more, perchance, does mine, nor his, nor
hers.

EARL OF KENT.
Sir, 'tis my occupation to be plain:
I have seen better faces in my time
Than stands on any shoulder that I see
Before me at this instant.

DUKE OF CORNWALL.
　　　　　　　This is some fellow,
Who, having been praised for bluntness, doth
affect
A saucy roughness, and constrains the garb
Quite from his nature: he cannot flatter, he,—
An honest mind and plain,—he must speak truth!
An they will take it, so; if not, he's plain.
These kind of knaves I know, which in this plain-
ness
Harbour more craft and more corrupter ends
Than twenty silly-ducking observants
That stretch their duties nicely.

EARL OF KENT.
Sir, in good sooth, in sincere verity,
Under the allowance of your great aspect,
Whose influence, like the wreath of radiant fire
On flickering Phœbus' front,—

DUKE OF CORNWALL.
　　　　　　What mean'st by this?

EARL OF KENT.
To go out of my dialect, which you discommend
so much. I know, sir, I am no flatterer: he that
beguiled you in a plain accent was a plain knave;
which, for my part, I will not be, though I should
win your displeasure to entreat me to't.

DUKE OF CORNWALL.
What was the offence you gave him?

OSWALD.
I never gave him any:
It pleased the king his master very late
To strike at me, upon his misconstruction;
When he, conjunct, and flattering his displeasure,
Tript me behind; being down, insulted, rail'd,
And put upon him such a deal of man,
That worthied him, got praises of the king
For him attempting who was self-subdued;
And, in the fleshment of this dread exploit,
Drew on me here again.

EARL OF KENT.
　　　　　None of these rogues and cowards
But Ajax is their fool.

DUKE OF CORNWALL.
　　　　　Fetch forth the stocks!—
You stubborn ancient knave, you reverend brag-
gart,
We'll teach you—

EARL OF KENT.
Sir, I am too old to learn:
Call not your stocks for me: I serve the king;
On whose employment I was sent to you:
You shall do small respect, show too bold malice
Against the grace and person of my master,
Stocking his messenger.

DUKE OF CORNWALL.
Fetch forth the stocks!—As I have life and honour,
There shall he sit till noon.

REGAN.
Till noon! till night, my lord; and all night too.

EARL OF KENT.
Why, madam, if I were your father's dog,
You should not use me so.

REGAN.
　　　　　Sir, being his knave, I will.

DUKE OF CORNWALL.
This is a fellow of the self-same colour
Our sister speaks of.—Come, bring away the
stocks!　　　　　[Stocks brought out.

EARL OF GLOSTER.
Let me beseech your Grace not to do so:
His fault is much, and the good king his master
Will check him for't: your purposed low correc-
tion
Is such as basest and contemned'st wretches
For pilferings and most common trespasses
Are punish'd with: the king must take it ill,
That he, so slightly valued in his messenger,
Should have him thus restrain'd.

DUKE OF CORNWALL.
　　　　　　　I'll answer that.

REGAN.
My sister may receive it much more worse,
To have her gentleman abused, assaulted,
For following her affairs.—Put in his legs.—
　　　　　　[KENT is put in the stocks.
Come, my good lord, away.
　　　　　[Exeunt all but GLOSTER and KENT.

EARL OF GLOSTER.
I am sorry for thee, friend; 'tis the duke's pleas-
ure,
Whose disposition, all the world well knows,
Will not be rubb'd nor stopt: I'll entreat for thee.

EARL OF KENT.

Pray, do not, sir: I have watcht, and travell'd hard;
Some time I shall sleep out, the rest I'll whistle.
A good man's fortune may grow out at heels:
Give you good morrow!

EARL OF GLOSTER.

The duke's to blame in this; 'twill be ill taken.

                       [*Exit.*

EARL OF KENT.

Good king, that must approve the common saw,—
Thou out of heaven's benediction comest
To the warm sun!
Approach, thou beacon to this under globe,
That by thy comfortable beams I may
Peruse this letter!—Nothing almost sees miracles
But misery:—I know 'tis from Cordelia,
Who hath most fortunately been inform'd
Of my obscured course; and shall find time
From this enormous state, seeking to give
Losses their remedies.—All weary and o'er-watcht,
Take vantage, heavy eyes, not to behold
This shameful lodging.
Fortune, good night: smile once more; turn thy
    wheel!   [*Sleeps.*

SCENE III.

The open country.

Enter EDGAR.

EDGAR.

I HEARD myself proclaim'd;
    And by the happy hollow of a tree
Escaped the hunt. No port is free; no place,
That guard, and most unusual vigilance,
Does not attend my taking. While I may scape,
I will preserve myself: and am bethought
To take the basest and most poorest shape
That ever penury, in contempt of man,
Brought near to beast: my face I'll grime with filth;
Blanket my loins; elf all my hair in knots;
And with presented nakedness out-face
The winds and persecutions of the sky.
The country gives me proof and precedent
Of Bedlam beggars, who, with roaring voices,
Strike in their numb'd and mortified bare arms
Pins, wooden pricks, nails, sprigs of rosemary;
And with this horrible object, from low farms,
Poor pelting villages, sheep-cotes, and mills,
Sometime with lunatic bans, sometime with pray-
    ers,
Enforce their charity.—'Poor Turlygod! poor
    Tom!'
That's something yet:—Edgar I nothing am. [*Exit.*

SCENE IV.

Before GLOSTER'S *castle;* KENT *in the stocks.*

Enter LEAR, FOOL, *and* GENTLEMAN.

KING LEAR.

'TIS strange that they should so depart from
    home,
And not send back my messenger.

GENTLEMAN.

                       As I learn'd,
The night before there was no purpose in them
Of this remove.

EARL OF KENT.

Hail to thee, noble master!

KING LEAR.

Ha!
Makest thou this shame thy pastime?

EARL OF KENT.

                       No, my lord.

FOOL.

Ha, ha! he wears cruel garters. Horses are tied by
the heads, dogs and bears by the neck, monkeys
by the loins, and men by the legs: when a man's
over-lusty at legs, then he wears wooden netherstocks.

KING LEAR.

What's he that hath so much thy place mistook
To set thee here?

EARL OF KENT.

                    It is both he and she,—
Your son and daughter.

KING LEAR.

No.

EARL OF KENT.

Yes.

KING LEAR.

No, I say.

EARL OF KENT.

I say, yea.

KING LEAR.

No, no, they would not.

EARL OF KENT.

Yes, they have.

KING LEAR.

By Jupiter, I swear, no.

EARL OF KENT.

By Juno, I swear, ay.

KING LEAR.

                They durst not do't;
They could not, would not do't; 'tis worse than
    murder,
To do upon respect such violent outrage:
Resolve me, with all modest haste, which way
Thou mightst deserve, or they impose, this
    usage,
Coming from us.

EARL OF KENT.

                My lord, when at their home
I did commend your highness' letters to them,
Ere I was risen from the place that show'd
My duty kneeling, came there a reeking post,
Stew'd in his haste, half breathless, panting forth
From Goneril his mistress salutations;
Deliver'd letters, spite of intermission,
Which presently they read: on whose contents,
They summon'd up their meiny, straight took
    horse;
Commanded me to follow, and attend
The leisure of their answer; gave me cold looks:
And meeting here the other messenger,
Whose welcome, I perceived, had poison'd
    mine,—
Being the very fellow which of late
Display'd so saucily against your highness,—
Having more man than wit about me, drew:
He raised the house with loud and coward cries.
Your son and daughter found this trespass worth
The shame which here it suffers.

FOOL.

Winter's not gone yet, if the wild-geese fly that way.

> Fathers that wear rags
> Do make their children blind;
> But fathers that bear bags
> Shall see their children kind.
> Fortune, that arrant whore,
> Ne'er turns the key to the poor.—

But, for all this, thou shalt have as many dolours for thy daughters as thou canst tell in a year.

KING LEAR.

O, how this mother swells up toward my heart!
Hysterica passio,—down, thou climbing sorrow,
Thy element's below!—Where is this daughter?

EARL OF KENT.

With the earl, sir, here within.

KING LEAR.

            Follow me not;
Stay here.   [*Exit.*

GENTLEMAN.

Made you no more offence but what you speak of?

EARL OF KENT.

None.

How chance the king comes with so small a train?

FOOL.

An thou hadst been set i'the stocks for that question, thou hadst well deserved it.

EARL OF KENT.

Why, fool?

FOOL.

We'll set thee to school to an ant, to teach thee there's no labouring i'the winter. All that follow their noses are led by their eyes but blind men; and there's not a nose among twenty but can smell him that's stinking. Let go thy hold when a great wheel runs down a hill, lest it break thy neck with following it; but the great one that goes up the hill, let him draw thee after. When a wise man gives thee better counsel, give me mine again: I would have none but knaves follow it, since a fool gives it.

> That sir which serves and seeks for gain,
> And follows but for form,
> Will pack when it begins to rain,
> And leave thee in the storm.
> But I will tarry; the fool will stay,
> And let the wise man fly:
> The knave turns fool that runs away;
> The fool no knave, perdy.

EARL OF KENT.

Where learn'd you this, fool?

FOOL.

Not i'the stocks, fool.

Enter LEAR *with* GLOSTER.

KING LEAR.

Deny to speak with me? They are sick? they are weary?
They have travell'd all the night? Mere fetches;
The images of revolt and flying-off.
Fetch me a better answer.

EARL OF GLOSTER.

            My dear lord,
You know the fiery quality of the duke;
How unremovable and fixt he is
In his own course.

KING LEAR.

Vengeance! plague! death! confusion!—
Fiery? what quality? Why, Gloster, Gloster,
I'ld speak with the Duke of Cornwall and his wife.

EARL OF GLOSTER.

Well, my good lord, I have inform'd them so.

KING LEAR.

Inform'd them! Dost thou understand me, man?

EARL OF GLOSTER.

Ay, my good lord.

KING LEAR.

The king would speak with Cornwall; the dear father
Would with his daughter speak, commands her service:
Are they inform'd of this?—My breath and blood!—
Fiery! the fiery duke!—Tell the hot duke that—
No, but not yet:—may be he is not well:
Infirmity doth still neglect all office
Whereto our health is bound; we are not ourselves
When nature, being opprest, commands the mind
To suffer with the body; I'll forbear;
And am faln out with my more headier will,
To take the indisposed and sickly fit
For the sound man.—Death on my state! where-
     fore   [*Looking on* KENT.
Should he sit here? This act persuades me
That this remotion of the duke and her
Is practice only. Give me my servant forth.
Go tell the duke and's wife I'ld speak with them,
Now, presently: bid them come forth and hear me,
Or at their chamber-door I'll beat the drum
Till it cry sleep to death.

EARL OF GLOSTER.

I would have all well betwixt you.   [*Exit.*

KING LEAR.

O me, my heart, my rising heart!—but, down!

FOOL.

Cry to it, nuncle, as the cockney did to the eels when she put 'em i'the paste alive; she knapt 'em o'the coxcombs with a stick, and cried, 'Down, wantons, down!' 'Twas her brother that, in pure kindness to his horse, butter'd his hay.

Enter CORNWALL, REGAN, GLOSTER, *and*
SERVANTS.

KING LEAR.

Good morrow to you both.

DUKE OF CORNWALL.

            Hail to your Grace!
           [KENT *here set at liberty.*

REGAN.

I am glad to see your highness.

KING LEAR.

Regan, I think you are; I know what reason
I have to think so: if thou shouldst not be glad,
I would divorce me from thy mother's tomb,
Sepulchring an adultress.—[*to* KENT] O, are you free?
Some other time for that.—Beloved Regan,
Thy sister's naught: O Regan, she hath tied
Sharp-tootht unkindness, like a vulture, here,—
           [*Points to his heart.*
I can scarce speak to thee; thou'lt not believe
Of how depraved a quality—O Regan!

REGAN.
I pray you, sir, take patience: I have hope
You less know how to value her desert
Than she to scant her duty.
KING LEAR.
Say, how is that?
REGAN.
I cannot think my sister in the least
Would fail her obligation: if, sir, perchance
She have restrain'd the riots of your followers,
'Tis on such ground, and to such wholesome end,
As clears her from all blame.
KING LEAR.
My curses on her!
REGAN.
O, sir, you are old;
Nature in you stands on the very verge
Of her confine: you should be ruled, and led
By some discretion that discerns your state
Better than you yourself. Therefore, I pray you,
That to our sister you do make return;
Say you have wrong'd her, sir.
KING LEAR.
Ask her forgiveness?
Do you but mark how this becomes the house:
'Dear daughter, I confess that I am old;
[Kneeling.
Age is unnecessary: on my knees I beg
That you'll vouchsafe me raiment, bed, and food.'
REGAN.
Good sir, no more; these are unsightly tricks:
Return you to my sister.
KING LEAR [rising].
Never, Regan:
She hath abated me of half my train;
Lookt black upon me; struck me with her tongue,
Most serpent-like, upon the very heart:—
All the stored vengeances of heaven fall
On her ingrateful top! Strike her young bones,
You taking airs, with lameness!
DUKE OF CORNWALL.
Fie, sir, fie!
KING LEAR.
You nimble lightnings, dart your blinding flames
Into her scornful eyes! Infect her beauty,
You fen-suckt fogs, drawn by the powerful sun,
To fall and blast her pride!
REGAN.
O the blest gods! so will you wish on me,
When the rash mood is on.
KING LEAR.
No, Regan, thou shalt never have my curse:
Thy tender-hefted nature shall not give
Thee o'er to harshness: her eyes are fierce; but
thine
Do comfort, and not burn. 'Tis not in thee
To grudge my pleasures, to cut off my train,
To bandy hasty words, to scant my sizes,
And, in conclusion, to oppose the bolt
Against my coming in: thou better know'st
The offices of nature, bond of childhood,
Effects of courtesy, dues of gratitude;
Thy half o'the kingdom hast thou not forgot,
Wherein I thee endow'd.
REGAN.
Good sir, to the purpose.

KING LEAR.
Who put my man i'the stocks? [Tucket within.
DUKE OF CORNWALL.
What trumpet's that?
REGAN.
I know't,—my sister's: this approves her letter,
That she would soon be here.
Enter OSWALD.
Is your lady come?
KING LEAR.
This is a slave, whose easy-borrow'd pride
Dwells in the fickle grace of her he follows.—
Out, varlet, from my sight!
DUKE OF CORNWALL.
What means your Grace?
KING LEAR.
Who stockt my servant? Regan, I have good hope
Thou didst not know on't.—Who comes here? O
heavens,
Enter GONERIL.
If you do love old men, if your sweet sway
Allow obedience, if yourselves are old,
Make it your cause; send down, and take my
part!—
[to GONERIL] Art not ashamed to look upon this
beard?—
O Regan, wilt thou take her by the hand?
GONERIL.
Why not by the hand, sir? How have I offended?
All's not offence that indiscretion finds
And dotage terms so.
KING LEAR.
O sides, you are too tough;
Will you yet hold?—How came my man i'the
stocks?
DUKE OF CORNWALL.
I set him there, sir: but his own disorders
Deserved much less advancement.
KING LEAR.
You! did you?
REGAN.
I pray you, father, being weak, seem so.
If, till the expiration of your month,
You will return and sojourn with my sister,
Dismissing half your train, come then to me:
I am now from home, and out of that provision
Which shall be needful for your entertainment.
KING LEAR.
Return to her, and fifty men dismist?
No, rather I abjure all roofs, and choose
To wage against the enmity o'the air;
To be a comrade with the wolf and owl,—
Necessity's sharp pinch! Return with her?
Why, the hot-blooded France, that dowerless took
Our youngest born, I could as well be brought
To knee his throne, and, squire-like, pension beg
To keep base life afoot.—Return with her?
Persuade me rather to be slave and sumpter
To this detested groom. [Pointing at OSWALD.
GONERIL.
At your choice, sir.
KING LEAR.
I prithee, daughter, do not make me mad:
I will not trouble thee, my child; farewell:
We'll no more meet, no more see one another:—
But yet thou art my flesh, my blood, my daughter;

Or rather a disease that's in my flesh,
Which I must needs call mine: thou art a boil,
A plague-sore, an embossed carbuncle,
In my corrupted blood. But I'll not chide thee;
Let shame come when it will, I do not call it:
I do not bid the thunder-bearer shoot,
Nor tell tales of thee to high-judging Jove:
Mend when thou canst; be better at thy leisure:
I can be patient; I can stay with Regan,
I and my hundred knights.

REGAN.
                Not altogether so:
I lookt not for you yet, nor am provided
For your fit welcome. Give ear, sir, to my sister;
For those that mingle reason with your passion
Must be content to think you old, and so—
But she knows what she does.

KING LEAR.
                Is this well spoken?

REGAN.
I dare avouch it, sir: what! fifty followers?
Is it not well? What should you need of more?
Yea, or so many, sith that both charge and danger
Speak 'gainst so great a number? How, in one
   house,
Should many people, under two commands,
Hold amity? 'Tis hard; almost impossible.

GONERIL.
Why might not you, my lord, receive attendance
From those that she calls servants or from mine?

REGAN.
Why not, my lord? If then they chanced to slack
   you,
We could control them. If you will come to me,—
For now I spy a danger,—I entreat you
To bring but five-and-twenty: to no more
Will I give place or notice.

KING LEAR.
I gave you all—

REGAN.
       And in good time you gave it.

KING LEAR.
Made you my guardians, my depositaries;
But kept a reservation to be follow'd
With such a number. What, must I come to you
With five-and-twenty, Regan? said you so?

REGAN.
And speak't again, my lord; no more with me.

KING LEAR.
Those wicked creatures yet do look well-favour'd,
When others are more wicked; not being the worst
Stands in some rank of praise.—[to GONERIL] I'll
   go with thee:
Thy fifty yet doth double five-and-twenty,
And thou art twice her love.

GONERIL.
           Hear me, my lord:
What need you five-and-twenty, ten, or five,
To follow in a house where twice so many
Have a command to tend you?

REGAN.
           What need one?

KING LEAR.
O, reason not the need: our basest beggars
Are in the poorest thing superfluous:
Allow not nature more than nature needs,

Man's life is cheap as beast's: thou art a lady;
If only to go warm were gorgeous,
Why, nature needs not what thou gorgeous wear'st,
Which scarcely keeps thee warm.—But, for true
   need,—
You heavens, give me that patience, patience I
   need!
You see me here, you gods, a poor old man,
As full of grief as age; wretched in both!
If it be you that stir these daughters' hearts
Against their father, fool me not so much
To bear it tamely; touch me with noble anger,
And let not women's weapons, water-drops,
Stain my man's cheeks!—No, you unnatural hags,
I will have such revenges on you both,
That all the world shall—I will do such things,—
What they are, yet I know not; but they shall be
The terrors of the earth. You think I'll weep;
No, I'll not weep:—
I have full cause of weeping; but this heart
Shall break into a hundred thousand flaws,
Or e'er I'll weep.—O fool, I shall go mad!
     [*Exeunt* LEAR, GLOSTER, KENT, *and* FOOL.
       Storm and tempest.

DUKE OF CORNWALL.
Let us withdraw; 'twill be a storm.

REGAN.
This house is little: the old man and his people
Cannot be well bestow'd.

GONERIL.
'Tis his own blame; 'hath put himself from rest,
And must needs taste his folly.

REGAN.
For his particular, I'll receive him gladly,
But not one follower.

GONERIL.
          So am I purposed.
Where is my Lord of Gloster?

DUKE OF CORNWALL.
Follow'd the old man forth:—he is return'd.
        Enter GLOSTER.

EARL OF GLOSTER.
The king is in high rage.

DUKE OF CORNWALL.
           Whither is he going?

EARL OF GLOSTER.
He calls to horse; but will I know not whither.

DUKE OF CORNWALL.
'Tis best to give him way; he leads himself.

GONERIL.
My lord, entreat him by no means to stay.

EARL OF GLOSTER.
Alack, the night comes on, and the bleak winds
Do sorely ruffle; for many miles about
There's scarce a bush.

REGAN.
       O, sir, to wilful men
The injuries that they themselves procure
Must be their schoolmasters. Shut up your doors:
He is attended with a desperate train;
And what they may incense him to, being apt
To have his ear abused, wisdom bids fear.

DUKE OF CORNWALL.
Shut up your doors, my lord; 'tis a wild night:
My Regan counsels well: come out o'the storm.
                       [*Exeunt.*

ACT III. SCENE I.

A heath.

Storm still. Enter KENT *and a* GENTLEMAN, *severally.*

EARL OF KENT.

WHO'S there, besides foul weather?

GENTLEMAN.

One minded like the weather, most unquietly.

EARL OF KENT.

I know you. Where's the king?

GENTLEMAN.

Contending with the fretful elements;
Bids the wind blow the earth into the sea,
Or swell the curled waters 'bove the main,
That things might change or cease; tears his white
    hair,
Which the impetuous blasts, with eyeless rage,
Catch in their fury, and make nothing of;
Strives in his little world of man to out-scorn
The to-and-fro-conflicting wind and rain.
This night, wherein the cub-drawn bear would
    couch,
The lion and the belly-pinched wolf
Keep their fur dry, unbonneted he runs,
And bids what will take all.

EARL OF KENT.

              But who is with him?

GENTLEMAN.

None but the fool; who labours to out-jest
His heart-struck injuries.

EARL OF KENT.

            Sir, I do know you;
And dare, upon the warrant of my note,'
Commend a dear thing to you. There is division,
Although as yet the face of it be cover'd
With mutual cunning, 'twixt Albany and Corn-
    wall;
Who have—as who have not, that their great stars
Throned and set high?—servants, who seem no
    less,
Which are to France the spies and speculations
Intelligent of our state; what hath been seen,
Either in snuffs and packings of the dukes;
Or the hard rein which both of them have borne
Against the old kind king; or something deeper,
Whereof perchance these are but furnishings;—
But, true it is, from France there comes a power
Into this scatter'd kingdom; who already,
Wise in our negligence, have secret feet
In some of our best ports, and are at point
To show their open banner.—Now to you:
If on my credit you dare build so far
To make your speed to Dover, you shall find
Some that will thank you, making just report
Of how unnatural and bemadding sorrow
The king hath cause to plain.
I am a gentleman of blood and breeding;
And, from some knowledge and assurance, offer
This office to you.

GENTLEMAN.

I will talk further with you.

EARL OF KENT.

             No, do not.
For confirmation that I am much more
Than my out-wall, open this purse, and take

What it contains. If you shall see Cordelia,—
As fear not but you shall,—show her this ring;
And she will tell you who your fellow is
That yet you do not know. Fie on this storm!
I will go seek the king.

GENTLEMAN.

Give me your hand: have you no more to say?

EARL OF KENT.

Few words, but, to effect, more than all yet,—
That, when we have found the king,—in which
    your pain
That way, I'll this,—he that first lights on him
Holla the other.   *[Exeunt severally.*

SCENE II.

Another part of the heath.

Storm still. Enter LEAR *and* FOOL.

KING LEAR.

BLOW, winds, and crack your cheeks! rage!
    blow!
You cataracts and hurricanoes, spout
Till you have drencht our steeples, drown'd the
    cocks!
You sulphurous and thought-executing fires,
Vaunt-couriers to oak-cleaving thunderbolts,
Singe my white head! And thou, all-shaking thun-
    der,
Strike flat the thick rotundity o'the world!
Crack nature's moulds, all germens spill at once,
That make ingrateful man!

FOOL.

O nuncle, court holy-water in a dry house is better
than this rain-water out o'door. Good nuncle, in,
and ask thy daughters' blessing: here's a night
pities neither wise man nor fool.

KING LEAR.

Rumble thy bellyful! Spit, fire! spout, rain!
Nor rain, wind, thunder, fire, are my daughters:
I tax not you, you elements, with unkindness;
I never gave you kingdom, call'd you children,
You owe me no subscription: then let fall
Your horrible pleasure; here I stand, your slave,
A poor, infirm, weak, and despised old man:—
But yet I call you servile ministers,
That have with two pernicious daughters join'd
Your high-engender'd battles 'gainst a head
So old and white as this! O! O! 'tis foul!

FOOL.

He that has a house to put's head in has a good
head-piece.

    The cod-piece that will house
        Before the head has any,
    The head and he shall louse;—
        So beggars marry many.
    The man that makes his toe
        What he his heart should make
    Shall of a corn cry woe,
        And turn his sleep to wake:
for there was never yet fair woman but she made
mouths in a glass.

KING LEAR.

No, I will be the pattern of all patience;
I will say nothing.

Enter KENT.

EARL OF KENT.

Who's there?

FOOL.

Marry, here's grace and a cod-piece; that's a wise
man and a fool.

EARL OF KENT.

Alas, sir, are you here? things that love night
Love not such nights as these; the wrathful skies
Gallow the very wanderers of the dark,
And make them keep their caves: since I was man,
Such sheets of fire, such bursts of horrid thunder,
Such groans of roaring wind and rain, I never
Remember to have heard: man's nature cannot
  carry
The affliction nor the fear.

KING LEAR.

        Let the great gods,
That keep this dreadful pother o'er our heads,
Find out their enemies now. Tremble, thou
  wretch,
That hast within thee undivulged crimes,
Unwhipt of justice: hide thee, thou bloody hand;
Thou perjured, and thou simular of virtue
That art incestuous: caitiff, to pieces shake,
That under covert and convenient seeming
Hast practised on man's life: close pent-up guilts,
Rive your concealing continents, and cry
These dreadful summoners grace.—I am a man
More sinn'd against than sinning.

EARL OF KENT.

        Alack, bare-headed!
Gracious my lord, hard by here is a hovel;
Some friendship will it lend you 'gainst the tem-
  pest:
Repose you there; while I to this hard house—
More harder than the stones whereof 'tis raised;
Which even but now, demanding after you,
Denied me to come in—return, and force
Their scanted courtesy.

KING LEAR.

        My wits begin to turn.—
Come on, my boy: how dost, my boy? art cold?
I am cold myself.—Where is this straw, my fellow?
The art of our necessities is strange,
That can make vile things precious. Come, your
  hovel.—
Poor fool and knave, I have one part in my heart
That's sorry yet for thee.

FOOL [*singing*].

He that has and a little tiny wit,—
    With hey, ho, the wind and the rain,—
Must make content with his fortures fit,
    Though the rain it raineth every day.

KING LEAR.

True, my good boy.—Come, bring us to this
  hovel.   [*Exeunt* LEAR *and* KENT.

FOOL.

This is a brave night to cool a courtezan.—I'll
speak a prophecy ere I go:
  When priests are more in word than matter;
  When brewers mar their malt with water;
  When nobles are their tailors' tutors;
  No heretics burn'd, but wenches' suitors;
  When every case in law is right;
  No squire in debt, nor no poor knight;

  When slanders do not live in tongues;
  Nor cutpurses come not to throngs;
  When usurers tell their gold i'the field;
  And bawds and whores do churches build;—
  Then shall the realm of Albion
  Come to great confusion:
  Then comes the time, who lives to see't,
  That going shall be used with feet.
This prophecy Merlin shall make; for I live be-
fore his time.   [*Exit.*

SCENE III.

GLOSTER'S *castle.*

Enter GLOSTER *and* EDMUND.

EARL OF GLOSTER.

ALACK, alack, Edmund, I like not this unnatural dealing. When I desired their leave
that I might pity him, they took from me the use
of mine own house; charged me, on pain of their
perpetual displeasure, neither to speak of him,
entreat for him, nor any way sustain him.

EDMUND.

Most savage and unnatural!

EARL OF GLOSTER.

Go to; say you nothing. There is division betwixt the dukes; and a worse matter than that: I
have received a letter this night;—'tis dangerous
to be spoken;—I have lockt the letter in my closet:
these injuries the king now bears will be revenged
home; there is part of a power already footed: we
must incline to the king. I will seek him, and
privily relieve him: go you, and maintain talk
with the duke, that my charity be not of him
perceived: if he ask for me, I am ill, and gone to
bed. Though I die for it, as no less is threaten'd
me, the king my old master must be relieved.
There is some strange thing toward, Edmund;
pray you, be careful.   [*Exit.*

EDMUND.

This courtesy, forbid thee, shall the duke
Instantly know; and of that letter too:—
This seems a fair deserving, and must draw me
That which my father loses,—no less than all:
The younger rises when the old doth fall.   [*Exit.*

SCENE IV.

The heath, before a hovel.

Enter LEAR, KENT, *and* FOOL.

EARL OF KENT.

HERE is the place, my lord; good my lord,
enter:
The tyranny of the open night's too rough
For nature to endure.   [*Storm still.*

KING LEAR.

        Let me alone.

EARL OF KENT.

Good my lord, enter here.

KING LEAR.

        Wilt break my heart?

EARL OF KENT.

I had rather break mine own. Good my lord,
enter.

KING LEAR.

Thou think'st 'tis much that this contentious
    storm
Invades us to the skin: so 'tis to thee;
But where the greater malady is fixt,
The lesser is scarce felt. Thou'ldst shun a bear;
But if thy flight lay toward the roaring sea,
Thou'ldst meet the bear i'the mouth. When the
    mind's free,
The body's delicate: the tempest in my mind
Doth from my senses take all feeling else
Save what beats there.—Filial ingratitude!
Is it not as this mouth should tear this hand
For lifting food to't?—But I will punish home:—
No, I will weep no more.—In such a night
To shut me out!—Pour on; I will endure:—
In such a night as this! O Regan, Goneril!—
Your old kind father, whose frank heart gave
    all,—
O, that way madness lies; let me shun that;
No more of that.

EARL OF KENT.
    Good my lord, enter here.

KING LEAR.
Prithee, go in thyself; seek thine own ease:
This tempest will not give me leave to ponder
On things would hurt me more.—But I'll go in.
[to the FOOL] In, boy; go first. You houseless
    poverty,—
Nay, get thee in. I'll pray, and then I'll sleep.—
                      [FOOL goes in.
Poor naked wretches, wheresoe'er you are,
That bide the pelting of this pitiless storm,
How shall your houseless heads and unfed sides,
Your loopt and window'd raggedness, defend
    you
From seasons such as these? O, I have ta'en
Too little care of this! Take physic, pomp;
Expose thyself to feel what wretches feel,
That thou mayst shake the superflux to them,
And show the heavens more just.

EDGAR [within].
Fathom and half, fathom and half!
Poor Tom!   [The FOOL runs out from the hovel.

FOOL.
Come not in here, nuncle, here's a spirit. Help me,
help me!

EARL OF KENT.
Give me thy hand.—Who's there?

FOOL.
A spirit, a spirit: he says his name's poor Tom.

EARL OF KENT.
What art thou that dost grumble there i'the
straw? Come forth.
    Enter EDGAR disguised as a madman.

EDGAR.
Away! the foul fiend follows me!—
    Through the sharp hawthorn blows the cold
        wind.—
Hum! go to thy cold bed, and warm thee.

KING LEAR.
Hast thou given all to thy two daughters?
And art thou come to this?

EDGAR.
Who gives any thing to poor Tom? whom the foul
fiend hath led through fire and through flame,
through ford and whirlpool, o'er bog and quagmire; that hath laid knives under his pillow, and
halters in his pew; set ratsbane by his porridge;
made him proud of heart, to ride on a bay trotting-
horse over four-incht bridges, to course his own
shadow for a traitor.—Bless thy five wits!—Tom's
a-cold,—O, do de, do de, do de.—Bless thee from
whirlwinds, star-blasting, and taking! Do poor
Tom some charity, whom the foul fiend vexes:—
there could I have him now,—and there—and
there again, and there.   [Storm still.

KING LEAR.
What, have his daughters brought him to this
    pass?—
Couldst thou save nothing? Didst thou give 'em
    all?

FOOL.
Nay, he reserved a blanket, else we had been all
shamed.

KING LEAR.
Now, all the plagues that in the pendulous air
Hang fated o'er men's faults light on thy daugh-
    ters!

EARL OF KENT.
He hath no daughters, sir.

KING LEAR.
Death, traitor! nothing could have subdued
    nature
To such a lowness but his unkind daughters.—
Is it the fashion, that discarded fathers
Should have thus little mercy on their flesh?
Judicious punishment! 'twas this flesh begot
Those pelican daughters.

EDGAR.
    Pillicock sat on Pillicock-hill:—
Halloo, halloo, loo, loo!

FOOL.
This cold night will turn us all to fools and madmen.

EDGAR.
Take heed o'the foul fiend: obey thy parents; keep
thy word justly; swear not; commit not with man's
sworn spouse; set not thy sweet heart on proud
array. Tom's a-cold.

KING LEAR.
What hast thou been?

EDGAR.
A servingman, proud in heart and mind; that
curl'd my hair; wore gloves in my cap; served the
lust of my mistress' heart, and did the act of darkness with her; swore as many oaths as I spake
words, and broke them in the sweet face of
heaven: one that slept in the contriving of lust,
and waked to do it: wine loved I deeply, dice
dearly; and in woman out-paramour'd the Turk:
false of heart, light of ear, bloody of hand; hog in
sloth, fox in stealth, wolf in greediness, dog in
madness, lion in prey. Let not the creaking of
shoes nor the rustling of silks betray thy poor
heart to woman: keep thy foot out of brothels, thy
hand out of plackets, thy pen from lenders' books,
and defy the foul fiend.—
    Still through the hawthorn blows the cold wind;
    Says suum, mun, ha, no, nonny.
Dolphin my boy, my boy, sessa! let him trot by.
                  [Storm still.

KING LEAR.

Why, thou wert better in thy grave than to answer
with thy uncover'd body this extremity of the
skies.—Is man no more than this? Consider him
well. Thou owest the worm no silk, the beast no
hide, the sheep no wool, the cat no perfume.—
Ha! here's three on's are sophisticated!—Thou
art the thing itself: unaccommodated man is no
more but such a poor, bare, forkt animal as thou
art.—Off, off, you lendings!—come, unbutton
here.   [*Tearing off his clothes.*

FOOL.

Prithee, nuncle, be contented; 'tis a naughty night
to swim in.—Now a little fire in a wild field were
like an old lecher's heart,—a small spark, all the
rest on's body cold.—Look, here comes a walking
fire.

Enter GLOSTER, *with a torch.*

EDGAR.

This is the foul fiend Flibbertigibbet: he begins
at curfew, and walks till the first cock; he gives the
web and the pin, squints the eye, and makes the
hare-lip; mildews the white wheat, and hurts the
poor creature of earth.

    Swithold footed thrice the old;
    He met the night-mare, and her nine-fold;
        Bid her alight,
        And her troth plight,
    And, aroint thee, witch, aroint thee!

EARL OF KENT.

How fares your Grace?

KING LEAR.

What's he?

EARL OF KENT.

Who's there? What is't you seek?

EARL OF GLOSTER.

What are you there?
Your names?

EDGAR.

Poor Tom; that eats the swimming frog, the toad,
the tadpole, the wall-newt and the water; that in
the fury of his heart, when the foul fiend rages,
eats cow-dung for sallets; swallows the old rat
and the ditch-dog; drinks the green mantle of the
standing pool; who is whipt from tithing to
tithing, and stock-punisht, and imprison'd; who
hath had three suits to his back, six shirts to his
body,

    Horse to ride, and weapon to wear;
    But mice, and rats, and such small deer,
    Have been Tom's food for seven long year.
Beware my follower.—Peace, Smulkin; peace,
thou fiend!

EARL OF GLOSTER.

What, hath your Grace no better company?

EDGAR.

The prince of darkness is a gentleman: Modo he's
call'd, and Mahu.

EARL OF GLOSTER.

Our flesh and blood, my lord, is grown so vile,
That it doth hate what gets it.

EDGAR.

Poor Tom's a-cold.

EARL OF GLOSTER.

Go in with me: my duty cannot suffer
T'obey in all your daughters' hard commands:

Though their injunction be to bar my doors,
And let this tyrannous night take hold upon
    you,
Yet have I ventured to come seek you out,
And bring you where both fire and food is ready.

KING LEAR.

First let me talk with this philosopher.—
What is the cause of thunder?

EARL OF KENT.

Good my lord, take his offer; go into the house.

KING LEAR.

I'll talk a word with this same learned Theban.—
What is your study?

EDGAR.

How to prevent the fiend, and to kill vermin.

KING LEAR.

Let me ask you one word in private.

EARL OF KENT.

Importune him once more to go, my lord;
His wits begin t'unsettle.

EARL OF GLOSTER.

            Canst thou blame him?
His daughters seek his death:—ah, that good
    Kent!—
He said it would be thus,—poor banisht man!—
Thou say'st the king grows mad; I'll tell thee,
    friend,
I am almost mad myself: I had a son,
Now outlaw'd from my blood; he sought my
    life,
But lately, very late: I loved him, friend,
No father his son dearer: true to tell thee,
            [*Storm still.*
The grief hath crazed my wits.—What a night's
this!—
I do beseech your Grace,—

KING LEAR.

          O, cry you mercy, sir.—
Noble philosopher, your company.

EDGAR.

Tom's a-cold.

EARL OF GLOSTER.

In, fellow, there, into the hovel: keep thee warm

KING LEAR.

Come, let's in all.

EARL OF KENT.

        This way, my lord.

KING LEAR.

                  With him;
I will keep still with my philosopher.

EARL OF KENT.

Good my lord, soothe him! let him take the fellow.

EARL OF GLOSTER.

Take him you on.

EARL OF KENT.

Sirrah, come on; go along with us.

KING LEAR.

Come, good Athenian.

EARL OF GLOSTER.

No words, no words: hush.

EDGAR.

    Child Rowland to the dark tower came;
    His word was still,—Fie, foh, and fum,
    I smell the blood of a British man.
                  [*Exeunt.*

SCENE V.

GLOSTER'S *castle.*

Enter CORNWALL *and* EDMUND.

DUKE OF CORNWALL.

I WILL have my revenge ere I depart his house.

EDMUND.

How, my lord, I may be censured, that nature thus gives way to loyalty, something fears me to think of.

DUKE OF CORNWALL.

I now perceive, it was not altogether your brother's evil disposition made him seek his death; but a provoking merit, set a-work by a reproveable badness in himself.

EDMUND.

How malicious is my fortune, that I must repent to be just! This is the letter he spoke of, which approves him an intelligent party to the advantages of France. O heavens! that this treason were not, or not I the detector!

DUKE OF CORNWALL.

Go with me to the duchess.

EDMUND.

If the matter of this paper be certain, you have mighty business in hand.

DUKE OF CORNWALL.

True or false, it hath made thee Earl of Gloster. Seek out where thy father is, that he may be ready for our apprehension.

EDMUND [*aside*].

If I find him comforting the king, it will stuff his suspicion more fully.—I will persever in my course of loyalty, though the conflict be sore between that and my blood.

DUKE OF CORNWALL.

I will lay trust upon thee; and thou shalt find a dearer father in my love.   [*Exeunt.*

SCENE VI.

A farmhouse adjoining the castle.

Enter LEAR, KENT, GLOSTER, FOOL, *and* EDGAR.

EARL OF GLOSTER.

HERE is better than the open air; take it thankfully. I will piece out the comfort with what addition I can: I will not be long from you.

EARL OF KENT.

All the power of his wits have given way to his impatience:—the gods reward your kindness!
     [*Exit* GLOSTER.

EDGAR.

Frateretto calls me, and tells me Nero is an angler in the lake of darkness.—Pray, innocent, and beware the foul fiend.

FOOL.

Prithee, nuncle, tell me whether a madman be a gentleman or a yeoman?

KING LEAR.

A king, a king!

FOOL.

No, he's a yeoman that has a gentleman to his son; for he's a mad yeoman that sees his son a gentleman before him.

KING LEAR.

To have a thousand with red burning spits
Come hissing in upon 'em,—

EDGAR.

The foul fiend bites my back.

FOOL.

He's mad that trusts in the tameness of a wolf, a horse's health, a boy's love, or a whore's oath.

KING LEAR.

It shall be done; I will arraign them straight.—
[*to* EDGAR] Come, sit thou here, most learned justicer;—
[*to the* FOOL] Thou, sapient sir, sit here.—Now, you she foxes!—

EDGAR.

Look, where he stands and glares!—Want'st thou eyes at trial, madam?
     Come o'er the bourn, Bessy to me.

FOOL.

     Her boat hath a leak,
     And she must not speak
Why she dares not come over to thee.

EDGAR.

The foul fiend haunts poor Tom in the voice of a nightingale. Hopdance cries in Tom's belly for two white herring. Croak not, black angel; I have no food for thee.

EARL OF KENT.

How do you, sir? Stand you not so amazed:
Will you lie down and rest upon the cushions?

KING LEAR.

I'll see their trial first.—Bring in the evidence.—
[*to* EDGAR] Thou robed man of justice, take thy place;—
[*to the* FOOL] And thou, his yoke-fellow of equity,
Bench by his side:—[*to* KENT] You are o'the commission,
Sit you too.

EDGAR.

Let us deal justly.
     Sleepest or wakest thou, jolly shepherd?
       Thy sheep be in the corn;
     And for one blast of thy minikin mouth
       Thy sheep shall take no harm.
Pur! the cat is gray.

KING LEAR.

Arraign her first; 'tis Goneril. I here take my oath before this honourable assembly, she kickt the poor king her father.

FOOL.

Come hither, mistress. Is your name Goneril?

KING LEAR.

She cannot deny it.

FOOL.

Cry you mercy, I took you for a joint-stool.

KING LEAR.

And here's another, whose warpt looks proclaim
What store her heart is made on.—Stop her there!
Arms, arms, sword, fire!—Corruption in the place!—
False justicer, why hast thou let her scape?

EDGAR.

Bless thy five wits!

EARL OF KENT.

O pity!—Sir, where is the patience now
That you so oft have boasted to retain?

EDGAR [aside].
My tears begin to take his part so much,
They'll mar my counterfeiting.
KING LEAR.
The little dogs and all,
Tray, Blanch, and Sweetheart, see, they bark at
me.
EDGAR.
Tom will throw his head at them.—Avaunt, you
curs!

Be thy mouth or black or white,
Tooth that poisons if it bite;
Mastiff, greyhound, mongrel grim,
Hound of spaniel, brach or lym,
Or bobtail tike or trundle-tail,—
Tom will make them weep and wail:
For, with throwing thus my head,
Dogs leap the hatch, and all are fled.

Do de, de, de. Sessa! Come, march to wakes and
fairs and market-towns.—Poor Tom, thy horn is
dry.
KING LEAR.
Then let them anatomize Regan; see what breeds
about her heart. Is there any cause in nature that
makes these hard hearts?—[to EDGAR] You, sir,
I entertain for one of my hundred; only I do not
like the fashion of your garments: you will say
they are Persian attire; but let them be changed.
EARL OF KENT.
Now, my good lord, lie here and rest awhile.
KING LEAR.
Make no noise, make no noise; draw the curtains:
so, so, so: we'll go to supper i'the morning: so, so,
so.
FOOL.
And I'll go to bed at noon.
Enter GLOSTER.
EARL OF GLOSTER.
Come hither, friend; where is the king my master?
EARL OF KENT.
Here, sir; but trouble him not,—his wits are gone.
EARL OF GLOSTER.
Good friend, I prithee, take him in thy arms;
I have o'erheard a plot of death upon him:
There is a litter ready; lay him in't,
And drive towards Dover, friend, where thou
shalt meet
Both welcome and protection. Take up thy mas-
ter:
If thou shouldst dally half an hour, his life,
With thine, and all that offer to defend him,
Stand in assured loss: take up, take up;
And follow me, that will to some provision
Give thee quick conduct.
EARL OF KENT.
Oppressed nature sleeps:—
This rest might yet have balm'd thy broken
sinews,
Which, if convenience will not allow,
Stand in hard cure.—[to the FOOL] Come, help
to bear thy master;
Thou must not stay behind.
EARL OF GLOSTER.
Come, come, away.
[Exeunt KENT, GLOSTER, and the FOOL,
bearing off LEAR.

EDGAR.
When we our betters see bearing our woes,
We scarcely think our miseries our foes.
Who alone suffers suffers most i'the mind,
Leaving free things and happy shows behind:
But then the mind much sufferance doth o'erskip,
When grief hath mates, and bearing fellowship.
How light and portable my pain seems now,
When that which makes me bend makes the king
bow,
He childed as I father'd!—Tom, away!
Mark the high noises; and thy self bewray,
When false opinion, whose wrong thoughts defile
thee,
In thy just proof, repeals and reconciles thee.
What will hap more to-night, safe scape the king!
Lurk, lurk. [Exit.

SCENE VII.

A room in GLOSTER'S castle.

Enter CORNWALL, REGAN, GONERIL,
EDMUND, and SERVANTS.

DUKE OF CORNWALL.
POST speedily to my lord your husband;
show him this letter:—the army of France is
landed.—Seek out the traitor Gloster.
[Exeunt some of the SERVANTS.
REGAN.
Hang him instantly.
GONERIL.
Pluck out his eyes.
DUKE OF CORNWALL.
Leave him to my displeasure.—Edmund, keep
you our sister company: the revenges we are
bound to take upon your traitorous father are not
fit for your beholding. Advise the duke, where
you are going, to a most festinate preparation: we
are bound to the like. Our posts shall be swift and
intelligent betwixt us. Farewell, dear sister:—
farewell, my Lord of Gloster.
Enter OSWALD.
How now! where's the king?
OSWALD.
My Lord of Gloster hath convey'd him hence:
Some five or six and thirty of his knights,
Hot questrists after him, met him at gate;
Who, with some other of the lords dependants,
Are gone with him towards Dover; where they
boast
To have well-armed friends.
DUKE OF CORNWALL.
Get horses for your mistress.
GONERIL.
Farewell, sweet lord, and sister.
DUKE OF CORNWALL.
Edmund, farewell.
[Exeunt GONERIL, EDMUND, and OSWALD.
Go seek the traitor Gloster,
Pinion him like a thief, bring him before us.
[Exeunt other SERVANTS.
Though well we may not pass upon his life
Without the form of justice, yet our power
Shall do a court'sy to our wrath, which men
May blame, but not control.—Who's there? the
traitor?

Enter GLOSTER, *brought in by two or three.*

REGAN.

Ingrateful fox! 'tis he.

DUKE OF CORNWALL.

Bind fast his corky arms.

EARL OF GLOSTER.

What mean your Graces?—Good my friends, consider

You are my guests: do me no foul play, friends.

DUKE OF CORNWALL.

Bind him, I say.   [SERVANTS *bind him.*

REGAN.

Hard, hard.—O filthy traitor!

EARL OF GLOSTER.

Unmerciful lady as you are, I'm none.

DUKE OF CORNWALL.

To this chair bind him.—Villain, thou shalt

find—   [REGAN *plucks his beard.*

EARL OF GLOSTER.

By the kind gods, 'tis most ignobly done

To pluck me by the beard.

REGAN.

So white, and such a traitor!

EARL OF GLOSTER.

Naughty lady,

These hairs, which thou dost ravish from my chin,

Will quicken, and accuse thee: I am your host:

With robbers' hands my hospitable favours

You should not ruffle thus. What will you do?

DUKE OF CORNWALL.

Come, sir, what letters had you late from France?

REGAN.

Be simple-answer'd, for we know the truth.

DUKE OF CORNWALL.

And what confederacy have you with the traitors

Late footed in the kingdom?

REGAN.

To whose hands have you sent the lunatic king?

Speak.

DUKE OF GLOSTER.

I have a letter guessingly set down,

Which came from one that's of a neutral heart,

And not from one opposed.

DUKE OF CORNWALL.

Cunning.

REGAN.

And false.

DUKE OF CORNWALL.

Where hast thou sent the king?

EARL OF GLOSTER.

To Dover.

REGAN.

Wherefore to Dover? Wast thou not charged at peril—

DUKE OF CORNWALL.

Wherefore to Dover? Let him answer that.

EARL OF GLOSTER.

I am tied to the stake, and I must stand the course.

REGAN.

Wherefore to Dover?

EARL OF GLOSTER.

Because I would not see thy cruel nails

Pluck out his poor old eyes; nor thy fierce sister

In his anointed flesh stick boarish fangs.

The sea, with such a storm as his bare head

In hell-black night endured, would have buoy'd up

And quencht the stelled fires:

Yet, poor old heart, he holp the heavens to rain.

If wolves had at thy gate howl'd that dern time,

Thou shouldst have said, 'Good porter, turn the key.'

All cruels else subscribed:—but I shall see

The winged vengeance overtake such children.

DUKE OF CORNWALL.

See't shalt thou never.—Fellows, hold the chair.—

Upon these eyes of thine I'll set my foot.

EARL OF GLOSTER.

He that will think to live till he be old,

Give me some help!—O cruel!—O you gods!

REGAN.

One side will mock another; the other too.

DUKE OF CORNWALL.

If you see vengeance,—

FIRST SERVANT.

Hold your hand, my lord:

I have served you ever since I was a child;

But better service have I never done you

Than now to bid you hold.

REGAN.

How now, you dog!

FIRST SERVANT.

If you did wear a beard upon your chin,

I'ld shake it on this quarrel. What do you mean?

DUKE OF CORNWALL.

My villain!   [*Draws.*

FIRST SERVANT.

Nay, then, come on, and take the chance of anger.

[*Draws. They fight.* CORNWALL *is wounded.*

REGAN.

Give me thy sword.—A peasant stand up thus!

[*Takes a sword from another* SERVANT, *and runs at* FIRST SERVANT *behind.*

FIRST SERVANT.

O, I am slain!—My lord, you have one eye left

To see some mischief on him.—O!   [*Dies.*

DUKE OF CORNWALL.

Lest it see more, prevent it.—Out, vile jelly!

Where is thy lustre now?

EARL OF GLOSTER.

All dark and comfortless.—Where's my son Edmund?

Edmund, enkindle all the sparks of nature

To quit this horrid act.

REGAN.

Out, treacherous villain!

Thou call'st on him that hates thee: it was he

That made the overture of thy treasons to us;

Who is too good to pity thee.

EARL OF GLOSTER.

O my follies!

Then Edgar was abused.—

Kind gods, forgive me that, and prosper him!

REGAN.

Go thrust him out at gates, and let him smell

His way to Dover. [*Exit one with* GLOSTER.] How is't, my lord? how look you?

DUKE OF CORNWALL.

I have received a hurt:—follow me, lady.—

Turn out that eyeless villain;—throw this slave

Upon the dunghill.—Regan, I bleed apace:
Untimely comes this hurt: give me your arm.

        [*Exit* CORNWALL, *led by* REGAN.

SECOND SERVANT.

I'll never care what wickedness I do,
If this man come to good.

THIRD SERVANT.

             If she live long,
And in the end meet the old course of death,
Women will all turn monsters.

SECOND SERVANT.

Let's follow the old earl, and get the Bedlam
To lead him where he would: his roguish madness
Allows itself to any thing.

THIRD SERVANT.

Go thou: I'll fetch some flax and whites of eggs
To apply to his bleeding face. Now, heaven help
   him!   [*Exeunt severally.*

ACT IV. SCENE I.

The heath.

Enter EDGAR.

EDGAR.

YET better thus, and known to be contemn'd,
  Than still contemn'd and flatter'd. To be
    worst,
The lowest and most dejected thing of fortune,
Stands still in esperance, lives not in fear:
The lamentable change is from the best;
The worst returns to laughter. Welcome, then,
Thou unsubstantial air that I embrace!
The wretch that thou hast blown unto the worst
Owes nothing to thy blasts.—But who comes
  here?

Enter GLOSTER, *led by an* OLD MAN.

My father, poorly led?—World, world, O world!
But that thy strange mutations make us hate
  thee,
Life would not yield to age.

OLD MAN.

            O, my good lord,
I have been your tenant, and your father's tenant,
These fourscore years.

EARL OF GLOSTER.

Away, get thee away; good friend, be gone:
Thy comforts can do me no good at all;
Thee they may hurt.

OLD MAN.

Alack, sir, you cannot see your way.

EARL OF GLOSTER.

I have no way, and therefore want no eyes;
I stumbled when I saw: full oft 'tis seen,
Our means secure us, and our mere defects
Prove our commodities.—O dear son Edgar,
The food of thy abused father's wrath!
Might I but live to see thee in my touch,
I'ld say I had eyes again!

OLD MAN.

          How now! Who's there?

EDGAR [*aside*].

O gods! Who is't can say, 'I am at the worst'?
I am worse than e'er I was.

OLD MAN.

         'Tis poor mad Tom.

EDGAR [*aside*].

And worse I may be yet: the worst is not
So long as we can say 'This is the worst.'

OLD MAN.

Fellow, where goest?

EARL OF GLOSTER.

          Is it a beggar-man?

OLD MAN.

Madman and beggar too.

EARL OF GLOSTER.

He has some reason, else he could not beg.
I'the last night's storm I such a fellow saw;
Which made me think a man a worm: my son
Came then into my mind; and yet my mind
Was then scarce friends with him: I have heard
  more since.
As flies to wanton boys, are we to the gods,—
They kill us for their sport.

EDGAR [*aside*].

            How should this be?—
Bad is the trade that must play fool to sorrow,
Angering itself and others.—Bless thee, master!

EARL OF GLOSTER.

Is that the naked fellow?

OLD MAN.

          Ay, my lord.

EARL OF GLOSTER.

Then, prithee, get thee gone: if, for my sake,
Thou wilt o'ertake us hence a mile or twain
I'the way toward Dover, do it for ancient love;
And bring some covering for this naked soul,
Which I'll entreat to lead me.

OLD MAN.

          Alack, sir, he is mad.

EARL OF GLOSTER.

'Tis the times' plague, when madmen lead the
  blind.
Do as I bid thee, or rather do thy pleasure;
Above the rest, be gone.

OLD MAN.

I'll bring him the best 'parel that I have,
Come on't what will.   [*Exit.*

EARL OF GLOSTER.

Sirrah, naked fellow,—

EDGAR.

Poor Tom's a-cold.—[*aside*] I cannot daub it further.

EARL OF GLOSTER.

Come hither, fellow.

EDGAR [*aside*].

And yet I must. Bless thy sweet eyes, they bleed.

EARL OF GLOSTER.

Know'st thou the way to Dover?

EDGAR.

Both stile and gate, horse-way and foot-path.
Poor Tom hath been scared out of his good wits:
—bless thee, good man's son, from the foul fiend!
—five fiends have been in poor Tom at once; of
lust, as Obidicut; Hobbididence, prince of dumbness; Mahu, of stealing; Modo, of murder; and
Flibbertigibbet, of mopping and mowing,—who
since possesses chambermaids and waiting-
women. So, bless thee, master!

EARL OF GLOSTER.

Here, take this purse, thou whom the heavens'
  plagues

Have humbled to all strokes: that I am wretched
Makes thee the happier:—heavens, deal so still!
Let the superfluous and lust-dieted man,
That slaves your ordinance, that will not see
Because he doth not feel, feel your power quickly;
So distribution should undo excess,
And each man have enough.—Dost thou know
  Dover?

EDGAR.

Ay, master.

EARL OF GLOSTER.

There is a cliff, whose high and bending head
Looks fearfully in the confined deep:
Bring me but to the very brim of it,
And I'll repair the misery thou dost bear
With something rich about me: from that place
I shall no leading need.

EDGAR.

          Give me thy arm:
Poor Tom shall lead thee.   [*Exeunt.*

SCENE II.

Before the DUKE OF ALBANY'S *palace.*

Enter GONERIL *and* EDMUND.

GONERIL.

WELCOME, my lord; I marvel our mild husband
Not met us on the way.

Enter OSWALD.

          Now, where's your master?

OSWALD.

Madam, within; but never man so changed.
I told him of the army that was landed;
He smiled at it: I told him you were coming;
His answer was, 'The worse:' of Gloster's treachery,
And of the loyal service of his son,
When I inform'd him, then he call'd me sot,
And told me I had turn'd the wrong side out:—
What most he should dislike seems pleasant to
  him;
What like, offensive.

GONERIL [*to* EDMUND].

          Then shall you go no further.
It is the cowish terror of his spirit,
That dares not undertake: he'll not feel wrongs,
Which tie him to an answer. Our wishes on the
  way
May prove effects. Back, Edmund, to my brother;
Hasten his musters and conduct his powers:
I must change arms at home, and give the distaff
Into my husband's hands. This trusty servant
Shall pass between us: ere long you are like to hear,
If you dare venture in your own behalf,
A mistress's command. Wear this; spare speech;
                    [*Giving a favour.*
Decline your head: this kiss, if it durst speak,
Would stretch thy spirits up into the air:—
Conceive, and fare thee well.

EDMUND.

Yours in the ranks of death.

GONERIL.

          My most dear Gloster!
          [*Exit* EDMUND.

O, the difference of man and man! To thee
A woman's services are due: my fool
Usurps my body.

OSWALD.

    Madam, here comes my lord. [*Exit.*
Enter ALBANY.

GONERIL.

I have been worth the whistle.

DUKE OF ALBANY.

          O Goneril!
You are not worth the dust which the rude wind
Blows in your face. I fear your disposition:
That nature which contemns its origin
Cannot be border'd certain in itself;
She that herself will sliver and disbranch
From her material sap, perforce must wither,
And come to deadly use.

GONERIL.

No more; the text is foolish.

DUKE OF ALBANY.

Wisdom and goodness to the vile seem vile:
Filths savour but themselves. What have you
  done?
Tigers, not daughters, what have you perform'd?
A father, and a gracious aged man,
Whose reverence the head-lugg'd bear would lick,
Most barbarous, most degenerate! have you
  madded.
Could my good brother suffer you to do it?
A man, a prince, by him so benefited!
If that the heavens do not their visible spirits
Send quickly down to tame these vile offences,
It will come,
Humanity must perforce prey on itself,
Like monsters of the deep.

GONERIL.

          Milk-liver'd man!
That bear'st a cheek for blows, a head for wrongs;
Who hast not in thy brows an eye discerning
Thine honour from thy suffering; that not
  know'st
Fools do those villains pity who are punisht
Ere they have done their mischief. Where's thy
  drum?
France spreads his banners in our noiseless land;
With plumed helm thy slayer begins threats;
Whiles thou, a moral fool, sitt'st still, and criest
'Alack, why does he so?'

DUKE OF ALBANY.

          See thyself, devil!
Proper deformity seems not in the fiend
So horrid as in woman.

GONERIL.

          O vain fool!

DUKE OF ALBANY.

Thou changed and self-cover'd thing, for shame,
Be-monster not thy feature. Were't my fitness
To let these hands obey my blood,
They are apt enough to dislocate and tear
Thy flesh and bones:—howe'er thou art a fiend,
A woman's shape doth shield thee.

GONERIL.

Marry, your manhood! mew!

Enter a MESSENGER.

DUKE OF ALBANY.

What news?

MESSENGER.

O, my good lord, the Duke of Cornwall's dead;
Slain by his servant, going to put out
The other eye of Gloster.

DUKE OF ALBANY.

Gloster's eyes!

MESSENGER.

A servant that he bred, thrill'd with remorse,
Opposed against the act, bending his sword
To his great master; who, thereat enraged,
Flew on him, and amongst them fell'd him dead;
But not without that harmful stroke which since
Hath pluckt him after.

DUKE OF ALBANY.

This shows you are above,
You justicers, that these our nether crimes
So speedily can venge!—But, O poor Gloster!
Lost he his other eye?

MESSENGER.

Both, both, my lord.—
This letter, madam, craves a speedy answer;
'Tis from your sister.

GONERIL [aside].

One way I like this well;
But being widow, and my Gloster with her,
May all the building in my fancy pluck
Upon my hateful life: another way
The news is not so tart.—I'll read, and answer.
[Exit.

DUKE OF ALBANY.

Where was his son when they did take his eyes?

MESSENGER.

Come with my lady hither.

DUKE OF ALBANY.

He is not here.

MESSENGER.

No, my good lord; I met him back again.

DUKE OF ALBANY.

Knows he the wickedness?

MESSENGER.

Ay, my good lord; 'twas he inform'd against him;
And quit the house on purpose, that their punish-
Might have the freer course.   [ment

DUKE OF ALBANY.

Gloster, I live
To thank thee for the love thou show'dst the king,
And to revenge thine eyes.—Come hither, friend:
Tell me what more thou know'st.   [Exeunt.

SCENE III.

The French camp near Dover.

Enter KENT *and a* GENTLEMAN.

EARL OF KENT.

WHY the King of France is so suddenly gone
back know you the reason?

GENTLEMAN.

Something he left imperfect in the state, which
since his coming forth is thought of; which imports to the kingdom so much fear and danger,
that his personal return was most required and
necessary.

EARL OF KENT.

Who hath he left behind him general?

GENTLEMAN.

The Marshal of France, Monsieur La Far.

EARL OF KENT.

Did your letters pierce the queen to any demonstration of grief?

GENTLEMAN.

Ay, sir; she took them, read them in my presence;
And now and then an ample tear trill'd down
Her delicate cheek: it seem'd she was a queen
Over her passion; who, most rebel-like,
Sought to be king o'er her.

EARL OF KENT.

O, then it moved her.

GENTLEMAN.

Not to a rage: patience and sorrow strove
Who should express her goodliest. You have seen
Sunshine and rain at once: her smiles and tears
Were like a better way: those happy smilets
That play'd on her ripe lip seem'd not to know
What guests were in her eyes; which parted thence
As pearls from diamonds dropt.—In brief,
Sorrow would be a rarity most beloved,
If all could so become it.

EARL OF KENT.

Made she no verbal question?

GENTLEMAN.

Faith, once or twice she heaved the name of
'father'
Pantingly forth, as if it prest her heart;
Cried 'Sisters, sisters!—Shame of ladies! sisters!
Kent! father! sisters! What, i'the storm? i'the night?
Let pity not be believed!'—There she shook
The holy water from her heavenly eyes,
And clamour moisten'd: then away she started
To deal with grief alone.

EARL OF KENT.

It is the stars,
The stars above us, govern our conditions;
Else one self mate and mate could not beget
Such different issues. You spoke not with her
since?

GENTLEMAN.

No.

EARL OF KENT.

Was this before the king return'd?

GENTLEMAN.

No, since.

EARL OF KENT.

Well, sir, the poor distressed Lear's i'the town;
Who sometime, in his better tune, remembers
What we are come about, and by no means
Will yield to see his daughter.

GENTLEMAN.

Why, good sir?

EARL OF KENT.

A sovereign shame so elbows him: his own un-
kindness,
That stript her from his benediction, turn'd her
To foreign casualties, gave her dear rights
To his dog-hearted daughters,—these things sting
His mind so venomously that burning shame
Detains him from Cordelia.

GENTLEMAN.

Alack, poor gentleman!

EARL OF KENT.

Of Albany's and Cornwall's powers you heard not?

GENTLEMAN.

'Tis so, they are a-foot.

EARL OF KENT.

Well, sir, I'll bring you to our master Lear,
And leave you to attend him: some dear cause
Will in concealment wrap me up awhile;
When I am known aright, you shall not grieve
Lending me this acquaintance. I pray you, go
Along with me.   [*Exeunt.*

SCENE IV.

The same. A tent.

Enter, with drum and colours, CORDELIA,
DOCTOR, *and* SOLDIERS.

CORDELIA.

ALACK, 'tis he: why, he was met even now
As mad as the vext sea; singing aloud;
Crown'd with rank fumiter and furrow-weeds,
With bur-docks, hemlock, nettles, cuckoo-flowers,
Darnel, and all the idle weeds that grow
In our sustaining corn.—A century send forth;
Search every acre in the high-grown field,
And bring him to our eye. [*Exit an* OFFICER.]—
     What can man's wisdom
In the restoring his bereaved sense?
He that helps him take all my outward worth.

DOCTOR.

There is means, madam:
Our foster-nurse of nature is repose,
The which he lacks; that to provoke in him
Are many simples operative, whose power
Will close the eye of anguish.

CORDELIA.

     All blest secrets,
All you unpublisht virtues of the earth,
Spring with my tears! be aidant and remediate
In the good man's distress!—Seek, seek for him;
Lest his ungovern'd rage dissolve the life
That wants the means to lead it.

Enter a MESSENGER.

MESSENGER.

     News, madam;
The British powers are marching hitherward.

CORDELIA.

'Tis known before; our preparation stands
In expectation of them.—O dear father,
It is thy business that I go about;
Therefore great France
My mourning and important tears hath pitied.
No blown ambition doth our arms incite,
But love, dear love, and our aged father's right:
Soon may I hear and see him!   [*Exeunt.*

SCENE V.

A room in GLOSTER'S *castle.*

Enter REGAN *and* OSWALD.

REGAN.

BUT are my brother's powers set forth?

OSWALD.

     Ay, madam.

REGAN.

Himself in person there?

OSWALD.

     Madam, with much ado:
Your sister is the better soldier.

REGAN.

Lord Edmund spake not with your lord at home?

OSWALD.

No, madam.

REGAN.

What might import my sister's letter to him?

OSWALD.

I know not, lady.

REGAN.

Faith, he is posted hence on serious matter.
It was great ignorance, Gloster's eyes being out,
To let him live: where he arrives he moves
All hearts against us: Edmund, I think, is gone,
In pity of his misery, to dispatch
His nighted life; moreover, to descry
The strength o'th'enemy.

OSWALD.

I must needs after him, madam, with my letter.

REGAN.

Our troops set forth to-morrow: stay with us;
The ways are dangerous.

OSWALD.

     I may not, madam:
My lady charged my duty in this business.

REGAN.

Why should she write to Edmund? Might not you
Transport her purposes by word? Belike,
Something—I know not what:—I'll love thee
Let me unseal the letter.   [much,

OSWALD.

     Madam, I had rather—

REGAN.

I know your lady does not love her husband;
I am sure of that: and at her late being here
She gave strange œilliades and most speaking looks
To noble Edmund. I know you are of her bosom.

OSWALD.

I, madam?

REGAN.

I speak in understanding; you are, I know't:
Therefore I do advise you, take this note:
My lord is dead; Edmund and I have talkt;
And more convenient is he for my hand
Than for your lady's:—you may gather more.
If you do find him, pray you, give him this;
And when your mistress hears thus much from
I pray, desire her call her wisdom to her.   [you,
So, fare you well.
If you do chance to hear of that blind traitor,
Preferment falls on him that cuts him off.

OSWALD.

Would I could meet him, madam! I would show
What party I do follow.

REGAN.

     Fare thee well.   [*Exeunt.*

SCENE VI.

The country near Dover.

Enter GLOSTER, *and* EDGAR *drest like a*
peasant.

EARL OF GLOSTER.

WHEN shall I come to the top of that same
hill?

EDGAR.

You do climb up it now: look, how we labour.

EARL OF GLOSTER.

Methinks the ground is even.

EDGAR.
                              Horrible steep.
Hark, do you hear the sea?
EARL OF GLOSTER.
                              No, truly.
EDGAR.
Why, then, your other senses grow imperfect
By your eyes' anguish.
EARL OF GLOSTER.
                              So may it be, indeed:
Methinks thy voice is alter'd; and thou speak'st
In better phrase and matter than thou didst.
EDGAR.
Y'are much deceived: in nothing am I changed
But in my garments.
EARL OF GLOSTER.
                              Methinks y'are better spoken.
EDGAR.
Come on, sir; here's the place:—stand still.—How
     fearful
And dizzy 'tis to cast one's eyes so low!
The crows and choughs that wing the midway air
Show scarce so gross as beetles: half way down
Hangs one that gathers samphire,—dreadful trade!
Methinks he seems no bigger than his head:
The fishermen, that walk upon the beach,
Appear like mice; and yond tall anchoring bark,
Diminish'd to her cock,—her cock, a buoy
Almost too small for sight: the murmuring surge,
That on the unnumber'd idle pebbles chafes,
Cannot be heard so high.—I'll look no more;
Lest my brain turn, and the deficient sight
Topple down headlong.
EARL OF GLOSTER.
                              Set me where you stand.
EDGAR.
Give me your hand:—you are now within a foot
Of the extreme verge: for all beneath the moon
Would I not leap upright.
EARL OF GLOSTER.
                              Let go my hand.
Here, friend, 's another purse; in it a jewel
Well worth a poor man's taking: fairies and gods
Prosper it with thee! Go thou further off;
Bid me farewell, and let me hear thee going.
EDGAR.
Now fare you well, good sir.
EARL OF GLOSTER.
                              With all my heart.
EDGAR [aside].
Why I do trifle thus with his despair
Is done to cure it.
EARL OF GLOSTER [kneeling].
                              O you mighty gods!
This world I do renounce, and, in your sights,
Shake patiently my great affliction off:
If I could bear it longer, and not fall
To quarrel with your great opposeless wills,
My snuff and loathed part of nature should
Burn itself out. If Edgar live, O, bless him!—
Now, fellow, fare thee well.
EDGAR.
                              Gone, sir:—farewell.
                    [GLOSTER falls forward.
[aside] And yet I know not how conceit may rob
The treasury of life, when life itself

Yields to the theft: had he been where he thought,
By this had thought been past.—Alive or dead?
Ho you, sir! friend!—Hear you, sir! speak!
[aside] Thus might he pass indeed: yet he re-
     vives.—
What are you, sir?
EARL OF GLOSTER.
                              Away, and let me die.
EDGAR.
Hadst thou been aught but gossamer, feathers, air,
So many fathom down precipitating,
Thou'dst shiver'd like an egg: but thou dost
     breathe;
Hast heavy substance; bleed'st not; speak'st; art
     sound.
Ten masts at each make not the altitude
Which thou hast perpendicularly fell:
Thy life's a miracle. Speak yet again.
EARL OF GLOSTER.
But have I faln, or no?
EDGAR.
From the dread summit of this chalky bourn.
Look up a-height;—the shrill-gorged lark so far
Cannot be seen or heard: do but look up.
EARL OF GLOSTER.
Alack, I have no eyes.—
Is wretchedness deprived that benefit
To end itself by death? 'Twas yet some comfort,
When misery could beguile the tyrant's rage,
And frustrate his proud will.
EDGAR.
                              Give me your arm:
Up:—so.—How is't? Feel you your legs? You
     stand.
EARL OF GLOSTER.
Too well, too well.
EDGAR.
                              This is above all strangeness.
Upon the crown o'the cliff, what thing was that
Which parted from you?
EARL OF GLOSTER.
                              A poor unfortunate beggar.
EDGAR.
As I stood here below, methought his eyes
Were two full moons; he had a thousand noses,
Horns whelkt and waved like the enridged sea:
It was some fiend; therefore, thou happy father,
Think that the clearest gods, who make them
     honours
Of men's impossibilities, have preserved thee.
EARL OF GLOSTER.
I do remember now: henceforth I'll bear
Affliction till it do cry out itself
'Enough, enough,' and die. That thing you speak
     of,
I took it for a man; often 'twould say
'The fiend, the fiend:' he led me to that place.
EDGAR.
Bear free and patient thoughts.—But who comes
     here?
Enter LEAR, fantastically drest with wild flowers.
The safer sense will ne'er accommodate
His master thus.
KING LEAR.
No, they cannot touch me for coining; I am the
king himself.

EDGAR [*aside*].
O thou side-piercing sight!
          KING LEAR.
Nature's above art in that respect.—There's your
press-money. That fellow handles his bow like a
crow-keeper: draw me a clothier's yard.—Look,
look, a mouse! Peace, peace;—this piece of
toasted cheese will do't.—There's my gauntlet;
I'll prove it on a giant.—Bring up the brown bills.
—O, well flown, bird!—i'the clout, i'the clout:
hewgh!—Give the word.
          EDGAR.
Sweet marjoram.
          KING LEAR.
Pass.
          EARL OF GLOSTER.
I know that voice.
          KING LEAR.
Ha! Goneril,—with a white beard!—They flatter'd me like a dog; and told me I had white hairs
in my beard ere the black ones were there.—To
say 'ay' and 'no' to every thing that I said!—'Ay'
and 'no' too was no good divinity. When the rain
came to wet me once, and the wind to make me
chatter; when the thunder would not peace at my
bidding; there I found 'em, there I smelt 'em out.
Go to, they are not men o' their words: they told me
I was every thing; 'tis a lie,—I am not ague-proof.
          EARL OF GLOSTER.
The trick of that voice I do well remember:
Is't not the king?
          KING LEAR.
          Ay, every inch a king:
When I do stare, see how the subject quakes!
I pardon that man's life.—What was thy cause?—
Adultery?
Thou shalt not die: die for adultery! No:
The wren goes to't, and the small gilded fly
Does lecher in my sight.
Let copulation thrive: for Gloster's bastard son
Was kinder to his father than my daughters
Got 'tween the lawful sheets.
To't, luxury, pell-mell! for I lack soldiers.
Behold yond simpering dame,
Whose face between her forks presages snow,
That minces virtue, and does shake the head
To hear of pleasure's name,—
The fitchew nor the soiled horse goes to't
With a more riotous appetite.
Down from the waist they are Centaurs,
Though women all above:
But to the girdle do the gods inherit,
Beneath is all the fiends';
There's hell, there's darkness, there's the sulphur-
ous pit,
burning, scalding, stench, consumption;—fie, fie,
fie! pah, pah! Give me an ounce of civet, good
apothecary, to sweeten my imagination: there's
money for thee.
          EARL OF GLOSTER.
O, let me kiss that hand!
          KING LEAR.
Let me wipe it first; it smells of mortality.
          EARL OF GLOSTER.
O ruin'd piece of nature! This great world
Shall so wear out to naught.—Dost thou know me?

          KING LEAR.
I remember thine eyes well enough. Dost thou
squiny at me? No, do thy worst, blind Cupid; I'll
not love.—Read thou this challenge; mark but
the penning on't.
          EARL OF GLOSTER.
Were all the letters suns, I could not see one.
          EDGAR [*aside*].
I would not take this from report;—it is,
And my heart breaks at it.
          KING LEAR.
Read.
          EARL OF GLOSTER.
What, with the case of eyes?
          KING LEAR.
O, ho, are you there with me? No eyes in your
head, nor no money in your purse? Your eyes are
in a heavy case, your purse in a light: yet you see
how this world goes.
          EARL OF GLOSTER.
I see it feelingly.
          KING LEAR.
What, art mad? A man may see how this world
goes with no eyes. Look with thine ears: see how
yond justice rails upon yond simple thief. Hark,
in thine ear: change places; and, handy-dandy,
which is the justice, which is the thief?—Thou
hast seen a farmer's dog bark at a beggar?
          EARL OF GLOSTER.
Ay, sir.
          KING LEAR.
And the creature run from the cur? There thou
mightst behold the great image of authority: a
dog's obey'd in office.—
Thou rascal beadle, hold thy bloody hand!
Why dost thou lash that whore? Strip thine own
    back;
Thou hotly lusts to use her in that kind
For which thou whipst her. The usurer hangs the
    cozener.
Through tatter'd clothes small vices do appear;
Robes and furr'd gowns hide all. Plate sin with
    gold,
And the strong lance of justice hurtless breaks;
Arm it in rags, a pigmy's straw does pierce it.
None does offend, none,—I say, none; I'll able 'em:
Take that of me, my friend, who have the power
To seal the accuser's lips. Get thee glass eyes;
And, like a scurvy politician, seem
To see the things thou dost not.—Now, now,
    now, now:
Pull off my boots:—harder, harder:—so.
          EDGAR [*aside*].
O, matter and impertinency mixt!
Reason in madness!
          KING LEAR.
If thou wilt weep my fortunes, take my eyes.
I know thee well enough; thy name is Gloster:
Thou must be patient; we came crying hither:
Thou know'st, the first time that we smell the air,
We wawl and cry.—I will preach to thee: mark.
          EARL OF GLOSTER.
Alack, alack the day!
          KING LEAR.
When we are born, we cry that we are come
To this great stage of fools.—This' a good block:—

It were a delicate stratagem to shoe
A troop of horse with felt: I'll put't in proof;
And when I have stoln upon these sons-in-law,
Then, kill, kill, kill, kill, kill, kill!

Enter a GENTLEMAN, *with* ATTENDANTS.

GENTLEMAN.

O, here he is: lay hand upon him.—Sir,
Your most dear daughter—

KING LEAR.

No rescue? What, a prisoner? I am even
The natural fool of fortune.—Use me well;
You shall have ransom. Let me have a surgeon;
I am cut to the brains.

GENTLEMAN.

            You shall have any thing.

KING LEAR.

No seconds? all myself?
Why, this would make a man a man of salt,
To use his eyes for garden water-pots,
Ay, and laying autumn's dust.

GENTLEMAN.

Good sir,—

KING LEAR.

I will die bravely, like a smug bridegroom.
   What!
I will be jovial: come, come; I am a king;
My masters, know you that.

GENTLEMAN.

You are a royal one, and we obey you.

KING LEAR.

Then there's life in't. Nay, an you get it, you
shall get it by running. Sa, sa, sa, sa.

     [*Exit running.* ATTENDANTS *follow.*

GENTLEMAN.

A sight most pitiful in the meanest wretch,
Past speaking of in a king!—Thou hast one
   daughter,
Who redeems nature from the general curse
Which twain have brought her to.

EDGAR.

Hail, gentle sir.

GENTLEMAN.

     Sir, speed you: what's your will?

EDGAR.

Do you hear aught, sir, of a battle toward?

GENTLEMAN.

Most sure and vulgar: every one hears that,
Which can distinguish sound.

EDGAR.

         But, by your favour,
How near's the other army?

GENTLEMAN.

Near and on speedy foot; the main descry
Stands on the hourly thought.

EDGAR.

     I thank you, sir: that's all.

GENTLEMAN.

Though that the queen on special cause is here,
Her army is moved on.

EDGAR.

     I thank you, sir.

     [*Exit* GENTLEMAN.

EARL OF GLOSTER.

You ever-gentle gods, take my breath from me;
Let not my worser spirit tempt me again
To die before you please!

EDGAR.

     Well pray you, father.

EARL OF GLOSTER.

Now, good sir, what are you?

EDGAR.

A most poor man, made tame to fortune's blows;
Who, by the art of known and feeling sorrows,
Am pregnant to good pity. Give me your hand,
I'll lead you to some biding.

EARL OF GLOSTER.

     Hearty thanks:
The bounty and the benison of heaven
To boot, and boot!

Enter OSWALD.

OSWALD.

     A proclaim'd prize! Most happy!
That eyeless head of thine was first framed flesh
To raise my fortunes.—Thou old unhappy traitor,
Briefly thyself remember:—the sword is out
That must destroy thee.

EARL OF GLOSTER.

     Now let thy friendly hand
Put strength enough to't.   [EDGAR *interposes.*

OSWALD.

     Wherefore, bold peasant
Darest thou support a publisht traitor? Hence;
Lest that the infection of his fortune take
Like hold on thee. Let go his arm.

EDGAR.

Chill not let go, zir, without vurther 'casion.

OSWALD.

Let go, slave, or thou diest!

EDGAR.

Good gentleman, go your gait, and let poor volk
pass. An chud ha' bin zwagger'd out of my life,
'twould not ha' bin zo long as 'tis by a vortnight.
Nay, come not near the old man; keep out, che
vor ye, or ise try whether your costard or my
ballow be the harder: chill be plain with you.

OSWALD.

Out, dunghill!

EDGAR.

Chill pick your teeth, zir: come; no matter vor
your foins.

     [*They fight, and* EDGAR *knocks him down.*

OSWALD.

Slave, thou hast slain me:—villain, take my purse:
If ever thou wilt thrive, bury my body;
And give the letters which thou find'st about me
To Edmund earl of Gloster; seek him out
Upon the English party:—O, untimely death!
Death!   [*Dies.*

EDGAR.

I know thee well: a serviceable villain;
As duteous to the vices of thy mistress
As badness would desire.

EARL OF GLOSTER.

     What, is he dead?

EDGAR.

Sit you down, father; rest you.—
Let's see his pockets: these letters that he speaks of
May be my friends.—He's dead; I am only sorry
He had no other death's-man.—Let us see:—
Leave, gentle wax; and, manners, blame us not:
To know our enemies' minds, we'ld rip their
   hearts;

Their papers, is more lawful.

[*Reads*] Let our reciprocal vows be remember'd.
You have many opportunities to cut him off:
if your will want not, time and place will be fruitfully offer'd. There is nothing done, if he return
the conqueror: then am I the prisoner, and his
bed my gaol; from the warmth loathed whereof
deliver me, and supply the place for your labour.
         Your—wife, so I would say—
         Affectionate servant,

                     GONERIL.

O undistinguisht space of woman's will!
A plot upon her virtuous husband's life;
And the exchange my brother!—Here, in the
     sands,
Thee I'll rake up, the post unsanctified
Of murderous lechers: and, in the mature time,
With this ungracious paper strike the sight
Of the death-practised duke: for him 'tis well
That of thy death and business I can tell.

              EARL OF GLOSTER.

The king is mad: how stiff is my vile sense,
That I stand up, and have ingenious feeling
Of my huge sorrows! Better I were distract:
So should my thoughts be sever'd from my griefs,
And woes, by wrong imaginations, lose
The knowledge of themselves.

                   EDGAR.

         Give me your hand: [*Drum afar off.*
Far off, methinks, I hear the beaten drum:
Come, father, I'll bestow you with a friend.
                           [*Exeunt.*

SCENE VII.

A tent in the French camp.

Enter CORDELIA, KENT, DOCTOR, *and*
GENTLEMAN.

                 CORDELIA.

O THOU good Kent, how shall I live and
     work,
To match thy goodness? My life will be too short,
And every measure fail me.

              EARL OF KENT.

To be acknowledged, madam, is o'erpaid.
All my reports go with the modest truth;
Nor more nor clipt, but so.

                 CORDELIA.

         Be better suited:
These weeds are memories of those worser hours:
I prithee, put them off.

              EARL OF KENT.

         Pardon, dear madam;
Yet to be known shortens my made intent:
My boon I make it, that you know me not
Till time and I think meet.

                 CORDELIA.

Then be't so, my good lord.—[*to the* DOCTOR]
     How does the king?

               DOCTOR.

Madam, sleeps still.

                 CORDELIA.

O you kind gods,
Cure this great breach in his abused nature!
Th'untuned and jarring senses, O, wind up
Of this child-changed father!

                 DOCTOR.

           So please your majesty
That we may wake the king: he hath slept long.

                 CORDELIA.

Be govern'd by your knowledge, and proceed
I'the sway of your own will. Is he array'd?

     Enter LEAR *in a chair carried by* SERVANTS.

              GENTLEMAN.

Ay, madam; in the heaviness of sleep
We put fresh garments on him.

                 DOCTOR.

Be by, good madam, when we do awake him;
I doubt not of his temperance.

                 CORDELIA.

               Very well.

               DOCTOR.

Please you, draw near.—Louder the music there!

                 CORDELIA.

O my dear father! Restoration hang
Thy medicine on my lips; and let this kiss
Repair those violent harms that my two sisters
Have in thy reverence made!

                 EARL OF KENT.

           Kind and dear princess!

                 CORDELIA.

Had you not been their father, these white flakes
Had challenged pity of them. Was this a face
To be opposed against the warring winds?
To stand against the deep dread-bolted thunder?
In the most terrible and nimble stroke
Of quick, cross lightning? to watch—poor per-
     du!—
With this thin helm? Mine enemy's dog,
Though he had bit me, should have stood that
     night
Against my fire; and wast thou fain, poor father,
To hovel thee with swine, and rogues forlorn,
In short and musty straw? Alack, alack!
'Tis wonder that thy life and wits at once
Had not concluded all.—He wakes; speak to him.

               DOCTOR.

Madam, do you: 'tis fittest.

                 CORDELIA.

How does my royal lord? how fares your majesty?

                 KING LEAR.

You do me wrong to take me out o'the grave:—
Thou art a soul in bliss; but I am bound
Upon a wheel of fire, that mine own tears
Do scald like molten lead.

                 CORDELIA.

           Sir, do you know me?

                 KING LEAR.

You are a spirit, I know: when did you die?

                 CORDELIA.

Still, still, far wide!

               DOCTOR.

He's scarce awake: let him alone awhile.

               KING LEAR.

Where have I been? Where am I?—Fair day-
     light?—
I am mightily abused.—I should e'en die with
     pity,
To see another thus.—I know not what to say.—
I will not swear these are my hands:—let's see;
I feel this pin prick. Would I were assured
Of my condition.

CORDELIA.
O, look upon me, sir,
And hold your hands in benediction o'er me:—
No, sir, you must not kneel.

KING LEAR.
Pray, do not mock me:
I am a very foolish fond old man,
Fourscore and upward, not an hour more nor
    less;
And, to deal plainly,
I fear I am not in my perfect mind.
Methinks I should know you, and know this man;
Yet I am doubtful: for I am mainly ignorant
What place this is; and all the skill I have
Remembers not these garments; nor I know not
Where I did lodge last night. Do not laugh at me;
For, as I am a man, I think this lady
To be my child Cordelia.

CORDELIA.
And so I am, I am.

KING LEAR.
Be your tears wet? yes, faith. I pray, weep not:
If you have poison for me, I will drink it.
I know you do not love me; for your sisters
Have, as I do remember, done me wrong:
You have some cause, they have not.

CORDELIA.
No cause, no cause.

KING LEAR.
Am I in France?

EARL OF KENT.
In your own kingdom, sir.

KING LEAR.
Do not abuse me.

DOCTOR.
Be comforted, good madam: the great rage,
You see, is kill'd in him: and yet it is danger
To make him even o'er the time he has lost.
Desire him to go in; trouble him no more
Till further settling.

CORDELIA.
Will't please your highness walk?

KING LEAR.
You must bear with me:
Pray you now, forget and forgive: I am old and
    foolish.
[*Exeunt all but* KENT *and* GENTLEMAN.

GENTLEMAN.
Holds it true, sir, that the Duke of Cornwall was
so slain?

EARL OF KENT.
Most certain, sir.

GENTLEMAN.
Who is conductor of his people?

EARL OF KENT.
As 'tis said, the bastard son of Gloster.

GENTLEMAN.
They say Edgar, his banisht son, is with the Earl
of Kent in Germany.

EARL OF KENT.
Report is changeable. 'Tis time to look about; the
powers of the kingdom approach apace.

GENTLEMAN.
The arbitrement is like to be bloody. Fare you
well, sir.
[*Exit.*

EARL OF KENT.
My point and period will be throughly wrought,
Or well or ill, as this day's battle's fought. [*Exit.*

ACT V. SCENE I.

The British camp, near Dover.

Enter, with drum and colours, EDMUND, REGAN,
OFFICERS, SOLDIERS, *and others.*

EDMUND.
KNOW of the duke if his last purpose hold,
    Or whether since he is advised by aught
To change the course: he's full of alteration
And self-reproving:—bring his constant pleasure.
[*To an* OFFICER, *who goes out.*

REGAN.
Our sister's man is certainly miscarried.

EDMUND.
'Tis to be doubted, madam.

REGAN.
Now, sweet lord,
You know the goodness I intend upon you:
Tell me,—but truly,—but then speak the truth,
Do you not love my sister?

EDMUND.
In honour'd love.

REGAN.
But have you never found my brother's way
To the forfended place?

EDMUND.
That thought abuses you.

REGAN.
I am doubtful that you have been conjunct
And bosom'd with her, as far as we call hers.

EDMUND.
No, by mine honour, madam.

REGAN.
I never shall endure her: dear my lord,
Be not familiar with her.

EDMUND.
Fear me not:—
She and the duke her husband!

Enter, with drum and colours, ALBANY,
GONERIL, *and* SOLDIERS.

GONERIL [*aside*].
I had rather lose the battle than that sister
Should loosen him and me.

DUKE OF ALBANY.
Our very loving sister, well be-met.—
Sir, this I hear,—the king is come to his daugh-
    ter,
With others whom the rigour of our state
Forced to cry out. Where I could not be honest,
I never yet was valiant: for this business,
It toucheth us, as France invades our land,
Not bolds the king, with others, whom, I fear,
Most just and heavy causes make oppose.

EDMUND.
Sir, you speak nobly.

REGAN.
Why is this reason'd?

GONERIL.
Combine together 'gainst the enemy;

For these domestic and particular broils
Are not the question here.
                    DUKE OF ALBANY.
                              Let's, then, determine
With the ancient of war on our proceedings.
                    EDMUND.
I shall attend you presently at your tent.
                    REGAN.
Sister, you'll go with us?
                    GONERIL.
No.
                    REGAN.
'Tis most convenient; pray you, go with us.
                    GONERIL [aside].
O, ho, I know the riddle.—I will go.
    As they are going out, enter EDGAR disguised.
                    EDGAR.
If e'er your Grace had speech with man so poor,
Hear me one word.
                    DUKE OF ALBANY.
                         I'll overtake you.—Speak.
        [Exeunt all but ALBANY and EDGAR.
                    EDGAR.
Before you fight the battle, ope this letter.
If you have victory, let the trumpet sound
For him that brought it: wretched though I
    seem,
I can produce a champion that will prove
What is avouched there. If you miscarry,
Your business of the world hath so an end,
And machination ceases. Fortune love you!
                    DUKE OF ALBANY.
Stay till I have read the letter.
                    EDGAR.
                         I was forbid it.
When time shall serve, let but the herald cry,
And I'll appear again.
                    DUKE OF ALBANY.
Why, fare thee well: I will o'erlook thy paper.
                              [Exit EDGAR.
            Enter EDMUND.
                    EDMUND.
The enemy's in view; draw up your powers.
Here is the guess of their true strength and forces
By diligent discovery;—but your haste
Is now urged on you.
                    DUKE OF ALBANY.
                    We will greet the time. [Exit.
                    EDMUND.
To both these sisters have I sworn my love;
Each jealous of the other, as the stung
Are of the adder. Which of them shall I take?
Both? one? or neither? Neither can be enjoy'd,
If both remain alive: to take the widow
Exasperates, makes mad her sister Goneril;
And hardly shall I carry out my side,
Her husband being alive. Now, then, we'll use
His countenance for the battle; which being
    done,
Let her who would be rid of him devise
His speedy taking off. As for the mercy
Which he intends to Lear and to Cordelia,—
The battle done, and they within our power,
Shall never see his pardon; for my state
Stands on me to defend, not to debate.   [Exit.

SCENE II.

A field between the two camps.

Alarum within. Enter, with drum and colours,
LEAR, CORDELIA, *and their* FORCES *over the*
stage; and exeunt.

            Enter EDGAR *and* GLOSTER.
                    EDGAR.
HERE, father, take the shadow of this tree
For your good host; pray that the right may
        thrive:
If ever I return to you again,
I'll bring you comfort.
                    EARL OF GLOSTER.
            Grace go with you, sir! [Exit EDGAR.
    Alarum and retreat within.   Enter EDGAR.
                    EDGAR.
Away, old man,—give me thy hand,—away!
King Lear hath lost, he and his daughter ta'en:
Give me thy hand; come on.
                    EARL OF GLOSTER.
No further, sir; a man may rot even here.
                    EDGAR.
What, in ill thoughts again? Men must endure
Their going hence, even as their coming hither:
Ripeness is all:—come on.
                    EARL OF GLOSTER.
            And that's true too.   [Exeunt.

SCENE III.

The British camp, near Dover.

Enter, in conquest, with drum and colours, ED-
MUND; LEAR *and* CORDELIA *as prisoners;*
OFFICERS, SOLDIERS, &c.
                    EDMUND.
SOME officers take them away: good guard,
Until their greater pleasures first be known
That are to censure them.
                    CORDELIA.
                    We are not the first
Who, with best meaning, have incurr'd the worst.
For thee, oppressed king, am I cast down;
Myself could else out-frown false fortune's
    frown.—
Shall we not see these daughters and these sisters?
                    KING LEAR.
No, no, no, no! Come, let's away to prison:
We two alone will sing like birds i'the cage:
When thou dost ask me blessing, I'll kneel down,
And ask of thee forgiveness: so we'll live,
And pray, and sing, and tell old tales, and laugh
At gilded butterflies, and hear poor rogues
Talk of court news; and we'll talk with them
    too,—
Who loses and who wins; who's in, who's out;—
And take upon's the mystery of things,
As if we were God's spies: and we'll wear out,
In a wall'd prison, packs and sects of great ones,
That ebb and flow by th'moon.
                    EDMUND.
                         Take them away.
                    KING LEAR.
Upon such sacrifices, my Cordelia,
The gods themselves throw incense. Have I
    caught thee?

He that parts us shall bring a brand from heaven,
And fire us hence like foxes. Wipe thine eyes;
The good-years shall devour them, flesh and fell,
Ere they shall make us weep; we'll see 'em starve
    first.
Come.   [*Exeunt* LEAR *and* CORDELIA, *guarded.*
                    EDMUND.
Come hither, captain; hark.
Take thou this note [*giving a paper*]; go follow
    them to prison:
One step I have advanced thee; if thou dost
As this instructs thee, thou dost make thy way
To noble fortunes: know thou this, that men
Are as the time is: to be tender-minded
Does not become a sword:—thy great employ-
    ment
Will not bear question; either say thou'lt do't,
Or thrive by other means.
                    OFFICER.
                        I'll do't, my lord.
                    EDMUND.
About it; and write happy when thou hast done.
Mark,—I say, instantly; and carry it so
As I have set it down.
                    OFFICER.
I cannot draw a cart, nor eat dried oats;
If it be man's work, I'll do't.   [*Exit.*
Flourish. Enter ALBANY, GONERIL, REGAN,
    OFFICERS, *and* ATTENDANTS.
                DUKE OF ALBANY.
Sir, you have shown to-day your valiant strain,
And fortune led you well: you have the captives
Who were the opposites of this day's strife:
We do require them of you, so to use them
As we shall find their merits and our safety
May equally determine.
                    EDMUND.
                        Sir, I thought it fit
To send the old and miserable king
To some retention and appointed guard;
Whose age has charms in it, whose title more,
To pluck the common bosom on his side,
And turn our imprest lances in our eyes
Which do command them. With him I sent the
    queen;
My reason all the same; and they are ready
To-morrow, or at further space, t'appear
Where you shall hold your session. At this time
We sweat and bleed: the friend hath lost his
    friend;
And the best quarrels, in the heat, are cursed
By those that feel their sharpness:—
The question of Cordelia and her father
Requires a fitter place.
                DUKE OF ALBANY.
                        Sir, by your patience,
I hold you but a subject of this war,
Not as a brother.
                    REGAN.
                That's as we list to grace him.
Methinks our pleasure might have been de-
    manded,
Ere you had spoke so far. He led our powers;
Bore the commission of my place and person;
The which immediacy may well stand up
And call itself your brother.

                    GONERIL.
                        Not so hot:
In his own grace he doth exalt himself,
More than in your addition.
                    REGAN.
                        In my rights
By me invested, he compeers the best.
                    GONERIL.
That were the most, if he should husband you.
                    REGAN.
Jesters do oft prove prophets.
                    GONERIL.
                        Holla, holla!
That eye that told you so lookt but a-squint.
                    REGAN.
Lady, I am not well; else I should answer
From a full-flowing stomach.—General,
Take thou my soldiers, prisoners, patrimony;
Dispose of them, of me; the walls are thine:
Witness the world that I create thee here
My lord and master.
                    GONERIL.
                Mean you to enjoy him?
                DUKE OF ALBANY.
The let-alone lies not in your good will.
                    EDMUND.
Nor in thine, lord.
                DUKE OF ALBANY.
                Half-blooded fellow, yes.
                REGAN [*to* EDMUND].
Let the drum strike, and prove my title thine.
                DUKE OF ALBANY.
Stay yet; hear reason.—Edmund, I arrest thee
On capital treason; and, in thy arrest,
This gilded serpent [*pointing to* GONERIL].—For
    your claim, fair sister,
I bar it in the interest of my wife;
'Tis she is sub-contracted to this lord,
And I, her husband, contradict your banns.
If you will marry, make your loves to me;
My lady is bespoke.
                    GONERIL.
                An interlude!
                DUKE OF ALBANY.
Thou art arm'd, Gloster:—let the trumpet sound:
If none appear to prove upon thy person
Thy heinous, manifest, and many treasons,
There is my pledge [*throwing down a glove*]; I'll
    prove it on thy heart,
Ere I taste bread, thou art in nothing less
Than I have here proclaim'd thee.
                    REGAN.
                        Sick, O, sick!
                GONERIL [*aside*].
If not, I'll ne'er trust medicine.
                    EDMUND.
There's my exchange [*throwing down a glove*]:
    what in the world is he
That names me traitor, villain-like he lies:
Call by thy trumpet: he that dares approach,
On him, on you, who not? I will maintain
My truth and honour firmly.
                DUKE OF ALBANY.
A herald, ho!
                    EDMUND.
        A herald, ho, a herald!

DUKE OF ALBANY.
Trust to thy single virtue; for thy soldiers,
All levied in my name, have in my name
Took their discharge.

REGAN.
            My sickness grows upon me.

DUKE OF ALBANY.
She is not well; convey her to my tent.
            [Exit REGAN, led.
            Enter a HERALD.
Come hither, herald,—Let the trumpet sound,—
And read out this.

OFFICER.
Sound, trumpet!   [A trumpet sounds.

HERALD [reads].
If any man of quality or degree within the lists of
the army will maintain upon Edmund, supposed
Earl of Gloster, that he is a manifold traitor, let
him appear by the third sound of the trumpet: he
is bold in his defence.

EDMUND.
Sound!   [First trumpet.

HERALD.
Again!   [Second trumpet.
Again!   [Third trumpet.
            [Trumpet answers within.
    Enter EDGAR, at the third sound, arm'd, a
            trumpet before him.

DUKE OF ALBANY.
Ask him his purposes, why he appears
Upon this call o'the trumpet.

HERALD.
            What are you?
Your name, your quality? and why you answer
This present summons?

EDGAR.
            Know, my name is lost;
By treason's tooth bare-gnawn and canker-bit:
Yet am I noble as the adversary
I come to cope.

DUKE OF ALBANY.
            Which is that adversary?

EDGAR.
What's he that speaks for Edmund earl of Gloster?

EDMUND.
Himself:—what say'st thou to him?

EDGAR.
            Draw thy sword,
That, if my speech offend a noble heart,
Thy arm may do thee justice: here is mine.
Behold, it is the privilege of mine honours,
My oath, and my profession: I protest,—
Maugre thy strength, youth, place, and eminence,
Despite thy victor sword and fire-new fortune,
Thy valour and thy heart,—thou art a traitor;
False to thy gods, thy brother, and thy father;
Conspirant 'gainst this high illustrious prince;
And, from th'extremest upward of thy head
To the descent and dust below thy foot,
A most toad-spotted traitor. Say thou 'no,'
This sword, this arm, and my best spirits are bent,
To prove upon thy heart, whereto I speak,
Thou liest.

EDMUND.
            In wisdom I should ask thy name;
But, since thy outside looks so fair and warlike,

And that thy tongue some say of breeding
            breathes,
What safe and nicely I might well delay
By rule of knighthood, I disdain and spurn:
Back do I toss these treasons to thy head;
With the hell-hated lie o'erwhelm thy heart;
Which,—for they yet glance by, and scarcely
            bruise,—
This sword of mine shall give them instant way,
Where they shall rest for ever.—Trumpets,
            speak!
            [Alarums. They fight. EDMUND falls.

DUKE OF ALBANY.
Save him, save him!

GONERIL.
            This is practice, Gloster:
By the law of arms thou wast not bound to answer
An unknown opposite; thou art not vanquisht,
But cozen'd and beguiled.

DUKE OF ALBANY.
            Shut your mouth, dame,
Or with this paper shall I stop it:—Hold, sir;
Thou worse than any name, read thine own
            evil:—
No tearing lady; I perceive you know it.
            [Gives the letter to EDMUND.

GONERIL.
Say, if I do,—the laws are mine, not thine:
Who can arraign me for't?

DUKE OF ALBANY.
            Most monstrous!
Know'st thou this paper?

GONERIL.
            Ask me not what I know. [Exit.

DUKE OF ALBANY.
Go after her: she's desperate; govern her.
            [To an OFFICER, who goes out.

EDMUND.
What you have charged me with, that have I done;
And more, much more; the time will bring it out:
'Tis past, and so am I.—But what art thou
That hast this fortune on me? If thou'rt noble,
I do forgive thee.

EDGAR.
            Let's exchange charity.
I am no less in blood than thou art, Edmund;
If more, the more thou hast wrong'd me.
My name is Edgar, and thy father's son.
The gods are just, and of our pleasant vices
Make instruments to plague us:
The dark and vicious place where thee he got
Cost him his eyes.

EDMUND.
            Thou hast spoken right, 'tis true;
The wheel is come full circle; I am here.

DUKE OF ALBANY.
Methought thy very gait did prophesy
A royal nobleness:—I must embrace thee:
Let sorrow split my heart, if ever I
Did hate thee or thy father!

EDGAR.
            Worthy prince,
I know't.

DUKE OF ALBANY.
Where have you hid yourself?
How have you known the miseries of your father?

EDGAR.
By nursing them, my lord.—List a brief tale;—
And when 'tis told, O, that my heart would
      burst!—
The bloody proclamation to escape,
That follow'd me so near,—O, our lives' sweet-
      ness!
That we the pain of death would hourly die
Rather than die at once!—taught me to shift
Into a madman's rags; t'assume a semblance
That very dogs disdain'd: and in this habit
Met I my father with his bleeding rings,
Their precious stones new lost; became his guide,
Led him, begg'd for him, saved him from despair;
Never—O fault!—reveal'd myself unto him,
Until some half-hour past, when I was arm'd;
Not sure, though hoping, of this good success,
I askt his blessing, and from first to last
Told him my pilgrimage: but his flaw'd heart,
Alack, too weak the conflict to support,
'Twixt two extremes of passion, joy and grief,
Burst smilingly.
            EDMUND.
            This speech of yours hath moved me,
And shall perchance do good: but speak you on;
You look as you had something more to say.
            DUKE OF ALBANY.
If there be more, more woeful, hold it in;
For I am almost ready to dissolve,
Hearing of this.
            EDGAR.
            This would have seem'd a period
To such as love not sorrow; but another,
To amplify too much, would make much more,
And top extremity.
Whilst I was big in clamour, came there a man,
Who, having seen me in my worst estate,
Shunn'd my abhorr'd society; but then, finding
Who 'twas that so endured, with his strong arms
He fasten'd on my neck, and bellow'd out
As he'ld burst heaven; threw him on my father;
Told the most piteous tale of Lear and him
That ever ear received: which in recounting
His grief grew puissant, and the strings of life
Began to crack: twice then the trumpets sounded,
And there I left him tranced.
            DUKE OF ALBANY.
                  But who was this?
            EDGAR.
Kent, sir, the banisht Kent; who in disguise
Follow'd his enemy king, and did him service
Improper for a slave.
      Enter a GENTLEMAN *with a bloody knife.*
            GENTLEMAN.
Help, help, O, help!
            EDGAR.
                  What kind of help?
            DUKE OF ALBANY.
                        Speak, man.
            EDGAR.
What means that bloody knife?
            GENTLEMAN.
                        'Tis hot, it smokes;
It came even from the heart of—O, she's dead!
            DUKE OF ALBANY.
Who dead? speak, man.

GENTLEMAN.
Your lady, sir, your lady: and her sister
By her is poisoned; she hath confest it.
            EDMUND.
I was contracted to them both: all three
Now marry in an instant.
            EDGAR.
                  Here comes Kent.
            DUKE OF ALBANY.
Produce their bodies, be they alive or dead:—
This judgement of the heavens, that makes us
      tremble,
Touches us not with pity.   [*Exit* GENTLEMAN.
            Enter KENT.
                  O, is this he?
The time will not allow the compliment
Which very manners urges.
            EARL OF KENT.
                        I am come
To bid my king and master aye good night:
Is he not here?
            DUKE OF ALBANY.
                  Great thing of us forgot!—
Speak, Edmund, where's the king? and where's
      Cordelia?—
            [*The bodies of* GONERIL *and* REGAN *are
                  brought in.*
See'st thou this object, Kent?
            EARL OF KENT.
Alack, why thus?
            EDMUND.
                  Yet Edmund was beloved:
The one the other poison'd for my sake,
And after slew herself.
            DUKE OF ALBANY.
Even so.—Cover their faces.
            EDMUND.
I pant for life: some good I mean to do,
Despite of mine own nature. Quickly send—
Be brief in it—to the castle; for my writ
Is on the life of Lear and on Cordelia:—
Nay, send in time.
            DUKE OF ALBANY.
                  Run, run, O, run!
            EDGAR.
To who, my lord?—Who hath the office? send
Thy token of reprieve.
            EDMUND.
Well thought on: take my sword;
Give it the captain.
            DUKE OF ALBANY.
                  Haste thee, for thy life. [*Exit* EDGAR.
            EDMUND.
He hath commission from thy wife and me
To hang Cordelia in the prison, and
To lay the blame upon her own despair,
That she fordid herself.
            DUKE OF ALBANY.
The gods defend her!—Bear him hence awhile.
                  [EDMUND *is borne off.*
      Enter LEAR, *with* CORDELIA *dead in his arms;*
            EDGAR, OFFICER, *and others.*
            KING LEAR.
Howl, howl, howl, howl!—O, you are men of
      stone:
Had I your tongues and eyes, I'ld use them so

That heaven's vault should crack.—She's gone
   for ever!—
I know when one is dead, and when one lives;
She's dead as earth.—Lend me a looking-glass;
If that her breath will mist or stain the stone,
Why, then she lives.
                     EARL OF KENT.
               Is this the promised end?
                     EDGAR.
Or image of that horror?
                     DUKE OF ALBANY.
                    Fall, and cease!
                     KING LEAR.
This feather stirs; she lives! if it be so,
It is a chance which does redeem all sorrows
That ever I have felt.
                     EARL OF KENT.
               O my good master! [*Kneeling.*
                     KING LEAR.
Prithee, away.
                     EDGAR.
         'Tis noble Kent, your friend.
                     KING LEAR.
A plague upon you, murderers, traitors all!
I might have saved her; now she's gone for ever!—
Cordelia, Cordelia! stay a little. Ha!
What is't thou say'st?—Her voice was ever soft,
Gentle, and low,—an excellent thing in woman.—
I kill'd the slave that was a-hanging thee.
                     OFFICER.
'Tis true, my lords, he did.
                     KING LEAR.
                Did I not, fellow?
I have seen the day, with my good biting falchion
I would have made them skip: I am old now,
And these same crosses spoil me.—Who are you?
Mine eyes are not o'the best:—I'll tell you straight.
                     EARL OF KENT.
If fortune brag of two she loved and hated,
One of them we behold.
                     KING LEAR.
This is a dull sight. Are you not Kent?
                     EARL OF KENT.
                         The same,
Your servant Kent.—Where is your servant Caius?
                     KING LEAR.
He's a good fellow, I can tell you that;
He'll strike, and quickly too:—he's dead and
   rotten.
                     EARL OF KENT.
No, my good lord; I am the very man,—
                     KING LEAR.
I'll see that straight.
                     EARL OF KENT.
That, from your first of difference and decay,
Have follow'd your sad steps.
                     KING LEAR.
                You are welcome hither.
                     EARL OF KENT.
Nor no man else:—all's cheerless, dark, and
   deadly.—

Your eldest daughters have fordone themselves,
And desperately are dead.
                     KING LEAR.
                     Ay, so I think.
                     DUKE OF ALBANY.
He knows not what he says; and vain is it
That we present us to him.
                     EDGAR.
                     Very bootless.
Enter an OFFICER.
                     OFFICER.
Edmund is dead, my lord.
                     DUKE OF ALBANY.
                     That's but a trifle here.—
You lords and noble friends, know our intent.
What comfort to this great decay may come
Shall be applied: for us, we will resign,
During the life of this old majesty,
To him our absolute power:—[*to* EDGAR *and*
   KENT] you, to your rights;
With boot, and such addition as your honours
Have more than merited.—All friends shall taste
The wages of their virtue, and all foes
The cup of their deservings.—O, see, see!
                     KING LEAR.
And my poor fool is hang'd! No, no, no life!
Why should a dog, a horse, a rat, have life,
And thou no breath at all? Thou'lt come no more,
Never, never, never, never, never!—
Pray you, undo this button:—thank you, sir.—
Do you see this? Look on her,—look, her lips,—
Look there, look there !—   [*Dies.*
                     EDGAR.
             He faints!—My lord, my lord!—
                     EARL OF KENT.
Break, heart; I prithee, break!
                     EDGAR.
                     Look up, my lord.
                     EARL OF KENT.
Vex not his ghost: O, let him pass! he hates him
That would upon the rack of this tough world
Stretch him out longer.
                     EDGAR.
             He is gone indeed.
                     EARL OF KENT.
The wonder is, he hath endured so long:
He but usurpt his life.
                     DUKE OF ALBANY.
Bear them from hence.—Our present business
Is general woe.—[*to* KENT *and* EDGAR] Friends
   of my soul, you twain
Rule in this realm, and the gored state sustain.
                     EARL OF KENT.
I have a journey, sir, shortly to go;
My master calls me,—I must not say no.
                     EDGAR.
The weight of this sad time we must obey;
Speak what we feel, not what we ought to say.
The oldest hath borne most: we that are young
Shall never see so much, nor live so long.
             [*Exeunt, with a dead march.*

ANTONY AND CLEOPATRA

DRAMATIS PERSONAE

MARK ANTONY,
OCTAVIUS CAESAR, } *triumvirs.*
M. AEMILIUS LEPIDUS, }
SEXTUS POMPEIUS.
DOMITIUS ENOBARBUS,
VENTIDIUS,
EROS,
SCARUS, } *friends to Antony.*
DERCETAS,
DEMETRIUS,
PHILO,
MAECENAS,
AGRIPPA,
DOLABELLA, } *friends to Cæsar.*
PROCULEIUS,
THYREUS,
GALLUS,
MENAS,
MENECRATES, } *friends to Pompey.*
VARRIUS,

TAURUS, *lieutenant-general to Cæsar.*
CANIDIUS, *lieutenant-general to Antony.*
SILIUS, *an officer in Ventidius' army.*
EUPHRONIUS, *an ambassador from Antony to Cæsar.*
ALEXAS, MARDIAN, SELEUCUS, and DIOMEDES, *attendants on Cleopatra.*
A SOOTHSAYER.
A CLOWN.

CLEOPATRA, *queen of Egypt.*
OCTAVIA, *sister to Cæsar and wife to Antony.*
CHARMIAN, } *attendants on Cleopatra.*
IRAS,

OFFICERS, SOLDIERS, MESSENGERS, *and other* ATTENDANTS.

SCENE—*In several parts of the Roman empire.*

ACT I. SCENE I.

Alexandria.   A room in CLEOPATRA'S *palace.*

Enter DEMETRIUS *and* PHILO.

PHILO.

NAY, but this dotage of our general's
O'erflows the measure: those his goodly eyes,
That o'er the files and musters of the war
Have glow'd like plated Mars, now bend, now turn,
The office and devotion of their view
Upon a tawny front: his captain's heart,
Which in the scuffles of great fights hath burst
The buckles on his breast, reneges all temper,
And is become the bellows and the fan
To cool a gipsy's lust. [*Flourish within.*] Look where they come:
Take but good note, and you shall see in him
The triple pillar of the world transform'd
Into a strumpet's fool: behold and see.

Enter ANTONY, CLEOPATRA, *her* LADIES, *the* TRAIN, *with* EUNUCHS *fanning her.*

CLEOPATRA.
If it be love indeed, tell me how much.

MARK ANTONY.
There's beggary in the love that can be reckon'd.

CLEOPATRA.
I'll set a bourn how far to be beloved.

MARK ANTONY.
Then must thou needs find out new heaven, new earth.

Enter an ATTENDANT.

ATTENDANT.
News, my good lord, from Rome.

MARK ANTONY.
            Grates me:—the sum.

CLEOPATRA.
Nay, hear them, Antony:
Fulvia perchance is angry; or, who knows
If the scarce-bearded Cæsar have not sent

His powerful mandate to you, 'Do this, or this;
Take in that kingdom, and enfranchise that;
Perform't, or else we damn thee.'

MARK ANTONY.
            How, my love!

CLEOPATRA.
Perchance! nay, and most like:—
You must not stay here longer,—your dismission
Is come from Cæsar; therefore hear it, Antony.—
Where's Fulvia's process? Cæsar's I would say?—both?—
Call in the messengers.—As I am Egypt's queen,
Thou blushest, Antony; and that blood of thine
Is Cæsar's homager: else so thy cheek pays shame
When shrill-tongued Fulvia scolds.—The messengers!

MARK ANTONY.
Let Rome in Tiber melt, and the wide arch
Of the ranged empire fall! Here is my space.
Kingdoms are clay: our dungy earth alike
Feeds beast as man: the nobleness of life
Is to do thus; when such a mutual pair
            [*Embracing.*
And such a twain can do't, in which I bind,
On pain of punishment, the world to weet
We stand up peerless.

CLEOPATRA.
            Excellent falsehood!
Why did he marry Fulvia, and not love her?—
I'll seem the fool I am not; Antony
Will be himself.

MARK ANTONY.
            But stirr'd by Cleopatra.—
Now, for the love of Love and her soft hours,
Let's not confound the time with conference harsh:
There's not a minute of our lives should stretch
Without some pleasure now:—what sport to-night?

CLEOPATRA.
Hear the ambassadors.

MARK ANTONY.
           Fie, wrangling queen!
Whom every thing becomes,—to chide, to laugh,
To weep; whose every passion fully strives
To make itself, in thee, fair and admired!
No messenger but thine; and all alone,   [note
To-night we'll wander through the streets, and
The qualities of people. Come, my queen;
Last night you did desire it:—speak not to us.
    [Exeunt ANTONY and CLEOPATRA with
        their TRAIN.

DEMETRIUS.
Is Cæsar with Antonius prized so slight?

PHILO.
Sir, sometimes, when he is not Antony,
He comes too short of that great property
Which still should go with Antony.

DEMETRIUS.
           I am full sorry
That he approves the common liar, who
Thus speaks of him at Rome: but I will hope
Of better deeds to-morrow. Rest you happy!
                    [Exeunt.

SCENE II.

The same. Another room.

Enter CHARMIAN, IRAS, ALEXAS, *and a*
SOOTHSAYER.

CHARMIAN.
LORD ALEXAS, sweet Alexas, most any thing
Alexas, almost most absolute Alexas, where's
the soothsayer that you praised so to the queen?
O, that I knew this husband, which, you say,
must charge his horns with garlands!

ALEXAS.
Soothsayer,—

SOOTHSAYER.
Your will?

CHARMIAN.
Is this the man?—Is't you, sir, that know things?

SOOTHSAYER.
In nature's infinite book of secrecy
A little I can read.

ALEXAS.
       Show him your hand.
Enter ENOBARBUS.

DOMITIUS ENOBARBUS.
Bring in the banquet quickly; wine enough
Cleopatra's health to drink.

CHARMIAN.
Good sir, give me good fortune.

SOOTHSAYER.
I make not, but forsee.

CHARMIAN.
Pray, then, foresee me one.

SOOTHSAYER.
You shall be yet far fairer than you are.

CHARMIAN.
He means in flesh.

IRAS.
No, you shall paint when you are old.

CHARMIAN.
Wrinkles forbid!

ALEXAS.
Vex not his prescience; be attentive.

CHARMIAN.
Hush!

SOOTHSAYER.
You shall be more beloving than beloved.

CHARMIAN.
I had rather heat my liver with drinking.

ALEXAS.
Nay, hear him.

CHARMIAN.
Good now, some excellent fortune! Let me be
married to three kings in a forenoon, and widow
them all: let me have a child at fifty, to whom
Herod of Jewry may do homage: find me to marry
me with Octavius Cæsar, and companion me
with my mistress.

SOOTHSAYER.
You shall outlive the lady whom you serve.

CHARMIAN.
O excellent! I love long life better than figs.

SOOTHSAYER.
You have seen and proved a fairer former fortune
Than that which is to approach.

CHARMIAN.
Then belike my children shall have no names:
prithee, how many boys and wenches must I
have?

SOOTHSAYER.
If every of your wishes had a womb,
And fertile every wish, a million.

CHARMIAN.
Out, fool! I forgive thee for a witch.

ALEXAS.
You think none but your sheets are privy to your
wishes.

CHARMIAN.
Nay, come, tell Iras hers.

ALEXAS.
We'll know all our fortunes.

DOMITIUS ENOBARBUS.
Mine, and most of our fortunes, to-night, shall be
—drunk to bed.

IRAS.
There's a palm presages chastity, if nothing else.

CHARMIAN.
E'en as the o'erflowing Nilus presageth famine.

IRAS.
Go, you wild bedfellow, you cannot soothsay.

CHARMIAN.
Nay, if an oily palm be not a fruitful prognostication, I cannot scratch mine ear.—Prithee, tell her
but a worky-day fortune.

SOOTHSAYER.
Your fortunes are alike.

IRAS.
But how, but how? give me particulars.

SOOTHSAYER.
I have said.

IRAS.
Am I not an inch of fortune better than she?

CHARMIAN.
Well, if you were but an inch of fortune better
than I, where would you choose it?

IRAS.
Not in my husband's nose.

CHARMIAN.

Our worser thoughts heavens mend!—Alexas,—
come, his fortune, his fortune!—O, let him marry
a woman that cannot go, sweet Isis, I beseech
thee! and let her die too, and give him a worse!
and let worse follow worse, till the worst of all
follow him laughing to his grave, fifty-fold a
cuckold! Good Isis, hear me this prayer, though
thou deny me a matter of more weight; good Isis,
I beseech thee!

IRAS.

Amen. Dear goddess, hear that prayer of the
people! for, as it is a heart-breaking to see a
handsome man loose-wived, so it is a deadly
sorrow to behold a foul knave uncuckolded:
therefore, dear Isis, keep decorum, and fortune
him accordingly!

CHARMIAN.

Amen.

ALEXAS.

Lo, now, if it lay in their hands to make me a
cuckold, they would make themselves whores but
they'ld do't!

DOMITIUS ENOBARBUS.

Hush! here comes Antony.

CHARMIAN.

Not he; the queen.

Enter CLEOPATRA.

CLEOPATRA.

Saw you my lord?

DOMITIUS ENOBARBUS.

No, lady.

CLEOPATRA.

Was he not here?

CHARMIAN.

No, madam.

CLEOPATRA.

He was disposed to mirth; but on the sudden
A Roman thought hath struck him.—Enobarbus,—

DOMITIUS ENOBARBUS.

Madam?

CLEOPATRA.

Seek him, and bring him hither.—Where's
Alexas?

ALEXAS.

Here, at your service.—My lord approaches.

CLEOPATRA.

We will not look upon him: go with us.   [*Exeunt.*
Enter ANTONY *with a* MESSENGER *and*
ATTENDANTS.

MESSENGER.

Fulvia thy wife first came into the field.

MARK ANTONY.

Against my brother Lucius?

MESSENGER.

Ay:
But soon that war had end, and the time's state
Made friends of them, jointing their force 'gainst
   Cæsar;
Whose better issue in the war from Italy
Upon the first encounter drave them.

MARK ANTONY.

Well, what worst?

MESSENGER.

The nature of bad news infects the teller.

MARK ANTONY.

When it concerns the fool or coward.—On:—
Things that are past are done with me.—'Tis
   thus;
Who tells me true, though in his tale lie death,
I hear him as he flatter'd.

MESSENGER.

Labienus—
This is stiff news—hath, with his Parthian force,
Extended Asia from Euphrates;
His conquering banner shook from Syria
To Lydia and to Ionia;
Whilst—

MARK ANTONY.

Antony, thou wouldst say,—

MESSENGER.

O, my lord!

MARK ANTONY.

Speak to me home, mince not the general tongue:
Name Cleopatra as she is call'd in Rome;
Rail thou in Fulvia's phrase; and taunt my faults
With such full licence as both truth and malice
Have power to utter. O, then we bring forth
   weeds
When our quick minds lie still; and our ills told us
Is as our earing. Fare thee well awhile.

MESSENGER.

At your noble pleasure.   [*Exit.*

MARK ANTONY.

From Sicyon, ho, the news! Speak there!

FIRST ATTENDANT.

The man from Sicyon,—is there such an one?

SECOND ATTENDANT.

He stays upon your will.

MARK ANTONY.

Let him appear.—
These strong Egyptian fetters I must break,
Or lose myself in dotage.
Enter another MESSENGER.
What are you?

SECOND MESSENGER.

Fulvia thy wife is dead.

MARK ANTONY.

Where died she?

SECOND MESSENGER.

In Sicyon:
Her length of sickness, with what else more
   serious
Importeth thee to know, this bears. [*Gives a letter.*

MARK ANTONY.

Forbear me.
      [*Exit* SECOND MESSENGER.
There's a great spirit gone! Thus did I desire it:
What our contempts do often hurl from us,
We wish it ours again; the present pleasure,
By revolution lowering, does become
The opposite of itself: she's good, being gone;
The hand could pluck her back that shoved her on.
I must from this enchanting queen break off:
Ten thousand harms, more than the ills I know,
My idleness doth hatch.—How now, Enobarbus!
Enter ENOBARBUS.

DOMITIUS ENOBARBUS.

What's your pleasure, sir?

MARK ANTONY.

I must with haste from hence.

DOMITIUS ENOBARBUS.

Why, then, we kill all our women: we see how mortal an unkindness is to them; if they suffer our departure, death's the word.

MARK ANTONY.

I must be gone.

DOMITIUS ENOBARBUS.

Under a compelling occasion, let women die: it were pity to cast them away for nothing; though, between them and a great cause, they should be esteem'd nothing. Cleopatra, catching but the least noise of this, dies instantly; I have seen her die twenty times upon far poorer moment: I do think there is mettle in death, which commits some loving act upon her, she hath such a celerity in dying.

MARK ANTONY.

She is cunning past man's thought.

DOMITIUS ENOBARBUS.

Alack, sir, no; her passions are made of nothing but the finest part of pure love: we cannot call her winds and waters sighs and tears; they are greater storms and tempests than almanacs can report: this cannot be cunning in her; if it be, she makes a shower of rain as well as Jove.

MARK ANTONY.

Would I had never seen her!

DOMITIUS ENOBARBUS.

O, sir, you had then left unseen a wonderful piece of work; which not to have been blest withal would have discredited your travel.

MARK ANTONY.

Fulvia is dead.

DOMITIUS ENOBARBUS.

Sir?

MARK ANTONY.

Fulvia is dead.

DOMITIUS ENOBARBUS.

Fulvia!

MARK ANTONY.

Dead.

DOMITIUS ENOBARBUS.

Why, sir, give the gods a thankful sacrifice. When it pleaseth their deities to take the wife of a man from him, it shows to man the tailors of the earth; comforting therein, that when old robes are worn out, there are members to make new. If there were no more women but Fulvia, then had you indeed a cut, and the case to be lamented: this grief is crown'd with consolation; your old smock brings forth a new petticoat:—and, indeed, the tears live in an onion that should water this sorrow.

MARK ANTONY.

The business she hath broached in the state Cannot endure my absence.

DOMITIUS ENOBARBUS.

And the business you have broached here cannot be without you; especially that of Cleopatra's, which wholly depends on your abode.

MARK ANTONY.

No more light answers. Let our officers Have notice what we purpose. I shall break The cause of our expedience to the queen, And get her leave to part. For not alone The death of Fulvia, with more urgent touches,

Do strongly speak to us; but the letters too Of many our contriving friends in Rome Petition us at home: Sextus Pompeius Hath given the dare to Cæsar, and commands The empire of the sea: our slippery people— Whose love is never linkt to the deserver Till his deserts are past—begin to throw Pompey the Great, and all his dignities, Upon his son; who, high in name and power, Higher than both in blood and life, stands up For the main soldier: whose quality, going on, The sides o' the world may danger: much is breeding,
Which, like the courser's hair, hath yet but life, And not a serpent's poison. Say, our pleasure, To such whose place is under us, requires Our quick remove from hence.

DOMITIUS ENOBARBUS.

I shall do't.   [Exeunt.

SCENE III.

The same.   Another room.

Enter CLEOPATRA, CHARMIAN, IRAS *and* ALEXAS.

CLEOPATRA.

WHERE is he?

CHARMIAN.

I did not see him since.

CLEOPATRA.

See where he is, who's with him, what he does:— I did not send you:—if you find him sad, Say I am dancing; if in mirth, report That I am sudden sick: quick, and return.

[*Exit* ALEXAS.

CHARMIAN.

Madam, methinks, if you did love him dearly, You do not hold the method to enforce The like from him.

CLEOPATRA.

What should I do I do not?

CHARMIAN.

In each thing give him way, cross him in nothing.

CLEOPATRA.

Thou teachest like a fool,—the way to lose him.

CHARMIAN.

Tempt him not so too far; I wish, forbear: In time we hate that which we often fear. But here comes Antony.

CLEOPATRA.

I am sick and sullen.

Enter ANTONY.

MARK ANTONY.

I am sorry to give breathing to my purpose,—

CLEOPATRA.

Help me away, dear Charmian; I shall fall: It cannot be thus long, the sides of nature Will not sustain it.

MARK ANTONY.

Now, my dearest queen,—

CLEOPATRA.

Pray you, stand further from me.

MARK ANTONY.

What's the matter?

CLEOPATRA.

I know, by that same eye, there's some good news.
What says the married woman?—You may go:
Would she had never given you leave to come!
Let her not say 'tis I that keep you here,—
I have no power upon you; hers you are.

MARK ANTONY.

The gods best know,—

CLEOPATRA.

        O, never was there queen
So mightily betray'd! yet at the first
I saw the treasons planted.

MARK ANTONY.

        Cleopatra,—

CLEOPATRA.

Why should I think you can be mine and true,
Though you in swearing shake the throned gods,
Who have been false to Fulvia? Riotous madness,
To be entangled with those mouth-made vows
Which break themselves in swearing!

MARK ANTONY.

        Most sweet queen,—

CLEOPATRA.

Nay, pray you, seek no colour for your going,
But bid farewell, and go: when you sued staying,
Then was the time for words: no going then;—
Eternity was in our lips and eyes,
Bliss in our brows' bent; none our parts so poor,
But was a race of heaven: they are so still,
Or thou, the greatest soldier of the world,
Art turn'd the greatest liar.

MARK ANTONY.

        How now, lady!

CLEOPATRA.

I would I had thy inches; thou shouldst know
There were a heart in Egypt.

MARK ANTONY.

        Hear me, queen:
The strong necessity of time commands
Our services awhile; but my full heart
Remains in use with you. Our Italy
Shines o'er with civil swords: Sextus Pompeius
Makes his approaches to the port of Rome:
Equality of two domestic powers
Breed scrupulous faction: the hated, grown to
    strength,
Are newly grown to love: the condemn'd Pompey,
Rich in his father's honour, creeps apace
Into the hearts of such as have not thrived
Upon the present state, whose numbers threaten;
And quietness, grown sick of rest, would purge
By any desperate change: my more particular,
And that which most with you should safe my
    going,
Is Fulvia's death.

CLEOPATRA.

Though age from folly could not give me freedom
It does from childishness:—can Fulvia die?

MARK ANTONY.

She's dead, my queen:
Look here, and, at thy sovereign leisure, read
The garboils she awaked; at the last, best:
See when and where she died.

CLEOPATRA.

        O most false love!
Where be the sacred vials thou shouldst fill

With sorrowful water? Now I see, I see,
In Fulvia's death, how mine received shall be.

MARK ANTONY.

Quarrel no more, but be prepared to know
The purposes I bear; which are, or cease,
As you shall give the advice: by the fire
That quickens Nilus' slime, I go from hence
Thy soldier, servant; making peace or war
As thou affect'st.

CLEOPATRA.

        Cut my lace, Charmian, come;—
But let it be:—I am quickly ill, and well,
So Antony loves.

MARK ANTONY.

        My precious queen, forbear;
And give true evidence to his love, which stands
An honourable trial.

CLEOPATRA.

        So Fulvia told me.
I prithee, turn aside, and weep for her;
Then bid adieu to me, and say the tears
Belong to Egypt: good now, play one scene
Of excellent dissembling; and let it look
Like perfect honour.

MARK ANTONY.

        You'll heat my blood: no more.

CLEOPATRA.

You can do better yet; but this is meetly.

MARK ANTONY.

Now, by my sword,—

CLEOPATRA.

        And target.—Still he mends;
But this is not the best:—look, prithee, Char-
    mian,
How this Herculean Roman does become
The carriage of his chafe.

MARK ANTONY.

I'll leave you, lady.

CLEOPATRA.

        Courteous lord, one word.
Sir, you and I must part,—but that's not it:
Sir, you and I have loved,—but there's not it;
That you know well: something it is I would,—
O, my oblivion is a very Antony,
And I am all forgotten.

MARK ANTONY.

        But that your royalty
Holds idleness your subject, I should take you
For idleness itself.

CLEOPATRA.

        'Tis sweating labour
To bear such idleness so near the heart
As Cleopatra this. But, sir, forgive me;
Since my becomings kill me, when they do not
Eye well to you: your honour calls you hence;
Therefore be deaf to my unpitied folly,
And all the gods go with you! upon your sword
Sit laurel victory! and smooth success
Be strew'd before your feet!

MARK ANTONY.

        Let us go. Come;
Our separation so abides, and flies,
That thou, residing here, go'st yet with me,
And I, hence fleeting, here remain with thee.
Away!   [*Exeunt.*

SCENE IV.

Rome.   An apartment in CAESAR'S *house.*

Enter OCTAVIUS CAESAR, *reading a letter,*
LEPIDUS, *and their* TRAIN.

OCTAVIUS CAESAR.

YOU may see, Lepidus, and henceforth know,
            [*Giving him a letter.*
It is not Cæsar's natural vice to hate
Our great competitor: from Alexandria
This is the news:—he fishes, drinks, and wastes
The lamps of night in revel; is not more manlike
Than Cleopatra, nor the queen of Ptolemy
More womanly than he; hardly gave audience, or
Vouchsafed to think he had partners: you shall
    find there
A man who is the abstract of all faults
That all men follow.

LEPIDUS.
          I must not think there are
Evils enow to darken all his goodness:
His faults, in him, seem as the spots of heaven,
More fiery by night's blackness; hereditary,
Rather than purchased; what he cannot change,
Than what he chooses.

OCTAVIUS CAESAR.
You are too indulgent. Let us grant, it is not
Amiss to tumble on the bed of Ptolemy;
To give a kingdom for a mirth; to sit
And keep the turn of tippling with a slave;
To reel the streets at noon, and stand the buffet
With knaves that smell of sweat; say this becomes
As his composure must be rare indeed   [him,—
Whom these things cannot blemish,—yet must
    Antony
No way excuse his soils, when we do bear
So great weight in his lightness. If he fill'd
His vacancy with his voluptuousness,
Full surfeits, and the dryness of his bones,
Call on him for't: but to confound such time,
That drums him from his sport, and speaks as loud
As his own state and ours,—'tis to be chid
As we rate boys, who, being mature in knowledge,
Pawn their experience to their present pleasure,
And so rebel to judgement.

Enter a MESSENGER.

LEPIDUS.
          Here's more news.

MESSENGER.
Thy biddings have been done; and every hour,
Most noble Cæsar, shalt thou have report
How 'tis abroad. Pompey is strong at sea;
And it appears he is beloved of those
That only have fear'd Cæsar: to the ports
The discontents repair, and men's reports
Give him much wrong'd.

OCTAVIUS CAESAR.
          I should have known no less.
It hath been taught us from the primal state,
That he which is was wisht until he were;
And the ebb'd man, ne'er loved till ne'er worth
    love,
Comes dear'd by being lackt. This common body,
Like to a vagabond flag upon the stream,
Goes to and back, lackeying the varying tide,
To rot itself with motion.

MESSENGER.
          Cæsar, I bring thee word,
Menecrates and Menas, famous pirates,
Make the sea serve them, which they ear and
    wound
With keels of every kind: many hot inroads
They make in Italy; the borders maritime
Lack blood to think on't, and flush youth revolt:
No vessel can peep forth, but 'tis as soon
Taken as seen; for Pompey's name strikes more
Than could his war resisted.

OCTAVIUS CAESAR.
          Antony,
Leave thy lascivious wassails. When thou once
Wast beaten from Modena, where thou slew'st
Hirtius and Pansa, consuls, at thy heel
Did famine follow; whom thou fought'st against,
Though daintily brought up, with patience more
Than savages could suffer: thou didst drink
The stale of horses, and the gilded puddle
Which beasts would cough at: thy palate then did
    deign
The roughest berry in the rudest hedge;
Yea, like the stag, when snow the pasture sheets,
The barks of trees thou browsed'st; on the Alps
It is reported thou didst eat strange flesh,
Which some did die to look on: and all this—
It wounds thine honour that I speak it now—
Was borne so like a soldier, that thy cheek
So much as lankt not.

LEPIDUS.
          It is pity of him.

OCTAVIUS CAESAR.
Let his shames quickly
Drive him to Rome: 'tis time we twain
Did show ourselves i'th'field; and to that end
Assemble we immediate council: Pompey
Thrives in our idleness.

LEPIDUS.
          To-morrow, Cæsar,
I shall be furnisht to inform you rightly
Both what by sea and land I can be able
To front this present time.

OCTAVIUS CAESAR.
          Till which encounter,
It is my business too. Farewell.

LEDIPUS.
Farewell, my lord; what you shall know meantime
Of stirs abroad, I shall beseech you, sir,
To let me be partaker.

OCTAVIUS CAESAR.
          Doubt not, sir;
I knew it for my bond.   [*Exeunt.*

SCENE V.

Alexandria.   A room in CLEOPATRA'S *palace.*

Enter CLEOPATRA, CHARMIAN, IRAS, *and*
MARDIAN.

CLEOPATRA.

CHARMIAN,—

CHARMIAN.
Madam?

CLEOPATRA.
Ha, ha!—
Give me to drink mandragora.

CHARMIAN.
　　　　　　Why, madam?
CLEOPATRA.
That I might sleep out this great gap of time
My Antony is away.
CHARMIAN.
　　　　You think of him too much.
CLEOPATRA.
O, 'tis treason!
CHARMIAN.
Madam, I trust, not so.
CLEOPATRA.
Thou, eunuch Mardian!
MARDIAN.
　　　　What's your highness' pleasure?
CLEOPATRA.
Not now to hear thee sing; I take no pleasure
In aught an eunuch has: 'tis well for thee,
That, being unseminar'd, thy freer thoughts
May not fly forth of Egypt. Hast thou affections?
MARDIAN.
Yes, gracious madam.
CLEOPATRA.
Indeed!
MARDIAN.
Not in deed, madam; for I can do nothing
But what indeed is honest to be done:
Yet have I fierce affections, and think
What Venus did with Mars.
CLEOPATRA.
　　　　　　O Charmian,
Where think'st thou he is now? Stands he, or sits
he?
Or does he walk? or is he on his horse?
O happy horse, to bear the weight of Antony!
Do bravely, horse! for wott'st thou whom thou
movest?
The demi-Atlas of this earth, the arm
And burgonet of men.—He's speaking now,
Or murmuring, 'Where's my serpent of old Nile?'
For so he calls me:—now I feed myself
With most delicious poison:—think on me,
That am with Phœbus' amorous pinches black,
And wrinkled deep in time? Broad-fronted Cæsar,
When thou wast here above the ground, I was
A morsel for a monarch; and great Pompey
Would stand, and make his eyes grow in my brow;
There would he anchor his aspect, and die
With looking on his life.
Enter ALEXAS.
ALEXAS.
　　　　　　Sovereign of Egypt, hail!
CLEOPATRA.
How much unlike art thou Mark Antony!
Yet, coming from him, that great medicine hath
With his tinct gilded thee.—
How goes it with my brave Mark Antony?
ALEXAS.
Last thing he did, dear queen,
He kist—the last of many doubled kisses—
This orient pearl:—his speech sticks in my heart.
CLEOPATRA.
Mine ear must pluck it thence.
ALEXAS.
　　　　　　'Good friend,' quoth he,
'Say, the firm Roman to great Egypt sends

This treasure of an oyster; at whose foot,
To mend the petty present, I will piece
Her opulent throne with kingdoms; all the east,
Say thou, shall call her mistress.' So he nodded,
And soberly did mount an arm-gaunt steed,
Who neigh'd so high, that what I would have spoke
Was beastly dumb'd by him.
CLEOPATRA.
　　　　　　What, was he sad or merry?
ALEXAS.
Like to the time o'the year between the extremes
Of hot and cold, he was nor sad nor merry.
CLEOPATRA.
O well-divided disposition!—Note him,
Note him, good Charmian, 'tis the man; but note
him:
He was not sad,—for he would shine on those
That make their looks by his; he was not merry,—
Which seem'd to tell them his remembrance lay
In Egypt with his joy; but between both:
O heavenly mingle!—Be'st thou sad or merry,
The violence of either thee becomes,
So does it no man else.—Mett'st thou my posts?
ALEXAS.
Ay, madam, twenty several messengers:
Why do you send so thick?
CLEOPATRA.
　　　　　　Who's born that day
When I forget to send to Antony,
Shall die a beggar.—Ink and paper, Charmian.—
Welcome, my good Alexas.—Did I, Charmian,
Ever love Cæsar so?
CHARMIAN.
　　　　　　O that brave Cæsar!
CLEOPATRA.
Be choked with such another emphasis!
Say, the brave Antony.
CHARMIAN.
　　　　　　The valiant Cæsar!
CLEOPATRA.
By Isis, I will give thee bloody teeth,
If thou with Cæsar paragon again
My man of men.
CHARMIAN.
　　　　　　By your most gracious pardon,
I sing but after you.
CLEOPATRA.
　　　　　　My salad days,
When I was green in judgement:—cold in blood,
To say as I said then!—But, come, away;
Get me ink and paper:
He shall have every day a several greeting,
Or I'll unpeople Egypt.　　　　　[*Exeunt.*

ACT II.　SCENE I.

Messina.　A room in POMPEY'S *house.*

Enter POMPEY, MENECRATES, *and* MENAS,
in warlike manner.

POMPEY.
IF the great gods be just, they shall assist
The deeds of justest men.
MENECRATES.
　　　　　　Know, worthy Pompey,
That what they do delay, they not deny.

POMPEY.
Whiles we are suitors to their throne, decays
The thing we sue for.
    MENECRATES.
      We, ignorant of ourselves,
Beg often our own harms, which the wise powers
Deny us for our good; so find we profit
By losing of our prayers.
    POMPEY.
      I shall do well:
The people love me, and the sea is mine;
My powers are crescent, and my auguring hope
Says it will come to the full. Mark Antony
In Egypt sits at dinner, and will make
No wars without doors: Cæsar gets money where
He loses hearts: Lepidus flatters both,
Of both is flatter'd; but he neither loves,
Nor either cares for him.
    MENAS.
      Cæsar and Lepidus
Are in the field; a mighty strength they carry.
    POMPEY.
Where have you this? 'tis false.
    MENAS.
      From Silvius, sir.
    POMPEY.
He dreams: I know they are in Rome together,
Looking for Antony. But all the charms of love,
Salt Cleopatra, soften thy waned lip!
Let witchcraft join with beauty, lust with both!
Tie up the libertine in a field of feasts,
Keep his brain fuming; Epicurean cooks
Sharpen with cloyless sauce his appetite;
That sleep and feeding may prorogue his honour
Even till a Lethe'd dulness!
    Enter VARRIUS.
      How now, Varrius!
    VARRIUS.
This is most certain that I shall deliver:—
Mark Antony is every hour in Rome
Expected: since he went from Egypt 'tis
A space for further travel.
    POMPEY.
      I could have given less matter
A better ear.—Menas, I did not think
This amorous surfeiter would have donn'd his
  helm
For such a petty war: his soldiership
Is twice the other twain: but let us rear
The higher our opinion, that our stirring
Can from the lap of Egypt's widow pluck
The ne'er-lust-wearied Antony.
    MENAS.
      I cannot hope
Cæsar and Antony shall well greet together:
His wife that's dead did trespasses to Cæsar;
His brother warr'd upon him; although, I think,
Not moved by Antony.
    POMPEY.
      I know not, Menas,
How lesser enmities may give way to greater.
Were't not that we stand up against them all,
'Twere pregnant they should square between
  themselves;
For they have entertained cause enough
To draw their swords: but how the fear of us

May cement their divisions, and bind up
The pettty difference, we yet not know.
Be't as our gods will have't! It only stands
Our lives upon to use our strongest hands.
Come, Menas.   [*Exeunt.*

SCENE II.

Rome. A room in the house of LEPIDUS.
  Enter ENOBARBUS *and* LEPIDUS.
    LEPIDUS.
GOOD Enobarbus, 'tis a worthy deed,
 And shall become you well, to entreat your
  captain
To soft and gentle speech.
    DOMITIUS ENOBARBUS.
      I shall entreat him
To answer like himself: if Cæsar move him,
Let Antony look over Cæsar's head,
And speak as loud as Mars. By Jupiter,
Were I the wearer of Antonius' beard,
I would not shave't to-day.
    LEPIDUS.
      'Tis not a time
For private stomaching.
    DOMITIUS ENOBARBUS.
      Every time
Serves for the matter that is then born in't.
    LEPIDUS
But small to greater matters must give way.
    DOMITIUS ENOBARBUS.
Not if the small come first.
    LEPIDUS.
      Your speech is passion:
But, pray you, stir no embers up. Here comes
The noble Antony.
    Enter ANTONY *and* VENTIDIUS.
    DOMITIUS ENOBARBUS.
      And yonder, Cæsar.
 Enter CAESAR, MAECENAS, *and* AGRIPPA.
    MARK ANTONY.
If we compose well here, to Parthia:
Hark, Ventidius.
    OCTAVIUS CAESAR.
      I do not know,
Mæcenas; ask Agrippa.
    LEPIDUS.
      Noble friends,
That which combined us was most great, and let
  not
A leaner action rend us. What's amiss,
May it be gently heard: when we debate
Our trivial difference loud, we do commit
Murder in healing wounds: then, noble part-
  ners,—
The rather, for I earnestly beseech,—
Touch you the sourest points with sweetest terms
Nor curstness grow to the matter.
    MARK ANTONY.
      'Tis spoken well.
Were we before our armies, and to fight,
I should do thus.   [*Flourish.*
    OCTAVIUS CAESAR.
Welcome to Rome.
    MARK ANTONY.
Thank you.

OCTAVIUS CAESAR.

Sit.

MARK ANTONY.

Sit, sir.

OCTAVIUS CAESAR.

Nay, then.

MARK ANTONY.

I learn, you take things ill which are not so,
Or being, concern you not.

OCTAVIUS CAESAR.

     I must be laught at,
If, or for nothing or a little, I
Should say myself offended, and with you
Chiefly i'the world; more laught at, that I should
Once name you derogately, when to sound your
 name
It not concern'd me.

MARK ANTONY.

     My being in Egypt, Cæsar,
What was't to you?

OCTAVIUS CAESAR.

No more than my residing here at Rome
Might be to you in Egypt: yet, if you there
Did practise on my state, your being in Egypt
Might be my question.

MARK ANTONY.

    How intend you, practised?

OCTAVIUS CAESAR.

You may be pleased to catch at mine intent
By what did here befall me. Your wife and
 brother
Made wars upon me; and their contestation
Was theme for you, you were the word of war.

MARK ANTONY.

You do mistake your business; my brother never
Did urge me in his act: I did inquire it;
And have my learning from some true reports,
That drew their swords with you. Did he not
 rather
Discredit my authority with yours;
And make the wars alike against my stomach,
Having alike your cause? Of this my letters
Before did satisfy you. If you'll patch a quarrel,
As matter whole you have not to make it with,
It must not be with this.

OCTAVIUS CAESAR.

     You praise yourself
By laying defects of judgement to me; but
You patcht up your excuses.

MARK ANTONY.

     Not so, not so;
I know you could not lack, I am certain on't,
Very necessity of this thought, that I,
Your partner in the cause 'gainst which he fought,
Could not with graceful eyes attend those wars
Which fronted mine own peace. As for my wife,
I would you had her spirit in such another:
The third o'the world is yours; which with a
 snaffle
You may pace easy, but not such a wife.

DOMITIUS ENOBARBUS.

Would we had all such wives, that the men might
go to wars with the women!

MARK ANTONY.

So much uncurbable, her garboils, Cæsar,
Made out of her impatience,—which not wanted

Shrewdness of policy too,—I grieving grant
Did you too much disquiet: for that you must
But say, I could not help it.

OCTAVIUS CAESAR.

     I wrote to you
When rioting in Alexandria; you
Did pocket up my letters, and with taunts
Did gibe my missive out of audience.

MARK ANTONY.

      Sir,
He fell upon me ere admitted: then
Three kings I had newly feasted, and did want
Of what I was i'the morning: but next day
I told him of myself; which was as much
As to have askt him pardon. Let this fellow
Be nothing of our strife; if we contend,
Out of our question wipe him.

OCTAVIUS CAESAR.

     You have broken
The article of your oath; which you shall never
Have tongue to charge me with.

LEPIDUS.

     Soft, Cæsar!

MARK ANTONY.

      No,
Lepidus, let him speak:
The honour is sacred which he talks on now,
Supposing that I lackt it.—But, on, Cæsar;
The article of my oath.

OCTAVIUS CAESAR.

To lend me arms and aid when I required them;
The which you both denied.

MARK ANTONY.

     Neglected, rather;
And then when poison'd hours had bound me up
From mine own knowledge. As nearly as I may,
I'll play the penitent to you: but mine honesty
Shall not make poor my greatness, nor my power
Work without it. Truth is, that Fulvia,
To have me out of Egypt, made wars here;
For which myself, the ignorant motive, do
So far ask pardon as befits mine honour
To stoop in such a case.

LEPIDUS.

     'Tis noble spoken.

MAECENAS.

If it might please you, to enforce no further
The griefs between ye: to forget them quite
Were to remember that the present need
Speaks to atone you.

LEPIDUS.

    Worthily spoken, Mæcenas.

DOMITIUS ENOBARBUS.

Or, if you borrow one another's love for the instant, you may, when you hear no more words of
Pompey, return it again: you shall have time to
wrangle in when you have nothing else to do.

MARK ANTONY.

Thou art a soldier only: speak no more.

DOMITIUS ENOBARBUS.

That truth should be silent I had almost forgot.

MARK ANTONY.

You wrong this presence; therefore speak no
 more.

DOMITIUS ENOBARBUS.

Go to, then; your considerate stone.

OCTAVIUS CAESAR.
I do not much dislike the matter, but
The manner of his speech; for't cannot be
We shall remain in friendship, our conditions
So differing in their acts. Yet, if I knew
What hoop should hold us stanch, from edge to
O'the world I would pursue it.   [edge

AGRIPPA.
Give me leave, Caesar,—

OCTAVIUS CAESAR.
Speak, Agrippa.

AGRIPPA.
Thou hast a sister by the mother's side,
Admired Octavia: great Mark Antony
Is now a widower.

OCTAVIUS CAESAR.
Say not so, Agrippa:
If Cleopatra heard you, your reproof
Were well deserved of rashness.

MARK ANTONY.
I am not married, Caesar: let me hear
Agrippa further speak.

AGRIPPA.
To hold you in perpetual amity,
To make you brothers, and to knit your hearts
With an unslipping knot, take Antony
Octavia to his wife; whose beauty claims
No worse a husband than the best of men;
Whose virtue and whose general graces speak
That which none else can utter. By this marriage,
All little jealousies, which now seem great,
And all great fears, which now import their dan-
    gers,
Would then be nothing: truths would be tales,
Where now half tales be truths: her love to both
Would each to other, and all loves to both,
Draw after her. Pardon what I have spoke;
For 'tis a studied, not a present thought,
By duty ruminated.

MARK ANTONY.
Will Caesar speak?

OCTAVIUS CAESAR.
Not till he hears how Antony is toucht
With what is spoke already.

MARK ANTONY.
What power is in Agrippa,
If I would say, 'Agrippa, be it so,'
To make this good?

OCTAVIUS CAESAR.
The power of Caesar, and
His power unto Octavia.

MARK ANTONY.
May I never
To this good purpose, that so fairly shows,
Dream of impediment!—Let me have thy hand:
Further this act of grace; and from this hour
The heart of brothers govern in our loves
And sway our great designs!

OCTAVIUS CAESAR.
There is my hand.
A sister I bequeath you, whom no brother
Did ever love so dearly: let her live
To join our kingdoms and our hearts; and never
Fly off our loves again!

LEPIDUS.
Happily, amen!

MARK ANTONY.
I did not think to draw my sword 'gainst Pompey;
For he hath laid strange courtesies and great
Of late upon me: I must thank him only,
Lest my remembrance suffer ill report;
At heel of that, defy him.

LEPIDUS.
Time calls upon's:
Of us must Pompey presently be sought,
Or else he seeks out us.

MARK ANTONY.
Where lies he?

OCTAVIUS CAESAR.
About the Mount Misenum.

MARK ANTONY.
What's his strength
By land?

OCTAVIUS CAESAR.
Great and increasing: but by sea
He is an absolute master.

MARK ANTONY.
So is the fame.
Would we had spoke together! Haste we for it:
Yet, ere we put ourselves in arms, dispatch we
The business we have talkt of.

OCTAVIUS CAESAR.
With most gladness;
And do invite you to my sister's view,
Whither straight I'll lead you.

MARK ANTONY.
Let us, Lepidus,
Not lack your company.

LEPIDUS.
Noble Antony,
Not sickness should detain me.
    [Flourish.   Exeunt CAESAR, ANTONY, and
    LEPIDUS.

MAECENAS.
Welcome from Egypt, sir.

DOMITIUS ENOBARBUS.
Half the heart of Caesar, worthy Maecenas!—
My honourable friend, Agrippa!—

AGRIPPA.
Good Enobarbus!

MAECENAS.
We have cause to be glad that matters are so well
digested. You stay'd well by't in Egypt.

DOMITIUS ENOBARBUS.
Ay, sir; we did sleep day out of countenance, and
made the night light with drinking.

MAECENAS.
Eight wild-boars roasted whole at a breakfast, and
but twelve persons there; is this true?

DOMITIUS ENOBARBUS.
This was but as a fly by an eagle: we had much
more monstrous matter of feast, which worthily
deserved noting.

MAECENAS.
She's a most triumphant lady, if report be square
to her.

DOMITIUS ENOBARBUS.
When she first met Mark Antony, she pursed up
his heart, upon the river of Cydnus.

AGRIPPA.
There she appear'd indeed; or my reporter devised well for her.

DOMITIUS ENOBARBUS.
I will tell you.
The barge she sat in, like a burnisht throne,
Burnt on the water: the poop was beaten gold;
Purple the sails, and so perfumed that
The winds were love-sick with them; the oars
  were silver,
Which to the tune of flutes kept stroke, and made
The water which they beat to follow faster,
As amorous of their strokes. For her own person,
It beggar'd all description: she did lie
In her pavilion—cloth-of-gold of tissue—
O'er-picturing that Venus where we see
The fancy outwork nature: on each side her
Stood pretty dimpled boys, like smiling Cupids,
With divers-colour'd fans, whose wind did seem
To glow the delicate cheeks which they did cool,
And what they undid did.

AGRIPPA.
                 O, rare for Antony!
DOMITIUS ENOBARBUS.
Her gentlewomen, like the Nereides,
So many mermaids, tended her i'the eyes,
And made their bends adornings: at the helm
A seeming mermaid steers: the silken tackle
Swell with the touches of those flower-soft hands,
That yarely frame the office. From the barge
A strange invisible perfume hits the sense
Of the adjacent wharfs. The city cast
Her people out upon her; and Antony,
Enthroned i'the market-place, did sit alone,
Whistling to the air; which, but for vacancy,
Had gone to gaze on Cleopatra too,
And made a gap in nature.

AGRIPPA.
               Rare Egyptian!
DOMITIUS ENOBARBUS.
Upon her landing, Antony sent to her,
Invited her to supper: she replied,
It should be better he became her guest;
Which she entreated: our courteous Antony,
Whom ne'er the word of 'No' woman heard
  speak,
Being barber'd ten times o'er, goes to the feast,
And for his ordinary pays his heart
For what his eyes eat only.

AGRIPPA.
               Royal wench!
She made great Cæsar lay his sword to bed:
He plough'd her, and she cropt.
DOMITIUS ENOBARBUS.
             I saw her once
Hop forty paces through the public street;
And having lost her breath, she spoke, and panted,
That she did make defect perfection,
And, breathless, power breathe forth.
MAECENAS.
Now Antony must leave her utterly.
DOMITIUS ENOBARBUS.
Never; he will not:
Age cannot wither her, nor custom stale
Her infinite variety: other women cloy
The appetites they feed; but she makes hungry
Where most she satisfies: for vilest things
Become themselves in her; that the holy priests
Bless her when she is riggish.

MAECENAS.
If beauty, wisdom, modesty, can settle
The heart of Antony, Octavia is
A blessed lottery to him.
AGRIPPA.
               Let us go.—
Good Enobarbus, make yourself my guest
Whilst you abide here.
DOMITIUS ENOBARBUS.
           Humbly, sir, I thank you.
                    [*Exeunt.*

SCENE III.

The same.   A room in CAESAR'S *house.*

Enter ANTONY, CAESAR, OCTAVIA *between
them; and* ATTENDANTS.

MARK ANTONY.
THE world and my great office will sometimes
Divide me from your bosom.
OCTAVIA.
               All which time
Before the gods my knee shall bow my prayers
To them for you.
MARK ANTONY.
          Good night, sir.—My Octavia,
Read not my blemishes in the world's report:
I have not kept my square; but that to come
Shall all be done by the rule. Good night, dear
  lady.
OCTAVIA.
Good night, sir.
OCTAVIUS CAESAR.
Good night.   [*Exeunt* CAESAR *and* OCTAVIA.
         Enter SOOTHSAYER.
MARK ANTONY.
Now, sirrah,—you do wish yourself in Egypt?
SOOTHSAYER.
Would I had never come from thence, nor you
thither!
MARK ANTONY.
If you can, your reason?
SOOTHSAYER.
I see it in my motion, have it not in my tongue:
but yet hie you to Egypt again.
MARK ANTONY.
Say to me
Whose fortunes shall rise higher, Cæsar's or mine?
SOOTHSAYER.
Cæsar's.
Therefore, O Antony, stay not by his side:
Thy demon, that's thy spirit which keeps thee, is
Noble, courageous, high, unmatchable,
Where Cæsar's is not; but, near him, thy angel
Becomes a fear, as being o'erpower'd: therefore
Make space enough between you.
MARK ANTONY.
            Speak this no more.
SOOTHSAYER.
To none but thee; no more, but when to thee.
If thou dost play with him at any game,
Thou art sure to lose; and, of that natural luck,
He beats thee 'gainst the odds: thy lustre thickens,
When he shines by: I say again, thy spirit
Is all afraid to govern thee near him;
But he away, 'tis noble.

MARK ANTONY.
               Get thee gone:
Say to Ventidius I would speak with him:—
               [*Exit* SOOTHSAYER.
He shall to Parthia.—Be it art or hap,
He hath spoken true: the very dice obey him;
And, in our sports, my better cunning faints
Under his chance: if we draw lots, he speeds;
His cocks do win the battle still of mine,
When it is all to naught; and his quails ever
Beat mine, inhoopt, at odds. I will to Egypt:
And though I make this marriage for my peace,
I'the east my pleasure lies.
       Enter VENTIDIUS.
               O, come, Ventidius,
You must to Parthia: your commission's ready;
Follow me, and receive't.   [*Exeunt.*

SCENE IV.

The same. A street.

Enter LEPIDUS, MAECENAS, *and* AGRIPPA.

LEPIDUS.

TROUBLE yourselves no further: pray you,
   hasten
Your generals after.
          AGRIPPA.
             Sir, Mark Antony
Will e'en but kiss Octavia, and we'll follow.
          LEPIDUS.
Till I shall see you in your soldier's dress,
Which will become you both, farewell.
          MAECENAS.
               We shall,
As I conceive the journey, be at the Mount
Before you, Lepidus.
          LEPIDUS.
            Your way is shorter;
My purposes do draw me much about:
You'll win two days upon me.
      MAECENAS *and* AGRIPPA.
              Sir, good success!
          LEPIDUS.
Farewell.   [*Exeunt.*

SCENE V.

Alexandria. A room in CLEOPATRA'S *palace.*

Enter CLEOPATRA, CHARMIAN, IRAS, *and*
ALEXAS.

CLEOPATRA.

GIVE me some music,—music, moody food
   Of us that trade in love.
        ATTENDANT.
             The music, ho!
      Enter MARDIAN.
        CLEOPATRA.
Let it alone; let's to billiards: come, Charmian.
        CHARMIAN.
My arm is sore; best play with Mardian.
        CLEOPATRA.
As well a woman with an eunuch play'd
As with a woman.—Come, you'll play with me,
   sir?
        MARDIAN.
As well as I can, madam.

CLEOPATRA.
And when good will is show'd, though't come too
   short,
The actor may plead pardon. I'll none now:—
Give me mine angle,—we'll to the river: there,
My music playing far off, I will betray
Tawny-finn'd fishes; my bended hook shall pierce
Their slimy jaws; and, as I draw them up,
I'll think them every one an Antony,
And say, 'Ah, ha! y'are caught.'
        CHARMIAN.
             'Twas merry when
You wager'd on your angling; when your diver
Did hang a salt-fish on his hook, which he
With fervency drew up.
        CLEOPATRA.
            That time,—O times!—
I laught him out of patience; and that night
I laught him into patience: and next morn,
Ere the ninth hour, I drunk him to his bed;
Then put my tires and mantles on him, whilst
I wore his sword Philippan.
      Enter a MESSENGER.
            O, from Italy!—
Ram thou thy fruitful tidings in mine ears,
That long time have been barren.
        MESSENGER.
             Madam, madam,—
        CLEOPATRA.
Antony's dead!—if thou say so, villain,
Thou kill'st thy mistress: but well and free,
If thou so yield him, there is gold, and here
My bluest veins to kiss,—a hand that kings
Have lipt, and trembled kissing.
        MESSENGER.
First, madam, he is well.
        CLEOPATRA.
            Why, there's more gold.
But, sirrah, mark, we use
To say the dead are well: bring it to that,
The gold I give thee will I melt and pour
Down thy ill-uttering throat.
        MESSENGER.
Good madam, hear me.
        CLEOPATRA.
            Well, go to, I will;
But there's no goodness in thy face: if Antony
Be free and healthful—so tart a favour
To trumpet such good tidings! If not well,
Thou shouldst come like a Fury crown'd with
   snakes,
Not like a formal man.
        MESSENGER.
            Will't please you hear me?
        CLEOPATRA.
I have a mind to strike thee ere thou speak'st:
Yet, if thou say Antony lives, is well,
Or friends with Cæsar, or not captive to him,
I'll set thee in a shower of gold, and hail
Rich pearls upon thee.
        MESSENGER.
          Madam, he's well.
        CLEOPATRA.
               Well said.
        MESSENGER.
And friends with Cæsar.

CLEOPATRA.
Th'art an honest man.
MESSENGER.
Cæsar and he are greater friends than ever.
CLEOPATRA.
Make thee a fortune from me.
MESSENGER.
But yet, madam,—
CLEOPATRA.
I do not like 'But yet,' it does allay
The good precedence; fie upon 'But yet'!
'But yet' is as a gaoler to bring forth
Some monstrous malefactor. Prithee, friend,
Pour out the pack of matter to mine ear,
The good and bad together: he's friends with
    Cæsar;
In state of health thou say'st; and thou say'st, free.
MESSENGER.
Free, madam! no; I made no such report:
He's bound unto Octavia.
CLEOPATRA.
For what good turn?
MESSENGER.
For the best turn i'the bed.
CLEOPATRA.
I am pale, Charmian.
MESSENGER.
Madam, he's married to Octavia.
CLEOPATRA.
The most infectious pestilence upon thee!
[Strikes him down.
MESSENGER.
Good madam, patience.
CLEOPATRA.
What say you?—Hence,
[Strikes him.
Horrible villain! or I'll spurn thine eyes
Like balls before me; I'll unhair thy head:
[She hales him up and down.
Thou shalt be whipt with wire, and stew'd in
    brine,
Smarting in lingering pickle.
MESSENGER.
Gracious madam,
I that do bring the news made not the match.
CLEOPATRA.
Say 'tis not so, a province I will give thee,
And make thy fortunes proud: the blow thou hadst
Shall make thy peace for moving me to rage;
And I will boot thee with what gift beside
Thy modesty can beg.
MESSENGER.
He's married, madam.
CLEOPATRA.
Rogue, thou hast lived too long.
[Draws a knife.
MESSENGER.
Nay, then I'll run.—
What mean you, madam? I have made no fault.
[Exit.
CHARMIAN.
Good madam, keep yourself within yourself:
The man is innocent.
CLEOPATRA.
Some innocents scape not the thunderbolt.—
Melt Egypt into Nile! and kindly creatures

Turn all to serpents!—Call the slave again:—
Though I am mad, I will not bite him:—call.
CHARMIAN.
He is afeard to come.
CLEOPATRA.
I will not hurt him.
[Exit CHARMIAN.
These hands do lack nobility, that they strike
A meaner than myself; since I myself
Have given myself the cause.
Enter CHARMIAN and MESSENGER.
Come hither, sir.
Though it be honest, it is never good
To bring bad news: give to a gracious message
An host of tongues; but let ill tidings tell
Themselves when they be felt.
MESSENGER.
I have done my duty.
CLEOPATRA.
Is he married?
I cannot hate thee worser than I do,
If thou again say 'Yes.'
MESSENGER.
He's married, madam.
CLEOPATRA.
The gods confound thee! dost thou hold there still?
MESSENGER.
Should I lie, madam?
CLEOPATRA.
O, I would thou didst,
So half my Egypt were submerged, and made
A cistern for scaled snakes! Go, get thee hence:
Hadst thou Narcissus in thy face, to me
Thou wouldst appear most ugly. He is married?
MESSENGER.
I crave your highness' pardon.
CLEOPATRA.
He is married?
MESSENGER.
Take no offence that I would not offend you:
To punish me for what you make me do
Seems much unequal: he's married to Octavia.
CLEOPATRA.
O, that his fault should make a knave of thee,
That art not what th'art sure of!—Get thee hence:
The merchandise which thou hast brought from
    Rome
Are all too dear for me: lie they upon thy hand,
And be undone by 'em!   [Exit MESSENGER.
CHARMIAN.
Good your highness, patience.
CLEOPATRA.
In praising Antony, I have dispraised Cæsar.
CHARMIAN.
Many times, madam.
CLEOPATRA.
I am paid for't now.
Lead me from hence;
I faint:—O Iras, Charmian!—'tis no matter.—
Go to the fellow, good Alexas; bid him
Report the feature of Octavia, her years,
Her inclination, let him not leave out
The colour of her hair:—bring me word quickly.
[Exit ALEXAS.
Let him for ever go:—let him not—Charmian,
Though he be painted one way like a Gorgon,

The other way's a Mars.—[to MARDIAN] Bid
　　you Alexas
Bring me word how tall she is.—Pity me,
　　Charmian,
But do not speak to me.—Lead me to my cham-
　　ber.　　　　　　　　　　　　　　[Exeunt.

SCENE VI.

Near Misenum.

Flourish.   Enter POMPEY *and* MENAS *at one door,
with drum and trumpet: at another,* CAESAR,
ANTONY, LEPIDUS, ENOBARBUS, MAECENAS,
with SOLDIERS *marching.*

POMPEY.

YOUR hostages I have, so have you mine;
　　And we shall talk before we fight.
OCTAVIUS CAESAR.
　　　　　　　　　　　　Most meet
That first we come to words; and therefore have we
Our written purposes before us sent;
Which, if thou hast consider'd, let us know
If 'twill tie up thy discontented sword,
And carry back to Sicily much tall youth
That else must perish here.
POMPEY.
　　　　　　　　To you all three,
The senators alone of this great world,
Chief factors for the gods,—I do not know
Wherefore my father should revengers want,
Having a son and friends; since Julius Cæsar,
Who at Philippi the good Brutus ghosted,
There saw you labouring for him. What was 't
That moved pale Cassius to conspire; and what
Made the all-honour'd, honest Roman, Brutus,
With the arm'd rest, courtiers of beauteous free-
　　dom,
To drench the Capitol, but that they would
Have one man but a man? And that is it
Hath made me rig my navy, at whose burden
The anger'd ocean foams; with which I meant
To scourge th'ingratitude that despiteful Rome
Cast on my noble father.
OCTAVIUS CAESAR.
　　　　　　　　Take your time.
MARK ANTONY.
Thou canst not fear us, Pompey, with thy sails;
We'll speak with thee at sea: at land, thou know'st
How much we do o'er-count thee.
POMPEY.
　　　　　　　　At land, indeed
Thou dost o'er-count me of my father's house:
But, since the cuckoo builds not for himself,
Remain in't as thou mayst.
LEPIDUS.
　　　　　　　　Be pleased to tell us—
For this is from the present—how you take
The offers we have sent you.
OCTAVIUS CAESAR.
　　　　　　　　There's the point.
MARK ANTONY.
Which do not be entreated to, but weigh
What it is worth embraced.
OCTAVIUS CAESAR.
　　　　　　　　And what may follow,
To try a larger fortune.

POMPEY.
　　　　　　　　You have made me offer
Of Sicily, Sardinia; and I must
Rid all the sea of pirates; then, to send
Measures of wheat to Rome; this greed upon,
To part with unhackt edges, and bear back
Our targes undinted.
OCTAVIUS CAESAR, MARK ANTONY, *and*
LEPIDUS.
　　　That's our offer.
POMPEY.
　　　　　　　　Know, then,
I came before you here a man prepared
To take this offer: but Mark Antony
Put me to some impatience:—though I lose
The praise of it by telling, you must know,
When Cæsar and your brother were at blows,
Your mother came to Sicily, and did find
Her welcome friendly.
MARK ANTONY.
　　　　　　　　I have heard it, Pompey;
And am well studied for a liberal thanks
Which I do owe you.
POMPEY.
　　　　　　　　Let me have your hand:
I did not think, sir, to have met you here.
MARK ANTONY.
The beds i'the east are soft; and thanks to you,
That call'd me, timelier than my purpose, hither;
For I have gain'd by't.
OCTAVIUS CAESAR.
　　　　　　　　Since I saw you last,
There is a change upon you.
POMPEY.
　　　　　　　　Well, I know not
What counts harsh fortune casts upon my face;
But in my bosom shall she never come,
To make my heart her vassal.
LEPIDUS.
　　　　　　　　Well met here.
POMPEY.
I hope so, Lepidus.—Thus we are agreed:
I crave our composition may be written,
And seal'd between us.
OCTAVIUS CAESAR.
　　　　　　　　That's the next to do.
POMPEY.
We'll feast each other ere we part; and let's
Draw lots who shall begin.
MARK ANTONY.
　　　　　　　　That will I, Pompey.
POMPEY.
No, Antony, take the lot: but, first
Or last, your fine Egyptian cookery
Shall have the fame. I have heard that Julius
　　Cæsar
Grew fat with feasting there.
MARK ANTONY.
　　　　　　　　You have heard much.
POMPEY.
I have fair meanings, sir.
MARK ANTONY.
　　　　　　　　And fair words to them.
POMPEY.
Then so much have I heard:
And I have heard, Apollodorus carried—

DOMITIUS ENOBARBUS.
No more of that:—he did so.

POMPEY.
What, I pray you?

DOMITIUS ENOBARBUS.
A certain queen to Cæsar in a mattress.

POMPEY.
I know thee now: how farest thou, soldier?

DOMITIUS ENOBARBUS.
Well;
And well am like to do; for I perceive
Four feasts are toward.

POMPEY.
Let me shake thy hand;
I never hated thee: I have seen thee fight,
When I have envied thy behaviour.

DOMITIUS ENOBARBUS.
Sir,
I never loved you much; but I ha' praised ye,
When you have well deserved ten times as much
As I have said you did.

POMPEY.
Enjoy thy plainness,
It nothing ill becomes thee.—
Aboard my galley I invite you all:
Will you lead, lords?

OCTAVIUS CAESAR, MARK ANTONY, *and*
LEPIDUS.
Show us the way, sir.

POMPEY.
Come.

[*Exeunt all but* MENAS *and* ENOBARBUS.
MENAS [*aside*].
Thy father, Pompey, would ne'er have made this
treaty.—You and I have known, sir.

DOMITIUS ENOBARBUS.
At sea, I think.

MENAS.
We have, sir.

DOMITIUS ENOBARBUS.
You have done well by water.

MENAS.
And you by land.

DOMITIUS ENOBARBUS.
I will praise any man that will praise me; though
it cannot be denied what I have done by land.

MENAS.
Nor what I have done by water.

DOMITIUS ENOBARBUS.
Yes, something you can deny for your own safety:
you have been a great thief by sea.

MENAS.
And you by land.

DOMITIUS ENOBARBUS.
There I deny my land service. But give me your
hand, Menas: if our eyes had authority, here they
might take two thieves kissing.

MENAS.
All men's faces are true, whatsoe'er their hands
are.

DOMITIUS ENOBARBUS.
But there is never a fair woman has a true face.

MENAS.
No slander; they steal hearts.

DOMITIUS ENOBARBUS.
We came hither to fight with you.

MENAS.
For my part, I am sorry it is turn'd to a drinking. Pompey doth this day laugh away his
fortune.

DOMITIUS ENOBARBUS.
If he do, sure, he cannot weep't back again.

MENAS.
Y'have said, sir. We lookt not for Mark Antony
here: pray you, is he married to Cleopatra?

DOMITIUS ENOBARBUS.
Cæsar's sister is called Octavia.

MENAS.
True, sir; she was the wife of Caius Marcellus.

DOMITIUS ENOBARBUS.
But she is now the wife of Marcus Antonius.

MENAS.
Pray ye, sir?

DOMITIUS ENOBARBUS.
'Tis true.

MENAS.
Then is Cæsar and he for ever knit together.

DOMITIUS ENOBARBUS.
If I were bound to divine of this unity, I would
not prophesy so.

MENAS.
I think the policy of that purpose made more in
the marriage than the love of the parties.

DOMITIUS ENOBARBUS.
I think so too. But you shall find, the band that
seems to tie their friendship together will be the
very strangler of their amity: Octavia is of a holy,
cold, and still conversation.

MENAS.
Who would not have his wife so?

DOMITIUS ENOBARBUS.
Not he that himself is not so; which is Mark
Antony. He will to his Egyptian dish again: then
shall the sighs of Octavia blow the fire up in
Cæsar; and, as I said before, that which is the
strength of their amity shall prove the immediate
author of their variance. Antony will use his
affection where it is: he married but his occasion
here.

MENAS.
And thus it may be. Come, sir, will you aboard?
I have a health for you.

DOMITIUS ENOBARBUS.
I shall take it, sir: we have used our throats in
Egypt.

MENAS.
Come, let's away.   [*Exeunt.*

SCENE VII.

On board POMPEY'S *galley, off Misenum.*

Music plays.   Enter two or three SERVANTS,
with a banquet.

FIRST SERVANT.
HERE they'll be, man. Some o'their plants are
ill-rooted already; the least wind i'the world
will blow them down.

SECOND SERVANT.
Lepidus is high-colour'd.

FIRST SERVANT.
They have made him drink alms-drink.

SECOND SERVANT.
As they pinch one another by the disposition, he cries out 'No more;' reconciles them to his entreaty, and himself to the drink.

FIRST SERVANT.
But it raises the greater war between him and his discretion.

SECOND SERVANT.
Why, this it is to have a name in great men's fellowship: I had as lief have a reed that will do me no service as a partisan I could not heave.

FIRST SERVANT.
To be call'd into a huge sphere, and not to be seen to move in't, are the holes where eyes should be, which pitifully disaster the cheeks.

A sennet sounded. Enter CAESAR, ANTONY, LEPIDUS, POMPEY, AGRIPPA, MAECENAS, ENOBARBUS, MENAS, *with other* CAPTAINS.

MARK ANTONY [*to* OCTAVIUS CAESAR].
Thus do they, sir: they take the flow o'the Nile
By certain scales i'the pyramid; they know,
By the height, the lowness, or the mean, if dearth
Or foison follow: the higher Nilus swells,
The more it promises: as it ebbs, the seedsman
Upon the slime and ooze scatters his grain,
And shortly comes to harvest.

LEPIDUS.
Y'have strange serpents there.

MARK ANTONY.
Ay, Lepidus.

LEPIDUS.
Your serpent of Egypt is bred now of your mud by the operation of your sun: so is your crocodile.

MARK ANTONY.
They are so.

POMPEY.
Sit,—and some wine!—A health to Lepidus!

LEPIDUS.
I am not so well as I should be, but I'll ne'er out.

DOMITIUS ENOBARBUS.
Not till you have slept; I fear me you'll be in till then.

LEPIDUS.
Nay, certainly, I have heard the Ptolemies' pyramises are very goodly things; without contradiction, I have heard that.

MENAS [*aside to* POMPEY].
Pompey, a word.

POMPEY [*aside to* MENAS].
Say in mine ear: what is't?

MENAS [*whispers in his ear*].
Forsake thy seat, I do beseech thee, captain,
And hear me speak a word.

POMPEY [*aside to* MENAS].
     Forbear me till anon.—
This wine for Lepidus!

LEPIDUS.
What manner o'thing is your crocodile?

MARK ANTONY.
It is shaped, sir, like itself; and it is as broad as it hath breadth; it is just so high as it is, and moves with its own organs: it lives by that which nourisheth it; and the elements once out of it, it transmigrates.

LEPIDUS.
What colour is it of?

MARK ANTONY.
Of its own colour too.

LEPIDUS.
'Tis a strange serpent.

MARK ANTONY.
'Tis so. And the tears of it are wet.

OCTAVIUS CAESAR.
Will this description satisfy him?

MARK ANTONY.
With the health that Pompey gives him, else he is a very epicure.

POMPEY [*aside to* MENAS].
Go hang, sir, hang! Tell me of that? away!
Do as I bid you.—Where's this cup I call'd for?

MENAS [*aside to* POMPEY].
If for the sake of merit thou wilt hear me,
Rise from thy stool.

POMPEY [*aside to* MENAS].
I think th'art mad. The matter?
     [*Rises, and walks aside.*

MENAS.
I have ever held my cap off to thy fortunes.

POMPEY.
Thou hast served me with much faith. What's else to say?—
Be jolly, lords.

MARK ANTONY.
     These quicksands, Lepidus,
Keep off them, for you sink.

MENAS.
Wilt thou be lord of all the world?

POMPEY.
      What say'st thou?

MENAS.
Wilt thou be lord of the whole world? That's twice.

POMPEY.
How should that be?

MENAS.
     But entertain it,
And though thou think me poor, I am the man
Will give thee all the world.

POMPEY.
     Hast thou drunk well?

MENAS.
No, Pompey, I have kept me from the cup.
Thou art, if thou darest be, the earthly Jove:
Whate'er the ocean pales, or sky inclips,
Is thine, if thou wilt ha't.

POMPEY.
     Show me which way.

MENAS.
These three world-sharers, these competitors,
Are in thy vessel: let me cut the cable;
And, when we are put off, fall to their throats:
All then is thine.

POMPEY.
     Ah, this thou shouldst have done,
And not have spoke on't! In me 'tis villainy;
In thee't had been good service. Thou must know,
'Tis not my profit that does lead mine honour;
Mine honour, it. Repent that e'er thy tongue
Hath so betray'd thine act: being done unknown,
I should have found it afterwards well done;
But must condemn it now. Desist, and drink.

MENAS [*aside*].
For this,
I'll never follow thy pall'd fortunes more.—
Who seeks, and will not take when once 'tis offer'd,
Shall never find it more.

POMPEY.
           This health to Lepidus!

MARK ANTONY.
Bear him ashore.—I'll pledge it for him, Pompey.

DOMITIUS ENOBARBUS.
Here's to thee, Menas!

MENAS.
         Enobarbus, welcome!

POMPEY.
Fill till the cup be hid.

DOMITIUS ENOBARBUS.
There's a strong fellow, Menas.
     [*Pointing to the* ATTENDANT *who carries
off* LEPIDUS.

MENAS.
Why?

DOMITIUS ENOBARBUS.
A' bears the third part of the world, man; see'st not?

MENAS.
The third part, then, is drunk: would it were all,
That it might go on wheels!

DOMITIUS ENOBARBUS.
Drink thou; increase the reels.

MENAS.
Come.

POMPEY.
This is not yet an Alexandrian feast.

MARK ANTONY.
It ripens towards it.—Strike the vessels, ho!—
Here's to Cæsar!

OCTAVIUS CAESAR.
        I could well forbear't.
It's monstrous labour, when I wash my brain,
And it grows fouler.

MARK ANTONY.
       Be a child o'the time.

OCTAVIUS CAESAR.
Possess it, I'll make answer:
But I had rather fast from all four days
Than drink so much in one.

DOMITIUS ENOBARBUS [*to* ANTONY].
        Ha, my brave emperor!
Shall we dance now the Egyptian Bacchanals,
And celebrate our drink?

POMPEY.
        Let's ha't, good soldier.

MARK ANTONY.
Come, let's all take hands,
Till that the conquering wine hath steept our sense
In soft and delicate Lethe.

DOMITIUS ENOBARBUS.
        All take hands.—
Make battery to our ears with the loud music:—
The while I'll place you: then the boy shall sing;
The holding every man shall bear as loud
As his strong sides can volley.
     [*Music plays.* ENOBARBUS *places them
hand in hand.*

The Song.
Come, thou monarch of the vine,
Plumpy Bacchus with pink eyne!
In thy fats our cares be drown'd,
With thy grapes our hairs be crown'd:
Cup us till the world go round,
Cup us till the world go round!

OCTAVIUS CAESAR.
What would you more?—Pompey, good night.—-
Good brother.
Let me request you off: our graver business
Frowns at this levity.—Gentle lords, let's part;
You see we have burnt our cheeks: strong Enobarb
Is weaker than the wine; and mine own tongue
Splits what it speaks: the wild disguise hath almost
Antickt us all. What needs more words? Good night.—
Good Antony, your hand.

POMPEY.
        I'll try you on the shore.

MARK ANTONY.
And shall, sir: give's your hand.

POMPEY.
          O Antony,
You have my father's house,—But, what? we are friends.
Come, down into the boat.

DOMITIUS ENOBARBUS.
        Take heed you fall not.
     [*Exeunt all except* ENOBARBUS *and* MENAS.
Menas, I'll not on shore.

MENAS.
        No, to my cabin.—
These drums!—these trumpets, flutes! what!—
Let Neptune hear we bid a loud farewell
To these great fellows: sound and be hang'd,
sound out!   [*Sound a flourish, with drums.*

DOMITIUS ENOBARBUS.
Hoo! says a'.—There's my cap.

MENAS.
Hoo!—Noble captain, come.   [*Exeunt.*

ACT III. SCENE I.

A plain in Syria.

Enter VENTIDIUS *as it were in triumph, with*
SILIUS *and other* ROMANS, OFFICERS, *and*
SOLDIERS; *the dead body of* PACORUS *borne
before him.*

VENTIDIUS.
NOW, darting Parthia, art thou struck; and now
Pleased fortune does of Marcus Crassus' death
Make me revenger.—Bear the king's son's body
Before our army.—Thy Pacorus, Orodes,
Pays this for Marcus Crassus.

SILIUS.
        Noble Ventidius,
Whilst yet with Parthian blood thy sword is warm,
The fugitive Parthians follow; spur through Media,
Mesopotamia, and the shelters whither
The routed fly: so thy grand captain Antony
Shall set thee on triumphant chariots, and
Put garlands on thy head.

VENTIDIUS.

         O Silius, Silius,
I have done enough: a lower place, note well,
May make too great an act; for learn this, Silius,—
Better to leave undone, than by our deed
Acquire too high a fame when him we serve's
    away.
Cæsar and Antony have ever won
More in their officer than person: Sossius,
One of my place in Syria, his lieutenant,
For quick accumulation of renown,
Which he achieved by the minute, lost his favour.
Who does i'the wars more than his captain can
Becomes his captain's captain: and ambition,
The soldier's virtue, rather makes choice of loss
Than gain which darkens him.
I could do more to do Antonius good,
But 'twould offend him; and in his offence
Should my performance perish.

SILIUS.

         Thou hast, Ventidius, that
Without the which a soldier, and his sword,
Grants scarce distinction. Thou wilt write to An-
tony?

VENTIDIUS.

I'll humbly signify what in his name,
That magical word of war, we have effected;
How, with his banners and his well-paid ranks,
The ne'er-yet-beaten horse of Parthia
We have jaded out o'the field.

SILIUS.

           Where is he now?

VENTIDIUS.

He purposeth to Athens: whither, with what
    haste
The weight we must convey with's will permit,
We shall appear before him.—On, there; pass
    along!   [*Exeunt.*

SCENE II.

Rome.   *An ante-chamber in* CAESAR'S *house.*

Enter AGRIPPA *at one door and* ENOBARBUS
at another.

AGRIPPA.

WHAT, are the brothers parted?

DOMITIUS ENOBARBUS.

They have dispatcht with Pompey; he is gone;
The other three are sealing. Octavia weeps
To part from Rome; Cæsar is sad; and Lepidus,
Since Pompey's feast, as Menas says, is troubled
With the green sickness.

AGRIPPA.

         'Tis a noble Lepidus.

DOMITIUS ENOBARBUS.

A very fine one: O, how he loves Cæsar!

AGRIPPA.

Nay, but how dearly he adores Mark Antony!

DOMITIUS ENOBARBUS.

Cæsar? Why, he's the Jupiter of men.

AGRIPPA.

What's Antony? The god of Jupiter.

DOMITIUS ENOBARBUS.

Spake you of Cæsar? How! the nonpareil!

AGRIPPA.

O Antony! O thou Arabian bird!

DOMITIUS ENOBARBUS.

Would you praise Cæsar, say 'Cæsar,'—go no further.

AGRIPPA.

Indeed, he plied them both with excellent praises.

DOMITIUS ENOBARBUS.

But he loves Cæsar best;—yet he loves Antony·
Hoo! hearts, tongues, figures, scribes, bards, poets,
    cannot
Think, speak, cast, write, sing, number,—
    hoo!—
His love to Antony. But as for Cæsar,
Kneel down, kneel down, and wonder.

AGRIPPA.

            Both he loves.

DOMITIUS ENOBARBUS.

They are his shards, and he their beetle. [*Trumpets within.*] So,—
This is to horse.—Adieu, noble Agrippa.

AGRIPPA.

Good fortune, worthy soldier; and farewell.

Enter CAESAR, ANTONY, LEPIDUS, *and*
OCTAVIA.

MARK ANTONY.

No further, sir.

OCTAVIUS CAESAR.

You take from me a great part of myself;
Use me well in't.—Sister, prove such a wife
As my thoughts make thee, and as my furthest
    band
Shall pass on thy approof.—Most noble Antony,
Let not the piece of virtue, which is set
Betwixt us as the cement of our love
To keep it builded, be the ram to batter
The fortress of it; for better might we
Have loved without this mean, if on both parts
This be not cherisht.

MARK ANTONY.

         Make me not offended
In your distrust.

OCTAVIUS CAESAR.

I have said.

MARK ANTONY.

           You shall not find,
Though you be therein curious, the least cause
For what you seem to fear: so, the gods keep
    you,
And make the hearts of Romans serve your ends!
We will here part.

OCTAVIUS CAESAR.

Farewell, my dearest sister, fare thee well:
The elements be kind to thee, and make
Thy spirits all of comfort! fare thee well.

OCTAVIA.

My noble brother!—

MARK ANTONY.

The April's in her eyes: it is love's spring,
And these the showers to bring it on.—Be cheerful.

OCTAVIA.

Sir, look well to my husband's house; and—

OCTAVIUS CAESAR.

              What, Octavia?

OCTAVIA.

I'll tell you in your ear.

MARK ANTONY.
Her tongue will not obey her heart, nor can
Her heart inform her tongue,—the swan's down-
    feather,
That stands upon the swell at full of tide,
And neither way inclines.

DOMITIUS ENOBARBUS [*aside to* AGRIPPA].
Will Cæsar weep?

AGRIPPA [*aside to* DOMITIUS ENOBARBUS].
                        He has a cloud in's face.

DOMITIUS ENOBARBUS [*aside to* AGRIPPA].
He were the worse for that were he a horse;
So is he being a man.

AGRIPPA [*aside to* DOMITIUS ENOBARBUS].
                                Why, Enobarbus,
When Antony found Julius Cæsar dead,
He cried almost to roaring; and he wept
When at Philippi he found Brutus slain.

DOMITIUS ENOBARBUS [*aside to* AGRIPPA].
That year, indeed, he was troubled with a rheum;
What willingly he did confound he wail'd,
Believe't, till I wept too.

OCTAVIUS CAESAR.
                        No, sweet Octavia,
You shall hear from me still; the time shall not
Out-go my thinking on you.

MARK ANTONY.
                        Come, sir, come;
I'll wrestle with you in my strength of love:
Look, here I have you; thus I let you go,
And give you to the gods.

OCTAVIUS CAESAR.
                    Adieu; be happy!

LEPIDUS.
Let all the number of the stars give light
To thy fair way!

OCTAVIUS CAESAR.
Farewell, farewell! [*Kisses* OCTAVIA.

MARK ANTONY.
                        Farewell!
                    [*Trumpets sound.   Exeunt.*

SCENE III.

Alexandria.   A room in CLEOPATRA's *palace.*

Enter CLEOPATRA, CHARMIAN, IRAS, *and*
ALEXAS.

CLEOPATRA.
WHERE is the fellow?

ALEXAS.
                    Half afeard to come.

CLEOPATRA.
Go to, go to.
        Enter the MESSENGER *as before.*
Come hither, sir.

ALEXAS.
                    Good majesty,
Herod of Jewry dare not look upon you
But when you are well pleased.

CLEOPATRA.
                        That Herod's head
I'll have: but how, when Antony is gone
Through whom I might command it?—Come
    thou near.

MESSENGER.
Most gracious majesty,—

CLEOPATRA.
                        Didst thou behold
Octavia?

MESSENGER.
Ay, dread queen.

CLEOPATRA.
Where?

MESSENGER.
                    Madam, in Rome;
I lookt her in the face, and saw her led
Between her brother and Mark Antony.

CLEOPATRA.
Is she as tall as me?

MESSENGER.
                    She is not, madam.

CLEOPATRA.
Didst hear her speak? is she shrill-tongued or low?

MESSENGER.
Madam, I heard her speak; she is low-voiced.

CLEOPATRA.
That's not so good:—he cannot like her long.

CHARMIAN.
Like her! O Isis! 'tis impossible.

CLEOPATRA.
I think so, Charmian: dull of tongue, and dwarf-
    ish!—
What majesty is in her gait? Remember,
If e'er thou looktst on majesty.

MESSENGER.
                            She creeps,—
Her motion and her station are as one;
She shows a body rather than a life,
A statue than a breather.

CLEOPATRA.
                    Is this certain?

MESSENGER.
Or I have no observance.

CHARMIAN.
                    Three in Egypt
Cannot make better note.

CLEOPATRA.
                    He's very knowing;
I do perceive't:—there's nothing in her yet:—
The fellow has good judgement.

CHARMIAN.
                        Excellent.

CLEOPATRA.
Guess at her years, I prithee.

MESSENGER.
                        Madam,
She was a widow,—

CLEOPATRA.
                    Widow!—Charmian, hark.

MESSENGER.
And I do think she's thirty.

CLEOPATRA.
Bear'st thou her face in mind? is't long or round?

MESSENGER.
Round even to faultiness.

CLEOPATRA.
For the most part, too, they are foolish that are
    so.—
Her hair, what colour?

MESSENGER.
                    Brown, madam: and her forehead
As low as she would wish it.

CLEOPATRA.
               There's gold for thee.
Thou must not take my former sharpness ill:—
I will employ thee back again; I find thee
Most fit for business: go make thee ready;
Our letters are prepared.   [*Exit* MESSENGER.

CHARMIAN.
            A proper man.

CLEOPATRA.
Indeed, he is so: I repent me much
That so I harried him. Why, methinks, by him,
This creature's no such thing.

CHARMIAN.
               Nothing, madam.

CLEOPATRA.
The man hath seen some majesty, and should
   know.

CHARMIAN.
Hath he seen majesty? Isis else defend,
And serving you so long!

CLEOPATRA.
I have one thing more to ask him yet, good Char-
   mian:
But 'tis no matter; thou shalt bring him to me
Where I will write. All may be well enough.

CHARMIAN.
I warrant you, madam.   [*Exeunt.*

SCENE IV.

Athens.   *A room in* ANTONY'S *house.*

Enter ANTONY *and* OCTAVIA.

MARK ANTONY.
NAY, nay, Octavia, not only that,—
    That were excusable, that, and thousands
     more
Of semblable import,—but he hath waged
New wars 'gainst Pompey; made his will, and read
   it
To public ear:
Spoke scantly of me: when perforce he could not
But pay me terms of honour, cold and sickly
He vented them; most narrow measure lent me:
When the best hint was given him, he not took't,
Or did it from his teeth.

OCTAVIA.
            O, my good lord,
Believe not all; or, if you must believe,
Stomach not all. A more unhappy lady,
If this division chance, ne'er stood between,
Praying for both parts:
The good gods will mock me presently,
When I shall pray, 'O, bless my lord and husband!'
Undo that prayer, by crying out as loud,
'O, bless my brother!' Husband win, win brother,
Prays, and destroys the prayer; no midway
'Twixt these extremes at all.

MARK ANTONY.
            Gentle Octavia,
Let your best love draw to that point, which seeks
Best to preserve it: if I lose mine honour,
I lose myself: better I were not yours
Than yours so branchless. But, as you requested,
Yourself shall go between's: the mean time, lady,

I'll raise the preparation of a war
Shall stay your brother: make your soonest haste;
So your desires are yours.

OCTAVIA.
            Thanks to my lord.
The Jove of power make me most weak, most
   weak,
Your reconciler! Wars 'twixt you twain would be
As if the world should cleave, and that slain men
Should solder up the rift.

MARK ANTONY.
When it appears to you where this begins,
Turn your displeasure that way; for our faults
Can never be so equal, that your love
Can equally move with them. Provide your going;
Choose your own company, and command what
   cost
Your heart has mind to.   [*Exeunt.*

SCENE V.

The same.   *Another room.*

Enter ENOBARBUS *and* EROS, *meeting.*

DOMITIUS ENOBARBUS.
HOW now, friend Eros!

EROS.
There's strange news come, sir.

DOMITIUS ENOBARBUS.
What, man?

EROS.
Cæsar and Lepidus have made wars upon Pompey.

DOMITIUS ENOBARBUS.
This is old: what is the success?

EROS.
Cæsar, having made use of him in the wars 'gainst
Pompey, presently denied him rivality; would not
let him partake in the glory of the action: and not
resting here, accuses him of letters he had formerly wrote to Pompey; upon his own appeal, seizes
him: so the poor third is up, till death enlarge his
confine.

DOMITIUS ENOBARBUS.
Then, world, thou hast a pair of chaps, no more;
And throw between them all the food thou hast,
They'll grind the one the other. Where's An-
tony?

EROS.
He's walking in the garden—thus; and spurns
The rush that lies before him; cries 'Fool Lepi-
dus!'
And threats the throat of that his officer
That murder'd Pompey.

DOMITIUS ENOBARBUS.
            Our great navy's rigg'd.

EROS.
For Italy and Cæsar. More, Domitius;
My lord desires you presently: my news
I might have told hereafter.

DOMITIUS ENOBARBUS.
            'Twill be naught:
But let it be.—Bring me to Antony.

EROS.
Come, sir.   [*Exeunt.*

SCENE VI.

Rome. A room in CAESAR'S *house.*

Enter CAESAR, AGRIPPA, *and* MAECENAS.

OCTAVIUS CAESAR.

CONTEMNING Rome, he has done all this
and more
In Alexandria: here's the manner of't:—
I'the market-place, on a tribunal silver'd,
Cleopatra and himself in chairs of gold
Were publicly enthroned; at the feet sat
Cæsarion, whom they call my father's son,
And all the unlawful issue that their lust
Since then hath made between them. Unto her
He gave the stablishment of Egypt; made her
Of lower Syria, Cyprus, Lydia,
Absolute queen.

MAECENAS.
This in the public eye?

OCTAVIUS CAESAR.
I'the common show-place, where they exercise.
His sons he there proclaim'd the kings of kings;
Great Media, Parthia, and Armenia,
He gave to Alexander; to Ptolemy he assign'd
Syria, Cilicia, and Phœnicia: she
In the habiliments of the goddess Isis
That day appear'd; and oft before gave audience,
As 'tis reported, so.

MAECENAS.
Let Rome be thus inform'd.

AGRIPPA.
Who, queasy with his insolence
Already, will their good thoughts call from him.

OCTAVIUS CAESAR.
The people know it; and have now received
His accusations.

AGRIPPA.
Who does he accuse?

OCTAVIUS CAESAR.
Cæsar: and that, having in Sicily
Sextus Pompeius spoil'd, we had not rated him
His part o'the isle: then does he say he lent me
Some shipping unrestored: lastly, he frets
That Lepidus of the triumvirate
Should be deposed; and, being, that we detain
All his revenue.

AGRIPPA.
Sir, this should be answer'd.

OCTAVIUS CAESAR.
'Tis done already, and the messenger gone.
I have told him, Lepidus was grown too cruel;
That he his high authority abused,
And did deserve his change: for what I have con-
quer'd,
I grant him part; but then, in his Armenia,
And other of his conquer'd kingdoms, I
Demand the like.

MAECENAS.
He'll never yield to that.

OCTAVIUS CAESAR.
Nor must not, then, be yielded to in this.

Enter OCTAVIA *with her* TRAIN.

OCTAVIA.
Hail, Cæsar, and my lord! hail, most dear Cæsar!

OCTAVIUS CAESAR.
That ever I should call thee castaway!

OCTAVIA.
You have not call'd me so, nor have you cause.

OCTAVIUS CAESAR.
Why have you stoln upon us thus? You come not
Like Cæsar's sister: the wife of Antony
Should have an army for an usher, and
The neighs of horse to tell of her approach
Long ere she did appear; the trees by the way
Should have borne men; and expectation fainted,
Longing for what it had not; nay, the dust
Should have ascended to the roof of heaven,
Raised by your populous troops: but you are
come
A market-maid to Rome; and have prevented
The ostentation of our love, which, left un-
shown
Is often left unloved: we should have met you
By sea and land; supplying every stage
With an augmented greeting.

OCTAVIA.
Good my lord,
To come thus was I not constrain'd, but did it
On my free will. My lord, Mark Antony,
Hearing that you prepared for war, acquainted
My grieved ear withal; whereon I begg'd
His pardon for return.

OCTAVIUS CAESAR.
Which soon he granted,
Being an obstruct 'tween his lust and him.

OCTAVIA.
Do not say so, my lord.

OCTAVIUS CAESAR.
I have eyes upon him,
And his affairs come to me on the wind.
Where is he now?

OCTAVIA.
My lord, in Athens.

OCTAVIUS CAESAR.
No, my most wronged sister; Cleopatra
Hath nodded him to her. He hath given his em-
pire
Up to a whore; who now are levying
The kings o'the earth for war: he hath assembled
Bocchus, the king of Libya; Archelaus,
Of Cappadocia; Philadelphos, king
Of Paphlagonia; the Thracian king, Adallas;
King Malchus of Arabia; King of Pont;
Herod of Jewry: Mithridates, king
Of Comagene; Polemon and Amyntas,
The kings of Mede and Lycaonia,
With a more larger list of sceptres.

OCTAVIA.
Ay me, most wretched,
That have my heart parted betwixt two friends
That do afflict each other!

OCTAVIUS CAESAR.
Welcome hither:
Your letters did withhold our breaking forth;
Till we perceived both how you were wrong led
And we in negligent danger. Cheer your heart:
Be you not troubled with the time, which drives
O'er your content these strong necessities;
But let determined things to destiny
Hold unbewail'd their way. Welcome to Rome;
Nothing more dear to me. You are abused
Beyond the mark of thought: and the high gods,

To do you justice, make them ministers
Of us and those that love you. Best of comfort;
And ever welcome to us.

AGRIPPA.
Welcome, lady.

MAECENAS.
Welcome, dear madam.
Each heart in Rome does love and pity you:
Only th'adulterous Antony, most large
In his abominations, turns you off;
And gives his potent regiment to a trull,
That noises it against us.

OCTAVIA.
Is it so, sir?

OCTAVIUS CAESAR.
Most certain. Sister, welcome: pray you,
Be ever known to patience: my dear'st sister!
[Exeunt.

SCENE VII.

ANTONY'S *camp, near Actium.*

Enter CLEOPATRA *and* ENOBARBUS.

CLEOPATRA.
I WILL be even with thee, doubt it not.

DOMITIUS ENOBARBUS.
But why, why, why?

CLEOPATRA.
Thou hast forspoke my being in these wars,
And say'st it is not fit.

DOMITIUS ENOBARBUS.
Well, is it, is it?

CLEOPATRA.
If not denounced against us, why should not we
Be there in person?

DOMITIUS ENOBARBUS [*aside*].
Well, I could reply:—
If we should serve with horse and mares together,
The horse were merely lost; the mares would bear
A soldier and his horse.

CLEOPATRA.
What is't you say?

DOMITIUS ENOBARBUS.
Your presence needs must puzzle Antony;
Take from his heart, take from his brain, from's
    time,
What should not then be spared. He is already
Traduced for levity; and 'tis said in Rome
That Photinus an eunuch and your maids
Manage this war.

CLEOPATRA.
Sink Rome, and their tongues rot
That speak against us! A charge we bear i'the war,
And, as the president of my kingdom, will
Appear there for a man. Speak not against it;
I will not stay behind.

DOMITIUS ENOBARBUS.
Nay, I have done.
Here comes the emperor.

Enter ANTONY *and* CANIDIUS.

MARK ANTONY.
Is it not strange, Canidius,
That from Tarentum and Brundusium
He could so quickly cut the Ionian sea,
And take in Toryne?—You have heard on't,
    sweet?

CLEOPATRA.
Celerity is never more admired
Than by the negligent.

MARK ANTONY.
A good rebuke,
Which might have well becomed the best of men,
To taunt at slackness.—Canidius, we
Will fight with him by sea.

CLEOPATRA.
By sea! what else?

CANIDIUS.
Why will my lord do so?

MARK ANTONY.
For that he dares us to't.

DOMITIUS ENOBARBUS.
So hath my lord dared him to single fight.

CANIDIUS.
Ay, and to wage this battle at Pharsalia,
Where Cæsar fought with Pompey: but these offers.
Which serve not for his vantage, he shakes off;
And so should you.

DOMITIUS ENOBARBUS.
Your ships are not well mann'd,—
Your mariners are muleters, reapers, people
Ingrost by swift impress; in Cæsar's fleet
Are those that often have 'gainst Pompey fought:
Their ships are yare; yours, heavy: no disgrace
Shall fall you for refusing him at sea,
Being prepared for land.

MARK ANTONY.
By sea, by sea.

DOMITIUS ENOBARBUS.
Most worthy sir, you therein throw away
The absolute soldiership you have by land;
Distract your army, which doth most consist
Of war-markt footmen; leave unexecuted
Your own renowned knowledge; quite forgo
The way which promises assurance; and
Give up yourself merely to chance and hazard,
From firm security.

MARK ANTONY.
I'll fight at sea.

CLEOPATRA.
I have sixty sails, Cæsar none better.

MARK ANTONY.
Our overplus of shipping will we burn;
And, with the rest full-mann'd, from the head of
    Actium
Beat the approaching Cæsar. But if we fail,
We then can do't at land.

Enter a MESSENGER.
Thy business?

MESSENGER.
The news is true, my lord; he is descried;
Cæsar has taken Toryne.

MARK ANTONY.
Can he be there in person? 'tis impossible;
Strange that his power should be.—Canidius,
Our nineteen legions thou shalt hold by land,
And our twelve thousand horse.—We'll to our
Away, my Thetis!   [ship:

Enter a SOLDIER.
How now, worthy soldier!

SOLDIER.
O noble emperor, do not fight by sea;
Trust not to rotten planks: do you misdoubt

This sword and these my wounds? Let the
  Egyptians
And the Phœnicians go a-ducking: we
Have used to conquer, standing on the earth,
And fighting foot to foot.

MARK ANTONY.
                 Well, well:—away!
[Exeunt ANTONY, CLEOPATRA, and
    ENOBARBUS.

SOLDIER.
By Hercules, I think I am i'the right.

CANIDIUS.
Soldier, thou art: but his whole action grows
Not in the power on't: so our leader's led,
And we are women's men.

SOLDIER.
               You keep by land
The legions and the horse whole, do you not?

CANIDIUS.
Marcus Octavius, Marcus Justeius,
Publicola, and Cælius, are for sea:
But we keep whole by land. This speed of Cæsar's
Carries beyond belief.

SOLDIER.
            While he was yet in Rome,
His power went out in such distractions as
Beguiled all spies.

CANIDIUS.
Who's his lieutenant, hear you?

SOLDIER.
They say, one Taurus.

CANIDIUS.
            Well I know the man.
Enter a MESSENGER.

MESSENGER.
The emperor calls Canidius.

CANIDIUS.
With news the time's with labour, and throes
  forth
Each minute some.   [Exeunt.

SCENE VIII.

A plain near Actium.

Enter CAESAR and TAURUS, with his army,
marching.

OCTAVIUS CAESAR.

TAURUS,—

TAURUS.
My lord?

OCTAVIUS CAESAR.
Strike not by land; keep whole: provoke not battle,
Till we have done at sea. Do not exceed
The prescript of this scroll: our fortune lies
Upon this jump.   [Exeunt.

SCENE IX.

Another part of the plain.

Enter ANTONY and ENOBARBUS.

MARK ANTONY.

SET we our squadrons on yond side o'the hill,
In eye of Cæsar's battle; from which place
We may the number of the ships behold,
And so proceed accordingly.   [Exeunt.

SCENE X.

Another part of the plain.

CANIDIUS *marcheth with his land army one way*
over the stage; and TAURUS, *the lieutenant of*
CAESAR, *the other way. After their going in, is*
heard the noise of a sea-fight.

Alarum. Enter ENOBARBUS.

DOMITIUS ENOBARBUS.

NAUGHT, naught, all naught! I can behold
  no longer:
Th'Antoniad, the Egyptian admiral,
With all their sixty, fly and turn the rudder:
To see't mine eyes are blasted.

Enter SCARUS.

SCARUS.
              Gods and goddesses,
All the whole synod of them!

DOMITIUS ENOBARBUS.
               What's thy passion?

SCARUS.
The greater cantle of the world is lost
With very ignorance; we have kist away
Kingdoms and provinces.

DOMITIUS ENOBARBUS.
            How appears the fight?

SCARUS.
On our side like the token'd pestilence,
Where death is sure. Yon ribaudred nag of
  Egypt,—
Whom leprosy o'ertake!—i'the midst o'the fight,
When vantage like a pair of twins appear'd,
Both as the same, or rather ours the elder,—
The breese upon her, like a cow in June,—
Hoists sails and flies.

DOMITIUS ENOBARBUS.
That I beheld:
Mine eyes did sicken at the sight, and could not
Endure a further view.

SCARUS.
            She once being looft,
The noble ruin of her magic, Antony,
Claps on his sea-wing, and, like a doting mallard,
Leaving the fight in height, flies after her:
I never saw an action of such shame;
Experience, manhood, honour, ne'er before
Did violate so itself.

DOMITIUS ENOBARBUS.
            Alack, alack!
Enter CANIDIUS.

CANIDIUS.
Our fortune on the sea is out of breath,
And sinks most lamentably. Had our general
Been what he knew himself, it had gone well:
O, he has given example for our flight
Most grossly by his own!

DOMITIUS ENOBARBUS.
            Ay, are you thereabouts?
Why, then, good night indeed.

CANIDIUS.
Toward Peloponnesus are they fled.

SCARUS.
'Tis easy to't; and there I will attend
What further comes.

CANIDIUS.
To Cæsar will I render
My legions and my horse: six kings already
Show me the way of yielding.
DOMITIUS ENOBARBUS.
I'll yet follow
The wounded chance of Antony, though my
reason
Sits in the wind against me.   [*Exeunt.*

SCENE XI.

Alexandria.   A room in CLEOPATRA'S *palace.*
Enter ANTONY *with* ATTENDANTS.

MARK ANTONY.
HARK! the land bids me tread no more
upon't,—
It is ashamed to bear me!—Friends, come hither:
I am so lated in the world, that I
Have lost my way for ever:—I have a ship
Laden with gold; take that, divide it; fly,
And make your peace with Cæsar.
ALL.
Fly! not we.
MARK ANTONY.
I have fled myself; and have instructed cowards
To run and show their shoulders.—Friends, be
gone;
I have myself resolved upon a course
Which has no need of you; be gone:
My treasure's in the harbour, take it.—O,
I follow'd that I blush to look upon:
My very hairs do mutiny; for the white
Reprove the brown for rashness, and they them
For fear and doting.—Friends, be gone: you shall
Have letters from me to some friends that will
Sweep your way for you. Pray you, look not sad,
Nor make replies of loathness: take the hint
Which my despair proclaims; let that be left
Which leaves itself: to the sea-side straightway:
I will possess you of that ship and treasure.
Leave me, I pray, a little: pray you now:—
Nay, do so; for, indeed, I have lost command,
Therefore I pray you:—I'll see you by and by.
[*Sits down.*
Enter CLEOPATRA *led by* CHARMIAN *and*
IRAS; EROS *following.*
EROS.
Nay, gentle madam, to him,—comfort him.
IRAS.
Do, most dear queen.
CHARMIAN.
Do! why, what else?
CLEOPATRA.
Let me sit down. O Juno!
MARK ANTONY.
No, no, no, no, no.
EROS.
See you here, sir?
MARK ANTONY.
O fie, fie, fie!
CHARMIAN.
Madam,—
IRAS.
Madam, O good empress,—

EROS.
Sir, sir,—
MARK ANTONY.
Yes, my lord, yes;—he at Philippi kept
His sword e'en like a dancer; while I struck
The lean and wrinkled Cassius; and 'twas I
That the mad Brutus ended: he alone
Dealt on lieutenantry, and no practice had
In the brave squares of war: yet now—No matter.
CLEOPATRA.
Ah, stand by.
EROS.
The queen, my lord, the queen.
IRAS.
Go to him, madam, speak to him:
He is unqualitied with very shame.
CLEOPATRA.
Well then,—sustain me:—O!
EROS.
Most noble sir, arise; the queen approaches:
Her head's declined, and death will seize her, but
Your comfort makes the rescue.
MARK ANTONY.
I have offended reputation,—
A most unnoble swerving.
EROS.
Sir, the queen.
MARK ANTONY.
O, whither hast thou led me, Egypt? See,
How I convey my shame out of thine eyes
By looking back what I have left behind
'Stroy'd in dishonour.
CLEOPATRA.
O my lord, my lord,
Forgive my fearful sails! I little thought
You would have follow'd.
MARK ANTONY.
Egypt, thou knew'st too well
My heart was to thy rudder tied by the strings,
And thou shouldst tow me after: o'er my spirit
Thy full supremacy thou knew'st, and that
Thy beck might from the bidding of the gods
Command me.
CLEOPATRA.
O, my pardon!
MARK ANTONY.
Now I must
To the young man send humble treaties, dodge
And palter in the shifts of lowness; who
With half the bulk o'the world play'd as I pleased,
Making and marring fortunes. You did know
How much you were my conqueror; and that
My sword, made weak by my affection, would
Obey it on all cause.
CLEOPATRA.
Pardon, pardon!
MARK ANTONY.
Fall not a tear, I say; one of them rates
All that is won and lost: give me a kiss;
Even this repays me.—We sent our school-
master;
Is a' come back?—Love, I am full of lead.—
Some wine. within there, and our viands!—
Fortune knows
We scorn her most when most she offers blows
[*Exeunt.*

SCENE XII.

CAESAR'S *camp in Egypt.*

Enter CAESAR, DOLABELLA, THYREUS, *with others.*

OCTAVIUS CAESAR.

LET him appear that's come from Antony.—
Know you him?

DOLABELLA.

Cæsar, 'tis his schoolmaster:
An argument that he is pluckt, when hither
He sends so poor a pinion of his wing,
Which had superfluous kings for messengers
Not many moons gone by.

Enter EUPHRONIUS, *ambassador from* ANTONY.

OCTAVIUS CAESAR.

Approach, and speak.

EUPHRONIUS.

Such as I am, I come from Antony:
I was of late as petty to his ends
As is the morn-dew on the myrtle-leaf
To his grand sea.

OCTAVIUS CAESAR.

Be't so:—declare thine office.

EUPHRONIUS.

Lord of his fortunes he salutes thee, and
Requires to live in Egypt: which not granted,
He lessens his requests; and to thee sues
To let him breathe between the heavens and
earth,
A private man in Athens: this for him.
Next, Cleopatra does confess thy greatness;
Submits her to thy might; and of thee craves
The circle of the Ptolemies for her heirs,
Now hazarded to thy Grace.

OCTAVIUS CAESAR.

For Antony,
I have no ears to his request. The queen
Of audience nor desire shall fail, so she
From Egypt drive her all-disgraced friend,
Or take his life there: this if she perform,
She shall not sue unheard. So to them both.

EUPHRONIUS.

Fortune pursue thee!

OCTAVIUS CAESAR.

Bring him through the bands.
[*Exit* EUPHRONIUS.

[*to* THYREUS] To try thy eloquence, now 'tis
time: dispatch;
From Antony win Cleopatra: promise,
And in our name, what she requires: add more,
From thine invention, offers: women are not
In their best fortunes strong; but want will per-
jure
The ne'er-toucht vestal: try thy cunning,
Thyreus;
Make thine own edict for thy pains, which we
Will answer as a law.

THYREUS.

Cæsar, I go.

OCTAVIUS CAESAR.

Observe how Antony becomes his flaw,
And what thou think'st his very action speaks
In every power that moves.

THYREUS.

Cæsar, I shall. [*Exeunt.*

SCENE XIII.

Alexandria. A room in CLEOPATRA'S *palace.*

Enter CLEOPATRA, ENOBARBUS, CHARMIAN,
and IRAS.

CLEOPATRA.

WHAT shall we do, Enobarbus?

DOMITIUS ENOBARBUS.

Think, and die

CLEOPATRA.

Is Antony or we in fault for this?

DOMITIUS ENOBARBUS.

Antony only, that would make his will
Lord of his reason. What though you fled
From that great face of war, whose several ranges
Frighted each other? why should he follow?
The itch of his affection should not then
Have nickt his captainship; at such a point,
When half to half the world opposed, he being
The mered question: 'twas a shame no less
Than was his loss, to course your flying flags,
And leave his navy gazing.

CLEOPATRA.

Prithee, peace.

Enter ANTONY *with* EUPHRONIUS, *the ambassador.*

MARK ANTONY.

Is that his answer?

EUPHRONIUS.

Ay, my lord.

MARK ANTONY.

The queen shall, then, have courtesy, so she
Will yield us up.

EUPHRONIUS.

He says so.

MARK ANTONY.

Let her know't.—
To the boy Cæsar send this grizzled head,
And he will fill thy wishes to the brim
With principalities.

CLEOPATRA.

That head, my lord?

MARK ANTONY.

To him again: tell him he wears the rose
Of youth upon him; from which the world should
note
Something particular: his coin, ships, legions,
May be a coward's; whose ministers would pre-
vail
Under the service of a child as soon
As i'the command of Cæsar: I dare him therefore
To lay his gay comparisons apart,
And answer me declined, sword against sword,
Ourselves alone. I'll write it: follow me.
[*Exeunt* ANTONY *and* EUPHRONIUS.

DOMITIUS ENOBARBUS [*aside*].

Yes, like enough, high-battled Cæsar will
Unstate his happiness, and be staged to the show,
Against a sworder! I see men's judgements are
A parcel of their fortunes; and things outward
Do draw the inward quality after them,
To suffer all alike. That he should dream,
Knowing all measures, the full Cæsar will
Answer his emptiness!—Cæsar, thou hast sub-
dued
His judgement too.

Enter an ATTENDANT.
ATTENDANT.
A messenger from Cæsar.
CLEOPATRA.
What, no more ceremony?—See, my women!—
Against the blown rose may they stop their nose
That kneel'd unto the buds.—Admit him, sir.
[*Exit* ATTENDANT.
DOMITIUS ENOBARBUS [*aside*].
Mine honesty and I begin to square.
The loyalty well held to fools does make
Our faith mere folly: yet he that can endure
To follow with allegiance a faln lord
Does conquer him that did his master conquer,
And earns a place i'the story.
Enter THYREUS.
CLEOPATRA.
Cæsar's will?
THYREUS.
Hear it apart.
CLEOPATRA.
None but friends: say boldly.
THYREUS.
So, haply, are they friends to Antony.
DOMITIUS ENOBARBUS.
He needs as many, sir, as Cæsar has;
Or needs not us. If Cæsar please, our master
Will leap to be his friend: for us, you know
Whose he is we are, and that is Cæsar's.
THYREUS.
So.—
Thus then, thou most renown'd: Cæsar entreats,
Not to consider in what case thou stand'st,
Further than he is Cæsar.
CLEOPATRA.
Go on: right royal.
THYREUS.
He knows that you embrace not Antony
As you did love, but as you fear'd him.
CLEOPATRA.
O!
THYREUS.
The scars upon your honour, therefore, he
Does pity, as constrained blemishes,
Not as deserved.
CLEOPATRA.
He is a god, and knows
What is most right: mine honour was not yielded,
But conquer'd merely.
DOMITIUS ENOBARBUS [*aside*].
To be sure of that,
I will ask Antony.—Sir, sir, thou art so leaky,
That we must leave thee to thy sinking, for
Thy dearest quit thee. [*Exit*.
THYREUS.
Shall I say to Cæsar
What you require of him? for he partly begs
To be desired to give. It much would please
him,
That of his fortunes you should make a staff
To lean upon: but it would warm his spirits,
To hear from me you had left Antony,
And put yourself under his shroud,
The universal landlord.
CLEOPATRA.
What's your name?

THYREUS.
My name is Thyreus.
CLEOPATRA.
Most kind messenger,
Say to great Cæsar this:—in deputation
I kiss his conquering hand: tell him, I am prompt
To lay my crown at's feet, and there to kneel:
Tell him, from his all-obeying breath I hear
The doom of Egypt.
THYREUS.
'Tis your noblest course.
Wisdom and fortune combating together,
If that the former dare but what it can,
No chance may shake it. Give me grace to lay
My duty on your hand.
CLEOPATRA.
Your Cæsar's father oft,
When he hath mused of taking kingdoms in,
Bestow'd his lips on that unworthy place,
As it rain'd kisses.
Enter ANTONY *and* ENOBARBUS.
MARK ANTONY.
Favours, by Jove that thunders!—
What art thou, fellow?
THYREUS.
One that but performs
The bidding of the fullest man, and worthiest
To have command obey'd.
DOMITIUS ENOBARBUS [*aside*].
You will be whipt.
MARK ANTONY.
Approach, there!—Ah, you kite!—Now, gods and
devils!
Authority melts from me: of late, when I cried 'Ho!'
Like boys unto a muss, kings would start forth,
And cry 'Your will?'—Have you no ears? I am
Antony yet.
Enter ATTENDANTS.
Take hence this Jack, and whip him.
DOMITIUS ENOBARBUS [*aside*].
'Tis better playing with a lion's whelp
Than with an old one dying.
MARK ANTONY.
Moon and stars!—
Whip him.—Were 't twenty of the greatest tribu-
taries
That do acknowledge Cæsar, should I find them
So saucy with the hand of she here,—what's her
name,
Since she was Cleopatra?—Whip him, fellows,
Till, like a boy, you see him cringe his face,
And whine aloud for mercy: take him hence.
THYREUS.
Mark Antony,—
MARK ANTONY.
Tug him away: being whipt,
Bring him again:—this Jack of Cæsar's shall
Bear us an errand to him.
[*Exeunt* ATTENDANTS *with* THYREUS.
You were half blasted ere I knew you:—ha!
Have I my pillow left unprest in Rome,
Forborne the getting of a lawful race,
And by a gem of women, to be abused
By one that looks on feeders?
CLEOPATRA.
Good, my lord,—

MARK ANTONY.
You have been a boggler ever:—
But when we in our viciousness grow hard,—
O misery on't!—the wise gods seal our eyes;
In our own filth drop our clear judgements; make us
Adore our errors; laugh at's, while we strut
To our confusion.

CLEOPATRA.
O, is't come to this?

MARK ANTONY.
I found you as a morsel cold upon
Dead Cæsar's trencher; nay, you were a fragment
Of Cneius Pompey's; besides what hotter hours,
Unregister'd in vulgar fame, you have
Luxuriously pickt out: for, I am sure,
Though you can guess what temperance should be,
You know not what it is.

CLEOPATRA.
Wherefore is this?

MARK ANTONY.
To let a fellow that will take rewards,
And say 'God quit you!' be familiar with
My playfellow, your hand; this kingly seal
And plighter of high hearts!—O, that I were
Upon the hill of Basan, to outroar
The horned herd! for I have savage cause;
And to proclaim it civilly, were like
A halter'd neck which does the hangman thank
For being yare about him.

Enter ATTENDANTS *with* THYREUS.
Is he whipt?

FIRST ATTENDANT.
Soundly, my lord.

MARK ANTONY.
Cried he? and begg'd a' pardon?

FIRST ATTENDANT.
He did ask favour.

MARK ANTONY.
If that thy father live, let him repent
Thou wast not made his daughter; and be thou
  sorry
To follow Cæsar in his triumph, since   [forth
Thou hast been whipt for following him: hence-
The white hand of a lady fever thee,
Shake thou to look on't.—Get thee back to Cæsar,
Tell him thy entertainment: look thou say
He makes me angry with him; for he seems
Proud and disdainful, harping on what I am,
Not what he knew I was: he makes me angry;
And at this time most easy 'tis to do't,
When my good stars, that were my former guides,
Have empty left their orbs, and shot their fires
Into th'abysm of hell. If he mislike
My speech and what is done, tell him he has
Hipparchus, my enfranched bondman, whom
He may at pleasure whip, or hang, or torture,
As he shall like, to quit me: urge it thou:
Hence with thy stripes, begone! [*Exit* THYREUS.

CLEOPATRA.
Have you done yet?

MARK ANTONY.
Alack, our terrene moon
Is now eclipst; and it portends alone
The fall of Antony!

CLEOPATRA.
I must stay his time.

MARK ANTONY.
To flatter Cæsar, would you mingle eyes
With one that ties his points?

CLEOPATRA.
Not know me yet?

MARK ANTONY.
Cold-hearted toward me?

CLEOPATRA.
Ah, dear, if I be so,
From my cold heart let heaven engender hail,
And poison it in the source; and the first stone
Drop in my neck: as it determines, so
Dissolve my life! The next Cæsarion smite!
Till, by degrees, the memory of my womb,
Together with my brave Egyptians all,
By the discandying of this pelleted storm,
Lie graveless,—till the flies and gnats of Nile
Have buried them for prey!

MARK ANTONY.
I am satisfied.
Cæsar sits down in Alexandria; where
I will oppose his fate. Our force by land
Hath nobly held; our sever'd navy too   [like.
Have knit again, and fleet, threatening most sea-
Where hast thou been, my heart?—Dost thou
  hear, lady?
If from the field I shall return once more
To kiss these lips, I will appear in blood;
I and my sword will earn our chronicle:
There's hope in't yet.

CLEOPATRA.
That's my brave lord!

MARK ANTONY.
I will be treble-sinew'd, hearted, breathed,
And fight maliciously: for when mine hours
Were nice and lucky, men did ransom lives
Of me for jests; but now I'll set my teeth,
And send to darkness all that stop me.—Come,
Let's have one other gaudy night: call to me
All my sad captains, fill our bowls; once more
Let's mock the midnight bell.

CLEOPATRA.
It is my birth-day:
I had thought t'have held it poor; but, since my
  lord
Is Antony again, I will be Cleopatra.

MARK ANTONY.
We will yet do well.

CLEOPATRA.
Call all his noble captains to my lord.

MARK ANTONY.
Do so, we'll speak to them; and to-night I'll force
The wine peep through their scars.—Come on,
  my queen;
There's sap in't yet. The next time I do fight,
I'll make death love me; for I will contend
Even with his pestilent scythe.
[*Exeunt all but* ENOBARBUS.

DOMITIUS ENOBARBUS.
Now he'll outstare the lightning. To be furious,
Is to be frighted out of fear; and in that mood
The dove will peck the estridge; and I see still,
A diminution in our captain's brain
Restores his heart: when valour preys on reason,
It eats the sword it fights with. I will seek
Some way to leave him.   [*Exit.*

ACT IV. SCENE I.

CAESAR'S *camp at Alexandria.*

Enter CAESAR, AGRIPPA, *and* MAECENAS, *with his army;* CAESAR *reading a letter.*

OCTAVIUS CAESAR.

HE calls me boy; and chides, as he had power
To beat me out of Egypt; my messenger
He hath whipt with rods; dares me to personal
  combat,
Cæsar to Antony:—let the old ruffian know
I have many other ways to die; meantime
Laugh at his challenge.

MAECENAS.
                    Cæsar must think,
When one so great begins to rage, he's hunted
Even to falling. Give him no breath, but now
Make boot of his distraction:—never anger
Made good guard for itself.

OCTAVIUS CAESAR.
                    Let our best heads
Know, that to-morrow the last of many battles
We mean to fight:—within our files there are,
Of those that served Mark Antony but late,
Enough to fetch him in. See it done:
And feast the army; we have store to do't,
And they have earn'd the waste. Poor Antony!
                                [*Exeunt.*

SCENE II.

Alexandria.   A room in CLEOPATRA'S *palace.*

Enter ANTONY, CLEOPATRA, ENOBARBUS,
  CHARMIAN, IRAS, ALEXAS, *with others.*

MARK ANTONY.

HE will not fight with me, Domitius.
        DOMITIUS ENOBARBUS.
                              No.
        MARK ANTONY.
Why should he not?
        DOMITIUS ENOBARBUS.
He thinks, being twenty times of better fortune,
He is twenty men to one.
        MARK ANTONY.
                    To-morrow, soldier,
By sea and land I'll fight: or I will live,
Or bathe my dying honour in the blood
Shall make it live again. Woo't thou fight well?
        DOMITIUS ENOBARBUS.
I'll strike, and cry 'Take all.'
        MARK ANTONY.
                    Well said; come on.—
Call forth my household servants: let's to-night
Be bounteous at our meal.
        Enter three or four SERVITORS.
                    Give me thy hand,
Thou hast been rightly honest;—so hast thou;—
Thou,—and thou,—and thou:—you have served
  me well,
And kings have been your fellows.
        CLEOPATRA [*aside to* ENOBARBUS].
                        What means this?
DOMITIUS ENOBARBUS [*aside to* CLEOPATRA].
'Tis one of those odd tricks which sorrow shoots
Out of the mind.

MARK ANTONY.
        And thou art honest too.
I wish I could be made so many men,
And all of you clapt up together in
An Antony, that I might do you service
So good as you have done.
        SERVANTS.
                    The gods forbid!
        MARK ANTONY.
Well, my good fellows, wait on me to-night:
Scant not my cups; and make as much of me
As when mine empire was your fellow too,
And suffer'd my command.
        CLEOPATRA [*aside to* ENOBARBUS].
                    What does he mean?
DOMITIUS ENOBARBUS [*aside to* CLEOPATRA].
To make his followers weep.
        MARK ANTONY.
                    Tend me to-night;
May be it is the period of your duty:
Haply you shall not see me more; or if,
A mangled shadow: perchance to-morrow
You'll serve another master. I look on you
As one that takes his leave. Mine honest friends,
I turn you not away; but, like a master
Married to your good service, stay till death:
Tend me to-night two hours, I ask no more,
And the gods yield you for't!
        DOMITIUS ENOBARBUS.
                    What mean you, sir,
To give them this discomfort? Look, they weep;
And I, an ass, am onion-eyed: for shame,
Transform us not to women.
        MARK ANTONY.
                    Ho, ho, ho!
Now the witch take me, if I meant it thus!
Grace grow where those drops fall! My hearty
  friends,
You take me in too dolorous a sense;
For I spake to you for your comfort,—did desire
  you
To burn this night with torches: know, my hearts,
I hope well of to-morrow; and will lead you
Where rather I'll expect victorious life
Than death and honour. Let's to supper, come,
And drown consideration.   [*Exeunt.*

SCENE III.

The same.   Before CLEOPATRA'S *palace.*

Enter a company of SOLDIERS.

FIRST SOLDIER.

BROTHER, good night: to-morrow is the day
        SECOND SOLDIER.
It will determine one way: fare you well.
Heard you of nothing strange about the streets?
        FIRST SOLDIER.
Nothing. What news?
        SECOND SOLDIER.
Belike 'tis but a rumour. Good night to you.
        FIRST SOLDIER.
Well, sir, good night.
        They meet other SOLDIERS.
        SECOND SOLDIER.
Soldiers, have careful watch.

THIRD SOLDIER.
And you. Good night, good night.

[*They place themselves in every corner of the stage.*

FOURTH SOLDIER.
Here we: and if to-morrow
Our navy thrive, I have an absolute hope
Our landmen will stand up.

THIRD SOLDIER.
'Tis a brave army,
And full of purpose.

[*Music of the hautboys as under the stage.*

FOURTH SOLDIER.
Peace! what noise?

FIRST SOLDIER.
List, list!

SECOND SOLDIER.
Hark!

FIRST SOLDIER.
Music i'the air.

THIRD SOLDIER.
Under the earth.

FOURTH SOLDIER.
It signs well, does it not?

THIRD SOLDIER.
No.

FIRST SOLDIER.
Peace, I say!
What should this mean?

SECOND SOLDIER.
'Tis the god Hercules, whom Antony loved,
Now leaves him.

FIRST SOLDIER.
Walk; let's see if other watchmen
Do hear what we do?

[*They advance to another post.*

SECOND SOLDIER.
How now, masters!

SOLDIERS [*speaking together*].
How now!
How now! do you hear this?

FIRST SOLDIER.
Ay; is't not strange?

THIRD SOLDIER.
Do you hear, masters? do you hear?

FIRST SOLDIER.
Follow the noise so far as we have quarter;
Let's see how it will give off.

SOLDIERS.
Content. 'Tis strange.   [*Exeunt.*

SCENE IV.

The same.   A room in CLEOPATRA'S *palace.*

Enter ANTONY *and* CLEOPATRA, CHARMIAN,
IRAS, *and others attending.*

MARK ANTONY.
EROS! mine armour, Eros!

CLEOPATRA.
Sleep a little.

MARK ANTONY.
No, my chuck.—Eros, come; mine armour, Eros!

Enter EROS *with armour.*
Come, good fellow, put mine iron on:—

If fortune be not ours to-day, it is
Because we brave her:—come.

CLEOPATRA.
Nay, I'll help too.
What's this for?

MARK ANTONY.
Ah, let be, let be! thou art
The armourer of my heart:—false, false; this, this.

CLEOPATRA.
Sooth, la, I'll help: thus it must be.

MARK ANTONY.
Well, well;
We shall thrive now.—Seest thou, my good fellow?
Go put on thy defences.

EROS.
Briefly, sir.

CLEOPATRA.
Is not this buckled well?

MARK ANTONY.
Rarely, rarely:
He that unbuckles this, till we do please
To daff't for our repose, shall hear a storm.—
Thou fumblest, Eros; and my queen's a squire
More tight at this than thou: dispatch.—O love,
That thou couldst see my wars to-day, and
    knew'st
The royal occupation! thou shouldst see
A workman in't.

Enter an arm'd SOLDIER.
Good morrow to thee; welcome:
Thou look'st like him that knows a warlike
    charge:
To business that we love we rise betime,
And go to't with delight.

SOLDIER.
A thousand, sir,
Early though't be, have on their riveted trim,
And at the port expect you.

[*Shout. Trumpets flourish.*
Enter CAPTAINS *and* SOLDIERS.

CAPTAIN.
The morn is fair.—Good morrow, general.

ALL.
Good morrow, general.

MARK ANTONY.
'Tis well blown, lads:
This morning, like the spirit of a youth
That means to be of note, begins betimes.—
So, so; come, give me that: this way; well said.—
Fare thee well, dame, whate'er becomes of me:
This is a soldier's kiss: rebukable,   [*Kisses her.*
And worthy shameful check it were, to stand
On more mechanic compliment; I'll leave thee
Now, like a man of steel.—You that will fight,
Follow me close; I'll bring you to't.—Adieu.

[*Exeunt* ANTONY, EROS, CAPTAINS, *and*
SOLDIERS.

CHARMIAN.
Please you, retire to your chamber.

CLEOPATRA.
Lead me.
He goes forth gallantly. That he and Cæsar
    might
Determine this great war in single fight!
Then, Antony,—but now—Well, on.   [*Exeunt.*

SCENE V.

ANTONY's camp near Alexandria.

Trumpets sound.   Enter ANTONY and EROS;
a SOLDIER meeting them.

SOLDIER.

THE gods make this a happy day to Antony!
MARK ANTONY.
Would thou and those thy scars had once pre-
vail'd
To make me fight at land!
SOLDIER.
                    Hadst thou done so,
The kings that have revolted, and the soldier
That has this morning left thee, would have still
Follow'd thy heels.
MARK ANTONY.
          Who's gone this morning?
SOLDIER.
                              Who!
One ever near thee: call for Enobarbus,
He shall not hear thee; or from Cæsar's camp
Say 'I am none of thine.'
MARK ANTONY.
                What say'st thou?
SOLDIER.
                              Sir,
He is with Cæsar.
EROS.
          Sir, his chests and treasure
He has not with him.
MARK ANTONY.
          Is he gone?
SOLDIER.
                    Most certain.
MARK ANTONY.
Go, Eros, send his treasure after; do it;
Detain no jot, I charge thee: write to him—
I will subscribe—gentle adieus and greetings;
Say that I wish he never find more cause
To change a master.—O, my fortunes have
Corrupted honest men!—Dispatch.—Enobarbus!
                              [*Exeunt.*

SCENE VI.

CAESAR's camp before Alexandria.

Flourish.   Enter CAESAR with AGRIPPA,
ENOBARBUS, and others.

OCTAVIUS CAESAR.

GO forth, Agrippa, and begin the fight:
  Our will is Antony be took alive;
Make it so known.
AGRIPPA.
Cæsar, I shall.   [*Exit.*
OCTAVIUS CAESAR.
The time of universal peace is near:
Prove this a prosperous day, the three-nookt world
Shall bear the olive freely.
Enter a MESSENGER.
MESSENGER.
                    Antony
Is come into the field.
OCTAVIUS CAESAR.
          Go charge Agrippa
Plant those that have revolted in the van,

That Antony may seem to spend his fury
Upon himself.   [*Exeunt all but ENOBARBUS.*
DOMITIUS ENOBARBUS.
Alexas did revolt; and went to Jewry on
Affairs of Antony; there did persuade
Great Herod to incline himself to Cæsar,
And leave his master Antony: for this pains
Cæsar hath hang'd him. Canidius, and the rest
That fell away, have entertainment, but
No honourable trust. I have done ill;
Of which I do accuse myself so sorely,
That I will joy no more.
Enter a SOLDIER of CAESAR's.
SOLDIER.
                    Enobarbus, Antony
Hath after thee sent all thy treasure, with
His bounty overplus: the messenger
Came on my guard; and at thy tent is now
Unloading of his mules.
DOMITIUS ENOBARBUS.
                I give it you.
SOLDIER.
Mock not, Enobarbus.
I tell you true: best you safed the bringer
Out of the host; I must attend mine office,
Or would have done't myself. Your emperor
Continues still a Jove.   [*Exit.*
DOMITIUS ENOBARBUS.
I am alone the villain of the earth,
And feel I am so most. O Antony,
Thou mine of bounty, how wouldst thou have paid
My better service, when my turpitude
Thou dost so crown with gold! This blows my
          heart:
If swift thought break it not, a swifter mean
Shall outstrike thought: but thought will do't, I
          feel.
I fight against thee!—No: I will go seek
Some ditch wherein to die; the foul'st best fits
My latter part of life.   [*Exit.*

SCENE VII.

Field of battle between the camps.

Alarum.   Drums and trumpets.   Enter AGRIPPA
and others.

AGRIPPA.

RETIRE, we have engaged ourselves too far:
  Cæsar himself has work, and our oppression
Exceeds what we expected.   [*Exeunt.*
Alarums.   Enter ANTONY, and SCARUS wounded.
SCARUS.
O my brave emperor, this is fought indeed!
Had we done so at first, we had driven them home
With clouts about their heads.
MARK ANTONY.
                Thou bleed'st apace.
SCARUS.
I had a wound here that was like a T,
But now 'tis made an H.
MARK ANTONY.
                They do retire.
SCARUS.
We'll beat 'em into bench-holes: I have yet
Room for six scotches more.

953

Enter EROS.

EROS.

They are beaten, sir; and our advantage serves
For a fair victory.

SCARUS.

Let us score their backs,
And snatch 'em up, as we take hares, behind:
'Tis sport to maul a runner.

MARK ANTONY.

I will reward thee
Once for thy spritely comfort, and tenfold
For thy good valour. Come thee on.

SCARUS.

I'll halt after. [*Exeunt.*

SCENE VIII.

Under the walls of Alexandria.

Alarums.   Enter ANTONY *again in a march;*
SCARUS, *with others.*

MARK ANTONY.

WE have beat him to his camp:—run one
before,
And let the queen know of our gests.—To-mor-
row,
Before the sun shall see's, we'll spill the blood
That has to-day escaped. I thank you all;
For doughty-handed are you, and have fought
Not as you served the cause, but as't had been
Each man's like mine; you have shown all Hectors.
Enter the city, clip your wives, your friends,
Tell them your feats; whilst they with joyful tears
Wash the congealment from your wounds, and
kiss
The honour'd gashes whole.—[*To* SCARUS] Give
me thy hand;

Enter CLEOPATRA, *attended.*

To this great fairy I'll commend thy acts,
Make her thanks bless thee.—[*To* CLEOPATRA]
O thou day o'the world,
Chain mine arm'd neck; leap thou, attire and all,
Through proof of harness to my heart, and there
Ride on the pants triumphing!

CLEOPATRA.

Lord of lords!
O infinite virtue, comest thou smiling from
The world's great snare uncaught?

MARK ANTONY.

My nightingale,
We have beat them to their beds. What, girl!
though gray
Do something mingle with our younger brown,
yet ha' we
A brain that nourishes our nerves, and can
Get goal for goal of youth. Behold this man;
Commend unto his lips thy favouring hand:—
Kiss it, my warrior:—he hath fought to-day
As if a god, in hate of mankind, had
Destroy'd in such a shape.

CLEOPATRA.

I'll give thee, friend,
An armour all of gold; it was a king's.

MARK ANTONY.

He hath deserved it, were it carbuncled
Like holy Phœbus' car.—Give me thy hand:—
Through Alexandria make a jolly march;

Bear our hackt targets like the men that owe them:
Had our great palace the capacity
To camp this host, we all would sup together,
And drink carouses to the next day's fate,
Which promises royal peril.—Trumpeters,
With brazen din blast you the city's ear;
Make mingle with our rattling tabourines;
That heaven and earth may strike their sounds
together,
Applauding our approach.   [*Exeunt.*

SCENE IX.

CAESAR'S camp.

SENTINELS *at their post.*

FIRST SOLDIER.

IF we be not relieved within this hour,
We must return to the court-of-guard: the night
Is shiny; and they say we shall embattle
By the second hour i'the morn.

SECOND SOLDIER.

This last day was
A shrewd one to's.

Enter ENOBARBUS.

DOMITIUS ENOBARBUS.

O, bear me witness, night,—

THIRD SOLDIER.

What man is this?

SECOND SOLDIER.

Stand close, and list him.

DOMITIUS ENOBARBUS.

Be witness to me, O thou blessed moon,
When men revolted shall upon record
Bear hateful memory, poor Enobarbus did
Before thy face repent!—

FIRST SOLDIER.

Enobarbus!

THIRD SOLDIER.

Peace!
Hark further.

DOMITIUS ENOBARBUS.

O sovereign mistress of true melancholy,
The poisonous damp of night disponge upon me,
That life, a very rebel to my will,
May hang no longer on me: throw my heart
Against the flint and hardness of my fault;
Which, being dried with grief, will break to
powder,
And finish all foul thoughts. O Antony,
Nobler than my revolt is infamous,
Forgive me in thine own particular;
But let the world rank me in register
A master-leaver and a fugitive.
O Antony! O Antony!   [*Dies.*

SECOND SOLDIER.

Let's speak
To him.

FIRST SOLDIER.

Let's hear him, for the things he speaks
May concern Cæsar.

THIRD SOLDIER.

Let's do so. But he sleeps.

FIRST SOLDIER.

Swounds rather; for so bad a prayer as his
Was never yet for sleep.

SECOND SOLDIER.
Go we to him.
THIRD SOLDIER.
Awake, sir, awake; speak to us.
SECOND SOLDIER.
Hear you, sir?
FIRST SOLDIER.
The hand of death hath raught him. [*Drums afar
off.*] Hark! the drums
Demurely wake the sleepers. Let us bear him
To the court-of-guard: he is of note: our hour
Is fully out.
THIRD SOLDIER.
Come on, then;
He may recover yet.   [*Exeunt with the body.*

SCENE X.

Ground between the two camps.

Enter ANTONY *and* SCARUS, *with their* ARMY.

MARK ANTONY.
THEIR preparation is to-day by sea;
We please them not by land.
SCARUS.
For both, my lord.
MARK ANTONY.
I would they'ld fight i'the fire or i'the air;
We'ld fight there too. But this it is; our foot
Upon the hills adjoining to the city—
Where their appointment we may best discover,
And look on their endeavour—
Shall stay with us: order for sea is given;
They have put forth the haven.   [*Exeunt.*

SCENE XI.

Another part of the same.

Enter CAESAR *and his* ARMY.

OCTAVIUS CAESAR.
BUT being charged, we will be still by land,
Which, as I take't, we shall; for his best force
Is forth to man his galleys. To the vales,
And hold our best advantage.   [*Exeunt.*

SCENE XII.

Another part of the same.

Enter ANTONY *and* SCARUS.

MARK ANTONY.
YET they are not join'd: where yond pine does
stand,
I shall discover all: I'll bring thee word
Straight, how 'tis like to go.   [*Exit.*
SCARUS.
Swallows have built
In Cleopatra's sails their nests: the augurers   [ly,
Say they know not,—they cannot tell;—look grim-
And dare not speak their knowledge. Antony
Is valiant, and dejected; and, by starts,
His fretted fortunes give him hope, and fear,
Of what he has, and has not.
[*Alarum afar off, as at a sea-fight.*
Enter ANTONY.
MARK ANTONY.
All is lost;
This foul Egyptian hath betrayed me:

My fleet hath yielded to the foe; and yonder
They cast their caps up, and carouse together
Like friends long lost.—Triple-turn'd whore! 'tis
thou
Hast sold me to this novice; and my heart
Makes only wars on thee.—Bid them all fly;
For when I am revenged upon my charm,
I have done all:—bid them all fly; begone.
[*Exit* SCARUS.
O sun, thy uprise shall I see no more:
Fortune and Antony part here; even here
Do we shake hands.—All come to this?—The
hearts
That spaniel'd me at heels, to whom I gave
Their wishes, do discandy, melt their sweets
On blossoming Cæsar; and this pine is barkt,
That overtopt them all. Betray'd I am:
O this false soul of Egypt! this grave charm,—
Whose eye beckt forth my wars, and call'd them
home;
Whose bosom was my crownet, my chief end,—
Like a right gipsy, hath, at fast and loose,
Beguiled me to the very heart of loss.—
What, Eros, Eros!
Enter CLEOPATRA.
Ah, thou spell! Avaunt!
CLEOPATRA.
Why is my lord enraged against his love?
MARK ANTONY.
Vanish, or I shall give thee thy deserving,
And blemish Cæsar's triumph. Let him take thee,
And hoist thee up to the shouting plebeians:
Follow his chariot, like the greatest spot
Of all thy sex; most monster-like, be shown
For poor'st diminutives, for doits; and let
Patient Octavia plough thy visage up
With her prepared nails.   [*Exit* CLEOPATRA.
'Tis well th'art gone,
If it be well to live; but better 'twere
Thou fell'st into my fury, for one death
Might have prevented many.—Eros, ho!—
The shirt of Nessus is upon me:—teach me,
Alcides, thou mine ancestor, thy rage:
Let me lodge Lichas on the horns o'the moon;
And with those hands, that graspt the heaviest
club,
Subdue my worthiest self. The witch shall die:
To the young Roman boy she hath sold me, and I
fall
Under this plot; she dies for't.—Eros, ho!   [*Exit.*

SCENE XIII.

Alexandria.   A room in CLEOPATRA'S *palace.*

Enter CLEOPATRA, CHARMIAN, IRAS, *and*
MARDIAN.

CLEOPATRA.
HELP me, my women! O, he is more mad
Than Telamon for his shield; the boar of
Thessaly
Was never so embost.
CHARMIAN.
To the monument!
There lock yourself, and send him word you are
dead.

The soul and body rive not more in parting
Than greatness going off.

CLEOPATRA.
To the monument!—
Mardian, go tell him I have slain myself;
Say, that the last I spoke was 'Antony,'
And word it, prithee, piteously: hence, Mardian,
And bring me how he takes my death.—To the
monument!   [*Exeunt.*

SCENE XIV.

The same.   Another room.

Enter ANTONY *and* EROS.

MARK ANTONY.
EROS, thou yet behold'st me?

EROS.
Ay, noble lord.

MARK ANTONY.
Sometime we see a cloud that's dragonish;
A vapour sometime like a bear or lion,
A tower'd citadel, a pendant rock,
A forked mountain, or blue promontory
With trees upon't, that nod unto the world,
And mock our eyes with air: thou hast seen these
signs;
They are black vesper's pageants.

EROS.
Ay, my lord.

MARK ANTONY.
That which is now a horse, even with a thought
The rack dislimns, and makes it indistinct
As water is in water.

EROS.
It does, my lord.

MARK ANTONY.
My good knave Eros, now thy captain is
Even such a body: here I am Antony;
Yet cannot hold this visible shape, my knave.
I made these wars for Egypt; and the queen,—
Whose heart I thought I had, for she had mine;
Which, whilst it was mine, had annext unto't
A million moe, now lost,—she, Eros, has
Packt cards with Cæsar, and false-play'd my glory
Unto an enemy's triumph.—
Nay, weep not, gentle Eros; there is left us
Ourselves to end ourselves.

Enter MARDIAN.
O, thy vile lady!
She has robb'd me of my sword.

MARDIAN.
No, Antony;
My mistress loved thee, and her fortunes mingled
With thine entirely.

MARK ANTONY.
Hence, saucy eunuch; peace!
She hath betray'd me, and shall die the death.

MARDIAN.
Death of one person can be paid but once,
And that she has discharged: what thou wouldst do
Is done unto thy hand: the last she spake
Was, 'Antony! most noble Antony!'
Then in the midst a tearing groan did break
The name of Antony; it was divided
Between her heart and lips: she render'd life,
Thy name so buried in her.

MARK ANTONY.
Dead, then?

MARDIAN.
Dead.

MARK ANTONY.
Unarm, Eros; the long day's task is done,
And we must sleep.—[*to* MARDIAN] That thou
depart'st hence safe,
Does pay thy labour richly; go. [*Exit* MARDIAN.
Off, pluck off:—
The seven-fold shield of Ajax cannot keep
The battery from my heart. O, cleave, my sides!
Heart, once be stronger than thy continent,
Crack thy frail case!—Apace, Eros, apace.—
No more a soldier:—bruised pieces, go;
You have been nobly borne.—From me awhile.
[*Exit* EROS.
I will o'ertake thee, Cleopatra, and
Weep for my pardon. So it must be, for now
All length is torture:—since the torch is out,
Lie down, and stray no farther, now all labour
Mars what it does; yea, very force entangles
Itself with strength: seal then, and all is done.—
Eros!—I come, my queen.—Eros!—Stay for me:
Where souls do couch on flowers, we'll hand in
hand,
And with our sprightly port make the ghosts gaze:
Dido and her Aeneas shall want troops,
And all the haunt be ours.—Come, Eros, Eros!

Enter EROS.

EROS.
What would my lord?

MARK ANTONY.
Since Cleopatra died,
I have lived in such dishonour, that the gods
Detest my baseness. I, that with my sword
Quarter'd the world, and o'er green Neptune's
back
With ships made cities, condemn myself to lack
The courage of a woman; less noble mind
Than she which by her death our Cæsar tells
'I am conqueror of myself.' Thou art sworn, Eros,
That, when the exigent should come,—which
now
Is come indeed,—when I should see behind me
Th'inevitable prosecution of
Disgrace and horror, that, on my command,
Thou then wouldst kill me: do't; the time is come:
Thou strikest not me, 'tis Cæsar thou defeat'st.
Put colour in thy cheek.

EROS.
The gods withhold me!
Shall I do that which all the Parthian darts,
Though enemy, lost aim, and could not?

MARK ANTONY.
Eros,
Wouldst thou be window'd in great Rome, and
see
Thy master thus with pleacht arms, bending
down
His corrigible neck, his face subdued
To penetrative shame, whilst the wheel'd seat
Of fortunate Cæsar, drawn before him, branded
His baseness that ensued?

EROS.
I would not see't.

MARK ANTONY.
Come, then; for with a wound I must be cured.
Draw that thy honest sword, which thou hast
          worn
Most useful for thy country.
                    EROS.
                              O, sir, pardon me!
          MARK ANTONY.
When I did make thee free, sworest thou not
          then
To do this when I bade thee? Do it at once;
Or thy precedent services are all
But accidents unpurposed. Draw, and come.
                    EROS.
Turn from me, then, that noble countenance,
Wherein the worship of the whole world lies.
          MARK ANTONY.
Lo thee!   [*Turning from him.*
                    EROS.
My sword is drawn.
          MARK ANTONY.
                    Then let it do at once
The thing why thou hast drawn it.
                    EROS.
                              My dear master,
My captain, and my emperor, let me say,
Before I strike this bloody stroke, farewell.
          MARK ANTONY.
'Tis said, man;—and farewell.
                    EROS.
Farewell, great chief. Shall I strike now?
          MARK ANTONY.
                              Now, Eros.
                    EROS.
Why, there then [*kills himself*]:—thus I do escape
          the sorrow
Of Antony's death.   [*Dies.*
          MARK ANTONY.
                    Thrice-nobler than myself!
Thou teachest me, O valiant Eros, what
I should, and thou couldst not. My queen and
          Eros
Have by their brave instruction got upon me
A nobleness in record: but I will be
A bridegroom in my death, and run into't
As to a lover's bed. Come, then; and, Eros,
Thy master dies thy scholar: to do thus
                    [*Falling on his sword.*
I learnt of thee. How! not dead? not dead?—
The guard, ho!—O, dispatch me!
          Enter DERCETAS *and* GUARD.
          FIRST GUARD.
                    What's the noise?
          MARK ANTONY.
I have done my work ill, friends: O, make an end
Of what I have begun.
          SECOND GUARD.
                    The star is faln.
          FIRST GUARD.
And time is at his period.
                    ALL.
                    Alas, and woe!
          MARK ANTONY.
Let him that loves me strike me dead.
          FIRST GUARD.
                    Not I.

          SECOND GUARD.
Nor I.
          THIRD GUARD.
Nor any one.   [*Exeunt* GUARD.
                    DERCETAS.
Thy death and fortunes bid thy followers fly.
This sword but shown to Cæsar, with this tid-
          ings,
Shall enter me with him.
          Enter DIOMEDES.
                    DIOMEDES.
Where's Antony?
          DERCETAS.
          There, Diomed, there.
                    DIOMEDES.
                              Lives he?
Wilt thou not answer, man?   [*Exit* DERCETAS.
          MARK ANTONY.
Art thou there, Diomed? Draw thy sword, and
          give me
Sufficing strokes for death.
                    DIOMEDES.
                    Most absolute lord,
My mistress Cleopatra sent me to thee.
          MARK ANTONY.
When did she send thee?
                    DIOMEDES.
                    Now, my lord.
          MARK ANTONY.
                              Where is she?
                    DIOMEDES.
Lockt in her monument. She had a prophesying
          fear
Of what hath come to pass: for when she saw—
Which never shall be found—you did suspect
She had disposed with Cæsar, and that your rage
Would not be purged, she sent you word she was
          dead;
But, fearing since how it might work, hath sent
Me to proclaim the truth; and I am come,
I dread, too late.
          MARK ANTONY.
Too late, good Diomed:—call my guard, I
          prithee.
                    DIOMEDES.
What, ho, the emperor's guard! The guard, what,
          ho!
Come, your lords calls!
          Enter four or five of the GUARD *of* ANTONY.
          MARK ANTONY.
Bear me, good friends, where Cleopatra bides;
'Tis the last service that I shall command you.
          FIRST GUARD.
Woe, woe are we, sir, you may not live to wear
All your true followers out.
                    ALL.
                    Most heavy day!
          MARK ANTONY.
Nay, good my fellows, do not please sharp fate
To grace it with your sorrows: bid that welcome
Which comes to punish us, and we punish it
Seeming to bear it lightly. Take me up:
I have led you oft: carry me now, good friends,
And have my thanks for all.
                    [*Exeunt, bearing* ANTONY.

SCENE XV.

The same.   A monument.

Enter CLEOPATRA *and her* MAIDS *aloft, with*
CHARMIAN *and* IRAS.

CLEOPATRA.

O CHARMIAN, I will never go from hence.
CHARMIAN.
Be comforted, dear madam.
CLEOPATRA.
No, I will not:
All strange and terrible events are welcome,
But comforts we despise; our size of sorrow
Proportion'd to our cause, must be as great
As that which makes it.
Enter, below, DIOMEDES.
How now! is he dead?
DIOMEDES.
His death's upon him, but not dead.
Look out o'the other side your monument;
His guard have brought him thither.
Enter, below, ANTONY, *borne by the* GUARD.
CLEOPATRA.
O sun,
Burn the great sphere thou mov'st in!—darkling
stand
The varying shore o'the world.—O Antony,
Antony, Antony!—Help, Charmian; help, Iras,
help;—
Help, friends below!—let's draw him hither.
MARK ANTONY.
Peace!
Not Cæsar's valour hath o'erthrown Antony,
But Antony's hath triumpht on itself.
CLEOPATRA.
So it should be, that none but Antony
Should conquer Antony; but woe 'tis so!
MARK ANTONY.
I am dying, Egypt, dying; only
I here importune death awhile, until
Of many thousand kisses the poor last
I lay upon thy lips.
CLEOPATRA.
I dare not, dear,—
Dear my lord, pardon,—I dare not,
Lest I be taken: not th'imperious show
Of the full-fortuned Cæsar ever shall
Be broocht with me; if knife, drugs, serpents, have
Edge, sting, or operation, I am safe:
Your wife Octavia, with her modest eyes
And still conclusion, shall acquire no honour
Demuring upon me.—But come, come, An-
tony,—
Help me, my women,—we must draw thee up;—
Assist, good friends.
MARK ANTONY.
O, quick, or I am gone.
CLEOPATRA.
Here's sport indeed!—How heavy weighs my
lord!
Our strength is all gone into heaviness;
That makes the weight: had I great Juno's power,
The strong-wing'd Mercury should fetch thee up,
And set thee by Jove's side. Yet come a little,—
Wishers were ever fools,—O, come, come, come;
[*They heave* ANTONY *aloft to* CLEOPATRA.

And welcome, welcome! die where thou hast
lived:
Quicken with kissing: had my lips that power,
Thus would I wear them out.
ALL.
A heavy sight!
MARK ANTONY.
I am dying, Egypt, dying:
Give me some wine, and let me speak a little.
CLEOPATRA.
No, let me speak; and let me rail so high,
That the false housewife Fortune break her
wheel,
Provoked by my offence.
MARK ANTONY.
One word, sweet queen:
Of Cæsar seek your honour, with your safety.—O!
CLEOPATRA.
They do not go together.
MARK ANTONY.
Gentle, hear me:
None about Cæsar trust but Proculeius.
CLEOPATRA.
My resolution and my hands I'll trust;
None about Cæsar.
MARK ANTONY.
The miserable change now at my end
Lament nor sorrow at; but please your thoughts
In feeding them with those my former fortunes,
Wherein I lived the greatest prince o'the world,
The noblest; and do now not basely die,
Not cowardly put off my helmet to
My countryman,—a Roman by a Roman
Valiantly vanquisht. Now my spirit is going;
I can no more.
CLEOPATRA.
Noblest of men, woo't die?
Hast thou no care of me? shall I abide
In this dull world, which in thy absence is
No better than a sty?—O, see, my women,
[ANTONY *dies.*
The crown o'the earth doth melt.—My lord!
O, wither'd is the garland of the war,
The soldiers' pole is faln: young boys and girls
Are level now with men; the odds is gone,
And there is nothing left remarkable
Beneath the visiting moon.   [*Faints.*
CHARMIAN.
O, quietness, lady!
IRAS.
She is dead too, our sovereign.
CHARMIAN.
Lady!
IRAS.
Madam!
CHARMIAN.
O madam, madam, madam!
IRAS.
Royal Egypt, Empress!
CHARMIAN.
Peace, peace, Iras!
CLEOPATRA.
No more, but e'en a woman, and commanded
By such poor passion as the maid that milks
And does the meanest chares.—It were for me
To throw my sceptre at the injurious gods;

To tell them that this world did equal theirs
Till they had stoln our jewel. All's but naught;
Patience is sottish, and impatience does
Become a dog that's mad; then is it sin
To rush into the secret house of death,
Ere death dare come to us?—How do you, women?
What, what! good cheer! Why, how now, Char-
  mian!
My noble girls! Ah, women, women, look,
Our lamp is spent, it's out! Good sirs, take
  heart:—
We'll bury him; and then, what's brave, what's
  noble,
Let's do it after the high Roman fashion,
And make death proud to take us. Come, away:
This case of that huge spirit now is cold:
Ah, women, women! come; we have no friend
But resolution, and the briefest end.

    [*Exeunt; those above bearing off* ANTONY'S
    body.

ACT V. SCENE I.

CAESAR'S *camp before Alexandria.*

Enter CAESAR, AGRIPPA, DOLABELLA,
MAECENAS, GALLUS, PROCULEIUS, *and others.*

OCTAVIUS CAESAR.

GO to him, Dolabella, bid him yield;
  Being so frustrate, tell him he mocks
The pauses that he makes.

DOLABELLA.
           Cæsar, I shall.   [*Exit.*
Enter DERCETAS, *with the sword of* ANTONY.
OCTAVIUS CAESAR.
Wherefore is that? and what art thou that darest
Appear thus to us?

DERCETAS.
    I am call'd Dercetas;
Mark Antony I served, who best was worthy
Best to be served: whilst he stood up and spoke,
He was my master; and I wore my life
To spend upon his haters. If thou please
To take me to thee, as I was to him
I'll be to Cæsar; if thou pleasest not,
I yield thee up my life.

OCTAVIUS CAESAR.
         What is't thou say'st?
DERCETAS.
I say, O Cæsar, Antony is dead.
OCTAVIUS CAESAR.
The breaking of so great a thing should make
A greater crack: the round world
Should have shook lions into civil streets,
And citizens to their dens. The death of Antony
Is not a single doom; in the name lay
A moiety of the world.

DERCETAS.
        He is dead, Cæsar;
Not by a public minister of justice,
Nor by a hired knife; but that self hand,
Which writ his honour in the acts it did,
Hath, with the courage which the heart did lend it,
Splitted the heart.—This is his sword;
I robb'd his wound of it; behold it stain'd
With his most noble blood.

OCTAVIUS CAESAR.
          Look you sad, friends?
The gods rebuke me, but it is a tidings
To wash the eyes of kings.

AGRIPPA.
          And strange it is
That nature must compel us to lament
Our most persisted deeds.

MAECENAS.
         His taints and honours
Waged equal with him.

AGRIPPA.
         A rarer spirit never
Did steer humanity: but you, gods, will give us
Some faults to make us men. Cæsar is toucht.

MAECENAS.
When such a spacious mirror's set before him,
He needs must see himself.

OCTAVIUS CAESAR.
          O Antony!
I have follow'd thee to this:—but we do lance
Diseases in our bodies: I must perforce
Have shown to thee such a declining day,
Or look on thine; we could not stall together
In the whole world: but yet let me lament,
With tears as sovereign as the blood of hearts,
That thou, my brother, my competitor
In top of all design, my mate in empire,
Friend and companion in the front of war,
The arm of mine own body, and the heart
Where mine his thoughts did kindle,—that our
Unreconciliable, should divide   [stars,
Our equalness to this.—Hear me, good friends,—
But I will tell you at some meeter season:
        Enter a MESSENGER.
The business of this man looks out of him;
We'll hear him what he says.—Whence are you?

MESSENGER.
A poor Egyptian yet. The queen my mistress,
Confined in all she has, her monument,
Of thy intents desires instruction,
That she preparedly may frame herself
To the way she's forced to.

OCTAVIUS CAESAR.
          Bid her have good heart:
She soon shall know of us, by some of ours,
How honourable and how kindly we
Determine for her; for Cæsar cannot live
To be ungentle.

MESSENGER.
        So the gods preserve thee! [*Exit.*
OCTAVIUS CAESAR.
Come hither, Proculeius. Go, and say
We purpose her no shame: give her what comforts
The quality of her passion shall require,
Lest, in her greatness, by some mortal stroke
She do defeat us; for her life in Rome
Would be eternal in our triumph: go,
And with your speediest bring us what she says,
And how you find of her.

PROCULEIUS.
        Cæsar, I shall.   [*Exit.*
OCTAVIUS CAESAR.
Gallus, go you along. [*Exit* GALLUS.] Where's
  Dolabella,
To second Proculeius?

AGRIPPA, MAECENAS, &c.
Dolabella!
OCTAVIUS CAESAR.
Let him alone, for I remember now
How he's employ'd: he shall in time be ready.
Go with me to my tent; where you shall see
How hardly I was drawn into this war;
How calm and gentle I proceeded still
In all my writings: go with me, and see
What I can show in this.   [*Exeunt.*

SCENE II.

Alexandria.   A room in the monument.

Enter CLEOPATRA, CHARMIAN, *and* IRAS.

CLEOPATRA.

MY desolation does begin to make
A better life. 'Tis paltry to be Cæsar;
Not being Fortune, he's but Fortune's knave,
A minister of her will: and it is great
To do that thing that ends all other deeds;
Which shackles accidents, and bolts up change;
Which sleeps, and never palates more the dug,
The beggar's nurse and Cæsar's.
Enter, to the gates of the monument, PROCULEIUS,
GALLUS, *and* SOLDIERS.
PROCULEIUS.
Cæsar sends greeting to the Queen of Egypt;
And bids thee study on what fair demands
Thou mean'st to have him grant thee.
CLEOPATRA.
      What's thy name?
PROCULEIUS.
My name is Proculeius.
CLEOPATRA.
      Antony
Did tell me of you, bade me trust you; but
I do not greatly care to be deceived,
That have no use for trusting. If your master
Would have a queen his beggar, you must tell
    him,
That majesty, to keep decorum, must
No less beg than a kingdom: if he please
To give me conquer'd Egypt for my son,
He gives me so much of mine own as I
Will kneel to him with thanks.
PROCULEIUS.
      Be of good cheer;
Y'are faln into a princely hand, fear nothing:
Make your full reference freely to my lord,
Who is so full of grace, that it flows over
On all that need: let me report to him
Your sweet dependency; and you shall find
A conqueror that will pray in aid for kindness,
Where he for grace is kneel'd to.
CLEOPATRA.
      Pray you, tell him
I am his fortune's vassal, and I send him
The greatness he has got. I hourly learn
A doctrine of obedience; and would gladly
Look him i'the face.
PROCULEIUS.
      This I'll report, dear lady.
Have comfort, for I know your plight is pitied
Of him that caused it.

GALLUS.
You see how easily she may be surprised:
[*Here* PROCULEIUS *and two of the* GUARD
*ascend the monument by a ladder placed
against a window, and, having descended,
come behind* CLEOPATRA. *Some of the*
GUARD *unbar and open the gates.*
[*to* PROCULEIUS *and the* GUARD] Guard her till
Cæsar come.   [*Exit.*
IRAS.
Royal queen!
CHARMIAN.
O Cleopatra! thou art taken, queen!
CLEOPATRA.
Quick, quick, good hands.   [*Drawing a dagger.*
PROCULEIUS.
      Hold, worthy lady, hold:
[*Seizes and disarms her.*
Do not yourself such wrong, who are in this
Relieved, but not betray'd.
CLEOPATRA.
      What, of death too,
That rids our dogs of languish?
PROCULEIUS.
      Cleopatra,
Do not abuse my master's bounty by
Th'undoing of yourself: let the world see
His nobleness well acted, which your death
Will never let come forth.
CLEOPATRA.
      Where art thou, death?
Come hither, come! come, come, and take a queen
Worth many babes and beggars!
PROCULEIUS.
      O, temperance, lady!
CLEOPATRA.
Sir, I will eat no meat, I'll not drink, sir;
If idle talk will once be necessary,
I'll not sleep neither: this mortal house I'll ruin,
Do Cæsar what he can. Know, sir, that I
Will not wait pinion'd at your master's court;
Nor once be chastised with the sober eye
Of dull Octavia. Shall they hoist me up,
And show me to the shouting varletry
Of censuring Rome? Rather a ditch in Egypt
Be gentle grave unto me! rather on Nilus' mud
Lay me stark-naked, and let the water-flies
Blow me into abhorring! rather make
My country's high pyramides my gibbet,
And hang me up in chains!
PROCULEIUS.
      You do extend
These thoughts of horror further than you shall
Find cause in Cæsar.
Enter DOLABELLA.
DOLABELLA.
      Proculeius,
What thou hast done thy master Cæsar knows,
And he hath sent for thee: for the queen,
I'll take her to my guard.
PROCULEIUS.
      So, Dolabella,
It shall content me best: be gentle to her.—
[*to* CLEOPATRA] To Cæsar I will speak what you
    shall please,
If you'll employ me to him.

CLEOPATRA.
Say, I would die.
[*Exeunt* PROCULEIUS *and* SOLDIERS.
DOLABELLA.
Most noble empress, you have heard of me?
CLEOPATRA.
I cannot tell.
DOLABELLA.
Assuredly you know me.
CLEOPATRA.
No matter, sir, what I have heard or known.
You laugh when boys or women tell their dreams;
Is't not your trick?
DOLABELLA.
I understand not, madam.
CLEOPATRA.
I dreamt there was an emperor Antony:—
O, such another sleep, that I might see
But such another man!
DOLABELLA.
If it might please ye,—
CLEOPATRA.
His face was as the heavens; and therein stuck
A sun and moon, which kept their course, and
The little O, the earth.   [lighted
DOLABELLA.
Most sovereign creature,—
CLEOPATRA.
His legs bestrid the ocean: his rear'd arm
Crested the world; his voice was propertied
As all the tuned spheres, and that to friends;
But when he meant to quail and shake the orb,
He was as rattling thunder. For his bounty,
There was no winter in't; an autumn 'twas
That grew the more by reaping: his delights
Were dolphin-like; they show'd his back above
The element they lived in: in his livery
Walkt crowns and crownets; realms and islands
were
As plates dropt from his pocket.
DOLABELLA.
Cleopatra,—
CLEOPATRA.
Think you there was, or might be, such a man
As this I dreamt of?
DOLABELLA.
Gentle madam, no.
CLEOPATRA.
You lie, up to the hearing of the gods.
But, if there be, or ever were, one such,
It's past the size of dreaming: nature wants stuff
To vie strange forms with fancy; yet, t'imagine
An Antony, were nature's piece 'gainst fancy,
Condemning shadows quite.
DOLABELLA.
Hear me, good madam.
Your loss is as yourself, great; and you bear it
As answering to the weight: would I might never
O'ertake pursued success, but I do feel,
By the rebound of yours, a grief that smites
My very heart at root.
CLEOPATRA.
I thank you, sir.
Know you what Cæsar means to do with me?
DOLABELLA.
I am loth to tell you what I would you knew.

CLEOPATRA.
Nay, pray you, sir,—
DOLABELLA.
Though he be honourable,—
CLEOPATRA.
He'll lead me, then, in triumph?
DOLABELLA.
Madam, he will; I know't.   [*Flourish and shout*
within,   'Make way there,—Cæsar!'
Enter CAESAR, GALLUS, PROCULEIUS, MAECE-
NAS, SELEUCUS, *and others of his* TRAIN.
OCTAVIUS CAESAR.
Which is the Queen of Egypt?
DOLABELLA.
It is the emperor, madam. [CLEOPATRA *kneels*.
OCTAVIUS CAESAR.
Arise, you shall not kneel:
I pray you, rise; rise, Egypt.
CLEOPATRA.
Sir, the gods
Will have it thus; my master and my lord
I must obey.
OCTAVIUS CAESAR.
Take to you no hard thoughts:
The record of what injuries you did us,
Though written in our flesh, we shall remember
As things but done by chance.
CLEOPATRA.
Sole sir o'the world,
I cannot project mine own cause so well
To make it clear; but do confess I have
Been laden with like frailties which before
Have often shamed our sex.
OCTAVIUS CAESAR.
Cleopatra, know,
We will extenuate rather than enforce:
If you apply yourself to our intents,—
Which towards you are most gentle,—you shall
find
A benefit in this change; but if you seek
To lay on me a cruelty, by taking
Antony's course, you shall bereave yourself
Of my good purposes, and put your children
To that destruction which I'll guard them from,
If thereon you rely. I'll take my leave.
CLEOPATRA.
And may, through all the world: 'tis yours; and we,
Your scutcheons and your signs of conquest, shall
Hang in what place you please. Here, my good
lord.
OCTAVIUS CAESAR.
You shall advise me in all for Cleopatra.
CLEOPATRA.
This is the brief of money, plate, and jewels,
I am possest of: 'tis exactly valued;
Not petty things omitted.—Where's Seleucus?
SELEUCUS.
Here, madam.
CLEOPATRA.
This is my treasurer: let him speak, my lord,
Upon his peril, that I have reserved
To myself nothing.—Speak the truth, Seleucus.
SELEUCUS.
Madam,
I had rather seal my lips than, to my peril,
Speak that which is not.

CLEOPATRA.
What have I kept back?

SELEUCUS.
Enough to purchase what you have made known.

OCTAVIUS CAESAR.
Nay, blush not, Cleopatra; I approve
Your wisdom in the deed.

CLEOPATRA.
See, Cæsar! O, behold,
How pomp is follow'd! mine will now be yours;
And, should we shift estates, yours would be
   mine.
The ingratitude of this Seleucus does
Even make me wild:—O slave, of no more trust
Than love that's hired!—What, goest thou back?
   thou shalt
Go back, I warrant thee; but I'll catch thine eyes,
Though they had wings: slave, soulless villain,
   dog!
O rarely base!

OCTAVIUS CAESAR.
Good queen, let us entreat you.

CLEOPATRA.
O Cæsar, what a wounding shame is this,—
That thou, vouchsafing here to visit me,
Doing the honour of thy lordliness
To one so meek, that mine own servant should
Parcel the sum of my disgraces by
Addition of his envy! Say, good Cæsar,
That I some lady trifles have reserved,
Immoment toys, things of such dignity
As we greet modern friends withal; and say,
Some nobler token I have kept apart
For Livia and Octavia, to induce
Their mediation; must I be unfolded
With one that I have bred? The gods! it smites me
Beneath the fall I have.—[to SELEUCUS] Prithee,
   go hence;
Or I shall show the cinders of my spirits
Through the ashes of my chance: wert thou a
   man,
Thou wouldst have mercy on me.

OCTAVIUS CAESAR.
Forbear, Seleucus. [Exit SELEUCUS.

CLEOPATRA.
Be it known that we, the greatest, are misthought
For things that others do; and, when we fall,
We answer others' merits in our name,
Are therefore to be pitied.

OCTAVIUS CAESAR.
Cleopatra,
Not what you have reserved, nor what acknow-
   ledged,
Put we i'the roll of conquest: still be't yours,
Bestow it at your pleasure; and believe,
Cæsar's no merchant, to make prize with you
Of things that merchants sold. Therefore be
   cheer'd;
Make not your thoughts your prisons: no, dear
   queen;
For we intend so to dispose you as
Yourself shall give us counsel. Feed, and sleep:
Our care and pity is so much upon you,
That we remain your friend; and so, adieu.

CLEOPATRA.
My master, and my lord!

OCTAVIUS CAESAR.
Not so. Adieu.
[Flourish. Exeunt CAESAR and his TRAIN.

CLEOPATRA.
He words me, girls, he words me, that I should
   not
Be noble to myself: but, hark thee, Charmian.
[Whispers CHARMIAN.

IRAS.
Finish, good lady; the bright day is done,
And we are for the dark.

CLEOPATRA.
Hie thee again:
I have spoke already, and it is provided;
Go put it to the haste.

CHARMIAN.
Madam, I will.

Enter DOLABELLA.

DOLABELLA.
Where is the queen?

CHARMIAN.
Behold, sir.   [Exit.

CLEOPATRA.
Dolabella!

DOLABELLA.
Madam, as thereto sworn by your command,
Which my love makes religion to obey,
I tell you this: Cæsar through Syria
Intends his journey; and, within three days,
You with your children will he send before:
Make your best use of this: I have perform'd
Your pleasure and my promise.

CLEOPATRA.
Dolabella,
I shall remain your debtor.

DOLABELLA.
I your servant.
Adieu, good queen; I must attend on Cæsar.

CLEOPATRA.
Farewell, and thanks.   [Exit DOLABELLA.
Now, Iras, what think'st thou?
Thou, an Egyptian puppet, shalt be shown
In Rome, as well as I: mechanic slaves,
With greasy aprons, rules, and hammers, shall
Uplift us to the view; in their thick breaths,
Rank of gross diet, shall we be enclouded,
And forced to drink their vapour.

IRAS.
The gods forbid!

CLEOPATRA.
Nay, 'tis most certain, Iras:—saucy lictors
Will catch at us, like strumpets; and scald rimers
Ballad us out o'tune: the quick comedians
Extemporally will stage us, and present
Our Alexandrian revels; Antony
Shall be brought drunken forth, and I shall see
Some squeaking Cleopatra boy my greatness
I'the posture of a whore.

IRAS.
O the good gods!

CLEOPATRA.
Nay, that's certain.

IRAS.
I'll never see't; for I am sure my nails
Are stronger than mine eyes.

CLEOPATRA.
             Why, that's the way
To fool their preparation, and to conquer
Their most absurd intents.
        Enter CHARMIAN.
              Now, Charmian!—
Show me, my women, like a queen:—go fetch
My best attires;—I am again for Cydnus,
To meet Mark Antony:—sirrah Iras, go.—
Now, noble Charmian, we'll dispatch indeed;
And, when thou hast done this chare, I'll give
    thee leave
To play till doomsday.—Bring our crown and all.
Wherefore's this noise?
        [*Exit* IRAS.   *A noise within.*
        Enter a GUARDSMAN.
         GUARDSMAN.
            Here is a rural fellow
That will not be denied your highness' presence:
He brings you figs.
         CLEOPATRA.
Let him come in.   [*Exit* GUARDSMAN.
           What poor an instrument
May do a noble deed! he brings me liberty.
My resolution's placed, and I have nothing
Of woman in me: now from head to foot
I am marble-constant; now the fleeting moon
No planet is of mine.
    Enter GUARDSMAN, *with* CLOWN *bringing in*
        a basket.
         GUARDSMAN.
        This is the man.
         CLEOPATRA.
Avoid, and leave him.   [*Exit* GUARDSMAN.
Hast thou the pretty worm of Nilus there,
That kills and pains not?
          CLOWN.
Truly I have him: but I would not be the party
that should desire you to touch him, for his biting
is immortal; those that do die of it do seldom or
never recover.
         CLEOPATRA.
Remember'st thou any that have died on't?
          CLOWN.
Very many, men and women too. I heard of one
of them no longer than yesterday: a very honest
woman, but something given to lie; as a woman
should not do, but in the way of honesty: how she
died of the biting of it, what pain she felt,—truly,
she makes a very good report o'the worm; but he
that will believe all that they say shall never be
saved by half that they do: but this is most falli-
able, the worm's an odd worm.
         CLEOPATRA.
Get thee hence; farewell.
          CLOWN.
I wish you all joy of the worm.
        [*Sets down his basket.*
         CLEOPATRA.
Farewell.
          CLOWN.
You must think this, look you, that the worm will
do his kind.
         CLEOPATRA.
Ay, ay; farewell.

         CLOWN.
Look you, the worm is not to be trusted but in
the keeping of wise people; for, indeed, there is no
goodness in the worm.
         CLEOPATRA.
Take thou no care; it shall be heeded.
         CLOWN.
Very good. Give it nothing, I pray you, for it is
not worth the feeding.
         CLEOPATRA.
Will it eat me?
          CLOWN.
You must not think I am so simple but I know
the devil himself will not eat a woman: I know
that a woman is a dish for the gods, if the devil
dress her not. But, truly, these same whoreson
devils do the gods great harm in their women;
for in every ten that they make, the devils mar
five.
         CLEOPATRA.
Well, get thee gone; farewell.
          CLOWN.
Yes, forsooth; I wish you joy o'the worm.   [*Exit.*
    Enter IRAS *with a robe, crown, &c.*
         CLEOPATRA.
Give me my robe, put on my crown; I have
Immortal longings in me: now no more
The juice of Egypt's grape shall moist this lip:—
Yare, yare, good Iras; quick.—Methinks I hear
Antony call; I see him rouse himself
To praise my noble act; I hear him mock
The luck of Cæsar, which the gods give men
To excuse their after wrath:—husband, I come:
Now to that name my courage prove my title!
I am fire and air; my other elements
I give to baser life.—So,—have you done?
Come then, and take the last warmth of my lips.
Farewell, kind Charmian;—Iras, long farewell.
        [*Kisses them.*   IRAS *falls and dies.*
Have I the aspic in my lips? Dost fall?
If thou and nature can so gently part,
The stroke of death is as a lover's pinch,
Which hurts, and is desired. Dost thou lie still?
If thus thou vanishest, thou tell'st the world
It is not worth leave-taking.
         CHARMIAN.
Dissolve, thick cloud, and rain; that I may say
The gods themselves do weep!
         CLEOPATRA.
            This proves me base:
If she first meet the curled Antony,
He'll make demand of her, and spend that kiss
Which is my heaven to have.—Come, thou mortal
    wretch,
    [*To an asp, which she applies to her breast.*
With thy sharp teeth this knot intrinsicate
Of life at once untie: poor venomous fool,
Be angry, and dispatch. O, couldst thou speak,
That I might hear thee call great Cæsar ass
Unpolicied!
         CHARMIAN.
        O eastern star!
         CLEOPATRA.
            Peace, peace!
Dost thou not see my baby at my breast,
That sucks the nurse asleep?

CHARMIAN.
O, break! O, break!
CLEOPATRA.
As sweet as balm, as soft as air, as gentle,—
O Antony!—Nay, I will take thee too:—
　　　　[*Applying another asp to her arm.*
What should I stay—　　　　　　[*Dies.*
CHARMIAN.
In this vile world?—So, fare thee well.—
Now boast thee, death, in thy possession lies
A lass unparallel'd.—Downy windows, close;
And golden Phœbus never be beheld
Of eyes again so royal!—Your crown's awry;
I'll mend it, and then play.
　　　　Enter the GUARD, *rushing in.*
FIRST GUARD.
Where is the queen?
CHARMIAN.
Speak softly, wake her not.
FIRST GUARD.
Cæsar hath sent—
CHARMIAN.
Too slow a messenger. [*Applies an asp.*
O, come apace, dispatch: I partly feel thee.
FIRST GUARD.
Approach, ho! All's not well: Cæsar's beguiled.
SECOND GUARD.
There's Dolabella sent from Cæsar; call him.
FIRST GUARD.
What work is here!—Charmian, is this well done?
CHARMIAN.
It is well done, and fitting for a princess
Descended of so many royal kings.
Ah, soldier!　　　　　　　　　ₗ*Dies.*
　　　　Enter DOLABELLA.
DOLABELLA.
How goes it here?
SECOND GUARD.
All dead.
DOLABELLA.
Cæsar, thy thoughts
Touch their effects in this: thyself art coming
To see perform'd the dreaded act which thou
So sought'st to hinder.
[*within,* 'A way there, a way for Cæsar!']
　　Enter CAESAR *and all his* TRAIN, *marching.*
DOLABELLA.
O sir, you are too sure an augurer;
That you did fear is done.

OCTAVIUS CAESAR.
Bravest at the last,
She levell'd at our purposes, and, being royal,
Took her own way.—The manner of their
　deaths?
I do not see them bleed.
DOLABELLA.
Who was last with them?
FIRST GUARD.
A simple countryman, that brought her figs:
This was his basket.
OCTAVIUS CAESAR.
Poison'd, then.
FIRST GUARD.
O Cæsar,
This Charmian lived but now; she stood and
　spake:
I found her trimming up the diadem
On her dead mistress; tremblingly she stood,
And on the sudden dropt.
OCTAVIUS CAESAR.
O noble weakness!—
If they had swallow'd poison, 'twould appear
By external swelling: but she looks like sleep,
As she would catch another Antony
In her strong toil of grace.
DOLABELLA.
Here, on her breast,
There is a vent of blood, and something blown:
The like is on her arm.
FIRST GUARD.
This is an aspic's trail: and these fig-leaves
Have slime upon them, such as the aspic leaves
Upon the caves of Nile.
OCTAVIUS CAESAR.
Most probable
That so she died; for her physician tells me
She hath pursued conclusions infinite
Of easy ways to die.—Take up her bed;
And bear her women from the monument:—
She shall be buried by her Antony:
No grave upon the earth shall clip in it
A pair so famous. High events as these
Strike those that make them; and their story is
No less in pity than his glory which
Brought them to be lamented. Our army shall
In solemn show attend this funeral;
And then to Rome.—Come, Dolabella, see
High order in this great solemnity.　　[*Exeunt.*

CORIOLANUS

DRAMATIS PERSONAE

CAIUS MARCIUS, *afterwards* CAIUS MARCIUS
   CORIOLANUS, *a noble Roman.*
TITUS LARTIUS, } *generals against the Volscians.*
COMINIUS,
MENENIUS AGRIPPA, *friend to Coriolanus.*
SICINIUS VELUTUS, } *tribunes of the people.*
JUNIUS BRUTUS,
YOUNG MARCIUS, *son to Coriolanus.*
A ROMAN HERALD.
TULLUS AUFIDIUS, *general of the Volscians.*
LIEUTENANT *to Aufidius.*
CONSPIRATORS *with Aufidius.*
A CITIZEN OF ANTIUM.
TWO VOLSCIAN GUARDS.

VOLUMNIA, *mother to Coriolanus.*
VIRGILIA, *wife to Coriolanus.*
VALERIA, *friend to Virgilia.*
GENTLEWOMAN *attending on Virgilia.*

ROMAN *and* VOLSCIAN SENATORS, PATRI-
CIANS, AEDILES, LICTORS, SOLDIERS, CITI-
ZENS, MESSENGERS, SERVANTS *to Aufidius,*
and other ATTENDANTS.

SCENE—*Partly Rome and its neighbourhood;*
partly Corioli and its neighbourhood; and partly
Antium.

ACT I. SCENE I.

Rome.   A street.

Enter a company of mutinous CITIZENS, *with*
staves, clubs, and other weapons.

FIRST CITIZEN.

BEFORE we proceed any further, hear me
speak.

CITIZENS.

Speak, speak.

FIRST CITIZEN.

You are all resolved rather to die than to famish?

CITIZENS.

Resolved, resolved.

FIRST CITIZEN.

First, you know Caius Marcius is chief enemy to
the people.

CITIZENS.

We know't, we know't.

FIRST CITIZEN.

Let us kill him, and we'll have corn at our own
price. Is't a verdict?

CITIZENS.

No more talking on't; let it be done: away, away!

SECOND CITIZEN.

One word, good citizens.

FIRST CITIZEN.

We are accounted poor citizens; the patricians,
good. What authority surfeits on would relieve
us: if they would yield us but the superfluity,
while it were wholesome, we might guess they
relieved us humanely; but they think we are too
dear: the leanness that afflicts us, the object of our
misery, is as an inventory to particularize their
abundance; our sufferance is a gain to them.—
Let us revenge this with our pikes, ere we become
rakes: for the gods know I speak this in hunger
for bread, not in thirst for revenge.

SECOND CITIZEN.

Would you proceed especially against Caius Marcius?

CITIZENS.

Against him first: he's a very dog to the commonalty.

SECOND CITIZEN.

Consider you what services he has done for his
country?

FIRST CITIZEN.

Very well; and could be content to give him good
report for't, but that he pays himself with being
proud.

SECOND CITIZEN.

Nay, but speak not maliciously.

FIRST CITIZEN.

I say unto you, what he hath done famously, he
did it to that end: though soft-conscienced men
can be content to say it was for his country, he did
it to please his mother, and to be partly proud;
which he is, even to the altitude of his virtue.

SECOND CITIZEN.

What he cannot help in his nature, you account
a vice in him. You must in no way say he is
covetous.

FIRST CITIZEN.

If I must not, I need not be barren of accusations;
he hath faults, with surplus, to tire in repetition.
[*Shouts within.*] What shouts are these? The other
side o' the city is risen: why stay we prating here?
to the Capitol!

CITIZENS.

Come, come.

FIRST CITIZEN.

Soft! who comes here?

SECOND CITIZEN.

Worthy Menenius Agrippa; one that hath always
loved the people.

FIRST CITIZEN.

He's one honest enough: would all the rest were so!

Enter MENENIUS AGRIPPA.

MENENIUS AGRIPPA.

What work's, my countrymen, in hand? where go
you
With bats and clubs? the matter? speak, I pray
you.

FIRST CITIZEN.

Our business is not unknown to the senate; they
have had inkling, this fortnight, what we intend
to do, which now we'll show 'em in deeds. They

say poor suitors have strong breaths: they shall
know we have strong arms too.

MENENIUS AGRIPPA.

Why, masters, my good friends, mine honest
  neighbours,
Will you undo yourselves?

FIRST CITIZEN.

We cannot, sir, we are undone already.

MENENIUS AGRIPPA.

I tell you, friends, most charitable care
Have the patricians of you. For your wants,
Your suffering in this dearth, you may as well
Strike at the heaven with your staves as lift them
Against the Roman state; whose course will on
The way it takes, cracking ten thousand curbs
Of more strong link asunder than can ever
Appear in your impediment: for the dearth,
The gods, not the patricians, make it; and
Your knees to them, not arms, must help. Alack,
You are transported by calamity
Thither where more attends you; and you slander
The helms o'th'state, who care for you like fathers,
When you curse them as enemies.

FIRST CITIZEN.

Care for us! True, indeed! They ne'er cared for
us yet:—suffer us to famish, and their store-
houses cramm'd with grain; make edicts for
usury, to support usurers; repeal daily any wholesome act establisht against the rich; and provide
more piercing statutes daily, to chain up and restrain the poor. If the wars eat us not up, they
will; and there's all the love they bear us.

MENENIUS AGRIPPA.

Either you must
Confess yourselves wondrous malicious,
Or be accused of folly. I shall tell you
A pretty tale: it may be you have heard it;
But, since it serves my purpose, I will venture
To stale't a little more.

FIRST CITIZEN.

Well, I'll hear it, sir: yet you must not think to
fob-off our disgrace with a tale: but, an't please
you, deliver.

MENENIUS AGRIPPA.

There was a time when all the body's members
Rebell'd against the belly; thus accused it:—
That only like a gulf it did remain
I'the midst o'the body, idle and unactive,
Still cupboarding the viand, never bearing
Like labour with the rest; where th'other instru-
  ments
Did see and hear, devise, instruct, walk, feel,
And, mutually participate, did minister
Unto the appetite and affection common
Of the whole body. The belly answer'd,—

FIRST CITIZEN.

Well, sir, what answer made the belly?

MENENIUS AGRIPPA.

Sir, I shall tell you.—With a kind of smile,
Which ne'er came from the lungs, but even thus—
For, look you, I may make the belly smile
As well as speak—it tauntingly replied
To the discontented members, the mutinous parts
That envied his receipt; even so most fitly
As you malign our senators for that
They are not such as you.

FIRST CITIZEN.

Your belly's answer? What!
The kingly-crowned head, the vigilant eye,
The counsellor heart, the arm our soldier,
Our steed the leg, the tongue our trumpeter,
With other muniments and petty helps
In this our fabric, if that they—

MENENIUS AGRIPPA.

What then?—
'Fore me, this fellow speaks!—what then? what
  then?

FIRST CITIZEN.

Should by the cormorant belly be restrain'd,
Who is the sink o'the body,—

MENENIUS AGRIPPA.

Well, what then?

FIRST CITIZEN.

The former agents, if they did complain,
What could the belly answer?

MENENIUS AGRIPPA.

I will tell you;
If you'll bestow a small—of what you have little—
Patience awhile, you'st hear the belly's answer.

FIRST CITIZEN.

Y'are long about it.

MENENIUS AGRIPPA.

Note me this, good friend;
Your most grave belly was deliberate,
Not rash like his accusers, and thus answer'd:
'True is it, my incorporate friends,' quoth he,
'That I receive the general food at first,
Which you do live upon; and fit it is,
Because I am the store-house and the shop
Of the whole body: but, if you do remember,
I send it through the rivers of your blood,
Even to the court, the heart,—to the seat o'the
  brain;
And, through the cranks and offices of man,
The strongest nerves and small inferior veins
From me receive that natural competency
Whereby they live: and though that all at once,
You, my good friends,'—this says the belly, mark
  me,—

FIRST CITIZEN.

Ay, sir; well, well.

MENENIUS AGRIPPA.

'Though all at once can not
See what I do deliver out to each,
Yet I can make my audit up, that all
From me do back receive the flour of all,
And leave me but the bran.'—What say you to't?

FIRST CITIZEN.

It was an answer: how apply you this?

MENENIUS AGRIPPA.

The senators of Rome are this good belly,
And you the mutinous members: for examine
Their counsels and their cares; digest things
  rightly
Touching the weal o'the common; you shall find,
No public benefit which you receive
But it proceeds or comes from them to you,
And no way from yourselves.—What do you
  think,—
You, the great toe of this assembly?

FIRST CITIZEN.

I the great toe? why the great toe?

MENENIUS AGRIPPA.
For that, being one o'the lowest, basest, poorest,
Of this most wise rebellion, thou go'st foremost:
Thou rascal, that art worst in blood to run,
Lead'st first to win some vantage.—
But make you ready your stiff bats and clubs:
Rome and her rats are at the point of battle;
The one side must have bale.
      Enter CAIUS MARCIUS.
                Hail, noble Marcius!
       CAIUS MARCIUS.
Thanks.—What's the matter, you dissentious
    rogues,
That, rubbing the poor itch of your opinion,
Make yourselves scabs?
       FIRST CITIZEN.
            We have ever your good word.
       CAIUS MARCIUS.
He that will give good words to thee will flatter
Beneath abhorring. What would you have, you
    curs,
That like nor peace nor war? the one affrights you,
The other makes you proud. He that trusts to you,
Where he should find you lions, finds you hares;
Where foxes, geese: you are no surer, no,
Than is the coal of fire upon the ice,
Or hailstone in the sun. Your virtue is,
To make him worthy whose offence subdues him,
And curse that justice did it. Who deserves great-
    ness
Deserves your hate; and your affections are
A sick man's appetite, who desires most that
Which would increase his evil. He that depends
Upon your favours swims with fins of lead,
And hews down oaks with rushes. Hang ye!
    Trust ye!
With every minute you do change a mind;
And call him noble that was now your hate,
Him vile that was your garland. What's the matter,
That in these several places of the city
You cry against the noble senate, who,
Under the gods, keep you in awe, which else
Would feed on one another?—What's their seek-
    ing?
       MENENIUS AGRIPPA.
For corn at their own rates; whereof, they say,
The city is well stored.
       CAIUS MARCIUS.
               Hang 'em! They say!
They'll sit by the fire, and presume to know
What's done i'the Capitol; who's like to rise,
Who thrives, and who declines; side factions, and
    give out
Conjectural marriages; making parties strong,
And feebling such as stand not in their liking
Below their cobbled shoes. They say there's grain
    enough!
Would the nobility lay aside their ruth,
And let me use my sword, I'ld make a quarry
With thousands of these quarter'd slaves, as high
As I could pick my lance.
       MENENIUS AGRIPPA.
Nay, these are almost thoroughly persuaded;
For though abundantly they lack discretion,
Yet are they passing cowardly. But, I beseech you,
What says the other troop?

       CAIUS MARCIUS.
           They are dissolved: hang 'em!
They said they were an-hungry: sigh'd forth pro-
    verbs,
That hunger broke stone walls, that dogs must
    eat,
That meat was made for mouths, that the gods
    sent not
Corn for the rich men only:—with these shreds
They vented their complainings; which being
    answer'd,
And a petition granted them, a strange one—
To break the heart of generosity,
And make bold power look pale—they threw
    their caps
As they would hang them on the horns o'the
    moon,
Shouting their emulation.
       MENENIUS AGRIPPA.
               What is granted them?
       CAIUS MARCIUS.
Five tribunes to defend their vulgar wisdoms,
Of their own choice: one's Junius Brutus,
Sicinius Velutus, and I know not—'Sdeath!
The rabble should have first unrooft the city,
Ere so prevail'd with me: it will in time
Win upon power, and throw forth greater themes
For insurrection's arguing.
       MENENIUS AGRIPPA.
               This is strange.
       CAIUS MARCIUS.
Go, get you home, you fragments!
      Enter a MESSENGER, *hastily.*
       MESSENGER.
Where's Caius Marcius?
       CAIUS MARCIUS.
             Here: what's the matter?
       MESSENGER.
The news is, sir, the Volsces are in arms.
       CAIUS MARCIUS.
I am glad on't; then we shall ha' means to vent
Our musty superfluity.—See, our best elders.
      Enter COMINIUS, TITUS LARTIUS, *with other*
      SENATORS; JUNIUS BRUTUS, *and* SICINIUS
      VELUTUS.
       FIRST SENATOR.
Marcius, 'tis true that you have lately told us,—
The Volsces are in arms.
       CAIUS MARCIUS.
           They have a leader,
Tullus Aufidius, that will put you to't.
I sin in envying his nobility;
And were I any thing but what I am,
I would wish me only he.
       COMINIUS.
           You have fought together.
       CAIUS MARCIUS.
Were half to half the world by the ears, and he
Upon my party, I'ld revolt, to make
Only my wars with him: he is a lion
That I am proud to hunt.
       FIRST SENATOR.
          Then, worthy Marcius,
Attend upon Cominius to these wars.
       COMINIUS.
It is your former promise.

CAIUS MARCIUS.

　　　　　　　Sir, it is;
And I am constant.—Titus Lartius, thou
Shalt see me once more strike at Tullus' face.
What, art thou stiff? stand'st out?

TITUS LARTIUS.

　　　　　　　　No, Caius Marcius;
I'll lean upon one crutch, and fight with t'other,
Ere stay behind this business.

MENENIUS AGRIPPA.

　　　　　　　O, true-bred!

FIRST SENATOR.

Your company to the Capitol; where, I know,
Our greatest friends attend us.

TITUS LARTIUS [to COMINIUS].

　　　　　　Lead you on.—
[to MARCIUS] Follow Cominius: we must follow
Right worthy you priority.　　　　　　[you;

COMINIUS.

　　　　　Noble Marcius!

FIRST SENATOR [to the CITIZENS].

Hence to your homes; be gone!

CAIUS MARCIUS.

　　　　　　　Nay, let them follow:
The Volsces have much corn; take these rats
　　thither
To gnaw their garners.—Worshipful mutiners,
Your valour puts well forth: pray, follow.
　　　[CITIZENS steal away.　Exeunt all but
　　　BRUTUS and SICINIUS.

SICINIUS VELUTUS.

Was ever man so proud as is this Marcius?

JUNIUS BRUTUS.

He has no equal.

SICINIUS VELUTUS.

When we were chosen tribunes for the people,—

JUNIUS BRUTUS.

Markt you his lip and eyes?

SICINIUS VELUTUS.

　　　　　　　Nay, but his taunts.

JUNIUS BRUTUS.

Being moved, he will not spare to gird the gods.

SICINIUS VELUTUS.

Be-mock the modest moon.

JUNIUS BRUTUS.

The present wars devour him! He is grown
Too proud to be so valiant.

SICINIUS VELUTUS.

　　　　　　　Such a nature,
Tickled with good success, disdains the shadow
Which he treads on at noon: but I do wonder
His insolence can brook to be commanded
Under Cominius.

JUNIUS BRUTUS.

　　　　　　　Fame, at the which he aims,—
In whom already he's well graced,—can not
Better be held, nor more attain'd, than by
A place below the first: for what miscarries
Shall be the general's fault, though he perform
To the utmost of a man; and giddy censure
Will then cry out of Marcius, 'O, if he
Had borne the business!'

SICINIUS VELUTUS.

　　　　　　　Besides, if things go well,
Opinion, that so sticks on Marcius, shall
Of his demerits rob Cominius.

JUNIUS BRUTUS.

　　　　　Come:
Half all Cominius' honours are to Marcius,
Though Marcius earn'd them not; and all his
　　faults
To Marcius shall be honours, though, indeed,
In aught he merit not.

SICINIUS VELUTUS.

　　　　　　Let's hence, and hear
How the dispatch is made; and in what fashion,
More than his singularity, he goes
Upon his present action.

JUNIUS BRUTUS.

　　　　　　Let's along.　　　[Exeunt.

SCENE II.

Corioli.　The Senate-house.

Enter TULLUS AUFIDIUS with SENATORS of
Corioli.

FIRST SENATOR.

SO, your opinion is, Aufidius,
　　That they of Rome are enter'd in our counsels,
And know how we proceed.

TULLUS AUFIDIUS.

　　　　　　Is it not yours?
What ever have been thought on in this state,
That could be brought to bodily act ere Rome
Had circumvention? 'Tis not four days gone
Since I heard thence: these are the words: I think
I have the letter here; yes, here it is:　　[Reads.
They have prest a power, but it is not known
Whether for east or west: the dearth is great;
The people mutinous: and it is rumour'd,
Cominius, Marcius your old enemy,—
Who is of Rome worse hated than of you,—
And Titus Lartius, a most valiant Roman,
These three lead on this preparation
Whither 'tis bent: most likely 'tis for you:
Consider of it.

FIRST SENATOR.

　　　　　　Our army's in the field:
We never yet made doubt but Rome was ready
To answer us.

TULLUS AUFIDIUS.

　　　　　　Nor did you think it folly
To keep your great pretences veil'd till when
They needs must show themselves; which in the
　　hatching,
It seem'd, appeared to Rome. By the discovery
We shall be shorten'd in our aim; which was,
To take in many towns, ere, almost, Rome
Should know we were afoot.

SECOND SENATOR.

　　　　　　Noble Aufidius,
Take your commission; hie you to your bands:
Let us alone to guard Corioli:
If they set down before's, for the remove
Bring up your army; but, I think, you'll find
Th'have not prepared for us.

TULLUS AUFIDIUS.

　　　　　　O, doubt not that;
I speak from certainties. Nay, more,
Some parcels of their power are forth already,
And only hitherward. I leave your honours.

If we and Caius Marcius chance to meet,
'Tis sworn between us, we shall ever strike
Till one can do no more.
                    ALL.
                    The gods assist you!
          TULLUS AUFIDIUS.
And keep your honours safe!
          FIRST SENATOR.
                    Farewell.
          SECOND SENATOR.
                              Farewell.
                    ALL.
Farewell.   [Exeunt.

                    SCENE III.

     Rome.   A room in MARCIUS' house.

Enter VOLUMNIA and VIRGILIA, mother and
     wife to MARCIUS: they set them down on two low
     stools, and sew.

                    VOLUMNIA.

I PRAY you, daughter, sing; or express your-
     self in a more comfortable sort: if my son were
my husband, I should freelier rejoice in that absence wherein he won honour than in the embracements of his bed where he would show most
love. When yet he was but tender-bodied, and
the only son of my womb; when youth with come-
liness pluckt all gaze his way; when, for a day of
kings' entreaties, a mother should not sell him an
hour from her beholding; I—considering how
honour would become such a person; that it was
no better than picture-like to hang by the wall, if
renown made it not stir—was pleased to let him
seek danger where he was like to find fame. To a
cruel war I sent him: from whence he return'd,
his brows bound with oak. I tell thee, daughter, I
sprang not more in joy at first hearing he was a
man-child than now in first seeing he had proved
himself a man.
                    VIRGILIA.
But had he died in the business, madam,—how
then?
                    VOLUMNIA.
Then his good report should have been my son; I
therein would have found issue. Hear me profess
sincerely, had I a dozen sons, each in my love
alike, and none less dear than thine and my good
Marcius, I had rather had eleven die nobly for
their country than one voluptuously surfeit out of
action.
          Enter a GENTLEWOMAN.
                    GENTLEWOMAN.
Madam, the Lady Valeria is come to visit you.
                    VIRGILIA.
Beseech you, give me leave to retire myself.
                    VOLUMNIA.
Indeed, you shall not.
Methinks I hear hither your husband's drum;
See him pluck Aufidius down by the hair;
As children from a bear, the Volsces shunning
     him;
Methinks I see him stamp thus, and call thus,—
'Come on, you cowards! you were got in fear,
Though you were born in Rome:' his bloody
     brow

With his mail'd hand then wiping, forth he goes,
Like to a harvest-man, that's taskt to mow
Or all, or lose his hire.
                    VIRGILIA.
His bloody brow! O Jupiter, no blood!
                    VOLUMNIA.
Away, you fool! it more becomes a man
Than gilt his trophy: the breasts of Hecuba,
When she did suckle Hector, lookt not lovelier
Than Hector's forehead when it spit forth blood
At Grecian sword, contemning.—Tell Valeria
We are fit to bid her welcome.
                    [Exit GENTLEWOMAN.
                    VIRGILIA.
Heavens bless my lord from fell Aufidius!
                    VOLUMNIA.
He'll beat Aufidius' head below his knee,
And tread upon his neck.
          Enter VALERIA with USHER and a
                    GENTLEWOMAN.
                    VALERIA.
My ladies both, good day to you.
                    VOLUMNIA.
Sweet madam.
                    VIRGILIA.
I am glad to see your ladyship.
                    VALERIA.
How do you both? you are manifest house-
keepers. What are you sewing here? A fine spot,
in good faith.—How does your little son?
                    VIRGILIA.
I thank your ladyship; well, good madam.
                    VOLUMNIA.
He had rather see the swords, and hear a drum,
than look upon his schoolmaster.
                    VALERIA.
O' my word, the father's son: I'll swear, 'tis a very
pretty boy. O'my troth, I lookt upon him o'
Wednesday half an hour together: has such a confirm'd countenance. I saw him run after a gilded
butterfly; and when he caught it, he let it go again;
and after it again; and over and over he comes,
and up again; catcht it again: or whether his fall
enraged him, or how 'twas, he did so set his teeth,
and tear it: O, I warrant, how he mammockt it!
                    VOLUMNIA.
One on's father's moods.
                    VALERIA.
Indeed, la, 'tis a noble child.
                    VIRGILIA.
A crack, madam.
                    VALERIA.
Come, lay aside your stitchery: I must have you
play the idle huswife with me this afternoon.
                    VIRGILIA.
No, good madam; I will not out of doors.
                    VALERIA.
Not out of doors!
                    VOLUMNIA.
She shall, she shall.
                    VIRGILIA.
Indeed, no, by your patience; I'll not over the
threshold till my lord return from the wars.
                    VALERIA.
Fie, you confine yourself most unreasonably:
come, you must go visit the good lady that lies in.

VIRGILIA.

I will wish her speedy strength, and visit her with
my prayers; but I cannot go thither.

VOLUMNIA.

Why, I pray you?

VIRGILIA.

'Tis not to save labour, nor that I want love.

VALERIA.

You would be another Penelope: yet, they say, all
the yarn she spun in Ulysses' absence did but fill
Ithaca full of moths. Come; I would your cambric
were sensible as your finger, that you might leave
pricking it for pity. Come, you shall go with us.

VIRGILIA.

No, good madam, pardon me; indeed, I will not
forth.

VALERIA.

In truth, la, go with me; and I'll tell you excellent
news of your husband.

VIRGILIA.

O, good madam, there can be none yet.

VALERIA.

Verily, I do not jest with you; there came news
from him last night.

VIRGILIA.

Indeed, madam?

VALERIA.

In earnest, it's true; I heard a senator speak it.
Thus it is:—The Volsces have an army forth;
against whom Cominius the general is gone, with
one part of our Roman power: your lord and
Titus Lartius are set down before their city
Corioli; they nothing doubt prevailing, and to
make it brief wars. This is true, on mine honour;
and so, I pray, go with us.

VIRGILIA.

Give me excuse, good madam; I will obey you in
every thing hereafter.

VOLUMNIA.

Let her alone, lady: as she is now, she will but
disease our better mirth.

VALERIA.

In troth, I think she would.—Fare you well, then.
—Come, good sweet lady.—Prithee, Virgilia, turn
thy solemness out o'door, and go along with us.

VIRGILIA.

No, at a word, madam; indeed, I must not. I wish
you much mirth.

VALERIA.

Well, then, farewell.　　　　　　　　　[Exeunt.

SCENE IV.

Before Corioli.

Enter MARCIUS, TITUS LARTIUS, *with drum and
colours, with* CAPTAINS *and* SOLDIERS, *as before the city Corioli: to them a* MESSENGER.

CAIUS MARCIUS.

YONDER comes news:—a wager they have
met.

TITUS LARTIUS.

My horse to yours, no.

CAIUS MARCIUS.

'Tis done.

TITUS LARTIUS.

Agreed.

CAIUS MARCIUS.

Say, has our general met the enemy?

MESSENGER.

They lie in view; but have not spoke as yet.

TITUS LARTIUS.

So, the good horse is mine.

CAIUS MARCIUS.

I'll buy him of you.

TITUS LARTIUS.

No, I'll nor sell nor give him; lend you him I will
For half a hundred years.—Summon the town.

CAIUS MARCIUS.

How far off lie these armies?

MESSENGER.

Within this mile and half.

CAIUS MARCIUS.

Then shall we hear their 'larum, and they ours.—
Now, Mars, I prithee, make us quick in work,
That we with smoking swords may march from
hence,
To help our fielded friends!—Come, blow thy
blast.

They sound a parley. Enter two SENATORS *with
others on the walls of Corioli.*

Tullus Aufidius, is he within your walls?

FIRST SENATOR.

No, nor a man that fears you less than he,
That's lesser than a little. [*Drum afar off.*] Hark,
our drums
Are bringing forth our youth! we'll break our
walls,
Rather than they shall pound us up: our gates,
Which yet seem shut, we have but pinn'd with
rushes;
They'll open of themselves. [*Alarum afar off.*]
Hark you, far off!
There is Aufidius; list, what work he makes
Amongst your cloven army.

CAIUS MARCIUS.

O, they're at it!

TITUS LARTIUS.

Their noise be our instruction.—Ladders, ho!

Enter the ARMY *of the* VOLSCES.

CAIUS MARCIUS.

They fear us not, but issue forth their city.
Now put your shields before your hearts, and
fight
With hearts more proof than shields.—Advance,
brave Titus:
They do disdain us much beyond our thoughts,
Which makes me sweat with wrath.—Come on,
my fellows:
He that retires, I'll take him for a Volsce,
And he shall feel mine edge.

Alarum. The ROMANS *are beat back to their
trenches.*

Enter MARCIUS, *cursing.*

CAIUS MARCIUS.

All the contagion of the south light on you,
You shames of Rome! you herd of—Boils and
plagues
Plaster you o'er; that you may be abhorr'd
Further than seen, and one infect another
Against the wind a mile! You souls of geese,
That bear the shapes of men, how have you run
From slaves that apes would beat! Pluto and hell!

All hurt behind; backs red, and faces pale
With flight and agued fear! Mend, and charge
   home,
Or, by the fires of heaven, I'll leave the foe,
And make my wars on you: look to't: come on;
If you'll stand fast, we'll beat them to their wives,
As they us to our trenches. Follow's.
    Another alarum, and MARCIUS *follows the*
      VOLSCES *to the gates, and is shut in.*
So, now the gates are ope:—now prove good
   seconds:
'Tis for the followers fortune widens them,
Not for the fliers: mark me, and do the like.
                 [Enters the gates.
       FIRST SOLDIER.
Fool-hardiness; not I.
        SECOND SOLDIER.
         Nor I.
       FIRST SOLDIER.
See, they have shut him in.
         ALL.
          To the pot, I warrant him.
                [Alarum continues.
     Enter TITUS LARTIUS.
       TITUS LARTIUS.
What is become of Marcius?
         ALL.
          Slain, sir, doubtless.
       FIRST SOLDIER.
Following the fliers at the very heels,
With them he enters; who, upon the sudden,
Clapt-to their gates: he is himself alone,
To answer all the city.
       TITUS LARTIUS.
         O noble fellow!
Who, sensible, outdares his senseless sword,
And, when it bows, stands up! Thou art left,
   Marcius:
A carbuncle entire, as big as thou art,
Were not so rich a jewel. Thou wast a soldier
Even to Cato's wish, not fierce and terrible
Only in strokes, but, with thy grim looks and
The thunder-like percussion of thy sounds,
Thou madest thine enemies shake, as if the world
Were feverous and did tremble.
     Enter MARCIUS, *bleeding, assaulted by the*
      enemy.
       FIRST SOLDIER.
         Look, sir.
       TITUS LARTIUS.
         O, 'tis Marcius!
Let's fetch him off, or make remain alike.
      [They fight, and all enter the city.

SCENE V.

Within Corioli. A street.

Enter certain ROMANS, *with spoils.*

       FIRST ROMAN.
THIS will I carry to Rome.
       SECOND ROMAN.
And I this.
       THIRD ROMAN.
A murrain on't! I took this for silver.
      [Alarum continues still afar off.

    Enter MARCIUS *and* TITUS LARTIUS *with a*
      trumpet.
       CAIUS MARCIUS.
See here these movers that do prize their hours
At a crackt drachma! Cushions, leaden spoons,
Irons of a doit, doublets that hangmen would
Bury with those that wore them, these base slaves,
Ere yet the fight be done, pack up:—down with
   them!—
And hark, what noise the general makes!—To him!
There is the man of my soul's hate, Aufidius,
Piercing our Romans: then, valiant Titus, take
Convenient numbers to make good the city;
Whilst I, with those that have the spirit, will haste
To help Cominius.
       TITUS LARTIUS.
         Worthy sir, thou bleed'st;
Thy exercise hath been too violent
For a second course of fight.
       CAIUS MARCIUS.
         Sir, praise me not;
My work hath yet not warm'd me: fare you well:
The blood I drop is rather physical
Than dangerous to me: to Aufidius thus
I will appear, and fight.
       TITUS LARTIUS.
         Now the fair goddess, Fortune,
Fall deep in love with thee; and her great charms
Misguide thy opposers' swords! Bold gentleman,
Prosperity be thy page!
       CAIUS MARCIUS.
         Thy friend no less
Than those she placeth highest! So, farewell.
       TITUS LARTIUS.
Thou worthiest Marcius!—   *[Exit* MARCIUS.
Go, sound thy trumpet in the market-place;
Call thither all the officers o'the town,
Where they shall know our mind: away! *[Exeunt.*

SCENE VI.

Near the camp of COMINIUS.

Enter COMINIUS, *as it were in retire, with*
      SOLDIERS.
       COMINIUS.
BREATHE you, my friends: well fought; we
   are come off
Like Romans, neither foolish in our stands
Nor cowardly in retire: believe me, sirs,
We shall be charged again. Whiles we have struck,
By interims and conveying gusts we have heard
The charges of our friends.—Ye Roman gods,
Lead their successes as we wish our own,
That both our powers, with smiling fronts en-
May give you thankful sacrifice!   [countering,
     Enter a MESSENGER.
              Thy news?
       MESSENGER.
The citizens of Corioli have issued,
And given to Lartius and to Marcius battle:
I saw our party to their trenches driven,
And then I came away.
       COMINIUS.
         Though thou speak'st truth,
Methinks thou speak'st not well. How long is't
   since?

MESSENGER.

Above an hour, my lord.

COMINIUS.

'Tis not a mile; briefly we heard their drums:
How couldst thou in a mile confound an hour,
And bring thy news so late?

MESSENGER.

Spies of the Volsces
Held me in chase, that I was forced to wheel
Three or four miles about; else had I, sir,
Half an hour since brought my report.

COMINIUS.

Who's yonder,
That does appear as he were flay'd? O gods!
He has the stamp of Marcius; and I have
Before-time seen him thus.

CAIUS MARCIUS [within].

Come I too late?

COMINIUS.

The shepherd knows not thunder from a tabor,
More than I know the sound of Marcius' tongue
From every meaner man.

Enter MARCIUS.

CAIUS MARCIUS.

Come I too late?

COMINIUS.

Ay, if you come not in the blood of others,
But mantled in your own.

CAIUS MARCIUS.

O, let me clip ye
In arms as sound as when I woo'd; in heart
As merry as when our nuptial day was done,
And tapers burnt to bedward!

COMINIUS.

Flower of warriors,
How is't with Titus Lartius?

CAIUS MARCIUS.

As with a man busied about decrees:
Condemning some to death, and some to exile;
Ransoming him or pitying, threatening the other;
Holding Corioli in the name of Rome,
Even like a fawning greyhound in the leash,
To let him slip at will.

COMINIUS.

Where is that slave
Which told me they had beat you to your
trenches?
Where is he? call him hither.

CAIUS MARCIUS.

Let him alone;
He did inform the truth: but for our gentlemen,
The common file—a plague!—tribunes for
them!—
The mouse ne'er shunn'd the cat as they did
budge
From rascals worse than they.

COMINIUS.

But how prevail'd you?

CAIUS MARCIUS.

Will the time serve to tell? I do not think.
Where is the enemy? are you lords o'the field?
If not, why cease you till you are so?

COMINIUS.

Marcius,
We have at disadvantage fought, and did
Retire, to win our purpose.

CAIUS MARCIUS.

How lies their battle? know you on which side
They have placed their men of trust?

COMINIUS.

As I guess, Marcius,
Their bands i'the vaward are the Antiates,
Of their best trust; o'er them Aufidius,
Their very heart of hope.

CAIUS MARCIUS.

I do beseech you,
By all the battles wherein we have fought,
By th'blood we have shed together, by the vows
We have made to endure friends, that you directly
Set me against Aufidius and his Antiates;
And that you not delay the present, but,
Filling the air with swords advanced and darts,
We prove this very hour.

COMINIUS.

Though I could wish
You were conducted to a gentle bath,
And balms applied to you, yet dare I never
Deny your asking: take your choice of those
That best can aid your action.

CAIUS MARCIUS.

Those are they
That most are willing.—If any such be here—
As it were sin to doubt—that love this painting
Wherein you see me smear'd; if any fear
Lesser his person than an ill report;
If any think brave death outweighs bad life,
And that his country's dearer than himself;
Let him alone, or so many so minded,
Wave thus, to express his disposition,
And follow Marcius.

[*They all shout, and wave their swords; take him
up in their arms, and cast up their caps.*

O, me alone! make you a sword of me?
If these shows be not outward, which of you
But is four Volsces? none of you but is
Able to bear against the great Aufidius
A shield as hard as his. A certain number,
Though thanks to all, must I select from all: the
rest
Shall bear the business in some other fight,
As cause will be obey'd. Please you to march;
And four shall quickly draw out my command,
Which men are best inclined.

COMINIUS.

March on, my fellows:
Make good this ostentation, and you shall
Divide in all with us.   [*Exeunt.*

SCENE VII.

The gates of Corioli.

TITUS LARTIUS, *having set a guard upon Corioli,
going with drum and trumpet toward* COMINIUS
and CAIUS MARCIUS, *enters with a* LIEUTEN-
ANT, *other* SOLDIERS, *and a* SCOUT.

TITUS LARTIUS.

SO, let the ports be guarded: keep your duties,
As I have set them down. If I do send, dis-
patch
Those centuries to our aid; the rest will serve
For a short holding: if we lose the field,
We cannot keep the town.

LIEUTENANT.
         Fear not our care, sir.
TITUS LARTIUS.
Hence, and shut your gates upon's.—
Our guider, come; to the Roman camp conduct us.
                    [*Exeunt.*

SCENE VIII.

*A field of battle between the Roman and the
Volscian camps.*

Alarum as in battle.   Enter MARCIUS *and*
AUFIDIUS *at several doors.*

CAIUS MARCIUS.
I'LL fight with none but thee; for I do hate thee
  Worse than a promise-breaker.
TULLUS AUFIDIUS.
            We hate alike:
Not Afric owns a serpent I abhor
More than thy fame I envy. Fix thy foot.
CAIUS MARCIUS.
Let the first budger die the other's slave,
And the gods doom him after!
TULLUS AUFIDIUS.
           If I fly, Marcius,
Halloo me like a hare.
CAIUS MARCIUS.
         Within these three hours, Tullus,
Alone I fought in your Corioli walls,
And made what work I pleased: 'tis not my blood
Wherein thou seest me maskt; for thy revenge
Wrench up thy power to the highest.
TULLUS AUFIDIUS.
            Wert thou the Hector
That was the whip of your bragg'd progeny,
Thou shouldst not scape me here.
    [*Here they fight, and certain* VOLSCES *come
      in the aid of* AUFIDIUS. MARCIUS
      fights till they be driven in breathless.*
Officious, and not valiant,—you have shamed me
In your condemned seconds.   [*Exeunt.*

SCENE IX.

The Roman camp.

Flourish.   *Alarum.*   *A retreat is sounded.*   Enter,
at one door, COMINIUS with the ROMANS; at
another door, MARCIUS, with his arm in a
scarf.

COMINIUS.
IF I should tell thee o'er this thy day's work,
  Thou'lt not believe thy deeds: but I'll report it,
Where senators shall mingle tears with smiles;
Where great patricians shall attend, and shrug,
I'the end admire; where ladies shall be frighted,
And, gladly quaked, hear more; where the dull
    tribunes,
That, with the fusty plebeians, hate thine hon-
    ours,
Shall say, against their hearts, 'We thank the
    gods
Our Rome hath such a soldier!'
Yet camest thou to a morsel of this feast,
Having fully dined before.

Enter TITUS LARTIUS, *with his power, from the
pursuit.*

TITUS LARTIUS.
         O general,
Here is the steed, we the caparison:
Hadst thou beheld—
CAIUS MARCIUS.
        Pray now, no more: my mother,
Who has a charter to extol her blood,
When she does praise me grieves me. I have
    done
As you have done,—that's what I can; induced
As you have been,—that's for my country:
He that has but effected his good will
Hath overta'en mine act.
COMINIUS.
          You shall not be
The grave of your deserving; Rome must know
The value of her own: 'twere a concealment
Worse than a theft, no less than a traducement,
To hide your doings; and to silence that,
Which, to the spire and top of praises voucht,
Would seem but modest: therefore, I beseech
    you—
In sign of what you are, not to reward
What you have done—before our army hear me.
CAIUS MARCIUS.
I have some wounds upon me, and they smart
To hear themselves remember'd.
COMINIUS.
           Should they not,
Well might they fester 'gainst ingratitude,
And tent themselves with death. Of all the
    horses,—
Whereof we have ta'en good, and good store,—of
    all
The treasure in this field achieved and city,
We render you the tenth; to be ta'en forth,
Before the common distribution,
At your only choice.
CAIUS MARCIUS.
         I thank you, general;
But cannot make my heart consent to take
A bribe to pay my sword: I do refuse it;
And stand upon my common part with those
That have beheld the doing.
    [*A long flourish.*   *They all cry, '*Marcius!
      Marcius!' *cast up their caps and lances:*
      COMINIUS *and* LARTIUS *stand bare.*
CAIUS MARCIUS.
May these same instruments, which you profane,
Never sound more! When drums and trumpets
    shall
I'the field prove flatterers, let courts and cities be
Made all of false-faced soothing! When steel
    grows
Soft as the parasite's silk, let him be made
A coverture for the wars! No more, I say!
For that I have not washt my nose that bled,
Or foil'd some debile wretch,—which, without
    note,
Here's many else have done,—you shout me
    forth
In acclamations hyperbolical;
As if I loved my little should be dieted
In praises sauced with lies.

COMINIUS.
Too modest are you;
More cruel to your good report than grateful
To us that give you truly: by your patience,
If 'gainst yourself you be incensed, we'll put
    you—
Like one that means his proper harm—in mana-
    cles,
Then reason safely with you. Therefore, be it
    known,
As to us, to all the world, that Caius Marcius
Wears this war's garland: in token of the which,
My noble steed, known to the camp, I give him,
With all his trim belonging; and from this
    time,
For what he did before Corioli, call him,
With all the applause and clamour of the host,
CAIUS MARCIUS CORIOLANUS.—Bear
The addition nobly ever!
          [*Flourish.   Trumpets sound and drums.*
ALL.
Caius Marcius Coriolanus!
CAIUS MARCIUS CORIOLANUS.
I will go wash;
And when my face is fair, you shall perceive
Whether I blush or no: howbeit, I thank you:—
I mean to stride your steed; and at all times,
To undercrest your good addition
To the fairness of my power.
COMINIUS.
So, to our tent;
Where, ere we do repose us, we will write
To Rome of our success.—You, Titus Lartius,
Must to Corioli back: send us to Rome
The best, with whom we may articulate,
For their own good and ours.
TITUS LARTIUS.
I shall, my lord.
CAIUS MARCIUS CORIOLANUS.
The gods begin to mock me. I, that now
Refused most princely gifts, am bound to beg
Of my lord general.
COMINIUS.
Take't; 'tis yours. What is't?
CAIUS MARCIUS CORIOLANUS.
I sometime lay, here in Corioli,
At a poor man's house; he used me kindly:—
He cried to me; I saw him prisoner;
But then Aufidius was within my view,
And wrath o'erwhelm'd my pity: I request you
To give my poor host freedom.
COMINIUS.
O, well begg'd!
Were he the butcher of my son, he should
Be free as is the wind.—Deliver him, Titus.
TITUS LARTIUS.
Marcius, his name?
CAIUS MARCIUS CORIOLANUS.
By Jupiter, forgot:—
I am weary; yea, my memory is tired.—
Have we no wine here?
COMINIUS.
Go we to our tent:
The blood upon your visage dries; 'tis time
It should be lookt to: come.   [*Exeunt.*

SCENE X.

The camp of the VOLSCES.

A flourish.   Cornets.   Enter TULLUS AUFIDIUS
bloody, with two or three SOLDIERS.

TULLUS AUFIDIUS.
THE town is ta'en!
FIRST SOLDIER.
'Twill be deliver'd back on good condition.
TULLUS AUFIDIUS.
Condition!—
I would I were a Roman; for I cannot,
Being a Volsce, be that I am.—Condition!
What good condition can a treaty find
I'the part that is at mercy?—Five times, Marcius,
I have fought with thee; so often hast thou beat me;
And wouldst do so, I think, should we encounter
As often as we eat.—By the elements,
If e'er again I meet him beard to beard,
He's mine, or I am his: mine emulation
Hath not that honour in't it had; for where
I thought to crush him in an equal force,
True sword to sword, I'll potch at him some way,
Or wrath or craft may get him.
FIRST SOLDIER.
He's the devil.
TULLUS AUFIDIUS.
Bolder, though not so subtle. My valour's poison'd
With only suffering stain by him; for him
Shall fly out of itself: nor sleep nor sanctuary,
Being naked, sick, nor fane nor Capitol,
The prayers of priests nor times of sacrifice,
Embarquements all of fury, shall lift up
Their rotten privilege and custom 'gainst
My hate to Marcius: where I find him, were it
At home, upon my brother's guard, even there,
Against the hospitable canon, would I
Wash my fierce hand in's heart. Go you to the city;
Learn how 'tis held; and what they are that must
Be hostages for Rome.
FIRST SOLDIER.
Will not you go?
TULLUS AUFIDIUS.
I am attended at the cypress grove: I pray you—
'Tis south the city mills—bring me word thither
How the world goes, that to the pace of it
I may spur on my journey.
FIRST SOLDIER.
I shall, sir.   [*Exeunt.*

ACT II.   SCENE I.

Rome.   A public place.

Enter MENENIUS, *with the two* TRIBUNES *of the
people,* SICINIUS *and* BRUTUS.

MENENIUS AGRIPPA.
THE augurer tells me we shall have news to-
night.
JUNIUS BRUTUS.
Good or bad?
MENENIUS AGRIPPA.
Not according to the prayer of the people, for they
love not Marcius.
SICINIUS VELUTUS.
Nature teaches beasts to know their friends.

MENENIUS AGRIPPA.
Pray you, who does the wolf love?
SICINIUS VELUTUS.
The lamb.
MENENIUS AGRIPPA.
Ay, to devour him; as the hungry plebeians would
the noble Marcius.
JUNIUS BRUTUS.
He's a lamb indeed, that baes like a bear.
MENENIUS AGRIPPA.
He's a bear indeed, that lives like a lamb. You
two are old men: tell me one thing that I shall ask
you.
BOTH.
Well, sir.
MENENIUS AGRIPPA.
In what enormity is Marcius poor in, that you two
have not in abundance?
JUNIUS BRUTUS.
He's poor in no one fault, but stored with all.
SICINIUS VELUTUS.
Especially in pride.
JUNIUS BRUTUS.
And topping all others in boasting.
MENENIUS AGRIPPA.
This is strange now: do you two know how you
are censured here in the city, I mean of us o'the
right-hand file? do you?
BOTH.
Why, how are we censured?
MENENIUS AGRIPPA.
Because you talk of pride now,—will you not be
angry?
BOTH.
Well, well, sir, well.
MENENIUS AGRIPPA.
Why, 'tis no great matter; for a very little thief of
occasion will rob you of a great deal of patience:
give your dispositions the reins, and be angry at
your pleasures; at the least, if you take it as a plea-
sure to you in being so. You blame Marcius for
being proud?
JUNIUS BRUTUS.
We do it not alone, sir.
MENENIUS AGRIPPA.
I know you can do very little alone; for your helps
are many, or else your actions would grow won-
drous single: your abilities are too infant-like for
doing much alone. You talk of pride:—O that you
could turn your eyes toward the napes of your
necks, and make but an interior survey of your
good selves! O that you could!
JUNIUS BRUTUS.
What then, sir?
MENENIUS AGRIPPA.
Why, then you should discover a brace of un-
meriting, proud, violent, testy magistrates, alias
fools, as any in Rome.
SICINIUS VELUTUS.
Menenius, you are known well enough too.
MENENIUS AGRIPPA.
I am known to be a humorous patrician, and one
that loves a cup of hot wine with not a drop of
allaying Tiber in't; said to be something imperfect
in favouring the first complaint; hasty and tinder-
like upon too trivial motion; one that converses

more with the buttock of the night than with the
forehead of the morning: what I think I utter and
spend my malice in my breath. Meeting two such
wealsmen as you are,—I cannot call you Lycur-
guses,—if the drink you give me touch my palate
adversely, I make a crooked face at it. I cannot say
your worships have deliver'd the matter well,
when I find the ass in compound with the major
part of your syllables: and though I must be content to bear with those that say you are reverend
grave men, yet they lie deadly that tell you you
have good faces. If you see this in the map of my
microcosm, follows it that I am known well enough
too? what harm can your bisson conspectuities
glean out of this character, if I be known well
enough too?
JUNIUS BRUTUS.
Come, sir, come, we know you well enough.
MENENIUS AGRIPPA.
You know neither me, yourselves, nor any thing.
You are ambitious for poor knaves' caps and legs:
you wear out a good wholesome forenoon in hearing a cause between an orange-wife and a fosset-
seller; and then rejourn the controversy of three-
pence to a second day of audience. When you are
hearing a matter between party and party, if you
chance to be pincht with the colic, you make faces
like mummers; set up the bloody flag against all
patience; and, in roaring for a chamber-pot, dismiss the controversy bleeding, the more entangled
by your hearing: all the peace you make in their
cause is, calling both the parties knaves. You are
a pair of strange ones.
JUNIUS BRUTUS.
Come, come, you are well understood to be a per-
fecter giber for the table than a necessary bencher
in the Capitol.
MENENIUS AGRIPPA.
Our very priests must become mockers, if they
shall encounter such ridiculous subjects as you
are. When you speak best unto the purpose, it is
not worth the wagging of your beards; and your
beards deserve not so honourable a grave as to
stuff a botcher's cushion, or to be entomb'd in an
ass's pack-saddle. Yet you must be saying, Marcius is proud; who, in a cheap estimation, is worth
all your predecessors since Deucalion; though
peradventure some of the best of 'em were hereditary hangmen. God-den to your worships: more
of your conversation would infect my brain, being
the herdsmen of the beastly plebeians: I will be
bold to take my leave of you.
[BRUTUS *and* SICINIUS *go aside.*
Enter VOLUMNIA, VIRGILIA, *and* VALERIA,
with ATTENDANTS.
How now, my as fair as noble ladies,—and the
moon, were she earthly, no nobler,—whither do
you follow your eyes so fast?
VOLUMNIA.
Honourable Menenius, my boy Marcius approaches; for the love of Juno, let's go.
MENENIUS AGRIPPA.
Ha! Marcius coming home!
VOLUMNIA.
Ay, worthy Menenius; and with most prosperous
approbation.

MENENIUS AGRIPPA.

Take my cap, Jupiter, and I thank thee.—Hoo!
Marcius coming home!

VIRGILIA *and* VALERIA.

Nay, 'tis true.

VOLUMNIA.

Look, here's a letter from him: the state hath
another, his wife another; and, I think, there's one
at home for you.

MENENIUS AGRIPPA.

I will make my very house reel to-night:—a letter
for me!

VIRGILIA.

Yes, certain, there's a letter for you; I saw't.

MENENIUS AGRIPPA.

A letter for me! it gives me an estate of seven
years' health; in which time I will make a lip at
the physician: the most sovereign prescription in
Galen is but empiricutic, and, to this preserva-
tive, of no better report than a horse-drench.—Is
he not wounded? he was wont to come home
wounded.

VIRGILIA.

O, no, no, no.

VOLUMNIA.

O, he is wounded; I thank the gods for't.

MENENIUS AGRIPPA.

So do I too, if it be not too much: brings a' victory
in his pocket? the wounds become him.

VOLUMNIA.

On's brows: Menenius, he comes the third time
home with the oaken garland.

MENENIUS AGRIPPA.

Has he disciplined Aufidius soundly?

VOLUMNIA.

Titus Lartius writes,—they fought together, but
Aufidius got off.

MENENIUS AGRIPPA.

And 'twas time for him too, I'll warrant him that:
an he had stay'd by him, I would not have been so
fidius'd for all the chests in Corioli, and the gold
that's in them. Is the senate possest of this?

VOLUMNIA.

Good ladies, let's go.—Yes, yes, yes; the senate
has letters from the general, wherein he gives my
son the whole name of the war: he hath in this
action out-done his former deeds doubly.

VALERIA.

In troth, there's wondrous things spoke of him.

MENENIUS AGRIPPA.

Wondrous! ay, I warrant you, and not without his
true purchasing.

VIRGILIA.

The gods grant them true!

VOLUMNIA.

True! pow, wow.

MENENIUS AGRIPPA.

True! I'll be sworn they are true.—Where is he
wounded?—[*to the* TRIBUNES] God save your
good worships! Marcius is coming home: he has
more cause to be proud.—Where is he wounded?

VOLUMNIA.

I'the shoulder and i'the left arm: there will be large
cicatrices to show the people, when he shall stand
for his place. He received in the repulse of Tarquin
seven hurts i'the body.

MENENIUS AGRIPPA.

One i'the neck, and two i'the thigh,—there's nine
that I know.

VOLUMNIA.

He had, before this last expedition, twenty-five
wounds upon him.

MENENIUS AGRIPPA.

Now it's twenty-seven: every gash was an enemy's
grave. [*A shout and flourish.*] Hark! the trumpets.

VOLUMNIA.

These are the ushers of Marcius: before him he
carries noise, and behind him he leaves tears:
Death, that dark spirit, in's nervy arm doth lie;
Which, being advanced, declines, and then men
die.

A sennet.   *Trumpets sound.*   *Enter* COMINIUS
the General and TITUS LARTIUS; *between them,*
COMINIUS, *crown'd with an oaken garland;*
with CAPTAINS *and* SOLDIERS, *and a* HERALD.

HERALD.

Know, Rome, that all alone Marcius did fight
Within Corioli gates: where he hath won,
With fame, a name to Caius Marcius; these
In honour follows Coriolanus.
Welcome to Rome, renowned Coriolanus!

                                 [*Flourish.*

ALL.

Welcome to Rome, renowned Coriolanus!

CAIUS MARCIUS CORIOLANUS.

No more of this, it does offend my heart;
Pray now, no more.·

COMINIUS.

           Look, sir, your mother!

CAIUS MARCIUS CORIOLANUS.

                                    O,

You have, I know, petition'd all the gods
For my prosperity.   [*Kneels.*

VOLUMNIA.

                Nay, my good soldier, up;
My gentle Marcius, worthy Caius, and
By deed-achieving honour newly named,—
What is it?—Coriolanus must I call thee?—
But, O, thy wife!

CAIUS MARCIUS CORIOLANUS.

                My gracious silence, hail!
Wouldst thou have laugh'd had I come coffin'd
    home,
That weep'st to see me triumph? Ah, my dear,
Such eyes the widows in Corioli wear,
And mothers that lack sons.

MENENIUS AGRIPPA.

                Now, the gods crown thee!

CAIUS MARCIUS CORIOLANUS.

And live you yet?—[*to* VALERIA] O my sweet
lady, pardon.

VOLUMNIA.

I know not where to turn:—O, welcome home;—
And welcome, general; and y'are welcome all.

MENENIUS AGRIPPA.

A hundred thousand welcomes:—I could weep,
And I could laugh; I am light and heavy:—wel-
    come:
A curse begin at very root on's heart
That is not glad to see thee!—You are three
That Rome should dote on: yet, by the faith of
    men,

We have some old crab-trees here at home that
    will not
Be grafted to your relish. Yet welcome, warriors:
We call a nettle but a nettle, and
The faults of fools but folly.
> COMINIUS.
>   Ever right.
> CAIUS MARCIUS CORIOLANUS.
Menenius ever, ever.
> HERALD.
Give way there, and go on!
> CAIUS MARCIUS CORIOLANUS [to VOLUMNIA
> and VIRGILIA].
>   Your hand, and yours:
Ere in our own house I do shade my head,
The good patricians must be visited;
From whom I have received not only greetings,
But with them change of honours.
> VOLUMNIA.
>   I have lived
To see inherited my very wishes,
And the buildings of my fancy: only there
Is one thing wanting, which I doubt not but
Our Rome will cast upon thee.
> CAIUS MARCIUS CORIOLANUS.
>   Know, good mother,
I had rather be their servant in my way
Than sway with them in theirs.
> COMINIUS.
>   On, to the Capitol!
[Flourish. Cornets. Exeunt in state, as before.
BRUTUS and SICINIUS come forward.
> JUNIUS BRUTUS.
All tongues speak of him, and the bleared sights
Are spectacled to see him: your prattling nurse
Into a rapture lets her baby cry
While she chats him: the kitchen malkin pins
Her richest lockram 'bout her reechy neck,
Clamb'ring the walls to eye him: stalls, bulks,
    windows,
Are smother'd up, leads fill'd, and ridges horsed
With variable complexions; all agreeing
In earnestness to see him: seld-shown flamens
Do press among tle popular throngs, and puff
To win a vulgar station: our veil'd dames
Commit the war of white and damask in
Their nicely-gawded cheeks to the wanton spoil
Of Phœbus' burning kisses: such a pother,
As if that whatsoever god who leads him
Were slily crept into his human powers,
And gave him graceful posture.
> SICINIUS VELUTUS.
>   On the sudden,
I warrant him consul.
> JUNIUS BRUTUS.
>   Then our office may,
During his power, go sleep.
> SICINIUS VELUTUS.
He cannot temperately transport his honours
From where he should begin and end; but will
Lose those he hath won.
> JUNIUS BRUTUS.
>   In that there's comfort.
> SICINIUS VELUTUS.
>   Doubt not
The commoners, for whom we stand, but they,

Upon their ancient malice, will forget,
With the least cause, these his new honours; which
That he will give them make I as little question
As he is proud to do't.
> JUNIUS BRUTUS.
>   I heard him swear,
Were he to stand for consul, never would he
Appear i'the market-place, nor on him put
The napless vesture of humility;
Nor, showing, as the manner is, his wounds
To the people, beg their stinking breaths.
> SICINIUS VELUTUS.
>   'Tis right.
> JUNIUS BRUTUS.
It was his word: O, he would miss it, rather
Than carry it but by the suit of the gentry to him,
And the desire of the nobles.
> SICINIUS VELUTUS.
>   I wish no better
Than have him hold that purpose, and to put it
In execution.
> JUNIUS BRUTUS.
>   'Tis most like he will.
> SICINIUS VELUTUS.
It shall be to him, then, as our good wills,
A sure destruction.
> JUNIUS BRUTUS.
>   So it must fall out
To him or our authorities. For an end,
We must suggest the people in what hatred
He still hath held them; that to's power he would
Have made them mules, silenced their pleaders,
    and
Dispropertied their freedoms; holding them,
In human action and capacity,
Of no more soul nor fitness for the world
Than camels in the war; who have their provand
Only for bearing burdens, and sore blows
For sinking under them.
> SICINIUS VELUTUS.
>   This, as you say, suggested
At some time when his soaring insolence
Shall touch the people,—which time shall not
If he be put upon't; and that's as easy   [want,
As to set dogs on sheep,—will be his fire
To kindle their dry stubble; and their blaze
Shall darken him for ever.
> Enter a MESSENGER.
> JUNIUS BRUTUS.
>   What's the matter?
> MESSENGER.
You are sent for to the Capitol. 'Tis thought
That Marcius shall be consul:
I have seen the dumb men throng to see him, and
The blind to hear him speak: matrons flung gloves,
Ladies and maids their scarfs and handkerchers,
Upon him as he past: the nobles bended,
As to Jove's statue; and the commons made
A shower and thunder with their caps and shouts:
I never saw the like.
> JUNIUS BRUTUS.
>   Let's to the Capitol;
And carry with us ears and eyes for the time,
But hearts for the event.
> SICINIUS VELUTUS.
>   Have with you. [Exeunt.

SCENE II.

The same. The Capitol.

Enter two OFFICERS, *to lay cushions, as it were, in the Capitol.*

FIRST OFFICER.

COME, come, they are almost here. How many stand for consulships?

SECOND OFFICER.

Three, they say: but 'tis thought of every one Coriolanus will carry it.

FIRST OFFICER.

That's a brave fellow; but he's vengeance proud, and loves not the common people.

SECOND OFFICER.

Faith, there have been many great men that have flatter'd the people, who ne'er loved them; and there be many that they have loved, they know not wherefore: so that, if they love they know not why, they hate upon no better a ground: therefore, for Coriolanus neither to care whether they love or hate him manifests the true knowledge he has in their disposition; and, out of his noble careless-ness, lets them plainly see't.

FIRST OFFICER.

If he did not care whether he had their love or no, he'd waved indifferently 'twixt doing them neither good nor harm: but he seeks their hate with greater devotion than they can render it him; and leaves nothing undone that may fully dis-cover him their opposite. Now, to seem to affect the malice and displeasure of the people is as bad as that which he dislikes,—to flatter them for their love.

SECOND OFFICER.

He hath deserved worthily of his country: and his ascent is not by such easy degrees as those who, having been supple and courteous to the people, bonneted, without any further deed to heave them at all into their estimation and report: but he hath so planted his honours in their eyes, and his actions in their hearts, that for their tongues to be silent, and not confess so much, were a kind of ingrateful injury; to report otherwise were a mal-ice, that, giving itself the lie, would pluck reproof and rebuke from every ear that heard it.

FIRST OFFICER.

No more of him; he's a worthy man: make way, they are coming.

A sennet. Enter the PATRICIANS *and the* TRIB-UNES *of the People,* LICTORS *before them:* CORIOLANUS, MENENIUS, COMINIUS *the Consul:* SICINIUS *and* BRUTUS *take their places by themselves:* CORIOLANUS *stands.*

MENENIUS AGRIPPA.

Having determined of the Volsces, and
To send for Titus Lartius, it remains,
As the main point of this our after-meeting,
To gratify his noble service that
Hath thus stood for his country: therefore, please you,
Most reverend and grave elders, to desire
The present consul, and last general
In our well-found successes, to report
A little of that worthy work perform'd
By Caius Marcius Coriolanus; whom

We meet here, both to thank, and to remember
With honours like himself.

FIRST SENATOR.

Speak, good Cominius:
Leave nothing out for length, and make us think
Rather our state's defective for requital
Than we to stretch it out.—[*to the* TRIBUNES]
Masters o'the people,
We do request your kindest ears; and, after,
Your loving motion toward the common body,
To yield what passes here.

SICINIUS VELUTUS.

We are convented
Upon a pleasing treaty; and have hearts
Inclinable to honour and advance
The theme of our assembly.

JUNIUS BRUTUS.

Which the rather
We shall be blest to do, if he remember
A kinder value of the people than
He hath hereto prized them at.

MENENIUS AGRIPPA.

That's off, that's off;
I would you rather had been silent. Please you
To hear Cominius speak?

JUNIUS BRUTUS.

Most willingly:
But yet my caution was more pertinent
Than the rebuke you give it.

MENENIUS AGRIPPA.

He loves your people;
But tie him not to be their bedfellow.—
Worthy Cominius, speak.—[CORIOLANUS *rises, and offers to go away.*] Nay, keep your place.

FIRST SENATOR.

Sit, Coriolanus; never shame to hear
What you have nobly done.

CAIUS MARCIUS CORIOLANUS.

Your honours' pardon:
I had rather have my wounds to heal again
Than hear say how I got them.

JUNIUS BRUTUS.

Sir, I hope
My words disbencht you not.

CAIUS MARCIUS CORIOLANUS.

No, sir: yet oft,
When blows have made me stay, I fled from words.
You sooth'd not, therefore hurt not: but your people,
I love them as they weigh.

MENENIUS AGRIPPA.

Pray now, sit down.

CAIUS MARCIUS CORIOLANUS.

I had rather have one scratch my head i'the sun,
When the alarum were struck, than idly sit
To hear my nothings monster'd.   [*Exit.*

MENENIUS AGRIPPA.

Masters of the people,
Your multiplying spawn how can he flatter—
That's thousand to one good one—when you now see
He had rather venture all his limbs for honour
Than one on's ears to hear't?—Proceed, Cominius.

COMINIUS.

I shall lack voice: the deeds of Coriolanus
Should not be utter'd feebly.—It is held

That valour is the chiefest virtue, and
Most dignifies the haver: if it be,
The man I speak of cannot in the world
Be singly counterpoised. At sixteen years,
When Tarquin made a head for Rome, he fought
Beyond the mark of others: our then dictator,
Whom with all praise I point at, saw him fight,
When with his Amazonian chin he drove
The bristled lips before him: he bestrid
An o'er-prest Roman, and i'the consul's view
Slew three opposers: Tarquin's self he met,
And struck him on his knee: in that day's feats,
When he might act the woman in the scene,
He proved best man i'the field, and for his meed
Was brow-bound with the oak. His pupil age
Man-enter'd thus, he waxed like a sea;
And, in the brunt of seventeen battles since,
He lurcht all swords of the garland. For this last,
Before and in Corioli, let me say,
I cannot speak him home: he stopt the fliers;
And by his rare example made the coward
Turn terror into sport: as weeds before
A vessel under sail, so men obey'd,
And fell below his stem: his sword, death's
    stamp
Where it did mark, it took; from face to foot
He was a thing of blood, whose every motion
Was timed with dying cries: alone he enter'd
The mortal gate of the city, which he painted
With shunless destiny; aidless came off,
And with a sudden re-enforcement struck
Corioli like a planet: now all's his:
When, by and by, the din of war gan pierce
His ready sense; then straight his doubled spirit
Re-quicken'd what in flesh was fatigate,
And to the battle came he; where he did
Run reeking o'er the lives of men, as if
'Twere a perpetual spoil: and till we call'd
Both field and city ours, he never stood
To ease his breast with panting.
        MENENIUS AGRIPPA.
                      Worthy man!
        FIRST SENATOR.
He cannot but with measure fit the honours
Which we devise him.
        COMINIUS.
                Our spoils he kickt at;
And lookt upon things precious as they were
The common muck of the world: he covets less
Than misery itself would give; rewards
His deeds with doing them; and is content
To spend the time to end it.
        MENENIUS AGRIPPA.
                  He's right noble:
Let him be call'd for.
        FIRST SENATOR.
                Call Coriolanus.
        OFFICER.
He doth appear.
        Enter CORIOLANUS.
        MENENIUS AGRIPPA.
The senate, Coriolanus, are well pleased
To make thee consul.
        CAIUS MARCIUS CORIOLANUS.
                I do owe them still
My life and services.

        MENENIUS AGRIPPA.
                It then remains
That you do speak to the people.
        CAIUS MARCIUS CORIOLANUS.
                  I do beseech you,
Let me o'erleap that custom, for I cannot
Put on the gown, stand naked, and entreat them,
For my wounds' sake, to give their suffrage: please
    you
That I may pass this doing.
        SICINIUS VELUTUS.
                  Sir, the people
Must have their voices; neither will they bate
One jot of ceremony.
        MENENIUS AGRIPPA.
                Put them not to't:—
Pray you, go fit you to the custom; and
Take to you, as your predecessors have,
Your honour with your form.
        CAIUS MARCIUS CORIOLANUS.
                  It is a part
That I shall blush in acting, and might well
Be taken from the people.
        JUNIUS BRUTUS [*to* SICINIUS].
                Mark you that?
        CAIUS MARCIUS CORIOLANUS.
To brag unto them,—thus I did, and thus;—
Show them th'unaching scars which I should hide,
As if I had received them for the hire
Of their breath only!—
        MENENIUS AGRIPPA.
                Do not stand upon't.—
We recommend to you, tribunes of the people,
Our purpose to them;—and to our noble consul
Wish we all joy and honour.
        SENATORS.
To Coriolanus come all joy and honour!
        [*Flourish of cornets. Exeunt all but* BRUTUS *and* SICINIUS.
        JUNIUS BRUTUS.
You see how he intends to use the people.
        SICINIUS VELUTUS.
May they perceive's intent! He will require them,
As if he did contemn what he requested
Should be in them to give.
        JUNIUS BRUTUS.
                Come, we'll inform them
Of our proceedings here: on the market-place
I know they do attend us.   [*Exeunt.*

SCENE III.

The same. The Forum.

Enter seven or eight CITIZENS.

        FIRST CITIZEN.
ONCE, if he do require our voices, we ought
not to deny him.
        SECOND CITIZEN.
We may, sir, if we will.
        THIRD CITIZEN.
We have power in ourselves to do it, but it is a
power that we have no power to do: for if he show
us his wounds, and tell us his deeds, we are to put
our tongues into those wounds, and speak for
them; so, if he tell us his noble deeds, we must

also tell him our noble acceptance of them. Ingratitude is monstrous: and for the multitude to
be ingrateful, were to make a monster of the
multitude; of the which we being members,
should bring ourselves to be monstrous members.

FIRST CITIZEN.
And to make us no better thought of, a little help
will serve; for once we stood up about the corn,
he himself stuck not to call us the many-headed
multitude.

THIRD CITIZEN.
We have been call'd so of many; not that our heads
are some brown, some black, some abram, some
bald, but that our wits are so diversely colour'd:
and truly I think, if all our wits were to issue out
of one skull, they would fly east, west, north,
south; and their consent of one direct way should
be at once to all the points o'th'compass.

SECOND CITIZEN.
Think you so? Which way do you judge my wit
would fly?

THIRD CITIZEN.
Nay, your wit will not so soon out as another
man's will,—'tis strongly wedged up in a blockhead; but if it were at liberty, 'twould, sure, southward.

SECOND CITIZEN.
Why that way?

THIRD CITIZEN.
To lose itself in a fog; where being three parts
melted away with rotten dews, the fourth would
return for conscience' sake, to help to get thee a
wife.

SECOND CITIZEN.
You are never without your tricks:—you may, you
may.

THIRD CITIZEN.
Are you all resolved to give your voices? But that's
no matter, the greater part carries it. I say, if he
would incline to the people, there was never a
worthier man.—Here he comes, and in the gown
of humility: mark his behaviour. We are not to
stay all together, but to come by him where he
stands, by ones, by twos, and by threes. He's to
make his requests by particulars; wherein every
one of us has a single honour, in giving him our
own voices with our own tongues: therefore follow
me, and I'll direct you how you shall go by him.

ALL.
Content, content.　　　　　　　　[Exeunt.
Enter CORIOLANUS, in a gown of humility, with
MENENIUS.

MENENIUS AGRIPPA.
O sir, you are not right: have you not known
The worthiest men have done't?

CAIUS MARCIUS CORIOLANUS.
　　　　　　　　What must I say?—
'I pray, sir,'—Plague upon't! I cannot bring
My tongue to such a pace. 'Look, sir, my wounds!
I got them in my country's service, when
Some certain of your brethren roar'd, and ran
From the noise of our own drums.'

MENENIUS AGRIPPA.
　　　　　　　　O me, the gods!
You must not speak of that: you must desire them
To think upon you.

CAIUS MARCIUS CORIOLANUS.
　　　　　　　　Think upon me! hang 'em!
I would they would forget me, like the virtues
Which our divines lose by 'em.

MENENIUS AGRIPPA.
　　　　　　　　You'll mar all:
I'll leave you: pray you, speak to 'em, I pray you,
In wholesome manner.

CAIUS MARCIUS CORIOLANUS.
　　　　　　　　Bid them wash their faces,
And keep their teeth clean. [Exit MENENIUS.]—
So, here comes a brace.
　　　Enter two of the CITIZENS.
You know the cause, sir, of my standing here.

FIRST CITIZEN.
We do, sir; tell us what hath brought you to't.

CAIUS MARCIUS CORIOLANUS.
Mine own desert.

SECOND CITIZEN.
Your own desert!

CAIUS MARCIUS CORIOLANUS.
Ay, not mine own desire.

FIRST CITIZEN.
How! not your own desire!

CAIUS MARCIUS CORIOLANUS.
No, sir, 'twas never my desire yet to trouble the
poor with begging.

FIRST CITIZEN.
You must think, if we give you any thing, we hope
to gain by you.

CAIUS MARCIUS CORIOLANUS.
Well, then, I pray, your price o'the consulship?

FIRST CITIZEN.
The price is, to ask it kindly.

CAIUS MARCIUS CORIOLANUS.
Kindly! Sir, I pray, let me ha't: I have wounds to
show you, which shall be yours in private.— Your
good voice, sir; what say you?

SECOND CITIZEN.
You shall ha't, worthy sir.

CAIUS MARCIUS CORIOLANUS.
A match, sir.—There's in all two worthy voices
begg'd.—I have your alms: adieu.

FIRST CITIZEN.
But this is something odd.

SECOND CITIZEN.
An 'twere to give again,—but 'tis no matter.
　　　　　　[Exeunt the two CITIZENS.
　　　Enter two other CITIZENS.

CAIUS MARCIUS CORIOLANUS.
Pray you now, if it may stand with the tune of
your voices that I may be consul, I have here the
customary gown.

THIRD CITIZEN.
You have deserved nobly of your country, and
you have not deserved nobly.

CAIUS MARCIUS CORIOLANUS.
Your enigma?

THIRD CITIZEN.
You have been a scourge to her enemies, you have
been a rod to her friends; you have not, indeed,
loved the common people.

CAIUS MARCIUS CORIOLANUS.
You should account me the more virtuous, that
I have not been common in my love. I will, sir,
flatter my sworn brother, the people, to earn a

dearer estimation of them; 'tis a condition they account gentle: and since the wisdom of their choice is rather to have my hat than my heart, I will practise the insinuating nod, and be off to them most counterfeitly; that is, sir, I will counterfeit the bewitchment of some popular man, and give it bountiful to the desirers. Therefore, beseech you I may be consul.

FOURTH CITIZEN.
We hope to find you our friend; and therefore give you our voices heartily.

THIRD CITIZEN.
You have received many wounds for your country.

CAIUS MARCIUS CORIOLANUS.
I will not seal your knowledge with showing them. I will make much of your voices, and so trouble you no further.

BOTH CITIZENS.
The gods give you joy, sir, heartily!   [Exeunt.

CAIUS MARCIUS CORIOLANUS.
Most sweet voices!—
Better it is to die, better to starve,
Than crave the hire which first we do deserve.
Why in this wolvish toge should I stand here,
To beg of Hob and Dick, that do appear,
Their needless vouches? Custom calls me to't:—
What custom wills, in all things should we do't,
The dust on antique time would lie unswept,
And mountainous error be too highly heapt
For truth to o'er-peer. Rather than fool it so,
Let the high office and the honour go
To one that would do thus.—I am half through;
The one part suffer'd, the other will I do.—
Here come moe voices.
          Enter three CITIZENS more.
Your voices: for your voices I have fought;
Watcht for your voices; for your voices bear
Of wounds two dozen odd; battles thrice six
I have seen, and heard of; for your voices have
Done many things, some less, some more: your
Indeed, I would be consul.   [voices:

FIFTH CITIZEN.
He has done nobly, and cannot go without any honest man's voice.

SIXTH CITIZEN.
Therefore let him be consul: the gods give him joy, and make him good friend to the people!

ALL THREE CITIZENS.
Amen, amen.—God save thee, noble consul!
          [Exeunt.

CAIUS MARCIUS CORIOLANUS.
Worthy voices!
Enter MENENIUS, with BRUTUS and SICINIUS.

MENENIUS AGRIPPA.
You have stood your limitation; and the tribunes
Endue you with the people's voice: remains
That, in the official marks invested, you
Anon do meet the senate.

CAIUS MARCIUS CORIOLANUS.
          Is this done?

SICINIUS VELUTUS.
The custom of request you have discharged:
The people do admit you; and are summon'd
To meet anon, upon your approbation.

CAIUS MARCIUS CORIOLANUS.
Where? at the senate-house?

SICINIUS VELUTUS.
          There, Coriolanus.

CAIUS MARCIUS CORIOLANUS.
May I change these garments?

SICINIUS VELUTUS.
          You may, sir.

CAIUS MARCIUS CORIOLANUS.
That I'll straight do; and, knowing myself again,
Repair to the senate-house.

MENENIUS AGRIPPA.
I'll keep you company.—Will you along?

JUNIUS BRUTUS.
We stay here for the people.

SICINIUS VELUTUS.
          Fare you well.
          [Exeunt CORIOLANUS and MENENIUS.
He has it now; and, by his looks, methinks
'Tis warm at's heart.

JUNIUS BRUTUS.
          With a proud heart he wore
His humble weeds.—Will you dismiss the people?
          Enter CITIZENS.

SICINIUS VELUTUS.
How now, my masters! have you chose this man?

FIRST CITIZEN.
He has our voices, sir.

JUNIUS BRUTUS.
We pray the gods he may deserve your loves.

SECOND CITIZEN.
Amen, sir:—to my poor unworthy notice,
He mockt us when he begg'd our voices.

THIRD CITIZEN.
          Certainly,
He flouted us downright.

FIRST CITIZEN.
No, 'tis his kind of speech,—he did not mock us.

SECOND CITIZEN.
Not one amongst us, save yourself, but says
He used us scornfully; he should have show'd us
His marks of merit, wounds received for's country.

SICINIUS VELUTUS.
Why, so he did, I am sure.

ALL THE CITIZENS.
          No, no; no man saw 'em.

THIRD CITIZEN.
He said he had wounds, which he could show in private;
And with his hat, thus waving it in scorn,
'I would be consul,' says he; 'aged custom
But by your voices will not so permit me;
Your voices therefore:' when we granted that,
Here was, 'I thank you for your voices,—thank you,—
Your most sweet voices:—now you have left your voices,
I have no further with you:'—was not this mockery?

SICINIUS VELUTUS.
Why either were you ignorant to see't,
Or, seeing it, of such childish friendliness
To yield your voices?

JUNIUS BRUTUS.
          Could you not have told him,
As you were lesson'd,—when he had no power,
But was a petty servant to the state,

He was your enemy; ever spake against
Your liberties, and the charters that you bear
I'the body of the weal; and now, arriving
A place of potency, and sway o'the state,
If he should still malignantly remain
Fast foe to the plebeii, your voices might
Be curses to yourselves? You should have said,
That as his worthy deeds did claim no less
Than what he stood for, so his gracious nature
Would think upon you for your voices, and
Translate his malice towards you into love,
Standing your friendly lord.

SICINIUS VELUTUS.
　　　　　　Thus to have said,
As you were fore-advised, had toucht his spirit
And tried his inclination; from him pluckt
Either his gracious promise, which you might,
As cause had call'd you up, have held him to;
Or else it would have gall'd his surly nature,
Which easily endures not article
Tying him to aught; so, putting him to rage,
You should have ta'en th'advantage of his choler,
And past him unelected.

JUNIUS BRUTUS.
　　　　　　Did you perceive
He did solicit you in free contempt,
When he did need your loves; and do you think
That his contempt shall not be bruising to you,
When he hath power to crush? Why, had your
　　bodies
No heart among you? or had you tongues to cry
Against the rectorship of judgement?

SICINIUS VELUTUS.
　　　　　　Have you,
Ere now, denied the asker? and now again,
Of him that did not ask, but mock, bestow
Your sued-for tongues?

THIRD CITIZEN.
He's not confirm'd; we may deny him yet.

SECOND CITIZEN.
And will deny him;
I'll have five hundred voices of that sound.

FIRST CITIZEN.
I twice five hundred, and their friends to piece 'em.

JUNIUS BRUTUS.
Get you hence instantly; and tell those friends
They have chose a consul that will from them take
Their liberties; make them of no more voice
Than dogs, that are as often beat for barking
As therefore kept to do so.

SICINIUS VELUTUS.
　　　　　　Let them assemble;
And, on a safer judgement, all revoke
Your ignorant election: enforce his pride,
And his old hate unto you: besides, forget not
With what contempt he wore the humble weed;
How in his suit he scorn'd you; but your loves,
Thinking upon his services, took from you
Th'apprehension of his present portance, which
Most gibingly, ungravely, he did fashion
After the inveterate hate he bears you.

JUNIUS BRUTUS.
　　　　　　Lay
A fault on us, your tribunes; that we labour'd,
No impediment between, but that you must
Cast your election on him.

SICINIUS VELUTUS.
　　　　　　Say you chose him
More after our commandment than as guided
By your own true affections; and that your minds,
Pre-occupied with what you rather must do
Than what you should, made you against the grain
To voice him consul: lay the fault on us.

JUNIUS BRUTUS.
Ay, spare us not. Say we read lectures to you,
How youngly he began to serve his country,
How long continued; and what stock he springs
　　of,—
The noble house o'the Marcians; from whence
　　came
That Ancus Marcius, Numa's daughter's son,
Who, after great Hostilius, here was king;
Of the same house Publius and Quintus were,
That our best water brought by conduits hither;
And Censorinus, nobly named so,
Twice being by the people chosen censor,
Was his great ancestor.

SICINIUS VELUTUS.
　　　　　　One thus descended,
That hath beside well in his person wrought
To be set high in place, we did commend
To your remembrances; but you have found,
Scaling his present bearing with his past,
That he's your fixed enemy, and revoke
Your sudden approbation.

JUNIUS BRUTUS.
　　　　　　Say you ne'er had done't—
Harp on that still—but by our putting on:
And presently, when you have drawn your num-
Repair to the Capitol. 　　　　　　[ber,

ALL THE CITIZENS.
　　　　　　We will so: almost all
Repent in their election. 　　　　　[Exeunt.

JUNIUS BRUTUS.
　　　　　　Let them go on;
This mutiny were better put in hazard,
Than stay, past doubt, for greater:
If, as his nature is, he fall in rage
With their refusal, both observe and answer
The vantage of his anger.

SICINIUS VELUTUS.
　　　　　　To the Capitol, come:
We will be there before the stream o'the people;
And this shall seem, as partly 'tis, their own,
Which we have goaded onward. 　　　[Exeunt.

ACT III.　SCENE I.

Rome.　A street.

Cornets.　Enter CORIOLANUS, MENENIUS, *all
the* GENTRY, COMINIUS, TITUS LARTIUS,
and other SENATORS.

CAIUS MARCIUS CORIÓLANUS.
TULLUS AUFIDIUS, then, had made new
　head?

TITUS LARTIUS.
He had, my lord; and that it was which caused
Our swifter composition.

CAIUS MARCIUS CORIÓLANUS.
So, then, the Volsces stand but as at first;
Ready, when time shall prompt them, to make
Upon's again. 　　　　　　　　[road

COMINIUS.
            They are worn, lord consul, so,
That we shall hardly in our ages see
Their banners wave again.
       CAIUS MARCIUS CORIOLANUS.
                Saw you Aufidius?
       TITUS LARTIUS.
On safe-guard he came to me; and did curse
Against the Volsces, for they had so vilely
Yielded the town: he is retired to Antium.
       CAIUS MARCIUS CORIOLANUS.
Spoke he of me?
       TITUS LARTIUS.
         He did, my lord.
       CAIUS MARCIUS CORIOLANUS.
                  How? what?
       TITUS LARTIUS.
How often he had met you, sword to sword;
That of all things upon the earth he hated
Your person most; that he would pawn his for-
     tunes
To hopeless restitution, so he might
Be call'd your vanquisher.
       CAIUS MARCIUS CORIOLANUS.
                At Antium lives he?
       TITUS LARTIUS.
At Antium.
       CAIUS MARCIUS CORIOLANUS.
I wish I had a cause to seek him there,
To oppose his hatred fully. Welcome home.
       Enter SICINIUS *and* BRUTUS.
Behold, these are the tribunes of the people,
The tongues o'th'common mouth: I do despise
For they do prank them in authority,   [them;
Against all noble sufferance.
       SICINIUS VELUTUS.
                Pass no further.
       CAIUS MARCIUS CORIOLANUS.
Ha! what is that?
       JUNIUS BRUTUS.
It will be dangerous to go on: no further.
       CAIUS MARCIUS CORIOLANUS.
What makes this change?
       MENENIUS AGRIPPA.
The matter?
       COMINIUS.
Hath he not past the noble and the common?
       JUNIUS BRUTUS.
Cominius, no.
       CAIUS MARCIUS CORIOLANUS.
          Have I had children's voices?
       FIRST SENATOR.
Tribunes, give way; he shall to the market-place.
       JUNIUS BRUTUS.
The people are incensed against him.
       SICINIUS VELUTUS.
                    Stop,
Or all will fall in broil.
       CAIUS MARCIUS CORIOLANUS.
            Are these your herd?—
Must these have voices, that can yield them now,
And straight disclaim their tongues?—What are
     your offices?
You being their mouths, why rule you not their
     teeth?
Have you not set them on?

MENENIUS AGRIPPA.
               Be calm, be calm.
       CAIUS MARCIUS CORIOLANUS.
It is a purposed thing, and grows by plot,
To curb the will of the nobility:
Suffer't, and live with such as cannot rule,
Nor ever will be ruled.
       JUNIUS BRUTUS.
             Call't not a plot:
The people cry you mockt them; and of late,
When corn was given them gratis, you repined;
Scandal'd the suppliants for the people,—call'd
     them
Time-pleasers, flatterers, foes to nobleness.
       CAIUS MARCIUS CORIOLANUS.
Why, this was known before.
       JUNIUS BRUTUS.
                Not to them all.
       CAIUS MARCIUS CORIOLANUS.
Have you inform'd them sithence?
       JUNIUS BRUTUS.
                How! I inform them!
       CAIUS MARCIUS CORIOLANUS.
You are like to do such business.
       JUNIUS BRUTUS.
                  Not unlike,
Each way, to better yours.
       CAIUS MARCIUS CORIOLANUS.
Why, then, should I be consul? By yond clouds,
Let me deserve so ill as you, and make me
Your fellow tribune.
       SICINIUS VELUTUS.
          You show too much of that
For which the people stir: if you will pass
To where you are bound, you must inquire your
     way,
Which you are out of, with a gentler spirit;
Or never be so noble as a consul,
Nor yoke with him for tribune.
       MENENIUS AGRIPPA.
               Let's be calm.
       COMINIUS.
The people are abused; set on. This paltering
Becomes not Rome; nor has Coriolanus
Deserved this so dishonour'd rub, laid falsely
I'the plain way of his merit.
       CAIUS MARCIUS CORIOLANUS.
             Tell me of corn!
This was my speech, and I will speak't again,—
       MENENIUS AGRIPPA.
Not now, not now.
       FIRST SENATOR.
           Not in this heat, sir, now.
       CAIUS MARCIUS CORIOLANUS.
Now, as I live, I will.—My nobler friends,
I crave their pardons:—
For the mutable, rank-scented meiny, let them
Regard me as I do not flatter, and
Therein behold themselves: I say again,
In soothing them, we nourish 'gainst our senate
The cockle of rebellion, insolence, sedition,
Which we ourselves have plough'd for, sow'd, and
     scatter'd,
By mingling them with us, the honour'd number;
Who lack not virtue, no, nor power, but that
Which they have given to beggars.

MENENIUS AGRIPPA.
Well, no more.
FIRST SENATOR.
No more words, we beseech you.
CAIUS MARCIUS CORIOLANUS.
How! no more!
As for my country I have shed my blood,
Not fearing outward force, so shall my lungs
Coin words t ll their decay against those measles,
Which we disdain should tetter us, yet sought
The very way to catch them.
JUNIUS BRUTUS.
You speak o'the people,
As if you were a god to punish, not
A man of their infirmity.
SICINIUS VELUTUS.
'Twere well
We let the people know't.
MENENIUS AGRIPPA.
What, what? his choler?
CAIUS MARCIUS CORIOLANUS.
Choler!
Were I as patient as the midnight sleep,
By Jove, 'twould be my mind!
SICINIUS VELUTUS.
It is a mind
That shall remain a poison where it is,
Not poison any further.
CAIUS MARCIUS CORIOLANUS.
Shall remain!—
Hear you this Triton of the minnows? mark you
His absolute 'shall'?
COMINIUS.
'Twas from the canon.
CAIUS MARCIUS CORIOLANUS.
'Shall'!
O good, but most unwise patricians! why,
You grave, but reckless senators, have you thus
Given Hydra here to choose an officer,
That with his peremptory 'shall,' being but
The horn and noise o'th'monster, wants not spirit
To say he'll turn your current in a ditch,
And make your channel his? If he have power,
Then vail your ignorance; if none, awake
Your dangerous lenity. If you are learn'd,
Be not as common fools; if you are not,
Let them have cushions by you. You are ple-
beians,
If they be senators: and they are no less,
When, both your voices blended, the great'st
taste
Most palates theirs. They choose their magistrate;
And such a one as he, who puts his 'shall,'
His popular 'shall,' against a graver bench
Than ever frown'd in Greece. By Jove himself,
It makes the consuls base! and my soul aches
To know, when two authorities are up,
Neither supreme, how soon confusion
May enter 'twixt the gap of both, and take
The one by th'other.
COMINIUS.
Well,—on to the market-place.
CAIUS MARCIUS CORIOLANUS.
Whoever gave that counsel, to give forth
The corn o'the storehouse gratis, as 'twas used
Sometime in Greece,—

MENENIUS AGRIPPA.
Well, well, no more of that.
CAIUS MARCIUS CORIOLANUS.
Though there the people had more absolute
power,—
I say, they nourisht disobedience, fed
The ruin of the state.
JUNIUS BRUTUS.
Why, shall the people give
One, that speaks thus, their voice?
CAIUS MARCIUS CORIOLANUS.
I'll give my reasons,
More worthier than their voices. They know the
corn
Was not their recompense, resting well assured
They ne'er did service for't: being prest to the
war,
Even when the navel of the state was toucht,
They would not thread the gates:—this kind of
service
Did not deserve corn gratis: being i'the war,
Their mutinies and revolts, wherein they show'd
Most valour, spoke not for them: th'accusation
Which they have often made against the senate,
All cause unborn, could never be the native
Of our so frank donation. Well, what then?
How shall this bosom multiplied digest
The senate's courtesy? Let deeds express
What's like to be their words:—'We did request it;
We are the greater poll, and in true fear
They gave us our demands:'—thus we debase
The nature of our seats, and make the rabble
Call our cares fears; which will in time
Break ope the locks o'the senate, and bring in
The crows to peck the eagles.
MENENIUS AGRIPPA.
Come, enough.
JUNIUS BRUTUS.
Enough, with over-measure.
CAIUS MARCIUS CORIOLANUS.
No, take more:
What may be sworn by, both divine and human,
Seal what I end withal!—This double worship,—
Where one part does disdain with cause, the other
Insult without all reason; where gentry, title,
wisdom,
Cannot conclude but by the yea and no
Of general ignorance,—it must omit
Real necessities, and give way the while
To unstable slightness: purpose so barr'd, it
follows,
Nothing is done to purpose. Therefore, beseech
you,—
You that will be less fearful than discreet,
That love the fundamental part of state
More than you doubt the change on't; that prefer
A noble life before a long, and wish
To jump a body with a dangerous physic
That's sure of death without it,—at once pluck
out
The multitudinous tongue; let them not lick
The sweet which is their poison: your dishonour
Mangles true judgement, and bereaves the state
Of that integrity which should become't;
Not having the power to do the good it would,
For th'ill which doth control't.

JUNIUS BRUTUS.
　　　　　　　　　'Has said enough.
SICINIUS VELUTUS.
'Has spoken like a traitor, and shall answer
As traitors do.
CAIUS MARCIUS CORIOLANUS.
　　　　　Thou wretch, despite o'erwhelm thee!—
What should the people do with these bald trib-
　unes?
On whom depending, their obedience fails
To the greater bench: in a rebellion,
When what's not meet, but what must be, was
　law,
Then were they chosen: in a better hour,
Let what is meet be said it must be meet,
And throw their power i'the dust.
　　　　　JUNIUS BRUTUS.
Manifest treason!
　　　　SICINIUS VELUTUS.
　　　　　This a consul? no.
　　　　　JUNIUS BRUTUS.
The ædiles, ho!
　　　　　Enter an AEDILE.
　　　　Let him be apprehended.
SICINIUS VELUTUS.
Go, call the people [*exit* AEDILE]:—in whose
　name myself
Attach thee as a traitorous innovator,
A foe to the public weal: obey, I charge thee,
And follow to thine answer.
　　　　CAIUS MARCIUS CORIOLANUS.
　　　　　　Hence, old goat!
　　　　　SENATORS, *&c.*
We'll surety him.
　　　　　COMINIUS.
　　　　Aged sir, hands off.
　　　CAIUS MARCIUS CORIOLANUS.
Hence, rotten thing! or I shall shake thy bones
Out of thy garments
　　　　SICINIUS VELUTUS.
　　　　　Help, ye citizens!
Enter a rabble of CITIZENS, *with the* AEDILES.
　　　　MENENIUS AGRIPPA.
On both sides more respect.
　　　　SICINIUS VELUTUS.
Here's he that would take from you all your power.
　　　　JUNIUS BRUTUS.
Seize him, ædiles!
　　　　　CITIZENS.
Down with him! down with him!
　　　　SENATORS, *&c.*
Weapons, weapons, weapons!
　　　[*They all bustle about* CORIOLANUS.
Tribunes!—Patricians!—Citizens!—What, ho!—
Sicinius!—Brutus!—Coriolanus!—Citizens!—
Peace, peace, peace!—Stay, hold, peace!
　　　　MENENIUS AGRIPPA.
What is about to be?—I am out of breath;
Confusion's near; I cannot speak.—You, tribunes
To the people!—Coriolanus, patience:—
Speak, good Sicinius.
　　　　SICINIUS VELUTUS.
　　　　　Hear me, people; peace!
　　　　　CITIZENS.
Let's hear our tribune: peace!—Speak, speak,
　speak.

SICINIUS VELUTUS.
You are at point to lose your liberties:
Marcius would have all from you; Marcius
Whom late you have named for consul.
　　　　MENENIUS AGRIPPA.
　　　　　　　Fie, fie, fie!
This is the way to kindle, not to quench.
　　　　　FIRST SENATOR.
To unbuild the city, and to lay all flat.
　　　　SICINIUS VELUTUS.
What is the city but the people?
　　　　　CITIZENS.
　　　　　　　True,
The people are the city.
　　　　JUNIUS BRUTUS.
By the consent of all, we were establisht
The people's magistrates.
　　　　　CITIZENS.
　　　　　You so remain.
　　　　MENENIUS AGRIPPA.
And so are like to do.
　　　　　COMINIUS.
That is the way to lay the city flat;
To bring the roof to the foundation,
And bury all, which yet distinctly ranges,
In heaps and piles of ruin.
　　　　SICINIUS VELUTUS.
　　　　　This deserves death.
　　　　JUNIUS BRUTUS.
Or let us stand to our authority,
Or let us lose it.—We do here pronounce,
Upon the part o'the people, in whose power
We were elected theirs, Marcius is worthy
Of present death.
　　　　SICINIUS VELUTUS.
　　　　　Therefore lay hold of him;
Bear him to the rock Tarpeian, and from thence
Into destruction cast him.
　　　　JUNIUS BRUTUS.
　　　　　Aediles, seize him!
　　　　　CITIZENS.
Yield, Marcius, yield!
　　　　MENENIUS AGRIPPA.
　　　　　Hear me one word!
Beseech you, tribunes, hear me but a word.
　　　　　AEDILES.
Peace, peace!
　　　　MENENIUS AGRIPPA.
Be that you seem, truly your country's friends,
And temperately proceed to what you would
Thus violently redress.
　　　　JUNIUS BRUTUS.
　　　　　Sir, those cold ways,
That seem like prudent helps, are very poisonous
Where the disease is violent.—Lay hands upon
　him,
And bear him to the rock.
　　　　CAIUS MARCIUS CORIOLANUS.
　　　　　No, I'll die here. [*Drawing his sword.*
There's some among you have beheld me fighting:
Come, try upon yourselves what you have seen me.
　　　　MENENIUS AGRIPPA.
Down with that sword!—Tribunes, withdraw
　awhile.
　　　　JUNIUS BRUTUS.
Lay hands upon him.

MENENIUS AGRIPPA.
              Help Marcius, help,
You that be noble; help him, young and old!
          CITIZENS.
Down with him! down with him!
   [*In this mutiny the* TRIBUNES, *the* AEDI-
    LES, *and the* PEOPLE *are beat in.*
       MENENIUS AGRIPPA.
Go, get you to your house; be gone, away!
All will be naught else.
      SECOND SENATOR.
             Get you gone.
        COMINIUS.
                Stand fast;
We have as many friends as enemies.
       MENENIUS AGRIPPA.
Shall it be put to that?
      FIRST SENATOR,
            The gods forbid!—
I prithee, noble friend, home to thy house;
Leave us to cure this cause.
       MENENIUS AGRIPPA.
          For 'tis a sore upon us,
You cannot tent yourself: be gone, beseech you.
        COMINIUS.
Come, sir, along with us.
   CAIUS MARCIUS CORIOLANUS.
I would they were barbarians, as they are,
Though in Rome litter'd; not Romans, as they
   are not,
Though calved i'the porch o'the Capitol.—
       MENENIUS AGRIPPA.
               Be gone;
Put not your worthy rage into your tongue;
One time will owe another.
   CAIUS MARCIUS CORIOLANUS.
           On fair ground
I could beat forty of them.
       MENENIUS AGRIPPA.
            I could myself
Take up a brace o'the best of them; yea, the two
   tribunes.
         COMINIUS.
But now 'tis odds beyond arithmetic;
And manhood is call'd foolery, when it stands
Against a falling fabric.—Will you hence,
Before the tag return? whose rage doth rend
Like interrupted waters, and o'erbear
What they are used to bear.
       MENENIUS AGRIPPA.
           Pray you, be gone:
I'll try whether my old wit be in request
With those that have but little: this must be
   patcht
With cloth of any colour.
        COMINIUS.
         Nay, come away.
  [*Exeunt* CORIOLANUS, COMINIUS, *and others.*
       FIRST PATRICIAN.
This man has marr'd his fortune.
       MENENIUS AGRIPPA.
His nature is too noble for the world:
He would not flatter Neptune for his trident,
Or Jove for's power to thunder. His heart's his
  mouth:
What his breast forges, that his tongue must vent;

And, being angry, does forget that ever
He heard the name of death.—   [*A noise within.*
Here's goodly work!
      SECOND PATRICIAN.
        I would they were a-bed!
       MENENIUS AGRIPPA.
I would they were in Tiber! What the vengeance
Could he not speak 'em fair?
  Enter BRUTUS *and* SICINIUS, *with the*
       rabble again.
       SICINIUS VELUTUS.
            Where is this viper,
That would depopulate the city, and
Be every man himself?
       MENENIUS AGRIPPA.
           You worthy tribunes,—
       SICINIUS VELUTUS.
He shall be thrown down the Tarpeian rock
With rigorous hands; he hath resisted law,
And therefore law shall scorn him further trial
Than the severity of the public power,
Which he so sets at naught.
       FIRST CITIZEN.
           He shall well know
The noble tribunes are the people's mouths,
And we their hands.
        CITIZENS.
         He shall, sure on't.
       MENENIUS AGRIPPA.
               Sir, sir,—
       SICINIUS VELUTUS.
Peace!
       MENENIUS AGRIPPA.
Do not cry havoc, where you should but hunt
With modest warrant.
       SICINIUS VELUTUS.
         Sir, how comes't that you
Have holp to make this rescue?
       MENENIUS AGRIPPA.
           Hear me speak:—
As I do know the consul's worthiness,
So can I name his faults,—
       SICINIUS VELUTUS.
         Consul!—what consul?
       MENENIUS AGRIPPA.
The consul Coriolanus.
       JUNIUS BRUTUS.
          He consul!
       CITIZENS.
No, no, no, no, no.
       MENENIUS AGRIPPA.
If, by the tribunes' leave, and yours, good people,
I may be heard, I'ld crave a word or two;
The which shall turn you to no further harm
Than so much loss of time.
       SICINIUS VELUTUS.
          Speak briefly, then;
For we are peremptory to dispatch
This viperous traitor: to eject him hence
Were but our danger; and to keep him here
Our certain death: therefore it is decreed
He dies to-night.
       MENENIUS AGRIPPA.
         Now the good gods forbid
That our renowned Rome, whose gratitude
Towards her deserved children is enroll'd

In Jove's own book, like an unnatural dam
Should now eat up her own!
SICINIUS VELUTUS.
He's a disease that must be cut away.
MENENIUS AGRIPPA.
O, he's a limb that has but a disease;
Mortal, to cut it off; to cure it, easy.
What has he done to Rome that's worthy death?
Killing our enemies, the blood he hath lost—
Which, I dare vouch, is more than that he hath,
By many an ounce—he dropt it for his country;
And what is left, to lose it by his country,
Were to us all, that do't and suffer it,
A brand to the end o'the world.
SICINIUS VELUTUS.
　　　　　　　This is clean kam.
JUNIUS BRUTUS.
Merely awry: when he did love his country,
It honour'd him.
MENENIUS AGRIPPA.
　　　　The service of the foot
Being once gangrened, is not then respected
For what before it was.
JUNIUS BRUTUS.
　　　　　We'll hear no more.—
Pursue him to his house, and pluck him thence;
Lest his infection, being of catching nature,
Spread further.
MENENIUS AGRIPPA.
　　　One word more, one word.
This tiger-footed rage, when it shall find
The harm of unscann'd swiftness, will, too late,
Tie leaden pounds to's heels. Proceed by process;
Lest parties—as he is beloved—break out,
And sack great Rome with Romans.
JUNIUS BRUTUS.
　　　　　　If it were so,—
SICINIUS VELUTUS.
What do ye talk?
Have we not had a taste of his obedience?
Our ædiles smote? ourselves resisted? Come,—
MENENIUS AGRIPPA.
Consider this:—he has been bred i'the wars
Since he could draw a sword, and is ill school'd
In bolted language; meal and bran together
He throws without distinction. Give me leave,
I'll go to him, and undertake to bring him
Where he shall answer, by a lawful form,—
In peace,—to his utmost peril.
FIRST SENATOR.
　　　　　　Noble tribunes,
It is the humane way: the other course
Will prove too bloody; and the end of it
Unknown to the beginning.
SICINIUS VELUTUS.
　　　　　Noble Menenius,
Be you, then, as the people's officer.—
Masters, lay down your weapons.
JUNIUS BRUTUS.
　　　　　　Go not home.
SICINIUS VELUTUS.
Meet on the market-place. We'll attend you
　there:
Where, if you bring not Marcius, we'll proceed
In our first way.

MENENIUS AGRIPPA.
　　　　I'll bring him to you.—
[to the SENATORS] Let me desire your company:
　he must come,
Or what is worst will follow.
FIRST SENATOR.
　　　　　Pray you, let's to him.
　　　　　　　　　[Exeunt.

SCENE II.
A room in CORIOLANUS' *house.*
Enter CORIOLANUS *and* PATRICIANS.
CAIUS MARCIUS CORIOLANUS.
LET them pull all about mine ears; present me
　Death on the wheel or at wild horses' heels;
Or pile ten hills on the Tarpeian rock,
That the precipitation might down stretch
Below the beam of sight; yet will I still
Be thus to them.
FIRST PATRICIAN.
　　　　You do the nobler.
CAIUS MARCIUS CORIOLANUS.
I muse my mother
Does not approve me further, who was wont
To call them woollen vassals, things created
To buy and sell with groats; to show bare heads
In congregations, to yawn, be still, and wonder,
When one but of my ordinance stood up
To speak of peace or war.
Enter VOLUMNIA.
　　　　　I talk of you:
Why did you wish me milder? would you have me
False to my nature? Rather say, I play
The man I am.
VOLUMNIA.
O, sir, sir, sir,
I would have had you put your power well on,
Before you had worn it out.
CAIUS MARCIUS CORIOLANUS.
　　　　　Let go.
VOLUMNIA.
You might have been enough the man you are,
With striving less to be so: lesser had been
The thwartings of your disposition, if
You had not show'd them how ye were disposed
Ere they lackt power to cross you.
CAIUS MARCIUS CORIOLANUS.
　　　　　Let them hang.
VOLUMNIA.
Ay, and burn too.
Enter MENENIUS *with the* SENATORS.
MENENIUS AGRIPPA.
Come, come, you have been too rough, something
　too rough;
You must return and mend it.
FIRST SENATOR.
　　　　　　There's no remedy;
Unless, by not so doing, our good city
Cleave in the midst, and perish.
VOLUMNIA.
　　　　　　Pray, be counsell'd:
I have a heart as little apt as yours,
But yet a brain that leads my use of anger
To better vantage.

MENENIUS AGRIPPA.
         Well said, noble woman!
Before he should thus stoop to the herd, but that
The violent fit o'the time craves it as physic
For the whole state, I would put mine armour on,
Which I can scarcely bear.
     CAIUS MARCIUS CORIOLANUS.
                 What must I do?
     MENENIUS AGRIPPA.
Return to the tribunes.
     CAIUS MARCIUS CORIOLANUS.
            Well, what then? what then?
     MENENIUS AGRIPPA.
Repent what you have spoke.
     CAIUS MARCIUS CORIOLANUS.
For them?—I cannot do it to the gods;
Must I, then, do't to them?
     VOLUMNIA.
            You are too absolute;
Though therein you can never be too noble,
But when extremities speak. I have heard you say,
Honour and policy, like unsever'd friends,
I'the war do grow together: grant that, and tell
     me,
In peace what each of them by th'other lose,
That they combine not there.
     CAIUS MARCIUS CORIOLANUS.
                 Tush, tush!
     MENENIUS AGRIPPA.
            A good demand.
     VOLUMNIA.
If it be honour in your wars to seem
The same you are not,—which, for your best ends,
You adopt your policy,—how is it less or worse,
That it shall hold companionship in peace
With honour, as in war; since that to both
It stands in like request?
     CAIUS MARCIUS CORIOLANUS.
            Why force you this?
     VOLUMNIA.
Because that now it lies you on to speak
To the people; not by your own instruction,
Nor by the matter which your heart prompts you,
But with such words that are but roted in
Your tongue, though but bastards, and syllables
Of no allowance to your bosom's truth.
Now, this no more dishonours you at all
Than to take in a town with gentle words,
Which else would put you to your fortune, and
The hazard of much blood.
I would dissemble with my nature, where
My fortunes and my friends at stake required
I should do so in honour: I am, in this,
Your wife, your son, these senators, the nobles;
And you will rather show our general louts
How you can frown than spend a fawn upon 'em,
For the inheritance of their loves, and safeguard
Of what that want might ruin.
     MENENIUS AGRIPPA.
            Noble lady!—
Come, go with us; speak fair: you may salve so,
Not what is dangerous present, but the loss
Of what is past.
     VOLUMNIA.
       I prithee now, my son,
Go to them, with this bonnet in thy hand;

And thus far having stretcht it,—here be with
     them,—
Thy knee bussing the stones,—for in such busi-
     ness
Action is eloquence, and the eyes of th'ignorant
More learned than the ears,—waving thy head,
Which often, thus, correcting thy stout heart,
Now humble as the ripest mulberry
That will not hold the handling,—or say to them,
Thou art their soldier, and, being bred in broils,
Hast not the soft way which, thou dost confess,
Were fit for thee to use, as they to claim,
In asking their good loves; but thou wilt frame
Thyself, forsooth, hereafter theirs, so far
As thou hast power and person.
     MENENIUS AGRIPPA.
            This but done,
Even as she speaks it, why, their hearts were
     yours;
For they have pardons, being askt, as free
As words to little purpose.
     VOLUMNIA.
            Prithee now,
Go, and be ruled: although I know thou hadst
     rather
Follow thine enemy in a fiery gulf
Than flatter him in a bower.—Here is Cominius.
            Enter COMINIUS.
     COMINIUS.
I have been i'the market-place; and, sir, 'tis fit
You make strong party, or defend yourself
By calmness or by absence: all's in anger.
     MENENIUS AGRIPPA.
Only fair speech.
     COMINIUS.
        I think 'twill serve, if he
Can thereto frame his spirit.
     VOLUMNIA.
            He must, and will.—
Prithee now, say you will, and go about it.
     CAIUS MARCIUS CORIOLANUS.
Must I go show them my unbarb'd sconce?
     must I
With my base tongue give to my noble heart
A lie that it must bear? Well, I will do't:
Yet, were there but this single plot to lose,
This mould of Marcius, they to dust should
     grind it,
And throw't against the wind.—To the market-
     place!—
You have put me now to such a part, which never
I shall discharge to the life.
     COMINIUS.
            Come, come, we'll prompt you.
     VOLUMNIA.
I prithee now, sweet son,—as thou has said
My praises made thee first a soldier, so,
To have my praise for this, perform a part
Thou hast not done before.
     CAIUS MARCIUS CORIOLANUS.
            Well, I must do't:
Away, my disposition, and possess me
Some harlot's spirit! my throat of war be turn'd,
Which quired with my drum, into a pipe
Small as an eunuch, or the virgin voice
That babies iulls asleep! the smiles of knaves

Tent in my cheeks; and schoolboys' tears take up
The glasses of my sight! a beggar's tongue
Make motion through my lips; and my arm'd
    knees,
Who bow'd but in my stirrup, bend like his
That hath received an alms!—I will not do't;
Lest I surcease to honour mine own truth,
And by my body's action teach my mind
A most inherent baseness.

            VOLUMNIA.
                    At thy choice, then:
To beg of thee, it is my more dishonour
Than thou of them. Come all to ruin: let
Thy mother rather feel thy pride than fear
Thy dangerous stoutness; for I mock at death
With as big heart as thou. Do as thou list.
Thy valiantness was mine, thou suck'dst it from
    me;
But owe thy pride thyself.

      CAIUS MARCIUS CORIOLANUS.
                  Pray, be content:
Mother, I am going to the market-place;
Chide me no more. I'll mountebank their loves,
Cog their hearts from them, and come home be-
    loved
Of all the trades in Rome. Look, I am going:
Commend me to my wife. I'll return consul;
Or never trust to what my tongue can do
I'the way of flattery further.

            VOLUMNIA.
                  Do your will.   [Exit.
            COMINIUS.
Away! the tribunes do attend you: arm yourself
To answer mildly; for they are prepared
With accusations, as I hear, more strong
Than are upon you yet.

      CAIUS MARCIUS CORIOLANUS.
The word is 'mildly:'—pray you, let us go:
Let them accuse me by invention, I
Will answer in mine honour.

       MENENIUS AGRIPPA.
                  Ay, but mildly.
      CAIUS MARCIUS CORIOLANUS.
Well, mildly be it, then,—mildly!   [Exeunt.

SCENE III.

The same. The Forum.

Enter SICINIUS *and* BRUTUS.

       JUNIUS BRUTUS.
IN this point charge him home,—that he affects
    Tyrannical power: if he evade us there,
Enforce him with his envy to the people;
And that the spoil got on the Antiates
Was ne'er distributed.

       Enter an AEDILE.
What, will he come?

           AEDILE.
        He's coming.
       JUNIUS BRUTUS.
                  How accompanied?
           AEDILE.
With old Menenius, and those senators
That always favour'd him.

       SICINIUS VELUTUS.
                  Have you a catalogue
Of all the voices that we have procured,
Set down by the poll?

           AEDILE.
          I have; 'tis ready.
       SICINIUS VELUTUS.
Have you collected them by tribes?

           AEDILE.
                  I have.
       SICINIUS VELUTUS.
Assemble presently the people hither:
And when they hear me say, 'It shall be so
I'th'right and strength o'th'commons,' be it either
For death, for fine, or banishment, then let them,
If I say fine, cry 'Fine,'—if death, cry 'Death;'
Insisting on the old prerogative
And power i'the truth o'the cause.

           AEDILE.
               I shall inform them.
       JUNIUS BRUTUS.
And when such time they have begun to cry,
Let them not cease, but with a din confused
Enforce the present execution
Of what we chance to sentence.

           AEDILE.
               Very well.
       SICINIUS VELUTUS.
Make them be strong, and ready for this hint,
When we shall hap to give't them.

       JUNIUS BRUTUS.
              Go about it.— [*Exit* AEDILE.
Put him to choler straight: he hath been used
Ever to conquer, and to have his worth
Of contradiction: being once chafed, he cannot
Be rein'd again to temperance; then he speaks
What's in his heart; and that is there which looks
With us to break his neck.

       SICINIUS VELUTUS.
               Well, here he comes.

Enter CORIOLANUS, MENENIUS, COMINIUS,
with SENATORS *and* PATRICIANS.

       MENENIUS AGRIPPA.
Calmly, I do beseech you.

      CAIUS MARCIUS CORIOLANUS.
Ay, as an ostler, that for the poorest piece
Will bear the knave by the volume.—The hon-
    our'd gods
Keep Rome in safety, and the chairs of justice
Supplied with worthy men! plant love among's!
Throng our large temples with the shows of
    peace,
And not our streets with war!

       FIRST SENATOR.
               Amen, amen.
       MENENIUS AGRIPPA.
A noble wish.

   Enter the AEDILE, *with* CITIZENS.
       SICINIUS VELUTUS.
Draw near, ye people.

           AEDILE.
List to your tribunes; audience! peace, I say!
      CAIUS MARCIUS CORIOLANUS.
First, hear me speak.

       BOTH TRIBUNES.
              Well, say.—Peace, ho!

CAIUS MARCIUS CORIOLANUS.
Shall I be charged no further than this present?
Must all determine here?

SICINIUS VELUTUS.
                              I do demand
If you submit you to the people's voices,
Allow their officers, and are content
To suffer lawful censure for such faults
As shall be proved upon you?

CAIUS MARCIUS CORIOLANUS.
                              I am content.

MENENIUS AGRIPPA.
Lo, citizens, he says he is content:
The warlike service he has done consider; think
Upon the wounds his body bears, which show
Like graves i'the holy churchyard.

CAIUS MARCIUS CORIOLANUS.
                              Scratches with briers,
Scars to move laughter only.

MENENIUS AGRIPPA.
                              Consider further,
That when he speaks not like a citizen,
You find him like a soldier: do not take
His rougher accents for malicious sounds,
But, as I say, such as become a soldier,
Rather than envy you.

COMINIUS.
                    Well, well, no more.

CAIUS MARCIUS CORIOLANUS.
What is the matter,
That being past for consul with full voice,
I am so dishonour'd, that the very hour
You take it off again?

SICINIUS VELUTUS.
                    Answer to us.

CAIUS MARCIUS CORIOLANUS.
Say, then: 'tis true, I ought so.

SICINIUS VELUTUS.
We charge you, that you have contrived to take
From Rome all season'd office, and to wind
Yourself into a power tyrannical;
For which you are a traitor to the people.

CAIUS MARCIUS CORIOLANUS.
How! traitor!

MENENIUS AGRIPPA.
                    Nay, temperately; your promise.

CAIUS MARCIUS CORIOLANUS.
The fires i'the lowest hell fold-in the people!
Call me their traitor!—Thou injurious tribune!
Within thine eyes sat twenty thousand deaths,
In thy hands clutcht as many millions, in
Thy lying tongue both numbers, I would say
'Thou liest' unto thee with a voice as free
As I do pray the gods.

SICINIUS VELUTUS.
                    Mark you this, people?

CITIZENS.
To the rock, to the rock with him!

SICINIUS VELUTUS.
                    Peace!
We need not put new matter to his charge:
What you have seen him do, and heard him speak,
Beating your officers, cursing yourselves,
Opposing laws with strokes, and here defying
Those whose great power must try him; even
    this,

So criminal, and in such capital kind,
Deserves th'extremest death.

JUNIUS BRUTUS.
                    But since he hath
Served well for Rome,—

CAIUS MARCIUS CORIOLANUS.
                    What do you prate of service?

JUNIUS BRUTUS.
I talk of that, that know it.

CAIUS MARCIUS CORIOLANUS.
                    You?

MENENIUS AGRIPPA.
Is this the promise that you made your mother?

COMINIUS.
Know, I pray you,—

CAIUS MARCIUS CORIOLANUS.
                    I'll know no further:
Let them pronounce the steep Tarpeian death,
Vagabond exile, flaying, pent to linger
But with a grain a day,—I would not buy
Their mercy at the price of one fair word;
Nor check my courage for what they can give,
To have't with saying 'Good morrow.'

SICINIUS VELUTUS.
                    For that he has,
As much as in him lies, from time to time
Envied against the people, seeking means
To pluck away their power; as now at last
Given hostile strokes, and that not in the presence
Of dreaded justice, but on the ministers
That do distribute it;—in the name o'the people,
And in the power of us the tribunes, we,
Even from this instant, banish him our city;
In peril of precipitation
From off the rock Tarpeian, never more
To enter our Rome gates: i'the people's name,
I say it shall be so.

CITIZENS.
                    It shall be so,
It shall be so; let him away: he's banisht,
And it shall be so.

COMINIUS.
Hear me, my masters and my common friends,—

SICINIUS VELUTUS.
He's sentenced; no more hearing.

COMINIUS.
                    Let me speak:
I have been consul, and can show for Rome
Her enemies' marks upon me. I do love
My country's good with a respect more tender,
More holy, and profound, than mine own life,
My dear wife's estimate, her womb's increase,
And treasure of my loins; then if I would
Speak that,—

SICINIUS VELUTUS.
                    We know your drift:—speak what?

JUNIUS BRUTUS.
There's no more to be said, but he is banisht,
As enemy to the people and his country:
It shall be so.

CITIZENS.
It shall be so, it shall be so.

CAIUS MARCIUS CORIOLANUS.
You common cry of curs! whose breath I hate
As reek o'the rotten fens, whose loves I prize
As the dead carcasses of unburied men

That do corrupt my air,—I banish you;
And here remain with your uncertainty!
Let every feeble rumour shake your hearts!
Your enemies, with nodding of their plumes,
Fan you into despair! Have the power still
To banish your defenders; till at length
Your ignorance, which finds not till it feels,
Making not reservation of yourselves,
Still your own foes, deliver you, as most
Abated captives, to some nation
That won you without blows! Despising,
For you, the city, thus I turn my back:
There is a world elsewhere.

    [*Exeunt* CORIOLANUS, COMINIUS, MENE-
    NIUS, SENATORS, *and* PATRICIANS.

            AEDILE.

The people's enemy is gone, is gone!

           CITIZENS.

Our enemy is banisht! he is gone!
Hoo! hoo!   [*They all shout and throw up their caps.*

       SICINIUS VELUTUS.

Go, see him out at gates, and follow him,
As he hath follow'd you, with all despite;
Give him deserved vexation. Let a guard
Attend us through the city.

          CITIZENS.

Come, come, let's see him out at gates; come:—
The gods preserve our noble tribunes!—come.

             [*Exeunt.*

ACT IV. SCENE I.

Rome.   Before a gate of the city.

Enter CORIOLANUS, VOLUMNIA, VIRGILIA,
MENENIUS, COMINIUS, *with the young* NO-
BILITY *of Rome.*

   CAIUS MARCIUS CORIOLANUS.

COME, leave your tears; a brief farewell:—the
   beast
With many heads butts me away.—Nay, mother,
Where is your ancient courage? you were used
To say extremity was the trier of spirits;
That common chances common men could bear;
That, when the sea was calm, all boats alike
Show'd mastership in floating; fortune's blows,
When most struck home, being gentle wounded,
  craves
A noble cunning: you were used to load me
With precepts that would make invincible
The heart that conn'd them.

         VIRGILIA.

O heavens! O heavens!

   CAIUS MARCIUS CORIOLANUS.

        Nay, I prithee, woman,—

        VOLUMNIA.

Now the red pestilence strike all trades in Rome,
And occupations perish!

   CAIUS MARCIUS CORIOLANUS.

        What, what, what!
I shall be loved when I am lackt. Nay, mother,
Resume that spirit, when you were wont to say,
If you had been the wife of Hercules,
Six of his labours you'ld have done, and saved
Your husband so much sweat.—Cominius,
Droop not; adieu.—Farewell, my wife,—my
  mother:

I'll do well yet.—Thou old and true Menenius,
Thy tears are salter than a younger man's,
And venomous to thine eyes.—My sometime
  general,
I have seen thee stern, and thou hast oft beheld
Heart-hard'ning spectacles; tell these sad women,
'Tis fond to wail inevitable strokes,
As 'tis to laugh at 'em.—My mother, you wot well
My hazards still have been your solace: and
Believe't not lightly,—though I go alone,
Like to a lonely dragon, that his fen
Makes fear'd and talkt of more than seen,—your
  son
Will or exceed the common, or be caught
With cautelous baits and practice.

        VOLUMNIA.

             My first son,
Whither wilt thou go? Take good Cominius
With thee awhile: determine on some course,
More than a wild exposure to each chance
That starts i'the way before thee.

   CAIUS MARCIUS CORIOLANUS.

            O the gods!

        COMINIUS.

I'll follow thee a month, devise with thee
Where thou shalt rest, that thou mayst hear of us,
And we of thee: so, if the time thrust forth
A cause for thy repeal, we shall not send
O'er the vast world to seek a single man;
And lose advantage, which doth ever cool
I'the absence of the needer.

   CAIUS MARCIUS CORIOLANUS.

         Fare ye well!
Thou hast years upon thee; and thou art too full
Of the wars' surfeits, to go rove with one
That's yet unbruised: bring me but out at gate.—
Come, my sweet wife, my dearest mother, and
My friends of noble touch; when I am forth,
Bid me farewell, and smile. I pray you, come.
While I remain above the ground, you shall
Hear from me still: and never of me aught
But what is like me formerly.

     MENENIUS AGRIPPA.

           That's worthily
As any ear can hear.—Come, let's not weep.—
If I could shake off but one seven years
From these old arms and legs, by the good gods,
I'ld with thee every foot.

   CAIUS MARCIUS CORIOLANUS.

         Give me thy hand:—
Come.   [*Exeunt.*

SCENE II.

The same.   A street near the gate.

Enter the two TRIBUNES, SICINIUS, BRUTUS,
with the AEDILE.

     SICINIUS VELUTUS.

BID them all home; he's gone, and we'll no
  further.—
The nobility are vext, whom we see have sided
In his behalf.

      JUNIUS BRUTUS.

      Now we have shown our power,
Let us seem humbler after it is done
Than when it was a-doing.

SICINIUS VELUTUS.
          Bid them home:
Say their great enemy is gone, and they
Stand in their ancient strength.
          JUNIUS BRUTUS.
                    Dismiss them home.
               [*Exit* AEDILE.
Here comes his mother.
          SICINIUS VELUTUS.
                    Let's not meet her.
          JUNIUS BRUTUS.
                              Why?
          SICINIUS VELUTUS.
They say she's mad.
          JUNIUS BRUTUS.
They have ta'en note of us: keep on your way.
Enter VOLUMNIA, VIRGILIA, *and* MENENIUS.
          VOLUMNIA.
O, y'are well met: the hoarded plague o'the gods
Requite your love!
          MENENIUS AGRIPPA.
               Peace, peace; be not so loud.
          VOLUMNIA.
If that I could for weeping, you should hear,—
Nay, and you shall hear some.—[*to* BRUTUS]
     Will you be gone?
          VIRGILIA [*to* SICINIUS VELUTUS].
You shall stay too: I would I had the power
To say so to my husband.
          SICINIUS VELUTUS.
                    Are you mankind?
          VOLUMNIA.
Ay, fool; is that a shame?—Note but this fool.—
Was not a man my father? Hadst thou foxship
To banish him that struck more blows for Rome
Than thou hast spoken words?—
          SICINIUS VELUTUS.
                    O blessed heavens!
          VOLUMNIA.
More noble blows than ever thou wise words;
And for Rome's good.—I'll tell thee what;—yet
     go:—
Nay, but thou shalt stay too:—I would my son
Were in Arabia, and thy tribe before him,
His good sword in his hand.
          SICINIUS VELUTUS.
                    What then?
          VIRGILIA.
                              What then!
He'ld make an end of thy posterity.
          VOLUMNIA.
Bastards and all.—
Good man, the wounds that he does bear for Rome!
          MENENIUS AGRIPPA.
Come, come, peace.
          SICINIUS VELUTUS.
I would he had continued to his country
As he began, and not unknit himself
The noble knot he made.
          JUNIUS BRUTUS.
                    I would he had.
          VOLUMNIA.
'I would he had'! 'Twas you incensed the rabble;—
Rats, that can judge as fitly of his worth
As I can of those mysteries which heaven
Will not have earth to know.

          JUNIUS BRUTUS.
                    Pray, let us go.
          VOLUMNIA.
Now, pray, sir, get you gone:
You have done a brave deed. Ere you go, hear
     this:—
As far as doth the Capitol exceed
The meanest house in Rome, so far my son,—
This lady's husband here, this, do you see,—
Whom you have banisht, does exceed you all.
          JUNIUS BRUTUS.
Well, well, we'll leave you.
          SICINIUS VELUTUS.
                    Why stay we to be baited
With one that wants her wits?
          VOLUMNIA.
                    Take my prayers with you.—
               [*Exeunt* TRIBUNES.
I would the gods had nothing else to do
But to confirm my curses! Could I meet 'em
But once a-day, it would unclog my heart
Of what lies heavy to't.
          MENENIUS AGRIPPA.
                    You have told them home;
And, by my troth, you have cause. You'll sup
     with me?
          VOLUMNIA.
Anger's my meat; I sup upon myself,
And so shall starve with feeding.—Come, let's go:
Leave this faint puling, and lament as I do,
In anger, Juno-like. Come, come, come.
          MENENIUS AGRIPPA.
Fie, fie, fie!   [*Exeunt.*

SCENE III.

A highway between Rome and Antium.

Enter a ROMAN *and a* VOLSCE, *meeting.*

          ROMAN.

I KNOW you well, sir, and you know me: your
     name, I think, is Adrian.
          VOLSCE.
It is so, sir: truly, I have forgot you.
          ROMAN.
I am a Roman; and my services are, as you are,
against 'em: know you me yet?
          VOLSCE.
Nicanor? no?
          ROMAN.
The same, sir.
          VOLSCE.
You had more beard when I last saw you; but
your favour is well approved by your tongue.
What's the news in Rome? I have a note from the
Volscian state, to find you out there: you have
well saved me a day's journey.
          ROMAN.
There hath been in Rome strange insurrections;
the people against the senators, patricians, and
nobles.
          VOLSCE.
Hath been! is it ended, then? Our state thinks not
so: they are in a most warlike preparation, and
hope to come upon them in the heat of their
division.

ROMAN.

The main blaze of it is past, but a small thing would make it flame again; for the nobles receive so to heart the banishment of that worthy Coriolanus, that they are in a ripe aptness to take all power from the people, and to pluck from them their tribunes for ever. This lies glowing, I can tell you, and is almost mature for the violent breaking out.

VOLSCE.

Coriolanus banisht!

ROMAN.

Banisht, sir.

VOLSCE.

You will be welcome with this intelligence, Nicanor.

ROMAN.

The day serves well for them now. I have heard it said, the fittest time to corrupt a man's wife is when she's faln out with her husband. Your noble Tullus Aufidius will appear well in these wars, his great opposer, Coriolanus, being now in no request of his country.

VOLSCE.

He cannot choose. I am most fortunate, thus accidentally to encounter you: you have ended my business, and I will merrily accompany you home.

ROMAN.

I shall, between this and supper, tell you most strange things from Rome; all tending to the good of their adversaries. Have you an army ready, say you?

VOLSCE.

A most royal one; the centurions and their charges, distinctly billeted, already in the entertainment, and to be on foot at an hour's warning.

ROMAN.

I am joyful to hear of their readiness, and am the man, I think, that shall set them in present action. So, sir, heartily well met, and most glad of your company.

VOLSCE.

You take my part from me, sir; I have the most cause to be glad of yours.

ROMAN.

Well, let us go together.   [*Exeunt.*

SCENE IV.

Antium.   *Before* AUFIDIUS' *house.*

Enter CORIOLANUS *in mean apparel, disguised and muffled.*

CAIUS MARCIUS CORIOLANUS.

A GOODLY city is this Antium.—City,
   'Tis I that made thy widows: many an heir
Of these fair edifices 'fore my wars
Have I heard groan and drop: then know me not;
Lest that thy wives with spits, and boys with
In puny battle slay me.   [stones,

Enter a CITIZEN.
       Save you, sir.

CITIZEN.

And you.

CAIUS MARCIUS CORIOLANUS.

Direct me, if it be your will,
Where great Aufidius lies: is he in Antium?

CITIZEN.

He is, and feasts the nobles of the state
At his house this night.

CAIUS MARCIUS CORIOLANUS.

      Which is his house, beseech you?

CITIZEN.

This, here, before you.

CAIUS MARCIUS CORIOLANUS.

      Thank you, sir: farewell.
          [*Exit* CITIZEN.

O world, thy slippery turns! Friends now fast sworn,
Whose double bosoms seems to wear one heart,
Whose hours, whose bed, whose meal, and exercise,
Are still together, who twin, as 'twere, in love
Unseparable, shall within this hour,
On a dissension of a doit, break out
To bitterest enmity: so, fellest foes,
Whose passions and whose plots have broke their sleep
To take the one the other, by some chance,
Some trick not worth an egg, shall grow dear friends
And interjoin their issues. So with me:
My birth-place hate I, and my love's upon
This enemy town.—I'll enter: if he slay me,
He does fair justice; if he give me way,
I'll do his country service.   [*Exit*

SCENE V.

The same.   *A hall in* AUFIDIUS' *house.*

Music plays.   *Enter a* SERVING-MAN.

FIRST SERVING-MAN.

W INE, wine, wine!—What service is here!
    I think our fellows are asleep.   [*Exit.*

Enter another SERVING-MAN.

SECOND SERVING-MAN.

Where's Cotus? my master calls for him.—
Cotus!   [*Exit.*

Enter CORIOLANUS.

CAIUS MARCIUS CORIOLANUS.

A goodly house: the feast smells well; but I
Appear not like a guest.

Enter the first SERVING-MAN.

FIRST SERVING-MAN.

What would you have, friend? whence are you?
Here's no place for you: pray, go to the door.
          [*Exit.*

CAIUS MARCIUS CORIOLANUS.

I have deserved no better entertainment
In being Coriolanus.

Enter second SERVING-MAN.

SECOND SERVING-MAN.

Whence are you, sir?—Has the porter his eyes in his head, that he gives entrance to such companions?—Pray, get you out.

CAIUS MARCIUS CORIOLANUS.

Away!

SECOND SERVING-MAN.

'Away!' get you away.

CAIUS MARCIUS CORIOLANUS.

Now th'art troublesome.

SECOND SERVING-MAN.

Are you so brave? I'll have you talkt with anon.

Enter a third SERVING-MAN. *The first
meets him.*

THIRD SERVING-MAN.

What fellow's this?

SECOND SERVING-MAN.

A strange one as ever I lookt on: I cannot get him
out o'the house: prithee, call my master to him.

THIRD SERVING-MAN.

What have you to do here, fellow? Pray you avoid
the house.

CAIUS MARCIUS CORIOLANUS.

Let me but stand; I will not hurt your hearth.

THIRD SERVING-MAN.

What are you?

CAIUS MARCIUS CORIOLANUS.

A gentleman.

THIRD SERVING-MAN.

A marvellous poor one.

CAIUS MARCIUS CORIOLANUS.

True, so I am.

THIRD SERVING-MAN.

Pray you, poor gentleman, take up some other
station; here's no place for you; pray you, avoid:
come.

CAIUS MARCIUS CORIOLANUS.

Follow your function, go, and batten on cold bits.
　　　　　　　　　　　　[Pushes him away from him.

THIRD SERVING-MAN.

What, you will not?—Prithee, tell my master
what a strange guest he has here.

SECOND SERVING-MAN.

And I shall.　　　　　　　　　　　　　　[*Exit.*

THIRD SERVING-MAN.

Where dwell'st thou?

CAIUS MARCIUS CORIOLANUS.

Under the canopy.

THIRD SERVING-MAN.

Under the canopy!

CAIUS MARCIUS CORIOLANUS.

Ay.

THIRD SERVING-MAN.

Where's that?

CAIUS MARCIUS CORIOLANUS.

I'th'city of kites and crows.

THIRD SERVING-MAN.

I'th'city of kites and crows!—What an ass it is!—
Then thou dwell'st with daws too?

CAIUS MARCIUS CORIOLANUS.

No, I serve not thy master.

THIRD SERVING-MAN.

How, sir! do you meddle with my master?

CAIUS MARCIUS CORIOLANUS.

Ay; 'tis an honester service than to meddle with
thy mistress: thou pratest, and pratest; serve with
thy trencher, hence!　　　　　　　　[*Beats him away.*

Enter AUFIDIUS *with the second* SERVING-
MAN.

TULLUS AUFIDIUS.

Where is this fellow?

SECOND SERVING-MAN.

Here, sir: I'ld have beaten him like a dog, but for
disturbing the lords within.　　　　　　　[*Retires.*

TULLUS AUFIDIUS.

Whence comest thou? what wouldst thou? thy
name?
Why speak'st not? speak, man: what's thy name?

CAIUS MARCIUS CORIOLANUS.

　　　　　　　　If, Tullus, [*Unmuffling.*
Not yet thou know'st me, and, seeing me, dost not
Think me for the man I am, necessity
Commands me name myself.

TULLUS AUFIDIUS.

　　　　　　　　What is thy name?

CAIUS MARCIUS CORIOLANUS.

A name unmusical to the Volscians' ears,
And harsh in sound to thine.

TULLUS AUFIDIUS.

　　　　　　　　Say, what's thy name?
Thou hast a grim appearance, and thy face
Bears a command in't; though thy tackle's torn,
Thou show'st a noble vessel: what's thy name?

CAIUS MARCIUS CORIOLANUS.

Prepare thy brow to frown:—know'st thou me
yet?

TULLUS AUFIDIUS.

I know thee not:—thy name?

CAIUS MARCIUS CORIOLANUS.

My name is Caius Marcius, who hath done
To thee particularly and to all the Volsces
Great hurt and mischief; thereto witness may
My surname, Coriolanus: the painful service,
The extreme dangers, and the drops of blood
Shed for my thankless country, are requited
But with that surname; a good memory,
And witness of the malice and displeasure
Which thou shouldst bear me: only that name
　　　remains;
The cruelty and envy of the people,
Permitted by our dastard nobles, who
Have all forsook me, hath devour'd the rest;
And suffer'd me by the voice of slaves to be
Whoopt out of Rome. Now, this extremity
Hath brought me to thy hearth; not out of hope—
Mistake me not—to save my life; for if
I had fear'd death, of all the men i'the world
I would have 'voided thee; but in mere spite,
To be full quit of those my banishers,
Stand I before thee here. Then if thou hast
A heart of wreak in thee, that wilt revenge
Thine own particular wrongs, and stop those
　　　maims
Of shame seen through thy country, speed thee
　　　straight,
And make my misery serve thy turn: so use it,
That my revengeful services may prove
As benefits to thee; for I will fight
Against my canker'd country with the spleen
Of all the under fiends. But if so be
Thou darest not this, and that to prove more
　　　fortunes
Th'art tired, then, in a word, I also am
Longer to live most weary, and present
My throat to thee and to thy ancient malice;
Which not to cut would show thee but a fool,
Since I have ever follow'd thee with hate,
Drawn tuns of blood out of thy country's breast,
And cannot live but to thy shame, unless
It be to do thee service.

TULLUS AUFIDIUS.

　　　　　　　　O Marcius, Marcius!
Each word thou hast spoke hath weeded from my
heart

A root of ancient envy. If Jupiter
Should from yond cloud speak divine things,
And say ''Tis true,' I'd not believe them more
Than thee, all-noble Marcius.—Let me twine
Mine arms about that body, where against
My grained ash an hundred times hath broke,
And scarr'd the moon with splinters: here I clip
The anvil of my sword; and do contest
As hotly and as nobly with thy love
As ever in ambitious strength I did
Contend against thy valour. Know thou first
I loved the maid I married; never man
Sigh'd truer breath; but that I see thee here,
Thou noble thing! more dances my rapt heart
Than when I first my wedded mistress saw
Bestride my threshold. Why, thou Mars! I tell thee,
We have a power on foot; and I had purpose
Once more to hew thy target from thy brawn,
Or lose mine arm for't: thou hast beat me out
Twelve several times, and I have nightly since
Dreamt of encounters 'twixt thyself and me;
We have been down together in my sleep,
Unbuckling helms, fisting each other's throat,
And waked half dead with nothing. Worthy
    Marcius,
Had we no quarrel else to Rome, but that
Thou art thence banisht, we would muster all
From twelve to seventy; and, pouring war
Into the bowels of ungrateful Rome,
Like a bold flood o'er-bear. O, come, go in,
And take our friendly senators by the hands;
Who now are here taking their leaves of me,
Who am prepared against your territories,
Though not for Rome itself.
      CAIUS MARCIUS CORIOLANUS.
                    You bless me, gods!
      TULLUS AUFIDIUS.
Therefore, most absolute sir, if thou wilt have
The leading of thine own revenges, take
The one half of my commission; and set down—
As best thou art experienced, since thou know'st
Thy country's strength and weakness—thine own
    ways;
Whether to knock against the gates of Rome,
Or rudely visit them in parts remote,
To fright them, ere destroy. But come in:
Let me commend thee first to those that shall
Say yea to thy desires. A thousand welcomes!
And more a friend than e'er an enemy;
Yet, Marcius, that was much. Your hand: most
    welcome!
    [*Exeunt* CORIOLANUS *and* AUFIDIUS.—
    The two SERVING-MEN *come forward.*
      FIRST SERVING-MAN.
Here's a strange alteration!
      SECOND SERVING-MAN.
By my hand, I had thought to have strucken him
with a cudgel; and yet my mind gave me his
clothes made a false report of him.
      FIRST SERVING-MAN.
What an arm he has! he turn'd me about with his
finger and his thumb as one would set up a top.
      SECOND SERVING-MAN.
Nay, I knew by his face that there was something
in him: he had, sir, a kind of face, methought,—I
cannot tell how to term it.

      FIRST SERVING-MAN.
He had so; looking as it were—Would I were
hang'd, but I thought there was more in him than
I could think.
      SECOND SERVING-MAN.
So did I, I'll be sworn: he is simply the rarest man
i'the world.
      FIRST SERVING-MAN.
I think he is: but a greater soldier than he you
wot on.
      SECOND SERVING-MAN.
Who, my master?
      FIRST SERVING-MAN.
Nay, it's no matter for that.
      SECOND SERVING-MAN.
Worth six on him.
      FIRST SERVING-MAN.
Nay, not so neither: but I take him to be the
greater soldier.
      SECOND SERVING-MAN.
Faith, look you, one cannot tell how to say that:
for the defence of a town our general is excellent.
      FIRST SERVING-MAN.
Ay, and for an assault too.
    Enter the third SERVING-MAN.
      THIRD SERVING-MAN.
O slaves, I can tell you news,—news, you rascals!
      FIRST *and* SECOND SERVING-MEN.
What, what, what? let's partake.
      THIRD SERVING-MAN.
I would not be a Roman, of all nations; I had as
lief be a condemn'd man.
      FIRST *and* SECOND SERVING-MEN.
Wherefore? wherefore?
      THIRD SERVING-MAN.
Why, here's he that was wont to thwack our
general,—Caius Marcius.
      FIRST SERVING-MAN.
Why do you say 'thwack our general'?
      THIRD SERVING-MAN.
I do not say 'thwack our general;' but he was
always good enough for him.
      SECOND SERVING-MAN.
Come, we are fellows and friends: he was ever too
hard for him; I have heard him say so himself.
      FIRST SERVING-MAN.
He was too hard for him directly, to say the troth
on't: before Corioli he scotcht him and notcht
him like a carbonado.
      SECOND SERVING-MAN.
An he had been cannibally given, he might have
broil'd and eaten him too.
      FIRST SERVING-MAN.
But, more of thy news?
      THIRD SERVING-MAN.
Why, he is so made on here within as if he were
son and heir to Mars; set at upper end o'the table;
no question askt him by any of the senators, but
they stand bald before him: our general himself
makes a mistress of him; sanctifies himself with's
hand, and turns up the white o'the eye to his discourse. But the bottom of the news is, our general
is cut i'the middle, and but one half of what he
was yesterday; for the other has half, by the entreaty and grant of the whole table. He'll go, he
says, and sowl the porter of Rome gates by the

ears: he will mow all down before him, and leave
his passage poll'd.

SECOND SERVING-MAN.

And he's as like to do't as any man I can imagine.

THIRD SERVING-MAN.

Do't! he will do't; for, look you, sir, he has as
many friends as enemies: which friends, sir, as it
were, durst not, look you, sir, show themselves,
as we term it, his friends whilst he's in directitude.

FIRST SERVING-MAN.

Directitude! what's that?

THIRD SERVING-MAN.

But when they shall see, sir, his crest up again,
and the man in blood, they will out of their bur-
rows, like conies after rain, and revel all with him.

FIRST SERVING-MAN.

But when goes this forward?

THIRD SERVING-MAN.

To-morrow; to-day; presently; you shall have the
drum struck up this afternoon: 'tis, as it were, a
parcel of their feast, and to be executed ere they
wipe their lips.

SECOND SERVING-MAN.

Why, then we shall have a stirring world again.
This peace is nothing, but to rust iron, increase
tailors, and breed ballad-makers.

FIRST SERVING-MAN.

Let me have war, say I; it exceeds peace as far as
day does night; it's spritely, waking, audible, and
full of vent. Peace is a very apoplexy, lethargy;
mull'd, deaf, sleepy, insensible; a getter of more
bastard children than war's a destroyer of men.

SECOND SERVING-MAN.

'Tis so: and as war, in some sort, may be said to
be a ravisher, so it cannot be denied but peace is a
great maker of cuckolds.

FIRST SERVING-MAN.

Ay, and it makes men hate one another.

THIRD SERVING-MAN.

Reason; because they then less need one another.
The wars for my money. I hope to see Romans as
cheap as Volscians.—They are rising, they are
rising.

ALL THREE.

In, in, in, in!   [*Exeunt.*

SCENE VI.

Rome.   A public place.

Enter the two TRIBUNES, SICINIUS *and*
BRUTUS.

SICINIUS VELUTUS.

WE hear not of him, neither need we fear him;
    His remedies are tame i'the present peace
And quietness of the people, which before
Were in wild hurry. Here do we make his friends
Blush that the world goes well; who rather had,
Though they themselves did suffer by't, behold
Dissentious numbers pest'ring streets, than see
Our tradesmen singing in their shops, and going
About their functions friendly.

JUNIUS BRUTUS.

We stood to't in good time.—Is this Menenius?

SICINIUS VELUTUS.

'Tis he, 'tis he: O, he is grown most kind
Of late. Hail, sir!

Enter MENENIUS.

JUNIUS BRUTUS.

Hail, sir!

MENENIUS AGRIPPA.

Hail to you both!

SICINIUS VELUTUS.

Your Coriolanus, sir, is not much mist
But with his friends: the commonwealth doth
    stand;
And so would do, were he more angry at it.

MENENIUS AGRIPPA.

All's well; and might have been much better, if
He could have temporized.

SICINIUS VELUTUS.

Where is he, hear you?

MENENIUS AGRIPPA.

Nay, I hear nothing: his mother and his wife
Hear nothing from him.

Enter three or four CITIZENS.

CITIZENS.

The gods preserve you both!

SICINIUS VELUTUS.

God-den, our neighbours.

JUNIUS BRUTUS.

God-den to you all, god-den to you all.

FIRST CITIZEN.

Ourselves, our wives, and children, on our knees,
Are bound to pray for you both.

SICINIUS VELUTUS.

Live, and thrive!

JUNIUS BRUTUS.

Farewell, kind neighbours: we wisht Coriolanus
Had loved you as we did.

CITIZENS.

Now the gods keep you!

BOTH TRIBUNES.

Farewell, farewell.   [*Exeunt* CITIZENS.

SICINIUS VELUTUS.

This is a happier and more comely time
Than when these fellows ran about the streets
Crying confusion.

JUNIUS BRUTUS.

Caius Marcius was
A worthy officer i'the war; but insolent,
O'ercome with pride, ambitious past all thinking,
Self-loving,—

SICINIUS VELUTUS.

And affecting one sole throne,
Without assistance.

MENENIUS AGRIPPA.

I think not so.

SICINIUS VELUTUS.

We should by this, to all our lamentation,
If he had gone forth consul, found it so.

JUNIUS BRUTUS.

The gods have well prevented it, and Rome
Sits safe and still without him.

Enter an AEDILE.

AEDILE.

Worthy tribunes,
There is a slave, whom we have put in prison,
Reports the Volsces with two several powers
Are enter'd in the Roman territories,
And with the deepest malice of the war
Destroy what lies before 'em.

MENENIUS AGRIPPA.
          'Tis Aufidius,
Who, hearing of our Marcius' banishment,
Thrusts forth his horns again into the world;
Which were inshell'd when Marcius stood for
And durst not once peep out.   [Rome,
      SICINIUS VELUTUS.
          Come, what talk you
Of Marcius?
      JUNIUS BRUTUS.
Go see this rumourer whipt.—It cannot be
The Volsces dare break with us.
      MENENIUS AGRIPPA.
          Cannot be!
We have record that very well it can;
And tl ree examples of the like hath been
Within my age. But reason with the fellow,
Before you punish him, where he heard this;
Lest you shall chance to whip your information,
And beat the messenger who bids beware
Of what is to be dreaded.
      SICINIUS VELUTUS.
          Tell not me:
I know this cannot be.
      JUNIUS BRUTUS.
          Not possible.
      Enter a MESSENGER.
      MESSENGER.
The nobles in great earnestness are going
All to the senate-house: some news is come
That turns their countenances.
      SICINIUS VELUTUS.
          'Tis this slave;—
Go whip him 'fore the people's eyes:—his raising;
Nothing but his report.
      MESSENGER.
          Yes, worthy sir,
The slave's report is seconded; and more,
More fearful, is deliver'd.
      SICINIUS VELUTUS.
          What more fearful?
      MESSENGER.
It is spoke freely out of many mouths—
How probable I do not know— that Marcius,
Join'd with Aufidius, leads a power 'gainst Rome,
And vows revenge as spacious as between
The young'st and oldest thing.
      SICINIUS VELUTUS.
          This is most likely!
      JUNIUS BRUTUS.
Raised only, that the weaker sort may wish
Good Marcius home again.
      SICINIUS VELUTUS.
          The very trick on't.
      MENENIUS AGRIPPA.
This is unlikely:
He and Aufidius can no more atone
Than violentest contrariety.
      Enter a second MESSENGER.
      SECOND MESSENGER.
You are sent for to the senate:
A fearful army, led by Caius Marcius
Associated with Aufidius, rages
Upon our territories; and have already
O'erborne their way, consumed with fire, and took
What lay before them.

      Enter COMINIUS.
      COMINIUS.
O, you have made good work!
      MENENIUS AGRIPPA.
          What news? what news?
      COMINIUS.
You have holp to ravish your own daughters, and
To melt the city leads upon your pates;
To see your wives dishonour'd to your noses,—
      MENENIUS AGRIPPA.
What's the news? what's the news?
      COMINIUS.
Your temples burned in their cement; and
Your franchises, whereon you stood, confined
Into an auger's bore.
      MENENIUS AGRIPPA.
          Pray now, your news?—
You have made fair work, I fear me.—Pray, your
    news?—
If Marcius should be join'd with Volscians,—
      COMINIUS.
             If!
He is their god: he leads them like a thing
Made by some other deity than nature,
That shapes man better; and they follow him,
Against us brats, with no less confidence
Than boys pursuing summer butterflies,
Or butchers killing flies.
      MENENIUS AGRIPPA.
          You have made good work,
You and your apron-men; you that stood so much
Upon the voice of occupation and
The breath of garlic-eaters!
      COMINIUS.
          He will shake
Your Rome about your ears.
      MENENIUS AGRIPPA.
          As Hercules
Did shake down mellow fruit.—You have made
    fair work!
      JUNIUS BRUTUS.
But is this true, sir?
      COMINIUS.
          Ay; and you'll look pale
Before you find it other. All the regions
Do smilingly revolt; and who resist
Are mockt for valiant ignorance,
And perish constant fools. Who is't can blame
    him?
Your enemies and his find something in him.
      MENENIUS AGRIPPA.
We are all undone, unless
The noble man have mercy.
      COMINIUS.
          Who shall ask it?
The tribunes cannot do't for shame; the people
Deserve such pity of him as the wolf
Does of the shepherds: for his best friends, if they
Should say, 'Be good to Rome,' they charged him
    even
As those should do that had deserved his hate,
And therein show'd like enemies.
      MENENIUS AGRIPPA.
          'Tis true:
If he were putting to my house the brand
That should consume it, I have not the face

To say, 'Beseech you, cease.'—You have made
    fair hands,
You and your crafts! you have crafted fair!

COMINIUS.
                You have brought
A trembling upon Rome, such as was never
So incapable of help.

BOTH TRIBUNES.
        Say not, we brought it.

MENENIUS AGRIPPA.
How! Was it we? we loved him; but, like beasts
And cowardly nobles, gave way unto your clusters,
Who did hoot him out o'the city.

COMINIUS.
           But I fear
They'll roar him in again. Tullus Aufidius,
The second name of men, obeys his points
As if he were his officer:—desperation
Is all the policy, strength, and defence,
That Rome can make against them.

Enter a troop of CITIZENS.

MENENIUS AGRIPPA.
          Here come the clusters.—
And is Aufidius with him?—You are they
That made the air unwholesome, when you cast
Your stinking greasy caps in hooting at
Coriolanus' exile. Now he's coming;
And not a hair upon a soldier's head
Which will not prove a whip: as many coxcombs
As you threw caps up will he tumble down,
And pay you for your voices. 'Tis no matter;
If he could burn us all into one coal,
We have deserved it.

CITIZENS.
Faith, we hear fearful news.

FIRST CITIZEN.
          For mine own part,
When I said, banish him, I said, 'twas pity.

SECOND CITIZEN.
And so did I.

THIRD CITIZEN.
And so did I; and, to say the truth, so did very
many of us; that we did, we did for the best; and
though we willingly consented to his banishment,
yet it was against our will.

COMINIUS.
Y'are goodly things, you voices!

MENENIUS AGRIPPA.
          You have made
Good work, you and your cry!—Shall's to the
    Capitol?

COMINIUS.
O, ay, what else?

[*Exeunt* COMINIUS *and* MENENIUS.

SICINIUS VELUTUS.
Go, masters, get you home; be not dismay'd:
These are a side that would be glad to have
This true which they so seem to fear. Go home,
And show no sign of fear.

FIRST CITIZEN.
The gods be good to us!—Come, masters, let's
home. I ever said we were i'the wrong when we
banish him.

SECOND CITIZEN.
So did we all. But, come, let's home.

[*Exeunt* CITIZENS.

JUNIUS BRUTUS.
I do not like this news.

SICINIUS VELUTUS.
Nor I.

JUNIUS BRUTUS.
Let's to the Capitol.—Would half my wealth
Would buy this for a lie!

SICINIUS VELUTUS.
          Pray, let us go.   [*Exeunt.*

SCENE VII.

A camp, at a small distance from Rome.

Enter AUFIDIUS *with his* LIEUTENANT.

TULLUS AUFIDIUS.
DO they still fly to the Roman?

LIEUTENANT.
I do not know what witchcraft's in him, but
Your soldiers use him as the grace 'fore meat,
Their talk at table, and their thanks at end;
And you are darken'd in this action, sir,
Even by your own.

TULLUS AUFIDIUS.
         I cannot help it now,
Unless, by using means, I lame the foot
Of our design. He bears himself more proudlier,
Even to my person, than I thought he would
When first I did embrace him: yet his nature
In that's no changeling; and I must excuse
What cannot be amended.

LIEUTENANT.
          Yet I wish, sir,—
I mean for your particular,—you had not
Join'd in commission with him; but either
Had borne the action of yourself, or else
To him had left it solely.

TULLUS AUFIDIUS.
I understand thee well; and be thou sure,
When he shall come to his account, he knows not
What I can urge against him. Although it seems,
And so he thinks, and is no less apparent
To the vulgar eye, that he bears all things fairly,
And shows good husbandry for the Volscian state,
Fights dragon-like, and does achieve as soon
As draw his sword; yet he hath left undone
That which shall break his neck or hazard mine,
Whene'er we come to our account.

LIEUTENANT.
Sir, I beseech you, think you he'll carry Rome?

TULLUS AUFIDIUS.
All places yield to him ere he sits down;
And the nobility of Rome are his:
The senators and patricians love him too:
The tribunes are no soldiers; and their people
Will be as rash in the repeal, as hasty
To expel him thence. I think he'll be to Rome
As is the osprey to the fish, who takes it
By sovereignty of nature. First he was
A noble servant to them; but he could not
Carry his honours even: whether 'twas pride,
Which out of daily fortune ever taints
The happy man; whether defect of judgement,
To fail in the disposing of those chances
Which he was lord of; or whether nature,
Not to be other than one thing, not moving

From the casque to the cushion, but commanding
Even with the same austerity and garb   [peace
As he controll'd the war; but one of these—
As he hath spices of them all, not all,
For I dare so far free him—made him fear'd,
So hated, and so banisht: but he has a merit,
To choke it in the utterance. So our virtues
Lie in the interpretation of the time;
And power, unto itself most commendable,
Hath not a tomb so evident as a chair
T'extol what it hath done.
One fire drives out one fire; one nail, one nail;
Rights by rights falter, strengths by strengths do
          fail.
Come, let's away. When, Caius, Rome is thine,
Thou'rt poor'st of all; then shortly art thou mine.
                              [*Exeunt*.

ACT V.   SCENE I.

Rome.   A public place.

Enter MENENIUS, COMINIUS, SICINIUS,
          BRUTUS, *and others*,

MENENIUS AGRIPPA.

NO, I'll not go: you hear what he hath said
    Which was sometime his general; who loved
          him
In a most dear particular. He call'd me father:
But what o'that? Go, you that banisht him;
A mile before his tent fall down, and knee
The way into his mercy: nay, if he coy'd
To hear Cominius speak, I'll keep at home.
COMINIUS.
He would not seem to know me.
MENENIUS AGRIPPA.
                              Do you hear?
COMINIUS.
Yet one time he did call me by my name:
I urged our old acquaintance, and the drops
That we have bled together. Coriolanus
He wou'd not answer to: forbade all names;
He was a kind of nothing, titleless,
Till he had forged himself a name o'the fire
Of burning Rome.
MENENIUS AGRIPPA.
          Why, so,—you have made good work!
A pair of tribunes that have rackt for Rome
To make coals cheap,—a noble memory!
COMINIUS.
I minded him how royal 'twas to pardon
When it was least expected: he replied,
It was a base petition of a state
To one whom they had punisht.
MENENIUS AGRIPPA.
                              Very well:
Could he say less?
COMINIUS.
I offer'd to awaken his regard
For's private friends: his answer to me was,
He could not stay to pick them in a pile
Of noisome musty chaff: he said 'twas folly,
For one poor grain or two, to leave unburnt,
And still to nose the offence.
MENENIUS AGRIPPA.
                    For one poor grain or two!
I am one of those; his mother, wife, his child,

And this brave fellow too, we are the grains;
You are the musty chaff; and you are smelt
Above the moon: we must be burnt for you.
SICINIUS VELUTUS.
Nay, pray, be patient: if you refuse your aid
In this so never-needed help, yet do not
Upbraid's with our distress. But, sure, if you
Would be your country's pleader, your good
          tongue,
More than the instant army we can make,
Might stop our countryman.
MENENIUS AGRIPPA.
                              No, I'll not meddle.
SICINIUS VELUTUS.
Pray you, go to him.
MENENIUS AGRIPPA.
                    What should I do?
JUNIUS BRUTUS.
Only make trial what your love can do
For Rome, towards Marcius.
MENENIUS AGRIPPA.
                    Well, and say that Marcius
Return me, as Cominius is return'd,
Unheard; what then?
But as a discontented friend, grief-shot
With his unkindness? say't be so?
SICINIUS VELUTUS.
                              Yet your good will
Must have that thanks from Rome, after the
          measure
As you intended well.
MENENIUS AGRIPPA.
                    I'll undertake't:
I think he'll hear me. Yet, to bite his lip
And hum at good Cominius, much unhearts me.
He was not taken well; he had not dined:
The veins unfill'd, our blood is cold, and then
We pout upon the morning, are unapt
To give or to forgive; but when we've stuft
These pipes and these conveyances of our blood
With wine and feeding, we have suppler souls
Than in our priest-like fasts: therefore I'll watch
          him
Till he be dieted to my request,
And then I'll set upon him.
JUNIUS BRUTUS.
You know the very road into his kindness,
And cannot lose your way.
MENENIUS AGRIPPA.
                    Good faith, I'll prove him,
Speed how it will: you shall ere long have know-
          ledge
Of my success.   [*Exit*.
COMINIUS.
He'll never hear him.
SICINIUS VELUTUS.
                    Not?
COMINIUS.
I tell you, he does sit in gold, his eye
Red as 'twould burn Rome; and his injury
The gaoler to his pity. I kneel'd before him;
'Twas very faintly he said 'Rise;' dismist me
Thus, with his speechless hand: what he would do,
He sent in writing after me; what he would not,
Bound with an oath to yield no fresh conditions:
So that all hope is vain,

Unless in's noble mother and his wife;
Who, as I hear, mean to solicit him
For mercy to his country. Therefore let's hence,
And with our fair entreaties haste them on.

                                    [Exeunt.

SCENE II.

The Volscian camp before Rome.
The SENTINELS *at their stations.*

Enter MENENIUS *to the* WATCH *or* GUARD.

               FIRST SENTINEL.

STAY: whence are you?
               SECOND SENTINEL.
                       Stand, and go back.
               MENENIUS AGRIPPA.
You guard like men; 'tis well: but, by your leave,
I am an officer of state, and come
To speak with Coriolanus.
               FIRST SENTINEL.
                     From whence?
               MENENIUS AGRIPPA.
                     From Rome.
               FIRST SENTINEL.
You may not pass, you must return: our general
Will no more hear from thence.
               SECOND SENTINEL.
You'll see your Rome embraced with fire, before
You'll speak with Coriolanus.
               MENENIUS AGRIPPA.
                Good my friends,
If you have heard your general talk of Rome,
And of his friends there, it is lots to blanks
My name hath toucht your ears: it is Menenius.
               FIRST SENTINEL.
Be it so; go back: the virtue of your name
Is not here passable.
               MENENIUS AGRIPPA.
               I tell thee, fellow,
Thy general is my lover: I have been
The book of his good acts, whence men have read
His fame unparallel'd, haply amplified;
For I have ever verified my friends—
Of whom he's chief—with all the size that verity
Would without lapsing suffer: nay, sometimes,
Like to a bowl upon a subtle ground,
I have tumbled past the throw; and in his praise
Have almost stampt the leasing: therefore, fellow,
I must have leave to pass.
               FIRST SENTINEL.
Faith, sir, if you had told as many lies in his behalf
as you have utter'd words in your own, you should
not pass here; no, though it were as virtuous to lie
as to live chastely. Therefore, go back.
               MENENIUS AGRIPPA.
Prithee, fellow, remember my name is Menenius,
always factionary on the party of your general.
               SECOND SENTINEL.
Howsoever you have been his liar, as you say you
have, I am one that, telling true under him, must
say you cannot pass. Therefore, go back.
               MENENIUS AGRIPPA.
Has he dined, canst thou tell? for I would not
speak with him till after dinner.
               FIRST SENTINEL.
You are a Roman, are you?

               MENENIUS AGRIPPA.
I am, as thy general is.
               FIRST SENTINEL.
Then you should hate Rome, as he does. Can you,
when you have pusht out your gates the very defender of them, and, in a violent popular ignorance, given your enemy your shield, think to front
his revenges with the easy groans of old women,
the virginal palms of your daughters, or with the
palsied intercession of such a decay'd dotant as
you seem to be? Can you think to blow out the intended fire your city is ready to flame in with such
weak breath as this? No, you are deceived; therefore, back to Rome, and prepare for your execution: you are condemn'd, our general has sworn
you out of reprieve and pardon.
               MENENIUS AGRIPPA.
Sirrah, if thy captain knew I were here, he would
use me with estimation.
               SECOND SENTINEL.
Come, my captain knows you not.
               MENENIUS AGRIPPA.
I mean, thy general.
               FIRST SENTINEL.
My general cares not for you. Back, I say, go; lest
I let forth your half-pint of blood;—back,—that's
the utmost of your having:—back.
               MENENIUS AGRIPPA.
Nay, but, fellow, fellow,—
          Enter CORIOLANUS *and* AUFIDIUS.
          CAIUS MARCIUS CORIOLANUS.
What's the matter?
               MENENIUS AGRIPPA.
Now, you companion, I'll say an errand for you:
you shall know now that I am in estimation; you
shall perceive that a Jack guardant cannot office
me from my son Coriolanus: guess, but by my
entertainment with him, if thou stand'st not i'the
state of hanging, or of some death more long in
spectatorship, and crueller in suffering; behold
now presently, and swound for what's to come
upon thee.—[*to* CORIOLANUS] The glorious gods
sit in hourly synod about thy particular prosperity, and love thee no worse than thy old father
Menenius does! O my son, my son! thou art preparing fire for us; look thee, here's water to quench
it. I was hardly moved to come to thee; but being
assured none but myself could move thee, I have
been blown out of our gates with sighs; and conjure thee to pardon Rome, and thy petitionary
countrymen. The good gods assuage thy wrath,
and turn the dregs of it upon this varlet here,—
this, who, like a block, hath denied my access to
thee.
          CAIUS MARCIUS CORIOLANUS.
Away!
               MENENIUS AGRIPPA.
How! away!
          CAIUS MARCIUS CORIOLANUS.
Wife, mother, child, I know not. My affairs
Are servanted to others: though I owe
My revenge properly, my remission lies
In Volscian breasts. That we have been familiar,
Ingrate forgetfulness shall prison, rather
Than pity note how much. Therefore, be gone.
Mine ears against your suits are stronger than

Your gates against my force. Yet, for I loved thee,
Take this along; I writ it for thy sake,
[Gives a letter.
And would have sent it. Another word, Menenius,
I will not hear thee speak.—This man, Aufidius,
Was my beloved in Rome: yet thou behold'st!

TULLUS AUFIDIUS.

You keep a constant temper.
[Exeunt CORIOLANUS and AUFIDIUS.

FIRST SENTINEL.

Now, sir, is your name Menenius?

SECOND SENTINEL.

'Tis a spell, you see, of much power: you know
the way home again.

FIRST SENTINEL.

Do you hear how we are shent for keeping your
greatness back?

SECOND SENTINEL.

What cause, do you think, I have to swound?

MENENIUS AGRIPPA.

I neither care for the world nor your general: for
such things as you, I can scarce think there's any,
y'are so slight. He that hath a will to die by himself fears it not from another: let your general do
his worst. For you, be that you are, long; and your
misery increase with your age! I say to you, as I
was said to, Away!   [Exit.

FIRST SENTINEL.

A noble fellow, I warrant him.

SECOND SENTINEL.

The worthy fellow is our general: he's the rock,
the oak not to be wind-shaken.   [Exeunt.

SCENE III.

The tent of CORIOLANUS.

Enter CORIOLANUS, AUFIDIUS, and others.

CAIUS MARCIUS CORIOLANUS.

WE will before the walls of Rome to-morrow
Set down our host.—My partner in this
    action,
You must report to the Volscian lords, how plainly
I have borne this business.

TULLUS AUFIDIUS.

             Only their ends
You have respected; stopt your ears against
The general suit of Rome; never admitted
A private whisper, no, not with such friends
That thought them sure of you.

CAIUS MARCIUS CORIOLANUS.

             This last old man,
Whom with a crackt heart I have sent to Rome,
Loved me above the measure of a father;
Nay, godded me, indeed. Their latest refuge
Was to send him; for whose old love I have,
Though I show'd sourly to him, once more offer'd
The first conditions, which they did refuse,
And cannot now accept; to grace him only
That thought he could do more, a very little
I have yielded to: fresh embassies and suits,
Nor from the state nor private friends, hereafter
Will I lend ear to.—Ha! what shout is this?
[Shout within.
Shall I be tempted to infringe my vow
In the same time 'tis made? I will not.

Enter, in mourning habits, VIRGILIA, VOLUM-
NIA, *leading* YOUNG MARCIUS, VALERIA,
with ATTENDANTS.

My wife comes foremost; then the honour'd
    mould
Wherein this trunk was framed, and in her hand
The grandchild to her blood. But out, affection!
All bond and privilege of nature, break!
Let it be virtuous to be obstinate.—
What is that curt'sy worth? or those doves' eyes,
Which can make gods forsworn?—I melt, and am
    not
Of stronger earth than others.—My mother
    bows;
As if Olympus to a molehill should
In supplication nod: and my young boy
Hath an aspect of intercession, which
Great nature cries 'Deny not.'—Let the Volsces
Plough Rome, and harrow Italy: I'll never
Be such a gosling to obey instinct; but stand,
As if a man were author of himself,
And knew no other kin.

VIRGILIA.

             My lord and husband!

CAIUS MARCIUS CORIOLANUS.

These eyes are not the same I wore in Rome.

VIRGILIA.

The sorrow that delivers us thus changed
Makes you think so.

CAIUS MARCIUS CORIOLANUS.

            Like a dull actor now,
I have forgot my part, and I am out,
Even to a full disgrace.—Best of my flesh,
Forgive my tyranny; but do not say,
For that, 'Forgive our Romans.' O, a kiss
Long as my exile, sweet as my revenge!
Now, by the jealous queen of heaven, that kiss
I carried from thee, dear; and my true lip
Hath virgin'd it e'er since.—You gods! I prate,
And the most noble mother of the world
Leave unsaluted: sink, my knee, i'the earth;
[Kneels.
Of thy deep duty more impression show
Than that of common sons.

VOLUMNIA.

            O, stand up blest!
Whilst, with no softer cushion than the flint,
I kneel before thee; and unproperly
Show duty, as mistaken all this while
Between the child and parent.   [Kneels

CAIUS MARCIUS CORIOLANUS.

             What is this?
Your knees to me? to your corrected son?
Then let the pebbles on the hungry beach
Fillip the stars; then let the mutinous winds
Strike the proud cedars 'gainst the fiery sun;
Murd'ring impossibility, to make
What cannot be, slight work.

VOLUMNIA.

            Thou art my warrior,
I holp to frame thee.—Do you know this lady?

CAIUS MARCIUS CORIOLANUS.

The noble sister of Publicola,
The moon of Rome; chaste as the icicle,
That's curdied by the frost from purest snow,
And hangs on Dian's temple:—dear Valeria!

VOLUMNIA.

This is a poor epitome of yours,
Which by the interpretation of full time
May show like all yourself.

CAIUS MARCIUS CORIOLANUS.

The god of soldiers,
With the consent of supreme Jove, inform
Thy thoughts with nobleness; that thou mayst
    prove
To shame unvulnerable, and stick i'the wars
Like a great sea-mark, standing every flaw,
And saving those that eye thee!

VOLUMNIA.

Your knee, sirrah.

CAIUS MARCIUS CORIOLANUS.

That's my brave boy!

VOLUMNIA.

Even he, your wife, this lady, and myself,
Are suitors to you.

CAIUS MARCIUS CORIOLANUS.

I beseech you, peace:
Or, if you'ld ask, remember this before,—
The things I have forsworn to grant may r ever
Be held by you denials. Do not bid me
Dismiss my soldiers, or capitulate
Again with Rome's mechanics:—tell me not
Wherein I seem unnatural: desire not
T'allay my rages and revenges with
Your colder reasons.

VOLUMNIA.

O, no more, no more!
You have said you will not grant us any thing;
For we have nothing else to ask, but that
Which you deny already: yet we will ask;
That, if you fail in our request, the blame
May hang upon your hardness: therefore hear us.

CAIUS MARCIUS CORIOLANUS.

Aufidius, and you Volsces, mark; for we'll
Hear naught from Rome in private.—Your re-
    quest?

VOLUMNIA.

Should we be silent and not speak, our raiment
And state of bodies would bewray what life
We have led since thy exile. Think with thyself
How more unfortunate than all living women
Are we come hither: since that thy sight, which
    should
Make our eyes flow with joy, hearts dance with
    comforts,
Constrains them weep, and shake with fear and
    sorrow;
Making the mother, wife, and child, to see
The son, the husband, and the father, tearing
His country's bowels out. And to poor we
Thine enmity's most capital: thou barr'st us
Our prayers to the gods, which is a comfort
That all but we enjoy; for how can we,
Alas, how can we for our country pray,   [tory,
Whereto we are bound,—together with thy vic-
Whereto we are bound? alack, or we must lose
The country, our dear nurse, or else thy person,
Our comfort in the country. We must find
An evident calamity, though we had
Our wish, which side should win; for either thou
Must, as a foreign recreant, be led
With manacles thorough our streets, or else

Triumphantly tread on thy country's ruin,
And bear the palm for having bravely shed
Thy wife and children's blood. For myself, son,
I purpose not to wait on fortune till
These wars determine: if I cannot persuade thee
Rather to show a noble grace to both parts
Than seek the end of one, thou shalt no sooner
March to assault thy country than to tread—
Trust to't, thou shalt not—on thy mother's womb
That brought thee to this world.

VIRGILIA.

Ay, and mine,
That brought you forth this boy, to keep your
    name
Living to time.

YOUNG MARCIUS.

A' shall not tread on me;
I'll run away till I am bigger, but then I'll fight.

CAIUS MARCIUS CORIOLANUS.

Not of a woman's tenderness to be,
Requires nor child nor woman's face to see.
I have sat too long.   [Rising.

VOLUMNIA.

Nay, go not from us thus.
If it were so that our request did tend
To save the Romans, thereby to destroy
The Volsces whom you serve, you might condemn
    us,
As poisonous of your honour: no; our suit
Is, that you reconcile them: while the Volsces
May say, 'This mercy we have show'd;' the
    Romans,
'This we received;' and each in either side
Give the all-hail to thee, and cry, 'Be blest
For making up this peace!' Thou know'st, great
    son,
The end of war's uncertain; but this certain,
That, if thou conquer Rome, the benefit
Which thou shalt thereby reap is such a name,
Whose repetition will be dogg'd with curses;
Whose chronicle thus writ,—'The man was noble,
But with his last attempt he wiped it out;
Destroy'd his country; and his name remains
To the ensuing age abhorr'd.' Speak to me, son:
Thou hast affected the fine strains of honour,
To imitate the graces of the gods;
To tear with thunder the wide cheeks o'the air,
And yet to charge thy sulphur with a bolt
That should but rive an oak. Why dost not speak?
Think'st thou it honourable for a noble man
Still to remember wrongs?—Daughter, speak you:
He cares not for your weeping.—Speak thou, boy:
Perhaps thy childishness will move him more
Than can our reasons.—There's no man in the
    world
More bound to's mother; yet here he lets me prate
Like one i'the stocks.—Thou hast never in thy life
Show'd thy dear mother any courtesy;
When she, poor hen, fond of no second brood,
Has cluckt thee to the wars, and safely home,
Loaden with honour. Say my request's unjust,
And spurn me back: but if it be not so,
Thou art not honest; and the gods will plague thee,
That thou restrain'st from me the duty which
To a mother's part belongs.—He turns away:
Down, ladies; let us shame him with our knees.

To his surname Coriolanus 'longs more pride
Than pity to our prayers. Down: an end;
This is the last:—so we will home to Rome,
And die among our neighbours.—Nay, behold's:
This boy, that cannot tell what he would have,
But kneels and holds up hands for fellowship,
Does reason our petition with more strength
Than thou hast to deny't.—Come, let us go:
This fellow had a Volscian to his mother;
His wife is in Corioli, and this child
Like him by chance.—Yet give us our dispatch:
I am husht until our city be a-fire,
And then I'll speak a little.

CAIUS MARCIUS CORIOLANUS [*holding her by*
the hand, silent].
     O mother, mother!
What have you done? Behold, the heavens do ope,
The gods look down, and this unnatural scene
They laugh at. O my mother, mother! O!
You have won a happy victory to Rome;
But, for your son, believe it, O, believe it,
Most dangerously you have with him prevail'd,
If not most mortal to him. But, let it come.—
Aufidius, though I cannot make true wars,
I'll frame convenient peace.—Now, good Aufi-
dius,
Were you in my stead, would you have heard
A mother less? or granted less, Aufidius?

TULLUS AUFIDIUS.
I was moved withal.

CAIUS MARCIUS CORIOLANUS.
     I dare be sworn you were:
And, sir, it is no little thing to make
Mine eyes to sweat compassion. But, good sir,
What peace you'll make, advise me: for my part
I'll not to Rome, I'll back with you; and pray you,
Stand to me in this cause.—O mother! wife!

TULLUS AUFIDIUS [*aside*].
I am glad thou hast set thy mercy and thy honour
At difference in thee: out of that I'll work
Myself a former fortune.

  [*The* LADIES *make signs to* CORIOLANUS.
CAIUS MARCIUS CORIOLANUS [*to* VOLUMNIA,
VIRGILIA, *&c.*].
     Ay, by and by;
But we will drink together; and you shall bear
A better witness back than words, which we,
On like conditions, will have counter-seal'd.
Come, enter with us. Ladies, you deserve
To have a temple built you: all the swords
In Italy, and her confederate arms,
Could not have made this peace. [*Exeunt.*

SCENE IV.

Rome.   A public place.

Enter MENENIUS *with* SICINIUS.

MENENIUS AGRIPPA.
SEE you yond coign o' the Capitol,—yond cor-
ner-stone?

SICINIUS VELUTUS.
Why, what of that?

MENENIUS AGRIPPA.
If it be possible for you to displace it with your
little finger, there is some hope the ladies of Rome,
especially his mother, may prevail with him. But

I say there is no hope in't: our throats are sentenced, and stay upon execution.

SICINIUS VELUTUS.
Is't possible that so short a time can alter the condition of a man?

MENENIUS AGRIPPA.
There is difference between a grub and a butterfly; yet your butterfly was a grub. This Marcius is
grown from man to dragon: he has wings; he's
more than a creeping thing.

SICINIUS VELUTUS.
He loved his mother dearly.

MENENIUS AGRIPPA.
So did he me: and he no more remembers his
mother now than an eight-year-old horse. The
tartness of his face sours ripe grapes: when he
walks, he moves like an engine, and the ground
shrinks before his treading: he is able to pierce a
corslet with his eye; talks like a knell, and his hum
is a battery. He sits in his state, as a thing made
for Alexander. What he bids be done, is finisht
with his bidding. He wants nothing of a god but
eternity, and a heaven to throne in.

SICINIUS VELUTUS.
Yes, mercy, if you report him truly.

MENENIUS AGRIPPA.
I paint him in the character. Mark what mercy his
mother shall bring from him: there is no more
mercy in him than there is milk in a male tiger;
that shall our poor city find: and all this is 'long of
you.

SICINIUS VELUTUS.
The gods be good unto us!

MENENIUS AGRIPPA.
No, in such a case the gods will not be good unto
us. When we banisht him, we respected not them;
and, he returning to break our necks, they respect
not us.

  Enter a MESSENGER.

MESSENGER.
Sir, if you'ld save your life, fly to your house:
The plebeians have got your fellow-tribune,
And hale him up and down; all swearing, if
The Roman ladies bring not comfort home,
They'll give him death by inches.

  Enter another MESSENGER.

SICINIUS VELUTUS.
     What's the news?

SECOND MESSENGER.
Good news, good news;—the ladies have pre-
vail'd,
The Volscians are dislodged, and Marcius gone:
A merrier day did never yet greet Rome,
No, not the expulsion of the Tarquins.

SICINIUS VELUTUS.
     Friend,
Art thou certain this is true? is it most certain?

SECOND MESSENGER.
As certain as I know the sun is fire:
Where have you lurkt, that you make doubt of it?
Ne'er through an arch so hurried the blown tide
As the recomforted through the gates. Why, hark
you!

  [*Trumpets hautboys, drums beat, all to-*
gether.

The trumpets, sackbuts, psalteries, and fifes,

Tabors, and cymbals, and the shouting Romans,
Make the sun dance. Hark you! [*A shout within.*

MENENIUS AGRIPPA.
      This is good news.
I will go meet the ladies. This Volumnia
Is worth of consuls, senators, patricians,
A city full; of tribunes, such as you,
A sea and land full. You have pray'd well to-day:
This morning for ten thousand of your throats
I'ld not have given a doit.—Hark, how they joy!
      [*Sound still with the shouts.*

SICINIUS VELUTUS.
First, the gods bless you for your tidings; next,
Accept my thankfulness.

SECOND MESSENGER.
      Sir, we have all
Great cause to give great thanks.

SICINIUS VELUTUS.
      They are near the city?

SECOND MESSENGER.
Almost at point to enter.

SICINIUS VELUTUS.
      We will meet them,
And help the joy.   [*Exeunt.*

SCENE V.

The same. A street near the gate.

Enter two SENATORS, *with* LADIES, *passing over
the stage; with other* LORDS.

FIRST SENATOR.
BEHOLD our patroness, the life of Rome!
 Call all your tribes together, praise the gods,
And make triumphant fires; strew flowers before
them:
Unshout the noise that banisht Marcius,
Repeal him with the welcome of his mother;
Cry, 'Welcome, ladies, welcome!'

ALL.
      Welcome, ladies,
Welcome!
 [*A flourish with drums and trumpets. Exeunt.*

SCENE VI.

Corioli. A public place.

Enter AUFIDIUS, *with* ATTENDANTS.

TULLUS AUFIDIUS.
GO tell the lords o'the city I am here:
 Deliver them this paper: having read it,
Bid them repair to the market-place; where I,
Even in theirs and in the commons' ears,
Will vouch the truth of it. Him I accuse
The city ports by this hath enter'd, and
Intends t'appear before the people, hoping
To purge himself with words: dispatch.
     [*Exeunt* ATTENDANTS.
Enter three or four CONSPIRATORS *of*
AUFIDIUS' *faction.*
      Most welcome!

FIRST CONSPIRATOR.
How is it with our general?

TULLUS AUFIDIUS.
      Even so
As with a man by his own alms empoison'd,
And with his charity slain.

SECOND CONSPIRATOR.
      Most noble sir,
If you do hold the same intent wherein
You wisht us parties, we'll deliver you
Of your great danger.

TULLUS AUFIDIUS.
      Sir, I cannot tell:
We must proceed as we do find the people.

THIRD CONSPIRATOR.
The people will remain uncertain whilst
'Twixt you there's difference; but the fall of either
Makes the survivor heir of all.

TULLUS AUFIDIUS.
      I know it;
And my pretext to strike at him admits
A good construction. I raised him, and I pawn'd
Mine honour for his truth: who being so height-
en'd,
He water'd his new plants with dews of flattery,
Seducing so my friends; and, to this end,
He bow'd his nature, never known before
But to be rough, unswayable, and free.

THIRD CONSPIRATOR.
      Sir, his stoutness
When he did stand for consul, which he lost
By lack of stooping,—

TULLUS AUFIDIUS.
     That I would have spoke of:
Being banisht for't, he came unto my hearth;
Presented to my knife his throat: I took him;
Made him joint-servant with me; gave him way
In all his own desires; nay, let him choose
Out of my files, his projects to accomplish,
My best and freshest men; served his designments
In mine own person; holp to reap the fame
Which he did end all his; and took some pride
To do myself this wrong: till, at the last,
I seem'd his follower, not partner; and
He waged me with his countenance, as if
I had been mercenary.

FIRST CONSPIRATOR.
      So did he, my lord,—
The army marvell'd at it; and, in the last,
When he had carried Rome, and that we lookt
For no less spoil than glory,—

TULLUS AUFIDIUS.
      There was it;—
For which my sinews shall be stretcht upon him.
At a few drops of women's rheum, which are
As cheap as lies, he sold the blood and labour
Of our great action: therefore shall he die,
And I'll renew me in his fall.—But, hark!
 [*Drums and trumpets sound, with great
shouts of the* PEOPLE.

FIRST CONSPIRATOR.
Your native town you enter'd like a post,
And had no welcomes home; but he returns,
Splitting the air with noise.

SECOND CONSPIRATOR.
      And patient fools,
Whose children he hath slain, their base throats
tear
With giving him glory.

THIRD CONSPIRATOR.
      Therefore, at your vantage,
Ere he express himself, or move the people

With what he would say, let him feel your
   sword,
Which we will second. When he lies along,
After your way his tale pronounced shall bury
His reasons with his body.
    TULLUS AUFIDIUS.
                Say no more:
Here come the lords.
    Enter the LORDS *of the city.*
        LORDS.
You are most welcome home.
    TULLUS AUFIDIUS.
             I have not deserved it.
But, worthy lords, have you with heed perused
What I have written to you?
        LORDS.
               We have.
    FIRST LORD.
             And grieve to hear't.
What faults he made before the last, I think
Might have found easy fines: but there to end
Where he was to begin, and give away
The benefit of our levies, answering us
With our own charge, making a treaty where
There was a yielding,—this admits no excuse.
    TULLUS AUFIDIUS.
He approaches: you shall hear him.
    Enter CORIOLANUS, *marching with drum and*
    colours; the COMMONERS *being with him.*
    CAIUS MARCIUS CORIOLANUS.
Hail, lords! I am return'd your soldier;
No more infected with my country's love
Than when I parted hence, but still subsisting
Under your great command. You are to know,
That prosperously I have attempted, and,
With bloody passage, led your wars even to
The gates of Rome. Our spoils we have brought
   home
Doth more than counterpoise a full third part
The charges of the action. We have made peace,
With no less honour to the Antiates
Than shame to the Romans: and we here deliver,
Subscribed by the consuls and patricians,
Together with the seal o'the senate, what
We have compounded on.
    TULLUS AUFIDIUS.
            Read it not, noble lords;
But tell the traitor, in the highest degree
He hath abused your powers.
    CAIUS MARCIUS CORIOLANUS.
Traitor!—how now!
    TULLUS AUFIDIUS.
          Ay, traitor, Marcius!
    CAIUS MARCIUS CORIOLANUS.
               Marcius!
    TULLUS AUFIDIUS.
Ay, Marcius, Caius Marcius: dost thou think
I'll grace thee with that robbery, thy stoln name
Coriolanus, in Corioli?—
You lords and heads o'the state, perfidiously
He has betray'd your business, and given up,
For certain drops of salt, your city Rome—
I say, your city—to his wife and mother;
Breaking his oath and resolution, like
A twist of rotten silk; never admitting
Counsel o'the war; but at his nurse's tears

He whined and roar'd away your victory;
That pages blusht at him, and men of heart
Lookt wond'ring each at other.
    CAIUS MARCIUS CORIOLANUS.
              Hear'st thou, Mars?
    TULLUS AUFIDIUS.
Name not the god, thou boy of tears!
    CAIUS MARCIUS CORIOLANUS.
                 Ha!
    TULLUS AUFIDIUS.
No more.
    CAIUS MARCIUS CORIOLANUS.
Measureless liar, thou hast made my heart
Too great for what contains it. Boy! O slave!—
Pardon me, lords, 'tis the first time that ever
I was forced to scold. Your judgements, my grave
   lords,
Must give this cur the lie: and his own notion—
Who wears my stripes imprest upon him; that
Must bear my beating to his grave—shall join
To thrust the lie unto him.
    FIRST LORD.
Peace, both, and hear me speak.
    CAIUS MARCIUS CORIOLANUS.
Cut me to pieces, Volsces; men and lads,
Stain all your edges on me.—Boy! false hound!
If you have writ your annals true, 'tis there,
That, like an eagle in a dove-cote, I
Flutter'd your Volscians in Corioli:
Alone I did it.—Boy!
    TULLUS AUFIDIUS.
            Why, noble lords,
Will you be put in mind of his blind fortune,
Which was your shame, by this unholy braggart,
'Fore your own eyes and ears?
    ALL THE CONSPIRATORS.
             Let him die for't!
    ALL THE PEOPLE.
Tear him to pieces!—Do it presently!—He kill'd
my son!—My daughter!—He kill'd my cousin
Marcus!—He kill'd my father!—
    SECOND LORD.
Peace, ho!—no outrage:—peace!
The man is noble, and his fame folds-in
This orb o'the earth. His last offences to us
Shall have judicious hearing.—Stand, Aufidius,
And trouble not the peace.
    CAIUS MARCIUS CORIOLANUS.
            O, that I had him,
With six Aufidiuses, or more, his tribe,
To use my lawful sword!
    TULLUS AUFIDIUS.
             Insolent villain!
    ALL THE CONSPIRATORS.
Kill, kill, kill, kill, kill him!
    [AUFIDIUS *and the* CONSPIRATORS *draw,*
    and kill CORIOLANUS, *who falls:* AUFI-
    DIUS *stands on him.*
        LORDS.
Hold, hold, hold, hold!
    TULLUS AUFIDIUS.
My noble masters, hear me speak.
    FIRST LORD.
               O Tullus,—
    SECOND LORD.
Thou hast done a deed whereat valour will weep.

THIRD LORD.
Tread not upon him.—Masters all, be quiet;
Put up your swords.

TULLUS AUFIDIUS.
My lords, when you shall know—as in this rage,
Provoked by him, you cannot—the great danger
Which this man's life did owe you, you'll rejoice
That he is thus cut off. Please it your honours
To call me to your senate, I'll deliver
Myself your loyal servant, or endure
Your heaviest censure.

FIRST LORD.
               Bear from hence his body,—
And mourn you for him:—let him be regarded
As the most noble corse that ever herald
Did follow to his urn.

SECOND LORD.
             His own impatience
Takes from Aufidius a great part of blame.
Let's make the best of it.

TULLUS AUFIDIUS.
            My rage is gone;
And I am struck with sorrow.—Take him up:—
Help, three o'the chiefest soldiers; I'll be one.—
Beat thou the drum, that it speak mournfully:
Trail your steel pikes.—Though in this city he
Hath widow'd and unchilded many a one,
Which to this hour bewail the injury,
Yet he shall have a noble memory.—
Assist.

       [*Exeunt, bearing the body of* MARCIUS. *A
       dead march sounded.*

TIMON OF ATHENS

DRAMATIS PERSONAE

TIMON, *a noble Athenian.*
LUCIUS,
LUCULLUS, } *two flattering lords.*
APEMANTUS, *a churlish philosopher.*
SEMPRONIUS, *another flattering lord.*
ALCIBIADES, *an Athenian captain.*
VENTIDIUS, *one of Timon's false friends.*
FLAVIUS, *steward to Timon.*
POET, PAINTER, JEWELLER, *and* MERCHANT.
AN OLD ATHENIAN.
FLAMINIUS,
LUCILIUS, } *servants to Timon.*
SERVILIUS,

CAPHIS,
PHILOTUS,
TITUS, } *servants to Timon's creditors.*
HORTENSIUS,
AND OTHERS,
A PAGE.   A FOOL.   THREE STRANGERS.

PHRYNIA, } *mistresses to Alcibiades.*
TIMANDRA,

CUPID *and* AMAZONS *in the mask.*

Other LORDS, SENATORS, OFFICERS, SOL-
DIERS, BANDITTI, *and* ATTENDANTS.

SCENE—*Athens and the woods adjoining.*

ACT I. SCENE I.

Athens.   A hall in TIMON'S *house.*

Enter POET, PAINTER, JEWELLER, MER-
CHANT, *and others, at several doors.*

POET.

GOOD day, sir.
          PAINTER.
I am glad y'are well.
          POET.
I have not seen you long: how goes the world?
          PAINTER.
It wears, sir, as it grows.
          POET.
                    Ay, that's well known:
But what particular rarity? what strange,
Which manifold record not matches? See,
Magic of bounty! all these spirits thy power
Hath conjured to attend. I know the merchant.
          PAINTER.
I know them both; the other's a jeweller.
          MERCHANT.
O, 'tis a worthy lord.
          JEWELLER.
                    Nay, that's most fixt.
          MERCHANT.
A most incomparable man; breathed, as it were
To an untirable and continuate goodness:
He passes.
          JEWELLER.
I have a jewel here—
          MERCHANT.
O, pray, let's see't: for the Lord Timon, sir?
          JEWELLER.
If he will touch the estimate: but, for that—
          POET.
'When we for recompense have praised the vile,
  It stains the glory in that happy verse
  Which aptly sings the good.'
          MERCHANT.
                    'Tis a good form.
          [*Looking at the jewel.*
          JEWELLER.
And rich: here is a water, look ye.

PAINTER.
You are rapt, sir, in some work, some dedication
To the great lord.
          POET.
                    A thing slipt idly from me.
Our poesy is as a gum, which oozes
From whence 'tis nourisht: the fire i'the flint
Shows not till it be struck; our gentle flame
Provokes itself, and, like the current, flies
Each bound it chafes.—What have you there?
          PAINTER.
A picture, sir.—When comes your book forth?
          POET.
Upon the heels of my presentment, sir.—
Let's see your piece.
          PAINTER.
'Tis a good piece.
          POET.
So 'tis: this comes off well and excellent.
          PAINTER.
Indifferent.
          POET.
                    Admirable: how this grace
Speaks his own standing! what a mental power
This eye shoots forth! how big imagination
Moves in this lip! to the dumbness of the gesture
One might interpret.
          PAINTER.
It is a pretty mocking of the life.
Here is a touch; is't good?
          POET.
                    I will say of it,
It tutors nature: artificial strife
Lives in these touches, livelier than life.
          Enter certain SENATORS, *and pass over.*
          PAINTER.
How this lord is follow'd!
          POET.
The senators of Athens:—happy man!
          PAINTER.
Look, moe!
          POET.
You see this confluence, this great flood of visitors.
I have, in this rough work, shaped out a man,

W :om this beneath-world doth embrace and hug
With amplest entertainment: my free drift
Halts not particularly, but moves itself
In a wide sea of wax: no levell'd malice
Infects one comma in the course I hold;
But flies an eagle flight, bold, and forth on,
Leaving no tract behind.

PAINTER.

How shall I understand you?

POET.

I will unbolt to you.
You see how all conditions, how all minds—
As well of glib and slippery creatures as
Of grave and austere quality—tender down
Their services to Lord Timon: his large fortune,
Upon his good and gracious nature hanging,
Subdues and properties to his love and tendance
All sorts of hearts; yea, from the glass-faced flat-
terer
To Apemantus, that few things loves better
Than to abhor himself: even he drops down
The knee before him, and returns in peace
Most rich in Timon's nod.

PAINTER.

I saw them speak together.

POET.

Sir,
I have upon a high and pleasant hill
Feign'd Fortune to be throned: the base o'the
mount
Is rankt with all deserts, all kind of natures,
That labour on the bosom of this sphere
To propagate their states: amongst them all,
Whose eyes are on this sovereign lady fixt,
One do I personate of Lord Timon's frame,
Whom Fortune with her ivory hand watts to her:
Whose present grace to present slaves and servants
Translates his rivals.

PAINTER.

'Tis conceived to scope.
This throne, this Fortune, and this hill, methinks,
With one man beckon'd from the rest below,
Bowing his head against the steepy mount
To climb his happiness, would be well exprest
In our condition.

POET.

Nay, sir, but hear me on.
All those which were his fellows but of late,—
Some better than his value,—on the moment
Follow his strides, his lobbies fill with tendance,
Rain sacrificial whisperings in his ear,
Make sacred even his stirrup, and through him
Drink the free air.

PAINTER.

Ay, marry, what of these?

POET.

When Fortune, in her shift and change of mood,
Spurns down her late beloved, all his dependants,
Which labour'd after him to the mountain's top,
Even on their knees and hands, let him slip down,
Not one accompanying his declining foot.

PAINTER.

'Tis common:
A thousand moral paintings I can show,
That shall demonstrate these quick blows of For-
tune's

More pregnantly than words. Yet you do well
To show Lord Timon that mean eyes have seen
The foot above the head.

Trumpets sound.   Enter LORD TIMON, *address-*
ing himself courteously to every SUITOR; *a*
SERVANT *of* VENTIDIUS *talking with him;*
LUCILIUS *and other* ATTENDANTS *following.*

TIMON.

Imprison'd is he, say you?

VENTIDIUS' SERVANT.

Ay, my good lord; five talents is his debt;
His means most short, his creditors most strait:
Your honourable letter he desires
To those have shut him up; which failing
Periods his comfort.

TIMON.

Noble Ventidius!—Well;
I am not of that feather to shake off
My friend when he must need me. I do know
him
A gentleman that well deserves a help,—
Which he shall have: I'll pay the debt, and free
him.

VENTIDIUS' SERVANT.

Your lordship ever binds him.

TIMON.

Commend me to him: I will send his ransom;
And, being enfranchised, bid him come to me:—
'Tis not enough to help the feeble up,
But to support him after.—Fare you well.

VENTIDIUS' SERVANT.

All happiness to your honour!   [*Exit.*

Enter an OLD ATHENIAN.

OLD ATHENIAN.

Lord Timon, hear me speak.

TIMON.

Freely, good father.

OLD ATHENIAN.

Thou hast a servant named Lucilius.

TIMON.

I have so: what of him?

OLD ATHENIAN.

Most noble Timon, call the man before thee.

TIMON.

Attends he here, or no?—Lucilius!

LUCILIUS [*coming forward*].

Here, at your lordship's service.

OLD ATHENIAN.

This fellow here, Lord Timon, this thy creature,
By night frequents my house. I am a man
That from my first have been inclined to thrift;
And my estate deserves an heir more raised
Than one which holds a trencher.

TIMON.

Well; what further?

OLD ATHENIAN.

One only daughter have I, no kin else,
On whom I may confer what I have got:
The maid is fair, o'the youngest for a bride,
And I have bred her at my dearest cost
In qualities of the best. This man of thine
Attempts her love: I prithee, noble lord,
Join with me to forbid him her resort;
Myself have spoke in vain.

TIMON.

The man is honest.

OLD ATHENIAN.
Therefore he will be, Timon:
His honesty rewards him in itself;
It must not bear my daughter.
TIMON.
Does she love him?
OLD ATHENIAN.
She is young and apt:
Our own precedent passions do instruct us
What levity's in youth.
TIMON [to LUCILIUS].
Love you the maid?
LUCILIUS.
Ay, my good lord; and she accepts of it.
OLD ATHENIAN.
If in her marriage my consent be missing,
I call the gods to witness, I will choose
Mine heir from forth the beggars of the world,
And dispossess her all.
TIMON.
How shall she be endow'd,
If she be mated with an equal husband?
OLD ATHENIAN.
Three talents on the present; in future, all.
TIMON.
This gentleman of mine hath served me long:
To build his fortune I will strain a little,
For 'tis a bond in men. Give him thy daughter:
What you bestow, in him I'll counterpoise,
And make him weigh with her.
OLD ATHENIAN.
Most noble lord,
Pawn me to this your honour, she is his.
TIMON.
My hand to thee; mine honour on my promise.
LUCILIUS.
Humbly I thank your lordship: never may
That state or fortune fall into my keeping,
Which is not owed to you!
[Exeunt LUCILIUS and OLD ATHENIAN.
POET.
Vouchsafe my labour, and long live your lordship!
TIMON.
I thank you, you shall hear from me anon:
Go not away.—What have you there, my friend?
PAINTER.
A piece of painting, which I do beseech
Your lordship to accept.
TIMON.
Painting is welcome.
The painting is almost the natural man;
For since dishonour traffics with man's nature,
He is but outside: these pencill'd figures are
Even such as they give out. I like your work;
And you shall find I like it: wait attendance
Till you hear further from me.
PAINTER.
The gods preserve ye!
TIMON.
Well fare you, gentleman: give me your hand;
We must needs dine together.—Sir, your jewel
Hath suffer'd under praise.
JEWELLER.
What, my lord! dispraise?
TIMON.
A mere satiety of commendations.

If I should pay you for't as 'tis extoll'd,
It would unclew me quite.
JEWELLER.
My lord, 'tis rated
As those which sell would give: but you well know,
Things of like value, differing in the owners,
Are prized by their masters· believe't, dear lord,
You mend the jewel by the wearing it.
TIMON.
Well mockt.
MERCHANT.
No, my good lord; he speaks the common tongue,
Which all men speak with him.
TIMON.
Look, who comes here:
Will you be chid?
Enter APEMANTUS.
JEWELLER.
We'll bear, with your lordship.
MERCHANT.
He'll spare none.
TIMON.
Good morrow to thee, gentle Apemantus.
APEMANTUS.
Till I be gentle, stay thou for thy good morrow;
When thou art Timon's dog, and these knaves
honest.
TIMON.
Why dost thou call them knaves? thou know'st
them not.
APEMANTUS.
Are they not Athenians?
TIMON.
Yes.
APEMANTUS.
Then I repent not.
JEWELLER.
You know me, Apemantus?
APEMANTUS.
Thou know'st I do; I call'd thee by thy name.
TIMON.
Thou art proud, Apemantus.
APEMANTUS.
Of nothing so much as that I am not like Timon.
TIMON.
Whither art going?
APEMANTUS.
To knock out an honest Athenian's brains.
TIMON.
That's a deed thou'lt die for.
APEMANTUS.
Right, if doing nothing be death by the law.
TIMON.
How likest thou this picture, Apemantus?
APEMANTUS.
The best, for the innocence.
TIMON.
Wrought he not well that painted it?
APEMANTUS.
He wrought better that made the painter; and yet
he's but a filthy piece of work.
PAINTER.
Y'are a dog.
APEMANTUS.
Thy mother's of my generation: what's she, if I
be a dog?

TIMON.
Wilt dine with me, Apemantus?

APEMANTUS.
No; I eat not lords.

TIMON.
An thou shouldst, thou'ldst anger ladies.

APEMANTUS.
O, they eat lords; so they come by great bellies.

TIMON.
That's a lascivious apprehension.

APEMANTUS.
So thou apprehend'st it: take it for thy labour.

TIMON.
How dost thou like this jewel, Apemantus?

APEMANTUS.
Not so well as plain-dealing, which will not cost
a man a doit.

TIMON.
What dost thou think 'tis worth?

APEMANTUS.
Not worth my thinking.—How now, poet!

POET.
How now, philosopher!

APEMANTUS.
Thou liest.

POET.
Art not one?

APEMANTUS.
Yes.

POET.
Then I lie not.

APEMANTUS.
Art not a poet?

POET.
Yes.

APEMANTUS.
Then thou liest: look in thy last work, where thou
hast feign'd him a worthy fellow.

POET.
That's not feign'd,—he is so.

APEMANTUS.
Yes, he is worthy of thee, and to pay thee for thy
labour: he that loves to be flatter'd is worthy o'the
flatterer. Heavens, that I were a lord!

TIMON.
What wouldst do then, Apemantus?

APEMANTUS.
E'en as Apemantus does now,—hate a lord with
my heart.

TIMON.
What, thyself?

APEMANTUS.
Ay.

TIMON.
Wherefore?

APEMANTUS.
That I had no angry wit to be a lord.—Art not
thou a merchant?

MERCHANT.
Ay, Apemantus.

APEMANTUS.
Traffic confound thee, if the gods will not!

MERCHANT.
If traffic do it, the gods do it.

APEMANTUS.
Traffic's thy god; and thy god confound thee!

Trumpet sounds. Enter a MESSENGER.

TIMON.
What trumpet's that?

MESSENGER.
'Tis Alcibiades, and some twenty horse,
All of companionship.

TIMON.
Pray, entertain them; give them guide to us.—
                     [*Exeunt some* ATTENDANTS.
You must needs dine with me: go not you hence
Till I have thankt you; and when dinner's done,
Show me this piece:—I am joyful of your sights.
        Enter ALCIBIADES *with the rest.*
Most welcome, sir!

APEMANTUS.
        So, so, there!—
Aches contract and starve your supple joints!—
That there should be small love 'mongst these
    sweet knaves,
And all this court'sy! The strain of man's bred
    out
Into baboon and monkey.

ALCIBIADES.
Sir, you have saved my longing, and I feed
Most hungerly on your sight.

TIMON.
              Right welcome, sir!
Ere we depart, we'll share a bounteous time
In different pleasures. Pray you, let us in.
        [*Exeunt all but* APEMANTUS.
        Enter two LORDS.

FIRST LORD.
What time o'day is't, Apemantus?

APEMANTUS.
Time to be honest.

FIRST LORD.
That time serves still.

APEMANTUS.
The more accursed thou, that still omitt'st it.

SECOND LORD.
Thou art going to Lord Timon's feast?

APEMANTUS.
Ay, to see meat fill knaves, and wine heat fools.

SECOND LORD.
Fare thee well, fare thee well.

APEMANTUS.
Thou art a fool to bid me farewell twice.

SECOND LORD.
Why, Apemantus?

APEMANTUS.
Shouldst have kept one to thyself, for I mean to
give thee none.

FIRST LORD.
Hang thyself!

APEMANTUS.
No, I will do nothing at thy bidding: make thy
requests to thy friend.

SECOND LORD.
Away, unpeaceable dog, or I'll spurn thee hence!

APEMANTUS.
I will fly, like a dog, the heels o'the ass.   [*Exit.*

FIRST LORD.
He's opposite to humanity.—Come, shall we in,
And taste Lord Timon's bounty? he outgoes
The very heart of kindness.

SECOND LORD.
He pours it out; Plutus, the god of gold,
Is but his steward: no meed but he repays
Sevenfold above itself; no gift to him
But breeds the giver a return exceeding
All use of quittance.
                    FIRST LORD.
                              The noblest mind he carries
That ever govern'd man.
                    SECOND LORD.
                              Long may he live
In fortunes!—Shall we in?
                    FIRST LORD.
                    I'll keep you company. [Exeunt.

SCENE II.

The same.   A room of state in TIMON'S *house.*

Hautboys playing loud music. A great banquet served in; FLAVIUS *and others attending; and then enter* LORD TIMON, ALCIBIADES, *the* STATES, *the Athenian* LORDS, VENTIDIUS *which* TIMON *redeem'd from prison. Then comes, dropping after all,* APEMANTUS, *discontentedly, like himself.*

                    VENTIDIUS.
MOST honour'd Timon,
        It hath pleased the gods to remember my
              father's age,
And call him to long peace.
He is gone happy, and has left me rich:
Then, as in grateful virtue I am bound
To your free heart, I do return those talents,
Doubled with thanks and service, from whose help
I derived liberty.
                    TIMON.
                    O, by no means,
Honest Ventidius; you mistake my love:
I gave it freely ever; and there's none
Can truly say he gives, if he receives:
If our betters play at that game, we must not dare
To imitate them; faults that are rich are fair.
                    VENTIDIUS.
A noble spirit!
                    TIMON.
                    Nay, my lords, ceremony
Was but devised at first
To set a gloss on faint deeds, hollow welcomes,
Recanting goodness, sorry ere 'tis shown;
But where there is true friendship, there needs
              none.
Pray, sit; more welcome are ye to my fortunes
Than my fortunes to me.   [They sit.
                    FIRST LORD.
My lord, we always have confest it.
                    APEMANTUS.
Ho, ho, confest it! hang'd it, have you not?
                    TIMON.
O, Apemantus,—you are welcome.
                    APEMANTUS.
                              No;
You shall not make me welcome:
I come to have thee thrust me out of doors.
                    TIMON.
Fie, th'art a churl; y'have got a humour there
Does not become a man; 'tis much to blame.—

They say, my lords, *Ira furor brevis est;*
But yond man is ever angry.—
Go, let him have a table by himself;
For he does neither affect company,
Nor is he fit for't, indeed.
                    APEMANTUS.
Let me stay at thine apperil, Timon:
I come to observe; I give thee warning on't.
                    TIMON.
I take no heed of thee; th'art an Athenian, there-
fore welcome: I myself would have no power; pri-
thee, let my meat make thee silent.
                    APEMANTUS.
I scorn thy meat; 'twould choke me, for I should
ne'er flatter thee.—O you gods, what a number of
men eats Timon, and he sees 'em not! It grieves
me to see so many dip their meat in one man's
blood; and all the madness is, he cheers them up
too.
I wonder men dare trust themselves with men:
Methinks they should invite them without knives;
Good for their meat, and safer for their lives.
There's much example for't; the fellow that sits
next him now, parts bread with him, pledges the
breath of him in a divided draught, is the readiest
man to kill him: 't has been proved. If I were a
huge man, I should fear to drink at meals;
Lest they should spy my windpipe's dangerous
              notes: [throats.
Great men should drink with harness on their
                    TIMON.
My lord, in heart; and let the health go round.
                    SECOND LORD.
Let it flow this way, my good lord.
                    APEMANTUS.
Flow this way! A brave fellow! he keeps his tides
well. Those healths will make thee and thy state
look ill, Timon. Here's that which is too weak to
be a sinner, honest water, which ne'er left man i'
the mire:
This and my food are equals; there's no odds:
Feasts are too proud to give thanks to the gods.
              APEMANTUS' *grace.*
Immortal gods, I crave no pelf,
I pray for no man but myself:
Grant I may never prove so fond,
To trust man on his oath or bond;
Or a harlot, for her weeping;
Or a dog, that seems a-sleeping;
Or a keeper with my freedom;
Or my friends, if I should need 'em.
Amen. So fall to't:
Rich men sin, and I eat root.
                              [Eats and drinks.
Much good dich thy good heart, Apemantus!
                    TIMON.
Captain Alcibiades, your heart's in the field now.
                    ALCIBIADES.
My heart is ever at your service, my lord.
                    TIMON.
You had rather be at a breakfast of enemies than
a dinner of friends.
                    ALCIBIADES.
So they were bleeding-new, my lord, there's no
meat like 'em: I could wish my best friend at such
a feast.

APEMANTUS.

Would all those flatterers were thine enemies,
then, that then thou mightst kill 'em, and bid me
to 'em!

FIRST LORD.

Might we but have that happiness, my lord, that
you would once use our hearts, whereby we might
express some part of our zeals, we should think
ourselves for ever perfect.

TIMON.

O, no doubt, my good friends, but the gods themselves have provided that I shall have much help
from you: how had you been my friends else? why
have you that charitable title from thousands, did
not you chiefly belong to my heart? I have told
more of you to myself than you can with modesty
speak in your own behalf; and thus far I confirm
you. O you gods, think I, what need we have any
friends, if we should ne'er have need of 'em? they
were the most needless creatures living, should
we ne'er have use for 'em; and would most resemble sweet instruments hung up in cases, that
keep their sounds to themselves. Why, I have often
wisht myself poorer, that I might come nearer to
you. We are born to do benefits: and what better
or properer can we call our own than the riches
of our friends? O, what a precious comfort 'tis,
to have so many, like brothers, commanding
one another's fortunes! O joy, e'en made away
ere't can be born! Mine eyes cannot hold out
water, methinks: to forget their faults, I drink to
you.

APEMANTUS.

Thou weep'st to make them drink, Timon.

SECOND LORD.

Joy had the like conception in our eyes,
And, at that instant, like a babe sprung up.

APEMANTUS.

Ho, ho! I laugh to think that babe a bastard.

THIRD LORD.

I promise you, my lord, you moved me much.

APEMANTUS.

Much!   [Tucket sounded within.

TIMON.

What means that trump?

Enter a SERVANT.

How now!

SERVANT.

Please you, my lord, there are certain ladies most
desirous of admittance.

TIMON.

Ladies! what are their wills!

SERVANT.

There comes with them a forerunner, my lord,
which bears that office, to signify their pleasures.

TIMON.

I pray, let them be admitted.

Enter CUPID.

CUPID.

Hail to thee, worthy Timon;—and to all
That of his bounties taste!—The five best senses
Acknowledge thee their patron; and come freely
To gratulate thy plenteous bosom:
The ear, taste, touch, smell, pleased from thy table
   rise.—
These only now come but to feast thine eyes.

TIMON.

They're welcome all; let 'em have kind admittance:—
Music, make their welcome!   [Exit CUPID.

FIRST LORD.

You see, my lord, how ample y'are beloved.

Music. Enter CUPID, with the Masque of LA-
DIES as Amazons with lutes in their hands, dancing and playing.

APEMANTUS.

Hoy-day, what a sweep of vanity comes this way!
They dance! they are mad women.
Like madness is the glory of this life,
As this pomp shows to a little oil and root.
We make ourselves fools, to disport ourselves;
And spend our flatteries, to drink those men,
Upon whose age we void it up agen,
With poisonous spite and envy.
Who lives, that's not depraved or depraves?
Who dies, that bears not one spurn to their graves
Of their friends' gift?
I should fear those that dance before me now
Would one day stamp upon me: 't has been done;
Men shut their doors against a setting sun.

The LORDS rise from table, with much adoring of
TIMON; and to show their loves, each singles out
an AMAZON, and all dance, men with women, a
lofty strain or two to the hautboys, and cease.

TIMON.

You have done our pleasures much grace, fair
Set a fair fashion on our entertainment,   [ladies,
Which was not half so beautiful and kind;
You have added worth unto't and lustre,
And entertain'd me with mine own device;
I am to thank you for't.

FIRST LADY.

My lord, you take us even at the best.

APEMANTUS.

Faith, for the worst is filthy; and would not hold
taking, I doubt me.

TIMON.

Ladies, there is an idle banquet attends you:
Please you to dispose yourselves.

ALL LADIES.

Most thankfully, my lord.

                         [Exeunt CUPID and LADIES.

TIMON.

Flavius,—

FLAVIUS.

My lord?

TIMON.

The little casket bring me hither.

FLAVIUS.

Yes, my lord.—[aside] More jewels yet!
There is no crossing him in's humour;
Else I should tell him,—well, i'faith, I should,—
When all's spent, he'ld be crost then, an he could.
'Tis pity bounty had not eyes behind,
That man might ne'er be wretched for his mind.

                                           [Exit.

FIRST LORD.

Where be our men?

SERVANT.

Here, my lord, in readiness.

SECOND LORD.

Our horses!

Enter FLAVIUS *with the casket.*
TIMON.
O my friends,
I have one word to say to you:—look you, my
good lord,
I must entreat you, honour me so much
As to advance this jewel; accept and wear it,
Kind my lord.
FIRST LORD.
I am so far already in your gifts,—
ALL.
So are we all.
Enter a SERVANT.
SERVANT.
My lord, there are certain nobles of the senate
newly alighted, and come to visit you.
TIMON.
They are fairly welcome.
FLAVIUS.
I beseech your honour, vouchsafe me a word; it
does concern you near.
TIMON.
Near! why, then, another time I'll hear thee: I
prithee, let's be provided to show them entertain-
ment.
FLAVIUS [*aside*].
I scarce know how.
Enter a second SERVANT.
SECOND SERVANT.
May it please your honour, Lord Lucius,
Out of his free love, hath presented to you
Four milk-white horses, trapt in silver.
TIMON.
I shall accept them fairly: let the presents
Be worthily entertain'd.
Enter a third SERVANT.
How now! what news?
THIRD SERVANT.
Please you, my lord, that honourable gentleman,
Lord Lucullus, entreats your company tomorrow
to hunt with him; and has sent your honour two
brace of greyhounds.
TIMON.
I'll hunt with him; and let them be received,
Not without fair reward.
FLAVIUS [*aside*].
What will this come to?
He commands us to provide, and give great gifts,
And all out of an empty coffer:
Nor will he know his purse; or yield me this,
To show him what a beggar his heart is,
Being of no power to make his wishes good:
His promises fly so beyond his state,
That what he speaks is all in debt; he owes
For every word: he is so kind, that he now
Pays interest for't; his land's put to their books.
Well, would I were gently put out of office,
Before I were forced out!
Happier is he that has no friend to feed
Than such that do e'en enemies exceed.
bleed inwardly for my lord. [*Exit.*
TIMON.
You do yourselves
Much wrong, you bate too much of your own
merits:—
Here, my lord, a trifle of our love.

SECOND LORD.
With more than common thanks I will receive it.
THIRD LORD.
O, he's the very soul of bounty!
TIMON.
And now I remember, my lord, you gave good
words the other day of a bay courser I rode on:
'tis yours, because you liked it.
FIRST LORD.
O, I beseech you, pardon me, my lord, in that.
TIMON.
You may take my word, my lord; I know, no man
can justly praise but what he does affect: I weigh
my friend's affection with mine own; I'll tell you
true.—I'll call to you.
ALL LORDS.
O, none so welcome.
TIMON.
I take all and your several visitations
So kind to heart, 'tis not enough to give;
Methinks, I could deal kingdoms to my friends,
And ne'er be weary.—Alcibiades,
Thou art a soldier, therefore seldom rich;
It comes in charity to thee: for all thy living
Is 'mongst the dead; and all the lands thou hast
Lie in a pitch'd field.
ALCIBIADES.
Ay, defiled land, my lord.
FIRST LORD.
We are so virtuously bound—
TIMON.
And so am I to you.
SECOND LORD.
So infinitely endear'd—
TIMON.
All to you.—Lights, more lights!
FIRST LORD.
The best of happiness, honour, and fortunes,
keep with you, Lord Timon!
TIMON.
Ready for his friends.
[*Exeunt all but* APEMANTUS *and* TIMON.
APEMANTUS.
What a coil's here!
Serving of becks, and jutting-out of bums!
I doubt whether their legs be worth the sums
That are given for 'em. Friendship's full of dregs:
Methinks, false hearts should never have sound
legs. [sies.
Thus honest fools lay out their wealth on court'-
TIMON.
Now, Apemantus, if thou were not sullen,
I would be good to thee.
APEMANTUS.
No, I'll nothing; for if I should be bribed too,
there would be none left to rail upon thee; and
then thou wouldst sin the faster. Thou givest so
long, Timon, I fear me thou wilt give away thy-
self in paper shortly: what needs these feasts,
pomps, and vain-glories?
TIMON.
Nay, an you begin to rail on society once, I am
sworn not to give regard to you. Farewell; and
come with better music. [*Exit.*
APEMANTUS.
So; thou wilt not hear me now,—

Thou shalt not then, I'll lock thy heaven from
O, that men's ears should be　　　　[thee.—
To counsel deaf, but not to flattery!　　　[*Exit.*

ACT II. SCENE I.

Athens.　A room in a SENATOR'S *house.*

Enter a SENATOR, *with papers in his hand.*

SENATOR.

AND late, five thousand;—to Varro and to
　　Isidore
He owes nine thousand;—besides my former sum,
Which makes it five-and-twenty.—Still in motion
Of raging waste? It cannot hold; it will not.
If I want gold, steal but a beggar's dog,
And give it Timon, why, the dog coins gold:
If I would sell my horse, and buy twenty moe
Better than he, why, give my horse to Timon,
Ask nothing, give it him, it foals me, straight,
And able horses: no porter at his gate;
But rather one that smiles, and still invites
All that pass by. It cannot hold; no reason
Can found his state in safety.—Caphis, ho!
Caphis, I say!

Enter CAPHIS.

CAPHIS.
　　Here, sir; what is your pleasure?

SENATOR.
Get on your cloak, and haste you to Lord Timon;
Importune him for my moneys; be not ceased
With slight denial; nor then silenced when—
'Commend me to your master'—and the cap
Plays in the right hand, thus:—but tell him, sirrah,
My uses cry to me, I must serve my turn
Out of mine own; his days and times are past,
And my reliances on his fracted dates
Have smit my credit: I love and honour him;
But must not break my back to heal his finger:
Immediate are my needs; and my relief
Must not be tost and turn'd to me in words,
But find supply immediate. Get you gone:
Put on a most importunate aspect,
A visage of demand; for, I do fear,
When every feather sticks in his own wing,
Lord Timon will be left a naked gull,
Which flashes now a phœnix. Get you gone.

CAPHIS.
I go, sir.

SENATOR.
　　Take the bonds along with you,
And have the dates in compt.

CAPHIS.
　　　　I will, sir.

SENATOR.
　　　　　　Go. [*Exeunt.*

SCENE II.

The same.　A hall in TIMON'S *house.*

Enter FLAVIUS, *with many bills in his hand.*

FLAVIUS.

NO care, no stop! so senseless of expense,
　　That he will neither know how to maintain it
Nor cease his flow of riot: takes no account
How things go from him; nor resumes no care
Of what is to continue: never mind

Was to be so unwise, to be so kind.
What shall be done? he will not hear, till feel:
I must be round with him, now he comes from
Fie, fie, fie, fie!　　　　　　　[hunting.

Enter CAPHIS, *and the* SERVANTS *of* ISIDORE
and VARRO.

CAPHIS.
Good even, Varro: what, you come for money?

VARRO'S SERVANT.
Is't not your business too?

CAPHIS.
It is:—and yours too, Isidore?

ISIDORE'S SERVANT.
It is so.

CAPHIS.
Would we were all discharged!

VARRO'S SERVANT.
I fear it.

CAPHIS.
Here comes the lord.

Enter TIMON, ALCIBIADES, *and* LORDS, &c.

TIMON.
So soon as dinner's done we'll forth again,
My Alcibiades.—With me? what is your will?

CAPHIS.
My lord, here is a note of certain dues.

TIMON.
Dues! Whence are you?

CAPHIS.
　　　　Of Athens here, my lord.

TIMON.
Go to my steward.

CAPHIS.
Please it your lordship, he hath put me off
To the succession of new days this month:
My master is awaked by great occasion
To call upon his own; and humbly prays you,
That with your other noble parts you'll suit
In giving him his right.

TIMON.
　　　　Mine honest friend,
I prithee, but repair to me next morning.

CAPHIS.
Nay, good my lord,—

TIMON.
　　　　Contain thyself, good friend.

VARRO'S SERVANT.
One Varro's servant, my good lord,—

ISIDORE'S SERVANT.
　　　　　　From Isidore
He humbly prays your speedy payment,—

CAPHIS.
If you did know, my lord, my master's wants,—

VARRO'S SERVANT.
'Twas due on forfeiture, my lord, six weeks and
past,—

ISIDORE'S SERVANT.
Your steward puts me off, my lord; and I am sent
expressly to your lordship.

TIMON.
Give me breath.—
I do beseech you, good my lords, keep on;
I'll wait upon you instantly.

　　　　[*Exeunt* ALCIBIADES *and* LORDS.
　　　　[*to* FLAVIUS] Come hither: pray you
How goes the world, that I am thus encounter'd

With clamorous demands of date-broke bonds,
And the detention of long-since-due debts,
Against my honour?

FLAVIUS.
                Please you, gentlemen,
The time is unagreeable to this business:
Your importunacy cease till after dinner;
That I may make his lordship understand
Wherefore you are not paid.

TIMON.
Do so, my friends. See them well entertain'd.
                              [*Exit.*

FLAVIUS.
Pray, draw near.   [*Exit.*
      Enter APEMANTUS *and* FOOL.

CAPHIS.
Stay, stay, here comes the fool with Apemantus:
let's ha' some sport with 'em.

VARRO'S SERVANT.
Hang him, he'll abuse us.

ISIDORE'S SERVANT.
A plague upon him, dog!

VARRO'S SERVANT.
How dost, fool?

APEMANTUS.
Dost dialogue with thy shadow?

VARRO'S SERVANT.
I speak not to thee.

APEMANTUS.
No, 'tis to thyself.—[*to the* FOOL] Come away.

ISIDORE'S SERVANT [*to* VARRO'S SERVANT].
There's the fool hangs on your back already.

APEMANTUS.
No, thou stand'st single, th'art not on him yet.

CAPHIS.
Where's the fool now?

APEMANTUS.
He last askt the question.—Poor rogues, and usurers' men! bawds between gold and want!

ALL SERVANTS.
What are we, Apemantus?

APEMANTUS.
Asses.

ALL SERVANTS.
Why?

APEMANTUS.
That you ask me what you are, and do not know
yourselves.—Speak to 'em, fool.

FOOL.
How do you, gentlemen?

ALL SERVANTS.
Gramercies, good fool: how does your mistress?

FOOL.
She's e'en setting on water to scald such chickens
as you are. Would we could see you at Corinth!

APEMANTUS.
Good! gramercy.

FOOL.
Look you, here comes my mistress' page.
          Enter PAGE.

PAGE [*to the* FOOL].
Why, how now, captain! what do you in this wise
company?—How dost thou, Apemantus?

APEMANTUS.
Would I had a rod in my mouth, that I might
answer thee profitably.

PAGE.
Prithee, Apemantus, read me the superscription
of these letters: I know not which is which.

APEMANTUS.
Canst not read?

PAGE.
No.

APEMANTUS.
There will little learning die, then, that day thou
art hang'd. This is to Lord Timon; this to Alcibiades. Go; thou wast born a bastard, and thou'lt
die a bawd.

PAGE.
Thou wast whelpt a dog, and thou shalt famish, a
dog's death. Answer not, I am gone.

APEMANTUS.
E'en so thou outrunn'st grace. [*Exit* PAGE.] Fool, I
will go with you to Lord Timon's.

FOOL.
Will you leave me there?

APEMANTUS.
If Timon stay at home.—You three serve three
usurers?

ALL SERVANTS.
Ay; would they served us!

APEMANTUS.
So would I,—as good a trick as ever hangman
served thief.

FOOL.
Are you three usurers' men?

ALL SERVANTS.
Ay, fool.

FOOL.
I think no usurer but has a fool to his servant: my
mistress is one, and I am her fool. When men
come to borrow of your masters, they approach
sadly, and go away merry; but they enter my mistress' house merrily, and go away sadly: the reason
of this?

VARRO'S SERVANT.
I could render one.

APEMANTUS.
Do it, then, that we may account thee a whoremaster and a knave; which notwithstanding, thou
shalt be no less esteem'd.

VARRO'S SERVANT.
What is a whoremaster, fool?

FOOL.
A fool in good clothes, and something like thee.
'Tis a spirit: sometime't appears like a lord;
sometime like a lawyer; sometime like a philosopher, with two stones moe than's artificial
one: he is very often like a knight; and, generally, in all shapes that man goes up and
down in from fourscore to thirteen, this spirit
walks in.

VARRO'S SERVANT.
Thou art not altogether a fool.

FOOL.
Nor thou altogether a wise man: as much foolery
as I have, so much wit thou lack'st.

APEMANTUS.
That answer might have become Apemantus.

ALL SERVANTS.
Aside, aside; here comes Lord Timon.

Enter TIMON *and* FLAVIUS.
APEMANTUS.
Come with me, fool, come.
FOOL.
I do not always follow lover, elder brother, and
woman; sometime the philosopher.
[*Exeunt* APEMANTUS *and* FOOL.
FLAVIUS.
Pray you, walk near: I'll speak with you anon.
[*Exeunt* SERVANTS.
TIMON.
You make me marvel: wherefore ere this time
Had you not fully laid my state before me;
That I might so have rated my expense
As I had leave of means?
FLAVIUS.
You would not hear me,
At many leisures I proposed.
TIMON.
Go to:
Perchance some single vantages you took,
When my indisposition put you back;
And that unaptness made your minister,
Thus to excuse yourself.
FLAVIUS.
O my good lord,
At many times I brought in my accounts,
Laid them before you; you would throw them off,
And say, you found them in mine honesty.
When, for some trifling present, you have bid me
Return so much, I have shook my head and wept;
Yea, 'gainst the authority of manners, pray'd you
To hold your hand more close: I did endure
Not seldom, nor no slight checks, when I have
Prompted you, in the ebb of your estate,
And your great flow of debts. My dear-loved lord,
Though you hear now—too late—yet now's a
time,
The greatest of your having lacks a half
To pay your present debts.
TIMON.
Let all my land be sold.
FLAVIUS.
'Tis all engaged, some forfeited and gone;
And what remains will hardly stop the mouth
Of present dues: the future comes apace:
What shall defend the interim? and at length
How goes our reckoning?
TIMON.
To Lacedæmon did my land extend.
FLAVIUS.
O my good lord, the world is but a word:
Were it all yours to give it in a breath,
How quickly were it gone!
TIMON.
You tell me true.
FLAVIUS.
If you suspect my husbandry or falsehood,
Call me before the exactest auditors,
And set me on the proof. So the gods bless me,
When all our offices have been opprest
With riotous feeders; when our vaults have wept
With drunken spilth of wine; when every room
Hath blazed with lights and bray'd with min-
l have retired me to a wasteful cock,   [strelsy;
And set mine eyes at flow.

TIMON.
Prithee, no more.
FLAVIUS.
Heavens, have I said, the bounty of this lord!
How many prodigal bits have slaves and peasants
This night englutted! Who is not Lord Timon's?
What heart, head, sword, force, means, but is
Lord Timon's?
Great Timon, noble, worthy, royal Timon!
Ah, when the means are gone that buy this praise,
The breath is gone whereof this praise is made:
Feast-won, fast-lost; one cloud of winter showers,
These flies are couch't.
TIMON.
Come, sermon me no further:
No villainous bounty yet hath past my heart;
Unwisely, not ignobly, have I given.
Why dost thou weep? Canst thou the conscience
lack,
To think I shall lack friends? Secure thy heart;
If I would broach the vessels of my love,
And try the argument of hearts by borrowing,
Men and men's fortunes could I frankly use
As I can bid thee speak.
FLAVIUS.
Assurance bless your thoughts!
TIMON.
And, in some sort, these wants of mine are
crown'd,
That I account them blessings; for by these
Shall I try friends: you shall perceive how you
Mistake my fortunes; I am wealthy in my
Within there! Flaminius! Servilius!   [friends.—
Enter FLAMINIUS, SERVILIUS, *and*
other SERVANTS.
SERVANTS.
My lord? my lord?—
TIMON.
I will dispatch you severally:—[*to* SERVILIUS]
you to Lord Lucius;—[*to* FLAMINIUS] to Lord
Lucullus you; I hunted with his honour to-day;—
[*to another* SERVANT] you to Sempronius: com-
mend me to their loves; and, I am proud, say, that
my occasions have found time to use 'em toward
a supply of money: let the request be fifty talents
FLAMINIUS.
As you have said, my lord.
[*Exit with* SERVILIUS *and another* SERVANT.
FLAVIUS [*aside*]—
Lord Lucius and Lucullus? hum!
TIMON [*to another* SERVANT].
Go you, sir, to the senators,—
Of whom, even to the state's best health, I have
Deserved this hearing; bid 'em send o'the instant
A thousand talents to me.   [*Exit* SERVANT.
FLAVIUS.
I have been bold—
For that I knew it the most general way—
To them to use your signet and your name;
But they do shake their heads, and I am here
No richer in return.
TIMON.
Is't true? can't be?
FLAVIUS.
They answer, in a joint and corporate voice,
That now they are at fall, want treasure, cannot

Do what they would; are sorry—you are honour-
    able—
But yet they could have wisht—they know not—
Something hath been amiss—a noble nature
May catch a wrench—would all were well—'tis
    pity;—
And so, intending other serious matters,
After distasteful looks and these hard fractions,
With certain half-caps and cold-moving nods
They froze me into silence.

TIMON.
                    You gods, reward them!—
Prithee, man, look cheerly. These old fellows
Have their ingratitude in them hereditary:
Their blood is caked, 'tis cold, it seldom flows;
'Tis lack of kindly warmth they are not kind;
And nature, as it grows again toward earth,
Is fashion'd for the journey, dull and heavy.—
[to another SERVANT] Go to Ventidius,—[to
    FLAVIUS] Prithee, be not sad,
Thou art true and honest; ingeniously I speak,
No blame belongs to thee:—[to the same SER-
    VANT] Ventidius lately
Buried his father; by whose death he's stept
Into a great estate: when he was poor,
Imprison'd, and in scarcity of friends,
I clear'd him with five talents: greet him from
    me;
Bid him suppose some good necessity
Touches his friend, which craves to be remem-
    ber'd
With those five talents.   [Exit SERVANT.
    [to FLAVIUS] That had, give't these fellows
To whom 'tis instant due. Ne'er speak, or think,
That Timon's fortunes 'mong his friends can
    sink.

FLAVIUS.
I would I could not think it: that thought is
    bounty's foe:
Being free itself, it thinks all others so.   [Exeunt.

ACT III. SCENE I.

Athens. A room in LUCULLUS' house.

FLAMINIUS *waiting to speak with* LUCULLUS
from his master, enters a SERVANT *to him.*

SERVANT.
I HAVE told my lord of you; he is coming
    down to you.

FLAMINIUS.
I thank you, sir.
              Enter LUCULLUS.

SERVANT.
Here's my lord.

LUCULLUS [aside].
One of Lord Timon's men? a gift, I warrant.
Why, this hits right; I dreamt of a silver basin and
ewer to-night.—Flaminius, honest Flaminius;
you are very respectively welcome, sir.—Fill me
some wine. [Exit SERVANT]—And how does
that honourable, complete, freehearted gentleman of Athens, thy very bountiful good lord and
master?

FLAMINIUS.
His health is well, sir.

LUCULLUS.
I am right glad that his health is well, sir: and
what hast thou there under thy cloak, pretty Flaminius?

FLAMINIUS.
Faith, nothing but an empty box, sir; which, in
my lord's behalf, I come to entreat your honour
to supply; who, having great and instant occasion
to use fifty talents, hath sent to your lordship to
furnish him, nothing doubting your present assistance therein.

LUCULLUS.
La, la, la, la,—'nothing doubting,' says he?
Alas, good lord! a noble gentleman 'tis, if he
would not keep so good a house. Many a time and
often I ha' dined with him, and told him on't; and
come again to supper to him, of purpose to have
him spend less, and yet he would embrace no
counsel, take no warning by my coming. Every
man has his fault, and honesty is his: I ha' told
him on't, but I could ne'er get him from't.
          Enter SERVANT, *with wine.*

SERVANT.
Please your lordship, here is the wine.

LUCULLUS.
Flaminius, I have noted thee always wise. Here's
to thee.

FLAMINIUS.
Your lordship speaks your pleasure.

LUCULLUS.
I have observed thee always for a towardly prompt
spirit,—give thee thy due,—and one that knows
what belongs to reason; and canst use the time
well, if the time use thee well: good parts in thee.
—[to SERVANT] Get you gone, sirrah. [Exit SER-
VANT]—Draw nearer, honest Flaminius. Thy
lord's a bountiful gentleman: but thou art wise;
and thou know'st well enough, although thou
comest to me, that this is no time to lend money;
especially upon bare friendship, without security.
Here's three solidares for thee: good boy, wink
at me, and say thou saw'st me not. Fare thee
well.

FLAMINIUS.
Is't possible the world should so much differ,
And we alive that lived? Fly, damned baseness,
To him that worships thee!
              [Throwing the money back.

LUCULLUS.
Ha! now I see thou art a fool, and fit for thy
master.   [Exit.

FLAMINIUS.
May these add to the number that may scald thee!
Let molten coin be thy damnation,
Thou disease of a friend, and not himself!
Has friendship such a faint and milky heart,
It turns in less than two nights? O you gods,
I feel my master's passion! This slave
Unto dishonour has my lord's meat in him:
Why should it thrive, and turn to nutriment,
When he is turn'd to poison?
O, may diseases only work upon't!
And, when he's sick to death, let not that part of
    nature
Which my lord paid for, be of any power
To expel sickness, but prolong his hour!   [Exit.

SCENE II.

The same.　A public place.

Enter LUCIUS, *with three* STRANGERS.

LUCIUS.

WHO, the Lord Timon? he is my very good friend, and an honourable gentleman.

FIRST STRANGER.

We know him for no less, though we are but strangers to him. But I can tell you one thing, my lord, and which I hear from common rumours,—now Lord Timon's happy hours are done and past, and his estate shrinks from him.

LUCIUS.

Fie, no, do not believe it; he cannot want for money.

SECOND STRANGER.

But believe you this, my lord, that, not long ago, one of his men was with the Lord Lucullus to borrow so many talents; nay, urged extremely for't, and show'd what necessity belong'd to't, and yet was denied.

LUCIUS.

How!

SECOND STRANGER.

I tell you, denied, my lord.

LUCIUS.

What a strange case was that! now, before the gods, I am ashamed on't. Denied that honourable man! there was very little honour show'd in't. For my own part, I must needs confess, I have received some small kindnesses from him, as money, plate, jewels, and such-like trifles, nothing comparing to his; yet, had he mistook him, and sent to me, I should ne'er have denied his occasion so many talents.

Enter SERVILIUS.

SERVILIUS.

See, by good hap, yonder's my lord; I have sweat to see his honour.—[*to* LUCIUS] My honour'd lord,—

LUCIUS.

Servilius! you are kindly met, sir. Fare thee well: commend me to thy honourable virtuous lord, my very exquisite friend.

SERVILIUS.

May it please your honour, my lord hath sent—

LUCIUS.

Ha! what has he sent? I am so much endear'd to that lord: he's ever sending: how shall I thank him, think'st thou? And what has he sent now?

SERVILIUS.

'Has only sent his present occasion now, my lord; requesting your lordship to supply his instant use with so many talents.

LUCIUS.

I know his lordship is but merry with me; He cannot want fifty-five hundred talents.

SERVILIUS.

But in the mean time he wants less, my lord. If his occasion were not virtuous, I should not urge it half so faithfully.

LUCIUS.

Dost thou speak seriously, Servilius?

SERVILIUS.

Upon my soul, 'tis true, sir.

LUCIUS.

What a wicked beast was I to disfurnish myself against such a good time, when I might ha' shown myself honourable! how unluckily it happen'd, that I should purchase the day before for a little part, and undo a great deal of honour!—Servilius, now, before the gods, I am not able to do,—the more beast, I say:—I was sending to use Lord Timon myself, these gentlemen can witness; but I would not, for the wealth of Athens, I had done't now. Commend me bountifully to his good lordship; and I hope his honour will conceive the fairest of me, because I have no power to be kind:— and tell him this from me, I count it one of my greatest afflictions, say, that I cannot pleasure such an honourable gentleman. Good Servilius, will you befriend me so far, as to use mine own words to him?

SERVILIUS.

Yes, sir, I shall.

LUCIUS.

I'll look you out a good turn, Servilius.

[*Exit* SERVILIUS.

True, as you said, Timon is shrunk indeed;
And he that's once denied will hardly speed.

[*Exit.*

FIRST STRANGER.

Did you observe this, Hostilius?

SECOND STRANGER.

Ay, too well.

FIRST STRANGER.

Why, this
Is the world's soul; and just of the same piece
Is every flatterer's spirit. Who can call him
His friend that dips in the same dish? for, in
My knowing, Timon has been this lord's
　　father,
And kept his credit with his purse;
Supported his estate; nay, Timon's money
Has paid his men their wages: he ne'er drinks,
But Timon's silver treads upon his lip;
And yet—O, see the monstrousness of man
When he looks out in an ungrateful shape!—
He does deny him, in respect of his,
What charitable men afford to beggars.

THIRD STRANGER.

Religion groans at it.

FIRST STRANGER.

For mine own part,
I never tasted Timon in my life,
Nor came any of his bounties over me,
To mark me for his friend; yet, I protest,
For his right noble mind, illustrious virtue,
And honourable carriage,
Had his necessity made use of me,
I would have put my wealth into donation,
And the best half should have return'd to him,
So much I love his heart: but I perceive
Men must learn now with pity to dispense;
For policy sits above conscience.　[*Exeunt.*

SCENE III.

The same.   A room in SEMPRONIUS' *house.*

Enter SEMPRONIUS, *and a* SERVANT *of* TIMON'S.

SEMPRONIUS.

MUST he needs trouble me in't,—hum!—'bove
all others?
He might have tried Lord Lucius or Lucullus;
And now Ventidius is wealthy too,
Whom he redeem'd from prison: all these
Owe their estates unto him.

SERVANT.
         My lord,
They have all been toucht, and found base metal;
They have all denied him.   [*for*

SEMPRONIUS.
         How! have they denied him?
Has Ventidius and Lucullus denied him?
And does he send to me? Three? hum!—
It shows but little love or judgement in him: [ans,
Must I be his last refuge? His friends, like physici-
Thrive, give him over: must I take th'cure upon me?
'Has much disgraced me in't; I'm angry at him,
That might have known my place: I see no sense
But his occasions might have woo'd me first; [for't,
For, in my conscience, I was the first man
That e'er received gift from him:
And does he think so backwardly of me now,
That I'll requite it last? No:
So it may prove an argument of laughter
To the rest, and 'mongst lords I be thought a fool.
I'd rather than the worth of thrice the sum,
'Had sent to me first, but for my mind's sake;
I'd such a courage to do him good. But now return,
And with their faint reply this answer join:
Who bates mine honour shall not know my coin.
         [*Exit.*

SERVANT.
Excellent! Your lordship's a goodly villain. The
devil knew not what he did when he made man
politic,—he crost himself by't: and I cannot think
but, in the end, the villainies of man will set him
clear. How fairly this lord strives to appear foul!
takes virtuous copies to be wicked; like those that,
under hot ardent zeal, would set whole realms on
fire:
Of such a nature is his politic love.
This was my lord's last hope; now all are fled,
Save the gods only: now his friends are dead,
Doors, that were ne'er acquainted with their wards
Many a bounteous year, must be employ'd
Now to guard sure their master.
And this is all a liberal course allows;
Who cannot keep his wealth must keep his house.
         [*Exit.*

SCENE IV.

The same.   A hall in TIMON'S *house.*

Enter two SERVANTS *of* VARRO, *and the* SERVANT
of LUCIUS, *meeting* TITUS, HORTENSIUS, *and
other* SERVANTS *of* TIMON'S *creditors, waiting
his coming out.*

VARRO'S FIRST SERVANT.

WELL met; good morrow, Titus and Hortensius.

TITUS.
The like to you, kind Varro.

HORTENSIUS.
         Lucius!
What, do we meet together?

LUCIUS' SERVANT.
         Ay, and I think
One business does command us all; for mine
Is money.

TITUS.
So is theirs and ours.

Enter PHILOTUS.

LUCIUS' SERVANT.
         And Sir Philotus too!

PHILOTUS.
Good day at once.

LUCIUS' SERVANT.
         Welcome, good brother.
What do you think the hour?

PHILOTUS.
         Labouring for nine.

LUCIUS' SERVANT.
So much?

PHILOTUS.
         Is not my lord seen yet?

LUCIUS' SERVANT.
         Not yet.

PHILOTUS.
I wonder on't; he was wont to shine at seven.

LUCIUS' SERVANT.
Ay, but the days are waxt shorter with him:
You must consider that a prodigal course
Is like the sun's;
But not, like his, recoverable. I fear
'Tis deepest winter in Lord Timon's purse;
That is, one may reach deep enough, and yet
Find little.

PHILOTUS.
         I am of your fear for that.

TITUS.
I'll show you how t'observe a strange event.
Your lord sends now for money.

HORTENSIUS.
         Most true, he does.

TITUS.
And he wears jewels now of Timon's gift,
For which I wait for money.

HORTENSIUS.
It is against my heart.

LUCIUS' SERVANT.
         Mark, how strange it shows,
Timon in this should pay more than he owes;
And e'en as if your lord should wear rich jewels,
And send for money for 'em.

HORTENSIUS.
I'm weary of this charge, the gods can witness:
I know my lord hath spent of Timon's wealth,
And now ingratitude makes it worse than stealth.

VARRO'S FIRST SERVANT.
Yes, mine's three thousand crowns: what's
yours?

LUCIUS' SERVANT.
Five thousand mine.

VARRO'S FIRST SERVANT.
'Tis much deep: and it should seem by the sum
Your master's confidence was above mine;
Else, surely, his had equall'd.

Enter FLAMINIUS.

TITUS.
One of Lord Timon's men.

LUCIUS' SERVANT.
Flaminius!—Sir, a word: pray, is my lord ready to
come forth?

FLAMINIUS.
No, indeed, he is not.

TITUS.
We attend his lordship; pray, signify so much.

FLAMINIUS.
I need not tell him that; he knows you are too diligent.　　　　　　　　　　　　　　　　　　　[*Exit.*

Enter FLAVIUS *in a cloak, muffled.*

LUCIUS' SERVANT.
Ha! is not that his steward muffled so?
He goes away in a cloud: call him, call him.

TITUS.
Do you hear, sir?

BOTH VARRO'S SERVANTS.
By your leave, sir,—

FLAVIUS.
What do ye ask of me, my friends?

TITUS.
We wait for certain money here, sir.

FLAVIUS.
　　　　　　　　　　　　　　　　　　　　Ay,
If money were as certain as your waiting,
'Twere sure enough.
Why then preferr'd you not your sums and bills
When your false masters eat of my lord's meat?
Then they could smile, and fawn upon his debts,
And take down the int'rest into their gluttonous
　　maws.
You do yourselves but wrong to stir me up;
Let me pass quietly:
Believe't, my lord and I have made an end;
I have no more to reckon, he to spend.

LUCIUS' SERVANT.
Ay, but this answer will not serve.

FLAVIUS.
If 'twill not serve, 'tis not so base as you;
For you serve knaves.　　　　　　　　　　[*Exit.*

VARRO'S FIRST SERVANT.
How! what does his cashier'd worship mutter?

VARRO'S SECOND SERVANT.
No matter what; he's poor, and that's revenge
enough. Who can speak broader than he that has
no house to put his head in? such may rail against
great buildings.

Enter SERVILIUS.

TITUS.
O, here's Servilius; now we shall know some answer.

SERVILIUS.
If I might beseech you, gentlemen, to repair
some other hour, I should derive much from't;
for, take't of my soul, my lord leans wondrously to
discontent: his comfortable temper has forsook
him; he's much out of health, and keeps his
chamber.

LUCIUS' SERVANT.
Many do keep their chambers are not sick:
And, if it be so far beyond his health,
Methinks he should the sooner pay his debts,
And make a clear way to the gods.

SERVILIUS.
　　　　　　　　　　　　　　　　Good gods!

TITUS.
We cannot take this for an answer, sir.

FLAMINIUS [*within*].
Servilius, help!—My lord! my lord!

Enter TIMON, *in a rage;* FLAMINIUS *following.*

TIMON.
What, are my doors opposed against my passage?
Have I been ever free, and must my house
Be my retentive enemy, my gaol?
The place which I have feasted, does it now,
Like all mankind, show me an iron heart?

LUCIUS' SERVANT.
Put in now, Titus.

TITUS.
My lord, here is my bill.

LUCIUS' SERVANT.
Here's mine.

HORTENSIUS.
And mine, my lord.

BOTH VARRO'S SERVANTS.
And ours, my lord.

PHILOTUS.
All our bills.

TIMON.
Knock me down with 'em: cleave me to the girdle.

LUCIUS' SERVANT.
Alas, my lord,—

TIMON.
Cut my heart in sums.

TITUS.
Mine, fifty talents.

TIMON.
Tell out my blood.

LUCIUS' SERVANT.
Five thousand crowns, my lord.

TIMON.
Five thousand drops pays that.—What yours?—
and yours?

VARRO'S FIRST SERVANT.
My lord,—

VARRO'S SECOND SERVANT.
My lord,—

TIMON.
Tear me, take me, and the gods fall upon you!
　　　　　　　　　　　　　　　　　　　　[*Exit.*

HORTENSIUS.
Faith, I perceive our masters may throw their caps
at their money: these debts may well be call'd desperate ones, for a madman owes 'em.　　[*Exeunt.*

Enter TIMON *and* FLAVIUS.

TIMON.
They have e'en put my breath from me, the slaves.
Creditors!—devils.

FLAVIUS.
My dear lord,—

TIMON.
What if it should be so?

FLAVIUS.
My lord,—

TIMON.
I'll have it so.—My steward!

FLAVIUS.
Here, my lord.

TIMON.
So fitly? Go, bid all my friends again,
Lucius, Lucullus, and Sempronius; all:
I'll once more feast the rascals.
FLAVIUS.
O my lord,
You only speak from your distracted soul;
There is not so much left to furnish out
A moderate table.
TIMON.
Be it not in thy care; go,
I charge thee, invite them all: let in the tide
Of knaves once more; my cook and I'll provide.
[*Exeunt.*

SCENE V.

The same.   The senate-house.

The Senate sitting.

FIRST SENATOR.
MY Lord, you have my voice to it; the fault's
Bloody; 'tis necessary he should die:
Nothing emboldens sin so much as mercy.
SECOND SENATOR.
Most true; the law shall bruise him.
Enter ALCIBIADES *attended.*
ALCIBIADES.
Honour, health, and compassion to the senate!
FIRST SENATOR.
Now, captain?
ALCIBIADES.
I am an humble suitor to your virtues;
For pity is the virtue of the law,
And none but tyrants use it cruelly.
It pleases time and fortune to lie heavy
Upon a friend of mine, who, in hot blood,
Hath stept into the law, which is past depth
To those that, without heed, do plunge into't.
He is a man, setting his fault aside,
Of comely virtues:
Nor did he soil the fact with cowardice,
An honour in him which buys out his fault;
But with a noble fury and fair spirit,
Seeing his reputation toucht to death,
He did oppose his foe:
And with such sober and unnoted passion
He did behave his anger, ere 'twas spent,
As if he had but proved an argument.
FIRST SENATOR.
You undergo too strict a paradox,
Striving to make an ugly deed look fair:
Your words have took such pains, as if they labour'd
To bring manslaughter into form, and set
Quarrelling upon the head of valour; which
Indeed is valour misbegot, and came
Into the world when sects and factions
Were newly born:
He's truly valiant that can wisely suffer
The worst that man can breathe; and make his
wrongs
His outsides,—to wear them like his raiment, care-
lessly;
And ne'er prefer his injuries to his heart,
To bring it into danger.
If wrongs be evils, and enforce us kill,
What folly 'tis to hazard life for ill!

ALCIBIADES.
My lord,—
FIRST SENATOR.
You cannot make gross sins look clear:
To revenge is no valour, but to bear.
ALCIBIADES.
My lords, then, under favour, pardon me,
If I speak like a captain:—
Why do fond men expose themselves to battle,
And not endure all threats? sleep upon't,
And let the foes quietly cut their throats,
Without repugnancy? If there be
Such valour in the bearing, what make we
Abroad? why, then, women are more valiant
That stay at home, if bearing carry it;
And the ass more captain than the lion; the felon
Loaden with irons wiser than the judge,
If wisdom be in suffering. O my lords,
As you are great, be pitifully good:
Who cannot condemn rashness in cold blood?
To kill, I grant, is sin's extremest gust;
But, in defence, by mercy, 'tis most just.
To be in anger is impiety;
But who is man that is not angry?
Weigh but the crime with this.
SECOND SENATOR.
You breathe in vain.
ALCIBIADES.
In vain! his service done
At Lacedæmon and Byzantium
Were a sufficient briber for his life.
FIRST SENATOR.
What's that?
ALCIBIADES.
Why, I say, my lords, 'has done fair service,
And slain in fight many of your enemies:
How full of valour did he bear himself
In the last conflict, and made plenteous wounds!
SECOND SENATOR.
He has made too much plenty with 'em,
He's a sworn rioter: he has a sin that often
Drowns him, and takes his valour prisoner:
If there were no foes, that were enough
To overcome him: in that beastly fury
He has been known to commit outrages
And cherish factions: 'tis inferr'd to us
His days are foul, and his drink dangerous.
FIRST SENATOR.
He dies.
ALCIBIADES.
Hard fate! he might have died in war.
My lords, if not for any parts in him,—
Though his right arm might purchase his own
time,
And be in debt to none,—yet, more to move you,
Take my deserts to his, and join 'em both:
And, for I know your reverend ages love
Security, I'll pawn my victories, all
My honour to you, upon his good returns.
If by this crime he owes the law his life,
Why, let the war receive't in valiant gore;
For law is strict, and war is nothing more.
FIRST SENATOR.
We are for law,—he dies: urge it no more,
On height of our displeasure: friend or brother,
He forfeits his own blood that spills another.

ALCIBIADES.
Must it be so? it must not be. My lords,
I do beseech you, know me.
         SECOND SENATOR.
How!
         ALCIBIADES.
Call me to your remembrances.
         THIRD SENATOR.
                 What!
         ALCIBIADES.
I cannot think but your age has forgot me;
It could not else be I should prove so base
To sue, and be denied such common grace:
My wounds ache at you.
         FIRST SENATOR.
              Do you dare our anger?
'Tis in few words, but spacious in effect;
We banish thee for ever.
         ALCIBIADES.
              Banish me!
Banish your dotage; banish usury,
That makes the senate ugly.
         FIRST SENATOR.
If after two days' shine Athens contain thee,
Attend our weightier judgement. And, not to
    swell our spirit,
He shall be executed presently.
               [*Exeunt* SENATORS.
         ALCIBIADES.
Now the gods keep you old enough; that you may
    live
Only in bone, that none may look on you!
I'm worse than mad: I have kept back their foes,
While they have told their money, and let out
Their coin upon large interest; I myself
Rich only in large hurts;—all those for this?
Is this the balsam that the usuring senate
Pours into captains' wounds? Banishment!
It comes not ill; I hate not to be banisht;
It is a cause worthy my spleen and fury,
That I may strike at Athens. I'll cheer up
My discontented troops, and lay for hearts.
'Tis honour with most lands to be at odds;
Soldiers should brook as little wrongs as gods.
                     [*Exit.*

SCENE VI.

The same.   *A magnificent room in* TIMON'S
house.

Music. Tables set out: SERVANTS *attending. Enter,*
at several doors, divers LORDS,—LUCIUS,
LUCULLUS, SEMPRONIUS,—SENATORS, *&c.,*
and VENTIDIUS.

         FIRST LORD.
THE good time of day to you, sir.
         SECOND LORD.
I also wish it to you. I think this honourable lord
did but try us this other day.
         FIRST LORD.
Upon that were my thoughts tiring when we encounter'd: I hope it is not so low with him as he
made it seem in the trial of his several friends.
         SECOND LORD.
It should not be, by the persuasion of his new feasting.

         FIRST LORD.
I should think so: he hath sent me an earnest inviting, which many my near occasions did urge me to
put off; but he hath conjured me beyond them,
and I must needs appear.
         SECOND LORD.
In like manner was I in debt to my importunate
business, but he would not hear my excuse. I am
sorry, when he sent to borrow of me, that my pro-
vision was out.
         FIRST LORD.
I am sick of that grief too, as I understand how all
things go.
         SECOND LORD.
Every man here's so. What would he have bor-
row'd of you?
         FIRST LORD.
A thousand pieces.
         SECOND LORD.
A thousand pieces!
         FIRST LORD.
What of you?
         SECOND LORD.
He sent to me, sir,—Here he comes.
      Enter TIMON *and* ATTENDANTS.
         TIMON.
With all my heart, gentlemen both:—and how fare
you—
         FIRST LORD.
Ever at the best, hearing well of your lordship.
         SECOND LORD.
The swallow follows not summer more willing
than we your lordship.
         TIMON [*aside*].
Nor more willingly leaves winter; such summer-
birds are men.—Gentlemen, our dinner will not
recompense this long stay: feast your ears with the
music awhile, if they will fare so harshly o'the
trumpet's sound; we shall to't presently.
         FIRST LORD.
I hope it remains not unkindly with your lordship,
that I return'd you an empty messenger.
         TIMON.
O, sir, let it not trouble you.
         SECOND LORD.
My noble lord,—
         TIMON.
Ah, my good friend,—what cheer?
         SECOND LORD.
My most honourable lord, I am e'en sick of shame,
that, when your lordship this other day sent to me
I was so unfortunate a beggar.
         TIMON.
Think not on't, sir.
         SECOND LORD.
If you had sent but two hours before,—
         TIMON.
Let it not cumber your better remembrance.—
Come, bring in all together.
             [*The banquet brought in.*
         SECOND LORD.
All cover'd dishes!
         FIRST LORD.
Royal cheer, I warrant you.
         THIRD LORD.
Doubt not that, if money and the season can yield it.

FIRST LORD.
How do you? What's the news?

THIRD LORD.
Alcibiades is banisht: hear you of it?

FIRST AND SECOND LORDS.
Alcibiades banisht!

THIRD LORD.
'Tis so, be sure of it.

FIRST LORD.
How! how!

SECOND LORD.
I pray you, upon what?

TIMON.
My worthy friends, will you draw near?

THIRD LORD.
I'll tell you more anon. Here's a noble feast to-ward.

SECOND LORD.
This is the old man still.

THIRD LORD.
Will't hold? will't hold?

SECOND LORD.
It does: but time will—and so—

THIRD LORD.
I do conceive.

TIMON.
Each man to his stool, with that spur as he would to the lip of his mistress: your diet shall be in all places alike. Make not a city feast of it, to let the meat cool ere we can agree upon the first place: sit, sit. The gods require our thanks.—
You great benefactors, sprinkle our society with thankfulness. For your own gifts, make yourselves praised: but reserve still to give, lest your deities be despised. Lend to each man enough, that one need not lend to another; for, were your godheads to borrow of men, men would forsake the gods. Make the meat be beloved more than the man that gives it. Let no assembly of twenty be without a score of villains: if there sit twelve women at the table, let a dozen of them be—as they are. The rest of your foes, O gods,—the senators of Athens, together with the common tag of people,—what is amiss in them, you gods, make suitable for destruction. For these my present friends—as they are to me nothing, so in nothing bless them, and to nothing are they welcome.—
Uncover, dogs, and lap.

[The dishes are uncovered, and seen to be full of warm water.

SOME SPEAK.
What does his lordship mean?

SOME OTHER.
I know not.

TIMON.
May you a better feast never behold,
You knot of mouth-friends! smoke and lukewarm water
Is your perfection. This is Timon's last:
Who, stuck and spangled with your flattery,
Washes it off, and sprinkles in your faces
[Throwing the water in their faces.
Your reeking villainy. Live loathed, and long,
Most smiling, smooth, detested parasites,
Courteous destroyers, affable wolves, meek bears,
You fools of fortune, trencher-friends, time's flies,

Cap and knee slaves, vapours, and minute-jacks!
Of man and beast the infinite malady
Crust you quite o'er!—What, dost thou go?
Soft! take thy physic first,—thou too,—and thou;—
Stay, I will lend thee money, borrow none.—
[Throws the dishes at them, and drives them out.
What, all in motion? Henceforth be no feast
Whereat a villain's not a welcome guest.
Burn, house! sink, Athens! henceforth hated be
Of Timon man and all humanity! [Exit.

Enter the LORDS, SENATORS, &c.

FIRST LORD.
How now, my lords!

SECOND LORD.
Know you the quality of Lord Timon's fury?

THIRD LORD.
Push! did you see my cap?

FOURTH LORD.
I have lost my gown.

FIRST LORD.
He's but a mad lord, and naught but humour
sways him. He gave me a jewel the other day, and
now he has beat it out of my hat:—did you see my
jewel?

THIRD LORD.
Did you see my cap?

SECOND LORD.
Here 'tis.

FOURTH LORD.
Here lies my gown.

FIRST LORD.
Let's make no stay.

SECOND LORD.
Lord Timon's mad.

THIRD LORD.
I feel't upon my bones.

FOURTH LORD.
One day he gives us diamonds, next day stones.
[Exeunt.

ACT IV. SCENE I.
Without the walls of Athens.
Enter TIMON.

TIMON.
LET me look back upon thee. O thou wall,
That girdlest in those wolves, dive in the earth,
And fence not Athens! Matrons, turn incontinent!
Obedience fail in children! slaves and fools,
Pluck the grave wrinkled senate from the bench,
And minister in their steads! to general filths
Convert o'the instant, green virginity,—
Do't in your parents' eyes! bankrupts, hold fast
Rather than render back, out with your knives,
And cut your trusters' throats! bound servants, steal!
Large-handed robbers your grave masters are,
And pill by law: maid, to thy master's bed,—
Thy mistress is o'the brothel! son of sixteen,
Pluck the lined crutch from thy old limping sire,
With it beat out his brains! piety, and fear,
Religion to the gods, peace, justice, truth,
Domestic awe, night-rest, and neighbourhood,
Instruction, manners, mysteries, and trades,
Degrees, observances, customs, and laws,

Decline to your confounding contraries,
And let confusion live!—Plagues incident to men,
Your potent and infectious fevers heap
On Athens, ripe for stroke! thou cold sciatica,
Cripple our senators, that their limbs may halt
As lamely as their manners! lust and liberty,
Creep in the minds and marrows of our youth,
That 'gainst the stream of virtue they may strive,
And drown themselves in riot! itches, blains,
Sow all the Athenian bosoms; and their crop
Be general leprosy! breath infect breath;
That their society, as their friendship, may
Be merely poison! Nothing I'll bear from thee
But nakedness, thou detestable town!
Take thou that too, with multiplying bans!
Timon will to the woods; where he shall find
The unkindest beast more kinder than mankind.
The gods confound—hear me, you good gods all—
The Athenians both within and out that wall!
And grant, as Timon grows, his hate may grow
To the whole race of mankind, high and low!
Amen.　　　　　　　　　　　　　　　　[*Exit.*

SCENE II.

Athens.　A room in TIMON'S *house.*

Enter FLAVIUS, *with two or three* SERVANTS.

FIRST SERVANT.

HEAR you, master steward,—where's our
master?
Are we undone? cast off? nothing remaining?

FLAVIUS.

Alack, my fellows, what should I say to you?
Let me be recorded by the righteous gods,
I am as poor as you.

FIRST SERVANT.

Such a house broke!
So noble a master faln! All gone! and not
One friend to take his fortune by the arm,
And go along with him!

SECOND SERVANT.

As we do turn our backs
From our companion thrown into his grave,
So his familiars from his buried fortunes
Slink all away; leave their false vows with him,
Like empty purses pickt; and his poor self,
A dedicated beggar to the air,
With his disease of all-shunn'd poverty,
Walks, like contempt, alone.—More of our fel-
lows.

Enter other SERVANTS.

FLAVIUS.

All broken implements of a ruin'd house.

THIRD SERVANT.

Yet do our hearts wear Timon's livery;
That see I by our faces; we are fellows still,
Serving alike in sorrow: leakt is our bark;
And we, poor mates, stand on the dying deck,
Hearing the surges threat: we must all part
Into this sea of air.

FLAVIUS.

Good fellows all,
The latest of my wealth I'll share amongst you,
Wherever we shall meet, for Timon's sake,
Let's yet be fellows; let's shake our heads, and say,
As 'twere a knell unto our master's fortunes,

'We have seen better days.' Let each take some;
　　　　　　　　　　　　　[*Giving them money.*
Nay, put out all your hands. Not one word more:
Thus part we rich in sorrow, parting poor.
　　　[SERVANTS *embrace, and part several ways.*
O, the fierce wretchedness that glory brings us!
Who would not wish to be from wealth exempt,
Since riches point to misery and contempt?
Who'ld be so mockt with glory? or to live
But in a dream of friendship?
To have his pomp, and all what state compounds,
But only painted, like his varnisht friends?
Poor honest lord, brought low by his own heart,
Undone by goodness! Strange, unusual blood,
When man's worst sin is, he does too much good!
Who, then, dares to be half so kind agen?
For bounty, that makes gods, does still mar men.
My dearest lord,—blest, to be most accurst,
Rich, only to be wretched,—thy great fortunes
Are made thy chief afflictions. Alas, kind lord!
He's flung in rage from this ingrateful seat
Of monstrous friends; nor has he with him to
Supply his life, or that which can command it.
I'll follow, and inquire him out:
I'll ever serve his mind with my best will;
Whilst I have gold, I'll be his steward still. [*Exit.*

SCENE III.

The woods.　Before TIMON'S *cave.*

Enter TIMON.

TIMON.

O BLESSED breeding sun, draw from the
earth
Rotten humidity; below thy sister's orb
Infect the air! Twinn'd brothers of one womb,—
Whose procreation, residence, and birth,
Scarce is dividant,—touch them with several for-
tunes;
The greater scorns the lesser: not nature,
To whom all sores lay siege, can bear great for-
Put by contempt of nature.　　　　　　[tune,
Raise me this beggar, and deny't that lord;
The senator shall bear contempt hereditary,
The beggar native honour.
It is the pasture lards the rother's sides,
The want that makes him lean. Who dares, who
dares,
In purity of manhood stand upright,
And say, 'This man's a flatterer'? if one be,
So are they all; for every grise of fortune
Is smooth'd by that below: the learned pate
Ducks to the golden fool: all is oblique;
There's nothing level in our cursed natures,
But direct villainy. Therefore, be abhorr'd
All feasts, societies, and throngs of men!
His semblable, yea, himself, Timon disdains:
Destruction fang mankind!—Earth, yield me
roots!　　　　　　　　　　　　　　[*Digging.*
Who seeks for better of thee, sauce his palate
With thy most operant poison!—What is here?
Gold? yellow, glittering, precious gold? No, gods,
I am no idle votarist: roots, your clear heavens!
Thus much of this will make black white; foul,
fair;

Wrong, right; base, noble; old, young; coward,
  valiant.
Ha, you gods! why this? what this, you gods?
  Why, this
Will lug your priests and servants from your sides;
Pluck stout men's pillows from below their heads:
This yellow slave
Will knit and break religions; bless th'accurst;
Make the hoar leprosy adored; place thieves,
And give them title, knee, and approbation,
With senators on the bench: this is it
That makes the wappen'd widow wed again;
She, whom the spital-house and ulcerous sores
Would cast the gorge at, this embalms and spices
To th'April day again. Come, damned earth,
Thou common whore of mankind, that putt'st
  odds
Among the rout of nations, I will make thee
Do thy right nature.—[*March within.*] Ha! a
  drum?—Th'art quick,
But yet I'll bury thee: thou'lt go, strong thief,
When gouty keepers of thee cannot stand:—
Nay, stay thou out for earnest. [*Keeping some gold.*
Enter ALCIBIADES, *with drum and fife, in warlike*
  manner; PHRYNIA *and* TIMANDRA.
                ALCIBIADES.
          What art thou there? speak.
                TIMON.
A beast, as thou art. The canker gnaw thy heart,
For showing me again the eyes of man!
                ALCIBIADES.
What is thy name? Is man so hateful to thee,
That art thyself a man?
                TIMON.
I am *misanthropos*, and hate mankind.
For thy part, I do wish thou wert a dog,
That I might love thee something.
                ALCIBIADES.
                    I know thee well;
But in thy fortunes am unlearn'd and strange.
                TIMON.
I know thee too; and more than that I know thee,
I not desire to know. Follow thy drum;
With man's blood paint the ground, gules, gules:
Religious canons, civil laws are cruel;
Then what should war be? This fell whore of
  thine
Hath in her more destruction than thy sword,
For all her cherubin look.
                PHRYNIA.
                    Thy lips rot off!
                TIMON.
I will not kiss thee; then the rot returns
To thine own lips again.
                ALCIBIADES.
How came the noble Timon to this change?
                TIMON.
As the moon does, by wanting light to give:
But then renew I could not, like the moon;
There were no suns to borrow of.
                ALCIBIADES.
Noble Timon, what friendship may I do thee?
                TIMON.
None, but to maintain my opinion.
                ALCIBIADES.
What is it, Timon?

                TIMON.
Promise me friendship, but perform none: if thou
wilt not promise, the gods plague thee, for thou
art a man! if thou dost perform, confound thee,
for thou art a man!
                ALCIBIADES.
I have heard in some sort of thy miseries.
                TIMON.
Thou saw'st them, when I had prosperity.
                ALCIBIADES.
I see them now; then was a blessed time.
                TIMON.
As thine is now, held with a brace of harlots.
                TIMANDRA.
Is this th'Athenian minion, whom the world
Voiced so regardfully?
                TIMON.
          Art thou Timandra?
                TIMANDRA.
Yes.
                TIMON.
Be a whore still: they love thee not that use thee;
Give them diseases, leaving with thee their lust.
Make use of thy salt hours: season the slaves
For tubs and baths; bring down rose-cheekt
  youth to
The tub-fast and the diet.
                TIMANDRA.
          Hang thee, monster!
                ALCIBIADES.
Pardon him, sweet Timandra; for his wits
Are drown'd and lost in his calamities.—
I have but little gold of late, brave Timon,
The want whereof doth daily make revolt
In my penurious band: I have heard, and grieved,
How cursed Athens, mindless of thy worth,
Forgetting thy great deeds, when neighbour states,
But for thy sword and fortune, trod upon them,—
                TIMON.
I prithee, beat thy drum, and get thee gone.
                ALCIBIADES.
I am thy friend, and pity thee, dear Timon.
                TIMON.
How dost thou pity him whom thou dost trouble?
I had rather be alone.
                ALCIBIADES.
          Why, fare thee well:
Here's some gold for thee.
                TIMON.
              Keep it, I cannot eat it.
                ALCIBIADES.
When I have laid proud Athens on a heap,—
                TIMON.
Warr'st thou 'gainst Athens?
                ALCIBIADES.
              Ay, Timon, and have cause.
                TIMON.
The gods confound them all in thy conquest;
And thee after, when thou hast conquer'd!
                ALCIBIADES.
              Why me, Timon?
                TIMON.
That, by killing of villains, thou wast born to
  conquer
My country.
Put up thy gold: go on,—here's gold,—go on,

Be as a planetary plague, when Jove
Will o'er some high-viced city hang his poison
In the sick air: let not thy sword skip one:
Pity not honour'd age for his white beard,—
He is an usurer: strike me the counterfeit
    matron,—
It is her habit only that is honest,
Herself's a bawd: let not the virgin's cheek [paps,
Make soft thy trenchant sword; for those milk-
That through the window-bars bore at men's eyes,
Are not within the leaf of pity writ,
But set down horrible traitors: spare not the babe,
Whose dimpled smiles from fools exhaust their
    mercy;
Think it a bastard, whom the oracle
Hath doubtfully pronounced thy throat shall cut,
And mince it s ns remorse: swear against objects;
Put armour on thine ears and on thine eyes,
Whose proof, nor yells of mothers, maids, nor
    babes,
Nor sight of priests in holy vestments bleeding,
Shall pierce a jot. There's gold to pay thy soldiers:
Make large confusion; and, thy fury spent,
Confounded be thyself! Speak not, be gone.

ALCIBIADES.
Hast thou gold yet? I'll take the gold thou givest
    me,
Not all thy counsel.

TIMON.
Dost thou, or dost thou not, heaven's curse upon
    thee!

PHRYNIA and TIMANDRA.
Give us some gold, good Timon: hast thou more?

TIMON.
Enough to make a whore forswear her trade,
And to make whores, a bawd. Hold up, you sluts,
Your aprons mountant: you are not oathable,—
Although, I know, you'll swear, terribly swear,
Into strong shudders and to heavenly agues,
Th'immortal gods that hear you,—spare your
    oaths,
I'll trust to your conditions: be whores still;
And he whose pious breath seeks to convert you,
Be strong in whore, allure him, burn him up;
Let your close fire predominate his smoke,
And be no turncoats: yet may your pains, six
    months,
Be quite contrary: and thatch your poor thin roofs
With burdens of the dead;—some that were
    hang'd,
No matter:—wear them, betray with them: whore
    still;
Paint till a horse may mire upon your face:
A pox of wrinkles!

PHRYNIA and TIMANDRA.
Well, more gold:—what then?—
Believe't, that we'll do any thing for gold.

TIMON.
Consumptions sow
In hollow bones of man; strike their sharp shins,
And mar men's spurring. Crack the lawyer's
    voice,
That he may never more false title plead,
Nor sound his quillets shrilly: hoar the flamen,
That scolds against the quality of flesh,
And not believes himself: down with the nose,

Down with it flat; take the bridge quite away
Of him that, his particular to foresee,
Smells from the general weal: make curl'd-pate
    ruffians bald;
And let the unscarr'd braggarts of the war
Derive some pain from you: plague all;
That your activity may defeat and quell
The source of all erection.—There's more gold:—
Do you damn others, and let this damn you,
And ditches grave you all!

PHRYNIA and TIMANDRA.
More counsel with more money, bounteous
    Timon.

TIMON.
More whore, more mischief first; I've given you
    earnest.

ALCIBIADES.
Strike up the drum towards Athens!—Farewell,
    Timon:
If I thrive well, I'll visit thee again.

TIMON.
If I hope well, I'll never see thee more.

ALCIBIADES.
I never did thee harm.

TIMON.
Yes, thou spokest well of me.

ALCIBIADES.
                    Call'st thou that harm?

TIMON.
Men daily find it. Get thee away, and take
Thy beagles with thee.

ALCIBIADES.
                    We but offend him.—Strike!
    [Drum beats. Exeunt ALCIBIADES, PHRY-
    NIA, and TIMANDRA.

TIMON.
That nature, being sick of man's unkindness,
Should yet be hungry!—Common mother, thou,
                    [Digging.
Whose womb unmeasurable, and infinite breast,
Teems, and feeds all; whose self-same mettle,
Whereof thy proud child, arrogant man, is puft,
Engenders the black toad and adder blue,
The gilded newt and eyeless venom'd worm,
With all th'abhorred births below crisp heaven
Whereon Hyperion's quickening fire both shine;
Yield him, who all thy human sons doth hate,
From forth thy plenteous bosom, one poor root!
Ensear thy fertile and conceptious womb,
Let it no more bring out ingrateful man!
Go great with tigers, dragons, wolves, and bears;
Teem with new monsters, whom thy upward face
Hath to the marbled mansion all above
Never presented!—O, a root,—dear thanks!—
Dry up thy marrows, vines, and plough-torn leas;
Whereof ingrateful man, with liquorish draughts
And morsels unctuous, greases his pure mind,
That from it all consideration slips!—

Enter APEMANTUS.
More man? plague, plague!

APEMANTUS.
I was directed hither: men report
Thou dost affect my manners, and dost use them.

TIMON.
'Tis, then, because thou dost not keep a dog,
Whom I would imitate: consumption catch thee!

APEMANTUS.

This is in thee a nature but infected;
A poor unmanly melancholy sprung
From change of fortune. Why this spade? this place?
This slave-like habit; and these looks of care?
Thy flatterers yet wear silk, drink wine, lie soft;
Hug their diseased perfumes, and have forgot
That ever Timon was. Shame not these woods,
By putting on the cunning of a carper.
Be thou a flatterer now, and seek to thrive
By that which has undone thee: hinge thy knee,
And let his very breath, whom thou'lt observe,
Blow off thy cap; praise his most vicious strain,
And call it excellent: thou wast told thus;
Thou gavest thine ears like tapsters that bid welcome
To knaves and all approachers: 'tis most just
That thou turn rascal; hadst thou wealth again,
Rascals should have't. Do not assume my likeness.

TIMON.

Were I like thee, I'ld throw away myself.

APEMANTUS.

Thou hast cast away thyself, being like thyself;
A madman so long, now a fool. What, think'st
That the bleak air, thy boisterous chamberlain,
Will put thy shirt on warm? will these moss'd trees,
That have outlived the eagle, page thy heels,
And skip when thou point'st out? will the cold brook,
Candied with ice, caudle thy morning taste,
To cure thy o'er-night's surfeit? Call the creatures
Whose naked natures live in all the spite
Of wreakful heaven, whose bare unhoused trunks,
To the conflicting elements exposed,
Answer mere nature, bid them flatter thee;
O, thou shalt find—

TIMON.

A fool of thee: depart.

APEMANTUS.

I love thee better now than e'er I did.

TIMON.

I hate thee worse.

APEMANTUS.

Why?

TIMON.

Thou flatter'st misery.

APEMANTUS.

I flatter not; but say thou art a caitiff.

TIMON.

Why dost thou seek me out?

APEMANTUS.

To vex thee.

TIMON.

Always a villain's office or a fool's.
Dost please thyself in't?

APEMANTUS.

Ay.

TIMON.

What! a knave too?

APEMANTUS.

If thou didst put this sour-cold habit on
To castigate thy pride, 'twere well: but thou
Dost it enforcedly; thou'ldst courtier be again,
Wert thou not beggar. Willing misery

Outlives incertain pomp, is crown'd before:
The one is filling still, never complete;
The other, at high wish: best state, contentless,
Hath a distracted and most wretched being,
Worse than the worst, content.
Thou shouldst desire to die, being miserable.

TIMON.

Not by his breath that is more miserable.
Thou art a slave, whom Fortune's tender arm
With favour never claspt; but bred a dog.
Hadst thou, like us from our first swath, proceeded
The sweet degrees that this brief world affords
To such as may the passive drugs of it
Freely command, thou wouldst have plunged thyself
In general riot; melted down thy youth
In different beds of lust; and never learn'd
The icy precepts of respect, but follow'd
The sugar'd game before thee. But myself,
Who had the world as my confectionary;
The mouths, the tongues, the eyes, and hearts of men
At duty, more than I could frame employment;
That numberless upon me stuck, as leaves
Do on the oak, have with one winter's brush
Fell from their boughs, and left me open, bare
For every storm that blows;—I, to bear this,
That never knew but better, is some burden:
Thy nature did commence in sufferance, time
Hath made thee hard in't. Why shouldst thou hate men?
They never flatter'd thee: what has thou given?
If thou wilt curse,—thy father, that poor rag,
Must be thy subject; who, in spite, put stuff
To some she-beggar, and compounded thee
Poor rogue hereditary. Hence, be gone!—
If thou hadst not been born the worst of men,
Thou hadst been a knave and flatterer.

APEMANTUS.

Art thou proud yet?

TIMON.

Ay, that I am not thee.

APEMANTUS.

I, that I was

No prodigal.

TIMON.

I, that I am one now:
Were all the wealth I have shut up in thee,
I'ld give thee leave to hang it. Get thee gone.—
That the whole life of Athens were in this!
Thus would I eat it.   [Gnawing a root.

APEMANTUS.

Here; I'll mend thy feast.
    [Offering him something.

TIMON.

First mend my company, take away thyself.

APEMANTUS.

So I shall mend mine own, by the lack of thine.

TIMON.

'Tis not well mended so, it is but botcht;
If not, I would it were.

APEMANTUS.

What wouldst thou have to Athens?

TIMON.

Thee thither in a whirlwind. If thou wilt,
Tell them there I have gold; look, so I have.

APEMANTUS.
Here is no use for gold.

TIMON.
The best and truest;
For here it sleeps, and does no hired harm.

APEMANTUS.
Where liest o'nights, Timon?

TIMON.
Under that's above me.
Where feed'st thou o'days, Apemantus?

APEMANTUS.
Where my stomach finds meat; or, rather, where
I eat it.

TIMON.
Would poison were obedient, and knew my mind!

APEMANTUS.
Where wouldst thou send it?

TIMON.
To sauce thy dishes.

APEMANTUS.
The middle of humanity thou never knewest, but
the extremity of both ends: when thou wast in thy
gilt and thy perfume they mockt thee for too
much curiosity; in thy rags thou know'st none,
but art despised for the contrary. There's a medlar for thee; eat it.

TIMON.
On what I hate I feed not.

APEMANTUS.
Dost hate a medlar?

TIMON.
Ay, though it look like thee.

APEMANTUS.
An th'hadst hated meddlers sooner, thou shouldst
have loved thyself better now. What man didst
thou ever know unthrift that was beloved after his
means?

TIMON.
Who, without those means thou talk'st of, didst
thou ever know beloved?

APEMANTUS.
Myself.

TIMON.
I understand thee; thou hadst some means to
keep a dog.

APEMANTUS.
What things in the world canst thou nearest compare to thy flatterers?

TIMON.
Women nearest; but men, men are the things
themselves. What wouldst thou do with the world,
Apemantus, if it lay in thy power?

APEMANTUS.
Give it the beasts, to be rid of the men.

TIMON.
Wouldst thou have thyself fall in the confusion of
men, and remain a beast with the beasts?

APEMANTUS.
Ay, Timon.

TIMON.
A beastly ambition, which the gods grant thee
t'attain to! If thou wert the lion, the fox would beguile thee: if thou wert the lamb, the fox would
eat thee: if thou wert the fox, the lion would suspect thee, when, peradventure, thou wert accused
by the ass: if thou wert the ass, thy dulness would

torment thee; and still thou livedst but as a breakfast to the wolf: if thou wert the wolf, thy greediness would afflict thee, and oft thou shouldst
hazard thy life for thy dinner: wert thou the unicorn, pride and wrath would confound thee, and
make thine own self the conquest of thy fury:
wert thou a bear, thou wouldst be kill'd by the
horse: wert thou a horse, thou wouldst be seized
by the leopard: wert thou a leopard, thou wert
german to the lion, and the spots of thy kindred
were jurors on thy life: all thy safety were remotion, and thy defence absence. What beast couldst
thou be, that were not subject to a beast? and
what a beast art thou already, that seest not thy
loss in transformation!

APEMANTUS.
If thou couldst please me with speaking to me,
thou mightst have hit upon it here: the commonwealth of Athens is become a forest of beasts.

TIMON.
How has the ass broke the wall, that thou art out
of the city?

APEMANTUS.
Yonder comes a poet and a painter: the plague of
company light upon thee! I will fear to catch it,
and give way: when I know not what else to do,
I'll see thee again.

TIMON.
When there is nothing living but thee, thou shalt
be welcome. I had rather be a beggar's dog than
Apemantus.

APEMANTUS.
Thou art the cap of all the fools alive.

TIMON.
Would thou wert clean enough to spit upon!

APEMANTUS.
A plague on thee, thou art too bad to curse!

TIMON.
All villains that do stand by thee are pure.

APEMANTUS.
There is no leprosy but what thou speak'st.

TIMON.
If I name thee.—
I'll beat thee, but I should infect my hands.

APEMANTUS.
I would my tongue could rot them off!

TIMON.
Away, thou issue of a mangy dog!
Choler does kill me that thou art alive;
I swound to see thee.

APEMANTUS.
Would thou wouldst burst!

TIMON.
Away, thou tedious rogue! I am sorry I shall lose
a stone by thee.   [Throws a stone at him.

APEMANTUS.
Beast!

TIMON.
Slave!

APEMANTUS.
Toad!

TIMON.
Rogue, rogue, rogue!
I am sick of this false world; and will love naught
But even the mere necessities upon't.
Then, Timon, presently prepare thy grave;

Lie where the light foam of the sea may beat
Thy grave-stone daily: make thine epitaph,
That death in me at others' lives may laugh.
O thou sweet king-killer, and dear divorce
                        [*Looking on the gold.*
'Twixt natural son and sire! thou bright defiler
Of Hymen's purest bed! thou valiant Mars!
Thou ever young, fresh, loved, and delicate wooer,
Whose blush doth thaw the consecrated snow
That lies on Dian's lap! thou visible god,
That solder'st close impossibilities,
And makest them kiss! that speak'st with every
    tongue,
To every purpose! O thou touch of hearts!
Think, thy slave man rebels; and by thy virtue
Set them into confounding odds, that beasts
May have the world in empire!

       APEMANTUS [*coming forward*].
                    Would 'twere so!—
But not till I am dead.—I'll say thou'st gold:
Thou wilt be throng'd to shortly.

       TIMON.
                Throng'd to!

       APEMANTUS.
                      Ay.

       TIMON.
Thy back, I prithee.

       APEMANTUS.
            Live, and love thy misery!

       TIMON.
Long live so, and so die! [*Exit* APEMANTUS.] I
    am quit.—
More things like men?—Eat, Timon, and abhor
    them.

       Enter BANDITTI.
       FIRST BANDIT.
Where should he have this gold? It is some poor
fragment, some slender ort of his remainder: the
mere want of gold, and the falling-from of his
friends, drove him into this melancholy.

       SECOND BANDIT.
It is noised he hath a mass of treasure.

       THIRD BANDIT.
Let us make the assay upon him: if he care not
for't, he will supply us easily; if he covetously reserve it, how shall's get it?

       SECOND BANDIT.
True; for he bears it not about him, 'tis hid.

       FIRST BANDIT.
Is not this he?

       BANDITTI.
Where?

       SECOND BANDIT.
'Tis his description.

       THIRD BANDIT.
He; I know him.

       BANDITTI.
Save thee, Timon.

       TIMON.
Now, thieves?

       BANDITTI.
Soldiers, not thieves.

       TIMON.
    Both too; and women's sons.

       BANDITTI.
We are not thieves, but men that much do want.

       TIMON.
Your greatest want is, you want much of meat
Why should you want? Behold, the earth hath
    roots;
Within this mile break forth a hundred springs;
The oaks bear mast, the briers scarlet hips;
The bounteous housewife, nature, on each bush
Lays her full mess before you. Want! why want?

       FIRST BANDIT.
We cannot live on grass, on berries, water,
As beasts and birds and fishes.

       TIMON.
Nor on the beasts themselves, the birds, and
    fishes;
You must eat men. Yet thanks I must you con,
That you are thieves profest; that you work not
In holier shapes: for there is boundless theft
In limited professions. Rascal thieves,
Here's gold. Go, suck the subtle blood o'the grape,
Till the high fever seethe your blood to froth,
And so scape hanging: trust not the physician;
His antidotes are poison, and he slays
More than you rob: take wealth and lives together;
Do villainy, do, since you protest to do't,
Like workmen. I'll example you with thievery:
The sun's a thief, and with his great attraction
Robs the vast sea: the moon's an arrant thief,
And her pale fire she snatches from the sun:
The sea's a thief, whose liquid surge resolves
The moon into salt tears: the earth's a thief,
That feeds and breeds by a composture stoln
From general excrement: each thing's a thief:
The laws, your curb and whip, in their rough
    power
Have uncheckt theft. Love not yourselves: away,
Rob one another. There's more gold. Cut throats;
All that you meet are thieves. To Athens go:
Break open shops; nothing can you steal, but
    thieves
Do lose it: steal not less for this I give you;
And gold confound you howsoe'er! Amen.

       THIRD BANDIT.
'Has almost charm'd me from my profession, by
persuading me to it.

       FIRST BANDIT.
'Tis in the malice of mankind that he thus advises
us; not to have us thrive in our mystery.

       SECOND BANDIT.
I'll believe him as an enemy, and give over my
trade.

       FIRST BANDIT.
Let us first see peace in Athens; there is no time
so miserable but a man may be true.
                     [*Exeunt* BANDITTI.
       Enter FLAVIUS.
       FLAVIUS.
O you gods!
Is yond despised and ruinous man my lord?
Full of decay and failing?
O monument and wonder of good deeds
Evilly bestow'd!
What an alteration of honour
Has desperate want made!
What viler thing upon the earth than friends
Who can bring noblest minds to basest ends!
How rarely does it meet with this time's guise,

When man was wisht to love his enemies!
Grant I may ever love, and rather woo
Those that would mischief me than those that
　do!—
'Has caught me in his eye: I will present
My honest grief unto him; and, as my lord,
Still serve him with my life.—My dearest master!

TIMON.

Away! what art thou?

FLAVIUS.

　　　　　Have you forgot me, sir?

TIMON.

Why dost ask that? I have forgot all men;
Then, if thou grant'st th'art man, I have forgot
　thee.

FLAVIUS.

An honest poor servant of yours.

TIMON.

Then I know thee not:
I never had honest man about me, I; all
I kept were knaves, to serve in meat to villains.

FLAVIUS.

The gods are witness,
Ne'er did poor steward wear a truer grief
For his undone lord than mine eyes for you.

TIMON.

What, dost thou weep?—come nearer;—then I
　love thee,
Because thou art a woman, and disclaim'st
Flinty mankind; whose eyes do never give
But thorough lust and laughter. Pity's sleeping:
Strange times, that weep with laughing, not with
　weeping!

FLAVIUS.

I beg of you to know me, good my lord,
T'accept my grief, and, whilst this poor wealth
　lasts,
To entertain me as your steward still.

TIMON.

Had I a steward
So true, so just, and now so comfortable?
It almost turns my dangerous nature mild.
Let me behold thy face. Surely, this man
Was born of woman.—
Forgive my general and exceptless rashness,
You perpetual-sober gods! I do proclaim
One honest man,—mistake me not,—but one;
No more, I pray,—and he's a steward.—
How fain would I have hated all mankind!
And thou redeem'st thyself: but all, save thee,
I fell with curses.
Methinks thou art more honest now than wise;
For, by oppressing and betraying me,
Thou mightst have sooner got another service:
For many so arrive at second masters,
Upon their first lord's neck. But tell me true,—
For I must ever doubt, though ne'er so sure,—
Is not thy kindness subtle-covetous,
A usuring kindness and, as rich men deal gifts,
Expecting in return twenty for one?

FLAVIUS.

No, my most worthy master; in whose breast
Doubt and suspect, alas, are placed too late:
You should have fear'd false times when you did
　feast:
Suspect still comes where an estate is least.

That which I show, heaven knows, is merely love,
Duty and zeal to your unmatched mind,
Care of your food and living; and, believe it,
My most honour'd lord,
For any benefit that points to me,
Either in hope or present, I'ld exchange
For this one wish,—that you had power and
　wealth
To requite me, by making rich yourself.

TIMON.

Look thee, 'tis so!—Thou singly honest man,
Here, take:—the gods, out of my misery,
Have sent thee treasure. Go, live rich and happy,
But thus condition'd:—thou shalt build from
　men;
Hate all, curse all; show charity to none;
But let the famisht flesh slide from the bone,
Ere thou relieve the beggar: give to dogs
What thou deny'st to men; let prisons swallow
　'em,
Debts wither 'em to nothing: be men like blasted
　woods,
And may diseases lick up their false bloods!
And so, farewell, and thrive.

FLAVIUS.

　　　　　　　　O, let me stay,
And comfort you, my master.

TIMON.

　　　　　　　　If thou hatest
Curses, stay not; fly, whilst thou art blest and
　free:
Ne'er see thou man, and let me ne'er see thee.
　　　　　　　　　　　[Exeunt severally.

ACT V.　SCENE I.

The woods.　Before TIMON'S *cave.*

Enter POET *and* PAINTER; TIMON *watching them
from his cave.*

PAINTER.

AS I took note of the place, it cannot be far
　where he abides.

POET.

What's to be thought of him? does the rumour
hold for true, that he's so full of gold?

PAINTER.

Certain: Alcibiades reports it; Phrynia and Timandra had gold of him: he likewise enricht poor
straggling soldiers with great quantity: 'tis said he
gave unto his steward a mighty sum.

POET.

Then this breaking of his has been but a try for
his friends.

PAINTER.

Nothing else: you shall see him a palm in Athens
again, and flourish with the highest. Therefore
'tis not amiss we tender our loves to him, in this
supposed distress of his: it will show honestly in
us; and is very likely to load our purposes with
what they travail for, if it be a just and true report
that goes of his having.

POET.

What have you now to present unto him?

PAINTER.

Nothing at this time but my visitation: only I will
promise him an excellent piece.

POET.

I must serve him so too,—tell him of an intent that's coming toward him.

PAINTER.

Good as the best. Promising is the very air o'the time; it opens the eyes of expectation: performance is ever the duller for his act; and, but in the plainer and simpler kind of people, the deed of saying is quite out of use. To promise is most courtly and fashionable: performance is a kind of will or testament which argues a great sickness in his judgement that makes it.

Enter TIMON *from his cave.*

TIMON [*aside*].

Excellent workman! thou canst not paint a man so bad as is thyself.

POET.

I am thinking what I shall say I have provided for him: it must be a personating of himself; a satire against the softness of prosperity, with a discovery of the infinite flatteries that follow youth and opulency.

TIMON [*aside*].

Must thou needs stand for a villain in thine own work? wilt thou whip thine own faults in other men? Do so, I have gold for thee.

POET.

Nay, let's seek him:
Then do we sin against our own estate,
When we may profit meet, and come too late.

PAINTER.

True;
When the day serves, before black-corner'd night,
Find what thou want'st by free and offer'd light.
Come.

TIMON [*aside*].

I'll meet you at the turn.—What a god's gold,
That he is worshipt in a baser temple
Than where swine feed!   [foam;
'Tis thou that rigg'st the bark and plough'st the
Settlest admired reverence in a slave:
To thee be worship! and thy saints for aye
Be crown'd with plagues, that thee alone obey!—
Fit I meet them.   [*Comes forward.*

POET.

Hail, worthy Timon!

PAINTER.

Our late noble master!

TIMON.

Have I once lived to see two honest men?

POET.

Sir,
Having often of your open bounty tasted,
Hearing you were retired, your friends faln off,
Whose thankless natures—O abhorred spirits!—
Not all the whips of heaven are large enough—
What! to you,
Whose star-like nobleness gave life and influence
To their whole being!—I am rapt, and cannot
    cover
The monstrous bulk of this ingratitude
With any size of words.

TIMON.

Let it go naked, men may see't the better:
You that are honest, by being what you are,
Make them best seen and known.

PAINTER.

              He and myself
Have travail'd in the great shower of your gifts,
And sweetly felt it.

TIMON.

Ay, you are honest men.

PAINTER.

We are hither come to offer you our service.

TIMON.

Most honest men! Why, how shall I requite you?
Can you eat roots, and drink cold water? no.

BOTH.

What we can do, we'll do, to do you service.

TIMON.

Y'are honest men: y'have heard that I have gold;
I am sure you have: speak truth; y'are honest men.

PAINTER.

So it is said, my noble lord: but therefore
Came not my friend nor I.

TIMON.

Good honest men!—Thou draw'st a counterfeit
Best in all Athens: th'art, indeed, the best;
Thou counterfeit'st most lively.

PAINTER.

          So, so, my lord.

TIMON.

E'en so, sir, as I say.—And, for thy fiction,
Why, thy verse swells with stuff so fine and
    smooth,
That thou art even natural in thine art.—
But, for all this, my honest-natured friends,
I must needs say you have a little fault:
Marry, 'tis not monstrous in you; neither wish I
You take much pains to mend.

BOTH.

          Beseech your honour
To make it known to us.

TIMON.

        You'll take it ill.

BOTH.

Most thankfully, my lord.

TIMON.

         Will you, indeed?

BOTH.

Doubt it not, worthy lord.

TIMON.

There's never a one of you but trusts a knave,
That mightily deceives you.

BOTH.

        Do we, my lord?

TIMON.

Ay, and you hear him cog, see him dissemble,
Know his gross patchery, love him, feed him,
Keep in your bosom: yet remain assured
That he's a made-up villain.

PAINTER.

I know none such, my lord.

POET.

         Nor I.

TIMON.

Look you, I love you well; I'll give you gold,
Rid me these villains from your companies:
Hang them or stab them, drown them in a
    draught,
Confound them by some course, and come to me,
I'll give you gold enough.

BOTH.
Name them, my lord, let's know them.
TIMON.
You that way, and you this,—but two in company:
Each man apart, all single and alone,
Yet an arch-villain keeps him company.
[to the PAINTER] If, where thou art, two villains
shall not be,
Come not near him.—[to the POET] If thou
wouldst not reside
But where one villain is, then him abandon.—
Hence, pack! there's gold,—you came for gold, ye
slaves:
[to the PAINTER] You have work for me, there's
payment: hence.—
[to the POET] You are an alchemist, make gold of
that:—
Out, rascal dogs!
[Beats and drives them out, and then retires
to his cave.
Enter FLAVIUS and two SENATORS.
FLAVIUS.
It is in vain that you would speak with Timon,
For he is set so only to himself,
That nothing but himself, which looks like man,
Is friendly with him.
FIRST SENATOR.
Bring us to his cave:
It is our pact and promise to th'Athenians
To speak with Timon.
SECOND SENATOR.
At all times alike
Men are not still the same: 'twas time and griefs
That framed him thus: time, with his fairer hand,
Offering the fortunes of his former days,
The former man may make him. Bring us to him.
And chance it as it may.
FLAVIUS.
Here is his cave.—
Peace and content be here! Lord Timon! Timon!
Look out, and speak to friends: th'Athenians,
By two of their most reverend senate, greet thee:
Speak to them, noble Timon.
Enter TIMON out of his cave.
TIMON.
Thou sun, that comfort'st, burn!—Speak, and be
hang'd:
For each true word, a blister! and each false
Be as a cauterizing to the root o'the tongue,
Consuming it with speaking!
FIRST SENATOR.
Worthy Timon,—
TIMON.
Of none but such as you, and you of Timon.
FIRST SENATOR.
The senators of Athens greet thee, Timon.
TIMON.
I thank them; and would send them back the
Could I but catch it for them. [plague,
FIRST SENATOR.
O, forget
What we are sorry for ourselves in thee.
The senators with one consent of love
Entreat thee back to Athens; who have thought
On special dignities, which vacant lie
For thy best use and wearing.

SECOND SENATOR.
They confess
Toward thee forgetfulness too general, gross:
Which now the public body,—which doth seldom
Play the recanter,—feeling in itself
A lack of Timon's aid, hath sense withal
Of it own fail, restraining aid to Timon;
And send forth us, to make their sorrow'd render,
Together with a recompense more fruitful
Than their offence can weigh down by the dram;
Ay, even such heaps and sums of love and wealth
As shall to thee blot out what wrongs were theirs,
And write in thee the figures of their love,
Ever to read them thine.
TIMON.
You witch me in it;
Surprise me to the very brink of tears:
Lend me a fool's heart and a woman's eyes,
And I'll beweep these comforts, worthy senators.
FIRST SENATOR.
Therefore, so please thee to return with us,
And of our Athens—thine and ours—to take
The captainship, thou shalt be met with thanks,
Allow'd with absolute power, and thy good name
Live with authority:—so soon we shall drive back
Of Alcibiades th'approaches wild;
Who, like a boar too savage, doth root up
His country's peace.
SECOND SENATOR.
And shakes his threat'ning sword
Against the walls of Athens.
FIRST SENATOR.
Therefore, Timon,—
TIMON.
Well, sir, I will; therefore, I will, sir; thus:—
If Alcibiades kill my countrymen,
Let Alcibiades know this of Timon,
That Timon cares not. But if he sack fair Athens,
And take our goodly aged men by the beards,
Giving our holy virgins to the stain
Of contumelious, beastly, mad-brain'd war,
Then let him know, and tell him Timon speaks it,
In pity of our aged and our youth
I cannot choose but tell him that I care not, [not,
And let him take't at worst; for their knives care
While you have throats to answer: for myself,
There's not a whittle in th'unruly camp
But I do prize it at my love, before
The reverend'st throat in Athens. So I leave you
To the protection of the prosperous gods,
As thieves to keepers.
FLAVIUS.
Stay not, all's in vain.
TIMON.
Why, I was writing of my epitaph;
It will be seen to-morrow: my long sickness
Of health and living now begins to mend,
And nothing brings me all things. Go, live still;
Be Alcibiades your plague, you his,
And last so long enough!
FIRST SENATOR.
We speak in vain.
TIMON.
But yet I love my country; and am not
One that rejoices in the common wrack,
As common bruit doth put it.

FIRST SENATOR.
            That's well spoke.

TIMON.
Commend me to my loving countrymen,—

FIRST SENATOR.
These words become your lips as they pass
   thorough them.

SECOND SENATOR.
And enter in our ears like great triumphers
In their applauding gates.

TIMON.
            Commend me to them;
And tell them that, to ease them of their griefs,
Their fears of hostile strokes, their aches, losses,
Their pangs of love, with other incident throes
That nature's fragile vessel doth sustain
In life's uncertain voyage, I will
Some kindness do them,—I'll teach them to pre-
Wild Alcibiades' wrath.   [vent

FIRST SENATOR.
I like this well: he will return again.

TIMON.
I have a tree, which grows here in my close,
That mine own use invites me to cut down,
And shortly must I fell it: tell my friends,
Tell Athens, in the sequence of degree,
From high to low throughout, that whoso please
To stop affliction, let him take his haste,
Come hither, ere my tree hath felt the axe,
And hang himself:—I pray you, do my greeting.

FLAVIUS.
Trouble him no further; thus you still shall find
   him.

TIMON.
Come not to me again: but say to Athens,
Timon hath made his everlasting mansion
Upon the beached verge of the salt flood;
Who once a day with his embossed froth
The turbulent surge shall cover: thither come,
And let my grave-stone be your oracle.—
Lips, let sour words go by, and language end:
What is amiss, plague and infection mend!
Graves only be men's works, and death their gain!
Sun, hide thy beams! Timon hath done his reign.
                         [Exit.

FIRST SENATOR.
His discontents are unremovably
Coupled to nature.

SECOND SENATOR.
Our hope in him is dead: let us return,
And strain what other means is left unto us
In our dear peril.

FIRST SENATOR.
         It requires swift foot.   [Exeunt.

SCENE II.

Before the walls of Athens.

Enter two SENATORS *and a* MESSENGER.

FIRST SENATOR.
THOU hast painfully discover'd: are his files
    As full as thy report?

MESSENGER.
         I have spoke the least:
Besides, his expedition promises
Present approach.

SECOND SENATOR.
We stand much hazard, if they bring not Timon.

MESSENGER.
I met a courier, one mine ancient friend;
Whom, though in general part we were opposed,
Yet our old love had a particular force,
And made us speak like friends:—this man was was
   riding
From Alcibiades to Timon's cave,
With letters of entreaty, which imported
His fellowship i'the cause against your city,
In part for his sake moved.

FIRST SENATOR.
          Here come our brothers.

Enter SENATORS *from* TIMON.

THIRD SENATOR.
No talk of Timon, nothing of him expect.
The enemies' drum is heard, and fearful scouring
Doth choke the air with dust: in, and prepare:
Ours is the fall, I fear; our foes the snare.
                         [Exeunt.

SCENE III.

The woods. TIMON'S *cave, and a rude
tomb seen.*

Enter a SOLDIER *in the woods, seeking* TIMON.

SOLDIER.
BY all description this should be the place.
    Who's here? speak, ho!—No answer?—What
   is this?
Timon is dead, who hath outstretcht his span:
Some beast rear'd this; here does not live a man.
Dead, sure; and this his grave.—
What's on this tomb I cannot read; the character
I'll take with wax:
Our captain hath in every figure skill,
An aged interpreter, though young in days:
Before proud Athens he's set down by this,
Whose fall the mark of his ambition is.   [Exit.

SCENE IV.

Before the walls of Athens.

Trumpets sound.   *Enter* ALCIBIADES *with his*
POWERS.

ALCIBIADES.
SOUND to this coward and lascivious town
    Our terrible approach.   [*A parley sounded.*

The SENATORS *appear upon the walls.*

Till now you have gone on, and fill'd the time
With all licentious measure, making your wills
The scope of justice; till now, myself, and such
As slept within the shadow of your power,
Have wander'd with our traversed arms, and
   breathed
Our sufferance vainly: now the time is flush,
When crouching marrow, in the bearer strong,
Cries, of itself, 'No more:' now breathless wrong
Shall sit and pant in your great chairs of ease;
And pursy insolence shall break his wind
With fear and horrid flight.

FIRST SENATOR.
           Noble and young,
When thy first griefs were but a mere conceit,
Ere thou hadst power, or we had cause of fear,

We sent to thee; to give thy rages balm,
To wipe out our ingratitude with loves
Above their quantity.

SECOND SENATOR.
　　　　　　So did we woo
Transformed Timon to our city's love
By humble message and by promised means:
We were not all unkind, nor all deserve
The common stroke of war.

FIRST SENATOR.
　　　　　　These walls of ours
Were not erected by their hands from whom
You have received your griefs; nor are they such
That these great towers, trophies, and schools
　　should fall
For private faults in them.

SECOND SENATOR.
　　　　　　Nor are they living
Who were the motives that you first went out;
Shame, that they wanted cunning, in excess,
Hath broke their hearts. March, noble lord,
Into our city, with thy banners spread:
By decimation, and a tithed death,—
If thy revenges hunger for that food
Which nature loathes,—take thou the destined
And by the hazard of the spotted die　　[tenth;
Let die the spotted.

FIRST SENATOR.
　　　　　　All have not offended;
For those that were, it is not square to take
On those that are, revenges: crimes, like lands,
Are not inherited. Then, dear countryman,
Bring in thy ranks, but leave without thy rage:
Spare thy Athenian cradle, and those kin
Which, in the bluster of thy wrath, must fall
With those that have offended: like a shepherd,
Approach the fold, and cull th'infected forth.
But kill not all together.

SECOND SENATOR.
　　　　　　What thou wilt,
Thou rather shalt enforce it with thy smile
Than hew to't with thy sword.

FIRST SENATOR.
　　　　　　Set but thy foot
Against our rampired gates, and they shall ope;
So thou wilt send thy gentle heart before,
To say thou'lt enter friendly.

SECOND SENATOR.
　　　　　　Throw thy glove,
Or any token of thine honour else,

That thou wilt use the wars as thy redress,
And not as our confusion, all thy powers
Shall make their harbour in our town, till we
Have seal'd thy full desire.

ALCIBIADES.
　　　　　　Then there's my glove;
Descend, and open your uncharged ports:
Those enemies of Timon's, and mine own,
Whom you yourselves shall set out for reproof,
Fall, and no more: and—to atone your fears
With my more noble meaning—not a man
Shall pass his quarter, or offend the stream
Of regular justice in your city's bounds,
But shall be render'd to your public laws
At heaviest answer.

SENATORS.
　　　　　　'Tis most nobly spoken.

ALCIBIADES.
Descend, and keep your words.
　　[The SENATORS descend, and open the gates.
　　　　　Enter a SOLDIER.

SOLDIER.
My noble general, Timon is dead;
Entomb'd upon the very hem o'the sea;
And on his grave-stone this insculpture, which
With wax I brought away, whose soft impression
Interprets for my poor ignorance.

ALCIBIADES [reads].
Here lies a wretched corse, of wretched soul be-
　　reft:
Seek not my name: a plague consume you wicked
　　caitiffs left!
Here lie I, Timon; who, alive, all living men did
　　hat
Pass b , and curse thy fill; but pass, and stay not
　　here thy gait.
These well express in thee thy latter spirits:
Though thou abhorr'dst in us our human griefs,
Scorn'dst our brain's flow, and those our droplets
　　which
From niggard nature fall, yet rich conceit
Taught thee to make vast Neptune weep for aye
On thy low grave, on faults forgiven. Dead
Is noble Timon: of whose memory
Hereafter more.—Bring me into your city,
And I will use the olive with my sword:
Make war breed peace; make peace stint war;
　　make each
Prescribe to other, as each other's leech.—
Let our drums strike.　　　　　[Exeunt.

PERICLES

DRAMATIS PERSONAE

ANTIOCHUS, *King of Antioch.*
PERICLES, *Prince of Tyre.*
HELICANUS,⎫ *two lords of Tyre.*
ESCANES, ⎭
SIMONIDES, *King of Pentapolis.*
CLEON, *governor of Tarsus.*
LYSIMACHUS, *governor of Mytilene.*
CERIMON, *a lord of Ephesus.*
THALIARD, *a lord of Antioch.*
PHILEMON, *servant to Cerimon.*
LEONINE, *servant to Dionyza.*
MARSHALL.
A PANDAR.
BOULT, *his servant.*

THE DAUGHTER OF ANTIOCHUS.
DIONYZA, *wife to Cleon.*
THAISA, *daughter to Simonides.*
MARINA, *daughter to Pericles and Thaisa.*
LYCHORIDA, *nurse to Marina.*
A BAWD.

LORDS, LADIES, KNIGHTS, GENTLEMEN,
SAILORS, PIRATES, FISHERMEN, *and*
MESSENGERS.

DIANA.

GOWER, *as* CHORUS.

SCENE—*Dispersedly in various countries.*

ACT I.

Enter GOWER.

Before the palace of Antioch.

GOWER.

TO sing a song that old was sung,
From ashes ancient Gower is come,
Assuming man's infirmities,
To glad your ear and please your eyes.
It hath been sung at festivals,
On ember-eves and holy-ales;
And lords and ladies in their lives
Have read it for restoratives:
The purchase is to make men glorious;
Et bonum quo antiquius, eo melius.
If you, born in these latter times,
When wit's more ripe, accept my rimes,
And that to hear an old man sing
May to your wishes pleasure bring,
I life would wish, and that I might
Waste it for you, like taper-light.—
This Antioch, then, Antiochus the Great
Built up, this city, for his chiefest seat;
The fairest in all Syria,—
I tell you what mine authors say:
This king unto him took a fere,
Who died and left a female heir,
So buxom, blithe, and full of face,
As heaven had lent her all his grace;
With whom the father liking took,
And her to incest did provoke:—
Bad child; worse father! to entice his own
To evil should be done by none:
But custom what they did begin
Was with long use account no sin.
The beauty of this sinful dame
Made many princes thither frame,
To seek her as a bed-fellow,
In marriage-pleasures play-fellow:
Which to prevent he made a law,—
To keep her still, and men in awe,—
That whoso askt her for his wife,
His riddle told not, lost his life:
So for her many a wight did die,

As yon grim looks do testify.
What now ensues, to the judgement of your eye
I give, my cause who best can justify. [*Exit.*

SCENE I.

Antioch. A room in the palace.

Enter ANTIOCHUS, PERICLES, *and* FOL-
LOWERS.

ANTIOCHUS.

YOUNG prince of Tyre, you have at large received
The danger of the task you undertake.

PERICLES.

I have, Antiochus, and, with a soul
Embolden'd with the glory of her praise,
Think death no hazard in this enterprise.

ANTIOCHUS.

Bring in our daughter, clothed like a bride,
For the embracements even of Jove himself;
At whose conception, till Lucina reign'd,
Nature this dowry gave, to glad her presence,
The senate-house of planets all did sit,
To knit in her their best perfections.
Music. Enter ANTIOCHUS' DAUGHTER.

PERICLES.

See where she comes, apparell'd like the spring,
Graces her subjects, and her thoughts the king
Of every virtue gives renown to men!
Her face the book of praises, where is read
Nothing but curious pleasures, as from thence
Sorrow were ever razed, and testy wrath
Could never be her mild companion.
You gods that made me man, and sway in love,
That have inflamed desire in my breast
To taste the fruit of yon celestial tree,
Or die in the adventure, be my helps,
As I am son and servant to your will,
To compass such a boundless happiness!

ANTIOCHUS.

Prince Pericles,—

PERICLES.

That would be son to great Antiochus.

ANTIOCHUS.

Before thee stands this fair Hesperides,
With golden fruit, but dangerous to be toucht;
For death-like dragons here affright thee hard:
Her face, like heaven, enticeth thee to view
Her countless glory, which desert must gain;
And which, without desert, because thine eye
Presumes to reach, all thy whole heap must die.
Yon sometimes famous princes, like thyself,
Drawn by report, adventurous by desire,
Tell thee, with speechless tongues and semblance
    pale,
That, without covering, save yon field of stars,
Here they stand martyrs, slain in Cupid's wars;
And with dead cheeks advise thee to desist
For going on death's net, whom none resist.

PERICLES.

Antiochus, I thank thee, who hath taught
My frail mortality to know itself,
And by those fearful objects to prepare
This body, like to them, to what I must;
For death remember'd should be like a mirror,
Who tells us life's but breath, to trust it error.
I'll make my will, then; and, as sick men do,
Who know the world, see heaven, but, feeling
    woe,
Gripe not at earthly joys, as erst they did;
So I bequeath a happy peace to you
And all good men, as every prince should do;
My riches to the earth from whence they came;—
But my unspotted fire of love to you.
        [To the DAUGHTER of ANTIOCHUS.
Thus ready for the way of life or death,
I wait the sharpest blow.

ANTIOCHUS.

Scorning advice,—read the conclusion, then:
Which read and not expounded, 'tis decreed,
As these before thee, thou thyself shalt bleed.

DAUGHTER OF ANTIOCHUS.

Of all 'say'd yet, mayst thou prove prosperous!
Of all 'say'd yet, I wish thee happiness!

PERICLES.

Like a bold champion, I assume the lists,
Nor ask advice of any other thought
But faithfulness and courage.   [Reads the riddle.
    I am no viper, yet I feed
    On mother's flesh which did me breed.
    I sought a husband, in which labour
    I found that kindness in a father:
    He's father, son, and husband mild;
    I mother, wife, and yet his child.
    How they may be, and yet in two,
    As you will live, resolve it you.
Sharp physic is the last: but, O you powers
That give heaven countless eyes to view men's
    acts,
Why cloud they not their sights perpetually,
If this be true, which makes me pale to read it?—
Fair glass of light, I loved you, and could still,
        [Takes hold of the hand of the PRINCESS.
Were not this glorious casket stored with ill:
But I must tell you,—now my thoughts revolt;
For he's no man on whom perfections wait
That, knowing sin within, will touch the gate.
You are a fair viol, and your sense the strings;
Who, finger'd to make man his lawful music,

Would draw heaven down, and all the gods, to
    hearken;
But being play'd upon before your time,
Hell only danceth at so harsh a chime.
Good sooth, I care not for you.

ANTIOCHUS.

Prince Pericles, touch not, upon thy life,
For that's an article within our law,
As dangerous as the rest. Your time's expired:
Either expound now, or receive your sentence.

PERICLES.

Great king,
Few love to hear the sins they love to act;
'Twould braid yourself too near for me to tell it.
Who has a book of all that monarchs do,
He's more secure to keep it shut than shown:
For vice repeated is like the wandering wind,
Blows dust in others' eyes, to spread itself;
And yet the end of all is bought thus dear,
The breath is gone, and the sore eyes see clear
To stop the air would hurt them. The blind mole
    casts
Copt hills towards heaven, to tell the earth is
    throng'd
By man's oppression; and the poor worm doth die
    for't.
Kings are earth's gods; in vice their law's their will;
And if Jove stray, who dares say Jove doth ill?
It is enough you know; and it is fit,
What being more known grows worse, to smother
    it.
All love the womb that their first being bred,
Then give my tongue like leave to love my head.

ANTIOCHUS [aside].

Heaven, that I had thy head! he has found the
    meaning:
But I will gloze with him.—Young prince of Tyre,
Though by the tenour of our strict edict, .
Your exposition misinterpreting,
We might proceed to cancel of your days;
Yet hope, succeeding from so fair a tree
As your fair self, doth tune us otherwise:
Forty days longer we do respite you;
If by which time our secret be undone,
This mercy shows we'll joy in such a son:
And until then your entertain shall be,
As doth befit our honour, and your worth.
        [Exeunt all but PERICLES.

PERICLES.

How courtesy would seem to cover sin,
When what is done is like an hypocrite,
The which is good in nothing but in sight!
If it be true that I interpret false,
Then were it certain you were not so bad
As with foul incest to abuse your soul;
Where now you're both a father and a son
By your untimely claspings with your child,—
Which pleasure fits a husband, not a father;
And she an eater of her mother's flesh
By the defiling of her parent's bed;
And both like serpents are, who though they feed
On sweetest flowers, yet they poison breed.
Antioch, farewell! for wisdom sees, those men
Blush not in actions blacker than the night,
Will shun no course to keep them from the light.
One sin, I know, another doth provoke;

Murder's as near to lust as flame to smoke:
Poison and treason are the hands of sin,
Ay, and the targets, to put off the shame:
Then, lest my life be cropt to keep you clear,
By flight I'll shun the danger which I fear. [*Exit.*

Enter ANTIOCHUS.

ANTIOCHUS.

He hath found the meaning, for the which we
  mean
To have his head.
He must not live to trumpet forth my infamy,
Nor tell the world Antiochus doth sin
In such a loathed manner;
And therefore instantly this prince must die;
For by his fall my honour must keep high.—
Who attends us there?

Enter THALIARD.

THALIARD.
                Doth your highness call?

ANTIOCHUS.

Thaliard,
You are of our chamber, and our mind partakes
Her private actions to your secrecy:
And for your faithfulness we will advance you.
Thaliard, behold, here's poison, and here's gold;
We hate the prince of Tyre, and thou must kill
  him:
It fits thee not to ask the reason why,
Because we bid it. Say, is it done?

THALIARD.
                   My lord,
'Tis done.

ANTIOCHUS.

Enough.

Enter a MESSENGER.

Let your breath cool yourself, telling your haste.

MESSENGER.

My lord, Prince Pericles is fled.   [*Exit.*

ANTIOCHUS.
                   As thou
Wilt live, fly after; and, like an arrow shot
From a well-experienced archer, hits the mark
His eye doth level at, so thou ne'er return
Unless thou say 'Prince Pericles is dead.'

THALIARD.

My lord,
If I can get him within my pistol's length,
I'll make him sure enough: so, farewell to your
  highness.

ANTIOCHUS.

Thaliard, adieu! [*Exit* THALIARD.] Till Pericles
  be dead
My heart can lend no succour to my head.   [*Exit.*

SCENE II.

Tyre. A room in the palace.

Enter PERICLES.

PERICLES [*to* LORDS *without*].

LET none disturb us.—Why should this charge
  of thoughts,
The sad companion, dull-eyed melancholy,
Be my so-used a guest as not an hour,
In the day's glorious walk or peaceful night,
The tomb where grief should sleep, can breed me
  quiet?

Here pleasures court mine eyes, and mine eyes
  shun them,
And danger, which I fear'd, is at Antioch,
Whose arm seems far too short to hit me here:
Yet neither pleasure's art can joy my spirits,
Nor yet the other's distance comfort me.
Then it is thus: the passions of the mind,
That have their first conception by mis-dread,
Have after-nourishment and life by care;
And what was first but fear what might be done,
Grows elder now, and cares it be not done.
And so with me:—the great Antiochus—
'Gainst whom I am too little to contend,
Since he's so great can make his will his act—
Will think me speaking, though I swear to silence;
Nor boots it me to say I honour him,
If he suspect I may dishonour him:
And what may make him blush in being known,
He'll stop the course by which it might be known:
With hostile forces he'll o'erspread the land,
And with th'ostent of war will look so huge,
Amazement shall drive courage from the state;
Our men be vanquisht ere they do resist,
And subjects punisht that ne'er thought offence:
Which care of them, not pity of myself,
Who am no more but as the tops of trees,
Which fence the roots they grow by and defend
  them,
Makes both my body pine and soul to languish,
And punish that before that he would punish.

Enter HELICANUS *and other* LORDS.

FIRST LORD.

Joy and all comfort in your sacred breast!

SECOND LORD.

And keep your mind, till you return to us,
Peaceful and comfortable!

HELICANUS.

Peace, peace, and give experience tongue.
They do abuse the king that flatter him:
For flattery is the bellows blows up sin;
The thing the which is flatter'd, but a spark,
To which that blast gives heat and stronger glow-
Whereas reproof, obedient, and in order,   [ing;
Fits kings, as they are men, for they may err.
When Signior Sooth here does proclaim a peace,
He flatters you, makes war upon your life.
Prince, pardon me, or strike me, if you please;
I cannot be much lower than my knees.

PERICLES.

All leave us else; but let your cares o'erlook
What shipping and what lading's in our haven,
And then return to us. [*Exeunt* LORDS.] Heli-
  canus, thou
Hast moved us: what seest thou in our looks?

HELICANUS.

An angry brow, dread lord.

PERICLES.

If there be such a dart in princes' frowns,
How durst thy tongue move anger to our face?

HELICANUS.

How dare the plants look up to heaven, from
  whence
They have their nourishment?

PERICLES.
               Thou know'st I have power
To take thy life from thee.

HELICANUS [*kneeling*].
I have ground the axe myself;
Do you but strike the blow.
            PERICLES.
                    Rise, prithee, rise.
Sit down: thou art no flatterer:
I thank thee for it; and heaven forbid
That kings should let their ears hear their faults
    chid!
Fit counsellor and servant for a prince,
Who by thy wisdom makest a prince thy servant,
What wouldst thou have me do?
            HELICANUS.
                        To bear with patience
Such griefs as you yourself do lay upon yourself.
            PERICLES.
Thou speak'st like a physician, Helicanus,
That minister'st a potion unto me
That thou wouldst tremble to receive thyself.
Attend me, then: I went to Antioch,
Where, as thou know'st, against the face of death,
I sought the purchase of a glorious beauty,
From whence an issue I might propagate,
Are arms to princes, and bring joys to subjects.
Her face was to mine eye beyond all wonder;
The rest—hark in thine ear—as black as incest:
Which by my knowledge found, the sinful father
Seem'd not to strike, but smooth: but thou know'st
    this,
'Tis time to fear when tyrants seem to kiss.
Which fear so grew in me, I hither fled,
Under the covering of a careful night,
Who seem'd my good protector; and, being here,
Bethought me what was past, what might succeed.
I knew him tyrannous; and tyrants' fears
Decrease not, but grow faster than the years:
And should he doubt it,—as no doubt he doth,—
That I should open to the listening air
How many worthy princes' bloods were shed,
To keep his bed of blackness unlaid ope,—
To lop that doubt, he'll fill this land with arms,
And make pretence of wrong that I have done him;
When all, for mine, if I may call offence,
Must feel war's blow, who spares not innocence:
Which love to all,—of which thyself art one,
Who now reprovest me for't,—
            HELICANUS.
Alas, sir!
            PERICLES.
Drew sleep out of mine eyes, blood from my
    cheeks,
Musings into my mind, with thousand doubts
How I might stop this tempest, ere it came;
And finding little comfort to relieve them,
I thought it princely charity to grieve them.
            HELICANUS.
Well, my lord, since you have given me leave to
Freely will I speak. Antiochus you fear,   [speak,
And justly too, I think, you fear the tyrant,
Who either by public war or private treason
Will take away your life.
Therefore, my lord, go travel for a while,
Till that his rage and anger be forgot,
Or till the Destinies do cut his thread of life.
Your rule direct to any; if to me,
Day serves not light more faithful than I'll be.

            PERICLES.
I do not doubt thy faith;
But should he wrong my liberties in my absence?
            HELICANUS.
We'll mingle our bloods together in the earth,
From whence we had our being and our birth.
            PERICLES.
Tyre, I now look from thee, then, and to Tarsus
Intend my travel, where I'll hear from thee;
And by whose letters I'll dispose myself.
The care I had and have of subjects' good
On thee I lay, whose wisdom's strength can bear it.
I'll take thy word for faith, not ask thine oath:
Who shuns not to break one will sure crack both:
But in our orbs we'll live so round and safe,
That time of both this truth shall ne'er convince,
Thou show'dst a subject's shine, I a true prince.
                                    [*Exeunt.*

SCENE III.

Tyre.   An ante-chamber in the palace.

Enter THALIARD.

            THALIARD.

SO, this is Tyre, and this the court. Here must
I kill King Pericles; and if I do it not, I am
sure to be hang'd at home: 'tis dangerous.—Well,
I perceive he was a wise fellow and had good discretion, that, being bid to ask what he would of
the king, desired he might know none of his
secrets: now do I see he had some reason for't; for
if a king bid a man be a villain, he's bound by the
indenture of his oath to be one.—Hush! here
come the lords of Tyre.

Enter HELICANUS *and* ESCANES, *with other*
            LORDS.
            HELICANUS.
You shall not need, my fellow peers of Tyre,
Further to question me of your king's departure:
His seal'd commission, left in trust with me,
Doth speak sufficiently he's gone to travel.
            THALIARD [*aside*].
How! the king gone!
            HELICANUS.
If further yet you will be satisfied,
Why, as it were unlicensed of your loves,
He would depart, I'll give some light unto you.
Being at Antioch,—
            THALIARD [*aside*].
                What from Antioch?
            HELICANUS.
Royal Antiochus—on what cause I know not—
Took some displeasure at him,—at least he judged
    so;
And doubting lest that he had err'd or sinn'd,
To show his sorrow, he'ld correct himself;
So puts himself unto the shipman's toil,
With whom each minute threatens life or death.
            THALIARD [*aside*].
Well, I perceive I shall not be hang'd now, al-
though I would; but since he's gone, the king's
seas must please,—he scaped the land, to perish
at the sea. I'll present myself.—Peace to the lords
of Tyre!
            HELICANUS.
Lord Thaliard from Antiochus is welcome.

THALIARD.

From him I come
With message unto princely Pericles;
But since my landing I have understood
Your lord has betook himself to unknown travels,
My message must return from whence it came.

HELICANUS.

We have no reason to desire it,
Commended to our master, not to us:
Yet, ere you shall depart, this we desire,—
As friends to Antioch, we may feast in Tyre.

[*Exeunt.*

SCENE IV.

Tarsus. *A room in the* GOVERNOR'S *house.*

Enter CLEON *the Governor of Tarsus, with his Wife* DIONYZA, *and others.*

CLEON.

MY Dionyza, shall we rest us here,
And by relating tales of others' griefs,
See if 'twill teach us to forget our own?

DIONYZA.

That were to blow at fire in hope to quench it;
For who digs hills because they do aspire
Throws down one mountain to cast up a higher.
O my distressed lord, even such our griefs are;
Here they are but felt, and seen with mischief's eyes,
But like to groves, being topt, they higher rise.

CLEON.

O Dionyza,
Who wanteth food, and will not say he wants it,
Or can conceal his hunger till he famish?
Our tongues and sorrows do sound deep our woes
Into the air; our eyes do weep, till tongues
Fetch breath that may proclaim them louder; that,
If heaven slumber while their creatures want,
They may awake their helps to comfort them.
I'll, then, discourse our woes, felt several years,
And, wanting breath to speak, help me with tears.

DIONYZA.

I'll do my best, sir.

CLEON.

This Tarsus, o'er which I have the government,
A city on whom Plenty held full hand,
For Riches strew'd herself even in the streets;
Whose towers bore heads so high they kist the clouds,
And strangers ne'er beheld but wonder'd at;
Whose men and dames so jetted and adorn'd,
Like one another's glass to trim them by:
Their tables were stored full, to glad the sight,
And not so much to feed on as delight;
All poverty was scorn'd, and pride so great,
The name of help grew odious to repeat.

DIONYZA.

O, 'tis too true.

CLEON.

But see what heaven can do! By this our change,
These mouths who but of late earth, sea, and air,
Were all too little to content and please,
Although they gave their creatures in abundance,
As houses are defiled for want of use,
They are now starved for want of exercise:
Those palates who, not yet two summers younger,

Must have inventions to delight the taste,
Would now be glad of bread, and beg for it:
Those mothers who, to nousle up their babes,
Thought naught too curious, are ready now
To eat those little darlings whom they loved.
So sharp are hunger's teeth, that man and wife
Draw lots who first shall die to lengthen life:
Here stands a lord, and there a lady weeping;
Here many sink, yet those which see them fall
Have scarce strength left to give them burial.
Is not this true?

DIONYZA.

Our cheeks and hollow eyes do witness it,

CLEON.

O, let those cities that of Plenty's cup
And her prosperities so largely taste,
With their superfluous riots, hear these tears!
The misery of Tarsus may be theirs.

Enter a LORD.

LORD.

Where's the lord governor?

CLEON.

Here.
Speak out thy sorrows which thou bring'st in haste,
For comfort is too far for us to expect.

LORD.

We have descried, upon our neighbouring shore,
A portly sail of ships make hitherward.

CLEON.

I thought as much.
One sorrow never comes but brings an heir,
That may succeed as his inheritor;
And so in ours: some neighbouring nation,
Taking advantage of our misery,
Hath stuft these hollow vessels with their power,
To beat us down, the which are down already;
And make a conquest of unhappy me,
Whereas no glory's got to overcome.

LORD.

That's the least fear; for, by the semblance
Of their white flags display'd, they bring us peace
And come to us as favourers, not as foes.

CLEON.

Thou speak'st like him's untutor'd to repeat:
Who makes the fairest show means most deceit.
But bring they what they will and what they can,
What need we fear?
The ground's the lowest, and we are half-way there.
Go tell their general we attend him here,
To know for what he comes, and whence he comes,
And what he craves.

LORD.

I go, my lord.   [*Exit.*

CLEON.

Welcome is peace, if he on peace consist;
If wars, we are unable to resist.

Enter PERICLES *with* ATTENDANTS.

PERICLES.

Lord Governor, for so we hear you are,
Let not our ships and number of our men
Be, like a beacon fired, t'amaze your eyes.
We have heard your miseries as far as Tyre,
And seen the desolation of your streets:

Nor come we to add sorrow to your tears,
But to relieve them of their heavy load;
And these our ships, you happily may think
Are like the Trojan horse was stuft within
With bloody veins, expecting overthrow,
Are stored with corn to make your needy bread,
And give them life whom hunger starved half dead.

ALL.
The gods of Greece protect you!
And we'll pray for you.

PERICLES.
　　　　　Arise, I pray you, rise:
We do not look for reverence, but for love,
And harbourage for ourself, our ships, and men.

CLEON.
The which when any shall not gratify,
Or pay you with unthankfulness in thought,
Be it our wives, our children, or ourselves,
The curse of heaven and men succeed their evils!
Till when,—the which I hope shall ne'er be
　　seen,—
Your Grace is welcome to our town and us.

PERICLES.
Which welcome we'll accept; feast here awhile,
Until our stars that frown lend us a smile.
　　　　　　　　　　　　　　[Exeunt.

ACT II.

Enter GOWER.

GOWER.
HERE have you seen a mighty king
His child, I wis, to incest bring;
A better prince, and benign lord,
That will prove awful both in deed and word.
Be quiet, then, as men should be,
Till he hath past necessity.
I'll show you those in troubles reign,
Losing a mite, a mountain gain.
The good in conversation—
To whom I give my benison—
Is still at Tarsus, where each man
Thinks all is writ he speken can;
And, to remember what he does,
Build his statue to make him glorious:
But tidings to the contrary
Are brought your eyes; what need speak I?
DUMB-SHOW.
Enter, at one door, PERICLES, *talking with* CLEON,
all the TRAIN *with them. Enter, at another door,
a* GENTLEMAN, *with a letter to* PERICLES;
PERICLES *shows the letter to* CLEON; *gives the*
MESSENGER *a reward, and knights him. Exit*
PERICLES *at one door, and* CLEON *at another.*
Good Helicane, that stay'd at home,
Not to eat honey like a drone
From others' labours; for though he strive
To killen bad, keep good alive;
And to fulfil his prince' desire,
Sends word of all that haps in Tyre:
How Thaliard came full bent with sin
And hid intent to murder him;
And that in Tarsus was not best
Longer for him to make his rest.
He, doing so, put forth to seas,
Where when men been, there's seldom ease;

For now the wind begins to blow;
Thunder above, and deeps below,
Make such unquiet, that the ship
Should house him safe is wrackt and split;
And he, good prince, having all lost,
By waves from coast to coast is tost:
All perishen of man, of pelf,
Ne aught escapen but himself;
Till fortune, tired with doing bad,
Threw him ashore, to give him glad:
And here he comes. What shall be next,
Pardon old Gower,—this longs the text. 　　[Exit.

SCENE I.

Pentapolis. 　　*An open place by the sea-side.*

Enter PERICLES, *wet.*

PERICLES.
YET cease your ire, you angry stars of heaven!
Wind, rain, and thunder, remember, earthly
　　man
Is but a substance that must yield to you;
And I, as fits my nature, do obey you:
Alas, the sea hath cast me on the rocks,
Washt me from shore to shore, and left me breath
Nothing to think on but ensuing death:
Let it suffice the greatness of your powers
To have bereft a prince of all his fortunes;
And having thrown him from your watery grave,
Here to have death in peace is all he'll crave.

Enter three FISHERMEN.

FIRST FISHERMAN.
What, ho, Pilch!

SECOND FISHERMAN.
Ha, come and bring away the nets!

FIRST FISHERMAN.
What, Patch-breech, I say!

THIRD FISHERMAN.
What say you, master?

FIRST FISHERMAN.
Look how thou stirr'st now! come away, or I'll
fetch thee with a wanion.

THIRD FISHERMAN.
Faith, master, I am thinking of the poor men that
were cast away before us even now.

FIRST FISHERMAN.
Alas, poor souls, it grieved my heart to hear what
pitiful cries they made to us to help them, when,
well-a-day, we could scarce help ourselves.

THIRD FISHERMAN.
Nay, master, said not I as much when I saw the
porpus, how he bounced and tumbled? they say
they're half-fish, half-flesh: a plague on them, they
ne'er come but I look to be washt. Master, I marvel how the fishes live in the sea.

FIRST FISHERMAN.
Why, as men do a-land,—the great ones eat up
the little ones: I can compare our rich misers to
nothing so fitly as to a whale; a' plays and tumbles,
driving the poor fry before him, and at last devours
them all at a mouthful: such whales have I heard
on o'the land, who never leave gaping till they've
swallow'd the whole parish, church, steeple, bells,
and all.

PERICLES [*aside*].
A pretty moral.

THIRD FISHERMAN.

But, master, if I had been the sexton, I would have been that day in the belfry.

SECOND FISHERMAN.

Why, man?

THIRD FISHERMAN.

Because he should have swallow'd me too: and when I had been in his belly, I would have kept such a jangling of the bells, that he should never have left, till he cast bells, steeple, church, and parish, up again. But if the good King Simonides were of my mind,—

PERICLES [aside].

Simonides!

THIRD FISHERMAN.

We would purge the land of these drones, that rob the bee of her honey.

PERICLES [aside].

How from the finny subject of the sea
These fishers tell the infirmities of men;
And from their watery empire recollect
All that may men approve or men detect!—
Peace be at your labour, honest fishermen.

SECOND FISHERMAN.

Honest! good fellow, what's that? If it be a day fits you, search out of the calendar, and nobody look after it.

PERICLES.

May see the sea hath cast upon your coast.

SECOND FISHERMAN.

What a drunken knave was the sea to cast thee in our way!

PERICLES.

A man whom both the waters and the wind,
In that vast tennis-court, have made the ball
For them to play upon, entreats you pity him;
He asks of you, that never used to beg.

FIRST FISHERMAN.

No, friend, cannot you beg? Here's them in our country of Greece gets more with begging than we can do with working.

SECOND FISHERMAN.

Canst thou catch any fishes, then?

PERICLES.

I never practised it.

SECOND FISHERMAN.

Nay, then thou wilt starve, sure; for here's nothing to be got now-a-days, unless thou canst fish for't.

PERICLES.

What I have been I have forgot to know;
But what I am, want teaches me to think on:
A man throng'd up with cold: my veins are chill,
And have no more of life than may suffice
To give my tongue that heat to ask your help;
Which if you shall refuse, when I am dead,
For that I am a man, pray see me buried.

FIRST FISHERMAN.

Die quoth-a? Now gods forbid't! And I have a gown here; come, put it on; keep thee warm. Now, afore me, a handsome fellow! Come, thou shalt go home, and we'll have flesh for holidays, fish for fasting-days, and moreo'er puddings and flap-jacks; and thou shalt be welcome.

PERICLES.

I thank you, sir.

SECOND FISHERMAN.

Hark you, my friend,—you said you could not beg.

PERICLES.

I did but crave.

SECOND FISHERMAN.

But crave! Then I'll turn craver too, and so I shall scape whipping.

PERICLES.

Why, are all your beggars whipt, then?

SECOND FISHERMAN.

O, not all, my friend, not all; for if all your beggars were whipt, I would wish no better office than to be beadle.—But, master, I'll go draw up the net.

[Exit with THIRD FISHERMAN.

PERICLES [aside].

How well this honest mirth becomes their labour!

FIRST FISHERMAN.

Hark you, sir,—do you know where ye are?

PERICLES.

Not well.

FIRST FISHERMAN.

Why, I'll tell you: this is call'd Pentapolis, and our king the good Simonides.

PERICLES.

The good Simonides, do you call him?

FIRST FISHERMAN.

Ay, sir; and he deserves so to be call'd for his peaceable reign and good government.

PERICLES.

He is a happy king, since he gains from his subjects the name of good by his government. How far is his court distant from this shore?

FIRST FISHERMAN.

Marry, sir, half a day's journey: and I'll tell you, he hath a fair daughter, and to-morrow is her birth-day; and there are princes and knights come from all parts of the world to just and tourney for her love.

PERICLES.

Were my fortunes equal to my desires, I could wish to make one there.

FIRST FISHERMAN.

O, sir, things must be as they may; and what a man cannot get, he may lawfully deal for—his wife's soul.

Enter SECOND and THIRD FISHERMEN, drawing up a net.

SECOND FISHERMAN.

Help, master, help! here's a fish hangs in the net, like a poor man's right in the law; 'twill hardly come out. Ha! bots on't, 'tis come at last, and 'tis turn'd to a rusty armour.

PERICLES.

An armour, friends! I pray you, let me see it.—
Thanks, fortune, yet, that, after all thy crosses,
Thou givest me somewhat to repair myself;
And though it was mine own, part of my heritage,
Which my dead father did bequeath to me,
With this strict charge, even as he left his life,
'Keep it, my Pericles; it hath been a shield
'Twixt me and death;'—and pointed to this brace;
'For that it saved me, keep it; in like necessity—
The which the gods protect thee from!—may defend thee.'
It kept where I kept, I so dearly loved it;

Till the rough seas, that spare not any man,
Took it in rage, though calm'd have given't again:
I thank thee for't; my shipwrack now's no ill,
Since I have here my father's gift in's will.

FIRST FISHERMAN.
What mean you, sir?

PERICLES.
To beg of you, kind friends, this coat of worth,
For it was sometime target to a king;
I know it by this mark. He loved me dearly,
And for his sake I wish the having of it;
And that you'ld guide me to your sovereign's
    court,
Where with it I may appear a gentleman;
And if that ever my low fortunes better,
I'll pay your bounties; till then rest your debtor.

FIRST FISHERMAN.
Why, wilt thou tourney for the lady?

PERICLES.
I'll show the virtue I have borne in arms.

FIRST FISHERMAN.
Why, do'e take it, and the gods give thee good
on't!

SECOND FISHERMAN.
Ay, but hark you, my friend; 'twas we that made
up this garment through the rough seams of the
waters: there are certain condolements, certain
vails. I hope, sir, if you thrive, you'll remember
from whence you had them.

PERICLES.
Believe't, I will.
By your furtherance I am clothed in steel;
And, spite of all the rapture of the sea,
This jewel holds his building on my arm:
Unto thy value I will mount myself
Upon a courser, whose delightful steps
Shall make the gazer joy to see him tread.—
Only, my friends, I yet am unprovided
Of a pair of bases.

SECOND FISHERMAN.
We'll sure provide: thou shalt have my best gown
to make thee a pair: and I'll bring thee to the
court myself.

PERICLES.
Then honour be but egal to my will,
This day I'll rise, or else add ill to ill.   [*Exeunt.*

SCENE II.

*The same. A public way or platform leading to the
lists. A pavilion by the side of it for the reception
of the* KING, PRINCESS, LORDS, *&c.*

Enter SIMONIDES, THAISA, LORDS, *and*
ATTENDANTS.

SIMONIDES.
ARE the knights ready to begin the triumph?

FIRST LORD.
They are, my liege;
And stay your coming to present themselves.

SIMONIDES.
Return them, we are ready; and our daughter,
In honour of whose birth these triumphs are,
Sits here, like beauty's child, whom nature gat
For men to see, and seeing wonder at.
     [*Exit a* LORD.

THAISA.
It pleaseth you, my royal father, to express
My commendations great, whose merit's less.

SIMONIDES.
It's fit it should be so; for princes are
A model, which heaven makes like to itself:
As jewels lose their glory if neglected,
So princes their renown if not respected.
'Tis now your honour, daughter, to explain
The labour of each knight in his device.

THAISA.
Which, to preserve mine honour, I'll perform.
The FIRST KNIGHT *passes by, and his* SQUIRE
presents his shield to the PRINCESS.

SIMONIDES.
Who is the first that doth prefer himself?

THAISA.
A knight of Sparta, my renowned father;
And the device he bears upon his shield
Is a black Aethiop reaching at the sun;
The word, *Lux tua vita mihi.*

SIMONIDES.
He loves you well that holds his life of you.
     [*The* SECOND KNIGHT *passes.*
Who is the second that presents himself?

THAISA.
A prince of Macedon, my royal father;
And the device he bears upon his shield
Is an arm'd knight that's conquer'd by a lady;
The motto thus in Spanish, *Piu por dulzura que
    por fuerza.*   [*The* THIRD KNIGHT *passes.*

SIMONIDES.
And what's the third?

THAISA.
         The third of Antioch;
And his device, a wreath of chivalry;
The word, *Me pompæ provexit apex.*
     [*The* FOURTH KNIGHT *passes.*

SIMONIDES.
What is the fourth?

THAISA.
A burning torch that's turned upside down;
The word, *Quod me alit, me extinguit.*

SIMONIDES.
Which shows that beauty hath his power and
    will,
Which can as well inflame as it can kill.
     [*The* FIFTH KNIGHT *passes.*

THAISA.
The fifth, an hand environed with clouds,
Holding out gold that's by the touchstone tried;
The motto thus, *Sic spectanda fides.*
     [*The* SIXTH KNIGHT *passes.*

SIMONIDES.
And what's
The sixth and last, the which the knight himself
With such a graceful courtesy deliver'd?

THAISA.
He seems to be a stranger; but his present is
A wither'd branch, that's only green at top;
The motto, *In hac spe vivo.*

SIMONIDES.
A pretty moral;
From the dejected state wherein he is,
He hopes by you his fortunes yet may flourish.

FIRST LORD.
He had need mean better than his outward
    show
Can any way speak in his just commend;
For, by his rusty outside, he appears
To have practised more the whipstock than the
    lance.
SECOND LORD.
He well may be a stranger, for he comes
To an honour'd triumph strangely furnished.
THIRD LORD.
And on set purpose let his armour rust
Until this day, to scour it in the dust.
SIMONIDES.
Opinion's but a fool, that makes us scan
The outward habit by the inward man.
But stay, the knights are coming: we'll with-
    draw
Into the gallery.   [*Exeunt.*
    [*Great shouts, and all cry* 'The mean knight!']

SCENE III.

The same.   A hall of state; a banquet prepared.

Enter SIMONIDES, THAISA, LADIES, LORDS,
    and KNIGHTS, *from tilting.*

SIMONIDES.
KNIGHTS,
    To say you're welcome were superfluous.
To place upon the volume of your deeds,
As in a title-page, your worth in arms,
Were more than you expect, or more than's fit,
Since every worth in show commends itself.
Prepare for mirth, for mirth becomes a feast:
You are princes and my guests.
THAISA.
But you, my knight and guest;
To whom this wreath of victory I give,
And crown you king of this day's happiness.
PERICLES.
'Tis more by fortune, lady, than my merit.
SIMONIDES.
Call it by what you will, the day is yours;
And here, I hope, is none that envies it.
In framing an artist, art hath thus decreed,
To make some good, but others to exceed;
And you are her labour'd scholar.—Come, queen
    o' the feast,—
For, daughter, so you are,—here take your place:
Marshal the rest, as they deserve their grace.
KNIGHTS.
We are honour'd much by good Simonides.
SIMONIDES.
Your presence glads our days: honour we love;
For who hates honour hates the gods above.
MARSHAL.
Sir, yonder is your place.
PERICLES.
                    Some other is more fit.
FIRST KNIGHT.
Contend not, sir; for we are gentlemen
That neither in our hearts nor outward eyes
Envy the great nor do the low despise.
PERICLES.
You are right courteous knights.
SIMONIDES.
                    Sit, sir, sit.—
By Jove, I wonder, that is king of thoughts,
These cates resist me, he not thought upon.
THAISA [*aside*].
By Juno, that is queen of marriage,
All viands that I eat do seem unsavoury,
Wishing him my meat.—Sure, he's a gallant gen-
    tleman.
SIMONIDES.
He's but a country gentleman:
Has done no more than other knights have done;
Has broken a staff or so; so let it pass.
THAISA [*aside*].
To me he seems like diamond to glass.
PERICLES [*aside*].
Yon king's to me like to my father's picture,
Which tells me in that glory once he was;
Had princes sit, like stars, about his throne,
And he the sun, for them to reverence;
None that beheld him, but, like lesser lights,
Did vail their crowns to his supremacy:
Where now his son like a glow-worm in the
    night,
The which hath fire in darkness, none in light:
Whereby I see that Time's the king of men,
For he's their parent, and he is their grave,
And gives them what he will, not what they
    crave.
SIMONIDES.
What, are you merry, knights?
FIRST KNIGHT.
Who can be other in this royal presence?
SIMONIDES.
Here, with a cup that's stored unto the brim,—
As you do love, fill to your mistress' lips,—
We drink this health to you.
KNIGHTS.
                    We thank your Grace.
SIMONIDES.
Yet pause awhile:
Yon knight doth sit too melancholy,
As if the entertainment in our court
Had not a show might countervail his worth.
Note it not you, Thaisa?
THAISA.
                    What is it
To me, my father?
SIMONIDES.
                    O, attend, my daughter:
Princes, in this, should live like gods above,
Who freely give to every one that comes
To honour them:
And princes not doing so are like to gnats,
Which make a sound, but kill'd are wonder'd at.
Therefore to make his entertain more sweet,
Here, say we drink this standing-bowl of wine to
    him.
THAISA.
Alas, my father, it befits not me
Unto a stranger knight to be so bold:
He may my proffer take for an offence,
Since men take women's gifts for impudence.
SIMONIDES.
How!
Do as I bid you, or you'll move me else.

THAISA [*aside*].
Now, by the gods, he could not please me better.
SIMONIDES.
And furthermore tell him, we desire to know of
him,
Of whence he is, his name and parentage.
THAISA
The king my father, sir, has drunk to you.
PERICLES.
I thank him.
THAISA.
Wishing it so much blood unto your life.
PERICLES.
I thank both him and you, and pledge him freely.
THAISA.
And further he desires to know of you,
Of whence you are, your name and parentage.
PERICLES.
A gentleman of Tyre,—my name, Pericles;
My education been in arts and arms;—
Who, looking for adventures in the world,
Was by the rough seas reft of ships and men,
And, after shipwrack, driven upon this shore.
THAISA.
He thanks your Grace; names himself Pericles,
A gentleman of Tyre,
Who only by misfortune of the seas
Bereft of ships and men, cast on this shore.
SIMONIDES.
Now, by the gods, I pity his misfortune,
And will awake him from his melancholy.—
Come, gentlemen, we sit too long on trifles,
And waste the time, which looks for other revels.
Even in your armours, as you are addrest,
Will very well become a soldier's dance.
I will not have excuse, with saying this
Loud music is too harsh for ladies' heads,
Since they love men in arms as well as beds.
[*The* KNIGHTS *dance.*
So, this was well askt, 'twas so well perform'd.—
Come, sir;
Here is a lady that wants breathing too:
And I have heard, you knights of Tyre
Are excellent in making ladies trip;
And that their measures are as excellent.
PERICLES.
In those that practise them they are, my lord.
SIMONIDES.
O, that's as much as you would be denied
Of your fair courtesy.
[*The* KNIGHTS *and* LADIES *dance.*
Unclasp, unclasp:
Thanks, gentlemen, to all; all have done well,
[*to* PERICLES] But you the best.—Pages and
lights, to conduct
These knights unto their several lodgings!—[*to*
PERICLES] Yours, sir.
We have given order to be next our own.
PERICLES.
I am at your Grace's pleasure.
SIMONIDES.
Princes, it is too late to talk of love;
And that's the mark I know you level at:
Therefore each one betake him to his rest;
To-morrow all for speeding do their best.
[*Exeunt.*

SCENE IV.

Tyre. A room in the GOVERNOR'S *house.*

Enter HELICANUS *and* ESCANES.

HELICANUS.

NO, Escanes; know this of me,—
Antiochus from incest lived not free:
For which, the most high gods not minding longer
To withhold the vengeance that they had in store,
Due to this heinous capital offence,
Even in the height and pride of all his glory,
When he was seated in a chariot
Of an inestimable value, and his daughter with
him,
A fire from heaven came, and shrivell'd up
Their bodies, even to loathing; for they so stunk,
That all those eyes adored them ere their fall
Scorn now their hand should give them burial.
ESCANES.
'Twas very strange.
HELICANUS.
And yet but justice; for though
This king were great, his greatness was no guard
To bar heaven's shaft, but sin had his reward.
ESCANES.
'Tis very true.
Enter two or three LORDS.
FIRST LORD.
See, not a man in private conference
Or council has respect with him but he.
SECOND LORD.
It shall no longer grieve without reproof.
THIRD LORD.
And curst be he that will not second it.
FIRST LORD.
Follow me, then.—Lord Helicane, a word.
HELICANUS.
With me? and welcome:—happy day, my lords.
FIRST LORD.
Know that our griefs are risen to the top,
And now at length they overflow their banks.
HELICANUS.
Your griefs! for what? wrong not the prince you
love.
FIRST LORD.
Wrong not yourself, then, noble Helicane;
But if the prince do live, let us salute him,
Or know what ground's made happy by his breath.
If in the world he live, we'll seek him out;
If in his grave he rest, we'll find him there;
And be resolved he lives to govern us,
Or dead, give's cause to mourn his funeral,
And leave us to our free election.
SECOND LORD.
Whose death's indeed the strongest in our cen-
sure:
And knowing this kingdom is without a head,—
Like goodly buildings left without a roof,
Soon fall to ruin,—your noble self,
That best know how to rule and how to reign,
We thus submit unto, our sovereign.
ALL.
Live, noble Helicane!
HELICANUS.
For honour's cause, forbear your suffrages:
If that you love Prince Pericles, forbear.

Take I your wish, I leap into the seas,
Where's hourly trouble for a minute's ease.
A twelvemonth longer, let me entreat you
To forbear the absence of your king;
If in which time expired, he not return,
I shall with aged patience bear your yoke.
But if I cannot win you to this love,
Go search like nobles, like noble subjects,
And in your search spend your adventurous
　　worth;
Whom if you find, and win unto return,
You shall like diamonds sit about his crown.
　　　　　FIRST LORD.
To wisdom he's a fool that will not yield;
And since Lord Helicane enjoineth us,
We with our travels will endeavour it.
　　　　　HELICANUS.
Then you love us, we you, and we'll clasp hands:
When peers thus knit, a kingdom ever stands.
　　　　　　　　　　　　[*Exeunt.*

SCENE V.

Pentapolis.　A room in the palace.

Enter SIMONIDES, *reading of a letter, at one
door: the* KNIGHTS *meet him.*

　　　　　FIRST KNIGHT.
GOOD morrow to the good Simonides.
　　　　　SIMONIDES.
Knights, from my daughter this I let you know,
That for this twelvemonth she'll not undertake
A married life.
Her reason to herself is only known,
Which yet from her by no means can I get.
　　　　　SECOND KNIGHT.
May we not get access to her, my lord?
　　　　　SIMONIDES.
Faith, by no means; she hath so strictly
Tied her to her chamber, that 'tis impossible.
One twelve moons more she'll wear Diana's
　　livery,
This by the eye of Cynthia hath she vow'd,
And on her virgin honour will not break it.
　　　　　THIRD KNIGHT.
Loth to bid farewell, we take our leaves.
　　　　　　　　　　　[*Exeunt* KNIGHTS.
　　　　　SIMONIDES.
So,
They are well dispatcht; now to my daughter's
　　letter:
She tells me here, she'll wed the stranger knight,
Or never more to view nor day nor light.
'Tis well, mistress; your choice agrees with mine;
I like that well:—nay, how absolute she's in't,
Not minding whether I dislike or no!
Well, I do commend her choice;
And will no longer have it be delay'd.—
Soft! here he comes: I must dissemble it.
　　　　　Enter PERICLES.
　　　　　PERICLES.
All fortune to the good Simonides!
　　　　　SIMONIDES.
To you as much, sir! I am beholding to you
For your sweet music this last night: I do
Protest my ears were never better fed
With such delightful pleasing harmony

　　　　　PERICLES.
It is your Grace's pleasure to commend;
Not my desert.
　　　　　SIMONIDES.
　　　　Sir, you are music's master.
　　　　　PERICLES.
The worst of all her scholars, my good lord.
　　　　　SIMONIDES.
Let me ask you one thing:
What do you think of my daughter, sir?
　　　　　PERICLES.
A most virtuous princess.
　　　　　SIMONIDES.
And she is fair too, is she not?
　　　　　PERICLES.
As a fair day in summer,—wondrous fair.
　　　　　SIMONIDES.
Sir, my daughter thinks very well of you;
Ay, so well, that you must be her master,
And she will be your scholar: therefore look to it.
　　　　　PERICLES.
I am unworthy for her schoolmaster.
　　　　　SIMONIDES.
She thinks not so; peruse this writing else.
　　　　　PERICLES [*aside*].
What's here?
A letter, that she loves the knight of Tyre!
'Tis the king's subtilty to have my life.—
O, seek not to entrap me, gracious lord,
A stranger and distressed gentleman,
That never aim'd so high to love your daughter,
But bent all offices to honour her.
　　　　　SIMONIDES.
Thou hast bewitcht my daughter, and thou art
A villain.
　　　　　PERICLES.
By the gods, I have not:
Never did thought of mine levy offence;
Nor never did my actions yet commence
A deed might gain her love or your displeasure.
　　　　　SIMONIDES.
Traitor, thou liest.
　　　　　PERICLES.
　　　　Traitor!
　　　　　SIMONIDES.
　　　　　　Ay, traitor.
　　　　　PERICLES.
Even in his throat—unless it be the king—
That calls me traitor, I return the lie.
　　　　　SIMONIDES [*aside*].
Now, by the gods, I do applaud his courage.
　　　　　PERICLES.
My actions are as noble as my thoughts,
That never relisht of a base descent.
I came unto your court for honour's cause,
And not to be a rebel to her state;
And he that otherwise accounts of me,
This sword shall prove he's honour's enemy.
　　　　　SIMONIDES.
No?
Here comes my daughter, she can witness it.
　　　　　Enter THAIAS.
　　　　　PERICLES.
Then, as you are as virtuous as fair,
Resolve your angry father, if my tongue

Did e'er solicit, or my hand subscribe
To any syllable that made love to you.
THAISA.
Why, sir, say if you had,
Who takes offence at that would make me glad?
SIMONIDES.
Yea, mistress, are you so peremptory?—
[*aside*] I am glad on't with all my heart.—
I'll tame you; I'll bring you in subjection.
Will you, not having my consent,
Bestow your love and your affections
Upon a stranger?—[*aside*] who, for aught I know,
May be—nor can I think the contrary—
As great in blood as I myself.—
Therefore hear you, mistress; either frame
Your will to mine,—and you, sir, hear you,
Either be ruled by me, or I'll make you—
Man and wife:
Nay, come, your hands and lips must seal it too;
And being join'd, I'll thus your hopes destroy;—
And for a further grief,—God give you joy!—
What, are you both pleased?
THAISA.
Yes,—if you love me, sir,
PERICLES.
Even as my life, or blood that fosters it.
SIMONIDES.
What, are you both agreed?
BOTH.
Yes, if't please your majesty.
SIMONIDES.
It pleaseth me so well, that I will see you wed;
And then with what haste you can get you to bed.
[*Exeunt.*

ACT III.

Enter GOWER.

GOWER.

NOW sleep yslaked hath the rout;
No din but snores the house about,
Made louder by the o'er-fed breast
Of this most pompous marriage-feast.
The cat, with eyne of burning coal,
Now couches fore the mouse's hole;
And crickets sing at the oven's mouth,
Aye the blither for their drouth.
Hymen hath brought the bride to bed,
Where, by the loss of maidenhead,
A babe is moulded.—Be attent,
And time that is so briefly spent
With your fine fancies quaintly eche:
What's dumb in show I'll plain with speech.

DUMB-SHOW.

Enter PERICLES *and* SIMONIDES, *at one door,
with* ATTENDANTS; *a* MESSENGER *meets them,
kneels, and gives* PERICLES *a letter:* PERICLES
shows it SIMONIDES; *the* LORDS *kneel to* PERI-
CLES. *Then enter* THAISA *with child, with*
LYCHORIDA, *a nurse: the* KING *shows her the
letter; she rejoices: she and* PERICLES *take leave
of her father, and depart with* LYCHORIDA *and
their* ATTENDANTS. *Then exeunt* SIMONIDES
and the rest.

By many a dern and painful perch
Of Pericles the careful search,

By the four opposing coigns
Which the world together joins,
Is made with all due diligence
That horse and sail and high expense
Can stead the quest. At last from Tyre—
Fame answering the most strange inquire—
To th'court of King Simonides
Are letters brought, the tenour these:—
Antiochus and his daughter dead;
The men of Tyrus on the head
Of Helicanus would set on
The crown of Tyre, but he will none:
The mutiny he there hastes t'oppress;
Says to 'em, if King Pericles
Come not home in twice six moons,
He, obedient to their dooms,
Will take the crown. The sum of this,
Brought hither to Pentapolis,
Yravished the regions round,
And every one with claps can sound,
'Our heir-apparent is a king!
Who dreamt, who thought of such a thing?'
Brief, he must hence depart to Tyre:
His queen with child makes her desire—
Which who shall cross?—along to go:—
Omit we all their dole and woe:—
Lychorida, her nurse, she takes,
And so to sea. Their vessel shakes
On Neptune's billow; half the flood
Hath their keel cut: but fortune's mood
Varies again; the grisled north
Disgorges such a tempest forth,
That, as a duck for life that dives,
So up and down the poor ship drives:
The lady shrieks, and, well-a-near,
Does fall in travail with her fear:
And what ensues in this fell storm
Shall for itself itself perform.
I nill relate, action may
Conveniently the rest convey;
Which might not what by me is told.
In your imagination hold
This stage the ship, upon whose deck
The sea-tost Pericles appears to speak. [*Exit.*

SCENE I.

Enter PERICLES, *a-shipboard.*

PERICLES.

THOU god of this great vast, rebuke these
surges,
Which wash both heaven and hell; and thou, that
hast
Upon the winds command, bind them in brass,
Having call'd them from the deep! O, still
Thy deafening, dreadful thunders; gently quench
Thy nimble, sulphurous flashes!—O, how, Ly-
chorida,
How does my queen?—Thou stormest venom-
ously;
Wilt thou spit all thyself?—The seaman's whistle
Is as a whisper in the ears of death,
Unheard.—Lychorida!—Lucina, O
Divinest patroness, and midwife gentle
To those that cry by night, convey thy deity

Aboard our dancing boat; make swift the pangs
Of my queen's travails!
    Enter LYCHORIDA, *with an* INFANT.
        Now, Lychorida!
         LYCHORIDA.
Here is a thing too young for such a place,
Who, if it had conceit, would die, as I
Am like to do: take in your arms this piece
Of your dead queen.
         PERICLES.
        How, how, Lychorida!
         LYCHORIDA.
Patience, good sir; do not assist the storm.
Here's all that is left living of your queen,—
A little daughter: for the sake of it,
Be manly, and take comfort.
         PERICLES.
        O you gods!
Why do you make us love your goodly gifts,
And snatch them straight away? We here below
Recall not what we give, and therein may
Vie honour with you.
         LYCHORIDA.
        Patience, good sir,
Even for this charge.
         PERICLES.
        Now, mild may be thy life!
For a more blusterous birth had never babe:
Quiet and gentle thy conditions! for
Thou art the rudeliest welcome to this world
That ever was prince's child. Happy what follows!
Thou hast as chiding a nativity
As fire, air, water, earth, and heaven can make,
To herald thee from the womb: even at the first
Thy loss is more than can thy portage quit,
With all thou canst find here.—Now, the good
    gods
Throw their best eyes upon't!
    Enter two SAILORS.
         FIRST SAILOR.
What courage, sir? God save you!
         PERICLES.
Courage enough: I do not fear the flaw;
It hath done to me the worst. Yet, for the love
Of this poor infant, this fresh-new seafarer,
I would it would be quiet.
         FIRST SAILOR.
Slack the bolins there!—Thou wilt not, wilt thou?
Blow, and split thyself.
         SECOND SAILOR.
But sea-room, an the brine and cloudy billow kiss
the moon, I care not.
         FIRST SAILOR.
Sir, your queen must overboard: the sea works
high, the wind is loud, and will not lie till the ship
be clear'd of the dead.
         PERICLES.
That's your superstition.
         FIRST SAILOR.
Pardon us, sir; with us at sea it hath been still ob-
served; and we are strong in custom. Therefore
briefly yield her; for she must overboard straight.
         PERICLES.
As you think meet.—Most wretched queen!
         LYCHORIDA.
Here she lies, sir.

         PERICLES.
A terrible childbed hast thou had, my dear;
No light, no fire: th'unfriendly elements
Forgot thee utterly; nor have I time
To give thee hallow'd to thy grave, but straight
Must cast thee, scarcely coffin'd, in the ooze;
Where, for a monument upon thy bones,
And aye-remaining lamps, the belching whale
And humming water must o'erwhelm thy
    corpse,
Lying with simple shells.—O Lychorida,
Bid Nestor bring me spices, ink and paper,
My casket and my jewels; and bid Nicander
Bring me the satin coffer: lay the babe
Upon the pillow: hie thee, whiles I say
A priestly farewell to her: suddenly, woman.
        [*Exit* LYCHORIDA.
         SECOND SAILOR.
Sir, we have a chest beneath the hatches, caulkt
and bitumed ready.
         PERICLES.
I thank thee.--Mariner, say what coast is this?
         SECOND SAILOR.
We are near Tarsus.
         PERICLES.
Thither, gentle mariner,
Alter thy course for Tyre. When canst thou reach
    it?
         SECOND SAILOR.
By break of day, if the wind cease.
         PERICLES.
O, make for Tarsus!—
There will I visit Cleon, for the babe
Cannot hold out to Tyrus: there I'll leave it
At careful nursing.—Go thy ways, good mariner:
I'll bring the body presently.   [*Exeunt.*

         SCENE II.

  Ephesus.   *A room in* CERIMON'S *house.*

 Enter CERIMON, *a* SERVANT, *and some* PER-
SONS *who have been shipwrackt.*
         CERIMON.
PHILEMON, ho!
      Enter PHILEMON.
         PHILEMON.
Doth my lord call?
         CERIMON.
Get fire and meat for these poor men:
'T has been a turbulent and stormy night.
         SERVANT.
I have been in many; but such a night as this,
Till now, I ne'er endured.
         CERIMON.
Your master will be dead ere you return;
There's nothing can be minister'd to nature
That can recover him.—[*to* PHILEMON] Give
    this to the pothecary,
And tell me how it works.
      [*Exeunt all but* CERIMON.
    Enter two GENTLEMEN.
         FIRST GENTLEMAN.
        Good morrow.
         SECOND GENTLEMAN.
Good morrow to your lordship.

CERIMON.   Gentlemen,
Why do you stir so early?
                    FIRST GENTLEMAN.
Sir,
Our lodgings, standing bleak upon the sea,
Shook as the earth did quake;
The very principals did seem to rend,
And all-to topple: pure surprise and fear
Made me to quit the house.
                    SECOND GENTLEMAN.
That is the cause we trouble you so early;
'Tis not our husbandry.
                    CERIMON.
                    O, you say well.
                    FIRST GENTLEMAN.
But I much marvel that your lordship, having
Rich tire about you, should at these early hours
Shake off the golden slumber of repose.
'Tis most strange,
Nature should be so conversant with pain,
Being thereto not compell'd.
                    CERIMON.
                    I hold it ever,
Virtue and cunning were endowments greater
Than nobleness and riches: careless heirs
May the two latter darken and expend;
But immortality attends the former,
Making a man a god. 'Tis known, I ever
Have studied physic, through which secret art,
By turning o'er authorities, I have—
Together with my practice—made familiar
To me and to my aid the blest infusions
That dwell in vegetives, in metals, stones;
And I can speak of the disturbances
That nature works, and of her cures; which doth
     give me
A more content in course of true delight
Than to be thirsty after tottering honour,
Or tie my treasure up in silken bags,
To please the fool and death.
                    SECOND GENTLEMAN.
Your honour has through Ephesus pour'd forth
Your charity, and hundreds call themselves
Your creatures, who by you have been restored:
And not your knowledge, your personal pain, but
     even
Your purse, still open, hath built Lord Cerimon
Such strong renown as time shall never—
     Enter two or three SERVANTS *with a chest.*
                    FIRST SERVANT.
So; lift there.
                    CERIMON.
What is that?
                    FIRST SERVANT.
                    Sir, even now
Did the sea toss upon our shore this chest:
'Tis of some wrack.
                    CERIMON.
                    Set't down, let's look upon't.
                    SECOND GENTLEMAN.
'Tis like a coffin, sir.
                    CERIMON.
                    Whate'er it be,
'Tis wondrous heavy. Wrench it open straight:
If the sea's stomach be o'ercharged with gold,

'Tis a good constraint of fortune it belches upon
     us.
                    SECOND GENTLEMAN.
'Tis so, my lord.
                    CERIMON.
                    How close 'tis caulkt and bitumed!—
Did the sea cast it up?
                    FIRST SERVANT.
I never saw so huge a billow, sir,
As tost it upon shore.
                    CERIMON.
                    Wrench it open;
Soft!—it smells most sweetly in my sense.
                    SECOND GENTLEMAN.
A delicate odour.
                    CERIMON.
As ever hit my nostril.—So, up with it.—
O you most potent gods! what's here? a corse!
                    FIRST GENTLEMAN.
Most strange!
                    CERIMON.
Shrouded in cloth of state; balm'd and entreasured
with full bags of spices! A passport too!—Apollo,
perfect me in the characters!   [*Reads from a scroll.*
     Here I give to understand,—
     If e'er this coffin drive a-land,—
     I, King Pericles, have lost
     This queen, worth all our mundane cost.
     Who finds her, give her burying;
     She was the daughter of a king:
     Besides this treasure for a fee,
     The gods requite his charity!
If thou livest, Pericles, thou hast a heart
That even cracks for woe!—This chanced to-night.
                    SECOND GENTLEMAN.
Most likely, sir.
                    CERIMON.
                    Nay, certainly to-night;
For look how fresh she looks!—They were too
     rough
That threw her in the sea.—Make a fire within:
Fetch hither all my boxes in my closet.—
                    [*Exit a* SERVANT.
Death may usurp on nature many hours,
And yet the fire of life kindle again
The o'erprest spirits. I heard of an Egyptian
That had nine hours lien dead,
Who was by good appliance recovered.
     Enter a SERVANT, *with boxes, napkins, and fire.*
Well said, well said; the fire and cloths.—
The rough and woeful music that we have,
Cause it to sound, beseech you.
The viol once more:—how thou stirr'st, thou
     block!—
The music there!—I pray you, give her air.—
Gentlemen, this queen will live: nature awakes;
A warmth breathes out of her: she hath not been
Entranced above five hours: see how she gins
To blow into life's flower again!
                    FIRST GENTLEMAN.
                    The heavens,
Through you, increase our wonder, and set up
Your fame for ever.
                    CERIMON.
                    She is alive; behold,
Her eyelids, cases to those heavenly jewels

Which Pericles hath lost, begin to part
Their fringes of bright gold; the diamonds
Of a most praised water do appear,
To make the world twice rich.—Live,
And make us weep to hear your fate, fair creature,
Rare as you seem to be!   [*She moves.*

     THAISA.
          O dear Diana,
Where am I? Where's my lord? What world is
  this?

     SECOND GENTLEMAN.
Is not this strange?

     FIRST GENTLEMAN.
        Most rare.

     CERIMON.
         Hush, my gentle neighbours!
Lend me your hands; to the next chamber bear
  her.
Get linen: now this matter must be lookt to,
For her relapse is mortal. Come, come;
And Aesculapius guide us!
     [*Exeunt, carrying out* THAISA.

SCENE III.

Tarsus.   A room in the GOVERNOR'S *house.*

Enter PERICLES, CLEON, DIONYZA, *and*
LYCHORIDA *with* MARINA *in her arms.*

     PERICLES.
MOST honour'd Cleon, I must needs be gone;
  My twelve months are expired, and Tyrus
  stands
In a litigious peace. You, and your lady,
Take from my heart all thankfulness! The gods
Make up the rest upon you!

     CLEON.
Your shafts of fortune, though they hurt you
  mortally,
Yet glance full wanderingly on us.

     DIONYZA.
         O your sweet queen!
That the strict Fates had pleased you had brought
  her hither,
To have blest mine eyes with her!

     PERICLES.
         We cannot but obey
The powers above us. Could I rage and roar
As doth the sea she lies in, yet the end
Must be as 'tis. My gentle babe Marina,—whom,
For she was born at sea, I have named so,—here
I charge your charity withal, leaving her
The infant of your care; beseeching you
To give her princely training, that she may be
Manner'd as she is born.

     CLEON.
        Fear not, my lord, but think
Your grace, that fed my country with your corn,—
For which the people's prayers still fall upon
  you,—
Must in your child be thought on. If neglection
Should therein make me vile, the common body,
By you relieved, would force me to my duty:
But if to that my nature need a spur,
The gods revenge it upon me and mine,
To the end of generation!

     PERICLES.
         I believe you;
Your honour and your goodness teach me to't,
Without your vows.—Till she be married,
  madam,
By bright Diana, whom we honour, all
Unscissar'd shall this hair of mine remain,
Though I show ill in't. So I take my leave.
Good madam, make me blessed in your care
In bringing up my child.

     DIONYZA.
         I have one myself,
Who shall not be more dear to my respect
Than yours, my lord.

     PERICLES.
     Madam, my thanks and prayers.

     CLEON.
We'll bring your Grace e'en to the edge o'th'shore,
Then give you up to the meek'st Neptune and
The gentlest winds of heaven.

     PERICLES.
         I will embrace
Your offer. Come, dearest madam.—O, no tears,
Lychorida, no tears:
Look to your little mistress, on whose grace
You may depend hereafter.—Come, my lord.
     [*Exeunt.

SCENE IV.

Ephesus.   A room in CERIMON'S *house.*

Enter CERIMON *and* THAISA.

     CERIMON.
MADAM, this letter, and some certain jewels,
  Lay with you in your coffer: which are
At your command. Know you the character?

     THAISA.
It is my lord's.
That I was shipt at sea, I well remember,
Even on my eaning time; but whether there
Delivered, by the holy gods,
I cannot rightly say. But since King Pericles,
My wedded lord, I ne'er shall see again,
A vestal livery will I take me to,
And never more have joy.

     CERIMON.
Madam, if this you purpose as ye speak,
Diana's temple is not distant far,
Where you may abide till your date expire.
Moreover, if you please, a niece of mine
Shall there attend you.

     THAISA.
My recompense is thanks, that's all;
Yet my good will is great, though the gift small.
     [*Exeunt.

ACT IV.

Enter GOWER.

     GOWER.
IMAGINE Pericles arrived at Tyre,
  Welcomed and settled to his own desire.
His woeful queen we leave at Ephesus,
Unto Diana there's a votaress.
Now to Marina bend your mind,
Whom our fast-growing scene must find
At Tarsus, and by Cleon train'd

In music, letters; who hath gain'd
Of education all the grace,
Which makes her both the heart and place
Of general wonder. But, alack,
That monster envy, oft the wrack
Of earned praise, Marina's life
Seeks to take off by treason's knife.
And in this kind hath our Cleon
One daughter, and a wench full grown,
Even ripe for marriage-rite; this maid
Hight Philoten: and it is said
For certain in our story, she
Would ever with Marina be:
Be't when she weaved the sleided silk
With fingers long, small, white as milk;
Or when she would with sharp needle wound
The cambric, which she made more sound
By hurting it; or when to the lute
She sung, and made the night-bird mute,
That still records with moan; or when
She would with rich and constant pen
Vail to her mistress Dian; still
This Philoten contends in skill
With absolute Marina: so
With the dove of Paphos might the crow
Vie feathers white. Marina gets
All praises, which are paid as debts,
And not as given. This so darks
In Philoten all graceful marks,
That Cleon's wife, with envy rare,
A present murderer does prepare
For good Marina, that her daughter
Might stand peerless by this slaughter.
The sooner her vile thoughts to stead,
Lychorida, our nurse, is dead:
And cursed Dionyza hath
The pregnant instrument of wrath
Prest for this blow. The unborn event
I do commend to your content:
Only I carry winged time
Post on the lame feet of my rime;
Which never could I so convey,
Unless your thoughts went on my way.—
Dionyza does appear,
With Leonine, a murderer.   [*Exit.*

SCENE I.

Tarsus.   An open place near the sea-shore.

Enter DIONYZA *and* LEONINE.

DIONYZA.

THY oath remember; thou hast sworn to do't:
'Tis but a blow, which never shall be known.
Thou canst not do a thing in the world so soon,
To yield thee so much profit. Let not conscience,
Which is but cold, inflame love in thy bosom,
Inflame too nicely; nor let pity, which
Even women have cast off, melt thee, but be
A soldier to thy purpose.

LEONINE.

I'll do't; but yet she is a goodly creature.

DIONYZA.

The fitter, then, the gods should have her.—Here
She comes weeping for her only nurse's death.—
Thou art resolved?

LEONINE.

I am resolved.

Enter MARINA, *with a basket of flowers.*

MARINA.

No, I will rob Tellus of her weed,
To strew thy green with flowers; the yellows,
   blues,
The purple violets, and marigolds,
Shall, as a carpet, hang upon thy grave,
While summer-days do last.—Ay me! poor maid,
Born in a tempest, when my mother died,
This world to me is like a lasting storm,
Whirring me from my friends.

DIONYZA.

How now, Marina! why do you keep alone?
How chance my daughter is not with you? Do not
Consume your blood with sorrowing: you have
A nurse of me. Lord, how your favour's changed
With this unprofitable woe! Come,
Give me your flowers, ere the sea mar it.
Walk with Leonine; the air is quick there,
And it pierces and sharpens the stomach.—Come,
Leonine, take her by the arm, walk with her.

MARINA.

No, I pray you;
I'll not bereave you of your servant.

DIONYZA.

                          Come, come;
I love the king your father, and yourself,
With more than foreign heart. We every day
Expect him here: when he shall come, and find
Our paragon to all reports thus blasted,
He will repent the breadth of his great voyage;
Blame both my lord and me, that we have taken
No care to your best courses. Go, I pray you,
Walk, and be cheerful once again; reserve
That excellent complexion, which did steal
The eyes of young and old. Care not for me;
I can go home alone.

MARINA.

                Well, I will go;
But yet I have no desire to it.

DIONYZA.

                          Come, come,
I know 'tis good for you.—
Walk half an hour, Leonine, at the least:
Remember what I have said.

LEONINE.

                     I warrant you, madam.

DIONYZA.

I'll leave you, my sweet lady, for a while:
Pray, walk softly, do not heat your blood:
What! I must have care of you.

MARINA.

                     My thanks, sweet madam.—
                          [*Exit* DIONYZA.
Is this wind westerly that blows?

LEONINE.

                          South-west.

MARINA.

When I was born, the wind was north.

LEONINE.

                               Was't so?

MARINA.

My father, as nurse said, did never fear,
But cried 'Good seamen!' to the sailors, galling

His kingly hands, haling ropes;
And, clasping to the mast, endured a sea
That almost burst the deck.

LEONINE.

When was this?

MARINA.

When I was born:
Never was waves nor wind more violent;
And from the ladder-tackle washes off
A canvas-climber. 'Ha!' says one, 'wilt out?'
And with a dropping industry they skip
From stem to stern: the boatswain whistles, and
The master calls, and trebles their confusion.

LEONINE.

Come, say your prayers.

MARINA.

What mean you?

LEONINE.

If you require a little space for prayer,
I grant it: pray; but be not tedious, for
The gods are quick of ear, and I am sworn
To do my work with haste.

MARINA.

         Why will you kill me?

LEONINE.

To satisfy my lady.

MARINA.

Why would she have me kill'd?
Now, as I can remember, by my troth,
I never did her hurt in all my life:
I never spake bad word, nor did ill turn
To any living creature: believe me, la,
I never kill'd a mouse, nor hurt a fly:
I trod upon a worm once 'gainst my will,
But I wept for it. How have I offended,
Wherein my death might yield her any profit,
Or my life imply her any danger?

LEONINE.

My commission
Is not to reason of the deed, but do't.

MARINA.

You will not do't for all the world, I hope.
You are well-favour'd, and your looks foreshow
You have a gentle heart. I saw you lately,
When you caught hurt in parting two that fought:
Good sooth, it show'd well in you: do so now:
Your lady seeks my life; come you between,
And save poor me, the weaker.

LEONINE.

         I am sworn,
And will dispatch.

Enter PIRATES.

FIRST PIRATE.

Hold, villain!   [LEONINE *runs away.*

SECOND PIRATE.

A prize! a prize!

THIRD PIRATE.

Half-part, mates, half-part. Come, let's have
her aboard suddenly.

[*Exeunt* PIRATES *with* MARINA.
Enter LEONINE.

LEONINE.

These roguing thieves serve the great pirate
Valdes;
And they have seized Marina. Let her go:

There's no hope she will return. I'll swear she's
dead,
And thrown into the sea.—But I'll see further:
Perhaps they will but please themselves upon her,
Not carry her aboard. If she remain,
Whom they have ravisht must by me be slain.

[*Exit.*

SCENE II.

Mytilene. A room in a brothel.

Enter PANDAR, BAWD, *and* BOULT.

PANDAR.

BOULT,—

BOULT.

Sir?

PANDAR.

Search the market narrowly; Mytilene is full of
gallants. We lost too much money this mart by
being too wenchless.

BAWD.

We were never so much out of creatures. We
have but poor three, and they can do no more
than they can do; and they with continual action
are even as good as rotten.

PANDAR.

Therefore let's have fresh ones, whate'er we pay
for them. If there be not a conscience to be used
in every trade, we shall never prosper.

BAWD.

Thou sayest true: 'tis not our bringing up of poor
bastards,—as, I think, I have brought up some
eleven,—

BOULT.

Ay, to eleven; and brought them down again.—
But shall I search the market?

BAWD.

What else, man? The stuff we have, a strong wind
will blow it to pieces, they are so pitifully sodden.

PANDAR.

Thou sayest true: they're too unwholesome, o'
conscience. The poor Transylvanian is dead, that
lay with the little baggage.

BOULT.

Ay, she quickly poopt him; she made him roast-
meat for worms.—But I'll go search the market.

[*Exit.*

PANDAR.

Three or four thousand chequins were as pretty a
proportion to live quietly, and so give over.

BAWD.

Why to give over, I pray you? is it a shame to get
when we are old?

PANDAR.

O, our credit comes not in like the commodity,
nor the commodity wages not with the danger:
therefore, if in our youths we could pick up some
pretty estate, 'twere not amiss to keep our door
hatcht. Besides, the sore terms we stand upon
with the gods will be strong with us for giving
o'er.

BAWD.

Come, other sorts offend as well as we.

PANDAR.

As well as we! ay, and better too; we offend
worse. Neither is our profession any trade; it's no
calling.—But here comes Boult.

Enter BOULT, *with the* PIRATES *and* MARINA.

BOULT [*to* MARINA].

Come your ways.—My masters, you say she's a virgin?

FIRST PIRATE.

O, sir, we doubt it not.

BOULT.

Master, I have gone through for this piece, you see: if you like her, so; if not, I have lost my earnest.

BAWD.

Boult, has she any qualities?

BOULT.

She has a good face, speaks well, and has excellent good clothes: there's no further necessity of qualities can make her be refused.

BAWD.

What's her price, Boult?

BOULT.

I cannot be bated one doit of a thousand pieces.

PANDAR.

Well, follow me, my masters, you shall have your money presently.—Wife, take her in; instruct her what she has to do, that she may not be raw in her entertainment. [*Exeunt* PANDAR *and* PIRATES.

BAWD.

Boult, take you the marks of her,—the colour of her hair, complexion, height, her age, with warrant of her virginity; and cry, 'He that will give most shall have her first.' Such a maidenhead were no cheap thing, if men were as they have been. Get this done as I command you.

BOULT.

Performance shall follow   [*Exit.*

MARINA.

Alack that Leonine was so slack, so slow!
He should have struck, not spoke; or that these pirates—
Not enough barbarous—had not o'erboard thrown me
For to seek my mother!

BAWD.

Why lament you, pretty one?

MARINA.

That I am pretty.

BAWD.

Come, the gods have done their part in you.

MARINA.

I accuse them not.

BAWD.

You are light into my hands, where you are like to live.

MARINA.

The more my fault
To scape his hands where I was like to die.

BAWD.

Ay, and you shall live in pleasure.

MARINA.

No.

BAWD.

Yes, indeed shall you, and taste gentlemen of all fashions: you shall fare well; you shall have the difference of all complexions. What! do you stop your ears?

MARINA.

Are you a woman?

BAWD.

What would you have me be, an I be not a woman?

MARINA.

An honest woman, or not a woman.

BAWD.

Marry, whip thee, gosling: I think I shall have something to do with you. Come, you're a young foolish sapling, and must be bow'd as I would have you.

MARINA.

The gods defend me!

BAWD.

If it please the gods to defend you by men, then men must comfort you, men must feed you, men must stir you up.—Boult's return'd.

Enter BOULT.

Now, sir, hast thou cried her through the market?

BOULT.

I have cried her almost to the number of her hairs; I have drawn her picture with my voice.

BAWD.

And I prithee tell me, how dost thou find the inclination of the people, especially of the younger sort?

BOULT.

Faith, they listen'd to me as they would have hearken'd to their father's testament. There was a Spaniard's mouth so water'd, that he went to bed to her very description.

BAWD.

We shall have him here to-morrow with his best ruff on.

BOULT.

To-night, to-night. But, mistress, do you know the French knight that cowers i'the hams?

BAWD.

Who, Monsieur Veroles?

BOULT.

Ay, he: he offer'd to cut a caper at the proclamation; but he made a groan at it, and swore he would see her to-morrow.

BAWD.

Well, well; as for him, he brought his disease hither: here he does but repair it. I know he will come in our shadow, to scatter his crowns in the sun.

BOULT.

Well, if we had of every nation a traveller, we should lodge them with this sign.

BAWD [*to* MARINA].

Pray you, come hither awhile. You have fortunes coming upon you. Mark me: you must seem to do that fearfully which you commit willingly, despise profit where you have most gain. To weep that you live as ye do makes pity in your lovers: seldom but that pity begets you a good opinion, and that opinion a mere profit.

MARINA.

I understand you not.

BOULT.

O, take her home, mistress, take her home: these blushes of hers must be quencht with some present practice.

BAWD.

Thou sayest true, i'faith, so they must; for your
bride goes to that with shame which is her way to
go with warrant.

BOULT.

Faith, some do, and some do not. But, mistress,
if I have bargain'd for the joint,—

BAWD.

Thou mayst cut a morsel off the spit.

BOULT.

I may so.

BAWD.

Who should deny it?—Come, young one, I like
the manner of your garments well.

BOULT.

Ay, by my faith, they shall not be changed yet.

BAWD.

Boult, spend thou that in the town: report what a
sojourner we have; you'll lose nothing by custom.
When nature framed this piece, she meant thee a
good turn; therefore say what a paragon she is,
and thou hast the harvest out of thine own report.

BOULT.

I warrant you, mistress, thunder shall not so
awake the beds of eels as my giving out her beauty
stir up the lewdly-inclined. I'll bring home some
to-night.

BAWD.

Come your ways; follow me.

MARINA.

If fires be hot, knives sharp, or waters deep,
Untied I still my virgin knot will keep.
Diana, aid my purpose!

BAWD.

What have we to do with Diana? Pray you, will
you go with us?   [*Exeunt.*

SCENE III.

Tarsus. A room in the GOVERNOR'S *house.*

Enter CLEON *and* DIONYZA.

DIONYZA.

WHY, are you foolish? Can it be undone?

CLEON.

O Dionyza, such a piece of slaughter
The sun and moon ne'er lookt upon!

DIONYZA.

                 I think

You'll turn a child again.

CLEON.

Were I chief lord of all this spacious world,
I'ld give it to undo the deed.—O lady,
Much less in blood than virtue, yet a princess
To equal any single crown o'the earth
I'the justice of compare!—O villain Leonine!
Whom thou hast poison'd too:
If thou hadst drunk to him, 't had been a kindness
Becoming well thy fact: what canst thou say
When noble Pericles shall demand his child?

DIONYZA.

That she is dead. Nurses are not the Fates,
To foster it, nor ever to preserve.
She died at night; I'll say so. Who can cross it?
Unless you play the pious innocent,
And for an honest attribute cry out
'She died by foul play.'

CLEON.

O, go to. Well, well,
Of all the faults beneath the heavens, the gods
Do like this worst.

DIONYZA.

Be one of those that think
The petty wrens of Tarsus will fly hence,
And open this to Pericles. I do shame
To think of what a noble strain you are,
And of how coward a spirit.

CLEON.

To such proceeding
Who ever but his approbation added,
Though not his prime consent, he did not flow
From honourable sources.

DIONYZA.

Be it so, then:
Yet none does know, but you, how she came dead,
Nor none can know, Leonine being gone.
She did distain my child, and stood between
Her and her fortunes: none would look on her,
But cast their gazes on Marina's face;
Whilst ours was blurted at, and held a malkin,
Not worth the time of day. It pierced me thor-
    ough;
And though you call my course unnatural,
You not your child well loving, yet I find
It greets me as an enterprise of kindness
Perform'd to our sole daughter.

CLEON.

              Heavens forgive it!

DIONYZA.

And as for Pericles,
What should he say? We wept after her hearse,
And yet we mourn: her monument
Is almost finisht, and her epitaphs
In glittering golden characters express
A general praise to her, and care in us
At whose expense 'tis done.

CLEON.

          Thou art like the harpy,
Which, to betray, dost, with thine angel's face,
Seize with thine eagle's talons.

DIONYZA.

You are like one that superstitiously
Doth swear to the gods that winter kills the flies:
But yet I know you'll do as I advise.   [*Exeunt.*

Enter GOWER, *before the monument of* MARINA
at Tarsus.

GOWER.

Thus time we waste, and longest leagues make
    short;
Sail seas in cockles, have and wish but for't;
Making—to take your imagination—
From bourn to bourn, region to region.
By you being pardon'd, we commit no crime
To use one language in each several clime
Where our scenes seem to live. I do beseech you
To learn of me, who stand i'th'gaps to teach you,
The stages of our story. Pericles
Is now again thwarting the wayward seas,
Attended on by many a lord and knight,
To see his daughter, all his life's delight.
Old Helicanus goes along: behind
Is left to govern it, you bear in mind,
Old Escanes, whom Helicanus late

Advanced in time to great and high estate.
Well-sailing ships and bounteous winds have
  brought
This king to Tarsus—think his pilot thought;
So with his steerage shall your thoughts grow
  on—
To fetch his daughter home, who first is gone.
Like motes and shadows see them move awhile;
Your ears unto your eyes I'll reconcile.

DUMB-SHOW.

Enter PERICLES, *at one door, with all his Train;*
CLEON *and* DIONYZA *at the other.* CLEON
shows PERICLES *the tomb; whereat* PERICLES
makes lamentation, puts on sackcloth, and in a
mighty passion departs. Then exeunt CLEON,
DIONYZA, *and the rest.*

See how belief may suffer by foul show!
This borrow'd passion stands for true old woe;
And Pericles, in sorrow all devour'd,
With sighs shot through and biggest tears o'er-
  shower'd,
Leaves Tarsus, and again embarks. He swears
Never to wash his face, nor cut his hairs:
He puts on sackcloth, and to sea. He bears
A tempest, which his mortal vessel tears,
And yet he rides it out. Now please you wit
The epitaph is for Marina writ
By wicked Dionyza.

[*Reads the inscription on* MARINA'S *monument.*

'The fairest, sweet'st, and best lies here,
Who wither'd in her spring of year.
She was of Tyrus the king's daughter,
On whom foul death hath made this slaughter;
Marina was she call'd; and at her birth,
Thetis, being proud, swallow'd some part o'th'
  earth:
Therefore the earth, fearing to be o'erflow'd,
Hath Thetis' birth-child on the heavens bestow'd:
Wherefore she does—and swears she'll never
  stint—
Make raging battery upon shores of flint.'
No visor doth become black villainy
So well as soft and tender flattery.
Let Pericles believe his daughter's dead,
And bear his courses to be ordered
By Lady Fortune; while our scene must play
His daughter's woe and heavy well-a-day
In her unholy service. Patience, then,
And think you now are all in Mytilen.   [*Exit.*

SCENE IV.

Mytilene. A street before the brothel.

Enter, from the brothel, two GENTLEMEN.

FIRST GENTLEMAN.

DID you ever hear the like?

SECOND GENTLEMAN.

No, nor never shall do in such a place as this, she
being once gone.

FIRST GENTLEMAN.

But to have divinity preacht there! did you ever
dream of such a thing?

SECOND GENTLEMAN.

No, no. Come, I am for no more bawdy-houses:
—shall's go hear the vestals sing?

FIRST GENTLEMAN.

I'll do any thing now that is virtuous; but I am
out of the road of rutting for ever.   [*Exeunt.*

SCENE V.

The same. A room in the brothel.

Enter PANDAR, BAWD, *and* BOULT.

PANDAR.

WELL, I had rather than twice the worth of
her she had ne'er come here.

BAWD.

Fie, fie upon her! she's able to freeze the god
Priapus, and undo a whole generation. We must
either get her ravisht, or be rid of her. When she
should do for clients her fitment, and do me the
kindness of our profession, she has me her
quirks, her reasons, her master reasons, her prayers, her knees; that she would make a puritan of
the devil, if he should cheapen a kiss of her.

BOULT.

Faith, I must ravish her, or she'll disfurnish us of
all our cavaliers, and make all our swearers
priests.

PANDAR.

Now, the pox upon her green-sickness for me!

BAWD.

Faith, there's no way to be rid on't but by the
way to the pox.—Here comes the Lord Lysimachus disguised.

BOULT.

We should have both lord and lown, if the peevish baggage would but give way to customers.

Enter LYSIMACHUS.

LYSIMACHUS.

How now! How a dozen of virginities?

BAWD.

Now, the gods to-bless your honour!

BOULT.

I am glad to see your honour in good health.

LYSIMACHUS.

You may so; 'tis the better for you that your re-
sorters stand upon sound legs. How now, wholesome iniquity! Have you that a man may deal
withal, and defy the surgeon?

BAWD.

We have here one, sir, if she would—but there
never came her like in Mytilene.

LYSIMACHUS.

If she'd do the deed of darkness, thou wouldst say.

BAWD.

Your honour knows what 'tis to say well enough.

LYSIMACHUS.

Well, call forth, call forth.

BOULT.

For flesh and blood, sir, white and red, you shall
see a rose; and she were a rose indeed, if she had
but—

LYSIMACHUS.

What, prithee?

BOULT.

O, sir, I can be modest.

LYSIMACHUS.

That dignifies the renown of a bawd, no less than
it gives a good report to a member to be chaste.

    [*Exit* BOULT.

BAWD.

Here comes that which grows to the stalk,—
never pluckt yet, I can assure you.

Enter BOULT *with* MARINA.

Is she not a fair creature?

LYSIMACHUS.

Faith, she would serve after a long voyage at sea.
Well, there's for you:—leave us.

BAWD.

I beseech your honour, give me leave: a word,
and I'll have done presently.

LYSIMACHUS.

I beseech you, do.

BAWD [*to* MARINA].

First, I would have you note, this is an honourable man.

MARINA.

I desire to find him so, that I may worthily note
him.

BAWD.

Next, he's the governor of this country, and a
man whom I am bound to.

MARINA.

If he govern the country, you are bound to him
indeed; but how honourable he is in that, I know
not.

BAWD.

Pray you, without any more virginal fencing, will
you use him kindly? He will line your apron with
gold.

MARINA.

What he will do graciously, I will thankfully receive.

LYSIMACHUS.

Ha' you done?

BAWD.

My lord, she's not paced yet: you must take some
pains to work her to your manage.—Come, we
will leave his honour and her together.—Go thy
ways.   [*Exeunt* BAWD, PANDAR, *and* BOULT.

LYSIMACHUS.

Now, pretty one, how long have you been at this
trade?

MARINA.

What trade, sir?

LYSIMACHUS.

Why, I cannot name't but I shall offend.

MARINA.

I cannot be offended with my trade. Please you
to name it.

LYSIMACHUS.

How long have you been of this profession?

MARINA.

E'er since I can remember.

LYSIMACHUS.

Did you go to't so young? Were you a gamester
at five or at seven?

MARINA.

Earlier too, sir, if now I be one.

LYSIMACHUS.

Why, the house you dwell in proclaims you to be
a creature of sale.

MARINA.

Do you know this house to be a place of such resort, and will come into't? I hear say you are of

honourable parts, and are the governor of this
place.

LYSIMACHUS.

Why, hath your principal made known unto you
who I am?

MARINA.

Who is my principal?

LYSIMACHUS.

Why, your herb-woman; she that sets seeds and
roots of shame and iniquity. O, you have heard
something of my power, and so stand aloof for
more serious wooing. But I protest to thee,
pretty one, my authority shall not see thee, or
else look friendly upon thee. Come, bring me to
some private place: come, come.

MARINA.

If you were born to honour, show it now;
If put upon you, make the judgement good
That thought you worthy of it.

LYSIMACHUS.

How's this? how's this?—Some more;—be sage.

MARINA.

                   For me,
That am a maid, though most ungentle fortune
Have placed me in this sty, where, since I came,
Diseases have been sold dearer than physic,—
O, that the gods
Would set me free from this unhallow'd place,
Though they did change me to the meanest bird
That flies i'the purer air!

LYSIMACHUS.

             I did not think
Thou couldst have spoke so well; ne'er dreamt
    thou couldst.
Had I brought hither a corrupted mind,
Thy speech had alter'd it. Hold, here's gold for
    thee:
Persever in that clear way thou goest,
And the gods strengthen thee!

MARINA.

           The good gods preserve you!

LYSIMACHUS.

For me, be you thoughten
That I came with no ill intent; for to me
The very doors and windows savour vilely.
Fare thee well. Thou art a piece of virtue, and
I doubt not but thy training hath been noble.—
Hold, here's more gold for thee.—
A curse upon him, die he like a thief,
That robs thee of thy goodness! If thou dost
Hear from me, it shall be for thy good.

Enter BOULT.

BOULT.

I beseech your honour, one piece for me.

LYSIMACHUS.

Avaunt, thou damned doorkeeper!
Your house, but for this virgin that doth prop it,
Would sink, and overwhelm you. Away!   [*Exit.*

BOULT.

How's this? We must take another course with
you. If your peevish chastity, which is not worth
a breakfast in the cheapest country under the
cope, shall undo a whole household, let me be
gelded like a spaniel. Come your ways.

MARINA.

Whither would you have me?

BOULT.

I must have your maidenhead taken off, or the
common hangman shall execute it. Come your
ways. We'll have no more gentlemen driven
away. Come your ways, I say.

Enter BAWD.

BAWD.

How now! what's the matter?

BOULT.

Worse and worse, mistress; she has here spoken
holy words to the Lord Lysimachus.

BAWD.

O abominable!

BOULT.

She makes our profession as it were to stink afore
the face of the gods.

BAWD

Marry, hang her up for ever!

BOULT.

The nobleman would have dealt with her like a
nobleman, and she sent him away as cold as a
snowball; saying his prayers too.

BAWD.

Boult, take her away; use her at thy pleasure:
crack the glass of her virginity, and make the rest
malleable.

BOULT.

An if she were a thornier piece of ground than
she is, she shall be plough'd.

MARINA.

Hark, hark, you gods!

BAWD.

She conjures: away with her! Would she had
never come within my doors!—Marry, hang
you!—She's born to undo us.—Will you not go
the way of women-kind? Marry, come up, my
dish of chastity with rosemary and bays!   [*Exit.*

BOULT.

Come, mistress; come your ways with me.

MARINA.

Whither wilt thou have me?

BOULT.

To take from you the jewel you hold so dear.

MARINA.

Prithee, tell me one thing first.

BOULT.

Come now, your one thing.

MARINA.

What canst thou wish thine enemy to be?

BOULT.

Why, I could wish him to be my master, or
rather, my mistress.

MARINA.

Neither of these are so bad as thou art,
Since they do better thee in their command.
Thou hold'st a place, for which the pained'st
   fiend
Of hell would not in reputation change:
Thou art the damned doorkeeper to every
Coistrel that comes inquiring for his Tib;
To the choleric fisting of every rogue
Thy ear is liable; thy food is such
As hath been belcht on by infected lungs.

BOULT.

What would you have me do? go to the wars,
would you? where a man may serve seven years

for the loss of a leg, and have not money enough
in the end to buy him a wooden one?

MARINA.

Do anything but this thou doest. Empty
Old receptacles, or common shores, of filth;
Serve by indenture to the common hangman:
Any of these ways are yet better than this;
For what thou professest, a baboon, could he
   speak,
Would own a name too dear.—O, that the gods
Would safely deliver me from this place!—
Here, here's gold for thee.
If that thy master would gain by me,
Proclaim that I can sing, weave, sew, and dance,
With other virtues, which I'll keep from boast;
And I will undertake all these to teach.
I doubt not but this populous city will
Yield many scholars.

BOULT.

But can you teach all this you speak of?

MARINA.

Prove that I cannot, take me home again,
And prostitute me to the basest groom
That doth frequent your house.

BOULT.

Well, I will see what I can do for thee: if I can
place thee, I will.

MARINA.

But amongst honest women.

BOULT.

Faith, my acquaintance lies little amongst them.
But since my master and mistress have bought
you, there's no going but by their consent: therefore I will make them acquainted with your purpose, and I doubt not but I shall find them tractable enough. Come, I'll do for thee what I can;
come your ways.   [*Exeunt.*

ACT V.

Enter GOWER.

GOWER.

MARINA thus the brothel scapes, and chances
Into an honest house, our story says.
She sings like one immortal, and she dances
As goddess-like to her admired lays;
Deep clerks she dumbs; and with her needle com-
   poses
Nature's own shape, of bud, bird, branch, or
   berry,
That even her art sisters the natural roses;
Her inkle, silk, twin with the rubied cherry:
That pupils lacks she none of noble race,
Who pour their bounty on her; and her gain
She gives the cursed bawd. Here we her place;
And to her father turn our thoughts again,
Where we left him, on the sea. We there him lost:
Whence, driven before the winds, he is arrived
Here where his daughter dwells; and on this
   coast
Suppose him now at anchor. The city strived
God Neptune's annual feast to keep: from
   whence
Lysimachus our Tyrian ship espies,
His banners sable, trimm'd with rich expense;
And to him in his barge with fervour hies.

In your supposing once more put your sight
Of heavy Pericles; think this his bark:
Where what is done in action, more, if might,
Shall be discover'd; please you, sit, and hark.
                         [*Exit.*

SCENE I.

On board PERICLES' *ship, off Mytilene. A pavilion
on deck, with a curtain before it;* PERICLES *within it, reclined on a couch. A barge lying beside the
Tyrian vessel.*

Enter two SAILORS, *one belonging to the Tyrian
vessel, the other to the barge; to them* HELICANUS.

TYRIAN SAILOR [*to the* SAILOR *of Mytilene*].

WHERE is Lord Helicanus? he can resolve
     you. O, here he is.—Sir, there is a barge
put off from Mytilene, and in it is Lysimachus the
governor, who craves to come aboard. What is
your will?

HELICANUS.

That he have his. Call up some gentlemen.

TYRIAN SAILOR.

Ho, gentlemen! my lord calls.

Enter two or three GENTLEMEN.

FIRST GENTLEMAN.

Doth your lordship call?

HELICANUS.

Gentlemen, there is some of worth would come
aboard: I pray, greet him fairly.

     [*The* GENTLEMEN *and the two* SAILORS
        descend, and go on board the barge.
Enter, from thence, LYSIMACHUS *and* LORDS,
   with the GENTLEMEN *and the two* SAILORS.

TYRIAN SAILOR.

Sir, this is the man that can, in aught you would,
resolve you.

LYSIMACHUS.

Hail, reverend sir! the gods preserve you!

HELICANUS.

And you, sir, to outlive the age I am,
And die as I would do.

LYSIMACHUS.

              You wish me well.
Being on shore, honouring of Neptune's triumphs,
Seeing this goodly vessel ride before us,
I made to it, to know of whence you are.

HELICANUS.

First, what is your place?

LYSIMACHUS.

             I am the governor
Of this place you lie before.

HELICANUS.

Sir,
Our vessel is of Tyre, in it the king;
A man who for this three months hath not spoken
To any one, nor taken sustenance
But to prorogue his grief.

LYSIMACHUS.

Upon what ground is his distemperature?

HELICANUS.

'Twould be too tedious to repeat;
But the main grief springs from the loss
Of a beloved daughter and a wife.

LYSIMACHUS.

May we not see him?

HELICANUS.

You may;
But bootless is your sight,—he will not speak
To any.

LYSIMACHUS.

Yet let me obtain my wish.

HELICANUS.

Behold him. [*Draws the curtains, and discovers*
    PERICLES.] This was a goodly person,
Till the disaster that, one mortal night,
Drove him to this.

LYSIMACHUS.

Sir king, all hail! the gods preserve you!
Hail, royal sir!

HELICANUS.

It is in vain; he will not speak to you.

FIRST LORD.

Sir,
We have a maid in Mytilen, I durst wager,
Would win some words of him.

LYSIMACHUS.

              'Tis well bethought.
She, questionless, with her sweet harmony
And other chosen attractions, would allure,
And make a battery through his deafen'd parts,
Which now are midway stopt:
She is all happy as the fairest of all,
And, with her fellow maids, is now upon
The leafy shelter that abuts against
The island's side.

       [*Whispers* FIRST LORD; *who goes off in the
            barge of* LYSIMACHUS.

HELICANUS.

Sure, all's effectless; yet nothing we'll omit
That bears recovery's name. But, since your kind-
   ness
We have stretcht thus far, let us beseech you
That for our gold we may provision have,
Wherein we are not destitute for want,
But weary for the staleness.

LYSIMACHUS.

              O, sir, a courtesy
Which if we should deny, the most just gods
For every graff would send a caterpillar,
And so inflict our province.—Yet once more
Let me entreat to know at large the cause
Of your king's sorrow.

HELICANUS.

             Sit, sir: I will recount it to you:—
But, see, I am prevented.

Enter, from the barge, FIRST LORD, *with* MARINA
          and a young LADY.

LYSIMACHUS.

              O, here is
The lady that I sent for.—Welcome, fair one!—
Is't not a goodly presence?

HELICANUS.

              She's a gallant lady.

LYSIMACHUS.

She's such a one, that, were I well assured
Came of a gentle kind and noble stock,
I'ld wish no better choice, and think me rarely
   wed.—
Fair one, all goodness that consists in bounty
Expect even here, where is a kingly patient:
If that thy prosperous and artificial feat

Can draw him but to answer thee in aught,
Thy sacred physic shall receive such pay
As thy desires can wish.

MARINA.
Sir, I will use
My utmost skill in his recovery,
Provided
That none but I and my companion maid
Be suffer'd to come near him.

LYSIMACHUS.
Come, let's leave her;
And the gods make her prosperous!

[MARINA sings.

LYSIMACHUS.
Markt he your music?

MARINA.
No, nor lookt on us.

LYSIMACHUS.
See, she will speak to him.

MARINA.
Hail, sir! my lord, lend ear.

PERICLES.
Hum, ha!

MARINA.
I am a maid,
My lord, that ne'er before invited eyes,
But have been gazed on like a comet: she speaks,
My lord, that, may be, hath endured a grief
Might equal yours, if both were justly weigh'd.
Though wayward fortune did malign my state,
My derivation was from ancestors
Who stood equivalent with mighty kings:
But time hath rooted out my parentage,
And to the world and awkward casualties
Bound me in servitude.—[aside] I will desist;
But there is something glows upon my cheek,
And whispers in mine ear, 'Go not till he speak.'

PERICLES.
My fortunes—parentage—good parentage—
To equal mine!—was it not thus? what say you?

MARINA.
I said, my lord, if you did know my parentage,
You would not do me violence.

PERICLES.
I do think so.—Pray you, turn your eyes upon
me.
You are like something that—What country-
woman?
Here of these shores?

MARINA.
No, nor of any shores:
Yet I was mortally brought forth, and am
No other than I appear.

PERICLES.
I am great with woe, and shall deliver weeping.
My dearest wife was like this maid, and such a
one
My daughter might have been: my queen's square
brows;
Her stature to an inch; as wand-like straight;
As silver-voiced; her eyes as jewel-like,
And cased as richly; in pace another Juno;
Who starves the ears she feeds, and makes them
hungry,
The more she gives them speech.—Where do you
live?

MARINA.
Where I am but a stranger: from the deck
You may discern the place.

PERICLES.
Where were you bred?
And how achieved you these endowments, which
You make more rich to owe?

MARINA.
If I should tell my history, it would seem
Like lies disdain'd in the reporting.

PERICLES.
Prithee, speak:
Falseness cannot come from thee; for thou look'st
Modest as Justice, and thou seem'st a palace
For the crown'd Truth to dwell in: I will believe
thee,
And make my senses credit thy relation
To points that seem impossible; for thou look'st
Like one I loved indeed. What were thy friends?
Didst thou not say, when I did push thee back,—
Which was when I perceived thee,—that thou
camest
From good descending?

MARINA.
So indeed I did.

PERICLES.
Report thy parentage. I think thou said'st
Thou hadst been tost from wrong to injury,
And that thou thought'st thy griefs might equal
mine,
If both were open'd.

MARINA.
Some such thing
I said, and said no more but what my thoughts
Did warrant me was likely.

PERICLES.
Tell thy story;
If thine consider'd prove the thousandth part
Of my endurance, thou art a man, and I
Have suffer'd like a girl: yet thou dost look
Like Patience gazing on kings' graves, and smil-
ing
Extremity out of act. What were thy friends?
How lost thou them? Thy name, my most kind
virgin?
Recount, I do beseech thee: come, sit by me.

MARINA.
My name is Marina.

PERICLES.
O, I am mockt,
And thou by some incensed god sent hither
To make the world to laugh at me.

MARINA.
Patience, good sir,
Or here I'll cease.

PERICLES.
Nay, I'll be patient,
Thou little know'st how thou dost startle me,
To call thyself Marina.

MARINA.
The name
Was given me by one that had some power,—
My father, and a king.

PERICLES.
How! a king's daughter?
And call'd Marina?

MARINA.
      You said you would believe me;
But, not to be a troubler of your peace,
I will end here.

PERICLES.
      But are you flesh and blood?
Have you a working pulse? and are no fairy?
Motion!—Well; speak on. Where were you born?
And wherefore call'd Marina?

MARINA.
        Call'd Marina
For I was born at sea.

PERICLES.
      At sea! what mother?

MARINA.
My mother was the daughter of a king;
Who died the minute I was born,
As my good nurse Lychorida hath oft
Deliver'd weeping.

PERICLES.
      O, stop there a little!—
[aside] This is the rarest dream that e'er dull sleep
Did mock sad fools withal: this cannot be:
My daughter's buried.—Well:—where were you
 bred?
I'll hear you more, to the bottom of your story,
And never interrupt you.

MARINA.
You scorn: believe me, 'twere best I did give o'er.

PERICLES.
I will believe you by the syllable
Of what you shall deliver. Yet, give me leave:—
How came you in these parts? where were you
 bred?

MARINA.
The king my father did in Tarsus leave me;
Till cruel Cleon, with his wicked wife,
Did seek to murder me: and having woo'd
A villain to attempt it, who having drawn to do't,
A crew of pirates came and rescued me;
Brought me to Mytilene. But, good sir,
Whither will you have me? Why do you weep? It
 may be
You think me an impostor: no, good faith;
I am the daughter to King Pericles,
If good King Pericles be.

PERICLES.
Ho, Helicanus!

HELICANUS.
Calls my lord?

PERICLES.
Thou art a grave and noble counsellor,
Most wise in general: tell me, if thou canst,
What this maid is, or what is like to be,
That thus hath made me weep?

HELICANUS.
      I know not; but
Here is the regent, sir, of Mytilene
Speaks nobly of her.

LYSIMACHUS.
      She never would tell
Her parentage; being demanded that,
She would sit still and weep.

PERICLES.
O Helicanus, strike me, honour'd sir;
Give me a gash, put me to present pain;

Lest this great sea of joys rushing upon me
O'erbear the shores of my mortality,
And drown me with their sweetness.—O, come
 hither,
Thou that begett'st him that did thee beget;
Thou that wast born at sea, buried at Tarsus,
And found at sea again!—O Helicanus,
Down on thy knees, thank the holy gods as loud
As thunder threatens us: this is Marina.—
What was thy mother's name? tell me but that,
For truth can never be confirm'd enough,
Though doubts did ever sleep.

MARINA.
      First, sir, I pray,
What is your title?

PERICLES.
I am Pericles of Tyre: but tell me now
My drown'd queen's name, as in the rest you said
Thou hast been godlike perfect:
Be heir of kingdoms, and another life
To Pericles thy father.

MARINA.
Is it no more to be your daughter than
To say my mother's name was Thaisa?
Thaisa was my mother, who did end
The minute I began.

PERICLES.
Now, blessing on thee! rise; thou art my child.—
Give me fresh garments.—Mine own, Heli-
 canus,—
She is not dead at Tarsus, as she should have
 been,
By savage Cleon: she shall tell thee all;
When thou shalt kneel, and justify in knowledge
She is thy very princess.—Who is this?

HELICANUS.
Sir, 'tis the governor of Mytilene,
Who, hearing of your melancholy state,
Did come to see you.

PERICLES.
I embrace you.
Give me my robes.—I am wild in my beholding.—
O heavens bless my girl!—But, hark, what
 music?—
Tell Helicanus, my Marina, tell him
O'er, point by point, for yet he seems to doubt,
How sure you are my daughter.—But, what
 music?

HELICANUS.
My lord, I hear none.

PERICLES.
None!
The music of the spheres!—List, my Marina.

LYSIMACHUS.
It is not good to cross him; give him way.

PERICLES.
Rarest sounds! Do ye not hear?

LYSIMACHUS.
      My lord, I hear. [Music.

PERICLES.
Most heavenly music!
It nips me unto listening, and thick slumber
Hangs upon mine eyes: let me rest.   [Sleeps.

LYSIMACHUS.
A pillow for his head:—
So, leave him all.—Well, my companion friends,

If this but answer to my just belief,
I'll well remember you.

                [Exeunt all but PERICLES.
              DIANA *appears.*

DIANA.

My temple stands in Ephesus: hie thee thither,
And do upon mine altar sacrifice.
There, when my maiden priests are met together,
Before the people all,
Reveal how thou at sea didst lose thy wife:
To mourn thy crosses, with thy daughter's, call,
And give them repetition to the life.
Or perform my bidding, or thou livest in woe;
Do it, and happy; by my silver bow!
Awake, and tell thy dream.   *[Disappears.*

PERICLES.

Celestial Dian, goddess argentine,
I will obey thee.—Helicanus!

Enter HELICANUS, LYSIMACHUS, MARINA, &c.

HELICANUS.
              Sir?

PERICLES.

My purpose was for Tarsus, there to strike
The inhospitable Cleon; but I am
For other service first: toward Ephesus
Turn our blown sails; eftsoons I'll tell thee why.—
[to LYSIMACHUS] Shall we refresh us, sir, upon
    your shore,
And give you gold for such provision
As our intents will need?

LYSIMACHUS.

Sir,
With all my heart; and, when you come ashore,
I have another suit.

PERICLES.
           You shall prevail,
Were it to woo my daughter; for it seems
You have been noble towards her.

LYSIMACHUS.
             Sir, lend me your arm.

PERICLES.

Come, my Marina.   *[Exeunt.*
Enter GOWER, *before the temple of* DIANA *at*
        Ephesus.

GOWER.

Now our sands are almost run;
More a little, and then dumb.
This, my last boon, give me,—
For such kindness must relieve me,
That you aptly will suppose
What pageantry, what feats, what shows,
What minstrelsy, and pretty din,
The regent made in Mytilin,
To greet the king. So he thrived,
That he is promised to be wived
To fair Marina; but in no wise
Till he had done his sacrifice,
As Dian bade: whereto being bound,
The interim, pray you, all confound.
In feather'd briefness sails are fill'd,
And wishes fall out as they're will'd.
At Ephesus, the temple see,
Our king, and all his company.
That he can hither come so soon,
Is by your fancies' thankful doom.   *[Exit.*

SCENE II.

The temple of DIANA *at Ephesus;* THAISA *standing
near the altar, as high priestess; a number of* VIR-
GINS *on each side;* CERIMON *and other* INHABI-
TANTS *of Ephesus attending.*

Enter PERICLES, *with his Train;* LYSIMACHUS,
    HELICANUS, MARINA, *and a* LADY.

PERICLES.

HAIL, Dian! to perform thy just command,
    I here confess myself the king of Tyre;
Who, frighted from my country, did wed
At Pentapolis the fair Thaisa.
At sea in childbed died she, but brought forth
A maid-child call'd Marina; who, O goddess,
Wears yet thy silver livery. She at Tarsus
Was nurst with Cleon; who at fourteen years
He sought to murder: but her better stars
Brought her to Mytilene; 'gainst whose shore
Riding, her fortunes brought the maid aboard us,
Where, by her own most clear remembrance, she
Made known herself my daughter.

THAISA.
             Voice and favour!—
You are, you are—O royal Pericles!—   *[Faints.*

PERICLES.

What means the nun? she dies! help, gentlemen!

CERIMON.

Noble sir,
If you have told Diana's altar true,
This is your wife.

PERICLES.
           Reverend appearer, no;
I threw her overboard with these very arms.

CERIMON.

Upon this coast, I warrant you.

PERICLES.
             'Tis most certain.

CERIMON.

Look to the lady;—O, she's but overjoy'd.—
Early one blustering morn this lady was
Thrown upon this shore. I oped the coffin,
Found there rich jewels; recover'd her, and placed
    her
Here in Diana's temple.

PERICLES.
           May we see them?

CERIMON.

Great sir, they shall be brought you to my house,
Whither I invite you.—Look, Thaisa is
Recover'd.

THAISA.
        O, let me look!
If he be none of mine, my sanctity
Will to my sense bend no licentious ear,
But curb it, spite of seeing.—O, my lord,
Are you not Pericles? Like him you speak,
Like him you are: did you not name a tempest,
A birth, and death?

PERICLES.
         The voice of dead Thaisa!

THAISA.

That Thaisa am I, supposed dead
And drown'd.

PERICLES.

Immortal Dian!

THAISA.
Now I know you better.—
When we with tears parted Pentapolis,
The king my father gave you such a ring.
[Shows a ring.

PERICLES.
This, this: no more, you gods! your present kind-
ness
Makes my past miseries sport: you shall do well,
That on the touching of her lips I may
Melt, and no more be seen.—O, come, be buried
A second time within these arms.

MARINA.
My heart
Leaps to be gone into my mother's bosom.
[Kneels to THAISA.

PERICLES.
Look, who kneels here! Flesh of thy flesh, Thaisa;
Thy burden at the sea, and call'd Marina
For she was yielded there.

THAISA.
Blest, and mine own!

HELICANUS.
Hail, madam, and my queen!

THAISA.
I know you not.

PERICLES.
You have heard me say, when I did fly from Tyre,
I left behind an ancient substitute:
Can you remember what I call'd the man?
I have named him oft.

THAISA.
'Twas Helicanus, then.

PERICLES.
Still confirmation:
Embrace him, dear Thaisa; this is he.
Now do I long to hear how you were found;
How possibly preserved; and who to thank,
Besides the gods, for this great miracle.

THAISA.
Lord Cerimon, my lord; this is the man,
Through whom the gods have shown their power,
  that can
From first to last resolve you.

PERICLES.
Reverend sir,
The gods can have no mortal officer
More like a god than you. Will you deliver
How this dead queen re-lives?

CERIMON.
I will, my lord.
Beseech you, first go with me to my house,
Where shall be shown you all was found with her;
How she came placed here in the temple;
No needful thing omitted.

PERICLES.
Pure Dian, bless thee for thy vision! I
Will offer night-oblations to thee,—Thaisa,
This prince, the fair-betrothed of your daughter,
Shall marry her at Pentapolis.—And now,
This ornament
Makes me look dismal will I clip to form;
And what this fourteen years no razor toucht,
To grace thy marriage-day, I'll beautify.

THAISA.
Lord Cerimon hath letters of good credit, sir,
My father's dead.

PERICLES.
Heavens make a star of him! Yet there, my
  queen,
We'll celebrate their nuptials, and ourselves
Will in that kingdom spend our following days:
Our son and daughter shall in Tyrus reign.—
Lord Cerimon, we do our longing stay
To hear the rest untold: sir, lead's the way.
[Exeunt.

Enter GOWER.

GOWER.
In Antiochus and his daughter you have heard
Of monstrous lust the due and just reward:
In Pericles, his queen and daughter, seen,
Although assail'd with fortune fierce and keen,
Virtue preserved from fell destruction's blast,
Led on by heaven, and crown'd with joy at last:
In Helicanus may you well descry
A figure of truth, of faith, of loyalty:
In reverend Cerimon there well appears
The worth that learned charity aye wears:
For wicked Cleon and his wife, when fame
Had spread their cursed deed, and honour'd
  name
Of Pericles, to rage the city turn,
That him and his they in his palace burn;
The gods for murder seemed so content
To punish them,—although not done, but meant.
So, on your patience evermore attending,
New joy wait on you! Here our play has ending.
[Exit·

CYMBELINE

DRAMATIS PERSONAE

CYMBELINE, *King of Britain.*
CLOTEN, *son to the Queen by a former husband.*
POSTHUMUS LEONATUS, *a gentleman, husband to Imogen.*
BELARIUS, *a banisht lord, disguised under the name of Morgan.*
GUIDERIUS, } *sons to Cymbeline, disguised under*
ARVIRAGUS, } *the names of Polydore and Cadwal, supposed sons of Belarius.*
PHILARIO, *friend to Posthumus,* } *Italians.*
IACHIMO, *friend to Philario,* }
A FRENCH GENTLEMAN, *friend to Philario.*
CAIUS LUCIUS, *general of the Roman forces.*
A ROMAN CAPTAIN.
TWO BRITISH CAPTAINS.
PISANIO, *servant to Posthumus.*
CORNELIUS, *a physician.*

TWO LORDS *of Cymbeline's court.*
TWO GENTLEMEN *of the same.*
TWO GAOLERS.

QUEEN, *wife to Cymbeline.*
IMOGEN, *daughter to Cymbeline by a former Queen.*
HELEN, *woman to Imogen.*

LORDS, LADIES, ROMAN SENATORS, TRIBUNES, *a* SOOTHSAYER, *a* DUTCH GENTLEMAN, *a* SPANISH GENTLEMAN, MUSICIANS, OFFICERS, CAPTAINS, SOLDIERS, MESSENGERS, *and* ATTENDANTS.

APPARITIONS.

SCENE—*Sometimes in Britain, sometimes in Italy.*

ACT I. SCENE I.

Britain.   The garden of CYMBELINE'S *palace.*

Enter two GENTLEMEN.

FIRST GENTLEMAN.

YOU do not meet a man but frowns: our bloods
No more obey the heavens than our courtiers
Still seem as does the king.

SECOND GENTLEMAN.
But what's the matter?

FIRST GENTLEMAN.
His daughter, and the heir of's kingdom, whom
He purposed to his wife's sole son—a widow
That late he married—hath referr'd herself
Unto a poor but worthy gentleman: she's wedded;
Her husband banisht; she imprison'd: all
Is outward sorrow; though, I think, the king
Be toucht at very heart.

SECOND GENTLEMAN.
None but the king?

FIRST GENTLEMAN.
He that hath lost her too: so is the queen,
That most desired the match: but not a courtier,
Although they wear their faces to the bent
Of the king's looks, hath a heart that is not
Glad at the thing they scowl at.

SECOND GENTLEMAN.
And why so?

FIRST GENTLEMAN.
He that hath mist the princess is a thing
Too bad for bad report: and he that hath her—
I mean, that married her, alack, good man!
And therefore banisht—is a creature such
As, to seek through the regions of the earth
For one his like, there would be something failing
In him that should compare:—I do not think
So fair an outward, and such stuff within,
Endows a man but he.

SECOND GENTLEMAN.
You speak him far.

FIRST GENTLEMAN.
I do extend him, sir, within himself;
Crush him together, rather than unfold
His measure duly.

SECOND GENTLEMAN.
What's his name and birth?

FIRST GENTLEMAN.
I cannot delve him to the root: his father
Was call'd Sicilius, who did join his honour
Against the Romans with Cassibelan,
But had his titles by Tenantius, whom
He served with glory and admired success,—
So gain'd the sur-addition Leonatus:
And had, besides this gentleman in question,
Two other sons, who, in the wars o'the time,
Died with their swords in hand; for which their father,
Then old and fond of issue, took such sorrow,
That he quit being; and his gentle lady,
Big of this gentleman our theme, deceased
As he was born. The king he takes the babe
To his protection; calls him Posthumus Leonatus;
Breeds him, and makes him of his bed-chamber;
Puts to him all the learnings that his time
Could make him the receiver of; which he took,
As we do air, fast as 'twas minister'd;
And in's spring became a harvest; lived in court—
Which rare it is to do—most praised, most loved;
A sample to the youngest; to the more mature
A glass that feated them; and to the graver
A child that guided dotards: to his mistress,
For whom he now is banisht,—her own price
Proclaims how she esteem'd him and his virtue;
By her election may be truly read
What kind of man he is.

SECOND GENTLEMAN.
I honour him
Even out of your report. But, pray you, tell me,
Is she sole child to the king?

FIRST GENTLEMAN.
His only child.
He had two sons,—if this be worth your hearing,
Mark it,—the eldest of them at three years old,
I'the swathing-clothes the other, from their nursery
Were stoln; and to this hour no guess in knowledge
Which way they went.

SECOND GENTLEMAN.
                    How long is this ago?
            FIRST GENTLEMAN.
Some twenty years.
            SECOND GENTLEMAN.
That a king's children should be so convey'd!
So slackly guarded! and the search so slow,
That could not trace them!
            FIRST GENTLEMAN.
                    Howsoe'er 'tis strange,
Or that the negligence may well be laught at,
Yet is it true, sir.
            SECOND GENTLEMAN.
                    I do well believe you.
            FIRST GENTLEMAN.
We must forbear: here comes the gentleman,
The queen, and princess.   [Exeunt.
Enter the QUEEN, POSTHUMUS, and IMOGEN.
                    QUEEN.
No, be assured you shall not find me, daughter,
After the slander of most stepmothers,
Evil-eyed unto you: you're my prisoner, but
Your gaoler shall deliver you the keys
That lock up your restraint.—For you, Posthu-
    mus,
So soon as I can win the offended king,
I will be known your advocate: marry, yet
The fire of rage is in him; and 'twere good
You lean'd unto his sentence with what patience
Your wisdom may inform you.
            POSTHUMUS LEONATUS.
                    Please your highness,
I will from hence to-day.
                    QUEEN.
                    You know the peril.—
I'll fetch a turn about the garden, pitying
The pangs of barr'd affections; though the king
Hath charged you should not speak together.
                                            [Exit.
            IMOGEN.
                                            O
Dissembling courtesy! How fine this tyrant
Can tickle where she wounds!—My dearest hus-
    band,
I something fear my father's wrath; but nothing—
Always reserved my holy duty—what
His rage can do on me: you must be gone;
And I shall here abide the hourly shot
Of angry eyes; not comforted to live,
But that there is this jewel in the world,
That I may see again.
            POSTHUMUS LEONATUS.
                    My queen! my mistress!
O lady, weep no more, lest I give cause
To be suspected of more tenderness
Than doth become a man! I will remain
The loyal'st husband that did e'er plight troth:
My residence in Rome at one Philario's;
Who to my father was a friend, to me
Known but by letter: thither write, my queen,
And with mine eyes I'll drink the words you send,
Though ink be made of gall.
            Enter QUEEN.
                    QUEEN.
                    Be brief, I pray you:
If the king come, I shall incur I know not

How much of his displeasure.—[aside] Yet I'll
    move him
To walk this way: I never do him wrong,
But he does buy my injuries, to be friends;
Pays dear for my offences.   [Exit.
            POSTHUMUS LEONATUS.
                    Should we be taking leave
As long a term as yet we have to live,
The loathness to depart would grow. Adieu!
            IMOGEN.
Nay, stay a little:
Were you but riding forth to air yourself,
Such parting were too petty. Look here, love;
This diamond was my mother's: take it, heart;
But keep it till you woo another wife,
When Imogen is dead.
            POSTHUMUS LEONATUS.
                    How, how! another?—
You gentle gods, give me but this I have,
And sear up my embracements from a next
With bonds of death!—Remain, remain thou here
                        [Putting on the ring.
While sense can keep it on! And, sweetest,
    fairest,
As I my poor self did exchange for you,
To your so infinite loss; so in our trifles
I still win of you: for my sake wear this;
It is a manacle of love; I'll place it
Upon this fairest prisoner.
            [Putting a bracelet upon her arm.
            IMOGEN.
                    O the gods!
When shall we see again?
            POSTHUMUS LEONATUS.
                    Alack, the king!
            Enter CYMBELINE and LORDS.
            CYMBELINE.
Thou basest thing, avoid! hence, from my sight!
If after this command thou fraught the court
With thy unworthiness, thou diest: away!
Thou'rt poison to my blood.
            POSTHUMUS LEONATUS.
                    The gods protect you!
And bless the good remainders of the court!
I am gone.   [Exit.
            IMOGEN.
                    There cannot be a pinch in death
More sharp than this is.
            CYMBELINE.
                    O disloyal thing,
That shouldst repair my youth, thou heap'st
A year's age on me!
            IMOGEN.
                    I beseech you, sir,
Harm not yourself with your vexation:
I am senseless of your wrath; a touch more rare
Subdues all pangs, all fears.
            CYMBELINE.
                    Past grace? obedience?
            IMOGEN.
Past hope, and in despair; that way, past grace.
            CYMBELINE.
That mightst have had the sole son of my queen!
            IMOGEN.
O blest, that I might not! I chose an eagle,
And did avoid a puttock.

CYMBELINE.
Thou took'st a beggar; wouldst have made my throne
A seat for baseness.

IMOGEN.
　　　　　No; I rather added
A lustre to it.

CYMBELINE.
　　　　O thou vile one!

IMOGEN.
　　　　　　　Sir,
It is your fault that I have loved Posthumus:
You bred him as my playfellow; and he is
A man worth any woman; overbuys me
Almost the sum he pays.

CYMBELINE.
　　　　　What, art thou mad!

IMOGEN.
Almost, sir: heaven restore me!—Would I were
A neat-herd's daughter, and my Leonatus
Our neighbour shepherd's son!

CYMBELINE.
　　　　　　Thou foolish thing!—
Enter QUEEN.
They were again together: you have done
Not after our command. Away with her,
And pen her up.

QUEEN.
　　　　　Beseech your patience.—Peace,
Dear lady daughter, peace!—Sweet sovereign,
Leave us to ourselves; and make yourself some
　　comfort
Out of your best advice.

CYMBELINE.
　　　　　Nay, let her languish
A drop of blood a day; and, being aged,
Die of this folly!
　　　　[Exeunt CYMBELINE and LORDS.

QUEEN.
　　　　　Fie! you must give way.
Enter PISANIO.
Here is your servant.—How now, sir! What news?

PISANIO.
My lord your son drew on my master.

QUEEN.
　　　　　　　　　　　Ha!
No harm, I trust, is done?

PISANIO.
　　　　　　There might have been,
But that my master rather play'd than fought,
And had no help of anger: they were parted
By gentlemen at hand.

QUEEN.
　　　　I am very glad on't.

IMOGEN.
Your son's my father's friend; he takes his part.—
To draw upon an exile!—O brave sir!—
I would they were in Afric both together;
Myself by with a needle, that I might prick
The goer-back.—Why came you from your
　　master?

PISANIO.
On his command: he would not suffer me
To bring him to the haven; left these notes
Of what commands I should be subject to,
When't pleased you to employ me.

QUEEN.
　　　　　　　This hath been
Your faithful servant: I dare lay mine honour
He will remain so.

PISANIO.
　　　I humbly thank your highness.

QUEEN.
Pray, walk awhile.

IMOGEN.
　　　About some half-hour hence,
I pray you, speak with me: you shall at least
Go see my lord aboard: for this time leave me.
　　　　　　　　　[Exeunt.

SCENE II.

The same.　A public place.

Enter CLOTEN *and two* LORDS.

FIRST LORD.
SIR, I would advise you to shift a shirt; the violence of action hath made you reek as a sacrifice: where air comes out, air comes in: there's none abroad so wholesome as that you vent.

CLOTEN.
If my shirt were bloody, then to shift it.—Have I hurt him?

SECOND LORD [aside].
No, faith; not so much as his patience.

FIRST LORD.
Hurt him! his body's a passable carcass, if he be not hurt: it is a thoroughfare for steel, if it be not hurt.

SECOND LORD [aside].
His steel was in debt; it went o'the backside the town.

CLOTEN.
The villain would not stand me.

SECOND LORD [aside].
No; but he fled forward still, toward your face.

FIRST LORD.
Stand you! You have land enough of your own: but he added to your having; gave you some ground.

SECOND LORD [aside].
As many inches as you have oceans.—Puppies!

CLOTEN.
I would they had not come between us.

SECOND LORD [aside].
So would I, till you had measured how long a fool you were upon the ground.

CLOTEN.
And that she should love this fellow, and refuse me!

SECOND LORD [aside].
If it be a sin to make a true election, she is damn'd.

FIRST LORD.
Sir, as I told you always, her beauty and her brain go not together: she's a good sign, but I have seen small reflection of her wit.

SECOND LORD [aside].
She shines not upon fools, lest the reflection should hurt her.

CLOTEN.
Come, I'll to my chamber. Would there had been some hurt done!

SECOND LORD [*aside*].
I wish not so; unless it had been the fall of an ass,
which is no great hurt.
CLOTEN.
You'll go with us?
SECOND LORD.
I'll attend your lordship.
CLOTEN.
Nay, come, let's go together.
SECOND LORD.
Well, my lord.   [*Exeunt.*

SCENE III.

A room in CYMBELINE'S *palace.*

Enter IMOGEN *and* PISANIO.

IMOGEN.
I WOULD thou grew'st unto the shores o'the
haven,
And question'dst every sail: if he should write,
And I not have it, 'twere a paper lost,
As offer'd mercy is. What was the last
That he spake to thee?
PISANIO.
It was, 'His queen, his queen!'
IMOGEN.
Then waved his handkerchief?
PISANIO.
And kist it, madam.
IMOGEN.
Senseless linen! happier therein than I!—
And that was all?
PISANIO.
No, madam; for so long
As he could make me with this eye or ear
Distinguish him from others, he did keep
The deck, with glove, or hat, or handkerchief,
Still waving, as the fits and stirs of's mind
Could best express how slow his soul sail'd on,
How swift his ship.
IMOGEN.
Thou shouldst have made him
As little as a crow, or less, ere left
To after-eye him.
PISANIO.
Madam, so I did.
IMOGEN.
I would have broke mine eye-strings; crackt them,
but
To look upon him; till the diminution
Of space had pointed him sharp as my needle;
Nay, follow'd him, till he had melted from
The smallness of a gnat to air; and then
Have turn'd mine eye, and wept.—But, good
Pisanio,
When shall we hear from him?
PISANIO.
Be assured, madam,
With his next vantage.
IMOGEN.
I did not take my leave of him, but had
Most pretty things to say: ere I could tell him
How I would think on him, at certain hours,
Such thoughts and such; or I could make him
swear
The shes of Italy should not betray

Mine interest and his honour; or have charged him,
At the sixth hour of morn, at noon, at midnight,
T'encounter me with orisons, for then
I am in heaven for him; or ere I could
Give him that parting kiss which I had set
Betwixt two charming words, comes in my father,
And, like the tyrannous breathing of the north,
Shakes all our buds from growing.

Enter a LADY.

LADY.
The queen, madam,
Desires you highness' company.
IMOGEN.
Those things I bid you do, get them dispatcht.—
I will attend the queen.
PISANIO.
Madam, I shall.   [*Exeunt.*

SCENE IV.

Rome. PHILARIO'S *house.*

Enter PHILARIO, IACHIMO, *a* FRENCHMAN, *a*
DUTCHMAN, *and a* SPANIARD.

IACHIMO.
BELIEVE it, sir, I have seen him in Britain:
he was then of a crescent note; expected to
prove so worthy as since he hath been allow'd the
name of: but I could then have lookt on him without the help of admiration, though the catalogue
of his endowments had been tabled by his side,
and I to peruse him by items.
PHILARIO.
You speak of him when he was less furnisht than
now he is with that which makes him both without and within.
FRENCHMAN.
I have seen him in France: we had very many
there could behold the sun with as firm eyes as he.
IACHIMO.
This matter of marrying his king's daughter—
wherein he must be weigh'd rather by her value
than his own—words him, I doubt not, a great
deal from the matter.
FRENCHMAN.
And then his banishment,—
IACHIMO.
Ay, and the approbation of those that weep this
lamentable divorce under her colours are wonder-
fully to extend him; be it but to fortify her judgement, which else an easy battery might lay flat,
for taking a beggar without less quality. But how
comes it he is to sojourn with you? how creeps acquaintance?
PHILARIO.
His father and I were soldiers together; to whom
I have been often bound for no less than my life.
—Here comes the Briton: let him be so entertain'd amongst you as suits, with gentlemen of
your knowing, to a stranger of his quality.

Enter POSTHUMUS.

I beseech you all, be better known to this gentleman; whom I commend to you as a noble friend
of mine: how worthy he is I will leave to appear
hereafter, rather than story him in his own hearing.

FRENCHMAN.
Sir, we have known together in Orleans.

POSTHUMUS LEONATUS.
Since when I have been debtor to you for courtesies, which I will be ever to pay, and yet pay still.

FRENCHMAN.
Sir, you o'er-rate my poor kindness: I was glad I did atone my countryman and you; it had been pity you should have been put together with so mortal a purpose as then each bore, upon importance of so slight and trivial a nature.

POSTHUMUS LEONATUS.
By your pardon, sir, I was then a young traveller; rather shunn'd to go even with what I heard than in my every action to be guided by others' experiences: but, upon my mended judgement,—if I offend not to say it is mended,—my quarrel was not altogether slight.

FRENCHMAN.
Faith, yes, to be put to the arbitrement of swords; and by such two that would, by all likelihood, have confounded one the other, or have faln both.

IACHIMO.
Can we, with manners, ask what was the difference?

FRENCHMAN.
Safely, I think: 'twas a contention in public, which may, without contradiction, suffer the report. It was much like an argument that fell out last night, where each of us fell in praise of our country mistresses; this gentleman at that time vouching, and upon warrant of bloody affirmation, his to be more fair, virtuous, wise, chaste, constant-qualified, and less attemptable, than any the rarest of our ladies in France.

IACHIMO.
That lady is not now living; or this gentleman's opinion, by this, worn out.

POSTHUMUS LEONATUS.
She holds her virtue still, and I my mind.

IACHIMO.
You must not so far prefer her fore ours of Italy.

POSTHUMUS LEONATUS.
Being so far provoked as I was in France, I would abate her nothing; though I profess myself her adorer, not her friend.

IACHIMO.
As fair and as good—a kind of hand-in-hand comparison—had been something too fair and too good for any lady in Britany. If she went before others I have seen, as that diamond of yours outlustres many I have beheld, I could not but believe she excell'd many: but I have not seen the most precious diamond that is, nor you the lady.

POSTHUMUS LEONATUS.
I praised her as I rated her: so do I my stone.

IACHIMO.
What do you esteem it at?

POSTHUMUS LEONATUS.
More than the world enjoys.

IACHIMO.
Either your unparagon'd mistress is dead, or she's outprized by a trifle.

POSTHUMUS LEONATUS.
You are mistaken: the one may be sold, or given, or if there were wealth enough for the purchase, or merit for the gift: the other is not a thing for sale, and only the gift of the gods.

IACHIMO.
Which the gods have given you?

POSTHUMUS LEONATUS.
Which, by their graces, I will keep.

IACHIMO.
You may wear her in title yours: but, you know, strange fowl light upon neighbouring ponds. Your ring may be stoln too: so, your brace of unprizable estimations, the one is but frail, and the other casual; a cunning thief, or a that-way-accomplisht courtier, would hazard the winning both of first and last.

POSTHUMUS LEONATUS.
Your Italy contains none so accomplisht a courtier to convince the honour of my mistress; if, in the holding or loss of that, you term her frail. I do nothing doubt you have store of thieves; notwithstanding, I fear not my ring.

PHILARIO.
Let us leave here, gentlemen.

POSTHUMUS LEONATUS.
Sir, with all my heart. This worthy signior, I thank him, makes no stranger of me; we are familiar at first.

IACHIMO.
With five times so much conversation, I should get ground of your fair mistress; make her go back, even to the yielding, had I admittance, and opportunity to friend.

POSTHUMUS LEONATUS.
No, no.

IACHIMO.
I dare thereupon pawn the moiety of my estate to your ring; which, in my opinion, o'ervalues it something: but I make my wager rather against your confidence than her reputation; and, to bar your offence herein too, I durst attempt it against any lady in the world.

POSTHUMUS LEONATUS.
You are a great deal abused in too bold a persuasion; and I doubt not you sustain what y'are worthy of by your attempt.

IACHIMO.
What's that?

POSTHUMUS LEONATUS.
A repulse: though your attempt, as you call it, deserve more,—a punishment too.

PHILARIO.
Gentlemen, enough of this: it came in too suddenly; let it die as it was born, and, I pray you, be better acquainted.

IACHIMO.
Would I had put my estate and my neighbour's on the approbation of what I have spoke!

POSTHUMUS LEONATUS.
What lady would you choose to assail?

IACHIMO.
Yours; whom in constancy you think stands so safe. I will lay you ten thousand ducats to your ring, that, commend me to the court where your lady is, with no more advantage than the opportunity of a second conference, and I will bring from thence that honour of hers which you imagine so reserved.

POSTHUMUS LEONATUS.

I will wage against your gold, gold to it: my ring
I hold dear as my finger; 'tis part of it.

IACHIMO.

You are afraid, and therein the wiser. If you buy
ladies' flesh at a million a dram, you cannot preserve it from tainting: but I see you have some
religion in you, that you fear.

POSTHUMUS LEONATUS.

This is but a custom in your tongue; you bear a
graver purpose, I hope.

IACHIMO.

I am the master of my speeches; and would undergo what's spoken, I swear.

POSTHUMUS LEONATUS.

Will you?—I shall but lend my diamond till your
return:—let there be covenants drawn between's:
my mistress exceeds in goodness the hugeness of
your unworthy thinking: I dare you to this match:
here's my ring.

PHILARIO.

I will have it no lay.

IACHIMO.

By the gods, it is one.—If I bring you no sufficient
testimony that I have enjoy'd the dearest bodily
part of your mistress, my ten thousand ducats are
yours; so is your diamond too: if I come off, and
leave her in such honour as you have trust in, she
your jewel, this your jewel, and my gold are yours;
provided I have your commendation for my more
free entertainment.

POSTHUMUS LEONATUS.

I embrace these conditions; let us have articles
betwixt us.—Only, thus far you shall answer: if
you make your voyage upon her, and give me
directly to understand you have prevail'd, I am
no further your enemy; she is not worth our debate: if she remain unseduced,—you not making
it appear otherwise,—for your ill opinion, and the
assault you have made to her chastity, you shall
answer me with your sword.

IACHIMO.

Your hand,—a covenant: we will have these things
set down by lawful counsel, and straight away for
Britain, lest the bargain should catch cold and
starve: I will fetch my gold, and have our two
wagers recorded.

POSTHUMOUS LEONATUS.

Agreed.   [*Exeunt* POSTHUMUS *and* IACHIMO.

FRENCHMAN.

Will this hold, think you?

PHILARIO.

Signior Iachimo will not from it. Pray, let us
follow 'em.   [*Exeunt.*

SCENE V.

Britain. A room in CYMBELINE'S *palace.*

Enter QUEEN, LADIES, *and* CORNELIUS.

QUEEN.

WHILES yet the dew's on ground, gather
    those flowers;
Make haste: who has the note of them?

FIRST LADY.

                      I, madam.

QUEEN.

Dispatch.—   [*Exeunt* LADIES.
Now, master doctor, have you brought those
    drugs?

CORNELIUS.

Pleaseth your highness, ay: here they are, madam:
                [*Presenting a small box.*
But I beseech your Grace, without offence,—
My conscience bids me ask,—wherefore you
    have
Commanded of me these most poisonous com-
    pounds,
Which are the movers of a languishing death;
But, though slow, deadly?

QUEEN.

              I wonder, doctor,
Thou ask'st me such a question. Have I not been
Thy pupil long? Hast thou not learn'd me how
To make perfumes? distil? preserve? yea, so
That our great king himself doth woo me oft
For my confections? Having thus far proceeded,
Unless thou think'st me devilish,—is't not meet
That I did amplify my judgement in
Other conclusions? I will try the forces
Of these thy compounds on such creatures as
We count not worth the hanging,—but none
    human,—
To try the vigour of them, and apply
Allayments to their act; and by them gather
Their several virtues and effects.

CORNELIUS.

                Your highness
Shall from this practice but make hard your heart:
Besides, the seeing these effects will be
Both noisome and infectious.

QUEEN.

             O, content thee.—
[*aside*] Here comes a flattering rascal; upon him
Will I first work: he's for his master,
And enemy to my son.—

            Enter PISANIO.

            How now, Pisanio!—
Doctor, your service for this time is ended;
Take your own way.

CORNELIUS [*aside*].

           I do suspect you, madam;
But you shall do no harm.

QUEEN [*to* PISANIO].

            Hark thee, a word.

CORNELIUS [*aside*].

I do not like her. She doth think she has
Strange lingering poisons: I do know her spirit,
And will not trust one of her malice with
A drug of such damn'd nature. Those she has
Will stupefy and dull the sense awhile;
Which first, perchance, she'll prove on cats and
    dogs,
Then afterward up higher: but there is
No danger in what show of death it makes,
More than the locking-up the spirits a time,
To be more fresh, reviving. She is fool'd
With a most false effect; and I the truer,
So to be false with her.

QUEEN.

       No further service, doctor,
Until I send for thee

CORNELIUS.
             I humbly take my leave. [*Exit.*
             QUEEN.
Weeps she still, say'st thou? Dost thou think in
             time
She will not quench, and let instructions enter
Where folly now possesses? Do thou work:
When thou shalt bring me word she loves my son,
I'll tell thee on the instant thou art then
As great as is thy master; greater,—for
His fortunes all lie speechless, and his name
Is at last gasp: return he cannot, nor
Continue where he is: to shift his being
Is to exchange one misery with another;
And every day that comes comes to decay
A day's work in him. What shalt thou expect,
To be depender on a thing that leans,—
Who cannot be new built, nor has no friends,
             [*The* QUEEN *drops the box:* PISANIO *takes it up.*
So much as but to prop him?—Thou takest up
Thou know'st not what; but take it for thy labour:
It is a thing I made, which hath the king
Five times redeem'd from death: I do not know
What is more cordial:—nay, I prithee, take it;
It is an earnest of a further good
That I mean to thee. Tell thy mistress how
The case stands with her; do't as from thyself.
Think what a chance thou chancest on; but think
Thou hast thy mistress still,—to boot, my son,
Who shall take notice of thee: I'll move the king
To any shape of thy preferment, such
As thou'lt desire; and then myself, I chiefly,
That set thee on to this desert, am bound
To load thy merit richly. Call my women:
Think on my words.   [*Exit* PISANIO.
             A sly and constant knave;
Not to be shaked; the agent for his master;
And the remembrancer of her to hold
The hand-fast to her lord.—I have given him that,
Which, if he take, shall quite unpeople her
Of liegers for her sweet; and which she after,
Except she bend her humour, shall be assured
To taste of too.
             Enter PISANIO *and* LADIES.
             So, so;—well done, well done:
The violets, cowslips, and the primroses,
Bear to my closet.—Fare thee well, Pisanio;
Think on my words.
             [*Exeunt* QUEEN *and* LADIES.
             PISANIO.
             And shall do:
But when to my good lord I prove untrue,
I'll choke myself: there's all I'll do for you. [*Exit.*

SCENE VI.

Another room in the palace.

Enter IMOGEN.

IMOGEN.
A FATHER cruel, and a step-dame false;
   A foolish suitor to a wedded lady,
That hath her husband banisht;—O, that husband!
My supreme crown of grief! and those repeated
Vexations of it! Had I been thief-stoln,
As my two brothers, happy! but most miserable
Is the desire that's glorious: blest be those,

How mean soe'er, that have their honest wills,
Which seasons comfort.—Who may this be? Fie!
   Enter PISANIO *and* IACHIMO.
             PISANIO.
Madam, a noble gentleman of Rome
Comes from my lord with letters.
             IACHIMO.
                      Change you, madam?
The worthy Leonatus is in safety,
And greets your highness dearly.
             [*Presents a letter.*
             IMOGEN.
                      Thanks, good sir:
You're kindly welcome.
             IACHIMO [*aside*].
All of her that is out of door most rich!
If she be furnisht with a mind so rare,
She is alone the Arabian bird; and I
Have lost the wager. Boldness be my friend!
Arm me, audacity, from head to foot!
Or, like the Parthian, I shall flying fight;
Rather, directly fly.
             IMOGEN [*reads*].
He is one of the noblest note, to whose kind-
nesses I am most infinitely tied. Reflect upon him
accordingly, as you value your trust—LEONATUS.
So far I read aloud:
But even the very middle of my heart
Is warm'd by the rest, and takes it thankfully.—
You are as welcome, worthy sir, as I
Have words to bid you; and shall find it so,
In all that I can do.
             IACHIMO.
             Thanks, fairest lady.—
What, are men mad? Hath nature given them eyes
To see this vaulted arch, and the rich crop
Of sea and land, which can distinguish 'twixt
The fiery orbs above, and the twinn'd stones
Upon the unnumber'd beach? and can we not
Partition make with spectacles so precious
'Twixt fair and foul?
             IMOGEN.
             What makes your admiration?
             IACHIMO.
It cannot be i'the eye; for apes and monkeys,
'Twixt two such shes, would chatter this way, and
Contemn with mows the other: nor i'the judge-
             ment;
For idiots, in this case of favour, would
Be wisely definite: nor i'the appetite;
Sluttery, to such neat excellence opposed,
Should make desire vomit emptiness,
Not so allured to feed.
             IMOGEN.
What is the matter, trow?
             IACHIMO.
             The cloyed will,—
That satiate yet unsatisfied desire, that tub
Both fill'd and running,—ravening first the lamb,
Longs after for the garbage.
             IMOGEN.
             What, dear sir,
Thus raps you? Are you well?
             IACHIMO.
Thanks, madam; well.—[*to* PISANIO] Beseech
you, sir,

Desire my man's abode where I did leave him:
He's strange and peevish.
PISANIO.
I was going, sir,
To give him welcome.   [*Exit.*
IMOGEN.
Continues well my lord? His health, beseech you?
IACHIMO.
Well, madam.
IMOGEN.
Is he disposed to mirth? I hope he is.
IACHIMO.
Exceeding pleasant; none a stranger there
So merry and so gamesome: he is call'd
The Briton reveller.
IMOGEN.
When he was here
He did incline to sadness, and oft-times
Not knowing why.
IACHIMO.
I never saw him sad.
There is a Frenchman his companion, one
An eminent monsieur, that, it seems, much loves
A Gallian girl at home; he furnaces
The thick sighs from him; whiles the jolly
    Briton—
Your lord, I mean—laughs from's free lungs,
    cries 'O,
Can my sides hold, to think that man—who knows
By history, report, or his own proof,
What woman is, yea, what she cannot choose
But must be—will his free hours languish for
Assured bondage?'
IMOGEN.
Will my lord say so?
IACHIMO.
Ay, madam; with his eyes in flood with laughter:
It is a recreation to be by,
And hear him mock the Frenchman. But, heavens
    know,
Some men are much to blame.
IMOGEN.
Not he, I hope.
IACHIMO.
Not he: but yet heaven's bounty towards him
    might
Be used more thankfully. In himself, 'tis much;
In you, which I account his, beyond all talents.
Whilst I am bound to wonder, I am bound
To pity too.
IMOGEN.
What do you pity, sir?
IACHIMO.
Two creatures heartily.
IMOGEN.
Am I one, sir?
You look on me: what wrack discern you in me
Deserves your pity?
IACHIMO.
Lamentable! What,
To hide me from the radiant sun, and solace
I'the dungeon by a snuff?
IMOGEN.
I pray you, sir,
Deliver with more openness your answers
To my demands. Why do you pity me?

IACHIMO.
That others do—
I was about to say—enjoy your—But
It is an office of the gods to venge it,
Not mine to speak on't.
IMOGEN.
You do seem to know
Something of me, or what concerns me: pray
    you—
Since doubting things go ill often hurts more
Than to be sure they do; for certainties
Either are past remedies, or, timely knowing,
The remedy then born—discover to me
What both you spur and stop.
IACHIMO.
Had I this cheek
To bathe my lips upon; this hand, whose touch,
Whose every touch, would force the feeler's soul
To the oath of loyalty; this object, which
Takes prisoner the wild motion of mine eye,
Fixing it only here;—should I—damn'd then—
Slaver with lips as common as the stairs
That mount the Capitol; join gripes with hands
Made hard with hourly falsehood—falsehood, as
With labour; then by-peeping in an eye
Base and illustrous as the smoky light
That's fed with stinking tallow;—it were fit
That all the plagues of hell should at one time
Encounter such revolt.
IMOGEN.
My lord, I fear,
Has forgot Britain.
IACHIMO.
And himself. Not I,
Inclined to this intelligence, pronounce
The beggary of his change; but 'tis your graces
That from my mutest conscience to my tongue
Charms this report out.
IMOGEN.
Let me hear no more.
IACHIMO.
O dearest soul, your cause doth strike my heart
With pity, that doth make me sick! A lady
So fair, and fasten'd to an empery
Would make the great'st king double, to be part-
    ner'd
With tomboys, hired with that self-exhibition
Which your own coffers yield! with diseased ven-
    tures
That play with all infirmities for gold
Which rottenness can lend nature! such boil'd
    stuff
As well might poison poison! Be revenged;
Or she that bore you was no queen, and you
Recoil from your great stock.
IMOGEN.
Revenged!
How should I be revenged? If this be true,—
As I have such a heart that both mine ears
Must not in haste abuse,—if it be true,
How should I be revenged?
IACHIMO.
Should he make me
Live, like Diana's priest, betwixt cold sheets,
Whiles he is vaulting variable ramps,
In your despite, upon your purse? Revenge it.

1069

I dedicate myself to your sweet pleasure;
More noble than that runagate to your bed;
And will continue fast to your affection,
Still close as sure.

IMOGEN.
What ho, Pisanio!

IACHIMO.
Let me my service tender on your lips.

IMOGEN.
Away!—I do condemn mine ears that have
So long attended thee.—If thou wert honourable,
Thou wouldst have told this tale for virtue, not
For such an end thou seek'st,—as base as strange.
Thou wrong'st a gentleman who is as far
From thy report as thou from honour; and
Solicit'st here a lady that disdains
Thee and the devil alike.—What ho, Pisanio!—
The king my father shall be made acquainted
Of thy assault: if he shall think it fit,
A saucy stranger, in his court, to mart
As in a Romish stew, and to expound
His beastly mind to us,—he hath a court
He little cares for, and a daughter who
He not respects at all.—What ho, Pisanio!—

IACHIMO.
O happy Leonatus! I may say:
The credit that thy lady hath of thee
Deserves thy trust; and thy most perfect goodness
Her assured credit.—Blessed live you long!
A lady to the worthiest sir that ever
Country call'd his! and you his mistress, only
For the most worthiest fit! Give me your pardon.
I have spoke this, to know if your affiance
Were deeply rooted; and shall make your lord,
That which he is, new o'er: and he is one
The truest manner'd; such a holy witch,
That he enchants societies into him;
Half all men's hearts are his.

IMOGEN.
You make amends.

IACHIMO.
He sits 'mongst men like a descended god:
He hath a kind of honour sets him off,
More than a mortal seeming. Be not angry,
Most mighty princess, that I have adventured
To try your taking of a false report; which hath
Honour'd with confirmation your great judgement
In the election of a sir so rare,
Which you know cannot err: the love I bear him
Made me to fan you thus; but the gods made
     you,
Unlike all others, chaffless. Pray, your pardon.

IMOGEN.
All's well, sir: take my power i'the court for yours.

IACHIMO.
My humble thanks. I had almost forgot
T'entreat your Grace but in a small request,
And yet of moment too, for it concerns
Your lord, myself, and other noble friends,
Are partners in the business.

IMOGEN.
Pray, what is't?

IACHIMO.
Some dozen Romans of us, and your lord—
The best feather of our wing—have mingled
sums

To buy a present for the emperor;
Which I, the factor for the rest, have done
In France: 'tis plate of rare device, and jewels
Of rich and exquisite form; their values great;
And I am something curious, being strange,
To have them in safe stowage: may it please you
To take them in protection?

IMOGEN.
Willingly;
And pawn mine honour for their safety: since
My lord hath interest in them, I will keep them
In my bedchamber.

IACHIMO.
They are in a trunk,
Attended by my men: I will make bold
To send them to you, only for this night;
I must aboard to-morrow.

IMOGEN.
O, no, no.

IACHIMO.
Yes, I beseech; or I shall short my word
By lengthening my return. From Gallia
I crost the seas on purpose and on promise
To see your Grace.

IMOGEN.
I thank you for your pains:
But not away to-morrow!

IACHIMO.
O, I must, madam:
Therefore I shall beseech you, if you please
To greet your lord with writing, do't to-night:
I have outstood my time; which is material
To the tender of our present.

IMOGEN.
I will write.
Send your trunk to me; it shall safe be kept,
And truly yielded you. You're very welcome.
                                        [Exeunt.

ACT II. SCENE I.

Britain.   Before CYMBELINE'S *palace.*

Enter CLOTEN *and two* LORDS.

CLOTEN.
WAS there ever man had such luck! when I
kist the jack, upon an up-cast to be hit away!
I had a hundred pound on't: and then a whoreson
jackanapes must take me up for swearing; as if I
borrow'd mine oaths of him, and might not spend
them at my pleasure.

FIRST LORD.
What got he by that? You have broke his pate
with your bowl.

SECOND LORD [*aside*].
If his wit had been like him that broke it, it would
have run all out.

CLOTEN.
When a gentleman is disposed to swear, it is not
for any standers-by to curtail his oaths, ha?

SECOND LORD.
No, my lord; [*aside*] nor crop the ears of them.

CLOTEN.
Whoreson dog! I give him satisfaction? Would he
had been one of my rank!

SECOND LORD [*aside*].
To have smelt like a fool.

CLOTEN.

I am not vext more at any thing in the earth: a pox
on't! I had rather not be so noble as I am; they
dare not fight with me, because of the queen my
mother: every Jack-slave hath his bellyful of
fighting, and I must go up and down like a cock
that nobody can match.

SECOND LORD [aside].

You are cock and capon too; and you crow, cock,
with your comb on.

CLOTEN.

Sayest thou?

SECOND LORD.

It is not fit your lordship should undertake every
companion that you give offence to.

CLOTEN.

No, I know that: but it is fit I should commit
offence to my inferiors.

SECOND LORD.

Ay, it is fit for your lordship only.

CLOTEN.

Why, so I say.

FIRST LORD.

Did you hear of a stranger that's come to court
to-night?

CLOTEN.

A stranger, and I not know on't!

SECOND LORD [aside].

He's a strange fellow himself, and knows it not.

FIRST LORD.

There's an Italian come; and, 'tis thought, one of
Leonatus' friends.

CLOTEN.

Leonatus! a banist rascal; and he's another,
whatsoever he be. Who told you of this stranger?

FIRST LORD.

One of your lordship's pages.

CLOTEN.

Is it fit I went to look upon him? is there no de-
rogation in't?

SECOND LORD.

You cannot derogate, my lord.

CLOTEN.

Not easily, I think.

SECOND LORD [aside].

You are a fool granted; therefore your issues,
being foolish, do not derogate.

CLOTEN.

Come, I'll go see this Italian: what I have lost to-
day at bowls I'll win to-night of him. Come, go.

SECOND LORD.

I'll attend your lordship.

[Exeunt CLOTEN and FIRST LORD.

That such a crafty devil as is his mother
Should yield the world this ass! a woman that
Bears all down with her brain; and this her son
Cannot take two from twenty, for his heart,
And leave eighteen. Alas, poor princess,
Thou divine Imogen, what thou endurest,
Betwixt a father by thy step-dame govern'd,
A mother hourly coining plots, a wooer
More hateful than the foul expulsion is
Of thy dear husband, than that horrid act
Of the divorce he'ld make! The heavens hold
firm
The walls of thy dear honour; keep unshaked

That temple, thy fair mind; that thou mayst
stand,
T'enjoy thy banist lord and this great land!

[Exit.

SCENE II.

IMOGEN'S *bedchamber: a trunk in one corner of it.*

Enter IMOGEN *in her bed, and a* LADY.

IMOGEN.

WHO'S there? my woman Helen?

LADY.

Please you, madam.

IMOGEN.

What hour is it?

LADY.

Almost midnight, madam.

IMOGEN.

I have read three hours, then: mine eyes are weak:
Fold down the leaf where I have left: to bed:
Take not away the taper, leave it burning;
And if thou canst awake by four o'the clock,
I prithee, call me. Sleep hath seized me wholly.

[Exit LADY.

To your protection I commend me, gods!
From fairies, and the tempters of the night,
Guard me, beseech ye!

[Sleeps. IACHIMO comes from the trunk.

IACHIMO.

The crickets sing, and man's o'er-labour'd sense
Repairs itself by rest. Our Tarquin thus
Did softly press the rushes, ere he waken'd
The chastity he wounded.—Cytherea,
How bravely thou becomest thy bed! fresh lily!
And whiter than the sheets! That I might touch!
But kiss; one kiss!—Rubies unparagon'd,
How dearly they do't!—'Tis her breathing that
Perfumes the chamber thus: the flame o'the taper
Bows towards her; and would under-peep her lids,
To see the enclosed lights, now canopied
Under these windows, white and azure, laced
With blue of heaven's own tinct.—But my design
To note the chamber: I will write all down:—
Such and such pictures;—there the window;—
such
The adornment of her bed;—the arras, figures,
Why, such and such;—and the contents o'the
story,—
Ah, but some natural notes about her body,
Above ten thousand meaner movables
Would testify, t'enrich mine inventory:—
O sleep, thou ape of death, lie dull upon her!
And be her sense but as a monument,
Thus in a chapel lying!—Come off; come off;—

[Taking off her bracelet.

As slippery as the Gordian knot was hard!—
'Tis mine; and this will witness outwardly,
As strongly as the conscience does within,
To the madding of her lord.—On her left breast
A mole cinque-spotted, like the crimson drops
I'the bottom of a cowslip: here's a voucher,
Stronger than ever law could make: this secret
Will force him think I have pickt the lock, and
ta'en
The treasure of her honour. No more. To what
end?

Why should I write this down, that's riveted,
Screw'd to my memory?—She hath been reading
  late
The tale of Tereus: here the leaf's turn'd down
Where Philomel gave up.—I have enough:
To the trunk again, and shut the spring of it.—
Swift, swift, you dragons of the night, that dawn-
  ing
May bare the raven's eye! I lodge in fear;
Though this a heavenly angel, hell is here.

                    [Clock strikes.

One, two, three,—Time, time!

    [Goes into the trunk.   Scene closes.

SCENE III.

An ante-chamber adjoining IMOGEN'S *apart-*
ments.

Enter CLOTEN *and* LORDS.

FIRST LORD.

YOUR lordship is the most patient man in
  loss, the most coldest that ever turn'd up
ace.

CLOTEN.

It would make any man cold to lose.

FIRST LORD.

But not every man patient after the noble temper
of your lordship. You are most hot and furious
when you win.

CLOTEN.

Winning will put any man into courage. If I
could get this foolish Imogen, I should have gold
enough. It's almost morning, is't not?

FIRST LORD.

Day, my lord.

CLOTEN.

I would this music would come: I am advised to
give her music o'mornings; they say it will penetrate.—

Enter MUSICIANS.

Come on; tune: if you can penetrate her with
your fingering, so; we'll try with tongue too: if
none will do, let her remain; but I'll never give
o'er. First, a very excellent good-conceited thing;
after, a wonderful sweet air, with admirable rich
words to it,—and then let her consider.

Song.

Hark, hark! the lark at heaven's gate sings,
  And Phœbus gins arise,
His steeds to water at those springs
  On chaliced flowers that lies;
And winking Mary-buds begin
    To ope their golden eyes:
With every thing that pretty is,
  My lady sweet, arise;
    Arise, arise!

CLOTEN.

So, get you gone. If this penetrate, I will consider your music the better: if it do not, it is a vice
in her ears, which horse-hairs and calves'-guts,
nor the voice of unpaved eunuch to boot, can
never amend.   *[Exeunt MUSICIANS.*

SECOND LORD.

Here comes the king.

CLOTEN.

I am glad I was up so late; for that's the reason I
was up so early; he cannot choose but take this
service I have done fatherly.

Enter CYMBELINE *and* QUEEN.

Good morrow to your majesty and to my gracious mother.

CYMBELINE.

Attend you here the door of our stern daughter?
Will she not forth?

CLOTEN.

I have assail'd her with musics; but she vouch-
safes no notice.

CYMBELINE.

The exile of her minion is too new;
She hath not yet forgot him: some more time
Must wear the print of his remembrance out,
And then she's yours.

QUEEN.

           You are most bound to the king,
Who lets go by no vantages that may
Prefer you to his daughter. Frame yourself
To orderly solicits, and be friended
With aptness of the season; make denials
Increase your services; so seem as if
You were inspired to do those duties which
You tender to her; that you in all obey her,
Save when command to your dismission tends,
And therein you are senseless.

CLOTEN.

                Senseless! not so.

Enter a MESSENGER.

MESSENGER.

So like you, sir, ambassadors from Rome;
The one is Caius Lucius.

CYMBELINE.

            A worthy fellow,
Albeit he comes on angry purpose now;
But that's no fault of his: we must receive him
According to the honour of his sender;
And towards himself, his goodness forespent on
  us,
We must extend our notice.—Our dear son,
When you have given good morning to your
  mistress,
Attend the queen and us; we shall have need
T'employ you towards this Roman.—Come, our
  queen.   *[Exeunt all but* CLOTEN.

CLOTEN.

If she be up, I'll speak with her; if not,
Let her lie still and dream.—By your leave, ho!—

                        [Knocks.

I know her women are about her: what
If I do line one of their hands? 'Tis gold
Which buys admittance; oft it doth; yea, and
  makes
Diana's rangers false themselves, yield up
Their deer to the stand o'the stealer; and 'tis gold
Which makes the true man kill'd, and saves the
  thief;
Nay, sometime hangs both thief and true man: what
Can it not do and undo? I will make
One of her women lawyer to me; for
I yet not understand the case myself.—
By your leave.   *[Knocks.*

Enter a LADY.

LADY.

Who's there that knocks?

CLOTEN.

           A gentleman.

LADY.

               No more?

CLOTEN.

Yes, and a gentlewoman's son.

LADY.

               That's more
Than some, whose tailors are as dear as yours,
Can justly boast of.   What's your lordship's
    pleasure?

CLOTEN.

Your lady's person: is she ready?

LADY.

          Ay,
To keep her chamber.

CLOTEN.

         There is gold for you;
Sell me your good report.

LADY.

How! my good name? or to report of you
What I shall think is good?—The princess!

Enter IMOGEN.

CLOTEN.

Good morrow, fairest: sister, your sweet hand.
              [*Exit* LADY.

IMOGEN.

Good morrow, sir. You lay out too much pains
For purchasing but trouble: the thanks I give
Is telling you that I am poor of thanks,
And scarce can spare them.

CLOTEN.

       Still, I swear I love you.

IMOGEN.

If you but said so, 'twere as deep with me:
If you swear still, your recompense is still
That I regard it not.

CLOTEN.

        This is no answer.

IMOGEN.

But that you shall not say, I yield being silent,
I would not speak. I pray you, spare me: faith,
I shall unfold equal discourtesy
To your best kindness: one of your great knowing
Should learn, being taught, forbearance.

CLOTEN.

To leave you in your madness, 'twere my sin:
I will not.

IMOGEN.

Fools are not mad folks.

CLOTEN.

        Do you call me fool?

IMOGEN.

As I am mad, I do:
If you'll be patient, I'll no more be mad;
That cures us both. I am much sorry, sir,
You put me to forget a lady's manners,
By being so verbal: and learn now, for all,
That I, which know my heart, do here pronounce,
By the very truth of it, I care not for you;
And am so near the lack of charity,—
To accuse myself,—I hate you; which I had rather
You felt than make't my boast.

CLOTEN.

               You sin against
Obedience, which you owe your father. For
The contract you pretend with that base wretch,—
One bred of alms, and foster'd with cold dishes,
With scraps o'the court,—it is no contract, none:
And though it be allow'd in meaner parties—
Yet who than he more mean?—to knit their
    souls—
On whom there is no more dependency
But brats and beggary—in self-figured knot;
Yet you are curb'd from that enlargement by
The consequence o'the crown; and must not
    foil
The precious note of it with a base slave,
A hilding for a livery, a squire's cloth,
A pantler, not so eminent.

IMOGEN.

           Profane fellow!
Wert thou the son of Jupiter, and no more
But what thou art besides, thou wert too base
To be his groom: thou wert dignified enough,
Even to the point of envy, if 'twere made
Comparative for your virtues, to be styled
The under-hangman of his kingdom; and hated
For being preferr'd so well.

CLOTEN.

          The south-fog rot him!

IMOGEN.

He never can meet more mischance than come
To be but named of thee. His meanest garment,
That ever hath but clipt his body, is dearer
In my respect than all the hairs above thee,
Were they all made such men.

Enter PISANIO.

           How now, Pisanio!

CLOTEN.

'His garment'! Now, the devil—

IMOGEN.

To Dorothy my woman hie thee presently—

CLOTEN.

'His garment'!

IMOGEN.

         I am sprited with a fool;
Frighted, and anger'd worse:—go bid my woman
Search for a jewel that too casually
Hath left mine arm: it was thy master's; shrew
    me,
If I would lose it for a revenue
Of any king's in Europe. I do think
I saw't this morning: confident I am
Last night 'twas on mine arm; I kist it:
I hope it be not gone to tell my lord
That I kiss aught but he.

PISANIO.

          'Twill not be lost.

IMOGEN.

I hope so: go and search.   [*Exit* PISANIO.

CLOTEN.

         You have abused me:—
'His meanest garment'!

IMOGEN.

          Ay, I said so, sir:
If you will make't an action, call witness to't.

CLOTEN.

I will inform your father.

IMOGEN.
Your mother too:
She's my good lady; and will conceive, I hope,
But the worst of me. So, I leave you, sir,
To the worst of discontent.   [*Exit.*
CLOTEN.
I'll be revenged:—
'His meanest garment'!—Well.   [*Exit.*

SCENE IV.

Rome. PHILARIO'S *house.*

Enter POSTHUMUS *and* PHILARIO.

POSTHUMUS LEONATUS.
FEAR it not, sir: I would I were so sure
To win the king, as I am bold her honour
Will remain hers.
PHILARIO.
What means do you make to him?
POSTHUMUS LEONATUS.
Not any; but abide the change of time;
Quake in the present winter's state, and wish
That warmer days would come: in these fear'd
I barely gratify your love; they failing,   [hopes,
I must die much your debtor.
PHILARIO.
Your very goodness and your company
O'erpays all I can do. By this, your king
Hath heard of great Augustus: Caius Lucius
Will do's commission throughly: and I think
He'll grant the tribute, send the arrearages,
Or look upon our Romans, whose remembrance
Is yet fresh in their grief.
POSTHUMUS LEONATUS.
I do believe—
Statist though I am none, nor like to be—
That this will prove a war; and you shall hear
The legions now in Gallia sooner landed
In our not-fearing Britain than have tidings
Of any penny tribute paid. Our countrymen
Are men more order'd than when Julius Cæsar
Smiled at their lack of skill, but found their
          courage
Worthy his frowning at: their discipline
Now mingled with their courages will make known
To their approvers they are people such
That mend upon the world.
PHILARIO.
See! Iachimo!

Enter IACHIMO.

POSTHUMUS LEONATUS.
The swiftest harts have posted you by land;
And winds of all the corners kist your sails,
To make your vessel nimble.
PHILARIO.
Welcome, sir.
POSTHUMUS LEONATUS.
I hope the briefness of your answer made
The speediness of your return.
IACHIMO.
Your lady
Is one of the fairest that I have lookt upon.
POSTHUMUS LEONATUS.
And therewithal the best; or let her beauty
Look through a casement to allure false hearts,
And be false with them.

IACHIMO.
Here are letters for you.
POSTHUMUS LEONATUS.
Their tenour good, I trust.
IACHIMO.
'Tis very like.
PHILARIO.
Was Caius Lucius in the Britain court
When you were there?
IACHIMO.
He was expected then,
But not approacht.
POSTHUMUS LEONATUS.
All is well yet.—
Sparkles this stone as it was wont? or is't not
Too dull for your good wearing?
IACHIMO.
If I had lost it,
I should have lost the worth of it in gold.
I'll make a journey twice as far, t'enjoy
A second night of such sweet shortness which
Was mine in Britain; for the ring is won.
POSTHUMUS LEONATUS.
The stone's too hard to come by.
IACHIMO.
Not a whit,
Your lady being so easy.
POSTHUMUS LEONATUS.
Make not, sir,
Your loss your sport: I hope you know that we
Must not continue friends.
IACHIMO.
Good sir, we must,
If you keep covenant. Had I not brought
The knowledge of your mistress home, I grant
We were to question further: but I now
Profess myself the winner of her honour,
Together with your ring; and not the wronger
Of her or you, having proceeded but
By both your wills.
POSTHUMUS LEONATUS.
If you can make't apparent
That you have tasted her in bed, my hand
And ring is yours: if not, the foul opinion
You had of her pure honour gains or loses
Your sword or mine, or masterless leaves both
To who shall find them.
IACHIMO.
Sir, my circumstances,
Being so near the truth as I will make them,
Must first induce you to believe: whose strength
I will confirm with oath; which, I doubt not,
You'll give me leave to spare, when you shall find
You need it not.
POSTHUMUS LEONATUS.
Proceed.
IACHIMO.
First, her bedchamber,—
Where, I confess, I slept not; but profess
Had that was well worth watching.—it was hang'd
With tapestry of silk and silver; the story
Proud Cleopatra, when she met her Roman,
And Cydnus swell'd above the banks, or for
The press of boats or pride: a piece of work
So bravely done, so rich, that it did strive
In workmanship and value; which I wonder'd

Could be so rarely and exactly wrought,
Since the true life on't was—
    POSTHUMUS LEONATUS.
                    This is true;
And this you might have heard of here, by me
Or by some other.
    IACHIMO.
              More particulars
Must justify my knowledge.
    POSTHUMUS LEONATUS.
                 So they must,
Or do your honour injury.
    IACHIMO.
              The chimney
Is south the chamber; and the chimney-piece
Chaste Dian bathing: never saw I figures
So lively to report themselves: the cutter
Was as another nature, dumb; outwent her,
Motion and breath left out.
    POSTHUMUS LEONATUS.
               This is a thing
Which you might from relation likewise reap,
Being, as it is, much spoke of.
    IACHIMO.
          The roof o'the chamber
With golden cherubins is fretted: her andirons—
I had forgot them—were two winking Cupids
Of silver, each on one foot standing, nicely
Depending on their brands.
    POSTHUMUS LEONATUS.
              This is her honour!—
Let it be granted you have seen all this,—and
    praise
Be given to your remembrance,—the description
Of what is in her chamber nothing saves
The wager you have laid.
    IACHIMO.
          Then, if you can,
        [Pulling out the bracelet.
Be pale: I beg but leave to air this jewel; see!—
And now 'tis up again: it must be married
To that your diamond; I'll keep them.
    POSTHUMUS LEONATUS.
              Jove!—
Once more let me behold it: is it that
Which I left with her?
    IACHIMO.
        Sir,—I thank her,—that:
She stript it from her arm; I see her yet;
Her pretty action did outsell her gift,
And yet enricht it too: she gave it me, and said
She prized it once.
    POSTHUMUS LEONATUS.
          May be she pluckt it off
To send it me.
    IACHIMO.
       She writes so to you, doth she?
    POSTHUMUS LEONATUS.
O, no, no, no! 'tis true. Here, take this too;
              [Gives the ring.
It is a basilisk unto mine eye,
Kills me to look on't.—Let there be no honour
Where there is beauty; truth, where semblance;
    love,
Where there's another man: the vows of women
Of no more bondage be to where they are made

Than they are to their virtues; which is nothing.—
O, above measure false!
    PHILARIO.
             Have patience, sir,
And take your ring again; 'tis not yet won:
It may be probable she lost it; or
Who knows if one of her women, being cor-
    rupted,
Hath stoln it from her?
    POSTHUMUS LEONATUS.
               Very true;
And so, I hope, he came by't.—Back my ring:
Render to me some corporal sign about her,
More evident than this; for this was stoln.
    IACHIMO.
By Jupiter, I had it from her arm.
    POSTHUMUS LEONATUS.
Hark you, he swears; by Jupiter he swears.
'Tis true,—nay, keep the ring,—'tis true: I am
    sure
She would not lose it: her attendants are
All sworn and honourable:—they induced to steal
    it!
And by a stranger!—No, he hath enjoy'd her:
The cognizance of her incontinency
Is this,—she hath bought the name of whore thus
    dearly.
There, take thy hire; and all the fiends of hell
Divide themselves between you!
    PHILARIO.
             Sir, be patient:
This is not strong enough to be believed
Of one persuaded well of—
    POSTHUMUS LEONATUS.
             Never talk on't;
She hath been colted by him.
    IACHIMO.
             If you seek
For further satisfying, under her breast—
Worthy the pressing—lies a mole, right proud
Of that most delicate lodging: by my life,
I kist it; and it gave me present hunger
To feed again, though full. You do remember
This stain upon her?
    POSTHUMUS LEONATUS.
          Ay, and it doth confirm
Another stain, as big as hell can hold,
Were there no more but it.
    IACHIMO.
           Will you hear more?
    POSTHUMUS LEONATUS.
Spare your arithmetic: never count the turns;
Once, and a million!
    IACHIMO.
      I'll be sworn—
    POSTHUMUS LEONATUS.
             No swearing.
If you will swear you have not done't, you lie:
And I will kill thee, if thou dost deny
Thou'st made me cuckold.
    IACHIMO.
           I'll deny nothing.
    POSTHUMUS LEONATUS.
O, that I had her here, to tear her limb-meal!
I will go there and do't: i'the court; before
Her father:—I'll do something—   *[Exit*

PHILARIO.

                      Quite besides
The government of patience!—You have won:
Let's follow him, and pervert the present wrath
He hath against himself.

IACHIMO.

             With all my heart. [*Exeunt.*

SCENE V.

Another room in PHILARIO'S *house.*

Enter POSTHUMUS.

POSTHUMUS LEONATUS.

IS there no way for men to be, but women
Must be half-workers? We are all bastards:
And that most venerable man which I
Did call my father, was I know not where
When I was stampt; some coiner with his tools
Made me a counterfeit: yet my mother seem'd
The Dian of that time: so doth my wife
The nonpareil of this.—O, vengeance, vengeance!
Me of my lawful pleasure she restrain'd,
And pray'd me oft forbearance; did it with
A pudency so rosy, the sweet view on't
Might well have warm'd old Saturn; that I
    thought her
As chaste as unsunn'd snow:—O, all the devils!—
This yellow Iachimo, in an hour,—was't not?—
Or less,—at first?—perchance he spoke not, but,
Like a full-acorn'd boar, a German one,
Cried 'O!' and mounted; found no opposition
But what he lookt for should oppose, and she
Should from encounter guard.—Could I find out
The woman's part in me! For there's no motion
That tends to vice in man, but I affirm
It is the woman's part: be it lying, note it,
The woman's; flattering, hers; deceiving, hers;
Lust and rank thoughts, hers, hers; revenges,
    hers;
Ambitions, covetings, change of prides, disdain,
Nice longing, slanders, mutability,
All faults that may be named, nay, that hell knows,
Why, hers, in part or all; but rather, all;
For even to vice
They are not constant, but are changing still
One vice, but of a minute old, for one
Not half so old as that. I'll write against them,
Detest them, curse them:—yet 'tis greater skill
In a true hate, to pray they have their will:
The very devils cannot plague them better. [*Exit.*

ACT III. SCENE I.

Britain. A room of state in CYMBELINE'S
palace.

Enter in state CYMBELINE, QUEEN, CLOTEN,
and LORDS *at one door, and at another* CAIUS
LUCIUS *and* ATTENDANTS.

CYMBELINE.

NOW say, what would Augustus Cæsar with
us?

CAIUS LUCIUS.

When Julius Cæsar, whose remembrance yet
Lives in men's eyes and will to ears and tongues
Be theme and hearing ever, was in this Britain

And conquer'd it, Cassibelan, thine uncle,—
Famous in Cæsar's praises, no whit less
Than in his feats deserving it,—for him
And his succession granted Rome a tribute,
Yearly three thousand pounds; which by thee
    lately
Is left untender'd.

QUEEN.

            And, to kill the marvel,
Shall be so ever.

CLOTEN.

           There be many Cæsars,
Ere such another Julius. Britain is
A world by itself; and we will nothing pay
For wearing our own noses.

QUEEN.

              That opportunity,
Which then they had to take from's, to resume
We have again.—Remember, sir, my liege,
The kings your ancestors, together with
The natural bravery of your isle, which stands
As Neptune's park, ribbed and paled in
With rocks unscalable and roaring waters;
With sands that will not bear your enemies' boats
But suck them up to the topmast. A kind of con-
    quest
Cæsar made here; but made not here his brag
Of 'Came, and saw, and overcame:' with
    shame—
The first that ever toucht him—he was carried
From off our coast, twice beaten; and his ship-
    ping—
Poor ignorant baubles!—on our terrible seas,
Like egg-shells moved upon their surges, crackt
As easily 'gainst our rocks: for joy whereof
The famed Cassibelan, who was once at point—
O giglot Fortune!—to master Cæsar's sword,
Made Lud's-town with rejoicing fires bright,
And Britons strut with courage.

CLOTEN.

Come, there's no more tribute to be paid: our
kingdom is stronger than it was at that time; and,
as I said, there is no moe such Cæsars: other of
them may have crookt noses; but to owe such
straight arms, none.

CYMBELINE.

Son, let your mother end.

CLOTEN.

We have yet many among us can gripe as hard as
Cassibelan: I do not say I am one; but I have a
hand.—Why tribute? why should we pay tribute?
If Cæsar can hide the sun from us with a blanket,
or put the moon in his pocket, we will pay him
tribute for light; else, sir, no more tribute, pray
you now.

CYMBELINE.

You must know,
Till the injurious Romans did extort
This tribute from's, we were free: Cæsar's ambi-
    tion,—
Which swell'd so much, that it did almost stretch
The sides o'the world,—against all colour, here
Did put the yoke upon's; which to shake off
Becomes a warlike people, whom we reckon
Ourselves to be. We do say, then, to Cæsar,
Our ancestor was that Mulmutius which

Ordain'd our laws,—whose use the sword of
　　Cæsar
Hath too much mangled; whose repair and fran-
　　chise
Shall, by the power we hold, be our good deed,
Though Rome be therefore angry;—Mulmutius
　　made our laws,
Who was the first of Britain which did put
His brows within a golden crown, and call'd
Himself a king.

　　　　　CAIUS LUCIUS.
　　　　　　　　I am sorry, Cymbeline,
That I am to pronounce Augustus Cæsar—
Cæsar, that hath moe kings his servants than
Thyself domestic officers—thine enemy:
Receive it from me, then:—war and confusion
In Cæsar's name pronounce I 'gainst thee: look
For fury not to be resisted.—Thus defied,
I thank thee for myself.

　　　　　CYMBELINE.
　　　　　　　Thou art welcome, Caius.
Thy Cæsar knighted me; my youth I spent
Much under him; of him I gather'd honour;
Which he to seek of me again, perforce,
Behoves me keep at utterance. I am perfect
That the Pannonians and Dalmatians for
Their liberties are now in arms,—a precedent
Which not to read would show the Britons cold:
So Cæsar shall not find them.

　　　　　CAIUS LUCIUS.
　　　　　　　　　Let proof speak.

　　　　　CLOTEN.
His majesty bids you welcome. Make pastime
with us a day or two, or longer: if you seek us
afterwards in other terms, you shall find us in our
salt-water girdle: if you beat us out of it, it is
yours; if you fall in the adventure, our crows shall
fare the better for you; and there's an end.

　　　　　CAIUS LUCIUS.
So, sir.

　　　　　CYMBELINE.
I know your master's pleasure, and he mine:
All the remain is 'Welcome.'　　　　　[Exeunt.

SCENE II.

Another room in the palace.

Enter PISANIO, with a letter.

　　　　　PISANIO.
HOW! of adultery? Wherefore write you not
　　What monster's her accuser? Leonatus!
O master! what a strange infection
Is faln into thy ear! What false Italian,
As poisonous-tongued as handed, hath prevail'd
On thy too ready hearing? Disloyal! No:
She's punisht for her truth; and undergoes,
More goddess-like than wife-like, such assaults
As would take in some virtue. O my master!
Thy mind to her is now as low as were
Thy fortunes. How! that I should murder her?
Upon the love, and truth, and vows, which I
Have made to thy command? I, her? her blood?
If it be so to do good service, never
Let me be counted serviceable. How look I,
That I should seem to lack humanity

So much as this fact comes to? [*reading*] 'Do't: the
　　letter
That I have sent her, by her own command
Shall give thee opportunity:'—O damn'd paper!
Black as the ink that's on thee! Senseless bauble,
Art thou a feodary for this act, and look'st
So virgin-like without?—Lo, here she comes.—
I am ignorant in what I am commanded.
　　　　　Enter IMOGEN.
　　　　　IMOGEN.
How now, Pisanio!
　　　　　PISANIO.
Madam, here is a letter from my lord.
　　　　　IMOGEN.
Who? thy lord? that is my lord,—Leonatus?
O, learn'd indeed were that astronomer
That knew the stars as I his characters;
He'ld lay the future open. You good gods,
Let what is here contain'd relish of love,
Of my lord's health, of his content,—yet not
That we two are asunder; let that grieve him:
Some griefs are medicinable; that is one of them,
For it doth physic love;—of his content
All but in that!—Good wax, thy leave: blest be
You bees that make these locks of counsel!
　　Lovers,
And men in dangerous bonds, pray not alike:
Though forfeiters you cast in prison, yet
You clasp young Cupid's tables.—Good news,
　　gods!　　　　　　　　　　　　　　　[*Reads.*
Justice, and your father's wrath, should he take
me in his dominion, could not be so cruel to me,
as you, O the dearest of creatures, would even
renew me with your eyes. Take notice that I am
in Cambria, at Milford-Haven: what your own
love will, out of this, advise you, follow. So, he
wishes you all happiness, that remains loyal to his
vow, and your, increasing in love,
　　　　　LEONATUS POSTHUMUS.
O, for a horse with wings! Hear'st thou, Pisanio?
He is at Milford-Haven: read, and tell me
How far 'tis thither. If one of mean affairs
May plod it in a week, why may not I
Glide thither in a day? Then, true Pisanio,—
Who long'st, like me, to see thy lord; who
　　long'st,—
O, let me bate,—but not like me;—yet long'st,
But in a fainter kind;—O, not like me;
For mine's beyond beyond,—say, and speak
　　thick,—
Love's counsellor should fill the bores of hearing,
To the smothering of the sense,—how far it is
To this same blessed Milford: and, by the way,
Tell me how Wales was made so happy as
T'inherit such a haven: but, first of all,
How we may steal from hence; and for the gap
That we shall make in time, from our hence-going
And our return, to excuse:—but first, how get
　　hence:
Why should excuse be born or e'er begot?
We'll talk of that hereafter. Prithee, speak,
How many score of miles may we well ride
'Twixt hour and hour?
　　　　　PISANIO.
　　　　　　　One score 'twixt sun and sun,
Madam, 's enough for you, and too much too.

IMOGEN.

Why, one that rode to's execution, man,
Could never go so slow: I have heard of riding
   wagers,
Where horses have been nimbler than the sands
That run i'the clock's behalf:—but this is foolery:—
Go bid my woman feign a sickness; say
She'll home to her father: and provide me pres-
   ently
A riding-suit, no costlier than would fit
A franklin's housewife.

PISANIO.
         Madam, you're best consider.

IMOGEN.

I see before me, man: nor here, nor here,
Nor what ensues, but have a fog in them,
That I cannot look through. Away, I prithee;
Do as I bid thee: there's no more to say;
Accessible is none but Milford way.   [Exeunt.

SCENE III.

Wales: a mountainous country with a cave.

Enter BELARIUS, GUIDERIUS, and ARVIRAGUS.

BELARIUS.

A GOODLY day not to keep house, with such
  Whose roof's as low as ours! Stoop, boys: this
   gate
Instructs you how t'adore the heavens, and bows
   you
To morning's holy office: the gates of monarchs
Are archt so high, that giants may jet through
And keep their impious turbans on, without
Good morrow to the sun.—Hail, thou fair heaven!
We house i'the rock, yet use thee not so hardly
As prouder livers do.

GUIDERIUS.
       Hail, heaven!

ARVIRAGUS.
               Hail, heaven!

BELARIUS.

Now for our mountain sport: up to yond hill,
Your legs are young; I'll tread these flats. Con-
   sider,
When you above perceive me like a crow,
That it is place which lessens and sets off;
And you may then revolve what tales I have told
   you
Of courts, of princes, of the tricks in war:
This service is not service, so being done,
But being so allow'd: to apprehend thus,
Draws us a profit from all things we see;
And often, to our comfort, shall we find
The sharded beetle in a safer hold
Than is the full-wing'd eagle. O, this life
Is nobler than attending for a check,
Richer than doing nothing for a bribe,
Prouder than rustling in unpaid-for silk:
Such gain the cap of him that makes 'em fine,
Yet keeps his book uncrost: no life to ours.

GUIDERIUS.

Out of your proof you speak: we, poor unfledged,
Have never wing'd from view o'the nest, nor know
   not
What air's from home. Haply this life is best,

If quiet life be best; sweeter to you
That have a sharper known; well corresponding
With your stiff age: but unto us it is
A cell of ignorance; travelling a-bed;
A prison for a debtor, that not dares
To stride a limit.

ARVIRAGUS.
        What should we speak of
When we are old as you? when we shall hear
The rain and wind beat dark December, how,
In this our pinching cave, shall we discourse
The freezing hours away? We have seen nothing;
We are beastly; subtle as the fox for prey;
Like warlike as the wolf for what we eat:
Our valour is to chase what flies; our cage
We make a quire, as doth the prison'd bird,
And sing our bondage freely.

BELARIUS.
             How you speak!
Did you but know the city's usuries,
And felt them knowingly: the art o'the court,
As hard to leave as keep; whose top to climb
Is certain falling, or so slippery that
The fear's as bad as falling: the toil o'the war,
A pain that only seems to seek out danger
I'the name of fame and honour; which dies i'the
   search;
And hath as oft a slanderous epitaph
As record of fair act; nay, many times
Doth ill deserve by doing well; what's worse,
Must court'sy at the censure:—O boys, this story
The world may read in me: my body's markt
With Roman swords; and my report was once
First with the best of note: Cymbeline loved me;
And when a soldier was the theme, my name
Was not far off: then was I as a tree
Whose boughs did bend with fruit: but in one
   night,
A storm or robbery, call it what you will,
Shook down my mellow hangings, nay, my leaves,
And left me bare to weather.

GUIDERIUS.
             Uncertain favour!

BELARIUS.

My fault being nothing,—as I have told you oft,—
But that two villains, whose false oaths prevail'd
Before my perfect honour, swore to Cymbeline
I was confederate with the Romans: so,
Follow'd my banishment; and, this twenty years,
This rock and these demesnes have been my world:
Where I have lived at honest freedom; paid
More pious debts to heaven than in all
The fore-end of my time.—But, up to the moun-
   tains!
This is not hunters' language:—he that strikes
The venison first shall be the lord o'the feast;
To him the other two shall minister;
And we will fear no poison, which attends
In place of greater state. I'll meet you in the
   valleys. [Exeunt GUIDERIUS and ARVIRAGUS.
How hard it is to hide the sparks of nature!
These boys know little they are sons to the king;
Nor Cymbeline dreams that they are alive.
They think they are mine; and, though train'd up
   thus meanly
I'the cave wherein they bow, their thoughts do hit

The roofs of palaces; and nature prompts them,
In simple and low things, to prince it much
Beyond the trick of others. This Polydore,—
The heir of Cymbeline and Britain, who
The king his father call'd Guiderius,—Jove!
When on my three-foot stool I sit, and tell
The warlike feats I have done, his spirits fly out
Into my story: say, 'Thus mine enemy fell,
And thus I set my foot on's neck;' even then
The princely blood flows in his cheek, he sweats,
Strains his young nerves, and puts himself in posture
That acts my words. The younger brother, Cadwal,—
Once Arviragus,—in as like a figure,
Strikes life into my speech, and shows much more
His own conceiving.—Hark, the game is roused!—
O Cymbeline! heaven and my conscience knows
Thou didst unjustly banish me: whereon,
At three and two years old, I stole these babes;
Thinking to bar thee of succession, as
Thou reft'st me of my lands. Euriphile,
Thou wast their nurse; they took thee for their mother,
And every day do honour to her grave:
Myself, Belarius, that am Morgan call'd,
They take for natural father.—The game is up.

                                 [*Exit.*

SCENE IV.
Near Milford-Haven.

Enter PISANIO *and* IMOGEN.

IMOGEN.

THOU told'st me, when we came from horse, the place
Was near at hand:—ne'er long'd my mother so
To see me first, as I have now:—Pisanio! man!
Where is Posthumus? What is in thy mind,
That makes thee stare thus? Wherefore breaks that sigh
From th'inward of thee? One, but painted thus,
Would be interpreted a thing perplext
Beyond self-explication: put thyself
Into a haviour of less fear, ere wildness
Vanquish my staider senses. What's the matter?
Why tender'st thou that paper to me, with
A look untender? If't be summer news,
Smile to't before; if winterly, thou need'st
But keep that countenance still.—My husband's hand!
That drug-damn'd Italy hath out-crafted him,
And he's at some hard point.—Speak, man: thy tongue
May take off some extremity, which to read
Would be even mortal to me.

PISANIO.
                       Please you, read;
And you shall find me, wretched man, a thing
The most disdain'd of fortune.

IMOGEN.
IMOGEN [*reads*].

Thy mistress, Pisanio, hath play'd the strumpet in my bed; the testimonies whereof lie bleeding in me. I speak not out of weak surmises; but from proof as strong as my grief, and as certain as I expect my revenge. That part thou, Pisanio, must act for me, if thy faith be not tainted with the breach of hers. Let thine own hands take away her life: I shall give thee opportunity at Milford-Haven: she hath my letter for the purpose: where, if thou fear to strike, and to make me certain it is done, thou art the pandar to her dishonour, and equally to me disloyal.

PISANIO.
What shall I need to draw my sword? the paper
Hath cut her throat already.—No, 'tis slander;
Whose edge is sharper than the sword; whose tongue
Outvenoms all the worms of Nile; whose breath
Rides on the posting winds, and doth belie
All corners of the world: kings, queens, and **states**,
Maids, matrons, nay, the secrets of the grave
This viperous slander enters.—What cheer, madam?

IMOGEN.
False to his bed! What is it to be false?
To lie in watch there, and to think on him?
To weep 'twixt clock and clock? if sleep charge nature,
To break it with a fearful dream of him,
And cry myself awake! that's false to's bed, it is?

PISANIO.
Alas, good lady!

IMOGEN.
I false! Thy conscience witness:—Iachimo,
Thou didst accuse him of incontinency;
Thou then look'dst like a villain; now, methinks,
Thy favour's good enough.—Some jay of Italy,
Whose mother was her painting, hath betray'd him:
Poor I am stale, a garment out of fashion;
And, for I am richer than to hang by the walls,
I must be ript:—to pieces with me!—O,
Men's vows are women's traitors! All good seeming,
By thy revolt, O husband, shall be thought
Put on for villainy; not born where't grows,
But worn a bait for ladies.

PISANIO.
                     Good madam, hear me.

IMOGEN.
True honest men being heard, like false Aeneas,
Were, in his time, thought false; and Sinon's weeping
Did scandal many a holy tear, took pity
From most true wretchedness: so thou, Posthumus,
Wilt lay the leaven on all proper men;
Goodly and gallant shall be false and perjured
From thy great fail.—Come, fellow, be thou honest:
Do thou thy master's bidding: when thou see'st him,
A little witness my obedience: look!
I draw the sword myself: take it, and hit
The innocent mansion of my love, my heart:
Fear not; 'tis empty of all things but grief:
Thy master is not there; who was, indeed,
The riches of it: do his bidding; strike.
Thou mayst be valiant in a better cause;
But now thou seem'st a coward.

PISANIO.
Hence, vile instrument!
Thou shalt not damn my hand.
IMOGEN.
Why, I must die;
And if I do not by thy hand, thou art
No servant of thy master's: 'gainst self-slaughter
There is a prohibition so divine
That cravens my weak hand. Come, here's my
heart:—
Something's afore't: soft, soft! we'll no defence;—
Obedient as the scabbard. What is here?
The scriptures of the loyal Leonatus
All turn'd to heresy? Away, away,
Corrupters of my faith! you shall no more
Be stomachers to my heart. Thus may poor fools
Believe false teachers: though those that are be-
tray'd
Do feel the treason sharply, yet the traitor
Stands in worse case of woe.
And thou, Posthumus, thou that didst set up
My disobedience 'gainst the king my father,
And make me put into contempt the suits
Of princely fellows, shalt hereafter find
It is no act of common passage, but
A strain of rareness: and I grieve myself
To think, when thou shalt be disedged by her
That now thou tirest on, how thy memory
Will then be pang'd by me.—Prithee, dispatch:
The lamb entreats the butcher: where's thy knife?
Thou art too slow to do thy master's bidding,
When I desire it too.
PISANIO.
O gracious lady,
Since I received command to do this business
I have not slept one wink.
IMOGEN.
Do't and to bed then.
PISANIO.
I'll wake mine eyeballs out first.
IMOGEN.
Wherefore, then,
Didst undertake it? Why hast thou abused
So many miles with a pretence? this place?
Mine action, and thine own? our horses' labour?
The time inviting thee? the perturb'd court
For my being absent, whereunto I never
Purpose return? Why hast thou gone so far,
To be unbent when thou hast ta'en thy stand,
Th'elected deer before thee?
PISANIO.
But to win time
To lose so bad employment; in the which
I have consider'd of a course. Good lady,
Hear me with patience.
IMOGEN.
Talk thy tongue weary; speak:
I have heard I am a strumpet; and mine ear,
Therein false struck, can take no greater wound,
Nor tent to bottom that. But speak.
PISANIO.
Then, madam,
I thought you would not back again.
IMOGEN.
Most like,
Bringing me here to kill me.

PISANIO.
Not so, neither:
But if I were as wise as honest, then
My purpose would prove well. It cannot be
But that my master is abused:
Some villain, ay, and singular in his art,
Hath done you both this cursed injury.
IMOGEN.
Some Roman courtezan.
PISANIO.
No, on my life.
I'll give but notice you are dead, and send him
Some bloody sign of it; for 'tis commanded
I should do so: you shall be mist at court,
And that will well confirm it.
IMOGEN.
Why, good fellow,
What shall I do the while? where bide? how live?
Or in my life what comfort, when I am
Dead to my husband?
PISANIO.
If you'll back to the court,—
IMOGEN.
No court, no father; nor no more ado
With that harsh, noble, simple nothing,—
That Cloten, whose love-suit hath been to me
As fearful as a siege.
PISANIO.
If not at court,
Then not in Britain must you bide.
IMOGEN.
Where then?
Hath Britain all the sun that shines? Day, night,
Are they not but in Britain? I'the world's volume
Our Britain seems as of it, but not in't;
In a great pool a swan's nest: prithee, think
There's livers out of Britain.
PISANIO.
I am most glad
You think of other place. Th'ambassador,
Lucius the Roman, comes to Milford-Haven
To-morrow: now, if you could wear a mind
Dark as your fortune is, and but disguise
That which, t'appear itself, must not yet be
But by self-danger, you should tread a course
Pretty and full of view; yea, happily, near
The residence of Posthumus,—so nigh at least
That though his actions were not visible, yet
Report should render him hourly to your ear
As truly as he moves.
IMOGEN.
O, for such means!
Though peril to my modesty, not death on't,
I would adventure.
PISANIO.
Well, then, here's the point:
You must forget to be a woman; change
Command into obedience; fear and niceness—
The handmaids of all women, or, more truly,
Woman it pretty self—into a waggish courage;
Ready in gibes, quick-answer'd, saucy, and
As quarrelous as the weasel; nay, you must
Forget that rarest treasure of your cheek,
Exposing it—but, O, the harder heart!
Alack, no remedy!—to the greedy touch
Of common-kissing Titan; and forget

Your laboursome and dainty trims, wherein
You made great Juno angry.
IMOGEN.
                 Nay, be brief:
I see into thy end, and am almost
A man already.
PISANIO.
           First, make yourself but like one.
Fore-thinking this, I have already fit—
'Tis in my cloak-bag—doublet, hat, hose. all
That answer to them: would you, in their serving,
And with what imitation you can borrow
From youth of such a season, fore noble Lucius
Present yourself, desire his service, tell him
Wherein you're happy,—which you'll make him
    know,
If that his head have ear in music,—doubtless
With joy he will embrace you; for he's honourable,
And, doubling that, most holy. Your means abroad,
You have me, rich; and I will never fail
Beginning nor supplyment.
IMOGEN.
           Thou art all the comfort
The gods will diet me with. Prithee, away:
There's more to be consider'd; but we'll even
All that good time will give us: this attempt
I am soldier to, and will abide it with
A prince's courage. Away, I prithee.
PISANIO.
Well, madam, we must take a short farewell,
Lest, being mist, I be suspected of
Your carriage from the court. My noble mistress,
Here is a box; I had it from the queen:
What's in't is precious; if you are sick at sea,
Or stomach-qualm'd at land, a dram of this
Will drive away distemper. To some shade,
And fit you to your manhood: may the gods
Direct you to the best!
IMOGEN.
          Amen: I thank thee. [*Exeunt.*

SCENE V.

A room in CYMBELINE'S *palace.*

Enter CYMBELINE, QUEEN, CLOTEN, LUCIUS,
and LORDS.

CYMBELINE.
THUS far; and so, farewell.
LUCIUS.
           Thanks, royal sir.
My emperor hath wrote; I must from hence;
And am right sorry that I must report ye
My master's enemy.
CYMBELINE.
          Our subjects, sir,
Will not endure his yoke; and for ourself
To show less sovereignty than they, must needs
Appear unkinglike.
LUCIUS.
          So, sir, I desire of you
A conduct overland to Milford-Haven.—
Madam, all joy befall your Grace, and you!
CYMBELINE.
My lords, you are appointed for that office;
The due of honour in no point omit.—
So, farewell, noble Lucius.

LUCIUS.
          Your hand, my lord.
CLOTEN.
Receive it friendly; but from this time forth
I wear it as your enemy.
LUCIUS.
          Sir, the event
Is yet to name the winner: fare you well.
CYMBELINE.
Leave not the worthy Lucius, good my lords,
Till he have crost the Severn.—Happiness!
          [*Exeunt* LUCIUS *and* LORDS.
QUEEN.
He goes hence frowning: but it honours us
That we have given him cause.
CLOTEN.
          'Tis all the better;
Your valiant Britons have their wishes in it.
CYMBELINE.
Lucius hath wrote already to the emperor
How it goes here. It fits us therefore ripely
Our chariots and our horsemen be in readiness:
The powers that he already hath in Gallia
Will soon be drawn to head, from whence he move
His war for Britain.
QUEEN.
          'Tis not sleepy business;
But must be lookt to speedily and strongly.
CYMBELINE.
Our expectation that it would be thus
Hath made us forward. But, my gentle queen,
Where is our daughter? She hath not appear'd
Before the Roman, nor to us hath tender'd
The duty of the day: she looks us like
A thing more made of malice than of duty:
We have noted it.—Call her before us; for
We have been too slight in sufferance.
          [*Exit an* ATTENDANT.
QUEEN.
          Royal sir,
Since the exile of Posthumus, most retired
Hath her life been; the cure whereof, my lord,
'Tis time must do. Beseech your majesty,
Forbear sharp speeches to her: she's a lady
So tender of rebukes, that words are strokes,
And strokes death to her.
Enter ATTENDANT.
CYMBELINE.
          Where is she, sir? How
Can her contempt be answer'd?
ATTENDANT.
          Please you, sir,
Her chambers are all lockt; and there's no answer
That will be given to the loud'st of noise we make.
QUEEN.
My lord, when last I went to visit her,
She pray'd me to excuse her keeping close;
Whereto constrain'd by her infirmity,
She should that duty leave unpaid to you,
Which daily she was bound to proffer: this
She wisht me to make known; but our great court
Made me to blame in memory.
CYMBELINE.
          Her doors lockt?
Not seen of late? Grant, heavens, that which I fear
Prove false!   [*Exit.*

QUEEN.
Son, I say, follow the king.
CLOTEN.
That man of hers, Pisanio, her old servant,
I have not seen these two days.
QUEEN.
Go, look after. [*Exit* CLOTEN.
Pisanio, thou that stand'st so for Posthumus!—
He hath a drug of mine; I pray his absence
Proceed by swallowing that; for he believes
It is a thing most precious. But for her,
Where is she gone? Haply, despair hath seized her;
Or, wing'd with fervour of her love, she's flown
To her desired Posthumus: gone she is
To death or to dishonour; and my end
Can make good use of either: she being down,
I have the placing of the British crown.
Enter CLOTEN.
How now, my son!
CLOTEN.
'Tis certain she is fled.
Go in and cheer the king: he rages; none
Dare come about him.
QUEEN [*aside*]
All the better: may
This night forestall him of the coming day! [*Exit.*
CLOTEN.
I love and hate her: for she's fair and royal,
And that she hath all courtly parts more exquisite
Than lady, ladies, woman; from every one
The best she hath, and she, of all compounded,
Outsells them all,—I love her therefore: but,
Disdaining me, and throwing favours on
The low Posthumus, slanders so her judgement,
That what's else rare is choked; and in that point
I will conclude to hate her, nay, indeed,
To be revenged upon her. For, when fools
Shall—
Enter PISANIO.
Who is here? What, are you packing, sirrah?
Come hither: ah, you precious pandar! Villain,
Where is thy lady? In a word; or else
Thou art straightway with the fiends.
PISANIO.
O, good my lord!—
CLOTEN.
Where is thy lady? or, by Jupiter—
I will not ask again. Close villain,
I'll have this secret from thy heart, or rip
Thy heart to find it. Is she with Posthumus?
From whose so many weights of baseness cannot
A dram of worth be drawn.
PISANIO.
Alas, my lord,
How can she be with him? When was she mist?
He is in Rome.
CLOTEN.
Where is she, sir? Come nearer;
No further halting: satisfy me home
What is become of her.
PISANIO.
O, my all-worthy lord!—
CLOTEN.
All-worthy villain!
Discover where thy mistress is at once,
At the next word,—no more of ' worthy lord;'

Speak, or thy silence on the instant is
Thy condemnation and thy death.
PISANIO.
Then, sir,
This paper is the history of my knowledge
Touching her flight. [*Presenting a letter.*
CLOTEN.
Let's see't.—I will pursue her
Even to Augustus' throne.
PISANIO [*aside*].
Or this, or perish.
She's far enough; and what he learns by this
May prove his travel, not her danger.
CLOTEN.
Hum!
PISANIO [*aside*].
I'll write to my lord she's dead. O Imogen,
Safe mayst thou wander, safe return agen!
CLOTEN.
Sirrah, is this letter true?
PISANIO.
Sir, as I think.
CLOTEN.
It is Posthumus' hand; I know't.—Sirrah, if thou
wouldst not be a villain, but do me true service,
undergo those employments wherein I should have
cause to use thee with a serious industry,—that is,
what villainy soe'er I bid thee do, to perform it
directly and truly,—I would think thee an honest
man: thou shouldst neither want my means for thy
relief, nor my voice for thy preferment.
PISANIO.
Well, my good lord.
CLOTEN.
Wilt thou serve me?—for since patiently and con-
stantly thou hast stuck to the bare fortune of that
beggar Posthumus, thou canst not, in the course of
gratitude, but be a diligent follower of mine,—
wilt thou serve me?
PISANIO.
Sir, I will.
CLOTEN.
Give me thy hand; here's my purse. Hast any of
thy late master's garments in thy possession?
PISANIO.
I have, my lord, at my lodging, the same suit he
wore when he took leave of my lady and mistress.
CLOTEN.
The first service thou dost me, fetch that suit
hither: let it be thy first service; go.
PISANIO.
I shall, my lord. [*Exit.*
CLOTEN.
Meet thee at Milford-Haven!—I forgot to ask him
one thing; I'll remember't anon:—even there,
thou villain Posthumus, will I kill thee.—I would
these garments were come. She said upon a time
—the bitterness of it I now belch from my heart—
that she held the very garment of Posthumus in
more respect than my noble and natural person,
together with the adornment of my qualities. With
that suit upon my back, will I ravish her: first kill
him, and in her eyes; there shall she see my valour,
which will then be a torment to her contempt. He
on the ground, my speech of insultment ended on
his dead body, and when my lust hath dined,—

which, as I say, to vex her I will execute in the
clothes that she so praised,—to the court I'll knock
her back, foot her home again. She hath despised
me rejoicingly, and I'll be merry in my revenge.

Enter PISANIO, *with the clothes.*

Be those the garments?

PISANIO.

Ay, my noble lord.

CLOTEN.

How long is't since she went to Milford-Haven?

PISANIO.

She can scarce be there yet.

CLOTEN.

Bring this apparel to my chamber; that is the
second thing that I have commanded thee: the
third is, that thou wilt be a voluntary mute to my
design. Be but duteous and true, preferment shall
tender itself to thee.—My revenge is now at
Milford: would I had wings to follow it!—Come,
and be true.   [*Exit.*

PISANIO.

Thou bidd'st me to my loss: for, true to thee
Were to prove false, which I will never be,
To him that is most true.—To Milford go,
And find not her whom thou pursuest.—Flow,
    flow,
You heavenly blessings, on her!—This fool's speed
Be crost with slowness; labour be his meed! [*Exit.*

SCENE VI.

Wales: before the cave of BELARIUS.

Enter IMOGEN, *in boy's clothes.*

IMOGEN.

I SEE a man's life is a tedious one:
  I have tired myself; and for two nights together
Have made the ground my bed. I should be sick,
But that my resolution helps me.—Milford,
When from the mountain-top Pisanio show'd
    thee,
Thou wast within a ken: O Jove! I think
Foundations fly the wretched; such, I mean,
Where they should be relieved. Two beggars told
    me
I could not miss my way: will poor folks lie,
That have afflictions on them, knowing 'tis
A punishment or trial? Yes; no wonder,
When rich ones scarce tell true: to lapse in full-
    ness
Is sorer than to lie for need; and falsehood
Is worse in kings than beggars.—My dear lord!
Thou art one o'the false ones: now I think on thee
My hunger's gone; but even before, I was
At point to sink for food.—But what is this?
Here is a path to't: 'tis some savage hold:
I were best not call; I dare not call: yet famine,
Ere clean it o'erthrow nature, makes it valiant.
Plenty and peace breeds cowards; hardness ever
Of hardiness is mother.—Ho! who's here?
If any thing that's civil, speak; if savage,
Take or lend. Ho!—No answer? then I'll enter.
Best draw my sword; and if mine enemy
But fear the sword like me, he'll scarcely look
    on't.
Such a foe,   [*Exit into the cave.*

Enter BELARIUS, GUIDERIUS, *and*
ARVIRAGUS.

BELARIUS.

You, Polydore, have proved best woodman, and
Are master of the feast: Cadwal and I
Will play the cook and servant; 'tis our match:
The sweat of industry would dry and die,
But for the end it works to. Come; our stomachs
Will make what's homely savoury: weariness
Can snore upon the flint, when resty sloth
Finds the down-pillow hard.—Now, peace be
    here,
Poor house, that keep'st thyself!

GUIDERIUS.

             I am throughly weary.

ARVIRAGUS.

I am weak with toil, yet strong in appetite.

GUIDERIUS.

There is cold meat i'the cave; we'll browse on
    that,
Whilst what we have kill'd be cookt.

BELARIUS.

               Stay; come not in.
            [*Looking into the cave.*
But that it eats our victuals, I should think
Here were a fairy.

GUIDERIUS.

           What's the matter, sir?

BELARIUS.

By Jupiter, an angel! or, if not,
An earthly paragon!—Behold divineness
No elder than a boy!

Enter IMOGEN.

IMOGEN.

Good masters, harm me not:
Before I enter'd here, I call'd; and thought
To have begg'd or bought what I have took: good
    troth,
I have stoln naught; nor would not, though I had
    found
Gold strew'd i'the floor. Here's money for my
    meat:
I would have left it on the board, so soon
As I had made my meal; and parted
With prayers for the provider.

GUIDERIUS.

               Money, youth?

ARVIRAGUS.

All gold and silver rather turn to dirt!
And 'tis no better reckon'd, but of those
Who worship dirty gods.

IMOGEN.

           I see you're angry:
Know, if you kill me for my fault, I should
Have died had I not made it.

BELARIUS.

             Whither bound?

IMOGEN.

To Milford-Haven.

BELARIUS.

What's your name?

IMOGEN.

Fidele, sir. I have a kinsman who
Is bound for Italy; he embarkt at Milford;

To whom being going, almost spent with hunger,
I am faln in this offence.

BELARIUS.
                Prithee, fair youth,
Think us no churls, nor measure our good minds
By this rude place we live in. Well encounter'd!
'Tis almost night: you shall have better cheer
Ere you depart; and thanks to stay and eat it.—
Boys, bid him welcome.

GUIDERIUS.
           Were you a woman, youth,
I should woo hard but be your groom:—in
honesty,
I bid for you as I do buy.

ARVIRAGUS.
             I'll make't my comfort
He is a man: I'll love him as my brother:—
And such a welcome as I'ld give to him
After long absence, such is yours: most wel-
come!
Be sprightly, for you fall 'mongst friends.

IMOGEN.
                'Mongst friends,
If brothers.—[aside] Would it had been so, that
they
Had been my father's sons! then had my prize
Been less; and so more equal ballasting
To thee, Posthumus.

BELARIUS.
          He wrings at some distress.

GUIDERIUS.
Would I could free't!

ARVIRAGUS.
          Or I; whate'er it be,
What pain it cost, what danger! Gods!

BELARIUS.
            Hark, boys. [Whispering.

IMOGEN.
Great men,
That had a court no bigger than this cave,
That did attend themselves, and had the virtue
Which their own conscience seal'd them,—laying
by
That nothing-gift of differing multitudes,—
Could not out-peer these twain. Pardon me,
gods!
I'ld change my sex to be companion with them,
Since Leonatus' false.

BELARIUS.
           It shall be so.
Boys, we'll go dress our hunt.—Fair youth, come
in:
Discourse is heavy, fasting; when we have supt,
We'll mannerly demand thee of thy story,
So far as thou wilt speak it.

GUIDERIUS.
           Pray, draw near.

ARVIRAGUS.
The night to the owl, and morn to the lark, less
welcome.

IMOGEN.
Thanks, sir.

ARVIRAGUS
I pray, draw near.   [Exeunt.

SCENE VII.

Rome. A public place.

Enter two SENATORS *and* TRIBUNES.

FIRST SENATOR.
THIS is the tenour of the emperor's writ,—
    That since the common men are now in action
'Gainst the Pannonians and Dalmatians;
And that the legions now in Gallia are
Full weak to undertake our wars against
The faln-off Britons; that we do incite
The gentry to this business. He creates
Lucius pro-consul: and to you the tribunes,
For this immediate levy, he commends
His absolute commission. Long live Cæsar!

FIRST TRIBUNE.
Is Lucius general of the forces?

SECOND SENATOR.
          Ay.

FIRST TRIBUNE.
Remaining now in Gallia?

FIRST SENATOR.
          With those legions
Which I have spoke of, whereunto your levy
Must be supplyant: the words of your commis-
sion
Will tie you to the numbers, and the time
Of their dispatch.

FIRST TRIBUNE.
          We will discharge our duty.
                    [Exeunt.

ACT IV. SCENE I.

Wales: the forest near the cave of BELARIUS.

Enter CLOTEN.

CLOTEN.
I AM near to the place where they should meet, if
  Pisanio have mapt it truly. How fit his garments
serve me! Why should his mistress, who was
made by him that made the tailor, not be fit too?
the rather—saving reverence of the word—for 'tis
said a woman's fitness comes by fits. Therein I
must play the workman. I dare speak it to myself,
—for it is not vainglory for a man and his glass to
confer; in his own chamber, I mean,—the lines of
my body are as well drawn as his; no less young,
more strong, not beneath him in fortunes, beyond
him in the advantage of the time, above him in
birth, alike conversant in general services, and
more remarkable in single oppositions: yet this
imperceiverant thing loves him in my despite.
What mortality is! Posthumus, thy head, which
now is growing upon thy shoulders, shall within
this hour be off; thy mistress enforced; thy garments cut to pieces before her face: and all this
done, spurn her home to her father; who may
happily be a little angry for my so rough usage;
but my mother, having power of his testiness,
shall turn all into my commendations. My horse
is tied up safe: out, sword, and to a sore purpose!
Fortune, put them into my hand! This is the very
description of their meeting-place; and the fellow
dares not deceive me.   [Exit.

SCENE II.

Before the cave of BELARIUS.

Enter BELARIUS, GUIDERIUS, ARVIRAGUS, *and*
IMOGEN *from the cave.*

BELARIUS [*to* IMOGEN].
YOU are not well: remain here in the cave;
  We'll come to you after hunting.

ARVIRAGUS [*to* IMOGEN].
              Brother, stay here:
Are we not brothers?

IMOGEN.
          So man and man should be;
But clay and clay differs in dignity,
Whose dust is both alike. I am very sick.

GUIDERIUS.
Go you to hunting; I'll abide with him.

IMOGEN.
So sick I am not,—yet I am not well;
But not so citizen a wanton as
To seem to die ere sick: so please you, leave me;
Stick to your journal course: the breach of cus-
  tom
Is breach of all. I am ill; but your being by me
Cannot amend me; society is no comfort
To one not sociable: I am not very sick,
Since I can reason of it. Pray you, trust me here:
I'll rob none but myself; and let me die,
Stealing so poorly.

GUIDERIUS.
        I love thee; I have spoke it:
How much the quantity, the weight as much,
As I do love my father.

BELARIUS.
          What? how! how!

ARVIRAGUS.
If it be sin to say so, sir, I yoke me
In my good brother's fault: I know not why
I love this youth; and I have heard you say,
Love's reason's without reason: the bier at door,
And a demand who is't shall die, I'ld say,
'My father, not this youth.'

BELARIUS [*aside*].
          O noble strain!
O worthiness of nature! breed of greatness!
Cowards father cowards, and base things sire
  base:
Nature hath meal and bran, contempt and grace.
I'm not their father; yet who this should be,
Doth miracle itself, loved before me.—
'Tis the ninth hour o'the morn.

ARVIRAGUS.
         Brother, farewell.

IMOGEN.
I wish ye sport.

ARVIRAGUS.
      You health.—So please you, sir.

IMOGEN [*aside*].
These are kind creatures. Gods, what lies I have
  heard!
Our courtiers say all's savage but at court:
Experience, O, thou disprovest report!
Th'imperious seas breed monsters; for the dish
Poor tributary rivers as sweet fish.
I am sick still; heart-sick:—Pisanio,
I'll now taste of thy drug.

GUIDERIUS.
         I could not stir him:
He said he was gentle, but unfortunate;
Dishonestly afflicted, but yet honest.

ARVIRAGUS.
Thus did he answer me: yet said, hereafter
I might know more.

BELARIUS.
        To the field, to the field!—
We'll leave you for this time: go in and rest.

ARVIRAGUS.
We'll not be long away.

BELARIUS.
         Pray, be not sick,
For you must be our housewife.

IMOGEN.
             Well or ill,
I am bound to you.

BELARIUS.
      And shalt be ever.
         [*Exit* IMOGEN *into the cave.*
This youth, howe'er distrest, appears he hath had
Good ancestors.

ARVIRAGUS.
        How angel-like he sings!

GUIDERIUS.
But his neat cookery! he cuts our roots in charac-
  ters;
And sauced our broths, as Juno had been sick,
And he her dieter.

ARVIRAGUS.
        Nobly he yokes
A smiling with a sigh,—as if the sigh
Was that it was for not being such a smile;
The smile mocking the sigh, that it would fly
From so divine a temple, to commix
With winds that sailors rail at.

GUIDERIUS.
           I do note
That grief and patience, rooted in him both,
Mingle their spurs together.

ARVIRAGUS.
          Grow, patience!
And let the stinking elder, grief, untwine
His perishing root with the increasing vine!

BELARIUS.
It is great morning. Come, away!—Who's there?

Enter CLOTEN.

CLOTEN.
I cannot find those runagates; that villain
Hath mockt me:—I am faint.

BELARIUS.
        'Those runagates'!
Means he not us? I partly know him; 'tis
Cloten, the son o'the queen. I fear some ambush.
I saw him not these many years, and yet
I know 'tis he.—We are held as outlaws: hence!

GUIDERIUS.
He is but one: you and my brother search
What companies are near: pray you, away;
Let me alone with him.
      [*Exeunt* BELARIUS *and* ARVIRAGUS.

CLOTEN.
        Soft!—What are you
That fly me thus? some villain mountaineers?
I have heard of such.—What slave art thou?

GUIDERIUS.
                     A thing
More slavish did I ne'er than answering
A slave without a knock.

CLOTEN.
                 Thou art a robber,
A law-breaker, a villain: yield thee thief.

GUIDERIUS.
To who? to thee? What art thou? Have not I
An arm as big as thine? a heart as big?
Thy words, I grant, are bigger; for I wear not
My dagger in my mouth. Say what thou art,
Why I should yield to thee.

CLOTEN.
                 Thou villain base,
Know'st me not by my clothes?

GUIDERIUS.
                 No, nor thy tailor, rascal,
Who is thy grandfather: he made those clothes,
Which, as it seems, make thee.

CLOTEN.
                 Thou precious varlet,
My tailor made them not.

GUIDERIUS.
                 Hence, then, and thank
The man that gave them thee. Thou art some fool;
I am loth to beat thee.

CLOTEN.
                 Thou injurious thief,
Hear but my name, and tremble.

GUIDERIUS.
                 What's thy name?

CLOTEN.
Cloten, thou villain.

GUIDERIUS.
Cloten, thou double villain, be thy name,
I cannot tremble at it: were it Toad, or Adder, Spider,
'Twould move me sooner.

CLOTEN.
                 To thy further fear,
Nay, to thy mere confusion, thou shalt know
I am son to the queen.

GUIDERIUS.
                 I am sorry for't; not seeming
So worthy as thy birth.

CLOTEN.
                 Art not afeard?

GUIDERIUS.
Those that I reverence, those I fear,—the wise:
At fools I laugh, not fear them.

CLOTEN.
                 Die the death:
When I have slain thee with my proper hand,
I'll follow those that even now fled hence,
And on the gates of Lud's-town set your heads:
Yield, rustic mountaineer.   [*Exeunt, fighting.*
Enter BELARIUS *and* ARVIRAGUS.

BELARIUS.
No company's abroad.

ARVIRAGUS.
None in the world: you did mistake him, sure.

BELARIUS.
I cannot tell:—long is it since I saw him,
But time hath nothing blurr'd those lines of favour

Which then he wore; the snatches in his voice,
And burst of speaking, were as his: I am absolute
'Twas very Cloten.

ARVIRAGUS.
                 In this place we left them:
I wish my brother make good time with him,
You say he is so fell.

BELARIUS.
                 Being scarce made up,
I mean, to man, he had not apprehension
Of roaring terrors; for defect of judgement
Is oft the cure of fear.—But, see, thy brother.
Enter GUIDERIUS *with* CLOTEN's *head.*

GUIDERIUS.
This Cloten was a fool, an empty purse,—
There was no money in't: not Hercules
Could have knockt out his brains, for he had none:
Yet I not doing this, the fool had borne
My head as I do his.

BELARIUS.
                 What hast thou done?

GUIDERIUS.
I am perfect what: cut off one Cloten's head,
Son to the queen, after his own report;
Who call'd me traitor, mountaineer; and swore
With his own single hand he'ld take us in,
Displace our heads where—thank the gods!—they grow,
And set them on Lud's-town.

BELARIUS.
                 We are all undone.

GUIDERIUS.
Why, worthy father, what have we to lose
But that he swore to take our lives? The law
Protects not us: then why should we be tender
To let an arrogant piece of flesh threat us,
Play judge and executioner all himself,
For we do fear the law? What company
Discover you abroad?

BELARIUS.
                 No single soul
Can we set eye on; but in all safe reason
He must have some attendants. Though his humour
Was nothing but mutation,—ay, and that
From one bad thing to worse; not frenzy, not
Absolute madness could so far have raved,
To bring him here alone: although, perhaps,
It may be heard at court, that such as we
Cave here, hunt here, are outlaws, and in time
May make some stronger head; the which he hearing—
As it is like him—might break out, and swear
He'ld fetch us in; yet is't not probable
To come alone, either he so undertaking,
Or they so suffering: then on good ground we fear,
If we do fear this body hath a tail,
More perilous than the head.

ARVIRAGUS.
                 Let ordinance
Come as the gods foresay it: howsoe'er,
My brother hath done well.

BELARIUS.
                 I had no mind
To hunt this day: the boy Fidele's sickness
Did make my way long forth.

GUIDERIUS.
　　　　　　　　With his own sword,
Which he did wave against my throat, I have ta'en
His head from him: I'll throw't into the creek
Behind our rock; and let it to the sea,
And tell the fishes he's the queen's son, Cloten:
That's all I reck.　　　　　　　　　[*Exit.*

BELARIUS.
　　　　I fear 'twill be revenged:
Would, Polydore, thou hadst not done 't! though
　valour
Becomes thee well enough.

ARVIRAGUS.
　　　　　　　　Would I had done't,
So the revenge alone pursued me!—Polydore,
I love thee brotherly; but envy much
Thou hast robb'd me of this deed: I would re-
　venges,
That possible strength might meet, would seek us
　through,
And put us to our answer.

BELARIUS.
　　　　Well, 'tis done:—
We'll hunt no more to-day, nor seek for danger
Where there's no profit. I prithee, to our rock;
You and Fidele play the cooks: I'll stay
Till hasty Polydore return, and bring him
To dinner presently.

ARVIRAGUS.
　　　　　Poor sick Fidele!
I'll willingly to him: to gain his colour
I'ld let a parish of such Clotens blood,
And praise myself for charity.　　　　[*Exit.*

BELARIUS.
　　　　　O thou goddess,
Thou divine Nature, how thyself thou blazon'st
In these two princely boys! They are as gentle
As zephyrs, blowing below the violet,
Not wagging his sweet head; and yet as rough,
Their royal blood enchafed, as the rudest wind,
That by the top doth take the mountain pine,
And make him stoop to the vale. 'Tis wonder
That an invisible instinct should frame them
To royalty unlearn'd; honour untaught;
Civility not seen from other; valour,
That wildly grows in them, but yields a crop
As if it had been sow'd. Yet still it's strange
What Cloten's being here to us portends,
Or what his death will bring us.
Enter GUIDERIUS.

GUIDERIUS.
　　　　　　Where's my brother?
I have sent Cloten's clotpoll down the stream,
In embassy to his mother: his body's hostage
For his return.　　　　　　　[*Solemn music.*

BELARIUS.
　　　My ingenious instrument!
Hark, Polydore, it sounds! But what occasion
Hath Cadwal now to give it motion? Hark!

GUIDERIUS.
Is he at home?

BELARIUS.
　　　He went hence even now.

GUIDERIUS.
What does he mean? since death of my dear'st
　mother

It did not speak before. All solemn things
Should answer solemn accidents. The matter?
Triumphs for nothing, and lamenting toys,
Is jollity for apes, and grief for boys.
Is Cadwal mad?

BELARIUS.
　　　Look, here he comes,
And brings the dire occasion in his arms
Of what we blame him for!
Enter ARVIRAGUS, *with* IMOGEN *as dead, bearing
her in his arms.*

ARVIRAGUS.
　　　　　The bird is dead
That we have made so much on. I had rather
Have skipt from sixteen years of age to sixty,
To have turn'd my leaping-time into a crutch,
Than have seen this.

GUIDERIUS.
　　　O sweetest, fairest lily!
My brother wears thee not the one half so well
As when thou grew'st thyself.

BELARIUS.
　　　　　O melancholy!
Who ever yet could sound thy bottom? find
The ooze, to show what coast thy sluggish crare
Might easiliest harbour in?—Thou blessed thing!
Jove knows what man thou mightst have made;
　but I,
Thou diedst, a most rare boy, of melancholy!—
How found you him?

ARVIRAGUS.
　　　Stark, as you see:
Thus smiling, as some fly had tickled slumber,
Not as death's dart, being laught at; his right
　check
Reposing on a cushion.

GUIDERIUS.
　　　　　Where?

ARVIRAGUS.
　　　　　O'the floor;
His arms thus leagued: I thought he slept; and put
My clouted brogues from off my feet, whose rude-
　ness
Answer'd my steps too loud.

GUIDERIUS.
　　　　Why, he but sleeps:
If he be gone, he'll make his grave a bed;
With female fairies will his tomb be haunted,
And worms will not come to't.

ARVIRAGUS.
　　　　With fairest flowers,
Whilst summer lasts, and I live here, Fidele,
I'll sweeten thy sad grave: thou shalt not lack
The flower that's like thy face, pale primrose; nor
The azured harebell, like thy veins; no, nor
The leaf of eglantine, whom not to slander,
Out-sweeten'd not thy breath: the ruddock would,
With charitable bill,—O bill, sore-shaming
Those rich-left heirs that let their fathers lie
Without a monument!—bring thee all this;
Yea, and furr'd moss besides, when flowers are
　none,
To winter-ground thy corse.

GUIDERIUS.
　　　　Prithee, have done;
And do not play in wench-like words with that

Which is so serious. Let us bury him,
And not protract with admiration what
Is now due debt.—To the grave!

ARVIRAGUS.
                Say, where shall's lay him?

GUIDERIUS.
By good Euriphile, our mother.

ARVIRAGUS.
                    Be't so:
And let us, Polydore, though now our voices
Have got the mannish crack, sing him to the
    ground,
As once our mother; use like note and words,
Save that Euriphile must be Fidele.

GUIDERIUS.
Cadwal,
I cannot sing: I'll weep, and word it with thee;
For notes of sorrow out of tune are worse
Than priests and fanes that lie.

ARVIRAGUS.
                   We'll speak it, then.

BELARIUS.
Great griefs, I see, medicine the less; for Cloten
Is quite forgot. He was a queen's son, boys:
And, though he came our enemy, remember
He was paid for that: though mean and mighty
    rotting
Together have one dust, yet reverence—
That angel of the world—doth make distinction
Of place 'tween high and low. Our foe was
    princely;
And though you took his life as being our foe,
Yet bury him as a prince.

GUIDERIUS.
              Pray you, fetch him hither.
Thersites' body is as good as Ajax',
When neither are alive.

ARVIRAGUS.
             If you'll go fetch him,
We'll say our song the whilst.—Brother, begin.
                     [*Exit* BELARIUS.

GUIDERIUS.
Nay, Cadwal, we must lay his head to th'east;
My father hath a reason for't.

ARVIRAGUS.
             'Tis true.

GUIDERIUS.
Come on, then, and remove him.

ARVIRAGUS.
               So.—Begin.

Song.

GUIDERIUS.
Fear no more the heat o'the sun,
    Nor the furious winter's rages;
Thou thy worldly task hast done,
    Home art gone, and ta'en thy wages:
Golden lads and girls all must,
As chimney-sweepers, come to dust.

ARVIRAGUS.
Fear no more the frown o'the great,
    Thou art past the tyrant's stroke;
Care no more to clothe and eat;
    To thee the reed is as the oak:
The sceptre, learning, physic, must
All follow this, and come to dust.

GUIDERIUS.
Fear no more the lightning-flash,

ARVIRAGUS.
Nor th'all-dreaded thunder-stone;

GUIDERIUS.
Fear not slander, censure rash;

ARVIRAGUS.
Thou hast finisht joy and moan:

BOTH.
All lovers young, all lovers must,
Consign to thee, and come to dust.

GUIDERIUS.
No exorciser harm thee!

ARVIRAGUS.
Nor no witchcraft charm thee!

GUIDERIUS.
Ghost unlaid forbear thee!

ARVIRAGUS.
Nothing ill come near thee!

BOTH.
Quiet consummation have;
And renowned be thy grave!

Enter BELARIUS *with the body of* CLOTEN.

GUIDERIUS.
We have done our obsequies: come, lay him
    down.

BELARIUS.
Here's a few flowers; but 'bout midnight, more:
The herbs that have on them cold dew o'the night
Are strewings fitt'st for graves.—Upon their
    faces.—
You were as flowers, now wither'd: even so
These herblets shall, which we upon you strow.—
Come on, away: apart upon our knees.
The ground that gave them first has them again:
Their pleasures here are past, so is their pain.
        [*Exeunt* BELARIUS, GUIDERIUS, *and*
              ARVIRAGUS.

IMOGEN [*awaking*].
Yes, sir, to Milford-Haven; which is the way?—
I thank you.—By yond bush?—Pray, how far
    thither?
'Ods pittikins! can it be six mile yet?—
I have gone all night:—faith, I'll lie down and
    sleep.
But, soft! no bedfellow:—O gods and goddesses!
             [*Seeing the body of* CLOTEN.
These flowers are like the pleasures of the world;
This bloody man, the care on't.—I hope I dream;
For so I thought I was a cave-keeper,
And cook to honest creatures: but 'tis not so;
'Twas but a bolt of nothing, shot at nothing,
Which the brain makes of fumes: our very eyes
Are sometimes like our judgements, blind. Good
    faith,
I tremble still with fear: but if there be
Yet left in heaven as small a drop of pity
As a wren's eye, fear'd gods, a part of it!
The dream's here still: even when I wake, it is
Without me, as within me; not imagined, felt.
A headless man!—The garments of Posthumus!
I know the shape of's leg: this is his hand;
His foot Mercurial; his Martial thigh;
The brawns of Hercules: but his Jovial face—
Murder in heaven?—How!—'Tis gone.—Pisanio,

All curses madded Hecuba gave the Greeks,
And mine to boot, be darted on thee! Thou,
Conspired with that irregulous devil, Cloten,
Hast here cut off my lord.—To write and read
Be henceforth treacherous!—Damn'd Pisanio
Hath with his forged letters,—damn'd Pisanio—
From this most bravest vessel of the world
Struck the main-top!—O Posthumus! alas,
Where is thy head? where's that? Ay me! where's
    that?
Pisanio might have kill'd thee at the heart,
And left thy head on.—How should this ber
    Pisanio?
'Tis he and Cloten: malice and lucre in them
Have laid this woe here. O, 'tis pregnant, preg-
    nant!
The drug he gave me, which he said was precious
And cordial to me, have I not found it
Murderous to the senses? That confirms it home:
This is Pisanio's deed and Cloten's: O!—
Give colour to my pale cheek with thy blood,
That we the horrider may seem to those
Which chance to find us: O, my lord, my lord!
                    [*Throws herself on the body.*
Enter LUCIUS, CAPTAINS, *and a* SOOTH-
                    SAYER.
            CAPTAIN.
To them the legions garrison'd in Gallia,
After your will, have crost the sea; attending
You here at Milford-Haven with your ships:
They are in readiness.
            CAIUS LUCIUS.
                    But what from Rome?
            CAPTAIN.
The senate hath stirr'd up the confiners
And gentlemen of Italy; most willing spirits,
That promise noble service: and they come
Under the conduct of bold Iachimo,
Sienna's brother.
            CAIUS LUCIUS.
                When expect you them?
            CAPTAIN.
With the next benefit o'the wind.
            CAIUS LUCIUS.
                        This forwardness
Makes our hopes fair. Command our present
    numbers
Be muster'd; bid the captains look to't.—Now,
    sir,
What have you dream'd of late of this war's pur-
    pose?
            SOOTHSAYER.
Last night the very gods show'd me a vision,—
I fast and pray'd for their intelligence,—thus:
I saw Jove's bird, the Roman eagle, wing'd
From the spongy south to this part of the west,
There vanisht in the sunbeams: which portends—
Unless my sins abuse my divination—
Success to the Roman host.
            CAIUS LUCIUS.
                    Dream often so,
And never false.—Soft, ho! what trunk is here
Without his top? The ruin speaks that sometime
It was a worthy building.—How! a page!—
Or dead, or sleeping on him? But dead, rather;
For nature doth abhor to make his bed

With the defunct, or sleep upon the dead.—
Let's see the boy's face.
            CAPTAIN.
            He's alive, my lord.
            CAIUS LUCIUS.
He'll, then, instruct us of this body.—Young one,
Inform us of thy fortunes; for it seems
They crave to be demanded. Who is this
Thou makest thy bloody pillow? Or who was he
That, otherwise than noble nature did,
Hath alter'd that good picture? What's thy in-
    terest
In this sad wrack? How came it? Who is it?
What art thou?
            IMOGEN.
            I am nothing; or if not,
Nothing to be were better. This was my master,
A very valiant Briton and a good,
That here by mountaineers lies slain:—alas!
There is no more such masters: I may wander
From east to occident, cry out for service,
Try many, all good, serve truly, never
Find such another master.
            CAIUS LUCIUS.
                    'Lack, good youth!
Thou movest no less with thy complaining than
Thy master in bleeding: say his name, good
    friend.
            IMOGEN.
Richard du Champ.—[*aside*] If I do lie, and do
No harm by it, though the gods hear, I hope
They'll pardon it.—Say you, sir?
            CAIUS LUCIUS.
                        Thy name?
            IMOGEN.
                        Fidele, sir.
            CAIUS LUCIUS.
Thou dost approve thyself the very same:
Thy name well fits thy faith, thy faith thy name.
Wilt take thy chance with me? I will not say
Thou shalt be so well master'd; but, be sure,
No less beloved. The Roman emperor's letters,
Sent by a consul to me, should not sooner
Than thine own worth prefer thee: go with me.
            IMOGEN.
I'll follow, sir. But first, an't please the gods,
I'll hide my master from the flies, as deep
As these poor pickaxes can dig: and when
With wild wood-leaves and weeds I ha' strew'd
    his grave,
And on it said a century of prayers,
Such as I can, twice o'er, I'll weep and sigh;
And leaving so his service, follow you,
So please you entertain me.
            CAIUS LUCIUS.
                        Ay good youth;
And rather father thee than master thee.—
My friends,
The boy hath taught us manly duties: let us
Find out the prettiest daisied plot we can,
And make him with our pikes and partisans
A grave: come, arm him.—Boy, he is preferr'd
By thee to us; and he shall be interr'd
As soldiers can. Be cheerful; wipe thine eyes:
Some falls are means the happier to arise.
                            [*Exeunt.*

SCENE III.

A room in CYMBELINE'S *palace.*

Enter CYMBELINE, LORDS, PISANIO, *and*
ATTENDANTS.

CYMBELINE.

AGAIN; and bring me word how 'tis with her.
A fever with the absence of her son;
                    [*Exit an* ATTENDANT.
A madness, of which her life's in danger,—
  Heavens,
How deeply you at once do touch me! Imogen,
The great part of my comfort, gone; my queen
Upon a desperate bed, and in a time
When fearful wars point at me; her son gone,
So needful for this present: it strikes me, past
The hope of comfort.—But for thee, fellow,
Who needs must know of her departure, and
Dost seem so ignorant, we'll enforce it from thee
By a sharp torture.

PISANIO.
                    Sir, my life is yours,
I humbly set it at your will: but, for my mistress,
I nothing know where she remains, why gone,
Nor when she purposes return. Beseech your
  highness
Hold me your loyal servant.

FIRST LORD.
                    Good my liege,
The day that she was missing he was here:
I dare be bound he's true, and shall perform
All parts of his subjection loyally. For Cloten,
There wants no diligence in seeking him,
And will, no doubt, be found.

CYMBELINE.
                    The time is troublesome.—
[*to* PISANIO] We'll slip you for a season; but our
  jealousy
Does yet depend.

FIRST LORD.
                    So please your majesty,
The Roman legions, all from Gallia drawn,
Are landed on your coast; with a supply
Of Roman gentlemen, by the senate sent.

CYMBELINE.
Now for the counsel of my son and queen!—
I am amazed with matter.

FIRST LORD.
                    Good my liege,
Your preparation can affront no less
Than what you hear of: come more, for more
  you're ready:
The want is, but to put those powers in motion
That long to move.

CYMBELINE.
                    I thank you. Let's withdraw;
And meet the time as it seeks us. We fear not
What can from Italy annoy us; but
We grieve at chances here.—Away!
                    [*Exeunt all but* PISANIO.

PISANIO.
I heard no letter from my master since
I wrote him Imogen was slain: 'tis strange:
Nor hear I from my mistress, who did promise
To yield me often tidings; neither know I
What is betid to Cloten; but remain

Perplext in all:—the heavens still must work.
Wherein I am false I am honest: not true, to be
  true:
These present wars shall find I love my country,
Even to the note o' the king, or I'll fall in them.
All other doubts, by time let them be clear'd:
Fortune brings in some boats that are not steer'd.
                    [*Exit.*

SCENE IV.

Wales: before the cave of BELARIUS.

Enter BELARIUS, GUIDERIUS, *and*
ARVIRAGUS.

GUIDERIUS.

THE noise is round about us.

BELARIUS.
                    Let us from it.

ARVIRAGUS.
What pleasure, sir, find we in life, to lock it
From action and adventure?

GUIDERIUS.
                    Nay, what hope
Have we in hiding us? This way, the Romans
Must or for Britons slay us, or receive us
For barbarous and unnatural revolts
During their use, and slay us after.

BELARIUS.
                    Sons,
We'll higher to the mountains; there secure us.
To the king's party there's no going: newness
Of Cloten's death—we being not known, not
  muster'd
Among the bands—may drive us to a render
Where we have lived; and so extort from's that
Which we have done, whose answer would be
  death
Drawn on with torture.

GUIDERIUS.
                    This is, sir, a doubt
In such a time nothing becoming you,
Nor satisfying us.

ARVIRAGUS.
                    It is not likely
That when they hear the Roman horses neigh,
Behold their quarter'd fires, have both their eyes
And ears so cloy'd importantly as now,
That they will waste their time upon our note,
To know from whence we are.

BELARIUS.
                    O, I am known
Of many in the army: many years,
Though Cloten then but young, you see, not wore
  him
From my remembrance. And, besides, the king
Hath not deserved my service nor your loves;
Who find in my exile the want of breeding,
The certainty of this hard life; aye hopeless
To have the courtesy your cradle promised,
But to be still hot summer's tanlings, and
The shrinking slaves of winter.

GUIDERIUS.
                    Than be so,
Better to cease to be. Pray, sir, to the army:
I and my brother are not known; yourself
So out of thought, and thereto so o'ergrown,
Cannot be question'd.

ARVIRAGUS.
             By this sun that shines,
I'll thither: what thing is it that I never
Did see man die! scarce ever lookt on blood,
But that of coward hares, hot goats, and venison!
Never bestrid a horse, save one that had
A rider like myself, who ne'er wore rowel
Nor iron on his heel! I am ashamed
To look upon the holy sun, to have
The benefit of his blest beams, remaining
So long a poor unknown.
GUIDERIUS.
             By heavens, I'll go:
If you will bless me, sir, and give me leave,
I'll take the better care; but if you will not,
The hazard therefore due fall on me by
The hands of Romans!
ARVIRAGUS.
             So say I,—Amen.
BELARIUS.
No reason I, since of your lives you set
So slight a valuation, should reserve
My crackt one to more care. Have with you, boys!
If in your country wars you chance to die,
That is my bed too, lads, and there I'll lie:
Lead, lead.—[aside] The time seems long; their
    blood thinks scorn,
Till it fly out, and show them princes born.
                    [Exeunt.

ACT V. SCENE I.

Britain. The Roman camp.

Enter POSTHUMUS *with a bloody handkerchief.*

POSTHUMUS LEONATUS.

YEA, bloody cloth, I'll keep thee; for I wisht
    Thou shouldst be colour'd thus. You mar-
    ried ones,
If each of you should take this course, how many
Must murder wives much better than themselves
For wrying but a little!—O Pisanio!
Every good servant does not all commands:
No bond but to do just ones.—Gods! if you
Should have ta'en vengeance on my faults, I never
Had lived to put on this: so had you saved
The noble Imogen to repent; and struck   [alack,
Me, wretch more worth your vengeance. But,
You snatch some hence for little faults; that's love,
To have them fall no more: you some permit
To second ills with ills, each elder worse,
And make them dread it, to the doers' thrift.
But Imogen is your own: do your best wills,
And make me blest to obey!—I am brought hither
Among the Italian gentry, and to fight
Against my lady's kingdom: 'tis enough
That, Britain, I have kill'd thy mistress; peace!
I'll give no wound to thee. Therefore, good
    heavens,
Hear patiently my purpose:—I'll disrobe me
Of these Italian weeds, and suit myself
As does a Briton peasant: so I'll fight
Against the part I come with; so I'll die
For thee, O Imogen, even for whom my life
Is, every breath, a death: and thus, unknown,
Pitied nor hated, to the face of peril
Myself I'll dedicate. Let me make men know

More valour in me than my habits show.
Gods, put the strength o'the Leonati in me!
To shame the guise o'the world, I will begin
The fashion,—less without and more within.
                    [Exit.

SCENE II.

A field between the British and Roman camps.

Enter LUCIUS, IACHIMO, IMOGEN, *and the*
ROMAN ARMY *at one door, and the* BRITON
ARMY *at another;* LEONATUS POSTHUMUS
*following, like a poor soldier. They march over
and go out. Then enter again, in skirmish,*
IACHIMO *and* POSTHUMUS: *he vanquisheth
and disarmeth* IACHIMO, *and then leaves him.*

IACHIMO.

THE heaviness and guilt within my bosom
    Takes off my manhood: I have belied a lady,
The princess of this country, and the air on't
Revengingly enfeebles me; or could this carl,
A very drudge of nature's, have subdued me
In my profession? Knighthoods and honours,
    borne
As I wear mine, are titles but of scorn.
If that thy gentry, Britain, go before
This lout as he exceeds our lords, the odds
Is that we scarce are men, and you are gods. [Exit.
The battle continues; the BRITONS *fly;* CYM-
BELINE *is taken: then enter, to his rescue,*
BELARIUS, GUIDERIUS, *and* ARVIRAGUS.
BELARIUS.
Stand, stand! We have the advantage of the
    ground;
The lane is guarded: nothing routs us but
The villainy of our fears.
GUIDERIUS *and* ARVIRAGUS.
             Stand, stand, and fight!
Enter POSTHUMUS, *and seconds the* BRITONS:
they rescue CYMBELINE, *and all exeunt. Then
enter* LUCIUS, IACHIMO, *and* IMOGEN.
CAIUS LUCIUS.
Away, boy, from the troops, and save thyself;
For friends kill friends, and the disorder's such
As war were hoodwinkt.
IACHIMO.
             'Tis their fresh supplies.
CAIUS LUCIUS.
It is a day turn'd strangely: or betimes
Let's re-inforce, or fly.   [Exeunt.

SCENE III.

Another part of the field.

Enter POSTHUMUS *and a Briton* LORD.

LORD.

CAMEST thou from where they made the
    stand?
POSTHUMUS LEONATUS.
                      I did:
Though you, it seems, come from the fliers.
LORD.
                      I did.
POSTHUMUS LEONATUS.
No blame be to you, sir; for all was lost,
But that the heavens fought: the king himself
Of his wings destitute, the army broken,

And but the backs of Britons seen, all flying
Through a strait lane; the enemy full-hearted,
Lolling the tongue with slaughtering, having
  work
More plentiful than tools to do't, struck down
Some mortally, some slightly toucht, some falling
Merely through fear; that the strait pass was
  damm'd
With dead men hurt behind, and cowards living
To die with lengthen'd shame.

LORD.
                    Where was this lane?

POSTHUMUS LEONATUS.
Close by the battle, ditcht, and wall'd with turf;
Which gave advantage to an ancient soldier,—
An honest one, I warrant; who deserved
So long a breeding as his white beard came to,
In doing this for's country:—athwart the lane,
He, with two striplings,—lads more like to run
The country base than to commit such slaughter;
With faces fit for masks, or rather fairer
Than those for preservation cased or shame,—
Made good the passage; cried to those that fled,
'Our Britain's harts die flying, not our men:
To darkness fleet, souls that fly backwards! Stand;
Or we are Romans, and will give you that
Like beasts, which you shun beastly, and may
  save,
But to look back in frown: stand, stand!'—These
  three,
Three thousand confident, in act as many,—
For three performers are the file when all
The rest do nothing,—with this word, 'Stand,
  stand,'
Accommodated by the place, more charming
With their own nobleness,—which could have
  turn'd
A distaff to a lance,—gilded pale looks,
Part shame, part spirit renew'd; that some,
  turn'd coward
But by example,—O, a sin in war,
Damn'd in the first beginners!—gan to look
The way that they did, and to grin like lions
Upon the pikes o'the hunters. Then began
A stop i'the chaser, a retire; anon
A rout, confusion-thick: forthwith they fly
Chickens, the way which they stoopt eagles;
  slaves,
The strides they victors made: and now our cow-
  ards—
Like fragments in hard voyages—became
The life o'the need: having found the back-door
  open
Of the unguarded hearts, heavens, how they
  wound!
Some slain before; some dying; some their friends
O'er-borne i'the former wave: ten, chased by one,
Are now each one the slaughter-man of twenty:
Those that would die or e'er resist are grown
The mortal bugs o'the field.

LORD.
                    This was strange chance,—
A narrow lane, an old man, and two boys!

POSTHUMUS LEONATUS.
Nay, do not wonder at it: you are made
Rather to wonder at the things you hear

Than to work any. Will you rime upon't,
And vent it for a mockery? Here is one:
'Two boys, an old man twice a boy, a lane,
Preserved the Britons, was the Romans' bane.'

LORD.
Nay, be not angry, sir.

POSTHUMUS LEONATUS.
                    'Lack, to what end?
Who dares not stand his foe, I'll be his friend;
For if he'll do as he is made to do,
I know he'll quickly fly my friendship too.
You have put me into rime.

LORD.
                    Farewell; you're angry.

POSTHUMUS LEONATUS.
Still going?   [Exit Lord.
This is a lord! O noble misery!
To be i'the field, and ask, what news, of me!
To-day how many would have given their hon-
  ours
To have saved their carcasses! took heel to do't,
And yet died too! I, in mine woe charm'd,
Could not find death where I did hear him groan,
Nor feel him where he struck: being an ugly mon-
  ster,
'Tis strange he hides him in fresh cups, soft
  beds,
Sweet words; or hath moe ministers than we
That draw his knives i'the war. Well, I will find
  him:
For being now a favourer to the Briton,
No more a Briton, I have resumed again
The part I came in: fight I will no more,
But yield me to the veriest hind that shall
Once touch my shoulder. Great the slaughter is
Here made by the Roman; great the answer be
Britons must take: for me, my ransom's death;
On either side I come to spend my breath;
Which neither here I'll keep nor bear agen,
But end it by some means for Imogen.

Enter two Briton CAPTAINS and SOLDIERS.

FIRST CAPTAIN.
Great Jupiter be praised! Lucius is taken:
'Tis thought the old man and his sons were angels.

SECOND CAPTAIN.
There was a fourth man, in a silly habit,
That gave the affront with them.

FIRST CAPTAIN.
                    So 'tis reported:
But none of 'em can be found.—Stand! who's
  there?

POSTHUMUS LEONATUS.
A Roman;
Who had not now been drooping here, if seconds
Had answer'd him.

SECOND CAPTAIN.
                    Lay hands on him; a dog!—
A leg of Rome shall not return to tell
What crows have peckt them here:—he brags his
  service
As if he were of note: bring him to the king.

Enter CYMBELINE, BELARIUS, GUIDERIUS,
ARVIRAGUS, PISANIO, and Roman CAPTIVES.
The CAPTAINS present POSTHUMUS to CYM-
BELINE, who delivers him over to a GAOLER:
then exeunt omnes.

SCENE IV.

A prison.

Enter POSTHUMUS *and two* GAOLERS.

FIRST GAOLER.

YOU shall not now be stoln, you have locks
  So graze as you find pasture.   [upon you;

SECOND GAOLER.

    Ay, or a stomach. [*Exeunt* GAOLERS.

POSTHUMUS LEONATUS.

Most welcome, bondage! for thou art a way,
I think, to liberty: yet am I better
Than one that's sick o'the gout; since he had rather
Groan so in perpetuity than be cured
By the sure physician, death; who is the key
T'unbar these locks. My conscience, thou art fet•
  ter'd
More than my shanks and wrists: you good gods,
  give me
The penitent instrument to pick that bolt,
Then free for ever! Is't enough I am sorry?
So children temporal fathers do appease;
Gods are more full of mercy. Must I repent?
I cannot do it better than in gyves,
Desired more than constrain'd: to satisfy,
If of my freedom 'tis the main part, take
No stricter render of me than my all.
I know you are more clement than vile men,
Who of their broken debtors take a third,
A sixth, a tenth, letting them thrive again
On their abatement: that's not my desire:
For Imogen's dear life take mine; and though
'Tis not so dear, yet 'tis a life; you coin'd it:
'Tween man and man they weigh not every stamp;
Though light, take pieces for the figure's sake:
You rather mine, being yours: and so, great
If you will take this audit, take this life,   [powers,
And cancel these cold bonds.—O Imogen!
I'll speak to thee in silence.   [*Sleeps.*

Solemn music. Enter, as in an apparition, SICI-
  LIUS LEONATUS, *father to* POSTHUMUS, *an
  old man, attired like a warrior; leading in his
  hand an ancient matron, his wife, and mother to
  *POSTHUMUS, *with music before them: then,
  after other music, follows the two young* LEO-
  NATI, *brothers to* POSTHUMUS, *with wounds as
  they died in the wars. They circle* POSTHUMUS
  round, as he lies sleeping.

SICILIUS LEONATUS.

No more, thou thunder-master, show
  Thy spite on mortal flies:
With Mars fall out, with Juno chide,
  That thy adulteries
    Rates and revenges.
Hath my poor boy done aught but well,
  Whose face I never saw?
I died whilst in the womb he stay'd
  Attending nature's law:
Whose father then, as men report
  Thou orphans' father art,
Thou shouldst have been, and shielded him
  From this earth-vexing smart.

MOTHER.

Lucina lent not me her aid,
  But took me in my throes;
That from me was Posthumus ript,

Came crying 'mongst his foes,
  A thing of pity!

SICILIUS LEONATUS.

Great nature, like his ancestry,
  Moulded the stuff so fair,
That he deserved the praise o'the world,
  As great Sicilius' heir.

FIRST BROTHER.

When once he was mature for man,
  In Britain where was he
That could stand up his parallel;
  Or fruitful object be
In eye of Imogen, that best
  Could deem his dignity?

MOTHER.

With marriage wherefore was he mockt,
  To be exiled, and thrown
From Leonati seat, and cast
  From her his dearest one,
    Sweet Imogen?

SICILIUS LEONATUS.

Why did you suffer Iachimo,
  Slight thing of Italy,
To taint his nobler heart and brain
  With needless jealousy;
And to become the geck and scorn
  O'the other's villainy?

SECOND BROTHER.

For this, from stiller seats we came,
  Our parents, and us twain,
That, striking in our country's cause,
  Fell bravely, and were slain;
Our fealty and Tenantius' right
  With honour to maintain.

FIRST BROTHER.

Like hardiment Posthumus hath
  To Cymbeline perform'd:
Then, Jupiter, thou king of gods,
  Why hast thou thus adjourn'd
The graces for his merits due;
  Being all to dolours turn'd?

SICILIUS LEONATUS.

Thy crystal window ope; look out;
  No longer exercise
Upon a valiant race thy harsh
  And potent injuries.

MOTHER.

Since, Jupiter, our son is good,
  Take off his miseries.

SICILIUS LEONATUS.

Peep through thy marble mansion; help;
  Or we poor ghosts will cry
To the shining synod of the rest
  Against thy deity.

BOTH BROTHERS.

Help, Jupiter; or we appeal,
  And from thy justice fly.

JUPITER *descends in thunder and lightning, sitting
upon an eagle: he throws a thunderbolt. The*
GHOSTS *fall on their knees.*

JUPITER.

No more, you petty spirits of region low,
  Offend our hearing; hush! How dare you
  ghosts
Accuse the thunderer, whose bolt, you know,
  Sky-planted, batters all rebelling coasts?

Poor shadows of Elysium, hence; and rest
   Upon your never-withering banks of flowers:
Be not with mortal accidents opprest;
   No care of yours it is; you know 'tis ours.
Whom best I love I cross; to make my gift,
   The more delay'd, delighted. Be content;
Your low-laid son our godhead will uplift:
   His comforts thrive, his trials well are spent.
Our Jovial star reign'd at his birth, and in
   Our temple was he married.—Rise, and fade!—
He shall be lord of lady Imogen,
   And happier much by his affliction made.
This tablet lay upon his breast; wherein
   Our pleasure his full fortune doth confine:
And so, away! no further with your din
   Express impatience, lest you stir up mine.—
   Mount, eagle, to my palace crystalline.
                        [*Ascends.*
      SICILIUS LEONATUS.
He came in thunder; his celestial breath
Was sulphurous to smell: the holy eagle
Stoopt, as to foot us: his ascension is
More sweet than our blest fields: his royal bird
Prunes the immortal wing, and cloys his beak,
As when his god is pleased.
       ALL.
               Thanks, Jupiter!
      SICILIUS LEONATUS.
The marble pavement closes, he is enter'd
His radiant roof.—Away! and, to be blest,
Let us with care perform his great behest.
             [*The* GHOSTS *vanish.*
    POSTHUMUS LEONATUS [*waking*].
Sleep, thou hast been a grandsire, and begot
A father to me; and thou hast created
A mother and two brothers: but—O scorn!—
Gone! they went hence so soon as they were born:
And so I am awake.—Poor wretches that depend
On greatness' favour dream as I have done;
Wake, and find nothing.—But, alas, I swerve:
Many dream not to find, neither deserve,
And yet are steept in favours; so am I,
That have this golden chance, and know not why.
What fairies haunt this ground? A book? O rare
   one!
Be not, as is our fangled world, a garment
Nobler than that it covers: let thy effects
So follow, to be most unlike our courtiers,
As good as promise.   [*Reads.*
Whenas a lion's whelp shall, to himself unknown,
without seeking find, and be embraced by a
piece of tender air; and when from a stately cedar
shall be lopt branches, which, being dead many
years, shall after revive, be jointed to the old
stock, and freshly grow; then shall Posthumus
end his miseries, Britain be fortunate, and flourish
in peace and plenty.
'Tis still a dream; or else such stuff as madmen
Tongue, and brain not: either both, or nothing:
Or senseless speaking, or a speaking such
As sense cannot untie. Be what it is,
The action of my life is like it, which
I'll keep, if but for sympathy.
       Enter FIRST GAOLER.
       FIRST GAOLER.
Come, sir, are you ready for death?

      POSTHUMUS LEONATUS.
Over-roasted rather; ready long ago.
       FIRST GAOLER.
Hanging is the word, sir: if you be ready for that,
you are well cookt.
      POSTHUMUS LEONATUS.
So, if I prove a good repast to the spectators, the
dish pays the shot.
       FIRST GAOLER.
A heavy reckoning for you, sir. But the comfort
is, you shall be call'd to no more payments, fear
no more tavern-bills; which are often the sadness
of parting, as the procuring of mirth: you come in
faint for want of meat, depart reeling with too
much drink; sorry that you have paid too much,
and sorry that you are paid too much; purse and
brain both empty,—the brain the heavier for being
too light, the purse too light being drawn of
heaviness: of this contradiction you shall now
be quit.—O, the charity of a penny cord! it
sums up thousands in a trice: you have no true
debitor and creditor but it; of what's past, is,
and to come, the discharge:—your neck, sir, is
pen, book, and counters; so the acquittance
follows.
      POSTHUMUS LEONATUS.
I am merrier to die than thou art to live.
       FIRST GAOLER.
Indeed, sir, he that sleeps feels not the toothache:
but a man that were to sleep your sleep, and a
hangman to help him to bed, I think he would
change places with his officer; for, look you, sir,
you know not which way you shall go.
      POSTHUMUS LEONATUS.
Yes, indeed do I, fellow.
       FIRST GAOLER.
Your death has eyes in's head, then; I have not
seen him so pictured: you must either be directed
by some that take upon them to know, or to
take upon yourself that which I am sure you
do not know; or jump the after-inquiry on your
own peril: and how you shall speed in your
journey's end, I think you'll never return to tell
one.
      POSTHUMUS LEONATUS.
I tell thee, fellow, there are none want eyes to
direct them the way I am going, but such as
wink and will not use them.
       FIRST GAOLER.
What an infinite mock is this, that a man should
have the best use of eyes to see the way of
blindness! I am sure hanging's the way of
winking.
       Enter a MESSENGER.
       MESSENGER.
Knock off his manacles; bring your prisoner to
the king.
      POSTHUMUS LEONATUS.
Thou bring'st good news,—I am call'd to be
made free.
       FIRST GAOLER.
I'll be hang'd, then.
      POSTHUMUS LEONATUS.
Thou shalt be then freer than a gaoler; no bolts
for the dead.
      [*Exeunt* POSTHUMUS *and* MESSENGER.

FIRST GAOLER.

Unless a man would marry a gallows, and beget
young gibbets, I never saw one so prone. Yet, on
my conscience, there are verier knaves desire to
live, for all he be a Roman: and there be some of
them too that die against their wills; so should I,
if I were one. I would we were all of one mind,
and one mind good; O, there were desolation of
gaolers and gallowses! I speak against my present
profit; but my wish hath a preferment in't.

[Exit.

SCENE V.

CYMBELINE'S *tent*.

Enter CYMBELINE, BELARIUS, GUIDERIUS,
ARVIRAGUS, PISANIO, LORDS, OFFICERS,
and ATTENDANTS.

CYMBELINE.

STAND by my side, you whom the gods have
made
Preservers of my throne. Woe is my heart
That the poor soldier, that so richly fought,
Whose rags shamed gilded arms, whose naked
breast
Stept before targes of proof, cannot be found:
He shall be happy that can find him, if
Our grace can make him so.

BELARIUS.

I never saw
Such noble fury in so poor a thing;
Such precious deeds in one that promised naught
But beggary and poor looks.

CYMBELINE.

No tidings of him?

PISANIO.

He hath been searcht among the dead and living,
But no trace of him.

CYMBELINE.

To my grief, I am
The heir of his reward; which I will add
To you, the liver, heart, and brain of Britain,
[*To* BELARIUS, GUIDERIUS, *and* ARVIRAGUS.
By whom I grant she lives. 'Tis now the time
To ask of whence you are:—report it.

BELARIUS.

Sir,
In Cambria are we born, and gentlemen:
Further to boast were neither true nor modest,
Unless I add we are honest.

CYMBELINE.

Bow your knees.
Arise my knights o'the battle; I create you
Companions to our person, and will fit you
With dignities becoming your estates.
Enter CORNELIUS *and* LADIES.
There's business in these faces.—Why so sadly
Greet you our victory? you look like Romans,
And not o'the court of Britain.

CORNELIUS.

Hail, great king!
To sour your happiness, I must report
The queen is dead.

CYMBELINE.

Who worse than a physician
Would this report become? But I consider

By medicine life may be prolong'd, yet death
Will seize the doctor too.—How ended she?

CORNELIUS.

With horror, madly dying, like her life;
Which, being cruel to the world, concluded
Most cruel to herself. What she confest
I will report, so please you: these her women
Can trip me, if I err; who with wet cheeks
Were present when she finisht.

CYMBELINE.

Prithee, say.

CORNELIUS.

First, she confest she never loved you; only
Affected greatness got by you, not you:
Married your royalty, was wife to your place;
Abhorr'd your person.

CYMBELINE.

She alone knew this;
And, but she spoke it dying, I would not
Believe her lips in opening it. Proceed.

CORNELIUS.

Your daughter, whom she bore in hand to love
With such integrity, she did confess
Was as a scorpion to her sight; whose life,
But that her flight prevented it, she had
Ta'en off by poison.

CYMBELINE.

O most delicate fiend!
Who is't can read a woman?—Is there more?

CORNELIUS.

More, sir, and worse. She did confess she had
For you a mortal mineral; which, being took,
Should by the minute feed on life, and, lingering,
By inches waste you: in which time she pur-
posed,
By watching, weeping, tendance, kissing, to
O'ercome you with her show; yes, and in time,
When she had fitted you with her craft, to work
Her son into the adoption of the crown:
But, failing of her end by his strange absence,
Grew shameless desperate; open'd, in despite
Of heaven and men, her purposes; repented
The evils she hatcht were not effected; so,
Despairing, died.

CYMBELINE.

Heard you all this, her women?

LADIES.

We did, so please your highness.

CYMBELINE.

Mine eyes
Were not in fault, for she was beautiful;
Mine ears, that heard her flattery; nor my heart,
That thought her like her seeming; it had been
vicious
To have mistrusted her: yet, O my daughter!
That it was folly in me, thou mayst say,
And prove it in thy feeling. Heaven mend all!
Enter LUCIUS, IACHIMO, *the* SOOTHSAYER,
and other Roman PRISONERS, *guarded;* POST-
HUMUS *behind, and* IMOGEN.
Thou comest not, Caius, now for tribute; that
The Britons have razed out, though with the loss
Of many a bold one; whose kinsmen have made
suit
That their good souls may be appeased with
slaughter

Of you their captives, which ourself have granted:
So think of your estate.

LUCIUS.

Consider, sir, the chance of war: the day
Was yours by accident; had it gone with us,
We should not, when the blood was cool, have
        threaten'd
Our prisoners with the sword. But since the
        gods
Will have it thus, that nothing but our lives
May be call'd ransom, let it come: sufficeth
A Roman with a Roman's heart can suffer:
Augustus lives to think on't: and so much
For my peculiar care. This one thing only
I will entreat; my boy, a Briton born,
Let him be ransom'd: never master had
A page so kind, so duteous-diligent,
So tender over his occasions, true,
So feat, so nurse-like: let his virtue join
With my request, which I'll make bold your high-
        ness
Cannot deny; he hath done no Briton harm,
Though he have served a Roman: save him, sir,
And spare no blood beside.

CYMBELINE.

                    I have surely seen him:
His favour is familiar to me.—
Boy, thou hast lookt thyself into my grace,
And art mine own.—I know not why, nor where-
        fore,
To say, 'Live, boy:' ne'er thank thy master; live:
And ask of Cymbeline what boon thou wilt,
Fitting my bounty and thy state, I'll give it;
Yea, though thou do demand a prisoner,
The noblest ta'en.

IMOGEN.

                    I humbly thank your highness.

LUCIUS.

I do not bid thee beg my life, good lad;
And yet I know thou wilt.

IMOGEN.

                    No, no: alack,
There's other work in hand: I see a thing
Bitter to me as death: your life, good master,
Must shuffle for itself.

LUCIUS.

                    The boy disdains me,
He leaves me, scorns me: briefly die their joys
That place them on the truth of girls and boys.—
Why stands he so perplext?

CYMBELINE.

                    What wouldst thou, boy?
I love thee more and more: think more and more
What's best to ask. Know'st him thou look'st on?
        speak,
Wilt have him live? Is he thy kin? thy friend?

IMOGEN.

He is a Roman; no more kin to me
Than I to your highness; who, being born your
        vassal,
Am something nearer.

CYMBELINE.

                    Wherefore eyest him so?

IMOGEN.

I'll tell you, sir, in private, if you please
To give me hearing.

CYMBELINE.

                    Ay, with all my heart,
And lend my best attention. What's thy name?

IMOGEN.

Fidele, sir.

CYMBELINE.

Thou'rt my good youth, my page;
I'll be thy master: walk with me; speak freely.
        [CYMBELINE and IMOGEN converse apart.

BELARIUS.

Is not this boy revived from death?

ARVIRAGUS.

                    One sand another
Not more resembles that sweet rosy lad
Who died, and was Fidele.—What think you?

GUIDERIUS.

The same dead thing alive.

BELARIUS.

Peace, peace! see further; he eyes us not; forbear;
Creatures may be alike: were't he, I am sure
He would have spoke to us.

GUIDERIUS.

                    But we saw him dead.

BELARIUS.

Be silent; let's see further.

PISANIO [aside].

                    It is my mistress:
Since she is living, let the time run on
To good or bad.
        [CYMBELINE and IMOGEN come forward.

CYMBELINE.

                    Come, stand thou by our side,
Make thy demand aloud.—[to IACHIMO] Sir,
        step you forth;
Give answer to this boy, and do it freely;
Or, by our greatness, and the grace of it,
Which is our honour, bitter torture shall   [him.
Winnow the truth from falsehood.—On, speak to

IMOGEN.

My boon is, that this gentleman may render
Of whom he had this ring.

POSTHUMUS LEONATUS [aside].

                    What's that to him?

CYMBELINE.

That diamond upon your finger, say
How came it yours?

IACHIMO.

Thou'lt torture me to leave unspoken that
Which, to be spoke, would torture thee.

CYMBELINE.

                                    How! me?

IACHIMO.

I am glad to be constrain'd to utter that
Which torments me to conceal. By villainy
I got this ring: 'twas Leonatus' jewel;
Whom thou didst banish; and—which more may
        grieve thee,
As it doth me—a nobler sir ne'er lived   [lord?
'Twixt sky and ground. Wilt thou hear more, my

CYMBELINE.

All that belongs to this.

IACHIMO.

                    That paragon, thy daughter,—
For whom my heart drops blood, and my false
        spirits
Quail to remember—Give me leave; I faint.

CYMBELINE.

My daughter! what of her? Renew thy strength:
I had rather thou shouldst live while nature will
Than die ere I hear more: strive, man, and speak.

IACHIMO.

Upon a time,—unhappy was the clock
That struck the hour!—it was in Rome,—accurst
The mansion where!—'twas at a feast,—O,
    would
Our viands had been poison'd, or at least
Those which I heaved to head!—the good Post-
    humus—
What should I say? he was too good to be
Where ill men were; and was the best of all
Amongst the rarest of good ones—sitting sadly,
Hearing us praise our loves of Italy
For beauty that made barren the swell'd boast
Of him that best could speak; for feature, laming
The shrine of Venus, or straight-pight Minerva,
Postures beyond brief nature; for condition,
A shop of all the qualities that man
Loves woman for; besides, that hook of wiving,
Fairness which strikes the eye,—

CYMBELINE.

                I stand on fire:
Come to the matter.

IACHIMO.

           All too soon I shall,
Unless thou wouldst grieve quickly.—This Post-
    humus,
Most like a noble lord in love, and one
That had a royal lover, took his hint;
And, not dispraising whom we praised,—therein
He was as calm as virtue,—he began
His mistress' picture; which by his tongue being
    made,
And then a mind put in't, either our brags
Were crackt of kitchen-trulls, or his description
Proved us unspeaking sots.

CYMBELINE.

          Nay, nay, to the purpose.

IACHIMO.

Your daughter's chastity—there it begins.
He spake of her, as Dian had hot dreams,
And she alone were cold: whereat I, wretch,
Made scruple of his praise; and wager'd with him
Pieces of gold 'gainst this which then he wore
Upon his honour'd finger, to attain
In suit the place of 's bed, and win this ring
By hers and mine adultery. He, true knight,
No lesser of her honour confident
Than I did truly find her, stakes this ring;
And would so, had it been a carbuncle
Of Phœbus' wheel; and might so safely, had it
Been all the worth of 's car. Away to Britain
Post I in this design:—well may you, sir,
Remember me at court; where I was taught
Of your chaste daughter the wide difference
'Twixt amorous and villainous. Being thus
    quencht
Of hope, not longing, mine Italian brain
Gan in your duller Britain operate
Most vilely; for my vantage, excellent:
And, to be brief, my practice so prevail'd
That I return'd with simular proof enough
To make the noble Leonatus mad,

By wounding his belief in her renown
With tokens thus and thus; averring notes
Of chamber-hanging, pictures, this her bracelet,—
O cunning, how I got it!—nay, some marks
Of secret on her person, that he could not
But think her bond of chastity quite crackt,
I having ta'en the forfeit. Whereupon—
Methinks, I see him now—

POSTHUMUS LEONATUS [coming forward].

            Ay, so thou dost,
Italian fiend!—Ay me, most credulous fool,
Egregious murderer, thief, any thing
That's due to all the villains past, in being,
To come!—O, give me cord, or knife, or poison,
Some upright justicer! Thou, king, send out
For torturers ingenious: it is I
That all the abhorred things o'the earth amend
By being worse than they. I am Posthumus,
That kill'd thy daughter:—villain-like, I lie;
That caused a lesser villain than myself,
A sacrilegious thief, to do't:—the temple
Of virtue was she; yea, and she herself.
Spit, and throw stones, cast mire upon me, set
The dogs o'the street to bay me: every villain
Be call'd Posthumus Leonatus; and
Be villainy less than 'twas!—O Imogen!
My queen, my life, my wife! O Imogen,
Imogen, Imogen!

IMOGEN.

        Peace, my lord; hear, hear—

POSTHUMUS LEONATUS.

Shall's have a play of this? Thou scornful page,
There lie thy part.   [Striking her: she falls.

PISANIO.

        O, gentlemen, help!
Mine and your mistress!—O, my lord Post-
    humus!
You ne'er kill'd Imogen till now.—Help, help!—
Mine honour'd lady!

CYMBELINE.

        Does the world go round?

POSTHUMUS LEONATUS.

How comes these staggers on me?

PISANIO.

           Wake, my mistress!

CYMBELINE.

If this be so, the gods do mean to strike me
To death with mortal joy.

PISANIO.

        How fares my mistress?

IMOGEN.

O, get thee from my sight;
Thou gavest me poison: dangerous fellow,
    hence!
Breathe not where princes are.

CYMBELINE.

        The tune of Imogen!

PISANIO.

Lady,
The gods throw stones of sulphur on me, if
That box I gave you was not thought by me
A precious thing; I had it from the queen.

CYMBELINE.

New matter still?

IMOGEN.

    It poison'd me.

CORNELIUS.
　　　　　　　　O gods!—
I left out one thing which the queen confest,
Which must approve thee honest: 'If Pisanio
Have,' said she, 'given his mistress that con-
　　fection
Which I gave him for cordial, she is served
As I would serve a rat.'
　　　　CYMBELINE.
　　　　　　　　What's this, Cornelius?
　　　　CORNELIUS.
The queen, sir, very oft importuned me
To temper poisons for her; still pretending
The satisfaction of her knowledge only
In killing creatures vile, as cats and dogs,
Of no esteem: I, dreading that her purpose
Was of more danger, did compound for her
A certain stuff, which, being ta'en, would cease
The present power of life; but in short time
All offices of nature should again
Do their due functions.—Have you ta'en of it?
　　　　IMOGEN.
Most like I did, for I was dead.
　　　　BELARIUS.
　　　　　　　　My boys,
There was our error.
　　　　GUIDERIUS.
　　　　　　　This is, sure, Fidele.
　　　　IMOGEN.
Why did you throw your wedded lady from you?
Think that you are upon a lock; and now
Throw me again. 　　　　[Embracing him.
　　　　POSTHUMUS LEONATUS.
　　　　　　Hang there like fruit, my soul,
Till the tree die!
　　　　CYMBELINE.
　　　　　　How now, my flesh, my child!
What, makest thou me a dullard in this act?
Wilt thou not speak to me?
　　　　IMOGEN.
　　　　　　　　Your blessing, sir.
　　　　　　　　　　[Kneeling.
　　　　BELARIUS.
Though you did love this youth, I blame ye not;
You had a motive for't.
　　　　[To GUIDERIUS and ARVIRAGUS.
　　　　CYMBELINE.
　　　　　　　My tears that fall
Prove holy water on thee! Imogen,
Thy mother's dead.
　　　　IMOGEN.
　　　　　　I am sorry for't, my lord.
　　　　CYMBELINE.
O, she was naught: and long of her it was
That we meet here so strangely: but her son
Is gone, we know not how nor where.
　　　　PISANIO.
　　　　　　　　My lord,
Now fear is from me, I'll speak troth. Lord
　　Cloten,
Upon my lady's missing, came to me
With his sword drawn; foam'd at the mouth, and
　　swore,
If I discover'd not which way she was gone,
It was my instant death. By accident,
I had a feigned letter of my master's

Then in my pocket; which directed him
To seek her on the mountains near to Milford;
Where, in a frenzy, in my master's garments,
Which he enforced from me, away he posts
With unchaste purpose, and with oath to vio-
　　late
My lady's honour: what became of him
I further know not.
　　　　GUIDERIUS.
　　　　　　Let me end the story:
I slew him there.
　　　　CYMBELINE.
　　　　　　Marry, the gods forfend!
I would not thy good deeds should from my lips
Pluck a hard sentence: prithee, valiant youth,
Deny't again.
　　　　GUIDERIUS.
　　　　　　I have spoke it, and I did it.
　　　　CYMBELINE.
He was a prince.
　　　　GUIDERIUS.
A most incivil one: the wrongs he did me
Were nothing prince-like; for he did provoke me
With language that would make me spurn the
　　sea,
If it could so roar to me: I cut off's head;
And am right glad he is not standing here
To tell this tale of mine.
　　　　CYMBELINE.
　　　　　　I am sorry for thee:
By thine own tongue thou art condemn'd, and
　　must
Endure our law: thou'rt dead.
　　　　IMOGEN.
　　　　　　　That headless man
I thought had been my lord.
　　　　CYMBELINE.
　　　　　　　Bind the offender,
And take him from our presence.
　　　　BELARIUS.
　　　　　　　Stay, sir king:
This man is better than the man he slew,
As well descended as thyself; and hath
More of thee merited than a band of Clotens
Had ever scar for.—[to the GUARD] Let his arms
　　alone:
They were not born for bondage.
　　　　CYMBELINE.
　　　　　　　Why, old soldier,
Wilt thou undo the worth thou art unpaid for,
By tasting of our wrath? How of descent
As good as we?
　　　　ARVIRAGUS.
　　　　　　In that he spake too far.
　　　　CYMBELINE.
And thou shalt die for't.
　　　　BELARIUS.
　　　　　　We will die all three:
But I will prove that two on's are as good
As I have given out him.—My sons, I must,
For mine own part, unfold a dangerous speech,
Though, haply, well for you.
　　　　ARVIRAGUS.
　　　　　　　Your danger's ours.
　　　　GUIDERIUS.
And our good his.

BELARIUS.
Have at it, then!—
By leave,—thou hadst, great king, a subject who
Was call'd Belarius.

CYMBELINE.
What of him? he is
A banisht traitor.

BELARIUS.
He it is that hath
Assumed this age: indeed, a banisht man;
I know not how a traitor.

CYMBELINE.
Take him hence:
The whole world shall not save him.

BELARIUS.
Not too hot:
First pay me for the nursing of thy sons;
And let it be confiscate all, so soon
As I have received it.

CYMBELINE.
Nursing of my sons!

BELARIUS.
I am too blunt and saucy: here's my knee:
Ere I arise, I will prefer my sons;
Then spare not the old father. Mighty sir,
These two young gentlemen, that call me father,
And think they are my sons, are none of mine;
They are the issue of your loins, my liege,
And blood of your begetting.

CYMBELINE.
How! my issue!

BELARIUS.
So sure as you your father's. I, old Morgan,
Am that Belarius whom you sometime banisht:
Your pleasure was my mere offence, my punishment
Itself, and all my treason; that I suffer'd
Was all the harm I did. These gentle princes—
For such and so they are—these twenty years
Have I train'd up: those arts they have as I
Could put into them; my breeding was, sir, as
Your highness knows. Their nurse, Euriphile,
Whom for the theft I wedded, stole these children
Upon my banishment: I moved her to't;
Having received the punishment before,
For that which I did then: beaten for loyalty
Excited me to treason: their dear loss,
The more of you 'twas felt, the more it shaped
Unto my end of stealing them. But, gracious sir,
Here are your sons again; and I must lose
Two of the sweet'st companions in the world.
The benediction of these covering heavens
Fall on their heads like dew! for they are worthy
To inlay heaven with stars.

CYMBELINE.
Thou weep'st, and speak'st.
The service that you three have done is more
Unlike than this thou tell'st. I lost my children:
If these be they, I know not how to wish
A pair of worthier sons.

BELARIUS.
Be pleased awhile.—
This gentleman, whom I call Polydore,
Most worthy prince, as yours, is true Guiderius:
This gentleman, my Cadwal, Arviragus,

Your younger princely son: he, sir, was lapt
In a most curious mantle, wrought by the hand
Of his queen-mother, which, for more probation,
I can with ease produce.

CYMBELINE.
Guiderius had
Upon his neck a mole, a sanguine star;
It was a mark of wonder.

BELARIUS.
This is he;
Who hath upon him still that natural stamp:
It was wise nature's end in the donation,
To be his evidence now.

CYMBELINE.
O, what, am I
A mother to the birth of three? Ne'er mother
Rejoiced deliverance more.—Blest pray you be,
That, after this strange starting from your orbs,
You may reign in them now!—O Imogen,
Thou hast lost by this a kingdom.

IMOGEN.
No, my lord;
I have got two worlds by't.—O my gentle
brothers,
Have we thus met? O, never say hereafter
But I am truest speaker: you call'd me brother,
When I was but your sister; I you brothers,
When ye were so indeed.

CYMBELINE.
Did you e'er meet?

ARVIRAGUS.
Ay, my good lord.

GUIDERIUS.
And at first meeting loved;
Continued so, until we thought he died.

CORNELIUS.
By the queen's dram she swallow'd.

CYMBELINE.
O rare instinct!
When shall I hear all through? This fierce abridgement
Hath to it circumstantial branches, which
Distinction should be rich in.—Where? how
lived you?
And when came you to serve our Roman captive?
How parted with your brothers? how first met
them?
Why fled you from the court? and whither?
These,
And your three motives to the battle, with
I know not how much more, should be demanded;
And all the other by-dependances,
From chance to chance: but nor the time nor
place
Will serve our long inter'gatories. See,
Posthumus anchors upon Imogen;
And she, like harmless lightning, throws her eye
On him, her brothers, me, her master, hitting
Each object with a joy: the counterchange
Is severally in all. Let's quit this ground,
And smoke the temple with our sacrifices.—
[to BELARIUS] Thou art my brother; so we'll
hold thee ever.

IMOGEN.
You are my father too; and did relieve me,
To see this gracious season.

CYMBELINE.
                    All o'erjoy'd,
Save these in bonds: let them be joyful too,
For they shall taste our comfort.
            IMOGEN.
                    My good master,
I will yet do you service.
            CAIUS LUCIUS.
                    Happy be you!
            CYMBELINE.
The forlorn soldier, that so nobly fought,
He would have well becomed this place, and
    graced
The thankings of a king.
            POSTHUMUS LEONATUS.
                    I am, sir,
The soldier that did company these three
In poor beseeming; 'twas a fitment for
The purpose I then follow'd.—That I was he,
Speak, Iachimo: I had you down, and might
Have made you finish.
            IACHIMO.
                    I am down again:
                            [Kneeling.
But now my heavy conscience sinks my knee,
As then your force did. Take that life, beseech
    you,
Which I so often owe: but your ring first;
And here the bracelet of the truest princess
That ever swore her faith.
            POSTHUMUS LEONATUS.
                    Kneel not to me:
The power that I have on you is to spare you;
The malice towards you to forgive you: live,
And deal with others better.
            CYMBELINE.
                    Nobly doom'd!
We'll learn our freeness of a son-in-law;
Pardon's the word to all.
            ARVIRAGUS.
                    You holp us, sir,
As you did mean indeed to be our brother;
Joy'd are we that you are.
            POSTHUMUS LEONATUS.
Your servant, princes.—Good my lord of Rome,
Call forth your soothsayer: as I slept, methought
Great Jupiter, upon his eagle backt,
Appear'd to me, with other spritely shows
Of mine own kindred: when I waked, I found
This label on my bosom; whose containing
Is so from sense in hardness, that I can
Make no collection of it: let him show
His skill in the construction.
            CAIUS LUCIUS.
                    Philarmonus,—
            SOOTHSAYER.
Here, my good lord.
            CAIUS LUCIUS.
                    Read, and declare the meaning.
            SOOTHSAYER [reads].
Whenas a lion's whelp shall, to himself un-
known, without seeking find, and be embraced by

a piece of tender air; and when from a stately
cedar shall be lopt branches, which, being dead
many years, shall after revive, be jointed to the
old stock, and freshly grow; then shall Posthumus
end his miseries, Britain be fortunate, and flour-
ish in peace and plenty.
Thou, Leonatus, art the lion's whelp:
The fit and apt construction of thy name,
Being Leo-natus, doth import so much:
[to CYMBELINE] The piece of tender air, thy vir-
    tuous daughter,
Which we call mollis aer; and mollis aer
We term it mulier: [to POSTHUMUS] which mulier
    I divine
Is thy most constant wife; who, even now,
Answering the letter of the oracle,
Unknown to you, unsought, were clipt about
With this most tender air.
            CYMBELINE.
                    This hath some seeming.
            SOOTHSAYER.
The lofty cedar, royal Cymbeline,
Personates thee: and thy lopt branches point
Thy two sons forth; who, by Belarius stoln,
For many years thought dead, are now revived,
To the majestic cedar join'd; whose issue
Promises Britain peace and plenty.
            CYMBELINE.
                    Well,
My peace we will begin:—and, Caius Lucius,
Although the victor, we submit to Cæsar,
And to the Roman empire; promising
To pay our wonted tribute, from the which
We were dissuaded by our wicked queen;
Whom heavens, in justice, both on her and hers,
Have laid most heavy hand.
            SOOTHSAYER.
The fingers of the powers above do tune
The harmony of this peace. The vision
Which I made known to Lucius, ere the stroke
Of this yet scarce-cold battle, at this instant
Is full accomplisht; for the Roman eagle,
From south to west on wing soaring aloft,
Lessen'd herself, and in the beams o'the sun
So vanisht; which foreshow'd our princely eagle,
Th'imperial Cæsar, should again unite
His favour with the radiant Cymbeline,
Which shines here in the west.
            CYMBELINE.
                    Laud we the gods;
And let our crooked smokes climb to their nos-
    trils
From our blest altars. Publish we this peace
To all our subjects. Set we forward: let
A Roman and a British ensign wave
Friendly together: so through Lud's-town
    march:
And in the temple of great Jupiter
Our peace we'll ratify; seal it with feasts.—
Set on there!—Never was a war did cease,
Ere bloody hands were washt, with such a peace.
                            [Exeunt.

THE WINTER'S TALE

DRAMATIS PERSONAE

LEONTES, *king of Sicilia.*
MAMILLIUS, *young prince of Sicilia.*
CAMILLO,
ANTIGONUS, } *four lords of Sicilia.*
CLEOMENES,
DION,
POLIXENES, *king of Bohemia.*
FLORIZEL, *prince of Bohemia.*
ARCHIDAMUS, *a lord of Bohemia.*
OLD SHEPHERD, *reputed father of Perdita.*
CLOWN, *his son.*
AUTOLYCUS, *a rogue.*
A MARINER.
GAOLER.

HERMIONE, *queen to Leontes.*
PERDITA, *daughter to Leontes and Hermione.*
PAULINA, *wife to Antigonus.*
EMILIA, *a lady attending on Hermione.*
MOPSA, } *Shepherdesses.*
DORCAS,

Other LORDS *and* GENTLEMEN, LADIES, OFFICERS, *and* SERVANTS, SHEPHERDS *and* SHEPHERDESSES.

TIME, *as* CHORUS.

SCENE—*Sometimes in Sicilia, sometimes in Bohemia.*

ACT I. SCENE I.

Sicilia. Antechamber in LEONTES' *palace.*

Enter CAMILLO *and* ARCHIDAMUS.

ARCHIDAMUS.

IF you shall chance, Camillo, to visit Bohemia, on the like occasion whereon my services are now on foot, you shall see, as I have said, great difference betwixt our Bohemia and your Sicilia.

CAMILLO.

I think, this coming summer, the King of Sicilia means to pay Bohemia the visitation which he justly owes him.

ARCHIDAMUS.

Wherein our entertainment shall shame us we will be justified in our loves; for, indeed,—

CAMILLO.

Beseech you,—

ARCHIDAMUS.

Verily, I speak it in the freedom of my knowledge: we cannot with such magnificence—in so rare—I know not what to say.—We will give you sleepy drinks, that your senses, unintelligent of our insufficience, may, though they cannot praise us, as little accuse us.

CAMILLO.

You pay a great deal too dear for what's given freely.

ARCHIDAMUS.

Believe me, I speak as my understanding instructs me, and as mine honesty puts it to utterance.

CAMILLO.

Sicilia cannot show himself over-kind to Bohemia. They were train'd together in their childhoods; and there rooted betwixt them such an affection, which cannot choose but branch now. Since their more mature dignities and royal necessities made separation of their society, their encounters, though not personal, hath been royally attorney'd with interchange of gifts, letters, loving embassies; that they have seem'd to be together, though absent; shook hands, as over a vast; and embraced, as it were, from the ends of opposed winds. The heavens continue their loves!

ARCHIDAMUS.

I think there is not in the world either malice or matter to alter it. You have an unspeakable comfort of your young prince Mamillius: it is a gentleman of the greatest promise that ever came into my note.

CAMILLO.

I very well agree with you in the hopes of him: it is a gallant child; one that, indeed, physics the subject, makes old hearts fresh: they that went on crutches ere he was born desire yet their life to see him a man.

ARCHIDAMUS.

Would they else be content to die?

CAMILLO.

Yes; if there were no other excuse why they should desire to live.

ARCHIDAMUS.

If the king had no son, they would desire to live on crutches till he had one. [*Exeunt.*

SCENE II.

A room of state in the same.

Enter LEONTES, POLIXENES, HERMIONE, MAMILLIUS, CAMILLO, *and* ATTENDANTS

POLIXENES.

NINE changes of the watery star hath been
The shepherd's note since we have left our throne
Without a burden: time as long again
Would be fill'd up, my brother, with our thanks;
And yet we should, for perpetuity,
Go hence in debt: and therefore, like a cipher,
Yet standing in rich place, I multiply
With one we-thank-you many thousands moe
That go before it.

LEONTES.

　　　Stay your thanks awhile,
And pay them when you part.

POLIXENES.

　　　　　Sir, that's to-morrow.
I am question'd by my fears, of what may chance
Or breed upon our absence: that may blow

No sneaping winds at home, to make us say,
'This is put forth too truly!' Besides, I have
   stay'd
To tire your royalty.

LEONTES.
        We are tougher, brother,
Than you can put us to't.

POLIXENES.
        No longer stay.

LEONTES.
One seven-night longer.

POLIXENES.
        Very sooth, to-morrow.

LEONTES.
We'll part the time between's, then: and in that
I'll no gainsaying.

POLIXENES.
        Press me not, beseech you, so.
There is no tongue that moves, none, none i'the
   world,
So soon as yours, could win me: so it should now,
Were there necessity in your request, although
'Twere needful I denied it. My affairs
Do even drag me homeward: which to hinder,
Were, in your love, a whip to me; my stay,
To you a charge and trouble: to save both,
Farewell, our brother.

LEONTES.
        Tongue-tied, our queen? speak you.

HERMIONE.
I had thought, sir, to have held my peace until
You had drawn oaths from him not to stay. You,
   sir,
Charge him too coldly. Tell him, you are sure
All in Bohemia's well; this satisfaction
The by-gone day proclaim'd: say this to him,
He's beat from his best ward.

LEONTES.
        Well said, Hermione.

HERMIONE.
To tell, he longs to see his son, were strong:
But let him say so then, and let him go;
But let him swear so, and he shall not stay,
We'll thwack him hence with distaffs.—
Yet of your royal presence I'll adventure
The borrow of a week. When at Bohemia
You take my lord, I'll give you my commission
To let him there a month behind the gest
Prefixt for's parting:—yet, good deed, Leontes,
I love thee not a jar o'the clock behind
What lady she her lord.—You'll stay?

POLIXENES.
        No, madam.

HERMIONE.
Nay, but you will?

POLIXENES.
I may not, verily.

HERMIONE.
Verily!
You put me off with limber vows; but I,
Though you would seek t'unsphere the stars with
   oaths,
Should yet say, 'Sir, no going.' Verily,
You shall not go: a lady's 'verily' is
As potent as a lord's. Will you go yet?
Force me to keep you as a prisoner,

Not like a guest; so you shall pay your fees
When you depart, and save your thanks. How say
   you?
My prisoner, or my guest? by your dread 'verily,'
One of them you shall be.

POLIXENES.
        Your guest, then, madam:
To be your prisoner should import offending;
Which is for me less easy to commit
Than you to punish.

HERMIONE.
        Not your gaoler, then,
But your kind hostess. Come, I'll question you
Of my lord's tricks and yours when you were
   boys:
You were pretty lordings then?

POLIXENES.
        We were, fair queen,
Two lads that thought there was no more behind
But such a day to-morrow as to-day,
And to be boy eternal.

HERMIONE.
Was not my lord the verier wag o'the two?

POLIXENES.
We were as twinn'd lambs that did frisk i'the sun,
And bleat the one at the other: what we changed
Was innocence for innocence; we knew not
The doctrine of ill-doing, no, nor dream'd
That any did. Had we pursued that life,
And our weak spirits ne'er been higher rear'd
With stronger blood, we should have answer'd
   heaven
Boldly, 'Not guilty;' the imposition clear'd
Hereditary ours.

HERMIONE.
        By this we gather
You have tript since.

POLIXENES.
        O my most sacred lady,
Temptations have since then been born to's; for
In those unfledged days was my wife a girl;
Your precious self had then not crost the eyes
Of my young playfellow.

HERMIONE.
        Grace to boot!
Of this make no conclusion, lest you say
Your queen and I are devils: yet, go on;
Th'offences we have made you do, we'll answer;
If you first sinn'd with us, and that with us
You did continue fault, and that you slipt not
With any but with us.

LEONTES.
        Is he won yet?

HERMIONE.
He'll stay, my lord.

LEONTES.
        At my request he would not.
Hermione, my dear'st, thou never spokest
To better purpose.

HERMIONE.
Never?

LEONTES.
        Never, but once.

HERMIONE.
What! have I twice said well? when was't before?
I prithee tell me; cram's with praise, and make's

As fat as tame things: one good deed dying
    tongueless
Slaughters a thousand waiting upon that.
Our praises are our wages: you may ride's
With one soft kiss a thousand furlongs, ere
With spur we heat an acre. But to the goal:—
My last good deed was to entreat his stay:
What was my first? it has an elder sister,
Or I mistake you: O, would her name were Grace!
But once before I spoke to the purpose: when?
Nay, let me have't; I long.

> LEONTES.
>   Why, that was when

Three crabbed months had sour'd themselves to
    death,
Ere I could make thee open thy white hand,
And clap thyself my love: then didst thou utter,
'I am yours for ever.'

> HERMIONE.
>   'Tis Grace indeed.—

Why, lo you now, I have spoke to the purpose
    twice:
The one for ever earn'd a royal husband;
Th'other for some while a friend.

>   [*Giving her hand to* POLIXENES.
> LEONTES [*aside*].
>   Too hot, too hot!

To mingle friendship far, is mingling bloods.
I have *tremor cordis* on me,—my heart dances;
But not for joy,—not joy.—This entertainment
May a free face put on; derive a liberty
From heartiness, from bounty's fertile bosom,
And well become the agent; 't may, I grant:
But to be paddling palms and pinching fingers,
As now they are; and making practised smiles,
As in a looking-glass; and then to sigh, as 'twere
The mort o'the deer; O, that is entertainment
My bosom likes not, nor my brows!—Mamillius,
Art thou my boy?

> MAMILLIUS.
>   Ay, my good lord.
> LEONTES.
>   I'fecks!

Why, that's my bawcock. What, hast smutch'd thy
nose?—
They say it is a copy out of mine. Come, captain,
We must be neat;—not neat, but cleanly, captain:
And yet the steer, the heifer, and the calf,
Are all call'd neat.—Still virginalling
Upon his palm?—How now, you wanton calf!
Art thou my calf?

> MAMILLIUS.
>   Yes, if you will, my lord.
> LEONTES.

Thou want'st a rough pash, and the shoots that I
have,
To be full like me:—yet they say we are
Almost as like as eggs; women say so,
That will say any thing: but were they false
As o'er-dyed blacks, as wind, as waters,—false
As dice are to be wisht by one that fixes
No bourn 'twixt his and mine; yet were it true
To say this boy were like me.—Come, sir page,
Look on me with your welkin eye: sweet villain!
Most dear'st! my collop!—Can thy dam?—may't
be?—

Affection! thy intention stabs the centre:
Thou dost make possible things not so held,
Communicatest with dreams;—how can this
    be?—
With what's unreal thou coactive art,
And fellow'st nothing: then 'tis very credent
Thou mayst co-join with something; and thou
    dost,
And that beyond commission, and I find it,—
And that to the infection of my brains
And hardening of my brows.

> POLIXENES.
>   What means Sicilia?
> HERMIONE.

He something seems unsettled.

> POLIXENES.
>   How, my lord!

What cheer? how is't with you, best brother?

> HERMIONE.
>   You look

As if you held a brow of much distraction:
Are you moved, my lord?

> LEONTES.
>   No, in good earnest.—

How sometimes nature will betray its folly,
Its tenderness, and make itself a pastime
To harder bosoms!—Looking on the lines
Of my boy's face, methoughts I did recoil
Twenty-three years; and saw myself unbreech'd,
In my green velvet coat; my dagger muzzled,
Lest it should bite its master, and so prove,
As ornaments oft do, too dangerous:
How like, methought, I then was to this kernel,
This squash, this gentleman.—Mine honest friend,
Will you take eggs for money?

> MAMILLIUS.

No, my lord, I'll fight.

> LEONTES.

You will? why, happy man be's dole!—My
    brother,
Are you so fond of your young prince as we
Do seem to be of ours?

> POLIXENES.
>   If at home, sir,

He's all my exercise, my mirth, my matter:
Now my sworn friend, and then mine enemy;
My parasite, my soldier, statesman, all:
He makes a July's day short as December;
And with his varying childness cures in me
Thoughts that would thick my blood.

> LEONTES.
>   So stands this squire

Officed with me. We two will walk, my lord,
And leave you to your graver steps.—Hermione,
How thou lovest us, show in our brother's wel-
    come;
Let what is dear in Sicily be cheap:
Next to thyself and my young rover, he's
Apparent to my heart.

> HERMIONE.
>   If you would seek us,

We are yours i'the garden: shall's attend you there?

> LEONTES.

To your own bents dispose you: you'll be found,
Be you beneath the sky.—[*aside*] I am angling
now,

Though you perceive me not how I give line.
Go to, go to!
How she holds up the neb, the bill to him!
And arms her with the boldness of a wife
To her allowing husband!

[*Exeunt* POLIXENES, HERMIONE, *and* AT-
TENDANTS.

Gone already!
Inch-thick, knee-deep, o'er head and ears a forkt
one!
Go, play, boy, play: thy mother plays, and I
Play too; but so disgraced a part, whose issue
Will hiss me to my grave: contempt and clamour
Will be my knell.—Go, play, boy, play.—There
have been,
Or I am much deceived, cuckolds ere now;
And many a man there is, even at this present,
Now while I speak this, holds his wife by th'arm,
That little thinks she has been sluiced in's ab-
sence,
And his pond fisht by his next neighbour, by
Sir Smile, his neighbour: nay, there's comfort in't,
Whiles other men have gates, and those gates
open'd,
As mine, against their will: should all despair
That have revolted wives, the tenth of mankind
Would hang themselves. Physic for't there's none;
It is a bawdy planet, that will strike
Where 'tis predominant; and 'tis powerful, think
it,
From east, west, north, and south: be it concluded,
No barricado for a belly; know't;
It will let in and out the enemy
With bag and baggage: many thousand on's
Have the disease, and feel't not.—How now, boy!

MAMILLIUS.
I am like you, they say.

LEONTES.
Why, that's some comfort.
What, Camillo there?

CAMILLO.
Ay, my good lord.

LEONTES.
Go, play, Mamillius; thou'rt an honest man.

[*Exit* MAMILLIUS.
Camillo, this great sir will yet stay longer.

CAMILLO.
You had much ado to make his anchor hold:
When you cast out, it still came home.

LEONTES.
Didst note it?

CAMILLO.
He would not stay at your petitions; made
His business more material.

LEONTES.
Didst perceive it?—
[*aside*] They're here with me already; whispering,
rounding,
'Sicilia is a—so-forth:' 'tis far gone,
When I shall gust it last.—How came't, Camillo,
That he did stay?

CAMILLO.
At the good queen's entreaty.

LEONTES.
At the queen's be't: 'good' should be pertinent;
But, so it is, it is not. Was this taken

By any understanding pate but thine?
For thy conceit is soaking, will draw in
More than the common blocks:—not noted, is't,
But of the finer natures? by some severals
Of head-piece extraordinary? lower messes
Perchance are to this business purblind? say.

CAMILLO.
Business, my lord! I think most understand
Bohemia stays here longer.

LEONTES.
Ha!

CAMILLO.
Stays here longer.

LEONTES.
Ay, but why?

CAMILLO.
To satisfy your highness, and the entreaties
Of our most gracious mistress.

LEONTES.
Satisfy
Th'entreaties of your mistress!—satisfy!—
Let that suffice. I have trusted thee, Camillo,
With all the nearest things to my heart, as well
My chamber-councils; wherein, priest-like, thou
Hast cleansed my bosom,—I from thee departed
Thy penitent reform'd: but we have been
Deceived in thy integrity, deceived
In that which seems so.

CAMILLO.
Be it forbid, my lord!

LEONTES.
To bide upon't,—thou art not honest; or,
If thou inclinest that way, thou art a coward,
Which hoxes honesty behind, restraining
From course required; or else thou must be
counted
A servant grafted in my serious trust,
And therein negligent; or else a fool
That seest a game play'd home, the rich stake
drawn,
And takest it all for jest.

CAMILLO.
My gracious lord,
I may be negligent, foolish, and fearful;
In every one of these no man is free,
But that his negligence, his folly, fear,
Among the infinite doings of the world,
Sometime puts forth. In your affairs, my lord,
If ever I were wilful-negligent,
It was my folly; if industriously
I play'd the fool, it was my negligence,
Not weighing well the end; if ever fearful
To do a thing, where I the issue doubted,
Whereof the execution did cry out
Against the non-performance, 'twas a fear
Which oft infects the wisest: these, my lord,
Are such allow'd infirmities that honesty
Is never free of. But, beseech your Grace,
Be plainer with me; let me know my trespass
By its own visage: if I then deny it,
'Tis none of mine.

LEONTES.
Ha' not you seen, Camillo,—
But that's past doubt, you have, or your eye-glass
Is thicker than a cuckold's horn,—or heard,—
For, to a vision so apparent, rumour

Cannot be mute,—or thought,—for cogitation
Resides not in that man that does not think,—
My wife is slippery? If thou wilt confess,—
Or else be impudently negative,
To have nor eyes nor ears nor thought,—then say
My wife's a hobby-horse; deserves a name
As rank as any flax-wench that puts-to
Before her troth-plight: say't, and justify't.

CAMILLO.
I would not be a stander-by to hear
My sovereign mistress clouded so, without
My present vengeance taken: 'shrew my heart,
You never spoke what did become you less
Than this; which to reiterate were sin
As deep as that, though true.

LEONTES.
               Is whispering nothing?
Is leaning cheek to cheek? is meeting noses?
Kissing with inside lip? stopping the career
Of laughter with a sigh?—a note infallible
Of breaking honesty;—horsing foot on foot?
Skulking in corners? wishing clocks more swift?
Hours, minutes? noon, midnight? and all eyes
Blind with the pin-and-web, but theirs, theirs
    only,
That would unseen be wicked? is this nothing?
Why, then the world and all that's in't is nothing;
The covering sky is nothing; Bohemia nothing;
My wife is nothing; nor nothing have these noth-
    ings,
If this be nothing.

CAMILLO.
          Good my lord, be cured
Of this diseased opinion, and betimes;
For 'tis most dangerous.

LEONTES.
            Say it be, 'tis true.

CAMILLO.
No, no, my lord.

LEONTES.
           It is; you lie, you lie.
I say thou liest, Camillo, and I hate thee;
Pronounce thee a gross lout, a mindless slave;
Or else a hovering temporizer, that
Canst with thine eyes at once see good and evil,
Inclining to them both; were my wife's liver
Infected as her life, she would not live
The running of one glass.

CAMILLO.
          Who does infect her?

LEONTES.
Why, he that wears her like his medal, hanging
About his neck, Bohemia: who—if I
Had servants true about me, that bare eyes
To see alike mine honour as their profits,
Their own particular thrifts,—they would do
    that
Which should undo more doing: ay, and thou,
His cupbearer,—whom I from meaner form
Have bencht, and rear'd to worship; who mayst
    see
Plainly, as heaven sees earth, and earth sees
    heaven,
How I am gall'd,—mightst bespice a cup,
To give mine enemy a lasting wink;
Which draught to me were cordial.

CAMILLO.
              Sir, my lord,
I could do this, and that with no rash potion,
But with a lingering dram, that should not work
Maliciously like poison: but I cannot
Believe this crack to be in my dread mistress,
So sovereignly being honourable.
I have loved thee,—

LEONTES.
        Make that thy question, and go rot!
Dost think I am so muddy, so unsettled,
To appoint myself in this vexation; sully
The purity and whiteness of my sheets,—
Which to preserve is sleep, which being spotted
Is goads, thorns, nettles, tails of wasps;
Give scandal to the blood o'the prince my son,—
Who I do think is mine, and love as mine,—
Without ripe moving to't? Would I do this?
Could man so blench?

CAMILLO.
           I must believe you, sir:
I do; and will fetch off Bohemia for't;
Provided that, when he's removed, your highness
Will take again your queen as yours at first,
Even for your son's sake; and thereby for sealing
The injury of tongues in courts and kingdoms
Known and allied to yours.

LEONTES.
          Thou dost advise me
Even so as I mine own course have set down:
I'll give no blemish to her honour, none.

CAMILLO.
My lord,
Go then; and with a countenance as clear
As friendship wears at feasts, keep with Bohemia
And with your queen. I am his cupbearer:
If from me he have wholesome beverage,
Account me not your servant.

LEONTES.
            This is all:—
Do't, and thou hast the one half of my heart;
Do't not, thou splitt'st thine own.

CAMILLO.
            I'll do't, my lord.

LEONTES.
I will seem friendly, as thou hast advised me. [Exit.

CAMILLO.
O miserable lady!—But, for me,
What case stand I in? I must be the poisoner
Of good Polixenes: and my ground to do't
Is the obedience to a master; one
Who, in rebellion with himself, will have
All that are his so too.—To do this deed,
Promotion follows: if I could find example
Of thousands that had struck anointed kings,
And flourisht after, I'ld not do't; but since
Nor brass nor stone nor parchment bears not one,
Let villainy itself forswear't. I must
Forsake the court: to do't, or no, is certain
To me a break-neck.—Happy star reign now!
Here comes Bohemia.

Enter POLIXENES.

POLIXENES.
          This is strange: methinks
My favour here begins to warp. Not speak?—
Good day, Camillo.

CAMILLO.
Hail, most royal sir!
POLIXENES.
What is the news i'the court?
CAMILLO.
None rare, my lord.
POLIXENES.
The king hath on him such a countenance
As he had lost some province, and a region
Loved as he loves himself: even now I met him
With customary compliment; when he,
Wafting his eyes to the contrary, and falling
A lip of much contempt, speeds from me; and
So leaves me, to consider what is breeding
That changes thus his manners.
CAMILLO.
I dare not know, my lord.
POLIXENES.
How! dare not! do not. Do you know, and dare not?
Be intelligent to me: 'tis thereabouts;
For, to yourself, what you do know, you must,
And cannot say you dare not. Good Camillo,
Your changed complexions are to me a mirror,
Which shows me mine changed too; for I must be
A party in this alteration, finding
Myself thus alter'd with't.
CAMILLO.
There is a sickness
Which puts some of us in distemper; but
I cannot name the disease; and it is caught
Of you that yet are well.
POLIXENES.
How! caught of me!
Make me not sighted like the basilisk:
I have lookt on thousands, who have sped the
better
By my regard, but kill'd none so. Camillo,—
As you are certainly a gentleman; thereto
Clerk-like experienced, which no less adorns
Our gentry than our parents' noble names,
In whose success we are gentle,—I beseech you,
If you know aught which does behove my know-
ledge
Thereof to be inform'd, imprison't not
In ignorant concealment.
CAMILLO.
I may not answer.
POLIXENES.
A sickness caught of me, and yet I well!
I must be answer'd.—Dost thou hear, Camillo,
I conjure thee, by all the parts of man
Which honour does acknowledge,—whereof the
least
Is not this suit of mine,—that thou declare
What incidency thou dost guess of harm
Is creeping toward me: how far off, how near;
Which way to be prevented, if to be;
If not, how best to bear it.
CAMILLO.
Sir, I will tell you;
Since I am charged in honour, and by him
That I think honourable: therefore mark my
counsel,
Which must be even as swiftly follow'd as
I mean to utter it, or both yourself and me
Cry 'lost,' and so good night!

POLIXENES.
On, good Camillo.
CAMILLO.
I am appointed him to murder you.
POLIXENES.
By whom, Camillo?
CAMILLO.
By the king.
POLIXENES.
For what?
CAMILLO.
He thinks, nay, with all confidence he swears,
As he had seen't, or been an instrument
To vice you to't, that you have toucht his queen
Forbiddenly.
POLIXENES.
O, then my best blood turn
To an infected jelly, and my name
Be yoked with his that did betray the Best!
Turn then my freshest reputation to
A savour that may strike the dullest nostril
Where I arrive, and my approach be shunn'd,
Nay, hated too, worse than the great'st infection
That e'er was heard or read!
CAMILLO.
Swear his thought over
By each particular star in heaven and
By all their influences, you may as well
Forbid the sea for to obey the moon,
As or by oath remove, or counsel shake
The fabric of his folly, whose foundation
Is piled upon his faith, and will continue
The standing of his body.
POLIXENES.
How should this grow?
CAMILLO.
I know not: but I am sure 'tis safer to
Avoid what's grown than question how 'tis born.
If, therefore, you dare trust my honesty,
That lies enclosed in this trunk, which you
Shall bear along impawn'd,—away to-night!
Your followers I will whisper to the business;
And will, by twos and threes, at several posterns,
Clear them o'the city: for myself, I'll put
My fortunes to your service, which are here
By this discovery lost. Be not uncertain;
For, by the honour of my parents, I
Have utter'd truth: which if you seek to prove,
I dare not stand by; nor shall you be safer
Than one condemn'd by the king's own mouth,
thereon
His execution sworn.
POLIXENES.
I do believe thee:
I saw his heart in's face. Give me thy hand:
Be pilot to me, and thy places shall
Still neighbour mine. My ships are ready, and
My people did expect my hence-departure
Two days ago.—This jealousy
Is for a precious creature: as she's rare,
Must it be great; and, as his person's mighty,
Must it be violent; and as he does conceive
He is dishonour'd by a man which ever
Profest to him, why, his revenges must
In that be made more bitter. Fear o'ershades me:
Good expedition be my friend, and comfort

The gracious queen, part of his theme, but noth-
ing
Of his ill-ta'en suspicion! Come, Camillo;
I will respect thee as a father, if
Thou bear'st my life off hence: let us avoid.
CAMILLO.
It is in mine authority to command
The keys of all the posterns: please your highness
To take the urgent hour: come, sir, away.
[*Exeunt.*

ACT II. SCENE I.

Sicilia. LEONTES' *palace.*

Enter HERMIONE, MAMILLIUS, *and* LADIES.

HERMIONE.
TAKE the boy to you: he so troubles me,
'Tis past enduring.
FIRST LADY.
Come, my gracious lord,
Shall I be your playfellow?
MAMILLIUS.
No, I'll none of you.
FIRST LADY.
Why, my sweet lord?
MAMILLIUS.
You'll kiss me hard, and speak to me as if
I were a baby still.—I love you better.
SECOND LADY.
And why so, my lord?
MAMILLIUS.
Not for because
Your brows are blacker, yet black brows, they say,
Become some women best, so that there be not
Too much hair there, but in a semicircle,
Or a half-moon made with a pen.
SECOND LADY.
Who taught ye this?
MAMILLIUS.
I learn'd it out of women's faces.—Pray now,
What colour are your eyebrows?
FIRST LADY.
Blue, my lord.
MAMILLIUS.
Nay, that's a mock: I have seen a lady's nose
That has been blue, but not her eyebrows.
FIRST LADY.
Hark ye;
The queen your mother rounds apace: we shall
Present our services to a fine new prince
One of these days; and then you'ld wanton with us,
If we would have you.
SECOND LADY.
She is spread of late
Into a goodly bulk; good time encounter her!
HERMIONE.
What wisdom stirs amongst you? Come, sir, now
I am for you again: pray you, sit by us,
And tell's a tale.
MAMILLIUS.
Merry or sad shall't be?
HERMIONE.
As merry as you will.
MAMILLIUS.
A sad tale's best for winter: I have one
Of sprites and goblins.

HERMIONE.
Let's have that, good sir.
Come on, sit down:—come on, and do your best
To fright me with your sprites; you're powerful
at it.
MAMILLIUS.
There was a man,—
HERMIONE.
Nay, come, sit down; then on.
MAMILLIUS.
Dwelt by a churchyard:—I will tell it softly;
Yond crickets shall not hear it.
HERMIONE.
Come on, then,
And give't me in mine ear.

Enter LEONTES, ANTIGONUS, LORDS,
and GUARDS.

LEONTES.
Was he met there? his train? Camillo with him?
FIRST LORD.
Behind the tuft of pines I met them; never
Saw I men scour so on their way: I eyed them
Even to their ships.
LEONTES.
How blest am I
In my just censure, in my true opinion!—
Alack, for lesser knowledge! how accurst
In being so blest!—There may be in the cup
A spider steept, and one may drink, depart,
And yet partake no venom; for his knowledge
Is not infected: but if one present
Th'abhorr'd ingredient to his eye, make known
How he hath drunk, he cracks his gorge, his
sides,
With violent hefts:—I have drunk, and seen the
spider.
Camillo was his help in this, his pandar:—
There is a plot against my life, my crown;
All's true that is mistrusted:—that false villain,
Whom I employ'd, was pre-employ'd by him:
He has discover'd my design, and I
Remain a pincht thing: yea, a very trick
For them to play at will.—How came the posterns
So easily open?
FIRST LORD.
By his great authority;
Which often hath no less prevail'd than so,
On your command.
LEONTES.
I know't too well.—
Give me the boy:—I am glad you did not nurse
him:
Though he does bear some signs of me, yet you
Have too much blood in him.
HERMIONE.
What is this? sport?
LEONTES.
Bear the boy hence; he shall not come about her;
Away with him!—and let her sport herself
[*Exit* MAMILLIUS *with some of the* GUARDS.
With that she's big with;—for 'tis Polixenes
Has made thee swell thus.
HERMIONE.
But I'ld say he had not,
And I'll be sworn you would believe my saying,
Howe'er you lean to the nayward.

LEONTES.
You, my lords,
Look on her, mark her well; be but about
To say, 'She is a goodly lady,' and
The justice of your hearts will thereto add,
''Tis pity she's not honest, honourable:'
Praise her but for this her without-door form,—
Which, on my faith, deserves high speech,—and
straight
The shrug, the hum, or ha,—these petty brands
That calumny doth use:—O, I am out,
That mercy does; for calumny will sear
Virtue itself:—these shrugs, these hums and ha's,
When you have said 'she's goodly,' come between
Ere you can say 'she's honest:' but be't known,
From him that has most cause to grieve it should
be,
She's an adultress.

HERMIONE.
Should a villain say so,
The most replenisht villain in the world,
He were as much more villain: you, my lord,
Do but mistake.

LEONTES.
You have mistook, my lady,
Polixenes for Leontes: O thou thing!
Which I'll not call a creature of thy place,
Lest barbarism, making me the precedent,
Should a like language use to all degrees,
And mannerly distinguishment leave out
Betwixt the prince and beggar!—I have said
She's an adultress; I have said with whom:
More, she's a traitor; and Camillo is
A feoderary with her; and one that knows,
What she should shame to know herself
But with her most vile principal, that she's
A bed-swerver, even as bad as those
That vulgars give bold'st titles; ay, and privy
To this their late escape.

HERMIONE.
No, by my life,
Privy to none of this. How will this grieve you,
When you shall come to clearer knowledge, that
You thus have publisht me! Gentle my lord,
You scarce can right me throughly then, to say
You did mistake.

LEONTES.
No; if I mistake
In those foundations which I build upon,
The centre is not big enough to bear
A schoolboy's top.—Away with her to prison!
He who shall speak for her is afar off guilty
But that he speaks.

HERMIONE.
There's some ill planet reigns:
I must be patient till the heavens look
With an aspect more favourable. Good my lords,
I am not prone to weeping, as our sex
Commonly are; the want of which vain dew
Perchance shall dry your pities; but I have
That honourable grief lodged here which burns
Worse than tears drown: beseech you all, my
lords,
With thoughts so qualified as your charities
Shall best instruct you, measure me; and so
The king's will be perform'd!

LEONTES [to the GUARDS].
Shall I be heard?

HERMIONE.
Who is't that goes with me? Beseech your high-
ness
My women may be with me; for, you see,
My plight requires it. Do not weep, good fools;
There is no cause: when you shall know your
mistress
Has deserved prison, then abound in tears
As I come out: this action I now go on
Is for my better grace. Adieu, my lord:
I never wisht to see you sorry; now
I trust I shall.—My women, come; you have
leave.

LEONTES.
Go, do our bidding; hence!
[Exeunt HERMIONE and LADIES, with
GUARDS.

FIRST LORD.
Beseech your highness, call the queen again.

ANTIGONUS.
Be certain what you do, sir, lest your justice
Prove violence; in the which three great ones
suffer,
Yourself, your queen, your son.

FIRST LORD.
For her, my lord,
I dare my life lay down, and will do't, sir,
Please you t'accept it, that the queen is spot-
less
I'the eyes of heaven and to you; I mean,
In this which you accuse her.

ANTIGONUS.
If it prove
She's otherwise, I'll keep my stables where
I lodge my wife; I'll go in couples with her;
Than when I feel and see her no further trust
her;
For every inch of woman in the world,
Ay, every dram of woman's flesh, is false,
If she be.

LEONTES.
Hold your peaces.

FIRST LORD.
Good my lord,—

ANTIGONUS.
It is for you we speak, not for ourselves:
You are abused, and by some putter-on,
That will be damn'd for't; would I knew the
villain,
I would land-damn him. Be she honour-flaw'd,—
I have three daughters; the eldest is eleven;
The second and the third, nine and some five;
If this prove true, they'll pay for't: by mine
honour,
I'll geld 'em all; fourteen they shall not see,
To bring false generations: they are co-heirs;
And I had rather glib myself than they
Should not produce fair issue.

LEONTES.
Cease; no more.
You smell this business with a sense as cold
As is a dead man's nose: but I do see't and feel't,
As you feel doing thus; and see withal
The instruments that feel.

ANTIGONUS.
If it be so,
We need no grave to bury honesty:
There's not a grain of it the face to sweeten
Of the whole dungy earth.

LEONTES.
What! lack I credit?

FIRST LORD.
I had rather you did lack than I, my lord,
Upon this ground; and more it would content
me
To have her honour true than your suspicion,
Be blamed for't how you might.

LEONTES.
Why, what need we
Commune with you of this, but rather follow
Our forceful instigation? Our prerogative
Calls not your counsels; but our natural good-
ness
Imparts this: which, if you—or stupefied,
Or seeming so in skill—cannot or will not
Relish a truth, like us, inform yourselves
We need no more of your advice: the matter,
The loss, the gain, the ordering on't, is all
Properly ours.

ANTIGONUS.
And I wish, my liege,
You had only in your silent judgement tried it,
Without more overture.

LEONTES.
How could that be?
Either thou art most ignorant by age,
Or thou wert born a fool. Camillo's flight,
Added to their familiarity,—
Which was as gross as ever toucht conjecture,
That lackt sight only, naught for approbation
But only seeing, all other circumstances
Made up to the deed,—doth push on this proceed-
ing:
Yet, for a greater confirmation,
For, in an act of this importance 'twere
Most piteous to be wild,—I have dispatcht in
post
To sacred Delphos, to Apollo's temple,
Cleomenes and Dion, whom you know
Of stuft sufficiency: now, from the oracle
They will bring all; whose spiritual counsel had
Shall stop or spur me. Have I done well?

FIRST LORD.
Well done, my lord.

LEONTES.
Though I am satisfied, and need no more
Than what I know, yet shall the oracle
Give rest to the minds of others; such as he
Whose ignorant credulity will not
Come up to the truth. So have we thought it
good
From our free person she should be confined,
Lest that the treachery of the two fled hence
Be left her to perform. Come, follow us;
We are to speak in public; for this business
Will raise us all.

ANTIGONUS [aside].
To laughter, as I take it,
If the good truth were known. [Exeunt.

SCENE II.

A prison.

Enter PAULINA *and* ATTENDANTS.

PAULINA.
THE keeper of the prison,—call to him;
Let him have knowledge who I am.
[*Exit an* ATTENDANT.
Good lady!
No court in Europe is too good for thee;
What dost thou, then, in prison?
Enter ATTENDANT, *with the* GAOLER.
Now, good sir,
You know me, do you not?

GAOLER.
For a worthy lady,
And one who much I honour.

PAULINA.
Pray you, then,
Conduct me to the queen.

GAOLER.
I may not, madam: to the contrary
I have express commandment.

PAULINA.
Here's ado,
To lock up honesty and honour from
Th'access of gentle visitors!—Is't lawful, pray
you,
To see her women? any of them? Emilia?

GAOLER.
So please you, madam,
To put apart these your attendants, I
Shall bring Emilia forth.

PAULINA.
I pray now, call her.—
Withdraw yourselves. [*Exeunt* ATTENDANTS

GOALER.
And, madam,
I must be present at your conference.

PAULINA.
Well, be't so, prithee. [*Exit* GAOLER
Here's such ado to make no stain a stain,
As passes colouring.
Enter GAOLER, *with* EMILIA.
Dear gentlewoman,
How fares our gracious lady?

EMILIA.
As well as one so great and so forlorn
May hold together: on her frights and griefs,—
Which never tender lady hath borne greater,—
She is something before her time deliver'd.

PAULINA.
A boy?

EMILIA.
A daughter; and a goodly babe,
Lusty, and like to live: the queen receives
Much comfort in't; says, 'My poor prisoner,
I am innocent as you.'

PAULINA.
I dare be sworn:—
These dangerous unsafe lunes i'the king, beshrew
them!
He must be told on't, and he shall: the office
Becomes a woman best; I'll take't upon me:
If I prove honey-mouth'd, let my tongue blister,
And never to my red-lookt anger be

The trumpet any more.—Pray you, Emilia,
Commend my best obedience to the queen:
If she dares trust me with her little babe,
I'll show't the king, and undertake to be
Her advocate to the loud'st.   We do not know
How he may soften at the sight o'the child:
The silence often of pure innocence
Persuades, when speaking fails.

                 EMILIA.
                     Most worthy madam,
Your honour and your goodness is so evident,
That your free undertaking cannot miss
A thriving issue: there is no lady living
So meet for this great errand. Please your lady-
ship
To visit the next room, I'll presently
Acquaint the queen of your most noble offer;
Who but to-day hammer'd of this design,
But durst not tempt a minister of honour,
Lest she should be denied.

                 PAULINA.
                    Tell her, Emilia,
I'll use that tongue I have: if wit flow from't,
As boldness from my bosom, let't not be doubted
I shall do good.

                 EMILIA.
             Now be you blest for it!
I'll to the queen: please you, come something
    nearer.

                 GAOLER.
Madam, if't please the queen to send the babe,
I know not what I shall incur to pass it,
Having no warrant.

                 PAULINA.
               You need not fear it, sir:
The child was prisoner to the womb, and is,
By law and process of great nature, thence
Freed and enfranchised; not a party to
The anger of the king, nor guilty of,
If any be, the trespass of the queen.

                 GAOLER.
I do believe it.

                 PAULINA.
Do not you fear: upon mine honour, I
Will stand betwixt you and danger.   [*Exeunt.*

SCENE III.
LEONTES' *palace.*

Enter LEONTES, ANTIGONUS, LORDS, *and*
ATTENDANTS.

                 LEONTES.
NOR night nor day no rest: it is but weakness
To bear the matter thus,—mere weakness. If
The cause were not in being,—part o'the cause,
She, the adultress; for the harlot king
Is quite beyond mine arm, out of the blank
And level of my brain, plot-proof; but she
I can hook to me:—say that she were gone,
Given to the fire, a moiety of my rest
Might come to me again.—Who's there?

      FIRST ATTENDANT [*advancing*].
                     My lord?

                 LEONTES.
How does the boy?

           FIRST ATTENDANT.
               He took good rest to-night;
'Tis hoped his sickness is discharged.

                 LEONTES.
To see his nobleness!
Conceiving the dishonour of his mother,
He straight declined, droopt, took it deeply,
Fasten'd and fixt the shame on't in himself,
Threw off his spirit, his appetite, his sleep,
And downright languisht.—Leave me solely:—
    go,
See how he fares. [*Exit* FIRST ATTENDANT.]—
    Fie, fie! no thought of him;—
The very thought of my revenges that way
Recoil upon me: in himself too mighty,
And in his parties, his alliance; let him be,
Until a time may serve: for present vengeance,
Take it on her. Camillo and Polixenes
Laugh at me, make their pastime at my sorrow:
They should not laugh, if I could reach them;
    nor
Shall she, within my power.

      Enter PAULINA, *with a Child.*

                 FIRST LORD.
                 You must not enter.

                 PAULINA.
Nay, rather, good my lords, be second to me:
Fear you his tyrannous passion more, alas,
Than the queen's life? a gracious innocent soul,
More free than he is jealous.

                 ANTIGONUS.
                 That's enough.

         SECOND ATTENDANT.
Madam, he hath not slept to-night; commanded
None should come at him.

                 PAULINA.
               Not so hot, good sir:
I come to bring him sleep. 'Tis such as you,—
That creep like shadows by him, and do sigh
At each his needless heavings,—such as you
Nourish the cause of his awaking: I
Do come, with words as medicinal as true,
Honest as either, to purge him of that humour
That presses him from sleep.

                 LEONTES.
               What noise there, ho?

                 PAULINA.
No noise, my lord; but needful conference
About some gossips for your highness.

                 LEONTES.
               How!—
Away with that audacious lady!—Antigonus,
I charged thee that she should not come about
    me:
I knew she would.

                 ANTIGONUS.
              I told her so, my lord,
On your displeasure's peril and on mine,
She should not visit you.

                 LEONTES.
             What, canst not rule her?

                 PAULINA.
From all dishonesty he can: in this,—
Unless he take the course that you have done,
Commit me for committing honour,—trust it,
He shall not rule me.

ANTIGONUS.
           La you now, you hear:
When she will take the rein, I let her run;
But she'll not stumble.
      PAULINA.
                Good my liege, I come,—
And, I beseech you, hear me, who profess
Myself your loyal servant, your physician,
Your most obedient counsellor; yet that dares
Less appear so, in comforting your evils,
Than such as most seem yours:—I say, I come
From your good queen.
      LEONTES.
             Good queen!
      PAULINA.
Good queen, my lord, good queen; I say good
    queen;
And would by combat make her good, so were I
A man, the worst about you.
      LEONTES.
                Force her hence.
      PAULINA.
Let him that makes but trifles of his eyes
First hand me: on mine own accord I'll off;
But first I'll do my errand.—The good queen—
For she is good—hath brought you forth a
    daughter;
Here 'tis; commends it to your blessing.
              [*Laying down the Child.*
      LEONTES.
                    Out!
A mankind witch! Hence with her, out o'door,—
A most intelligencing bawd!
      PAULINA.
               Not so:
I am as ignorant in that as you
In so entitling me; and no less honest
Than you are mad; which is enough, I'll warrant,
As this world goes, to pass for honest.
      LEONTES.
               Traitors!
Will you not push her out?—Give her the bas-
    tard:—
[*to* ANTIGONUS] Thou dotard, thou art woman-
    tired, unroosted
By thy Dame Partlet here:—take up the bastard;
Take't up, I say; give't to thy crone.
      PAULINA.
               For ever
Unvenerable be thy hands, if thou
Takest up the princess by that forced baseness
Which he has put upon't!
      LEONTES.
              He dreads his wife.
      PAULINA.
So I would you did; then 'twere past all doubt
You'ld call your children yours.
      LEONTES.
               A nest of traitors!
      ANTIGONUS.
I am none, by this good light.
      PAULINA.
             Nor I; nor any,
But one, that's here, and that's himself; for he
The sacred honour of himself, his queen's,
His hopeful son's, his babe's, betrays to slander,

Whose sting is sharper than the sword's; and will
    not—
For, as the case now stands, it is a curse;
He cannot be compell'd to't—once remove
The root of his opinion, which is rotten
As ever oak or stone was sound.
      LEONTES.
               A callet
Of boundless tongue, who late hath beat her
    husband,
And now baits me!—This brat is none of mine;
It is the issue of Polixenes:
Hence with it, and together with the dam
Commit them to the fire!
      PAULINA.
              It is yours;
And, might we lay the old proverb to your charge,
So like you, 'tis the worse.—Behold, my lords,
Although the print be little, the whole matter
And copy of the father,—eye, nose, lip;
The trick of's frown; his forehead; nay, the valley,
The pretty dimples of his chin and cheek; his
    smiles;
The very mould and frame of hand, nail, finger:—
And thou, good goddess Nature, which hast made
    it
So like to him that got it, if thou hast
The ordering of the mind too, 'mongst all colours
No yellow in't, lest she suspect, as he does,
Her children not her husband's!
      LEONTES.
               A gross hag!—
And, losel, thou art worthy to be hang'd,
That wilt not stay her tongue.
      ANTIGONUS.
             Hang all the husbands
That cannot do that feat, you'll leave yourself
Hardly one subject.
      LEONTES.
             Once more, take her hence.
      PAULINA.
A most unworthy and unnatural lord
Can do no more.
      LEONTES.
            I'll ha'thee burnt.
      PAULINA.
               I care not:
It is an heretic that makes the fire,
Not she which burns in't. I'll not call you tyrant;
But this most cruel usage of your queen—
Not able to produce more accusation
Than your own weak-hinged fancy—something
    savours
Of tyranny, and will ignoble make you,
Yea, scandalous to the world.
      LEONTES.
             On your allegiance
Out of the chamber with her! Were I a tyrant,
Where were her life? she durst not call me so,
If she did know me one. Away with her!
      PAULINA.
I pray you do not push me; I'll be gone.—
Look to your babe, my lord; 'tis yours: Jove send
    her
A better-guiding spirit!—What needs these hands?
You, that are thus so tender o'er his follies,

Will never do him good, not one of you.
So, so:—farewell; we are gone.   [*Exit.*
          LEONTES.
Thou, traitor, has set on thy wife to this.—
My child? away with't!—even thou, that hast
A heart so tender o'er it, take it hence,
And see it instantly consumed with fire;
Even thou, and none but thou. Take it up straight.
Within this hour bring me word 'tis done,
And by good testimony; or I'll seize thy life,
With what thou else call'st thine. If thou refuse,
And wilt encounter with my wrath, say so;
The bastard-brains with these my proper hands
Shall I dash out. Go, take it to the fire;
For thou sett'st on thy wife.
          ANTIGONUS.
                I did not, sir:
These lords, my noble fellows, if they please,
Can clear me in't.
          LORDS.
         We can:—my royal liege,
He is not guilty of her coming hither.
          LEONTES.
You're all liars.
          FIRST LORD.
Beseech your highness, give us better credit:
We have always truly served you; and beseech
So to esteem of us: and on our knees we beg,
As recompense of our dear services
Past and to come, that you do change this purpose,
Which being so horrible, so bloody, must
Lead on to some foul issue: we all kneel.
          LEONTES.
I am a feather for each wind that blows:
Shall I live on, to see this bastard kneel
And call me father? better burn it now
Than curse it then. But be it; let it live.
It shall not neither.—You, sir, come you hither;
                     [*to* ANTIGONUS.
You that have been so tenderly officious
With Lady Margery, your midwife, there,
To save this bastard's life,—for 'tis a bastard,
So sure as this beard's gray,—what will you ad-
    venture
To save this brat's life?
          ANTIGONUS.
             Any thing, my lord,
That my ability may undergo,
And nobleness impose: at least, thus much,—
I'll pawn the little blood which I have left
To save the innocent:—any thing possible.
          LEONTES.
It shall be possible. Swear by this sword
Thou wilt perform my bidding.
          ANTIGONUS.
                I will, my lord.
          LEONTES.
Mark, and perform it; seest thou? for the fail
Of any point in't shall not only be
Death to thyself, but to thy lewd-tongued wife,
Whom for this time we pardon. We enjoin thee,
As thou art liegeman to us, that thou carry
This female bastard hence; and that thou bear it
To some remote and desert place, quite out
Of our dominions; and that there thou leave it,
Without more mercy, to it own protection

And favour of the climate. As by strange fortune
It came to us, I do in justice charge thee,
On thy soul's peril and thy body's torture,
That thou commend it strangely to some place
Where chance may nurse or end it. Take it up.
          ANTIGONUS.
I swear to do this, though a present death
Had been more merciful.—Come on, poor babe:
Some powerful spirit instruct the kites and ravens
To be thy nurses! Wolves and bears, they say,
Casting their savageness aside, have done
Like offices of pity.—Sir, be prosperous
In more than this deed does require!—and bless-
    ing,
Against this cruelty, fight on thy side,
Poor thing, condemn'd to loss! [*Exit with the Child.*
          LEONTES.
             No, I'll not rear
Another's issue.
         Enter a SERVANT.
          SERVANT.
        Please your highness, posts
From those you sent to the oracle are come
An hour since: Cleomenes and Dion,
Being well arrived from Delphos, are both landed
Hasting to the court.
          FIRST LORD.
         So please you, sir, their speed
Hath been beyond account.
          LEONTES.
           Twenty-three days
They have been absent: 'tis good speed; foretells
The great Apollo suddenly will have
The truth of this appear. Prepare you, lords;
Summon a session, that we may arraign
Our most disloyal lady; for, as she hath
Been publicly accused, so shall she have
A just and open trial. While she lives,
My heart will be a burden to me. Leave me;
And think upon my bidding.   [*Exeunt.*

ACT III. SCENE I.

Sicilia. A street in some town.

Enter CLEOMENES *and* DION.

          CLEOMENES.
THE climate's delicate; the air most sweet;
    Fertile the isle; the temple much surpassing
The common praise it bears.
          DION.
             I shall report,
For most it caught me, the celestial habits—
Methinks I so should term them—and the rever-
    ence
Of the grave wearers. O, the sacrifice!
How ceremonious, solemn, and unearthly
It was i'the offering!
          CLEOMENES.
         But, of all, the burst
And the ear-deafening voice o'the oracle,
Kin to Jove's thunder, so surprised my sense,
That I was nothing.
          DION.
          If the event o'the journey
Prove as successful to the queen,—O, be't so!—

As it has been to us rare, pleasant, speedy,
The time is worth the use on't.

CLEOMENES.
                  Great Apollo
Turn all to the best! These proclamations,
So forcing faults upon Hermione,
I little like.

DION.
The violent carriage of it
Will clear or end the business: when the oracle—
Thus by Apollo's great divine seal'd up—
Shall the contents discover, something rare
Even then will rush to knowledge.—Go; fresh
    horses!
And gracious be the issue!   [*Exeunt.*

SCENE II.

A Court of Justice.

Enter LEONTES, LORDS, *and* OFFICERS.

LEONTES.
THIS sessions—to our great grief, we pro-
    nounce—
Even pushes 'gainst our heart; the party tried,
The daughter of a king, our wife, and one
Of us too much beloved. Let us be clear'd
Of being tyrannous, since we so openly
Proceed in justice; which shall have due course,
Even to the guilt or the purgation.—
Produce the prisoner.

FIRST OFFICER.
It is his highness' pleasure that the queen
Appear in person here in court. Silence!

HERMIONE *is brought in guarded;* PAULINA
and LADIES *attending.*

LEONTES.
Read the indictment.

FIRST OFFICER [*reads*].
Hermione, queen to the worthy Leontes, king of
Sicilia, thou art here accused and arraign'd of high
treason, in committing adultery with Polixenes,
king of Bohemia, and conspiring with Camillo to
take away the life of our sovereign lord the king,
thy royal husband: the pretence whereof being by
circumstances partly laid open, thou, Hermione,
contrary to the faith and allegiance of a true subject, didst counsel and aid them, for their better
safety, to fly away by night.

HERMIONE.
Since what I am to say must be but that
Which contradicts my accusation, and
The testimony on my part no other
But what comes from myself, it shall scarce boot
    me
To say, 'Not guilty:' mine integrity
Being counted falsehood, shall, as I express it,
Be so received. But thus: if powers divine
Behold our human actions, as they do,
I doubt not, then, but innocence shall make
False accusation blush, and tyranny
Tremble at patience. You, my lord, best know,
Who least will seem to do so, my past life
Hath been as continent, as chaste, as true,
As I am now unhappy: which is more
Than history can pattern, though devised
And play'd to take spectators; for, behold me,—

A fellow of the royal bed, which owe
A moiety of the throne, a great king's daughter,
The mother to a hopeful prince,—here standing
To prate and talk for life and honour 'fore
Who please to come and hear. For life, I prize it
As I weigh grief, which I would spare: for honour,
'Tis a derivative from me to mine,
And only that I stand for. I appeal
To your own conscience, sir, before Polixenes
Came to your court, how I was in your grace,
How merited to be so; since he came,
With what encounter so uncurrent I
Have strain'd, t'appear thus: if one jot beyond
The bound of honour, or in act or will
That way inclining, harden'd be the hearts
Of all that hear me, and my near'st of kin
Cry 'Fie' upon my grave!

LEONTES.
            I ne'er heard yet
That any of these bolder vices wanted
Less impudence to gainsay what they did
Than to perform it first.

HERMIONE.
           That's true enough;
Though 'tis a saying, sir, not due to me.

LEONTES.
You will not own it.

HERMIONE.
           More than mistress of
Which comes to me in name of fault, I must not
At all acknowledge. For Polixenes,—
With whom I am accused,—I do confess
I loved him, as in honour he required;
With such a kind of love as might become
A lady like me; with a love even such,
So and no other, as yourself commanded:
Which not to have done, I think had been in me
Both disobedience and ingratitude
To you and toward your friend; whose love had
    spoke,
Even since it could speak, from an infant, freely,
That it was yours. Now, for conspiracy,
I know not how it tastes; though it be disht
For me to try how: all I know of it
Is, that Camillo was an honest man;
And why he left your court, the gods themselves,
Wotting no more than I, are ignorant.

LEONTES.
You knew of his departure, as you know
What you have underta'en to do in's absence.

HERMIONE.
Sir,
You speak a language that I understand not:
My life stands in the level of your dreams,
Which I'll lay down.

LEONTES.
           Your actions are my dreams;
You had a bastard by Polixenes,
And I but dream'd it: as you were past all shame,—
Those of your fact are so,—so past all truth:
Which to deny concerns more than avails; for as
Thy brat hath been cast out, like to itself,
No father owning it,—which is, indeed,
More criminal in thee than it,—so thou
Shalt feel our justice; in whose easiest passage
Look for no less than death.

HERMIONE.

                Sir, spare your threats:
The bug which you would fright me with I seek.
To me can life be no commodity:
The crown and comfort of my life, your favour,
I do give lost; for I do feel it gone,
But know not how it went: my second joy
And first-fruits of my body, from his presence
I am barr'd, like one infectious: my third comfort,
Starr'd most unluckily, is from my breast,
The innocent milk in it most innocent mouth,
Haled out to murder: myself on every post
Proclaimed a strumpet; with immodest hatred
The child-bed privilege denied, which 'longs
To women of all fashion; lastly, hurried
Here to this place, i'the open air, before
I have got strength of limit. Now, my liege,
Tell me what blessings I have here alive,
That I should fear to die? Therefore, proceed.
But yet hear this; mistake me not:—for life,
I prize it not a straw; but for mine honour,
Which I would free, if I shall be condemn'd
Upon surmises, all proofs sleeping else,
But what your jealousies awake,—I tell you,
'Tis rigour, and not law.—Your honours all,
I do refer me to the oracle:
Apollo be my judge!

FIRST LORD.

          This your request
Is altogether just:—therefore, bring forth,
And in Apollo's name, his oracle,

        [*Exeunt certain* OFFICERS.

HERMIONE.

The Emperor of Russia was my father:
O, that he were alive, and here beholding
His daughter's trial! that he did but see
The flatness of my misery,—yet with eyes
Of pity, not revenge!

Enter OFFICERS, *with* CLEOMENES *and* DION.

FIRST OFFICER.

You here shall swear upon this sword of justice,
That you, Cleomenes and Dion, have
Been both at Delphos; and from thence have
   brought
This seal'd-up oracle, by the hand deliver'd
Of great Apollo's priest; and that, since then,
You have not dared to break the holy seal,
Nor read the secrets in't.

CLEOMENES *and* DION.

          All this we swear.

LEONTES.

Break up the seals, and read.

FIRST OFFICER [*reads*].

Hermione is chaste; Polixenes blameless; Camillo a true subject; Leontes a jealous tyrant; his innocent babe truly begotten; and the king shall live without an heir, if that which is lost be not found.

LORDS.

Now blessed be the great Apollo!

HERMIONE.

             Praised!

LEONTES.

Hast thou read truth?

FIRST OFFICER.

         Ay, my lord; even so
As it is here set down.

LEONTES.

There is no truth at all i'the oracle:
The sessions shall proceed: this is mere falsehood.

Enter an ATTENDANT *hastily.*

ATTENDANT.

My lord the king, the king!

LEONTES.

            What is the business?

ATTENDANT.

O sir, I shall be hated to report it!
The prince your son, with mere conceit and fear
Of the queen's speed, is gone.

LEONTES.

           How! gone!

ATTENDANT.

               Is dead.

LEONTES.

Apollo's angry; and the heavens themselves
Do strike at my injustice. [HERMIONE *faints*.]
  How now, there!

PAULINA.

This news is mortal to the queen:—look down,
And see what death is doing.

LEONTES.

          Take her hence:
Her heart is but o'ercharged; she will recover:—
I have too much believed mine own suspicion:—
Beseech you, tenderly apply to her
Some remedies for life.

      [*Exeunt* PAULINA *and* LADIES, *with*
        HERMIONE.

           Apollo, pardon
My great profaneness 'gainst thine oracle!
I'll reconcile me to Polixenes;
New woo my queen; recall the good Camillo,
Whom I proclaim a man of truth, of mercy;
For, being transported by my jealousies
To bloody thoughts and to revenge, I chose
Camillo for the minister, to poison
My friend Polixenes: which had been done,
But that the good mind of Camillo tardied
My swift command, though I with death and with
Reward did threaten and encourage him,
Not doing it and being done: he, most humane,
And fill'd with honour, to my kingly guest
Unclaspt my practice; quit his fortunes here,
Which you knew great; and to the certain hazard
Of all incertainties himself commended,
No richer than his honour:—how he glisters
Thorough my rust! and how his piety
Does my deeds make the blacker!

Enter PAULINA.

PAULINA.

             Woe, the while!
O, cut my lace, lest my heart, cracking it,
Break too!

FIRST LORD.

What fit is this, good lady?

PAULINA.

What studied torments, tyrant, hast for me?
What wheels? racks? fires? what flaying? boiling?
In leads or oils? what old or newer torture
Must I receive, whose every word deserves
To taste of thy most worst? Thy tyranny
Together working with thy jealousies,—
Fancies too weak for boys, too green and idle

For girls of nine,—O, think what they have done,
And then run mad indeed,—stark mad! for all
Thy by-gone fooleries were but spices of it.
That thou betray'dst Polixenes, 'twas nothing,—
That did but show thee, of a fool, inconstant,
And damnable ingrateful; not was't much,
Thou wouldst have poison'd good Camillo's
   honour,
To have him kill a king;—poor trespasses,
More monstrous standing by: whereof I reckon
The casting forth to crows thy baby daughter,
To be or none, or little,—though a devil
Would have shed water out of fire ere done't;
Nor is't directly laid to thee, the death
Of the young prince, whose honourable thoughts—
Thoughts high for one so tender—cleft the heart
That could conceive a gross and foolish sire
Blemisht his gracious dam: this is not, no,
Laid to thy answer: but the last,—O lords,
When I have said, cry, 'Woe,'—the queen, the
   queen,
The sweet'st, dear'st creature's dead; and venge-
   ance for't
Not dropt down yet.

FIRST LORD.
      The higher powers forbid!

PAULINA.
I say she's dead; I'll swear't. If word nor oath
Prevail not, go and see: if you can bring
Tincture or lustre in her lip, her eye,
Heat outwardly or breath within, I'll serve you
As I would do the gods.—But, O thou tyrant!
Do not repent these things; for they are heavier
Than all thy woes can stir: therefore betake
   thee
To nothing but despair. A thousand knees
Ten thousand years together, naked, fasting,
Upon a barren mountain, and still winter
In storm perpetual, could not move the gods
To look that way thou wert.

LEONTES.
      Go on, go on:
Thou canst not speak too much; I have deserved
All tongues to talk their bitterest.

FIRST LORD.
      Say no more:
Howe'er the business goes, you have made fault
I'the boldness of your speech.

PAULINA.
      I am sorry for't:
All faults I make, when I shall come to know
   them,
I do repent. Alas, I have show'd too much
The rashness of a woman! he is toucht
To the noble heart.—What's gone, and what's
   past help,
Should be past grief: do not receive affliction
At my petition; I beseech you, rather
Let me be punisht, that have minded you
Of what you should forget. Now, good my liege,
Sir, royal sir, forgive a foolish woman:
The love I bore your queen,—lo, fool again!—
I'll speak of her no more, nor of your children;
I'll not remember you of my own lord,
Who is lost too: take your patience to you,
And I'll say nothing.

LEONTES.
      Thou didst speak but well,
When most the truth; which I receive much better
Than to be pitied of thee. Prithee, bring me
To the dead bodies of my queen and son:
One grave shall be for both; upon them shall
The causes of their death appear, unto
Our shame perpetual. Once a day I'll visit
The chapel where they lie; and tears shed there
Shall be my recreation: so long as nature
Will bear up with this exercise, so long
I daily vow to use it. Come, and lead me
To these sorrows.   [*Exeunt.*

SCENE III.

Bohemia.   A desert country near the sea.

Enter ANTIGONUS *with the Child, and a*
MARINER.

ANTIGONUS.
THOU art perfect, then, our ship hath toucht
   upon
The deserts of Bohemia?

MARINER.
      Ay, my lord; and fear
We have landed in ill time: the skies look grimly,
And threaten present blusters. In my conscience,
The heavens with that we have in hand are angry,
And frown upon's.

ANTIGONUS.
Their sacred wills be done!—Go, get aboard;
Look to thy bark: I'll not be long before
I call upon thee.

MARINER.
Make your best haste; and go not
Too far i'the land: 'tis like to be loud weather;
Besides, this place is famous for the creatures
Of prey that keep upon't.

ANTIGONUS.
      Go thou away.
I'll follow instantly.

MARINER.
      I am glad at heart
To be rid so o'the business.   [*Exit.*

ANTIGONUS.
      Come, poor babe:—
I have heard,—but not believed,—the spirits o'the
   dead
May walk again: if such thing be, thy mother
Appear'd to me last night; for ne'er was dream
So like a waking. To me comes a creature,
Sometimes her head on one side, some another;
I never saw a vessel of like sorrow,
So fill'd and so becoming: in pure white robes,
Like very sanctity, she did approach
My cabin where I lay; thrice bow'd before me;
And, gasping to begin some speech, her eyes
Became two spouts: the fury spent, anon
Did this break from her: 'Good Antigonus,
Since fate, against thy better disposition,
Hath made thy person for the thrower-out
Of my poor babe, according to thine oath,—
Places remote enough are in Bohemia,
There weep, and leave it crying; and, for the babe
Is counted lost for ever, Perdita,

I prithee, call't. For this ungentle business,
Put on thee by my lord, thou ne'er shalt see
Thy wife Paulina more:'—and so, with shrieks,
She melted into air. Affrighted much,
I did in time collect myself; and thought
This was so, and no slumber. Dreams are toys:
Yet, for this once, yea, superstitiously,
I will be squared by this. I do believe
Hermione hath suffer'd death; and that
Apollo would, this being indeed the issue
Of king Polixenes, it should here be laid,
Either for life or death, upon the earth
Of its right father.—Blossom, speed thee well!
　　　[*Laying down the* CHILD, *with a scroll.*
There lie; and there thy character: there these;
　　　　　　[*Laying down a bundle.*
Which may, if fortune please, both breed thee,
　　pretty,
And still rest thine.—The storm begins:—poor
　　wretch,　　　　　　　[*Thunder.*
That, for thy mother's fault, art thus exposed
To loss and what may follow!—Weep I cannot,
But my heart bleeds: and most accurst am I
To be by oath enjoin'd to this.—Farewell!—
The day frowns more and more:—thou'rt like to
　　have
A lullaby too rough:—I never saw
The heavens so dim by day.—A savage clamour!—
　　　[*Noise of hunters, dogs, and bears within.*
Well may I get aboard!—This is the chase:
I am gone for ever.　　[*Exit, pursued by a bear.*
　　　　Enter an old SHEPHERD.

SHEPHERD.
I would there were no age between ten and three-
and-twenty, or that youth would sleep out the
rest; for there is nothing in the between but getting wenches with child, wronging the ancientry,
stealing, fighting—Hark you now!—Would any
but these boil'd brains of nineteen and two-and-
twenty hunt this weather? They have scared away
two of my best sheep, which I fear the wolf will
sooner find than the master: if any where I have
them, 'tis by the sea-side, browzing of ivy. Good
luck, an't be thy will! what have we here? [*Seeing
the* CHILD.] Mercy on's, a barne; a very pretty
barne! A boy or a child, I wonder? A pretty one;
a very pretty one: sure, some scape: though I am
not bookish, yet I can read waiting-gentlewoman
in the scape. This has been some stair-work,
some trunk-work, some behind-door-work: they
were warmer that got this than the poor thing is
here. I'll take it up for pity: yet I'll tarry till my
son come; he hallooed but even now.—Whoa, ho,
hoa!

CLOWN [*within*].
Hilloa, loa!

SHEPHERD.
What, art so near? If thou'lt see a thing to talk on
when thou art dead and rotten, come hither.
　　　　Enter CLOWN.
What ail'st thou, man?

CLOWN.
I have seen two such sights, by sea and by land!—
but I am not to say it is a sea, for it is now the sky:
betwixt the firmament and it you cannot thrust a
bodkin's point.

SHEPHERD.
Why, boy, how is it?

CLOWN.
I would you did but see how it chafes, how it
rages, how it takes up the shore!—but that's not
to the point. O, the most piteous cry of the poor
souls! sometimes to see 'em, and not to see 'em;
now the ship boring the moon with her main-
mast, and anon swallow'd with yest and froth, as
you'ld thrust a cork into a hogshead. And then for
the land-service,—to see how the bear tore out his
shoulder-bone; how he cried to me for help, and
said his name was Antigonus, a nobleman:—but
to make an end of the ship,—to see how the sea
flap-dragon'd it:—but, first, how the poor souls
roar'd, and the sea mockt them;—and how the
poor gentleman roar'd, and the bear mockt him,
both roaring louder than the sea or weather.

SHEPHERD.
Name of mercy, when was this, boy?

CLOWN.
Now, now; I have not winkt since I saw these
sights: the men are not yet cold under water, nor
the bear half dined on the gentleman,—he's at it
now.

SHEPHERD.
Would I had been by, to have helpt the nobleman.

CLOWN.
I would you had been by the ship-side, to have
helpt her: there your charity would have lackt
footing.

SHEPHERD.
Heavy matters! heavy matters! but look thee here,
boy. Now bless thyself: thou met'st with things
dying, I with things new-born. Here's a sight for
thee; look thee, a bearing-cloth for a squire's
child! look thee here; take up, take up, boy; open't.
So, let's see: it was told me I should be rich by
the fairies; this is some changeling: open't. What's
within, boy?

CLOWN.
You're a made old man: if the sins of your youth
are forgiven you, you're well to live. Gold! all
gold!

SHEPHERD.
This is fairy gold, boy, and 'twill prove so; up
with't, keep it close: home, home, the next way.
We are lucky, boy; and to be so still, requires
nothing but secrecy.—Let my sheep go:—come,
good boy, the next way home.

CLOWN.
Go you the next way with your findings. I'll go
see if the bear be gone from the gentleman, and
how much he hath eaten: they are never curst, but
when they are hungry: if there be any of him left,
I'll bury it.

SHEPHERD.
That's a good deed. If thou mayst discern by that
which is left of him what he is, fetch me to the
sight of him.

CLOWN.
Marry, will I; and you shall help to put him i'the
ground.

SHEPHERD.
'Tis a lucky day, boy, and we'll do good deeds
on't.　　　　　　　　　　　　　[*Exeunt.*

ACT IV.

Enter TIME, *the* CHORUS.

TIME.

I,—that please some, try all; both joy and terror
Of good and bad; that masks and unfolds
  error,—
Now take upon me, in the name of Time,
To use my wings. Impute it not a crime
To me or my swift passage, that I slide
O'er sixteen years, and leave the growth untried
Of that wide gap; since it is in my power
To o'erthrow law, and in one self-born hour
To plant and o'erwhelm custom. Let me pass
The same I am, ere ancient'st order was,
Or what is now received: I witness to
The times that brought them in; so shall I do
To the freshest things now reigning, and make
  stale
The glistering of this present, as my tale
Now seems to it. Your patience this allowing,
I turn my glass, and give my scene such growing
As you had slept between. Leontes leaving,
The effects of his fond jealousies so grieving
That he shuts up himself,—imagine me,
Gentle spectators, that I now may be
In fair Bohemia; and remember well,
I mention'd a son o'the king's, which Florizel
I now name to you; and with speed so pace
To speak of Perdita, now grown in grace
Equal with wond'ring: what of her ensues,
I list not prophesy; but let Time's news
Be known when 'tis brought forth:—a shepherd's
  daughter,
And what to her adheres, which follows after,
Is the argument of Time. Of this allow,
If ever you have spent time worse ere now;
If never, yet that Time himself doth say
He wishes earnestly you never may.   [*Exit.*

SCENE I.

Bohemia. POLIXENES' *palace.*

Enter POLIXENES *and* CAMILLO.

POLIXENES.

I PRAY thee, good Camillo, be no more importunate: 'tis a sickness denying thee any thing; a
death to grant this.

CAMILLO.

It is fifteen years since I saw my country: though
I have, for the most part, been air'd abroad, I desire to lay my bones there. Besides, the penitent
king, my master, hath sent for me; to whose feeling sorrows I might be some allay, or I o'erween
to think so,—which is another spur to my departure.

POLIXENES.

As thou lovest me, Camillo, wipe not out the rest
of thy services by leaving me now: the need I
have of thee, thine own goodness hath made; better not to have had thee than thus to want thee:
thou, having made me businesses which none
without thee can sufficiently manage, must either
stay to execute them thyself, or take away with
thee the very services thou hast done; which if I

have not enough consider'd,—as too much I cannot,—to be more thankful to thee shall be my
study; and my profit therein, the heaping friend-
ships. Of that fatal country Sicilia, prithee speak
no more; whose very naming punishes me with
the remembrance of that penitent, as thou call'st
him, and reconciled king, my brother; whose loss
of his most precious queen and children are even
now to be afresh lamented. Say to me, when saw'st
thou the Prince Florizel, my son? Kings are no
less unhappy, their issue not being gracious, than
they are in losing them when they have approved
their virtues.

CAMILLO.

Sir, it is three days since I saw the prince. What
his happier affairs may be, are to me unknown:
but I have missingly noted, he is of late much retired from court, and is less frequent to his princely exercises than formerly he hath appear'd.

POLIXENES.

I have consider'd so much, Camillo, and with
some care; so far, that I have eyes under my service which look upon his removedness; from whom
I have this intelligence:—that he is seldom from
the house of a most homely shepherd; a man, they
say, that from very nothing, and beyond the
imagination of his neighbours, is grown into an
unspeakable estate.

CAMILLO.

I have heard, sir, of such a man, who hath a
daughter of most rare note: the report of her is
extended more than can be thought to begin from
such a cottage.

POLIXENES.

That's likewise part of my intelligence; but I fear
the angle that plucks our son thither. Thou shalt
accompany us to the place; where we will, not appearing what we are, have some question with
the shepherd; from whose simplicity I think it not
uneasy to get the cause of my son's resort thither.
Prithee, be my present partner in this business,
and lay aside the thoughts of Sicilia.

CAMILLO.

I willingly obey your command.

POLIXENES.

My best Camillo!—We must disguise ourselves.
                              [*Exeunt.*

SCENE II.

A road near the SHEPHERD'S *cottage.*

Enter AUTOLYCUS, *singing.*

WHEN daffodils begin to peer,
    With hey! the doxy over the dale,
Why, then comes in the sweet o'the year;
    For the red blood reigns in the winter's pale.

The white sheet bleaching on the hedge,
    With hey! the sweet birds, O, how they sing!
Doth set my pugging tooth on edge;
    For a quart of ale is a dish for a king.

The lark, that tirra-lirra chants,
    With hey! with hey! the thrush and the jay,
Are summer songs for me and my aunts,
    While we lie tumbling in the hay.

I have served Prince Florizel, and, in my time, wore three-pile; but now I am out of service:

> But shall I go mourn for that, my dear?
>   The pale moon shines by night:
> And when I wander here and there,
>   I then do most go right.
>
> If tinkers may have leave to live,
>   And bear the sow-skin budget,
> Then my account I well may give,
>   And in the stocks avouch it.

My traffic is sheets; when the kite builds, look to lesser linen. My father named me Autolycus; who being, as I am, litter'd under Mercury, was likewise a snapper-up of unconsider'd trifles. With die and drab I purchased this caparison; and my revenue is the silly cheat: gallows and knock are too powerful on the highway; beating and hanging are terrors to me; for the life to come, I sleep out the thought of it.—A prize! a prize!

Enter CLOWN.

CLOWN.
Let me see:—every 'leven wether tods; every tod yields pound and odd shilling: fifteen hundred shorn, what comes the wool to?

AUTOLYCUS [*aside*].
If the springe hold, the cock's mine.

CLOWN.
I cannot do't without counters.—Let me see; what am I to buy for our sheep-shearing feast? Three pound of sugar; five pound of currants; rice—what will this sister of mine do with rice? But my father hath made her mistress of the feast, and she lays it on. She hath made me four-and-twenty nosegays for the shearers,—three-man songmen all, and very good ones; but they are most of them means and bases; but one puritan amongst them, and he sings psalms to hornpipes. I must have saffron, to colour the warden-pies; mace; dates,—none, that's out of my note; nutmegs, seven; a race or two of ginger,—but that I may beg; four pound of prunes, and as many of raisins o'the sun.

AUTOLYCUS.
O, that ever I was born!

[*Grovelling on the ground.*

CLOWN.
I'the name of me,—

AUTOLYCUS.
O, help me, help me! pluck but off these rags; and then, death, death!

CLOWN.
Alack, poor soul! thou hast need of more rags to lay on thee, rather than have these off.

AUTOLYCUS.
O sir, the loathsomeness of them offend me more than the stripes I have received, which are mighty ones and millions.

CLOWN.
Alas, poor man! a million of beating may come to a great matter.

AUTOLYCUS.
I am robb'd, sir, and beaten; my money and apparel ta'en from me, and these detestable things put upon me.

CLOWN.
What, by a horseman or a footman?

AUTOLYCUS.
A footman, sweet sir, a footman.

CLOWN.
Indeed, he should be a footman by the garments he has left with thee: if this be a horseman's coat, it hath seen very hot service. Lend me thy hand, I'll help thee: come, lend me thy hand.

[*Helping him up.*

AUTOLYCUS.
O, good sir, tenderly, O!

CLOWN.
Alas, poor soul!

AUTOLYCUS.
O, good sir, softly, good sir! I fear, sir, my shoulder-blade is out.

CLOWN.
How now! canst stand?

AUTOLYCUS.
Softly, dear sir [*picks his pocket*]; good sir, softly. You ha'done me a charitable office.

CLOWN.
Dost lack any money? I have a little money for thee.

AUTOLYCUS.
No, good sweet sir; no, I beseech you, sir: I have a kinsman not past three quarters of a mile hence, unto whom I was going; I shall there have money, or any thing I want: offer me no money, I pray you,—that kills my heart.

CLOWN.
What manner of fellow was he that robb'd you?

AUTOLYCUS.
A fellow, sir, that I have known to go about with troll-my-dames: I knew him once a servant of the prince: I cannot tell, good sir, for which of his virtues it was, but he was certainly whipt out of the court.

CLOWN.
His vices, you would say; there's no virtue whipt out of the court: they cherish it, to make it stay there; and yet it will no more but abide.

AUTOLYCUS.
Vices, I would say, sir. I know this man well: he hath been since an ape-bearer; then a process-server,—a bailiff; then he compast a motion of the Prodigal Son, and married a tinker's wife within a mile where my land and living lies; and, having flown over many knavish professions, he settled only in rogue: some call him Autolycus.

CLOWN.
Out upon him! prig, for my life, prig: he haunts wakes, fairs, and bear-baitings.

AUTOLYCUS.
Very true, sir; he, sir, he; that's the rogue that put me into this apparel.

CLOWN.
Not a more cowardly rogue in all Bohemia; if you had but lookt big and spit at him, he'ld have run.

AUTOLYCUS.
I must confess to you, sir, I am no fighter; I am false of heart that way; and that he knew, I warrant him.

CLOWN.
How do you now?

AUTOLYCUS.

Sweet sir, much better than I was; I can stand and walk: I will even take my leave of you, and pace softly towards my kinsman's.

CLOWN.

Shall I bring thee on the way?

AUTOLYCUS.

No, good-faced sir; no, sweet sir.

CLOWN.

Then fare thee well: I must go buy spices for our sheep-shearing.

AUTOLYCUS.

Prosper you, sweet sir! [*Exit* CLOWN.] Your purse is not hot enough to purchase your spice. I'll be with you at your sheep-shearing too: if I make not this cheat bring out another, and the shearers prove sheep, let me be unroll'd, and my name put in the book of virtue!   [*Sings.*

Jog on, jog on, the footpath way,
    And merrily hent the stile-a:
A merry heart goes all the day,
    Your sad tires in a mile-a.   [*Exit.*

SCENE III.

Before the SHEPHERD'S *cottage.*

Enter FLORIZEL *and* PERDITA.

FLORIZEL.

THESE your unusual weeds to each part of you
    Do give a life: no shepherdess; but Flora
Peering in April's front. This your sheep-shear-
    ing
Is as a meeting of the petty gods,
And you the queen on't.

PERDITA.

                    Sir, my gracious lord,
To chide at your extremes, it not becomes me,—
O, pardon that I name them!—your high self,
The gracious mark o'the land, you have obscured
With a swain's wearing; and me, poor lowly maid,
Most goddess-like prankt up: but that our feasts
In every mess have folly, and the feeders
Digest it with a custom, I should blush
To see you so attired; swoon, I think,
To show myself a glass.

FLORIZEL.

                    I bless the time
When my good falcon made her flight across
Thy father's ground.

PERDITA.

                    Now Jove afford you cause!
To me the difference forges dread; your greatness
Hath not been used to fear. Even now I tremble
To think your father, by some accident,
Should pass this way, as you did: O, the Fates!
How would he look, to see his work, so noble,
Vilely bound up? What would he say? Or how
Should I, in these my borrow'd flaunts, behold
The sternness of his presence?

FLORIZEL.

                    Apprehend
Nothing but jollity. The gods themselves,
Humbling their deities to love, have taken
The shapes of beasts upon them: Jupiter
Became a bull, and bellow'd; the green Neptune

A ram, and bleated; and the fire-robed god,
Golden Apollo, a poor humble swain,
As I seem now:—their transformations
Were never for a piece of beauty rarer,—
Nor in a way so chaste, since my desires
Run not before mine honour, nor my lusts
Burn hotter than my faith.

PERDITA.

                    O, but, sir,
Your resolution cannot hold, when 'tis
Opposed, as it must be, by the power of the king:
One of these two must be necessities.
Which then will speak,—that you must change
    this purpose,
Or I my life.

FLORIZEL.

                    Thou dearest Perdita,
With these forced thoughts, I prithee, darken not
The mirth o'the feast: or I'll be thine, my fair,
Or not my father's; for I cannot be
Mine own, nor any thing to any, if
I be not thine: to this I am most constant,
Though destiny say no. Be merry, gentle;
Strangle such thoughts as these with any thing
That you behold the while. Your guests are com-
    ing:
Lift up your countenance, as it were the day
Of celebration of that nuptial which
We two have sworn shall come.

PERDITA.

                    O Lady Fortune,
Stand you auspicious!

FLORIZEL.

                    See, your guests approach:
Address yourself to entertain them sprightly,
And let's be red with mirth.

Enter SHEPHERD, *with* POLIXENES *and* CAMIL-
    LO *disguised;* CLOWN, MOPSA, DORCAS, *and*
    other SHEPHERDS *and* SHEPHERDESSES.

SHEPHERD.

Fie, daughter! when my old wife lived, upon
This day she was both pantler, butler, cook;
Both dame and servant; welcomed all; served all;
Would sing her song and dance her turn; now
    here,
At upper end o'the table, now i'the middle;
On his shoulder, and his; her face o'fire
With labour, and the thing she took to quench it,
She would to each one sip. You are retired,
As if you were a feasted one, and not
The hostess of the meeting: pray you, bid
These unknown friends to's welcome; for it is
A way to make us better friends, more known.
Come, quench your blushes, and present yourself
That which you are, mistress o'the feast: come on,
And bid us welcome to your sheep-shearing,
As your good flock shall prosper.

PERDITA [*to* POLIXENES].

                    Sir, welcome:—
It is my father's will I should take on me
The hostess-ship o'the day.—[*to* CAMILLO]
    You're welcome, sir.—
Give me those flowers there, Dorcas.—Reverend
    sirs,
For you there's rosemary and rue; these keep
Seeming and savour all the winter long:

Grace and remembrance be to you both,
And welcome to our shearing!
              POLIXENES.
                        Shepherdess,—
A fair one are you,—well you fit our ages
With flowers of winter.
              PERDITA.
                Sir, the year growing ancient,—
Not yet on summer's death, nor on the birth
Of trembling winter,—the fairest flowers o'the
   season
Are our carnations, and streakt gillyvors,
Which some call nature's bastards: of that kind
Our rustic garden's barren; and I care not
To get slips of them.
             POLIXENES.
               Wherefore, gentle maiden,
Do you neglect them?
             PERDITA.
               For I have heard it said,
There is an art which, in their piedness, shares
With great creating nature.
             POLIXENES.
                Say there be;
Yet nature is made better by no mean,
But nature makes that mean: so, over that art
Which you say adds to nature, is an art
That nature makes. You see, sweet maid, we
   marry
A gentler scion to the wildest stock,
And make conceive a bark of baser kind
By bud of nobler race: this is an art
Which does mend nature,—change it rather; but
The art itself is nature.
             PERDITA.
          So it is.
             POLIXENES.
Then make your garden rich in gillyvors,
And do not call them bastards.
             PERDITA.
                   I'll not put
The dibble in earth to set one slip of them;
No more than, were I painted, I would wish
This youth should say, 'twere well, and only
   therefore
Desire to breed by me.—Here's flowers for you;
Hot lavender, mints, savory, marjoram;
The marigold, that goes to bed wi'the sun,
And with him rises weeping: these are flowers
Of middle summer, and, I think, they are given
To men of middle age. Y'are very welcome.
             CAMILLO.
I should leave grazing, were I of your flock,
And only live by gazing.
             PERDITA.
               Out, alas!
You'ld be so lean, that blasts of January
Would blow you through and through.—Now,
   my fair'st friend,
I would I had some flowers o'the spring that
   might
Become your time of day;—and yours, and yours,
That wear upon your virgin branches yet
Your maidenheads growing:—O Proserpina,
For the flowers now, that, frighted, thou lett'st
   fall

From Dis's wagon! daffodils,
That come before the swallow dares, and take
The winds of March with beauty; violets dim,
But sweeter than the lids of Juno's eyes
Or Cytherea's breath; pale primroses,
That die unmarried, ere they can behold
Bright Phœbus in his strength,—a malady
Most incident to maids; bold oxlips and
The crown-imperial; lilies of all kinds,
The flower-de-luce being one! O, these I lack,
To make you garlands of; and my sweet friend,
To strew him o'er and o'er!
             FLORIZEL.
                   What, like a corse?
             PERDITA.
No, like a bank for love to lie and play on;
Not like a corse; or if,—not to be buried,
But quick, and in mine arms.—Come, take your
   flowers:
Methinks I play as I have seen them do
In Whitsun pastorals: sure, this robe of mine
Does change my disposition.
             FLORIZEL.
                   What you do
Still betters what is done. When you speak, sweet,
I'ld have you do it ever: when you sing,
I'ld have you buy and sell! so; so give alms;
Pray so; and, for the ord'ring your affairs,
To sing them too: when you do dance, I wish you
A wave o'the sea, that you might ever do
Nothing but that; move still, still so,
And own no other function: each your doing,
So singular in each particular,
Crowns what you are doing in the present deeds,
That all your acts are queens.
             PERDITA.
                 O Doricles,
Your praises are too large: but that your youth,
And the true blood which peeps fairly through't,
Do plainly give you out an unstain'd shepherd,
With wisdom I might fear, my Doricles,
You woo'd me the false way.
             FLORIZEL.
                I think you have
As little skill to fear as I have purpose
To put you to't.—But, come; our dance, I pray:
Your hand, my Perdita: so turtles pair,
That never mean to part.
             PERDITA.
               I'll swear for 'em.
             POLIXENES.
This is the prettiest low-born lass that ever
Ran on the green-sward: nothing she does or seems
But smacks of something greater than herself,
Too noble for this place.
             CAMILLO.
               He tells her something
That makes her blood look out: good sooth, she is
The queen of curds and cream.
             CLOWN.
                 Come on, strike up!
             DORCAS.
Mopsa must be your mistress: marry, garlic,
To mend her kissing with!
             MOPSA.
               Now, in good time!

CLOWN.

Not a word, a word; we stand upon our manners.—
Come, strike up!

[*Music. Here a dance of Shepherds and
Shepherdesses.*

POLIXENES.

Pray, good shepherd, what fair swain is this
Which dances with your daughter?

SHEPHERD.

They call him Doricles; and boasts himself
To have a worthy feeding: I but have it
Upon his own report, and I believe it;
He looks like sooth. He says he loves my daugh-
ter:
I think so too; for never gazed the moon
Upon the water, as he'll stand, and read,
As 'twere, my daughter's eyes: and, to be plain,
I think there is not half a kiss to choose
Who loves another best.

POLIXENES.

　　　　　She dances featly.

SHEPHERD.

So she does any thing; though I report it,
That should be silent: if young Doricles
Do light upon her, she shall bring him that
Which he not dreams of.

Enter a SERVANT.

SERVANT.

O master, if you did but hear the pedlar at the
door, you would never dance again after a tabor
and pipe; no, the bagpipe could not move you:
he sings several tunes faster than you'll tell money;
he utters them as he had eaten ballads, and all
men's ears grew to his tunes.

CLOWN.

He could never come better; he shall come in:
I love a ballad but even too well, if it be doleful
matter merrily set down, or a very pleasant thing
indeed and sung lamentably.

SERVANT.

He hath songs for man or woman, of all sizes.—
no milliner can so fit his customers with gloves:—
he has the prettiest love-songs for maids; so without
bawdry, which is strange; with such delicate
burdens of 'dildos' and 'fadings,' 'jump her and
thump her;' and where some stretch-mouth'd
rascal would, as it were, mean mischief, and break
a foul jape into the matter, he makes the maid to
answer, 'Whoop, do me no harm, good man;'
puts him off, slights him, with 'Whoop, do me no
harm, good man.'

POLIXENES.

This is a brave fellow.

CLOWN.

Believe me, thou talkest of an admirable-conceited
fellow. Has he any unbraided wares?

SERVANT.

He hath ribands of all the colours i'the rainbow;
points more than all the lawyers in Bohemia can
learnedly handle, though they come to him by
the gross; inkles, caddisses, cambrics, lawns: why,
he sings 'em over, as they were gods or goddesses;
you would think a smock were a she-angel, he so
chants to the sleeve-hand, and the work about the
square on't.

CLOWN.

Prithee, bring him in; and let him approach singing.

PERDITA.

Forewarn him that he use no scurrilous words in's
tunes.　　　　　　　　　　　[*Exit SERVANT.*

CLOWN.

You have of these pedlars, that have more in them
than you'ld think, sister.

PERDITA.

Ay, good brother, or go about to think.

Enter AUTOLYCUS, singing.

Lawn as white as driven snow;
Cyprus black as e'er was crow;
Gloves as sweet as damask roses;
Masks for faces and for noses;
Bugle-bracelet, necklace-amber,
Perfume for a lady's chamber;
Golden quoifs and stomachers,
For my lads to give their dears;
Pins and poking-sticks of steel,
What maids lack from head to heel:
Come buy of me, come; come buy, come buy;
Buy, lads, or else your lasses cry:
Come buy.

CLOWN.

If I were not in love with Mopsa, thou shouldst
take no money of me; but being enthrall'd as I am,
it will also be the bondage of certain ribands and
gloves.

MOPSA.

I was promised them against the feast; but they
come not too late now.

DORCAS.

He hath promised you more than that, or there be
liars.

MOPSA.

He hath paid you all he promised you: may be, he
has paid you more,—which will shame you to
give him again.

CLOWN.

Is there no manners left among maids? will they
wear their plackets where they should bear their
faces? Is there not milking-time, when you are
going to bed, or kiln-hole, to whistle-off these
secrets, but you must be tittle-tattling before all
our guests? 'tis well they are whispering. Clamour
your tongues, and not a word more.

MOPSA.

I have done. Come, you promised me a tawdry-
lace and a pair of sweet gloves.

CLOWN.

Have I not told thee how I was cozen'd by the
way, and lost all my money?

AUTOLYCUS.

And, indeed, sir, there are cozeners abroad; therefore it behoves men to be wary.

CLOWN.

Fear not thou, man, thou shalt lose nothing here.

AUTOLYCUS.

I hope so, sir; for I have about me many parcels
of charge.

CLOWN.

What hast here? ballads?

MOPSA.

Pray now, buy some; I love a ballet in print a-life,
for then we are sure they are true.

AUTOLYCUS.

Here's one to a very doleful tune, How a usurer's wife was brought to bed of twenty money-bags at a burden, and how she long'd to eat adders' heads and toads carbonadoed.

MOPSA.

Is it true, think you?

AUTOLYCUS.

Very true; and but a month old.

DORCAS.

Bless me from marrying a usurer!

AUTOLYCUS.

Here's the midwife's name to't, one Mistress Taleporter, and five or six honest wives that were present. Why should I carry lies abroad?

MOPSA.

Pray you now, buy it.

CLOWN.

Come on, lay it by: and let's first see moe ballads; we'll buy the other things anon.

AUTOLYCUS.

Here's another ballad, Of a fish, that appear'd upon the coast on Wednesday the fourscore of April, forty thousand fadom above water, and sung this ballad against the hard hearts of maids: it was thought she was a woman, and was turn'd into a cold fish for she would not exchange flesh with one that loved her: the ballad is very pitiful, and as true.

DORCAS.

Is it true too, think you?

AUTOLYCUS.

Five justices' hands at it, and witnesses more than my pack will hold.

CLOWN.

Lay it by too: another.

AUTOLYCUS.

This is a merry ballad, but a very pretty one.

MOPSA.

Let's have some merry ones.

AUTOLYCUS.

Why, this is a passing merry one, and goes to the tune of, 'Two maids wooing a man:' there's scarce a maid westward but she sings it; 'tis in request, I can tell you.

MOPSA.

We can both sing it: if thou'lt bear a part, thou shalt hear; 'tis in three parts.

DORCAS.

We had the tune on't a month ago.

AUTOLYCUS.

I can bear my part; you must know 'tis my occupation: have at it with you!

Song.

AUTOLYCUS.

Get you hence, for I must go;
Where, it fits not you to know.

DORCAS.

Whither?

MOPSA.

O, whither?

DORCAS.

Whither?

MOPSA.

It becomes thy oath full well,
Thou to me thy secrets tell:

DORCAS.

Me too, let me go thither.

MOPSA.

Or thou go'st to the grange or mill:

DORCAS.

If to either, thou dost ill.

AUTOLYCUS.

Neither.

DORCAS.

What, neither?

AUTOLYCUS.

Neither.

DORCAS.

Thou hast sworn my love to be;

MOPSA.

Thou hast sworn it more to me:
Then, whither go'st? say, whither?

CLOWN.

We'll have this song out anon by ourselves: my father and the gentlemen are in sad talk, and we'll not trouble them.—Come, bring away thy pack after me.—Wenches, I'll buy for you both.—Pedlar, let's have the first choice.—Follow me, girls.   [*Exit with* DORCAS *and* MOPSA.

AUTOLYCUS.

And you shall pay well for 'em.—   [*Singing.*

Will you buy any tape,
Or lace for your cape,
My dainty duck, my dear-a?
Any silk, any thread,
Any toys for your head,
Of the new'st and fin'st, fin'st wear-a?
Come to the pedlar;
Money's a meddler,
That doth utter all men's ware-a.   [*Exit.*

Enter SERVANT.

SERVANT.

Master, there is three carters, three shepherds, three neat-herds, three swine-herds, that have made themselves all men of hair,—they call themselves Saltiers: and they have a dance which the wenches say is a gallimaufry of gambols, because they are not in't; but they themselves are o'the mind,—if it be not too rough for some that know little but bowling,—it will please plentifully.

SHEPHERD.

Away! we'll none on't: here has been too much homely foolery already.—I know, sir, we weary you.

POLIXENES.

You weary those that refresh us: pray, let's see these four threes of herdsmen.

SERVANT.

One three of them, by their own report, sir, hath danced before the king; and not the worst of the three but jumps twelve foot and a half by the squier.

SHEPHERD.

Leave your prating: since these good men are pleased, let them come in; but quickly now.

SERVANT.

Why, they stay at door, sir.   [*Exit.*

Here a dance of twelve Satyrs.

POLIXENES.
O, father, you'll know more of that hereafter.—
[*to* CAMILLO] Is it not too far gone? 'Tis time to
    part them.
He's simple and tells much.—How now, fair shep-
    herd!
Your heart is full of something that does take
Your mind from feasting. Sooth, when I was
    young,
And handed love as you do, I was wont
To load my she with knacks: I would have ran-
    sackt
The pedlar's silken treasury, and have pour'd it
To her acceptance; you have let him go,
And nothing marted with him. If your lass
Interpretation should abuse, and call this
Your lack of love or bounty, you were straited
For a reply, at least if you make care
Of happy holding her.

FLORIZEL.
                    Old sir, I know
She prizes not such trifles as these are:
The gifts she looks from me are packt and lockt
Up in my heart; which I have given already,
But not deliver'd.—O, hear me breathe my life
Before this ancient sir, who, it should seem,
Hath sometime loved! I take thy hand,—this hand,
As soft as dove's down and as white as it,
Or Ethiopian's tooth, or the fann'd snow that's
    bolted
By the northern blasts twice o'er.

POLIXENES.
                    What follows this?—
How prettily the young swain seems to wash
The hand was fair before!—I have put you out:—
But to your protestation; let me hear
What you profess.

FLORIZEL.
Do, and be witness to't.

POLIXENES.
And this my neighbour too?

FLORIZEL.
                    And he, and more
Than he, and men, the earth, the heavens, and
    all:—
That, were I crown'd the most imperial monarch,
Thereof most worthy; were I the fairest youth
That ever made eye swerve; had force and know-
    ledge
More than was ever man's,—I would not prize
    them
Without her love; for her employ them all;
Commend them, and condemn them, to her
    service,
Or to their own perdition.

POLIXENES.
                    Fairly offer'd.

CAMILLO.
This shows a sound affection.

SHEPHERD.
                    But, my daughter,
Say you the like to him?

PERDITA.
                    I cannot speak
So well, nothing so well; no, nor mean better:

By the pattern of mine own thoughts I cut out
The purity of his.

SHEPHERD.
                    Take hands, a bargain!—
And, friends unknown, you shall bear witness to't:
I give my daughter to him, and will make
Her portion equal his.

FLORIZEL.
                    O, that must be
I'the virtue of your daughter: one being dead,
I shall have more than you can dream of yet:
Enough then for your wonder. But, come on,
Contract us 'fore these witnesses.

SHEPHERD.
                    Come, your hand;—
And, daughter, yours.

POLIXENES.
                    Soft, swain, awhile, beseech you;
Have you a father?

FLORIZEL.
                    I have: but what of him?

POLIXENES.
Knows he of this?

FLORIZEL.
                    He neither does nor shall.

POLIXENES.
Methinks a father
Is, at the nuptial of his son, a guest
That best becomes the table. Pray you, once more;
Is not your father grown incapable
Of reasonable affairs? is he not stupid
With age and alt'ring rheums? can he speak? hear?
Know man from man? dispute his own estate?
Lies he not bed-rid? and again does nothing
But what he did being childish?

FLORIZEL.
                    No, good sir;
He has his health, and ampler strength indeed
Than most have of his age.

POLIXENES.
                    By my white beard,
You offer him, if this be so, a wrong
Something unfilial: reason my son
Should choose himself a wife; but as good reason
The father,—all whose joy is nothing else
But fair posterity,—should hold some counsel
In such a business.

FLORIZEL.
                    I yield all this;
But, for some other reasons, my grave sir,
Which 'tis not fit you know, I not acquaint
My father of this business.

POLIXENES.
                    Let him know't.

FLORIZEL.
He shall not.

POLIXENES.
                    Prithee, let him.

FLORIZEL.
                    No, he must not.

SHEPHERD.
Let him, my son; he shall not need to grieve
At knowing of thy choice.

FLORIZEL.
                    Come, come, he must not.—
Mark our contract.

1123

POLIXENES.

Mark your divorce, young sir,
[*Discovering himself.*
Whom son I dare not call; thou art too base
To be acknowledged: thou a sceptre's heir,
That thus affects a sheep-hook!—Thou old traitor,
I am sorry that, by hanging thee, I can but
Shorten thy life one week.—And thou, fresh piece
Of excellent witchcraft, who, of force, must know
The royal fool thou copest with,—

SHEPHERD.

O, my heart!

POLIXENES.

I'll have thy beauty scratcht with briers, and made
More homely than thy state.—For thee, fond boy,
If I may ever know thou dost but sigh
That thou no more shalt see this knack,—as never
I mean thou shalt,—we'll bar thee from succession;
Not hold thee of our blood, no, not our kin,
Far' than Deucalion off:—mark thou my words:—
Follow us to the court.—Thou churl, for this time,
Though full of our displeasure, yet we free thee
From the dead blow of it.—And you, enchantment,
Worthy enough a herdsman; yea, him too
That makes himself, but for our honour therein,
Unworthy thee,—if ever henceforth thou
These rural latches to his entrance open,
Or hoop his body more with thy embraces,
I will devise a death as cruel for thee
As thou art tender to't.   [*Exit.*

PERDITA.

Even here undone!
I was not much afeard; for once or twice
I was about to speak, and tell him plainly,
The selfsame sun that shines upon his court
Hides not his visage from our cottage, but
Looks on alike. [*to* FLORIZEL] Will't please you, sir, be gone?
I told you what would come of this: beseech you,
Of your own state take care: this dream of mine,—
Being now awake, I'll queen it no inch further,
But milk my ewes and weep.

CAMILLO.

Why, how now, father!
Speak ere thou diest.

SHEPHERD.

I cannot speak, nor think,
Nor dare to know that which I know.—[*to* FLORIZEL] O sir,
You have undone a man of fourscore three,
That thought to fill his grave in quiet,—yea,
To die upon the bed my father died,
To lie close by his honest bones! but now
Some hangman must put on my shroud, and lay me
Where no priest shovels-in dust.—[*to* PERDITA]
O cursed wretch,
That knew'st this was the prince, and wouldst adventure
To mingle faith with him!—Undone! undone!
If I might die within this hour, I have lived
To die when I desire.   [*Exit.*

FLORIZEL.

Why look you so upon me?
I am but sorry, not afeard; delay'd,
But nothing alter'd: what I was, I am;
More straining on for plucking back; not following
My leash unwillingly.

CAMILLO.

Gracious my lord,
You know your father's temper: at this time
He will allow no speech,—which I do guess
You do not purpose to him;—and as hardly
Will he endure your sight as yet, I fear:
Then, till the fury of his highness settle,
Come not before him.

FLORIZEL.

I not purpose it.
I think Camillo?

CAMILLO.

Even he, my lord.

PERDITA.

How often have I told you 'twould be thus!
How often said my dignity would last
But till 'twere known!

FLORIZEL.

It cannot fail but by
The violation of my faith; and then
Let nature crush the sides o'the earth together,
And mar the seeds within!—Lift up thy looks:—
From my succession wipe me, father! I
Am heir to my affection.

CAMILLO.

Be advised.

FLORIZEL.

I am,—and by my fancy: if my reason
Will thereto be obedient, I have reason;
If not, my senses, better pleased with madness,
Do bid it welcome.

CAMILLO.

This is desperate, sir.

FLORIZEL.

So call it: but it does fulfil my vow;
I needs must think it honesty. Camillo,
Not for Bohemia, nor the pomp that may
Be thereat glean'd; for all the sun sees, or
The close earth wombs, or the profound seas hide
In unknown fadoms, will I break my oath
To this my fair beloved: therefore, I pray you,
As you have ever been my father's honour'd friend,
When he shall miss me,—as, in faith, I mean not
To see him any more,—cast your good counsels
Upon his passion: let myself and fortune
Tug for the time to come. This you may know,
And so deliver,—I am put to sea
With her who here I cannot hold on shore;
And, most opportune to her need, I have
A vessel rides fast by, but not prepared
For this design. What course I mean to hold
Shall nothing benefit your knowledge, nor
Concern me the reporting.

CAMILLO.

O my lord,
I would your spirit were easier for advice,
Or stronger for your need!

FLORIZEL.
Hark, Perdita.—[*Taking her aside.*
[*to* CAMILLO] I'll hear you by and by.
CAMILLO.
              He's irremovable,
Resolved for flight. Now were I happy, if
His going I could frame to serve my turn;
Save him from danger, do him love and honour;
Purchase the sight again of dear Sicilia,
And that unhappy king my master, whom
I so much thirst to see.
FLORIZEL.
            Now, good Camillo,
I am so fraught with curious business, that
I leave out ceremony.
CAMILLO.
            Sir, I think
You have heard of my poor services, i'the love
That I have borne your father?
FLORIZEL.
             Very nobly
Have you deserved: it is my father's music
To speak your deeds; not little of his care
To have them recompensed as thought on.
CAMILLO.
            Well, my lord,
If you may please to think I love the king,
And, through him, what's nearest to him, which is
Your gracious self, embrace but my direction,—
If your more ponderous and settled project
May suffer alteration,—on mine honour
I'll point you where you shall have such receiving
As shall become your highness; where you may
Enjoy your mistress,—from the whom, I see,
There's no disjunction to be made, but by,
As heavens forfend! your ruin;—marry her;
And—with my best endeavours in your absence—
Your discontenting father strive to qualify,
And bring him up to liking.
FLORIZEL.
           How, Camillo,
May this, almost a miracle, be done?
That I may call thee something more than man,
And, after that, trust to thee.
CAMILLO.
           Have you thought on
A place whereto you'll go?
FLORIZEL.
           Not any yet:
But as the unthought-on accident is guilty
To what we wildly do, so we profess
Ourselves to be the slaves of chance, and flies
Of every wind that blows.
CAMILLO.
           Then list to me:
This follows,—if you will not change your pur-
    pose,
But undergo this flight,—make for Sicilia;
And there present yourself and your fair prin-
    cess—
For so I see she must be—'fore Leontes:
She shall be habited as it becomes
The partner of your bed. Methinks I see
Leontes opening his free arms, and weeping
His welcomes forth; asks thee, the son, forgive-
ness,

As 'twere i'the father's person; kisses the hands
Of your fresh princess; o'er and o'er divides him
'Twixt his unkindness and his kindness,—the one
He chides to hell, and bids the other grow
Faster than thought or time.
FLORIZEL.
           Worthy Camillo,
What colour for my visitation shall I
Hold up before him?
CAMILLO.
          Sent by the king your father
To greet him and to give him comforts. Sir,
The manner of your bearing towards him, with
What you, as from your father, shall deliver,
Things known betwixt us three, I'll write you
    down:
The which shall point you forth at every sitting
What you must say; that he shall not perceive
But that you have your father's bosom there,
And speak his very heart.
FLORIZEL.
          I am bound to you:
There is some sap in this.
CAMILLO.
          A course more promising
Than a wild dedication of yourselves
To unpath'd waters, undream'd shores, most cer-
    tain
To miseries enough: no hope to help you;
But, as you shake off one, to take another:
Nothing so certain as your anchors; who
Do their best office, if they can but stay you
Where you'll be loth to be: besides, you know
Prosperity's the very bond of love,
Whose fresh complexion and whose heart together
Affliction alters.
PERDITA.
         One of these is true:
I think affliction may subdue the cheek,
But not take in the mind.
CAMILLO.
         Yea, say you so?
There shall not, at your father's house, these seven
    years
Be born another such.
FLORIZEL.
         My good Camillo,
She's as forward of her breeding as she is
I'the rear o'her birth.
CAMILLO.
         I cannot say 'tis pity
She lacks instructions, for she seems a mistress
To most that teach.
PERDITA.
        Your pardon, sir, for this;
I'll blush you thanks.
FLORIZEL.
        My prettiest Perdita!—
But, O, the thorns we stand upon!—Camillo,—
Preserver of my father, now of me,
The medicine of our house!—how shall we do?
We are not furnish like Bohemia's son,
Nor shall appear in Sicilia.
CAMILLO.
        My lord,
Fear none of this: I think you know my fortunes

Do all lie there: it shall be so my care
To have you royally appointed as if
The scene you play were mine. For instance, sir,
That you may know you shall not want,—one
word.   [*They talk aside.*
                Enter AUTOLYCUS.
                AUTOLYCUS.
Ha, ha! what a fool Honesty is! and Trust, his
sworn brother, a very simple gentleman! I have
sold all my trumpery; not a counterfeit stone, not
a riband, glass, pomander, brooch, table-book,
ballad, knife, tape, glove, shoe-tie, bracelet, horn-
ring, to keep my pack from fasting: they throng
who should buy first, as if my trinkets had been
hallow'd, and brought a benediction to the
buyer: by which means I saw whose purse was
best in picture; and what I saw, to my good use I
remember'd. My clown—who wants but something to be a reasonable man—grew so in love
with the wenches' song, that he would not stir
his pettitoes till he had both tune and words;
which so drew the rest of the herd to me, that all
their other senses stuck in ears: you might have
pincht a placket,—it was senseless; 'twas nothing
to geld a codpiece of a purse,—I would have filed
keys off that hung in chains: no hearing, no feeling, but my sir's song, and admiring the nothing
of it. So that, in this time of lethargy, I pickt and
cut most of their festival purses; and had not the
old man come in with a whoobub against his
daughter and the king's son, and scared my
choughs from the chaff, I had not left a purse
alive in the whole army.
        [CAMILLO, FLORIZEL, *and* PERDITA
                come forward.
                CAMILLO.
Nay, but my letters, by this means being there
So soon as you arrive, shall clear that doubt.
                FLORIZEL.
And those that you'll procure from King Leon-
tes,—
                CAMILLO.
Shall satisfy your father.
                PERDITA.
                        Happy be you!
All that you speak shows fair.
                CAMILLO.
                        Who have we here?
                        [*Seeing* AUTOLYCUS.
We'll make an instrument of this; omit
Nothing may give us aid.
        AUTOLYCUS [*aside*].
If they have overheard me now,—why, hanging.
                CAMILLO.
How now, good fellow! why shakest thou so? Fear
not, man; here's no harm intended to thee.
                AUTOLYCUS.
I am a poor fellow, sir.
                CAMILLO.
Why, be so still; here's nobody will steal that
from thee: yet, for the outside of thy poverty, we
must make an exchange; therefore discase thee
instantly,—thou must think there's a necessity
in't,—and change garments with this gentleman
though the pennyworth on his side be the worst,
yet hold thee, there's some boot.   [*Giving money.*

                AUTOLYCUS.
I am a poor fellow, sir.—[*aside*] I know ye well
enough.
                CAMILLO.
Nay, prithee, dispatch: the gentleman is half
flay'd already.
                AUTOLYCUS.
Are you in earnest, sir?—[*aside*] I smell the trick
on't.
                FLORIZEL.
Dispatch, I prithee.
                AUTOLYCUS.
Indeed, I have had earnest; but I cannot with
conscience take it.
                CAMILLO.
Unbuckle, unbuckle.—
        [FLORIZEL *and* AUTOLYCUS *exchange garments.*
Fortunate mistress,—let my prophecy
Come home to ye!—you must retire yourself
Into some covert: take your sweetheart's hat,
And pluck it o'er your brows; muffle your face;
Dismantle you; and, as you can, disliken
The truth of your own seeming; that you may—
For I do fear eyes over—to shipboard
Get undescried.
                PERDITA.
                I see the play so lies
That I must bear a part.
                CAMILLO.
                        No remedy.—
Have you done there?
                FLORIZEL.
                Should I now meet my father,
He would not call me son.
                CAMILLO.
                        Nay, you shall have no hat,—
                        [*Giving it to* PERDITA.
Come, lady, come.—Farewell, my friend.
                AUTOLYCUS.
                                Adieu, sir.
                FLORIZEL.
O Perdita, what have we twain forgot!
Pray you, a word.   [*They converse apart.*
                CAMILLO [*aside*].
What I do next, shall be to tell the king
Of this escape, and whither they are bound;
Wherein, my hope is, I shall so prevail
To force him after: in whose company
I shall review Sicilia, for whose sight
I have a woman's longing.
                FLORIZEL.
                        Fortune speed us!—
Thus we set on, Camillo, to the sea-side.
                CAMILLO.
The swifter speed the better.
        [*Exeunt* FLORIZEL, PERDITA, *and* CAMILLO.
                AUTOLYCUS.
I understand the business, I hear it: to have an
open ear, a quick eye, and a nimble hand, is
necessary for a cut-purse; a good nose is re-
quisite also, to smell out work for the other
senses. I see this is the time that the unjust man
doth thrive. What an exchange had this been
without boot! what a boot is here with this exchange! Sure, the gods do this year connive at us,
and we may do any thing extempore. The prince

himself is about a piece of iniquity,—stealing away from his father with his clog at his heels: if I thought it were not a piece of honesty to acquaint the king withal, I would do't: I hold it the more knavery to conceal it; and therein am I constant to my profession.

Enter CLOWN *and* SHEPHERD.

Aside, aside;—here is more matter for a hot brain: every lane's end, every shop, church, session, hanging, yields a careful man work.

CLOWN.

See, see; what a man you are now! There is no other way but to tell the king she's a changeling, and none of your flesh and blood.

SHEPHERD.

Nay, but hear me.

CLOWN.

Nay, but hear me.

SHEPHERD.

Go to, then.

CLOWN.

She being none of your flesh and blood, your flesh and blood has not offended the king; and so your flesh and blood is not to be punisht by him. Show those things you found about her; those secret things, all but what she has with her: this being done, let the law go whistle; I warrant you.

SHEPHERD.

I will tell the king all, every word, yea, and his son's pranks too,—who, I may say, is no honest man neither to his father nor to me, to go about to make me the king's brother-in-law.

CLOWN.

Indeed, brother-in-law was the furthest off you could have been to him; and then your blood had been the dearer by I know not how much an ounce.

AUTOLYCUS [*aside*].

Very wisely, puppies!

SHEPHERD.

Well, let us to the king: there is that in this fardel will make him scratch his beard.

AUTOLYCUS [*aside*].

I know not what impediment this complaint may be to the flight of my master.

CLOWN.

Pray heartily he be at palace.

AUTOLYCUS [*aside*].

Though I am not naturally honest, I am so sometimes by chance:—let me pocket up my pedlar's excrement. [*Takes off his false beard.*]—How now, rustics! whither are you bound?

SHEPHERD.

To the palace, an it like your worship.

AUTOLYCUS.

Your affairs there? what? with whom? the condition of that fardel, the place of your dwelling, your names, your ages, of what having, breeding, and any thing that is fitting to be known, discover.

CLOWN.

We are but plain fellows, sir.

AUTOLYCUS.

A lie; you are rough and hairy. Let me have no lying: it becomes none but tradesmen, and they often give us soldiers the lie: but we pay them for it with stampt coin, not stabbing steel; therefore they do not give us the lie.

CLOWN.

Your worship had like to have given us one, if you had not taken yourself with the manner.

SHEPHERD.

Are you a courtier, an't like you, sir?

AUTOLYCUS.

Whether it like me or no, I am a courtier. See'st thou not the air of the court in these enfoldings? hath not my gait in it the measure of the court? receives not thy nose court-odour from me? reflect I not on thy baseness court-contempt? Think'st thou, for that I insinuate, or toaze from thee thy business, I am therefore no courtier? I am courtier cap-a-pe; and one that will either push on or pluck back thy business there: whereupon I command thee to open thy affair.

SHEPHERD.

My business, sir, is to the king.

AUTOLYCUS.

What advocate hast thou to him?

SHEPHERD.

I know not, an't like you.

CLOWN [*aside to* SHEPHERD].

Advocate's the court-word for a pheasant: say you have none.

SHEPHERD.

None, sir; I have no pheasant, cock nor hen.

AUTOLYCUS.

How blest are we that are not simple men! Yet nature might have made me as these are, Therefore I will not disdain.

CLOWN [*aside to* SHEPHERD].

This cannot be but a great courtier.

SHEPHERD [*aside to* CLOWN].

His garments are rich, but he wears them not handsomely.

CLOWN [*aside to* SHEPHERD].

He seems to be the more noble in being fantastical: a great man, I'll warrant; I know by the picking on's teeth.

AUTOLYCUS

The fardel there? what's i'the fardel? Wherefore that box?

SHEPHERD.

Sir, there lies such secrets in this fardel and box, which none must know but the king; and which he shall know within this hour, if I may come to the speech of him.

AUTOLYCUS.

Age, thou hast lost thy labour.

SHEPHERD.

Why, sir?

AUTOLYCUS.

The king is not at the palace; he is gone aboard a new ship to purge melancholy and air himself: for, if thou be'st capable of things serious, thou must know the king is full of grief.

SHEPHERD.

So 'tis said, sir,—about his son, that should have married a shepherd's daughter.

AUTOLYCUS.

If that shepherd be not in hand-fast, let him fly: the curses he shall have, the tortures he shall feel, will break the back of man, the heart of monster.

CLOWN.

Think you so, sir?

AUTOLYCUS.

Not he alone shall suffer what wit can make heavy and vengeance bitter; but those that are germane to him, though removed fifty times, shall all come under the hangman: which though it be great pity, yet it is necessary. An old sheep-whistling rogue, a ram-tender, to offer to have his daughter come into grace! Some say he shall be stoned; but that death is too soft for him, say I: draw our throne into a sheep-cote! all deaths are too few, the sharpest too easy.

CLOWN.

Has the old man e'er a son, sir, do you hear, an't like you, sir?

AUTOLYCUS.

He has a son,—who shall be flay'd alive; then, 'nointed over with honey, set on the head of a wasps' nest; then stand till he be three quarters and a dram dead; then recover'd again with aqua-vitæ or some other hot infusion; then, raw as he is, and in the hottest day prognostication proclaims, shall he be set against a brick-wall, the sun looking with a southward eye upon him,—where he is to behold him with flies blown to death. But what talk we of these traitorly rascals, whose miseries are to be smiled at, their offences being so capital? Tell me—for you seem to be honest plain men—what you have to the king: being something gently consider'd, I'll bring you where he is aboard, tender your persons to his presence, whisper him in your behalfs; and if it be in man besides the king to effect your suits, here is man shall do it.

CLOWN [aside to SHEPHERD].

He seems to be of great authority: close with him; give him gold: and though authority be a stubborn bear, yet he is oft led by the nose with gold: show the inside of your purse to the outside of his hand, and no more ado. Remember,—stoned, and flay'd alive.

SHEPHERD.

An't please you, sir, to undertake the business for us, here is that gold I have: I'll make it as much more, and leave this young man in pawn till I bring it you.

AUTOLYCUS.

After I have done what I promised?

SHEPHERD.

Ay, sir.

AUTOLYCUS.

Well, give me the moiety.—Are you a party in this business?

CLOWN.

In some sort, sir: but though my case be a pitiful one, I hope I shall not be flay'd out of it.

AUTOLYCUS.

O, that's the case of the shepherd's son:—hang him, he'll be made an example.

CLOWN [aside to SHEPHERD].

Comfort, good comfort! We must to the king, and show our strange sights: he must know 'tis none of your daughter nor my sister; we are gone

else.—Sir, I will give you as much as this old man does, when the business is perform'd; and remain, as he says, your pawn till it be brought you.

AUTOLYCUS.

I will trust you. Walk before toward the sea-side; go on the right hand: I will but look upon the hedge, and follow you.

CLOWN [aside to SHEPHERD].

We are blest in this man, as I may say, even blest.

SHEPHERD [aside to CLOWN].

Let's before, as he bids us: he was provided to do us good.   [Exeunt SHEPHERD and CLOWN.

AUTOLYCUS.

If I had a mind to be honest, I see Fortune would not suffer me: she drops booties in my mouth. I am courted now with a double occasion,—gold, and a means to do the prince my master good; which who knows how that may turn back to my advancement? I will bring these two moles, these blind ones, aboard him: if he think it fit to shore them again, and that the complaint they have to the king concerns him nothing, let him call me rogue for being so far officious; for I am proof against that title, and what shame else belongs to't. To him will I present them: there may be matter in it.   [Exit.

ACT V. SCENE I.

Sicilia. LEONTES' palace.

Enter LEONTES, CLEOMENES, DION, PAULINA, and others.

CLEOMENES.

SIR, you have done enough, and have performed
A saint-like sorrow: no fault could you make,
Which you have not redeem'd; indeed, paid down
More penitence than done trespass: at the last,
Do as the heavens have done, forget your evil;
With them, forgive yourself.

LEONTES.   Whilst I remember
Her and her virtues, I cannot forget
My blemishes in them; and so still think of
The wrong I did myself: which was so much,
That heirless it hath made my kingdom; and
Destroy'd the sweet'st companion that e'er man
Bred his hopes out of.

PAULINA.   True, too true, my lord:
If, one by one, you wedded all the world,
Or from the all that are took something good,
To make a perfect woman, she you kill'd
Would be unparallel'd.

LEONTES.   I think so.   Kill'd!
She I kill'd! I did so: but thou strikest me
Sorely, to say I did; it is as bitter
Upon thy tongue as in my thought: now, good now,
Say so but seldom.

CLEOMENES.
Not at all, good lady:
You might have spoken a thousand things that would

Have done the time more benefit, and graced
Your kindness better.

PAULINA.
You are one of those
Would have him wed again.

DION.
If you would not so,
You pity not the state, nor the remembrance
Of his most sovereign name; consider little
What dangers, by his highness' fail of issue,
May drop upon his kingdom, and devour
Incertain lookers-on. What were more holy
Than to rejoice the former queen is well?
What holier than,—for royalty's repair,
For present comfort, and for future good,—
To bless the bed of majesty again
With a sweet fellow to't?

PAULINA.
There is none worthy,
Respecting her that's gone. Besides, the gods
Will have fulfill'd their secret purposes;
For has not the divine Apollo said,
Is't not the tenour of his oracle,
That King Leontes shall not have an heir
Till his lost child be found? which that it shall,
Is all as monstrous to our human reason
As my Antigonus to break his grave
And come again to me; who, on my life,
Did perish with the infant. 'Tis your counsel
My lord should to the heavens be contrary,
Oppose against their wills.—[to LEONTES] Care
not for issue;
The crown will find an heir: great Alexander
Left his to the worthiest; so his successor
Was like to be the best.

LEONTES.
Good Paulina,
Who hast the memory of Hermione,
I know, in honour,—O, that ever I
Had squared me to thy counsel!—then, even now,
I might have lookt upon my queen's full eyes;
Have taken treasure from her lips,—

PAULINA.
And left them
More rich for what they yielded.

LEONTES.
Thou speak'st truth.
No more such wives; therefore, no wife: one
worse,
And better used, would make her sainted spirit
Again possess her corpse, and on this stage—
Where we offend her now—appear soul-vext,
And begin, 'Why to me?'

PAULINA.
Had she such power
She had just cause.

LEONTES.
She had; and would incense me
To murder her I married.

PAULINA.
I should so.
Were I the ghost that walkt, I'ld bid you mark
Her eye, and tell me for what dull part in't
You chose her; then I'ld shriek, that even your ears
Should rift to hear me; and the words that follow'd
Should be, 'Remember mine.'

LEONTES.
Stars, stars,
And all eyes else dead coals!—fear thou no wife;
I'll have no wife, Paulina.

PAULINA.
Will you swear
Never to marry but by my free leave?

LEONTES.
Never, Paulina; so be blest my spirit!

PAULINA.
Then, good my lords, bear witness to his oath.

CLEOMENES.
You tempt him over-much.

PAULINA.
Unless another,
As like Hermione as is her picture,
Affront his eye.

CLEOMENES.
Good madam,—

PAULINA.
I have done.
Yet, if my lord will marry,—if you will, sir,
No remedy, but you will,—give me the office
To choose you a queen: she shall not be so young
As was your former; but she shall be such
As, walkt your first queen's ghost, it should take joy
To see her in your arms.

LEONTES.
My true Paulina,
We shall not marry till thou bidd'st us.

PAULINA.
That
Shall be when your first queen's again in breath;
Never till then.

Enter a GENTLEMAN.

GENTLEMAN.
One that gives out himself Prince Florizel,
Son of Polixenes, with his princess,—she
The fairest I have yet beheld,—desires access
To your high presence.

LEONTES.
What with him? he comes not
Like to his father's greatness: his approach,
So out of circumstance and sudden, tells us
'Tis not a visitation framed, but forced
By need and accident. What train?

GENTLEMAN.
But few,
And those but mean.

LEONTES.
His princess, say you, with him?

GENTLEMAN.
Ay, the most peerless piece of earth, I think,
That e'er the sun shone bright on.

PAULINA.
O Hermione,
As every present time doth boast itself
Above a better gone, so must thy grave
Give way to what's seen now! Sir, you yourself
Have said and writ so; but your writing now
Is colder than that theme, 'She had not been,
Nor was not to be equall'd;'—thus your verse
Flow'd with her beauty once: 'tis shrewdly ebb'd
To say you have seen a better.

GENTLEMAN.
Pardon, madam:
The one I have almost forgot,—your pardon;

The other, when she has obtain'd your eye,
Will have your tongue too. This is a creature,
Would she begin a sect, might quench the zeal
Of all professors else; make proselytes
Of who she but bid follow.

PAULINA.
　　　　　　How! not women?

GENTLEMAN.
Women will love her, that she is a woman
More worth than any man; men, that she is
The rarest of all women.

LEONTES.
　　　　　Go, Cleomenes;
Yourself, assisted with your honour'd friends,
Bring them to our embracement.

[Exeunt CLEOMENES and others.
　　　　　　Still, 'tis strange
He thus should steal upon us.

PAULINA.
　　　　　Had our prince,
Jewel of children, seen this hour, he had pair'd
Well with this lord: there was not full a month
Between their births.

LEONTES.
　　　　Prithee, no more; cease; thou know'st
He dies to me again when talkt of: sure,
When I shall see this gentleman, thy speeches
Will bring me to consider that which may
Unfurnish me of reason.—They are come.

Enter CLEOMENES and others, with FLORIZEL
and PERDITA.
Your mother was most true to wedlock, prince;
For she did print your royal father off,
Conceiving you: were I but twenty-one,
Your father's image is so hit in you,
His very air, that I should call you brother,
As I did him, and speak of something wildly
By us perform'd before. Most dearly welcome!
And your fair princess-goddess!—O, alas,
I lost a couple, that 'twixt heaven and earth
Might thus have stood, begetting wonder, as
You, gracious couple, do! and then I lost—
All mine own folly—the society,
Amity too, of your brave father, whom,
Though bearing misery, I desire my life
Once more to look on him.

FLORIZEL.
　　　　　By his command
Have I here toucht Sicilia, and from him
Give you all greetings, that a king, at friend,
Can send his brother; and, but infirmity—
Which waits upon worn times—hath something
　　seized
His wisht ability, he had himself
The lands and waters 'twixt your throne and his
Measured to look upon you; whom he loves—
He bade me say so—more than all the sceptres,
And those that bear them, living.

LEONTES.
　　　　　　O my brother,
Good gentleman, the wrongs I have done thee stir
Afresh within me; and these thy offices,
So rarely kind, are as interpreters
Of my behindhand slackness!—Welcome hither,
As is the spring to the earth. And hath he too
Exposed this paragon to the fearful usage—

At least ungentle—of the dreadful Neptune,
To greet a man not worth her pains, much less
The adventure of her person?

FLORIZEL.
　　　　　　Good my lord,
She came from Libya.

LEONTES.
　　　　　Where the warlike Smalus,
That noble honour'd lord, is fear'd and loved?

FLORIZEL.
Most royal sir, from thence; from him, whose
　　daughter
His tears proclaim'd his, parting with her: thence,
A prosperous south-wind friendly, we have crost
To execute the charge my father gave me,
For visiting your highness: my best train
I have from your Sicilian shores dismist;
Who for Bohemia bend, to signify
Not only my success in Libya, sir,
But my arrival, and my wife's, in safety
Here where we are.

LEONTES.
　　　　　The blessed gods
Purge all infection from our air whilst you
Do climate here! You have a holy father,
A graceful gentleman; against whose person,
So sacred as it is, I have done sin:
For which the heavens, taking angry note,
Have left me issueless; and your father's blest,
As he from heaven merits it, with you,
Worthy his goodness. What might I have been,
Might I a son and daughter now have lookt on,
Such goodly things as you!

Enter a LORD.

LORD.
　　　　　Most noble sir,
That which I shall report will bear no credit,
Were not the proof so nigh. Please you, great sir,
Bohemia greets you from himself by me;
Desires you to attach his son, who has—
His dignity and duty both cast off—
Fled from his father, from his hopes, and with
A shepherd's daughter.

LEONTES.
　　　Where's Bohemia? speak.

LORD.
Here in your city; I now came from him:
I speak amazedly; and it becomes
My marvel and my message. To your court
Whiles he was hastening,—in the chase, it seems,
Of this fair couple,—meets he on the way
The father of this seeming lady, and
Her brother, having both their country quitted
With this young prince.

FLORIZEL.
　　　　Camillo has betray'd me;
Whose honour and whose honesty till now
Endured all weathers.

LORD.
　　　　Lay't so to his charge:
He's with the king your father.

LEONTES.
　　　　　Who? Camillo?

LORD.
Camillo, sir; I spake with him; who now
Has these poor men in question. Never saw I

Wretches so quake: they kneel, they kiss the earth;
Forswear themselves as often as they speak:
Bohemia stops his ears, and threatens them
With divers deaths in death.

PERDITA.
                O my poor father!
The heaven set spies upon us, will not have
Our contract celebrated.

LEONTES.
               You are married?

FLORIZEL.
We are not, sir, nor are we like to be;
The stars, I see, will kiss the valleys first:—
The odds for high and low's alike.

LEONTES.
                   My lord,
Is this the daughter of a king?

FLORIZEL.
                 She is,
When once she is my wife.

LEONTES.
That 'once,' I see by your good father's speed,
Will come on very slowly. I am sorry,
Most sorry, you have broken from his liking,
Where you were tied in duty; and as sorry
Your choice is not so rich in worth as beauty,
That you might well enjoy her.

FLORIZEL.
              Dear, look up:
Though Fortune, visible an enemy,
Should chase us, with my father, power no jot
Hath she to change our loves.—Beseech you, sir,
Remember since you owed no more to time
Than I do now: with thought of such affections,
Step forth mine advocate; at your request
My father will grant precious things as trifles.

LEONTES.
Would he do so, I'ld beg your precious mistress,
Which he counts but a trifle.

PAULINA.
              Sir, my liege,
Your eye hath too much youth in't: not a month
'Fore your queen died, she was more worth such
    gazes
Than what you look on now.

LEONTES.
           I thought of her,
Even in these looks I made.—[to FLORIZEL] But
    your petition
Is yet unanswer'd. I will to your father;
Your honour not o'erthrown by your desires,
I am friend to them and you: upon which errand
I now go toward him; therefore follow me,
And mark what way I make: come, good my lord.
                         [Exeunt.

SCENE II.

Before LEONTES' *palace.*

Enter AUTOLYCUS *and a* GENTLEMAN.

AUTOLYCUS.

BESEECH you sir, were you present at this
relation?

FIRST GENTLEMAN.
I was by at the opening of the fardel, heard the old
shepherd deliver the manner how he found it:
whereupon, after a little amazedness, we were all

commanded out of the chamber; only this, methought I heard the shepherd say he found the
child.

AUTOLYCUS.
I would most gladly know the issue of it.

FIRST GENTLEMAN.
I make a broken delivery of the business;—but the
changes I perceived in the king and Camillo were
very notes of admiration: they seem'd almost, with
staring on one another, to tear the cases of their
eyes; there was speech in their dumbness, language
in their very gesture; they lookt as they had heard
of a world ransom'd, or one destroy'd: a notable
passion of wonder appear'd in them; but the wisest
beholder, that knew no more but seeing, could not
say if the importance were joy or sorrow,—but in
the extremity of the one, it must needs be.—Here
comes a gentleman that happily knows more.

Enter another GENTLEMAN.

The news, Rogero?

SECOND GENTLEMAN.
Nothing but bonfires: the oracle is fulfill'd; the
king's daughter is found: such a deal of wonder is
broken out within this hour, that ballad-makers
cannot be able to express it.—Here comes the
Lady Paulina's steward: he can deliver you more.

Enter a third GENTLEMAN.

How goes it now, sir? this news, which is call'd
true, is so like an old tale, that the verity of it is in
strong suspicion: has the king found his heir?

THIRD GENTLEMAN.
Most true, if ever truth were pregnant by circumstance: that which you hear you'll swear you see,
there is such unity in the proofs. The mantle of
Queen Hermione's; her jewel about the neck of it;
the letters of Antigonus, found with it, which they
know to be his character; the majesty of the creature, in resemblance of the mother; the affection of
nobleness, which nature shows above her breeding; and many other evidences,—proclaim her
with all certainty to be the king's daughter. Did
you see the meeting of the two kings?

SECOND GENTLEMAN.
No.

THIRD GENTLEMAN.
Then have you lost a sight, which was to be seen,
cannot be spoken of. There might you have beheld
one joy crown another, so and in such manner,
that it seem'd sorrow wept to take leave of them,—
for their joy waded in tears. There was casting up
of eyes, holding up of hands, with countenance of
such distraction, that they were to be known by
garment, not by favour. Our king, being ready to
leap out of himself for joy of his found daughter,
as if that joy were now become a loss, cries, 'O,
thy mother, thy mother!' then asks Bohemia forgiveness; then embraces his son-in-law; then again
worries he his daughter with clipping her, now he
thanks the old shepherd, which stands by like a
weather-bitten conduit of many kings' reigns. I
never heard of such another encounter, which
lames report to follow it, and undoes description
to do it.

SECOND GENTLEMAN.
What, pray you, became of Antigonus, that carried
hence the child?

THIRD GENTLEMAN.
Like an old tale still, which will have matter to
rehearse, though credit be asleep, and not an ear
open.   He was torn to pieces with a bear: this a-
vouches the shepherd's son; who has not only his
innocence, which seems much, to justify him, but a
handkerchief and rings of his, that Paulina knows.
FIRST GENTLEMAN.
What became of his bark and his followers?
THIRD GENTLEMAN.
Wrackt the same instant of their master's death,
and in view of the shepherd: so that all the instruments which aided to expose the child were even
then lost when it was found. But, O, the noble
combat that, 'twixt joy and sorrow, was fought in
Paulina! She had one eye declined for the loss of
her husband, another elevated that the oracle was
fulfill'd: she lifted the princess from the earth; and
so locks her in embracing, as if she would pin her
to her heart, that she might no more be in danger
of losing.
FIRST GENTLEMAN.
The dignity of this act was worth the audience
of kings and princes, for by such was it acted.
THIRD GENTLEMAN.
One of the prettiest touches of all, and that which
angled for mine eyes—caught the water, though
not the fish—was when, at the relation of the
queen's death, with the manner how she came
to't,—bravely confest and lamented by the king,—
how attentiveness wounded his daughter; till,
from one sign of dolour to another, she did, with
an 'Alas,' I would fain say, bleed tears; for I am
sure my heart wept blood.   Who was most marble
there changed colour; some swownded, all sorrow'd: if all the world could have seen't, the
woe had been universal.
FIRST GENTLEMAN.
Are they return'd to the court?
THIRD GENTLEMAN.
No: the princess hearing of her mother's statue,
which is in the keeping of Paulina,—a piece many
years in doing, and now newly perform'd by that
rare Italian master, Julio Romano, who, had he
himself eternity, and could put breath into his
work, would beguile Nature of her custom, so perfectly he is her ape: he so near to Hermione hath
done Hermione, that they say one would speak to
her, and stand in hope of answer:—thither with all
greediness of affection are they gone; and there
they intend to sup.
SECOND GENTLEMAN.
I thought she had some great matter there in hand;
for she hath privately twice or thrice a day, ever
since the death of Hermione, visited that removed
house. Shall we thither, and with our company
piece the rejoicing?
FIRST GENTLEMAN.
Who would be thence that has the benefit of access? every wink of an eye, some new grace will be
born: our absence makes us unthrifty to our knowledge. Let's along.   [Exeunt GENTLEMEN.
AUTOLYCUS.
Now, had I not the dash of my former life in me,
would preferment drop on my head. I brought the
old man and his son aboard the prince; told him I

heard them talk of a fardel, and I know not what:
but he at that time, overfond of the shepherd's
daughter,—so he then took her to be,—who began
to be much sea-sick, and himself little better, extremity of weather continuing, this mystery remain'd undiscover'd. But 'tis all one to me; for had
I been the finder-out of this secret, it would not
have relisht among my other discredits.—Here
come those I have done good to against my will,
and already appearing in the blossoms of their
fortune.
        Enter SHEPHERD and CLOWN.
SHEPHERD.
Come, boy; I am past moe children, but thy sons
and daughters will be all gentlemen born.
CLOWN.
You are well met, sir. You denied to fight with me
this other day, because I was no gentleman born.
See you these clothes? say you see them not, and
think me still no gentleman born: you were best
say these robes are not gentlemen born: give me
the lie, do; and try whether I am not now a gentleman born.
AUTOLYCUS.
I know you are now, sir, a gentleman born.
CLOWN.
Ay, and have I been so any time these four hours.
SHEPHERD.
And so have I, boy.
CLOWN.
So you have:—but I was a gentleman born before
my father; for the king's son took me by the hand,
and call'd me brother; and then the two kings
call'd my father brother; and then the prince my
brother and the princess my sister call'd my father
father; and so we wept,—and there was the first
gentleman-like tears that ever we shed.
SHEPHERD.
We may live, son, to shed many more.
CLOWN.
Ay; or else 'twere hard luck, being in so preposter-
ous estate as we are.
AUTOLYCUS.
I humbly beseech you, sir, to pardon me all the
faults I have committed to your worship, and to
give me your good report to the prince my master.
SHEPHERD.
Prithee, son, do; for we must be gentle, now we
are gentlemen.
CLOWN.
Thou wilt amend thy life?
AUTOLYCUS.
Ay, an it like your good worship.
CLOWN.
Give me thy hand: I will swear to the prince thou
art as honest a true fellow as any is in Bohemia.
SHEPHERD.
You may say it, but not swear it.
CLOWN.
Not swear it, now I am a gentleman? Let boors
and franklins say it, I'll swear it.
SHEPHERD.
How if it be false, son?
CLOWN.
If it be ne'er so false, a true gentleman may swear
it in the behalf of his friend:—and I'll swear to the

prince thou art a tall fellow of thy hands, and that
thou wilt not be drunk; but I know thou art no tall
fellow of thy hands, and that thou wilt be drunk:
but I'll swear it; and I would thou wouldst be a tall
fellow of thy hands.

AUTOLYCUS.
I will prove so, sir, to my power.

CLOWN.
Ay, by any means prove a tall fellow: if I do not
wonder how thou darest venture to be drunk, not
being a tall fellow, trust me not.—[*Trumpets within.*] Hark! the kings and the princes, our kindred,
are going to see the queen's picture. Come, follow
us: we'll be thy good masters.   [*Exeunt.*

SCENE III.

A chapel in PAULINA'S *house.*

Enter LEONTES, POLIXENES, FLORIZEL, PER-
DITA, CAMILLO, PAULINA, LORDS, *and* AT-
TENDANTS.

LEONTES.
O GRAVE and good Paulina, the great comfort
That I have had of thee!

PAULINA.
What, sovereign sir,
I did not well, I meant well. All my services
You have paid home: but that you have vouch-
safed
With your crown'd brother and these your con-
tracted
Heirs of your kingdoms my poor house to visit,
It is a surplus of your grace, which never
My life may last to answer.

LEONTES.
O, Paulina,
We honour you with trouble:—but we came
To see the statue of our queen: your gallery
Have we past through, not without much content
In many singularities; but we saw not
That which my daughter came to look upon,
The statue of her mother.

PAULINA.
As she lived peerless,
So her dead likeness, I do well believe,
Excels whatever yet you lookt upon,
Or hand of man hath done; therefore I keep it
Lonely, apart. But here it is: prepare
To see the life as lively mockt as ever
Still sleep mockt death: behold, and say 'tis well.
[PAULINA *draws back a curtain, and dis-
covers* HERMIONE *standing as a statue.*
I like your silence,—it the more shows off
Your wonder: but yet speak;—first, you, my liege:
Comes it not something near?

LEONTES.
Her natural posture!—
Chide me, dear stone, that I may say indeed
Thou art Hermione; or rather, thou art she
In thy not chiding, for she was as tender
As infancy and grace.—But yet, Paulina,
Hermione was not so much wrinkled, nothing
So aged as this seems.

POLIXENES.
O, not by much.

PAULINA.
So much the more our carver's excellence;
Which lets go by some sixteen years, and makes
her
As she lived now.

LEONTES.
As now she might have done,
So much to my good comfort, as it is
Now piercing to my soul. O, thus she stood,
Even with such life of majesty,—warm life,
As now it coldly stands,—when first I woo'd her!
I am ashamed: does not the stone rebuke me
For being more stone than it?—O royal piece,
There's magic in thy majesty; which has
My evils conjured to remembrance, and
From thy admiring daughter took the spirits,
Standing like stone with thee!

PERDITA.
And give me leave,
And do not say 'tis superstition that
I kneel, and then implore her blessing.—Lady,
Dear queen, that ended when I but began,
Give me that hand of yours to kiss.

PAULINA.
O, patience!
The statue is but newly fixt, the colour's
Not dry.

CAMILLO.
My lord, your sorrow was too sore laid on,
Which sixteen winters cannot blow away,
So many summers dry: scarce any joy
Did ever so long live; no sorrow
But kill'd itself much sooner.

POLIXENES.
Dear my brother,
Let him that was the cause of this have power
To take off so much grief from you as he
Will piece up in himself.

PAULINA.
Indeed, my lord,
If I had thought the sight of my poor image
Would thus have wrought you,—for the stone is
mine,—
I'ld not have show'd it.

LEONTES.
Do not draw the curtain.

PAULINA.
No longer shall you gaze on't, lest your fancy
May think anon it moves.

LEONTES.
Let be, let be.—
Would I were dead, but that, methinks, already
What was he that did make it?—See, my lord,
Would you not deem it breathed? and that those
veins
Did verily bear blood?

POLIXENES.
Masterly done:
The very life seems warm upon her lip.

LEONTES.
The fixture of her eye has motion in't,
As we are mockt with art.

PAULINA.
I'll draw the curtain:
My lord's almost so far transported, that
He'll think anon it lives.

LEONTES.
           O sweet Paulina.
Make me to think so twenty years together!
No settled senses of the world can match
The pleasure of that madness. Let't alone.

PAULINA.
I am sorry sir, I have thus far stirr'd you; but
I could afflict you further.

LEONTES.
           Do, Paulina;
For this affliction has a taste as sweet
As any cordial comfort.—Still, methinks,
There is an air comes from her: what fine chisel
Could ever yet cut breath? Let no man mock me,
For I will kiss her.

PAULINA.
           Good my lord, forbear:
The ruddiness upon her lip is wet;
You'll mar it, if you kiss it; stain your own
With oily painting. Shall I draw the curtain?

LEONTES.
No, not these twenty years.

PERDITA.
           So long could I
Stand by, a looker-on.

PAULINA.
           Either forbear,
Quit presently the chapel, or resolve you
For more amazement. If you can behold it,
I'll make the statue move indeed, descend
And take you by the hand: but then you'll think,—
Which I protest against,— I am assisted
By wicked powers.

LEONTES.
           What you can make her do,
I am content to look on; what to speak,
I am content to hear; for 'tis as easy
To make her speak as move.

PAULINA.
           It is required
You do awake your faith. Then all stand still;
Or those that think it is unlawful business
I am about, let them depart.

LEONTES.
           Proceed:
No foot shall stir.

PAULINA.
           Music, awake her; strike!—[Music.
'Tis time; descend; be stone no more; approach;
Strike all that look upon with marvel. Come;
I'll fill your grave up: stir; nay, come away;
Bequeath to death your numbness, for from him
Dear life redeems you.—You perceive she stirs:
     [HERMIONE comes down from the pedestal.
Start not; her actions shall be holy as
You hear my spell is lawful: do not shun her,
Until you see her die again; for then
You kill her double. Nay, present your hand:
When she was young, you woo'd her; now in age
Is she become the suitor.

LEONTES.
           O, she's warm! [Embracing her.
If this be magic, let it be an art
Lawful as eating.

POLIXENES.
           She embraces him.

CAMILLO.
She hangs about his neck:
If she pertain to life, let her speak too.

POLIXENES.
Ay, and make't manifest where she has lived,
Or how stolen from the dead.

PAULINA.
           That she is living,
Were it but told you, should be hooted at
Like an old tale: but it appears she lives,
Though yet she speak not. Mark a little while.--
Please you to interpose, fair madam; kneel,
And pray your mother's blessing.—Turn, good
     lady;
Our Perdita is found.
    [Presenting Perdita, who kneels to HERMIONE.

HERMIONE.
           You gods, look down,
And from your sacred vials pour your graces
Upon my daughter's head!— Tell me, mine
     own,
Where hast thou been preserved? where lived? how
     found
Thy father's court? for thou shalt hear that I,—
Knowing by Paulina that the oracle
Gave hope thou wast in being,—have preserved
Myself to see the issue.

PAULINA.
           There's time enough for that;
Lest they desire, upon this push, to trouble
Your joys with like relation.—Go together,
You precious winners all; your exultation
Partake to every one. I, an old turtle,
Will wing me to some wither'd bough, and there
My mate, that's never to be found again,
Lament till I am lost.

LEONTES.
           O, peace, Paulina!
Thou shouldst a husband take by my consent,
As I by thine a wife: this is a match,
And made between's by vows. Thou hast found
     mine;
But how, is to be question'd; for I saw her,
As I thought, dead; and have, in vain, said many
A prayer upon her grave. I'll not seek far,—
For him, I partly know his mind,—to find thee
An honourable husband. Come, Camillo,
And take her by the hand; whose worth and
     honesty
Is richly noted; and here justified
By us, a pair of kings.—Let's from this place.—
What! look upon my brother:—both your par-
     dons,
That e'er I put between your holy looks
My ill suspicions.—This your son-in-law,
And son unto the king, whom heavens directing,
Is troth-plight to your daughter.—Good Paulina,
Lead us from hence; where we may leisurely
Each one demand, and answer to his part
Perform'd in this wide gap of time, since first
We were dissever'd; hastily lead away.   [Exeunt.

THE TEMPEST

DRAMATIS PERSONAE

ALONSO, *King of Naples.*
SEBASTIAN, *his brother.*
PROSPERO, *the right Duke of Milan.*
ANTONIO, *his brother, the usurping Duke of Milan.*
FERDINAND, *son to the King of Naples.*
GONZALO, *an honest old counsellor.*
ADRIAN, } *lords.*
FRANCISCO, }
CALIBAN, *a savage and deformed slave.*
TRINCULO, *a jester.*
STEPHANO, *a drunken butler.*
MASTER OF A SHIP, BOATSWAIN, *and* MARINERS.

MIRANDA, *daughter to Prospero.*

ARIEL, *an airy spirit.*
IRIS,
CERES,
JUNO, } *presented by spirits.*
NYMPHS,
REAPERS,

OTHER SPIRITS ATTENDING ON PROSPERO.

SCENE—*A ship at sea; afterwards an island.*

ACT I. SCENE I.

A ship at sea: a tempestuous noise of thunder and lightning heard.

Enter a SHIP-MASTER *and a* BOATSWAIN.

SHIP-MASTER.
BOATSWAIN!
BOATSWAIN.
Here, master: what cheer?
SHIP-MASTER.
Good, speak to the mariners: fall to't yarely, or we run ourselves a-ground: bestir, bestir. [*Exit.*
Enter MARINERS.
BOATSWAIN.
Heigh, my hearts! cheerly, cheerly, my hearts! yare, yare! Take in the topsail! Tend to the master's whistle! [*Exeunt* MARINERS.]—Blow, till thou burst thy wind, if room enough!
Enter ALONSO, SEBASTIAN, ANTONIO, FERDINAND, GONZALO, *and others.*
ALONSO.
Good boatswain, have care. Where's the master? Play the men.
BOATSWAIN.
I pray now, keep below.
ANTONIO.
Where is the master, boatswain?
BOATSWAIN.
Do you not hear him? You mar our labour: keep your cabins: you do assist the storm.
GONZALO.
Nay, good, be patient.
BOATSWAIN.
When the sea is. Hence! What cares these roarers for the name of king? To cabin: silence! trouble us not.
GONZALO.
Good, yet remember whom thou hast aboard.
BOATSWAIN.
None that I more love than myself. You are a counsellor; if you can command these elements to silence, and work the peace of the present, we will not hand a rope more; use your authority: if you cannot, give thanks you have lived so long, and make yourself ready in your cabin for the mischance of the hour, if it so hap.—Cheerly, good hearts!—Out of our way, I say. [*Exit.*

GONZALO.
I have great comfort from this fellow: methinks he hath no drowning-mark upon him; his complexion is perfect gallows. Stand fast, good Fate, to his hanging! make the rope of his destiny our cable, for our own doth little advantage! If he be not born to be hang'd, our case is miserable.
[*Exeunt.*

Enter BOATSWAIN.
BOATSWAIN.
Down with the topmast! yare; lower, lower! Bring her to try with main-course! [*A cry within.*] A plague upon this howling! they are louder than the weather or our office.
Enter SEBASTIAN, ANTONIO, *and* GONZALO.
Yet again! what do you here? Shall we give o'er, and drown? Have you a mind to sink?
SEBASTIAN.
A pox o'your throat, you bawling, blasphemous, incharitable dog!
BOATSWAIN.
Work you, then.
ANTONIO.
Hang, cur, hang! you whoreson, insolent noise-maker, we are less afraid to be drown'd than thou art.
GONZALO.
I'll warrant him for drowning; though the ship were no stronger than a nutshell, and as leaky as an unstanch'd wench.
BOATSWAIN.
Lay her a-hold, a-hold! set her two courses off to sea again: lay her off!
Enter MARINERS *wet.*
MARINERS.
All lost! to prayers, to prayers! all lost!
BOATSWAIN.
What, must our mouths be cold?
GONZALO.
The king and prince at prayers! let's assist them, For our case is as theirs.
SEBASTIAN.
I'm out of patience.
ANTONIO.
We are merely cheated of our lives by drunkards: This wide-chopt rascal,—would thou mightst lie The washing of ten tides! [*drowning,*

GONZALO.
           He'll be hang'd yet,
Though every drop of water swear against it,
And gape at widest to glut him.
    [*A confused noise within,*—'Mercy on us!'—
'We split, we split!'—'Farewell, my wife and children!'—
'Farewell, brother!'—'We split, we split, we split!']

ANTONIO.
Let's all sink with the king.

SEBASTIAN.
           Let's take leave of him.
    [*Exeunt* ANTONIO *and* SEBASTIAN.

GONZALO.
Now would I give a thousand furlongs of sea for
an acre of barren ground,—long heath, broom,
furze, anything. The wills above be done! but I
would fain die a dry death.   [*Exeunt.*

SCENE II.

The island: before PROSPERO'S *cell.*

Enter PROSPERO *and* MIRANDA.

MIRANDA.
IF by your art, my dearest father, you have
  Put the wild waters in this roar, allay them.
The sky, it seems, would pour down stinking pitch,
But that the sea, mounting to the welkin's cheek,
Dashes the fire out. O, I have suffer'd
With those that I saw suffer! a brave vessel,
Who had, no doubt, some noble creature in her,
Dash'd all to pieces. O, the cry did knock
Against my very heart! Poor souls, they perish'd!
Had I been any god of power, I would
Have sunk the sea within the earth, or ere
It should the good ship so have swallow'd, and
The fraughting souls within her.

PROSPERO.
           Be collected;
No more amazement: tell your piteous heart
There's no harm done.

MIRANDA.
           O, woe the day!

PROSPERO.
                No harm.
I have done nothing but in care of thee,
Of thee, my dear one, thee, my daughter, who
Art ignorant of what thou art, naught knowing
Of whence I am, nor that I am more better
Than Prospero, master of a full poor cell,
And thy no greater father.

MIRANDA.
           More to know
Did never meddle with my thoughts.

PROSPERO.
           'Tis time
I should inform thee further. Lend thy hand,
And pluck my magic garment from me. So:
          [*Lays down his mantle.*
Lie there, my art. Wipe thou thine eyes; have comfort.
The direful spectacle of the wrack, which touch'd
The very virtue of compassion in thee,
I have with such provision in mine art

So safely order'd, that there is no soul—
No, not so much perdition as an hair
Betid to any creature in the vessel
Which thou heard'st cry, which thou saw'st sink.
  Sit down;
For thou must now know further.

MIRANDA.
           You have often
Begun to tell me what I am; but stopt,
And left me to a bootless inquisition,
Concluding, 'Stay, not yet.'

PROSPERO.
           The hour's now come;
The very minute bids thee ope thine ear:
Obey, and be attentive. Canst thou remember
A time before we came unto this cell?
I do not think thou canst, for then thou wast not
Out three years old.

MIRANDA.
           Certainly, sir, I can.

PROSPERO.
By what? by any other house or person?
Of any thing the image tell me that
Hath kept with thy remembrance.

MIRANDA.
           'Tis far off,
And rather like a dream than an assurance
That my remembrance warrants. Had I not
Four or five women once that tended me?

PROSPERO.
Thou hadst, and more, Miranda. But how is it
That this lives in thy mind? What see'st thou else
In the dark backward and abysm of time?
If thou remember'est aught ere thou camest here,
How thou camest here thou mayst.

MIRANDA.
           But that I do not.

PROSPERO.
Twelve year since, Miranda, twelve year since,
Thy father was the Duke of Milan, and
A prince of power.

MIRANDA.
           Sir, are not you my father?

PROSPERO.
Thy mother was a piece of virtue, and
She said thou wast my daughter; and thy father
Was Duke of Milan; thou his only heir,
And princess, no worse issued.

MIRANDA.
           O the heavens!
What foul play had we, that we came from thence?
Or blessed was't we did?

PROSPERO.
           Both, both, my girl:
By foul play, as thou say'st, were we heaved thence;
But blessedly holp hither.

MIRANDA.
           O, my heart bleeds
To think o'the teen that I have turn'd you to,
Which is from my remembrance! Please you, further.

PROSPERO.
My brother, and thy uncle, call'd Antonio,—
I pray thee, mark me,—that a brother should
Be so perfidious!—he whom, next thyself,

Of all the world I loved, and to him put
The manage of my state; as, at that time,
Through all the signiories it was the first,
And Prospero the prime duke, being so reputed
In dignity, and for the liberal arts
Without a parallel: those being all my study,
The government I cast upon my brother,
And to my state grew stranger, being transported
And rapt in secret studies. Thy false uncle—
Dost thou attend me?

       MIRANDA.
           Sir, most heedfully,

       PROSPERO.
Being once perfected how to grant suits,
How to deny them, who t'advance, and who
To trash for over-topping, new created
The creatures that were mine, I say, or changed
     'em,
Or else new-form'd 'em; having both the key
Of officer and office, set all hearts i'the state
To what tune pleased his ear; that now he was
The ivy which had hid my princely trunk,
And suck'd my verdure out on't. Thou attend'st
     not.

       MIRANDA.
O, good sir, I do.

       PROSPERO.
           I pray thee, mark me.
I, thus neglecting worldly ends, all dedicate
To closeness, and the bettering of my mind
With that which, but by being so retired,
O'er-prized all popular rate, in my false brother
Awaked an evil nature; and my trust,
Like a good parent, did beget of him
A falsehood, in its contrary as great
As my trust was; which had indeed no limit,
A confidence sans bound. He being thus lorded,
Not only with what my revenue yielded,
But what my power might else exact, like one
Who having into truth, by telling of it,
Made such a sinner of his memory,
To credit his own lie, he did believe
He was indeed the duke; out o'the substitution,
And executing the outward face of royalty,
With all prerogative:—hence his ambition grow-
     ing,—
Dost thou hear?

       MIRANDA.
           Your tale, sir, would cure deafness.

       PROSPERO.
To have no screen between this part he play'd
And him he play'd it for, he needs will be
Absolute Milan. Me, poor man, my library
Was dukedom large enough: of temporal royalties
He thinks me now incapable; confederates—
So dry he was for sway—with the King of Naples
To give him annual tribute, do him homage,
Subject his coronet to his crown, and bend
The dukedom, yet unbow'd,—alas, poor
     Milan!—
To most ignoble stooping.

       MIRANDA.
           O the heavens!

       PROSPERO.
Mark his condition, and the event; then tell me
If this might be a brother.

       MIRANDA.
           I should sin
To think but nobly of my grandmother:
Good wombs have borne bad sons.

       PROSPERO.
           Now the condition.
This King of Naples, being an enemy
To me inveterate, hearkens my brother's suit;
Which was, that he, in lieu o'the premises,—
Of homage, and I know not how much tribute,—
Should presently extirpate me and mine
Out of the dukedom, and confer fair Milan,
With all the honours, on my brother: whereon,
A treacherous army levied, one midnight
Fated to the purpose, did Antonio open
The gates of Milan; and, i'the dead of darkness,
The ministers for the purpose hurried thence
Me and thy crying self.

       MIRANDA.
           Alack, for pity!
I, not rememb'ring how I cried out then,
Will cry it o'er again: it is a hint
That wrings mine eyes to't.

       PROSPERO.
           Hear a little further,
And then I'll bring thee to the present business
Which now's upon's; without the which this story
Were most impertinent.

       MIRANDA.
           Wherefore did they not
That hour destroy us?

       PROSPERO.
           Well demanded, wench:
My tale provokes that question. Dear, they durst
     not,
So dear the love my people bore me, nor set
A mark so bloody on the business; but
With colours fairer painted their foul ends.
In few, they hurried us aboard a bark,
Bore us some leagues to sea; where they prepared
A rotten carcass of a butt, not rigg'd,
Nor tackle, sail, nor mast; the very rats
Instinctively have quit it: there they hoist us,
To cry to the sea that roar'd to us; to sigh
To the winds, whose pity, sighing back again,
Did us but loving wrong.

       MIRANDA.
           Alack, what trouble
Was I then to you!

       PROSPERO.
           O, a cherubin
Thou wast that did preserve me! Thou didst
     smile,
Infused with a fortitude from heaven,
When I have deck'd the sea with drops full salt,
Under my burden groan'd; which raised in me
An undergoing stomach, to bear up
Against what should ensue.

       MIRANDA.
           How came we ashore?

       PROSPERO.
By Providence divine.
Some food we had, and some fresh water, that
A noble Neapolitan, Gonzalo,
Out of his charity (who being then appointed
Master of this design), did give us, with

Rich garments, linens, stuffs, and necessaries,
Which since have steaded much; so, of his gentle-
　　ness,
Knowing I loved my books, he furnish'd me,
From mine own library, with volumes that
I prize above my dukedom.
MIRANDA.
　　　　　　Would I might
But ever see that man!
PROSPERO.
　　　　　　Now I arise:
　　　　　　[*Resuming his mantle.*
Sit still, and hear the last of our sea-sorrow.
Here in this island we arrived; and here
Have I, thy schoolmaster, made thee more profit
Than other princess' can, that have more time
For vainer hours, and tutors not so careful.
MIRANDA.
Heavens thank you for't! And now, I pray you,
　　sir,
For still 'tis beating in my mind, your reason
For raising this sea-storm?
PROSPERO.
　　　　　　Know thus far forth.
By accident most strange, bountiful Fortune,
Now my dear lady, hath mine enemies
Brought to this shore; and by my prescience
I find my zenith doth depend upon
A most auspicious star, whose influence
If now I court not, but omit, my fortunes
Will ever after droop. Here cease more questions:
Thou art inclined to sleep; 'tis a good dulness,
And give it way: I know thou canst not chuse.—
　　　　　　[*MIRANDA sleeps.*
Come away, servant, come! I am ready now:
Approach, my Ariel; come!
Enter ARIEL.
ARIEL.
All hail, great master! grave sir, hail! I come
To answer thy best pleasure; be't to fly,
To swim, to dive into the fire, to ride
On the curl'd clouds,—to thy strong bidding task
Ariel and all his quality.
PROSPERO.
　　　　　　Hast thou, spirit,
Perform'd to point the tempest that I bade thee?
ARIEL.
To every article.
I boarded the king's ship; now on the beak,
Now in the waist, the deck, in every cabin,
I flamed amazement: sometime I'ld divide,
And burn in many places; on the topmast,
The yards, and bowsprit, would I flame distinctly,
Then meet, and join. Jove's lightnings, the pre-
　　cursors
O'the dreadful thunder-claps, more momentary
And sight-outrunning were not: the fire, and
　　cracks
Of sulphurous roaring, the most mighty Neptune
Seem to besiege, and make his bold waves
　　tremble,
Yea, his dread trident shake.
PROSPERO.
　　　　　　My brave spirit!
Who was so firm, so constant, that this coil
Would not infect his reason?

ARIEL.
　　　　　　Not a soul
But felt a fever of the mad, and play'd
Some tricks of desperation. All but mariners
Plunged in the foaming brine, and quit the vessel,
Then all a-fire with me: the king's son, Ferdi-
　　nand,
With hair up-staring,—then like reeds, not hair,—
Was the first man that leapt; cried, 'Hell is empty,
And all the devils are here.'
PROSPERO.
　　　　　　Why, that's my spirit!
But was not this nigh shore?
ARIEL.
　　　　　　Close by, my master.
PROSPERO.
But are they, Ariel, safe?
ARIEL.
　　　　　　Not a hair perish'd;
On their sustaining garments not a blemish,
But fresher than before: and, as thou bad'st me,
In troops I have dispersed them 'bout the isle.
The king's son have I landed by himself;
Whom I left cooling of the air with sighs
In an odd angle of the isle, and sitting,
His arms in this sad knot.
PROSPERO.
　　　　　　Of the king's ship
The mariners, say how thou hast disposed,
And all the rest o'the fleet.
ARIEL.
　　　　　　Safely in harbour
Is the king's ship; in the deep nook, where once
Thou call'dst me up at midnight to fetch dew
From the still-vext Bermoothes, there she's hid:
The mariners all under hatches stow'd;
Who, with a charm join'd to their suffer'd labour,
I have left asleep: and for the rest o'the fleet,
Which I dispersed, they all have met again,
And are upon the Mediterranean flote,
Bound sadly home for Naples;
Supposing that they saw the king's ship wrackt,
And his great person perish.
PROSPERO.
　　　　　　Ariel, thy charge
Exactly is perform'd; but there's more work.
What is the time o'the day?
ARIEL.
　　　　　　Past the mid season.
PROSPERO.
At least two glasses. The time 'twixt six and now
Must by us both be spent most preciously.
ARIEL.
Is there more toil? Since thou dost give me pains,
Let me remember thee what thou hast promised,
Which is not yet perform'd me.
PROSPERO.
　　　　　　How now? moody?
What is't thou canst demand?
ARIEL.
　　　　　　My liberty.
PROSPERO.
Before the time be out? no more!
ARIEL.
　　　　　　I prithee,
Remember I have done thee worthy service;

Told thee no lies, made thee no mistakings,
served
Without or grudge or grumblings; thou did
promise
To bate me a full year.

PROSPERO.
           Dost thou forget
From what a torment I did free thee?

ARIEL.
                No.

PROSPERO.
Thou dost; and think'st it much to tread the ooze
Of the salt deep,
To run upon the sharp wind of the north,
To do me business in the veins o'the earth
When it is baked with frost.

ARIEL.
           I do not, sir.

PROSPERO.
Thou liest, malignant thing! Hast thou forgot
The foul witch Sycorax, who with age and envy
Was grown into a hoop? hast thou forgot her?

ARIEL.
No, sir.

PROSPERO.
    Thou hast. Where was she born? speak; tell me.

ARIEL.
Sir, in Argier.

PROSPERO.
         O, was she so? I must
Once in a month recount what thou hast been,
Which thou forgett'st. This damn'd witch Syco-
rax,
For mischiefs manifold, and sorceries terrible
To enter human hearing, from Argier,
Thou know'st, was banish'd: for one thing she
did
They would not take her life. Is not this true?

ARIEL.
Ay, sir.

PROSPERO.
This blue-eyed hag was hither brought with
child,
And here was left by the sailors. Thou, my slave,
As thou report'st thyself, was then her servant;
And, for thou wast a spirit too delicate
To act her earthy and abhorr'd commands,
Refusing her grand hests, she did confine thee,
By help of her more potent ministers,
And in her most unmitigable rage,
Into a cloven pine; within which rift
Imprison'd, thou didst painfully remain
A dozen years; within which space she died,
And left thee there; where thou didst vent thy
groans
As fast as mill-wheels strike. Then was this
island—
Save for the son that she did litter here,
A freckled whelp hag-born—not honour'd with
A human shape.

ARIEL.
       Yes, Caliban, her son.

PROSPERO.
Dull thing, I say so; he, that Caliban,
Whom now I keep in service. Thou best know'st
What torment I did find thee in; thy groans

Did make wolves howl, and penetrate the breasts
Of ever-angry bears: it was a torment
To lay upon the damn'd, which Sycorax
Could not again undo: it was mine art,
When I arrived and heard thee, that made gape
The pine, and let thee out.

ARIEL.
          I thank thee, master.

PROSPERO.
If thou more murmur'st, I will rend an oak,
And peg thee in his knotty entrails, till
Thou'st howl'd away twelve winters.

ARIEL.
              Pardon, master:
I will be correspondent to command,
And do my spriting gently.

PROSPERO.
           Do so; and after two days
I will discharge thee.

ARIEL.
         That's my noble master!
What shall I do? say what; what shall I do?

PROSPERO.
Go make thyself like a nymph o'the sea: be sub-
ject
To no sight but thine and mine: invisible
To every eyeball else. Go take this shape,
And hither come in't: go; hence with diligence!
                      [*Exit* ARIEL.
Awake, dear heart, awake! thou hast slept well;
Awake!

MIRANDA [*waking*].
    The strangeness of your story put
Heaviness in me.

PROSPERO.
         Shake it off. Come on;
We'll visit Caliban my slave, who never
Yields us kind answer.

MIRANDA.
          'Tis a villain, sir,
I do not love to look on.

PROSPERO.
           But, as 'tis,
We cannot miss him: he does make our fire,
Fetch in our wood; and serves in offices
That profit us.—What, ho! slave! Caliban!
Thou earth, thou! speak.

CALIBAN [*within*].
        There's wood enough within.

PROSPERO.
Come forth, I say! there's other business for thee:
Come, thou tortoise, when?
     Enter ARIEL *like a water-nymph.*
Fine apparition! My quaint Ariel,
Hark in thine ear.

ARIEL.
     My lord, it shall be done. [*Exit.*

PROSPERO.
Thou poisonous slave, got by the devil himself
Upon thy wicked dam, come forth!
           Enter CALIBAN.

CALIBAN.
As wicked dew as e'er my mother brush'd
With raven's feather from unwholesome fen
Drop on you both! a south-west blow on ye,
And blister you all o'er!

PROSPERO.
For this, be sure, to-night thou shalt have
    cramps,
Side-stitches that shall pen thy breath up;
    urchins
Shall, for that vast of night that they may work,
All exercise on thee; thou shalt be pinch'd
As thick as honeycomb, each pinch more stinging
Than bees that made 'em.

CALIBAN.
                I must eat my dinner.
This island's mine, by Sycorax my mother,
Which thou takest from me. When thou camest
    first,
Thou strokedst me, and made much of me;
    wouldst give me
Water with berries in't; and teach me how
To name the bigger light, and how the less,
That burn by day and night: and then I loved thee,
And show'd thee all the qualities o'the isle,
The fresh springs, brine-pits, barren place and
    fertile:
Cursed be I that did so! All the charms
Of Sycorax, toads, beetles, bats, light on you!
For I am all the subjects that you have,
Which first was mine own king: and here you sty
    me
In this hard rock, whiles you do keep from me
The rest o'the island.

PROSPERO.
             Thou most lying slave,
Whom stripes may move, not kindness! I have
    used thee,
Filth as thou art, with human care, and lodged thee
In mine own cell, till thou didst seek to violate
The honour of my child.

CALIBAN.
O ho, O ho! would't had been done!
Thou didst prevent me; I had peopled else
This isle with Calibans.

PROSPERO.
             Abhorred slave,
Which any print of goodness wilt not take,
Being capable of all ill! I pitied thee,
Took pains to make thee speak, taught thee each
    hour
One thing or other: when thou didst not, savage,
Know thine own meaning, but wouldst gabble
    like
A thing most brutish, I endow'd thy purposes
With words that made them known. But thy vile
    race,
Though thou didst learn, had that in't which
    good natures
Could not abide to be with; therefore wast thou
Deservedly confined into this rock,
Who hadst deserved more than a prison.

CALIBAN.
You taught me language; and my profit on't
Is, I know how to curse. The red plague rid you
For learning me your language!

PROSPERO.
             Hag-seed, hence!
Fetch us in fuel; and be quick, thou'rt best,
To answer other business. Shrugg'st thou,
    malice?

If thou neglect'st, or dost unwillingly
What I command, I'll rack thee with old cramps,
Fill all thy bones with aches, make thee roar,
That beasts shall tremble at thy din.

CALIBAN.
             No, 'pray thee.—
[aside] I must obey: his art is of such power,
It would control my dam's god, Setebos,
And make a vassal of him.

PROSPERO.
           So, slave; hence! [Exit CALIBAN.
Enter ARIEL, *invisible, playing and singing;*
    FERDINAND *following.*

ARIEL'S *song.*
Come unto these yellow sands,
    And then take hands:
Court'sied when you have and kist,—
    The wild waves whist,—
Foot it featly here and there;
And, sweet sprites, the burden bear.
    Hark, hark!
        [Burden, dispersedly, within. Bow, wow.]
    The watch-dogs bark:
        [Burden, dispersedly, within. Bow, wow.]
    Hark, hark! I hear
    The strain of strutting chanticleer.
        [Cry: Cock-a-diddle-dow.]

FERDINAND.
Where should this music be? i'the air or the
    earth?
It sounds no more:—and, sure, it waits upon
Some god o'the island. Sitting on a bank,
Weeping again the king my father's wrack,
This music crept by me upon the waters,
Allaying both their fury and my passion
With its sweet air: thence I have follow'd it,
Or it hath drawn me rather:—but 'tis gone.
No, it begins again.

ARIEL *sings.*
Full fadom five thy father lies;
    Of his bones are coral made;
Those are pearls that were his eyes;
    Nothing of him that doth fade
But doth suffer a sea-change
Into something rich and strange.
Sea-nymphs hourly ring his knell:
    [Burden within. Ding-dong.]
Hark! now I hear them,—Ding-dong, bell.

FERDINAND.
The ditty does remember my drown'd father:—
This is no mortal business, nor no sound
That the earth owes:—I hear it now above me.

PROSPERO.
The fringed curtains of thine eye advance,
And say what thou see'st yond.

MIRANDA.
             What is't? a spirit?
Lord, how it looks about! Believe me, sir,
It carries a brave form:—but 'tis a spirit.

PROSPERO.
No, wench; it eats, and sleeps, and hath such
    senses
As we have, such. This gallant which thou see'st
Was in the wrack; and, but he's something stain'd
With grief, that's beauty's canker, thou mightst
    call him

A goodly person: he hath lost his fellows,
And strays about to find 'em.

MIRANDA.
              I might call him
A thing divine; for nothing natural
I ever saw so noble.

PROSPERO [aside].
              It goes on, I see,
As my soul prompts it.—Spirit, fine spirit! I'll
    free thee
Within two days for this.

FERDINAND.
           Most sure, the goddess
On whom these airs attend!—Vouchsafe my
    prayer
May know if you remain upon this island;
And that you will some good instruction give
How I may bear me here: my prime request,
Which I do last pronounce, is, O you wonder!
If you be maid or no?

MIRANDA.
          No wonder, sir;
But certainly a maid.

FERDINAND.
          My language! heavens!
I am the best of them that speak this speech,
Were I but where 'tis spoken.

PROSPERO.
            How! the best!
What wert thou, if the King of Naples heard thee?

FERDINAND.
A single thing, as I am now, that wonders
To hear thee speak of Naples. He does hear me;
And that he does I weep: myself am Naples;
Who with mine eyes, never since at ebb, beheld
The king my father wrackt.

MIRANDA.
          Alack! for mercy!

FERDINAND.
Yes, faith, and all his lords; the Duke of Milan
And his brave son being twain.

PROSPERO [aside].
          The Duke of Milan
And his more braver daughter could control thee,
If now 'twere fit to do't. At the first sight
They have changed eyes. Delicate Ariel,
I'll set thee free for this!—A word, good sir;
I fear you have done yourself some wrong: a word.

MIRANDA.
Why speaks my father so ungently? This
Is the third man that e'er I saw; the first
That e'er I sigh'd for: pity move my father
To be inclined my way!

FERDINAND.
          O, if a virgin,
And your affection not gone forth, I'll make you
The queen of Naples.

PROSPERO.
         Soft, sir! one word more.—
[aside] They are both in either's powers: but this
    swift business
I must uneasy make, lest too light winning
Make the prize light.—One word more; I charge
    thee
That thou attend me: thou dost here usurp
The name thou owest not; and hast put thyself

Upon this island as a spy, to win it
From me, the lord on't.

FERDINAND.
          No, as I am a man.

MIRANDA.
There's nothing ill can dwell in such a temple:
If the ill spirit have so fair a house,
Good things will strive to dwell with't.

PROSPERO.
              Follow me.
Speak not you for him; he's a traitor. Come;
I'll manacle thy neck and feet together:
Sea-water shalt thou drink; thy food shall be
The fresh-brook mussels, wither'd roots, and
    husks
Wherein the acorn cradled. Follow.

FERDINAND.
               No;
I will resist such entertainment till
Mine enemy has more power.
        [Draws, and is charm'd from moving.

MIRANDA.
          O dear father,
Make not too rash a trial of him, for
He's gentle, and not fearful.

PROSPERO.
           What, I say,
My foot my tutor! Put thy sword up, traitor;
Who makest a show, but darest not strike, thy
    conscience
Is so possest with guilt: come from thy ward;
For I can here disarm thee with this stick,
And make thy weapon drop.

MIRANDA.
          Beseech you, father!—

PROSPERO.
Hence! hang not on my garments.

MIRANDA.
          Sir, have pity;
I'll be his surety.

PROSPERO.
         Silence! one word more
Shall make me chide thee, if not hate thee. What,
An advocate for an impostor! hush!
Thou think'st there are no more such shapes as he,
Having seen but him and Caliban: foolish wench!
To the most of men this is a Caliban,
And they to him are angels.

MIRANDA.
          My affections
Are, then, most humble; I have no ambition
To see a goodlier man.

PROSPERO.
         Come on; obey:
Thy nerves are in their infancy again,
And have no vigour in them.

FERDINAND.
         So they are:
My spirits, as in a dream, are all bound up.
My father's loss, the weakness which I feel,
The wrack of all my friends, nor this man's threats
To whom I am subdued, are but light to me,
Might I but through my prison once a day
Behold this maid: all corners else o'the earth
Let liberty make use of; space enough
Have I in such a prison.

PROSPERO [*aside*].
It works.—Come on.— [*To* FERDINAND.
Thou hast done well, fine Ariel!—Follow me.—
[*To* FERDINAND.
Hark what thou else shalt do me.   [*To* ARIEL.

MIRANDA.
Be of comfort;
My father's of a better nature, sir,
Than he appears by speech: this is unwonted
Which now came from him.

PROSPERO.
Thou shalt be as free
As mountain winds: but then exactly do
All points of my command.

ARIEL.
To the syllable.

PROSPERO.
Come, follow.—Speak not for him.   [*Exeunt.*

ACT II. SCENE I.

Another part of the island.

Enter ALONSO, SEBASTIAN, ANTONIO, GON-
ZALO, ADRIAN, FRANCISCO, *and others.*

GONZALO.
BESEECH you, sir, be merry; you have cause,
So have we all, of joy; for our escape
Is much beyond our loss. Our hint of woe
Is common; every day some sailor's wife,
The masters of some merchant, and the mer-
chant,
Have just our theme of woe; but for the miracle,
I mean our preservation, few in millions
Can speak like us: then wisely, good sir, weigh
Our sorrow with our comfort.

ALONSO.
Prithee, peace.

SEBASTIAN.
He receives comfort like cold porridge.

ANTONIO.
The visitor will not give him o'er so.

SEBASTIAN.
Look, he's winding up the watch of his wit; by
and by it will strike.

GONZALO.
Sir,—

SEBASTIAN.
One: tell.

GONZALO.
When every grief is entertain'd that's offer'd,
Comes to the entertainer—

SEBASTIAN.
A dollar.

GONZALO.
Dolour comes to him, indeed; you have spoken
truer than you purposed.

SEBASTIAN.
You have taken it wiselier than I meant you
should.

GONZALO.
Therefore, my lord,—

ANTONIO.
Fie, what a spendthrift is he of his tongue!

ALONSO.
I prithee, spare.

GONZALO.
Well, I have done: but yet,—

SEBASTIAN.
He will be talking.

ANTONIO.
Which, of he or Adrian, for a good wager, first
begins to crow?

SEBASTIAN.
The old cock.

ANTONIO.
The cockerel.

SEBASTIAN.
Done! The wager?

ANTONIO.
A laughter.

SEBASTIAN.
A match!

ADRIAN.
Though this island seem to be desert,—

SEBASTIAN.
Ha, ha, ha!

ANTONIO.
So: you've paid.

ADRIAN.
Uninhabitable, and almost inaccessible,—

SEBASTIAN.
Yet,—

ADRIAN.
Yet,—

ANTONIO.
He could not miss't.

ADRIAN.
It must needs be of subtle, tender, and delicate
temperance.

ANTONIO.
Temperance was a delicate wench.

SEBASTIAN.
Ay, and a subtle; as he most learnedly deliver'd.

ADRIAN.
The air breathes upon us here most sweetly.

SEBASTIAN.
As if it had lungs, and rotten ones.

ANTONIO.
Or as 'twere perfumed by a fen.

GONZALO.
Here is everything advantageous to life.

ANTONIO.
True; save means to live.

SEBASTIAN.
Of that there's none, or little.

GONZALO.
How lush and lusty the grass looks! how
green!

ANTONIO.
The ground, indeed, is tawny.

SEBASTIAN.
With an eye of green in't.

ANTONIO.
He misses not much.

SEBASTIAN.
No; he doth but mistake the truth totally.

GONZALO.
But the rariety of it is,—which is indeed almost
beyond credit,—

SEBASTIAN.
As many voucht rarieties are.

GONZALO.

That our garments, being, as they were, drencht
in the sea, hold, notwithstanding, their freshness
and glosses, being rather new-dyed than stain'd
with salt water.

ANTONIO.

If but one of his pockets could speak, would it not
say he lies?

SEBASTIAN.

Ay, or very falsely pocket up his report.

GONZALO.

Methinks our garments are now as fresh as when
we put them on first in Afric, at the marriage of the
king's fair daughter Claribel to the King of Tunis.

SEBASTIAN.

'Twas a sweet marriage, and we prosper well in
our return.

ADRIAN.

Tunis was never graced before with such a paragon to their queen.

GONZALO.

Not since widow Dido's time.

ANTONIO.

Widow! a pox o'that! How came that widow in?
widow Dido!

SEBASTIAN.

What if he had said 'widower Aeneas' too? Good
Lord, how you take it!

ADRIAN.

Widow Dido, said you? you make me study of
that: she was of Carthage, not of Tunis.

GONZALO.

This Tunis, sir, was Carthage.

ADRIAN.

Carthage!

GONZALO.

I assure you, Carthage.

ANTONIO.

His word is more than the miraculous harp.

SEBASTIAN.

He hath raised the wall, and houses too.

ANTONIO.

What impossible matter will he make easy next?

SEBASTIAN.

I think he will carry this island home in his
pocket, and give it his son for an apple.

ANTONIO.

And, sowing the kernels of it in the sea, bring
forth more islands.

GONZALO.

Ay.

ANTONIO.

Why, in good time.

GONZALO.

Sir, we were talking that our garments seem now
as fresh as when we were at Tunis at the marriage
of your daughter, who is now queen.

ANTONIO.

And the rarest that e'er came there.

SEBASTIAN.

Bate, I beseech you, widow Dido.

ANTONIO.

O, widow Dido: ay, widow Dido.

GONZALO.

Is not, sir, my doublet as fresh as the first day I
wore it? I mean, in a sort.

ANTONIO.

That sort was well fish'd for.

GONZALO.

When I wore it at your daughter's marriage?

ALONSO.

You cram these words into mine ears against
The stomach of my sense. Would I had never
Married my daughter there! for, coming thence,
My son is lost; and, in my rate, she too,
Who is so far from Italy removed,
I ne'er again shall see her. O thou mine heir
Of Naples and of Milan, what strange fish
Hath made his meal on thee?

FRANCISCO.

                    Sir, he may live:
I saw him beat the surges under him,
And ride upon their backs; he trod the water,
Whose enmity he flung aside, and breasted
The surge most swoln that met him; his bold
    head
'Bove the contentious waves he kept, and oar'd
Himself with his good arms in lusty stroke
To the shore, that o'er his wave-worn basis bow'd,
As stooping to relieve him: I not doubt
He came alive to land.

ALONSO.

            No, no, he's gone.

SEBASTIAN.

Sir, you may thank yourself for this great loss,
That would not bless our Europe with your
    daughter,
But rather lose her to an African;
Where she, at least, is banish'd from your eye,
Who hath cause to wet the grief on't.

ALONSO.

                    Prithee, peace.

SEBASTIAN.

You were kneel'd to, and importuned otherwise,
By all of us; and the fair soul herself
Weigh'd, between loathness and obedience, at
Which end o'the beam should bow. We have lost
    your son,
I fear, for ever: Milan and Naples have
Moe widows in them of this business' making
Than we bring men to comfort them:
The fault's your own.

ALONSO.

            So is the dear'st o'the loss.

GONZALO.

My lord Sebastian,
The truth you speak doth lack some gentleness,
And time to speak it in: you rub the sore,
When you should bring the plaster.

SEBASTIAN.

            Very well.

ANTONIO.

And most chirurgeonly.

GONZALO.

It is foul weather in us all, good sir,
When you are cloudy.

SEBASTIAN.

            Foul weather!

ANTONIO.

                    Very foul.

GONZALO.

Had I plantation of this isle, my lord,—

ANTONIO.
He'd sow't with nettle-seed.
SEBASTIAN.
               Or docks, or mallows.
GONZALO.
And were the king on't, what would I do?
SEBASTIAN.
Scape being drunk for want of wine.
GONZALO.
I'the commonwealth I would by contraries
Execute all things; for no kind of traffic
Would I admit; no name of magistrate;
Letters should not be known; riches, poverty,
And use of service, none; contract, succession,
Bourn, bound of land, tilth, vineyard, none;
No use of metal, corn, or wine, or oil;
No occupation; all men idle, all;
And women too,—but innocent and pure;
No sovereignty,—
SEBASTIAN.
        Yet he would be king on't.
ANTONIO
The latter end of his commonwealth forgets the
beginning.
GONZALO.
All things in common nature should produce
Without sweat or endeavour: treason, felony,
Sword, pike, knife, gun, or need of any engine,
Would I not have; but nature should bring
    forth,
Of it own kind, all foison, all abundance,
To feed my innocent people.
SEBASTIAN.
No marrying 'mong his subjects?
ANTONIO.
None, man; all idle; whores and knaves.
GONZALO.
I would with such perfection govern, sir,
T'excel the golden age.
SEBASTIAN.
       'Save his majesty!
ANTONIO.
Long live Gonzalo!
GONZALO.
      And,—do you mark me, sir?—
ALONSO.
Prithee, no more: thou dost talk nothing to me.
GONZALO.
I do well believe your highness; and did it to
minister occasion to these gentlemen, who are of
such sensible and nimble lungs that they always
use to laugh at nothing.
ANTONIO.
'Twas you we laugh'd at.
GONZALO.
Who in this kind of merry fooling am nothing to
you: so you may continue, and laugh at nothing
still.
ANTONIO.
What a blow was there given!
SEBASTIAN.
An it had not fallen flat-long.
GONZALO.
You are gentlemen of brave mettle; you would
lift the moon out of her sphere, if she would con-
tinue in it five weeks without changing.

Enter ARIEL, *invisible, playing solemn music.*
SEBASTIAN.
We would so, and then go a bat-fowling.
ANTONIO.
Nay, good my lord, be not angry.
GONZALO.
No, I warrant you; I will not adventure my dis-
cretion so weakly. Will you laugh me asleep, for I
am very heavy?
ANTONIO.
Go sleep, and hear us.
    [*All sleep except* ALONSO, SEBASTIAN,
      and ANTONIO.
ALONSO.
What, all so soon asleep! I wish mine eyes
Would, with themselves, shut up my thoughts: I
    find
They are inclined to do so.
SEBASTIAN.
           Please you, sir,
Do not omit the heavy offer of it:
It seldom visits sorrow; when it doth,
It is a comforter.
ANTONIO.
        We two, my lord,
Will guard your person while you take your rest,
And watch your safety.
ALONSO.
       Thank you.—Wondrous heavy.
    [ALONSO *sleeps.*   *Exit* ARIEL.
SEBASTIAN.
What a strange drowsiness possesses them!
ANTONIO.
It is the quality o'the climate.
SEBASTIAN.
           Why
Doth it not, then, our eyelids sink? I find not
Myself disposed to sleep.
ANTONIO.
        Nor I; my spirits are nimble.
They fell together all, as by consent;
They dropt, as by a thunder-stroke. What might,
Worthy Sebastian, O, what might?—No more:—
And yet methinks I see it in thy face,
What thou shouldst be: the occasion speaks thee;
    and
My strong imagination sees a crown
Dropping upon thy head.
SEBASTIAN.
        What, art thou waking?
ANTONIO.
Do you not hear me speak?
SEBASTIAN.
        I do; and surely
It is a sleepy language, and thou speak'st
Out of thy sleep. What is it thou didst say?
This is a strange repose, to be asleep
With eyes wide open; standing, speaking, moving,
And yet so fast asleep.
ANTONIO.
       Noble Sebastian,
Thou lett'st thy fortune sleep,—die, rather; wink'st
Whiles thou art waking.
SEBASTIAN.
        Thou dost snore distinctly;
There's meaning in thy snores.

ANTONIO.
I am more serious than my custom: you
Must be so too, if heed me; which to do
Trebles thee o'er.

SEBASTIAN.
    Well, I am standing water.

ANTONIO.
I'll teach you how to flow.

SEBASTIAN.
    Do so: to ebb
Hereditary sloth instructs me.

ANTONIO.
    O,
If you but knew how you the purpose cherish
Whiles thus you mock it! how, in stripping it,
You more invest it! Ebbing men, indeed,
Most often do so near the bottom run
By their own fear or sloth.

SEBASTIAN.
    Prithee, say on:
The setting of thine eye and cheek proclaim
A matter from thee; and a birth, indeed,
Which throes thee much to yield.

ANTONIO.
    Thus, sir:
Although this lord of weak remembrance, this,
Who shall be of as little memory
When he is earth'd, hath here almost per-
    suaded,—
For he's a spirit of persuasion, only
Professes to persuade,—the king his son's alive,
'Tis as impossible that he's undrown'd
As he that sleeps here swims.

SEBASTIAN.
    I have no hope
That he's undrown'd.

ANTONIO.
O, out of that 'no hope'
What great hope have you! no hope, that way, is
Another way so high a hope that even
Ambition cannot pierce a wink beyond,
But doubts discovery there. Will you grant with
    me
That Ferdinand is drown'd?

SEBASTIAN.
    He's gone.

ANTONIO.
    Then, tell me,
Who's the next heir of Naples?

SEBASTIAN.
    Claribel.

ANTONIO.
She that is queen of Tunis; she that dwells
Ten leagues beyond man's life; she that from
    Naples
Can have no note, unless the sun were post,—
The man-i'the-moon's too slow,—till new-born
    chins
Be rough and razorable; she that—from whom
We all were sea-swallow'd, though some cast again;
And, by that destiny, to perform an act
Whereof what's past is prologue; what to come,
In yours and my discharge.

SEBASTIAN.
    What stuff is this!—How say you?
'Tis true, my brother's daughter's queen of Tunis;

So is she heir of Naples; 'twixt which regions
There is some space.

ANTONIO.
    A space whose every cubit
Seems to cry out, 'How shall that Claribel
Measure us back to Naples? Keep in Tunis,
And let Sebastian wake!'—Say, this were death
That now hath seized them; why, they were no
    worse
Than now they are. There be that can rule Naples
As well as he that sleeps; lords that can prate
As amply and unnecessarily
As this Gonzalo; I myself could make
A chough of as deep chat. O, that you bore
The mind that I do! what a sleep were this
For your advancement! Do you understand me?

SEBASTIAN.
Methinks I do.

ANTONIO.
    And how does your content
Tender your own good fortune?

SEBASTIAN.
    I remember
You did supplant your brother Prospero.

ANTONIO.
    True:
And look how well my garments sit upon me;
Much feater than before: my brother's servants
Were then my fellows; now they are my men.

SEBASTIAN.
But, for your conscience,—

ANTONIO.
Ay, sir; where lies that? if 'twere a kibe,
'Twould put me to my slipper: but I feel not
This deity in my bosom: twenty consciences,
That stand 'twixt me and Milan, candied be they,
And melt, ere they molest! Here lies your brother,
No better than the earth he lies upon,
If he were that which now he's like, that's dead;
Whom I, with this obedient steel, three inches of
    it,
Can lay to bed for ever; whiles you, doing thus,
To the perpetual wink for aye might put
This ancient morsel, this Sir Prudence, who
Should not upbraid our course. For all the rest,
They'll take suggestion as a cat laps milk;
They'll tell the clock to any business that
We say befits the hour.

SEBASTIAN.
    Thy case, dear friend,
Shall be my precedent; as thou gott'st Milan,
I'll come by Naples. Draw thy sword: one stroke
Shall free thee from the tribute which thou pay'st;
And I the king shall love thee.

ANTONIO.
    Draw together;
And when I rear my hand, do you the like,
To fall it on Gonzalo.

SEBASTIAN.
    O, but one word.
Enter ARIEL, *invisible, with music and song.*

ARIEL.
My master through his art foresees the danger
That you, his friend, are in; and sends me forth,—
For else his project dies,—to keep them living.
            [*Sings in* GONZALO'S *ear.*

While you here do snoring lie,
    Open-eyed conspiracy
        His time doth take.
If of life you keep a care,
Shake off slumber, and beware:
        Awake, awake!

ANTONIO.

Then let us both be sudden.

GONZALO [*waking*].

                    Now, good angels
Preserve the king! Why, how now? ho, awake!
Why are you drawn? wherefore this ghastly
    looking?

ALONSO [*waking*].

What's the matter?

SEBASTIAN.

Whiles we stood here securing your repose,
Even now, we heard a hollow burst of bellowing
Like bulls, or rather lions: did't not wake you?
It struck mine ear most terribly.

ALONSO.

                  I heard nothing.

ANTONIO.

O, 'twas a din to fright a monster's ear,
To make an earthquake! sure, it was the roar
Of a whole herd of lions.

ALONSO.

           Heard you this, Gonzalo?

GONZALO.

Upon mine honour, sir, I heard a humming,
And that a strange one too, which did awake me:
I shaked you, sir, and cried: as mine eyes open'd,
I saw their weapons drawn:—there was a noise,
That's verily. 'Tis best we stand upon our guard,
Or that we quit this place: let's draw our weapons.

ALONSO.

Lead off this ground; and let's make further
    search
For my poor son.

GONZALO.

          Heavens keep him from these beasts!
For he is, sure, i'the island.

ALONSO.

              Lead away.

ARIEL.

Prospero my lord shall know what I have done:—
So, king, go safely on to seek thy son.   [*Exeunt.*

SCENE II.

Another part of the island.

Enter CALIBAN *with a burden of wood. A noise of
thunder heard.*

CALIBAN.

ALL the infections that the sun sucks up
From bogs, fens, flats, on Prosper fall, and
    make him
By inch-meal a disease! His spirits hear me,
And yet I needs must curse. But they'll nor pinch,
Fright me with urchin-shows, pitch me i'the mire,
Nor lead me, like a firebrand, in the dark
Out of my way, unless he bid 'em: but
For every trifle are they set upon me;
Sometime like apes, that mow and chatter at me,
And after bite me; then like hedgehogs, which

Lie tumbling in my barefoot way, and mount
Their pricks at my footfall; sometime am I
All wound with adders, who with cloven tongues
Do hiss me into madness. Lo, now, lo!
Here comes a spirit of his; and to torment me
For bringing wood in slowly. I'll fall flat;
Perchance he will not mind me.

Enter TRINCULO.

TRINCULO.

Here's neither bush nor shrub, to bear off any
weather at all, and another storm brewing; I hear
it sing i' the wind: yond same black cloud, yond
huge one, looks like a foul bombard that would
shed his liquor. If it should thunder as it did before, I know not where to hide my head: yond
same cloud cannot choose but fall by pailfuls.—
What have we here? a man or a fish? dead or
alive? A fish: he smells like a fish; a very ancient
and fish-like smell; a kind of, not of the newest,
Poor-John. A strange fish! Were I in England
now, as once I was, and had but this fish painted,
not a holiday fool there but would give a piece of
silver: there would this monster make a man; any
strange beast there makes a man: when they will
not give a doit to relieve a lame beggar, they will
lay out ten to see a dead Indian. Legg'd like a
man! and his fins like arms! Warm, o' my troth!
I do now let loose my opinion, hold it no longer,
—this is no fish, but an islander, that hath lately
suffer'd by a thunderbolt. [*Thunder.*] Alas, the
storm is come again! my best way is to creep
under his gaberdine; there is no other shelter
hereabout: misery acquaints a man with strange
bedfellows. I will here shroud till the dregs of the
storm be past.

[*Creeps under* CALIBAN'S *gaberdine.*
Enter STEPHANO, *singing; a bottle in his hand.*

STEPHANO.

    I shall no more to sea, to sea,
        Here shall I die ashore,—
This is a very scurvy tune to sing at a man's
funeral: well, here's my comfort.   [*Drinks.*
    The master, the swabber, the boatswain, and I,
        The gunner, and his mate,
    Loved Mall, Meg, and Marian, and Margery,
        But none of us cared for Kate;
        For she had a tongue with a tang,
        Would cry to a sailor, Go hang!
    She loved not the savour of tar nor of pitch;
        Yet a tailor might scratch her where'er she did
          itch.
    Then, to sea, boys, and let her go hang!
This is a scurvy tune too: but here's my comfort.
                           [*Drinks.*

CALIBAN.

Do not torment me:—O!

STEPHANO.

What's the matter? Have we devils here? Do you
put tricks upon's with salvages and men of Inde?
ha! I have not scaped drowning, to be afeard now
of your four legs; for it hath been said, As proper
a man as ever went on four legs cannot make him
give ground; and it shall be said so again, while
Stephano breathes at nostrils.

CALIBAN.

The spirit torments me:—O!

STEPHANO.

This is some monster of the isle with four legs, who hath got, as I take it, an ague. Where the devil should he learn our language? I will give him some relief, if it be but for that. If I can recover him, and keep him tame, and get to Naples with him, he's a present for any emperor that ever trod on neat's-leather.

CALIBAN.

Do not torment me, prithee; I'll bring my wood home faster.

STEPHANO.

He's in his fit now, and does not talk after the wisest. He shall taste of my bottle: if he have never drunk wine afore, it will go near to remove his fit. If I can recover him, and keep him tame, I will not take too much for him; he shall pay for him that hath him, and that soundly.

CALIBAN.

Thou dost me yet but little hurt; thou wilt anon, I know it by thy trembling: now Prosper works upon thee.

STEPHANO.

Come on your ways; open your mouth; here is that which will give language to you, cat: open your mouth; this will shake your shaking, I can tell you, and that soundly: you cannot tell who's your friend: open your chaps again.

TRINCULO.

I should know that voice: it should be—but he is drown'd; and these are devils:—O, defend me!

STEPHANO.

Four legs and two voices,—a most delicate monster! His forward voice, now, is to speak well of his friend; his backward voice is to utter foul speeches and to detract. If all the wine in my bottle will recover him, I will help his ague. —Come,—Amen! I will pour some in thy other mouth.

TRINCULO.

Stephano!—

STEPHANO.

Doth thy other mouth call me?—Mercy, mercy! This is a devil, and no monster: I will leave him; I have no long spoon.

TRINCULO.

Stephano!—if thou be'st Stephano, touch me, and speak to me; for I am Trinculo,—be not afeard,—thy good friend, Trinculo.

STEPHANO.

If thou be'st Trinculo, come forth: I'll pull thee by the lesser legs: if any be Trinculo's legs, these are they. [Draws TRINCULO out by the legs.]— Thou art very Trinculo indeed! How camest thou to be the siege of this moon-calf? can he vent Trinculos?

TRINCULO.

I took him to be kill'd with a thunder-stroke.— But art thou not drown'd, Stephano? I hope, now, thou art not drown'd. Is the storm overblown? I hid me under the dead moon-calf's gaberdine for fear of the storm. And art thou living, Stephano? O Stephano, two Neapolitans scaped!

STEPHANO.

Prithee, do not turn me about; my stomach is not constant.

CALIBAN [aside].

These be fine things, an if they be not sprites. That's a brave god, and bears celestial liquor: I will kneel to him.

STEPHANO.

How didst thou scape? How camest thou hither? swear, by this bottle, how thou camest hither. I escaped upon a butt of sack, which the sailors heaved o'erboard, by this bottle! which I made of the bark of a tree with mine own hands, since I was cast ashore.

CALIBAN.

I'll swear, upon that bottle, to be thy true subject; for the liquor is not earthly.

STEPHANO.

Here; swear, then, how thou escapedst.

TRINCULO.

Swum ashore, man, like a duck: I can swim like a duck, I'll be sworn.

STEPHANO.

Here, kiss the book. Though thou canst swim like a duck, thou art made like a goose.

TRINCULO.

O Stephano, hast any more of this?

STEPHANO.

The whole butt, man: my cellar is in a rock by the sea-side, where my wine is hid.—How now, moon-calf! how does thine ague?

CALIBAN.

Hast thou not dropt from heaven?

STEPHANO.

Out o'the moon, I do assure thee: I was the man-i'-the-moon when time was.

CALIBAN.

I have seen thee in her, and I do adore thee: my mistress show'd me thee, and thy dog, and thy bush.

STEPHANO.

Come, swear to that; kiss the book:—I will furnish it anon with new contents:—swear.

TRINCULO.

By this good light, this is a very shallow monster!—I afeard of him!—a very weak monster:— the man-i'the-moon!—a most poor credulous monster!—Well drawn, monster, in good sooth.

CALIBAN.

I'll show thee every fertile inch o'the island; and I will kiss thy foot: I prithee, be my god.

TRINCULO.

By this light, a most perfidious and drunken monster! when's god's asleep, he'll rob his bottle.

CALIBAN.

I'll kiss thy foot; I'll swear myself thy subject.

STEPHANO.

Come on, then; down, and swear.

TRINCULO.

I shall laugh myself to death at this puppyheaded monster: a most scurvy monster! I could find in my heart to beat him,—

STEPHANO.

Come kiss.

TRINCULO.

But that the poor monster's in drink: an abominable monster!

CALIBAN.

I'll show thee the best springs; I'll pluck thee
   berries;
I'll fish for thee, and get thee wood enough.
A plague upon the tyrant that I serve!
I'll bear him no more sticks, but follow thee,
Thou wondrous man.

TRINCULO.

A most ridiculous monster, to make a wonder of
a poor drunkard!

CALIBAN.

I prithee, let me bring thee where crabs grow;
And I with my long nails will dig thee pig-nuts;
Show thee a jay's nest, and instruct thee how
To snare the nimble marmoset; I'll bring thee
To clustering filberts, and sometimes I'll get
   thee
Young scamels from the rock. Wilt thou go with
   me?

STEPHANO.

I prithee now, lead the way, without any more
talking.—Trinculo, the king and all our company
else being drown'd, we will inherit here. Here,
bear my bottle: fellow Trinculo, we'll fill him by
and by again.

CALIBAN [sings drunkenly].

Farewell, master; farewell, farewell!

TRINCULO.

A howling monster; a drunken monster!

CALIBAN.

No more dams I'll make for fish;
   Nor fetch in firing
     At requiring;
Nor scrape trenchering, nor wash dish:
   'Ban, 'Ban, Ca-Caliban
     Has a new master: get a new man.
Freedom, high-day! high-day, freedom! freedom, high-day, freedom!

STEPHANO.

O brave monster! lead the way.   [Exeunt.

ACT III. SCENE I.

Before PROSPERO'S *cell.*

Enter FERDINAND, *bearing a log.*

FERDINAND.

THERE be some sports are painful, and their
   labour
Delight in them sets off: some kinds of baseness
Are nobly undergone; and most poor matters
Point to rich ends. This my mean task
Would be as heavy to me as odious, but
The mistress which I serve quickens what's
   dead,
And makes my labours pleasures: O, she is
Ten times more gentle than her father's crabb'd;
And he's composed of harshness. I must remove
Some thousands of these logs, and pile them up,
Upon a sore injunction: my sweet mistress
Weeps when she sees me work; and says such
   baseness
Had never like executor. I forget:

But these sweet thoughts do even refresh my
   labour;
Most busiless when I do it.

Enter MIRANDA; *and* PROSPERO *behind.*

MIRANDA.

               Alas, now, pray you,
Work not so hard: I would the lightning had
Burnt up those logs that you are enjoin'd to pile!
Pray, set it down, and rest you: when this burns,
'Twill weep for having wearied you. My father
Is hard at study; pray, now, rest yourself:
He's safe for these three hours.

FERDINAND.

             O most dear mistress,
The sun will set before I shall discharge
What I must strive to do.

MIRANDA.

            If you'll sit down,
I'll bear your logs the while: pray, give me that;
I'll carry it to the pile.

FERDINAND.

           No, precious creature;
I had rather crack my sinews, break my back,
Than you should such dishonour undergo,
While I sit lazy by.

MIRANDA.

          It would become me
As well as it does you: and I should do it
With much more ease; for my good will is to it,
And yours it is against.

PROSPERO [aside].

         Poor worm, thou art infected!
This visitation shows it.

MIRANDA.

         You look wearily.

FERDINAND.

No, noble mistress; 'tis fresh morning with me
When you are by at night. I do beseech you,—
Chiefly that I might set it in my prayers,—
What is your name?

MIRANDA.

        Miranda:—O my father,
I've broke your hest to say so!

FERDINAND.

          Admired Miranda!
Indeed the top of admiration; worth
What's dearest to the world! Full many a lady
I have eyed with best regard; and many a time
The harmony of their tongues hath into bondage
Brought my too diligent ear: for several virtues
Have I liked several women; never any
With so full soul, but some defect in her
Did quarrel with the noblest grace she owed,
And put it to the foil: but you, O you,
So perfect and so peerless, are created
Of every creature's best!

MIRANDA.

        I do not know
One of my sex; no woman's face remember,
Save, from my glass, mine own; nor have I seen
More that I may call men, than you, good
   friend,
And my dear father: how features are abroad,
I'm skilless of; but, by my modesty,—
The jewel in my dower,—I would not wish
Any companion in the world but you;

Nor can imagination form a shape,
Besides yourself, to like of. But I prattle
Something too wildly, and my father's precepts
I therein do forget.

FERDINAND.
                I am, in my condition,
A prince, Miranda; I do think, a king,—
I would not so!—and would no more endure
This wooden slavery than to suffer
The flesh-fly blow my mouth. Hear my soul
    speak:
The very instant that I saw you, did
My heart fly to your service; there resides
To make me slave to it; and for your sake
Am I this patient log-man.

MIRANDA.
                Do you love me?

FERDINAND.
O heaven, O earth, bear witness to this sound,
And crown what I profess with kind event,
If I speak true! if hollowly, invert
What best is boded me to mischief! I,
Beyond all limit of what else i' the world,
Do love, prize, honour you.

MIRANDA.
                I am a fool
To weep at what I am glad of.

PROSPERO [aside].
                Fair encounter
Of two most rare affections! Heavens rain grace
On that which breeds between 'em!

FERDINAND.
                Wherefore weep you?

MIRANDA.
At mine unworthiness, that dare not offer
What I desire to give; and much less take
What I shall die to want. But this is trifling;
And all the more it seeks to hide itself,
The bigger bulk it shows. Hence, bashful cun-
    ning!
And prompt me, plain and holy innocence!
I am your wife, if you will marry me;
If not, I'll die your maid: to be your fellow
You may deny me; but I'll be your servant,
Whether you will or no.

FERDINAND.
                My mistress, dearest;
And I thus humble ever.

MIRANDA.
                My husband, then?

FERDINAND.
Ay, with a heart as willing
As bondage e'er of freedom: here's my hand.

MIRANDA.
And mine, with my heart in't: and now farewell
Till half an hour hence.

FERDINAND.
                A thousand thousand!
[Exeunt FERDINAND and MIRANDA severally.

PROSPERO.
So glad of this as they I cannot be,
Who are surprised withal; but my rejoicing
At nothing can be more. I'll to my book;
For yet, ere supper-time, must I perform
Much business appertaining.   [Exit.

SCENE II.

Another part of the island.

Enter CALIBAN, STEPHANO, and TRINCULO.

STEPHANO.
TELL not me; when the butt is out, we will
drink water; not a drop before: therefore bear
up, and board 'em. Servant-monster, drink to
me.

TRINCULO.
Servant-monster! the folly of this island! They
say there's but five upon this isle: we are three of
them; if the other two be brain'd like us, the
state totters.

STEPHANO.
Drink, servant-monster, when I bid thee: thy
eyes are almost set in thy head.

TRINCULO.
Where should they be set else? he were a brave
monster indeed, if they were set in his tail.

STEPHANO.
My man-monster hath drown'd his tongue in
sack: for my part, the sea cannot drown me; I
swam, ere I could recover the shore, five-and-
thirty leagues off and on, by this light.—Thou
shalt be my lieutenant, monster, or my standard.

TRINCULO.
Your lieutenant, if you list; he's no standard.

STEPHANO.
We'll not run, Monsieur Monster.

TRINCULO.
Nor go neither: but you'll lie, like dogs; and yet
say nothing neither.

STEPHANO.
Moon-calf, speak once in thy life, if thou be'st a
good moon-calf.

CALIBAN.
How does thy honour? Let me lick thy shoe. I'll
not serve him, he is not valiant.

TRINCULO.
Thou liest, most ignorant monster: I am in case
to justle a constable. Why, thou debosh'd fish,
thou, was there ever man a coward that hath
drunk so much sack as I to-day? Wilt thou tell a
monstrous lie, being but half a fish and half a
monster?

CALIBAN.
Lo, how he mocks me! wilt thou let him, my
lord?

TRINCULO.
'Lord,' quoth he!—that a monster should be such
a natural!

CALIBAN.
Lo, lo, again! bite him to death, I prithee.

STEPHANO.
Trinculo, keep a good tongue in your head: if you
prove a mutineer, the next tree! The poor monster's my subject, and he shall not suffer indignity.

CALIBAN.
I thank my noble lord. Wilt thou be pleased to
hearken once again to the suit I made to thee?

STEPHANO.
Marry, will I: kneel and repeat it; I will stand,
and so shall Trinculo.

Enter ARIEL [*invisible*].

CALIBAN.

As I told thee before, I am subject to a tyrant,—a sorcerer, that by his cunning hath cheated me of the island.

ARIEL.

Thou liest.

CALIBAN.

Thou liest, thou jesting monkey, thou: I would my valiant master would destroy thee! I do not lie.

STEPHANO.

Trinculo, if you trouble him any more in's tale, by this hand, I will supplant some of your teeth.

TRINCULO.

Why, I said nothing.

STEPHANO.

Mum, then, and no more.—Proceed.

CALIBAN.

I say, by sorcery, he got this isle; From me he got it. If thy greatness will, Revenge it on him, for I know thou darest, But this thing dare not,—

STEPHANO.

That's most certain.

CALIBAN.

Thou shalt be lord of it, and I'll serve thee.

STEPHANO.

How now shall this be compast? Canst thou bring me to the party?

CALIBAN.

Yea, yea, my lord: I'll yield him thee asleep, Where thou mayst knock a nail into his head.

ARIEL.

Thou liest; thou canst not.

CALIBAN.

What a pied ninny's this! Thou scurvy patch! I do beseech thy greatness, give him blows, And take his bottle from him: when that's gone, He shall drink naught but brine; for I'll not show him Where the quick freshes are.

STEPHANO.

Trinculo, run into no further danger: interrupt the monster one word further, and, by this hand I'll turn my mercy out o'doors, and make a stockfish of thee.

TRINCULO.

Why, what did I? I did nothing. I'll go further off.

STEPHANO.

Didst thou not say he lied?

ARIEL.

Thou liest.

STEPHANO.

Do I so? take thou that [*Strikes* TRINCULO]. As you like this, give me the lie another time.

TRINCULO.

I did not give the lie.—Out o'your wits, and hearing too?—A pox o' your bottle! this can sack and drinking do—A murrain on your monster, and the devil take your fingers!

CALIBAN.

Ha, ha, ha!

STEPHANO.

Now, forward with your tale.—Prithee, stand further off.

CALIBAN.

Beat him enough: after a little time, I'll beat him too.

STEPHANO.

Stand further.—Come, proceed.

CALIBAN.

Why, as I told thee, 'tis a custom with him I'the afternoon to sleep: then thou mayst brain him, Having first seized his books; or with a log Batter his skull, or paunch him with a stake, Or cut his wesand with thy knife: remember, First to possess his books; for without them He's but a sot, as I am, nor hath not One spirit to command: they all do hate him As rootedly as I:—burn but his books. He has brave utensils,—for so he calls them,— Which, when he has a house, he'll deck withal: And that most deeply to consider is The beauty of his daughter; he himself Calls her a nonpareil: I never saw a woman, But only Sycorax my dam and she; But she as far surpasseth Sycorax As great'st does least.

STEPHANO.

Is it so brave a lass?

CALIBAN.

Ay, lord; she will become thy bed, I warrant, And bring thee forth brave brood.

STEPHANO.

Monster, I will kill this man: his daughter and I will be king and queen,—save our graces!—and Trinculo and thyself shall be viceroys.—Dost thou like the plot, Trinculo?

TRINCULO.

Excellent.

STEPHANO.

Give me thy hand: I am sorry I beat thee, but, while thou livest, keep a good tongue in thy head.

CALIBAN.

Within this half hour will he be asleep: Wilt thou destroy him then?

STEPHANO.

Ay, on mine honour.

ARIEL.

This will I tell my master.

CALIBAN.

Thou makest me merry; I am full of pleasure: Let us be jocund: will you troll the catch You taught me but while-ere?

STEPHANO.

At thy request, monster, I will do reason, any reason.—Come on, Trinculo, let us sing.   [*Sings*.

'Flout 'em and scout 'em, and scout 'em and flout 'em; Thought is free.'

CALIBAN.

That's not the tune.

[ARIEL *plays a tune on a tabor and pipe.*

STEPHANO.

What is this same?

TRINCULO.

This is the tune of our catch, played by the picture of Nobody.

STEPHANO.

If thou be'st a man, show thyself in thy likeness: if thou be'st a devil, take't as thou list.

TRINCULO.
O, forgive me my sins!
STEPHANO.
He that dies pays all debts: I defy thee.—Mercy
upon us!
CALIBAN.
Art thou afeard?
STEPHANO.
No, monster, not I.
CALIBAN.
Be not afeard; the isle is full of noises,
Sounds, and sweet airs, that give delight, and hurt
not.
Sometimes a thousand twangling instruments
Will hum about mine ears; and sometime voices,
That, if I then had waked after long sleep,
Will make me sleep again: and then, in dreaming,
The clouds methought would open, and show
riches
Ready to drop upon me; that, when I waked,
I cried to dream again.
STEPHANO.
This will prove a brave kingdom to me, where I
shall have my music for nothing.
CALIBAN.
When Prospero is destroy'd.
STEPHANO.
That shall be by and by: I remember the story.
TRINCULO.
The sound is going away; let's follow it, and after
do our work.
STEPHANO.
Lead, monster; we'll follow.—I would I could
see this taborer! he lays it on.
TRINCULO.
Wilt come? I'll follow, Stephano.　　[Exeunt.

SCENE III.

Another part of the island.

Enter ALONSO, SEBASTIAN, ANTONIO, GON-
ZALO, ADRIAN, FRANCISCO, *and others.*

GONZALO.
BY'R lakin, I can go no further, sir;
My old bones ache! here's a maze trod, in-
deed,
Through forth-rights and meanders! by your
patience,
I needs must rest me.
ALONSO.
Old lord, I cannot blame thee,
Who am myself attach'd with weariness,
To the dulling of my spirits: sit down, and
rest.
Even here I will put off my hope, and keep it
No longer for my flatterer: he is drown'd
Whom thus we stray to find; and the sea mocks
Our frustrate search on land. Well, let him go.
ANTONIO [*aside to* SEBASTIAN].
I am right glad that he's so out of hope.
Do not, for one repulse, forgo the purpose
That you resolved t'effect.
SEBASTIAN [*aside to* ANTONIO].
The next advantage
Will we take throughly.

ANTONIO [*aside to* SEBASTIAN].
Let it be to-night;
For, now they are oppress'd with travel, they
Will not, nor cannot, use such vigilance
As when they are fresh.
SEBASTIAN [*aside to* ANTONIO].
I say, to-night: no more.
[*Solemn and strange music.*
ALONSO.
What harmony is this?—My good friends, hark!
GONZALO.
Marvellous sweet music!
Enter PROSPERO, *above, invisible. Enter, below,
several strange Shapes, bringing in a banquet:
they dance about it with gentle actions of saluta-
tion; and, inviting the King, &c., to eat, they de-
part.*
ALONSO.
Give us kind keepers, heavens!—What were these?
SEBASTIAN.
A living drollery. Now I will believe
That there are unicorns; that in Arabia
There is one tree, the phœnix' throne; one phœnix
At this hour reigning there.
ANTONIO.
I'll believe both;
And what does else want credit, come to me,
And I'll be sworn 'tis true: travellers ne'er did lie,
Though fools at home condemn 'em.
GONZALO.
If in Naples
I should report this now, would they believe me?
If I should say, I saw such islanders,—
For, certes, these are people of the island,—
Who, though they are of monstrous shape, yet,
note,
Their manners are more gentle-kind than of
Our human generation you shall find
Many, nay, almost any.
PROSPERO [*aside*].
Honest lord,
Thou hast said well; for some of you there present
Are worse than devils.
ALONSO.
I cannot too much muse
Such shapes, such gesture, and such sound, ex-
pressing—
Although they want the use of tongue—a kind
Of excellent dumb discourse.
PROSPERO [*aside*].
Praise in departing.
FRANCISCO.
They vanish'd strangely.
SEBASTIAN.
No matter, since
They have left their viands behind; for we have
stomachs.—
Will't please you taste of what is here?
ALONSO.
Not I.
GONZALO.
Faith, sir, you need not fear. When we were boys,
Who would believe that there were mountaineers
Dew-lapp'd like bulls, whose throats had hanging
at 'em
Wallets of flesh? or that there were such men

Whose heads stood in their breasts? which now
  we find
Each putter-out of five for one will bring us
Good warrant of.

ALONSO.

          I will stand to, and feed,
Although my last: no matter, since I feel
The best is past.—Brother, my lord the duke,
Stand to, and do as we.

Thunder and lightning. Enter ARIEL, *like a
  harpy; claps his wings upon the table; and, with a
  quaint device, the banquet vanishes.*

ARIEL.

You are three men of sin, whom Destiny,—
That hath to instrument this lower world
And what is in't,—the never-surfeited sea
Hath caused to belch up you; and on this island,
Where man doth not inhabit,—you 'mongst men
Being most unfit to live. I have made you mad;
And even with such-like valour men hang and
  drown
Their proper selves.   [*They draw their swords.*
          You fools! I and my fellows
Are ministers of Fate: the elements,
Of whom your swords are temper'd, may as well
Wound the loud winds, or with bemock'd-at stabs
Kill the still-closing waters, as diminish
One dowle that's in my plume: my fellow-ministers
Are like invulnerable. If you could hurt,
Your swords are now too massy for your strengths,
And will not be uplifted. But remember,—
For that's my business to you,—that you three
From Milan did supplant good Prospero;
Exposed unto the sea, which hath requit it,
Him and his innocent child: for which foul deed
The powers, delaying, not forgetting, have
Incensed the seas and shores, yea, all the creatures,
Against your peace. Thee of thy son, Alonso,
They have bereft; and do pronounce, by me,
Lingering perdition—worse than any death
Can be at once—shall step by step attend
You and your ways; whose wraths to guard you
  from,—
Which here, in this most desolate isle, else falls
Upon your heads,—is nothing but heart's sorrow
And a clear life ensuing.

*He vanishes in thunder; then, to soft music, enter the
  Shapes again, and dance, with mocks and mows,
  and carrying out the table.*

PROSPERO [*aside*].

Bravely the figure of this harpy hast thou
Perform'd, my Ariel; a grace it had, devouring:
Of my instruction hast thou nothing bated
In what thou hadst to say: so, with good life
And observation strange, my meaner ministers
Their several kinds have done. My high charms
  work,
And these, mine enemies, are all knit up
In their distractions: they now are in my power;
And in these fits I leave them, while I visit
Young Ferdinand,—whom they suppose is
  drown'd,—
And his and mine loved darling.   [*Exit above.*

GONZALO.

I'the name of something holy, sir, why stand you
In this strange stare?

ALONSO.

        O, it is monstrous, monstrous!
Methought the billows spoke, and told me of it;
The winds did sing it to me; and the thunder,
That deep and dreadful organ-pipe, pronounced
The name of Prosper: it did bass my trespass.
Therefore my son i'the ooze is bedded; and
I'll seek him deeper than e'er plummet sounded,
And with him there lie mudded.   [*Exit.*

SEBASTIAN.

          But one fiend at a time,
I'll fight their legions o'er.

ANTONIO.

          I'll be thy second.
[*Exeunt* SEBASTIAN *and* ANTONIO.

GONZALO.

All three of them are desperate: their great guilt,
Like poison given to work a great time after,
Now 'gins to bite the spirits.—I do beseech you,
That are of suppler joints, follow them swiftly,
And hinder them from what this ecstasy
May now provoke them to.

ADRIAN.

      Follow, I pray you. [*Exeunt.*

ACT IV. SCENE I.

Before PROSPERO'S *cell.*

Enter PROSPERO, FERDINAND, *and* MIRANDA.

PROSPERO.

IF I have too austerely punish'd you,
  Your compensation makes amends; for I
Have given you here a thread of mine own life,
Or that for which I live: who once again
I tender to thy hand: all thy vexations
Were but my trials of thy love, and thou
Hast strangely stood the test: here, afore Heaven,
I ratify this my rich gift. O Ferdinand,
Do not smile at me that I boast her off,
For thou shalt find she will outstrip all praise,
And make it halt behind her.

FERDINAND.

          I do believe it
Against an oracle.

PROSPERO.

Then, as my gift, and thine own acquisition
Worthily purchased, take my daughter: but
If thou dost break her virgin-knot before
All sanctimonious ceremonies may
With full and holy rite be minister'd,
No sweet aspersion shall the heavens let fall
To make this contract grow; but barren hate,
Sour-eyed disdain, and discord, shall bestrew
The union of your bed with weeds so loathly
That you shall hate it both: therefore take heed,
As Hymen's lamps shall light you.

FERDINAND.

            As I hope
For quiet days, fair issue, and long life,
With such love as 'tis now,—the murkiest den,
The most opportune place, the strong'st sugges-
  tion
Our worser Genius can, shall never melt
Mine honour into lust; to take away
The edge of that day's celebration,

When I shall think, or Phœbus' steeds are foun-
   der'd,
Or Night kept chain'd below.
            PROSPERO.
                   Fairly spoke.
Sit, then, and talk with her; she is thine own.—
What, Ariel! my industrious servant, Ariel!
         Enter ARIEL.
            ARIEL.
What would my potent master? here I am.
            PROSPERO.
Thou and thy meaner fellows your last service
Did worthily perform; and I must use you
In such another trick. Go bring the rabble,
O'er whom I give thee power, here, to this place:
Incite them to quick motion; for I must
Bestow upon the eyes of this young couple
Some vanity of mine art: it is my promise,
And they expect it from me.
            ARIEL.
                 Presently?
           PROSPERO.
Ay, with a twink.
            ARIEL.
Before you can say, 'Come,' and 'Go,'
And breathe twice, and cry, 'So, so,'
Each one, tripping on his toe,
Will be here with mop and mow.
Do you love me, master? no?
           PROSPERO.
Dearly, my delicate Ariel. Do not approach
Till thou dost hear me call
           ARIEL.
             Well, I conceive. [*Exit.*
          PROSPERO.
Look thou be true; do not give dalliance
Too much the rein; the strongest oaths are straw
To the fire i'the blood: be more abstemious,
Or else good night your vow!
          FERDINAND.
               I warrant you, sir;
The white-cold virgin snow upon my heart
Abates the ardour of my liver.
          PROSPERO.
                Well.—
Now come, my Ariel! bring a corollary,
Rather than want a spirit: appear, and pertly!
No tongue; all eyes; be silent.   [*Soft music.*
         Enter IRIS.
           IRIS.
Ceres, most bounteous lady, thy rich leas
Of wheat, rye, barley, vetches, oats, and pease;
Thy turfy mountains, where live nibbling sheep,
And flat meads thatch'd with stover, them to keep;
Thy banks with pioned and twilled brims,
Which spongy April at thy hest betrims,
To make cold nymphs chaste crowns; and thy
   broom-groves,
Whose shadow the dismissed bachelor loves,
Being lass-lorn; thy pole-clipt vineyard;
And thy sea-marge, sterile and rocky-hard,
Where thou thyself dost air;—the queen o' the
   sky,
Whose watery arch and messenger am I,
Bids thee leave these; and with her sovereign
   grace,

Here on this grass-plot, in this very place,
To come and sport:—her peacocks fly amain:
Approach, rich Ceres, her to entertain.
         Enter CERES.
          CERES.
Hail, many-colour'd messenger, that ne'er
Dost disobey the wife of Jupiter;
Who, with thy saffron wings, upon my flowers
Diffusest honey-drops, refreshing showers;
And with each end of thy blue bow dost crown
My bosky acres and my unshrubb'd down,
Rich scarf to my proud earth;—why hath thy
   queen
Summon'd me hither, to this short-grass'd green?
           IRIS.
A contract of true love to celebrate;
And some donation freely to estate
On the bless'd lovers.
          CERES.
            Tell me, heavenly bow,
If Venus or her son, as thou dost know,
Do now attend the queen? Since they did plot
The means that dusky Dis my daughter got,
Her and her blind boy's scandall'd company
I have forsworn.
           IRIS.
            Of her society
Be not afraid: I met her deity
Cutting the clouds towards Paphos, and her son
Dove-drawn with her. Here thought they to have
   done
Some wanton charm upon this man and maid,
Whose vows are, that no bed-rite shall be paid
Till Hymen's torch be lighted: but in vain;
Mars's hot minion is return'd again;
Her waspish-headed son has broke his arrows,
Swears he will shoot no more, but play with spar-
   rows,
And be a boy right out.
          CERES.
            Highest queen of state,
Great Juno, comes; I know her by her gait.
         Enter JUNO.
          JUNO.
How does my bounteous sister? Go with me
To bless this twain, that they may prosperous be,
And honour'd in their issue.
          Song.
          JUNO.
Honour, riches, marriage-blessing,
Long continuance, and increasing,
Hourly joys be still upon you!
Juno sings her blessings on you.
          CERES.
Earth's increase, foison plenty,
Barns and garners never empty;
Vines with clustering bunches growing;
Plants with goodly burden bowing;
Spring come to you at the farthest
In the very end of harvest!
Scarcity and want shall shun you;
Ceres' blessing so is on you.
         FERDINAND.
This is a most majestic vision, and
Harmonious charmingly. May I be bold
To think these spirits?

PROSPERO.

Spirits, which by mine art
I have from their confines call'd to enact
My present fancies.

FERDINAND.

Let me live here ever;
So rare a wonder'd father, and a wife,
Makes this place Paradise.

[JUNO and CERES whisper, and send IRIS
on employment.

PROSPERO.

Sweet, now, silence!
Juno and Ceres whisper seriously;
There's something else to do; hush, and be mute,
Or else our spell is marr'd.

IRIS.

You nymphs, call'd Naiades, of the windring
   brooks,
With your sedged crowns and ever-harmless
   looks,
Leave your crisp channels, and on this green land
Answer your summons; Juno does command:
Come, temperate nymphs, and help to celebrate
A contract of true love; be not too late.

Enter certain NYMPHS.

You sunburn'd sicklemen, of August weary,
Come hither from the furrow, and be merry:
Make holiday; your rye-straw hats put on,
And these fresh nymphs encounter every one
In country footing.

Enter certain REAPERS, properly habited: they join
with the NYMPHS in a graceful dance; towards
the end whereof PROSPERO starts suddenly, and
speaks; after which, to a strange, hollow, and
confused noise, they heavily vanish.

PROSPERO [aside].

I had forgot that foul conspiracy
Of the beast Caliban and his confederates
Against my life: the minute of their plot
Is almost come.—[to the SPIRITS] Well done;—
avoid,—no more.

FERDINAND.

This is strange: your father's in some passion
That works him strongly.

MIRANDA.

Never till this day
Saw I him touch'd with anger so distemper'd.

PROSPERO.

You do look, my son, in a moved sort,
As if you were dismay'd: be cheerful, sir.
Our revels now are ended. These our actors,
As I foretold you, were all spirits, and
Are melted into air, into thin air:
And, like the baseless fabric of this vision,
The cloud-capp'd towers, the gorgeous palaces,
The solemn temples, the great globe itself,
Yea, all which it inherit, shall dissolve,
And, like this insubstantial pageant faded,
Leave not a rack behind. We are such stuff
As dreams are made on; and our little life
Is rounded with a sleep.—Sir, I am vext;
Bear with my weakness; my old brain is troubled:
Be not disturb'd with my infirmity:
If you be pleased, retire into my cell,
And there repose: a turn or two I'll walk,
To still my beating mind.

FERDINAND and MIRANDA.

We wish your peace. [Exeunt.

PROSPERO [to ARIEL].

Come with a thought!—I thank thee, Ariel, come!

Enter ARIEL.

ARIEL.

Thy thoughts I cleave to. What's thy pleasure?

PROSPERO.

Spirit,
We must prepare to meet with Caliban.

ARIEL.

Ay, my commander: when I presented Ceres,
I thought to have told thee of it; but I fear'd
Lest I might anger thee.

PROSPERO.

Say again, where didst thou leave these varlets?

ARIEL.

I told you, sir, they were red-hot with drinking;
So full of valour that they smote the air
For breathing in their faces; beat the ground
For kissing of their feet; yet always bending
Towards their project. Then I beat my tabor;
At which, like unback'd colts, they prick'd their
   ears,
Advanced their eyelids, lifted up their noses
As they smelt music: so I charm'd their ears,
That, calf-like, they my lowing follow'd through
Tooth'd briers, sharp furzes, pricking goss, and
   thorns,
Which enter'd their frail shins: at last I left them
I'the filthy-mantled pool beyond your cell,
There dancing up to the chins, that the foul lake
O'erstunk their feet.

PROSPERO.

This was well done, my bird.
Thy shape invisible retain thou still:
The trumpery in my house, go bring it hither,
For stale to catch these thieves.

ARIEL.

I go, I go. [Exit.

PROSPERO.

A devil, a born devil, on whose nature
Nurture can never stick; on whom my pains,
Humanely taken, all, all lost, quite lost;
And as with age his body uglier grows,
So his mind cankers. I will plague them all,
Even to roaring.

Enter ARIEL, loaden with glistering apparel, &c.

Come, hang them on this line.

PROSPERO and ARIEL remain, invisible. Enter
CALIBAN, STEPHANO, and TRINCULO, all wet.

CALIBAN.

Pray you, tread softly, that the blind mole may not
Hear a foot fall: we now are near his cell.

STEPHANO.

Monster, your fairy, which you say is a harmless
fairy, has done little better than play'd the Jack
with us.

TRINCULO.

Monster, I do smell all horse-piss; at which my
nose is in great indignation.

STEPHANO.

So is mine.—Do you hear, monster? If I should
take a displeasure against you, look you,—

TRINCULO.

Thou wert but a lost monster.

CALIBAN.

Good my lord, give me thy favour still.
Be patient, for the prize I'll bring thee to
Shall hoodwink this mischance: therefore speak
　　softly;—
All's hush'd as midnight yet.

TRINCULO.

Ay, but to lose our bottles in the pool,—

STEPHANO.

There is not only disgrace and dishonour in that,
monster, but an infinite loss.

TRINCULO.

That's more to me than my wetting: yet this is
your harmless fairy, monster.

STEPHANO.

I will fetch off my bottle, though I be o'er ears
for my labour.

CALIBAN.

Prithee, my king, be quiet. See'st thou here,
This is the mouth o'the cell: no noise, and enter.
Do that good mischief which may make this
　　island
Thine own for ever, and I, thy Caliban,
For aye thy foot-licker.

STEPHANO.

Give me thy hand. I do begin to have bloody
thoughts.

TRINCULO.

O King Stephano! O peer! O worthy Stephano!
look what a wardrobe here is for thee!

CALIBAN.

Let it alone, thou fool; it is but trash.

TRINCULO.

O, ho, monster! we know what belongs to a frip-
pery.—O King Stephano!

STEPHANO.

Put off that gown, Trinculo: by this hand, I'll
have that gown.

TRINCULO.

Thy grace shall have it.

CALIBAN.

The dropsy drown this fool! what do you mean
To dote thus on such luggage? Let's along,
And do the murder first: if he awake,
From toe to crown he'll fill our skins with pinches,
Make us strange stuff.

STEPHANO.

Be you quiet, monster.—Mistress line, is not this
my jerkin? Now is the jerkin under the line: now,
jerkin, you are like to lose your hair, and prove a
bald jerkin.

TRINCULO.

Do, do: we steal by line and level, an't like your
grace.

STEPHANO.

I thank thee for that jest; here's a garment for't:
wit shall not go unrewarded while I am king of
this country. 'Steal by line and level' is an excellent pass of pate; there's another garment for't.

TRINCULO.

Monster, come, put some lime upon your fingers,
and away with the rest.

CALIBAN.

I will have none on't: we shall lose our time,
And all be turn'd to barnacles, or to apes
With foreheads villainous low.

STEPHANO.

Monster, lay-to your fingers: help to bear this
away where my hogshead of wine is, or I'll turn
you out of my kingdom: go to, carry this.

TRINCULO.

And this.

STEPHANO.

Ay, and this.

A noise of hunters heard.　Enter divers SPIRITS,
　in shape of dogs and hounds, hunting them about;
　PROSPERO *and* ARIEL *setting them on.*

PROSPERO.

Hey, Mountain, hey!

ARIEL.

Silver! there it goes, Silver!

PROSPERO.

Fury, Fury! there, Tyrant, there! hark, hark!

[CALIBAN, STEPHANO, *and* TRINCULO
　are driven out.

Go charge my goblins that they grind their joints
With dry convulsions; shorten up their sinews
With aged cramps; and more pinch-spotted make
　them
Than pard or cat-o'-mountain.

ARIEL.

　　　　　　　　　　　　Hark, they roar!

PROSPERO.

Let them be hunted soundly. At this hour
Lie at my mercy all mine enemies:
Shortly shall all my labours end, and thou
Shalt have the air at freedom: for a little
Follow, and do me service.　　　　　　[*Exeunt.*

ACT V.　SCENE I.

Before the cell of PROSPERO.

Enter PROSPERO *in his magic robes, and* ARIEL.

PROSPERO.

NOW does my project gather to a head:
My charms crack not; my spirits obey; and
　　Time
Goes upright with his carriage. How's the day?

ARIEL.

On the sixth hour; at which time, my lord,
You said our work should cease.

PROSPERO.

　　　　　　　　　　　　　I did say so,
When first I raised the tempest. Say, my spirit,
How fares the king and's followers?

ARIEL.

　　　　　　　　　　　　Confined together
In the same fashion as you gave in charge.
Just as you left them; all prisoners, sir,
In the line-grove which weather-fends your cell;
They cannot budge till your release. The king,
His brother, and yours, abide all three distracted;
And the remainder mourning over them,
Brimful of sorrow and dismay; but chiefly
Him that you term'd, sir, 'The good old lord,
　　Gonzalo';
His tears run down his beard, like winter's drops
From eaves of reeds. Your charm so strongly
　　works 'em,
That if you now beheld them, your affections
Would become tender.

PROSPERO.
Dost thou think so, spirit?
ARIEL.
Mine would, sir, were I human.
PROSPERO.
And mine shall.
Hast thou, which art but air, a touch, a feeling
Of their afflictions, and shall not myself,
One of their kind, that relish all as sharply,
Passion as they, be kindlier moved than thou art?
Though with their high wrongs I am struck to the
quick,
Yet, with my nobler reason, 'gainst my fury
Do I take part: the rarer action is
In virtue than in vengeance: they being penitent,
The sole drift of my purpose doth extend
Not a frown further. Go release them, Ariel:
My charms I'll break, their senses I'll restore,
And they shall be themselves.
ARIEL.
I'll fetch them, sir. [*Exit.*
PROSPERO.
Ye elves of hills, brooks, standing lakes, and
groves;
And ye that on the sands with printless foot
Do chase the ebbing Neptune, and do fly him
When he comes back; you demi-puppets that
By moonshine do the green sour ringlets make,
Whereof the ewe not bites; and you whose pastime
Is to make midnight mushrumps, that rejoice
To hear the solemn curfew; by whose aid—
Weak masters though ye be—I have bedimm'd
The noontide sun, call'd forth the mutinous
winds,
And 'twixt the green sea and the azured vault
Set roaring war: to the dread-rattling thunder
Have I given fire, and rifted Jove's stout oak
With his own bolt: the strong-based promontory
Have I made shake; and by the spurs pluck'd up
The pine and cedar: graves at my command
Have waked their sleepers, oped, and let 'em forth
By my so potent art. But this rough magic
I here abjure; and, when I have required
Some heavenly music,—which even now I do,—
To work mine end upon their senses that
This airy charm is for, I'll break my staff,
Bury it certain fadoms in the earth,
And deeper than did ever plummet sound
I'll drown my book.   [*Solemn music.*
Here enters ARIEL *before: then* ALONSO, *with a
frantic gesture, attended by* GONZALO; SEBAS-
TIAN *and* ANTONIO *in like manner, attended by*
ADRIAN *and* FRANCISCO: *they all enter the
circle which* PROSPERO *had made, and there
stand charm'd; which* PROSPERO *observing,
speaks.*
A solemn air, and the best comforter
To an unsettled fancy, cure thy brains,
Now useless, boil'd within thy skull! There stand,
For you are spell-stopt.
Holy Gonzalo, honourable man,
Mine eyes, even sociable to the show of thine,
Fall fellowly drops. The charm dissolves apace;
And as the morning steals upon the night,
Melting the darkness, so their rising senses
Begin to chase the ignorant fumes that mantle

Their clearer reason. O good Gonzalo,
My true preserver, and a loyal sir
To him thou follow'st! I will pay thy graces
Home both in word and deed. Most cruelly
Didst thou, Alonso, use me and my daughter:
Thy brother was a furtherer in the act;
Thou art pinch'd for't now, Sebastian. Flesh and
blood,
You, brother mine, that entertain'd ambition,
Expell'd remorse and nature; who, with Sebas-
tian,—
Whose inward pinches therefore are most
strong,—
Would here have kill'd your king; I do forgive
thee,
Unnatural though thou art.—Their understanding
Begins to swell; and the approaching tide
Will shortly fill the reasonable shore,
That now lies foul and muddy. Not one of them
That yet looks on me, or would know me:—Ariel,
Fetch me the hat and rapier in my cell:—
I will discase me, and myself present
As I was sometime Milan:—quickly, spirit;
Thou shalt ere long be free.
ARIEL *sings and helps to attire him.*
Where the bee sucks, there suck I:
In a cowslip's bell I lie;
There I couch when owls do cry.
On the bat's back I do fly
After summer merrily.
Merrily, merrily shall I live now
Under the blossom that hangs on the bough.
PROSPERO.
Why, that's my dainty Ariel! I shall miss thee;
But yet thou shalt have freedom:—so, so, so.—
To the king's ship, invisible as thou art:
There shalt thou find the mariners asleep
Under the hatches; the master and the boatswain
Being awake, enforce them to this place,
And presently, I prithee.
ARIEL.
I drink the air before me, and return
Or e'er your pulse twice beat.   [*Exit.*
GONZALO.
All torment, trouble, wonder, and amazement,
Inhabit here: some heavenly power guide us
Out of this fearful country!
PROSPERO.
Behold, sir king,
The wronged Duke of Milan, Prospero:
For more assurance that a living prince
Does now speak to thee, I embrace thy body;
And to thee and thy company I bid
A hearty welcome.
ALONSO.
Whe'r thou be'st he or no,
Or some enchanted trifle to abuse me,
As late I have been, I not know: thy pulse
Beats, as of flesh and blood; and, since I saw thee,
The affliction of my mind amends, with which,
I fear, a madness held me: this must crave
(An if this be at all) a most strange story.
Thy dukedom I resign, and do entreat
Thou pardon me my wrongs.—But how should
Prospero
Be living and be here?

PROSPERO.
First, noble friend,
Let me embrace thine age, whose honour cannot
Be measured or confined.
GONZALO.
Whether this be
Or be not, I'll not swear.
PROSPERO.
You do yet taste
Some subtilties o'the isle, that will not let you
Believe things certain.—Welcome, my friends all:—
[aside to SEBASTIAN and ANTONIO] But you, my
brace of lords, were I so minded,
I here could pluck his highness' frown upon you,
And justify you traitors: at this time
I will tell no tales.
SEBASTIAN [aside].
The devil speaks in him.
PROSPERO.
No.—
For you, most wicked sir, whom to call brother
Would even infect my mouth, I do forgive
Thy rankest fault,—all of them; and require
My dukedom of thee, which perforce, I know,
Thou must restore.
ALONSO.
If thou be'st Prospero,
Give us particulars of thy preservation;
How thou hast met us here, who three hours since
Were wrack'd upon this shore; where I have lost—
How sharp the point of this remembrance is!—
My dear son Ferdinand.
PROSPERO.
I'm woe for't, sir.
ALONSO.
Irreparable is the loss; and patience
Says it is past her cure.
PROSPERO.
I rather think
You have not sought her help; of whose soft grace,
For the like loss I have her sovereign aid,
And rest myself content.
ALONSO.
You the like loss!
PROSPERO.
As great to me as late; and, supportable
To make the dear loss, have I means much weaker
Than you may call to comfort you; for I
Have lost my daughter.
ALONSO.
A daughter!
O heavens, that they were living both in Naples,
The king and queen there! that they were, I wish
Myself were mudded in that oozy bed
Where my son lies. When did you lose your
daughter?
PROSPERO.
In this last tempest. I perceive, these lords
At this encounter do so much admire,
That they devour their reason, and scarce think
Their eyes do offices of truth, their words
Are natural breath: but, howsoe'er you have
Been justled from your senses, know for certain
That I am Prospero, and that very duke
Which was thrust forth of Milan; who most
strangely

Upon this shore, where you were wrack'd, was
landed,
To be the lord on't. No more yet of this;
For 'tis a chronicle of day by day,
Not a relation for a breakfast, nor
Befitting this first meeting. Welcome, sir;
This cell's my court: here have I few attendants,
And subjects none abroad: pray you, look in.
My dukedom since you have given me again,
I will requite you with as good a thing;
At least bring forth a wonder, to content ye
As much as me my dukedom.
Here PROSPERO *discovers* FERDINAND *and*
MIRANDA *playing at chess.*
MIRANDA.
Sweet lord, you play me false.
FERDINAND.
No, my dearest love,
I would not for the world.
MIRANDA.
Yes, for a score of kingdoms you should wrangle,
And I would call it fair play.
ALONSO.
If this prove
A vision of the island, one dear son
Shall I twice lose.
SEBASTIAN.
A most high miracle!
FERDINAND.
Though the seas threaten, they are merciful:
I have cursed them without cause.
[Kneels to ALONSO.
ALONSO.
Now all the blessings
Of a glad father compass thee about!
Arise, and say how thou camest here.
MIRANDA.
O, wonder!
How many goodly creatures are there here!
How beauteous mankind is! O brave new world,
That has such people in't!
PROSPERO.
'Tis new to thee.
ALONSO.
What is this maid with whom thou wast at play?
Your eld'st acquaintance cannot be three hours:
Is she the goddess that hath sever'd us,
And brought us thus together?
FERDINAND.
Sir, she's mortal;
But by immortal Providence she's mine:
I chose her when I could not ask my father
For his advice, nor thought I had one. She
Is daughter to this famous Duke of Milan,
Of whom so often I have heard renown,
But never saw before; of whom I have
Received a second life; and second father
This lady makes him to me.
ALONSO.
I am hers:
But, O, how oddly will it sound that I
Must ask my child forgiveness!
PROSPERO.
There, sir, stop:
Let us not burden our remembrances
With a heaviness that's gone.

GONZALO.
I have inly wept,
Or should have spoke ere this.—Look down, you
gods,
And on this couple drop a blessed crown!
For it is you that have chalk'd forth the way
Which brought us hither.

ALONSO.
I say, Amen, Gonzalo!

GONZALO.
Was Milan thrust from Milan, that his issue
Should become kings of Naples? O, rejoice
Beyond a common joy! and set it down
With gold on lasting pillars,—In one voyage
Did Claribel her husband find at Tunis;
And Ferdinand, her brother, found a wife
Where he himself was lost; Prospero, his dukedom
In a poor isle; and all of us, ourselves
When no man was his own.

ALONSO [to FERDINAND and MIRANDA].
Give me your hands:
Let grief and sorrow still embrace his heart
That doth not wish you joy!

GONZALO.
Be it so! Amen!
Enter ARIEL, *with the* MASTER *and* BOAT-
SWAIN *amazedly following.*

O, look, sir, look, sir! here is more of us:
I prophesied, if a gallows were on land,
This fellow could not drown.—Now, blasphemy,
That swear'st grace o'erboard, not an oath on
shore?
Hast thou no mouth by land? What is the news?

BOATSWAIN.
The best news is, that we have safely found
Our king and company; the next, our ship—
Which, but three glasses since, we gave out split—
Is tight, and yare, and bravely rigg'd, as when
We first put out to sea.

ARIEL [aside to PROSPERO].
Sir, all this service
Have I done since I went.

PROSPERO [aside to ARIEL].
My tricksy spirit!

ALONSO.
These are not natural events; they strengthen
From strange to stranger.—Say, how came you
hither?

BOATSWAIN.
If I did think, sir, I were well awake,
I'ld strive to tell you. We were dead of sleep,
And—how we know not—all clapt under hatches;
Where, but even now, with strange and several
noises
Of roaring, shrieking, howling, jingling chains,
And more diversity of sounds, all horrible,
We were awaked; straightway, at liberty:
Where we, in all her trim, freshly beheld
Our royal, good, and gallant ship; our master
Capering to eye her: on a trice, so please you,
Even in a dream, were we divided from them,
And were brought moping hither.

ARIEL [aside to PROSPERO].
Was't well done?

PROSPERO [aside to ARIEL].
Bravely, my diligence. Thou shalt be free.

ALONSO.
This is as strange a maze as e'er men trod;
And there is in this business more than nature
Was ever conduct of: some oracle
Must rectify our knowledge.

PROSPERO.
Sir, my liege,
Do not infest your mind with beating on
The strangeness of this business; at pick'd leisure,
Which shall be shortly, single I'll resolve you—
Which to you shall seem probable—of every
These happen'd accidents: till when, be cheerful,
And think of each thing well.—[aside to ARIEL]
Come hither, spirit:
Set Caliban and his companions free;
Untie the spell. [Exit ARIEL.]—How fares my
gracious sir?
There are yet missing of your company
Some few odd lads that you remember not.
Enter ARIEL, *driving in* CALIBAN, STEPHANO,
and TRINCULO, *in their stolen apparel.*

STEPHANO.
Every man shift for all the rest, and let no man
take care for himself; for all is but fortune.—Coragio, bully-monster, coragio!

TRINCULO.
If these be true spies which I wear in my head,
here's a goodly sight.

CALIBAN.
O Setebos, these be brave spirits indeed!
How fine my master is! I am afraid
He will chastise me.

SEBASTIAN.
Ha, ha!
What things are these, my lord Antonio?
Will money buy 'em?

ANTONIO.
Very like; one of them
Is a plain fish, and, no doubt, marketable.

PROSPERO.
Mark but the badges of these men, my lords,
Then say if they be true.—This mis-shapen
knave,—
His mother was a witch; and one so strong
That could control the moon, make flows and ebbs,
And deal in her command, without her power.
These three have robb'd me; and this demi-
devil—
For he's a bastard one—had plotted with them
To take my life: two of these fellows you
Must know and own; this thing of darkness I
Acknowledge mine.

CALIBAN.
I shall be pinch'd to death.

ALONSO.
Is not this Stephano, my drunken butler?

SEBASTIAN.
He is drunk now: where had he wine?

ALONSO.
And Trinculo is reeling ripe: where should they
Find this grand liquor that hath gilded 'em?—
How camest thou in this pickle?

TRINCULO.
I have been in such a pickle, since I saw you last,
that, I fear me, will never out of my bones: I shall
not fear fly-blowing.

SEBASTIAN.
Why, how now, Stephano!

STEPHANO.
O, touch me not:—I am not Stephano, but a cramp.

PROSPERO.
You'ld be king o'the isle, sirrah?

STEPHANO.
I should have been a sore one, then.

ALONSO.
This is a strange thing as e'er I look'd on.
[Pointing to CALIBAN.

PROSPERO.
He is as disproportion'd in his manners
As in his shape.—Go, sirrah, to my cell;
Take with you your companions; as you look
To have my pardon, trim it handsomely.

CALIBAN.
Ay, that I will; and I'll be wise hereafter,
And seek for grace. What a thrice-double ass
Was I, to take this drunkard for a god,
And worship this dull fool!

PROSPERO.
Go to; away!

ALONSO.
Hence, and bestow your luggage where you found
it.

SEBASTIAN.
Or stole it, rather.
[Exeunt CALIBAN, STEPHANO, and TRIN-
CULO.

PROSPERO.
Sir, I invite your highness and your train
To my poor cell, where you shall take your rest
For this one night; which, part of it, I'll waste
With such discourse as, I doubt not, shall make it
Go quick away; the story of my life,
And the particular accidents gone by
Since I came to this isle: and in the morn
I'll bring you to your ship, and so to Naples,
Where I have hope to see the nuptial

Of these our dear-beloved solemnized;
And thence retire me to my Milan, where
Every third thought shall be my grave.

ALONSO.
I long
To hear the story of your life, which must
Take the ear strangely.

PROSPERO.
I'll deliver all;
And promise you calm seas, auspicious gales,
And sail so expeditious, that shall catch
Your royal fleet far off.—[aside to ARIEL] My
Ariel,—chick,—
That is thy charge: then to the elements
Be free, and fare thou well!—Please you, draw
near. [Exeunt.

EPILOGUE.

SPOKEN BY PROSPERO.

NOW my charms are all o'erthrown,
And what strength I have's mine own,—
Which is most faint: now, 'tis true,
I must be here confined by you,
Or sent to Naples. Let me not,
Since I have my dukedom got,
And pardon'd the deceiver, dwell
In this bare island by your spell;
But release me from my bands
With the help of your good hands:
Gentle breath of yours my sails
Must fill, or else my project fails,
Which was to please: now I want
Spirits to enforce, art to enchant;
And my ending is despair,
Unless I be relieved by prayer,
Which pierces so, that it assaults
Mercy itself, and frees all faults.
As you from crimes would pardon'd be,
Let your indulgence set me free.

KING HENRY THE EIGHTH

DRAMATIS PERSONAE

KING HENRY THE EIGHTH.
CARDINAL WOLSEY.
CARDINAL CAMPEIUS.
CAPUCIUS, *Ambassador from the Emperor Charles V.*
CRANMER, *Archbishop of Canterbury.*
DUKE OF NORFOLK.
DUKE OF BUCKINGHAM.
DUKE OF SUFFOLK.
EARL OF SURREY.
LORD CHAMBERLAIN.
LORD CHANCELLOR.
GARDINER, *Bishop of Winchester.*
BISHOP OF LINCOLN.
LORD ABERGAVENNY.
LORD SANDS.
SIR HENRY GUILDFORD.
SIR THOMAS LOVELL.
SIR ANTHONY DENNY.
SIR NICHOLAS VAUX.
SECRETARIES *to Wolsey.*
CROMWELL, *servant to Wolsey.*
GRIFFITH, *gentleman-usher to Queen Katharine.*

THREE GENTLEMEN.
DOCTOR BUTTS, *Physician to the King.*
GARTER KING-AT-ARMS.
SURVEYOR *to the Duke of Buckingham.*
BRANDON, *and a* SERGEANT-AT-ARMS.
DOORKEEPER *of the Council chamber.* PORTER, *and his* MAN.
PAGE *to Gardiner.* A CRIER.

QUEEN KATHARINE, *wife to King Henry, afterwards divorced.*
ANNE BULLEN, *her maid of honour, afterwards Queen.*
AN OLD LADY, *friend to Anne Bullen.*
PATIENCE, *woman to Queen Katharine.*

Several BISHOPS, LORDS, *and* LADIES *in the Dumb-shows;* WOMEN *attending upon the Queen;* SCRIBES, OFFICERS, GUARDS, *and other* ATTENDANTS.

SPIRITS.

SCENE—*Chiefly in London and Westminster; once at Kimbolton.*

PROLOGUE.

I COME no more to make you laugh: things now,
That bear a weighty and a serious brow,
Sad, high, and working, full of state and woe,
Such noble scenes as draw the eye to flow,
We now present. Those that can pity, here
May, if they think it well, let fall a tear;
The subject will deserve it. Such as give
Their money out of hope they may believe,
May here find truth too. Those that come to see
Only a show or two, and so agree
The play may pass, if they be still and willing,
I'll undertake may see away their shilling
Richly in two short hours. Only they
That come to hear a merry bawdy play,
A noise of targets, or to see a fellow
In a long motley coat guarded with yellow,
Will be deceived; for, gentle hearers, know,
To rank our chosen truth with such a show
As fool and fight is, beside forfeiting
Our own brains, and the opinion that we bring,
To make that only true we now intend,
Will leave us ne'er an understanding friend.
Therefore, for goodness' sake, and as you are known
The first and happiest hearers of the town,
Be sad, as we would make ye: think ye see
The very persons of our noble story
As they were living; think you see them great,
And follow'd with the general throng and sweat
Of thousand friends; then, in a moment, see
How soon this mightiness meets misery:
And, if you can be merry then, I'll say
A man may weep upon his wedding-day.

ACT I. SCENE I.

London. An ante-chamber in the palace.

Enter the DUKE OF NORFOLK *at one door; at the other, the* DUKE OF BUCKINGHAM *and the* LORD ABERGAVENNY.

DUKE OF BUCKINGHAM.
GOOD morrow, and well met. How have ye done
Since last we saw in France?

DUKE OF NORFOLK.
     I thank your Grace,
Healthful; and ever since a fresh admirer
Of what I saw there.

DUKE OF BUCKINGHAM.
    An untimely ague
Stay'd me a prisoner in my chamber, when
Those suns of glory, those two lights of men,
Met in the vale of Andren.

DUKE OF NORFOLK.
    'Twixt Guines and Arde:
I was then present, saw them salute on horseback;
Beheld them, when they lighted, how they clung
In their embracement, as they grew together;
Which had they, what four throned ones could have weigh'd
Such a compounded one?

DUKE OF BUCKINGHAM.
    All the whole time
I was my chamber's prisoner.

DUKE OF NORFOLK.
    Then you lost
The view of earthly glory: men might say,
Till this time pomp was single, but now married
To one above itself. Each following day

Became the next day's master, till the last
Made former wonders its: to-day, the French,
All clinquant, all in gold, like heathen gods,
Shone down the English; and, to-morrow, they
Made Britain India; every man that stood
Show'd like a mine. Their dwarfish pages were
As cherubins, all gilt: the madams too,
Not used to toil, did almost sweat to bear
The pride upon them, that their very labour
Was to them as a painting: now this mask
Was cried incomparable; and the ensuing night
Made it a fool and beggar. The two kings,
Equal in lustre, were now best, now worst,
As presence did present them; him in eye,
Still him in praise: and, being present both,
'Twas said they saw but one; and no discerner
Durst wag his tongue in censure. When these
 suns—
For so they phrase 'em—by their heralds chal-
 lenged
The noble spirits to arms, they did perform
Beyond thought's compass; that former fabulous
 story,
Being now seen possible enough, got credit,
That Bevis was believed.

DUKE OF DUCKINGHAM.
   O, you go far.

DUKE OF NORFOLK.
As I belong to worship, and affect
In honour honesty, the tract of every thing
Would by a good discourser lose some life,
Which action's self was tongue to. All was royal;
To the disposing of it naught rebell'd.
Order gave each thing view; the office did
Distinctly his full function.

DUKE OF BUCKINGHAM.
     Who did guide,
I mean, who set the body and the limbs
Of this great sport together, as you guess?

DUKE OF NORFOLK.
One, certes, that promises no element
In such a business.

DUKE OF BUCKINGHAM.
    I pray you, who, my lord?

DUKE OF NORFOLK.
All this was order'd by the good discretion
Of the right-reverend Cardinal of York.

DUKE OF BUCKINGHAM.
The devil speed him! no man's pie is freed
From his ambitious finger. What had he
To do in these fierce vanities? I wonder
That such a keech can with his very bulk
Take up the rays o'the beneficial sun,
And keep it from the earth.

DUKE OF NORFOLK.
    Surely, sir,
There's in him stuff that puts him to these ends;
For, being not propt by ancestry, whose grace
Chalks successors their way; nor call'd upon
For high feats done to the crown; neither allied
To eminent assistants; but, spider-like,
Out of his self-drawing web, he gives us note
The force of his own merit makes his way;
A gift that heaven gives; which buys for him
A place next to the king.

LORD ABERGAVENNY.
    I cannot tell
What heaven hath given him,—let some graver
 eye
Pierce into that; but I can see his pride
Peep through each part of him: whence has he
 that?
If not from hell, the devil is a niggard;
Or has given all before, and he begins
A new hell in himself.

DUKE OF BUCKINGHAM.
    Why the devil,
Upon this French going-out, took he upon him,
Without the privity o'the king, t'appoint
Who should attend on him? He makes up the file
Of all the gentry; for the most part such
To whom as great a charge as little honour
He meant to lay upon; and his own letter,
The honourable board of council out,
Must fetch him in the papers.

LORD ABERGAVENNY.
    I do know
Kinsmen of mine, three at the least, that have
By this so sicken'd their estates, that never
They shall abound as formerly.

DUKE OF BUCKINGHAM.
    O, many
Have broke their backs with laying manors on 'em
For this great journey. What did this vanity
But minister communication of
A most poor issue?

DUKE OF NORFOLK.
    Grievingly I think,
The peace between the French and us not values
The cost that did conclude it.

DUKE OF BUCKINGHAM.
    Every man,
After the hideous storm that follow'd, was
A thing inspired; and, not consulting, broke
Into a general prophecy,—That this tempest,
Dashing the garment of this peace, aboded
The sudden breach on't.

DUKE OF NORFOLK.
    Which is budded out;
For France hath flaw'd the league, and hath attacht
Our merchants' goods at Bourdeaux.

LORD ABERGAVENNY.
    Is it therefore
The ambassador is silenced?

DUKE OF NORFOLK.
    Marry, is't.

LORD ABERGAVENNY.
A proper title of a peace; and purchased
At a superfluous rate!

DUKE OF BUCKINGHAM.
    Why, all this business
Our reverend cardinal carried.

DUKE OF NORFOLK.
    Like it your Grace,
The state takes notice of the private difference
Betwixt you and the cardinal. I advise you,—
And take it from a heart that wishes towards you
Honour and plenteous safety,—that you read
The cardinal's malice and his potency
Together; to consider further, that
What his high hatred would effect wants not

A minister in his power. You know his nature,
That he's revengeful; and I know his sword
Hath a sharp edge: it's long, and, 't may be said,
It reaches far; and where 'twill not extend,
Thither he darts it. Bosom up my counsel,   [rock
You'll find it wholesome.—Lo, where comes that
That I advise your shunning.

Enter CARDINAL WOLSEY, *the purse borne before*
him; certain of the GUARD, *and two* SECRETAR-
IES *with papers. The* CARDINAL *in his passage*
fixeth his eye on BUCKINGHAM, *and* BUCKING-
HAM *on him, both full of disdain.*

CARDINAL WOLSEY.
The Duke of Buckingham's surveyor, ha?
Where's his examination?

FIRST SECRETARY.
                    Here, so please you.

CARDINAL WOLSEY.
Is he in person ready?

FIRST SECRETARY.
                    Ay, please your Grace.

CARDINAL WOLSEY.
Well, we shall then know more; and Buckingham
Shall lessen this big look.
                    [*Exeunt* WOLSEY *and his* TRAIN.

DUKE OF BUCKINGHAM.
This butcher's cur is venom-mouth'd, and I
Have not the power to muzzle him; therefore best
Not wake him in his slumber. A beggar's book
Outworths a noble's blood.

DUKE OF NORFOLK.
                    What, are you chafed?
Ask God for temperance; that's the appliance only
Which your disease requires.

DUKE OF BUCKINGHAM.
                    I read in's looks
Matter against me; and his eye reviled
Me, as his abject object: at this instant
He bores me with some trick: he's gone to the king;
I'll follow, and outstare him.

DUKE OF NORFOLK.
                    Stay, my lord,
And let your reason with your choler question
What 'tis you go about: to climb steep hills
Requires slow pace at first: anger is like
A full-hot horse, who being allow'd his way,
Self-mettle tires him. Not a man in England
Can advise me like you: be to yourself
As you would to your friend.

DUKE OF BUCKINGHAM.
                    I'll to the king;
And from a mouth of honour quite cry down
This Ipswich fellow's insolence; or proclaim
There's difference in no persons.

DUKE OF NORFOLK.
                    Be advised;
Heat not a furnace for your foe so hot
That it do singe yourself: we may outrun,
By violent swiftness, that which we run at,
And lose by over-running. Know you not,
The fire that mounts the liquor till't run o'er,
In seeming t'augment it wastes it? Be advised:
I say again, there is no English soul
More stronger to direct you than yourself,
If with the sap of reason you would quench,
Or but allay, the fire of passion.

DUKE OF BUCKINGHAM.
                    Sir,
I'm thankful to you; and I'll go along
By your prescription: but this top-proud fellow,—
Whom from the flow of gall I name not, but
From sincere motions,—by intelligence,
And proofs as clear as founts in July, when
We see each grain of gravel, I do know
To be corrupt and treasonous.

DUKE OF NORFOLK.
                    Say not, treasonous.

DUKE OF BUCKINGHAM.
To the king I'll say't; and make my vouch as
                    strong
As shore of rock. Attend. This holy fox,
Or wolf, or both,—for he is equal ravenous
As he is subtle, and as prone to mischief
As able to perform't; his mind and place
Infecting one another, yea, reciprocally,—
Only to show his pomp as well in France
As here at home, suggests the king our master
To this last costly treaty, the interview,
That swallow'd so much treasure, and like a glass
Did break i'the rinsing.

DUKE OF NORFOLK.
                    Faith, and so it did.

DUKE OF BUCKINGHAM.
Pray, give me favour, sir. This cunning cardinal
The articles o'the combination drew
As himself pleased; and they were ratified
As he cried, 'Thus let be:' to as much end
As give a crutch to the dead: but our count-
                    cardinal
Has done this, and 'tis well; for worthy Wolsey
Who cannot err, he did it. Now this follows,—
Which, as I take it, is a kind of puppy
To the old dam, treason,—Charles the emperor,
Under pretence to see the queen his aunt,—
For 'twas indeed his colour, but he came
To whisper Wolsey,—here makes visitation:
His fears were, that the interview betwixt
England and France might, through their amity,
Breed him some prejudice; for from this league
Peept harms that menaced him: he privily
Deals with our cardinal; and, as I trow,—
Which I do well; for, I am sure, the emperor
Paid ere he promised; whereby his suit was granted
Ere it was askt;—but when the way was made,
And paved with gold, the emperor thus desired,—
That he would please to alter the king's course,
And break the foresaid peace. Let the king know—
As soon he shall by me—that thus the cardinal
Does buy and sell his honour as he pleases,
And for his own advantage.

DUKE OF NORFOLK.
                    I am sorry
To hear this of him; and could wish he were
Something mistaken in't.

DUKE OF BUCKINGHAM.
                    No, not a syllable:
I do pronounce him in that very shape
He shall appear in proof.

Enter BRANDON, *a* SERGEANT-AT-ARMS *before*
him, and two or three of the GUARD.

BRANDON.
Your office, sergeant; execute it.

SERGEANT.
              Sir,
My lord the Duke of Buckingham and Earl
Of Hereford, Stafford, and Northampton, I
Arrest thee of high treason, in the name
Of our most sovereign king.

DUKE OF BUCKINGHAM.
            Lo, you, my lord,
The net has faln upon me! I shall perish
Under device and practice.

BRANDON.
              I am sorry
To see you ta'en from liberty, to look on
The business present: 'tis his highness' pleasure
You shall to the Tower.

DUKE OF BUCKINGHAM.
          It will help me nothing
To plead mine innocence; for that dye is on me
Which makes my whitest part black. The will of
    heaven
Be done in this and all things!—I obey.—
O my Lord Aberga'ny, fare you well!

BRANDON.
Nay, he must bear you company.—[to ABERGA-
VENNY] The king
Is pleased you shall to the Tower, till you know
How he determines further.

LORD ABERGAVENNY.
            As the duke said,
The will of heaven be done, and the king's pleasure
By me obey'd!

BRANDON.
         Here is a warrant from
The king t'attach Lord Montacute; and the bodies
Of the duke's confessor, John de la Car,
One Gilbert Peck, his chancellor,—

DUKE OF BUCKINGHAM.
              So, so;
These are the limbs o'the plot:—no more, I hope.

BRANDON.
A monk o'the Chartreux.

DUKE OF BUCKINGHAM.
         O, Nicholas Hopkins?

BRANDON.
                  He.

DUKE OF BUCKINGHAM.
My surveyor is false; the o'er-great cardinal
Hath show'd him gold; my life is spann'd already:
I am the shadow of poor Buckingham,
Whose figure even this instant cloud puts on,
By darkening my clear sun.—My lord, farewell.
                        [Exeunt.

SCENE II.

The same. The council-chamber.

Cornets. Enter KING HENRY, leaning on the
CARDINAL'S shoulder; the NOBLES and SIR
THOMAS LOVELL: the CARDINAL places him-
self under the KING'S feet on his right side.

KING HENRY.
MY life itself, and the best heart of it,
Thanks you for this great care: I stood i'the
    level
Of a full-charged confederacy, and give thanks
To you that choked it. Let be call'd before us
That gentleman of Buckingham's: in person

I'll hear him his confessions justify;
And point by point the treasons of his master
He shall again relate.
A noise within, crying 'Room for the Queen!'
    Enter QUEEN KATHARINE, usher'd by the
    DUKES OF NORFOLK and SUFFOLK: she kneels.
    The KING riseth from his state, takes her up,
    kisses and placeth her by him.

QUEEN KATHARINE.
Nay, we must longer kneel: I am a suitor.

KING HENRY.
Arise, and take place by us:—half your suit
Never name to us; you have half our power:
The other moiety, ere you ask, is given;
Repeat your will, and take it.

QUEEN KATHARINE.
           Thank your majesty.
That you would love yourself, and in that love
Not unconsider'd leave your honour, nor
The dignity of your office, is the point
Of my petition.

KING HENRY.
        Lady mine, proceed.

QUEEN KATHARINE.
I am solicited, not by a few,
And those of true condition, that your subjects
Are in great grievance: there have been commis-
    sions
Sent down among 'em, which hath flaw'd the
    heart
Of all their loyalties: wherein, although,
My good lord cardinal, they vent reproaches
Most bitterly on you, as putter-on
Of these exactions, yet the king our master,—
Whose honour heaven shield from soil!—even he
    escapes not
Language unmannerly, yea, such which breaks
The sides of loyalty, and almost appears
In loud rebellion.

DUKE OF NORFOLK.
         Not almost appears;
It doth appear; for, upon these taxations,
The clothiers all, not able to maintain
The many to them longing, have put off
The spinsters, carders, fullers, weavers, who,
Unfit for other life, compell'd by hunger
And lack of other means, in desperate manner
Daring the event to the teeth, are all in uproar,
And danger serves among them.

KING HENRY.
              Taxation!
Wherein? and what taxation?—My lord Cardinal,
You that are blamed for it alike with us,
Know you of this taxation?

CARDINAL WOLSEY.
          Please you, sir,
I know but of a single part, in aught
Pertains to the state; and front but in that file
Where others tell steps with me.

QUEEN KATHARINE.
          No, my lord,
You know no more than others: but you frame
Things that are known alike; which are not
    wholesome
To those which would not know them, and yet
    must

Perforce be their acquaintance. These exactions,
Whereof my sovereign would have note, they are
Most pestilent to the hearing; and, to bear 'em,
The back is sacrifice to the load. They say
They are devised by you; or else you suffer
Too hard an exclamation.

KING HENRY.
                            Still exaction!
The nature of it? in what kind, let's know,
Is this exaction?

QUEEN KATHARINE.
                    I am much too venturous
In tempting of your patience; but am bolden'd
Under your promised pardon. The subjects'
    grief
Comes through commissions, which compel from
    each
The sixth part of his substance, to be levied
Without delay; and the pretence for this
Is named, your wars in France: this makes bold
    mouths:
Tongues spit their duties out, and cold hearts
    freeze
Allegiance in them; their curses now
Live where their prayers did: and it's come to
    pass,
That tractable obedience is a slave
To each incensed will. I would your highness
Would give it quick consideration, for
There is no primer business.

KING HENRY.
                        By my life,
This is against our pleasure.

CARDINAL WOLSEY.
                        And for me,
I have no further gone in this than by
A single voice; and that not past me but
By learned approbation of the judges. If I am
Traduced by ignorant tongues, which neither
    know
My faculties nor person, yet will be
The chronicles of my doing,—let me say
'Tis but the fate of place, and the rough brake
That virtue must go through. We must not stint
Our necessary actions, in the fear
To cope malicious censurers; which ever,
As ravenous fishes, do a vessel follow
That is new-trimm'd, but benefit no further
Than vainly longing. What we oft do best,
By sick interpreters, once weak ones, is
Not ours, or not allow'd; what worst, as oft,
Hitting a grosser quality, is cried up
For our best action. If we shall stand still,
In fear our motion will be mockt or carpt at,
We should take root here where we sit, or sit
State-statues only.

KING HENRY.
                    Things done well,
And with a care, exempt themselves from fear;
Things done without example, in their issue
Are to be fear'd. Have you a precedent
Of this commission? I believe, not any.
We must not rend our subjects from our laws,
And stick them in our will. Sixth part of each?
A trembling contribution! Why, we take
From every tree lop, bark, and part o'the timber;

And, though we leave it with a root, thus hackt,
The air will drink the sap. To every county
Where this is question'd send our letters, with
Free pardon to each man that has denied
The force of this commission: pray, look to't;
I put it to your care.

CARDINAL WOLSEY [to the SECRETARY].
A word with you.
Let there be letters writ to every shire,
Of the king's grace and pardon. The grieved
    commons
Hardly conceive of me; let it be noised
That through our intercession this revokement
And pardon comes: I shall anon advise you
Further in the proceeding.   [Exit SECRETARY.

Enter SURVEYOR.

QUEEN KATHARINE.
I am sorry that the Duke of Buckingham
Is run in your displeasure.

KING HENRY.
                    It grieves many:
The gentleman is learn'd, and a most rare
    speaker;
To nature none more bound; his training such,
That he may furnish and instruct great teachers,
And never seek for aid out of himself.
Yet see,
When these so noble benefits shall prove
Not well disposed, the mind growing once cor-
    rupt,
They turn to vicious forms, ten times more ugly
Than ever they were fair. This man so complete,
Who was enroll'd 'mongst wonders, and when we,
Almost with ravisht listening, could not find
His hour of speech a minute; he, my lady,
Hath into monstrous habits put the graces
That once were his, and is become as black
As if besmear'd in hell. Sit by us; you shall
    hear—
This was his gentleman in trust—of him
Things to strike honour sad. Bid him recount
The fore-recited practices; whereof
We cannot feel too little, hear too much.

CARDINAL WOLSEY.
Stand forth, and with bold spirit relate what you,
Most like a careful subject, have collected
Out of the Duke of Buckingham.

KING HENRY.
                        Speak freely.

SURVEYOR.
First, it was usual with him, every day
It would infect his speech,—that if the king
Should without issue die, he'll carry it so
To make the sceptre his: these very words
I've heard him utter to his son-in-law,
Lord Aberga'ny; to whom by oath he menaced
Revenge upon the cardinal.

CARDINAL WOLSEY.
                    Please your highness, note
His dangerous conception in this point.
Not friended by his wish, to your high person
His will is most malignant; and it stretches
Beyond you, to your friends.

QUEEN KATHARINE.
                    My learn'd lord Cardinal,
Deliver all with charity.

KING HENRY.
Speak on:
How grounded he his title to the crown,
Upon our fail? to this point hast thou heard him
At any time speak aught?

SURVEYOR.
He was brought to this
By a vain prophecy of Nicholas Henton.

KING HENRY.
What was that Henton?

SURVEYOR.
Sir, a Chartreux friar,
His confessor; who fed him every minute
With words of sovereignty.

KING HENRY.
How know'st thou this?

SURVEYOR.
Not long before your highness sped to France,
The duke being at the Rose, within the parish
Saint Lawrence Poultney, did of me demand
What was the speech among the Londoners
Concerning the French journey: I replied,
Men fear'd the French would prove perfidious,
To the king's danger. Presently the duke
Said, 'twas the fear, indeed; and that he doubted
'Twould prove the verity of certain words
Spoke by a holy monk; 'that oft,' says he,
'Hath sent to me, wishing me to permit
John de la Car, my chaplain, a choice hour
To hear from him a matter of some moment:
Whom after, under the confession's seal,
He solemnly had sworn, that what he spoke
My chaplain to no creature living but
To me should utter, with demure confidence
This pausingly ensued,—'Neither the king nor's
    heirs,
Tell you the duke, shall prosper: bid him strive
To gain the love o'the commonalty: the duke
Shall govern England.'

QUEEN KATHARINE.
If I know you well,
You were the duke's surveyor, and lost your
    office
On the complaint o'the tenants: take good heed
You charge not in your spleen a noble person,
And spoil your nobler soul: I say, take heed;
Yes, heartily beseech you.

KING HENRY.
Let him on.
Go forward.

SURVEYOR.
On my soul, I'll speak but truth.
I told my lord the duke, by the devil's illusions
The monk might be deceived; and that 'twas dan-
    gerous for him
To ruminate on this so far, until
It forged him some design, which, being believed,
It was much like to do: he answer'd, 'Tush,
It can do me no damage;' adding further,
That, had the king in his last sickness fail'd,
The Cardinal's and Sir Thomas Lovell's heads
Should have gone off.

KING HENRY.
Ha! what, so rank? Ah-ha!
There's mischief in this man:—canst thou say
    further?

SURVEYOR.
I can, my liege.

KING HENRY.
Proceed.

SURVEYOR.
Being at Greenwich,
After your highness had reproved the duke
About Sir William Blomer,—

KING HENRY.
I remember
Of such a time:—being my sworn servant,
The duke retain'd him his.—But on; what hence?

SURVEYOR.
'If,' quoth he, 'I for this had been committed,
As, to the Tower, I thought, I would have play'd
The part my father meant to act upon
The usurper Richard; who, being at Salisbury,
Made suit to come in's presence; which if granted,
As he made semblance of his duty, would
Have put his knife into him.'

KING HENRY.
A giant traitor!

CARDINAL WOLSEY.
Now, madam, may his highness live in freedom,
And this man out of prison?

QUEEN KATHARINE.
God mend all!

KING HENRY.
There's something more would out of thee; what
say'st?

SURVEYOR.
After 'the duke his father,' with 'the knife,'
He stretch him, and, with one hand on his dagger,
Another spread on's breast, mounting his eyes,
He did discharge a horrible oath; whose tenour
Was,—were he evil used, he would outgo
His father by as much as a performance
Does an irresolute purpose.

KING HENRY.
There's his period,
To sheathe his knife in us. He is attacht;
Call him to present trial: if he may
Find mercy in the law, 'tis his; if none,
Let him not seek't of us: by day and night!
He's traitor to the height.   [Exeunt.

SCENE III.
An antechamber in the palace.

Enter the LORD CHAMBERLAIN *and* LORD
SANDS.

LORD CHAMBERLAIN.
IS'T possible the spells of France should juggle
Men into such strange mysteries?

LORD SANDS.
New customs,
Though they be never so ridiculous,
Nay, let 'em be unmanly, yet are follow'd.

LORD CHAMBERLAIN.
As far as I see, all the good our English
Have got by the late voyage is but merely
A fit or two o'the face; but they are shrewd ones;
For when they hold 'em, you would swear
    directly
Their very noses had been counsellors
To Pepin or Clotharius, they keep state so.

LORD SANDS.

They have all new legs, and lame ones: one would
  take it,
That never saw 'em pace before, the spavin
Or springhalt reign'd among 'em.

LORD CHAMBERLAIN.

               Death! my lord,
Their clothes are after such a pagan cut too,
That, sure, th'have worn out Christendom.

Enter SIR THOMAS LOVELL.

               How now!
What news, Sir Thomas Lovell?

SIR THOMAS LOVELL.

               Faith, my lord,
I hear of none, but the new proclamation
That's clapt upon the court-gate.

LORD CHAMBERLAIN.

               What is't for?

SIR THOMAS LOVELL.

The reformation of our travell'd gallants,
That fill the court with quarrels, talk, and tailors.

LORD CHAMBERLAIN.

I'm glad 'tis there: now I would pray our mon-
  sieurs
To think an English courtier may be wise,
And never see the Louvre.

SIR THOMAS LOVELL.

            They must either—
For so run the conditions—leave those remnants
Of fool and feather, that they got in France,
With all their honourable points of ignorance
Pertaining thereunto,—as fights and fireworks;
Abusing better men than they can be,
Out of a foreign wisdom,—renouncing clean
The faith they have in tennis, and tall stockings,
Short blister'd breeches, and those types of
  travel,
And understand again like honest men;
Or pack to their old playfellows: there, I take it,
They may, *cum privilegio*, wear away
The lag end of their lewdness, and be laugh'd at.

LORD SANDS.

'Tis time to give 'em physic, their diseases
Are grown so catching.

LORD CHAMBERLAIN.

            What a loss our ladies
Will have of these trim vanities!

SIR THOMAS LOVELL.

               Ay, marry,
There will be woe indeed, lords: the sly whore-
  sons
Have got a speeding trick to lay down ladies;
A French song and a fiddle has no fellow.

LORD SANDS.

The devil fiddle 'em! I am glad they are going;
For, sure, there's no converting of 'em: now
An honest country lord, as I am, beaten
A long time out of play, may bring his plain-song,
And have an hour of hearing; and, by'r lady,
Held current music too.

LORD CHAMBERLAIN.

            Well said, Lord Sands;
Your colt's tooth is not cast yet.

LORD SANDS.

               No, my lord;
Nor shall not, while I have a stump.

LORD CHAMBERLAIN.

               Sir Thomas,
Whither were you a-going?

SIR THOMAS LOVELL.

             To the cardinal's:
Your lordship is a guest too.

LORD CHAMBERLAIN.

             O, 'tis true:
This night he makes a supper, and a great one,
To many lords and ladies; there will be
The beauty of this kingdom, I'll assure you.

SIR THOMAS LOVELL.

That churchman bears a bounteous mind indeed,
A hand as fruitful as the land that feeds us;
His dews fall every where.

LORD CHAMBERLAIN.

            No doubt he's noble;
He had a black mouth that said other of him.

LORD SANDS.

He may, my lord,—'has wherewithal; in him
Sparing would show a worse sin than ill doctrine:
Men of his way should be most liberal;
They are set here for examples.

LORD CHAMBERLAIN.

            True, they are so;
But few now give so great ones. My barge stays;
Your lordship shall along.—Come, good Sir
  Thomas,
We shall be late else; which I would not be,
For I was spoke to, with Sir Henry Guildford,
This night to be comptrollers.

LORD SANDS.

           I'm your lordship's. [*Exeunt.*

SCENE IV.

The presence-chamber in York-Place.

Hautboys. A small table under a state for the
CARDINAL, *a longer table for the guests. Then*
enter ANNE BULLEN *and divers other* LADIES
and GENTLEWOMEN, *as guests, at one door; at*
another door, enter SIR HENRY GUILDFORD.

SIR HENRY GUILDFORD.

LADIES, a general welcome from his Grace
  Salutes ye all; this night he dedicates
To fair content and you: none here, he hopes,
In all this noble bevy, has brought with her
One care abroad; he would have all as merry
As, first, good company, good wine, good welcome,
Can make good people—

Enter LORD CHAMBERLAIN, LORD SANDS,
and SIR THOMAS LOVELL.

          O, my lord, y'are tardy:
The very thought of this fair company
Clapt wings to me.

LORD CHAMBERLAIN.

        You are young, Sir Harry Guildford.

LORD SANDS.

Sir Thomas Lovell, had the cardinal
But half my lay thoughts in him, some of these
Should find a running banquet ere they rested,
I think would better please 'em: by my life,
They are a sweet society of fair ones.

SIR THOMAS LOVELL.

O, that your lordship were but now confessor
To one or two of these!

LORD SANDS.
               I would I were;
They should find easy penance.
          SIR THOMAS LOVELL.
                     Faith, how easy?
          LORD SANDS.
As easy as a down-bed would afford it.
          LORD CHAMBERLAIN.
Sweet ladies, will it please you sit?—Sir Harry,
Place you that side; I'll take the charge of this:
His Grace is entering.—Nay, you must not
     freeze;
Two women placed together makes cold
     weather:—
My Lord Sands, you are one will keep 'em
     waking;
Pray, sit between these ladies.
          LORD SANDS.
                  By my faith,
And thank your lordship.—By your leave, sweet
     ladies:
If I chance to talk a little wild, forgive me;
I had it from my father.
          ANNE BULLEN.
               Was he mad, sir?
          LORD SANDS.
O, very mad, exceeding mad, in love too:
But he would bite none; just as I do now,—
He would kiss you twenty with a breath.
                          [Kisses her.
          LORD CHAMBERLAIN.
               Well said, my lord.—
So, now y'are fairly seated.—Gentlemen,
The penance lies on you, if these fair ladies
Pass away frowning.
          LORD SANDS.
               For my little cure,
Let me alone.
Hautboys. Enter CARDINAL WOLSEY, attended,
     and takes his state.
          CARDINAL WOLSEY.
Y'are welcome, my fair guests: that noble lady,
Or gentleman, that is not freely merry,
Is not my friend: this, to confirm my welcome;
And to you all, good health.   [Drinks.
          LORD SANDS.
              Your Grace is noble:—
Let me have such a bowl may hold my thanks,
And save me so much talking.
          CARDINAL WOLSEY.
               My Lord Sands,
I am beholding to you: cheer your neighbours.—
Ladies, you are not merry:—gentlemen,
Whose fault is this?
          LORD SANDS.
             The red wine first must rise
In their fair cheeks, my lord; then we shall have
     'em
Talk us to silence.
          ANNE BULLEN.
             You are a merry gamester,
My Lord Sands.
          LORD SANDS.
          Yes, if I make my play.
Here's to your ladyship: and pledge it, madam,
For 'tis to such a thing,—

ANNE BULLEN.
          You cannot show me.
          LORD SANDS.
I told your Grace they would talk anon.
     [Drum and trumpet; chambers discharged.
          CARDINAL WOLSEY.
                   What's that?
          LORD CHAMBERLAIN.
Look out there, some of ye.   [Exit a SERVANT.
          CARDINAL WOLSEY.
               What warlike voice,
And to what end, is this?—Nay, ladies, fear not;
By all the laws of war y'are privileged.
          Enter SERVANT.
          LORD CHAMBERLAIN.
How now! what is't?
          SERVANT.
           A noble troop of strangers,—
For so they seem: th'have left their barge, and
     landed;
And hither make, as great ambassadors
From foreign princes.
          CARDINAL WOLSEY.
           Good lord chamberlain,
Go, give 'em welcome; you can speak the French
     tongue;
And, pray, receive 'em nobly, and conduct 'em
Into our presence, where this heaven of beauty
Shall shine at full upon them.—Some attend him.
     [Exit CHAMBERLAIN, attended.   All rise,
     and tables removed.
You have now a broken banquet; but we'll mend
     it.
A good digestion to you all: and once more
I shower a welcome on ye;—welcome all.
Hautboys. Enter KING and others, as MASKERS,
     habited like shepherds, usher'd by the LORD
     CHAMBERLAIN. They pass directly before the
     CARDINAL, and gracefully salute him.
A noble company! what are their pleasures?
          LORD CHAMBERLAIN.
Because they speak no English, thus they pray'd
To tell your Grace,—that, having heard by fame
Of this so noble and so fair assembly
This night to meet here, they could do no less,
Out of the great respect they bear to beauty,
But leave their flocks; and, under your fair con-
     duct,
Crave leave to view these ladies, and entreat
An hour of revels with 'em.
          CARDINAL WOLSEY.
            Say, lord chamberlain,
They have done my poor house grace; for which I
     pay 'em
A thousand thanks, and pray 'em take their
     pleasures.
     [They choose LADIES. The KING chooses
     ANNE BULLEN.
          KING HENRY.
The fairest hand I ever toucht! O beauty,
Till now I never knew thee!   Music. Dance.
          CARDINAL WOLSEY.
My lord,—
          LORD CHAMBERLAIN.
          Your Grace?

CARDINAL WOLSEY.
Pray, tell 'em thus much from me:—
There should be one amongst 'em, by his person,
More worthy this place than myself; to whom,
If I but knew him, with my love and duty
I would surrender it.
LORD CHAMBERLAIN.
I will, my lord.
[Whispers the MASKERS.
CARDINAL WOLSEY.
What say they?
LORD CHAMBERLAIN.
Such a one, they all confess,
There is indeed; which they would have your
Grace
Find out, and he will take it.
CARDINAL WOLSEY.
Let me see, then.
[Comes from his state.
By all your good leaves, gentlemen;—here I'll
make
My royal choice.
KING HENRY.
Ye have found him, Cardinal:
[Unmasking.
You hold a fair assembly; you do well, lord:
You are a churchman, or, I'll tell you, Cardinal,
I should judge now unhappily.
CARDINAL WOLSEY.
I am glad
Your Grace is grown so pleasant.
KING HENRY.
My lord chamberlain,
Prithee, come hither: what fair lady's that?
LORD CHAMBERLAIN.
An't please your Grace, Sir Thomas Bullen's
daughter,—
The Viscount Rochford,—one of her highness'
women.
KING HENRY.
By heaven, she is a dainty one.—Sweetheart,
I were unmannerly, to take you out,
And not to kiss you [kisses her].—A health, gentle-
men!
Let it go round.
CARDINAL WOLSEY.
Sir Thomas Lovell, is the banquet ready
I'the privy chamber?
SIR THOMAS LOVELL.
Yes, my lord.
CARDINAL WOLSEY.
Your Grace,
I fear, with dancing is a little heated.
KING HENRY.
I fear, too much.
CARDINAL WOLSEY.
There's fresher air, my lord,
In the next chamber.
KING HENRY.
Lead in your ladies, every one: sweet partner,
I must not yet forsake you: let's be merry:
Good my lord Cardinal, I have half a dozen healths
To drink to these fair ladies, and a measure
To lead 'em once again; and then let's dream
Who's best in favour.—Let the music knock it.
[Exeunt with trumpets.

ACT II. SCENE I.

London. A street.

Enter two GENTLEMEN, at several doors.

FIRST GENTLEMAN.
WHITHER away so fast?
SECOND GENTLEMAN.
O,—God save ye!
Ev'n to the hall, to hear what shall become
Of the great Duke of Buckingham.
FIRST GENTLEMAN.
I'll save you
That labour, sir. All's now done, but the ceremony
O᾿ bringing back the prisoner.
SECOND GENTLEMAN.
Were you there?
FIRST GENTLEMAN.
Yes, indeed, was I.
SECOND GENTLEMAN.
Pray, speak what has happen'd.
FIRST GENTLEMAN.
You may guess quickly what.
SECOND GENTLEMAN.
Is he found guilty?
FIRST GENTLEMAN.
Yes, truly is he, and condemn'd upon't.
SECOND GENTLEMAN.
I am sorry for't.
FIRST GENTLEMAN.
So are a number more.
SECOND GENTLEMAN.
But, pray, how past it?
FIRST GENTLEMAN.
I'll tell you in a little. The great duke
Came to the bar; where to his accusations
He pleaded still, not guilty, and alleged
Many sharp reasons to defeat the law.
The king's attorney, on the contrary,
Urged on the examinations, proofs, confessions
Of divers witnesses; which the duke desired
To have brought, viva voce, to his face:
At which appear'd against him his surveyor;
Sir Gilbert Peck his chancellor; and John Car,
Confessor to him; with that devil-monk,
Hopkins, that made this mischief.
SECOND GENTLEMAN.
That was he
That fed him with his prophecies?
FIRST GENTLEMAN.
The same.
All these accused him strongly; which he fain
Would have flung from him, but, indeed, he
could not:
And so his peers, upon this evidence,
Have found him guilty of high treason. Much
He spoke, and learnedly, for life; but all
Was either pitied in him or forgotten.
SECOND GENTLEMAN.
After all this, how did he bear himself?
FIRST GENTLEMAN.
When he was brought again to the bar, to hear
His knell rung out, his judgement,—he was stirr'
With such an agony, he sweat extremely,
And something spoke in choler, ill, and hasty:
But he fell to himself again, and sweetly
In all the rest show'd a most noble patience.

SECOND GENTLEMAN.
I do not think he fears death.

FIRST GENTLEMAN.
                Sure, he does not,—
He never was so womanish; the cause
He may a little grieve at.

SECOND GENTLEMAN.
             Certainly
The cardinal is the end of this.

FIRST GENTLEMAN.
             'Tis likely,
By all conjectures: first, Kildare's attainder,
Then deputy of Ireland; who removed,
Earl Surrey was sent thither, and in haste too,
Lest he should help his father.

SECOND GENTLEMAN.
           That trick of state
Was a deep envious one.

FIRST GENTLEMAN.
          At his return
No doubt he will requite it. This is noted,
And generally,—whoever the king favours,
The cardinal instantly will find employment,
And far enough from court too.

SECOND GENTLEMAN.
          All the commons
Hate him perniciously, and, o'my conscience,
Wish him ten fadom deep: this duke as much
They love and dote on; call him bounteous
    Buckingham,
The mirror of all courtesy,—

FIRST GENTLEMAN.
         Stay there, sir,
And see the noble ruin'd man you speak of.

Enter BUCKINGHAM *from his arraignment; tip-
staves before him; the axe with the edge towards
him; halberds on each side: accompanied with* SIR
THOMAS LOVELL, SIR NICHOLAS VAUX,
SIR WILLIAM SANDS, *and common People,
&c.*

SECOND GENTLEMAN.
Let's stand close, and behold him.

DUKE OF BUCKINGHAM.
         All good people,
You that thus far have come to pity me,
Hear what I say, and then go home and lose me.
I have this day received a traitor's judgement,
And by that name must die: yet, heaven bear
    witness,
And if I have a conscience, let it sink me,
Even as the axe falls, if I be not faithful!
The law I bear no malice for my death;
'T has done, upon the premises, but justice:
But those that sought it I could wish more
    Christians:
Be what they will, I heartily forgive 'em:
Yet let 'em look they glory not in mischief,
Nor build their evils on the graves of great men;
For then my guiltless blood must cry against 'em.
For further life in this world I ne'er hope,
Nor will I sue, although the king have mercies
More than I dare make faults. You few that loved
    me,
And dare be bold to weep for Buckingham,
His noble friends and fellows, whom to leave
Is only bitter to him, only dying,

Go with me, like good angels, to my end;
And, as the long divorce of steel falls on me,
Make of your prayers one sweet sacrifice,
And lift my soul to heaven.—Lead on, o'God's
    name.

SIR THOMAS LOVELL.
I do beseech your Grace, for charity,
If ever any malice in your heart
Were hid against me, now to forgive me frankly.

DUKE OF BUCKINGHAM.
Sir Thomas Lovell, I as free forgive you
As I would be forgiven: I forgive all;
There cannot be those numberless offences
'Gainst me that I cannot take peace with: no black
    envy
Shall mark my grave.—Commend me to his
    Grace;
And, if he speak of Buckingham, pray, tell him
You met him half in heaven: my vows and
    prayers
Yet are the king's; and, till my soul forsake,
Shall cry for blessings on him: may he live
Longer than I have time to tell his years!
Ever beloved and loving may his rule be!
And when old time shall lead him to his end,
Goodness and he fill up one monument!

SIR THOMAS LOVELL.
To the water-side I must conduct your Grace;
Then give my charge up to Sir Nicholas Vaux,
Who undertakes you to your end.

SIR NICHOLAS VAUX.
            Prepare there,
The duke is coming: see the barge be ready;
And fit it with such furniture as suits
The greatness of his person.

DUKE OF BUCKINGHAM.
          Nay, Sir Nicholas,
Let it alone; my state now will but mock me.
When I came hither, I was lord high constable
And Duke of Buckingham; now, poor Edward
    Bohun:
Yet I am richer than my base accusers,
That never knew what truth meant: I now seal it;
And with that blood will make 'em one day groan
    for't.
My noble father, Henry of Buckingham,
Who first raised head against usurping Richard,
Flying for succour to his servant Banister,
Being distrest, was by that wretch betray'd,
And without trial fell; God's peace be with him!
Henry the Seventh succeeding, truly pitying
My father's loss, like a most royal prince,
Restored me to my honours, and, out of ruins,
Made my name once more noble. Now his son,
Henry the Eighth, life, honour, name, and all
That made me happy, at one stroke has taken
For ever from the world. I had my trial,
And, must needs say, a noble one; which makes
    me
A little happier than my wretched father:
Yet thus far we are one in fortunes,—both
Fell by our servants, by those men we loved most;
A most unnatural and faithless service!
Heaven has an end in all: yet, you that hear me,
This from a dying man receive as certain:—
Where you are liberal of your loves and counsels

Be sure you be not loose; for those you make
   friends
And give your hearts to, when they once perceive
The least rub in your fortunes, fall away
Like water from ye, never found again
But where they mean to sink ye. All good people,
Pray for me! I must now forsake ye: the last
   hour
Of my long weary life is come upon me.
Farewell: and when you would say something
   that is sad,
Speak how I fell.—I have done; and God forgive
   me!   [*Exeunt* BUCKINGHAM *and* TRAIN.

FIRST GENTLEMAN.
O, this is full of pity!—Sir, it calls,
I fear, too many curses on their heads
That were the authors.

SECOND GENTLEMAN.
               If the duke be guiltless,
'Tis full of woe: yet I can give you inkling
Of an ensuing evil, if it fall,
Greater than this.

FIRST GENTLEMAN.
            Good angels keep it from us!
What may it be? You do not doubt my faith, sir?

SECOND GENTLEMAN.
This secret is so weighty, 'twill require
A strong faith to conceal it.

FIRST GENTLEMAN.
              Let me have it;
I do not talk much.

SECOND GENTLEMAN.
           I am confident;
You shall, sir: did you not of late days hear
A buzzing of a separation
Between the king and Katharine?

FIRST GENTLEMAN.
           Yes, but it held not:
For when the king once heard it, out of anger
He sent command to the lord mayor straight
To stop the rumour, and allay those tongues
That durst disperse it.

SECOND GENTLEMAN.
           But that slander, sir,
Is found a truth now: for it grows again
Fresher than e'er it was; and held for certain
The king will venture at it. Either the cardinal,
Or some about him near, have, out of malice
To the good queen, possess him with a scruple
That will undo her: to confirm this too,
Cardinal Campeius is arrived, and lately;
As all think, for this business.

FIRST GENTLEMAN.
           'Tis the cardinal;
And merely to revenge him on the emperor
For not bestowing on him, at his asking,
The archbishopric of Toledo, this is purposed.

SECOND GENTLEMAN.
I think you have hit the mark: but is't not cruel
That she should feel the smart of this? The car-
   dinal
Will have his will, and she must fall.

FIRST GENTLEMAN.
           'Tis woful.
We are too open here to argue this;
Let's think in private more.   [*Exeunt.*

SCENE II.
An ante-chamber in the palace.

Enter the LORD CHAMBERLAIN, *reading this
letter.*

LORD CHAMBERLAIN.
'MY lord, the horses your lordship sent for,
with all the care I had, I saw well chosen,
ridden, and furnish't. They were young and handsome, and of the best breed in the north. When
they were ready to set out for London, a man of
my lord Cardinal's, by commission and main
power, took 'em from me; with this reason,—His
master would be served before a subject, if not
before the king; which stopt our mouths, sir.'
I fear he will indeed: well, let him have them:
He will have all, I think.

Enter to the LORD CHAMBERLAIN *the* DUKES
OF NORFOLK *and* SUFFOLK.

DUKE OF NORFOLK.
Well met, my lord chamberlain.

LORD CHAMBERLAIN.
Good day to you both, your Graces.

DUKE OF SUFFOLK.
How is the king employ'd?

LORD CHAMBERLAIN.
           I left him private,
Full of sad thoughts and troubles.

DUKE OF NORFOLK.
              What's the cause?

LORD CHAMBERLAIN.
It seems the marriage with his brother's wife
Has crept too near his conscience.

DUKE OF SUFFOLK.
            No, his conscience
Has crept too near another lady.

DUKE OF NORFOLK.
             'Tis so:
This is the cardinal's doing, the king-cardinal:
That blind priest, like the eldest son of fortune,
Turns what he list. The king will know him one
   day.

DUKE OF SUFFOLK.
Pray God he do! he'll never know himself else.

DUKE OF NORFOLK.
How holily he works in all his business!
And with what zeal! for, now he has crackt the
   league
'Tween us and the emperor, the queen's great
   nephew,
He dives into the king's soul, and there scatters
Dangers, doubts, wringing of the conscience,
Fears, and despairs,—and all these for his mar-
   riage:
And out of all these to restore the king,
He counsels a divorce; a loss of her
That, like a jewel, has hung twenty years
About his neck, yet never lost her lustre;
Of her that loves him with that excellence
That angels love good men with; even of her
That, when the greatest stroke of fortune falls,
Will bless the king: and is not this course pious?

LORD CHAMBERLAIN.
Heaven keep me from such counsel! 'Tis most true
These news are everywhere; every tongue speaks
   'em,

And every true heart weeps for't: all that dare
Look into these affairs see this main end,—
The French king's sister. Heaven will one day
          open
The king's eyes, that so long have slept upon
This bold bad man.
          DUKE OF SUFFOLK.
                    And free us from his slavery.
          DUKE OF NORFOLK.
We had need pray,
And heartily, for our deliverance;
Or this imperious man will work us all
From princes into pages: all men's honours
Lie like one lump before him, to be fashion'd
Into what pitch he please.
          DUKE OF SUFFOLK.
                    For me, my lords,
I love him not, nor fear him; there's my creed:
As I am made without him, so I'll stand,
If the king please; his curses and his blessings
Touch me alike, th'are breath I not believe in.
I knew him, and I know him; so I leave him
To him that made him proud, the Pope.
          DUKE OF NORFOLK.
                              Let's in;
And with some other business put the king
From these sad thoughts, that work too much
          upon him:—
My lord, you'll bear us company?
          LORD CHAMBERLAIN.
                              Excuse me;
The king has sent me otherwhere: besides,
You'll find a most unfit time to disturb him:
Health to your lordships!
          DUKE OF NORFOLK.
          Thanks, my good lord chamberlain.
[*Exit* LORD CHAMBERLAIN; *and the* KING
draws the curtain and sits reading pensively.
          DUKE OF SUFFOLK.
How sad he looks! sure, he is much afflicted.
          KING HENRY.
Who's there, ha?
          DUKE OF NORFOLK.
          Pray God he be not angry.
          KING HENRY.
Who's there, I say? How dare you thrust your-
          selves
Into my private meditations?
Who am I, ha?
          DUKE OF NORFOLK.
A gracious king that pardons all offences
Malice ne'er meant: our breach of duty this way
Is business of estate; in which we come
To know your royal pleasure.
          KING HENRY.
                    Ye are too bold:
Go to; I'll make ye know your times of business:
Is this an hour for temporal affairs, ha?
          Enter WOLSEY *and* CAMPEIUS, *with a
          commission.*
Who's there? my good lord Cardinal?—O my
          Wolsey,
The quiet of my wounded conscience;
Thou art a cure fit for a king.—[*to* CAMPEIUS]
          You're welcome,
Most learned reverend sir, into our kingdom:

Use us and it.—[*to* WOLSEY] My good lord, have
          great care
I be not found a talker.
          CARDINAL WOLSEY.
                    Sir, you cannot.
I would your Grace would give us but an hour
Of private conference.
          KING HENRY [*to* DUKES OF NORFOLK
                    and SUFFOLK].
                    We are busy; go.
          DUKE OF NORFOLK [*aside to* DUKE OF
                    SUFFOLK].
This priest has no pride in him!
          DUKE OF SUFFOLK [*aside to* DUKE OF
                    NORFOLK].
                              Not to speak of:
I would not be so sick though for his place:
But this cannot continue.
          DUKE OF NORFOLK [*aside to* DUKE OF
                    SUFFOLK].
                              If it do,
I'll venture one have-at-him.
          DUKE OF SUFFOLK [*aside to* DUKE OF
                    NORFOLK].
                    I another.
          [*Exeunt* NORFOLK *and* SUFFOLK.
          CARDINAL WOLSEY.
Your Grace has given a precedent of wisdom
Above all princes, in committing freely
Your scruple to the voice of Christendom:
Who can be angry now? what envy reach you?
The Spaniard, tied by blood and favour to her,
Must now confess, if they have any goodness,
The trial just and noble. All the clerks,
I mean the learned ones, in Christian kingdoms
Have their free voices: Rome, the nurse of judge-
Invited by your noble self, hath sent   [ment,
One general tongue unto us, this good man,
This just and learned priest, Cardinal Cam-
          peius,—
Whom once more I present unto your highness.
          KING HENRY.
And once more in mine arms I bid him welcome,
And thank the holy conclave for their loves:
They have sent me such a man I would have
          wisht for.

          CARDINAL CAMPEIUS.
Your Grace must needs deserve all strangers' loves,
You are so noble. To your highness' hand
I tender my commission; by whose virtue,
The court of Rome commanding, you, my lord
Cardinal of York, are join'd with me their servant
In the unpartial judging of this business.
          KING HENRY.
Two equal men. The queen shall be acquainted
Forthwith for what you come. Where's Gardiner?
          CARDINAL WOLSEY.
I know your majesty has always loved her
So dear in heart, not to deny her that
A woman of less place might ask by law,—
Scholars allow'd freely to argue for her.
          KING HENRY.
Ay, and the best she shall have; and my favour
To him that does best: God forbid else. Cardinal,
Prithee, call Gardiner to me, my new secretary:
I find him a fit fellow.   [*Exit* WOLSEY.

Enter WOLSEY, *with* GARDINER.

CARDINAL WOLSEY [*aside to* GARDINER].
Give me your hand: much joy and favour to you;
You are the king's now.

GARDINER [*aside to* CARDINAL WOLSEY].
           But to be commanded
For ever by your Grace, whose hand has raised me.

KING HENRY.
Come hither, Gardiner.   [*Walks and whispers.*

CARDINAL CAMPEIUS.
My Lord of York, was not one Doctor Pace
In this man's place before him?

CARDINAL WOLSEY.
           Yes, he was.

CARDINAL CAMPEIUS.
Was he not held a learned man?

CARDINAL WOLSEY.
           Yes, surely.

CARDINAL CAMPEIUS.
Believe me, there's an ill opinion spread, then,
Even of yourself, lord Cardinal.

CARDINAL WOLSEY.
           How! of me?

CARDINAL CAMPEIUS.
They will not stick to say you envied him;
And fearing he would rise, he was so virtuous,
Kept him a foreign man still; which so grieved
    him,
That he ran mad and died.

CARDINAL WOLSEY.
           Heaven's peace be with him!
That's Christian care enough: for living mur-
    murers
There's places of rebuke. He was a fool;
For he would needs be virtuous: that good fellow,
If I command him, follows my appointment:
I will have none so near else. Learn this, brother,
We live not to be griped by meaner persons.

KING HENRY.
Deliver this with modesty to the queen.
           [*Exit* GARDINER.
The most convenient place that I can think of
For such receipt of learning is Black-Friars;
There ye shall meet about this weighty busi-
    ness:—
My Wolsey, see it furnisht.—O, my lord
Would it not grieve an able man to leave
So sweet a bedfellow? But, conscience, con-
    science,—
O, 'tis a tender place! and I must leave her.
           [*Exeunt.*

SCENE III.

An ante-chamber in the QUEEN'S *apartments.*

Enter ANNE BULLEN *and an old* LADY.

ANNE BULLEN.
NOT for that neither: here's the pang that
    pinches:—
His highness having lived so long with her, and she
So good a lady that no tongue could ever
Pronounce dishonour of her,—by my life,
She never knew harm-doing;—O, now, after
So many courses of the sun enthroned,
Still growing in a majesty and pomp,—the which
To leave a thousand-fold more bitter than

'Tis sweet at first t'acquire,—after this process,
To give her the avaunt! it is a pity
Would move a monster.

OLD LADY.
           Hearts of most hard temper
Melt and lament for her.

ANNE BULLEN.
           O, God's will! much better
She ne'er had known pomp: though 't be temporal
Yet, if that quarrel, fortune, do divorce
It from the bearer, 'tis a sufferance panging
As soul and body's severing.

OLD LADY.
           Alas, poor lady!
She's a stranger now again.

ANNE BULLEN.
           So much the more
Must pity drop upon her. Verily,
I swear, 'tis better to be lowly born,
And range with humble livers in content,
Than to be perkt up in a glistering grief,
And wear a golden sorrow.

OLD LADY.
           Our content
Is our best having.

ANNE BULLEN.
           By my troth and maidenhead,
I would not be a queen.

OLD LADY.
           Beshrew me, I would,
And venture maidenhead for't; and so would you,
For all this spice of your hypocrisy:
You, that have so fair parts of woman on you,
Have too a woman's heart; which ever yet
Affected eminence, wealth, sovereignty;
Which, to say sooth, are blessings; and which
    gifts—
Saving your mincing—the capacity
Of your soft cheveril conscience would receive,
If you might please to stretch it.

ANNE BULLEN.
           Nay, good troth,—

OLD LADY.
Yes, troth, and troth;—you would not be a queen?

ANNE BULLEN.
No, not for all the riches under heaven.

OLD LADY.
'Tis strange; a three-pence bow'd would hire me,
Old as I am, to queen it: but, I pray you,
What think you of a duchess? have you limbs
To bear that load of title?

ANNE BULLEN.
           No, in truth.

OLD LADY.
Then you are weakly made: pluck off a little;
I would not be a young count in your way,
For more than blushing comes to: if your back
Cannot vouchsafe this burden, 'tis too weak
Ever to get a boy.

ANNE BULLEN.
           How you do talk!
I swear again, I would not be a queen
For all the world.

OLD LADY.
           In faith, for little England
You'ld venture an emballing: I myself

Would for Carnarvonshire, although there long'd
No more to the crown but that.—Lo, who comes
here?
   Enter the LORD CHAMBERLAIN.
    LORD CHAMBERLAIN.
Good morrow, ladies. What were't worth to know
The secret of your conference?
    ANNE BULLEN.
       My good lord,
Not your demand; it values not your asking:
Our mistress' sorrows we were pitying.
    LORD CHAMBERLAIN.
It was a gentle business, and becoming
The action of good women: there is hope
All will be well.
    ANNE BULLEN.
   Now, I pray God, amen!
    LORD CHAMBERLAIN.
You bear a gentle mind, and heavenly blessings
Follow such creatures. That you may, fair lady,
Perceive I speak sincerely, and high note's
Ta'en of your many virtues, the king's majesty
Commends his good opinion to you, and
Does purpose honour to you no less flowing
Than Marchioness of Pembroke; to which title
A thousand pound a year, annual support,
Out of his grace he adds.
    ANNE BULLEN.
     I do not know
What kind of my obedience I should tender;
More than my all is nothing: nor my prayers
Are not words duly hallow'd, nor my wishes
More worth than empty vanities; yet prayers and
 wishes
Are all I can return. Beseech your lordship,
Vouchsafe to speak my thanks and my obedience,
As from a blushing handmaid, to his highness;
Whose health and royalty I pray for.
    LORD CHAMBERLAIN.
        Lady,
I shall not fail t'approve the fair conceit
The king hath of you.—[*aside*] I have perused her
 well;
Beauty and honour in her are so mingled,
That they have caught the king: and who knows yet
But from this lady may proceed a gem
To lighten all the isle?—I'll to the king,
And say I spoke with you.
    ANNE BULLEN.
     My honour'd lord.
   [*Exit* LORD CHAMBERLAIN.
    OLD LADY.
Why, this it is; see, see!
I have been begging sixteen years in court,—
Am yet a courtier beggarly,—nor could
Come pat betwixt too early and too late
For any suit of pounds; and you, O fate!
A very fresh-fish here,—fie, fie, fie upon
This compell'd fortune!—have your mouth fill'd
 up
Before you open it.
    ANNE BULLEN.
   This is strange to me.
    OLD LADY.
How tastes it? is it bitter? forty pence, no.
There was a lady once—'tis an old story—

That would not be a queen, that would she not,
For all the mud in Egypt: have you heard it?
    ANNE BULLEN.
Come, you are pleasant.
    OLD LADY.
     With your theme, I could
O'ermount the lark. The Marchioness of Pem-
 broke!
A thousand pounds a year—for pure respect!
No other obligation! By my life,
That promises moe thousands: honour's train
Is longer than his foreskirt. By this time
I know your back will bear a duchess:—say,
Are you not stronger than you were?
    ANNE BULLEN.
       Good lady,
Make yourself mirth with your particular fancy,
And leave me out on't. Would I had no being,
If this salute my blood a jot: it faints me,
To think what follows.
The queen is comfortless, and we forgetful
In our long absence: pray, do not deliver
What here y'have heard to her.
    OLD LADY.
     What do you think me?
         [*Exeunt.*

SCENE IV.

A hall in Black-Friars.

Trumpets, sennet, and cornets. Enter two VERGERS,
with short silver wands; next them, two SCRIBES,
in the habit of doctors; after them, the ARCH-
BISHOP OF CANTERBURY *alone; after him, the*
BISHOPS OF LINCOLN, ELY, ROCHESTER, *and*
SAINT ASAPH; *next them, with some small distance, follows a* GENTLEMAN *bearing the purse,
with the great seal, and a cardinal's hat; then
two* PRIESTS, *bearing each a silver cross; then a*
GENTLEMAN-USHER *bare-headed, accompanied
with a* SERGEANT-AT-ARMS *bearing a silver
mace; then two* GENTLEMEN *bearing two great
silver pillars; after them, side by side, the two*
CARDINALS; *two* NOBLEMEN *with the sword
and mace. The* KING *takes place under the cloth
of state; the two* CARDINALS *sit under him as
judges. The* QUEEN *takes place some distance
from the* KING. *The* BISHOPS *place themselves
on each side the court, in manner of a consistory;
below them, the* SCRIBES. *The* LORDS *sit next
the* BISHOPS. *The rest of the* ATTENDANTS
stand in convenient order about the hall.

    CARDINAL WOLSEY.
WHILST our commission from Rome is read,
  Let silence be commanded.
    KING HENRY.
       What's the need?
It hath already publicly been read,
And on all sides the authority allow'd;
You may, then, spare that time.
    CARDINAL WOLSEY.
       Be't so.—Proceed.
    SCRIBE.
Say, Henry King of England, come into the court.
    CRIER.
King Henry of England, &c.

KING HENRY.

Here.

SCRIBE.

Say, Katharine Queen of England, come into the court.

CRIER.

Katharine Queen of England, &c.

[*The* QUEEN *makes no answer, rises out of her chair, goes about the court, comes to the* KING, *and kneels at his feet; then speaks.*

QUEEN KATHARINE.

Sir, I desire you do me right and justice;
And to bestow your pity on me: for
I am a most poor woman, and a stranger,
Born out of your dominions; having here
No judge indifferent, nor no more assurance
Of equal friendship and proceeding. Alas, sir,
In what have I offended you? what cause
Hath my behaviour given to your displeasure,
That thus you should proceed to put me off,
And take your good grace from me? Heaven witness,
I have been to you a true and humble wife,
At all times to your will conformable;
Ever in fear to kindle your dislike,
Yea, subject to your countenance,—glad or sorry,
As I saw it inclined. When was the hour
I ever contradicted your desire,
Or made it not mine too? Or which of your friends
Have I not strove to love, although I knew
He were mine enemy? what friend of mine
That had to him derived your anger, did I
Continue in my liking? nay, gave notice
He was from thence discharged? Sir, call to mind
That I have been your wife, in this obedience,
Upward of twenty years, and have been blest
With many children by you: if, in the course
And process of this time, you can report,
And prove it too, against mine honour aught,
My bond to wedlock, or my love and duty,
Against your sacred person, in God's name,
Turn me away; and let the foul'st contempt
Shut door upon me, and so give me up
To the sharp'st kind of justice. Please you, sir,
The king, your father, was reputed for
A prince most prudent, of an excellent
And unmatch't wit and judgement: Ferdinand,
My father, king of Spain, was reckon'd one
The wisest prince that there had reign'd by many
A year before: it is not to be question'd
That they had gather'd a wise council to them
Of every realm, that did debate this business,
Who deem'd our marriage lawful. Wherefore I humbly
Beseech you, sir, to spare me, till I may
Be by my friends in Spain advised; whose counsel
I will implore: if not, i' the name of God,
Your pleasure be fulfill'd!

CARDINAL WOLSEY.

You have here, lady,—
And of your choice,—these reverend fathers; men
Of singular integrity and learning,
Yea, the elect o' the land, who are assembled
To plead your cause: it shall be therefore bootless
That longer you defer the court; as well

For your own quiet, as to rectify
What is unsettled in the king.

CARDINAL CAMPEIUS.

His Grace
Hath spoken well and justly: therefore, madam,
It's fit this royal session do proceed;
And that, without delay, their arguments
Be now produced and heard.

QUEEN KATHARINE.

Lord Cardinal,—
To you I speak.

CARDINAL WOLSEY.

Your pleasure, madam?

QUEEN KATHARINE.

Sir,
I am about to weep; but, thinking that
We are a queen,—or long have dream'd so,—certain
The daughter of a king, my drops of tears
I'll turn to sparks of fire.

CARDINAL WOLSEY.

Be patient yet.

QUEEN KATHARINE.

I will, when you are humble; nay, before,
Or God will punish me. I do believe,
Induced by potent circumstances, that
You are mine enemy; and make my challenge
You shall not be my judge: for it is you
Have blown this coal betwixt my lord and me,—
Which God's dew quench! Therefore I say again,
I utterly abhor, yea, from my soul
Refuse you for my judge; whom, yet once more,
I hold my most malicious foe, and think not
At all a friend to truth.

CARDINAL WOLSEY.

I do profess
You speak not like yourself; who ever yet
Have stood to charity, and display'd the effects
Of disposition gentle, and of wisdom
O'ertopping woman's power. Madam, you do me wrong:
I have no spleen against you; nor injustice
For you or any: how far I have proceeded,
Or how far further shall, is warranted
By a commission from the consistory,
Yea, the whole consistory of Rome. You charge me
That I have blown this coal: I do deny it:
The king is present: if it be known to him
That I gainsay my deed, how may he wound,
And worthily, my falsehood! yea, as much
As you have done my truth. But if he know
That I am free of your report, he knows
I am not of your wrong. Therefore in him
It lies to cure me: and the cure is, to
Remove these thoughts from you: the which before
His highness shall speak in, I do beseech
You, gracious madam, to unthink your speaking,
And to say no more.

QUEEN KATHARINE.

My lord, my lord,
I am a simple woman, much too weak
T'oppose your cunning. Y'are meek and humble-mouth'd;
You sign your place and calling, in full seeming,
With meekness and humility: but your heart

Is cramm'd with arrogancy, spleen, and pride.
You have, by fortune, and his highness' favours,
Gone slightly o'er low steps, and now are mounted
Where powers are your retainers, and your wards
(Domestics to you); serve your will as't please
Yourself pronounce their office. I must tell you,
You tender more your person's honour than
Your high profession spiritual: that again
I do refuse you for my judge; and here,
Before you all, appeal unto the Pope,
To bring my whole cause 'fore his holiness,
And to be judged by him.

[*She curtsies to the* KING, *and offers to depart.*

CARDINAL CAMPEIUS.
                    The queen is obstinate,
Stubborn to justice, apt to accuse it, and
Disdainful to be tried by't: 'tis not well.
She's going away.

KING HENRY.
Call her again.

CRIER.
Katharine Queen of England, come into the court.

GENTLEMAN USHER.
Madam, you are call'd back.

QUEEN KATHARINE.
What need you note it? pray you, keep your way:
When you are call'd, return.—Now, the Lord
    help,
They vex me past my patience!—Pray you, pass
    on:
I will not tarry; no, nor ever more
Upon this business my appearance make
In any of their courts.

[*Exeunt* QUEEN *and her* ATTENDANTS.

KING HENRY.
                    Go thy ways, Kate:
That man i'the world who shall report he has
A better wife, let him in naught be trusted,
For speaking false in that: thou art, alone—
If thy rare qualities, sweet gentleness,
Thy meekness saint-like, wife-like government,
Obeying in commanding, and thy parts
Sovereign and pious else, could speak thee out—
The queen of earthly queens:—she's noble born;
And, like her true nobility, she has
Carried herself towards me.

CARDINAL WOLSEY.
                    Most gracious sir,
In humblest manner I require your highness,
That it shall please you to declare, in hearing
Of all these ears,—for where I am robb'd and
    bound,
There must I be unloosed; although not there
At once and fully satisfied,—whether ever I
Did broach this business to your highness; or
Laid any scruple in your way, which might
Induce you to the question on't? or ever
Have to you—but with thanks to God for such
A royal lady—spake one the least word that might
Be to the prejudice of her present state,
Or touch of her good person?

KING HENRY.
                    My lord Cardinal,
I do excuse you; yea, upon mine honour,
I free you from't. You are not to be taught
That you have many enemies, that know not

Why they are so, but, like to village-curs,
Bark when their fellows do: by some of these
The queen is put in anger. Y'are excused:
But will you be more justified? you ever
Have wisht the sleeping of this business; never
Desired it to be stirr'd; but oft have hinder'd, oft,
The passages made toward it:—on my honour,
I speak my good lord Cardinal to this point,
And thus far clear him. Now, what moved me to't,
I will be bold with time and your attention:—
Then mark the inducement. Thus it came;—give
    head to't:—
My conscience first received a tenderness,
Scruple, and prick, on certain speeches utter'd
By the Bishop of Bayonne, then French ambas-
    sador;
Who had been hither sent on the debating
A marriage 'twixt the Duke of Orleans and
Our daughter Mary: i'the progress of this business,
Ere a determinate resolution, he—
I mean the bishop—did require a respite;
Wherein he might the king his lord advertise
Whether our daughter were legitimate,
Respecting this our marriage with the dowager,
Sometimes our brother's wife. This respite shook
The bottom of my conscience, enter'd me,
Yea, with a splitting power, and made to tremble
The region of my breast; which forced such way,
That many mazed considerings did throng,
And prest in with this caution. First, methought
I stood not in the smile of heaven; who had
Commanded nature, that my lady's womb,
If it conceived a male child by me, should
Do no more offices of life to't than
The grave does to the dead; for her male issue
Or died where they were made, or shortly after
This world had air'd them: hence I took a thought,
This was a judgement on me; that my kingdom,
Well worthy the best heir o'the world, should not
Be gladded in't by me: then follows, that
I weigh'd the danger which my realms stood in
By this my issue's fail; and that gave to me
Many a groaning throe. Thus hulling in
The wild sea of my conscience, I did steer
Toward this remedy, whereupon we are
Now present here together; that's to say,
I meant to rectify my conscience—which
I then did feel full sick, and yet not well—
By all the reverend fathers of the land
And doctors learn'd. First I began in private
With you, my Lord of Lincoln; you remember
How under my oppression I did reek,
When I first moved you.

BISHOP OF LINCOLN.
                    Very well, my liege.

KING HENRY.
I have spoke long: be pleased yourself to say
How far you satisfied me.

BISHOP OF LINCOLN.
                    So please your highness,
The question did at first so stagger me,—
Bearing a state of mighty moment in't,
And consequence of dread,—that I committed
The daring'st counsel which I had to doubt;
And did entreat your highness to this course
Which you are running here.

KING HENRY.
                    I then moved you,
My Lord of Canterbury; and got your leave
To make this present summons:—unsolicited
I left no reverend person in this court;
But by particular consent proceeded
Under your hands and seals: therefore, go on;
For no dislike i'the world against the person
Of the good queen, but the sharp thorny points
Of my alleged reasons, drive this forward:
Prove but our marriage lawful, by my life
And kingly dignity, we are contented
To wear our mortal state to come with her,
Katharine our queen, before the primest creature
That's paragon'd o'the world.

CARDINAL CAMPEIUS.
               So please you highness,
The queen being absent, 'tis a needful fitness
That we adjourn this court till further day:
Meanwhile must be an earnest motion
Made to the queen, to call back her appeal
She intends unto his holiness. [*They rise to depart.*

KING HENRY [*aside*].
                   I may perceive
These cardinals trifle with me: I abhor
This dilatory sloth and tricks of Rome.
My learn'd and well-beloved servant, Cranmer,
Prithee, return: with thy approach, I know,
My comfort comes along.—Break up the court:
I say, set on.   [*Exeunt in manner as they enter'd.*

ACT III. SCENE I.

London.   The QUEEN'S *apartments.*

Enter QUEEN *and her* WOMEN *as at work.*

QUEEN KATHARINE.
TAKE thy lute, wench: my soul grows sad with
    troubles;
Sing, and disperse 'em, if thou canst: leave work-
    ing.

Song.
Orpheus with his lute made trees,
And the mountain-tops that freeze,
    Bow themselves, when he did sing:
To his music plants and flowers
Ever sprung; as sun and showers
    There had made a lasting spring.

Every thing that heard him play,
Even the billows of the sea,
    Hung their heads, and then lay by.
In sweet music is such art,
Killing care and grief of heart
    Fall asleep, or hearing, die.

Enter a GENTLEMAN.

QUEEN KATHARINE.
How now!

GENTLEMAN.
An't please your Grace, the two great cardinals
Wait in the presence.

QUEEN KATHARINE.
            Would they speak with me?

GENTLEMAN.
They will'd me say so, madam.

QUEEN KATHARINE.
               Pray their Graces
To come near. [*Exit* GENTLEMAN.] What can be
    their business
With me, a poor weak woman, faln from favour?
I do not like their coming, now I think on't.
They should be good men; their affairs as right-
    eous:
But all hoods make not monks.

Enter the two CARDINALS, WOLSEY *and*
CAMPEIUS.

CARDINAL WOLSEY.
              Peace to your highness!

QUEEN KATHARINE.
Your Graces find me here part of a housewife:
I would be all, against the worst may happen.
What are your pleasures with me, reverend lords?

CARDINAL WOLSEY.
May it please you, noble madam, to withdraw
Into your private chamber, we shall give you
The full cause of our coming.

QUEEN KATHARINE.
              Speak it here;
There's nothing I have done yet, o'my conscience,
Deserves a corner: would all other women
Could speak this with as free a soul as I do!
My lords, I care not,—so much I am happy
Above a number,—if my actions
Were tried by every tongue, every eye saw 'em,
Envy and base opinion set against 'em,
I know my life so even. If your business
Seek me out, and that way I am wise in,
Out with it boldly: truth loves open dealing.

CARDINAL WOLSEY.
*Tanta est erga te mentis integritas, regina serenis-
sima,—*

QUEEN KATHARINE.
O, good my lord, no Latin;
I am not such a truant since my coming,
As not to know the language I have lived in:
A strange tongue makes my cause more strange,
    suspicious;
Pray, speak in English: here are some will thank
    you,
If you speak truth, for their poor mistress' sake,—
Believe me, she has had much wrong: lord Cardinal,
The willing'st sin I ever yet committed
May be absolved in English.

CARDINAL WOLSEY.
              Noble lady,
I am sorry my integrity should breed—
And service to his majesty and you—
So deep suspicion, where all faith was meant.
We come not by the way of accusation,
To taint that honour every good tongue blesses,
Nor to betray you any way to sorrow,—
You have too much, good lady; but to know
How you stand minded in the weighty difference
Between the king and you; and to deliver,
Like free and honest men, our just opinions,
And comforts to your cause.

CARDINAL CAMPEIUS.
             Most honour'd madam,
My Lord of York,—out of his noble nature,
Zeal and obedience he still bore your Grace,—
Forgetting, like a good man, your late censure

Both of his truth and him, which was too far,—
Offers, as I do, in a sign of peace,
His service and his counsel.

QUEEN KATHARINE [*aside*].
　　　　　　To betray me.
My lords, I thank you both for your good wills;
Ye speak like honest men,—pray God, ye prove
　　so!—
But how to make ye suddenly an answer,
In such a point of weight, so near mine honour,—
More near my life, I fear,— with my weak wit,
And to such men of gravity and learning,
In truth, I know not. I was set at work
Among my maids; full little, God knows, looking
Either for such men or such business.
For her sake that I have been,— for I feel
The last fit of my greatness,—good your Graces,
Let me have time and counsel for my cause:
Alas, I am a woman, friendless, hopeless!

CARDINAL WOLSEY.
Madam, you wrong the king's love with these fears:
Your hopes and friends are infinite.

QUEEN KATHARINE.
　　　　　　In England
But little for my profit: can you think, lords,
That any Englishman dare give me counsel?
Or be a known friend, 'gainst his highness'
　　pleasure,—
Though he be grown so desperate to be honest,—
And live a subject? Nay, forsooth, my friends,
They that must weigh out my afflictions,
They that my trust must grow to, live not here:
They are, as all my other comforts are, far hence,
In mine own country, lords.

CARDINAL CAMPEIUS.
　　　　　　I would your Grace
Would leave your griefs, and take my counsel.

QUEEN KATHARINE.
　　　　　　How, sir?

CARDINAL CAMPEIUS.
Put your main cause into the king's protection;
He's loving and most gracious: 'twill be much
Both for your honour better and your cause;
For if the trial of the law o'ertake ye,
You'll part away disgraced.

CARDINAL WOLSEY.
　　　　　　He tells you rightly.

QUEEN KATHARINE.
Ye tell me what ye wish for both, my ruin:
Is this your Christian counsel? out upon ye!
Heaven is above all yet; there sits a Judge
That no king can corrupt.

CARDINAL CAMPEIUS.
　　　　　　Your rage mistakes us.

QUEEN KATHARINE.
The more shame for ye: holy men I thought ye,
Upon my soul, two reverend cardinal virtues;
But cardinal sins and hollow hearts I fear ye;
Mend 'em, for shame, my lords. Is this your com-
　　fort?
The cordial that ye bring a wretched lady,—
A woman lost among ye, laugh'd at, scorn'd?
I will not wish ye half my miseries;
I have more charity: but say, I warn'd ye;
Take heed, for heaven's sake, take heed, lest at once
The burden of my sorrows fall upon ye.

CARDINAL WOLSEY.
Madam, this is a mere distraction;
You turn the good we offer into envy.

QUEEN KATHARINE.
Ye turn me into nothing: woe upon ye,
And all such false professors! Would you have
　　me—
If you have any justice, any pity,
If ye be any thing but churchmen's habits—
Put my sick cause into his hands that hates me?
Alas, has banisht me his bed already,—
His love, too long ago! I am old, my lords,
And all the fellowship I hold now with him
Is only my obedience. What can happen
To me above this wretchedness? all your studies
Make me a curse like this.

CARDINAL CAMPEIUS.
　　　　　　Your fears are worse.

QUEEN KATHARINE.
Have I lived thus long—let me speak myself,
Since virtue finds no friends—a wife, a true one?
A woman—I dare say, without vain-glory—
Never yet branded with suspicion?
Have I with all my full affections
Still met the king? loved him next heaven? obey'd
　　him?
Been, out of fondness, superstitious to him?
Almost forgot my prayers to content him?
And am I thus rewarded? 'tis not well, lords.
Bring me a constant woman to her husband,
One that ne'er dream'd a joy beyond his pleasure;
And to that woman, when she has done most,
Yet will I add an honour,—a great patience.

CARDINAL WOLSEY.
Madam, you wander from the good we aim at.

QUEEN KATHARINE.
My lord, I dare not make myself so guilty,
To give up willingly that noble title
Your master wed me to: nothing but death
Shall e'er divorce my dignities.

CARDINAL WOLSEY.
　　　　　　Pray, hear me.

QUEEN KATHARINE.
Would I had never trod this English earth,
Or felt the flatteries that grow upon it!
Ye have angels' faces, but heaven knows your
　　hearts.
What will become of me now, wretched lady!
I am the most unhappy woman living.—
[*to her* WOMEN] Alas, poor wenches, where are
　　now your fortunes!
Shipwrackt upon a kingdom, where no pity,
No friends, no hope; no kindred weep for me;
Almost no grave allow'd me:—like the lily,
That once was mistress of the field and flourish,
I'll hang my head and perish.

CARDINAL WOLSEY.
　　　　　　If your Grace
Could but be brought to know our ends are honest,
You'ld feel more comfort. Why should we, good
　　lady,
Upon what cause, wrong you? alas, our places,
The way of our profession is against it:
We are to cure such sorrows, not to sow 'em.
For goodness' sake, consider what you do;
How you may hurt yourself, ay, utterly

Grow from the king's acquaintance, by this car-
riage.
The hearts of princes kiss obedience,
So much they love it; but to stubborn spirits
They swell, and grow as terrible as storms.
I know you have a gentle, noble temper,
A soul as even as a calm: pray, think us
Those we profess, peace-makers, friends, and
servants.

CARDINAL CAMPEIUS.

Madam, you'll find it so. You wrong your virtues
With these weak women's fears: a noble spirit,
As yours was put into you, ever casts
Such doubts, as false coin, from it. The king
loves you;
Beware you lose it not: for us, if please you
To trust us in your business, we are ready
To use our utmost studies in your service.

QUEEN KATHARINE.

Do what ye will, my lords: and, pray, forgive me,
If I have used myself unmannerly;
You know I am a woman, lacking wit
To make a seemly answer to such persons.
Pray, do my service to his majesty:
He has my heart yet; and shall have my prayers
While I shall have my life. Come, reverend fathers,
Bestow your counsels on me: she now begs,
That little thought, when she set footing here,
She should have bought her dignities so dear.

[*Exeunt.*

SCENE II.

Ante-chamber to the KING'S *apartment.*

Enter the DUKE OF NORFOLK, *the* DUKE OF
SUFFOLK, *the* EARL OF SURREY, *and the*
LORD CHAMBERLAIN.

DUKE OF NORFOLK.

IF you will now unite in your complaints,
And force them with a constancy, the cardinal
Cannot stand under them: if you omit
The offer of this time, I cannot promise
But that you shall sustain more new disgraces,
With these you bear already.

EARL OF SURREY.

I am joyful
To meet the least occasion that may give me
Remembrance of my father-in-law, the duke,
To be revenged on him.

DUKE OF SUFFOLK.

Which of the peers
Have uncontemn'd gone by him, or at least
Strangely neglected? when did he regard
The stamp of nobleness in any person
Out of himself?

LORD CHAMBERLAIN.

My lords, you speak your pleasures:
What he deserves of you and me I know;
What we can do to him,—though now the time
Gives way to us,—I much fear. If you cannot
Bar his access to the king, never attempt
Any thing on him; for he hath a witchcraft
Over the king in's tongue.

DUKE OF NORFOLK.

O, fear him not;
His spell in that is out: the king hath found

Matter against him that for ever mars
The honey of his language. No, he's settled,
Not to come off, in his displeasure.

EARL OF SURREY.

Sir,
I should be glad to hear such news as this
Once every hour.

DUKE OF NORFOLK.

Believe it, this is true:
In the divorce his contrary proceedings
Are all unfolded; wherein he appears
As I would wish mine enemy.

EARL OF SURREY.

How came
His practices to light?

DUKE OF SUFFOLK.

Most strangely.

EARL OF SURREY.

O, how, how?

DUKE OF SUFFOLK.

The cardinal's letters to the Pope miscarried,
And came to the eye o'the king: wherein was
read,
How that the cardinal did entreat his holiness
To stay the judgement o'the divorce; for if
It did take place, 'I do,' quoth he, 'perceive
My king is tangled in affection to
A creature of the queen's, Lady Anne Bullen.'

EARL OF SURREY.

Has the king this?

DUKE OF SUFFOLK.

Believe it.

EARL OF SURREY.

Will this work?

LORD CHAMBERLAIN.

The king in this perceives him, how he coasts
And hedges his own way. But in this point
All his tricks founder, and he brings his physic
After his patient's death: the king already
Hath married the fair lady.

EARL OF SURREY.

Would he had!

DUKE OF SUFFOLK.

May you be happy in your wish, my lord!
For, I profess, you have it.

EARL OF SURREY.

Now, all my joy
Trace the conjunction!

DUKE OF SUFFOLK.

My amen to't!

DUKE OF NORFOLK.

All men's!

DUKE OF SUFFOLK.

There's order given for her coronation:
Marry, this is yet but young, and may be left
To some ears unrecounted.—But, my lords,
She is a gallant creature, and complete
In mind and feature: I persuade me, from her
Will fall some blessing to this land, which shall
In it be memorized.

EARL OF SURREY.

But, will the king
Digest this letter of the cardinal's?
The Lord forbid!

DUKE OF NORFOLK.

Marry, amen!

DUKE OF SUFFOLK.
No, no;
There be more wasps that buzz about his nose
Will make this sting the sooner. Cardinal Campeius
Is stoln away to Rome; hath ta'en no leave;
Has left the cause o'the king unhandled; and
Is posted, as the agent of our cardinal,
To second all his plot. I do assure you
The king cried 'Ha!' at this.
LORD CHAMBERLAIN.
Now, God incense him,
And let him cry 'Ha!' louder!
DUKE OF NORFOLK.
But, my lord,
When returns Cranmer?
DUKE OF SUFFOLK.
He is return'd in his opinions; which
Have satisfied the king for his divorce,
Together with all famous colleges
Almost in Christendom: shortly, I believe,
His second marriage shall be publisht, and
Her coronation. Katharine no more
Shall be call'd queen, but princess dowager
And widow to Prince Arthur.
DUKE OF NORFOLK.
This same Cranmer's
A worthy fellow, and hath ta'en much pain
In the king's business.
DUKE OF SUFFOLK.
He has; and we shall see him
For it an archbishop.
DUKE OF NORFOLK.
So I hear.
DUKE OF SUFFOLK.
'Tis so.—
The cardinal!
Enter WOLSEY and CROMWELL.
DUKE OF NORFOLK.
Observe, observe, he's moody.
CARDINAL WOLSEY.
The packet, Cromwell,
Gave't you the king?
CROMWELL.
To his own hand, in's bedchamber.
CARDINAL WOLSEY.
Lookt he o'the inside of the papers?
CROMWELL.
Presently
He did unseal them: and the first he view'd,
He did it with a serious mind; a heed
Was in his countenance. You he bade
Attend him here this morning.
CARDINAL WOLSEY.
Is he ready
To come abroad?
CROMWELL.
I think, by this he is.
CARDINAL WOLSEY.
Leave me awhile. [Exit CROMWELL.
It shall be to the Duchess of Alençon,
The French king's sister: he shall marry her.—
Anne Bullen! No; I'll no Anne Bullens for him:
There's more in't than fair visage.—Bullen!
No, we'll no Bullens.—Speedily I wish [broke!
To hear from Rome.—The Marchioness of Pem-

DUKE OF NORFOLK.
He's discontented.
DUKE OF SUFFOLK.
May be, he hears the king
Does whet his anger to him.
EARL OF SURREY.
Sharp enough,
Lord, for thy justice!
CARDINAL WOLSEY.
The late queen's gentlewoman, a knight's
daughter,
To be her mistress' mistress! the queen's queen!—
This candle burns not clear: 'tis I must snuff it;
Then out it goes.—What though I know her virtuous
And well deserving? yet I know her for
A spleeny Lutheran; and not wholesome to
Our cause, that she should lie i'the bosom of
Our hard-ruled king. Again there is sprung up
An heretic, an arch one, Cranmer; one
Hath crawl'd into the favour of the king,
And is his oracle.
DUKE OF NORFOLK.
He's vext at something.
EARL OF SURREY.
I would 'twere something that would fret the
string,
The master-cord on's heart!
DUKE OF SUFFOLK.
The king, the king!
Enter KING, reading of a schedule, and LOVELL.
KING HENRY.
What piles of wealth hath he accumulated
To his own portion! and what expense by the
hour
Seems to flow from him! How, i'the name of
thrift,
Does he rake this together?—Now, my lords,—
Saw you the cardinal?
DUKE OF NORFOLK.
My lord, we have
Stood here observing him: some strange commotion
Is in his brain: he bites his lip, and starts;
Stops on a sudden, looks upon the ground,
Then lays his finger on his temple; straight
Springs out into fast gait; then stops again,
Strikes his breast hard; and anon he casts
His eye against the moon: in most strange postures
We have seen him set himself.
KING HENRY.
It may well be;
There is a mutiny in's mind. This morning
Papers of state he sent me to peruse,
As I required: and wot you what I found
There,—on my conscience, put unwittingly?
Forsooth, an inventory, thus importing,—
The several parcels of his plate, his treasure,
Rich stuffs, and ornaments of household; which
I find at such proud rate, that it out-speaks
Possession of a subject.
DUKE OF NORFOLK.
It's heaven's will:
Some spirit put this paper in the packet,
To bless your eye withal.

KING HENRY.
                    If we did think
His contemplation were above the earth,
And fixt on spiritual objects, he should still
Dwell in his musings: but I am afraid
His thinkings are below the moon, not worth
His serious considering.
          [KING *takes his seat; whispers* LOVELL,
            who goes to the CARDINAL.
          CARDINAL WOLSEY.
                    Heaven forgive me!—
Ever God bless your highness!
          KING HENRY.
                    Good my lord,
You are full of heavenly stuff, and bear the in-
     ventory
Of your best graces in your mind; the which
You were now running o'er: you have scarce time
To steal from spiritual leisure a brief span
To keep your earthly audit: sure, in that
I deem you an ill husband, and am glad
To have you therein my companion.
          CARDINAL WOLSEY.
                    Sir,
For holy offices I have a time; a time
To think upon the part of business which
I bear i'the state; and nature does require
Her times of preservation, which perforce
I, her frail son, amongst my brethren mortal,
Must give my tendance to.
          KING HENRY.
                    You have said well.
          CARDINAL WOLSEY.
And ever may your highness yoke together,
As I will lend you cause, my doing well
With my well saying!
          KING HENRY.
                    'Tis well said again;
And 'tis a kind of good deed to say well:
And yet words are no deeds. My father loved you:
He said he did; and with his deed did crown
His word upon you. Since I had my office,
I have kept you next my heart; have not alone
Employ'd you where high profits might come
     home,
But pared my present havings, to bestow
My bounties upon you.
          CARDINAL WOLSEY [*aside*].
                    What should this mean?
          EARL OF SURREY [*aside*].
The Lord increase this business!
          KING HENRY.
                    Have I not made you
The prime man of the state? I pray you, tell me,
If what I now pronounce you have found true:
And, if you may confess it, say withal,
If you are bound to us or no. What say you?
          CARDINAL WOLSEY.
My sovereign, I confess your royal graces,
Shower'd on me daily, have been more than could
My studied purposes requite; which went
Beyond all man's endeavours:—my endeavours
Have ever come too short of my desires,
Yet filed with my abilities: mine own ends
Have been mine so, that evermore they pointed
To the good of your most sacred person and

The profit of the state. For your great graces
Heapt upon me, poor undeserver, I
Can nothing render but allegiant thanks;
My prayers to heaven for you; my loyalty,
Which ever has and ever shall be growing,
Till death, that winter, kill it.
          KING HENRY.
                    Fairly answer'd;
A loyal and obedient subject is
Therein illustrated: the honour of it
Does pay the act of it; as, i'the contrary,
The foulness is the punishment. I presume
That, as my hand has open'd bounty to you,
My heart dropt love, my power rain'd honour,
     more
On you than any; so your hand and heart,
Your brain, and every function of your power,
Should, notwithstanding that your bond of duty,
As 'twere in love's particular, be more
To me, your friend, than any.
          CARDINAL WOLSEY.
                    I do profess
That for your highness' good I ever labour'd
More than mine own; that am, have, and will be,—
Though all the world should crack their duty to
     you,
And throw it from their soul; though perils did
Abound, as thick as thought could make 'em, and
Appear in forms more horrid,—yet my duty,
As doth a rock against the chiding flood,
Should the approach of this wild river break,
And stand unshaken yours.
          KING HENRY.
                    'Tis nobly spoken.—
Take notice, lords, he has a loyal breast,
For you have seen him open't.—Read o'er this;
          [*Giving him papers.*
And after, this: and then to breakfast with
What appetite you have.
          [*Exit* KING, *frowning upon* WOLSEY: *the*
            NOBLES *throng after him, smiling and*
            whispering.
          CARDINAL WOLSEY.
                    What should this mean?
What sudden anger's this? how have I reapt it?
He parted frowning from me, as if ruin
Leapt from his eyes: so looks the chafed lion
Upon the daring huntsman that has gall'd him;
Then makes him nothing. I must read this paper;
I fear, the story of his anger.—'Tis so;
This paper has undone me:—'tis the account
Of all that world of wealth I have drawn together
For mine own ends; indeed, to gain the Popedom,
And fee my friends in Rome. O negligence,
Fit for a fool to fall by! what cross devil
Made me put this main secret in the packet
I sent the king?—Is there no way to cure this?
No new device to beat this from his brains?
I know 'twill stir him strongly; yet I know
A way, if it take right, in spite of fortune,
Will bring me off again.—What's this?—'To the
     Pope'!
The letter, as I live, with all the business
I writ to's holiness. Nay, then, farewell!
I have toucht the highest point of all my great-
     ness;

And, from that full meridian of my glory,
I haste now to my setting: I shall fall
Like a bright exhalation in the evening,
And no man see me more.

Enter to WOLSEY *the* DUKES OF NORFOLK *and*
SUFFOLK, *the* EARL OF SURREY, *and the* LORD
CHAMBERLAIN.

DUKE OF NORFOLK.
Hear the king's pleasure, Cardinal; who com-
   mands you
To render up the great seal presently
Into our hands; and to confine yourself
To Asher-house, my Lord of Winchester's,
Till you hear further from his highness.

CARDINAL WOLSEY.
                      Stay,—
Where's your commission, lords? words cannot
   carry
Authority so weighty.

DUKE OF SUFFOLK.
               Who dare cross 'em,
Bearing the king's will from his mouth expressly?

CARDINAL WOLSEY.
Till I find more than will or words to do it,—
I mean your malice,—know, officious lords,
I dare and must deny it. Now I feel
Of what coarse metal ye are moulded,—envy:
How eagerly ye follow my disgraces,
As if it fed ye! and how sleek and wanton
Ye appear in every thing may bring my ruin!
Follow your envious courses, men of malice;
You have Christian warrant for 'em, and, no
   doubt,
In time will find their fit rewards. That seal,
You ask with such a violence, the king—
Mine and your master—with his own hand gave
   me;
Bade me enjoy it, with the place and honours,
During my life; and, to confirm his goodness,
Tied it by letters-patents:—now, who'll take it?

EARL OF SURREY.
The king, that gave it.

CARDINAL WOLSEY.
             It must be himself, then.

EARL OF SURREY.
Thou art a proud traitor, priest.

CARDINAL WOLSEY.
            Proud lord, thou liest:
Within these forty hours Surrey durst better
Have burnt that tongue than said so.

EARL OF SURREY.
                  Thy ambition,
Thou scarlet sin, robb'd this bewailing land
Of noble Buckingham, my father-in-law:
The heads of all thy brother cardinals—
With thee and all thy best parts bound together—
Weigh'd not a hair of his. Plague of your policy!
You sent me deputy for Ireland;
Far from his succour, from the king, from all
That might have mercy on the fault thou gavest
   him;
Whilst your great goodness, out of holy pity,
Absolved him with an axe.

CARDINAL WOLSEY.
           This, and all else
This talking lord can lay upon my credit,

I answer is most false. The duke by law
Found his deserts: how innocent I was
From any private malice in his end,
His noble jury and foul cause can witness.
If I loved many words, lord, I should tell you
You have as little honesty as honour;
That I in the way of loyalty and truth
Toward the king, my ever royal master,
Dare mate a sounder man than Surrey can be,
And all that love his follies.

EARL OF SURREY.
              By my soul,
Your long coat, priest, protects you; thou shouldst
   feel
My sword i'the life-blood of thee else.—My lords,
Can ye endure to hear this arrogance?
And from this fellow? If we live thus tamely,
To be thus jaded by a piece of scarlet,
Farewell nobility; let his Grace go forward,
And dare us with his cap like larks.

CARDINAL WOLSEY.
               All goodness
Is poison to thy stomach.

EARL OF SURREY.
            Yes, that goodness
Of gleaning all the land's wealth into one,
Into your own hands, Cardinal, by extortion;
The goodness of your intercepted packets
You writ to the Pope against the king: your good-
   ness,
Since you provoke me, shall be most notorious.—
My Lord of Norfolk,—as you are truly noble,
As you respect the common good, the state
Of our despised nobility, our issues,
Whom, if he live, will scarce be gentlemen,—
Produce the grand sum of his sins, the articles
Collected from his life:—I'll startle you
Worse than the sacring bell, when the brown
   wench
Lay kissing in your arms, lord Cardinal.

CARDINAL WOLSEY.
How much, methinks, I could despise this man,
But that I'm bound in charity against it!

DUKE OF NORFOLK.
Those articles, my lord, are in the king's hand:
But, thus much, they are foul ones.

CARDINAL WOLSEY.
            So much fairer
And spotless shall mine innocence arise,
When the king knows my truth.

EARL OF SURREY.
          This cannot save you:
I thank my memory, I yet remember
Some of these articles; and out they shall.
Now, if you can blush, and cry guilty, Cardinal,
You'll show a little honesty.

CARDINAL WOLSEY.
            Speak on, sir;
I dare your worst objections: if I blush,
It is to see a nobleman want manners.

EARL OF SURREY.
I had rather want those than my head.—Have at
   you.
First, that, without the king's assent or knowledge
You wrought to be a legate; by which power
You maim'd the jurisdiction of all bishops.

DUKE OF NORFOLK.
Then, that in all you writ to Rome, or else
To foreign princes, *Ego et Rex meus*
Was still inscribed; in which you brought the king
To be your servant.

DUKE OF SUFFOLK.
Then, that, without the knowledge
Either of king or council, when you went
Ambassador to the emperor, you made bold
To carry into Flanders the great seal.

EARL OF SURREY.
Item, you sent a large commission
To Gregory de Cassalis, to conclude,
Without the king's will or the state's allowance,
A league between his highness and Ferrara.

DUKE OF SUFFOLK.
That, out of mere ambition, you have caused
Your holy hat to be stampt on the king's coin.

EARL OF SURREY.
Then, that you have sent innumerable sub-
    stance—
By what means got, I leave to your own con-
    science—
To furnish Rome, and to prepare the ways
You have for dignities; to the mere undoing
Of all the kingdom. Many more there are;
Which, since they are of you, and odious,
I will not taint my mouth with.

LORD CHAMBERLAIN.
O my lord,
Press not a falling man too far! 'tis virtue:
His faults lie open to the laws; let them,
Not you, correct him. My heart weeps to see him
So little of his great self.

EARL OF SURREY.
I forgive him.

DUKE OF SUFFOLK.
Lord Cardinal, the king's further pleasure is,—
Because all those things you have done of late,
By your power legatine, within this kingdom,
Fall into the compass of a *præmunire*,—
That therefore such a writ be sued against you;
To forfeit all your goods, lands, tenements,
Chattels, and whatsoever, and to be
Out of the king's protection:—this is my charge.

DUKE OF NORFOLK.
And so we'll leave you to your meditations
How to live better. For your stubborn answer
About the giving back the great seal to us,
The king shall know it, and, no doubt, shall thank
    you.
So fare you well, my little good lord Cardinal.
    [*Exeunt all but* WOLSEY.

CARDINAL WOLSEY.
So farewell to the little good you bear me.
Farewell, a long farewell, to all my greatness!
This is the state of man: to-day he puts forth
The tender leaves of hope; to-morrow blossoms,
And bears his blushing honours thick upon him;
The third day comes a frost, a killing frost,
And—when he thinks, good easy man, full surely
His greatness is a-ripening—nips his root,
And then he falls, as I do. I have ventured,
Like little wanton boys that swim on bladders,
This many summers in a sea of glory;
But far beyond my depth: my high-blown pride

At length broke under me; and now has left me,
Weary and old with service, to the mercy
Of a rude stream, that must for ever hide me.
Vain pomp and glory of this world, I hate ye:
I feel my heart new open'd. O, how wretched
Is that poor man that hangs on princes' favours!
There is, betwixt that smile we would aspire to,
That sweet aspect of princes, and their ruin,
More pangs and fears than wars or women have;
And when he falls, he falls like Lucifer,
Never to hope again.
    Enter CROMWELL, *standing amazed.*
Why, how now, Cromwell!

CROMWELL.
I have no power to speak, sir.

CARDINAL WOLSEY.
What, amazed
At my misfortunes? can thy spirit wonder
A great man should decline? Nay, an you weep,
I am faln indeed.

CROMWELL.
How does your Grace?

CARDINAL WOLSEY.
Why, well;
Never so truly happy, my good Cromwell.
I know myself now; and I feel within me
A peace above all earthly dignities,
A still and quiet conscience. The king has cured
    me,
I humbly thank his Grace; and from these shoul-
    ders,
These ruin'd pillars, out of pity, taken
A load would sink a navy,—too much honour:
O, 'tis a burden, Cromwell, 'tis a burden
Too heavy for a man that hopes for heaven!

CROMWELL.
I am glad your Grace has made that right use of it.

CARDINAL WOLSEY.
I hope I have: I am able now, methinks—
Out of a fortitude of soul I feel—
To endure more miseries and greater far
Than my weak-hearted enemies dare offer.—
What news abroad?

CROMWELL.
The heaviest and the worst
Is your displeasure with the king.

CARDINAL WOLSEY.
God bless him!

CROMWELL.
The next is, that Sir Thomas More is chosen
Lord Chancellor in your place.

CARDINAL WOLSEY.
That's somewhat sudden:
But he's a learned man. May he continue
Long in his highness' favour, and do justice
For truth's sake and his conscience; that his
    bones,
When he has run his course and sleeps in bless-
    ings,
May have a tomb of orphans' tears wept on 'em!—
What more?

CROMWELL.
That Cranmer is return'd with welcome,
Install'd lord archbishop of Canterbury.

CARDINAL WOLSEY.
That's news indeed.

CROMWELL.
            Last, that the Lady Anne,
Whom the king hath in secrecy long married,
This day was view'd in open as his queen,
Going to chapel; and the voice is now
Only about her coronation.

CARDINAL WOLSEY.
There was the weight that pull'd me down. O
    Cromwell,
The king has gone beyond me: all my glories
In that one woman I have lost for ever:
No sun shall ever usher forth mine honours,
Or gild again the noble troops that waited
Upon my smiles. Go, get thee from me, Crom-
    well;
I am a poor faln man, unworthy now
To be thy lord and master: seek the king;
That sun, I pray, may never set! I have told him
What and how true thou art: he will advance thee;
Some little memory of me will stir him—
I know his noble nature—not to let
Thy hopeful service perish too: good Cromwell,
Neglect him not; make use now, and provide
For thine own future safety.

CROMWELL.
           O my lord,
Must I, then, leave you? must I needs forgo
So good, so noble, and so true a master?
Bear witness, all that have not hearts of iron,
With what a sorrow Cromwell leaves his lord.
The king shall have my service; but my prayers
For ever and for ever shall be yours.

CARDINAL WOLSEY.
Cromwell, I did not think to shed a tear
In all my miseries; but thou hast forced me,
Out of thy honest truth, to play the woman.
Let's dry our eyes: and thus far hear me, Crom-
    well;
And—when I am forgotten, as I shall be,
And sleep in dull cold marble, where no mention
Of me more must be heard of—say, I taught thee,
Say, Wolsey—that once trod the ways of glory,
And sounded all the depths and shoals of honour—
Found thee a way, out of his wrack, to rise in;
A sure and safe one, though thy master mist it.
Mark but my fall, and that that ruin'd me.
Cromwell, I charge thee, fling away ambition:
By that sin fell the angels; how can man, then,
The image of his Maker, hope to win by it?
Love thyself last; cherish those hearts that hate
    thee;
Corruption wins not more than honesty,
Still in thy right hand carry gentle peace,
To silence envious tongues. Be just, and fear not:
Let all the ends thou aim'st at be thy country's,
Thy God's, and truth's: then if thou fall'st, O
    Cromwell,
Thou fall'st a blessed martyr! Serve the king;
And,—prithee, lead me in:
There take an inventory of all I have,
To the last penny; 'tis the king's: my robe,
And my integrity to heaven, is all
I dare now call mine own. O Cromwell, Cromwell!
Had I but served my God with half the zeal
I served my king, He would not in mine age
Have left me naked to mine enemies.

CROMWELL.
Good sir, have patience.

CARDINAL WOLSEY.
         So I have. Farewell
The hopes of court! my hopes in heaven do dwell.
                          [*Exeunt.*

ACT IV. SCENE I.

A street in Westminster.

Enter two GENTLEMEN, *meeting one another.*

FIRST GENTLEMAN.
Y'ARE well met once again.

SECOND GENTLEMAN.
So are you.

FIRST GENTLEMAN.
You come to take your stand here, and behold
The Lady Anne pass from her coronation?

SECOND GENTLEMAN.
'Tis all my business. At our last encounter
The Duke of Buckingham came from his trial.

FIRST GENTLEMAN.
'Tis very true: but that time offer'd sorrow;
This, general joy.

SECOND GENTLEMAN.
        'Tis well: the citizens,
I am sure, have shown at full their royal minds—
As, let 'em have their rights, they are ever for-
    ward—
In celebration of this day with shows,
Pageants, and sights of honour.

FIRST GENTLEMAN.
              Never greater,
Nor, I'll assure you, better taken, sir.

SECOND GENTLEMAN.
May I be bold to ask what that contains,
That paper in your hand?

FIRST GENTLEMAN.
           Yes; 'tis the list
Of those that claim their offices this day
By custom of the coronation.
The Duke of Suffolk is the first, and claims
To be high-steward; next, the Duke of Norfolk,
He to be earl marshal: you may read the rest.

SECOND GENTLEMAN.
I thank you, sir: had I not known those customs,
I should have been beholding to your paper.
But, I beseech you, what's become of Katharine,
The princess dowager? how goes her business?

FIRST GENTLEMAN.
That I can tell you too. The archbishop
Of Canterbury, accompanied with other
Learned and reverend fathers of his order,
Held a late court at Dunstable, six miles off
From Ampthill, where the princess lay; to which
She was often cited by them, but appear'd not:
And, to be short, for not appearance and
The king's late scruple, by the main assent
Of all these learned men she was divorced,
And the late marriage made of none effect:
Since which she was removed to Kimbolton,
Where she remains now sick.

SECOND GENTLEMAN.
       Alas, good lady!— [*Trumpets.*
The trumpets sound: stand close, the queen is
    coming.

THE ORDER OF THE CORONATION.

A lively flourish of trumpets.   Then enter,

1. *Two* JUDGES.
2. LORD CHANCELLOR, *with the purse and mace before him.*
3. CHORISTERS, *singing.*   [*Music.*
4. MAYOR OF LONDON, *bearing the mace. Then* GARTER, *in his coat of arms, and on his head he wore a gilt copper crown.*
5. MARQUESS DORSET, *bearing a sceptre of gold, on his head a demi-coronal of gold. With him, the* EARL OF SURREY, *bearing the rod of silver with the dove, crown'd with an earl's coronet. Collars of SS.*
6. DUKE OF SUFFOLK, *in his robe of estate, his coronet on his head, bearing a long white wand, as high-steward. With him, the* DUKE OF NORFOLK, *with the rod of marshalship, a coronet on his head. Collars of SS.*
7. *A canopy borne by four of the* CINQUE-PORTS; *under it, the* QUEEN *in her robe, in her hair richly adorn'd with pearl, crown'd. On each side of her, the* BISHOPS OF LONDON *and* WINCHESTER.
8. *The old* DUCHESS OF NORFOLK, *in a coronal of gold, wrought with flowers, bearing the* QUEEN'S *train.*
9. *Certain* LADIES *or* COUNTESSES, *with plain circlets of gold without flowers.*
          [*Exeunt, first passing over the stage in order and state; and then a great flourish of trumpets.*

A royal train, believe me.—These I know:—
Who's that that bears the sceptre?

          FIRST GENTLEMAN.
                    Marquess Dorset:
And that the Earl of Surrey, with the rod.

          SECOND GENTLEMAN.
A bold brave gentleman.—That should be
The Duke of Suffolk?

          FIRST GENTLEMAN.
                    'Tis the same,—high-steward.

          SECOND GENTLEMAN.
And that my Lord of Norfolk?

          FIRST GENTLEMAN.
                              Yes.

SECOND GENTLEMAN [*looking on the* QUEEN].
                    Heaven bless thee!
Thou hast the sweetest face I ever lookt on.—
Sir, as I have a soul, she is an angel;
Our king has all the Indies in his arms,
And more and richer, when he strains that lady:
I cannot blame his conscience.

          FIRST GENTLEMAN.
                    They that bear
The cloth of honour over her are four barons
Of the Cinque-ports.

          SECOND GENTLEMAN.
Those men are happy; and so are all are near
     her.
I take it, she that carries up the train
Is that old noble lady, Duchess of Norfolk.

          FIRST GENTLEMAN.
It is; and all the rest are countesses.

          SECOND GENTLEMAN.
Their coronets say so. These are stars indeed;
And sometimes falling ones.

          FIRST GENTLEMAN.
                    No more of that.
          Enter a third GENTLEMAN.
God save you, sir! where have you been broiling?

          THIRD GENTLEMAN.
Among the crowd i'the abbey; where a finger
Could not be wedged in more : I am stifled
With the mere rankness of their joy.

          SECOND GENTLEMAN.
                              You saw
The ceremony?

          THIRD GENTLEMAN.
                    That I did.

          FIRST GENTLEMAN.
                    How was it?

          THIRD GENTLEMAN.
Well worth the seeing.

          SECOND GENTLEMAN.
                    Good sir, speak it to us.

          THIRD GENTLEMAN.
As well as I am able. The rich stream
Of lords and ladies, having brought the queen
To a prepared place in the choir, fell off
A distance from her; while her Grace sat down
To rest awhile, some half an hour or so,
In a rich chair of state, opposing freely
The beauty of her person to the people.
Believe me, sir, she is the goodliest woman
That ever lay by man: which when the people
Had the full view of, such a noise arose
As the shrouds make at sea in a stiff tempest,
As loud, and to as many tunes: hats, cloaks,—
Doublets, I think,—flew up; and had their faces
Been loose, this day they had been lost. Such joy
I never saw before. Great-bellied women,
That had not half a week to go, like rams
In the old time of war, would shake the press,
And make 'em reel before 'em. No man living
Could say, 'This is my wife,' there; all were
     woven
So strangely in one piece.

          SECOND GENTLEMAN.
                    But what follow'd?

          THIRD GENTLEMAN.
At length her Grace rose, and with modest paces
Came to the altar; where she kneel'd, and, saint-
     like,
Cast her fair eyes to heaven, and pray'd devoutly:
Then rose again, and bow'd her to the people:
When by the archbishop of Canterbury
She had all the royal makings of a queen;
As holy oil, Edward Confessor's crown,
The rod, and bird of peace, and all such emblems
Laid nobly on her: which perform'd, the choir,
With all the choicest music of the kingdom,
Together sung *Te Deum.* So she parted,
And with the same full state paced back again
To York-place, where the feast is held.

          FIRST GENTLEMAN.
                              Sir,
You must no more call it York-place, that's past;
For, since the cardinal fell, that title's lost:
'Tis now the king's, and call'd Whitehall.

THIRD GENTLEMAN.
                       I know it;
But 'tis so lately alter'd, that the old name
Is fresh about me.

SECOND GENTLEMAN.
           What two reverend bishops
Were those that went on each side of the queen?

THIRD GENTLEMAN.
Stokesly and Gardiner; the one of Winchester,
Newly preferr'd from the king's secretary;
The other, London.

SECOND GENTLEMAN.
              He of Winchester
Is held no great good lover of the archbishop's,
The virtuous Cranmer.

THIRD GENTLEMAN.
                 All the land knows that:
However, yet there is no great breach; when it
    comes,
Cranmer will find a friend will not shrink from him.

SECOND GENTLEMAN.
Who may that be, I pray you?

THIRD GENTLEMAN.
               Thomas Cromwell;
A man in much esteem with the king, and truly
A worthy friend. The king
Has made him master o'the jewel-house,
And one, already, of the privy-council.

SECOND GENTLEMAN.
He will deserve more.

THIRD GENTLEMAN.
            Yes, without all doubt.—
Come, gentlemen, ye shall go my way, which
Is to the court, and there ye shall be my guests:
Something I can command. As I walk thither,
I'll tell ye more.

BOTH.
     You may command us, sir. [*Exeunt.*

SCENE II.

Kimbolton.

Enter KATHARINE, *dowager, sick; led between*
GRIFFITH, *her gentleman-usher, and* PATIENCE,
her woman.

GRIFFITH.
HOW does your Grace?

KATHARINE.
           O Griffith, sick to death!
My legs, like loaden branches, bow to the earth,
Willing to leave their burden. Reach a chair:—
So,—now, methinks, I feel a little ease.
Didst thou not tell me, Griffith, as thou ledd'st me,
That the great child of honour, Cardinal Wolsey,
Was dead?

GRIFFITH.
      Yes, madam; but I think your Grace,
Out of the pain you suffer'd, gave no ear to't.

KATHARINE.
Prithee, good Griffith, tell me how he died:
If well, he stept before me, happily,
For my example.

GRIFFITH.
          Well, the voice goes, madam:
For after the stout Earl Northumberland

Arrested him at York, and brought him forward—
As a man sorely tainted—to his answer,
He fell sick suddenly, and grew so ill
He could not sit his mule.

KATHARINE.
           Alas, poor man!

GRIFFITH.
At last, with easy roads, he came to Leicester,
Lodged in the abbey; where the reverend abbot,
With all his covent, honourably received him;
To whom he gave these words,—'O father abbot,
An old man, broken with the storms of state,
Is come to lay his weary bones among ye;
Give him a little earth for charity!'
So went to bed; where eagerly his sickness
Pursued him still: and, three nights after this,
About the hour of eight,—which he himself
Foretold should be his last,—full of repentance,
Continual meditations, tears, and sorrows,
He gave his honours to the world again,
His blessed part to heaven, and slept in peace.

KATHARINE.
So may he rest; his faults lie gently on him!
Yet thus far, Griffith, give me leave to speak
    him,
And yet with charity. He was a man
Of an unbounded stomach, ever ranking
Himself with princes; one that by suggestion
Tithed all the kingdom: simony was fair-play;
His own opinion was his law: i'the presence
He would say untruths; and be ever double
Both in his words and meaning: he was never,
But where he meant to ruin, pitiful:
His promises were, as he then was, mighty;
But his performance, as he is now, nothing:
Of his own body he was ill, and gave
The clergy ill example.

GRIFFITH.
          Noble madam,
Men's evil manners live in brass; their virtues
We write in water. May it please your highness
To hear me speak his good now?

KATHARINE.
             Yes, good Griffith;
I were malicious else.

GRIFFITH.
          This cardinal,
Though from an humble stock, undoubtedly
Was fashion'd to much honour from his cradle.
He was a scholar, and a ripe and good one;
Exceeding wise, fair-spoken, and persuading:
Lofty and sour to them that lov'd him not;
But to those men that sought him sweet as
    summer.
And though he were unsatisfied in getting,—
Which was a sin.—yet in bestowing, madam,
He was most princely: ever witness for him
Those twins of learning that he raised in you,
Ipswich and Oxford! one of which fell with him,
Unwilling to outlive the good that did it;
The other, though unfinisht, yet so famous,
So excellent in art, and still so rising,
That Christendom shall ever speak his virtue.
His overthrow heapt happiness upon him;
For then, and not till then, he felt himself,
And found the blessedness of being little:

And, to add greater honours to his age
Than man could give him, he died fearing God.
KATHARINE.
After my death I wish no other herald,
No other speaker of my living actions,
To keep mine honour from corruption,
But such an honest chronicler as Griffith.
Whom I most hated living, thou hast made me,
With thy religious truth and modesty,
Now in his ashes honour: peace be with him!—
Patience, be near me still; and set me lower:
I have not long to trouble thee.—Good Griffith,
Cause the musicians play me that sad note
I named my knell, whilst I sit meditating
On that celestial harmony I go to.
          [Sad and solemn music.
GRIFFITH.
She is asleep: good wench, let's sit down quiet,
For fear we wake her:—softly, gentle Patience.
*The vision. Enter, solemnly tripping one after an-
other, six personages, clad in white robes, wearing
on their heads garlands of bays, and golden vizards on their faces; branches of bays or palm in
their hands. They first congee unto her, then
dance; and, at certain changes, the first two hold
a spare garland over her head; at which the other
four make reverent curtsies; then the two that
held the garland deliver the same to the other
next two, who observe the same order in their
changes, and holding the garland over her head:
which done, they deliver the same garland to the
last two, who likewise observe the same order; at
which (as it were by inspiration) she makes in her
sleep signs of rejoicing, and holdeth up her hands
to heaven: and so in their dancing they vanish,
carrying the garland with them. The music con-
tinues.*
KATHARINE.
Spirits of peace, where are ye? are ye all gone,
And leave me here in wretchedness behind ye?
GRIFFITH.
Madam, we are here.
KATHARINE.
          It is not you I call for:
Saw ye none enter since I slept?
GRIFFITH.
               None, madam.
KATHARINE.
No? Saw you not, even now, a blessed troop
Invite me to a banquet; whose bright faces
Cast thousand beams upon me, like the sun?
They promised me eternal happiness;
And brought me garlands, Griffith, which I feel
I am not worthy yet to wear: I shall,
Assuredly.
GRIFFITH.
I am most joyful, madam, such good dreams
Possess your fancy.
KATHARINE.
          Bid the music leave;
They are harsh and heavy to me.   *[Music ceases.*
PATIENCE [aside].
          Do you note
How much her Grace is alter'd on the sudden?
How long her face is drawn? how pale she looks,
And of an earthy colour? Mark her eyes!

GRIFFITH [aside].
She is going, wench: pray, pray.
PATIENCE [aside].
          Heaven comfort her!
Enter a MESSENGER.
MESSENGER.
An't like your Grace,—
KATHARINE.
          You are a saucy fellow:
Deserve we no more reverence?
GRIFFITH.
          You are to blame,
Knowing she will not lose her wonted greatness,
To use so rude behaviour: go to, kneel.
MESSENGER.
I humbly do entreat your highness' pardon;
My haste made me unmannerly. There's staying
A gentleman, sent from the king, to see you.
KATHARINE.
Admit him entrance, Griffith: but this fellow
Let me ne'er see again.
          [Exeunt GRIFFITH and MESSENGER.
Enter GRIFFITH, with CAPUCIUS.
          If my sight fail not,
You should be lord ambassador from the em-
    peror,
My royal nephew, and your name Capucius.
CAPUCIUS.
Madam, the same,—your servant.
KATHARINE.
          O my lord,
The times and titles now are alter'd strangely
With me since first you knew me. But, I pray you,
What is your pleasure with me?
CAPUCIUS.
          Noble lady,
First, mine own service to your Grace; the next,
The king's request that I would visit you;
Who grieves much for your weakness, and by me
Sends you his princely commendations,
And heartily entreats you take good comfort.
KATHARINE.
O my good lord, that comfort comes too late;
'Tis like a pardon after execution:
That gentle physic, given in time, had cured me;
But now I am past all comforts here, but prayers.
How does his highness?
CAPUCIUS.
          Madam, in good health.
KATHARINE.
So may he ever do! and ever flourish,
When I shall dwell with worms, and my poor name
Banisht the kingdom!—Patience, is that letter,
I caused you write, yet sent away?
PATIENCE.
          No, madam,
          [Giving it to KATHARINE.
KATHARINE.
Sir, I most humbly pray you to deliver
This to my lord the king;—
CAPUCIUS.
          Most willing, madam.
KATHARINE.
In which I have commended to his goodness
The model of our chaste loves, his young
    daughter,—

The dews of heaven fall thick in blessings on
　her!—
Beseeching him to give her virtuous breeding;—
She is young, and of a noble modest nature;
I hope she will deserve well;—and a little
To love her for her mother's sake, that loved him,
Heaven knows how dearly. My next poor petition
Is, that his noble Grace would have some pity
Upon my wretched women, that so long
Have follow'd both my fortunes faithfully:
Of which there is not one, I dare avow,—
And now I should not lie,—but will deserve,
For virtue and true beauty of the soul,
For honesty and decent carriage,
A right good husband, let him be a noble;
And, sure, those men are happy that shall have
　'em.
The last is, for my men;—they are the poorest,
But poverty could never draw 'em from me,—
That they may have their wages duly paid 'em,
And something over to remember me by:
If heaven had pleased to have given me longer life
And able means, we had not parted thus.
These are the whole contents:—and, good my lord,
By that you love the dearest in this world,
As you wish Christian peace to souls departed,
Stand these poor people's friend, and urge the king
To do me this last right.

CAPUCIUS.
　　　　　　By heaven, I will,
Or let me lose the fashion of a man!

KATHARINE.
I thank you, honest lord. Remember me
In all humility unto his highness:
Say his long trouble now is passing
Out of this world; tell him, in death I blest him,
For so I will.—Mine eyes grow dim.—Farewell,
My lord.—Griffith, farewell.—Nay, Patience,
You must not leave me yet: I must to bed;
Call in more women.—When I'm dead, good
　wench,
Let me be used with honour: strew me over
With maiden flowers, that all the world may know
I was a chaste wife to my grave: embalm me,
Then lay me forth; although unqueen'd, yet like
A queen, and daughter to a king, inter me.
I can no more.　　[Exeunt, leading KATHARINE.

ACT V.　SCENE I.

London.　A gallery in the palace.

Enter GARDINER, bishop of Winchester, a PAGE
with a torch before him, met by SIR THOMAS
LOVELL.

GARDINER.
IT'S one o'clock, boy, is't not?
BOY.
　　　　　　　　It hath struck.
GARDINER.
These should be hours for necessities,
Not for delights; times to repair our nature
With comforting repose, and not for us
To waste these times.—Good hour of night, Sir
　Thomas!
Whither so late?

SIR THOMAS LOVELL.
　　　　Came you from the king, my lord?
GARDINER.
I did, Sir Thomas; and left him at primero
With the Duke of Suffolk.
SIR THOMAS LOVELL.
　　　　　　　　I must to him too,
Before he go to bed. I'll take my leave.
GARDINER.
Not yet, Sir Thomas Lovell. What's the matter?
It seems you are in haste: an if there be
No great offence belongs to't, give your friend
Some touch of your late business: affairs that
　walk—
As they say spirits do—at midnight have
In them a wilder nature than the business
That seeks dispatch by day.
SIR THOMAS LOVELL.
　　　　　　　　My lord, I love you;
And durst commend a secret to your ear
Much weightier than this work. The queen's in
　labour,
They say, in great extremity; and fear'd
She'll with the labour end.
GARDINER.
　　　　　　The fruit she goes with
I pray for heartily, that it may find
Good time, and live: but for the stock, Sir Thomas,
I wish it grubb'd up now.
SIR THOMAS LOVELL.
　　　　　　　　Methinks I could
Cry the amen; and yet my conscience says
She's a good creature, and, sweet lady, does
Deserve our better wishes.
GARDINER.
　　　　　　But, sir, sir,—
Hear me, Sir Thomas: y'are a gentleman
Of mine own way; I know you wise, religious;
And, let me tell you, it will ne'er be well,—
'Twill not, Sir Thomas Lovell, take't of me,—
Till Cranmer, Cromwell, her two hands, and she,
Sleep in their graves.
SIR THOMAS LOVELL.
　　　　　　Now, sir, you speak of two
The most remarkt i'the kingdom. As for Crom-
　well,—
Beside that of the jewel-house, is made master
O'the rolls, and the king's secretary; further, sir,
Stands in the gap and trade of moe preferments,
With which the time will load him. The arch-
　bishop
Is the king's hand and tongue; and who dare speak
One syllable against him?
GARDINER.
　　　　　　Yes, yes, Sir Thomas,
There are that dare; and I myself have ventured
To speak my mind of him: and, indeed, this day—
Sir, I may tell it you, I think—I have
Incensed the lords o'the council that he is—
For so I know he is, they know he is—
A most arch heretic, a pestilence
That does infect the land: with which they moved,
Have broken with the king; who hath so far
Given ear to our complaint,—of his great grace
And princely care, foreseeing those fell mischiefs
Our reasons laid before him,—hath commanded

To-morrow morning to the council-board
He be convented. He's a rank weed, Sir Thomas,
And we must root him out. From your affairs
I hinder you too long: good night, Sir Thomas.

SIR THOMAS LOVELL.
Many good nights, my lord: I rest your servant.
　　　　　　　[Exeunt GARDINER and PAGE.
　　　Enter KING and SUFFOLK.
KING HENRY.
Charles, I will play no more to-night;
My mind's not on't; you are too hard for me.

DUKE OF SUFFOLK.
Sir, I did never win of you before.

KING HENRY.
But little, Charles;
Nor shall not, when my fancy's on my play.—
Now, Lovell, from the queen what is the news?

SIR THOMAS LOVELL.
I could not personally deliver to her
What you commanded me, but by her woman
I sent your message; who return'd her thanks
In the great'st humbleness, and desired your
　　highness
Most heartily to pray for her.

KING HENRY.
　　　　　　What say'st thou, ha?
To pray for her? what, is she crying out?

SIR THOMAS LOVELL.
So said her woman; and that her suff'rance made
Almost each pang a death.

KING HENRY.
　　　　　　Alas, good lady!

DUKE OF SUFFOLK.
God safely quit her of her burden, and
With gentle travail, to the gladding of
Your highness with an heir!

KING HENRY.
　　　　　　'Tis midnight, Charles;
Prithee, to bed; and in thy prayers remember
The estate of my poor queen. Leave me alone;
For I must think of that which company
Would not be friendly to.

DUKE OF SUFFOLK.
　　　　　　I wish your highness
A quiet night; and my good mistress will
Remember in my prayers.

KING HENRY.
　　　　Charles, good night. [Exit SUFFOLK.
　　Enter SIR ANTHONY DENNY.
Well, sir, what follows?

SIR ANTHONY DENNY.
Sir, I have brought my lord the archbishop
As you commanded me.

KING HENRY.
　　　　　　Ha! Canterbury?

SIR ANTHONY DENNY.
Ay, my good lord.

KING HENRY.
　　　　'Tis true: where is he, Denny?

SIR ANTHONY DENNY.
He attends your highness' pleasure.

KING HENRY.
Bring him to us. [Exit DENNY.

SIR THOMAS LOVELL [aside].
This is about that which the bishop spake:
I am happily come hither.

　　Enter CRANMER and DENNY.
KING HENRY.
Avoid the gallery. [LOVELL seems to stay]. Ha! I
　　have said. Be gone.
What!　　　　[Exeunt LOVELL and DENNY.

CRANMER [aside].
　　I am fearful:—wherefore frowns he thus?
'Tis his aspect of terror. All's not well.

KING HENRY.
How now, my lord! you do desire to know
Wherefore I sent for you.

CRANMER [kneeling].
　　　　　　It is my duty
T'attend your highness' pleasure.

KING HENRY.
　　　　　　Pray you, arise,
My good and gracious Lord of Canterbury.
　　　　　　　[CRANMER rises.
Come, you and I must walk a turn together;
I have news to tell you: come, come, give me
　　your hand.
Ah, my good lord, I grieve at what I speak,
And am right sorry to repeat what follows:
I have, and most unwillingly, of late
Heard many grievous, I do say, my lord,
Grievous complaints of you; which, being con-
　　sider'd,
Have moved us and our council, that you shall
This morning come before us; where, I know,
You cannot with such freedom purge yourself,
But that, till further trial in those charges
Which will require your answer, you must take
Your patience to you, and be well contented
To make your house our Tower: you a brother of
　　us,
It fits we thus proceed, or else no witness
Would come against you.

CRANMER [kneeling].
　　　　　　I humbly thank your highness;
And am right glad to catch this good occasion
Most thoroughly to be winnowed, where my
　　chaff
And corn shall fly asunder: for, I know,
There's none stands under more calumnious
　　tongues
Than I myself, poor man.

KING HENRY.
　　　　　　Stand up, good Canterbury:
Thy truth and thy integrity is rooted
In us, thy friend: give me thy hand, stand up:
Prithee, let's walk. Now, by my holy-dame,
　　　　　　　[CRANMER rises.
What manner of man are you! My lord, I lookt
You would have given me your petition, that
I should have ta'en some pains to bring together
Yourselves and your accusers: and to have heard
　　you,
Without indurance, further.

CRANMER.
　　　　　　Most dread liege,
The good I stand on is my truth and honesty:
If they shall fail, I, with mine enemies,
Will triumph o'er my person; which I weigh not,
Being of those virtues vacant. I fear nothing
What can be said against me.

KING HENRY.
                              Know you not
How your state stands i'the world, with the
    whole world?
Your enemies are many, and not small; their
    practices
Must bear the same proportion; and not ever
The justice and the truth o'the question carries
The due o'the verdict with it: at what ease
Might corrupt minds procure knaves as corrupt
To swear against you! such things have been
    done.
You are potently opposed; and with a malice
Of as great size. Ween you of better luck,
I mean, in perjured witness, than your Master,
Whose minister you are, whiles here He lived
Upon this naughty earth? Go to, go to;
You take a precipice for no leap of danger,
And woo your own destruction.

CRANMER.
                              God and your majesty
Protect mine innocence, or I fall into
The trap is laid for me!

KING HENRY.
                              Be of good cheer;
They shall no more prevail than we give way to.
Keep comfort to you; and this morning see
You do appear before them. If they shall chance,
In charging you with matters, to commit you,
The best persuasions to the contrary
Fail not to use, and with what vehemency
The occasion shall instruct you: if entreaties
Will render you no remedy, this ring
Deliver them, and your appeal to us
There make before them.—Look, the good man
    weeps!
He's honest, on mine honour. God's blest
    mother!
I swear he is true-hearted; and a soul
None better in my kingdom.—Get you gone,
And do as I have bid you. [*Exit* CRANMER.] He
    has strangled
His language in his tears.

Enter OLD LADY.

GENTLEMAN [*within*].
Come back: what mean you?

OLD LADY.
I'll not come back; the tidings that I bring
Will make my boldness manners.—Now, good
    angels
Fly o'er thy royal head, and shade thy person
Under their blessed wings!

KING HENRY.
                              Now, by thy looks
I guess thy message. Is the queen deliver'd?
Say ay; and of a boy.

OLD LADY.
                              Ay, ay, my liege;
And of a lovely boy: the God of heaven
Both now and ever bless her!—'tis a girl,—
Promises boys hereafter. Sir, your queen
Desires your visitation, and to be
Acquainted with this stranger: 'tis as like you
As cherry is to cherry.

KING HENRY.
                              Lovell!

Enter LOVELL.

SIR THOMAS LOVELL.
                              Sir?

KING HENRY.
Give her an hundred marks. I'll to the queen.
                              [*Exit.*

OLD LADY.
An hundred marks! By this light, I'll ha' more.
An ordinary groom is for such payment.
I will have more, or scold it out of him.
Said I for this, the girl was like to him?
I will have more, or else unsay't; and now,
While it is hot, I'll put it to the issue. [*Exeunt.*

SCENE II.

Before the council-chamber.

Enter CRANMER; PURSUIVANTS, PAGES, *and*
                              FOOTBOYS.

CRANMER.
I HOPE I am not too late; and yet the gentleman,
    That was sent to me from the council, pray'd
    me
To make great haste.—All fast? what means this?—
    Ho!
Who waits there?—Sure, you know me?

Enter KEEPER.

KEEPER.
                              Yes, my lord;
But yet I cannot help you.

CRANMER.
Why?

KEEPER.
Your Grace must wait till you be call'd for.

Enter DOCTOR BUTTS.

CRANMER.
                              So.

DOCTOR BUTTS [*aside*].
This is a piece of malice. I am glad
I came this way so happily: the king
Shall understand it presently. [*Exit.*

CRANMER [*aside*].
                              'Tis Butts,
The king's physician: as he past along,
How earnestly he cast his eyes upon me!
Pray heaven, he sound not my disgrace! For cer-
    tain,
This is of purpose laid by some that hate me—
God turn their hearts! I never sought their
    malice—
To quench mine honour: they would shame to
    make me
Wait else at door, a fellow-counsellor,
Among boys, grooms, and lackeys. But their
    pleasures
Must be fulfill'd, and I attend with patience.

Enter the KING *and* BUTTS *at a window above.*

DOCTOR BUTTS.
I'll show your Grace the strangest sight—

KING HENRY.
                              What's that, Butts?

DOCTOR BUTTS.
I think your highness saw this many a day.

KING HENRY.
Body o'me, where is it?

DOCTOR BUTTS.

There, my lord:
The high promotion of his Grace of Canterbury;
Who holds his state at door, 'mongst pursuivants,
Pages, and footboys.

KING HENRY.

Ha! 'tis he, indeed:
Is this the honour they do one another?
'Tis well there's one above 'em yet. I had thought
They had parted so much honesty among 'em—
At least, good manners—as not thus to suffer
A man of his place, and so near our favour,
To dance attendance on their lordships' pleasures,
And at the door too, like a post with packets.
By holy Mary, Butts, there's knavery:
Let 'em alone, and draw the curtain close;
We shall hear more anon.   [*Curtain drawn.*
*A council-table brought in with chairs and stools
and placed under the state. Enter* LORD CHAN-
CELLOR, *places himself at the upper end of the
table on the left hand; a seat being left void above
him, as for* CANTERBURY'S *seat;* DUKE OF
SUFFOLK, DUKE OF NORFOLK, SURREY,
LORD CHAMBERLAIN, GARDINER, *seat
themselves in order on each side.* CROMWELL
at lower end, as secretary.

LORD CHANCELLOR.

Speak to the business, master secretary:
Why are we met in council?

CROMWELL.

Please your honours,
The chief cause concerns his Grace of Canterbury.

GARDINER.

Has he had knowledge of it?

CROMWELL.

Yes.

DUKE OF NORFOLK.

Who waits there?

KEEPER.

Without, my noble lords?

GARDINER.

Yes.

KEEPER.

My lord archbishop;
And has done half an hour, to know your pleasures.

LORD CHANCELLOR.

Let him come in.

KEEPER.

Your Grace may enter now.
[CRANMER *approaches the council-table.*

LORD CHANCELLOR.

My good lord archbishop, I'm very sorry
To sit here at this present, and behold
That chair stand empty: but we all are men,
In our own natures frail and culpable;
Of one flesh; few are angels: out of which frailty
And want of wisdom, you, that best should teach
us,
Have misdemean'd yourself, and not a little,
Toward the king first, then his laws, in filling
The whole realm, by your teaching and your
chaplains,—
For so we are inform'd,—with new opinions,
Divers and dangerous; which are heresies,
And, not reform'd, may prove pernicious.

GARDINER.

Which reformation must be sudden too,
My noble lords; for those that tame wild horses
Pace 'em not in their hands to make 'em gentle,
But stop their mouths with stubborn bits, and
spur 'em,
Till they obey the manage. If we suffer—
Out of our easiness, and childish pity
To one man's honour—this contagious sickness,
Farewell all physic: and what follows then?
Commotions, uproars, with a general taint
Of the whole state: as, of late days, our neigh-
bours,
The upper Germany, can dearly witness,
Yet freshly pitied in our memories.

CRANMER.

My good lords, hitherto, in all the progress
Both of my life and office, I have labour'd,
And with no little study, that my teaching
And the strong course of my authority
Might go one way, and safely; and the end
Was ever, to do well: nor is there living—
I speak it with a single heart, my lords—
A man that more detests, more stirs against,
Both in his private conscience and his place,
Defacers of a public peace, than I do.
Pray heaven, the king may never find a heart
With less allegiance in it! Men that make
Envy and crooked malice nourishment
Dare bite the best. I do beseech your lordships
That, in this case of justice, my accusers,
Be what they will, may stand forth face to face,
And freely urge against me.

DUKE OF SUFFOLK.

Nay, my lord,
That cannot be: you are a counsellor,
And, by that virtue, no man dare accuse you.

GARDINER.

My lord, because we have business of more mo-
ment,
We will be short with you. 'Tis his highness'
pleasure,
And our consent, for better trial of you,
From hence you be committed to the Tower;
Where, being but a private man again,
You shall know many dare accuse you boldly,
More than, I fear, you are provided for.

CRANMER.

Ah, my good Lord of Winchester, I thank you;
You are always my good friend; if your will pass,
I shall both find your lordship judge and juror,
You are so merciful: I see your end,—
'Tis my undoing: love and meekness, lord,
Become a churchman better than ambition:
Win straying souls with modesty again,
Cast none away. That I shall clear myself,
Lay all the weight ye can upon my patience,
I make as little doubt, as you do conscience
In doing daily wrongs. I could say more,
But reverence to your calling makes me modest.

GARDINER.

My lord, my lord, you are a sectary,
That's the plain truth: your painted gloss discovers,
To men that understand you, words and weakness.

CROMWELL.
My Lord of Winchester, you are a little,
By your good favour, too sharp; men so noble,
However faulty, yet should find respect
For what they have been: 'tis a cruelty
To load a falling man.
GARDINER.
                    Good master secretary,
I cry your honour mercy; you may, worst
Of all this table, say so.
CROMWELL.
                    Why, my lord?
GARDINER.
Do not I know you for a favourer
Of this new sect? ye are not sound.
CROMWELL.
                              Not sound?
GARDINER.
Not sound, I say.
CROMWELL.
                    Would you were half so honest!
Men's prayers then would seek you, not their
     fears.
GARDINER.
I shall remember this bold language.
CROMWELL.
                                   Do.
Remember your bold life too.
LORD CHANCELLOR.
                         This is too much;
Forbear, for shame, my lords.
GARDINER.
                         I have done.
CROMWELL.
                                   And I.
LORD CHANCELLOR.
Then thus for you, my lord:—it stands agreed,
I take it, by all voices, that forthwith
You be convey'd to the Tower a prisoner;
There to remain till the king's further pleasure
Be known unto us: are you all agreed, lords?
ALL.
We are.
CRANMER.
     Is there no other way of mercy,
But I must needs to the Tower, my lords?
GARDINER.
                              What other
Would you expect? you are strangely trouble-
     some.—
Let some o'the guard be ready there!
          Enter GUARD.
CRANMER.
                              For me?
Must I go like a traitor thither?
GARDINER.
                         Receive him,
And see him safe i'the Tower.
CRANMER.
                    Stay, good my lords,
I have a little yet to say. Look there, my lords;
By virtue of that ring I take my cause
Out of the gripes of cruel men, and give it
To a most noble judge, the king my master.
LORD CHANCELLOR.
This is the king's ring.

EARL OF SURREY.
               'Tis no counterfeit.
DUKE OF SUFFOLK.
'Tis the right ring, by heaven: I told ye all,
When we first put this dangerous stone a-rolling,
'Twould fall upon ourselves.
DUKE OF NORFOLK.
                    Do you think, my lords,
The king will suffer but the little finger
Of this man to be vext?
LORD CHANCELLOR.
                    'Tis now too certain:
How much more is his life in value with him!
Would I were fairly out on't!
CROMWELL.
                         My mind gave me,
In seeking tales and informations
Against this man,—whose honesty the devil
And his disciples only envy at,—
Ye blew the fire that burns ye: now have at ye!
     Enter KING, *frowning on them; takes his seat.*
GARDINER.
Dread sovereign, how much are we bound to
     heaven
In daily thanks, that gave us such a prince;
Not only good and wise, but most religious:
One that, in all obedience, makes the church
The chief aim of his honour; and, to strengthen
That holy duty, out of dear respect,
His royal self in judgement comes to hear
The cause betwixt her and this great offender.
KING HENRY.
You were ever good at sudden commendations,
Bishop of Winchester. But know, I come not
To hear such flatteries now, and in my presence;
They are too thin and bare to hide offences.
To me, you cannot reach, you play the spaniel,
And think with wagging of your tongue to win me;
But, whatsoe'er thou takest me for, I'm sure
Thou hast a cruel nature and a bloody.—
[*to* CRANMER] Good man, sit down. Now let me
     see the proudest
He, that dares most, but wag his finger at thee:
By all that's holy, he had better starve
Than but once think this place becomes thee not.
EARL OF SURREY.
May it please your Grace,—
KING HENRY.
                    No, sir, it does not please me.
I had thought I had had men of some understand-
     ing
And wisdom of my council; but I find none.
Was it discretion, lords, to let this man,
This good man,—few of you deserve that title,—
This honest man, wait like a lousy footboy
At chamber-door? and one as great as you are?
Why, what a shame was this! Did my commission
Bid ye so far forget yourselves? I gave ye
Power as he was a counsellor to try him,
Not as a groom: there's some of ye, I see,
More out of malice than integrity,
Would try him to the utmost, had ye mean;
Which ye shall never have while I live.
LORD CHANCELLOR.
                              Thus far,
My most dread sovereign, may it like your Grace

To let my tongue excuse all. What was purpo ed
Concerning his imprisonment, was rather—
If there be faith in men—meant for his trial,
And fair purgation to the world, than malice,—
I'm sure, in me.

KING HENRY.
            Well, well, my lords, respect him;
Take him, and use him well, he's worthy of it.
I will say thus much for him,—if a prince
May be beholding to a subject, I
Am, for his love and service, so to him.
Make me no more ado, but all embrace him:
Be friends, for shame, my lords!—My Lord of
    Canterbury,
I have a suit which you must not deny me;
That is, a fair young maid that yet wants bap-
    tism,
You must be godfather, and answer for her.

CRANMER.
The greatest monarch now alive may glory
In such an honour: how may I deserve it,
That am a poor and humble subject to you?

KING HENRY.
Come, come, my lord, you'ld spare your spoons:
you shall have two noble partners with you; the
old Duchess of Norfolk, and Lady Marquess
Dorset: will these please you?—
Once more, my Lord of Winchester, I charge
    you,
Embrace and love this man.

GARDINER.
            With a true heart
And brother-love I do it.

CRANMER.
            And let heaven
Witness, how dear I hold this confirmation.

KING HENRY.
Good man, those joyful tears show thy true heart:
The common voice, I see, is verified
Of thee, which says thus, 'Do my Lord of Canter-
    bury
A shrewd turn, and he is your friend for ever.'—
Come, lords, we trifle time away; I long
To have this young one made a Christian.
As I have made ye one, lords, one remain;
So I grow stronger, you more honour gain.
                       [*Exeunt.*

SCENE III.

The palace-yard.

Noise and tumult within.   Enter PORTER *and his*
MAN.

PORTER.
YOU'LL leave your noise anon, ye rascals: do
you take the court for Parish-garden? ye rude
slaves, leave your gaping.
[*within*] Good master porter, I belong to the
larder.

PORTER.
Belong to the gallows, and be hang'd, ye rogue! is
this a place to roar in?—Fetch me a dozen crab-
tree staves, and strong ones: these are but
switches to 'em.—I'll scratch your heads: you
must be seeing christenings! do you look for ale
and cakes here, you rude rascals?

MAN.
Pray, sir, be patient: 'tis as much impossible—
Unless we sweep 'em from the door with can-
    nons—
To scatter 'em, as 'tis to make 'em sleep
On May-day morning; which will never be:
We may as well push against Powle's as stir 'em.

PORTER.
How got they in, and be hang'd?

MAN.
Alas, I know not; how gets the tide in?
As much as one sound cudgel of four foot—
You see the poor remainder—could distribute,
I made no spare, sir.

PORTER.
            You did nothing, sir.

MAN.
I am not Samson, nor Sir Guy, nor Colbrand,
To mow 'em down before me: but if I spared any
That had a head to hit, either young or old,
He or she, cuckold or cuckold-maker,
Let me ne'er hope to see a chine again;
And that I would not for a cow, God save her!
    [*within*] Do you hear, master porter?

PORTER.
I shall be with you presently, good master puppy.
—Keep the door close, sirrah.

MAN.
What would you have me do?

PORTER.
What should you do, but knock 'em down by the
dozens? Is this Moorfields to muster in? or have
we some strange Indian with the great tool come
to court, the women so besiege us? Bless me,
what a fry of fornication is at door! On my Christian conscience, this one christening will beget a
thousand; here will be father, godfather, and all
together.

MAN.
The spoons will be the bigger, sir. There is a
fellow somewhat near the door,—he should be a
brazier by his face, for, o'my conscience, twenty
of the dog-days now reign in's nose; all that stand
about him are under the line, they need no other
penance: that fire-drake did I hit three times on
the head, and three times was his nose discharged
against me: he stands there, like a mortar-piece,
to blow us. There was a haberdasher's wife of
small wit near him, that rail'd upon me, till her
pinkt porringer fell off her head, for kindling such
a combustion in the state. I mist the meteor once,
and hit that woman, who cried out 'Clubs!' when
I might see from far some forty truncheoners
draw to her succour, which were the hope o'the
Strond, where she was quarter'd. They fell on; I
made good my place: at length they came to the
broomstaff to me; I defied 'em still: when suddenly a file of boys behind 'em, loose shot, deliver'd such a shower of pebbles, that I was fain
to draw mine honour in, and let 'em win the work:
the devil was amongst 'em, I think, surely.

PORTER.
These are the youths that thunder at a playhouse,
and fight for bitten apples; that no audience, but
the Tribulation of Tower-hill, or the Limbs of
Limehouse, their dear brothers, are able to en-

dure. I have some of 'em in *Limbo Patrum*, and
there they are like to dance these three days; besides the running banquet of two beadles that is
to come.

    Enter the LORD CHAMBERLAIN.
        LORD CHAMBERLAIN.
Mercy o'me, what a multitude are here!
They grow still too: from all parts they are coming,
As if we kept a fair here! Where are these porters,
These lazy knaves?—Y'have made a fine hand,
   fellows:
There's a trim rabble let in: are all these
Your faithful friends o'the suburbs? We shall
   have
Great store of room, no doubt, left for the ladies,
When they pass back from the christening.
        PORTER.
              An't please your honour,
We are but men; and what so many may do,
Not being torn a-pieces, we have done:
An army cannot rule 'em.
        LORD CHAMBERLAIN.
           As I live,
If the king blame me for't, I'll lay ye all
By the heels, and suddenly; and on your heads
Clap round fines for neglect: y'are lazy knaves;
And here ye lie baiting of bombards, when
Ye should do service. Hark! the trumpets sound;
Th'are come already from the christening:
Go, break among the press, and find a way out
To let the troop pass fairly; or I'll find
A Marshalsea shall hold ye play these two months.
        PORTER.
Make way there for the princess!
        MAN.
              You great fellow,
Stand close up, or I'll make your head ache!
        PORTER.
You i'the chamblet,
Get up o'the rail; I'll peck you o'er the pales else!
                    [*Exeunt.*

SCENE IV.

The palace.

Enter trumpets, sounding; then two ALDERMEN,
LORD MAYOR, GARTER, CRANMER, DUKE
OF NORFOLK, *with his marshal's staff,* DUKE
OF SUFFOLK, *two* NOBLEMEN *bearing great
standing-bowls for the christening-gifts; then four*
NOBLEMEN *bearing a canopy, under which the*
DUCHESS OF NORFOLK, *godmother, bearing
the* CHILD *richly habited in a mantle, etc., train
borne by a* LADY; *then follows the* MARCHION-
ESS OF DORSET, *the other godmother, and*
LADIES. *The* TROOP *pass once about the stage
and* GARTER *speaks.*

        GARTER.
HEAVEN, from thy endless goodness, send
    prosperous life, long, and ever happy, to the
high and mighty princess of England, Elizabeth!
   Flourish.   *Enter* KING *and* GUARD.
        CRANMER [*kneeling*].
And to your royal Grace, and the good queen,
My noble partners and myself thus pray;—
All comfort, joy, in this most gracious lady,

Heaven ever laid up to make parents happy,
May hourly fall upon ye!
        KING HENRY.
         Thank you, good lord Archbishop:
What is her name?
        CRANMER.
   Elizabeth.
        KING HENRY.
              Stand up, lord.—
        [*The* KING *kisses the* CHILD.
With this kiss take my blessing: God protect thee!
Into whose hand I give thy life.
        CRANMER.
               Amen.
        KING HENRY.
My noble gossips, y'have been too prodigal:
I thank ye heartily; so shall this lady,
When she has so much English.
        CRANMER.
               Let me speak, sir,
For heaven now bids me; and the words I utter
Let none think flattery, for they'll find 'em truth.
This royal infant—heaven still move about her!—
Though in her cradle, yet now promises
Upon this land a thousand thousand blessings,
Which time shall bring to ripeness: she shall be—
But few now living can behold that goodness—
A pattern to all princes living with her,
And all that shall succeed: Saba was never
More covetous of wisdom and fair virtue
Than this pure soul shall be: all princely graces,
That mould up such a mighty piece as this is,
With all the virtues that attend the good,
Shall still be doubled on her: truth shall nurse her,
Holy and heavenly thoughts still counsel her:
She shall be loved and fear'd: her own shall bless
   her;
Her foes shake like a field of beaten corn,
And hang their heads with sorrow: good grows
   with her:
In her days every man shall eat in safety,
Under his own vine, what he plants; and sing
The merry songs of peace to all his neighbours:
God shall be truly known; and those about her
From her shall read the perfect ways of honour,
And by those claim their greatness, not by blood.
Nor shall this peace sleep with her: but as when
The bird of wonder dies, the maiden phœnix,
Her ashes new create another heir,
As great in admiration as herself;
So shall she leave her blessedness to one,
When heaven shall call her from this cloud of
   darkness,
Who from the sacred ashes of her honour
Shall star-like rise, as great in fame as she was,
And so stand fixt: peace, plenty, love, truth,
   terror,
That were the servants to this chosen infant,
Shall then be his, and like a vine grow to him:
Wherever the bright sun of heaven shall shine,
His honour and the greatness of his name
Shall be, and make new nations: he shall flourish,
And, like a mountain cedar, reach his branches
To all the plains about him:—our children's chil-
   dren
Shall see this, and bless heaven.

KING HENRY.
                Thou speakest wonders.
              CRANMER.
She shall be, to the happiness of England,
An aged princess; many days shall see her,
And yet no day without a deed to crown it.
Would I had known no more! but she must die,—
She must, the saints must have her,— yet a virgin;
A most unspotted lily shall she pass
To the ground, and all the world shall mourn her.
             KING HENRY.
O lord Archbishop,
Thou hast made me now a man! never before
This happy child did I get any thing:
This oracle of comfort has so pleased me,
That when I am in heaven I shall desire
To see what this child does, and praise my
   Maker.—
I thank ye all.—To you, my good lord mayor,
And your good brethren, I am much beholding;
I have received much honour by your presence,
And ye shall find me thankful.—Lead the way,
   lords:—

Ye must all see the queen, and she must thank ye;
She will be sick else. This day no man think
'Has business at his house; for all shall stay:
This little one shall make it holiday.   [Exeunt.

EPILOGUE.

'TIS ten to one this play can never please
   All that are here: some come to take their
      ease,
And sleep an act or two; but those, we fear,
W'have frighted with our trumpets; so, 'tis clear,
They'll say 'tis naught: others, to hear the city
Abused extremely, and to cry, 'That's witty!'
Which we have not done neither: that, I fear,
All the expected good w'are like to hear
For this play at this time, is only in
The merciful construction of good women;
For such a one we show'd 'em: if they smile,
And say 'twill do, I know, within a while
All the best men are ours; for 'tis ill hap,
If they hold when their ladies bid 'em clap.

VENUS AND ADONIS

Vilia miretur vulgus : mihi flavus Apollo
Pocula Castalia plena ministret aqua.

TO THE RIGHT HONOURABLE HENRY WRIOTHESLEY,

EARL OF SOUTHAMPTON, AND BARON OF TITCHFIELD.

RIGHT HONOURABLE,

I KNOW not how I shall offend in dedicating my unpolisht lines to your Lordship, nor how the world will censure me for choosing so strong a prop to support so weak a burthen: only if your Honour seem but pleased, I account myself highly praised, and vow to take advantage of all idle hours, till I have honour'd you with some graver labour. But if the first heir of my invention prove deform'd, I shall be sorry it had so noble a godfather: and never after ear so barren a land, for fear it yield me still so bad a harvest. I leave it to your honourable survey, and your Honour to your heart's content which I wish may always answer your own wish, and the world's hopeful expectation.

Your Honour's in all duty,
WILLIAM SHAKESPEARE.

EVEN as the sun with purple-colour'd face
Had ta'en his last leave of the weeping morn,
Rose cheekt Adonis hied him to the chase;
Hunting he loved, but love he laught to scorn:
   Sick-thoughted Venus makes amain unto him,
   And like a bold-faced suitor gins to woo him.

'Thrice-fairer than myself,' thus she began,
'The field's chief flower, sweet above compare,
Stain to all nymphs, more lovely than a man,
More white and red than doves or roses are;
   Nature that made thee, with herself at strife,
   Saith that the world hath ending with thy life.

'Vouchsafe, thou wonder, to alight thy steed,
And rein his proud head to the saddle-bow;
If thou wilt deign this favour, for thy meed
A thousand honey secrets shalt thou know:
   Here come and sit, where never serpent hisses,
   And being set, I'll smother thee with kisses;

'And yet not cloy thy lips with loath'd satiety,
But rather famish them amid their plenty,
Making them red and pale with fresh variety;
Ten kisses short as one, one long as twenty:
   A summer's day will seem an hour but short,
   Being wasted in such time-beguiling sport.'

With this she seizeth on his sweating palm,
The precedent of pith and livelihood,
And, trembling in her passion, calls it balm,
Earth's sovereign salve to do a goddess good:
   Being so enraged, desire doth lend her force
   Courageously to pluck him from his horse.

Over one arm the lusty courser's rein,
Under her other was the tender boy,
Who blusht and pouted in a dull disdain,
With leaden appetite, unapt to toy;
   She red and hot as coals of glowing fire,
   He red for shame, but frosty in desire.

The studded bridle on a ragged bough
Nimbly she fastens:—O, how quick is love!—
The steed is stalled up, and even now

To tie the rider she begins to prove:
   Backward she pusht him, as she would be
     thrust,
   And govern'd him in strength, though not in
     lust.

So soon was she along as he was down,
Each leaning on their elbows and their hips:
Now doth she stroke his cheek, now doth he
   frown,
And gins to chide, but soon she stops his lips;
   And kissing speaks, with lustful language
     broken,
   'If thou wilt chide, thy lips shall never open.'

He burns with bashful shame; she with her tears
Doth quench the maiden burning of his cheeks;
Then with her windy sighs and golden hairs
To fan and blow them dry again she seeks:
   He saith she is immodest, blames her miss;
   What follows more she murders with a kiss.

Even as an empty eagle, sharp by fast,
Tires with her beak on feathers, flesh, and bone,
Shaking her wings, devouring all in haste,
Till either gorge be stuft, or prey be gone;
   Even so she kist his brow, his cheek, his chin,
   And where she ends she doth anew begin.

Forced to content, but never to obey,
Panting he lies, and breatheth in her face;
She feedeth on the steam as on a prey,
And calls it heavenly moisture, air of grace;
   Wishing her cheeks were gardens full of
     flowers,
   So they were dew'd with such distilling
     showers.

Look how a bird lies tangled in a net,
So fasten'd in her arms Adonis lies;
Pure shame and awed resistance made him fret,
Which bred more beauty in his angry eyes:
   Rain added to a river that is rank
   Perforce will force it overflow the bank.

Still she entreats, and prettily entreats,
And to a pretty ear she tunes her tale;
Still is he sullen, still he lours and frets,
'Twixt crimson shame and anger ashy-pale;
   Being red, she loves him best; and being white,
   Her best is better'd with a more delight.

Look how he can, she cannot choose but love;
And by her fair immortal hand she swears,
From his soft bosom never to remove,
Till he take truce with her contending tears,
   Which long have rain'd, making her cheeks all
      wet;
   And one sweet kiss shall pay this comptless
      debt.

Upon this promise did he raise his chin,
Like a dive-dapper peering through a wave,
Who, being lookt on, ducks as quickly in;
So offers he to give what she did crave;
   But when her lips were ready for his pay,
   He winks, and turns his lips another way.

Never did passenger in summer's heat
More thirst for drink than she for this good turn.
Her help she sees, but help she cannot get;
She bathes in water, yet her fire must burn:
   'O, pity,' gan she cry, 'flint-hearted boy!
   'Tis but a kiss I beg; why art thou coy?

'I have been woo'd, as I entreat thee now,
Even by the stern and direful god of war,
Whose sinewy neck in battle ne'er did bow,
Who conquers where he comes in every jar;
   Yet hath he been my captive and my slave,
   And begg'd for that which thou unaskt shalt
      have.

'Over my altars hath he hung his lance,
His batter'd shield, his uncontrolled crest,
And for my sake hath learnt to sport and dance,
To toy, to wanton, dally, smile, and jest;
   Scorning his churlish drum and ensign red,
   Making my arms his field, his tent my bed.

'Thus he that overruled I overswayed,
Leading him prisoner in a red-rose chain:
Strong-temper'd steel his stronger strength
   obeyed,
Yet was he servile to my coy disdain.
   O, be not proud, nor brag not of thy might,
   For mast'ring her that foil'd the god of fight!

'Touch but my lips with those fair lips of thine,—
Though mine be not so fair, yet are they red,—
The kiss shall be thine own as well as mine:—
What see'st thou in the ground? hold up thy head:
   Look in mine eyeballs, there thy beauty lies;
   Then why not lips on lips, since eyes in eyes?

'Art thou ashamed to kiss? then wink again,
And I will wink; so shall the day seem night;
Love keeps his revels where there are but twain;
Be bold to play, our sport is not in sight:
   These blue-vein'd violets whereon we lean
   Never can blab, nor know not what we mean.

'The tender spring upon thy tempting lip
Shows thee unripe; yet mayst thou well be tasted:
Make use of time, let not advantage slip;
Beauty within itself should not be wasted:
   Fair flowers that are not gather'd in their prime
   Rot and consume themselves in little time.

'Were I hard-favour'd, foul, or wrinkled-old,
Ill-nurtured, crooked, churlish, harsh in voice,
O'erworn, despised, rheumatic, and cold,
Thick-sighted, barren, lean, and lacking juice,
   Then mightst thou pause, for then I were not
      for thee;
   But having no defects, why dost abhor me?

'Thou canst not see one wrinkle in my brow;
Mine eyes are gray, and bright, and quick in
   turning;
My beauty as the spring doth yearly grow,
My flesh is soft and plump, my marrow burning;
   My smooth moist hand, were it with thy hand
      felt,
   Would in thy palm dissolve, or seem to melt.

'Bid me discourse, I will enchant thine ear,
Or, like a fairy, trip upon the green,
Or, like a nymph, with long dishevell'd hair,
Dance on the sands, and yet no footing seen:
   Love is a spirit all compact of fire,
   Not gross to sink, but light, and will aspire.

'Witness this primrose bank whereon I lie;
These forceless flowers like sturdy trees support
   me;
Two strengthless doves will draw me through the
   sky,
From morn till night, even where I list to sport me:
   Is love so light, sweet boy, and may it be
   That thou should think it heavy unto thee?

'Is thine own heart to thine own face affected?
Can thy right hand seize love upon thy left?
Then woo thyself, be of thyself rejected,
Steal thine own freedom, and complain on theft.
   Narcissus so himself himself forsook,
   And died to kiss his shadow in the brook.

'Torches are made to light, jewels to wear,
Dainties to taste, fresh beauty for the use,
Herbs for their smell, and sappy plants to bear;
Things growing to themselves are growth's abuse:
   Seeds spring from seeds, and beauty breedeth
      beauty;
   Thou wast begot; to get it is thy duty.

'Upon the earth's increase why shouldst thou feed,
Unless the earth with thy increase be fed?
By law of nature thou art bound to breed,
That thine may live when thou thyself art dead;
   And so, in spite of death, thou dost survive,
   In that thy likeness still is left alive.'

By this, the love-sick queen began to sweat,
For, where they lay, the shadow had forsook them,
And Titan, tired in the mid-day heat,
With burning eye did hotly overlook them;
   Wishing Adonis had his team to guide
   So he were like him, and by Venus' side.

And now Adonis, with a lazy sprite,
And with a heavy, dark, disliking eye,
His louring brows o'erwhelming his fair sight,
Like misty vapours when they blot the sky,—
    Souring his cheeks, cries, 'Fie, no more of love!
    The sun doth burn my face; I must remove.'

'Ay me,' quoth Venus, 'young, and so unkind?
What bare excuses makest thou to be gone!
I'll sigh celestial breath, whose gentle wind
Shall cool the heat of this descending sun:
    I'll make a shadow for thee of my hairs;
    If they burn too, I'll quench them with my
      tears.

'The sun that shines from heaven shines but warm,
And, lo, I lie between that sun and thee:
The heat I have from thence doth little harm,
Thine eye darts forth the fire that burneth me;
    And were I not immortal, life were done
    Between this heavenly and earthly sun.

'Art thou obdurate, flinty, hard as steel,
Nay, more than flint, for stone at rain relenteth?
Art thou a woman's son, and canst not feel
What 'tis to love? how want of love tormenteth?
    O, had thy mother borne so hard a mind,
    She had not brought forth thee, but died un-
      kind.

'What am I, that thou shouldst contemn me this?
Or what great danger dwells upon my suit?
What were thy lips the worse for one poor kiss?
Speak, fair; but speak fair words, or else be mute:
    Give me one kiss, I'll give it thee again,
    And one for interest, if thou wilt have twain.

'Fie, lifeless picture, cold and senseless stone,
Well-painted idol, image dull and dead,
Statue contenting but the eye alone,
Thing like a man, but of no woman bred!
    Thou art no man, though of a man's com-
      plexion,
    For men will kiss even by their own direction.'

This said, impatience chokes her pleading tongue,
And swelling passion doth provoke a pause;
Red cheeks and fiery eyes blaze forth her wrong;
Being judge in love, she cannot right her cause:
    And now she weeps, and now she fain would
      speak,
    And now her sobs do her intendments break.

Sometime she shakes her head, and then his hand,
Now gazeth she on him, now on the ground;
Sometime her arms infold him like a band:
She would, he will not in her arms be bound;
    And when from thence he struggles to be gone,
    She locks her lily fingers one in one.

'Fondling,' she saith, 'since I have hemm'd thee
    here
Within the circuit of this ivory pale,
I'll be a park, and thou shalt be my deer;
Feed where thou wilt, on mountain or in dale:
    Graze on my lips; and if those hills be dry,
    Stray lower, where the pleasant fountains lie.

'Within this limit is relief enough,
Sweet bottom-grass, and high delightful plain,
Round rising hillocks, brakes obscure and rough,
To shelter thee from tempest and from rain:
    Then be my deer, since I am such a park;
    No dog shall rouse thee, though a thousand
      bark.'

At this Adonis smiles as in disdain,
That in each cheek appears a pretty dimple:
Love made those hollows, if himself were slain,
He might be buried in a tomb so simple;
    Foreknowing well, if there he came to lie,
    Why, there Love lived, and there he could not
      die.

These lovely caves, these round enchanting pits,
Open'd their mouths to swallow Venus' liking.
Being mad before, how doth she now for wits?
Struck dead at first, what needs a second striking?
    Poor queen of love, in thine own law forlorn,
    To love a cheek that smiles at thee in scorn!

Now which way shall she turn? what shall she say?
Her words are done, her woes the more increas-
    ing;
The time is spent, her object will away,
And from her twining arms doth urge releasing.
    'Pity,' she cries, 'some favour, some remorse!'
    Away he springs, and hasteth to his horse.

But, lo, from forth a copse that neighbours by,
A breeding jennet, lusty, young, and proud,
Adonis' trampling courser doth espy,
And forth she rushes, snorts, and neighs aloud:
    The strong neckt steed, being tied unto a tree,
    Breaketh his rein, and to her straight goes he.

Imperiously he leaps, he neighs, he bounds,
And now his woven girths he breaks asunder;
The bearing earth with his hard hoof he wounds,
Whose hollow womb resounds like heaven's
    thunder;
    The iron bit he crusheth 'tween his teeth,
    Controlling what he was controlled with.

His ears up-prickt; his braided hanging mane
Upon his compast crest now stand on end;
His nostrils drink the air, and forth again,
As from a furnace, vapours doth he send;
    His eye, which scornfully glisters like fire,
    Shows his hot courage and his high desire.

Sometime he trots, as if he told the steps,
With gentle majesty and modest pride;
Anon he rears upright, curvets and leaps,
As who should say, 'Lo, thus my strength is tried,
    And this I do to captivate the eye
    Of the fair breeder that is standing by.'

What recketh he his rider's angry stir,
His flattering 'Holla' or his 'Stand, I say'?
What cares he now for curb or pricking spur?
For rich caparisons or trapping gay?
    He sees his love, and nothing else he sees,
    For nothing else with his proud sight agrees.

Look, when a painter would surpass the life
In limning out a well-proportion'd steed,
His art with nature's workmanship at strife,
As if the dead the living should exceed;
　　So did this horse excel a common one
　　In shape, in courage, colour, pace, and bone.

Round-hooft, short-jointed, fetlocks shag and
　　long,
Broad breast, full eye, small head, and nostril wide,
High crest, short ears, straight legs, and passing
　　strong,
Thin mane, thick tail, broad buttock, tender hide:
　　Look, what a horse should have he did not lack,
　　Save a proud rider on so proud a back.

Sometime he scuds far off, and there he stares;
Anon he starts at stirring of a feather;
To bid the wind a base he now prepares,
And whe'r he run or fly they know not whether;
　　For through his mane and tail the high wind
　　　　sings,
　　Fanning the hairs, who wave like feath'red
　　　　wings.

He looks upon his love, and neighs unto her;
She answers him, as if she knew his mind:
Being proud, as females are, to see him woo her,
She puts on outward strangeness, seems unkind;
　　Spurns at his love, and scorns the heat he feels,
　　Beating his kind embracements with her heels.

Then, like a melancholy malcontent,
He vails his tail, that, like a falling plume,
Cool shadow to his melting buttock lent:
He stamps, and bites the poor flies in his fume.
　　His love, perceiving how he is enraged,
　　Grew kinder, and his fury was assuaged.

His testy master goeth about to take him;
When, lo, the unbackt breeder, full of fear,
Jealous of catching, swiftly doth forsake him,
With her the horse, and left Adonis there:
　　As they were mad, unto the wood they hie them,
　　Out-stripping crows that strive to over-fly them.

All swoln with chafing, down Adonis sits,
Banning his boist'rous and unruly beast:
And now the happy season once more fits,
That love-sick Love by pleading may be blest;
　　For lovers say, the heart hath treble wrong
　　When it is barr'd the aidance of the tongue.

An oven that is stopt, or river stay'd,
Burneth more hotly, swelleth with more rage:
So of concealed sorrow may be said;
Free vent of words love's fire doth assuage;
　　But when the heart's attorney once is mute,
　　The client breaks, as desperate in his suit.

He sees her coming, and begins to glow,
Even as a dying coal revives with wind,
And with his bonnet hides his angry brow;
Looks on the dull earth with disturbed mind;
　　Taking no notice that she is so nigh,
　　For all askance he holds her in his eye.

O, what a sight it was, wistly to view
How she came stealing to the wayward boy!
To note the fighting conflict of her hue,
How white and red each other did destroy!
　　But now her cheek was pale, and by and by
　　It flasht forth fire, as lightning from the sky.

Now she was just before him as he sat,
And like a lowly lover down she kneels;
With one fair hand she heaveth up his hat,
Her other tender hand his fair cheek feels:
　　His tenderer cheek receives her soft hand's print,
　　As apt as new-faln snow takes any dint.

O, what a war of looks was then between them!
Her eyes petitioners to his eyes suing;
His eyes saw her eyes as they had not seen them;
Her eyes woo'd still, his eyes disdain'd the wooing:
　　And all this dumb-play had his acts made plain
　　With tears, which, chorus-like, her eyes did
　　　　rain.

Full gently now she takes him by the hand,
A lily prison'd in a goal of snow,
Or ivory in an alabaster band;
So white a friend engirts so white a foe:
　　This beauteous combat, wilful and unwilling,
　　Show'd like two silver doves that sit a-billing.

Once more the engine of her thoughts began:
'O fairest mover on this mortal round,
Would thou wert as I am, and I a man,
My heart all whole as thine, thy heart my wound;
　　For one sweet look thy help I would assure thee,
　　Though nothing but my body's bane would
　　　　cure thee.'

'Give me my hand,' saith he; 'why dost thou feel
　　it?'
'Give me my heart,' saith she, 'and thou shalt
　　have it;
O, give it me, lest thy hard heart do steel it,
And being steel'd, soft sighs can never grave it:
　　Then love's deep groans I never shall regard,
　　Because Adonis' heart hath made mine hard.'

'For shame,' he cries, 'let go, and let me go;
My day's delight is past, my horse is gone,
And 'tis your fault I am bereft him so:
I pray you hence, and leave me here alone;
　　For all my mind, my thought, my busy care
　　Is how to get my palfrey from the mare.'

Thus she replies: 'Thy palfrey, as he should,
Welcomes the warm approach of sweet desire:
Affection is a coal that must be cool'd;
Else, suffer'd, it will set the heart on fire:
　　The sea hath bounds, but deep desire hath none;
　　Therefore no marvel though thy horse be gone.

'How like a jade he stood, tied to the tree,
Servilely master'd with a leathern rein!
But when he saw his love, his youth's fair fee,
He held such petty bondage in disdain;
　　Throwing the base thong from his bending crest,
　　Enfranchising his mouth, his back, his breast.

'Who sees his true-love in her naked bed,
Teaching the sheets a whiter hue than white,
But, when his glutton eye so full hath fed,
His other agents aim at like delight?
    Who is so faint, that dares not be so bold
    To touch the fire, the weather being cold?

'Let me excuse thy courser, gentle boy;
And learn of him, I heartily beseech thee,
To take advantage on presented joy;
Though I were dumb, yet his proceedings teach
    thee:
    O, learn to love; the lesson is but plain,
    And once made perfect, never lost again.'

'I know not love,' quoth he, 'nor will not know it,
Unless it be a boar, and then I chase it;
'Tis much to borrow, and I will not owe it;
My love to love is love but to disgrace it;
    For I have heard it is a life in death,
    That laughs, and weeps, and all but with a
    breath.

'Who wears a garment shapeless and unfinisht?
Who plucks the bud before one leaf put forth?
If springing things be any jot diminisht,
They wither in their prime, prove nothing worth:
    The colt that's backt and burden'd being
    young
    Loseth his pride, and never waxeth strong.

'You hurt my hand with wringing; let us part,
And leave this idle theme, this bootless chat:
Remove your siege from my unyielding heart;
To love's alarms it will not ope the gate:
    Dismiss your vows, your feigned tears, your
    flatt'ry;
    For where a heart is hard they make no batt'ry.'

'What! canst thou talk?' quoth she, 'hast thou a
    tongue?
O, would thou hadst not, or I had no hearing!
Thy mermaid's voice hath done me double
    wrong;
I had my load before, now prest with bearing:
    Melodious discord, heavenly tune harsh-
    sounding,
    Ear's deep-sweet music, and heart's deep-sore
    wounding.

'Had I no eyes but ears, my ears would love
That inward beauty and invisible;
Or were I deaf, thy outward parts would move
Each part in me that were but sensible:
    Though neither eyes nor ears, to hear nor see,
    Yet should I be in love by touching thee.

'Say, that the sense of feeling were bereft me,
And that I could not see, nor hear, nor touch,
And nothing but the very smell were left me,
Yet would my love to thee be still as much;
    For from the stillitory of thy face excelling
    Comes breath perfumed, that breedeth love by
    smelling.

'But, O, what banquet wert thou to the taste,
Being nurse and feeder of the other four!
Would they not wish the feast might ever last,
And bid Suspicion double-lock the door,
    Lest Jealousy, that sour unwelcome guest,
    Should, by his stealing in, disturb the feast?'

Once more the ruby-colour'd portal open'd,
Which to his speech did honey passage yield;
Like a red morn, that ever yet betoken'd
Wrack to the seaman, tempest to the field,
    Sorrow to shepherds, woe unto the birds,
    Gusts and foul flaws to herdmen and to herds.

This ill presage advisedly she marketh:
Even as the wind is husht before it raineth,
Or as the wolf doth grin before he barketh,
Or as the berry breaks before it staineth,
    Or like the deadly bullet of a gun,
    His meaning struck her ere his words begun.

And at his look she flatly falleth down,
For looks kill love, and love by looks reviveth:
A smile recures the wounding of a frown;
But blessed bankrout, that by love so thriveth!
    The silly boy, believing she is dead,
    Claps her pale cheek, till clapping makes it
    red;

And all-amazed brake off his late intent,
For sharply he did think to reprehend her,
Which cunning love did wittily prevent:
Fair fall the wit that can so well defend her!
    For on the grass she lies as she were slain,
    Till his breath breatheth life in her again.

He wrings her nose, he strikes her on the cheeks,
He bends her fingers, holds her pulses hard,
He chafes her lips; a thousand ways he seeks
To mend the hurt that his unkindness marr'd:
    He kisses her; and she, by her good will,
    Will never rise, so he will kiss her still.

The night of sorrow now is turn'd to day:
Her two blue windows faintly she up-heaveth,
Like the fair sun, when in his fresh array
He cheers the morn, and all the earth relieveth:
    And as the bright sun glorifies the sky,
    So is her face illumined with her eye;

Whose beams upon his hairless face are fixt,
As if from thence they borrow'd all their shine.
Were never four such lamps together mixt,
Had not his clouded with his brow's repine;
    But hers, which through the crystal tears gave
    light,
    Shone like the moon in water seen by night.

'O, where am I?' quoth she; 'in earth or heaven,
Or in the ocean drencht, or in the fire?
What hour is this? or morn or weary even?
Do I delight to die, or life desire?
    But now I lived, and life was death's annoy;
    But now I died, and death was lively joy.

'O, thou didst kill me: kill me once again:
Thy eyes' shrewd tutor, that hard heart of thine,
Hath taught them scornful tricks, and such dis-
    dain,
That they have murder'd this poor heart of mine;
    And these mine eyes, true leaders to their queen,
    But for thy piteous lips no more had seen.

'Long may they kiss each other, for this cure!
O, never let their crimson liveries wear!
And as they last, their verdure still endure,
To drive infection from the dangerous year!
    That the star-gazers, having writ on death,
    May say, the plague is banisht by thy breath.

'Pure lips, sweet seals in my soft lips imprinted,
What bargains may I make, still to be sealing?
To sell myself I can be well contented,
So thou wilt buy, and pay, and use good dealing;
    Which purchase if thou make, for fear of slips
    Set thy seal-manual on my wax-red lips.

'A thousand kisses buys my heart from me;
And pay them at thy leisure, one by one.
What is ten hundred touches unto thee?
Are they not quickly told and quickly gone?
    Say, for non-payment that the debt should
        double,
    Is twenty hundred kisses such a trouble?'

'Fair queen,' quoth he, 'if any love you owe me,
Measure my strangeness with my unripe years:
Before I know myself, seek not to know me;
No fisher but the ungrown fry forbears:
    The mellow plum doth fall, the green sticks fast,
    Or being early pluckt is sour to taste.

'Look, the world's comforter, with weary gait,
His day's hot task hath ended in the west;
The owl, night's herald, shrieks; 'tis very late;
The sheep are gone to fold, birds to their nest;
    And coal black clouds that shadow heaven's
        light
    Do summon us to part and bid good night.

'Now let me say "Good night," and so say you;
If you will say so, you shall have a kiss.'
'Good night,' quoth she; and, ere he says 'Adieu,'
The honey fee of parting tender'd is:
    Her arms do lend his neck a sweet embrace;
    Incorporate then they seem; face grows to face:

Till, breathless, he disjoin'd, and backward drew
The heavenly moisture, that sweet coral mouth,
Whose precious taste her thirsty lips well knew,
Whereon they surfeit, yet complain on drouth:
    He with her plenty prest, she faint with dearth,
    Their lips together glued, fall to the earth.

Now quick desire hath caught the yielding prey,
And glutton-like she feeds, yet never filleth;
Her lips are conquerors, his lips obey,
Paying what ransom the insulter willeth;
    Whose vulture thought doth pitch the price so
        high,
    That she will draw his lips' rich treasure dry:

And having felt the sweetness of the spoil,
With blindfold fury she begins to forage;
Her face doth reek and smoke, her blood doth boil,
And careless lust stirs up a desperate courage;
    Planting oblivion, beating reason back,
    Forgetting shame's pure blush and honour's
        wrack.

Hot, faint, and weary with her hard embracing,
Like a wild bird being tamed with too much
    handling,
Or as the fleet-foot roe that's tired with chasing,
Or like the froward infant still'd with dandling,
    He now obeys, and now no more resisteth,
    While she takes all she can, not all she listeth.

What wax so frozen but dissolves with temp'ring,
And yields at last to every light impression?
Things out of hope are compast oft with vent'ring,
Chiefly in love, whose leave exceeds commission:
    Affection faints not like a pale-faced coward,
    But then woos best when most his choice is
        froward.

When he did frown, O, had she then gave over,
Such nectar from his lips she had not suckt.
Foul words and frowns must not repel a lover;
What though the rose have prickles, yet 'tis pluckt;
    Were beauty under twenty locks kept fast,
    Yet love breaks through and picks them all at last.

For pity now she can no more detain him;
The poor fool prays her that he may depart:
She is resolved no longer to restrain him;
Bids him farewell, and look well to her heart,
    The which, by Cupid's bow she doth protest,
    He carries thence incaged in his breast.

'Sweet boy,' she says, 'this night I'll waste in
    sorrow,
For my sick heart commands mine eyes to watch.
Tell me, Love's master, shall we meet to-morrow?
Say, shall we? shall we? wilt thou make the match?'
    He tells her, no; to-morrow he intends
    To hunt the boar with certain of his friends.

'The boar!' quoth she: whereat a sudden pale,
Like lawn being spread upon the blushing rose,
Usurps her cheek; she trembles at his tale,
And on his neck her yoking arms she throws:
    She sinketh down, still hanging by his neck,
    He on her belly falls, she on her back.

Now is she in the very lists of love,
Her champion mounted for the hot encounter:
All is imaginary she doth prove,
He will not manage her, although he mount her;
    That worse than Tantalus' is her annoy,
    To clip Elysium, and to lack her joy.

Even so poor birds, deceived with painted grapes,
Do surfeit by the eye and pine the maw:
Even so she languisheth in her mishaps
As those poor birds that helpless berries saw.
    The warm effects which she in him finds missing
    She seeks to kindle with continual kissing.

But all in vain; good queen, it will not be:
She hath assay'd as much as may be proved;
Her pleading hath deserved a greater fee;
She's Love, she loves, and yet she is not loved.
    'Fie, fie,' he says, 'you crush me; let me go;
    You have no reason to withhold me so.'

'Thou hadst been gone,' quoth she, 'sweet boy,
    ere this,
But that thou told'st me thou wouldst hunt the
    boar.
O, be advised! thou know'st not what it is
With javelin's point a churlish swine to gore,
    Whose tushes never-sheathed he whetteth still,
    Like to a mortal butcher bent to kill.

'On his bow-back he hath a battle set
Of bristly pikes, that ever threat his foes;
His eyes, like glow-worms, shine when he doth fret;
His snout digs sepulchres where'er he goes;
    Being moved, he strikes whate'er is in his way,
    And whom he strikes his crooked tushes slay.

'His brawny sides, with hairy bristles armed,
Are better proof than thy spear's point can enter;
His short thick neck cannot be easily harmed;
Being ireful, on the lion he will venter:
    The thorny brambles and embracing bushes,
    As fearful of him, part; through whom he rushes.

'Alas, he naught esteems that face of thine,
To which Love's eyes pays tributary gazes;
Nor thy soft hands, sweet lips, and crystal eyne,
Whose full perfection all the world amazes;
    But having thee at vantage,—wondrous dread!—
    Would root these beauties as he roots the mead.

'O, let him keep his loathsome cabin still;
Beauty hath naught to do with such foul fiends:
Come not within his danger by thy will;
They that thrive well take counsel of their friends.
    When thou didst name the boar, not to dis-
      semble,
    I fear'd thy fortune, and my joints did tremble.

'Didst thou not mark my face? was it not white?
Saw'st thou not signs of fear lurk in mine eye?
Grew I not faint? and fell I not downright?
Within my bosom, whereon thou dost lie,
    My boding heart pants, beats, and takes no rest,
    But, like an earthquake, shakes thee on my
      breast.

'For where Love reigns, disturbing Jealousy
Doth call himself Affection's sentinel;
Gives false alarms, suggesteth mutiny,
And in a peaceful hour doth cry "Kill, kill!"
    Distemp'ring gentle Love in his desire,
    As air and water do abate the fire.

'This sour informer, this bate-breeding spy,
This canker that eats up Love's tender spring,
This carry-tale, dissentious Jealousy,
That sometime true news, sometime false doth
    bring,
    Knocks at my heart, and whispers in mine ear,
    That if I love thee, I thy death should fear:

'And more than so, presenteth to mine eye
The picture of an angry-chafing boar,
Under whose sharp fangs on his back doth lie
An image like thyself, all stain'd with gore;
    Whose blood upon the fresh flowers being shed
    Doth make them droop with grief and hang the
      head.

'What should I do, seeing thee so indeed,
That tremble at the imagination?
The thought of it doth make my faint heart bleed,
And fear doth teach it divination:
    I prophesy thy death, my living sorrow,
    If thou encounter with the boar to-morrow.

'But if thou needs wilt hunt, be ruled by me;
Uncouple at the timorous flying hare,
Or at the fox which lives by subtlety,
Or at the roe which no encounter dare:
    Pursue these fearful creatures o'er the downs,
    And on thy well-breathed horse keep with thy
      hounds.

'And when thou hast on foot the purblind hare,
Mark the poor wretch, to overshoot his troubles
How he outruns the wind, and with what care
He cranks and crosses with a thousand doubles:
    The many musets through the which he goes
    Are like a labyrinth to amaze his foes.

'Sometime he runs among a flock of sheep,
To make the cunning hounds mistake their smell,
And sometime where earth-delving conies keep,
To stop the loud pursuers in their yell;
    And sometime sorteth with a herd of deer:
    Danger deviseth shifts; wit waits on fear:

'For there his smell with others being mingled,
The hot scent-snuffing hounds are driven to
    doubt,
Ceasing their clamorous cry till they have singled
With much ado the cold fault cleanly out;
    Then do they spend their mouths: Echo replies,
    As if another chase were in the skies.

'By this, poor Wat, far off upon a hill,
Stands on his hinder legs with list'ning ear,
To hearken if his foes pursue him still:
Anon their loud alarums he doth hear;
    And now his grief may be compared well
    To one sore sick that hears the passing-bell.

'Then shalt thou see the dew-bedabbled wretch
Turn, and return, indenting with the way;
Each envious brier his weary legs doth scratch,
Each shadow makes him stop, each murmur stay;
    For misery is trodden on by many,
    And being low never relieved by any.

'Lie quietly, and hear a little more;
Nay, do not struggle, for thou shalt not rise:
To make thee hate the hunting of the boar,
Unlike myself thou hear'st me moralize,
    Applying this to that, and so to so;
    For love can comment upon every woe.

'Where did I leave?' 'No matter where,' quoth he;
' Leave me, and then the story aptly ends:
The night is spent.' 'Why, what of that?' quoth
   she.
'I am,' quoth he, 'expected of my friends;
   And now 'tis dark, and going I shall fall.'
   'In night,' quoth she, 'desire sees best of all.

'But if thou fall, O, then imagine this,
The earth, in love with thee, thy footing trips,
And all is but to rob thee of a kiss.
Rich preys make true-men thieves; so do thy lips
   Make modest Dian cloudy and forlorn,
   Lest she should steal a kiss, and die forsworn.

'Now of this dark night I perceive the reason:
Cynthia for shame obscures her silver shine,
Till forging Nature be condemn'd of treason,
For stealing moulds from heaven that were divine;
   Wherein she framed thee, in high heaven's
      despite,
   To shame the sun by day, and her by night.

'And therefore hath she bribed the Destinies
To cross the curious workmanship of Nature,
To mingle beauty with infirmities,
And pure perfection with impure defeature;
   Making it subject to the tyranny
   Of mad mischances and much misery;

'As burning fevers, agues pale and faint,
Life-poisoning pestilence, and frenzies wood,
The marrow-eating sickness, whose attaint
Disorder breeds by heating of the blood:
   Surfeits, imposthumes, grief, and damn'd
      despair,
   Swear Nature's death for framing thee so fair.

'And not the least of all these maladies
But in one minute's fight brings beauty under:
Both favour, savour, hue, and qualities,
Whereat the impartial gazer late did wonder,
   Are on the sudden wasted, thaw'd, and done,
   As mountain snow melts with the midday sun.

'Therefore, despite of fruitless chastity,
Love-lacking vestals, and self-loving nuns,
That on the earth would breed a scarcity
And barren dearth of daughters and of sons,
   Be prodigal: the lamp that burns by night
   Dries up his oil to lend the world his light.

'What is thy body but a swallowing grave,
Seeming to bury that posterity
Which by the rights of time thou needs must have,
If thou destroy them not in dark obscurity?
   If so, the world will hold thee in disdain,
   Sith in thy pride so fair a hope is slain.

'So in thy self thyself art made away;
A mischief worse than civil home-bred strife,
Or theirs whose desperate hands themselves do
   slay,
Or butcher-sire that reaves his son of life.
   Foul-cank'ring rust the hidden treasure frets,
   But gold that's put to use more gold begets.'

'Nay, then,' quoth Adon, 'you will fall again
Into your idle over-handled theme:
The kiss I gave you is bestow'd in vain,
And all in vain you strive against the stream;
   For, by this black-faced night, desire's foul
      nurse,
   Your treatise makes me like you worse and
      worse.

'If love have lent you twenty thousand tongues,
And every tongue more moving than your own,
Bewitching like the wanton mermaid's songs,
Yet from mine ear the tempting tune is blown;
   For know, my heart stands armed in mine ear,
   And will not let a false sound enter there;

'Lest the deceiving harmony should run
Into the quiet closure of my breast;
And then my little heart were quite undone,
In his bedchamber to be barr'd of rest.
   No, lady, no; my heart longs not to groan,
   But soundly sleeps, while now it sleeps alone.

'What have you urged that I cannot reprove?
The path is smooth that leadeth on to danger:
I hate not love, but your device in love,
That lends embracements unto every stranger.
   You do it for increase: O strange excuse,
   When reason is the bawd to lust's abuse!

'Call it not love, for Love to heaven is fled,
Since sweating Lust on earth usurpt his name;
Under whose simple semblance he hath fed
Upon fresh beauty, blotting it with blame;
   Which the hot tyrant stains and soon bereaves,
   As caterpillars do the tender leaves.

'Love comforteth like sunshine after rain,
But Lust's effect is tempest after sun;
Love's gentle spring doth always fresh remain,
Lust's winter comes ere summer half be done;
   Love surfeits not, Lust like a glutton dies;
   Love is all truth, Lust full of forged lies.

'More I could tell, but more I dare not say;
The text is old, the orator too green.
Therefore, in sadness, now I will away;
My face is full of shame, my heart of teen:
   Mine ears, that to your wanton talk attended,
   Do burn themselves for having so offended.'

With this, he breaketh from the sweet embrace
Of those fair arms which bound him to her breast,
And homeward through the dark laund runs apace;
Leaves Love upon her back deeply distrest.
   Look, how a bright star shooteth from the sky,
   So glides he in the night from Venus' eye;

Which after him she darts, as one on shore
Gazing upon a late-embarked friend,
Till the wild waves will have him see no more,
Whose ridges with the meeting clouds contend:
   So did the merciless and pitchy night
   Fold-in the object that did feed her sight.

Whereat amazed, as one that unaware
Hath dropt a precious jewel in the flood,
Or stonisht as night-wanderers often are,
Their light blown out in some mistrustful wood;
  Even so confounded in the dark she lay,
  Having lost the fair discovery of her way.

And now she beats her heart, whereat it groans,
That all the neighbour caves, as seeming troubled,
Make verbal repetition of her moans;
Passion on passion deeply is redoubled:
  'Ay me!' she cries, and twenty times, 'Woe,
    woe!'
  And twenty echoes twenty times cry so.

She, marking them, begins a wailing note,
And sings extemporally a woeful ditty;
How love makes young men thrall, and old men
    dote;
How love is wise in folly, foolish-witty:
  Her heavy anthem still concludes in woe,
  And still the choir of echoes answer so.

Her song was tedious, and outwore the night,
For lovers' hours are long, though seeming short:
If pleased themselves, others, they think, delight
In such-like circumstance, with such-like sport:
  Their copious stories, oftentimes begun,
  End without audience, and are never done.

For who hath she to spend the night withal,
But idle sounds resembling parasites;
Like shrill-tongued tapsters answering every call,
Soothing the humour of fantastic wits?
  She says ''Tis so:' they answer all, ''Tis so;'
  And would say after her, if she said 'No.'

Lo, here the gentle lark, weary of rest,
From his moist cabinet mounts up on high,
And wakes the morning, from whose silver breast
The sun ariseth in his majesty;
  Who doth the world so gloriously behold,
  That cedar-tops and hills seem burnisht gold.

Venus salutes him with this fair good-morrow:
'O thou clear god, and patron of all light,
From whom each lamp and shining star doth
    borrow
The beauteous influence that makes him bright,
  There lives a son, that suckt an earthly mother,
  May lend thee light, as thou dost lend to other.'

This said, she hasteth to a myrtle grove,
Musing the morning is so much o'erworn,
And yet she hears no tidings of her love:
She hearkens for his hounds and for his horn:
  Anon she hears them chant it lustily,
  And all in haste she coasteth to the cry.

And as she runs, the bushes in the way
Some catch her by the neck, some kiss her face,
Some twined about her thigh to make her stay:
She wildly breaketh from their strict embrace,
  Like a milch doe, whose swelling dugs do ache,
  Hasting to feed her fawn hid in some brake.

By this, she hears the hounds are at a bay:
Whereat she starts, like one that spies an adder
Wreathed up in fatal folds just in his way,
The fear whereof doth make him shake and
    shudder;
  Even so the timorous yelping of the hounds
  Appals her senses and her spirit confounds.

For now she knows it is no gentle chase,
But the blunt boar, rough bear, or lion proud,
Because the cry remaineth in one place,
Where fearfully the dogs exclaim aloud:
  Finding their enemy to be so curst,
  They all strain court'sy who shall cope him first

This dismal cry rings sadly in her ear,
Through which it enters to surprise her heart;
Who, overcome by doubt and bloodless fear,
With cold-pale weakness numbs each feeling part:
  Like soldiers, when their captain once doth
    yield,
  They basely fly, and dare not stay the field.

Thus stands she in a trembling ecstasy;
Till, cheering up her senses all dismay'd,
She tells them 'tis a causeless fantasy,
And childish error, that they are afraid;
  Bids them leave quaking, bids them fear no
    more:—
  And with that word she spied the hunted boar;

Whose frothy mouth, bepainted all with red,
Like milk and blood being mingled both togither,
A second fear through all her sinews spread,
Which madly hurries her she knows not whither:
  This way she runs, and now she will no further,
  But back retires to rate the boar for murther.

A thousand spleens bear her a thousand ways;
She treads the path that she untreads again;
Her more than haste is mated with delays,
Like the proceedings of a drunken brain,
  Full of respects, yet naught at all respecting;
  In hand with all things, naught at all effecting.

Here kennell'd in a brake she finds a hound,
And asks the weary caitiff for his master;
And there another licking of his wound,
'Gainst venom'd sores the only sovereign plaster:
  And here she meets another sadly scowling,
  To whom she speaks, and he replies with howl-
    ing.

When he hath ceased his ill-resounding noise,
Another flap-mouth'd mourner, black and grim,
Against the welkin volleys out his voice;
Another and another answer him,
  Clapping their proud tails to the ground below,
  Shaking their scratcht ears, bleeding as they go.

Look how the world's poor people are amazed
At apparitions, signs, and prodigies,
Whereon with fearful eyes they long have gazed,
Infusing them with dreadful prophecies;
  So she at these sad signs draws up her breath,
  And, sighing it again, exclaims on Death.

'Hard-favour'd tyrant, ugly, meagre, lean,
Hateful divorce of love.'—thus chides she
    Death,—
'Grim-grinning ghost, earth's worm, what dost
    thou mean
To stifle beauty and to steal his breath,
    Who when he lived, his breath and beauty set
    Gloss on the rose, smell to the violet?

'If he be dead,—O no, it cannot be,
Seeing his beauty, thou shouldst strike at it;—
O yes, it may; thou hast no eyes to see,
But hatefully at random dost thou hit.
    Thy mark is feeble age; but thy false dart
    Mistakes that aim, and cleaves an infant's heart.

'Hadst thou but bid beware, then he had spoke,
And, hearing him, thy power had lost his power.
The Destinies will curse thee for this stroke;
They bid thee crop a weed, thou pluck'st a flower:
    Love's golden arrow at him should have fled,
    And not Death's ebon dart, to strike him dead.

'Dost thou drink tears, that thou provokest such
    weeping?
What may a heavy groan advantage thee?
Why hast thou cast into eternal sleeping
Those eyes that taught all other eyes to see?
    Now Nature cares not for thy mortal vigour,
    Since her best work is ruin'd with thy rigour.'

Here overcome, as one full of despair,
She vail'd her eyelids, who, like sluices, stopt
The crystal tide that from her two cheeks fair
In the sweet channel of her bosom dropt;
    But through the flood-gates breaks the silver
      rain,
    And with his strong course opens them again.

O, how her eyes and tears did lend and borrow!
Her eye seen in the tears, tears in her eye;
Both crystals, where they view'd each other's
    sorrow,—
Sorrow that friendly sighs sought still to dry;
    But like a stormy day, now wind, now rain,
    Sighs dry her cheeks, tears make them wet
      again.

Variable passions throng her constant woe,
As striving who should best become her grief;
All entertain'd, each passion labours so,
That every present sorrow seemeth chief,
    But none is best: then join they all together,
    Like many clouds consulting for foul weather.

By this, far off she hears some huntsman hollo;
A nurse's song ne'er pleased her babe so well:
The dire imagination she did follow
This sound of hope doth labour to expel;
    For now reviving joy bids her rejoice,
    And flatters her it is Adonis' voice.

Whereat her tears began to turn their tide,
Being prison'd in her eye like pearls in glass;
Yet sometimes falls an orient drop beside,
Which her cheek melts, as scorning it should pass,
    To wash the foul face of the sluttish ground,
    Who is but drunken when she seemeth drown'd.

O hard-believing love, how strange it seems
Not to believe, and yet too credulous!
Thy weal and woe are both of them extremes;
Despair and hope makes thee ridiculous:
    The one doth flatter thee in thoughts unlikely,
    In likely thoughts the other kills thee quickly.

Now she unweaves the web that she hath wrought;
Adonis lives, and Death is not to blame;
It was not she that call'd him all to-naught:
Now she adds honours to his hateful name;
    She clepes him king of graves, and grave for
      kings,
    Imperious supreme of all mortal things.

'No, no,' quoth she, 'sweet Death, I did but jest;
Yet pardon me I felt a kind of fear
Whenas I met the boar, that bloody beast
Which knows no pity, but is still severe:
    Then, gentle shadow,— truth I must confess,—
    I rail'd on thee, fearing my love's decease.

''Tis not my fault: the boar provoked my tongue;
Be wreakt on him, invisible commander;
'Tis he, foul creature, that hath done thee wrong;
I did but act, he's author of thy slander:
    Grief hath two tongues; and never woman yet
    Could rule them both without ten women's wit.'

Thus hoping that Adonis is alive,
Her rash suspect she doth extenuate;
And that his beauty may the better thrive,
With Death she humbly doth insinuate;
    Tells him of trophies, statues, tombs, and
      stories
    His victories, his triumphs, and his glories.

'O Jove,' quoth she, 'how much a fool was I
To be of such a weak and silly mind
To wail his death who lives, and must not die
Till mutual overthrow of mortal kind!
    For he being dead, with him is beauty slain,
    And, beauty dead, black chaos comes again.

'Fie, fie, fond love, thou art as full of fear
As one with treasure laden hemm'd with thieves;
Trifles, unwitnessed with eye or ear,
Thy coward heart with false bethinking grieves.'
    Even at this word she hears a merry horn,
    Whereat she leaps that was but late forlorn.

As falcons to the lure, away she flies;
The grass stoops not, she treads on it so light;
And in her haste unfortunately spies
The foul boar's conquest on her fair delight;
    Which seen, her eyes, as murder'd with the
      view,
    Like stars ashamed of day, themselves with-
      drew;

Or as the snail, whose tender horns being hit,
Shrinks backward in his shelly cave with pain,
And there, all smother'd up, in shade doth sit,
Long after fearing to creep forth again;
    So at his bloody view her eyes are fled
    Into the deep-dark cabins of her head:

Where they resign their office and their light
To the disposing of her troubled brain;
Who bids them still consort with ugly night,
And never wound the heart with looks again;
    Who, like a king perplexed in his throne,
    By their suggestion gives a deadly groan,

Whereat each tributary subject quakes;
As when the wind, imprison'd in the ground,
Struggling for passage, earth's foundation shakes,
Which with cold terror doth men's minds con-
    found.
    This mutiny each part doth so surprise,
    That from their dark beds once more leap her
    eyes;

And, being open'd, threw unwilling light
Upon the wide wound that the boar had trencht
In his soft flank; whose wonted lily white
With purple tears, that his wound wept, was
    drencht:
    No flower was nigh, no grass, herb, leaf, or weed,
    But stole his blood, and seem'd with him to
    bleed.

This solemn sympathy poor Venus noteth;
Over one shoulder doth she hang her head:
Dumbly she passions, franticly she doteth;
She thinks he could not die, he is not dead:
    Her voice is stopt, her joints forget to bow;
    Her eyes are mad that they have wept till now.

Upon his hurt she looks so steadfastly,
That her sight dazzling makes the wound seem
    three;
And then she reprehends her mangling eye,
That makes more gashes where no breach should
    be:
    His face seems twain, each several limb is
    doubled;
    For oft the eye mistakes, the brain being
    troubled.

'My tongue cannot express my grief for one,
And yet,' quoth she, 'behold two Adons dead!
My sighs are blown away, my salt tears gone,
Mine eyes are turn'd to fire, my heart to lead:
    Heavy heart's lead, melt at mine eyes' red fire!
    So shall I die by drops of hot desire.

'Alas, poor world, what treasure hast thou lost!
What face remains alive that's worth the viewing?
Whose tongue is music now? what canst thou
    boast
Of things long since, or any thing ensuing?
    The flowers are sweet, their colours fresh and
    trim;
    But true-sweet beauty lived and died with him.

'Bonnet nor veil henceforth no creature wear!
Nor sun nor wind will ever strive to kiss you:
Having no fair to lose, you need not fear;
The sun doth scorn you, and the wind doth hiss
    you:
    But when Adonis lived, sun and sharp air
    Lurkt like two thieves, to rob him of his fair:

'And therefore would he put his bonnet on,
Under whose brim the gaudy sun would peep;
The wind would blow it off, and, being gone,
Play with his locks: then would Adonis weep;
    And straight, in pity of his tender years,
    They both would strive who first should dry his
    tears.

'To see his face the lion walkt along
Behind some hedge, because he would not fear
    him;
To recreate himself when he hath sung,
The tiger would be tame, and gently hear him;
    If he had spoke, the wolf would leave his prey,
    And never fright the silly lamb that day.

'When he beheld his shadow in the brook,
The fishes spread on it their golden gills;
When he was by, the birds such pleasure took,
That some would sing, some other in their bills
    Would bring him mulberries and ripe-red
    cherries;
    He fed them with his sight, they him with
    berries.

'But this foul, grim, and urchin-snouted boar,
Whose downward eye still looketh for a grave,
Ne'er saw the beauteous livery that he wore;
Witness the entertainment that he gave:
    If he did see his face, why then I know
    He thought to kiss him, and hath kill'd him so.

''Tis true, 'tis true; thus was Adonis slain:
He ran upon the boar with his sharp spear,
Who did not whet his teeth at him again,
But by a kiss thought to persuade him there;
    And nuzzling in his flank, the loving swine
    Sheathed, unaware, the tusk in his soft groin.

'Had I been tooth'd like him, I must confess,
With kissing him I should have kill'd him first;
But he is dead, and never did he bless
My youth with his; the more am I accurst.'
    With this, she falleth in the place she stood,
    And stains her face with his congealed blood.

She looks upon his lips, and they are pale;
She takes him by the hand, and that is cold;
She whispers in his ears a heavy tale,
As if they heard the woeful words she told;
    She lifts the coffer-lids that close his eyes,
    Where, lo, two lamps, burnt out, in darkness
    lies;

Two glasses, where herself herself beheld
A thousand times, and now no more reflect;
Their virtue lost, wherein they late excell'd,
And every beauty robb'd of his effect:
    'Wonder of time,' quoth she, 'this is my spite,
    That, thou being dead, the day should yet be
    light.

'Since thou art dead, lo, here I prophesy
Sorrow on love hereafter shall attend:
It shall be waited on with jealousy,
Find sweet beginning, but unsavoury end;
    Ne'er settled equally, but high or low;
    That all love's pleasure shall not match his woe.

'It shall be fickle, false, and full of fraud;
Bud and be blasted in a breathing-while;
The bottom poison, and the top o'erstraw'd
With sweets that shall the truest sight beguile:
   The strongest body shall it make most weak,
   Strike the wise dumb, and teach the fool to
     speak.

'It shall be sparing and too full of riot,
Teaching decrepit age to tread the measures;
The staring ruffian shall it keep in quiet,
Pluck down the rich, enrich the poor with treas-
     ures;
   It shall be raging-mad and silly-mild,
   Make the young old, the old become a child.

'It shall suspect where is no cause of fear;
It shall not fear where it should most mistrust;
It shall be merciful and too severe,
And most deceiving when it seems most just;
   Perverse it shall be where it shows most toward,
   Put fear to valour, courage to the coward.

'It shall be cause of war and dire events,
And set dissension 'twixt the son and sire;
Subject and servile to all discontents,
As dry combustious matter is to fire:
   Sith in his prime Death doth my love destroy,
   They that love best their loves shall not enjoy.'

By this, the boy that by her side lay kill'd
Was melted like a vapour from her sight;
And in his blood, that on the ground lay spill'd,
A purple flower sprung up, chequer'd with white,

Resembling well his pale cheeks, and the blood
Which in round drops upon their whiteness
   stood.

She bows her head the new-sprung flower to
   smell,
Comparing it to her Adonis' breath;
And says within her bosom it shall dwell,
Since he himself is reft from her by Death:
   She crops the stalk, and in the breach appears
   Green-dropping sap, which she compares to
     tears.

'Poor flower,' quoth she, 'this was thy father's
   guise,—
Sweet issue of a more sweet-smelling sire,—
For every little grief to wet his eyes:
To grow unto himself was his desire,
   And so 'tis thine; but know, it is as good
   To wither in my breast as in his blood.

'Here was thy father's bed, here in my breast;
Thou art the next of blood, and 'tis thy right:
Lo, in this hollow cradle take thy rest,
My throbbing heart shall rock thee day and night:
   There shall not be one minute in an hour
   Wherein I will not kiss my sweet love's flower.'

Thus weary of the world away she hies,
And yokes her silver doves; by whose swift aid
Their mistress, mounted, through the empty skies
In her light chariot quickly is convey'd;
   Holding their course to Paphos, where their
     queen
   Means to immure herself and not be seen.

LUCRECE

TO THE RIGHT HONOURABLE HENRY WRIOTHESLEY,

EARL OF SOUTHAMPTON, AND BARON OF TITCHFIELD.

THE love I dedicate to your Lordship is without end; whereof this pamphlet, without beginning, is but a superfluous moiety. The warrant I have of your honourable disposition, not the worth of my untutor'd lines, makes it assured of acceptance. What I have done is yours; what I have to do is yours; being part in all I have, devoted yours. Were my worth greater, my duty would show greater; meantime, as it is, it is bound to your Lordship, to whom I wish long life, still lengthen'd with all happiness.

Your Lordship's in all duty,

WILLIAM SHAKESPEARE.

THE ARGUMENT.

LUCIUS TARQUINIUS (for his excessive pride surnamed Superbus), after he had caused his own father-in-law Servius Tullius to be cruelly murder'd, and, contrary to the Roman laws and customs, not requiring or staying for the people's suffrages, had possest himself of the kingdom, went, accompanied with his sons and other noblemen of Rome, to besiege Ardea. During which siege the principal men of the army meeting one evening at the tent of Sextus Tarquinius, the king's son, in their discourses after supper every one commended the virtues of his own wife; among whom Collatinus extoll'd the incomparable chastity of his wife Lucretia. In that pleasant humour they all posted to Rome; and intending, by their secret and sudden arrival, to make trial of that which every one had before avoucht, only Collatinus finds his wife, though it were late in the night, spinning amongst her maids: the other ladies were all found dancing and revelling, or in several disports. Whereupon the noblemen yielded Collatinus the victory, and his wife the fame. At that time Sextus Tarquinius being inflamed with Lucrece' beauty, yet smothering his passions for the present, departed with the rest back to the camp; from whence he shortly after privily withdrew himself, and was (according to his estate) royally entertain'd and lodged by Lucrece at Collatium. The same night he treacherously stealeth into her chamber, violently ravisht her, and early in the morning speedeth away. Lucrece, in this lamentable plight, hastily dispatcheth messengers, one to Rome for her father, another to the camp for Collatine. They came, the one accompanied with Junius Brutus, the other with Publius Valerius; and finding Lucrece attired in mourning habit, demanded the cause of her sorrow. She, first taking an oath of them for her revenge, reveal'd the actor, and whole manner of his dealing, and withal suddenly stabb'd herself. Which done, with one consent they all vow'd to root out the whole hated family of the Tarquins; and bearing the dead body to Rome, Brutus acquainted the people with the doer and manner of the vile deed, with a bitter invective against the tyranny of the king: wherewith the people were so moved, that with one consent and a general acclamation the Tarquins were all exiled, and the state government changed from kings to consuls.

FROM the besieged Ardea all in post,
Borne by the trustless wings of false desire,
Lust-breathed Tarquin leaves the Roman host,
And to Collatium bears the lightless fire
Which, in pale embers hid, lurks to aspire
  And girdle with embracing flames the waist
  Of Collatine's fair love, Lucrece the chaste.

Haply that name of 'chaste' unhap'ly set
This bateless edge on his keen appetite;
When Collatine unwisely did not let
To praise the clear unmatched red and white
Which triumpht in that sky of his delight,
  Where mortal stars, as bright as heaven's
    beauties,
  With pure aspects did him peculiar duties.

For he the night before, in Tarquin's tent,
Unlockt the treasure of his happy state;
What priceless wealth the heavens had him lent
In the possession of his beauteous mate;
Reckoning his fortune at such high-proud rate,
  That kings might be espoused to more fame,
  But king nor peer to such a peerless dame.

O happiness enjoy'd but of a few!
And, if possest, as soon decay'd and done
As is the morning's silver-melting dew
Against the golden splendour of the sun!
An expired date, cancell'd ere well begun:
  Honour and beauty, in the owner's arms,
  Are weakly fortrest from a world of harms.

Beauty itself doth of itself persuade
The eyes of men without an orator;
What needeth, then, apologies be made,
To set forth that which is so singular?
Or why is Collatine the publisher
  Of that rich jewel he should keep unknown
  From thievish ears, because it is his own?

Perchance his boast of Lucrece' sovereignty
Suggested this proud issue of a king;
For by our ears our hearts oft tainted be:
Perchance that envy of so rich a thing,
Braving compare, disdainfully did sting
  His high-pitcht thoughts, that meaner men
    should vaunt
  That golden hap which their superiors want.

But some untimely thought did instigate
His all-too-timeless speed, if none of those:
His honour, his affairs, his friends, his state,
Neglected all, with swift intent he goes
To quench the coal which in his liver glows.
    O rash-false heat, wrapt in repentant cold,
    Thy hasty spring still blasts, and ne'er grows old!

When at Collatium this false lord arrived,
Well was he welcomed by the Roman dame,
Within whose face Beauty and Virtue strived
Which of them both should underprop her fame:
When Virtue bragg'd, Beauty would blush for
    shame;
    When Beauty boasted blushes, in despite
    Virtue would stain that o'er with silver white.

But Beauty, in that white intituled,
From Venus' doves doth challenge that fair field:
Then Virtue claims from Beauty Beauty's red,
Which Virtue gave the golden age to gild
Their silver cheeks, and call'd it then their shield;
    Teaching them thus to use it in the fight,—
    When shame assail'd, the red should fence the
    white.

This heraldry in Lucrece' face was seen,
Argued by Beauty's red and Virtue's white:
Of either's colour was the other queen,
Proving from world's minority their right:
Yet their ambition makes them still to fight;
    The sovereignty of either being so great,
    That oft they interchange each other's seat.

This silent war of lilies and of roses,
Which Tarquin view'd in her fair face's field,
In their pure ranks his traitor eye encloses;
Where, lest between them both it should be kill'd,
The coward captive vanquished doth yield
    To those two armies that would let him go,
    Rather than triumph in so false a foe.

Now thinks he that her husband's shallow
    tongue,—
The niggard prodigal that praised her so,—
In that high task hath done her beauty wrong,
Which far exceeds his barren skill to show:
Therefore that praise which Collatine doth owe
    Enchanted Tarquin answers with surmise,
    In silent wonder of still-gazing eyes.

This earthly saint, adored by this devil,
Little suspecteth the false worshipper;
For unstain'd thoughts do seldom dream on evil;
Birds never limed no secret bushes fear:
So guiltless she securely gives good cheer
    And reverend welcome to her princely guest,
    Whose inward ill no outward harm exprest:

For that he colour'd with his high estate,
Hiding base sin in plaits of majesty;
That nothing in him seem'd inordinate,
Save sometime too much wonder of his eye,
Which, having all, all could not satisfy;
    But, poorly rich, so wanteth in his store,
    That, cloy'd with much, he pineth still for more.

But she, that never coped with stranger eyes,
Could pick no meaning from their parling looks,
Nor read the subtle-shining secrecies
Writ in the glassy margents of such books:
She toucht no unknown baits, nor fear'd no hooks;
    Nor could she moralize his wanton sight,
    More than his eyes were open'd to the light.

He stories to her ears her husband's fame,
Won in the fields of fruitful Italy;
And decks with praises Collatine's high name,
Made glorious by his manly chivalry
With bruised arms and wreaths of victory:
    Her joy with heaved-up hand she doth express,
    And, wordless, so greets heaven for his success.

Far from the purpose of his coming thither,
He makes excuses for his being there:
No cloudy show of stormy blustering weather
Doth yet in his fair welkin once appear;
Till sable Night, mother of dread and fear,
    Upon the world dim darkness doth display,
    And in her vaulty prison stows the Day.

For then is Tarquin brought unto his bed,
Intending weariness with heavy sprite;
For, after supper, long he questioned
With modest Lucrece, and wore out the night:
Now leaden slumber with life's strength doth fight,
    And every one to rest themselves betake,
    Save thieves, and cares, and troubled minds,
    that wake.

As one of which doth Tarquin lie revolving
The sundry dangers of his will's obtaining;
Yet ever to obtain his will resolving,
Though weak-built hopes persuade him to ab-
    staining:
Despair to gain doth traffic oft for gaining;
    And when great treasure is the meed proposed,
    Though death be adjunct, there's no death sup-
    posed.

Those that much covet are with gain so fond,
That what they have not, that which they possess,
They scatter and unloose it from their bond,
And so, by hoping more, they have but less;
Or, gaining more, the profit of excess
    Is but to surfeit, and such griefs sustain,
    That they prove bankrout in this poor-rich gain.

The aim of all is but to nurse the life
With honour, wealth, and ease, in waning age;
And in this aim there is such thwarting strife,
That one for all, or all for one we gage;
As life for honour in fell battle's rage;
    Honour for wealth; and oft that wealth doth cost
    The death of all, and all together lost.

So that in vent'ring ill we leave to be
The things we are for that which we expect;
And this ambitious foul infirmity,
In having much, torments us with defect
Of that we have: so then we do neglect
    The thing we have; and, all for want of wit,
    Make something nothing by augmenting it.

Such hazard now must doting Tarquin make,
Pawning his honour to obtain his lust;
And for himself himself he must forsake:
Then where is truth, if there be no self-trust?
When shall he think to find a stranger just,
    When he himself himself confounds, betrays
    To slanderous tongues and wretched hateful
      days?

Now stole upon the time the dead of night,
When heavy sleep had closed up mortal eyes:
No comfortable star did lend his light,
No noise but owls' and wolves' death-boding ries;
Now serves the season that they may surprise
    The silly lambs: pure thoughts are dead and
      still,
    While lust and murder wakes to stain and kill.

And now this lustful lord leapt from his bed,
Throwing his mantle rudely o'er his arm;
Is madly tost between desire and dread;
Th'one sweetly flatters, th'other feareth harm;
But honest fear, bewitcht with lust's foul charm,
    Doth too-too oft betake him to retire,
    Beaten away by brain-sick rude desire.

His falchion on a flint he softly smiteth,
That from the cold stone sparks of fire do fly;
Whereat a waxen torch forthwith he lighteth,
Which must be lode-star to his lustful eye;
And to the flame thus speaks advisedly,
    'As from this cold flint I enforced this fire,
    So Lucrece must I force to my desire.'

Here pale with fear he doth premeditate
The dangers of his loathsome enterprise,
And in his inward mind he doth debate
What following sorrow may on this arise:
Then looking scornfully, he doth despise
    His naked armour of still-slaughter'd lust,
    And justly thus controls his thoughts unjust:

'Fair torch, burn out thy light, and lend it not
To darken her whose light excelleth thine:
And die, unhallow'd thoughts, before you blot
With your uncleanness that which is divine;
Offer pure incense to so pure a shrine:
    Let fair humanity abhor the deed
    That spots and stains love's modest snow-
      white weed.

'O shame to knighthood and to shining arms!
O foul dishonour to my household's grave!
O impious act, including all foul harms!
A martial man to be sort fancy's slave!
True valour still a true respect should have;
    Then my digression is so vile, so base,
    That it will live engraven in my face.

'Yea, though I die, the scandal will survive,
And be an eye-sore in my golden coat;
Some loathsome dash the herald will contrive,
To cipher me how fondly I did dote;
That my posterity, shamed with the note,
    Shall curse my bones, and hold it for no sin
    To wish that I their father had not bin.

'What win I, if I gain the thing I seek?
A dream, a breath, a troth o fleeting joy.
Who buys a minute's mirth o wail a week?
Or sells eternity to get a toy?
For one sweet grape who will the vine destroy?
    Or what fond begger, but to touch the crown,
    Would with the sceptre straight be strucken
      down?

'If Collatinus dream of my intent,
Will he not wake, and in a desperate rage
Post hither, this vile purpose to prevent?
This siege that hath engirt his marriage,
This blur to youth, this sorrow to the sage,
    This dying virtue, this surviving shame,
    Whose crime will bear an ever-during blame?

'O, what excuse can my invention make,
When thou shalt charge me with so black a deed?
Will not my tongue be mute, my frail joints shake,
Mine eyes forgo their light, my false heart bleed?
The guilt being great, the fear doth still exceed;
    And extreme fear can neither fight nor fly,
    But coward-like with trembling terror die.

'Had Collatinus kill'd my son or sire,
Or lain in ambush to betray my life,
Or were he not my dear friend, this desire
Might have excuse to work upon his wife,
As in revenge or quittal of such strife:
    But as he is my kinsman, my dear friend,
    The shame and fault finds no excuse nor end.

'Shameful it is;—ay, if the fact be known:
Hateful it is;—there is no hate in loving:
I'll beg her love;—but she is not her own:
The worst is but denial and reproving:
My will is strong, past reason's weak removing
    Who fears a sentence or an old man's saw
    Shall by a painted cloth be kept in awe.'

Thus, graceless, holds he disputation
'Tween frozen conscience and hot burning will,
And with good thoughts makes dispensation,
Urging the worser sense for vantage still;
Which in a moment doth confound and kill
    All pure effects, and doth so far proceed,
    That what is vile shows like a virtuous deed.

Quoth he, 'She took me kindly by the hand,
And gazed for tidings in my eager eyes,
Fearing some hard news from the warlike band,
Where her beloved Collatinus lies.
O, how her fear did make her colour rise!
    First red as roses that on lawn we lay,
    Then white as lawn, the roses took away.

'And how her hand, in my hand being lockt,
Forced it to tremble with her loyal fear!
Which struck her sad, and then it faster rockt,
Until her husband's welfare she did hear;
Whereat she smiled with so sweet a cheer,
    That had Narcissus seen her as she stood,
    Self-love had never drown'd him in the flood.

'Why hunt I, then, for colour or excuses?
All orators are dumb when beauty pleadeth;
Poor wretches have remorse in poor abuses;
Love thrives not in the heart that shadows dread-
  eth:
Affection is my captain, and he leadeth;
  And when his gaudy banner is display'd,
  The coward fights, and will not be dismay'd.

'Then, childish fear avaunt! debating die!
Respect and reason wait on wrinkled age!
My heart shall never countermand mine eye:
Sad pause and deep regard beseems the sage;
My part is youth, and beats these from the stage:
  Desire my pilot is, beauty my prize;
  Then who fears sinking where such treasure
    lies?'

As corn o'ergrown by weeds, so heedful fear
Is almost choked by unresisted lust.
Away he steals with open listening ear,
Full of foul hope and full of fond mistrust;
Both which, as servitors to the unjust,
  So cross him with their opposite persuasion,
  That now he vows a league, and now invasion.

Within his thought her heavenly image sits,
And in the self-same seat sits Collatine:
That eye which looks on her confounds his wits;
That eye which him beholds, as more divine,
Unto a view so false will not incline;
  But with a pure appeal seeks to the heart,
  Which once corrupted takes the worser part;

And therein heartens up his servile powers,
Who, flatter'd by their leader's jocund show,
Stuff up his lust, as minutes fill up hours;
And as their captain, so their pride doth grow,
Paying more slavish tribute than they owe.
  By reprobate desire thus madly led,
  The Roman lord marcheth to Lucrece' bed.

The locks between her chamber and his will,
Each one by him enforced, retires his ward;
But, as they open, they all rate his ill,
Which drives the creeping thief to some regard:
The threshold grates the door to have him heard;
  Night-wandering weasels shriek to see him
    there;
  They fright him, yet he still pursues his fear.

As each unwilling portal yields him way,
Through little vents and crannies of the place
The wind wars with his torch to make him stay,
And blows the smoke of it into his face,
Extinguishing his conduct in this case;
  But his hot heart, which fond desire doth scorch,
  Puffs forth another wind that fires the torch:

And being lighted, by the light he spies
Lucretia's glove, wherein her needle sticks:
He takes it from the rushes where it lies,
And griping it, the needle his finger pricks;
As who should say, 'This glove to wanton tricks
  Is not inured; return again in haste;
  Thou see'st our mistress' ornaments are chaste.'

But all these poor forbiddings could not stay him;
He in the worst sense consters their denial:
The doors, the wind, the glove, that did delay him,
He takes for accidental things of trial;
Or as those bars which stop the hourly dial,
  Who with a lingering stay his course doth let,
  Till every minute pays the hour his debt.

'So, so,' quoth he, 'these lets attend the time,
Like little frosts that sometime threat the spring,
To add a more rejoicing to the prime,
And give the sneaped birds more cause to sing.
Pain pays the income of each precious thing;
  Huge rocks, high winds, strong pirates, shelves
    and sands,
  The merchant fears, ere rich at home he lands.'

Now is he come unto the chamber-door
That shuts him from the heaven of his thought,
Which with a yielding latch, and with no more,
Hath barr'd him from the blessed thing he sought.
So from himself impiety hath wrought,
  That for his prey to pray he doth begin,
  As if the heavens should countenance his sin.

But in the midst of his unfruitful prayer,
Having solicited th'eternal power
That his foul thoughts might compass his fair fair,
And they would stand auspicious to the hour,
Even there he starts:—quoth he, 'I must deflower:
  The powers to whom I pray abhor this fact,
  How can they, then, assist me in the act?

'Then Love and Fortune be my gods, my guide!
My will is backt with resolution:
Thoughts are but dreams till their effects be tried;
The blackest sin is clear'd with absolution;
Against love's fire fear's frost hath dissolution.
  The eye of heaven is out, and misty night
  Covers the shame that follows sweet delight.'

This said, his guilty hand pluckt up the latch,
And with his knee the door he opens wide.
The dove sleeps fast that this night-owl will catch:
Thus treason works ere traitors be espied.
Who sees the lurking serpent steps aside;
  But she, sound sleeping, fearing no such thing,
  Lies at the mercy of his mortal sting.

Into the chamber wickedly he stalks,
And gazeth on her yet-unstained bed.
The curtains being close, about he walks,
Rolling his greedy eyeballs in his head:
By their high treason is his heart misled;
  Which gives the watch-word to his hand full
    soon
  To draw the cloud that hides the silver moon.

Look, as the fair and fiery-pointed sun,
Rushing from forth a cloud, bereaves our sight;
Even so, the curtain drawn, his eyes begun
To wink, being blinded with a greater light:
Whether it is that she reflects so bright,
  That dazzleth them, or else some shame sup-
    posed;
  But blind they are, and keep themselves en-
    closed.

O, had they in that darksome prison died!
Then had they seen the period of their ill;
Then Collatine again, by Lucrece' side,
In his clear bed might have reposed still:
But they must ope, this blessed league to kill;
　　And holy-thoughted Lucrece to their sight
　　Must sell her joy, her life, her world's delight.

Her lily hand her rosy cheek lies under,
Cozening the pillow of a lawful kiss;
Who, therefore angry, seems to part in sunder,
Swelling on either side to want his bliss;
Between whose hills her head entombed is:
　　Where, like a virtuous monument, she lies,
　　To be admired of lewd unhallow'd eyes.

Without the bed her other fair hand was,
On the green coverlet; whose perfect white
Show'd like an April daisy on the grass,
With pearly sweat, resembling dew of night.
Her eyes, like marigolds, had sheathed their light,
　　And canopied in darkness sweetly lay,
　　Till they might open to adorn the day.

Her hair, like golden threads, play'd with her
　　breath;
O modest wantons! wanton modesty!
Showing life's triumph in the map of death,
And death's dim look in life's mortality:
Each in her sleep themselves so beautify,
　　As if between them twain there were no strife,
　　But that life lived in death, and death in life.

Her breasts, like ivory globes circled with blue,
A pair of maiden worlds unconquered,
Save of their lord no bearing yoke they knew,
And him by oath they truly honoured.
These worlds in Tarquin new ambition bred;
　　Who, like a foul usurper, went about
　　From this fair throne to heave the owner out.

What could he see but mightily he noted?
What did he note but strongly he desired?
What he beheld, on that he firmly doted,
And in his will his wilful eye he tired.
With more than admiration he admired
　　Her azure veins, her alabaster skin,
　　Her coral lips, her snow-white dimpled chin.

As the grim lion fawneth o'er his prey,
Sharp hunger by the conquest satisfied,
So o'er this sleeping soul doth Tarquin stay,
His rage of lust by gazing qualified;
Slackt, not supprest; for standing by her side,
　　His eye, which late this mutiny restrains,
　　Unto a greater uproar tempts his veins:

And they, like straggling slaves for pillage fighting,
Obdurate vassals fell exploits effecting,
In bloody death and ravishment delighting,
Nor children's tears nor mothers' groans respect-
　　ing,
Swell in their pride, the onset still expecting:
　　Anon his beating heart, alarum striking,
　　Gives the hot charge, and bids them do their
　　liking.

His drumming heart cheers up his burning eye,
His eye commends the leading to his hand;
His hand, as proud of such a dignity,
Smoking with pride, marcht on to make his stand
On her bare breast, the heart of all her land;
　　Whose ranks of blue veins, as his hand did scale,
　　Left their round turrets destitute and pale.

They, mustering to the quiet cabinet
Where their dear governess and lady lies,
Do tell her she is dreadfully beset,
And fright her with confusion of their cries:
She, much amazed, breaks ope her lockt-up eyes,
　　Who, peeping forth this tumult to behold,
　　Are by his flaming torch dimm'd and controll'd.

Imagine her as one in dead of night
From forth dull sleep by dreadful fancy waking,
That thinks she hath beheld some ghastly sprite,
Whose grim aspect sets every joint a-shaking;
What terror 'tis! but she, in worser taking,
　　From sleep disturbed, heedfully doth view
　　The sight which makes supposed terror true.

Wrapt and confounded in a thousand fears,
Like to a new-kill'd bird she trembling lies;
She dares not look; yet, winking, there appears
Quick-shifting antics, ugly in her eyes:
Such shadows are the weak brain's forgeries;
　　Who, angry that the eyes fly from their lights,
　　In darkness daunts them with more dreadful
　　sights.

His hand, that yet remains upon her breast,—
Rude ram, to batter such an ivory wall!—
May feel her heart—poor citizen!—distrest,
Wounding itself to death, rise up and fall,
Beating her bulk, that his hand shakes withal.
　　This moves in him more rage, and lesser pity,
　　To make the breach, and enter this sweet city.

First, like a trumpet, doth his tongue begin
To sound a parley to his heartless foe;
Who o'er the white sheet peers her whiter chin,
The reason of this rash alarm to know,
Which he by dumb demeanour seeks to show;
　　But she with vehement prayers urgeth still
　　Under what colour he commits this ill.

Thus he replies: 'The colour in thy face—
That even for anger makes the lily pale,
And the red rose blush at her own disgrace—
Shall plead for me, and tell my loving tale:
Under that colour am I come to scale
　　Thy never-conquer'd fort: the fault is thine,
　　For those thine eyes betray thee unto mine.

'Thus I forestall thee, if thou mean to chide:
Thy beauty hath ensnared thee to this night,
Where thou with patience must my will abide;
My will that marks thee for my earth's delight,
Which I to conquer sought with all my might;
　　But as reproof and reason beat it dead,
　　By thy bright beauty was it newly bred.

'I see what crosses my attempt will bring;
I know what thorns the growing rose defends;
I think the honey guarded with a sting;
All this beforehand counsel comprehends:
But will is deaf, and hears no heedful friends;
    Only he hath an eye to gaze on beauty,
    And dotes on what he looks, 'gainst law or duty.

'I have debated, even in my soul,
What wrong, what shame, what sorrow I shall
    breed;
But nothing can affection's course control,
Or stop the headlong fury of his speed.
I know repentant tears ensue the deed,
    Reproach, disdain, and deadly enmity;
    Yet strive I to embrace mine infamy.'

This said, he shakes aloft his Roman blade,
Which, like a falcon towering in the skies,
Coucheth the fowl below with his wings' shade,
Whose crooked beak threats if he mount he dies:
So under his insulting falchion lies
    Harmless Lucretia, marking what he tells
    With trembling fear, as fowl hear falcon's bells.

'Lucrece,' quoth he, 'this night I must enjoy thee:
If thou deny, then force must work my way,
For in thy bed I purpose to destroy thee:
That done, some worthless slave of thine I'll slay,
To kill thine honour with thy life's decay;
    And in thy dead arms do I mean to place him,
    Swearing I slew him, seeing thee embrace him.

'So thy surviving husband shall remain
The scornful mark of every open eye;
Thy kinsmen hang their heads at this disdain,
Thy issue blurr'd with nameless bastardy:
And thou, the author of their obloquy,
    Shalt have thy trespass cited up in rimes,
    And sung by children in succeeding times.

'But if thou yield, I rest thy secret friend:
The fault unknown is as a thought unacted;
A little harm done to a great good end
For lawful policy remains enacted.
The poisonous simple sometime is compacted
    In a pure compound; being so applied,
    His venom in effect is purified.

'Then, for thy husband and thy children's sake,
Tender my suit: bequeath not to their lot
The shame that from them no device can take,
The blemish that will never be forgot;
Worse than a slavish wipe or birth-hour's blot:
    For marks descried in men's nativity
    Are nature's faults, not their own infamy.'

Here with a cockatrice' dead-killing eye
He rouseth up himself, and makes a pause;
While she, the picture of true piety,
Like a white hind under the gripe's sharp claws,
Pleads, in a wilderness where are no laws,
    To the rough beast that knows no gentle right,
    Nor aught obeys but his foul appetite.

But when a black-faced cloud the world doth
    threat,
In his dim mist the aspiring mountains hiding,
From earth's dark womb some gentle gust doth
    get,
Which blows these pitchy vapours from their bid-
    ing,
Hindering their present fall by this dividing;
    So his unhallow'd haste her words delays,
    And moody Pluto winks while Orpheus plays.

Yet, foul night-waking cat, he doth but dally,
While in his hold-fast foot the weak mouse
    panteth:
Her sad behaviour feeds his vulture folly,
A swallowing gulf that even in plenty wanteth:
His ear her prayers admits, but his heart granteth
    No penetrable entrance to her plaining:
    Tears harden lust, though marble wear with
    raining.

Her pity-pleading eyes are sadly fixed
In the remorseless wrinkles of his face;
Her modest eloquence with sighs is mixed,
Which to her oratory adds more grace.
She puts the period often from his place;
    And midst the sentence so her accent breaks,
    That twice she doth begin ere once she speaks.

She conjures him by high almighty Jove,
By knighthood, gentry, and sweet friendship's
    oath,
By her untimely tears, her husband's love,
By holy human law, and common troth,
By heaven and earth, and all the power of both,
    That to his borrow'd bed he make retire,
    And stoop to honour, not to foul desire.

Quoth she, 'Reward not hospitality
With such black payment as thou hast pretended;
Mud not the fountain that gave drink to thee;
Mar not the thing that cannot be amended;
End thy ill aim before thy shoot be ended;
    He is no woodman that doth bend his bow
    To strike a poor unseasonable doe.

'My husband is thy friend,—for his sake spare
    me;
Thyself art mighty,—for thine own sake leave
    me;
Myself a weakling,—do not, then, ensnare me;
Thou look'st not like deceit,—do not deceive me.
My sighs, like whirlwinds, labour hence to heave
    thee:
    If ever man were moved with woman's moans,
    Be moved with my tears, my sighs, my groans:

'All which together, like a troubled ocean,
Beat at thy rocky and wrack-threatening heart,
To soften it with their continual motion;
For stones dissolved to water do convert.
O, if no harder than a stone thou art,
    Melt at my tears, and be compassionate!
    Soft pity enters at an iron gate.

'In Tarquin's likeness I did entertain thee:
Hast thou put on his shape to do him shame?
To all the host of heaven I complain me,
Thou wrong'st his honour, wound'st his princely
    name.
Thou art not what thou seem'st; and if the same,
    Thou seem'st not what thou art, a god, a king;
    For kings like gods should govern every thing.

'How will thy shame be seeded in thine age,
When thus thy vices bud before thy spring!
If in thy hope thou darest do such outrage,
What darest thou not when once thou art a king?
O, be remember'd, no outrageous thing
    From vassal actors can be wiped away;
    Then kings' misdeeds cannot be hid in clay.

'This deed will make thee only loved for fear;
But happy monarchs still are fear'd for love:
With foul offenders thou perforce must bear,
When they in thee the like offences prove:
If but for fear of this, thy will remove;
    For princes are the glass, the school, the book,
    Where subjects' eyes do learn, do read, do look.

'And wilt thou be the school where Lust shall learn?
Must he in thee read lectures of such shame?
Wilt thou be glass wherein it shall discern
Authority for sin, warrant for blame,
To privilege dishonour in thy name?
    Thou back'st reproach against long-living laud,
    And makest fair reputation but a bawd.

'Hast thou command? by him that gave it thee,
From a pure heart command thy rebel will:
Draw not thy sword to guard iniquity,
For it was lent thee all that brood to kill.
Thy princely office how canst thou fulfil,
    When, pattern'd by thy fault, foul Sin may say,
    He learnt to sin, and thou didst teach the way?

'Think but how vile a spectacle it were,
To view thy present trespass in another.
Men's faults do seldom to themselves appear;
Their own transgressions partially they smother:
This guilt would seem death-worthy in thy
    brother.
    O, how are they wrapt in with infamies
    That from their own misdeeds askance their
    eyes!

'To thee, to thee, my heaved-up hands appeal,
Not to seducing lust, thy rash relier;
I sue for exiled majesty's repeal;
Let him return, and flattering thoughts retire:
His true respect will prison false desire,
    And wipe the dim mist from thy doting eyne,
    That thou shalt see thy state, and pity mine.'

'Have done,' quoth he: 'my uncontrolled tide
Turns not, but swells the higher by this let.
Small lights are soon blown out, huge fires abide,
And with the wind in greater fury fret:
The petty streams that pay a daily debt
    To their salt sovereign, with their fresh falls'
    haste
    Add to his flow, but alter not his taste.'

'Thou art,' quoth she, 'a sea, a sovereign king;
And, lo, there falls into thy boundless flood
Black lust, dishonour, shame, misgoverning,
Who seek to stain the ocean of thy blood.
If all these petty ills shall change thy good,
    Thy sea within a puddle's womb is hearsed,
    And not the puddle in thy sea dispersed.

'So shall these slaves be king, and thou their slave;
Thou nobly base, they basely dignified;
Thou their fair life, and they thy fouler grave:
Thou loathed in their shame, they in thy pride:
The lesser thing should not the greater hide;
    The cedar stoops not to the base shrub's foot,
    But low shrubs wither at the cedar's root.

'So let thy thoughts, low vassals to thy state'—
'No more,' quoth he; 'by heaven, I will not hear
    thee:
Yield to my love; if not, enforced hate,
Instead of love's coy touch, shall rudely tear thee;
That done, despitefully I mean to bear thee
    Unto the base bed of some rascal groom,
    To be thy partner in this shameful doom.'

This said, he sets his foot upon the light,
For light and lust are deadly enemies:
Shame folded up in blind-concealing night,
When most unseen, then most doth tyrannize.
The wolf hath seized his prey, the poor lamb
    cries;
    Till with her own white fleece her voice con-
    troll'd
    Entombs her outcry in her lips' sweet fold:

For with the nightly linen that she wears
He pens her piteous clamours in her head;
Cooling his hot face in the chastest tears
That ever modest eyes with sorrow shed.
O, that prone lust should stain so pure a bed!
    The spots whereof could weeping purify,
    Her tears should drop on them perpetually.

But she hath lost a dearer thing than life,
And he hath won what he would lose again:
This forced league doth force a further strife;
This momentary joy breeds months of pain;
This hot desire converts to cold disdain:
    Pure Chastity is rifled of her store,
    And Lust, the thief, far poorer than before.

Look, as the full-fed hound or gorged hawk,
Unapt for tender smell or speedy flight,
Make slow pursuit, or altogether balk
The prey wherein by nature they delight;
So surfeit-taking Tarquin fares this night:
    His taste delicious, in digestion souring,
    Devours his will, that lived by foul devouring

O, deeper sin than bottomless conceit
Can comprehend in still imagination!
Drunken Desire must vomit his receipt,
Ere he can see his own abomination.
While Lust is in his pride, no exclamation
    Can curb his heat, or rein his rash desire,
    Till, like a jade, Self-will himself doth tire.

And then with lank and lean discolour'd cheek,
With heavy eye, knit brow, and strengthless pace,
Feeble Desire, all recreant, poor, and meek,
Like to a bankrout beggar wails his case:
The flesh being proud, Desire doth fight with
    Grace,
    For there it revels; and when that decays,
    The guilty rebel for remission prays.

So fares it with this faultful lord of Rome,
Who this accomplishment so hotly chased;
For now against himself he sounds this doom,—
That through the length of times he stands dis-
    graced:
Besides, his soul's fair temple is defaced;
    To whose weak ruins muster troops of cares,
    To ask the spotted princess how she fares.

She says, her subjects with foul insurrection
Have batter'd down her consecrated wall,
And by their mortal fault brought in subjection
Her immortality, and made her thrall
To living death and pain perpetual:
    Which in her prescience she controlled still,
    But her foresight could not forestall their will.

Even in this thought through the dark night he
    stealeth,
A captive victor that hath lost in gain;
Bearing away the wound that nothing healeth,
The scar that will, despite of cure, remain;
Leaving his spoil perplext in greater pain.
    She bears the load of lust he left behind,
    And he the burthen of a guilty mind.

He like a thievish dog creeps sadly thence;
She like a wearied lamb lies panting there;
He scowls, and hates himself for his offence;
She, desperate, with her nails her flesh doth tear;
He faintly flies, sweating with guilty fear;
    She stays, exclaiming on the direful night;
    He runs, and chides his vanisht, loathed
        delight.

He thence departs a heavy convertite;
She there remains a hopeless castaway;
He in his speed looks for the morning light;
She prays she never may behold the day,
'For day,' quoth she, 'night's scapes doth open lay,
    And my true eyes have never practised how
    To cloak offences with a cunning brow.

'They think not but that every eye can see
The same disgrace which they themselves behold;
And therefore would they still in darkness be,
To have their unseen sin remain untold;
For they their guilt with weeping will unfold,
    And grave, like water that doth eat in steel,
    Upon my cheeks what helpless shame I feel.'

Here she exclaims against repose and rest,
And bids her eyes hereafter still be blind.
She wakes her heart by beating on her breast,
And bids it leap from thence, where it may find
Some purer chest to close so pure a mind.
    Frantic with grief thus breathes she forth her
        spite
    Against the unseen secrecy of night:

'O comfort-killing Night, image of hell!
Dim register and notary of shame!
Black stage for tragedies and murders fell!
Vast sin-concealing chaos! nurse of blame!
Blind muffled bawd! dark harbour for defame!
    Grim cave of death! whispering conspirator
    With close-tongued treason and the ravisher!

'O hateful, vaporous, and foggy Night!
Since thou art guilty of my cureless crime,
Muster thy mists to meet the eastern light,
Make war against proportion'd course of time;
Or if thou wilt permit the sun to climb
    His wonted height, yet ere he go to bed,
    Knit poisonous clouds about his golden head.

'With rotten damps ravish the morning air;
Let their exhaled unwholesome breaths make sick
The life of purity, the supreme fair,
Ere he arrive his weary noon-tide prick;
And let thy misty vapours march so thick,
    That in their smoky ranks his smother'd light
    May set at noon, and make perpetual night.

'Were Tarquin Night, as he is but Night's child,
The silver-shining queen he would distain;
Her twinkling handmaids too, by him defiled,
Through Night's black bosom should not peep
    again:
So should I have co-partners in my pain;
    And fellowship in woe doth woe assuage,
    As palmers' chat makes short their pilgrimage.

'Where now I have no one to blush with me,
To cross their arms, and hang their heads with
    mine,
To mask their brows, and hide their infamy;
But I alone alone must sit and pine,
Seasoning the earth with showers of silver brine,
    Mingling my talk with tears, my grief with
        groans,
    Poor wasting monuments of lasting moans.

'O Night, thou furnace of foul-reeking smoke,
Let not the jealous Day behold that face
Which underneath thy black all-hiding cloak
Immodestly lies martyr'd with disgrace!
Keep still possession of thy gloomy place,
    That all the faults which in thy reign are made
    May likewise be sepulchred in thy shade!

'Make me not object to the tell-tale Day!
The light will show, character'd in my brow,
The story of sweet chastity's decay,
The impious breach of holy wedlock vow:
Yea, the illiterate, that know not how
    To cipher what is writ in learned books,
    Will quote my loathsome trespass in my looks.

'The nurse, to still her child, will tell my story,
And fright her crying babe with Tarquin's name;
The orator, to deck his oratory,
Will couple my reproach to Tarquin's shame;
Feast-finding minstrels, tuning my defame,
    Will tie the hearers to attend each line,
    How Tarquin wronged me, I Collatine.

'Let my good name, that senseless reputation,
For Collatine's dear love be kept unspotted:
If that be made a theme for disputation,
The branches of another root are rotted,
    That is as clear from this attaint of mine
    As I, ere this, was pure to Collatine.

'O unseen shame! invisible disgrace!
O unfelt sore! crest-wounding, private scar!
Reproach is stampt in Collatinus' face,
And Tarquin's eye may read the mot afar,
    How he in peace is wounded, not in war.
    Alas, how many bear such shameful blows,
    Which not themselves, but he that gives them
    knows!

'If, Collatine, thine honour lay in me,
From me by strong assault it is bereft.
My honey lost, and I, a drone-like bee,
Have no perfection of my summer left,
But robb'd and ransackt by injurious theft:
    In thy weak hive a wandering wasp hath crept,
    And suckt the honey which thy chaste bee kept.

'Yet am I guilty of thy honour's wrack,—
Yet for thy honour did I entertain him;
Coming from thee, I could not put him back,
For it had been dishonour to disdain him:
Besides, of weariness he did complain him,
    And talkt of virtue:—O unlookt-for evil,
    When virtue is profaned in such a devil!

'Why should the worm intrude the maiden bud?
Or hateful cuckoos hatch in sparrows' nests?
Or toads infect fair founts with venom mud?
Or tyrant folly lurk in gentle breasts?
Or kings be breakers of their own behests?
    But no perfection is so absolute,
    That some impurity doth not pollute.

'The aged man that coffers-up his gold
Is plagued with cramps and gouts and painful fits;
And scarce hath eyes his treasure to behold,
And like still-pining Tantalus he sits,
And useless barns the harvest of his wits;
    Having no other pleasure of his gain
    But torment that it cannot cure his pain.

'So then he hath it when he cannot use it,
And leaves it to be master'd by his young;
Who in their pride do presently abuse it:
Their father was too weak, and they too strong,
To hold their cursed-blessed fortune long.
    The sweets we wish for turn to loathed sours
    Even in the moment that we call them ours.

'Unruly blasts wait on the tender spring;
Unwholesome weeds take root with precious
    flowers;
The adder hisses where the sweet birds sing;
What virtue breeds iniquity devours:
We have no good that we can say is ours,
    But ill-annexed Opportunity
    Or kills his life or else his quality.

'O Opportunity, thy guilt is great!
'Tis thou that executest the traitor's treason;
Thou sett'st the wolf where he the lamb may get;
Whoever plots the sin, thou point'st the season;
'Tis thou that spurn'st at right, at law, at reason;
    And in thy shady cell, where none may spy him,
    Sits Sin, to seize the souls that wander by him.

'Thou makest the vestal violate her oath;
Thou blow'st the fire when temperance is thaw'd;
Thou smother'st honesty, thou murder'st troth;
Thou foul abettor! thou notorious bawd!
Thou plantest scandal, and displacest laud:
    Thou ravisher, thou traitor, thou false thief,
    Thy honey turns to gall, thy joy to grief!

'Thy secret pleasure turns to open shame,
Thy private feasting to a public fast,
Thy smoothing titles to a ragged name,
Thy sugar'd tongue to bitter wormwood taste:
Thy violent vanities can never last.
    How comes it, then, vile Opportunity,
    Being so bad, such numbers seek for thee?

'When wilt thou be the humble suppliant's friend,
And bring him where his suit may be obtained?
When wilt thou sort an hour great strifes to end?
Or free that soul which wretchedness hath
    chained?
Give physic to the sick, ease to the pained?
    The poor, lame, blind, halt, creep, cry out for
    thee;
    But they ne'er meet with Opportunity.

'The patient dies while the physician sleeps;
The orphan pines while the oppressor feeds;
Justice is feasting while the widow weeps;
Advice is sporting while infection breeds:
Thou grant'st no time for charitable deeds:
    Wrath, envy, treason, rape, and murder's rages,
    Thy heinous hours wait on them as their pages.

'When Truth and Virtue have to do with thee,
A thousand crosses keep them from thy aid:
They buy thy help; but Sin ne'er gives a fee,
He gratis comes; and thou art well appaid
As well to hear as grant what he hath said.
    My Collatine would else have come to me
    When Tarquin did, but he was stay'd by thee.

'Guilty thou art of murder and of theft,
Guilty of perjury and subornation,
Guilty of treason, forgery, and shift,
Guilty of incest, that abomination;
An accessary by thine inclination
    To all sins past, and all that are to come,
    From the creation to the general doom.

'Mis-shapen Time, copesmate of ugly Night,
Swift subtle post, carrier of grisly care,
Eater of youth, false slave to false delight,
Base watch of woes, sin's pack-horse, virtue's
    snare;
Thou nursest all, and murder'st all that are:
    O, hear me, then, injurious, shifting Time!
    Be guilty of my death, since of my crime.

'Why hath thy servant Opportunity
Betray'd the hours thou gavest me to repose,
Cancell'd my fortunes, and enchained me
To endless date of never-ending woes?
Time's office is to fine the hate of foes;
   To eat up errors by opinion bred,
   Not spend the dowry of a lawful bed.

'Time's glory is to calm contending kings,
To unmask falsehood, and bring truth to light,
To stamp the seal of time in aged things,
To wake the morn, and sentinel the night,
To wrong the wronger till he render right,
   To ruinate proud buildings with thy hours,
   And smear with dust their glittering golden
     towers;

'To fill with worm-holes stately monuments,
To feed oblivion with decay of things,
To blot old books and alter their contents,
To pluck the quills from ancient ravens' wings,
To dry the old oak's sap . and cherish springs,
   To spoil antiquities of hammer'd steel,
   And turn the giddy round of Fortune's wheel;

'To show the beldam daughters of her daughter,
To make the child a man, the man a child,
To slay the tiger that doth live by slaughter,
To tame the unicorn and lion wild,
To mock the subtle in themselves beguiled,
   To cheer the ploughman with increaseful crops,
   And waste huge stones with little water-drops.

'Why work'st thou mischief in thy pilgrimage,
Unless thou couldst return to make amends?
One poor retiring minute in an age
Would purchase thee a thousand thousand friends,
Lending him wit that to bad debtors lends:
   O, this dread night, wouldst thou one hour
     come back,
   I could prevent this storm, and shun thy wrack!

'Thou ceaseless lackey to eternity,
With some mischance cross Tarquin in his flight:
Devise extremes beyond extremity,
To make him curse this cursed crimeful night:
Let ghastly shadows his lewd eyes affright;
   And the dire thought of his committed evil
   Shape every bush a hideous shapeless devil.

'Disturb his hours of rest with restless trances,
Afflict him in his bed with bedrid groans;
Let there bechance him pitiful mischances,
To make him moan; but pity not his moans:
Stone him with harden'd hearts, harder than
    stones;
   And let mild women to him lose their mildness,
   Wilder to him than tigers in their wildness.

'Let him have time to tear his curled hair,
Let him have time against himself to rave,
Let him have time of Time's help to despair,
Let him have time to live a loathed slave,
Let him have time a beggar's orts to crave,
   And time to see one that by alms doth live
   Disdain to him disdained scraps to give.

'Let him have time to see his friends his foes,
And merry fools to mock at him resort;
Let him have time to mark how slow time goes
In time of sorrow, and how swift and short
His time of folly and his time of sport;
   And ever let his unrecalling crime
   Have time to wail th' abusing of his time.

'O Time, thou tutor both to good and bad,
Teach me to curse him that thou taught'st this ill!
At his own shadow let the thief run mad,
Himself himself seek every hour to kill!
Such wretched hands such wretched blood should
    spill;
   For who so base would such an office have
   As slanderous death's-man to so base a slave?

'The baser is he, coming from a king,
To shame his hope with deeds degenerate:
The mightier man, the mightier is the thing
That makes him honour'd, or begets him hate;
For greatest scandal waits on greatest state.
   The moon being clouded presently is mist,
   But little stars may hide them when they list.

'The crow may bathe his coal-black wings in mire,
And unperceived fly with the filth away;
But if the like the snow-white swan desire,
The stain upon his silver down will stay.
Poor grooms are sightless night, kings glorious
    day:
   Gnats are unnoted wheresoe'er they fly,
   But eagles gazed upon with every eye.

'Out, idle words, servants to shallow fools!
Unprofitable sounds, weak arbitrators!
Busy yourselves in skill-contending schools;
Debate where leisure serves with dull debaters:
To trembling clients be you mediators:
   For me, I force not argument a straw,
   Since that my case is past the help of law.

'In vain I rail at Opportunity,
At Time, at Tarquin, and uncheerful Night;
In vain I cavil with mine infamy,
In vain I spurn at my confirm'd despite:
This helpless smoke of words doth me no right.
   The remedy indeed to do me good
   Is to let forth my foul defiled blood.

'Poor hand, why quiver'st thou at this decree?
Honour thyself to rid me of this shame;
For if I die, my honour lives in thee;
But if I live, thou livest in my defame:
Since thou couldst not defend thy loyal dame,
   And wast afeard to scratch her wicked foe,
   Kill both thyself and her for yielding so.'

This said, from her betumbled couch she starteth,
To find some desperate instrument of death:
But this no slaughter-house no tool imparteth
To make more vent for passage of her breath;
Which, thronging through her lips, so vanisheth
   As smoke from Aetna, that in air consumes,
   Or that which from discharged cannon fumes.

'In vain,' quoth she, 'I live, and seek in vain
Some happy mean to end a hapless life.
I fear'd by Tarquin's falchion to be slain,
Yet for the self-same purpose seek a knife:
But when I fear'd I was a loyal wife:
    So am I now:—O no, that cannot be;
    Of that true type hath Tarquin rifled me.

'O, that is gone for which I sought to live,
And therefore now I need not fear to die.
To clear this spot by death, at least I give
A badge of fame to slander's livery;
A dying life to living infamy:
    Poor helpless help, the treasure stoln away,
    To burn the guiltless casket where it lay!

'Well, well, dear Collatine, thou shalt not know
The stained taste of violated troth;
I will not wrong thy true affection so,
To flatter thee with an infringed oath;
This bastard graff shall never come to growth:
    He shall not boast who did thy stock pollute
    That thou art doting father of his fruit.

'Nor shall he smile at thee in secret thought,
Nor laugh with his companions at thy state;
But thou shalt know thy interest was not bought
Basely with gold, but stoln from forth thy gate.
For me, I am the mistress of my fate,
    And with my trespass never will dispense,
    Till life to death acquit my forced offence.

'I will not poison thee with my attaint,
Nor fold my fault in cleanly-coin'd excuses;
My sable ground of sin I will not paint,
To hide the truth of this false night's abuses:
My tongue shall utter all; mine eyes, like sluices,
    As from a mountain-spring that feeds a dale,
    Shall gush pure streams to purge my impure
        tale.'

By this, lamenting Philomel had ended
The well-tuned warble of her nightly sorrow,
And solemn night with slow sad gait descended
To ugly hell; when, lo, the blushing morrow
Lends light to all fair eyes that light will borrow:
    But cloudy Lucrece shames herself to see,
    And therefore still in night would cloister'd be.

Revealing day through every cranny spies,
And seems to point her out where she sits weeping;
To whom she sobbing speaks: 'O eye of eyes,
Why pry'st thou through my window? leave thy
        peeping:
Mock with thy tickling beams eyes that are sleep-
        ing:
    Brand not my forehead with thy piercing light,
    For day hath naught to do what's done by night.'

Thus cavils she with every thing she sees:
True grief is fond and testy as a child,
Who wayward once, his mood with naught agrees:
Old woes, not infant sorrows, bear them mild;
Continuance tames the one; the other wild,
    Like an unpractised swimmer plunging still,
    With too much labour drowns for want of skill.

So she, deep-drenched in a sea of care,
Holds disputation with each thing she views,
And to herself all sorrow doth compare;
No object but her passion's strength renews;
And as one shifts, another straight ensues:
    Sometime her grief is dumb, and hath no words;
    Sometime 'tis mad, and too much talk affords.

The little birds that tune their morning's joy
Make her moans mad with their sweet melody:
For mirth doth search the bottom of annoy;
Sad souls are slain in merry company;
Grief best is pleased with grief's society:
    True sorrow then is feelingly sufficed
    When with like semblance it is sympathized.

'Tis double death to drown in ken of shore;
He ten times pines that pines beholding food;
To see the salve doth make the wound ache more;
Great grief grieves most at that would do it good;
Deep woes roll forward like a gentle flood,
    Who, being stopt, the bounding banks o'erflows;
    Grief dallied with nor law nor limit knows.

'You mocking birds,' quoth she, 'your tunes en-
        tomb
Within your hollow swelling feather'd breasts,
And in my hearing be you mute and dumb:
My restless discord loves no stops nor rests;
A woeful hostess brooks not merry guests:
    Relish your nimble notes to pleasing ears;
    Distress likes dumps when time is kept with
        tears.

'Come, Philomel, that sing'st of ravishment,
Make thy sad grove in my dishevell'd hair:
As the dank earth weeps at thy languishment,
So I at each sad strain will strain a tear,
And with deep groans the diapason bear;
    For burthen-wise I'll hum on Tarquin still,
    While thou on Tereus descant'st better skill.

'And whiles against a thorn thou bear'st thy part,
To keep thy sharp woes waking, wretched I,
To imitate thee well, against my heart
Will fix a sharp knife, to affright mine eye;
Who, if it wink, shall thereon fall and die.
    These means, as frets upon an instrument,
    Shall tune our heart-strings to true languish-
        ment.

'And for, poor bird, thou sing'st not in the day,
As shaming any eye should thee behold,
Some dark-deep desert, seated from the way,
That knows not parching heat nor freezing cold,
Will we find out; and there we will unfold
    To creatures stern sad tunes, to change their
        kinds:
    Since men prove beasts, let beasts bear gentle
        minds.'

As the poor frighted deer, that stands at gaze,
Wildly determining which way to fly,
Or one encompast with a winding maze,
That cannot tread the way out readily;
So with herself is she in mutiny,
    To live or die, which of the twain were better,
    When life is shamed, and death reproach's
        debtor.

'To kill myself,' quoth she, 'alack, what were it,
But with my body my poor soul's pollution?
They that lose half with greater patience bear it
Than they whose whole is swallow'd in confusion.
That mother tries a merciless conclusion
    Who, having two sweet babes, when death takes one,
    Will slay the other, and be nurse to none.

'My body or my soul, which was the dearer,
When the one pure, the other made divine?
Whose love of either to myself was nearer,
When both were kept for heaven and Collatine?
Ay me! the bark pill'd from the lofty pine,
    His leaves will wither, and his sap decay;
    So must my soul, her bark being pill'd away.

'Her house is sackt, her quiet interrupted,
Her mansion batter'd by the enemy;
Her sacred temple spotted, spoil'd, corrupted,
Grossly engirt with daring infamy:
Then let it not be call'd impiety,
    If in this blemisht fort I make some hole
    Through which I may convey this troubled soul.

'Yet die I will not till my Collatine
Have heard the cause of my untimely death;
That he may vow, in that sad hour of mine,
Revenge on him that made me stop my breath.
My stained blood to Tarquin I'll bequeath,
    Which by him tainted shall for him be spent,
    And as his due writ in my testament.

'My honour I'll bequeath unto the knife
That wounds my body, so dishonoured.
'Tis honour to deprive dishonour'd life;
The one will live, the other being dead:
So of shame's ashes shall my fame be bred;
    For in my death I murder shameful scorn:
    My shame so dead, mine honour is new-born.

'Dear lord of that dear jewel I have lost,
What legacy shall I bequeath to thee?
My resolution, love, shall be thy boast,
By whose example thou revenged mayst be.
How Tarquin must be used, read it in me:
    Myself, thy friend, will kill myself, thy foe,
    And, for my sake, serve thou false Tarquin so.

'This brief abridgement of my will I make:—
My soul and body to the skies and ground;
My resolution, husband, do thou take;
Mine honour be the knife's that makes my wound;
My shame be his that did my fame confound;
    And all my fame that lives disbursed be
    To those that live, and think no shame of me.

'Thou, Collatine, shalt oversee this will;
How was I overseen that thou shalt see it!
My blood shall wash the slander of mine ill;
My life's foul deed, my life's fair end shall free it.
Faint not, faint heart, but stoutly say "So be it:"
    Yield to my hand; my hand shall conquer thee:
    Thou dead, both die and both shall victors be.'

This plot of death when sadly she had laid,
And wiped the brinish pearl from her bright eyes,
With untuned tongue she hoarsely calls her maid,
Whose swift obedience to her mistress hies;
For fleet-wing'd duty with thought's feathers flies.
    Poor Lucrece' cheeks unto her maid seem so
    As winter meads when sun doth melt their snow.

Her mistress she doth give demure good-morrow,
With soft-slow tongue, true mark of modesty,
And sorts a sad look to her lady's sorrow,
For why her face wore sorrow's livery;
But durst not ask of her audaciously
    Why her two suns were cloud-eclipsed so,
    Nor why her fair cheeks overwasht with woe.

But as the earth doth weep, the sun being set,
Each flower moisten'd like a melting eye,
Even so the maid with swelling drops gan wet
Her circled eyne, enforced by sympathy
Of those fair suns set in her mistress' sky,
    Who in a salt-waved ocean quench their light,
    Which makes the maid weep like the dewy night.

A pretty while these pretty creatures stand,
Like ivory conduits coral cisterns filling:
One justly weeps; the other takes in hand
No cause, but company, of her drops spilling:
Their gentle sex to weep are often willing;
    Grieving themselves to guess at others' smarts,
    And then they drown their eyes, or break their hearts.

For men have marble, women waxen, minds,
And therefore are they form'd as marble will;
The weak opprest, the impression of strange kinds
Is form'd in them by force, by fraud, or skill:
Then call them not the authors of their ill,
    No more than wax shall be accounted evil
    Wherein is stampt the semblance of a devil.

Their smoothness, like a goodly champaign plain,
Lays open all the little worms that creep;
In men, as in a rough-grown grove, remain
Cave-keeping evils that obscurely sleep:
Through crystal walls each little mote will peep:
    Though men can cover crimes with bold stern looks,
    Poor women's faces are their own faults' books.

No man inveigh against the wither'd flower,
But chide rough winter that the flower hath kill'd:
Not that devour'd, but that which doth devour,
Is worthy blame. O, let it not be hild
Poor women's faults, that they are so fulfill'd
    With men's abuses: those proud lords, to blame,
    Make weak-made women tenants to their shame.

The precedent whereof in Lucrece view,
Assail'd by night with circumstances strong
Of present death, and shame that might ensue
By that her death, to do her husband wrong:
Such danger to resistance did belong,
    That dying fear through all her body spread;
    And who cannot abuse a body dead?

By this, mild patience bid fair Lucrece speak
To the poor counterfeit of her complaining:
'My girl,' quoth she, 'on what occasion break
Those tears from thee, that down thy cheeks are
    raining?
If thou dost weep for grief of my sustaining,
    Know, gentle wench, it small avails my mood:
    If tears could help, mine own would do me
    good.

'But tell me, girl, when went'—and there she
    stay'd
Till after a deep groan—'Tarquin from hence?'
'Madam, ere I was up,' replied the maid,
'The more to blame my sluggard negligence:
Yet with the fault I thus far can dispense,—
    Myself was stirring ere the break of day,
    And ere I rose was Tarquin gone away.

'But, lady, if your maid may be so bold,
She would request to know your heaviness.'
'O, peace!' quoth Lucrece: 'if it should be told,
The repetition cannot make it less,
For more it is than I can well express:
    And that deep torture may be call'd a hell
    When more is felt than one hath power to tell.

'Go, get me hither paper, ink, and pen,—
Yet save that labour, for I have them here.
What should I say?—One of my husband's men
Bid thou be ready, by and by, to bear
A letter to my lord, my love, my dear:
    Bid him with speed prepare to carry it;
    The cause craves haste, and it will soon be writ.'

Her maid is gone, and she prepares to write,
First hovering o'er the paper with her quill:
Conceit and grief an eager combat fight;
What wit sets down is blotted straight with will;
This is too curious-good, this blunt and ill:
    Much like a press of people at a door,
    Throng her inventions, which shall go before.

At last she thus begins: 'Thou worthy lord
Of that unworthy wife that greeteth thee,
Health to thy person! next vouchsafe t'afford—
If ever, love, thy Lucrece thou wilt see—
Some present speed to come and visit me.
    So, I commend me from our house in grief:
    My woes are tedious, though my words are
    brief.'

Here folds she up the tenour of her woe,
Her certain sorrow writ uncertainly.
By this short schedule Collatine may know
Her grief, but not her grief's true quality:
She dares not thereof make discovery,
    Lest he should hold it her own gross abuse,
    Ere she with blood had stain'd her stain'd
    excuse.

Besides, the life and feeling of her passion
She hoards, to spend when he is by to hear her;
When sighs and groans and tears may grace the
    fashion
Of her disgrace, the better so to clear her
From that suspicion which the world might bear
    her.
    To shun this blot, she would not blot the letter
    With words, till action might become them
    better.

To see sad sights moves more than hear them
    told;
For then the eye interprets to the ear
The heavy motion that it doth behold,
When every part a part of woe doth bear.
'Tis but a part of sorrow that we hear:
    Deep sounds make lesser noise than shallow
    fords,
    And sorrow ebbs, being blown with wind of
    words.

Her letter now is seal'd, and on it writ,
'At Ardea to my lord with more than haste.'
The post attends, and she delivers it,
Charging the sour-faced groom to hie as fast
As lagging fowls before the northern blast:
    Speed more than speed but dull and slow she
    deems:
    Extremity still urgeth such extremes.

The homely villain court'sies to her low;
And, blushing on her, with a steadfast eye
Receives the scroll without or yea or no,
And forth with bashful innocence doth hie.
But they whose guilt within their bosoms lie
    Imagine every eye beholds their blame;
    For Lucrece thought he blusht to see her
    shame:

When, silly groom! God wot, it was defect
Of spirit, life, and bold audacity.
Such harmless creatures have a true respect
To talk in deeds, while others saucily
Promise more speed, but do it leisurely:
    Even so this pattern of the worn-out age
    Pawn'd honest looks, but laid no words to gage.

His kindled duty kindled her mistrust,
That two red fires in both their faces blazed;
She thought he blusht, as knowing Tarquin's
    lust,
And, blushing with him, wistly on him gazed;
Her earnest eye did make him more amazed:
    The more she saw the blood his cheeks re-
    plenish,
    The more she thought he spied in her some
    blemish.

But long she thinks till he return again,
And yet the duteous vassal scarce is gone.
The weary time she cannot entertain,
For now 'tis stale to sigh, to weep, and groan:
So woe hath wearied woe, moan tired moan,
    That she her plaints a little while doth stay,
    Pausing for means to mourn some newer way.

At last she calls to mind where hangs a piece
Of skilful painting, made for Priam's Troy;
Before the which is drawn the power of Greece,
For Helen's rape the city to destroy,
Threatening cloud-kissing Ilion with annoy;
    Which the conceited painter drew so proud,
    As heaven, it seem'd, to kiss the turrets bow'd.

A thousand lamentable objects there,
In scorn of nature, art gave lifeless life:
Many a dry drop seem'd a weeping tear,
Shed for the slaughter'd husband by the wife:
The red blood reekt, to show the painter's strife;
    And dying eyes gleam'd forth their ashy lights,
    Like dying coals burnt out in tedious nights.

There might you see the labouring pioner
Begrimed with sweat, and smeared all with dust;
And from the towers of Troy there would appear
The very eyes of men through loop-holes thrust,
Gazing upon the Greeks with little lust:
    Such sweet observance in this work was had,
    That one might see those far-off eyes look sad.

In great commanders grace and majesty
You might behold, triumphing in their faces;
In youth, quick bearing and dexterity;
And here and there the painter interlaces
Pale cowards, marching on with trembling paces;
    Which heartless peasants did so well resemble
    That one would swear he saw them quake and
        tremble.

In Ajax and Ulysses, O, what art
Of physiognomy might one behold!
The face of either cipher'd either's heart;
Their face their manners most expressly told:
In Ajax' eyes blunt rage and rigour roll'd;
    But the mild glance that sly Ulysses lent
    Show'd deep regard and smiling government.

There pleading might you see grave Nestor stand,
As 'twere encouraging the Greeks to fight:
Making such sober action with his hand,
That it beguiled attention, charm'd the sight:
In speech, it seem'd, his beard, all silver white,
    Wagg'd up and down, and from his lips did fly
    Thin winding breath, which purl'd up to the
        sky.

About him were a press of gaping faces,
Which seem'd to swallow up his sound advice;
All jointly listening, but with several graces,
As if some mermaid did their ears entice,
Some high, some low,—the painter was so nice;
    The scalps of many, almost hid behind,
    To jump up higher seem'd, to mock the mind.

Here one man's hand lean'd on another's head,
His nose being shadow'd by his neighbour's ear;
Here one, being throng'd, bears back, all boln and
    red;
Another, smother'd, seems to pelt and swear;
And in their rage such signs of rage they bear,
    As, but for loss of Nestor's golden words,
    It seem'd they would debate with angry swords.

For much imaginary work was there;
Conceit deceitful, so compact, so kind,
That for Achilles' image stood his spear,
Griped in an armed hand; himself, behind,
Was left unseen, save to the eye of mind:
    A hand, a foot, a face, a leg, a head,
    Stood for the whole to be imagined.

And from the walls of strong-besieged Troy
When their brave hope, bold Hector, marcht to
    field,
Stood many Trojan mothers, sharing joy
To see their youthful sons bright weapons wield;
And to their hope they such odd action yield,
    That through their light joy seemed to appear,
    Like bright things stain'd, a kind of heavy
        fear.

And from the strond of Dardan, where they
    fought,
To Simois' reedy banks the red blood ran,
Whose waves to imitate the battle sought
With swelling ridges; and their ranks began
To break upon the galled shore, and than
    Retire again, till meeting greater ranks,
    They join, and shoot their foam at Simois'
        banks.

To this well-painted piece is Lucrece come,
To find a face where all distress is stell'd.
Many she sees where cares have carved some,
But none where all distress and dolour dwell'd,
Till she despairing Hecuba beheld,
    Staring on Priam's wounds with her old eyes,
    Which bleeding under Pyrrhus' proud foot
        lies.

In her the painter had anatomized
Time's ruin, beauty's wrack, and grim care's
    reign:
Her cheeks with chops and wrinkles were dis-
    guised;
Of what she was no semblance did remain:
Her blue blood changed to black in every vein,
    Wanting the spring that those shrunk pipes
        had fed,
    Show'd life imprison'd in a body dead.

On this sad shadow Lucrece spends her eyes,
And shapes her sorrow to the beldam's woes,
Who nothing wants to answer her but cries,
And bitter words to ban her cruel foes:
The painter was no god to lend her those;
    And therefore Lucrece swears he did her
        wrong,
    To give her so much grief, and not a tongue.

'Poor instrument,' quoth she, 'without a sound,
I'll tune thy woes with my lamenting tongue;
And drop sweet balm in Priam's painted wound,
And rail on Pyrrhus that hath done him wrong;
And with my tears quench Troy that burns so
    long;
    And with my knife scratch out the angry eyes
    Of all the Greeks that are thine enemies.

'Show me the strumpet that began this stir,
That with my nails her beauty I may tear.
Thy heat of lust, fond Paris, did incur
This load of wrath that burning Troy doth bear:
Thy eye kindled the fire that burneth here;
    And here in Troy, for trespass of thine eye,
    The sire, the son, the dame, and daughter die.

'Why should the private pleasure of some one
Become the public plague of many moe?
Let sin, alone committed, light alone
Upon his head that hath transgressed so;
Let guiltless souls be freed from guilty woe:
    For one's offence why should so many fall,
    To plague a private sin in general?

'Lo, here weeps Hecuba, here Priam dies,
Here manly Hector faints, here Troilus swounds,
Here friend by friend in bloody channel lies,
And friend to friend gives unadvised wounds,
And one man's lust these many lives confounds:
    Had doting Priam checkt his son's desire,
    Troy had been bright with fame, and not with
      fire.'

Here feelingly she weeps Troy's painted woes:
For sorrow, like a heavy-hanging bell,
Once set on ringing, with his own weight goes;
Then little strength rings out the doleful knell:
So Lucrece, set a-work, sad tales doth tell
    To pencill'd pensiveness and colour'd sorrow;
    She lends them words, and she their looks doth
      borrow.

She throws her eyes about the painting round,
And who she finds forlorn she doth lament.
At last she sees a wretched image bound,
That piteous looks to Phrygian shepherds lent:
His face, though full of cares, yet show'd content;
    Onward to Troy with the blunt swains he goes,
    So mild that Patience seem'd to scorn his woes.

In him the painter labour'd with his skill
To hide deceit, and give the harmless show
An humble gait, calm looks, eyes wailing still,
A brow unbent, that seem'd to welcome woe;
Cheeks neither red nor pale, but mingled so
    That blushing red no guilty instance gave,
    Nor ashy pale the fear that false hearts have.

But, like a constant and confirmed devil,
He entertain'd a show so seeming just,
And therein so ensconced his secret evil,
That jealousy itself could not mistrust
False-creeping craft and perjury should thrust
    Into so bright a day such black-faced storms,
    Or blot with hell-born sin such saint-like forms.

The well-skill'd workman this mild image drew
For perjured Sinon, whose enchanting story
The credulous old Priam after slew;
Whose words, like wildfire, burnt the shining glory
Of rich-built Ilion, that the skies were sorry,
    And little stars shot from their fixed places,
    When their glass fell wherein they view'd their
      faces.

This picture she advisedly perused,
And chid the painter for his wondrous skill,
Saying, some shape in Sinon's was abused;
So fair a form lodged not a mind so ill:
And still on him she gazed; and gazing still,
    Such signs of truth in his plain face she spied,
    That she concludes the picture was belied.

'It cannot be,' quoth she, 'that so much guile'—
She would have said 'can lurk in such a look;'
But Tarquin's shape came in her mind the while,
And from her tongue 'can lurk' from 'cannot'
    took:
'It cannot be' she in that sense forsook,
    And turn'd it thus, 'It cannot be, I find,
    But such a face should bear a wicked mind:

'For even as subtle Sinon here is painted,
So sober-sad, so weary, and so mild,
As if with grief or travail he had fainted,
To me came Tarquin armed; so beguiled
With outward honesty, but yet defiled
    With inward vice: as Priam him did cherish,
    So did I Tarquin; so my Troy did perish.

'Look, look, how listening Priam wets his eyes,
To see those borrow'd tears that Sinon sheeds!
Priam, why art thou old, and yet not wise?
For every tear he falls a Trojan bleeds:
His eye drops fire, no water thence proceeds;
    Those round clear pearls of his, that move thy
      pity,
    Are balls of quenchless fire to burn thy city.

'Such devils steal effects from lightless hell;
For Sinon in his fire doth quake with cold,
And in that cold hot-burning fire doth dwell;
These contraries such unity do hold,
Only to flatter fools, and make them bold:
    So Priam's trust false Sinon's tears doth
      flatter,
    That he finds means to burn his Troy with
      water.'

Here, all enraged, such passion her assails,
That patience is quite beaten from her breast.
She tears the senseless Sinon with her nails,
Comparing him to that unhappy guest
Whose deed hath made herself herself detest:
    At last she smilingly with this gives o'er;
    'Fool, fool!' quoth she, 'his wounds will not be
      sore.'

Thus ebbs and flows the current of her sorrow,
And time doth weary time with her complaining.
She looks for night, and then she longs for
    morrow,
And both she thinks too long with her remain-
    ing;
Short time seems long in sorrow's sharp sustain-
    ing:
    Though woe be heavy, yet it seldom sleeps;
    And they that watch see time how slow it
      creeps.

Which all this time hath overslipt her thought,
That she with painted images hath spent;
Being from the feeling of her own grief brought
By deep surmise of others' detriment;
Losing her woes in shows of discontent.
    It easeth some, though none it ever cured,
    To think their dolour others have endured.

But now the mindful messenger, come back,
Brings home his lord and other company:
Who finds his Lucrece clad in mourning black;
And round about her tear-distained eye
Blue circles stream'd, like rainbows in the sky:
    These water-galls in her dim element
    Foretell new storms to those already spent.

Which when her sad-beholding husband saw,
Amazedly in her sad face he stares:
Her eyes, though sod in tears, lookt red and raw,
Her lively colour kill'd with deadly cares.
He hath no power to ask her how she fares;
    Both stood, like old acquaintance in a trance,
    Met far from home, wondering each other's
    chance.

At last he takes her by the bloodless hand,
And thus begins: 'What uncouth ill event
Hath thee befaln, that thou dost trembling
    stand?
Sweet love, what spite hath thy fair colour spent?
Why art thou thus attired in discontent?
    Unmask, dear dear, this moody heaviness,
    And tell thy grief, that we may give redress.'

Three times with sighs she gives her sorrow fire,
Ere once she can discharge one word of woe:
At length addrest to answer his desire,
She modestly prepares to let them know
Her honour is ta'en prisoner by the foe;
    While Collatine and his consorted lords
    With sad attention long to hear her words.

And now this pale swan in her watery nest
Begins the sad dirge of her certain ending:
'Few words,' quoth she, 'shall fit the trespass best,
Where no excuse can give the fault amending:
In me moe woes than words are now depending;
    And my laments would be drawn out too long,
    To tell them all with one poor tired tongue.

'Then be this all the task it hath to say:
Dear husband, in the interest of thy bed
A stranger came, and on that pillow lay
Where thou wast wont to rest thy weary head;
And what wrong else may be imagined
    By foul enforcement might be done to me,
    From that, alas, thy Lucrece is not free.

'For in the dreadful dead of dark midnight,
With shining falchion in my chamber came
A creeping creature, with a flaming light,
And softly cried, "Awake, thou Roman dame,
And entertain my love; else lasting shame
    On thee and thine this night I will inflict,
    If thou my love's desire do contradict.

' "For some hard-favour'd groom of thine,"
    quoth he,
"Unless thou yoke thy liking to my will,
I'll murder straight, and then I'll slaughter thee,
And swear I found you where you did fulfil
The loathsome act of lust, and so did kill
    The lechers in their deed: this act will be
    My fame, and thy perpetual infamy."

'With this, I did begin to start and cry;
And then against my heart he set his sword,
Swearing, unless I took all patiently,
I should not live to speak another word;
So should my shame still rest upon record,
    And never be forgot in mighty Rome
    Th' adulterate death of Lucrece and her groom.

'Mine enemy was strong, my poor self weak,
And far the weaker with so strong a fear:
My bloody judge forbade my tongue to speak;
No rightful plea might plead for justice there:
His scarlet lust came evidence to swear
    That my poor beauty had purloin'd his eyes;
    And when the judge is robb'd, the prisoner dies.

'O, teach me how to make mine own excuse!
Or, at the least, this refuge let me find,—
Though my gross blood be stain'd with this abuse,
Immaculate and spotless is my mind;
That was not forced; that never was inclined
    To accessary yieldings, but still pure
    Doth in her poison'd closet yet endure.'

Lo, here, the hopeless merchant of this loss,
With head declined, and voice damm'd up with
    woe,
With sad-set eyes, and wretched arms across,
From lips new-waxen pale begins to blow
The grief away that stops his answer so:
    But, wretched as he is, he strives in vain;
    What he breathes out his breath drinks up again.

As through an arch the violent roaring tide
Outruns the eye that doth behold his haste,
Yet in the eddy boundeth in his pride
Back to the strait that forced him on so fast;
In rage sent out, recall'd in rage, being past:
    Even so his sighs, his sorrows, make a saw,
    To push grief on, and back the same grief draw.

Which speechless woe of his poor she attendeth,
And his untimely frenzy thus awaketh:
'Dear lord, thy sorrow to my sorrow lendeth
Another power; no flood by raining slaketh.
My woe too sensible thy passion maketh
    More feeling-painful: let it, then, suffice
    To drown one woe, one pair of weeping eyes.

'And for my sake, when I might charm thee so,
For she that was thy Lucrece,—now attend me:
Be suddenly revenged on my foe,
Thine, mine, his own: suppose thou dost defend
    me
From what is past: the help that thou shalt lend me
    Comes all too late, yet let the traitor die;
    For sparing justice feeds iniquity.

'But ere I name him, you fair lords,' quoth she,
Speaking to those that came with Collatine,
'Shall plight your honourable faiths to me,
With swift pursuit to venge this wrong of mine;
For 'tis a meritorious fair design
   To chase injustice with revengeful arms:
   Knights, by their oaths, should right poor
     ladies' harms.'

At this request, with noble disposition
Each present lord began to promise aid,
As bound in knighthood to her imposition,
Longing to hear the hateful foe bewray'd.
But she, that yet her sad task hath not said,
   The protestation stops. 'O, speak,' quoth she,
   'How may this forced stain be wiped from me?

'What is the quality of mine offence,
Being constrain'd with dreadful circumstance?
May my pure mind with the foul act dispense,
My low-declined honour to advance?
May any terms acquit me from this chance?
   The poison'd fountain clears itself again;
   And why not I from this compelled stain?'

With this, they all at once began to say,
Her body's stain her mind untainted clears;
While with a joyless smile she turns away
The face, that map which deep impression bears
Of hard misfortune, carved in it with tears.
   'No, no,' quoth she, 'no dame, hereafter living,
   By my excuse shall claim excuse's giving.'

Here with a sigh, as if her heart would break,
She throws forth Tarquin's name: 'He, he,' she
   says,
But more than 'he' her poor tongue could not
   speak;
Till after many accents and delays,
Untimely breathings, sick and short assays,
   She utters this, 'He, he, fair lords, 'tis he
   That guides this hand to give this wound to me.'

Even here she sheathed in her harmless breast
A harmful knife, that thence her soul unsheathed:
That blow did bail it from the deep unrest
Of that polluted prison where it breathed:
Her contrite sighs unto the clouds bequeathed
   Her winged sprite, and through her wounds
    doth fly
   Life's lasting date from cancell'd destiny.

Stone-still, astonisht with this deadly deed,
Stood Collatine and all his lordly crew;
Till Lucrece' father, that beholds her bleed,
Himself on her self-slaughter'd body threw;
And from the purple fountain Brutus drew
   The murderous knife, and, as it left the place,
   Her blood, in poor revenge, held it in chase;

And bubbling from her breast, it doth divide
In two slow rivers, that the crimson blood
Circles her body in on every side,
Who, like a late-sackt island, vastly stood
Bare and unpeopled in this fearful flood.
   Some of her blood still pure and red remain'd,
   And some lookt black, and that false Tarquin
   stain'd.

About the mourning and congealed face
Of that black blood a watery rigol goes,
Which seems to weep upon the tainted place:
And ever since, as pitying Lucrece' woes,
Corrupted blood some watery token shows;
   And blood untainted still doth red abide,
   Blushing at that which is so putrefied.

'Daughter, dear daughter,' old Lucretius cries,
'That life was mine which thou hast here de-
   prived.
If in the child the father's image lies,
Where shall I live now Lucrece is unlived?
Thou wast not to this end from me derived.
   If children pre-decease progenitors,
   We are their offspring, and they none of ours.

'Poor broken glass, I often did behold
In thy sweet semblance my old age new born;
But now that fair fresh mirror, dim and old,
Shows me a bare-boned death by time outworn:
O, from thy cheeks my image thou hast torn,
   And shiver'd all the beauty of my glass,
   That I no more can see what once I was.

'O time, cease thou thy course, and last no longer,
If they surcease to be that should survive.
Shall rotten death make conquest of the stronger,
And leave the faltering feeble souls alive?
The old bees die, the young possess their hive:
   Then live, sweet Lucrece, live again, and see
   Thy father die, and not thy father thee.'

By this, starts Collatine as from a dream,
And bids Lucretius give his sorrow place;
And then in key-cold Lucrece' bleeding stream
He falls, and bathes the pale fear in his face,
And counterfeits to die with her a space;
   Till manly shame bids him possess his breath,
   And live to be revenged on her death.

The deep vexation of his inward soul
Hath served a dumb arrest upon his tongue;
Who, mad that sorrow should his use control,
Or keep him from heart-easing words so long,
Begins to talk; but through his lips do throng
   Weak words, so thick come in his poor heart's
    aid,
   That no man could distinguish what he said.

Yet sometime 'Tarquin' was pronounced plain,
But through his teeth, as if the name he tore.
This windy tempest, till it blow up rain,
Held back his sorrow's tide, to make it more;
At last it rains, and busy winds give o'er:
   The son and father weep with equal strife
   Who should weep most, for daughter or for
    wife.

The one doth call her his, the other his,
Yet neither may possess the claim they lay.
The father says 'She's mine.' 'O, mine she is,'
Replies her husband: 'do not take away
My sorrow's interest; let no mourner say
   He weeps for her, for she was only mine,
   And only must be wail'd by Collatine.'

'O,' quoth Lucretius, 'I did give that life
Which she too early and too late hath spill'd.'
'Woe, woe,' quoth Collatine, 'she was my wife,
I owed her, and 'tis mine that she hath kill'd.'
'My daughter' and 'my wife' with clamours fill'd
    The dispersed air, who, holding Lucrece' life,
    Answer'd their cries, 'my daughter ' and 'my
        wife.'

Brutus, who pluckt the knife from Lucrece' side,
Seeing such emulation in their woe,
Began to clothe his wit in state and pride,
Burying in Lucrece' wound his folly's show.
He with the Romans was esteemed so
    As silly-jeering idiots are with kings,
    For sportive words and uttering foolish things:

But now he throws that shallow habit by,
Wherein deep policy did him disguise;
And arm'd his long-hid wits advisedly,
To check the tears in Collatinus' eyes.
'Thou wronged lord of Rome,' quoth he, 'arise:
    Let my unsounded self, supposed a fool,
    Now set thy long-experienced wit to school.

'Why, Collatine, is woe the cure for woe?
Do wounds help wounds, or grief help grievous
        deeds?
Is it revenge to give thyself a blow
For his foul act by whom thy fair wife bleeds?
Such childish humour from weak minds pro-
        ceeds:
    Thy wretched wife mistook the matter so,
    To slay herself, that should have slain her foe.

'Courageous Roman, do not steep thy heart
In such relenting dew of lamentations;
But kneel with me, and help to bear thy part,
To rouse our Roman gods with invocations,
That they will suffer these abominations,
    Since Rome herself in them doth stand dis-
        graced,
    By our strong arms from forth her fair streets
        chased.

'Now, by the Capitol that we adore,
And by this chaste blood so unjustly stained,
By heaven's fair sun that breeds the fat earth's
        store,
By all our country rights in Rome maintained,
And by chaste Lucrece' soul that late complained
    Her wrongs to us, and by this bloody knife,
    We will revenge the death of this true wife.'

This said, he struck his hand upon his breast,
And kist the fatal knife, to end his vow;
And to his protestation urged the rest,
Who, wondering at him, did his words allow:
Then jointly to the ground their knees they bow;
    And that deep vow, which Brutus made before,
    He doth again repeat, and that they swore.

When they had sworn to this advised doom,
They did conclude to bear dead Lucrece thence,
To show her bleeding body thorough Rome,
And so to publish Tarquin's foul offence:
Which being done with speedy diligence,
    The Romans plausibly did give consent
    To Tarquin's everlasting banishment.

SONNETS

To the Onlie Begetter of
These Insving Sonnets
Mr. W. H. All Happinesse
and that Eternitie
Promised by
Ovr Ever-Living Poet
Wisheth
The Well-Wishing
Adventvrer in
Setting
Forth

T. T.

1.

FROM fairest creatures we desire increase,
That thereby beauty's Rose might never die,
But as the riper should by time decease,
His tender heir might bear his memory:
But thou, contracted to thine own bright eyes,
Feed'st thy light's flame with self-substantial fuel,
Making a famine where abundance lies,
Thyself thy foe, to thy sweet self too cruel.
Thou that art now the world's fresh ornament,
And only herald to the gaudy spring,
Within thine own bud buriest thy content,
And, tender churl, makest waste in niggarding.
  Pity the world, or else this glutton be,
  To eat the world's due, by the grave and thee.

2.

When forty winters shall besiege thy brow,
And dig deep trenches in thy beauty's field,
Thy youth's proud livery, so gazed on now,
Will be a totter'd weed, of small worth held:
Then being askt where all thy beauty lies,
Where all the treasure of thy lusty days;
To say, within thine own deep-sunken eyes,
Were an all-eating shame and thriftless praise.
How much more praise deserved thy beauty's use,
If thou couldst answer, 'This fair child of mine
Shall sum my count, and make my old excuse,'
Proving his beauty by succession thine!
  This were to be new made when thou art old,
  And see thy blood warm when thou feel'st it
    cold.

3.

Look in thy glass, and tell the face thou viewest
Now is the time that face should form another;
Whose fresh repair if now thou not renewest,
Thou dost beguile the world, unbless some
    mother.
For where is she so fair whose unear'd womb
Disdains the tillage of thy husbandry?
Or who is he so fond will be the tomb
Of his self-love, to stop posterity?
Thou art thy mother's glass, and she in thee
Calls back the lovely April of her prime:
So thou through windows of thine age shalt see,
Despite of wrinkles, this thy golden time.
  But if thou live, remember'd not to be,
  Die single, and thine image dies with thee.

4.

Unthrifty loveliness, why dost thou spend
Upon thyself thy beauty's legacy?
Nature's bequest gives nothing, but doth lend;
And, being frank, she lends to those are free.
Then, beauteous niggard, why dost thou abuse
The bounteous largess given thee to give?
Profitless usurer, why dost thou use
So great a sum of sums, yet canst not live?
For having traffic with thyself alone,
Thou of thyself thy sweet self dost deceive.
Then how, when nature calls thee to be gone,
What acceptable audit canst thou leave?
  Thy unused beauty must be tomb'd with thee,
  Which, used, lives th' executor to be.

5.

Those hours, that with gentle work did frame
The lovely gaze where every eye doth dwell,
Will play the tyrants to the very same,
And that unfair which fairly doth excel:
For never-resting time leads summer on
To hideous winter and confounds him there;
Sap checkt with frost, and lusty leaves quite gone,
Beauty o'ersnow'd, and bareness every where:
Then, were not summer's distillation left,
A liquid prisoner pent in walls of glass,
Beauty's effect with beauty were bereft,
Nor it, nor no remembrance what it was:
  But flowers distill'd, though they with winter
    meet,
  Leese but their show; their substance still lives
    sweet.

6.

Then let not winter's ragged hand deface
In thee thy summer, ere thou be distill'd:
Make sweet some vial; treasure thou some place
With beauty's treasure, ere it be self-kill'd.
That use is not forbidden usury,
Which happies those that pay the willing loan;
That's for thyself to breed another thee,
Or ten times happier, be it ten for one;
Ten times thyself were happier than thou art,
If ten of thine ten times refigured thee:
Then what could death do, if thou shouldst depart,
Leaving thee living in posterity?
  Be not self-will'd, for thou art much too fair
  To be death's conquest and make worms thine
    heir.

7.

Lo, in the orient when the gracious light
Lifts up his burning head, each under eye
Doth homage to his new-appearing sight,
Serving with looks his sacred majesty;
And having climb'd the steep-up heavenly hill,
Resembling strong youth in his middle age,
Yet mortal looks adore his beauty still,
Attending on his golden pilgrimage;
But when from highmost pitch, with weary car,
Like feeble age, he reeleth from the day,
The eyes, 'fore duteous, now converted are
From his low tract and look another way:
　　So thou, thyself outgoing in thy noon,
　　Unlookt on diest, unless thou get a son.

8.

Music to hear, why hear'st thou music sadly?
Sweets with sweets war not, joy delights in joy.
Why lovest thou that which thou receivest not
　　gladly,
Or else receivest with pleasure thine annoy?
If the true concord of well-tuned sounds,
By unions married, do offend thine ear,
They do but sweetly chide thee, who confounds
In singleness the parts that thou shouldst bear.
Mark how one string, sweet husband to another,
Strikes each in each by mutual ordering;
Resembling sire and child and happy mother,
Who, all in one, one pleasing note do sing:
　　Whose speechless song, being many, seeming
　　　one,
　　Sings this to thee, 'Thou single wilt prove none.'

9.

Is it for fear to wet a widow's eye
That thou consumest thyself in single life?
Ah! if thou issueless shalt hap to die,
The world will wail thee, like a makeless wife;
The world will be thy widow, and still weep
That thou no form of thee hast left behind,
When every private widow well may keep
By children's eyes her husband's shape in mind.
Look, what an unthrift in the world doth spend
Shifts but his place, for still the world enjoys it;
But beauty's waste hath in the world an end,
And kept unused, the user so destroys it.
　　No love toward others in that bosom sits
　　That on himself such murd'rous shame com-
　　　mits.

10.

For shame deny that thou bear'st love to any,
Who for thyself art so unprovident.
Grant, if thou wilt, thou art beloved of many,
But that thou none lovest is most evident;
For thou art so possest with murd'rous hate,
That 'gainst thyself thou stick'st not to conspire,
Seeking that beauteous roof to ruinate,
Which to repair should be thy chief desire.
O, change thy thought, that I may change my
　　mind!
Shall hate be fairer lodged than gentle love?
Be, as thy presence is, gracious and kind,
Or to thyself, at least, kind-hearted prove:
　　Make thee another self, for love of me,
　　That beauty still may live in thine or thee.

11.

As fast as thou shalt wane, so fast thou grow'st
In one of thine, from that which thou departest;
And that fresh blood which youngly thou be-
　　stow'st
Thou mayst call thine when thou from youth con-
　　vertest.
Herein lives wisdom, beauty, and increase;
Without this, folly, age, and cold decay:
If all were minded so, the times should cease,
And threescore year would make the world away.
Let those whom Nature hath not made for store,
Harsh, featureless, and rude, barrenly perish:
Look, whom she best endow'd she gave the more;
Which bounteous gift thou shouldst in bounty
　　cherish:
　　She carved thee for her seal, and meant thereby
　　Thou shouldst print more, not let that copy die.

12.

When I do count the clock that tells the time,
And see the brave day sunk in hideous night;
When I behold the violet past prime,
And sable curls all silver'd o'er with white;
When lofty trees I see barren of leaves,
Which erst from heat did canopy the herd,
And summer's green, all girded up in sheaves,
Borne on the bier with white and bristly beard;
Then of thy beauty do I question make,
That thou among the wastes of time must go,
Since sweets and beauties do themselves forsake,
And die as fast as they see others grow;
　　And nothing 'gainst Time's scythe can make
　　　defence
　　Save breed, to brave him when he takes thee
　　　hence.

13.

O that you were yourself! but, love, you are
No longer yours than you yourself here live:
Against this coming end you should prepare,
And your sweet semblance to some other give.
So should that beauty which you hold in lease
Find no determination; then you were
Yourself again, after yourself's decease,　　[bear.
When your sweet issue your sweet form should
Who lets so fair a house fall to decay,
Which husbandry in honour might uphold
Against the stormy gusts of winter's day
And barren rage of death's eternal cold?
　　O, none but unthrifts: dear my love, you know
　　You had a father; let your son say so.

14.

Not from the stars do I my judgement pluck;
And yet methinks I have astronomy,
But not to tell of good or evil luck,
Of plagues, of dearths, or seasons' quality;
Nor can I fortune to brief minutes tell,
Pointing to each his thunder, rain, and wind,
Or say with princes if it shall go well,
By oft predict that I in heaven find:
But from thine eyes my knowledge I derive,
And, constant stars, in them I read such art,
As truth and beauty shall together thrive,
If from thyself to store thou wouldst convert;
　　Or else of thee this I prognosticate:
　　Thy end is truth's and beauty's doom and date.

15.

When I consider every thing that grows
Holds in perfection but a little moment,
That this huge stage presenteth naught but shows
Whereon the stars in secret influence comment;
When I perceive that men as plants increase,
Cheered and checkt even by the self-same sky,
Vaunt in their youthful sap, at height decrease,
And wear their brave state out of memory;
Then the conceit of this inconstant stay
Sets you most rich in youth before my sight,
Where wasteful Time debateth with Decay,
To change your day of youth to sullied night;
    And, all in war with Time, for love of you,
    As he takes from you, I engraft you new.

16.

But wherefore do not you a mightier way
Make war upon this bloody tyrant, Time?
And fortify yourself in your decay
With means more blessed than my barren rime?
Now stand you on the top of happy hours;
And many maiden gardens, yet unset,
With virtuous wish would bear your living flowers,
Much liker than your painted counterfeit:
So should the lines of life that life repair,
Which this, Time's pencil, or my pupil pen,
Neither in inward worth nor outward fair,
Can make you live yourself in eyes of men.
    To give away yourself keeps yourself still;
    And you must live, drawn by your own sweet
      skill.

17.

Who will believe my verse in time to come,
If it were fill'd with your most high deserts?
Though yet, heaven knows, it is but as a tomb
Which hides your life, and shows not half your
    parts.
If I could write the beauty of your eyes,
And in fresh numbers number all your graces,
The age to come would say, 'This poet lies,
Such heavenly touches ne'er toucht earthly faces.'
So should my papers, yellow'd with their age,
Be scorn'd, like old men of less truth than tongue;
And your true rights be term'd a poet's rage,
And stretched metre of an antique song:
    But were some child of yours alive that time,
    You should live twice, in it and in my rime.

18.

Shall I compare thee to a summer's day?
Thou art more lovely and more temperate:
Rough winds do shake the darling buds of May,
And summer's lease hath all too short a date:
Sometime too hot the eye of heaven shines,
And often is his gold complexion dimm'd;
And every fair from fair sometime declines,
By chance, or nature's changing course, un-
    trimm'd;
But thy eternal summer shall not fade,
Nor lose possession of that fair thou ow'st;
Nor shall Death brag thou wander'st in his shade,
When in eternal lines to time thou grow'st:
    So long as men can breathe, or eyes can see,
    So long lives this, and this gives life to thee.

19.

Devouring Time, blunt thou the lion's paws,
And make the earth devour her own sweet brood;
Pluck the keen teeth from the fierce tiger's jaws,
And burn the long-lived phœnix in her blood;
Make glad and sorry seasons as thou fleets,
And do whate'er thou wilt, swift-footed Time,
To the wide world and all her fading sweets;
But I forbid thee one most heinous crime:
O, carve not with thy hours my love's fair brow,
Nor draw no lines there with thine antique pen;
Him in thy course untainted do allow
For beauty's pattern to succeeding men.
    Yet, do thy worst, old Time: despite thy wrong,
    My love shall in my verse ever live young.

20.

A woman's face, with Nature's own hand painted,
Hast thou, the master-mistress of my passion;
A woman's gentle heart, but not acquainted
With shifting change, as is false women's fashion;
An eye more bright than theirs, less false in rolling,
Gilding the object whereupon it gazeth;
A man in hew all *Hews* in his controlling,
Which steals men's eyes, and women's souls
    amazeth.
And for a woman wert thou first created;
Till Nature, as she wrought thee, fell a-doting,
And by addition me of thee defeated,
By adding one thing to my purpose nothing.
    But since she prickt thee out for women's
      pleasure,
    Mine be thy love, and thy love's use their
      treasure.

21.

So is it not with me as with that Muse
Stirr'd by a painted beauty to his verse,
Who heaven itself for ornament doth use,
And every fair with his fair doth rehearse;
Making a couplement of proud compare,
With sun and moon, with earth and sea's rich gems,
With April's first-born flowers, and all things rare
That heaven's air in this huge rondure hems.
O, let me, true in love, but truly write,
And then believe me, my love is as fair
As any mother's child, though not so bright
As those gold candles fixt in heaven's air:
    Let them say more that like of hearsay well;
    I will not praise that purpose not to sell.

22.

My glass shall not persuade me I am old,
So long as youth and thou are of one date;
But when in thee time's furrows I behold,
Then look I death my days should expiate.
For all that beauty that doth cover thee
Is but the seemly raiment of my heart,
Which in my breast doth live, as thine in me:
How can I, then, be elder than thou art?
O, therefore, love, be of thyself so wary
As I, not for myself, but for thee will;
Bearing thy heart, which I will keep so chary
As tender nurse her babe from faring ill.
    Presume not on thy heart when mine is slain;
    Thou gavest me thine, not to give back again.

23.

As an unperfect actor on the stage,
Who, with his fear is put besides his part,
Or some fierce thing replete with too much rage,
Whose strength's abundance weakens his own
So I, for fear of trust, forget to say   [heart;
The perfect ceremony of love's rite,
And in mine own love's strength seem to decay,
O'ercharged with burthen of mine own love's
        might.
O, let my books be, then, the eloquence
And dumb presagers of my speaking breast;
Who plead for love, and look for recompense,
More than that tongue that more hath more ex-
        prest.
  O, learn to read what silent love hath writ:
  To hear with eyes belongs to love's fine wit.

24.

Mine eye hath play'd the painter, and hath stell'd
Thy beauty's form in table of my heart;
My body is the frame wherein 'tis held,
And perspective it is best painter's art.
For through the painter must you see his skill,
To find where your true image pictured lies;
Which in my bosom's shop is hanging still,
That hath his windows glazed with thine eyes.
Now see what good turns eyes for eyes have done:
Mine eyes have drawn thy shape, and thine for me
Are windows to my breast, where-through the sun
Delights to peep, to gaze therein on thee;
  Yet eyes this cunning want to grace their art,
  They draw but what they see, know not the heart.

25.

Let those who are in favour with their stars
Of public honour and proud titles boast,
Whilst I, whom fortune of such triumph bars,
Unlookt for joy in that I honour most.
Great princes' favourites their fair leaves spread
But as the marigold at the sun's eye;
And in themselves their pride lies buried,
For at a frown they in their glory die.
The painful warrior famoused for fight,
After a thousand victories once foil'd,
Is from the book of honour razed quite,
And all the rest forgot for which he toil'd:
  Then happy I, that love and am beloved
  Where I may not remove nor be removed.

26.

Lord of my love, to whom in vassalage
Thy merit hath my duty strongly knit,
To thee I send this written ambassage,
To witness duty, not to show my wit:
Duty so great, which wit so poor as mine
May make seem bare, in wanting words to show it,
But that I hope some good conceit of thine
In thy soul's thought, all naked, will bestow it;
Till whatsoever star that guides my moving,
Points on me graciously with fair aspect,
And puts apparel on my totter'd loving,
To show me worthy of thy sweet respect:
  Then may I dare to boast how I do love thee;
  Till then not show my head where thou mayst
  prove me.

27.

Weary with toil, I haste me to my bed,
The dear repose for limbs with travel tired;
But then begins a journey in my head,
To work my mind, when body's work's expired:
For then my thoughts, from far where I abide,
Intend a zealous pilgrimage to thee,
And keep my drooping eyelids open wide,
Looking on darkness which the blind do see:
Save that my soul's imaginary sight
Presents thy shadow to my sightless view,
Which, like a jewel hung in ghastly night,
Makes black night beauteous, and her old face new.
  Lo, thus, by day my limbs, by night my mind,
  For thee and for myself no quiet find.

28.

How can I, then, return in happy plight,
That am debarr'd the benefit of rest?
When day's oppression is not eased by night,
But day by night, and night by day, opprest?
And each, though enemies to either's reign,
Do in consent shake hands to torture me;
The one by toil, the other to complain
How far I toil, still farther off from thee.
I tell the day, to please him thou art bright,
And dost him grace when clouds do blot the
        heaven:
So flatter I the swart-complexion'd night,
When sparkling stars twire not thou gild'st the
        even.
  But day doth daily draw my sorrows longer,
  And night doth nightly make grief's strength
  seem stronger.

29.

When, in disgrace with fortune and men's eyes,
I all alone beweep my outcast state,
And trouble deaf heaven with my bootless cries,
And look upon myself, and curse my fate,
Wishing me like to one more rich in hope,
Featured like him, like him with friends possest,
Desiring this man's art, and that man's scope,
With what I most enjoy contented least;
Yet in these thoughts myself almost despising,
Haply I think on thee,—and then my state,
Like to the lark at break of day arising
From sullen earth, sings hymns at heaven's gate;
  For thy sweet love remember'd such wealth
  brings,
  That then I scorn to change my state with kings.

30.

When to the sessions of sweet silent thought
I summon up remembrance of things past,
I sigh the lack of many a thing I sought,
And with old woes new wail my dear time's waste,
Then can I drown an eye, unused to flow,
For precious friends hid in death's dateless night,
And weep afresh love's long-since-cancell'd woe,
And moan the expense of many a vanisht sight:
Then can I grieve at grievances foregone,
And heavily from woe to woe tell o'er
The sad account of fore-bemoaned moan,
Which I new pay as if not paid before.
  But if the while I think on thee, dear friend,
  All losses are restored, and sorrows end.

31.

Thy bosom is endeared with all hearts,
Which I by lacking have supposed dead;
And there reigns love, and all love's loving parts,
And all those friends which I thought buried.
How many a holy and obsequious tear
Hath dear religious love stoln from mine eye,
As interest of the dead, which now appear
But things removed, that hidden in thee lie!
Thou art the grave where buried love doth live,
Hung with the trophies of my lovers gone,
Who all their parts of me to thee did give;
That due of many now is thine alone:
    Their images I loved I view in thee,
    And thou, all they, hast all the all of me.

32.

If thou survive my well-contented day,
When that churl Death my bones with dust shall
    cover,
And shalt by fortune once more re-survey
These poor rude lines of thy deceased lover:
Compare them with the bettering of the time,
And though they be outstript by every pen,
Reserve them for my love, not for their rime,
Exceeded by the height of happier men.
O, then vouchsafe me but this loving thought:
'Had my friend's Muse grown with this growing
    age,
A dearer birth than this his love had brought,
To march in ranks of better equipage:
    But since he died, and poets better prove,
    Theirs for their style I'll read, his for his love.'

33.

Full many a glorious morning have I seen
Flatter the mountain-tops with sovereign eye,
Kissing with golden face the meadows green,
Gilding pale streams with heavenly alchemy;
Anon permit the basest clouds to ride
With ugly rack on his celestial face,
And from the forlorn world his visage hide,
Stealing unseen to west with this disgrace:
Even so my sun one early morn did shine
With all-triumphant splendour on my brow;
But, out, alack! he was but one hour mine,
The region cloud hath maskt him from me now.
    Yet him for this my love no whit disdaineth;
    Suns of the world may stain when heaven's sun
      staineth.

34.

Why didst thou promise such a beauteous day,
And make me travel forth without my cloak,
To let base clouds o'ertake me in my way,
Hiding thy bravery in their rotten smoke?
'Tis not enough that through the cloud thou break,
To dry the rain on my storm-beaten face,
For no man well of such a salve can speak
That heals the wound, and cures not the disgrace:
Nor can thy shame give physic to my grief;
Though thou repent, yet I have still the loss:
The offender's sorrow lends but weak relief
To him that bears the strong offence's cross.
    Ah, but those tears are pearl which thy love
      sheeds,
    And they are rich, and ransom all ill deeds.

35.

No more be grieved at that which thou hast done:
Roses have thorns, and silver fountains mud;
Clouds and eclipses stain both moon and sun,
And loathsome canker lives in sweetest bud.
All men make faults, and even I in this,
Authorizing thy trespass with compare,
Myself corrupting, salving thy amiss,
Excusing 'their sins more than thy sins are';
For to thy sensual fault I bring in sense,—
Thy adverse party is thy advocate,—
And 'gainst myself a lawful plea commence:
Such civil war is in my love and hate,
    That I an accessary needs must be
    To that sweet thief which sourly robs from me.

36.

Let me confess that we two must be twain,
Although our undivided loves are one:
So shall those blots that do with me remain,
Without thy help, by me be borne alone.
In our two loves there is but one respect,
Though in our lives a separable spite,
Which though it alter not love's sole effect,
Yet doth it steal sweet hours from love's delight.
I may not evermore acknowledge thee,
Lest my bewailed guilt should do thee shame;
Nor thou with public kindness honour me,
Unless thou take that honour from thy name:
    But do not so; I love thee in such sort,
    As, thou being mine, mine is thy good report.

37.

As a decrepit father takes delight
To see his active child do deeds of youth,
So I, made lame by Fortune's dearest spite,
Take all my comfort of thy worth and truth;
For whether beauty, birth, or wealth, or wit,
Or any of these all, or all, or more,
Entitled in their parts do crowned sit,
I make my love engrafted to this store:
So then I am not lame, poor, nor despised,
Whilst that this shadow doth such substance give,
That I in thy abundance am sufficed,
And by a part of all thy glory live.
    Look, what is best, that best I wish in thee:
    This wish I have; then ten times happy me!

38.

How can my Muse want subject to invent,
While thou dost breathe, that pour'st into my
    verse
Thine own sweet argument, too excellent
For every vulgar paper to rehearse?
O, give thyself the thanks, if aught in me
Worthy perusal stand against thy sight;
For who's so dumb that cannot write to thee,
When thou thyself dost give invention light?
Be thou the tenth Muse, ten times more in worth
Than those old nine which rimers invocate;
And he that calls on thee, let him bring forth
Eternal numbers to outlive long date.
    If my slight Muse do please these curious days,
    The pain be mine, but thine shall be the praise.

39.

O, how thy worth with manners may I sing,
When thou art all the better part of me?
What can mine own praise to mine own self bring?
And what is't but mine own when I praise thee?
Even for this let us divided live,
And our dear love lose name of single one,
That by this separation I may give
That due to thee which thou deservest alone.
O absence, what a torment wouldst thou prove,
Were it not thy sour leisure gave sweet leave
To entertain the time with thoughts of love,
Which time and thoughts so sweetly doth deceive,
    And that thou teachest how to make one twain,
    By praising him here who doth hence remain!

40.

Take all my loves, my love, yea, take them all;
What hast thou then more than thou hadst before?
No love, my love, that thou mayst true love call;
All mine was thine before thou hadst this more.
Then, if for my love thou my love receivest,
I cannot blame thee for my love thou usest;
But yet be blamed, if thou this self deceivest
By wilful taste of what thyself refusest.
I do forgive thy robbery, gentle thief,
Although thou steal thee all my poverty;
And yet, love knows, it is a greater grief
To bear love's wrong than hate's known injury.
    Lascivious grace, in whom all ill well shows,
    Kill me with spites; yet we must not be foes.

41.

Those pretty wrongs that liberty commits,
When I am sometime absent from thy heart,
Thy beauty and thy years full well befits,
For still temptation follows where thou art.
Gentle thou art, and therefore to be won,
Beauteous thou art, therefore to be assailed;
And when a woman woos, what woman's son
Will sourly leave her till she have prevailed?
Ay me! but yet thou mightst my seat forbear,
And chide thy beauty and thy straying youth,
Who lead thee in their riot even there
Where thou art forced to break a twofold truth,—
    Hers, by thy beauty tempting her to thee,
    Thine, by thy beauty being false to me.

42.

That thou hast her, it is not all my grief,
And yet it may be said I loved her dearly;
That she hath thee, is of my wailing chief,
A loss in love that touches me more nearly.
Loving offenders, thus I will excuse ye:—
Thou dost love her, because thou know'st I love
    her;
And for my sake even so doth she abuse me,
Suff'ring my friend for my sake to approve her.
If I lose thee, my loss is my love's gain,
And losing her, my friend hath found that loss;
Both find each other, and I lose both twain,
And both for my sake lay on me this cross:
    But here's the joy; my friend and I are one;
    Sweet flattery! then she loves but me alone.

43.

When most I wink, then do mine eyes best see,
For all the day they view things unrespected;
But when I sleep, in dreams they look on thee,
And, darkly bright, are bright in dark directed.
Then thou, whose shadow shadows doth make
    bright,
How would thy shadow's form form happy show
To the clear day with thy much clearer light,
When to unseeing eyes thy shade shines so!
How would, I say, mine eyes be blessed made
By looking on thee in the living day,
When in dead night thy fair imperfect shade
Through heavy sleep on sightless eyes doth stay!
    All days are nights to see till I see thee,
    And nights bright days when dreams do show
        thee me.

44.

If the dull substance of my flesh were thought,
Injurious distance should not stop my way;
For then, despite of space, I would be brought,
From limits far remote, where thou dost stay.
No matter then although my foot did stand
Upon the farthest earth removed from thee;
For nimble thought can jump both sea and land,
As soon as think the place where he would be.
But, ah, thought kills me, that I am not thought,
To leap large lengths of miles when thou art gone,
But that, so much of earth and water wrought,
I must attend time's leisure with my moan;
    Receiving naught by elements so slow
    But heavy tears, badges of either's woe.

45.

The other two, slight air and purging fire,
Are both with thee, wherever I abide;
The first my thought, the other my desire,
These present-absent with swift motion slide.
For when these quicker elements are gone
In tender embassy of love to thee,
My life, being made of four, with two alone
Sinks down to death, opprest with melancholy;
Until life's composition be recured
By those swift messengers return'd from thee,
Who even but now come back again, assured
Of thy fair health, recounting it to me:
    This told, I joy; but then no longer glad,
    I send them back again, and straight grow sad.

46.

Mine eye and heart are at a mortal war,
How to divide the conquest of thy sight;
Mine eye my heart thy picture's sight would bar,
My heart mine eye the freedom of that right.
My heart doth plead that thou in him dost lie—
A closet never pierced with crystal eyes—
But the defendant doth that plea deny,
And says in him thy fair appearance lies.
To cide this title is impanneled
A quest of thoughts, all tenants to the heart;
And by their verdict is determined
The clear eye's moiety and the dear heart's part:
    As thus; mine eye's due is thy outward part,
    And my heart's right thy inward love of heart.

47.

Betwixt mine eye and heart a league is took,
And each doth good turns now unto the other:
When that mine eye is famisht for a look,
Or heart in love with sighs himself doth smother,
With my love's picture then my eye doth feast,
And to the painted banquet bids my heart;
Another time mine eye is my heart's guest,
And in his thoughts of love doth share a part:
So, either by thy picture or my love,
Thyself away art present still with me;
For thou not farther than my thoughts canst move,
And I am still with them, and they with thee;
 Or, if they sleep, thy picture in my sight
 Awakes my heart to heart's and eye's delight.

48.

How careful was I, when I took my way,
Each trifle under truest bars to thrust,
That to my use it might unused stay
From hands of falsehood, in sure wards of trust!
But thou, to whom my jewels trifles are,
Most worthy comfort, now my greatest grief,
Thou, best of dearest, and mine only care,
Art left the prey of every vulgar thief.
Thee have I not lockt up in any chest,
Save where thou art not, though I feel thou art,
Within the gentle closure of my breast,
From whence at pleasure thou mayst come and part;
 And even thence thou wilt be stoln, I fear,
 For truth proves thievish for a prize so dear.

49.

Against that time, if ever that time come,
When I shall see thee frown on my defects,
Whenas thy love hath cast his utmost sum,
Call'd to that audit by advised respects;
Against that time when thou shalt strangely pass,
And scarcely greet me with that sun, thine eye,
When love, converted from the thing it was,
Shall reasons find of settled gravity;
Against that time do I ensconce me here
Within the knowledge of mine own desert,
And this my hand against myself uprear,
To guard the lawful reasons on thy part:
 To leave poor me thou hast the strength of laws,
 Since why to love I can allege no cause.

50.

How heavy do I journey on the way,
When what I seek—my weary travel's end—
Doth teach that ease and that repose to say,
'Thus far the miles are measured from thy friend!'
The beast that bears me, tired with my woe,
Plods dully on, to bear that weight in me,
As if by some instinct the wretch did know
His rider loved not speed, being made from thee:
The bloody spur cannot provoke him on
That sometimes anger thrusts into his hide;
Which heavily he answers with a groan,
More sharp to me than spurring to his side;
 For that same groan doth put this in my mind;
 My grief lies onward, and my joy behind.

51.

Thus can my love excuse the slow offence
Of my dull bearer when from thee I speed:
From where thou art why should I haste me thence?
Till I return, of posting is no need.
O, what excuse will my poor beast then find,
When swift extremity can seem but slow?
Then should I spur, though mounted on the wind,
In winged speed no motion shall I know:
Then can no horse with my desire keep pace;
Therefore desire, of perfect'st love being made,
Shall neigh, no dull flesh in his fiery race;
But love, for love, thus shall excuse my jade,—
 Since from thee going he went wilful-slow,
 Towards thee I'll run, and give him leave to go.

52.

So am I as the rich, whose blessed key
Can bring him to his sweet up-locked treasure,
The which he will not every hour survey,
For blunting the fine point of seldom pleasure.
Therefore are feasts so solemn and so rare,
Since, seldom coming, in the long year set,
Like stones of worth they thinly placed are,
Or captain jewels in the carcanet.
So is the time that keeps you, as my chest,
Or as the wardrobe which the robe doth hide,
To make some special instant special blest,
By new unfolding his imprison'd pride.
 Blessed are you, whose worthiness gives scope,
 Being had, to triumph, being lackt, to hope.

53.

What is your substance, whereof are you made,
That millions of strange shadows on you tend?
Since every one hath, every one, one shade,
And you, but one, can every shadow lend.
Describe Adonis, and the counterfeit
Is poorly imitated after you;
On Helen's cheek all art of beauty set,
And you in Grecian tires are painted new:
Speak of the spring, and foison of the year;
The one doth shadow of your beauty show,
The other as your bounty doth appear;
And you in every blessed shape we know.
 In all external grace you have some part,
 But you like none, none you, for constant heart.

54.

O, how much more doth beauty beauteous seem
By that sweet ornament which truth doth give!
The rose looks fair, but fairer we it deem
For that sweet odour which doth in it live.
The canker-blooms have full as deep a dye
As the perfumed tincture of the roses,
Hang on such thorns, and play as wantonly
When summer's breath their masked buds discloses:
But, for their virtue only is their show,
They live unwoo'd, and unrespected fade;
Die to themselves. Sweet roses do not so;
Of their sweet deaths are sweetest odours made:
 And so of you, beauteous and lovely youth,
 When that shall vade, my verse distils your truth.

55.

Not marble, nor the gilded monuments
Of princes, shall outlive this powerful rime;
But you shall shine more bright in these contents
Than unswept stone, besmear'd with sluttish time.
When wasteful war shall statues overturn,
And broils root out the work of masonry,
Nor Mars his sword nor war's quick fire shall burn
The living record of your memory.
'Gainst death and all-oblivious enmity
Shall you pace forth; your praise shall still find
　　room
Even in the eyes of all posterity
That wears this world out to the ending doom.
　　So, till the judgement that yourself arise,
　　You live in this, and dwell in lovers' eyes.

56.

Sweet love, renew thy force; be it not said
Thy edge should blunter be than appetite,
Which but to-day by feeding is allay'd,
To-morrow sharpen'd in his former might:
So, love, be thou; although to-day thou fill
Thy hungry eyes even till they wink with fullness,
To-morrow see again, and do not kill
The spirit of love with a perpetual dullness.
Let this sad int'rim like the ocean be
Which parts the shore, where two contracted new
Come daily to the banks, that, when they see
Return of love, more blest may be the view;
　　Or call it winter, which, being full of care,
　　Makes summer's welcome thrice more wisht,
　　　more rare.

57.

Being your slave, what should I do but tend
Upon the hours and times of your desire?
I have no precious time at all to spend,
Nor services to do, till you require.
Nor dare I chide the world-without-end hour
Whilst I, my sovereign, watch the clock for you,
Nor think the bitterness of absence sour
When you have bid your servant once adieu;
Nor dare I question with my jealous thought
Where you may be, or your affairs suppose,
But, like a sad slave, stay and think of nought
Save, where you are how happy you make those.
　　So true a fool is love, that in your Will,
　　Though you do any thing, he thinks no ill.

58.

That god forbid that made me first your slave,
I should in thought control your times of
　　pleasure,
Or at your hand the account of hours to crave,
Being your vassal, bound to stay your leisure!
O, let me suffer, being at your beck,
The imprison'd absence of your liberty;
And patience, tame to sufferance, bide each check,
Without accusing you of iniury.
Be where you list, your charter is so strong,
That you yourself may privilege your time
To what you will; to you it doth belong
Yourself to pardon of self-doing crime.
　　I am to wait, though waiting so be hell;
　　Not blame your pleasure, be it ill or well.

59.

If there be nothing new, but that which is
Hath been before, how are our brains beguiled,
Which, labouring for invention, bear amiss
The second burden of a former child!
O, that record could with a backward look,
Even of five hundred courses of the sun,
Show me your image in some antique book,
Since mind at first in character was done!
That I might see what the old world could say
To this composed wonder of your frame;
Whether we are mended, or whe'r better they,
Or whether revolution be the same.
　　O, sure I am, the wits of former days
　　To subjects worse have given admiring praise.

60.

Like as the waves make towards the pebbled shore,
So do our minutes hasten to their end;
Each changing place with that which goes before,
In sequent toil all forwards do contend.
Nativity, once in the main of light,
Crawls to maturity, wherewith being crown'd,
Crooked eclipses 'gainst his glory fight,
And Time that gave doth now his gift confound.
Time doth transfix the flourish set on youth,
And delves the parallels in beauty's brow;
Feeds on the rarities of nature's truth,
And nothing stands but for his scythe to mow:
　　And yet, to times in hope my verse shall stand,
　　Praising thy worth, despite his cruel hand.

61.

Is it thy will thy image should keep open
My heavy eyelids to the weary night?
Dost thou desire my slumbers should be broken,
While shadows like to thee do mock my sight?
Is it thy spirit that thou send'st from thee
So far from home into my deeds to pry,
To find out shames and idle hours in me,
The scope and tenour of thy jealousy?
O, no! thy love, though much, is not so great:
It is my love that keeps mine eye awake;
Mine own true love that doth my rest defeat,
To play the watchman ever for thy sake:
　　For thee watch I whilst thou dost wake else-
　　　where,
　　From me far off, with others all too near.

62.

Sin of self-love possesseth all mine eye,
And all my soul, and all my every part;
And for this sin there is no remedy,
It is so grounded inward in my heart.
Methinks no face so gracious is as mine,
No shape so true, no truth of such account;
And for myself mine own worth do define,
As I all other in all worths surmount.
But when my glass shows me myself indeed,
Beated and chopt with tann'd antiquity,
Mine own self-love quite contrary I read;
Self so self-loving were iniquity.
　　'Tis thee, myself, that for myself I praise,
　　Painting my age with beauty of thy days.

63.

Against my love shall be, as I am now,
With Time's injurious hand crusht and o'erworn;
When hours have drain'd his blood, and fill'd his
brow
With lines and wrinkles; when his youthful morn
Hath travell'd on to age's steepy night;
And all those beauties whereof now he's king
Are vanishing or vanisht out of sight,
Stealing away the treasure of his spring;
For such a time do I now fortify
Against confounding age's cruel knife,
That he shall never cut from memory
My sweet love's beauty, though my lover's life:
   His beauty shall in these black lines be seen,
   And they shall live, and he in them still green.

64.

When I have seen by Time's fell hand defaced
The rich proud cost of outworn buried age;
When sometime lofty towers I see down-razed,
And brass eternal slave to mortal rage;
When I have seen the hungry ocean gain
Advantage on the kingdom of the shore,
And the firm soil win of the watery main,
Increasing store with loss, and loss with store;
When I have seen such interchange of state,
Or state itself confounded to decay;
Ruin hath taught me thus to ruminate,—
That Time will come and take my love away.
   This thought is as a death, which cannot choose
   But weep to have that which it fears to lose.

65.

Since brass, nor stone, nor earth, nor boundless
sea,
But sad mortality o'ersways their power,
How with this rage shall beauty hold a plea,
Whose action is no stronger than a flower?
O, how shall summer's honey breath hold out
Against the wrackful siege of battering days,
When rocks impregnable are not so stout,
Nor gates of steel so strong, but Time decays?
O fearful meditation! where, alack,
Shall Time's best jewel from Time's chest lie hid?
Or what strong hand can hold his swift foot back?
Or who his spoil of beauty can forbid?
   O, none, unless this miracle have might,
   That in black ink my love may still shine bright.

66.

Tired with all these, for restful death I cry,—
As, to behold Desert a beggar born,
And needy Nothing trimm'd in jollity,
And purest Faith unhappily forsworn,
And gilded Honour shamefully misplaced,
And maiden Virtue rudely strumpeted,
And right Perfection wrongfully disgraced,
And Strength by limping Sway disabled,
And Art made tongue-tied by Authority,
And Folly, doctor-like, controlling Skill,
And simple Truth miscall'd Simplicity,
And captive Good attending captain Ill:
   Tired with all these, from these would I be gone,
   Save that, to die, I leave my love alone.

67.

Ah, wherefore with infection should he live,
And with his presence grace impiety,
That sin by him advantage should achieve,
And lace itself with his society?
Why should false painting imitate his cheek,
And steal dead seeing of his living hue?
Why should poor beauty indirectly seek
Roses of shadow, since his rose is true?
Why should he live, now Nature bankrout is,
Beggar'd of blood to blush through lively veins?
For she hath no exchequer now but his,
And, proud of many, lives upon his gains.
   O, him she stores, to show what wealth she had
   In days long since, before these last so bad.

68.

Thus is his cheek the map of days outworn,
When beauty lived and died as flowers do now,
Before these bastard signs of fair were born,
Or durst inhabit on a living brow;
Before the golden tresses of the dead,
The right of sepulchres, were shorn away,
To live a second life on second head;
Ere beauty's dead fleece made another gay:
In him those holy antique hours are seen,
Without all ornament, itself, and true,
Making no summer of another's green,
Robbing no old to dress his beauty new;
   And him as for a map doth Nature store,
   To show false Art what beauty was of yore.

69.

Those parts of thee that the world's eye doth view
Want nothing that the thought of hearts can mend;
All tongues, the voice of souls, give thee that due,
Uttering bare truth, even so as foes commend.
Thy outward thus with outward praise is crown'd;
But those same tongues, that give thee so thine
own,
In other accents do this praise confound
By seeing farther than the eye hath shown.
They look into the beauty of thy mind,
And that, in guess, they measure by thy deeds;
Then, churls, their thoughts, although their eyes
were kind,
To thy fair flower add the rank smell of weeds:
   But why thy odour matcheth not thy show,
   The soil is this, that thou dost common grow.

70.

That thou art blamed shall not be thy defect,
For slander's mark was ever yet the fair;
The ornament of beauty is suspect,
A crow that flies in heaven's sweetest air.
So thou be good, slander doth but approve
Thy worth the greater, being woo'd of time;
For canker vice the sweetest buds doth love,
And thou present'st a pure unstained prime.
Thou hast past by the ambush of young days,
Either not assail'd, or victor being charged;
Yet this thy praise cannot be so thy praise,
To tie up envy evermore enlarged:
   If some suspect of ill maskt not thy show,
   Then thou alone kingdoms of hearts shouldst
   owe.

71.

No longer mourn for me when I am dead
Than you shall hear the surly sullen bell
Give warning to the world that I am fled
From this vile world, with vilest worms to dwell:
Nay, if you read this line, remember not
The hand that writ it; for I love you so,
That I in your sweet thoughts would be forgot,
If thinking on me then should make you woe.
O, if, I say, you look upon this verse
When I perhaps compounded am with clay,
Do not so much as my poor name rehearse;
But let your love even with my life decay;
   Lest the wise world should look into your moan,
   And mock you with me after I am gone.

72.

O, lest the world should task you to recite
What merit lived in me, that you should love,
After my death, dear love, forget me quite,
For you in me can nothing worthy prove;
Unless you would devise some virtuous lie,
To do more for me than mine own desert,
And hang more praise upon deceased I
Than niggard truth would willingly impart:
O, lest your true love may seem false in this,
That you for love speak well of me untrue,
My name be buried where my body is,
And live no more to shame nor me nor you.
   For I am shamed by that which I bring forth,
   And so should you, to love things nothing
     worth.

73.

That time of year thou mayst in me behold
When yellow leaves, or none, or few, do hang
Upon those boughs which shake against the cold,
Bare ruin'd choirs, where late the sweet birds sang.
In me thou see'st the twilight of such day
As after sunset fadeth in the west;
Which by and by black night doth take away,
Death's second self, that seals up all in rest.
In me thou see'st the glowing of such fire,
That on the ashes of his youth doth lie,
As the death-bed whereon it must expire,
Consumed with that which it was nourish'd by.
   This thou perceivest, which makes thy love
     more strong,
   To love that well which thou must leave ere
     long.

74.

But be contented: when that fell arrest
Without all bail shall carry me away,
My life hath in this line some interest,
Which for memorial still with thee shall stay.
When thou reviewest this, thou dost review
The very part was consecrate to thee:
The earth can have but earth, which is his due;
My spirit is thine, the better part of me:
So, then, thou hast but lost the dregs of life,
The prey of worms, my body being dead;
The coward conquest of a wretch's knife,
Too base of thee to be remembered.
   The worth of that is that which it contains,
   And that is this, and this with thee remains.

75.

So are you to my thoughts as food to life,
Or as sweet-season'd showers are to the ground;
And for the peace of you I hold such strife
As 'twixt a miser and his wealth is found;
Now proud as an enjoyer, and anon
Doubting the filching age will steal his treasure;
Now counting best to be with you alone,
Then better'd that the world may see my pleasure:
Sometime all full with feasting on your sight,
And by and by clean starved for a look;
Possessing or pursuing no delight,
Save what is had or must from you be took.
   Thus do I pine and surfeit day by day,
   Or gluttoning on all, or all away.

76.

Why is my verse so barren of new pride,
So far from variation or quick change?
Why, with the time, do I not glance aside
To new-found methods and to compounds
    strange?
Why write I still all one, ever the same,
And keep invention in a noted weed,
That every word doth almost tell my name,
Showing their birth, and where they did proceed?
O, know, sweet love, I always write of you,
And you and love are still my argument;
So all my best is dressing old words new,
Spending again what is already spent:
   For as the sun is daily new and old,
   So is my love still telling what is told.

77.

Thy glass will show thee how thy beauties wear,
Thy dial how thy precious minutes waste;
The vacant leaves thy mind's imprint will bear,
And of this book this learning mayst thou taste.
The wrinkles which thy glass will truly show,
Of mouthed graves will give thee memory;
Thou by thy dial's shady stealth mayst know
Time's thievish progress to eternity.
Look, what thy memory cannot contain,
Commit to these waste blanks, and thou shalt find
Those children nursed, deliver'd from thy brain
To take a new acquaintance of thy mind.
   These offices, so oft as thou wilt look,
   Shall profit thee, and much enrich thy book.

78.

So oft have I invoked thee for my Muse,
And found such fair assistance in my verse,
As every alien pen hath got my use,
And under thee their poesy disperse.
Thine eyes, that taught the dumb on high to sing,
And heavy ignorance aloft to fly,
Have added feathers to the learned's wing,
And given grace a double majesty.
Yet be most proud of that which I compile,
Whose influence is thine, and born of thee:
In others' works thou dost but mend the style,
And arts with thy sweet graces graced be;
   But thou art all my art, and dost advance
   As high as learning my rude ignorance.

79.

Whilst I alone did call upon thy aid,
My verse alone had all thy gentle grace;
But now my gracious numbers are decay'd,
And my sick Muse doth give another place.
I grant, sweet love, thy lovely argument
Deserves the travail of a worthier pen;
Yet what of thee thy poet doth invent
He robs thee of, and pays it thee again.
He lends thee virtue, and he stole that word
From thy behaviour; beauty doth he give,
And found it in thy cheek; he can afford
No praise to thee but what in thee doth live.
    Then thank him not for that which he doth say,
    Since what he owes thee thou thyself dost pay.

80.

O, how I faint when I of you do write,
Knowing a better spirit doth use your name,
And in the praise thereof spends all his might,
To make me tongue-tied, speaking of your fame!
But since your worth, wide as the ocean is,
The humble as the proudest sail doth bear,
My saucy bark, inferior far to his,
On your broad main doth wilfully appear.
Your shallowest help will hold me up afloat,
While he upon your soundless deep doth ride;
Or, being wrackt, I am a worthless boat,
He of tall building and of goodly pride:
    Then if he thrive, and I be cast away,
    The worst was this; my love was my decay.

81.

Or I shall live your epitaph to make,
Or you survive when I in earth am rotten;
From hence your memory death cannot take,
Although in me each part will be forgotten.
Your name from hence immortal life shall have,
Though I, once gone, to all the world must die:
The earth can yield me but a common grave,
When you entombed in men's eyes shall lie.
Your monument shall be my gentle verse,
Which eyes not yet created shall o'er-read;
And tongues to be your being shall rehearse,
When all the breathers of this world are dead;
    You still shall live—such virtue hath my pen—
    Where breath most breathes, even in the mouths
      of men.

82.

I grant thou wert not married to my Muse,
And therefore mayst without attaint o'erlook
The dedicated words which writers use
Of their fair subject, blessing every book.
Thou art as fair in knowledge as in hue,
Finding thy worth a limit past my praise;
And therefore art enforced to seek anew
Some fresher stamp of the time-bettering days.
And do so, love; yet when they have devised
What strained touches rhetoric can lend,
Thou truly fair wert truly sympathized
In true plain words by thy true-telling friend;
    And their gross painting might be better used
    Where cheeks need blood; in thee it is abused.

83.

I never saw that you did painting need,
And therefore to your fair no painting set;
I found, or thought I found, you did exceed
The barren tender of a poet's debt:
And therefore have I slept in your report,
That you yourself, being extant, well might show
How far a modern quill doth come too short,
Speaking of worth, what worth in you doth grow.
This silence for my sin you did impute,
Which shall be most my glory, being dumb;
For I impair not beauty, being mute,
When others would give life, and bring a tomb.
    There lives more life in one of your fair eyes
    Than both your poets can in praise devise.

84.

Who is it that says most? which can say more
Than this rich praise, that you alone are you?
In whose confine immured is the store
Which should example where your equal grew.
Lean penury within that pen doth dwell
That to his subject lends not some small glory;
But he that writes of you, if he can tell
That you are you, so dignifies his story:
Let him but copy what in you is writ,
Not making worse what nature made so clear,
And such a counterpart shall fame his wit,
Making his style admired everywhere.
    You to your beauteous blessings add a curse,
    Being fond on praise, which makes your praises
      worse.

85.

My tongue-tied Muse in manners holds her still,
While comments of your praise, richly compiled,
Reserve their character with golden quill,
And precious phrase by all the Muses filed.
I think good thoughts, whilst other write good
    words,
And, like unletter'd clerk, still cry 'Amen'
To every hymn that able spirit affords
In polish'd form of well-refined pen.
Hearing you praised, I say ''Tis so, 'tis true,'
And to the most of praise add something more;
But that is in my thought, whose love to you,
Though words come hindmost, holds his rank
    before.
    Then others for the breath of words respect,
    Me for my dumb thoughts, speaking in effect.

86.

Was it the proud full sail of his great verse,
Bound for the prize of all-too-precious you,
That did my ripe thoughts in my brain inhearse,
Making their tomb the womb wherein they grew?
Was it his spirit, by spirits taught to write
Above a mortal pitch, that struck me dead?
No, neither he, nor his compeers by night
Giving him aid, my verse astonished.
He, nor that affable familiar ghost
Which nightly gulls him with intelligence,
As victors, of my silence cannot boast;
I was not sick of any fear from thence:
    But when your countenance fill'd up his line,
    Then lackt I matter; that enfeebled mine.

87.

Farewell! thou art too dear for my possessing,
And like enough thou know'st thy estimate:
The charter of thy worth gives thee releasing;
My bonds in thee are all determinate.
For how do I hold thee but by thy granting?
And for that riches where is my deserving?
The cause of this fair gift in me is wanting,
And so my patent back again is swerving.
Thyself thou gavest, thy own worth then not
    knowing,
Or me, to whom thou gavest it, else mistaking;
So thy great gift, upon misprision growing,
Comes home again, on better judgement making.
    Thus have I had thee, as a dream doth flatter,
    In sleep a king, but waking no such matter.

88.

When thou shalt be disposed to set me light,
And place my merit in the eye of scorn,
Upon thy side against myself I'll fight,
And prove thee virtuous, though thou art forsworn.
With mine own weakness being best acquainted,
Upon thy part I can set down a story
Of faults conceal'd, wherein I am attainted;
That thou, in losing me, shalt win much glory:
And I by this will be a gainer too;
For bending all my loving thoughts on thee,
The injuries that to myself I do,
Doing thee vantage, double-vantage me.
    Such is my love, to thee I so belong,
    That for thy right myself will bear all wrong.

89.

Say that thou didst forsake me for some fault,
And I will comment upon that offence:
Speak of my lameness, and I straight will halt,
Against thy reasons making no defence.
Thou canst not, love, disgrace me half so ill,
To set a form upon desired change,
As I'll myself disgrace: knowing thy will,
I will acquaintance strangle, and look strange;
Be absent from thy walks; and in my tongue
Thy sweet beloved name no more shall dwell,
Lest I, too much profane, should do it wrong,
And haply of our old acquaintance tell.
    For thee, against myself I'll vow debate,
    For I must ne'er love him whom thou dost
        hate.

90.

Then hate me when thou wilt; if ever, now;
Now, while the world is bent my deeds to cross,
Join with the spite of fortune, make me bow,
And do not drop in for an after-loss:
Ah, do not, when my heart hath scaped this
    sorrow,
Come in the rearward of a conquer'd woe;
Give not a windy night a rainy morrow,
To linger out a purposed overthrow.
If thou wilt leave me, do not leave me last,
When other petty griefs have done their spite,
But in the onset come: so shall I taste
At first the very worst of fortune's might;
    And other strains of woe, which now seem woe,
    Compared with loss of thee will not seem so.

91.

Some glory in their birth, some in their skill,
Some in their wealth, some in their bodies' force;
Some in their garments, though new-fangled ill;
Some in their hawks and hounds, some in their
    horse;
And every humour hath his adjunct pleasure,
Wherein it finds a joy above the rest:
But these particulars are not my measure;
All these I better in one general best.
Thy love is better than high birth to me,
Richer than wealth, prouder than garments' cost,
Of more delight than hawks or horses be;
And having thee, of all men's pride I boast:
    Wretched in this alone, that thou mayst take
    All this away, and me most wretched make.

92.

But do thy worst to steal thyself away,
For term of life thou art assured mine;
And life no longer than thy love will stay,
For it depends upon that love of thine.
Then need I not to fear the worst of wrongs,
When in the least of them my life hath end.
I see a better state to me belongs
Than that which on thy humour doth depend:
Thou canst not vex me with inconstant mind,
Since that my life on thy revolt doth lie.
O, what a happy title do I find,
Happy to have thy love, happy to die!
    But what's so blessed-fair that fears no blot?
    Thou mayst be false, and yet I know it not.

93.

So shall I live, supposing thou art true,
Like a deceived husband; so love's face
May still seem love to me, though alter'd new;
Thy looks with me, thy heart in other place:
For there can live no hatred in thine eye,
Therefore in that I cannot know thy change.
In many's looks the false heart's history
Is writ in moods and frowns and wrinkles strange;
But heaven in thy creation did decree
That in thy face sweet love should ever dwell;
Whate'er thy thoughts or thy heart's workings be,
Thy looks should nothing thence but sweetness
    tell.
    How like Eve's apple doth thy beauty grow,
    If thy sweet virtue answer not thy show!

94.

They that have power to hurt and will do none,
That do not do the thing they most do show,
Who, moving others, are themselves as stone,
Unmoved, cold, and to temptation slow;
They rightly do inherit heaven's graces,
And husband nature's riches from expense;
They are the lords and owners of their faces,
Others but stewards of their excellence.
The summer's flower is to the summer sweet,
Though to itself it only live and die,
But if that flower with base infection meet,
The basest weed outbraves his dignity:
    For sweetest things turn sourest by their deeds;
    Lilies that fester smell far worse than weeds.

95.

How sweet and lovely dost thou make the shame
Which, like a canker in the fragrant rose,
Doth spot the beauty of thy budding name!
O, in what sweets dost thou thy sins enclose!
That tongue that tells the story of thy days,
Making lascivious comments on thy sport,
Cannot dispraise but in a kind of praise;
Naming thy name blesses an ill report.
O, what a mansion have those vices got
Which for their habitation chose out thee,
Where beauty's veil doth cover every blot,
And all things turn to fair that eyes can see!
   Take heed, dear heart, of this large privilege;
   The hardest knife ill-used doth lose his edge.

96.

Some say, thy fault is youth, some wantonness;
Some say, thy grace is youth and gentle sport;
Both grace and faults are loved of more and less:
Thou makest faults graces that to thee resort.
As on the finger of a throned queen
The basest jewel will be well esteem'd,
So are those errors that in thee are seen
To truths translated, and for true things deem'd.
How many lambs might the stern wolf betray,
If like a lamb he could his looks translate!
How many gazers mightst thou lead away,
If thou wouldst use the strength of all thy state!
   But do not so; I love thee in such sort,
   As thou being mine, mine is thy good report.

97.

How like a winter hath my absence been
From thee, the pleasure of the fleeting year!
What freezings have I felt, what dark days seen!
What old December's bareness every where!
And yet this time removed was summer's time;
The teeming autumn, big with rich increase,
Bearing the wanton burden of the prime,
Like widow'd wombs after their lords' decease:
Yet this abundant issue seem'd to me
But hope of orphans and unfather'd fruit;
For summer and his pleasures wait on thee,
And, thou away, the very birds are mute;
   Or, if they sing, 'tis with so dull a cheer,
   That leaves look pale, dreading the winter's
     near.

98.

From you have I been absent in the spring,
When proud-pied April, drest in all his trim,
Hath put a spirit of youth in every thing,
That heavy Saturn laught and leapt with him.
Yet nor the lays of birds, nor the sweet smell
Of different flowers in odour and in hue,
Could make me any summer's story tell,
Or from their proud lap pluck them where they
   grew;
Nor did I wonder at the lily's white,
Nor praise the deep vermilion in the rose;
They were but sweet, but figures of delight,
Drawn after you,—you pattern of all those.
   Yet seem'd it winter still, and, you away,
   As with your shadow I with these did play.

99.

The forward violet thus did I chide:
Sweet thief, whence didst thou steal thy sweet
   that smells,
If not from my love's breath? The purple pride
Which on thy soft cheek for complexion dwells
In my love's veins thou hast too grossly dyed.
The lily I condemned for thy hand;
And buds of marjoram had stoln thy hair:
The roses fearfully on thorns did stand,
One blushing shame, another white despair;
A third, nor red nor white, had stoln of both,
And to his robbery had annext thy breath;
But, for his theft, in pride of all his growth
A vengeful canker eat him up to death.
   More flowers I noted, yet I none could see
   But sweet or colour it had stoln from thee.

100.

Where art thou, Muse, that thou forgett'st so long
To speak of that which gives thee all thy might?
Spend'st thou thy fury on some worthless song,
Dark'ning thy power to lend base subjects light?
Return, forgetful Muse, and straight redeem
In gentle numbers time so idly spent;
Sing to the ear that doth thy lays esteem,
And gives thy pen both skill and argument.
Rise, resty Muse, my love's sweet face survey,
If Time have any wrinkle graven there;
If any, be a satire to decay,
And make Time's spoils despised everywhere.
   Give my love fame faster than Time wastes life;
   So thou prevent'st his scythe and crooked knife.

101.

O truant Muse, what shall be thy amends
For thy neglect of truth in beauty dyed?
Both truth and beauty on my love depends;
So dost thou too, and therein dignified.
Make answer, Muse: wilt thou not haply say,
'Truth needs no colour, with his colour fixt;
Beauty no pencil, beauty's truth to lay;
But best is best, if never intermixt'?
Because he needs no praise, wilt thou be dumb?
Excuse not silence so: for't lies in thee
To make him much outlive a gilded tomb,
And to be praised of ages yet to be.
   Then do thy office, Muse; I teach thee how
   To make him seem long hence as he shows now.

102.

My love is strengthen'd, though more weak in
   seeming;
I love not less, though less the show appear:
That love is merchandized whose rich esteeming
The owner's tongue doth publish everywhere.
Our love was new, and then but in the spring,
When I was wont to greet it with my lays;
As Philomel in summer's front doth sing,
And stops her pipe in growth of riper days:
Not that the summer is less pleasant now
Than when her mournful hymns did hush the
   night,
But that wild music burdens every bough,
And sweets grown common lose their dear delight.
   Therefore, like her, I sometime hold my tongue,
   Because I would not dull you with my song.

103.

Alack, what poverty my Muse brings forth,
That having such a scope to show her pride,
The argument, all bare, is of more worth
Than when it hath my added praise beside!
O, blame me not, if I no more can write!
Look in your glass, and there appears a face
That overgoes my blunt invention quite,
Dulling my lines, and doing me disgrace.
Were it not sinful, then, striving to mend,
To mar the subject that before was well?
For to no other pass my verses tend
Than of your graces and your gifts to tell;
    And more, much more, than in my verse can sit,
    Your own glass shows you when you look in it.

104.

To me, fair friend, you never can be old,
For as you were when first your eye I eyed,
Such seems your beauty still. Three winters' cold
Have from the forests shook three summers' pride;
Three beauteous springs to yellow autumn turn'd
In process of the seasons have I seen,
Three April perfumes in three hot Junes burn'd,
Since first I saw you fresh, which yet are green.
Ah, yet doth beauty, like a dial-hand,
Steal from his figure, and no pace perceived;
So your sweet hue, which methinks still doth stand,
Hath motion, and mine eye may be deceived:
    For fear of which, hear this, thou age unbred,—
    Ere you were born was beauty's summer dead.

105.

Let not my love be call'd idolatry,
Nor my beloved as an idol show,
Since all alike my songs and praises be
To one, of one, still such, and ever so.
Kind is my love to-day, to-morrow kind,
Still constant in a wondrous excellence;
Therefore my verse to constancy confined,
One thing expressing, leaves out difference.
Fair, kind, and true, is all my argument,—
Fair, kind, and true, varying to other words;
And in this change is my invention spent,
Three themes in one, which wondrous scope
    affords.
    Fair, kind, and true, have often lived alone,
    Which three till now never kept seat in one.

106.

When in the chronicle of wasted time
I see descriptions of the fairest wights,
And beauty making beautiful old rime
In praise of ladies dead and lovely knights,
Then, in the blazon of sweet beauty's best,
Of hand, of foot, of lip, of eye, of brow,
I see their antique pen would have exprest
Even such a beauty as you master now.
So all their praises are but prophecies
Of this our time, all you prefiguring;
And, for they lookt but with divining eyes,
They had not skill enough your worth to sing:
    For we, which now behold these present days,
    Have eyes to wonder, but lack tongues to
    praise.

107.

Not mine own fears, nor the prophetic soul
Of the wide world dreaming on things to come,
Can yet the lease of my true love control,
Supposed as forfeit to a confined doom.
The mortal moon hath her eclipse endured,
And the sad augurs mock their own presage;
Incertainties now crown themselves assured,
And peace proclaims olives of endless age.
Now with the drops of this most balmy time
My love looks fresh, and Death to me subscribes,
Since, spite of him, I'll live in this poor rime,
While he insults o'er dull and speechless tribes:
    And thou in this shalt find thy monument,
    When tyrants' crests and tombs of brass are
    spent.

108.

What's in the brain, that ink may character,
Which hath not figured to thee my true spirit?
What's new to speak, what new to register,
That may express my love, or thy dear merit?
Nothing, sweet boy; but yet, like prayers divine,
I must each day say o'er the very same;
Counting no old thing old, thou mine, I thine,
Even as when first I hallow'd thy fair name.
So that eternal love in love's fresh case
Weighs not the dust and injury of age,
Nor gives to necessary wrinkles place,
But makes antiquity for aye his page;
    Finding the first conceit of love there bred,
    Where time and outward form would show it
    dead.

109.

O, never say that I was false of heart,
Though absence seem'd my flame to qualify.
As easy might I from myself depart
As from my soul, which in thy breast doth lie:
That is my home of love: if I have ranged,
Like him that travels I return again,
Just to the time, not with the time exchanged,
So that myself bring water for my stain.
Never believe, though in my nature reign'd
All frailties that besiege all kinds of blood,
That it could so preposterously be stain'd,
To leave for nothing all thy sum of good;
    For nothing this wide universe I call,
    Save thou, my Rose; in it thou art my all.

110.

Alas, 'tis true I have gone here and there,
And made myself a motley to the view,
Gored mine own thoughts, sold cheap what is
    most dear,
Made old offences of affections new;
Most true it is that I have lookt on truth
Askance and strangely: but, by all above,
These blenches gave my heart another youth,
And worse essays proved thee my best of love.
Now all is done, have what shall have no end:
Mine appetite I never more will grind
On newer proof, to try an older friend,
A god in love, to whom I am confined.
    Then give me welcome, next my heaven the
    best,
    Even to thy pure and most most loving breast.

III.

O, for my sake do you with Fortune chide,
The guilty goddess of my harmful deeds,
That did not better for my life provide
Than public means which public manners breeds.
Thence comes it that my name receives a brand;
And almost thence my nature is subdued
To what it works in, like the dyer's hand:
Pity me, then, and wish I were renew'd;
Whilst, like a willing patient, I will drink
Potions of eisel 'gainst my strong infection;
No bitterness that I will bitter think,
Nor double penance, to correct correction.
  Pity me, then, dear friend, and I assure ye
  Even that your pity is enough to cure me.

112.

Your love and pity doth the impression fill
Which vulgar scandal stampt upon my brow;
For what care I who calls me well or ill,
So you o'er-green my bad, my good allow?
You are my all-the-world, and I must strive
To know my shames and praises from your
    tongue;
None else to me, nor I to none alive,
That my steel'd sense or changes right or wrong.
In so profound abysm I throw all care
Of others' voices, that my adder's sense
To critic and to flatterer stopped are.
Mark how with my neglect I do dispense:
  You are so strongly in my purpose bred,
  That all the world besides methinks are dead.

113.

Since I left you, mine eye is in my mind;
And that which governs me to go about
Doth part his function, and is partly blind,
Seems seeing, but effectually is out;
For it no form delivers to the heart
Of bird, of flower, or shape, which it doth latch:
Of his quick objects hath the mind no part,
Nor his own vision holds what it doth catch;
For if it see the rudest or gentlest sight,
The most sweet favour or deformed'st creature,
The mountain or the sea, the day or night,
The crow or dove, it shapes them to your feature:
  Incapable of more, replete with you,
  My most true mind thus maketh mine untrue.

114.

Or whether doth my mind, being crown'd with
    you,
Drink up the monarch's plague, this flattery?
Or whether shall I say, mine eye saith true,
And that your love taught it this alchemy,
To make of monsters and things indigest
Such cherubins as your sweet self resemble,
Creating every bad a perfect best,
As fast as objects to his beams assemble?
O, 'tis the first; 'tis flatt'ry in my seeing,
And my great mind most kingly drinks it up:
Mine eye well knows what with his gust is greeing,
And to his palate doth prepare the cup:
  If it be poison'd, 'tis the lesser sin
  That mine eye loves it, and doth first begin.

115.

Those lines that I before have writ do lie,
Even those that said I could not love you dearer:
Yet then my judgement knew no reason why
My most full flame should afterwards burn clearer.
But reckoning Time, whose million'd accidents
Creep in 'twixt vows, and change decrees of kings,
Tan sacred beauty, blunt the sharp'st intents,
Divert strong minds to the course of alt'ring things;
Alas, why, fearing of Time's tyranny,
Might I not then say, 'Now I love you best,'
When I was certain o'er incertainty,
Crowning the present, doubting of the rest?
  Love is a babe; then might I not say so,
  To give full growth to that which still doth
    grow.

116.

Let me not to the marriage of true minds
Admit impediments. Love is not love
Which alters when it alteration finds,
Or bends with the remover to remove:
O, no! it is an ever-fixed mark,
That looks on tempests, and is never shaken,
It is the star to every wandering bark,
Whose worth's unknown, although his height be
    taken.
Love's not Time's fool, though rosy lips and cheeks
Within his bending sickle's compass come;
Love alters not with his brief hours and weeks,
But bears it out even to the edge of doom.
  If this be error, and upon me proved,
  I never writ, nor no man ever loved.

117.

Accuse me thus: that I have scanted all
Wherein I should your great deserts repay;
Forgot upon your dearest love to call,
Whereto all bonds do tie me day by day;
That I have frequent been with unknown minds,
And given to time your own dear-purchased right;
That I have hoisted sail to all the winds
Which should transport me farthest from your
    sight.
Book both my wilfulness and errors down,
And on just proof surmise accumulate;
Bring me within the level of your frown,
But shoot not at me in your waken'd hate;
  Since my appeal says I did strive to prove
  The constancy and virtue of your love.

118.

Like as, to make our appetites more keen,
With eager compounds we our palate urge;
As, to prevent our maladies unseen,
We sicken to shun sickness when we purge;
Even so, being full of your ne'er-cloying sweetness,
To bitter sauces did I frame my feeding;
And, sick of welfare, found a kind of meetness
To be diseased, ere that there was true needing.
Thus policy in love, t'anticipate
The ills that were not, grew to faults assured,
And brought to medicine a healthful state,
Which, rank of goodness, would by ill be cured:
  But thence I learn, and find the lesson true,
  Drugs poison him that so fell sick of you.

119.

What potions have I drunk of Siren tears,
Distill'd from limbecks foul as hell within,
Applying fears to hopes, and hopes to fears,
Still losing when I saw myself to win!
What wretched errors hath my heart committed,
Whilst it hath thought itself so blessed never!
How have mine eyes out of their spheres been
    fitted
In the distraction of this madding fever!
O benefit of ill! now I find true
That better is by evil still made better;
And ruin'd love, when it is built anew,
Grows fairer than at first, more strong, far greater.
    So I return rebuked to my content,
    And gain by ill thrice more than I have spent.

120.

That you were once unkind befriends me now,
And for that sorrow which I then did feel
Needs must I under my transgression bow,
Unless my nerves were brass or hammer'd steel.
For if you were by my unkindness shaken,
As I by yours, y'have past a hell of time;
And I, a tyrant, have no leisure taken
To weigh how once I suffer'd in your crime.
O, that our night of woe might have remember'd
My deepest sense, how hard true sorrow hits,
And soon to you, as you to me then, tender'd
The humble salve which wounded bosoms fits!
    But that, your trespass, now becomes a fee;
    Mine ransoms yours, and yours must ransom
    me.

121.

'Tis better to be vile than vile esteemed,
When not to be receives reproach of being;
And the just pleasure lost, which is so deemed
Not by our feeling, but by others' seeing:
For why should others' false adulterate eyes
Give salutation to my sportive blood?
Or on my frailties why are frailer spies,
Which in their wills count bad what I think good?
No, I am that I am; and they that level
At my abuses reckon up their own:
I may be straight, though they themselves be bevel;
By their rank thoughts my deeds must not be
    shown;
    Unless this general evil they maintain—
    All men are bad, and in their badness reign.

122.

Thy gift, thy tables, are within my brain
Full character'd with lasting memory,
Which shall above that idle rank remain,
Beyond all date, even to eternity:
Or, at the least, so long as brain and heart
Have faculty by nature to subsist;
Till each to razed oblivion yield his part
Of thee, thy record never can be mist.
That poor retention could not so much hold,
Nor need I tallies thy dear love to score;
Therefore to give them from me was I bold,
To trust those tables that receive thee more:
    To keep an adjunct to remember thee
    Were to import forgetfulness in me.

123.

No, Time, thou shalt not boast that I do change:
Thy pyramids built up with newer might
To me are nothing novel, nothing strange;
They are but dressings of a former sight.
Our dates are brief, and therefore we admire
What thou dost foist upon us that is old;
And rather make them born to our desire
Than think that we before have heard them told.
Thy registers and thee I both defy,
Not wondering at the present nor the past;
For thy records and what we see doth lie,
Made more or less by thy continual haste.
    This I do vow, and this shall ever be,
    I will be true, despite thy scythe and thee.

124.

If my dear love were but the child of state,
It might for Fortune's bastard be unfather'd,
As subject to Time's love or to Time's hate,
Weeds among weeds, or flowers with flowers
    gather'd.
No, it was builded far from accident;
It suffers not in smiling pomp, nor falls
Under the blow of thralled discontent,
Whereto the inviting time our fashion calls:
It fears not policy, that heretic,
Which works on leases of short-number'd hours,
But all alone stands hugely politic,
That it nor grows with heat nor drowns with
    showers.
    To this I witness call the fools of Time,
    Which die for goodness, who have lived for
    crime.

125.

Were't aught to me I bore the canopy,
With my extern the outward honouring,
Or laid great bases for eternity,
Which proves more short than waste or ruining?
Have I not seen dwellers on form and favour
Lose all, and more, by paying too much rent,
For compound sweet foregoing simple savour,
Pitiful thrivers, in their gazing spent?
No, let me be obsequious in thy heart,
And take thou my oblation, poor but free,
Which is not mixt with seconds, knows no art,
But mutual render, only me for thee.
    Hence, thou suborn'd informer! a true soul
    When most impeacht stands least in thy control.

126.

O thou, my lovely boy, who in thy power
Dost hold Time's fickle glass, his sickle-hour;
Who hast by waning grown, and therein show'st
Thy lovers withering, as thy sweet self grow'st;
If Nature, sovereign mistress over wrack,
As thou goest onwards, still will pluck thee back,
She keeps thee to this purpose, that her skill
May Time disgrace, and wretched minutes kill.
Yet fear her, O thou minion of her pleasure!
She may detain, but not still keep, her treasure:
Her audit, though delay'd, answer'd must be,
And her quietus is to render thee.

127.

In the old age black was not counted fair,
Or if it were, it bore not beauty's name;
But now is black beauty's successive heir,
And beauty slander'd with a bastard shame:
For since each hand hath put on nature's power,
Fairing the foul with art's false borrow'd face,
Sweet beauty hath no name, no holy bower,
But is profaned, if not lives in disgrace.
Therefore my mistress' eyes are raven black,
Her eyes so suited, and they mourners seem
At such who, not born fair, no beauty lack,
Slandering creation with a false esteem:
    Yet so they mourn, becoming of their woe,
    That every tongue says beauty should look so.

128.

How oft, when thou, my music, music play'st,
Upon that blessed wood whose motion sounds
With thy sweet fingers, when thou gently sway'st
The wiry concord that mine ear confounds,
Do I envy those jacks that nimble leap
To kiss the tender inward of thy hand,
Whilst my poor lips, which should that harvest reap,
At the wood's boldness by thee blushing stand!
To be so tickled, they would change their state
And situation with those dancing chips,
O'er whom thy fingers walk with gentle gait,
Making dead wood more blest than living lips.
    Since saucy jacks so happy are in this,
    Give them thy fingers, me thy lips to kiss.

129.

The expense of spirit in a waste of shame
Is lust in action; and till action, lust
Is perjured, murd'rous, bloody, full of blame,
Savage, extreme, rude, cruel, not to trust;
Enjoy'd no sooner but despised straight;
Past reason hunted; and no sooner had,
Past reason hated, as a swallow'd bait,
On purpose laid to make the taker mad:
Mad in pursuit, and in possession so;
Had, having, and in quest to have, extreme;
A bliss in proof, and proved, a very woe;
Before, a joy proposed; behind, a dream.
    All this the world well knows; yet none knows well
    To shun the heaven that leads men to this hell.

130.

My mistress' eyes are nothing like the sun;
Coral is far more red than her lips' red:
If snow be white, why then her breasts are dun;
If hairs be wires, black wires grow on her head.
I have seen roses damaskt, red and white,
But no such roses see I in her cheeks;
And in some perfumes is there more delight
Than in the breath that from my mistress reeks.
I love to hear her speak, yet well I know
That music hath a far more pleasing sound:
I grant I never saw a goddess go;
My mistress, when she walks, treads on the ground.
    And yet, by heaven, I think my love as rare
    As any she belied with false compare.

131.

Thou art as tyrannous, so as thou art,
As those whose beauties proudly make them cruel;
For well thou know'st to my dear doting heart
Thou art the fairest and most precious jewel.
Yet, in good faith, some say that thee behold,
Thy face hath not the power to make love groan.
To say they err I dare not be so bold,
Although I swear it to myself alone.
And, to be sure that is not false I swear,
A thousand groans, but thinking on thy face,
One on another's neck, do witness bear
Thy black is fairest in my judgement's place.
    In nothing art thou black save in thy deeds,
    And thence this slander, as I think, proceeds.

132.

Thine eyes I love, and they, as pitying me,
Knowing thy heart torments me with disdain,
Have put on black, and loving mourners be,
Looking with pretty ruth upon my pain.
And truly not the morning sun of heaven
Better becomes the gray cheeks of the east,
Nor that full star that ushers in the even
Doth half that glory to the sober west,
As those two mourning eyes become thy face:
O, let it, then, as well beseem thy heart
To mourn for me, since mourning doth thee grace,
And suit thy pity like in every part.
    Then will I swear Beauty herself is black,
    And all they foul that thy complexion lack.

133.

Beshrew that heart that makes my heart to groan
For that deep wound it gives my friend and me!
Is't not enough to torture me alone,
But slave to slavery my sweet'st friend must be?
Me from myself thy cruel eye hath taken,
And my next self thou harder hast engrossed:
Of him, myself, and thee, I am forsaken;
A torment thrice threefold thus to be crossed.
Prison my heart in thy steel bosom's ward,
But then my friend's heart let my poor heart bail;
Whoe'er keeps me, let my heart be his guard;
Thou canst not then use rigour in my jail.
    And yet thou wilt; for I, being pent in thee,
    Perforce am thine, and all that is in me.

134.

So, now I have confest that he is thine,
And I myself am mortgaged to thy will,
Myself I'll forfeit, so that other mine
Thou wilt restore, to be my comfort still:
But thou wilt not, nor he will not be free,
For thou art covetous, and he is kind;
He learn'd but, surety-like, to write for me,
Under that bond that him as fast doth bind.
The statute of thy beauty thou wilt take,
Thou usurer, that putt'st forth all to use,
And sue a friend came debtor for my sake;
So him I lose through my unkind abuse.
    Him have I lost; thou hast both him and me:
    He pays the whole, and yet am I not free.

135.

Whoever hath her wish, thou hast thy *Will*,
And *Will* to boot, and *Will* in overplus;
More than enough am I that vex thee still,
To thy sweet will making addition thus.
Wilt thou, whose will is large and spacious,
Not once vouchsafe to hide my will in thine?
Shall will in others seem right gracious,
And in my will no fair acceptance shine?
The sea, all water, yet receives rain still,
And in abundance addeth to his store;
So thou, being rich in *Will*, add to thy *Will*
One will of mine, to make thy large *Will* more.
   Let no unkind, no fair beseechers kill;
   Think all but one, and me in that one *Will*.

136.

If thy soul check thee that I come so near,
Swear to thy blind soul that I was thy *Will*,
And will, thy soul knows, is admitted there;
Thus far for love my love-suit, sweet, fulfil.
Will will fulfil the treasure of thy love,
Ay, fill it full with wills, and my will one.
In things of great receipt with ease we prove
Among a number one is reckon'd none:
Then in the number let me pass untold,
Though in thy store's account I one must be;
For nothing hold me, so it please thee hold
That nothing me, a something, sweet, to thee:
   Make but my name thy love, and love that still,
   And then thou lovest me, for my name is *Will*.

137.

Thou blind fool, Love, what dost thou to mine eyes,
That they behold, and see not what they see?
They know what beauty is, see where it lies,
Yet what the best is take the worst to be.
If eyes, corrupt by over-partial looks,
Be anchor'd in the bay where all men ride,
Why of eyes' falsehood hast thou forged hooks,
Whereto the judgement of my heart is tied?
Why should my heart think that a several plot
Which my heart knows the wide world's common place?
Or mine eyes seeing this, say this is not,
To put fair truth upon so foul a face?
   In things right-true my heart and eyes have erred,
   And to this false plague are they now transferred.

138.

When my love swears that she is made of truth,
I do believe her, though I know she lies,
That she might think me some untutor'd youth,
Unlearned in the world's false subtleties.
Thus vainly thinking that she thinks me young,
Although she knows my days are past the best,
Simply I credit her false-speaking tongue:
On both sides thus is simple truth supprest.
But wherefore says she not she is unjust?
And wherefore say not I that I am old?
O, love's best habit is in seeming trust,
And age in love loves not to have years told:
   Therefore I lie with her and she with me,
   And in our faults by lies we flatter'd be.

139.

O, call not me to justify the wrong
That thy unkindness lays upon my heart;
Wound me not with thine eye, but with thy tongue;
Use power with power, and slay me not by art.
Tell me thou lovest elsewhere; but in my sight,
Dear heart, forbear to glance thine eye aside:
What need'st thou wound with cunning, when thy might
Is more than my o'erprest defence can bide?
Let me excuse thee: ah, my love well knows
Her pretty looks have been mine enemies;
And therefore from my face she turns my foes,
That they elsewhere might dart their injuries:
   Yet do not so; but since I am near slain,
   Kill me outright with looks, and rid my pain.

140.

Be wise as thou art cruel; do not press
My tongue-tied patience with too much disdain;
Lest sorrow lend me words, and words express
The manner of my pity-wanting pain.
If I might teach thee wit, better it were,
Though not to love, yet, love, to tell me so;
As testy sick men, when their deaths be near,
No news but health from their physicians know;
For, if I should despair, I should grow mad,
And in my madness might speak ill of thee:
Now this ill-wresting world is grown so bad,
Mad slanderers by mad ears believed be.
   That I may not be so, nor thou belied,
   Bear thine eyes straight, though thy proud heart go wide.

141.

In faith, I do not love thee with mine eyes,
For they in thee a thousand errors note;
But 'tis my heart that loves what they despise,
Who, in despite of view, is pleased to dote;
Nor are mine ears with thy tongue's tune delighted;
Nor tender feeling to base touches prone,
Nor taste, nor smell, desire to be invited
To any sensual feast with thee alone:
But my five wits nor my five senses can
Dissuade one foolish heart from serving thee,
Who leaves unsway'd the likeness of a man,
Thy proud heart's slave and vassal wretch to be:
   Only my plague thus far I count my gain,
   That she that makes me sin awards me pain.

142.

Love is my sin, and thy dear virtue hate,
Hate of my sin, grounded on sinful loving:
O, but with mine compare thou thine own state,
And thou shalt find it merits not reproving;
Or, if it do, not from those lips of thine,
That have profaned their scarlet ornaments
And seal'd false bonds of love as oft as mine,
Robb'd others' beds' revenues of their rents.
Be it lawful I love thee, as thou lovest those
Whom thine eyes woo as mine importune thee:
Root pity in thy heart, that, when it grows,
Thy pity may deserve to pitied be.
   If thou dost seek to have what thou dost hide,
   By self-example mayst thou be denied!

143.

Lo, as a careful housewife runs to catch
One of her feather'd creatures broke away,
Sets down her babe, and makes all swift dispatch
In pursuit of the thing she would have stay;
Whilst her neglected child holds her in chase,
Cries to catch her whose busy care is bent
To follow that which flies before her face,
Not prizing her poor infant's discontent:
So runn'st thou after that which flies from thee,
Whilst I thy babe chase thee afar behind;
But if thou catch thy hope, turn back to me,
And play the mother's part, kiss me, be kind:
    So will I pray that thou mayst have thy *Will*,
    If thou turn back, and my loud crying still.

144.

Two loves I have of comfort and despair,
Which like two spirits do suggest me still:
The better angel is a man right fair,
The worser spirit a woman colour'd ill.
To win me soon to hell, my female evil
Tempteth my better angel from my side,
And would corrupt my saint to be a devil,
Wooing his purity with her foul pride.
And whether that my angel be turn'd fiend
Suspect I may, yet not directly tell;
But being both from me, both to each friend,
I guess one angel in another's hell:
    Yet this shall I ne'er know, but live in doubt,
    Till my bad angel fire my good one out.

145.

Those lips that Love's own hand did make
Breathed forth the sound that said 'I hate'
To me that languisht for her sake:
But when she saw my woeful state,
Straight in her heart did mercy come,
Chiding that tongue that ever sweet
Was used in giving gentle doom;
And taught it thus anew to greet;
'I hate' she alter'd with an end,
That follow'd it as gentle day
Doth follow night, who like a fiend
From heaven to hell is flown away;
    'I hate' from hate away she threw,
    And saved my life, saying—'Not you.'

146.

Poor soul, the centre of my sinful earth—
My sinful earth these rebel powers array—
Why dost thou pine within and suffer dearth,
Painting thy outward walls so costly gay?
Why so large cost, having so short a lease,
Dost thou upon thy fading mansion spend?
Shall worms, inheritors of this excess,
Eat up thy charge? is this thy body's end?
Then, soul, live thou upon thy servant's loss,
And let that pine to aggravate thy store;
Buy terms divine in selling hours of dross;
Within be fed, without be rich no more:
    So shalt thou feed on Death, that feeds on men,
    And Death once dead, there's no more dying
      then.

147.

My love is as a fever, longing still
For that which longer nurseth the disease;
Feeding on that which doth preserve the ill,
The uncertain sickly appetite to please.
My reason, the physician to my love,
Angry that his prescriptions are not kept,
Hath left me, and I desperate now approve
Desire is death, which physic did except.
Past cure I am, now reason is past care,
And frantic-mad with evermore unrest;
My thoughts and my discourse as madmen's are,
At random from the truth vainly exprest;
    For I have sworn thee fair, and thought thee
      bright,
    Who art as black as hell, as dark as night.

148.

O me, what eyes hath Love put in my head,
Which have no correspondence with true sight!
Or, if they have, where is my judgement fled,
That censures falsely what they see aright?
If that be fair whereon my false eyes dote,
What means the world to say it is not so?
If it be not, then love doth well denote
Love's eye is not so true as all men's: no.
How can it? O, how can Love's eye be true,
That is so vext with watching and with tears?
No marvel, then, though I mistake my view;
The sun itself sees not till heaven clears.
    O cunning Love! with tears thou keep'st me
      blind,
    Lest eyes well-seeing thy foul faults should find.

149.

Canst thou, O cruel! say I love thee not,
When I, against myself, with thee partake?
Do I not think on thee, when I forgot
Am of myself, all tyrant for thy sake?
Who hateth thee that I do call my friend?
On whom frown'st thou that I do fawn upon?
Nay, if thou lour'st on me, do I not spend
Revenge upon myself with present moan?
What merit do I in myself respect,
That is so proud thy service to despise,
When all my best doth worship thy defect,
Commanded by the motion of thine eyes?
    But, love, hate on, for now I know thy mind;
    Those that can see thou lovest, and I am blind.

150.

O, from what power hast thou this powerful might
With insufficiency my heart to sway?
To make me give the lie to my true sight,
And swear that brightness doth not grace the day?
Whence hast thou this becoming of things ill,
That in the very refuse of thy deeds
There is such strength and warrantise of skill,
That, in my mind, thy worst all best exceeds?
Who taught thee how to make me love thee more,
The more I hear and see just cause of hate?
O, though I love what others do abhor,
With others thou shouldst not abhor my state:
    If thy unworthiness raised love in me,
    More worthy I to be beloved of thee.

151.

Love is too young to know what conscience is;
Yet who knows not conscience is born of love?
Then, gentle cheater, urge not my amiss,
Lest guilty of my faults thy sweet self prove:
For, thou betraying me, I do betray
My nobler part to my gross body's treason;
My soul doth tell my body that he may
Triumph in love; flesh stays no farther reason;
But, rising at thy name, doth point out thee
As his triumphant prize. Proud of this pride,
He is contented thy poor drudge to be,
To stand in thy affairs, fall by thy side.
   No want of conscience hold it that I call
   Her 'love' for whose dear love I rise and fall.

152.

In loving thee thou know'st I am forsworn,
But thou art twice forsworn, to me love swearing;
In act thy bed-vow broke, and new faith torn
In vowing new hate after new love bearing.
But why of two oaths' breach do I accuse thee,
When I break twenty? I am perjured most;
For all my vows are oaths but to misuse thee,
And all my honest faith in thee is lost:
For I have sworn deep oaths of thy deep kindness,
Oaths of thy love, thy truth, thy constancy;
And, to enlighten thee, gave eyes to blindness,
Or made them swear against the thing they see;
   For I have sworn thee fair; more perjured I,
   To swear against the truth so foul a lie!

153.

Cupid laid by his brand, and fell asleep:
A maid of Dian's this advantage found,
And his love-kindling fire did quickly steep
In a cold valley-fountain of that ground;
Which borrow'd from this holy fire of Love
A dateless lively heat, still to endure,
And grew a seething bath, which yet men prove
Against strange maladies a sovereign cure.
But at my mistress' eye Love's brand new-fired,
The boy for trial needs would touch my breast;
I, sick withal, the help of bath desired,
And thither hied, a sad distemper'd guest,
   But found no cure: the bath for my help lies
   Where Cupid got new fire,—my mistress' eyes.

154.

The little Love-god lying once asleep
Laid by his side his heart-inflaming brand,
Whilst many nymphs that vow'd chaste life to keep
Came tripping by; but in her maiden hand
The fairest votary took up that fire
Which many legions of true hearts had warm'd;
And so the general of hot desire
Was sleeping by a virgin hand disarm'd.
This brand she quenched in a cool well by,
Which from Love's fire took heat perpetual,
Growing a bath and healthful remedy
For men diseased; but I, my mistress' thrall,
   Came there for cure, and this by that I prove,
   Love's fire heats water, water cools not love.

A LOVER'S COMPLAINT

FROM off a hill whose concave womb re-worded
    A plaintful story from a sistering vale,
My spirits t'attend this double voice accorded,
And down I laid to list the sad-tuned tale;
Ere long espied a fickle maid full pale,
Tearing of papers, breaking rings a-twain,
Storming her world with sorrow's wind and rain.

Upon her head a platted hive of straw,
Which fortified her visage from the sun,
Whereon the thought might think sometime it
    saw
The carcass of a beauty spent and done:
Time had not scythed all that youth begun,
Nor youth all quit; but, spite of heaven's fell rage,
Some beauty peept through lattice of sear'd age.

Oft did she heave her napkin to her eyne,
Which on it had conceited characters,
Laundering the silken figures in the brine
That season'd woe had pelleted in tears,
And often reading what contents it bears;
As often shrieking undistinguisht woe,
In clamours of all size, both high and low.

Sometimes her levell'd eyes their carriage ride,
As they did battery to the spheres intend;
Sometime diverted their poor balls are tied
To th' orbed earth; sometimes they do extend
Their view right on; anon their gazes lend
To every place at once, and, nowhere fixt,
The mind and sight distractedly commixt.

Her hair, nor loose nor tied in formal plat,
Proclaim'd in her a careless hand of pride;
For some, untuckt, descended her sheaved hat,
Hanging her pale and pined cheek beside;
Some in her threaden fillet still did bide,
And, true to bondage, would not break from
    thence,
Though slackly braided in loose negligence.

A thousand favours from a maund she drew
Of amber, crystal, and of beaded jet,
Which one by one she in a river threw,
Upon whose weeping margent she was set;
Like usury, applying wet to wet,
Or monarch's hands that lets not bounty fall
Where want cries some, but where excess begs all.

Of folded schedules had she many a one,
Which she perused, sigh'd, tore, and gave the
    flood;
Crackt many a ring of posied gold and bone,
Bidding them find their sepulchres in mud;
Found yet moe letters sadly penn'd in blood,
With sleided silk feat and affectedly
Enswathed, and seal'd to curious secrecy.

These often bathed she in her fluxive eyes,
And often kist, and often gan to tear;
Cried, 'O false blood, thou register of lies,
What unapproved witness dost thou bear!

Ink would have seem'd more black and damned
    here!'
This said, in top of rage the lines she rents,
Big discontent so breaking their contents.

A reverend man that grazed his cattle nigh—
Sometime a blusterer, that the ruffle knew
Of court, of city, and had let go by
The swiftest hours, observed as they flew—
Towards this afflicted fancy fastly drew,
And, privileged by age, desires to know
In brief the grounds and motives of her woe.

So slides he down upon his grained bat,
And comely-distant sits he by her side;
When he again desires her, being sat,
Her grievance with his hearing to divide:
If that from him there may be aught applied
Which may her suffering ecstasy assuage,
'Tis promised in the charity of age.

'Father,' she says, 'though in me you behold
The injury of many a blasting hour,
Let it not tell your judgement I am old;
Not age, but sorrow, over me hath power:
I might as yet have been a spreading flower,
Fresh to myself, if I had self-applied
Love to myself, and to no love beside.

'But, woe is me! too early I attended
A youthful suit—it was to gain my grace—
Of one by nature's outwards so commended,
That maidens' eyes stuck over all his face:
Love lackt a dwelling, and made him her place;
And when in his fair parts she did abide,
She was new lodged, and newly deified.

'His browny locks did hang in crooked curls;
And every light occasion of the wind
Upon his lips their silken parcels hurls.
What's sweet to do, to do will aptly find:
Each eye that saw him did enchant the mind·
For on his visage was in little drawn
What largeness thinks in Paradise was sawn

'Small show of man was yet upon his chin;
His phœnix down began but to appear,
Like unshorn velvet, on that termless skin,
Whose bare out-bragg'd the web it seem'd to
    wear:
Yet show'd his visage by that cost more dear
And nice affections wavering stood in doubt
If best were as it was, or best without.

'His qualities were beauteous as his form,
For maiden-tongued he was, and thereof free;
Yet, if men moved him, was he such a storm
As oft 'twixt May and April is to see,
When winds breathe sweet, unruly though they
    be.
His rudeness so with his authorized youth
Did livery falseness in a pride of truth.

'Well could he ride, and often men would say,
"That horse his mettle from his rider takes:
Proud of subjection, noble by the sway,
What rounds, what bounds, what course, what
    stop he makes!"
And controversy hence a question takes,
Whether the horse by him became his deed,
Or he his manage by the well-doing steed.

'But quickly on this side the verdict went:
His real habitude gave life and grace
To appertainings and to ornament,
Accomplisht in himself, not in his case:
All aids, themselves made fairer by their place,
Came for additions; yet their purposed trim
Pieced not his grace, but were all graced by him.

'So on the tip of his subduing tongue
All kind of arguments and question deep,
All replication prompt, and reason strong,
For his advantage still did wake and sleep:
To make the weeper laugh, the laugher weep,
He had the dialect and different skill,
Catching all passions in his craft of will:

'That he did in the general bosom reign
Of young, of old; and sexes both enchanted,
To dwell with him in thoughts, or to remain
In personal duty, following where he haunted:
Consents bewitcht, ere he desire, have granted;
And dialogued for him what he would say,
Askt their own wills, and made their wills obey.

'Many there were that did his picture get,
To serve their eyes, and in it put their mind;
Like fools that in th' imagination set
The goodly objects which abroad they find
Of lands and mansions, theirs in thought assign'd;
And labouring in moe pleasures to bestow them
Than the true gouty landlord which doth owe
    them:

'So many have, that never toucht his hand,
Sweetly supposed them mistress of his heart.
My woeful self, that did in freedom stand,
And was my own fee-simple, not in part,
What with his art in youth, and youth in art,
Threw my affections in his charmed power,
Reserved the stalk, and gave him all my flower.

'Yet did I not, as some my equals did,
Demand of him, nor being desired yielded;
Finding myself in honour so forbid,
With safest distance I mine honour shielded:
Experience for me many bulwarks builded
Of proofs new-bleeding, which remain'd the foil
Of this false jewel, and his amorous spoil.

'But, ah, who ever shunn'd by precedent
The destined ill she must herself assay?
Or forced examples, 'gainst her own content,
To put the by-past perils in her way?
Counsel may stop awhile what will not stay;
For when we rage, advice is often seen
By blunting us to make our wits more keen.

'Nor gives it satisfaction to our blood,
That we must curb it upon others' proof;
To be forbod the sweets that seem so good,
For fear of harms that preach in our behoof.
O appetite, from judgement stand aloof!
The one a palate hath that needs will taste,
Though Reason weep, and cry, "It is thy last."

'For further I could say, "This man's untrue,"
And knew the patterns of his foul beguiling;
Heard where his plants in others' orchards grew,
Saw how deceits were gilded in his smiling;
Knew vows were ever brokers to defiling;
Thought characters and words merely but art,
And bastards of his foul adulterate heart.

'And long upon these terms I held my city,
Till thus he gan besiege me: "Gentle maid,
Have of my suffering youth some feeling pity,
And be not of my holy vows afraid:
That's to ye sworn to none was ever said;
For feasts of love I have been call'd unto,
Till now did ne'er invite, nor never woo.

' "All my offences that abroad you see
Are errors of the blood, none of the mind;
Love made them not; with acture they may be,
Where neither party is nor true nor kind:
They sought their shame that so their shame did
    find;
And so much less of shame in me remains,
But how much of me their reproach contains.

' "Among the many that mine eyes have seen,
Not one whose flame my heart so much as warmed,
Or my affection put to the smallest teen,
Or any of my leisures ever charmed:
Harm have I done to them, but ne'er was harmed;
Kept hearts in liveries, but mine own was free,
And reign'd, commanding in his monarchy.

' "Look here, what tributes wounded fancies sent
    me,
Of paled pearls and rubies red as blood;
Figuring that they their passions likewise lent me
Of grief and blushes, aptly understood
In bloodless white and the encrimson'd mood;
Effects of terror and dear modesty,
Encampt in hearts, but fighting outwardly.

' "And, lo, behold these talents of their hair,
With twisted metal amorously impleacht,
I have received from many a several fair—,
Their kind acceptance weepingly beseecht,—
With the annexions of fair gems enricht,
And deep-brain'd sonnets that did amplify
Each stone's dear nature, worth, and quality.

' "The diamond,—why, 'twas beautiful and hard,
Whereto his invised properties did tend;
The deep-green emerald, in whose fresh regard
Weak sights their sickly radiance do amend;
The heaven-hued sapphire, and the opal blend
With objects manifold: each several stone,
With wit well blazon'd, smiled or made some
    moan.

' "Lo, all these trophies of affections hot,
Of pensived and subdued desires the tender,
Nature hath charged me that I hoard them not,
But yield them up where I myself must render,
That is, to you, my origin and ender;
For these, of force, must your oblations be,
Since I their altar, you enpatron me.

' "O, then, advance of yours that phraseless hand,
Whose white weighs down the airy scale of praise;
Take all these similes to your own command,
Hallow'd with sighs that burning lungs did raise;
What me your minister, for you obeys,
Works under you; and to your audit comes
Their distract parcels in combined sums.

' "Lo, this device was sent me from a nun,
A sister sanctified, of holiest note;
Which late her noble suit in court did shun,
Whose rarest havings made the blossoms dote;
For she was sought by spirits of richest coat,
But kept cold distance, and did thence remove,
To spend her living in eternal love.

' "But, O my sweet, what labour is't to leave
The thing we have not, mastering what not
     strives,—
Paling the place which did no form receive,
Playing patient sports in unconstrained gyves?
She that her fame so to herself contrives,
The scars of battle scapeth by the flight,
And makes her absence valiant, not her might.

' "O, pardon me, in that my boast is true:
The accident which brought me to her eye
Upon the moment did her force subdue,
And now she would the caged cloister fly:
Religious love put out Religion's eye:
Not to be tempted, would she be immured,
And now, to tempt all, liberty procured.

' "How mighty, then, you are, O, hear me tell!
The broken bosoms that to me belong
Have emptied all their fountains in my well,
And mine I pour your ocean all among:
I strong o'er them, and you o'er me being strong,
Must for your victory us all congest,
As compound love to physic your cold breast.

' "My parts had power to charm a sacred nun,
Who, disciplined, ay, dieted in grace,
Believed her eyes when they t'assail begun,
All vows and consecrations giving place:
O most potential love! vow, bond, nor space,
In thee hath neither sting, knot, nor confine,
For thou art all, and all things else are thine.

' "When thou impressest, what are precepts worth
Of stale example? When thou wilt inflame,
How coldly those impediments stand forth
Of wealth, of filial fear, law, kindred, fame!
Love's arms are peace, 'gainst rule, 'gainst sense,
     'gainst shame:
And sweetens, in the suffering pangs it bears,
The aloes of all forces, shocks, and fears.

' "Now all these hearts that do on mine depend,
Feeling it break, with bleeding groans they pine;
And supplicant their sighs to you extend,
To leave the battery that you make 'gainst mine,
Lending soft audience to my sweet design,
And credent soul to that strong-bonded oath
That shall prefer and undertake my troth."

'This said, his watery eyes he did dismount,
Whose sights till then were levell'd on my face;
Each cheek a river running from a fount
With brinish current downward flow'd apace:
O, how the channel to the stream gave grace!
Who glazed with crystal gate the glowing roses
That flame through water which their hue en-
     closes.

'O father, what a hell of witchcraft lies
In the small orb of one particular tear!
But with the inundation of the eyes
What rocky heart to water will not wear?
What breast so cold that is not warmed here?
O cleft effect! cold modesty, hot wrath,
Both fire from hence and chill extincture hath.

'For, lo, his passion, but an art of craft,
Even there resolved my reason into tears;
There my white stole of chastity I daft,
Shook off my sober guards and civil fears;
Appear to him, as he to me appears,
All melting; though our drops this difference bore
His poison'd me, and mine did him restore.

'In him a plenitude of subtle matter,
Applied to cautels, all strange forms receives,
Of burning blushes, or of weeping water,
Or swounding paleness; and he takes and leaves,
In either's aptness, as it best deceives,
To blush at speeches rank, to weep at woes,
Or to turn white and swound at tragic shows:

'That not a heart which in his level came
Could scape the hail of his all-hurting aim,
Showing fair nature is both kind and tame;
And, veil'd in them, did win whom he would
     maim:
Against the thing he sought he would exclaim;
When he most burnt in heart-wisht luxury,
He preacht pure maid, and praised cold chastity.

'Thus merely with the garment of a Grace
The naked and concealed fiend he cover'd;
That th' unexperient gave the tempter place,
Which, like a cherubin, above them hover'd.
Who, young and simple, would not be so lover'd?
Ay me! I fell; and yet do question make
What I should do again for such a sake.

'O, that infected moisture of his eye,
O, that false fire which in his cheek so glow'd,
O, that forced thunder from his heart did fly,
O, that sad breath his spongy lungs bestow'd,
O, all that borrow'd motion seeming ow'd,
Would yet again betray the fore-betray'd,
And new pervert a reconciled maid!'

THE PASSIONATE PILGRIM

1.

WHEN my love swears that she is made of
    truth,
I do believe her, though I know she lies,
That she might think me some untutor'd youth,
Unskilful in the world's false forgeries.
Thus vainly thinking that she thinks me young,
Although I know my years be past the best,
I smiling credit her false-speaking tongue,
Outfacing faults in love with love's ill rest.
But wherefore says my love that she is young?
And wherefore say not I that I am old?
O, love's best habit is a soothing tongue,
And age, in love, loves not to have years told.
    Therefore I'll lie with love, and love with me,
    Since that our faults in love thus smother'd be.

2.

Two loves I have, of comfort and despair,
That like two spirits do suggest me still;
My better angel is a man right fair,
My worser spirit a woman colour'd ill.
To win me soon to hell, my female evil
Tempteth my better angel from my side,
And would corrupt my saint to be a devil,
Wooing his purity with her fair pride.
And whether that my angel be turn'd fiend,
Suspect I may, yet not directly tell:
For being both to me, both to each friend,
I guess one angel in another's hell:
    The truth I shall not know, but live in doubt,
    Till my bad angel fire my good one out.

3.

Did not the heavenly rhetoric of thine eye,
'Gainst whom the world could not hold argument,
Persuade my heart to this false perjury?
Vows for thee broke deserve not punishment.
A woman I forswore; but I will prove,
Thou being a goddess, I forswore not thee:
My vow was earthly, thou a heavenly love;
Thy grace being gain'd cures all disgrace in me.
My vow was breath, and breath a vapour is;
Then, thou fair sun, that on this earth doth shine,
Exhale this vapour vow; in thee it is:
If broken, then it is no fault of mine.
    If by me broke, what fool is not so wise
    To break an oath, to win a paradise?

4.

Sweet Cytherea, sitting by a brook
With young Adonis, lovely, fresh and green,
Did court the lad with many a lovely look,
Such looks as none could look but beauty's queen.
She told him stories to delight his ear,
She show'd him favours to allure his eye;
To win his heart, she toucht him here and there;
Touches so soft still conquer chastity.
But whether unripe years did want conceit,
Or he refused to take her figured proffer,
The tender nibbler would not touch the bait,
But smile and jest at every gentle offer:
    Then fell she on her back, fair queen, and to-
      ward:
    He rose and ran away; ah, fool too froward.

5.

If love make me forsworn, how shall I swear to
    love?
O never faith could hold, if not to beauty vowed:
Though to myself forsworn, to thee I'll constant
    prove;
Those thoughts, to me like oaks, to thee like osiers
    bowed
Study his bias leaves, and makes his book thine
    eyes,
Where all those pleasures live that art can com-
    prehend.
If knowledge be the mark, to know thee shall
    suffice;
Well learned is that tongue that well can thee
    commend:
All ignorant that soul that sees thee without
    wonder;
Which is to me some praise, that I thy parts admire:
Thine eye Jove's lightning seems, thy voice his
    dreadful thunder,
Which, not to anger bent, is music and sweet fire.
    Celestial as thou art, O do not love that wrong,
    To sing heaven's praise with such an earthly
      tongue.

6.

Scarce had the sun dried up the dewy morn,
And scarce the herd gone to the hedge for shade,
When Cytherea, all in love forlorn,
A longing tarriance for Adonis made
Under an osier growing by a brook,
A brook where Adon used to cool his spleen:
Hot was the day; she hotter that did look
For his approach, that often there had been.
Anon he comes, and throws his mantle by,
And stood stark naked on the brook's green brim:
The sun lookt on the world with glorious eye,
Yet not so wistly as this queen on him.
    He, spying her, bounced in, whereas he stood:
    'O Jove,' quoth she, 'why was not I a flood!'

7.

Fair is my love, but not so fair as fickle,
Mild as a dove, but neither true nor trusty,
Brighter than glass and yet, as glass is, brittle,
Softer than wax and yet as iron rusty:
    A lily pale, with damask dye to grace her,
    None fairer, nor none falser to deface her.

Her lips to mine how often hath she joined,
Between each kiss her oaths of true love swearing!
How many tales to please me hath she coined,
Dreading my love, the loss whereof still fearing!
    Yet in the midst of all her pure protestings,
    Her faith, her oaths, her tears, and all were
      jestings.

She burnt with love, as straw with fire flameth;
She burnt out love, as soon as straw out-burneth;
She framed the love, and yet she foil'd the fram-
    ing;
She bade love last, and yet she fell a-turning.
    Was this a lover, or a lecher whether?
    Bad in the best, though excellent in neither.

8.

If music and sweet poetry agree,
As they must needs, the sister and the brother,
Then must the love be great 'twixt thee and me,
Because thou lovest the one and I the other.
Dowland to thee is dear, whose heavenly touch
Upon the lute doth ravish human sense;
Spenser to me, whose deep conceit is such
As passing all conceit needs no defence.
Thou lovest to hear the sweet melodious sound
That Phœbus' lute, the queen of music, makes;
And I in deep delight am chiefly drown'd
Whenas himself to singing he betakes.
  One god is god of both, as poets feign;
  One knight loves both, and both in thee remain.

9.

Fair was the morn when the fair queen of love,
.   .   .   .   .
Paler for sorrow than her milk-white dove,
For Adon's sake, a youngster proud and wild;
Her stand she takes upon a steep-up hill:
Anon Adonis comes with horn and hounds;
She, silly queen, with more than love's good will,
Forbade the boy he should not pass those grounds:
'Once,' quoth she, 'did I see a fair sweet youth
Here in these brakes deep-wounded with a boar,
Deep in the thigh, a spectacle of ruth!
See, in my thigh,' quoth she, 'here was the sore.'
  She showed hers: he saw more wounds than
    one,
  And blushing fled, and left her all alone.

10.

Sweet rose, fair flower, untimely pluckt, soon
  vaded,
Pluckt in the bud and vaded in the spring!
Bright orient pearl, alack, too timely shaded!
Fair creature, kill'd too soon by death's sharp
  sting!
  Like a green plum that hangs upon a tree,
  And falls through wind before the fall should be.

I weep for thee and yet no cause I have;
For why thou left'st me nothing in thy will:
And yet thou left'st me more than I did crave;
For why I craved nothing of thee still:
  O yes, dear friend, I pardon crave of thee,
  Thy discontent thou didst bequeath to me.

11.

Venus, with young Adonis sitting by her
Under a myrtle shade, began to woo him:
She told the youngling how god Mars did try her,
And as he fell to her, so fell she to him.
'Even thus,' quoth she, 'the warlike god em-
  braced me,'
And then she clipt Adonis in her arms;
'Even thus,' quoth she, 'the warlike god unlaced
  me,'
As if the boy should use like loving charms;
'Even thus,' quoth she, 'he seized on my lips,'
And with her lips on his did act the seizure:
And as she fetched breath, away he skips,
And would not take her meaning nor her pleasure.
  Ah, that I had my lady at this bay,
  To kiss and clip me till I run away!

12.

Crabbed age and youth cannot live together:
Youth is full of pleasance, age is full of care;
Youth like summer morn, age like winter weather;
Youth like summer brave, age like winter bare.
Youth is full of sport, age's breath is short;
  Youth is nimble, age is lame;
Youth is hot and bold, age is weak and cold;
  Youth is wild, and age is tame.
Age, I do abhor thee; youth, I do adore thee;
  O, my love, my love is young!
Age, I do defy thee: O, sweet shepherd, hie thee,
  For methinks thou stay'st too long.

13.

Beauty is but a vain and doubtful good;
A shining gloss that vadeth suddenly;
A flower that dies when first it gins to bud;
A brittle glass that's broken presently:
  A doubtful good, a gloss, a glass, a flower,
  Lost, vaded, broken, dead within an hour.

And as goods lost are seld or never found,
As vaded gloss no rubbing will refresh,
As flowers dead lie wither'd on the ground,
As broken glass no cement can redress,
  So beauty blemisht once for ever lost,
  In spite of physic, painting, pain and cost.

14.

Good night, good rest. Ah, neither be my share:
She bade good night that kept my rest away;
And daft me to a cabin hang'd with care,
To descant on the doubts of my decay. [morrow:'
  'Farewell,' quoth she, 'and come again to-
  Fare well I could not, for I supt with sorrow.

Yet at my parting sweetly did she smile,
In scorn or friendship, nill I conster whether:
'T may be, she joy'd to jest at my exile,
'T may be, again to make me wander thither:
  'Wander,' a word for shadows like myself,
  As take the pain, but cannot pluck the pelf.

15.

Lord, how mine eyes throw gazes to the east!
My heart doth charge the watch; the morning rise
Doth cite each moving sense from idle rest.
Not daring trust the office of mine eyes,
  While Philomela sits and sings, I sit and mark,
  And wish her lays were tuned like the lark;

For she doth welcome daylight with her ditty,
And drives away dark dreaming night:
The night so packt, I post unto my pretty;
Heart hath his hope and eyes their wished sight;
  Sorrow changed to solace and solace mixt with
    sorrow; [morrow.
  For why she sigh'd, and bade me come to-

Were I with her, the night would post too soon;
But now are minutes added to the hours;
To spite me now, each minute seems a moon;
Yet not for me, shine sun to succour flowers!
  Pack night, peep day; good day, of night now
    borrow:
  Short, night, to-night, and length thyself to-
    morrow.

SONNETS TO SUNDRY NOTES
OF MUSIC.

1.

IT was a lording's daughter, the fairest one of
   three,
That liked of her master as well as well might be,
Till looking on an Englishman, the fair'st that eye
   could see,
   Her fancy fell a-turning.
Long was the combat doubtful that love with love
   did fight,
To leave the master loveless, or kill the gallant
   knight:
To put in practice either, alas, it was a spite
   Unto the silly damsel!
But one must be refused; more mickle was the
   pain
That nothing could be used to turn them both to
   gain,
For of the two the trusty knight was wounded
   with disdain:
   Alas, she could not help it!
Thus art with arms contending was victor of the
   day,
Which by a gift of learning did bear the maid away:
Then, lullaby, the learned man hath got the lady
   gay;
   For now my song is ended.

2.

On a day, alack the day!
Love, whose month was ever May,
Spied a blossom passing fair,
Playing in the wanton air:
Through the velvet leaves the wind
All unseen gan passage find;
That the lover, sick to death,
Wisht himself the heaven's breath,
'Air,' quoth he, 'thy cheeks may blow;
Air, would I might triumph so!
But, alas! my hand hath sworn
Ne'er to pluck thee from thy thorn:
Vow, alack! for youth unmeet:
Youth, so apt to pluck a sweet.
Thou for whom Jove would swear
Juno but an Ethiope were;
And deny himself for Jove,
Turning mortal for thy love.'

3.

My flocks feed not,
My ewes breed not,
My rams speed not;
   All is amiss:
Love's denying,
Faith's defying,
Heart's renying,
   Causer of this.
All my merry jigs are quite forgot,
All my lady's love is lost, God wot:
Where her faith was firmly fixt in love,
There a nay is placed without remove.
   One silly cross
   Wrought all my loss;

O frowning Fortune, cursed, fickle dame!
   For now I see
   Inconstancy
More in women than in men remain.

   In black mourn I,
   All fears scorn I,
   Love hath forlorn me,
     Living in thrall:
   Heart is bleeding,
   All help needing,
   O cruel speeding,
     Fraughted with gall.
My shepherd's pipe can sound no deal:
My wether's bell rings doleful knell;
My curtal dog, that wont to have play'd,
Plays not at all, but seems afraid;
   My sighs so deep
   Procure to weep,
In howling wise, to see my doleful plight.
   How sighs resound
   Through heartless ground,
Like a thousand vanquisht men in bloody fight!

   Clear wells spring not,
   Sweet birds sing not,
   Green plants bring not
     Forth their dye;
   Herds stand weeping,
   Flocks all sleeping,
   Nymphs back peeping
     Fearfully:
All our pleasure known to us poor swains,
All our merry meetings on the plains,
All our evening sport from us is fled,
All our love is lost, for Love is dead.
   Farewell, sweet lass,
   Thy like ne'er was
For a sweet content, the cause of all my moan:
   Poor Corydon
   Must live alone;
Other help for him I see that there is none.

4.

Whenas thine eye hath chose the dame,
And stall'd the deer that thou shouldst strike,
Let reason rule things worthy blame,
As well as fancy partial like:
   Take counsel of some wiser head,
   Neither too young nor yet unwed.

And when thou comest thy tale to tell,
Smooth not thy tongue with filed talk,
Lest she some subtle practice smell,—
A cripple soon can find a halt;—
   But plainly say thou lovest her well,
   And set thy person forth to sell.

What though her frowning brows be bent,
Her cloudy looks will calm ere night:
And then too late she will repent
That thus dissembled her delight;
   And twice desire, ere it be day,
   That which with scorn she put away.

What though she strive to try her strength,
And ban and brawl, and say thee nay,
Her feeble force will yield at length,
When craft hath taught her thus to say:
   'Had women been so strong as men,
   In faith, you had not had it then.'

And to her will frame all thy ways;
Spare not to spend, and chiefly there
Where thy desert may merit praise,
By ringing in thy lady's ear:
   The strongest castle, tower and town,
   The golden bullet beats it down.

Serve always with assured trust,
And in thy suit be humble true;
Unless thy lady prove unjust,
Press never thou to choose anew:
   When time shall serve, be thou not slack
   To proffer, though she put thee back.

The wiles and guiles that women work,
Dissembled with an outward show,
The tricks and toys that in them lurk,
The cock that treads them shall not know.
   Have you not heard it said full oft,
   A woman's nay doth stand for nought?

Think women still to strive with men,
To sin and never for to saint:
There is no heaven, by holy then,
When time with age shall them attaint.
   Were kisses all the joys in bed,
   One woman would another wed.

But, soft! enough—too much, I fear—
Lest that my mistress hear my song:
She will not stick to round me on the ear,
To teach my tongue to be so long:
   Yet will she blush, here be it said,
   To hear her secrets so bewray'd.

5.

Live with me, and be my love,
And we will all the pleasures prove
That hills and valleys, dales and fields,
And all the craggy mountains yields.

There will we sit upon the rocks,
And see the shepherds feed their flocks,
By shallow rivers, by whose falls
Melodious birds sing madrigals.

There will I make thee a bed of roses,
With a thousand fragrant posies,
A cap of flowers, and a kirtle
Embroider'd all with leaves of myrtle.

A belt of straw and ivy buds,
With coral clasps and amber studs;
And if these pleasures may thee move,
Then live with me and be my love.

LOVE'S ANSWER.

If that the world and love were young,
And truth in every shepherd's tongue,
These pretty pleasures might me move
To live with thee and be thy love.

6.

As it fell upon a day
In the merry month of May,
Sitting in a pleasant shade
Which a grove of myrtles made,
Beasts did leap and birds did sing,
Trees did grow and plants did spring;
Every thing did banish moan,
Save the nightingale alone:
She, poor bird, as all forlorn,
Lean'd her breast up-till a thorn,
And there sung the dolefull'st ditty,
That to hear it was great pity:
'Fie, fie, fie,' now would she cry;
'Tereu, Tereu!' by and by;
That to hear her so complain,
Scarce I could from tears refrain;
For her griefs so lively shown
Made me think upon mine own.
Ah, thought I, thou mourn'st in vain!
None takes pity on thy pain:
Senseless trees they cannot hear thee;
Ruthless beasts they will not cheer thee:
King Pandion he is dead;
All thy friends are lapt in lead;
All thy fellow birds do sing,
Careless of thy sorrowing.
Even so, poor bird, like thee,
None alive will pity me.
Whilst as fickle Fortune smiled,
Thou and I were both beguiled.

   Every one that flatters thee
Is no friend in misery.
Words are easy, like the wind;
Faithful friends are hard to find:
Every man will be thy friend
Whilst thou hast wherewith to spend:
But if store of crowns be scant,
No man will supply thy want.
If that one be prodigal,
Bountiful they will him call,
And with such-like flattering,
'Pity but he were a king;'
If he be addict to vice,
Quickly him they will entice;
If to women he be bent,
They have at commandement:
But if Fortune once do frown,
Then farewell his great renown;
They that fawn'd on him before
Use his company no more.
He that is thy friend indeed,
He will help thee in thy need:
If thou sorrow, he will weep;
If thou wake, he cannot sleep;
Thus of every grief in heart
He with thee doth bear a part.
These are certain signs to know
Faithful friend from flattering foe.

THE PHŒNIX AND TURTLE

LET the bird of loudest lay,
On the sole Arabian tree,
Herald sad and trumpet be,
To whose sound chaste wings obey.

But thou shrieking harbinger,
Foul precurrer of the fiend,
Augur of the fever's end,
To this troop come thou not near!

From this session interdict
Every fowl of tyrant wing,
Save the eagle, feather'd king:
Keep the obsequy so strict.

Let the priest in surplice white,
That defunctive music can,
Be the death-divining swan,
Lest the requiem lack his right.

And thou treble-dated crow,
That thy sable gender makest
With the breath thou givest and takest,
'Mongst our mourners shalt thou go.

Here the anthem doth commence:
Love and constancy is dead;
Phœnix and the turtle fled
In a mutual flame from hence.

So they loved, as love in twain
Had the essence but in one;
Two distincts, division none:
Number there in love was slain.

Hearts remote, yet not asunder;
Distance, and no space was seen
'Twixt the turtle and his queen:
But in them it were a wonder.

So between them love did shine,
That the turtle saw his right
Flaming in the phœnix' sight;
Either was the other's mine.

Property was thus appalled,
That the self was not the same;
Single nature's double name
Neither two nor one was called.

Reason, in itself confounded,
Saw division grow together,
To themselves yet either neither,
Simple were so well compounded;

That it cried, How true a twain
Seemeth this concordant one!
Love hath reason, reason none,
If what parts can so remain.

Whereupon it made this threne
To the phœnix and the dove,
Co-supremes and stars of love,
As chorus to their tragic scene.

THRENOS.

Beauty, truth, and rarity,
Grace in all simplicity,
Here enclosed in cinders lie.

Death is now the phœnix' nest;
And the turtle's loyal breast
To eternity doth rest,

Leaving no posterity:
'Twas not their infirmity,
It was married chastity.

Truth may seem, but cannot be;
Beauty brag, but 'tis not she;
Truth and beauty buried be.

To this urn let those repair
That are either true or fair;
For these dead birds sigh a prayer.

GLOSSARY

References are given only where a word has more than one meaning, the first occurrence of each sense being then noted.

Abate, *v.t.* to diminish. M.N.D III. 2. 432. Deduct, except. L.L.L. v. 2. 539. Cast down. Cor. III. 3. 134. Blunt. R III. v. 5. 35. Deprive. Lear, II. 4. 159.

Abatement, *sb.* diminution. Lear, I. 4. 59. Depreciation. Tw. N. I. 1. 13.

Abjects, *sb.* outcasts, servile persons.

Able, *v.t.* to warrant.

Abode, *v.t.* to forebode. 3 H VI. v. 6. 45.

Abode, *sb.* stay, delay. M. of V. II. 6. 77.

Abodements, *sb.* forebodings.

Abram, *adj.* auburn.

Abridgement, *sb.* short entertainment, for pastime.

Abrook, *v.t.* to brook, endure.

Absey book, *sb.* ABC book, or primer.

Absolute, *adj.* resolved. M. for M. III 1 5. Positive. Cor. III. 2. 39. Perfect. H V. III. 7. 26. Complete. Tp. I. 2. 109; Lucr 853.

Aby, *v.t.* to atone for, expiate.

Accite, *v.t.* to cite, summon.

Acknown, cognisant.

Acture, *sb.* performance.

Addition, *sb.* title, attribute.

Adoptious, *adj.* given by adoption.

Advice, *sb.* consideration.

Aery, *sb.* eagle's nest or brood. R III. I. 3. 265, 271. Hence generally any brood. Ham. II. 2. 344.

Affectioned, *p.p.* affected.

Affeered, *p.p.* sanctioned, confirmed.

Affiance, *sb.* confidence, trust.

Affined, *p.p.* related. T. & C. I. 3. 25. Bound. Oth. I. I 39.

Affront, *v.t.* to confront, meet.

Affy, *v.t.* to betroth. 2 H VI. IV. 1. 80. *v.t.* to trust. T.A. I. 1. 47.

Aglet-baby, *sb.* small figure cut on the tag of a lace (Fr. *aiguillette*). T. of S. I. 2. 78.

Agnize, *v.t.* to acknowledge, confess.

Agood, *adv.* much.

Aim, *sb.* a guess.

Aim, to cry aim, to encourage, an archery term.

Alderliefest, *adj.* most loved of all.

Ale, *sb.* alehouse.

All amort, completely dejected (Fr. *à la mort*).

Allicholy, melancholy.

Allow, *v.t.* to approve

Allowance, *sb.* acknowledgment, approval.

Ames-ace, *sb.* the lowest throw of the dice.

Anchor, *sb.* anchorite, hermit.

Ancient, *sb.* ensign, standard. 1 H IV. IV. 2. 32. Ensign ensign-bearer. 1 H IV. IV. 2. 24.

Ancientry, antiquity, used of old people, W.T. III. 3. 62. Of the gravity which belongs to antiquity, M.A. II. 1. 75.

Angel, *sb.* gold coin, worth about 10s.

Antic, *adj.* fantastic. Ham. 1. 5. 172.

Antick, *v.t.* to make a buffoon of. A. & C. II. 7. 126.

Antick, *sb.* buffoon of the old plays.

Appeal, *sb.* impeachment.

Appeal, *v.t.* to impeach.

Apperil, *sb.* peril.

Apple-john, *sb.* a shrivelled winter apple.

Argal, corruption of the Latin *ergo*, therefore.

Argo, corruption of *ergo*, therefore.

Aroint thee, begone, get thee gone.

Articulate, *v.i.* to make articles of peace. Cor. I. 9. 75. *v.t.* to set forth in detail. 1 H IV. v. 1. 72.

Artificial, *adj.* working by art.

Askance, *v.t.* to make look askance or sideways, make to avert.

Aspic, *sb.* asp.

Assured, *p.p.* betrothed.

Atone, *v.t.* to reconcile. R II. I. 1. 202. Agree. As v. 4. 112.

Attorney, *sb.* proxy, agent.

Attorneyed, *p.p.* done by proxy. W.T. I. 1. 28. Engaged as an attorney. M. for M. v. 1. 383.

Attribute, *sb.* reputation.

Avail, *sb.* profit.

Avise, *v.t.* to inform. 'Are you avised?' = 'Do you know?'

Awful, *adj.* filled with regard for authority.

Awkward, *adj.* contrary.

Baby, *sb.* a doll.

Baccare, go back, a spurious Latin word.

Back-trick, a caper backwards in dancing.

Baffle, *v.t.* to disgrace (a recreant knight).

Bale, *sb* evil, mischief.

Ballow, *sb.* cudgel.

Ban, *v t.* curse. 2 H VI. II 4. 25. *sb.* a curse Ham. III 2 269.

Band, *sb* bond.

Bank, *v.t.* sail along the banks of.

Bare, *v.t.* to shave.

Barn, *v.t* to put in a barn.

Barn, or Barne, *sb.* bairn, child.

Base, *sb* a rustic game 'Bid the base' = Challenge to a race. Two G. I 2. 97

Bases, *sb.* knee-length skirts worn by mounted knights.

Basilisco-like, Basilisco, a character in the play of *Soliman and Perseda*.

Basilisk, *sb.* a fabulous serpent. H V. v. 2. 17. A large cannon. 1 H V. II. 3. 57.

Bate, *sb.* strife.

Bate, *v.i.* flutter as a hawk. 1 H IV. IV. 1. 99. Diminish. H IV. III. 3. 2.

Bate, *v.t.* abate. Tp. I. 2. 250. Beat down, weaken. M. of V. III. 3. 32.

Bavin, *adj.* made of bavin or brushwood. 1 H IV. III. 2. 61.

Bawbling, *adj.* trifling, insignificant.

Baw-cock, *sb.* fine fellow (Fr. *beau coq*). H V. III. 2. 25.

Bay, *sb.* space between the main timbers in a roof.

Beadsman, *sb.* one who is hired to offer prayers for another.

Bearing-cloth, *sb.* the cloth in which a child was carried to be christened.

Bear in hand, to deceive with false hopes.

Beat, *v.i.* to meditate. 2 H IV. II. 1. 20. Throb. Lear, III. 4. 14.

Becoming, *sb.* grace.

Beetle, *sb.* a heavy mallet. 2 H IV. I. 2. 235.

Beetle-headed = heavy, stupid. T. of S. IV. 1. 150.

Behave, *v.t.* to control.

Behest, *sb.* command.

Behove, *sb.* behoof.

Be-lee'd, *p.p.* forced to lee of the wind.

Bench, *v.i.* to seat on the bench of justice. Lear, III. 6. 38.

Bench, *v.t.* to elevate to the bench. W.T. I. 2. 313.

Bench-hole, the hole of a privy.

Bergomask, a rustic dance, named from Bergamo in Italy.

Beshrew, *v.t.* to curse; but not used seriously.

Besort, *v.t.* to fit, suit.

Bestraught, *adj.* distraught.

Beteem, *v.t.* to permit, grant.

Bezonian, *sb.* a base and needy fellow.

Bias, *adj.* curving like the bias side of a bowling bowl.

Biggen, *sb* a nightcap.

Bilbo, *sb.* a Spanish rapier, named from Bilbao or Bilboa.

Bilboes, *sb* stocks used for punishment on shipboard

Birdbolt, *sb* a blunt-headed arrow used for birds

Bisson, *sb* dim-sighted Cor. II. 1. 65. 'Bisson rheum' = blinding tears. Ham II 2 514.

Blacks, *sb* black mourning clothes.

Blank, *sb.* the white mark in the centre of a target.

Blank, *v.t.* to blanch, make pale.

Blanks, *sb.* royal charters left blank to be filled in as occasion dictated.

Blench, *sb.* a swerve, inconsistency.

Blistered, *adj.* padded out, puffed.

Block, *sb.* the wood on which hats are made. M.A. I. I. 71. Hence, the style of a hat. Lear, IV. 6. 185.

Blood-boltered, *adj.* clotted with blood.

Blowse, *sb.* a coarse beauty.

Bob, *sb.* smart rap, jest.

Bob, *v.t.* to beat hard, thwack. R III. V. 3. 335. To obtain by fraud, cheat. T. & C. III. 1. 69.

Bodge, to budge.

Bodkin, *sb.* small dagger, stiletto.

Boggle, *v.i.* to swerve, shy, hesitate.

Boggler, *sb.* swerver.

Boln, *adj.* swollen.

Bolt, *v.t.* to sift, refine.

Bolter, *sb.* a sieve.

Bombard, *sb.* a leathern vessel for liquor.

Bona-robas, *sb.* flashily dressed women of easy virtue.

Bonnet, *v.i.* to doff the hat, be courteous.

Boot, *sb.* profit. 1 H VI. IV. 6. 52.

Boot, that which is given over and above. R III. IV. 4. 65.

Boot, *sb.* booty. 2 H VI. IV. 1. 13.

Boots, *sb.* 'Give me not the boots' = do not inflict on me the torture of the boots, which were employed to wring confessions.

Bosky, *adj.* woody.

Botcher, *sb.* patcher of old clothes.

Bots, *sb.* small worms in horses.

Brabble, *sb.* quarrel, brawl.

Brabbler, *sb.* a brawler.

Brach, *sb.* a hound-bitch.

Braid, *adj.* deceitful.

Braid, *v.t.* to upbraid, reproach.

Brain, *v.t.* to conceive in the brain.

Brazed, *p.p.* made like brass, perhaps hardened in the fire.

Breeched, *p.p.* as though wearing breeches.

Breeching, *adj.* liable to be breeched for a flogging.

Breese, *sb.* a gadfly.

Bribe-buck, *sb.* perhaps a buck distributed in presents.

Brock, *sb.* badger.

Broken, *adj.* of a mouth with some teeth missing.

Broker, *sb.* agent, go-between.

Brownist, a follower of Robert Brown, the founder of the sect of Independents.

Buck, *v.t.* to wash and beat linen.

Buck-basket, *sb.* a basket to take linen to be bucked.

Bucking, *sb.* washing.

Buckle, *v.i.* to encounter hand to hand, cope. 1 H VI. I. 2. 95. To bow. 2 H VI. I. 1. 141.

Budget, *sb.* a leather scrip or bag.

Bug, *sb.* bugbear, a thing causing terror.

Bugle, *sb.* a black bead.

Bully, *sb.* a swaggering fellow.

Bully-rook. *sb.* a swaggering cheater.

Bung, *sb.* pickpocket.

Burgonet, *sb.* close-fitting Burgundian helmet.

Busky, *adj.* woody.

By-drinkings, *sb.* drinks taken between meals.

Caddis, *sb.* worsted trimming, galloon.

Cade, *sb.* cask, barrel.

Caitiff, *sb.* captive, slave, a wretch. As *adj.* R II. 1. 2. 53.

Caliver, *sb.* musket.

Callet, *sb.* trull, drab.

Calling, *sb.* appellation.

Calm, *sb.* qualm.

Canary = quandary.

Canary, *v.i.* to dance canary.

Canker, *sb.* the dog-rose or wild-rose. 1 H IV. 1. 3. 176. A worm that destroys blossoms. M.N.D. II. 2. 3.

Canstick, *sb.* candlestick.

Cantle, *sb.* piece, slice.

Canton, *sb.* canto.

Canvass, *v.t.* shake as in a sieve, take to task.

Capable, *adj.* sensible. As, III. 5. 23. Sensitive, susceptible. Ham. III. 4. 128. Comprehensive. Oth. III. 3. 459. Able to possess. Lear, II. 1. 85.

Capocchia, *sb.* the feminine of capocchio (Ital.), simpleton.

Capriccio, *sb.* caprice, fancy.

Captious, *adj.* either a contraction of capacious or a coined word meaning 'capable of receiving.'

Carack, *sb.* a large merchant ship.

Carbonado, *sb.* meat scotched for boiling. *v.t.* to hack like a carbonado.

Card, *sb.* a cooling card = a sudden and decisive stroke.

Card, *v.t.* to mix (liquids).

Cardecu, *sb.* quarter of a French crown (*quart d'écu*).

Care, *v.i.* to take care.

Careire, *sb.* a short gallop at full speed.

Carlot, *sb.* peasant.

Carpet consideration, On, used of those made knights for court services, not for valour in the field.

Carpet-mongers, *sb.* carpet-knights.

Carpets, *sb.* tablecloths.

Case, *v.t.* to strip off the case or skin of an animal. A.W. III. 6. 103. Put on a mask. 1 H IV. II. 2. 55.

Case, *sb.* skin of an animal. Tw.N. V. 1. 163. A set, as of musical instruments, which were in fours. H V. III. 2. 4.

Cashiered, *p.p.* discarded; in M.W. I. 1. 168 it probably means relieved of his cash.

Cataian, *sb.* a native of Cathay, a Chinaman; a cant word.

Cater-cousins, good friends, incorrectly derived from *quatre cousin.*

Catlings, *sb.* catgut strings for musical instruments.

Cautel, *sb.* craft, deceit, stratagem.

Cautelous, *adj.* crafty, deceitful.

Ceased, *p.p.* put off.

Censure, *sb.* opinion, judgment.

Certify, *v.t.* to inform, make certain.

Cess, *sb.* reckoning; out of all cess = immoderately.

Cesse = cease.

Champain, *sb.* open country.

Channel, *sb.* gutter.

Chape, *sb.* metal end of a scabbard.

Chapless, *adj.* without jaws.

Charact, *sb.* a special mark or sign of office.

Chare, *sb.* a turn of work.

Charge, *sb.* weight, importance. W. T. IV. 3. 258. Cost, expense. John I. 1. 49.

Chaudron, *sb.* entrails.

Check, *sb.* rebuke, reproof.

Check, *v.t.* to rebuke, chide.

Check, *v.i.* to start on sighting game.

Cherry-pit, *sb.* a childish game consisting of pitching cherry-stones into a small hole.

Cheveril, *sb.* leather of kid skin. R. & J. II. 3. 85. As adjective. Tw.N. III. 1. 12.

Che vor ye = I warn you.

Chewet, *sb.* chough. 1 H IV. V. 1. 29. (Fr. *chouette* or *chutte*). Perhaps with play on other meaning of chewet, *i.e.*, a kind of meat pie.

Childing, *adj.* fruitful.

Chop, *v.t.* to clop, pop.

Chopine, *sb.* shoe with a high sole.

Choppy, *adj.* chapped.

Christendom, *sb.* Christian name.

Chuck, *sb.* chick, term of endearment.

Chuff, *sb.* churl, boor.

Cinque pace, a slow stately dance. M.A. II. 1. 72. Compare sink-a-pace in Tw.N. I. 3. 126.

Cipher, *v.t.* to decipher.

Circumstance, *sb.* particulars, details. Two G. I. 1. 36. Ceremonious phrases. M. of V. I. 1. 154.

Circumstanced, *p.p.* swayed by circumstance.

Citizen, *adj.* town bred, effeminate.

Cittern, *sb.* guitar.

Clack-dish, *sb.* wooden dish carried by beggars.

Clamour, *v.t.* to silence.

Clapper-claw, *v.t.* to thrash, drub.

Claw, *v.t.* to scratch, flatter.

Clepe, *v.t.* to call.

Cliff, *sb.* clef, the key in music.

Cling, *v.t.* to make shrivel up.

Clinquant, *adj.* glittering with gold or silver lace or decorations.

Close, *sb.* cadence in music. R II. II. 1. 12. *adj.* secret. T. of S. Ind. I. 127. *v.i.* to come to an agreement, make terms. Two G. II. 5. 12.

Closely, *adv.* secretly.

Clout, *sb.* bull's-eye of a target.

Clouted, *adj.* hobnailed (others explain as patched).

Cobloaf, *sb.* a crusty, ill-shapen loaf.

Cockered, *p.p.* pampered.

Cockle, *sb.* the corncockle weed.

Cockney, *sb.* a city-bred person, a foolish wanton.

Cock-shut time, *sb*. twilight.

Codding, *adj*. lascivious.

Codling, *sb*. an unripe apple.

Cog, *v.i.* to cheat. R III I. 3. 48. *v.t.* to get by cheating, filch. Cor. III. 2. 133.

Coistrel, *sb*. groom.

Collection, *sb*. inference.

Col'ied, *p.p.* blackened, darkened.

Colour, *sb*. pretext. Show no colour, or bear no colour = allow of no excuse.

Colours, fear no colours = fear no enemy, be afraid of nothing.

Colt, *v.t.* to make a fool of, gull.

Combinate, *adj*. betrothed.

Combine, *v.t.* to bind.

Comfect, *sb*. comfit.

Commodity, *sb*. interest, advantage. John, II. 1. 573. Cargo of merchandise. Tw.N. III. 1. 46.

Comparative, *adj*. fertile in comparisons. 1 H IV. 1. 2. 83.

Comparative, *sb*. a rival in wit. 1 H IV. III. 2. 67.

Compassed, *adj*. arched, round.

Complexion, *sb*. temperament.

Comply, *v.i.* to be ceremonious.

Composition, *sb*. agreement, consistency.

Composture, *sb*. compost.

Composure, *sb*. composition. T. & C. II. 3. 238; A. & C. I. 4. 22.

Compact. T. & C. II. 3. 100.

Compt, *sb*. account, reckoning.

Comptible, *adj*. susceptible, sensitive.

Con, *v.t.* to study, learn; con thanks = give thanks.

Conceptious, *adj*. apt at conceiving.

Conclusion, *sb*. experiment.

Condolement, *sb*. lamentation. Ham. I. 2. 93. Consolation, Per. II. 1. 150.

Conduce, *v.i.* perhaps, to tend to happen.

Conduct, *sb*. guide, escort.

Confiners, *sb*. border peoples.

Confound, *v.t.* to waste. 1 H IV. I. 3. 100. Destroy. M. of V. III. 2. 278.

Congied, *p.p.* taken leave (Fr. congé).

Consent, *sb*. agreement, plot.

Consist, *v.i.* to insist.

Consort, *sb*. company, fellowship. Two G. III. 2. 84; IV. 1. 64. *v.t.* to accompany. C. of E. I. 2. 28.

Conspectuity, *sb*. power of vision.

Constant, *adj*. consistent.

Constantly, *adv*. firmly, surely.

Conster, *v.t.* to construe, interpret.

Constringed, *p.p.* compressed.

Consul, *sb*. senator.

Containing, *sb*. contents.

Contraction, *sb*. the making of the marriage-contract.

Contrive, *v.t.* to wear out, spend. T. of S. I. 2. 273. Conspire. J.C. II. 3. 16.

Control, *v.t.* to check, contradict.

Convent, *v.t.* to summon.

Convert, *v.i.* to change.

Convertite, *sb*. a penitent.

Convince, *v.t.* to overcome. Mac.

I. 7. 64. Convict. T. & C. II. 2. 130.

Convive, *v.i.* to banquet together.

Convoy, *sb*. conveyance, escort.

Copatain hat, *sb*. a high-crowned hat.

Cope, *v.t.* to requite. M. of V. IV. 1. 412. Encounter. As. II. 1. 67.

Copesmate, *sb*. a companion.

Copped, *adj*. round-topped.

Copulatives, *sb*. persons desiring to be coupled in marriage.

Copy, *sb*. theme, text. C. of E. V. 1. 62. Tenure. Mac. III. 2. 37.

Coranto, *sb*. a quick, lively dance.

Corky, *adj*. shrivelled (with age).

Cornet, *sb*. a band of cavalry.

Corollary, *sb*. a supernumerary.

Cosier, *sb*. botcher, cobbler.

Costard, *sb*. an apple, the head (slang).

Cote, *v.t.* to come up with, pass on the way.

Cot-quean, *sb*. a man who busies himself in women's affairs.

Couch, *v.t.* to make to cower.

Counter, *adv*. to run or hunt counter is to trace the scent of the game backwards.

Counter, *sb*. a metal disk used in reckoning.

Counter-caster, *sb*. one who reckons by casting up counters.

Countermand, *v.t.* to prohibit, keep in check. C. of E. IV. 2. 37. Contradict. Lucr. 276.

Countervail, *v.t.* to outweigh.

Couplet, *sb*. a pair.

Courser's hair, a horse's hair laid in water was believed to turn into a serpent.

Court holy-water, *sb*. flattery.

Courtship, *sb* courtly manners.

Covent, *sb*. a convent.

Cox my passion = God's passion.

Coy, *v.t.* to fondle, caress. M.N.D. IV. 1. 2. *v.i.* to disdain. Cor. V. 1. 6.

Crack, *v.i.* to boast. *sb*. an urchin.

Crank, *sb*. winding passage. *v.i.* to wind, twist.

Crants, *sb*. garland, chaplet.

Crare, *sb*. a small sailing vessel.

Crisp, *adj*. curled.

Cross, *sb*. a coin (stamped with a cross).

Cross-row, *sb*. alphabet.

Crow-keeper, *sb*. a boy, or scarecrow, to keep crows from the corn.

Cullion, *sb*. a base fellow.

Cunning, *sb*. knowledge, skill. *adj*. knowing, skilful, skilfully wrought.

Curb, *v.i* to bow, cringe obsequiously.

Curdied, *p.p.* congealed.

Curiosity, *sb*. scrupulous nicety.

Curst, *adj*. bad-tempered.

Curtal, *adj*. having a docked tail. *sb*. a dock-tailed horse.

Customer, *sb*. a loose woman.

Cut, *sb*. a bobtailed horse.

Cuttle, *sb*. a bully.

Daff, *v.t.* to doff. Daff aside = thrust aside in a slighting manner.

Darreign, *v.t.* to arrange, order the ranks for battle.

Dash, *sb*. mark of disgrace.

Daubery, *sb*. false pretence, cheat.

Day-woman, *sb*. dairy woman.

Debosht, *p.p.* debauched.

Deem, *sb*. doom; opinion.

Defeat, *v.t.* to disguise. Oth. I. 3. 333. Destroy. Oth. IV. 2. 160.

Defeature, *sb*. disfigurement.

Defend, *v.t.* to forbid.

Defuse, *v.t.* to disorder and make unrecognizable.

Defused, *p.p.* disordered, shapeless.

Demerit, *sb*. desert.

Dern, *adj*. secret, dismal.

Detect, *v.t.* to discover, disclose.

Determinate, *p.p.* determined upon. Tw.N. II. 1. 10. Decided. Oth. IV. 2. 229. Ended. Sonn. LXXXVII. 4. *v.t.* bring to an end. R II. I. 3.

Dich, *v.i.* do to, happen to.

Diet, *v.t.* keep strictly, as if by a prescribed regimen.

Diffidence, *sb*. distrust, suspicion.

Digression, *sb*. transgression.

Diminutives, *sb*. the smallest of coins.

Directitude, *sb*. a blunder for some word unknown. Cor. IV. 5. 205

Disanimate, *v.t.* to discourage.

Disappointed, *p.p.* unprepared.

Discandy, *v.i.* to thaw, melt.

Discipled, *p.p.* taught.

Disclose, *v.t.* to hatch. *sb*. the breaking of the shell by the chick on hatching.

Disme, *sb*. a tenth.

Distain, *v.t.* to stain, pollute.

Dive-dapper, *sb*. the dabchick or didaper.

Dividant, *adj*. separate, different.

Dotant, *sb*. dotard.

Doubt, *sb*. fear, apprehension.

Dout, *v.t.* to extinguish.

Dowlas, *sb*. coarse linen.

Dowle, *sb*. down, the soft plumage of a feather.

Down-gyved, *adj*. hanging down about the ancle like gyves.

Dribbling, *adj*. weakly shot.

Drugs, *sb*. drudges.

Drumble, *v.i.* to be sluggish or clumsy.

Dry-beat, *v.t.* to cudgel, thrash.

Dry-foot. To draw dry-foot, track by scent.

Dudgeon, *sb*. the handle of a dagger.

Due, *v.t.* to endue.

Dump, *sb*. a sad strain.

Dup, *v.t.* to open.

Ean, *v.i.* to yean, lamb.

Ear, to plough, till.

Eche, *v.t.* to eke out.

Eftest, *adv*. readiest.

Eftsoons, *adv*. immediately

Egal, *adj*. equal.

Egally, *adv*. equally.

Eisel, *sb*. vinegar.

Elf, *v.t.* to mat hair in a tangle; believed to be the work of elves.

Emballing, *sb.* investiture with the crown and sceptre.

Embarquement, *sb.* hindrance, restraint.

Ember-eves, *sb.* vigils of Ember days—four periods of prayer and fasting in the four seasons of the year.

Embowelled, *p.p.* emptied, exhausted.

Emmew, *v.t.* perhaps, to mew up.

Empiricutic, *adj.* empirical, quackish.

Emulation, *sb.* jealous rivalry.

Enacture, *sb.* enactment, performance.

Encave, *v.t.* to hide, conceal

Encumbered, *p.p.* folded.

End, *sb.* still an end = continually.

End, *v.t.* to get in the harvest.

Englut, *v.t.* to swallow.

Enlargement, *sb.* liberty, liberation.

Enormous, *adj.* out of the norm, monstrous.

Enseamed, *p.p.* defiled, filthy.

Ensear, *v.t.* to sear up, make dry.

Enshield, *adj.* enshielded, protected.

Entertain, *v.t.* to take into one's service.

Entertainment, *sb.* service.

Entreat, *v.t.* to treat.

Entreatments, *sb.* invitations.

Ephesian, *b.* boon companion.

Eryngoes, *sb.* roots of the sea-holly, a supposed aphrodisiac.

Escot, *v.t.* to pay for.

Espial, *sb.* a spy.

Even Christian, *sb.* fellow Christian.

Excrement, *sb.* anything that grows out of the body, as hair, nails, etc. Used of the beard. M. of V. III. 2. 84. Of the hair. C. of E. II. 2. 79. Of the moustache. L.L.L. v. I. 98.

Exhibition, *sb.* allowance, pension.

Exigent, *sb.* end. I H VI. II. 5. 9. Exigency, critical need. J. C. v. I. 19.

Exion, *sb.* blunder for action.

Expiate, *v.t.* to terminate. Sonn. XXII. 4

Expiate, *p.p.* ended. R III. III. 3. 24.

Exsufflicate, *adj.* inflated, both literally and metaphorically.

Extent, *sb.* seizure. As, III. I. 17. Violent attack. Tw.N.IV.I.51. Condescension, favour. Ham. II. 2. 377. Display. T.A. IV. 4. 3.

Extraught, *p.p.* extracted.

Extravagancy, *sb.* vagrancy, aimless wandering about.

Eyas, *sb.* a nestling, a young hawk just taken from the nest.

Eyas-musket, *sb.* the young sparrow-hawk.

Eye, *v.i.* to appear, look to the eye.

Facinerious, *adj.* facinorous, wicked.

Fadge, *v.i.* to succeed, suit.

Fading, *sb.* the burden of a song.

Fair, *v.t.* to make beautiful.

Fairing, *sb.* a gift.

Faitor, *sb.* evil-doer

Fangled, *adj.* fond of novelties.

Fap, *adj.* drunk.

Farced, *p.p.* stuffed out.

Fardel, *sb.* a burden, bundle.

Fat, *adj.* cloying. *sb.* vat.

Favour, *sb.* outward appearance, aspect. In pl. = features.

Fear, *v.t.* to frighten. 3 H VI. III. 3. 226. Fear for. M. of V III. 5. 3.

Feat, *adj.* neat, dexterous.

Feat, *v.t.* to fashion, form.

Fee, *sb.* worth, value.

Feeder, *sb.* servant.

Fee-farm, *sb.* a tenure without limit of time.

Fellowly, *adj.* companionable, sympathetic.

Feodary, *sb.* confederate.

Fere, *sb.* spouse, consort.

Ferret, *v.t.* to worry.

Festinate, *adj.* swift, speedy.

Fet, *p.p.* fetched.

Fico, *sb.* a fig (Span.).

File, *sb.* list.

File, *v.t.* to defile. Mac. III. I.65. Smooth, polish. L.L.L. v. I. II. *v.i.* to walk in file. H VIII. III. 2. 171.

Fill-horse, *sb.* a shaft-horse.

Fills, *sb.* shafts.

Fineless, *adj.* endless, infinite.

Firago, *sb.* virago.

Firk, *v.t.* to beat.

Fitchew, *sb.* pole-cat.

Fitment, *sb.* that which befits.

Flap-dragon, *sb.* snap-dragon, or small burning object, lighted and floated in a glass of liquor, to be swallowed burning. L.L.L. v. I. 43. 2 H IV. II. 4. 244. *v.t.* to swallow like a flapdragon. W. T. III. 3. 100.

Flaw, *sb.* gust of wind. Ham. v. I. 223 Small flake of ice. 2 H IV. IV. 4. 35. Passionate outburst. M. for M. II. 3. 11. A crack. Lear, II. 4. 288. *v.t.* make a flaw in, break. H VIII. I. I. 95; I. 2. 21.

Fleer, *sb.* sneer. Oth. IV. I. 83. *v.i.* to grin; sneer. L.L.L. v. 2. 109.

Fleshment, *sb.* encouragement given by first success.

Flewed, *p.p.* with large hanging chaps.

Flight, *sb.* a long light arrow.

Flighty, *adj.* swift.

Flirt-gill, *sb.* light wench.

Flote, *sb.* sea.

Flourish, *v.t.* to ornament, gloss over.

Fobbed, *p.p.* cheated, deceived.

Foil, *sb.* defeat. I H VI. III. 3. 11. *v.t.* to defeat, mar. Pass. P. 99.

Foin, *v.i.* to thrust (in fencing).

Fopped, *p.p.* cheated, fooled.

Forbod, *p.p.* forbidden.

Fordo, *v.t.* to undo, destroy.

Foreign, *adj.* dwelling abroad.

Fork, *sb.* the forked tongue of a snake. M. for M. III. I. 16. The barbed head of an arrow. Lear, I. I. 146. The junction of the legs with the trunk. Lear, IV 6. 120.

Forked, *p.p* barbed. As, II. I 24 Horned as a cuckold. T. & C. I. 2. 164.

Forslow, *v.i.* to delay.

Forspeak, *v.t.* to speak against.

Fosset-seller, *sb.* a seller of taps.

Fox, *sb.* broadsword.

Foxship, *sb.* selfish and ungrateful cunning.

Fracted, *p.p.* broken.

Frampold, *adj.* turbulent, quarrelsome.

Frank, *v.t.* to pen in a frank or sty. R III. I. 3. 314. Frank, *sb.* a sty. 2 H IV. II. 2. 145. *adj.* liberal. Lear, III. 4. 20.

Franklin, *sb.* a yeoman.

Fraught, *sb.* freight, cargo, load. Tw. N. v. I. 59. *v.t.* to load, burden. Cym. I. I. 126. *p.p.* laden. M. of V. II. 8. 30. Stored. Two G. III. 2. 70.

Fraughtage, *sb.* cargo. C. of E. IV. I. 8.

Fraughting, *part. adj.* constituting the cargo.

Frize, *sb.* a kind of coarse woollen cloth with a nap.

Frontier, *sb.* an outwork in fortification. I H IV. II. 3. 56. Used figuratively. I H IV. I. 3. 19.

Fruitful, *adj.* bountiful, plentiful.

Frush, *v.t.* to bruise, batter.

Frutify, blunder for certify. M. of V. ii. 2. 132.

Fubbed off, *p.p.* put off with excuses. 2 H IV. II. I. 34.

Fullams, *sb.* a kind of false dice.

Gad, *sb.* a pointed instrument. T.A. IV. I. 104. Upon the gad = on the spur of the moment, hastily. Lear, I. 2. 26

Gage, *v.t.* to pledge.

Gaingiving, *sb.* misgiving.

Galliard, *sb.* a lively dance.

Gallimaufry, *sb.* medley, jumble.

Gallow, *v.t.* to frighten.

Gallowglass, *sb.* heavy-armed Irish foot-soldier.

Gallows, *sb.* a rogue, one fit to be hung.

Gallows-bird, *sb.* one that merits hanging.

Garboil, *sb.* uproar, commotion.

Gaskins, *sb.* loose breeches.

Gastness, *sb.* ghastliness, terror.

Geck, *sb.* dupe.

Generation, *sb.* offspring.

Generous, *adj.* nobly born.

Gennet, *sb.* a Spanish horse.

Gentry, *sb.* rank by birth. M. W. II. I. 51. Courtesy. Ham II. 2. 22.

German, *sb.* a near kinsman.

Germen, *sb.* germ, seed.

Gest, *sb.* a period of sojourn; originally the halting place in a royal progress (Fr. *gite*).

Gib, *sb.* an old tom-cat.

Gibbet, *v.t.* to hang, as a barrel when it is slung.

Gib-cat, *sb.* an old tom-cat.

Gig, *sb.* top.

Giglot, *adj.* wanton. I H VI. IV. 7. 41. *sb.* M. for M. V. I. 345.

Gillyvors, *sb.* gillyflowers.

Gimmal-bit, a double bit, or one made with double rings.

Gimmer, *sb.* contrivance, mechanical device.

Ging, *sb.* gang, pack.

Gird, *sb.* a scoff, jest. 2 H VI. III. I. 131. *v.t.* to taunt, gibe at. 2 H IV. I. 2. 6.

Gleek, *sb.* scoff. I H VI. IV. 2. 123. *v.i.* to scoff. M.N.D. III. I. 145.

Glib, *v.t.* to geld.

Gloze, *v.i.* to comment. H V. I. 2. 40. T. & C. II. 2. 165. To use flattery. R II. II. I. 10; T.A. IV. 4. 35.

Gnarling, *pr.p.* snarling.

Godden, *sb.* good even.

God'ild, God vield, God reward.

Good-jer = good-year.

Good-year, *sb.* a meaningless interjection. M.A. I. 3. I. Some malific power. Lear, V. 3. 24.

Goss, *sb.* gorse.

Gossip, *sb.* sponsor. Two G. III. I. 269. *v.t.* to stand sponsor for. A.W. I. I. 176.

Gorbellied, *adj.* big-bellied.

Graff, *sb.* graft, scion. *v.t.* to graft.

Grain, *sb.* a fast colour.

Gratility, *sb.* gratuity.

Gratulate, *adj.* gratifying.

Greek, *sb.* boon companion.

Grise, *sb.* a step.

Guard, *v.t.* to trim, ornament.

Guardant, *sb.* sentinel, guard.

Guidon, *sb.* standard, banner.

Gules, *adj.* red, in heraldry.

Gust, *sb.* taste. *v.t.* to taste.

Hackney, *sb.* loose woman.

Haggard, *sb.* untrained hawk.

Haggled, *p.p.* hacked, mangled.

Hair, *sb.* texture, nature. I H IV. IV. I. 61. Against the hair = against the grain. R. & J. II. 3. 97.

Handfast, *sb.* betrothal, contract. Cym. I. 5. 78. Custody. W.T. IV. 3. 778.

Handsaw, *sb.* corruption of heronshaw, a heron.

Hardiment, *sb.* daring deed.

Harlot, *adj.* lewd, base.

Hatched, *p.p.* closed with a hatch or half door. Per. IV. 2. 33. Engraved. T. & C. I. 3. 65.

Havoc, to cry havoc = cry no quarter. John, II. I. 357. *v.t.* cut to pieces, destroy. H V. I. 2. 193.

Hawking, *adj.* hawk-like.

Hay, *sb.* a round dance. L.L.L. V. I. 147. A term in fencing when a hit is made (Ital. *hai*, you have it). R. & J. II. 4. 27

Hebenon, *sb.* perhaps the yew (Germ. *Eiben*). Ebony and henbane have been suggested.

Hefts, *sb.* heavings.

Helm, *v.t.* to steer.

Helpless, *adj.* not helping, useless.

Hent, *sb.* grasp, hold. Ham. III. 3. 88. *v.t.* to hold, pass. M. for M. IV. 6. 14.

Hermit, *sb.* beadsman, one bound to pray for another.

Hild = held.

Hilding, *sb.* menial, drudge.

Hoar, *adj.* mouldy, R. & J. II. 3. 136. *v.i.* to become mouldy. R. & J. II. 3. 142.

Hoar, *v.t.* to make hoary or white, as with leprosy.

Hobby-horse, *sb.* a principal figure in the old morris dance. L.L.L. III. I. 30. A light woman. M.A. III. 2. 68.

Hob-nob, have or not have, hit or miss.

Hold in, *v.i.* to keep counsel.

Holding, *sb.* the burden of a song. A. & C. II. 7. 112. Fitness, sense. A.W. IV. 2. 27.

Holy-ales, rural festivals.

Honest, *adj.* chaste.

Honesty, *sb.* chastity. M.W.W. II. 2. 234. Decency. Tw.N. II. 3. 85. Generosity, liberality. Tim. III. I. 30.

Honey-seed, blunder for homicide. 2 H IV. II. I. 52.

Honey-suckle, blunder for homicidal. 2 H IV. II. I. 50

Hoodman, *sb.* the person blinded in the game of hoodman-blind.

Hoodman-blind, *sb.* blindman's buff.

Hot at hand, not to be held in.

Hot-house, *sb.* bagnio, often in fact a brothel as well.

Hox, *v.t.* to hough, hamstring.

Hoy, *sb.* a small coasting vessel.

Hugger-mugger, In, stealthily and secretly.

Hull, *v.i.* to float.

Hulling, *pr.p.* floating at the mercy of the waves.

Ignomy, *sb.* ignominy.

Imbar, *v.t.* to bar in, make secure H V. I. 2. 94.

Imboss, *v.t.* to hunt to death.

Imbossed, *p.p.* swollen. As, II. 7. 67. Foaming at the mouth. T. of S. Ind. I. 16.

Immanity, *sb.* savageness, ferocity.

Immoment, *adj.* insignificant.

Immures, *sb.* surrounding walls.

Imp, *v.t.* to graft new feathers to a falcon's wing.

Impair, *adj.* unsuitable, inappropriate.

Impale, *v.t.* to encircle.

Impart, *v.t.* to afford, grant. Lucr. 1039; Sonn. LXXII. 8. *v.i.* to behave oneself. Ham. I. 2. 112.

Imperceiverant, *adj.* lacking in perception.

Impeticos, *v.t.* to put in the petticoat or pocket.

Importance, *sb.* importunity. John, II. I. 7. Import. W.T. V. 2. 19.

Question at issue, that which is imported. Cym. I. 5. 40.

Imposition, *sb.* command, injunction. M. of V. I. 2. 106. Penalty. M. for M. I. 2. 186.

Imposthume, *sb.* abscess.

Imprese, *sb.* device with a motto.

Include, *v.t.* to conclude, end.

Incontinent, *adj.* immediate.

Incony, *adj.* dainty, delicate.

Indent, *v.i.* to make terms.

Index, *sb.* introduction (in old books the index came first).

In-differency, *sb.* impartiality.

In-directly, *adv.* wrongly, unjustly.

Indurance, *sb.* durance, imprisonment.

Infest, *v.t.* to vex, trouble.

Inherit, *v.t.* to possess. Tp. IV. I. 154. To cause to possess, put in possession. R II. I. I. 85. *v.i.* to take possession. Tp. II. 2. 182.

Inheritor, *sb.* possessor.

Injury, *sb.* insult.

Inkhorn mate, *sb.* bookworm.

Inkle, *sb.* coarse tape.

Insisture, *sb.* persistence.

Intenible, *adj.* incapable of holding.

Intention, *sb.* aim, direction.

Intermissive, *adj.* intermitted, interrupted.

Intrinse, *adj.* tightly drawn.

Invised, *adj.* unseen, a doubtful word.

Irregulous, *adj.* lawless.

Jack, *sb.* figure that struck the bell in old clocks. R III. IV. 2. 114. A term of contempt. R III. I. 3. 72. The small bowl aimed at in the game of bowls. Cym. II. I. 2.

Jacks, *sb.* the keys of a virginal. Sonn. CXXVIII. 5. A drinking vessel. T. of S. IV. I. 48.

Jade, *v.t.* to play the jade with, run away with. Tw.N. II. 5. 164. Drive like a jade. A. & C. III. I. 34. Treat with contempt. H VIII. III. 2. 280.

Jakes, *sb.* a privy.

Jar, *sb.* a tick of the clock. W.T. I. 2. 43.

Jar, *v.t.* to tick. R II. V. 5. 51. *v.i.* to guard. I H VI. III. I. 70. *sb.* a quarrel. I H VI. I. I. 44.

Jesses, *sb.* straps attaching the legs of a hawk to the fist.

Jet, *v.i.* to strut. Tw.N. II. 4. 32. Advance threateningly. R III. II. 4. 51.

Journal, *adj.* diurnal, daily.

Jowl, *v.t.* to knock, dash.

Kam, *adj.* crooked, away from the point.

Keech, *sb.* a lump of tallow or fat.

Keel, *v.t.* explained by some as meaning to cool; by others, to scum or skim.

Ken, *sb.* perception, sight. *v.t.* to know.

Kern, *sb*. light-armed foot-soldier of Ireland.

Kibe, *sb*. chilblain on the heel.

Kicky-wicky, *sb*. a pet name.

Killen = to kill.

Kiln-hole, *sb*. the fireplace of an oven or kiln.

Kind, *sb*. nature. M. of V. I. 3. 84. *adj*. natural. Lucr. 1423. *adv*. kindly. Tim. I. 2. 224.

Kindle, *v.t*. to bring forth young. As, III. 2. 343. Incite. As, I. I. 179.

Knack, *sb*. a pretty trifle.

Knap, *v.t*. to gnaw, nibble. M. of V. III. I. 9. Rap. Lear, II. 4. 123.

Laboursome, *adj*. elaborate.

Laced mutton, *sb*. slang for courtesan.

Lade, *v.t*. to empty, drain.

Land-damn. Unrecognizably corrupted word in W.T. II. I. 143.

Lapsed, *p.p.* caught, surprised. Tw.N. III. 3. 36.

Latch, *v.t*. to catch, lay hold of.

Latten, *sb*. a mixture of copper and tin. M.W.W. I. I. 153.

Lavolt, *sb*. a dance in which two persons bound high and whirl round.

Lay for, *v.t*. to strive to win.

Leasing, *sb*. lying, falsehood.

Leave, *sb*. liberty, license.

Leese, *v.t*. to lose.

Leet, *sb*. a manor court. T. of S. Ind. 'I. 87. The time when such is held. Oth. III. 3. 140.

Leiger, *sb*. ambassador.

Length, *sb*. delay.

Let, *v.t*. to hinder. Tw.N. v. I. 246; Ham. I. 4. 85. Detain. W.T. I. 2. 41. Forbear. Lucr. 10. *p.p.* caused. Ham. IV. 6. 11. *sb*. hindrance. H V. v. 2. 65.

Let-alone, *sb*. hindrance, prohibition.

Level, *sb*. aim, line of fire. R. & J. III. 3. 102. *v.i*. to aim. R III. IV. 4. 202. Be on the same level. Oth. I. 3. 239. *adv*. evenly. Tw.N. II. 4. 32.

Lewd, *adj*. base, vile.

Libbard, *sb*. leopard.

Liberal, *adj*. licentious. Liberal conceit = elaborate design. Ham. v. 2. 152. *adv*. freely, openly. Oth. v. 2. 220.

Lieger, *sb*. ambassador.

Lifter, *sb*. thief.

Light, *p.p*. lighted.

Likelihood, *sb*. sign, indication.

Lime *v.t*. to put lime into liquor. M.W.W. I. 3. 14. Smear with bird-lime. 2 H VI. I. 3. 86. Catch with bird-lime. Tw.N. III. 4. 75. Cement. 3 H VI. V. I. 84.

Limit, *sb*. appointed time. R II. I. 3. 151. *v.t*. to appoint. John, v. 2. 123.

Line, *v.t*. to draw, paint. As, III. 2, 93. Strengthen, fortify. I H IV. II. 3. 85.

Line-grove, *sb*. a grove of ime trees.

Linsey-woolsey, *sb*. gibberish (literally, mixed stuff).

Lipsbury pinfold. Perhaps = between the teeth.

List, *sb*. desire, inclination. Oth. II. I. 105. Limit, boundary. I H IV. IV. I. 51. Lists for combat. Mac. III. I. 70.

Lither, *adj*. flexible, gentle.

Livery, *sb*. delivery of a freehold into the possession of the heir.

Lob, *sb*. lubber, lout.

Lockram, *sb*. coarse linen.

Lodge, *v.t*. to lay flat, beat down.

Loggats, *sb*. a game somewhat resembling bowls.

Loof, *v.t*. to luff, bring close to the wind.

Losel, *sb*. a wasteful, worthless fellow.

Lout, *v.t*. to make a lout or fool of.

Lown, *sb*. base fellow.

Luce, *sb*. pike or jack.

Lurch, *v.t*. to win a love set at a game; bear off the prize easily. Cor. II. 2. 102. *v.i*. to skulk. M.W.W. II. 2. 25.

Lym, *sb*. bloodhound; so called from the leam or leash used to hold him.

Maggot-pie, *sb*. magpie.

Main, *sb*. a hand at dice. I H IV. IV. I. 47. Mainland. Lear, III. I. 6. The chief power. Ham. v. 4. 15.

Main-course, *sb*. mainsail.

Makeless, *adj*. mateless, widowed.

Malkin, *sb*. slattern.

Mallard, *sb*. a wild drake.

Mallecho, *sb*. mischief (Span. *malhecho*).

Malt-horse, *sb*. brewer's horse.

Mammering, *pr.p*. hesitating.

Mammet, *sb*. a doll.

Mammock, *v.t*. to tear in pieces.

Manakin, *sb*. little man.

Mankind, *adj*. masculine, applied to a woman.

Manner, with the = in the fact, red-handed.

Mare, *sb*. nightmare. To ride the wild mare = play at see-saw.

Mark, *sb*. thirteen shillings and fourpence.

Mart, *v.i*. to market, traffic. Cym. I. 6. 150. *v.t*. to vend, traffic with. J.C. IV. 3. 11.

Mastic, *sb*. used to stop decayed teeth.

Match, *sb*. compact, bargain. M. of V. III. I. 40. Set a match = make an appointment. I H IV. I. 2. 110.

Mate, *v.t*. to confound, make bewildered. C. of E. III. 2. 54. Match, cope with. H VIII. III. 2. 274.

Material, *adj*. full of matter.

Maugre, in spite of.

Maund, *sb*. a basket.

Mazzard, *sb*. skull.

Meacock, *adj*. spiritless, pusillanimous.

Mealed, *p.p.* mingled, compounded.

Mean, *sb*. the intermediate part between the tenor and treble.

Meiny, *sb*. attendants, retinue.

Mell, *v.i*. to meddle.

Mered, He being the mered question = the question concerning him alone. A. & C. III. 13. 10.

Mess, *sb*. a set of four. L.L.L. IV. 3. 204. Small quantity. 2 H IV. II. I. 95. Lower messes = inferiors, as messing at the lower end of the table. W.T. I. 2. 226.

Mete, *v.i*. to mete at = aim at.

Metheglin, *sb*. a kind of mead, made of honey and water.

Micher, *sb*. truant.

Miching, *adj*. sneaking, stealthy.

Mineral, *sb*. a mine.

Minikin, *adj*. small, pretty.

Minion, *sb*. darling, favourite. John, II. I. 392. Used contemptuously. 2 H VI. I. 3. 82. A pert, saucy person. 2 H VI. I. 3. 136.

Mirable, *adj*. admirable.

Mire, *v.i*. to be bemired, sink as into mire.

Misdread, *sb*. fear of evil.

Misprision, *sb*. mistake. M.N.D. III. 2. 90. Contempt. A.W. II. 3. 153.

Misproud, *adj*. viciously proud.

Miss, *sb*. misdoing.

Missingly, *adv*. regretfully.

Missive, *sb*. messenger.

Misthink, *v.t*. to misjudge.

Mobled, *p.p.* having the face or head muffled.

Modern, commonplace, trite.

Module, *sb*. mould, form.

Moldwarp, *sb*. mole.

Mome, *sb*. blockhead, dolt.

Momentany, *adj*. momentary, lasting an instant.

Monster, *v.t*. to make monstrous.

Month's mind, *sb*. intense desire or yearning.

Moralize, *v.t*. to interpret, explain.

Mort, *sb*. trumpet notes blown at the death of the deer.

Mortal, *adj*. deadly.

Mortified, *p.p.* deadened, insensible.

Mot, *sb*. motto, device.

Mother, *sb*. the disease *hysterica passio*.

Motion, *v.t*. to propose, counsel. I H VI. I. 3. 63. *sb*. a puppet show. W.T. IV. 3. 96. A puppet. Two G. II. I. 91. Solicitation, proposal, suit. C. of E. I. I. 60. Emotion, feeling, impulse. Tw.N. II. 4. 18.

Motive, *sb*. a mover, instrument, member.

Mountant, *adj*. lifted up.

Mow, *sb*. a grimace. *v.i*. to grimace.

Moy, *sb*. probably some coin.

Muleter, *sb.* muleteer.

Mulled, *p.p.* flat, insipid.

Mummy, *sb.* a medical or magical preparation originally made from mummies.

Murdering-piece, *sb.* a cannon loaded with chain-shot.

Murrion, *adj.* infected with the murrain.

Muse, *v.i.* to wonder. John, III. I. 317. *v.t.* to wonder at. Tp. III. 3. 36.

Muset, *sb.* a gap or opening in a hedge.

Muss, *sb.* scramble.

Mutine, *sb.* mutineer.

Mystery, *sb.* profession. M. for M. IV. 2. 28. Professional skill. A.W. III. 6. 65.

Nayword, *sb.* pass-word. M.W.W. II. 2. 126. A by-word. Tw.N. II. 3. 132.

Neat, *adj.* trim, spruce.

Neb, *sb.* bill or beak.

Neeld, *sb.* needle.

Neeze, *v.i.* to sneeze.

Neif, *sb.* fist.

Next, *adj.* nearest.

Nick, *sb.* out of all nick, beyond all reckoning.

Night-rule, *sb.* revelry.

Nill = will not.

Nine-men's-morris, *sb.* a rustic game, often played in the open air.

Note, *sb.* list, catalogue. W.T. IV. 2. 47. Note of expectation = list of expected guests. Mac. III. 3. 10. Stigma, mark of reproach. R II. I. I. 43. Distinction. Cym. II. 3. 12. Knowledge, observation. Lear, III. I. 18.

Nott-pated, *adj.* crop-headed.

Nousle, *v.t.* to nurse, nourish delicately.

Nowl, *sb.* noddle.

Nuthook, *sb.* slang for catchpole.

Oathable, *adj.* capable of taking an oath.

Objects, *sb.* anything presented to the sight; everything that comes in the way.

Obsequious, *adj.* regardful of funeral rites. 3 H VI. II. 5. 118. Funereal, having to do with obsequies. T.A. V. 3. 153.

Observance, *sb.* observation. Oth. III. 3. 151. Homage. 2 H IV. IV. 3. 15. Ceremony. M. of V. II. 2. 194.

Obstacle, *sb.* blunder for 'obstinate.'

Occupation, *sb.* trade (in contemptuous sense). Cor. IV. I. 14. Voice of occupation = vote of working men. Cor. IV. 6. 98.

Odd, *adj.* unnoticed. Tp. I. 2. 223. At odds. T. & C. IV. 5. 265.

Oeillades, *sb.* amorous glances.

O'ergrown, *p.p.* bearded. Cym. IV. 4. 33. Become too old. M. for M. I. 3. 22.

O'erstrawed, *p.p.* overstrewn.

Office, *v.t.* to office all = do all the domestic service. A.W. III. 2. 128. Keep officiously. Cor. v. 2. 61.

Oneyers, *sb.* unexplained word.

Opposition, *sb.* combat, encounter.

Orb, *sb.* orbit. R. & J. II. I. 151. Circle. M.N.D. II. I. 9. A heavenly body. M. of V. V. I. 60. The earth. Tw.N. III. I. 39.

Ordinant, *adj.* ordaining, controlling.

Ordinary, *sb.* a public dinner at which each man pays for his own share.

Ort, *sb.* remnant, refuse.

Ouphs, *sb.* elves, goblins.

Outrage, *sb.* outburst of rage.

Overscutcht, *p.p.* over-whipped, over-switched (perhaps in a wanton sense).

Overture, *sb.* disclosure. W.T. II. I. 172. Declaration. Tw.N. I. 5. 208.

Owe, *v.t.*, to own, possess.

Packing, *sb.* plotting, conspiracy.

Paddock, *sb.* toad. Ham. III. 4. 191. A familiar spirit in the form of a toad. Mac. I. I. 9.

Pajock, *sb.* term of contempt, by some said to mean peacock.

Pale, *sb.* enclosure, confine.

Palliament, *sb.* robe.

Parcel-bawd, *sb.* half-bawd.

'Paritor, *sb.* apparitor, an officer of the Bishops' Court.

Part, *sb.* party, side.

Partake, *v.t.* to make to partake, impart. W.T. V. 3. 132. To share. J.C. II. I. 305.

Parted, *p.p.* endowed.

Partisan, *sb.* a kind of pike.

Pash, *sb.* a grotesque word for the head. W.T. I. 2. 128. *v.t.* to smite, dash. T. & C. II. 3. 202.

Pass, *v.t.* to pass sentence on. M. for M. II. I. 19. Care for. 2 H VI. IV. 2. 127. Represent. L.L.L. V. I. 123. Make a thrust in fencing. Tw.N. III. I. 44.

Passage, *sb.* passing to and fro. C. of E. III. I. 99. Departure, death. Ham. III. 3. 86. Passing away. 1 H VI. II. 5. 108. Occurrence. A.W. I. I. 19. Process, course. R. & J. Prol. 9. Thy passages of life = the actions of thy life. 1 H IV. III. 2. 8. Passages of grossness = gross impositions. Tw.N. III. 2. 70. Motion. Cor. V. 6. 76.

Passant. In heraldry, the position of an animal walking.

Passionate, *v.t.* to express with emotion. T.A. III. 2. 6. *adj.* displaying emotion. 2 H VI. I. I. 104. Sorrowful. John, II. I. 544.

Passy measures, a corruption of the Italian *passamezzo*, denoting a stately and measured step in dancing.

Patch, *sb.* fool.

Patchery, *sb.* knavery, trickery.

Patronage, *v.t.* to patronize, protect.

Pavin, *sb.* a stately dance of Spanish or Italian origin.

Pawn, *sb.* a pledge.

Peach, *v.t.* to impeach, accuse.

Peat, *sb.* pet, darling.

Pedascule, *sb.* pedant, schoolmaster.

Peevish, *adj.* childish, silly. 1 H VI. V. 3. 186. Fretful, wayward. M. of V. I. I. 86.

Peise, *v.t.* to poise, balance. John, II. I. 575. Retard by making heavy. M. of V. III. 2. 22. Weigh down. R III. V. 3. 106.

Pelt, *v.i.* to let fly with words of opprobrium.

Pelting, *adj.* paltry.

Penitent, *adj.* doing penance.

Periapt, *sb.* amulet.

Period, *sb.* end, conclusion. A. & C. IV. 2. 25. *v.t.* to put an end to. Tim. I. I. 103.

Perked up, dressed up.

Perspective, *sb.* glasses so fashioned as to create an optical illusion.

Pert, *adj.* lively, brisk.

Pertaunt-like, *adv.* word unexplained and not yet satisfactorily amended. L.L.L. V. 2. 67.

Pervert, *v.t.* to avert, turn aside.

Pettitoes, *sb.* feet; properly pig's feet.

Pheeze, *v.t.* beat, chastise, torment.

Phisnomy, *sb.* physiognomy.

Phraseless, *adj.* indescribable.

Physical, *adj.* salutary, wholesome.

Pia mater, *sb.* membrane that covers the brain; used for the brain itself.

Pick, *v.t.* to pitch, throw.

Picked, *p.p.* refined, precise.

Picking, *adj.* trifling, small.

Piece, *sb.* a vessel of wine.

Pight, *p.p.* pitched.

Piled, *p.p.* = peeled, bald, with quibble on 'piled' of velvet.

Pill, *v.t.* to pillage, plunder.

Pin, *sb.* bull's-eye of a target.

Pin-buttock, *sb.* a narrow buttock.

Pioned, *adj.* doubtful word: perhaps covered with marsh-marigold, or simply 'dug.'

Pip, *sb.* a spot on cards. 'A pip out' = intoxicated, with reference to a game called 'one and thirty.'

Pitch, *sb.* the height to which a falcon soars, height.

Placket, *sb.* opening in a petticoat, or a petticoat.

Planched, *adj.* made of planks.

Plantage, *sb.* plants, vegetation.

Plantation, *sb.* colonising.

Plausive, *adj.* persuasive, pleasing.

Pleached, *adj.* interlaced, folded.

Plurisy, *sb.* superabundance.

Point-devise, *adj.* precise, finical. L.L.L. V. I. 19. *adv.* Tw.N. II. 5. 162.

Poking-sticks, *sb.* irons for setting out ruffs.

Pole-clipt, *adj.* used of vineyards in which the vines are grown around poles.

Polled, *adj.* clipped, laid bare.

Pomander, *sb.* a ball of perfume.

Poor-John, *sb.* salted and dried hake.

Porpentine, *sb.* porcupine.

Portable, *adj.* supportable, endurable.

Portage, *sb.* port-hole. H V. III. 1. 10. Port-dues. Per. III. 1. 35.

Portance, *sb.* deportment, bearing.

Posset, *v.t.* to curdle.

Posy, *sb.* a motto on a ring.

Potch, *v.i.* to poke, thrust.

Pottle, *sb.* a tankard; strictly a two-quart measure.

Pouncet-box, *sb.* a box for perfumes, pierced with holes.

Practice, *sb.* plot.

Practisant, *sb.* accomplice.

Practise, *v.i.* to plot, use stratagems. Two G. IV. 1. 47. *v.t.* to plot. John, IV. 1. 20.

Precedent, *sb.* rough draft. R III. III. 6. 7. Prognostic, indication. V. & A. 26.

Prefer, *v.t.* to promote, advance. Two G. II. 4. 154. Recommend. Cym. II. 3. 50. Present, offer. M.N.D. IV. 2. 37.

Pregnant, *adj.* ready-witted, clever. Tw.N. II. 2. 28. Full of meaning. Ham. II. 2. 209. Ready. Ham. III. 2. 66. Plain, evident. M. for M. II. 1. 23.

Prenzie, *adj.* demure.

Pretence, *sb.* project, scheme.

Prick, *sb.* point on a dial. 3 H VI. I. 4. 34. Bull's-eye. L.L.L. IV. 1. 132. Prickle. As. III. 2. 113. Skewer. Lear, II. 3. 16.

Pricket, *sb.* a buck of the second year.

Prick-song, *sb.* music sung from notes.

Prig, *sb.* a thief.

Private, *sb.* privacy. Tw.N. III. 4. 90. Private communication. John, IV. 3. 16.

Prize, *sb.* prize-contest. T.A. I. 1. 399. Privilege. 3 H VI. I. 4. 59. Value. Cym. III. 6. 76.

Probal, *adj.* probable, reasonable.

Proditor, *sb.* traitor.

Proface, *int.* much good may it do you!

Propagate, *v.t.* to augment.

Propagation, *sb.* augmentation.

Proper-false, *adj.* handsome and deceitful.

Property, *sb.* a tool or instrument. M.W.W. III. 4. 10. *v.t.* to make a tool of. John, v. 2. 79

Pugging, *adj.* thievish.

Puisny, *adj.* unskilful, like a tyro.

Pun, *v.t.* to pound.

Punk, *sb.* strumpet.

Purchase, *v.t.* to acquire, get. *sb.* acquisition, booty.

Pursuivant, *sb.* a herald's attendant or messenger.

Pursy, *adj.* short-winded, asthmatic.

Puttock, *sb.* a kite.

Puzzle, *sb.* a filthy drab (Italian *puzzolente*).

Quaintly, *adv.* ingeniously, deliberately.

Qualification, *sb.* appeasement.

Quality, *sb.* profession, calling, especially that of an actor. Two G. IV. 1. 58. Professional skill. Tp. 1. 2. 193.

Quarter, *sb.* station. John, v. 5. 20. Keep fair quarter = keep on good terms with, be true to. C. of E. II. 1. 108. In quarter = on good terms. Oth. II. 3. 176.

Quat, *sb.* pimple.

Quatch-buttock, *sb.* a squat or flat buttock.

Quean, *sb.* wench, hussy.

Queasy, *adj.* squeamish, fastidious. M.A. II. 1. 368. Disgusted. A. & C. III. 6. 20.

Queasiness, *sb.* nausea, disgust.

Quell, *sb.* murder.

Quest, *sb.* inquest, jury. R III. 1. 4. 177. Search, inquiry, pursuit. M. of V. I. 1. 172. A body of searchers. Oth. I. 2. 46.

Questant, *sb.* aspirant, candidate.

Quicken, *v.t.* to make alive. A.W. II. 1. 76. Refresh, revive. M. of V. II. 7. 52. *v.i.* to become alive, revive. Lear, III. 7. 40.

Quietus, *sb.* settlement of an account.

Quillet, *sb.* quibble.

Quintain, *sb.* a figure set up for tilting at.

Quire, *sb.* company.

Quittance, *v.i.* to requite. 1 H. VI. II. 1. 14. *sb.* acquittance. M.W.W. I. 1. 10. Requital. 2 H IV. I. 1. 108.

Quoif, *sb.* cap.

Quoit, *v.t.* to throw.

Quote, *v.t.* to note, examine.

Rabato, *sb.* a kind of ruff.

Rabbit-sucker, *sb.* sucking rabbit.

Race, *sb.* root. W.T. IV. 3. 48. Nature, disposition. M. for M. II. 4. 160. Breed. Mac. II. 4. 15.

Rack, *v.t.* stretch, strain. M. of V. I. 1. 181. Strain to the utmost. Cor. V. 1. 16.

Rack, *sb.* a cloud or mass of clouds. Ham. II. 2. 492. *v.i.* move like vapour. 3 H VI. II. 1. 27.

Rampired, *p.p.* fortified by a rampart.

Ramps, *sb.* wanton wenches.

Ranges, *sb* ranks.

Rap, *v.t.* to transport.

Rascal, *sb.* a deer out of condition.

Raught, *impf.* & *p.p.* reached.

Rayed, *p.p.* befouled. T. of S. IV. 1. 3. In T. of S. III. 2. 52 it means perhaps arrayed, attacked.

Raze, *sb.* root.

Razed, *p.p.* slashed.

Reave, *v.t.* to bereave.

Rebate, *v.t.* to make dull, blunt.

Recheat, *sb.* a set of notes sounded to call the dogs off from a false scent.

Rede, *sb.* counsel.

Reechy, *adj.* smoky, grimy.

Refell, *v.t.* to refute.

Refuse, *sb.* rejection, disowning. *v.t.* to reject, disown.

Reguerdon, *v.t.* to reward, guerdon.

Remonstrance, *sb.* demonstration.

Remotion, *sb.* removal.

Renege, *v.t.* to deny.

Renying, *pres. p.* denying.

Replication, *sb.* echo. J.C. I. 1. 50 Reply. Ham. IV. 2. 12.

Rere-mice, *sb.* bats.

Respected, blunder for suspected.

Respective, *adj.* worthy of regard. Two G. IV. 4. 197. Showing regard. John, I. 1. 188. Careful. M. of V. V. 1. 156.

Respectively, *adv.* respectfully.

Rest, *sb.* set up one's rest is to stand upon the cards in one's hand, be fully resolved.

Resty, *adj.* idle, lazy.

Resume, *v.t.* to take.

Reverb, *v.t.* to resound.

Revolt, *sb.* rebel.

Ribaudred, *adj.* ribald, lewd.

Rid, *v.t.* to destroy, do away with.

Riggish, *adj.* wanton.

Rigol, *sb.* a circle.

Rim, *sb.* midriff or abdomen.

Rivage, *sb.* shore.

Rival, *sb.* partner, companion. M.N.D. III. 2. 156. *v.i.* to be a competitor. Lear, I. 1. 191.

Rivality, *sb.* partnership, participation.

Rivelled, *adj.* wrinkled.

Road, *sb.* roadstead, port. Two G. II. 4. 185. Journey. H VIII. IV. 2. 17. Inroad, incursion. H V. I. 2. 138.

Roisting, *adj.* roistering, blustering

Romage, *sb.* bustle, turmoil.

Ronyon, *sb.* scurvy wretch.

Rook, *v.r.* to cower, squat.

Ropery, *sb.* roguery.

Rope-tricks, *sb.* knavish tricks.

Roping, *pr.p.* dripping.

Roted, *p.p.* learned by heart.

Rother, *sb.* an ox, or animal of the ox kind.

Round, *v.i.* to whisper. John, II. 1. 566. *v.t.* to surround. M. N.D. IV. 1. 52.

Round, *adj.* straightforward, blunt, plainspoken. C. of E. II. 1. 82.

Rouse, *sb.* deep draught, bumper.

Rout, *sb.* crowd, mob. C. of E. III. 1. 101. Brawl. Oth. II. 3. 210.

Row, *sb.* verse or stanza.

Roynish, *adj.* scurvy; hence coarse, rough.

Rub, *v.i.* to encounter obstacles. L. L. L. IV. 1. 139. 'Rub on,' of a bowl that surmounts the obstacles in its course. T. & C. III. 2. 49.

Rub, *sb.* impediment, hindrance; taken from game of bowls. John, III. 4. 128.

Ruddock, *sb.* the redbreast.

Rudesby, *sb.* a rude fellow.

Rump-fed, *adj.* pampered; perhaps fed on offal; or else fat-rumped.

Running banquet, a hasty refreshment (fig.).

Rush aside, *v.t.* to pass hastily by, thrust aside.

Rushling, blunder for rustling.

Sad, *adj.* grave, serious. M. of V. II. 2. 195. Gloomy, sullen. R II. v. 5. 70.

Sagittary, *sb.* a centaur. T. & C. v. 5. 14. The official residence in the arsenal at Venice. Oth. I. I. 160.

Sallet, *sb.* a close-fitting helmet. 2 H VI. IV. 10. 11. A salad. 2 H VI. IV. 10. 8.

Salt, *sb.* salt-cellar. Two G. III. I. 354. *adj.* lecherous. M. for M. v. I. 399. Stinging, bitter. T. & C. I. 3. 371.

Salutation, *sb.* give salutation to my blood = make my blood rise.

Salute, *v.t.* to meet. John, II. I. 590. To affect. H VIII. II. 3. 103.

Sanded, *adj.* sandy-coloured.

Sarcenet, *sb.* fine silk.

Say, *sb.* a kind of silk.

Scald, *adj.* scurvy, scabby. H V. v. I. 5.

Scale, *v.t.* to put in the scales, weigh.

Scall = Scald. M. W. W. III. I. 115.

Scamble, *sb.* scramble.

Scamel, *sb.* perhaps a misprint for seamell, or seamew.

Scantling, *sb.* a scanted or small portion.

Scape, *sb.* freak, escapade.

Sconce, *sb.* a round fort. H V. III. 6. 73. Hence a protection for the head. C. of E. II. 2. 37. Hence the skull. Ham. v. I. 106. *v.t.* to ensconce, hide. Ham. III. 4. 4.

Scotch, *sb.* notch. *v.t.* to cut, slash.

Scrowl, *v.t.* perhaps for to scrawl.

Scroyles, *sb.* scabs, scrofulous wretches.

Scrubbed, *adj.* scrubby, paltry.

Scull, *sb.* shoal of fish.

Seal, *sb.* to give seals = confirm, carry out.

Seam, *sb.* grease, lard.

Seconds, *sb.* an inferior kind of flour.

Secure, *adj.* without care, confident.

Security, *sb.* carelessness, want of caution.

Seedness, *sb.* sowing with seed.

Seel, *v.t.* to close up a hawk's eyes.

Self-admission, *sb.* self-approbation.

Semblative, *adj.* resembling, like.

Sequestration, *sb.* separation.

Serpigo, *sb.* tetter or eruption on the skin.

Sessa, exclamation urging to speed.

Shard-borne, *adj.* borne through the air on shards.

Shards, *sb.* the wing cases of beetles. A. & C. III. 2. 20. Potsherds. Ham. v. I. 254.

Sharked up, gathered indiscriminately.

Shealed, *p.p.* shelled.

Sheep-biter, *sb.* a malicious, niggardly fellow.

Shent, *p.p.* scolded, rebuked. M.W.W. I. 4. 36.

Shive, *sb.* slice.

Shog, *v.i.* to move, jog.

Shrewd, *adj.* mischievous, bad.

Shrewdly, *adv.* badly.

Shrewdness, *sb.* mischievousness.

Shrieve, *sb.* sheriff.

Shore, *sb.* a sewer.

Shrowd, *sb.* shelter, protection.

Siege, *sb.* seat. M. for M. IV. 2. 98. Rank. Ham. IV. 7. 75. Excrement. Tp. II. 2. 111.

Significant, *sb.* sign, token.

Silly, *adj.* harmless, innocent. Two G. IV. I. 72. Plain, simple. Tw.N. II. 4. 46.

Simular, *adj.* simulated, counterfeited. Cym. v. 5. 20. *sb.* simulator, pretender. Lear, III. 2. 54.

Sith, *adv.* and *conj.* since.

Skains-mates, *sb.* knavish companions.

Slab, *adj.* slabby, slimy.

Sleeve-band, *sb.* wristband.

Sleided, *adj.* untwisted.

Slipper, *adj.* slippery.

Slobbery, *adj.* dirty.

Slubber, *v.t.* to slur over, do carelessly.

Smatch, *sb.* smack, taste.

Sneak-cup, *sb.* a fellow who shirks his liquor.

Sneap, *v.t.* to pinch, nip. L.L.L. I. I. 100. *sb.* snub, reprimand. 2 H IV. II. I. 125.

Sneck up, contemptuous expression = go and be hanged.

Snuff, *sb.* quarrel. Lear, III. I. 26. Smouldering wick of a candle. Cym. I. 6. 87. Object of contempt. A.W. I. 2. 60. Take in snuff = take offence at. L.L.L. v. 2. 22.

Sob, *sb.* a rest given to a horse to regain its wind.

Solidare, *sb.* a small coin.

Sonties, *sb.* corruption of 'santé' or 'sanctity' or 'saints.'

Sooth, *sb.* flattery.

Soothers, *sb.* flatterers.

Sophy, *sb.* the Shah of Persia.

Sore, *sb.* a buck of the fourth year.

Sorel, *sb.* a buck of the third year.

Sort, *sb.* rank. M.A. I. I. 6. Set, company. R III. v. 3. 316. Manner. M. of V. I. 2. 105. Lot. T. & C. I. 3. 376.

Sort, *v.t.* to pick out. Two G. III. 2. 92. To rank. Ham. II. 2. 270. To arrange, dispose. R III. II. 2. 148. To adapt. 2 H VI. II. 4. 68. *v.i.* to associate. V. & A. 689. To be fitting.

T. & C. I. I. 109. Fall out, happen. M.N.D. III. 2. 352.

Souse, *v.t.* to swoop down on, as a falcon.

Sowl, *v.t.* to lug, drag by the ears.

Span-counter, *sb.* boy's game of throwing a counter so as to strike, or rest within a span of, an opponent's counter.

Speed, *sb.* fortune, success.

Speken = speak.

Sperr, *v.t.* to bar.

Spital, *sb.* hospital.

Spital house, *sb.* hospital.

Spleen, *sb.* quick movement. M.N.D. I. I. 146. Fit of laughter. L.L.L. III. I. 76.

Spot, *sb.* pattern in embroidery.

Sprag, *adj.* sprack, quick, lively.

Spring, *sb.* a young shoot.

Springhalt, *sb.* a lameness in horses.

Spurs, *sb.* the side roots of a tree.

Squandering, *adj.* roving, random. As, II. 7. 57.

Square, *sb.* the embroidery about the bosom of a smock or shift. W.T. IV. 3. 212. 'Most precious square of sense' = the most sensitive part. Lear, I. I. 74.

Square, *v.i.* to quarrel.

Squash, *sb.* an unripe peascod.

Squier, *sb.* square, rule.

Squiny, *v.i.* to look asquint.

Staggers, *sb.* giddiness, bewilderment. A.W. II. 3. 164. A disease of horses. T. of S. III. 2. 53.

Stale, *sb.* laughing stock, dupe. 3 H VI. III. 3. 260. Decoy. T. of S. III. I. 90. Stalking-horse. C. of E. II. I. 101. Prostitute. M.A. II. 2. 24. Horse-urine. A. & C. I. 4. 62.

Stamp, *v.t.* to mark as genuine, give currency to.

Standing, *sb.* duration, continuance. W.T. I. 2. 430. Attitude. Tim. I. I. 34.

Standing-tuck, *sb.* a rapier standing on end.

Staniel, *sb.* a hawk, the kestrel.

Stare, *v.i.* to stand on end.

State, *sb.* attitude. L.L.L. IV. 3. 183. A chair of state. I H IV. II. 4. 390. Estate, fortune. M. of V. III. 2. 258. States (pl.) = persons of high position. John, II. I. 395.

Statute-caps, *sb.* woollen caps worn by citizens as decreed by the act of 1571.

Stead, *v.t.* to help.

Stead up, *v.t.* to take the place of.

Stelled, *p.p.* fixed. Lucr. 1444. Sonn. XXIV. I. Starry. Lear, III. 7. 62.

Stickler-like, *adj.* like a stickler, whose duty it was to separate combatants.

Stigmatic, *adj.* marked by deformity.

Stillitory, *sb.* a still.

Stint, *v.t.* to stop, cease. R. & J. I. 3. 48. *v.t.* to check, stop. T. & C. IV. 5. 93.

Stock, *sb.* stocking. I H IV. II. 4. 118. A thrust in fencing

M. W.W. II. 3. 24. *v.t.* to put in the stocks. Lear, II. 2. 133.

Stomach, *sb.* courage. 2 H IV. I. I. 129. Pride. T. of S. v. 2. 177.

Stomaching, *sb.* resentment.

Stone-bow, *sb.* a cross-bow for shooting stones.

Stoop, *sb.* a drinking vessel

Stricture, *sb.* strictness.

Stride, *v.t.* to overstep.

Stover, *sb.* cattle fodder.

Stuck, *sb.* a thrust in fencing.

Subject, *sb.* subjects, collectively.

Subscribe, *v.i.* to be surety. A. W. III. 6. 84. Yield, submit. 1 H VI. II. 4. 44. *v.t.* to admit acknowledge. M.A. v. 2. 58.

Subtle, *adj.* deceptively smooth.

Successantly, *adv.* in succession.

Sufferance, *sb.* suffering. M. for M. II. 2. 167. Patience. M. of V. I. 3. 109. Loss. Oth. II. 1. 23. Death penalty. H V. II. 2. 158.

Suggest, *v.t.* to tempt.

Suit, *sb.* service, attendance. M. for M. IV. 4. 19. Out of suits with fortune=out of fortune's service.

Supervise, *sb.* inspection.

Suppliance, *sb.* pastime.

Sur-addition, *sb.* an added title.

Surmount, *v.i.* to surpass, exceed. 1 H VI. v. 3. 191. *v.t.* to surpass. L.L.L. v. 2. 677.

Sur-reined, *p.p.* overridden.

Suspect, *sb.* suspicion.

Swarth, *adj.* black. T.A. II. 3. 71. *sb.* swath. Tw.N. II. 3. 145.

Swoopstake, *adv.* in one sweep, wholesale.

Tag, *sb.* rabble.

Take, *v.t.* to captivate. W.T. IV. 3. 119. Strike. M.W.W. IV. 4. 32. Take refuge in. C. of E. v. 1. 36. Leap over. John, v. 2. 138. Take in=conquer. A. & C. I. 1. 23. Take out=copy. Oth. III. 3. 296. Take thought =feel grief for. J.C. II. 1. 187. Take up=get on credit. 2 H VI. IV. 7. 125. Reconcile. Tw.N. III. 4. 294. Rebuke. Two G. I. 2. 134.

Tallow-keech, *sb.* a vessel filled with tallow.

Tanling, *sb.* one tanned by the sun. John, IV. 1. 117. Incite. Ham. II. 2. 358.

Taste, *sb.* trial, proof. *v.t.* to try, prove.

Tarre, *v.t.* to set on dogs to fight.

Tawdry-lace, *sb.* a rustic necklace.

Taxation, *sb.* satire, censure. As, I. 2. 82. Claim, demand. Tw.N. I. 5. 210.

Teen, *sb.* grief.

Tenable, *adj.* capable of being kept.

Tend, *v.i.* to wait, attend. Ham. I. 3. 83. Be attentive. Tp. I. 1. 6. *v.t.* to tend to, regard. 2 H VI. I. 1. 204. Wait upon. A. & C. II. 2. 212.

Tendance, *sb.* attention. Tim.

I. 1. 60. Person attending. Tim. I. 1. 74.

Tender, *v.t.* to hold dear, regard. R III. I. 1. 44. *sb.* care, regard. 1 H IV. v. 4. 49.

Tender-hefted, *adj.* set in a delicate handle or frame.

Tent, *sb.* probe. T. & C. II. 2. 16. *v.t.* to probe. Ham. II. 2. 608. Cure. Cor. I. 9. 31.

Tercel, *sb.* male goshawk.

Termless, *adj.* not to be described.

Testerned, *p.p.* presented with sixpence.

Testril, *sb.* sixpence.

Tetchy, *adj.* touchy, irritable.

Tetter, *sb.* skin eruption. Ham. I. 5. 71. *v.t.* to infect with tetter. Cor. III. 1. 79.

Than=then.

Tharborough, *sb.* third borough, constable.

Thick, *adv.* rapidly, close.

Thirdborough, *sb.* constable.

Thisne, perhaps=in this way. M.N.D. I. 2. 48.

Thoughten, *p.p.* be you thoughten =entertain the thought.

Thrall, *sb.* thraldom, slavery. Pass. P. 266. *adj.* enslaved. V.&A. 837.

Three-man beetle, a rammer operated by three men.

Three-man songmen, three-part glee-singers.

Three-pile, *sb.* the finest kind of velvet.

Three-piled, *adj.* having a thick pile. M. for M. I. 2. 32. Superfine (met.). L.L.L. v. 2. 407.

Tickle, *adj.* unstable. 2 H VI. I. 1. 216. Tickle of the sere, used of lungs readily, prompted to laughter; literally hair-triggered. Ham. II. 2. 329.

Ticklish, *adj.* wanton.

Tight, *adj.* swift, deft. A. & C. IV. 4. 15. Water-tight, sound. T. of S. II. 1. 372.

Tightly, *adv.* briskly, smartly.

Time-pleaser, *sb.* time server, one who complies with the times.

Tire, *sb.* headdress, Two G. IV. 4. 187. Furniture. Per. II. 2. 21.

Tire, *v.i.* to feed greedily. 3 H VI. I. 1. 269. *v.t.* make to feed greedily. Lucr. 417.

Tisick, *sb.* phthisic, a cough.

Toaze, *v.t.* to draw out, untangle.

Tod, *sb.* Twenty-eight pounds of wool. *v.t.* to yield a tod.

Toged, *adj.* wearing a toga.

Toll, *v.i.* to pay toll. A.W. v. 3. 147. *v.t.* to take toll. John, III. 1. 154.

Touch, *sb.* trait. As, v. 4. 27. Dash, spice. R III. IV. 4. 157. Touchstone. R III. IV. 2. 8. Of noble touch=of tried nobility. Cor. IV. 1. 49. Brave touch =fine test of valour. M.N.D. III. 2. 70. Slight hint. H VIII. v. 1. 13. Know no touch=have no skill. R II. 1. 3. 165.

Touse, *v.t.* to pull, tear.

Toy, *sb.* trifle, idle fancy, folly.

Tract, *sb.* track, trace. Tim. I. 1. 53. Course. H VIII. I. 1. 40.

Train, *v.t.* to allure, decoy. 1 H VI. I. 3. 25. *sb.* bait, allurement. Mac. IV. 3. 118.

Tranect, *sb.* ferry, a doubtful word.

Translate, *v.t.* to transform.

Trash, *v.t.* lop off branches. Tp. I. 2. 81. Restrain a dog by a trash or strap. Oth. II. 1. 307.

Traverse, *v.i.* to march to the right or left.

Tray-trip, *sb.* a game at dice, which was won by throwing a trey.

Treatise, *sb.* discourse.

Treachors, *sb.* traitors.

Trench, *v.t.* to cut. Two G. III. 2. 7. Divert from its course by digging. H IV. III. 1. 112.

Troll-my-dames, *sb.* the French game of *trou madame*, perhaps akin to bagatelle.

Tropically, *adv.* figuratively.

True-penny, *sb.* an honest fellow. Ham. I. 5. 150.

Try, *sb.* trial, test. Tim. vi 1. 9. 'Bring to try=bring a ship as close to the wind as possible. Tp. I. 1. 35.

Tub, *sb.* and tubfast, *sb.* a cure of venereal disease by sweating and fasting.

Tuck, *sb.* rapier.

Tun-dish, *sb.* funnel.

Turk, to turn Turk=to be a renegade. M.A. III. 4. 52. Turk Gregory=Pope Gregory VII 1 H IV. v. 3. 125.

Twiggen, *adj.* made of twigs or wicker.

Twilled, *adj.* perhaps, covered with sedge or reeds.

Twire, *v.i.* to twinkle.

Umber, *sb.* a brown colour.

Umbered, *p.p.* made brown, darkened.

Umbrage, *sb.* a shadow.

Unaneled, *adj.* not having received extreme unction.

Unbarbed, *adj.* not wearing armour, bare.

Unbated, *adj.* unblunted.

Unbraced, *adj.* unbuttoned.

Uncape, *v.i.* to uncouple, throw off the hounds.

Uncase, *v.i.* to undress.

Unclew, *v.t.* to unwind, undo.

Uncolted, *p.p.* deprived of one's horse. 1 H IV. II. 2. 41.

Uncomprehensive, *adj.* incomprehensible.

Unconfirmed, *adj.* inexperienced.

Undercrest, *v.t.* to wear upon the crest.

Undertaker, *sb.* agent, person responsible to another for something.

Underwrite, *v.t.* to submit to.

Undistinguished, *adj.* not to be seen distinctly, unknowable.

Uneath, *adv.* hardly, with difficulty.

Unfolding, *adj.* unfolding star, the star at whose rising the shepherd lets the sheep out of the fold.

Unhappy, *adj.* mischievous, unlucky.

Unhatcht, *pp.* unhacked. Tw.N. III.
4. 234. Undisclosed. Oth. III.
4 140.

Unhouseled, *adj.* without having
received the sacrament.

Union, *sb.* large pearl.

Unkind, *adj.* unnatural. Lear, I.
I. 261. Childless. V & A. 204.

Unlived, *p.p.* deprived of life.

Unpaved, *adj.* without stones.

Unpinked, *adj.* not pinked, or
pierced with eyelet holes.

Unraked, *adj.* not made up for the
night.

Unrecuring, *adj.* incurable.

Unrolled, *p.p.* struck off the role.

Unseeming, *pr.p.* not seeming.

Unseminared, *p.p.* deprived of seed
or virility.

Unset, *adj.* unplanted.

Unshunned, *adj.* inevitable.

Unsifted, *adj.* untried, inexperienced.

Unsquared, *adj.* unsuitable.

Unstate, *v.t.* to deprive of dignity.

Untented, *adj.* incurable.

Unthrift, *sb.* prodigal. *adj.* good for
nothing.

Untraded, *adj.* unhackneyed.

Unyoke, *v.i.* to put off the yoke,
take ease after labour. Ham.
v. I. 55. *v.t.* to disjoin. John,
III. I. 241.

Up-cast, *sb.* a throw at bowls; perhaps the final throw.

Upshoot, *sb.* decisive shot.

Upspring, *sb.* a bacchanalian dance.

Upstaring, *adj.* standing on end.

Urchin, *sb.* hedgehog. T.A. II.
3. 101. A goblin. M.W. IV.
4. 49.

Usance, *sb.* interest.

Use, *sb.* interest. M.A. II. 1. 269.
Usage, M. for M. I. 1. 40. In
use=in trust. M. of V. IV. I.
383.

Use, *v.r.* to behave oneself.

Uses, *sb.* manners, usages.

Utis, *sb.* boisterous merriment.

Vade, *v.i.* to fade.

Vail, *sb.* setting (of the sun). T. &
C. v. 8. 7. *v.t.* to lower, let fall.
I H VI. v. 3. 25. *v.i.* to bow.
Per. IV. Prol. 29.

Vails, *sb.* a servant's perquisites.

Vain, for vain=to no purpose.

Vantbrace, *sb.* armour for the fore-
arm.

Vast, *adj.* waste, desolate, boundless.

Vaunt-couriers, *sb.* fore-runners.

Vaward, *sb.* vanguard. I H VI. I.
I. 132. The first part. M.N.
D. IV. I. 106.

Vegetives, *sb.* plants.

Velvet-guards, *sb.* velvet linings,
used metaphorically of those who
wear them. I H IV. III. I. 256.

Veney, *sb.* or venew, *sb.* a fencing
bout, a hit.

Venge, *v.t.* to avenge.

Vent, *sb.* discharge. 'Full of vent'
=effervescent like wine.

Via *interj.* away, on!

Vice, *sb.* the buffoon in old morality plays. R III. III. 1. 82.
v.t. to screw (met.) W.T. I. 2.
415.

Vinewedst, *adj.* mouldy, musty.

Violent, *v.i.* to act violently, rage.

Virginalling, *p.p.* playing with the
fingers as upon the virginals.

Virtuous, *adj.* efficacious, powerful.
Oth. III. 4. 110. Essential. M.
N.D. II. 2. 367. 'Virtuous
season' = benignant influence.
M. for M. II. 2. 168.

Vouch, *sb.* testimony, guarantee.
I H VI. v. 3. 71. *v.i.* to assert,
warrant.

Waft, *v.t.* to beckon. C. of E. II.
2. 108. To turn. W.T. I. 2.
371.

Wag, *v.i.* and *v.t.* to move, stir.
R III. III. 5. 7. To go one's way.
M.A. v. 1. 16.

Wage, *v.t.* to stake, risk. I H IV.
v.i. to contend. Lear, II. 4. 210.
Wage equal=be on an equality
with. A. & C. v. 1. 31.

Wanion, *sb.* with a wanion=with
a vengeance.

Wanton, *sb.* one brought up in
luxury, an effeminate person.
John, v. 1. 70. *v.i.* to dally,
play. W.T. II. 1. 18.

Wappened, *p.p.* of doubtful meaning, perhaps worn out, stale.

Ward, *sb.* guardianship. A.W. I.
1. 5. Defence. L.L.L. III. 1. 131.
Guard in fencing. I H IV.
II. 4. 198. Prison, custody.
2 H VI. v. I. 112. Lock, bolt.
Tim. III. 3. 38. *v.t.* to guard.
R III. v. 3. 254.

Warden-pies, *sb.* pies made with
the warden, a large baking pear.

Warrantize, *sb.* security, warranty.

Warrener, *sb.* keeper of a warren,
gamekeeper.

Watch, *sb.* a watch candle which
marked the hours.

Watch, *v.t.* to tame by keeping
from sleep.

Waters, *sb.* 'for all waters'=ready
for anything.

Wealsmen, *sb.* statesmen.

Web and pin, *sb.* cataract of the eye.

Weeding, *sb.* weeds.

Weet, *v.t.* to know.

Welkin, *sb.* the blue, the sky.
Tw.N. II. 3. 61. *adj.* sky blue.
W.T. I. 2. 136.

Whiffler, *sb.* one who cleared the
way for a procession, carrying
the whiffle or staff of his office.

Whist, *adj.* still, hushed.

Whittle, *sb.* a clasp-knife.

Whoobub, *sb.* hubbub.

Widowhood, *sb.* rights as a widow.

Wilderness, *sb.* wildness.

Wimpled, *p.p.* blindfolded. (A
wimple was a wrap or handkerchief for the neck.)

Winchester goose, *sb.* a venereal
swelling in the groin, the brothels
of Southwark being in the
jurisdiction of the Bishop of
Winchester.

Window-bars, *sb.* lattice-like embroidery worn by women across
the breast.

Windring, *adj.* winding.

Wink, *sb.* a closing of the eyes,
sleep. Tp. II. I. 281. *v.i.* to
close the eyes, be blind, be in
the dark. C. of E. III. 2. 58.

Winter-ground, *v.t.* to protect a
plant from frost by bedding it
with straw.

Wipe, *sb.* a brand, mark of shame.

Wise-woman, *sb.* a witch.

Witch, *sb.* used of a man also;
wizard.

Woman, *v.t.* woman me=make
me show my woman's feelings.

Woman-tired, *adj.* henpecked.

Wondered, *p.p.* performing wonders.

Wood, *adj.* mad.

Woodman, *sb.* forester, hunter.
M.W.W. v. 5. 27. In a bad
sense, a wencher. M. for M.
IV. 4. 163.

Woollen, to lie in the=either to
lie in the blankets, or to be
buried in flannel, as the law in
Shakespeare's time prescribed.

Word, *sb.* to be at a word=to be
as good as one's word.

Word, *v.t.* to represent. Cym.
I. 4. 15. To deceive with words.
A. & C. v. 2. 191.

World, *sb.* to go to the world=to
be married. A woman of the
world—a married woman. A
world to see=a marvel to behold.

Wrangler, *sb.* an opponent, a tennis
term.

Wreak, *sb.* revenge. T.A. IV.
3. 33. *v.t.* to revenge. T.A.
IV. 3. 51.

Wreakful, *adj.* revengeful.

Wrest, *sb.* a tuning-key.

Wring, *v.i.* to writhe.

Write, *v.t.* to describe oneself,
claim to be. 'Writ as little beard'
=claimed as little beard. A.W.
II. 3. 62.

Writhled, *adj.* shrivelled up, wrinkled.

Wry, *v.i.* to swerve.

Yare, *adj.* and *adv.* ready, active,
nimble.

Yarely, *adv.* readily, briskly.

Yearn, *v.t.* and *v.i.* to grieve.

Yellows, *sb.* jaundice in horses.

Yerk, *v.t.* to lash out at, strike
quickly.

Yest, *sb.* froth, foam.

Yesty, *adj.* foamy, frothy.

Younker, *sb.* a stripling, youngster,
novice.

Yslaked, *p.p.* brought to rest.

Zany, *sb.* a fool, buffoon.